INDEX OF DEATH NOTICES

APPEARING IN

DER CHRISTLICHE APOLOGETE

A National German Methodist Newspaper

1839 – 1899

INDEX OF DEATH NOTICES

APPEARING IN

DER CHRISTLICHE APOLOGETE

A National German Methodist Newspaper

1839 – 1899

Indexed by

Jeffrey G. Herbert

HAMILTON COUNTY CHAPTER OF
THE OHIO GENEALOGICAL SOCIETY

Cincinnati, Ohio
2016

Published by the
Hamilton County Chapter, OGS
P.O. Box 15865
Cincinnati, OH 45215-0865
513-956-7078
http://hcgsohio.org

Printed in the United States of America.
ISBN-13: 978-0692679630
LCCN 2016938734

Table of Contents

Introduction   iii

Example Death Notices   ix

Suggested Further Readings   xiii

Index of Death Notices by Surname   1

Introduction

This index is based on information extracted from the original hardbound copies of the German Methodist newspaper, *Der Christliche Apologete,* that are stored at the Cincinnati History Library and Archives (CHLA) located in the Cincinnati Museum Center. CHLA has the most complete and comprehensive collection of this historic newspaper which was published for over 100 years, as a weekly newspaper in order to promote the Methodist religion for the newly arriving German immigrants. Articles typically contained sermons, current events both local, national, and in Europe, notices of upcoming religious conferences, advertisements, articles of advice to help in daily life, and most important to researchers today, death notices reported from fellow Methodist ministers from around the various German Methodist congregations in the United States.

Since German Methodism was introduced in the United States by Reverend Wilhelm Nast, the early members were converts once they arrived in the United States, and were typically previously members of the Roman Catholic, German Evangelical or German Lutheran churches and were typically originally baptized there. Over 85% of the death notices reported on a weekly basis in this newspaper contain the date and town of birth, typically in Germany, as well as a small biography of the individual and their family.

Der Christliche Apologete, or The Christian Apologist in English, was begun in 1839 by Rev. Wilhelm Nast, who was a minister in the Cincinnati, Ohio and mid-western area, and was the founder of the German Methodist religious movement in the United States. He was born in 1807 in Stuttgart, Baden-Württemberg, Germany, and immigrated to the United States in 1828. He began his work organizing German Methodist churches in 1837 in the Cincinnati and surrounding areas. His first church was located on Race Street in Cincinnati, Ohio. The present building was designed and built in 1881 by architect Samuel Hannaford on the original site, and still stands today, and is known today as the

> Nast Trinity United Methodist Church
> 1310 Race Street
> Cincinnati, Ohio 45202.

The issues used for this index are the hardbound original newspapers located at the Cincinnati History Library and Archives. These copies have never been microfilmed, and are currently only available from the library in paper, hardbound format. Copies of individual death notices can be requested. The current address and contact information for this repository is:

	Cincinnati Historical Library and Archives
Address:	1301 Western Avenue
	Cincinnati, Ohio 45203
Phone:	(513) 287-7030
Email:	library@cincymuseum.org
Website:	www.cincymuseum.org/library

The original hardbound newspapers are part of the Nippert manuscript collection. The call number for this collection is **MSS 873,** and the newspaper collection runs from Box 5-70 (Volume 1 – 1839) through Box 5-125 (Volume 103 – 1941). There are occasional missing issues, but for the most part, the issues are intact and complete for the years 1839 through 1941 with no major gaps in the collection. CHLA also has a finding aid as part of their collection that provides more detailed information of what is part of the collection. It also provides a detailed list by year as to what is included in each box. This index contains death notice extractions from the first issue in January 1839 through December 1899. An index of the subsequent years from 1900 through 1941 may be a future project. Please contact CHLA for more information on obtaining copies of the death notices and the current costs. The name of the deceased, publication date and page number should be included with any request for copies.

This index has over 26,800 deaths, which were reported and published before 1899 throughout the United States, with the majority of them from the Midwest area. As Reverend Nast's influence in the Cincinnati area spread, he recruited many more ministers to support the German Methodist movement, and the founding of many more local churches in the area, which eventually expanded to include most of the United States and Europe. The death notices contained in this index therefore include people that lived in all parts of the United States in the 19th and early 20th century, and also include approximately 85% of the towns of birth in the death notice. This makes the index of benefit to researchers throughout the United States looking for the place of birth of their German ancestors, as well as researchers in Germany trying to find what happened to relatives that left the area and settled in the United States in the 19th century.

The original paper started life in January 1839 as a 4 page newspaper, and by 1840 had over 100 subscribers. In 1847, the paper was resized to a 12" x 17" format and counted 1700 subscribers. In 1852, the format was enlarged to a 14" x 19" format to allow for more news content. In 1861 the news coverage and topics were expanded to an 8 page format. The typical format was 4 pages were devoted to religious content, 2 pages for political items and commentary, and 2 pages for news items from the United States and Europe. At this point, more detail was now typically provided in the obituaries, and in some instances there were also details given on the date and place of their conversion to Methodism and by whom. It also might list other places of residence once the deceased person and their family arrived in America, place of marriage and to whom, and any surviving family members. In 1887 the format was again changed. The paper now was a much smaller, more readable 11" x 17" page format, and enlarged to 16 pages per week. At this point there was a standardization of the obituary content and a limit of 20 lines or 120 words for each death notice. This new format only lasted for a few years, and then reverted back to a larger format with additional information about the deceased, their family and survivors, and their journeys in America, and continued through 1899.

The original text of the newspaper is in German and also uses the old German or Gothic script letters. To facilitate finding the correct name, the original German letters and names have been extracted. The unique German letters and their usual English equivalents are listed below as an aid to the reader.

ä translated into English as 'ae'
ö translated into English as 'oe'

ü translated into English as 'ue'
ß translated into English as 'ss'

In the original death notices that were published, there could be a wide variety of information given on the individual. All of this valuable information could not be included in this index, and much more information could be provided by reading and translating the death notice. The information that has been extracted and provided in this index is: full name of the deceased, date when the notice was published in the newspaper, date of death, age of the deceased, page number where the death notices appears, maiden name (if a married woman), reported place of death, and place of birth. More details on each of the fields is listed below.

Name of Deceased - In many cases individuals had 2, 3 or sometimes even 4 given names in the 19th century. They might be known by any of these given or baptismal names or sometimes even went by a nick name that was totally different from their baptismal name. Last or family names were extracted in their original German spelling and sorted alphabetically according to this spelling.

Age - The age was extracted or calculated as given in the death notice. A simple number would indicate age in years. If a full age was provided, it is displayed in year, month and day format (YY-MM-DD). In many cases an exact date of birth was given in the death notice, but a simple subtraction of the year of death from the year of birth was used as a calculation for an age in years in this index.

In the 1840s when the newspaper first began, there were sometimes inquiries published on persons who came to the United States, but whose whereabouts were lost. In some cases, they stopped sending letters back to Germany, or they had ventured on to another city farther west, and their family members published an inquiry to see if anyone knew what happened to them. These are denoted by the word "Inquiry" in the age column, and do not indicate that the person died on that date, but merely that someone was looking for them and published an inquiry, usually with relevant family information and their original place of birth to help identify them. The place of death in this case is the last place where the individual was known to have lived.

Place of Death – The place of death is the reported place of death given in the obituary. Since this index comprises obituaries from all over the United States, both the town where the pastor reported the death is listed, as well as the two letter abbreviation for the specific state. It is usually given as the town where the church or minister was located, and the actual place of death was most likely on a nearby farm or if in a city, in a nearby neighborhood. In rare cases, the individual may have died in another location, and the death notice was written and reported by the local minister and that place of death was extracted. A few examples could be the death of a soldier in battle, the death of a person suffering from tuberculosis, and they were recently sent to a warmer southern state and they died there, or someone died while travelling or visiting family members in another state. The two letter abbreviation for the state is the official code used by the United States Post Office. The list of the 50 states and their abbreviations are listed below as a convenience for the researcher.

AL	Alabama	LA	Louisiana	OH	Ohio
AK	Alaska	ME	Maine	OK	Oklahoma
AZ	Arizona	MD	Maryland	OR	Oregon
AR	Arkansas	MA	Massachusetts	PA	Pennsylvania
CA	California	MI	Michigan	RI	Rhode Island
CO	Colorado	MN	Minnesota	SC	South Carolina
CT	Connecticut	MS	Mississippi	SD	South Dakota
DE	Delaware	MO	Missouri	TN	Tennessee
FL	Florida	MT	Montana	TX	Texas
GA	Georgia	NE	Nebraska	UT	Utah
HI	Hawaii	NV	Nevada	VT	Vermont
ID	Idaho	NH	New Hampshire	VA	Virginia
IL	Illinois	NJ	New Jersey	WA	Washington
IN	Indiana	NM	New Mexico	WV	West Virginia
IA	Iowa	NY	New York	WI	Wisconsin
KS	Kansas	NC	North Carolina	WY	Wyoming
KY	Kentucky	ND	North Dakota		

And there were also a few notices from other countries. The 2-digit abbreviation codes used for these five countries are listed below.

CD	Canada	GE	Germany	SW	Switzerland
CN	China	TK	Turkey		

Of the reported places of death listed in the various states in the obituaries, the top seven states are listed below in Figure 1 for reference. They collectively represent over two-thirds of the obituaries reported, and are contained within what is commonly known as the "German Triangle", with vertices at St. Louis, Missouri, Milwaukee, Wisconsin, and Cincinnati, Ohio. The remaining 30% are spread over 27 states as well as locations in Canada, Germany and Switzerland.

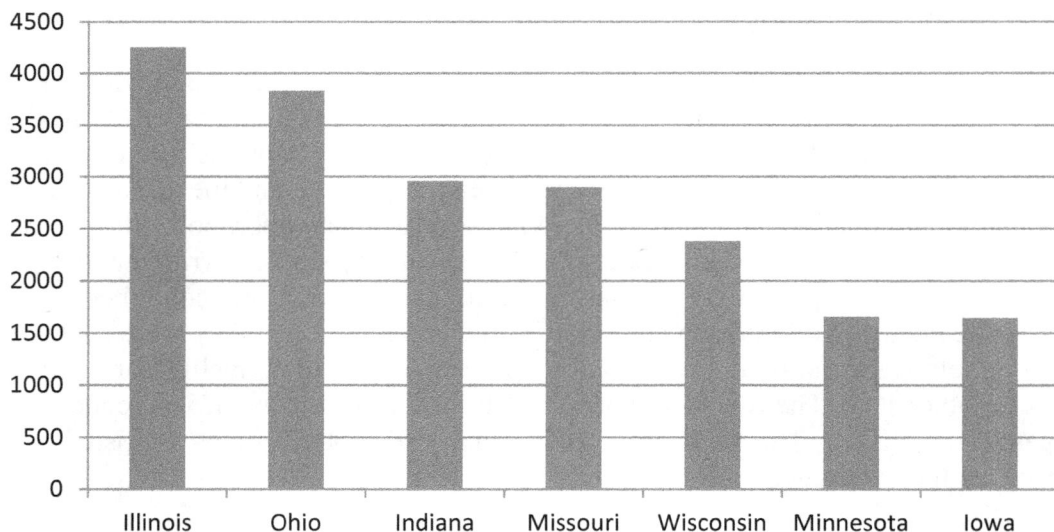

Figure 1

Place of Birth – If the place of birth was mentioned in the death notice, these were extracted and listed as part of the index. The information is recorded as the smallest town or village where the birth or church of baptism occurred, followed by the next largest administrative district, and then by the state, kingdom or province that the town belonged to at the time of death. In the case where the name of a town is popular, and could occur in many states the town is sometimes referred to by the name of the river it is near. Some examples are: Neustadt an der Haardt, Neustadt an der Donau, Neustadt an der Orla, or Frankfurt am Main, Frankfurt an der Oder. In these cases to save space on the page, this is sometimes abbreviated as "a. d. Haardt", "a. d. Donau", or "a. d. Oder", for example, and these abbreviations are quite common in Germany.

Obviously over the time span of 100 years, there were many different states or provinces for a given town, and the information was recorded exactly as was written in the death notice at the time. There were large administrative changes and reorganizations in 1871 when the German Empire was formed and acquired most of present day Germany and Poland, and later after World War I ended. In some cases, the place of birth is no longer within the present borders of modern Germany, and could now reside within the borders of France, Austria, Poland, Denmark, or the Czech Republic.

Of the places of birth listed in Europe in the death notices, the top eight kingdoms, states, provinces, duchies, etc. are listed below in the Figure 2 graph for reference. They collectively represent over half of the places of birth mentioned in the death notices. The remaining 50% are spread over 120 provinces, duchies, smaller kingdoms, and various states in America. Of the various states listed for place of birth, most are in the Midwestern area (i.e. Ohio, Indiana, Illinois, Missouri, and Wisconsin) and are for children of the original emigrants.

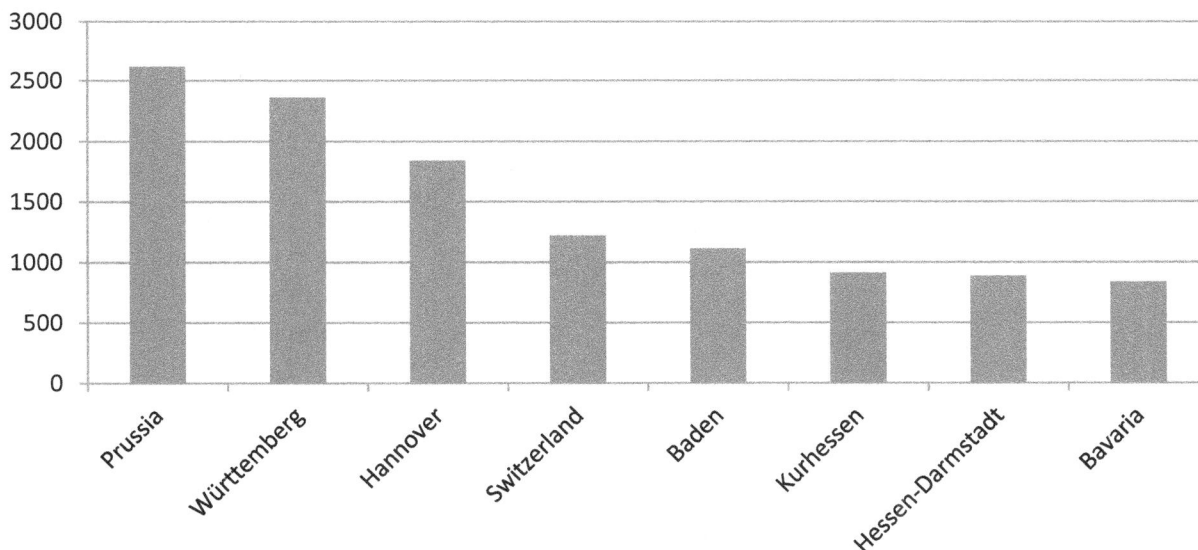

Figure 2

The 16 Bundesländer (federal states) in present day Germany are listed below in English (and German in parenthesis if a different name) are:

Baden-Württemberg	Lower Saxony (Niedersachsen)
Bavaria (Bayern)	North Rhine-Westphalia (Nordrhein-Westfalen)
Berlin – city-state	Rhineland-Palatinate (Rheinland-Pfalz)
Brandenburg	Saarland
Bremen – city-state	Saxony (Sachsen)
Hamburg – city-state	Saxony-Anhalt (Sachsen-Anhalt)
Hesse (Hessen)	Schleswig-Holstein
Mecklenburg-Vorpommern	Thuringia (Thüringen)

The following is a sample list of locations of birth given in obituaries, and a rough equivalent of where these previous duchies, kingdoms, fürstdoms, and principalities were located. Some of these areas which were previously considered part of the German-speaking confederation of states are now located in neighboring countries.

Province	Modern State
Baden	Baden-Württemberg
Baiern	Bavaria
Böhmen	Bohemia, Czech Republic
Brandenburg	Brandenburg
Braunschweig	Lower Saxony
Elsaß	Alsace-Lorraine, France
Frankreich	France
Hannover	Lower Saxony
Hessen	Hesse
Hinterpommern	Pomerania, Poland
Holstein	Schleswig-Holstein
Kurhessen	Hesse
Lippe-Detmold	Westphalia
Lippe-Schaumburg	Westphalia
Mecklenburg-Schwerin	Mecklenburg-Vorpommern
Mecklenburg-Strelitz	Mecklenburg-Vorpommern
Oldenburg	Oldenburg
Ostfriesland	Lower Saxony
Ost Preußen	Russia
Osterreich	Austria
Pommern	Pomerania, Poland
Preußen	Prussia
Reuß	Thüringia
Rheinkreis Baiern	Bavaria
Rheinpfalz Baiern	Rhineland-Palatinate

Rußland	Russia
Sachsen	Saxony
Sachsen-Gotha	Thüringia
Sachsen-Weimar	Thüringia
Schwarzburg-Rudolstadt	Thüringia
Schwarzburg-Sondershausen	Thüringia
Schweiz	Switzerland
Silesien	Silesia, Poland
Thüringen	Thüringia
Ungarn	Hungary
VorPommern	Mecklenburg-Vorpommern
Waldeck	Hesse
West Preußen	Poland
Westphalen	Westphalia
Württemberg	Baden-Württemberg

Some typical examples of obituaries that were placed in this newspaper are given below as well as an approximate translation of the original text. Only the name of the deceased, maiden name if a married woman, the death date, the obituary date, place of death, and place of birth have been extracted and included in this index, but as these few examples show, there may be much more valuable information contained in the original texts.

The following are some typical examples of the death notices that are reported in various issues of the newspaper.

Example Obituary #1

Schönebaum – Henriette Schönebaum, nee Meierford, was born in Stemmen, Lippe-Detmold on 30, March 1833. In 1855 she married Ernst Schönebaum, who died suddenly 8 year ago. The Lord blessed this marriage with 4 children, of which 3 are alive and cared for their mother during her 8 month illness. Under the leadership of Brother M. Röder, both her and her husband joined the church, and found peace with God. She died on 29, November 1888 at the age of 55 years, 7 months, and 29 days of pneumonia.

Warrenton, MO   G. Enzeroth

Christliche Apologete 27, December, 1888 pg. 330

Schönebaum — Henriette Schöne=
baum, geb. Meierford, wurde geboren zu
Stemmen, Lippe=Detmold, den 30. März
1833. 1855 verehelichte sie sich mit Ernst
Schönebaum, der ihr vor 8 Jahren durch
einen schnellen Tod voranging. Der Herr
segnete diese Ehe mit 4 Kinder; 3 noch le=
bende Kinder pflegten die Mutter während
ihrem 8 Monate langem Leiden auf das
Zärtlichste. Unter der Amtsführung von
Br. M. Röder schloß sie sich mit ihrem
Gatten der Kirche an, und fanden bald
hernach Frieden mit Gott. Sie starb den
29. November 1888, im Alter von 55 J., 7
M. und 29 T. an der Wassersucht. Bereit
und fertig, ging sie im seligen Bewußtsein
heim zu Jesu.
     Warrenton, Mo.   G. Enzeroth.

Example Obituary #2

Pahl – Henry Pahl was born at Alt Waldmoden, Hannover on 7, February 1844, and died in peace with his heavenly father on the 19, January 1895. He came to this land as a 9 year old boy. He was the oldest of seven children in his family. Three are still living: August, William, and Christian Pahl, all living in St. Louis. As a 17 year old he lost his pious mother; soon after her death, he arose, searched, and found his salvation in the forgiveness of his sins, and remained true until he was called home. On 2, July 1865, he was married with Barbara Baumgarten, his now grieving wife. Four children were born to them, of which two died in childhood, and the others, Mrs. Emma Schlagenhauf and Harry Pahl, along with their mother are mourning their father's too early death. Brother Pahl was converted under the work of Brother Böshenz, in the church on the corner of 8th and Soulard Streets, remained a true and active member of the church, and served the last four years as a trustee. Our loss is his gain, he was ready.

St. Louis, MO, Memorial Parish   J. L. J. Barth

Christliche Apologete 21, February 1895 pg. 126

Pahl — Henry Pahl wurde geboren zu Alt Waldmoden, Hannover, den 7. Februar 1844, und starb im Frieden mit seinem himmlischen Vater am 19. Januar 1895. Schon als neunjähriger Knabe kam er in dieses Land. Von den sieben Geschwistern seiner Familie war er der Aelteste. Drei sind noch am Leben: August, William und Christian Pahl, alle wohnhaft in St. Louis. Als 17jähriger Jüngling verlor er seine fromme Mutter; bald nach ihrem Tode machte er sich auf, suchte und fand seinen Heiland in der Vergebung seiner Sünden, und blieb ihm treu, bis er ihn zu sich rief. Am 2. Juli 1865 verehelichte er sich mit Barbara Baumgarten, seiner nun trauernden Gattin. Es wurden ihnen vier Kinder geboren, wovon zwei in früher Kindheit starben, und die Andern, Frau Emma Schlagenhauf und Harry Pahl, mit der Mutter den allzufrühen Tod des Vaters beweinen. Br. Pahl war seit seiner Bekehrung unter der Arbeit von Br. Böshenz, in der Kirche an der Achten und Soulard Str., ein treues, zuverlässiges Glied der Kirche und diente derselben seit vielen Jahren als Beamter. Unser Verlust ist sein Gewinn, denn er war bereit.

St. Louis, Mo., Memorial Gemeinde.
J. L. J. Barth.

Example Obituary # 3

Death Reports

Blessed are they, who die in the Lord.

Memoir of Sister Rosine Schneider

Sister Rosine Schneider entered into the rest of God's people at the age of 76 years and 8 days. She was born on 17, August 1823 in Rümlingen, Kanton Baselland, Switzerland. In 1840 she entered into marriage with Ed. Schneider. In 1844 they emigrated to Texas, and four years later joined the German Episcopal Methodist Church. In 1849 Brother Schneider entered the ministry and was sent to Fredericksburg, (Texas). For many years Mrs. Schneider shared the joys and sorrows of a travelling minister. In the 80s Brother Schneider joined the list of retired ministers, and in 1890 preceded his wife in death. Sister Schneider survived her husband by almost nine years, and on 25, August 1899 followed him into eternal rest. At our last camp meeting in July she was still quite well, indeed she remarked, she must participate in this meeting, but it would be her last. And so it has become. On 26, August we laid her body in the bowels of the earth amidst a large gathering. She leaves behind eight children, 55 grandchildren, and 29 great-grandchildren, along with three sisters in Texas, as well as a brother and a sister living in Switzerland.

Perry, Texas   Th. Havekost

Der Christliche Apologete 28, September 1899 pg. 623

Todesberichte.

Selig sind, die in dem Herrn sterben.

Memoire von Schw. Rosine Schneider.

Schw. Rosine Schneider ging im Alter von 76 Jahren und acht Tagen zur Ruhe des Volkes Gottes ein. Sie wurde geboren am 17. August 1823 in Rümlingen, Kanton Baselland, Schweiz. In 1840 schloß sie den Ehebund mit Ed. Schneider. In 1844 wanderten sie aus nach Texas, und vier Jahre später schlossen sie sich der Deutschen Bisch. Methodistenkirche an. In 1849 trat Br. Schneider in das Predigtamt und wurde nach Fredricksburg gesandt. Manches Jahr teilte Schw. Schneider mit ihrem Gatten die Freuden und Leiden des Reisepredigtamts. In den 80er Jahren ließ Br. Schneider sich auf die Liste der alterschwachen Prediger setzen und ging in 1890 seiner Gattin im Tode voran. Schw. Schneider überlebte ihren Gatten noch beinahe neun Jahre, um dann am 25. August 1899 ihm in die ewige Ruhe zu folgen. Auf unserer letzten Lagerversammlung im Juli war sie noch recht wohl, doch meinte sie, sie müsse diese Lagerversammlung noch mitmachen, es möchte die letzte sein. Und so ist es geworden. Am 26. August betteten wir ihren Leib unter großer Beteiligung in den Schoß der Erde. Sie hinterläßt acht Kinder, 55 Enkel und 29 Urenkel, nebst diesen noch drei Schwestern in Texas, sowie einen Bruder und eine Schwester in der Schweiz.

Perry, Tex.   Th. Havekost.

Example Obituary # 4

Klebs – Brother Johann Christian Klebs was born on 22, April 1850 at Sydowswyse, Lebuser County, in the Province of Brandenburg, Prussia, and died in the hope of eternal life on 9, September 1884 in the town of Germania, Todd County, Minnesota. He was converted to God by the work of W. H. Träger in Clingo, Minnesota. He has been sick since last year, and endured difficult pain. He suffered in particular in his head and stomach. Since the past six months, he has been blind; indeed he carried his sufferings with patience and offered them up to God. He leaves behind his wife and four children, and other close relatives to mourn his too early death.

Wadena, Minn   L. J. Brenner

Der Christliche Apologete 29, September 1884
Page 7

Klebs—Br. Johann Christian Klebs wurde den 22. April 1850 zu Sydowswyse, Lebuser Kreis, Provinz Brandenburg, Preußen, geboren und starb in der Hoffnung des ewigen Lebens den 9. Sept. 1884 in Town Germania, Todd Co., Minn. Unter der Arbeit von W. H. Träger wurde er in Clingo, Minn., zu Gott bekehrt. Seit einem Jahre war er krank und hatte schwer und beständig zu leiden. Er litt besonders im Kopf und Magen. Seit einem halben Jahre war er auch blind; doch er trug sein Leiden mit vieler Geduld und war immer Gott ergeben, so lange er seinen Verstand hatte. Er hinterläßt seine Gattin und vier Kinder, nebst andern nahen Anverwandten, seinen frühen Tod zu betrauern.

Wadena, Minn.   L. J. Brenner.

Suggested further reading on the topic of the history of the German Methodist Church in America

----, Nast-Trinity United Methodist Church, The Mother of German Methodism – 150th Anniversary 1835 – 1985, ----, 1985

Dixon, Barbara, A Forgotten Heritage – The German Methodist Church, Little Miami Publishing Co., Milford, Ohio, 2011

Overton, Julie M., Ministers and Churches of the Central German Methodist Conference 1835 – 1907, Jennings & Graham, Cincinnati, OH 1975

Riemenschneider, Engelhardt, Engelhardt Riemenschneider – Memoirs of a German Methodist Pioneer, Translated by Edwin A. Riemenschneider and edited by Don Heinrich Tolzmann, Milford, Ohio, Little Miami Publishing Co., 2015

Wittke, Carl Frederick, William Nast, Patriarch of German Methodism, Wayne State University Press, Detroit, MI, 1959

All of these books are available at the Public Library of Cincinnati and Hamilton County in the Genealogy and Local History Department.

Christliche Apologete Death Notices --- 1839 - 1899

Name of Deceased	Notice Date	Death Date	Age	Page	Maiden Name	Place of Death	Place of Birth
Abbit, Louise	3, Mar. 1887	31, Jan.	22	142	Hugel	Boonville, IN	Warrick County, Indiana
Abe, Maria	22, Sept 1879	6, Sept	84	303		Allegheny City, PA	Mühledorf, Solothurn, Schweiz
Abegg, Anton	12, Mar. 1883	20, Feb.	73-11m	87		Lansing, IA	Canton Unterwalden, Schweiz
Abegg, Jakob	3, Aug. 1854	10, July	62	124		Blakesburg, IA	Kanton Zürich, Schweiz
Abel , Johan Gerhart	8, Dec. 1892	15, Nov.	82	782		St. Paul, MN	Oldenburg
Abel, Blondine	24, Aug. 1874	27, July	51	273	Stohmann	Quincy, IL	Helmstedt, Braunschweig
Abel, C.E.	12, June 1871	24, May	79- 5m-13d	191		Galena, IL	Oldenburg, Oldenburg
Abel, Christian	11, Dec. 1890	21, Nov.	78- 3m	798		Quincy, IL	OberEschbach, Hessen-Darmstadt
Abel, Elisabeth	13, Mar. 1862	16, Feb.	19	44	Wenzel	Quincy, IL	Quincy, Illinois
Abel, Heinrich	31, Mar. 1873	7, Mar.	32- 7m	103		Quincy, IL	Quincy, Illinois
Abel, Johann H.	14, July 1862	29, May	45	112		Lawrence, KS	Westerbeck, Hannover
Abel, Johanna Friederike D.	15, Dec. 1892	23, Nov.	33	798	Hoffmann	Quincy, IL	Roseville, Michigan
Abel, Jonas	24, Feb. 1873	30, Jan.	26	63		Quincy, IL	Quincy, Illinois
Abel, Rebecca	9, Apr. 1891		34- 4m-25d	238	Mayer	Marshall, IL	Marshall, Illinois
Abele, Carl	19, Apr. 1888	1, Apr.	63- 2m- 4d	254		Wheeling, WV	Rothwiel, Württemberg
Abele, Christine	1, Oct. 1891	2, Sept	58	638		Wheeling, WV	Kolmetsch, Sachsen-Weimar
Abele, Heinrich	10, Apr. 1876	25, Mar.	17	118		Saginaw, MI	
Abele, Maria Elisabeth	1, Sept 1892	31, July	56	558	Kirschner	New York City, NY	Dodenhausen, Kurhessen
Abelmann, Friedrke	18, Dec. 1882	30, Nov.	68- -27d	407		Chester, IL	Winslow, Hannover
Abendroth, M. Sophia Charlotte	18, Oct. 1880	30, Sept	40	335	Klanke	Schulenburg, TX	Lempferde, Hannover
Abers, Henry	11, Jan. 1894	24, Dec.	70	30		Smithton, MO	Hollendorf, Zeven, Hannover
Abicht, Johan Wilhelm	19, Mar. 1883	1, Mar.	75- 4m-11d	95		Marietta, OH	Erfurt, Preußen
Abilgaard, (Mrs)	25, July 1889	19, May	50	478		Cucamonga, CA	
Abitz, Wilhelmine	27, Oct. 1887	2, Oct.	32- 8m-24d	686	Schell	Swanton, NE	Drelitz, Pommern
Abplanalp, Andreas	25, Aug. 1892	28, July	99	542		Madison, IN	Brunin, Bern, Schweiz
Abplanalp, Anna	8, Feb. 1869	23, Jan.	25- 4m-17d	47		Batesville, IN	Ripley County, Indiana
Abplanalp, Melchior	15, Apr. 1872	7, Dec.	77-11m-15d	127		Jeffersonville, NY	Eblingen, Interlaken, Bern, Schweiz
Abplanalp, Peter	27, June 1864	2, June	53- 1m	104		Batesville, IN	Brienz, Interlaken, Bern, Schweiz
Abraham, Anna Catharina	1, June 1893	1, May	57	350	VonEssen	Jerusalem, NY	Vielstädt, Delmenhorst, Oldenburg
Abrahams, Dorothea Johanna Julia	13, Jan. 1887	23, Dec.	40	30	Wenken	Pekin, IL	Fürden, Ostfriesland
Abrahams, Dorothea Johanna Julia	27, Jan. 1887	23, Dec.	40	62	Weeken	Pekin, IL	Emden, Ostfriesland
Abrahams, Heinrich	25, Oct. 1844	13, Sept		164		New York, NY	Vadel, Oldenburg
Abt, Franz Joseph	21, Apr. 1884	2, Apr.	35	7		Ft. Dodge, IA	Ravensburg, Württemberg
Achenbach, (Mrs)	10, Jan. 1876		77- 2m	15		Forest Bay, WI	Niederdieten, Hessen-Darmstadt
Achenbach, Anna Elisabeth	17, Nov. 1887	9, Oct.	78	734		Charles City, IA	Niederdieten, Liedenkopf, Hessen
Achenbach, Bertha	14, Jan. 1886	22, Dec.	75	7	Hapes	Flood Creek, IA	Hebbron, Hemerten, Westphalen
Achenbach, Georg Heinrich	1, Feb. 1894	15, Jan.	22	78		Lebanon, MO	
Achenbach, Jost	27, Nov. 1865	1, Nov.	60	192		Fond du Lac, WI	Nieder-Dieten, Hessen-Darmstadt
Achenbach, Maria Elisabeth	15, Dec. 1887	19, Oct.	85-11m-10d	798	Achenbach	Forest, WI	Nieder-Dieten, Hessen
Achepohl, Wilhelm	27, Dec. 1894	2, Dec.	16	836		Quincy, IL	
Achilles, Katharina Dorothea	8, May 1890	8, Apr.	73	302	Behrens	Angelica, NY	Leiferde, Gifhorn, Hannover
Achilles, Sophia	2, Apr. 1891	11, Nov.	61	222	Laue	Wellsville, NY	Hannover
Acker, Johan Friedrich	27, Jan. 1879	28, Dec.	79	31		Louisville, KY	Edekosen, Rheinpfalz Baiern
Acker, Maria Magdalena	23, Apr. 1865	31, Mar.	63	68	Vogt	Louisville, KY	Böchingen, Edehofen, Rheinkreis Baiern
Acker, Mary D.	12, Nov. 1896	18, Oct.	68	734	Goßmann	Iowa City, IA	Almersbach, Württemberg
Ackeret, Jakob	22, Aug. 1861	23, July	37	136		Seymour, IN	Seuzach, Zürich, Schweiz

Christliche Apologete Death Notices --- 1839 - 1899

Name of Deceased	Notice Date	Death Date	Age	Page	Maiden Name	Place of Death	Place of Birth
Ackermann, Agnes	17, July 1876	30, June	72	231	Deiß	Buffalo, NY	Unterbrüden, Backnang, Württemberg
Ackermann, Anna	7, Jan. 1867	3, Dec.	28	6	Bohnenberger	Kendallville, IN	
Ackermann, Anna Christina	1, May 1876	12, Apr.	60	143	Gonnermann	Vermillion, OH	Berneburg, Rodenburg, Kurhessen
Ackermann, Barbara	19, July 1880	2, July		231	Siegel	Yankton, SD	Baiern
Ackermann, Christine	1, July 1867	16, June	29	206		Lancaster, NY	Lambsheim, Rheinkreis Baiern
Ackermann, Christoph	10, June 1867	27, May	69	182		Lancaster, NY	Unterbrüden, Backnang, Württemberg
Ackermann, Eduard	30, July 1883	5, July	23	247		Quincy, IL	Quincy, Illinois
Ackermann, Emma	26, June 1882	9, June	14	207		West Point, NE	
Ackermann, Engelhart	5, Mar. 1877	9, Feb.	74	79		Nobletown, IA	Hernefelde, Spangenberg, Kurhessen
Ackermann, Franz Salis	16, Mar. 1899	11, Jan.	75	175		White Creek, IN	Wolfwyl, Solothurn, Schweiz
Ackermann, Johan	2, Mar. 1899	12, Jan.	63	143		Kendallville, IN	Bartenbach, Göppingen, Württemberg
Ackermann, Johan Adam	20, Oct. 1873	15, Sept	67- 1m- 1d	335		Marion, OH	Oberbrüden, Backnang, Württemberg
Ackermann, John	5, Oct. 1899	17, Aug.	72	639		Petersburg, IL	Strockholt, Aurich, Ostfriesland
Ackermann, Louise	23, Oct. 1890	17, Sept	24- 4m- 2d	686	Christmann	New Metamoras, OH	
Ackert, Dorothea	30, Apr. 1896	9, Apr.	77	286	Woerley	Seymour, IN	
Ackert, Eduard	5, Feb. 1877	20, Jan.	32	47		Seymour, IN	
Ackert, Friederike	11, Aug. 1884	28, July	40	7		Brooklyn, NY	
Ackert, Maria	20, Dec. 1860	2, Dec.	9	204		Seymour, IN	
Ackmann, Henrietta Bertha	12, June 1882	10, May	45- 7m-11d	191	Marks	Smiths Creek, MO	
Adae, Christiane	10, Mar. 1884	5, Feb.	42- - 5d	7	Nuding	Marion, OH	Heutensbach, Backnang, Württemberg
Adam, (Mrs)	14, Dec. 1893	17, Nov.	81- 1m-16d	798		Lowell, WI	Oberhofen, Elsaß
Adam, Anna Maria	3, Aug. 1874	17, July	43- 2m-12d	247	Dörr	Charlestown, IN	Luttweiler, Rheinkreis Baiern
Adam, Catharina	17, Feb. 1873	31, Jan.	49- 9m-29d	53	Schäfer	Cincinnati, OH	Naunheim, Hessen-Darmstadt
Adam, Elisabeth	28, Mar. 1889	18, Feb.	78	206	Dauenhauer	New Haven, CT	Nothweiler, RheinPfalz Baiern
Adam, Ernst	30, Dec. 1897	9, Dec.	69	828		Kansas City, KS	Krenzendorf, Schlesien
Adam, G.	21, June 1875	28, May	66	199		Lowell, WI	Oberhoffen, Bischweiler, Elsaß
Adam, Heinrich	5, Feb. 1877	25, Dec.	51- 6m	47		Tea Creek, IN	Bettweiler, Rheinpfalz Baiern
Adam, Helena	21, June 1875	8, June	42	199		Cincinnati, OH	Borkum Island, Holland
Adam, Maria	8, Aug. 1870	20, July	20	255		Seymour, IN	Cincinnati, Hamilton County, Ohio
Adam, Maria	26, Jan. 1880	19, Jan.	39	31		Wyandotte, KS	St. Louis , Missouri
Adam, Wilhelm	1, Feb. 1894	18, Feb.	77	78		Baltimore, MD	Kirchhofbach, Bischhausen, Kurhessen
Adami, Adam	14, Jan. 1878	20, Dec.	53	15		Bradford, IN	Niederweisel, Friedberg, Hessen-Darmstadt
Adams, Emma L.	30, June 1892	28, Apr.	30	414	Kreinhop	Emporia, KS	Quincy, Illinois
Adams, Georg	18, Apr. 1895	1, Mar.		254		San Francisco, CA	Niederweisel, Hessen-Darmstadt
Adams, Heinrich Dietrich	2, Apr. 1891	12, Feb.	18- 3m- 5d	222		Nokomis, IL	Macoupin County, Illinois
Adams, Maria Katharina	13, Nov. 1876	26, Oct.	72	367	Krauß	Dayton, OH	Allendorf, Koblenz, Preußen
Adams, Minnie	24, May 1888	2, May	26- 3m- 5d	334	Heine	Freeport, IL	Freeport, Illinois
Adams, Sophia	3, Aug. 1899	17, July	44	495	Skär	Kansas City, MO	Merxheim a. d. Nahe, RheinPreußen
Adamy, Martin	2, Nov. 1863	10, Oct.	58	176		St. Louis, MO	Kemmenau, Nassau
Addicks, Lydia	13, Mar. 1890	24, Feb.	25	174	Baumgartner	Geneseo, IL	Geneseo, Illinois
Addicks, Maria	1, Aug. 1881	13, July	58- 6m -20d	247		Geneseo, IL	Linsburg, Amt Wolpe, Hannover
Addison, Joseph	11, Jan. 1839			8			
Aden, Gesche J.	8, Oct. 1883	31, Aug.	31- 6m-24d	327	Meiners	Osceola, NE	Amt Aurich, Ostfriesland
Aden, Habbo Lübben	21, Oct. 1897	2, Oct.	80	671		Duncan, NE	Holtrup, Aurich, Ostfriesland
Aden, Hiskea	17, May 1894	18, Apr.	43	326		Osceola, NE	Flachsmeer, Ostfriesland
Aden, John	25, Apr. 1889	29, Mar.	46	270		Osceola, NE	Ostfriesland

Christliche Apologete Death Notices --- 1839 - 1899

Name of Deceased	Notice Date	Death Date	Age	Page	Maiden Name	Place of Death	Place of Birth
Aden, Töpke Janzen	10, Oct. 1895	24, Sept	72	654	Frerichs	Duncan, NE	Holtrup, Aurich, Ostfriesland
Adler, Christian Friedrich	14, July 1898	15, June	68	447		Lemars, IA	Besigheim, Württemberg
Adler, Eduard Ludwig	6, Dec. 1880	20, Nov.	9	391		Lemars, IA	
Adler, Elisabeth Margaretha	18, Nov. 1872	19, Oct.	59	375		Toledo, OH	Weißenburg, Altdorf, Baiern
Adler, Ernst	27, Nov. 1876	8, Nov.	59	383		Brooklyn, NY	Markowitz, Preußen
Adler, Johan Gottlieb	6, Dec. 1880	22, Nov.	7	391		Lemars, IA	
Adler, R.	14, June 1888	21, May	69	382	Stoffel	Ft. Scott, KS	Reininghausen bei Köln, Preußen
Adlof, Frieda	2, Sept 1897	3, Aug.	14	559		Lexington, TX	
Adolf, Anna Barbara	3, Sept 1883	12, Aug.	53	287	Brunner	Oregon, MO	Augen, Mühlheim, Baden
Adolph, Agnes Maria	19, Apr. 1875	1, Apr.	38- 9m-11d	127	Gruensfelder	San Jose, IL	Reilingen, Schwetzingen, Baden
Adolph, Jakob	8, July 1852	6, June	30	112		Pekin, IL	Baden
Adres, Johan Adam	20, Jan. 1868	24, Dec.	27	22		New Bremen, IL	Königswald, Kurhessen
Adrion, Christine	13, Aug. 1891	27, July	59- 2m- 4d	526		Akron, OH	Betzweiler, Berndorf, Württemberg
Aebi, Friedrich	25, Jan. 1894	29, Dec.	52	62		Lyona, KS	Walkringen, Heimiswyl, Bern, Schweiz
Aeft, F.	21, Sept 1885	5, Sept	67	7		Rose Hill, TX	Kaßdorf, Frostfelden, Braunschweig
Aendes, Jakob	2, Feb. 1888		54	78		Boonville, IN	Heimbach, Trier, Preußen
Aepperle, Michael	26, Mar. 1866	24, Feb.	62	102		Platteville, WI	Streich, Schorndorf, Württemberg
Aerchbach, Elisabeth	4, Mar.1872	17, Jan.	52	79		New York City, NY	Kanton Baselland, Schweiz
Affeld, Richard	19, Aug. 1878	28, June	30	263		Holden, MO	Deutschkrone, West Preußen
Afflerbach, Dorothea	15, Mar. 1875	14, Feb.	43	87	Hahnecke	Brenham, TX	Großbrensen, Preußen
Afflerbach, Elias	4, Sept 1876	25, June	62	287		Fayette Co., PA	Berghausen bei Berleburg, Preußen
Afholder,	8, Apr. 1858	16, Mar.	77	56		Newark, OH	Kopingen, Bern, Schweiz
Aflerbach, Heinrich	15, Nov. 1880		22-11m- 6d	367		Brenham, TX	Austin County, Texas
Afterhaide, Laura Auguste	25, Nov. 1886	5, Nov.	25- 1m- 9d	7	Delbrüge	Boody, IL	
Ahlbrand, Maria Elisabeth	4, Sept 1865	9, Aug.	74	144		Seymour, IN	Hurdelbrink, Osterkappeln, Osnabrück, Hannover
Ahlbrecht, Augustus	7, Dec. 1893	19, Nov.	83	782		Iowa City, IA	Aalfeld, Hannover
Ahlers, (Mr)	6, July 1868	17, June	64- 8m-29d	215		Red Wing, MN	Thätro, Mecklenburg-Schwerin
Ahlers, Anna Margaretha	24, Mar. 1892	29, Feb.	89	190		St. Paul, MN	Hamberg, Kurhessen
Ahlers, Elisabeth	18, Aug. 1898	6, July	75	527	Rüther	Rushville, NE	
Ahlers, Louisa	21, May 1857	23, Apr.	45	84		Red Wing, MN	Meienburg, Potsdam, Preußen
Ahlers, Wilhelm	14, Dec. 1893	28, Nov.	78	798		Rushville, NE	Uepsen zu Asendorf, Altenhausen, Germany
Ahlers, Wilhelm Ludwig	27, July 1863	4, June	19	120		Dayton, OH	
Ahnemann, Maria	13, Sept 1894	31, July	64	598	Steinheim	Cincinnati, OH	Entinghausen, Braunschweig
Ahrend, Johann Wilhelm	17, Nov. 1853	21, Aug.	35	184		Clayton County, MO	Bomde, Amt Wiedlage, Hannover
Ahrendt, Margaretha	21, Apr. 1873		23	127	Buerz	Beaver Falls, MN	Buffalo, New York
Ahrens, (child)	26, July 1860	11, June	5	120		Pittsfield, IL	
Ahrens, Anna	3, Apr. 1865	2, Feb.		56	Held	Dunkirk, NY	Oberbalzheim, Laubheim, Württemberg
Ahrens, Anna Elisabeth	2, Dec. 1897	10, Nov.	67- 7m- 4d	767	Faupel	Lakeside, OH	Hessen
Ahrens, Casten	28, May 1883	2, May	78	175		Sandusky, OH	Kuhstedt, Beverstedt, Hannover
Ahrens, Catharina	17, Mar 1873	4, Mar.	40	87	Vesper	Quincy, IL	Münden, Waldeck
Ahrens, Christian	24, Aug. 1893	10, June	77	542		Hay Creek, MN	Bazlow, Preußen
Ahrens, Gesche	4, Mar. 1878	9, Feb.	61	71		New York City, NY	Benken, Hannover
Ahrens, Heinrich	3, Mar. 1879	13, Jan.	57	71		Attica, IN	Bergstadt, Hannover
Ahrens, Heinrich Wilhelm	10, July 1865	17, Mar.	16- 8m	112		Warsaw, IL	
Ahrens, Henry J.	9, Feb. 1893	5, Jan.	77	94		Mt. Hope, KS	Germany
Ahrens, Johan	8, May 1876	2, Apr.	54- 8m- 3d	151		Dunkirk, NY	Marin, Mecklenburg-Schwerin

Christliche Apologete Death Notices --- 1839 - 1899

Name of Deceased	Notice Date	Death Date	Age	Maiden Name	Page	Place of Death	Place of Birth
Ahrens, Karl Heinrich	24, Aug. 1874	29, July	63-10m- 9d		273	New York City, NY	Rautendorf, Amt Ottersberg, Hannover
Ahrens, Mathilde	14, Jan. 1892	18, Dec.	68	Drake	30	Indianapolis, IN	Minden, Preußen
Ahrens, Wilhelm	22, Dec. 1873	15, Oct.	23		407	Decatur, IL	Beardstown, Illinois
Ahrensfeld, Anna Rosa	8, Jan. 1891	16, Dec.	22		30	Arlington Heights, IL	
Ahrensfeld, Christoph	17, Apr. 1882	17, Mar.	56		127	Evanston, IL	Bramstedt, Amt Hagen, Hannover
Ahrensfeld, Heinrich	23, Dec. 1897	5, Dec.	61		815	Chicago, IL	Dresede bei Bremerhafen, Germany
Ahms, Adolph Johan	4, Jan. 1875	17, Dec.	17-10m-24d		7	Sandusky, OH	Ottawa County, Ohio
Ahmy, Salomon	17, Dec. 1877	1, Nov.	25		407	Lancaster, MO	Canton Solothurn, Schweiz
Aicher, Rumuald	5, June 1882	23, Apr.	57- 2m-10d		183	Flint Creek, IA	Waldstetten, Spaichingen, Württemberg
Aigeltinger, Leopold	4, Nov. 1886	7, June	61		7	San Francisco, CA	Württemberg
Aigner, Matheis	11, May 1899	15, Apr.	71		302	Delaware, OH	Illingen, Maulbronn, Württemberg
Aker, Marie	11, Sept 1882	11, July	64	Größinger	295	Schnectady, NY	Rottenaker, Ehningen, Württemberg
Akermann, (Mr)	6, Aug. 1883	19, July	41- 6m-14d		255	Lewis, IA	Landefeld, Kurhessen
Alber, Anna Maria	20, June 1895	19, May	25		398	Sharon, MI	Silwen, Michigan
Alber, Eva Katharina	16, June 1879	11, May	81	Weiderich	191	Franciscoville, MI	Fünfbronn, Württemberg
Albers, Anna	3, Dec. 1896	27, Oct.	90		782	Moweaqua, IL	Wißt, Zevsu, Hannover
Albers, Anna C.	21, Feb. 1870	3, Feb.	61- 2m-20d	Reineberg	63	Batesville, IN	Kleinen Kneten, Wildeshausen, Oldenburg
Albers, C. Henry	14, June 1888	22, May	52		382	Junction City, KS	
Albers, Gretje	14, Feb. 1895	10, Jan.	58	Jansen	110	Emden, IL	Nord-Dumum, Esens, Ostfriesland
Albers, Heinrich	16, Feb. 1885	30, Jan.	50		7	Boody, IL	Westedt, Hannover
Albers, Magdalena	18, July 1864	26, June	38	Beckmann	116	Pekin, IL	Mordorf, Amt Aurich, Hannover
Albers, Mary	7, Jan. 1878	15, Dec.	33- 9m- 9d	Müller	7	Junction City, KS	
Albers, Rebekka	30, July 1896	9, July	79	Knoop	495	Warsaw, IL	Oldendorf, Hannover
Alberswerth, Friederika	17, Aug. 1863	14, July	21	Fleer	132	Herman, MO	Laa bei Herfort, Preußen
Alberswerth, Jürgen Heinrich	26, May 1873	2, May	76- 7m-18d		167	Herman, MO	
Alberswerth, Margaretha Elisabetha	18, Jan. 1869	6, Jan.	71- 2m- 2d		23	Herman, MO	Osnabrück, Hannover
Albert, Anna Maria	13, Jan. 1898	20, Dec.	34	Gehner	31	Chester, IL	New Palestine, Randolph County, Illinois
Albert, Anna Maria Elisabeth	2, Sept 1886	15, Aug.	20	Severling	7	Wilber, NE	Nebraska City, Nebraska
Albert, Johan David	30, July 1891	6, July	77- 8m-24d		494	Wilber, NE	Wester, Oldendorf bei Melle, Hannover
Albert, Jürgen	24, Oct. 1895	22, Sept	78		686	Chester, IL	Petersdorf, Insel Fehmar, Holstein
Albert, Katharine Gertrud	24, Feb. 1887	5, Feb.	75- 5m	Kienker	126	Clatonia, NE	Westeroldendorf, Hannover
Albert, Louis	25, Apr. 1870	30, Mar.	19- 9m- 9d		135	Randolph County, Illinois	Randolph County, Illinois
Albert, Louise Friederike	2, Jan. 1896	27, Nov.	77	Petersen	14	Chester, IL	Petersdorf, Insel Fehmar, Germany
Albert, Wilhelm	22, June 1899	2, June	37		399	Chester, IL	Sternberg, Randolph County, Illinois
Alberts, Albert	24, Mar. 1879	8, Mar.	72		95	Emden, IL	Barkhold, Essens, Ostfriesland
Alberts, Emma Sophia	1, Jan. 1891	28, Nov.	46	Gode	14	Wilber, NE	Hambergen bei Bremen, Germany
Alberts, Jatje R.	28, June 1880	24, May	35- 2m	Rieken	207	Emden, IL	Groot Husen, Emden, Ostfriesland
Alberts, Petrus Johannes	5, Apr. 1880	12, Mar.	36		111	Emden, IL	Loquard, Amt Emden, Ostfriesland
Albertsen, John H.	16, Mar. 1874	19, Feb.	53		87	Pekin, IL	Rysum, Ostfriesland
Alberwerth, Friedrich	28, Apr. 1859	9, Apr.	36		68	Herman, MO	Dissen, Amt Osnabrück, Hannover
Albietz, Pauline	5, Aug. 1897		37- 2m-12d		495	Cleveland, OH	Oberhausen, Reublingen, Württemberg
Albrecht, Anna Franziska	25, June 1896	9, June	34		415	Indianapolis, IN	Indianapolis, Marion County, Indiana
Albrecht, Anna Sophia Carolina	27, July 1868	8, July	36	Seekamp	239	Indianapolis, IN	Emsten, Aachen, Hannover
Albrecht, August Friedrich	25, Feb. 1892	27, Jan.	72		126	Spencerville, OH	Heutlingsheim, Ludwigsburg, Württemberg
Albrecht, Barbara	31, Oct. 1889	28, Sept	81	Klöpfel	702	Iowa City, IA	Breitenbach a. d. Fulda, Kurhessen
Albrecht, Catharina	15, May 1871	6, Jan.	21- 8m- 9d		159	Eudora, KS	Columbus, Ohio

Christliche Apologete Death Notices --- 1839 - 1899

Name of Deceased	Notice Date	Death Date	Age	Page	Maiden Name	Place of Death	Place of Birth
Albrecht, Dina Hulda	12, May 1892	19, Apr.	33	302	Parten	Indianapolis, IN	Indianapolis, Marion County, Indiana
Albrecht, Elisabeth	1, Nov. 1880	17, Oct.	35	351		Peoria, IL	RheinPreußen
Albrecht, Friedrich	25, Aug. 1898	22, July	85	543		Tainter, WI	Hansfelde, Stettin, Pommern
Albrecht, Gustav	25, Apr. 1895	10, Mar.	38	270		Wausau, WI	Bromberg, West Preußen
Albrecht, Heinrich	5, Mar. 1883	16, Feb.	77	79		Iowa City, IA	Alfeld, Hannover
Albrecht, Ida	7, Feb. 1895	14, Jan.	26	94	Kißner	Morgan, MN	Sleepy Eye , Minnesota
Albrecht, Johan	25, Mar. 1897		79-10m-15d	190		Des Moines, IA	Halle, Sachsen
Albrecht, Johann	15, Feb. 1864	12, Jan.	59	28		Cincinnati, OH	Feelbow, Kreis Mechlenburg, Preußen
Albrecht, Johanna	29, Jan. 1877	20, Dec.	46- 6m	39		Sherrills Mount, IA	Hoheneggelsen, Hannover
Albrecht, Johanna Caroline	3, Mar. 1892	11, Feb.	77	142	Haack	Des Moines, IA	Fichtenwerther, Brandenburg
Albrecht, Louise	18, Feb. 1897	1, Feb.	44	111	Beh	Cincinnati, OH	Cincinnati, Hamilton County, Ohio
Albrecht, Louise	13, Dec. 1880	12, Nov.	53-11m-25d	399		Menomonie, WI	Hansfelde, Stettin, Pommern
Albrecht, Maria	19, June 1865	12, May	72	100	Weber	Delaware, OH	Oberdorf, Basel, Schweiz
Albrecht, Michael	14, Sept 1893	18, Aug.	77	590		Spring Lake, WI	Hofenstein, Stolp, Pommern
Albrecht, Michael	8, June 1893	1, Apr.	28	366		Aurora, IL	Kuchen, Württemberg
Albrecht, Peter	12, Mar. 1857	18, Nov.		44		Auburn, OH	Cumberland County, Pennsylvania
Albrecht, Sophia	25, Jan. 1869	4, Jan.	62	31	Schultz	Cincinnati, OH	Tützpatz, Kreis Demmin, Preußen
Albrecht, Wilhelm Friedrich	5, Aug. 1897	12, July	20	495		Mankato, MN	Winnebago, Faribault County, Minnesota
Albrecht, Wilhelmine	10, Feb. 1898	15, Jan.	40	94	Krauße	Newton, KS	Lakendorf, West Preußen
Alef, Katharina	20, Oct. 1887	12, Sept	47- 6m- 3d	670		Great Bend, KS	Köln, Preußen
Alefs, John	23, Feb. 1888	31, Jan.	34	126		Great Bend, KS	Roseville, Michigan
Alefs, Louise D.	29, Jan. 1883	14, Dec.	41	39	Dendel	Great Bend, KS	Kleinsteinbach, Durlach, Baden
Alion, Caroline	21, June 1880	30, May	77	199	Bäcker	Salem, ---	Geisingen, Württemberg
Allbrecht, Gottlieb Friedrich	3, Aug. 1868	12, July	74	247		Delaware, OH	Dietenhausen, Pforzheim, Baden
Allean, Elisabeth	17, Nov. 1879	3, Nov.	73	367	Sähmann	Henderson, KY	Württemberg
Allen, Maria Christina	13, Feb. 1896	21, Jan.	72	110	Schultz	Kendallville, IN	Falkenberg, Preußen
Allendorf, Johan Friedrich	7, Feb. 1895	16, Jan.	44	94		Bloomington, IL	Hochelheim, Preußen
Allendörfer, Katharina	3, Mar. 1879	28, Jan.	35	71	Althen	Town Falls, IA	
Allerdorf, Carl	4, Jan. 1864	16, Dec.	83	4		Milan, IN	
Allers, Anna	8, Apr. 1886	21, Jan.	46	7		Marietta, OH	Obensen, Gilden, Hannover
Allers, Johann	5, Dec. 1850	13, Aug.	71	196		Marietta, OH	Abbensenn, Hannover
Allers, Philipp	8, June 1863	9, May	81	92		New York, NY	Muschenheim, Hessen-Darmstadt
Allersmeier, Ludwig	25, Jan. 1894	23, Dec.	16	62		Dallas, TX	Faldorf, Vlotho, Herfurt, Preußen
Allersmeier, Wilhelmina	29, May 1876	22, Apr.	21	175		New Haven, MO	Warren County, Missouri
Allert, Carolina	22, Apr. 1867	31, Mar.		126	Borcharding	Sherrills Mount, IA	Jackson County, Indiana
Allert, Elisabeth	13, Jan. 1879	19, Dec.		15		Sherrills Mount, IA	Lippe-Detmold
Allert, Emil Theodor	26, Sept 1889	25, Aug.	6m- 4d	619		Sherrills Mount, IA	Bega, Amt Allverdissen, Lippe-Detmold
Allert, Heinrich August	30, Oct. 1871	8, Oct.	30- 7m-19d	351		Robinson, KS	Robinson, Kansas
Alley, Christina	17, Nov. 1884	8, Aug.	23	7	Weil	Santa Claus, IN	Lauffen am Neckar, Besigheim, Württemberg
Allinger, Catharina Elisabeth	25, July 1881	10, July	60	239	Schaaf	Cannelton, IN	
Allinger, Georg Leonhart	28, Sept 1874	25, Aug.	7	311		Santa Claus, IN	Lauffen a. Neckar, Besigheim, Württemberg
Allinger, Heinrich	28, July 1873	5, July	63- 4m-28d	239		Santa Claus, IN	Marietta, Ohio
Allis, Heinrich	21, Jan. 1886	6, Jan.	44	7		Marietta, OH	
Allison, Emilie Fr.	13, Jan. 1887	27, Dec.	23	30	Hosp	Boonville, MO	
Almendinger, Anna Maria	1, Oct. 1877	17, Sept	79- - 5d	319		Cleveland, OH	Heiningen, Göppingen, Württemberg
Almendinger, David	18, Mar. 1886	3, Feb.	77	7		Marion, OH	Horrheim, Vaihingen, Württemberg

Christliche Apologete Death Notices -- 1839 - 1899

Name of Deceased	Notice Date	Death Date	Age	Maiden Name	Page	Place of Death	Place of Birth
Allmendinger, Elias	24, Feb. 1868	24, Jan.	36		63	Cleveland, OH	Heiningen, Göppingen, Württemberg
Allmendinger, Elisabeth	20, Nov. 1865	3, Sept	56		188	Bethlehem, OH	Hefnerhaßlich, Württemberg
Allmendinger, Elisabeth Katharina	24, Jan. 1871	8, Sept	80	Fritz	31	Ann Arbor, MI	Lindorf, Kirchheim u. T., Württemberg
Allmendinger, Elisabeth M.	6, Nov. 1890	18, Oct.	70-9m-30d		718	Marion, OH	Horheim, Vaihingen, Württemberg
Allmendinger, Gottlieb	2, Apr. 1891	15, Mar.	82		222	Marion, OH	Horheim, Württemberg
Allmendinger, Jakob	25, June 1883	31, May	65-7m-21d		207	Marion, OH	Horheim, Vaihingen an der Enz, Württemberg
Allmendinger, Louisa	22, Dec. 1887	3, Dec.	70-10m-26d	Bensler	814	Marion, OH	Horheim an der Enz, Vaihingen, Württemberg
Allmendinger, Louise	10, June 1886	14, Apr.	26	Hoch	7	Marion, OH	Marion County, Ohio
Allmendinger, Maria E.	27, Nov. 1890	5, Nov.	28		766	Berea, OH	Wellsville, Ohio
Allmendinger, Philipp	18, Nov. 1878	8, Nov.	31-6m-29d		367	Marion, OH	Marion County, Ohio
Allmendinger, Sophie	27, July 1885	1, July	18-9m-20d	Romoser	7	Marion, OH	
Allmendinger, William P.	18, Nov. 1886	8, Sept	26		7	Cleveland, OH	Wellsville, Columbiana County, Ohio
Almendinger, Anton	14, Apr. 1892		29		238	Marion, OH	Pleasant Twp., Marion County, Ohio
Almendinger, Bartholomäus	4, Oct. 1855	16, Sept	61- 7m		160	Rockport, OH	Denna, Göppingen, Württemberg
Alnor, Nicolai Heinrich	3, Dec. 1896	4, Nov.	64		782	New York City, NY	Eckensund, Schleswig-Holstein
Alomang, Rebekka	10, Apr. 1856	23, Dec.	39		60	Auburn, IN	
Alt , Wilhelmine	22, June 1899	25, May	69	Schmit	399	Grand Island, NY	Rüdigheim, Hanau, Germany
Alt, Heinrich	17, Apr. 1890	13, Mar.	54- 5m-17d		254	St. Louis, MO	Wetzlosgehag, Lauterbach, Hessen
Alt, John	29, Aug. 1881	10, Aug.	65- 1m- 7d		279	Carrollton, MO	Busenborn, Nidda, Hessen-Darmstadt
Alt, Karl	21, Feb. 1870	11, Dec.	18- 1m-19d		63	Warrenton, MO	
Alt, Katharina	4, Apr. 1889	21, Feb.	63	Wagner	222	Bogard, MO	Harreshausen, Offenbach, Hessen-Darmstadt
Alt, Sophie	5, June 1865	22, May	13- 8m-19d		92	Manchester, MO	
Altenbernd, David	18, June 1896	24, May	37		399	Lena, IL	Lena, Illinois
Altenbernd, Edward	22, Sept 1887	4, Sept	32		606	Lena, IL	Lena , Illinois
Altenburg, Emma	1, Apr. 1872	11, Mar.	21		111	Galena, IL	Bibra bei Naumberg, Merseburg, Preußen
Altenburg, Heinrich	23, Feb. 1885	6, Feb.	26		7	Allegheny City, PA	Pittsburg, Pennsylvania
Altenburg, Johannetta	29, Dec. 1873	10, Nov.	48- 8m-10d	Hahn	415	Allegheny City, PA	Eisenach, Sachsen-Weimar
Altenburg, John	29, Mar. 1888	13, Mar.	31		206	Milwaukee, WI	Pittsburg, Pennsylvania
Altenburg, Maria Rosina	13, Aug. 1896	24, July	86	Kulbe	527	Galena, Il	Gatterstadt, Merseburg, Preußen
Altenburg, Katharina	24, Aug. 1899	5, Aug.	37		543	Alton, IL	Basdorf, Wöhl, Hessen
Altesellemeier, Anna Catharina	12, Feb. 1877	21, Dec.	75	Steinhage	55	Ft. Wayne, IN	Linnen, Tecklenburg, Münster, Preußen
Attesellmeyer, Heinrich Jakob	6, Sept 1844		Inquiry		136		Lienen, Tecklenburg, Preußen
Athart, Georg	11, Mar.1872	22, Feb.	45		87	Pittsburg, PA	Dorheim, Fritzlar, Jeßberg, Hessen-Kassel
Althoff, Henriette L.	25, June 1883	7, June	63- 4m	Karel	207	Yellow Creek, IL	Jemgum, Ostfriesland
Althoff, Ude	29, Apr. 1878	1, Apr.	55- -13d		135	Yellow Creek, IL	Hotland, Stickhausen,
Altmann, Auguste	13, Sept 1869	26, Aug.	37		295	New York, NY	
Altmann, Johan B.	26, Jan. 1899	22, Dec.	83		62	West Unity, OH	Columbiana County, Ohio
Alton, Anna Johanna	17, Dec. 1877	20, Nov.	21- 5m-10d	Drächsel	407	Junction City, MO	
Altörfer, Jacob	11, Apr. 1870	25, Mar.	87- 3m-15d		119	Washington, MN	Kanton Zürich, Schweiz
Altörfer, Ottilie Friederika Johanna	13, June 1889	25, May	53-10m-27d	Retzlaff	382	Houston, TX	West Preußen
Altroge, Maria Louise	12, Sept 1889	16, Aug.	61	Hamann	590	Watertown, WI	Sonnenborn, Alverdissen, Lippe-Detmold
Altrogge, Friedrich	1, Sept 1879	4, Aug.	24		279	Watertown, WI	Salem,
Altrogge, H.	14, Oct. 1878	17, Sept	25		327	Watertown, WI	Salem, Wisconsin
Altrogge, Heinrich	31, May 1894	10, May	69-11m- 6d		358	Watertown, WI	Bega, Lippe-Detmold
Altrogge, Konrad	19, Jan. 1899	4, Dec.	77		47	Warren, MO	Schnorbeck, Nalhof, Germany
Altrup, (Mr)	22, Aug. 1881	1, Aug.	70		271	Warren, MO	

Christliche Apologete Death Notices --- 1839 - 1899

Name of Deceased	Notice Date	Death Date	Age	Page	Maiden Name	Place of Death	Place of Birth
Altrup, (Mrs)	2, Mar. 1863	26, Jan.	63	36		Warrenton, MO	Line, Preußen
Altrup, Katharina	4, Apr. 1889	27, Feb.	75	222		Edwardsville, IL	Lienen, Tecklenburg, Preußen
Altschwager, Andreas	21, Apr. 1873	2, Apr.	91	127		Columbus, WI	Nantrow, Neubuckow, Mecklenburg-Schwerin
Altschwager, Edwin	1, June 1893	6, May	20	350		Columbus, WI	York, Dane County, Wisconsin
Altschwager, Friedrich	21, Sept 1899	4, Sept	72	607		Columbus, WI	Nandrow, Mecklenburg-Schwerin
Altsellemeier, Friederike	2, June 1887	29, Apr.	53	350		Bunker Hill, IL	Lienen, Tecklenburg, Westphalen
Atttrug, Margaretha Charl.	21, July 1848		Inquiry	119		Marthasville, MO	
Altvatter, Susanna Elisabeth	20, Mar. 1865	8, Nov.	80	48		Callicoon, NY	Lindheim, Hessen
Alves, Heinrich	21, June 1888	23, May	80	398		Kenosha, WI	Hannover
Alves, Marie	8, Apr. 1897	21, Mar.	83- 7m-20d	222	Kinni	Kenosha, WI	Graubünden, Schweiz
Alwes, Heinrich	22, Mar. 1888	24, Feb.	63- 7m- 8d	190		Seymour, IN	Wilfel, Hannover
Ambacher, Sophia Friederike	5, July 1894	7, June	63	438	Bezner	New York City, NY	Kehbinn, Brackenheim, Württemberg
Ambel, (Mrs)	5, Apr. 1880	16, Mar.	75- 4m-23d	111	Trautmann	Pittsburg, PA	Bärenthal, Lothringen
Amborn, Louis	3, Nov. 1898	4, Oct.	17	703		Morris, MN	Wabasha County, Minnesota
Amborn, Susanna Margaretha	21, July 1887	29, June	73- 1m-11d	462		Zumbro Falls, MN	Kurhessen
Amende, Therese	29, Mar. 1888	3, Feb.	19	206		Lake Creek, MO	
Amendt, Carl	5, Mar. 1896	13, Feb.	54- 7m	158		Scranton, PA	Obernbül, Coblenz, RheinPreußen
Amerine, Anna Maria	11, July 1881	20, June	80- 1m-26d	223		Davenport, IA	Erksdorf, Kurhessen
Ammann, Elisabeth	16, Mar. 1893	22, Feb.	67	174		Decatur, IL	Bernold, Aargau, Schweiz
Ammos, Maria Dorothea	2, Sept 1867	21, Aug.	48	278	Peyer	Columbus, OH	
Anacker, Friedrich	5, Nov. 1891	19, Sept	27	718	Jennewein	Brooklyn, NY	Herrenbreitungen, Schmalkalden, Germany
Ande, Catharine	23, Jan. 1875	25, Dec.	55	31		Elizabeth, NJ	Röthenau, Frankenberg, Kurhessen
Ander, Maria	10, May 1888	21, Mar.	69- 7m-19d	302	Schwarz	Brooklyn, NY	Kirchharth, Baden
Anderegg, Anna Barbara	30, Aug. 1869	11, Aug.	78	279	Born	Columbus, OH	Nieder-Bipp, Wangen, Bern, Schweiz
Andermann, G.	30, Nov. 1893	28, Oct.	65	766	Schmit	Palatine, IL	Hannover
Anders, Albert	19, Mar. 1866	17, Feb.	36	94		Golconda, IL	
Anders, Elisabeth Sophia	19, Mar. 1877	3, Mar.	61	95	Lehmann	Summerfield, IL	Stargard, Mecklenburg-Schwerin
Anders, Eva Elisabeth	20, June 1881	10, June	80- 9m-12d	199		Marietta, OH	Seeheim, Hessen-Darmstadt
Anders, Friedrich	27, July 1885	3, July	73	7		Jordan, MN	Heminghausen, Westphalen
Anderson, Jacob	14, Nov. 1895	11, Sept	81	734		Lawrenceburg, IN	Amsterdam, Holland
Anderson, Jacob	7, Nov. 1895	11, Sept	81	718		Lawrenceburg, IN	Amsterdam, Holland
Anderson, Pauline	13, Mar. 1890	23, Feb.	32	174		Newport, KY	
Andert, Helene	27, Jan. 1898	6, Jan.	73	63		Morris, MN	Mecklenburg-Schwerin
Andre, Christine	31, Jan. 1881	17, Jan.	46- 8m	39	Scheurer	Burlington, IA	Albany, New York
Andreas, Georg	27, June 1870		76-10m-26d	207		Mascoutah, IL	Weingarten, Rheinkreis Baiern
Andree, Elisabeth	2, June 1892	11, Apr.	45- -23d	350	Mahler	Marietta, OH	Preston, Ontario, Canada
Andree, Johan Gottlob	13, Sept 1894	19, Aug.	76- 1m-20d	598		Los Angeles, CA	Berlinchen, Preußen
Andree, Wilhelm	12, Oct. 1899	22, Sept	27	655		Los Angeles, CA	Perris, Canada
Andres, Anna Maria	19, Apr. 1894	29, Mar.	86	262	Bettenhausen	Tinley Park, IL	Königswald, Kurhessen
Andres, Chr. Friedrich Th.	28, Apr. 1879	12, Apr.	61-4m- 4d	135		Milan, IN	Groß Wehnendorf, Güstrow, Mecklenburg
Andres, Conrad	19, Aug. 1897	28, July	64	527		Tinley Park, IL	Königswald, Kurhessen
Andres, Elisabeth	23, June 1887	2, June	49	398	Stephan	New Bremen, IL	Rautenhausen, Kurhessen
Andres, Francisca	29, May 1882	14, May		175	Saumweber	Philadelphia, PA	Fellheim, Baiern
Andres, Grethge Maria	15, Apr. 1897	23, Mar.	61	238	Gerdes	Beman, KS	Wittmont, Germany
Andres, Johan Ludwig	28, July 1879	28, June		239		Lansing, IA	Dölzig, Brandenburg, Preußen
Andres, Johann Georg	13, July 1863	5, June	25	112		Bremen, IL	Königswald, Kurhessen

Christliche Apologete Death Notices --- 1839 - 1899

Name of Deceased	Notice Date	Death Date	Age	Page	Maiden Name	Place of Death	Place of Birth
Andres, John	6, June 1870	16, May	20- 7m- 9d	183		Bremen, IL	Königswald, Kurhessen
Andres, Maria	22, Nov. 1875	5, Nov.	34	375	Grünsfelder	San Jose, IL	Reilingen, Schwetzingen, Baden
Andres, Maria	9, May 1870	22, Apr.	1- -17d	151		Bremen, IL	
Andres, Mathilde	30, Sept 1886	15, Sept	51	7	Lehr	Rock Island, IL	Stürsdorf, Schleswig-Holstein
Andres, Meinrad	18, May 1893	29, Apr.	64	318		Philadelphia, PA	Zähringen, Baden
Andres, Paulus	17, Apr. 1882	30, Mar.	71-11m-15d	127		Bremen, IL	
Andres, S.M.	29, Jan. 1857	31, Dec.	34	20	Häring	Mascoutah, IL	Haßloch bei Neustadt, Germany
Andres, Samuel	26, Nov. 1891	6, Nov.	19	766		Enterprise, KS	Champaign City, Champaign County, Illinois
Angenthaler, Juliane	14, June 1880	1, June	56-10m-12d	191		Brooklyn, NY	Rothenburg, Kurhessen
Ankerholz, Wilhelmina Carolina F.	3, Sept 1891	9, Aug.	40	574	Borgwart	Huntsville, KS	Lassentin, Pommern
Anliker, Elisabeth	14, Feb. 1895	28, Jan.	70	110	Biegler	Aurora, IL	Worb, Bern, Schweiz
Anliker, Johannes	16, July1883	22, June	65- 6m-17d	231		Toledo, OH	Gundeswühl, Bern, Schweiz
Annecker, Jakob	28, June 1869	8, June	32- 8m-12d	207		Secor, IL	
Annschütz, Elisabeth	22, Sept 1892	28, July	78	606		Baltimore, MD	Center County, Pennsylvania
Ansbach, Hester	23, Aug. 1894	21, May	86	550	Trautmann	Stryker, OH	Rudi, Bern, Schweiz
Anschitz, Magdalena	18, Feb. 1867	20, Jan.	61- 3m	54		Clarington, IL	Chillicothe, Ross County, Ohio
Anschuetz, Emma	28, July 1887	5, July	15	478		Kansas City, MO	Zinsweiler, Elsaß
Anschuetz, Margaretha Elisabeth	6, Sept 1875	17, Aug.	71	287	Anschuetz	Baresville, OH	Hessen-Kassel
Anschütz, Caroline	14, Feb. 1895	16, Jan.	53	110		Kansas City, KS	Karlsruhe, Baden
Anschutz, Christine	22, June 1899	29, May	60	399	Burkart	Cleveland, OH	
Anschütz, Karl	12, Jan. 1899	16, Dec.	66	30		Chicago, IL	Monroe County, Ohio
Anschütz, Louisa	18, June 1896	30, May	47	399		Baresville, OH	
Anschütz, Philipp Christian	7, Aug. 1865	22, May	23- 6m-24d	128		Clarington, OH	Grindelwald, Bern, Schweiz
Anthony, Susanna	2, July 1891	21, Apr.	39	430	Blauer	Harper, IA	Istorf, Amt Barenholz, Lippe-Detmold
Antlang, Ernst H.	2, Feb. 1874	5, Jan.	50	39		Hopewell, MO	Schleswig
Antoni, Margaretha Dorothea	16, Feb. 1888	25, Jan.	75	110		New Ulm, MN	Waldorf, Baden
Antoni, Maria Barbara	5, July 1880	16, June	48	215		Cleveland, OH	Württemberg
Antonis, Dorothea	4, Oct. 1860	8, Sept	39	160		Muscatine, IA	
Antonsen, John H.	29, Nov. 1875	9, Nov.	25- 8m	383		Le Sueur, MN	Husum, Hannover
Antonsen, Karolina	18, Sept 1856	19, Aug.	10- 9m	152		Le Sueur, MN	Rausbach, Amt Lausa, Sachsen
Antonsen, Louise	3, Jan. 1889	3, Dec.	62	14	Kahle	Le Sueur, MN	Lauterberg am Harz, Hannover
Anweiler, Christiana Sophia	13, Oct. 1879	14, Sept	60-11m	327	Nagler	Freeport, MI	Lauterberg am Harz, Germany
Apel, Caroline	20, Jan. 1873	27, Dec.	62	23	Gattermann	Quincy, IL	Neuenstadt, Neckarsulm, Württemberg
Apel, Christian Ferdinand	31, July 1876	16, July	63	247		Quincy, IL	Brianz, Bern, Schweiz
Apfelbach, Herman Gotthilf	6, Aug. 1891	13, July	22- 5m-29d	510		Sandwich, IL	
Aplanalp, Melchior	2, Oct. 1865	13, Sept	62	160		Lawrenceburg, IN	
Aplin, Elisabeth	9, Apr. 1891	18, Mar.	21	238	Walter	Waltersburg, IL	
Appel, Ferdinand	27, Sept 1860	5, Sept	33-10m- 5d	156		Cincinnati, OH	Ubstadt, Bruchsal, Baden
Appel, Anna Maria	24, Nov. 1879	2, Oct.	64	375		Alton, IL	Fredericks County, Maryland
Appel, Flora Alice	22, Sept 1887	4, Sept	13	606		Bushton, KS	Nokomis, Illinois
Appel, G. Adam	15, Sept 1853	27, July	53	148		Mascoutah, IL	Spitzaltheim, Kreis Dieburg, Hessen
Appel, John H. (Rev)	9, June 1892	7, May	83	366		Alton, IL	Spitz-Altenheim, Dieburg, Hessen-Darmstadt
Appel, Jost	5, July 1888	7, June	84	430		Sandwich, IL	Neunkirchen, Nassau
Appel, Margaretha	18, May 1893	3, May	57	318	Peußer	Sandwich, IL	Neunkirchen, Nassau
Appel, Margaretha E.	23, June 1898	27, May	70	399	Maurer	Sandwich, IL	Hüblingen, Rennerod, Nassau
Appel, Maria	18, Apr. 1870	20, Mar.	72	127		St. Louis, MO	Marienberg, Nassau

Christliche Apologete Death Notices --- 1839 - 1899

Name of Deceased	Notice Date	Death Date	Age	Page	Maiden Name	Place of Death	Place of Birth
Appel, Regina	19, Aug. 1897	30, July	65- 3m- 5d	527		St. Louis, MO	Altheim, Hessen-Darmstadt
Appel, Sophia Elisabeth	17, Feb. 1898	8, Jan.	50	111	Dal	Chicago, IL	Freiburg an der Unstrut, Baden
Appel, Susanna	30, Aug. 1849	29, July	46	140		Mascoutah, IL	
Appel, Walter Louis	2, Feb. 1888	8, Jan.	15	78		Covington, KY	Chicago, Cook County, Illinois
Appel, Wilhelm	13, Feb. 1871	31, Jan.	45	55		Sandwich, IL	Neuenkirchen, Amt Remeroth, Nassau
Appelhaus, Clara	12, Apr. 1860	22, Mar.	60	60		Cincinnati, OH	Rapper, Witlage, Hannover
Appelt, (Mrs)	25, Aug. 1884	8, Aug.	69	7	Hornburg	Minneapolis, MN	Stephanhagen, Mecklenburg-Schwerin
Appelt, Christian	15, Aug. 1889	27, July	72	526		Minneapolis, MN	Mecklenburg-Strelitz
Appelt, Emil	25, July 1895	5, July	57	478		Wilmington, CA	Comitz, West Preußen
Appenzeller, Karl Friedrich	20, Jan. 1873	5, Jan.	19	23		New Albany, IN	Neumöhl, Amt Kork, Baden
Appi, Anna	1, May 1882	16, Mar.	83	143		Jeffersonville, NY	Wichtrach, Bern, Schweiz
Apple, Lucretia	9, Aug. 1849	10, July		128		Smooth Prairie, ---	
Apple, W.	9, Aug. 1849	10, July		128		Smooth Prairie, ---	
Arans, Dorothea	18, Aug. 1884	8, Aug.	25- 7m-25d	7	Mentz	Altamont, IL	Nicollet County, Minnesota
Arb, Margaretha C.	25, July 1881	8, July	37	239	Thomsen	Lena, IL	Holstein
Arbogast, Magdalena	27, Jan. 1859	18, June	78	16		Big Mount, IA	Rittershofer, Sulz, Schweiz
Arch, Caspar	12, Aug. 1878	26, July	77- 2m-12d	255		Jeffersonville, NY	Watzenborn, Hessen
Arend, Anna M. Gertrud	29, Nov. 1894	12, Nov.	62	774	Helwig	Delhi, MI	Haddamar, Fritzlar, Kurhessen
Arend, Johan Georg	26, Jan. 1899	24, Dec.	72	62		Holt, MI	Haddam, Fritzlar, Kurhessen
Arend, Mina	3, July 1871	18, June	30- 9m-13d	215	Redger	Bunker Hill, IL	Wolfhagen, Gandersheim, Braunschweig
Arends, Friedrich	5, Oct. 1893	17, Aug.	20	638		Kansas City, KS	Kansas City, Kansas
Arends, Trinke Maria	6, Aug. 1896	20, July	78	511	Poplin	Melvin, IL	Ostfriesland
Arensman, Julchen	25, May 1893	11, May	84	334	Domhofs	Huntingburg, IN	Schledehausen, Osnabrück, Hannover
Arensmann, Carl H.	9, Feb. 1874	18, Jan.	26	47		Mt. Vernon, IN	Cincinnati, Hamilton County, Ohio
Arensmann, Elenora Elise	27, Sept 1880	3, Sept	30	311	Reineking	Metropolis, IL	Cincinnati, Hamilton County, Ohio
Argleben, Caroline	19, Dec. 1870	22, Nov.	56	407		Detroit, MI	Peters Waldau, Schlesien, Preußen
Argleben, Ernst Friedrich	2, Nov. 1863	1, July	18- 4m	176			Langenbielau, Schlesien, Preußen
Argleben, Ferdinand	24, Sept 1877	27, Aug.	66-10m-27d	311		Dearborn, MI	Langenbielau, Breslau, Preußen
Arhart, John Albert	7, Mar. 1895	3, Feb.	25	158		Fairfax, MN	West Newton, Nicollet County, Minnesota
Arhelger, Eva Elisabeth	7, Apr. 1879	15, Mar.	74	111	Weber	Friendship, WI	Kleingladenbach, Biedenkopf, Hessen-Darmstadt
Arhelger, Johan	7, Feb. 1881	78- 8m-16d	47		Friendship, WI	Breidenbach, Biedenkopf, Hessen	
Aring, Heinrich	26, Feb. 1883	5, Feb.	67	71		Santa Claus, IN	Altendorf, Grünberg, Hannover
Arit, Augusta	10, Oct. 1895	30, Aug.	69	654	Grauer	Sturgeon Bay, WI	
Arman, Georg	12, Jan. 1874	19, Dec.	25- 6m- 6d	15		Clarington, OH	
Armann, Regina	6, Sept 1888	7, Aug.	66- 9m- 7d	574	Schanz	Wheeling, WV	Oelbronn, Maulbronn, Württemberg
Armbrust, Albert Georg	30, July 1896	11, July	20	495		Scranton, PA	
Armbrust, Ella Maria	13, Dec. 1880	9, Nov.	19- 7m-12d	399		Scranton, PA	
Armbrust, Margaretha	12, Mar. 1857	21, Jan.	37	44	Breitenbach	Waverly, OH	Lizel, Beiver, Kurhessen
Armbruster, Anna Maria	2, Apr. 1891	6, Mar.	72- 6m-16d	222	Morlock	Spencerville, OH	Ispringen, Pforzheim, Baden
Armbruster, Augusta	16, Feb. 1899	25, Jan.	40	110	Stemmler	Spencerville, OH	Ispingen, Baden
Armbruster, Barnabas	17, Oct. 1881	5, Oct.	68- 3m-24d	335		Mt. Vernon, IN	Oberkirch, Baden
Armbruster, Johann Philipp	8, Aug. 1864	23, May	83- 3m- 5d	128		Kossuth, OH	Singen, Amt Durlach, Baden
Armbruster, John	20, May 1897	3, May	80	318		Ann Arbor, MI	Dettingen, Hohenzollern
Armbruster, Joseph	18, Apr. 1889	19, Mar.	79	254		Ann Arbor, MI	Dettingen, Glatt, Hohenzollern
Armbruster, Katharine	21, June 1894	5, June	75	406	Haas	Mt. Vernon, IN	Lohweiler, Rheinkreis Baiern
Armbruster, Maria	1, Sept 1853	9, June	36	140		Detroit, MI	Freudenstadt, Württemberg

Christliche Apologete Death Notices --- 1839 - 1899

Name of Deceased	Notice Date	Death Date	Age	Page	Maiden Name	Place of Death	Place of Birth
Armbruster, Philipp	25, Aug. 1887	12, Aug.	73- 9m- 2d	542		Spencerville, OH	Singen, Durlach, Baden
Armorust, Katharina	22, Mar. 1875	12, Feb.	44	95		Waverly, OH	Neuhofen bei Mutterstadt, Baiern
Arnds, Gottlieb	16, Dec. 1878	21, Nov.	33	399		Quincy, IL	Ardorf, Wittmund, Ostfriesland
Arndt, Anna Ottilie	22, Dec. 1892	30, Nov.	20	814		Michigan City, IN	Michigan City, Indiana
Arndt, Johanna	22, Mar. 1888	16, Feb.	48	190	Kleist	Michigan City, IN	Kodezoesen, Posen
Arndt, Johanna Sophia Friederike	31, Dec. 1896	11, Dec.	64	844	Reinke	Billings, MO	Mecklenburg
Arndt, Lizzie	3, June 1886	18, May	22	7		Berea, OH	
Arndt, Margaretha	27, Sept 1875	12, Sept		311	Schuler	New Albany, IN	Prinzheim, Buckweiler, Elsaß
Arndt, Michael	1, Oct 1883	17, Sept	49- 8m-12d	319		Berea, OH	Vollstein, Posen
Arndt, Sarah	6, May 1897	16, Apr.	29	287	Höhle	Sheboygan, WI	Scott, Sheboygan County, Wisconsin
Arni, Anna	12, Mar. 1891	12, Feb.	84	174		Queen City, MO	Schweiz
Arni, J.	17, Mar.1873	12, Feb.	63- 3m	87		Etna, MO	Liberen, Solothurn, Schweiz
Arnika, Margaretha	8, July 1867	16, June	51	214		Jefferson City, MO	Bunde, Ostfriesland
Arnike, August P.	3, June 1867	4, May	40	174		Jefferson City, MO	Halle bei Aurich, Hannover
Arning, Emma	22, Apr. 1872	24, Feb.	16- 6m	135		Roseville, MI	
Arning, Heinrich	20, Apr. 1874	6, Feb.	23	127		Roseville, MI	
Arning, Johan Bernard	13, Sept 1875	12, Aug.	60	295		Roseville, MI	Wildeswick, Holland
Arning, John	24, Jan. 1881	5, Jan.	23- 4m- 8d	31		Roseville, MI	
Arning, Katharina	25, Jan. 1894	31, Dec.	78	62	Tiewinkel	Wheeling, IL	Winteswick, Holland
Arnold, Anna Maria	13, Apr. 1854	11, Mar.	28- 4m-24d	60	Schneider	East Grove, IL	
Arnold, Caspar	27, July 1885	4, July	67- 1m-18d	7		New Bremen, IL	Muttersholz, Elsaß
Arnold, Catharina	3, Feb. 1873	5, Jan.	41	39	Mühlhausen	Giard, IA	Weisenhafel, Kurhessen
Arnold, Christian	17, Nov. 1879	29, Oct.	60- 7m-10d	367		Brownton, MN	Meißenheim, Amt Lahr, Baden
Arnold, Christian H.	24, Nov. 1887	7, Nov.	63	750		Morrison, MO	Neckarwestheim, Württemberg
Arnold, Eberhart Friedrich	19, June 1890	20, May	66	398		Oshkosh, WI	Biedigheim, Württemberg
Arnold, Friedrich	15, Sept 1873	21, July	62	295		Oshkosh, WI	Kaubenheim, Baiern
Arnold, Gottfried	22, Oct. 1877	7, Oct.	39	343		Buffalo, NY	Großen, Burschla, Preußen
Arnold, Jakob	14, July 1887	26, June	60- 9m-24d	446		New Bremen, IL	Mitterode, Kurhessen
Arnold, John	27, Oct. 1884	17, Sept	77	7		Batesville, IN	Homburg, Baiern
Arnold, Louise Catharine	11, May 1874	24, Apr.	75- 8m- 9d	151	Klensch	Batesville, IN	Karlsberg, Erbach, Homburg, Baiern
Arnold, Margarete Barbara	6, Apr. 1899	8, Mar.	83	222	Mark	Oshkosh, WI	Uffenheim, Baiern
Arnold, Margaretha	26, Nov. 1883	20, Sept	58	383	Scheuch	Iowa City, IA	Kohlberg, Nürtingen, Württemberg
Arnold, Rosina	23, Dec. 1886	26, Nov.	36	7	Kenzler	Newark, NJ	Friedinger, Baden
Arnolt, Friedrich	23, Nov. 1893	22, Oct.	76	750		Chillicothe, OH	Längenfeld, Waldeck
Arns, Maria Katharina	27, Jan. 1887	11, Jan.	49	62	Weiand	Aurora, IL	Thronecke, Trier, Preußen
Arnsheimer, Lina	4, July 1889	18, June	73	430		New York City, NY	Darmstadt, Hessen-Darmstadt
Arnsmann, Adam	27, Mar. 1882	19, Jan.	73- -25d	103		Enterprise, IL	Schledehausen, Hannover
Arnsmann, Carolina	14, Aug. 1890	15, July	26- 9m-24d	526		Enterprise, IL	AltSchledehausen, Osnabrück, Hannover
Arnsmann, Clammer Wilhelm	3, Aug. 1899	3, July	78	495		Louisville, KY	Schlendehausen, Hannover
Arnsmann, Heinrich Ludwig	27, Mar. 1871	12, Feb.	66- -17d	103		Huntingburg, IN	Wilmeroth, Rennerod, Nassau
Arnsmann, Sophia	3, Apr. 1882	19, Mar.	59-11m	111	Helwig	Sandoval, IL	Waldorf, Vlotho, Herfort, Minden, Preußen
Arnsmeier, Wilhelmine	17, Feb. 1887	19, Jan.	55- 8m	110	Lenger	Hopewell, MO	Württemberg
Arnsperger, Magdalene	29, Nov. 1875	1, Oct.	73	383		Canaan, MO	Geneseo, Illinois
Arnsperger, Mathilde Lydia	16, Oct. 1890	19, 2m-21d	19- 2m-21d	670		Salisbury, MO	Pekin, Illinois
Arrens, Margaretha Johanna	10, Apr. 1882	14, Feb.	16 -3m- 7d	119		Storm Lake, IA	
Artus, Eva Christina	24, Mar. 1892	2, Mar.	56	190	Fischer	LaCrosse, WI	Wernshausen, Meiningen, Sachsen-Meiningen

Christliche Apologete Death Notices --- 1839 - 1899

Name of Deceased	Notice Date	Death Date	Age	Maiden Name	Page	Place of Death	Place of Birth
Artz, Elisabeth	6, May 1878	11, Apr.	35	Hofmann	143	Charlestown, IN	Bettweiler, Rheinkreis Baiern
Artz, Eva	6, Dec. 1844	29, Oct.	24		188	Woodville, OH	
Artz, Friedrich Philipp	5, Dec. 1881	16, Aug.			391	Le Sueur, MN	Belle Plaine, Scott County, Minnesota
Artz, Johan Philipp	5, Sept 1881	19, Aug.	74- 8m-14d		287	Charlestown, IN	Nordheim, Hessen
Artz, Margaretha	26, Sept 1889	30, Aug.	84- 6m- 17d		619	Charlestown, IN	GroßRohrheim, Hessen-Darmstadt
Arx, Anna	23, Apr. 1883	3, Apr.	68-10m- 4d	Schaub	135	St. Elma, IL	Anvil, Siffach, Baselland, Schweiz
Arz, Simon	28, Mar. 1870	13, Mar.	53-10m-22d		103	Lansing, MI	Nordheim, Hessen-Darmstadt
Arzd, Johan David	15, Apr. 1878	10, Mar.	70- 8m-10d		119	Canton, OH	Stöcken, Sachsen-Weimar
Arzt, Friederike Eleonore	21, Sept 1863	22, Aug.	4		152	Shakopee, MN	
Arzt, Gottfried	19, June 1882	2, June	66		199	Lafayette, IN	Rosenfeld bei Halle an der Saale, Preußen
Arzt, Walpurga	15, July 1886	4, June	41	Andrist	7	Wheeling, WV	Behringen, Urach, Württemberg
Asche, Emilie Pauline	7, July 1884	18, June	19		7	Ft. Atkinson, WI	
Asche, John N.	8, June 1868	26, May	52-10m		183	Milan, IN	Bruchhausen, Hannover
Aschelmann, Mary	21, Nov. 1864	2, Oct.			188	Edgerton, OH	Nenekofen, Solothurn, Schweiz
Aschemeier, Wilhelm	18, Aug. 1898	1, Aug.	64		527	Baltimore, MD	Holzhausen, Preußen
Aschke, Rosette	11, Mar. 1878	17, Feb.	18- 9m-15d		79	Ft. Atkinson, WI	
Asel, Wilhelm	27, Feb. 1896	6, Feb.	70		142	New York City, NY	Rastätten, Nassau
Asling, Caroline	13, Mar. 1876	31, Jan.	24- -21d	Rockemann	87	Lyona, KS	Cincinnati, Hamilton County, Ohio
Asling, E.	17, Apr. 1876	27, Mar.	39- 2m-23d		127	Lyona, KS	Asken, Amt Diepholz, Hannover
Asling, Ernst Heinrich	28, Feb. 1895	26, Jan.	46		142	Lyona, KS	Batesville, Indiana
Asmann, Eduard	15, Dec. 1873	3, Nov.	14		399	Liberty, MO	
Asmus, Carl Friedrich	11, Dec. 1882	22, Sept	60- 2m		399	Hoboken, NJ	Einbeck, Hannover
Aspelmeier, Anna Maria Elisabeth	26, Mar. 1896	6, Mar.	21		206	Ft. Hunter, NY	Montgomery County, New York
Aspelmeier, Marie	26, Mar. 1896	23, Feb.	47	Wittemeier	206	Ft. Hunter, NY	Hille, Preußen
Assel, Henriette	16, June 1887	28, Mar.	66- 5m-25d	Deichmüller	382	Brooklyn, NY	Vacha, Sachsen-Weimar
Atkins, Anna	7, Mar. 1881	7, Feb.	32	Fischer	79	Liberty, MO	Willmandingen, Württemberg
Attig, Adam	22, Mar. 1894	28, Feb.			198	Des Moines, IA	Liebesbach, Heppenheim, Hessen-Darmstadt
Atzel, Tobias	23, Dec. 1867	11, Nov.	21- 6m-22d		406	Chicago, IL	Canton Bischwiller bei Straßburg, Frankreich
Aubel, Georg	15, Dec. 1862	22, Nov.	25- 9m- 9d		200	Lefargeville, NY	
Aubel, Katharina	15, Sept 1887	28, Aug.	58- 9m		590	Pittsburg, PA	
Aubel, Konrad	5, May 1898	13, Apr.	76		287	Allegheny, PA	Eifershausen, Hessen-Kassel
Aubel, Sophia	21, Aug. 1890	18, July	76- 5m	Vaught	542	Allegheny City, PA	Melzungen, Cassel, Kurhessen
Auch, Elisabeth Friederike	27, Mar. 1882	8, Mar.	34	Lämle	103	Chillicothe, OH	Ross County, Ohio
Auch, Johan Georg	7,May 1883	20, Apr.	56- 4m-21d		151	Chicago, IL	Obersilmingen, Stuttgart, Württemberg
Aude, Johan	12, May 1873	19, Apr.	55		151	Elizabeth City, NJ	Sumpler, Hessen-Kassel
Auer, Anna B.	14, Dec. 1885	25, Nov.	69	Weiß	7	Decatur, IL	Neudorf bei Ansbach, Mittelfranken, Baiern
Auer, Georg	9, June 1892	17, May	66		366	Chicago, IL	Unter-hallau, Schaffhausen, Schweiz
Auer, Johan Paulus	17, June 1897	17, May	79		383	Decatur, IL	Leutershausen, Mittelfranken, Baiern
Auer, M. Sophia	20, Nov. 1871	10, Oct.	17- - 5d		375	Decatur, IL	Manchester, Carroll County, Maryland
AufdemOrte, Heinrich	6, Mar. 1871	11, Feb.	50- 6m		79	New Orleans, LA	Hannover
AufderHaide, Wilhelm	9, June 1862	23, Mar.	51		92	Decatur, IL	Aschendorf, Amt Iburg, Hannover
Aufderheide, Herman	2, Feb. 1899	31, Dec.	22		79	Kansas City, MO	Scholen, Sulingen, Hannover
Aufderher, Wilhelm	28, Mar. 1895	25, Feb.	50		206	New Knoxville, OH	Ladbergen, Tecklenburg, Germany
Aufenkam, Elisabetha	12, Mar. 1847	10, Nov.	52- -14d		43	Herman, MO	Borkhorst, Preußen
Aufrecht, Anna Emilie	3, Mar. 1898	30, Jan.	14		143	Big Spring, NE	Seward County, Nebraska
Aufrecht, Christina Louise	5, July 1894	14, June	38		438	Waco, NE	Unterbrüden, Backnang, Württemberg

Christliche Apologete Death Notices --- 1839 - 1899

Name of Deceased	Notice Date	Death Date	Age	Maiden Name	Page	Place of Death	Place of Birth
Aufrecht, Johannes	23, Aug. 1888	25, June	77		542	Lansing, MI	Oelbronn, Maulbronn, Württemberg
Augenstein, Katharina	19, Jan. 1860	19, Dec.		Rabb	12	Marshall, MI	Roßway, O.A. Vaihingen, Württemberg
Augenstein, Matthias	22, Sept 1848		Inquiry		155	Poughkeepsie, NY	Eissingen, Amt Pforzheim, Baden
Augenthaler, Caspar	10, Feb. 1887	27, Jan.	60		94	Brooklyn, NY	Offenbach bei Frankfurt, Germany
Augsbach, Charlotte	4, Jan. 1864	30, Nov.	37		4	Saginaw, MI	Hornberg, Baden
Augsbach, Heinrich Gustav	25, Dec. 1882	3, Dec.	56		415	Toledo, OH	Domischow bei Warsaw, Rußland
Augusten, Hanna	28, Dec. 1854	27, Nov.	63-6m	Haug	208	German Creek, IA	Württemberg
Augustin, Christian	20, June 1889	2, June	62		398	Hebron, IA	Rheinpfalz Baiern
Augustin, John	22, Oct. 1896	27, Sept	73		687	Winona, MN	Ottensen, Hannover
Augustin, Margaretha	25, June 1883	6, June	57- 5m		207	Winona, MN	Notendorf, Hannover
Augustin, Margaretha B.	6, Dec. 1894	5, Nov.	32		790	Winona, MN	Winona County, Minnesota
Augustin, Michael	21, Nov. 1864	13, Oct.	78		188	German Creek, IA	Meinsheim, Brackenheim, Württemberg
Aukes, Fentge	12, Jan. 1874	15, Dec.	75- 1m- 7d	Bakker	15	Roberts, IL	Hinte, Ostfriesland
Aukstein, Carl	3, June 1858	9, May	48		88	Pekin, IL	Rastatt, Baden
Aulemann, Catharina	16, May 1881	2, Mar.	81		159	Newton, IA	Mühlen, Nassau
Aulenbacher, Georg	1, Feb. 1894	9, Jan.	75		78	Yonkers, NY	Altenglahn, Baiern
Aumann, Louise	11, Aug. 1887	24, July	35	Harsen	510	Nokomis, IL	Marlow, Mecklenburg-Schwerin
Aumann, Marie Philippine	29, May 1876	21, Apr.	32	Heine	175	Nokomis, IL	Polkdorf, Lippe-Schaumburg
Aupperle, Adam	2, Sept 1867	13, Aug.	22- 1m-23d		278	Platteville, WI	Pennsylvania
Aupperle, Anna Margaretha	7, Apr. 1879	22, Mar.	96- 1m- 4d		111	Lancaster, PA	Streich, Schorndorf, Württemberg
Aupperle, Catharine	12, May 1884	30, Apr.	13		7	Odebolt, IA	Grant County, Wisconsin
Aupperle, Elisabeth	15, Aug. 1889	18, July	75	Hartmann	526	Stitzer, WI	
Aupperle, Gottlieb	14, Feb. 1889	30, Jan.	73		110	Stitzer, WI	
Aupperle, Johannes	2, Oct. 1876	15, Sept	52- 5m-20d		319	Lancaster, WI	Oberamt Schorndorf, Württemberg
Aupperle, Karl	9, Sept 1886	19, Aug.	67- 5m-25d		7	Schenectady, NY	Birkenweißbuch, Schorndorf, Württemberg
Ausiker, Friedrich	17, June 1867	8, Apr.	12		190	Schenectady, NY	Nettelstedt, Lübbecke, Minden, Preußen
Aussicker, Friedrich Wilhelm	14, Apr. 1898	7, Mar.	50		239	Schenectady, NY	Nettelstedt, Lübecke, Minden, Preußen
Aussicker, Friedrich Wilhelm	4, Aug. 1898	9, Mar.	50		495	Schenectady, NY	Nettelstedt, Lübeck, Minden, Preußen
Aussicker, Ida	9, Apr. 1896	16, Mar.	33	Engelbrecht	238	Schenectady, NY	Herne, Bochum, Westphalen
Aussicker, Sophie	9, Aug. 1894	2, July	67	Drahn	518	Schenectady, NY	Großmockern, Yetrow, Mecklenburg-Schwerin
Austermann, Anna	25, June 1896	31, May	37	Heitzmann	415	Drake, MO	Gasconade County, Missouri
Austermann, Christine	6, Oct. 1887	18, Aug.	21- 7m-11d		638	St. Louis, MO	
Austermann, Florentine	28, Dec. 1899	8, Dec.	77	Sünkel	828	Drake, MO	Nienhagen, Lage , Lippe-Detmold
Austermühle, Karl W.	25, June 1891	15, May	70		414	Madison, IN	Liebenau, Kurhessen
Austermüller, Maria	9, Oct. 1871	11, Sept	25	Kampe	327	Madison, IN	Liebenau, Kreis Hofgeismar, Preußen
Auts, Lizzie	4, May 1885	5, Apr.	27- -16d		7	Graham, MO	
Ave, Sophia	6, Apr. 1899	19, Feb.	71	Wieting	222	Charleston, WI	Nukow, Mecklenburg-Schwerin
Awe, Friedrich	29, Sept 1884	6, Sept	47-11m- 1d		7	Alden, IA	Mecklenburg-Schwerin
Awe, Sophia	6, Feb. 1882	21, Jan.	41- 1m- 1d		47	Oshkosh, WI	Goldebee, Mecklenburg-Schwerin
Axt, Elisabeth	5, Dec. 1889	21, Oct.	38	Roth	782	Anaheim, CA	Charleston, Lee County, Iowa
Axter, Elisabeth	7, May 1877	18, Apr.	65	Steiner	151	Allegheny City, PA	Bonfeld, Heilbronn, Württemberg
Baab, Sophia H.	22, May 1890	28, Apr.	27- -16d	Schlinger	334	Junction City, KS	St. Charles, Missouri
Baar, Johanna Friederike	14, Jan. 1892	2, Dec.	51	Kortkamp	30	Green Bay, WI	Krausin, Pommern
Baars, Johann R.F.	25, Nov. 1858	15, Sept	47		188	Wawaka, IN	Lüdershoff, Mecklenburg-Schwerin
Baartz, Maria Anna	1, Apr. 1872	15, Mar.	24- 6m-16d	Rebstock	111	Buffalo, NY	

Christliche Apologete Death Notices --- 1839 - 1899

Name of Deceased	Notice Date	Death Date	Age	Maiden Name	Page	Place of Death	Place of Birth
Babel, Lena	7, June 1888	1, May	16-10m- 8d		366	Lancaster, NY	Griesheim, Hessen-Darmstadt
Babel, Ottilie	28, July 1892	5, July	56	Nothnagel	478	Sweet Home, NY	Questin, Neu-Buckow, Mecklenburg-Schwerin
Babenderd, Wilhelm	27, Feb. 1882	12, Jan.	16- 8m-11d		71	Roseville, MI	Friederichsdorf, Mecklenburg-Schwerin
Babenehr, Dettloff Heinrich	31, Oct. 1889	23, Sept	79		702	Roseville, MI	Herford bei Minden, Preußen
Babenhausen, Herman	28, Jan. 1892	3, Jan.	60		62	Jacksonville, IL	Nesse, Hannover
Babikon, Lucia Christine	1, Apr. 1897	28, Feb.	66	Schmidt	206	Baltimore, MD	Niederkirchen bei Neustadt an der Haardt, Baiern
Bäbinger, Abraham	26, Dec. 1861	25, Nov.	81		208	Cincinnati, OH	
Bach, Adam	19, Apr. 1860	27, Mar.			64	Stillwater, MN	Highland Station, Illinois
Bach, Anna	2, Feb. 1874	5, Jan.	30		39	Nauvoo, IL	Lawrenceburg, Dearborn County, Indiana
Bach, Anna Margaretha	26, July 1888	12, July	46	Mulfinger	478	Crown Point, IN	Caperdessen bei Osnabrück, Preußen
Bach, Charlotte	6, Aug. 1847	20, July	23	Dormann	127	St. Louis, MO	
Bach, Clara	26, Dec. 1889	1, Dec.	24		830	Washington, ---	Wernsdorf bei Weißenfels, Sachsen
Bach, Gottlob	14, May 1883	20, Apr.	71		159	Cedar Lake, IN	Breddorf, Amt Ottersberg, Hannover
Bach, Margaretha	11, Mar. 1852	9, Feb.		Henning	44	St. Louis, MO	Niederkirchen, Neustadt, Rheinkreis Baiern
Bach, Martin	4, Aug. 1892	11, July	76		494	St. Paul, MN	Niederkirchen, Rheinkreis Baiern
Bach, Nicholas	8, Feb. 1894	18, Jan.	76		94	St. Paul, MN	Schwarzburg, Schwarzburg-Sondershausen
Bächle, Dorothea	4, Feb. 1867	24, Dec.	29	Kappel	38	Williamsburg, NY	Münsingen, Bern, Schweiz
Bächler, Anna	25, Aug. 1862	4, Aug.	39	Hodel	136	Buffalo Co, WI	Menzingen, Bern, Schweiz
Bächler, Rosina	19, Dec. 1864	16, Nov.	26	Hodel	204		
Bachman, William H.	5, Dec. 1881	14, Nov.	30- - 4d		391	Mt. Vernon, IN	Wiederhöen, Kreis Eschweig, Kurhessen
Bachmann, Christian	18, Oct. 1875	25, Sept	34		335	Allegan, MI	Perouse, Württemberg
Bachmann, Christina	25, Feb. 1892	21, Jan.	67	Heritier	126	Washington, MN	Rengshausen, Rothenburg, Kurhessen
Bachmann, Conrad Wilhelm	28, Jan. 1892	7, Jan.	70		62	Decatur, IL	Oberdorla, Mühlheim, Erfurt, Preußen
Bachmann, Friedrich	27, Mar. 1890	3, Mar.	54- 4m-18d		206	Columbus, IL	Zeller, Hannover
Bachmann, Heinrich	25, June 1883	5, June	43		207	Wausau, WI	Saginaw, Michigan
Bachmann, Jakob	12, Apr. 1880	31, Mar.	27		119	St. Paul, MN	Bielefeld, Preußen
Bachmann, Julius	20, Nov. 1882	2, July	35		375	Decatur, IL	Carmi, Illinois
Bachmann, Käthe	23, Feb. 1893	30, Sept	19		126	St. Philip, IN	Oberhelrogen, Preußen
Bachmann, Maria	25, Dec. 1871	30, Nov.	42	Schactschobel	415	Washington, MN	Baltimore, Maryland
Bachmann, Maria	20, Nov. 1882	3, Oct.	28		375	Decatur, IL	
Bachmann, Maria Elisabeth	26, Aug. 1886	5, Aug.		Wolf	7	Columbus, IL	Neustadt , Baden
Bachmann, Sophia	25, Sept 1856	2, Sept	34- 3m	Meier	156	New Haven, CT	Schloßbeinlingen, Preußen
Bachmann, Wilhelm	18, Mar. 1897	23, Feb.	76		174	Washington, Mn	Baltimore, Maryland
Bachmann, Wilhelm Heinrich	20, Nov. 1882	14, Nov.	31		375	Decatur, IL	
Bachmeier, Caroline	26, May 1892	1, May	62	Treiber	334	Philadelphia, PA	Franklin County, Missouri
Bächmeyer, Anna Maria	15, Mar. 1888	8, Feb.	26	Tölke	174	Beaufort, MO	Wald, Zürich, Schweiz
Bächtold, Anna Elisabeth	10, Nov. 1884	23, Oct.	63	Egli	7	Cannelton, IN	Jefferson County, Kentucky
Bächtold, Carrie	17, July 1890	22, June	40		462	Louisville, KY	
Bäck, Jakob Georg	19, May 1873	15, Mar.	4-10m- 3d		159	Marion, OH	Weserdeich, Bern, Preußen
Bäck, John	2, Mar. 1874	11, Feb.	37-11m-24d		71	Goshen, IN	Baden
Bäck, Maria Sarah	19, May 1873	7, Apr.	6- 7m-10d		159	Marion, OH	Overbeck, Preußen
Backenköhler, Heinrich Christian D.	26, May 1898	2, May	54	Able	335	Peoria, IL	Holzhausen, Lübbeke, Minden, Preußen
Bäcker, Catharina	26, July 1880		43		239	Rome, OH	Metzungen, Amt Adelshausen, Kurhessen
Bäcker, Ernst	19, Feb. 1857	24, Jan.	37		32	Highland, IL	
Bäcker, Friedrich	25, Aug. 1843		Inquiry		135	St. Louis, MO	
Bäcker, Gertraud Elisabeth	19, Oct. 1863	23, Aug.		Koch	168	New Knoxville, OH	

- 13 -

Christliche Apologete Death Notices --- 1839 - 1899

Name of Deceased	Notice Date	Death Date	Age	Maiden Name	Page	Place of Death	Place of Birth
Bäcker, Hanna	10, Mar. 1853	31, Jan.	28		40	Wheeling, VA	Schwegenheim, Rheinkreis Baiern
Bäcker, Jacob	23, Oct. 1856	19, Sept	38- 2m		172	Portsmouth, OH	Mannheim, Baden
Bäcker, Jacob	16, Oct. 1856	16, Sept	37		168		Allenbach, Preußen
Bäcker, Johan Jakob	4, Sept 1865	23, May			144	Platteville, WI	Hagen, Preußen
Bäcker, Karl	18, May 1893	28, Apr.	71		318	Boston, MA	Wisconsin
Bäcker, Karoline	2, Apr. 1883	13, Mar.	32- 6m- 6d	Riebe	111	Hokah, MN	WaldHambach, Drüllingen, Elsaß
Bäcker, Peter	2, June 1898	30, Apr.			351	Chicago, IL	Bruchsal, Baden
Bäcker, Philipp Jacob	12, Sept 1870	28, Aug.	81		295	Mansfield, OH	Scioto County, Ohio
Bäcker, Sarah	9, Feb. 1888	23, Jan.	19- 9m		94	Portsmouth, OH	Norga, Rußland
Bäcker, Wilhelm	13, Apr. 1899	11, Mar.	69		238	Bison, KS	Winning bei Labes, Pommern
Backhaus, Anna Sophia	25, Dec. 1876	10, Dec.	71	Hinz	413	Milwaukee, WI	Preußen
Backhaus, Beata	1, July 1842	2, June	48		103	Marietta, OH	
Backhaus, Charley	29, Aug. 1870		41		279	Lincoln, NE	Farbezien bei Naugard, Pommern
Backhaus, Gottfried	7,May 1883	24, Apr.	85- 3m		151	Milwaukee, WI	
Backhaus, Heinrich	7, Feb. 1889		26- 5m		94	Hopewell, MO	
Backhaus, Heinrich Christian	6, Sept 1875	9, Aug.	57		287	Lansing Ridge, IA	Burgdorf, Medingen, Hannover
Backhaus, Johan David	31, Jan. 1876	20, Nov.	62- 1m- 2d		39	Chippewa Falls, WI	Naugard, Stettin, Pommern
Backhaus, John G.	3, Nov. 1862	12, Oct.	50		176	Dayton, OH	Grosdorf, Hannover
Backhaus, Maria Wilhelmine Magd.	11, Sept 1890		55	Zeibig	590	Chicago, IL	Berlin , Preußen
Backhaus, Wilhelmine Friederike	14, Oct. 1852	7, Sept	35		168	Fond du Lac, WI	Wismar, Mecklenburg
Backley,	3, Aug. 1854	7, July	52- 5m-23d		124	Cedar Lake, IN	Reusten, Herrenberg, Württemberg
Backus, Peter	19, Sept 1889	21, Aug.	74		606	Scranton, PA	Bürgenfeld, Oldenburg
Bade, Dorothea	14, Mar. 1889	24, Jan.	77	Kammann	174	Menominee, MI	Oppershausen, Hannover
Bade, Johan Heinrich	9, Feb. 1888	6, Jan.	87- 9m- 3d		94	Menominee, MI	Hannover
Bader, Bartholomäus	2, Oct. 1865	9, Sept	22		160	Cleveland, OH	Oberhausen, Württemberg
Bader, Emma	2, Apr. 1896	13, Mar.	21		222	Hokah, MN	Hokah, Minnesota
Bader, Gottlob	20, Aug. 1896	6, Aug.	31		543	Chicago, IL	Stuttgart, Württemberg
Bader, Heinrich	20, Nov. 1871	1, Nov.			375	Piqua, OH	Müllum, Amt Strade, Hannover
Bader, Johan	31, Aug. 1893	8, Aug.	62		558	Chicago, IL	Michelbach an der Haid, Württemberg
Bader, Joseph	26, Apr. 1880	2, Apr.	73		135	Jacksonville, IL	Zaden, Freiburg, Baden
Badzeli, Maria	22, Feb. 1875	26, Jan.	26- 1m- 3d	Margoot	63	Highland, IL	
Baer, J.A.	14, Apr. 1884	13, Mar.	55-10m-27d		7	Greenville, NJ	Ittlingen, Sinzheim, Baden
Baer, Louise	25, July 1864	28, June	30- 5m-25d	Achard	120	New York, NY	
Baerhold, Johan F.	23, Nov. 1885	1, Nov.	66- 9m-28d		7	Columbus, WI	Naumburg, Preußen
Baerholt, Luise	29, June 1899	7, June	91		415	Columbus, WI	Steinbach, Sachsen
Bagemann, Anton	1, Sept 1884	14, Aug.	77		7	Stitzer, WI	Helberg, Hohenhausen, Lippe-Detmold
Bahlmann, Luise	14, Sept 1899	4, Aug.	67	Wegener	591	Gonzales, TX	
Bahr, Anna Christina	27, Feb. 1896	8, Feb.	76	Radke	142	Bedford, IN	Zeilgenau, Preußen
Bähr, Dorothea Elisabeth	16, Aug. 1888	26, July	80	Rütz	526	Manitowoc, WI	Neustetten, Pommern
Bähr, Ernst	9, Nov. 1893	20, Sept	78		718	Brooklyn, NY	Golzwarden, Oldenburg
Bähr, Friedrich	17, June 1872	15, May	67- 1m- 5d		199	Cannon, MO	Kleinbüdde, Kreis Neustettin, Preußen
Bähr, Jacob	5, June 1876	3, May	82- 2m-21d		183	Cleveland, OH	Kettenheim, Alzei, Hessen-Darmstadt
Bähr, Jakob	30, Sept 1872	3, Sept	41		319	New Haven, CT	Lambsheim, Baiern
Bähr, Joh. F. Ernst	17, Aug. 1854	10, July	80	Kastner	132	Sheboygan, WI	Sachsenhagen, Bückeburgischen, Hannover
Bähr, Maria	2, July 1891	9, June	38		430	Minneapolis, MN	Freeport, Illinois
Bähr, Nicolaus	25, July 1889	25, June	76		478	Blooming Grove, MN	Rodach, Sachsen-Coburg

Christliche Apologete Death Notices -- 1839 - 1899

Name of Deceased	Notice Date	Death Date	Age	Maiden Name	Page	Place of Death	Place of Birth
Bähr, Rosina	4, Feb. 1892	29, Dec.	74		78	Brighton, IL	Ofdringen, Schweiz
Bahr, Wilhelm	13, Feb. 1896	24, Jan.	75		110	Bedford, IN	Grabin, Preußen
Bahrat, Christiana	13, Dec. 1888	24, Oct.	27- 3m		798	Portland, OR	
Bahrenburg, Adelheid	12, Nov. 1883	29, Oct.	67- 7m-18d	Oelkers	367	Marietta, OH	Breddorf, Ottersberg, Hannover
Bahrenburg, Johan Peter	16, July 1877	24, June	94- 6m		231	Marietta, OH	Wieersdorf, Amt Zeven, Hannover
Bahrenburg, John P.	26, Aug. 1878	31, July	31- 2m-13d		271	Salem, Washington County, Ohio	Salem, Washington County, Ohio
Bahrenburg, Louise Augusta Georgine	2, Apr. 1883	14, Mar.	28- 6m-23d	Engel	111	Hoboken, NJ	
Bahrenburg, Margaretha	14, Feb. 1870	15, Jan.	31- 8m-21d		55	New York City, NY	Fischerhude, Amt Rothenburg, Hannover
Bahrenburg, Wilhelmine	22, Feb. 1875	5, Feb.	88- 4m-10d	Meier	63	Bonn, OH	Wargedorf, Ottersberg, Hannover
Bährens, Katharina Johanna	8, Jan. 1877	22, Nov.	71- 7m- 2d	Eggelte	15	Canton, OH	Amsterdam, Holland
Bährens, Katharine	16, Feb. 1874	6, Feb.	46		55	Dayton, OH	Antwörn, Hannover
Bährens, Maria Margaretha Christine	3, Sept 1896	12, Aug.	45	Reichel	575	Canton, OH	Bremen, Germany
Bahret, Andreas	15, Mar. 1880		78		87	Poughkeepsie, NY	Wolffölden, Marbach, Württemberg
Bahret, Christine	11, Aug. 1898	25, June	88		510	Poughkeepsie, NY	Wolffölden, Marbach, Württemberg
Bahret, Dorothea	13, Sept 1849	9, Aug.	41		148	Poughkeepsie, NY	Wolfstettin, Marbach, Württemberg
Bahret, Jakob	6, Mar. 1865	3, Jan.	55- 6m		40	Poughkeepsie, NY	Kornthal, Württemberg
Bahret, Louise Gottlieba	14, Oct. 1878	3, Oct.	58		327	Poughkeepsie, NY	
Bährwald, Eteretta	27, Nov. 1882	20, Oct.	28- 7m	Tochtermann	383	Oregon, MO	Jefferson County, Missouri
Baier, Anna S.	20, Apr. 1899	26, Feb.	35	Williams	254	Honey Creek, WI	Dover, Wisconsin
Baier, Johan Jakob	22, Aug. 1889	30, July	81- 7m-22d		542	Pittsburg, PA	Bredach, Weinsberg, Württemberg
Baier, Katharina	26, Feb. 1891	25, Jan.	16		142	Boelus, NE	Waterford, Rosine County, Wisconsin
Baier, Maria	28, Aug. 1851	12, Aug.	33	Elenberger	140	Cleveland, OH	
Baier, Maria	13, Apr. 1874	10, Mar.	42- 6m-11d	Kling	119	Columbus, IL	
Baier, Sophia	9, Sept 1872		63		295	Kossuth, OH	Dietlingen, Pforzheim, Baden
Bailey, Maria	11, Dec. 1871	22, Nov.	21- -11d	Wegner	399	Laporte, IN	
Baisch, Catharina	6, Feb. 1890	20, Jan.		Kraft	94	Spencerville, OH	Schönthal, Marbach, Württemberg
Baisch, Eberhart Gottlieb	19, June 1876	26, May	73		199	Kossuth, OH	Hedelfingen, Cannstadt, Württemberg
Bakenhausen, Anna Carolina	20, Oct. 1879	4, Oct.	59	Steur	335	Baltimore, MD	Emden, Ostfriesland
Bakenhus, Wilhelmine	12, Dec. 1889	14, Nov.	42	Kemper	798	Chicago, IL	North Northfield, Cook County, Illinois
Bakenhus, Wilhelmine	14, May 1891	25, Apr.	39	Münz	318	Chicago, IL	Münsingen, Donau, Württemberg
Bäker, Heinrich	22, Feb. 1864	28, Jan.	41- 8m-28d		32	Baltimore, MD	Aufleide bei Homberg an der Ohm, Baden
Bäker, Katharina R.	21, Feb. 1870	28, Nov.	23- 5m- 7d	Laible	63	Kansas City, MO	Lake County, Illinois
Baker, Theresia	17, Nov. 1879	29, Aug.	42-11m	Daak	367	Silver Creek, IL	
Baker, Wibka Engelina	5, Dec. 1864	28, Oct.	33		196	Alton, IL	Logers Fehl, Hannover
Bäker, Wilhelmina	17, Feb. 1873	24, Jan.	63	Albers	53	Highland, IL	Westphalen
Bald, Elisabeth	16, Oct. 1871	2, Sept	26- -25d	Harely	335	Red Bud, IL	
Bald, Georg	27, May 1878	8, May	59- 7m- 1d		167	Red Bud, IL	Hessen-Darmstadt
Bald, Karl	7, June 1880	21, May	17		183	Red Bud, IL	St. Clair County, Illinois
Bald, Margaretha Barbara	17, Oct. 1877	20, Nov.	58	Dressel	407	Red Bud, IL	Geubisch, Amt Sonnenberg, Sachsen-Meiningen
Baldauf, Heinrich	20, Mar. 1846		Inquiry		47	Madison, IN	Ricken, Tieburg, Hessen-Darmstadt
Baldauf, Valentin	20, Mar. 1846		Inquiry		47	Madison, IN	Ricken, Tieburg, Hessen-Darmstadt
Balde, Sybilla	29, Aug. 1850	2, Aug.	29- 6m		140	Louisville, KY	Hessen-Darmstadt
Baldes, Jacob	23, Aug. 1880	26, July			271	Milwaukee, WI	Kindelheim, Koblenz, Simmern, Preußen
Baldt, Wilhelmine Albertine H.	30, Aug. 1880	15, Aug.	22- 4m-22d	Marotz	279	Red Wing, MN	Standemin, Belgard, Hinterpommern
Balet, Margarethe	22, Dec. 1859	1, Nov.	67- 7m-17d		204	Herman, MO	Ochsenburg, Brakenheim, Württemberg
Balk, Antje	25, July 1864	18, June	44	Uhnken	120	Petersburg, IL	Engerhafen, Amt Aurich, Ost-Friesland, Hannover

Christliche Apologete Death Notices --- 1839 - 1899

Name of Deceased	Notice Date	Death Date	Age	Maiden Name	Page	Place of Death	Place of Birth
Balk, Dirk	8, July 1897	20, June	69		431	Lamberton, MN	Süd-Fitterburg, Aurich, Hannover
Balk, Emma	21, Apr. 1887	28, Mar.			254	Melvin, IL	
Balke, Heinrich Friedrich	21, Jan. 1892	26, Dec.	72		46	St. Joseph, MO	Duenna, Buende, Herford, Preußen
Balke, Henriette	9, Mar. 1893	20, Feb.	76		158	Sioux City, IA	Vlotho, Herford , Westphalen
Ball, Katharine	22, Sept 1898	6, Sept	68		607	Louisville, KY	Albersweiler bei Londau, Baiern
Ballentien, Dorothea Louise	15, Jan. 1872	28, Dec.	83- 6m-13d	Kanne	23	Waseca, MN	Nordhausen bei Königsberg, Neumark, Preußen
Bällner, Elenore Elsebein	30, Aug. 1849	18, July	41		140	Beardstown, IL	Wimmer, Hannover
Bällner, Heinrich Wilhelm	30, Aug. 1849	19, July	24		140	Beardstown, IL	Schledehausen bei Osnabrück, Hannover
Ballowsky, Karl	26, Oct. 1899	3, Oct.	82		687	Seguin, TX	Wischwill, Reguit, Preußen
Ballschmider, Jensina	15, Apr. 1872	24, Mar.	30-10m-11d	Dau	127	Fond du Lac, WI	Björt bei Kolding, Dänemark
Ballschmider, Margaretha	22, May 1876	6, May	23	Musgat	167	Fond du Lac, WI	Fache an der Werra, Sachsen-Weimar
Bals, Anton	20, May 1872	23, Apr.	82		167	Lafayette, IN	Friele, Preußen
Bals, Margaretha	22, Sept 1879	28, Aug.	57	Meier	303	Lafayette, IN	Rilsheim, Rheinkreis Baiern
Balser, Maria Louise Friederika	29, Jan. 1857	21, Dec.	21		20	Dayton, OH	Linderhofen, Lippe-Detmold
Balsiger, Lydia	21, Apr. 1898	26, May	19		255	Crandon, SD	Sand Ridge, Cook County, Illinois
Balster, (Mr)	29, Apr. 1872	4, Apr.	44-10m-19d		143	Graham, MO	Marn, Amt Friedburg, Hannover
Balster, Catharina Moderna	9, Oct. 1876	9, Sept	50		327	Alton, IL	Westeraccum, Ostfriesland
Balt, Wilhelm	20, July 1868	30, June	27		231	Red Bud, IL	
Balten, Friedrich	7, Aug. 1871		21		255	Des Moines, IA	Schwalingen, Neuenkirchen, Hannover
Balten, Maria	7, Aug. 1871		52		255	Des Moines, IA	Schwalingen, Neuenkirchen, Hannover
Balten, Peter	7, Aug. 1871		51		255	Des Moines, IA	Schwalingen, Neuenkirchen, Hannover
Baltensperger, Jakob	19, Nov. 1877	4, Nov.	37- 3m		375	Nebraska City, NE	Wülflingen, Zürich, Schweiz
Baltes, Georg	18, Mar. 1872	29, Feb.	63		95	Milwaukee, WI	Kreidelheim, Alt-Simmern, Coblenz, Preußen
Baltes, Georg J.	3, Oct. 1895	5, Sept	56		638	Milwaukee, WI	Keitelheim, RheinPreußen
Baltes, Johan Peter	21,May 1883	5, May	48		167	Milwaukee, WI	Archenthal, Preußen
Baltes, Margarete	17, Nov. 1898	17, Oct.	81	Wickert	735	Milwaukee, WI	Keutelheim, Koblenz, RheinPreußen
Baltes, Maria Margaretha	21, Apr. 1859	1, Apr.	52- 3m-24d	Klumb	64	St. Louis, MO	Ellren, Koblenz, Preußen
Balthaser, Emilie Louisa	25, Nov. 1897	30, Oct.	27	Koch	751	St. Louis, MO	Franklin County, Missouri
Baltzer, Eva	1, Aug. 1870	4, June	22		247	German Creek, IA	Burlington, Iowa
Balzer, Andreas	25, Aug. 1887	12, Aug.	73		542	Harper, IA	Schiers, Graubünden, Schweiz
Balzer, Barbara	16, Dec. 1886	23, Nov.	74	Hartmann	7	Des Moines, IA	Kanton Graubünden, Schweiz
Balzer, Dorothea E.	19, Feb. 1866	29, Jan.	32		62	Lowell, WI	Zorndorf, Preußen
Balzer, Elisabeth	21, Dec. 1893	24, Nov.	85		814	Harper, IA	St. Antonian, Graubünden, Schweiz
Balzer, Florian	13, Feb. 1896	21, Jan.	57	Hartmann	110	Des Moines, IA	Schiers, Graubünden, Schweiz
Balzer, Wilhelm	8, May 1865	19, Mar.	37		76	Watertown, WI	Ziecher bei Königsberg, Preußen
Bamberg, Albertina	22, Dec. 1898	25, Nov.	30	Bader	815	New Haven, CT	Affoltern, Zürich, Schweiz
Bamberg, Anna Barbara	18, Nov. 1886	28, Oct.	89- 8m		7	New Haven, CT	Tachbach, Sachsen-Meiningen
Bamberg, Anna Barbara	9, Dec. 1886	28, Oct.	89- 8m		7	New Haven, CT	Tachbach, Sachsen-Meiningen
Bamberg, Henry	25, Jan. 1894	10, Dec.	20		62	New Haven, CT	
Bamberg, Karolina	22, June 1899	30, May	70	Euerle	399	New Haven, CT	Groß-Aßbach bei Backnang, Württemberg
Bamberg, Wilhelm M.	9, Oct. 1890	31, Aug.	17		654	New Haven, CT	New Haven, Connecticut
Bamberger, Joseph	14, Dec. 1863	25, Oct.	39		200	St. Louis, MO	Buchenau, Bidenkopf, Hessen-Darmstadt
Bambrock, Louise	27, June 1861	26, May	23- 2m-11d	Steinike	104	New Knoxville, OH	Königsberg Miswald, Alt-Preußen, Preußen
Bamfort, Sophia	6, Apr. 1874	18, Mar.	56-11m-11d		111	Burlington, IA	Minden, Preußen
Bandel, Christian	26, May 1873	11, Mar.	33		167	Troy, NY	Weiler, Schorndorf, Württemberg
Bandel, Katharina	22, Dec. 1898	7, Nov.	47	Ningle	815	Pasadena, CA	Oberamt Rothenburg, Württemberg

Christliche Apologete Death Notices --- 1839 - 1899

Name of Deceased	Notice Date	Death Date	Age	Maiden Name	Page	Place of Death	Place of Birth
Bandelow, Carl	1, Aug. 1889	23, June	14- - 4d		494	Forest, WI	
Bandelow, Gusta	1, Aug. 1889	7, July	16- 8m- 3d		494	Forest, WI	
Bandelow, Karl W.	8, Dec. 1892	7, Nov.	62		782	Fond du Lac, WI	Klein Holzendorf bei Prenzlau, Brandenburg
Bandelow, William	8, Aug. 1889	25, July	12		510	Forest, WI	Forest, Wisconsin
Bandi, Nikolaus	14, Dec. 1893	11, Nov.	60		798	Allegheny City, PA	Oberwyl, Bern, Schweiz
Bandow, Karl	19, May 1884	26, Apr.	67		7	Decorah, IA	Seehausen, Preußen
Bandow, Maria	15, Aug. 1889	24, July	67- 2m-24d		526	Decorah, IA	Ludwigsluft, Mecklenburg-Schwerin
Bang, Emma Emilie	15, Sept 1873	22, Aug.	14- 4m		295	Red Wing, MN	
Bang, Heinrich	14, June 1894	29, May	70		390	Red Wing, MN	Langolan, Erfurt, Preußen
Bang, Ida	19, July 1875	2, July	12- - 3d		231	Red Wing, MN	
Bang, Margaretha	11, Aug. 1884	22, July	64		7	Brooklyn, NY	Kaiserslautern, Rheinkreis Baiern
Bang, Minnie	9, Sept 1897	19, Aug.	32	Kreß	575	Red Wing, MN	Featherstone, Minnesota
Bang, Wesley	20, Nov. 1882	6, Nov.	21		375	Red Wing, MN	
Bank, Dorothea	6, Mar. 1890	10, Feb.	78- 9m	Witt	158	Swanton, NE	Dölitz, Piritz, Hinterpommern
Banker, Eduard	6, Apr. 1874	13, Feb.	14		111	Rockford, MN	
Bannmeyer, Caroline	20, Nov. 1882	21, Aug.	59	Schlagenhauff	375	Greenfield, MA	Oberdegesheim, Balingen, Württemberg
Banthauer, Henriette	19, May 1887	23, Apr.	68	Fitzan	318	Canton, MO	Gräfenhainchen, Sachsen
Bantz, Anna Maria	11, Sept 1882	24, Aug.	66	Brunner	295	Evansville, IN	Klingen, Rheinkreis Baiern
Bantz, Barbara	14, Feb. 1889	8, Jan.	62		110	Evansville, IN	Mosbach, Hessen-Darmstadt
Bantz, Christine Rosine	21, July 1884	28, June	38	Allinger	7	Evansville, IN	Laufen, Württemberg
Banz, Elisabeth	22, Dec. 1853	11, Nov.	46	Bitzmann	204	Shelbyville, IN	Engelsheim bei Weißenburg, Elsaß
Banze, Anna	11, Apr. 1895	10, Mar.	69	Henkes	238	Giard, IA	Kassel, Hessen-Nassau
Banzhaf, Pauline	2, Dec. 1886	5, Nov.	34- -13d	Beiser	7	Humboldt, NE	Heiden, Appelzell, Schweiz
Bänziger, Bertha	12, Jan. 1899	30, Nov.	51	Tobler	30	Seguin, TX	Reichenberg, Baiern
Bär, Babette	2, Nov. 1899	29, Sept	58	Heer	703	Clay Center, KS	Aarburg, Aargau, Schweiz
Bär, Jacob	19, Nov. 1896	26, Oct.	80		750	Alton, IL	Ostheim, Elsaß
Bär, Salome	29, June 1885		49	Fröhlich	7	Toledo, OH	Knebecke, Rußland
Barcart, Emilia	29, July 1897	29, June	53		479	Independence, MO	Tecklenburg, Münster, Preußen
Bardelmeier, Eberhard	29, July 1872	13, July	72		247	Bunker Hill, IL	
Bardels, Anna	6, Mar. 1882	12, Feb.	16- 2m-15d		79	Buffalo, NY	GräfenLeinchen, Sachsen
Bardhauer, Amalia	12, Sept 1889	22, Aug.	39	Just	590	Peace Creek, KS	
Bareis, Albert	4, Oct. 1888	21, Sept	15- 9m- 1d		638	Platteville, WI	Breitenfürst, Welzheim, Württemberg
Bareis, Gilbert	20, July 1885	2, July	55		7	Platteville, WI	Nashville, Tennessee
Bargatzi, Florian	8, Apr. 1897		37		222	Nashville, TN	Sandhatten, Oldenburg
Barkmann, Anna	19, Sept 1870	3, Jan.	68- 2m- 6d	Rolle	303	Newark, OH	Nierstadt, Oldenburg
Barkmeier, Hermann G.	2, Oct. 1865	4, Sept	72		160	Pekin, IL	Sandhatten, Oldenburg
Barkmeier, Tolke	2, Oct. 1865	28, July	52	Addei	160	Pekin, IL	Sullivan County, New York
Barkhöfer, Louise Wilhelmine Karoline	18, Nov. 1878	29, Oct.	48		367	St. Louis, MO	Hille, Minden, Preußen
Barkoff, W. Charlotte Louise	8, Dec. 1898	18, Nov.	67		783	Wapello, IA	Basel, Fairfield County, Ohio
Barlau, Christian	19, Apr. 1869	28, Mar.	80		127	Benton, MN	Garten, Oldenburg
Bärnd, Carolina F.W.	30, July 1877	11, July	60-10m	Tietz	247	Red Wing, MN	Loharst, Germany
Barner, Friedrich Wilhelm	31, Aug. 1874	8, July	85- 7m		279	Herman, MO	Linnofko, Kreis Beret, Danzig, Preußen

Christliche Apologete Death Notices --- 1839 - 1899

Name of Deceased	Notice Date	Death Date	Age	Maiden Name	Page	Place of Death	Place of Birth
Barnes, Georg Sanford	18, June 1891	2, June	26		398	Pekin, IL	Washington, Illinois
Barnett, Johan	19, Jan. 1885	13, Dec.	82		7	Montrose, MN	
Barnhart, Christine	27, Dec. 1880	6, Dec.	23	Cranick	415	Zilwaukee, MI	Haberschlacht, Württemberg
Barnitz, Elisabeth	31, May 1860	5, Apr.	61		88	New Oxford, PA	
Barrett, Maria	13, Nov. 1882	17, Oct.	23- 8m- 8d	Huser	367	Oxford, NE	Meißenheim, Lahr, Baden
Bärstecher, Johanna	23, June 1884	4, Mar.	29- -11d		7	Toledo, OH	Bondorf, Herrenberg, Württemberg
Barteit, Friedrich	2, May 1881	7, Apr.	28-10m- 7d		143	Lena, IL	Succow a. d. Ihne, Pommern
Bartel, Caroline	13, Oct. 1884	20, Aug.	80	Kayser	7	Humboldt, NE	Blumberg, Pieritz, Pommern
Bartel, Johan Fr. Theo.	28, June 1880	6, June	62- 1m- 9d		207	Pomeroy, OH	Breitwisch, Vorpommern
Bartel, Louisa	26, Sept 1881	11, Sept	79- 8m- 9d		311	Tomah, WI	Watenbruch an der Warte, Preußen
Bartelheim, Heinrich	22, Oct. 1896	5, Oct.	69		687	Belleville, IL	Binghofen, Preußen
Bartels, Christian	13, July 1863	22, June	64- 2m- 6d		112	Jackson, MO	Schleweke, Lather am Bahrenberge, Braunschweig
Bartels, Christine L.	17, Dec. 1883	23, Nov.	89		7	Pomeroy, OH	Eldachsen, Petershagen, Westphalen
Bartels, Dorothea Maria Elisabeth	13, Sept 1888	25, Aug.	82- 6m-19d	Broockmeier	590	Jackson, MO	Groß-Hehre, Hannover
Bartels, Georg Gerhard	9, June 1879	21, May	19- 7m-22d	Vrehee	183	Quincy, IL	Warsaw, Illinois
Bartels, Heinrich	11, Oct. 1894	3, Aug.	75		662	Buffalo, NY	Weidendorf, Woland, Mecklenburg-Schwerin
Bartels, Heinrich	8, Dec. 1884	17, Nov.	50-10m- 7d		7	Jackson, MO	Schleweke, Luther, Braunschweig
Bartels, Louise	18, Nov. 1897	30, Oct.	62	Klenke	735	Lexington, MO	Lüntorf, Gronde, Hannover
Bartels, Wilhelm	7, Dec. 1863				196	Charleston, VA	
Bartels, Wilhelmine	16, Feb. 1885	21, Dec.	58	Knape	7	Dalton, MO	Lenzen an der Elbe, Preußen
Bartelsmeier, Friedrich	19, Mar. 1866	18, Feb.	63-11m		94	Union, MO	Bierkirchen, Minden, Preußen
Bartelsmeier, Wilhelmine	22, Jan. 1877	26, Dec.	37	Krüger	31	Nashville, IL	Unterlabe, Preußen
Bartelsmeyer, Heinrich	11, Sept 1890	25, July	80- 5m		590	Hoyleton, IL	Hartenhausen, Minden, Preußen
Bartelt, Ferdinand A.	3, July 1890	17, June	42		430	Lena, IL	Sucow , Pommern
Bartelt, Maria Therese	7, Oct. 1897	14, Sept	28	Dehnert	639	Oconomowoc, WI	Concord, Wisconsin
Bartelt, Wilhelmine	14, Jan. 1892	16, Dec.	69	Walter	30	Lena, IL	Succow a. d. Ihna, Satzig, Pommern
Barth,	29, Oct. 1847	8, Oct.	43- - 8d		175	Williamsburg, NY	
Barth, Adam	6, Mar. 1865	4, Feb.	55		40	Lafayette, IN	Kirchbormbach, Hessen-Darmstadt
Barth, Barbara	10, Apr. 1876	21, Mar.	63	Kritschgau	118	Milwaukee, WI	Langenzenn, Baiern
Barth, Franz Christoph	31, Oct. 1895	3, Oct.	63		702	Rochester, NY	Nielingen, Baden
Barth, Friederike	31, Jan. 1889		54	Mahler	78	Carthage, OH	Dürmens, Maulbrunn, Württemberg
Barth, Georg J.	1, Oct. 1896	24, Aug.	31- 1m- 8d		639	Grand Rapids, MI	Philadelphia, Pennsylvania
Barth, J. H. (Rev)	30, Mar. 1899	4, Mar.	78		207	Indianapolis, IN	Kirchbrombach, Hessen-Darmstadt
Barth, Joseph	31, May 1855	17, Apr.			88	Mills Prarie, IL	
Barth, Mamie	7, Nov. 1889	13, Oct.	24- 1m-29d	Blochstedt	718	New Albany, IN	Nashville, Tennessee
Barth, Maria Catharina	3, Mar.1873	2, Feb.	61- -15d	Gremme	71	Canton, MO	Schelterhausen, Hannover
Barth, Ottilie	27, Sept 1894	24, Aug.	25		630	Decorah, IA	Wallace, Porth County, Ontario, Canada
Barth, Ottilie Maria	23, Jan. 1846	21, Oct.	1m		15	Burlington, MO	Cole County, Missouri
Barth, Peter	6, Apr. 1899	18, Feb.	64		222	Toledo, OH	Oberalben, Rheinkreis Baiern
Barth, Philipp	22, Mar. 1894	1, Mar.	76		198	Burlington, IA	Brumbach, Hessen-Darmstadt
Barth, Sophia Ottilie	26, Sept 1846	5, Sept	24		155	Louisville, KY	Hirschfeld, Kurhessen
Barth, Wilhelmine C. C.	14, June 1894	27, May	21		390	Grand Rapids, MI	Philadelphia, Pennsylvania
Bartheimes, Johan Georg	24, Nov. 1862	27, July			188	Roxbury, MA	
Barthelheim, Ernst	17, June 1886				7	St. Paul, MN	
Barthelheim, Friedrich	27, June 1864		37		104	Belleville, IL	Böninghausen, Lübeke, Minden, Preußen
Barthels, Albertine Friederika	20, Dec. 1875	9, Nov.			407	Tomah, WI	Neuberlinchen, Brandenburg, Preußen

Christliche Apologete Death Notices --- 1839 - 1899

Name of Deceased	Notice Date	Death Date	Age	Maiden Name	Page	Place of Death	Place of Birth
Barthelsmeyer, Friedrich	10, Aug. 1863	17, May	23- 5m- 2d		128	Union, MO	Bergkirchen, Minden, Preußen
Barthelsmeyer, Maria	6, Apr. 1885		74- 4m		7	Hoyleton, IL	
Barthold, Carl Friedrich	21, Oct. 1852				172	Beardstown, IL	
Bartholdi-Bennefeld, John	10, Aug. 1899	9, July	78		511	Red Wing, MN	Wehrendorf, Minden, Preußen
Bartholmeß, Johan Georg	15, Apr. 1867	21, Mar.	80		118	Roxbury, MA	Oestheim, Baiern
Bartholomäus, Anna Katharina	11, Apr. 1870	11, Mar.	68	Trimber	119	East Troy, WI	Höhnebach, Rothenburg, Hessen-Kassel
Bartholomäus, Karoline	15, Oct. 1883	24, Sept	46- 2m-19d	Benseler	335	Warrenton, MO	Beyenrode, Hannover
Bartholomeus, Barbara	19, July 1860		68		116	Boston, MA	
Bartlelt, Friedrich	4, June 1891	10, May	56		366	Oconomowoc, WI	Farbezin bei Naugard, Germany
Bartling, Friedrich	23, Apr. 1891	30, Mar.	65- -21d		270	Pittsburg, PA	Borstiel bei Hagen, Hannover
Bartling, Friedrich Karl	21, Sept 1885	17, Aug.	30		7	Schnectady, NY	Hille, Minden, Preußen
Bartling, Wilhelmine	19, Nov. 1891	19, Oct.		Sündermann	750	Hebron, IA	Bentrob, Hohenhausen, Lippe-Detmold
Barton, Maria E.	14, July 1884	23, June	25		7	Lawrenceburg, IN	Lawrenceburg, Dearborn County, Indiana
Bartruf, Louise	11, Mar. 1886	25, Feb.	18		7	Cincinnati, OH	Cincinnati, Hamilton County, Ohio
Bartruff, Karl	16, May 1895		66		318	Cincinnati, OH	Unterbrüten, Württemberg
Bartrum, Konrad	6, Sept 1839		Inquiry		143	Livingston, IL	
Bärtschi, Elisabeth	12, Jan. 1899	26, Dec.	73- - 9d		30	Chicago, IL	Unterbreitsbach, Sachsen-Weimar
Bartz,	10, Apr. 1882				119		
Bartz, Arthur	1, Sept 1898	20, June	12		559	Stevens Point, WI	Cas County, Wisconsin
Bartz, Bertha	30, Apr. 1891	19, Mar.	37- 7m-28d	Wölfel	286	Buffalo, NY	Massau, Preußen
Bartz, Christian	27, Dec. 1880	16, Nov.	66- 6m-15d		415	Buffalo, NY	Stepen, Pommern
Bartz, Margaretha Barbara	21, Jan. 1878	3, Jan.	52	Hammer	23	Oregon, MO	Fischbach, Rheinkreis Baiern
Bartz, Regina	9, Mar. 1863	27, Jan.	73		40	Jeffersonville, NY	Aichschieß, Eßlingen, Württemberg
Bartz, Wilhelmina	18, Oct. 1894		65- 9m-11d	Lüdke	678	Ahnapee, WI	suckoushoff, Treptow an der Rega, Pommern
Bartz, Wilhelmine	22, Jan. 1891	22, Dec.	35	Hannemann	62	Buffalo, NY	Kritzkow, Mecklenburg-Schwerin
Barz, Christreich Alb. Ludwig	17, June 1897	10, May	46		383	Redfield, SD	Groß-Jestin, Fürstenthum, Köslin, Pommern
Barz, Frank	17, June 1897	10, May	19		383	Redfield, SD	Roberts, Illinois
Barz, Franz Friedrich Ferdinand C.	17, June 1897	10, May	54		383	Redfield, SD	Groß-Jestin, Fürstenthum, Köslin, Pommern
Barz, Reinhold	17, June 1897	10, May	20		383	Redfield, SD	Roberts, Illinois
Bäsel, Jakob	30, May 1895	10, May	74		350	Berea, OH	Keshofen, Rheinpfalz Baiern
Bäsel, Sophia	11, Feb. 1892	18, Jan.	74	Weier	94	Milwaukee, WI	Jarin, Collberg, Pommern
Baselt, Auguste	2, June 1879	4, May	31- 3m- 9d	Magdsick	175	Chicago, IL	Zewitz, Hinterpommern
Basler, Verona	5, Apr. 1894	25, Feb.	75	Hauri	230	Buffalo, NY	Hirschtal, Aargau, Schweiz
Baßler, Friederika	20, Sept 1888	7, Sept	55- -12d		606	Milwaukee, WI	
Bast, Augusta	16, Apr. 1891	20, Mar.	38	Blank	254	Wadena, MN	Repzin, Pommern
Bast, Margaretha	1, July 1878	13, June	78- 5m- 7d	Thomas	207	Llano, TX	Unzenberg, Rheinpreußen
Bastian, Emil F.	1, Oct. 1896	29, Aug.	21		639	Redfield, SD	Roberts, Ford County, Illinois
Bastian, Friedrich	14, Feb. 1889	17, Jan.	77- 4m		110	Ft. Dodge, IA	Mecklenburg-Schwerin
Bastian, Ida Wilhelmina	2, June 1898	9, May	70	Schulz	351	Chicago, IL	Stralsund, Pommern
Bastian, Irvin Benjamin	23, Jan. 1896		37		62	Redfield, SD	Roberts, Ford County, Illinois
Bastian, Johanne	12, Dec. 1889	8, Nov.	43	Grobe	798	Redfield, SD	Neuenkirchen, Mecklenburg-Strelitz
Bastian, Katharina	19, July 1894	1, July	90	Steener	470	Pekin, IL	Union County, Pennsylvania
Bastian, Ludwig	13, Feb. 1871	27, Jan.	65		55	Charleston, WI	Boddin, Mecklenburg-Schwerin
Bastian, Maria	15, Dec. 1879	26, Sept	64- 9m	Wackerow	399	Flood Creek, IA	Klenz, Mecklenburg-Schwerin
Bath, Carl	14, May 1891	21, Apr.	74- - 7d		318	Storm Lake, IA	
Bath, Clara Bernardine	16, June 1884	27, May	74	Konerding	7	Sac County, IA	Oldenburg

Christliche Apologete Death Notices --- 1839 - 1899

Name of Deceased	Notice Date	Death Date	Age	Page	Maiden Name	Place of Death	Place of Birth
Bathel, Anton	22, Sept 1898	30, Aug.	61	607	Hamm	Kramer, NE	Soltau, Boizenburg, Mecklenburg-Schwerin
Batschelet, (Mrs)	26, July 1860	17, June		120	Maurer	East Troy, WI	
Batschelet, Elisabeth	16, June 1859	21, May	52- 3m-15d	96		East Troy, WI	Sutz, Bern, Schweiz
Batschelet, Louise	9, June 1887	14, May	57	366	Uebele	Burlington, WI	Pfahlbronn, Württemberg
Batschelet, Maria	19, Jan. 1899	23, Dec.	89	47	Strupp	Burlington, WI	Schweiz
Bätschelet, Rudolph	18, July 1870	13, June	68	231		East Troy, WI	Sutz, Ober Amt Niedau, Bern, Schweiz
Batschlet, Rudolph	20, Jan. 1879	5, Jan.	38- 8m-29d	23		Burlington, WI	Nidau, Bern, Schweiz
Battaglia, Christian	24, Mar. 1873	23, Feb.	58- 6m- 3d	95		Liberty, MO	
Battaglia, Elias	1, Mar. 1880	8, Feb.	28- 1m- 8d	71		Liberty, MO	
Batzer, Elisabeth	8, Aug. 1861	20, May	68- 6m	128	Schmidt	East Troy, WI	Chirschen, Graubünden, Schweiz
Bau , Henrietta	22, Nov. 1888	28, Oct.	58- 8m-26d	750	Koerner	Baltimore, MD	Braunwalde, Sachsen-Altenburg
Bau, Catharina	8, Oct. 1857	17, Sept	22	164		Baltimore, MD	Bürgel, Kurhessen
Bau, Heinrich	3, Feb. 1873	15, Jan.	44	39		Baltimore, MD	Schönstadt, Kreis Marburg, Kurhessen
Baub, Chr.	12, Mar. 1883	20, Feb.	58	87		Burlington, WI	Canton Graubünden, Schweiz
Bauchhans, Catharina	12, Nov. 1847	25, Aug.	50	183		New Orleans, LA	
Baue , Karoline	17, Feb. 1898	1, Feb.	49	111	Dunsing	Chester, IL	Zelle, Hannover
Bauenpohl, Charlotte Louise	24, Apr. 1871	6, Apr.	67-1m	135		Greenville, OH	Levern, Minden, Preußen
Bauer , Caroline	21, Apr. 1892	2, Apr.	59- 1m- 7d	254		Louisville, KY	Weiler, Weinsberg, Württemberg
Bauer , Johan Georg	20, Aug. 1896	26, July	51	542		Hedwigs Hill, TX	Dettenhausen, Tübingen, Württemberg
Bauer , Rosine	25, Feb. 1892	23, Jan.	83	126	Durst	Hedwigs Hill, TX	Dettenhausen, Württemberg
Bauer, (Mrs)	20, Oct. 1879	23, Aug.	63- -25d	335		Montgomery, ---	Birmensdorf, Zürich, Schweiz
Bauer, (Mrs)	31, May 1869			175		Boonville, MO	
Bauer, A.	12, Jan. 1860	27, Nov.	38	8		Ft. Riley, KS	Klein-Vora, Preußen
Bauer, Abraham	26, July 1875	10, July	55	239		Toledo, OH	Oberhofen, Bern, Schweiz
Bauer, Adam	8, Aug. 1864	30, June	24	128		Blue Island, IL	
Bauer, Alvina	23, Aug. 1894	6, Aug.	70	550	Kruspe	Salem, NE	Mühltroff, Sachsen
Bauer, Anke Jansen	23, Jan. 1862	2, Dec.	32	16	Dickman	Lyona, KS	Strackholt, Amt Aurich, Hannover
Bauer, Anna Catharine	12, Mar. 1896	8, Feb.	63- 5m-24d	175	Schmidt	Lyona, KS	Gotha, Sachsen
Bauer, Anna Christine	19, July 1894	29, June	57	470	Kürner	Dallas, TX	Neuffen, Nartigen, Württemberg
Bauer, Anna Elisabeth	8, Dec. 1879	24, Nov.	63	391		Wilton, IA	Geismar, Fritzlar, Kurhessen
Bauer, Anna Katharina	13, June 1870	7, May	60- 8m-15d	191		Webster, OH	Reckershausen, Simmer, Koblenz, Preußen
Bauer, Anna Maria	3, May 1894	14, Apr.	73	294	Gorth	Yonkers, NY	Offstein, Rhein-Hessen
Bauer, Anton	7, Sept 1868	25, Aug.	49	287		Aurora, IL	Mistelholz, Böhmen
Bauer, Auguste	24, May 1880	20, Apr.	32- 5m- 8d	167		Chicago, IL	Eggesin, Pommern
Bauer, Bertha	26, Jan. 1899	21, Dec.	53- 2m- 5d	62	Träger	Minneapolis, MN	Freiburg, Sachsen
Bauer, Catharina	6, May 1878	12, Mar.	52	143		Baraboo, WI	Bieber, Baiern
Bauer, Christian	16, Aug. 1888	23, July	68	526		Waco, TX	Klein-Bottwar, Marbach, Württemberg
Bauer, Christiane Katharine	15, Nov. 1888	22, Oct.	80	734	Krämer	Lexington, TX	Unterkessach, Baden
Bauer, Dietrich	16, Aug. 1849	30, June	25	132		Dayton, OH	Edelfingen, Württemberg
Bauer, Dora Emma	11, Nov. 1897	14, Oct.	22	719		Wheelersburg, OH	Wheelersburg, Ohio
Bauer, Dorothea	6, Jan. 1887	14, Dec.	65	14	Hauck	York, NE	Pleidelsheim, Marbach, Württemberg
Bauer, Elisabeth	4, Aug. 1887	20, July	64	494	Schmollwein	Louisville, KY	Gemminen, Eppingen, Baden
Bauer, Elisabeth	5, Apr. 1860	15, Nov.		56	Walter	St. Louis, MO	
Bauer, Elisabeth	10, Sept 1877	11, Aug.	50- 9m	295	Young	Farmington, MO	
Bauer, Elisabeth D.	2, Mar. 1899	22, Jan.	51	143	Krumme	St. Joseph, MO	Baltimore, Maryland
Bauer, Ernst Friedrich	2, May 1895	5, Apr.	46	286		Mt. Olive, IL	Eibenstock, Sachsen

Christliche Apologete Death Notices --- 1839 - 1899

Name of Deceased	Notice Date	Death Date	Age	Maiden Name	Page	Place of Death	Place of Birth
Bauer, Eva Susanna	18, Sept 1890	14, Aug.	64	Weitbrenner	606	Mt. Vernon, IN	Oberschüpf, Boxberg, Baden
Bauer, Francisca Juliane	18, Mar. 1897	26, Feb.	30	Gatt	174	Hedwigs Hill, TX	Llano County, Texas
Bauer, Friederika	25, Oct. 1875	21, Sept	55		343	Dayton, OH	Erdmanshausen, Marbach, Württemberg
Bauer, Friedrich	28, Nov. 1881	9, Nov.	21- 7m-24d		383	Chillicothe, OH	Neussen, Nürtingen, Württemberg
Bauer, Friedrich	6, Dec. 1894	26, Oct.	50		790	Evansville, IN	Elpersheim, Württemberg
Bauer, Friedrich August	6, Oct. 1887	18, Sept	71		638	Pittsburg, PA	Mühltroff, Sachsen
Bauer, Friedrich Wilhelm	24, Oct. 1881	12, Oct.	21		343	Portsmouth, OH	Gebhart's Station, Scioto County, Ohio
Bauer, Georg	23, Nov. 1874	23, Nov.	64		375	Blue Island, IL	Wankheim, Württemberg
Bauer, Gottlieb	7, Apr. 1879	15, Mar.	28- 4m		111	Llano, TX	Fredericksburg, Gillespie County, Texas
Bauer, Heinrich	31, July 1890	28, June	71		494	De Soto, MO	Lichtenau, Hessen-Kassel
Bauer, Johan	27, Sept 1880	10, Sept	68- 3m-29d		311	Nashville, TN	Neckarthailfingen, Nürtingen, Württemberg
Bauer, Johan	24, Jan. 1871	6, Jan.	47		31	St. Louis, MO	Horkheim bei Heilbronn, Württemberg
Bauer, Johan Christian	18, Oct. 1875	29, Sept	76		335	Marietta, OH	Oberriexingen, Vaihingen, Württemberg
Bauer, Johan F.	27, July 1893	30, June	69- 4m-10d		478	Leeds, WI	Grotenbins, Mecklenburg-Schwerin
Bauer, Johann	12, Mar. 1883	20, Feb.	82		87	Baraboo, WI	Grün, Weißenbrunn, Baiern
Bauer, John Wilhelm	17, Jan. 1876	26, Dec.	40- -11d		23	Portsmouth, OH	Neckarshausen, Simmern, Preußen
Bauer, Karl	6, Sept 1869	6, Sept	53		287	St. Louis, MO	Philadelphia, Pennsylvania
Bauer, Karoline	3, Mar. 1884	3, Mar.	21- -26d		7	Mt. Vernon, IN	
Bauer, Katharina	22, Nov. 1894	4, Nov.	70		758	Aurora, IL	Vaihingen, Böblingen, Württemberg
Bauer, Louis	27, May 1886	15, May	30		7	St. Louis, MO	St. Louis, Missouri
Bauer, Louise	29, Dec. 1898	2, Dec.	60	Götz	828	Cincinnati, OH	Flein, Heilbronn, Württemberg
Bauer, Lydia A.	23, May 1895	3, May	25- 2m- 6d		334	Louisville, KY	Louisville, Jefferson County, Kentucky
Bauer, M.	7, June 1894		86		374	Hedwigs Hill, TX	Dettenhausen, Tübingen, Württemberg
Bauer, Magdalena	25, May 1863	29, Apr.	44	Schmidt	84	Louisville, KY	Guntalingen, Stammheim, Zürich, Schweiz
Bauer, Magdalena	18, Feb. 1884	26, Jan.	31- 8m-22d	Walther	7	Chicago, IL	Blue Island, Cook County, Illinois
Bauer, Margaretha	24, Apr. 1890	30, Mar.	64	Blöche	270	Wathena, KS	Untermußbach, Freudenstadt, Württemberg
Bauer, Margaretha	23, Aug. 1869	23, July	60		271	Nashville, TN	Echterdingen, Württemberg
Bauer, Maria M.	19, June 1890	31, May	81		398	Philadelphia, PA	Nürtingen, Württemberg
Bauer, Michael	9, Apr. 1891	17, Mar.	52		238	Chicago, IL	Wankheim, Württemberg
Bauer, Philipp	1, May 1871	21, Apr.	84- 1m-13d		143	Marion, OH	Ellmerdingen, Pforzheim, Baden
Bauer, Rosina	2, Jan. 1896	13, Dec.	80	Schuster	14	Galion, OH	Oedenhart, Waiblingen, Württemberg
Bauer, Rosine Margarethe	21, July 1884	7, July	27		7	Geneva Lake, WI	Württemberg
Bauer, Sophia	21, June 1880	31, May	25		199	Louisville, KY	
Bauer, Wilhelm	13, Dec. 1894	24, Nov.	69		806	Jamestown, MO	Ober-Ingelheim, Hessen-Darmstadt
Bauerfeld, Georg Julius	14, Jan. 1892	23, Dec.	13		30	Cincinnati, OH	Covington, Kenton County, Kentucky
Bäuerle, Georg	20, Aug. 1883	7, Aug.	46- 2m-27d		271	Columbus, OH	Heiningen, Backnang, Württemberg
Bäuerle, Johannes	7, Feb. 1881	18, Jan.	54- 6m- 2d		47	Columbus, OH	Hainingen, Backnang, Württemberg
Bäuerle, Julie	10, May 1855	27, Apr.	31- -16d	Knoderer	76	Columbus, OH	
Bäuerle, Louise Caroline	10, Feb. 1868	17, Jan.	13		47	Columbus, OH	
Bäuerle, Magdalena	31, Dec. 1883	15, Dec.	69	Eichelberger	7	Menomonie, WI	Münchweiler an der Alsenz, RheinPfalz Baiern
Bäuerle, Tobias	25, Apr. 1864	25, Jan.	43		68	Dayton, OH	Königsbrunn, Heidenheim, Württemberg
Bäuerlein, Johan	5, Nov. 1877	2, Oct.	49- 5m-24d		359	Chicago, IL	Roth am See, Gerabronn, Württemberg
Bauermann, Arjen	30, July 1896	7, July	64		495	Chicago, IL	Norden, Ostfriesland
Bauerrichter, Johan Friedrich	4, Apr. 1881	18, Mar.	75		111	Hopewell, MO	Valdorf, Minden, Westphalen, Preußen
Bauerrichter, Karoline M.	22, Nov. 1880	1, Nov.	22		375	Hopewell, MO	Warren County, Missouri
Bauersax, Hanna	1, May 1882	16, Apr.	24- 2m-18d		143	Woodville, OH	Sandusky County, Ohio

Christliche Apologete Death Notices --- 1839 - 1899

Name of Deceased	Notice Date	Death Date	Age	Maiden Name	Place of Death	Page	Place of Birth
Bauersfeld, Henriette	9, Dec. 1886	23, Nov.	78	Otto	Covington, KY	7	Schlesien
Bauersfeld, Johanne	2, May 1895	18, Apr.	76	Nelter	Rock Island, IL	286	Otterbach, Rheinkreis Baiern
Baug, Louis	6, July 1893	19, June	37- 9m-19d		Cincinnati, OH	430	Sharon, LeSueur County, Minnesota
Bauleke, Wilhelmine Henriette	27, Dec. 1894	2, Dec.	29		Le Sueur, MN	836	Norden bei Göttingen, Hannover
Baulke, Wilhelm	25, Nov. 1878	8, Nov.	67- 3m-27d		St. Paul, MN	375	Wantagh, Queens County, New York
Baulser, Henriette Auguste Caroline	7, Mar. 1895	24, Jan.	31	Stehl	Hicksville, NY	158	Impflingen, Rheinpfalz Baiern
Baulwitz, Barbara	24, Aug. 1874	4, Aug.		Peterson	Cincinnati, OH	273	Weisenheim (am Berg), Baiern
Baum , Elisabeth	22, Sept 1853	18, Aug.			Boonville, IN	152	Schloßvigpach, Sachsen-Weimar
Baum , Elisabeth Magdalena	7, Dec. 1893	17, Nov.	81	Schimmel	Chicago, IL	782	Dauphin County, Pennsylvania
Baum, Michael	1, Sept 1873	11, Aug.	55- 3m-23d		Edgerton, OH	279	Oberamt Künzelsau, Württemberg
Bauman, Andreas	7, June 1894	7, May	86			374	Herblingen, Bern, Schweiz
Bauman, Christian	3, May 1894	28, Mar.	51		Denver, CO	294	Diesbach, Bern, Schweiz
Bauman, Magdalena	14, Apr. 1892	24, Mar.	51	Wütherich	Vermillion, OH	238	Birmingham, Erie County, Ohio
Baumann, Anna	22, June 1893	1, June	20		Denver, CO	398	Kassel, Kurhessen
Baumann, Caroline	16, July 1891	25, June	67	Müller	Tacoma, WA	462	Bern, Schweiz
Baumann, Christian	25, Aug. 1879	8, Aug.	80		Blue Island, IL	271	Remptendorf, Reuß-Greiz
Baumann, Christiana	23, Aug. 1888	7, Aug.	70- 5m-25d	Nestler	Jordan, MN	542	Rheingönheim, Rheinkreis Baiern
Baumann, Christoph	7, Dec. 1854	12, Oct.	55		Weston, MO	196	Hessenrode, Kurhessen
Baumann, Chrstine	26, Oct. 1893	25, Sept	55	Münzdorf	Allegheny City, PA	686	Aarau, Aargau, Schweiz
Baumann, Elisabeth	4, Apr. 1881	20, Feb.	78	Bannhofer	Warsaw, IL	111	Kanton Bern, Schweiz
Baumann, Elisabeth	7, Oct. 1872	14, Sept	64- 4m		Vermillion, OH	327	New York
Baumann, Emma	19, May 1887	17, Apr.	36	Scheerer	Hartford, CT	318	Neuhofen, Rheinkreis Baiern
Baumann, Eva Elisabetha	13, Sept 1849	21, Aug.	17- 6m	Brenner	Platte County, MO	148	
Baumann, Georg	14, Jan. 1884		46		St. Philip, IN	7	
Baumann, Georg A. M.	8, Aug. 1889	13, July	77		Marrs, IN	510	Kocherstetten, Künzelsau, Württemberg
Baumann, Georg Herman	12, Mar. 1896	6, Jan.	65		Ripon, WI	174	Heide, Holstein
Baumann, Gerhard Eilers	2, Oct. 1871	11, Sept	33		Edwardsville, IL	319	Schwertinsdorf, Ostfriesland
Baumann, J.L.	12, June 1876	23, May	47		Nokomis, IL	191	Ickelheim, Baiern
Baumann, Johan	7, Oct. 1878	14, Sept	82		Boonville, MO	319	Schweiz
Baumann, Johan Christian	9, Sept 1897	5, Aug.	67		Clarence, IA	575	Kaierberg, Baiern
Baumann, Johann	26, May 1853	7, May	61- 7m		Dubuque, IA	84	Unfind, Hofheim, Baiern
Baumann, Johannes	10, Feb. 1873	3, Jan.	71		St. Joseph, MO	47	Mittelschönthal, Backnang, Württemberg
Baumann, Johannes Wendel	14, Oct. 1878	19, Sept	71- 7m-26d		Mascoutah, IL	327	Hasloch bei Neustadt, Baiern
Baumann, John	23, Nov. 1899	31, Oct.	77		Sherrills Mount, IA	751	Uefind, Königsberg, Baiern
Baumann, Joseph	8, Sept 1892	18, Aug.	56		St. Philip, IN	574	Schafersheim, Lindsburg, Aargau, Schweiz
Baumann, Julia	20, Mar. 1890	2, Feb.	15		Evansville, IN	190	
Baumann, Karolina	13, Aug. 1891	27, July	75- 1m	Blaser	Spencer Co, IN	526	Maisdorf, Künzelau, Württemberg
Baumann, Magdalena	7, Apr. 1879	23, Mar.	68		Blue Island, IL	111	Trub, Bern, Schweiz
Baumann, Margaretha Barbara	27, Dec. 1880	7, Dec.	88- 9m- 7d		Sherrills Mount, IA	415	Unfind, Baiern
Baumann, Maria	9, Apr. 1883	24, Mar.	79		Boonville, MO	119	Lauberdorf, Ballstall, Solothurn, Schweiz
Baumann, Maria Christina	29, May 1882	4, May	82	Wenz	Summerfield, IL	175	Hasloch, Rheinkreis Baiern
Baumann, Mina P.	17, May 1875	10, Apr.		Koch	Jersey City, NJ	159	Deistel, Hofgeismar, Karshafen, Kurhessen
Baumann, Nikolaus	16, Feb. 1880	28, Jan.	73- 3m-19d		Henrietta, OH	55	Herblingen, Oberdiesbach, Bern, Schweiz
Baumann, Ottilia	24, May 1888	27, Apr.	81		Kansas City, MO	334	Rheingonheim, Mutterstadt, Rheinkreis Baiern
Baumann, Peter	10, May 1855	15, Apr.	27		Weston, MO	76	
Baumann, Peter A.	26, Aug. 1897	31, July	41		Lincoln, NE	543	Holland

- 22 -

Christliche Apologete Death Notices --- 1839 - 1899

Name of Deceased	Notice Date	Death Date	Age	Page	Maiden Name	Place of Death	Place of Birth
Baumbach, Christine	26, Jan. 1893	25, Dec.	72	62	Jäck	Brooklyn, NY	Kornweiler, Neuenburg, Württemberg
Baumbach, Johan Georg	5, Mar. 1896	13, Feb.	77	158		Newport, KY	Gehaus, Eisenach, Sachsen-Weimar
Baumbach, Ottilie	29, Apr. 1897	8, Apr.	76	271	Mertz	Newport, KY	Gehaus, Eisenach, Sachsen-Weimar
Baumberger, Christina	3, Jan. 1889	28, Nov.	93- 2m-14d	14	Lanz	Clarington, OH	Canton Bern, Schweiz
Baumeister, Johan Dietrich	21, Mar. 1889	1, Mar.	55	190		Michigan City, IN	Weiler, Baden
Baumeister, Selma	4, May 1893	9, Apr.	42	286	Rocher	Michigan City, IN	Sachsen
Baumgardner,	20, Oct. 1892	24, Sept	12	670		Freeport, IL	Stephenson County, Illinois
Baumgarten, Anna Maria	23, May 1870	25, Apr.	72	167	Barth	Frankfort, IL	Obtigen, Amt Aarberg, Bern, Schweiz
Baumgarten, Carl	17, Dec. 1891	11, Nov.	80	814		Jordan, MN	Baumgart bei Gülzow, Pommern
Baumgarten, Caroline	15, Sept 1884	16, Aug.	70	7	Höfs	Lydia, MN	Plathe, Stargard, Pommern
Baumgarten, David	28, Apr. 1898	19, Mar.	67	271		Blooming Grove, MN	Barkow, Mecklenburg-Schwerin
Baumgarten, Friedrich	26, Feb. 1866	26, Jan.	20	70		LaCrosse, WI	Barkow, Mecklenburg-Schwerin
Baumgarten, Heinrich	30, Jan. 1882	7, Jan.	17- 7m-18d	39		Tomah, WI	
Baumgarten, Johan Christian	14, June 1894	28, Apr.	61	390		Belleville, IL	Barkow, Neustadt, Mecklenburg-Schwerin
Baumgarten, Maria	9, Apr. 1883	17, Jan.	17- 3m- 5d	119		Tomah, WI	
Baumgarten, Mathilde	30, Jan. 1882	5, Jan.	15- 1m- 5d	39		Tomah, WI	
Baumgarten, Regina Maria	17, Apr. 1865	11, Mar.	58	64	Hochstraßen	Staunton, IL	Dietweil, Aargau, Schweiz
Baumgärtner, (boy)	7, Feb. 1861	17, Dec.	13	24		Canton, MO	
Baumgärtner, (Mrs)	19, Nov. 1891	20, Sept	40	750	Vogel	Chillicothe, OH	Mariette, Ohio
Baumgärtner, Barbara	15, June 1874	23, May	62- -11d	191	Sommer	St. Louis, MO	Neumühl, Amt Kork, Baden
Baumgärtner, Gottlieb	11, Feb. 1884	22, Jan.	62	7		Marietta, OH	KleinSachsenheim, Vaihnigen, Württemberg
Baumgärtner, Henrietta	5, Feb. 1891	7, Jan.	48	94	Stephan	Mt. Pleasant, IA	Katzenellenbogen, Nassau
Baumgärtner, Johan Gottfried	12, Oct. 1868	28, Sept	67	327		Yellow Creek, IL	Schwaigern bei Heilbronn, Württemberg
Baumgärtner, Johan Ulrich	3, Apr. 1882	16, Mar.	68- 4m	111		Canton, MO	St. Gallen, Altstätten, Schweiz
Baumgärtner, Joseph	9, July 1877	19, June	49- 6m-24d	223		Geneseo, IL	Kerbingen, Neresheim, Württemberg
Baumgärtner, Maria	31, Aug. 1874	14, Aug.	34- 3w- 3d	279	Frankhauser	Laporte, IN	Lewville, Jefferson County, New York
Baumgärtner, Maria Rosina	18, Mar. 1872	4, Mar.	66	95	Plunier	Laporte, IN	Biel, Bern, Schweiz
Baumgärtner, Susanna	28, June 1880	17, June	65	207		Canton, MO	
Baumgras, Jacob J.G.	16, Oct. 1890	24, Sept	75- 2m-14d	670		DeWitt, MI	Schmalenberg, Pirmasens, Rheinpfalz Baiern
Baumgras, Maria Katharina	29, Dec. 1898		79	828	Trumm	Lansing, MI	Scheidweiler, Baiern
Baumhardt, Anna Martha	23, Mar. 1874	7, Mar.	76- 5m	95	Gleim	Vermillion, OH	Mecklar, Kurhessen
Baumhardt, Elias	11, May 1874	19, Apr.	80- 6m-20d	151		Vermillion, OH	Mecklar, Kurhessen
Baumhart, Emilie	14, Apr. 1873	18, Mar.	22-10m- 2d	119	Lutz	Vermillion, OH	Braunheim, Ohio
Baumhart, Margarethe	18, Nov. 1897	17, Oct.	56	735	Klaus	Vermillion, OH	Brownhelm Township, Lorain County, Ohio
Baumle, Albert	17, Nov. 1898	23, Oct.	26	735		Burlington, IA	Burlington, Iowa
Baur, Adolph	29, Sept 1884	4, Sept	20	7		Toledo, OH	Oberhofen, Bern, Schweiz
Baur, Conrad	18, Dec. 1890	19, Nov.	47	814		Humboldt, NE	Unterjettingen, Herrenberg, Württemberg
Baur, Jakob M.	16, Aug. 1880	6, July	28	263		Danbury, CT	Enzingen, Württemberg
Baur, Samuel Wilhelm	10, Feb. 1887	25, Jan.	18	94		Cincinnati, OH	Cincinnati, Hamilton County, Ohio
Baur, Susanna	24, June 1886	8, June	37	7	Hertig	Toledo, OH	Oberhofen, Thun, Bern, Germany
Baurichter, Wilhelmine	6, May 1897	27, Mar.	74	287	Kölling	Pinckney, MO	Bohnenberg, Blole, Germany
Bausch, Leonhart	17, Apr. 1876	4, Apr.	53	127		Sandusky, OH	Holzhausen, Württemberg
Bauschliger, William F.	28, Sept 1893	23, Aug.	27	622		Bucyrus, OH	
Bause, Johan Friedrich Albert	4, Feb. 1892	13, Jan.	19	78		Odebolt, IA	Richmond, Indiana
Bax, Heinrich	31, Mar. 1884	7, Mar.	66	7		Mt. Healthy, OH	Realkirche, Geder, Lippe-Detmold
Bax, Karoline	7, Oct. 1897	11, Sept	73	639	Ebker	Mt. Healthy, OH	Igexen, Lippe-Detmold

Christliche Apologete Death Notices --- 1839 - 1899

Name of Deceased	Notice Date	Death Date	Age	Maiden Name	Page	Place of Death	Place of Birth
Bax, Sarah Rebekka	7, Apr. 1887	24, Mar.	21		222	Hamilton, OH	Mt. Healthy, Hamilton County, Ohio
Bay, Elisabeth Susanna	19, Aug. 1867	2, Aug.			262	Marietta, OH	
Bay, Sabina	14, Feb. 1881	2, Feb.	75- 5m- 8d		55	Marietta, OH	Affalterbach, Marbach, Württemberg
Bay, Thomas	5, Apr. 1888	11, Mar.	90- 1m-19d		222	Marietta, OH	Erdmannshausen, Marbach, Württemberg
Bayer, Anna Elisabeth	24, Dec. 1891	26, Nov.	73	Brauch	830	Wheeling, WV	RheinPreußen
Bayer, Friedrich	1, June 1868	15, May	12- 2m-12d		175	Birmingham, PA	
Bayer, Johanna	18, Mar. 1886	2, Mar.	72	Münzing	7	Pittsburg, PA	Flem, Heilbronn, Württemberg
Bayer, Wilhelmina	21, Apr. 1873	22, Mar.	21-10m		127	Allegheny City, PA	Flein, Württemberg
Beach, Elisabeth	11, July 1895	17, June	78	Becker	446	Spencerville, OH	Nauheim, Hessen
Beare, Christian	31, Jan. 1895	6, Jan.	78		78	Ellis Grove, IL	Schwarzeneck, Bern, Schweiz
Beare, Johan	16, June 1892	27, May	69- 2m- 3d		382	Ellis Grove, IL	Canton Bern, Schweiz
Bebermeier, (Mrs)	3, Aug. 1854	9, July	43- 2m		124	St. Charles, MO	Reine, Amt Sternberg, Lippe
Bebermeyer, Anton	28, Feb. 1889	28, Jan.	78		142	Warren, MO	Schönhagen, Sternberg, Lippe-Detmold
Bebermeyer, Heinrich	30, Jan. 1890	1, Jan.	68		78	Warren, MO	Schönhagen, Sternberg, Lippe-Detmold
Bebermeyer, Wilhelm	6, Nov. 1876	13, Oct.	52-10m-23d		359	Washington, MN	Schönhagen, Lippe-Detmold
Bebinger, Katharina	16, Oct. 1851	11, Oct.	64		168	Cincinnati, OH	Becherbach, Hessen-Darmstadt
Becher, Johan	24, Dec. 1891	2, Dec.	70		830	Ft. Atkinson, WI	Unterschwanningen, Baiern
Becherer, Jakobine	20, Aug. 1883	3, Aug.			271	Boston, MA	
Bechthold, Heinrich	2, Nov. 1868	8, Oct.	50		351	Warsaw, IL	Dudenhofen, Kreis Wetzlar, Preußen
Bechthold, Peter	17, Apr. 1882	21, Mar.	43		127	Chicago, IL	Schleitheim, Schaffhausen, Schweiz
Bechtholt, Johannes	4, Feb. 1858	14, Dec.			20	Louisville, KY	Altenhaslau, Kurhessen
Bechtle, Caroline	27, Sept 1869	2, Sept	36	Möll	311	Evansville, IN	Evansville, Indiana
Bechtle, John	4, Dec. 1890	17, Nov.	65- 1m- 7d		782	Marion, OH	Rüppur, Karlsruhe, Baden
Bechtle, Joseph	23, Feb. 1885	1, Feb.	56		7	Perrysburg, OH	Geisbach, Baden
Bechtler, Christina	9, Aug. 1869	10, July	61- 9m- 2d	Münsinger	255	Pittsburg, PA	Schmiren, Maulbronn, Württemberg
Bechtold, Elise	21, Mar. 1889	5, Mar.	36- 7m	Niesenägger	190	Duncan, NE	Roggwyl, Bern, Schweiz
Bechtold, Wilhelm	5, Nov. 1891	16, Oct.	70- 8m-15d		718	Yellow Creek, IL	Lebanon County, Pennsylvania
Beck, Maria	2, Oct. 1856	17, Sept	6-10m-14d		160	Lafayette, IN	
Beck, Amanda	4, Apr. 1889	6, June	64	Lerch	222	Terre Haute, IN	Dauphin County, Pennsylvania
Beck, Anna Maria	21, June 1888	6, June	52	Gebhard	398	Marion, OH	Roßwaag, Vaihingen, Württemberg
Beck, Anna Maria	4, Mar.1872	15, Jan.	14		79	Pittsburg, PA	
Beck, Barbara	20, Oct. 1887	18, Sept	63-11m-10d	Kohl	670	New Albany, IN	Nürnberg, Baiern
Beck, Christine	2, Dec. 1872	11, Nov.	53	Anselm	391	Quincy, IL	Altenheim, Baden
Beck, Conrad	18, July 1895	7, June	52		462	Columbus, OH	Roßwag, Vaihingen, Württemberg
Beck, Eberhard Friedrich	13, Oct. 1859	29, Sept	30- 9m		164	Pittsburg, PA	Urach, Württemberg
Beck, Elisabeth	10, July 1882	11, June	49	Seibold	223	Howard, NE	Erzhausen, Hessen-Darmstadt
Beck, Elisabeth	16, Feb. 1880	21, Dec.	77	Yost	55	Toledo, OH	Heimiswiel, Bern, Schweiz
Beck, Frances	20, June 1895	24, May	92- -11d		398	Ada, MN	Anna, Dumphreys County, Scotland
Beck, Helene	23, Feb. 1888	6, Feb.	28	Miller	126	Ironton, OH	Lawrence County, Ohio
Beck, Mary	2, Feb. 1874	31, Dec.			39	Flint Creek, IA	Burlington, Iowa
Beck, Pauline	14, Aug. 1882	22, July	20	Magthold	263	New York City, NY	
Beck, Philippina Katharina	23, July 1877	4, July	54- 9m	Kraft	239	Farmington, MO	
Beck, Rose	24, Jan. 1871	12, Dec.	4- - 6d		31	Columbus, OH	
Beck, Samuel	24, Nov. 1879	27, Oct.	19- 6m-20d		375	Pittsburg, PA	Pittsburg, Pennsylvania
Beck, Wilhelmine	22, Nov. 1894	25, Oct.	38		758	Wheeling, WV	Kainsdorf bei Zwickau, Sachsen
Beckemeier, William	10, Sept 1866	23, Aug.	32		294	St. Louis, MO	Minden, Preußen

- 24 -

Christliche Apologete Death Notices --- 1839 - 1899

Name of Deceased	Notice Date	Death Date	Age	Maiden Name	Page	Place of Death	Place of Birth
Beckenbach, Balthasar	16, Oct. 1876	29, Sept	47- 2m-19d		335	New York City, NY	Wennings, Hessen-Darmstadt
Beckenbach, Philipp	12, Oct. 1899	29, Aug.	80		655	Minneapolis, MN	Wiesbaden, Baden
Beckendorf, August	26, Oct. 1885	13, Oct.	72		7	Rose Hill, TX	Kalbe bei Magdeburg, Preußen
Becker, A. Elisabeth	3, July 1851		53- 6m		108	Galion, OH	Waldgiermer, Hessen-Darmstadt
Becker, Agathe	3, Dec. 1866	21, Oct.	35	Meier	390	Alton, IL	
Becker, Anna	1, Dec. 1879	14, Nov.	25		383	Brenham, TX	Reichenbach, Preußen
Becker, Anna	29, Dec. 1884	14, Dec.	36	Koppen	7	Concordia, MO	Westphalen
Becker, Anna Margaretha	12, Dec. 1895	17, Nov.		Schneider	798	Cincinnati, OH	Langendorf, Kurhessen
Becker, Anna Maria	2, Jan. 1871	7, Dec.	71- -16d		7	Freedom, MO	Böeninghausen, Lübke, Minden, Preußen
Becker, Anna Maria	16, Feb. 1880	30, Jan.	32-11m- 2d	Schäfer	55	Menomonie, WI	Steinheim, Hessen-Darmstadt
Becker, Anna Maria	17, Jan. 1881	12, Dec.	65		23	Columbia City, IN	Germany
Becker, Anna Martha	4, Feb. 1897	5, Jan.	72	Berlip	79	Vermillion, OH	Eltmanshausen, Kurhessen
Becker, Barbara	16, Dec. 1897	14, Oct.	46	Bertenhausen	799	Marietta, OH	Königswald, Hessen
Becker, Bernard	29, Sept 1873	14, Sept	33		311	Peoria, IL	Klinsiel, Amt Widmund, Ostfriesland
Becker, Bernhard	23, Sept 1886	28, Aug.	55		7	Santa Barbara, CA	Angbil, Glarus, Schweiz
Becker, Carl Friedrich	1, May 1882	6, Mar.	71- 2m- 1d		143	Peoria, IL	Poppendorf, Sachsen-Weimar
Becker, Catharina	22, May 1865	1, May	90	Boling	84	Malay, OH	Hanstedt, Amt Heven, Hannover
Becker, Chr. Fr.	21, Sept 1874	20, Aug.	44- 6m-18d		303	Aurora, IL	
Becker, Christian	5, June 1876	12, May	70- 5m-15d		183	Herman, MO	Nordhemmern, Hartum, Preußen
Becker, Christine	20, Sept 1869	21, Aug.	62- 6m-15d	Andres	303	Portsmouth, OH	Weingarten, Rheinkreis Baiern
Becker, Christine	1, Jan. 1866	30, Nov.	27	Kich	303	New Bremen, IL	Königswald, Kurhessen
Becker, Eli	1, Mar. 1869	14, Jan.	28	Wagner	6	Evansville, IN	
Becker, Elisabeth	19, Jan. 1899	13, Dec.	49	Balk	71	Nokomis, IL	Süd-Fitterburg, Aurich, Hannover
Becker, Elisabeth	19, Nov. 1896	6, Oct.	72	Heller	47	Baltimore, MD	Echzel, Hessen-Darmstadt
Becker, Elise	16, Feb. 1893	20, Jan.	87	Fries	750	Kenosha, WI	Derschen, Coblenz, Preußen
Becker, Eva Katharina	10, May 1849	24, Apr.	29	Klein	110	Wheeling, VA	Hopfgarten, Hessen-Darmstadt
Becker, Friedrich A.	15, Dec. 1892	26, Oct.	65		76	Portsmouth, OH	Niederwartet, Hagenburg, Nassau
Becker, Friedrich Charles	28, July 1892	15, June	34		798	New York City, NY	New York
Becker, Georg	13, Apr. 1874	11, Mar.	16		478	Taylorsville, IA	
Becker, Georg	20, July 1885	18, May	86		119	St. Louis, MO	
Becker, Georg Willie	10, Oct. 1889	10, Aug.	19		7	Kenosha, WI	Kenosha, Wisconsin
Becker, Hanna Christina	29, May 1876	26, Apr.	68- 2m-23d		654	Monee, IL	Rudelsdorf, Preußen
Becker, Henrietta	13, Apr. 1874	19, Mar.			175	Taylorsville, IA	
Becker, Henriette Emilie Louise	12, May 1887	23, Apr.	20- 6m		119	Taylorsville, IA	
Becker, Henry	18, Dec. 1882	26, Nov.			302	Grand Island, NE	
Becker, Henry Carl	5, Sept 1895	5, Aug.	60		407	Pittsburg, PA	Obernbeck, Herford, Preußen
Becker, Ida	5, July 1883	12, Jan.	17- 6m-15d		574	St. Louis, MO	Sanct Urnual bei Saarbrücken, Preußen
Becker, Ilsebein	30, Mar. 1885	27, Feb.	72- 3m-22d	Bohn	47	Herman, MO	
Becker, Jacob	31, Aug. 1874	20, Aug.	75		7	Galion, OH	Hille, Minden, Preußen
Becker, Johan	6, July 1899	22, May	45		279	Galion, OH	Naunheim bei Gießen, Hessen-Darmstadt
Becker, Johan	11, May 1893	23, Apr.	61		431	Highland, IL	St. Jacob, Illinois
Becker, Johan Georg	15, July 1878	10, June	48- 8m-11d		302	Yellow Creek, IL	Cashagen, Pommern
Becker, Johan Heinrich	28, Apr. 1892	16, Mar.	74		223	Galion, OH	Waldgirmes, Hessen-Darmstadt
Becker, Johan Volrath	2, Sept 1897	6, Aug.	53		270	Neerstedt, GE	Neerstedt, Oldenburg
Becker, Johanne Fr.	24, July 1890	9, July	86	Klugen	559	Sun Prairie, WI	Lebin, Stettin, Preußen
Becker, Johannes	8, Aug. 1895	19, July	67		478	Watertown, WI	Ludwigsruh, Soldin, Preußen
					510	Nauvoo, IL	Kesselbach, Giesen, Hessen-Darmstadt

Christliche Apologete Death Notices --- 1839 - 1899

Name of Deceased	Notice Date	Death Date	Age	Page	Maiden Name	Place of Death	Place of Birth
Becker, John	2, Nov. 1885	10, Oct.	59- 6m-25d	7		Vermillion, OH	Bebera, Rothenburg, Kurhessen
Becker, John	18, Oct. 1875	25, Sept	23- -17d	335		Pekin, IL	
Becker, Karolina Johanna	13, Apr. 1899	20, Feb.	76	238	Geier	Stitzer, WI	Schwarzburg-Rudolstadt
Becker, Katharina Elisabeth	4, Dec. 1890	7, Nov.	90-10m- 2d	782	Eckert	St. Louis, MO	Großbeberau, Hessen-Darmstadt
Becker, Katharine	10, Sept 1883	22, Aug.	71	295		New York City, NY	Waldirmes, Hessen-Darmstadt
Becker, Lizzie	17, May 1875	29, Apr.	19	159		Evansville, IN	Evansville, Indiana
Becker, Louise	8, May 1876	22, Apr.	19- 7m- 9d	151		Clarington, OH	
Becker, Lydia	6, Aug. 1883	19, July	14- 8m-14d	255		Hokah, MN	Union, Houston County, Minnesota
Becker, Magdalena	24, Nov. 1884	17, Sept	19	7		Clarington, OH	Monroe County, Ohio
Becker, Margaretha	15, May 1856	28, Mar.	50	80		Herman, MO	Nordhemmern, Münden, Preußen
Becker, Margaretha	26, Feb. 1872	31, Jan.	67	71	Vagts	Wheeling, WV	Rade, Amt Zeven, Hannover
Becker, Margaretha	13, Nov. 1890	24, Oct.	59	734	Dietz	El Paso, IL	Spielberg, Durlach, Baden
Becker, Maria E.	17, Nov. 1892	18, Oct.	80	734	Siebert	Evansville, IN	Schledhausen, Hannover
Becker, Mary	8, Aug. 1881	14, July	68	255		Atlanta, IL	Ober-Ohmbach, Kaiserslautern, Baiern
Becker, Mary Elisabeth	11, Feb. 1878	23, Jan.	13- 5m-25d	47		Evansville, IN	
Becker, Mathilde Emilie	14, June 1880	8, May	15- 6m- 1d	191		West Point, IA	
Becker, Mina	31, Mar. 1887	13, Mar.	30	206	Wahrenbrock	Concordia, MO	Concordia, Missouri
Becker, Nikolaus	2, Apr. 1866		67	110		Washington, OH	Hamstedt am Zevern, Hannover
Becker, Samuel	27, Jan. 1868	23, Dec.	65- 2m	31		Brighton, IL	Niederswyl, Aarau, Schweiz
Becker, Sophia	16, Nov. 1863	29, Oct.	51	184	Hollmann	Dayton, OH	Greifenstein, Preußen
Becker, Susanna	19, Apr. 1869	27, Mar.	44	127	Schmidt	Nashville, TN	Hasloch, Rheinkreis Baiern
Becker, Therese	2, Aug. 1888	14, July	37- 4m- 5d	494	Schwenborn	Sun Prairie, WI	Tattewitz, Olmütz, Mähren, Oesterreich
Becker, Valentin	3, June 1886		64	7		Clarington, OH	Maar, Lauderbach, Hessen-Darmstadt
Becker, Valentin	28, Apr. 1898	3, Apr.	67	271		Hamilton, OH	Zell , Rheinpfalz Baiern
Becker, Wilhelm	25, Apr. 1861	11, Mar.	7- 1m	68		St. Louis, MO	
Becker, Wilhelmina	6, Mar. 1890	5, Feb.	48	158	Baumann	Kenosha, WI	Schotso bei Treptow a.d. Tolens, Preußen
Beckley, J.W.	13, Nov. 1865	20, Oct.	28	184		Blue Island, IL	
Beckley, Katharina	17, Aug. 1854	17, July	52	132	Muzer	Cedar Lake, IN	Reusten, Herrenberg, Württemberg
Beckley, Lydia	27, Apr. 1874	24, Mar.	16- 1m- 8d	135		Cannon River, MN	Cedar Lake, Lake County, Indiana
Beckley, Wilhelm	2, Feb. 1863	6, Dec.	22	20		Cannon City, MN	Freiburg, Hannover
Beckmann, Anna Christina Dorothea	4, Aug. 1887	17, July	67- 6m-11d	494	Ahlf	Muscatine, IA	
Beckmann, Anna Wilhelmine	7, Dec. 1893	5, Nov.	19	782		Quincy, IL	
Beckmann, Christian	1, Mar. 1894	8, Feb.	86	150		Altamont, IL	Dizenbach, Hessen-Darmstadt
Beckmann, Erwin	28, Oct. 1872	5, Oct.	52	351		New Albany, IN	Oberrode, Hessen
Beckmann, Gottfried	25, Feb. 1892	30, Jan.	21	126		Roseville, MI	Winterfelde, Pommern
Beckmann, Heinrich	24, Apr. 1876	28, Mar.	21	135		Morrison, MO	Holstein, Warren County, Missouri
Beckmann, Ludwig	22, Aug. 1850	13, July	62	136		Laughery, IN	Fußgenheim, Rheinkreis Baiern
Beckmann, Ludwig	22, Oct. 1891		66	686		Quincy, IL	
Beckmann, Margaretha Maria	17, July 1890	27, June	38	462	Kemp	Muscatine, IA	Allwarden, Hannover
Beckmann, Susanna Margaretha	20, Aug. 1896	30, July	89- 1m- 3d	542		Altamont, IL	Dutzenbach, Hessen-Darmstadt
Becky, Christ. Dorothea Friederika	25, Apr. 1870	7, Apr.	47	135		Chicago, IL	Winnenden, Württemberg
Bedei, Johan Heinrich	2, Oct. 1890	12, Sept	58	638		Grand Ridge, IL	Schleswig-Holstein
Bedenbender, A. Elisabeth	20, Nov. 1882	3, Nov.	71- 9m-17d	375	Schäfer	Beardstown, IL	Wandelbach, Nassau
Bedenbender, Johan August	23, Feb. 1880	6, Feb.	44-10m- 1d	63		Rushville, IL	Manderbach, Dillenburg, Nassau
Bedenbinder, Johan Heinrich	7, Jan. 1886	15, Dec.	77	7		Bushnell, IL	Manderbach, Dillenburg, Hessen-Nassau
Beder, (boy)	13, May 1867	22, Apr.		150		Brooklyn, NY	

Christliche Apologete Death Notices --- 1839 - 1899

Name of Deceased	Notice Date	Death Date	Age	Maiden Name	Place of Death	Page	Place of Birth
Beder, (girl)	13, May 1867	13, Apr.	5-10m		Brooklyn, NY	150	Bremen, Germany
Beder, Eleonore	13, May 1867	25, Mar.	31	Hepke	Brooklyn, NY	150	Bega, Amt Alverdissen, Lippe-Detmold
Bedig, Wilhelm	29, Dec. 1873	5, Dec.	51		Yellow Creek, IL	415	
Bedinger, Elisabeth	15, Jan. 1877	31, Dec.	30-8m	Gumbel	Warsaw, IL	23	Schwenningen, Württemberg
Beeler, Johannes	1, Dec. 1862	3, Nov.			Helena, AR	192	
Beesch, Agathe	21, Jan. 1884	1, Jan.	45	Weiler	Rochester, NY	7	
Beesch, Anna	4, Feb. 1867	28, Dec.	11- 1m		Rochester, NY	38	
Beese, Anna	11, Dec. 1890	3, Nov.	22	Reineke	Blooming Grove, MN	798	Blooming Grove, Minnesota
Beese, Friedrich	27, Feb. 1890	28, Jan.	54		Blooming Grove, MN	142	Sietow, Mecklenburg-Schwerin
Beesse, Friederike	6, Dec. 1888	29, Oct.	61- 2m-20d	Klakow	Blooming Grove, MN	782	Farenhold, Mecklenburg-Schwerin
Beets, Johan	24, Apr. 1882	12, Nov.	26- 6m- 9d		Cleveland, OH	135	Lanzenheim, Hessen-Darmstadt
Beetz, Maria	27, May 1897	8, May	59	Fetzer	Aurora, IL	335	Amon-Schönbrunn, Baiern
Beffert, Georg Jacob	7, May 1891	5, Apr.	76		Newark, NJ	302	Biegenbrunn, Pforzheim, Baden
Beffert, Katharina	26, Jan. 1899	14, Dec.	78	Seger	Newark, NJ	63	Reichenbach, Württemberg
Begemann, Bonrad	13, Oct. 1873	5, Sept	64		Allegan, MI	327	Leopoldsthal, Lippe-Detmold
Begemann, Dorothea	26, May 1898	18, Apr.	50		Morrison, MO	335	Besingfeld, Lippe-Detmold
Begemann, Dorothea	12, Nov. 1896	16, Oct.	58	Heuer	Truxton, MO	734	Stemme, Lippe-Detmold
Begemann, Elisabeth Margaete	12, Jan. 1899	18, Dec.	37	Miller	Chester, IL	30	Hannover
Begemann, Friedrika	15, Apr. 1867	28, Mar.	34	Wehrmann	Warren, MO	118	
Begemann, Herman Heinrich Friedrich	19, Feb. 1891	31, Jan.	42		Morrison, MO	126	Reine bei Alverdissen, Lippe-Detmold
Begemann, Karoline	29, Jan. 1866	9, Jan.	39	Römer	Warren, MO	38	Lincoln County, Missouri
Begemann, Karoline	11, May 1893	14, Apr.	34	Düewel	Warren, MO	302	Helberg, Lüdenhausen, Lippe-Detmold
Begemann, Wilhelm F.	4, Mar. 1886	21, Jan.			Lancaster, WI	7	Mecklenburg-Schwerin
Begemann, Wilhelmine	30, June 1892	9, June	72	Pann	Stitzer, WI	414	Wesbeck, Waldeck
Behle, Carl W.	3, May 1880	11, Apr.	28- 6m- 9d		Lawrence, KS	143	
Behle, Wilhelm	16, Oct. 1876	26, Sept	38		Boody, IL	335	
Behlendorf, Heinrich Fr.	15, Jan. 1872	29, Dec.	58- 1m-13d		Wheeling, IL	23	Gifhorn, Hannover
Behling, Johan Christoph Ludwig	14, Apr. 1898	23, Mar.	68		Milwaukee, WI	239	Drosedow bei Colberg, Germany
Behlmeyer, Christine	27, Jan. 1887	30, Dec.	30		Giard, IA	62	Elkport, Iowa
Behn, Frederike	31, Aug. 1874	13, Aug.	69	Werth	Buffalo, NY	279	Sonnenberg, Preußen
Behn, Emilie	24, June 1897	5, June	32		New York City, NY	399	Altenau bei Hamburg, Germany
Behne, Christoph	8, Dec. 1884	12, Nov.	56-11m-22d		Owatonna, MN	7	Kohlenfeld, Hannover
Behne, Johanna	5, May 1892	18, Mar.	55	Müller	Blooming Grove, MN	286	Mohr, Mecklenburg-Schwerin
Behne, Wilhelm	29, Nov. 1860	22, Sept	36		Zumbro, MN	192	Colenfeld, Hannover
Behneke, Henriette	2, Feb. 1888	17, Jan.	68- 8m		Berea, OH	78	Filehne, Posen
Behner, Jacob Friedrich	7, Dec. 1874	20, Nov.	31		Berea, OH	391	Liverpool, Medina County, Ohio
Behnke, Christ.	18, Oct. 1888	15, July	49		Arlington, MN	670	
Behnke, Christine	15, Dec. 1887	26, Nov.	59	Fröhling	Michigan City, IN	798	Pyritz, Pommern
Behnke, Friederike	24, May 1894	2, May	89	Laborn	Louisville, KY	342	Neukalden, Schwerin
Behnke, Wilhelmine	9, June 1892	25, May	45	Bartelt	Kenaskum, WI	366	Farbezien, Hinterpommern
Behr, Johan Friedrich	30, Sept 1897	14, Sept	68		Fredericksburg, TX	623	Stettendorf, Hannover
Behre, Elisabeth	26, May 1853	2, May	34	Thöle	Quincy, IL	84	Sutrup, Thüne, Hannover
Behrend, Gottfried	13, Jan. 1887	20, Dec.	72- 2m-17d		Red Wing, MN	30	
Behrend, Karoline	2, Oct. 1871	3, Sept	67- 3m	Schultz	Junction City, KS	319	Sonnenburg, Preußen
Behrends, Hermine	20, Apr. 1893	28, Mar.	69	Wintkam	Emden, IL	254	Ostfriesland
Behrens, Anna Margaretha	10, Jan. 1881	25, Dec.	72- 8m		Portsmouth, OH	15	Safen, Hannover

Christliche Apologete Death Notices --- 1839 - 1899

Name of Deceased	Notice Date	Death Date	Age	Page	Maiden Name	Place of Death	Place of Birth
Behrens, Anna Margaretha	1, Nov. 1894	7, Oct.	38	710		Farmington, IA	Hannover
Behrens, Berend	23, Dec. 1872	5, Dec.	36	415		San Jose, IL	Rysum, Amt Emden, Ostfriesland
Behrens, Christoph	8, Apr. 1867	25, Mar.	27	110		Laporte, IN	Charlottenhof, Mecklenburg-Schwerin
Behrens, Johann	22, Jan. 1857	10, Jan.	50	16		Portsmouth, OH	Borchesmohr, Rothenberg, Hannover
Behrens, Johannes	7, Sept 1893	25, Aug.	75	574		Dayton, OH	Schwerin, Darpun, Mecklenburg
Behrens, Louise	12, Sept 1864	6, Aug.	13	148		Angelica, NY	Vollbüttel, Amt Gifhorn, Hannover
Behrens, Louise	14, Oct. 1886	25, Sept	56	7	Hammeister	Milwaukee, WI	Poppendorf, Mecklenburg-Schwerin
Behrens, Maria	26, Nov. 1896	15, Oct.	68	766	Schröder	Stevens Point, WI	Germany
Behrens, Maria Elisabeth	26, July 1875	24, June	16-10m- 9d	239		Portsmouth, OH	
Behrensmeyer, Karl Friedrich	22, Oct. 1877	28, Sept	54- 4m	343		Quincy, IL	Eidinghausen, Preußen
Behinger, Barbara	5, Aug. 1872	17, July	63	255		Lafayette, IN	Schlierbach, Göppingen, Württemberg
Behinger, Catharina	26, Oct. 1868	27, Sept	84- 7m	343		Louisville, KY	Oelbronn, Maulbronn, Württemberg
Behinger, Christian	26, June 1882	25, June	58	207		Yellow Creek, IL	Schweigern, Württemberg
Behinger, Elisabeth	8, Sept 1892	31, July	37	574	Rentz	Perry, TX	Freestone County, Texas
Behinger, Emma Auguste	7, July 1898	2, June	34	431	Sommerfeld	Perry, TX	Parlinek, Posen
Behinger, Heinricke	5, Nov. 1865		24	180	Barthe	Lafayette, IN	
Behinger, Jakob	30, Dec. 1872	10, Dec.	30	423		Lafayette, IN	Schlierbach, Göppingen, Württemberg
Behinger, Jakob Friedrich	26, Oct. 1854	27, Aug.	42	172		Lafayette, IN	Schlierbach, Göppingen, Württemberg
Behinger, Johan Ernst	3, Dec. 1896	11, Nov.	71	782		Perry, TX	Teschlingen, Baden
Behinger, Margaretha	18, Sept 1871	25, July	68	303	Biebinger	Pomeroy, OH	Oppau, Frankenthal, Baiern
Behinger, Susanna	12, Aug. 1872	26, July	15- 1m-10d	263		Yellow Creek, IL	
Behrnds, Anna Selma	5, Nov. 1891	17, July	13	718		Springfield, MN	Schneidlingen, Preußen
Behrnds, Martha Louise	5, Nov. 1891	28, July	15	718		Springfield, MN	Schneidlingen, Preußen
Beiderwill, Dietrich	27, Mar. 1856	10, Feb.	48	52		Evansport, OH	Wersen, Preußen
Beidewill, Friedrich Wilhelm	3, Apr. 1871	9, Mar.	9	111		Defiance, OH	Defiance County, Ohio
Beier, Charlotte	23, Apr. 1891	29, Mar.	79	270	Schwichtenberg	Garner, IA	Naugard, Pommern
Beier, Georg Benjamin	15, Nov. 1894	28, Oct.	15	742		Klemme, IA	
Beier, Karl	9, Sept 1878	23, Aug.	51	287		Dallas, TX	Bunzlau, Preußen
Beier, Wilhelm	13, Dec. 1880	19, Nov.	27- -20d	399		Detroit, MI	Hardenbeck, Brandenburg
Beierbach, (Mrs)	7, Dec. 1874	15, Nov.	73- 1m-19d	391		Allegheny City, PA	Eschenau, Weinsberg, Württemberg
Beiermeister, Barbara	3, Aug. 1893	22, June	61-10m-19d	494	Schlosser	Troy, NY	Lambrecht, Rheinkreis Baiern
Beiersdorf, William H.	19, Jan. 1888		32- 4m-17d	46		Sheboygan, WI	Westbend, Washington County, Wisconsin
Beile, Friedrich	27, July 1885	10, July	48	7		South Bend, IN	Iptingen, Vaihingen, Württemberg
Beilharz, Margaretha	26, Aug. 1886	5, Aug.	24	7		Poughkeepsie, NY	
Beine, Christoph	10, July 1890	27, June	77- 8m	446		Lena, IL	Belle, Lippe-Detmold
Beine, Friedrich Heinrich Wilhelm	18, Sept 1890	21, Aug.	73	606		Lawrence, KS	Belle, Schieder, Lippe-Detmold
Beine, Heinrich	23, May 1850	6, May	34	84		St. Louis, MO	Jertzen bei Detmold, Lippe
Beine, Karl	20, July 1863	1, July	49	116		Freeport, IL	Belle, Lippe-Detmold
Beine, Louise	2, May 1889	16, Apr.	73- 8m-30d	286		Lena, IL	Berre, Lippe-Detmold
Beinhardt, Maria	23, Aug. 1869	8, Aug.	20	271		German Creek, IA	Keokuk County, Iowa
Beinhart, Andreas	22, Mar. 1875	2, Mar.		95		German Creek, IA	
Beinhart, Christina	9, Aug. 1894	12, July	40	518		Harper, IA	German Township, Keokuk County, Iowa
Beinhart, Johan	12, Jan. 1899	17, Dec.	82	30		Harper, IA	Kehl, Baden
Beinhart, Julia	13, Apr. 1893	23, Feb.	33	238		Harper, IA	
Beinhart, Louisa Friederika	29, Jan. 1877	17, Jan.	46	39	Gais	Harper, IA	Mühlfeld, Müllerichstadt, Baiern
Beisel, Pauline	25, May 1899	5, May	39	335	Lorenz	LaCrosse, WI	Prausa, Böhmen, Oesterreich

- 28 -

Christliche Apologete Death Notices --- 1839 - 1899

Name of Deceased	Notice Date	Death Date	Age	Maiden Name	Place of Death	Page	Place of Birth
Beiser, Gottfried	8, Nov. 1869	22, Oct.	36		Clarington, OH	359	Brucken, Kirchheim, Württemberg
Beisser, Barbara	6, Feb. 1896	7, Dec.	78		Clarington, OH	94	Immenhausen, Württemberg
Beisser, Georg	19, Feb. 1891	11, Jan.	73		Akron, NY	126	Dettingen am Main, Württemberg
Beißer, Georg Adam	11, Mar. 1886	5, Dec.	66		Clarington, OH	7	Brocken, Württemberg
Beißer, Katharina	28, Jan. 1878	7, Jan.	56- - 1d	Kurtz	Lancaster, NY	31	Jessingen, Kirchheim, Württemberg
Beißer, Sophia Dorothea	14, Feb. 1881	27, Dec.	89- 2m-15d	Attinger	Clarington, OH	55	Brucken bei Kirchheim an der Teck, Germany
Beißwenger, Friedrich	10, Feb. 1859	10, Dec.	68- 2m			24	Alfdorf, Welzheim, Württemberg
Beiswanger, Christina	5, Dec. 1870	23, Nov.			Streator, IL	391	
Beiswanger, Georg	3, Mar. 1873	14, Feb.	45		Peru, IL	71	Neustadt, Waiblingen, Württemberg
Beitel, Julius T.	26, May 1892	29, Apr.	67		Sandwich, IL	334	Nazareth, Pennsylvania
Beitschert, Wilhelm	4, May 1885		74		Toledo, OH	7	Großblumberg, in der Neumark, Preußen
Beitz, Jacob	8, Jan. 1877	19, Dec.	53		Lena, IL	15	Nußloch, Heidelberg, Baden
Beitz, Wilhelm	5, Feb. 1877	16, Jan.			Charles City, IA	47	
Bekedorf, August	25, Aug. 1887	29, July	27		Olpe, KS	542	Hittfeld, Embsen, Hannover
Beker, Wilhelmine	24, Oct. 1895	29, Sept	49- 8m- 2d	Beker	Sun Prairie, WI	686	Rafenstein, Satzig, Pommern
Belau, Anna	5, Mar. 1891		72	Mittelstätt		158	West Preußen
Belger, Johan Heinrich	11, Feb. 1897	19, Jan.	94		Galion, OH	94	Neuenheim, Hessen-Darmstadt
Belger, Heinrich Friedrich	13, July 1899	12, June	82		Akron, NY	447	Denstädt, Lenagensalza, Preußen
Bell, Maria	31, May 1875	8, May	83		New York City, NY	175	
Beller, Maria Elisabeth	8, Apr. 1886		79- 4m		Weston, MO	7	Möringen, Baden
Bellmer, Dorothea	29, Sept 1853	14, July	40		Florence, MO	156	Hoya, Hannover
Bellmer, Gesche	7, Apr. 1884	26, Mar.	46	Knopp	Sedalia, MO	7	Benton County, Missouri
Bellmer, John F.	21, Jan. 1892	29, Dec.	58		Sedalia, MO	46	Aschwarm, Hagen, Hannover
Belser, Friedrich	27, Aug. 1866	8, Aug.	49		Hamilton, OH	278	Mühlacker, Maulbronn, Württemberg
Belser, Lena	27, Aug. 1866	7, Aug.	40	Küstner	Hamilton, OH	278	Ilshofen, Hall, Württemberg
Belte, Heinrich	17, Aug. 1863	7, July	33		Perry, IL	132	Bleichenbach, Kreis Nidda, Hessen
Beltz, Anna Louise	19, July 1888	27, June	49- 8m- 3d	Draheim	Beaver Falls, MN	462	Kurrasch Zawo, Germany
Belz, Ferdinand	24, Dec. 1877	26, Nov.	47		Beaver Falls, MN	415	Kauwolwe, Bromberg, Preußen
Belz, Heinrich	29, Mar. 1894	12, Feb.	41		Auburn, IN	214	Alt-Brunslar, Kurhessen
Bendel, Jakob	12, Dec. 1870	21, Nov.	58		LaCrosse, WI	399	Günthersdorf, Tetschen, Böhmen
Bender, Albert	27, Nov. 1876	4, Nov.	28		Milwaukee, WI	383	Rehberg, Pommern
Bender, Barbara	1, Dec. 1892	4, Nov.	82	Schmidt	Baraboo, WI	766	Metzingen, Württemberg
Bender, Eva Margaretha	7, Aug. 1871	16, July	71	Müller	Portsmouth, OH	255	Sandhofen, Baden
Bender, Johan Christoph Gottfried	26, Jan. 1888	2, Jan.	75			62	Beckingen, Württemberg
Bender, Johanna Susanna	14, Mar. 1861	17, Feb.	34		Wheeling, VA	44	Dambach, Baiern
Bender, Johannes	2, Dec. 1872	5, Nov.	68		Peterson, IA	391	Kirchardt, Baden
Bender, John C.	30, Jan. 1882	3, Jan.	66- 6m-11d		Cleveland, OH	39	Merzhausen, Usingen, Nassau
Bender, John L.	7, May 1896	12, Apr.	72		Freeport, IL	302	Baden
Bender, Margaretha	23, May 1881	3, May	70- 3m-16d	Tilken	Francisco, MI	167	Langen, Derbstedt, Lehe, Hannover
Bender, Margaretha	24, June 1886	3, June	63- 9m-14d		Sandusky, OH	7	
Bender, Philipp	2, Jan. 1896	2, Dec.	41		Marion, OH	14	Waldo Township, Marion County, Ohio
Bendheimer, Mathilda Augusta	11, Apr. 1881	25, Mar.	29- 9m-11d	Grützmacher	Watertown, WI	119	
Bendix, Wilhelm	17, Apr. 1890	30, Mar.	73- 4m-27d		Redwood, MN	254	Gottberg, Pommern
Benecke, Jürgen Heinrich Wilhelm	14, Dec. 1893	15, Nov.	15		Bushton, KS	798	Leer, Ostfriesland
Benefeld, Maria Anna	21, Jan. 1897	27, Dec.	30		Red Wing, MN	46	Hay Creek, Minnesota
Beneke, Ludwig	27, Oct. 1873	8, Oct.	68- 7m-23d		Goshen, IN	343	Glasowitz bei Güstrow, Mecklenburg-Schwerin

Christliche Apologete Death Notices --- 1839 - 1899

Name of Deceased	Notice Date	Death Date	Age	Page	Maiden Name	Place of Death	Place of Birth
Beneke, Martin	19, Sept 1895	2, Sept	74	606		Rochester, MN	Gensmarch bei Cestrin, Preußen
Bengel, Elisabeth	7, July 1859	25, June	22	108	Gonheimer	Pomeroy, OH	Niedigheim, Rheinkreis Baiern
Bengel, Heinrich	15, Aug. 1864	9, June	38	132		Newport, MI	Hessen-Darmstadt
Bengel, Ida May	19, Nov. 1896	23, Oct.	14- 8m-27d	750		Pomeroy, OH	Dirmstein, Rheinpfalz, Baiern
Bengel, Magdalena	26, Apr. 1875	29, Mar.	75	135	Keck	Pomeroy, OH	Washington County, Ohio
Bengel, Margaretha	30, July 1896	4, July	57	495	Roth	Pomeroy, OH	
Bengerin, Sara	30, Oct. 1840	25, Sept		171	Schaad	Columbus, OH	
Bengs, (Mr)	1, Nov. 1880	9, Oct.	31	351		Nebraska City, NE	Brügge, Soldin, Preußen
Benitsch, Katharina	9, Sept 1886	6, Aug.	66	7		Dodgeville, IA	Griesheim bei Darmstadt, Hessen-Darmstadt
Benker, Anton	2, Mar. 1874	8, Feb.	11	71		Rockford, MN	
Benker, Wilhelm	2, Mar. 1874	7, Feb.	10	71		Rockford, MN	Henderson, Minnesota
Bennefeld, Christine	7, Feb. 1889	10, Jan.	59- -29d	94		Red Wing, MN	Wehrendorf, Minden, Preußen
Bennefeld, Friedrich	11, Nov. 1886	24, Oct.	31	7		Big Stone City, SD	Martinsville, Missouri
Benner, Anna M.	2, Mar. 1893	21, Jan.	68	142	Guvendal	Atchison, KS	Hessen-Kassel
Benner, Philipp	16, Dec. 1897	16, Nov.	62	799		Burlington, IA	St. Charles, Missouri
Bennet, E.	2, Oct. 1865	13, Sept	63-10m- 2d	160		Cleveland, OH	Schopp, Rheinkreis Baiern
Bennett, Andreas	2, Jan. 1865	7, Dec.	72- 7m	4		Cleveland, OH	UnterUebenthal, Freiburg, Baden
Bennicke, Wilhelm	29, Jan. 1872	26, Nov.	16	39		Galena, IL	
Bennien, Wilhelm	15, Apr. 1872	15, Mar.	58- 4m	127		Chicago, IL	Briest, Kreis Angermünde, Preußen
Benninger, Eva Katharina	5, June 1876	21, May	66	183		Cincinnati, OH	Freistett, Baden
Benoit, Anna Rosine	10, Dec. 1866	9, Oct.	64	398		Petersburg, IL	Liebenau, Amt Hofkreismar, Hessen-Kassel
Bentel, Elisabeth Margaretha	8, Apr. 1872	5, Mar.	78- 5m-15d	119		Matamoras, OH	Weissach, Maulbronn, Württemberg
Benter, Christoph	3, July 1882	12, June	69- 5m-18d	215		Francisco, MI	Hoffe, Amt Dorum, Hannover
Benter, Florentina	19, Sept 1870	23, Aug.	35	303	Hoppe	Winona, MN	Sodel, Amt Lehe, Hannover
Bentlage, Catharina	30, Apr. 1877	26, Mar.	52	143	Brune	Canaan, MO	Kleve, Minden, Preußen
Bentz, Elisabeth	9, May 1895	20, Apr.	72	302	Bentz	Independence, MO	Welflingen, Schweiz
Bentz, Eva Barbara	5, Oct. 1893	27, Aug.	71	638		Pomeroy, OH	Schwetzingen, Baden
Bentz, Georg	20, Nov. 1865	3, Nov.	22	188		Canal Dover, OH	
Bentz, Heinrich	28, Mar. 1889	12, Mar.	65	206		Armourdale, KS	Merzheim bei Landau, Rheinkreis Baiern
Benz, Barbara	25, Nov. 1872	20, Sept	46- 1m- 8d	383	Bolli	Hudson City, NJ	Beringen, Schaffhausen, Schweiz
Benz, Edward	25, Sept 1890	27, Aug.	18- 7m-13d	622		Charles City, IA	
Benz, Heinrich Gottfried	31, May 1869	29, Apr.	18	175		Hudson City, NJ	Schaffhausen, Schweiz
Benz, Jakob	1, June 1854	12, Mar.	67	88		Canal Dover, OH	Neulusheim, Baden
Benz, Magdalena	8, June 1868	5, May		183	Süß	Waterloo, IA	Oppau, Frankenthal, Baiern
Benz, Marie Caroline	27, June 1895	26, May	56	414		Elgin, IL	Biel, Bern, Schweiz
Benz, Selma	22, July 1897	28, June	27	463		Dubuque, IA	Dubuque, Iowa
Benz, Sophia	24, Nov. 1892	1, Nov.	52	750	Köhler	Dayton, OH	Orschweier, Ettenheim, Baden
Benz, Susanna	27, May 1886	12, May	37	7		Mt. Vernon, NY	Hoffenheim bei Zinsheim, Baden
Benzel, Johan	29, June 1899	18, June	64	415	Nasse	Bedford, IN	Moschütz, Preußen
Benzel, Matilda Klara	5, Oct. 1899	29, Aug.	31	639		Seymour, IN	Bartholomew County, Indiana
Benzel, Michael	4, May 1893	29, Mar.	89	286		Bedford, IN	Burgendorf, Preußen
Benzler, Katharina Maria	8, Jan. 1877	6, Dec.	82- 9m-19d	15		Marion, OH	Horheim, Vaihingen, Württemberg
Bepper, Johan Heinrich	3, Oct. 1889	8, Sept	26- 6m- 2d	638		Pittsburg, PA	Pittsburg, Pennsylvania
Berck, Mina	27, Oct. 1887	21, Sept	18-10m-14d	686		Howard, NE	Osage County, Missouri
Berck, Mina	13, Oct. 1887	23, Sept	18-10m-14d	654		Howard, NE	
Berdel, Maria K.	22, Aug. 1881	22, July	66	271	Layer	Lansing, IA	Brombach, Heidelberg, Baden

- 30 -

Christliche Apologete Death Notices --- 1839 - 1899

Name of Deceased	Notice Date	Death Date	Age	Page	Maiden Name	Place of Death	Place of Birth
Berenstecher, (Mr)	7, June 1855	18, May		92		Baltimore, MD	
Berenstecher, Katharina	17, Apr. 1865			64		Baltimore, MD	
Berg , Balthasar	8, July 1858	19, June	66-10m	108		Milan, IN	Niederamstadt, Waschbach, Hessen-Darmstadt
Berg, Adam	17, Mar. 1892	16, Feb.	66-9m	174		Stockton, CA	Ober-Appenfeld, Kurhessen
Berg, Anna Christina	3, July 1876	8, June	85	215	Krugen	Cedar Grove, IN	Niederamstadt, Hessen-Darmstadt
Berg, Anna Maria	16, June 1843	12, May	36	95		Chester, OH	
Berg, Apollonia	9, Sept 1867	20, Aug.	35-10m	286	Redinger	Batesville, IN	Pilot Grove, Missouri
Berg, Barbara	31, May 1894	8, May	30	358	Mayer	Norwich, KS	
Berg, Catharina	10, Mar. 1848	28, Feb.	13	43		Cincinnati, OH	Remsfeld, Kurhessen
Berg, Elisabeth	5, Oct. 1874	17, Sept	84	319		Giard, IA	
Berg, Georg Adam	29, Oct. 1847	21, Oct.	40-10m	175		Cincinnati, OH	
Berg, Heinrich	28, May 1866	3, Mar.	16-3m-16d	174		Batesville, IN	
Berg, Jakob	20, Apr. 1854	25, Mar.		64		Elyria, OH	Altenkirchen, Waltmar, Rheinkreis Baiern
Berg, Jakob	3, July 1876	25, May	66	215		Pomeroy, OH	Lambsheim, Rheinkreis Baiern
Berg, Margaretha	21, Apr. 1879	30, Mar.	88	127	Dreißigacker	Weston, MO	Gries, Zweibrücken, Rheinkreis Baiern
Berg, Margaretha	24, Nov. 1887	7, Nov.	82	750	Strott	Lemars, IA	Schlüctern, Kurhessen
Berg, Maria	5, Jan. 1899	2, Dec.	87- 7m-24d	14		Watertown, WI	Konstantinopel, Pommern
Berg, Maria	25, Dec. 1865	21, Oct.	80	208	Uhe	Marthasville, MO	Rehme, Preußen
Berg, Maria	22, Apr. 1886	23, Mar.	51	7	Mann	Jacksonville, OR	Captina, Ohio
Berg, Michael Friedrich	18, Nov. 1897	20, Oct.	60	735		Lowell, WI	Dölitz, Pieritz, Pommern
Berg, Oskar E.	23, June 1887	27, May	14- 3m	398		Portland, OR	Giard, Clayton County, Iowa
Berg, Pauline Auguste	26, July 1894	1, July	37	486	Krüger	Rochester, MN	Ele Drowe, Posen
Berg, Wilhelmine	15, June 1899	23, May	69	383		Lowell, WI	Arnswalde, Brandenburg
Bergdoll, Christiana	2, June 1898	24, Apr.	67	351	Sankel	Seymour, IN	Ewertsheim, Rheinpfalz Baiern
Bergdoll, Conrad	25, Apr. 1895	9, Mar.	68	270		White Creek, IN	Dannstadt, Rheinpfalz Baiern
Bergdoll, Conrad Wilhelm	12, July 1875	1, June	10- 2m	223		White Creek, IN	
Bergdoll, Elisabeth	9, Oct. 1876	21, Sept	51	327	Heinz	White Creek, IN	Ogau, Frankenthal, Rheinkreis Baiern
Bergdoll, Jacob	17, Sept 1866	28, Aug.	14- 5m-11d	302		Seymour, IN	Etna Furnace, Lawrence County, Ohio
Bergdoll, Jakob	20, Jan. 1873	15, Dec.	72	23		Seymour, IN	Dannstadt, Rheinkreis Baiern
Bergdoll, Susanna	17, Mar. 1873	24, Jan.	72	87	Remer	Seymour, IN	Dannstedt, Rheinkreis Baiern
Bergen, Gertrud	19, Dec. 1870	6, Dec.	35- 9m- 5d	407		St. Paul, MN	Hitzkirchen, Hessen-Darmstadt
Bergen, Johan	17, Oct. 1889	20, Aug.	60	670		St. Paul, MN	Hessen-Darmstadt
Berger, Maria E.	23, Sept 1852	10, Sept	29- 1m-25d	156	Blankertz	Sandusky, OH	
Berger, Anna Wilhelmina	5, Mar. 1877	5, Jan.	48-10m- 5d	79	Wenger	Detroit, MI	Steffigsburg, Thun, Bern, Schweiz
Berger, Barbara	14, Sept 1885	30, Aug.	79	7		Baresville, OH	Moline, Illinois
Berger, Benjamin Franklin	18, July 1889	16, June		462		Wausau, WI	Wiesbaden, Hessen-Nassau
Berger, Carl	18, June 1891	24, May	59	398		Newark, NJ	
Berger, Carolina M.	14, Feb. 1881	12, Jan.	51- 2m	55	Hax	Sandusky, OH	Schafsheim, Dieburg, Hessen
Berger, Carolina M.	31, Jan. 1881	12, Jan.	51- 2m	39	Hax	Sandusky, OH	Umstadt, Dieburg, Hessen
Berger, Christian	15, Nov. 1888	19, Oct.	61	734		Baresville, OH	Steffisburg, Thun, Bern, Schweiz
Berger, Christian	10, Feb. 1879	27, Jan.	76- 5m	47		Winona, MN	Canton Bern, Schweiz
Berger, Christian	8, Jan. 1872	13, Dec.	42-11m-15d	15		Baresville, OH	
Berger, Christiane	12, June 1890	15, May	45	382		Covington, KY	Palsterkamp, Amt Iburg, Osnabrück, Hannover
Berger, Elisabeth	30, Oct. 1871	11, Oct.	51- 8m	351	Springmeier	Blue Island, IL	Gerbenhagen, Kurhessen
Berger, Eva	29, Jan. 1866	24, Dec.	33	38	Häusner	Marine City, MI	Weiblingen, Württemberg
Berger, Friederike	16, Aug. 1894	25, July	67- 2m-12d	534		Newark, NJ	

Christliche Apologete Death Notices --- 1839 - 1899

Name of Deceased	Notice Date	Death Date	Age	Maiden Name	Page	Place of Death	Place of Birth
Berger, Heinrich	5, Mar. 1877	12, Jan.	6		79	Detroit, MI	Güsmannsdorf bei Reichenbach, Schlesien
Berger, Karl August	30, Sept 1867	30, Aug.	48		310	Toledo, OH	Schlesien
Berger, Karl Ernst E.	27, July 1899	24, June	77		479	Marine City, MI	Altbach, Eßlingen, Württemberg
Berger, Louise Margaretha	8, Jan. 1872			Frick	15	Baresville, OH	
Berger, Nikolaus	22, Aug. 1861	13, July	45		136	Blue Island, IL	Steffisburg, Bern, Schweiz
Berger, Rosa	17, Mar. 1892	28, Jan.	26		174	Cannelton, IN	Steffisburg, Bern, Schweiz
Berger, Samuel	6, Oct. 1892	2, Aug.	68		638	Cannelton, IN	Indiana
Berger, Wilhelm	1, June 1863	2, May	21		88	Blue Island, IL	Canton Graubünden, Schweiz
Berger, Wilhelmine	11, Feb. 1884	26, Jan.	75	Flütsch	7	Clayton, IA	
Bergers, Rosine Helena	22, Jan. 1852	21, Dec.	61- 6m-14d		16	St. Clair, MI	Siebstock, Ostfriesland
Berghaus, Friedrich	5, Oct. 1874	20, Sept	33- 8m-18d		319	Edwardsville, IL	
Berghorn, Emilie	16, Apr. 1883	30, Mar.	21- 8m	Lindelmann	127	Long Grove, IL	Ela , Illinois
Berghorn, Heinrich D.	18, Oct. 1894	20, Sept	40		678	Arlington Heights, IL	Anemolten, Hannover
Berghorn, Maria	5, Mar. 1866			Krieger	78	Wheeling, IL	Kanterhagen, Bunzlow, Mecklenburg-Schwerin
Berghorn, Sophia Dorothea Christine	9, July 1896	7, June	42	Klingeberg	447	Arlington Heights, IL	Frelsdorfmühlen, Alt-Luneberg, Ostfriesland
Bergmann, Anna Sophia	7, May 1857	18, Apr.	75	Köster	76	Watertown, WI	Rehlingen, Hannover
Bergmann, Dorothea Carolina Maria	10, May 1880	27, Feb.	42	Willer	151	Odebolt, IA	
Bergmann, John	7, Aug. 1876	15, July	26		255	Schnectady, NY	Sievershütten, Sülfelt, Schleswig-Holstein
Bergmann, Margaretha Maria	15, Dec. 1879	29, Nov.	13- 6m	Wessel	399	Chillicothe, OH	Bitzow, Mecklenburg-Schwerin
Bergmann, Maria	25, Dec. 1871	7, Dec.	35		415	Chicago, IL	Schnectady , New York
Bergmann, Sophia Rebecca	4, June 1891	17, Apr.	20		366	Schnectady, NY	Fraurenth, Sachsen
Bergner, Arthur	7, May 1896	7, Mar.	20		302	Lawrence, MA	Langenwetzendorf, Sachsen
Bergner, Chrisiana Rosine	8, Aug. 1889	17, July	81		510	Wheeling, WV	Triebes, Sachsen
Bergner, Gustav	3, Sept 1891	12, Aug.	30		574	Wheeling, WV	
Bergschicker, Maria	12, Aug. 1858	28, July	43- 4m-12d	Heß	128	Pomeroy, OH	Hoffenheim, Baden
Beringer, Stephan	1, Sept 1848	25, July	42- 2m-15d		144	Pomeroy, OH	Oppau, Rheinkreis Baiern
Berkemeier, Ernst G.H.	21, Mar. 1881	1, Mar.	68- 6m-25d		95	Seymour, IN	Mittenhügel, Minden, Preußen
Berkenbrück, Heinrich	1, Sept 1862	11, June	34		140	Quincy, IL	Herford, Preußen
Berkholz, Ernestine Wilhelmine	1, Aug. 1895	4, July	66	Köpke	494	Oconomowoc, WI	Sukow, Pieritz, Pommern
Berkholz, Wilhelm	23, Feb. 1899	5, Feb.	73- 7m-26d		126	Oconomowoc, WI	Megor, Piritz, Stettin, Pommern
Berlau, Conrad	19, Oct. 1874	1, Oct.	77- -13d		335	Clarington, OH	Re-wod, Alsfeld, Hessen-Darmstadt
Berlau, G.C.	20, Feb. 1846	23, Jan.	21- 8m-17d		31	Lawrenceburg, IN	
Berlau, Katharina	5, Apr. 1860	25, Feb.	60		56	Captina, OH	Braunschwend, Hessen
Berlepp, Georg	12, Nov. 1847	5, Sept	27		183	New Orleans, LA	Hoboken, New Jersey
Berlin, Heinrich	3, May 1880	15, Apr.	15- 9m- 9d		143	Nora Springs, IA	
Beritt, Augusta	10, May 1849	14, Feb.	38		76	Captina, OH	
Bernd, Maria E.	24, Oct. 1881	27, Sept	77		343	Jersey City, NJ	Gries bei Kaiserslauten, Rheinkreis Baiern
Berndt, Caroline	19, Dec. 1895	26, Nov.	70		814	Aurora, IL	Zabelsberg, Fürstenau, Hinterpommern
Berndt, Caroline Christine D.	15, Apr. 1878	2, Apr.	32		119	Milwaukee, WI	Fritzow, Pommern
Berndt, Ernst Friedrich	2, May 1887	2, Apr.	86- 7m-28d		286	Wausau, WI	Schönfließ, Neumark, Preußen
Berndt, Henriette	31, Aug. 1899	14, Aug.	88	Lehmgold	559	Wausau, WI	Germany
Berndt, Karl	2, Jan. 1882	12, Dec.	46- 6m-12d		7	Toledo, OH	Bitow, Hinterpommern
Berndt, Maria	25, June 1883	26, May	51		207	Kearney, MO	Hirlingen, Rottenburg, Württemberg
Berner, Anna Maria	11, Feb. 1897	23, Jan.	55	Eggly	94	Prescott, WI	Maienrieth, Bern, Schweiz
Berner, Franziska Henriette	7, Mar. 1864	12, Dec.	66- 6m		40	Chester, IL	
Berner, Gottlieb	21, July 1898	4, July	71		463	Indianapolis, IN	Grunbach, Schorndorf, Württemberg

Christliche Apologete Death Notices --- 1839 - 1899

Name of Deceased	Notice Date	Death Date	Age	Maiden Name	Page	Place of Death	Place of Birth
Berner, Johan	17, Jan. 1870	21, Dec.	69		23	Rochester, MN	Wensenrambs, Mecklenburg-Schwerin
Berner, Maria	28, Jan. 1886	17, Jan.	45	Henkel	7	Cincinnati, OH	Zichopau,
Berner, Maria	30, Sept 1872	5, Sept			319	Chicago, IL	
Bernet, Albert Wilhelm	5, May 1879	23, Apr.	18 - -20d		143	LaCrosse, WI	Grindelwald, Interlaken, Bern, Schweiz
Bernet, Elisabeth	6, Nov. 1871	16, Oct.	45	Bernet	359	LaCrosse, WI	Lacrosse, Wisconsin
Bernet, Ella	22, Apr. 1878	30, Mar.	24	Markle	127	St. Louis, MO	Grindelwald, Bern, Schweiz
Bernet, Gottlieb	6, Feb. 1882	18, Oct.	28		47	St. Louis, MO	Grindelwald, Interlaken, Bern, Schweiz
Bernet, Johan	25, July 1895	30, June	77		478	LaCrosse, WI	
Bernet, Maria Elisabeth	12, Mar. 1883	16, Feb.	16		87	LaCrosse, WI	Grindelwald, Bern, Schweiz
Bernet, Peter	23, Nov. 1899	1, Nov.	47		751	New York, NY	Arnsheim, Kurhessen
Bernhard, Anna Katharina	8, June 1863	24, Nov.			92	Chicago, IL	
Bernhard, Georg Jakob	24, May 1875	26, Apr.	35		167	Clayton, IA	Kremen, Amt Dorum, Hannover
Bernhard, Helena	6, Apr. 1863	5, Mar.	26	Wichmann	56	Toledo, OH	Lindau am Bodensee, Baiern
Bernhard, Johan Georg	16, Feb. 1874	28, Jan.	66		55	Milwaukee, OR	Untervaz, Graubünden, Schweiz
Bernhard, Johan Luzius	8, Dec. 1898	31, Oct.	59		783	Clayton, IA	Ellerstadt, Rheinkreis Baiern
Bernhardt, Johann Heinrich	12, May 1862	12, Apr.	86		76	Clayton, IA	Klein-Schifferstadt, Rheinkreis Baiern
Bernhardt, Anna Margaretha	4, Nov. 1872	13, Oct.	73	Stahl	359	San Francisco, CA	Darmstadt, Rheinkreis Baiern
Bernhardt, C.J.	24, Nov. 1887	31, Aug.	79- 4m-21d		750	Tioga Center, NY	Wangen, Elsaß
Bernhardt, Christian	24, Sept 1877	23, July	72		311	Faimount, KS	New Bedford, Coshocton County, Ohio
Bernhardt, Friedrich	10, Jan. 1889	24, Dec.	41- 4m- 9d		30	Giard, IA	Niederhülsa, Homberg, Kurhessen
Bernhardt, Johan A.	30, Aug. 1888	11, Aug.	52- 8m-27d		558	Giard, IA	Aghlasterhausen, Mosbach, Baden
Bernhardt, Johan Georg	18, Feb. 1886	28, Jan.	65		7	Clayton, IA	Aglasterhausen, Amt Mosbach, Baden
Bernhardt, John	2, May 1870	12, Apr.	52		143	Lawrenceburg, IN	Dannstadt , Baiern
Bernhart, A.B.	23, Aug. 1849	15, July	69		136	Louisville, KY	Geten, Hessen-Darmstadt
Bernhart, Katharina Christiana	28, Dec. 1899	12, Dec.	78	Derfeld	828	Giard, IA	Ebenfeld bei Herzfeld, Hessen-Darmstadt
Bernhart, Katherine Louise	26, Oct. 1893	17, Sept	55	Müller	686	Toledo, OH	Oberamsen, Solothurn, Schweiz
Bernholt, Maria	14, Mar. 1881	18, Jan.	73	Mullet	87	Dodgeville, IA	Gehrde, Hannover
Bernholt, Johan	15, Mar. 1880	28, Feb.	80		87	Schnectady, NY	Eickhorst, Minden, Preußen
Berning, Friedrich Wilhelm	16, Mar. 1899	15, Feb.	74		174	Ft. Hunter, NY	Hille, Minden, Preußen
Berning, Karolina	8, May 1890	21, Apr.	46 -2m-25d		302	Ft. Hunter, NY	Hille, Minden, Preußen
Berning, Maria	17, Apr. 1890	23, Mar.	69- - 6d	Wittemeier	254	Ft. Hunter, NY	Eickhorst, Minden, Preußen
Berning, Wihelm	15, Nov. 1888	16, Oct.	78- 9m-16d		734	Flint Creek, IA	Badbergen, Hannover
Bernold, (Mrs)	31, Jan. 1876	22, Dec.	77	Kemper	39	Batesville, IN	
Bernreuter, Katharina	1, June 1893	24, Apr.		Stulken	350	Nashville, IL	
Berns, Gerhard	1, Aug. 1870	2, July	68		247	Evansville, IN	Friemersheim, Grefels, Preußen
Bersch, Christian	14, Sept 1885	16, Aug.	69		7	Baltimore, MD	Marburg, Hessen-Kassel
Bersch, Maria	22, Apr. 1886	1, Mar.	53	Marquart	7	New York City, NY	Darmstadt, Hessen-Darmstadt
Bersch, Wilhelmine	21, Mar. 1864	5, Mar.	80		48	West Baltimore, MD	Marburg, Kurhessen
Berscheid, Philipp	7, Mar. 1889	31, Jan.	62		158	Ft. Dodge, IA	Oberengelheim, Hessen-Darmstadt
Berstler, Susanna	28, Sept 1893	25, Aug.	69	Deutsch	622	Batesville, IN	Maudach, Mutterstadt, Baiern
Bert, Elisabeth Barbara	13, Feb. 1882		72		55	Quincy, IL	Großbiberau bei Darmstadt, Hessen-Darmstadt
Bert, John Philipp	22, Mar. 1860		56		48	Quincy, IL	Haan, Rohrbach, Dieburg, Hessen-Darmstadt
Bert, Karolina	29, Aug. 1889	6, Aug.	51	Trippe	558	Quincy, IL	Baltimore, Maryland
Berteloth, (Mr)	22, Nov. 1869	6, Nov.			375	Belleville, IL	Gewiesenruh, Geismar, Kurhessen
Berthold, Anna Rosalie	22, Sept 1884	9, Sept	41	Zürcher	7	Bible Grove, IL	Bern, Schweiz
Berthold, Wilhelm M.	9, Oct. 1890	5, June	35		654	Billings, MO	St. Francis County, Missouri

Christliche Apologete Death Notices --- 1839 - 1899

Name of Deceased	Notice Date	Death Date	Age	Page	Maiden Name	Place of Death	Place of Birth
Bertloth, Ida	31, Oct. 1895	16, Oct.	49	702		Belleville, IL	St. Clair County, Illinois
Bertram, Christian	30, Mar. 1863	24, Feb.	60	52		Canton, MO	Elbers, Braunschweig
Bertram, Dorothea	22, Apr. 1867	6, Apr.	37	126	Eckerlebe	Etna, MO	Rene, Amt Wohlenberg, Hildesheim, Hannover
Bertram, Eduard	27, Apr. 1893	28, Mar.	35	270		Quincy, IL	Quincy, Illinois
Bertram, Ferdinand	4, May 1899	17, Apr.	74	287		Stryker, OH	Magdeburg, Germany
Bertram, Frieda	22, Sept 1884	28, Aug.	47	7		Boston, MA	Carlsruhe, Germany
Bertram, Gustav	13, July 1899	1, July	23- -14d	447		Louisville, KY	Louisville, Jefferson County, Kentucky
Bertram, Gustav (Rev)	29, Sept 1898	10, Sept	75	623		Ypsilanti, MI	Leuchlingen, Düsseldorf, Sollingen, Preußen
Bertram, Maria Sophia	5, Mar. 1891	14, Feb.	74	158	Schwaneberg	Stryker, OH	Hillersleben, Magdeburg, Sachsen
Bertram, Wilhelm	23, Apr. 1896	6, Apr.	75	270		Quincy, IL	Leuchlingen, Düsseldorf, Solingen, Preußen
Bertsch, Catharine	20, Nov. 1882	4, Nov.	65	375		Baltimore, MD	Giltersberg, Germany
Bertsch, Christian	27, Dec. 1875	2, Dec.	64	415		Buffalo, NY	Metzingen, Herrenberg, Württemberg
Bertsch, Christian	12, May 1887	17, Apr.	30	302		Santa Rosa, CA	Erie County, New York
Bertsch, Malwine	17, Mar. 1887	24, Feb.	27	174		St. Joseph, MO	Niedersommerskau, Danzig, West Preußen
Bertz, Regina	27, Mar. 1876	28, Feb.	80	103	Fuß	Grand Rapids, MI	Hohenwettersbach, Baden
Bertz, Salome	31, Oct. 1895		78	702	Faulheber	Gulare, CA	Lichtenau, Germany
Bertz, Salome	30, May 1895		48	350		Tulare, CA	Lichtenau, Baden
Bertz, John Chr.	7, July 1879	14, Feb.	21	215		Bushnell, IL	Bushnell, Illinois
Bertz, Margaretha Elisabeth	1, July 1878	24, May	14- 5m- 1d	207	Hahne	Bushnell, IL	
Bertz, Sophia	4, July 1870	7, June	49- 8m	215	Lutz	Bushnell, IL	Siewesen, Amt Hildesheim, Hannover
Besch, Anna Margaretha	16, Nov. 1863	14, Oct.	27	184		Berea, OH	Sondelfingen, Urach, Württemberg
Bese, Elisabeth	14, Jan. 1897		76	31		Pittsburg, PA	Berleburg, Witgenstein, Westphalen
Besecke, Henriette	28, May 1891	9, Apr.	44- 6m-16d	350	Lühring	Arlington, MN	
Besecke, Katharine	28, June 1888	6, June	88	414		Arlington, MN	Wellen, Sachsen
Beseke, Andreas Heinrich	24, Nov. 1884	6, Nov.	87	7		Arlington, MN	Wellen, Wollmirstedt, Sachsen
Beseke, Carl	4, Aug. 1879	1, July	52	247		Henderson, MN	Wollen, Wolminstedt, Magdeburg, Preußen
Beseke, Louise	9, Mar. 1868	12, Feb.	15	79		Henderson, MN	
Bessege, Matthias	7, Sept 1863	23, July		144		Camp Sherman, MS	
Best, Georg	1, May 1876	9, Apr.	61	143		Carrollton, MO	
Best, Georg Peter	16, Apr. 1891	29, Mar.	72- 6m	254		Kansas City, KS	
Best, Johannes	11, Dec. 1890	4, Nov.	70- 7m- 8d	798		Black River Falls, WI	
Best, Karl	2, June 1898	4, May	67	351		Saginaw, MI	
Best, Mathilde	6, Sept 1894	12, Aug.	23	582		Nokomis, IL	
Best, Philipp	2, Aug. 1894	12, July	69	502		Toledo, OH	
Beste, Christina	17, Oct. 1881	22, Sept	40- 3m	335		Mt. Vernon, IN	Osthofen, Hessen-Darmstadt
Beste, Friedrich Wilhelm	29, Mar. 1888	14, Feb.	58	206		Mt. Vernon, IN	Osthofen, Hessen
Bethe, Sophia Rosina Elisabeth	29, Sept 1859	14, Sept	59- 5m-10d	156	Beuermann	Manchester, MO	Asel bei Voehl, Hessen-Darmstadt
Betsch, Anna Barbara	1, May 1865	12, Apr.	18- - 4d	72		Farmington, IA	Detroff, Mecklenburg-Schwerin
Betsch, Johan	20, May 1872	5, Mar.	25- 6m-26d	167		St. Charles, MO	Worfelden, Hessen-Darmstadt
Bettenhausen, Adam	27, May 1867	13, May		166		New Bremen, IL	Oberschümpf, Boxberg, Baden
Bettenhausen, Adam	17, Sept 1891	23, Aug.	12	606		Frankfort Station, IL	Dissen, Hannover
Bettenhausen, Anna Martha	27, Feb. 1865	11, Feb.	76	36	Boley	New Bremen, IL	Jühnde, Hannover
Bettenhausen, Karoline	19, Nov. 1896	26, Oct.	72	750	Göbel	Lockport, IL	Grabs, St. Gallen, Schweiz
Bettenhausen, Katharina Elisabeth	24, Apr. 1890	24, Mar.	30	270		Frankfort, IL	Königswald, Kurhessen
Bettenhausen, Margaretha	24, Jan. 1889	4, Jan.	26	62	Telten	Frankfort, IL	Königswald, Kurhessen
Bettenhausen, Margarethe	21, Feb. 1889	4, Jan.	27	126	Telten	Frankfort, IL	Rainhartshausen, Waldeck

- 34 -

Christliche Apologete Death Notices --- 1839 - 1899

Name of Deceased	Notice Date	Death Date	Age	Maiden Name	Page	Place of Death	Place of Birth
Bettenhausen, Sabina	18, May 1899	11, Apr. 1899	42	Brandau	319	Frankfort, IL	Orland
Bettenhausen, William	16, Apr. 1891	1, Apr. 1891	18		254	Frankfort Station, IL	Orland, Cook County, Illinois
Bettger, Anna Catharina	28, May 1883	24, Apr. 1883	34- 2m-21d	Schwab	175	Mendota, IL	
Bettien, Jul. M.	31, Dec. 1896	3, Dec. 1896	47		844	Klemme, IA	Rosenfelde, Schlochau, Preußen
Bettien, Martin	21, Mar. 1895	20, Feb. 1895	81		190	Klemme, IA	
Bettin, Michael	4, Apr. 1895	13, Mar. 1895	60		222	Napoleon, MO	Klewitzdorf bei Guesen, Mogitno, Preußen
Bettin, Robert	5, July 1888	4, June 1888	30- 1m-19d		430	Duluth, MN	
Bettinger, Jacob	28, Jan. 1897	8, Jan. 1897	75		62	Boonville, IN	Trier, Preußen
Betz, Anna	13, Oct. 1884	8, Sept 1884	13		7	Virginia, IL	
Betz, Emilie	7, Nov. 1881	9, Sept 1881	17- 4m-26d		359	Beardstown, IL	Ashland,
Betz, Friedrich	23, Aug. 1869	25, July 1869	37		271	St. Charles, MO	Vaterstadt, Württemberg
Betz, Gustav	28, Mar. 1889	7, Mar. 1889	72- - 2d		206	Pepin, WI	Thunsenreuth, Baiern
Betz, Johannes	6, Jan. 1868	8, Dec. 1868	38- - 5d		6	Hudson City, NJ	Rottman, Sonnenberg, Sachsen-Meiningen
Betz, Wesley	23, Aug. 1869	18, July 1869	9m- 8d		271	St. Charles, MO	
Beuerle, Margaretha B.	25, July 1861	10, July 1861	47- 7m- 2d		120	Frederick City, MO	Neustadt an der Aisch, Baiern
Beuheit, Heinrich	29, Sept 1887	13, Sept 1887	77		622	Louisville, KY	Pirmasens, RheinPfalz Baiern
Beukmann, Johan Konrad	2, Mar. 1899	22, Jan. 1899	83		143	Seymour, IN	Husum, Hannover
Beukmann, Regine Margaretha	23, July 1891	30, June 1891	70- 8m-20d	Wonning	478	Seymour, IN	Bramsche, Hannover
Beunk, Andreas	29, June 1863	24, May 1863	45		104	Brunswick, MO	Holland
Beuse, Catharina	13, Dec. 1860	23, Nov. 1860	27	Stickrad	200	Covington, KY	Hessen-Kassel
Beutel, Maria Elisabeth	14, Feb. 1881	27, Jan. 1881	80- 1m-10d	Bache	55	Columbus, IL	Langel bei Mühlhausen, Preußen
Beutel, Martha	19, Jan. 1880	31, Dec. 1880	80	Kellermann	23	Quincy, IL	OberDora bei Mühlhausen, Preußen
Beutel, Mattheus	27, May 1878	8, May 1878	84- 7m-20d		167	Jersey City, NJ	Steinbach, Backnang, Württemberg
Beutel, Sebastian	2, Dec. 1878	14, Nov. 1878	79- 3m-18d		383	Columbus, IL	Oberdurloch bei Mühlhausen, Erfurt, Preußen
Beutel, Wilhelm	26, Aug. 1886	5, July 1886	66		7	Columbus, IL	Oberdorla, Mühlhausen, Erfurt, Preußen
Beutler, Karl	22, Feb. 1869	19, Jan. 1869	35- 3m- 3d		63	Ann Arbor, MI	Allensteig, Nagold, Württemberg
Beuttel, Wilhelmine	22, Aug. 1889	29, July 1889	40	Hosch	542	San Jose, CA	Fulton County, Ohio
Bevers, Catharina	23, May 1870	22, Nov. 1870	82- 6m-22d		167	Petersburg, IL	
Bewig, Dorothea	23, July 1877	4, July 1877	61- 5m-11d		239	Belleville, IL	Goßmar, Hannover
Bewig, H.	16, June 1859	30, May 1859	68		96	Belleville, IL	Soßmar, Hannover
Bewig, Heinrich	11, Nov. 1897	21, Oct. 1897	19- 9m-10d		719	Belleville, IL	Sosmer, Hannover
Bexten, Anna Emilie	17, Oct. 1881	3, Oct. 1881	37		335	Quincy, IL	
Beyer, Auguste Albertine	11, Jan. 1894				30	Grand Rapids, MI	Bromberg, West Preußen
Beyer, Carl	1, June 1893	10, May 1893	29		350	Cleveland, OH	Brachhorst, Vorpommern
Beyer, Elisabeth	3, Aug. 1893	15, July 1893	67	Grans	494	Pittsburg, PA	Zweiflingen, Württemberg
Beyer, Friederike	11, May 1899	17, Mar. 1899	64	Braun	302	Faribault, MN	Langenhagen, Pommern
Beyer, Magdalena	15, Dec. 1879	22, Nov. 1879	64- 4m- 4d		399	Buffalo, NY	Lothringen, Elsaß
Beyer, Matthias	16, Sept 1886	14, Aug. 1886	77		7	Buffalo, NY	Weiler, Marbach, Württemberg
Beyer, Salome	14, Oct. 1858	19, Sept 1858	39		164	Buffalo, NY	Mietesheim, Elsaß
Beyerley, Margaretha	28, Oct. 1858	28, Aug. 1858	36		172	New Albany, IN	
Beyersdorf, Wilhelm	11, July 1895	27, May 1895	75- 5m-26d		446	Plymouth, WI	Falkenwalde, Brandenburg
Beyhl, Heinrich	17, Jan. 1881	20, Dec. 1881	72-10m-28d		23	Dubuque, IA	Lauffen, Besigheim, Württemberg
Bez, Margaretha	5, May 1898	9, Apr. 1898	67	Kast	287	Louisville, KY	Kirweiler, Elsaß
Biber, Jakob	7, Apr. 1887	19, Mar. 1887	31		222	Topeka, KS	Berks County, Pennsylvania
Bibighäuser, Christian	16, Oct. 1871	23, Sept 1871	59- 6m- 9d		335	Washington, MN	Dodenau, Hessen-Darmstadt
Bichele, Dora	2, Aug. 1880	5, July 1880	38	Haberer	247	Detroit, MI	Rothenberg, Württemberg

Christliche Apologete Death Notices --- 1839 - 1899

Name of Deceased	Notice Date	Death Date	Age	Maiden Name	Page	Place of Death	Place of Birth
Bichele, Katharina Margaretha	16, Apr. 1877	21, Mar.	71- 11d	Quack	127	Detroit, MI	Schaadt, Grevenbroich, Düsseldorf, Preußen
Bick, Andreas	23, Aug. 1860	5, Aug.	62- 3m		136	Iowa City, IA	Immshausen, Hannover
Bick, Anna	23, Apr. 1866	2, Apr.	27- 2m-11d	Spreckler	134	Iowa City, IA	
Bick, August	4, Mar. 1897	27, Jan.	71		143	York, NE	Imbshausen, Hannover
Bick, Heinrich	17, Jan. 1895	27, Oct.	67		46	Des Moines, IA	
Bick, Johanne	3, Mar. 1859	27, Jan.	57		36	Iowa City, IA	Imshausen, Hannover
Bick, Julius	31, July 1851	13, Mar.	26- 6m		124	Iowa City, IA	Nordheim, Hannover
Bick, Katharina	20, Apr. 1899	24, Mar.	67	Sinn	254	Canton, MO	Zeiskamm, Germersheim, Rheinpfalz Baiem
Bick, Louis Wesley	11, Aug. 1887	29, July	27		510	Canton, MO	Iowa City, Iowa
Bickel, Anna Elisabeth	3, Nov. 1898	15, Oct.	76	Schwarz	703	Giard, IA	Ersrode, Rotenburg, Preußen
Bickel, Charlotte	5, June 1871	29, Apr.	36- 4m		183	St. Louis, MO	Eidinghausen, Preußen
Bickel, Christine	12, Oct. 1899	16, Sept	71	Walter	655	Scranton, PA	Hesselhurst, Baden
Bickel, Daniel	2, Nov. 1899	8, Oct.	82		703	Giard, IA	Nausis, Rothenberg, Kurhessen
Bickel, Johan Georg	2, Dec. 1878	18, Nov.	63- 2m- 1d		383	Lancaster, WI	Dorf Elsof, Wittgenstein, Preußen
Bickel, Karl Friedrich	30, Apr. 1891	8, Apr.	54		286	Chicago, IL	Malterdingen, Baden
Bickel, Katharina	30, Mar. 1885	5, Mar.	89		7	Newark, OH	Geisenberg, Baiem
Bickel, Magdalena	15, Mar. 1894	1, Mar.	56	Wiedling	182	Chicago, IL	Broggingen, Kensingen, Baden
Bickel, Nellie	14, Jan. 1886	18, Dec.	17		7	Toledo, OH	
Bickelmann, Charlotte	1, Mar. 1888	17, Jan.	61	Hardt	142	Brooklyn, NY	Berzhain, Nassau
Bickenbach, August	31, Oct. 1870	20, Sept	18		351	Hedwigs Hill, TX	
Bickenbach, Daniel	18, Apr. 1881	4, Apr.	86 - 4m		127	Llano, TX	Oelroth, Köln, Preußen
Bickenbach, Heinrich	13, June 1895	11, May	82		382	Burlington, IA	Schnellenbach, Humersbach, Köln, Preußen
Bickenbach, Julius	11, Aug. 1892	19, July	30		510	Llano, TX	Beaver Creek, Mason County, Texas
Bickenbach, Lisette	13, June 1881	14, May	61- 6m	Riemerschüdt	191	Burlington, IA	Schnellenbach, Köln, Preußen
Bickenbach, Otto Bismarck	17, July 1890	24, June	21		462	Albert Lea, MN	Burlington, Iowa
Bickenbach, Sophie	4, May 1874	4, Apr.	19- 6m-14d		143	Mason, TX	
Bicker, Fr. Wilhelm	5, Feb. 1877	9, Dec.	63		47	Drake, MO	Lüde, Lippe
Bicker, Friedrich	20, Oct. 1862	1, Oct.	45		168	Freeport, IL	Bendorf, Amt Varenholz, Lippe
Bicker, Sophia	12, Apr. 1875	21, Mar.	36	Rethemeyer	119	Drake, MO	Valdorf, Amt Vlotho, Minden, Preußen
Bidel, Wilhelmina Elisabeth	25, Apr. 1870	4, Apr.	69- 3m- 5d	Leweke	135	Gasconade Co, MO	Lippe-Detmold
Bidel, Zacharias	29, Nov. 1860	17, Sept	62		192	Columbus, IL	
Bieber, Anna Katharina	10, Oct. 1895	23, Sept	58	Diebel	654	Billings, MO	Niederaula, Hersfeld, Kurhessen
Bieber, Johan Heinrich	20, May 1897	14, Apr.	64		318	Eldora, IL	Niederante, Hirschfeld, Kurhessen
Biebighäuser, Heinrich Christian	1, Apr. 1878	14, Mar.	35		103	Washington, MN	Dodenau, Hessen-Darmstadt
Biebinger, Barbara	19, July 1860	30, May	30-10m		116	Milan, IN	
Biebinger, Heinrich	25, Dec. 1856	21, Nov.	56		208	Pomeroy, OH	Obba, Rheinkreis Baiem
Biecheler, Anna Friederika	14, Mar. 1870	13, Feb.	71		87	Dover, OH	Plieringen, Stuttgart, Württemberg
Bied, Margarethe Clara	5, Sept 1889	20, Aug.	27- 1m-28d	Wohlberg	574	Chicago, IL	Sheboygan County, Wisconsin
Biedebach, C. H.	20, July 1899	24, June	73		463	Pasadena, CA	Mommershausen, Kurhessen
Biedebach, Emma M.	26, Apr. 1880	31, Mar.	12-11m- 9d		135	Victor, IA	Muscatine County, Iowa
Biedenkapp, John	9, Sept 1878	24, Aug.	67- 4m-10d		287	Brooklyn, NY	Weltersdorf, Hessen-Darmstadt
Bieder, Anna Barbara	19, Apr. 1869	22, Mar.	88	Glaser	127	Shakopee, MN	Binningen, Basel, Schweiz
Bieder, Jakob Friedrich	21, Feb. 1895	22, Jan.	68		126	Jordan, MN	Basel, Schweiz
Bieder, Rudolph	30, Dec. 1886	13, Dec.	63		7	Jordan, MN	Binningen, Basel, Schweiz
Biedermann, August	13, Oct. 1879	25, Sept	74		327	Blue Island, IL	Gangloffsimmern, Erfurt, Preußen
Biedermann, Barbara	19, July 1880	12, June	65- 2m	Briner	231	Philadelphia, PA	Ufter, Zürich, Schweiz

Christliche Apologete Death Notices --- 1839 - 1899

Name of Deceased	Notice Date	Death Date	Age	Page	Maiden Name	Place of Death	Place of Birth
Biedermann, Bertha	9, Apr. 1883	20, Mar.	32- 6m-16d	119	Bulling	Jerusalem, NY	Schwieberdingen, Württemberg
Biedermann, Wilhelmina	28, Feb. 1881	15, Feb.	62	71	Rinkenberger	Blue Island, IL	Stuchow, Pommern
Biegert, Auguste Wilhelmine	1, Nov. 1894	27, Sept	51	710	Staalz	Lyona, KS	Davis County, Kansas
Biegert, Eddie	8, Sept 1887	20, Aug.	16	574		Lyona, KS	Lyons Creek, Davis County, Kansas
Biegert, Emilie Louise	30, June 1884	10, June	16	7		Lyona, KS	Davis County, Kansas
Biegert, Emma	25, Aug. 1887	5, Aug.	19	542		Lyona, KS	Lyona, Kansas
Biegert, Lydia Ella	2, Jan. 1896	7, Dec.	20	14		Woodbine, KS	
Biegler, Georg Leonhard	13, Apr. 1899	25, Mar.	77	238		Terre Haute, IN	Bierbach, Baiern
Biegler, Rosina	12, May 1873	20, Apr.	43- - 3d	151		Terre Haute, IN	Württemberg
Biehl, Abigail	18, May 1899	21, Apr.	66	319		Lancaster, NY	Alabama, New York
Biehl, Dorothea Carolina	2, July 1891	30, May	75	430	Rau	San Diego, CA	Remstatt bei Michelbach, Nassau
Biehl, Elisabeth	9, Mar. 1899	10, Feb.	48	158	Strack	Clay Center, KS	Klingenbach, Nassau
Biehl, Maria	23, Dec. 1867	14, Nov.	27	406		Bucyrus, OH	
Biehl, Phil. Wilhelm	30, June 1884	14, June	67	7		Clay Center, KS	Katzenellenbogen, Nassau
Biehler, Hugo	20, June 1864	12, May	27	100		Buffalo, NY	Herrenzimmer, Rottweil, Württemberg
Biehm, Anna	11, May 1899	18, Apr.	84	302		Troy, NY	
Biel, Carl	26, Feb. 1891	28, Jan.	65- 6m- 8d	142		San Antonio, TX	Norden, Ostfriesland
Biel, Charlotte	24, Feb. 1853	11, Feb.	65	32		Cincinnati, OH	Zweibrücken, Rheinkreis Baiern
Biel, Johan Friedrich	31, Jan. 1870	19, Dec.	46	39		Waverly, OH	Prötlin, Preußen
Biel, Mary	10, Dec. 1883	14, Nov.	20- 8m-19d	7		Scranton, PA	Scranton, Pennsylvania
Bielefeld, Gustav	19, Oct. 1863	3, July	50	168		New Knoxville, OH	Ladbergen, Kreis Tecklenburg, Preußen
Bieler, Joseph	9, Sept 1886	28, Aug.	80	7		Cincinnati, OH	Spaichingen, Württemberg
Bier, Gottlieb Herman	18, Nov. 1897	28, Oct.	76	735		Hoboken, NJ	FreiRhoda bei Leipzig, Sachsen
Bier, Heinrich	20, Jan. 1868	31, Dec.	80- 7m	22		Pittsburg, PA	
Bier, Johan Conrad	25, June 1896	26, May	80	415		Greenville, OH	Altmorschen, Spangenberg, Melsungen, Germany
Bier, John	10, Sept 1891	18, Aug.	71-11m-25d	590		Pittsburg, PA	Altmorschen, Melsungen, Kurhessen
Bier, Susanne	2, June 1859	8, May	72	88	Miller	Pittsburg, PA	
Bierbaum, Conrad	1, Nov. 1888	16, Oct.	87	702		Bunker Hill, IL	Lienen, Westphalen
Bierbaum, Ernst	30, Mar. 1899	2, Mar.	67	207		Brighton, IL	Lienen, Westphalen
Bierbaum, Johan Friedrich	19, Feb. 1883	4, Feb.	54	63		Dayton, OH	Stockum, Osnabrück, Hannover
Bierbaum, Katharina Sophia	19, Apr. 1888	27, Mar.	61- 8m-15d	254	AltSellmeier	Bunker Hill, IL	Lienen, Westphalen
Bierbaum, Maria Gertrud	26, Jan. 1885	26, Dec.	58	7		Marshall, IL	
Bierbrauer, Christian Ferdinand	14, Jan. 1897	4, Dec.	72	31		Wausau, WI	Schiefelbein, Pommern
Biedemann, August	19, July 1894	17, June	85	470		Grand Ridge, IL	Langenhagen bei Harm, Hannover
Biering, Friedrich	20, Dec. 1849		Inquiry	203		St. Louis, MO	Mengeringhausen,
Bierle, Johannes	8, May 1856	16, Apr.	61	76		Sidney, OH	Essingen, Rheinkreis Baiern
Bierlein, Barbara	2, May 1870	29, Mar.	67- 9m-29d	143	Glaser	St. Johns, OH	
Biermann, Catharina	2, Sept 1872	6, June	26	287	Schwarz	Angelica, NY	
Biermann, Dietrich	7, Nov. 1864	17, Oct.	53- 1m- 7d	180		Santa Claus, IN	Borstel, Amt Nienburg, Hannover
Biermann, Dore Elisabeth	18, Nov. 1886	18, Oct.	78	7		Angelica, NY	Leiferde, Gifhorn, Germany
Biermann, Dorothea	18, Apr. 1895	20, Feb.	81	254	Hoffmeyer	Santa Claus, IN	Nienburg, Hannover
Biermann, H.	3, Dec. 1877	2, Nov.	55	391		Ballwin, MO	Wiershausen, Hannover
Biermann, Heinrich	13, Mar. 1865	10, Feb.	26- 9m- 6d	44		Wellsville, NY	Leiferde, Amt Gifhorn, Hannover
Biermann, Johan Heinrich	15, Aug. 1881	29, July	76- 4m- 3d	263		Angelica, NY	Leiferde, Hannover
Biermann, Margaretha	15, May 1851	20, Apr.	38- 6m	80		Laughery, IN	Rathlosen, Hannover
Biermann, Maria	23, Oct. 1876	12, Sept	20	343	Kreuz	Cannon, MN	Rice County, Minnesota

- 37 -

Christliche Apologete Death Notices --- 1839 - 1899

Name of Deceased	Notice Date	Death Date	Age	Page	Maiden Name	Place of Death	Place of Birth
Biermann, Wilhelm	29, Mar. 1880	12, Mar.	21	103		Manitowoc, WI	Rapids, Manitowoc County, Wisconsin
Bierschwal, Christian	4, Apr. 1861	14, Mar.	32	56		Jackson, MO	
Bierwirth, Henry	19, Sept 1889	28, Aug.	55	606		Scranton, PA	Weißenborn, Hessen-Kassel
Biesemeier, Anna	10, June 1897	30, Apr.	39	367	Burton	Warren, MO	Lincoln County, Missouri
Biesemeier, Wilhelmine Amalia	14, Apr. 1898	8, Mar.	18-5m-19d	239		Warren, MO	
Biesemeyer, Amalia	16, Dec. 1867	14, Oct.	43	398		Warren, MO	Wöbbel, Lippe
Biesemeyer, Elisabeth	7, Nov. 1895	5, Oct.	54	718	Feldmann	Warren, MO	Warren County, Missouri
Biesemeyer, Friedrich	14, Apr. 1862	11, Mar.	39	60		Warren, MO	Schönhagen, Amt Sternberg, Lippe
Bigler, Friedrich	24, Nov. 1892	7, Nov.	49	750		Girard, KS	Schweiz
Bigler, Verene	30, July 1877	11, July	6-3m-4d	247	Waber	Cleveland, OH	Schwarzeneck, Bern, Schweiz
Bihler, Christian	28, Apr. 1862	17, Mar.	20-2m	68		Grand Rapids, MI	Ingbenhausen, Göppingen, Württemberg
Bihler, Leonhard	7, Oct. 1897	18, Sept	78	639		Grand Rapids, MI	Klein-Eislingen, Göppingen, Württemberg
Bihr, Augusta	26, Mar. 1883	7, Mar.	29	103	Bahr	Cincinnati, OH	Ludwigkowo bei Cromberg, Preußen
Bilderbeck, Rudolf	8, Sept 1898	14, Aug.	68	575		Alton, IL	Rorichan, Emden, Hannover
Bilderbeck, Sophia Louise	6, Aug. 1883	12, July	34-2m-8d	255	Gabriel	Alton, IL	
Bilderbeck, Talea	29, July 1878	9, July	42	239	Hemmen	Alton, IL	Collinghorst, Stickhausen, Ostfriesland
Bilderbeck, Wenderke	13, Feb. 1871	20, Jan.	72-7m	55	Schmidt	Alton, IL	Rorschum, Amt Emden, Ostfriesland
Bilderbek, Jost	17, Sept 1877	28, Aug.	79	305		Alton, IL	Rorichum, Emden, Ostfriesland
Bill, J. Jakob	27, Sept 1888	5, Sept	87-2m-1d	622		Bradford, IN	Niederweisel, Butschbach, Friedberg, Hessen
Bill, Jakob	22, May 1876	2, May	69	167		Chicago, IL	Münchenbuchsee, Bern, Schweiz
Bill, Karolina	23, Aug. 1869	10, June	62-11m-28d	271	Merrci	Milan, IN	Roppenheim, Bisweiler, Frankreich
Billau, Martin	5, Jan. 1874	13, Dec.	28	7		Toledo, OH	Northeim, Hessen-Darmstadt
Billenstein, Catharina	30, Oct. 1851	19, Oct.	38-6m	176	Ringel	Cincinnati, OH	Trautskirchen, Baiern
Billenstein, Georg	30, Apr. 1877	14, Apr.	34-3m-26d	143		Cincinnati, OH	Cincinnati, Hamilton County, Ohio
Billenstein, Johan Michael	5, Mar. 1877	23, Feb.	64--10d	79		Cincinnati, OH	Buch, Mittelfranken, Baiern
Billenstein, John	19, Oct. 1885	29, Sept	41	7		Newport, KY	Cincinnati, Hamilton County, Ohio
Billenstein, William	20, Sept 1888	29, Aug.	18	606		Newport, KY	
Billing, Leonard	2, Feb. 1893	25, Dec.	82	78		Sterling, NE	Ansbach bei Nürnburg, Baiern
Billing, Peter	28, Dec. 1893			828		Ansbach, GE	Ansbach, Baiern
Biltemeier, Heinrich August	28, Feb. 1895	5, Feb.	32	142		Indianapolis, IN	Greenville, Ohio
Bitz, Albert	22, Mar. 1888	10, Feb.	14	190		Newport, KY	
Bitz, Eduard	30, Dec. 1867	Dec.		414		Cincinnati, OH	
Bitz, Louisa	4, June 1891	16, May	58	366	Venemann	Cincinnati, OH	Hannover
Bitz, Margaretha	25, Mar.1872	11, Mar.	52	103		Newport, KY	
Bitz, Wilhelm	30, Dec. 1867	Dec.		414		Cincinnati, OH	
Bilz, Philipp Jakob	11, Mar. 1897	24, Feb.	83	158		Summerfield, IL	Haßloch a. M., Unterfranken, Germany
Binde, Heinrich	12, June 1882	11, May	23-3m-22d	191		New York City, NY	
Bindenagel, Carolina Friederika	26, July 1875	3, July	25	239	Bonneß	Roberts, IL	Zarben, Pommern
Bing, Caspar	16, Mar. 1893	21, Feb.	84	174		Chicago, IL	Salzungen, Sachsen-Meiningen
Bing, Elisabeth	2, Apr. 1891	11, Mar.	88	222	Schevel	Chicago, IL	Salzungen, Sachsen-Meiningen
Bingenheimer, Theodor August	27, July 1885	6, July	19	7		Lemars, IA	Liberty, Grant County, Wisconsin
Binggeli, Verena	7, Dec. 1893	16, Nov.	23	782		Bloomington, IL	Schwarzenburg, Bern, Schweiz
Binkert, Sylvester	20, Oct. 1853	3, Oct.	28	168		Nauvoo, IL	
Binkhölter, (Mrs)	29, Mar. 1880	1, Mar.	28	103	Edinghaus	Drake, MO	Germany
Binmiker, Johan	22, Mar. 1875	2, Mar.	64- 7m- 2d	95		St. Joseph, MO	Bergenheim, Württemberg
Binnicker, Georg	3, Nov. 1848		Inquiry	179		Bloomington, IL	Oberamt Mergentheim, Württemberg

Christliche Apologete Death Notices --- 1839 - 1899

Name of Deceased	Notice Date	Death Date	Age	Page	Maiden Name	Place of Death	Place of Birth
Binniker, Barbara	8, Dec. 1859	29, Oct.	54- 7m- 6d	196	Busch	St. Joseph, MO	Burgstal, Württemberg
Binniker, Regine	28, Mar. 1864	20, Oct.	45	52	Bartels	St. Joseph, MO	Bäckede, Amt Bissendorf, Hannover
Bintz, Anna Christina	19, Mar. 1896		33	190	Ackermann	Monroefield, OH	Benwood, Marsh County, West Virginia
Bintz, Georg J.	30, Apr. 1896	13, Apr.	40	286		Monroefield, OH	Monroefield, Ohio
Binz, Elisabeth	12, May 1853		64- 7m- 6d	76		Buckhill, OH	Rumpach, Rheinkreis Baiern
Binz, Elisabetha	24, Mar. 1853	11, Feb.		48		Malaga,	
Binz, Franz Anton	14, Nov. 1895	23, Oct.	72	734		Pomeroy, OH	Forchheim in Breisgau, Baden
Birbaum, Maria	5, Mar. 1866		60	78		Alton, IL	
Birk, Jakobine	4, July 1889	13, June	62- 1m-17d	430	Dittmann	Cincinnati, OH	Sieglingen, Neckarsulm, Württemberg
Birk, Johan Christoph	27, Mar. 1882	9, Mar.	60	103		Cincinnati, OH	Bubenorbis, Hall, Württemberg
Birkemeier, Margaretha	2, Sept 1858	7, Aug.	78- 7m- 1d	140		Louisville, KY	Beutelspach, Schorndorf, Württemberg
Birkenbäuel, Peter	11, May 1863	3, Apr.	45-11m-21d	76		Florence, MO	Hemmelzen, Kreis Altkirchen, Preußen
Birkenmayer, Philipp Jacob	12, Apr. 1860	11, Mar.	67	60			Beutelsbach, Schorndorf, Württemberg
Birkholz, Dorothea Sophia	10, Jan. 1881	20, Dec.	44- 7m-25d	15	Burchard	Oconomowoc, WI	Schönewerde, Piritz, Pommern
Birkholz, Ferdinand	3, Oct. 1895	21, Aug.	42	638		Burlington, IA	Arnswalde, Brandenburg
Birkholz, Herman	10, Oct. 1895	27, Aug.	50	654		Boelus, NE	Cratznik, Arnswalde, Brandenburg
Birkle, Katharina	5, Oct. 1854	23, Sept	32	160		Louisville, KY	Nagold, Württemberg
Birkle, Margaretha	19, Apr. 1880	25, Mar.	76- 3m- 7d	127	Großhans	Lafayette, IN	Aichhalten, Calw, Württemberg
Birnbaum, Johann Christian	1, Mar. 1860	2, Feb.	47	36		Cannon City, MN	Reetze, Amt Lüchwo, Hannover
Birr, Reinhold	15, Apr. 1886		22	7		Chicago, IL	
Bischmann, Dorothea Louise	26, Apr. 1888	3, Mar.	22	270	Breitenfeld	White, SD	Reuhmde, Frankfurt a .d. Oder, Preußen
Bischof, Louise	1, June 1868	8, May	5	175	Volland	Chicago, IL	
Bischoff, Carolina	13, Aug. 1883	24, July	53- 5m-29d	263	Tiemann	Brenham, TX	
Bischoff, Georg Theodor	24, Mar. 1848		Inquiry	51		Chicago, IL	
Bischoff, Magdalena	27, Apr. 1899	22, Mar.	73	271		Orlando, OK	Kolmar, Elsaß
Bisemeier, Friedrich	27, Oct. 1887	11, Oct.	30	686		Warren Co, MO	Warren County, Missouri
Bisemeier, Louise	16, Mar. 1885	5, Mar.	32	7	Knipmeier	Warrenton, MO	Warren County, Missouri
Bisseger, Anton	1, Dec. 1862	29, Oct.	28	192		Chillicothe, OH	Sulgen, Thurgau, Schweiz
Bissenger, Maria Margaretha	11, June 1877	15, May	20- 5m-16d	191		Ripley, OH	Adams County, Ohio
Bissig, Margaretha	13, Feb. 1890	20, Jan.	36	110		Appleton, WI	Schweiz
Bissinger, Anna Rosina	5, Nov. 1877	5, Oct.	10	359		Ripley, OH	
Bitsch, Katharina	11, Feb. 1892	21, Jan.	85	94	Sulzer	Galion, OH	Gau Angerloch, Baden
Bitschy, Ettie	10, July 1890	13, Feb.	29- 7m- 7d	446	Schwarz	Canal Dover, OH	Berlin, Holmes County, Ohio
Bittaway, Elisabeth	27, June 1895	25, May	29	414	Neu	Buffalo, NY	Zweibrücken, Rheinpfalz Baiern
Bitter, Christina Maria Elisabeth	16, Dec. 1858	11, Oct.	50- 5m-11d	200		Brunswick, MO	Veltheim, Preußen
Bitter, Karolina	8, Jan. 1888	6, Feb.	69- 6m-22d	158		Boody, IL	
Bittickhofer, John	29, Jan. 1883	17, Jan.	46	39		Kendallville, IN	
Bittner, Barbara	8, Sept 1892	25, Aug.	65	574	Rose	New Palestine, IN	Canton Bern, Schweiz
Bittner, Dora	21, Apr. 1887	11, Mar.	47- 6m	254		Union Hill, NY	Mark Erlbach, Baiern
Bittner, Elisabeth	25, Aug. 1879	27, July	39	271		Jerusalem, IA	
Bittner, Ernestine	1, May 1890	15, Apr.	74	286	Heischke	Lawrence, MA	Rheinpreußen
Bittner, Ernst	7, June 1894	12, May	31	374		Echo, MN	Pollischen, Landsberg, Preußen
Bittner, Johannes	27, Aug. 1891	1, Aug.	65- 8m-25d	558		New Palestine, IN	Burschendorf, Baiern
Bitz, Theresa	25, May 1885		63	7	Neuhausen	Lena, IL	Oberweyer, Lahr, Baden
Bitzer, Conrad	20, June 1895	26, Apr.	65	398		Crown Point, IN	Württemberg
Bitzer, Dorothea	14, Jan. 1878	9, Dec.	32- 9m-17d	15		Glencoe, MN	Weil im Schönbuch, Böblingen, Württemberg

- 39 -

Christliche Apologete Death Notices --- 1839 - 1899

Name of Deceased	Notice Date	Death Date	Age	Page	Maiden Name	Place of Death	Place of Birth
Bitzer, Eva	18, May 1899	17, Apr.	70	319	Postel	Cincinnati, OH	Ingeheim, Baiern
Bitzer, Jakob Heinrich	10, Mar. 1898	16, Feb.	23	158		Pittsburg, PA	Pittsburg, Pennsylvania
Bitzer, Johan	21, Jan. 1886	8, Jan.	77- 3m	7		Minneapolis, MN	Pfaffingen, Balingen, Württemberg
Bitzer, Johan Martin	4, Aug. 1898	15, July	36	495		Greenfield, MA	Burgfelden, Balingen, Württemberg
Bitzer, Martin	16, Sept 1897	25, Aug.	23	591		Greenfield, MA	Burgfelden, Balingen, Württemberg
Bjick, Maria	12, Jan. 1885	21, Dec.	23- 3m-16d	7	Durkisk	Chicago, IL	New Brunswick,
Blackburn, Katie	4, Aug. 1884	18, June	20	7		Evansville, IN	Vanderburg County, Indiana
Blackletge, Joseph P.	3, Aug. 1863	3, July	23	124		Winchester, VA	
Blangers, Karolina	20, May 1886	3, May	52	7	Wagner	Topeka, KS	Gertwiller, Barr, Elsaß
Blank, Anna Maria	5, Oct. 1893	15, Sept	71	638	Völbel	Brooklyn, NY	Forsthaus bei Dürkheim, Rheinkreis Baiern
Blank, Catharina	4, Aug. 1879	15, July	81	247	Zollmann	De Soto, MN	Mansfelden, Amt Limburg, Nassau
Blank, Catharine	21, Apr. 1873	5, Apr.	61	127		Muscatine, IA	Otterstein, Amt Ottersberg, Hannover
Blank, Elisabeth Ernestine	14, July 1892	13, June	24	446		Beardstown, IL	Sandridge, Cook County, Illinois
Blank, Heinrich	11, Apr. 1895	4, Mar.	71	238		Rossbach, IA	Martinsfeld bei Heiligenstadt, Preußen
Blank, Maria Catharina	25, Apr. 1889	25, Mar.	63- -16d	270	Pister	De Soto, MO	Ellar, Nassau
Blank, Sarah Wilhelmine	3, Feb. 1887	5, Jan.	25- 9m-12d	78		De Soto, MO	
Blank, Wilhelm	29, Apr. 1886	6, Apr.	56	7		De Soto, MN	Mensfelden, Nassau
Blanke, Anna Elisabeth	3, Aug. 1885	20, July	67	7	Brinkmeyer	St. Louis, MO	Frotheim, Westphalen
Blanke, Caroline	8, Sept 1887	20, Aug.	36	574		Burlington, IA	Herfort, Preußen
Blanke, H. (Rev)	17, Feb. 1873	21, Jan.		53		Second Creek, MO	
Blanke, Heinrich	23, Aug. 1880	6, Aug.	56- 5m-23d	271		St. Louis, MO	Altena, Westphalen, Preußen
Blanke, Henriette	3, Oct. 1895	25, Aug.	74	638	Dressel	Garden City, KS	Altena bei Iserlohn, Preußen
Blanke, J.H.	13, Aug. 1883	15, July	80- 6m	263		St. Louis, MO	Ravensbergen bei Buchholzhausen, Preußen
Blankemeyer, Sophia	10, Mar. 1879	26, Jan.	28	79	Goebel	Toledo, OH	Toledo, Lucas County, Ohio
Blanken, Hermann	28, Apr. 1862	25, Mar.	26- 5m-25d	68	Brandau	Charles City, IA	Webstet, Amt Ottersberg, Hannover
Blankenbach, Elisabeth	27, Jan. 1898	1, Jan.	92	63		Wheeling, VA	Königswald, Kurhessen
Blankenber, Heinrich	18, Feb. 1842		Inquiry	27		Melrose, NY	
Blankenburg, Wilhelm Christian	28, Jan. 1886		21-11m- 8d	7		Philadelphia, PA	
Blankenhorn, Katharina	2, Apr. 1891	27, Feb.	80	222		Toledo, OH	Ulm, Württemberg
Blankenmeyer, Sophia	17, Feb. 1879	26, Jan.	28	55	Grebel	Falls Co, TX	Toledo, Lucas County, Ohio
Blankenstein, Dorothea	27, Feb. 1882	30, Jan.	55	71		Ft. Dodge, IA	Badeleben, Preußen
Blase, August Herman	22, Sept 1892	30, Aug.	36	606		St. Paul, MN	West St. Paul, Minnesota
Blase, Heinrich	26, Jan. 1885		56	7		St. Paul, MN	
Blase, Sophia	29, May 1871	12, May	20- -22d	175	Niepold	Lafayette, IN	Quincy, Illinois
Blaser, Christoph	16, June 1892	25, May	65	382		Chicago, IL	Sparwiese, Württemberg
Bläser, Dorothea	11, Feb. 1897	24, Jan.	85	94		Newton, KS	Esselborth, Hessen-Darmstadt
Bläser, Emma	21, Sept 1893	28, Aug.	20	606		Golconda, IL	Austin, Texas
Blaser, Maria	30, Oct. 1876	15, Oct.	77	351	Künk	Princeton, IL	Oberamt Nagold, Württemberg
Blaser, Samuel	29, May 1856	23, Mar.	52	88		Amourdale, KS	Biglen, Bern, Schweiz
Blaß, Anna K.	3, Jan. 1889	30, Nov.	43	14	Kleinschmidt	Canal Dover, OH	Niederlau bei Mühlhausen, Thüringen
Blaßer, Elisabeth	10, July 1865	24, June	68	112		Milwaukee, WI	
Bläßer, Peter	7, July 1898	6, June	44	431		Golconda, IL	Hesselborn, Hessen-Darmstadt
Blatter, Anna Barbara	27, Oct. 1884	9, Oct.	76	7		Wheeling, VA	Eich, Tübingen, Württemberg
Blätter, Anna Maria	23, Apr. 1857	3, Apr.	26	68		Waltersburg, IL	Dettwyler, Schweiz
Blatter, Heinrich	23, Oct. 1890	1, Oct.	68	686		Pueblo, CO	Dettweiler, Elsaß
Blatter, Johan	20, Apr. 1893	24, Mar.	66	254			Preußen

- 40 -

Christliche Apologete Death Notices --- 1839 - 1899

Name of Deceased	Notice Date	Death Date	Age	Maiden Name	Place of Death	Page	Place of Birth
Blättler, Friedrich	7, Dec. 1868	19, Nov.	21- 6m-17d		Clarington, OH	391	Bern, Schweiz
Blättler, Jakob	24, July 1882	4, July	84- -25d		Clarington, OH	239	Kanton Bern, Schweiz
Blättler, Johannes	13, Oct. 1887	12, Sept	71- 7m- 7d		Wheeling, WV	654	
Blattler, Maria	27, Sept 1849	22, Aug.	45		Captina, OH	156	
Blattner, Erwin Wilhelm	12, Mar. 1896	18, Feb.	28		Highland, IL	174	Highland, Illinois
Blättner, Heinrich	1, Apr. 1897	3, Mar.	64		Pittsburg, PA	206	Nieder-Grenzenbach, Kurhessen
Blättner, Marie	20, June 1870	2, June	42	Bretz	Chicago, IL	199	Sebbederode, Amt Treisa, Ziegenhain, Kurhessen
Blatz, Peter	25, Jan. 1894	16, Dec.	65		New York City, NY	62	Kilsheim an der Tauber, Baden
Blaufus, Jacob	23, July 1857	25, June			Quincy, IL	120	
Blaum, Catharina	3, May 1880	17, Apr.	54		Henrietta, OH	143	Fürth, Lindenfels, Hessen
Blaus, Anna Katharina	11, Mar. 1886	28, Feb.	86	Betz	Brooklyn, NY	7	Steinberg, Württemberg
Beck, Robert J.	5, May 1892	2, Apr.	22		Colbey, KS	286	Preußen
Beck, Wilhelmine	28, May 1877	6, Apr.	37- 2m- 5d	Naß	Maple Creek, WI	175	Hillerse, Gifhorn, Hannover
Beckwide, Heinrich	30, Sept 1886	4, Sept	21		Caneadea, NY	7	
Beeker, Wiardus	29, Nov. 1888	7, Nov.	19- 9m-17d		Bible Grove, IL	766	Bucheberg, Solothurn, Schweiz
Beier, Magdalena	5, Feb. 1872	21, Jan.	74	Drittebach	Davenport, IA	47	Schäftersheim, Mergentheim, Württemberg
Beil, Barbara	27, June 1889	17, May	62	Stahl	Detroit, MI	414	Erlingheim, Württemberg
Beil, Christina R.	29, Dec. 1859	15, Dec.			Detroit, MI	208	
Bleimayer, Emil	10, Oct. 1870	14, Sept	21-11m-18d		Grand Rapids, MI	327	Attenasienhof bei Samunalschin, Preußen
Bleimeier, Anna	16, Sept 1886	1, Sept	67- 5m-14d	Golbeck	Grand Rapids, MI	7	Tetten, Oldenburg
Bleker, Eduard	1, July 1878	13, June	57- 5m-15d		New Orleans, LA	207	Ladbergen, Tecklenburg, Preußen
Blemker, Elise	2, Feb. 1899	3, Jan.			Evansville, IN	79	
Blemker, Jakob E.R.	1, Jan. 1883	10, Dec.	45- -15d		Huntingburg, IN	7	Ladbergen, Tecklenburg, Preußen
Blemker, Marie Louise	3, Sept 1883	23, Aug.	39- 3m-16d	Brinkmeier	Evansville, IN	287	Huntingburg, Indiana
Blemker, Samuel E.	19, July 1880	30, June	17- 5m-14d		Huntingburg, IN	231	Ladbergen, Preußen
Blemker, Sophia C.	19, Oct. 1893	1, Oct.	60	Bremer	Huntingburg, IN	670	New Orleans, Louisiana
Blesch, Flora M.C.	2, July1883	16, June	31-11m-16d		Mt. Vernon, IN	215	Schillingstadt am Boxberg, Baden
Blesch, John Peter	22, Oct. 1883	14, Oct.	61- 3m- 1d		Evansville, IN	343	Esens, Ostfriesland
Blesene, Johan	9, Feb. 1880	20, Jan.	60		Red Bud, IL	47	Holzhausen, Minden, Preußen
Blesse, Heinrich	12, May 1892	3, Apr.	56		St. Charles, MO	302	Ehrenberg, Kreis Soldien,
Blessien, F.	9, Feb. 1874	12, Jan.	73		Lowell, WI	47	Blankensee, Pommern
Blessin, Louise	22, Sept 1884	5, Sept	79- 7m	Lemke	Lowell, WI	7	Chicago, Cook County, Illinois
Bletsch, Charles Fr.	10, Oct. 1881	2, Oct.	19		Covington, KY	327	Lambsheim, Rheinkreis Baiern
Bletsch, Elisabeth	8, Sept 1898	19, Aug.	67	Yost	Chicago, IL	575	Waldorf, Baden
Bletsch, Peter	13, Jan. 1898	19, Dec.	64		Waco, TX	31	Spring Prairie, Wisconsin
Bletsch, Rose Erzelia	12, Feb. 1891	12, Jan.	23	Funk	Chicago, IL	110	
Bletscher, Maria Dorothea	19, Feb. 1857	12, Feb.		Schneider	Galion, OH	32	Neustadt, Württemberg
Bleuler, Mathilde	12, May 1873	9, Apr.	39	Maichel	Jacksonville, IL	151	Pommern
Bleymeier, Rudolph	19, June 1871	17, May	52- -20d		Grand Rapids, MI	199	Altheim, Dieburg, Hessen-Darmstadt
Blickhahn, Georg	27, May 1886	13, May	77		St. Louis, MO	7	St. Gallen, Schweiz
Blickhahn, Luise Maria	23, Mar. 1899	23, Feb.	81	Werkmeister	St. Louis, MO	190	Undingen, Reutlingen, Württemberg
Blickle, Anna Maria	23, Feb. 1885	2, Feb.	64		Grand Rapids, MI	7	
Blickle, Catharina	1, June 1863	21, Mar.	8- 6m		Grand Rapids, MI	88	Undingen, Reutlingen, Württemberg
Blickle, Jakob	22, June 1893	3, June	67		Grand Rapids, MI	398	Undingen, Reutlingen, Württemberg
Blickle, Johan Georg	8, Mar. 1860	21, Feb.	28		Grand Rapids, MI	40	Independence, Ohio
Blickle, Magdalena	16, Mar. 1893	24, Feb.	33	Heßler	Grand Rapids, MI	174	

Christliche Apologete Death Notices --- 1839 - 1899

Name of Deceased	Notice Date	Death Date	Age	Page	Maiden Name	Place of Death	Place of Birth
Blickle, Maria	19, Aug. 1886	29, July	55	7	Kalmbach	Grand Rapids, MI	Edelweiler, Freudenstadt, Württemberg
Blickle, Maria	10, Nov. 1887	21, Sept	23- 9m-19d	718		Grand Rapids, MI	Undingen, Württemberg
Blickvede, Dora H.	26, Aug. 1897	25, July	60	543		Wellsville, NY	Diterson, Hannover
Blickwede, Friedrich	16, Oct. 1876	24, Sept	18	335		Angelica, NY	
Bliese, August	2, Feb. 1874	3, Jan.	54	39		Milwaukee, WI	Pinnow, Pommern
Bliese, Emilie	20, July 1885	11, June	30	7	Schneck	Milwaukee, WI	Milwaukee, Wisconsin
Bliese, Friedrich Wilhelm	29, June 1885	11, June	28	7		Milwaukee, WI	Cölpien, Pommern
Bliffert, Johann	5, Apr. 1869	22, Mar.	47	111		Farmington, WI	Fürstenfelde, Preußen
Binn, Margaretha	20, Aug. 1896	28, June	69	542	Gegenheimer	Brooklyn, NY	Ottenheusen, Württemberg
Binn, Philipp	28, June 1888	10, June	64	414		Brooklyn, NY	Winterbach, Rheinkreis Baiern
Binne, August	29, Sept 1887	7, Sept	30	622		Drake, MO	Drake, Missouri
Binne, Henriette	18, Aug. 1892	27, July	73	526	Schröder	Drake, MO	Lippe-Detmold
Binne, Karl	18, Feb. 1886	25, Jan.	71	7		Drake, MO	Belle, Lippe-Detmold
Bliß, Sophia	15, Dec. 1892	28, Nov.	27	798	Bruhe	Chicago, IL	Flensburg, Schleswig
Blöcher, Elise	13, Sept 1875	31, Aug.	42	295	Weigel	Friendship, WI	Oberdieten, Biedenkopf, Hessen-Darmstadt
Blöcher, Yost	13, Jan. 1868	17, Dec.	39	14		Fond du Lac, WI	Ober-Dierhen, Biedenkopf, Hessen-Darmstadt
Block, Bernhard	20, Mar. 1871	23, Jan.	59	95		De Soto, MO	Paderborn, Westphalen
Block, Catharina	8, Jan. 1877	26, Dec.	75	15		Boston, MA	
Block, Elisabeth	1, Dec. 1898	10, Nov.	81	766	Rätzlaf	Willow City, ND	Pommern
Block, Franz	5, Aug. 1886	3, July	36	7		New York City, NY	Zischen, Waldeck
Block, Johan	18, Oct. 1894	17, Sept	67	678		Marietta, OH	Ritterhude, Ottersberg bei Bremen, Germany
Block, Louise	26, July 1869	12, July	24	239		Oconomowoc, WI	Kannenberg, Preußen
Block, Wilhelm	24, June 1872	6, June	52- 2m-11d	207		Beaver Dam, WI	
Blocks, Theresa	13, June 1889	4, May	46- 4m- 5d	382	Weinreich	Wilmette, IL	
Blohm, (Mrs)	26, Mar. 1866	6, Feb.	66	102		Shakopee, MN	Mecklenburg-Schwerin
Blohm, Bertha	21, Sept 1899	31, Aug.	36	607	Lorenz	Needville, TX	Reichenau, Sachsen
Blohm, Christian	3, Feb. 1868	17, Jan.	42- 8m- 7d	39		Wabasha, MN	Steinhagen, Mecklenburg-Schwerin
Blom, Christine	17, Mar. 1884	28, Feb.	58	7	Bau	Keokuk, IA	Neuweiler, Böblingen, Württemberg
Blom, Katharine	8, Nov. 1880	18, Oct.	18- 1m-16d	359		Keokuk, IA	
Blomberg, Anna	26, Apr. 1888	17, Mar.	25	270	Ropp	Beaufort, MO	Franklin County, Missouri
Blomberg, Anna	17, May 1888	17, Mar.	25	318	Sopp	Beaufort, MO	Franklin County, Missouri
Blomberg, Carolina	16, Apr. 1896	18, Mar.	32	254	Froelker	Owensville, MO	Jeffriesburg, Franklin County, Missouri
Blomberg, Charles	12, Nov. 1866	12, Oct.	10- 7m	366		Union, MO	
Blomberg, Dorothea	3, Mar. 1884	8, Feb.	63	7		Red Oak, MO	Meiersfeld, Lippe-Detmold
Blomberg, Friedrich C.	18, Dec. 1882	29, Nov.	48- -15d	407		St. Louis, MO	Sternberg, Lippe-Detmold
Blomberg, Heinrich	8, Oct. 1896		74- 6m	655		Nashville, IL	Lippe-Detmold
Blome, Dorothea Louise Charlotte	8, July 1897	18, June	77	431	Steutelneul	Marysville, CA	Blomberg, Lippe-Detmold
Blome, Simon	26, Sept 1870	5, Aug.	47	311		Warren, MO	Meinberg, Lippe-Detmold
Blömeke, Bernhard	1, Sept 1898	30, May	72	559		Springfield, MN	Büren, Westphalen
Blomeyer, Heinrich	19, Nov. 1896	24, Oct.	73- 1m-20d	750		Farmington, MO	Sohlingen, Uslaer, Hannover
Blomeyer, Henriette	18, Feb. 1897	29, Dec.	71- 9m-26d	111	Krull	Farmington, MO	Aschlauer, Hannover
Blömker, Elisabeth	13, Oct. 1873	24, Aug.	14	327		Huntingburg, IN	
Blömker, Ernst Wilhelm	9, Dec. 1878	18, Nov.	81-10m-15d	391		Huntingburg, IN	Lienen, Tecklenburg, Preußen
Blömker, Maria E.	2, Sept 1867	19, Aug.	70	278	Twente	Huntingburg, IN	Lengerich, Tecklenburg, Preußen
Blömker, Rudolf	28, June 1875	12, June	53	207		Huntingburg, IN	Lienen, Münster, Preußen
Blommeier, Carl	9, Aug. 1855	15, July	9- 6m	128		Hanging Rock, OH	

Christliche Apologete Death Notices --- 1839 - 1899

Name of Deceased	Notice Date	Death Date	Age	Page	Maiden Name	Place of Death	Place of Birth
Blommeier, Heinrich	9, Aug. 1855	7, July	3- 6m	128		Hanging Rock, OH	Des Moines, Iowa
Bloom, Herman Heinrich	12, Jan. 1893	15, Dec.	19	30		Des Moines, IA	Mecklenburg-Schwerin
Bloom, Sophia	29, Mar. 1894	6, Mar.	78	214		Oakfield, NY	
Bloompot, Jebke	23, Jan. 1875	18, Dec.	30- -12d	31		Pekin, IL	
Blösch, Abraham	21, Apr. 1879		55	127		Waco, TX	Möringen, Niedau, Bern, Schweiz
Blösch, Maria	31, July 1871	16, July	66	247	Zeisinger	Nashville, TN	Canton Bern, Schweiz
Blöser, Elisabeth	23, Dec. 1897	3, Dec.	74	815	Fischer	St. Charles, MO	Oberbärbach, Hessen-Darmstadt
Blöser, Georg	5, Nov. 1883	15, Oct.	56	359		St. Charles, MO	Oberbärbach, Hessen-Darmstadt
Blosfeld, Mathilde Lydia	7, Feb. 1895	16, Jan.	20	94		Mt. Vernon, IN	Mt. Vernon, Indiana
Bluece, Johan	16, May 1881	30, Apr.	60	159		Petersburg, IL	Aarau, Aargau, Schweiz
Blueß, Minna	8, June 1899	13, May	15	367		Akron, OH	Niederweiler, Baden
Bluhm, Adelheid	25, Feb. 1892	11, Feb.	81	126	Röhrs	Smithton, MO	Wilstedt, Hannover
Bluhm, Franz	29, May 1890	24, Apr.	28	350		Zumbro Falls, MN	West Albany, Wabasha County, Minnesota
Bluhm, Henriette	22, Dec. 1887	23, Nov.	13	814		Perry, TX	Zionsville, Washington County, Texas
Bluhm, John	12, Apr. 1894	15, Mar.	76	246		Lake Creek, MO	Rohmerode, Lichtenau, Germany
Bluhm, Katharine	7, May 1896	8, Apr.	52	302	Göhrs	Sedalia, MO	Morgan County, Missouri
Bluhm, Wilhelm	20, Nov. 1882	28, Oct.	50	375		Wadena, MN	Alsdorf, Mecklenburg-Schwerin
Bluhm, Wilhelm	22, Oct. 1891	3, Sept	27	686		Wadena, MN	Stammgarten, Vorpommern
Bluhm, Heinrich	15, Apr. 1897	23, Mar.	56	238		Culbertson, NE	Fürstenhagen, Hessen
Blum, Christina Magdalena	21, Apr. 1898	8, Mar.	83	255	Jung	Newport, KY	Erdmanhausen, Württemberg
Blum, Dorothea	4, Oct. 1880	28, Aug.	82- 5m	319	Horn	Jeffersonville, NY	Karlshafen, Kurhessen
Blum, E.	26, June 1882	10, June	69 -5m	207		St. Paul, MN	Canton Argau, Schweiz
Blum, Eleanora Emilie	15, Feb. 1864	6, Oct.		28		Spakopee, MN	
Blum, Heinrich	15, Feb. 1864	12, Sept	14	28		Spakopee, MN	
Blum, Henrietta Susanna	23, Apr. 1883	23, Mar.	61- 1m-10d	135	Jaimet	Pinckneyville, IL	Württemberg
Blum, Jacob	9, Mar. 1893	30, Jan.	72	158		New Rochelle, NY	Schandern, Baiern
Blum, Jakob	25, Dec. 1876	19, Nov.	69	413		Bloomington, IL	Weißweil, Baden
Blum, Johannes	19, Jan. 1899	23, Nov.	87	47		Covington, KY	Erdmannshausen, Württemberg
Blum, Julia	18, Aug. 1879	4, Aug.	22	263	Myer	Oregon, MO	Holt County, Missouri
Blum, Kurtihle	11, Nov. 1886	26, Sept	88	7		Petersburg, IL	Libenau, Hofgeismar, Kurhessen
Blum, Louisa Catharina	13, Nov. 1871	25, Sept	20- 5m- 7d	367		Pills Fork, —	
Blum, Magdalena	10, Feb. 1887	20, Jan.	84	94		Higginsport, OH	Hildingsheim, Württemberg
Blum, Maria Elisabeth	13, Jan. 1868	24, Dec.	86	14	Staube	St. Joseph, MO	Röhrenfeld, Kurhessen
Blum, Peter	30, Nov. 1874	30, Oct.	67- 6m-23d	383		Mountain Lake, MN	Bilden, Glarus, Schweiz
Blum, Philippine	5, Dec. 1889	25, Ot.	37	782	Jokisch	Arenzville, IL	Bluff Springs, Illinois
Blum, Sophia	27, Apr. 1893	16, Mar.	63	270		Bertha, MN	Altenwillershagen, Germany
Blumberg, Georg	3, Nov. 1873	7, Oct.	14	351		Indianapolis, IN	
Blumberg, Karl	3, Sept 1883	19, Aug.	21- 4m-27d	287		Indianapolis, IN	Monroe Furnace, Jackson County, Ohio
Blumberg, Louis	9, Feb. 1893	12, Jan.	24	94		Guadalupe Valley, TX	Guadalupe County, Texas
Blume, Christine	22, May 1865	19, Apr.	39	84	Dierking	Collensville, MO	Esperke, Amt Neustadt, Hannover
Blume, Ernestine	8, Apr. 1872	5, Mar.	17- 8m-11d	119		Jordan, MN	Bloomington, Illinois
Blume, Friedrich	14, Feb. 1870	12, Jan.	24	55		Sand Creek, MN	Brodenbeck, Hannover
Blume, H.L. (Rev)	6, Mar. 1876	15, Feb.	64- -21d	79		Edwardsville, IL	
Blume, Heinrich Wilhelm	25, Sept 1890	27, Aug.	23	622	Stunkel	Edwardsville, IL	Collinsville, Illinois
Blume, Maria Sophia	13, Sept 1875	28, Aug.	49	295		Edwardsville, IL	Bosse, Neustatt a.d. R..
Blume, Sophie Christina	25, Mar. 1897	3, Mar.	75	190	Vestring	Jordan, MN	Hüpede, Kallenberg, Hannover

- 43 -

Name of Deceased	Notice Date	Death Date	Age	Maiden Name	Page	Place of Death	Place of Birth
Blume, Wilhelm F.A.	21, May 1896	2, May	38-3m-7d		334	Jordan, MN	Mackendorf, Braunschweig
Blume, William Louis	23, Sept 1897	5, Sept	68		607	Wellsville, NY	Rapper, Amt Witlage, Hannover
Blumenkamp, Clara	10, Aug. 1868	1, Aug.	80		255	Dayton, OH	Salzberg, Kurhessen
Blumenstiel, Margaretha	6, Sept 1894	18, Aug.	77	Hüßner	582	Charles City, IA	Knittlingen, Maulbronn, Württemberg
Blumer, Bernhardt	2, Oct. 1890	8, Sept	70-3m-5d		638	Philadelphia, PA	Schweiz
Blumer, Regula	13, Apr. 1874	15, Mar.	30-7m-6d	Wintsch	119	New York City, NY	Heilbronn,
Blumer, Susanna	18, July 1871	5, July	48	Wolpert	231	Philadelphia, PA	Middelton, Ohio
Blumkamp, Johan	16, Feb. 1893	27, Jan.	31- -23d		110	Baltimore, MD	Watertown, Wisconsin
Blümke, Emma	11, Mar. 1886	16, Feb.	17		7	Watertown, WI	
Blymeyer, A. (Dr)	18, Dec. 1882	2, Dec.	79		407	Delaware, OH	
Böbel, Christiana Catharina	12, Mar. 1896	22, Feb.	51	Pfeifer	174	Clay Center, KS	Oberamt Hessigheim, Württemberg
Bober, Anna Louise	28, Apr. 1892	31, Mar.	15		270	Hedwigs Hill, TX	Mason County, Texas
Böber, Friedrich	23, Apr. 1891	5, Apr.	73		270	Blue Island, IL	Tannroda, Sachsen-Weimar
Bobilin, Christian	10, Dec. 1891	15, Nov.	59-6m-7d		798	Ft. Hunter, NY	Gundelfingen, Freiburg, Baden
Bobilin, Friedrich	25, Feb. 1892	17, Feb.	22-1m-2d		126	Berea, OH	
Bobinhaus, Johan Heinrich	11, Jan. 1864	6, July	20		8	Blooming Grove, MN	Debrack bei Hartfurt, Preußen
Bobzien, Ernst	28, May 1891	7, Apr.	83		350	Indianapolis, IN	Gurnen, Mecklenburg-Schwerin
Bock, Anna Elisabeth	8, Dec. 1862	17, Nov.	27	Traub	196	Wheeling, WV	Seuzach, Zürich, Schweiz
Bock, Arnold	24, Jan. 1895	28, Dec.	52		62	New York, NY	Badbergen, Hannover
Bock, Christian	24, June 1867	14, May	63		198	New York City, NY	Oker vor dem Harz, Germany
Bock, Christine	9, Dec. 1897	16, Nov.	67	Möß	783	Indianapolis, IN	Schorndorf, Württemberg
Bock, Elisabeth	1, May 1871	21, Mar.	3		143	Detroit, MI	
Bock, John	4, May 1893	5, Apr.	83		286	Indianapolis, IN	Holzburg, Ziegenhain, Kurhessen
Bock, Karl	1, May 1871	5, Mar.	10-4m-5d		143	Indianapolis, IN	
Bock, Karolina	1, May 1871	14, Mar.	4- 7m-17d		143	Indianapolis, IN	
Bock, Katharina	7, May 1877	17, Apr.	83	Ringel	151	Detroit, MI	Weizendorf, Heidelbach, Alsfeld, Hessen-Darmstadt
Bock, Katharina	2, May 1881	10, Apr.	38-5m-14d	Haas	143	Indianapolis, IN	Dearborn County, Indiana
Bock, Lisette	11, Aug. 1884	23, July	33		7	Le Sueur, MN	
Bock, Louise	22, July 1886	18, Apr.	26-3m-18d		7	Iowa Falls, IA	
Bock, M. Dorothea	11, Mar. 1867	5, Feb.	46		78	Wausau, WI	Grapzon, Preußen
Bock, Margaretha	12, Mar. 1891	4, Jan.	79		174	Pomeroy, OH	Baiern
Bock, Maria	2, Aug. 1888	10, July	66	Brand	494	Chicago, IL	KleinLukow, Mecklenburg-Schwerin
Bock, Wilhelm	14, Feb. 1889	20, Jan.	70		110	Milwaukee, WI	Klein Ritzerow, Mecklenburg-Schwerin
Bock, Wilhelmine	30, Apr. 1891	30, Mar.	58		286	Milwaukee, WI	Becksen, Lippe-Detmold
Böcker, Auguste	31, Jan. 1870	13, Dec.	41-5m	Koch	39	New York City, NY	Nansen, Braunschweig
Böcker, Christina	6, Apr. 1874	22, Jan.	21-10m-3d	Weidemann	111	Sandridge, IL	
Böcker, Louise	12, Oct. 1863	3, Sept	76- 8m		164	Petersburg, IL	Dassel, Hannover
Böcker, Ludwig Heinrich	9, Aug. 1880	21, July	63-3m		255	Petersburg, IL	Helmarshausen, Kurhessen
Böcking, Anna M.K.	6, Apr. 1868	17, Mar.	77		111	Lowell, WI	Kirtorf bei Alsfeld, Hessen-Darmstadt
Böcklin, Katharina	2, May 1889	18, Apr.	64-1m-22d	Vetterli	286	Toledo, OH	Wagenhausen, Thurgau, Schweiz
Bocksch, Karl Ernst	20, Aug. 1896	31, July	64		542	San Jose, CA	Schmolz bei Breslau, Preußen
Bockstahler, Barbara	28, Apr. 1859	9, Apr.	56		68	Santa Claus, IN	Lörrach, Baden
Bockstahler, J. Georg	5, July 1869	13, June	71-5m		215	Santa Claus, IN	Echeringen, Amt Lörrach, Baden
Bockstahler, Jesse Virgil Lee A.	12, Aug. 1886	30, July	15		7	Marrs, IN	Newark, Ohio
Bockstahler, John	20, Jan. 1879	19, Dec.	41-8m-8d		23	Santa Claus, IN	Ripley County, Indiana
Bockstruck, Maria	31, Aug. 1893	16, Aug.	86	Brunn	558	Highland, IL	Barnhausen, Halle, Minden, Preußen

Christliche Apologete Death Notices --- 1839 - 1899

Name of Deceased	Notice Date	Death Date	Age	Maiden Name	Page	Place of Death	Place of Birth
Bockwitz, Alwina	17, May 1888	22, Apr.	59- 5m-27d	Bornschein	318	San Jose, IL	Wangen, Merseburg, Preußen
Bockwitz, Georg Wilhelm	10, Feb. 1873	12, Jan.	78		47	San Jose, IL	Heinleben, Preußen
Bockwitz, Wilhelm	5, July 1888	16, June	70-10m- 7d		430	San Jose, IL	Hemleben, Merseburg, Preußen
Bod, Joachim	10, Apr. 1876	26, Mar.	35- 6m-23d		118	Summerfield, IL	Russo, Mecklenburg
Boddien, Anna	31, Dec. 1896	15, Nov.	71	Hase	844	Kendallville, IN	Gagelow, Mecklenburg-Schwerin
Bode, Auguste	17, Aug. 1899	28, July	43	Leifeste	527	Hedwigs Hill, TX	Castell, Texas
Bode, Friedrich	28, June 1869	9, June	27		207	Cincinnati, OH	Uesen, Amt Achim, Hannover
Bode, J.	14, Oct. 1878	2, Oct.			327	St. Joseph, MO	Hümme, Hofgeismar, Kurhessen
Bode, Margaretha Elisabeth	15, Sept 1884	26, Aug.	84		7	Cincinnati, OH	Schwam, Hannover
Bode, Wilhelmina	12, June 1871	6, May	71	Koch	191	St. Joseph, MO	Hümme, Kreis Hofgeismar, Kurhessen
Bödecker, Albert J.	25, Aug. 1898	8, Aug.	22		543	Newport, KY	
Bödecker, Emilie	28, Sept 1899	5, Sept	16		623	Ballwin, MO	Ballwin, Missouri
Bödecker, Heinrich	3, May 1888	20, Jan.	24		286	Morris, MN	
Bödecker, Maria	11, Mar. 1867	22, Jan.	29- 5m		78	De Soto, MO	
Bödeke, Louise	8, Mar. 1880	22, Feb.	77-10m- 6d	Bode	79	Wapello, IA	Hille, Minden, Preußen
Bödeker, Friedrich W.	4, Nov. 1897	19, Oct.	27		703	Senate Grove, MO	Red Oak, Gasconade County, Missouri
Bödeker, Heinrich	3, Apr. 1876	9, Mar.	74		111	Wapello, IA	Büne, Minden, Preußen
Bödeker, Johan Dietrich	18, May 1893	24, Apr.	46		318	Rochester, NY	Delmenhorst, Oldenburg
Bödeker, Louise	30, Oct. 1876	6, Oct.	42		351	Columbus, TX	Salzuflen, Lippe-Detmold
Bodemer, Anna	21, July 1887	26, June	90- 2m-26d		462	Jamestown, MO	Württemberg
Bodendorfer, Maria	25, Apr. 1870	23, Feb.	38		135	Oshkosh, WI	Montgomery County, New York
Bodenhausen, Carolina	31, Mar. 1884	14, Feb.	74		7	Cosby, MO	Helmighausen, Waldeck
Bodenhöfer, Christina	8, June 1874	5, May	52	Zimmermann	183	Kendallville, IN	Mähringen, Tübingen, Württemberg
Bodenhöfer, Georg F.	1, Mar. 1888	28, Jan.	77- - 2d	Diegel	142	Kendallville, IN	Hofen, Tubingen, Württemberg
Bodenschatz, Johannes	12, Oct. 1854	30, Sept			164	Allegheny, PA	
Bodenstein, Auguste	27, Dec. 1855	5, Dec.	50- 9m	Schmidt	208	Louisville, KY	Seesen, Braunschweig
Bodenstein, Elisabeth	23, Oct. 1890	14, Sept	53	Rost	686	Newport, KY	Zweibrücken, Rheinkreis Baiern
Bodenstein, John Friedrich	18, Mar. 1878	2, Mar.	75		87	Jeffersonville, IN	Seesen, Braunschweig
Bodenstein, Karl	5, Sept 1850	31, July	18- 9m		144	Louisville, KY	Susen, Braunschweig
Bodin, Christian J. Friedrich H.	31, May 1869	7, May	76		175	Kendallville, IN	Laase, Mecklenburg-Schwerin
Bodinus, Heinrich	1, June 1893	4, May	59		350	Toledo, OH	Coburg, Sachsen
Bodmer, Gottlieb	20, June 1881	30, May	63		199	Milwaukee, WI	Mehrstetten, Balingen, Württemberg
Bodmer, Heinrich G.	29, Apr. 1872	14, Apr.	6- 5m-24d		143	Bay City, MI	
Bodmer, Katharina	5, Dec. 1881	13, Nov.	62	Fritz	391	Milwaukee, WI	Meßstetten, Vaiingen, Württemberg
Boecker, Carl Christoph Friedrich	12, Apr. 1880	30, Mar.	19- 9m- 6d		119	Laporte, IN	
Boecker, Friedrich	16, Apr. 1877	24, Mar.	55		127	Petersburg, IL	Helmershausen, Karlshafen, Kurhessen
Boehlke, Herman	13, Nov. 1871	20, Aug.	26- 7m		367	Waseca, MN	Warsin, Pommern
Boehm, Johanna Louise	28, Mar. 1881	13, Feb.	76-10m-20d	Bick	103	Herman, MO	
Boehmer, Katharina M.E.	22, Mar. 1888	31, Jan.	75- 5m-28d	Grewe	190	Warrenton, MO	
Boehrer, John L.	2, June 1898	28, Apr.	22		351	Chicago, IL	Unterschwanigen, Baiern
Boekenkamp, Johan Heinrich	23, Nov. 1885	4, Nov.	57		7	St. Louis, MO	Neukirchen bei Melle, Hannover
Boeker, Elisabeth	18, Nov. 1886	25, Oct.	80	Kammin	7	San Jose, IL	
Boelts, Gerd	9, June 1898	9, May	65		367	Grand Island, NE	Edewecht, Oldenburg
Boerger, Georg Wilhelm	28, Feb. 1881	27, Jan.	18- 3m- 6d		71	Muscatine, IA	Muscatine County, Iowa
Boerger, James	28, Mar. 1881	10, Mar.	27- -15d		103	Muscatine, IA	
Boerner, Paul Moritz	31, July 1882	6, July	32		247	Rose Hill, TX	Altstädt, Sachsen-Weimar

Christliche Apologete Death Notices -- 1839 - 1899

Name of Deceased	Notice Date	Death Date	Age	Maiden Name	Page	Place of Death	Place of Birth
Boesch, Jacob Heinrich	14, June 1888	21, May	21		382	Chicago, IL	Mogelsberg, St. Gallen, Schweiz
Boese, August	7, Oct. 1886	9, Sept	42		7	St. Louis, MO	Hannover
Boese, H.	5, Apr. 1880	21, Mar.	68- 7m-27d		111	Lawrenceburg, IN	Achim bei Bremen, Germany
Boese, Rebecca Maria	28, Apr. 1884	27, Mar.	48- 5m- 6d	Seebeck	6	Baltimore, MD	
Boese, Sophie Elisabeth	26, Sept 1881	30, Sept	41	Hunsche	311	Kenosha, WI	
Boeshenz, Georg	14, Oct. 1886	24, Sept	41		7	Summerfield, IL	St. Louis, Missouri
Boeshenz, George (Rev)	21, Jan. 1884	17, Dec.	66-11m-15d		7	St. Louis, MO	Bobenheim am Berg, Rheinkreis Baiern
Boeshing, Elisabeth	5, Aug. 1886	19, June	37	Eisenmeyer	7	Summerfield, IL	Milwaukee, Wisconsin
Boest, Anna	29, July 1867	14, July	23- 4m-14d	Offermann	238	Cleveland, OH	
Bevers, Friedrich Karl	1, Apr. 1886	7, Mar.	68		7	Algona, IA	Pollhagen, Lippe-Schaumburg
Böge, Margaretha	4, Mar. 1878	15, Feb.	31		71	Winona, MN	St. Michaelis Donn, Schleswig-Holstein
Bogen, Emanuel	5, May 1898	7, Apr.	71		287	Lemars, IA	Stepanof, Ungarn
Bogener, Friedrich	13, Oct. 1884	17, Sept	46		7	Canton, MO	Sachsenhausen, Waldeck
Boger, Anna M.	17, Nov. 1887	27, Oct.	27- 8m- 4d	Wißmeyer	734	Hamilton, OH	Hamilton, Butler County, Ohio
Boger, Christian	1, May 1890	31, Mar.	67- 6m-12d		286	Junction City, KS	Leeheim, Hessen-Darmstadt
Boger, Emma	24, Oct. 1895	2, Oct.	33		686	Junction City, KS	Davis County, Kansas
Böger, Karl Wilhelm	21, Nov. 1889	18, Oct.	75- 1m- 2d		750	Schulenburg, TX	Lage, Lippe-Detmold
Boger, Rosine	14, Apr. 1884	18, Mar.	76	Heckler	7	Marietta, OH	Schweigern, Brackenheim, Württemberg
Bogner, Christian	3, June 1897	19, May	84		351	Kendallville, IN	Württemberg
Bogner, Margaretha	7, Dec. 1893	6, Nov.	66	Weingart	782	Kendallville, IN	Rattenharz, Welsheim, Württemberg
Bogner, Stephan	3, Mar. 1884	28, Jan.	60		7	Buffalo, NY	Pattenhofen, Aldorf, Baiern
Böhl, Christian	20, June 1861	11, June	57		100	Blue Island, IL	Schwarzenau, Preußen
Bohl, Nicholaus	6, Feb. 1890	11, Jan.	76- 8m-24d		94	Sprague, NE	Wachenheim, Baiern
Bohlander, Anna Maria	8, Apr. 1886	21, Mar.	74- 2m- 2d	Emig	7	Mascoutah, IL	Falkenstein, Rheinkreis Baiern
Bohlander, Christina Louisa	16, Jan. 1896	18, Dec.	52		46	Mascoutah, IL	Meßlingen, Minden, Preußen
Bohländer, Jakob	3, Jan. 1870	8, Dec.			7	Mascoutah, IL	Imsbach, Baiern
Bohle, (Mr)	2, Mar. 1863	2, Feb.	71		36	Warrenton, MO	Reine, Hannover
Böhle, Anna	16, Feb. 1860	13, Nov.	37- 9m-17d	Kroß	28	Newark, NJ	Krummwegen, Stade, Hannover
Bohlen, Gesina	3, Feb. 1868	10, Jan.	29	Rose	39	New York, NY	Wöhldorf, Amt Lehe, Hannover
Bohley, William	31, May 1894	19, Apr.	57		358	Linton, IN	Greene County, Ohio
Bohling, Anna	13, Jan. 1853	7, Nov.	37-10m-12d		8	Florence, MO	Altenbulstedt, Amt Otterburg, Hannover
Bohling, Anna	29, Aug.1895	29, July	69	Benken	558	Lake Creek, MO	Taken, Ottersberg, Hannover
Bohling, Cord	27, Oct. 1862	20, Sept	44		172	Florence, MO	Hepstedt, Amt Ottersberg, Hannover
Bohling, Heinrich	21, Jan. 1884	5, Jan.	31		7	Lake Creek, MO	Morgan County, Missouri
Bohling, J.	1, Nov. 1875	15, Aug.	56		351	Lake Creek, MO	Westertimbke, Hannover
Bohling, Marx	12, Apr. 1844		Inquiry		59	Port Clinton, OH	Amt Sefenrode, Hannover
Böhm, Barbara	9, May 1881	13, Mar.	68		151	Baltimore, MD	Oberalbach, Baiern
Böhm, Dorothea	12, May 1898	2, Apr.	81	Woltemath	303	Warrenton, MO	Coppenbrügge, Germany
Böhm, Ferdinand	24, Dec. 1877	1, Dec.	65-11m- 6d		415	Sun Prairie, WI	Großtriebendorf, Olmütz, Oesterreich
Bohm, Georg	4, Feb. 1884	15, Jan.	76		7	Pittsburg, PA	Chester, Oberrhein, Frankreich
Böhm, Gottfried	17, Sept 1877	23, Aug.	74- 2m-21d		305	Herman, MO	Suhl bei Erfurt, Sachsen
Böhm, Herman	7, May 1896	21, Mar.	41		302	Fond du Lac, WI	Denso, Templin, Potsdam, Preußen
Böhm, Joseph	21, Apr. 1892	2, Apr.	54		254	Pomeroy, OH	Kolmar, Elsaß
Bohm, L.	20, Apr. 1874	1, Apr.	24- 5m-13d		127	Edwardsville, IL	
Böhm, Theresa	16, Feb. 1880	31, Jan.	67	Weiß	55	Sun Prairie, WI	Groß-Triedendorf, Oesterreich
Böhm, Wilhelmine	26, Apr. 1888	30, Mar.	37- 5m-10d	Huxol	270	Herman, MO	Gasconade County, Missouri

Christliche Apologete Death Notices --- 1839 - 1899

Name of Deceased	Notice Date	Death Date	Age	Maiden Name	Page	Place of Death	Place of Birth
Bohmbach, Anna Metta	11, Feb. 1886	4, Jan.	40	Bolland	7	Minneola, MN	Helmste, Hannover
Bohmbach, Maria	11, Oct. 1894	20, Sept	16		662	Warrenton, MO	Red Wing, Minnesota
Böhme, Anton	14, Dec. 1893	23, Nov.	89		798	Farmington, IA	Bettmer, Braunschweig
Böhme, August	7, May 1891	25, Mar.	52		302	Troy, NY	Lossow bei Frankfurt a. d. Oder, Germany
Böhmer, Anna Friederike	1, Dec. 1898	1, Nov.	70	Kipp	766	Senate Grove, MO	Altenhagen, Bielefeld, Preußen
Böhmer, Eva Lena	21, Jan. 1897	27, Dec.	30	Friedrich	46	Chippewa Falls, WI	Lafette, Wisconsin
Böhmer, Gerhard Heinrich	25, Aug. 1884	29, July	74- 6m- 3d		7	Warrenton, MO	Otter bei Osnabrück, Hannover
Böhmer, Heinrich Gerhard	27, July 1899		69		479	Warren, MO	Germany
Böhmer, Henriette Carolina	2, May 1889	18, Mar.	72- 9m-20d	Nebelsick	286	Beaufort, MO	Werl, Schölmar, Lippe-Detmold
Böhmer, Johan Friedrich	21, Dec. 1885	2, Dec.	67		7	Port Hudson, MO	Lockhausen, Schottmer, Lippe-Detmold
Bohmfalk, (Mr)	22, Aug. 1895	16, July	35		542	Perry, TX	New Fountain, Texas
Böhnke, Franz	23, Sept 1872	21, Aug.	50- 6m		311	New York City, NY	Greß, Mecklenburg-Schwerin
Böhmler, Anna Maria	7, Sept 1863	11, Aug.	63		144	Mansfield, OH	Eltingen, Leonberg, Württemberg
Böhmler, Maria	15, Sept 1862	15, Aug.	14- -14d		148	Mansfield, OH	
Bohn, Carl Wilhelm	8, Dec. 1892	30, Sept	70		782	Rockham, SD	Collien, Hinterpommern
Bohn, Catharina	5, May 1862	31, Mar.	28	Hüblitz	72	Summerfield, MO	Zweibrücken, Rheinkreis Baiern
Bohn, Friedrich	27, Sept 1880	23, Aug.	48		311	Goshen, IN	Efthal, Rheinkreis Baiern
Bohn, Johan Friedrich	11, Nov. 1897	20, Oct.	50		719	Bristol, WI	Puntow, Pieritz, Pommern
Bohn, Johanne	4, Mar.1872	13, Feb.	27		79	Kenosha, WI	Pandow, Kreis Pienitz, Preußen
Bohn, Katharina	29, Nov. 1894	30, Oct.	54- 3m-27d	Schwan	774	Perry, TX	Spring Creek, Harrison County, Texas
Bohn, Minna	29, Nov. 1894	4, Nov.	36	Pinkart	774	Perry, TX	Warren County, Missouri
Bohn, Sophia	21, Mar. 1895	27, Feb.	44	Freede	190	Warrenton, MO	Sandhorst, Amt Aurich, Ostfriesland
Bohne, Johanna	7, June 1869	11, Apr.	28- 5m-14d	Harms	183	Red Bud, IL	Hille, Germany
Bohne, Maria Louise	17, Dec. 1883	29, Oct.	54		7	Ft. Hunter, NY	Holzhausen, Preußen
Bohne, Wilhelm	9, May 1870	23, Mar.	38		151	Red Bud, IL	Herford, Westphalen
Bohnenkamp, Johan Philipp	7, Jan. 1886	15, Dec.	76		7	Port Hudson, MO	Cape Girardeau County, Missouri
Bohnsack, Albert	10, Jan. 1881	11, Dec.	27		15	Jackson, MO	Hannover
Bohnsack, Amalia	4, Jan. 1869	20, Nov.	35		7	Jackson, MO	Cape Girardeau, Missouri
Bohnsack, Auguste	31, May 1875	26, Apr.	25	Brase	175	Jackson, MO	Opperhausen, Braunschweig
Bohnsack, Christian	5, May 1892	27, Mar.	73		286	Jackson, MO	Hajeshausen, Amt Gandersheim, Braunschweig
Bohnsack, Friedrich	13, Mar. 1871	25, Jan.	43- - 8d		87	Jackson, MO	Cape Girardeau County, Missouri
Bohnsack, Henrietta	1, Apr. 1872	2, Mar.	23	Nothdurst	111	Jackson, MO	Cape Girardeau County, Missouri
Bohnsack, John	13, June 1870	3, May	17		191	Jackson, MO	Cape Girardeau, Missouri
Bohnsack, Karoline	27, Jan. 1868	4, Jan.	48		31	Jackson, MO	Helmscherode, Gandersheim, Braunschweig
Bohnsack, Katharine	24, Feb. 1879	22, Jan.	59- 5m		63	Jackson, MO	Rothheim v. d. Höhe, Frankfurt am Main, Germany
Bohrer, Louise	25, Jan. 1864	9, Nov.	29		16	Boonville, IN	Birkenfeld, Oldenburg
Böhringer, Joh. Engelhard	13, Oct. 1843	19, Sept	31- 8m- 8d		163	Louisville, KY	Oelbronn, Maulbronn, Württemberg
Bohn, Elisabeth	28, May 1877	9, Apr.	65- 9m-13d	Fehtern	175	Herman, MO	
Bohsen, Antonie R. C.	27, Oct. 1884	12, Oct.	32	Swane	7	Sleepy Eye, MN	Flensburg, Schleswig
Boise, Anna Margaretha	19, Nov. 1847	1, Nov.	62- 6m		187	Mascoutah, IL	Ruchheim, Baiern
Boise, Catharina	17, Jan. 1850	17, Dec.	23	Merkel	12	Mascoutah, IL	Hessen-Darmstadt
Boise, Salome	15, Mar. 1880	27, Feb.	59- 7m-19d	Cafti	87	Chicago, IL	Hohentrins, Graubünden, Schweiz
Bokel, Eva Elisabeth	18, June 1883	5, June	74- 3m- 8d		199	Charles City, IA	
Bökenkamp, Amanda	24, Oct. 1881	3, Oct.	16- - 6d		343	St. Louis, MO	
Böker, Georg	3, May 1875	12, Apr.	20- 1m-25d		143	Petersburg, IL	
Böker, Karl	4, Dec. 1882	30, Oct.	16		391	Petersburg, IL	Menard County, Illinois

Christliche Apologete Death Notices --- 1839 - 1899

Name of Deceased	Notice Date	Death Date	Age	Maiden Name	Page	Place of Death	Place of Birth
Böker, Katharina Mathilda	15, Jan. 1891	16, Dec.	23- 7m- 1d		46	Tallula, IL	Sandridge, Illinois
Böker, Sophie	8, Jan. 1891	12, Dec.	60	Gusewelle	30	St. Louis, MO	Lippe-Schaumburg
Böker, Tibka	6, Aug. 1891	11, July	73	Mahnken	510	Lake Creek, MO	Wilstedt, Hannover
Böker, Wilhelm	1, July 1897	3, June	77		414	Smithton, MO	Lockum, Hannover
Bokermann, W.	5, June 1890	16, Apr.	61-11m-20d		366	Beaufort, MO	Schildesche, Bielefeld, Westphalen
Bokus, Karl	15, Mar. 1888	17, Feb.	76-11m-12d		174	St. Louis, MO	Osterburg, Preußen
Bolander, Stella	23, July1883				239	Cincinnati, OH	
Bold, Abraham	2, Aug. 1894	12, July	74		502	Beatrice, NE	West Preußen
Bolden, Charley	12, Jan. 1880	13, Nov.	7-10m		15	Minneapolis, MN	
Bolden, Frank	12, Jan. 1880	22, Nov.	2-10m		15	Minneapolis, MN	
Bolden, Willy	12, Jan. 1880	1, Dec.	5- 2m		15	Minneapolis, MN	
Boldt, August	26, Jan. 1888	6, Nov.	42- 5m		62	Schnectady, NY	Dorothean-Höh, Naugard, Stettin, Preußen
Boldt, Emilie L.	6, Sept 1894	26, July	13		582	Bushton, KS	Rice County, Kansas
Boldt, Friederike	26, Apr. 1888	5, Apr.	67	Dassow	270	Green Bay, WI	Pommern
Boldt, Helena K.	10, May 1880	27, Mar.	51	Nehls	151	Platteville, WI	Padingbüttel, Dorum, Hannover
Boldt, Mina L.	28, Nov. 1889	22, Oct.	17		766	Bushton, KS	Topeka, Kansas
Boldt, Robert H.	4, May 1899		12- 1m-16d		287	Bushton, KS	
Boldt, Wilhelm Ernst	11, Apr. 1889	15, Mar.	67		238	Green Bay, WI	Dumzien, HinterPommern
Boldt, Wilhelm Friedrich Johan	2, Jan. 1890	13, Dec.	68		14	Bushton, KS	Rahbuhn, Hinterpommern
Bole, Christian	2, May 1870	11, Mar.	61- 8m-27d		143	Terre Haute, IN	Eberschütz, Hofgeismar, Kurhessen
Boley, John	23, June 1862	1, June	21		100	Dodgeville, IA	
Bolick, Amos	12, July 1880	31, Apr.	64	Meier	223	Milwaukee, WI	Lincoln County, North Carolina
Bölke, Caroline	24, Nov. 1892	3, Nov.	91		750	Milwaukee, WI	
Bölke, J. Louis	8, June 1893	17, May	52		366	Milwaukee, WI	Beger, Bromberg, Preußen
Böker, Stephan	1, Mar. 1880	10, Feb.	78		71	Milwaukee, WI	
Bollacker, Caroline Marie	14, July 1892	14, June	71- 5m-22d		446	Schnectady, NY	Hille, Minden, Preußen
Bollacker, Christian Heinrich	31, Aug. 1868	13, July	17		279	Schnectady, NY	Hille, Preußen
Bollacker, Cort Heinrich	24, Jan. 1895	4, Jan.	75		62	Schnectady, NY	Hille, Minden, Preußen
Bollacker, Friedrich	23, Feb. 1863	25, Jan.	57		32	Schnectady, NY	Hille, Minden, Preußen
Bollacker, Louise	17, Aug. 1868	29, July	22		263	Schnectady, NY	Hille, Preußen
Bollbach, Hugo	19, Aug. 1897	6, July	41		527	Lafayette, IN	Lübsch, Preußen
Bolle, Susanna	30, Oct. 1890	5, Oct.	71		702	St. Louis, MO	Neuwied am Rhein, Coblenz, RheinPreußen
Boller, Adam	24, Feb. 1868	10, Feb.	45- -13d		63	Evansville, IN	Höchst, Hessen-Darmstadt
Boller, Katharina	29, June 1899	6, June	77	Roth	415	Evansville, IN	Langstadt, Hessen-Darmstadt
Bolli, Jacob	25, Nov. 1872	29, Oct.	37- 9m-27d		383	Hudson City, NJ	Beringen, Schaffhausen, Schweiz
Bolliger, Elisabeth	21, May 1896	6, May	66		334	Chicago, IL	Canton Aargau, Schweiz
Bolliger, Jakob	11, Jan. 1894	22, Dec.	64		30	St. Paul, MN	Schmiedrud, Aargau, Schweiz
Bolliger, Samuel	29, Nov. 1888	23, Oct.	21		766	St. Paul, MN	Kirchroth, Aargau, Schweiz
Bolliger, Samuel	19, Jan. 1885	25, Dec.	48		7	St. Paul, MN	Kirchruth, Aargau, Schweiz
Bollin, Friederike	17, Oct. 1881	22, Sept	66		335	Detroit, MI	Zelasen, Lauenburg, Preußen
Bolling, Maria Anna	24, Mar. 1879	22, Feb.		Rages	95	Lake Creek, MO	
Bollinger, Barbara	12, Apr. 1888	10, Mar.	75- 2m- 8d	Rost	238	Seymour, IN	Beringen, Schweiz
Bollinger, Conrad	1, Mar. 1875	13, Feb.	70		71	Seymour, IN	Beringen, Schaffhausen, Schweiz
Böllinger, J. H.	19, July 1894	28, June	33		470	Toledo, OH	
Böllingen, Jakob	16, Nov. 1885	21, Sept	30		7	Algona, IA	Löhlingen, Schaffhausen, Schweiz
Bollinger, Jakob	7, Dec. 1863				196	Charleston, VA	

Christliche Apologete Death Notices --- 1839 - 1899

Name of Deceased	Notice Date	Death Date	Age	Maiden Name	Page	Place of Death	Place of Birth
Bollinger, Karl A.	15, Nov. 1880	2, Nov.	31		367	Poughkeepsie, NY	Burgstall, Marbach, Württemberg
Bollinger, Kaspar	20, Sept 1894	1, Sept	64- 5m-24d		614	Toledo, OH	Beringen, Schaffhausen, Schweiz
Bollinger, Margaretha	22, Aug. 1895	1, Aug.	78		542	Burt, IA	Loehningen, Schaffhausen, Schweiz
Bollinger, Maria Sarah	18, Aug. 1887	2, Aug.	77-11m-12d	Steichele	526	Poughkeepsie, NY	Rudersberg, Welsheim, Württemberg
Bollinger, Wilhelm A.	13, May 1897	29, Mar.	38-10m- 3d		303	San Francisco, CA	Sacramento, California
Bollmann, Elisabeth	21, Jan. 1892	30, Dec.	80- 9m-16d	Kätker	46	Edwardsville, IL	Lienen, Westphalen
Bollmann, Ernst	16, Feb. 1899	3, Jan.	69		110	Edwardsville, IL	Liene, Germany
Bollmann, Karolina	4, Feb. 1892	18, Jan.	40	Kriege	78	Edwardsville, IL	Edwardsville, Illinois
Bollmann, Lydia	30, June 1887	15, June	17		414	Dayton, OH	
Bollmann, Wilhelm	9, Apr. 1883	24, Mar.	63		119	Dayton, OH	Schwarm, Bruchhausen, Hannover
Bölner, (Mr)	17, Aug. 1868				263	Hannibal, MO	
Bölner, Katharina Elsebein	30, Jan. 1890	9, Jan.	88- 8m- 3d	Henning	78	San Jose, IL	Lengerich, Preußen
Boly , Simon	8, June 1893	15, May	61		366		Behring, Schaffhausen, Schweiz
Boly, M.	7, Jan. 1897	17, Dec.	64		15		Zürich, Schweiz
Böim, Friedrich C.	11, Apr. 1895	19, Mar.	34- 3m- 9d	Bauer	238	Stockton, CA	Warren County, Missouri
Bolsiger, Nikolaus	11, Apr. 1895	21, Mar.	79		238	Warrenton, MO	Gurten, Könitz, Bern, Schweiz
Bolsinger, Katharina	17, May 1888	27, Apr.	68		318	Chicago, IL	Kanton Bern , Schweiz
Bolte, Tiolina	23, Feb. 1899	4, Feb.	44	Afolder	126	Blue Island, IL	Bagband, Leer, Ostfriesland
Bolti, Katharina Margaretha	2, June 1873	2, Apr.	65	Oltmanns	175	Nokomis, IL	Griets, Predelbach, Württemberg
Bolting, Carl Friedrich	24, July 1865	9, July	57	Weiß	120	Roseville, MI	Löhne, Preußen
Boltz, Benjamin	28, Jan. 1897	1, Jan.	54		62	Linton, IN	Amalienruh, OstPreußen
Boly, Katharina	26, Apr. 1869	3, Feb.	15		135	South Bend, IN	Poland, Clay County, Indiana
Bolz, Karl Gustav	6, Feb. 1896	1, Jan.	44		94	Terre Haute, IN	Liedolsheim, Baden
Bolz, Louise	14, Feb. 1889	13, Jan.	36	Hahn	110	Cleveland, OH	Weilburg, Nassau
Bolze, Dorothea	11, Apr. 1870	15, Mar.	73- 6m-11d	Lindemann	119	St. Joseph, MO	Sauingen, Braunschweig
Bolzinger, Margareha	2, Mar. 1885	12, Feb.	45	Boeckler	7	Bunker Hill, IL	Königsbrunn, Württemberg
Bommert, Anna	9, Mar. 1885	16, Feb.	38- 6m-25d	Schimmel	7	Clay Center, KS	Dobern, Böhmen, Oesterreich
Bondel, Maria Dorothea	20, Feb. 1890	25, Jan.	70		126	Minneapolis, MN	Murr, Marbach, Württemberg
Bondeli, Eduard	8, Jan. 1866	19, Dec.	65- 9m		14	Springfield, IL	Bern, Schweiz
Bone, William	23, Apr. 1883	24, Mar.	31		135	Sandusky, OH	New Orleans, Louisiana
Bonefeld, Dorothea	2, June 1887	9, May	55		350	New Orleans, LA	Lemgo, Lippe-Detmold
Boner, Jacobine	5, July 1860	11, June	77	Weil	108	Evansville, IN	Albisheim an der Pfremm, Rheinkreis Baiem
Bongers, Elisabeth	13, Apr. 1874	28, Mar.	74	Schumacher	119	Newark, OH	Issen, Düsseldorf, Rheinpreußen
Bongers, Helena	6, Apr. 1854	22, Mar.	18- 9m- 3d		56	Milwaukee, WI	
Bonk, Tholea F.	8, Apr. 1872	29, Feb.	25- 3m-22d	Neef	119	Milwaukee, WI	Loquard, Ostfriesland
Bonn, Arthur	24, Dec. 1891	17, Nov.	10- 8m- 4d		830	Pekin, IL	
Bonn, Johanne	11, Aug. 1896	22, May	62	Meier	383	Keokuk, IA	Tuchtfeld, Braunschweig
Bonn, Maria Katharina	21, Aug. 1876	14, May	73	Schmidt	271	Fredericksburg, TX	Cappel, Kreis Zell, Coblenz , Preußen
Bonn, Nicholaus	20, Sept 1880	20, Aug.	83		303	Scranton, PA	Lautzenhausen, Preußen
Bonn, Sophie	13, Dec. 1869	23, Nov.	13- 8m		399	Scranton, PA	
Bönning, Peter	29, Aug.1895		26		558	Edwardsville, IL	Germany
Bontz, Katharina	25, Apr. 1881	4, Apr.	31	Jesen	135	Oklahoma City, OK	Erfde, Vogelholm, Schleswig-Holstein
Bontz, Katharine	18, Apr. 1881	4, Apr.	31	Jesen	127	Oregon, MO	Schleswig-Holstein
Book, John	18, May 1893	20, Aug.	82		318	Oregon, MO	Württemberg
Book, Karl Ch. G.	3, Nov. 1898	21, Oct.	56		703	Spencerville, OH	Volmersstadt, Magdeburg, Preußen
Boos, Jakob	26, Sept 1864	5, Sept	58		156	Schnectady, NY	Einseldumm, Baiem
						Roxbury, MA	

Name of Deceased	Notice Date	Death Date	Age	Page	Maiden Name	Place of Death	Place of Birth
Booth, Verena	23, Feb. 1899	15, Jan.	55	126		Salem, OR	He--gen, Glarus, Schweiz
Bopp, Johan	13, Oct. 1887	17, Aug.	30-11m-15d	654		Beaufort, MO	St. Louis, Missouri
Bopp, Johann Heinrich	29, Aug. 1861	2, Aug.	33- 9m- 2d	140		Manchester, MO	Bermuthsham, Niddau, Hessen-Darmstadt
Bopp, Julia Louise	18, July 1895	8, June	22	462		Ballwin, MO	Ballwin, Missouri
Bopp, Kunigunde	2, Nov. 1899	15, Oct.	81	703	Haas	Bradford, IN	Hartenberg, Baiern
Bopp, Maria	17, Dec. 1891	20, Nov.	63	814	Mild	Ballwin, MO	Altenheim am Rhein, Preußen
Bopp, Maria	27, Dec. 1855	9, Dec.	45-9m	208	König	Galena, IL	Rohrbach , Hessen-Darmstadt
Bopp, Sebastian	19, Aug. 1897	30, July	73	527		Canal Dover, OH	Gerksheim, Baden
Bopp, Sebastian	27, Dec. 1894	25, Nov.	72	836		Ballwin, MO	Hessen-Darmstadt
Bopp, Wilhelmina	5, Apr. 1894	28, Feb.	36	230	Heinz	Bradford, IN	New Salisbury, Indiana
Borberg, Otto	2, Nov. 1863	19, Sept	24	176		Laporte, IN	Schweiz
Borchardt, Emilie	15, Dec. 1887	20, Nov.	33	798	Sellin	Lyona, KS	Geiglitz-Regenwalde an der Rega, Pommern
Borchardt, Friedrich	13, Mar. 1890	7, Feb.	80	174		Mankato, MN	Witznitz, Pommern
Borchardt, Friedrich Carl	1, Nov. 1894	8, Oct.	69	710		Jordan, MN	Minden, Naugard, Pommern
Borchardt, Wilhelmine	3, June 1886	22, Mar.	62	7	Kuhfahl	Maine, WI	Braschendorf, Hinterpommern
Borchart, Ernst Friedrich Martin	22, Oct. 1883	3, Oct.	44-10m-21d	343		Jordan, MN	
Borcheld, John	10, Jan. 1881	26, Dec.	62- - 1d	15		Lancaster, NY	Stavenhagen, Mecklenburg-Schwerin
Borcherding, Adelheid	15, Sept 1859	20, Aug.	61- 6m	148		Wapello, IA	Achim, Hannover
Borcherding, Anna Louise	7, Jan. 1884	17, Dec.	75- 5m-23d	7	Zahn	Cincinnati, OH	Ueffeln, Hannover
Borcherding, Charles Louis	28, July 1884	5, July	15-10m-13d	7		Cincinnati, OH	Santa Claus, Indiana
Borcherding, Conrad	17, June 1867	1, June	18	190		Cincinnati, OH	
Borcherding, Emma C.	4, Apr. 1895	7, Mar.	68	222		Cincinnati, OH	Großvarlingen, Melpe, Hannover
Borcherding, Johan Rudolph	8, Feb. 1875	21, Jan.	16- 3m- 5d	47		Cleveland, OH	
Borcherding, Johann Friedrich	17, Feb. 1868	4, Feb.	64	55		Cincinnati, OH	Ueffeln, Osnabrück, Hannover
Borcherding, Katharina	8, Aug. 1861	27, July	67-11m	128		Madison, IN	Großvailingen, Amt Wölpe, Hannover
Borcherding, Louise	20, Nov. 1890		53	750	Kunkel	Madison, IN	Fläschbach, Biber, Kurhessen
Borcherding, Maria	18, May 1868	2, May	25	159		Cincinnati, OH	Cincinnati, Hamilton County, Ohio
Borcherding, Maria	28, Dec. 1854	10, Sept	50	208		Huntingburg, IN	Großvarlingen am Wölpe, Hannover
Borcherding, Wilhelm	22, Jan. 1861	1, Jan.	49	16	Miller	Seymour, IN	Brokoloh, Hannover
Borcherding, Wilhelm	19, May 1892	30, Mar.	54	80		Seymour, IN	Linsburg, Amt Welge, Hannover
Borcherding, William	13, June 1864	19, Apr.	58	96		Herman, MO	Hartum, Minden, Preußen
Borchert, Anna Louise	4, Jan. 1869	23, Dec.	27	7		Seymour, IN	Jackson County, Indiana
Borchert, Johanna	26, Feb. 1883	27, Jan.	52- 7m- 3d	71	Priebe	Eldora, IA	Neuwasser, Seebuckow, Hinterpommern
Borchert, Maria	23, Apr. 1883	11, Apr.	67- -27d	135	Vetter	Lancaster, NY	Dukow, Demmin, Mecklenburg
Borchert, Wilhelmine	7, May 1883	28, Mar.	84	151	Witt	Sandusky, OH	Kittendorf, Mecklenburg-Schwerin
Borck, Elisabeth	13, Oct. 1887	25, Sept	29- 3m-13d	654	Joerke	Akron, NY	Scharpzow, Mecklenburg-Schwerin
Borer, Anna Elisabeth	28, Feb. 1861	15, Dec.	82	36		Sheboygan, WI	Blankenburg, Preußen
Borgeld, Louise	11, Oct. 1869	19, Sept	40	327		Eudora, KS	Dänike, Basel, Schweiz
Borgelt, Franz	13, June 1864	19, May	18	96		St. Charles, MO	
Borgelt, Katharina Louisa	25, Jan. 1869	9, Dec.	55	31		Saltburg, MO	Mellen, Amt Greneberg, Preußen
Borgen, Daniel	8, June 1868	3, May	45	183	Maschmeier	St. Charles, MO	Mellen, Amt Greneberg, Preußen
Börger, Mary	19, June 1876	30, May	23	199		St. Paul, MN	Athens County, Ohio
Borgeß, Helena Elisa	14, June 1880	30, May	24- 2m-26d	191		Muscatine, IA	Muscatine County, Iowa
Borgraefe, Friedrich	10, June 1886	22, Apr.	73	7	Meinige	New York City, NY	Nienburg, Hannover
Borgmann, Edward A.	29, Dec. 1884	13, Dec.	52	7		St. Louis, MO	Elberfeld, RheinPreußen
	23, Apr. 1891	17, Mar.	31	270		Spokane, WA	St. Charles, Missouri

Christliche Apologete Death Notices --- 1839 - 1899

Name of Deceased	Notice Date	Death Date	Age	Maiden Name	Place of Death	Page	Place of Birth
Borgmann, Heinrich	25, June 1857	27, May	45		Marthasville, MO	104	Westerkappel, Tecklenburg, Preußen
Borgmann, Wilhelmine Regine Louise	20, Sept 1875	1, Sept		Krüger	Henderson, KY	303	Unter-Lübbe, Minden, Preußen
Böringer, Katharina	2, Sept 1858	12, Aug.	37		Louisville, KY	140	Heitensbach, Württemberg
Bork, Maria	24, July 1871	16, June	55- 3m- 7d	Turbier	Sheboygan, WI	239	Granzow, Ufermark, Preußen
Borkmeyer, Gert	25, Aug. 1898		70- 9m- 7d		Storm Lake, IA	543	Ostfriesland
Borkmeyer, Margaretha Johanna	6, Mar. 1882	14, Feb.	16 -3m- 7d		Storm Lake, IA	79	Pikan, Illinois
Borlesch, Johan	5, Mar. 1877	3, Feb.	64		St. Louis, MO	79	Bixow, Köslin, Preußen
Borman, Wilhelm	22, Nov. 1888	30, Oct.	64- 4m-24d		Garner, IA	750	Westerode, Harzburg, Braunschweig
Bormann, Heinrich	8, Oct. 1896	4, Sept	54- 8m- 3d		Greenville, OH	655	Osnabrück, Wittlage, Hannover
Born, (Mrs)	12, May 1862	18, Apr.	59		Mascoutah, IL	76	Hömberg, Nassau
Born, Anna Rosina	11, July 1881	23, June	79	Siegismund	Allegheny City, PA	223	Zilsendorf, Schlesien
Born, Elisabeth	19, Jan. 1854	1, Dec.	42		Newark, OH	12	Bitzberg, Bern, Schweiz
Born, Elisabeth	28, June 1880	15, June	47- 2m-14d		Mascoutah, IL	207	
Born, Henriette	4, July 1881	22, June	67	Scheel	Watertown, WI	215	Neumark
Born, Johan Friedrich	13, Dec. 1888	13, Nov.	50- 9m-10d		Kampeska, SD	798	Petznick, Pommern
Born, Johan Gottfried	15, Apr. 1872	2, Apr.	69- 5m-20d		Allegheny City, PA	127	
Born, Johanne C. F.	14, Apr. 1879	16, Mar.	57- 7m-15d	Vogel	Menomonie, WI	119	
Born, Jost	14, Sept 1899	17, Aug.	63		St. Paul, MN	591	Hämberg, Nassau
Born, Karoline	23, July1883	14, June	62- 5m-10d	Leistikow	Sheboygan, WI	239	Samenthür, Brandenburg
Born, Michael	5, Nov. 1896	1, Oct.	85		Summit, WI	719	Petznick, Piritz, Pommern
Born, Sophia	23, Feb. 1874		14- -21d		Menomonie, WI	63	
Borne, Elisabeth	4, Feb. 1886	18, Jan.	59	Frauenfeld	Warsaw, IL	7	Flaach, Zürich, Schweiz
Borne, Henriette	28, Apr. 1873	7, Apr.	54	Orth	Burlington, IA	135	Fußgönheim, Rheinkreis Baiern
Borne, Minna	13, Jan. 1887	18, Dec.	33	Steinmeyer	Keokuk, IA	30	Farmington, Iowa
Bornefeld, Josua	1, Mar. 1869	27, Jan.	38		Evansville, IN	71	Dühn, Preußen
Bornemann, (Mr)	10, Nov. 1873	21, Oct.	73		Cincinnati, OH	359	Sud-Hemmern, Westphalen
Bornemann, Anna Katharina	12, May 1873	26, Apr.	40	Kaufmann	Cleveland, OH	151	Haltingen, Baden
Bornemann, Anna Margaretha	10, Sept 1891	22, Aug.	76- 1m- 6d		St. Louis, MO	590	
Bornemann, Carl	5, June 1890	16, May	70- 6m-27d		St. Louis, MO	366	Oelsdorf, Waldeck
Bornemann, Christiana	11, Aug. 1873	27, July	65- 9m	Mayer	Cincinnati, OH	255	Nordhämmern, Hartum, Preußen
Bornemann, Maria	8, Dec. 1887	23, Nov.	58- 5m-24d	Vergu	Cleveland, OH	782	Duwenbeck, Vorpommern
Bornemann, Martha Katharina	1, Apr. 1842	24, Feb.	39- -10d		Middletown, CT	51	Helmanshausen,
Bornemann, Wilhelmina	15, July 1878	6, June	49	Oestmann	Cleveland, OH	223	Neuhof, Amt Feldberg, Mecklenburg-Strelitz
Bornemann, Wilhelmina	29, July 1878	6, June	43-11m- 2d	Oestmann	Cleveland, OH	239	Neuhof, Amt Feldberg, Mecklenburg-Strelitz
Bornholdt, Metta	24, Apr. 1882	18, Mar.	56	Sahts	Minneapolis, MN	135	Bockelzis, Holstein
Börnke, Karl Friedrich August	30, Apr. 1896	24, Mar.	76		Taegesville, WI	286	Spring bei Roggen, Pommern
Bornschein, Johan Gottlob	28, Jan. 1892	21, Dec.	72		Danville, IL	62	Großwangen, Preußen
Bornschein, Justina	10, Nov. 1898	3, Oct.	80	Schmidt	Danville, IL	719	Oberschmond, Preußen
Bornscheuer, Lydia	8, Dec. 1884	23, Nov.	22- 8m-22d		Danville, IL	7	Waverly, Pike County, Ohio
Bornscheuer, Conrad	4, Aug. 1884	30, June	67- 6m- 5d		Newark, NJ	7	Altenhainer, Kurhessen
Bornscheuer, Friedrich Konrad	25, May 1885	2, May	26		Newark, NJ	7	Newark, New Jersey
Borpagel, Karoline	25, Dec. 1876		49	Scheibe	Burlington, WI	413	B---, Kreis Dramburg, Preußen
Börsch, Johan Peter	20, Feb. 1871	26, Dec.	83		Red Bud, IL	63	Philadelphia, Pennsylvania
Borschel,	29, Sept 1873	10, Sept	28- -16d	Kall	Baden, NE	311	Johnston County, Iowa
Borschel, Caroline Wilhelmine	20, Aug. 1891	13, July	20		Lincoln, NE	542	
Borschel, Martin	22, May 1882	5, May	87		Iowa City, IA	167	Weiderode, Kurhessen

Christliche Apologete Death Notices --- 1839 - 1899

Name of Deceased	Notice Date	Death Date	Age	Maiden Name	Place of Death	Page	Place of Birth
Borschen, Claus	30, Sept 1858	18, July	70		Florence, MO	156	Worgedorf, Amt Ottersberg, Hannover
Borst, Johan	17, May 1894	9, Apr.	57		Burlington, IA	326	Württemberg
Bort, Friederika Dina	16, July 1896	19, June	33	Lippold	Bunker Hill, IL	463	Westphalen
Borth, Albert	21, July 1892	29, June	53		Dallas, TX	462	Nehmer bei Colberg, Pommern
Bösch, Anna Maria	30, Aug. 1875	9, Aug.	70		Burlington, IA	279	Reinberg, Preußen
Bösch, Anna Maria	25, Nov. 1872	1, Nov.	24-10m- 8d		Burlington, IA	383	
Bösch, Christian Ludwig	12, Aug. 1897	19, July	81	Deichert	Burlington, IA	511	Hüllhorst, Münden, Preußen
Bösch, F.	19, June 1865	28, Mar.			Burlington, IA	100	
Bösche, Wilhelm	20, Sept 1888	20, Aug.	64		Scranton, PA	606	Lagesbüttel, Gifhorn, Hannover
Böschel, Caroline Wilhelmine	6, Aug. 1891	13, July	20		Lincoln, NE	510	Johnston County, Iowa
Böschen, Anna Margaretha	9, June 1879	29, May	22		St. Louis, MO	183	Morgan County, Missouri
Böschen, Carolina	11, Dec. 1865	5, Oct.	19-10m		San Francisco, CA	200	Wolfersheim, Rheinkreis Baiern
Böschen, Heinrich	18, Mar. 1878	1, Feb.	23- 9m-22d		St. Louis, MO	87	Morgen County, Missouri
Böse, Christian	24, Nov. 1898	4, Nov.	72		Chicago, IL	751	Altenwerder, Pommern
Böse, Frank Ferdinand	29, Sept 1879	5, Sept	17- 7m-23d		Chicago, IL	311	Chicago, Cook County, Illinois
Böse, Gottlob	21, Aug. 1876	28, July	20		Lansing, MI	271	
Böse, Johan Conrad	7, Feb. 1881	14, Jan.	85- 3m-20d		Kenosha, WI	47	Südhemmern, Minden, Preußen
Böse, Julius	14, Nov. 1895	24, Sept	63		Plymouth, IA	734	Gellin bei Stettin, Pommern
Böse, Karl Friedrich	26, Feb. 1877	31, Jan.	59- 7m- 5d		Caseville, MI	71	Unterweißach, Backnang, Württemberg
Böse, Maria Luise	23, Mar. 1899	19, Feb.	63	Cordes	Long Island City, NY	190	Fischerhude, Ottersberg, Hannover
Böse, Peter	13, Mar. 1862	20, Jan.	68		Defiance, OH	44	Withselders, Amt Ransbach, Nassau
Böse, Wilhelm	7, May 1891	20, Mar.	18- 7m- 5d		Hart's Island, NY	302	Bremen, Germany
Böshens, Conrad	26, Oct. 1874	6, Oct.	42- 5m-24d		St. Louis, MO	343	
Boß, Elisabeth	15, Nov. 1888	19, Oct.	33	Braward	Harper, IA	734	Gründelwald, Bern, Schweiz
Boß, Johan	29, Dec. 1887	6, Dec.	84		New Orleans, LA	830	Langenau, Bern, Schweiz
Boß, Sophie	5, Sept 1895		77		Madison, WI	574	Isenburg bei Frankfurt am Main, Preußen
Bossard, Johan Rudolf	16, Mar. 1899	12, Feb.	71		Denver, CO	174	Köliken, Aargau, Schweiz
Bosse, Anna Katharina	6, Feb. 1896	21, Dec.	75	Ritz	Troy, NY	94	Fuldt, Kurhessen
Bosse, Bernhard	15, Sept 1884	28, Aug.	61		St. Paul, MN	7	Osnabrück, Hannover
Bosse, Frank	17, Mar. 1884	5, Mar.	52- 8m-22d		St. Paul, MN	7	
Bosse, Herman Heinrich	20, Feb. 1890	27, Jan.	60		Fairfax, MN	126	Lengerich, Tecklenburg, Preußen
Böße, Margaretha Barbara	6, Apr. 1868	21, Mar.	56- 6m-11d	Muffinger		111	Neuzenheim, Baiern
Bossert, Carl Ludwig	30, May 1870	4, Apr.	42- 2m-10d		Dundee, IL	175	Bauschlot, Pforzheim, Baden
Boßhart, Johan	21, Jan. 1892	20, Dec.	43		Louisville, KY	46	Laubheim, Württemberg
Bossie, Henriette	22, Jan. 1891		25- - 4d		Chicago, IL	62	
Bostian, Karoline	19, Apr. 1894	4, Apr.	72	Persohn	Brillion, WI	262	Kaiseko, Demmin, Pommern
Böstle, Margaretha	29, Aug. 1881	12, Aug.	64		Batesville, IN	279	
Both, Ellen	12, May 1873	19, Apr.		Brodbeck	Portsmouth, OH	151	Portsmouth, Scioto County, Ohio
Both, Johan Friedrich	7, June 1888	12, May			De Soto, MO	366	Siedenbollentin, Pommern
Both, Maria	12, Nov. 1857	5, Oct.			Valley Mines, MO	184	Siebenhollentin, Pommern
Bothe, Friedrich Chr.	6, Oct. 1898	23, Aug.	69		Washington, MN	639	Renie, Hannover
Bothe, Hannah	26, Oct. 1874	7, Oct.	42	Hensch	Chicago, IL	343	
Bothe, Heinrich August	7, Dec. 1893	9, Nov.	52		Warrenton, MO	782	Reine bei Hameln, Hannover
Bothe, Louise	14, July 1884	26, June	83	Heidemann	Warrenton, MO	7	Griese, Harmel, Hannover
Bothenweiler, Anna Maria	8, Jan. 1866	24, Oct.	74		Washington, MN	14	Halle, Minden, Preußen
Bott, Charles Wilhelm	22, Jan. 1883	26, Dec.	27- 8m-19d		Warsaw, IL	31	Warsaw, Illinois

Christliche Apologete Death Notices --- 1839 - 1899

Name of Deceased	Notice Date	Death Date	Age	Page	Maiden Name	Place of Death	Place of Birth
Böttcher, Adelheid	29, June 1899	3, June	70	415	Drücker	Owensville, MO	Leste, Sieke, Hannover
Böttcher, Anna	9, Feb. 1885	2, Jan.		7	Knesebeck	Chicago, IL	Blekede bei Lüneburg, Hannover
Böttcher, Conrad	17, Mar. 1884	3, Mar.	83-4m-13d	7		Le Sueur, MN	Lichtenberg, Braunschweig
Böttcher, Fr.	5, Jan. 1893	10, Nov.	23-10m-22d	14		Burlington, IA	Germany
Böttcher, Fritz	18, May 1863	27, Apr.	7-4m-8d	80		Rochester, NY	
Böttcher, H.L.	24, Oct. 1861	4, July	12	172		Liberty, MO	
Böttcher, Heinrich	5, Oct. 1885	9, Sept	70	7		Bland, MO	Leeste am Syke, Hannover
Böttcher, Heinrich	2, Dec. 1897	28, June	50	767		Lorton, NE	Leste, Hannover
Böttcher, Johan	19, Jan. 1880	27, Dec.	27-5m-11d	23		Third Creek, MO	Leeste, Amt Sieke, Hannover
Böttcher, John	11, Feb. 1897	6, Jan.	36	94		Le Sueur, MN	LeSueur, Minnesota
Böttcher, Karl Johan Theodor	14, Feb. 1895	23, Jan.	55	110		Marine City, MI	Wamelow, Mecklenburg-Schwerin
Böttcher, Lydia	20, May 1897	1, May	35	318		St. Paul, MN	Blooming Grove, Minnesota
Böttcher, Maria	19, Feb. 1883	30, Jan.	57-6m-19d	63		Chicago, IL	Leistow, Preußen
Böttcher, Sophia	28, Mar. 1881	23, Feb.	19-2m-16d	103		Bland, MO	Gasconade, Missouri
Böttcher, Wilhelm	5, Nov. 1896	4, Oct.	68	719		Owensville, MO	Barrien, Syke, Germany
Bottemiller, Casper Heinrich	14, May 1896	20, Apr.	70	318		Milwaukee, OR	Brockagen bei Halle, Germany
Bottemiller, Friedrich Wilhelm	26, Jan. 1888	19, Nov.	23-9m-13d	62		Santa Rosa, CA	Chisago County, Minnesota
Bottemüller, Charlotte	17, Jan. 1856	11, Nov.	22	12		Wapello, IA	
Bottenus, Anna Maria	27, Apr. 1868	13, Apr.	42- -4d	135	Pflieger	Red Wing, MN	Darmsheim, Böblingen, Württemberg
Bottenus, Peter	13, July 1863	21, June	65- 3m	112		Red Wing, MN	Mülheim bei Cöln am Rhein,
Bötger, Amalia	2, Oct. 1882	3, Sept	15- 8m	319		New York City, NY	
Bötger, Caroline	20, May 1897	29, Apr.	70	318	Flach	Sea Cliff, NY	Treptow a. d. Tollense, Vorpommern
Bötger, Karl Friedrich	30, Dec. 1897	6, Dec.	69	828		Sea Cliff, NY	Schildau, Sachsen
Böttger, Mina	17, Apr. 1882	19, Mar.	39- 7m	127	Mantel	New York City, NY	Erfurt, Preußen
Böttner, Catharina	11, Mar. 1878	27, Feb.	25	79	Flauhausin	Baresville, OH	Virginia
Böttner, Katharina	18, Mar. 1867	24, Feb.	39	86	Vaubel	Clarington, OH	Reichensachsen, Kurhessen
Böttner, Katharine	2, Sept 1897	6, Aug.	81	559	Wettstein	Clarington, OH	Reickesachsen, Eschwege, Kurhessen
Böttner, Maria	15, June 1899	18, May	42	383		Clarington, OH	Baresville, Monroe County, Ohio
Bottorf, Jefferson	23, Jan. 1882	20, Nov.	24- -20d	31		New Albany, IN	
Böttscher, Henriette Carolina	7, Apr. 1873	22, Mar.	18- 2m- 2d	111		Le Sueur, MN	Cape Girardeau County, Missouri
Bötzel, Regina	4, Jan. 1875	12, Dec.	64	7	Eberwein	Watertown, WI	Vaihingen, Württemberg
Boub, Caroline	25, Apr. 1881	5, Apr.	23	135	Scherer	Burlington, WI	Milwaukee, Wisconsin
Boub, Chr.	26, Mar. 1883	20, Feb.	58	103		Burlington, WI	Canton Graubünden, Schweiz
Bouget, Johan	15, Apr. 1886		58	7		Peru, IL	Hessen-Darmstadt
Böver, Marie	25, Oct. 1894	21, Sept	31	694	Dau	Burt, IA	
Bövers, Anna Dorothea	5, Apr. 1894		76- -26d	230	Kastendick	Billings, MO	Morsum, Hannover
Bowman, Anna	5, Jan. 1893	14, Dec.	68	14		Ft. Hunter, NY	Mecklenburg
Bowman, Friedrich	8, Sept 1892	9, Aug.	65	574		Ft. Hunter, NY	Hille, Minden, Preußen
Boyer, Ephraim Daniel	3, Dec. 1857	10, Nov.	23	196		Brookville, IN	Schuylkill County, Pennsylvania
Boyer, Friedrich	9, Apr. 1866	21, Mar.	17	118		Buffalo, NY	Williamsville, New York
Boyer, Wilhelm	11, Nov. 1872	28, Oct.	27	367		Buffalo, NY	Amherst, Erie County, New York
Bozenhard, Georg Albert	24, Mar. 1884	1, Mar.	24-5m-17d	7		Toledo, OH	Birmingham, Pennsylvania
Bozenhard, Louise	1, Apr. 1897	13, Mar.	37	206	Wehle	Dayton, OH	Indianapolis, Marion County, Indiana
Bozeth, Elisabeth	24, Mar. 1884	12, Mar.	72	7	Deubler	Austin, TX	Osterode, Hannover
Braase, August	22, Sept 1898	16, Aug.	28	607		Gordonville, MO	Gordonville, Missouri
Braats, Sarah	6, July 1893	13, June	29	430	Rätz	Winona, MN	Buffalo County, Wisconsin

Name of Deceased	Notice Date	Death Date	Age	Maiden Name	Page	Place of Death	Place of Birth
Braband, Wilhelm	25, Mar. 1897	13, Feb.	47		190	New York City, NY	Muschen, Germany
Bracher, Frenor	14, Oct. 1886	24, Sept	75		7	Davenport, IA	Kanton Bern, Schweiz
Brachold, Johan Georg	13, Apr. 1874		47- 6m-18d		119	Chillicothe, OH	Herbrechdingen, Heidenheim, Württemberg
Brachmann, Maria Margarete	2, Feb. 1899	10, Jan.	76	Hartmann	79	Wheeling, WV	Niedringhausen, Hessen-Darmstadt
Bracht, Anna Maria	1, Oct. 1857	1, Sept			160	Warren, MO	
Bracht, Friedrich Wilhelm	10, Sept 1896	20, Aug.	74		591	Truxton, MO	Hummersbruch, Sternberg, Lippe-Detmold
Bracht, Heinrich	11, Aug. 1862	10, July	34		128	St. Paul, MN	Rhoden, Waldeck
Brachwitz, Gottlieb	1, Dec. 1873	10, Nov.	46		383	Nabbs Creek, TX	Klicken, Preußen
Brackebusch, Louise	8, May 1890	24, Apr.	54- 4m-14d	Ahrens	302	Highland, IL	Groß-Rhüden, Hannover
Brackemeier, Susanna Katharina	6, Feb. 1882	10, Jan.	14- 6m		47	Spraytown, IN	
Brackmann, Christina R.	19, Apr. 1875	2, Apr.	22	Topp	127	Wheeling, WV	Nauenförde, Hannover
Bracksick, Christina Elisabeth	23, Aug. 1849	26, July	22- 6m	Haberkamp	136	Knoxville, OH	Burgsteinford, Preußen
Bracksick, Johann H.	23, Aug. 1849	31, July	27		136	Knoxville, OH	Hille, Münden, Preußen
Bracksieck, Anna Maria Elisabeth	27, Mar. 1871	11, Mar.	75	VonAhe	103	New Knoxville, OH	Arensmor, Hannover
Bradehöft, Christina	11, July 1895	20, June	63	Reifinger	446	Nebraska City, NE	Uchte, Hannover
Brädemeyer, Wilhelm	6, Apr. 1885	5, Mar.	75		7	Huntingburg, IN	Rothemühle, Hannover
Bradherig, Dorothea Regine	11, Jan. 1894	17, Dec.	80	Ahrns	30	Fredericksburg, TX	
Brahmstedt, Henriette	11, Dec. 1876	22, Nov.	34		399	Chicago, IL	
Braje, Gerd	25, May 1899	6, May	57		335	Mt. Olive, IL	Westerloy, Westerstede, Oldenburg
Brakemeyer, Christina	30, Sept 1897	11, Sept	37	Wegener	623	Concordia, MO	Warren County, Missouri
Brakemyer, Caroline	4, July 1881	30, May	24	Wegner	215	Hopewell, MO	
Brakensiek, Henrietta	2, Apr. 1883	10, Jan.	63		111	Carthage, IL	Beeten, Lippe-Detmold
Braker, Dorothea	18, Apr. 1895	23, Mar.	84		254	Montague, MI	Mecklenburg-Strelitz
Bramstädt, Ludwig	22, Sept 1898	31, Aug.	76		607	Akron, NY	Schimp, Mecklenburg-Schwerin
Brand , Arthur	25, May 1893	9, Apr.	25		334	St. Louis, MO	Mascoutah, Illinois
Brand , Conrad Heinrich	11, Feb. 1892	24, Dec.	81		94	Murray Co, MN	Herford, Münden, Preußen
Brand, (Mrs)	3, Apr. 1871	12, Mar.	44	Ebker	111	Second Creek, MO	
Brand, Anna Catharina	29, May 1890	3, May	40- 7m- 8d	Dols	350	Hicksville, NY	Wellen, Hannover
Brand, Johan Heinrich Christian	8, Apr. 1886		87- 5m-21d		7	Allegan, MI	Peitzier, Mecklenburg-Schwerin
Brand, Karl Heinrich	24, Mar. 1879	20, Feb.	44		95	Brunswick, MO	Eisbergen, Minden, Preußen
Brand, Leonhard	10, Nov. 1884	2, Oct.	48		7	Jerusalem, NY	Baiern
Brand, Maria	12, Apr. 1880	24, Mar.	77	Puls	119	Allegan, WI	Pritzier, Mecklenburg-Schwerin
Brand, Sarah	19, Mar. 1877	20, Feb.	21	Huscher	95	Concordia, MO	
Brand, Sophia	16, Oct. 1882	8, Sept	69		335	Herman, MO	Oberhausen, Lippe-Detmold
Brandau, Andreas	8, Jan. 1891	19, Dec.	72		30	Vermillion, OH	Aßmußhausen, Kurhessen
Brandau, Catharina	28, Jan. 1878	15, Jan.	69		31	Huntingdale, MO	Germany
Brandau, Cathe	15, Sept 1879		6- 3m-11d		295	Charles City, IA	
Brandau, Elisabeth	15, Mar. 1894	19, Feb.	77	Sippel	182	Frankfort, IL	Königswald, Kurhessen
Brandau, Elizabeth	9, Feb. 1893	20, Jan.	60	Boley	94	Vermillion, OH	Königswalde, Kurhessen
Brandau, Katharina Elisabeth	20, Dec. 1880	30, Nov.	55- 6m-24d	Hasenpflug	407	Huntingdale, MO	Asmushausen, Rothenburg, Kurhessen
Brandau, Netha	15, Sept 1879		9-10m- 3d		295	Charles City, IA	
Brandenberger, Ernestina Johanna	9, July 1896	6, June	75	Appelt	447	Hedwigs Hill, TX	Sagan, Schlesien
Brandenberger, Fritz	30, Sept 1897	5, Sept	74		623	Hedwigs Hill, TX	Kanton Bern, Schweiz
Brandenberger, Gottlieb	16, Feb. 1899	14, Jan.	74		110	Hedwigs Hill, TX	Kanton Bern, Schweiz
Brandenberger, Heinrich	17, Apr. 1876		58		127	Henderson, KY	Bäretschwiel, Zürich, Schweiz
Brandenberger, Jakob	5, Sept 1889	10, Aug.	61- 1m-20d		574	Denton, TX	Flaach, Zürich, Schweiz

Name of Deceased	Notice Date	Death Date	Age	Page	Maiden Name	Place of Death	Place of Birth
Brandenberger, Magdalena	22, Dec. 1879	24, Nov.	54	407	Schury	Henderson, KY	Schärly, Cönitz, Bern, Schweiz
Brandenberger, Mary	20, Sept 1888	17, Aug.	36	606	Newmaster	Evansville, IN	
Brandenburg, Johan	9, Sept 1878	22, Aug.	74	287		Brunswick, MO	Strelow bei Grimmen, Pommern
Brandenburg, Johan H.	16, Nov. 1885	26, Oct.	47	7		Crandon, SD	Hinterpommern
Brandenburg, Maria Louise	29, Jan. 1883	25, Dec.	77	39	Sponholz	Salisbury, MO	Strelow, Grimmen, Stralsund, Preußen
Brandenburg, Matthäus Heinrich	19, Apr. 1888	26, Mar.	61	254		Minneapolis, MN	Osnabrück, Hannover
Brandenburger, Anna Maria	10, Aug. 1893	27, June	85	510	Vogel	Drake, MO	Werdote, Preußen
Brandenstein, Clara Jeanette Elis.	18, Oct. 1888	26, Sept	73	670	Evert	Bushton, KS	Wabern, Fritzlar, Kurhessen
Brandenstein, Johannes	17, May 1888	25, Apr.	69	318		Huntingburg, IN	Guxhagen, Melsungen, Kurhessen
Brandenstein, Otto	19, Feb. 1866	27, Jan.	22	62		Huntingburg, IN	Guxhagen, Kurhessen
Brandes, Christian	28, May 1891	6, May	75	350		Chicago, IL	Kleinbrunsrode, Braunschweig
Brandes, Dietrich	30, Aug. 1880	2, Aug.	28	279		Angelica, NY	
Brandes, Dorothea	3, Aug. 1854	22, June	44- 1m-20d	124		Grove Center, NY	Hillerse, Amt Giffhorn, Hannover
Brandes, Dorothea	8, May 1882	6, Apr.	64- 4m-15d	151		Garner, IA	Peine, Hannover
Brandes, Elisabeth Dorothea	2, June 1892	5, May	75	350	Bethge	Chicago, IL	Rethen, Hannover
Brandes, Elsa	21, Jan. 1892	8, Dec.	81	46	Garms	Angelica, NY	Gillerse, Giffhorn, Hannover
Brandes, Friedrich Dietrich Karl	29, Apr. 1897	5, Apr.	46	271		Wellesville, NY	Hillerse, Giffhorn, Hannover
Brandes, Johan Heinrich	31, Aug. 1868	23, July	84- 5m-21d	279		Angelica, NY	Hillerse, Amt Gifhorn, Hannover
Brandes, Johan Heinrich	17, Nov. 1879	31, Oct.	72	367		Concord, IA	Abbensen, Peine, Hannover
Brandes, Maria	24, Aug. 1899	8, Aug.	74	543		San Antonio, TX	Buxtehude, Hannover
Brandhorst, Anna Sophie	21, Oct. 1872	22, Sept		343		Kanaan, MO	Frotheim, Kreis Lübbeke, Minden, Preußen
Brandhorst, Caroline	5, Feb. 1872	12, Jan.	57	47		Columbus, OH	Hille, Minden, Preußen
Brandhorst, Friedrich Wilhelm	5, May 1884	18, Apr.	48	7		Nashville, IL	Jartum bei Minden, Preußen
Brandhorst, Louise	7, Aug. 1876	19, July	24	255	Wege	Schnectady, NY	Bohnhorst, Hannover
Brandmeier, Magdalena	5, Jan. 1893	12, Dec.	77	14	Hippler	Madison, IN	Weiler, Zinsheim, Baden
Brandner, Elisabeth	5, July 1880		24- 8m-11d	215	Morsch	Sandwich, IL	Freedom, Lasalle County, Illinois
Brandstätner, Gottfried	10, Nov. 1879	23, Oct.	48	359		Frankfort, IL	Demmin, Germany
Brandt, (Mr)	28, Apr. 1862	15, Mar.		68		Wausau, WI	
Brandt, Anna	27, Nov. 1882	10, Nov.	27-10m	383	Meier	Evansville, IN	New York
Brandt, Anna	17, July 1876	29, June	14- -21d	231		St. Louis, MO	
Brandt, August	1, July 1897	12, June	54- 8m-26d	414		Waseca, MN	
Brandt, Caroline Ernestine	30, June 1887	15, June	35	414	Fieker	Dalton, MO	Chariton County, Missouri
Brandt, Christian	10, Feb. 1887	26, Jan.	41	94		Schnectady, NY	Hille, Minden, Preußen
Brandt, Dorothea Sophia Christina	19, Dec. 1881	9, Nov.	57	407	Schulz	Nebraska City, NE	Kossow, Mecklenburg-Schwerin
Brandt, Emma	11, Mar. 1886	9, Feb.	26	7		Springfield, MN	Pennsylvania
Brandt, Friederika	11, Apr. 1895	7, Mar.	54	238	Wehmeyer	Drake, MO	Amte Floto, Preußen
Brandt, Friederika Elisabeth	14, June 1880	26, May	61	191	Trappe	St. Louis, MO	Altenau, Ahrenberg, West Preußen
Brandt, Friedrich	20, Dec. 1894	2, Dec.	51	822		Detroit, MI	Rehberg, Mecklenburg-Strelitz
Brandt, Georg	3, Aug. 1874	26, May	21	247		Louisville, KY	
Brandt, Gustav	2, Jan. 1896	14, Dec.	77	14		Lamberton, MN	Dachwig, Erfurt, Preußen
Brandt, Joachim	7, Aug. 1882	18, July	69- 2m-10d	255		St. Louis, MO	
Brandt, Joachim Christian	23, Feb. 1880	3, Feb.	57	63		Nebraska City, NE	Kossow, Mecklenburg-Schwerin
Brandt, Johan H.D.	4, Feb. 1878	12, Jan.	71	39		Third Creek, MO	Rünthe, Westphalen
Brandt, Johan Wilhelm Carl	13, Sept 1894	21, Aug.	54	598		St. Louis, MO	
Brandt, John	25, May 1874	27, Apr.	15	167		Portsmouth, OH	Portsmouth, Scioto County, Ohio
Brandt, John Gill	29, May 1890	30, Apr.	31	350		Parsons, KS	Louisville, Jefferson County, Kentucky

Christliche Apologete Death Notices --- 1839 - 1899

Name of Deceased	Notice Date	Death Date	Age	Maiden Name	Page	Place of Death	Place of Birth
Brandt, Karl	8, Apr. 1897	30, Dec.	76		222	Parsons, KS	Pollhagen, Lippe-Schaumburg
Brandt, Maria	1, Dec. 1879	14, Nov.	76	Mensing	383	Milwaukee, WI	Röbel, Mecklenburg-Schwerin
Brandt, Sophie	27, June 1861	6, June	37	Mohns	104	Louisville, KY	Hagenburg, Lippe-Schaumburg
Brandt, Wilhelm	3, Mar. 1887	19, Feb.	25		142	Dalton, MO	
Brange, Christiane	15, Dec. 1859	25, Sept	54		200	German Creek, IA	Pommern
Brantz, Augusta	7, Mar. 1895	6, Feb.	40-6m	Reinke	158	Big Spring, NE	Brockeloh, Amt Wölpe, Hannover
Brase, Dietrich	13, Oct. 1859	23, Sept	51		164	Jackson, MO	Goldhausen, Waldeck
Brase, Maria Charlotte	3, Oct. 1870	8, Sept	49		319	Jackson, MO	Wölpe, Hannover
Brasen, Maria	30, May 1850	2, Mar.	33-2m		88	Jackson, MO	Oberg, Peine, Hannover
Brathering, Johan Heinrich Christoph	4, Apr. 1881	16, Mar.	65		111	Fredericksburg, TX	Claushagen bei Boitzenburg, Preußen
Bratsch, Friederike	21, Oct. 1872	21, Sept	23	Schulz	343	Le Sueur, MN	Birkholz, Neumark
Bratsch, Julia Johanna	11, Aug. 1892	9, June	37		510	Ripon, WI	Burghagen,
Brau, Christian	17, Feb. 1887	6, Jan.	54		110	Paige, TX	Lade, Minden, Preußen
Brauch, Friedrike	10, Aug. 1899	22, July	54	Sackhoff	511	Bushnell, IL	
Brauer, Cecilie	12, Aug. 1878	27, June	21-5m	Riedel	255	Madison, IN	Hamswerum, Emden, Ostfriesland
Brauer, Epke Maria	27, Mar. 1882	5, Mar.	21-4m-7d	Gabranz	103	Emden, IL	Leer an der Ems, Ostfriesland
Brauer, Jakob	19, Nov. 1877	31, Oct.	67		375	Golconda, IL	Westerode, Hannover
Bräuer, Johan	22, Sept 1898	14, Aug.	82		607	Seattle, WA	
Brauer, John	20, Aug. 1883				271	San Jose, IL	
Brauer, Maggie	13, Oct. 1898	31, Aug.	43		655	Bloomington, IL	Peoria, Illinois
Braumiller, Samuel	6, Apr. 1863	16, Feb.	42-9m-27d		56	Delaware, OH	Berks County, Pennsylvania
Braun, Anna	31, May 1849		Inquiry		87	Brighton, IA	Vestenberg, Amt Anspach, Baiern
Braun, Barbara	10, Sept 1896	17, Aug.	63	Daicker	591	Cincinnati, OH	Stein, Hechingen, Hohenzollern
Braun, Carolina	4, Oct. 1880	20, Sept	56-6m-2d	Heintz	319	Marietta, OH	Schwedelbach, Kaiserslautern, Rheinkreis Baiern
Braun, Catharina	11, Nov. 1872	20, Oct.	62-3m		367	Evansville, IN	Lengerich, Münster, Preußen
Braun, Christian	13, Jan. 1887	Jan.	24		30	Turners Falls, MA	Sachsen-Meiningen
Braun, Elisabeth	20, Oct. 1892	25, Sept	63	Stoffel	670	St. Joseph, MO	
Braun, Emilie	30, Jan. 1896	10, Jan.	42	Michaelis	78	Fairbault, MN	Langen-Hagen, Pommern
Braun, Georg	2, Feb. 1893	27, Dec.	62		78	Defiance, OH	Biedenkopf, Hessen-Darmstadt
Braun, Gottlieb	3, May 1894	1, Apr.	16		294	Clay Center, KS	
Braun, Heinrich Abraham	17, July 1882	26, June	11-11m-1d		231	Defiance, OH	
Braun, Henriette	15, Mar. 1894	24, Feb.	93		182	Warsaw, IL	Sagefeld bei Schneidemühl, Preußen
Braun, Herman	7, Mar. 1895	7, Feb.	27		158	Brownton, MN	Henderson, Minnesota
Braun, Jakob	14, May 1896	18, Mar.	78		318	Marietta, OH	Randsditschweiler, Rheinpfalz Baiern
Braun, John	3, Dec. 1866	11, Nov.	31		390	Leavenworth, KS	Murrhard, Württemberg
Braun, Julius E.	22, July 1897	8, July	49	Zoller	463	Louisville, KY	Wartburg, Tennessee
Braun, Karl August	6, Mar. 1882	6, Feb.	21		79	Secor, IL	Westpoint, New York
Braun, Lizzie	26, Jan. 1893	26, Dec.	18		62	New Haven, CT	
Braun, Louisa	4, Nov. 1897	3, Oct.	50	Schall	703	Otisco, IN	Mainz, Germany
Braun, Louise	28, July 1884	11, July	39	Malott	7	Faribault, MN	Walko, Preußen
Braun, Magdalena	12, Aug. 1897	16, July	78		511	Denison, IA	Canton Bern, Schweiz
Braun, Margaretha	27, Mar. 1890	11, Mar.	32- -2d	Hill	206	Kansas City, MO	Niederofleiden, Allsfeld, Hessen-Darmstadt
Braun, Margaretha Barbara	22, Nov. 1894	20, Oct.	69		758		Frohndorf, Württemberg
Braun, Maria	2, Oct. 1871	11, Sept	58	Stork	319	Louisville, KY	Meisenheim, Amt Lahr, Baden
Braun, Maria Anna	10, Nov. 1873	10, Oct.	23-10m-13d	Rementer	359	Sibewaing, MI	Otterstatt, Rheinpfalz Baiern
Braun, Maria Margaretha	31, May 1849		Inquiry		87	Brighton, IA	Vestenberg, Amt Anspach, Baiern

Christliche Apologete Death Notices --- 1839 - 1899

Name of Deceased	Notice Date	Death Date	Age	Maiden Name	Page	Place of Death	Place of Birth
Braun, Matthias	24, Sept 1891		79- 2m- 9d		622	Rapids, NY	Ossenheim, Hessen-Darmstadt
Braun, Michael	14, July 1898	23, June	69		447	Summerfield, IL	Gladbach bei Trier, Wittlich, Preußen
Braun, Michael	12, Oct. 1868	19, Sept	56		327	Louisville, KY	Menster, Hessen-Darmstadt
Braun, Philipp	2, Oct. 1876	6, Sept	85- 3m-10d		319	Defiance, OH	Biedenkopf, Hessen-Darmstadt
Braun, Simon	13, Oct. 1884	25, Sept	57		7	Nashville, TN	Friesenheim, Lahr, Baden
Braun, Susanna	14, Aug. 1876	30, July	64	Hastedt	263	Mt. Pleasant, IA	Kleinhammersen, Sittens, Hannover
Braun, Theodor Traugott	11, Feb. 1886	21, Jan.	11- 5m- 6d		7	Santa Cruz, CA	Baresville, Ohio
Braun, Veronika	16, June 1862	9, Apr.	67		96	Baresville, OH	Heimberg, Bern, Schweiz
Braun, Wilhelm H.	20, Oct. 1887	29, Sept	38		670	Champaign, IL	Indiana
Brauneker, Wilhelmine	4, Oct. 1880		37		319	Lawrenceburg, IN	Feuerbach bei Stuttgart, Württemberg
Braunfield, Georg	11, Mar. 1852	1, Sept	25		44	Boonville, MO	Wangen bei Stuttgart, Württemberg
Bräuning, Heinrich	5, Jan. 1899	10, Dec.	18		14	Lawrence, KS	Alemakee County, Iowa
Braunsroth, Emma Leonora	28, Aug. 1890	28, July	23- 5m-28d		558	Bismark, IA	
Braunsroth, Lenora	11, Nov. 1886	14, Oct.	63- -11d	Erbstößer	7	Addison, NE	Thenstedd bei Langensalza, Preußen
Brauser, Maria Elisabeth	28, Jan. 1884	11, Jan.	22-11m-20d		7	Mt. Vernon, IN	
Bräutigam, Barbara	24, Sept 1878	1, Sept	57- 8m	Künzi	303	Bay City, MI	
Bräutigam, Friedrich	22, July 1897	2, July	77		463	Bay City, MI	Eisfeldt, Sachsen
Bräutigam, Johan David	17, Nov. 1879	28, Oct.	53		367	Wheeling, WV	
Bräutigam, Maria	12, Oct. 1874		41	Händel	327	Indianapolis, IN	Eisfeld, Sachsen-Meiningen
Bräutigam, Maria	24, Feb. 1868	20, Sept	36- 7m- 1d	Bergfled	63	Summerfield, IL	
Bräutigam, Michael	18, Apr. 1881	2, Apr.	57		127	Fillmore, WI	Zechernitz bei Schmölle, Sachsen-Altenburg
Braxmeier, Bernhard	24, Mar. 1853	4, Mar.	30		48	Dayton, OH	Ober-Sasbach, Amt Achern, Baden
Breager, Maria Karolina	5, Mar. 1896	12, Jan.	73	Volkmann	158	VanDyne, WI	Robe, Germany
Brech, Catharina	22, Oct. 1864	7, Oct.	31	Ulrich	172	Beardstown, IL	Neuhof, Nassau
Brech, Karl	7, Jan. 1892	21, Oct.	63		14	Beardstown, IL	Neuhof, Nassau
Brech, Philippina	5, Dec. 1864	21, Oct.	12- 9m		196	Beardstown, IL	
Brecher, Jacob	27, July 1893	6, July	53		478	Sandwich, IL	Willingen, Nassau
Brechner, Kunigunda	8, Apr. 1886	11, Mar.	81- -12d		7	St. Louis, MO	
Brecht, Bernhard Gottfried	18, Nov. 1867	11, Oct.	36- 2m-17d		366	Richardson Co, NE	Unterröwisheim, Baden
Breckenfeld, Andreas Heinrich	29, Dec. 1887	3, Dec.	58- 9m-15d		830		Osterholm, Germany
Brecke, Dorothea Luise	14, Nov. 1895	24, Oct.	82		734	Oconomowoc, WI	Mellentin Pieritz, Pommern
Brede, John	24, May 1869	4, May	39		167	Cassville, WI	Ehringshausen, Kurhessen
Bredeker, (Mrs)	27, Sept 1849	18, July	68		156	Manchester, MO	
Bredeker, Anton	27, Sept 1849	23, July			156	Manchester, MO	
Bredeker, Anton	27, Sept 1849	19, July	10		156	Manchester, MO	
Bredeker, Heinrich	27, Sept 1849	18, July	10		156	Manchester, MO	
Bredeker, Louise	27, Sept 1849	23, July			156	Manchester, MO	
Bredeker, Ph.	27, Sept 1849	17, July	43		156	Manchester, MO	
Bredemeier, Karl August	15, Feb. 1894	18, Jan.	57		110	Moberly, MO	Minden, Preußen
Bredhorst, Anna Maria	26, May 1853	28, Apr.	40		84	Herman, MO	Levern, Amt Raden, Preußen
Bredow, Johan Friedrich	29, Dec. 1884	10, Dec.	69		7	Junction City, KS	Lölhöfel bei Pieritz, Pommern
Breek, Caroline	9, Oct. 1890	13, Sept	85- 7m-11d	Rust	654	Ft. Hunter, NY	Hille, Minden, Preußen
Breek, Caroline Wilhelmine L.	29, Sept 1873	6, Sept	35	Brandhorst	311	Schnectady, NY	Hille, Minden, Preußen
Breek, Friedrich Wilhelm	20, Dec. 1880	18, Nov.	78- 1m- 3d		407	Ft. Hunter, NY	Hille, Minden, Preußen
Breek, Karoline	17, Nov. 1898	9, Oct.	48	Steinhauer	735	Schnectady, NY	Westphalen
Breh, Caroline	22, Apr. 1897	20, Mar.	79	Sommerfeld	254	Arlington, MN	Neu-Hoferwiese, Preußen

Christliche Apologete Death Notices --- 1839 - 1899

Name of Deceased	Notice Date	Death Date	Age	Maiden Name	Page	Place of Death	Place of Birth
Breh, Jakob	5, Jan. 1899	18, Nov.	80		14	Arlington, MN	Edenbach, Müllheim, Baden
Brehm, Anton	28, Oct. 1886	29, Sept	62- - 4d		7	Hinton, IA	Savian, Graubünden, Schweiz
Brehm, Menga	10, May 1880	8, Apr.	51		151	Melbourne, IA	Madon, Graubünden, Schweiz
Breibarth, Katharina E.	23, Aug. 1849	28, July	57		136	Quincy, IL	
Breidert, Karl	19, June 1865	2, Apr.	15		100	Chicago, IL	
Breidert, Katharina	18, Nov. 1886	4, Nov.	63	Schwarz	7	Chicago, IL	Braunshardt, Hessen-Darmstadt
Breidert, Philipp	13, Mar. 1882	20, Feb.	64- 7m-29d		87	Chicago, IL	Erzhausen, Hessen-Darmstadt
Breiding, Dorothea	26, July 1894	8, July	83	Werner	486	Goshen, IN	Ellingerrode, Kurhessen
Breier, Dora	29, Dec. 1898	2, Dec.	37	Brüggemann	828	St. Louis, MO	Gehlenbeck, Lübbeke, Westphalen
Breier, Maria Elisabeth	1, Aug. 1889	18, June	57	Pilgrim	494	St. Louis, MO	Heuerling in Jeggen, Schledehausen, Germany
Breihan, H. A.	11, Feb. 1897	13, Jan.	90		94	Industry, TX	Upen, Hannover
Breiling, Franz	29, Aug.1895	25, July	44		558	Newport, KY	Cincinnati, Hamilton County, Ohio
Breiling, Franz	21, May 1891	2, May	70-5m-23d		334	Cincinnati, OH	Ergenzingen, Württemberg
Breiling, Henriette	10, Jan. 1876	27, Dec.	56	Zeller	15	Cincinnati, OH	Erzingen, Württemberg
Breine, Elisabeth	1, Aug. 1870				247	St. Paul, MN	Oelber, Braunschweig
Breiner, Johannes (Mrs)	6, Feb. 1846	22, Jan.		Peter	23	Rockford, IN	Stadel, Zürich, Schweiz
Breitenbach, Anton	5, Feb. 1857	28, Dec.			24	Cincinnati, OH	Oberrad, Frankfurt am Main, Germany
Breitenbach, Katharina	5, Aug. 1858	15, July	56		124	Watertown, WI	
Breitenbach, Maria	23, Dec. 1886	5, Dec.	66		7	Belleville, IL	Badenstein, Baiern
Breitenfeld, Wilhelmina	17, Jan. 1876	17, Dec.	26	Neuf	23	Wausau, WI	Sheboygan Falls, Wisconsin
Breitenpöhler, C.	30, Jan. 1882	14, Jan.	46	Hoffschmit	39	Nashville, IL	Lippe-Detmold
Breitenpöhler, Delphie	5, Jan. 1899	9, Dec.	16		14	St. Louis, MO	
Breitenstein, Elisabeth	9, May 1895	3, Apr.	69	Günder	302	Etna, MO	Wallen, Hessen-Darmstadt
Breitenstein, Lorenz	20, Dec. 1855	18, Nov.	40		204	Palestine, IN	Melzen, Spangenberg, Kurhessen
Breiter, Dorothea	1, Feb. 1875	17, Jan.	33- 2m-14d	Bodin	39	Kendallville, IN	Groß-Raden, Sternberg, Mecklenburg-Schwerin
Breiter, Hans Jacob	1, June 1893		17		350		Flaach
Breithaupt, Sophia Dorothea Louise	22, Apr. 1897	26, Mar.	75	Griese	254	Chester, IL	Schloß Ricklingen, Hannover
Breitkreutz, Gesche	25, Mar. 1897	28, Feb.	42	Feldmann	190	Arlington, MN	Benton County, Missouri
Breitkreutz, Wilhelm	9, June 1884	1, May	61		7	Arlington, MN	Neuhöfen, Tscharnikow, Preußen
Breitung, Georg	19, Dec. 1881	23, Nov.	55- 6m- 2d		407	Chicago, IL	Henneberg, Sachsen
Breitung, Theresia	22, Sept 1879	4, Sept	34	Heinze	303	Poughkeepsie, NY	Remte, Sachsen-Weimar
Bremer , Friedrich Heinrich	27, July 1893	6, July	16		478	Boelus, NE	Howard County, Nebraska
Bremer, Carl	12, Nov. 1847	14, Sept			183	New Orleans, LA	
Bremer, Carolina	1, Feb. 1875	22, Dec.	64	Vogt	39	Stanton, NE	Briesun, Schieffelbein, Preußen
Bremer, Elisabeth Wilhelmine	6, Aug. 1896	10, July	25- 8m- 1d	Stock	511	Green Bay, WI	Lowell, Dodge County, Wisconsin
Bremer, Karl	11, Feb. 1848	14, Sept	31		27	New Orleans, LA	Waldung, Preußen
Bremer, Sophia	5, Apr. 1875	20, Mar.	25	Ackmann	111	Swanville, NE	Rolfshagen, Oberkirchen, Schaumburg, Hessen
Bremermann, Anna Margaretha	6, Apr. 1893	10, Mar.	72	Asendorf	222	Auburn, IN	Schwarm bei Bremen, Germany
Brendel, Michael	12, Mar. 1891	17, Jan.	78		174	Cincinnati, OH	Reichenau, Baiern
Brendel, Paul	11, Apr. 1881	16, Feb.	46		119	Vermilion, OH	Blankenheim, Rothenburg, Preußen
Brendle, Sebastian	9, Oct. 1882	8, Sept	55		327	Edwardsville, IL	Appenweier, Offenburg, Baden
Brenke, Fr. Chr.	2, Feb. 1880	9, Jan.	72		39	Third Creek, MO	Belle, Amt Schiede, Lippe-Detmold
Brenn, Bertha	20, Apr. 1893	27, Feb.	28	Schweitzer	254	Laporte, IN	Gönningen, Tübingen, Württemberg
Brennecke, Anna	17, Aug. 1885	29, July	35	Kühle	7	Jackson, MO	Cape Girardeau County, Missouri
Brennecke, Wilhelmine	27, Apr. 1874	19, Mar.	68		135	Jackson, IL	Wiershausen, Hannover
Brenneke, August	30, Oct. 1856	8, Oct.	54		176	Jackson, MO	Seberen, Amt Westerhoff, Hannover

- 58 -

Christliche Apologete Death Notices --- 1839 - 1899

Name of Deceased	Notice Date	Death Date	Age	Maiden Name	Page	Place of Death	Place of Birth
Brenner, (Mr)	28, Oct. 1852	24, Sept			176	Baltimore, MD	
Brenner, (Mrs)	9, Apr. 1877	24, Feb.	76- 2m- 6d		119	Freeport, IL	
Brenner, Adam	6, Feb. 1871	13, Jan.	18		47	Giard, IA	
Brenner, Anna	14, Mar. 1889	21, Feb.	35	Balyour	174	Champaign, IL	Rohr, Hameln, Hannover
Brenner, Anna Sibilla	2, Sept 1878	21, Aug.	71		279	Red Beanson, MO	Germany
Brenner, Christine	23, Mar. 1899	2, Feb.	67- 7m		190	Wathena, KS	Dunkerson, Minden, Preußen
Brenner, Elisabetha	30, Oct. 1856	28, Sept	22- -14d		176	Dayton, OH	Großgerau, Hessen-Darmstadt
Brenner, Emilie	17, Nov. 1898	29, Oct.	58	Köthe	735	Charles City, IA	Großen-Vorra, Schwarzburg-Sondershausen
Brenner, Jakob	5, May 1873	26, Mar.	73		143	Chicago, IL	Rapperswyl, Aargau, Schweiz
Brenner, Johan Heinrich	3, Apr. 1865	8, Mar.	75- 6m- 9d		56	Wyandotte, KS	Neuhofen, Rheinpfalz Baiern
Brenner, Johann	27, Dec. 1844		Inquiry		200	Cincinnati, OH	Dettweiler, Elsaß
Brenner, John D.W.	7, Nov. 1889	17, Oct.	20		718	St. Louis, MO	
Brenner, Katharine	20, May 1858	8, May	39- 2m-18d	Kaucher	80	Ripley, OH	Stein, Amt Bretten, Baden
Brenner, Louis Frank Rudolph	26, June 1890	3, June	17		414	Kansas City, KS	Platte County, Missouri
Brenner, Lydia	17, May 1888	26, Apr.	2- 7m-18d		318	Freeman, SD	
Brenner, Magdalena	28, July 1862	1, June	38	Klamm	120	Liberty, MO	Rheingönheim, Rheinkreis Baiern
Brenner, Margaretha	19, Nov. 1866	28, Oct.	85		374	Belleville, IL	Aldorf, Welzheim, Württemberg
Brenner, Margaretha Christine	25, Feb. 1892	4, Feb.	29		126	St. Joseph, MO	Burlington, Iowa
Brenner, Philipp	23, Jan. 1882	31, Dec.	43-10m-25d		31	Kearney, MO	Neuhofen, Rheinkreis Baiern
Brenner, Susanne	22, Oct. 1877	4, Oct.	78	Hoffmann	343	Liberty, MO	Neuhofen, Rheinkreis Baiern
Brenner, Wilhelm	11, Nov. 1886	15, Oct.	30- 2m		7	Delhi, MI	
Brenner, Wilhelm Friedrich	12, Mar. 1891	13, Feb.	29		174	LaCrosse, WI	Brownsville, Minnesota
Brenzikofer, Christian	5, Feb. 1891	11, Jan.	67		94	Baresville, OH	Mensingen, Bern, Schweiz
Brenzikofer, Peter	5, Mar. 1891	8, Feb.	65		158	Baresville, OH	Mensingen, Bern, Schweiz
Brenzikofer, Rebekka	7, Dec. 1893	9, Nov.	35	Göring	782	Baresville, OH	Monroe County, Ohio
Brenzikofer, Susanna	9, Feb. 1893	11, Dec.	64-10m- 6d	Rubin	94	Hannibal, OH	Reichenbach, Bern, Schweiz
Bresemle, John	11, Mar. 1878	2, Feb.	35		79	Franciscoville, MI	Schönengründ, Freudenstadt, Württemberg
Bretall, Ernst Wilhelm Bogeslaw	22, Sept 1892	5, Sept	35		606		Steinorth, Schlawe, Germany
Breth, Christina Clara	17, June 1867	30, May	60- 1m- 3d	Best	190	Chillicothe, OH	Osthofen, Hessen-Darmstadt
Brethauer, Heinrich	5, Mar. 1896	5, Feb.	76		158	Stryker, OH	Rotterode, Hersford, Kurhessen
Brethorst, Katharina	26, May 1887	2, May	57	Klein	334	Herman, MO	Halle, Germany
Brett, Heinrich	18, Apr. 1864	1, Mar.	33-11m-11d		64	Chillicothe, OH	
Bretthauer, Johannes	25, June 1883	21, May	66- 1m-25d		207	Stryker, OH	Rotteroda, Kurhessen
Bretthauer, Nancy	7, Dec. 1854	16, Nov.	29	Altmann	196	West Unity, OH	Columbiana County, Ohio
Brettmann, Therese	7, Jan. 1858	11, Dec.			4	Cincinnati, OH	Nörten bei Göttingen, Germany
Bretzinger, Catharine	26, Dec. 1850	6, Dec.	67		208	Greenville, OH	Heiterbach, Württemberg
Breuer, Friedrich	10, May 1875	23, Apr.	30		151	Pittsfield, IL	Heimsen, Windheim, Minden, Preußen
Breuling, Jakob	8, Feb. 1855	26, Dec.	2- -27d		24	St. Joseph, MO	
Breuling, Margaretha	8, Apr. 1858	7, Mar.	34	Scheid	56	Weston, MO	Hessen-Darmstadt
Breunig, Adam	2, Mar. 1874	16, Feb.	30	Buchhammer	71	Chillicothe, OH	Darmstadt, Hessen-Darmstadt
Breunig, Anna Maria	26, Feb. 1891	3, Feb.	70- 1m-15d	Schneider	142	Chillicothe, OH	Freischbach, Germersheim, Rheinpfalz Baiern
Breunig, Georg A. (Rev)	19, Nov. 1896	1, Nov.	86- 7m-21d		750	Indianapolis, IN	Mechenhart, Klingenberg, Baiern
Breunig, Josephine	7, Dec. 1854	17, Nov.	11- 2m		196	Indianapolis, IN	
Breunig, Katharina	9, Aug. 1894	20, July	81	Jung	518	Indianapolis, IN	Schellhütte, Backnang, Württemberg
Brewe, Wilhelmine	25, Oct. 1875	10, Oct.	45	Henschen	343	Edwardsville, IL	Linen, Westphalen
Breyfogel, Clinton	16, Sept 1858	20, July	19		148	Delaware, OH	

Christliche Apologete Death Notices --- 1839 - 1899

Name of Deceased	Notice Date	Death Date	Age	Page	Maiden Name	Place of Death	Place of Birth
Brezius, Johan	5, Apr. 1894		60	230		Canal Dover, OH	Ransweiler, Rackenhausen, Baiern
Brick, Friedrich	22, Mar. 1888	27, Feb.	68	190		Marietta, OH	Grandorf, Holdorf, Oldenburg
Brickbiller, Sarah	2, Dec. 1878	17, Nov.	77	383		St. Louis, MO	Ostheim, Elsaß
Bricker, Carl	14, Sept 1874	28, Aug.	78- 5m- 8d	295		Warsaw, OH	Hermanstein, Kreis Gießen, Hessen
Bricker, Christina Elisabeth	16, July 1891	24, June	94- 7m-29d	462	Schäfer	Warsaw, IL	Naunheim, Hessen-Darmstadt
Brickwade, Friedrich	5, Apr. 1888	27, Feb.	68	222		Marietta, OH	Grandorf, Holdorf, Oldenburg
Brickwäde, Wilhelmine	13, Apr. 1868	25, Mar.	22	119	Meyer	Marietta, OH	
Brickwede, Anna Katharina	20, June 1864	30, May	26	100	Meyer	Marietta, OH	Wheeling, Virginia
Brickwede, Julia Mallie	12, Mar. 1891	15, Feb.	25	174		Marietta, OH	Marietta, Ohio
Brickwedel,	29, Jan. 1847	1, Jan.		19		Carrolton, ---	
Brickwedel, Elisa	29, Oct. 1857	10, Sept	26	176		New York City, NY	Drangstadt, Amt Bedakesa, Hannover
Brickwedel, Elisabeth Maria	21, Mar. 1895	19, Jan.	53	190		New York City, NY	Segehorn, Oldenburg
Brickwedel, Maria Katharina	1, Jan. 1883	30, Nov.	73	7	Yost	Hoboken, NJ	Drangstedt, Lehe, Hannover
Briesch, Friedrich	28, Dec. 1868		62	415		Marion, OH	Häfnerhasloch, Brackenheim, Württemberg
Briker, Joseph	15, Feb. 1864	19, May	22-10m	28		Warsaw, IL	
Briks, Wilhelmine	24, Mar. 1879	19, Feb.	88	95		Hopewell, MO	Rohle, Holzminden, Preußen
Brill, Friedericke	31, Jan. 1876	16, Jan.	37	39	Moses	Boston Highlands, MA	Ilbesheim, Baiern
Bringmann, Johan D.	20, Aug. 1891	18, July	63	542		Quincy, IL	Schwarzenmoor, Herford, Westphalen
Bringmann, Maria	29, Sept 1887	13, Sept	18- 4m- 5d	622		Pittsfield, IL	
Brink, Maria	7, May 1891	31, Mar.	59	302	Gerken	North Prairie, IL	Hepstedt, Zewen, Hannover
Brink, Christian	24, Feb. 1873	28, Jan.	55	63		Nashville, IL	Rothenuffeln, Minden, Preußen
Brink, Ernst Friedrich Wilhelm	4, July 1889	11, June	69	430		Hoyleton, IL	Eiksen, Rothenusseln, Minden, Preußen
Brink, Louise	5, Nov. 1891	19, Oct.	37	718	Heitmeyer	North Prairie, IL	Hüllhorst, Lübbecke, Preußen
Brinker, Christine Sophie	31, July 1876	2, July	43- 4m	247	Lutterbein	Golconda, IL	Ladbergen, Tecklenburg, Preußen
Brinker, Margaretha Adelheid	13, Oct. 1873	18, Sept	47	327	Kleinschmidt	Golconda, IL	Klosterschule, Tecklenburg, Preußen
Brinkmann, Adelheid	12, Mar. 1891	28, Jan.	68	174	Hüneke	Spokane Falls, WA	Morsum, Hannover
Brinkmann, Anna Maria	12, May 1892	3, Mar.	80	302	Wortmann	Drake, MO	
Brinkmann, Bertha Alwina	26, Oct. 1885	9, Oct.	11	7		Newport, KY	
Brinkmann, Carl	6, Apr. 1885	21, Mar.	20	7		Newport, KY	Newport, Campbell County, Kentucky
Brinkmann, Caroline	5, July 1869	16, May	28- 1m-14d	215	Wessel	Schnectady, NY	Hille, Preußen
Brinkmann, Caroline	21, Feb. 1876	13, Nov.	14	63		Schnectady, NY	
Brinkmann, Catharine	12, Nov. 1857	9, Oct.	32	184	Renner	Menona, IA	Dannstadt, Rheinkreis Baiern
Brinkmann, Eduard	21, Feb. 1876	7, Dec.		63		Schnectady, NY	
Brinkmann, Elisabeth	20, Feb. 1882	11, Jan.	31	63	Burmeister	Denison, IA	Hille, Minden, Westphalen
Brinkmann, Emma	22, July 1878	13, July	19- 9m-23d	231		Cincinnati, OH	
Brinkmann, Friedrich	22, Apr. 1867	20, Mar.	40	126		Schnectady, NY	Eickhorst, Preußen
Brinkmann, Heinrich	27, May 1886	14, May	73	7		St. Louis, MO	Bornum, Sesen, Braunschweig
Brinkmann, Heinrich	11, June 1877	21, May	57	191		Cincinnati, OH	Bremen, Germany
Brinkmann, Henriette	22, May 1876	22, Apr.	28	167	Blinne	Drake, MO	
Brinkmann, Johannes	14, Oct. 1878	16, Sept	54- 9m-26d	327		Summerfield, IL	Wintershausen, Witzenhausen, Kurhessen
Brinkmann, Louise	24, Aug. 1899	23, June	69	543	Wessel	Schnectady, NY	Hille, Minden, Preußen
Brinkmann, Maria Gertrude	4, Mar. 1842	18, Jan.	1- 6m	34		Belleville, IL	
Brinkmann, Rebecca	15, Dec. 1887	26, Nov.	32- 8m- 8d	798	Sülthaus	Drake, MO	Gasconade County, Missouri
Brinkmann, Sophia	13, May 1897	24, Apr.	77	303	Krieger	St. Louis, MO	Nordhausen, Lübeck, Westphalen
Brinkmann, Wilhelm	5, Nov. 1896	20, Oct.	58	719		Newport, KY	Bünge, Westphalen
Brinkmeier, Wilhelmina	26, Sept 1881	23, Aug.	21-10m-12d	311	Brinkmann	Morrison, MO	Minden, Preußen

Christliche Apologete Death Notices --- 1839 - 1899

Name of Deceased	Notice Date	Death Date	Age	Maiden Name	Page	Place of Death	Place of Birth
Brinkmeyer, Friedrike	20, Jan. 1868	1, Jan.	44- 5m-24d		22	Union, MO	Vlotho, Preußen
Brinkmeyer, Kartharina	27, Aug. 1866	14, July	13- 2m-25d		278	Evansville, IN	
Brinkmeyer, Willie	29, Oct. 1877	7, Oct.	13- 4m-23d		351	Evansville, IN	
Brischar, Susie	26, Jan. 1899	5, Jan.	19		63	Chicago, IL	Aurora, Illinois
Briscoe, Catharine	29, Jan. 1872	17, Dec.	25	Stutz	39	Pinckneyville, IL	
Brissel, Philipp	1, May 1876	9, Feb.	60		143	Carmi, IL	Bechtheim, Hessen-Darmstadt
Brissel, Philipp	24, Apr. 1876	9, Feb.	59- 7m-15d		135	Carmi, IL	
Britsch, Carolina	11, Feb. 1884	1, Feb.	25	Döhner	7	Covington, KY	Covington, Kenton County, Kentucky
Britsch, Friedrich	29, June 1874	7, June	26- 8m-27d		207	Marion, OH	Bethlehem, Marion County, Ohio
Britsch, Mary	13, Oct. 1892	14, Sept	37		654	Marion, OH	Pleasant Twp., Marion County, Ohio
Britt, Bernhard H.	23, Nov. 1863	13, Aug.			188	Charlestown, IN	Südwalde, Amt Bruckhausen, Hannover
Brock, Catharine	20, Nov. 1890	27, Oct.	74-10m- 5d	Dubla	750	Morrison, MO	Schweiz
Brock, Emma Carolina	20, Oct. 1879	2, Sept	16		335	Chamois, MO	Lancaster, Pennsylvania
Brock, Heinrich	13, Jan. 1879	4, Dec.	29		15	Morrison, MO	Kanton Aargau, Schweiz
Brock, Maria Elisabeth	26, Jan. 1888	5, Jan.	32	Grannemann	62	Morrison, MO	DeSoto, Missouri
Brock, Maria Louise	26, Mar. 1883	5, Mar.	40-11m- 6d		103	Morrison, MO	Canton Aargau, Schweiz
Brock, Simon	9, Feb. 1880	18, Jan.	26- 7m-27d		47	Morrison, MO	Lancaster, Pennsylvania
Brocke, Heinrich	12, Oct. 1863	8, Sept	53		164	Perrysburg, OH	Lauenberg, Amt Ekesburg, Hannover
Bröcke, Friedrich	27, May 1878	6, May	54		167	Stillwater, MN	Bünde, Herford, Preußen
Bröcker, Karl	9, Apr. 1883	11, Mar.	24		119	Clayton, IL	Clempenow, Lando, Stettin, Preußen
Bröcker, Margarethe	8, Sept 1892	13, Aug.	73	Greimann	574	Stillwater, MN	Quernheim, Herford, Minden, Preußen
Bröckmann, Emma	10, Nov. 1892	19, Oct.	13		718	Rock Island, IL	Rock Island, Illinois
Brockmann, Hanna Friederike	14, Sept 1899	23, Aug.	80	Wittenberg	591	Nokomis, IL	Blecke, Werther, Halle, West Preußen
Brockmann, Lisette	15, May 1876	13, Apr.	27	Dolling	159	Nokomis, IL	Lienen, Tecklenburg, Preußen
Brockmann, Louise	23, June 1887	19, May	25	Döhring	398	Mt. Olive, IL	Madison County, Illinois
Brockmann, Susanna Margaretha	15, Jan. 1872	21, Dec.	23	Zier	23	Melrose, NY	Lindheim, Hessen
Brockmeier, Adelheid Mary	8, Jan. 1891	7, Nov.	35	Krümpel	30	Colesburg, IA	Brockhausen, Hannover
Brockmeier, Christian	22, Jan. 1877	3, Jan.	29		31	Chicago, IL	Paderborn, Westphalen, Preußen
Brockmeier, Christiana	9, July 1857	28, June	39-11m-21d	Weckel	112	Marietta, OH	Zückra, Clodra, Sachsen-Weimar
Brockmeier, Lina	1, Aug. 1889	6, July	18		494	Pinckneyville, IL	Hartum, Minden, Preußen
Brockride, Christina Elisabeth	26, May 1898	15, Apr.	71	Zwick	335	Huntingburg, IN	Germany
Brockriede, Wilhelm	20, May 1872	25, Apr.	56- 6m	Blomeier	167	Huntingburg, IN	Ladbergen, Germany
Brod, Marie	3, Sept 1847	22, July	34	Puvogel	143	Mt. Vernon, IN	Baden
Brodbeck, Abraham	4, Dec. 1890	15, Nov.	79		782	Paige, TX	Eschenz, Thurgau, Schweiz
Brodbeck, Adolph	27, Nov. 1876	12, Nov.	26- 9m- 4d		383	Giddings, TX	Lagrange, Texas
Brodbeck, Anna Maria	18, June 1877	6, June	37		199	Portsmouth, OH	New York
Brodbeck, Hannah Maria	6, Feb. 1896	15, Jan.	44	Mees	94	Portsmouth, OH	Hanging Rock, Ohio
Brodbeck, Johan Georg	26, Dec. 1881	11, Dec.	60- 3m-19d		415	Lawrenceburg, IN	Walsheim, Baiern
Brodbeck, Katharina	28, Jan. 1886	13, Jan.	36		7	Portsmouth, OH	Hostet, Thedinghausen, Braunschweig
Brodbeck, Michael	19, Jan. 1863	1, Dec.	20- 7m		12	Dunkirk, NY	
Brodbeck, Otilde	7, June 1888	16, May	74		366	Portsmouth, OH	Oppau, Frankenthal, Baiern
Brodbeck, Peter	2, Oct. 1890	7, Sept	71- 3m- 4d		638	Portsmouth, OH	Bingen, Stauffen, Baden
Brodbeck, Peter	22, Oct. 1864	30, Sept	17- 7m-16d		172	Portsmouth, OH	
Brodbeck, Peter Franzis	29, Aug. 1845	18, Aug.	1- 1m- 8d		139	Portsmouth, OH	Oberschopfheim, Amt Lahr, Baden
Brodbeck, Rosa	12, Feb. 1857	29, Jan.	37- 5m		28	Portsmouth, OH	Yora County, Pennsylvania
Brodbeck, Sophia	16, Apr. 1883	29, Mar.	72	Otstatt	127	Portsmouth, OH	

Christliche Apologete Death Notices --- 1839 - 1899

Name of Deceased	Notice Date	Death Date	Age	Page	Maiden Name	Place of Death	Place of Birth
Brodbeck, Vincent	3, Aug. 1899	4, July	82	495		Portsmouth, OH	Bingen am Rhein, Preußen
Brodbeck, William H.	18, Sept 1890	22, Aug.	22- 8m	606		Portsmouth, OH	
Bröder, Anna Barbara	10, Oct. 1881	19, Sept	63	327	Bar	Jamestown, MO	Nassau
Bröder, Philipp	4, Sept 1882	19, Aug.	64- 7m-30d	287		Jamestown, MO	
Broderick, Joh. Rudolph	3, Apr. 1871	17, Mar.		111		Cleveland, OH	
Brodersen, Emma Margaretha	4, Aug. 1898	16, July	29	495	Kück	Lutman, MO	
Brodmann, Catharina Elisabeth	19, Apr. 1894	30, Mar.	69	262		Hartford, CT	Tuttlingen, Württemberg
Brodmann, Margaretha	6, Nov. 1876	16, Oct.	56- 3m-26d	359	Witt	Davenport, IA	Insel Vermehen, Schleswig-Holstein
Brodt, Louise	7, Apr. 1873	24, Mar.	42	111	Klemp	Hamilton, OH	Rothweil, Weißenburg, Elsaß
Brodt, Maria J.	23, May 1881	13, May	20- 8m- 7d	167		Ripley, OH	North Liberty, Adams County, Ohio
Brodwolf, Friederike	23, Sept 1897	8, Aug.	79	607	Meier	White Cloud, KS	Welze, Hannover
Brodwolf, Johan B.	20, Oct. 1887	3, Oct.	77- 7m- 3d	670		Atchison, KS	Alexandermühl, Baiern
Broecker, Walter Eduard	6, Sept 1894	22, Aug.	14	582			Frankonia Townshp Chicago County, Minnesota
Brogle, Simon	24, Aug. 1868	7, Aug.	71- 9m-17d	271		Lowell, WI	Wegenstädten, Rheinfelden, Aargau, Schweiz
Brogli, Petronelle	10, May 1875	28, Apr.	63	151		Beaver Dam, WI	St. Plaisia, Baden
Broich, Fr. W.	8, May 1882	10, Apr.	49	151		New Ulm, MN	Neuß, Köln, Preußen
Broke, Charlotte	4, Nov. 1886	18, Oct.	67	7	Schütte		Badenhausen am Säsen, Braunschweig
Bröker, Anna Maria	27, Aug. 1883	6, Aug.	68- 5m-24d	279	Lueking	St. Louis, MO	Blasheim, Westphalen
Bröker, Eva	30, Oct. 1871	5, Oct.	24- 2m- 1d	351	Schuhmann	Beardstown, IL	Sulzbach, Amt Weinheim, Baden
Bröker, Louise	8, Feb. 1875	23, Jan.	13- -21d	47		Stillwater, MN	
Bröker, Maria Magdalena	1, Apr. 1872	7, Mar.	26- -14d	111	Rentz	Washington, MN	Perouse, Württemberg
Brokmeier, Mina	7, July 1879	22, May	21- 4m-16d	215	Schwichtenberg	Colesburg, IA	
Brokmüller, Adolf	31, May 1888	10, May	8	350		Sun Prairie, WI	
Brokmüller, Heinrich	8, Mar. 1888	6, Feb.	91- 7m- 6d	158		Sun Prairie, WI	Wehlau, Mecklenburg-Schwerin
Bromdau, Paul	4, Mar.1872		70	79		New Bremen, IL	Siefershausen, Kreis Rodenburg, Kurhessen
Bromm, Carolina	24, Jan. 1876	8, Jan.	29	31		Saginaw, MI	Tuscarawas County, Ohio
Bromme, Dorothea	19, Nov. 1891	30, Oct.	75	750	Lehmann	Eldorado, WI	Ober-Grünberg, Sachsen
Bromme, Georg	25, Feb. 1892	2, Feb.	80	126		Friendship, WI	Sachsen-Altenburg
Brommelsick, August	16, Jan. 1896	22, Dec.	92	46		Eudora, KS	Bergshausen, Borgholzhausen, Minden, Preußen
Brommelsick, Franziska	2, Oct. 1890	12, Sept	81	638		Warrenton, MO	
Brömmelsick, Friedrich	9, Jan. 1865	23, Dec.	17- 8m-12d	8		Union, MO	
Brommelsick, Hanna Wilhelmine	11, Feb. 1878	26, Jan.	40- 7m-26d	47	Heidbrecher	Herman, MO	Elferdissen, Herford, Preußen
Brömmelsick, Katharine Charlotte	18, July 1871	12, June	56	231	Landwehr	Union, MO	Frosmold, Minden, Preußen
Bromme, Margaretha	11, Feb. 1878	23, Jan.	58- 8m-18d	47		Yellow Creek, IL	Grandstaid, Hannover
Brönneke, Gottlieb	28, Jan. 1878	14, Jan.	57	31		Yellow Creek, IL	Listringen, Hildesheim, Hannover
Brönnemann, Gottlieb	23, Nov. 1885	31, Oct.	39	7		Watertown, WI	Rubigen, Bern, Schweiz
Brönniman, Wilhelmina	3, May 1855	27, Mar.	28- 6m	72		Rossville, MI	
Brönnimann, John	30, Aug. 1855	12, June	53	140		Rossville, MI	
Brösamie, Friedrich	14, Jan. 1878	29, Dec.	54- 3m-15d	15		Cincinnati, OH	Obermusbach, Freudenstadt, Württemberg
Brösamle, Martin	8, July 1858	26, June	24-10m- 4d	108		Cincinnati, OH	Kälberbrunn, Freudenstadt, Württemberg
Brosch, Sophia Dorothea	5, July 1869	30, May	30	215	Stephan	Louisville, KY	Burbach bei Saaarbrücken,
Brose, Barbara	8, May 1871	31, Mar.	72	151	Akola	La Grange, MO	Glaris, Graubünden auf Davos, Schweiz
Brose, Barbara	11, Feb. 1892	18, Jan.	84	94	Hagen	Quincy, IL	Warmensteinach, Baiern
Brose, Carolina	2, June 1879	11, May	27	175	Barth	Canton, MO	
Brose, Franz	3, Nov. 1887	17, Oct.	22	702	Gebhardt	Beaver Dam, WI	Brietzig, Pieritz, Pommern
Brosi, Anna Katharina	21, May 1877	13, Apr.	34	166		Quincy, IL	Weidenberg, Oberfranken, Baiern

Christliche Apologete Death Notices --- 1839 - 1899

Name of Deceased	Notice Date	Death Date	Age	Maiden Name	Page	Place of Death	Place of Birth
Brosi, Johan Heinrich	26, Feb. 1872	11, Feb.	78- 6m- 8d		71	Lagrange, MO	Klosters, Graubündten, Schweiz
Brosi, Maria	5, May 1862	15, Apr.	71- 3m	Fönze	72	Canton, MO	Closter, Graubünden, Schweiz
Brosi, Peter	18, Jan. 1864	16, Dec.	45- 9m		12	Canton, MO	Kloster, Graubunden, Schweiz
Brosius, Catharine	5, May 1862	9, Mar.		Biehl	72	Baltimore, MD	Straßburg, Elsaß
Brosius, Jakob	7, May 1877	22, Feb.	59		151	Baltimore, MD	Frankreich
Brosius, Jakob	5, Apr. 1869	2, Mar.	92		111	Baltimore, MD	
Brosius, Louise	13, Feb. 1890	21, Jan.	72- 6m-27d	Schmidt	110	Baltimore, MD	Langensteinbach, Baden
Brost, Margaretha	4, June 1896	2, Apr.	72	Merkle	367	Wheeling, WV	
Brost, Sophia	27, May 1872		24- 6m-19d		175	Sandusky, OH	
Brotherson, Gertrud	11, June 1896	3, May	51	Wilde	383	Merrill, WI	Fehmern, Schleswig
Brotherson, Gesche	31, May 1880	2, May	28	Meyer	175	Lake Creek, MO	Morgan County, Missouri
Brötje, Augusta	2, Dec. 1872	19, Oct.	36	Schuchardt	391	Belleville, IL	
Brotzmann, Johan	12, Nov. 1866				366	Chicago, IL	Eisenach, Amt Dermbach, Sachsen-Weimar
Brotzmann, Wilhelm Ernst	12, Nov. 1866				366	Chicago, IL	Eisenach, Amt Dermbach, Sachsen-Weimar
Brown, Friedrich	1, July 1897	14, June	72		414	Brownton, MN	Orlinghausen, Lippe-Detmold
Brown, George	22, Sept 1884	30, Aug.	84		7	Sherrills Mount, IA	Durham County, England
Brown, Wilhelmine	31, Dec. 1896	15, Dec.	70	Siekmann	844	Brownton, MN	Orlinghausen, Lippe-Detmold
Broxmeier, Emilie Friederike	9, July 1866	25, May	15-11m		222	Dayton, OH	Groß-Almerode bei Kassel, Hessen
Brubach, Friedrich	13, Jan. 1887	29, Dec.	67		30	Toledo, OH	Keichsweiler, Sandwendel, Trier, Rheinpreußen
Brücker, Elisabeth	16, Nov. 1874	15, Oct.	70		367	Columbus, WI	Mutterstadt, Baiern
Brücker, Elisabeth	2, June 1887	14, May	53	Schwerdfeger	350	Summerfield, IL	Gerlin, Köslin, Pommern, Preußen
Brüchert, Wilhelmine	15, Feb. 1875	6, Jan.	50	Patzwald	55	Kewaunee, WI	Süßenborn, Sachsen-Weimar
Bruchlos, Johanna Dorothea	6, Mar. 1882	20, Feb.	62- 7m		79	Hoboken, NJ	Frienersheim, Crefeld, Düsseldorf, Preußen
Bruchsen, Helene	18, May 1874	18, Mar.	52- - 3d	Berns	159	Evansville, IN	Rödchen, Hessen
Brück , Wilhelm	3, Jan. 1895	22, Nov.	56		14	Oakland, CA	Bobenhausen, Kurhessen
Brück, Louise	12, Mar. 1857	31, Dec.	58	Spamer	44	Chicago, IL	Salo bei Friedlin, Mecklenburg-Strelitz
Brückert, Ludwig	27, Feb. 1896	11, Nov.	68		142	Akron, NY	Lembach, Baden
Buckle, Anton	13, Oct. 1859	20, Aug.	47		164	Upper Alton, IL	Eikhoff, Mecklenburg
Brückman, Maria Dorothea Regina	5, Apr. 1894	1, Mar.	76		230	Laporte, IN	Walkerton, Indiana
Brückman, Marie Elisabeth	25, Apr. 1895	15, Mar.	19		270	Laporte, IN	New York City, New York
Brückmann, Dorothea Elisabeth	24, Oct. 1881	30, Sept	23- -11d		343	Warsaw, IL	Schwasdorf, Mecklenburg-Schwerin
Brückmann, Louis	22, Mar. 1880	6, Mar.	64		95	Laporte, IN	Fechtel, Fürstenau, Hannover
Bruckmeyer, Anna Margaretha	8, Jan. 1877	25, Dec.	60	Harbecken	15	Colesburg, IA	Tränskirchen, Baiern
Brückner, Anna Margaretha	2, Oct. 1876	4, Sept	61		319	Dayton, OH	Wartenberg bei Breslau, Schlesien, Preußen
Bruder, Robert	10, Nov. 1873	17, Oct.	30		359	Pekin, IL	
Bruebach, Rosine Katharine	16, June 1873	2, May	11- 8m		191	Toledo, OH	
Bruehl, R.A.W.	21, June 1894	19, June	66		401	Covington, KY	Ratibor, Germany
Bruehl, Rudolph August Wilhelm	5, July 1894	19, June	66		438	Covington, KY	Ratibor, Schlesien
Brüggemann, Wilhelm	26, May 1862	27, Apr.	40		84	Herman, MO	Lübbeke, Preußen
Brüger, Robert	14, Dec. 1885	15, Nov.	41- 7m-12d		7	Schulenburg, TX	
Brüggemann, Friedrich	13, Sept 1875	11, Aug.	60		295	Waco, TX	Stendal, Magdeburg, Preußen
Brüggemann, Friedrich August	29, July 1878	22, June	58		239	Alton, IL	Lemgo, Lippe-Detmold
Brüggemann, Maria	29, Apr. 1878	2, Apr.	22-10m-18d		135	Crawfish, WI	
Brüggemann, Maria Elisabeth	10, Jan. 1889	18, Dec.	51	Breitenbach	30	Watertown, WI	Nickweiler bei Bingen am Rhein, Germany
Brüger, Heinrich Friedrich Wilhelm	4, Sept 1876	3, Aug.	2		287	Hamburg, IA	
Brühl, Jessie Emma	3, Mar. 1892	24, Jan.	29		142	Appleton, MO	Appleton, Missouri

Christliche Apologete Death Notices --- 1839 - 1899

Name of Deceased	Notice Date	Death Date	Age	Page	Maiden Name	Place of Death	Place of Birth
Bruhl, Wilhelmine	11, Feb. 1867	6, Jan.	21	46	Günter	Jackson, MO	Schallbach, Elsaß
Brühschwein, Nänse	31, May 1888	5, May	33	350	Wolf	LaMouse, SD	Stinfelde, Ostfriesland
Brum, Jakob	28, Feb. 1889	16, Jan.	61	142		Junction City, KS	Logan County, Illinois
Brumlive, Johan Mennon	27, July 1899	21, June	70	479		Brighton, IL	
Brummer, Nettie	9, Mar. 1893	8, Feb.	22	158		Emden, IL	Leidensdorf, Mecklenburg-Schwerin
Brümmer, Sophia	13, Mar. 1890	30, Jan.	76	174	Westphal	Manitowoc, WI	Leidensdorf, Mecklenburg-Schwerin
Brümmer, Sophie	27, Feb. 1890	30, Jan.	85-10m-14d	142	Westphal	Manitowoc, WI	Immerndall bei Golnow, Pommern
Brummond, Anna Sophia	28, Sept 1893	20, Aug.	72- 9m-17d	622	Kleon	Wittenberg, WI	Eberstadt, Baden
Brun, Johann	30, Dec. 1858	1, Aug.	22	208		Madora, IN	Washington County, Illinois
Brun, Louise Elisabeth	10, July 1890	8, June	21- 4m- 2d	446	Könemann	Mt. Vernon, MO	
Brunasky, Friedrich	4, Jan. 1864	2, Dec.		4		Elizabeth, NJ	
Brune, Anna Maria	24, Dec. 1877	13, Dec.	86- 2m	415	Sirp	Lawrence, KS	Bokell, Minden, Preußen
Brune, Katharina Charlotte	29, Dec. 1898	1, Dec.	67	828	Rieke	Lawrence, KS	Dissen, Hannover
Bruner, Jakob	28, Oct. 1886	10, Oct.	78- 1m	7		Galena, IL	Gränichen, Aargau, Schweiz
Brunerkant, Balbina	15, Sept 1884	23, Aug.	57- 5m-12d	7		Ft. Wayne, IN	Wallenbrück, Minden, Preußen
Bruning, Herman Heinrich	14, Apr. 1898	21, Mar.	87- 7m-27d	239		Warren, MO	Spenge, Heerfurth, Preußen
Bruning, Johan H.	7, Jan. 1884	18, Dec.	22	7		Warrenton, MO	
Brunk, Ernst Theodor	12, Nov. 1896	1, Oct.	17	734		Grand Island, NE	
Brunkau, Mathilda	31, Jan. 1895	10, Jan.	29	78	Albrecht	Ada, MN	New Ulm, Minnesota
Brunkhorst, Anna Margaretha	9, Apr. 1896	19, Mar.	62	238	Miller	Sandusky, OH	Wildershausen, Oldenburg
Brunkhorst, Johan Heinrich	5, Feb. 1883	18, Jan.	85- 8m- 4d	47		Lake Creek, MO	Bötersen, Rodenberg, Hannover
Brunkhorst, Maria Elisabeth	24, Apr. 1876	6, Apr.	21	135	Holst	Belvedere, MN	Knoxville, Ohio
Brunkhost, Gesche	12, May 1879	12, Apr.	48	151	Lück	Lake Creek, MO	Grasberg, Hannover
Brunkow, Christian Friedrich	27, June 1895	10, June	77	414		Pepin, WI	Dölitz, Pommern
Brunkow, David	14, May 1896	22, Apr.	65	318		Pepin, WI	Doelitz, Pommern
Brunnemann, Christian	2, June 1887	2, May	80	350		Roseville, MI	Canton Bern, Schweiz
Brunner, Anna Maria	27, Jan. 1859	23, Dec.	28	16	Scheiermann	Ripley, OH	Niederkirchen, Dürkheim, Rheinpfalz Baiern
Brunner, Anna Maria	28, July 1873	12, July	83-10m- 8d	239	Stephan	Evansville, IN	Klingen, Bergzabern, Baiern
Brunner, Barbara Elisabeth	12, Jan. 1888	18, Dec.	40	30	Stiedenroth	Columbus, OH	Erzhausen, Darmstadt, Hessen-Darmstadt
Brunner, Barbara Katharina	10, June 1878	23, May	68- 2m-19d	183		Washington, MN	Langwiesen, Zürich, Schweiz
Brunner, Friedrich Wilhelm	7, Jan. 1884	6, Dec.	31	7			
Brunner, Heinrich	27, Aug. 1891	1, Aug.	74	558		West Point, NE	Greening, Zürich, Schweiz
Brunner, Johan Adam	22, Sept 1879	10, Sept	66- 3m-14d	303		Woodbury, MN	Langwiesen, Zürich, Schweiz
Bruning, Johan Heinrich	3, Feb. 1887	15, Jan.	60	78		Warren, MO	Helgen, Wallenbrück, Preußen
Brunold, Anna	17, July 1890	28, June	72-11m- 5d	462	Staub	Nashville, TN	Brimmis, Graubünden, Schweiz
Bruns, Elisabeth	7, May 1877	15, Apr.	62- 7m	151	Spahn	St. Louis, MO	Inghausen, Baiern
Bruns, Gesche	16, Aug. 1888	2, Aug.	36- 7m- 4d	526	Rosenbrock	New York City, NY	Fischerhude, Hannover
Bruns, Heinrich	23, Mar. 1893	15, Feb.	80	190		Sherrills Mount, IA	Hoheneggelesen, Steinbrück, Hannover
Bruns, Heinrich	30, Nov. 1893	30, Oct.	71- 2m-17d	766		Papillion, NE	Vahlbruch, Hannover
Bruns, Johan	17, July 1876	30, May	63	231		St. Louis, MO	
Bruns, Louise	17, Nov. 1887	17, Oct.	35	734	Zwick	Zumbro Falls, MN	Williamsburg, New York
Bruns, Maria Carolina	24, July 1871	17, June	26- 3m-13d	239	Bork	Sheboygan, WI	Blankenburg, Ufermark, Preußen
Bruntrup, Wilhelm	31, Jan. 1889	4, Jan.	53	78		Brownton, MN	Wahrburg, Lippe-Detmold
Bruntz, Johan Georg	25, July 1895	22, June	20	478		Turkey Creek, NE	Merkel, Rußland
Brusch, Gottfried Joachim Otto	19, May 1879	26, Apr.	58	159		Blooming Grove, MN	Benwisch bei Rostock, Mecklenburg-Schwerin
Brüschert, Johan	31, Dec. 1896	15, Dec.	33	844		Phillips, WI	Manitowoc County, Wisconsin

Christliche Apologete Death Notices --- 1839 - 1899

Name of Deceased	Notice Date	Death Date	Age	Maiden Name	Place of Death	Page	Place of Birth
Brush, Emilie	18, May 1899	9, Apr.	39	Reinhart	Morristown, MN	319	Blooming Grove, Minnesota
Brüß, Christina	10, Oct. 1895	19, Sept	85	Stiem	Lowell, WI	654	Zülsdorf, Arenswalde, Neumark, Brandenburg
Brüß, Friedrich	7, Nov. 1895	26, Oct.	84		Columbus, WI	718	Rietzig, Brandenburg
Brüßmann, John	11, Apr. 1881	2, Mar.	21- 7m		Oregon, MO	119	Falkenberg, Neumark
Brüssow, Johanna	16, Nov. 1893	7, Sept	82	Carow	Parsons, KS	734	Ostheim, Kreis Hanau, Kurhessen
Brust, Caspar	5, Dec. 1870	25, Nov.	55-10m- 2d		Baltimore, MD	391	Dübendorf, Zürich, Schweiz
Brütsch, Louisa	19, July 1888	6, June	32	Bietenholz	Los Angeles, CA	462	Kleine, West Preußen
Brutsch, Marie	8, Jan. 1866	10, Nov.	20- 7m- 8d	Steffen		14	Oberdorf, Grenzingen, Elsaß
Bruwer, Magdalena	27, Sept 1869	17, May	79		Etna, MO	311	Hasloch, RheinPfalz Baiern
Bub, Susanna Katharina	26, Jan. 1880	23, Dec.	71- 6m-21d	Leonard	Bunker Hill, IL	31	Cannstadt, Württemberg
Bubeck, Friedrich Wilhelm	5, Dec. 1895	14, Nov.	47		Akron, OH	782	Stettin, Preußen
Bubeitz, Wilhelm	15, Nov. 1888	20, Oct.	46		Chicago, IL	734	Halsdorf, Rauschenburg, Kirchheim, Kurhessen
Bubenheim, Heinrich	10, Mar. 1879	21, Feb.	56		Hamilton, OH	79	Groß-Rambin bei Belgrad, Pommern
Bublitz, Auguste	25, June 1883	28, May	41- -27d	Jech	Lansing, IA	207	Breitenfelde, Stettin, Preußen
Bublitz, Louise	30, Aug. 1875	28, July	49		Menomonie, WI	279	Minneapolis, Minnesota
Bublitz, Louise Emilie	9, Aug. 1894	11, July	26	Baumeister	Ada, MN	518	Petzeick, Germany
Bublitz, Wilhelmina Francisca	20, May 1897	28, Mar.	34	Schwandt	Menomonie, WI	318	Samenthausen bei Heiligenberg, Baden
Buchacker, Christoph	19, Feb. 1872	4, Feb.	71		Platteville, WI	63	
Buchacker, Maria L.	12, Jan. 1885	5, Dec.	31	Haas	Stitzer, WI	7	Zittenfeld, Amerbach, MittelBaiern, Baiern
Buchard, Blasius	8, Aug. 1889	18, July	73		Decatur, IL	510	Hamburg, Germany
Buche, Ida Henriette Eleonore A.	21, May 1891	29, Apr.	21	Metzner	Chicago, IL	334	
Bucheit, Maria	25, Nov. 1842		Inquiry		Wheeling, VA	187	Dortmund, Preußen
Büchel, Charles	13, Apr. 1899	6, Mar.	59	Afenmark	Wichita, KS	238	Dettingen, Heidenheim, Württemberg
Büchel, Johanna Barbara	27, Apr. 1893	23, Mar.	85- 3m-24d		Pepin, WI	270	Memmingen, Baiern
Büchele, E.	21, Aug. 1890	2, July	43- 4m-28d		Junction City, KS	542	Württemberg
Büchele, Ferdinand	12, May 1898	11, Apr.	74		Detroit, MI	303	Memmingen, Baiern
Büchele, Gottfried	12, July 1894	7, June	65		Evansville, IN	454	Zürich, Schweiz
Büchele, Robert	13, Sept 1869	19, Aug.	42		Detroit, MI	295	Biglen, Bern, Schweiz
Bucher, Herman (Rev)	2, Dec. 1886		26- 2m-10d			7	Hannover, Hannover
Bucher, John	10, Dec. 1891	1, Nov.	15	Achilles	Zumbro Falls, MN	798	Portsmouth, Scioto County, Ohio
Bucher, Katharine	4, Feb. 1886	18, Jan.	68		Fond du Lac, WI	7	Amerbach, Baiern
Buchert, Anna M.	7, July 1892	6, June	22- 4m-27d	Brand	Portsmouth, OH	430	Trafös, Steiermark, Oesterreich
Buchert, Maria Anna	12, Feb. 1891	12, Jan.	73-10m-25d	Hartmann	Decatur, IL	110	Altfeld, Hannover
Buchheim, Urban	28, Jan. 1884	4, Jan.	68		Los Angeles, CA	7	Allen, New York
Buchheister, Auguste M.	18, Jan. 1894	24, Dec.	69		Plainville, KS	46	Oestringen, Bruchsal, Baden
Buchheister, Louise Dorothea	28, Nov. 1889	5, Nov.	36	Achilles	Angelica, NY	766	Wachsfelde, Brandenburg
Bucheit, Brigitta	14, Sept 1899	23, Aug.	82	Körner	Louisville, KY	591	Nesselgrund, Preußen
Buchholtz, Karl Friedrich	2, Nov. 1899	7, Sept	69		Appleton, WI	703	Zeden, Neumark, Brandenburg
Buchholz, (Mr)	31, Aug. 1868	4, Aug.	84		Cannon River, MN	279	Zadelow, Pommern
Buchholz, Auguste	7, Sept 1899	6, Aug.	71	Köhler	Melrose, ID	575	Belvedere, Goodhue County, Minnesota
Buchholz, Carl	25, Jan. 1894	10, Jan.	71		Columbus, WI	62	Hotteln, Hannover
Buchholz, Carl Theodor	15, Nov. 1894	24, Oct.	37		Crandon, SD	742	Osceola, NE
Buchholz, Conrad Christian	26, Sept 1889	30, Aug.	42		Osceola, NE	619	Cooper's Grove, Cook County, Illinois
Buchholz, Dietrich	12, Jan. 1899	15, Dec.	41		Altamont, IL	30	Brandenburg
Buchholz, Dorothea Elisabeth	14, May 1896	8, Apr.	85- - 8d	Behred	Morris, MN	318	Sporsee, Reustettin, Pommern, Preußen
Buchholz, Emilie	28, May 1877	10, May	22- 1m-10d		San Jose, IL	175	

- 65 -

Name of Deceased	Notice Date	Death Date	Age	Maiden Name	Page	Place of Death	Place of Birth
Buchholz, Friederike Louise	21, June 1875	26, May	20		199	Columbus, WI	Moderow, Kreis Saatzig, Pommern
Buchholz, Gottlieb	4, Nov. 1897	28, Sept	85		703	Morris, MN	Brandenburg
Buchholz, Johan Heinrich Fr. (Rev)	17, Dec. 1883	25, Nov.	26		7	Belleville, IL	Coppers Grove, Cook County, Illinois
Buchholz, Karl	15, July 1852	11, Apr.	15		116	Dubuque, IA	Kleinkamin, Kreis Frankfurt, Preußen
Buchholz, Maria Anna	16, Mar. 1899	17, Feb.	35	Graf	174	Crandon, SD	Columbus, Wisconsin
Buchholz, Minna	18, June 1891	30, May	20- -23d		398	Chicago, IL	Grabow, Bromberg, Posen
Buchholz, Rebekka	11, Dec. 1882	17, Nov.	41- 8m-14d	Schmekpeper	399	Altamont, IL	Wechhold, Hoya, Hannover
Buchholz, Rosette	21, Nov. 1881		17-11m-15d	Fritz	375	Altamont, IL	Grand Prairie, Effingham County, Illinois
Buchholz, Wilhelm	4, May 1899	6, Apr.	61		287	Altamont, IL	Schweringen, Matfeld, Hannover
Büchler, Christian	23, June 1879	4, June	43		199	Poughkeepsie, NY	Darmstadt, Hessen-Darmstadt
Büchler, Christina	3, Sept 1866		31	Schöttli	286	St. Louis, MO	Wildberg, Nagold, Württemberg
Büchler, Friederike	7, Mar. 1864	18, Feb.	31- 3m- 3d		40	Canal Dover, OH	
Büchler, Georg	12, Oct. 1893	9, Sept	36		654	Bradford, IN	Harrison County, Indiana
Büchler, Jacob	12, Mar. 1896		73		174	San Diego, CA	Geislingen, Württemberg
Buchmann, Ottilie	8, Jan. 1872	29, Nov.	21		15	Milwaukee, WI	Milwaukee, Wisconsin
Buchmann, Rahel M.	30, July1883	8, July	13		247	Cannon River, MN	Goodhue County, Minnesota
Büchner, Edward	8, May 1890	15, Apr.	52- 3m- 8d		302	Cameron, MO	
Büchner, Friedrich August Albert	21, Nov. 1881	23, Oct.	33		375	Cameron, MO	Großida, Sachsen
Büchner, Rosina Maria	10, Apr. 1890	18, Mar.	77	Sommer	238	Cameron, MO	
Büchner, Wilhelm	23, June 1862	13, Feb.	30		100	Liberty, MO	Mansdorf bei Zeitz, Preußen
Büchner, Wilhelm	22, Mar. 1888	17, Feb.			190	Cameron, MO	
Buchs, Johannes	14, Sept 1893	21, Aug.	29-11m-21d		590	Vermillion, OH	Lenk, Bern, Schweiz
Buchs, Peter	19, Sept 1889	20, July	61- 4m-22d		606	Vermillion, OH	Mellen, Regenwalde, Preußen
Bucht, Wilhelm F.	31, Mar. 1887	18, Mar.	60		206	Oconomowoc, WI	
Buchwald, Louise	21, Jan. 1886	1, Dec.			7	Heilbronn, GE	
Buchwald, Luise	4, Mar. 1886	1, Dec.	17- 6m		7	Heilbronn, GE	
Buck, (Mrs)	22, June 1899	11, May	79		399	South Grove, IL	Hochelheim, Koblenz, Preußen
Buck, Friedrich	14, Nov. 1889	17, Oct.	68- 5m-14d		734	Saginaw, MI	Dummersdorf, Mecklenburg-Schwerin
Buck, Gerhard Heinrich	25, Nov. 1867	8, Nov.	25		374	Hamilton, OH	Schlethausen, Amt Osnabrück, Hannover
Buck, Johan Heinrich	1, June 1899	11, May	75		351	San Jose, CA	Hannover
Buck, Katharina Wilhelmina	8, May 1890	20, Apr.	66- 2m-18d		302	Cincinnati, OH	Altdorf bei Melle, Pommern
Buck, Maria	13, Feb. 1890	21, Jan.	68-10m-16d	Brand	110	Saginaw, MI	Klingdorf, Mecklenburg-Schwerin
Buckendal, Katharine Dorothea Louise	5, Apr. 1894		58	Roeber	230	Lansing, IA	Hansstaed, Epsdorf, Hannover
Bücker, Anna Elisabeth	25, Oct. 1888	22, Sept	89- 2m- 9d		686	Saginaw, MI	Oerlinghausen, Lippe-Detmold
Bücker, Maria	24, Jan. 1871	8, Dec.	23		31	Saginaw, MI	
Buckmann, Michael Dietrich	6, Dec. 1875	11, Nov.	73		391	Pomeroy, OH	Woldhoff, Preußen
Bucksath, Caroline	14, Dec. 1885	28, Nov.	55	Brandt	7	Dalton, MO	Eisbergen, Minden, Westphalen, Preußen
Bucksath, Sophia	5, June 1856	16, Apr.	23		92	Brunswick, MO	Eisberge, Minden, Preußen
Budde , Emma	20, May 1897	29, Apr.	31		319	Gladbrook, IA	
Budde, Ernst H.	24, Dec. 1891	24, Nov.	64		830	Red Bud, IL	Werther, Halle, Westphalen
Budde, Frank	20, Sept 1888	13, Aug.	23- 4m-17d		606	Charles City, IA	Madison, Wisconsin
Budde, Wilhelm	13, Dec. 1888	28, Aug.	19- 6m- 9d		798	Charles City, IA	Madison, Wisconsin
Buddeberg, August	6, Dec. 1888	16, Nov.	66- 2m-10d		782	Elizabeth, NJ	Halle, Westphalen
Buddemeier, Luise A.	2, Sept 1897	24, July	65	Hermsmeier	559	Champaign, IL	Langenholzhausen, Lippe-Detmold
Budden, Margaretha	28, May 1866	17, Mar.	40	Prediger	174	Clifton, WI	Baiern
Buddenbaum, Emil	16, June 1892	16, May	19		382	Bay City, MI	Grand Rapids, Michigan

- 66 -

Christliche Apologete Death Notices --- 1839 - 1899

Name of Deceased	Notice Date	Death Date	Age	Maiden Name	Page	Place of Death	Place of Birth
Buddenbaum, Heinrich (Rev)	21, May 1896	28, Apr.	60		334	Detroit, MI	Holzhausen, Hartum, Minden, Preußen
Buddenbaum, Heinrich Wilhelm	18, Aug. 1892	25, July	24		526	Bay City, MI	Cincinnati, Hamilton County, Ohio
Buddenbaum, Karl Edwin	15, Apr. 1897	19, Mar.	19		238	Bay City, MI	Goshen, Indiana
Buddenbaum, Oskar Walter	14, Mar. 1895	5, Feb.	19		174	Bay City, MI	Roseville, Michigan
Buddensick, Emilie Helene	12, Dec. 1889	14, Nov.	28	Schmidt	798	Minneola, MN	Balkow, Hinterpommern
Bude, (Mrs)	10, Feb. 1873	2, Dec.	57		47	Madison, WI	
Bude, Heinrich	11, July 1870	31, May	68		223	Arena, WI	Landwehrhagen, Amt Münden, Preußen
Budlitz, Emilie	27, Jan. 1868	17, Nov.	18		31	Fountain City, WI	Daber, Kreis naugardt, Pommern
Budwig, Anna Maria	26, July 1888	5, July	73		478	Detroit, MI	Unterberg, Marienwerder, Preußen
Buerdemann, Dorada	31, Mar. 1887	12, Mar.	40	Janke	206	Colbex, KS	Egelsbach, Hessen-Darmstadt
Buerdemann, Dorada	28, Apr. 1887	12, Mar.	40	Schlapp	270	Colbey, KS	Egelsbach, Hessen-Darmstadt
Buermann, Ludwig	23, Feb. 1880	3, Feb.	45	Schlapp	63	Ballwin, MO	Wiershausen, Minden, Hannover
Buerstatte, Heinrich M.	1, Dec. 1887	15, Nov.	69-10m- 6d		766	Manitowoc, WI	Bielefeld, Westphalen
Buese, Henrietta	3, June 1878	16, May	44- 6m- 8d	Fehr	175	Waverly, OH	Schachten, Kurhessen
Bufort, Maria	6, Dec. 1894	4, Nov.	27		790	Ballwin, MO	
Büge, (Mrs)	23, May 1870	3, May	46- 8m- 6d		167	Allegan, MI	Kolberg, HinterPommern, Preußen
Bugge, Wilhelmine	4, July 1889	5, June	79	Witthun	430	Milwaukee, WI	Klein-Lukff in der Ukermark, Preußen
Buhl, Georg Theodor Wilhelm	2, Mar. 1893	12, Feb.	30		142	Dayton, OH	Allendorf auf der Ulm, Wetzlar, Preußen
Buhl, Heinrich	10, Mar. 1884	18, Feb.	64		7	Dayton, OH	Dayton, Montgomery County, Ohio
Buhl, Karl	25, Jan. 1894	9, Jan.	26		62	Dayton, OH	Gersfeld, Baiern
Buhl, Kunigunde	7, Nov. 1850	19, Sept			180	Mt. Vernon, IN	Allendorf auf der Ulm, Koblenz, Preußen
Buhl, Maria	4, Feb. 1886	17, Jan.	58		7	Dayton, OH	Stuttgart, Württemberg
Buhl, Scharlotte Sophia	14, Mar. 1889	9, Feb.	29- 8m-18d	Haller	174	Galion, OH	Derschen, Coblenz, Germany
Buhl, Wilhelmine	1, July 1897	17, June	76	Johannes	414	Kenosha, WI	Dayton, Montgomery County, Ohio
Buhl, William	8, May 1890	24, Apr.	17- 8m-11d		302	Dayton, OH	Baden
Bühler, (Mrs)	21, Sept 1885	29, Aug.	76		7	Sterling, NE	Seedorf, Bern, Schweiz
Bühler, Anna	11, Jan. 1849	1, Dec.	68- 6m		8	Madison, IN	Diedenhäusen, Pforzheim, Baden
Bühler, Anna Maria	23, Sept 1867	7, Aug.	36	Kies	302	Kossuth, OH	Lycoming County, Pennsylvania
Bühler, Anna Maria	29, Nov. 1880	11, Nov.	24-11m-25d	Kürgis	383	Firth, NE	Schwanden, Bern, Schweiz
Bühler, Christian	8, Nov. 1855	27, July	74		180	Madison, IN	Nußloch, Baden
Bühler, Conrad	14, June 1894	4, May	80		390	Ritzville, WA	Sterling, Nebraska
Bühler, Dorothea	16, Mar. 1899	23, Feb.	20		174	Sterling, NE	Reusten, Herrenberg, Württemberg
Bühler, Georg	12, Aug. 1886	26, June	36		7	Odebolt, IA	Minneapolis, Minnesota
Bühler, Georg Johan	14, Jan. 1892	16, Dec.	22		30	Minneapolis, MN	Reusten, Herrenberg, Württemberg
Bühler, Jacob	5, Apr. 1894	7, Mar.	85		230	Odebolt, IA	Nußloch bei Heidelberg, Germany
Bühler, Jacob	8, Mar. 1855	17, Jan.	70- 6m		40	Canton, MO	Reusten, Herrenberg, Württemberg
Bühler, John	15, Dec. 1862	2, Nov.	24		200	Cedar Lake, IN	Reusten, Herrenberg, Württemberg
Bühler, Lucia	8, Sept 1892	17, Aug.	72	Musbach	574	Lemars, IA	Reusten, Herrenberg, Württemberg
Bühler, Margaretha	6, July 1854	4, June	33-10m		108	Madison, IN	
Bühler, Maria Catharina	25, Sept 1876	31, Aug.	66-10m-15d	Sauter	311	Storm Lake, IA	Reusten, Herrenberg, Württemberg
Bühler, Martha Magdalena	9, Feb. 1899	12, Jan.	66	Wyß	95	Garrett, IN	Bern, Schweiz
Bühler, Peter	25, Sept 1876	21, Aug.	62- 1m-16d		311	Dwight, IL	Reusten, Herrenberg, Württemberg
Bühler, Sebastian	6, Apr. 1899	12, Mar.	55		222	Odebolt, IA	Reusten, Herrenberg, Württemberg
Bühlmaier, Henry L.	8, Apr. 1897	23, Mar.	28		222	New York City, NY	Ernsbach, Oehringen, Württemberg
Buhlmeyer, Fr. J. (Rev)	12, Mar. 1896	2, Feb.	30- 9m- 6d		174	Redfield, SD	Bramsche, Hannover
Buhner, Anna R.	10, Mar. 1887	22, Feb.	73- 8m-18d	Liemann	158	Seymour, IN	

Name of Deceased	Notice Date	Death Date	Age	Page	Maiden Name	Place of Death	Place of Birth
Bühner, Charles	27, Oct. 1892	5, Sept	69	686		Sauk City, WI	Bruck, Welzheim, Württemberg
Bühner, Edward	9, Oct. 1882	25, Sept	18-10m-25d	327		Higginsville, MO	Warsaw, Illinois
Bühner, Elisabeth	8, May 1876	5, Apr.	16- 4m-12d	151		Sauk City, WI	
Bühner, Georg	15, Sept 1884	24, Aug.	28	7		Higginsville, MO	Cincinnati, Hamilton County, Ohio
Buhner, Johann Heinrich	29, Aug. 1881	12, Aug.	77-10m	279		Seymour, IN	Bramsche, Amt Malgarten, Hannover
Bühner, Louise	10, June 1886	28, May	30	7	Stelter	Seymour, IN	Louisville, Jefferson County, Kentucky
Buhr, Babette	15, June 1899	19, May	62	383	Hetzel	Chicago, IL	Dinkelsbühl, Baiern
Buhre, Friedrich W.	11, June 1891	11, Apr.	80	382		Burlington, WI	Bremen, Germany
Bühren, Wilhelm (Rev)	3, Mar. 1898	1, Feb.	88	143		San Jose, CA	Hilden, Germany
Bührer, Katharina	15, Nov. 1894	19, Oct.	42	742		Berea, OH	Lohn, Schaffhausen, Schweiz
Bührer, Maria	25, June 1883	24, May	29	207		Toledo, OH	Bibern, Schaffhausen, Schweiz
Bührig, Heinrich	10, Dec. 1877	21, Nov.	72	399		Cleveland, OH	Linma, Braunschweig
Bühmann, Carl	16, Oct. 1890	11, Sept	43	670		Elizabeth, NJ	Gandersheim, Braunschweig
Buhmeister, Heinrich	23, Feb. 1863	12, Dec.	31	32		Schnectady, NY	Hille, Minden, Preußen
Buhmeister, Louis Heinrich	16, Feb. 1888	13, Jan.	20	110		Hoyleton, IL	Nashville, Illinois
Buhmeister, Wilhelm	7, Feb. 1895	13, Dec.	42	94		Kline, IA	
Buhrmester, August	14, Aug. 1876	27, July	25	263		Schnectady, NY	Hille, Preußen
Buhrmester, Louise	2, Feb. 1885	15, Jan.	42	7	Krüger	Schnectady, NY	Hille, Minden, Preußen
Buhrmester, Sophia Louisa	22, Jan. 1872	27, Dec.	62	31	Pranger	Burlington, IA	Dankerson, Minden, Preußen
Buhrow, F.	15, Mar. 1894	14, Jan.	24	182		Ripon, WI	Wollen, Preußen
Buhsmann, Amalia	1, Apr. 1897	4, Mar.	46	206	Holste	Yellow Creek, IL	Blumberg, Lippe-Detmold
Buk, Anna Carolina	30, May 1889	5, May	13- 7m-13d	350		Saginaw, MI	
Büker, Adolph	24, June 1886	26, May	78	7		Drake, MO	Dehlintrop, Lippe-Detmold
Büker, Anton	30, May 1895	22, Feb.	95	350		Saginaw, MI	Preußen
Büker, Lena W.	1, Apr. 1897	13, Mar.	31	206		Higginsville, MO	Lage, Lippe-Detmold
Büker, Sophia	12, Apr. 1894	22, Feb.	76	246		Drake, MO	
Bulgrin, Albertine	22, May 1871	30, Apr.	35	167	Maier	Marine City, MI	Lickow, Kreis Schiefelbein, Köslin, Pommern
Bulgrin, Henrietta	4, Mar. 1897	23, Jan.	69	143	Bohn	Moor, MI	Pommern
Bulgrün, Karl Albert	15, Aug. 1881	16, July	49	263		Marine City, MI	Simmatzig, Schiefelbein, Pommern
Bullgrin, August	20, Aug. 1883	2, Aug.	61-11m-19d	271		Marine City, MI	Simatzig, Schiefelbein, Hinterpommern
Butling, (Mrs)	29, July 1897	25, June	73	479	Hilbert	Jerusalem, NY	Grötzingen, Baden
Butling, Burkard Nikolaus	7, Apr. 1862	19, Mar.	9	56		Williamsburg, NY	
Bution, Philipp	26, Mar. 1896	6, Mar.	79	206		Brooklyn, NY	Mönichzell, Baden
Bullweiler, Friedrich	18, Oct. 1849		Inquiry	167		New York, NY	Germersheim, Rheinkreis Baiern
Bullwinkel, Karsten	23, Oct. 1882	3, Oct.	66	343		Brooklyn, NY	Löhe, Hagen, Hannover
Bülow, Georg	6, May 1897	30, Mar.	70	287		Ripon, WI	Neubrandenburg, Mecklenburg-Strelitz
Büttemann, Heinrich Christian	24, Jan. 1895	6, Jan.	78	62		Cape Girardeau, MO	Schleweke, Braunschweig
Büttemann, Wilhlemina Christina	7, Apr. 1892	13, Mar.	21	222		Jackson, IL	Cape Girardeau County, Missouri
Butman, Wilhelmina	14, July 1892	10, June	70	446	Schlörling	Golconda, IL	Wetscherhort, Diepholz, Hannover
Bund, Karl	7, Aug. 1882	24, July	32	255		Brooklyn, NY	Eßlingen, Württemberg
Bünemann, Herman Heinrich	14, Aug. 1882	30, July	72	263		St. Paul, MN	Seeste, Tecklenburg, Preußen
Bünemann, Katharina Isabella	17, Aug. 1893	30, July	76	526	Hellwig	St. Louis, MO	Westerkappeln, Tecklenburg, Preußen
Bunert, Johann Gottlieb	6, Sept 1855	22, Aug.	59	144		Evansville, IN	Peilau, Kreis Reichenbach, Schlesien
Bunge, Friedrich Wilhelm	10, Oct. 1895	16, Sept	74	654		Evansville, IN	Polau, Oldenstadt, Hannover
Bünger, Anna	9, Mar. 1899	3, Feb.	66	158	Rosky	Industry, TX	Preußen
Bünger, Christoph	13, Apr. 1885	13, Mar.	84	7		Milwaukee, WI	Klopzow, Mecklenburg-Schwerin

Christliche Apologete Death Notices --- 1839 - 1899

Name of Deceased	Notice Date	Death Date	Age	Page	Maiden Name	Place of Death	Place of Birth
Bünger, Sophia	24, Mar. 1887	3, Mar.	76	190	Winkel	Milwaukee, WI	Klopzow, Mecklenburg-Schwerin
Bunk, Garette	2, Apr. 1891	13, Mar.	86	222		Dalton, MO	
Bünnemann, Johan H.	15, Oct. 1877	28, Sept	70- 5m-21d	335		St. Louis, MO	WesterKappeln, Tecklenburg, Münster, Preußen
Bunsen, Mina	20, Dec. 1875	2, Dec.	44-11m-23d	407	Zimmermann	St. Joseph, MO	
Buntrock, Friederike	29, July 1886	8, July	32	7		Lansing, IA	Schaale, Preußen
Bünz, Friedrich	18, Mar. 1878	10, Feb.		87		Wathena, KS	Hohenfelde, Holstein
Bunz, Margaretha	19, Aug. 1872	3, Aug.	35	271	Tusch	Oregon, MO	Elbershausen, Kreis Frankenberg, Hessen
Bunz, Margaretha	24, Apr. 1871	4, Mar.	36- 3m- 6d	135	Baunert	Oregon, MO	Käßboffen bei Zweibrücken, Baiern
Burcker, Jacob	23, Oct. 1856	19, Sept	42	172		Muscatine, IA	Niederhochstadt, Rheinkreis Baiern
Burg , Henriette	4, Sept 1851	25, July	22	144	Müller	Burlington, IA	
Burg, Margaretha	8, July 1878	21, June	77- 3m- 8d	215	Hiliox	Burlington, IA	Burlington, Iowa
Burg, Margaretha Anna	23, Sept 1897	8, Aug.	42	607		Burlington, IA	Hergesweiler, Bergzabern, Rheinpfalz Baiern
Burg, Margarethe	22, July 1878	21, June	77- 3m- 8d	231	Ziliox	Burlington, IA	Hohenegelsen, Hannover
Burgdorf, Ferdinand	16, May 1895	13, Apr.	84	318		Sherrills Mount, IA	Hohenegeben, Hannover
Burgdorf, Johanna	18, Mar. 1878	23, Feb.	67- 9m-13d	87		Sherrills Mount, IA	Einbeck, Hannover
Burgdorf, Juliana Dorothea	6, Feb. 1851	20, Jan.	27- 4m	24	Wächter	Cincinnati, OH	Eißnerberg, Wittlage, Hannover
Burge, Gerhard Heinrich	22, Dec. 1892	6, Nov.	58	814		DeWitt, MI	
Bürger, Louise	28, July 1884	4, July	67-10m- 3d	7		St. Louis, MO	
Burger, Regina Matilda	14, Nov. 1895		40	734	Dettmer	Dallas, TX	Industry, Austin County, Texas
Burgert, Friedrich	16, Feb. 1893	14, Jan.	67	110		Kendallville, IN	Geneven, Crilwitz, Mecklenburg-Schwerin
Burgert, Johan Heinrich	9, Mar. 1885	20, Feb.	60- 3m-28d	7		Kendallville, IN	Kambs, Mecklenburg-Schwerin
Burghard, Friederika	4, July 1881	15, June	68	215		Watertown, WI	Neugat, Pommern
Burghardt, Anna Maria	9, Nov. 1885	20, Oct.	45- 9m-20d	7	Guthier	Belleville, IL	Fehlheim, Hessen-Darmstadt
Burghardt, Johan Christian	13, Apr. 1885	21, Mar.	50	7		Bunker Hill, IL	Wöllnitz bei Jena, Sachsen-Weimar
Burghardt, Karl	8, Aug. 1889	23, July	75	510		Bushnell, IL	Neustadt an der Oder, Sachsen-Weimar
Burghardt, Louis	29, Jan. 1883	22, Dec.	81- 1m-12d	39		Bridgeport, CT	Jägersburg, Homburg, Rheinkreis Baiern
Burghart, Lizzie	12, Jan. 1888		37	30		Louisville, KY	
Burghart, Michael Theobald	20, June 1895	27, May	62-11m-15d	398		Bridgeport, CT	Jägersburg, Rheinpfalz Baiern
Burgnis, Wilhelm Rudolph	11, Nov. 1897	22, Oct.	32	719		Cleveland, OH	Miamisburg, Montgomery County, Ohio
Burgstahler, Maria	25, Nov. 1897	26, Oct.	71	751	Husser	Buffalo Lake, MN	Munzenheim bei Collmar, Elsaß
Burgtorf, Friedrich	30, Mar. 1863	12, Mar.	51- 8m-15d	52		St. Louis, MO	
Burgtorf, Marie Louise	27, Apr. 1868	16, Apr.	20	135		Cincinnati, OH	Cincinnati, Hamilton County, Ohio
Burgtorf, Sophia	5, Feb. 1883	29, Dec.	70	47	Winters	Cincinnati, OH	Hannover
Burhen, Gertrude	26, Oct. 1893	4, Oct.	60	686		Scranton, PA	Lautenbach, Kurhessen
Burk, Anna Maria	17, Mar. 1853	22, Feb.	50	44		Pennsylvanienburg, IN	Kippenheimweiler, Baden
Burk, Barbara	16, Dec. 1854	20, Nov.	24	200		Pennsylvanienburg, IN	Kippenheim , Baden
Burke, Conrad Heinrich	18, Apr. 1881		58	127		DeWitt, MI	Essenerberg, Amt Wittlage, Hannover
Burkel, Caroline	20, Jan. 1873	6, Jan.	18- 9m- 6d	23		Newport, KY	
Bürkemayer, Nancy	18, Oct. 1855	18, Sept	62	168	Dreisbach	Union, MO	Westphalen
Burkhardt, Friederika	22, Aug. 1889	28, July	56	542		Louisville, KY	Württemberg
Burkhardt, Margaretha	18, Jan. 1894	30, Dec.	56	46	Gröde	Chicago, IL	Westhoven, Germany
Burkhardt, Maria	2, Mar. 1885	30, Jan.	86	7		Edon, OH	Schöneich, Württemberg
Burkhardt, Maria S.	11, July 1889	15, June	72- 1m- 3d	446	Schimmel	New Bremen, IL	Vippach, Sachsen-Weimar
Burkhardt, Rosina	2, Jan. 1882	18, Dec.	79	7		Galion, OH	Unterhausen, Württemberg
Burkhardt, Sarah	6, June 1881	18, May	73-10m-17d	183		Edon, OH	Lycoming County, Pennsylvania
Burkhardt, Wilhelm	6, May 1897	30, Mar.	96- 6m-21d	287		Belleville, IL	Oberdorla, Erfurt, Preußen

Name of Deceased	Notice Date	Death Date	Age	Maiden Name	Page	Place of Death	Place of Birth
Burkhardtd, Sophia	5, Dec. 1870	30, Oct.			391	Dubuque, IA	Heilbronn, Württemberg
Burkhart, Anna	24, June 1867	19, Apr.	65- -11d		198	Evansville, IN	SchloßVibach, Sachsen-Weimar
Burkhart, Gustav	19, Oct. 1893	6, Sept	18		670	Owatonna, MN	Württemberg
Burkhart, Lorenz	26, Jan. 1880	9, Jan.	64- 7m- 1d		31	New Bremen, IL	
Burkhart, Margaretha	8, Mar. 1880	12, Feb.	85	Zanger	79	Galion, OH	
Burkhart, Michael	12, June 1890		81		382	Cincinnati, OH	Odessa, Rußland
Burkhart, Regina	23, July1883	12, July	50	Laybold	239	Terre Haute, IN	Bleningen, Württemberg
Burkhartsmayer, Joseph	10, Apr. 1876	22, Mar.	47		118	Louisville, KY	Steinreinach, Waiblingen, Württemberg
Bürkle, Johan Georg	3, Mar. 1884	7, Feb.	75		7	Wheeling, WV	Schmieden, Cannstatt, Württemberg
Bürkle, Maria Catharina	17, Mar. 1879	22, Feb.	65- 3m-11d	Schanz	87	Wheeling, WV	Oelbronn, Maulbronn, Württemberg
Bürkle, Pauline	27, Nov. 1890	28, Oct.	62- 1m-19d	Schneck	766	Seymour, IN	Osweil, Ludwigsburg, Württemberg
Bürky, Anna Elisabeth	11, Aug. 1898	19, July	75	Joß	510	Billings, MO	Kanton Bern, Schweiz
Bürky, Johan	4, June 1896	10, May	64		367	Billings, MO	Hütlingen, Bern, Schweiz
Burlisch, Mina	20, July 1885	24, June	26	Brandhorst	7	Bland, MO	Gasconade County, Missouri
Burmann, F.G.	1, Nov. 1875	25, Sept	78- -16d		351	Forestville, MI	
Bürmann, Johan Friedrich	18, Feb. 1867	22, Jan.	55		54	Quincy, IL	Burr bei Osnabrück, Hannover
Bürmann, Maria Christine Wilhelmine	26, Apr. 1888	9, Apr.	63	Schrader	270	Quincy, IL	Wiershausen, Hannover
Burmeister, Carolina	16, July 1891	4, May	76	Schütte	462	Schnectady, NY	Hille, Minden, Preußen
Burmeister, Karl Heinrich	16, June 1873	22, May	69- 4m-12d		191	Burlington, IA	Dankersen, Preußen
Burmeister, Louisa	31, Dec. 1891	22, Aug.	25	Brinkmann	846	Schnectady, NY	Watervliet,
Burmeister, Louise Henriette	4, Dec. 1876	9, July	43-11m- 8d		391	New Orleans, LA	Nordassel, Braunschweig
Burmeister, Martha Maria	14, Sept 1899	29, Aug.	23	Wegehaupt	591	Milwaukee, WI	Klein-Elguth, Schlesien
Burmester, C.W.	15, Mar. 1875	31, Jan.	48- 2m- 5d		87	Nashville, IL	Hille, Minden, Preußen
Burmester, Christ F.	20, Nov. 1882	5, Sept	28- 7m- 5d		375	Schnectady, NY	Hille, Minden, Preußen
Burmester, Katie	28, July 1884	18, Apr.	26	Kihn	7	Schnectady, NY	Cannelton, Indiana
Burmester, Maria	27, Sept 1860	26, Aug.	41	Eckersberg	156	Shotwell, MO	Einhorst bei Preußisch Minden, Preußen
Burow, Gottfried	6, Mar. 1890	12, Feb.	60- 9m		158	Humboldt, NE	Blumberg, Pyritz, Stettin, Preußen
Burow, Marie Chrstine	31, Dec. 1883	15, Dec.	69-11m-24d	Brunk	7	Oconomowoc, WI	Megow, Pieritz, Preußen
Burrucker, Friedrich Carl	31, Dec. 1896	11, Dec.	83		844	Brooklyn, NY	Kleinheubach, Baiern
Bursch, Martin	6, Oct. 1887	19, Sept	64		638	Stillwater, MN	Dombrowke, Schübin, Bromberg, Posen
Bürsing, Heinrich	5, Jan. 1874	17, Oct.	62		7	Effingham, IL	Wedde, Gröningen, Holland
Bürstler, Adam	8, July 1878	10, May	59		215	Lawrenceville, IN	Maudach, Mutterstadt, Baiern
Bürstler, Maria	28, Nov. 1881	7, Nov.	17- 1m-27d		383	Batesville, IN	
Bus, Anna	26, Aug. 1897	7, Aug.	43	Horstmann	543	St. Louis, MO	Franklin County, Missouri
Bus, William F.	9, June 1898	23, May	21		367	St. Louis, MO	St. Louis, Missouri
Busacker, Anna	6, June 1895	27, Apr.	94		366	Golden City, MO	Grebs, Dürwitz, Mecklenburg-Schwerin
Busacker, John	10, Mar. 1884	29, Feb.	80		7	Belleville, IL	Grebs, Demitz, Mecklenburg-Schwerin
Busacker, Theodor	7, Aug. 1882	5, July	21- 5m-17d		255	Bunker Hill, IL	Belleville, St. Clair County, Illinois
Busch, Catharine	7, Nov. 1881	21, Oct.	75- -16d		359	Salem, MN	Ruschwehl, Hannover
Busch, Diedrich	12, Oct. 1893	13, Sept	66	Rinck	654	Davenport, IA	Hamminkeln bei Düsseldorf, Preußen
Busch, Elisabeth	2, Oct. 1865	28, Aug.	31		160	Davenport, IA	Isselburg, Preußen
Busch, Fritz	27, Nov. 1876	1, Nov.	39- 6m		383	Seymour, IN	Hüllhorst, Kreis Lübbecke, Preußen
Busch, Heinrich Louis	10, May 1880	25, Apr.	41		151	Seymour, IN	Hilhorst, Lübbecke, Minden, Preußen
Busch, Hendrina	8, Nov. 1880	27, Oct.	75- -13d		359	Davenport, IA	Haminkeln, RheinPreußen
Busch, J.J.	5, Feb. 1872	15, Jan.	54- 1m-11d		47	Batesville, IN	Kalkreise, Engter, Hannover
Busch, Johan	22, Oct. 1883	25, Sept	74- 4m		343	Salem, MN	

Christliche Apologete Death Notices --- 1839 - 1899

Name of Deceased	Notice Date	Death Date	Age	Page	Maiden Name	Place of Death	Place of Birth
Busch, Johann	12, Mar. 1883	15, Feb.	40	87		Salem, MN	Ft. Madison, Iowa
Busch, Johann Wilhelm	29, Mar. 1860	6, Mar.	34	52		Burlington, IA	Lübeck, Germany
Busch, Karl Friedrich	25, Oct. 1875	11, Oct.	73	343		Seymour, IN	Lübbecke, Minden, Preußen
Busch, Louise	13, Oct. 1873	26, Sept	71	327	Trepp	Mt. Vernon, IN	Landau, Rheinkreis Baiern
Büsch, Rahel	9, Feb. 1885	23, Jan.	70	7	Valer	Nauvoo, IL	Davos, Graubünden, Schweiz
Busch, Wilhelmina	27, June 1864	21, May	17 - - 6d	104		Defiance, OH	
Busche, Maria Dorothea	21, Nov. 1864	28, Sept	64	188	Mayfeld	Cape Girardeau, MO	Dolgen, Amt Ilton, Hannover
Büscher, Gretchen Y.	29, Apr. 1878	13, Apr.	21- -38d	135		Springfield, IL	
Büscher, Heinrich	29, Dec. 1892	28, Nov.	63	828		Chester, IL	
Busching, Barbara	26, Mar. 1891	22, Feb.	51- 1m-13d	206	Steiner	Cincinnati, OH	Erlenbach, Rheinpfalz Baiern
Busching, Heinrich	23, Aug. 1849	15, July		136		Quincy, IL	Amtstolzen, Hannover
Büsching, Katharina	4, Apr. 1870	15, Mar.	70	111	Strohmann	Cincinnati, OH	Genhorst, Amt Solzenau, Hannover
Buschke, John Fr.	29, Mar. 1880	17, Mar.	35	103		Columbus, WI	Chodziesen, Posen, Preußen
Buschke, Maria Elisabeth	20, Nov. 1871	7, Nov.	25	375	Strehlow	Columbus, WI	
Büschle, Maria	18, June 1891	16, May	57	398	Schneider	Berne, MI	Oberfeld, Frütigen, Bern, Schweiz
Buschmann, Dina Wilhelmina	31, Mar. 1859	25, Dec.	18	52		Red Bud, IL	Kirchdorf, Ostfriesland
Buschmann, Meta	25, Feb. 1884	10, Jan.	22	7	Gerken	Bland, MO	Gasconade County, Missouri
Buschmann, Sophia Henriette	2, Feb. 1888	9, Jan.	17	78		Covington, KY	
Buse, Karl	15, Nov. 1869	29, Oct.	68- 7m-26d	367		Red Wing, MN	Marchin, Mecklenburg-Schwerin
Busehrus, Philipp	31, Jan. 1889	9, Jan.	63- 3m	78		Hopewell, MO	Valldorf, Floda, Germany
Busekrutz, Louise	7, Apr. 1873	22, Nov.	43	111	Mische	Hopewell, MO	Humfeld, Lippe-Detmold
Buser, Anna	22, Oct. 1891	30, Sept	67	686	Schäfer	Burlington, IA	Sellisberg, Liesthal, Baselland, Schweiz
Buser, Edwin	7, Oct. 1897	10, Sept	36	639		New York City, NY	Omarlingen, Basel, Schweiz
Buser, Heinrich	10, May 1894	3, Apr.	72	310		Burlington, IA	Hemiken Canton Basel, Schweiz
Buser, Herman	3, Aug. 1893	19, June	23	494		New York City, NY	Ornalingen, Schweiz
Busett, Christine	9, Apr. 1891	11, Mar.	61	238	Teut	Minneapolis, MN	Mecklenburg-Schwerin
Busian, Friedrich	17, Feb. 1887	30, Dec.		110		Dover Center, MN	Brostowo, Posen
Busiek, Johanna	23, Sept 1897	29, Aug.	32	607		Belleville, IL	
Busiek, Wilhelm	19, June 1890	15, May	64- - 8d	398		Belleville, IL	Lienen, Tecklenburg, Münster, Preußen
Büsing, Martha	5, June 1876		54	183		Bible Grove, IL	Termünten, Groningen, Holland
Buske, Henriette	29, July 1886	2, July	69-10m- 8d	7		Anson, WI	Kowantz, Pommern
Busmann, Tobbi	16, Feb. 1879	16, May	43	191		Emden, IL	Dorum, Berum, Ostfriesland
Buß, Margaretha	16, Feb. 1899	26, Jan.	59	110		Keokuk, IA	
Buß, Friedrich	28, Aug. 1876	12, Aug.	69	279		Watertown, WI	Meesow, Regenwalde, Pommern
Buß, Hanna Wilhelmina Friedrika	19, Nov. 1896	4, Oct.	81	750	Buß	Rockham, SD	GroßBenz, Naugard, Pommern
Buß, Hilka Johanna	29, May 1882	3, May	50- 5m- 6d	175		San Jose, IL	Midlum, Reuterland, Ostfriesland
Buß, Luppe Luppen	28, Oct. 1897	8, Oct.	72	687		San Jose, IL	Neuefehn, Ostfriesland
Buß, Margarethe	26, June 1882	7, June	62	207		Elizabeth City, NJ	Mainz, Hessen
Buß, Wilhelm	10, Sept 1891	12, Aug.	65	590		Odebolt, IA	Lippe-Detmold
Buß, William	9, Mar. 1899	11, Feb.	52	158		Kewaskum, WI	Plantikow, Pommern
Bußaker, Catharina	3, Feb. 1873	30, Dec.	54	39		Bunker Hill, IL	Greps, Mecklenburg-Schwerin
Bußaker, Helene	24, Feb. 1873	23, Jan.	21	63		Bunker Hill, IL	Belleville, Illinois
Bussard, Lorette	8, Sept 1887	20, Aug.	17	574			Darke County, Ohio
Busse, (Mrs)	10, May 1849	30, Mar.	52- 2m	76		Monroe, IL	
Busse, Anna	12, Mar. 1866	19, Jan.	65	86		Milwaukee, WI	Stafelde, Preußen
Busse, Anton	11, Apr. 1864	15, Jan.	62	60		Red Bud, IL	Illse, Minden, Preußen

Christliche Apologete Death Notices --- 1839 - 1899

Name of Deceased	Notice Date	Death Date	Age	Page	Maiden Name	Place of Death	Place of Birth
Busse, Charles	22, Mar. 1888	8, Feb.	50	190		Chicago, IL	Gnesen, Posen
Busse, Heinrich	20, Jan. 1879	1, Jan.	18- 1m-18d	23		Clayton, WI	Milwaukee, Wisconsin
Busse, John	25, Mar. 1897	25, Feb.	72	190		Appleton, WI	Craatzen, Brandenburg
Busse, Karl	23, Apr. 1865	16, Mar.	28	68		Milwaukee, WI	Craazel, Neumark
Busse, Katharina Elisabeth	23, Apr. 1865	1, Apr.		68	Pagenhart	Blue Island, IL	Hombressen, Amt Hofgeismar, Kurhessen
Buße, Martin F.	18, Feb. 1884	28, Jan.	90	7		Clayton, IA	Uckermark, Preußen
Busse, Therese Barbara Elisabeth	19, Apr. 1860	3, Apr.	28	64	Langbein	Red Bud, IL	
Bußhaker, Ludwig	13, Aug. 1883	23, July	65- -16d	263		Red Bud, IL	Grebs, Eldena, Mecklenburg-Schwerin
Bussian, Henriette	18, Sept 1876	21, Aug.	68	303	Sänger	Rochester, MN	Posen
Bußman, Antonie Katharine	3, May 1894	12, Apr.	27	294		Yellow Creek, IL	Haselüne, Hannover
Bußmann, Adina	29, Dec. 1884	7, Dec.	25-11m-17d	7		Beardstown, IL	
Bußmann, Claumer Adolph	25, Feb. 1892	23, Jan.	70	126		Beardstown, IL	Osnabrück, Hannover
Bußmann, Geske	25, Sept 1890	3, Sept	75- 9m	622		Mascoutah, IL	Kirchdorf, Aurich, Ostfriesland
Bußmann, Joseph Franklin	17, Sept 1883	16, Aug.	28	303		Beardstown, IL	Beardstown, Illinois
Bußmann, Sina	26, Nov. 1891	2, Nov.	91- 6m-19d	766	Chellie	Wilber, NE	Bunde, Ostfriesland
Bußmann, Wilhelm	27, Dec. 1869	13, Dec.	60	415		Mascoutah, IL	Kirchdorf, Amt Aurich, Hannover
Bußmann, Wilhelmine F.	28, May 1891	27, Apr.	38- 8m- 5d	350		Mascoutah, IL	Kirchdorf, Aurich, Ostfriesland
Bußmann, William A.	13, Oct. 1898	25, Sept	24	655		Winona, MN	New Memphis, Clinton County, Illinois
Bustrin, Lina	12, Jan. 1899	20, Dec.	28	30	Kölliker	Golden City, MO	Thalweil, Zürich, Schweiz
Büthe, Heinrich Gerhard	27, Mar. 1882	6, Mar.	79- 6m	103		Schulenburg, TX	Delfshausen, Rastede, Oldenburg
Buthmann, Annette	17, Sept 1883	27, Aug.	47	303		Concordia, MO	Quelkhorn, Zeven, Hannover
Buthmann, Cordt	25, Oct. 1875	12, Oct.	43	343		Concordia, MO	Surheide bei Quarqaer, Ottersberg, Hannover
Buthmann, Katharina	2, Oct. 1876	18, Sept	64- 8m	319		Concordia, MO	Bredenau, Hannover
Buthmann, Meta	4, Sept 1890	31, July	25	574		Warrenton, MO	Surheide, Zeven, Hannover
Buthoff, Heinrich	2, Oct. 1890	3, Aug.	14	638		Cincinnati, OH	Covington, Kenton County, Kentucky
Butler, William (Rev)	24, Aug. 1899		81	536		Old Orchard, ME	Ireland
Buttelmann, Herman	20, Apr. 1899	4, Mar.	76	254		Montague, MI	Schlambeck, Hannover
Buttenhoff, Henriette	20, Oct. 1898	31, Aug.	83	670	Gründemann	Lewis, IA	Nehmer bei Kolberg, Germany
Buttke, Clara Martha	8, Nov. 1894	17, Oct.	11	726		Willow Creek, WI	Poysippi, Wisconsin
Buttke, Johan	19, Jan. 1899	2, Dec.	64	47		Willow Creek, WI	Deutschkron, West Preußen
Buttke, Minnie	13, Aug. 1896	20, July	18	527		Neenah, WI	Poysippi, Waushora County, Wisconsin
Buttlemann, Maria Friederike W.	30, Nov. 1893	3, Nov.	64	766		Montague, MI	Preußen
Büttner, (Mr)	2, Nov. 1854	20, Oct.	56- 2m	176		Morrisania, NJ	Neuenkirchen bei Melle, Amt Groneberg, Hannover
Büttner, Anna Katharina	24, May 1880	4, May	70- 6m	167		New York City, NY	Blatz, Baiern
Büttner, Anna Maria	7, Mar. 1864	21, Feb.		40	Honnecker	Aurora, IN	Maudach, Baiern
Büttner, Christina	31, Jan. 1889	11, Jan.	38- 6m- 7d	78		Chicago, IL	Heurote, Kurhessen
Büttner, Eduard	4, Aug. 1892	5, July	28	494		Portsmouth, OH	Portsmouth, Scioto County, Ohio
Büttner, Elisabeth	19, July 1880	27, June	58- 2m-25d	231	Kanz	Clarington, OH	
Büttner, Elisabethe	5, Nov. 1865	20, Oct.	51	180		Lawrenceburg, IN	Maudach, Baiern
Büttner, John	27, Nov. 1865	11, Nov.	53	192		Lawrenceburg, IN	Maudach, Rheinkreis Baiern
Büttner, John A.	28, Mar. 1895	5, Mar.	76	206		Baltimore, MD	Darmstadt, Hessen-Darmstadt
Büttner, Magdalena	1, Sept 1884	11, Aug.	74- 2m-15d	7	Heintzen	Toledo, OH	Oppau, Frankenthal, Rheinkreis Baiern
Büttner, Ursual	23, June 1859	9, May		100		St. Louis, MO	
Buttschau, Peter	23, July 1877	3, June	67- 2m-25d	239		Davenport, IA	Insel Behmen, Germany
Butz, Andreas	17, June 1878	28, May	51	191		Kendallville, IN	Greißheim, Württemberg
Butz, Catharina	2, June 1887	10, May	39	350	Kolbe	Marietta, OH	Odendorf, Geilsdorf, Württemberg

- 72 -

Christliche Apologete Death Notices --- 1839 - 1899

Name of Deceased	Notice Date	Death Date	Age	Maiden Name	Page	Place of Death	Place of Birth
Butz, Maria Anna	23, Dec. 1897	25, Nov.	85	Nagel	815	Cincinnati, OH	Kanton Basel, Schweiz
Butz, Theobald	20, May 1897	26, Apr.	79		319	Decorah, IA	Renchen, Baden
Butzke, Wilhelmine	27, Oct. 1892		76	Schild	686	Salina, KS	Ukermark-Sehausen bei Brentzlau, Germany
Buxmann, Georg	21, May 1896		28		334	Columbus, OH	Groß-Lieberau, Hessen-Darmstadt
Buyer, Catharina	19, Dec. 1889	28, Nov.	67- 8m-27d	Bahnmüller	814	Louisville, KY	Beutelsbach, Württemberg
Byron, Maria Sophia	20, Oct. 1884	16, Sept	84- 7m	Jordan	7	Iron Ridge, WI	Alt-Litzegericke, Königsberg, Brandenburg
Cadonau, Maria Virginia	4, Mar. 1886	18, Jan.	6		7	Taylor Bridge, OH	
Caflisch, David	17, July 1890	3, May	57		462	Brillion, WI	Hohentrinß, Graubünden, Schweiz
Caflisch, Jakob	5, Sept 1881	19, Aug.	79- 6m- 1d		287	Brillion, WI	Hohentrins, Graubündten, Schweiz
Caflisch, Ursula	26, Sept 1889	18, Aug.	82	Colonder	619	Brillion, WI	Hohendring, Graubünden, Schweiz
Cagney, Christina	11, Apr. 1881	26, Mar.	29- 3m-22d	Eisenhart	119	Waverly, OH	
Cagney, Christina	18, Apr. 1881		57- 1m- 8d	Eisenhart	127	Waverly, OH	
Cahl, Anna Catharina	19, Dec. 1864	24, Nov.	15		204	Charlestown, IN	Diedenbergen, Amt Hochheim, Nassau
Calmerten, Johannes	18, Apr. 1881	25, Feb.	19- 3m-22d		127	Sheboygan, WI	
Campel, Maria	21, May 1877	15, Apr.	72-11m- 1d	Menger	166	Delhi, MI	Dayton, Montgomery County, Ohio
Campmann, Elisabeth	26, Oct. 1885	11, Oct.	58		7	Pekin, IL	Hittenhausen, Erfurt, Minden, Preußen
Camus, Maria Dorothea	16, June 1862	28, May	35	Teke	96	Chicago, IL	
Canman, Leopold	7, June 1849	19, May	8- 6m- 5d		92	St. Louis, MO	St. Louis, Missouri
Cantieny, Dominic	17, June 1872	14, May	42- 3m-18d		199	St. Louis, MO	Andeer, Graubünden, Schweiz
Cantieny, Nicolaus	1, Feb. 1875	15, Jan.	39		39	Lima, OH	Reischen, Graubünden, Schweiz
Cantieny, Philipp	5, July 1869	10, June	33		215	St. Louis, MO	
Canton, Maria	16, Apr. 1857	31, Mar.			64	Galena, IL	
Capelle, Carl	15, Aug. 1850	2, Aug.			132	Columbus, OH	
Carl, Anna Maria	20, Nov. 1871	2, Nov.		Hartmann	375	Warsaw, IL	Retha, Preußen
Carl, Johannes	1, Dec. 1892	14, Nov.	55		766	Warsaw, IL	Oberscheid, Dillenburg, Nassau
Carl, Louisa	7, Mar. 1889	3, Feb.	73		158	Mt. Vernon, NY	Katzenfurt, Wetzlar, Koblenz, Preußen
Carl, Rosanna M.	21, Jan. 1897	26, Dec.	24	Würfel	46	Jeffersonville, IN	Braunfels, RheinPreußen
Carmann, Margaretha	24, May 1894	14, Apr.	45	Stetter	342	New York City, NY	Louisville, Jefferson County, Kentucky
Carpenter, Gabriel	10, July 1882	25, June	49- 6m-17d		223	Junction City, KS	Kirchart, Sinsheim, Baden
Carpenter, Wilhelm	17, Apr. 1882	5, Apr.	18- 2m		127	Junction City, KS	
Carr, Pauline	8, Aug. 1889	29, June	50		510	Randolph, KS	
Carrell, Johann	18, Mar. 1867	21, Feb.	39		86	Red Wing, MN	Hochdorf, Weiblingen, Württemberg
Carson, Margaretha	12, July 1894	20, June	40- 1m-26d	Ziegler	454	Marrs, IN	Gundersheim bei Worms, Hessen-Darmstadt
Case, Catharina	17, June 1872	2, Feb.	35	Buttermeier	199	San Francisco, CA	St. Louis, Missouri
Casebeer, Isaac	9, July 1877	23, June	76		223	Blue Springs, NE	Sommerset County, Pennsylvania
Cash, Karolina	1, Nov. 1875	10, Oct.	23	Roggenfüß	351	Boonville, MO	St. Charles, Missouri
Casper, Magdalena	13, June 1870	30, May	48		191	Wyandotte, KS	Vackerade, Kurhessen
Casse, Luise	2, Mar. 1899	7, Feb.	74	Beckemeier	143	Warren, MO	Alverdiesen, Sternberg, Lippe-Detmold
Casse, Luise	16, Mar. 1899	7, Feb.	74	Beckemeier	175	Warren, MO	Alverdiesen, Sternberg, Lippe-Detmold
Caynor, Lucette Mina	3, Aug. 1899	24, July	27	Rauschkolb	495	St. Louis, MO	Belleville, Illinois
Cehrs, Christian	9, Feb. 1893	15, Dec.	75- 6m-14d		94	Hannibal, OH	Reutigen, Bern, Schweiz
Cehrs, Heinrich	14, Apr. 1887	27, Mar.	18		238	Baresville, OH	Monroe County, Ohio
Cerkemeyer, Elisa	20, Nov. 1876	29, July	76		375	Highland, IL	Seftigen, Bern, Schweiz
Chapmann, Edwin	8, Jan. 1883	15, Dec.	59		15	Oconomowoc, WI	
Charles, Anna Elisabeth	9, Sept 1878	24, Aug.	67		287	Eudora, KS	Packebusch, Magdeburg, Preußen

Christliche Apologete Death Notices --- 1839 - 1899

Name of Deceased	Notice Date	Death Date	Age	Maiden Name	Page	Place of Death	Place of Birth
Chers, Barbara	28, July 1898	28, June	69	Berger	479	Hannibal, OH	Steffesburg, Bern, Schweiz
Chickedanz, Catharina	6, May 1878	16, Apr.	68	Wenzen	143	Delaware, OH	Hessen-Darmstadt
Chilius, Kasper	23, Mar. 1899	8, Feb.	84		190	Jeffersonville, NY	Reichshofen, Gießen, Hessen-Darmstadt
Choitz, Anna	3, Nov. 1892	8, Oct.	25		702	Menominee, MI	Brick Creek, Michigan
Christ, Auguste	15, Oct. 1896	15, Sept		Hoh	671	Scranton, PA	Bausa, Sachsen
Christ, Dorothea	3, Nov. 1873	8, Oct.	25- 9m-24d	Schenk	351	Rochester, NY	Sulz, Württemberg
Christ, Maria Margaretha	11, Sept 1865	28, July	56	Adam	148	Dayton, OH	Allendorf, Preußen
Christ, Wilhelmine Karoline	28, July 1898	6, July	70		479	Owatonna, MN	Chur, Graubünden, Schweiz
Christberger, Catharina Elisabeth	10, May 1875	22, Apr.	44		151	Warsaw, IL	Garbenheim, Kreis Wetzlar, Preußen
Christel, Johan Georg	1, Aug. 1870	15, July	77		247	Wathena, KS	Weißdorf bei Schurgast, Falkenberg, Schlesien
Christel, Johanna Christiana	21, Jan. 1884	5, Jan.	73		7	Wathena, KS	
Christen, Johanna	14, Oct. 1878	29, Sept	39	Schreiber	327	Summerfield, IL	Freudenberg, Westphalen
Christensen, Andreas	28, June 1894	16, Apr.	57		422	Clarks, OR	Hadensleben, Schleswig
Christian, Ernst	11, Feb. 1878	21, Jan.	50		47	Wausau, WI	Hermannsdorf, Naugart, Stettin, Preußen
Christian, Rosina	4, Nov. 1867	16, Oct.	21- 6m		350	Canal Dover, OH	
Christian, Wilhelm	9, June 1873	25, May	30		183	Warsaw, IL	Liebelsheim, Kreis Alzey, Hessen
Christianer, Jobst A.	29, June 1874	5, June	78		207	Beardstown, IL	Güsede, Essen, Amt Wittlage, Hannover
Christianer, Johan Friedrich	11, Aug. 1898	12, July	77		510	Arenzville, IL	Hüsede, Wittlage, Hannover
Christianer, Maria Engel	1, Feb. 1869	6, Jan.	75	Adams	39	Beardstown, IL	Harpenfeld, Essen, Hannover
Christianer, Wilhelm Eduard	19, Mar. 1891	18, Feb.	28		190	Arenzville, IL	
Christiani, Christine	12, Mar. 1877	20, Feb.	57	Horstmann	87	Batesville, IN	Stemmer, Minden, Preußen
Christiansen, O.C.	14, Mar. 1889	21, Feb.	44		174	Des Moines, IA	Kopenhagen, Dänemark
Christiene, L.	30, Aug. 1875	14, Aug.	65		279	Cincinnati, OH	Dannstadt, Mutterstadt, Preußen
Christina, Albert	18, Sept 1890	1, Aug.	30		606	Indianapolis, IN	Lawrenceburg, Dearborn County, Indiana
Christina, Dietrich	18, Jan. 1849	28, Dec.	26		12	Cincinnati, OH	
Christina, Georg Michael	9, Jan. 1862		68		8	Monona, IA	Dannstadt, Rheinkreis Baiern
Christina, Jacob	7, Mar. 1895	18, Feb.	66		158	Des Moines, IA	Mutterstadt, Rheinkreis Baiern
Christina, Joseph E.	22, Apr. 1886	31, Mar.	20		7	Lawrenceburg, IN	
Christina, Margaretha	1, Mar. 1875	12, Feb.	74	Gärtner	71	Giard, IA	Mutterstadt, Rheinkreis Baiern
Christina, Margaretha	1, Aug. 1889	12, July	62- 5m- 2d	Marquardt	494	Indianapolis, IN	Hochdorf, Württemberg
Christina, Maria	1, July 1867	12, June	53		206	Cincinnati, OH	Neustadt, Hannover
Christina, Maria Catharina	16, Dec. 1854	27, Oct.	63- 9m		200	Pennsylvanienburg, IN	Dannstadt, Rheinkreis Baiern
Christina, Martin	12, Sept 1850	25, Aug.	24		148	Lawrenceburg, IN	Mutterstadt, Rheinkreis Baiern
Christina, Sarah	23, Oct. 1890	2, Oct.	64	Smith	686	Des Moines, IA	Rohrau, Herrenberg, Württemberg
Christina, Valentin	29, Sept 1848	22, June	17		160	Lawrenceburg, IN	
Christine, Maria	27, Dec. 1894	21, Nov.	51		836	Cincinnati, OH	Cincinnati, Hamilton County, Ohio
Christlieb, Th.	12, Sept 1889	16, Aug.	56		585	Bonn, GE	
Christman, John	11, Oct. 1894	23, Sept	33	Neff	662	Topeka, KS	Wallerstädten, Groß-Gerau, Hessen-Darmstadt
Christmann, Anna Maria	18, Jan. 1869	2, Jan.	22		23	Bucyrus, OH	Lycomen County, Pennsylvania
Christmann, Barbara Elisabeth	7,May 1883	24, Apr.	64	Bender	151	Topeka, KS	Wallerstädten, Hessen-Darmstadt
Christmann, Eva	26, June 1890	31, May	73- 2m-14d	Reichert	414	Brookville, IN	Kries, Brumpt , Elsaß
Christmann, Martin	17, Feb. 1887		70		110	Batesville, IN	Oberhofen bei Bischweiler, Elsaß
Christmann, Peter	1, Jan. 1877	28, Nov.	29- 6m		7	Carroll Co., MO	
Christmann, Philipp	4, May 1854	6, Apr.	47		72	Brunswick, MO	Milsenbach, Baiern
Christnagel, Margaretha	8, July 1886	14, June	74		7	Fond du Lac, WI	
Christoffer, Heinrich	2, Feb. 1893	11, Jan.	66		78	Huntingburg, IN	Legenich, Tekenburg, Münster, Preußen

Christliche Apologete Death Notices --- 1839 - 1899

Name of Deceased	Notice Date	Death Date	Age	Page	Maiden Name	Place of Death	Place of Birth
Christoffer, Herman	9, Aug. 1888	18, July	25	510		Denver, CO	Bremerhaven, Germany
Christoffer, Louis Ora	26, Nov. 1896	28, Oct.	18	766		Gibson Co, IN	Huntingburg, Dubois County, Indiana
Christoffer, Louisa Carolina	27, Apr. 1893	12, Apr.	30	270	Rademacher	Huntingburg, IN	Pike County, Indiana
Christophel, Abraham	26, Jan. 1885	26, Dec.	53- 6m-11d	7		Herscher, IL	Alsheim, Hessen-Darmstadt
Chytraus, Karl	17, May 1894	5, May	40	326		Batesville, IN	Beslau, Schlesien
Claassen, Heinrich Janßen	27, Aug. 1896	6, Aug.	17	559		San Jose, IL	Hartsburg, Illinois
Clantz, John Albert	11, Dec. 1882	7, Oct.	24-11m-15d	399		Chicago, IL	Carrol County, Missouri
Clarenbach, Wilhelmina	13, Dec. 1869	21, Nov.	60	399		Jefferson City, MO	Rade vorm Wald, Preußen
Clark, Christian Friedrich	18, Feb. 1897	25, Jan.	39	111		Greenville, OH	Pikeville, Darke County, Ohio
Clark, John	6, Feb. 1890	16, Jan.	64	94		Aurora, IN	Erfurt, Preußen
Clarke, Marie	2, Nov. 1854	17, Oct.	17	176		Aurora, IN	
Claß, Christian	6, Mar. 1890	17, Feb.	46	158		Lafayette, IN	Zeingen, Urach, Württemberg
Claß, Christiane	21, Aug. 1890	23, July	41	542	Gassert	Newport, KY	Hochberg, Württemberg
Claß, Elisabeth Jane	3, Nov. 1884	21, Aug.	16	7		Greenfield, MA	
Claß, Margarethe	19, Oct. 1899	29, Sept	57	671	Seibert	Greenfield, MA	Waldlaubersheim, Kreuzach, RheinPreußen
Classe, Carl	28, July 1887	12, July	44	478		Seguin, TX	Liebenwalde bei Berlin, Germany
Classen, Catharina Margaretha	1, Feb. 1869	5, Jan.	41- 7m-28d	39		San Jose, IL	Eversmer, Amt Essens, Ostfriesland
Classen, Ida Augusta	27, July 1893	23, June	17	478		Toledo, OH	Kiel, Schleswig-Holstein
Claus, August	11, Mar.1872	17, Feb.	43	87		Kingston, IL	Bielefeld, Preußen
Claus, Catharine	22, Feb. 1875	3, Feb.	65- 1m-22d	63	Grünewald	Vermillion, OH	Obermöllrich, Kreis Fritzlar, Kurhessen
Claus, Gottfried	18, May 1863	29, Apr.	68	80		Blue Island, IL	Weißensee, Erfurt, Preußen
Claus, Maria Barbara	17, June 1886	3, June	72	7	Jakob	Baltimore, MD	Württemberg
Claus, Maria Elisabeth	2, Mar. 1899	9, Feb.	48	143	Biltz	Newport, KY	Newport, Campbell County, Kentucky
Claus, Nikolaus	10, Nov. 1892	15, Sept	80	718		Monroefield, OH	Herfeld, Spangenberg, Melsungen, Hessen
Clausen, Heinrich	10, Aug. 1899	21, July	75	511		Faribault, MN	Westertreia, Schleswig-Holstein
Clausen, Theodor	6, Aug. 1877	3, July		255		Sheboygan, WI	
Clausewitz, Gustav	30, June 1884	7, June	81	7		Hochheim, TX	Burg, Sachsen
Clausing, Friedrich	24, July 1890	1, July	18- 6m	478		Portsmouth, OH	Portsmouth, Scioto County, Ohio
Clausing, Friedrich	18, Sept 1871	27, Aug.	67	303		Portsmouth, OH	Heringhausen,
Clauß, Magdalena	9, Nov. 1893	21, Oct.	62	718	Seeger	Elizabeth, NJ	Böchingen, Rheinpfalz Baiern
Clauter, Apollonia	28, Nov. 1864	21, Sept	27	192	Falter	Jerseyville, IL	Eppelsheim, Hessen-Darmstadt
Clemenz, Dorothea Elisabeth	6, Feb. 1882	7, Jan.	81- -26d	47		Batesville, IN	Ordmanhausen, Sachsen-Weimar
Clemens, Ernst	17, Nov. 1873	11, Oct.	33	367		Chicago, IL	
Clemens, Heinrich	21, Apr. 1884	30, Mar.	20	7		Fond du Lac, WI	Treplin, Köslin, Pommern
Clemens, Karoline	26, May 1884	10, May	41	7	Behringer	Lafayette, IN	Schlierbach, Göppingen, Württemberg
Clemens, Magdalena	15, Nov. 1880	21, Oct.	62- 2m-21d	367		Faribault, MN	Canton Bern, Schweiz
Clements, (Mrs)	24, July 1865	25, May	76- 1m- 6d	120		Batesville, IN	Ilbesheim, Landau, Baiern
Clemenz, Johannes	14, May 1891	22, Apr.	35	318		Brookville, IN	
Clewe, Karoline	2, Nov. 1863	15, Sept	31	176	Bruns	Jackson, MO	Wolfenbüttel, Braunschweig
Clifford, Sophia D.	17, July 1890	27, June	49- 6m-21d	462		Chicago, IL	Suelten, Mecklenburg-Schwerin
Clobes, Georg	2, Apr. 1896		49-1m-14d	222		Muscatine, IA	Rindau, Melsungen, Hessen-Kassel
Clobes, Hermine	2, Apr. 1896		37- 6m	222	Schilling	Muscatine, IA	
Cloes, Heinrich	15, Mar. 1860	2, Nov.	28	44		Kenosha, IL	Mirkenbach, Amt Herborn, Nassau
Cloes, Hiram	15, Mar. 1860	3, Dec.		44		Kenosha, IL	
Cloes, Katharine Elisabeth	19, Feb. 1872	26, Jan.	68	63	Dietrich	Lamonte, MO	Merkenbach, Herborn, Nassau
Close, Maria Elisabeth	23, Oct. 1890	3, Oct.	39-11m-13d	686	Meyers	Edgerton, OH	Milford Township, Defiance County, Ohio

- 75 -

Christliche Apologete Death Notices -- 1839 - 1899

Name of Deceased	Maiden Name	Place of Death	Page	Age	Death Date	Notice Date	Place of Birth
Cloßmann, Maria		Lemars, IA	7	73	26, Oct.	17, Nov. 1884	Hof Grabow, Crewitz, Mecklenburg-Schwerin
Clotz, Fr.		St. Louis, MO	95	83	28, Feb.	22, Mar. 1880	Vaihingen an der Enz, Württemberg
Clump, Anna Maria		Freeport, IL	39	74	17, Jan.	3, Feb. 1873	Freudenstadt, Württemberg
Clut, Helena		Alden, IA	254	26	25, Mar.	21, Apr. 1887	Naugard, Hinterpommern
Clute, Anna Charlotte Sophia	Wegner	Fairbault, MN	7	34-10m-20d	18, Feb.	3, Mar. 1884	Neuenkirchen, Freudenberg, Hannover
Clymer, Heinrich Landes	Gronewald	St. Louis, MO	350	46- 7m	13, May	2, June 1887	Richland, Pennsylvania
Coates, Ella A.		St. Louis, MO	686	33	8, Oct.	25, Oct. 1888	Burlington, Iowa
Coender, Anna Maria	Koeneke	Cleveland, OH	78	78	26, Dec.	30, Jan. 1896	Bauigen, Bern, Schweiz
Coffmann, Isaak	Rauch	Omaha, NE	311	46	1, Sept	27, Sept 1875	Union County, Pennsylvania
Cohlmeier, Christina		Nashville, IL	72	9	8, Mar.	5, May 1862	
Cohlmeyer, Carl Friedrich Wilhelm		Hoyleton, IL	398	68	12, May	20, June 1895	Husbergen, Germany
Cohlmeyer, Christine	Meyer	Hoyleton, IL	543	77	2, Aug.	24, Aug. 1899	
Colberg, Wilhelmine	Schulz	Sheboygan, WI	124	34	20, June	4, Aug. 1862	Eichstedt, Preußen
Coleman, Wilhemine Maria	Berg	Monroe, WI	718	59- 8m- 6d	14, Sept	10, Nov. 1892	Dölitz, Preußen
Colihan, Emilie	Wendler	Elmore, OH	510	26	18, July	7, Aug. 1890	Woodville, Sandusky County, Ohio
Collmann, Gredge	Gerdes	Tecumseh, NE	31	30	23, Dec.	23, Jan. 1875	Aurich, Foßberg, Hannover
Collmann, Hege H.		Macon, NE	582	66	17, Aug.	6, Sept 1894	Strakholt, Aurich, Ostfriesland
Collmann, Mootyes	Fockenga	Humboldt, NE	215	82	1, May	5, July 1880	Aurich, Ostfriesland
Colonius, Catharina Elisabeth	Maxeimer	Alton, IL	8	61- 7m	29, Oct.	10, Jan. 1856	Werlau, Saar, Preußen
Colonius, Elisabeth	Knoblauch	St. Louis, MO	127			15, Apr. 1872	Steinau, Schlichten, Kurhessen
Colonius, Elisabeth M.	Meffert	Alton, IL	558	71- 8m-11d	1, Aug.	29, Aug.1895	Steinsberg, Diez, Nassau
Colonius, Johan Philip		Nokomis, IL	606	73-11m- 8d	25, Aug.	18, Sept 1890	Lierschied, St. Goarshausen, Nassau
Colonius, Maria Katharina	Hübinger	St. Charles, MO	144	31	26, July	8, Sept 1859	Reigehein, Hessen-Kassel
Colonius, Peter Karl		Alton, IL	7	62	9, Mar.	24, Mar. 1884	Lürschied, St. Goarshausen, Nassau
Combrink, Wilhelmina	Vombrok	Secor, IL	135	52	21, Feb.	23, Apr. 1877	Bergholzhausen, Minden, Preußen
Conrad, Barbara	Blaum	Elizabeth, NJ	7	68	22, Mar.	15, Apr. 1886	Rockenhausen, Baiern
Conrad, Elisabeth	Kaus	Mankato, MN	814	43	30, Oct.	18, Dec. 1890	Weickartshain, Grünberg, Hessen-Darmstadt
Conrad, Elise Rebekka	VonHäfen	Bristol, WI	751	80	26, Oct.	24, Nov. 1898	Hammelwarden, Oldenburg
Conrad, Ernestina	Kaufmann	Watertown, WI	31	40	3, Jan.	24, Jan. 1876	
Conrad, Fr. Wilhelm (Rev)		Watertown, WI	80	25	8, Apr.	16, May 1864	Batzlow, Preußen
Conrad, Franz		St. Louis, MO	814	38- 3m-19d	21, Nov.	18, Dec. 1890	Ruschinowitz, Schlesien
Conrad, Gottfried		Sheboygan, WI	382	80	3, Nov.	26, Nov. 1866	Dölzig, Preußen
Conrad, Johanna Charlotte	Conrad	Kewaunee, WI	71	83- 5m- 3d	21, Jan.	26, Feb. 1883	Dölzig, Preußen
Conrad, John		Elizabeth, NJ	575	78	1, Aug.	3, Sept 1896	Dielkirchen, Rheinpfalz Baiern
Conrad, Karl		St. Louis, MO	302	53	11, Apr.	7, May 1896	Ruschinewitz, Schlesien
Conrad, Karl		Ann Arbor, MI	7	75	1, Apr.	15, Apr. 1886	Ruppur, Baden
Conrad, Maria	Brethauer	Elizabeth, NJ	510	39	17, July	10, Aug. 1893	Oberlaufungen bei Cassel, Germany
Conrad, Minnie	Thek	Lamberton, MN	719	42	18, Oct.	10, Nov. 1898	Wisconsin
Conradi, Anna Katharina Sophia		Newark, NJ	351	13	25, Sept	1, Nov. 1869	Marbach, Marburg, Kurhessen
Conradi, Johan		Newark, NJ	47	67	16, Dec.	19, Jan. 1899	Dothenhausen, Frankenberg, Kurhessen
Conradi, John		Newark, NJ	231	17	1, July	17, July 1882	
Conradi, Lilli		Newark, NJ	359	11- 9m-11d		5, Nov. 1877	Newark, New Jersey
Conradi, Maria Caroline		Newark, NJ	135	15-10m-27d	8, Apr.	28, Apr. 1879	
Conrady, C.A. (Dr)		Stockton, CA	46		16, Dec.	18, Jan. 1894	
Conrath, Barbara	Leonhardt	Ann Arbor, MI	447	63	20, June	9, July 1896	Dingenhausen, Baden
Conzmann, Katharina		Terre Haute, IN	319	69	25, Apr.	18, May 1899	Echterdingen, Württemberg

Christliche Apologete Death Notices --- 1839 - 1899

Name of Deceased	Notice Date	Death Date	Age	Maiden Name	Page	Place of Death	Place of Birth
Cook, Bonne Moritz	7, July 1873	11, May	80- 4m-12d		215	Peoria, IL	Ostdörp, Ostfriesland
Cook, Georg W.	23, Feb. 1899	3, Feb.	68		126	Red Wing, MN	Adolfsdorf, Lilienthal bei Bremen, Germany
Cook, Sophrana	11, Feb. 1867	14, Jan.	24- 11d	Meier	46	Red Wing, MN	Schweiz
Coors, Karl Louis	22, Apr. 1872		20- 1m-13d		135	Muskegon, MI	Chicago, Cook County, Illinois
Cordes, Catharine	1, June 1874	30, Apr.	62	Mahnden	175	Lake Creek, MO	Wilstett, Amt Ottersberg, Hannover
Cordes, Christian	11, Jan. 1849		Inquiry		7	St. Louis, MO	Kleinfahlingen, Amt Wölpe,
Cordes, Dorothea	21, Dec. 1868	23, Nov.	73	Krumwiede	407	Lake Creek, MO	Wenden, Amt Wölpe, Hannover
Cordes, Friedrich	7, Apr. 1879	9, Mar.	55		111	Lake Creek, MO	Wenden, Amt Walpern, Hannover
Cordes, Heinrich Georg	9, May 1895	13, Apr.	46		302	Ansley, NE	Ahausen, Hannover
Cordes, Henry	14, May 1891	18, Apr.	47		318	Concordia, MO	Wilsted, Hannover
Cordes, Herman	26, May 1884	26, Apr.	34- 3m-15d		7	Denver, CO	Willstedt, Hannover
Cordes, Johan Heinrich	21, Apr. 1879	22, Mar.	70		127	Sedalia, MO	Ottersberg, Hannover
Cordes, Lüder	20, June 1895	30, May			398	Bloomington, IL	Nesse, Lohn, Hannover
Cordes, Trine	7, Apr. 1879	10, Mar.	49	Ringe	111	Lake Creek, MO	Breddorf, Hannover
Corelis, Louise	28, Apr. 1862	28, Mar.	33- 1m	Brinkmann	68	Newport, KY	Holzhausen, Amt Lübbeke, Preußen
Corleissen, Anna Maria	26, Apr. 1894	29, Mar.		Pfefinger	278	Florence, MO	Vermosa, Canada
Cornelius, Maria	2, Feb. 1899	4, Jan.	81	Dilk	79	Duluth, MN	Spießen, Preußen
Cornelius, Valentin	4, Aug. 1879	10, July	60		247	Newport, KY	Nußdorf bei Landau, Rheinpfalz Baiern
Cortes, Luzia	19, May 1887	30, Apr.	67	Janner	318	Cincinnati, OH	Mainfeld, Graubündten, Schweiz
Corvey, Sophia Wilhelmina	29, Sept 1892	1, Sept	34	Tempel	622	Nashville, TN	Smiths Creek, Warren County, Missouri
Corvey, William	18, Dec. 1890	7, Nov.	76		814	Big Spring, MO	Lemgo, Lippe-Detmold
Corweg, Willie	23, Mar. 1893	6, Mar.	14		190	Big Spring, MO	
Cott, Anna	9, Apr. 1896	12, Mar.	51		238	New Florence, MO	
Courts, Franz Arnold	9, Apr. 1866	23, Jan.	63		118	Dubuque, IA	Württemberg
Crack, Eva	8, Dec. 1862	17, Nov.	62	Bachmann	196	Burlington, IA	Pohlhausen, RheinPreußen
Cramer, Augusta	14, May 1896	15, Apr.	74	Margrander	318	Galion, OH	Hempfield, Westmoreland County, Pennsylvania
Cramer, Friedrich (Rev)	2, Sept 1897	6, Aug.	55- 5m- 4d		559	East St. Louis, IL	Karlsruhe, Baden
Cramer, Heinrich Wilhelm	26, Aug. 1897	10, Aug.	25		543	Newport, KY	Hasbergen, Oldenburg
Cramer, Jakob Herron	8, July 1872	7, May	50		223	Batesville, IN	Dörtendorf, Sachsen-Weimar
Crämer, Margaretha	23, Nov. 1874	3, Nov.	44		375	Beardstown, IL	Norden, Ostfriesland
Cramm, Margaretha	23, Jan. 1896	2, Jan.	43	Steiner	62	St. Louis, MO	England
Cramm, Sophia	5, Apr. 1888	10, Mar.	38	Surmann	222	Bushton, KS	Malaus, St. Gallen, Schweiz
Craß, Johanna	22, Mar. 1888	27, Feb.	80- 7m	Eggelte	190	Bushton, KS	Huntingburgh, Indiana
Credi, Emma	17, Nov. 1898	25, Oct.	57	Clarenbach	735	Sandusky, OH	Amsterdam, Holland
Cree, Sophia	23, Oct. 1890	24, Sept	84- 7m		686	Jefferson City, MO	Westphalia, Osage County, Missouri
Cremer, Gretje	20, June 1889	2, June	69- 4m-20d	Menninga	398	Goshen, IN	Mecklenburg-Schwerin
Cremer, Heinrich	16, Aug. 1875	17, July	57		263	Clatonia, NE	Folkum, Essens, Ostfriesland
Crepon, Caroline	18, July 1889	24, June	39- 4m-29d		462	San Jose, IL	Arle, Amt Berum, Ostfriesland
Crepon, Eleonore	4, Apr. 1889	13, Mar.	65- 9m-12d		222	Muscatine, IA	Trenton, Ohio
Creß, Sophia	22, Sept 1887	2, Sept	40-11m- 4d	Schaaf	606	Muscatine, IA	Beuren, Kurhessen
Creß, Ursula	29, July 1867	25, June	34	Bruner	238	Warsaw, IL	Frankenstein, RheinPfalz Baiern
Cresson, Georg	19, Sept 1861	28, Aug.	47		152	Warsaw, IL	Cincinnati, Hamilton County, Ohio
Crick, Anna Maria	3, Nov. 1892	16, Oct.	80- 6m-24d		702	Muscatine, IA	Altenbraunslar, Melsungen, Kurhessen
Croll, H.C.	16, Sept 1886	20, Aug.	66- 4m		7	Chillicothe, OH	Lampertheim, Hessen-Darmstadt
Crolow, Louise M.	14, Mar. 1889	18, Feb.	71	Feltmann	174	Eudora, KS	
Croman, Salome	22, Oct. 1896	20, Sept	85	Schweitzer	687	Huntingburg, IN	Hilgenbach, Westphalen
						Francisco, MI	Canton St. Gallen, Schweiz

Name of Deceased	Notice Date	Death Date	Age	Maiden Name	Page	Place of Death	Place of Birth
Cromann, Abraham	21, Feb. 1876	3, Feb.	88		63	Francisco, MI	Pennsylvania
Croshaus, Katharina	28, Oct. 1867	21, Sept	68- 8m-13d		342	Valparaiso, IN	Nagold, Württemberg
Croßman, Eduard Louis	3, Mar. 1887	17, Feb.	44		142	Toledo, OH	Funkstadt, Hessen-Darmstadt
Crovas, Johanna	10, Mar. 1879	2, Feb.	45	Man	79	Roberts, IL	Lehstin, Rügen, Pommern, Preußen
Crusius, Georg	5, Apr. 1880	6, Mar.	43		111	El Paso, IL	Kroppen, Rheinkreis Baiern
Cruwel, Sophia L.	23, Dec. 1878	26, Sept	29- 7m-12d	Schowengardt	407	Morrison, MO	Warren County, Missouri
Cuebeman, (Mr)	23, Aug. 1855	28, July	81-11m		136	New Albany, IN	Harspe bei Bramsche, Hannover
Cuininga, John	12, Aug. 1897	18, June	59		511	Hokah, MN	Petersbürum, Holland
Cull, Jacob Wesley	2, July 1891	9, June	24- 9m-29d		430	Marion, OH	Marion, Ohio
Cullen, Maria	9, July 1847	13, June	63		111	Pinckney, MO	Buhre, Hannover
Cumber, Georg	22, Jan. 1861	4, Dec.	27		16	Woodville, OH	
Curtin, Anna Maria	16, Apr. 1877	25, Mar.	31	Schäfer	127	Allegheny City, PA	Glasewitz, Amt Gustrow, Mecklenburg-Schwerin
Curtis, Sophia	24, Jan. 1876	10, Jan.	43	Behnke	31	Goshen, IN	Berlin, Germany
Custerer, Wilhelmine	9, Mar. 1893	9, Feb.	67	Koch	158	Baltimore, MD	Honesdale, Pennsylvania
Czerwinski, Anna Maria	6, Mar. 1876	10, Feb.	24	Heckmann	79	Scranton, PA	
Daab, Rosina	15, Jan. 1883	28, Dec.	43	Frank	23	White Creek, IN	Holmes County, Ohio
Daake, Henriette	16, Mar. 1893	23, Feb.	19		174	Flood Creek, IA	Ulster, Floyd County, Iowa
Dab, Ludwig	4, Apr. 1864	20, Mar.			56	Hamilton, CD	
Dabbert, Auguste Philippine	30, Sept 1878	3, Sept	35	Brimmer	311	Dunkirk, NY	Liepen, Stavenhagen, Mecklenburg
Däbel, Friedrich	30, Apr. 1891	8, Apr.	70		286	Toledo, OH	Katzow, Templin, Uckermark, Preußen
Däbel, Wilhelmina	2, Apr. 1891	14, Mar.	70	Müller	222	Toledo, OH	Rutenberg, Templin, Preußen
Daberkow, Franz	18, Nov. 1897	30, Oct.	23		735	Grand Island, NE	Voigtshagen bei Daber, Hinterpommern
Daberkow, Friederike	16, Mar. 1899	31, Jan.	68	Ulrich	174	Grand Island, NE	Leimhaggen, Grimm, Preußen
Dabler, Hanna Elisabeth	28, Dec. 1899	31, Oct.	69	Nehls	828	Waterford, WI	Boll, Göppingen, Württemberg
Dachroth, Angelika	15, May 1871	19, Apr.	50- 2m	Getty	159	Nauvoo, IL	Portsmouth, Scioto County, Ohio
Daehler, Dina Catharina	28, Apr. 1887	10, Apr.	26- 1m-29d		270	Portsmouth, OH	
Daehler, John Peter	16, Jan. 1890	24, Dec.	18- 6m-14d		46	Portsmouth, OH	
Daeling, Louis	23, May 1889	4, May	37		334	Red Bud, IL	
Dagit, Anna	29, Nov. 1880	24, Sept 1896	23- 4m-11d	Schneider	383	Summerfield, IL	Merxheim, RheinPreußen
Dagit, Jakob	22, Oct. 1896	24, Sept	87- 8m- 5d		687	Summerfield, IL	Merxheim, Rheinpreußen
Dagit, Louise Christina	6, Jan. 1879	21, Dec.	68- 8m-12d	Skaer	7	Summerfield, IL	Merzheim, Rheinkreis Baiern
Dagit, Michael	1, Apr. 1897	9, Mar.	62		206	Summerfield, IL	Mitweida, Sachsen
Dahde, Johanna Helene	4, Aug. 1887	18, July	70	Niederwever	494	Le Sueur, MN	Erbsloe, Lennup, Preußen
Dahl, Abraham	19, Apr. 1888	31, Mar.	67- 4m-21d		254	Le Sueur, MN	
Dahl, Anna Katharina	8, May 1876	22, Apr.	17- 2m-17d		151	Boston Highlands, MA	Oberrotterbach, Rheinkreis Baiern
Dahl, Catharina Margaretha	4, May 1874	2, Apr.	64		143	Boston, MA	
Dahl, Friedrich Wilhelm	22, Sept 1887	5, Sept	17		606	Boston, MA	Ober-Otterbach, Bergzabern, Rheinpfalz Baiern
Dahl, Heinrich	15, Oct. 1896	13, Sept	61		671	Le Sueur, MN	Hornberg, Württemberg
Dahl, Katharine	12, Nov. 1877	22, Oct.	56	Schaeff	367	Boston, MA	Oberotterbach, Rheinkreis Baiern
Dahl, Lorenz	20, Mar. 1882	15, Feb.	40-11m-13d		95	Le Sueur, MN	
Dahl, Marie E.	3, May 1875	29, Apr.	18		143	Marine City, MI	Giesdorf, Preußen
Dahlenburg, Maria	30, Apr. 1877	13, Apr.	74- - 5d		143	Portsmouth, OH	Kreidach, Heppenheim, Hessen-Darmstadt
Dähler, Anna Katharine	12, July 1894	26, June	60		454	Portsmouth, OH	Portsmouth, Ohio
Dähler, Margaretha Ella	14, Oct. 1886	22, Sept	24		7		Jungerwenning, Neuhaus, Hannover
Dähling, Marie	18, Dec. 1882	17, Nov.	70- 9m-17d	Engel	407	Red Bud, IL	

Christliche Apologete Death Notices --- 1839 - 1899

Name of Deceased	Notice Date	Death Date	Age	Page	Maiden Name	Place of Death	Place of Birth
Dahlte, Wilhelmine Christiane	3, Aug. 1868	7, July	51- 6m- 5d	247	Hoff	Buffalo, NY	Bärenwalder Glashütte, Schlochau, Preußen
Dahms, Anna M.E.	9, Jan. 1890	17, Dec.	35	30	Brunn	Defiance, OH	Kopenhagen, Dänemark
Dahn, Gesina	27, Nov. 1882	30, Oct.	58- -30d	383	Feiß	Brooklyn, NY	Morsum, Achim bei Bremen, Germany
Dähn, Johan	9, Jan. 1882	27, Dec.	64	15		Milwaukee, WI	Mühlenhagen, Demin, Vorpommern
Dahn, John A.	27, July 1899	22, Jan.	69	479		Brooklyn, NY	Oberndorf, Neuhaus an der Oster, Germany
Dähnert, Ottilie	11, Apr. 1881	20, Mar.	47- 3m-17d	119	Burow	Oconomowoc, WI	Megow, Piritz, Pommern
Dahnke, Frieda Johanna	17, May 1888	26, Apr.	16	318		Blue Island, IL	
Dahnke, John	19, Mar. 1896	17, Feb.	80	190		Palmer, TX	Malcow, Mecklenburg-Schwerin
Dahnke, Marie	19, Oct. 1899	15, Sept	23	671		Dallas, TX	Melvin, Ford County, Illinois
Dahnken, Cordt	14, Sept 1885	17, Aug.	43	7		Brooklyn, NY	Kloster-Moor, Lilienthal, Hannover
Dais, Anna Katharina	24, Mar. 1879	9, Mar.	50	95	Mäder	Madison, WI	Gannenbach, Mühlheim, Baden
Dais, Emilie	6, Sept 1894	14, Aug.	41	582	Weiner	Madison, WI	Bernsdorf bei Bieverau, Sachsen
Dais, Gottlieb	9, Oct. 1890	1, Sept	71	654		Madison, WI	Ober-Urbach, Schorndorf, Württemberg
Dais, J.J.	23, Aug. 1875		5-	271		Cincinnati, OH	Schmollenmühl, Oberbrüder, Württemberg
Daiß, Anna Barbara	7, Nov. 1870	2, Oct.	79	359	Schiek	Bonn, OH	Oberurbach, Schorndorf, Württemberg
Daiß, Christina	31, Aug. 1874	5, Aug.	67	279	Bückel	Milwaukee, WI	Oberurbach, Schorndorf, Württemberg
Daiß, Emma	26, Oct. 1885	7, Oct.	29	7	Jung	Wichita, KS	Columbus, Franklin County, Ohio
Daiß, Friederike	10, Nov. 1898	16, Oct.	91	719	Horn	Mt. Healthy, OH	Schmollenmühl, Backnang, Württemberg
Daiß, Georg	24, Mar. 1892	3, Mar.	84- 8m- 9d	190		Mt. Healthy, OH	Unterbrüden, Backnang, Württemberg
Daiß, Gottlieb	11, Nov. 1867	14, Oct.	58	358		Cincinnati, OH	Unterbrüden, Backnang, Württemberg
Daiß, Johann	1, Nov. 1844	20, Oct.	26	168		Cincinnati, OH	Unterbrüden, Backnang, Württemberg
Daiß, John Georg	5, May 1862	15, Apr.	68- 6m	72		Pomeroy, OH	Oberurbach, Schorndorf, Württemberg
Dal, Jacob (Rev)	8, Aug. 1895	18, July	72	510		Chicago, IL	Schönau, Baden
Dalenburg, Georg	6, Jan. 1859	13, Dec.	62	4		Newport, MI	
Dällenbach, Christian	22, Feb. 1875	15, Jan.	63- 3m	63		Highland, IL	Canton Bern, Schweiz
Dallenbach, Karl Gottfried	19, Oct. 1874	16, Sept	23-11m-22d	335		Hickland, IL	Canton Bern, Schweiz
Dallner, Effa Barbara	15, Nov. 1894	16, Oct.	18	742		Mt. Pleasant, IA	Lockridge Township, Jefferson County, Iowa
Dallner, Georg	4, Sept 1882	13, July	60- 1m-15d	287		Walnut Creek, IA	Aschbach, Rezat, Baiern
Dallwig, Anna Katharina	21, Jan. 1867	8, Jan.	62	22		Cincinnati, OH	Sandheim, Kreis Homberg, Kurhessen
Dallwig, Johann Heinrich	27, Dec. 1860	28, Nov.	58	208		Cincinnati, OH	
Dam, Dittmar	2, Feb. 1880	3, Jan.	12	39		Daytonville, IA	Geismar, Fritzlar, Kurhessen
Damaske, August	23, Feb. 1893	24, Jan.	75- 8m- 9d	126		Bloomington, IL	
Damaske, Charlotte W.	21, Nov. 1895	6, Nov.	55	750		St. Louis, MO	Dissen , Hannover
Damaske, Friedrich A.	28, Mar. 1881	12, Mar.	38	103		Bloomington, IL	Gerbro, Pommern
Damaski, Ernestine	8, Oct. 1891	1, Sept	72- 3m	654	Bock	Bloomington, IL	Charbrow, Lauenburg, Hinterpommern
Dambach, Christine Barbara	19, Jan. 1874	2, Jan.	24- 2m	23	Zimmermann	Newark, NJ	Koengen, Württemberg
Dambach, Elisabeth	13, Oct. 1898	15, Sept	72	655		Newark, NJ	Kingen, Württemberg
Damke, Anna Dorothea	14, Apr. 1884	13, Mar.	48	7	Lamme	Western, NE	Neuendorf am Speck, Magdeburg, Preußen
Damkroeger, Lidie	22, Dec. 1887	15, Nov.	29	814		San Francisco, CA	St. Paul, Minnesota
Damkröger, Anna Maria Louise C.	28, Mar. 1870	28, Feb.	34	103	Grumbach	St. Paul, MN	Blasheim, Preußen
Damkröger, Catharina	23, June 1873	23, May	36- 1m-17d	199		San Francisco, CA	Heddinghausen, Holzhausen, Preußen
Damkröger, Margaretha	28, Aug. 1876		40- 8m-21d	279	Hottendorf	San Francisco, CA	
Damm , Valentin	12, Oct. 1899	20, Aug.	80	655		Jeffersonville, NY	Greisfeld, Rheinkreis Baiern
Damm, Christian	12, Aug. 1858	19, May	40	128		Lansing, MI	Friedberg, Hessen-Darmstadt
Damm, Gottfried	10, Dec. 1883	6, Nov.	17	7		Buffalo, NY	
Damm, Johan Albert	15, Sept 1884	31, Aug.	36	7		Wheeling, WV	Wheeling, West Virginia

Christliche Apologete Death Notices --- 1839 - 1899

Name of Deceased	Notice Date	Death Date	Age	Maiden Name	Page	Place of Death	Place of Birth
Damm, Johan Heinrich	26, July 1875	7, July	66		239	Wheeling, WV	Dorle, Kurhessen
Damm, Karl	17, June 1878	31, May	47- 3m-28d		191	Buffalo, NY	
Damm, Katharina	23, Feb. 1893	17, Jan.	52	Adam	126	Brooklyn, NY	Nothweiler, Rheinpfalz Baiern
Damm, Luise	11, May 1899	2, Apr.	86	Wühlert	302	Jeffersonville, NY	Kammerborn, Schönhagen, Hannover
Damm, Magdalena	12, May 1892	18, Apr.	74- 1d	Hellerriegel	302	Jeffersonville, NY	Katzweiler, Baiern
Damm, Mathilde	1, Sept 1879	12, Aug.			279	---, WV	
Damman, Anna Katharina	1, May 1876	22, Mar.	69	Pörtner	143	Blairstown, IA	Großlafferde, Hannover
Dammann, Christian	26, Apr. 1888	8, Apr.	62		270	Seguin, TX	Schumansville, Guadalupe County, Texas
Dammann, Emilie Auguste	21, Sept 1899	26, Aug.	34	Kroms	607	Seguin, TX	Spenge, Minden, Preußen
Dammann, Herman Heinrich	19, Jan. 1888	1, Jan.	59-7m		46	Petersburg, IL	Kasperstillan, Schleswig-Holstein
Dammann, Katharina	4, Aug. 1892	13, July	72	Brammann	494	Garrett, IN	Pommern
Dammann, Rudolf	27, July 1899	5, July	47		479	St. Louis, MO	Auburn, Indiana
Dammann, Sophia	18, June 1891	27, May	30- 4m-24d	Steffen	398	Garrett, IN	Cremson, Piritz, Pommern
Dams, Dorothea Sophia Caroline	5, June 1890	6, May	25	Beyer	366	Oconomowoc, WI	Poppenweiler, Ludwigsburg, Württemberg
Danenhoever, Christine	29, Dec. 1884	18, May	84		7	Rockport, NY	Amsterdam, Holland
Danens, Elisabeth	11, Aug. 1887	18, July	40	Hofenaar	510	St. Paul, MN	Heimehausen, Bern, Schweiz
Dangel, Anna Barbara	12, Nov. 1891	24, Oct.	55	Ingold	734	Clarington, OH	Brucken, Kirchheim, Württemberg
Dangel, Anna Katharina	9, Nov. 1874	4, Oct.	74- 3m- 2d	Beiser	359	Baresville, OH	Unter-Leningen, Württemberg
Dangel, Christian	9, Nov. 1893	13, Oct.	66		718	Hannibal, OH	Unterlinningen, Kircheim, Württemberg
Dangel, Jakob	28, Sept 1899	3, Sept	64		623	Baresville, OH	Monroe County, Ohio
Dangel, John	20, Aug. 1896	24, July	33		542	Baresville, OH	
Dangel, John	16, June 1862	6, Apr.	20		96	Baresville, OH	
Dangel, Magdalena	2, May 1895	6, Apr.	65	Rothacher	286	Mt. Vernon, NY	Blumenstein, Bern, Schweiz
Daniel, Caroline	8, Dec. 1892	16, Oct.	78	Almuß	782	Ironton, OH	Odenheim, Rheinpfalz Baiern
Daniel, Friedrich Wilhelm	8, Sept 1898	25, Aug.	54		575	Newport, KY	Pfeffelbach, RheinPreußen
Daniel, Peter	23, Nov. 1854	21, Oct.	38		188	Clayton, WI	Greifenstein, Kreis Wetzlar, Preußen
Danke, Johanna S.C.	10, July 1890	12, June	68	Schulz	446	Clayton, WI	Wulfsahl, Mecklenburg-Schwerin
Danker, Anna Catharina	29, Apr. 1852	28, Mar.	61-11m	Rosenbrock	72		Tüschendorf, Hannover
Danker, Christina	14, Jan. 1892	19, Dec.	85- 1m-10d		30	Marietta, OH	Wahldriens, Württemberg
Danker, Klaus Heinrich	23, May 1881	12, May	61		167	Marietta, OH	Tüschendorf, Ottersberg, Hannover
Danker, Wilhelm	8, Nov. 1880	26, Sept	81		359	Bremen, ---	Zeven, Hannover
Danklefs, Anna Chr.	10, June 1886	21, May	45		7	Seguin, TX	Boesbüll, Schleswig-Holstein
Dankward, (boy)	30, Mar. 1863		5		52	Wabasha, MN	
Dankwerth, Karl	5, Nov. 1883	28, July	72- 9m-25d		359	Clarington, OH	Borenfede, Hannover
Dankwerth, Maria Christina	6, Mar. 1851	5, Feb.	74		40	Herman, MO	Bodenfelde, Amt Lauenforde, Hannover
Danne, (Mr)	19, July 1860	12, June	65		116	Brunswick, MO	Brelingen, Amt Bissendorf, Hannover
Danne, Sophia	23, Oct. 1865	29, Aug.	64- 8m- 9d		172	Brunswick, MO	Hannover
Danneberg, Justine	6, Sept 1875	16, Aug.	53	Hofmeier	287	Schnectady, NY	Barkhausen bei Münden, Preußen
Dannecker, Maria Magdalena	8, Sept 1853	16, Aug.	62-11m		144	New Albany, IN	Kircheim-Bolanden, Rheinkreis Baiern
Dannenberg, Katharina	29, July 1878	15, July	37	Bühler	239	Odebolt, IA	Reusten, Herrenberg, Württemberg
Dannenbrink, Karolina	18, Sept 1882	1, Sept	30- 8m	Wente	303	Chester, IL	
Dannenbrink, Louis	1, Sept 1898	20, Aug.	57		559	Chester, IL	Randolph County, Illinois
Dannenfelser, John	17, July 1865	8, Mar.			116	Wausau, WI	Dischendorf, Preußen
Dannenhauer, Magdalena	26, Aug. 1878	13, Aug.	87		271	Canton, MO	Hoheneck, Ludwigsburg, Württemberg
Dannenhauer, Samuel	10, July 1882	May	30		223	Canton, MO	
Dannenhauser, Sarah Susanna	27, Nov. 1876	22, Sept	16		383	Canton, MO	Winchester County, Ohio

Christliche Apologete Death Notices --- 1839 - 1899

Name of Deceased	Notice Date	Death Date	Age	Maiden Name	Page	Place of Death	Place of Birth
Dannenmann, Josephine	3, Sept 1891	4, Aug.	19		574	New Orleans, LA	Waterprove, Louisiana
Danner, Anna Maria	10, Nov. 1862	14, Oct.	42		180	Cincinnati, OH	Sulz, Württemberg
Danner, Christian	24, July 1871	31, May	50		239	Chicago, IL	
Danner, Johan Georg	22, Apr. 1897	15, Mar.	67		254	El Paso, IL	Weiden, Sulz, Württemberg
Danner, John	6, Apr. 1899	15, Mar.	75- 4m-22d		222	Wrayville, IL	Langenau, Ulm, Württemberg
Dannhaus, Barbara Elisabeth	7, Aug. 1871	30, June	46- 4m- 5d	Enzeroth	255	Warsaw, IL	
Dannheim, Ernst	8, May 1871	10, Apr.	65		151	Hedwigs Hill, TX	Burgdorf, Hannover
Dannheim, Heinrich	1, July 1878	11, June	63- 10m-20d		207	Lafayette, MN	Neubokel, Gifhorn, Hannover
Dannheim, Minna	23, Apr. 1891	29, Mar.	36	Lemburg	270	Hedwigs Hill, TX	Mason County, Texas
Dannies, Joachim	3, June 1878	28, Apr.	38		175	Flint Creek, IA	Qaarebeck, Gardelegen, Magdeburg, Preußen
Dannoar, Elisabeth Philippine	25, Sept 1882	9, Aug.	29- 2m- 5d	Jakobi	311	Brighton, IL	
Danz, Emil	7, Nov. 1881	20, Oct.	20		359	Montague, MI	
Danzberger, Anna Elisabeth	27, May 1897	22, Mar.	74		335	New York City, NY	Reisendrei, Kurhessen
Dapp, Daad	20, Sept 1894	2, Sept	48		614	Portland, OR	Adelboden, Bern, Schweiz
Darb, Margaretha	23, Oct. 1871	9, Oct.	41		343	Seymour, IN	Berlenbach, Elsaß
Darstein, Anna Maria	12, Nov. 1847	Sept			183	New Orleans, LA	
Dasbach, Maria	7, July 1892	16, June	64	Schaller	430	Quincy, IL	Sachsenhausen, Waldeck
Dasch, Bertha	1, May 1890	19, Apr.	18		286	Newport, KY	
Dasow, Friedrich	19, July 1894	26, June	71		470	Germanville, --	Neuenkirchen, Mecklenburg-Strelitz
Dasow, Henriette	18, Oct. 1894	23, Sept	71	Kulo	678	Germanville, --	Lindo, Mecklenburg-Strelitz
Datisman, Michael	28, Oct. 1897	4, Oct.	86		687	Sherrills Mount, IA	Ernsbach, Oehringen, Württemberg
Datismann, Gazena	2, Feb. 1899	2, Jan.	53	Krümpel	79	Dubuque, IA	Bippen, Fürstenau, Hannover
Datismann, Karolina	3, May 1875	18, Apr.	64	Höfner	143	Sherrills Mount, IA	Ernsbach, Ering, Württemberg
Datismann, Louise F.	1, Mar. 1894	10, Feb.	70		150	Giard, IA	Beidingen, Hessen-Darmstadt
Datismann, Rosina Catharina	27, Feb. 1862	9, Feb.	9- 2m-27d		36	Sherrills Mount, IA	
Daub, Conrad	13, Aug. 1877	16, July	72- 3m-21d		263	Arenzville, IL	Rüfenrod, Alsfeld, Hessen-Darmstadt
Daub, Katharina	27, Dec. 1880	17, Nov.	69	Pfeil	415	Arenzville, IL	Arenshausen, Alsfeld, Hessen-Darmstadt
Däuber, Anna Maria	30, Dec. 1858	8, Dec.	43	Scharf	208	Freeport, IL	Schwäbisch Hall, Württemberg
Dauch, Barbara	20, Nov. 1871	29, Oct.	52	Brand	375	Jerusalem, NY	Reichenberg bei Würzburg, Baiern
Dauernheimer, Carrie	1, June 1893	7, May	35		350	Delaware, OH	Holzhausen , Hessen-Darmstadt
Daugs, John	7, Mar. 1895	29, Jan.	72		158	Ft. Atkinson, WI	Ziezeneff, Schiefelbein, Preußen
Daum, August Adolph	12, Nov. 1891	14, Oct.	28		734	Higginsport, OH	Higginsport, Ohio
Daum, Catharina	24, Feb. 1887	5, Feb.	62		126	Chicago, IL	
Daum, Christine	11, Nov. 1858	22, Sept	67- 6m		180	Ripley, OH	Ipsingen bei Pforzheim, Baden
Daum, Johan Friedrich	7, Dec. 1863	13, Nov.	73		196	West Union, OH	Almendingen, Württemberg
Daum, Wilhelm Heinrich	1, July 1897	30, May	28		414	Poughkeepsie, NY	
Däumler, Anna Maria	2, June 1898	7, May	42	Stäuble	351	Columbus, OH	Mengen, Freiberg, Baden
Dauser, Maria	14, Oct. 1886	2, Oct.	27	Sieber	7	Grand Rapids, MI	Aetigen, Schweiz
Dauth, Elenora	5, Feb. 1877	24, Jan.	69- 6m- 2d		47	Cincinnati, OH	Billigheim, Rheinpfalz Baiern
Davies, Rosaline	27, Aug. 1877	10, Aug.	23		279	Delaware, OH	Delaware, Ohio
Davitsen, Juliane	26, July 1869	17, June	21- 4m-10d	Fischer	239	Chicago, IL	Böhmen
Deal, Katharina	7, Oct. 1886	15, Sept	66	Krüger	7	Edon, OH	Holmes County, Ohio
Debb, Elisabeth	1, June 1899	19, Apr.	25		351	Bethany, OR	Adelboden, Bern, Schweiz
DeBoben, Auguste Maria	29, Dec. 1873	8, Dec.	56- 10m	Friedrich	415	Dayton, OH	Dittelsheim, Hessen-Darmstadt
Debus, Elisabeth	15, July 1852	3, June	51		116	East Baltimore, MD	Josbach, Kirchheim, Kurhessen
Debus, Maria Wilhelmina E.	19, Apr. 1880	4, Apr.	42	Vohs	127	Cannelton, IN	Längerich, Tecklenburg, Preußen

Christliche Apologete Death Notices --- 1839 - 1899

Name of Deceased	Notice Date	Death Date	Age	Page	Maiden Name	Place of Death	Place of Birth
Dechtmeyer, Helena	21, Oct. 1858	27, Sept	55	168		Santa Claus, IN	Oberkirchen, Hessen
Decken, Maria Wilhelmina Bertha	13, July 1899	30, May	32	447	Köpke	Burt, IA	Janesville, Wisconsin
Deckendorf, Valentin	4, Nov. 1878	10, Oct.	53	351		Morris, MN	Baiern
Decker, Anna Engel	7, June 1860	24, Apr.	40	92		Santa Claus, IN	Preußisch Minden, Preußen
Decker, Catharina Babetta	9, Nov. 1885	18, Oct.	20	7	Ehnes	Boston, MA	Diebach, Mittelfranken, Baiern
Decker, Georg	24, Nov. 1873	7, Nov.	76-10m-7d	375		Vermillion, OH	Riederich, Urach, Württemberg
Decker, Georg	20, Apr. 1854	5, Mar.	30	64		Vermillion, OH	Riedrich, Württemberg
Decker, Jakob	25, Aug. 1892	22, July	67	542		Cleveland, OH	Ritherich, Urach, Württemberg
Decker, Karl Gustav	17, Nov. 1898	30, Oct.	21	735		Vermillion, OH	Lorain County, Ohio
Decker, Louis Arthur	14, Nov. 1895	25, Oct.	13	734		Vermillion, OH	Lorain County, Ohio
Decker, M.	4, Aug. 1859	13, July	72-10m-10d	124		Columbus, OH	Dauphin County, Pennsylvania
Decker, Ottilie	3, Sept 1891	4, Aug.	39	574		Evansville, IN	Evansville, Indiana
Decker, Phil.	4, Nov. 1897		82	703		Evansville, IN	Eckelsheim, Hessen-Darmstadt
Dedert, (Mrs)	19, Nov. 1883	2, Nov.	90	375		Quincy, IL	Höchel, Hannover
Deerhake, Christina Sophia	1, Feb. 1875	10, Jan.	19	39		Huntingburg, IN	
DeFrese, Everdine	30, Nov. 1885	10, Nov.	17- 8m	7		Brenham, TX	
DeFries, Christina	13, May 1878	18, Apr.	35	151	Heil	Roberts, IL	Cleestadt, Hessen-Darmstadt
DeFries, Gerhard G.	15, Apr. 1897	26, Mar.	70	238		Melvin, IL	Theener, Ostfriesland
Degen, Adam	13, May 1878	14, Apr.	100	151		Faribault, MN	
Degen, Elisabeth	15, July 1878	20, June	42	223	Schmutz	Faribault, MN	Obenheim, Elsaß
Degenfelder, Johanna	9, Dec. 1858	5, Oct.	23	196		New York City, NY	Vaihingen, Stuttgart, Württemberg
Degering, Adolph	7, Feb. 1895	24, Dec.	34	94		Toledo, OH	Celle, Hannover
Degiescher, Rosina	13, Aug. 1877	24, July	11- 1m-28d	263		Terre Haute, IN	
Deglow, Carl	19, Aug. 1886	6, Aug.	49	7		Beaver Dam, WI	Wotsick, Piritz, Pommern
Deglow, Johan	10, Apr. 1890	3, Mar.	88	238		Beaver Dam, WI	Zitten, Preußen
Degner, Carl	1, Mar. 1894	17, Jan.	66	150		Kewaskum, WI	Plantikow, Stettin, Preußen
Degner, Michael F.	11, Nov. 1878	5, Oct.	79- -19d	359		Newton, IA	Cramersdorf, Pommern
Degner, W.	25, July 1864	24, June	51- 8m- 2d	120		Red Bud, IL	Nepke, Amt Wölpke, Hannover
Degner, Wilhelmine	28, Jan. 1892	29, Dec.	63	62	Sell	Storm Lake, IA	Falkenberg, Pommern
Degner, Wilhelmine	27, Nov. 1865	15, Oct.	72	192		Milan, IN	Nöpke, Hannover
DeGrave, Rintius	6, June 1864	Nov.	35	92		Rochester, NY	Petkam, Hannover
Dehn, Christian F.	27, July 1893	2, July	55	478		Clearwater, MN	Berlin, Brandenburg
Dehn, John	20, Mar. 1876	23, Feb.	25	95		St. Charles, MO	Lancaster County, Pennsylvania
Dehn, Maria	7, July 1898	20, June	74	431		St. Louis, MO	Frissenhausen, Hasenheim, Mittelfranken, Baiern
Dehne, Franz	11, Aug. 1898	31, July	68	510		Brighton, IL	Holtensen, Hannover
Dehnert, Christine	20, Sept 1888	4, Sept	17- 8m-11d	606		Oconomowoc, WI	Briezig, Pommern
Dehnhardt, Elisabeth	7, Apr. 1873	18, Mar.	51	111	Dehnhardt	New Bremen, IL	Statthosbach, Kurhessen
Dehnhardt, Peter	15, Sept 1887	25, Aug.	69	590		New Bremen, IL	Stadthosbach, Kurhessen
Dehnhart, Mary	20, June 1881	3, June	24- -15d	199		New Bremen, IL	Orland, Cook County, Illinois
Dehning, Katharine	21, Dec. 1885	27,Nov.	48	7		Lansing, IA	Velgen, Hannover
Deibel, Barbara	24, Nov. 1873	6, Nov.	41	375	Braun	New Orleans, LA	Jockgrimm am Rhein, Baden
Deible, Hanna	5, Oct. 1874	18, Sept	32- 1m-10d	319	Weingart	Kendallville, IN	
Deichmann, Andreas	17, Mar. 1898	25, Feb.	35	175		Belleville, IL	New Athens Township, St. Clair County, Illinois
Deichmann, Valentin Carl	26, Apr. 1888	29, Mar.	89	270		Altamont, IL	Ermershausen, Baiern
Deigel, Johannes	8, Mar. 1855	16, Feb.	10	40		Brunswick, MO	
Deik, Wilhelmina	30, Apr. 1891	10, Apr.	51	286	Sowatzky	Hartford, CT	Goringen, West Preußen

Christliche Apologete Death Notices --- 1839 - 1899

Name of Deceased	Notice Date	Death Date	Age	Maiden Name	Page	Place of Death	Place of Birth
Deike, Fr.	21, Mar. 1881	6, Mar.	37		95	New Haven, CT	Braunschweig, Germany
Deike, Karl Heinrich	16, June 1898	18, Apr.	77		383	New York City, NY	Reihen, Sinsheim, Baden
Dein, Jonas	27, Nov. 1882	29, Oct.	60		383	Brooklyn, NY	Emskirchen, Baiern
Deindörfer, Anna	3, Mar. 1859	31, Jan.	59		36	Baltimore, MD	Oberheinrich, Württemberg
Deininger, Barbara	1, May 1890	5, Mar.	87- 2m- 5d	Schwarz	286	Brooklyn, NY	Ober-Heinrieth, Heinbronn, Württemberg
Deininger, Gottlieb	15, Aug. 1861	3, June	64		132	New Haven, CT	Klauberbach, Heilbronn, Württemberg
Deininger, Gottlieb	15, Sept 1853		23		148	New York, NY	Gifford, New York
Deininger, Mary	4, Sept 1890	4, Aug.	46- 7m-23d	Addison	574	Schnectady, NY	Ober-Gruppenbach, Heilbronn, Württemberg
Deininger, Wilhelm J.	26, May 1879	7, May	40		167	Brooklyn, NY	Straßburg, Elsaß
Deis, Amalie	15, Aug. 1850	24, July	46- 6m		132	Columbus, OH	Sieboldingen, Landau, Rheinpfalz Baiern
Deisel, Eva C.	15, Sept 1892	6, Aug.	77	Keller	590	Boston, MA	Baiern
Deiß, Christina	16, June 1898	27, May	77	Scheydt	383	Laurel, IN	Enzberg, Maulbronn, Württemberg
Deiß, Elisabeth Katharina	18, Sept 1876	10, Sept	56- 4m- 6d	Schülz	303	Covington, KY	Württemberg
Deiß, John F.	27, July 1893	13, June	80		478	Carlisle, IN	Enzberg, Württemberg
Deiß, John G.	4, Sept 1890		45-10m-18d		574	Covington, KY	Enzberg, Maulbronn, Württemberg
Deiß, Jonas	5, Dec. 1889	9, Nov.	72		782	Covington, KY	York County, Pennsylvania
Deiß, Katharine	12, Jan. 1893	23, Dec.	86- 3m-12d		30	Columbus, OH	Unterdürkheim, Cannstatt, Württemberg
Deiß, Wilhelmine Elisabeth	23, June 1884	25, May	69	Häfner	7	Carlisle, IN	
Deitzel, Louis	29, Aug. 1870				279	Lincoln, NE	
Deke, Heinrich	14, Mar. 1881	31, Jan.	83- 6m- 6d		87	Freeport, IL	Essen, Oldenburg
Dekoben, Anna Elisabeth	9, Sept 1867	22, Aug.	56- 8m-12d		286	Dayton, OH	Dittelsheim, Kreis Worms, Hessen-Darmstadt
DeLaRue, Joseph August	26, Oct. 1899	7, Oct.	74		687	Quincy, IL	Benzheim, Hessen-Darmstadt
DelaRue, Karl Ernst	20, Aug. 1891	27, July	15		542	Chicago, IL	Cleveland, Ohio
DelaRue, Louise	20, Apr. 1893	26, Mar.	49	Rasch	254	Chicago, IL	Berlin, Germany
Delbrügge, Wilhelmine	3, July 1890	16, June	66- 2m-26d		430	Boody, IL	
Deling, Heinrich	13, Aug. 1896	17, July	81		527	Red Bud, IL	Grebs, Döhmitz, Mecklenburg
Delker, Heinrich	4, Nov. 1886	26, Sept	61		7	Lyona, KS	Dalhorn, Blomberg, Lippe-Detmold
Delker, Johan Jakob	25, Mar. 1878	7, Mar.	67- 9m-10d	Müller	95	Vermillion, OH	Mickelfeld, Sinsheim, Baden
Delker, Louise	20, Nov. 1876	29, Oct.	38		375	Lyona, KS	Ripley County, Indiana
Delker, Margaretha	10, May 1894	13, Apr.	81-11m- 1d	Seburger	310	Vermillion, OH	
Delker, Martha	28, Jan. 1867	5, Dec.	17- 4m- 2d		30	Vermillion, OH	
Delker, Michael	18, July 1864	27, May	18- 5m-11d		116	Vermillion, OH	Michelfeld, Amt Sinsheim, Baden
Dell, (Mrs)	3, May 1880	10, Feb.	84		143	Little Creek, MO	NiederMosheim, Lauterbach, Hessen-Darmstadt
Dell, Anna Maria	9, Jan. 1896	18, Dec.	64	Gansly	30	Holt, MI	Waldorf, Nagold, Württemberg
Dell, Johann	19, May 1892	19, Apr.	19		80	Canton, MO	
Dell, Margaretha	4, Nov. 1878	7, Oct.	36	Ried	351	Delhi, MI	Rothenburg, Baiern
Dell, Maria Josephine	28, Aug. 1882	27, July			279		
Dellenbach, Elisabeth	27, Jan. 1887	6, Jan.	66-10m-15d		62	Kendallville, IN	Bern, Schweiz
Demand, Dorothea	2, Feb. 1874	25, Dec.	88		39	Lake Creek, MO	Wilstedt, Amt Ottersberg, Hannover
Demand, Herman	6, Oct. 1898	18, Sept	76		639	Smithton, MO	Willstedt, Hannover
DeMarce, Alexander E.	31, Oct. 1889	10, Oct.	55		702	Harper, IA	Priscott County, Canada
Demby, Christina	17, Nov. 1887	14, Oct.	57	Knodel	734	Milwaukee, WI	Niefern, Pforzheim, Baden
Demland, Emma	5, Nov. 1896	14, Oct.	20		719	Defiance, OH	
Demmler, Anna Rägli	4, Dec. 1890	1, Nov.	56- 1m-10d	Mor	782	Lemars, IA	
Demus, Johann	27, Oct. 1859	28, Mar.			172	Smithland, KY	Nänikow, Usler, Zürich, Schweiz
Demuth, Anna	24, Jan. 1876	4, Jan.	27	Pax	31	Houston, TX	

Christliche Apologete Death Notices --- 1839 - 1899

Name of Deceased	Notice Date	Death Date	Age	Maiden Name	Page	Place of Death	Place of Birth
Demuth, Anna Maria	2, Feb. 1874	31, Dec.	71- 1m-21d	Hauser	39	Pittsburg, PA	Schriesheim, Baden
Dendel, Dorothea	22, Jan. 1852	22, Dec.	23- 1m-16d		16	St. Clair, MI	
Dendel, Friedrich	22, Dec. 1853	25, Nov.	37- 6m		204	Roseville, MI	Rosenfeld, Württemberg
Dendel, Jacob	12, June 1865	29, May	76- 4m-17d		96	Detroit, MI	Rosenfeld, Sulz, Württemberg
Dendel, Johan Peter	4, Oct. 1894	13, Sept	60		646	Allegan, MI	Rosenfeld, Württemberg
Dendel, Johan Peter	18, Oct. 1894	13, Sept	75		678	Allegan, MI	Rosenfeld, Württemberg
Dendel, Katharina	17, Aug. 1854	2, Aug.	32-10m	Kunge	132	Roseville, MI	Rosenfeld, Württemberg
Dendel, Magdalena	7, Nov. 1889	15, Oct.	24- 2m-15d	Löw	718	Allegan, MI	Clarington, Ohio
Dendel, Maria Friederike	5, Nov. 1896	15, Oct.	63	Brandt	719	Allegan, MI	Britzier, Mecklenburg-Schwerin
Denekas, Margaretha	6, Feb. 1890	5, Jan.	77	Pailler	94	New York City, NY	Manheim, Baden
Deneke, Friederike	9, Mar. 1899	16, Jan.	36	Hartmann	158	Gordonville, MO	Cape Girardeau County, Missouri
Deneke, Louise	2, Apr. 1877	13, Mar.	30	Ahrens	111	Jackson, MO	Cape Girardeau County, Missouri
Deneke, Maria Magdalena	25, Aug. 1887	13, Aug.	86- 5m- 6d	Oberbeck	542	Jackson, MO	KleinRhüden, Braunschweig
Denert, Gottfried	8, Mar. 1869	16, Feb.	33- 1-28d		79	Oconomowoc, WI	Pritzig, Kreis Piritz, Pommern
DeNeve, John	3, Mar. 1859	6, Feb.			36	St. Louis, MO	
Denker, Johanna	25, Oct. 1875	26, Sept	51- 7m- 4d	Mainz	343	Bishop Station, IL	Turn, Ostfriesland
Denkwerth, Heinrich	1, May 1871	1, Apr.	21- -10d		143	Clarington, OH	
Denner, Maria Margaretha	31, Jan. 1895	20, Dec.	74		78	Saginaw, MI	Westheim, Baiern
Dennerlein, Katharina Maria	3, Feb. 1873	19, Jan.	18		39	Indianapolis, IN	
Dennig, Caroline Maria	20, Mar. 1890	25, Feb.	44	Habermann	190	Galion, OH	Langendulack, Kurhessen
Dennig, Magdalena	17, July 1890	6, July	78	Schlittenhart	462	Galion, OH	Elmendingen, Pforzheim, Baden
Dennig, Maria Christina	18, Oct. 1860	3, Sept			168	Schnectady, NY	Eikhorst bei Preußisch Minden, Preußen
Denning, Karl D.	28, May 1883	11, May	53		175	St. Charles, MO	Herfort, Preußen
Denninger, Emma Sophia	17, Aug. 1885	28, July	20		7	Ellis Grove, IL	
Denninger, Maria	1, Sept 1884	11, Aug.	16		7	Ellis Grove, IL	
Dennler, Anna Rägli	25, Dec. 1890	2, Nov.	56- 1m-10d	Morf	830	Lemars, IA	Nänikow, Usler, Zürich, Schweiz
Dennler, Maria	3, Jan. 1889	8, Dec.	71	Gloger	14	Laporte, IN	Langenthal, Bern, Schweiz
Densch, Erhard	30, June 1862	14, June	16- 9m-13d		104	Golconda, IL	Pope County, Illinois
Densch, Johan	17, Apr. 1865	23, Mar.	57		64	Golconda, IL	Weidnitz, Weismann, Baiern
Denzel, Johan Georg	31, Mar. 1884	16, Mar.	60		7	Cleveland, OH	Ehrenstein, Ulm, Württemberg
Denzel, Sebastian	15, Mar. 1888	6, Feb.	54- -16d		174	Vermillion, OH	Ehrenstein, Ulm, Württemberg
Denzel, Sophia Dorothea	1, Sept 1898	14, Aug.	71	Muldner	559	Cleveland, OH	Waldkappel bei Kassel, Kurhessen
Denzinger, Louise	7, Mar. 1881	1, Feb.	17		79	Louisville, KY	
Denzler, Casper	17, Nov. 1873	2, Nov.	43-11m-25d		367	Jeffersonville, IN	Debendorf, Zürich, Schweiz
Denzler, Charley	19, Aug. 1886	2, Aug.	22		7	Jeffersonville, IN	Jeffersonville, Indiana
DePinal, Sophia	3, Sept 1877	23, Aug.	49- 6m- 2d	Bührmann	287	Cincinnati, OH	Nipke, Hannover
Deppe, Bertha Emilia	21, Feb. 1876	6, Jan.	27- 8m-23d	Luß	63	DePere, WI	Meesow, Rügenwalde, Preußen
Deppe, Bertha Emilia	20, Mar. 1876	6, Jan.	27- 8m-23d	Buss	95	DePere, WI	Regenwalde, Preußen
Deppe, Car.	25, June 1883	15, May	39- 5m-15d	Reuter	207	Drake, MO	Lageonia County, Pennsylvania
Deppe, Car.	16, July1883	15, May	39- 5m-15d	Reuter	231	Drake, MO	Lageonia County, Pennsylvania
Deppe, Carolina Wilhelmine	1, Dec. 1884	7, Nov.	18		7	Drake, MO	Oerlinghausen, Lippe-Detmold
Deppe, Friedrich	5, Nov. 1877	13, Sept	68		359	Petersburg, IL	Sommerhell, Lippe-Detmold
Deppe, Heinrich	10, Dec. 1866	18, Oct.	45		398	Wapello, IA	Lippe-Detmold
Deppe, Heinrich	21, Dec. 1893	2, Oct.	55		814	Lowell, WI	Portland, Dodge County, Wisconsin
Deppe, Henry Louis	18, Jan. 1894	28, Dec.	38		46	Watertown, WI	Sebeck, Lippe-Detmold
Deppe, Herman	9, Mar. 1899	15, Feb.	86		158		

Christliche Apologete Death Notices --- 1839 - 1899

Name of Deceased	Notice Date	Death Date	Age	Maiden Name	Page	Place of Death	Place of Birth
Deppe, Louis	8, Nov. 1880	22, Oct	25- 1m-26d	Hansmeier	359	Petersburg, IL	Beardstown, Illinois
Deppe, Louise	12, Apr. 1880	29, Mar.	20- 6m- 9d		119	Petersburg, IL	Zeven, Hannover
Deppe, Rebecca	28, Apr. 1873	29, Mar.	40	Hinners	135	Petersburg, IL	Portland, Dodge County, Wisconsin
Deppe, W. Karl	7, Apr. 1887	25, Mar.	24		222	Lowell, KS	Barntrup, Lippe-Detmold
Deppe, Wilhelm	10, Feb. 1859	29, Dec.	58		24	Beardstown, IL	Horn, Lippe-Detmold
Deppe, Wilhelm	23, Sept 1886	10, Sept	64		7	Portland, WI	Waterloo, Wisconsin
Deppe, Wilhelm	29, July 1886	2, June	32		7	Watertown, WI	Waterloo, Wisconsin
Deppe, Wilhelm	30, Sept 1886	2, June	32		7	Watertown, WI	Rohrbach, RheinPfalz Baiern
Deprez, Maria Elisabeth	3, Oct. 1881	16, Sept	78		319		
Derbisch, Carl	11, Feb. 1897	18, Jan.	15		94	Columbus, OH	Kleinfahner, Sachsen-Coburg-Gotha
Dernow, Johan Hieronymus	28, Aug. 1871	9, July	75		279	Wellsville, OH	Farmersheim, Hessen-Darmstadt
Dersch, Eva	30, Nov. 1874		24-11m	Wagner	383	St. Joseph, MO	Wollmar, Marburg, Kurhessen
Dersch, Heinrich	25, June 1891	19, Apr.	44		414	St. Joseph, MO	Montabaur, Nassau
Dersch, Helene	12, Jan. 1899	15, Dec.	44	LaBonta	30	St. Joseph, MO	Wolmer, Kreis Marburg, Kurhessen
Dersch, Johan Jacob	17, June 1872	28, May	58- 5m-25d		199	St. Joseph, MO	
Dersch, Louise	12, May 1879	16, Apr.	19- 1m-14d		151	St. Joseph, MO	
Deschler, Catharina	30, Apr. 1891	13, Mar.	85	Wendel	286	New Metamoras, OH	Württemberg
Desentz, Johanna	4, Sept 1890	18, Aug.	49	Fick	574	Detroit, MI	Lauenburg, Pommern
Desponds, Charles E.	6, Nov. 1882	12, Aug.	27- 5m-22d		359	San Francisco, CA	Schweiz
Deters, Gerhard	20, Feb. 1871	23, Jan.			63	Waterloo, IA	Schale, Tecklenburg, Preußen
Deters, Katharina Adelheid	6, Apr. 1885	20, Mar.	75	Meiners	7	Lansing, IA	Schaele, Tecklenburg, Preußen
Dethloff, Philipp	4, Feb. 1892	13, Jan.	82		78	Altamont, IL	Trifzow, Pommern
Detsch, Magdalena Juliane	6, July 1893	17, June	70		430	Philadelphia, PA	Zottishofen, Kingelsau, Württemberg
Detsch, Martin	15, Dec. 1892	28, Nov.	71- 2m-21d		798	Philadelphia, PA	Hof, Baiern
Dettmar, Antoinette	14, Mar. 1881	28, Feb.	15- 3m-20d		87	Dallas, TX	Lickwegen, Kurhessen
Dettmer, Heinrich	6, Mar. 1890	3, Feb.	62		158	Louisville, KY	Steinbeck, Lippe-Schaumburg
Dettmer, Henriette	9, May 1881	17, Apr.	65	Drißmeier	151	Louisville, KY	Industry, Texas
Dettmer, Johanna	3, Nov. 1879	19, Oct.	18		351	Dallas, TX	Bickwegen, Amt Oberkirchen, Kurhessen
Dettmer, Marie	9, Mar. 1863	10, Feb.	81	Ilsemon	40	Charlestown, IN	Canton Argau, Schweiz
Dettweiler, Catharine	19, Oct. 1874	4, Oct.	63	Kohl	335	Wheeling, WV	Hannover
Detyn, Engel	15, Mar. 1860	10, Feb.	58- 5m		44	Winona, MN	Hierlingen, Württemberg
Deubler, Anton	31, July 1876	4, July	68- 4m-26d		247	New Lisbon, IN	Hoheneck, Ludwigsburg, Württemberg
Deubler, Barbara	22, Sept 1879	30, July	83- 3m		303		Huntingburg, Dubois County, Indiana
Deuper, Charles H.	20, Oct. 1898	31, Aug.	32		670	Huntingburg, IN	Mühlhausen am Neckar, Kannstatt, Württemberg
Deupner, Christina Katharina	22, Apr. 1872	11, Apr.	54	Vander	135	Greenville, OH	Binde, Osterburg, Magdeburg, Preußen
Deutsch, Catharina Dor.	6, Mar. 1876	11, Feb.	75	Schernikau	79	Bloomington, IL	
Deutsch, Dorothea	26, May 1873	14, May	32	Krieger	167	Bloomington, IL	
Devos, Emma	14, Sept 1893	21, Aug.		Griese	590	Evansville, IN	
Devos, Iman	20, May 1858	9, May	51		80	Evansville, IN	Kapelle, Neu-Seeland, Holland
DeVos, Jakob	7, June 1869	15, Apr.	33		183	Evansville, IN	Kapelle, Zeeland, Holland
Devos, Louis	9, Apr. 1892	16, Mar.	50		238	Louisville, KY	Holland
DeVos, Maria	25, Feb. 1892	30, Jan.	49		126	Louisville, KY	Gleichenbach, Hessen
Devos, Maria Elsebein	12, June 1871	11, May	67	Brinkmeyer	191	Evansville, IN	Ladbergen, Tecklenburg, Münster, Preußen
Devose, Maatje	8, Feb. 1855	Oct.	38	Bom	24	Mt. Vernon, IN	Capelle, Seeland, Holland
DeVries, Katharina	26, June 1890	14, June	45- 1m- 4d		414	Peoria, IL	Groothusen, Hannover
DeVries, Steven George	1, July 1897	7, June	22- -20d		414	Pekin, IL	

Christliche Apologete Death Notices --- 1839 - 1899

Name of Deceased	Notice Date	Death Date	Age	Page	Maiden Name	Place of Death	Place of Birth
DeVries, Wilhelm	2, May 1889	21, Apr.	55	286		Macon, NE	Timmel, Ostfriesland
Dewein, Heinrich	27, Nov. 1871	23, Oct.	23	383		Burlington, IA	Hörgersweiler, Bergzabern, Baiern
Dewein, Johannes	27, Nov. 1871	14, Oct.	68-10m-11d	383		Burlington, IA	Burlington, Iowa
Dewein, Lulu	14, June 1894	26, May	14	390		Burlington, IA	PikeTown, Ohio
Dewein, Maria	14, Apr. 1873	22, Mar.	35	119	Reif	Flint Creek, IA	
Dewein, Maria Lydia	12, Oct. 1899	24, Sept	16	655		St. Louis, MO	
Dexheimer,	4, Jan. 1849		Inquiry	3			
Dexheimer, Johan	20, Feb. 1890	28, Jan.	66	126		Louisville, KY	Osthofen, Rhein-Hessen
Dexheimer, Phil	12, July 1894	21, June	69- 2m	454		Lawrenceburg, IN	Osthofen, Hessen-Darmstadt
Dexheimer, Susanna Mina	25, Aug. 1879	1, Aug.	55- 5m	271	Kern	Dillsborough, IN	Frankenthal, Rheinkreis Baiern
Deyemann, Heinrich	16, Dec. 1878	29, Nov.	62	399		Warren, MO	Schönhagen, Sternberg, Lippe-Detmold
Dick , Christian	28, July 1859	14, July	71	120		New Albany, IN	Tützenstein, NiederRhein, Elsaß
Dick, Augusta Carolina	5, Jan. 1880	6, Dec.	47	7	Drege	Harrison, IN	
Dick, Daniel	18, May 1893	21, Apr.	31	318		Seattle, WA	Indiana
Dick, Henry	26, Aug. 1867	3, Aug.	20	270		Peru, IL	Harrison County, Indiana
Dick, Wilhelm C.	28, Dec. 1899	10, Nov.	28	828		Norwich, KS	Decatur, Illinois
Dickel, Magdalena	4, Apr. 1895	13, Mar.	63	222	Frank	Philadelphia, PA	Sachsenhausen, Preußen
Dicker, Michael	10, Mar. 1848	4, Feb.	10	43		Williamsburg, NY	
Dickgräfe, Friedrich	19, Nov. 1877	5, Oct.	50	375		Bland, MO	Altenau, Westphalen
Dickhaut, Anna Maria	17, Nov. 1898	21, Oct.	81	735	Schmitt	Marrs, IN	Schrecksbach, Kurhessen
Dickhaut, Elisabeth	6, Jan. 1873	2, Dec.	63	7	Koch	Cincinnati, OH	Homberg, Kurhessen
Dickhaut, Heinrich	10, Feb. 1898	15, Jan.	79	94		Marrs, IN	Schrecksbach, Neukirchen, Kurhessen
Dickhaut, Ludwig	5, Jan. 1899	1, Dec.	50	14		Marrs, IN	Schrecksbach, Kurhessen
Dickhof, Ella	15, Nov. 1894	12, Oct.	38	742	Krumminger	Emden, IL	Gaundersum, Ostfriesland
Dickhoff, J.	1, Mar. 1880	15, Feb.	83- 7m- 7d	71		Beaver Dam, WI	Prizig, Pommern
Dickhut, Anna Barbara	16, Mar. 1899	20, Feb.	67	174	Kinsly	Quincy, IL	Mogingen, Württemberg
Dickhut, Anna Catharine	23, May 1861	7, Apr.	27	84	Dinkelbein	Quincy, IL	
Dickhut, Augusta	19, Oct. 1885	29, Sept	48	7	Misselwitz	Columbus, IL	Löbichau, Altenburg, Sachsen
Dickhut, Catharina	17, Aug. 1893	21, July	79	526	Wengert	Quincy, IL	Mühlhausen, Preußen
Dickhut, Christian C.	23, July 1896	2, July	67	479		Quincy, IL	Mühlhausen, Thüringen
Dickhut, Christian Gottlob	26, Aug. 1878	12, Aug.	74- 7m- 6d	271		Quincy, IL	Mühlhausen, Thüringen
Dickhut, Christoph W.	19, Mar. 1877	23, Feb.	70	95		Quincy, IL	Mühlhausen, Germany
Dickhut, Johan Andreas Adolf	23, Mar. 1899	22, Feb.	76	190		Columbus, IL	Mühlhausen, Thüringen, Preußen
Dickhut, Johanna E.	14, Sept 1885	18, Aug.	75- 6m-10d	7	Schmidt	Quincy, IL	Mühlhausen beim Thuringer Wald, Preußen
Dickhut, John Christian	9, Sept 1872	20, Aug.	52	295		Washington, MN	
Dickhut, Margarethe	3, July 1856	6, June	28	108	Maus	Quincy, IL	
Dickhut, Maria	8, Apr. 1858	7, Mar.	21- 5m	56		Quincy, IL	
Dickhut, Maria Caroline	28, July 1879	11, July	74	239	Schmidt	Quincy, IL	Mühlhausen, Preußen
Dickhut, Wilhelm	29, Sept 1892	7, Sept	83- 4m-23d	622		Quincy, IL	Mühlhausen, Thüringen
Dickman, Emma Ch.	1, Oct. 1896	14, Sept	20	639		Defiance, OH	Lippe-Detmold
Dickmann, Wilhelm	12, Dec. 1889	2, Nov.	72- 5m- 3d	798	Donges	St. Paul, MN	
Dickmann, Anna	28, July 1879	27, June		239		Ballwin, MO	
Dickmann, Dorothea	26, Dec. 1870	1, Dec.	72	415	Rathert	Batesville, IN	Todtenhausen, Minden, Preußen
Dickmann, Elisabeth Sophia Rebekka	16, Apr. 1896	31, Mar.	34	254	Buckholz	Altamont, IL	Cook County, Illinois
Dickmann, Georg Friedrich	28, Nov. 1895	11, Nov.	78	766		Covington, KY	Wagenfeld, Diepholz, Hannover
Dickmann, Gustav Adolph	22, Apr. 1886	30, Mar.	19	7		St. Paul, MN	Inver Grove, Dakota County, Minnesota

Christliche Apologete Death Notices --- 1839 - 1899

Name of Deceased	Notice Date	Death Date	Age	Maiden Name	Page	Place of Death	Place of Birth
Dickmann, Johan Rudolph	11, Feb. 1892	19, Jan.	69		94	Defiance, OH	Loote, Münster, Preußen
Dickmann, Katharina	17, Mar. 1898	11, Feb.	69		175	Altamont, IL	Kurhessen
Dickmann, Maria	12, Apr. 1880	13, Mar.	70		119	Quincy, IL	Holzhausen, Amt Hartum, Minden, Preußen
Diddens, Heiko	17, Apr. 1882	11, Mar.	80- 5m- 8d		127	Melvin, IL	Bunde, Amt Weener, Ostfriesland
Didzun, Anna	22, Sept 1887	10, Sept	57	Zielert	606	Fairbury, IL	OstPreußen
Diebag, Johannes	8, May 1890	11, Apr.	64-11m- 8d	Lemke	302	Menomonie, WI	Schwenz, Kammin, Pommern
Diebag, John	24, May 1894	27, Apr.	16		342	Menomonie, WI	
Diebel, Friedrich	13, May 1872	28, Apr.	55		159	Detroit, MI	Rakoldshausen, Kurhessen
Diebel, Louis	17, Nov. 1879	3, Nov.	30- 6m		367	Brooklyn, NY	Reinboldshausen, Kurhessen
Diebel, Wilhelmine	18, Feb. 1897	13, Jan.	80	Schuch	111	Detroit, MI	Raboldshausen, Hessen
Diebold, Anna	29, Mar. 1888	28, Feb.	60- - 3d		206	Aurora, IL	Sontheim an der Brenz, Württemberg
Diebold, Christian	4, Feb. 1886	17, Jan.	68		7	Aurora, IL	Sontheim an der Brenz, Württemberg
Diebold, Ulrich	27, Oct. 1884	5, Oct.	68		7	Aurora, IL	Sontheim a. d. Brenz, Württemberg
Dieckmann, Assa	1, Nov. 1875	1, Oct.	6m		351	Defiance, OH	
Dieder, Anna Margaretha	3, Nov. 1892	9, Oct.	34		702	Chillicothe, OH	Chillicothe, Ross County, Ohio
Diederich, (Mrs)	19, Jan. 1888	27, Dec.	62	Bollmann	46	Laporte, IN	Demmin, Preußen
Diederich, Georg	2, Mar. 1863	5, Feb.	36- 2m-25d		36	Columbus, IN	Oberkaufungen, Kreis Kassel, Kurhessen
Diederich, Johan Georg	15, Apr. 1886	31, Mar.	36		7	Lemars, IA	Milwaukee, Wisconsin
Diedrich, August	12, June 1876	21, May	42- -14d		191	New Ulm, MN	Schiffelbach, Kirchheim, Kurhessen
Diedrich, Elisabeth	31, Mar. 1879	12, Mar.	27- 1m- 1d	Bletsch	103	Columbus, OH	
Diedrich, Friedrich	6, Dec. 1894	30, Sept	16		790	Ripon, WI	
Diedrich, Georg	31, Oct. 1895	3, Oct.	78		702	Bradford, IN	Diedenbergen, Hoheim, Nassau
Diedrich, Heinrich	8, Jan. 1872	20, Nov.			15	Etna, MO	Holzburg, Ziegenhain, Kurhessen
Diedrich, Karolina Louisa	18, July 1864	12, May	23	Kruse	116	St. Paul, MN	Halen, Minden, Preußen
Diedrich, Katharina Margaretha	14, Feb. 1870	3, Jan.	58- 7m- 8d		55	New Albany, IN	Diedenbergen, Amt Hochheim, Nassau
Diedrich, Margaretha	2, Apr. 1877	16, Mar.	38-11m-27d	Harz	111	Jeffersonville, IN	Wachenheim, Kreis Worms, Hessen-Darmstadt
Diedrich, Maria Magaretha	5, Sept 1889		65- 8m-11d	Weber	574	Bradford, IN	Diedenbergen, Hochheim, Nassau
Diefenbach, Anna Barbara	3, Aug. 1868	13, July	59- 2m- 3d	Rinkenberger	247	Valparaiso, IN	Schwieberdingen, Württemberg
Diefenbach, Charlotte	27, Aug. 1866	27, July	24- 6m- 8d	Berkler	278	Blue Island, IL	
Diefenbach, Christian	28, Aug. 1876	12, Aug.	30		279	Caseville, MI	Kesselbach, Amt Wehen, Nassau
Diefenbach, Christian	5, Sept 1864	18, July	45		144	Cassville, MI	Limbach, Kesselbach, Nassau
Diefenbach, Johannes Georg	12, July 1869	11, June	69- 8m12d		223	Valparaiso, IN	Dietzingen, Württemberg
Diefenbach, Lydia Louise	23, June 1892	18, May	17		398	Berne, MI	Windsor, Huron County, Michigan
Diefenbacher, Johan Adam	25, Feb. 1878	22, Jan.	74- 4m-13d		63	Richmond, IN	Mühlbach, Baden
Diefenbacher, Rosina	26, June 1890	18, May	82- 5m- 3d		414	Indianapolis, IN	Mühlbach, Baden
Diehl, Anna Katharina	9, Nov. 1874	5, Sept	67- 8m-24d	Schwalms	359	Cleveland, OH	Kreußenberg, Eudorf, Neukirchen, Kurhessen
Diehl, Caspar	29, Jan. 1866	15, Dec.	57		38	Piqua, OH	Kleinenrechtenbach, Coblenz, Wetzlar, Preußen
Diehl, Johan	30, Apr. 1891	10, Apr.	77- 4m-26d		286	Charlestown, IN	Nordheim, Hessen-Darmstadt
Diehl, Johann	21, June 1855	20, Apr.	62-10m-10d		100	Kingston, IL	Oberseemen, Kreis Nidda, Hessen-Darmstadt
Diehl, Joseph	14, July 1892	16, May	21		446	Danville, IL	Allentown, Pennsylvania
Diehl, Ludwig	18, Mar. 1897	21, Feb.	91		174	Cleveland, OH	Elbenrod bei Asfeld, Hessen-Darmstadt
Diehl, Magdalena	25, Nov. 1886	17, Oct.	80		7	Allegheny, PA	Bätschdorf, Elsaß
Diehl, Maria	16, Dec. 1878	16, Nov.	53	Förtsch	399	Madison, WI	Hitzacker, Hannover
Diehl, Paulina	31, May 1875	12, May	26- 5m-10d		175	Etna, MO	
Diehl, Philipp	15, July 1886	24, June	72- 1m-25d		7	Delhi, MI	Nordheim, Hessen
Diehl, Samuel	30, Mar. 1863	31, Dec.	22		52	Cleveland, OH	Karl County, Ohio

Christliche Apologete Death Notices --- 1839 - 1899

Name of Deceased	Notice Date	Death Date	Age	Page	Maiden Name	Place of Death	Place of Birth
Diehl, Wilhelm C.	17, Jan. 1881	31, Dec.	21- 9m- 3d	23		Dayton, OH	Warren County, Indiana
Diehle, Katharina	15, Dec. 1892	25, Sept	60	798	Schwammbach	Marrs, IN	Wiesweiler, St. Wendel, Preußen
Diehlmann, D.	10, Dec. 1877	20, Nov.		399	Hafner	Baltimore, MD	
Diehm, Elisabeth Margaretha	16, June 1892	18, May	33	382		St. Louis, MO	Hammelbach, Hessen
Diehm, Franz	26, Jan. 1899	10, Jan.	83	63		Cincinnati, OH	Edesheim, Rheinpfalz Baiern
Diehm, John	17, Oct. 1864	1, Oct.	14- 7m- 7d	168		Cincinnati, OH	
Diehm, Margaretha	17, June 1897	1, June	72	383	Pinger	Cincinnati, OH	Framersheim, Hessen-Darmstadt
Diehn, Heinrich	20, Feb. 1890		30- 8m	126		New Ulm, MN	Polz bei Dömitz, Mecklenburg-Schwerin
Diekmann, H.	12, Jan. 1880	22, Dec.	76	15		St. Paul, MN	L--rse, Lippe-Detmold
Diekmann, John Wesley	7, May 1877	14, Apr.	13- 7m-22d	151		Defiance, OH	
Diel, John	3, Nov. 1887	21, Oct.	58	702		Storm Lake, IA	Hessen-Darmstadt
Dielenberg, Margarethe	5, Jan. 1863	6, Dec.		4		St. Louis, MO	Schupbach, Amt Runkel, Nassau
Dielschneider, Mina	26, Apr. 1894	5, Apr.	25	278	Gethman	Gladbrook, IA	Tama County, Iowa
Diem, Elisabeth	25, Jan. 1894		81	62	Heß	Marine City, MI	Limbach, Rheinkreis Baiern
Diem, Elisabeth	30, Aug. 1855	1, July	64- 6m	140		Bellriver, MI	
Diem, Gottfried	7, Sept 1899	22, Aug.	82	575		Marine City, MI	Piramesens, Baiern
Diem, Gottfried	19, Dec. 1881	20, Nov.	29- 4m-13d	407		Marine City, MI	
Diem, Heinrich	28, July 1884	5, July	23	7		China, MI	China, St. Clair County, Michigan
Diem, Jac.	3, June 1858	4, May	20	88		Belles River, MI	
Diem, Magdalena	28, Dec. 1868	27, Nov.	50	415		Marine City, MI	
Diem, Margaretha	10, May 1880	22, Apr.	62	151	Schreiwer	Marine City, MI	
Diener, (Mrs)	12, Jan. 1874	24, Nov.	71	15		Liberty, MO	Mathissen, Fischenthal, Zürich, Schweiz
Diercks, Johan Christian	25, Mar. 1886	25, Feb.	38	7		Menominee, MI	Struvenhütten, Segeberg, Holstein
Dierigo, Maria	27, Feb. 1882	4, Feb.	24	71	Moll	Lancaster, MO	Schuyler County, Missouri
Dieringer, Friederika	31, Mar. 1898	6, Mar.	72	207	Finkeldei	Boonville, MO	Essen, West Preußen
Dierking, Anna Barbara	8, Mar. 1894	15, Feb.	64	166	Eriling	Jeffersonville, IN	
Dierking, Charley	23, Feb. 1888	30, Jan.	35- 2m-12d	126		New Albany, IN	Bierde, Minden, Preußen
Dierking, Conrad	2, Sept 1878	5, Aug.	48	279		New Albany, IN	Schloß Valkenberg, Kurhessen
Dierking, Elisabeth	24, June 1867	13, June		198	Horn	New Albany, IN	Binode, Preußen
Dierking, Friedrich	31, Dec. 1883	14, Dec.	66	7		Jeffersonville, IN	Hannover
Dierking, Friedrich	22, Mar. 1894	25, Feb.	72	198		Atchison, KS	Wendenborstel, Stimbke, Hannover
Dierking, Heinrich Christian	7, Mar. 1895	11, Feb.	81	158		Chester, IL	
Dierking, Heinrich Friedrich	19, Oct. 1885	29, Sept	33	7		Council Grove, KS	Dünsen, Neustadt, Hannover
Dierking, Heinrich Wilhelm	26, Aug. 1886	9, Aug.	72- 6m-22d	7		Nerstrand, MN	
Dierking, Hester	29, May 1856	2, May	22- 8m	88	Knauer	New Albany, IN	Wentenbostel, Hannover
Dierking, John Wesley	12, Nov. 1883	10, Oct.	27-10m	367		Jeffersonville, IN	
Dierking, Maria	29, Dec. 1898	30, Nov.	78	828	Wiegmann	Chester, IL	Stuttgart, Württemberg
Dierking, Maria	15, Dec. 1843	23, Nov.	17	199		Louisville, KY	Steinecke, Amt Wölbe, Hannover
Dierking, Rosina	8, Dec. 1887	27, Sept	65	782	Leib	Jeffersonville, IN	Hammelwörden, Freiburg an der Elbe, Hannover
Dierking, Sophia	3, Dec. 1866		53	390		Weston, MO	Sandusky, Ohio
Dierks, Karsten Heinrich	30, June 1898	5, June	61	415		Muscatine, IA	Mainz, Hessen-Darmstadt
Diers, Fred A.	21, Jan. 1892	22, Dec.	24- 3m-18d	46		Cincinnati, OH	Mutterstadt, Rheinkreis Baiern
Diers, Margaretha	28, Nov. 1889		60	766	Otto	Cincinnati, OH	Chillicothe, Ross County, Ohio
Diesque, Barbara	14, Apr. 1859	18, Mar.	45	60		Lawrenceburg, IN	
Dieter, Caroline	23, Nov. 1893	22, Oct.	32	750		Columbus, OH	
Dieter, Emma	28, July 1887	26, June	21	478		Chillicothe, OH	

- 88 -

Christliche Apologete Death Notices --- 1839 - 1899

Name of Deceased	Notice Date	Death Date	Age	Maiden Name	Page	Place of Death	Place of Birth
Dieter, Maria	2, Apr. 1877	20, Feb.	17		111	St. Paul, MN	Kendall County, Illinois
Dieter, Wilhelm Ferdinand	14, May 1896	19, Apr.	68		318	Arenzville, IL	Berka an der Vera, Sachsen
Dieterich, Anna Catharina	25, Jan. 1864	8, Dec.	60	Schreiber	16	Sandwich, IL	Holzburg, Amt Neukirchen, Kurhessen
Dieterich, Charles	22, Dec. 1898	16, Nov.	29		815		
Dieterich, Georg	23, Jan. 1896	24, Dec.	57		62	Victor, IA	Schönau bei Heidelberg, Baden
Dieterich, Johannes	18, June 1891	29, Mar.	87		398	Etna, MO	Holsburg, Ziegenheim, Kurhessen
Dieterich, Louretta Florinta	3, May 1888	12, Apr.	16		286	Aurora, IL	
Dieterich, Valentin Friedrich	26, Feb. 1891	5, Feb.	28		142	Sandwich, IL	Aurora,
Dietewich, Maria	19, Apr. 1860	4, Apr.	31		64	Chicago, IL	Niedersaulheim, Hessen
Dietewig, Andreas	18, Feb. 1878	28, Jan.	80		55	Chicago, IL	Niedersaulheim, Wörrstadt, Alzey, Rhein-Hessen
Dietewig, Andreas	12, May 1879	19, Apr.	70-6m		151	Chicago, IL	Niedersaulheim, Hessen
Dietewig, Eduard	21, May 1883	3, May	20		167	Chicago, IL	Chicago, Cook County, Illinois
Diether, Bernhard	25, Dec. 1876	30, Nov.	47		413	St. Paul, MN	Neuenstadt, Neckarsulm, Württemberg
Diether, Frances Myrtle	28, July 1898	28, May	18		479	St. Paul, MN	St. Paul, Minnesota
Diether, J. Franz	15, May 1865	11, Apr.	69		80	Bucyrus, OH	Neuenstadt, Weinsberg, Württemberg
Diether, Karl F.	11, Mar. 1897	13, Feb.	85		158	Ft. Wayne, IN	Neuenstadt, Württemberg
Diether, Karoline	26, May 1898	12, Apr.	71	Sommer	335	Philadelphia, PA	Baumerlebach, Oehringen, Württemberg
Diether, Maria Katharina	9, Feb. 1899	15, Dec.	70	Gärtner	95	Columbus, OH	Waldmissibach, Hessen-Darmstadt
Diether, Robert	23, Nov. 1874	6, Nov.	25- 3m-10d		375	Allegheny City, PA	Neuenstadt, Neckarsulm, Württemberg
Dietrich, Barbara	13, Mar. 1871	8, Feb.	65-11m-17d		87	Chillicothe, OH	Wachenheim, Rheinpfalz Baiern
Dietrich, Caroline	14, Mar. 1889	22, Feb.	76- -10d		174	Baltimore, MD	Braunschweig
Dietrich, Christine	20, Aug. 1896	26, May	77		542	New York City, NY	Württemberg
Dietrich, Emilie	1, Nov. 1880	9, Oct.	24- -5d		351	Santa Claus, IN	Spencer County, Indiana
Dietrich, Fabian	15, June 1893	21, May	56		382	New Haven, CT	
Dietrich, Franklin Otto	3, Mar. 1884	15, Feb.	12		7	Indianapolis, IN	Indianapolis, Marion County, Indiana
Dietrich, Georg Michael	26, July 1888	8, July	79-11m- 2d		478	Jordan, MN	Windelsbach, Mittelfranken, Baiern
Dietrich, Gertraud	20, Mar. 1876	20, Feb.	86		95	Carrollton, MO	Ringelshausen, Kurhessen
Dietrich, Heinrich	19, Feb. 1872	30, Jan.	44		63	Chillicothe, OH	Wachenheim, Rheinkreis Baiern
Dietrich, Heinrich	13, Jan. 1887	27, Dec.	90		30	Pittsburg, PA	Ehlen, Wolfhagen, Kurhessen
Dietrich, Johan	23, Aug. 1888	30, July	57		542	Sterling, NE	Grünewalde, Liebenwerda, Preußen
Dietrich, Johan Friedrich	30, Mar. 1885	18, Mar.	65		7	Ellis Grove, IL	Menzingen, Bretten, Baden
Dietrich, Johan Georg	29, Oct. 1857	24, Sept	48		176	Cedar Lake, IN	Unterrammerdorf, Baiern
Dietrich, John	30, Mar. 1874	14, Mar.	76-9m		103	Lexington, ---	Härdingshausen, Amt Kassel, Kurhessen
Dietrich, John	21, Apr. 1892	11, Mar.	72		254	Jeffersonville, IN	Diedbergen, Nassau
Dietrich, Julius	14, July 1887	21, June	25		446	Sterling, NE	Bromberg, Posen
Dietrich, Katharina Maria	29, Jan. 1877	12, Jan.	76- 1m		39	Oregon, MO	Dietz, Nassau
Dietrich, Louise	28, Jan. 1897	23, Dec.	62	Dörr	62	Kramer, NE	Grünewolden, Preußen
Dietrich, Margaretha	21, Mar. 1895	2, Mar.	43	Meyer	190	Chicago, IL	Naterdeich, Schleswig-Holstein
Dietrich, Sarah	20, Apr. 1899	12, Mar.	62		254	Hannibal, OH	Monroe County, Ohio
Dietrichs, Carolina	25, July 1850	6, July	6- 6m		120	Louisville, KY	
Dietrichs, Ernst	25, July 1850	July	4- -19d		120	Louisville, KY	
Dietrichs, Ernst	25, July 1850	10, July	38-9m		120	Louisville, KY	
Dietrichs, Maria Anna	25, July 1850	3, July	11- -20d		120	Louisville, KY	
Dietricht, Caroline	7, Feb. 1845	14, Jan.	67		67	Boonville, IN	Birkenfeld, Oldenburg
Dietsch, Friedrich Wilhelm	11, Nov. 1878	7, Oct.	33-4m-12d		359	New Orleans, LA	Unersirken bei Pausa, Sachsen
Dietsch, Georg	25, Jan. 1894	3, Dec.	53		62	Marion, OH	Richland Township, Marion County, Ohio

Name of Deceased	Notice Date	Death Date	Age	Maiden Name	Page	Place of Death	Place of Birth
Dietsch, Georg	17, Apr. 1890	30, Jan.	17- 1m- 1d		254	Marion, OH	Heidelsheim, Bruchsal, Baden
Dietz, Andreas	1, Aug. 1881	21, May	74- 4m-28d		247	San Francisco, CA	Ruderhausen, Sachsen-Weimar
Dietz, August	1, Jan. 1866		61		6	Chicago, IL	Sindelfingen, Böblingen, Württemberg
Dietz, Christina Magdalena	25, Aug. 1862	1, June	32	Pflüger	136	Philadelphia, PA	Gretern, Baiern
Dietz, Elisabeth	23, Sept 1897	28, Aug.	39	Berenz	607	Bloomington, IL	Siedenbollentin, Preußen
Dietz, Friederika	6, Oct. 1898	20, Sept	58	Haas	639	Firth, NE	Spielberg, Durlach, Baden
Dietz, Friedrich	15, Oct. 1866	19, Sept	42		334	Sicori, IL	Spielberg bei Carlsruhe, Baden
Dietz, Heinrich	21, Apr. 1853	11, Mar.	38- 3m		64	Marion, OH	Ellendingen, Pforzheim, Baden
Dietz, Karl F.	24, Nov. 1884		72- 6m-10d		7	Marshall, IL	Heidelsheim, Baden
Dietz, Katharina	6, Sept 1888	6, Aug.	74- 9m- 1d	Papst	574	San Francisco, CA	Hohenhausen, Hessen-Kassel
Dietz, Maria	19, Jan. 1860	13, Oct.	52		12	East Troy, WI	Jefferson County, Indiana
Dietz, Maria	23, Aug. 1888	29, July	33- 4m-17d	Lippot	542	Madison, IN	Holmes County, Ohio
Dietz, Maria	29, Apr. 1897	8, Apr.	80	Krieger	271	Edon, OH	Sommerset County, Pennsylvania
Dietz, Samuel	28, Sept 1854	2, Sept	42- 6m		156	Bryan, OH	
Dietzel, Bertha	15, June 1874		4- 2w		191	Caseville, MI	Chursdorf, Sachsen-Weimar
Dietzel, Ernestine	12, Nov. 1891	16, Oct.	45		734	Berne, MI	Triebes, Reuß
Dietzel, Friedrich Wilhelm	12, Mar. 1896	18, Feb.	59		174	Lawrence, MA	Hohenleuben, Gera, Reuß
Dietzel, Henry	20, Oct. 1892	27, Sept			670	Hohenleuben, GE	Dörtendorf, Sachsen-Weimar
Dietzel, Johan Gottfried	11, Dec. 1876	17, Nov.	42- 2m-16d		399	Caseville, MI	Driebes, Sachsen
Dietzel, Paulina	30, Sept 1886	31, Aug.	47	Dietzel	7	Lawrence, MA	Hohenleuben, Reuß
Dietzel, Wilhelmine	3, Aug. 1874	24, June	31- 6m-27d	Weidner	247	Scranton, PA	Weisenborn, Kurhessen
Diezel, Anna	27, Aug. 1877	11, Aug.	60- 5m- 3d		279	Goshen, IN	Hobach, Elsaß
Diffor, Johan	30, Nov. 1893	19, Oct.	72		766	Buffalo, MN	Halenbeck, Lohe, Nienburg, Hannover
Dikmann, F.	17, May 1869	22, Apr.	75		159	Effingham, IL	Lotte, Tecklenburg, Münster, Preußen
Dikmann, Johan Heinrich	24, May 1875	3, May	58		167	Defiance, OH	Cook County, Illinois
Dikmann, Marie	10, Mar. 1879	26, Jan.	23		79	Altamont, IL	Kindenheim, Frankenthal, Baiern
Dilg, Katharina	19, Jan. 1888	20, Dec.	77- 2m- 5d	Simon	46	Edon, OH	St. Joseph Twp, Williams County, Ohio
Dilgs, Karoline	9, June 1892	11, May	37	Stork	366	Edon, OH	Medina County, Ohio
Dilgs, Katharina	6, Mar. 1890	17, Feb.	27	Schutt	158	Edgerton, OH	Göllheim, Rheinkreis Baiern
Dilgs, Peter	16, June 1892	20, May	82- 1m-14d		382	Edon, OH	Schwarzenfels, Kurhessen
Dilk, Elisabeth	16, Jan. 1896	17, Dec.	82	Iring	46	Graham, MO	
Dilk, Harvey E.	15, Sept 1884	10, July	11- 4m-15d		7	Madison, IN	
Dilk, Jacob Ludwig	7, Nov. 1895	19, Oct.	68		718	Madison, In	
Dilk, Katharina Elisabeth	14, June 1860	16, Apr.	75	Küfer	96	Patriot, IN	Spiesen, RheinPreußen
Dilk, Margaretha	16, Jan. 1890	21, Dec.	58		46	Madison, IN	Spisen, Preußen
Dilk, Nickolaus	20, Apr. 1893	20, Mar.	72	Augustin	254	Graham, MO	Saarlouis, Preußen
Dill, Maria Katharina	17, Nov. 1898	29, Oct.	78 - 8d		735	Evansville, IN	RheinPreußen
Dille, Caspar	27, Sept 1849		44		156	Manchester, MO	Baden
Diller, Louise	12, Feb. 1891	23, Jan.		Heller	110	Freeport, IL	
Dilling, Heinrich	29, Jan. 1866	9, Sept	22		38	Fond du Lac, WI	Klein-Gladenbach, Hessen-Darmstadt
Dilling, Johannes	16, Feb. 1885	1, Feb.	40		7	Fond du Lac, WI	Kleingladenbach, Hessen-Darmstadt
Dillman, Gottlieb Friedrich	23, Apr. 1896	3, Apr.	34		270	Madison, WI	Vaihingen, Württemberg
Dinger, David	24, Feb. 1873	31, Jan.	67-11m-19d		63	Baresville, OH	Zwirdschen, Sachsen
Dinger, Friedrich Wilhelm	16, May 1895	26, Apr.	74		318	Baltimore, MD	Aarau, Aargau, Schweiz
Dinger, Julia Charlotte	27, Mar. 1890	10, Mar.	36- 7m-18d	Becker	206	Wheeling, WV	Wheeling, West Virginia
Dinger, Louise	17, Nov. 1879	2, Nov.	47- 5m-12d	Eisenhardt	367	Wheeling, WV	Wheeling, WV

Christliche Apologete Death Notices --- 1839 - 1899

Name of Deceased	Notice Date	Death Date	Age	Maiden Name	Page	Place of Death	Place of Birth
Dinger, Maria Rosina	1, Jan. 1877	29, Nov.	69-10m-19d	Geselbarth	7	Baresville, OH	Gauern, Sachsen-Altenburg
Dingersen, Wilhelm Heinrich A.	17, Mar. 1898	17, Feb.	24		175	Beaufort, MO	Port Hudson , Missouri
Dingerson, Emma D.	7, July 1873	8, June	3		215	Beaufort, MO	
Dingwerth, Charlotte	28,May 1883	9, May	68- 4m-19d	Jahn	175	Decatur, Il	Oldendorf, Borgholzhausen, Minden, Preußen
Dingwerth, Herman	25, June 1866	2, June	38		206	Decatur, IL	Backaloh, Kreis Halle, Minden, Preußen
Dinkelmann, Maria	2, Nov. 1899		17- 4m- 8d		703	Schnectady, NY	
Dinniger, Catharina	8, Apr. 1867	17, Feb.	65	Hukenduckler	110	Chester, IL	
Dinsch, Margaretha	7, June 1888	20, May	30	Knaup	366	Beaver Dam, WI	Großhausen, Hessen-Darmstadt
Dinse, Albertine Catharina	14, Mar. 1889	29, Jan.		Schwichtenberg	174	Sedalia, MO	Pommern
Dinse, Caroline Albertine	2, May 1889	29, Jan.		Schwichtenberg	286	Colesburg, IA	Retschtrow, Pommern
Dinse, Joachim Christoph	8, July 1897	9, June	75		431	Klemme, IA	Stepnitz, Pommern
Dippe, Friederike	7, Apr. 1887	21, Mar.	71		222	Harper, IA	Holzkamp bei Ehrichhausen, Lippe-Detmold
Dippel, Elisabeth	23, May 1881	27, Apr.	28	Spielhof	167	Indianapolis, IN	
Dippert, Josephine	3, Nov. 1898	20, Aug.	67	Ambs	703	Des Moines, IA	Pforzheim, Baden
Dippius, Wilhelm	17, Feb. 1898		73		111	Lena, IL	Baden
Dippon, Mary	18, Jan. 1894	22, Dec.	18		46	Newark, NJ	Waiblingen, Württemberg
Dirking, Christian	18, Dec. 1890	26, Nov.	65- 6m-15d		814	New Albany, IN	Bierden, Preußen
Dirks, Anna Maria	6, Apr. 1899	17, Mar.	73	Schuler	222	Crow River, MN	Waldorf, Nagold, Württemberg
Dirks, Auguste	24, June 1897		30	Götsch	399	New Ulm, MN	
Dirks, Conrad	1, Mar. 1894	1, Feb.	61		150	New Ulm, MN	Frommhausen, Lippe-Detmold
Dirks, Friedrich	2, Feb. 1888	18, Dec.	66		78	Summerfield, IL	Wittmund, Hannover
Dirks, Johan	24, Mar. 1884	8, Mar.	70		7	Humboldt, NE	Wiesede, Repshold, Ostfriesland
Dirr, Catharine	24, Dec. 1891	23, Nov.	22- 3m		830	Defiance, OH	Henry County, Ohio
Dirr, Georg	2, June 1879	12, May	73- 9m-24d		175	Defiance, OH	Wankheim, Tübingen, Württemberg
Dirr, Katharina	12, May 1862	9, Apr.		Gortener	76	Defiance, OH	Niederbecksbach, Humburg, Rheinkreis Baiern
Dirr, Katharina	9, Dec. 1878	23, Nov.	66- 9m- 5d		391	Defiance, OH	Oberauerbach, Baiern
Dirscheit, C.	5, Dec. 1870	15, Nov.	42	Flor	391	Webster City, IA	Jugendheim, Hessen
Disch , Margaretha	30, Mar. 1893	16, Feb.	68	Kundert	206	St. Paul, MN	Elm, Glarus, Schweiz
Disch, Andreas	7, Apr. 1887	9, Mar.	68		222	Galena, IL	Elm, Glarus, Schweiz
Discher, Anna Maria	10, Nov. 1892	13, Oct.	59	Bode	718	Cincinnati, OH	Uesen, Achim, Hannover
Discher, Dietrich	9, June 1898	27, Apr.	75- 4m-12d		367	Cincinnati, OH	Bremen, Germany
Discher, Heinrich	9, May 1881	27, Apr.	16		151	Cincinnati, OH	
Discher, Helene	29, July 1897	5, July	36		479	Cincinnati, OH	Cincinnati, Hamilton County, Ohio
Dischinger, Charlotte	10, Dec. 1896	4, Nov.	51	Suehrbei	798	Elmore, OH	Lusewitz, Mecklenburg
Dischinger, Minna	26, Sept 1895	10, Aug.	25	Kuensting	622	Elmore, OH	Elmore, Ohio
Disque, Johannes	22, Oct. 1864	15, June			172	Batesville, IN	
Diß, Karoline	3, Oct. 1895	9, Aug.	33	Groh	638	Cincinnati, OH	Cincinnati, Hamilton County, Ohio
Dissen, Anna Gertrud	7, Jan. 1884	13, Dec.	38		7	Madison, IN	Oberdurlach bei Mühlhausen, Preußen
Distel, Georg	29, Aug.1895	3, Aug.	69		558	Madison, IN	Wächtersbach, Gelnhausen, Hannau, Kurhessen
Distelhorst, Friedrike	12, Aug. 1872	27, July	80	Vos	263	Sheboygan, WI	Lachen, Hannover
Distler, Elise	29, Sept 1887	27, July	34	Baukel	622	Brooklyn, NY	Lauf, Baiern
Ditewig, Katharina	21, Sept 1899	3, Sept	75		607	Chicago, IL	Niedersaulheim, Hessen-Darmstadt
Ditewig, Magdalena	9, Dec. 1872	23, Sept	80	Kröhle	399	Chicago, IL	Niedersaulheim bei Mainz, Preußen
Ditmeier, Theresia	14, June 1875	25, May	45	Wusler	191	Freeport, IL	
Ditsch, Johannes Friedrich	22, Sept 1887	7, Sept	40- 7m- 7d		606	Marion, OH	Marion, Ohio
Dittbenner, Johan Siegfried	23, Dec. 1897	24, Nov.	51		815	Morgan, MN	Claushagen, Neustettin, Köslin, Hinterpommern

Christliche Apologete Death Notices --- 1839 - 1899

Name of Deceased	Notice Date	Death Date	Age	Maiden Name	Place of Death	Page	Place of Birth
Dittbenner, Johanna Caroline W.	4, Apr. 1889	10, Mar.	68	Krüger	Sleepy Eye, MN	222	Klockow, Belgard, Germany
Dittbenner, Karolina Maria	10, Sept 1896	16, Aug.	48	Simonbit	Morgan, MN	591	Lamsheim, Leonberg, Württemberg
Dittbenner, Therese Louise	13, Sept 1888	17, Aug.	23	Fischer	Sleepy Eye, MN	590	Hohenwalde, Pommern
Dittbenner, Johan Friedrich W.	16, Apr. 1896	21, Mar.	83		Morgan, MN	254	Klöppenfür, Pommern
Ditters, Wilhelmine	15, Feb. 1864	23, Dec.	25- 1m- 2d	Luedwich	Carver, MN	28	Langenholzhausen, Lippe
Dittes, Wilhelmine	30, Dec. 1878	1, Dec.	33	Siegrist	Cincinnati, OH	415	Niederdorf, Basel, Schweiz
Dittman, Charlotte	3, Sept 1896	13, Aug.	82		Davenport, IA	575	Wiehe, Sachsen
Dittmann, Christoph Heinrich	30, Nov. 1868	21, Oct.	19-11m-19d		Cincinnati, OH	383	Sieglingen, Nekarsulm, Württemberg
Dittmann, Georg Friedrich	2, Sept 1886	15, Aug.	22		Cincinnati, OH	7	Cincinnati, Hamilton County, Ohio
Dittmann, Herman	17, Nov. 1892	8, Oct.	22		Washington, MN	734	Oakdale, Washington County, Minnesota
Dittmann, Joh. Peter	13, Apr. 1874	28, Mar.	56		Cincinnati, OH	119	Sichlingen, Neckarsulm, Württemberg
Dittmann, Johan Christian	24, Dec. 1866	2, Dec.	20		Cincinnati, OH	414	Siglingen, Neckarsulm, Württemberg
Dittmann, Karl Peter	23, Oct. 1882	30, Sept	25- 6m-27d		Cincinnati, OH	343	
Dittmann, Pauline	22, Apr. 1878	29, Mar.	46		Washington, MN	127	Bonin, Köslin, Hinterpommern
Dittmar, Georg	29, June 1885	10, June	86		Lena, IL	7	Maßbach, Baiern
Dittmar, Margaretha	4, Apr. 1864	12, Mar.	53	Gräbner	Rush Creek, IL	56	Zell, Schweinfurth, Baiern
Dittmer, Anna Maria	18, Feb. 1878	27, Jan.	47	Redlingshöfer	Colesburg, IA	55	Nürnberg, Baiern
Dittmer, Johanne	3, Sept 1877	25, Mar.	57		Belleville, IL	287	Bielefeld, Westphalen
Dittmer, Kezia S.	19, Aug. 1897	31, July	68		Colesburg, IA	527	Logan Twp, Center County, Pennsylvania
Dittmer, Martin	1, Aug. 1881	8, July	75- 3m- 5d		Wheeling, WV	247	Eubach, Kurhessen
Ditzel, Georg	13, Oct. 1887		12- 8m-27d		Charlestown, Indiana	654	Charlestown, Indiana
Ditzel, Heinrich	29, Sept 1887	13, Sept	30- 5m- 7d		Charlestown, IN	622	Züntersbach, Schlüchtern, Kurhessen
Ditzel, Konrad	28, Feb. 1889	16, Feb.	55		Charlestown, IN	142	Zündersbach, Schwarzenfels, Kurhessen
Dixon, Catharina	10, June 1897	18, May	41	Ziegler	Marrs, IN	367	West Franklin, Posey County, Indiana
Doble, Wilhelmine	8, Feb. 1875	9, Jan.	24	Madelung	Freeport, IL	47	
Dobler, Regina	24, Feb. 1879	11, Feb.	79	Sauer	Poughkeepsie, NY	63	Groß-Aspach, Backnang, Württemberg
Dobratz, Heinrich	13, Dec. 1880	6, Nov.	83		Milwaukee, WI	399	Lekow, Schiefelbein, Pommern
Dochan, Caroline	31, Oct. 1895	9, Oct.	41		Berea, OH	702	Hilmersdorf, Sachsen
Dock, Dorothea	1, Feb. 1894	18, Dec.	38		Troy, NY	78	Merzweiler, Elsaß
Dockweiler, John	6, Oct. 1892	16, Sept	58		Indianapolis, IN	638	Neuhausen, Tuttlingen, Württemberg
Doderer, Ernst Friedrich	13, Feb. 1890	11, Jan.	60- 2m- 4d		Mason City, IA	110	Waiblingen, Württemberg
Doehtli, Karoline	7, June 1875	16, May	29	Noll	St. Louis, MO	183	
Doelfield, Friedrich	27, Sept 1888	6, Sept	81- 2m-18d		Baltimore, MD	622	
Döeller, Gottfried	22, June 1893	21, May	43		Hamilton, OH	398	
Doemland, Margarethe Selma	12, Aug. 1886	30, July	34	Buser	Burlington, IA	7	Pratteln, Baselland, Schweiz
Doere, August	31, Aug. 1854	7, Aug.	4		Highland, IL	140	
Doere, Karl	31, Aug. 1854	3, Aug.	7		Highland, IL	140	
Doere, Mina	31, Aug. 1854	3, Aug.	34		Highland, IL	140	
Doering, Christina Elisabeth	20, Mar. 1882	7, Mar.	64- 7m- 1d	Braksiks	Greenville, OH	95	Feldbergen, Hannover
Doering, Emilie	9, Aug. 1888	20, June	22- -19d		Farwell, IL	510	Burg Steinfurt, Preußen
Doern, Maria Katharina	11, June 1883	20, May	75		Louisville, KY	191	Mansfelden, Nassau
Doerr, John	29, Oct. 1891	3, Oct.	77		Poughkeepsie, NY	702	Raien, Sinsheim, Baden
Doerr, Margaretha	14, Aug. 1865	15, June	47- 6m-19d		Seymour, IN	132	Gotzing, Baiern
Doerrle, Emma Sophia	23, Apr. 1891	29, Mar.	28	Westenkühler	Dalton, MO	270	St. Charles, Missouri
Doersam, Georg	21, July 1884		25		Scranton, PA	7	
Doescher, Hermine	8, Oct. 1896	14, Sept	40	Bäcker	New York City, NY	655	New York

Christliche Apologete Death Notices --- 1839 - 1899

Name of Deceased	Notice Date	Death Date	Age	Page	Maiden Name	Place of Death	Place of Birth
Döge, Carl Fr. W.	13, Feb. 1896	15, Jan.	73	110		Eldora, IA	Meseritz, Schieferbein, Pommern
Döhle, Johan	21, Jan. 1897	26, Dec.	40	46		Sioux City, IA	OberNeuland bei Bremen, Germany
Dohmann, Sophia	30, July1883	17, July	61- 1m- 7d	247		Chicago, IL	Bentzin, Pommern
Döhner, Barbara	15, July 1858	25, June	20-10m-25d	112	Hob	Covington, KY	Steinkirchen, Künzelsau, Württemberg
Döhner, Johan	30, Nov. 1885	17, Nov.	59	7		Covington, KY	Steinkirchen, Kinzelsau, Württemberg
Dohrmann, Dorothea	26, May 1853	20, Apr.	34	84	Grote	Des Moines, IA	
Dohrmann, Elisabeth Anna	6, Jan. 1887	24, Dec.	58	14		Brooklyn, NY	
Dohrmann, Johan	21, Apr. 1887	6, Apr.	74- 8m-24d	254		Nauvoo, IL	Brümmerhaft, Hannover
Dohrmann, Johan Dietrich	5, Dec. 1889	21, Oct.	33	782		Brooklyn, NY	Elmlohe, Hannover
Dohrmann, Johan Friedrich	20, Dec. 1894	21, Aug.	29	822		Covington, KY	Covington, Kenton County, Kentucky
Dohrmann, Maria Elisabeth	11, Feb. 1884		64	7	Reser	Nauvoo, IL	Baiern
Dohrmann, Sophia Elisa	7, Mar. 1895	28, Jan.	34	158		Covington, KY	
Dökel, Sophie	18, Nov. 1897	15, Oct.	86	735	Heine	Perry, TX	Rehburg, Hannover
Dold, Anna Maria	1, Nov. 1880	15, Aug.		351	Scharde	Decatur, IL	Kestrich, Alsfeld, Hessen
Dold, Maria	6, Sept 1880	15, Aug.	83-11m-13d	287		St. Louis, MO	Hessen
Döfeld, Elisabeth	18, Mar. 1897	22, Feb.	88	174	Mortell	St. Paul, MN	Thalmischweiler, Pirmasens, Rheinpfalz Baiern
Döfeld, Peter	29, Apr. 1852	5, Apr.	10- 8m-17d	72		Baltimore, MD	Neustadt an der Aisch, Baiern
Dolhage, Katharina Elisabeth	23, Jan. 1875	30, Dec.	62	31	Büscher	Hopewell, MO	Lienen, Tecklenburg, Preußen
Döker, Johan	17, Aug. 1893	28, July	100- 3m-22d	526		Farmington, IA	Schopfloch, Württemberg
Döker, Maria	7, June 1880	18, May	66	183	Blesinger	Farmington, IA	Waiblingen, Württemberg
Doll, Georg	20, May 1886	27, Apr.	24	7		Milwaukee, WI	St. Louis, Missouri
Doll, John George	22, Sept 1892	16, Aug.	56	606		New York City, NY	Schluchten, Eppingen, Baden
Dölle, Andreas	26, Sept 1864	3, Sept	72- 8m-27d	156		Burlington, IA	
Döllenbach, (Mrs)	29, Oct. 1877	22, Sept	72	351		Highland, IL	Fechingen, Bern, Schweiz
Döller, Katharina Elisabeth	18, Mar. 1886	27, Feb.	86- 2m- 4d	7			Röhrenfurth, Kurhessen
Döling, Dina	31, May 1875	10, May	24	175		Nokomis, IL	Lienen, Tecklenburg, Preußen
Dollinger, Franz	23, May 1895		66	334		Champaign, IL	Baden
Dols, Martin	29, Oct. 1891	18, Sept	72	702		Jerusalem, NY	Wellen, Hannover
Dömland, Joachim Andreas	21, Aug. 1876	1, Aug.	76	271		Defiance, OH	Preußen
Dömland, John	20, Mar. 1865	Dec.	22- 1m	48		Defiance, OH	Wiebke, Magdeburg, Preußen
Donerth, Lisette Justine	16, Aug. 1880	23, July	27- 8m	263		Winona, MN	Fountain City, Wisconsin
Donges, (Mr)	29, Apr. 1886	10, Apr.	84	7		St. Louis, MO	Sinkershausen, Biedenkopf, Hessen-Darmstadt
Donges, Fr. Wilhelm	26, Feb. 1877	30, Jan.	63	71		Elizabeth, NJ	Selters, Nassau
Donges, Katharina	2, Oct. 1871	31, Aug.	69	319	Jung	Ballwin, MO	Singershausen, Biedenkopf, Hessen-Darmstadt
Dönges, Kilian	25, May 1863	11, Apr.	29	84		Springfield, IL	Gudensberg, Kurhessen
Donges, Ludwig	15, Mar. 1888	5, Feb.	62- 2m-27d	174		Ballwin, MO	Sinkerhausen, Biedenkopf, Hessen-Darmstadt
Dönges, Maria	29, Dec. 1898	6, Dec.	86	828	Straube	Springfield, IL	Magdeburg, Preußen
Donner, Barbara	21, Oct. 1886	15, Sept	71	7	Baumann	Marrs, IN	Kocherstetten, Künzelsau, Württemberg
Donner, Heinrich	3, Jan. 1895	5, Dec.	82- 4m-24d	14		Marrs, IN	Kocherstetten, Künzelsau, Württemberg
Donop, Alexander	18, June 1891	21, May	16- 2m-21d	398		Hedwigs Hill, TX	Lage, Lippe-Detmold
Donop, Otto	1, Nov. 1875	5, Oct.	46	351		Mason, TX	
Döpel, Johan Gottlob	12, Jan. 1899	12, Dec.	82	31		Mt. Vernon, NY	Hellborn, Sachsen-Altenburg
Döpker, Caroline	3, June 1872	8, May	17	183		Indianapolis, IN	
Döpling, Clara Margaretha	18, Nov. 1878		59	367	Hekermann	St. Louis, MO	Hördinghausen, Wittlage, Osnabrück, Hannover
Dopp, Peter Friedrich	22, Sept 1887	1, Sept	26	606		Sandwich, IL	Jürgenshagen, Mecklenburg-Schwerin
Doren, Frank Jansen	18, Nov. 1897	25, Oct.	89	735		Petersburg, IL	Strackholt, Aurich, Ostfriesland

- 93 -

Christliche Apologete Death Notices --- 1839 - 1899

Name of Deceased	Notice Date	Death Date	Age	Maiden Name	Page	Place of Death	Place of Birth
Dorer, Salome	1, May 1876	25, Jan.	75	Uhlerich	143	Brooklyn, NY	Ottmarsingen, Aargau, Schweiz
Dörfling, Johan	1, Mar. 1894	19, Jan.	75		150	Belleville, Il	Parchim, Mecklenburg-Schwerin
Dorfmeister, Albert	25, Feb. 1878	21, Apr.	24		63	Storm Lake, IA	Washington County, Wisconsin
Döring, Anna Katharine	12, May 1873	21, Apr.	65	Schnell	151	Peoria, IL	Niedervorschütz, Melsungen, Hessen-Kassel
Döring, Anna Maria	17, Mar. 1892	28, Feb.	81	Erbskorn	174	Ironton, OH	Bibra, Rodenburg, Kurhessen
Döring, Rosa	28, Aug. 1890	14, Aug.	62	Lindner	558	Chicago, IL	
Doring, Sophia	11, June 1883		25	Kinum	191	Schnectady, NY	
Dorl, Mathilde	21, June 1894	1, June	73		406	Brooklyn, NY	Coßwig bei Bernburg, Germany
Dorman, Friederike	26, Jan. 1888	26, Dec.	85- 7m-24d		62	Davenport, IA	Ildehausen, Seefen, Braunschweig
Dorman, Wilhelmine	22, Oct. 1896	3, Oct.	65	Henze	687	Davenport, IA	Ildehausen, Braunschweig
Dormann, Christian	19, Feb. 1877	28, Jan.	75		63	Buffalo, IA	Senate Grove, Missouri
Dömann, Herman	10, June 1897	24, May	46		367	Senate Grove, MO	Strackholt, Aurich, Ostfriesland
Dorn, Anna	6, Dec. 1888	12, Nov.	75- 3m-26d	Lobinus	782	Petersburg, IL	Brand bei Golnnow, Hinterpommern
Dorn, Augustine	12, Nov. 1896	23, Sept	75	Zaudtle	734	Jordan, MN	Egenhausen, Nagold, Württemberg
Dorn, Christine	4, Aug. 1862	16, July	36- 9m- 9d	Stickel	124	Nauvoo, IL	Ohio
Dorn, Kate	18, July 1889	27, June	30	Erdmann	462	Chicago, IL	Sand Creek Twp, Scott County, Minnesota
Dorn, Wilhelm Albert	7, July 1898	27, May	16		431	Jordan, MN	Niederhausen, Dieburg, Hessen-Darmstadt
Dornbusch, Heinrich	24, Apr. 1890	6, Apr.	64- 7m-23d		270	Dayton, OH	Holzburg, Kreis Ziegenhain, Kurhessen
Dörr, Adam	8, May 1871	11, Mar.	52- 4m		151	Beardstown, IL	Grombach, Freudenstadt, Württemberg
Dorr, Agatha	25, Dec. 1890	3, Dec.	58	Rentschler	830	Perrysburg, OH	Riblingen, Schaffhausen, Schweiz
Dorr, Anna	22, Sept 1859	2, July	25	Willberger	152	Woodville, OH	Steinsfurth, Zinsheim, Baden
Dörr, Anna Maria	23, Jan. 1882	6, Nov.	68	Klenger	31	Baltimore, MD	Markelsheim, Württemberg
Dorr, Caspar Joseph	5, Dec. 1895	10, Nov.	71		782	Toledo, OH	Frischborn, Hessen-Darmstadt
Dörr, Christine	4, Feb. 1884	12, Jan.	63		7	Bardstown, IL	Müssen, Armsberg, Preußen
Dörr, Friedrich	22, Feb. 1875	24, Dec.	65		63	Evansville, IN	Lettweiler, Obermarschel, Baiern
Dörr, Jakob	18, Aug. 1887	31, July	86- 2m		526	Charlestown, IN	Landau, Rheinkreis Baiern
Dörr, Johan Valentin	20, Sept 1894	16, Aug.	63		614	Portsmouth, OH	
Dörr, Louise Friederike	21, Jan. 1892	31, Dec.	25		46	Santa Claus, IN	
Dörr, M.	11, Oct. 1875	6, Sept	71- 6m		327	Ripon, WI	Weiler, Schorndorf, Württemberg
Dörr, Margaretha	7, Oct. 1878	17, Sept	25- 7m- 9d	Grim	319	Defiance, OH	
Dörr, Wilhelm	23, July 1877	6, July	64		239	Baltimore, MD	Steinford, Baden
Dörre, Heinrich	30, Apr. 1866	23, Feb.	49		142	St. Charles, MO	
Dorrer, Margaetha	13, Oct. 1884	21, Sept	64	Köchel	7	Jeffersonville, NY	Gumbrechtshofen, Elsaß
Dorrer, Peter	17, Aug. 1899	30, July	83- 1m-14d		527	Jeffersonville, NY	Gumbrechtshofen, Elsaß
Dorres, Salome	14, Mar. 1889	23, Feb.	78	Diemer	174	Jeffersonville, NJ	Guntershoffen, Elsaß
Dörrie, Juliana	4, Feb. 1867	18, Jan.	77		38	Highland, IL	Bierbergen, Hannover
Dorris, Heinrich	31, Aug. 1893	2, Aug.	77- 4m-28d		558	Holt, MI	Lidhorst, Hannover
Dös, Katharina	10, Aug. 1899	11, July	71	Müller	511	Clarington, OH	Ilsfeld, Besigheim, Württemberg
Dosbach, Elisabeth	1, Dec. 1879	14, Nov.	27- 2m	Sander	383	Quincy, IL	
Doscher, Friedrich	24, Nov. 1862	20, Sept	47		188	Williamsburg, NY	Kappen, Hannover
Döscher, Herman Heinrich	2, Feb. 1893	28, Dec.	88- 6m- 6d		78	San Francisco, CA	Dorum, Hannover
Döse, Ernestine	10, May 1894	19, Apr.	39	Habek	310	Elkport, IA	Speck, Golnov,
Doser, Johanna Maria	5, Nov. 1877	26, Sept	27		359	Washington, KS	Iowa City, Iowa
Doser, Johanna Maria	10, Dec. 1877	26, Sept	27	Jacky	399	Washington, KS	Iowa City, Iowa
Döß, Friedrich	23, Apr. 1891	31, Jan.	26		270	Clarington, OH	Cincinnati, Hamilton County, Ohio
Dota, Karl	30, May 1864	3, May	65		88	Captina, OH	Commantirola, Tessin, Schweiz

Christliche Apologete Death Notices --- 1839 - 1899

Name of Deceased	Notice Date	Death Date	Age	Maiden Name	Place of Death	Page	Place of Birth
Dothage, Charlotte	27, Oct. 1879	10, Oct.	28- 1m- 19d	Marcks	Hopewell, MO	343	Warren County, Missouri
Dothage, Emma	18, Apr. 1889	28, Mar.	15-10m-11d		Hopewell, MO	254	Warren County, Missouri
Dothage, Herman	15, Oct. 1891	28, Aug.	12		Hopewell, MO	670	Smiths Creek, Warren County, Missouri
Dotta, John	29, June 1863	9, June	24		Captina, OH	104	Monroe County, Ohio
Dotta, Karl	31, Jan. 1889	5, Jan.	53-10m- 2d		Clarington, OH	78	Switzer, Monroe County, Ohio
Dotta, Maria	24, Mar. 1862	24, Jan.	52- 9m- 3d		Captina, OH	48	Oberamt Waiblingen, Württemberg
Döttweiler, John	16, June 1862	6, Apr.	35		Baresville, OH	96	Höllstein, Basel, Schweiz
Drachsel, Jakob	8, Dec. 1898	21, Oct.	62		Bethany, OR	783	Zwischenbach, Bern, Schweiz
Draeger, Anna Christine	17, Aug. 1885	3, Aug.	73		Fredericksburg, TX	7	Kamionka, Bromberg, Preußen
Dräger, Gottlieb	16, Apr. 1896	30, Mar.	78		Spencer, IA	254	Klosterfelde, Friedeberg, Neumark
Dräger, Johanna	22, Dec. 1887	25, Nov.	42	Henke	Spencer, IA	814	Ziedötzel, Pommern
Dräger, Louise Pauline	25, Feb. 1886	15, Jan.	23- 7m-23d	Berg		7	
Dräger, Mina	11, Mar. 1897	16, Feb.	63		Milwaukee, WI	158	Stargard, Pommern
Dräger, Wilhelmine	19, Mar. 1896	2, Mar.	76	Höst	Spencer, IA	190	Schönfeld, Friedeberg, Neumark
Dragowsky, Julius	8, June 1899	17, Apr.	58		Detroit, MI	367	Groß Tromnau, West Preußen
Dräher, Engelbert	3, Dec. 1891	6, Nov.	79		Berne, MI	782	Aixsheim, Spaichingen, Württemberg
Drake, Heinrich Daniel	10, July 1865	18, June	83- 5m-22d		Dayton, OH	112	Primont, Waldeck
Drake, Maria Elisabeth	11, Sept 1865	19, Aug.	70- 2m-20d	Hoffmeister	Dayton, OH	148	
Dräke, Wilhelm	7, Apr. 1887	21, Mar.	1- -10d		San Antonio, TX	222	
Dralle, Virlinda	3, Feb. 1853	23, Oct.	33- 1m- 4d	Apton	Farmington, IA	20	Virginia
Draves, Sophia Maria	18, Oct. 1875	8, Sept	82		Batesville, IN	335	Limme, Amt Brake, Lippe-Detmold
Drawantz, Bertha	13, June 1881	15, May	15		Lyona, KS	191	
Drechsel, Georg	3, July 1871	28, May	31		Junction City, KS	215	
Dreckshage, Henriette	1, Sept 1887	14, Aug.	72- 4m- 2d	Lücking	Pittsfield, IL	558	Weil, Schöttmar, Lippe-Detmold
Dreckshage, Simon Heinrich	29, Mar. 1869	5, Jan.	56- 8m- 5d		Pittsfield, IL	103	
Drecksler, Louis	18, Mar. 1897	13, Feb.	67		Quincy, IL	174	Wiede, Braunschweig
Dreeke, Christian	21, Nov. 1889	20, Oct.	44		San Antonio, TX	750	Neundorf, Stolzenau, Hannover
Dreher, Bibiana	17, Sept 1896	29, Aug.	75		Newark, NJ	607	Hecklingen, Baden
Dreher, Christine Dorothea	2, Sept 1872	27, July	67		Newark, NJ	287	Lahr, Baden
Dreher, Jakob	24, Nov. 1862	6,Nov.	30		Columbus, OH	188	Pitsburg, Bern, Schweiz
Dreher, Wilhelm	2, Sept 1872	27, July	17		Newark, NJ	287	
Dreidoppelt, Margaretha	25, Oct. 1875	31, Aug.	21- 8m-21d		Louisville, KY	343	Louisville, Jefferson County, Kentucky
Dreier, Anton Heinrich	11, Aug. 1848		Inquiry		Cincinnati, OH	131	Lippe-Detmold
Dreier, Elisabeth	20, Oct. 1887	4, Oct.	45	Gros	Scranton, PA	670	Oberjäckenbach, RheinPreußen
Dreier, John	13, Oct. 1873	9, Sept	20		Cleveland, OH	327	
Dreier, Louise	8, May 1865	13, Apr.	78	Seuwald	Mt. Pleasant, OH	76	Westdorf, Amt Hohenhausen, Lippe-Detmold
Dreier, Philipp	25, Aug. 1898	29, July	67		Scranton, PA	543	Nobohlenbach, Germany
Dreisbach, Margaretha	26, June 1846		75		Louisville, KY	103	Westphalen
Dreiske, Auguste	10, Dec. 1896	15, Nov.	41	Radke	Chicago, IL	798	Kleinlazikow, Neumark
Dreiske, Bertha A.E.	2, Mar. 1893	21, Jan.	35		Chicago, IL	142	
Dreiske, Ferdinand	7, Feb. 1870	19, Dec.	45-10m		Chicago, IL	47	Langenböse, HinterPommern
Dreiske, Louise	4, Jan. 1869	8, Dec.	5		Chicago, IL	7	
Dreiske, Wilhelm	1, July 1897	7, June	68		Chicago, IL	414	Langebäse, Lauenburg, Hinterpommern
Dreiske, Wilhelm Friedrich	2, July1883	9, June	24		Chicago, IL	215	
Dreitzler, Dorothea	18, Nov. 1886	13, Oct.	72- 2m- 6d	Auch	Spraytown, IN	7	Heuwadten, Stuttgart, Württemberg
Drejer, Maria Charlotte	17, Feb. 1887	26, Jan.	77	Martens	Lexington, MO	110	Cappeln, Tecklenburg, Preußen

Christliche Apologete Death Notices --- 1839 - 1899

Name of Deceased	Notice Date	Death Date	Age	Page	Maiden Name	Place of Death	Place of Birth
Dreke, Heinrich	2, June 1898	12, May	61	351		Winona, MN	Neundorf, Stolznau, Hannover
Dreke, Karoline H.	22, June 1899	27, Apr.	63	399		Winona, MN	Hannover
Dreke, Lina	9, Dec. 1878	15, Nov.	14- 8m-12d	391		Winona, MN	Nenndorf, Amt Stolzenau, Hannover
Drentlau, Emilie	28, June 1875	3, June	41	207	Damke	Prairie Creek, MN	Schlomawanakel, Bromberg, Preußen
Drentlau, Maria	3, Nov. 1873	5, Oct.	15	351		Prairie Creek, MN	
Drentlau, Sarah Sibily	22, July 1886	24, June	59- 1m-13d	7	Müller	Northfield, MN	
Drescher, Emma	7, June 1894	19, May	29- 3m-24d	374	Seefeld	Watertown, WI	Kewaskum, Washington County, Wisconsin
Drescher, Emma Hulda	27, Apr. 1899	1, Apr.	43	271		Milwaukee, WI	Farmington, Washington County, Wisconsin
Drescher, Jacob	29, Dec. 1879	15, Dec.	71	415		Carrolton, MO	Höringhausen, Amt Vöhl, Hessen-Darmstadt
Drescher, Karl Oswald	20, Jan. 1898	22, Dec.	15	47		Milwaukee, WI	
Drescher, Margaretha	13, Apr. 1874	28, Feb.	70	119	Schies	Lexington, MO	Messelhausen, Gellersheim, Baden
Dressel, Bertha Wilhelmine	26, Jan. 1888	1, Jan.	21	62	Kröl	Peace Creek, KS	Rock Island County, Illinois
Dressel, Dorothea	22, Dec. 1879	25, Nov.	54	407	Hagemann	Red Bud, IL	Blickershausen, Kurhessen
Dressel, Emilie	10, Mar. 1898	9, Feb.	41	158		Le Sueur, MN	Nicolet, Minnesota
Dressel, Ernst	21, May 1896	21, Apr.	70	334		Red Bud, IL	Sachsen
Dressel, Maria	13, Apr. 1885	22, Mar.	75	7	Nething	Baresville, OH	Beuren, Nürtingen, Württemberg
Dresselmeyer, Herman	25, Mar. 1886	20, Feb.	65	7		Mathena, KS	Hannover
Dreßler, Elisabeth	23, May 1870	11, May	59	167		Portsmouth, OH	Edigheim, Rheinpfalz Baiern
Dreßler, Maria	14, Mar. 1870	16, Feb.	17	87		New Rochelle, NY	
Dreßler, Wilhelm (Rev)	21, Dec. 1885	3, Dec.	79	7		Portsmouth, OH	Flomersheim, Rheinkreis Baiern
Dreßmann, Nettje	11, Feb. 1878	25, Jan.	38	47	Sampen	Pekin, IL	Rysum, Ostfriesland
Dreve, Simon August	23, Sept 1867	11, Sept	76	302		Batesville, IN	Brundorf, Honhausen, Lippe-Detmold
Dreves, Christina Wilhelmine	10, May 1875	11, Apr.	16	151		Batesville, IN	
Dreves, D.H.	20, Dec. 1875	4, Dec.	18	407		Batesville, IN	
Dreves, F. Conrad	8, Mar. 1888	4, Feb.	33	158		Batesville, IN	Cincinnati, Hamilton County, Ohio
Dreves, Wilhelmine	25, Apr. 1889		65	270			Wälsdorf, Talle, Hornhausen, Lippe-Detmold
Drewes, Friederike	11, Dec. 1882	22, Nov.	66	399	Jünger	Columbus, WI	Glockziehn, Neu-Brandenburg, Preußen
Drewes, Ludwig	11, Dec. 1882	17, Nov.	69	399		Columbus, WI	Prasdorf, Mecklenburg-Strelitz
Drewes, Sophia Maria	7, Mar. 1870	17, Feb.	15-10m- 3d	79		Batesville, IN	
Drewing, Louis	19, May 1884	3, May	61- -19d	7		Wilber, NE	
Drewnowske, Auguste	1, July 1897	15, June	35	414	Krieger	Detroit, MI	Bayenden, Göttingen, Hannover
Drews, Caroline	3, Feb. 1873	26, Dec.	63- 4m-14d	39	Koester	Marine City, MI	Rosenum, West Preußen
Drews, Caroline	16, Feb. 1885	30, Jan.	56- 5m- 3d	7		Laporte, IN	Wolkow, Neu Pommern, Preußen
Drews, Christoph	2, Feb. 1885	19, Jan.	72	7		Laporte, IN	Waren, Mecklenburg-Schwerin
Drews, Louisa	4, Apr. 1870	30, Jan.	25	111		Laporte, IN	Zwidorf, Mecklenburg-Schwerin
Drews, Ludwig	8, Aug. 1870	27, July	42-10m	255		Columbus, WI	
Dreyer, Anna Barbara	17, June 1852	28, May	13- 3m-12d	100		Columbus, OH	
Dreyer, Carl	17, Mar. 1892	21, Feb.	45	174		Lexington, MO	Schweiz
Dreyer, Christian	16, Aug. 1849	18, July	76- 7m-13d	132		Cincinnati, OH	
Dreyer, Dorothea	13, Jan. 1879	14, Dec.	28- 6m-14d	15	Kroh	Industry, TX	Bösingfeld,
Dreyer, Elisabeth	18, Nov. 1867	22, Oct.	69	366		Batesville, IN	Klein-Sißbeck, Braunschweig
Dreyer, Elisabeth B.	25, Feb. 1897	5, Feb.	53- 9m- 3d	126	Steininger	Kansas City, KS	Erlenbach bei Landau, Rheinkreis Baiern
Dreyer, Ferdinand	3, Apr. 1882	5, Mar.	73	111		Cleveland, OH	Nimmersdorf bei Baireuth, Baiern
Dreyer, Franz	30, Nov. 1893	5, Nov.	23	766		Boonville, IN	Friedrichswald, Rindel, Kurhessen
Dreyer, Georg	19, Nov. 1847	25, Oct.	67	187		Rockford, IN	Eckendorf, Bielefeld, Preußen
Dreyer, Hanna Friederike	22, July 1886	4, July		7	Plöger	Boonville, IN	Heepen bei Bielefeld, Preußen

Christliche Apologete Death Notices --- 1839 - 1899

Name of Deceased	Notice Date	Death Date	Age	Maiden Name	Page	Place of Death	Place of Birth
Dreyer, Heinrich	17, Sept 1896	20, July	77		607	Perry, TX	Germany
Dreyer, Johan H.	26, Nov. 1877		77		383	Industry, TX	Gensdorf, Braunschweig
Dreyer, Johan Rudolph	12, Feb. 1883	11, Jan.	75		55	Bunker Hill, IL	Lotte, , Preußen
Dreyer, Katharina	28, Dec. 1893	9, Nov.	63		828	Berea, OH	München, Baiern
Dreyer, Maria	20, Nov. 1890	20, Oct.	29- 4m-12d	Kuhns	750	Boonville, IN	
Dreyer, Meta M.	2, Sept 1878	20, Aug.	68- 6m- 1d	Kübortz	279	Covington, KY	Schoff, Bremen, Germany
Dreyer, Metta	30, Jan. 1882	16, Jan.	17	Hardendorf	39	Covington, KY	
Dreyer, Theodor	23, Jan. 1890	19, Dec.	24		62	Denver, CO	
Driesel, Ottilie	21, June 1894	28, May	77	Fitz	406	Cross, OK	Sulzfeld, Meiningen, Sachsen-Meiningen
Driftmeyer, Maria	28, Mar. 1870	14, Feb.	62	Twente	103	Woodville, OH	Langerich, Tecklenburg, Preußen
Drinkhahn, Christina	23, July 1891	27, June	70-11m-20d	Pätow	478	Roseville, MI	Warlitz, Mecklenburg-Schwerin
Drinkhahn, Karl	11, Feb. 1878	14, Jan.	50		47	Roseville, MI	Pretzler, Mecklenburg-Schwerin
Drobisch, Carl	4, Mar. 1897	18, Jan.	15		143	Columbus, OH	
Dröge, August	1, Oct. 1866	6, Sept	62		318	Charlestown, IN	Sesen am Harz, Braunschweig
Dröge, Magdalena	15, Nov. 1894	22, Oct.	82	Lopan	742	Rocky, TX	Esingen, Holstein
Droll, Simon	13, Feb. 1862	8, Jan.	26		28	Wheeling, IL	Axheim, Spaichingen, Württemberg
Dromms, Caroline Wilhelmine	11, June 1896	15, May	48	Horstmann	383	Schenectady, NY	Süd-Hemmen, Minden, Preußen
Droselmeyer, Wilhelm	19, Oct. 1874	29, July	63		335	Warren, MO	Holzhausen, Amt Melle, Hannover
Droß, Henriette	16, May 1889	2, May	60- 7m-23d	Adam	318	Dayton, OH	Allendorf, Wetzlar, Koblenz, Preußen
Droß, Johanette	19, Aug. 1858	8, Aug.	41	Buhl	132	Dayton, OH	Allendorf auf der Ulm, Weßlar, Preußen
Droß, Wilhelm	28, Feb. 1881	12, Feb.	53- 7m-11d		71	Dayton, OH	Allendorf auf der Ulm, Wetzler, Koblenz, Preußen
Drosselmeier, Heinrich	4, Jan. 1864	Oct.	19		4	Columbus, KS	Barkhausen, Bur, Amt Krönenberg, Hannover
Drosselmeier, Klara Louisa	30, Mar. 1885	10, Mar.	68		7	Warrenton, MO	Burr, Melle, Hannover
Drosselmeier, Wilhelmina	27, Aug. 1891	10, Aug.	71	Meier	558	Wathena, KS	Minden, Preußen
Droste, Louise	11, Apr. 1895	13, Mar.	66	Hoppmann	238	Freelandville, IN	Hille, Minden, Preußen
Drücker, Friedricke	26, Jan. 1854	27, Nov.			16	New Orleans, LA	Preußen
Drücker, William A.	29, Dec. 1873	9, Nov.	25		415	New Orleans, LA	New Orleans, Louisiana
Drüeke, H.	3, Dec. 1857	12, Nov.	28		196	Burlington, IA	
Drum, Johan Martin	11, Dec. 1876	13, Nov.	75-10m-10d		399	Lexington, MO	Lekow, Schiefelbein, Pommern
Drum, Katharina	6, Apr. 1899	9, Mar.	76	Fischer	222	Stryker, OH	Herschberg, Baiern
Drum, Peter	9, Aug. 1880	23, July	68-11m-10d		255	West Unity, OH	Ulmeth, Baiern
Drumm, Amalia	2, June 1898	27, Apr.	60	Vollheim	351	Muskegon, MI	Bremen, Germany
Drumm, Dorothea Caroline	21, Feb. 1895	17, Jan.	86- 4m- 2d		126	Lexington, MO	Williamsport, Lycoming County, Pennsylvania
Drumm, Elisabeth	29, Oct. 1891	3, Oct.	45- 4m- 8d	Kern	702	West Unity, OH	Kirweiler, Grombach, Preußen
Drumm, Elisabeth Catharina	23, Jan. 1862	28, Oct.	75- -19d		16	Defiance, OH	Rützow, Pommern
Drumm, Samuel Julius Ulrich	28, Nov. 1889	30, Oct.	55		766	Lexington, MO	Warren County, Missouri
Drünert, Christian Conrad Louis	1, Nov. 1894	30, Sept	28		710	Warren, MO	Lüdenhausen, Amt Hohenhausen, Lippe-Detmold
Drünert, Dorothea	1, July 1867	31, May	57	Richterberg	206	Warren, MO	Schönhagen, Lippe-Detmold
Drünert, Friedrich Christian	4, Dec. 1865	11, Nov.	56- 8m		196	Warren, MO	Hönel, Amt Melle, Hannover
Drünert, Maria	13, July 1868	26, May	28- 8m		223	Warren, MO	Lüdenhausen, Hohenhausen, Lippe-Detmold
Drünert, Wilhelmina Henrietta	15, Feb. 1894	30, Dec.	59	Drünert	110	Warren, MO	Egge, Hameln, Hannover
Drünert, Willie	22, Nov. 1888	31, Oct.	84	Deikert	750	Warren, MO	Schönhagen, Amt Sternberg, Lippe-Detmold
Drunnert, Conrad	6, Mar. 1865	23, Sept	30		40	Warrenton, MO	Poppelatz, Pommern
Druß, Ferdinand	15, May 1871	1, May	37		159	Second Creek, MO	Czarnikau, Posen
Dryer, Friederika Amalia	8, May 1882	11, Apr.	23		151	Troy, NY	Nieder-Stocken, Bern, Schweiz
Dubach, Adolph	7, Apr. 1862	26, Feb.	18		56	Columbus, WI	

Christliche Apologete Death Notices --- 1839 - 1899

Name of Deceased	Notice Date	Death Date	Age	Page	Maiden Name	Place of Death	Place of Birth
Dubach, Benjamin	26, June 1890	24, May	80- 9m-17d	414		Fairview, KS	Juragebirge, St. Imerthal, Bern, Schweiz
Dubach, Elisabeth	18, Mar. 1878	23, Feb.	65	87	Schindler	Wathena, KS	Niederwichtrach, Bern, Schweiz
Dubach, Emma	12, June 1876	18, May	25	191	Nahrung	Wathena, KS	Cumberland, Maryland
Dubach, Kleophas	7, Jan. 1892	15, Dec.	77	14		Wathena, KS	Santimer, Bern, Schweiz
Dubach, Rosina Barbara	17, June 1886	2, June	61	7	Bendel	Baresville, OH	Eptingen, Maulbronn, Württemberg
Dubach, Susanna	4, Aug. 1892	17, July	44	494	Schwarz	Hannibal, MO	Monroe County, Ohio
Dubbermann, Johanna Elenora	2, June 1879	27, Apr.	85	175	Beer	Chicago, IL	Oberwaldenburg, Preußen
Dube, Wilhelmine	24, Jan. 1870	14, Dec.	43	31		Milwaukee, WI	
Dubler, Anna	18, May 1899	26, Apr.	29	319		Dubuque, IA	
Dubler, Sophie	15, Aug. 1881	27, July	41	263	Biermann	Galena, IL	Galena, Illinois
Dubratz, Karoline	8, Oct. 1883	12, Sept	48-10m-19d	327		Ahnapee, WI	Ziemotzel bei Kolberg, Preußen
Duchardt, Christian	4, Feb. 1892	6, Jan.	74	78		Brownstown, IL	Lauterbach, Hessen-Darmstadt
Dücker, Anna Barbara	26, Feb. 1857	18, Jan.	23	36	Gokel	Monroe, IL	Unter-Althausen, Hessen
Dücker, Friederike	9, Mar. 1893	19, Feb.	40	158	Edler	Big Spring, MO	Flahda, Preußen
Dücker, Heinrich	29, Oct. 1877	11, Oct.	47	351		Red Bud, IL	Herford, Minden, Preußen
Duckhard, Anna Maria	29, Mar. 1888	10, Mar.	70	206	Nelsch	Beardstown, IL	Dürnen, Göppingen, Württemberg
Dude, Karl	18, Nov. 1886	23, Oct.	58	7		Edwardsville, IL	Obernburg, Vöhl, Hessen-Darmstadt
Duden, Claus	26, July 1875	9, July	68	239		Marietta, OH	Groß-Wohnstätt, Hannover
Duden, Johanna	11, July 1864	19, June	50	112	Fischer	Marietta, OH	Metzingen, Herrenberg, Württemberg
Duden, Magdalena	19, Mar. 1841	2, Mar.	39	43			
Duden, Magdalena	26, Mar. 1841	2, Mar.	39	47			
Duebbe, Louise	6, Oct. 1884	28, Aug.	74	7	Diesing	Rocky Hill, TX	
Düecker, Friedrich	16, June 1859	6, Apr.	36	96		Red Bud, IL	
Düehn, Johanne Sophia Caroline	24, Dec. 1877		18- 3m-18d	415		Ahnapee, WI	Unterlübe, Minden, Preußen
Dueker, Friederika	15, Mar. 1880		60- -26d	87		Hoyleton, IL	
Dueker, Wilhelm C.	21, Feb. 1889	29, Jan.	32- -24d	126		Red Bud, IL	Baiern
Duerr, Anna Margaretha	28, Apr. 1898	27, Feb.	78	271	Kundel	Beaufort, MO	Ostfriesland
Duerre, Margaretha	17, Sept 1891	6, July	17	606	Hillens	Osceola, NE	Rostock, Mecklenburg-Schwerin
Duewall, Rudolph	19, Mar. 1891	17, Feb.	51	190		Lexington, TX	Schledehausen, Osnabrück, Hannover
Dufendach, Maria Elisabeth	23, June 1873	16, May	68	199		Huntingburg, IN	Preußen
Dühning, Henriette	3, Oct. 1889	31, Aug.	61	638	Giesen	Seward, NE	Werner, Ostfriesland
Duin, Christian	26, May 1898	21, Apr.	87	335	Dreesmann	Prospect Park, CA	Weener, Ostfriesland
Duin, Etje	11, Apr. 1889	23, Feb.	79-11m-11d	238	Martens	Los Angeles, CA	Felde, Holtrop, Schleswig-Holstein
Duis, Antji Marie	15, Dec. 1887	24, July	32	798		Humboldt, NE	Leer , Ostfriesland
Duis, Bernhard	20, Sept 1894	26, Aug.	68	614		Ironton, OH	Strackholt, Ostfriesland, Hannover
Düis, C.	17, Oct. 1861	25, Aug.	48	168		Petersburg, IL	
Duis, Catharina	12, Nov. 1877	6, Oct.	16- 5m-22d	367		Portsmouth, OH	Hilden, Amt Iburg, Hannover
Duis, Charlotte	10, Sept 1866	30, June	30	294	Landwehr	Portsmouth, OH	
Duis, Johanna Friederike	15, Dec. 1887	24, Oct.	3m	798		Humboldt, NE	
Duis, Marie Magdalena	15, Dec. 1887	11, July	2	798		Humboldt, NE	
Duis, Rosina	14, Mar. 1881		76- 6m-12d	87	Grube	Ironton, OH	Detern, Ostfriesland
Duisdieler, Auguste	4, Aug. 1892	12, June	43	494		Pekin, IL	Dayton, Montgomery County, Ohio
Dulitz, Katharina	28, Apr. 1898	6, Apr.	65	271	Aspacher	Grand Island, NE	Brukhof, Gaildof, Württemberg
Dümmer, Dorothea	3, May 1894	13, Apr.	24	294		Decorah, IA	
Dümon, Philipp	20, Oct. 1879	26, Sept	75	335		Bradford, IN	Hochweisel, Hessen-Darmstadt
Dunken, Christina	15, Nov. 1880	15, Oct.	28- 9m-26d	367	Breth	Chillicothe, OH	

Christliche Apologete Death Notices --- 1839 - 1899

Name of Deceased	Notice Date	Death Date	Age	Maiden Name	Page	Place of Death	Place of Birth
Dunker, Carl Friedrich	14, June 1888	21, May	66		382	Delhi, MI	Espelkamp, Rahde, Preußen
Dunker, El.	10, Mar. 1879	12, Feb.	77		79	Detroit, MI	Schwerin
Dunker, Fr. G.	3, Jan. 1876	12, Dec.	38- 1m- 1d		7	St. Louis, MO	Oldendorf, Preußen
Dunker, Lydia Katharina	22, Mar. 1894	27, Feb.	27- 3m- 7d	Kramer	198	St. Louis, MO	St. Louis, Missouri
Dupke, Carl Friedrich	1, Jan. 1872	15, Dec.	54		7	Milwaukee, WI	Weizenhagen, Kreis Naugard, Pommern
Dupke, Louise W.H.	5, Feb. 1883	18, Jan.	66- 4m-20d	Ninnemann	47	Milwaukee, WI	Claushagen bei Wangerin, Preußen
Durbahn, August	6, June 1881	17, May	13		183	Lafayette, MN	
Durbahn, Dorothea Pauline	23, June 1884	24, May	50	Antoni	7	New Ulm, MN	Süd-Ditmarschen, Holstein
Durbahn, Emilie	6, June 1881	12, May	15		183	Lafayette, MN	
Durbahn, Ernst	11, July 1881	11, June	16		223	Lafayette, MN	Albersdorf, Holstein
Durbahn, Jürgen	27, Sept 1894	7, Sept	61		630	New Ulm, MN	
Durbahn, Ludwig	6, June 1881	27, May	11		183	Lafayette, MN	
Dürbaum, Katharina Philippine	26, Oct. 1885	7, Oct.	75- 9m-19d		7	Belleville, IL	Nassau
Durhake, Heinrich Ernst	8, Jan. 1891	12, Dec.	65		30	Huntingburg, IN	Ladbergen, Preußen
Dürig, Sophia	8, July 1886	18, June	51	Low	7	Clarington, OH	Monroe County, Ohio
Düringer, Heinrich	31, Dec. 1896	29, Nov.	52		844	Melvin, IL	Hanau, Kurhessen
Dürr, Anton	29, Apr. 1897	30, Mar.	68		271	Lemars, IA	Mutzenhausen, Hochfeldern, Elsaß
Dürr, Benjamin	25, Feb. 1886	2, Feb.	35		7	Bucyrus, OH	Crawford County, Ohio
Dürr, Elias	26, July 1894	4, July	33		486	Bucyrus, OH	Chatfield Township, Crawford County, Ohio
Dürr, Elisabeth	22, Jan. 1872		23- 9m-19d	Fauser	31	Bucyrus, OH	Crawford County, Ohio
Dürr, Elisabeth	20, Mar. 1871	28, Feb.	44- 5m- 3d	Jacoby	95	Bucyrus, OH	Marion County, Ohio
Dürr, Ernestine	13, May 1897	23, Apr.	70	Heinzelmann	303	Kendallville, IN	Württemberg
Dürr, Etta Jane	8, Oct. 1883	22, Sept	30		327	Amboy, MN	Wisconsin
Dürr, Hannah	21, Aug. 1890	7, Aug.	56-10m	McPeek	542	Bucyrus, OH	Guernsey County, Ohio
Dürr, Wilhelmine Dorothea Chr.	13, Nov. 1871	13, Oct.	49	Kron	367	Kendallville, IN	Loitz, Stralsund, Preußen
Dürrstein, Christian	7, July 1898	13, June	68		431	Freeport, IL	Zeilfeld, Sachsen-Meiningen
Dürrwächter, Jonathan	4, May 1863	4, Apr.	70- 3m		72		Maulbronn, Württemberg
Dürsken, Sophia E.G.	16, Aug. 1894	24, July	30	VonDeest	534	Columbus, NE	Leer, Preußen
Durst, Adam	31, May 1875	5, May	27		175	Detroit, MI	Canada
Durst, Anna Maria	1, Mar. 1888	30, Jan.	58- 8m-29d	Betz	142	Cleveland, OH	Lanzenhain, Lauterbach, Hessen-Darmstadt
Durst, Catharina	19, Apr. 1869	27, Mar.	61	Marti	127	New Orleans, LA	Glarus, Schweiz
Durst, Christine Margaretha	3, Feb. 1887	16, Jan.	85- 2m-12d	Binder	78	Fredericksburg, TX	Dettenhausen, Tübingen, Württemberg
Durst, Johan Bernard	9, May 1889	18, Apr.	48		302	Llano, TX	Dettenhausen, Tübingen, Württemberg
Durst, Johannes	21, Nov. 1870	14, Oct.	71- 7m-20d		375	Llano, TX	Dettenhausen, Amt Tübingen, Württemberg
Dürwächter, Katharina Barbara	1, Jan. 1891	21, Nov.	81- 1m- 2d	Niedemeier	14	LaCrosse, WI	Knittlingen, Maulbronn, Württemberg
Düsenberg, Emma C.	15, Oct. 1896	19, Sept	34	Völker	671	Flood Creek, IA	LaCrosse, Wisconsin
Dusenberg, Margaetha	5, May 1898	13, Apr.	33	Beyer	287	Flood Creek, IA	Sterbfritz, Schlüchtern, Kurhessen
Düssel, Katharine E.	18, Mar. 1897	3, Mar.	89	Fiehler	174	Eudora, KS	Hönebach, Hessen-Kassel
Dutcher, Katie	25, June 1896	3, June		Betz	415	Pepin, WI	Stockholm, Pepin County, Wisconsin
Dutismann, Carolina Catharina	30, Jan. 1862	18, Jan.	15-10m		20	Sherrills Mount, IA	
Dutler, Anna	11, Mar. 1867	9, Feb.	46	Hösle	78	Highland, IL	Haslen, Glarus, Schweiz
Dütscher, Henrietta	9, Feb. 1880	28, Nov.	72	Küster	47	Herman, MO	Braunschweig
Duttenhofer, Gottliebe	4, Feb. 1886		46	Schulz	7	Montague, MI	Remmingsheim, Rottenburg, Württemberg
Duttweiler, Heinrich	11, July 1889	17, June	72- 6m-27d		446	Jeffersonville, NY	Wehnthal, Regensburg, Zürich, Schweiz
Duttweiler, Maria	5, June 1882	10, Mar.	33	Mann	183	Walnut Creek, IA	Jefferson County, Iowa
Duttwyler, Anna	1, Nov. 1888	5, Aug.	69	Meyer	702	Jeffersonville, IN	Niederhasli, Zürich, Schweiz

- 99 -

Christliche Apologete Death Notices --- 1839 - 1899

Name of Deceased	Notice Date	Death Date	Age	Page	Maiden Name	Place of Death	Place of Birth
Düwel, Heinrich Konrad	30, July 1896	29, June	60	495	Bebermeyer	Truxton, MO	Egge, Hannover
Düwel, Sophia	11, Mar. 1878	15, Feb.	40	79		Warren, MO	Schönhagen, Lippe-Detmold
Duwenick, Dietrich	21, July 1879	16, June	74- 6m	231		Jamestown, MO	
Duwenick, Elisabeth	30, Aug. 1875	6, July	76	279	Gerkewermann	Boonville, MO	Lintorf, Amt Wittlage, Hannover
Eastmann, Rosa	13, Oct. 1879	5, Sept	24	327	Deagoes	Poughkeepsie, NY	Poughkeepsie, New York
Ebbert, Klara Elisabeth	6, Oct. 1892	3, Sept	33	638	Hermann	Allegheny City, PA	Butler County, Pennsylvania
Ebel, (Mrs)	26, Sept 1870	30, Aug.	52	311		Rockford, MN	Spandau, Preußen
Ebel, Andreas	25, Jan. 1864	29, Dec.	5- 3m- 7d	16		Cannon City, MN	
Ebel, Carl Heinrich	12, June 1882	14, May	65- 3m-29d	191		Nerstrand, MN	Graben, Baden
Ebel, Christina	24, Nov. 1884	14, Sept	63	7	Scholl	Cannon River, MN	Graben, Baden
Ebel, Friedrich Andreas Paul	26, June 1882	10, May	33	207		Schulenburg, TX	Magdeburg, Preußen
Ebel, Hermann	6, July 1868	31, May	20- 2m- 7d	215		Crow River, MN	Berlin, Germany
Ebel, Maria Magdalena	20, June 1895	4, May	20	398	Foos	Bison, KS	Friedenfeld, Rußland
Ebeling, Anna	29, Dec. 1887	20, Nov.	30- 1m-20d	830		San Jose, IL	Hagen, Lippe-Detmold
Ebeling, Conrad	6, Oct. 1892	23, Aug.	50	638		Farmington, IA	Adenstett, Hannover
Ebeling, Heinrich	5, Sept 1881	17, Aug.	77	287		Belleville, IL	Sosmar, Hannover
Ebeling, Katharina	2, Mar. 1885	16, Feb.	77	7	Tase	Belleville, IL	Rödinghausen, Bünde, Herrfurt, Minden, Preußen
Ebenheck, John	9, Apr. 1857	27, Mar.	27	60		Madison, IN	Poppendorf, Baiern
Ebenstein, Johann Gottfried	7, Oct. 1858	7, Sept	65	160		Greenville, OH	Kleinenhausen, Sachsen-Weimar
Ebenstein, Susanna Maria	28, Oct. 1858	10, Oct.	67	172	Reisin	Greenville, OH	Kleinneuhausen, Sachsen-Weimar
Eberbach, Anna Maria	29, Dec. 1873	15, Dec.	27- -29d	415	Heyn	New Albany, IN	Feldhausen, Holstein
Eberbach, Dorothea	10, July 1871	17, June	43	223	Krieger	New Albany, IN	Buxweiler, Elsaß
Eberbach, Elisabeth Rosina	26, Mar. 1866	22, Feb.	31- 2m-22d	102	Maier	Louisville, KY	Hausen bei Brackenheim, Württemberg
Eberbach, Johann	27, June 1864	17, May	27	104		New Albany, IN	Hausen an der Zaber, Brackenheim, Württemberg
Eberhard, Anna Katharina	18, Jan. 1894	3, Dec.	33	46		Arthur, IL	Marion County, Illinois
Eberhard, Carl	15, June 1854	10, May	20-11m- 4d	96		Manitowoc, WI	Hagenburg, Bückeburg, Lippe-Schaumburg
Eberhard, Elisabeth	15, Dec. 1898	15, Nov.	67	799		Lancaster, NY	Germany
Eberhard, H. Philipp	3, Nov. 1873	19, Sept	71- 4m-17d	351		Mt. Prairie, MN	Steg, Preußen
Eberhard, Jakob	21, Sept 1863	1, July	25	152		Milwaukee, WI	
Eberhard, Karl	27, July 1868	8, May	66- - 8d	239		Newtonburg, WI	Bückeburg, Lippe-Schaumburg
Eberhard, Maria C.	23, Apr. 1877	2, Apr.	20	135		Canton, MO	
Eberhardt, Anna	25, Feb. 1878	4, Feb.	39	63	Siegenthaler	Decatur, IL	Konolfingen, Bern, Schweiz
Eberhardt, Anna Katharine	6, May 1886	2, Apr.	69	7	Artz	Salina, KS	Osthofen, Hessen-Darmstadt
Eberhardt, Charles W.	1, June 1893	19, Apr.	33	350		Minneapolis, MN	Ahnapee, Wisconsin
Eberhardt, Christina	20, June 1895	16, May	73	398	Pfefferle	Springfield, IL	Ober-Iflingen, Württemberg
Eberhardt, Edward	9, Jan. 1896	10, Dec.	22	30		Moweaqua, IL	
Eberhardt, Elise	9, Aug. 1894	20, June	33	518		Moweaqua, IL	
Eberhardt, Fr. W.	13, Sept 1880	21, Aug.	22- 2m-16d	295		Canton, MO	Canton Bern, Schweiz
Eberhardt, George	21, Feb. 1881	2, Feb.	19	63		Decatur, IL	Marion County, Illinois
Eberhardt, Johanna	30, Nov. 1893	28, Oct.	74	766	Zenker	Lawrence, MA	Steinpleis bei Werdau, Sachsen
Eberhardt, Matthias	25, Nov. 1867	18, Aug.	48	374		Springfield, IL	Büchenberg, Freudenstadt, Württemberg
Eberhardt, Sophia	31, May 1894	25, Apr.	93	358		Manitowoc, WI	Hagenburg, Lippe-Schaumburg
Eberhardt, Theophil	18, Apr. 1881	9, Mar.	53- 3m-10d	127		Hochheim, TX	Hessen-Darmstadt
Eberhardt, Valentin	20, Mar. 1890	13, Feb.	85	190		Salina, KS	Gundersblum, Hessen-Darmstadt
Eberhart, Augusta Amalia	24, Oct. 1895	9, Oct.	19	686		New York City, NY	New York City, New York

Christliche Apologete Death Notices --- 1839 - 1899

Name of Deceased	Notice Date	Death Date	Age	Page	Maiden Name	Place of Death	Place of Birth
Eberhart, Alfred Valentin	15, Apr. 1886	26, Mar.	11	7		Albert Lea, MN	
Eberhart, Anna	18, Dec. 1890	18, Nov.	13	814		Moweaqua, IL	
Eberhart, Nikolaus	14, Feb. 1870	29, Jan.	63	55		Clarington, OH	Schüpfen, Bern, Schweiz
Eberle, Bernhard	7, May 1891	10, Apr.	75-10m-13d	302		San Jose, IL	Baden
Eberle, Christine	6, Oct. 1873	19, July	53	319	Wittwer	San Jose, IL	Großeichholzhausen, Baden
Eberle, Ernestina	31, Jan. 1876	17, Jan.	20	39		Laporte, IN	
Eberle, Gottfried	20, Oct. 1873	25, Sept	65- 9m	335		Laporte, IN	Dittlingen, Pforzheim, Baden
Eberle, Johan	1, Dec. 1898	10, Nov.	83	767		Chillicothe, OH	Lampertheim, Hessen-Darmstadt
Eberle, Johan	27, Apr. 1893	9, Apr.	71	270		Perrysburg, OH	Watenheim bei Worms, Germany
Eberle, Joseph	3, Mar. 1879	12, Jan.	77- 6m-17d	71		New York City, NY	Wiesenbach, Baden
Eberle, Lizzie	30, May 1895	10, May	37	350		New Haven, CT	New York
Eberle, Philippine Sophie	19, Sept 1895	31, Aug.	39	606	Birnstiel	New Haven, CT	Utica, New York
Eberle, Rosine	4, Aug. 1898	3, July	74	495		Toledo, OH	Weinheim, Baden
Eberle, Sophia	9, Apr. 1891	6, Mar.		238	Faulhaber	New Haven, CT	Dürkheim a.d. Hardt, Rheinkreis Baiern
Eberlein, Maria	16, June 1898	3, June	45	383		Sheboygan, WI	Hannover
Eberlein, Maria	12, Jan. 1893	4, Dec.	24	30	Volander	Greenfield, MA	
Eberli, Katharina	24, July 1871	26, June		239		Louisville, KY	
Eberlin, Maria Katharine	17, Nov. 1892	28, Oct.	67	734	Hamm	Graham, MO	Ingenheim , Elsaß
Eberlin, Theobald	23, Oct. 1871	28, Sept	17- 2m-28d	343	III	Oregon, MO	Pendleton, Niagra County, New York
Eberlin, Theobald H.	18, Mar. 1897	28, Feb.	71	174		Graham, MO	Melzheim, Elsaß
Eberling, Louise	22, May 1882	26, Feb.	78	167	Brügmann	Etna, MO	Kleinhöre, Hannover
Eberly, Josephina	2, Aug. 1849	26, June	30	124		St. Louis, MO	
Ebers, Wilhelm Konrad	23, Nov. 1899	8, Nov.	79- 3m-24d	751		Lexington, TX	Helmstädt, Braunschweig
Ebersbach, Eva Katharina	2, Jan. 1896	2, Dec.	84	14		Pomeroy, OH	Edigheim, Baiern
Ebersbach, Jak.	8, Aug. 1881	12, July	72	255		Pomeroy, OH	Oppau, Frankenthal, Rheinpfalz Baiern
Ebersbach, Sophie	25, Mar. 1897	26, Feb.	57	190		Pomeroy, OH	Rielingshausen, Marbach, Württemberg
Ebert, Albert Friedrich	7, May 1896	17, Apr.	24	302		Clarington, OH	Monroe County, Ohio
Ebert, Anna	18, Feb. 1897	31, Jan.	46	111	Brandenstein	Bushton, KS	Huntingburg, Dubois County, Indiana
Ebert, Carl Friedrich	23, Sept 1897	25, Aug.	62	607		Menomonie, WI	Henderson, Sypply County, Minnesota
Ebert, Catharina	16, Aug. 1849	8, July	37	132		Dayton, OH	Lübecke, Münden, Preußen
Ebert, Christian	8, Nov. 1894	16, Oct.	78	726		Menominee, MI	Werden a. d. Elbe, Osterburg, Preußen
Ebert, Christine	30, July 1896	9, July	75	495	Rautenberg	Beaver Dam, WI	Brietzing, Pommern
Ebert, Fanny	9, July 1877	2, June	29	223	George	Nauvoo, IL	Augusta County, Virginia
Ebert, Jacob	18, Dec. 1882	25, Nov.	55	407		Quincy, IL	Schweigern, Brackenheim, Württemberg
Ebert, Johann F.	8, Sept 1862	20, Aug.	43- 6m-10d	144		Allegheny City, PA	Obermeisungen, Kurhessen
Ebert, Johannes	22, Oct. 1891	3, Oct.	57	686		Tell City, IN	Belmeden, Kurhessen
Ebert, Katharina	10, Apr. 1849	2, Feb.	42	76		Captina, OH	
Ebert, Konrad	21, Apr. 1892	30, Mar.	27	254		Tell City, IN	Burfehnde, Hannover
Ebert, Lena	24, Nov. 1892	29, Oct.	21	750	Matthews	St. Paul, MN	Deer Park, Wisconsin
Ebert, Ludwig	8, Jan. 1883	12, Dec.	82- 1m- 3d	15		Clarington, OH	Lembach, Weißenburg, Elsaß
Ebert, Maria Dorothea Ida	22, Aug. 1895	28, June	21	542		Berne, MI	Berne, Michigan
Eberwein, John	20, July 1885	2, July	69	7		Chili, OH	Oberlauringen, Baiern
Ebinger, Margaretha	23, May 1895	26, Apr.	87	334	Breitenstein	Chicago, IL	Schönau bei Heidelberg, Baden
Ebke, Wilhelm	28, Apr. 1873	5, Apr.	47	135		Petersburg, IL	Sile, Kreis Herfort, Preußen
Ebker, Ernst	9, Apr. 1896	17, Mar.	75	238		Mt. Healthy, OH	Gerxen, Lage. Lippe-Detmold
Eble, Anton	16, Feb. 1860	9, Nov.	58	28		Newark, NJ	Hohen-Wortersbach, Baden

Christliche Apologete Death Notices --- 1839 - 1899

Name of Deceased	Notice Date	Death Date	Age	Page	Maiden Name	Place of Death	Place of Birth
Echterdick, Louisa	23, June 1862		17-10m	100		New York, NY	
Echterdick, Wilhelmina	5, Oct. 1863	4, Sept	25	160		New York, NY	Lippe-Detmold
Echterdieck, Elise	14, May 1891	30, Mar.	89	318	Fischer	New York City, NY	
Echterdieck, Elise	7, May 1866	23, Mar.	20	150		New York, NY	Königshafen an der Tauber, Baden
Eck, Anton	25, Feb. 1897	22, Jan.	74	126		Jersey City, NJ	Hergersweiler, Rheinkreis Baiern
Eck, Johan	28, Mar. 1889	28, Feb.	30- 3m	206		Jersey City, NJ	Leinsweiler, Rheinpfalz Baiern
Eck, Peter	16, May 1864	22, Apr.	27	80		Cincinnati, OH	Washington County, Ohio
Eck, Philipp	3, Jan. 1861	30, Nov.	81	4		Boonville, IN	Lauchröden bei Eisenach, Sachsen-Weimar
Eckart, Adolph	31, Jan. 1895	29, Dec.	39	78		Trail Run, OH	Ipsheim, Baiern
Eckart, Catharine	11, Apr. 1889	1, Feb.	60	238		Galena, IL	Niedersachswerfen, Hannover
Eckart, Johan Sebastian	9, July 1877	16, June	57	223		Matamoras, OH	
Ecke, Andreas	30, June 1853	2, June	53	104		Pittsburg, PA	
Ecke, Carl	11, Mar.1872	10, Dec.	34- 4m	87		Chicago, IL	
Eckel, Anna	22, Apr. 1878	3, Apr.	37- 3m- 9d	127	Horst	Fond du Lac, WI	Neckar-Kreis, Vaihingen, Württemberg
Eckel, Elisabeth Katharina	19, Oct. 1885	28, Sept	81	7	Hofmann	Fairmount, KS	Roßwaag, Vaihingen an der Enz, Württemberg
Eckel, Friedrich	3, Apr. 1871		75	111		Leavenworth, KS	
Eckel, Friedrich	17, Apr. 1871	15, Mar.		127			Durbach bei Offenburg, Baden
Eckenfels, Maria	19, May 1898	25, Apr.	64	319	Fritz	Ada, MN	
Eckermann, Lizzie	16, Dec. 1872	27, Oct.	13	407		Cleveland, OH	Grosgumpen, Hessen-Darmstadt
Eckermann, Sophia	7, Jan. 1858	21, Dec.	26	4		Cleveland, OH	Benickenstein, Nordhausen am Harz, Preußen
Eckert, Anna Elisabetha	20, Aug.1847	25, July	26	135	Nicklas	St. Louis, MO	Alt-Wißloch, Baden
Eckert, August	26, Feb. 1872	24, Jan.	36	71		Camp Point, ---	Hitzkirchen, Hessen-Darmstadt
Eckert, Burkhart	10, Aug. 1899	12, July	76	511		Billings, MO	Niederkeinsbach, Hessen-Darmstadt
Eckert, Conrad	12, July 1888	28, June	65	446	Eidmüller	East Liberty, PA	
Eckert, Elisabeth	15, July 1878	27, June	46	223	Rieflin	Canton, MO	Hach, Mühlheim, Baden
Eckert, Elisabeth	22, Aug. 1895	4, Aug.	51- 7m- 8d	542		Decatur, IL	Holzhausen, Minden, Preußen
Eckert, John	13, June 1889	1, Apr.	57	382		Decatur, IL	Plantikow, Pommern
Eckert, Maria	22, Aug. 1889	3, Aug.	69	542	Scholle	Quincy, IL	Illsdorf, Kreis Grimberg, Hessen-Darmstadt
Eckert, Wilhelmine Dora	16, Feb. 1888	9, Jan.	56- 1m-29d	110	Gall	Oconomowoc, WI	Gersungen, Melsungen, Kurhessen
Eckhard, Johann	25, Jan. 1864	31, Dec.	72	16		Arenzville, IL	Großzimmern, Hessen-Darmstadt
Eckhardt, Martha	16, Feb. 1885		65	7		Goshen, IN	
Eckhart, Georg	7, Dec. 1874	16, Nov.	61- 6m-16d	391		Toledo, OH	Birlenbach, Elsaß
Eckmann, Johan Georg	18, May 1893	31, Mar.	63	318		Bischweiler, GE	Columbus, Wisconsin
Eckmann, Magdalena	21, Jan. 1892	28, Dec.	73	46	Ungerer	Cincinnati, OH	Holzhausen, Sachsen-Meiningen
Eckstein, Emilie	17, Aug. 1885	25, July	21	7	Wegner	Chicago, IL	Alshausen, Württemberg
Eckstein, Johan F. C.	24, June 1897	6, June	70	399		Prescott, WI	UnterHeinrieth, Württemberg
Eckstein, Maria	22, June 1899	1, Apr.	62	399	Lehmann	Brooklyn, NY	Rinteln, Kurhessen
Eckstein, Martin Johan	30, July 1896	4, July	73	495		Lancaster, NY	Knusten, Herrenberg, Württemberg
Eckstine, Sophia	15, Jan. 1872	14, Dec.	41- 5m- 7d	23		Brooklyn, NY	Wildbad, Württemberg
Eckstine, Barbara	10, July 1876	4, June	41	223	Oster	Prescott, WI	Kleinhindorn, Amt Blumenau, Hannover
Edel, Anna Louise Karoline	3, Mar. 1898	22, Jan.	82	143	Rivieius	New York City, NY	Friedeburg, Hannover
Edeler, (Mrs)	5, Sept 1864	2, Aug.	31	144	Hufschmidt	Sheboygan, WI	Büttelborn, Gerau, Hessen-Darmstadt
Eden, Margaretha Catharina	16, June 1873	31, May	25-10m- 4d	191	Renken	Peterson, IA	Louisville, Jefferson County, Kentucky
Eder, Elisabeth	17, Mar. 1879	16, Feb.	70	87	Jungheim	Montague, WI	Dürrmenz, Württemberg
Edinger, John Rozel	19, Nov. 1896	17, Sept	21	750		Louisville, KY	
Edinger, Rosina Katharina	27, Nov. 1876	11, Nov.	61- 8m-20d	383	Schneider	Louisville, KY	

Christliche Apologete Death Notices --- 1839 - 1899

Name of Deceased	Notice Date	Death Date	Age	Page	Maiden Name	Place of Death	Place of Birth
Edler, Friedrich	25, June 1891	16, May	67- 1m-20d	414		Wellington Co, ON	Rommerod, Alsfeld, Hessen
Edler, Josephina	21, Oct. 1872		26	343	Keßler	New Albany, IN	New Albany, Indiana
Edler, Louise	19, Mar. 1891	21, Feb.	46	190	Gutbub	New Albany, IN	Neuweiler, Elsaß
Edtling, Mary	25, Dec. 1890	24, Nov.	86	830		St. Louis, MO	
Egbert, (Mr)	5, Feb. 1883	31, Dec.	66	47		Newark, OH	Hundeburg, Hannover
Egbert, Johan Friedrich Wilhelm	25, Apr. 1895	23, Jan.	78	270		Etna, MO	Huteburg, Witlagen, Hannover
Egbert, Louise	23, Dec. 1872	30, Nov.	19- 3m-17d	415		Newark, NJ	
Egbert, Sophie	3, Jan. 1876	14, Dec.	57	7	Möhlenhage	Dresden, OH	Haslinge, Burlage, Lemförde, Hannover
Egeley, James	18, July 1889	26, June	72	462		Lawrence, KS	Berks County, Pennsylvania
Egenberger, Andreas	13, Dec. 1888	25, Oct.	87	798		West Bend, WI	Grabs, St. Gallen, Schweiz
Eger, Elisabeth	1, Oct. 1883	6, Sept	83-11m-21d	319	Borkholder	De Soto, MO	Höningen, Grünstadt, Rheinkreis Baiern
Eger, Johan	4, Oct. 1894		78- 2m- 2d	646		Louisville, KY	Empfingen, Hohenzollern, Württemberg
Egge, Wilhelmine	19, Apr. 1894	6, Mar.	24	262		Eudora, KS	Wabaunee County, Kansas
Eggeling, Johan Heinrich Christian	18, Nov. 1878	2, Nov.	67	367		Chicago, IL	Vordorf, Hannover
Eggelmann, Wilhelm	26, Aug. 1897	29, July		543		Hoboken, NJ	Eicklingen, Hannover
Eggemann, David Bernhard	10, Feb. 1879	2, Jan.	65	47		Detroit, MI	Thun, Bern, Schweiz
Eggensperger, Elisabeth	2, Apr. 1877	6, Feb.	70	111	Golder	Brooklyn, NY	Schluchtern, Württemberg
Eggers, Maria Magdalena	9, Sept 1878	12, Aug.	63- 7m-11d	287	Heim	Wathena, KS	
Eggestein, Elisabeth Maria	5, Apr. 1894	27, Feb.	16	230		Etna, MO	
Eggler, Johan	20, Nov. 1876	19, Oct.	13- 2m-13d	375		LaCrosse, WI	
Eggler, Lena B.	30, Jan. 1896	9, Jan.	30- 5m-11d	78		LaCrosse, WI	
Eggler, Margaretha	22, Feb. 1875	28, Jan.	15	63		Batesville, IN	
Egle, (Mrs)	14, Apr. 1884	28, Feb.	25	7	Koch	St. Louis, MO	
Egli, Anna	18, Jan. 1869	4, Jan.	77	23	Hartmann	Burlington, IA	St. Anthony, Schweiz
Egly, Eduard Peter	25, Dec. 1882	3, Dec.	15	415		Toledo, OH	Lansing, Michigan
Egly, Emma Adeline	23, Oct. 1890	4, Oct.	24	686		Delaware, OH	Auburn, Indiana
Egly, Heinrich	7, Jan. 1892	11, Dec.	63	14		San Jose, CA	
Egly, Lizzie	7, Apr. 1884	19, Mar.	19-11m-27d	7		Toledo, OH	Lancaster County, Pennsylvania
Egly, Peter	8, Aug. 1889	5, July	56	510	Lander	Warsaw, IL	Oberkeinsbach, Hessen-Darmstadt
Eha, Sophia	29, Nov. 1888	13, Nov.	64	766	Dönnerlein	Cincinnati, OH	Schönberg, Rottweil, Württemberg
Ehemann, Elisabeth	19, June 1856	1, June	31- 3m	100		Indianapolis, IN	Kemnath, Baiern
Ehlebe, Heinrich	15, Jan. 1893	21, May	38	382		Warsaw, IL	Warsaw, Illinois
Ehlen, Rebekka	11, Sept 1851	7, Sept	37- 9m	148	Peper	Cincinnati, OH	Brümmelhof, Amt Zevern, Hannover
Ehlers, Agnes	6, June 1889	17, May	71-11m	366	Buchhold	New York City, NY	Barnekow, Mecklenburg-Schwerin
Ehlers, Brün	27, July 1854	23, June	24	120		Dayton, OH	
Ehlers, Catharina	27, July 1854	28, June	27	120		Dayton, OH	Otterberg, Hannover
Ehlers, Catharine Sophia	18, Apr. 1889	19, Mar.	53	254	Schlichting	Roseville, MI	Mecklenburg-Schwerin
Ehlers, Dietrich	27, July 1854	28, June	17	120		Dayton, OH	
Ehlers, Henry	16, Nov. 1893	25, Oct.	27	734		Detroit, MI	Lenox Township, McComb County, Michigan
Ehlers, Herman	23, July 1896	3, July	35	479		Winona, MN	Winona, Minnesota
Ehlers, Jakob	11, Nov. 1878	19, Oct.		359		Greenville, OH	Helmste, Harsefeld, Hannover
Ehlers, Joachim Christian	14, Apr. 1887	2, Mar.	70	238		New York City, NY	Breitendorf, Mecklenburg-Schwerin
Ehlers, Johan	26, Apr. 1869	3, Apr.	40	135		Effingham, IL	Hollen, Martfeld, Amt Hoya, Hannover
Ehlers, Johan Dietrich	27, July 1854	25, June	55	120		Dayton, OH	Linsen, Amt Thedinghausen, Braunschweig
Ehlers, Johan Heinrich	5, Sept 1889	5, Aug.	64	574		Lexington, MO	Raden, Hannover
Ehlers, John	14, Feb. 1895	25, Jan.	67	110		Winona, MN	Alt-Benebeck, Ckrope, Schleswig-Holstein

Christliche Apologete Death Notices --- 1839 - 1899

Name of Deceased	Notice Date	Death Date	Age	Page	Maiden Name	Place of Death	Place of Birth
Ehlers, Louise Elisabeth	19, July 1894	26, June	23	470	Hirtzel	Altamont, IL	Effingham County, Illinois
Ehlers, Paul	24, Feb. 1887	1, Feb.	50	126		Greenville, OH	Helmste, Hasefeld, Hannover
Ehlers, Rebecca	17, Jan. 1881	3, Jan.	75	23		Cincinnati, OH	Morsum, Hannover
Ehlert, (girl)	18, Sept 1882	26, Aug.		303		Patterson, TX	
Ehlert, Auguste Johanna Emilia	11, Sept 1890	20, Aug.	21- 1m-26d	590		Chicago, IL	Chicago, Cook County, Illinois
Ehlert, Frank	7, Jan. 1884	22, Dec.	20	7		Chicago, IL	Danzig, Preußen
Ehlert, Friederika	11, Dec. 1856	23, Oct.	60	200		Herman, MO	Belle, Lippe-Detmold
Ehlert, Friedrich	30, Sept 1872	6, Sept	76	319		Altamont, IL	Belle, Amt Schiedes, Lippe-Detmold
Ehlert, Friedrich H.	30, Dec. 1886	11, Dec.	76	7		---, TX	Brockum, Lemförde, Hannover
Ehlert, Johan Friedrich Wilhelm	11, Aug. 1892	16, July	85	510		Pepin, WI	Lazig, Belgart, Pommern
Ehlert, Maria	15, June 1863	20, May	44	96	Clausmeier	Second Creek, MO	Niese, Amt Schwalenberg, Lippe-Detmold
Ehlert, Maria Louise	6, Feb. 1882	22, Jan.	66	47	Brandhorst	Brenham, TX	Herman, Missouri
Ehlert, Paulina	9, June 1892	13, May	25	366		Owensville, MO	Belle, Schieder, Lippe-Detmold
Ehlert, Wilhelm Friedrich	17, Dec. 1883	29, Nov.	62	7		Drake, MO	Amt Rhodenburg, Hannover
Ehling, J.H.	25, Apr. 1864	24, Mar.	45	68		Watertown, WI	
Ehmann, D.	3, Oct. 1864	19, Sept	44	160		Indianapolis, IN	Speichersdof, Kämath, Oberpfalz, Baiern
Ehrensberger, Frank	4, Aug. 1887	27, May	47- 8m-24d	494	Fiel	Indianapolis, IN	Mutaschingen, Waldshut, Baden
Ehrensperger, Georgie	1, May 1890	8, Apr.	25- - 4d	286	Neu	Indianapolis, IN	Indianapolis, Marion County, Indiana
Ehresmann, Katharina	18, Aug. 1892	25, July	70	526		Allegheny City, PA	Großenmohr, Hinfeld, Kurhessen
Ehret, Elisabeth	6, Jan. 1887	17, Dec.	51	14	German	Jeffersonville, NY	Kanton Thurgau, Schweiz
Ehrhard, Anna	3, Aug. 1893	13, July	92- 9m-19d	494	Fuhrmann	Louisville, KY	Haag, Baiern
Ehrhard, Georg	7, Aug. 1876		80	255		New Albany, IN	Hauendorf, Bayreuth, Baiern
Ehrhard, Lena	3, May 1875	9, Feb.	72	143		New York City, NY	
Ehrhardt, Balthasar Karl	13, Oct. 1898	29, Sept	58	655		Chicago, IL	Birkenherd, Rheinpfalz Baiern
Ehrhardt, Heinrich	8, Apr. 1897	23, Mar.	33	222		McKeesport, PA	Hessen-Darmstadt
Ehrich, Christoph	1, Oct. 1896	11, Sept	64	639		Enterprise, KS	Kleinswangen, Querfurt, Merseburg, Preußen
Ehrich, Christoph	22, Oct. 1896	11, Sept	67	687		Enterprise, KS	Kleinswangen, Querfurt, Merseburg, Preußen
Ehrich, Louisa	5, Jan. 1880	16, Apr.	39- -17d	7	Voltz	New York City, NY	New York
Ehringer, Elisabeth	19, Apr. 1888	29, Mar.	77	254	Karlin	Quincy, IL	Lörrach, Baden
Ehrke, Joachim	14, Aug. 1865			132		Manitowoc, WI	Nemilson, Pommern, Preußen
Ehrlicher, Johan Andreas	13, Dec. 1888	22, Nov.	63- 3m-23d	798		Pekin, IL	Schorndof, Baiern
Ehrlicher, Maria Katharina	16, Feb. 1899	1, Jan.	67	110	Hotze	Pekin, IL	Salza, Nordhausen, Preußen
Ehrmann, Margaretha B.	13, July 1899	26, June	64	447		Terre Haute, IN	Weingarten, Baden
Ehrmann, Max	11, May 1893	14, Apr.	63	302		Terre Haute, IN	Nußloch bei Heidelberg, Baden
Ehrsam, Anna	2, Feb. 1888	12, Jan.	73	78	Bikli	Enterprise, KS	Bützberg, Bern, Schweiz
Ehrsam, Friedrich	29, Oct. 1891	2, Oct.	61	702		Enterprise, KS	Vanwyl, Bern, Schweiz
Ehrsam, Maria	12, Aug. 1897	27, July	61	511	Keller	Clay Center, KS	Herzogenbuchsee, Bern, Schweiz
Eib, Margaretha	22, May 1876	10, Apr.	45- 2m	167	Schweizer		Obermoß, Hessen-Darmstadt
Eibel, Johan	31, Dec. 1877	24, Nov.	60-11m-18d	423		Giard, IA	Geißmar, Kurhessen
Eibelmeser, Ernestine	23, Sept 1867	7, Sept	70- 8m	302		Vandalia, IL	
Eichacker, Elisabeth	15, Apr. 1878	22, Mar.	33	119	Eitelwein	Batesville, IN	Ripley County, Indiana
Eichberg, Johan Wilhelm	9, July 1891	23, June	80	446		Columbus, WI	Bernstein, Brandenburg
Eichele, (Mrs)	21, Nov. 1850	18, July	70	188		New Orleans, LA	Württemberg
Eichenauer, Elisabeth	19, Oct. 1899	31, Aug.	53	671	Göbel	Quincy, IL	Alsheim, Rheinpfalz Baiern
Eichenauer, Minnie P.	23, July 1891	3, July	18	478	Sachs	Brooklyn, NY	
Eichenberger, Christian	1, Oct. 1896	13, Sept	41	639		Redfield, SD	Durb, Schweiz

Christliche Apologete Death Notices --- 1839 - 1899

Name of Deceased	Notice Date	Death Date	Age	Page	Maiden Name	Place of Death	Place of Birth
Eichenberger, J.J.	23, Nov. 1893	23, Aug.	56- 9m	750		Clay County, MO	Canton Aargau, Schweiz
Eichenberger, Martha	3, Apr. 1890	11, Mar.	42- 5m-17d	222	Schmidt	Lexington, MO	Morgan County, Missouri
Eichenberger, Sarah Lydia	22, Nov. 1888	30, Oct.	18	750		Cameron, MO	Lexington, Missouri
Eichenberger, Sophie	26, Apr. 1888	31, Mar.	34- 7m- 9d	270	Singenthaler	Redfield, SD	Oberemmenthal, Schweiz
Eichhorn, Anna	12, June 1890	12, May	26	382	Ludwig	Lawrence, MA	Neundorf, Reuß
Eichhorn, Anna Amalia	20, May 1897	1, May	29	318	Böttcher	St. Paul, MN	Salem, Minnesota
Eichhorn, Christoph	29, Nov. 1894	22, Oct.	52	774		Ft. Dodge, IA	Kudringen bei Landau, Rheinpfalz Baiern
Eichler, Pauline	11, Dec. 1882	24, Nov.		399	Pucklitsch	Lawrence, MA	
Eichmann, Johanna Friederike	23, July 1896	3, July	72	479	Gronow	Chicago, IL	Zewitz, Lauenburg, Pommern
Eichmeier, Herman	6, July 1874	5, June	74	215		Flood Creek, IA	Almina, Lippe-Detmold
Eichmeyer, Louise Magdalena	20, Feb. 1882	28, Jan.	12- 4m-18d	63		Hopewell, MO	Marthasville, Warren County, Missouri
Eichmüller, Michael	18, Feb. 1858	29, Dec.	41	28		Carver, MN	Stemmenreuth, Pegnitz, Baiern
Eickelman, Hermine	20, Apr. 1893	22, Mar.	66	254	Schaue	Danville, IL	Baden, Minden, Preußen
Eickhoff, Catharine	1, Oct. 1896	15, Aug.	52- - 5d	639	Riebel	Denver, CO	Chester, Meigs County, Ohio
Eickhoff, Sophia	30, Nov. 1893	5, Nov.	43	766		Cass County, NE	Dölitz bei Pyritz, Pommern
Eickmann, Henry William	6, May 1886	18, Apr.	18- 2m-15d	7		St. Louis, MO	
Eidelwein, Susanna	13, Aug. 1883	29, July	70- 5m	263	Beckmann	Batesville, IN	Fußgangheim, Pfalz, Baiern
Eier, Georg	12, Aug. 1842		Inquiry	127		Belmont County, OH	
Eiermann, Heinrich	19, Mar. 1877	5, Mar.	51- 3m- 9d	95		St. Louis, MO	Dittersdorf, Schleiz, Sachsen
Eiermann, Johan Nikolaus Christ.	22, Aug. 1881		14- 9m	271		St. Louis, MO	Spitzaltheim, Kreis Dieburg, Hessen
Eiermann, Margaretha	21, Feb. 1856	9, Jan.	25- 3m	32	Sauerwein	Mascoutah, IL	St. Louis, Missouri
Eiermann, Wilhelmine Katharine	4, Mar. 1897	14, Feb.	71	143	Pöttger	St. Louis, MO	Zanesville, Ohio
Eifele, Dina	3, Dec. 1896	5, Nov.	21	782		Columbus, OH	Connefeld, Spangenberg, Melsungen, Kurhessen
Eifer, Fred.	21, Aug. 1882	27, July	45	271		Burlington, IA	Reisenbach, Sachsen
Eifert, John E.W.	24, Apr. 1890	5, Mar.	61	270		Delhi, MI	Wernges, Hessen
Eifert, Maria	27, Jan. 1879	8, Jan.	42- 7m	31		Rushville, IL	Langenkursdorf, Waldenburg, Sachsen
Eifert, Wilhelmine	2, Mar. 1899	26, Jan.	66	143	Helwig	Holt, MI	Ellweiler, Birkenfeld, Oldenburg
Eifert, Carolina Louisa	25, Dec. 1865	5, Dec.	43	208	Werrz	Boonville, IN	Heimbach, RheinPreußen
Eifler, Elisabeth	29, May 1890	25, Apr.	67- 3m-12d	350		Beaver Dam, WI	Cedern, Birkenfeld, Oldenburg
Eifler, Jacob	29, Aug. 1881	18, Aug.	70- -15d	279		Boonville, ---	West Bend, Wisconsin
Eifler, Julius	2, June 1873	10, May	9- -28d	175		Ahnapee, WI	Westenheim, Rheinkreis Baiern
Eifler, Katharina	25, Jan. 1864	27, Dec.	36	16		Boonville, IN	Sötern, Oldenburg
Eifler, Nicolaus (Rev)	25, Mar. 1897	25, Apr.	72	190		Beaver Dam, WI	Häffner-Haslach, Brackenheim, Württemberg
Eigner, Elisabetha	7, Sept 1863	21, Aug.	25- 6m- 6d	144	Schock	Delaware, OH	Bielefeld, Minden, Preußen
Eikelmann, Wilhelm	13, July 1899	12, June	74	447		Danville, IL	Winschoten, Holland
Eikema, Harmke	8, May 1890	21, Apr.	50	302	Venekamp	Pekin, IL	
Eilber, Agnes	12, Nov. 1896	18, Oct.	72- 2m- 9d	734	Gunther	Crediton, CD	Baiersbronn, Freudenstadt, Baiern
Eilber, Christian	9, Sept 1897	13, Aug.	65	575		Columbus, OH	Reichenbach, Freudenstadt, Württemberg
Eilers, Friedrich G.	21, Oct. 1897	6, Oct.	62	671		Evansville, IN	Westerstede, Oldenburg
Eilers, Heinrich	5, Jan. 1864	7, Nov.	61	4		Sherrills Mount, IA	Hohenergelsen, Amt Steinbrück, Hannover
Eilhart, Friedrich	2, May 1870	13, Apr.	69	143		Cincinnati, OH	Bennien, Amt Melle, Osnabrück, Hannover
Eilhart, Maria Elisabeth	29, May 1882	14, May	65-10m-20d	175	Beckmann	Cincinnati, OH	Bennien, Amt Melle, Osnabrück, Hannover
Eilrich, Friedrich Wilhelm	23, Feb. 1874	5, Feb.	70	63		Chicago, IL	Ganz bei Lauenburg, HinterPommern
Einsele, Fanny	18, Dec. 1856	27, Nov.	9- 7m	204		Louisville, KY	
Einsele, Katharina	8, Dec. 1892	10, Nov.		782	Jakobi	Louisville, KY	
Einske, Fannie	27, Sept 1888	21, July	16- 5m- 6d	622		Louisville, KY	Buschweiler, Elsaß

Christliche Apologete Death Notices --- 1839 - 1899

Name of Deceased	Notice Date	Death Date	Age	Maiden Name	Page	Place of Death	Place of Birth
Einsle, Catharina	28, Sept 1874	12, Sept	19- -12d	Harm	311	Nashville, ---	Gut Tesdorf bei Oldenburg, Holstein
Einspaar, Dora	21, Jan. 1878	3, Jan.	19- 8m-3d		23	Cedar Lake, IN	Wesselbuhren, Holstein
Einspahr, August Johan	15, Mar. 1894	11, Feb.	51		182	Crown Point, IN	Westlingbuhren, Holstein
Einspahr, Friedrich	22, Nov. 1875	29, Oct.	59		375	Cedar Lake, IN	Blue Island, Cook County, Illinois
Einspahr, Wilhelm	11, Jan. 1894	14, Dec.	35		30	Crown Point, IN	Wangen bei Cannstatt, Württemberg
Eisele, (Mrs)	24, Apr. 1882	5, Apr.	64		135	Lawrence, KS	Markt Essingen, Württemberg
Eisele, Anna Catharina	13, Nov. 1871	17, Oct.	80-3m	Hindermann	367	Chicago, IL	South Bend, Indiana
Eisele, Christian Albert	27, Feb. 1890	4, Feb.	20- 1m-12d		142	Minneapolis, MN	Waiblingen, Württemberg
Eisele, Christine Pauline	17, May 1869	6, May	20- 4m-28d		159	Cincinnati, OH	Bretten, Baden
Eisele, Ernestine	29, Sept 1873	11, Sept	33	Dittes	311	Cincinnati, OH	Denkendorf, Eßlingen, Württemberg
Eisele, J.G.	4, May 1863	7, Apr.	50- 3m-7d		72	Logan, OH	Oberbäbingen, Gmünd, Württemberg
Eisele, Jakob Wilhelm	4, Jan. 1864	7, Dec.	78		4	Chicago, IL	Backnang, Württemberg
Eisele, Louise	30, May 1889	13, May	53- 5m-19d		350	St. Paul, MN	Isingen, Kirchheim, Württemberg
Eisele, Maria Barbara	21, Dec. 1868	9, Dec.	26	Nägele	407	Birmingham, PA	Oppo, Frankenthal, Rheinkreis Baiern
Eiselstein, Johannes	26, Jan. 1885	15, Jan.	84		7	Pomeroy, OH	Oppau, Frankenthal , Rheinkreis Baiern
Eiselstein, Katharina	3, July 1882	13, June	77- 3m-28d		215	Pomeroy, OH	Oppau, Frankenthal, Pfalz, Baiern
Eiselstein, Valentin	27, Dec. 1875	2, Dec.	44		415	Pomeroy, OH	Galena, Illinois
Eisemann, Wilhelm Heinrich	19, Oct. 1899	1, Oct.	23		671	Galena, IL	Berg, Preußen
Eisemenger, Ferdinand	10, Oct. 1864	16, June			164	Schnectady, NY	Frank , Rußland
Eisenach, Johannes	15, Apr. 1897	26, Mar.	67		238	Culbertson, NE	Kolb, Rußland
Eisenach, Maria Elisabeth	8, May 1890	27, Mar.	65- 9m- 1d	Meininger	302	Culbertson, NE	Sylvan, Washtenau County, Michigan
Eisenbeiser, Maria	13, Dec. 1888	29, Sept	25-10m- 2d	Kalmbach	798	Francisco, MI	Arolsen, Waldeck
Eisenberg, Fr.	4, May 1863	1, Apr.	32		72	Appleton, MO	Deringhausen, Amt Arollson, Waldeck
Eisenberg, Friederika	12, June 1871	11, May	65- 3m-11d	Schreier	191	Appleton, MO	Brendorf, Waldeck
Eisenberg, Heinrich	27, Dec. 1880	1, Dec.	80-11m- 5d		415	Cape Girardeau, MO	Berndorf, Waldeck
Eisenberg, J. H.	10, Mar. 1879	16, Feb.	51- 3m-15d		79	Cape Girardeau, MO	
Eisenberg, Maria Elisabeth	16, Apr. 1877	11, Mar.	12		127	Bloomington, IL	Westheim, Germersheim, Rheinkreis Baiern
Eisenhart, Maria Eva	2, Jan. 1890	13, Oct.	73- 5m-27d	Mees	14	Chillicothe, OH	Westheim, Germersheim, RheinPfalz Baiern
Eisenhart, Melcher	11, Feb. 1886	9, Jan.	75		7	Waverly, OH	Pike County, Ohio
Eisenhart, Sarah Emeline	27, Oct. 1879	9, Oct.	26- 7m-29d	Rhoades	343	Waverly, OH	Wittlinsweiler, Freudenstadt, Württemberg
Eisenheis, John M.	27, Apr. 1868	9, Apr.	29		135	Allegheny City, PA	Haßloch, Rheinkreis Baiern
Eisenmayer, Conrad	9, May 1889	13, Apr.	73		302	Nashville, IL	Imsbach bei Winnweiler, Rheinkreis Baiern
Eisenmayer, Margaretha	22, Nov. 1894	27, Oct.	71	Emig	758	Mascoutah, IL	Haßloch, Rheinkreis Baiern
Eisenmeier, Phillip Heinrich	17, Nov. 1887	24, Oct.	70- 5m-18d		734	Mascoutah, IL	Haßloch, Rheinkreis Baiern
Eisenmenger, Louise Magdalena	23, Feb. 1893	23, Jan.	29-2m-16d	Laufer	126	Louisville, KY	Haßloch, RheinPfalz Baiern
Eisenmeyer, Elisabeth	8, Dec. 1884	24, Nov.	67		7	Mascoutah, IL	Niederschlesien, Germany
Eisenmeyer, Jakob	8, Sept 1873	19, Aug.	39		287	Mascoutah, IL	
Eisert, Carl	25, Nov. 1886		67		7	Blooming Grove, MN	
Eisert, Helena	17, Apr. 1882	26, Mar.	14-11m-23d	Hennemann	127	Blooming Grove, MN	Herschweiler, Germany
Eisle, Katharine	13, Oct. 1898	18, Sept	67	Kimmich	655	Hooker, NE	Kleinsachsenheim, Vaihingen, Württemberg
Eißler, Margaretha Elisabetha	3, June 1867	4, May	72- 1m-14d		174	Louisville, KY	Ehningen, Württemberg
Eitel, Daniel	26, Mar. 1847	4, Nov.	69		51	New Orleans, LA	Belle, Lippe-Detmold
Eitel, Henriette	11, Aug. 1898	16, July	76	Deppe	510	Warrenton, MO	
Eitel, Katie E.	9, May 1881	23, Apr.	21- 7m-15d	Schramm	151	Indianapolis, IN	Madison, Indiana
Eitel, Susanna Lisetta	2, June 1887	3, May	14		350	Madison, IN	New York
Eitelgeorg, Anna	29, Sept 1879	11, Sept	31		311	Aurora, IL	

Christliche Apologete Death Notices --- 1839 - 1899

Name of Deceased	Notice Date	Death Date	Age	Maiden Name	Page	Place of Death	Place of Birth
Eitelgoerge, Johanne	3, Mar.1873	22, Jan.	74		71	Aurora, IL	Rottleben, Frankenhausen, Schwarzburg-Rudolstadt
Eitelgörge, Johanna	22, Mar. 1875	6, Mar.	43-11m-10d	Stolberg	95	Aurora, IL	Rottleben, Frankenhausen, Schwarzburg-Rudolstadt
Eitelwein, Andreas	15, Dec. 1879	28, Nov.	78		399	Batesville, IN	Altleiningen, Rheinkreis Baiern
Ekam, Peter	26, Oct. 1854	26, Sept	53- 2m		172	Delaware, OH	Oberhausen, Hessen
Ekam, Wilhelm	19, June 1865		25- 9m		100	Delaware, OH	
Ekam, Wilhelmine	29, Aug. 1850	6, Aug.	15- 5m		140	Columbus, OH	
Ekert, (Mrs)	21, Sept 1874	8, Sept	57- 5m- 6d	Bühler	303	Fillmore, MI	Nußbach, Amt Heidelberg, Baden
Eklin, Elisabeth	5, Oct. 1899	23, Sept	79	Schrodin	639	Indianapolis, IN	Sexau auf der Lerch, Baden
Elebracht, Heinrich Wilhelm Ernst	22, July 1897	24, June	62		463	Chase, WI	Lemjo, Westphalen
Elfeld, Marie	28, Nov. 1870	26, Oct.	20		383	Centreville, NE	
Elfers, Anna Elisabeth	26, Oct. 1868	6, Oct.	63		343	Quincy, IL	Eiterdam, Amt Achim, Hannover
Elfert, Cord	31, July 1851	12, July	49- 1m-12d		124	Quincy, IL	Hassel, Achim, Hannover
Elfmann, Auguste	8, Nov. 1888	15, Oct.	37	Timm	718	Sleepy Eye, MN	Gornitz, Scharniko, Germany
Elfring, John Gerhard	13, Oct. 1892	13, Sept	72-11m-23d		654		Schale, Westphalen
Elfrink, Anna Katharina	3, Feb. 1898	5, Jan.	82	Tasche	79	Bensonville, IL	Schaale, Westphalen
Elger, Bertha	25, Aug. 1892	2, Aug.	20	Neitzel	542	Burt, IA	Großtriechen, Belgrad, Hinterpommern
Elger, Ferdinand	21, Mar. 1881	5, Mar.	52- 9m		95	Chicago, IL	Heinesdorf bei Reichenberg, Böhmen
Elger, Gustav Carl	10, Sept 1896	15, July	46		591	St. Paul, MN	Pößneck, Sachsen-Meiningen
Elk, Katharina Margaretha	20, Aug. 1891	16, July	66	Weidmann	542	Garner, IA	Ernsthofen, Niederwaldau, Hessen-Darmstadt
Ellebracht, Friedrich	6, Nov. 1882	20, Oct.	73- 6m-28d		359	Llano, TX	Rosenthal, Lippe-Schaumburg, Kurhessen
Ellebracht, Sophie	5, Feb. 1872	12, Jan.	65	Stemme	47	Llano, TX	Ranneberg, Hessen
Ellebrecht, Joseph	2, Aug. 1875	10, July	46		247	Quincy, IL	Vorbeke, Warburg, Minden, Preußen
Ellemund, Wilhelm	15, Apr. 1858	25, Mar.	49		60	Cincinnati, OH	Oldendorf , Preußen
Ellemund, Wilhelmine	17, Dec. 1891	29, Nov.	77		814	Dayton, OH	Levera, Preußen
Ellen, Fenje	28, July 1873	3, July	80	Saathof	239	Blue Grass, IA	Altendorf, Amt Aurich, Ostfriesland
Ellenberger, Elisabeth	21, Oct. 1878	3, Oct.	63- 3m- 5d		335	Newark, NJ	Inkenbach, Baiern
Ellenberger, Jacob	25, July 1864	20, May	56		120	Newark, NJ	Neundorf, Baden
Ellensohn, Emilie	2, Oct. 1890	29, June	29- - 3d		638	Santa Cruz, CA	LaCrosse County, Wisconsin
Ellenson, Eduard	2, Sept 1897	24, July	44		559	Santa Cruz, CA	Wilkesbarre, Luzern County, Pennsylvania
Ellenson, Elise	28, Jan. 1897	26, Dec.	74		62	Santa Cruz, CA	Constanz, Germany
Ellerbeck, Maria	28, Sept 1897	28, Sept	71- 2m- 28d	Reckmeyer	687	Burlington, IA	Bokel, Halle, Westphalen
Ellerbeck, Wilhelmina	10, Feb. 1873		38	Kamp	47		Halle, Minden, Preußen
Ellerbrock, Carolina	9, Feb. 1885	24, Jan.	36	Trük	7	St. Louis, MO	Freudenstadt, Württemberg
Ellermann, Johan	30, Aug. 1875	12, Aug.	60		279	St. Louis, MO	Fenne, Hannover
Ellers, Anna Elisabeth	21, Feb. 1876	30, Jan.	44	Dubbels	63	Schnectady, NY	Deinsten, Hannover
Eley, Gustav (Rev)	12, Jan. 1899	14, Nov.	82- 5m- 3d		30	Seguin, TX	Schmiedeberg, Erzgeburge, Sachsen
Eley, Henrietta	16, Mar. 1899	20, Feb.	38		174	Seguin, TX	New Fountain, Texas
Elling, Anna	5, Aug. 1878	14, July	40	Klingenberg	247	Concordia, MO	Walkenbrück, Bünde, Preußen
Elling, Anna Maria	15, Jan. 1872	22, Dec.	60		23	Watertown, WI	
Elling, David W.	18, Mar. 1897	3, Mar.			174	Higginsville, MO	Concordia, Missouri
Elling, Wilhelm	15, Feb. 1875	30, Jan.	26- 7m		55	Concordia, MO	Spenger, Minden, Preußen
Ellinger, Elisabeth	2, Jan. 1890	16, Dec.	76	Werner	14	Giard, IA	Württemberg
Ellinger, Elisabetha	28, May 1866	7, May		Haas	174	Allegan, MI	
Ellinger, Ernestine	15, Jan. 1883	28, Dec.	86		23	Almond, WI	Saalfeld, Sachsen-Meiningen
Ellinger, Johan Georg	21, May 1877	28, Apr.	66		166	Giard, IA	Eutendorf, Württemberg
Ellinger, Johan Joseph	12, Jan. 1899	3, Dec.	68		31	Allegan, MI	Thalmessing, Baiern

Christliche Apologete Death Notices --- 1839 - 1899

Name of Deceased	Notice Date	Death Date	Age	Page	Maiden Name	Place of Death	Place of Birth
Ellinger, Maria Elisabeth	14, Oct. 1878	25, Sept		327	Merz	Allegan, MI	Oberisigheim bei Hanau, Kurhessen
Ellinger, Walburga	3, Aug. 1874	14, July	81- 6m- 8d	247		Allegan, MI	Thalmessing, Baiern
Elliott, Carolina	18, Sept 1890	26, Aug.	43- 4m-26d	606	Tönges	New Bremen, IL	Reinhartshausen, Waldeck
Ellis, Pauline Louise	23, July1883	9, July		239	Loeble	New York City, NY	Beilstein, Württemberg
Elrich, Anna E.	21, Mar. 1895	1, Mar.	40	190	Ritter	Boody, IL	Poland, Clay County, Indiana
Elsässer, Friedrich	29, Sept 1884	31, Aug.	56	7		Cleveland, OH	Brettach, Neckarsulm, Württemberg
Elwanger, Barbara	26, May 1873	9, May	63- 4m-19d	167	Schiller	East Rush, NY	Großheppach, Waiblingen, Württemberg
Elwanger, Emanuel Andr.	26, Sept 1881	29, Aug.	73-10m	311		Rochester, NY	
Elmer, Jacob	3, July 1890	13, June	57- 5m- 5d	430		Milwaukee, WI	Elm, Glarus, Schweiz
Elmer, Rudolph	12, Nov. 1883		20- 7m-23d	367		Highland, OR	Kansas
Elmers, Anna Maria	17, Apr. 1865	17, Mar.	18	64	Niemeier	Staunton, IL	Hohenmoor, Altenbruchhausen, Hannover
Elmers, August	13, Nov. 1890	21, Oct.	32	734		Moweaqua, IL	Madison County, Illinois
Els, Ludwig	5, Feb. 1866	16, Dec.	30	46		Washington, MN	Preußen
Elsäßer, Adam	23, Sept 1872	15, Aug.	57	311		Troy, NY	Vaihingen bei Stuttgart, Württemberg
Elsässer, Dorothea	11, Sept 1871	29, Aug.	72	295	Ulmer	Buffalo, NY	Piederhausen, Welzheim, Württemberg
Elsäster, Rosina Gottliebin	17, Sept 1857	8, Aug.	14	152		Melrose, NY	Vaihingen bei Stuttgart, Württemberg
Elsebach, Johan	3, Apr. 1890	13, Mar.	65	222		Terre Haute, IN	Birken Bringhausen, Frankenberg, Kurhessen
Eisenheimer, Peter D.	9, Nov. 1893	23, Oct.	74	718		Norwich, KS	Altenheim , Nassau
Elser, Maria Charlotte	18, Oct. 1894	28, Sept	39	678	Schutz	Boonville, IN	Newburgh, Warrick County, Indiana
Elsesser, Gottlieb Friedrich	27, Dec. 1880	10, Dec.	25- 2m-18d	415		Omaha, NE	Vaihingen, Württemberg
Elske, (Mrs)	22, Dec. 1873	24, Nov.	67	407	Stull	Oconomowoc, WI	Warsten, Pommern
Elsner, Georg Walter	12, Jan. 1885	18, Dec.	4- 2m-13d	7		Arlington, NE	
Ewing, Emilie	17, Mar. 1892	29, Feb.	26	174		Milwaukee, WI	Neustadt, Eberswalde, Brandenburg
Eizenheimer, Hugo Adolph	23, Feb. 1885	5, Feb.	23	7		Moweaqua, IL	
Elzer, Georg Jacob	26, Dec. 1881	13, Dec.	49- - 1d	415		Boonville, IN	Wertheim, Germershausen, RheinPfalz Baiern
Elzer, Maria	21, Feb. 1889	31, Jan.	18	126		Warsaw, IL	Amana, Iowa
Emch, Anna Barbara	24, July 1856	18, June	33- 5m	120	Flükiger	Woodville, OH	
Emch, Franziska	9, Feb. 1863	18, Dec.		24	Helferich	Perrysburg, OH	Waltenheim, Hessen-Darmstadt
Emch, Magdalena	20, Jan. 1859	23, Dec.	46- 3m	12	Ami	Woodville, OH	Lütterswyl, Solothurn, Schweiz
Emch, Margaretha	9, Feb. 1863	13, Nov.		24	Hoffmann	Woodville, OH	Lacha , Neustadt an der Hardt, Rheinkreis Baiern
Emch, Nicklaus	16, Oct. 1882	27, Sept	63- 6m-24d	335		Perrysburg, OH	Liedonville, Solothurn, Schweiz
Emde, Jakob	30, July 1857	18, June		124		Canton, IL	Höringshausen, Voehl, Hessen
Emde, Katharina	26, Sept 1861	29, July	59	156	Gerold	Baltimore, MD	
Emerich, Dorothea	14, Feb. 1881	26, Jan.	76	55	Neun	Matamoras, OH	Bleichenfeld, Nidda, Hessen-Darmstadt
Emich, Adam	9, Jan. 1882	25, Dec.	52- 2m-16d	15		Zanesville, OH	Zätzelbach, Hessen-Darmstadt
Emich, Jakob	21, Mar. 1881	25, Feb.	27- 1m-18d	95		Woodville, OH	
Emig, Friedrich Theobald	19, Mar. 1891	17, Feb.	76- 1m-23d	190		Marine City, MI	Jägersburg, Rheinkreis Baiern
Emig, Katharina	14, July 1898	13, June	65	447	Wagner	Mascoutah, IL	Kriegsfeld, Rheinpfalz Baiern
Emig, Magdalena	5, Feb. 1866	14, Jan.	40- 7m- 4d	46		Mascoutah, IL	Imsbach, Rheinpfalz Baiern
Emke, Johanna Henriette	8, July 1886	13, June	41	7	Voge	Owatonna, MN	Reetz, Arnswalde, Brandenburg
Emke, Katharina Elisabeth	27, Sept 1888	22, Aug.	35- 3m-12d	622	Scherb	Richmond, IN	Cincinnati, Hamilton County, Ohio
Emke, Mina	2, Jan. 1871	30, Oct.	24-11m-28d	7	Sommer	Fairbault, MN	Radwönke, Bromberg, Posen
Emkee, Wilhelmine	24, June 1872	7, June	28-11m	207	Voge	Cannon River, MN	Cornraden, Preußen
Emley, Philipp Heinrich	26, Oct. 1893	25, Sept	39	686		West Bend, WI	Pleasant, Marion County, Ohio
Emmel, Maria	6, Sept 1875	15, Aug.	81- 3m	287		Baltimore, MD	
Emmerich, Johan Martin	20, Jan. 1887	20, Dec.	57	46		New Haven, CT	Geisig, Nassau

- 108 -

Christliche Apologete Death Notices --- 1839 - 1899

Name of Deceased	Notice Date	Death Date	Age	Page	Maiden Name	Place of Death	Place of Birth
Emmerich, Johannes	12, Sept 1881	23, Aug.	84	295		New Matamoras, OH	Bleichenbach, Hessen-Darmstadt
Emmerick, Helena	21, Feb. 1895	26, Jan.	66	126	Rothhaar	New Haven, CT	Kastelaun bei Kreuznach, Germany
Emmert, Friederike	3, Mar. 1884	18, Feb.	67	7	Schiek	Terre Haute, IN	Vanarotha, Sachsen-Weimar
Emmert, Johan Ludwig	21, July 1884	31, May	72	7		San Francisco, CA	Klein-Aschbach, Marbach, Württemberg
Emmig, Hattie	24, Oct. 1881	30, Sept	20- 5m- 5d	343	Hammacher	Marine City, MI	
Emmrich, Daniel	14, June 1875	30, May	61- 3m- 4d	191		Portsmouth, OH	Kusel, Rheinkreis Baiern
Emrich, Anna Katharina	15, Nov. 1869	29, Sept	52-10m-24d	367	Hanter	Waverly, OH	Muttersbach, Wetzlar, Preußen
Emrich, Christian	7, May 1866		66	150		New Albany, IN	Fökelburg, Rheinpfalz, Baiern
Emrich, El. Margaretha	8, Feb. 1875		77	47	Rosebeke	Le Sueur, MN	Rothheim, Hessen-Darmstadt
Emrich, Emilie Karoline	4, Apr. 1870	19, Mar.	35	111	Bozenhart	Waverly, OH	Rockenhausen, Rheinpfalz Baiern
Emrich, Karl	8, Jan. 1883	19, Dec.	78- 1m	15		Ripley, OH	Kusel, Rheinkreis Baiern
Emrich, Maria Anna	21, Apr. 1892	15, Mar.	74	254	Müller	Waverly, OH	Niedermohr, Rheinkreis Baiern
Emrich, Susanna Elisabeth	21, June 1888	5, June	86	398	Hodum	Columbus, OH	Mauchenheim, Rheinkreis Baiern
Emrich, Theobald	28, Sept 1893	4, Sept	83-10m-25d	622			Vekelberg bei Kusel, Rheinkreis Baiern
Emrich, Valentin	28, Jan. 1884	24, Dec.	86-10m-16d	7		Columbus, OH	Illesheim, Rheinkreis Baiern
Ems, Clara	27, Sept 1888	30, Nov.	65	622	Siebel	Louisville, KY	Weilbach, Hochheim, Hessen-Nassau
Ems, Johan	1, Jan. 1877	13, Dec.	58- 3m	7		Bradford, IN	Weilbach, Hochheim, Nassau
Ems, Peter	11, Feb. 1892	19, Jan.	76- 1m- 4d	94		Louisville, KY	Weilbach, Hochheim, Nassau
Ems, Philipp	13, Apr. 1899	24, Mar.	46	238		Bradford, IN	Weilbach, Nassau
Endelmann, Anna M.	19, Mar. 1883		52- 1m-20d	95		Clatonia, NE	
Enderle, Karl	1, Feb. 1894	10, Jan.	67	78		Brooklyn, NY	Pforzheim, Baden
Endorf, Carolina M.	7, Feb. 1881	1, Nov.	74- 9m-28d	47	Speigel	Prescott, WI	
Endriß, Andreas	25, Feb. 1886	28, Jan.	43- 7m- 6d	7		Colesburg, IA	Mosbach, Baiern
Endriß, Johan Martin Theodor	5, Mar. 1896	17, Feb.	19	158		Colesburg, IA	Jo Davis County, Illinois
Endriß, Mary E.	9, Oct. 1882	28, Sept	30	327	Schultz	Galena, IL	Guilford, Jo Daviess County, Illinois
Enes, Carl Lurker	29, Dec. 1879	2, Dec.	13	415		Waymansville, IN	Brown County, Indiana
Enes, Johan Adam	29, Dec. 1879	13, Nov.	21	415		Waymansville, IN	Brown County, Indiana
Enes, Susanna Margaretha	22, Aug. 1881	2, Aug.	19	271		Waymansville, IN	
Engehausen, Maria	6, Feb. 1882	21, Jan.	22	47	Uebergall	Chicago, IL	Himmelpforten, Hannover
Engel, (Mrs)	9, Sept 1878	24, Aug.	77	287		Canal Dover, OH	Desloch, Homburg, Hessen
Engel, Anna Maria	22, May 1890	28, Apr.	47-11m-17d	334	Blankemeyer	Pomeroy, OH	Halle, Hannover
Engel, August	31, Dec. 1883	4, Dec.	62	7		Pomeroy, OH	Neubatzdorf, Hobelschwert, Schlesien
Engel, Bernhard	18, Sept 1871	18, Aug.	60	303		Jordan, MN	Esch, Amt Idstein, Nassau
Engel, Bernhard	10, Feb. 1843		Inquiry	23		Persia, NY	
Engel, Carl Friedrich	22, Mar. 1888	28, Feb.	83	190		Sandusky, OH	Weingarten, Durlach, Baden
Engel, Eddie	3, Nov. 1898	18, Oct.	22	703		Lyona, KS	
Engel, Elisabeth	19, Nov. 1866	21, Sept	23- 4m	374		Sandusky, OH	Freyenstein, Brandenburg
Engel, Friedrich	23, Mar. 1899	2, Mar.	73	190		Berlin, OH	Holzheim, Gießen, Hessen-Darmstadt
Engel, Friedrich	27, Feb. 1890	21, Jan.	49	142		Bloomington, IL	Esch, Amt Idstein, Nassau
Engel, Friedrich	10, July 1865	12, June	66- 8m	112		Pepin, WI	Desloch, Meisenheim, Homburg, Hessen
Engel, Friedrich Carl	27, July 1893		67	478		Lake City, MN	Edigheim, Frankenthal, Rheinkreis Baiern
Engel, Georg Heinrich	2, June 1892	29, Apr.	51	350		Chicago, IL	Rinzenberg, Birkenfeld, Oldenburg
Engel, Helene	14, Feb. 1870	7, Jan.	19	55		Sand Creek, MN	
Engel, Jakob	27, Mar. 1890	28, Feb.	69- 4m-13d	206		Canal Dover, OH	
Engel, Johan	12, Mar. 1891	31, Jan.	69	174		Pomeroy, OH	
Engel, Johan Karl	21, Nov. 1881	7, Nov.	51- 4m-19d	375		Laporte, IN	

Christliche Apologete Death Notices --- 1839 - 1899

Name of Deceased	Notice Date	Death Date	Age	Maiden Name	Page	Place of Death	Place of Birth
Engel, Johannes	6, Apr. 1874	7, Mar.	73		111	Belleville, IL	Ernsthausen, Kurhessen
Engel, John	23, Jan. 1890	5, Jan.	54		62	Allegan, MI	Bebra, Rothenburg, Kurhessen
Engel, Katharina	26, Mar. 1877	17, Mar.	28- 9m-14d		103	Louisville, KY	
Engel, Katharina Barbara	3, Sept 1891	15, July	81	Rohrbacher	574	Sandusky, OH	Weingarten, Baden
Engel, Katharine	1, Mar. 1869	4, Feb.	50	Goos	71	Boonville, IN	Wollmar, Amt Wetter, Marburg, Kurhessen
Engel, Lydia Amalie	22, Jan. 1877	28, Dec.	17		31	Covington, KY	
Engel, Margaretha	8, Jan. 1891	5, Dec.	66	Bäker	30	Canal Dover, OH	Defsloch, Homburg, Hessen
Engel, Margaretha	24, Mar. 1884	10, Mar.	64	Lemmel	7	Louisville, KY	Imbsheim, Elsaß
Engel, Margaretha	3, July 1865	14, June	9		108	Pomeroy, OH	
Engel, Maria	20, May 1878	4, May	66- 1m-29d		159	Jordan, MN	Esch, Amt Idstein, Nassau
Engel, Maria Katharina	6, Sept 1894		52	Kaiser	582	Friend, NE	Colonie Golg, Kacomiech, Rußland
Engel, Mathilde Elisabeth	19, Dec. 1870	11, Nov.	19		407	Covington, KY	
Engel, Rosine	31, Jan. 1870	22, Dec.	38	Woody	39	Pomeroy, OH	Oppau, Baiern
Engel, Rosine Sophie Wilhelmine	11, Jan. 1864	29, Dec.	18		8	Cincinnati, OH	Ebingen, Württemberg
Engel, Sarah	3, Sept 1896	7, Aug.	68	Bohl	575	Covington, KY	Pirmasens, Rheinpfalz Baiern
Engel, Wilhelm	27, Mar. 1865	21, Mar.	45		50		Eblingen, Balingen, Württemberg
Engel, Wilhelm August	24, May 1875	10, May	20-11m-10d		167	Covington, KY	
Engel, Winnie	29, July 1897	5, July	14		479	Allegheny, PA	Allegheny, Pennsylvania
Engelbrecht, Albert	19, Jan. 1885	2, Jan.	17- 3m		7	Jefferson City, MO	
Engelbrecht, Anna Margaretha	2, July 1896	15, June	86	Merkel	431	Jefferson City, MO	Kemnitz, Baiern
Engelbrecht, Casper	5, Feb. 1877	4, Jan.	42		47	Drake, MO	Nieder-Gollenbeck, Minden, Preußen
Engelbrecht, Charlotte	9, Oct. 1876	15, Sept	55- 7m- 6d	Brodbeck	327	Portsmouth, OH	Bingen, Baden
Engelbrecht, Johan Adam	8, Jan. 1872	21, Dec.	73		15	Boonville, MO	Untersteinach bei Bayreuth, Baiern
Engelbrecht, Margaretha	8, Apr. 1872	13, Mar.	30		119	Vermillion, OH	
Engelhardt, Anna Maria	25, Mar. 1886	11, Mar.	64- -24d	Reim	7	Wheeling, WV	Oeschingen, Schwarzwald, Württemberg
Engelhardt, Jakob	22, Dec. 1862	8, Nov.	68		204	Terre Haute, IN	Roßwag, Vaihingen, Württemberg
Engelhardt, Katharina	3, Mar. 1879	17, Jan.	42- - 7d		71	New York City, NY	Enzweihingen, Vaihingen, Württemberg
Engelhardt, Lisette	31, Jan. 1895	9, Jan.	48- 4m-27d		78	Brighton, IL	Linn bei Osnabrück, Hannover
Engelhardt, Peter	29, Jan. 1883	15, Jan.	67- 9m- 6d		39	Metamoras, OH	Nordheim, Hessen
Engelhart, Anna Elisabeth	10, Oct. 1864	12, Sept	14-10m-12d		164	Lease Run, OH	Wheeling Island, Virginia
Engelhorn, Anna Eva	16, Aug. 1894	13, June	77	Barthel	534	Edwardsville, IL	Beerbach, Heilsbron bei Nürnberg, Baiern
Engeling, Anna Margaretha Elisabeth	12, Jan. 1888	18, Dec.	77	Sewing	30	Edwardsville, IL	Schielsche, Jarford, Preußen
Engeling, Herman Heinrich	30, Apr. 1877	16, Apr.	74		143	Nebraska City, NE	Herford, Minden, Preußen
Engelke, Louise	21, Oct. 1878	5, Oct.	74	Schmalte	335	Nebraska City, NE	Brügge bei Soldin, Preußen
Engelking, Heinrich	30, Aug. 1880	11, Aug.	39		279	Aurora, MN	Bückeburg, Lippe-Schaumburg
Engelkirch, Kilian	20, Oct. 1862	30, Sept	15		168	Watertown, WI	Föhrden, Hohn, Schleswig
Engelland, Doetlef	19, Sept 1881	2, Sept	69		303	Cedar Lake, IN	Krogg, Schleswig-Holstein
Engelland, Margaretha	18, Aug. 1892	24, July	65	Reve	526	Crown Point, IN	Sehlem, Hannover
Engelmann, (Mrs)	15, Nov. 1860	22, Oct.	60- 9m-22d		184	Appleton, MO	Lexington, Missouri
Engelmann, Carl Friedrich	5, May 1884	3, Apr.	28		7	Concordia, MO	
Engelmann, Caroline Emilie	6, Mar. 1882	18, Feb.	17- 8m-24d		79	Concordia, MO	Sohlen, Hannover
Engelmann, Ernst	10, Aug. 1863	13, June	23		128	Appleton, MO	Wallenbruck, Herfort, Preußen
Engelmann, Franz	29, Sept 1898	16, Sept	81		623	Concordia, MO	Sehlem, Hannover
Engelmann, Heinrich	15, Nov. 1860	22, Oct.	30- 8m-16d		184	Appleton, MO	Delaware County, Iowa
Engelmann, Minna Hanna	9, Mar. 1899	7, Feb.	33	Kuhlmann	158	Colesburg, IA	Holzhausen, Tecklenburg, Westphalen
Engelmann, Sophia	27, Apr. 1899	9, Apr.	42	Brockmeier	271	Nokomis, IL	

Christliche Apologete Death Notices --- 1839 - 1899

Name of Deceased	Notice Date	Death Date	Age	Maiden Name	Place of Death	Page	Place of Birth
Engels, Nathaniel	20, Oct. 1892	28, Aug.	80		St. Louis, MO	670	Laporte, Indiana
Engelsberger, Lizzie	31, May 1888	5, May	22		Hartford, CT	350	Portsbach bei Kaiserslautern, Baiern
Engelskircher, Leonard	12, Aug. 1878	1, Aug.	59- -24d		Lowell, WI	255	Chicago, Cook County, Illinois
Enghausen, Caroline	3, Aug. 1885	15, July	18		Chicago, IL	7	Solingen, Preußen
Engler, Augustine	18, Sept 1882	30, Aug.	61	Knecht	Harper, IA	303	Erlingen, Saulgau, Württemberg
Engler, Moritz	5, Jan. 1899	16, Dec.	57		Nashville, TN	14	Mt. Prairie, Minnesota
Engler, Rosa	23, Feb. 1893	22, Jan.	18		St. Louis, MO	126	Hoffenheim, Sinsheim, Baden
Enne, Elisabeth	10, Nov. 1884		34-10m- 8d		Mt. Vernon, NY	7	Drullingen, Elsaß
Ensminger, Philipp	6, May 1852	13, Apr.	70- -29d		Langgrove, IL	76	Wulfsahl, Mecklenburg-Schwerin
Enterich, Friederika	13, Apr. 1899	21, Mar.	67		Columbus, WI	238	Hedem, Westphalen
Enters, Charlotte	3, May 1888	17, Apr.	79- 2m- 1d	Schroeder	Jordan, MN	286	Milwaukee, Wisconsin
Entzminger, Johan	25, May 1899	5, May	34		Almond, WI	335	
Enz, Agathe L.	12, Oct. 1874	24, Sept	25		Kenosha, WI	327	Döffingen, Böblingen, Württemberg
Enz, Johan Christian	28, Mar. 1864	2, Jan.	44- 5m- 5d		Milwaukee, WI	52	Edigheim, Frankenthal, Rheinkreis Baiern
Enzenauer, Anna Maria	3, Sept 1891	20, July	59		Pomeroy, OH	574	Bergheim, Kreis Melsungen, Kurhessen
Enzeroth, Anna Barbara	3, June 1867	6, Apr.	64	Liebau	Warsaw, IL	174	Bussick, Gießen, Hessen
Enzeroth, Elisabeth	16, Apr. 1883	23, Mar.	78- 1m-23d	Stephan	Warsaw, IL	127	St. Charles, Missouri
Enzeroth, H. Wilhelm	30, Oct. 1871	9, Oct.	5- 9m-14d		Beardstown, IL	351	Schnellrode, Spangenberg, Kurhessen
Enzeroth, Johan Heinrich	25, June 1883	26, May	81- 4m- 1d		Warsaw, IL	207	Bergheim, Spangenberg, Kurhessen
Enzeroth, Justus	19, July 1875	26, June	39		Warsaw, IL	231	WesternCappeln, Kreis Tecklenburg, Preußen
Enzeroth, Wilhelmine	30, Nov. 1863	21, Oct.	23- 3m	Wallenbrock	Warsau, IL	192	Brucken, Kirchheim a. d. Teck, Württemberg
Enzinger, Johan Adam	6, Apr. 1893	13, Mar.	82		Hannibal, OH	222	Nortmoor, Ostfriesland
Ephusen, Bertha	12, July 1875	14, June	39- 8m-21d	Lüken	St. Louis, MO	223	Hersen, Lippe-Detmold
Epker, Amalia	13, Mar. 1856	3, Feb.	16- 1m		Herman, MO	44	Midlum, Landewurfen, Dorum, Hannover
Epmeyer, Henriette	16, Oct. 1890	16, Aug.	43	Böse	Boston, MA	670	Lansing Township, Allamakee County, Iowa
Epner, Flora Ann	14, Mar. 1895	13, Feb.	17		Allamakee Co, IA	174	Oberkrummbach, Bruchsal, Baden
Eppele, Johann	6, Sept 1860	20, Aug.	35		Troy, NY	144	
Eppele, John	11, Nov. 1878	21, Oct.	16		Troy, NY	359	Rohtt bei Landau, Baiern
Eppelhäuser, Elisabeth	27, Feb. 1882	14, Feb.	51	Heintz	Peoria, IL	71	Sinsheim, Baden
Eppensteiner, Elisabeth	6, Jan. 1853	29, Nov.	69		Saugerties, NY	4	Darsin, Cöslin, Preußen
Eppert, Johanna	20, Sept 1860	12, Sept	62- 3m	Mazischke	Sandusky, OH	152	Olmsted Falls, Cuyahoga County, Ohio
Eppink, Arnold Johan	23, May 1881	4, May	13- 2m-23d		Olmstead Falls, OH	167	Buchhold, Westphalen
Eppink, Arnold Johan	7, Oct. 1886	20, Sept	63		Berea, OH	7	
Epple, Anna Barbara	19, Mar. 1877	24, Feb.	39	Weimann	Rockford, MN	95	Isingen, Sulz, Württemberg
Eppler, Andreas	12, Jan. 1893	27, Nov.	14		Muskoda, MN	30	Ebensweiler, Neustadt, Kurhessen
Erb, Anna Catharina	3, Oct. 1864	1, Sept	54		Lafayette, IN	160	Schwallungen, Meiningen, Sachsen-Meiningen
Erb, Georg Simon	5, Mar. 1857	13, Dec.	46		Hazel Green, WI	40	Friesenheim, Baden
Erb, Lorenz	29, Mar. 1888	10, Mar.	75		Lafayette, IN	206	Sundhausen, Elsaß
Erb, Magdalena	5, Jan. 1860	7, Dec.	51- 4m		Wheeling, VA	4	New Orleans, Louisiana
Erbach, Frank H.	18, July 1895	1, July	26		New Orleans, LA	462	Filehne, Posen, Preußen
Erbe, Barbara Elisabeth	5, July 1875	11, June	85		Faribault, MN	215	Barchfeld, Schamlkalden, Kurhessen
Erbe, Caroline	16, Apr. 1883	1, Apr.	76- 8m- 4d	Volkert	Pittsburg, PA	127	Pittsburg, Pennsylvania
Erbe, Louise	18, Oct. 1894	25, Sept	49	Wellemeyer	Pittsburg, PA	678	Veikazein, Hessen-Darmstadt
Erbes, Louis	26, Mar. 1891	19, Feb.	44		Los Angeles, CA	206	
Erdel, (Mrs)	12, Jan. 1874	22, Dec.	67		Schnectady, NY	15	Nördlingen, Baiern
Erdlen, Friedrich Maximilian	11, Sept 1876	28, Aug.	52		Marion, OH	295	

Christliche Apologete Death Notices --- 1839 - 1899

Name of Deceased	Notice Date	Death Date	Age	Page	Maiden Name	Place of Death	Place of Birth
Erdmann, Albert Friedrich	17, Dec. 1891	14, Nov.	19	814		Stillwater, MN	Treptow, Pommern
Erdmann, Anna Alwina	9, June 1898	9, May	24	367		Panola, MN	Panola, Minnesota
Erdmann, Emil	24, Mar. 1884	3, Mar.	7- 2m	7		Wausau, WI	
Erdmann, Ernst	25, Aug. 1898	9, Aug.	62	543		Chicago, IL	Steinach, Thüringen
Erdmann, Gottlieb Ferdinand Martin	6, Oct. 1879	21, Sept	74- 1m- 2d	319		Herman, MO	Jargelin, Mangard, Pommern
Erdmann, Heinrich Johan	8, Mar. 1880	19, Feb.	22	79		Columbus, IL	
Erdmann, Johan Heinrich	22, Apr. 1867	13, Mar.	58-10m-17d	126	Köpsel	Columbus, IL	Oberdorla, Mülhausen, Preußen
Erdmann, Johanna	11, Mar. 1897	20, Feb.	86	158		West Bend, WI	Gergelin, Preußen
Erdmann, John	18, Dec. 1890	15, Nov.	25- 3m	814		Chicago, IL	Chicago, Cook County, Illinois
Efffmeier, Karoline	26, Jan. 1880	29, Dec.	46- 1m-27d	31		Sandusky, OH	Minden, Preußen
Erfurth, Anna E.	29, July 1897	27, June	26	479		Independence, MO	Maciesbort, Pennsylvania
Erfurth, Johan Christian Traugott	25, Feb. 1878	14, Feb.	62	63		Chicago, IL	Kiebitz, Sachsen
Erhardt, Auguste	10, Mar. 1898	22, Feb.	58	158	Niemeier	Chicago, IL	Halle bei Bielefeld, Germany
Erhardt, Barbara	3, Feb. 1887	12, Jan.	74	78		Moweaqua, IL	
Erich, Gustav	18, Aug. 1898	20, July	78	527		Chillicothe, OH	Kleinwangen, Germany
Erich, Johan Christoph	6, Apr. 1854	5, Mar.	62	56		Waverly, OH	Eckartsberga zu Saubach, Preußen
Erich, Karl M.	16, June 1879		27	191		Waverly, OH	Waverly, Ohio
Erich, Rosina Elisabeth	31, July 1882	5, July	89- 7m-13d	247		Waverly, OH	Querfurt, Merseburg, Preußen
Erich, Sarah Magdalena	10, Jan. 1889	23, Dec.	20	30		Chillicothe, OH	Pike County, Ohio
Ericson, Elise	18, Apr. 1895	30, Mar.	29	254	Grünewald	St. Paul, MN	Greisenberg, Pommern
Erion, Maria Kunigunde	12, Dec. 1889	24, Nov.	54	798	Morhart	Bay City, MI	Altensteig, Nagold, Württemberg
Erker, Karoline	25, May 1885	6, May	44- 2m-24d	7		St. Louis, MO	Friedberg, Hessen
Erlenbusch, Maria M.	11, Apr. 1881	10, Mar.	75- 2m-18d	119	Härtle	Columbus, OH	Mauren, Hartburg, Baiern
Erlenmeier, Dorothea	6, July 1899	9, June	65- 3m-20d	431	Timper	Schnectady, NY	
Erling, Emilie	9, July 1891	16, June	63	446	Schuhmann	Baltimore, MD	Ronneburg, Sachsen-Altenburg
Erling, Marie	23, Jan. 1890	9, Jan.	33- - 2d	62		Baltimore, MD	
Erling, Wilhelm	26, June 1890	8, June	69- 3m- 5d	414		Baltimore, MD	Marne, Schleswig-Holstein
Ermann, Lydia	23, Oct. 1876	24, Sept	13- 5m-20d	343		Jacksonville, IL	
Ermel, Johan Christian	4, Nov. 1897	2, Oct.	56	703		Perry, TX	Knielingen, Baden
Ermlich, Amalie	25, Apr. 1864	9, Mar.	15- 6m-28d	68		Marietta, OH	Montreal, Canada
Ermlich, Johan Friedrich	6, June 1895	22, Apr.	78	366		Marietta, OH	Neustadt bei Stolpen, Sachsen
Erni, Sophia Anna	19, Apr. 1875	26, Mar.	20	127		Jeffersonville, IN	Thundorf, Thurgau, Schweiz
Ernst, Anna Katharina	11, Aug. 1892	9, July	83- 6m-29d	510	Magdlung	Newport, KY	Lengsfeld, Sachsen-Weimar
Ernst, Anna Maria	14, June 1894	25, Apr.	90	390	Beinguns	Madison, IN	Obendorf, Welzheim, Württemberg
Ernst, Anna Maria	12, July 1894	25, Apr.	90	454	Benignus	Madison, IN	Obendorf, Welzheim, Württemberg
Ernst, Eva	9, Sept 1858	14, Aug.	41	144		Rochester, IN	Hackmath, Elsaß
Ernst, Friedrich	8, Aug. 1850	14, July		128			Württemberg
Ernst, Johannes	5, Aug. 1886	18, July	66	7		Sandusky, OH	Arwangen, Bern, Schweiz
Ernst, Johannes	26, Apr. 1860	20, Mar.	37	68		Mt. Vernon, IN	Epfenbach, Baden
Ernst, Katharina	2, Dec. 1867	1, Nov.		382	Schmidt	New Braunfels, TX	Beilstein, Amt Herborn, Nassau
Ernst, Margaretha	26, Sept 1881		75	311		Philadelphia, PA	
Ernst, Mathilda	19, Oct. 1881	23, Oct.	36	407	Sauer	Marion, OH	Marion County, Ohio
Ernst, Mathilde	12, Jan. 1899	19, Dec.	57	31	Kriofsky	Chicago, IL	Friedrichsberg bei Flato, Germany
Ernsthausen, Caspar H.	8, Apr. 1886	18, Mar.	58	7		Elmore, OH	Weimar, Germany
Ernsthausen, Dorothea	26, Mar. 1896	25, Feb.	69	206	Gerwin	Elmore, OH	Baumte, Hannover
Ernsthausen, John	10, Nov. 1887	16, Oct.	33	718		Elmore, OH	Toledo, Lucas County, Ohio

- 112 -

Christliche Apologete Death Notices --- 1839 - 1899

Name of Deceased	Notice Date	Death Date	Age	Page	Maiden Name	Place of Death	Place of Birth
Ernstmeyer, Wilhelm	18, Aug. 1873	16, July	67	263		Warrenton, MO	Palar, Minden, Preußen
Ersenhard, Anton	11, Aug. 1862	17, July	21	128		Waverly, OH	Westheim, Rheinkreis Baiern
Ertel, Leonard	16, Mar. 1893	18, Jan.	88	174		Amsterdam, NY	Breitenstein, Baiern
Erven, Anna	1, Dec. 1884	19, Nov.	24	7	Großjohn	Lebanon, IL	Lebanon, Illinois
Esch, Johan Bernard Heinrich	6, Feb. 1882	16, Jan.	14	47		Evanston, IL	
Esch, Katharina	14, Jan. 1858	15, Dec.	16	8		Rockford, IN	Holmes County, Ohio
Eschbacher, Samuel	15, Feb. 1894	28, Jan.	60	110		Graham, MO	Eggewyl, Bern, Schweiz
Esche, Albert	19, Mar. 1883	11, Feb.	22	95		Marrs, IN	
Esche, Heinrich	10, May 1875	18, Apr.	43	151		Marrs, IN	Siebershausen, Braunschweig
Eschelbach, Heinrich Conrad	30, May 1895	4, May	17	350		Cincinnati, OH	Mosbach, Baden
Eschelbach, Louise	8, Aug. 1895	12, July	39	510	Baier	Cincinnati, OH	Schefflenz, Baden
Eschmann, Barbara	4, Sept 1871	2, July	51	287		Newark, NJ	Lammsheim, Rheinkreis Baiern
Eschmann, Friederika Sophia	14, Nov. 1889	12, Oct.	70-10m-15d	734	Schulte	Canal Dover, OH	Tecklenburg, Westphalen, Preußen
Eschmann, Herman Heinrich	21, Mar. 1881	4, Mar.	67	95		Newark, OH	Ladbergen, Tecklenburg, Westphalen, Preußen
Eschmann, Johan	27, July 1893	6, July	74	478		Newark, NJ	Dentersheim, Rheinpfalz Baiern
Eschstruth, Elisabeth	27, July 1868	7, July	59	239		Wheeling, WV	Ulfen, Amt Sondra, Kurhessen
Eschstruth, Mary	6, Nov. 1882	22, Oct.	42- 7m-11d	359	Top	Wheeling, WV	Wheeling, West Virginia
Eske, Ernestina	22, Aug. 1895	2, Aug.	51	542	Wörpel	Redfield, SD	Dobbenpful, Pommern
Esmann, Eggert Heinrich	14, Nov. 1881		60	367		Bland, MO	Heiligenfelde, Amt Sike, Hannover
Esmeier, Elisabeth	30, Sept 1872	25, Aug.	30	319	Nippert	Portsmouth, OH	Monroe County, Ohio
Esmeyer, Hermann	1, May 1865	2, Apr.	67	72		Baresville, OH	Ladbergen, Tecklenburg, Preußen
Espenlaub, Margaretha	29, Apr. 1867	16, Apr.	61	134		Evansville, IN	
Essig, Auguste	1, June 1899	9, May	27	351	Dräger	Springfield, MN	Lafayette, Nicolette County, Minnesota
Essig, Johan Friedrich	20, Feb. 1896	25, Jan.	85	126		Springfield, MN	Maubron bei Linzingen, Württemberg
Essig, Magdalena	3, Mar. 1859	18, Jan.	80- -12d	36		Ripley, OH	Affalterbach, Marbach, Württemberg
Essinger, Martin	4, July 1881	24, June	72- 9m- 9d	215		Portsmouth, OH	Altingen, Spaichingen, Württemberg
Eßlinger, Christian	23, June 1873	13, May	20	199		Canton, MO	
Eßlinger, Johannes	16, Nov. 1885	18, Oct.	64	7		Canton, MO	Hopfau, Sulz, Württemberg
Eßmann, Margaretha M.	16, Oct. 1890	14, Sept	31	670	Gleize	Bland, MO	Maries County, Missouri
Eßmeier, Marie	7, May 1891	26, Mar.	26- 3m- 1d	302	Zeller	Evansville, IN	
Eßmeyer, Elisabeth	4, May 1874	7, Apr.	72	143		Bonn, OH	Tecklenburg bei Münster, Preußen
Eßmeyer, Heinrich	20, Oct. 1892	27, Sept	24- 7m-29d	670		Evansville, IN	New York
Eßmeyer, Priscilla Ellen	8, Apr. 1878	3, Mar.	39	111		Wittens, OH	
Esterle, David	9, Dec. 1872	27, Nov.	20	399		Buffalo, NY	Lancaster, New York
Esterle, Rosine	25, May 1899	9, May	35	335	Yoos	LaCrosse, WI	Kirchenhirnberg, Württemberg
Etelwein, Anna Maria	28, July 1887	2, July	43	478	Röder	Batesville, IN	Ripley County, Indiana
Etschel, Eleonore	24, Jan. 1889	17, Dec.		62		Troy, NY	Wittenberg, Germany
Etschel, Libbie	29, Jan. 1891	24, Dec.	26	78		Troy, NY	Troy, New York
Etter, Elisabeth	22, Oct. 1891	2, Sept	74	686	Beck	Wadena, MN	Kuiftlingen, Maulbronn, Württemberg
Etter, Maggie	24, Sept 1891	1, Sept		622		Pittsburg, PA	Pittsburg, Pennsylvania
Etzel, Savina	10, Mar. 1879	19, Feb.	73	79	Fleischmann	Baltimore, MD	Wilhelmsdorf, Baiern
Etzold, Anna	16, Dec. 1872	1, Dec.	21	407		Buffalo, NY	
Etzold, Auguste Emma	3, Nov. 1884	12, Oct.	16	7		Lancaster, NY	Akron, New York
Etzold, Johan	3, Oct. 1895	22, Aug.	79	638		Akron, NY	Gartschütz, Sachsen-Altenburg
Euerle, (Mrs)	24, Mar. 1887	7, Mar.	60	190	Burghart	Bridgeport, CT	Jägersburg, Rheinkreis Baiern
Euerle, Georg Michael	3, Dec. 1883	2, Nov.	52	391		Bridgeport, CT	Großasbach, Backnang, Württemberg

- 113 -

Name of Deceased	Notice Date	Death Date	Age	Page	Maiden Name	Place of Death	Place of Birth
Euerle, Gottlieb	13, Feb. 1890	16, Jan.	61	110	Horning	Boston, MA	Ornburg, Württemberg
Euler, Katharina	8, Dec. 1859	26, Nov.	35	196		Iowa City, IA	Michelbach, Württemberg
Euler, Louise	24, Feb. 1873	24, Jan.	30- 7m	63	Wiegant	New Rochelle, NY	Kirchheim, Kurhessen
Euler, Maria	10, Mar.1873	15, Feb.	32	79		Rushville, IL	
Eulig, Sophia	3, Feb. 1868	2, Jan.	30	39	Dreyer	St. Joseph, MO	Liebenau, Hannover
Eull, Gertrud	8, Feb. 1894	30, Nov.	69	94	Ulm	Quincy, IL	Rothenburg, Kurhessen
Evans, Louise	30, Apr. 1883	24, Mar.	29- 2m- 2d	143	Traser	Nauvoo, IL	LaHarve, Illinois
Eventhal, Barbara Anna	28, May 1891	21, Apr.	36	350		Ironton, OH	
Evers, Christian E.	19, Dec. 1881	30, Nov.	81	407		Fredericksburg, TX	Söhlde, Hannover
Evers, Dorothea	22, June 1899	1, June	89	399	Müller	Fredericksburg, TX	Halchtern, Braunschweig
Eversmeier, Carolina	21, Jan. 1884	28, Dec.	33	7	Schlomann	Warrenton, MO	Warren County, Missouri
Eversmeier, Johan Adolph	8, Mar. 1888	10, Feb.	59	158		Warren, MO	Lotte, Westphalen
Eversmeier, Anna Margaretha	21, June 1894	7, May	61	406	Schäper	Warren, MO	Spenge, Preußen
Eversmeier, Bernhard Heinrich	4, June 1891	19, Apr.	66	366		Muscatine, IA	Vlotho, Westphalen
Eversmeyer, Elisabeth	9, Sept 1886	18, Aug.	43	7	Martin	Wapello, IA	Dorf-Geismar, Kurhessen
Eversmeyer, Friedrich Wilhelm	8, May 1890	14, Apr.	47- 3m-18d	302		Warren, MO	Indian Camp, Warren County, Missouri
Eversmeyer, Margaretha Catharina	6, Feb. 1890	5, Jan.	23	94		Warren, MO	Indian Camp, Warren County, Missouri
Eversmeyer, Maria	10, Nov. 1873	5, Sept	21	359		Warren, MO	
Evert, Friedrich	12, Jan. 1893	16, Oct.		30		Tomah, WI	
Evesmeyer, Herman Heinrich	18, Dec. 1876	29, Nov.	49	407		Wapello, TX	Steinbründorf, Amt Vlotho, Preußen
Ewald, Christoph	15, May 1876	26, Apr.	50	159		Columbus, WI	Bartelsen, Bromberg, Preußen
Ewald, Jakob	28, Mar. 1870	19, Feb.	73	103		Charlestown, IN	Mölsbach, Pfeddersheim, Worms, Rheinpfalz Baiern
Ewalt, John	6, July 1868	14, June	35	215		Baltimore, MD	Schlierbach, Kreis Fritzlar, Kurhessen
Ewersmeyer, Louisa	16, Aug. 1860	2, Aug.	26	132	Schlerf	Muscatine, IA	
Ewert, Katharine	17, Feb. 1898	28, Jan.	56	111	Schwartz	Goshen, IN	Mutterstadt bei Speier, Rheinpfalz Baiern
Ewinger, Heinrich	17, June 1897	22, May	70	383		Burlington, IA	Langenkandel, Rheinpfalz Baiern
Ewinger, Katharina	5, Aug. 1878	22, July	50- 1m-21d	247	Burg	Burlington, IA	Hergersweiler, Rheinpfalz Baiern
Ewinger, Wilhelm	23, Jan. 1896	26, Dec.	27	62		Burlington, IA	Langekandel, Rheinpfalz Baiern
Eyer, Johan	5, May 1898	8, Apr.	47	287		Newport, KY	Newport, Campbell County, Kentucky
Faas, Anna Maria	24, Dec. 1866	20, Nov.	71	414	Wacker	Pittsburg, PA	Engelsbrand, Württemberg
Faas, Katharina	3, Feb. 1898	16, Jan.	68	79	Schmid	Chicago, IL	Auenstein, Marbach, Württemberg
Faber, Christina	31, Oct. 1864		83- 3m-13d	176		Bonn, OH	Osweiler, Frankreich
Faber, H.	22, May 1856	1, May	59	84		Bremen, ---	Hastedt, Bremen
Faber, Heinrich	29, June 1863	17,Mar.	85	104		Washington, OH	Lamprecht, Rheinkreis Baiern
Faber, Jakobine	29, Mar. 1888	25, Feb.	79- -10d	206		Sandwich, IL	Gabenzberg, Württemberg
Faber, Margaretha	24, Jan. 1881	12, Jan.	85	31		Newport, KY	Speckenholz, Edelsen, Hannover
Faber, Sophia	20, June 1889	9, May	66- 4m-23d	398	Adel	Woodsfield, OH	Sachsen
Fabian, Christian	22, Mar. 1875	5, Feb.	70	95		Tomah, WI	Lozine, Schlesien, Preußen
Fabre, Louis	22, June 1893	11, May	76	398		Belleville, IL	Dornholzhausen, Homburg, Hessen
Fabry, Elisabeth Maria Caroline	7, Feb. 1881	14, Jan.	18	47		Schnectady, NY	
Fabry, Friedrich W.	16, July 1891	17, Apr.	83	462		Schnectady, NY	Minden, Preußen
Fabry, Maria	29, July 1872	11, July	36- 6m	247	Lamb	Schnectady, NY	
Fache, Ursula	17, June 1886	30, May	52	7		Stitzer, WI	Thalheim, Württemberg
Fader, Christian	7, Nov. 1895	22, Oct.	79	718		Quincy, IL	Sulgau, Oberndorf, Württemberg
Fader, Sophia	24, Jan. 1895	28, Dec.	82	62	Sindlinger	Quincy, IL	Mötzingen, Württemberg

Christliche Apologete Death Notices --- 1839 - 1899

Name of Deceased	Notice Date	Death Date	Age	Maiden Name	Page	Place of Death	Place of Birth
Fadt, Anna Maria	27, July 1899	11, July	53	Reutinger	479	Wapello, IA	Wollmatinen, Konstanz, Baden
Faggusch, August	2, Feb. 1885	11, Jan.	42		7	Detroit, MI	Fakabau, West Preußen
Fahl, Ida Henriette	30, June 1892	12, June	12-10m-29d		414	Sheboygan, WI	
Fahl, Susanne Elisabeth	20, Apr. 1899	23, Mar.	49		254	Dotyville, WI	Frankfurt am Main, Preußen
Fähnel, Christine	19, Mar. 1883	26, Feb.	69- 1m-28d	Heller	95	Parker, SD	Sandow, Pommern
Fahr, Georg	1, May 1865	23, Mar.	55		72	Santa Claus, IN	Pirmasens, Rheinkreis Baiern
Fahr, Louise	18, Dec. 1890	9, Nov.	81	Schnaithmann	814	Santa Claus, IN	Felbach, Cannstadt, Württemberg
Fahrenholz, Johan	22, Sept 1898	22, Aug.	66		607	Warsaw, IL	Sagehorn, Achim, Hannover
Fahrenhorst, Johann H.	1, Sept 1859	18, Aug.	55		140	Decatur, IL	Versmold, Minden, Preußen
Fahrig, Georg Wilhelm	6, June 1881	22, May	78- 1m-21d		183	Galena, IL	Preußen
Fahnwald, Herman	31, July 1882	9, July	18-11m		247	Green Isle, MN	
Fähns, Robert	1, May 1876	19, Mar.	25- 3m-19d		143	Edgewood, IL	Schöstland, Aargau, Schweiz
Faigle, Sophia	19, July 1880	29, June	76		231	New York City, NY	Knittlingen, Maulbronn, Württemberg
Fails, Anna	4, Feb. 1892	6, Jan.	29	Stahl	78	Buffalo, NY	Jerseyville, Illinois
Falch, Jeremias	9, Aug. 1849		Inquiry		127	Chicago, IL	Eßlingen, Württemberg
Falk, Auguste	20, Feb. 1896	20, Jan.	29- 6m-28d	Mewes	126	Parkston, SD	
Falk, Charles H.	1, June 1899	18, Apr.	25		351	Louisville, KY	Louisville, Jefferson County, Kentucky
Falk, Theodor	24, Dec. 1891	20, Nov.			830	Bloomington, IL	Lütz, Mecklenburg-Schwerin
Falk, Wilhelmina	30, May 1895	29, Apr.	68	Jerke	350	Menominee, MI	Temnek, Pommern
Falke, Jakob	13, July 1874	28, Apr.	73		223	Lexington, MO	Höringhausen, Hessen-Darmstadt
Falke, Jakob	12, Apr. 1875	18, Mar.	39- 5m		119	Carroll, MO	Hähringshausen, Vöhle, Hessen
Faller, (Mrs)	15, Dec. 1862	17, Nov.	70	Ronshausen	200	Baraboo, WI	Altmorschen, Melsungen, Kurhessen
Faller, Emma	9, Oct. 1876	23, Sept	23- - 8d		327	Baraboo, WI	Pittsburg, Pennsylvania
Faller, Georg	26, June 1890	1, June	39		414	Baraboo, WI	Pittsburg, Pennsylvania
Faller, Heinrich	1, May 1890	14, Apr.	74		286	Baraboo, WI	Kurhessen
Faller, John	13, June 1881	17, May	38- 7m-25d		191	Baraboo, WI	Pittsburg, Pennsylvania
Faller, Maria Elisabeth	27, Feb. 1890	1, Feb.	72	Horn	142	Baraboo, WI	Altmorschen, Hessen-Kassel
Faller, Pauline Henriette	2, Feb. 1899	4, Jan.	47	Ristau	79	Baraboo, WI	
Falty, Marie	28, Apr. 1853	3, Apr.	22		68	Louisville, KY	Leiweile, Metz, Frankreich
Fankhausen, Louis	22, July 1867	2, July	23		230	Clarington, OH	Monroe County, Ohio
Fankhauser, Elisabeth	30, Oct. 1890	3, Oct.	48- 3m	Blätter	702	Clarington, OH	Monroe County, Ohio
Fankhauser, Jacob	12, Mar. 1891	15, Feb.	41		174	Clarington, OH	
Fanslow, Wilhelm	19, June 1876	23, May	49- 1m- 7d		199	Cannon River, MN	Altlüpke, Bromberg, Preußen
Färber, Anna Elisabeth	7, Oct. 1872	30, Aug.	71- 2m-21d	Boshold	327	Vermillion, OH	Gleicher, Kurhessen
Färber, Christina	25, Nov. 1872	29, Oct.	70		383	Scranton, PA	Wilstedt, Baden
Färber, Dorothea	17, Sept 1896	2, Sept	88		607	Brooklyn, NY	Fistingen, Baden
Färber, Elisabeth	29, July 1878	11, July	69		239	Junction City, KS	Baiern
Färber, Jakob	19, Dec. 1889	26, Nov.	94- 2m-21d	Trossel	814	Scranton, PA	Willstädt, Baden
Färber, Marie	16, Feb. 1874	18, Jan.	29		55	Brooklyn, NY	Willamsburg, Long Island, New York
Farner, Joh. F.	25, Apr. 1864	13, Mar.	19		68	Connersville, IN	Connersville, Fayette County, Indiana
Farner, Johan Xaver	28, July 1884	13, July	48		7	Stuart, NE	Nebikon, Luzern, Schweiz
Farnlacher, Johan Georg	13, Oct. 1879	13, Sept	70- 1m-20d		327	Cleveland, OH	Burghasloch bei Kleisenberg, Baiern
Farnlacher, Susanna	2, May 1889	9, Apr.	68- 1m- 5d		286	Buffalo, NY	Ziegenbach, Baiern
Fäs, Samuel	3, Nov. 1862	15, Oct.	22		176	Highland, IL	Schöftland, Aargau, Schweiz
Faßbinder, Peter Arnold	29, Aug. 1870	18, May	68		279	Burlington, IA	Winkelhausen, Lemp, Düsseldorf, Preußen
Fasse, Bertha	24, May 1894	27, Apr.	30	Aufderhar	342	Warren, MO	Holstein, Warren County, Missouri

Christliche Apologete Death Notices --- 1839 - 1899

Name of Deceased	Notice Date	Death Date	Age	Maiden Name	Place of Death	Page	Place of Birth
Fasse, Charles	9, Feb. 1899	3, Jan.	47		Junction City, KS	95	Alverdiesen, Sternberg, Lippe-Detmold
Fasse, Fr.	26, Nov. 1883	5, Nov.	52-10m		Warren, MO	383	Alberdiesen, Lippe-Detmold
Fassel, Frank A.	26, May 1892	4, Apr.	45		Pasadena, CA	334	Baden
Faßen, Louise	7, Mar. 1861	16, Feb.			Cheviot, OH	40	Lippe
Fäßler, Johannes	6, Apr. 1899	9, Mar.	61		Moberly, MO	222	Bechetobel, Appenzell, Schweiz
Fasterling, Karl	4, Mar.1872	29, Dec.	22- -20d		Le Sueur, MN	79	Jackson, Missouri
Fath, Karoline	26, May 1884	8, May	53	Weidmann	Wapello, IA	7	Berg, Elsaß
Fathauer, Wilhelmine	31, Aug. 1874	3, Aug.	66-10m-13d	Drooß	S. Dover, ---	279	Gortschoff, West Priegnitz, Preußen
Fatke, Anna Maria	1, Mar. 1869	12, Feb.	71		Blue Island, IL	71	Reichensachsen, Kurhessen
Faubel, Georg	10, Sept 1896	18, July	62		Wheeling, WV	591	
Faubel, Georg	25, Sept 1846	10, Aug.	19- 4m		Monroe Co, ---	165	
Faud, Friederika Maria Elis.	25, June 1866				Indianapolis, IN	206	Totenhauße, Minden, Preußen
Fauk, Gustav	24, Mar. 1892	1, Mar.	57		Dayton, OH	190	Ulm, Württemberg
Faul, Elisabeth	31, Oct. 1895	3, Oct.	58		Dayton, OH	702	Albig, Rhein-Hessen
Faul, Louis	7, June 1894	22, May	70		Dayton, OH	374	Ulm an der Donau, Württemberg
Faul, Wilhelm	30, May 1864	30, Apr.	34		Dayton, OH	88	Ulm, Württemberg
Faulhaber, Friedrich	20, May 1897	29, Apr.	54		Edon, OH	319	Zweibrücken, Baiern
Faulwetter, Anna Maria	26, Dec. 1881	11, Nov.	33-10m-11d	Krieg	Covington, KY	415	
Faulwetter, Elise Sophie	15, Aug. 1881	6, Aug.	66- 7m- 5d	Neujork	Covington, KY	263	Bremen, Germany
Faulwetter, Karl Heinrich	9, Feb. 1893	15, Jan.	76		Covington, KY	94	Rhoda, Sachsen
Faupel, Heinrich	30, May 1889	5, Apr.	59		Wheeling, WV	350	Reichensachsen, Kurhessen
Faupel, Johan Peter	25, Oct. 1869	30, Aug.	50		Clarington, OH	343	Reicherssachsen, Kurhessen
Faupel, Ludwig Conrad	27, Sept 1875	2, Sept	14- 5m-17d		Baltimore, MD	311	
Fauser, Magdalena	29, July 1872	18, June	7- 3m-21d		Bucyrus, OH	247	
Fausser, Paulina	7, Dec. 1874	29, Sept	20		Bucyrus, OH	391	Crawford County, Ohio
Faust, Anna Maria	22, Aug. 1895	28, June			Poughkeepsie, NY	542	Uhlbach, Frankenberg, Kurhessen
Faust, Franciska	22, Jan. 1861	3, Jan.	30	Eppsteiner	Poughkeepsie, NY	16	Sinsheim, Baden
Faust, Friedericka	29, Oct. 1896	14, Oct.	53		Cincinnati, OH	703	Geisberg bei Stuttgart, Württemberg
Faust, Friedrika S.	11, Oct. 1894	23, Sept	46	Sorg	Kansas City, KS	662	Bettenhausen, Sachsen-Meiningen
Faust, P.	3, Apr. 1882	21, Mar.	40- 3m- 2d	Dörr	Poughkeepsie, NY	111	Kirchardt, Sinsheim, Baden
Faut, Anna B.	9, Jan. 1871	6, Dec.			Melrose, NY	15	Seibersbach, Coblenz, Preußen
Faut, Daniel	23, June 1884	5, June			New Palestine, IN	7	New Palestine, Indiana
Faut, Friederike C.S.	22, Jan. 1872	1, Jan.			New Palestine, IN	31	Lerbeck, Minden, Preußen
Fauth, Katharina	13, Mar. 1890	18, Feb.	48- 3m-17d	Raabe	New Palestine, IN	174	Dehme, Rehme, Minden, Preußen
Fauth, Katharina	27, May 1878	9, May	73	Stuffer	New Knoxville, OH	167	Feldrennach, Neuenbürg, Württemberg
Fauzel, Johan Peter	17, June 1878	9, May	73	Roffer	New Knoxville, OH	191	Feldrennach, Neuenbürg, Württemberg
Febiger, Gottlob	13, Sept 1869	30, Aug.	76		Clarington, OH	295	Reichensachsen, Kurhessen
Fecht, Etta	5, July 1880	16, May	84- 8m-26d	Ferichs	San Jose, CA	215	Bautzen, Sachsen
Federmann, Ludwig	2, May 1895	12, Apr.	62- 4m		Alton, IL	286	Hollen, Ostfriesland
Fedewald, Friedrich	5, Apr. 1894	10, Mar.	75		Milwaukee, WI	230	Güstrow, Mecklenburg-Schwerin
Fedewald, H. Wilhelm	11, Oct. 1869	4, Sept	57		Herman, MO	327	Holzhausen, Hartum, Preußen
Fedinga, Martinus	28, Mar. 1870	18- 4m			Herman, MO	103	
Fedler, Wilhelmine	17, Feb. 1873	20, Jan.	27		Pekin, IL	53	Uplewald, Amt Emden, Ostfriesland
Fegebusch, Maria Regina	6, May 1886	17, Apr.	55	Wieland	Sheboygan, WI	7	Uckermark bei Prenzlow, Preußen
Fegel, Karl Friedrich	26, Oct. 1868	26, Sept	82-10m-26d		Louisville, KY	343	Oelbronn, Maulbronn, Württemberg
	1, July 1897	13, June	74		Schnectady, NY	414	Hille, Minden, Preußen

- 116 -

Christliche Apologete Death Notices --- 1839 - 1899

Name of Deceased	Notice Date	Death Date	Age	Page	Maiden Name	Place of Death	Place of Birth
Fegel, Karolina	18, Sept 1882	16, Aug.	38	303	Hellinger	Schnectady, NY	Eikhorst, Minden, Preußen
Fegenbusch, Tobias	10, Mar.1873	12, Jan.	92	79		Louisville, KY	
Fegert, Ellena	29, Apr. 1878	7, Apr.	13- 6m-21d	135		Bay City, MI	
Fehler, Michael	8, Nov. 1888	21, Oct.	81- 2m- 4d	718		Lena, IL	Weigolshausen, Schweinfurt, Baiern
Fehlewald, Maria	9, May 1895	16, Apr.	81	302		Senate Grove, MO	Nord-Hemmen, Preußen
Fehlis, Gesine	8, Nov. 1888	20, Oct.	53	718		New York City, NY	Amtönighausen, Braunschweig
Fehmer, Albert	14, July 1898	18, June	21	447		Morristown, MN	
Fehmer, Carl	11, Feb. 1886	21, Jan.	19	7		Blooming Grove, MN	Waukesha County, Wisconsin
Fehmer, Christian	19, July 1880	1, July	82	231		Blooming Grove, MN	Malfitz, Mecklenburg-Schwerin
Fehmer, Franz Albert	11, Apr. 1889	14, Mar.	24- 9m-23d	238		Big Stone City, SD	
Fehmer, Georg	6, June 1889	15, May	18	366		Blooming Grove, MN	Deerfield, Minnesota
Fehmer, Georg Christian	26, July 1894	24, June	23	486		Big Stone City, SD	Obertouno, Steele County, Minnesota
Fehmer, Hatty	4, Feb. 1892	21, Dec.	19	78		Blooming Grove, MN	
Fehmer, Johanna	25, Aug. 1887		82	542	Lau	Blooming Grove, MN	Jabel, Mecklenburg-Schwerin
Fehmer, Josephine	25, May 1885	1, May	21- -16d	7		Blooming Grove, MN	
Fehr, Anna	26, Feb. 1891	30, Dec.	70	142	Mühlhaupt	Schnectady, NY	Brunslar, Melsungen, Hessen-Kassel
Fehr, Anna Elisabeth	22, Jan. 1877	30, Dec.	56	31	Gabriel	Etna, MO	Culte, Waldeck
Fehr, Elisabeth	6, Mar. 1871	21, Jan.	74	79	Stricker	Waverly, OH	Wollroden, Amt Melsungen, Hessen
Fehr, Heinrich	22, Jan. 1872	3, Jan.	42- 3m	31		Pittsburg, PA	Kurhessen
Fehr, Johan	19, July 1880	25, May	69	231		Etna, MO	
Fehr, Johan Konrad	8, Sept 1898	15, Aug.	56	575		Indianapolis, IN	Flaach, Zürich, Schweiz
Fehr, Johannes	27, Dec. 1875	8, Dec.	80	415		Buffalo, NY	Kirchhart, Amt Sinsheim, Baden
Fehr, Lisette	6, Jan. 1868	9, Dec.	34	6	Brennwald	Kabbscreek, TX	Mänedorf, Zürich, Schweiz
Feige, Georg J.	3, Nov. 1898	2, Oct.	69	703		Des Moines, IA	Höhlmühle, hitzerode, Kurhessen
Feige, Gertrud	25, Mar. 1897		64-10m-27d	190		Des Moines, IA	Wichtmannshausen, Eschwege, Kurhessen
Feigenspahn, G. Gustav	16, Dec. 1867	8, Nov.	29- 9m	398		Quincy, IL	Mühlhausen, Preußen
Feiger, Elisa Maria	11, Aug. 1892	23, July	26	510		Lawrenceburg, IN	Lawrenceburg, Dearborn County, Indiana
Feik, Christina	19, Aug. 1867	25, July	76- 3m-23d	262		Defiance, OH	Northhampton County, Pennsylvania
Feikert, Sophia	1, Mar. 1875		88	71		Liberty, MO	Kriegsheim, Alzey, Hessen-Darmstadt
Feil, Elisabeth	29, Jan. 1866	12, Dec.	21	38		Boonville, IN	Ebingen, Baden
Feilbach, Anton	30, Nov. 1863	20, Oct.	44	192		Freeport, IL	Mühle, Amt Nassau, Nassau
Feiler, Philipp Jakob	8, Apr. 1878	17, Mar.	60	111		Valparaiso, IN	Flacht, Leonberg, Württemberg
Feiler, Regina Catharine	23, June 1884	5, June	69- 5m- 5d	7	Schrag	Hobart, IN	Wurmberg, Maulbronn, Württemberg
Fein, Anna Margaretha	4, Jan. 1894	5, Dec.	79	14	Diedrich	Bradford, IN	Dietenbergen, Nassau
Fein, Franz Jakob	26, Apr. 1888	29,Mar.	68- -19d	270		Bradford, IN	Diedenbergen, Hochheim, Nassau
Fein, Maria Elisabeth	28, Nov. 1870	31, Oct.	22	383		Bradford, IN	Diedenbergen, Amt Hochheim, Nassau
Feinauer, Maria	30, Sept 1897	1, Sept	67	623	Walther	Chillicothe, OH	Gedelsbach, Württemberg
Feininger, Wilhelmine	20, Aug. 1891	13, July	53	542		Troy, NY	Schildbach, Baden
Feisel, Jakob	6, June 1895	16, May	83	366		Quincy, NY	Dodenau, Hessen-Darmstadt
Feißt, Gottfried	7, Dec. 1885	19, Sept	20- 1m- 3d	7		Baresville, OH	Monroe County, Ohio
Feistkorn, Florentin	24, Oct. 1889	29, Sept	65	686		Blue Island, IL	Ellersleben, Buttstädt, Sachsen-Weimar
Feith, Herman	27, June 1895	25, May	69	414		Warren Co.,MO	Meierburg, Alverdissen, Lippe-Detmold
Felber, A. Barbara	6, Aug. 1883	20, July	82	255	Kummerer	Baraboo, WI	Großwyl, Bern, Schweiz
Felber, Jacob A.	14, Aug. 1865		23	132		Baraboo, WI	Fairfield County, Ohio
Felber, Oswald	19, Apr. 1894	27, Mar.	41	262		Anaheim, CA	Sonvillier, Bern, Schweiz
Felber, Rebecka	10, Jan. 1881	17, Dec.	34-11m-11d	15		Baraboo, WI	Atna, Marion County, Ohio

Christliche Apologete Death Notices --- 1839 - 1899

Name of Deceased	Notice Date	Death Date	Age	Page	Maiden Name	Place of Death	Place of Birth
Feldbaum, Klara Bertha	15, Dec. 1898	19, Nov.	22	799	Paul	Taegesville, WI	Stettin, Marathon County, Wisconsin
Felde, Johanne	24, May 1880	23, Apr.	44	167	Hardwig	Canton, MO	
Felden, Daniel	6, Mar. 1871	19, Feb.	65- 3m	79		Kendallville, IN	Bernin, Amt Kriwitz, Mecklenburg-Schwerin
Felder, Ludwig Friedrich	17, July 1876	7, June	45-11m-29d	231		Rochester, IN	Böblingen, Württemberg
Feldhäuser, (Mrs)	11, Feb. 1884	17, Jan.	64	7	Stützmann	Los Angeles, CA	Steinbach, RheinPreußen
Feldhauser, Philipp	11, Nov. 1886	19, Oct.	68- - 3d	7		Denver, CO	Neun-Kirchen, RheinPreußen
Feldmann, August Wilhelm	2, Aug. 1894	10, July	22	502		Etna, MO	Clark County, Missouri
Feldmann, Diena	8, Jan. 1872		21	15		Etna, MO	Rehne, Amt Wollenburg, Hannover
Feldmann, H.	25, Nov. 1878	16, Oct.	65- 8m-13d	375		Illinois City, IL	
Feldmann, Johan	16, Jan. 1882	7, Dec.	77	23		Etna, MO	Broistadt, Salder, Braunschweig
Feldmann, Johan Friedrich	5, Jan. 1899	25, Nov.	82	14		Arlington, MN	Seehausen, Ottensberg, Hannover
Feldmann, Johanna	2, June 1892	8, May	23	350		Etna, MO	Kahoka, Missouri
Feldmann, Margaretha	22, Sept 1892	18, Aug.	22	606		Bushton, KS	Leer , Ostfriesland
Feldmann, Margaretha Louise	25, Mar. 1878	17, Mar.	58-10m- 6d	95	Kardes	Illinois City, IL	Gellenbeck, Lübbecke, Westphalen
Feldmann, Rosina	15, June 1899	14, May	27	383	Schlegel	Arlington, MN	LeSueur, Minnesota
Feldmann, Willie	19, July 1894	21, June	79	470	Jäger	Crow River, MN	Kolmbach, Neuenburg, Württemberg
Feldmeier, Conrad Heinrich	27, Mar. 1890	25, Feb.	69	206		Huntingburg, IN	Lengerich, Tecklenburg, Münster, Preußen
Feldmeier, Elisabeth	15, Sept 1887	25, July	66- 4m- 4d	590		Baltimore, MD	
Feldmeier, Maria Elisabeth	11, Feb. 1897	10, Jan.	68	94	Blemker	Huntingburg, IN	Lienen, Germany
Feldmeyer, Dorothea	8, Mar. 1894	11, Feb.	65	166		Annapolis, MD	Hildesheim, Germany
Feldner, Elisabeth	14, June 1869	11, May	70- 3m- 9d	191	Neuhard	Baresville, OH	Nothweiler, Rheinkreis Baiern
Feldner, Philipp	4, Feb. 1867	30, Dec.	71	38		Baresville, OH	Nothweiler, Rheinkreis Baiern
Feldschneider, Wilhelm	17, Jan. 1881	31, Dec.	67- 8m	23		Portland, WI	Horn, Lippe-Detmold
Feldschneider, Wilhelmine	21, July 1884	30, June	66- 9m-22d	7	Hagemeister	Waterloo, WI	Distelbrug, Lippe-Detmold
Feldt, Christian Friedrich	25, June 1896	22, May	80	415		Chase, WI	Jakobsdorff, Saazig, Stettin, Pommern
Feldwesch, Christina	9, Feb. 1854	21, Jan.	38- 4m	24	Rikelmann	Huntingburg, IN	Ladbergen, Preußen
Feldwisch, Caroline	13, Oct. 1873	2, Sept	14- 5m	327		Huntingburg, IN	
Feldwisch, Christina	21, Feb. 1876	4, Feb.	53	63	Voskuhle	Huntingburg, IN	Ladbergen, Tecklenburg, Preußen
Feldwisch, Heinrich Wilhelm	7, Aug. 1865	6, Mar.	22	128		Huntingburg, IN	Dubois County, Indiana
Felicht, Karl	8, Mar. 1894	16, Feb.	54	166		Rudd, IA	Stockhausen , Schwarzburg-Sondershausen
Fell, Anna Maria	10, Nov. 1887	23, Sept	31	718	Streicher	Detroit, MI	Detroit, Wayne County, Michigan
Fell, Dorothea	6, Oct. 1879	29, Aug.	79	319	Trefz	Dallas, TX	Groß-Asbach, Brackenheim, Württemberg
Fell, Friederika	8, Nov. 1894	4, July	62	726	Hoch	Victoria, TX	Oberschenau, Schmalkalten, Kurhessen
Fellemende, Barbara	21, Mar. 1889	1, Feb.	71	190		Mt. Vernon, IN	
Fellemende, Elisabeth	24, Oct. 1861	7, Sept	14	172		Parker, IN	
Fellemende, Friedrich	28, Oct. 1878	8, Oct.	56	343		Mt. Vernon, IN	Wachenheim, Hessen-Darmstadt
Feller, Katharina	19, Oct. 1899	1, Oct.	54	671	Lebold	Canal Dover, OH	Lorenz Township, Tuscarawas County, Ohio
Feller, Katharine	19, Nov. 1896	21, Oct.	78	750	Rathmann	Winona, MN	Steesien, Schleswig-Holstein
Feller, Lisetta Carolina	22, Aug. 1889	29, July	11	542		Chili, OH	Chili, Ohio
Feller, Ludwig Philipp	16, Jan. 1896	26, Dec.	79	46		Winona, MN	Kropp, Schleswig-Holstein
Feller, Tellsche Christine	20, Aug. 1896	30, July	32	542		Winona, MN	Erfde, Schleswig-Holstein
Fellicht, Johan	10, Feb. 1873	23, Jan.	62- 3m-22d	47		Yellow Creek, IL	Stockhausen, Schwarzburg-Sondershausen
Fellmann, Abraham	30, Jan. 1896	27, Dec.	81	78		Red Wing, MN	Brühl, Schwetzingen, Baden
Fellmann, Julia	20, Feb. 1896	2, Feb.	28	126	Golder	Red Wing, MN	Stuben County, New York
Fellmann, Sophia Dorothea	27, Oct. 1892	12, Oct.	74	686	Spernagel	Red Wing, MN	Schwitzingen, Schwitzingen, Baden
Felsing, Walter	19, Dec. 1895	10, Nov.	18	814		Oshkosh, WI	Kewaskum, Washington County, Wisconsin

Christliche Apologete Death Notices --- 1839 - 1899

Name of Deceased	Notice Date	Death Date	Age	Maiden Name	Page	Place of Death	Place of Birth
Felten, Maria	14, May 1896	24, Apr.	66	Feil	318	Chicago, IL	Kotweiler, Baiern
Feltens, Karl Friedrich	5, Jan. 1880	20, Dec.	16-10m-7d		7	Laporte, IN	
Feltens, Wilhelmine	5, Jan. 1880	7, Dec.	13-4m-8d		7	Laporte, IN	
Feltman, Emma	18, Dec. 1890	8, Nov.	29		814	Los Angeles, CA	Kenosha, Wisconsin
Felton, Johan Jacob	1, Dec. 1892	13, Nov.	64		766	Laporte, IN	Raversbeuern, RheinPreußen
Femmer, Edward	27, Mar. 1890	6, Mar.	26-5m-6d		206	Warren, MO	Eudora, Kansas
Femmer, Katharina Charlotte	11, Oct. 1860	18, Sept	20-7m-29d	Brommelsiek	164	Lawrence, KS	
Fenber, Wilhelm	1, Nov. 1888	7, Oct.	57		702	Covington, KY	Brockum, Lemförder, Hannover
Fendenheim, Katharina	2, Nov. 1885	19, Oct.	79	Hotum	7	Columbus, OH	Mauchenheim in der Pfalz, Baiern
Fender, Anna Christina	28, Sept 1874	30, Aug.	76-8m	Kröger	311	Manitowoc, WI	Dalow bei Tramburg, HinterPommern
Fender, Friedrich	18, May 1893	23, Apr.	59		318	Manitowoc, WI	Gershagen, Pommern
Fender, Gottlieb	1, Sept 1873	18, Aug.	85- -25d		279	Manitowoc, WI	Gerzhagen, Regenwalde, Pommern
Fender, Katharine	31, Mar. 1898	8, Mar.	80	Ulrich	207	Manitowoc, WI	Wildeshausen, Oldenburg
Fengel, Anna Margaretha	6, Feb. 1896	12, Jan.	81		94	Burlington, IA	Dudenhofen, Offenbach, Hessen-Darmstadt
Feniwein, Maria Dorothea	9, Aug. 1849		52		128	Columbus, OH	Benswangen, Donau, Württemberg
Fennemann, Maria	23, Feb. 1860	25, Jan.	13- 5m		32	Huntingburg, IN	
Fenschel, Ernst	4, Mar. 1853	7, Feb.	10		36	Burlington, ---	
Fenschel, Johanna	4, Mar. 1853	8, Feb.	2		36	Burlington, ---	
Fenska, Emilie	12, Oct. 1874		13- 4m-17d		327	Kenosha, WI	
Fenske, Anna Rosina	17, June 1897	22, May	71	Steinker	383	Berlin, WI	Floth, Schaniko, Holland
Fenske, Dorothea Louisa	6, June 1889	17, Apr.	52	Schreiber	366	Kenosha, WI	Replin bei Stargard, Pommern
Fenske, Emma	9, Apr. 1896	6, Mar.	21		238	New Ulm, MN	
Fenske, Heinrich	23, Feb. 1888	14, Jan.	50		126	Kenosha, WI	Jayertow bei Polzin, Belgart, Pommern
Fenske, Josie	9, Apr. 1896	2, Mar.	19		238	New Ulm, MN	
Fenske, Justine	14, Feb. 1889	15, Jan.	84	Brunk	110	New Ulm, MN	Deutschkuden, West Preußen
Fenske, Pauline	6, Apr. 1863	18, Mar.	13		56	St. Paul, MN	Friedland, Marienwerder, Preußen
Fenske, Wilhelmine	24, July 1890	6, June	48	Pofahl	478	Kenosha, WI	Klakshagen, Preußen
Fensky, Johan Gottfried	16, Aug. 1875	30, July	74-10m-24d		263	New Ulm, MN	Friedland, Westphalen
Fenster, August	17, Mar. 1892	2, Mar.	29		174	Madison, WI	Washington, Sauk County, Wisconsin
Fenstermacher, Johan Wilhelm	22, July 1886	20, June	75- 7m-10d		7	Barton, WI	
Fentzlaff, Wilhelmine	21, Oct. 1897	27, Sept	53	Steindorf	671	Watertown, WI	Fürstensee, Pommern
Ferkel, Jacob	26, Apr. 1880	14, Apr.	54- 7m-6d		135	Jeffersonville, NY	Willstadt, Baden
Ferkel, Katharina	11, May 1899	31, Mar.	90		302	Jeffersonville, NY	Kanton Bern, Schweiz
Ferle, Heinrich	26, July 1894	21, June	61		486	Lansing, MI	Ramsthal, Hessen-Nassau
Fern, Catharine	3, Nov. 1884	24, Oct.	79		7	Scranton, PA	Lauterbach, Hessen-Kassel
Fern, Christoph	25, July 1871	10, July	61		239	Scranton, PA	Lauterbach, Kurhessen
Fern, Heinrich	3, July 1871	25, May	28		215	Scranton, PA	Lautenbach, Amt Lichtenau, Hessen-Kassel
Ferregut, Nette	9, Mar. 1868	19, Feb.	24	Bodenhausen	79	St. Joseph, MO	Helmighausen, Waldeck
Feser, Kaspar	17, Mar. 1892	16, Feb.	80		174	Lyons, WI	Baiern
Feske, Wilhelm	7, Jan. 1897	9, Dec.	63		15	Lemars, IA	Granow, Neumark
Feske, Wilhelm	14, Jan. 1897	9, Dec.	64		31	Parker, SD	Germany
Feßler, Georg A.	26, May 1892	23, Apr.	67		334	Philadelphia, PA	
Fessler, Louis	13, June 1861	16, Apr.	3-11m		96	Philadelphia, PA	
Fessler, Wilhem	13, June 1861	25, May	5- 8m		96	Philadelphia, PA	
Feth, Elisabeth	22, May 1890	7, May	65	Schäfer	334	Cincinnati, OH	Naunheim, Gießen, Hessen-Darmstadt
Feth, Heinrich	22, Sept 1898	3, Sept	61		607	Hamilton, OH	Naunheim bei Wetzlar, Kurhessen

Name of Deceased	Notice Date	Death Date	Age	Maiden Name	Page	Place of Death	Place of Birth
Fetsch, Jakob	12, July 1880	29, June	56- 5m-28d		223	Lancaster, NY	Kohtitz, Sachsen-Altenburg
Fett, Eva Katharina	8, Nov. 1888	4, Oct.	81	Sonntag	718	Ft. Atkinson, WI	NeuFreistadt, Baden
Fett, Georg	19, Feb. 1866	20, Jan.	64-11m		62	Portland, WI	Waldböckelheim, Koblenz, Preußen
Fett, Georg	24, Feb. 1887	5, Feb.	48		126	Madison, WI	Waldbekelheim, Preußen
Fetter, Maria F.	7, Dec. 1893	19, Nov.	75	Tietz	782	Clearwater, MN	Mecklenburg
Fettkenheuer, Friedrich	6, Aug. 1891	12, July	34		510	Storm Lake, IA	Großwaglin, Pommern
Feucht, Charles	9, Sept 1886	24, Aug.	34		7	Pittsburg, PA	Winnenren, Württemberg
Feucht, Friederike C.	21, June 1875	20, May	57		199	Pittsburg, PA	Winnenden, Württemberg
Feucht, Friedrich	21, Jan. 1892	19, Nov.	74		46	Alta Vista, KS	Bretsach, Weinsberg, Württemberg
Feucht, Rosina	30, June 1887	16, June	68		414	Hoboken, NJ	Osweil, Württemberg
Feuchter, Katharina	20, Mar. 1865	11, Feb.	12- 3m-29d		48	Cleveland, OH	
Feuchter, Ludwig	20, Mar. 1865	1, Mar.	7-10m-26d		48	Cleveland, OH	
Feuchter, Maria	28, Feb. 1895	70- 7m-24d		Hammin	142	Cleveland, OH	Lobenhausen, Gerabronn, Württemberg
Feuchter, Michael	9, Dec. 1886	17, Nov.	69		7	Cleveland, OH	Marienkappel, Kreilsheim, Württemberg
Feustel, Wilhelmina	7, Mar. 1895	14, Feb.	52	Kehl	158	Lawrence, MA	Langenwetzendorf, Reuß
Fey, Johan Ulrich	19, June 1882	16, May	60		199	Toledo, OH	Canton Thurgau, Schweiz
Fey, Katharina Elisabeth	27, May 1897	15, May	65	Wilhelm	335	Chicago, IL	Eschwege, Hessen
Ficher, Jakob	8, Aug. 1850	20, July	76- 9m		128	Louisville, KY	
Fichs, Jakob	20, Sept 1894	25, Aug.	61		614	Mt. Vernon, IN	Edenkoben, Rheinpfalz Baiern
Fichter, Michael	24, Mar. 1892	6, Mar.	66		190	Lawrenceburg, IN	Zinsweiler, Niederrhein, Elsaß
Fichter, Sophia	22, Feb. 1894	5, Feb.	63	Wagner	126	Lawrenceburg, IN	Grumbach, Baden
Fichtner, (Mr	6, Mar. 1856		55		40	German Creek, IA	
Fichtner, Bertha	21, Dec. 1893	1, Dec.	78	Hallenbeck	814	Harper, IA	
Fichtner, Christina	11, June 1847	20, Apr.	43- 6m-12d		95	Walnut Creek, IA	Vegesack, Hannover
Fichtner, Marie	17, June 1886	21, Mar.	29- 8m	Hert	7	Rochester, NY	Kottenweiler, Backnang, Württemberg
Fick, Dorothea	2, Nov. 1899	7, Oct.	80	Frenz	703	Willow City, ND	Kaup, Küßling, Germany
Fick, Auguste	24, Aug. 1893	30, July	45	Schuth	542	Chicago, IL	Pannwitz, Lauenburg, Pommern
Fick, Christian	20, May 1897	3, Apr.	77		319	Manitowoc, WI	Pfau, Mecklenburg-Schwerin
Fick, Christian	30, Mar. 1863		6		52	Wabasha, MN	
Fick, Dorothea	24, Apr. 1890	3, Apr.	65- 2m- 8d		270	Manitowoc, WI	Plau, Mecklenburg-Schwerin
Fick, Friedrich	20, Sept 1888	31, Aug.	44	Grußendorf	606	Caldwell, TX	
Fick, Herman	9, Oct. 1890	15, Sept	25	Jahn	654	Baraboo, WI	Hohenbenz, Pommern
Fick, Johanna	5, Oct. 1874		27		319	Chicago, IL	Garzigaw, Pommern, Preußen
Fick, Karl Friedrich Wilhelm	28, July 1887	10, July	54		478	Baraboo, WI	Wittenfelde, Naugard, Pommern
Fick, Sophia Louise	25, Dec. 1882	1, Dec.	78	Gädeke	415	Lyona, KS	Groß-Zappin, Pommern
Fickel, Bernhard	7, July 1884	12, June	67		7	Brooklyn, NY	Bardenfleth, Oldenburg
Fickel, Johanne	16, Sept 1897	29, Aug.	37	Bauchhenz	591	Grassyville, TX	Grassesach, Bastrop County, Texas
Fickel, Wilhelmina Johanna F.	28, July 1884	26, June	61		7	Knoxville, OH	Clausthal am Harz, Hannover
Ficken, (Mrs)	11, Oct. 1849	1, Oct.	42		164	Allegheny City, PA	Wehn, Amt Raden, Preußen
Ficken, Amalia Barbara	10, May 1869	21, Apr.	12- 8m-18d	Bauchhenz	151	Lacrosse, KS	Hancock County, Indiana
Ficken, Anna Katharina	14, Mar. 1889	22, Feb.	87	Bötzen	174	Toledo, OH	Reßum, Ottersberg, Hannover
Ficken, Barbara	3, July 1890	4, June	70- -25d		430	Huntingburg, IN	Knittelsheim, Rheinkreis Baiern
Ficken, Daniel	1, Mar. 1869	9, Feb.	12-11m		71	Sedalia, MO	
Ficken, Gesina	13, Feb. 1882	23, Dec.	36		55	Greenville, OH	
Ficken, Gretchen	26, Jan. 1888	29, Dec.	41- 1m-25d	Meinders	62	Piqua, OH	Hesepe, Nordhorn, Hannover
Ficken, Hanna Maria	14, Sept 1899	27, Aug.	20		591		Piqua, Miami County, Ohio

- 120 -

Christliche Apologete Death Notices --- 1839 - 1899

Name of Deceased	Notice Date	Death Date	Age	Maiden Name	Place of Death	Page	Place of Birth
Ficken, Heinrich	17, Feb. 1868	13, Jan.	72		Luke Creek, MO	55	Wilstädt, Amt Ottersberg, Hannover
Ficken, Jakob	10, Jan. 1889	19, Dec.	70-10m		Huntingburg, IN	30	Wehldorf, Safen, Hannover
Ficken, Johan	10, Oct. 1889	19, Sept	74- 6m- 4d		Greenville, OH	654	Levenstedt, Bördeschingen, Zeben, Hannover
Ficken, John N.	30, Dec. 1897	17, Dec.	48- 5m- 6d		Chicago, IL	828	Helte, Lele, Hannover
Ficken, Louise	22, Dec. 1887	29, Nov.	30	Meyer	Chicago, IL	814	Briest, Preußen
Ficken, Martha	6, Oct. 1898	2, Sept	63	Kahrs	Bison, KS	639	Neuenbüllstedt, Hannover
Ficken, Matta	18, Aug. 1892	29, June	77	Ahrensfeld	Chicago, IL	526	Bramstadt, Hannover
Ficken, Sophie	3, Sept 1891	13, Aug.	25	Meier	LaCrosse, KS	574	Gasconade County, Missouri
fickenscher, Carolina	1, Aug. 1864	3, June	57		Waterloo, MI	124	Rohbach, Rudolstadt,
Ficker, William	6, Mar. 1876	16, Feb.	25- 6m		Brunswick, MO	79	
Fickler, Christian	15, Apr. 1886	31, Mar.	67		Kewaskum, WI	7	Magersdorf, Sachsen-Altenburg
Fieber, Elisabeth	17, Apr. 1865	29, Mar.	74-3m	Knauber	Cincinnati, OH	64	Steinweiler, Rheinkreis Baiern
Fieber, Simon	25, Feb. 1867	12, Dec.	79		Cincinnati, OH	62	Steinweiler, Rheinkreis Baiern
Fiechtner, Wilhelm	29, Nov. 1888	1, Nov.	38		Wichita, KS	766	Wattenweiler, Backnang, Württemberg
Fiedel, Christoph	24, Aug. 1854	11, July	39		Detroit, MI	136	Hegersdorf, Sachsen
Fiedler, Andreas	14, Aug. 1876	24, July	51		Bloomington, IL	263	Rügheim, Baiern
Fiedler, Charlotte	25, Mar.1872	2, Mar.	49- 2m-25d	Schröder	Bloomington, IL	103	Hohenhausen, Lippe-Detmold
Fiedler, Elisabeth	1, Apr. 1852	Nov.	22		St. Louis, MO	56	Richheim, Baiern
Fiedler, Jacob G.	27, Oct. 1887	23, Sept	21		Lyona, KS	686	Kosciusko County, Indiana
Fiedler, Johannes	27, Feb. 1851		55- 8m-15d		Bloomington,	36	Rügheim, Baiern
Fiedler, Kunigunde	27, Sept 1855	12, Aug.	53- 9m	Herr	Lyona, KS	156	Rüchheim, Unter-Franken, Baiern
Fiedler, Maria	22, Sept 1887	25, Aug.	21	Schultz	Lyona, KS	606	Hanover, Canada
Fiedler, Nicolaus	12, Sept 1850	19, July	16		St. Louis, MO	148	Riegheim bei Wüzburg, Baiern
Fiedler, Rosina	2, Dec. 1886	13, Nov.	59	Gugler	Lyona, KS	7	Wangen, Cannstatt, Württemberg
Fiedler, William	22, Sept 1887	6, Sept	23		Lyona, KS	606	Kosciusko County, Indiana
Fiefelmann, Christine	7, Apr. 1873	16, Mar.			Herman, MO	111	
Fiege, Ernst Friedrich	6, Sept 1875	13, Aug.	66		Pomeroy, OH	287	Offensen, Amt Uslar, Hannover
Fiege, Marie Louise	3, Apr. 1871	1, Feb.	18		Pomeroy, OH	111	Pittsburg, Pennsylvania
Fiege, Wessel	7, Aug. 1882	5, July	88		Bremen, ——	255	
Fiegenbaum, Adolph	29, Jan. 1877	11, Jan.	84		Garner, IA	39	Ladbergen, Münster, Preußen
Fiegenbaum, Anna Elisabeth	15, Oct. 1877	22, Sept	40	Krümpel	Garner, IA	335	Hannover
Fiegenbaum, Christina	16, Oct. 1871	17, Sept	75	Peterjohann	Giard, IA	335	Ladbergen, Münster, Preußen
Fiegenbaum, Clara	30, Sept 1897	2, Sept	74	Kastenbudt	St. Joseph, MO	623	Osnabrück, Hannover
Fiegenbaum, Emilie Maria	25, Apr. 1895	3, Apr.	41		Edwardsville, IL	270	Edwardsville, Illinois
Fiegenbaum, Julia Gillespie	8, Apr. 1886	18, Mar.	29- 8m		Edwardsville, IL	7	
Fiegenbaum, Luelle	15, Nov. 1894	14, Oct.	15-10m-16d		Garner, IA	742	
Fieger, Magdalena	6, Apr. 1899	10, Mar.	63		Pittsburg, PA	222	Niedersteinbach, Elsaß
Fieger, Maria	15, Dec. 1862	11, Nov.	3- 4m		Cleveland, OH	200	
Fieger, Maria Carolina	29, Nov. 1888	31, Oct.	78		Pomeroy, OH	766	Offensen, Asler, Hannover
Fiehler, Johan	30, Apr. 1891	7, Apr.	57		Eudora, KS	286	Hönebach, Rothenburg, Kurhessen
Fiehn, Heinrich	11, Aug. 1892	27, July	72		Freeport, IL	510	Holstein
Fieker, Ernestine Katharine Maria	24, Mar. 1879	12, Feb.	60	Manse	Brunswick, MO	95	Eisbergen, Minden, Preußen
Fieker, Friedrich	16, Feb. 1893	25, Jan.	76		Mt. Vernon, MO	110	Oberlübbe, Bergkirchen, Minden, Westphalen
Fieker, Johan Friedrich	13, Apr. 1885	28, Mar.	80		Dalton, MO	7	Eisbergen, Germany
Field, David	2, July 1896	30, May	37		Goshen, IN	431	Goshen, Indiana
Fieler, Johan	14, Nov. 1870	13, Oct.	9- 9m-21d		Eudora, KS	367	

Name of Deceased	Notice Date	Death Date	Age	Maiden Name	Place of Death	Page	Place of Birth
Fleltner, Friedrich	24, Jan. 1856	3, Dec.	55		German Creek, IA	16	Kottenweiler, Bocknang, Württemberg
Fierle, Georg	10, July 1890	12, June	66- 1m-18d		Holt, MI	446	Romsthal, Kurhessen
Fieselmann, Friedrich	2, May 1870	12, Mar.	47		St. Charles, MO	143	Hille, Minden, Preußen
Fieselmann, John	29, July 1872	8, June	41- 5m- 5d		Herman, MO	247	Holte, Amt Osnabrück, Hannover
Fieselmann, Josephina	19, Dec. 1870	17, Nov.	15- -19d		St. Charles, MO	407	
Fieselmann, Maria	26, May 1873	14, Apr.	15- 7m		Herman, MO	167	Holzburg, Neu Kirchen, Kurhessen
Fieser, Georg Heinrich	18, Apr. 1895	27, Mar.			Norwich, KS	254	Alberdissen, Lippe-Detmold
Fieth, Friedrich Wilhelm	27, Aug. 1896		76		Warren, MO	559	Faribault, Minnesota
Filbert, Eduard Michael	14, Nov. 1881	16, Oct.	18- 9m-18d		Buffalo, NY	367	
Filbert, Eva	21, June 1875	5, June	32- 7m	Fraas	Palatine, IL	199	
Filbert, Helena Regina	3, Nov. 1879	7, Oct.	40	Klimper	Preston Lake, MN	351	Buffalo, New York
Filbert, Jakob Peter	30, Jan. 1882	13, Jan.	75		Palatin, IL	39	Klein-Heibach bei Würzburg, Baiern
Fild, Maria Dorothea	14, Apr. 1887	27, Mar.	64	Krauslach	Goshen, IN	238	Gellershausen, Sachsen
Filenius, Wilhelmine	6, Mar. 1890	6, Feb.	47	Ruske	Oconomowoc, WI	158	Megow, Piritz, Preußen
Fike, (Mrs)	8, Apr. 1867	9, Feb.	45		Horicon, WI	110	Schillersdorf, VorPommern, Preußen
Fill, Amanda	3, Mar. 1884	17, Feb.	20		Seymour, IN	7	Seymour, Jackson County, Indiana
Fill, Christian	30, Mar. 1893	24, Feb.	69		Seymour, IN	206	Sonnenfeld bei Wiesbaden, Nassau
Fill, Johan	29, Oct. 1883	16, Oct.	30		Seymour, IN	351	
Fill, Johan Christian	22, Dec. 1884	7, Dec.	25- 9m-27d		Seymour, IN	7	Jackson County, Indiana
Fill, Phillip	3, Feb. 1887	16, Jan.	35		Seymour, IN	78	
Fill, Wilhelm	12, Aug. 1878	26, July	28- 1m- 7d		Seymour, IN	255	Alt-Morschen, Melzungen, Kurhessen
Fillhauer, Anna Gertrude	6, Oct. 1887	7, Sept	63	Oswald	Baraboo, WI	638	Pittsburg, Pennsylvania
Fillhouer, Katharina	19, Apr. 1894	15, Mar.	48	Nippert	Baraboo, WI	262	
Filter, Friederika Wilhelmina	19, June 1882	3, June	57- 7m-18d	Reddant	Manitowoc, WI	199	Enge bei Bielefeld, Preußen
Finck, Anna M.	26, July 1849	27, June	42		St. Louis, MO	120	St. Louis, Missouri
Fincke, Carolina Mathilde	7, Nov. 1895	11, Oct.	39	Grütter	Quincy, IL	718	Könbronn, Gerabronn, Württemberg
Findeisen, Margaretha Barbara	14, June 1894	12, May	70	Hoffmann	Green Bay, WI	390	Kurhessen
Finder, Martha Elisabeth	25, May 1885	29, Apr.	55	Bachmann	Troy, NY	7	Essigheim bei Hanau am Main, Germany
Finder, William	18, Oct. 1894	28, Aug.			Troy, NY	678	
Finding, Anna Maria	16, Aug. 1849		37		Pomeroy, OH	132	Oppen, Baiern
Finding, Dorothea	29, July 1872	28, June	58	Urban	Pomeroy, OH	247	Ungstein, Rheinkreis Baiern
Finding, Heinrich	3, Apr. 1871	16, Feb.	19		Pomeroy, OH	111	Pomeroy, Ohio
Finding, Heinrich	3, Sept 1847	23, Oct.	5m- 9d		Pomeroy, OH	143	
Finding, Louisa	7, Dec. 1893	1, Sept	42	Fries	Marion, OH	782	Rüppur, Karlsruhe, Baden
Finding, Louise	7, Oct. 1867		27	Geier	Indianapolis, IN	318	
Finding, Magdalena	3, Mar. 1879	16, Feb.	72		Pomeroy, OH	71	Oppau, Frankenthal, Baiern
Finding, Matthäus	4, Feb. 1878	14, Jan.	72- 3m-21d		Pomeroy, OH	39	Oppau, Rheinkreis Baiern
Finding, Philipp	8, Aug. 1864	26, May	24- 6m		Pomeroy, OH	128	
Finding, Wilhelmina	27, Jan. 1873	30, Dec.	28	Lock	Pomeroy, OH	31	KlosterHeiningen, Hannover
Finding, Wilhelmina	24, Feb. 1873			Bock	Lancaster, NY	63	
Findt, Johan Georg	27, Dec. 1875	5, Dec.	83		Swanville, NE	415	Kleinbakenheim, Baiern
Finger, Michael Friedrich	21, May 1891	7, Apr.	78- 8m- 2d		Appleton, WI	334	Steinwege, Pommern
Fingerhut, Anna	10, Apr. 1890	12, Mar.	32	Ulrich	Jackson, MO	238	Cape Girardeau County, Missouri
Finis, Johan Conrad	21, Mar. 1889	25, Feb.	62		Guthrie, IL	190	Ersen, Hofgeismar, Kurhessen
Fink, (Mr)	7, Apr. 1862	15, Feb.	60- -23d		Perrysburg, OH	56	
Fink, Anna	24, Nov. 1879	21, Oct.	16- -18d		Julietta, IN	375	

- 122 -

Christliche Apologete Death Notices --- 1839 - 1899

Name of Deceased	Notice Date	Death Date	Age	Page	Maiden Name	Place of Death	Place of Birth
Fink, Catharina	22, Mar. 1888	23, Feb.	23-10m-13d	190	Weber	New Palestine, IN	Askerg, Ludwigsburg, Württemberg
Fink, Christian Friedrich	25, July 1889	21, June	57	478		Pittsburg, PA	Kircheim a. N., Württemberg
Fink, Christina Magdalena	20, Mar. 1876	12, Feb.	75	95	Klepser	Buffalo, NY	Marschall, Michigan
Fink, Christine Caroline	7, Mar. 1895		40	158	Katz	Grand Rapids, MI	Schadeck, Amt Runkel, Nassau
Fink, Friedrich	21, Jan. 1867	27, Dec.	70	22		Louisville, KY	Rödinghaus, Preußen
Fink, Friedrich	5, Jan. 1863	15, Dec.	60-9m	4		St. Louis, MO	Hessen-Darmstadt
Fink, Heinrich	15, Dec. 1892	28, Nov.	70	798		Indianapolis, IN	Buffalo, New York
Fink, Henry Georg	11, Feb. 1897	21, Jan.	23	94		Buffalo, NY	Belsenberg, Württemberg
Fink, J.P.	23, June 1873	31, May	43-5m-21d	199		St. Joseph, MO	Schadek, Nassau
Fink, Jakob	2, Sept 1872	8, Aug.	33	287		Louisville, KY	Perrysburg, Ohio
Fink, Johan	20, Mar. 1882	4, Mar.	36-6m-24d	95		Perrysburg, OH	Kircheim am Neckar, Württemberg
Fink, Johan Jakob	21, Apr. 1898	2, Apr.	62	255		Buffalo, NY	Echtorf, Pickeburg, Germany
Fink, Leonore	28, Mar. 1850	30, Jan.	52	52		Monroe, IL	Schadek, Runkel, Nassau
Fink, Louisa	4, Mar. 1886	22, Feb.	86	7	Schmidt	Louisville, KY	Widdersheim, Preußen
Fink, Louise Eleonore	13, Aug. 1891	11, June	71	526	Miller	New Palestine, IN	Barby bei Magdaburg, Preußen
Fink, Louise Emilie	21, Nov. 1881	30, Oct.	28	375	Blankenstein	Falls Mission, TX	Tonawanda, New York
Fink, Magdalena	2, May 1881	8, Apr.	40-8m	143	Jakob	Buffalo, NY	Altloßheim, Amt Schwetzingen, Baden
Fink, Paulina	25, Oct. 1869	22, Sept	30	343	Schwegheimer	Lansing, MI	Stark County, Ohio
Fink, Samuel	11, May 1863	4, Feb.	29	76		Galion, OH	Wackernheim, Hessen-Darmstadt
Fink, Wilhelmine	22, May 1865	6, Apr.	27-10m-28d	84	Klippel	St. Joseph, MO	Königshagen, Waldeck
Finke, Christian H.	15, Dec. 1884	1, Dec.	31-9m-6d	7		Quincy, IL	
Finke, Dorothea	17, Mar. 1879	24, Feb.	62-3m-10d	87		St. Louis, MO	Valdorf, Amt Vlotho, Herford, Minden, Preußen
Finke, Friederike	23, Apr. 1877	18, Mar.	60	135	Schalk	Herman, MO	
Finke, Friederike	14, May 1896	14, Apr.	75-6m	318	Sundermann	Huntingburg, IN	
Finke, H.E.	31, July 1876	15, July	58-3m-6d	247		Huntingburg, IN	
Finke, Heinrich Wilhelm	23, June 1873	11, May	59	199		Nashville, IL	Schröttinghausen, Lübbeke, Minden, Preußen
Finke, Herman	1, Oct. 1877	2, Sept	52	319		Herman, MO	Valdorf, Kreis Herford, Minden, Preußen
Finke, Johan Heinrich	9, Jan. 1896	21, Dec.	70-11m-7d	30		Hamline, MN	
Finke, Karl	31, July 1882	4, July	81-5m-2d	247		Red Bud, IL	Rusbend, Bückeburg, Lippe-Schaumburg
Finke, Maria E.	24, May 1875	26, Apr.	62	167	Hacke	Nashville, IL	Amt Wittlage, Hannover
Finkeldei, Margarethe	26, July 1855	30, June		120		West Baltimore, MD	
Finken, Anna Katharina	3, Nov. 1884	7, Oct.	31	7	Ahrens	Locust Point, OH	Danbury, Ottawa County, Ohio
Finken, Louise	7, Aug. 1876	4, July	46	255	Widdnakel	Second Creek, MO	Polle an der Weser, Amt Polle, Hannover
Finsel, Justus	25, Dec. 1876	27, Nov.	72	413		Wheeling, WV	Everhausen, Hannover
Finstermann, Anna Elsbein	11, Feb. 1878	26, Jan.	35-4m	47	Wessel	Charles City, IA	Oldendorf, Amt Aurich, Ostfriesland
Fintel, Hilke	15, Feb. 1875	30, Jan.	53	55	Ellen	Wilton, IA	Hannover
Fintel, Peter C.	29, Sept 1887	11, Sept	64	622		Davenport, IA	Kornweiler, Neuenburg, Württemberg
Finter, Elisabeth	8, Dec. 1887	17, Oct.	74	782	Vauth	Jeffersonville, IN	Oberniebelsbach, Neuenburg, Württemberg
Finter, Georg	27, Feb. 1882	12, Feb.	70	71		Jefferonville, IN	Oberrein, Bern, Schweiz
Fintig, Katharina	6, Sept 1875	9, Aug.	60	287	Blaser	Muscatine, IA	Poß, Pieritz, Pommern
Firchow, Johan Friedrich	9, May 1889	5, Apr.	67	302		Kenosha, WI	Melgershausen, Melzungen, Kurhessen
Firmkäs, Maria	19, Aug. 1858	5, June	38	132		Beardstown, IL	Langenfalz, Preußen
Fisch, Johannes	9, Feb. 1893	13, Jan.	70	94		Muscatine, IA	
Fischbach, Christina Karolina	11, Feb. 1892	19, Jan.	60	94	Kimmel	Rossville, OH	
Fischbach, Emma	8, Dec. 1887	17, Nov.	32	782		Ansonia, OH	Dayton, Montgomery County, Ohio
Fischbach, Friedrich Wilhelm	10, Jan. 1876	19, Dec.	41	15		Dayton, OH	Baltimore, Maryland

Name of Deceased	Notice Date	Death Date	Age	Maiden Name	Page	Place of Death	Place of Birth
Fischbach, Heinrich Phil.	16, May 1889	26, Apr.	36- 9m-17d		318	Dayton, OH	Klein-Germes, Preußen
Fischbach, Lorenz	2, Apr. 1857	21, Mar.	79		56	Dayton, OH	Greifenstein, Wetzlar, Coblenz, Preußen
Fischbach, Philipp	16, Jan. 1896	16, Nov.	78		46	Dayton, OH	Greifenstein, Wetzlar, Preußen
Fischbach, Philippine	3, June 1858	26, May	67		88	Dayton, OH	Milwaukee, Wisconsin
Fischbach, Wilhelm Eduard	12, May 1898	3, Mar.	18	Metzger	303	Ripon, WI	
Fischer, (Mrs)	25, Oct. 1894	30, Sept	81		694	Danville, IL	Württemberg
Fischer, Alois	28, Mar. 1895	20, Feb.	86		206	Dunkirk, NY	
Fischer, Anna Augusta	13, Oct. 1873	13, Aug.	13		327	New York City, NY	Hockenheim, Schwetzingen, Baden
Fischer, Anna Elisabeth	18, Mar.1872	11, Feb.	34	Hirth	95	Waterloo, IA	Bittenfeld, Waiblingen, Württemberg
Fischer, Anna Maria	10, Apr. 1876	21, Jan.	87- 8m-11d	Stum	118	Sandusky, OH	Neuhofen, Rheinkreis Baiern
Fischer, Anna Maria	17, May 1855	2, Apr.	16		80	Defiance, OH	Ladbergen, Westphalen
Fischer, Anna Maria	17, Jan. 1881	2, Dec.	60- 7m-28d	Bothemüller	23	Nerstrand, MN	Neuendettelsau, Baiern
Fischer, Barbara K.	3, Apr. 1890	9, Mar.	54- 1m-12d		222	Sprague, NE	Stargard, Pommern
Fischer, Carl	28, Dec. 1893	29, Nov.	33		828	Hammond, IN	Adelhausen, Schoppheim, Baden
Fischer, Cecilia	18, Aug. 1887	3, Aug.	76- 8m-11d	Weber	526	Watertown, WI	Louisville, Jefferson County, Kentucky
Fischer, Charles Edward	12, Oct. 1899	2, Aug.	46- 8m		655	Louisville, KY	Unterbruden, Backnang, Württemberg
Fischer, Christina Barbara	31, Mar. 1873	4, Mar.	76- 5m-27d	Wieland	103	Buffalo, NY	Liedolsheim, Baden
Fischer, Christine	11, July 1864	24, June	69		112	Detroit, MI	Oberstedten, Homburg, Hessen
Fischer, Christoph	8, Mar. 1894	5, Feb.	44		166	Bradford, IN	Oberbreitenbach, Alsfeld, Hessen-Darmstadt
Fischer, Conrad	19, May 1892	4, May	26	Thompson	80	Captina, OH	Norberg, Insel Alson, Schleswig-Holstein
Fischer, Dorothea	31, Dec. 1883	16, Nov.	65		7	Enterprise, KS	Willmandingen, Reutlingen, Württemberg
Fischer, Elisabeth	13, Sept 1888	24, July	50- 9m- 5d	Heinz	590	Cameron, MO	Anweiler, Waiblingen, Württemberg
Fischer, Elisabeth	20, May 1872	29, Apr.	77- 4m-20d		167	Ann Arbor, MI	Oberstetten, Homburg, Hessen
Fischer, Elisabeth	11, June 1883	12, May	70	Racke	191	Bradford, IN	Roethen, Mundschau, Germany
Fischer, Elisabeth	11, Dec. 1890		27	Kreuz	798	Cibolo, TX	Ohmbach, Amt Kusel, Baiern
Fischer, Elisabeth	23, July 1866	6, July	28		238	Marietta, OH	Kölken, Aargau, Schweiz
Fischer, Emil	25, Feb. 1897	16, Jan.	79- 1m-16d	Feik	126	Hammond, IN	Ostfriesland
Fischer, Emilia Catharina	7, Nov. 1881	22, Oct.	39	Palma	359	St. Louis, MO	Kankelfitz, Pommern
Fischer, Emilie	15, Mar. 1888	13, Feb.	16	Hübner	174	Watertown, WI	
Fischer, Ernst	27, Feb. 1882	2, Feb.	64		71	Warren, MO	Kulmbach, Baiern
Fischer, Eva	11, Oct. 1880	16, Sept	32		327	De Soto, MO	Steinweiler, Rheinpfalz Baiern
Fischer, Eva Catharina	1, Jan. 1866	9, Dec.	52	Hauck	6	Laporte, IN	Heidesbach, Heidelberg, Baden
Fischer, Eva Katharina	6, Oct. 1892	15, Sept	67		638	Lansing, IA	Beiersdorf, Sachsen
Fischer, Ferdinand Lebrecht	2, July1883	12, June	34- -14d		215	Jordan, MN	
Fischer, Friedrich	8, May 1882	25, Apr.	60- 3m-26d		151	Lancaster, WI	Mandorf, Hannover
Fischer, G.L.	1, Dec. 1884	11, Nov.	34		7	Olive Branch, NE	ribnitz, Mecklenburg-Schwerin
Fischer, Gesina	3, Sept 1866	26, Aug.	82- 5m	Henken	286	Cincinnati, OH	Kirchdorf bei Aurich, Ostfriesland, Preußen
Fischer, Gottlieb Johan Christoph	18, Sept 1871	24, Aug.	12- 2m-28d		303	Chicago, IL	Gräfenstein, Kurhessen
Fischer, Greta Catharina	5, Oct. 1868	28, Aug.	60		319	Mascoutah, IL	Hirschberg, Bermersheim, Rheinkreis Baiern
Fischer, Heinrich	9, Feb. 1893	3, Dec.	69- -13d		94	Brooklyn, NY	Louisville, Jefferson County, Kentucky
Fischer, Jakob	28, Apr. 1879	4, Apr.	53		135	Louisville, KY	Leun, Wetzlar, Preußen
Fischer, Jakob	2, July 1896	12, June	56		431	Louisville, KY	Willmandingen, Württemberg
Fischer, Jakob	15, Sept 1879	22, Aug.	77		295	Marietta, OH	Pommern
Fischer, Johan	12, Jan. 1893	1, Aug.	35		30	Kearney, MO	Hohenwalde, Pommern
Fischer, Johan Friedrich Wilhelm	16, Sept 1897	6, May	30		591	Bertha, MN	
Fischer, Johan Gottlieb	9, June 1892				366	Sleepy Eye, MN	

Christliche Apologete Death Notices --- 1839 - 1899

Name of Deceased	Notice Date	Death Date	Age	Maiden Name	Place of Death	Place of Birth	Page
Fischer, Johann Leonhard	21, Feb. 1861	6, Dec.	53		Indianapolis, IN	Metzingen , Württemberg	32
Fischer, Johann Ludwig	17, Jan. 1861	25, Dec.	83		Detroit, MI	Lückenheim, Baden	12
Fischer, Johanna	29, Mar. 1888	9, Mar.	74	Metz	Chicago, IL	Liedolsheim, Baden	206
Fischer, Johanne	5, May 1892	27, Mar.	70	Koch	Sleepy Eye, MN	Barsfließ, Fürstensee, Pommern	286
Fischer, Johannes	26, Jan. 1860	9, Jan.	70		Sandusky, OH	Bitterfeld, O.A. Waiblingen, Württemberg	16
Fischer, Johannes	19, July 1894	24, May	62		Minneapolis, MN	Minfeld, Kandel, Rheinpfalz Baiern	470
Fischer, Johannes	1, July 1886	23, June	64		Lansing, IA	Canton Basel, Schweiz	7
Fischer, John	21, Nov. 1889	28, Oct.	86-10m-10d		Sherrills Mount, IA	Weidenthal, Rheinkreis Baiern	750
Fischer, John	10, Jan. 1889	16, Nov.	68		Allegheny City, PA	Martinroda, Sachsen-Weimar	30
Fischer, John C.	18, July 1870	30, June	40		Cedar Lake, IN	Sonnhausen, Elsaß	231
Fischer, Joseph	6, Mar. 1865	14, Feb.	64		Chicago, IL	Wodinan, Böhmen	40
Fischer, Karl	8, Oct. 1896	29, Aug.	38		Columbus, OH	Columbus, Franklin County, Ohio	655
Fischer, Karl	23, Sept 1858	26, Aug.	32- 8m- 6d		Covington, KY	Steinbach, Amt Bühl, Baden	152
Fischer, Karl	15, Dec. 1873	21, Nov.	48		Boody, IL	Menzingen, Baden	399
Fischer, Karl Friedrich	20, Nov. 1882	28, Oct.	70- 2m- 7d		Detroit, MI	Wichmannsdorf, Brandenburg, Preußen	375
Fischer, Karl Peter	10, May 1888	28, Mar.	44		St. Paul, MN	Berlin, Preußen	302
Fischer, Karolina	11, July 1881		28- 9m-23d		Lancaster, WI		223
Fischer, Karoline	18, Sept 1871	5, Sept	34	Kant	Lowell, WI	Glockziehn, Kreis Pieritz, Preußen	303
Fischer, Katharina	22, July 1872	7, July	33- -15d	Kolmer	Kossuth, OH	Roßwaag, Vaihingen, Württemberg	239
Fischer, Katharina	18, June 1891	29, Mar.	55	Müller	Baltimore, MD	Schönstedt, Kurhessen	398
Fischer, Katharine	7, Apr. 1853	21, Mar.	48		Marietta, OH	Mözingen, Amt Herrenberg, Württemberg	56
Fischer, Katharine	26, Sept 1895	3, Sept	76		Lexington, MO	Reinrod, Hessen-Darmstadt	622
Fischer, Katharine Wilhelmine	9, Feb. 1899	11, Jan.	34	Sundermann	Corder, MO	Amsterdam, Holland	95
Fischer, Leopold Samuel	21, Jan. 1886	7, Jan.	34-11m		Chicago, IL		7
Fischer, Lewis Emory	27, Aug. 1896	17, July	30		Bradford, IN	Clark County, Indiana	559
Fischer, Louis	25, July 1889	5, July	14		Watertown, WI	Watertown, Wisconsin	478
Fischer, Ludwig	8, Nov. 1875	21, Oct.	66		Wheeling, IL	Linkenheim, Amt Karlsruhe, Baden	359
Fischer, Ludwig Friedrich	19, Dec. 1889	24, Nov.	66		Columbus, OH	Unterweisach, Backnang, Württemberg	814
Fischer, Luisa	30, Oct. 1856		2		Ripley, OH		176
Fischer, M.	30, Apr. 1866	16, Apr.	54		St. Louis, MO	Langenstein, Kurhessen	142
Fischer, Magdalena	6, Nov. 1871	9, Oct.	78-11m- 9d	Kolmer	Kossuth, OH	Roßwag, Vaihingen, Württemberg	359
Fischer, Maria	26, Mar. 1877	11, Mar.	36- -22d	Winzler	Toledo, OH	Bartsheim, Schaffhausen, Schweiz	103
Fischer, Maria	13, Oct. 1887	26, Sept	88		Davenport, IA	GroßAspach, Württemberg	654
Fischer, Martin H.	28, Feb. 1881	10, Sept	11- 7m- 5d		New Memphis, IL	Anbrechtis, Böhmen	335
Fischer, Mary	8, Feb. 1869	22, Sept	25		Berea, OH	Böhmen	671
Fischer, Mary E.	19, Apr. 1894	26, Jan.	19		Chicago, IL	Uttram, Kurhessen	47
Fischer, Maria Catharina	25, July 1889	19, June	65	Vater	Brooklyn, NY	Roßwag, Vaihingen, Württemberg	262
Fischer, Maria Henriette	21, Oct. 1897	8, Sept	54		Steinhagen, MO	Spórthauen, Preußen	671
Fischer, Maria Juliane	18, Oct. 1875	4, Oct.	79	Michel	Marietta, OH	Leun, Kreis Wetzlar, Preußen	335
Fischer, Mathias	18, Oct. 1875	30, Mar.	17- 6m-22d		Bradford, IN	Kirchdorf, Amt Aurich, Ostfriesland	399
Fischer, Mathias	21, Oct. 1897	6, Mar.	23-11m-10d		Hatton, ND	Atlantic Ocean	262
Fischer, Melinda	29, Mar. 1880	25, Oct.	69- 8m-25d		Liberty, MO	Rochester, Olmstead County, Minnesota	103
Fischer, Nikolaus	2, July1883	20, June	44- 7m-13d	Daniel	Minneapolis, MN	Oberstetten, Homburg, Hessen	215
Fischer, Olive	14, Apr. 1853	15, Oct.	56		Henry County, OH	Summet County, Ohio	60
	8, Mar. 1880	15, Feb.	33- 6m-15d	Friedler	Toledo, OH	Oberottenbach, Rheinkreis Baiern	79
						Schmellen, Sachsen	

Name of Deceased	Notice Date	Death Date	Age	Page	Maiden Name	Place of Death	Place of Birth
Fischer, Rosina	12, May 1862	10, Apr.	76	76		Bucyrus, OH	Steinach, Waiblingen, Württemberg
Fischer, Rosina	20, Feb. 1862	31, Jan.	19	32		Dunkirk, NY	
Fischer, Susanna	19, Dec. 1889	18, Nov.	84- 5m-23d	814	Laubscher	Sherrills Mount, IA	Weidenthal, Rheinkreis Baiern
Fischer, Theresia	27, May 1897	12, May	74	335	Speyer	Louisville, KY	Güntersthal, Freiburg, Baden
Fischer, Theresia	1, Apr. 1897	7, Mar.	30	206	Rau	Dunkirk, NY	Dorfen, Württemberg
Fischer, Traugott	29, Sept 1898	15, Sept	77	623		Bracken, TX	Oberlinda, Lauhon, Preußen
Fischer, Verena	6, Oct. 1884	17, Sept	71	7	Waldvogel	Toledo, OH	Stetten, Schaffhausen, Schweiz
Fischer, Wilhelm	13, Dec. 1894	20, Nov.	75	806		Marietta, OH	Leun bei Braunfels, Preußen
Fischer, Wilhelmine M.H.	7, Feb. 1881	17, Jan.	45	47	Lütke		Gifhorn, Hannover
Fisches, Johan Friedrich	9, Nov. 1885	26, Oct.	58	7			Oberlinningen, Württemberg
Fisches, Juliane Christina	22, Nov. 1880	8, Nov.	43	375	Specht	Industry, TX	Widdem an der Jaxt, Neckarsulm, Württemberg
Fischhauser, Christian	29, June 1868	3, June	24	207		Industry, TX	Sevelen, St. Gallen, Schweiz
Fisher, Emma	4, June 1896	9, May	38	367	Ringler	Ellis Grove, IL	Ellis Grove, Illinois
Fisher, Margaretha	21, June 1894	17, May	39	406	Price	Victor, IA	Weberschreit, Germany
Fissel, Johan L.	19, Aug. 1897	31, July	20	527		Lemars, IA	Plymouth County, Iowa
Fissel, Katharina	22, Dec. 1884	23, Nov.	35	7	Fissel	Stryker, OH	
Fisser, Maria Elisabeth	6, Nov. 1890	14, Oct.	72- 3m-27d	718	Schmidt	Wilber, NE	Rogenstede, Esens, Ostfriesland
Fitschen, Martha	16, Jan. 1862	22, Dec.	71	12	Ditschen	Marietta, OH	Tist, Hannover
Fitzke, Wilhelmina	20, Sept 1875	9, July	47	303	Wuswat	Flint Creek, IA	Mittelfeld, Preußen
Fitzner, Carl	30, Dec. 1878	8, Dec.	63	415		West Bend, WI	Großrosen, Schlesien
Fitzner, Ernst H.F.	8, Sept 1892	8, Aug.	53	574		West Bend, WI	Pilgramsheim, Preußen
Fitzner, Willie Friedrich	31, Mar. 1884	11, Mar.	12	7		Milwaukee, WI	Platteville, Wisconsin
Fix, Caroline	3, Mar. 1887	7, Feb.	66- - 6d	142	Steckle	New Albany, IN	Stein, Bretten, Baden
Fix, Emma	18, Dec. 1890	14, Nov.	21- 7m-26d	814		Kramer, NE	Illinois
Fix, Georg	10, Mar. 1873	14, Jan.	5	79		Trenton, IL	
Fix, Jacob	14, Mar. 1881	16, Feb.	42- 5m-11d	87			Ilbesheim, Rheinkreis Baiern
Fix, Johan	10, Mar. 1873	18, Feb.	13	79			Ilbesheim, Rheinkreis Baiern
Fix, Johan Adam	26, Nov. 1896	8, Nov.	65	766	Nahm	Summerfield, IL	Unterhalau, Schaffhausen, Schweiz
Fix, Margaretha	4, Feb. 1884	15, Jan.	48	7		Crete, NE	Ilbesheim bei Landau, Baiern
Fix, Thomas	11, Dec. 1876	21, Nov.	67	399		Summerfield, IL	
Fix, Wilhelmine	10, Mar. 1873	10, Jan.	7	79		Trenton, IL	
Flaccus, Anna Katharina	28, Nov. 1895	11, Nov.	74	766	Rudolph	Pittsburg, PA	Niederellenbach, Rothenburg, Kurhessen
Flaceus, Ph. Wilhelm	28, Nov. 1870	11, Nov.	55	383		Pittsburg, PA	Ottweiler, Trier, RheinPreußen
Flach, Heinrich	3, June 1878		68- 5m-17d	175		Weston, MO	Wölflingen, Zürich, Schweiz
Flacus, Maria	5, Oct. 1868	2, Aug.	11	319		Pittsburg, PA	
Flad, Anna Maria	27, Sept 1855	7, Sept	31	156		Rochester, NY	Neuhausen an der Ems, Urach, Württemberg
Flad, Elias	5, Feb. 1891	5, Jan.	73- 3m-25d	94		Rochester, NY	Neuhausen an der Ems, Urach, Württemberg
Flad, Gottfried	19, Sept 1895	25, Aug.	68	606		Rochester, NY	Neuhausen, Urach, Württemberg
Flad, Johan Georg	21, Oct. 1897	10, Sept	52	671		Rochester, NY	Neuhausen an der Ems, Urach, Württemberg
Flad, Johan Ulrich	20, Feb. 1896	3, Feb.	66	126		Rochester, NY	Odernheim, Rheinkreis Baiern
Flad, Maria	21, Dec. 1893	29, Nov.	76	814		Rochester, NY	Neuhausen an der Elm, Württemberg
Fladd, Elisabeth	7, Aug. 1890	16, July	71- 8m-24d	510	Schäfer	Dallas City, IL	Dallas City, Illinois
Flag, Anna	7, Feb. 1895	4, Jan.	27	94		Dallas City, IL	
Flagge, Heinrich	3, Jan. 1881	8, Dec.	78- 5m-28d	7		Batestown, IL	Margoldendorf, Hannover
Flaig, Anna	28, Feb. 1895	4, Jan.	27	142		Dallas City, IL	Dallas City, Illinois
Flaig, Anna Barbara	20, Apr. 1863	2, Apr.	38	64	Schiedinger	Nauvoo, IL	Oberbothingen, Nürtingen, Württemberg

Christliche Apologete Death Notices --- 1839 - 1899

Name of Deceased	Notice Date	Death Date	Age	Maiden Name	Page	Place of Death	Place of Birth
Flaig, Katharina Wilhelmina	8, Dec. 1898	13, Nov.	26		783	Dallas City, IL	KleinKursdorf bei Glaubach, Sachsen
Flaming, Friedrich	14, Aug. 1890	22, July	39- 3m- 6d		526	Holt, MI	
Flamm, Gottfried	31, May 1869	18, Apr.	44- 7m- 7d		175	Cincinnati, OH	
Flater, Jakob	4, July 1895	9, June	55		430	Kewaskum, WI	Oberscham, Werdenberg, St. Gallen, Schweiz
Flath, Maria	28, July 1892	12, July	30		478	Pekin, IL	Pekin, Illinois
Flauaus, Johannes	10, Oct. 1850	27, Sept	23--8m-23d		164	Wheeling, VA	Hopfengarten, Hessen-Darmstadt
Fleck, Anna Emilia	28, May 1896	9, May	17		350	Indianapolis, IN	
Fleck, Georg	3, Nov. 1884	17, Oct.	36- 5m-29d		7	Indianapolis, IN	Tressau, Weitenberg, Baiern
Fleckner, Franz	5, Nov. 1865	12, Oct.	36		180	Poughkeepsie, NY	Herboldsheim, Baden
Fleckner, John	22, Oct. 1864	20, Aug.	28		172	Delaware, OH	Rohrbach, Büdingen, Hessen-Darmstadt
Fleder, Maria	17, Sept 1866	19, Aug.	36		302	Seymour, IN	Sonnenberg, Nassau
Fleiner, Johann Gottlieb	4, Apr. 1861	4, Mar.	27		56	Allegheny City, PA	Willsbach, Weinsberg, Württemberg
Fleischhauer, Andreas Rauch	20, Dec. 1880	6, June	23		407	Lafayette, IN	Vöhingen, Sultz am Neckar, Württemberg
Fleischhauer, Maria Magdalena	18, Oct. 1888	29, Sept	66		670	Lafayette, IN	
Fleischhauer, Sarah	2, Feb. 1880	11, Jan.	14		39	Lafayette, IN	Dalhausen, Kreis Höxter, Preußen
Fleischhauer, Wilhelm	9, Nov. 1868	8, Oct.	22		359	Lafayette, IN	Dahlhausen, Preußen
Fleischheuer, Ernst	4, Feb. 1878	16, Jan.	34		39	Lafayette, IN	Reichshofen, Niederbrunn, Elsaß
Fleischmann, Barbara	1, Aug. 1881	14, July	71	Machin	247	Terre Haute, IN	Indian Creek, Osage County, Missouri
Fleischmann, Bertha Maria	18, Jan. 1894	8, Oct.	18		46	Bland, MO	
Fleischmann, Friedrich	9, Jan. 1871	2, Dec.	70		15	Flint Creek, IA	
Fleischmann, Johan Georg	12, Apr. 1894	14, Mar.	50		246	Bland, MO	Ermershausen, Baiern
Fleischmann, Margaretha	17, Dec. 1877	17, Nov.	77- 3m	Heimstadt	407	Bloomington, IL	Hessen-Darmstadt
Fleming, Katharina	24, Mar. 1879	2, Mar.	46	Schmidt	95	Kendallville, IN	Haaskirchen, Elsaß
Flesch, Barbara	9, Sept 1897	6, Aug.	59	Schmidt	575	Amsterdam, NY	Bodingen, Emmendingen, Baden
Fleßner, Fentje Minken	15, May 1876	9, Mar.	71- 2m		159	Roberts, IL	Amt Aurich, Ostfriesland
Flickinger, Friedrich	24, Dec. 1883	27, Nov.	31		7	Caseville, MI	Kanton Bern, Schweiz
Flickinger, Ida Auguste	4, Feb. 1884	27, Nov.	29	Roeder	7	Caseville, MI	Landeck, West Preußen
Flickinger, John	20, Nov. 1876	29, Oct.	68-11m- 7d		375	Caseville, MI	Rohrbach, Bern, Schweiz
Fliedner, (Pastor)	5, Dec. 1864	4, Oct.			194		
Flindt, George	29, Apr. 1897	10, Mar.	21		271	Albert Lea, MN	Manchester, Freeborn County, Minnesota
Flindt, Johan M.	13, Oct. 1898	23, Sept	31		655	Albert Lea, MN	Manchester, Minnesota
Flindt, John	9, Dec. 1897	10, Nov.	56		783	Albert Lea, Mn	Kiel, Schleswig-Holstein
Flitsch, John	25, Apr. 1889	28, Mar.	74- 1m		270	Harper, IA	St. Antoine, Graubünden, Schweiz
Flocken, Amanda Elisabeth	21, Mar. 1881	19, Feb.	14- -30d		95	Bucyrus, OH	
Flocken, F.W.	6, Apr. 1893	24, Feb.	62		222	Brooklyn, NY	Odessa, Rußland
Flocken, Johannes	6, June 1890	6, Apr.			183	Tultscha, TK	Albersweiler bei Landau, Rheinkreis Baiern
Flocken, Michael	25, Sept 1890	1, Sept	61- 4m-21d		622	Bucyrus, OH	Rheinpfalz Baiern
Flohr, Amanda Maria	6, Jan. 1898	29, Nov.	32		15	Clyman, WI	Clyman, Wisconsin
Flohr, Ernst Heinrich	30, Apr. 1866		64- 6m-23d		142	Lowell, WI	Auleben, Preußen
Flokenstein, Katharina	27, May 1878	10, May			167	Louisville, KY	
Floreth, C. Wilhelm (Rev)	23, Mar. 1899	21, Feb.	68		190	St. Louis, MO	Zimmerschied, Nassau
Floreth, Elise	16, Feb. 1885	27, Jan.	43	Zürcher	7	Chester, IL	Canton Bern, Schweiz
Floreth, Karl Albert	16, Aug. 1888	1, Aug.	19		526	Summerfield, IL	Chester, Illinois
Floreth, Philipp	7, Apr. 1884	10, Mar.	55		7	Peoria, IL	Zimmerschied, Nassau
Flörke, Charlotte	27, July 1863	1, June	77- 2m		120	Omaha, NE	Lübke, Minden, Preußen
Flörke, Elisabeth	30, July 1896	3, July	69	Wölel	495	Omaha, NE	Bremen, Germany

Christliche Apologete Death Notices -- 1839 - 1899

Name of Deceased	Notice Date	Death Date	Age	Page	Maiden Name	Place of Death	Place of Birth
Flörte, David	18, Sept 1865	2, Aug.	32	152		St. Louis, MO	Hessen
Flottmann, Heinrich	24, June 1897	24, May	55	399		Altamont, IL	Bremen, Germany
Fluck, Ottilie	8, Aug. 1889	23, June	42	510	Reichart	Lafayette, IN	Lehigh County, Pennsylvania
Flückiger, Anna Elisabeth	9, Aug. 1880	31, July	28- 7m	255	Stein	Nashville, TN	Rimbach, Hessen-Darmstadt
Flückiger, Ulrich	2, Nov. 1854	16, Oct.	65	176		Woodville, OH	Rohrbach, Bern, Schweiz
Flückinger, Samuel	8, Apr. 1886	18, Mar.	59	7		Elmore, OH	Canton Solothurn, Schweiz
Fluegel, Wihelm	8, July 1886	21, June	62	7		Goshen, IN	Hagenohsen, Hameln, Hannover
Flügel, August	19, Oct. 1885	11, Sept	40	7		Morris, MN	Heeßten, Lippe-Detmold
Flükiger, Anna Barbara	21, Sept 1863	16, Apr.	70	152		Woodville, OH	Rohrbach, Bern, Schweiz
Fluth, Georg	30, Mar. 1885	28, Feb.	52	7		St. Louis, MO	Ostfriesland
Fluth, Jac. J.	30, May 1881	8, May	76-10m-28d	175		De Soto, MO	Loquard, Ostfriesland
Fluth, Maria Philippine	17, Aug. 1899	4, Aug.	55	527	Zollmann	St. Louis, MO	Mannsfelden, Nassau
Fluth, Sarah Katharina	4, Mar. 1872	16, Feb.	71	79		De Soto, MO	Norden, Ostfriesland
Focken, Gerd Jansen	10, Apr. 1882	25, Mar.	74- -13d	119		San Jose, IL	Neudorf, Amt Esen, Ostfriesland
Focken, Hilka	24, Apr. 1882	2, Apr.	62	135	Barels	San Jose, IL	Neudorf, Amt Esen, Ostfriesland
Foebel, Catharine	22, July 1867	11, July	43	230	Zilles	Covington, KY	Nordheim, Hessen
Föell, Georg A.	4, Dec. 1876		73	391		Rockwell, IA	Erlach, Württemberg
Föell, Johanna	14, May 1877		72	159		Rockwell, IA	Oberamt Weinsberg, Württemberg
Föhl, Phobe	27, Oct. 1892	1, Oct.	26- - 8d	686		Terre Haute, IN	
Föhling, Susanna	23, Oct. 1876	5, Oct.	44	343	Stephan	Baraboo, WI	Sieglingen, Neckarsulm, Württemberg
Folkers, J.H.	30, May 1864	7, Apr.	36	88		Petersburg, IL	Sandhorst, Aurich, Ostfriesland, Hannover
Föll, Carolina	15, Oct. 1891	14, Sept	66	670	Belz	DeWitt, MI	Steinbach, Backnang, Württemberg
Fongard, Andreas	22, Nov. 1874	22, Nov.	61	399		Troy, NY	Hertingshausen bei Marburg, Kurhessen
Fongart, Katharina	11, May 1899	21, Apr.	84	302		Troy, NY	Langendorf, Rauschenberg, Kurhessen
Förderer, Margarethe	23, May 1881	20, May	52-11m-21d	167		San Francisco, CA	Weiler, Sinsheim, Baden
Förderer, Stephen	16, July 1877	25, June	18	231		Cincinnati, OH	Weiler, Sinsheim, Baden
Forderhase, Emma Elisa	12, Apr. 1888	25, Mar.	18	238		Warren Co, MO	Warren County, Missouri
Forderhase, Heinrich	13, Apr. 1863	21, Mar.	52	60		Warren Co., MO	Wesen, Kreis Tecklenburg, Preußen
Forderhase, Johan	6, Mar. 1890	18, Feb.	38-11m- 7d	158		Berger, MO	New Melle, Missouri
Forderhase, Maria Elisabeth	3, Feb. 1859	16, Jan.	74	20		Warren, MO	Wersen, Preußen
Forderhase, Rudolph	22, Apr. 1878	2, Apr.	65- 3m- 7d	127		Herman, MO	Wesen, Tecklenburg, Münster, Preußen
Förding, (Mrs)	21, Nov. 1861	20, Oct.	48	188		Louisville, KY	
Forell, Christine	16, Sept 1897	27, Aug.	73	591	Mayor	Louisville, KY	Herzbach bei Martöbel, Winecke, Kurhessen
Forell, Johan	23, Mar. 1899	2, Mar.	77	190		Louisville, KY	Marköbel, Windeke, Kurhessen
Forger, John	11, Aug. 1884	7, July	15- 9m- 7d	7		Pittsburg, PA	
Forkert, Johan Karl Ernst	29, Nov. 1888	6, Nov.	63- 8m-28d	766		Batesville, IN	Schlesien
Forman, Henrietta	26, Aug. 1897	11, Aug.	54	543	Walter	Watersburg, IL	Dietrichsfeld, Aurich, Hannover
Förschler, Andreas	14, Sept 1899	20, Aug.	72	591		Poughkeepsie, NY	Köndringen, Emmendingen, Baden
Förschler, Anna Maria	21, July 1879	6, July	50	231	Koch	Poughkeepsie, NY	Köndringen, Emmendingen, Baden
Förschler, August	22, June 1899	6, June	74-10m-25d	399		Junction City, KS	Köndringen, Emmendingen, Baden
Förschler, Emilie	10, Nov. 1884	20, Oct.	26	7	Grüninger	Wyandotte, KS	
Förschler, Louis A.	10, Nov. 1898	23, Oct.	20	719		Kansas City, KS	Poughkeepsie, New York
Först, Friedrich	8, May 1871	17, Mar.	31	151		Canton, MO	Zinskam, Germersheim, Rheinpfalz Baiern
Förster, (son of Johann Tobias)	15, Apr. 1852	Mar.	1- 5m	64		Dayton, OH	
Förster, Constantin	11, Jan. 1864	13, Nov.	33	8		Milwaukee, WI	Gläsendorf, Kreis Grottkau, Preußen
Forster, Friedrich	22, Oct. 1896	2, Sept	79	687			Elbuxen, Germany

- 128 -

Christliche Apologete Death Notices --- 1839 - 1899

Name of Deceased	Notice Date	Death Date	Age	Page	Maiden Name	Place of Death	Place of Birth
Förster, Johann Tobias	15, Apr. 1852	19, Mar.	44	64		Dayton, OH	Markt Neuhof, Baiern
Försterling, Meta Adelheid	9, Feb. 1893	13, Jan.	85	94	Niebuhr	Weatherby, OR	Bremen, Germany
Fortmann, Carolina	23, Feb. 1863	2, Feb.	10	32		Louisville, KY	
Fös, Samuel	17, Apr. 1882	8, Mar.	71	127		Effingham, IL	Schöftland, Aargau, Schweiz
Fosbrink, Maria Katharina	29, Apr. 1886	26, Mar.	74- 5m- 7d	7	Westendorf	Seymour, IN	
Fosloh, Heinrich Fr. Chr.	7, Feb. 1876	22, Jan.	50	47		Golconda, IL	Wulfhagen, Windheim, Preußen
Foß, Ernst	20, Apr. 1885	29, Mar.	83	7		Lancaster, NY	Scharpsow, Staffenhagen, Mecklenburg-Schwerin
Fotens, Sophia	22, Oct. 1896	15, Sept	70	687		Manitowoc, WI	
Fotsch, (Mrs)	12, May 1887	23, Apr.	58	302	Fund	Wrayville, IL	Unterhallau, Schaffhausen, Schweiz
Fotsch, John Jakob	25, June 1877	27, May	18	207		Illinois City, IL	Unterhalau, Schaffhausen, Schweiz
Fotsch, Louise Wilhelmine	11, Oct. 1894	23, Sept	12	662		Brighton, IL	Rock Island, Illinois
Foucar, Eduard	21, Mar. 1870	5, Feb.	45	95		Frankfurt am Main, GER	
Fox, Susanna	6, Mar. 1871	15, Jan.	42	79	Michael	Edgerton, OH	Pennsylvania
fraedrich, Christian	19, Dec. 1889	22, Nov.	90	814		Chicago, IL	Voigtshagen bei Daber, Naugard, Preußen
Framcke, Maria	19, Oct. 1885	18, Sept	52	7	Neumann	Los Angeles, CA	OstPreußen
Frandrech, Salomi	29, Sept 1875	29, Sept	46	335	Keller	Chicago, IL	Elsaß
Fränk, Adam	8, July 1897	18, June	63	431		Indianapolis, IN	Oderbach, Hessen-Darmstadt
Frank, Anna	7, June 1888	17, May	56- 9m-23d	366		Louisville, KY	
Frank, Anna C.	30, Sept 1897	14, Sept	46	623	Arensmann	Louisville, KY	New Albany, Indiana
Frank, August	25, July 1889	26, June	29- 6m- 8d	478		Sun Prairie, WI	Blumberg, Stettin, Randow, Preußen
Fränk, Catharina	20, Mar. 1876	23, Feb.	40- 1m-16d	95	Jensen	Allegan, MI	Gausthal, Norway
Frank, Catharine	22, Feb. 1875	19, Dec.	44- 3m	63	Schilling	Troy, NY	Grumstadt, Hessen-Darmstadt
Frank, Elisabeth	30, Nov. 1893	3, Nov.	55	766	Dohn	St. Joseph, MO	Beaver, Jackson County, Ohio
Frank, Elisabeth	18, Feb. 1858	24, Dec.	22	28	Kinkel	Quincy, IL	
Frank, Ernstina	3, Dec. 1877	17, Sept	17- 3m- 7d	391		Tecumseh, NE	
Frank, Friedrich	12, Sept 1889	22, Aug.	58- 2m- 9d	590		Allegan, MI	Dorflas, Baiern
Frank, Friedrich August	7, Oct. 1897	11, Sept	56	639		Philadelphia, PA	Böl bei Plauen, Sachsen
Frank, Friedrich Conrad	20, Dec. 1869	27, Nov.	58- 7m-17d	407		Huntingburg, IN	Salz, Münchberg, Baiern
Frank, Georg	14, Feb. 1870	25, Jan.	19- 5m-23d	55		Sand Creek, MN	
Frank, Gottfried Wilhelm	10, Mar. 1898	14, Feb.	80	158		Hobart, IN	Lehm, Weinsfeld, Württemberg
Frank, Heinerike Wilhelmine	21, Dec. 1863	28, Nov.	14	204		Sand Creek, MN	Weil im Schönbuch, Böblingen, Württemberg
Frank, Heinrich	14, Feb. 1870	19, Jan.	13	55		Sand Creek, MN	Weil im Schönbuch, Böblingen, Württemberg
Frank, Helene	15, Apr. 1886	15, Mar.	46	7	Frank	Menominee, MI	Albany, New York
Frank, Henriette	14, Feb. 1870	21, Jan.	3- 6m	55		Sand Creek, MN	Weil im Schönbuch, Böblingen, Württemberg
Frank, Henriette Wilhelmine	11, Oct. 1888	24, Sept	68	654	Laib	Jordan, MN	Weil, Schönbuch, Böblingen, Württemberg
Frank, Jakob	12, Feb. 1866	19, Jan.	41- 8m	54		Columbus, OH	Streich, Schorndorf, Württemberg
Frank, Jakob Theobald	12, Nov. 1896	21, Oct.	71	734		Louisville, KY	Langmeil, Kaiserslautern, Baiern
Frank, Johanna Louise	22, Aug. 1886	2, Apr.	63	7	Burow	Humboldt, NE	Blumberg, Pieritz, Pommern
Frank, Johannes	2, Aug. 1888	29, June	66	494		Brooklyn, NY	Ittlingen, Eppingen, Baden
Frank, Joseph	8, July 1897			431		Kramer, NE	Goes, Ungarn
Frank, Katharina Luise	8, June 1899	14, May	28- 6m	367	Dein	Brooklyn, NY	
Frank, Katharine	27, Aug. 1896	8, Aug.	75- 7m	559		Scranton, PA	
Frank, Katie	6, Sept 1880	20, Aug.	16	287		Allegan, MI	
Frank, Lizzie	28, Oct. 1897	9, Oct.	21	687		Indianapolis, IN	Indianapolis, Marion County, Indiana
Frank, Louise	30, July 1896	12, July	45	495		Brooklyn, NY	Zitzlingen, Württemberg
Frank, Lydia L.	31, Aug. 1899	21, July	22	559		Baltimore, MD	Belgard, Pommern

Christliche Apologete Death Notices --- 1839 - 1899

Name of Deceased	Notice Date	Death Date	Age	Page	Maiden Name	Place of Death	Place of Birth
Frank, Margaretha	2, Aug. 1888	8, July	90- 6m- 2d	494		Santa Claus, IN	Rittershausen, Baiern
Frank, Margaretha	1, Nov. 1888	5, Oct.	73	702		Marine City, MI	
Fränk, Maria	29, July 1897	5, July	52	479	Green	Indianapolis, IN	Flensungen, Hessen-Darmstadt
Frank, Maria A.	10, Oct. 1881	28, Aug.	34- 1m-21d	327		Columbus, OH	New York
Frank, Maria Elisabeth	27, July 1899	10, June	80-10m-15d	479	Oehm	Jeffersonville, IN	Helburg, Sachsen
Frank, Maria Elisabeth	10, Mar.1873	15, Feb.	7	79		Zaleski, OH	Pomeroy, Ohio
Frank, Maria Theresa	1, Dec. 1884	31, Oct.	32	7	Koplitz	Friendship, WI	Black Wolf, Winnebago County, Wisconsin
Frank, Marie	19, June 1890	8, May	38	398	Beckmann	Humboldt, NE	Quincy, Illinois
Frank, Mary	14, Feb. 1870	28, Jan.	15- 1m-23d	55		Sand Creek, MN	
Frank, Moses	4, Jan. 1875	16, Dec.	22- 3m-20d	7		Valparaiso, IN	Michigan
Frank, Peter Wilhelm	26, Oct. 1899	24, Sept	46	687		Bushton, KS	Washtenaw County, Michigan
Frank, Philippina	6, Aug. 1877	22, July	42- 8m-25d	255	Weis	Louisville, KY	
Frank, Rosina K.	27, May 1878	3, May	22- 8m- 7d	167		Hebron, IA	Langenweiler, Baiern
Frank, Valentin	26, Mar. 1866	2, Mar.	77	102		Louisville, KY	
Frank, Wilhelm	31, Oct. 1881	12, Oct.	13	351		Allegan, MI	
Franke, Mathilda Pauline C.	20, Oct. 1892	24, Sept	53	670	Krampe	Baltimore, MD	Darkow, Belgard, Hinterpommern
Franke, Rebecca	27, Jan. 1873		23	31	Schneider	Pittsburg, PA	
Franke, Rosina	16, June 1873	19, May	14	191		Pittsburg, PA	Monroe County, Ohio
Frankenstein, Eduard	12, Sept 1889	25, July	30-11m- 4d	590		Parker, SD	Neustadt, West Preußen
Frankenstein, Johan August	10, Jan. 1876	10, Dec.	58	15		Pensaukee, WI	Poganitz, Stolpe, Pommern, Preußen
Frankenstein, Wilhelm	11, Aug. 1898	13, July	68	511		Parker, SD	Lauenburg, Pommern
Frankhauser, Barbara	19, Apr. 1869	5, Apr.	50	127	Kurtz	Clarington, OH	Pfechingen, Bern, Schweiz
Frankhauser, David	17, Jan. 1889	1, Jan.	81	46		St. Paul, MN	Biel, Bern, Schweiz
Frankhauser, Emma	16, Mar. 1885	20, Feb.	39- 1m-24d	7	Movies	Big Stone City, SD	
Frankhauser, Johannes	5, Nov. 1883	22, Oct.	59-11m	359	Serbeck	Mankato, MN	Micheln, Merseburg, Preußen
Frankhauser, Werner	21, Mar. 1889	17, Feb.	79- - 7d	190		Clarington, OH	Canton Bern, Schweiz
Franz, Anna Margaretha	24, Nov. 1887	6, Nov.	69	750	Thonner	Switzer, OH	Einertzhausen, Hessen
Franz, Christiane Sophie	12, Jan. 1885	27, Dec.	50	7	Hirsch	Lawrence, MA	Triebes, Reuß
Franz, Friedrich	13, Feb. 1890	23, Jan.	63- 2m-10d	110		Louisville, KY	Burbach, Saarbrücken, RheinPreußen
Franz, Jakob	19, Jan. 1893	2, Jan.	64	46		Indianapolis, IN	Dornhain, Sulz, Württemberg
Franz, Lizzie	31, Jan. 1889	18, Oct.	14	78		Boonville, IN	
Franz, Louis	14, Jan. 1886		54	7		St. Louis, MO	Gießen, Hessen-Darmstadt
Franz, Margaretha	25, Feb. 1886	6, Feb.	48	15		Louisville, KY	Erlinghausen, Kurhessen
Franz, Maria Magdalena	7, Jan. 1897	11, Dec.	65	15		Boonville, IN	Germany
Franz, Mattie	31, Jan. 1889	25, Oct.	17	78		Boonville, IN	
Franz, Sophia	25, Feb. 1892	14, Nov.	64	126	Scheibe	Ironton, OH	Triebes, Schleitz, Sachsen
Franz, Willy	12, Aug. 1872	16, July	10- 1m	263		Ballwin, MO	
Franzlau, Friedrich	7, Mar. 1864	14, Dec.	68	40		Chester, IL	Eilse, Bückeburg, Lippe-Schaumburg
Franzlau, Friedrich	9, Nov. 1893	11, Oct.	48- 9m-21d	718		Nashville, IL	Eilsen, Bückeburg, Germany
Franzlau, Mina	4, Apr. 1895	14, Mar.	48	222	Krumwiede	Nashville, IL	Stöckse, Steimbke, Hannover
Franzman, Sophie	5, Nov. 1899	24, Nov.	72	14	Reiman	Butte, MT	Waldlaubersheim, Preußen
Franzmann, Carl	8, Feb. 1894	16, Dec.	68	94		Minneapolis, MN	Schweppenhausen, Kreuznach, Preußen
Fratscher, Christian	3, Aug. 1854		47	124		Saugerties, NY	Oltisleben, Sachsen-Weimar
Frauer, Caroline	6, Nov. 1882	28, Oct.	39	359		Indianapolis, IN	Schnaith, Schorndorf, Württemberg
Frauer, Christiana	6, Oct. 1892	10, Sept	78	638	Mensch	Indianapolis, IN	Weinsberg, Württemberg
Frauer, Emanuel Christian	17, Mar. 1879	2, Mar.	74	87		Indianapolis, IN	Truchtelfingen, Balingen, Württemberg

Christliche Apologete Death Notices -- 1839 - 1899

Name of Deceased	Notice Date	Death Date	Age	Page	Maiden Name	Place of Death	Place of Birth
Frauer, Margaretha	12, May 1892	18, Apr.	49	302	Meß	Indianapolis, IN	Heimertshausen, Hessen-Darmstadt
Frautschi, Anna	24, May 1888		78-11m-10d	334	Lugenbut	Toledo, OH	Oberwyl, Bern, Schweiz
Frautschi, Magdalena	22, Aug. 1881	7, Aug.	37	271		Toledo, OH	Oberweil, Schweiz
Frebert, Catharine	22, Aug. 1881	1, Aug.	26- 4m-24d	271	Ewinger	Burlington, IA	Burlington, Iowa
Frebert, Conrad	28, May 1896	20, Apr.	71	350		Burlington, IA	Seilbeck, Lippe-Detmold
Frebisch, Maria Josephina	22, May 1876	30, Apr.	30	167	Haueisen	Baresville, OH	Monroe County, Ohio
Frech, Catharina	7, Feb. 1889	7, Jan.	70- 2m-26d	94	Mahn	De Soto, MO	Nack, Alzey, Hessen-Darmstadt
Frech, Christian	14, Nov. 1881	23, Oct.	40	367		Seymour, IN	Sonnenberg, Nassau
Frech, Christoph Fr.	23, Feb. 1863		60	32		Franciscoville, MI	Degerloch, Stuttgart, Württemberg
Frech, Dorothea	22, Jan. 1883	1, Jan.	78- 2m-11d	31	Reiser	Francisco, MI	Stuttgart, Württemberg
Frech, Konrad	3, May 1869	10, Apr.	47	143		St. Charles, MO	Kettenheim, Kreis Allzei, Hessen
Frech, Philippine	9, Mar. 1893	15, Feb.	35- 6m- 2d	158		De Soto, MO	
Frede, Dorothea	19, Nov. 1896	29, Oct.	68	750		Warrenton, MO	Reinerbeck, Hannover
Fredeking, Carolina	27, Feb. 1865	9, Feb.	33	36	Röckemann	Nashville, TN	Hahle bei Minden, Preußen
Frederich, Dorothea Louise	22, Jan. 1891	7, Jan.	51- 3m-14d	62	Hübner	Columbus, WI	
Fredrich, Hulda	10, Sept 1891	8, June		590	Hinz	Almond, WI	
Frees, Christian	28, Nov. 1881	23, Oct.	40	383		Seymour, IN	Sonnenberg, Nassau
Freese, Elisabeth	26, July 1880	9, July	49- 8m-29d	239	Hofer	Laporte, IN	Bern, Schweiz
Freese, Heinrich	10, June 1872	19, May	52- 3m	191		Terre Haute, IN	WesterKappeln, Westphalen, Preußen
Freese, Richard C.	19, Jan. 1880	14, Dec.	61	23		Roberts, IL	
Frei, Anna Maria Elisabeth	29, May 1856	7, May	30	88	Schäfer	Furnace, OH	Amt Wittlage, Hannover
Frei, Charles G.	9, Apr. 1896	10, Mar.	65	238		Baltimore, MD	Kirchheim, Teck, Württemberg
Frei, Johan	15, Feb. 1894	27, Jan.	79	110		Champaign, IL	Nonnenweier, Baden
Frei, Friedrich	27, Nov. 1856	5, Nov.	24	192		Wheeling, IL	Feldbach, Kannstadt, Württemberg
Frei, John	13, Jan. 1887		65	30		Chicago, IL	Hochhausen, Mosbach, Baden
Frei, Katharine	16, Nov. 1885	30, Oct.	57- 4m-12d	7		Chicago, IL	Hochhausen, Baden
Frei, Ludwig	21, July 1892	29, June	63	462		Dayton, OH	Dillheim, Wetzlar, Koblenz, Preußen
Frei, Marie	18, Aug. 1884	1, Aug.	38- 4m-25d	7	Güntert	Des Moines, IA	Büsingen, Baden
Freiberger, Barbara	3, Apr. 1876	20, Mar.	67	111		Francisco, MI	Eckenweiler, Rotenburg, Württemberg
Freienwalde, Carl	21, Jan. 1897	28, Nov.	32	46		Portland, OR	Stegnitz, Pommern
Freier, Engel	20, Dec. 1860	18, Nov.	50	204		Woodville, OH	
Freiermuth, Catharina	3, Nov. 1887	14, Oct.	68	702	Schnell	Wrayville, IL	Adamswiller, Drulingen, Elsaß
Freihofer, Heinrich	14, Apr. 1862	7, Mar.	20- 1m-12d	60		Santa Claus, IN	Jackson County, Indiana
Freihofer, Jakob	20, Dec. 1849	28, Nov.	18	204		Rockford, IN	Veltheim, Zürich, Schweiz
Freimuth, Sophia	4, Apr. 1889	6, Mar.	40	222	Altrup	Edwardsville, IL	Pennsylvania
Freise, Maria Wilhelmina Friedrike	18, Jan. 1894	16, Dec.	39	46		Ritzville, WA	Naudemin bei Belgrad, Pommern
Freistein, Eleonora Friederike	28, Mar. 1881	5, Mar.	60	103		Quincy, IL	
Freitag, Adolph	4, July 1864	12, May	25	108		Washington, DC	Langenholzhausen, Lippe-Detmold
Freitag, Adolph	20, June 1864	11, May	25	100		White River, MI	Langenhausen, Lippe-Detmold
Freitag, Beat	6, Apr. 1885	20, Mar.	57	7		Friendship, WI	Elm, Glarus , Schweiz
Freitag, Charlotte	2, Dec. 1858	9, Aug.	11- 6m	192		Cedar Lake, IN	
Freitag, Conrad	17, Nov. 1887	31, Oct.	68	734		Crandon, SD	Langenholzhausen, Lippe-Detmold
Freitag, Conrad	1, Mar. 1869	27, July		71		Grand Rapids, MI	Gottien, Preußen
Freitag, Daniel Gottfried	14, Sept 1893	16, Aug.	73	590		Watertown, WI	Weibstadt, Neckar-Bischofsheim, Baden
Freitag, Hanna	20, Nov. 1876	30, Oct.	36	375	Wacker	White Hall, MI	
Freitag, Heinrich	4, Feb. 1867	15, Oct.	40	38		Junction City, KS	Altkothen, Kreis Langensalza, Preußen

Christliche Apologete Death Notices --- 1839 - 1899

Name of Deceased	Notice Date	Death Date	Age	Maiden Name	Page	Place of Death	Place of Birth
Freitag, Heinrich	22, Sept 1853	29, July	30		152	Portsmouth, OH	Groß-Goskow bei Lito, Pommern
Freitag, Henriette	27, Nov. 1890	5, Nov.	73		766	Nerstrand, MN	Langenholzhausen, Farrenholz, Lippe-Detmold
Freitag, Henry	10, Feb. 1898	12, Jan.	72		94	Montague, MI	
Freitag, Hermann	5, Feb.1847	22, Jan.	32- -21d		23	Captina, OH	Gutkur, Rodenberg, Hessen
Freitag, Johan	12, Mar. 1896	17, Jan.	84		174	Swanton, NE	
Freitag, Johannes	10, Apr. 1846		Inquiry		59	Wheeling, PA	
Freitag, Magdalena	29, May 1856	3, May	23-10m	Schäfer	88	Portsmouth, OH	
Freitag, Verina	8, Aug. 1889	24, June	74- 3m-17d		510	Montague, MI	Umiken, Brugg, Schweiz
Freling, Susanna	12, June 1890	22, May	78		382	Milwaukee, WI	Schwerdorf, Lothringen
Frels, Friederike Dorothea	8, June 1893	2, May	47	Müller	366	Geneseo, IL	Angern, Wilmerstadt, Magdeburg, Preußen
Fremder, Edward	14, Jan. 1892	26, Dec.	70		30	Wheeling, WV	Deissel, Kurhessen
Frense, Georg	9, Oct. 1890	23, Aug.	59- 7m-21d		654	Goshen, IN	
Frentrop, Heinrich	29, May 1890	8, May	69		350	Pekin, IL	Bünde, Herford, Preußen
Frenzel, Augusta Bertha	27, July 1885	25, June	26		7	Bloomington, Illinois	Bloomington, Illinois
Frenzel, Wilhelmine	18, Apr. 1889	17, Mar.	63	Gemsleben	254	Bloomington, IL	Hornburg, Braunschweig
Frerichs, Harm	25, Nov. 1872	9, Nov.	53		383	Mascoutah, IL	Aurich, Hannover
Frers, Bertha	26, Mar. 1896	3, Feb.	32		206	Brooklyn, NY	
Frers, Johan	15, June 1899	18, May	74		383	Brooklyn, NY	Staden, Lehe, Hannover
Frers, Sylvester Tuttle	20, May 1886	5, May	2		7	Brooklyn, NY	
Freudenberg, Elisabeth	13, July 1893	20, June	67	Sippel	446	Pittsburg, PA	Uensterode, Hessen-Kassel
Freudenberg, Karl	17, Oct. 1889	30, Sept	37- 9m-11d		670	Pittsburg, PA	Baltimore, Maryland
Freudenberger, Johann	7, Jan. 1858	3, Dec.	45		4	Boonville, IN	
Freudiger, Anna Maria	6, Sept 1880	21, Aug.	38- 9m- 3d	Sepp	287	Clarington, OH	Monroe County, Ohio
Freudiger, Carolina	14, Aug. 1851	12, July	15		132	Captina, OH	
Freudiger, Caroline Josephine	16, June 1879	20, May	15- 5m-17d		191	Clarington, IL	Wiedlisbach, Bern, Schweiz
Freudiger, Elisabeth	27, Mar. 1871	3, Mar.	66		103	Clarington, OH	Schirmsdorf, Baiern
Freudiger, Elisabeth	13, Feb. 1890	19, Jan.	73- 2m- 3d		110	Clarington, OH	Clarington, Monroe County, Ohio
Freudiger, Maria Elisabeth	25, Nov. 1897	28, Oct.	30		751	Clarington, OH	Niederbib, Bern, Schweiz
Freudinger, Johan	12, Apr. 1894	21, Mar.	86		246	Clarington, OH	Dayton, Montgomery County, Ohio
Freuer, Marie Louise	21, July 1879	26, June	37	Meyer	231	Indianapolis, IN	New Haven, Connecticut
Freund, Helena Eleonora	7, Dec. 1885	18, Nov.	21		7	Newark, NJ	
Freund, Jean Paul	1, Feb. 1869	24, Jan.			39	Philadelphia, PA	
Freund, John	24, Jan. 1856	4, Dec.	53		16	German Creek, IA	Schlichten, Kurhessen
Frevert, Charlotte	6, Apr. 1868	24, Mar.	31	Hölsmann	111	St. Louis, MO	Blasheim, Kreis Lübbecke, Minden, Preußen
Frevert, Sophia	4, Feb. 1886	29, Dec.	65	Kluckhohn	7	Odebolt, IA	Bavenhausen, Hoenhausen, Lippe-Detmold
Frewert, Wilhelmine Karoline	6, Sept 1880	21, Aug.	23- 2m-18d	Petersmeyer	287	Odebolt, IA	Cedar Lake, Indiana
Frewert, Wilhelmina	26, Nov. 1866	1, Nov.	51		382	Cleveland, OH	Rott, Bremke, Lippe-Detmold
Frey , Georg Daniel	28, Dec. 1854	5, Dec.	68		208	Wheeling, IL	Fellbach, Kannstadt, Württemberg
Frey, Anna Katharine	12, Jan. 1893	23, Dec.	84	Gründfelder	30	Pekin, IL	Reilingen, Schwetzingen, Baden
Frey, Catharine	2, Dec. 1858	3, Nov.	34		192	Lawrenceburg, IN	Litzelhausen, Kurhessen
Frey, Charlotte	12, Sept 1850	13, Aug.	34		148	Mt. Vernon, IN	
Frey, Edward	5, Mar. 1883	16, Feb.	22		79	Sandusky, OH	Hamilton, Butler County, Ohio
Frey, Friederike	28, May 1866	18, Apr.	71- 1m- 4d		174	Chicago, IL	Fellbach, Cannstadt, Württemberg
Frey, H.	26, Jan. 1874	31, Dec.	47- 8m-22d		31	Crete, NE	Arenshorst, Amt Wittlage, Hannover
Frey, Heinrich	13, Feb. 1890	21, Jan.	55- 8m-13d		110	Dayton, OH	Dillheim, Wetzlar, Koblenz, Preußen
Frey, Henriette	17, Nov. 1859	1, Nov.	34	Tews	184	Milwaukee, WI	Planton, Preußen

Christliche Apologete Death Notices --- 1839 - 1899

Name of Deceased	Notice Date	Death Date	Age	Maiden Name	Place of Death	Page	Place of Birth
Frey, Jakob	24, Mar. 1884	2, Mar.	23		Odebolt, IA	7	Lea County, Illinois
Frey, Johan Georg	3, Oct. 1895	10, Sept	84		Kendallville, IN	638	Eislingen, Württemberg
Frey, Johan H.	15, Feb. 1869	9, Jan.	49		Furnace, OH	55	Bleckrieden, Kötten, Hannover
Frey, Johan Karl Friedrich Gottlieb	27, July 1899	8, July	78		Milwaukee, WI	479	Lasbeck, Pommern
Frey, John	13, Feb. 1882	24, Jan.	54		Cannelton, IN	55	Grove, Alleghany County, New York
Frey, John M.	4, June 1877	22, May	61		Covington, KY	183	Eichstettin, Emmendingen, Baden
Frey, John M.	14, Mar. 1895	25, Feb.	26		Madison, WI	174	Madison , Wisconsin
Frey, Katharina	18, Feb. 1867	6, Jan.	48	Jack	Saugerties, NY	54	Conweiler, Neüenbürg, Württemberg
Frey, Louise	19, May 1884	8, May	67	Leyer	Louisville, KY	7	Eichelbach, Backnang, Württemberg
Frey, Louise F.	24, Mar. 1879	22, Dec.	30		Newark, NJ	95	Altensteig, Württemberg
Frey, Margaretha	22, Jan. 1891	30, Dec.	79- - 8d	Neileft	Burlington, IA	62	Graefenfeld, Baiern
Frey, Margaretha	17, Apr. 1890	19, Mar.	47- 1m- 2d		Louisville, KY	254	
Frey, Maria	6, May 1852	24, Mar.	33	Weber	Liberty, OH	76	Kanton Aargau, Schweiz
Frey, Maria Agnes	30, May 1895	19, Apr.	29	Metzger	Dayton, OH	350	
Frey, Nick	21, Sept 1874	20, Aug.	63- 6m-11d		Lawrenceburg, IN	303	Dannstadt, Rheinkreis Baiern
Frey, Rosine	10, Jan. 1881	21, Dec.	17- 5m-12d		Dayton, OH	15	
Frey, Susanna	22, Jan. 1883	2, Jan.	47	Köhler	Lafayette, IN	31	Gelnhausen, Kurhessen
Frey, Wilhelm	27, May 1886	29, Apr.	21		Odebolt, IA	7	Sublette, Lee County, Illinois
Frey, Wilhelm	21, Oct. 1878	1, Oct.	17- 9m- 9d		Danville, MN	335	Lee County, Illinois
Freyer, Barbara	17, Apr. 1871	3, Mar.	21	Arz	Lansing, MI	127	
Freyer, Friedrich	14, July 1853	16, June	59-10m-20d		Woodville, OH	112	Osnabrück, Hannover
Freyer, Louis	17, Apr. 1871	13, Mar.			Lansing, MI	127	
Freyermuth, Jakob	6, Apr. 1899	19, Mar.	90		Wrayville, IL	222	Weer, Drullingen, Elsaß
Freygang, Friedrike	22, Mar. 1869	15, Jan.	54	Wier	Davenport, IA	95	Altmark, Preußen
Freyhofer, Jakob	26, May 1898	27, Apr.	92		Kansas City, KS	335	Veltheim bei Winterthur, Schweiz
Freyhofer, Susanna	9, Mar. 1863	11, Feb.	59	Aegeter	Santa Claus, IN	40	Veltheim, Zürich, Schweiz
Freytag, Katharine	22, June 1868	4, June	61	Becker	Cincinnati, OH	199	Alsheim, Kreis Worms, Hessen-Darmstadt
Friauf, Hannah	30, Jan. 1896	12, Jan.	75	Hansohm	Louisville, KY	78	Eschershausen, Braunschweig
Frick, Johann A.	25, Oct. 1855	15, Aug.	57		Mt. Vernon, IN	172	Büchigt, Baden
Frick, Julius	6, Apr. 1863	14, Feb.	83		Omaha, NE	56	Süppling, Helberstedt, Braunschweig
Frick, Katharina	23, Feb. 1893	3, Feb.	78	Höhn	Kearney, MO	126	Niederhausen, Koblenz, Rheinpfalz Baiern
Frick, Katharina B.	13, Aug. 1891	21, July	72	Meyer	Evansville, IN	526	Grünwettersbach, Durlach, Baden
Frick, Nicolaus	17, July 1890	7, Apr.	77		Cameron, MO	462	Tuchroth, Obermoschel, Baiern
Frick, Wilhelm	1, Aug. 1895	5, July	85		Warrenton, MO	494	duchroth, obermosel, Rheinkreis Baiern
Fricke, Dorothea	27, Sept 1894		69- 6m- 7d		Clatonia, NE	630	Ziegenhagen, Witzenhausen, Kurhessen
Fricke, F.	9, Jan. 1882	9, Dec.	57			15	Ziegenhagen, Witzenhausen, Kurhessen
Fricke, Louis	16, Aug. 1894	30, July	63		Seymour, IN	534	Mariendorf, Kurhessen
Fricke, Louise	16, Jan. 1862	2, Dec.	58- 9m	Prast	Sheboygan, WI	12	Dorndorf bei Naumberg,
Fricke, Ludwig	21, June 1860	23, May	48- 2m- 3d		Sheboygan, WI	100	Oldendorf, Hessen
Fricke, Wilhelmine	2, Nov. 1893	14, Oct.	63	Nolde	Seymour, IN	702	Kurhessen
Fried, Hannah	13, July 1893	24, May	59	Kurle	Kendallville, IN	446	New York City, New York
Friedch, Anton	27, Dec. 1880		56-11m		Lyona, KS	415	
Friederich, Auguste Julianne W.	11, June 1896	8, May	69		Ray, MI	383	Landeck, Marienwerder, West Preußen
Friederich, Carolina Henriette Amanda	12, July 1888	25, June	38	Schenk	Madison, WI	446	Zorndorf, Preußen
Friederich, Eva Margaretha	23, May 1895	2, May	61- 5m-22d	Reinold	Chippewa Falls, WI	334	Mühlbach, Baden
Friederich, Johan Conrad	9, Apr. 1896	22, Mar.	71		Chippewa Falls, WI	238	Mühlbach, Baden

Christliche Apologete Death Notices --- 1839 - 1899

Name of Deceased	Notice Date	Death Date	Age	Page	Maiden Name	Place of Death	Place of Birth
Friederich, Wilhelmine	3, Nov. 1873	20, Oct.	36	351	Röhl	Marshall, WI	Pröbitz, Pommern
Friedhofer, (Mrs)	2, May 1889		76	286		Denver, CO	Bökingen, Heilbronn, Württemberg
Friedhoff, Henriette Friederike	30, Apr. 1877			143	Schüttler	Edwardsville, IL	Linnen, Münster, Preußen
Friedhoff, Katharina El.	8, Dec. 1873	22, Nov.	34- 1m- 1d	391	Hunsche	Edwardsville, IL	Madison County, Illinois
Friedhoff, Maria	18, Feb. 1884	24, Jan.	26	7	Peters	Edwardsville, IL	Ohlinghausen, Germany
Friedhoff, Wilhelm F.	8, Dec. 1898	18, Nov.	63	783		Edwardsville, IL	Bannwill, Arwangen, Bern, Schweiz
Friedle, Andreas	13, Nov. 1865	29, Sept	53	184		Ft. Wayne, IN	Lindelbach, Baden
Friedlein, Michael	18, Apr. 1889	21, Mar.	23	254		Sterling, NE	
Friedrich, Abraham	16, Apr. 1857	20, Mar.	65	64		Warsaw, IL	
Friedrich, Anna Louise	3, Dec. 1891	23, Oct.	19-11m-18d	782		Clyman, WI	
Friedrich, Augustine	1, June 1899		71	351	Utech	Lyona, KS	Meesow, Pommern
Friedrich, Catharina	16, June 1873	13, May	76- 3m- 2d	191	Seitz	Warsaw, IL	
Friedrich, Charlotte	12, July 1880	9, June		223			
Friedrich, Elisabeth	15, July 1867	8, June	34	222	Riebel	Ripley, OH	Hessen
Friedrich, Emma Elisabeth	24, Apr. 1890	3, Apr.	16- 2m-28d	270		Beaver Dam, WI	
Friedrich, Johan Friedrich	26, Feb. 1883	7, Feb.	63- 3m- 1d	71		Beaver Dam, WI	Zorndorf, Königsberg, Brandenburg
Friedrich, John W.	1, Oct. 1896	22, Aug.	34	639		Los Angeles, CA	Lowell, Dodge County, Wisconsin
Friedrich, Louis August	24, Apr. 1890	30, Mar.	5- 2m-30d	270		Beaver Dam, WI	
Friedrich, Marie	13, Oct. 1873	22, Sept	52- 5m-11d	327	Baumann	Allegan, MI	Ettenheim, Baden
Friedrich, Michael	11, Dec. 1871	4, Oct.	77	399		Allegan, MI	
Friedrich, Peter	4, Oct. 1888	1, Sept	58-11m-14d	638		Roseville, MI	Hillsheim, Hessen
Friedrich, Philippine	3, Mar. 1879	30, Jan.	66- 1m	71	Euler	Kansas City, MO	Singhofen, Nassau
Friedrichsohn, Magdalena	10, July 1856	10, June	19	112		Newark, NJ	Nürtingen, Württemberg
Friegel, Christine	3, Aug. 1899	15, July	76	495	Eichenhofer	Indianapolis, IN	Gusenstadt, Heidenheim, Württemberg
Frieling, (Mr)	19, Jan. 1893	2, Nov.	29	46		Ritzville, WA	Oster, Aurich, Germany
Frieling, Anna Catharina	19, Jan. 1893	9, Dec.		46	Bänger	Ritzville, WA	
Fries, (Mr)	30, Aug. 1860	29, July	63- 5m-13d	140		Jeffersonville, NY	Neckarbischofsheim, Baden
Fries, Carolina	24, Mar. 1884	11, Mar.	25	7	Huber	Chicago, IL	Mettmenstetten, Zürich, Schweiz
Fries, Charlotte	6, June 1870	23, May	70	183		Scranton, PA	Fülme, Preußen
Fries, Elisabeth	8, June 1893	19, May	73	366	Schwegler	Marion, OH	Baden
Friese, Anna	26, Jan. 1899	21, Nov.	20	63	Weigers	Schaller, IA	Mohrdorf, Aurich, Ostfriesland
Frieß, Katharina	14, Nov. 1881	13, Oct.	31- 5m-13d	367	Stumpf	Buffalo, NY	Baden
Frieß, Maria	2, Apr. 1891	3, Mar.	51	222	Muskop	Brookville, IN	White Township, Pennsylvania
Frikhöfer, Johan Wilhelm	9, Mar. 1885	21, Feb.	85- 1m- 5d	7		Charlestown, IN	Münzfelden, Lümburg, Nassau
Frill, Anna	30, Aug. 1894	11, June	66	566		Scotch Hill, PA	
Frillmann, Dorothea	25, Jan. 1894	10, Dec.	81- 6m- 8d	62	Kammeyer	Columbus, OH	Lahrhorst, Westphalen
Frillmann, Heinrich	26, Jan. 1899	11, Jan.	85	63		Columbus, OH	Lippika, Westphalen
Frischknecht, Hans Ulrich	1, Oct. 1896	6, Sept	71	639		Hoboken, NJ	Canton Zürich, Schweiz
Fritsch, Heinrich	28, Feb. 1856	24, Oct.	60	36		Louisville, KY	Treisa, Kurhessen
Fritsch, John	15, Apr. 1872	26, Mar.	58	127		Louisville, KY	
Fritsch, Juliana	17, Feb. 1879	28, Jan.	57	55	Friedrichs	Bushnell, IL	Klein-Himstedt, Steinbrück, Hannover
Fritsche, Christine	22, Nov. 1875	20, Oct.	54	375		Kewaunee, WI	Mecklenburg-Schwerin
Fritsche, Louis	20, May 1878	4, May	31	159		Industry, TX	
Fritsche, Louisa Auguste	28, July 1859	16, July		120	Berger	Portsmouth, OH	Güttmansdorf bei Reichenbach, Preußen
Fritsche, Susanne Helene	5, June 1871	15, May	83- 3m-25d	183	Berger	Toledo, OH	Güttmannsdorf bei Reichenbach, Schlesien
Fritz, Adam	27, Dec. 1855	23, Oct.	43- 9m	208		Mt. Vernon, IN	Belbach, Meisenheim, Homburg, Hessen

Name of Deceased	Notice Date	Death Date	Age	Page	Maiden Name	Place of Death	Place of Birth
Fritz, Anna	24, Feb. 1887	5, Feb.	29- 9m- 8d	126	Mänz	Altamont, IL	Massenbach, Brackenheim, Württemberg
Fritz, Christina	15, Apr. 1897	27, Mar.	80	239	Zöller	Wheelersburg, OH	Langsdorf, Gießen, Hessen
Fritz, Elisabeth	4, July 1889	16, June	78	430	Kneipp	Nashville, TN	Oberbrüden, Württemberg
Fritz, Georg	27, June 1850	5, May	66	104		Bethlehem, OH	Gündelbach, Maulbronn, Württemberg
Fritz, Gottlieb	16, Aug. 1855	24, July	27- 9m- 2d	132		Delaware, OH	Korb, Waiblingen, Württemberg
Fritz, Gottlieb	23, Oct. 1882	10, Oct.	71	343		Portsmouth, OH	Delaware, Ohio
Fritz, Gottlieb	14, May 1891	22, Apr.	37- 2m-10d	318		Hay Creek, MN	Dogwood Ridge, Ohio
Fritz, Juliana Elisabeth	7, July 1898	15, June	40	431		Wheelersburg, OH	Pittsburg, Pennsylvania
Fritz, Karl Heinrich	26, Jan. 1874	25, Dec.	18- 4m- 9d	31		Portsmouth, OH	Hilpertsau, Baden
Fritz, Lorenz	16, May 1881	8, Apr.	51- 8m	159		Newark, NJ	Liepen, Anklam, Pommern
Fritz, Maria Dorothea Friedrike	12, May 1879	11, Apr.	52- 8m- 5d	151	Siewert	Schumway, IL	
Fritz, Maria Louise	30, Dec. 1858	29, Nov.	8	208		Bridgeport, CT	
Fritz, Otto	5, Aug. 1886	17, July	19- 9m-24d	7		Altamont, IL	Atzenbach, Baden
Fritz, S. F. (Rev)	16, Mar. 1899	5, Mar.	59	169		Chicago, IL	Atzenbach, Baden
Fritz, Seraphin F. (Rev)	30, Mar. 1899	5, Mar.	59	207		Chicago, IL	
Fritze, Anna Maria	7, July 1887	17, June	23	430	Schlattmann	St. Paul, MN	
Fritze, Clara Louise	8, Jan. 1883	25, Dec.	1- 4m- 8d	15		Mountain Lake, MN	Lützlow, Angermünde, Potsdam, Preußen
Fritze, Gottfried	24, Feb. 1879	6, Feb.	63-10m- 5d	63		St. Paul, MN	Espenstadt, Frankenhausen, Preußen
Fritze, Johan Carl Christian	2, June 1892	12, May	70	350		Washington, MN	Detroit, Michigan
Fritze, Paul Wesley	21, May 1877	29, Apr.	26- 2m-23d	166		St. Paul, MN	Steinberg, Württemberg
Fritze, Rosina	25, Mar. 1886	12, Mar.	71	7	Schmidt	Bloomington, IL	Neustadt an der Orla, Sachsen-Weimar
Fritzschler, Bernhard	27, Sept 1855	31, July		156		Beardstown, IL	Naza, Sachsen-Gotha
Fröbe, Heinrich	21, Nov. 1861	29, Oct.	40	188		Beardstown, IL	Beardstown, Illinois
Fröbe, Karl	5, Oct. 1874		17- 6m	319		San Jose, IL	Hitzhausen, Hannover
Fröbe, Maria	22, Apr. 1858	31, Mar.	33	64	Steiner	Peoria, IL	Schweiz
Fröbisch, Barbara	17, Dec. 1896	17, Nov.	83	814		Trail Run, OH	Schweiz
Fröbisch, Barbara	14, Jan. 1897	27, Nov.	83	814		Trail Run, OH	Monroe County, Ohio
Fröbisch, Maggie	24, Mar. 1884	10, Mar.	20	7	Heinlein	Trail Run, OH	Bern, Schweiz
Fröbisch, Marie	8, Mar. 1860	21, Jan.	36- 8m- 9d	40	Krummer	Hannibal, OH	Unterurbach, Schorndorf, Württemberg
Fröbisch, Rosina	1, Mar. 1869	17, Jan.	73	71	Walter	Woodville, OH	Babenhausen, Amt Seesen, Braunschweig
Fröbose, August	15, Feb. 1864	15, Nov.	23	28		Perrysburg, OH	Rehme, Minden, Preußen
Frodermann, Christine	30, Apr. 1896	1, Apr.	73	286	Steinkämper	Berger, MO	
Frodermann, Ernst Friedrich	29, Dec. 1873	25, Nov.	25- 6m-23d	415		Herman, MO	Schnectady, New York
Frödert, Maria Louise	23, Aug. 1880	1, Aug.	28	271	Müller	Delhi, MI	
Froebe, Clara	17, Apr. 1882	5, Mar.	18- 4m	127		Pekin, IL	Eltingen, Leonberg, Württemberg
Froeschle, John	23, June 1887	21, May	65	398		Higginsville, MO	Mahrdorf, Kurhessen
Froewerd, Charlotte	11, Dec. 1856	9, Nov.	27	200	Kleinschmidt	St. Louis, MO	Zouny, Posen, Preußen
Fröhlich, Catharina Elisabeth	19, Aug. 1867	24, July	36	262	Gutheil	Giard, IA	Wagenfeld, Amt Diebholz, Hannover
Fröhlich, Eduard A.	15, Nov. 1875	1, Nov.	71- 6m- 5d	367		Kendallville, IN	Baßfeld, Hamberg, Kurhessen
Fröhlich, Georg	31, Aug. 1868	13, July	43	279		Metropolis, IL	Gumbrechofen, Niederbronn, Elsaß
Fröhlich, Heinrich	10, Sept 1896	6, Aug.	84	591		Giard, IA	Heringen, Hersfeld, Kurhessen
Fröhlich, Jakob	19, May 1892	23, Apr.	69- 5m- 2d	80		Captina, OH	Dielsdorf, Zürich, Schweiz
Fröhlich, Katharina	8, Nov. 1875	4, Oct.	74	359		Cincinnati, OH	Ober-Durla, Preußen
Fröhly, Heinrich	15, May 1851	28, Apr.	39- 5m	80		Louisville, KY	Zinsweiler, Elsaß
Frohn, Valentin	17, Feb. 1859	7, Dec.	32- 3m- 3d	28		Canton, MO	
Frölig, Maria Elisabeth	30, Dec. 1878	13, Dec.	86	415	Schauerin	Clarington, OH	

Christliche Apologete Death Notices --- 1839 - 1899

Name of Deceased	Notice Date	Death Date	Age	Maiden Name	Page	Place of Death	Place of Birth
Fröll, Christian	10, July 1846	10, Dec.	Inquiry		111	Baltimore, MD	Württemberg
Frommel, Friedrich Theodor	9, Feb. 1874		62		47	Buffalo, NY	Kirchberg, Koblenz, Preußen
Frömming, Engel	2, May 1895	15, Apr.	83	Schultz	286	Ahnapee, WI	Rowe, Hinterpommern
Frömming, Karl	19, Apr. 1894	15, Mar.	18		262	Ahnapee, WI	Ahnapee, Wisconsin
Frömming, Karoline	1, Aug. 1870	29, Apr.	24	Pflughöft	247	Ahnapee, WI	Camin bei Treptow, HinterPommern
Frop, Margaretha	24, Jan. 1871	23, Dec.	50		31	Leland, MI	
Frosch, Peter	18, June 1891	26, May	65		398	Peoria, IL	KlosterHimmelkron, Germany
Fröschle, Frieda	2, Feb. 1893	16, Jan.	68- 3m-29d	Rindel	78	Higginsville, MO	Eldingen, Lehrberg, Württemberg
Fröse, Martin	12, Aug. 1886	25, July	26		7	Detroit, MI	Neu-Rognischen, West Preußen
Fröwert, Herman	6, May 1872	17, Mar.	45		151	St. Louis, MO	Oberhausen, Lippe-Detmold
Frühling, Friedrich	19, Sept 1895	27, Aug.	66		606	Warsaw, IL	Rheden, Gronau, Hannover
Frühling, Maria	13, Aug. 1877	21, July	31	Orth	263	Warsaw, IL	
Frühling, Wilhelm	13, Oct. 1898	20, Sept	68		655	San Jose, CA	Glittendorf bei Breslau, Germany
Frühling, Wilhelm Friedrich	6, Aug. 1891	27, June	26		510	Burlington, IA	
Fründ, John	7, Apr. 1884	19, Mar.	61		7	Baraboo, WI	Groß-Gören, Mecklenburg-Schwerin
Frutig, Katharine	24, Jan. 1876	9, Sept		Blasser	31	Muscatine, IA	
Fry, Benjamin St.James (Rev)	11, Feb. 1892	5, Feb.	67		88	St. Louis, MO	Rutland, Tennessee
Fry, Eduard	28, July 1898	28, June	28		479	Madison, IN	
Fry, Eva	31, Dec. 1883	17, Dec.	47- 7m-14d		7	Hooker, NE	
Fuchs, Adam	13, June 1864	14, Apr.	18		96	Seymour, IN	Mössingen, Rothenburg, Württemberg
Fuchs, Agnes	23, June 1892	31, May	63	Reth	398	Hannibal, Mo	
Fuchs, Anna	8, Oct. 1891	21, Sept	35- 2m-12d	Klein	654	Rome, IN	Nordheim bei Worms, Hessen-Darmstadt
Fuchs, Anna Margaretha	22, Nov. 1869	27, Oct.	60	Held	375	Clarington, OH	Oberlenningen, Kirchheim, Württemberg
Fuchs, Anna Maria	25, June 1877	30, May	76- 5m-22d	Reichle	207	Norborne, MO	
Fuchs, Elisabeth	22, Mar. 1880	5, Mar.	70	Sachsen	95	Rochester, NY	Rochester, New York
Fuchs, Friedrich	6, Apr. 1899	18, Feb.	39		222	Hannibal, OH	Oberlinningen, Württemberg
Fuchs, Gottlieb	19, Oct. 1899	5, Oct.	62		671	Seymour, IN	
Fuchs, Heinrich	26, June 1871	6, June	23- 1m		207	Lexington, KY	
Fuchs, Heinrich	28, Oct. 1872	29, Sept	35-11m- 4d		351	Oregon, MO	
Fuchs, Johannes	18, Nov. 1878	2, Nov.	57		367	Charlestown, IN	Auggen, Mühlheim, Baden
Fuchs, John	14, Nov. 1881	5, July	28		367	Lexington, MO	Taycheedah, Fon du Lac County, Wisconsin
Fuchs, John	30, Apr. 1891	1, Apr.	65		286	Oakland, CA	Monsheim, Worms, Hessen-Darmstadt
Fuchs, John	13, July 1874	27, June	66- 6m- 2d		223	Cincinnati, OH	Mainzlar bei Gießen, Hessen
Fuchs, Julie M.	4, June 1891	18, Apr.	30- 7m- 4d		366	Marion, OH	
Fuchs, Karl Ludwig	21, Dec. 1893	20, Nov.	39	Engelhart	814	San Francisco, CA	Cüstrin, Preußen
Fuchs, Katharina	8, May 1865	30, Mar.	31	Ammann	76	Marion, OH	Roßwak, Vaihingen, Württemberg
Fuchs, Katharine	9, Aug. 1869	11, July	43- 3m-18d		255	Chicago, IL	Lanschied, Homburg, Hessen
Fuchs, Magdalena Susanna	8, Jan. 1877	22, Dec.	88- 7m-16d		15	Hannibal, MO	Häffnerhaslach, Brakenheim, Württemberg
Fuchs, Margaretha	1, Jan. 1866	10, Dec.	68- 5m- 8d	Hof	6	Cincinnati, OH	Basel, Schweiz
Fuchs, Maria Katharina	9, Feb. 1899	8, Jan.	70	Gwinner	95	Allegheny City, PA	Liebenzell, Calw, Württemberg
Fuchs, Sophie	30, Oct. 1890	13, Oct.	53		702	Edewecht, GE	Uchte, Hannover
Fuegli, Johan Caspar	11, Nov. 1878	20, Oct.	68		359	Allegheny City, PA	Zürich, Zürich, Schweiz
Füffstück, Wilhelm	23, Apr. 1896	22, Feb.	74	Reif	270	Allegheny City, PA	Nestebach, Zürich, Schweiz
Fügli, Margaretha	20, July 1885	30, June	83		7	St. Louis, MO	AltStatten bei Zürich, Schweiz
Fügli, Pauline	15, Nov. 1888	15, Oct.	42- 1m- 7d		734		Melle, Gröneberg, Hannover
Fuhe, Johanna Maria Dorothea	4, Sept 1890	7, Aug.	86		574		

Christliche Apologete Death Notices --- 1839 - 1899

Name of Deceased	Notice Date	Death Date	Age	Maiden Name	Page	Place of Death	Place of Birth
Fuhlmann, Wilhelmine	25, Mar. 1897	7, Mar.	84		190	Wrayville, IL	Beitiko bei Prenzlau, Germany
Fuhr, Friedrich	10, Nov. 1879	25, Oct.	68		359	Spencer, IA	Neunkirchen, Amt Rennerod, Nassau
Fuhr, Louise	25, Feb. 1867	25, Jan.	16		62	Sandwich, IL	Neukirchen, Nassau
Führer, Andreas	30, May 1889	12, May	63		350	Dalton, MO	Elsaß
Führer, August	22, Sept 1884	31, Aug.	75		7	New Robinson, OH	Hohensolms, Wetzlar, Coblenz, RheinPreußen
Führer, Elisabeth	2, Apr. 1877	11, Mar.	67- 8m	Führer	111	Galion, OH	Hohensolms, Wetzlar, Coblenz, Preußen
Führer, Heinrich	21, Mar. 1864	17, Nov.	20-4m- 2d		48	Galion, OH	
Fuhrmann, Anna Margaretha	9, May 1895	9, Apr.	55	Alles	302	Muskegon, MI	Unterschwarz, Hessen
Fuhrmann, Heinrich Louis	26, Apr. 1880	8, Apr.	22		135	Milwaukee, WI	Kirchheim, Wisconsin
Fuhrmann, Joachim	27, Nov. 1871	11, Nov.	77		383	Columbus, WI	Muchow, Amt Neustadt, Mecklenburg-Schwerin
Fuhrmann, Joachim Friedrich	31, Oct. 1864	5, Oct.	47		176	Columbus, WI	Barkow, Amt Neustadt, Mecklenburg-Schwerin
Fuhrmann, Johan	10, Sept 1866		44		294	Columbus, WI	Muchow, Mecklenburg-Schwerin
Fülle, Rosina	16, May 1864	12, Apr.	39		80	Wheeling, WV	Culmitzsch, Neustätter, Sachsen-Weimar
Fulmer, Sophia	22, July 1872	1, June	56		239	San Jose, CA	Paderborn, Preußen
Funck, Maria Margaret	2, Dec. 1897	28, Oct.	84	Kriechbauen	767	Burlington, IA	Oberhausen, Hessen-Darmstadt
Funk, L.	21, Nov. 1889	25, Oct.	44	Krauß	750	St. Paul, MN	
Funk, Anna	1, Nov. 1894	4, Oct.	34	Wichmann	710	Mascoutah, IL	
Funk, Anna M.	13, May 1886	22, Apr.	29	Farow	7	St. Paul, MN	Galena, Illinois
Funk, Charlotte Wilhelmine	30, Dec. 1878	28, Mar.	53		415	Madison, WI	Straßburg, Uckermark, Preußen
Funk, Christoph	6, May 1878	28, Mar.	69- 8m		143	Fox Lake, WI	Nierenstein, Hessen-Darmstadt
Funk, Daniel M.	28, Jan. 1886	5, Jan.	57		7	Wilton, IA	Pennsylvania
Funk, Dietrich	11, Oct. 1875	29, Sept	49		327	Pinckneyville, IL	Amt Eppingen, Baden
Funk, Jacob	9, Sept 1886	16, Aug.	78		7	East Troy, WI	Schwind, Galdorf, Württemberg
Funk, Jane	13, June 1895	22, May	54- 2m-14d		382	Hamline, MN	
Funk, Johan Adam	18, June 1877	8, May	70		199	Burlington, IA	Altheim, Hessen-Darmstadt
Funk, Johan Heinrich	28, Dec. 1899	7, Nov.	53		828	Muscatine, IA	Neuland, Freiburg, Hannover
Funk, Karolina	25, Dec. 1890	1, Dec.	79- 8m- 1d	Hamm	830	East Troy, WI	Engenheim bei Straßburg, Elsaß
Funk, Katharine	8, Dec. 1892		36	Hersch	782	Clay Center, KS	Gibelstadt, Baiem
Funk, Louisa Maria	30, June 1892	4, May	28	Fenske	414	Kenosha, WI	Bristol, Kenosha County, Wisconsin
Funk, Philipp (Rev)	26, Apr. 1894	3, Apr.	75- 6m-28d		278	St. Paul, MN	Spitzaltheim, Dieburg, Hessen-Darmstadt
Funk, Rosina	12, Aug. 1858	11, July	16		128	East Troy, WI	
Funk, Rosine	3, Sept 1883	16, Aug.	80- 5m- 1d		287	East Troy, WI	Spielhof, Gaildorf, Württemberg
Funk, Wilhelm Fr.	12, Aug. 1878	17, July	34		255	East Troy, WI	Philadelphia, Pennsylvania
Funke, Josepha	7, Nov. 1889	10, Oct.	60	Barthels	718	Seguin, TX	Hausten-Eichsfeld, Sachsen
Funkler, Wilhelmine	1, Dec. 1884	14, Nov.	65		7	Danville, IL	Groß Breitenbach, Schwarzburg-Sondershausen
Fürbaum, Catharina Elisabeth	30, Nov. 1868	13, Nov.	52- 8m- 5d	Gunstmann	383	Birmingham, PA	Niedermeiser, Gräbenstein, Kurhessen
Furman, Rosa	25, June 1883	11, May	27		207	Wawaka, IN	Chautauqua County, New York
Furmann, Catharina	24, June 1858	31, May	64		100	New Albany, IN	Haag, bei Baireuth, Baiem
Furrer, Dorothea	10, June 1897	4, May	28		367	Houston, TX	Catspring, Texas
Furrer, Elisabeth	9, Oct. 1882	26, Sept	36	Huber	327	Waco, TX	Fehradorf, Zürich, Schweiz
Furrer, Emma	20, Nov. 1882	2, Oct.			375	Savannah, GA	
Fürst, Elisabeth	18, Feb. 1867	24, Jan.	39	Boß	54	Buffalo, IA	Krindelwald, Bern, Schweiz
Fürst, Georg Jacob	2, Feb. 1893	6, Jan.	85		78	Canton, MO	Zeiskam, Germersheim, Rheinpfalz Baiem
Fürst, Sabina	15, Mar. 1888	16, Feb.	75		174	Champaign, IL	Cumberland County, Pennsylvania
Fürste, Friedrich	27, Aug. 1866	13, Aug.	37		278	Cincinnati, OH	Dielingen, Kreis Libke, Preußen
Fürste, Julie	19, Nov. 1896	24, Oct.	59		750	Cincinnati, OH	Annweiler, Rheinpfalz Baiem

Christliche Apologete Death Notices --- 1839 - 1899

Name of Deceased	Notice Date	Death Date	Age	Page	Maiden Name	Place of Death	Place of Birth
Fürstenau, Heinrich Theodor	11, July 1889	15, May	6	446		Elkton, SD	Devin, Pommern
Fürstenberg, Johan Carl Christian	30, Jan. 1871	24, Dec.	52	39		Charlestown, WI	Wiesloch, Baden
Fürstenberger, Franz	11, Oct. 1894		68	662		Terre Haute, IN	Lehigh County, Pennsylvania
Fürstenberger, Sophia	10, July 1890	14, June	62	446	Schneider	Terre Haute, IN	Ammendorf, Kadolsburg, Mittel-Franken, Baiern
Fürster, Peter Johan	6, Apr. 1863	9, Feb.	33	56		LaCrosse, WI	Louisville, Jefferson County, Kentucky
Furter, Hieronymus	29, Sept 1887	18, Sept	19	622		Louisville, KY	Hohenwettersbach, Durlach, Baden
Fuß, Elisabeth	11, Oct. 1855	24, May	51	164		Newark, NJ	Weißenburg, Elsaß
Fuß, Magdalena	8, Nov. 1880	16, Sept	45- 8m-10d	359	Lipp	Newark, NJ	
Fuß, Rosine	9, June 1862	1, May	59- 6m-18d	92		Newark, NJ	
Füßele, Agatha	1, Dec. 1898	29, Oct.	72	767	Harlin	Dallas City, IL	Schuflenheim, Frankreich
Füßler, Anna Elisabeth Wilhelmina	9, Feb. 1874	27, Jan.	70	47	Holzhauser	Terre Haute, IN	Kreis Nassau, Preußen
Füßler, Johan Adam	10, May 1880	15, Apr.	79	151		Terre Haute, IN	Bischofsheim, Hessen-Darmstadt
Füßler, Louise	30, June 1873	8, June	40	207	Wedemeier	Terre Haute, IN	Herenhausen bei Seesen, Braunschweig
Gaas, Henriette	27, July 1854	30, June	52	120		Dayton, OH	Culmbach, Baiern
Gabardeal, Katharina	14, Feb. 1850	26, Jan.	22- 4m	28	Rühle	Delaware, OH	
Gabathuler, Margaretha	22, July 1878	9, July	29- 6m- 3d	231		Morrison, MO	Graubündten, Schweiz
Gabbert, Mina	8, Sept 1887	23, July	31	574	Badtcke	LaCrosse, WI	Großchensen, Filehne, Preußen
Gäbe, Heinrich	10, Feb. 1898	21, Jan.	69	94		Nashville, IL	Arrenkamp, Dielingen, Minden, Preußen
Gabel , Maria Magdalena	24, Sept 1891	2, Sept	65	622	Umdenstock	Pekin, IL	Mittelweyh, Elsaß
Gabel, Johan	18, Mar. 1878	24, Feb.	42	87		Lexington, MO	Nieste, Kaufungen, Kurhessen
Gabel, Sarah Lydia	4, Nov. 1872	1, Oct.	14- 6m	359		Pekin, IL	
Gäbele, Johan M.	15, Dec. 1884	2, Nov.		7		Alma, WI	
Gäbele, Michael	27, Oct. 1887	18, Sept	28-10m-18d	686		Buffalo Co, WI	Neuburg Lauben, Schwaben, Baiern
Gabelmann, Martha Louise	12, Nov. 1891	23, Oct.	24-11m	734		Portsmouth, OH	Belvedere, Buffalo County, Wisconsin
Gabelmann, Philipp	27, Jan. 1898	6, Jan.	74	63		Portsmouth, OH	Rechenhausen, Rheinpfalz Baiern
Gaberdiel, Susanna	11, Aug. 1853	23, July	28- 1m	128	Jacoby	Bethlehem,	
Gabirel, Susanna	3, Jan. 1861	18, Dec.	28- - 2d	4	Keagy	Wilton, IA	Bedford County, Pennsylvania
Gabler, Dorothea	26, June 1876	31, May	78- 3m-15d	207	März	Marion, OH	Mühlhausen am Neckar, Cannstadt, Württemberg
Gabler, Dorothea	10, July 1876	31, May	78- 3m-15d	223	Wörz	Marion, OH	Mühlhausen am Neckar, Cannstadt, Württemberg
Gabler, Friedrich	5, Apr. 1888	16, Mar.	68- 6m-23d	222		Portsmouth, OH	Mühlhausen, Cannstatt, Württemberg
Gabler, Jakob	31, July 1876	16, July	21- 9m-22d	247		Portsmouth, OH	
Gabler, Johan Georg	4, Sept 1882	7, Aug.	86- 3m-11d	287		Marion, OH	Mühlhausen am Neckar, Cannstatt, Württemberg
Gabler, Wilhelm Wesley	26, Nov. 1896	2, Oct.	13	766		Wheelersburg, OH	Wheelersburg, Ohio
Gabrants, Johan	29, Nov. 1894	20, Oct.	61	774		Emden, IL	Schwerum, Ostfriesland
Gabriel, Anna Elisabeth	13, Sept 1875	18, Aug.	53	295		Victor, IA	Bottegern, Kurhessen
Gabriel, David	7, Dec. 1874	13, Nov.	40- 4m-25d	391		Friendship, WI	Lux, Amt Rheinbischofsheim, Baden
Gabriel, Elisabeth	31, May 1880	29, Apr.	93	175		Wilton, IA	Altenbrunslar, Kurhessen
Gabriel, Elisabeth	12, Oct. 1893	3, Sept	34	654	Fisch	Victor, IA	Muscatine County, Iowa
Gabriel, Elise	17, Apr. 1882	22, Mar.	38	127	Schneider	Eudora, KS	Spietz, Bern, Schweiz
Gabriel, Heinrich	31, May 1880	2, May	55	175		Wilton, IA	Altenbrunslar, Kurhessen
Gabriel, Maria Rosine	6, Nov. 1871	28, Sept	67	359		Eudora, KS	Werrwitz, Schlesien, Preußen
Gackstetter, Wilhelm Johan	25, July 1895	10, July	33	478		Salem, MN	InverGrove, Dakota County, Minnesota
Gaebe, Louise	3, Dec. 1896		40- 9m-10d	782	Kiepe	Farmington, MO	Farmington, Missouri
Gaffner, Abraham	10, July 1890	20, June	58-11m-27d	446		Highland, IL	St. Beatenberg, Bern, Schweiz
Gaffner, Abraham	11, Oct. 1880	25, Sept	42	327		Highland, IL	St. Beatenberg, Bern, Schweiz

Christliche Apologete Death Notices --- 1839 - 1899

Name of Deceased	Notice Date	Death Date	Age	Page	Maiden Name	Place of Death	Place of Birth
Gaffner, Christian	19, Oct. 1893	26, Aug.	50	670		Highland, IL	Badenberg, Bern, Schweiz
Gaffner, Elisabeth	1, Mar. 1894	7, Feb.		150	Almen	Highland, IL	St. Beatenberg, Bern, Schweiz
Gaffner, Jakob	15, Sept 1887	10, Aug.	49-4m	590		Highland, IL	St. Beienberg, Hinderlache, Bern, Schweiz
Gaffner, Jakob	20, Jan. 1879	27, Dec.	67-3m-16d	23		Highland, IL	St. Reutenberg, Bern, Schweiz
Gaffner, Rosa	19, Oct. 1874	18, Sept	22-7m-20d	335	Weber	Hickland, IL	Menzken, Aargau, Schweiz
Gägel, Johan Friedrich	11, Nov. 1897	19, Oct.	76	719		Louisville, KY	Bedstadt, Baiern
Gagel, John Heinrich	16, Apr. 1883	4, Mar.	24	127		Louisville, KY	Louisville, Jefferson County, Kentucky
Gagstetter, Amanda Julia	27, July 1899	10, July	27	479		Minneapolis, MN	Empire, Dakota County, Minnesota
Gagstetter, Johan Michael	11, Feb. 1897	16, Jan.	87	94		Salem, MN	Breden, Württemberg
Gahl, Adolph Lewis	17, July 1890	15, June	51-8m-27d	462		Albert Lea, MN	Wolgast, Vorpommern
Gahl, Wilhelmine	3, May 1894	3, Apr.	73	294	Siegert	Albert Lea, MN	Futzow, Vorpommern
Gahn, Adam	21, Oct. 1878	4, Oct.	71	335		Charlestown, IN	Worms, Hessen-Darmstadt
Gahn, Adam	29, Aug. 1850	11, Aug.	10	140		Columbus, OH	
Gahn, Conrad	17, Aug. 1893	27, July	75	526		Tiffin, OH	Nordheim, Hessen-Darmstadt
Gahn, Elisabeth	4, Jan. 1894	5, Dec.	89	14	Ordt	Sandusky, OH	Nordheim, Lensheim, Hessen-Darmstadt
Gahn, Margaretha	10, Nov. 1887	25, Oct.	78-2m-7d	718		Charlestown, IN	
Gährs, Meta Margaretha	29, June 1874	10, June	62	207	Papen	Lake Creek, MO	Dermstein, Rheinkreis Baiern
Gaier, Wilhelm	17, Oct. 1870	25, Sept	71	335		Woodville, OH	Wettad, Hessen-Homburg, Kurhessen
Gaiersbach, Dorothea	5, Aug. 1878	16, July	40	247	Glaßer	Delhi, MI	Aach, Amt Stockach, Baden
Gaißer, Amalia	17, Feb. 1859	20, Jan.	25	28		Lawrenceburg, IN	Waldheim, Sachsen
Gaitzsch, John Fr.	17, Feb. 1887	31, Jan.	40	110		Red Bud, IL	
Gall, Agnes	21, Apr. 1887	27, Mar.	78	254	Fiesel	Lansing, MI	Remmingsheim bei Rottenburg, Württemberg
Gall, Elisabeth	5, Mar. 1891	11, Feb.	75	158	Rieger	Chicago, IL	Wilhelmshuld bei Danzig, West Preußen
Gall, Hanna	22, Apr. 1897	31, Mar.	98-7m-29d	254	Degener	Oconomowoc, WI	Plantikow, Naugard, Pommern
Gall, Heinrich	10, Jan. 1895	11, Dec.	24	30		Milwaukee, WI	Milwaukee, Wisconsin
Gall, Johan Friedrich	29, Mar. 1880		77	103		St. Paul, MN	Plantikow, Germany
Gall, Leonhardt	25, May 1893	26, Apr.	87	334		Lansing, MI	Affalterbach, Marbach, Württemberg
Gall, Louise	27, Nov. 1871	11, Nov.	70	383	Barfknecht	St. Paul, MN	Finkenwald bei Alt-Stettin, VorPommern
Gall, Marie	13, Dec. 1888	15, Nov.	84-9m-13d	798	Klett	Galena, IL	Dußlingen, Tüblingen, Württemberg
Gall, Mathilde	14, May 1896	19, Apr.	22	318		Milwaukee, WI	
Galles, Julius	13, Nov. 1890	24, Oct.	66	734		Lawrence, KS	
Gallmann, Louise	29, Sept 1898	24, Aug.	59	623	Deschler	Buffalo, NY	Erkenbrechsweiler, Württemberg
Galopp, Johan	29, Apr. 1878	11, Apr.	80	135		Milwaukee, WI	Buchholz, Vorpommern
Galtz, Anna Wilhelmine	7, Mar. 1889	26, Jan.	69-7m-1d	158		Zumbro Falls, MN	Koppesin, Wongrowitz, Bromberg, Posen
Gamber, Anna Maria	10, July 1871	26, May	53	223	Abel	Waverly, OH	Mechtersheim bei Sprien, Rheinpfalz Baiern
Gamer, Margaretha	14, Mar. 1870	17, Feb.	53	87		Chicago, IL	Graben, Baden
Games, Karl Ludwig	25, Nov. 1867		59	374		Wheeling, IL	Graben, Amt Karlsruhe, Baden
Gammerdinger, Elisabeth	23, Feb. 1899		47-6m-28d	127	Krämer	Columbus, OH	Columbus, Franklin County, Ohio
Gammesdinger, Flora Elisabeth	2, Jan. 1896	10, Nov.	21	14		Columbus, OH	
Gamp, Karl August	23, Nov. 1899	3, Nov.	77	751		Des Moines, IA	Stettin, Preußen
Gäng, Alois	23, Feb. 1899	11, Jan.	80	127		Lansing, IA	Buch, Walzhut, Baden
Gäng, Magdalena	20, Nov. 1876	6, Nov.		375	Tröndle	Lansing, IA	Buch, Amt Waldshut, Baden
Gangloff, Marie Dorothea	12, Jan. 1860	14, Aug.	80	8	Grünblatt	Laporte, IN	Dehlingen, Elsaß
Gans, Amelie	3, Sept 1896	3, Aug.	76	575		Cincinnati, OH	Heisebeck, Kurhessen
Ganschier, Catharina	31, Mar. 1873	11, Mar.	80	103	Ganscher	Madison, IN	Dietendorf, Trulingen, Elsaß
Ganschier, John Nikolaus	25, Feb. 1884	6, Feb.	92-1m	7		Madison, IN	Bischdorf, Elsaß

Christliche Apologete Death Notices --- 1839 - 1899

Name of Deceased	Notice Date	Death Date	Age	Page	Maiden Name	Place of Death	Place of Birth
Gansel, Frank H.	22, Oct. 1891	4, Sept	16	686		West Bend, WI	Patavia, Wisconsin
Gansel, Franz	8, Oct. 1891	4, Sept	16- 8m- 4d	654		Scott, WI	Scott, Sheboygan County, Wisconsin
Gansel, Franz	19, Nov. 1896	19, Oct.	75	750		Milwaukee, WI	Preußen
Ganske, Dorothea Sophia	22, Apr. 1872	11, Feb.	58	135	Tank	Kenosha, WI	Brallenthin, Pommern
Gänsle, Bernhard	19, Dec. 1870	3, Dec.	53	407		Greenville, OH	Messingen, Württemberg
Ganß, Heinrich Wilhelm	23, June 1862	25, Mar.	44- 2m-22d	100		Mt. Pleasant, OH	Geisselwerder, Amt Weckerhagen, Kurhessen
Ganß, Karolina	19, Mar. 1877	22, Feb.	59- 6m- 5d	95		Cincinnati, OH	Hesebeck, Kurhessen
Gänßle, Gottlob	11, June 1896	20, May	56	383		Holt, MI	Waldorf, Nagold, Württemberg
Gänßle, Katharine	24, Nov. 1884	9, Nov.	64	7	Hoch	Greenville, OH	Möstringen, Rottenburg, Württemberg
Ganßly, Maria	1, Jan. 1891	30, Nov.	23- 8m-23d	14		Lansing, MI	
Gantschier, Johann	26, May 1859	17, Feb.	44	84		Madison, IN	Elsaß
Gantz, Gottfried	17, Apr. 1882	3, Mar.	48- 3m	127		New York City, NY	Homberg bei Kassel, Hessen
Gantz, Johanna	14, July 1887	29, June	54- - 5d	446		New York City, NY	Kleinwaldstädt, Baiern
Gantz, Margaretha	15, Mar. 1888	11, Feb.	76	174	Schmidt	Marietta, OH	Vorden-Windenthal, Baiern
Ganz, August	10, Aug. 1863	22, May	19- 2m-20d	128		Union, MO	
Ganz, Christina Wilhelmine	19, Sept 1870	24, July	84	303		Indianapolis, IN	Kesselwerther, Kurhessen
Ganz, Georg	15, May 1890		75- 5m-18d	318		Bonn, OH	Dolar, Wetzlar, Preußen
Ganzel, Ambrose	8, Apr. 1886	16, Mar.	34	7		---, WI	Johnstown, Fulton County, New York
Ganzhorn, Friederike	29, Mar. 1888	14, Mar.	64	206	Finter	Jeffersonville, IN	Oberniebelsbach, Neuenkirch, Württemberg
Ganzhorn, Gottlieb	9, Oct. 1876	4, Sept	51	327		Jeffersonville, IN	Unterniebelsbach, Neuenbürg, Württemberg
Gapizinski, Auguste	11, Sept 1882	10, June	37	295	Streewer	Schnectady, NY	Hamburg, Germany
Gapp, Friedrich	3, Aug. 1893	20, June	28- 4m-13d	494		Troy, NY	Lothringen
Gar, Johanne	12, Jan. 1863	14, Sept	68	8		Valparaiso, IN	
Garber, Geske	4, Mar. 1886	4, Feb.	72	7		Petersburg, IL	Moordorf, Aurich, Ostfriesland
Garbers, Marie	6, Oct. 1862	5, Sept	7- 4m	160		Petersburg, IL	
Garbig, Maria S.	25, June 1896	3, June	66	415	Lotz	Greenville, OH	Haitz bei Gelnhausen, Kurhessen
Garbig, Nicolaus	10, July 1890	15, June	75- 7m-15d	446		Greenville, OH	Belstein, Neustadt, Hessen-Darmstadt
Gardner, Georg Thomas	12, Mar. 1877	28, Jan.	22-11m-13d	87		St. Charles, MO	Mittelbach, Baiern
Gardner, Katharina	27, Mar. 1856	21, Jan.	56	52		Poplar Ridge, OH	Ulmit, Kusel, Baiern
Gares, John	26, June 1890		80- 3m-27d	414		Stryker, OH	Tiffin Township, Defiance County, Ohio
Gares, Mary	28, Oct. 1897	15, Oct.	60	687	Heckmann	West Unity, OH	Baiern
Gares, Peter	21, Oct. 1897	30, Sept	61	671		West Unity, OH	Ulmeht, Kusel, Rheinpfalz Baiern
Gares, Sarah	7, Oct. 1897	15, Sept	81	639	Drumm	Stryker, OH	Blue Island, Illinois
Gargen, Minnie	30, Aug. 1894	8, Aug.	31	566	Senn	Milwaukee, WI	Schiers, Graubündten, Schweiz
Gäring, Barbara	2, Feb. 1874	12, Jan.	33	39	Balzer	German Creek, IA	Sachsen-Gotha
Gäring, Heinrich	7, Dec. 1874	19, Nov.	66	391		Dallas, IA	
Garmhausen, Dietrich Heinrich	15, Dec. 1873	20, Nov.	65	399		Batesville, IN	Kolerota, Amt Harbstädt, Hannover
Garms, Elisabeth	28, Feb. 1870	2, Feb.	44	71		New York City, NY	Leifferde, Amt Gifhorn, Hannover
Garms, Friedrich Wilhelm	17, Dec. 1883	26, Nov.	14	7		New York City, NY	New York
Garms, Jost	21, Dec. 1863	18, Oct.		204		Lansing, MI	Rhode, Hannover
Garms, Rosina	22, Dec. 1887	18, Feb.		814		Bellevue, MI	
Garner, Louisa Karolina	18, Nov. 1897	30, Oct.	54	735	Feldschneider	Chicago, IL	Lippe-Detmold
Garner, Minnie	23, Mar. 1893	24, Jan.	27	190	Menmann	Davenport, IA	Davenport, Iowa
Garnholz, Dietrich	25, Oct. 1894	29, Sept	71	694		Hoyleton, IL	Altenkamp, Oldenburg
Garnholz, Elise	11, Oct. 1894	22, Sept	55	662	Hake	Boody, IL	Edewecht, Oldenburg
Gärrmann, Christian	7, Oct. 1858	7, Sept		160		Huntingburg, IN	Bern, Schweiz

Christliche Apologete Death Notices --- 1839 - 1899

Name of Deceased	Notice Date	Death Date	Age	Maiden Name	Page	Place of Death	Place of Birth
Garstmann, (boy)	9, Mar. 1863		5		40	Quincy, IL	
Garstmann, (girl)	9, Mar. 1863		7		40	Quincy, IL	
Garstmann, Margaretha Elisabetha	28, Nov. 1864	12, Nov.	70	Hackmann	192	Quincy, IL	Sögeln, Amt Vörden, Hannover
Gärstner, Louise	27, Apr. 1874	19, Mar.	19- 5m	Bär	135	Greenville, NY	
Gartmann, Josua	20, June 1870	18, May	55		199	Madison, IN	Sculms, Graubünden, Schweiz
Gartmann, Ursula	14, Oct. 1878	24, Sept	79- 7m- 1d		327	Arena, WI	Sevelen, St. Gallen, Schweiz
Gärtner, Christian	30, Oct. 1890	27, Aug.	49- 7m		702	Schnectady, NY	Hille, Minden, Preußen
Gartz, Gottlieb	10, July 1890	20, June	62		446	Toledo, OH	Kleindipsow, Hinterpommern
Gartz, Louisa	11, Oct. 1875	18, Sept	73	Wedemeyer	327	Burlington, IA	Salzwedel, Magdeburg, Preußen
Gartz, Mathilda Charlotta A.	20, Oct. 1887	28, Sept	16		670	Toledo, OH	Starnitz, Pommern
Garz, J. Carl	15, Apr. 1852	20, Mar.	39		64	Cincinnati, OH	Havelberg, Preußen
Gas, Katharina	3, Aug. 1899	17, June	57	Metzger	495	Rochester, NY	Malterdingen, Baden
Gäschel, Christiana Friederika	15, June 1874	26, May	66- -14d		191	Saginaw, MI	Kirchberg, Sachsen
Gaß, Daniel	29, May 1876	10, May	55- 1m-10d		175	Pinckneyville, IL	Sachsen-Meiningen
Gaß, Friedrich Georg Frank	13, June 1895	20, May	25		382	Aurora, IL	Aurora , Illinois
Gaß, Ida Jola	6, Aug. 1891	12, July	23- 9m-13d		510	Aurora, IL	Aurora, Illinois
Gassel, Friedrich D.	20, Oct. 1898	30, Sept	29		670	Jordan, MN	Spring Lake Township, Scott County, Minnesota
Gasser, Johan	4, Sept 1890	16, Aug.	34		574	Kansas City, MO	Trutticken, Zürich, Schweiz
Gasser, Johan Georg	1, Dec. 1884	13, Nov.	46		7	Quincy, IL	Bahlingen, Ammendingen, Baden
Gasser, Nanke H.	29, May 1890	11, May	42	Aden	350	Osceola, NE	Holtrup , Hannover
Gassert, Martin	23, Oct. 1865	13, Aug.	26		172	Hokah, MN	
Gast, Justus	9, Jan. 1865	3, Aug.	25		8	Covington, KY	Salz-Uflen, Lippe-Detmold
Gast, Lena	20, Dec. 1894	20, Nov.	24	Stille	822	Klemme, IA	
Gast, Maria Hanna Sophie	26, Jan. 1893	21, Dec.	49	Krüger	62	Garner, IA	Atl-Steinorth, Hinterpommern
Gast, Minna	27, July 1885		11		7	Garner, IA	
Gastel, Anna Maria	14, Jan. 1878	19, Dec.	75		15	Pomeroy, OH	Oppra, Baiern
Gathmann, Johan Albert	21, Aug. 1882	6, Aug.	69		271	Batesville, IN	Wachendorf, Zicke, Hannover
Gatschet, Anna Maria	31, May 1869	13, May	57- 4m		175	Boonville, MO	
Gatt, Adolph Lorenz	1, Sept 1898	10, Aug.	26		559	Hedwigs Hill, TX	Llano County, Texas
Gatz, Fr.	21, Apr. 1873	20, Mar.	71		127	Burlington, IA	Brome, Hannover
Gatzke, Ida	30, Dec. 1886	16, Dec.	9		7	Grand Island, NE	
Gätzke, Louise	28, Mar. 1895	7, Mar.	39	Rhüde	206	Los Angeles, CA	Brownstown, Indiana
Gauck, Caroline	25, Apr. 1889	2, Apr.	41		270	Lawrence, KS	Barth, Pommern
Gaudian, Wilhelm Theodor	1, Jan. 1891	13, Nov.	30- 9m- 2d		14	Dallas, TX	
Gauding, Anna Maria	28, Feb. 1895	1, Feb.	72	Niemann	142	Baresville, OH	Engter, Hannover
Gauding, Caroline Maria	1, Jan. 1891	6, Dec.	74	Landwer	14	Greenville, OH	Melle, Osnabrück, Hannover
Gauding, Heinrich	5, Nov. 1891	23, Oct.	49		718	Indianapolis, IN	Cincinnati, Hamilton County, Ohio
Gauding, Katie	21, Apr. 1873	25, Mar.	14- 1m-16d		127	Richmond, IN	
Gauding, Louise	31, July 1871	9, Apr.	17		247	Baresville, OH	
Gauding, Wilhelmina Augustina	26, Mar. 1891	4, Mar.	32	Hartlieb	206	Baresville, OH	Balzholz, Nierlingen, Württemberg
Gauger, Wilhelm	21, Sept 1885	19, Aug.	55		7	Flood Creek, IA	Triglaff, Greifenberg, Pommern
Gaulke, Karoline	29, Oct. 1896	1, Oct.	80	Boneß	703	Spencer, IA	Gandelin bei Rolberg, Pommern
Gaulke, Mathilda	18, May 1893	27, Apr.	20		318	Oshkosh, WI	
Gaulke, Wilhelm	23, July1883	4, June	72		239	Sheldon, IA	Drose, Kößlin, Preußen
Gaumitz, Eleonora	21, Dec. 1893	30, Oct.	30	Michael	814	Merton, SD	
Gaumitz, Gottlieb	21, Jan. 1892	1, Dec.			46	Merton, SD	Sachsen

Christliche Apologete Death Notices --- 1839 - 1899

Name of Deceased	Notice Date	Death Date	Age	Page	Maiden Name	Place of Death	Place of Birth
Gaus, Heinrich	15, June 1854	6, May	35	96		Boonville, IN	Heezen, Kreis Bielefeld, Preußen
Gausmann, Friedrich	15, May 1890	25, Apr.	58	318		Washington, MO	Blasheim, Lübbecke, Minden, Preußen
Gauweiler, Margarethe	16, July 1891	27, June	61	462		Quincy, IL	Schwegenheim, Germersheim, Rheinpfalz Baiern
Gaverdiehl, Maria Eva	28, Feb. 1895	4, Feb.		142	Schaub	Spencerville, OH	Wiesloh, Baden
Gay, Christine	13, Dec. 1888	8, Nov.	72- 2m	798		New York City, NY	Grambath, Württemberg
Gayer, John G.	18, May 1899	22, Apr.	83	319		Spencerville, OH	Rosway, Vaihingen, Württemberg
Gebauer, Jacob	17, Apr. 1876	28, Mar.	37	127		Chicago, IL	Seigertshausen, Amt Neukirchen, Hessen-Kassel
Gebauer, Katharine Barbara	14, Aug. 1890	18, July	36	526		Waltersburg, IL	Pope County, Illinois
Gebaur, Johan Georg	29, Apr. 1872	12, Apr.	48	143		Golconda, IL	Häringen, Amt Friedewalt, Kurhessen
Gebbie, Emilie	23, Apr. 1891	2, Apr.	48- 4m-28d	270	Böshenz	Mascoutah, IL	St. Louis, Missouri
Gebelein, Bernhard	6, Aug. 1883	29, June	21-11m-25d	255		Rib Falls, WI	Lowmeyre, Wisconsin
Gebelein, Leonhart	18, Nov. 1878	3, Oct.	17	367		Wausau, WI	Ruttlitz, Brandenburg
Gebert, Dorothea	2, Oct. 1890	10, Sept	59- 6m-12d	638	Wolterdorf	Crow River, MN	Unter-Selbach, Oehringen, Württemberg
Gebert, Elizabeth	23, Jan. 1896		36-11m	62		Lawrence, MA	Liemelang, Brandenburg
Gebert, John	6, July 1899	18, May	69	431		Greenwood, MN	
Gebhard, Christian (Rev)	27, Feb. 1896	13, Jan.	67	142		Flora, MN	Pferdsfeld, RheinPreußen
Gebhard, Jacob	4, Oct. 1894	9, Sept	87	646		Marion, OH	Roswaag, Vaihingen an der Enz, Württemberg
Gebhard, Johan	11, Apr. 1889	14, Mar.	63	238		Giard, IA	Planig, Hessen-Darmstadt
Gebhard, Johan	11, Dec. 1890	17, Nov.	28	798		New Ulm, MN	Pferdsfeld, Preußen
Gebhard, Katharina	15, Nov. 1869	23, Oct.	36	367	Schuh	Minneapolis, MN	Rhaunen, Trier, RheinPreußen
Gebhard, Marie	6, Aug. 1866		34- 5m	254	Krois	Clayton, IA	
Gebhardt, Frank	25, Nov. 1886	29, Oct.	21- 5m	7		Beardstown, IL	Kuntlam, Vilzhofen, Baiern
Gebhardt, Friedrich Wilhelm	24, Sept 1883	3, Sept	14- 8m-12d	311		Beardstown, IL	Cass County, Illinois
Gebhardt, Johan	15, Dec. 1862	28, Jan.	22	200		Marion, OH	
Gebhart, Caroline	23, Feb. 1893	8, Apr.	18-1m-24d	126		Giard, IA	Roswaag, Vaihingen, Württemberg
Gebhart, Katharina	23, June 1887	19, Mar.	40	398	Baab	Canal Dover, OH	
Gebhart, Maria	27, Apr. 1899	29, Mar.	81	271	Rühl	Lansing, MI	Tuscarawas County, Ohio
Gebhart, Maria Sarah	19, Apr. 1880	23, Oct.	70- 5m-20d	127	Etzel	Marion, OH	Alteckendorf, Elsaß
Gebike, Albert Johan Friedrich	9, Nov. 1874	9, Jan.	57	359		Marietta, OH	Nußdorf, Vaihingen, Württemberg
Geckler, Elisabeth	25, Feb. 1892	9, July	51	126	Niemeier	Indianapolis, IN	Esperstadt, Schwarzburg-Rudolstadt
Geckler, Elisabeth	26, Sept 1850	21, Mar.	22- 3m	156		Waverly, OH	Hagerstown, Maryland
Geerdes, Bertha	6, Apr. 1885	18, Mar.	47	7	Braner	Sterling, NE	Strockhold, Ostfriesland
Geerken, Herman	14, Apr. 1873	11, July	33	119		Canaan, MO	Liesum, Amt Blumenthal, Hannover
Geertz, Christine	28, July 1892	18, Feb.	80	478	Jäger	Davenport, IA	Gut Aschberg, Holstein
Gegenheimer, Philipp	17, Mar. 1898	5, Nov.	78	175		Vermillion, OH	Ittersbach, Pforzheim, Baden
Gegenheimer, Susanna Katharina	27, Apr. 1899	3, Dec.	74	271		Vermillion, OH	Ittersbach, Pforzheim, Baden
Geggus, Jakob	11, Dec. 1846	17, Nov.	1- 5m	209		Louisville, KY	Lübeck, Germany
Geggus, Johanna	30, Dec. 1858	16, Nov.	39	208	Boldt	Louisville, KY	Oberamt Durlach, Baden
Geggus, Katharina	11, Dec. 1846	31, Mar.	61- 9m	209		Louisville, KY	Weingarten, Durlach, Baden
Geggus, Louis	7, Dec. 1893	17, Oct.	19- -17d	782		Louisville, KY	Sachsen-Weimar
Gegus, Jakob	13, Apr. 1885	19, June	74	7		Louisville, KY	
Gehb, Heinrich G.	7, Nov. 1881	25, Jan.	64- 2m-14d	359		New York City, NY	
Gehlken, Rebekka	14, July 1898		80	447	Bluhm	Smithton, MO	Bülsted, Otterberg, Hannover
Gehnheimer, Katharina Elisabeth	10, Feb. 1879		72	47	Klees	New Orleans, LA	
Gehri, Nikolaus	25, June 1883	4, June	64- 6m- 3d	207		Wheeling, WV	Seedorf, Beierberg, Bern, Schweiz
Gehrig, Katharina	29, Dec. 1879	13, Dec.	21	415	Spring	Hannibal, OH	New York

Christliche Apologete Death Notices --- 1839 - 1899

Name of Deceased	Notice Date	Death Date	Age	Page	Maiden Name	Place of Death	Place of Birth
Gehring, (Mr)	7, Oct. 1858	6, Sept		160		Oregon, MO	Brielingen, Amt Kissendorf, Hannover
Gehring, Carolina Dorothea	23, Feb. 1893	31, Jan.	69	126	Süsser	Rock Creek, SD	Althengstett, Calw, Württemberg
Gehring, Johan Michael	5, Nov. 1866	12, Sept	62	385		Wheeling, WV	Katzendorf, Sachsen-Weimar
Gehring, Karl Georg	20, July 1893	30, June	40	462		Rock Creek, SD	Alt-Hengstätt, Calw, Württemberg
Gehring, Rudolph	14, Aug. 1890	27, July	25	526		Waco, TX	Großziethen, Germany
Gehring, Sophia	9, May 1870	18, Mar.	69	151	Tillemann	Union, MO	Steinegge, Amt Sternberg, Lippe-Detmold
Gehring, Wilhelm	1, Jan. 1877		82	7		Beaufort, MO	Minden, Preußen
Gehring, William F.	20, July 1893	17, June	28	462		Wheeling, WV	Wheeling, West Virginia
Gehrke, Augusta	29, Sept 1887	16, Sept	51- 7m-21d	622	Kroschel	Minneapolis, MN	Altenflies, Brandenburg
Gehrke, Charlotte	21, Jan. 1886	24, Dec.	60	7	Bartelt	Maine, WI	Franz-Felde bei Golnau, Pommern
Gehrke, Lybbie	2, Apr. 1891	7, Mar.	35	222	Thaurer	Watertown, WI	Emmet, Dodge County, Wisconsin
Gehrke, Wilhelm G.	29, Jan. 1877	7, Jan.	65	39		Wausau, WI	Gamelsdorf bei Masow, Pommern
Gehrling, M. Magdalena Katharina	14, Apr. 1898	23, Mar.	74	239	Naumann	St. Louis, MO	Lüneburg, Hannover
Gehrmann, Philipp	20, Feb. 1890	26, Jan.	70	126		Quincy, IL	Alsbach, Hessen-Darmstadt
Gehrt, Emilie	3, Feb. 1898	11, Jan.	43	79	Berendt	Aurora, IL	Zerene, Kestlin, Pommern
Geib, Anna	19, Mar. 1896	28, Feb.	62	190	Moyer	Canal Dover, OH	Berks County, Pennsylvania
Geib, Augustine	21, Dec. 1893		52	814	Sander	Arlington, MN	
Geib, Karl	16, Apr. 1883	30, Mar.	33	127		Canal Dover, OH	Erie, Pennsylvania
Geibel, Anna Maria	22, Jan. 1861	4, Jan.	18-10m- 3d	16		Detroit, MI	Wachenheim, Dürkheim, Baiern
Geibel, Jeanette	15, Jan. 1866	25, Dec.	68	22		Detroit, MI	Schweiz
Geide, Jakob	20, Jan. 1873	16, Nov.	45	23		Canaan, IL	Obereisenhausen, Hessen-Darmstadt
Geier, Anna Maria	25, Feb. 1858		9	32		Platteville, WI	Bünzwangen, Württemberg
Geier, Christian	4, Feb. 1892	12, Jan.	76	78		Ellis Grove, IL	Waltersdorf, Sachsen-Weimar
Geier, Christiana	4, May 1874	12, Apr.	55	143	Rohleder	Florence, IL	Waltersdorf, Sachsen-Weimar
Geier, Christine	8, Sept 1898	28, July	72	575	Huber	Philadelphia, PA	Niederhofen, Brackenheim, Württemberg
Geier, Ferdinand	1, June 1863	20, Apr.	19	88		Red Bud, IL	Waltersdorf, Sachsen-Weimar
Geier, Georg	20, Sept 1869	14, Aug.	77	303		New Knoxville, OH	Litzelstein, Elsaß
Geige, August	29, July 1897	9, June	56	479		Troy, NY	Wildenbruch bei Bahn, Greiffenhagen, Pommern
Geiger, Adam	16, May 1881	21, Apr.	31	159		Red Bud, IL	Bieber bei Gelnhausen, Kurhessen
Geiger, Adam Georg	12, Dec. 1881	7, Nov.	68- 1d	399		Red Bud, IL	Johnson County, Kansas
Geiger, August	30, Jan. 1896	10, Jan.	30	78		Kansas City, KS	Obermuschelbach, Pforzheim, Baden
Geiger, Christina	21, July 1879	22, June	41- 5m- 8d	231	Roser	Carmi, IL	Ahstedt, Steinbrück, Hannover
Geiger, Christine	17, Dec. 1891	23, Nov.	65	814	Könnecker	Red Bud, IL	Heidingsheim, Württemberg
Geiger, Georg Friedrich	18, Dec. 1897	25, Jan.	70	111		Brooklyn, NY	Röhrich, Bieber, Hessen
Geiger, Gertrud	5, Nov. 1857	10, Oct.	71	180		Monroe, IL	
Geiger, Johan Peter	6, Sept 1894	19, Aug.	84	582		Spokane, WA	Quarten, St. Gallen, Schweiz
Geiger, Joseph	11, May 1874	8, Feb.	51-11m	151		Oregon, MO	Sulz, Lahr, Baden
Geiger, Karolina	11, May 1874	16, Feb.	41- 7m-29d	151	Holzworth	Oregon, MO	Waldenstein, Welzheim, Württemberg
Geiger, Katharina	30, Nov. 1868	20, Oct.	69	383	Veigel	Defiance, OH	Großingersheim, Württemberg
Geiger, Phillippine	14, Mar. 1889	14, Feb.	59	174	Mann	Stryker, OH	NiederAlben, RheinPreußen
Geile, Catharine	7, Apr. 1862	12, Mar.	72	56		Nashville, TN	Gechingen, Caln, Württemberg
Geils, Anna	23, Jan. 1890	2, Jan.	42	62		New Rochelle, NY	
Geinitz, Friedrich G.	26, May 1879	2, May	17- 9m-10d	167	Schötler	Roseville, MI	Oberschönhagen, Lippe-Detmold
Geise, Louise	3, May 1875	28, Dec.	53	143		Waterloo, WI	Dodge County, Wisconsin
Geise, Otto	30, June 1898	27, May	40	415		Castlewood, SD	
Geisel, (Mrs)	21, June 1855	5, May	79	100		Nashville, IL	Mörshausen, Spangenberg, Kurhessen

Christliche Apologete Death Notices --- 1839 - 1899

Name of Deceased	Notice Date	Death Date	Age	Maiden Name	Page	Place of Death	Place of Birth
Geisel, Anna Elisabeth	5, June 1871	8, May	64-7m	Nadler	183	Nashville, IL	Württemberg
Geisel, Dorothea	10, Jan. 1870	9, Sept	62		15	San Francisco, CA	Cincinnati, Hamilton County, Ohio
Geisel, Heinrich	18, Sept 1865	2, Sept	29		152	Nashville, IL	Mörschausen, Kurhessen
Geisel, Johan	11, Aug. 1879	25, July	72- 6m-17d		255	Mascoutah, IL	
Geisel, Johannes	11, Apr. 1870	20, Mar.	20- 6m-10d		119	Nashville, IL	
Geisel, John Conrad	6, Oct. 1887	8, Sept	19- 8m- 7d		638	New Palestine, IN	
Geisel, Justus	27, Aug. 1896	9, Aug.	66		559	Mascoutah, IL	Mörshausen, Melsungen, Kurhessen
Geisendörfer, Johan Michael	31, Dec. 1896	6, Dec.	69		844	Vermilion, OH	Kustenlohr, Baiern
Geiser, Abraham	9, Jan. 1871	24, Dec.	72- 8m-22d		15	Warrenton, MO	
Geiser, Maria	12, May 1892	9, Apr.	46		302	Pittsburg, PA	Canton Bern, Schweiz
Geiser, Susanna C.	15, Sept 1873	12, Aug.		Kloßner	295	Warrenton, MO	Dimtigen, Bern, Schweiz
Geißenhöfer, Rosina	25, Oct. 1869	24, Sept	66		343	Lansing, MI	Lippoldsweiler, Württemberg
Geißman, Jakob	10, Nov. 1884	30, Oct.	64		7	Louisville, KY	Niederlenz, Aargau, Schweiz
Geister, Friederike	25, Apr. 1870	25, Mar.	27- 3m-27d	Köttelhön	135	Sand Creek, MN	Eldena, Mecklenburg-Schwerin
Geistlich, G.	1, Feb. 1875	17, Jan.	78		39	Davenport, IA	Zimmersrode, Kreis Ziegenhain, Kurhessen
Geistweidt, Helene	10, Aug. 1899	11, July	67	Schammeier	511	Hedwigs Hill, TX	Arnsberg, Preußen
Geistweidt, Johan Heinrich	1, Oct. 1891	10, Sept	62		638	Llano, TX	Erntebrück, Arnsberg, Bitchenstein, Preußen
Geitz, Auguste	10, Aug. 1854	16, July	39	Baumann	128	Warsaw, IL	Kupferzell, Württemberg
Geitz, Sophia	9, Mar. 1899	13, Feb.	77	Lorenz	159	Warsaw, IL	Kitzingen, Baiern
Geiwitz, Heinrich	1, Nov. 1888	5, Oct.	70		702	Jordan, MN	
Gekle, Jakob Fr.	15, Sept 1884	23, Aug.	56		7	Bloomfield, NJ	Bernbach, Neuenbürg, Württemberg
Gekus, Louise	16, Aug. 1849	24, July	38		132	Cincinnati, OH	
Gelbreth, Anna Maria	14, Feb. 1870	16, Jan.	31- 8m-14d		55	Madison, IN	Cincinnati, Hamilton County, Ohio
Gelhaus, Wilhelm	21, Oct. 1852	4, July	30- - 8d		172	Evansville, IN	Silbach, Lippe
Gellert, Anna	28, Jan. 1897	3, Dec.	41	Inderstroodt	62	Brenham, TX	Cincinnati, Hamilton County, Ohio
Geltmeier, Caroline	1, Oct. 1891	12, Sept	22	Möller	638	Perry, TX	Germany
Gemecker, Johan Konrad	17, Aug. 1885	11, July	74		7	Bradford, IN	Stanheim, Hessen
Gemeker, Andreas	14, May 1891	23, Apr.	79		318	Oregon, MO	Gundersheim, Hessen-Darmstadt
Gemeker, Maria B.	27, July 1893	11, July	74		478	Oregon, MO	
Gemke, Anton	27, Mar. 1876	2, Mar.	65		103	Rosemount, MN	Finsenbeck, Preußen
Gemlich, Georg	20, Feb. 1862	1, Feb.	13- -22d		32	Boonville, IN	
Gemlich, Heinrich	27, May 1858	25, Apr.	32- 7m		84	Boonville, MO	Kirchheim, Grienstadt, Rheinkreis Baiern
Gemlich, Karl	9, Apr. 1883	27, Mar.	21- 7m-10d		119	Boonville, IN	
Gemlich, Maria Magdalena	4, Oct. 1894	7, Sept	32	Franz	646	Boonville, IN	Spencer County, Indiana
Gemlich, Peter Phillip	3, Jan. 1876	10, Dec.	52- 9m-18d		7	Boonville, IN	Kirchheim an der Eck, Rheinkreis Baiern
Gemmecke, Wilhelm	4, Dec. 1865	8, Oct.	64		196	Poland, IN	Hombressen, Hessen-Kassel
Gemmecker, Margaretha	19, May 1884		78	Bickel	7	Bradford, IN	Bleichenbach, Nida, Hessen-Darmstadt
Gemmer, August	26, Dec. 1861	16, Oct.	18- 1m-23d		208	Decatur, IL	
Gemmer, Christina	23, June 1862	6, June	14- 5m		100	Decatur, IL	
Gemming, August	26, Feb. 1883	1, Feb.	71		71	Beardstown, IL	Mußbach bei Neustadt an der Haardt, Preußen
Gemming, Katharina	22, Aug. 1889	9, Aug.	84- 9m- 4d	Buchmüller	542	Beardstown, IL	Musbach, Neustadt a. d. Hardt, Rheinkreis Baiern
Geng, Anna Maria	10, Dec. 1891	10, Sept	44	Kraft	798	New Haven, CT	Breitenholz, Herrenberg, Württemberg
Genheimer, Agnes Madora	13, Sept 1894	20, Aug.	17-10m- 7d		598	Pomeroy, OH	Pomeroy, Ohio
Genheimer, Barbara	22, Aug. 1850	3, Aug.	18-11m		136	Pomeroy, OH	
Genheimer, Hanna	13, Nov. 1856	30, Sept	25		184	Washington, ---	Marmheim, Rheinkreis Baiern
Genheimer, Katharina	9, Feb. 1885	27, Jan.	78	Schlägel	7	Pomeroy, OH	Edigheim, Frankenthal, Rheinkreis Baiern

- 144 -

Christliche Apologete Death Notices --- 1839 - 1899

Name of Deceased	Notice Date	Death Date	Age	Page	Maiden Name	Place of Death	Place of Birth
Genheimer, Sophia	11, Apr. 1881	22, Mar.	68	119		Portsmouth, OH	Oppau, Rheinkreis Baiern
Gennich, August	11, Feb. 1892	13, Jan.	59	94		Milwaukee, WI	Breitenfeld, Preußen
Gennit, Anna	6, June 1895		78-10m- 6d	366		Stockton, CA	Kukelhausen, Westphalen
Genofsky, Catharina	6, Aug. 1896	2, July	55	511	Stumpf	Schnectady, NY	Hessen-Kassel
Genrich, Emilie Henriette	28, Mar. 1895	6, Mar.	33- 1m-13d	206	Gelbke	Milwaukee, WI	
Genrich, Friedrich	29, Dec. 1884	29, Nov.	76	7		Defiance, OH	
Genrich, Johanne Wilhelmine A.	20, Nov. 1890	12, Oct.	51- 9m-24d	750	Behling	Milwaukee, WI	Colberg, Preußen
Genrich, Maria Margaretha	24, Sept 1878	1, Sept	66	303		Defiance, OH	Hillersleben, Preußen
Genßle, Rosa Lydia	1, July 1897	8, June	26	414		Lansing, MI	
Genthner, Jakob	30, July1883	15, July	64- 3m- 7d	247		Saugerties, NY	Feldrinach, Neuenbürg, Württemberg
Genthner, Regina	15, Jan. 1877	26, Dec.	65- 9m	23	Jäck	Saugerties, NY	Consweiler, Neuenbürg, Württemberg
Gentner, Katharina	30, June 1884	7, June	73- 1m-23d	7	Liebherz	Philadelphia, PA	Württemberg
Genz, Heinrich	30, Oct. 1871	30, Sept	7	351		Colesburg, IA	
Genzlinger, Katharina Christine	12, Dec. 1895	19, Nov.	59	798	Auwärter	Yonkers, NY	Schlichten bei Schorndorf, Württemberg
Georg, Gertrude	24, Nov. 1887	29, Oct.	83-11m-19d	750	Sippel	Long Point, IL	Rotenburg an der Fulda, Hessen
Georg, Heinrich	27, June 1870	30, Sept	77	207		Nauvoo, IL	Weißenhasel, Kurhessen
Georg, Magdalena	3, Dec. 1841	27, Oct.	24	191		New Albany, IN	
George, Heinrich	26, Aug. 1897	7, July	19	543		Hampton, NE	Neusatz, Rußland
George, Johannes	15, Jan. 1883	27, Dec.	79	23		Nauvoo, IL	Weißenhasel, Rotenburg, Kurhessen
George, John G.	3, Apr. 1865	24, Jan.		56		Nauvoo, IL	Weißenhasel, Amt Neutershausen, Kurhessen
George, Katharina	15, Jan. 1883	21, Dec.	77	23	Kube	Nauvoo, IL	Weißenhasel, Rotenburg, Kurhessen
George, Maria	9, Jan. 1890	19, Nov.	32	30	Heep	Trenton, IL	
Gephart, Katharine	5, Mar. 1891	2, Feb.	43- 4m	158	Ried	Canal Dover, OH	Coshocton County, Ohio
Geppert, Gottlieb	23, Feb. 1880	10, Feb.	54	63		Wabasha, MN	Großaurau, Falkenberg, Schlesien, Preußen
Geppert, Johanna	6, Sept 1855	13, July	26	144	Hillebrecht	Ironton, OH	Hannover
Gerber, Daniel	29, May 1840			83		Perry County, PA	
Gerber, Elisa	3, May 1888	24, Jan.	32- 4m-23d	286		Mt. Olive, IL	
Gerber, Elisabeth	15, Apr. 1867	10, Mar.	73	118		Roxbury, MA	Neufirmel, Ostfriesland
Gerber, Elisabeth	17, Nov. 1879	4, Nov.	71-11m-16d	367	Sägesser	Sandwich, IL	Weiningen, Bern, Schweiz
Gerber, Elisabeth	28, Feb. 1895	28, Jan.	70	142	Owen	Bedford, IN	Arwangen, Bern, Schweiz
Gerber, Frederika	26, July 1888	4, July	81	478	Fickel	Waco, TX	Bedford, Indiana
Gerber, Johann	24, Jan. 1850	7, Dec.		16		Versailles, MO	Schneeberg bei Lindenau, Preußen
Gerber, Johannes	4, Sept 1890	14, Aug.	85-11m- 1d	574		Sandwich, IL	Hannover
Gerber, Louis	5, Apr. 1894	12, Mar.	72	230		Bedford, IN	Aarwangen, Bern, Schweiz
Gerber, Maria	3, Dec. 1877	16, Nov.	24	391	Behringer	Lafayette, IN	Reinbach, Baden
Gerber, Marie	2, Dec. 1897	13, Nov.	69	767	Hoßner	Duncan, NE	Schlierbach, Württemberg
Gerbing, Johan G.M.	20, July 1885	26, June	71- 6m	7		Newark, NJ	Madiswiel, Bern, Schweiz
Gerbracht, Anna Katharina	7, Apr. 1887	26, Jan.	57	222	Rosenkrantz	Jackson, MN	Roth am See, Gerabronn, Württemberg
Gerdes, (Mrs)	18, Sept 1871	22, Aug.	69	303	Hermann	Petersburg, IL	Wobern, Fritzlar, Kurhessen
Gerdes, Etti	18, Apr. 1895	25, Mar.	68	254		Humboldt, NE	Strakholt, Hannover
Gerdes, G.H.	17, May 1860	25, Apr.	61	80		Petersburg, IL	Strakholt, Aurich, Ostfriesland
Gerdes, Heere	10, Apr. 1876	5, Mar.	45	118		Petersburg, IL	Remels, Amt Stickhausen, Hannover
Gerdes, Herman	27, Oct. 1892	6, Oct.	71	686		Wilber, NE	Zwischenbergen, Amt Aurich, Ostfriesland
Gerdes, Maria	16, Mar. 1868	28, Feb.	66	87	Rese	Laporte, IN	Norden, Ostfriesland
Gerding, August Herman	2, Sept 1878	13, Aug.	15- 2m	279		New Haven, MO	
Gerding, Auguste	27, July 1885	1, July	21- 3m-17d	7	Greiwer	Ironton, OH	

Christliche Apologete Death Notices --- 1839 - 1899

Name of Deceased	Notice Date	Death Date	Age	Maiden Name	Page	Place of Death	Place of Birth
Gerding, Cort	24, June 1872	24, May	61- 6m		207	Schnectady, NY	Hannover
Gerding, Johan F.	11, Mar. 1897	15, Jan.	78		158	Wheelersburg, OH	Nepersdorf, Mecklenburg-Schwerin
Gerding, Julia	16, June 1887	30, May	45	Schulz	382	Wyandotte, KS	Ladschke, Magdeburg, Preußen
Gereke, Katharina Elisabeth	20, July 1868	22, June	54	Kleinau	231	Flint Creek, IA	Marinette, Wisconsin
Gergensky, Lydia Augusta	9, June 1898		17		367	Menominee, MI	Königsberg, Preußen
Gerginski, (Mrs)	13, Nov. 1882	26, Oct.	81-11m	Stab	367	Menominee, MI	Gi_sch, West Preußen
Gerginsky, Augusta	8, Dec. 1884	13, Nov.	50	Haase	7	Menominee, MI	Brausen bei Rosenberg, West Preußen
Gerginsky, Wilhelm	30, May 1889	2, May	23		350	Menomonie, WI	Dobitschen, Sachsen-Altenburg
Gerhardt, Gottlieb	7, Apr. 1892	9, Mar.	80		222	West Bend, WI	Burgbrecht, Hessen-Darmstadt
Gerhardt, Heinrich	23, Jan. 1896	19, Nov.	66		62	Edon, OH	Reichstädt, Sachsen-Altenburg
Gerhardt, Sophie	8, Jan. 1891	13, Dec.	62- 6m	Fritschen	30	West Bend, WI	Volkholz, Preußen
Gerhart, Louise	20, Dec. 1888	29, Nov.	59	Schneider	814	Cibolo, TX	Gunzenau, Lauterbach, Germany
Gerheart, (Mrs)	4, Oct. 1888	9, Sept	88- 6m- 9d		638	Stitzer, WI	Jugendheim, Hessen-Darmstadt
Gerisch, Christian	6, July 1893	14, June	83		430	Warsaw, IL	Grumbach, Odenwald, Hessen-Darmstadt
Gerisch, Christine	1, June 1868	3, May	48- 8m	Frey	175	Warsaw, IL	Greene, Braunschweig
Gerish, Caroline	29, June 1885	27, May	59	Berline	7	Warsaw, IL	
Gerjets, Metta	11, May 1874	26, Apr.	26- 3m- 3d		151	Nokomis, IL	Bierbergen, Hannover
Gerke, Christine	15, June 1899	22, Apr.	87	Dörrie	383	Highland, IL	Obernbeck, Mennighüffen, Westphalen
Gerkemeyer, J.F. Wilhelm	9, July1883	20, June	80		223	Highland, IL	
Gerken, Anna Maria	7, Aug. 1846	17, June	40-10m		127	Woodville, OH	Werrendorf, Hannover
Gerken, Christine	26, Nov. 1896	30, Oct.	93	Driftmeyer	766	Elmore, OH	LaPorte, Indiana
Gerken, Emma	11, Aug. 1892	19, July	26		510	Milwaukee, WI	Wright City, Missouri
Gerken, Ernst Heinrich	23, Feb. 1893	13, Jan.	19	Senn	126	Warren, MO	
Gerken, G. Willie	27, Nov. 1882	9, Nov.	2-10m		383	St. Louis, MO	
Gerken, Georg	4, Dec. 1890		20		782	Bland, MO	
Gerken, Heinrich	31, Oct. 1870	13, Sept	74		351	Lake Creek, MO	Heppstädt, Amt Otterberg, Hannover
Gerken, Henry	4, Dec. 1890		22		782	Bland, MO	
Gerken, J. Henry	27, Nov. 1882	9, Nov.	8- 2m		383	St. Louis, MO	
Gerken, J.F.	12, Apr. 1880	24, Mar.	76		119	Woodville, OH	Bohmke, Amt Wittlage, Hannover
Gerken, Johan Christian	18, Aug. 1887	27, July	71		526	Hebron, IA	Heiligen-Bruch, Ride, Syke, Hannover
Gerken, Johnny	4, Dec. 1890		26		782	Bland, MO	Hepstedt, Amt Ottersberg, Hannover
Gerken, Katharina	29, July 1858	17, May	68		120	Florence, MO	Heinrode
Gerken, Louis	4, Dec. 1890		15		782	Bland, MO	
Gerken, Margaretha	1, May 1890	9, Apr.	75- 5m-15d	Wehmken	286	Drake, MO	Bremerhaven, Germany
Gerken, Mary	4, Dec. 1890		26		782	Bland, MO	
Gerken, Mette	13, Apr. 1893	8, Mar.	74	Hillmann	238	Hebron, IA	Hannover
Gerken, Pet.	16, Feb. 1885	24, Jan.	66		7	Warrenton, MO	Kirchtimke, Zeven, Hannover
Gerlach, August	13, Aug. 1896	27, July	65		527	Pinckneyville, IL	Hainrode, Preußen
Gerlach, Augustus	5, June 1876	15, May	38		183	Red Bud, IL	Eilvese, Hannover
Gerlach, H.	6, Apr. 1868	9, Mar.	42		111	Muskegon, MI	Eifesehs, Hagen, Amt Wölpe, Hannover
Gerlach, Heinrich	7, Jan. 1888	12, May	87		366	Delaware, OH	Horheim, Vaihingin, Württemberg
Gerlach, Jakob	21, Jan. 1848		Inquiry		15	Columbus, OH	Walburg, Hessen-Kassel
Gerlach, Johannes	2, Oct. 1890	10, Sept	70- 6m- 3d		638	Franciscoville, MI	Groß Sachsenheim, Vaihingen, Württemberg
Gerlach, Johannes Friedrich	1, Nov. 1860	26, Sept	32		176	Oakdale, IL	Hannover
Gerlach, Ludwig	7, May 1891	28, Feb.	59		302	Red Bud, IL	
Gerlach, Maria	31, July 1865	15, July		Tegtmeier	124		

Christliche Apologete Death Notices --- 1839 - 1899

Name of Deceased	Notice Date	Death Date	Age	Maiden Name	Page	Place of Death	Place of Birth
Gerlemann, Regina Elsbein	6, Apr. 1863	1, Mar.	61-11m	Bergisch	56	Warsaw, IL	Westerkappeln, Münster, Preußen
Gerling, Elisabeth	29, Mar. 1888	27, Feb.	68- 5m-16d	Droste	206	St. Louis, MO	Hille, Minden, Preußen
Gerling, Karl Friedrich	12, Jan. 1880	4, Dec.	59		15	Dodgeville, IA	Hille, Minden, Preußen
Gerling, Karl Heinrich	22, Mar. 1894	5, Mar.	52		198	Ft. Hunter, NY	Hille, Preußen
Gerling, Karolina Maria Ilsabein	15, Oct. 1877	22, Sept	54- 8m-22d	Tiemann	335	Flint Creek, IA	Hille, Minden, Preußen
Gerling, Louisa	18, Feb. 1878	1, Feb.	63- 7m-25d		55	Schnectady, NY	Lovelsloh, Hannover
Gerling, Sophia Friederika	12, June 1882	16, May	44- 1m- 2d	Utlaut	191	Highland, IL	Lienen, Westphalen
Gerling, Wilhelm	22, Apr. 1897	4, Apr.	75		254	Allegheny City, PA	Ströhen, Minden, Preußen
German, Johannes	19, Aug. 1872	28, July	30		271	Blue Island, IL	
Germann, Anna Maria	17, Nov. 1892	21, Oct.	68	Brenner	734	Quincy, IL	Heil, Hannover
Germann, Katharina	14, Dec. 1885	26, Nov.	75	Stoll	7	Blue Island, IL	Dilburg, Nassau
Germann, Mariana	6, July 1854	13, June	19	Dreyer	108	Huntingburg, IN	
Germolus, Wilhelmine	30, Apr. 1896	2, Apr.	77		286	Ada, MN	Germany
Gerner, Johan	16, Dec. 1878	13, Nov.	55		399	Red Bud, IL	Nimmersdorf, Baiern
Gerner, Katharina	6, Oct. 1892	1, Sept	59	Denninger	638	Ellis Grove, IL	Elsaß
Gernlein, Katharina	3, May 1894	11, Apr.	70	Schmidt	294	Louisville, KY	Dossenheim, Elsaß
Gernlein, Wilhelm Friedrich	27, Oct. 1884	15, Oct.	20		7	Louisville, KY	Louisville, Jefferson County, Kentucky
Gerreis, Cornelius	29, June 1868	14, Oct.	62- 1m- 2d		207	Industry, TX	Oldenburg
Gerspacher, Bertha	25, July 1889	23, June	21		478	St. Louis, MO	St. Louis, Missouri
Gerst, Maria	18, Nov. 1878	28, Oct.	67	Lutz	367	New Rochelle, NY	Kirchheim, Kurhessen
Gerst, Wiegandt	13, July 1893	24, June	82		446	New Rochelle, NY	Kirchheim, Kurhessen
Gerstenhauer, W. J.	24, June 1872	28, May	17- 4m- 3d		207	Chicago, IL	Milwaukee, Wisconsin
Gerstmann, Hermann Heinrich	20, Oct. 1862	26, Aug.	37		168	Quincy, IL	Segeln, Amt Vörden, Hannover
Gerstner, Georg	7, Nov. 1889	8, Oct.	83- 8m- 2d		718	Peoria, IL	Heddesheim, Ladenburg, Baden
Gerth, Ludwig	26, Feb. 1877		69- 7m-20d		71	Galion, OH	Hohensolms, Wetzlar, Preußen
Gerth, Margaretha	15, Mar. 1888		88		174	Galion, OH	Hohensolms, Wetzlar, Coblenz, Preußen
Gerthäffner, Nikolaus	23, Aug. 1888	8, Aug.	67		542	Chicago, IL	Blankenborn, Landau, Rheinkreis Baiern
Gertz, Heinrich	28, July 1887	6, July	68		478	Lockland, OH	Mecklenburg-Schwerin
Gerwin, Katharina Julian	7, July 1892	7, June	76		430	Elmore, OH	Hannover
Gerwin, Maria	1, Aug. 1881		23- 1m- 2d		247	Woodville, OH	
Gerwin, Sarha Dorothea Elisabeth	4, June 1877	13, May	74	Hunter	183	Woodville, OH	Bordnau, Amt Neustadt, Hannover
Gesberg, Bernhard	17, Aug. 1885	24, July	58		7	Iowa City, IA	Kurhessen
Geske, Caroline Christine	19, Dec. 1881	27, Nov.	43- -17d	Stock	407	Concord, WI	Megow, Piritz, Stettin, Pommern
Geske, Wilhelm F.	10, May 1880	18, Apr.	15- 5m- 5d		151	Oconomowoc, WI	Meegow bei Piritz, Pommern
Gesser, Katharina Gertraud	29, Aug. 1850	10, Aug.			140	Louisville, KY	
Gessinger, Louis A.	22, Mar. 1888	7, Feb.	19		190	Chicago, IL	
Geßmann, Maria Sophia	17, Jan. 1861	1, Jan.	24		12	Detroit, MI	Erligheim, Besigheim, Württemberg
Geßner, Emma	25, July 1881	18, June	22- 4m- 5d		239	Madison, WI	
Geßner, Johanna Elisabeth	8, Apr. 1878	4, Mar.		Horlein	111	Beaver Dam, WI	Horicon, Wisconsin
Geßner, Lydia Hulda	29, July 1886	4, July	22		7		Singlis, Germany
Gethart, Anna Katharina	2, Mar. 1899	4, Feb.	76	Töpfer	143	Charles City, IA	
Gethmann, Anna Maria	2, Oct. 1890	13, Sept	9- 8m -1d		638	Gladbrook, IA	Crystal, Tama County, Iowa
Gethmann, Heinrich J.	1, Sept 1898	19, Aug.	25		559	Gladbrook, IA	Udorf, Brilon, Germany
Gethmann, J. L.	27, Feb. 1896	29, Jan.	50		142	Gladbrook, IA	
Gethmann, Louis	2, Feb. 1888	9, Jan.	69		78	Gladbrook, IA	
Gethmann, Mary	19, June 1890	21, May	22- 6m- 1d		398	Gladbrook, IA	Champagne-Mühle, Wetterburg, Aralsen, Waldeck

Christliche Apologete Death Notices --- 1839 - 1899

Name of Deceased	Notice Date	Death Date	Age	Page	Maiden Name	Place of Death	Place of Birth
Getke, Christian	8, May 1882	30, Mar.	64- -7d	151		Salina, KS	Schwerin, Mecklenburg
Getz, Johan Nepomuk	27, Feb. 1896	28, Jan.	77	142		Chicago, IL	Truntheim, Norway
Getzke, Ferdinand	13, Oct. 1898	9, Sept	66- 2m-11d	655		Baltimore, MD	Belgard, Preußen
Geule, Amalia	25, July 1895	29, June	28	478		Ironton, OH	Ironton, Ohio
Geule, Carolina	27, Feb. 1896	2, Feb.	66	142	Fischer	Ironton, OH	Dinkelhausen, Isler, Hannover
Geule, Friedrike	16, Feb. 1893	20, Jan.	24	110		Ironton, OH	Ironton, Ohio
Gewehr, Katharina Sophia	6, Apr. 1893	20, Feb.	71	222	Kammann	Menominee, MI	Oppersheim, Zeller, Hannover
Geyer, (Mr)	10, Apr. 1876	24, Mar.	62	118		Platteville, WI	Metzingen, Urach, Württemberg
Geyer, Anna Maria	8, Sept 1879	22, Aug.	76	287	Keck	Pomeroy, OH	Diermstein, Rheinkreis Baiern
Geyer, Anna Maria	3, Sept 1847	19, July	6m-18d	143		Pomeroy, OH	
Geyer, Anna Maria	26, Mar. 1857	12, Feb.	15- 6m	52		Woodville, OH	
Geyer, Edward Lincoln	10, Apr. 1882	16, Mar.	16- 9m-14d	119		Pomeroy, OH	
Geyer, Elisabeth	25, Oct. 1875	5, Sept	88	343	Stamler	Kossuth, OH	Eckartsweiler, Elsaß
Geyer, Friederike	31, Jan. 1850	10, Jan.		20	Mack	Bethlehem, OH	
Geyer, Georg Wilhelm	29, Oct. 1866	14, Oct.	12- 5m-12d	350		New Knoxville, OH	Diermstein, Rheinkreis Baiern
Geyer, Johann	3, Aug. 1854	3, July	76	124		Pomeroy, OH	
Geyer, Johann	26, July 1849	12, July	41	120		Cincinnati, OH	
Geyer, John J.	8, Dec. 1892	10, Oct.	62	782		San Diego, CA	Schweiz
Geyer, Karoline	4, May 1885	18, Apr.	50	7		Platteville, WI	Almirsbach, Marbach, Württemberg
Geyer, Katharina	3, Sept 1891	25, July	48	574	Ohlinger	Pomeroy, OH	Chester, Meigs County, Ohio
Geyer, Magdalena	28, Nov. 1845	19, Sept	23- 3m-28d	191			Dirmstein, Rheinkreis Baiern
Geyer, Margaretha	21, May 1877	6, May	69	166	Nuhfer	Woodville, OH	Dirmstein, Rheinkreis Baiern
Geyer, N.	5, Jan. 1880	14, Dec.	24-11m- 6d	7		Ellis Grove, IL	Randolph County, Illinois
Geyer, Philipp	22, Oct. 1891	24, Sept	74	686		New Knoxville, OH	Ergottsweiler, Elsaß
Geyer, Salomon	22, Oct. 1866	7, Oct.	15	342		New Knoxville, OH	St. Johns, Auglaize County, Ohio
Geyer, Susanna Elisabeth	17, Dec. 1847	13, Nov.	25	203	Ihle	Pomeroy, OH	Edigheim, Rheinkreis Baiern
Geyer, Willie	7, Sept 1899	7, Aug.	77	575	Herbst	New Knoxville, OH	Hannover
Geymann, Anna B.	8, Apr. 1867	24, Mar.		110	Braun	Baraboo, WI	Buch, Baiern
Gfeller, Christ.	4, May 1893	4, Apr.		286		Jamestown, MO	
Gfeller, Maria	13, Feb. 1896	17, Jan.	69	110		Jamestown, MO	Kanton Bern, Schweiz
Ghemaehle, Catharine	19, Jan. 1860	29, Nov.	64	12		Red Bud, IL	
Gickler, Johan	5, Sept 1881	10, Aug.	56-10m- 3d	287		Waverly, OH	Württemberg
Giebe, Maria	23, Aug. 1894	28, July	35	550		Chicago, IL	Ardorf, Waldeck
Gieck, Auguste	24, Mar. 1873	7, Mar.	36	95	Arnsperger	Canaan, MO	Eßlingen, Württemberg
Gieck, Caroline	29, July 1897	15, June	58	479	Brand	Bland, MO	Ludwighurst, Germany
Gieck, Georg	27, Oct. 1873	5, Sept	28	343		Canaan, MO	
Gieck, Johan A.	8, Nov. 1888	28, Sept	28	718		Bland, MO	Osage County, Missouri
Gieck, Johan Georg	27, July 1885	1, July	50	7		Bland, MO	Dippah, Baiern
Gieck, Johan Gottfried	3, Nov. 1859	10, Oct.		176		Indian Creek, MO	Dippach, Hofheim, Baiern
Gieck, John	28, Aug. 1890	12, July	64	558		Bland, MO	Dippach, Hofheim, Baiern
Gieck, Katharine Elisabeth	29, Oct. 1896	2, Oct.	65	703	Roesner	Bland, MO	Birkenfeld, Baiern
Gieger, Maria Elisabeth	3, May 1880	26, Mar.	67	143	Kunsmann	Galion, OH	Weinheim, Baden
Giegerich, G.	15, July 1878	25, June	49	223		Canton, MO	Niederkeinsbach, Hessen-Darmstadt
Giehl, Friedrich Ludwig August	25, Sept 1876	13, Aug.	36	311		Perre Creek, IA	
Giehl, Jakob	27, Apr. 1863		3- 3m	68		Williamsburg, NY	
Giehl, Katharina	27, Apr. 1863		6m	68		Williamsburg, NY	

Name of Deceased	Notice Date	Death Date	Age	Maiden Name	Page	Place of Death	Place of Birth
Giehl, Maria	27, Apr. 1863		5		68	Williamsburg, NY	
Giehl, Peter	27, Apr. 1863		7		68	Williamsburg, NY	
Gielow, Christian	20, Jan. 1887	31, Dec.	74		46	Manitowoc, WI	Kittendorf, Mecklenburg-Schwerin
Giem, (Mrs)	29, Dec. 1898	14, Aug.	58		828	Denver, CO	Jugermünde, Pommern
Giem, Elisabeth	4, July 1881	30, May	48- 9m-18d	Müller	215	Rochester, MN	Ohio
Giem, Hannah	15, May 1871	18, Apr.	33	Vorden	159	Wabasha, MN	
Giem, Johan Christian	15, Apr. 1872	30, Mar.	68- -21d		127	Rochester, MN	Columbiana County, Ohio
Giem, Sophie	8, Feb. 1869	8, Dec.	14-11m		47	Rochester, MN	Cennern, Preußen
Giercher, Valentin	12, June 1876	12, Apr.	44- 8m- 4d		191	Highland, IL	
Giermann, Emilie Louise	8, Sept 1884	27, Aug.	32		7	Charles City, IA	Libbesike, Brandenburg
Gieschen, Johan	30, Mar. 1885	9, Mar.	53		7	Lake Creek, MO	Glentzstett, Zarwen, Hannover
Giese , Wilhelm R.	13, Dec. 1894	24, Nov.	36		806	Edwardsville, IL	Madison County, Illinois
Giese, August	22, May 1890	4, May	78- -28d		334	Lena, IL	Langenhagen, Pommern
Giese, Dorothea	7, July 1884	10, May	66		7	Alma, WI	Großkiesel, Preußen
Giese, Friedrich M.	31, Dec. 1883	29, Nov.	81		7	Freeport, IL	Repplin, Pieritz, Pommern
Giese, Gottlieb	15, Apr. 1897	11, Feb.	61		239	Roseville, MI	Brünken, Stettin, Pommern
Giese, Herman	26, Jan. 1899	24, Dec.	68		63	Edwardsville, IL	Germany
Giesebrecht, Franz Ernst	8, Mar. 1888	11, Feb.	33		158	New York City, NY	
Gieseke, Caroline Sophia	12, Nov. 1896	28, Oct.	77	Soelhorst	734	Appleton, MO	Maize, Dissendorf, Germany
Gieseke, Wilhelm	11, Apr. 1889		70		238	Appleton, MO	Meitze, Bissendorf, Hannover
Gieseking, Hannah Elisabeth	16, Aug. 1894	30, July	26		534	Altamont, IL	Freemington, Effingham County, Texas
Gieseking, Wilhelm	17, Feb. 1887	30, Jan.	60		110	Altamont, IL	Quetzen, Minden, Preußen
Gieselmann, (Mr)	22, Dec. 1859		56		204	Marthasville, MO	Reme, Preußen
Gieselmann, Anna Katharina Ilsabein	8, Sept 1879	22, Aug.	61- 6m-20d		287	Concordia, MO	Spenger, Herfort, Minden, Preußen
Gieselmann, Anna Katharina M.	22, Oct. 1891	23, Sept	76	Neimeier	686	Burlington, IA	Göllenbeck, Bielefeld, Minden, Westphalen
Gieselmann, Sophia	12, Nov. 1896	23, Oct.	87		734	St. Louis, MO	Windheim, Minden, Westphalen
Giesen, Johanna	28, Feb. 1895	4, Feb.	67		142	Chicago, IL	Barmen, Preußen
Gieser, Jakob	26, Jan. 1899	3, Jan.	65		63	Pearl City, IL	Hockenheim, Baden
Giesker, Margaretha	26, July 1849	6, July	13- 6m		120	St. Louis, MO	
Giesler, Katharina	29, June 1885	6, June	58	Schröder	7	Milwaukee, WI	Lidfeld, Westphalen
Giesler, Martin	19, May 1879	18, Apr.	67- 3m-28d		159	Scranton, PA	Wellingerode, Eschwege, Kurhessen
Giesmann, G.W.	18, Oct. 1888	14, Sept	51- 7m-12d		670	Billings, MO	Nürnberg, Mittelfranken, Baiern
Giesmann, Katharine Wilhelmine	27, Jan. 1898	26, Dec.	78		63	New Melle, MO	Buchholzhauen, Hannover
Giesregen, Margaretha	18, Mar. 1897	26, Feb.	69	Deindörfer	174	Brooklyn, NY	Fürth, Baiern
Giesselmann, Heinrich	6, Aug. 1896	18, July	38		511	Kansas City, MO	Wittmar, Burgwedel, Hannover
Gießler, Catharina	11, Mar. 1886	25, Feb.	59	Suck	7	Scranton, PA	
Gießmann, Joseph Heinrich	12, Oct. 1899	20, Sept	71		655	New Melle, MO	Buer, Hannover
Giezendanner, Margarethe	29, Nov. 1894		47	Junge	774	Madison, WI	Wrack bei Kellinghusen, Schleswig-Holstein
Gigerich, Margaretha	1, Apr. 1886	10, Feb.	48-5m	Röder	7	New York City, NY	Frommbach bei Darmstadt, Hessen-Darmstadt
Gilbert, Anna	14, Jan. 1856	27, Jan.	51- 8m-15d		28	New Haven, CT	
Gildehouse, Henry	26, Jan. 1885	10, Jan.	21- - 4d		7	Hamilton, OH	
Gildemann, Florentine Maria	13, Apr. 1854		38	Schollen	60	Aurora, IN	Selingdorf, Buren, Grüneberg, Hannover
Gildner, Juliane	11, Apr. 1870	11, Mar.	34-10m- 5d	Schnarr	119	Nora Springs, IA	Grabenau, Ahlsfeld, Hessen-Darmstadt
Gilfort, Martha	24, Jan. 1870	6, Jan.	76		31	Pittsburg, PA	Nieder-Ellenbach, Rothenburg, Kurhessen
Gilfort, Nikolaus	1, Sept 1848	7, Aug.			144	Pittsburg, PA	Niederalmbach, Kurhessen
Gilgen, Elisabeth	28, Aug. 1876	28, July	59- 9m-14d	Brühling	279	West Unity, OH	Höchst bei Damstadt, Hessen-Darmstadt

Christliche Apologete Death Notices --- 1839 - 1899

Name of Deceased	Notice Date	Death Date	Age	Maiden Name	Page	Place of Death	Place of Birth
Gilgert, John George	17, Mar. 1884	7, Dec.	56		7	Stockton, CA	Meiersberg bei Bayreuth, Baiern
Gille, A.H.J.	4, Apr. 1895	5, Mar.	88		222	Jansen, NE	Berneberg, Preußen
Gille, Chrsitian	6, July 1893	1, June	80		430	Columbus, WI	Stafelde, Neumark
Gillert, Nettie	8, Dec. 1892	20, Nov.	33		782	Highland, IL	Hillsboro, Montgomery County, Illinois
Gils, Heinrich	28, Mar. 1889	4, Mar.	62		206	Chicago, IL	Kalberlah, Hannover
Gisdorf, Heinrich Peter	6, Apr. 1893	1, Mar.	69		222	Portsmouth, OH	Archenthal, Simmern, Rheinkreis Baiern
Gilson, Louise	15, Sept 1879	1, Sept	23	Zickgraf	295	Zoar, OH	
Gilz, Friedrich	12, Sept 1889	20, Aug.	76- 5m-12d		590	Chicago, IL	GroßWonschien, Stolpe, Preußen
Gilz, Maria	7, Jan. 1884	20, Dec.	80		7	Chicago, IL	Lauenburg, Hinterpommern
Gizer, Emilie	29, July 1878	16, July	16- 9m-19d		239	Waverly, OH	
Gimbel, Heinrich	7, Apr. 1873	22, Mar.	21- 5m-16d		111	Warsaw, IL	Marburg, Kurhessen
Gimbel, Wigand	1, June 1868	14, Apr.	51		175	Warsaw, IL	Hepsisau, Württemberg
Ginger, Johan Christian	3, July 1890	18, June	47		430	Chicago, IL	Canton, Missouri
Gingrich, Peter	19, Nov. 1883	25, Oct.	29		375	Canton, MO	Eulau, West Preußen
Ginski, Karoline	30, Mar. 1885	8, Feb.	61	Krückhahn	7	Detroit, MI	Schippenwiel, Königsberg, Preußen
Ginski, Otto Hemran	17, Dec. 1883	23, Nov.	54		7	Detroit, MI	Baltimore, Maryland
Ginter, Christina	13, Sept 1894	24, July	40	Hack	598	Baltimore, MD	Flotz, Preußen
Girke, Louise	25, Feb. 1892	1, Feb.	67	Kahlo	126	Defiance, OH	Minneapolis, Minnesota
Girrbach, Esther Philippine	9, July 1896	14, June	17		447	Minneapolis, MN	Minneapolis, Minnesota
Girrbach, Wilhelm	16, Feb. 1893	30, Jan.	26		110	Minneapolis, MN	Niederaulau, Kurhessen
Gischer, Johannes	16, May 1864	24, Jan.	39- 1m- 7d		80	New York, NY	New York
Gisebrech, Louise	29, Dec. 1884	16, Nov.	25	Theiß	7	New York City, NY	Schweiz
Gisel, Georg	9, Dec. 1897	29, Oct.	36		783	St. Louis, MO	
Glaesmann, Bertha Albertine	28, Apr. 1884	2, Apr.	10		7	New Ulm, MN	
Glaeßer, Johan Caspar	4, Oct. 1894	4, July	81		646	Columbus, IL	Dodenau, Battenberg, Hessen-Darmstadt
Glander, Anton	3, Jan. 1876	11, Dec.	61- 8m-22d		7	German Creek, IA	Varel, Oldenburg
Glander, Louise	28, Apr. 1898	6, Apr.	39	Neumann	271	St. Paul, MN	Oconomowoc, Wisconsin
Glander, Susanna	4, Dec. 1882	2, Nov.	72		391	Harper, IA	Krohn bei Vegesack, Hannover
Glanz, Christina	21, Dec. 1893	29, Nov.	73		814	Harper, IA	Lorbach, Büdingen, Hessen-Darmstadt
Glanz, Heinrich	25, Dec. 1865	21, Nov.			208	Valley, IA	
Glanz, Peter	23, June 1898	24, May	73		399	Holt, MI	Heingründau, Büdingen, Hessen-Darmstadt
Glänzer, Maria Louisa	16, Sept 1858	16, Aug.	54		148	Poland, IN	Hombressen, Amt Hofgeismar, Kurhessen
Gläser, Adolph	28,May 1883	14, May	25		175	Seguin, TX	Flensburg, Schlesien
Gläser, Anna Maria	4, Feb. 1886	16, Nov.	70	Rinke	7	Saginaw, MI	Dittmannsdorf, Schlesien
Gläser, Auguste Wilhelmine	5, Oct. 1899	5, Sept	38	Drülsch	639	South Bend, IN	Albernan, Sachsen
Gläser, Johan Ehrenfried	10, Feb. 1887	22, Jan.	59- 7m-20d		94	Seguin, TX	Bad Flinsberg, Schlesien
Glaser, Wilhelm	19, Jan. 1863	14, Sept	55		12	Dunkirk, NY	Stafforth bei Karlsruhe, Baden
Glasing, Heinrich	13, Mar. 1876	16, Feb.	75		87	Seguin, TX	Hildesheim, Hannover
Glaßmann, (child)	7, Nov. 1881				359	Lafayette, MN	
Glättle, Pauline	25, Nov. 1886	7, Nov.	31	Dilger	7	New York City, NY	Winterbach, Württemberg
Glatz, Anna	10, June 1897	15, May	32	Schneider	367	Waco, TX	Indianapolis, Marion County, Indiana
Glause, Marie	20, Apr. 1899	29, Mar.	72	Otto	255	Grand Island, NE	Hohenmokow, Demmin, Pommern
Glebb, Elisabeth	7, Jan. 1897		79	Hoffmann	15	Cleveland, OH	Hadebach, Herschfeld, Preußen
Glebb, Valentin	1, May 1890	11, Apr.	75		286	Cleveland, OH	Monchshausen, Hirschfeld, Kurhessen
Glees, Heinrich	26, Apr. 1880	25, Mar.	57- 1m- 1d		135	Junction Creek, MO	Landau am Harz, Hannover
Gleich, Ferdinand	4, Aug. 1898	15, July	80		495	Marine City, MI	Götchendorf, Potsdam, Brandenburg

Christliche Apologete Death Notices --- 1839 - 1899

Name of Deceased	Notice Date	Death Date	Age	Maiden Name	Page	Place of Death	Place of Birth
Gleichman, Georg	5, Sept 1895	9, Aug.	58		574	Owatonna, MN	Dennmar, Sachsen-Meiningen
Gleichmann, Anna Barbara	25, Apr. 1870	5, Apr.	74	Langbein	135	Evansville, IN	
Gleichmann, Gottlieb	17, Mar. 1884	21, Feb.	17- 6m		7	Blooming Grove, MN	
Glendmeier, Wilhelmine	26, May 1884	28, Apr.	25		7	Schnectady, NY	Grißen, Preußen
Glendmeier, William F. F.	2, Nov. 1899	4, Oct.	24		703	Schnectady, NY	
Glenz, Wilhelm	4, Dec. 1865	15, Oct.			196	Valley, IA	
Gliendmeier, Matthias	10, Feb. 1868	11, Jan.	47		47	Calhoun, IL	Eburg, Hannover
Glinger, Catharina	20, Oct. 1887	29, Sept	77	Wessauer	670	Pomeroy, OH	Edigheim, Frankenthal, Baiern
Glock, Catharine	13, Dec. 1855	19, Nov.		Fischer	200	Greenfield, OH	
Glock, Johanna	24, July 1890	9, July	34	Nagel	478	Osceola, NE	Hoheneck, Württemberg
Glock, Louise	6, Aug. 1847	18, July	19		127	Ft. Wayne, IN	
Gloninger, Maria	11, Aug. 1859	21, July	66-10m-23d		128	Canal Dover, OH	Lebanon, Pennsylvania
Glor, Sophia	23, Apr. 1877	9, Apr.	45	Schulz	135	Cannon River, MN	Pölitz, Mecklenburg-Schwerin
Glöser, Heinrich	1, Sept 1884	8, Aug.	75		7	Wichita, KS	Dodenau, Marburg, Hessen-Darmstadt
Gloß, Regine	26, Dec. 1864	4, Dec.	45		208	Baltimore, MD	Wurmberg, Maulbronn, Württemberg
Glück, Regina	25, Nov. 1878	7, Nov.	63- 9m-16d		375	Evansville, IN	Helmsheim, Baden
Gluckhohn, Sophie	23, Aug. 1894	29, July	72	Gluckhorn	550	Reddick, IL	Bovenhausen, Lippe-Detmold
Gluth, Christoph	15, May 1871	27, Apr.	66- 4m		159	New Ulm, MN	Schwerte, Preußen
Gmünder, Magdalena	29, Nov. 1894	13, Nov.	29	Neff	774	Newport, KY	Appenzell, Schweiz
Gnadt, Auguste	3, Nov. 1887	18, Oct.	52- - 2d	Taube	702	Chicago, IL	Felstow, Lauenburg, Hinterpommern
Gnäge, Friedrich	5, Sept 1864	3, Aug.	19- 4m		144	New Knoxville, OH	
Gnägi, Elisabeth	18, Aug. 1892	22, July	71		526	Spencerville, OH	Koppingen, Bern, Schweiz
Gnägi, Jakob	29, May 1890	21, Apr.	74- 1m- 5d		350	New Knoxville, OH	Hochstätten, Bern, Schweiz
Gnase, Dorothea	30, Mar. 1893	8, Mar.	79	Peters	206	Eudora, KS	Ost-Prünetz, Preußen
Gnase, Julius H.	13, Dec. 1894	16, Nov.	18		806	Eudora, KS	
Gnüther, Gerd Harms	10, Apr. 1882	22, Mar.	49-11m- 1d		119	San Jose, IL	Westerfold, Amt Esen, Ostfriesland
Göber, Albrecht Heinrich	30, Oct. 1882		77- 9m-11d		351	Allegheny City, PA	Bücken, Hoya, Hannover
Göbel, Christian	6, Apr. 1868	12, Mar.	56		111	Spencerville, OH	Friedmannsdorf, Eisenach, Sachsen-Weimar
Göbel, Cornelius	13, Mar. 1865	14, Feb.	32- 5m-21d		44	Canal Dover, OH	Epterode bei Hessen-Kassel, Hessen
Göbel, Friedrich	11, July 1861	14, June	31		112	Golconda, IL	Heerta, Sachsen-Weimar
Göbel, Johan	25, Oct. 1875	2, Oct.	53- 9m- 9d		343	Mascoutah, IL	Harpertshausen, Hessen
Göbel, Johan Emil	5, Sept 1895	13, Aug.	34		574	Mascoutah, IL	Mascoutah, Illinois
Göbel, Julia Maria	7, Mar. 1889	14, Feb.	26		158	Toledo, OH	
Göbel, Maria	14, Dec. 1874	30, Nov.	72- 1m-10d	Deisinger	399	Warsaw, IL	Alsheim, Rheinpfalz Baiern
Göbels, Jakob	28, Feb. 1889	13, Feb.	83		142	Warsaw, IL	Geroldsheim, RheinPfalz Baiern
Gödecke, Catharina	11, June 1866	28, May	26- 1m-22d	Mühlbach	190	Baltimore, MD	Poppenweiler, Ludwigsburg, Württemberg
Gödeke, Louise	21, May 1877	27, Apr.	32	Ekhard	166	Baltimore, MD	
Godel, Eberhard	25, Aug. 1887	10, Aug.			542	Peoria, IL	Feierbach, Württemberg
Godel, Eberhardt	15, Sept 1887	10, Aug.	51		590	Peoria, IL	Monmouth, Illinois
Godel, Georg Gottlieb	2, June 1898	7, May	50		351	Peoria, IL	
Goeckler, Anna Barbara	3, May 1880	10, Apr.	75- 3m- 5d	Böw	143	Hannibal, OH	Brucken, Kirchheim, Württemberg
Goehring, Wilhelm	13, Oct. 1887	23, Sept	76		654	Tuscola, IL	
Goeres, Jakob	11, Dec. 1876	28, Nov.	70		399	Stryker, OH	Ulmeth, Baiern
Goeres, Louise	4, Apr. 1881	14, Mar.	25		111	West Unity, OH	Williams County, Ohio
Goeres, Maria Elisabeth	19, Oct. 1885	19, Sept	75	Drum	7	Stryker, OH	Ulmet bei Kaiserslautern, Rheinkreis Baiern
Goering, Susanna	5, Apr. 1888	8, Mar.	54	Beck	222	Chicago, IL	Ernstrode, Sachsen-Coburg-Gotha

Christliche Apologete Death Notices --- 1839 - 1899

Name of Deceased	Notice Date	Death Date	Age	Maiden Name	Place of Death	Place of Birth
Goeschel, Emilie	21, July 1884	4, July	28		Saginaw, MI	Neustadt, Preußen
Goeß, Margaretha	31, Dec. 1883	10, Nov.	72- -15d		Brooklyn, NY	
Goetz, Charles	3, Apr. 1876	8, Feb.	23		Fond du Lac, WI	Fond du Lac, Wisconsin
Goetz, Edward	29, Oct. 1883	13, Oct.	20		Fond du Lac, WI	Fond du Lac, Wisconsin
Goetz, Friederike	12, Aug. 1886	26, July	70	Sieb	Michigan City, IN	Bernbach, Württemberg
Goetz, Henry A.	11, Aug. 1887	5, July	37		Lake View, IL	Bremen, Germany
Goetz, John	17, Jan. 1876	30, Dec.	53		Fond du Lac, WI	Rheinkreis Baiern
Goetz, Philipp	25, June 1877	13, June	21		Fond du Lac, WI	Fond du Lac, Wisconsin
Goetz, Rosa	20, Dec. 1888	29, Nov.	21- 1m-26d	Varwig	St. Louis, MO	
Goetzke, Catharina	14, Nov. 1895	21, Oct.	64	Toenges	Albert Lea, MN	Rheinbartshausen, Waldeck
Goevert, Heinrich Herman	11, Aug. 1884	28, July	81- 3m- 7d		Arenzville, IL	Restrup, Osnabrück, Hannover
Gogel, Barbara	20, Oct. 1873	23, Sept	76- 2m		Red Wing, MN	
Göhring, Barbara	12, Dec. 1889	21, Nov.	65-10m-19d		Cannelton, IN	Mühlhausen, Preußen
Göhrs, Herman	20, Dec. 1869	18, Nov.	63		Lake Creek, MO	Graßdorf, Amt Otterberg, Hannover
Gökeler, Johannes	15, Mar. 1888	19, Feb.	51- 1m- 6d		Clarington, OH	Burken, Kirchheim, Württemberg
Gökeler, John	21, July 1892	1, July	21		Wheeling, WV	
Göking, Katharina Elisabeth	16, Nov. 1893	10, Oct.	39		St. Joseph, MO	Brownstown, Jackson County, Indiana
Golden, Amalie	5, Jan. 1860	12, Dec.	20- 8m- 5d		Wheeling, VA	
Goldenberger, Anna	23, Apr. 1883	17, Mar.	50- - 7d	Höhnlie	Mascoutah, IL	Reitnau, Aargau, Schweiz
Goldenstein, Gertjen Harms	19, Oct. 1885	20, Aug.	72	Stromann	Dornum, CO	
Goldenstein, Johanne	15, Apr. 1897	18, Feb.	50		Dornum, CO	
Goldenstein, Marie Gesine	15, Dec. 1898	22, Nov.	19		Chicago, IL	Ochtersum, Ostfriesland
Goldenstein, Richard	24, Mar. 1892	26, Feb.	42		Terre Haute, IN	Widdern, Neckarsulm, Württemberg
Golder, Theodor	16, Feb. 1899	12, Jan.	44		Mt. Olive, IL	
Goightly, Dorothea	26, Feb. 1883	9, Feb.	23	Ahrens	Galena, IL	Lambard, Illinois
Golke, Maria	15, Mar. 1888	15, Feb.	38	Boß	Madison, WI	Niederwenden, Gerabronn, Württemberg
Göller, Margaretha	12, Apr. 1844		Inquiry		Circleville, OH	Edersbach, Baden
Göller, Philippine	28, Jan. 1886	29, Dec.	39		Newark, ---	
Gollmar, Anna Maria	17, Mar. 1884	25, Feb.	72		Allegheny City, PA	Württemberg
Gollmer, Friedrike	8, Nov. 1894	14, Oct.	76		Industry, TX	Wisconsin
Goltz, Emma	6, Dec. 1894	5, Nov.	25	Unlauf	Waseca, MN	Schwennigen, Württemberg
Gölz, Catharina	1, Mar. 1875	5, Feb.	38- 1m- 2d	Würthner	Erie, PA	Zichen, Kreis Soldin, Frankfurt, Preußen
Golz, Henriette	13, July 1854	28, June	39	Buchholz	Galena, IL	Menbach, Rheinkreis Baiern
Gölzer, Catharina	29, Apr. 1878	28, Mar.	88	Götzer	Cannelton, IN	Minbach bei Zweibrücken, Rheinpfalz Baiern
Gölzer, Joh. Daniel	26, Oct. 1854	28, Aug.	73- 2m-12d		Grove Center, NY	St. Maurice, Decatur County, Indiana
Gommel, Georg Eduard	18, Jan. 1894	21, Dec.	27		Detroit, MI	Groß-Sachsenheim, Vaihingen, Württemberg
Gommel, Katharine Friederike	25, June 1891	30, May	72		Batesville, IN	
Gompert, Daniel	14, Feb. 1870	19, Dec.	18- 4m-25d		Jeffersonville, NY	Steppach, Amt Eppingen, Baden
Gönawein, Anna Maria	31, Mar. 1859	15, Mar.	60- 2m- 1d		Ripley, OH	Annweiler, RheinPfalz Baiern
Gönawein, Maria	12, Sept 1881	3, Sept	33- 9m- 5d	Seibel	Cincinnati, OH	Niederhofen, Brackenheim, Württemberg
Gonawein, Matthias	23, Apr. 1877	8, Apr.	68- 4m-11d		Birmingham, PA	Thurnhosbach, Kurhessen
Gondermann, Benjamin	2, July 1877	30, May	75- 4m-26d		Chicago, IL	Hof an der Saal, Baiern
Gönel, Margaretha	7, Mar. 1895	18, Feb.	66	Strobel	Cincinnati, OH	Holzhausen, Minden, Preußen
Gönewein, Maria	20, Oct. 1873	26, Sept	60		Pomeroy, OH	Opau, RheinPfalz Baiern
Gönheimer, Heinrich	19, May 1887	4, May	77		Pomeroy, OH	Opau, RheinPfalz Baiern
Gönheimer, Johannes	19, May 1887	2, May	80			

Christliche Apologete Death Notices --- 1839 - 1899

Name of Deceased	Notice Date	Death Date	Age	Maiden Name	Place of Death	Place of Birth
Gönheimer, Wendel	6, June 1889	10, May	80		Ironton, OH	Oppau, RheinPfalz Baiern
Gönnel, Gottlob Fr.	4, Mar.1872	23, Jan.	61		Chicago, IL	Schönheide bei Eibenstock, Sachsen
Good, Emanuel	26, Feb. 1891	5, Feb.	66		St. Paul, MN	Pennsylvania
Good, Henrietta	15, Mar. 1894	21, Feb.	58		Plainfield, IA	Werdau, Sachsen
Goodbub, Mary A.	14, Apr. 1898	16, Mar.	45		New Albany, IN	New Albany, Indiana
Goos, J.E.	18, Feb. 1867	23, Dec.	35- 6m-27d		Second Creek, MO	Island Föhr, Schleswig-Holstein
Göpel, Andreas	24, Dec. 1896	4, Dec.	63		Waltersburg, IL	Heerda bei Berka, Sachsen-Weimar
Göpel, Anna Maria	4, Nov. 1897	9, Oct.	62	Mähler	Waltersburg, IL	Reinau bei Berta an der Werra, Sachsen
Göpfert, Friederike	27, Oct. 1892	5, Oct.	57	Maier	Berne, MI	Wonnsdorf, Hannover
Gordner, Julia	8, Mar. 1888	10, Feb.	59	Eppinghaus	Boonville, IN	Birkenfeld, Oldenburg
Göres, Johannes	10, Nov. 1862	1, Oct.	20		Defiance, OH	
Görhke, Friedrich	5, Nov. 1865	5, Oct.	47		Portland, WI	Parkewitz, Stargart, Vorpommern, Preußen
Göring, Anna Maria	7, Apr. 1884	11, Mar.	66	Fröhlich	Chicago, IL	Wahlwinkel, Sachsen-Gotha
Goring, Johan Heinrich	7,May 1883	18, Apr.	65- 6m- 3d		Chicago, IL	Ernstroda, Sachsen-Gotha
Göringer, Helene	14, Nov. 1870	27, Oct.	19	Krummel	Batesville, IN	Dearborn County, Indiana
Gorke, Anna	22, May 1871	2, May	28	Karg	Baltimore, MD	Hessen-Darmstadt
Görken, Catharina	28, Apr. 1862	7, Apr.	18		Evansville, IN	
Görner, Gottfried	22, Feb. 1869	8, Jan.	55		Philadelphia, PA	Pfitzhof, Heilbronn, Württemberg
Görts, Maria Elisabeth	10, Oct. 1870	30, Aug.	21		Defiance, OH	Williams County, Ohio
Görtz, Jakob	15, May 1890	22, Apr.	83- 6m- 8d		Columbus, IL	Dambach, Idstein, Nassau
Gosch, Henry	21, Sept 1868	14, Aug.			San Francisco, CA	Holstein, Germany
Gosch, Marie	4, Aug. 1884	20, July	45	Kaufmann	Wichita, KS	Warsaw, Illinois
Göschel, Friedrich Wilhelm	16, Aug. 1875	23, July	72		Saginaw, MI	Kirchberg, Sachsen
Göschel, Louise Maria	19, Aug. 1878	1, Aug.	41- 6m	Burger	Saginaw, MI	Eßlingen, Württemberg
Gosejohann, Catharina M.	27, Oct. 1873	4, Oct.	60	Hartmann	St. Louis, MO	Westerkappeln, Preußen
Gosejohann, Herman Heinrich	24, Jan. 1871	29, Dec.	44- 3m-16d		St. Louis, MO	Westerkappeln, Münster, Preußen
Gösker, Heinrich L.	19, May 1884	28, Apr.	12		Huntingburg, IN	
Göß, Karl	21, Jan. 1892	26, Dec.	80		Brooklyn, NY	Langenfeld, Baiern
Göß, Martin	21, Nov. 1881	10, Sept	17- -17d		Brooklyn, NY	
Gössel, Konrad August	11, Nov. 1886	1, Oct.	61		Newark, NJ	
Gösser, Christian	19, Feb. 1877	7, Feb.	18		Cincinnati, OH	Bickenbach, Preußen
Gost, Johan	5, Dec. 1870	5, Nov.	18		Nora Springs, IA	
Goth, John William	10, Apr. 1871	30, Nov.	58- 7m- 4d	Groh	Giard, IA	Ripley County, Indiana
Goth, Margaretha	10, Jan. 1889	18, Dec.	75-10m- 7d		Giard, IA	Erlenbach, Rheinkreis Baiern
Goth, Valentin	2, Feb. 1880	16, Jan.	67		Dillsboro, IN	Mutterstadt, RheinPfalz Baiern
Goth, Valentine	7, June 1894	14, May	69		Indianapolis, IN	
Götsch, August	23, Feb. 1899	9, Jan.	52	Gihring	New Ulm, MN	Harnbeck, Brandenburg
Gotsch, Marie Friederike	11, Mar. 1897	13, Feb.	60	Gerstung	Baltimore, MD	Tübingen, Württemberg
Gottbehüt, Katharina	17, July 1893	18, July	77- 3m-27d		St. Paul, MN	Wendershausen bei Tann, Baiern
Götte, David	18, Jan. 1869	21, Dec.	66		Madison, IN	Liebenau, Hofgeimar, Kurhessen
Götte, Elisabeth	5, Aug. 1886	8, July	66		Madison, IN	Sachsen-Coburg
Göttel, Karl	24, Nov. 1898	23, Oct.	21- 4m- 9d		Rochester, NY	Altenglan, Kusel, Rheinpfalz Baiern
Göttel, Ottilie	8, Apr. 1878	14, Mar.	16		Rochester, NY	Rochester, New York
Göttel, Willie	26, Oct. 1899	12, Sept	68- 4m		Rochester, NY	Rochester, New York
Gotter, Catharina	8, Feb. 1875	8, Feb.	69	Roth	Warsaw, IL	Marenheim, RheinPfalz Baiern
Göttert, Maria Katharina	28, Dec. 1893	7, Aug.		Manhinweg	Muscatine, IA	Rininger, Leonberg, Württemberg

Christliche Apologete Death Notices --- 1839 - 1899

Name of Deceased	Notice Date	Death Date	Age	Maiden Name	Page	Place of Death	Place of Birth
Gottfried, Peter	17, Nov. 1887	31, Oct.	30		734	Bucyrus, OH	Crawford County, Ohio
Göttgen, Margaretha	20, Aug. 1883	8, July	50-8m	Borchers	271	New York City, NY	Neulande, Hannover
Göttler, Elisabeth	8, May 1882	10, Apr.	31-10m	Schade	151	Secor, IL	Niederaula, Kurhessen
Göttler, Melchior	31, Oct. 1881	5, Oct.	60- - 3d		351	Hannibal, MO	Aldorf, Horb, Württemberg
Gottschalk, (Mr)	4, Dec. 1865	17, Nov.	67		196	Mt. Vernon, IN	Rauschenberg, Kurhessen
Gottschalk, Benjamin Theophilus	20, Apr. 1893	22, Mar.	16		254	Chicago, IL	Watertown, Wisconsin
Gottschalk, Carolina	27, Aug. 1877	15, Aug.	37		279	Milwaukee, WI	Krokow, Pommern
Gottschalk, Christine	25, May 1899	26, Apr.	86		335	Webster, SD	Muttrin, Belgrad, Hinterpommern
Gottschalk, Emma Louisa	11, Aug. 1892	23, July	20-6 m-23d		510	Chicago, IL	Oshkosh, Wisconsin
Gottschalk, Ernestine	12, May 1879	24, Apr.	75	Wippler	151	Brunswick, MO	Buckholz, Lippe-Schaumburg
Gottschalk, Johan	8, Apr. 1886	8, Mar.	86		7	Chicago, IL	Tütspaz, Vorpommern
Gottschalk, Katharina Elisabeth	24, Feb. 1868	28, Jan.	72		63	Mt. Vernon, IN	Rauschenberg bei Marburg, Kurhessen
Gottschalk, Maria Catharina	8, Aug. 1864	19, July	58		128	Milwaukee, WI	Altenhagen, Kreis Temin, Preußen
Gottschalk, Sophia	20, July 1885	5, June	77	Keding	7	Milwaukee, WI	Tützpatz, Pommern
Gottschämer, John	19, Dec. 1895	1, Dec.	69		814	St. Paul, MN	Frankfurt a. Main, Preußen
Göttschammer, Christine	28, Jan. 1878		29-11m- 9d	Schmidt	31	St. Louis, MO	Hainbom bei Brunbach, Baiern
Gottschammer, Hayes	19, Nov. 1891	27, Oct.	15		750	St. Louis, MO	St. Louis, Missouri
Gottschammer, Johanna	10, Mar. 1887	22, Feb.	60	Jost	158	St. Louis, MO	Götzenhain, Hessen-Darmstadt
Gottschammer, Maria	28, July 1873	11, July	24- 2m- 7d		239	St. Louis, MO	Nauvoo, Illinois
Gottschammer, Philipp	26, May 1898	7, May	55		335	St. Louis, MO	Getzenheim, Hessen-Darmstadt
Gottselig, Adam	16, Feb. 1885	8, Feb.	50- 5m-10d		7	Indianapolis, IN	Haubersbronn, Schorndorf, Württemberg
Gottwald, Minnie	2, Apr. 1896	5, Mar.	29	Schütz	222	Garner, IA	Bloomington, Illinois
Götz, Georg	16, Feb. 1899	20, Jan.	76		110	Allegheny City, PA	Bärenthal, Elsaß
Götz, Isaak	31, July 1890	13, July	106		494	St. Louis, MO	Hemmeshofen, Schaffhausen, Schweiz
Götz, Jakob	5, Apr. 1875	7, Mar.	57- 1m- 3d		111	Canal Dover, OH	Zeiningen, Urach, Württemberg
Götz, John	29, Jan. 1872	14, Jan.	24		39	Fond du Lac, WI	Dodge County, Wisconsin
Götz, Julianne	28, Mar. 1870	19, Jan.	65	Hornung	103	Industry, TX	Unter-Kersach, baden
Götz, Katharine Dorothea	4, Feb. 1886	19, Jan.	61- 4m-23d		7	Ellis Grove, IL	Mackmühl, Neckarsulm, Württemberg
Götz, Margaretha	24, Oct. 1895	16, Sept	70		686	Minneapolis, MN	Württemberg
Götz, Maria A.	12, Aug. 1878	20, June	69		255	Baltimore, MD	Schweiz
Götz, Wilford	23, June 1887	1, June	25		398	Minneapolis, MN	Fond Du Lac County, Wisconsin
Götze, Cilia	12, Feb. 1883	23, Jan.	16		55	Chicago, IL	Chicago, Cook County, Illinois
Götze, Georg	29, July 1878	16, July	100- 3m		239	Wyandotte, KS	
Göyert, Alice Luise	18, May 1899	27, Apr.	28		319	Waltersburg, IL	Massao County, Illinois
Goyert, Luise	3, Aug. 1899	12, July	63	Wellmann	495	Waltersburg, IL	Dillingen, Hannover
Graaf, Maria	2, June 1873	12, May	83		175	Clarington, OH	Canton Aarau, Schweiz
Graas, Maria	5, June 1846	15, May	2- 7m-15d		91	Lawrenceburg, IN	
Grab, Catharina	6, Oct. 1873	29, Aug.		Zoller	319	New Rochelle, NY	
Grab, Friedrich	21, Dec. 1885	1, Dec.	75		7	Freeport, IL	Brietzig, Pyritz, Stettin, Preußen
Grabener, Gustav August	9, Dec. 1872	20, Oct.	20		399	Charles City, IA	Darlington, Wisconsin
Gräber, Johan	26, Jan. 1885	8, Jan.			7	Minneapolis, MN	Erdmanshausen, Württemberg
Gräber, Wilhelm H.	8, Aug. 1864	19, June	18- 6m		128	Platteville, WI	
Grabert, Christiane	24, Feb. 1859	8, Feb.	42		32	Roxbury, MA	Schnaith, Schorndorf, Württemberg
Grabhorn, Caroline	15, Oct. 1866	4, Sept	35	Kuhne	334	Manhattan, KS	Gofeld, Preußen
Grabhorn, Johanna	22, Aug. 1870	3, Aug.	40	Kuhne	271	Randolph, KS	Gofeld, Minden, Preußen
Grabhorn, Telke Helena	13, Oct. 1862	23, Sept	65	Koch	164	Evansville, IN	Westerstede, Oldenburg

Christliche Apologete Death Notices -- 1839 - 1899

Name of Deceased	Notice Date	Death Date	Age	Maiden Name	Page	Place of Death	Place of Birth
Grabinske, Augusta Emilie	13, Sept 1894	19, Aug.	66- 5m- 3d	Korduan	598	--, SD	Zorndorf, Germany
Grabinski, Amalia	30, Mar. 1893	1, Mar.	36- 3m- 6d		206	Miller, SD	
Grabow, Gottlieb	13, June 1889	22, May	75		382	Sleepy Eye, MN	Schwinden, Flatow, West Preußen
Grade, Elisabeth	23, May 1889	15, Apr.	75- 6m	Voß	334	Roseville, MI	Selzin, Mecklenburg-Schwerin
Grade, Johan	20, Feb. 1882	26, Jan.	72- 9m-25d		63	Roseville, MI	Selzin, Mecklenburg-Schwerin
Gradert, Heinrich	21, Dec. 1893	7, Nov.	65- 5m-12d		814	Crown Point, IN	Hanzühn, Schleswig-Holstein
Graf, Ursula	5, May 1898	1, Apr.	64	Meier	287	Montague, MI	Unterhallau, Schaffhausen, Schweiz
Graf, Agnes	22, Jan. 1883	6, Jan.	76- 7m		31	New Albany, IN	Schaffhausen, Schweiz
Graf, Anna Margaretha	5, Jan. 1880	18, Dec.	75	Kissel	7	Portsmouth, OH	Umstadt, Hessen
Graf, Barbara	8, Dec. 1884	19, Nov.	29- 8m- 7d	Rabenstein	7	Aurora, IN	Aurora, Dearborn County, Indiana
Graf, Eva	3, Apr. 1865	13, Mar.	82		56	New Albany, IN	
Graf, Franz	25, Dec. 1856	23, Nov.	49		208	New Albany, IN	Oppenrode, Hessen-Darmstadt
Graf, Friederika	22, Nov. 1875	5, Nov.	48- 6m- 6d		375	Canal Dover, OH	
Graf, Jost	3, Dec. 1896	8, Nov.	82		782	Blue Island, IL	Nonnenroth, Hessen-Darmstadt
Graf, Leon	20, Mar. 1865	Oct.	21		48	New York, NY	Schnefingen, Argau, Schweiz
Graf, Rudolf	9, May 1889	25, Apr.	20		302	Wilton, IA	Baden-Baden, Baden
Graf, Sarah	17, May 1888	11, Apr.	27- 1m-25d	Trautmann	318	Tonawanda, NY	
Graf, Wilhelmine	11, Aug. 1879	7, July	65- 5m- 3d		255	Eudora, KS	Solingen, Düsseldorf, Preußen
Graf, Wilhelmine	23, Dec. 1872	23, Nov.	36	Ruchotzky	415	Columbus, WI	Grabiona, Bromberg, Preußen
Gräfe, Gottfried	14, June 1894	26, May	90		390	Louisville, KY	Wintersdorf, Sachsen-Altenburg
Gräfer, Wilhelm Robert	25, Apr. 1881	1, Apr.	31- 4m		135	Menomonie, WI	Zwickau, Sachsen
Graff, (girl)	14, Aug. 1840	3, Aug.	16- 3m		127	Monroe Co, OH	
Graff, C. Elsworth	29, Jan. 1891	1, Jan.	26		78	Delaware, OH	Delaware, Ohio
Graff, Ida	13, Oct. 1887	28, Sept	17		654	Crandon, SD	Fountain Prairie, Columbia County, Wisconsin
Graff, Johan	10, May 1888	15, Apr.	73		302	Boonville, IN	Oberamt Lutz, Württemberg
Graff, Karoline	8, July 1878	23, June	76-10m-16d	Wemmer	215	Delaware, OH	Gündelbach, Maulbronn, Württemberg
Graff, Katharine	24, Nov. 1892	1, Nov.	61	Schneider	750	Galion, OH	Hohensolms, Wetzlar, Preußen
Graff, Susanna	25, Mar. 1858	24, Feb.	67		48	Wapello, IA	
Grafius, Margaretha	4, Nov. 1872	1, Oct.	21		359	Pittsburg, PA	Inkenbach bei Meisenheim, Preußen
Gräfnitz, Karl Friedrich	31, July 1890	9, July			494	Detroit, MI	Sipke bei Barth, Vorpommern
Gralapp, Christian Wilhelm	31, Oct. 1895	12, Oct.	62		702	Lemars, IA	Nauenheim bei Geitheim, Sachsen
Gram, Albert	19, Jan. 1880	4, Nov.	5-10m		23	Pittsburg, PA	
Gram, Mathilde	20, Nov. 1882	7, Nov.	20-10m-13d	Ambell	375	Pittsburg, PA	
Gramer, Christoph	27, June 1864	12, June	62- 3m- 7d		104	Bucyrus, OH	Münzingen, Bretten, Baden
Gramkow, Herman Christian	27, July 1899	26, June	29		479	Parker, SD	Ahnapee, Wisconsin
Gramlich, Georg	16, Dec. 1897	16, Nov.	86		799	Lansing, IA	Adelsheim, Baden
Gramlich, Mina Karoline	21, May 1891	27, Apr.	22- 5m- 5d		334	Lansing, IA	Allamakee County, Iowa
Gramm, Jakob	28, Oct. 1878	7, Sept	67		343	Jamestown, MO	Bothnang, Württemberg
Gramm, Oskar Eugen	6, Oct. 1898	25, Sept	18		639	Ironton, OH	Lafayette County, Missouri
Gramp, Magdalena	25, June 1866		20		206	St. Louis, MO	
Gramph, Georg	15, May 1882	26, Apr.	61- 2m- 2d		159	St. Louis, MO	Freistadt, Baiern
Grampp, Charles A.	30, Oct. 1890	7, Oct.	31- 3m-17d		702	St. Louis, MO	St. Louis, Missouri
Grampp, Georg	12, June 1882	26, Apr.	61- 2m- 2d		191	St. Louis, MO	Freistadt, Baiern
Grampp, Rosina	21, Feb. 1895	12, Jan.	74		126	St. Louis, MO	Baden-Baden, Baden
Grandjot, Henriette	14, June 1894	12, May	75		390	Chicago, IL	Kreiswald, Pommern
Grandt, Louisa Emma	3, Nov. 1892	17, Oct.	28		702	Fond du Lac, WI	

Christliche Apologete Death Notices --- 1839 - 1899

Name of Deceased	Notice Date	Death Date	Age	Page	Maiden Name	Place of Death	Place of Birth
Granemann, Maria	23, June 1879	4, June	52	199	Niemeyer	Morrison, MO	Hille bei Minden, Preußen
Graner, Wilhelm Friedrich	21, Jan. 1892	19, Dec.	47	46		Toledo, OH	Nürtingen am Neckar, Württemberg
Granget, Johan Stephen	1, Apr. 1872	23, Feb.	63	111		Mt. Vernon, IN	Pallenbach, Durlach, Baden
Granget, Justina	15, Apr. 1878	10, Mar.	60	119		Mt. Vernon, IN	Grünwettersbach, Durlach, Baden
Grannamann, C.H.	20, Aug. 1891	1, Aug.	69	542		Morrison, MO	Nordhämmern, Minden, Preußen
Grannemann, Anna Rosina	27, Sept 1875	5, Sept	23	311		Morrison, MO	
Grannemann, John H.	28, Apr. 1873	15, Mar.	55	135		Jefferson City, MO	Nordhemmern, Minden, Preußen
Grannemann, Maria	25, Feb. 1878	1, Feb.	60- 5m- 4d	63	VonWehren	Morrison, MO	Nord-Hemmern, Minden, Preußen
Grannemann, Maria	4, Jan. 1864	7, Nov.	50	4	Südmeyer	Herman, MO	Nordhemmern, Minden, Preußen
Grannemann, Malinda Louise	5, Feb. 1891	13, Jan.	33	94	Thee	Morrison, MO	Big Springs, Montgomery County, Missouri
Graper, Gottfried	12, Sept 1861	13, July	67	148		Monterey, WI	Landon, Pommern, Preußen
Graper, Herman Friedrich	6, July 1899	15, June	52	431		Oconomowoc, WI	Schönwärder, Piritz, Pommern
Graper, Maria	12, Sept 1889	19, Aug.	65	590		Oconomowoc, WI	Schönwerder, Piritz, Pommern
Graper, Wilhelm Fr.	17, Aug. 1863	5, July	26	132		Monterey, WI	Seinow, Arnswalte in der Neumark, Preußen
Gräpler, Carl	12, Nov. 1896	23, Oct.	52	734		Alden, IA	Neuhof, Mecklenburg-Schwerin
Grasdorf, Elisabeth	19, May 1884	1, May	74- 1m	7		Angelica, NY	Gifhorn, Hannover
Gräser, Jakob	9, Nov. 1863	23, Sept	39- 6m-16d	180			Mantel bei Kreutznach, Preußen
Graske, Christina	4, May 1874	17, Feb.	80	143		Brunswick, MO	Brandeburg, Preußen
Gräsle, Philipp	15, Oct. 1857	23, Sept	23	168		Marion, OH	
Gräsle, Sophia	15, Oct. 1857	17, Sept	49	168		Marion, OH	Ellmendingen, Pforzheim, Baden
Graß, Heinrich Wilhelm	17, Apr. 1890	26, Mar.	82	254		Sandusky, OH	Dietz, Nassau
Graßdorf, Gottlieb	28, Jan. 1867	11, Jan.		30		Wellsville, NY	Leiferde, Amt Gifhorn, Hannover
Graßhof, Herman O.	7, Mar. 1881	5, Feb.	59	79		Schulenburg, TX	Naumburg am Cober, Schlesien
Graßhoff, Herman	8, Nov. 1894	14, Oct.	32	726		Freyburg, TX	
Graßhoff, Maria Wilhelmine	4, Jan. 1894	10, Dec.	68	14	Warsang	Freiburg, TX	Halbau, Schlesien
Gräßle, Bernhard	2, July 1896	10, June	93- 4m-28d	431		Spencerville, OH	Elmendingen, Pfortzheim, Baden
Gräßle, Christine Amalie	12, Feb. 1891	19, Jan.	46	110	Knöller	Michigan City, IN	Neusatz, Neubürg, Württemberg
Gräßle, Jacob Friedrich	10, Sept 1896	17, Aug.	90	591		Marion, OH	Elmendingen, Pfortzheim, Baden
Gräßle, Juliana	17, Aug. 1899	29, July	65	527	Sitterley	Wellsville, NY	Newark, Ohio
Gräßle, Regina	6, Dec. 1888	11, Nov.	65	782	Müller	Boonville, MO	Blüderhausen, Welzheim, Württemberg
Graßmück, Adam	15, Sept 1892	6, July	63	590		New York City, NY	König , Hessen-Darmstadt
Graßtorf, Clara	4, June 1891	9, May	28-11m-16d	366		Angelica, NY	
Grastorf, August Wilhelm	9, July 1891	26, May	39	446		Angelica, NY	Wellsville, New York
Grastorf, Christoph J.	25, Jan. 1894	29, Dec.	26	62		Wellsville, NY	Wellsville, New York
Grastorf, Elisabeth	8, May 1865	9, Apr.	20- 3m- 8d	76		Angelica, NY	
Grastorf, Johan Heinrich	10, May 1888	5, Apr.	75	302		Wellsville, NY	Leiferde, Gifhorn, Hannover
Grastorf, Johan Heinrich	24, May 1875	14, Mar.	70	167		Boonville, MO	Gifhorn, Hannover
Grastorf, John	29, Dec. 1873	23, Nov.	65	415		Angelica, NY	Leiferde, Amt Gifhorn, Hannover
Gratz, Francis G. (Rev)	20, May 1897	21, Apr.	74	318		Boston, MA	Grundbach, Neuenburg, Württemberg
Grätz, Friederike L.	4, Apr. 1889	23, Feb.	79	222		Rochester, MN	Pensilvanien, Staudenberg, Preußen
Grätz, Louis Wilmot	17, July 1890	20, June	26	462		Spokane Falls, WA	Rochester, Minnesota
Grau, Gottlieb	6, Dec. 1875	19, Nov.	54	391		Concord, IA	Schudischen, Wilhelmsberg, OstPreußen
Grau, Sophie	8, Jan. 1891	9, Dec.	66- 8m- 9d	30	Rätz	Milwaukee, WI	Gondelsheim, Betten, Baden
Graubner, Gustav	18, Dec. 1851	31, Aug.	25	204		Quincy, IL	
Graue, Karoline	6, Sept 1860		22- 6m-15d	144		Greencastle, IN	Easttown, Pennsylvania
Grauel, Charlotte	6, June 1861	14, May	66	92	Mäurer	Pittsburg, PA	Großkerbach, Rheinkreis Baiern

Christliche Apologete Death Notices --- 1839 - 1899

Name of Deceased	Notice Date	Death Date	Age	Maiden Name	Page	Place of Death	Place of Birth
Grauel, Lena Anna	26, Jan. 1899	1, Jan.	27	Misse	63	St. Paul, MN	Arnsberg, Preußen
Graul, Philipp Adolph	9, May 1889	27, Feb.	17		302	St. Paul, MN	Goodhue County, Minnesota
Grauwinkel, Dorothea Sophie	19, Sept 1861	11, Aug.	75		152	Wapello, IA	Hudemühlen, Amt Aller, Hannover
Grauwinkel, Elisabeth	10, Feb. 1898	2, Jan.	41		95	Wapello, IA	Gründelhardt, Grailsheim, Württemberg
Grauwinkel, Friedrich	3, Dec. 1877	17, Nov.	34- 4m		391	Morrison, MO	Thola, Hohenhausen, Minden, Preußen
Gräve, Anna	14, Mar. 1864	5, Feb.	42	Herzog	44	Aurora, IN	Laufenholz, Nürnberg, Baiern
Grawe, Lena	26, Jan. 1880	10, Jan.	24		31	St. Louis, MO	Ballwin, Missouri
Gray, Anna	28, Jan. 1884	8, Dec.	31	Bödecker	7	Chicago, IL	Baden
Grazcikowski, Therese Augusta	5, Apr. 1894	13, Mar.	23		230	Detroit, MI	Berlin, Preußen
Gräzel, Frank	21, Oct. 1897	28, Aug.	39		671	Ft. Atkinson, WI	Miford, Jefferson County, Wisconsin
Gräzel, Martha	10, Feb. 1898	2, Jan.	19	Kugath	95	Ft. Atkinson, WI	Miford, Jefferson County, Wisconsin
Grebe, Anna Emilie	9, Mar. 1899	2, Feb.	72	Tödtemann	159	Warren County, MO	Warren County, Missouri
Grebe, August	10, Nov. 1887	21, Oct.	64		718	Springfield, IL	Springfield, Illinois
Grebe, August Siegesmund	26, Feb. 1891	26, Jan.	22		142	Dallas, TX	Obernkirchen, Hessen
Grebe, Charlotte	9, Jan. 1890	26, Dec.	66	Kölling	30	Warrenton, MO	Bonneberg, Minden, Westphalen
Grebe, Christian	19, Aug. 1878	3, Aug.	19- 8m-10d		263	Dallas, TX	Osage, Illinois
Grebe, Dorothea	6, Dec. 1894	20, Nov.	29	Neubig	790	Springfield, IL	Schwarzenberg, Namberg, Württemberg
Grebe, Friedrich Ludwig	29, Mar. 1880	12, Mar.	73		103	Bucyrus, OH	Rehme, Minden, Preußen
Grebe, Heinrich	14, Mar. 1881	1, Mar.	81- 5m-27d		87	Warrenton, MO	Beatenkopf, Hessen-Darmstadt
Grebe, Johan	19, Oct. 1899	19, Sept	50- 6m		671	Springfield, IL	Rhoden , Waldeck
Grebe, Johan Jacob Christian	8, Aug. 1881	25, July	68		255	Madison, IN	Berndorf, Waldeck
Grebe, Maria	8, Mar. 1880	23, Feb.	27		79	Appleton, MO	Neustadt, Schweiz
Grebe, Marianna	18, June 1877	24, May		Bühler	199		
Grebien, Christina	1, Nov. 1880	1, Nov.		Reinmuth	351	Madison, IN	
Grebner, Katharina	30, Mar. 1863	11, Feb.		Riedel	52	Hebron, IA	Heidenheim, Württemberg
Grebner, Mary L.	12, Jan. 1893	20, Dec.		Tieman	30	Dresden, OH	
Greeman, Elisa	3, Apr. 1882	12, Mar.	32	Hülscher	111	Dresden, OH	Hilter, Amt Iburg, Osnabrück, Hannover
Greemann, Elise	16, Sept 1886	21, Aug.	55		7	Batesville, IN	Cincinnati, Hamilton County, Ohio
Greemann, Klara Ilsabein	8, Sept 1898	12, Aug.	55- 6m-14d	Jockheck	575	Batesville, IN	Gettmold, Oldendorf, Leibecke, Westphalen
Green, Andreas W.	7, June 1894	14, May	30		374	Batesville, IN	
Green, Maria M.	7, Jan. 1886	2, Dec.	69	Grieshaber	7	Peoria, IL	
Greene, Malinda	27, Nov. 1890	3, Nov.	34		766	Peoria, IL	Sulz am Neckar, Württemberg
Greffin, Charlotte Sophia	22, June 1899	24, Apr.	54- 3m- 2d		399	Owensville, MO	Gasconade County, Missouri
Greibe, Maria	29, May 1865	4, May	42- 10m- 3d		88	Blair, NE	Brotzen, West Preußen
Greife, Anna Louise	20, July 1874	12, June	76	Meyer	231	St. Louis, MO	Oldenburg, Hannover
Greife, Wilhelm Friedrich	18, Sept 1890	31, July	50- 5m-20d		606	Beaufort, MO	Laar, Herfort, Minden, Preußen
Greife, Wilhelmina Karolina	24, Mar. 1887	26, Feb.	33-10m		190	Beaufort, MO	Franklin County, Missouri
Greims, Elisabeth	21, Oct. 1886	5, Oct.	21- 2m-10d	Heß	7	Beaufort, MO	Gasconade County, Missouri
Greims, Johan	6, Dec. 1875	10, Oct.	13- 9m-21d		391	Lafayette, IN	Pennsylvania
Grein, Anna Martha	19, Apr. 1875	26, Mar.	68- 5m		127	Warrensburg, MO	Weißdorf, Baiern
Grein, Georg Heinrich	1, July 1867	20, June	37- 3m-18d		206	Pittsburg, PA	Pittsburg, Pennsylvania
Grein, Johannes	26, Jan. 1863	27, Dec.	17		16	Indianapolis, IN	Hancock County, Indiana
Greiner, Georg Jakob	27, Sept 1894	30, Aug.	23		630	Indianapolis, IN	Zell, Hessen-Darmstadt
Greiner, Gottlieb	25, July 1850	6, July	55		120	Batesville, IN	Niederbron, Elsaß
Greiner, Johannes	7, Oct. 1872	15, Sept	72- 8m-15d		327	Burlington, ---	Michelbach, Brackenheim, Württemberg
Greiner, Johannes	30, July 1857	25, May	28		124	Buffalo, NY	Steinenberg, Schorndorf, Württemberg

Christliche Apologete Death Notices -- 1839 - 1899

Name of Deceased	Notice Date	Death Date	Age	Maiden Name	Page	Place of Death	Place of Birth
Greiner, Johannes Konrad	10, Nov. 1898	17, Oct.	67		719	Delaware, OH	Bissingen, Kirchheim, Württemberg
Greiner, Karoline	8, May 1882	5, Apr.	29	Schill	151	Toledo, OH	Stuttgart, Württemberg
Greiner, Katharina	29, Oct. 1883	11, Oct.			351	St. Paul, MN	Fichtenberg, Gaildorf, Württemberg
Greiner, Philippine	7, Mar. 1881	17, Feb.	44- 7m	Schaf	79	Chicago, IL	Merkenbach, Nassau
Greiner, Sophie	28, Apr. 1879	6, Apr.	79- 1m-11d	Flumm	135	Grand Rapids, MI	Cappel, Oehringen, Württemberg
Greinhardt, Mathilda	17, Dec. 1877	29, Nov.	36	Witthuhn	407	Clayton, WI	Stolzenburg, Stettin, Preußen
Greischer, Fr. W.	7, Aug. 1865	9, July	26		128	Galion, OH	
Greive, Elisabeth	26, July 1849	27, June	38		120	St. Louis, MO	Schlethausen, Hannover
Greiwe, Adam Heinrich	16, Sept 1872	12, Apr.	62		303	Lake Creek, MO	Schlederhausen, Amt Osnabrück, Hannover
Greiwe, Anna Maria	8, Jan. 1877	21, Dec.	69- -14d	Kleinschmidt	15	St. Louis, MO	Blasheim, Minden, Preußen
Greiwe, Herman Heinrich	25, Dec. 1856	5, Dec.	13-10m		208	St. Louis, MO	Belm bei Osnabrück, Hannover
Greiwe, Johan Adam	24, Jan. 1871	11, Jan.	63		31	St. Louis, MO	Bohmte, Amt Wittlage, Osnabrück, Hannover
Greiwer, Friedrich	27, Dec. 1875	14, Dec.	55-11m		415	Portsmouth, OH	
Grelle, Heinrich	19, Nov. 1866	30, Oct.	70- 4m-25d		374	Wheeling, IL	Gifhorn, Hannover
Grelle, Marie	23, Oct. 1871	11, Sept	76- 9m		343	Wheeling, IL	
Grembels, H.	7, Apr. 1879	23, Mar.	61- 1m- 6d		111	St. Joseph, MO	Reinbach, Lauterbach, Hessen
Gremm, Otilia	11, Feb. 1892	21, Jan.	87	Schmier	94	Decorah, IA	
Gremmels, Karl	9, Oct. 1876	2, Sept	15- 4m- 6d		327	St. Joseph, MO	Hausem, Thurgau, Schweiz
Gremminger, Jacob	2, Aug. 1855	28, June	26		124	Chillicothe, OH	
Grener, Magdalena	18, Feb. 1884	22, Jan.		Schäfer	7	Galion, OH	Allmershausen, Kurhessen
Grenzenbach, Jakob	17, Aug. 1893	29, July	45		526	Cleveland, OH	Ulmershausen, Hirschfeld, Kurhessen
Grenzenbach, Johannes	3, Aug. 1899	5, July	60		495	Cleveland, OH	Waldburg, Edenheim, Baden
Greschbach, Justina	16, Apr. 1891	27, Mar.	60	Bürkle	254	Warsaw, IL	
Greßly, Carolina	21, Apr. 1848	1, Feb.	39		68	Bethlehem, OH	Maple Lake, Minnesota
Grest, Anna	23, Feb. 1880	1, Feb.	19		63	Clearwater, MN	Waldangelloch, Baden
Greth, Friederike	18, July 1889	31, May	69- 3m-23d	Thumm	462	Nashville, TN	
Gretschbach, Julia	29, Dec. 1873	16, Dec.	16-11m- 3d		415	Warsaw, IL	Wolfölden, Württemberg
Grettenberger, Anna Maria	18, Dec. 1871	30, Nov.	58- 4m- 5d		407	Lansing, MI	Affalterbach, Marbach, Württemberg
Grettenberger, Georg Jakob	6, Jan. 1898	10, Dec.	59		15	Holt, MI	Canton Waadt, Schweiz
Greub, Eugene	16, July 1891	7, June	56	Suter	462	Lorin, CA	
Grev, Friederika	23, Oct. 1882	4, Oct.	28- 6m- 8d		343	Ann Arbor, MI	Göttelfingen, Freudenstadt, Württemberg
Greve, Anna	12, Jan. 1888	15, Dc.	19- 4m-19d	Zollinger	30	Sherburnville, IL	Bohmte, Amt Osnabrück, Hannover
Greve, Christina Barbara	12, June 1871		20- 8m- 1d		191	Ann Arbor, MI	Urtannen, Bern, Schweiz
Greve, Friedrich	12, Oct. 1874	28, Sept	46		327	Cleveland, OH	Ann Arbor, Michigan
Greve, Maria	19, Dec. 1864	1, Dec.	27- 2m- 3d		204	Cleveland, OH	
Greve, Wilhelm	14, July 1892	29, June	30		446	Ann Arbor, MI	Stockhausen, Lübecke, Minden, Preußen
Grewe, Charlotte	30, Nov. 1893	7, Nov.	83	Schultze	766	St. Paul, MN	Hertlinghausen, Minden, Preußen
Grewe, Johan Heinrich	2, Sept 1872	21, Aug.	58		287	St. Paul, MN	
Grieb, Gottlieb Friedrich	23, Oct. 1871		71- 1m		343	San Francisco, CA	Chicago, Cook County, Illinois
Grieb, Ida Christina Elisabeth	3, Jan. 1889	21, Dec.	16		14	Chicago, IL	Veilsdorf, Amt Hilburghausen, Sachsen
Griebel, Dorothea	27, Dec. 1869	2, Nov.	73	Trier	415	Wapello, IA	Schwabenroth, Hessen-Darmstadt
Griebel, Katharine	8, May 1882	22, Apr.	51- 4m-22d	Scheuer	151	Wapello, IA	Heide, Sachsen-Meiningen
Griebel, Michael	1, July 1886	5, June	86		7	Wapello, IA	Altmark, Preußen
Grieger, Anna Dorothea Friederike	30, Dec. 1886	15, Dec.		Buchholz	7	Kansas City, MO	Pennsylvania
Griehof, Johannes	29, Apr. 1852	15, Jan.	55		72	Liverpool, —	Estein, Hannover
Griepenstroh, Johan Friedrich	13, Jan. 1898	26, Dec.	96		31	Waltersburg, IL	

Christliche Apologete Death Notices -- 1839 - 1899

Name of Deceased	Notice Date	Death Date	Age	Page	Maiden Name	Place of Death	Place of Birth
Griepenstroh, Marg. Lisabetha	21, Oct. 1867	6, Oct.	27- 1m	334	Nordemann	Golconda, IL	Fürstenau, Hannover
Griepentrog, Fr.	15, Mar. 1875	25, Feb.	48- 7m-27d	87		Clayton, WI	Rosenow, Stettin, Pommern
Gries, Barbara	10, Sept 1866	11, Apr.	76	294		Ludwigsburg, GE	
Gries, Friederika	6, May 1872	17, Apr.	47- 9m-21d	151	Rießler	Davenport, IA	
Griesinger, Margaretha	8, Mar. 1894	19, Feb.	69	166	Hagmann	Arena, WI	Tobel, St. Gallen, Schweiz
Grieß, Lizzie Mathilda	14, Sept 1893	26, Aug.	17	590		Pittsburg, PA	Pittsburg, Pennsylvania
Griewe, Johan Heinrich Christian	16, Jan. 1896	10, Dec.	68	46		Colesburg, IA	Eldena, Mecklenburg-Schwerin
Griewe, Maria	11, Feb. 1892	13, Jan.	68	94	Scheid	Garner, IA	Eildena, Grabow, Mecklenburg-Schwerin
Grigrisch, Elisabeth	20, July 1868	23, May	63	231	Altörfer	St. Paul, MN	Langwiesen, Zürich, Schweiz
Grill, Hans Christian	30, Oct. 1890	22, Sept	59	702		Larned, KS	Schenefeld, Rendsburg, Holstein
Grim, Peter	1, Aug. 1850	2, June	56	124		Defiance, OH	Mittelbach bei Zweibrücken, Rheinkreis Baiern
Grimm, Adam	20, Sept 1888	13, July	68	606		Newark, NJ	Bernbach, Neuenburg, Württemberg
Grimm, Albert C. F.	23, Dec. 1897	9, Nov.	33	815		New York City, NY	New York
Grimm, Anna Maria Mathilda	1, Oct. 1891	22, Aug.	25	638	Bentrup	Newark, NJ	
Grimm, Barbara Catharina	3, Feb. 1868	8, Jan.	55	39	Gundrum	Indianapolis, IN	Zell, Kreis Alsfeld, Hessen-Darmstadt
Grimm, Friedrika	15, July 1867	22, June		222		Philadelphia, PA	
Grimm, Gottlieb Friedr. Ferdinand	27, May 1867	3, May	33	166		Newark, NJ	Bernbach, Amt Neuenbürg, Württemberg
Grimm, Johan Friedrich	24, Mar. 1892	6, Mar.	71	190		Wheeling, WV	Unterneuendorf, Sachsen
Grimm, Johan Matheus	8, July 1878	28, May	60	215		Newark, NJ	Bernbach, Neuenbürg, Württemberg
Grimm, Karl	11, Sept 1882	7, Aug.	78	295			Triebes, Reuß-Schleiz
Grimm, Katharina	24, July 1890	30, June	59	478	Nachtigall	Sun Prairie, WI	Rümmelsheim, Kreuznach, RheinPreußen
Grimm, Mary Katharine	21, July 1892	5, July	38	462	Schwerer	Dallas City, IL	Fiatt County, Ohio
Grimm, Mathias F.	9, May 1895	20, Apr.	53	302		Newark, NJ	Bernbach, Württemberg
Grimm, Rosa Carolina	2, Feb. 1893	7, Jan.	36- 9m- 3d	78	Pepper	Schnectady, NY	
Grimm, Rosine	3, July 1890	10, June	70- 3m- 4d	430	Pfeiffer	Newark, NJ	Bernbach, Neuenbürg, Württemberg
Grimm, Wilhelmine	9, July1883	13, June	38	223	Joels	Oconomowoc, WI	Hinterpommern
Grimme, Anna Adelheid	23, Feb. 1899	25, Dec.	85	127	Lürs	Indianapolis, IN	Weihe, Syke, Hannover
Grimme, Georg	15, Oct. 1877	13, Sept	63	335		Hebron, IA	Hannover
Grimme, Georg	22, Jan. 1861	12, Dec.	7	16		Des Moines, IA	
Grimme, Louis	22, Jan. 1861	19, Dec.	15	16		Des Moines, IA	
Grimme, (girl)	21, June 1855	29, May	3	100		East Baltimore, MD	
Grimme, Carolina	7, Sept 1874	22, Aug.	16- 5m	287		Baltimore, MD	
Grimmel, Elisabeth	19, Nov. 1883	30, Oct.	38	375	Rieß	Baltimore, MD	Frauen Aurach, Erlangen, Baiern
Grimmel, Jakob	10, Feb. 1887	4, Jan.	66	94		Baltimore, MD	Schönstadt, Marburg, Kurhessen
Grimmel, Louis	27, May 1886	18, Apr.	30	7		Baltimore, MD	Baltimore, Maryland
Grimmel, Louis	21, June 1855	29, May	6	100		East Baltimore, MD	
Grimmel, Nikolaus	13, Feb. 1890	21, Jan.	21	110		Baltimore, MD	
Grimmel, Susanne	22, June 1899	6, June	72	399	Klingelhöfer	Baltimore, MD	Niederwetter, Kurhessen
Grimmer, Anna Maria	2, Feb. 1880	14, Jan.	56	39	Hochgräfe	Columbus, IL	Oberdorla, Mühlhausen, Erfurt, Preußen
Grimmer, Christina	5, Oct. 1868	17, Aug.	12- 4m-17d	319		Columbus, IL	
Grimmer, Maria	23, May 1895	9, Apr.	51	334	Schäfer	Quincy, IL	Ginkelsheim, Büdingen, Frankfort am Main
Grimpe, Ida	17, June 1897	29, May	42	383	Brasche	Warsaw, IL	Warsaw, Illinois
Grison, Elisa Bertha	26, Nov. 1877	11, Nov.	42	383		Belleville, IL	Fürstenau, Hannover
Griver, Charles	10, June 1897	25, May	36	367		Wheelersburg, OH	Pine Grove Furnace, Lawrence County, Ohio
Grob, Konrad	10, Jan. 1895	2, Dec.	54	30		Elizabeth, NJ	Zürich, Schweiz
Grob, Maria	4, Aug. 1873	6, June	49	247	Spenner	Union, MO	Todenhausen, Kreis Marbach, Kurhessen

Christliche Apologete Death Notices --- 1839 - 1899

Name of Deceased	Notice Date	Death Date	Age	Page	Maiden Name	Place of Death	Place of Birth
Grob, Matthäus	17, Nov. 1898	15, Sept	80	735		Vermillion, OH	Neckarkreis, Ingersheim, Besigheim, Württemberg
Grob, Susanna	22, Dec. 1892	19, Nov.	64	814	Fehr	Columbus, OH	Berg am Irgel, Zürich, Schweiz
Grob, Werner	21, Jan. 1892	30, Dec.	14- 5m-15d	46		Elizabeth, NJ	Zürich, Schweiz
Gröbe, Charles	26, Dec. 1889	9, Nov.	17- 3m- 9d	830		Chicago, IL	
Gröbe, Christoph	2, Nov. 1874	14, Oct.	76	351		Blue Island, IL	Westhofen, Kries Worms , Hessen-Darmstadt
Grobe, John	2, Feb. 1888	13, Jan.	70	78		Redfield, SD	Neuenkirchen, Mecklenburg-Strelitz
Grobe, Magdalena	26, May 1884	16, Apr.	81	7		Cameron, MO	Döllstädt, Sachsen-Gotha
Gröbe, Magdalena	28, Apr. 1879	11, Apr.	76	135		Blue Island, IL	Niederflörsheim, Worms, Hessen-Darmstadt
Gröbe, Philipp	14, Dec. 1885	24, Nov.	50	7		Blue Island, IL	Westhofen, Worms, Hessen-Darmstadt
Grochowski, D.	28, Nov. 1889	4, Nov.	70	766		Milwaukee, WI	Randen, Graudenz, Preußen
Groebe, Charley	12, Dec. 1889	9, Nov.	17- 3m- 9d	798		Chicago, IL	Lyons, Cook County, Illinois
Groen, Trinke Margaretha	27, Aug. 1877	6, Aug.	25- 1m	279		Pekin, IL	West Dunum, Ostfriesland
Groh, Heinrich	2, Jan. 1882		21- 8m-19d	7		Cincinnati, OH	Cincinnati, Hamilton County, Ohio
Groh, Johanna Mathilde	20, Dec. 1888	8, Dec.	14	814		Chicago, IL	
Groh, John	4, Nov. 1878	16, Oct.	38- - 4d	351		Chicago, IL	Dandürkheim, Hessen-Darmstadt
Groh, John Jakob	3, June 1878	20, May	72	175		Batesville, IN	Canton Kandel, Rheinpfalz Baiern
Groh, Maria Elisabeth	1, July 1897	5, June	76	414	Brenner	Fairmount, KS	Neuhofen, Baiern
Groh, Michael	9, June 1898	16, May	57	367		Alton, IL	Columbus, Franklin County, Ohio
Groh, Philipp Heinrich	29, Mar. 1894	28, Feb.	77	214		Clay County, MO	Rheingönheim, Mutterstadt, Baiern
Grohs, Philipp Heinrich	20, Feb. 1890	27, Dec.	58	126		Mascoutah, IL	Homberg, Nassau
Grokowski, D.	26, Dec. 1889		70	830		Milwaukee, WI	Randen, Graudenz, West Preußen
Grokowsky, Albert	1, Nov. 1894	21, Sept	32	710		Minneapolis, MN	Milwaukee, Wisconsin
Groll, Anna Maria	20, Nov. 1882	18, Oct.	72	375	Groll	Greenfield, MA	Zillhausen, Balingen, Württemberg
Groll, Regina	6, Dec. 1894	16, Nov.	40	790	Wiesenfeld		Hessen-Kassel
Grollmann, Maria	10, May 1869	22, Mar.	23	151		St. Louis, MO	Kolberg, Hinterpommern, Preußen
Grollmann, Maria	17, May 1869	22, Mar.	23	159		St. Louis, MO	Bavenhausen, Hohenhausen, Lippe-Detmold
Gröltz, Louise	19, Mar. 1877	25, Feb.	50	95	Behte	Burlington, IA	Bavenhausen, Lippe-Detmold
Groman, Karoline	6, Dec. 1869	17, Nov.	40- 2m- 9d	391	Kluckhohn	Cedar Lake, IN	
Gromann, Sophia	25, Feb. 1897	5, Feb.	55	127	Orthmeyer		
Grondenberg, Carolina	25, May 1863	4, May	32	84	Fröhe	Crown Point, IN	Herdecke a.d. Ruhr, Westphalen
Grondenberg, Charles H.	28, Nov. 1889	27, Oct.	69	766		Chicago, IL	Westphalen
Grondenberg, Friedrich	4, Mar. 1852	3, Feb.	27- 7m	40		Monroe, IL	Hörde bei Herdeke, Preußen
Grondenberg, Kath. Elis. M. Charlotte	28, Apr. 1884	23, Mar.	96	7		Pekin, IL	Waldorf, Baden
Grondkowsky, Franziska	21, Apr. 1892	24, Mar.	56	254	Bletsch	Michigan City, IN	
Gronemeier, Karl	18, Mar. 1886	25, Feb.	28	7		Mt. Vernon, IN	
Gronemeier, Karl Otto	3, Mar. 1884	19, Feb.	8- 2m-24d	7		Mt. Vernon, IN	Mt. Vernon, Indiana
Gronemeier, Simon	9, Apr. 1866	20, Mar.	47	118		Mt. Vernon, IN	Welstorf, Lippe-Detmold
Gronemeier, Sophia C.	5, May 1892	16, Apr.	67	286	Brinkmann	Mt. Vernon, IN	Kirchenheide, Hohnhausen, Lippe-Detmold
Gronemeyer, Henriette	15, Jan. 1864	3, Jan.	45- -12d	28	Brinkmann	Mt. Vernon, IN	Kirchheide, Amt Hohenhausen, Lippe-Detmold
Gronert, Maria	5, Jan. 1899	15, Dec.	76- 7m-22d	14	Schröder	Chicago, IL	Stolpe, Insel Usedom, Preußen
Gronewald, Herman	28, Feb. 1889	3, Feb.	37	206		Faribault, MN	Neuenkirchen, Hannover
Gronewald, Johan Friedrich	4, Feb. 1884	17, Jan.	80	7		Faribault, MN	Harmhausen, Ehrenberg, Hannover
Gronewald, Margarethe	28, Feb. 1889	27, Jan.		142		Faribault, MN	
Grönig, Gustav	21, June 1875	27, May	42- 5m-10d	199		Sleepy Eye, MN	Podanin, Bromberg, Preußen
Gröning, Henrietta Friedericka	9, Apr. 1877	24, Mar.	33- 1m-21d	119	Pitzner	Columbus, WI	Neuhoff, Kreis Dramburg, Preußen
Gröninger, Christina	30, Apr. 1883	9, Apr.	76	143	Köhler	Bradford, IN	Ilbersheim, Landau, RheinPfalz Baiern

Christliche Apologete Death Notices --- 1839 - 1899

Name of Deceased	Notice Date	Death Date	Age	Page	Maiden Name	Place of Death	Place of Birth
Gröninger, Matthias	3, Mar. 1873	4, Feb.	76	71		Bradford, IN	Linden-Bruner Hof, Bergzabern, Rheinpfalz Baiern
Grönlof, Anna Maria	7, Feb. 1881		70- 6m-17d	47		Francisco, MI	Langen, Baldbergen, Hannover
Groose, Christian Friedrich	20, Apr. 1899	20, Mar.	82	255		Beaver Dam, WI	Pomptow, Stettin, Pommern
Groose, Ferdinand Elias	8, Aug. 1895	21, July	25	510		Oconomowoc, WI	Concord, Jefferson County, Wisconsin
Groose, Ida	20, Apr. 1893	22, Mar.	33	254		Beaver Dam, WI	Monterey, Wisconsin
Groothuis, Lüpke J.	12, Oct. 1874	14, Aug.	55	327		Altamont, IL	Olderhum, Amt Emden, Ostfriesland
Gropf, Emma	7, June 1869	1, May	2- 2m-10d	183		Sheboygan, WI	
Gropf, Georg	7, June 1869	30, Apr.	16-11m	183		Sheboygan, WI	
Gropp, Friedrich	21, Apr. 1887	6, Apr.	61	254		Hartford, CT	Katzhütte, Rudolstadt, Sachsen
Grosch, Elisabeth	12, May 1859	15, Apr.	18- 2m- 8d	76		Golconda, IL	Nessenborn, Amt Marburg, Kurhessen
Grosch, Johanna	20, July 1874	2, July	61	231	Hammer	Elizabeth, NJ	Kinzelsau, Württemberg
Grösch, Lorenz	11, Mar. 1858	14, Feb.	24	40		New Albany, IN	Dalherda, Baiern
Groschon, Elise	22, Jan. 1857	6, Dec.		16		Fulton, IN	Bern, Schweiz
Groshans, Anna Elisabeth	12, July 1888	18, June	56- 8m-27d	446	Homburg	Baltimore, MD	Fürstenwald, Hessen-Kassel
Groshans, Jakob	9, June 1884	22, May	63	7		Baltimore, MD	Fürstenwald, Hessen-Kassel
Groß , Louisa	9, Apr. 1891	24, Mar.	44-10m- 6d	238	Helfrich	New Albany, IN	Winstadt, Baden
Groß, A. Dorothea	5, Mar. 1877	20, Dec.	57	79	Schreiber	Waco, TX	Alberoda, Eschwege, Kurhessen
Groß, Catharina	8, Nov. 1880	10, Oct.	64-10m-15d	359	Lambert	Fremont, OH	Dürrenbach, Elsaß
Groß, Christian	9, July 1896	7, June	73	447		Dayton, OH	Rothheim bei Gießen, Hessen-Darmstadt
Groß, Christian	19, Nov. 1857	30, Oct.	80	188		Grove Center, NY	Minbach, Rheinkreis Baiern
Groß, Dorothea	3, Mar. 1892	8, Feb.	80- 2m-23d	142	Baur	St. Paul, MN	Neustadt, Elsaß
Groß, Edward	20, Nov. 1890	27, Oct.	18	750		Dalton, MO	
Groß, Emma Rebecca	9, Mar. 1893	16, Feb.	21	158		New Albany, IN	Higginsport, Ohio
Groß, Emma Sophia	15, Apr. 1872	8, Mar.	28	127	Fraas	Dayton, OH	Saalfeld an der Saale, Sachsen-Meiningen
Groß, Friederike	30, May 1881	8, May	45	175	Klein	Lawrenceburg, IN	Oberlenningen, Württemberg
Groß, Friederike	2, May 1889	17, Apr.	60	286		Cincinnati, OH	Magdeburg, Preußen
Groß, Gottfried	19, Apr. 1888	30, Mar.	61	254		Fairbury, IL	Memmleben, Preußen
Groß, Heinrich	6, Feb. 1882	17, Sept	82	47		Ellis Grove, IL	Borne-Roth, Lauterbach, Hessen-Darmstadt
Groß, Heinrich	9, Sept 1897	24, July	87	575		Salem, MN	Neustadt, Elsaß
Groß, Henry P.	18, Feb. 1886	25, Jan.	25	7		Milwaukee, WI	Milwaukee, Wisconsin
Groß, Jacob	23, Aug. 1894	7, Aug.	50	550		Pittsburg, PA	Tärningen, Baden
Groß, Johan Georg	18, Mar. 1886	13, Feb.	80- 3m-24d	7		Des Moines, IA	Mühlau, Nassau
Groß, Karoline Henriette	19, Nov. 1896	24, Oct.	80	750	Wagner	Quincy, IL	Oberdollar, Mühlhausen, Germany
Groß, Katharina	30, May 1895	28, Apr.	52	350	Magly	Cincinnati, OH	Rohrbach, Baiern
Groß, Katharina Elisabeth	12, Apr. 1869	20, Mar.	64	119	Hauf	Summerfield, IL	Böhl, Neustadt a. d. Haardt, Rheinkreis Baiern
Groß, Katharina Elisabeth	21, June 1869	20, Mar.	64	199	Hauk	Summerfield, IL	Böhl, Neustadt a. d. Haardt, Rheinkreis Baiern
Groß, Konrad	26, Feb. 1883	7, Feb.	49- -18d	71		Cincinnati, OH	Lorch, Welzheim, Württemberg
Groß, Louise	30, Aug. 1888	21, May	58	558		Farmington, MN	Diedenshausen, Westphalen
Groß, Luise	12, Jan. 1899	17, Dec.	51	31		Pittsburg, PA	Emmerdingen, Baden
Groß, Maria	17, Dec. 1866	29, Nov.	37	406	Herzog	Dayton, OH	Plech, Oberfranken, Baiern
Groß, Maria	17, May 1888	16, Apr.	68- 7m- 3d	318	Polster	Warrenton, MO	Oberschützen, Ungarn
Groß, Maria Katharine	5, Apr. 1888	11, Mar.	42	222	Stull	DeWitt, MI	Sandusky County, Ohio
Groß, Martha Elisabeth	12, May 1898	28, Apr.	68	303		Allegheny, PA	Schellbach, Hessen-Kassel
Groß, Philipp Jakob	21, Aug. 1882	2, Aug.	80- 5m- 22d	271		Summerfield, IL	Böhl, Rheinkreis Baiern
Groß, Salomina	11, June 1877	26, May	28	191	Walzer	Summerfield, IL	St. Clair County, Illinois
Groß, Sarah	4, Aug. 1887	5, July	30	494	Brandes	Northfield, MN	St. Peter, Minnesota

Christliche Apologete Death Notices --- 1839 - 1899

Name of Deceased	Notice Date	Death Date	Age	Maiden Name	Page	Place of Death	Place of Birth
Große, Friedrich	1, Dec. 1879	8, Nov.	61-11m-12d	Ahlers	383	Red Wing, MN	Neu Hardenberg, Liebus, Brandenburg
Große, Wilhelmine	27, Apr. 1893	3, Apr.	43		270	Red Wing, MN	Mayenburg, Preußen
Grossebacher, Elisabeth	24, July 1882	4, July	70	Lichte	239	Batesville, IN	Hochstätten, Konolfingen, Bern, Schweiz
Grossebacher, Jakob	16, June 1884	21, May	82- 7m		7	Baresville, OH	Wichtrag, Burgdorf, Bern, Schweiz
Grossenbacher, Anna Maria	26, Dec. 1895	21, Nov.			828	Toledo, OH	Kinßau, Bern, Schweiz
Großenbacher, Louise M.	15, July 1886	1, July	25	Göbel	7	Toledo, OH	Toledo, Lucas County, Ohio
Großenbacher, Maria	18, May 1899	8, Feb.	57	Eichenberger	319	Jamestown, MO	Goldbach, Lützelflüh, Bern, Schweiz
Grossenbacher, Samuel	16, July1883	16, June	59		231	Toledo, OH	Signau, Bern, Schweiz
Großenbacher, Samuel	5, Dec. 1864	3, Nov.	17- -13d		196	Toledo, OH	
Großenbacher, Stephan	13, Jan. 1887	2, Jan.	81	Fries	30	Baresville, OH	Kanton Bern, Schweiz
Großglaus, Elisabeth	16, Nov. 1893	3, Nov.	35		734	Marion, OH	Ruppur, Baden
Großglauser, Johan	19, Feb. 1891	25, Jan.	35		126	Jamestown, MO	Aeschlen, Bern, Schweiz
Großmann, Angelica	29, Jan. 1891	10, Nov.	60	Ritter	78	Marrs, IN	Wonsheim, Alzei, Hessen-Darmstadt
Großmann, Eleonora	23, Dec. 1878	11, Nov.			407	Cincinnati, OH	Hessen-Darmstadt
Großmann, Gottlieb	25, Jan. 1869	3, Jan.			31	Defiance, OH	Horrheim, Vaihingen, Württemberg
Großmann, Johan Philipp	4, June 1896	13, May	70		367	Marrs, IN	Zuhöfen, Neuburg, Württemberg
Großmann, John	24, June 1867	5, June	47- 5m-17d		198	Mt. Vernon, IN	Höfen, Neuenburg, Württemberg
Großmann, Katharina	28, Sept 1863	23, July	73- 7m		156	Posey Co, IN	Neuenburg, Württemberg
Großmann, Philippine	1, Dec. 1887	28, Oct.	28	Werry	766	Boonville, IN	
Großmann, Wilhelm F.	24, Feb. 1873	26, Dec.	26-11m- 4d		63	Marrs, IN	Posey County, Indiana
Großwinkler, Adelheid	6, May 1872		80		151	Green Bay, WI	
Grote, Anna Maria Elisabeth	22, Mar. 1888	15, Feb.	35- 3m-21d		190	Hickman, NE	Hüde, Hannover
Grote, Fr.	7, Mar. 1895	10, Feb.	63		158	Rocky, TX	
Grote, Friedrich Wilhelm	2, Dec. 1867	5, Nov.	20- 6m		382	Hoyleton, IL	Halle bei Bielefeld, Preußen
Grote, Henriette Auguste	27, Nov. 1871	30, Oct.	50	Lohofer	383	Nashville, IL	Fürstenhagen, Amt Ußlar, Hannover
Grote, Justus Friedrich	8, July 1867		71		214	Baresville, OH	Melle, Hannover
Grote, Kasper Friedrich Wilhelm	28, Sept 1899	13, Sept	84		623	Hoyleton, IL	Belm, Hannover
Grote, Wilhelm	23, Feb. 1860	5, Feb.	45		32	Vandalia, IL	Ottenstein, Amt Ottenstein, Preußen
Grotejohn, August	30, Oct. 1876		64	Demkes	351	Summerfield, IL	Dinxperlo, Gelderland, Holland
Grotenhuis, Hendrika	25, Feb. 1886	11, Feb.	44		7	Berea, OH	Bremen, Germany
Groth, , John	2, Nov. 1893	14, Oct.	79		702	Platteville, WI	Thüringen, Altbreisach, Baden
Groth, Barbara	13, Feb. 1871	25, Jan.	34- 9m-18d	Birmelie	55	Chicago, IL	Mecklenburg-Schwerin
Groth, Catharina	3, Dec. 1866	26, Sept	44- 5m		390	Giard, IA	Hannover
Groth, Gesine	21, Mar. 1889	23, Feb.	77- 5m-17d	Hannemann	190	Platteville, WI	Ponzow,
Groth, Johan Karl	17, Aug. 1885	28, July	59		7	Perry, TX	Neuenlibke, Vor-Pommern, Preußen
Groth, Maria	29, Oct. 1866	17, Oct.	42	Ludewig	350	Chicago, IL	Nordhausen, Preußen
Grothe, Friederika	3, Apr. 1865	16, Feb.	56	Beitz	56	Cincinnati, OH	Herzfelde, Brandenburg
Grothe, Maria	19, Jan. 1893	17, Dec.	34		46	Fond du Lac, WI	Illinois
Grothus, Louis	7, Sept 1893	1, Aug.	15		574	Swanton, NE	Grunde, Hannover
Grotjohn, Friederike	17, Nov. 1891	1, Nov.	77	Siever	814	Summerfield, IL	Fürstenhagen, Hannover
Grotte, Charlotte	22, Mar. 1880	26, Feb.	84- 2m-26d		95	New Metamoras, OH	Dornhahn, Sulz, Württemberg
Grotthaus, Anna Maria	2, Dec. 1878	19, Nov.	55- 5m-26d	Bosseden	383	Santa Claus, IN	Rattenharz, Welzheim, Württemberg
Grötzmyer, Anna Catharina	11, Nov. 1872	3, Oct.	60	Seng	367	Kendallville, IN	Warsau, Illinois
Grtiz, Ernst	22, Nov. 1880	12, Nov.	26		375	Warsau, IL	
Grub, Christian	13, May 1878	18, Apr.	76- 7m-25d		151	Terre Haute, IN	Ulmet, Kusel, Rheinkreis Baiern
Grub, Jakob	19, May 1873	28, Apr.	33-10m- 3d		159	Edgerton, OH	Massillion, Stark County, Ohio

Christliche Apologete Death Notices --- 1839 - 1899

Name of Deceased	Notice Date	Death Date	Age	Maiden Name	Page	Place of Death	Place of Birth
Grub, Katharine	21, May 1891	19, Apr.	64	Kaufmann	334	Terre Haute, IN	Kefenroth, Büdingen, Hessen-Darmstadt
Grub, Maria Elisabeth	18, Jan. 1869	22, Dec.	57- -29d		23	Edgerton, OH	Erdesbach, Ulmeth, Baiern
Grub, Philipp	13, June 1881	22, May	56- 5m-24d		191	Baraboo, WI	Kronenberg, RheinPfalz Baiern
Grub, Wilhelm	12, Feb. 1883	20, Jan.	24		55	Baraboo, WI	Freedom, Wisconsin
Grube , Catharina Elisa	5, July 1860	16, June	9- 4m- 9d		108	Hazel Green, WI	
Grube, D.G.	1, Jan. 1866	3, Dec.	35		6	Springfield, IL	Abbehausen, Oldenburg
Grube, Elisabeth	12, Dec. 1870	21, Oct.	31- 1m- 7d		399	Cape Girardeau, MO	Landau, , Waldeck
Grube, Friederika	13, Sept 1875	30, Aug.	77- 5w	Dietrich	295	Grand Rapids, MI	Zetzow, Mecklenburg-Strelitz
Grube, Johanna	17, Aug. 1874	5, Aug.	53	Dasso	263	Roberts, IL	Neuenkirchen, Mecklenburg-Strelitz
Grube, Karl	13, Mar. 1871	23, Feb.	76		87	Peru, IL	Neuenkirchen, Mecklenburg-Schwerin
Grube, Louisa Anna	19, Sept 1895	26, Aug.	40	Zahn	606	Glenwood, KS	Farm Ridge, Lasalle County, Illinois
Grube, Rebecca	16, Nov. 1874		23		367	Schnectady, NY	
Gruber, Anna Maria	29, Mar. 1880	20, Feb.	72		103	Delhi, MI	Nordheim, Hessen-Darmstadt
Gruber, Jakob	28, June 1860		82		104		Bucks County, Pennsylvania
Gruber, Maria Elisabeth	15, Oct. 1891	8, Sept	55-11m- 8d	Bartles	670	Des Moines, IA	
Gruettey, Georg Friedrich	24, July 1871	27, Apr.	22- 2m-27d		239	Baltimore, MD	
Grüewaldt, Minna	5, May 1892	6, Apr.	29		286	Dalton, MO	
Grulke, Maria Elisabeth	17, May 1894	15, Apr.	36	Hübner	326	Beaver Dam, WI	Monterey, Wisconsin
Grün, Anna Catharina	4, Oct. 1880	4, Sept	70- 2m-25d		319	New Albany, IN	Dietenbergen, Höchst, Nassau
Grün, Barbara	22, Aug. 1850	31, July	43		136	New Albany, IN	Cevenne, Frankreich
Grün, Johan	2, July 1891	10, June	54		430	Indianapolis, IN	Flinsungen, Hessen-Darmstadt
Grün, Johan Jakob	14, Dec. 1874	20, Oct.	73		399	New Albany, IN	Osweil, Amt Ludwigsburg, Württemberg
Grün, John	29, May 1876	9, Mar.	61- 2m-12d		175	Bradford, IN	Osweil, Ludwigsburg, Württemberg
Grün, Maria	6, Feb. 1882	15, Jan.	26- -16d	Heiligtag	47	Marine City, MI	Casko Township, St. Clair County, Michigan
Grün, Philipp	12, Jan. 1880	22, Dec.	76		15	Highland, IL	Brezenheim bei Kreuznach, Preußen
Grün, Thomas	3, Apr. 1865	31, Jan.	24		56	Morgan Co., IN	
Grund, Anna	2, Aug. 1888	14, July	75	Hoffmann	494	Milwaukee, WI	Karlshof bei Riezen, Preußen
Grund, Heinrich Matthias	3, Oct. 1870	6, Sept	46		319	Kendallville, IN	Gadebusch, Mecklenburg-Schwerin
Grund, Maria	5, Dec. 1889	10, Nov.	70		782	Toledo, OH	Buch, Waiblingen, Württemberg
Grund, Maria Catharina	27, May 1872	27, Apr.	55	Heidel	175	Kendallville, IN	Knöse, Amt Gadebusch, Mecklenburg-Schwerin
Grund, Wilhelm	7, Aug. 1876	13, June	58- 1m- 7d		255	Waterloo, WI	
Grundenberg, Kath. Elis. M. Charlotte	7, Apr. 1884	23, Mar.	96		7	Pekin, IL	Hörde bei Herdeke, Preußen
Grundgrüper, Ernestine	31, Jan. 1895	2, Jan.	71	Generich	78	Menominee, MI	Breitenfelde, Naugard , Preußen
Grundkowsky, Anton	21, Apr. 1887	5, Apr.	77		254	Michigan City, IN	Ust, Posen
Grundprieper, Wilhelm	19, Mar. 1896		73		190	Menomonie, WI	Meesow, Pommern
Gruner, Catharine	21, Apr. 1862	2, Apr.	28- 2m	Henny	64	Detroit, MI	Ostheim, Elsaß
Gruner, Maria	24, Feb. 1887	8, Feb.	60	Werner	126	New Haven, CT	Kirchentellersforth, Württemberg
Gruner, Martin	13, Feb. 1896	27, Jan.	74		110	New Haven, CT	Kirchentellinsfurth, Tübingen, Württemberg
Gruner, Peter	1, Oct. 1866		36- 2m-21d		318	Ann Arbor, MI	Niedertorfallden, Kurhessen
Gruner, Wilhelm C.	13, Oct. 1873	28, Aug.	50		327	Farmington, MO	Niederdorffelden, Kurhessen
Grünert, Dorothea	23, Sept 1872	3, Aug.	63	Neibert	311	Muscatine, IA	
Grunett, Louis	17, Aug. 1874	30, July	20		263	Watertown, WI	Langenkandel am Rhein, Baiern
Grünert, Michael	12, Jan. 1863	13, Nov.	61		8	Valparaiso, IN	Siebelskamp, Merscheid, Solingen, Germany
Grünewald, Amalia	27, Feb. 1890	4, Feb.	67- 7m-18d		142	St. Louis, MO	
Grünewald, Charles	15, Sept 1884	22, Aug.	28- -27d		7	New York City, NY	
Grunewald, Friedrich F.	9, Sept 1897	14, Aug.	60		575	Larned, KS	Heinrichshof, Naugard, Stettin, Germany

Christliche Apologete Death Notices --- 1839 - 1899

Name of Deceased	Notice Date	Death Date	Age	Page	Maiden Name	Place of Death	Place of Birth
Grünewald, Jacob	11, Nov. 1867	28, Oct.	56-10m	358		St. Louis, MO	Elberfeld, Preußen
Grünewald, Johan August Karl	20, Sept 1894	1, Sept	70	614		Jordan, MN	Barkow, Greifenberg, Pommern
Grünewald, Johan P.	24, Dec. 1891	28, Nov.	70	830		St. Louis, MO	Regensburg, Baiern
Grünewald, W. J.	7, Oct. 1872	13, Sept	65	327		Nokomis, IL	Niederklingen, Hessen-Darmstadt
Grünewald, Wilhelmina Johanna	11, Apr. 1895	21, Mar.		238	Ackermann	Jordan, MN	Zetlin, Greifenberg, Pommern
Grüninger, Jacob Friedrich	27, Nov. 1876	25, Oct.	58- 3m	383		Wyandotte, KS	Osweil, Württemberg
Gruninger, Laura Henriette	7, July 1892	15, June	16-7m-15d	430		Baltimore, MD	
Grüninger, Martha	21, Dec. 1874	20, Nov.	15	407		Wyandotte, KS	Westport, Missouri
Grunow, Johanna Gottlieba	24, Apr. 1890	28, Mar.	72	270		East Troy, WI	Sulz am Neckar, Württemberg
Grünsfelder, Johan	27, Feb. 1896	2, Feb.	84	142		San Jose, IL	Reilingen bei Schwetzingen, Baden
Grünsfelder, Philipp	8, Sept 1853	9, Aug.	34- 2m	144		Pekin, IL	Reilingen, Baden
Grünwald, Heinrich F.T.	26, Feb. 1872	9, Feb.	30	71		Jordan, MN	Neuenhagen, Regenwalden, HinterPommern
Grünwald, Heinrich L.	3, Nov. 1892	9, Sept	42	702		Jordan, MN	Hinterpommern
Grupe, Diedrich	21, Jan. 1897	4, Jan.	73	46		Schnectady, NY	Morsum, Hannover
Grusendorf, Fritz	4, Mar. 1897	7, Feb.	78	143		Lexington, TX	Gifhorn, Hannover
Grusendorff, Auguste	23, Jan. 1896	28, Dec.	62	62		Lexington, TX	Michelstadt, Hessen-Darmstadt
Grussendorf, Caroline	4, Mar. 1878	11, Feb.	62	71	Inze	Houston, TX	Klein-Schwöpler, Hannover
Grußendorf, Christine	17, Jan. 1881	8, Nov.	57-10m- 8d	23	Hartung	Giddings, TX	Schallenburg bei Erfurt, Preußen
Grussendorf, H.	30, May 1881	4, May	64	175		Schulenburg, TX	Gifhorn, Hannover
Grußendorf, Heinrich	20, Aug. 1883	15, July	10	271		New Ulm, MN	
Grußendorf, Johanna Catharina	4, June 1877	8, May	82	183	Wolfram	Giddings, TX	Gifhorn, Hannover
Grussendorf, Maria	7, Nov. 1881		15- 9m	359		Lafayette, MN	Calberlah, Gifhorn, Hannover
Grüther, Louise	16, Apr. 1866	29, Mar.	35- -15d	126	Tribbe	Quincy, IL	Hunteburg, Hannover
Grütter, Anna Margaretha	1, Dec. 1873	13, Nov.	48- 2m-16d	383	Scheer	Quincy, IL	
Grütter, Georg	29, May 1882		56	175		Quincy, IL	Darmstadt, Hessen-Darmstadt
Grütter, Sophie	3, Oct. 1864	16, Sept	13- 5m-20d	160		Quincy, IL	
Grützer, (Mrs)	1, Aug. 1861	10, July	54	124	Warneboldt	Warsaw, IL	Netingen, Amt Steinbruck, Hannover
Grützmacher, August	16, Apr. 1891	14, Mar.	37	254		Watertown, WI	Lübkow, Preußen
Grützmacher, Carl G.	8, Aug. 1861	22, July	58	128		East Troy, WI	Wangeritz bei Stettin, Preußen
Grützmacher, Christoph J.	1, Apr. 1897	15, Mar.	73	206		Klemme, IA	Remin bei Wismer, Germany
Grützmacher, Eduard Karl	10, Sept 1877	16, Aug.	20- 7m-13d	295		Watertown, WI	Waterloo, Wisconsin
Grützmacher, Friedrich Karl (Rev)	19, May 1898	1, May	39	319		Chicago, IL	York near Columbus, Wisconsin
Grützmacher, Friedrich Wilhem	26, July 1880	11, July	56- -19d	239		Watertown, WI	Lüdtow bei Stargard, Pyritz, Preußen
Grützmacher, Heinrich J.	8, Nov. 1888	8, Oct.	29-7m-26d	718		Watertown, WI	
Grützmacher, Karl	1, June 1863	1, May	29	88		East Troy, WI	Wangritz, Kreis Naugard, Pommern, Preußen
Gschwind, Gustav	16, Mar. 1885	10, Feb.	47	7		Triumph, NE	Freiburg, Baden
Guck, Anna	3, June 1878	6, May	25- 1m- 9d	175		Brooklyn, NY	
Gucker, Johannes	7, Aug. 1846	28, Apr.	52	127		Monroe Co., ---	
Guckes, Philipp	30, May 1864	8, Apr.	59- -11d	88		Dayton, OH	Albig, Rhein-Hessen
Guderian, Lydia Ida	21, Apr. 1898	25, Mar.	16- 4m- 7d	255		Rochester, MN	
Guertler, Wilhem	5, May 1887	16, Apr.	59	286		Beardstown, IL	Ebersbach, Oberlausitz, Sachsen
Guese, Gustav Adolph	17, Jan. 1876	10, Dec.	6	23		Herman, MO	
Guese, Paulina Wilhelmine	6, Dec. 1875	19, Oct.	11	391		Herman, MO	
Guetler, C.F. Wilhelm	6, May 1886	17, Apr.	29	7		Green Bay, WI	Pittsfield, Wisconsin
Gugel, Georg	23, Sept 1858	2, Sept	65- 2m-22d	152		Allegheny City, PA	Oberlindach, Baiern
Gugel, Magdalena B.	17, Mar. 1879	14, Feb.	85- 7m- 4d	87	Schuh	Marion, OH	Donderflein, Baiern

Christliche Apologete Death Notices --- 1839 - 1899

Name of Deceased	Notice Date	Death Date	Age	Page	Maiden Name	Place of Death	Place of Birth
Guger, Anna Mary	19, Apr. 1875	31, Mar.	44	127	Hanhardt	New Orleans, LA	Zürich, Schweiz
Gugholz, Johan	9, Feb. 1885	1, Jan.	38	7		Perry, TX	Sinsheim, Baden
Gugler, Jakob	29, Sept 1898	26, Aug.	67	623		Lyona, KS	Wangen, Cannstadt, Württemberg
Gugler, Johan Louis	2, Aug. 1888	17, July	62-2m-7d	494		Galion, OH	Ochsenbach, Baden
Gugler, John A.	2, Dec. 1886	9, Nov.	25	7		Lyona, KS	Lyona, Dickinson County, Kansas
Gugus, Katharina E.	16, Dec. 1878	2, Dec.	14	399		Dayton, OH	Bornheim, Mainz, Rhein-Hessen
Guillaume, Theodor	29, May 1876	23, Mar.	46	175		Cannelton, IN	Schüttringen, Luxemburg
Gülzer, Carl Friedrich	6, Mar. 1871	23, Jan.	21-8m-7d	79		Waverly, OH	Altflemmingen, Neuenburg a.d. Saale, Preußen
Gülzer, Julius	6, Dec. 1880	20, Nov.	66	391		Waverly, OH	Waverly, Ohio
Gummig, Gottfried	14, June 1888	20, May	19-3m-4d	382		Wathena, KS	Geniegwitz, Schlesien
Gummig, Gottfried	16, July 1877	19, June	38	231		Wathena, KS	
Gummig, Maria Anna	14, Apr. 1862	22, Mar.	33	60	Hauser	Columbus, KS	Heidelsheim, Amt Bruchtal, Baden
Gummig, Wilhelm	12, Apr. 1894	18, Mar.		246		Wathena, KS	Doniphan County, Kansas
Gumming, Christina	13, Nov. 1865	23, Sept		184	Meng	Columbus, KS	Rothenbach, Oberndorf, Württemberg
Gums, Karoline	25, Sept 1871	2, July	25-11m	311	Mathwes	Grand Rapids, MI	Wladislowo, Kreis Bromberg, Preußen
Gums, Karoline	16, Oct. 1871	2, July	25-11m	335	Mathwes	Grand Rapids, MI	Wladislowo, Kreis Bromberg, Preußen
Gundel, John M.	25, Aug. 1898	29, July	71	543		Berea, OH	Külsheim, Baiern
Gundermann, Johannette	24, Dec. 1866	28, Nov.	30-8m-7d	414		Birmingham, Pa	
Gundlach, Anna Eva	24, Aug. 1868	28, July	50	271	Fink	Roseville, MI	
Gundlach, Conrad	17, Aug. 1863	1, July	19-8m-2d	132		Detroit, MI	Grebenhagen, Kreis Humberg, Kurhessen
Gundlach, Ernst	28, June 1880	26, May	62-9m-3d	207		Champaign, IL	
Gundlach, Peter	26, Nov. 1877	17, Oct.	18	383		Scranton, PA	
Gundlach, Wilhelm	21, Jan. 1886	31, Dec.	42--22d	7		St. Paul, MN	Hundelshausen, Witzenhausen, Cassel, Preußen
Gundlach, Wilhelm	14, Aug. 1865	21, May	70-9m-17d	132		Wheeling, WV	
Gundrum, Conrad	29, Aug. 1889	8, Aug.	24	558		New Palestine, IN	Zell, Alsfeld, Hessen-Darmstadt
Gundrum, Edward	9, July 1883	22, June	69	223		New Palestine, IN	New Palestine, Indiana
Gundrum, Elisabeth	22, Sept 1887	5, Sept	69	606	Gommel	New Palestine, IN	Zell, Hessen-Darmstadt
Gundrum, Elisabeth	6, Oct. 1887	5, Sept	40-4m-6d	638	Gemmel	New Palestine, IN	Zell, Hessen-Darmstadt
Gundrum, Maria E.	3, Dec. 1891	23, Oct.	24	782		New Palestine, IN	
Gundrum, Wilhelm	5, Dec. 1881	21, Nov.	20	391		New Palestine, IN	Hancock County, Indiana
Gundum, Conrad	19, Jan. 1874	26, Dec.	73-6m-9d	23		Waco, NE	
Gunlach, Christian	18, Apr. 1889	24, Mar.	52	254		Waco, NE	Williamsburg, Vorpommern
Gunlach, Wilhelmine	12, Aug. 1897	15, July		511		Mt. Pleasant, KY	Pommern
Günßel, Sophie	24, Feb. 1853	12, Feb.		32		Santa Claus, IN	Beilstein, Marbach, Württemberg
Günter, Anna M.E.	13, Nov. 1876	25, Oct.	76	367	Kokomohr	Appleton, MO	Drohne, Dielingen, Preußen
Günter, Elisabeth	22, Feb. 1869	3, Jan.	60	63	Sander	Beman, KS	Schleweke, Braunschweig
Günter, Hannah	4, Jan. 1894	1, Nov.	50	14	Hansen	Lyona, KS	Trittelfitz, Förchen, Pommern
Günter, Karl	6, May 1878	10, Apr.	48-10m-20d	143		Galion, OH	Schönfeld, Demen, Pommern
Günther, Abraham	28, Feb. 1861	12, Feb.	67	36		Chillicothe, OH	Möhringen, Stuttgart, Württemberg
Günther, Abraham	28, Apr. 1879	11, Apr.	30	135		Chillicothe, OH	Möhringen, Stuttgart, Württemberg
Günther, Adelia	11, Sept 1876	31, Aug.	41-5m-28d	295	Brett	Delhi, MI	
Günther, Anna Margaretha	4, Apr. 1881	9, Mar.	67	111	Faß	Evansville, IN	Rodenbergen, Kurhessen
Günther, August	13, Mar. 1882	2, Mar.	71	87		St. Paul, MN	Schlarpe, Hardegsen, Hannover
Günther, August	25, Sept 1890	4, Sept	41-3m	622		Decatur, IL	Lutters, Hannover
Günther, Barbara	14, Apr. 1862		62	60		New Albany, IN	Bargen, Baden
Günther, Carolina	13, Aug. 1896			527	Hofmeister		Hannover

Christliche Apologete Death Notices --- 1839 - 1899

Name of Deceased	Notice Date	Death Date	Age	Page	Maiden Name	Place of Death	Place of Birth
Günther, Christina Elisabeth	14, Mar. 1889	17, Feb.	52	174	Ohmberger	Chillicothe, OH	Wasser, Emmendingen bei Freiburg, Baden
Günther, Christine	12, May 1879	22, Apr.	56-4m	151		Galion, OH	Mosbach, Freudenstadt, Württemberg
Günther, Eduard	12, May 1884	28, Apr.	22	7		Evansville, IN	
Günther, Friedrike	18, Apr. 1895	18, Mar.	72	254	Paul	Summerfield, IL	Plau, Mecklenburg-Schwerin
Günther, Georg	2, Apr. 1866	13, Mar.	23-1m	110		Chillicothe, OH	Chillicothe, Ross County, Ohio
Günther, Gerhard Heinrich	11, Aug. 1848		Inquiry	131		Manchester, MO	Dilgen, Amt Raden, Preußen
Günther, Johan	6, Dec. 1869	20, Nov.	69-9m-3d	391		Peru, IL	Giltingen, Nagold, Württemberg
Günther, Johan Heinrich Ludwig	16, May 1881	21, Apr.	86	159		Santa Claus, IN	Dielingen, Amt Rathen, Preußen
Günther, Louise	10, May 1860	5, Apr.	31-7m	76	Schwemmer		Plau, Mecklenburg-Schwerin
Günther, Magdalena	12, Nov. 1891	27, Oct.	60	734	Wilbert	Pittsburg, PA	Hibsack, Schandorf, Württemberg
Günther, Maria	1, Oct. 1883	14, Sept	29-11m-14d	319		Galion, OH	Marion County, Ohio
Günther, Maria Dorothea	3, Feb. 1887	18, Jan.	65	78	Diedrich	Laporte, IN	Großen Wilberg, Pommern
Günther, Mathias	28, Nov. 1881	15, Nov.	43-1m-9d	383		Chillicothe, OH	Wasser, Emmendingen, Baden
Günther, Reent Ehlen	26, Oct. 1899	22, Sept	32	687		San Jose, IL	Barkholt, Esens, Ostfriesland
Günther, Sarah Elisabeth	15, Apr. 1872	31, Mar.	55	127	Strohhecker	Chillicothe, OH	Murr, Marbach, Württemberg
Günther, Wesley	21, May 1891	16, Apr.	15	334		Evansville, IN	
Günther, Wilhelm	20, June 1861	20, May	45- -11d	100		Dunkirk, Ny	Nienhagenhütte, Mecklenburg-Schwerin
Günthert, Valentin	20, Feb. 1882	8, Feb.	53-3m-25d	63		Washington, IL	Nußdorf bei Landau, Rheinkreis Baiern
Guntle, Ulrich	28, Feb. 1895	27, Jan.	86	142		Kewaskum, WI	Burgerau, St. Gallen, Schweiz
Guntly, Ursula	21, Jan. 1897		81	46	Mindner	Kewaskum, WI	Burgerau, St. Gallen, Schweiz
Guntz, Maria	3, Mar. 1898	3, Feb.	78-10m-6d	143		Baltimore, MD	Ballenheim, Baiern
Gürthler, Wilhelmina	21, Jan. 1858	6, Dec.	22	12	Rode	Beardstown, IL	Dolan, Blomberg, Lippe-Detmold
Gürtler, Johan	2, Sept 1878	21, Aug.	29-2m-12d	279		Pittsfield, WI	Golem, Mecklenburg-Strelitz
Gurtler, Rahel	21, Oct. 1852	3, Jan.		172		Beardstown, IL	
Gürtler, Wilhelmine	16, June 1879	28, May	74	191	Riechart	Pittsfield, WI	
Gusche, Emma Karoline	8, June 1899	27, Apr.	26	367	Wilkeming	Elkhart, IN	
Güsewelle, Anna Maria	13, Dec. 1869	18, Nov.	21	399	Kunz	Edwardsville, IL	Canton Solothurn, Schweiz
Güsewelle, Caroline	8, Mar. 1880	17, Feb.	79- -7d	79		Edwardsville, MO	Pallhagen, Lippe-Schaumburg
Gusewelle, Friedrich Christian	11, Nov. 1878	25, Oct.	82	359		Edwardsville, IL	Pollhagen, Lippe-Schaumburg
Guseweller, Friedrich Wilhelm	5, Jan. 1880	16, Dec.	44	7		Edwardsville, IL	Lippe-Schaumburg
Güß, Magdalena	6, May 1897	14, Apr.	62	287	Stegmeier	Mt. Vernon, NY	Gemmingen, Baden
Gußmann, August Fr.	2, Aug. 1894	11, July	45	502		Minneapolis, MN	Syndelfingen, Württemberg
Gust, Wilhelm	10, Sept 1896	9, Aug.	75	591		Sheboygan, WI	Köslin, Hinterpommern
Gustorf, Henriette	29, Feb. 1864	1, Feb.	61	36		Wapello, IA	Raydt, Düsseldorf, Preußen
Gutberlet, Anna	25, July 1889	8, June	16-4m-14d	478		Woodsfield, OH	
Gutberlet, Heinrich (Dr)	26, Mar. 1891	27, Dec.	95-1m-13d	206		New Metamoras, OH	Sträerklos, Hersfled, Kurhessen
Gutberlet, Lusinda Elisabeth	25, July 1889	9, Feb.	20-7m	478		Woodsfield, OH	
Gutbub, Elisabeth	27, Oct. 1892	1, Oct.	79	686	Gottfried	New Albany, NY	Neuweiler, Elsaß
Gutbub, Sarah Maria	5, Aug. 1872	14, July	33	255		New Albany, NY	Hüttenheim, Rheinpfalz Baiern
Gutchett, Pauline	28, May 1896	11, Apr.	40	350	Fischer	Jamestown, MO	Zeitzs, Sachsen
Gutekunst, Anna Maria	10, May 1860	21, Apr.	51	76		Greenfield, OH	Schielingen bei Nagold, Württemberg
Gutekunst, Elisabeth Katharina	31, May 1880	30, Apr.	75	175	Allmendinger	State Center, IA	Börnstein, Waiblingen, Württemberg
Gutekunst, Katharina	28, Jan. 1897	29, Dec.	75	62	Fitzemeyer	Bloomington, IL	Großaschbach, Backnang, Württemberg
Gutfried, Jakob	4, Dec. 1876	23, Nov.	66	391		New Albany, IN	Neuweiler, Lützelstein, Zabern, Elsaß
Gutgesell, Georg	1, Mar. 1875	13, Feb.	70-11m-1d	71		Jeffersonville, NY	Freiburg, Baden
Guth, Catharine	26, Oct. 1854	30, Sept	12-6m	172		Evansville, IN	

Christliche Apologete Death Notices --- 1839 - 1899

Name of Deceased	Notice Date	Death Date	Age	Page	Maiden Name	Place of Death	Place of Birth
Guth, Emma C.	31, July 1890	19, July	14- 7m- 1d	494		Santa Claus, IN	Santa Claus, Spencer County, Indiana
Guth, Johan Georg	14,May 1883	27, Apr.	70	159		Santa Claus, IN	Zierolshofen, Rheinbischofsheim, Baden
Guth, Margaretha	15, Jan. 1883	26, Dec.	29	23	Schnücker	Santa Claus, IN	Posey County, Indiana
Guth, Maria K.	13, Oct. 1887	21, Sept	19- 3m- 8d	654		Mascoutah, IL	
Guth, Maria Magdalena	24, Mar. 1892	28, Feb.	77	190	Schütterle	Santa Claus, IN	Kehl, Baden
Guth, Susan	10, Jan. 1861	15, Dec.	53	8	Schmidt	Nashville, IL	
Guthardt, Johan Georg	25, Mar. 1897	27, Feb.	79	190		Charles City, IA	Verna, Homburg, Hessen
Guthberlet, Lydia	10, Aug. 1893	10, July	59	510	Schell	New Metamoras, OH	Malaga Township, Monroe County, Ohio
Guthberlet, Lydia	3, Aug. 1893	10, July	59	494		Washington Co, OH	Monroe County, Ohio
Gutheil, Elisabeth	9, Aug. 1880	20, June	44	255		Edgewood, IA	Pittsburg, Pennsylvania
Gutheil, Georg	4, Oct. 1888	28, Aug.	55	638		Colesburg, IA	
Güther, Karolina Wilhemina	15, Jan. 1877	24, Dec.	56	23	Brandt	Galena, IL	Wedderwarden, Amt Dorum, Hannover
Guthmann, Jakob	17, Dec. 1847	13, Nov.	63- 7m-21d	203		Glasboro, NJ	
Guthmüller, Ida Frances	15, Sept 1892	28, July	41	590	Sabestrom	New York City, NY	Wraule, Preußen
Gutknecht, Heinrich	26, Oct. 1885	24, Sept	73- 9m-22d	7		Mooretown, MI	Podewelz, Belgard, Preußen
Gutmann, Bertha	23, Feb. 1860	7, Jan.	4- 1m	32		Defiance, OH	
Gutmann, Katharina Elisabeth	28, Jan. 1886	26, Dec.	76	7	Bürmann	Quincy, IL	Buhr, Hannover
Gutmann, Philipp	27, Apr. 1899	21, Mar.	56	271		Louisville, KY	Büdingen, Hessen-Damstadt
Gutmann, Wilhelmine	18, Apr. 1895	27, Mar.	68	254		Chicago, IL	Trein, Sachsen
Gutor, Guior	20, Aug. 1896	13, June	69	542	Gnädig	Gonzales, TX	Bangenbrück, Habelschwerdt, Germany
Guttmann, Julius Moritz	13, Apr. 1863	12, Feb.	19	60		New Albany, IN	Mellauen, Preußen
Gutwein, Magdalena	15, Mar. 1880	21, Feb.	73	86	Berdel	Chicago, IL	Geiselberg, Waldfischbach, RheinPfalz Baiern
Gutzmer, Christian Friedrich	4, Jan. 1869	29, Oct.	20- 8m-13d	7		Lincoln, NE	Dölitz, Kreis Pyritz, Pommern
Gutzmer, Daniel	22, Sept 1892	30, Aug.	68	606		Humboldt, NE	Schwanenbeck, Pommern
Gutzmer, Johan Friedrich	10, Sept 1891	17, July	72	590		Humboldt, NE	Brunkow, Pommern
Gutzmer, Maria	3, June 1897	9, May	78	351	Zabel	Swanton, NE	Dölitz, Piritz, Pommern
Gutzmer, Wilhelm Friedrich	6, Aug. 1891	17, July	72	510		Humboldt, NE	Dölitz, Pierritz, Pommern
Gutzmer, Wilhelm Friedrich	25, May 1899	25, Apr.	77	335		Swanton, NE	Dölitz, Pieritz, Pommern
Gutzmer, Wilhelmine	3, Mar. 1892	11, Feb.	57- 4m-27d	142	Körber	Humboldt, NE	Cohlenfeld, Hannover
Guyer, August	28, Aug. 1890	3, Aug.	28	558		Dallas, TX	Zürich, Schweiz
Guyer, J.	15, Sept 1884	17, July	50	6		Austin, TX	Canton Zürich, Schweiz
Gwinn, Christian	7, June 1880	2, May	62	183		Charlestown, IN	Liebelsberg, Calw, Württemberg
Gyr, August	28, Dec. 1893	11, Dec.	55	828		Tell City, IN	Einsiedeln, Schweiz
Gyse, Christian	1, Jan. 1883	9, Dec.	76- - 9d	7		Madison, ---	Untersee, Bern, Schweiz
Haack, Friederike Auguste	22, July 1886	3, July	29	7		Redfield, SD	Helle, Insel Rügen, Preußen
Haacke, M.	7, Dec. 1863	15, Dec.		196		Charleston, VA	
Haag, Daniel	30, Sept 1878	5, Sept	25- 4m-25d	311		Lawrence, KS	Altheim, Meßkirch, Baden
Haag, Dinnis	15, July 1886	28, June	52- 4m	7		Scranton, PA	
Haag, Emilie	16, Mar. 1899	20, Feb.	33	174		West Bend, WI	Scott, Sheboygan County, Wisconsin
Haag, Ernestine	12, Apr. 1875	27,Mar.	59	119	Bauer	Fillmore, WI	Ellmentingen, Pforzheim, Baden
Haag, Jakob	24, Oct. 1881	6, Oct.	77- 2m-11d	343		Fillmore, WI	Auerbach, Durchlach, Baden
Haag, Jakob	17, Apr. 1865	6, Feb.	25	64		Farmington, IA	Marion County, Ohio
Haag, Johan M.	25, May 1868	10, May	49- 5m- 4d	167		Grand Rapids, MI	Eguarhofen, Baiern
Haag, Karoline	26, Oct. 1893	1, Oct.	62	686	Kurz	Fosterburg, IL	Erbstetten, Württemberg
Haag, Margarethe	16, Feb. 1860	28, Jan.	58	28	Schnäbele	Kewaskum, WI	Auerbach, Baden

Christliche Apologete Death Notices --- 1839 - 1899

Name of Deceased	Notice Date	Death Date	Age	Page	Maiden Name	Place of Death	Place of Birth
Haag, Maria Elisabeth	6, Nov. 1890	10, Oct.	75	718	Häge	Belleville, IL	Hasloch, Rheinpfalz Baiern
Haag, Minna	5, Jan. 1899	10, Dec.	41	14		Brighton, IL	Madison County, Illinois
Haag, Nicolaus	24, Dec. 1877	15, Nov.	9- -25d	415		San Francisco, CA	Boonville, Missouri
Haag, Philipp	7, Jan. 1884	20, Dec.	70	7		West Bend, WI	Auerbach, Durlach, Baden
Haag, Wilhelmine	18, May 1885	2, May	72	7	Waldmann	Sheboygan, WI	Landringhausen, Hannover
Haak, Henriette	22, Feb. 1894	3, Feb.	57	126	Globke	Hokah, MN	Großbuschpohl, Lauenburg, Pommern
Haak, Isabella	20, Feb. 1862	20, Jan.	38- 6m	32		Edgerton, OH	
Haak, Karl	1, Mar. 1894	11, Feb.	63	150		Hokah, MN	Perleberg, Brandenburg
Haake, Friedrike Wilhelmine	20, Dec. 1894	27, Nov.	69	822	Krause	Jersey City, NJ	Hamburg, Germany
Haardt, Laura	9, Apr. 1896	5, Mar.	18	238		Dubuque, IA	Siegen, Westphalen
Haas , Ida Auguste	21, July 1898	14, June	32	463	Krafofsky	Burlington, WI	Burlington, Wisconsin
Haas, Rosina	8, Mar. 1894	31, Jan.		166	Henzel	St. Louis, MO	Elsaß
Haas, (Mrs)	15, Dec. 1892	18, Nov.	91	798		Sterling, NE	Cessin, Preußen
Haas, Amalie	17, Mar.1873	21, Feb.	31	87	Göhring	Lowell, WI	Voigtstadt, Merseburg, Preußen
Haas, Amalie	7, Apr. 1873			111	Göhring		
Haas, Anna Maria	17, Dec. 1877	28, Nov.	70	407		Santa Claus, IN	Battelestat, Baiern
Haas, Anna Maria Catharina	17, June 1852	23, Apr.	76	100		Perry, IL	Eckartshorn, Hessen-Darmstadt
Haas, Anton	18, Aug. 1873	24, July	50	263		Mt. Vernon, IN	Lohenweiler, Rheinkreis Baiern
Haas, Anton	10, Oct. 1864	8, Aug.	11- 5m- 6d	164		Nashville, TN	
Haas, Carl	8, Dec. 1892	16, Nov.	76	782		Mt. Vernon, IN	Miesenheim, Rheinkreis Baiern
Haas, Carolina Emilie	30, Apr. 1877	12, Apr.	41	143		St. Paul, MN	
Haas, Catharina	5, June 1851	1, May	26	92	Kiefer	Delaware, OH	Harrheim, Vaihingen, Württemberg
Haas, Catharina	3, Mar. 1879	30, Jan.	68-11m-9d	71		Downers Grove, IL	Matta, Elsaß
Haas, Elisabeth	16, Jan. 1896	18, Sept	54	46		Cincinnati, OH	Gernsheim am Rhein, Hessen
Haas, Elisabeth Margaretha	3, Apr. 1882	12, Mar.	68- 4m-12d	111	Adam	Dayton, OH	Allendorf, Koblenz, Preußen
Haas, Ella Nora Cordilie	16, June 1887		26	382	Kaufmann	Halstead, KS	Warsaw, Illinois
Haas, Ellen	2, Nov. 1868	6, Oct.	23	351		Mt. Vernon, IN	Defiance County, Ohio
Haas, Georg	8, Mar. 1888	9, Feb.	72	158		St. Paul, MN	Stattmatten, Elsaß
Haas, Georg	4, Sept 1882	19, Aug.	18- 4m-29d	287		Muscatine, IA	Muscatine, Iowa
Haas, Gottfried	23, Oct. 1882	13, Sept	76	343		Pekin, IL	Martern, Bischville, Elsaß
Haas, Heinrich	18, July 1889	14, June	56- 9m-26d	462		Dayton, OH	Holzhausen, Preußen
Haas, Jacob	6, June 1895	28, Apr.		366		Los Angeles, CA	Auswyl, Rohrbach, Schweiz
Haas, Jakob	13, Nov. 1865	13, Oct.	65	184		Ft. Wayne, IN	Walleswill, Bern, Schweiz
Haas, Johan	1, Mar. 1869	6, Feb.	37	71		Santa Claus, IN	Dannstadt, Rheinkreis Baiern
Haas, Johan	19, Dec. 1870	22, Nov.	77	407		Bradford, IN	Grubbach, Altdorf, Baiern
Haas, Johan Peter	17, Dec. 1866	18, Nov.	55	406		Dayton, OH	Allendorf, Coblenz, Preußen
Haas, Johanna Friederika	14, July 1859	26, May	40	112		Ripley, OH	Niederhofen, Brackenheim, Württemberg
Haas, John	16, June 1862	28, May	75	96		Kingston, IL	Wippenbach, Kreis Nieda, Hessen-Darmstadt
Haas, John	2, Oct. 1878	16, Sept	45- -11d	383		St. Louis, MO	Allenheim, Baden
Haas, Katharina	26, Oct. 1868	24, Aug.	24-10m-24d	343	Becker	New Albany, IN	
Haas, Katharina Eva	14, Feb. 1895	21, Jan.	86	110	Raas	Kendallville, IN	Bischweiler, Elsaß
Haas, Kunigunda	22, Sept 1859	9, Sept	74	152		New Albany, IN	Nalzberg, Herschbruck, Baiern
Haas, Lisette	18, Aug. 1873	22, July	56	263		Mt. Vernon, IN	Meisenheim, Rheinkreis Baiern
Haas, Margaretha	3, Feb. 1887	30, Nov.	43	78	Wührmann	Santa Claus, IN	Cincinnati, Hamilton County, Ohio
Haas, Maria Catharina	15, Jan. 1852	5, Oct.	57-10m	12		Marietta, OH	Württemberg
Haas, Maria E.	21, Mar. 1864	25, Feb.	35	48	Kruse	St. Paul, MN	Hannover

- 168 -

Christliche Apologete Death Notices --- 1839 - 1899

Name of Deceased	Notice Date	Death Date	Age	Maiden Name	Place of Death	Place of Birth
Haas, Mathias	17, Dec. 1877	25, Nov.	45		Belleville, IL	Altenheim, Baden
Haas, Nikolaus	20, Jan. 1898	1, Jan.	58		Buffalo, NY	Folsheit, Reding, Luxemburg
Haas, Sophia	9, Mar. 1899	18, Feb.	33		Mt. Vernon, IN	Mt. Vernon, Indiana
Haas, Wilhelm	6, Aug. 1847	24, June	45		Laughery, IN	Dannstadt, Mutterstadt, Speier, Rheinpfalz Baiern
Haase, Caroline	30, Apr. 1896	12, Apr.	56	Bröker	Neenah, WI	Mewgen, Stettin, Germany
Haase, Christine	30, June 1898	3, June	85	Johanning	Pinckney, MO	Rehme, Minden, Preußen
Haase, Dorothea Elisabeth	30, June 1887	16, June	89- 4m-25d		Freeport, IL	Treptow an der Rega, Preußen
Haase, Emilie	9, Aug. 1888	27, July	40	Pfeil	Oshkosh, WI	Behle, Posen
Haase, Emma Magdalena	3, Feb. 1887	20, Jan.	19- - 1d		Freeport, IL	
Haase, Ferdinand Gustav	1, Dec. 1873	15, Nov.	35		New Ulm, MN	Samoczin, Posen, Preußen
Haase, Friedrich	30, Dec. 1878	14, Dec.	77		Lincoln, NE	Sieden-Bollentin, Demmin, Stettin, Pommern
Haase, Karl	9, Jan. 1882		81		Hopewell, MO	Rahme, Minden, Preußen
Haase, Karl F.	15, Dec. 1892	18, Nov.	62		Oshkosh, WI	Treptow an der Rega, Pommern
Haase, Karl Joseph	14, Dec. 1893	18, Nov.	48		Bedford, IN	Deutschruden, Bromberg, Preußen
Haase, Karolina Ernestina	14, July 1892	11, June	57	Pautzke	Freeport, IL	Nürnberg, Germany
Haase, Magdalena Friederike	19, Nov. 1896	4, Nov.	64		Newport, KY	Urach, Württemberg
Haase, Maria	29, Apr. 1867	29, Mar.	69			Gittmansdorf, Reichenbach, Schlesien
Haase, Maria	26, Jan. 1880	7, Jan.	52	Laabs	Oshkosh, WI	Rega, Preußen
Habeck, Bertha	6, May 1897	13, Apr.	20		Kewaunee, WI	
Habegger, Margaretha	24, Aug. 1893	24, July	72	Hermann	St. Paul, MN	Basel, Schweiz
Habegger, Rudolph	13, Apr. 1893	19, Mar.	48		Jordan, MN	Basel, Schweiz
Habenich, Ernestina	15, Sept 1862	26, Aug.	25- 2m	Löffel	Evansville, IN	Boll bei Hechingen, Hoherzollern, Preußen
Habenicht, (Mrs)	26, Nov. 1896	31, Oct.	70	Schönewolf	Laporte, IN	Elbersdorf, Germany
Habenicht, E.H.L.	27, June 1870	30, May	32- 2m-21d		Evansville, IN	Ruthen Muffeln, Preußen
Haber, Philipp Heinrich	21, Aug. 1876	28, July	50		Berea, OH	Helmarshausen, Kurhessen
Haber, Rosina	20, Dec. 1888	2, Dec.	65	Peter	Olmstead Falls, OH	Mösbach, Achern, Baden
Haberkamp, Joh. H.A.	23, Aug. 1849	23, July	57		Knoxville, OH	West Lattbergen, Preußen
Haberkamp, Wilhelm	23, Aug. 1849	28, July	30		Knoxville, OH	
Haberland, Sophie	22, May 1890	26, Apr.	34- 3m-27d		New York City, NY	Ratzebur, Pommern
Häberle, Catharine Dorothea	5, Feb. 1891	1, Jan.	76	Mayer	New Haven, CT	Baum Ehrlenbach, Oehringen, Württemberg
Häberle, Georg Friedrich	8, Feb. 1894		76		New Haven, CT	Württemberg
Habermann, Barbara	13, Mar. 1890	18, Feb.	89- 2m-28d	Brack	Spencerville, OH	Hüttengefäß, Langenselbolt, Kurhessen
Habermann, Heinrich	6, Mar. 1871	12, Feb.	14- 7m-19d		Marion, OH	
Habermann, John	25, Sept 1890	1, Sept	13		Marion, OH	
Habermann, Rosina	22, Sept 1898	23, Sept	31-10m- 8d	Britsch	Marion, OH	
Haberstich, Daniel	9, Feb. 1888	12, Jan.	77		New Orleans, LA	Ober Entfelden, Aargau, Schweiz
Habicht, Heinrich	18, Oct. 1894	2, Oct.	42		Hoboken, NJ	Schleitz, Hessen
Habicht, Maria	2, Mar. 1885	12, Feb.	93	Schmermund	Mankato, MN	Hessen-Darmstadt
Habighorst, Heinrich	26, May 1892	13, Apr.	68		Portland, OR	Brockhagen bei Bielefeld, Westphalen
Habighorst, Katharina	9, Apr. 1891	8, Mar.	67	Warmann	Portland, OR	Blasheim, Minden, Preußen
Hablitzel, John	22, Sept 1898	30, Aug.	35		Clay Center, KS	Wilkingen, Schaffhausen, Schweiz
Habschid, Anton	27, Oct. 1877	14, Oct.	17- 9m-14d		Lancaster, NY	Weißkirchen, Ungarn
Hachmeister, Hanna S.	12, May 1879	28, Apr.	45	Bockhorst	Boonville, IN	Heepen, Bielefeld, Minden, Westphalen
Hachmeister, Maria Elisabeth	6, Aug. 1896	8, July	34	Roth	Boonville, IN	Warrick County, Indiana
Hachmeister, Wilhelm	7, Aug. 1890	22, July	36		Boonville, IN	Heben, Bielefeld, Westphalen
Hack, Elisabeth	24, Nov. 1853	31, Oct.	41		West Baltimore, MD	Leinzingen, Maulbronn, Württemberg

Christliche Apologete Death Notices --- 1839 - 1899

Name of Deceased	Notice Date	Death Date	Age	Page	Maiden Name	Place of Death	Place of Birth
Hack, Georg	27, Oct. 1879	26, Sept	79	343		Baltimore, MD	Baiern
Hack, Georg Nikolaus	13, Dec. 1888	16, Nov.	67- 5m-26d	798		Allegheny City, PA	Unterköst, Heckstadt, Baiern
Hack, Heinrich	14, Dec. 1885	18, Nov.	71	7		Pittsburg, PA	Unterköft, Höchstadt, Oberfranken, Baiern
Hack, Karoline Elenorie	6, June 1889	12, May	69	366		Salina, KS	Breslau, Preußen
Hack, Ludwig	5, July 1894	5, June	37	438		New York City, NY	Städten, Rheinkreis Baiern
Hack, Marie	1, Apr. 1872	14, Mar.	15	111		Pittsburg, PA	Pittsburg, Alleghany County, Pennsylvania
Hackathorn, Martha	18, Apr. 1889	14, Mar.	74	254	Selig	Woodsfield, OH	Rockenfuß, Sondra, Rotenburg, Hessen-Kassel
Hackbart, Julius Karl Conrad	5, Feb. 1891		50- 8m- 9d	94		Kenosha, WI	Zadtkow, Belgard, Preußen
Hackbart, Maria	10, Nov. 1892	10, Sept	26	718	Trantow	Merrill, WI	Maine, Wisconsin
Hacke, Anna Franzisca	30, Oct. 1871	16, Oct.	6- 7m-13d	351		Hartin, IL	Aurora, Indiana
Hacke, Friedrich	10, Mar. 1848	1, Mar.	60	43		Cincinnati, OH	
Hacke, Susanna Justina	27, Aug. 1891	29, July	28	558		Hoyleton, IL	N. Prairie, Washington County, Illinois
Häckel, Magdalena	18, Aug. 1884	2, Aug.	54	7	Hofmann	Clay Center, KS	Gailenkirchen, Württemberg
Hackemann, (Mr)	3, Jan. 1881	16, Dec.	85	7		Menominee, MI	Oppershausen bei Celle, Hannover
Hackemann, Karolina	10, Mar. 1898	8, Feb.	61	158	Oberkirchner	Menominee, MI	New York
Hackemann, Wilhelm	24, Nov. 1892	24, Oct.	72	750		Menominee, MI	Oppershausen bei Zelle, Hannover
Hacker, Andreas	18, May 1893	24, Apr.	27	318		Quincy, IL	Baden
Hacker, Barbara	23, July 1896	6, July	47-10m- 1d	479	Dreiber	Denver, CO	Wayne bei Kewaskum, Wisconsin
Hacker, Kunigunde	24, June 1872	27, May	67	207		Nauvoo, IL	Crecz bei Baireuth, Baiern
Hacker, Maria Dorothea Caroline	26, Aug. 1878	3, Aug.	46- -14d	271	Kutzbach	Wadena, MN	Hildebrandshausen, Prenzlow, Preußen
Hackmann, (Mrs)	8, Feb. 1869		43	47	Steinhage	Edwardsville, IL	
Hackmann, Anna Dor.	23, June 1848	17, May	36- 6m	104		Williamsburg, NY	
Hackmann, Catharina Elsebain	30, Nov. 1854	21, Oct.	58- 8m	192		Defiance, OH	
Hackmann, Catharina St.	27, Oct. 1862	14, Sept	56	172	Hack	Defiance, OH	
Hackmann, Edwin Wilhelm	8, Mar. 1880	23, Feb.	22- 4m-22d	79		Arenzville, IL	Westerkappeln, Seeste, Preußen
Hackmann, Emma Melinda	7, Feb. 1881	21, Jan.	21- 5m-20d	47		Arenzville, IL	Westerkappeln, Preußen
Hackmann, Frank	22, Sept 1879	9, Sept	31	303		Arenzville, IL	Cass County, Illinois
Hackmann, Friedrich	20, Oct. 1879	3, Oct.	61	335		Edwardsville, IL	Cass County, Illinois
Hackmann, Friedrich	6, Feb. 1896	16, Jan.	79	94		Arenzville, IL	Westerkappeln, Münster, Tecklenburg, Preußen
Hackmann, Friedrich	22, Oct. 1896	17, Sept	84	687		Truxton, MO	Vehrte, Osnabrück, Hannover
Hackmann, Georg	29, Jan. 1877	10, Jan.	75	39		West Unity, OH	Cappeln, Preußen
Hackmann, Gerhard	18, May 1863	22, Apr.	49	80		Arenzville, IL	WesterKappeln, Westphalen, Preußen
Hackmann, Gerhard	7, Feb. 1889	16, Jan.	68- - 7d	94		Hopewell, MO	Vehrte, Belm, Osnabrück, Hannover
Hackmann, Heinrich	3, July 1856	14, May	57	108		Evansport, OH	WesterKappeln, Westphalen, Preußen
Hackmann, Johan Heinrich	18, Apr. 1870	24, Mar.	37	127		Defiance, OH	Westerkabel, Preußen
Hackmann, Johan Heinrich	18, May 1874	18, Apr.	50	159		Arenzville, IL	Wester-Kappeln, Westphalen, Preußen
Hackmann, Johan Heinrich	22, Sept 1892	4, Sept	69	606		New Melle, MO	Fährte, Belm, Osnabrück, Hannover
Hackmann, Katharina Elsebein	4, Mar. 1872	7, Feb.	71	79	Stegemann	Defiance, OH	Gehrden bei Melle, Hannover
Hackmann, Lizzie	6, Aug. 1877	26, May	16	255		Edwardsville, IL	WesterKappeln, Westphalen, Preußen
Hackmann, Louisa	13, Aug. 1877		40	263	Jokisch	Arenzville, IL	Beardstown, Cass County, Illinois
Hackmann, Maria	15, Sept 1887	9, Aug.	70	590		Jacksonville, IL	Osterkappeln, Wittlage, Osnabrück, Hannover
Hackmann, Maria	5, Sept 1861	18, Aug.	71	144	Strive	Beardstown, IL	Haltern, Belme, Osnabrück, Hannover
Hackmann, Maria	6, Mar. 1882	16, Feb.	83- 3m	79	Beiderwill	West Unity, OH	Wesen, Tecklenburg, Preußen
Hackmann, Maria	26, July 1849	24, June	26	120		St. Louis, MO	Westerkappel , Preußen
Hackmann, Maria	2, May 1881	12, Apr.	49	143		Warren, MO	
Hackmann, Rosina Alwina	25, Nov. 1886	6, Nov.	20	7		Beaver Falls, MN	Rice County, Minnesota

Christliche Apologete Death Notices --- 1839 - 1899

Name of Deceased	Notice Date	Death Date	Age	Maiden Name	Page	Place of Death	Place of Birth
Hackmann, Stephan H.	12, Apr. 1880	9, Mar.	75		119	Defiance, OH	Westphalen, Preußen
Hackmeister, Barbara	19, May 1873	27, Apr.	35	Boehm	159	Red Bud, IL	Schrotzberg, Württemberg
Hackmeister, Dorothea	9, May 1870	28, Mar.	50		151	Red Bud, IL	Pfinhorst, Amt Langenhage, Hannover
Hackmeister, Karl	9, Aug. 1875	25, July	33		255	Red Bud, IL	Monroe County, Illinois
Hackmeister, Wilhelm E.	21, July 1879	2, July	17		231	Red Bud, IL	Neuendorf, Greisenhagen, Stettin
Hackstein, August	18, May 1893	13, Apr.	49- 4m		318	Willow Springs, KS	Romansau, Pyritz, Pommern
Hackstein, Henriette	17, Feb. 1898	18, Jan.	55	Lübke	111	Willow Springs, KS	Münster, Elsaß
Hadel, G.	14, June 1880		70		191	Lawrenceburg, IN	LeSueur, Minnesota
Hademeck, Lydia Maria	28, Feb. 1895	30, Jan.	22		142	Le Sueur, MN	Mecklenburg-Schwerin
Hader, Sophia	4, Nov. 1872	15, Oct.	70		359	Effington, IL	Pennington, Indiana
Hadler, Charles Lud.	13, Mar. 1890	9, Feb.	20-10m- 5d		174	Brookville, IN	Lindheim, Hessen-Darmstadt
Hadtert, Marie	19, May 1884		82		7	Melrose, NY	Mecklenburg-Schwerin
Haeker, Karl F.	12, Mar. 1883	13, Feb.	27	Feuerbach	87	Lawrence, KS	Woodland, Barry County, Michigan
Haenes, Conrad	25, Nov. 1886	9, Nov.	31		7		Neckargartach, Württemberg
Haerle, Georg	25, July 1881	9, July	82- 7m-22d		239	Quincy, IL	Temmen, Dissen, Hannover
Hafe, Friedrich	2, June 1873	5, May	39		175	St. Louis, MO	
Hafen, Martha	22, Mar. 1880	26, Feb.	14		95	Los Angeles, CA	
Hafendörfer, Johan Gottlieb	4, Dec. 1876	21, Sept	77		391	Louisville, KY	Bönigheim, Besigheim, Württemberg
Hafendörfer, Katharina Dorothea	4, Dec. 1876	8, Nov.	78	Heiges	391	Louisville, KY	Bönigheim, Besigheim, Württemberg
Hafer, Amalia Elisabeth	2, Feb. 1863	18, Jan.	5- 6m-19d		20	Reading, OH	
Hafer, Christian	30, Aug. 1880	11, Aug.	63-10m-25d		279	Allegheny City, PA	NeuMorschen, Spangeberg, Kurhessen
Hafer, Friederika Augusta	13, Nov. 1882	64- 4m-13d		Blickwedel	367	Allegheny City, PA	Braunschweig, Preußen
Haffer, Julia	20, July 1885	27- 7m-16d			7	Allegheny City, PA	
Häffle, Gottfried	22, May 1871	28, Apr.	66		167	Platteville, WI	Affalterbach, Württemberg
Häffner, Jakobine H.	6, Feb. 1882	1, Dec.	58		47	Baltimore, MD	
Häffner, Johan Michael	27, Dec. 1880	7, Dec.	53		415	Minneapolis, MN	Zisch, Preußen
Häffner, Adam John	27, Aug. 1896	13, Aug.	29		559	Batesville, IN	Ironton, Ohio
Häfner, Anna Maria	9, Mar. 1885		79	Kopfmann	7	Sherrills Mount, IA	Nimburg, Emmendingen, Baden
Hafner, Carolina Friederika Louisa	9, Mar. 1893	2, Feb.	38	Grebe	158	Chicago, IL	Ardorf, Waldeck
Hafner, Catharina	9, Aug. 1894	23, July	16		518	Batesville, IN	Lawrenceville, Dearborn County, Indiana
Häfner, Elisabeth	21, June 1875	11, June	28	Keller	199	Chicago, IL	Malterdingen, Baden
Häfner, Elisabeth	23, May 1895	30, Apr.	55	Mann	334	Louisville, KY	Monroe County, Ohio
Häfner, Karl	7, Jan. 1886	24, Dec.	60		7	Cincinnati, OH	Eberstadt, Baden
Häfner, Karoline	5, May 1892	13, Feb.	53- 5m-19d	Mann	286	Giard, IA	Monroe County, Ohio
Häfner, Maria	12, Apr. 1880	21, June	61		119	St. Joseph, MO	Solitude, Leonberg, Württemberg
Häfner, Nettie	30, Oct. 1882	27, Sept	4- 7m- 3d		351	Giard, IA	
Häfner, Wilhelm H.	23, Nov. 1899	1, Nov.	86		751	Sherrills Mount, IA	Ersbach, Oehringen, Württemberg
Hage, Friederika	15, Aug. 1889	20, July	70- 6m- 1d		526	Sun Prairie, WI	Brunsen, Braunschweig
Hage, Johanna Maria Justina	6, Jan. 1879	21, Dec.	75	Wille	7	Sun Prairie, WI	Brunsen, Braunschweig
Hagebuch, Christian	24, Apr. 1882		63- 6m		135	Clay Center, KS	Tuttendorf, Schleswig-Holstein
Hagedorn, Carl	7, July 1892	21, June	71		430	Mankato, MN	Rothenberg, Württemberg
Hagedorn, Christine	13, Nov. 1876	26, Oct.		Osiander	367	Grand Rapids, IL	Johnsville, Bartholomew County, Indiana
Hagedorn, Emilie	15, July 1886	15, June	26	Hackmann	7	Beaver Falls, MN	Poughkeepsie, New York
Hagedorn, Friedrich	5, June 1882	10, May	29- 5m		183	Poughkeepsie, NY	Langenhagen, Hannover
Hagedorn, Friedrich	7, May 1896	28, Mar.	59		302	Papillion, NE	Vinnhorst, Hannover
Hagedorn, Heinrich	23, Dec. 1886	30, Nov.	73- 3m-14d		7	Grand Ridge, IL	

Christliche Apologete Death Notices --- 1839 - 1899

Name of Deceased	Notice Date	Death Date	Age	Maiden Name	Page	Place of Death	Place of Birth
Hagedorn, Louise	22, Dec. 1879	1, Dec.	19	Rieth	407	Grand Rapids, IL	Troy Grove, Illinois
Hagelgans, Wilhelmine Mathilde	15, Dec. 1887	22, Nov.	33	Kammeier	798	Wyandotte, KS	Berger Station, Franklin County, Missouri
Hagemann, Friederike	17, June 1858	21, May	36- 5m	Münzemeier	96	Peoria, IL	Obereßlingen, Württemberg
Hagemann, John	29, Jan. 1891	22, Dec.	16		78	Bloomington, IL	Bloomington, Illinois
Hagemann, Maria	4, Jan. 1875	14, Dec.	39- 6m	Troß	7	Louisville, KY	Thalhausen, Coblenz, Preußen
Hagemann, Wilhelm	29, Jan. 1866	26, Nov.	58- 2m-20d		38	Manchester, MO	
Hagemeyer, J. C. Wilhelm	20, July 1899	3, July	78		463	Covington, KY	Bremen, Germany
Hagen, Elisabeth	23, May 1889	22, Apr.	70- 8m-21d	Trinkhan	334	Roseville, MI	Mecklenburg-Schwerin
Hagen, Heinrich Gottfried	25, May 1885	30, Apr.	67		7	Roseville, MI	Warlitz, Mecklenburg-Schwerin
Hagen, Tönjes Johan	10, Aug. 1899	26, July	80		511	Emden, IL	Kloster-Cymönken, Emden, Ostfriesland
Hagen, Wilhelmine	24, Mar. 1884	4, Mar.	29	Kruse	7	Roseville, MI	Holf Malchow, Mecklenburg
Hagemann, Magdalena	27, May 1872	24, Apr.	44- 6m-16d	Sipfle	175	Bloomington, IL	Diedelsheim, Baden
Häger, Christoph	14, Jan. 1886	18, Dec.	75		7	Watertown, WI	Erdbruch, Lippe-Detmold
Hager, Ernestine	17, Nov. 1873	7, Oct.	38	Weige	367	Leavenworth, MN	Frankfurt a. d. Oder, Preußen
Häger, Katharina	23, Apr. 1877	20, Feb.	80		135	New Knoxville, OH	Leimen, Baden
Häger, Philipp	26, Feb. 1877	6, Feb.	76		71	New Knoxville, OH	Leimen bei Heidelberg, Baden
Hager, Robert Roland	29, Nov. 1888	30, Oct.	17		766	Sleepy Eye, MN	Eden, Minnesota
Hager, Sophia	27, Oct. 1892	9, Oct.	62		686	Salem, OR	Seffingen bei Thun, Bern, Schweiz
Hagmann, John J.	1, July 1886	13, June	48		7	Redfield, SD	Canton Appenzell, Schweiz
Hagmeier, Jakob	22, Apr. 1897	22, Feb.	66		254	Columbus, IL	Ulm, Württemberg
Hagmeyer, Martha	23, Feb. 1899	1, Feb.	67	Heller	127	Columbus, IL	Oberdorla bei Mühlhausen, Germany
Hählen, Elisabeth	24, Dec. 1891	26, Nov.		Zbäaren	830	De Soto, MO	
Hahn, (Mr)	30, Dec. 1878	10, Oct.	60		415	Storm Lake, IA	Berlin, Preußen
Hahn, (Mrs)	19, Aug. 1878	6, Aug.	44- 6m- 7d	Lattemann	263	Giard, IA	Dorf Besse, Kurhessen
Hahn, Adam C.	10, Nov. 1887	21, Oct.	62		718	Marrs, IN	Alten-Kronau, Kurhessen
Hahn, Andreas	4, Nov. 1878	27, Sept	17- 3m-25d		351	Boston, MA	South Dedham, Massachuetts
Hahn, Anna Gertrude	13, July 1899	24, June	64	Gertenbach	447	Muscatine, IA	Zenneren, Fritzlar, Hessen-Kassel
Hahn, Anna Katharina	12, June 1871	12, May	47- 7m	Bartholomä	191	Boston, MA	Oberöstheim, Rothenburg, Baiern
Hahn, Anna Magdalena Maria	1, Mar. 1880	16, Feb.	71	Kobel	71	Milwaukee, WI	Rostock, Mecklenburg-Schwerin
Hahn, Anton	22, Jan. 1866	2, Jan.	56- 7m- 8d		30	Chicago, IL	Schierheim, Elsaß
Hahn, August	14, Aug. 1876	25, July	61		263	Michigan City, IN	Prezin, Pommern, Preußen
Hahn, Barbara Elisabeth	7, Oct. 1878	4, Aug.	74	Mendel	319	Kendallville, IN	Salzberg, Homberg, Kurhessen
Hahn, Caroline	2, Aug. 1888	21, June	56	Kautz	494	St. Philip, IN	New Orleans, Louisiana
Hahn, Catharina	11, Oct. 1875	23, Sept	28	Nun	327	Vermillion, OH	Vermillion, Erie County, Ohio
Hahn, Catharina	8, Apr. 1867	20, Mar.	53	Tenny	110	Chicago, IL	Fagweiler, Elsaß
Hahn, Christina	4, Mar. 1878	4, Feb.	18-11m-12d		71	Giard, IA	
Hahn, Christoph Ernst	30, Apr. 1896		76		286	Stitzer, WI	Dahme, Brandenburg
Hahn, Conrad	8, Feb. 1855	30, Sept	20- 4m-28d		24	Mt. Vernon, IN	
Hahn, Dorothea	19, Jan. 1885	8, Dec.	27- 4m- 4d		7	New York City, NY	New York City, New York
Hahn, Elisabeth	21, June 1875	20, Apr.	81		199	Canton, MO	
Hahn, Emilie Pauline	1, May 1890	4, Mar.	66- 9m- 8d	Wruch	286	San Jose, CA	Birnbaum bei Bromberg, Posen
Hahn, Friederika	31, Aug. 1863	5, Aug.	19		140	Michigan City, IN	
Hahn, Georg	27, Feb. 1890	22, Jan.	48- 6m-17d		142	Vermillion, OH	Lorain County, Ohio
Hahn, George	6, May 1878	15, Apr.	58		143	New York City, NY	Lange, Hannover
Hahn, George	4, July 1881	14, June	22- 4m		215	New York City, NY	
Hahn, Heinrich	2, Feb. 1860	2, Sept	13- 4m		20	Mt. Vernon, IN	

- 172 -

Christliche Apologete Death Notices --- 1839 - 1899

Name of Deceased	Notice Date	Death Date	Age	Maiden Name	Page	Place of Death	Place of Birth
Hahn, Johan Adam	1, Apr. 1886	28, Feb.	71		7	St. Philip, IN	AltenGroßenau, Schwarzenfels, Kurhessen
Hahn, Johan Adam	9, Jan. 1865	11, Dec.	79		8	Mt. Vernon, IN	Allengonnan, Schwarzenfels, Kurhessen
Hahn, Johan Adam	13, Oct. 1892	30, Aug.	77		654	Boston, MA	Wolfsau, Baiern
Hahn, Johan Peter	27, Apr. 1885	10, Apr.	66-11m-10d		7	Vermillion, OH	Presdorf, Sachsen-Weimar
Hahn, Johanna Louise	5, Apr. 1894	12, Mar.	71	Hecht	230	Stitzer, WI	Schlenzer bei Jüterbock, Brandenburg
Hahn, John C.	27, Nov. 1890	6, Aug.	61		766	Marrs, IN	Altgramau, Hessen-Kassel
Hahn, Katharina	5, May 1879	19, Apr.	74-10m-11d	Schüßler	143	Marrs, IN	Altengronau, Schwarzenfels, Kurhessen
Hahn, Margaretha	30, Dec. 1897	1, Dec.	20		828	Marrs, IN	Posey County, Indiana
Hahn, Margarethe	20, June 1895	30, May	54- 8m		398	Boston, MA	Diebach, Baiern
Hahn, Maria	31, Oct. 1895	1, Oct.	64	Pepper	702	New York City, NY	Depstedt, Lehe, Hannover
Hahn, Maria Elisabeth	6, Dec. 1880	18, Nov.	44		391	Milwaukee, WI	Wicks, Schopfheim, Baden
Hahn, Maria M.	1, Sept 1887	10, Aug.	36	Decker	558	Vermillion, OH	Oberndorf, Schwarzwald, Württemberg
Hahn, Mathilde	17, Feb. 1873	24, Jan.	35		53	Chicago, IL	Mutten, Kreis Schlüchtern, Kurhessen
Hahn, Nikolaus	12, June 1865	11, May	65-10m-11d		96	Evansville, IN	Rosendale, Fond du Lac County, Wisconsin
Hahn, Otilda Amelia Louise	3, Feb. 1898	31, Oct.	22		79	Ripon, WI	Lippe-Detmold
Hahn, Sophie	9, Oct. 1882	15, Sept	59- -3d	Dohmeyer	327	Storm Lake, IA	Hall, Württemberg
Hahn, Susanna Magdalena	3, Mar. 1892	6, Jan.	73	Kübler	142	Poughkeepsie, NY	Wehe, Nassau
Hahn, Wilhelmine	13, May 1886	20, Apr.	57	Kaltwasser	7	Brillion, WI	Totenhausen, Minden, Preußen
Hahne, Christine	27, May 1897	9, May	77	Rathert	335	Senate Grove, MO	
Hahne, Franz	17, Jan. 1876	10, Dec.	18- 4m- 6d		23	Herman, MO	
Hahne, Friedrich	9, Mar. 1868	4, Feb.	36- 6m		79	Union, MO	Hemer, Minden, Preußen
Hahne, Louis	2, May 1889	13, Apr.	59		286	New Haven, MO	Ribbesbüttel, Gifhorn, Hannover
Hahnebuth, Friedrich	22, Mar. 1888	23, Feb.	50		190	Cannelton, MN	Platendorf, Gischorn, Hannover
Hahnebuth, Marie	8, Mar. 1875	20, Feb.	50	Fricke	79	Cannelton, IN	
Hahnhardt, Emma	16, Jan. 1882	27, Dec.	24- 4m		23	Winona, MN	Lenk, Bern, Schweiz
Hähnlein, Samuel	23, Feb. 1899	2, Jan.	34		127	Chicago, IL	
Haibener, Ludwig	18, Feb. 1842		Inquiry		27	Wheeling, VA	
Haidle, Mina	8, Sept 1879	27, Aug.	12-10m-27d		287	Blissfield, MI	Walstädten, Balingen, Württemberg
Haigis, Johan	17, June 1872	3, June	47- 3m-17d		199	Tuneis Falls, MA	Louisville, Kentucky
Haim, Marie Elisabeth	18, Aug. 1859	23, July	18- 8m- 3d		132	Newark, OH	Nordsehl, Bückeburg, Lippe-Schaumburg
Haine, Christian	3, Feb. 1873	13, Jan.	70- 3m		39	Muscatine, IA	Dubuque, Iowa
Haisch, Friedrich	9, June 1898	16, May	20		367	Dubuque, IA	Heinde, Hannover
Haise, Johan Heinrich G.	11, Dec. 1882	15, Nov.	77		399	Cape Girardeau, MO	Rochester, New York
Haiseman, Katharina	14, Apr. 1892	29, Mar.	39	Teufel	238	Rochester, NY	Waldlaubersheim, Preußen
Haist, Margaretha	8, Mar. 1894		62	Poß	166	Freeport, IL	Portenheim, Hessen-Darmstadt
Haith, Maria	7, Jan. 1867	10, Nov.	75		6	Chicago, IL	Hördinghausen, Lintorf, Wittlage, Hannover
Hake, Fr. W.	29, Aug. 1881	6, Aug.	77- 6m- 8d		279	Hoyleton, IL	Lintorf, Wittlage, Hannover
Hake, Henriette	10, Apr. 1882	21, Mar.	84- 1m-21d	Jepker	119	Hoyleton, IL	Sternberg , Lippe-Detmold
Hake, Luise Karolina	24, Aug. 1899	9, Aug.	62- 1m-15d	Blomberg	543	Hoyleton, IL	West Preußen
Haker, Caroline	22, Mar. 1888	11, Feb.	67- 7m-14d	Möllmann	190	Effington, MN	Engter, Hannover
Hakmann, Elisabeth	19, May 1859	8, Apr.	22		80	Rockford, IN	Fowler, Adams County, Illinois
Hakmeyer, Johan Eduard Wesley	19, Jan. 1886	23, Dec.	15- -16d		46	Columbus, IL	Mißburg, Hannover
Halberstadt, Conrad	28, Jan. 1886	27, Dec.	68		7	Robinson, KS	Kintz, Preußen
Halberstadt, Maria	19, Feb. 1872	23, Dec.	73- 7m-18d		63	Washington, MN	Geradstetten, Württemberg
Halbgewachs, Pauline	5, June 1890	9, May	43- 2m- 2d	Hottmann	366	Eustis, NE	Norden, Ostfriesland
Halbohm, Adelheid	30, Oct. 1890	6, Oct.	71	Wayers	702	Bushnell, IL	

Christliche Apologete Death Notices --- 1839 - 1899

Name of Deceased	Notice Date	Death Date	Age	Page	Maiden Name	Place of Death	Place of Birth
Halbritter, Johanna Charlotte	1, Jan. 1877	14, Dec.	40- 2m-23d	7		Cleveland, OH	Erfurt, Sachsen
Halgi, Anna	23, Apr. 1891	2, Apr.	70	270	Gallmann	Baltimore, MD	Mettmenstetten, Zürich, Schweiz
Hall, Dorothea Maria	8, Aug. 1881	29, July	64- 7m	255		Sandusky, OH	Mosbill, Schleswig-Holstein
Hall, Maria	23, Apr. 1891	5, Apr.	62	270	Vetterli	Oshkosh, WI	
Hall, Phobe	5, May 1884	8, Apr.	26	7	Kellermeier	Stryker, OH	Defiance County, Ohio
Hallbach, Catharina	26, Mar. 1866	22, Feb.	64	102	Hollinger	Louisville, KY	Santenet, Rheinkreis Baiern
Hallbach, Henrietta	21, Oct. 1872	19, Aug.	36	343	Stolz	Louisville, KY	Lobsan, Sulz, Elsaß
Hallbach, Louis	24, Mar. 1873	27, Feb.	37	95		Louisville, KY	Bruchmühlbach, Rheinkreis Baiern
Halle, Maria	26, May 1887	10, Feb.	27- 8m- 3d	334	Gralapp	Eldorado, WI	Friendship, Fond du Lac County, Wisconsin
Hallenberger, Anna Catharina	26, Mar. 1877	11, Mar.	50- 4m-15d	103	Müller	Danville, IL	Nieder-Asphe, Marburg, Kurhessen
Hallenscheidt, Lisette	27, Oct. 1873	3, Oct.	29	343		Second Creek, MO	
Haller, Anna Elisabeth	15, Mar. 1894	22, Feb.	81	182	Kyburtz	East Troy, WI	Ober-Entfelden, Aargau, Schweiz
Haller, Elisabeth	28, July 1873	13, July	67- 8m-23d	239		Bucyrus, OH	Offenbach bei Landau, Baiern
Haller, Ernst	25, Oct. 1855	17, Sept	36	172		Bucyrus, OH	Roswaag, Vaihingen, Württemberg
Haller, Johan	20, Apr. 1874	26, Mar.	46	127		Bloomington, IL	Schückingen, Maulbronn, Württemberg
Haller, Johan Jakob	25, Oct. 1894	1, Oct.	85	694		Honey Creek, WI	Zetzwiel, Aargau, Schweiz
Haller, John	14, Sept 1893	7, Aug.	83	590		Jeffersonville, IN	Offenthal, Hessen-Darmstadt
Haller, Maria	7, Dec. 1893	10, Nov.	79	782	Loneman		Osnabrück, Hannover
Haller, Martin	14, Sept 1863	29, Aug.	39	148		New Haven, CT	Gillstein, Herrenberg, Württemberg
Hallewedel, Sophia	17, Dec. 1866	12, Sept	50	406		Batesville, IN	Larien, Amt Syke, Hannover
Hällfrisch, Friedrich	4, June 1883	16, Mar.		183		Manitowoc, WI	Sechselbach, Mergentheim, Württemberg
Hällfrisch, Johan	16, June 1884	15, May	28	7		Cairo, WI	
Halsenberg, Anna Maria Elsabein	7, Jan. 1878	25, Dec.	32- 2m-20d	7	Hoberg	Morrison, MO	Vlotho, Minden, Preußen
Halste, Christoph Heinrich	5, Mar. 1883	9, Feb.	68- 9m-25d	79		Le Sueur, MN	Strühen, Rahden, Westphalen
Halstenberg, Carl Friedrich Gottlieb	1, Jan. 1891	7, Dec.	53	14		Morrison, MO	Minden, Preußen
Halter, Adam	3, July 1865	15, Mar.	20- -12d	108		De Soto, MO	
Halter, Margaretha	27, Sept 1888	3, Sept	70- 7m-22d	622		De Soto, MO	Langendiebach bei Hanau, Kurhessen
Halter, Mina	18, June 1891	29, May	30	398	Kleinschmidt	De Soto, MO	
Haman, (Mrs)	6, Nov. 1851	19, Aug.	42	180		Bethlehem, OH	Kleinfischlingen, Rheinkreis Baiern
Haman, Barbara	19, Jan. 1888	30, Dec.	54-11m-23d	46	Nischwitz	Cape Girardeau, MO	Hemsbach, Weinheim, Baden
Haman, H. Ph.	29, Sept 1887	12, Sept	58- 8m-13d	622		Cape Girardeau, MO	Hary, Woldenberg, Hannover
Haman, Ida Augusta	21, May 1896	25, Apr.	30	334		Cape Girardeau, MO	Cape Girardeau County, Missouri
Haman, Katharina Magdalena	17, Oct. 1889	20, Aug.	76- 4m- 9d	670	Schill	Brookville, IN	Erbhausen, Nagold, Württemberg
Haman, Katharine Elisabeth	25, Feb. 1897	31, Jan.	71	127	Oberbeck	Cape Girardeau, MO	Woltershausen, Germany
Hamann,	6, Aug. 1857	19, July	32	128		Jackson, MO	Lutter am Badenberge, Braunschweig
Hamann, Anna Louise	8, Dec. 1879	19, Oct.	82- 5m-27d	391	Horn	Vernon, WI	Belgen, Brandenburg
Hamann, Karl	22, Mar. 1880	9, Feb.	79-11m-25d	95		Vernon, WI	Adamsdof, Brandenburg
Hamburg, Friederika	26, Apr. 1875	7, Apr.	20- 5m-29d	135	Schlick	Waco, TX	New York
Hamilton, Caroline	21, Dec. 1893	17, Oct.	27	814	Zölling	Crown Point, IN	Will County, Illinois
Hamm, Anna Maria	3, June 1897	28, Apr.	57	351	Ehmrich	Portsmouth, OH	Portmouth, Scioto County, Ohio
Hamm, Anna Ellenora	10, June 1886	24, May	41	7	Meis	Dubuque, IA	Preußen
Hamm, Eva	4, Dec. 1890	9, Nov.	81	782	Frömmer	East Troy, WI	Eckwartsheim, Elsaß
Hamm, J.	24, Nov. 1892	20, Oct.	46	750		Arlington, MN	Kwastenheim bei Straßburg, Elsaß
Hamm, Johan	11, Nov. 1897	5, Oct.	90	719		Honey Creek, WI	Ingenheim, Hochfelten, Elsaß
Hamm, Karoline	26, Jan. 1893	23, Dec.	27	62	Fink	Buffalo, NY	Boston, Erie County, New York
Hamm, Maria	17, Nov. 1898	27, Oct.	69	735	Härrer	Anaheim, CA	Pennsylvania

Christliche Apologete Death Notices --- 1839 - 1899

Name of Deceased	Notice Date	Death Date	Age	Maiden Name	Place of Death	Page	Place of Birth
Hammann, Barbara	6, Feb. 1882	13, Jan.	66		Meredosia, IL	47	Schwegenheim, Rheinkreis Baiern
Hammann, Charly	3, Nov. 1862	21, Sept	5- 9m		St. Paul, MN	176	
Hammann, Doris	3, Nov. 1862	1, Oct.	4- 6m		St. Paul, MN	176	
Hammann, Friedrich	13, Dec. 1860	23, Nov.	32		Peoria, IL	200	Hallwangen, Freudenstadt, Württemberg
Hammann, Heinrich	11, May 1874	29, Apr.	82		Cape Girardeau, MO	151	Dallon, Amt Lampspringe, Hannover
Hammann, Heinrich	21, Feb. 1876	30, Jan.	69		Jacksonville, IL	63	Neustadt a.H., Baiern
Hammann, Johan Conrad	24, Sept 1883	15, May	54- 6m-24d		Stockton, CA	311	Reinhorn, Hessen
Hammel, (Mr)	23, Apr. 1866	17, Mar.	83		De Soto, MO	134	Hohebach, Münster, Württemberg
Hammel, Heinrich Jakob	15, Dec. 1873	27, Nov.	78		Nauvoo, IL	399	Niederocke, Amt Böhl, Hessen
Hammel, John Daniel	22, Oct. 1896	8, Sept	74		Warsaw, IL	687	Niederocke, Hessen-Darmstadt
Hammel, John Phil.	9, Nov. 1893	15, Oct.	33		Nauvoo, IL	718	Nauvoo, Illinois
Hammel, Maria	21, Feb. 1876	1, Feb.	56	Knoche	St. Louis, MO	63	Buchenberg, Hessen-Darmstadt
Hammel, Mina	11, Sept 1876	22, Aug.	30- 7m-12d	Börger	Warsaw, IL	295	Buchenberg, Wähl, Hessen-Darmstadt
Hammell, John	5, Nov. 1883	12, Oct.	36- 9m-20d		St. Louis, MO	359	Holtingen, Baden
Hammer, Catharina	11, July 1870	6, June	57		Boston, MA	223	Heimerdingen, Leonberg, Württemberg
Hammer, Christine	19, Oct. 1893	21, Sept	92- 4m- 4d	Meierheinrich	Hokah, MN	670	Beutelsbach, Württemberg
Hammer, Friedrich Ludwig	3, Sept 1883	18, Aug.	78- 9m-26d		Jacksonville, IL	287	Efringen, Amt Lörrach, Baden
Hammer, Johan Georg	26, Sept 1864	25, Aug.	67		Roxbury, MA	156	Kunzelsau, Württemberg
Hammer, Margaretha	20, Sept 1860	30, Aug.	67		Elizabeth, NJ	152	Breinersfeld, Oberfranken, Baiern
Hammerand, Anna	30, Sept 1872	4, Sept	45	Widmann	Sherrills Mount, IA	319	Buseck, Gießen, Hessen
Hammerle, Caspar	14, Jan. 1858	20, Dec.	55		St. Louis, MO	8	Harrison County, Indiana
Hämmerle, Emma Karoline	2, Sept 1878	20, Aug.	22- -21d	Dick	Marshall, IL	279	Großenroda bei Mooringen, Hannover
Hämmerling, Karoline	15, Mar. 1869	12, Feb.	43	Lorberg	Lowell, WI	87	Berlin, Preußen
Hämmerly, Bertha	23, Dec. 1878	10, Dec.	46	Schmidt	Dallas, TX	407	Hirschau, Württemberg
Hämmerly, Valentin	12, Mar. 1896	7, Feb.	77		Chillicothe, OH	174	Binder, Bockenem, Hannover
Hammerschmidt, Caroline Henrietta C.	4, Dec. 1882	14, Nov.	48- - 9d	Rump	Champaign, IL	391	Chicago, Cook County, Illinois
Hammler, Emma E.	17, Aug. 1885	4, Aug.	17	Salzer	Topeka, KS	7	
Hammon, Mich.	2, July 1847	10, June			New York, NY	107	
Hammond, Ella C.	30, Nov. 1893	21, Sept	30		Troy, NY	766	Troy, New York
Hamon, Nancy L.	27, Feb. 1882	7, Feb.	28- 7m-16d	Rinker	Ellinwood, KS	71	
Hamp, Gottliebin	12, May 1887	1, Apr.	64		Beilstein, GE	302	
Hamp, Louise	22, July 1858	11, July	58	Bleck	Dayton, OH	116	Löwen, Preußen
Hamscher, Anna Maria	27, July 1893	20, June	77	Opp	Dillsboro, IN	478	Freimersheim, Hessen-Darmstadt
Hamscher, Christian	31, Dec. 1891	6, July	68		Dillsboro, OH	846	Germany
Hancock, Louise Emma	11, Apr. 1881	23, Mar.	21	Miller	Seymour, IN	119	Jackson County, Indiana
Handel, Maria Agnes	14, Apr. 1884	16, Mar.	89	Salzer	Lenox, IA	7	Dettingen, Urach, Württemberg
Handerich, Maria Barbara	8, June 1899	26, Apr.	85		Belleville, IL	367	Schauernheim, Rheinpfalz Baiern
Händiges, Barbara	18, May 1899	28, Mar.	48	Link	Newark, NJ	318	Rainham, Ontario, Canada
Handke, Helena	27, Jan. 1887	10, Jan.	64		Chicago, IL	62	
Handrich, Wilhelm	18, July 1895	30, June	82		Highland, IL	462	Schauenheim, Rheinpfalz Baiern
Handstein, Wilhelm	16, Feb. 1874	2, Jan.	54-11m- 1d		Jeffersonville, NY	55	Eifersee, Hannover
Hanebut, Carl	25, Dec. 1876	6, Dec.	51- 6m		Hopewell, MO	413	Großsenmarpe, Blomberg, Lippe-Detmold
Haneisen, Amalia	14, Sept 1893	12, Aug.	70	Gelser	Marshall, IL	590	Canton Drülingen, Frankreich
Hänel, Margaretha	10, Mar. 1887	21, Feb.	57		Pekin, IL	158	Roth, Baden
Hanfman, Peter	21, Sept 1899	4, Sept	89		New York City, NY	607	
Hanft, Adam	27, June 1889	12, June	79- -19d		Greenville, OH	414	Redwitz, Lichtenfels, Oberfranken, Baiern

Christliche Apologete Death Notices -- 1839 - 1899

Name of Deceased	Death Date	Age	Page	Maiden Name	Place of Death	Place of Birth	Notice Date
Hanft, Katharina	18, Oct.	40- 8m-17d	351		Greenville, OH	Lockport, Ohio	31, Oct. 1881
Hangardner, Jakob	28, Mar.	52	271		Marion, WI	Altstetten, Schweiz	29, Apr. 1897
Hangbühl, Joseph	7, Feb.	40	48		Highland, IL	Melle, Hannover	22, Mar. 1860
Hanhardt, Emilie	1, Sept		303		New Orleans, LA	Zürich, Schweiz	24, Sept 1878
Hanhardt, Maria Saloma	13, Jan.	65	94	Morbach	Winona, MN	Kunheim, Elsaß	9, Feb. 1893
Hanhart, Maria	24, Apr.	45	334	Schlüter	Ballwin, MO		23, May 1895
Hanhart, Maria Elisabeth	29, Mar.	26	334		Ballwin, MO		23, May 1895
Hanke, Anton Heinrich	16, Oct.	49	783		Pinckney, MO	Warren County, Missouri	8, Dec. 1898
Hanke, Christine	10, Nov.	33	204	Allersmeyer	Marthasville, MO	Valdorf, Amt Flote, Preußen	19, Dec. 1861
Hanke, Friederika	24, Aug.	46	590	Potthap	Hopewell, MO	Bösingfeld, Lippe-Detmold	11, Sept 1890
Hanke, Friederike C.	14, Jan.	35- 5m-20d	78		Hopewell, MO		31, Jan. 1889
Hanke, Friedrich Simon August	18, Feb.	40	190		Warren, MO	Heidelbeck, Lippe-Detmold	23, Mar. 1899
Hanke, Louise	11, Mar.	62	127	Kampmeier	Cedar Lake, IN	Talle, Amt Hohenhausen, Lippe-Detmold	20, Apr. 1868
Hanke, W. Heinrich Herman	28, Nov.	20-11m-10d	798		Hopewell, MO	Heidelbeck, Lippe-Detmold	15, Dec. 1887
Hanke, Wilhelm	14, June	36	462		Larned, KS	Drake, Gasconade County, Missouri	18, July 1889
Hanke, Wilhelmine Dorothea	10, July	37	495	Austermann	Pinckney, MO	Lippe-Detmold	30, July 1896
Hankemeyer, Heinrich	10, Nov.	72	844		Warrenton, MO		31, Dec. 1896
Hanna, Wilhelmine Friederika	4, Oct.	81	703	Buß	Rockham, SD	Groß Benz, Naugard, Pommern	29, Oct. 1896
Hanne, Luise	5, Dec.	59	14		Lincoln, NE		5, Jan. 1899
Hannemann, Dietrich	14, July	63	247		Columbus, WI	Neuenkirchen, Mecklenburg-Strelitz	29, July 1872
Hannemann, Friedrich Wilhelm	16, Jan.	59	39		Union, MO	Hamlingdorf, Halle, Westphalen	4, Feb. 1878
Hannemann, Katharina	2, Nov.	69- 6m	814		Beaufort, MO		20, Dec. 1888
Hannen, Metta	7, Feb.	65	158		Humboldt, NE		8, Mar. 1888
Hannes, Anna Maria	30, July	48	271		Toledo, OH	Osnabrück, Hannover	22, Aug. 1881
Hannes, Georg Paul	26, Oct.	76	750		Toledo, OH	Hersbruch, Baiern	21, Nov. 1895
Hannes, Mary	2, May	26	350		Toledo, OH	Toledo, Lucas County, Ohio	1, June 1893
Hänni, Jakob	28, Feb.	36	7		Austin, TX	Canton Bern, Schweiz	11, Mar. 1886
Hanning, Johan Dietrich Conrad	29, Nov.	28	4		Santa Claus, IN	Diepholz, Hannover	4, Jan. 1864
Hanning, Johanna Karolina Christiana	25, Oct.	18- 4m	192		Huntingburg, IN		27, Nov. 1856
Häny, Christian	17, July	54	128		Highland, IL	Seftigen, Bern, Schweiz	10, Aug. 1854
Hany, Daniel	17, June	75	108		Captina, OH	Kanton Bern, Schweiz	5, July 1855
Häny, Elissa	9, June	36	100		Captina, OH	Münstingen, Bern, Schweiz	23, June 1859
Hans, Georg Michael	8, Aug.	65	543		Mascoutah, IL	Langenkandel, Rheinkreis Baiern	25, Aug. 1898
Hans, David	16, Feb.	90	142		Arlington Heights, IL	Hunneweier, Elsaß	3, Mar. 1892
Hans, J. Phil	12, Mar.	41	206		Golconda, IL	Plaggenburg, Aurich, Ostfriesland	31, Mar. 1887
Hansa, Eva Maria	25, Aug.	76	327	Klaß	Schnectady, NY	Greifswalde, Pommern	10, Oct. 1881
Hansche, Wilhelm	7, Jan.	68	22		Kenosha, WI	Lienen, Westphalen	21, Jan. 1867
Hansel, Karoline C. S.	17, July	47	511	Bastian	Dallas, TX	Conitz, Mecklenburg-Schwerin	11, Aug. 1898
Hansel, Wilhelm	15, Jan.	43	126		Ft. Dodge, IA	Neukirchen, Mecklenburg-Strelitz	19, Feb. 1891
Hanselmann, Johan	14, Aug.	61	279		Greenville, OH	Hartz bei Gelnhausen, Kurhessen	27, Aug. 1883
Hansen, Anna Catharina		2w	319		Hokah, MN		2, Oct. 1876
Hansen, Elisabeth	2, Sept	49	311		Brooklyn, NY	Gesterberg, Kurhessen	27, Sept 1875
Hansen, Georg Friedrich		3	319		Hokah, MN		2, Oct. 1876
Hansen, Katharina	20, Mar.	38	334		Davenport, IA	Hannover	23, May 1889
Hanser, Barbara	15, Nov.	65	782	Fröhlich	Detroit, MI	Ostheim, Elsaß	3, Dec. 1889
Hansmeyer, Antin	28, Dec.	68- 9m-11d	46	Tholen	Jacksonville, IL	Norden, Ostfriesland	15, Jan. 1891

Name of Deceased	Notice Date	Death Date	Age	Page	Maiden Name	Place of Death	Place of Birth
Hanstein, Elisabeth	22, Feb. 1894	25, Jan.	72	126	Altvater	Jeffersonville, NY	Lindheim, Hessen-Darmstadt
Hanstein, Heinrich	6, May 1897	24, Jan.	80	287		New York City, NY	Lindheim, Hessen-Darmstadt
Häny, Katharina	16, May 1861	2, May	47- 1m	80		Canal Dover, OH	Ober-Haßle, Bern, Schweiz
Hänzel, (Mrs)	13, Apr. 1874	28, Mar.	73	119	Neiger	Wabasha, MN	Niendorf bei Lübeck,
Happel, Elisabeth	7, May 1896	10, Apr.	82	302	Busch	Rose Hill, TX	Retterode, Hessen-Kassel
Happel, Johanna	16, Feb. 1899	24, Jan.	76	111	Möller	Cape Girardeau, MO	Hannover
Happel, Karl Louis	3, May 1894	14, Apr.	18	294	Bierschwal	Cape Girardeau, MO	Cape Girardeau County, Missouri
Happel, Maria M.	19, Jan. 1888	27, Dec.	46	46	Barth	New Metamoras, OH	Schmidt-Hagelbach, Preußen
Happel, Theodor	18, Feb. 1886	25, Jan.	27- -10d	7		Cape Girardeau, MO	
Happel, Theodor Martin	10, May 1894	20, Apr.	14	310		Cape Girardeau, MO	
Harbeson, Minna S.	27, Oct. 1884	13, Oct.	26	7	Källke	Mt. Vernon, MO	
Harck, Chrstian Friedrich	3, May 1894	28, Mar.	76- 3m-11d	294		Chippewa Falls, WI	Kannenberg bei Freienwalde, Pommern
Harck, Wilhelmine	31, Mar. 1887	4, Feb.	66- 2m-15d	206		Wheaton, WI	Plantikow bei Daber, Pommern
Hardar, Sophia Johanna Magdalena	5, Sept 1870	12, Aug.	45	287	Boddin	Kendallville, IN	Gr. Radon, Sternberg, Mecklenburg-Schwerin
Harde, Katharina	6, Jan. 1898	10, Dec.	79	15		Red Bud, IL	Germany
Hardel, Martin	5, Dec. 1895	7, Nov.	70	782	Morgentaler	Bethany, MO	Zbosse, Flatow, Marienwerder, Pommern
Harder, Karl F.W	4, July 1881	19, June	55- 1m	215		Kendallville, IN	Planz-Recknitz, Mecklenburg-Schwerin
Harderle, John	20, Mar. 1882	18, Feb.	47- 8m-16d	95		Buffalo, NY	Württemberg
Hardert, Anna Margarethe	29, July 1897	6, July	63	479	Zier	New York City, NY	Lindheim, Brietingen, Hessen
Hardis, Wilhelmine	10, Dec. 1891	27, Sept	37-10m- 5d	798	Crutz	Ft. Hunter, NY	Wodtke, Cöslin, Lauenburg, Hinterpommern
Hardt, Casper	13, June 1870	15, Apr.		191		Troy, NY	
Hardt, Henriette	13, July 1899	24, June	72	447	Stratmann	Galena, IL	Kronenberg, West Preußen
Hardt, Jennie	24, Nov. 1898	8, Oct.	43	751	Frentrop	Pekin, IL	
Hardt, Johannette	1, Mar. 1888	25, Dec.	89- 4m	142	Rosert	Brooklyn, NY	Berzhain, Nassau
Härdy, Johannes	27, Nov. 1882	18, Oct.	70	383		Red Bud, IL	Hunsischweil, Aargau, Schweiz
Hardy, John	22, Nov. 1888	27, Oct.	45-10m- 1d	750		Red Bud, IL	Deutschhügel, St.Clair County, Illinois
Hardy, Marie	16, May 1881	30, Apr.	35	159	Bald	Red Bud, IL	
Hardy, Susanna	27, Mar. 1865	11, Feb.	65	52	Rohr	Red Bud, IL	Staufen, Aargau, Württemberg
Hardy, William	15, Mar. 1880	21, Feb.	30- 4m-29d	86		Victoria, TX	
Härer, Friedericke	28, Feb. 1876	15, Feb.	67	71	Reinhardt	Bucyrus, OH	Eberstadt, Württemberg
Harff, Jacob	28, Oct. 1858	2, Oct.	62	172		Charlestown, IN	Diedenbergen, Amt Hochheim, Nassau
Harff, Lisette	21, Aug. 1876	4, Aug.		271	Schulz	Kenosha, WI	Ludwigsluft, Mecklenburg-Schwerin
Hargersheimer, Friedrich Jakob	16, Sept 1897	30, Aug.	82	591		Louisville, KY	Ruppertsweiler, Rheinpfalz Baiern
Hargesheimer, Lydia	14, Oct. 1878	15, Sept	57	327	Brannamann	Louisville, KY	Knox County, Ohio
Harland, Johanna	6, Apr. 1893	11, Mar.	70	222	Henner	Toledo, OH	Lüthofen,
Härle, Helene Friederike	17, Mar.1873	27, Feb.	73	87	Krebs	Quincy, IL	Ellhofen, Weinsberg, Württemberg
Harley, Regina E.	25, Sept 1880	30, Sept	55- 4m-16d	343	Wagenknecht	Defiance, OH	Stavenhagen, Mecklenburg-Schwerin
Harloff, Friederika	29, July 1897	7, July	55	479		Akron, NY	Jörgensdorf, Steffernhagen, Mecklenburg-Schwerin
Harloff, Friedrich Johan Christian	29, Aug. 1889	30, June	36	558		Akron, NY	Wermelskirchen, Lennep, Preußen
Hartloff, Friedrich W.	25, Nov. 1886	9, Nov.	71	7		Santa Claus, IN	Ruppertsweiler, Rheinpfalz Baiern
Harmann, Heinrich	11, Feb. 1886	21, Jan.	61	7		Milwaukee, WI	Kelpin bei Greifenberg, Hinterpommern
Harmel, Charlotte	26, Feb. 1883	6, Feb.	81- 7m-15d	71		Boody, IL	Kalis, Preußen
Harmel, Luther	20, Jan. 1879	4, Jan.	10- 3m- 3d	23		Belleville, IL	
Harmeling, Christian	14, Mar. 1850	24, Jan.	29	44		Cincinnati, OH	
Harmeling, Dorothea	15, Jan. 1872	23, Dec.	62	23	Meyer	New Albany, IN	Erichshagen, Amt Wölpe, Hannover
Harmeling, J.F. Heinrich	18, Oct. 1875	20, Sept	67	335		New Albany, IN	Erichshagen, Hannover

Christliche Apologete Death Notices --- 1839 - 1899

Name of Deceased	Notice Date	Death Date	Age	Page	Maiden Name	Place of Death	Place of Birth
Harmeyer, Gerhard	8, Mar. 1855	18, Jan.	21	40		Wheelersburg, OH	Hannover
Harms, Adele	29, Sept 1898	4, Sept	23	623		Jersey City, NJ	Hemling, Hannover
Harms, Anna Maria Elisabeth	30, June 1859	23, May	70- 3m- 5d	104		Florence, MO	Schweringen, Amt Hoya, Hannover
Harms, Christoph	12, Mar. 1857	7, Feb.	53	44		Kingston, IL	Nindern, Amt Rödel, Preußen
Harms, Friedrich	29, Aug. 1870	29, July	74	279		Lake Creek, MO	Schweringen, Amt Hoya, Hannover
Harms, Haucke	14, Oct. 1858	31, Aug.	65	164		Monroe, IL	Grisiehl, Ostfriesland
Harms, Heere	14, Oct. 1858	11, Sept	80- 6m	164		Monroe, IL	Wollinghausen, Ostfriesland
Harms, Helena	29, Jan. 1872	8, Jan.	66	39	Post	Lebanon, IL	Amt Aurich, Hannover
Harms, Herman	20, Jan. 1879	6, Jan.	15	23		Red Bud, IL	
Harms, Ilke	22, Jan. 1883	6, Jan.	36- 9m- 5d	31	Kruse	Mascoutah, IL	Extum, Amt Aurich, Ostfriesland
Harms, Klaus Heinrich	7, Sept 1899	22, Aug.	69	575		Sheboygan, WI	Kürstadt, Hannover
Harms, Maria	20, June 1895	25, May	41	398	Seng	Lyona, KS	Washington, Tazewell County, Illinois
Harms, Martha	14, Mar. 1881	10, Jan.	35	87	Rönik	Toledo, OH	Merksleben, Preußen
Harms, Sophia Wilhelmina	23, Aug. 1888	4, Aug.	38	542		Kansas City, MO	Kingston, Adams County, Illinois
Harms, Wilhelm	14, Oct. 1858	2, Sept	28	164		Monroe, IL	
Harms, Wilhelmine	18, Aug. 1873	16, June	20	263		Oregon, MO	Chatham, Illinois
Harnisch, Carl Ernst	21, May 1891	19, Apr.	37	334		Lawrence, MA	Annaberg, Sachsen
Harrels, Maria	11, June 1896	11, May	22	383		Bellvella, IA	Minonk, Illinois
Harrenstein, Fanna	6, May 1886	21, Apr.	64- 2m- 4d	7	Dirksen	Yellow Creek, IL	Twixlum, Emden, Ostfriesland
Harrenstein, Johan	10, July 1890	21, June	68	446		Yellow Creek, IL	Hannover
Harris, Margaretha	6, Sept 1894	8, Aug.	21- 8m- 8d	582		San Jose, IL	Hilgermissen, Hannover
Harris, Martha Elisabeth	27, May 1867	23, Apr.	24	166	Stöber	Hazel Green, WI	Mühlhausen, Thüringen
Harris, Pauline	6, Aug. 1877	19, July	22	255	Hoffmann	Chicago, IL	Galena, Illinois
Harsch, Anna Maria	30, Apr. 1896	15, Apr.	57	286	Koppert	Newark, OH	Waldorf , Baden
Harsch, Heinrich	12, Feb. 1872	15, Jan.	16- 8m-19d	55		Davenport, IA	
Harsch, Johannes	23, Oct. 1851	8, Sept	56	172		Clay County, IN	
Harsch, Margaretha	28, Apr. 1884	4, Apr.	68	7	Karmann	Davenport, IA	Zweibrücken, Rheinkreis Baiern
Harseim, Carl August	20, Sept 1849	23, Aug.	11- 3m-21d	152		Milwaukee, WI	
Hart, Anna Theresa	5, Dec. 1889	10, Nov.	29	782	Stollberg	Toledo, OH	Toledo, Lucas County, Ohio
Härtel, Eva Barbara	10, Jan. 1889	29, Nov.	74	30	Hessel	Cameron, MO	Oberhausen, Bergzabern, Rheinkreis Baiern
Härtel, Friedrich	10, Apr. 1890	4, Mar.	82	238		Cameron, MO	
Härtel, Jakob	8, Nov. 1875	14, Oct.	26	359		Liberty, MO	
Harsch, Peter	30, Jan. 1882	16, Jan.	79- 7m-22d	39		Kearney, MO	Freimersheim, Alzei, Hessen-Darmstadt
Hartel, Wilhelm (Rev)	6, June 1895	14, Apr.	37	366		---, MO	Clay County, Missouri
Hartenstein, Wilhelm	6, Feb. 1890	9, Jan.	24-10m- 4d	94		Dallas City, IL	Dallas City, Illinois
Hartge, Conrad	24, Jan. 1895	4, Nov.	49	62		Senate Grove, MO	
Harth, Maria	29, Dec. 1873	7, Dec.	43	415	Niestöckel	Wheeling, IL	Müttersholz, Elsaß
Hartig, Elisabeth	16, Nov. 1893	30, Oct.	83	734		Louisville, KY	Rankendorf, Kalkost, Mecklenburg
Hartig, Adam Friedrich	25, Sept 1865	25, Aug.	28- 9m-14d	156		Farmington, IA	Meladers, Graubünden, Schweiz
Hartink, Bernard	21, June 1894	24, May	76	406		Covington, KY	Söhlde, Hannover
Hartje, Johan Friedrich	13, Oct. 1887	28, Sept	64	654	Saak	Covington, KY	Buschhausen, Osterholz, Hannover
Hartje, Sophia Charlotte	4, Oct. 1877	16, Sept	71	646		Baresville, OH	Hohenhausen, Lippe-Detmold
Hartkopf, Christina	1, Jan. 1877	26, Oct.	60	7	Pretzinger	Kochville, MI	Heiterbach, Nagold, Württemberg
Hartleb, Heinrich Christian	- 14, May 1883	4, Apr.	37- 3m-13d	159		Kochville, MI	Schwarzburg, Almenhausen, Sachsen
Hartleb, Heinrich Johan	20, Jan. 1898	24, Dec.	45	47		Roseville, MI	Roseville, Michigan
Hartley, Andreas Chr.	17, Aug. 1854	28, July	44	132			

- 178 -

Christliche Apologete Death Notices --- 1839 - 1899

Name of Deceased	Notice Date	Death Date	Age	Page	Maiden Name	Place of Death	Place of Birth
Hartlieb, Christine	27, Apr. 1899	23, Mar.	81	271	Nething	Hannibal, OH	Beuren, Nürtingen, Württemberg
Hartloff, Amalie	19, July 1875	22, June	28- 2m-19d	231	Johann	Evansville, IN	Wermelskirchen, Preußen
Hartloff, Friederike	9, May 1864	12, Apr.	47- 4m	76		Cannelton, IN	Thun, Kreis Lennep, Preußen
Hartman, Charley F.	10, Oct. 1889	14, Aug.	9	654		New Albany, IN	New Albany , Indiana
Hartmann, (Mr)	13, June 1861	10, May	56	96		German Creek, IA	Schweiz
Hartmann, (Mrs)	30, Apr. 1866	30, Mar.	29	142		Jackson, MO	Klein Rhüden, Braunschweig
Hartmann, (Mrs)	3, May 1875	16, Apr.	40- -26d	143	Menger	St. Peters, MO	Wernigerode, Preußen
Hartmann, Albertine Emelie Maria	22, Mar. 1894	25, Feb.	48	198	Glasow	Milwaukee, WI	Neukolden, Mecklenburg-Schwerin
Hartmann, Andreas	9, Aug. 1888	20, July	67	510		Hokah, MN	Knittlingen, Maulbronn, Württemberg
Hartmann, Andreas G.	12, Feb. 1877	20, Jan.	65	55		Wittens, OH	Hehlingen, Preußen
Hartmann, Anna	8, Oct. 1891	23, Sept	85 - 4m- 8d	654		Louisville, KY	Meistern, Kalw, Württemberg
Hartmann, Anna	6, Oct. 1892	1, Sept	70	638		Denver, CO	Canton Graubünden, Schweiz
Hartmann, Anna C.	9, Oct. 1882	19, Sept	20	327	Harland	Toledo, OH	Toledo, Lucas County, Ohio
Hartmann, Anna Catharina	5, May 1892		78	286	Sauer	Ballwin, MO	Hessen bei Eschwege, Germany
Hartmann, Anna Catharina	1, Oct. 1877	15, Sept	72- 6m-11d	319	Aupperle	Lancaster, WI	Obermosau,
Hartmann, August	19, Oct. 1885	7, Oct.	54	7		Jackson, MO	Mechtshausen, Hannover
Hartmann, Auguste	8, Mar. 1880	23, Feb.	22	79	Lambrecht	Waymansville, IN	Klein-Wiesseck, Preußen
Hartmann, Barbara	29, Dec. 1873	10, Dec.	34- - 6d	415	Metz	Cottleville, MO	Jockgrimm, Langen-Kandel, Rheinkreis Baiem
Hartmann, Bernhardine	2, Apr. 1891	8, Mar.	55	222	Peterson	Brooklyn, NY	Ysstadt, Schweden
Hartmann, Carl	6, Sept 1844	9, Aug.	16m- 5d	136		New York, NY	
Hartmann, Carl Moritz	29, Mar. 1894	2, Mar.	67	214		Pepin, WI	Barntrup, Lippe-Detmold
Hartmann, Catharina	13, Oct. 1879	26, Sept	83	327	Deckeroß	Concord, IA	Gierweiler bei Saarbrücken, West Preußen
Hartmann, Catharina	18, July 1895	24, June	47	462	Kernkamp		Wehdel, Hannover
Hartmann, Catharina Engel	16, Feb. 1888	18, Nov.	72-11m-21d	110	Kruwel	White Creek, IN	
Hartmann, Catharina Maria	30, May 1861	7, May	63	88	Meyer	Union, MO	Disten, Hannover
Hartmann, Charles F.	26, Feb. 1891	31, Jan.	67	142		Enterprise, KS	Mühlheim, Baden
Hartmann, Christian	31, Mar. 1862	1, Mar.	32	52		Cape Girardeau, MO	
Hartmann, Christina	3, May 1875	2, Mar.	71	143		New York City, NY	
Hartmann, Conrad	1, July 1872	12, June	71	215		Charlestown, IN	Hefferich, Nassau
Hartmann, Dorothea	5, Jan. 1874	2, Dec.	68	7	Meier	Etna, MO	Rettmar, Amt Soldern, Braunschweig
Hartmann, Dorothea	14, Nov. 1895	25, Oct.	61	734		Cincinnati, OH	Dransfeld, Hannover
Hartmann, Edward	28, Aug. 1876	12, Aug.	22- 4m	279		White Creek, IN	
Hartmann, Elisabeth	26, Apr. 1875	11, Apr.	38	135	Steinmetz	Muscatine, IA	Nieder-Möllerich, Kurhessen
Hartmann, Emma Margaretha	29, May 1890	27, Nov.	29	350	Moschler	Bradford, IN	Harrison County, Indiana
Hartmann, Emma Mathilde	13, May 1897	24, Apr.	33	303	Lukemeier	Bradford, IN	Louisville, Jefferson County, Kentucky
Hartmann, F.W.	5, Sept 1895	19, Aug.	80	574		Cincinnati, OH	Enger bei Osnabrück, Hannover
Härtmann, Fanny	1, Apr. 1867	9, Mar.	70	102		Wheeling, VA	Fülmachen, Bern, Schweiz
Hartmann, Franz Karl	16, Jan. 1896	25, Dec.	61- 2m	46		Scranton, PA	Börsink, Trier, RheinPreußen
Hartmann, Friederika	23, Nov. 1874	6, Oct.	6- 4m	375		Hokah, MN	
Hartmann, Friederike	15, Sept 1879	31, Aug.	51-4m-16d	295	Peter	Brighton, IL	Salzuflen, Lippe-Detmold
Hartmann, Friedrich	25, Dec. 1856	15, Dec.	34-10m	208		Portsmouth, OH	Königsfeld, Amt Billingen, Baden
Hartmann, Friedrich	5, Aug. 1867	3, July	31- 9m	246		Union, MO	
Hartmann, Gerhard	26, July 1849	12, July	38	120		Cincinnati, OH	
Hartmann, Gottlieb	30, Aug. 1894	9, Aug.	69	566		Brooklyn, NY	Berwangen, Baden
Hartmann, Heinrich	25, Oct. 1875	5, Oct.	71	343		Nashville, IL	Hartenhausen, Bergkirchen, Preußen
Hartmann, Heinrich	7, May 1883	14, Apr.	56- -12d	151		Warsaw, IL	Oberscheid, Dillenburg, Nassau

Christliche Apologete Death Notices --- 1839 - 1899

Name of Deceased	Notice Date	Death Date	Age	Maiden Name	Page	Place of Death	Place of Birth
Hartmann, Heinrich	12, May 1898	28, Apr.	73		303	Bradford, IN	Hettenhausen, Baiern
Hartmann, Heinrich	24, Jan. 1881	14, Jan.	18		31	Bradford, IN	
Hartmann, Henriette	27, June 1895	10, June	81	Büssing	414	Pittsburg, PA	Löhr, Brandenburg
Hartmann, Henriette Christine	16, Feb. 1863	26, Jan.	30	Wischen	28	Columbus, IN	Ellerode, Amt Moringen, Hannover
Hartmann, Herman H.	10, Jan. 1876	28, Dec.	52		15	White Creek, IN	Engter bei Osnabrück, Hannover
Hartmann, Johan F.	24, Sept 1878	1, Aug.	32		303	White Creek, IN	Cincinnati, Hamilton County, Ohio
Hartmann, Johan Friedrich	14, Apr. 1873	28, Mar.	76		119	Fond du Lac, WI	Ebersroda, Naumburg an der Saale, Preußen
Hartmann, Johanna Augusta	14, Sept 1885		74	Melle	7	Covington, KY	Bremen, Germany
Hartmann, Johanna Maria Elisabeth	25, Oct. 1894	28, Sept	85	Längricht	694	Fond du Lac, WI	Eberschrote bei Freiburg, Preußen
Hartmann, John Louis	1, Dec. 1873	14, Nov.	22- -15d		383	White Creek, IN	
Hartmann, Julianna	24, Nov. 1853	28, Oct.	1- 7m		188	Cincinnati, OH	
Hartmann, Karl Friedrich	10, Aug. 1868	6, June	63		255	Etna, MO	Broistedt, Amt Salder, Braunschweig
Hartmann, Karolina	21, May 1891	3, May	67	Sommer	334	Warsaw, IL	Constantin, Russisch-Polen
Hartmann, Karoline	4, Apr. 1850	13, Mar.		Behlen	56	Louisville, KY	Hagenburg, Lippe-Schaumburg
Hartmann, Katharina	9, Sept 1897	23, Aug.	60	Horn	575	Louisville, KY	Osthofen, Hessen-Darmstadt
Hartmann, Katharina	5, Jan. 1885	28, Nov.	87- 3m-18d	Koch	7	Louisville, KY	Weingarten, Baden
Hartmann, Leonhard	15, Jan. 1891	1, Jan.	57- 9m		46	Chicago, IL	Trimmis, Graubünden, Schweiz
Hartmann, Louis	23, Oct. 1871	3, Oct.	46		343	Seymour, IN	
Hartmann, Louis	3, Oct. 1881	7, Sept	16- 8m-10d		319	New Albany, IN	
Hartmann, Louise	3, Sept 1896	31, July	40		575	Harper, IA	German Township, Keokuk County, Iowa
Hartmann, Louise	29, Aug. 1850	9, Aug.	23		140	Louisville, KY	
Hartmann, Louise	29, Nov. 1860		9		192	Nashville, IL	
Hartmann, Lucy	2, Nov. 1893	18, Sept	78	Egly	702	Burlington, IA	St. Antoenien, Graubünden, Schweiz
Hartmann, Lucy	27, Apr. 1899	23, Mar.	88	Fluor	271	Harper, IA	Kanton Graubünden, Schweiz
Hartmann, Magdalena	4, Aug. 1879	12, July	53	Brucker	247	Louisville, KY	Döttingen, Künzelsau, Württemberg
Hartmann, Magdalena	16, Nov. 1893	17, Oct.	65		734	Garner, IA	Gersweiler, Saarbrücken, Preußen
Hartmann, Maria	7, Feb. 1876	20, Jan.	54	Stexen	47	Louisville, KY	Reburg, Hannover
Hartmann, Maria	23, Oct. 1876	16, Aug.	21		343	Wittens, OH	
Hartmann, Maria Anna	19, Jan. 1863	10, Dec.	10- 4m-12d		12	Seymour, IN	
Hartmann, Maria Magdalena	7, Mar. 1881		55	Wolf	79	Bradford, IN	Burweiler, Niederrhein, Elsaß
Hartmann, Marie Luise	22, Apr. 1897	4, Apr.	71	Kaustatter	254	Brooklyn, NY	Württemberg
Hartmann, Nikolaus	12, July 1869	9, June	20		223	German Creek, IA	Burlington, Iowa
Hartmann, Peter	28, Mar. 1895	7, Mar.	71		206	Warsaw, IL	Oberschild, Dillenburg, Nassau
Hartmann, Philipp K.	2, July 1896	14, June	62		431	Charlestown, IN	Mensfelden, Nassau
Hartmann, Rudolph	20, June 1864	9, May	72		100	Wheeling, VA	Fillmachem, Bruck, Aargau, Schweiz
Hartmann, Susanna Beata	8, Sept 1892	24, Aug.	67	Moser	574	Brooklyn, NY	Bernwangen, Baden
Hartmann, Theresia	17, Apr. 1865	27, Mar.	24		64	New Albany, IN	
Hartmann, Tobias	8, Apr. 1872	11, Mar.	64		119	Burlington, IA	St. Antonia, Graubünden, Schweiz
Hartmann, Wilhelm	14, June 1888	24, May	21- 8m-21d		382	Garner, IA	
Hartmann, Wilhelm F.	2, Jan. 1882	27, Nov.	14		7	Bradford, IN	Harrison County, Indiana
Hartmann, Wilhelm Louis	21, Apr. 1873	21, Mar.	19		127	Seymour, IN	Jackson County, Indiana
Hartmann, Wilhelmina	7, May 1891	13, Apr.	83	Horstmann	302	North Prairie, IL	Frotheim, Zöllenbeck, Minden, Preußen
Hartmann, Wilhelmina Sophia	29, Oct. 1891	8, Oct.	17		702	Chicago, IL	Jeffersonville, Indiana
Hartmann, Wilhelmine	23, Nov. 1874	11, Oct.	13		375	Hokah, MN	Knittlingen, Maulbronn, Württemberg
Hartmann, Wilhelmine Caroline	26, Dec. 1874	16, Nov.	33	Deneke	828		Cape Girardeau County, Missouri
Hartmeyer, Franz	18, Jan. 1849	10, Jan.	58		12	Cincinnati, OH	

Christliche Apologete Death Notices --- 1839 - 1899

Name of Deceased	Notice Date	Death Date	Age	Maiden Name	Page	Place of Death	Place of Birth
Hartmus, Johannes	12, Apr. 1849	31, Mar.	70		60	Pike County, OH	Westheim, Rheinkreis Baiern
Hartmuß, (Mrs)	26, Jan. 1885	30, Dec.	66		7	Greenfield, OH	Westheim, RheinPfalz Baiern
Hartnagel, Bertha Ottilia	30, June 1884	14, June	27		7	St. Paul, MN	St. Paul, Minnesota
Hartnagel, Christiana M.	21, Aug. 1851	3, July	68- 2m-28d		136	Belleville, IL	Michelbach, Gerabronn, Württemberg
Hartnagel, Friedrich	28, Mar. 1889	4, Mar.	72		206	Belleville, IL	Kreilsheim, Württemberg
Hartnagel, Georg	16, Apr. 1877		68		127	St. Louis, MO	Michelbach, Gerabronn, Württemberg
Hartnagel, Georg	19, Dec. 1895		29- 5m- 4d		814	Belleville, IL	Belleville, Illinois
Hartnagel, Julius	12, Feb. 1883	25, Jan.	19		55	Belleville, IL	Belleville, St. Clair County, Illinois
Hartnagel, Leonhard	24, Apr. 1856	7, Apr.	45		68	Belleville, IL	Michelstadt, Württemberg
Hartnagel, Maria	20, Jan. 1873	15, Dec.	46	Alt	23	Nashville, IL	Metzosgehag, Hessen-Darmstadt
Hartnagel, Michael	17, Mar. 1892	19, Feb.	87- 7m- 5d		174	Belleville, IL	Michelbach, Württemberg
Hartnagel, Michael	24, Nov. 1843	5, Sept	68-11m-19d		187	Belleville, IL	
Hartnagel, Regina	20, Jan. 1898	26, Dec.	84	Lächler	47	Belleville, IL	Steinbach am Walde, Kreuzheim, Württemberg
Hartnagel, Susanna	17, Dec. 1883	25, Nov.	58	Schobe	7	St. Paul, MN	Basel, Schweiz
Härtner, Ursula	3, June 1897	8, May	81		351	Topeka, KS	Sonstetten, Heidenheim, Württemberg
Hartsang, (Mr)	11, Sept 1865	22, Aug.	73		148	St. Louis, MO	Tettisfeld, Coblenz, RheinPreußen
Hartwich, Maria	12, Jan. 1899	7, Dec.	59	Stautke	31	Decatur, IL	Groß-Glogau, Schlesien
Hartung, Anna Carolina	15, Sept 1884	27, Aug.	42		7	Charles City, IA	Marietta, Ohio
Hartung, August	17, June 1886	1, June	72		7	Burlington, IA	Tadtenberg, Minsterhorst, Magdeburg, Preußen
Hartung, Barbara Elisa	16, Feb. 1888	28, Jan.	71	Knaben	110	St. Paul, MN	Longula bei Mühlhausen, Thüringen
Hartung, Dorothea	28, Apr. 1898	18, Mar.	77- 1m-13d	Giese	271	Burlington, IA	Dannefeld, Preußen
Hartung, Henriette	1, Apr. 1897	13, Mar.	82	Otto	207	Geneseo, IL	Zeigefeld, Merseberg, Preußen
Hartung, Johan Carl	25, Sept 1890	4, Sept	70		622	Geneseo, IL	Nißmitz, Freiburg, Querfurt, Merseburg, Germany
Hartwich, Anna Maria	9, June 1873	26, May	46	Ott	183	Galena, IL	Sargans, St. Gallen, Schweiz
Hartwich, Anna Sophia	12, Jan. 1888	9, Dec.	80		30	Danville, MN	Genschmar, Preußen
Hartwick, Conrad	14, Aug. 1890	27, July	79		526	Giard, IA	Schellbach, Homberg, Kurhessen
Hartwig, Anna Elisabeth	9, June 1873	25, May	57	Schneider	183	Giard, IA	Relwehausen, Kreis Homberg, Kurhessen
Hartwig, Anna Friedrika Maria	5, Aug. 1897	10, July	76	Engel	495	Marine City, MI	Gamehl bei Wismar, Mecklenburg-Schwerin
Hartwig, Carl F.	9, Jan. 1896	18, Nov.	38- 6m-18d		30	Madison, WI	Rosenfelde, Pieritz, Pommern
Hartwig, Christian Joachim	8, Dec. 1884	26, Nov.	74		7	Roseville, MI	Alt-Karin, Neu-Bukow, Mecklenburg-Schwerin
Hartwig, Friederike	19, Jan. 1860	28, Dec.	42		12	Galena, IL	
Hartwig, Johan Ch. W.	19, Apr. 1880		30		127	Roseville, MI	Clasdorf bei Neubugo, Mecklenburg-Schwerin
Hartwig, Johan Joachim Christoph	2, July 1891	11, June	62		430	Roseville, MI	Alt-Karin, Mecklenburg-Schwerin
Hartwig, Johan Martin	18, Oct. 1875	28, Sept	28		335	Roseville, MI	
Hartwig, Sophia Maria Dorothea	1, June 1893	3, Apr.	76	Miller	350	Marine City, MI	Altkarrin, Mecklenburg-Schwerin
Hartwig, Wilhelmine	31, May 1888	12, May	55	Gottschalk	350	Sun Prairie, WI	Garz, Peritz, Pommern
Hartz, Amalia	13, Nov. 1890	9, Sept	74		734	Charleston, SC	Lippe-Detmold
Harwick, Minnie	8, Dec. 1884	31, Oct.	65		7	Perry, IL	
Harz, Christina	23, Sept 1858	24, Aug.	53- 9m	Schäfer	152	Charlestown, IN	Oberflehrsheim, Worms, Hessen-Darmstadt
Harz, Georg	21, Nov. 1895	31, Oct.	88- 4m-12d		750	Jeffersonville, IN	
Harzmann, Anna Luise	4, May 1899	6, Apr.	72	Heinrichs	287	Great Bend, KS	Dorfzinna, Preußen
Harzmeier, (girl)	12, Nov. 1866	12, Sept	12		366	St. Louis, MO	Vahdel, Hannover
Harzmeier, Heinrich	12, Nov. 1866	12, Sept			366	St. Louis, MO	Varel, Hannover
Harzmeier, W.	12, Oct. 1874	13, Sept	28		327	St. Louis, MO	
Hasch, (boy)	13, Nov. 1851	24, Oct.	13- 6m		184	Terre Haute, IN	
Hasch, Catharina	30, Jan. 1862	12, Jan.	59-10m	Schmidt	20	Poland, IN	Mundelsheim, Besigheim, Württemberg

Christliche Apologete Death Notices --- 1839 - 1899

Name of Deceased	Notice Date	Death Date	Age	Page	Maiden Name	Place of Death	Place of Birth
Häschenmüller, Maria E.	28, June 1855		56	104		New Orleans, LA	Latten, Tecklenburg, Preußen
Hase, J. Friedrich	16, Jan. 1882	27, Dec.	15- 5m-11d	23		St. Louis, MO	
Haselo, Margaretha	4, June 1891	7, Apr.	54	366	Meyer	Schenectady, NY	Eichhorst, Westphalen
Hasenjäger, Friedrich	10, June 1897	26, Apr.	77	367		Chicago, IL	Beckedorf, Schaumburg, Kurhessen
Hasenjäger, Friedrich W.	16, Feb. 1880	25, Jan.	71-10m-16d	55		Burlington, IA	Melbergen, Minden, Preußen
Hasenjäger, Maria	30, Nov. 1868	15, Nov.	64	383	Prange	Burlington, IA	Dangsen, Minden, Preußen
Hasenkamp, H.C.	13, July 1868	27, June	61	223		Cincinnati, OH	Fahrenhorst, Kreis Salzwedel, Preußen
Hasenkamp, Johan	21, Apr. 1884	Mar.	33- 1m-16d	7		Cincinnati, OH	
Hasenpflug, Elisabeth	15, Dec. 1892	25, Nov.	70- 1m-17d	798	Heußner	Berea, OH	Kalkobes, Kurhessen
Hasenwinkel, (Mrs)	13, July 1863	9, June	54	112		Bloomington, IL	Güber, Kreis Salzwedel, Magdeburg, Preußen
Hasenwinkel, Fr.	13, July 1863	22, May	30- 6m-20d	112		Bloomington, IL	
Hasenwinkel, Henry	13, July 1863			112		Bloomington, IL	
Hasenwinkel, Hermann	13, July 1863			112		Bloomington, IL	
Hashoff, Heinrich C.	5, Sept 1889	9, Aug.	24- 1m- 1d	574		Arlington, NE	Siek, Hannover
Hasilmann, Margarethe	1, Oct. 1883	31, Aug.	78- 7m-29d	319	Garbs	Junction City, KS	
Haß, August Michael	24, Dec. 1883	26, Nov.	12-11m-12d	7		Wausau, WI	Dittelsheim, Hessen-Darmstadt
Haß, Barbara	12, Feb. 1883	22, Jan.	34-11m-22d	55	Roll	Troy, NY	Skorracheve, Wirsitz, Bromberg, Preußen
Haß, Gottlieb	14, Feb. 1881	1, Feb.	42	55		Wausau, WI	Aschaffenburg, Baiern
Haß, Margarethe	8, Dec. 1853	20, Oct.	52	196	Korn	Mt. Vernon, IN	Nienstedt bei Hildesheim, Kronau, Hannover
Hasse, Heinrich	24, May 1880	27, Apr.	70	167		Llano, TX	Schwarme, Hannover
Hasse, Margaretha	2, June 1887	11, May	37	350	Esborn	Saginaw, MI	Lehmstädt, Braunschweig
Hasse, Sophie	14, July 1892	25, June	82	446	Heuer	Hedwigs Hill, TX	Horn, Lippe-Detmold
Hasselmann, Friedrich	23, June 1862	8, Apr.		100		Freeport, IL	Rüps, Kronach, Baiern
Hasselmann, Heinrich	6, Jan. 1887	12, Dec.	57	14		New Haven, CT	Weidenthal, Neustadt, Rheinkreis Baiern
Hassen, Elisabeth	23, Dec. 1886	1, Dec.	52- 9m-25d	7	Schmidt	New Albany, IN	Engelthal, Friedberg, Hessen
Hassinger, Margarete	9, Mar. 1899	14, Feb.	70	159		Newark, NJ	
Haßler, Maria	2, Aug. 1849	5, July	10- 4m- 5d	124		St. Louis, MO	
Haßler, Jacob	8, Jan. 1891	16, Dec.	84	30		Louisville, KY	Buß, Basel, Schweiz
Hassler, Jakob	18, June 1877	1, May	57	199		Louisville, KY	Maladers, Graubünden, Schweiz
Haßler, M. Barbara	22, Jan. 1861	10, Dec.	73- 3m-23d	16		Galion, OH	Graben, Baden
Haßler, Maria	8, May 1882	22, Apr.	76	151	Frei	Charlestown, IN	Leui, Basel, Schweiz
Häßler, Melchior	2, Oct. 1871	25, Aug.	73	319		Charles City, IA	Canton Glarus, Schweiz
Hattwig, Carl	26, July 1849	28, June		120		St. Louis, MO	
Hatz, Dorothea	9, Apr. 1891	25, Feb.	77- 4m- 8d	238	Accola	Honey Creek, WI	Schweiz
Hau, Gottlieb	11, Nov. 1878	23, Oct.	52- 6m-20d	359		St. Joseph, MO	Leonberg, Württemberg
Haub, Katharina	1, Sept 1887	22, July	59	558		Pittsburg, PA	Beuern, Gießen, Hessen-Darmstadt
Haub, Konrad	30, June 1873	6, June	15- 2m	207		Bradford, IN	
Haubeil, Christina	13, July 1866	24, July	72	262		Waverly, OH	Biedesheim, Baiern
Haubold, Maria	2, Apr. 1891	15, Mar.	68- 6m	222	Kalter	Newport, KY	Sitzelhausen, Kurhessen
Haubold, Sarah	1, Oct. 1883	19, sept	40	319	Arzt	Newport, KY	Hessville, Sandusky County, Ohio
Hauck, Charlotte	15, Mar. 1894	2, Feb.	42	182	Schlichte	Nashville, IL	Decatur, Illinois
Hauck, Christine Barbara	29, Nov. 1869	8, Nov.	79	383	Vouth	St. Joseph, MO	Niederluststadt, Germersheim, Rheinkreis Baiern
Hauck, J. Adam	17, Oct. 1861	30, Sept	61- 7m- 8d	168		Edgerton, OH	
Hauck, J.G.	16, Aug. 1849	21, July		132		Brookville, IN	Stammheim,
Hauck, Jacob	21, July 1892	22, June	72- -12d	462		St. Joseph, MO	Steinweiler bei Landau, Rheinkreis Baiern
Hauck, John P.	20, Dec. 1894	3, Dec.	60	822		Terre Haute, IN	Neckarbischofsheim, Baden

Christliche Apologete Death Notices --- 1839 - 1899

Name of Deceased	Notice Date	Death Date	Age	Maiden Name	Page	Place of Death	Place of Birth
Hauck, Lydia	10, Feb. 1873	7, Jan.	19-10m		47	St. Joseph, MO	
Hauck, Maria Anna	3, Oct. 1861	27, Sept	67- 9m		160	Cincinnati, OH	
Hauck, Michael	30, May 1881	6, May	71		175	Defiance, OH	Oberseebach, Elsaß
Haucke, Maria Magdalena	22, Mar. 1888	24, Feb.	74	Moeller	190	Ahnapee, WI	Rudolstadt, Schwarzburg
Haude, John	11, Jan. 1864	9, Dec.	49		8	Dunkirk, NY	Schlesien
Haudenschild, Johan	3, Nov. 1892	11, Sept	67		702	Hannibal, MO	Schweiz
Haudenschild, John	24, Nov. 1892	11, Sept	67		750	Monroe Co, OH	Germany
Haueisen, John M.	9, Jan. 1896	11, Dec.	69- 9m-27d		30	Cleveland, OH	Berwangen bei Eppingen, Baden
Hauenstein, Barbara	17, May 1855	28, Apr.	31		80	Rochester, NY	
Hauenstein, Lizzie	25, Sept 1876	10, Sept			311	Waco, TX	
Hauff, Rosine	17, Jan. 1895	14, Dec.	75		46	Baltimore, MD	Neustadt, OstPreußen
Hauffe, Wilhelmina	15, June 1893	21, May	72	Wunsch	382	Bloomington, IL	Posen
Haug, Maria	3, Nov. 1892	13, Oct.	58	Trautmann	702	Chicago, IL	Teningen, Emmendingen, Baden
Haug, Christina	27, Aug. 1877		85- 5m-22d	Reichart	279	Delaware, OH	Illingen, Maulbronn, Württemberg
Haug, Elisabeth	19, Jan. 1888	24, Dec.	55	Schlegel	46	Bloomington, IL	Honau, Reutlingen, Württemberg
Haug, Friederike	23, Aug. 1880	3, Aug.	56- 5m-26d	Jeans	271	Michigan City, IN	Ribnitz, Mecklenburg-Schwerin
Haug, Heinrich	11, Apr. 1845		Inquiry		59	Leonberg, ---	Eßlingen, Württemberg
Haug, Johan Jakob	8, May 1871	17, Apr.	69- 2m-28d		151	Delaware, OH	Illingen, Maulbronn, Württemberg
Haug, Maria	26, July 1849	1, July	35		120	St. Louis, MO	
Haug, Maria Louise	31, May 1894	7, May	41	Börn	358	Sheboygan, WI	Debberport, Pommern
Haug, Peter	26, July 1849	29, June	37		120	St. Louis, MO	Warmling, Württemberg
Haug, Rosina	25, Aug. 1887	28, July	54	Lemppen	542	Wathena, KS	Canton Bern, Schweiz
Haugk, Christine Wilhelmine	7, July 1884	22, June	59		7	Mt. Olive, IL	Niederhaßlau, Sachsen
Haugstörfer, Gottlieb	22, Aug. 1870	3, Aug.	50-10m-15d		271	Allegheny City, PA	Gündelbach, Maulbronn, Württemberg
Hauhardt, H.	24, May 1880	20, Mar.	42		167	Ballwin, MO	Oldinghausen, Minden, Preußen
Hauk, (Mr)	14, July 1862	2, June	76		112	Mascoutah, IL	
Hauk, August	7, Dec. 1868	2, Nov.	24		391	Terre Haute, IN	Brookville, Franklin County, Indiana
Hauk, Charlotte	4, July 1889	June	21-11m-10d	Grotteguth	430	Jerauld Co, SD	
Hauk, Eva Margaretha	18, Jan. 1864	30, Oct.	49	Junker	12	Defiance, OH	Steinfelz, Weißenburg, Ober-Elsaß, Frankreich
Hauk, Johan Adolph	15, July 1867	29, June	19- 7m-13d		222	Poland, IN	
Hauk, Johannes Zacharias	10, June 1886	24, Apr.	84		7	Illinois City, IL	Breitenau, Baiem
Haunschild, Johan Conrad	25, Apr. 1881		50		135	Seymour, IN	Friedenwalde, Westphalen
Haupt, Carolina	1, June 1893	29, Apr.		Rutherhenke	350	Chamois, MO	
Haupt, Friedericke	31, Jan. 1876	14, Dec.	35		39	Morrison, MO	
Haupt, Henry John	4, Feb. 1892	13, Jan.	26		78	Beatrice, NE	
Haupt, Louise	17, May 1869	18, Apr.	25- 8m- 5d	Spreckelmeier	159	Union, MO	Gasconade County, Missouri
Haupt, Mathilde Katharina	21, Feb. 1895		21- 7m-16d		126	Clatonia, NE	Peoria, Illinois
Haupt, Th.	15, Apr. 1878	30, Mar.	37- 2m-29d		119	Morrison, MO	Cape Girardeau County, Missouri
Hauptmann, Anna Katharina Elsebein	3, Aug. 1893	12, July	84	Rolf	494	Nebraska City, NE	Jöllenbeck, Bielefeld, Germany
Hauptmann, Heinrich Peter	20, Mar. 1890	4, Mar.	54		190	Nebraska City, NE	Jolenbeck, Münden, Preußen
Hauptmann, Herman Heinrich	23, Dec. 1886	30, Nov.	83-10m		7	Nebraska City, NE	Nieder-Jöllenbeck, Bielefeld, Preußen
Hauptmann, Kaspar	12, June 1890	19, May	57		382	Nebraska City, NE	Nieder-Jöllenbeck, Bielefeld, Preußen
Haure, Anna Maria	16, Sept 1852	27, July	35	Ritzmann	152	Aurora, ---	Mutterstedt, Baiem
Haurie, Jane	1, May 1871	21, Feb.	10	Mahler	143	Red Wing, MN	
Haurie, Johan	31, Mar. 1879	16, Feb.	22- 2m-27d		103	Red Wing, MN	
Haurmer, Sophia	1, Nov. 1894	12, Oct.	67	Voskuhlen	710	Huntingburg, IN	Ladbergen, Tecklenburg, Preußen

Christliche Apologete Death Notices --- 1839 - 1899

Name of Deceased	Notice Date	Death Date	Age	Maiden Name	Page	Place of Death	Place of Birth
Haury, Albert	22, July 1886	2, July	15		7	Nashville, TN	Nashville, Tennessee
Haury, Henriette	11, June 1896	16, May	43- 7m-25d	Vogt	383	Nashville, TN	Bromstett, Holstein
Haus, Catharine	22, Dec. 1892	24, Nov.	54	Hartmann	814	Michigan City, IN	Hohensolms, Preußen
Haus, Margaretha	28, July 1898	7, July	81	Gerth	479	Galion, OH	
Hausam, Charlotte	14, Aug. 1851	7, July	25- 3m- 5d	Schneider	132	St. Charles, MO	Ruckheim, Baiern
Hausam, Jacob	30, Apr. 1896	11, Apr.	74		286	Kansas City, MO	Buchheim, Baiern
Hausam, Johan	8, Oct. 1896	11, Sept	75		655	Nebraska City, NE	Ruchheim, Baiern
Hausam, John	31, Oct. 1870	6, Oct.	79- 9m-20d		351	St. Charles, MO	Heppenheim an der Wiß, Hessen-Darmstadt
Hausam, Maria	12, Mar. 1883	24, Feb.	53	Methisheimer	87	Sedalia, MO	Rucheim, Rheinkreis Baiern
Hausam, Peter	30, Aug. 1894	13, Aug.	77		566	Sedalia, MO	
Hauschield, Martha Rebecca Elis.	27, Dec. 1894	2, Dec.	18- 9m		836	LaCarne, OH	
Hauschild, Christina	15, June 1874	2, May	56- 9m-10d	Köhnson	191	New York City, NY	Bremen,
Hauschild, Johan Heinrich	16, June 1887	24, May	64		382	New York City, NY	Eißeln, Hannover
Hauschildt, Hannah Josephine	26, June 1882	4, June	13- 9m-15d		207	New York City, NY	
Häuselmann, Christine	6, Aug. 1883	7, July	60	Futzi	255	Toledo, OH	Rüderswyl, Bern, Schweiz
Hausener, Anna Maria	27, July 1893	2, July	30	Albitz	478	St. Paul, MN	Rockford, Wright County, Minnesota
Hausener, Christian	29, Dec. 1862	10, Oct.	42		208	Canal Dover, OH	Rüggisberg, Amt Seftigen, Schweiz
Hauser, Beanka	15, Sept 1887	12, Aug.	29	Volkland	590	Bushton, KS	Fond Du Lac County, Wisconsin
Hauser, Christian	24, Nov. 1898	2, Nov.	64		751	Rochester, NY	Württemberg
Hauser, David	28, July 1898	2, July	71		479	Woonsocket, SD	Sinnbronn, Ulm, Württemberg
Häuser, G.M.	8, Dec. 1879	23, Nov.	53		391	Platteville, WI	Allmersbach, Marbach, Württemberg
Häuser, Jakob	1, May 1871	29, Mar.	63		143	Lancaster, MO	Monroe County, Pennsylvania
Hauser, John	5, Mar. 1883	20, Jan.	63		79	St. Helena, CO	Stadel, Schweiz
Hauser, Leonhard	18, Feb. 1884	31, Jan.	57		7	Chicago, IL	Trasadingen, Schaffhausen, Schweiz
Hauser, Maria	9, Apr. 1891	11, Mar.	61	Keinarth	238	Pittsburg, PA	Dattingen, Urach, Württemberg
Hauser, Marie	25, Mar. 1886	2, Mar.	27	Urban	7	St. Paul, MN	Wien, Oesterreich
Hauser, Philippine	23, Sept 1897	16, Aug.	66	Herb	607	Rochester, NY	Langenalt, Pforzheim, Preußen
Häuser, Sigismund G.H.	13, Mar. 1876	13, Feb.	63		87	Newport, KY	Langelselwald, Hessen
Häusermann, Elisabeth Magdalena	4, May 1899	28, Mar.	59- 8m-18d	Scheihing	287	Junction City, KS	Unter-Türkheim, Kannstadt, Württemberg
Häusermann, Katharine Barbara	3, May 1894	4, Apr.	92	Ramhofer	294	Junction City, KS	Aldingen am Neckar, Ludwigsburg, Württemberg
Häusermann, Magdalena	26, May 1884	6, May	20		7	Madison, IN	Madison, Indiana
Häusler, Juliana Catharine	3, Oct. 1864	22, Sept	21		160	Cincinnati, OH	Weil im Schönbuch, Böblingen, Württemberg
Hausmann, Albert	27, July 1885	8, July	50		7	St. Louis, MO	Frielingshausen, Lennep, Düsseldorf, Preußen
Hausmann, Barbara	22, June 1899	10, Apr.	60	Hetzel	399	Salem, IN	Kork, Baden
Hausmann, Herman	21, June 1888	5, June	40		398	St. Louis, MO	Frielinghausen, Düsseldorf, RheinPreußen
Hausmann, Katharina W.	31, Jan. 1889	13, Dec.	35	Ammon	78	Bunker Hill, IL	Calhoun County, Illinois
Hausmann, Margaretha	14, June 1855	31, May	30- 5m-14d		96	Vandalia, IL	Little York, Pennsylvania
Hausmann, Peter	6, Nov. 1890	19, Oct.	52-11m- 5d		718	Evansville, IN	Arnsheim, Hessen-Darmstadt
Hausmann, Wilhelm Eduard	19, Apr. 1894	26, Mar.	67		262	Lansing, IA	Treptow an der Rega, Pommern
Hausmann, Wilhelmine	8, Apr. 1897	19, Mar.	73	Oloff	222	Lansing, IA	Triebes bei Treptow an der Rega , Preußen
Hauß, John A.	3, Jan. 1895	3, Dec.	66		14	West Albany, IN	Geinsheim, Neustadt, Rheinkreis Baiern
Häußer, Christine	22, Apr. 1897	3, Apr.	62	Schiek	254	Duncan, NE	Oberamt Schorndorf, Württemberg
Häußer, Heinrich	26, July 1849	20, June	37		120	St. Louis, MO	Büdingen, Hessen-Darmstadt
Hausser, Samuel	25, Mar. 1897	3, Mar.	71		190	Chillicothe, OH	Kirnbach, Bretten, Germany
Häußermann, Albert	26, Oct. 1893	2, Oct.	26		686	Columbus, OH	Madison, Indiana
Häußermann, Fletcher	28, Oct. 1897	9, Oct.	22		687	Columbus, OH	Columbus, Franklin County, Ohio

Christliche Apologete Death Notices --- 1839 - 1899

Name of Deceased	Notice Date	Death Date	Age	Page	Maiden Name	Place of Death	Place of Birth
Häußermann, Paul	4, Apr. 1895	21, Feb.	25	222		Columbus, OH	Delaware, Ohio
Häussermann, Richard Erasmus	30, June 1887	14, June	13	414		Columbus, OH	Columbus, Franklin County, Ohio
Häußler, Friederike	19, Jan. 1899	29, Dec.	81	47		Dayton, OH	Weiler, Brackenheim, Württemberg
Häußler, Jakob Heinrich	21, Nov. 1881	8, Nov.	71- 3m-13d	375	Mächtle	Cincinnati, OH	Weil im Schönbuch, Böblingen, Württemberg
Häußler, Wilhelmine Jakobine	19, Aug. 1886	4, Aug.	29	7		Dayton, OH	Cincinnati, Hamilton County, Ohio
Haußmann, Elisabeth	17, Mar.1873	15, Feb.	39	87	Martin	Marrs, IN	Armsheim, Hessen-Darmstadt
Haußner, Caroline	2, June 1873	11, May	24- 3m- 8d	175	Ohl	Roseville, MI	
Haußner, John	24, Sept 1878	5, Aug.	37	303		St. Louis, MO	Schenklingsfeld, Hersfeld, Kurhessen
Haustein, Albin Friedrich	25, Feb. 1897	26, Jan.	36	127		Mt. Olive, IL	OberHohendorf, Sachsen
Hauswald, Georg	12, July 1880	6, June	61-11m-28d	223		New Albany, IN	Elsaß
Hauswirth, Anna Christina	31, Mar. 1859	22, Nov.	8	52		Red Bud, IL	
Hauswirth, Franz	9, May 1870	3, Apr.	56- 6m	151		Red Bud, IL	Hasloch, Pfalz, Baiern
Hauswirth, Katharina	9, Oct. 1882	19, Sept	67- 1m-26d	327		Oregon, MO	Augen, Müllheim, Baden
Hauswirth, Konrad	19, Sept 1864	25, Aug.	19- 2m-17d	152		Red Bud, IL	
Hauswirth, Maria Magdalena	2, Apr. 1866	14, Feb.	40	110	Merkel	Red Bud, IL	Diburg, Hessen
Hautzenröder, Wilhelm	7, June 1894	22, May	63	374		Wathena, KS	Herbstein, Hessen-Darmstadt
Havendörfer, Rosina	25, Dec. 1865	29, Nov.	36	208	Lenz	Boonville, IN	Schmüd, Württemberg
Haverbeck, Heinrich	22, Mar. 1888	28, Feb.	57-10m-18d	190		Pittsburg, PA	Hannover
Haverkampf, Johanna	6, Nov. 1876	22, Oct.	38- 5m-18d	359		Arlington Heights, IL	Holland, Germany
Haverland, Friedrich	11, Apr. 1881	28, Mar.	42	119		Frankfort, IL	Unze bei Perleberg, Preußen
Hawkins, Anna Margaretha	31, Oct. 1850	14, Sept	34	176	Engel	Mascoutah, IL	Schafheim, Hessen-Darmstadt
Hayenga, Geertje	15, Nov. 1869	21, Sept	31- 9m-17d	367	Tammäus	San Jose, IL	Upleward, Amt Enden, Ostfriesland
Hebbel, Caroline	10, Nov. 1887	24, Oct.	30	718	Mill	Des Moines, IA	Ichenheim, Baden
Hebecker, Dorothea	24, Jan. 1889	1, Jan.	81	62	Heideke	Manitowoc, WI	Rhode, Sachsen-Anhalt
Hebecker, Samuel	11, May 1863	9, Apr.	78	76		Manitowoc, WI	Dietensdorf, Roßla, Preußen
Heber, Wilhelmine	29, May 1890	10, May	56	350	Baader	Arlington Heights, IL	Marbach, Württemberg
Heberle, Catharina	20, Feb. 1882	4, Feb.	56	574	Kimbel	Lincoln, NE	Reppigsheim, Schotten, Hessen-Darmstadt
Heberlein, Emilie	14, Jan. 1878	26, Dec.	32	15		Melrose, NY	Osterrode, Hannover
Hebig, Heinrich	2, July 1896	15, June	20	431		Indianapolis, IN	Sebach, Rheinpfalz Baiern
Hebner, Jacob	27, Mar. 1876	10, Mar.	59- 3m	103		Mascoutah, IL	Kemmau, Nassau
Hechler, Christina	15, May 1890	1, May	78	318	Betz	Marietta, OH	Feierfeld, Heilbronn, Württemberg
Hechler, Christoph	7, Aug. 1871	8, July	19- 4m-28d	255		Marietta, OH	
Hechler, Georg	24, Aug. 1899	19, July	53	543		Wheeling, WV	Georgenhausen, Hessen-Darmstadt
Hechler, Gottfried	6, Sept 1888	19, Aug.	85	574		Marietta, OH	Schweigern, Württemberg
Hecht, Friedrich Wilhelm	12, Dec. 1870	24, Sept	25	399		LaCrosse, WI	
Hecht, Johan	23, Mar. 1899	19, Feb.	85	190		Marine City, MI	Mecklenburg-Schwerin
Hecht, Julius	5, May 1873	17, Apr.	19- 8m-28d	143		Tomah, WI	
Hechter, Auguste	27, Aug. 1877	28, July	59- 3m	279	Bokus	St. Louis, MO	
Heck, Joseph	10, Oct. 1895	15, Sept	73	654		Pittsfield, IL	Dumersheim, Rastatt, Baden
Heck, Anna Caroline	20, Nov. 1882	30, Oct.	33- 9m-12d	375	Wolfangel	Baltimore, MD	
Heck, Dorothea	29, Oct. 1896	17, Sept	38	703	Rinkel	Nashville, TN	Ausbüttel, Gifhorn, Hannover
Heck, Johan	2, Feb. 1885	13, Jan.	26	7		Pittsfield, IL	
Heck, Johan Adam	7, Jan. 1878	21, Dec.	66- 9m- 3d	7		Freeport, IL	Gondelsheim, Bretten, Baden
Heck, Rosa	29, Jan. 1891	14, Jan.	61- 5m	78		Pittsfield, IL	Dormersheim, Raschstadt, Baden
Heck, Sophiana	17, Nov. 1892		23	734		Englewood, IL	St. Joseph, Tazewell County, Illinois
Heck, Verena	29, July 1897	6, July	62- 9m-10d	479		Toledo, OH	Siblengen, Schaffhausen, Schweiz

Christliche Apologete Death Notices --- 1839 - 1899

Name of Deceased	Notice Date	Death Date	Age	Maiden Name	Page	Place of Death	Place of Birth
Heck, Wilhelm	2, Sept 1872	13, Aug.	48		287	Wathena, KS	Gnichwitz, Breslau, Schlesien
Heckedon, Martin	9, Feb. 1860	19, Oct.			24	Vandalia, IL	Basel, Schweiz
Heckel, Barbara	30, July 1891	6, July	55- 8m	Laudenschlägel	494	Cleveland, OH	Eichstädt, Baden
Heckel, Elisabeth	24, Apr. 1890	28, Jan.	52	Mathies	270	Brooklyn, NY	Meissenheim an der Glan, Hessen-Darmstadt
Heckelmann, Johanna	11, Oct. 1888	28, Sept	75	Schirmer	654	Ironton, OH	Osterhagen, Hannover
Heckendorn, A.K.	4, May 1868		13		143	Baresville, OH	
Heckenleibli, Rosina	4, Nov. 1878	18, Oct.	78- 6m		351	St. Joseph, MO	
Hecker, Agnes Mathilde	18, Sept 1882	24, Aug.	13- 6m- 2d		303	Concordia, MO	
Hecker, Anna	29, Dec. 1873	4, Dec.		Schmidt	415	Mt. Vernon, IN	Häringshausen, Amt Wittlage, Hannover
Hecker, Anna	30, Aug. 1860	29, July	18		140	Mt. Vernon, IN	
Hecker, George	22, Oct. 1896		24		687	Marion, OH	Marion County, Ohio
Hecker, Jacob	25, Oct. 1869	16, Sept	61		343	Marion, OH	Wiesloch, Baden
Hecker, Karl David	29, Aug. 1889	13, Aug.	28- 1m- 1d		558	New York City, NY	Weingarten bei Durchloch, Baden
Hecker, Louis	18, Nov. 1878	22, Oct.	18- 4m-24d		367	Marion, OH	
Hecker, Maria S.	28, Dec. 1899	26, Oct.	38	Romoser	828	Marion, OH	Marion County, Ohio
Hecker, Rosa Melinda	27, July 1885	5, July	20- 5m-19d	Burland	7	Marion, OH	Weisloch bei Heidelberg, Baden
Hecker, Rudolph	6, June 1895	15, May	69		366	Marion, OH	Wiesloch, Baden
Hecker, Susanna	5, June 1865	6, Apr.	37		92	Marion, OH	Jettmund, Oldendorf, Preußen
Heckermann, Anna Maria Clara	26, Apr. 1880	3, Apr.	66		135	St. Louis, MO	Oldendorf, Preußen
Heckermann, Friedrich Wilhelm	29, May 1876	16, May	63		175	St. Louis, MO	Baden
Heckler, Friedrich	11, Oct. 1880	22, Sept	41- 6m- 8d		327	Laporte, IN	
Heckman, Anna Christina	8, Aug. 1895	22, July	40	Weber	510	Dayton, OH	Virma, Hannover
Heckman, Elisabeth M.	13, June 1895	17, May	66	Plümer	382	Dayton, OH	Willstadt, Baden
Heckmann, Elisabeth	21, Sept 1893	2, Sept	70- 8m	Färber	606	Scranton, PA	Böchingen bei Landau, Rheinpfalz Baiern
Heckmann, Georg	23, July 1896	7, June	31		479	Indianapolis, IN	Handschucksheim, Baden
Heckmann, Georg J.	29, Dec. 1898	10, Oct.	67		828	Pekin, IL	Freudenstadt, Württemberg
Heckmann, Margaretha Dorothea	10, Feb. 1898	19, Jan.	67	Schmeetzle	95	San Francisco, CA	
Heckmann, Peter	10, Nov. 1879	3, Oct.	77		359	Newark, NJ	Eisenbühl bei Wilkenburg, Baiern
Heckmann, Thomas H.	26, Dec. 1895	23, Nov.	67		828	San Francisco, CA	Dayton, Montgomery County, Ohio
Heckmann, Wilhelm	1, Mar. 1894	8, Feb.	34		150	Dayton, OH	Hochstetten, Rheinpfalz Baiern
Heddesheimer, Elisabeth	16, June 1898	1, June	74	Schütz	383	Akron, OH	Dietersdorf, Sachsen
Hedecker, Gottfried	24, Mar. 1892	18, Feb.	87		190	Manitowoc, WI	
Hedler, Friederike	6, June 1889	18, May	75		366	Chicago, IL	Apolda, Sachsen-Weimar
Hedler, Gustav	5, June 1871	4, May	26- 5m		183	Chicago, IL	
Hedrich, Alletta Martine	29, Dec. 1873	9, Nov.	43- 1m-11d		415	Scranton, PA	Aßler, Preußen
Hedrich, Caspar	27, Aug. 1866	11, Aug.	38		278	Scranton, PA	Aßler, Preußen
Hedrich, Philipp	15, June 1893	8, May	65- 3m-19d		263	Scranton, PA	Monroe County, Illinois
Heene, Anna F.	29, Aug. 1889	6, Aug.	32	Rippen	558	Mascoutah, IL	Schaffhausen, Schweiz
Heer, Konrad	11, Aug. 1898	21, July	27		511	St. Louis, MO	Lohrhaupten, Kurhessen
Heerd, Anna Maria	11, July 1881	25, June	49- 7m- 7d		223	Baltimore, MD	Tannenhausen, Amt Aurich, Ostfriesland
Heeren, Johan Jakob	11, Oct. 1875	13, Sept	28		327	Red Bud, IL	Gormsen, Hannover
Heers, Christine Elisabeth	28, Sept 1899	8, Sept	91	Röhr	623	Wellsville, NY	Morenholz, Hannover
Heers, Johan Heinrich Christoph	15, Aug. 1881	29, July	78-10m- 9d		263	Angelica, NY	Buhr, Osnabrück, Hannover
Heffelmire, Maria Elisabeth	26, Aug. 1897	4, Aug.	79	Licking	543	Cincinnati, OH	Elsaß
Heffner, Katharina	3, June 1897	11, May	79		351	Minneapolis, MN	La Chapelle, Rougomaunt, Frankreich
Hefner, Louise Maria	28, Apr. 1887	12, Apr.	52	Haller	270	Lockland, OH	

Christliche Apologete Death Notices --- 1839 - 1899

Name of Deceased	Notice Date	Death Date	Age	Maiden Name	Page	Place of Death	Place of Birth
Hegemann, Johan Christoph	21, Jan. 1897	22, Dec.	83		46	Andrew Co, MO	Grabo, Lucho, Hannover
Heger, Elisabeth	4, Dec. 1865	13, Oct.	23- -17d		196	Kossuth, OH	
Heger, Friederike Sophia Henriette	26, Jan. 1880	11, Jan.	56	Gräßle	31	Watertown, WI	Kufeld, Amt Sternberg, Lippe
Heger, Johan	22, June 1893	30, May	68		398	Nebraska City, NE	Motzingen, Herrenburg, Württemberg
Hegnauer, Anna	14, Sept 1885	26, Aug.	70		7	Burlington, IA	Trimmis, Graubünden, Schweiz
Hehmann, J.H.	14, June 1888	23, Apr.	57		382	Kansas City, KS	Münster, Tecklenburg, Preußen
Hehn, Maria	4, Apr. 1881	17, Mar.	25- 1m-16d		111	Farmington, IA	Farmington, Iowa
Hehner, Bertha Susanna	23, Nov. 1899		20-10m- 7d		751	Warsaw, IL	Brighton, Illinois
Hehner, Katharina Elisa	23, July 1891	21, June	52	Lafrenz	478	Brighton, IL	New Orleans, Louisiana
Hehner, Peter	6, Oct. 1892	12, Sept	71		638	St. Louis, MO	Zimmerschied, Nassau
Hehner, Phil Ludwig	5, May 1884	20, Apr.	59		7	Belleville, IL	Kemmenau, Nassau
Heibeck, Katharina Magdalena	30, Apr. 1896	10, Apr.	35	Disqui	286	Batesville, IN	Lawrenceville, Indiana
Heid, Elisabeth	7, Mar. 1895	9, Feb.		Horne	158	Ironton, OH	Württemberg
Heid, Fritz	4, Nov. 1886	12, Oct.	37		7	Chillicothe, OH	Chillicothe, Ross County, Ohio
Heid, Margaretha	27, July 1885	7, July	37	Scholl	7	Chillicothe, OH	
Heid, Philipp	31, Oct. 1870	13, Oct.	19		351	Cincinnati, OH	
Heid, Sophia	29, May 1865	6, May	42	Huppert	88	Ft. Antasen, WI	Güdingen, Saarbrücken, Preußen
Heidbreder, Peter	23, Feb. 1880	3, Feb.	69		63	Herman, MO	Elferdissen, Herford, Preußen
Heidel, August	1, Feb. 1864	1, Jan.	60		20	St. Paul, MN	Reden, Hannover
Heidel, Heinrich	19, July 1875	9, June	31		231	Woodbury, MN	Rheden, Hannover
Heidel, Joachim H.	14, Apr. 1884		56		7	Kendallville, IN	Sandfeld, Mecklenburg-Schwerin
Heidel, Margaretha Dorothea Magd.	8, July 1897	7, June	70	Rodemüller	431	St. Paul, MN	Dissen, Iborch, Hannover
Heidel, Maria	4, Aug. 1873	4, July	38	Ziffarth	247	St. Paul, MN	Langula, Mühlhausen, Thüringen, Preußen
Heidelberger, J. Heinrich	25, May 1863	24, Mar.	21		84	Herman, MO	Elferdissen, Herfort, Preußen
Heidemann, Caroline	11, Nov. 1878	28, Oct.	53		359	Milwaukee, WI	Neuwedel, Mecklenburg-Schwerin
Heidemann, Karl	7, June 1888	9, May	58- 3m-16d		366	Milwaukee, WI	
Heiden, Hilda	24, Aug. 1893	15, May	25		542	Wessel, IL	Galena, Illinois
Heiden, Hilda	8, June 1893	15, May	25		366	Wessel, IL	
Heiden, Johan Christian Theodor	14, May 1896	3, Apr.	74		318	Vermillion, OH	
Heiden, Karl	21, Feb. 1881	31, Jan.	17		63	Vermillion, OH	
Heiden, Maria	10, Nov. 1884	20, Oct.	87- 8m- 8d	Hahker	7	Milwaukee, WI	Seltz, Pommern
Heiden, Wilhelmine	15, Oct. 1883	14, Sept	55- 8m- 1d	Pollow	335	Milwaukee, WI	Gnewekow, Vorpommern
Heidke, Elisabeth	28, Apr. 1884	20, Apr.	63- 7m-18d		7	Almond, WI	
Heidland, Carolina Henriette W.	5, May 1887	3, Apr.	32	Sommers	286	Beaufort, MO	Herford, Westphalen
Heidland, Gottlieb Fr.	28, Apr. 1892	5, Apr.	38		270	Beaufort, MO	Altenhagen, Heppen, Preußen
Heidlauf, Johan Michael	8, Sept 1884	9, Aug.	61		7	Canal Dover, OH	Güllstein, Herrenberg, Württemberg
Heidloff, Karl Martin	5, Jan. 1893	2, Dec.	18		14	Vermillion, OH	
Heidloff, Willie	5, May 1892	6, Apr.	16		286	Vermillion, OH	Vermillion, Erie County, Ohio
Heidloff, Willie	5, Jan. 1893	6, Apr.	16		14	Vermillion, OH	
Heidner, Franz August	29, Dec. 1873	1, Dec.	21- 9m- 8d		415	Chicago, IL	Blecker, New York
Heidom, Edward L.	27, Nov. 1871	Nov.	20		383	Warrenton, MO	
Heidom, Heinrich	4, Apr. 1881	9, Mar.	61- 3m- 3d		111	St. Louis, MO	Eilwesen, Neustadt, Hannover
Heidom, Heinrich	19, May 1859	6, Apr.	59		80	Brookville, IN	Hannover
Heidom, Heinrich	1, Jan. 1872	28, Nov.	9- 6m		7	Clement, IL	
Heidom, Minnie	5, Nov. 1896	13, Sept	76	Hochmeister	719	St. Louis, MO	Emgde, Neustadt, Hannover
Heidt, Anna Catharina	12, May 1879	26, Apr.	77	Eberhardt	151	Cincinnati, OH	Hobin, Baden

Christliche Apologete Death Notices --- 1839 - 1899

Name of Deceased	Notice Date	Death Date	Age	Maiden Name	Place of Death	Page	Place of Birth
Heidt, Georg	18, Aug. 1892	19, July	64		Oakland, CA	526	Linx, Baden
Heidt, Margaretha	28, July 1879	4, July	57	Grampp	Cincinnati, OH	239	Rheinbischofsheim, Baden
Heidt, Michael	13, Sept 1894	26, Aug.	63- 7m-26d		Batesville, IN	598	Hobbin, Baden
Heidt, Therese	28, Nov. 1889	2, Nov.	29	Adams	Cincinnati, OH	766	Brookville, Indiana
Heinenberg, Heinrich Conrad	1, July 1886	14, June	73		West Point, IA	7	Rosenthal, Hannover
Heier, Karolina	21, May 1877	7, May	41	Sauer	New Knoxville, OH	166	Erbstätten, Marbach, Württemberg
Heiermann, Bernhard	16, Dec. 1886	16, Nov.	56		Arenzville, IL	7	Flühn, RheinPreußen
Heiermann, Maria L.	13, July 1899	10, June	38	Winklehake	Arenzville, IL	447	Palmyra, Marion County, Missouri
Heigold, Maria Katharina	14, Apr. 1873	2, Mar.	57	Koch	Petersburg, IL	119	Aidlingen, Böblingen, Württemberg
Heiking, August	14, Apr. 1898	8, Mar.	58		Ft. Atkinson, WI	239	Stolzenhagen, Pommern
Heil, Albert	17, Nov. 1892	27, Oct.	27		Louisville, KY	734	Karlshafen an der Weser, Hessen
Heil, Anna Barbara	8, Sept 1892	13, July	70	Großmann	St. Philip, IN	574	Hofen, Neuenburg, Württemberg
Heil, Elisabeth	2, Apr. 1891	1, Mar.	81		Platteville, WI	222	Landenau, Hessen-Darmstadt
Heil, (Mr)	30, Sept 1886	10, Aug.	78		Georgetown, WI	7	Niedermodan, Hessen-Darmstadt
Heil, Henriette	10, Aug. 1893	30, June	36	Reviol	Baltimore, MD	510	
Heil, Peter	10, Jan. 1876	20, Dec.	59		Pittsburg, PA	15	Reichenhausen, Sachsen-Weimar
Heilemann, Gottfried	9, Mar. 1863	22, Jan.	25- 4m-15d		Cincinnati, OH	40	Lorch, Welzheim, Württemberg
Heilemann, Johan Jacob	7, July 1892	14, June	59		Covington, KY	430	Lorch, Welzheim, Württemberg
Heilemann, Johannes	9, Aug. 1855	5, July	49		Cincinnati, OH	128	Lorch, Welzheim, Württemberg
Heilemann, Karoline	23, Feb. 1899	10, Jan.	45	Deiß	Covington, KY	127	Covington, Kenton County, Kentucky
Heilemann, Louise	5, Nov. 1883	6, Oct.	49- 6m	Hochstadt	New York City, NY	359	Eichen, Kurhessen
Heilemann, Maria	15, Mar. 1860	27, Feb.	19	Kätter	Cincinnati, OH	44	New Bremen, Ohio
Heilemann, Mathilda Magdalena	26, Feb. 1883	21, Nov.	38- 1m-13d	Konrad	Covington, KY	71	Pirmasenz, Rheinpfalz Baiern
Heilemann, Wilhelmine	6, Dec. 1875	28, Feb.	49	Schnüring	Covington, KY	391	Duebenau, Hannover
Heiligtag, Cariene	22, Mar. 1888	2, Feb.	24		Marine City, MI	190	
Heiligtag, Maria Friederika Dorothea	19, Mar. 1891		58- 7m- 8d	Schlottmann	Marine City, MI	190	Grabbin, Mecklenburg-Schwerin
Heill, Heinrich	4, Nov. 1867		53- 9m		Quincy, IL	350	UnterMainkreis, Brückenau, Baiern
Heilmann, A. Maria	23, Oct. 1876	14, Oct.	67		Covington, KY	343	Bruck, Welzheim, Württemberg
Heilmann, Casimir	5, Oct. 1868	7, Aug.	55		Beardstown, IL	319	Büdingen, Kreis Büdingen, Hessen
Heilmann, Christine	5, Mar. 1877	3, Feb.	15		Junction City, KS	79	
Heilmann, Gottlieb	17, Mar. 1887	18, Feb.	78- 5m		Friendship, WI	174	Wernsdorf bei Böhnig, Sachsen
Heilmann, Henriette	13, Oct. 1887	15, Sept	63	Maas	Friendship, WI	654	Langenhagen bei Treptow, Pommern
Heilmann, Henriette Fr.	16, Feb. 1893	30, Jan.	59	Bublitz	Merrill, WI	110	Langenhagen, Preußen
Heilmann, Johan Jacob	30, Apr. 1891	21, Apr.	91		Giard, IA	286	Oelbrunn, Württemberg
Heilmann, Juliana	28, Mar. 1881	3, Mar.	59	Naumann	Beardstown, IL	103	Bindsachsen, Büdington, Hessen
Heilmann, Louis	28, Apr. 1892	7, Apr.	39		Oshkosh, WI	270	Friendship, Fond du Lac County, Wisconsin
Heilmann, Nicholas	16, July 1896	29, June	77		St. Louis, MO	463	Ash, Oesterreich
Heilmann, Rosine	16, Aug. 1875	3, Aug.	72	Fischer	Clayton, IA	263	Kleinvillar, Maulbronn, Württemberg
Heim, Angelica	30, May 1881	16, May	23	Müller	Blue Island, IL	175	Turners Junction, Illinois
Heim, Anna Dorothea	21, Mar. 1881	3, Mar.	54	Wagner	Blue Island, IL	95	Atzhausen, Unterfranken, Baiern
Heim, Barbara	3, Mar. 1848	15, Feb.	83		Columbus, OH	39	
Heim, Barbara	23, Aug. 1869	28, Apr.	63		Jacksonville, IL	271	
Heim, Elisabeth	9, Feb. 1888	28, Jan.	92	Döll	Blue Island, IL	94	
Heim, Friederika	26, Jan. 1863	13, Oct.	49		Newark, OH	16	Eichfeld, Unterfranken, Baiern
Heim, Katharine	2, Feb. 1899	19, Dec.	28	Beck	Pittsburg, PA	79	Beutelsbach, Württemberg
Heim, Martin	11, Oct. 1869	15, Sept	46		Berea, OH	327	Bischofsheim a. d. Rhon, Baiern

Christliche Apologete Death Notices --- 1839 - 1899

Name of Deceased	Notice Date	Death Date	Age	Page	Maiden Name	Place of Death	Place of Birth
Heim, Nancy	13, Jan. 1868	23, Dec.	23- 9m-10d	14	Stumpf	Indianapolis, IN	Kückelhausen, Westphalen
Heimbeck, Julius	2, Dec. 1897	4, Nov.	80	767		Menomonie, WI	
Heimberger, Johan Jakob	5, Sept 1889	14, Aug.	27	574		Menomonie, WI	Walleraks, Hildburghausen, Sachsen-Meiningen
Heimbrodt, Anna Carolina	19, Dec. 1895	1, Dec.	69	814	Schad	Giard, IA	Amannsweier, Baden
Heimburger, Andreas	9, May 1864	12, Jan.	75- 2m-10d	76		Dunkirk, NY	
Heimerdinger, Eva	28, Feb. 1861	7, Feb.	53	36	Weber	Canal Dover, OH	Württemberg
Heimers, Maria D.	9, Apr. 1891	18, Mar.	81	238		Louisville, KY	Syracuse, New York
Heimlich, Katharine	25, Oct. 1894	4, Oct.	38	694	Heßler	Syracuse, NY	Nohl, Zürich, Schweiz
Heimlicher, Elisabeth	19, Feb. 1891	2, Feb.	61	126		Defiance, OH	Dortmund, West Preußen
Heimscher, Diedrich	6, Mar. 1890	14, Feb.	52	158		Watertown, WI	Watertown, Wisconsin
Heimüller, Heinrich	24, Nov. 1862	3, Nov.	14	188		Watertown, WI	Pansin, Pommern
Hein, Anna	28, Sept 1893	9, Sept	78	622	Priipp	Columbus, WI	Oberstedten bei Homburg, Hessen
Hein, Christine Elisabeth	18, Aug. 1892	29, June	62	526	Fischer	Bradford, IN	
Heinäck, Lilia	22, Jan. 1861	31, Dec.	2- 2m-12d	16		Burr Oak Valley, WI	
Heinaik, Frank	1, Nov. 1860	8, Oct.	4- 6m- 1d	176		LaCrosse, WI	
Heine, Wilhelmine	19, Apr. 1888	22, Mar.	79- 1m-23d	254		Muscatine, IA	Lippe-Schaumburg
Heineck, Christian	11, June 1883	25, Mar.	39-10m-19d	191		Portland, OR	Sachsen-Meiningen
Heineck, Georg Friedrich	18, May 1893	17, Apr.	77	318		Montana, WI	Wernshausen, Sachsen-Meiningen
Heinekamp, Flora	27, Nov. 1890	24, Oct.	18	766		Quincy, IL	
Heinemanan, Apollonia	12, Feb. 1866	1, Feb.	27	54		Covington, KY	
Heinemann, A. Catharina Friedrike	17, May 1860	13, Apr.	35	80	Sickendiek	Union, MO	Dissen bei Osnabrück, Hannover
Heinemann, Andreas	29, Nov. 1855	18, Nov.	19	192		Greenville, OH	Bubsheim, Spaichingen, Württemberg
Heinemann, Anna Elisabeth	2, Apr. 1891	5, Mar.	55	222	Hupfeld	Chicago, IL	Germerode, Hessen-Kassel
Heinemann, Emma	6, Feb. 1882	25, Jan.	19	47		Covington, KY	
Heinemann, Heinrich	28, Nov. 1864	8, Oct.	22- 3m- 8d	192		New York, NY	Schönstein, Ziegenhain, Amt Treysa, Kurhessen
Heinemann, Johan	17, Mar. 1892	22, Feb.	71	174		Ballwin, MO	Schönstein, Eisenhütte, Zingenheim, Germany
Heinemann, Marcellus	17, June 1867	3, June	38	190		Covington, KY	
Heiner, Emilie	17, Mar. 1859	11, Jan.	5-11m- 4d	44		Newark, NJ	
Heiner, Ernst	3, May 1880	15, Apr.	45	143		Cleveland, OH	Belzig, Sachsen-Altenburg
Heiner, Joseph	12, Jan. 1854	5, June	8- 5m- 3d	8		Newark, NJ	
Heiners, Josephine	27, Jan. 1879	5, Dec.	32	31		Louisville, KY	Louisville, Jefferson County, Kentucky
Heinlein, Adam	20, Apr. 1874	31, Mar.	61- 5m-18d	127		Bonn, OH	MainKlein, Weißmain, Oberfranken, Baiern
Heinlein, Anna M.	19, Sept 1889	13, Aug.	9	606	Ettmyer	Woodsfield, OH	Windelsbach, Baiern
Heinlein, Ella	11, Sept 1890	9, July	9	590		St. Paul, MN	
Heinlein, Ellen	30, Jan. 1890	23, Jan.	26- 9m- 7d	78	Heythorn	Woodsfield, OH	Perry Township, Monroe County, Ohio
Heinlein, John	1, Apr. 1897	13, Mar.	49	207		Trail Run, OH	Mainklein, Weismein, Oberfranken, Baiern
Heinlein, Laura	11, Sept 1890	7, July	14	590		St. Paul, MN	
Heinlein, Louis D.	14, Aug. 1890	12, July	29	526		Woodsfield, OH	Trail Run, Monroe County, Ohio
Heinlein, Louisa	8, Apr. 1878	21, Feb.	24	111		Wittens, OH	
Heinlein, Maria	11, Nov. 1869			15			
Heinlein, Sarah	11, Feb. 1886	9, Jan.	34	7	Fröbisch	Miltonsburg, OH	Trail Run, Monroe County, Ohio
Heinmöller, Elisabeth	31, Mar. 1879	22, Feb.	79- 9m-12d	103	Häcker	Baltimore, MD	Mengsberg, Kurhessen
Heinold, Elisabetha	21, May 1857		33	84		Cincinnati, OH	Kirchheim am Neckar, Württemberg
Heinold, Marie	11, Apr. 1889	7, Mar.	61	238	Kaiser	Sidney, OH	Oberflachs, Aargau, Schweiz
Heinold, Willimna Katharina	14, Apr. 1898	11, Mar.	20	239		Woonsocket, SD	Eallow Creek, Illinois
Heinrich, Anna Bertha	9, Nov. 1893	7, Oct.	58	718	Später	Brooklyn, NY	Eckhartsberg, Sachsen

Christliche Apologete Death Notices --- 1839 - 1899

Name of Deceased	Notice Date	Death Date	Age	Page	Maiden Name	Place of Death	Place of Birth
Heinrich, Anna M.	19, May 1887	22, Apr.	74	318	Eichele	Marietta, OH	Deckenpfronn, Calw, Württemberg
Heinrich, Johann Gottlob	23, Apr. 1883	20, Mar.	80- 5m- 6d	135		Jordan, MN	Oberneukirch, Sachsen
Heinrich, Johanna Rosina	23, Nov. 1885	4, Nov.	84	7		Jordan, MN	Klein-Morau, Schlesien, Oesterreich
Heinrich, Josepha	24, Nov. 1884	27, Oct.	20- 7m- 9d	7		St. Paul, NE	
Heinrich, Leonhard Carl	20, Nov. 1871	8, Sept	1- 8m-21d	375		Williamsburg, NY	
Heinrich, Luisa	30, Jan. 1896	17, Dec.	56- 8m-17d	78	Reigel	Blissfield, MI	
Heinrich, Margaretha Maria	21, Sept 1874	30, Aug.	58	303	Vogel	Sherrills Mount, IA	Oppenweiler, Backnang, Württemberg
Heinrich, Samuel	18, June 1847	13, May	74	99			
Heins, Arand Christ.	25, Jan. 1869	12, Nov.	64	31		Shakopee, MN	Hadste, Amt Zeven, Hannover
Heins, Elisabeth	2, July 1877	15, June	31	215	Schausten	Blue Island, IL	Hermeskeil, Trier, Preußen
Heins, Elisabetha	4, Apr. 1864	6, Mar.	22	56	Schmidt	Washington, OH	Meikelsen, Amt Zefen, Hannover
Heins, John H.	12, Jan. 1863	5, Dec.	27	8		Colesburg, IA	Meierberg, Sternberg, Lippe-Detmold
Heins, Louisa	13, May 1897	23, Apr.	60	303	Nolting	Jordan, MN	Grabe, Erfurt, Preußen
Heins, Margaretha	1, June 1874	30, Apr.	71- 3m-14d	175	Doreiter	Rochester, MN	Red Wing, Minnesota
Heinselmann, Catharina	28, June 1855	4, June	36	104	Cook	New Orleans, LA	
Heintz, Alice	27, Feb. 1896	19, Jan.	26	142	Brünning	Red Wing, MN	
Heintz, Catharina Maria	16, Sept 1872	30, Aug.	52	303	Schieferstein	St. Louis, MO	Hochelheim bei Wetzlar, Preußen
Heintz, Christine	28, Sept 1863	17, Apr.	79- 3m- 2d	286		Manitowoc, WI	Holzhausen, Homberg, Kurhessen
Heintz, Johnny	1, May 1890	13, Sept	11- 7m-13d	156		Cincinnati, OH	Volkensen, Amt Zerme, Hannover
Heintzmann, Heinrich	14, Dec. 1868	10, Apr.	75	286		Wapello, IA	Esselborn, Hessen-Darmstadt
Heintz, A.C.	2, May 1895	12, Nov.	61	399		Milwaukee, WI	Oldendorf, Hannover
Heintz, Adam	29, Jan. 1883	9, Jan.	52	39		Hannibal, OH	Lexington, Missouri
Heintz, Ahrend	5, Apr. 1880	15, Mar.	80- 5m- 2d	111		Kansas City, MO	Metzbach, Baiern
Heintz, Alwine Sophia	21, Mar. 1889	18, Feb.	26	190	Meyer	New York City, NY	Walerwillt, Schweiz
Heinz, Anna Margarethe	16, Dec. 1897	2, Nov.	59	799	Hüls	Cosby, MO	Römersberg, Homberg, Kurhessen
Heinz, Anna Maria	29, Oct. 1891	4, Oct.	59	702	Marolf	Winona, MN	Duheim, Germany
Heinz, Catharina	28, Nov. 1870	11, Nov.	28	383	Schmidt	Elkton, SD	
Heinz, Chr. Friedrich	19, Oct. 1893	29, Sept	66	670		St. Louis, MO	
Heinz, Christoph	3, July 1890	9, June	69	430		Baltimore, MD	Alt-Schmittelfeld, Geildorf, Württemberg
Heinz, Elisabeth	24, June 1897	26, May	70	399	Horlacher	Cincinnati, OH	Roth bei Landau, RheinPfalz Baiern
Heinz, Elisabeth	2, Feb. 1880	21, Jan.	57	39		Delhi, MI	
Heinz, Friedrich	23, Dec. 1878	7, Nov.	79	407		Des Moines, IA	Großheppach, Württemberg
Heinz, G. Ph.	5, May 1884	11, Apr.	77- 6m	7		Aurora, IL	Karlstadt, Rheinkreis Baiern
Heinz, George	23, Feb. 1888	5, Feb.	27- - 8d	126		New York City, NY	Flonheim, Alzei, Hessen-Darmstadt
Heinz, Henry	26, Mar. 1896	2, Mar.	69	206		Bradford, IN	Niederweisel, Hessen-Darmstadt
Heinz, Johan	6, Nov. 1882	19, Oct.	27- 8m	359		Bradford, IN	Niederweisel, Hessen-Darmstadt
Heinz, Johan Georg	16, Dec. 1886	1, Nov.	66	7		Wapello, IA	
Heinz, John	14, Dec. 1868	26, Nov.		399		Winona, MN	
Heinz, Joseph	14, Dec. 1868	19, Nov.	31	399		St. Joseph, MO	
Heinz, Katharina	3, Jan. 1895	14, Dec.	84	14	Möck	Schnectady, NY	Dobern, Kreis Leitmeritz, Böhmen
Heinz, Ludwig F.	26, Jan. 1888	8, Dec.	69	62		Wapello, IA	Willmandingen, Reutlingen, Württemberg
Heinz, M.E.	9, Nov. 1868	18, Oct.	61	359	Gerken	Bradford, IN	Hogah, Hannover
Heinz, Margaretha	9, Aug. 1888	16, July	62- -12d	510	Haub	New Metamoras, OH	Volkensen, Amt Zerme, Hannover
Heinz, Maria Ellen	26, Aug. 1886	31, July	49	7	Boos		Niederweisel, Butzbach, Hessen-Darmstadt
Heinz, Maria Eva	8, Jan. 1883	16, Dec.	50- 6m-11d	15	Hoffheinz	New York City, NY	Speeck bei Karlsruhe, Baden
Heinz, Meta Catharina	4, June 1877	28, Apr.	78	183	Ohstedt	Wittens, OH	Grasberg, Ottersberg, Preußen

Christliche Apologete Death Notices --- 1839 - 1899

Name of Deceased	Notice Date	Death Date	Age	Maiden Name	Page	Place of Death	Place of Birth
Heinz, Peter	11, Mar.1872	20, Feb.	38		87	Milwaukee, WI	Iffelborn, Kreis Alzei, Hessen-Darmstadt
Heinz, Philipp	24, Nov. 1898	27, Oct.	31		751	Bradford, IN	Harrison County, Indiana
Heinz, William	19, Sept 1889	15, Aug.	52- 2m-16d		606	Woodsfield, OH	Marietta, Ohio
Heinze , Henriette	15, Mar. 1894	15, Jan.	72	Donath	182	Poughkeepsie, NY	Wallendorf, Sachsen-Meiningen
Heinze, Christiana Maria	25, July 1895	6, July	63	Buchheim	478	Lawrence, MA	Steingrub bei Asch, Böhmen
Heinze, Ernst	9, Jan. 1865	15, Dec.	42- 1m- 8d		8	New York, NY	Remda, Sachsen-Weimar
Heinze, Ferdinand	29, Apr. 1872	16, Feb.	19- 5m-13d		143	Poughkeepsie, NY	Remda, Sachsen-Weimar
Heinzelmann, Dorothea	31, Aug. 1854	14, Aug.	22-10m-11d		140	Cincinnati, OH	
Heinzelmann, John A.	20, Sept 1869	31, Aug.	59		303	Belleville, IL	Grünthal, Freudenstadt, Württemberg
Heinzelmann, Katharina	11, Jan. 1894	11, Dec.	69	Alt	30	Belleville, IL	Metzlosgehag, Lauterbach, Hessen-Darmstadt
Heinzelmann, Katharine	6, Sept 1860	21, Aug.	47	Haüsermann	144	Belleville, IL	Wolfsölden, Württemberg
Heinzelmann, Peter	20, Dec. 1855		64		204	New Orleans, LA	Reichenbach, Freudenstadt, Württemberg
Heinzelmann, Sybille	1, Nov. 1855		51		176	Laporte, IN	Hallstadt, Rheinkreis Baiern
Heinzmann, Gottfried	27, Mar. 1876	3, Mar.	64		103	Columbus, WI	Pantow, Pommern
Heise, Johanna Augusta	4, Apr. 1895	7, Feb.	61	Krüger	222	Taegesville, WI	Pammin, Arnswalde, Pommern
Heise, Sophia Amalie	19, Aug. 1878	4, Aug.	71- 5m-17d	Ossenkopp	263	Cape Girardeau, MO	Heinde, Hannover
Heiser, Georg Adam	9, Feb. 1860	18, Jan.	27		24	Baltimore, MD	Gaiberg, Baden
Heisig, Emil	14, June 1888	28, Jan.	22		382	Brenham, TX	
Heisig, Sophie	7, Jan. 1878	16, Dec.	32	Breihan	7	Brenham, TX	
Heislein, (Mrs)	22, Apr. 1872	29, Mar.	37- 4m-20d		135	Baltimore, MD	Diebenau, Hannover
Heismann, Mina	15, Jan. 1872	22, Dec.	14		23	Watertown, WI	
Heisner, Maria	17, June 1867	23, May	77-11m		190	Amherst, OH	Heenes bei Hirschfeld, Kurhessen
Heiß, Anna Maria	21, Jan. 1892	29, Dec.	77		46	Lansing, IA	Heddesbach, Heidelberg, Baden
Heiß, Caroline	15, Oct. 1866	26, June	30- 4m-28d	Fischer	334	New York, NY	
Heiß, Elisabeth	4, Feb. 1878	12, Jan.	78		39	New York City, NY	
Heiß, Johan Michael	29, May 1865	21, Apr.	61-10m-28d		88	New York, NY	
Heiß, Lewis	18, July 1870	2, July	57		231	Dayton, OH	
Heißner, Johan Christoph	8, Dec. 1892	17, Nov.	81		782	Allegan, MI	Meinersen, Hannover
Heißner, Peter	17, Aug. 1874	2, Aug.	49- -18d		263	Frankfort, IL	Rothenburg, Amt Sontra, Königswald, Kurhessen
Heitkamp, Catharina	13, Sept 1849	24, Aug.			148	Pittsburg, PA	
Heitkamp, Friedrich	13, Sept 1849	27, Aug.			148	Pittsburg, PA	
Heitke, E.F. Wilhelm	20, Aug. 1866	9, Apr.	51		270	Watertown, WI	Pommern
Heitloff, Elisabeth	8, Apr. 1878	18, Mar.	31- 2m-28d	Schellhaas	111	Vermilion, OH	Brownhelm, Loraine County, Ohio
Heitmann, Louise	2, Aug. 1894	12, July	47		502	Davenport, IA	Meinersen, Hannover
Heitmeyer, Maria Dorothea	8, Dec. 1892	2, Nov.	66	Kraas	782	DeWitt, MI	Husum, Völpe, Hannover
Heitz, Andreas	20, Dec. 1894	15, Oct.	74		822	Bushnell, IL	Baden
Heitz, Eduard	25, Jan. 1864	4, Dec.	3- 6m		16	Rushville, IL	
Heitz, Elisabeth Margaretha	22, Mar. 1880	1, Mar.	74- 5m-21d	Haubert	95	Rushville, IL	Nonnenweier, Amt Lahr, Baden
Heitz, Eva	31, Mar. 1879	17, Feb.	81		103	Rushville, IL	Namenweier, Lahr, Baden
Heitz, Julie	10, July 1890	9, June	31		446	Charles City, IA	Joe Davis County, Illinois
Heitz, Karl	25, Jan. 1864	1, Dec.	6- 3m-10d		16	Rushville, IL	
Heitz, Louise	4, Apr. 1864	9, Mar.	48- 5m-22d	Schuler	56	Rush Creek, IL	Sondheim bei Kehl, Amt Kork, Baden
Heitz, Louise	25, Jan. 1864		10- -24d		16	Rushville, IL	
Heitzmann, Elisabeth	17, June 1897	20, May			383	Quincy, IL	Heidelsheim, Bruchsaal, Baden
Heker, Louise Albertine	24, July 1871	27, June		Falke	239	Pekin, IL	Saleske, Schlawels, HinterPommern
Hekethier, Johan Christoph	20, July 1893	29, June	75		462	Baraboo, WI	Andisleben, Preußen

Name of Deceased	Notice Date	Death Date	Age	Maiden Name	Page	Place of Death	Place of Birth
Hekle, J. Fr.	14, Mar. 1850	18, Jan.			44	Warren, MO	Steinbündorf, Preußen
Hekmann, Philippina	15, July 1886	30, June	63	Ammann	7	Pittsburg, PA	Ottenbach, Rheinkreis Baiern
Helber, Agatha	7, June 1894	18, May	71	Schreivogel	374	Ann Arbor, MI	Rothenburg, Württemberg
Helbert, Christian	17, Apr. 1865	27, Feb.	38		64	De Soto, MO	
Helbig, John	25, Apr. 1889	2, Apr.	63		270	Greenfield, MA	Steinbach, Sachsen-Meiningen
Helbig, Karl	10, May 1888	20, Apr.	69		302	Mt. Vernon, NY	Groß Obitz, Sachsen
Helbling, Elisabethe	29, Dec. 1862	9, Dec.	31	Weber	208	Evansville, IN	Niederkeinspach, Erbach, Hessen-Darmstadt
Helbling, Karl Joseph	2, Nov. 1893	5, Oct.	25		702		
Held, Christ	22, Jan. 1877	19, Nov.	42		31		Vlotho, Minden, Preußen
Held, Elisabetha	18, Apr. 1864	23, Mar.	22- 3m- 6d		64	Aurora, IN	Louisville, Jefferson County, Kentucky
Held, Friedrich Ludwig	15, Nov. 1869	13, Oct.	44- 2m-17d		367	Mulburn, IA	Langenbach, Amt Hachenburg, Nassau
Held, Johan Heinrich	19, May 1884	6, May	83		7	Covington, KY	Darmstedt, Hessen-Darmstadt
Held, John N.	4, Mar. 1897	15, Feb.	65		143	Burlington, IA	Deckenau, Baden
Held, Maria	24, Apr. 1890	28, Mar.	57	Heiden	270	Lemars, IA	Friedrichsruhe, Mecklenburg-Schwerin
Held, Mathilde Elisabeth	29, Nov. 1894	24, Nov.	25- - 3d	Wanner	774	Laporte, IN	Laporte, Indiana
Heldberg, Frieda Hermine Dorothea	5, Jan. 1893	17, Nov.	18		14	Industry, TX	Isenbüttel, Germany
Helder, Sophia	28, Jan. 1878	8, Jan.	37	Siegel	31	Boonville, IN	Birkenfeld, Oldenburg
Heldmeier, Martin	16, Dec. 1886	19, Nov.	62- 9m-17d		7	Minneapolis, MN	Weil im Schönburch, Böblingen, Württemberg
Heldstab, Georg	23, June 1873	13, May	60- 2m-17d		199	Canton, MO	Klosters, Graubünden, Schweiz
Helfenstein, Karolina	13, June 1881	24, May	43- 8m-14d	Raschke	191	Harrison, KS	Gluschins, Hinterpommern
Helfenstein, Franz Jakob	4, May 1899	5, Apr.	19		287	Pekin, IL	Kirchberg, RheinPreußen
Helge, Friedrich	7, June 1880	8, May	60		183	Louisville, KY	Neuenkirchen, Hannover
Helge, Wallburga	25, June 1896	3, June	54	Thiergärtner	415	Louisville, KY	Reutern, Baiern
Heling, Auguste	29, Aug. 1870	16, Aug.		Beheke	279	Muskegon, MI	
Hell, Auguste Carolina	22, Mar. 1880	9, Mar.	14		95	Platteville, WI	Alt-Stidnitz, Hinterpommern
Hell, Herman	11, Aug. 1892	19, July	62		510	Platteville, WI	Schönfeld, Preußen
Helle, Charlotte	29, May 1871	9, May	51- 6m		175	Greenville, OH	Minden, Preußen
Hellenscheidt, Auguste	24, Mar. 1873	11, Jan.	15		95	Second Creek, MO	
Heller, (child of F.)	13, Nov. 1846				193	New Albany, IN	
Heller, Alvine Francisca	3, Apr. 1865	23, Feb.	8- 5m		56	Oconomowoc, WI	
Heller, Augusta	24, Aug. 1885	6, Aug.	18	Albrecht	7	Sun Prairie, WI	
Heller, Christian	29, May 1865	9, May	64		88	Muscatine, IA	Löstnitz, Sachsen
Heller, Heinrich	28, May 1891	8, May	71- 5m-22d		350	Baltimore, MD	Achzel, Hessen-Darmstadt
Heller, Johan	7, Oct. 1897	13, Aug.	81		639	Baltimore, MD	Echzell, Nidda, Hessen-Darmstadt
Heller, Karl	25, Nov. 1872	31, Oct.	18		383	Green Bay, WI	Semro, Pommern
Heller, Katharine A.	15, Mar. 1888	19, Feb.	29	Hohl	174	Hamilton, OH	Wolfshalden, Appenzell, Schweiz
Heller, Lea	29, Aug. 1870	6, Aug.	53- 5m-13d		279	Edgerton, OH	Pennsylvania
Heller, Lydia	28, Mar. 1881	13, Mar.	31- 9m- 7d		103	Wabasha, MN	
Heller, Maria Sophia	2, May 1870	10, Apr.	63		143	Seymour, IN	Wever, Amt Runkel, Nassau
Heller, Philippine	14, July 1848	23, June	15- 5m-24d		116	Boonville, IN	
Helleriegel, Wilhelm	15, Dec. 1892	21, Nov.	70		798	Freeport, MI	Langula, Erfurt, Preußen
Hellermann, Wilhelm	6, Mar. 1865	28, Jan.	27		40	St. Paul, MN	Wechselbach, Mergentheim, Württemberg
Hellfrisch, Jacob	18, Aug. 1892	16, July	73		526	Manitowoc, WI	Preußen
Heling, Joseph	2, Nov. 1868	3, Sept	50-10m- 4d		351	Birmingham, PA	Rotteridda, Kurhessen
Heling, Maria	25, Mar. 1867		39	Weidling	94	Vermillion, OH	Nenndorf, Ostfriesland
Hellmann, Ahlrich	25, Sept 1882		54-11m-19d		311	Melvin, IL	

Christliche Apologete Death Notices --- 1839 - 1899

Name of Deceased	Notice Date	Death Date	Age	Maiden Name	Page	Place of Death	Place of Birth
Hellmann, Amke A.	4, Apr. 1895	10, Mar.	79	Sathof	222	San Jose, IL	Nenndorf, Wittmund, Ostfriesland
Hellmann, Daniel	6, May 1878		21		143	Quincy, IL	
Hellmann, Elisabeth	25, Dec. 1890	13, Oct.	32- 8m- 2d		830	San Jose, IL	Niederlustadt, Landau, Rheinkreis Baiern
Hellmann, Georg	21, Aug. 1882	8, Aug.	47- 6m-29d		271	Weston, MO	Niederlußtadt, Rheinkreis Baiern
Hellmann, Johan Herman	31, Aug. 1874	18, Aug.	73		279	Chillicothe, OH	Sandhofen, Mannheim, Baden
Hellmann, Katharine	3, Nov. 1898	13, Oct.	71	Wehe	703	Kansas City, KS	Melle, Hannover
Hellmann, Louise	24, Aug. 1874	13, July	69- 1m-23d		273	Prairie Creek, MN	
Hellmig, Elisabetha	26, July 1849	30, June	29		120	St. Louis, MO	
Hellweg, Martha	17, Mar. 1898	18, Feb.	75- 3m	Danker	175	Garner, IA	Bremen, Hannover
Hellweg, Peter	25, Feb. 1897	5, Feb.	80		126	Garner, IA	Assel, Hannover
Hellwig, Georg H.	23, Apr. 1865	31, Mar.	18- 4m- 4d		68	Galena, IL	
Helmbock, Karoline	25, Aug. 1884	15, Aug.	67- -28d	Schneider	7	Columbus, OH	Neuwied, RheinPreußen
Helmboldt, Carolina	25, Feb. 1886	27, Jan.	21		7	Bunker Hill, IL	
Helmbrecht, Anna Gertraut	28, Apr. 1873	20, Mar.	58- 8m-12d	Hoheditz	135	Des Moines, IA	Sielen, Kurhessen
Helmbrecht, Heinrich	26, Sept 1881	9, Sept	60		311	Perrysburg, OH	Launenberg, Eimbeck, Hannover
Helmbrecht, Sophie	10, Oct. 1881	27, Sept	16- 6m-25d		327	Perrysburg, OH	
Helmer, (Mrs)	4, Feb. 1858	5, Jan.	32	Winpenn	20	Lancaster, WI	Flögen, Hannover
Helmer, Daniel	21, Feb. 1895	18, Jan.	78		126	Mason City, IA	Pumprow, Pyritz, Germany
Helmer, Gesche	23, Dec. 1886	21, Nov.	11		7	LaHarpe, WI	
Helmer, Heinrich Christopher	7, Mar. 1881	14, Feb.	67		79	Platteville, WI	Deichsende, Spicka, Dorum, Hannover
Helmer, Wilhelm Friedrich	1, Nov. 1894	11, Oct.	37		710	Mason City, IA	Jefferson County, Wisconsin
Helmers, Elisabeth	12, June 1876	19, Apr.		Traser	191	Nauvoo, IL	Arheilingen, Hessen-Darmstadt
Helmers, Elisabeth	3, July 1876	19, Apr.	30	Traser	215	Nauvoo, IL	Arheilingen, Hessen-Darmstadt
Helmholz, Wilhelmine	19, Feb. 1872	19, Jan.	42	Lohmann	63	Ahnapee, WI	Braunschweig
Helmick, Catharine	26, Jan. 1888	25, Sept	87		62	Burlington, IA	Kaplen bei Tecklenburg, Westphalen
Helmig, Maria Catharina	10, Dec. 1877	21, Nov.	75- 5m- 8d	Nagel	399	Allegheny City, PA	Holzgerlingen, Böblingen, Württemberg
Helmig, Mary	3, Mar. 1884	15, Feb.	33	Gehrs	7	Lake Creek, MO	
Helmig, Sebina	18, Apr. 1870	6, Mar.	33		127	Lake Creek, MO	
Helmig, Stephan H.	4, Apr. 1889	11, Mar.	75		222	Lake Creek, MO	Westkappel, Westphalen
Helmkamp, Friedrich G.	27, Nov. 1882	31, Oct.	42- 6m-28d		383	St. Louis, MO	Engter, Föhren, Hannover
Helmkamp, W. Henriette	29, Oct. 1877	15, Oct.	33-10m-20d	Kriete	351	St. Louis, MO	
Helmke, Heinrich C.	15, Apr. 1897	11, Mar.	59- 9m-21d		239	Sun Prairie, WI	Stroit, Braunschweig
Helmke, John	22, Oct. 1883	30, Sept	19- 2m- 4d		343	Toledo, OH	
Helmke, Maria	16, Feb. 1893	17, Jan.	67	Schneider	110	Sun Prairie, WI	Klein-Pramsen, Schlesien
Helmker, Frank Georg	8, May 1890	20, Apr.	19		302	Toledo, OH	Branau, Böhmen
Helmker, Josephina	26, Nov. 1891	1, Nov.	53		766	Toledo, OH	Lauenberg, Hannover
Helmker, Lea N.	29, Oct. 1866	12, Oct.	60		350	Toledo, OH	Niederhofen, Württemberg
Helmle, (Mrs)	9, Jan. 1882	16, Dec.	63	Dieter	15	Ripley, OH	Niederhofen, Brackenheim, Württemberg
Helmle, Christian F.	27, June 1881	12, June	69- 4m-29d		207	Ripley, OH	Fredelsloh, Amt Moringen, Hannover
Helmrer, Louise	23, Nov. 1868	14, Nov.	51- 3m-13d		375	Toledo, OH	Chelsea, Washtenau County, Michigan
Helmrich, Gustav Adolf	26, Sept 1889	20, Aug.	20- 7m-27d		619	Francisco, MI	Mecklenburg-Schwerin
Helmrich, Henriette	18, Nov. 1897	27, Oct.	73	Schultz	735	Francisco, MI	Neustadt a. O., Sachsen-Weimar
Helmrich, Karl August	26, Mar. 1896	18, Feb.	72		206	Francisco, MI	Winfen, Hannover
Helms, August	30, July 1896	9, July	56		495	Sheboygan, WI	Batavia, Sheboygan County, Wisconsin
Helms, Bertha Catharina	21, Mar. 1889	3, Mar.	18		190	Sheboygan, WI	Rühmberg, Neustadt, Hannover
Helms, Charlotte S.	11, Apr. 1881	7, Mar.	79		119	Smithton, MO	

Christliche Apologete Death Notices --- 1839 - 1899

Name of Deceased	Notice Date	Death Date	Age	Page	Maiden Name	Place of Death	Place of Birth
Helms, Friedrich	10, Feb. 1898	21, Jan.	60	95		Chicago, IL	Gifhorn, Hannover
Helms, Georg	4, Nov. 1872	5, Sept	53	359		Concordia, MO	
Helms, Louise	16, Apr. 1896	1, Apr.	60	254		Chicago, IL	Giffond, Hannover
Helscher, Henry	2, July 1891	25, May	49	430		Harper, IA	Burlington, Iowa
Helscher, Johan	24, Aug. 1899	5, Aug.	55	543		Harper, IA	Burlington, Iowa
Helt, Margaretha	28, Jan. 1892	21, Dec.	72	62	Reif	Portsmouth, OH	Mergnes, Bodenstein, Oberfranken, Baiem
Helwig, Anna	16, Dec. 1872	24, Nov.	46	407	Winkler	Bonn, OH	Hagerbuch, Turkau, Schweiz
Helwig, Anna Louise	8, Oct. 1896	4, Sept	23	655		Cannelton, IN	German, Perry County, Indiana
Helwig, Anton	13, Oct. 1879	25, Aug.	83- 4m- 6d	327		Indianapolis, IN	Westphalen
Helwig, Caroline	24, June 1858	9, May	38	100	Hartmann	Morrisania, NY	Westphalen
Helwig, Charlotte	8, Nov. 1880	19, Oct.	47	359	Witt	Oregon, MO	Anclam, Pommern
Helwig, Eva	4, June 1883	18, May	67- 6m	183	Schuster	Lancaster, NY	Sesenheim, Bischweiler, Elsaß
Helwig, Georg	27, May 1842	13, May	53- 6m-17d	83		Marietta, OH	
Helwig, Georg	27, Feb. 1890	1, Feb.	14-11m- 7d	142		Lancaster, NY	
Helwig, Hanna	6, May 1872	20, Apr.	73	151		Allegheny City, PA	Lachte, Minden, Preußen
Helwig, Julius	11, Aug. 1892		58	510		Cannelton, IN	Hückeswagen, Lennep, Düsseldorf, Preußen
Helwig, Karl	12, Aug. 1878	19, July	18- 6m-21d	255		Giard, IA	
Helwig, Wilhelm	8, Nov. 1869	7, Oct.	16	359		Lancaster, NY	
Helzer, Johannes	17, Sept 1866	22, Aug.	56- 8m-10d	302		Jeffersonville, IN	Oberzell, Schlichtern, Kurhessen
Hemke, Christian	6, Nov. 1876	21, Oct.		359		Oconomowoc, WI	Dölitz, Kreis Pieritz, Preußen
Hemman, Christiana	13, Apr. 1874	30, Mar.	43	119	Pieler	Wheeling, WV	Culnitzsch, Weida, Neustadt, Sachsen-Weimar
Hemman, Georg Edward	7, May 1891	17, Apr.	19- 5m	302		Wheeling, WV	Ladbergen, Preußen
Hemmer, Anna Christine Elisabeth	1, June 1899		89	351		Huntingburg, IN	
Hemmer, Emilie	19, Sept 1870	1, Sept	15- 5m-13d	303		Huntingburg, IN	
Hemmer, Ernst Heinrich	7, Dec. 1885	21, Nov.	21	7		Huntingburg, IN	Price County, Indiana
Hemmer, H. Wilhelm	31, May 1880	12, May	28-11m- 1d	175		Huntingburg, IN	Cincinnati, Hamilton County, Ohio
Hemmer, Johan Friedrich	23, Apr. 1896	2, Mar.	49	270		Huntingburg, IN	Dubois County, Indiana
Hemmer, Josephine	4, Aug. 1873	1, July	28- 1m-10d	247	Rhein	Evansville, IN	
Hemmer, Maria	17, Feb. 1879	2, Feb.	25- -22d	55	Lammers	Huntingburg, IN	
Hemmer, Wilhelm	23, Dec. 1867	27, Nov.	49	406		Evansville, IN	Ladbergen, Decklinburg, Preußen
Hemmesatt, Joh. Fr.	21, July 1848		Inquiry	119		Marthasville, MO	
Hemmingen, Christian Friedrich	10, Mar. 1879		80- 5m-10d	79		Roseville, MI	Melzow, Preußen
Hemminger, Catharina	28, Jan. 1878	15, Jan.	47	31	Sehner	Morrison, MO	Starr County, Ohio
Hemminger, Auguste	30, June 1887	9, June	29	414	Miller	Lawrence, MA	Falkenhain, Preußen
Hempel, Carolina	29, Jan. 1891	23, Dec.	44	78	Niebuhr	Bartlett, TX	Brohme, Isenhagen, Germany
Hempel, H. L. Wilhelmine	20, Nov. 1865	28, Sept	34	188	Berkholz	Lowell, WI	Megow bei Pyritz, Pommern, Preußen
Hempel, Maria Louise	13, Sept 1894	24, Aug.	36	598	Bräuning	Scranton, PA	Ludwigsburg, Württemberg
Hempel, Otto	31, Mar. 1884	7, Feb.	23	7		Beaver Dam, WI	Watertown, Wisconsin
Hempel, Otto E.	3, Mar. 1884	7, Feb.	24	7		Beaver Dam, WI	Watertown, Wisconsin
Hempen, Anna Margaretha	28, Jan. 1884	26, Dec.	39	7	Reil	Gladbrook, IA	Dämkhorst, Oldenburg
Hempfling, Johan Louis	20, Feb. 1890	1, Feb.	17- 2m- 5d	126		Baltimore, MD	Baltimore, Maryland
Hempfling, John	19, Oct. 1893	19, Sept	71	670		Baltimore, MD	Gravendoberach, Baiem
Hempfling, Margaretha	8, Jan. 1866	20, Dec.	52	14		Baltimore, MD	Losau, Baiem
Hemrich, Catharina	4, Nov. 1886	20, Oct.		7	Mautner	Le Sueur, MN	Elisabetzel, Baiem
Hemschemeyer, (Mrs)	20, Feb. 1862	21, Jan.	59- 6m-15d	32	Rexer	Manitowoc, WI	Langenbrand, Weinsberg, Württemberg
Hemschemeyer, Heinrich	28, Aug. 1876	10, Aug.	74	279		Manitowoc, WI	Stolzenau, Hoya, Bruchhagen, Hannover

Christliche Apologete Death Notices --- 1839 - 1899

Name of Deceased	Notice Date	Death Date	Age	Maiden Name	Page	Place of Death	Place of Birth
Henchel, Mina	13, Aug. 1896	24, July	40	Poppe	527	Princeton, MN	Chicago, Cook County, Illinois
Hencke, Amelie Christine	19, Jan. 1899	1, Oct.	50		47	St. Paul, MN	Schiefelbein, Pommern
Hendrecker, Friedrich	29, Oct. 1896	23, Sept	93		703	Arenzville, IL	Schlütringen, Osnabrück, Hannover
Hendrickson, Heinrich	7, Feb. 1861	23, Jan.	42		24	Troy, NY	Finnland
Hendriker, Conrad	24, May 1875	7, May	33-8m		167	Beardstown, IL	
Hendriker, Elisabeth	3, Feb. 1868	6, Jan.	51	Kuhl	39	Beardstown, IL	Bindsachsen, Hessen-Darmstadt
Hene, Elisabeth Regine	16, Apr. 1896	5, Mar.	83	Britsch	254	Spencerville, OH	Häfnershasloch, Brakenheim, Württemberg
Heneise, Jakob	26, July 1860	25, June	37		120	Ripley, OH	Zaberfeld, Brackenheim, Württemberg
Henel, Konrad	11, Nov. 1897	25, Oct.	76		719	Arley, MO	Oberhausen, Rheinkreis Baiern
Henenberg, Auguste	11, Mar. 1867	13, Feb.	53	Linkmeier	78	Henderson, MN	Valdorf bei Vlotho, Herford, Minden, Preußen
Hengen, Anna Margaretha	14, Jan. 1884	26, Dec.	39	Reil	7	Gladbrook, IA	Dämkhorst, Oldenburg
Henk, A.F.	11, Jan. 1894	24, Dec.	50		30	Beaver Dam, WI	Klausdorf, Solden, Neumark
Henke, Anna Louisa	28, Mar. 1850	21, Feb.	70		52	Wheeling, VA	
Henke, Christoph	20, May 1886	25, Apr.	69		7	West Bend, WI	Drosebow, Hinterpommern
Henke, Elisabeth	18, Jan. 1894	2, Jan.	75	Magnus	46	Blue Island, IL	Schwering , Hannover
Henke, Ernst J.	26, Jan. 1880	12, Jan.	58- 7m-10d		31	Woodbury, MN	Ziegenhagen in Reetz, Pommern
Henke, F.	10, Nov. 1873	13, Oct.	21		359	Berea, OH	
Henke, Friedrich	28, July 1887	18, June	74		478	Blue Island, IL	Schweringen, Hannover
Henke, Friedrich	21, Jan. 1867	4, Jan.	74		22	Hazel Green, WI	Widewarm, Hannover
Henke, Henry	6, May 1886	16, Apr.	74		7		Lauenförde, Hannover
Henke, Johanna Sophie Wilhelmine	3, Dec. 1883	19, Nov.	68- 7m-10d		391	West Bend, WI	Drosidan, Pommern
Henke, Justina	30, Sept 1852	28, Aug.	36	Dankwerth	160	Pomeroy, OH	Bodenfelde, Amt Nienofer, Hannover
Henke, Martha	15, June 1899	25, May	39	Luschei	383	St. Joseph, MO	Bogdahnen, Niedrung, OstPreußen
Henke, Martin	18, Aug. 1892	31, July	74		526	Milford, SD	Posen
Henkel, Christine	25, June 1883	30, May	61	Wagner	207	Jersey City, NJ	Niefern, Pforzheim, Baden
Henkel, Georg	29, Aug. 1889	8, Aug.	67		558	Kansas City, KS	Mengshausen, Kurhessen
Henkel, John Nicholaus	24, Mar. 1892		68		190	St. Louis, MO	Wichtshausen bei Suhl, Sachsen
Henkel, Ludwig	30, Apr. 1896	30, Mar.	58		286	Tiffin, OH	Bessungen, Darmstadt, Hessen-Darmstadt
Henkel, Maria	10, Dec. 1891	23, Nov.	67- 6m-11d		798	St. Louis, MO	Sachsen
Henkelmann, Elisabeth	9, Aug. 1880	11, July	43-10m- 2d	Becker	255	Ft. Atkinson, WI	Nieder-Eschbach, Hessen-Darmstadt
Henken, Elisa	18, June 1883	4, June	27- 4m	Kanable	199	Lake Creek, MO	Morgan County, Missouri
Henken, Herman	15, Feb. 1875	27, Jan.	77		55	Lake Creek, MO	Altenbulstädt, Ottersberg, Hannover
Henmann, Johan Gottfried	22, Apr. 1886	30, Mar.	66		7	Wheeling, WV	Kulmitsch, Sachsen-Weimar
Henn, Elisabeth	31, Mar. 1898	4, Mar.	59	Schmitt	207	Wellman, IA	Germany
Henn, Philipp	24, Apr. 1882	12, Mar.	60		135	Brighton, IL	
Henne, Anna	5, July 1888	31, May	74- 1m-11d	Klaßing	430	Hopewell, MO	Lippe-Detmold
Henne, Anna Margaretha	31, Oct. 1864	17, Aug.	34		176	New Albany, IN	
Henne, Elisabeth	25, Feb. 1867	2, Feb.	33	Gerlach	62	Allegheny City, PA	Elm, Kreis Schlichten, Kurhessen
Henne, Friedrich	11, Feb. 1892	10, Jan.	83- 6m-24d		94	Spencerville, OH	Haslach, Württemberg
Henne, John Fr.	3, Sept 1896	9, Aug.	16		575	Spencerville, OH	Spencerville, Ohio
Henneberg, Anna Elisabeth	1, May 1882	29, Mar.	63- 6m- 3d	Wagner	143	St. Paul, MN	Mutterstadt, Rheinkreis Baiern
Henneberg, Heinrich	9, June 1892	11, Apr.	88		366	Arlington, MN	Theseberg bei Blankenburg, Braunschweig
Henneck, Katharine	19, Jan. 1899	15, Dec.	87- 5m-10d	Kaiser	47	Cleveland, OH	Hermannsdof, Baiern
Hennel, Carolina	5, Aug. 1878	23, July	22- 7m-20d	Großmann	247	Evansville, IN	
Hennemann, Katharina Dorothea	28, Dec. 1893	3, Dec.	76- 4m- 2d	Maxeiner	828	Chippewa Falls, WI	Schönborn, Dietz, Nassau
Hennich, Johann M.	24, Sept 1857	25, Aug.	20-11m		156	Menona, IA	

Christliche Apologete Death Notices --- 1839 - 1899

Name of Deceased	Notice Date	Death Date	Age	Maiden Name	Page	Place of Death	Place of Birth
Hennig, Auguste	2, Sept 1897	1, Aug.	79	Keiser	559	Hannibal, MO	Zanzie, Brandenburg
Hennig, Christian	12, July 1875	24, June	80- 9m- 7d		223	West Bend, WI	Dewenzimmer, Brackenheim, Württemberg
Hennig, Friedrich Wilhelm	13, Feb. 1882	26, Jan.	18- 2m- 3d		55	Iron Ridge, WI	
Hennig, Heinrich	4, Nov. 1886	18, Oct.	59		7	West Bend, WI	
Hennig, Alfred	10, June 1897	15, May	16		367	Dalton, MO	Dalton, Missouri
Henning, Andreas	27, Feb. 1862	8, Jan.	20-11m- 4d		36	Columbus, IL	Oberdorla, Mühlhausen, Erfurt, Preußen
Henning, Carolina	12, Apr. 1888	27, Mar.	57		238	Chicago, IL	Starnitz, Hinterpommern
Henning, Charlotte Louise	16, Nov. 1874	1, Oct.	68	Truhn	367	Woodville, OH	Viteröse, Köslin, Pommern, Preußen
Henning, Christine Justine	5, Sept 1864	7, June	31	Kletzin	144	Sheboygan, WI	Granzow, Uckermark, Preußen
Henning, Dorothea	15, Aug. 1881	25, July	35- 6m-10d	Camus	263	Chicago, IL	Osterholz, Hannover
Henning, Elisabeth	29, Dec. 1879	16, Dec.	48	May	415	Dalton, MO	Wehrheim, Ufingen, Nassau
Henning, Ernst	3, Mar. 1879	7, Feb.	62		71	Sandusky, OH	Malzkow, Cöslin, Preußen
Henning, Ferdinand	14, Apr. 1887	27, Mar.	63		238	DeWitt, MI	Alt-Malzkow, Cöslin, Preußen
Henning, Friedrich	25, Sept 1890	5, Sept	54		622	Chicago, IL	Meckroth, Lamberg, Pommern
Henning, Friedrich	24, Aug. 1854	9, July	44		136	Detroit, MI	Willmar, Pommern
Henning, Gottfried	20, Jan. 1868	31, Dec.	72-11m-16d		22	Columbus, IL	Oberdorla bei Mühlhausen, Preußen
Henning, Henriette	6, Jan. 1887	20, Dec.	72	Kahnow	14	Manitowoc, WI	Schönermark, Preußen
Henning, Hermann Friedrich	27, July 1868	17, May			239	Newtonburg, WI	
Henning, Joachim	27, Mar. 1871	8, Mar.	78		103	Henderson, MN	Stukenbosta, Amt Ottersberg, Hannover
Henning, Johan Albert	10, Nov. 1887	13, Oct.	47		718	DeWitt, MI	Malzhow, Ceslin, Preußen
Henning, John D.	1, Nov. 1888	23, Sept	82		702	Evansville, IN	Diepholz, Hannover
Henning, Louise Amalie Henriette	25, Mar. 1867	1, Mar.	19		94	Manitowoc, WI	Harnbeck, Ukermark
Henning, M.	18, Sept 1882	25, Aug.	61		303	Sheboygan, WI	Zieghof, Uckermark, Preußen
Henning, Margaretha	25, Feb. 1884	9, Feb.	87	Vogt	7	Arlington, MN	Boorf, Ottersberg, Hannover
Henning, Margaretha Dorothea	13, Dec. 1855	10, Oct.		Nepper	200	Huntingburg, IN	Diepholz, Hannover
Henning, Maria	23, Jan. 1875	19, Dec.	19- 1m		31	Sheboygan, WI	
Henning, Maria Katharina	7, Apr. 1873	9, Mar.	67	Letz	111	Columbus, IL	Langela, Preußen
Henning, Maria Louise	12, Oct. 1893	14, Aug.	26		654	DeWitt, MI	Fremont, Ohio
Henning, Wilhelmina	24, Aug. 1854	14, July	14		136	Detroit, MI	
Henning, Wilhelmine	21, Jan. 1897	30, Dec.	39	Buth	46	Milwaukee, WI	Groß Sabow, Pommern
Henninger, Anna Maria	10, Apr. 1882	18, Feb.	84		119	Bradford, IN	Buckingen, Mühlheim, Baden
Henninger, Johan	28, Sept 1899		76		623	Chillicothe, OH	Baden
Henningsen, Marcus	17, Sept 1891	29, Aug.	34-11m-19d		606	Omaha, NE	Krusebill, Tondern, Schleswig
Hennrich, Fritz	22, Mar. 1888	27, Feb.	50		190	Doe Run, MO	Niederhausen a. d. Nah, RheinPreußen
Hennrich, Karl	6, May 1886	14, Apr.	17		7	St. Francois Co, MO	
Hennrich, Margaretha	16, Mar. 1885	1, Mar.	84	Roth	7	Farmington, MO	Niederhausen an der Nahe, RheinPreußen
Henny, Catharine	12, Feb. 1883	17, Jan.	73	Umbdenstick	55	Detroit, MI	Ostheim, Elsaß
Henny, Elisabeth	7, Nov. 1850	20, Oct.	62- 5m-10d		180	Mt. Vernon, IN	Hurssellen, Bern, Schweiz
Henry, Friederike Dorothea	18, Dec. 1865	2, Dec.	19	Vögel	204	Detroit, MI	Gemerichheim, Württemberg
Henry, Margaretha	13, Dec. 1880	18, Nov.	46- -23d	Baumann	399	Detroit, MI	Erbstadt, Windecken, Kurhessen
Henoch, Karoline	30, Oct. 1890	9, Oct.	80- 1m-25d	Michaels	702	Cincinnati, OH	Sonnenburg, Preußen
Henop, Albert Ernst	17, June 1897	26, May	14		383	Abrams, WI	
Henrice, Katharina	11, May 1899	16, Apr.	63	Freudenberger	302	Philadelphia, PA	Schillingstadt, Boxberg, Baden
Henrich, Johan Heinrich	21, Sept 1885	5, Sept	39		7	Ft. Atkinson, WI	Bruchsal, Baden
Henrichs, Anna Maria	14, May 1891	23, Apr.	72	Threseler	318	Jordan, MN	Dorfsgrottingshausen, Oltendorf, Lüpke, Preußen
Henrichs, Johan	20, Feb. 1890	26, Jan.	44		126	Rochester, MN	Rebshold, Wittmund, Hannover

Christliche Apologete Death Notices --- 1839 - 1899

Name of Deceased	Notice Date	Death Date	Age	Maiden Name	Page	Place of Death	Place of Birth
Henrichs, Uhlrich H.	15, Sept 1887	21, Aug.	51		590	Frankfort, IL	Aldenburg, Germany
Henny, Minnie	1, Feb. 1894	13, Jan.	23	Böttscher	78	Burlington, IA	
Hensch, Friedrich	12, June 1882		32- 7m-28d		191	Marine City, MI	
Henschel, F. M.	19, Oct. 1893	25, Sept	72		670	Waco, TX	Germersheim, Baiern
Henschel, Gustav	3, Sept 1883	8, Aug.	44- -20d		287	Toledo, OH	Posen, Posen, Germany
Henschel, Henry	24, July 1890	8, July	21- 9m-16d		478	Clearwater, MN	Princeton, Minnesota
Henschel, Karl	2, Nov. 1899	12, Oct.	34		703	Clearwater, MN	Lebuser, Preußen
Henschel, Karl Ludwig	26, May 1892	6, May	64		334	Clearwater, MN	Princeton, Minnesota
Henschel, Lydia	18, Sept 1890	16, Aug.	18- 6m- 6d		606	Clearwater, MN	
Henschen, Friedrike	30, Mar. 1868	2, Mar.	40	Schmiederjohann	103	Herman, MO	Linnen, Tecklenburg, Preußen
Henschen, Heinrich	28, June 1888	6, June	24		414	Nokomis, IL	Edwardsville, Illinois
Henschen, Maria Elisabeth	8, Apr. 1886	18, Mar.	91	Heemann	7	Nokomis, IL	Lienen, Westphalen
Henscher, Franz August Herman	25, Jan. 1869	24, Dec.	49		31	De Soto, MO	Wanzleben bei Magdeburg,
Hensel, Charlotte Karoline	21, Sept 1899	5, Sept	60	Zybell	607	Bristol, WI	Zadtkow, Belgard, Pommern
Henseler, Maria	9, Mar. 1885	15, Feb.	90	Marge	7	Beaver Dam, WI	Neudam, Brandenburg
Henske, Johanna Louise	7, Mar. 1895	31, Jan.	84	Berg	158	Sun Prairie, WI	Liptow, Pieritz, Pommern
Hensler, Christina	5, May 1892	24, Mar.	63		286	Cincinnati, OH	Obereggenen, Baden
Hensohn, August	28, Nov. 1850	10, Aug.	32		192	Evansville, IN	Dassel, Hannover
Henßel, Carl Friedrich	10, May 1894	19, Apr.	29		310	Dayton, OH	Dayton, Montgomery County, Ohio
Henze, August	18, Mar. 1897	2, Feb.	73		174	Herman, MO	Hannover
Henze, Karl W.J.	22, Jan. 1883	3, Jan.	16		31	Wabasha, MN	Pipin County, Wisconsin
Heob, Heinrich	12, Nov. 1891	20, Oct.	20		734	St. Louis, MO	Ellis Grove, Illinois
Hepp, F. C. (Rev0	2, July 1896	4, June	6- 9m-10d		431	Boonville, IN	Birkenfeld, Oldenburg
Hepp, Georg	21, Apr. 1853		31		64	Indianapolis, IN	Ermershausen bei Aschaffenburg, Baiern
Hepp, Maria Henriette	12, Jan. 1885	27, Dec.	84- 6m-17d	Schmitt	7	Boonville, IN	Birkenfeld, Oldenburg
Hepp, Wilhelm	5, Dec. 1889	15, Oct.	24- 3m		782	Indianapolis, IN	
Heppe, (Mrs)	27, Sept 1875	8, Sept	25- 4m	Grein	311	Muscatine, IA	
Heppe, Elisabeth	15, Mar. 1888	25, Feb.	34- 7m-27d	Beck	174	Muscatine, IA	
Heppe, Emma Katharina	27, June 1895	27, May	26		414	Muscatine, IA	Muscatine, Iowa
Herbel, August	8, Jan. 1877	17, Dec.	19-10m-20d		15	Pittsburg, PA	
Herbel, Heinrich	17, Oct. 1889	26, Sept	82- - 5d		670	Baraboo, WI	Breitenbach, Wetzlar, Koblenz, Preußen
Herbel, Philippine	19, Apr. 1888	25, Mar.	80	Clößner	254	Baraboo, WI	Katzenfurt, Wetzlar, Preußen
Herber, Johan Adam	3, Jan. 1876	8, Dec.	63- -27d		7	Pomeroy, OH	Dill, Kreis Simmern, Rheinpfalz Baiern
Herber, Conrad	17, Jan. 1845		Inquiry		11	Zanesville, OH	Kurhessen
Herbert, Karl	3, June 1878	1, May	73- -20d		175	New Orleans, LA	Ecklingerode, Worbis, Erfurt, Preußen
Herbig, Günther Friedrich Carl	2, Sept 1872	1, Aug.	52- 8m-28d		287	Yellow Creek, IL	Groß-Furra, Schwarzburg-Sondershausen
Herbold, Christina	25, Feb. 1892	18, Jan.	69	Beutekam	126	Ironton, OH	Hombressen, Hofgeismar, Kurhessen
Herbold, Georg	10, Apr. 1882	20, Mar.	14		119	Mt. Pleasant, IA	Hombressen, Hofgeismar, Kurhessen
Herbold, John H.	20, Sept 1860	9, July	70		152	Poland, OH	
Herbold, Maria	31, Jan. 1881	23, Dec.	40- 4m-22d	Wicke	39	Ironton, OH	
Herbrechtsmeyer, Louise Amalie F.	28, Dec. 1893	8, Dec.	77		828	Charles City, IA	Hambressen, Hofgeismar, Kurhessen
Herbrig, Johan Christlieb	10, Aug. 1899	17, July	82		511	Industry, TX	Varenholz, Lippe-Detmold
Herbst, Maria Anna	2, Mar. 1885	27, Dec.	59		7	New York City, NY	Taubenheim, Sachsen
Herbst, Marianna	30, Mar. 1885	27, Dec.	59		7	New York City, NY	Schweiz
Herbst, William	6, Dec. 1875	3, Nov.	56		391	Kossuth, OH	Sachsen
Herbstreidt, John	3, Mar. 1873	18, Jan.	21- 5m- 4d		71	Trenton, IL	Walbrechtshausen, Hannover

Christliche Apologete Death Notices --- 1839 - 1899

Name of Deceased	Notice Date	Death Date	Age	Maiden Name	Page	Place of Death	Place of Birth
Herbstreit, Katharine	24, Dec. 1896	4, Dec.	67	Upmeier	831	Summerfield, IL	Brochterbeck, Münster, Preußen
Herche, Caspar	28, Dec. 1868	7, Dec.	68		415	Rushville, IL	Schlüchtern, Kurhessen
Herdach, Jakob	28, Jan. 1878	11, Jan.	38- 1m-12d		31	Minneapolis, MN	Niederurneu, Schweiz
Herder, Anna Maria	5, Sept 1889	10, Aug.	63- 6m-10d	Dörr	574	Portsmouth, OH	Niederhochstadt, RheinPfalz Baiern
Herder, Georg Heinrich	4, Feb. 1897	6, Jan.	63		79	Portsmouth, OH	Niederlustadt bei Germersheim, Rheinkreis Baiern
Herder, Katharina	11, Oct. 1894	18, Aug.	71	Wellmann	662	Portsmouth, OH	Niederlustadt bei Germersheim, Rheinkreis Baiern
Herder, Maria Louisa	28, Aug. 1876	4, Aug.	87	Bußen	279	Red Wing, MN	Grabow, West Priegnitz, Preußen
Herdt, Benedict	12, July 1875	6, May	47		223	Rochester, NY	Messen, Solothurn, Schweiz
Hereth, Margaretha	17, Mar. 1884	25, Feb.	66		7	Indianapolis, IN	Heiderbach, Württemberg
Hergenröther, Magdalena	23, Apr. 1877	11, Apr.	56		135	Louisville, KY	Hessen-Darmstadt
Herger, Carolina	27, Feb. 1890	4, Feb.	86- 1m- 8d	Kirchner	142	Bucyrus, OH	Heinerit, Weinsberg, Württemberg
Hergersheimer, Sophie	24, Feb. 1879	26, Jan.	20- 1m- 3d	Dreidoppell	63	Louisville, KY	
Herhold, Maria Friederika	31, Mar. 1873	3, Mar.	23- 9m- 6d		103	Junction City, KS	Posewalk, Preußen
Herholz, Albert	16, Mar. 1899	16, Jan.	65		175	Lansing, MI	
Herholz, Emilie	1, Mar. 1894	16, Jan.	57		150	Roseville, MI	
Herholz, Wilhelmine	22, Aug. 1895	31, July	34	Jenß	542	Berne, MI	Glausow, Mecklenburg-Schwerin
Hering, Louise	26, Nov. 1896	6, Nov.	45	Baumstark	766	Buffalo, NY	Buffalo, New York
Heritier, Friederike	5, Feb. 1866	1, Jan.	75		46	Washington, MN	Heimerdingen, Württemberg
Herke, Ernst	13, Aug. 1877	6, July	55- 7m- 6d		263	Angelica, NY	Gamsen, Amt Gifhorn, Hannover
Herker, Louise Albertine	10, July 1871	27, June	22-13m- 4d		223	Pekin, IL	Gresgande, Preußen
Herlein, Wilhelmine	20, June 1895	25, May	66	Krüger	398	Wrayville, IL	Schleppkau, Preußen
Herling, Emil	2, Nov. 1885	15, Oct.	19		7	Enterprise, KS	
Herman, Christine	3, Sept 1891	8, Aug.	63- 6m-24d	Sieder	574	Santa Claus, IN	Eversbach, Württemberg
Herman, Gerhard	16, July 1891	29, June	72- 3m-23d		462	St. Louis, MO	Zweifall, Aachen, Preußen
Herman, Anna	21, Mar. 1895	15, Jan.	15		190	Troy, NY	
Hermann, Anna Agnes	23, Feb. 1893	13, Feb.	86-10m- 6d	Köhler	126	Cincinnati, OH	Offenbach, Hessen-Darmstadt
Hermann, Anna Catharina	19, May 1873	28, Apr.		Ott	159	Oregon, MO	Krumbach bei Gießen, Hessen-Darmstadt
Hermann, Anna Maria	12, July 1875	4, June	73- 4m- 8d	Schmitt	223	Flint Creek, IA	Marburg, Caltern, Hessen
Hermann, Anna Maria	6, Feb. 1882	24, Jan.	62- -12d		47	St. Louis, MO	Weisenheim, Baden
Hermann, Barbara	26, Feb. 1866	6, Feb.	64		70	Lawrence, KS	Cleversulzbach, Neckarsulm, Württemberg
Hermann, Barbara	1, Apr. 1886	5, Mar.	67- 3m-17d	Ferbert	7	Nebraska City, NE	Langsheim, Rheinkreis Baiern
Hermann, Barbara	12, Mar. 1877	12, Feb.	71	Seiler	87	Allegheny City, PA	Bottmingen, Basel, Schweiz
Hermann, Barbara	30, Aug. 1888	31, July	78- 6m-26d	Lux	558	Spring Lake, IL	Feuerbach, Württemberg
Hermann, Carolina	4, Aug. 1892	11, July	83		494	Lansing, MI	Hohenzieritz, Mecklenburg-Strelitz
Hermann, Catharina Friederike	16, Feb. 1880	29, Jan.	68- 4m-22d	Krämer	55	Santa Claus, IN	Mundelsheim, Marbach, Württemberg
Hermann, Christiana	2, Mar. 1899	1, Feb.	80- 5m- 4d		143	Hope, MO	
Hermann, Christina	21, Jan. 1867	23, Sept	17		22	Allegheny City, PA	Alleghany City, Pennsylvania
Hermann, Eckhardt	22, Sept 1879	16, Aug.	63- 5m-18d		303	Red Wing, MN	Homberg, Kurhessen
Hermann, Elisabeth	19, Jan. 1888		80		46	Mt. Vernon, NY	
Hermann, Friedrich	22, Apr. 1897	26, Mar.	81		254	Morrison, MO	Seifhennersdorf, Sachsen
Hermann, Georg W.	3, Feb. 1873	10, Jan.	45		39	Jewells Prairie, IL	Hessen-Kassel
Hermann, Heinrich	17, Sept 1883	28, Aug.	83- -17d		303	Allegheny City, PA	Biel & Benken, Baselland, Schweiz
Hermann, Helena	14, Sept 1868	16, Aug.		Krümel	295	St. Louis, MO	Zweifall, Kreis Montjoie, Preußen
Hermann, Jacob Georg	26, Dec. 1881	3, Dec.	66-10m		415	Pittsburg, PA	Bettenfeld bei Rodenburg, Baiern
Hermann, Jakob	25, Dec. 1876	12, Dec.	32		413	Burlington, IA	Einhausen bei Marburg, Kurhessen
Hermann, Johan Jacob	15, Sept 1879	24, Aug.	73- -12d		295	Santa Claus, IN	Meinsheim, Brackenheim, Württemberg

Christliche Apologete Death Notices --- 1839 - 1899

Name of Deceased	Notice Date	Death Date	Age	Maiden Name	Page	Place of Death	Place of Birth
Hermann, Johan Ulrich	23, Dec. 1886		98- 6m-27d		7	Jordan, MN	Binnigen, Basel, Schweiz
Hermann, Katharina	25, Apr. 1864	3, Apr.	64	Marmein	68	Warsaw, IL	Neuhof, Künzelsau, Württemberg
Hermann, Kunigunde	8, Dec. 1892	8, Nov.	70	Weidner	782	Pittsburg, PA	Schonweisen, Baiern
Hermann, Lillie	14, July 1879	25, June	21- -22d		223	Woodbine, IL	Woodbine, Daviss County, Illinois
Hermann, Louis	12, Oct. 1899	9, Sept	26		655	Santa Claus, IN	Santa Claus, Indiana
Hermann, Louise	17, Feb. 1879	22, Jan.	22- 8m-22d	Christ	55	Toole City, UT	St. Louis, Missouri
Hermann, Margarethe	6, May 1886	10, Mar.	66		7	Dillenburg, —	
Hermann, Maria	21, Apr. 1898	19, Mar.	52	Springer	255	Lake City, MN	Löffenbach, Zürich, Schweiz
Hermann, Michael	12, July 1849		Inquiry		111	Monroe, OH	Hirschthal, Baiern
Hermann, Mina	1, Dec. 1892	11, Nov.	64	Kurtz	766	Dodgeville, IA	Wermuthskirche, Preußen
Hermann, Phröne Katharina	7, Apr. 1873	17, Mar.	31- - 7d	Oberst	111	Toledo, OH	Gersbach, Amt Schopfheim, Baden
Hermann, Rosina	3, Feb. 1887	18, Jan.	64	Spohn	78	Osceola, NE	Blächstetten, Urach, Württemberg
Hermann, Susanna E.	10, Jan. 1889	29, Dec.	54-10m-17d		30	Allegheny City, PA	Seckbach bei Frankfurt am Main, Germany
Herms, Rosa E.	8, Dec. 1887	25, Nov.	41- 7m-20d	Brodbeck	782	Portsmouth, OH	
Herms, Wesley	29, Mar. 1888	1, Mar.	17- 4m-10d		206	Portsmouth, OH	Portsmouth, Scioto County, Ohio
Hermsmeier, Friedrich (Rev)	29, Sept 1898	3, Sept	73		623	Waseca, MN	Lippe-Detmold
Hermsmeier, Wilhelm	22, Mar. 1869	18, Feb.	21		95	Le Sueur, MN	Marthasville, Warren County, Missouri
Herner, Lydia	10, Sept 1866	14, Aug.	25		294	Brookville, IN	
Herpel, Agnes Virginia	16, July 1883	4, June	16- 5m		231	Baltimore, MD	
Herpel, Anna Martha	9, Mar. 1885	20, Feb.	25- 8m-13d		7	Baltimore, MD	
Herpel, J.H.	8, May 1890				302	Baltimore, MD	
Herpel, Johan Heinrich	6, Nov. 1890	17, Sept	65- 5m-20d		718	Baltimore, MD	Hessen-Nassau
Herr, Caspar	20, Nov. 1851	25, Jan.	44		188	St. Louis, MO	St. Louis, Missouri
Herr, John	26, Feb. 1866	18, Feb.	15		70	Peru, IL	Straßburg, Elsaß
Herr, Margaretha	12, Mar. 1891	10, Aug.	72	Knob	174	Wellman, IA	Ehze, Hannover
Herr, Sophia	1, Sept 1848	24, Jan.	19		144	Newark, NJ	
Herre, David	29, Apr. 1897	5, Mar.	75- 4m-18d		271	Philadelphia, PA	Ruith, Stuttgart, Württemberg
Herrenleben, Anna	28, June 1855	30, Jan.	49		104	Boonville, MO	
Herrenleben, Christian	27, Mar. 1871		73- 5m-16d		103	Boonville, MO	Ebermanstadt, Albertshof, Baiern
Herrman, Charlotte	23, Apr. 1896	12, Mar.	66	Zimp	270	New Rochelle, NY	Bertelsdorf, Lauben, Liegnitz, Preußen
Herrman, Luise	11, Aug. 1898	16, July	47	Ott	511	Toledo, OH	Monroe, Michigan
Herrman, Ursula	16, July 1891	3, June	60		462	Enterprise, KS	Werdenberg, Schweiz
Herrmann, Albert	10, Nov. 1898	25, Oct.	64		719	Troy, NY	Rastatt, Baden
Herrmann, Anna	25, Mar. 1886	20, Feb.		Stegemann	7	Montrose, MN	
Herrmann, Anna Ottilie	31, Aug. 1899	13, Aug.	28- -13d	Hafner	559	Lincoln, NE	St. Joseph, Missouri
Herrmann, Bruno	11, Mar. 1897	Feb.	43		158	Lexington, TX	Chemnitz, Sachsen
Herrmann, Elisabeth	28, July 1862	23, June	27-11m- 8d		120	Allegheny City, PA	Biel, Basel, Schweiz
Herrmann, Franziska	22, Sept 1884	7, Sept	22		7	Caldwell, TX	Industry, Austin County, Texas
Herrmann, Friederike	5, Oct. 1863	17, Sept	33- 6m-17d	Pape	160	Waikerton, IN	Oberamt Ravensburg, Württemberg
Herrmann, Julius	12, Oct. 1899	24, Sept	37		655		Ohnastädten, Urach, Württemberg
Hermleben, Elisabeth	21, July 1879	5, July	56- 4m- 4d		231	Jamestown, MO	Fürstenhagen, Kurhessen
Herrschaft, Elisa	9, Nov. 1874	21, Oct.	40- 2m		359	New Haven, CT	KleinHeilbach, Aschaffenburg, Baiern
Herrschaft, Franz	31, Oct. 1889	9, Sept	58		702	Brooklyn, NY	
Herrschaft, Gottlieb	31, Jan. 1861	21, Nov.	8		20	New Haven, CT	
Herrstein, Christian	26, June 1871	10, June	78- 5m- 3d		207	De Soto, MO	Battenberg, Grünstadt, Baiern
Herwig, Gottlieb	24, Nov. 1843	30, Aug.	63		187		

Christliche Apologete Death Notices -- 1839 - 1899

Name of Deceased	Notice Date	Death Date	Age	Page	Maiden Name	Place of Death	Place of Birth
Herschberger, Clara	21, Oct. 1897	24, Aug.	85-11m-21d	671		Bucyrus, OH	Lancaster County, Pennsylvania
Herschberger, Jacob	25, Sept 1882	17, Nov.	65	311		Bucyrus, OH	Lancaster County, Pennsylvania
Herschberger, Jakob	11, Nov. 1897	18, Mar.	37	719		Bucyrus, OH	Lancaster County, Pennsylvania
Herschberger, Samuel	7, Apr. 1873	14, Aug.	50	111		Marrs, IN	Vanderburgh County, Indiana
Herschelman, Andreas	7, Sept 1899	1, June	84	575		Marrs, IN	Frankenstein bei Kaiserslautern, Germany
Herschelmann, Andreas	24, June 1897	18, June	37	399	Baumann	St. Philip, IN	
Herschelmann, Magdalena	10, Sept 1891	31, Aug.	35-6m-8d	590	Leibold	Mt. Vernon, IN	Elbersheim, Mergentheim, Württemberg
Herschelmann, Sophia Margaretha	30, Sept 1858	18, Nov.	39	156		Newark, OH	Lienen, Kreis Wallendorf, Preußen
Hersmann, Friedrich Jakob	21, Jan. 1867	25, July	64	22		De Soto, MO	Eppstein, Frankenthal, Rheinkreis Baiern
Herstein, (Mrs)	11, Aug. 1884	15, July	75	7		De Soto, MO	Battenberg, Baiern
Herstein, Peter	3, Aug. 1893	8, June	66-10m-13d	494		Vermillion, OH	Tann, Kurhessen
Hert, Jakob	30, June 1887	29, Feb.	63	414		Osage Bluff, MO	Bibern, Solothurn, Schweiz
Hert, Johannes	18, Mar. 1872	28, July	31	95		Vermillion, OH	
Hert, Martha	27, Aug. 1891	20, July	8	558	Baumhart		
Hertel, Augustus	15, Dec. 1862	26, Jan.	84	200		Jeffersonville, NY	Lancaster, New York
Hertel, Catharina	28, Feb. 1895	26, Aug.	61-8m-9d	142	Brua	Belleville, IL	Niederstinzel, Finstingen, Lothringen
Hertel, Christine	10, Sept 1883	10, Jan.	84	295	Schneider	Ft. Atkinson, WI	Gündigen, Saarbrücken, Trier, Preußen
Hertel, Johan	16, Mar. 1899	25, Oct.	64	175		Ft. Atkinson, WI	Güdingen, Saarbrücken, RheinPreußen
Hertel, Karl	10, Nov. 1884	15, May	82	7		Belleville, IL	Niederstinzel, Finstingen, Lothringen
Hertel, Maria	12, June 1865	11, Apr.	21-6m	96	Michel	Clay County, MO	Flumborn, Kreis Alzet, Hessen-Darmstadt
Hertel, Theresa	21, July 1859	11, Dec.	77-8m-25d	116	Reimert	St. Louis, MO	
Hertenstein, Anna Maria	19, Mar. 1883	12, Jan.	80-6m-7d	95		Delaware, OH	Hugsweier, Lahr, Baden
Hertenstein, Jakob	12, Jan. 1885	28, Sept	23	7		Spencerville, OH	Hugsweier, Lahr, Baden
Herter, Bertha	8, Nov. 1888	21, Mar.	60	718	Walter	Clay Center, KS	Wilchingen, Schaffhausen, Schweiz
Herter, Elisabeth	14, Apr. 1898	7, Nov.	58	239	Kunz	Culbertson, NE	Winterthur, Schweiz
Herter, Margaretha	29, Nov. 1888	20, Dec.		766	Keller	Clay Center, KS	Wulflingen, Zürich, Schweiz
Hetfelder, Wilhelm F. H.	10, Jan. 1895	27, Dec.	87- 2m-17d	30		Terre Haute, IN	
Hethel, Franziska	16, Jan. 1882	24, Jan.	39	23		Boston, MA	Sibeldingen, Rheinkreis Baiern
Hertrich, Caroline	6, Mar. 1876	21, Oct.	20	79	Weise	Howard Lake, MN	Schwarzbach, Sachsen-Weimar
Hertter, Anna Christine	21, Nov. 1889	20, Nov.	34- 1m- 6d	750	Manßen	Waltersburg, IL	Schleuß, Wittmund, Ostfriesland
Hertter, Charles Friedrich	8, Dec. 1887	17, July	24-7m-24d	782		Golconda, IL	
Hertter, Otto Robert	8, Aug. 1889	17, Jan.	34	510		Golconda, IL	
Hertz, Carl Johan Joachim	15, Feb. 1894	13, Oct.	19	110		Charles City, IA	Oberhof, Mecklenburg-Schwerin
Hertzel, Rebecca	27, Nov. 1876	6, Feb.	62	383		Nashville, IL	Nashville, Illinois
Hertzler, Daniel	7, Mar. 1895	6, Apr.	22	158		Halstead, KS	Ramsen, Rheinpfalz Baiern
Hertzler, Heinrich	26, May 1862	12, June	65	84		Burlington, IA	Ramsen, Rheinpfalz Baiern
Hertzler, John	13, July 1893	2, Mar.	28	446		Burlington, IA	Ramsen, Rheinpfalz Baiern
Hertzler, Lydia	24, Mar. 1892	10, Nov.	20	190	Kammermeyer	Davenport, IA	Paris, Iowa
Herwehe, Maria Anna	27, Nov. 1871	11, Mar.	20	383	Wernz	Des Moines, IA	Sendhofen, Amt Ladenburg, Baden
Herwig, Bertha L.	25, Mar. 1897	26, Oct.	73	190		Nokomis, IL	
Herwig, Friedrich	23, Nov. 1893	1, June	21	750		Bushnell, IL	Lade, Minden, Preußen
Herwig, Heinrich	29, June 1899	26, June	36	415		Chicago, IL	Chicago, Cook County, Illinois
Herwig, Heinrich	21, July 1862	13, May	69	116		Chicago, IL	
Herwig, Karl	28, May 1877	8, July	39	175			Windheim, Preußen
Herwig, Katharine	14, Aug. 1871	2, Sept	74	263	Schade	Chicago, IL	Hirschfeld, Kurhessen
Herwig, Louis	24, Sept 1896			623		Chicago, IL	Drentelburg, Kurhessen

Christliche Apologete Death Notices --- 1839 - 1899

Name of Deceased	Notice Date	Death Date	Age	Maiden Name	Page	Place of Death	Place of Birth
Herwig, Wilhelm	14, Jan. 1884		72- 2m-16d		7	Nokomis, IL	Albungen, Hessen
Herz, Friedrich Jacob L.	14, June 1888	31, May	21- -15d		382	Farmington, MO	Maine, LaMotte, Missouri
Herz, Johan Friedrich	2, July 1883	18, June	54		215	Mt. Vernon, NY	Oberhoff, Mecklenburg-Schwerin
Herz, Karl	27, Feb. 1890	30, Jan.	53		142	Flood Creek, IA	Mecklenburg-Schwerin
Herzberg, Carolina	24, Jan. 1871	1, Jan.	22- 8m-7d	Arz	31	Lansing, MI	
Herzberg, Carolina	17, Apr. 1871	1, Jan.			127	Lansing, MI	
Herzberg, Dorothea Friederike	8, Nov. 1894	8, Oct.	61	Kamin	726	Willow Creek, WI	Giesebitz, Germany
Herzberg, Frida	10, Feb. 1898	25, Jan.	26- 5m- 8d	Edelmann	95	Allegheny, PA	
Herzer, Angeline	30, June 1884	3, June	48	Landes	7	Francisco, MI	Ypsilanti, Michigan
Herzer, Christoph Friedrich	12, Nov. 1877	11, Oct.	69		367	Franciscoville, MI	Neustadt, Sachsen-Weimar
Herzer, Friederike	16, May 1881	27, Apr.	52- 7m-22d	Brösamle	159	Francisco, MI	Schöngrund, Freudenstadt, Württemberg
Herzer, Friedrich G.	19, Apr. 1880	14, Mar.	51- -13d		127	Francisco, MI	Neustadt an der Orla, Sachsen-Weimar
Herzer, Georg	15, Jan. 1866	16, Dec.	18		22	Muscatine, IA	Bretten, Baden
Herzer, Margaretha	3, Sept 1857	24, Mar.		Frank	144	Detroit, MI	
Herzer, Milton	13, May 1897	7, Sept	23		303	Columbus, OH	Louisville, Jefferson County, Kentucky
Herzer, Richard	7, Mar. 1864	30, May	21		40	Ann Arbor, MI	Neustadt an der Orla, Sachsen-Weimar
Herzer, Wilhelmina	12, June 1871	17, Mar.	63	Götze	191	Franciscoville, MI	Neustadt an der Orlg, Sachsen-Weimar
Herzig, Johan	7, Apr. 1892	4, Jan.	47		222	Jamestown, MO	Uttingen, Bern, Schweiz
Herzig, Rosa	13, Feb. 1896	7, Aug.	16		110	Jamestown, MO	Jamestown, Missouri
Herzog, Anna Kunigunda	29, Aug. 1870	18, Mar.	81		279	Dayton, OH	Markblech, Baiern
Herzog, Catharina	12, Apr. 1869	20, Nov.	25	Jotter	119	Warsaw, IL	Maxenheim, Kirchheimholanden, Rheinkreis Baiern
Herzog, Georg	4, Jan. 1894	4, Sept	77		14	Neustadt, NJ	Arnsheim, Hessen-Darmstadt
Herzog, Heinrich Oscar	27, Sept 1894	4, Dec.	28		630	Warsaw, IL	Warsaw, Illinois
Herzog, Josef	2, Jan. 1896	16, July			14	Marysville, CA	Schweiz
Herzog, Katharina	18, Aug. 1892	12, Apr.	69	Pfeiffer	526	Jeffersonville, IN	Hochsaal, Baden
Herzog, Louise	9, May 1895	9, May	24	Bollmann	302	Nokomis, IL	
Herzog, Maria Engel	23, May 1881	9, Nov.	79	Gerwin	167	Woodville, OH	Sandusky County, Ohio
Herzog, Maria Magdalena	3, Dec. 1896	19, Nov.	76	Maus	782	Akron, NY	Wallertheim, Hessen-Darmstadt
Herzog, Peter	10, Dec. 1891	9, Aug.	25		798	Brooklyn, NY	Roßwiller bei Kusel, Rheinkreis Baiern
Heselschwerdt, Lydia	8, Sept 1898	1, Apr.	70		575	Drake, MO	Sharon, Waschtenaw County, Michigan
Hesemann, Wilhelmine	27, Apr. 1899	31, Jan.	30	Vetter	271	LaCrosse, WI	Hochholzhausen, Halle, Germany
Heß, Andreas	23, Feb. 1893	8, Dec.	20		126	Louisville, KY	Germany
Heß, Anna Christina	11, Jan. 1894	27, Oct.	47	Panke	30	Louisville, KY	Louisville, Jefferson County, Kentucky
Heß, Anna Maria Magdalena	29, Jan. 1857	24, Nov.	35		20		
Heß, Christian Ludwig	10, Dec. 1896	19, Apr.	91- 3m		798		Ogersheim, Ludwigshafen, Rheinpfalz Baiern
Heß, Dorothea Catharina	9, June 1887	23, Feb.	85	Schmidt	366	Spraytown, IN	Mackensen, Hannover
Heß, Elisabeth	10, Mar. 1879	8, Jan.	63-11m-7d	Konrad	79	Bloomington, IL	Hüffweiler, Rheinpfalz Baiern
Heß, Elisabeth	5, Feb. 1883	30, Oct.	69	Schüler	47	Clayton, WI	Mandeln, Dillenburg, Nassau
Heß, Elisabeth	5, Jan. 1874	17, Mar.	71		7	Galveston, TX	Storbeck, Preußen
Heß, Elisabeth	13, May 1897	13, Apr.	36- 5m-23d	Eck	303	Canton, MO	Lambach, Baiern
Heß, Elisabeth M.	2, May 1895	20, Dec.	30	Ahrens	286	Lake Side, OH	
Heß, Emma	9, Jan. 1896	11, June	19	Ruegg	30	Hoboken, NJ	Bubikow, Zürich, Schweiz
Heß, Franziska	25, June 1896	26, July	17		104	Portsmouth, OH	
Heß, Friedrich	17, Aug. 1854	18, Apr.	16		132	Roseville, MI	Okersheim, Ludwigshafen, Rheinpfalz Baiern
Heß, Georg	1, May 1890	24, Mar.	53- -20d		286	Louisville, KY	Nidda, Hessen
Heß, Georg	20, Apr. 1868				127	Columbus, IL	

Christliche Apologete Death Notices --- 1839 - 1899

Name of Deceased	Notice Date	Death Date	Age	Maiden Name	Page	Place of Death	Place of Birth
Heß, Georg	22, May 1876	11, Apr.	26		167	Baltimore, MD	
Heß, Heinrich	17, Aug. 1854	30, July	29		132	Roseville, MI	Harxheim, Rheinkreis Baiern
Heß, Henry	7, Mar. 1889	6, Feb.	62		158	Scranton, PA	
Heß, J. Christoph	17, Aug. 1854	28, July	67		132	Roseville, MI	Bleichenbach, Nidda, Hessen
Heß, Johan Heinrich	10, Jan. 1870	12, Dec.	78		15	Louisville, KY	Reutlingen, Württemberg
Heß, Johan Jacob	26, Mar. 1866	10, Mar.	18		102	Philadelphia, PA	Württemberg
Heß, John	15, Jan. 1877	3, Dec.	69		23	White Creek, IN	Three Oaks, Michigan
Heß, John L.	25, July 1889	22, June	25		478	Laporte, IN	Bleichenbach, Lüdingen, Hessen-Darmstadt
Heß, Jonas	8, Dec. 1898	16, Nov.	81		783	Louisville, KY	Bleichenbach, Hessen-Darmstadt
Heß, Jonas	2, Nov. 1893	13, Oct.	70		702	Canton, MO	
Heß, Jonas	11, Apr. 1889	15, Mar.	29		238	Canton, MO	Bleichenbach, Nidda, Hessen-Darmstadt
Heß, Katharina	12, May 1859	9, Apr.	64- 9m- 7d	Mägley	76	Kingston, IL	Cincinnati, Hamilton County, Ohio
Heß, Katharina	25, Sept 1882	16, Sept	36- 9m-26d		311	Cincinnati, OH	Freaking, Baiern
Heß, Leonhard	24, Aug. 1893	28, July	66		542	Newark, NJ	Grünstadt, Baiern
Heß, Magdalena	27, Oct. 1873	10, Oct.	55		343	Columbus, IL	New Jersey
Heß, Margaretha	10, Oct. 1870	24, Sept	35	Steuernagel	327	Scranton, PA	
Heß, Margaretha Louise	4, May 1868	16, Apr.	22		143	Louisville, KY	Relbehausen, Kurhessen
Heß, Maria	5, May 1892	11, Mar.	72		286	Giard, IA	Bleichenbach, Hessen
Heß, Maria	25, Sept 1856	18, Aug.	23	Renn	156	Quincy, IL	Maßbach, Baiern
Heß, Maria	19, May 1898	28, Apr.	61		319	Freeport, IL	
Heß, Marie	17, Aug. 1854	26, July	57		132	Roseville, MI	Bleichenbach, Hessen-Darmstadt
Heß, Martha Emmeline	2, Feb. 1880	12, Jan.	1- 5m-24d		39	Halstead, KS	Pekin, Illinois
Heß, Philipp	12, Feb. 1883	28, Jan.	59- 2m-15d		55	Columbus, ---	Brenekenstein, Preußen
Heß, Wilhelm	29, Nov. 1888	3, Nov.	22		766	Pekin, IL	Liberty, Missouri
Hesse, Karl Wilhelm	21, Jan. 1884	9, Jan.	65		7	Chicago, IL	Kearny, Clay County, Missouri
Hessel, Bertha Drusilla	16, Apr. 1896	21, Mar.	28	Weber	254	Arley, MO	Neu-Baiern, Germany
Hessel, Jakob	8, Oct. 1883	15, Sept	25- 4m-18d		327	Baltimore, MD	
Hessel, Jakob	29, Aug. 1881	12, Aug.	57		279	Liberty, MO	
Hessel, Marie	8, Nov. 1875	13, Oct.	17		359	Liberty, MO	
Hesselbacher, Carolina	21, June 1855	26, Jan.	4		100	Baltimore, MD	Meiston, Kalb, Württemberg
Hesselschwerdt, Jakob	27, Dec. 1894	22, Nov.	66		836	Chelsea, MI	Posey County, Indiana
Hessenauer, Andreas	21, May 1896		28		334	Salem, IN	Hummersen, Lippe
Hessenauer, Dorothea	30, Sept 1858	7, Sept	45- 7m- 7d	Mühlenbein	156	Mt. Vernon, IN	Lohbach, Hasserstatter, Künzelsau, Württemberg
Hessennauer, Georg H.	19, Dec. 1881	2, Dec.	69- 8m-23d		407	Marrs, IN	
Hesser, Carl	24, Nov. 1843	12, Oct.	35-11m- 7d		187	Northumberland Co, PA	Clinbach, Elsaß
Hessig, Georg	11, Aug. 1898	10, May	72		511	Santa Claus, IN	Heiningen, Göppingen, Württemberg
Heßler, Gottlieb	7, June 1894	24, Apr.	65		374	Grand Rapids, MI	Neunstetten, Krautheim, Baden
Heßlöhl, Barbara	6, Sept 1869	28, Aug.	36- 6m- 5d		287	Cincinnati, OH	
Heßlöhl, Georg	28, Aug. 1890	14, Aug.	76- - 8d		558	Cincinnati, OH	
Heßner, Katharina	29, July 1878	13, June	77- 1m-13d		239	Allegheny City, PA	Weisenheim, Dürkheim, RheinPfalz Baiern
Hetsch, Heinrich	19, Nov. 1883	5, Nov.	76		375	Newport, KY	Waisenheim, Dürheim,
Hetsch, Johannes	12, Feb. 1891	19, Jan.	65- 6m- 2d		110	Newport, KY	
Hetsch, Samuel	6, Feb. 1890	17, Jan.	22		94	Newport, KY	Baden
Hettinger, Georg	5, Nov. 1865	13, Sept	56		180	Muscatine, IA	Hessen-Darmstadt
Hettinger, Margarethe	2, Oct. 1856	13, Sept	46	Buck	160	Muscatine, IA	Unterhambach, Hessen-Darmstadt
Hettinger, Philipp	21, Nov. 1864	3, Aug.	25- 4m		188	Muscatine, IA	

Christliche Apologete Death Notices --- 1839 - 1899

Name of Deceased	Notice Date	Death Date	Age	Maiden Name	Page	Place of Death	Place of Birth
Hetzel, Georg	9, May 1895	17, Apr.	62		302	Milwaukee, WI	Archenthal, Simmern, Coblenz, Preußen
Hetzel, Georg J.	23, July 1891	6, July	30		478	Sinton, PA	
Hetzel, Jacob	7, Apr. 1887	22, Mar.	63		222	Evansville, IN	Röthenberg, Oberndorf, Württemberg
Hetzel, Lizzie	21, Feb. 1881	19, Jan.	17- 4m-27d		63	Scranton, PA	
Hetzel, Paul	22, Dec. 1859	10, Nov.	34		204	Highland, IL	Winseln, Oberndorf, Württemberg
Hetzemann, Christina	27, Aug. 1866	18, Aug.	73		278	Cincinnati, OH	Neuenknick, Windheim, Minden, Preußen
Hetzemann, Friedrich	2, June 1862	5, May	69		88	Cincinnati, OH	
Heubach, Elisabeth Margaretha	6, Sept 1869	22, Aug.	71- 9m-26d		287	Louisville, KY	Beutelsbach, Schorndorf, Württemberg
Heuckendorff, Herman	19, Aug. 1886	3, Aug.	37		7	Denton, TX	Hamburg, Germany
Heuduck, Elisabeth	1, June 1863	12, May	24		88	Nashville, IL	Söllingen, Amt Denbach, Baden
Heuer, Anna Maria	18, Nov. 1886	25, Oct.	74		7	Blue Island, IL	Hömmel, Heide, Nord-Ditmarschen, Preußen
Heuer, Auguste	3, Feb. 1873	11, Dec.	44	Küster	39	Alton, IL	
Heuer, Auguste	4, June 1891	13, May	33-10m-18d	Dreger	366	Oshkosh, WI	Jarrenwisch, Schleswig-Holstein
Heuer, Detlef	20, Dec. 1888	20, Nov.	69		814	Blue Island, IL	Warnitz, Gardelegen, Preußen
Heuer, Friedrich Wilhelm Herman	19, Apr. 1888	24, Mar.	25		254	Dodgeville, IA	
Heuer, Heinrich	24, Apr. 1882	24, Mar.	60		135	Brighton, IL	
Heuer, John Bernard	30, Mar. 1863	8, Oct.	32		52	Alton, IL	Bippen, Hannover
Heuer, Louis	3, Aug. 1899	17, July	42		495	Brighton, IL	Fosterburg, Madison County, Illinois
Heuer, Sophia	10, July 1865	12, June			112	Manitowoc, WI	Schönhagel, Naugard, Preußen
Heukel, Anna Barbara	5, July 1880	21, June	56-10m-26d	König	215	Wyandotte, KS	Menschausen, Kurhessen
Heuschen, Friedrich Wilhelm	2, Apr. 1891	16, Feb.	20- 8m-12d		222	Nokomis, IL	
Heuser, Anna Margaretha	3, July 1890	14, June	82- 9m-26d	Demond	430	Nashville, TN	Hessen-Darmstadt
Heuser, Jacob	6, Jan. 1887	18, Dec.	81-10m		14	Nashville, TN	Niederweißel, Hessen-Darmstadt
Heuser, Johannes	24, Dec. 1891	27, Nov.	33		830	Louisville, KY	
Heuser, Margaretha	16, Dec. 1886	8, Nov.	30	Schmidt	7	Bradford, IN	Neuweiler, Elsaß
Heuser, Wilhelm	26, Nov. 1877	29, Oct.	46		383	St. Louis, MO	Holthausen, Müllheim an der Ruhr, Preußen
Heusi, Georg	26, May 1892	3, May	62-11m-20d		334	Laporte, IN	Kur, Schweiz
Heusi, Johan	4, Aug. 1884	18, July	62- 5m-23d		7	Denver, CO	
Heusi, Johannes	18, Dec. 1856	30, Nov.	36- 1m-23d		204	Nauvoo, IL	Canton Schaffhausen, Schweiz
Heusi, Katharina	2, Apr. 1891	11, Mar.	67		222	Chicago, IL	Schleitheim, Schaffhausen, Schweiz
Heusler, Maria	16, June 1898	24, May	50- 8m-11d	Hummel	383	Chicago, IL	Eblingen, Württemberg
Heusner, Barbara Elisabeth	1, May 1871	8, Apr.	43		143	St. Louis, MO	Schenglengsfeld, Kurhessen
Heusner, Georg L.	19, Nov. 1891	27, Oct.	19		750	Clay Center, KS	St. Louis, Missouri
Heussel, Ludwig	15, July 1872	19, June	42-11m		231	St. Louis, MO	Schenklengsfeld, Kurhessen
Heussel, Margaretha	27, Oct. 1873	7, Oct.	22		343	Mascoutah, IL	
Heußner, Adam	13, Apr. 1893	11, Mar.	72- 9m- 6d		238	Henrietta, OH	Kalckobes, Kurhessen
Heußner, Johan Adam	29, Jan. 1883	5, Dec.	35- 4m-16d		39	S. Amherst, OH	
Heußner, Maria Elisabeth	16, June 1879	17, May	26- 2m- 1d		191	Henrietta, OH	
Heußner, Martha Elisabeth	27, Feb. 1890	31, Jan.	18		142	Frankfort, IL	
Heverly, Christina	12, Aug. 1878	10, July	67- 8m-13d	Miller	255	Winchester, OH	New Lenox, Illinois
Hey, Clementina	19, May 1888	22, Apr.	66		318	Sterling, IL	Württemberg
Heybach, Esther	8, Dec. 1898	20, Nov.	55		783	Newport, KY	Oberkreis , Baden
Heybeck, Friedrich	16, Nov. 1863	18, Sept	45		184	Batesville, IN	Wilhelmsdorf, Baiern
Heyde, Albert	24, Aug. 1874	3, Aug.	74		273	Mascoutah, IL	Dispeck, Neustadt an der Eich, Baiern
Heyde, Anna M.	3, Feb. 1879		54- 8m- 4d		39	Mascoutah, IL	Dresden, Sachsen
Heyer, Adam	31, July 1882	15, July	42- 5m-11d		247	Colesburg, IA	Walhausen, Preußen
							Gersdorf, Hirschfeld, Kurhessen

Christliche Apologete Death Notices --- 1839 - 1899

Name of Deceased	Notice Date	Death Date	Age	Maiden Name	Page	Place of Death	Place of Birth
Heyer, Charlotte	6, July 1868	19, June	33	Wehmeyer	215	Cincinnati, OH	Wehnen, Kreis Lipke, Preußen
Heyer, Christina	9, June 1853		24	Lang	92	Jackson, MO	Igis, Graubündten, Schweiz
Heyer, Dorothea	29, Nov. 1875	24, Sept	75		383	Third Creek, MO	Stapelnburg, Preußen
Heyer, Jakob	28, May 1877	13, May	46		175	New Knoxville, OH	Enzweihingen, Maulbronn, Württemberg
Heyer, Peter	4, Feb. 1892	15, Jan.	15		78	Brighton, IL	Hille, Münden, Preußen
Heyer, Th. (Mrs)	3, July 1856	6, May	28- 6m	Waßmann	108	Vandalia, IL	
Heyer, Thomas	20, Aug. 1891	4, July	48		542	Brighton, IL	Dobern, Benzen, Kreis Leibaer, Böhmen
Hickel, Theresa	6, July 1863	3, May	23	Ritschel	108	LaCrosse, WI	Güntersdorf, Bensen, Böhmen
Hickel, Theresia	21, July 1879	6, July	75		231	LaCrosse, WI	Gensdorf, Böhmen
Hickisch, Theresa	2, July 1896	12, June	46		431	Lansing, MI	Wolferborn, Kurhessen
Hicks, Johan	29, Nov. 1880	25, Oct.	46		383	Odebolt, IA	Groß-Niedersheim, Rheinkreis Baiern
Hieber, Eva	4, Oct. 1888	22, Sept	51- 7m-26d	Schmahl	638	Baltimore, MD	Lehnenberg, Waiblingen, Württemberg
Hieber, Johanna	11, Feb. 1886	29, Jan.	80	Doberer	7	Cincinnati, OH	Dippach, Hofheim, Baiern
Hieck, John	7, Aug. 1890	12, July	64		510	Bland, MO	Großjober, Bensen, Böhmen
Hiekel, Francisca	15, Feb. 1894	24, Jan.	66	Werner	110	LaCrosse, WI	Stephanshausen, Nassau
Hierholzer, Magdalene	10, Nov. 1898	22, Oct.	60	Arnold	719	Bracken, TX	Schillersdorf, Elsaß
Hieronimus, Catharina	5, Dec. 1870	24, Oct.	66 - 6d	Merkling	391	Boston, MA	Posey County, Indiana
Hieronimus, Elisabeth	31, May 1888	23, Mar.	24	Beste	350	Mt. Vernon, IN	Elberfeld, Preußen
Hieronimus, Lisette	26, Apr. 1880	9, Apr.	60		135	Mt. Vernon, IN	
Hieronimus, Michael	3, Sept 1883	21, Aug.	82		287	Boston, MA	Oberniederberg, Hessen-Nassau
Hieronimus, Philipp	8, Oct. 1883	24, Sept	58-10m- 3d		327	Mt. Vernon, IN	Oberstetten, Gerabronn, Württemberg
Hiersch, Philipp	25, Sept 1851	24, Aug.	31- 6m		156	Platteville, WI	Suhr, Aargau, Schweiz
Hilbe, Verena	13, May 1897	27, Apr.	66	Vogel	303	Chicago, IL	Neu-Lusheim, Schwetzing, Baden
Hilbert, Eva Margaretha	12, Nov. 1891	17, Oct.	69	Langloz	734	Higginsport, OH	Cincinnati, Hamilton County, Ohio
Hilbert, Rosina	7, Jan. 1886	24, Dec.	28-10m-14d		7	Higginsport, OH	Burlington, Iowa
Hilburn, Emilia H.	26, May 1879	8, May	27	Walther	167	Quincy, IL	Rushville, Pennsylvania
Hild, Elisabeth	11, Apr. 1895	19, Mar.	74	Staufer	238	Chillicothe, OH	Lehnbach, Elsaß
Hild, Elisabeth	15, Nov. 1875	29, Oct.	81	Treiber	367	Louisville, KY	
Hildebrand, Andreas	7, Aug. 1865	24, Apr.	13		128	Louisville, KY	Stockton, Pennsylvania
Hildebrand, Anna Katharina	23, Apr. 1896	11, Mar.	21		270	Passaic, NJ	Hürbe, Waldeck
Hildebrand, Christian	20, Aug. 1883	3, Aug.	70		271	Ida Grove, IA	Nevensen, Moringen-Hardegsen, Hannover
Hildebrand, Friederika	6, Sept 1888	6, Aug.	67- 3m- 2d		574	Cannon River, MN	Mittelhausen, Rudelstädt, Sachsen-Weimar
Hildebrand, Friedrich Wilhelm J.	13, Nov. 1876	25, Oct.	50		367	Madison, WI	Aldenbuch,
Hildebrand, Georg	3, July 1851	9, June	17- 8m- 9d		108	St. Louis, MO	Magdeburg, Preußen
Hildebrand, Ida Friederika	1, July 1878	15, June	57	Brachvogel	207	Woodbine, IL	
Hildebrand, John	7, Aug. 1865	17, Apr.	19		128	Louisville, KY	New Rochelle, New York
Hildebrand, John Adam	14, June 1894	28, May	33		390	New Rochelle, NY	Walbrechthausen, Hannover
Hildebrand, Karl	21, Jan. 1892	1, Jan.	81		46	Nerstrand, MN	Ober-Maßfeld, Sachsen-Meiningen
Hildebrand, Ottilie	11, Feb. 1867	25, Jan.	67	Spieß	46	Burlington, IA	Niederweisel, Freiberg, Hessen-Darmstadt
Hildebrand, Wenzel	28, Aug. 1890	2, Aug.	73		558	Bradford, IN	Schönau vor dem Walde, Sachsen-Coburg
Hildebrandt,	17, Mar. 1892	15, Feb.	63		174	Granger, MO	Tattenitz, Oesterreich
Hildebrandt, Franz	25, Nov. 1897	29, Oct.	50		751	Corder, MO	Prairie Creek, Rice County, Minnesota
Hildebrandt, Friedrich	24, Aug. 1899	31, July	24		543	Cannon River, MN	Hevensen, Moringen, Hannover
Hildebrandt, John	23, Mar. 1893	10, Feb.	80		190	Nerstrand, MN	Lillebeck, Lippe-Detmold
Hildebrandt, Louise Wilhelmine	30, June 1879	15, June		Holste	207	Farmington, WI	Dürnau, Göppingen, Württemberg
Hildenbrand, Charlotte	14, Feb. 1856	2, Jan.	32		28	Arenzville, IL	

Christliche Apologete Death Notices --- 1839 - 1899

Name of Deceased	Notice Date	Death Date	Age	Maiden Name	Page	Place of Death	Place of Birth
Hildenbrand, Fritz	10, Aug. 1885	27, July	34		7	Lancaster, WI	Ittlingen, Eppingen, Baden
Hildenbrand, Louis	10, May 1888	24, Mar.	34		302	Brooklyn, NY	West Hoboken, New Jersey
Hildenbrand, Louise	1, Dec. 1892	5, Nov.	31		766	Lancaster, NY	Brooklyn, New York
Hildenbrand, Margarethe	29, Aug. 1850	12, Aug.	31		140	Louisville, KY	
Hildenbrandt, Elisabeth	24, Nov. 1862	13, Oct.	36		188	Williamsburg, NY	Herschberg, Rheinpfalz Baiern
Hildenbrandt, Joseph	21, Oct. 1897	4, Oct.	68		671	Jacksonville, IL	Oberkirch, Baden
Hildesheimer, Georg	1, Sept 1892	16, Aug.	83		558	Newark, NJ	Coppebrigge, Hannover
Hildesheimer, Louisa	10, Nov. 1879	26, Sept			359	Newark, NJ	
Hilfinger, Christina	28, Dec. 1874	9, Dec.	64	Haller	415	Buffalo, NY	Schenningen, Rottweil, Württemberg
Hilfinger, John	17, Nov. 1862	1, Oct.	25		184	Buffalo, NY	
Hilfinger, Martin	6, Feb. 1871	18, Jan.	60		47	Buffalo, NY	Schwenningen, Rottweil, Württemberg
Hilge, Wilhelm	14, July 1862	16, June	25		112	Edwardsville, IL	Tecklenburg, Preußen
Hilgedick, Alexander	23, Aug. 1888	7, Aug.	32- 7m-18d		542	Minneapolis, MN	Ramsey County, Minnesota
Hilgedick, Conrad	6, Jan. 1868	15, Dec.	73		6	Salem, MN	Lienen, Preußen
Hilgedick, Friderika	5, Aug. 1878	22, July	53	Bartelmeier	247	Staunton, IL	Lienen, Preußen
Hilgedick, Heinrich	27, May 1878	7, Apr.	36- 5m		167		Lienen, Warendorf, Münster, Preußen
Hilgedick, Maria	3, Dec. 1883	20, Nov.	71- 9m-20d		391	Minneapolis, MN	Tecklenburg, Münster, Preußen
Hilgedick, Rudolph	7, Oct. 1878		55		319	Staunton, IL	
Hilgedick, Sarah	19, Mar. 1883	15, Feb.	18		95	Minneapolis, MN	
Hilgemann, Christina Elisabeth	20, Aug. 1877	1, Aug.	76-10m-20d		271	Huntingburg, IN	Ladbergen, Preußen
Hilgemann, Rudolph	10, July 1846		20		111	New Orleans, LA	Liengen, Warendorf, Preußen
Hilgemann, Sophie	12, Nov. 1847	28, Aug.	26		183	New Orleans, LA	
Hilgen, Wilhelmine Katharine	9, June 1892	1, May	32	Gieseler	366	Milwaukee, WI	Milwaukee, Wisconsin
Hilgenberg, Elizabeth	27, Mar. 1890	14, Feb.	72	Herwig	206	Moweaqua, IL	Gensungen, Felsburg, Melzungen, Kurhessen
Hilgenberg, Heinrich	5, Feb. 1883	11, Jan.	73- 6m-11d		47	Moweaqua, IL	Gensungen, Melzungen, Felsberg, Kurhessen
Hilgenberg, Martin	12, Jan. 1899	12, Dec.	24		31	St. Paul, MN	Kassel, Hessen
Hilgenberg, Wilhelm	28, Feb. 1870	12, Feb.	30- 7m-10d		71	Springfield, IL	Gessungen, Kurhessen
Hilgendorf, Johanna Dorothea	28, May 1891	5, May	67	Schwichtenberg	350	Elkport, IA	Naugarten, Pommern
Hilke, Elisabeth	13, Oct. 1892	25, Sept			654	Baltimore, MD	
Hilkemann, Maria Chr.	7, Dec. 1863	15, Nov.	19- 2m	Storck	196	Evansville, IN	Ladbergen, Preußen
Hilker, Anton Friedrich Eduard	6, Mar. 1890	11, Feb.	62		158	Watertown, WI	Barntrup, Lippe-Detmold
Hilker, Charlotte	3, Dec. 1866	25, Nov.	32- 5m		390	Covington, KY	Lippe-Detmold
Hilker, Freddie	3, June 1886	5, May	14		7	Denver, CO	Cincinnati, Hamilton County, Ohio
Hilker, Friederike	19, Dec. 1889	30, Nov.	55- 2m- 3d	Saak	814	Indianapolis, IN	Hohenhausen, Lippe-Detmold
Hilker, Heinrich	7, June 1888	11, May	53- 4m-18d		366	Indianapolis, IN	Asendorf, Lippe-Detmold
Hilker, Lulu	19, Dec. 1895	29, Nov.	27		814	Covington, KY	Covington, Kenton County, Kentucky
Hilker, Simon August	20, Jan. 1887	7, Jan.	49		46	Covington, KY	Asendorf, Hohnhausen, Lippe-Detmold
Hill, Anna Barbara	30, Oct. 1876	14, Oct.	51- 8m-21d	Speidel	351	Covington, KY	Bodelshausen, Württemberg
Hill, Heinrich	30, July 1857	12, June	36		124	Jackson, MO	Nordasse, Braunschweig
Hill, Katharine Dorothea	4, Feb. 1892	16, Jan.	42	Enz	78	Decorah, IA	Doffingen, Boblingen, Württemberg
Hill, Susanna M.	15, Jan. 1877	26, Dec.	82- 7m-22d	Reichenbach	23	Roberts, IL	Asbach, Sachsen-Coburg-Gotha
Hille, (Mrs)	27, Feb. 1865	29, Jan.	60		36	Cape Girardeau, MO	Blumberg, Salter, Braunschweig
Hille, Frank	22, May 1882	8, May	40- 4m- 2d		167	New Orleans, LA	Lingen, Hannover
Hille, Heinrich	15, Sept 1873	5, Aug.	76		295	Jackson, MO	Nordassel, Braunschweig
Hillebrand, Friedrich	15, Sept 1879	1, Sept	68		295	Freeport, IL	Barenholz, Lippe-Detmold
Hillebrand, Henriette	21, Sept 1885	3, Sept	32-11m- 8d	Meyer	7	Boody, IL	Ohlendorf, Liebenburg, Hannover

Christliche Apologete Death Notices --- 1839 - 1899

Name of Deceased	Notice Date	Death Date	Age	Page	Maiden Name	Place of Death	Place of Birth
Hillebrandt, Caroline	5, Dec. 1895	13, Nov.	78	782	Bürgersmeier	Freeport, IL	Varenholz, Lippe-Detmold
Hillebrenner, Friedrich	9, May 1861	15, Feb.	35	76		Perry, IL	Kriegerheide, Schöppner, Lippe-Detmold
Hiller, Johan	13, June 1881	13, May	40	191		Industry, TX	Gursewo, Grewitz, Posen
Hiller, Johan David	29, July 1886	9, July	68	7		Minneapolis, MN	Dembogora bei Exin, Posen
Hiller, Sigmund	16, Feb. 1880	2, Feb.	62- 9m-13d	55		Muscatine, IA	Radolphzell, Baden
Hillerns, Ense	2, Aug. 1894	10, July	55	502	Glassen	Osceola, NE	Ochtersum, Ostfriesland
Hillmann, Ernestine	5, Feb. 1891	15, Jan.	52- 6m-21d	94	Stöcker	Bay City, MI	Pebenow, Mecklenburg-Schwerin
Hillme, Julius	24, Apr. 1882	30, Mar.	52- 7m-13d	135		Pittsburg, PA	Löbau, Sachsen
Hillmer, Christine	28, July 1884	19, May	61	7		Lena, IL	Streckhausen, Oevergonne, Oldenburg
Hilmer, Friedrich	18, Feb. 1886	19, Jan.	59	7		Gladbrook, IA	Steinbergen, Lippe-Schaumburg
Hilmer, Johan Heinrich Christophel	6, May 1886	23, Mar.	73	7		St. Paul, NE	Kirchweihe, Oldenstadt, Hannover
Hilmes, Anna Catharina	19, Jan. 1888	22, Dec.	70	46		Chicago, IL	Witzenhausen, Hessen-Kassel
Hilmes, Maria K.	21, May 1891	28, Apr.	33	334	Breidert	Chicago, IL	Chicago, Cook County, Illinois
Hilmes, Martha	21, July 1887	6, July	32	462	Wilk	Chicago, IL	Harmutsachlen, Kurhessen
Hilmes, Philipp	27, Aug. 1891	24, July	18- 9m	558		Omaha, NE	Bunker Hill, Illinois
Hils, Emma	15, May 1890	13, Mar.	22	318		Danville, IL	Covington, Indiana
Hils, Helene	22, Sept 1879	1, Sept	69	303		New York City, NY	
Hilscher, Karl	22, Oct. 1896	25, Sept	70	687		Enterprise, KS	Wenigrakovitz, Schlesien
Hilsemann, Heinrich Eduard	5, May 1879	19, Apr.	29- 7m -5d	143		Evansville, IN	Westerwisch bei Hamburg, Germany
Hilsenbeck, Sophia Elisabeth	29, May 1882	16, May	19- 8m- 6d	175		Colesburg, IA	Dover, Bureau County, Illinois
Hilsmann, Sophia Katharina	15, July 1872	18, Apr.	53	231		New Orleans, LA	Lienen, Preußen
Hilti, Bartholomäus	5, Dec. 1864	17, Nov.	56- 6m-12d	196		Highland, IL	
Hilti, Elisabeth	9, Mar. 1899	14, Feb.	61- 9m- 8d	159	Tischhauser	Highland, IL	
Hilti, Johannes	1, Mar. 1894	8, Feb.	72	150		Highland, IL	Grabs, St. Gallen, Schweiz
Hilti, Margaretha	28, July 1879	10, July	67	239	Schlegel	Highland, IL	Grab, Werdenberg, St. Gallen, Schweiz
Himmler, Georg	1, Mar. 1875	8, Feb.	55	71		Seymour, IN	Gembronn, Württemberg
Himstedt, Christine	4, Feb. 1884	15, Jan.	28-10m-28d	7		Quincy, IL	Ft. Madison, Iowa
Himstedt, Karl	16, May 1889	30, Apr.	70- 5m-26d	318		Papillion, NE	Hoheneggelien, Steinbrück, Hannover
Himstedt, Rosamunda	20, Feb. 1896	3, Nov.	76	126	Grobe	Papillion, IA	Hoheneggelsen, Hannover
Hinde, Alice	29, Nov. 1888	3, Nov.	76- 9m- 8d	766		Sherrills Mount, IA	Ince, England
Hinde, Jane	13, Mar. 1890	14, Feb.	80- 1m	174		Sherrills Mount, IA	Isle of Man, England
Hinde, Thomas	15, May 1890	9, Apr.	54	318		Sherrills Mount, IA	Ince, Cheshire, England
Hinderer, Marie Friederike	29, Sept 1884	16, Sept	90- 8m-22d	7	Plagge	Columbus, OH	Oberwelten, Württemberg
Hink, Wilhelmine	29, Nov. 1888	4, Nov.	33	766	Müller	Gordonville, MO	Cape Girardeau County, Missouri
Hinke, Gesche Margaretha Sophia	6, Aug. 1896	9, Apr.	38	511		Mayville, WI	Groß Sotrum, Rothenburg, Hannover
Hinkel, Katharine	4, Feb. 1867	13, Jan.		38		Lafayette, IN	Bocklet, Baiern
Hinken, Tipke	22, Sept 1892	20, Aug.	88- 6m	606	Possels	German Creek, IA	Wilstedt, Ottersberg, Hannover
Hinnah, Wilhelm	14, Nov. 1881	27, Oct.	17-10m-18d	367		Waco, TX	Indianapolis, Marion County, Indiana
Hinnant, Mathilde Wilhelmine	18, Aug. 1892	29, July	20	526	Schneider	Petersburg, IL	Oldendorf, Amt Zeven, Hannover
Hinners, Anna	19, Feb. 1857	2, Dec.	66	32	Ditmer	Arenzville, IL	Badenstadt, Amt Zeven, Hannover
Hinners, Heinrich	16, Dec. 1867	18, Nov.	36	398		Meredosia, IL	Budenstedt, Hannover
Hinners, John	28, Feb. 1895	8, Feb.	67	142		Pekin, IL	Bentzin, Vorpommern
Hinners, Wilhelmine	26, Nov. 1891	6, Nov.	41	766	Witt	New Orleans, LA	Norden, Ostfriesland
Hinrichs, Tjark	9, May 1895	20, Apr.	53	302		Brooklyn, NY	Oldenburg
Hinsch, Friederike	3, May 1894	16, Apr.	48	294	Oehlmann	Brooklyn, NY	New York
Hinsch, William	6, Dec. 1894	16, Nov.	24	790		Brooklyn, NY	

Christliche Apologete Death Notices --- 1839 - 1899

Name of Deceased	Notice Date	Death Date	Age	Page	Maiden Name	Place of Death	Place of Birth
Hinske, Daniel	10, Oct. 1881	17, Sept	77- 6m- 4d	327		Sun Prairie, WI	Pompow, Pieritz, Pommern
Hinter, Johan Zacharias	30, Jan. 1896	5, Jan.	68	78		Hokah, MN	Wyl, Schweiz
Hintz, August	24, Aug. 1863		18- 3m	136		Watertown, WI	Neudorf, Posen, Preußen
Hintz, Henrietta Christina Maria	22, July 1897		73	463	Warnke	Grand Rapids, MI	Wismar, Mecklenburg
Hintz, Karl	24, Mar. 1892	28, Feb.	61	190		Chicago, IL	Rogatz, Stolp, Kößlin, Pommern
Hintz, Wilhelmina	15, Feb. 1894	21, Jan.	81	110		Oshkosh, WI	Altgurkhofsbauch, Neumark
Hintzen, Emilie	5, Feb. 1866	13, Jan.	28- 6m-21d	46		Louisville, KY	Ohio
Hintzen, Johan Heinrich	7, Feb. 1881	17, Jan.	80- 6m-17d	47		Louisville, KY	Rheidt, Düsseldorf, Preußen
Hintzmann, Maria	16, July 1896	15, June	65	463		Menomonie, WI	Replin, Piritz, Preußen
Hintzmann, Michael Friedrich	10, Oct. 1889	14, Sept	61- 8m-12d	654		Menomonie, WI	Pitznick, Pommern
Hinz, Adeline Malvine	22, Sept 1898	30, Aug.	29	607		Willow City, ND	DeBänke, Bromberg, Posen
Hinz, Johan	14, Feb. 1889	15, Jan.	83- 5m-11d	110		Zumbro Falls, MN	Niemdorf bei Lübeck, Germany
Hinz, Johanna	10, Sept 1891	12, July	64	590		Almond, WI	Barko, Pommern
Hinze, Caroline Christine W.	3, Nov. 1892		82	702	Friederich	Eustis, NE	Labes, Regenwalde, Pommern
Hinze, Michael Friedrich	4, Feb. 1884	17, Jan.	75	7		Oxford, NE	Kunow, Regenwalde, Pommern
Hinzen, Maria S.	5, Sept 1864	11, Aug.	66	144		Wapello, IA	Rheidt, Düsseldorf, Preußen
Hinzmann, Maria Wilhelmine	20, Mar. 1876	29, Feb.	42	95	Witt	Oconomowoc, WI	Petznick, Stettin, Preußen
Hippen, Anna Christine	23, July 1891	4, July	75	478	Jans	Pekin, IL	Auri, Ostfriesland
Hirn, Regina	28, Feb. 1881	19, Dec.	72	71		San Francisco, CA	
Hirny, Jacob	19, Aug. 1858	30, July	46	132		Canal Dover, OH	Armille, Bern, Schweiz
Hirs, Maria Margaretha	18, May 1893		28	318	Schmid	Bern, SW	
Hirsch, Albert Oscar	10, Sept 1891	22, Aug.	15	590		Lemars, IA	Charles City, Iowa
Hirsch, Anna	19, Apr. 1875	1, Apr.	16- -22d	127		Charles City, IA	
Hirsch, Bertha Augusta	27, June 1881	5, June	23- 4m- 3d	207	Doege	Alden, IA	Neuwerder bei Kolberg, Köslin, Hinterpommern
Hirsch, Catharina	8, Aug. 1861	21, July	31	128	Haag	Kewaskum, WI	Auerbach, Durlach, Baden
Hirsch, Dora	6, July 1899	4, June	59	431		Louisville, KY	Emmendingen, Baden
Hirsch, Friedrich	19, Apr. 1888	25, Mar.	79	254		Eldora, IA	Mannhagen, Lübeck, Schleswig-Holstein
Hirschberger, Georg	5, Nov. 1891	24- 6m- 2d		718		Bucyrus, OH	Crawford County, Ohio
Hirschberger, Gottfried	15, Mar. 1875	20, Feb.	80- -10d	87		German Creek, IA	Rothensohl, Württemberg
Hirschberger, Rosa	29, Apr. 1897	4, Apr.	29	271	Schultheis	Cincinnati, OH	Hainweiher, Baiern
Hirschbiehl, Louise Wilhelmina	3, May 1880	7, Apr.	17- 7m-24d	143		Danville, IL	
Hirschbiel, Juliane	5, Nov. 1866	23, Oct.	64- 2m-23d	385	Dreher	Cincinnati, OH	Annweiler, Rheinpfalz, Baiern
Hirschbrenner, Margaretha	18, Sept 1871	29, Aug.	63	303	Bielmann	Canal Dover, OH	Groß Hochstattin, Schloßweil, Schweiz
Hirschel, Heinrich	10, Sept 1877	25, Aug.	58	295		Roberts, IL	Riegen, Umstadt, Hessen-Darmstadt
Hirschelmann, Elisabeth	1, Aug. 1850	14, July	27- 7m-12d	124		Evansville, IN	Bechtheim, Hessen-Darmstadt
Hirschelmann, Regina	4, May 1868	29, Mar.	88	143		St. Peters, IN	Erlingshausen, Rheinpfalz Baiern
Hirschinger, (Mr)	14, Apr. 1853	20, Mar.	67	60		Baraboo, WI	Elsaß
Hirschinger, Saloma	22, Mar. 1880	29, Feb.	82-11m-19d	95		Baraboo, WI	Malzthal, Währt, Elsaß
Hirschinger, Salome	11, June 1866	14, May	28	190	Nippert	Wingville, WI	Ohio
Hirschleber, Julius	21, Sept 1893	29, Aug.	68	606			Illeben, Sachsen-Gotha
Hirschvogel, Michael	17, Nov. 1879	3, Oct.	79	367		Lake Creek, MO	Wallem, Oesterreich
Hirt , Jacob	25, Mar. 1858	25, Feb.	67	48		St. Louis, MO	
Hirt, Cary	27, Jan. 1879	14, Dec.	12	31		Quincy, IL	
Hirt, Jackey	23, Aug. 1880	21, July	11	271		Quincy, IL	
Hirt, Katharina	29, Nov. 1888	16, Nov.	52	766	Zeitler	Lansing, IA	Oberfranken, Baiern
Hirt, Maria	19, Dec. 1895		65- 9m	814	Rueter	Chicago, IL	Hille, Minden, Preußen

Christliche Apologete Death Notices -- 1839 - 1899

Name of Deceased	Notice Date	Death Date	Age	Page	Maiden Name	Place of Death	Place of Birth
Hirt, Peter	13, Feb. 1896	13, Dec.	82	110		Quincy, IL	Kurhessen
Hirth, Christina	6, July 1893	4, June	63	430	Zeitler	Lansing, IA	Oberfrankenkreis, Baiern
Hirth, Katharina	3, Aug. 1874	13, July	25	247	Leppert	Lansing, MI	New York
Hirth, Katharine Elisabeth	16, Sept 1872	23, Aug.	43	303	Maus	Quincy, IL	Großbieberauer, Hessen-Darmstadt
Hirth, Sophia	27, Sept 1849	19, July	34	156		Manchester, MO	
Hirth, Sybilla	26, Mar. 1857	3, Mar.	65- 8m	52	Bauchhenz	St. Louis, MO	Bellheim, Rheinpfalz Baiern
Hirtzel, Luella Florenz	14, Sept 1893	13, Aug.	29	590	Devore	Altamont, IL	Dexter, Effingham County, Illinois
Hirz, Anna Maria	18, Nov. 1872	27, Oct.	70- -23d	375	Wurst	Columbus, OH	Waldenstein, Welzheim, Württemberg
Hirz, Catharina	12, May 1862		33	76		Bucyrus, OH	Althütten, Backnang, Württemberg
Hiß, Georg Jakob	23, June 1887	6, May	41	398		Chicago, IL	Köndringen, Emmendingen, Baden
Hiß, Louise	27, Oct. 1879	28, Sept	33- 8m-26d	343	Heß	Chicago, IL	Theningen, Emmendingen, Baden
Hiß, Louise	18, Aug. 1887	27, July	18- 7m	526		Chicago, IL	
Hittner, Maria	26, Apr. 1888	20, Feb.	30- 7m	270	Lehmann	Larned, KS	
Hitz, (Mrs)	28, Apr. 1892			270		Menominee, MI	
Hitz, Alice	10, June 1886	19, May	10- 7m-29d	7		Indianapolis, IN	
Hitz, Margaretha	28, June 1894	12, June	79	422	Arnold	Madison, IN	Neudorf, Mittelfranken, Baiern
Hitz, Maria	22, Mar. 1880	12, Feb.	80	95	Tontz	Polk City, IA	
Hitz, Maria Louise Auguste	25, Dec. 1882	18, Nov.	17- 1m-28d	415		Menominee, MI	
Hitzfeld, Johann Jürgen Heinrich	9, June 1859	28, Apr.	65- 1m	92		Lawrenceburg, IN	Cincinnati, Hamilton County, Ohio
Hitzfeld, Maria Carolina	15, Dec. 1884	29, Nov.	53	7	Homberger	Lawrenceburg, IN	Zettel, Oldenburg
Hobbe, Gert	23, Feb. 1888	30, Jan.	80	126		Macon, NE	Felde, Ostfriesland
Hobbie, Wilhelm	15, Mar. 1880	22, Feb.	39	87		Petersburg, IL	Mecklenburg-Schwerin
Hobe, Carl Heinrich Friedrich Otto	28, May 1891		46	350		Bath, SD	Buffalo, New York
Hobe, Katharina	13, Apr. 1899	20, Feb.	42	238	Hickmann	St. Paul, MN	Eininghausen, Westphalen
Hobelmann, Anna Maria	10, Oct. 1889	11, Sept	20	654	Schlacke	Clatonia, NE	Vlotho, Minden, Kreis Herford, Preußen
Hoberg, August	16, Mar. 1863	24, Jan.	57	44		Marthasville, MO	
Hoberg, Elsabein	15, Sept 1859		64	148		Marthasville, MO	Vlotho, Westphalen
Hoberg, Friedrich	22, May 1856	13, Apr.	65- 1m-12d	84		Marthasville, MO	
Hobert, Elisabeth	25, Aug. 1884		22- 3m- 7d	7	Ritz	Charles City, IA	Vacha an der Werra, Sachsen-Weimar
Höbinger, Georgina	25, Aug. 1879	1, Aug.	53	271		Bay City, MI	Pesth, Ungarn
Hobstetter, Peter	14, Mar. 1889	28, Feb.	77- 2m- 1d	174		Ironton, OH	Ditschweiler, RheinPfalz Baiern
Hoch, Barbara	31, Oct. 1889	29, Sept	18- - 7d	702	Wenz	Galena, IL	Gräfenhausen, Neuenbirk, Württemberg
Höch, Dorothea Maria	14, May 1891	29, Apr.	66	318	Ulrich	Warrenton, MO	Nazza, Sachsen-Gotha
Höch, Kalr Eduard	14, May 1896	14, Apr.	37	318		Truxton, MO	
Hoch, Katharine	23, Feb. 1854	29, Dec.	64	32		Newport, KY	Pirmasens, Rheinkreis Baiern
Hoch, Margaretha Elisabetha	11, Jan. 1864	23, Oct.	39	8	Vollmer	Clayton, IA	Mandel, RheinPreußen
Hoch, Marie	3, Oct. 1889	10, Sept	82	638		Newport, KY	
Hoch, Valentin	24, July 1890	7, July	18	478		Yoakum, TX	
Hoch, Wilhelm	8, Aug. 1861	29, June	29- 6m-28d	128		Sherrills Mount, IA	Ober-Schönau, Germany
Hochgräfe, Katharina	2, Nov. 1883	16, Mar.	71- 2m- 5d	111		Columbus, IL	Crawford County, Ohio
Hochstadt, Katharina	21, Nov. 1881	7, Nov.	68	375	Doerr	Detroit, MI	Adams County, Illinois
Hockemeyer, Cat. Maria	4, Nov. 1872	9, Aug.	58	359		Union, MO	Eichen, Hessen
Hockemeyer, Willie	16, Feb. 1899	19, Dec.	76	111		St. Louis, MO	Osnabrück, Hannover
Höcker, Karolina	16, Mar. 1868	4, Feb.	28-11m- 5d	87	Hehner	Freedom, MO	Blomberg, Lippe-Detmold
Höckert, Emilie Lisette Amanda	20, July 1885	4, July	72	7		Berea, OH	Pittsburg, Pennsylvania
Hodan, Hanna Sophia	2, Apr. 1866	19, Nov.		110		Waverly, OH	Steinberg, Preußen

Christliche Apologete Death Notices --- 1839 - 1899

Name of Deceased	Notice Date	Death Date	Age	Page	Maiden Name	Place of Death	Place of Birth
Hodapp, Bertha Maria	8, Apr. 1886	25, Mar.	63	7		Seymour, IN	Oberkirch, Baden
Hodapp, Martin	18, Dec. 1890	11, Nov.	79- -12d	814		Seymour, IN	Thiergarten, Oberkirch, Baden
Höde, Amalia Friederike	3, May 1894	9, Apr.	87	294	Möbels		Kunnersdorf, Frankfurt an der Oder, Preußen
Höde, Karl Julius	12, Jan. 1893	17, Dec.	89	30		Terre Haute, IN	Tschetzschenow, Frankfurt a. d. Oder, Preußen
Hodel, Barbara	24, July 1876	10, July	67	239	Burg	Lawrenceburg, IN	Honsbach, Elsaß
Hodel, Christian	22, Sept 1859	7, Aug.	74	152		Baresville, OH	Kanton Bern, Schweiz
Hodel, Margaretha	20, Jan. 1859	3, Dec.	15	12		Lawrenceburg, IN	
Hodsdon, Fannie R.	4, May 1899	19, Mar.	32	287	Zellmer	Oshkosh, WI	Oshkosh, Wisconsin
Hoebinger, Friedricke	20, Feb. 1882	27, Jan.	49	63		Bay City, MI	Ortenburg, Baiern
Hoeft, Carl Friedrich	26, Mar. 1891	22, Feb.	66-11m- 2d	206		Ripon, WI	Barkenbrück, Arnswalde, Preußen
Hoenes, Anna Catharina	10, July 1876	21, June		223		Fillmore, MI	Münchingen, Leonberg, Württemberg
Hoenes, Conrad	10, June 1858	28, Apr.		92		Woodland, MI	Münchingen, Leonberg, Württemberg
Hoerer, Andreas	22, Dec. 1884	23, Nov.	78	7		Canton, MO	Metterzimmern, Besigheim, Württemberg
Hoerer, Christian Gottlieb	5, Aug. 1886	10, July	44	7		Salem, ---	Metterzimmern, Neckar, Besigheim, Württemberg
Hoerig, Emilie	16, June 1887	2, June	31- 4m-25d	382	Boettger	New York City, NY	St. Louis, Missouri
Hoerr, George	20, Feb. 1896	28, Jan.	50	126		Burlington, IA	
Hoerreth, Rosina	29, Sept 1853	19, Sept	25-10m	156	Niklaus	Indianapolis, IN	Minschen Mier, Bern, Schweiz
Hoersemann, Julia	1, Dec. 1884	27, Oct.	31	7	Hoppen	Wyandotte, KS	Wheeling, West Virginia
Hoerster, Maria	23, Apr. 1883	2, Apr.	26- 2m- 8d	135	Seip	Llano, TX	Fredericksburg, Gillespie County, Texas
Hoesle, Maria Louise	26, Apr. 1888	1, Apr.	43- 4m-21d	270	Stoeber	Garner, IA	Hazelgren, Wisconsin
Hof , Henriette	2, May 1889	13, Apr.	93- 3m-21d	286	Stegemann	Watertown, WI	Legenitz, Uckermark, Preußen
Hofacker, Maria	10, Dec. 1866	10, Oct.	43- -16d	398	Krauß	Woodville, OH	Baleberg, Krautheim, Baden
Hofeditz, Elisabeth	19, Nov. 1866	15, Oct.	19	374	Gilgen	Highland, IL	Kanton Bern, Schweiz
Hofeditz, Friedrich Wilhelm	14, July 1887		55	446		Linton, IN	Kurhessen
Hofeditz, Johan Christoph	8, Dec. 1879	24, Nov.	68	391		Highland, IL	Sielen, Hofgeißmar, Kurhessen
Hofeditz, Susanna	13, Oct. 1887	22, Scpt	39- 2m	654	Stadtbacher	Parsons, KS	
Hofen, Sebastian	2, Sept 1872	22, July	74	287		Etna, MO	Rodersheim, Dürkheim, Rheinpfalz Baiern
Hofer, Christina	7, Jan. 1886	20, Dec.	70	7		Richmond, IN	Württemberg
Höfer, Eva K.	10, Sept 1891	13, Aug.	79	590		Hillsboro, KS	Nassau
Höfer, Johannes	7, June 1844	12, May		95		Louisville, KY	Obermainkreis, Baiern
Höfer, Karl Michael	9, Feb. 1899	27, Dec.	65	95		Miltonvale, KS	Nassau
Höfer, Margaretha Emilie	15, Dec. 1873	24, Nov.	21- 8m-23d	399	Müller	Cincinnati, OH	
Höfer, Nicolaus	21, Mar. 1864		58	48		Sauk City, WI	Nassau
Hoff, Johan Friedrich	5, Apr. 1894	26, Jan.	93	230		Santa Claus, IN	Eberschütz, Geismar, Kurhessen
Hoff,	19, Apr. 1860	14, Mar.	40	64		Poland, IN	Eberschütz, Hofgeismar, Kurhessen
Hoff, Friedrich	8, Feb. 1869	18, Jan.	47-10m	47		Giard, IA	Plochingen, Eßlingen, Württemberg
Hoff, Martha Elisabeth	13, Jan. 1853	10, Dec.	52	8		Terre Haute, IN	Eberschütz, Hofgeismar, Kurhessen
Hoffer, Anna Maria	24, Oct. 1881	14, Oct.	73- 4m-18d	343		Ft. Wayne, IN	Banwil, Bern, Schweiz
Hoffer, Jakob	20, Mar. 1865	4, Mar.	58- -17d	48		Perrysburg, OH	Niederwiel, Argau, Schweiz
Hoffer, Maria	21, Oct. 1872		63- 4m-29d	343	Müller	Perrysburg, OH	Rügen, Schweiz
Hofferberth, Georg	27, Apr. 1899	11, Apr.	66	271		Brooklyn, NY	Etzengefäß, Hessen-Darmstadt
Hoffert, Johan Jakob	9, Feb. 1899	8, Jan.	74	95		Jordan, MN	Munsenheim, Elsaß
Hoffert, Maria	1, Jan. 1872	27, Nov.	16	7		Carver Co., MN	
Höffle, Helen Wilhelmine	17, May 1869	24, Apr.	62	159	Trischmann	Charles City, IA	Elberfeld, Preußen
Höfflinger, Georg Friedrich	24, July 1876	5, July	52	239		Woodville, OH	Eichstetten, Emmendingen, Baden
Hoffmaier, Ludwig	4, Apr. 1895	8, Mar.	70	222		Rochester, NY	Pletzk, Hinterpommern

Christliche Apologete Death Notices --- 1839 - 1899

Name of Deceased	Notice Date	Death Date	Age	Maiden Name	Page	Place of Death	Place of Birth
Hoffmann,	16, Oct. 1890	7, Sept	79		670	Harper, IA	Ahorn, Sachsen-Coburg
Hoffmann, (Mrs)	27, Dec. 1894	21, Nov.	30	Baltrusch	836	Rockham, SD	Schönwald, Lippe-Detmold
Hoffmann, A. Chr.	19, Apr. 1875		38- 2m-26d		127	Cincinnati, OH	Herborn, Nassau
Hoffmann, A. M. Elisabeth	12, Sept 1850	16, Aug.	71		148	St. Louis, MO	Geismar, Hannover
Hoffmann, Agnes	24, May 1888	4, May	73		334	Tomah, WI	Wermsdorf, Sachsen
Hoffmann, Amalie	4, Jan. 1864	31, Oct.	13		4	Waverly, OH	Hornsemmer, Preußen
Hoffmann, Anna Elisabeth	25, May 1899	21, Apr.	72	Heimeling	335	Paige, TX	Georgenzell, Wasungen, Sachsen
Hoffmann, Anna Katharina	25, Oct. 1880	7, Oct.	53- 3m- 6d		343	Brooklyn, NY	Niederaula, Kurhessen
Hoffmann, Anna Maria	28, Apr. 1884	16, Apr.	54		7	Chillicothe, OH	Schwegenheim, Rheinkreis Baiern
Hoffmann, Anna Maria	17, Feb. 1873	27, Jan.	68		53	Charlestown, IN	Lettweiler, Rheinkreis Baiern
Hoffmann, Anna Maria	25, Aug. 1873	1, Aug.	70	Gärich	271	Mt. Vernon, IN	Blankenloch, Baden
Hoffmann, August	6, Oct. 1884	22, Sept	59		7	Columbus, WI	Bromberg, Preußen
Hoffmann, Auguste Elise	20, Dec. 1880		15		407	New York City, NY	
Hoffmann, Aurelia	4, July 1895	15, June	63	Trojer	430	Tea Creek, IN	Holmes County, Ohio
Hoffmann, Barbara	7, Feb. 1881	18, Jan.	58	Schuh	47	Chicago, IL	Steigenthal, Mergentheim, Württemberg
Hoffmann, Carl	29, Mar. 1888	1, Mar.	55		206	Quincy, IL	Bliedungen, Nordhausen, Preußen
Hoffmann, Carl Gottlieb	22, Sept 1873	29, Aug.	28		303	Galena, IL	Crumbach, Hessen
Hoffmann, Carolina	1, Mar. 1880	24, Jan.	27- 7m-14d	Bettinger	71	Boonville, IN	Kalberau, Alzenau, Baiern
Hoffmann, Catharina	1, July 1867	3, June	46	Barreiter	206	Cincinnati, OH	Krailsheim, Württemberg
Hoffmann, Charley	4, Oct. 1888		9- 7m-24d		638	Quincy, IL	
Hoffmann, Christian	22, Oct. 1896	28, Sept	71		687	Dunkirk, NY	Ober-Riexingen, Württemberg
Hoffmann, Christina	17, Mar. 1892	22, Feb.	73- -29d	Basler	174	Stitzer, WI	Buchs, St. Gallen, Schweiz
Hoffmann, Christine	1, Feb. 1894	15, Jan.	73	Lang	78	Mt. Olive, IL	Gailenkirchen, Hall, Württemberg
Hoffmann, Christoph	24, July 1851	12, July	84		120	St. Louis, MO	
Hoffmann, Conrad	31, Mar. 1898	22, Feb.	72		207	Milwaukee, OR	Herborn, Nassau
Hoffmann, David	18, Nov. 1897	15, Oct.	65		735	Clay Center, KS	Oppbau, Rheinkreis Baiern
Hoffmann, Eduard M.	24, Dec. 1877	5, Dec.	15-10m- 1d		415	German Creek, IA	Bästs, Werdenberg, St. Gallen, Schweiz
Hoffmann, Edward	27, Feb. 1896	7, Jan.	62		142	Cincinnati, OH	Kerner, Sachsen-Gotha
Hoffmann, Elisabeth	8, Mar. 1855	2, Feb.	68		40	Wheelersburg, OH	Niederhochstadt, Landau, Rheinpfalz Baiern
Hoffmann, Elsbeth	22, July 1886	5, July	56		7	Enterprise, KS	Rheingönheim, Rheinkreis Baiern
Hoffmann, Ernst	8, Dec. 1898	13, Nov.	67		783	Saginaw, MI	Weinsberg, Württemberg
Hoffmann, Eva Catharina	30, Nov. 1885	16, Nov.	63	Gutzler	7	Covington, KY	Gersdorf, Köslin, Damburg, Pommern
Hoffmann, Eva Elisabeth	30, Aug. 1855	2, Aug.	56	Frech	140	Galena, IL	Hochstall, Baiern
Hoffmann, Friederike	3, May 1888	12, Apr.	74	Schäfer	286	Berger, MO	
Hoffmann, Friederike Hanna Maria	29, Dec. 1892		67	Prochnow	828	Seguin, TX	
Hoffmann, Friedrich	17, July 1882	28, June	81- -10d		231	Chillicothe, OH	Gailenkirchen, Hall, Württemberg
Hoffmann, Friedrike	25, Jan. 1869		13- 3m		31	Oregon, IA	Edekofen, Rheinpfalz Baiern
Hoffmann, Fritz	25, Mar. 1897	3, Mar.	60		190	Clay Center, KS	
Hoffmann, Georg	25, Jan. 1869	20, Dec.	43		31	Cincinnati, OH	Arrau, Argau, Schweiz
Hoffmann, Georg	3, Feb. 1868	4, Nov.	22		39	New York, NY	
Hoffmann, Gottlieb	26, June 1890	30, May	70- 8m-10d		414	Paterson, NJ	Hannover
Hoffmann, Hanna Margaretha	6, Dec. 1880	29, Oct.	64		391	Canton, MO	Lettweiler, Obermoschel, Rheinkreis Baiern
Hoffmann, Hannah	8, Apr. 1886	24, Mar.		Koch	7	Kearney, MO	Ufeln-Bergkirchen, Minden, Preußen
Hoffmann, Heinrich	24, Feb. 1887	7, Feb.	51- 2m- 1d		126	Charlestown, IN	
Hoffmann, Heinrich	12, May 1887	16, Apr.	82		302	Hoyleton, IL	
Hoffmann, Heinrich	19, Dec. 1881	1, Dec.	62		407	Seguin, TX	

Christliche Apologete Death Notices --- 1839 - 1899

Name of Deceased	Notice Date	Death Date	Age	Maiden Name	Page	Place of Death	Place of Birth
Hoffmann, J.M.	6, Aug. 1877	19, July	70		255	Canton, MO	Viernau, Erfurt, Preußen
Hoffmann, Jacob	11, Feb. 1892	18, Jan.	62		94	Lovett, IN	Bettweiler, Obermorschel, Rheinkreis Baiern
Hoffmann, Jacob	22, Mar. 1888	25, Feb.	15		190	Marietta, OH	
Hoffmann, Jakob	25, Oct. 1894		73- 5m- 7d		694	Cleveland, OH	Hadebach, Herschfeld, Preußen
Hoffmann, Jakob	23, June 1879	2, June	75		199	Highland, IL	Buchs, St. Gallen, Schweiz
Hoffmann, Joh. Dietrich	19, Nov. 1847	30, Oct.	36		187	Mascoutah, IL	Schafheim, Hessen-Darmstadt
Hoffmann, Johan Adam	30, May 1881	2, May	78		175	Schnectady, NY	Neuekirchen, Baden
Hoffmann, Johan August	9, Oct. 1890	8, Sept	27		654	Nashville, IL	Washington County, Illinois
Hoffmann, Johan Friedrich	18, May 1885	27, Apr.	61		7	Chillicothe, OH	Wasserthalleben, Schwarzburg-Sondershausen
Hoffmann, Johan Georg	3, July 1882	18, June	74- 8m-17d		215	Pomeroy, OH	Egenhausen, Leutershausen, Baiern
Hoffmann, Johan Gottfried	1, Apr. 1886	14, Mar.	61		7	Belleville, IL	Hausdorf bei Frankenberg, Sachsen
Hoffmann, Johan Michael	29, Apr. 1886	5, Apr.	77- 6m-11d		7	Herman, MO	Ellhofen, Weinsberg, Württemberg
Hoffmann, Johann	6, Aug. 1857	17, July	20-10m		128	Boonville, MO	
Hoffmann, Johann Friedrich	29, Sept 1853	10, Sept	55		156	Erie, MI	Körner, Sachsen-Gotha
Hoffmann, John	9, Oct. 1890	9, Sept	27- -10d		654	Tacoma, WA	Nashville, Illinois
Hoffmann, John M.	3, Dec. 1877		44		391	Canton, MO	Viernau, Erfurt, Preußen
Hoffmann, Joseph	3, Apr. 1876	17, Mar.	49	Brink	111	New Rochelle, NY	Floria, Schweinitz, Preußen
Hoffmann, Karolina	9, Dec. 1897	19, Nov.	67		783	Hoyleton, IL	Eilsen, Rotenuffeln, Minden, Westphalen
Hoffmann, Karolina	2, Aug. 1849	23, June	28		124	St. Louis, MO	
Hoffmann, Katharina	9, Aug. 1855	20, July	37	Kalb	128	Indianapolis, IN	Zwingenberg, Hessen-Darmstadt
Hoffmann, Katharina	10, Mar. 1884		96		7	Marine City, MI	Waldmohr, Rheinkreis Baiern
Hoffmann, Katharina	19, May 1887	27, Apr.	39- 8m-25d	Schmidt	318	Allegan, MI	Dingern, Karlstadt, Baiern
Hoffmann, Katharina	18, Sept 1882	6, Aug.	57	Rheinhart	303	Schnectady, NY	Neunkirchen, Baden
Hoffmann, Katharina Elisabeth	4, May 1874	19, Apr.	18		143	Cleveland, OH	
Hoffmann, Kunigunde	14, May 1857	1, May	32		80	Mt. Pleasant, OH	Burgstahl, Mitwitz, Baiern
Hoffmann, Louise F.H.	22, Apr. 1878	6, Apr.	59	Müller	127	Oregon, MO	Schweigern, Brackenheim, Württemberg
Hoffmann, Magdalena	14, Apr. 1848	30, Jan.	34		64	Mascoutah, IL	
Hoffmann, Magdalena B.	14, Mar. 1870	26, Feb.	80	Nudinger	87	Marble Rock, IA	Elpersheim, Mergentheim, Württemberg
Hoffmann, Margaretha	12, Feb. 1872	27, Jan.	64		55	Birmingham, PA	Reinwartshofen, Greding, Baiern
Hoffmann, Maria	10, June 1897	23, Apr.	44	Braun	367	Marietta, OH	Salem Township, Washington County, Ohio
Hoffmann, Maria	30, June 1879	17, June	74	Colemann	207	Dallas, TX	Dauphin County, Pennsylvania
Hoffmann, Maria	24, Nov. 1898	21, Oct.	66- 4m-24d	Hartmann	751	Cincinnati, OH	Meistern, Calw, Württemberg
Hoffmann, Maria	31, Aug. 1863	18, Aug.	22- 5m- 5d		140	Chillicothe, OH	Chillicothe, Ohio
Hoffmann, Maria	16, Sept 1872	30, Aug.		Lindemuth	303	Quincy, IL	
Hoffmann, Maria	23, Feb. 1880	11, Feb.	17- 2m		63	Mt. Vernon, IN	
Hoffmann, Maria Elise	4, Aug. 1898	15, July	33	Ladiges	495	Omaha, NE	Wedel, Holstein
Hoffmann, Maria Magdalena	22, Jan. 1872	5, Dec.	53	Koch	31	Chicago, IL	Dettelsheim, Kreis Worms, Hessen-Darmstadt
Hoffmann, Matthäus	12, May 1876	2, May	68- 7m-22d		191	Highland, IL	Bucks, St. Gallen, Schweiz
Hoffmann, Paul	17, Nov. 1884	30, Oct.	22-10m-14d		7	Hurricane, IL	Lafayette County,
Hoffmann, Paul Albert	11, Oct. 1880	13, Sept	4		327		Maquoketa, Jackson County, Iowa
Hoffmann, Peter	19, Feb. 1883	28, Jan.	67		63	Lancaster, WI	Krumbach, Hessen-Darmstadt
Hoffmann, Philipp Jakob	30, Mar. 1899	14, Feb.	78		207		Edenkoven, Rheinpfalz Baiern
Hoffmann, Rosina	21, Apr. 1862	4, Apr.	35	Bollinger	64	Chillicothe, OH	Hofen, Besigheim, Württemberg
Hoffmann, Rosina	31, Mar. 1879	3, Mar.	27- 8m-22d	Feuchter	103	Cleveland, OH	
Hoffmann, Sarah	3, June 1867	12, May			174	Canada West	
Hoffmann, Sophie Christine	13, Apr. 1899	16, Mar.	76	Eisenach	238	Chillicothe, OH	Greuß, Germany

- 211 -

Christliche Apologete Death Notices --- 1839 - 1899

Name of Deceased	Notice Date	Death Date	Age	Page	Maiden Name	Place of Death	Place of Birth
Hoffmann, Susanne	27, Feb. 1896	1, Feb.	78	142	Schmitt	Chillicothe, OH	Canton Uri, Schweiz
Hoffmann, Wilhelm	18, Aug. 1879	6, Aug.	24- -17d	263		Saginaw, MI	Roseville, Michigan
Hoffmann, Wilhelm	27, Nov. 1882	8, Nov.	23- 6m-9d	383		Clatonia, NE	
Hoffmann, Wilhelmina Philippina	31, Mar. 1873	13, Mar.	81	103	Moser	Cincinnati, OH	Edenkoven bei Landau, Rheinkreis Baiern
Hoffmarch, Wilhelm	3, Sept 1866	23, Aug.	16- 2m-7d	286		Cincinnati, OH	Bremen,
Hoffmeier, A. H.	11, Feb. 1897	2, Jan.	69	94		Santa Claus, IN	Essenerberge, Hannover
Hoffmeier, Heinrich	9, June 1887	18, May	49	366		Covington, KY	Wuelpe, Hannover
Hoffmeier, Ludwig	4, May 1874	22, Apr.	65	143		Covington, KY	Linsburg, Amt Wölpe, Hannover
Hoffmeier, Sophia	1, Jan. 1872	19, Dec.		7	Harmeling	Covington, KY	Erichshagen, Hannover
Hoffmeier, Sophie	1, May 1865	27, Mar.	84-10m-27d	72	Knoke	Santa Claus, IN	Linsburg, Amt Nienburg, Hannover
Hoffmeister, (Mr)	18, Aug. 1879	29, July	69- 4m-23d	263		Flood Creek, IA	Obbenrode, Halberstadt, Preußen
Hoffmeister, Elisabeth	8, Mar. 1888	5, Feb.	54	158	Diel	Columbus, IL	Westmoreland County, Pennsylvania
Hoffmeister, Johannes	21, Nov. 1895		77	750			
Hoffmeister, Margaretha	3, Aug. 1874	20, Apr.	43	247	Lutz	Mt. Vernon, IN	Stemshorn, Lemförde, Hannover
Hoffmeyer, Carolina	7, Feb. 1876	18, Jan.	44	47	Röttger	Santa Claus, IN	
Hoffmeyer, Magdalene	21, Apr. 1892	4, Apr.		254	Schmitt	Denton, TX	
Hoffmeyer, Sophie	24, Mar. 1873	19, Dec.	63	95	Harmeling		Erichshagen, Hannover
Hoffmeyer, Wilhelmine	15, Sept 1884	21, Aug.	33	7		Covington, KY	Scheffinghausen, Nienburg, Germany
Hoffrogge, (Mrs)	3, Aug. 1868	27, June	27	247	Rennebohn	New York, NY	Kirchhüchting, Bremen, Germany
Hoffrogge, Lydia Sophia Louisa	8, Nov. 1875	7, Oct.	3- 5m- 7d	359		Baltimore, MD	
Hoffrogge, William Edward	27, Dec. 1894	28, Nov.	24- 1m- 4d	836		Baltimore, MD	Rochester, Monroe County, New York
Hoffschmidt, (Mrs)	13, Mar. 1882	15, Feb.		87	Meyer	Maine, WI	
Hoffschmidt, Heinrich	3, Mar. 1898	27, Jan.	52	143		Marion, WI	Kleinheydorn, Germany
Hoffstädt, Friedrich	13, Apr. 1893	11, Mar.	72	238		Clatonia, NE	Gaiz, Pommern
Hofheinz, Katharina	16, July 1891	26, June	41- 4m-26d	462		Philadelphia, PA	Golzhausen, Bretten, Baden
Hofius, Anna Maria	13, Dec. 1855	10, Sept	64	200	Schmidt	Jefferson City, MO	Hilchenbach, Westphalen, Preußen
Höflin, Christina	9, Mar. 1863	21, Feb.	63	40	Riecker	Quincy, IL	Baden
Höflina, Eberhart	18, Sept 1865	18, July	56	152		Charlestown, IN	Neidorf, Mittelfranken, Baiern
Hofmann, Christian	25, June 1896	31, May	51	415		St. Louis, MO	Hessen-Darmstadt
Hofmann, Christina	4, Nov. 1858	20, Oct.	26	176		Yorktown, IL	
Hofmann, Johan	12, Dec. 1889	19, Nov.	55- 5m- 8d	798		Marion, OH	Argenstein, Marburg, Kurhessen
Hofmann, Johan Nikolaus	7, Mar. 1870	6, Feb.	60	79		Furnace, OH	Rittershausen, RheinPreußen
Hofmann, Maria Christine	10, Mar. 1884	21, Feb.	59	7		Clay Center, KS	Gailenkirchen, Württemberg
Hofmann, Peter	27, Sept 1855	30, Aug.	60- 3m-10d	156		Rockford, IN	
Hofmeister, Carolina	17, Nov. 1862	23, Oct.	48	184		Kingston, IL	Einnellen, Baiern
Hofmeister, Hedwig	3, Feb. 1879	19, Jan.		39	Mahnkopf	Newport, KY	Hagenstädt, Bokenen, Hannover
Hofmeister, Joahnne	5, May 1884	25, Mar.	73	7	Hartmann	Flood Creek, IA	Vakenstedt, Wernigrode, Sachsen
Hofmeister, Ludwig	29, Apr. 1852	4, Apr.		72		Newport, KY	Hackenstedt, Amt Waldenberg, Hannover
Hofmeister, Wilhelm	27, Mar. 1890	1, Mar.	38- 9m-21d	206		Charlestown, IN	Charlestown, Indiana
Hofmeyer, Henriette	3, Oct. 1895	4, Sept	42-11m- 1d	638	Schmieken	Santa Claus, IN	Santa Claus, Indiana
Höfner, Rosine	9, Dec. 1872	22, Nov.	18	399		Giard, IA	
Hofritz, Johan Jakob	20, Feb. 1896	31, Jan.	84	126		Grand Ridge, IL	Berneck, Oberfranken, Baiern
Hofrock, Anna Luise	17, Aug. 1899	2, Aug.	22	527	Kreie	Brownton, MN	Sumter, Minnesota
Hofschmidt, Dorothea	21, Jan. 1892	23, Dec.	84	46		Quincy, IL	Mesmerode, Hannover
Hofschmidt, Heinrich	15, July 1878	2, July	77- 1m- 7d	223		Sheboygan, WI	Bokeloh, Hannover
Hofsommer, Clara Catharina	18, Apr. 1889	27, Mar.	45	254	Pfaff	Scranton, PA	Aslar, RheinPreußen

- 212 -

Christliche Apologete Death Notices --- 1839 - 1899

Name of Deceased	Notice Date	Death Date	Age	Page	Maiden Name	Place of Death	Place of Birth
Hofstätter, Margaretha	8, May 1865	3, Apr.	70- 6m-5d	76		Galion, OH	Brunnentobel, Leutkirch, Württemberg
Hofstetter, Marianna	7, Mar. 1881	20, Feb.	47- 7m-3d	79	Heß	Cincinnati, OH	Herbatzofen, Leutkirch, Württemberg
Hofstetter, Stephan	6, Aug. 1866	23, July	39	254		Cincinnati, OH	Neustadt, Mecklenburg-Schwerin
Höft, Anna Maria	10, Feb. 1898	17, Jan.	17	95	Boldt	Oshkosh, WI	
Hoge, Otto	25, Aug. 1887	4, Aug.	16	542		Chicago, IL	
Hoge, Wilhelm Friedrich	26, July 1869	14, July	46	239		Oconomowoc, WI	Petznick, Kreis Piritz, Pommern
Högel, Jacob	26, Jan. 1893	28, Dec.	44- 2m-5d	62		Boonville, IN	Warrick County, Indiana
Höger, Eleonore	18, Mar.1872	8, Feb.	65	95	Höger	Kossuth, OH	Leimen bei Heidelberg, Baden
Hogg, Margaret	27, Jan. 1898	23, Dec.	83	63		Hokah, MN	Dover Forge, Norfolk County, Canada
Hogrefe, Andreas	26, May 1879	20, Apr.	56	167		Winona, MN	Winzlar, Hannover
Hogrefe, Clara Dorothea Christina	2, Sept 1872	9, Aug.	10	287		Quincy, IL	Oberdurlach, Preußen
Hogrefe, Friedrich (Rev)	6, May 1886	14, Apr.	68	7		Faribault, MN	Wabasha, Minnesota
Hogrefe, Heinrich	1, Dec. 1898	10, Oct.	20-11m-4d	766		Fairbault, MN	Winzler, Hannover
Hogreve, Emma Elisabeth Engelein	3, Dec. 1877	28, Apr.	1	391		Winona, MN	
Hogreve, Friedrich Louis	21, June 1875	1, May	9	199		Wabasha, MN	
Hogue, John	21, June 1875	13, Nov.	27	199		Wabasha, MN	
Hohago, Wilhelm	29, Dec. 1898	6, May	64- 4m-11d	828		St. Philip, IN	Ohle, Preußen
Hohaus, (Mrs)	23, June 1873	25, Feb.	52	199		Minneapolis, MN	Moleshein, Württemberg
Hohaus, Joh.	15, Mar. 1875	15, Jan.	29- 6m-11d	526	Schnaufer	Marietta, OH	
Hohaus, Johan	16, Aug. 1888	29, May	62	94		Marietta, OH	Hünfeld, Hessen-Kassel
Hohaus, Maximillian (Rev)	10, Feb. 1887	15, Sept	33-7m	96		Washington, MO	
Hohf, Barbara Anna	13, June 1861	16, Feb.	51	670	Katz	Parker, SD	Hochdorf, Horb, Württemberg
Hohf, Michael	16, Oct. 1890	3, Apr.	62	158		Allegan, MI	Baerl, Preußen
Höhl, Elisabeth	10, Mar. 1898	17, Feb.	69	270		Danville, IL	Erfelden am Rhein, Hessen-Darmstadt
Hohl, Jacob Heinrich (Dr)	26, Apr. 1888	6, Apr.	58- 9m-10d	103		Mt. Vernon, IN	Wolfhalden, Appenzell, Schweiz
Hohl, John H.	29, Mar. 1869	20, Mar.	21	124		Nauvoo, IL	Schönstein, Ziegenhain, Kurhessen
Hohlstädt, Martha Henrietta	4, Aug. 1862	21, Dec.	21	222		Flood Creek, IA	
Hohmann, Chr.	7, Apr. 1892		Inquiry	83	Kircher	Marion, OH	
Hohmann, Katharina	23, May 1849		28	47	Bauer	Louisville, KY	
Hohmann, Katharina Barbara	5, Feb. 1877	21, Sept	71	343		Buffalo, NY	Neckar-Gemünd, Baden
Hohmann, William	22, Oct. 1877	10, Apr.	11-10m-26d	286		Blossom, NY	
Höhn, Elisabeth	2, May 1889	2, Apr.	82	334		Bradford, IN	
Höhn, Jakob Ulrich	23, May 1895	15, Nov.	50- 4m-7d	7		Marion, OH	Fauerbach, Hessen-Darmstadt
Höhn, Johan Phil.	14, Dec. 1885	27, Jan.	47- 8m-2d	110		San Francisco, CA	Berneck, Nagold, Württemberg
Höhn, Katharina	16, Feb. 1888	5, Apr.	30	7		Bradford, IN	Kleeberg, Nassau
Höhn, Katharina	13, May 1886	22, Feb.	76	207		Cincinnati, OH	New Salisbury, Indiana
Höhn, Maria	31, Mar. 1898	23, Aug.	78	590		Davenport, IA	Hessen-Darmstadt
Höhn, Philipp	15, Sept 1887	26, Dec.	77	158		Bradford, IN	Kurhessen
Höhne, Friedrich	5, Mar. 1891	13, Feb.	16-11m-25d	79		Industry, TX	Feuerbach, Butschbach, Hessen-Darmstadt
Höhnes, Conrad	5, Mar. 1877	9, Feb.	45- 1m-3d	95		Grand Rapids, MI	Münchingen, Leonberg, Württemberg
Höhns, Claus Heinrich	20, Mar. 1871	19, Apr.	65- 5m	167		New York City, NY	Hellweg, Rothenburg, Hannover
Hoins, Marie	23, May 1881	8, May	16	191		Lake Creek, MO	
Höisly, Heinrich	13, June 1870	29, Apr.	67	422		Milwaukee, WI	Diesbach, Glarus, Schweiz
Hoist, Friedrike	28, June 1894	4, Jan.	78	39		Buffalo, NY	
Hoist, John	3, Feb. 1879	8, Apr.	20- 6m-25d	135		Freeport, IL	

Christliche Apologete Death Notices --- 1839 - 1899

Name of Deceased	Notice Date	Death Date	Age	Page	Maiden Name	Place of Death	Place of Birth
Hokamp, Joseph Heinrich	7, Oct. 1897	7, Sept	66	639		Burlington, IA	Aikump, Westphalen
Hold, Emilie Magdalena	22, May 1871	28, Apr.	18- 8m- 8d	167		Melrose, NY	
Hold, Mathilde Rebecka	10, Sept 1891	19, Aug.	66	590	Straldmann	New York City, NY	Rodekirche, Oldenburg
Holdefer, Carolina	4, Dec. 1890	8, Nov.	84	782	Hamann	Farmington, IA	Braunschweig
Holder, Elisabeth	18, Aug. 1887	1, Aug.	72	526	Kutschman	Brookville, IN	Wälzikow, Zürich, Schweiz
Holderbach, Anna Maria Justine	1, Sept 1898	16, Aug.	64	559	Drach	Cincinnati, OH	Wertheim, Baden
Holderith, Daniel	23, Sept 1886	6, Sept	69	7		New Orleans, LA	Münchhausen, Selz, Elsaß
Holdimann, Jakob	5, Jan. 1885	11, Dec.	75	7		Greenville, OH	Mahountuage, Schuylkill County, Pennsylvania
Holdkamp, Christina Elsabein	9, Feb. 1854		59	24	Stork		Ladbergen, Münster, Preußen
Hölke, (Mr)	30, Oct. 1876	19, Oct.	68	351		Seymour, IN	Venne, Amt Wittlage, Hannover
Hoke, (Mrs)	21, Apr. 1884	10, Apr.	90	7	Lupold	Burlington, WI	Weilheim, Balingen, Württemberg
Holl, Heinrich	22, Feb. 1869	27, Dec.	70	63		St. Louis, MO	Odenhausen, Hessen-Darmstadt
Holldorb, Joh. Carsten	7, Oct. 1858	26, Sept	29	160		Cincinnati, OH	Neubruchhausen, Hannover
Hole, Katharina	13, Feb. 1890	8, Jan.	24-11m-19d	110		Mt. Healthy, OH	
Hole, Anna Catharina	2, Apr. 1883	12, Mar.	41- 1m- 4d	111	Mack	Mt. Healthy, OH	Wertheim am Main, Baden
Hole, Christian Friedrich	30, Apr. 1891	10, Apr.	57	286		Mt. Healthy, OH	Rohden, Münden, Hannover
Hollen, Therese	3, Sept 1896	12, Aug.	46	575	Brunner	New York City, NY	
Hollewedel, Arthur C.	7, Mar. 1870	24, Feb.	72	79		Batesville, IN	Syke, Hannover
Holliger, Anna	29, May 1876	4, May		175	Wyttenbach	Rochester, NY	Seegen, Aargau, Schweiz
Holliger, Katharina	9, Apr. 1883	11, Mar.	36	119	Neitz	Toledo, OH	Snyder County, Pennsylvania
Hollmann, Arnold	4, Apr. 1889	17, Mar.	57- 8m-18d	222		Minneapolis, MN	Salzuflen, Lippe-Detmold
Hollmann, F.W. Ernst	1, July 1878	24, May	27- 7m- 9d	207		Union, MO	Bexter-Hagen, Schöttmar, Lippe-Detmold
Hollmann, Friederike	15, Jan. 1891	31, Dec.	80- 4m-18d	46	Brinkmann	St. Louis, MO	Düssen, Hannover
Hollmann, Georg	25, Aug. 1879	4, Aug.	77	271		St. Louis, MO	Belm bei Osnabrück, Hannover
Hollmann, Louise	4, Apr. 1895	8, Mar.	81	222	Niermeier	Morris, MN	Hille, Minden, Preußen
Hollmann, Mina Carolina	2, Apr. 1896	16, Feb.	30	222	Hockemeyer	St. Louis, MO	Franklin County, Missouri
Hollmann, Wilhelm	17, Apr. 1871	21, Feb.	35	127		Lincoln, NE	Deepholz, Preußen
Hollmann, Wilhelm A.	21, Aug. 1890	28, July	24	542		Warren, MO	Warren County, Missouri
Hölscher, Anna Maria	8, Oct. 1891	28, Aug.	80	654	Maneke	Huntingburg, IN	Ladbergen, Tecklenburg, Westphalen
Hölscher, Friedrich Wilhelm	31, Mar. 1887	13, Mar.	60	206		Evansville, IN	Ladbergen, Tecklenburg, Hannover
Hölscher, Lydia	23, Mar. 1899	22, Feb.	25	191	Bunte	Bushton, KS	Gasconade County, Missouri
Hölscher, Wilhelmine	26, Jan. 1854	19, Dec.	21	16	Röse	Evansville, IN	Rosenthal, Frankenberg, Kurhessen
Hölsker, Dina	10, June 1878	27, May	50- 5m-23d	183	Holtgröve	Edwardsville, IL	
Holst, Anna	23, May 1881	6, May	43- 1m- 4d	167		Marietta, OH	Apensen, Hannover
Holst, Anna	4, Nov. 1878	1, Oct.	21	351		Belvidere, IA	
Holst, Anna	18, Nov. 1878	1, Oct.	21	367		Belvidere, IA	
Holst, Ernst	26, Nov. 1891	22, Oct.	90	766		Red Wing, MN	Goldback, Delm, Hannover
Holst, Joachim	5, Dec. 1864	21, Sept	25	196		Red Wing, MN	Apensch, Hannover
Holst, John	13, Mar. 1865	23, Feb.	69- 6m- 5d	44		Marietta, OH	Mankels, Zittens, Amt Zevern, Hannover
Holst, Louise	23, Apr. 1883	6, Apr.	21	135		Red Wing, MN	
Holst, Margaretha Christina	25, Feb. 1878	7, Feb.	82- 7m- 3d	63	Ficken	Marietta, OH	Mankels, Zittens, Hannover
Holst, Maria	19, May 1898	17, Apr.	92	319	Heinßen	Red Wing, MN	Hannover
Holste, Anna Maria Louise	30, Jan. 1896	22, Dec.	81	78	Klicker	Le Sueur, MN	Rahden, Germany
Holste, Philipp	24, Aug. 1868	10, Aug.	74	271		Watertown, WI	Grossenmarpe, Lippe-Detmold
Holstein, Anna Kunigunde	11, June 1877	18, May	74	191	Wagner	New Bremen, IL	Raubenhausen, Rothenburg, Kurhessen
Holstein, Emma Catharina	14, Feb. 1881	24, Jan.	14- 7m	55		Sherrills Mount, IA	

- 214 -

Christliche Apologete Death Notices --- 1839 - 1899

Name of Deceased	Notice Date	Death Date	Age	Page	Maiden Name	Place of Death	Place of Birth
Holstein, Georg	16, July 1866	1, July	67	230	Miller	New Bremen, IL	Rockenfuß, Kurhessen
Holstein, Maria Louisa	24, Jan. 1895	29, Dec.	64	62	Stough	Trail Run, OH	Alfeld, Hannover
Holstein, Sarah	24, June 1858	11, June	25-10m-23d	100		Sherrills Mount, IA	
Holt , Fr.	10, Aug. 1893	8, July	57	510		Flora, MN	Lüneburg, Minden, Preußen
Holtcamp, Augusta	11, Jan. 1894	12, Dec.	29	30	Hausman	St. Louis, MO	St. Louis, Missouri
Holte, Justina	28, Oct. 1878	28, July	74-1m	343		Ballwin, MO	Lippe-Detmold
Holtegel, Johanna	13, Jan. 1873	29, Dec.	29-4m-18d	15	Zehe	Milan, IN	
Holtegel, Wilhelm	17, Mar. 1884	4, Mar.	84	7		Dillsboro, IN	Vernuwahlshausen, Kurhessen
Hölter, Anna Eva	2, Feb. 1863	13, Jan.	45- - 1d	20		Boonville, IN	Itar, Oldenburg
Holtgreve, Christina	7, Mar. 1881	20, Feb.	25	79	Wille	Oregon, MO	Troy, Madison County, Illinois
Holtkamp, Anna Maria	26, July 1860	10, July	54	120		Pittsfield, IL	
Holtkamp, Caroline	1, Apr. 1872	4, Mar.	35	111	Büsching	Pittsfield, IL	Harrienstädt, Amt Stolzenau, Hannover
Holtkamp, Hermann Heinrich	12, July 1869	22, June	72	223		Evansville, IN	Ladbergen, Westphalen, Preußen
Holtkamp, Johan Friedrich	9, July 1896		81- 1m- 2d	447		Elmore, OH	Stätefreund, Westphalen
Holtkamp, Katharina E.	25, Apr. 1870	19, Mar.	72	135	Flederjohann	Evansville, IN	Ladbergen, Tecklenburg, Preußen
Holtkamp, Kobus	10, Dec. 1891	5, Nov.	18	798		Oakford, IL	Süd-Georgs Fehn, Germany
Holtkamp, Maria Engel	3, Apr. 1871	6, Mar.	66-1m	111	Schäfer	Woodville, OH	Boneberg, Amt Vlotho, Valdorf, Preußen
Holtz, C.F.	4, Feb. 1892	7, Jan.	51-10m-19d	78		Swanton, NE	
Holtz, Christian Friedrich	9, July1883	23, June	63	223		Redfield, MN	Blumberg, Pommern
Holtz, Franz	12, June 1890	17, May	72	382		Wichita, KS	Schillingsfürst, Baiern
Holtz, Joachim Heinrich	12, Mar. 1857	25, Feb.	59- 3m	44		Columbus, WI	Redenten, Mecklenburg, Mecklenburg-Schwerin
Holweger, Marie Agnes	12, Nov. 1883	22, Oct.	77- - 7d	367	Doßter	Madison, IN	Riederich, Urach, Württemberg
Holwegner, Georg Fr.	21, Apr. 1873	24, Mar.	71	127		Madison, IN	Bempflingen, Urach, Württemberg
Holz, Anna Christina	19, Dec. 1861	27, Nov.		204	Hoeft	Watertown, WI	Reppeln bei Stargard, Pommern
Holz, August	20, Mar. 1876	1, Mar.	17-10m	95		Minnesota Lake, MN	Milford, Wisconsin
Holz, Elisabeth	15, Oct. 1877	25, Sept	73	335		Columbus, WI	Blowitz, Radentin, Mecklenburg-Schwerin
Holz, Ernestine Wilhelmina	13, May 1897	25, Apr.	56	303	Hintz	Swanton, NE	Dölitz, Pommern
Holz, Friedrich	9, Feb. 1874	13, Jan.	47	47		Columbus, WI	Blowatz, Redentsin, Mecklenburg-Schwerin
Holz, Katharine	24, Jan. 1870	25, Dec.	56- 1m-24d	31	Herr	Bradford, IN	Schillingsfürst, Mittelfranken, Baiern
Holz, Rieke	28, Oct. 1878	30, Sept	15	343		Columbus, WI	Portland, Dodge County, Wisconsin
Holz, Therese	20, Oct. 1879	26, Sept	24	335		Bradford, IN	New Albany, Indiana
Holzapfel, Nicolaus	14, May 1891	17, Apr.	64	318		Eudora, KS	Winschhausen, Marburg, Werder, Kurhessen
Holzbeierlein, (Mrs)	14, June 1860	19, May	62	96	Ott	Jefferson City, MO	Bayreuth, Baiern
Holzbeierlein, Andreas	4, Nov. 1897	16, Oct.	71	703		Medford, OK	Mühle bei Untersteinach, Weiderberg, Baiern
Holzbeierlein, Heinrich	19, Feb. 1852	23, Jan.	22- 1m-11d	32		Jefferson City, MO	
Holzbeierlein, Lydia Caroline	28, Jan. 1884	1, Jan.		7		Wyandotte, KS	
Holzberger, David Michael	27, Mar. 1890	3, Mar.	21-4m- 9d	206		Brookville, IN	Lawrenceville, Indiana
Holzberger, Michael	25, June 1891	3, June		414		Brookville, IN	Diespeck bei Neustadt, Baiern
Holzbog, Johan Georg	30, Dec. 1897	9, Dec.	75	828		Jeffersonville, IN	Kornwestheim, Ludwigsburg, Württemberg
Holzebosch, Margaretha Barbara	21, May 1891	21, Apr.	51- 6m	334	Frey	Newark, NJ	Altentaig, Nagold, Württemberg
Hölzer, Catharine	10, Nov. 1884	28, Oct.	72	7	Eiring	Charlestown, IN	Schwarzenfels, Schlichtern, Hessen
Holzinger, Anna Katharina	15, Mar. 1888	14, Feb.	31	174		Stitzer, WI	
Holzinger, Johan	18, Nov. 1878	30, Oct.	40	367		Austin, TX	
Holzinger, Leonhard	10, Dec. 1896	16, Nov.	80	798		Stitzer, WI	Lerchenbühl bei Ettingen, Baiern
Holzinger, Maria	2, Oct. 1871		41	319	Schmidt	Charles City, IA	Hachtel, Gerabronn, Württemberg
Hölzle, Georg	7, Aug. 1846	15, June	34	127		Monroe Co., ---	

- 215 -

Christliche Apologete Death Notices --- 1839 - 1899

Name of Deceased	Notice Date	Death Date	Age	Page	Maiden Name	Place of Death	Place of Birth
Hölzle, Johan	14, Feb. 1895	17, Jan.	85	110		Denison, IA	Summiswald, Bern, Schweiz
Hölzle, Maria Margaretha	14, Feb. 1895	19, Jan.	72	110	Balsiger	Denison, IA	Kleinwabern, Bern, Schweiz
Holzmann, Dina	24, Feb. 1868	11, Jan.	23- 6m	63		Pekin, Il	
Holzt, Heinrich	10, Feb. 1887	15, Jan.	60	94		Marietta, OH	Maeckels, Zeven, Hannover
Holzward, Christian	3, Aug. 1863	26, May	27	124		Cedar Lake, IN	Rietenau, Backnang, Württemberg
Holzworth, Matthäus	7, Apr. 1879	1, Mar.	80- 4m-19d	111		Cedar Lake, IN	Allmirsbach, Backnang, Württemberg
Homann, Johan Friedrich August	20, Aug. 1896	2, Aug.	74	542		St. Louis, MO	Neuenkirchen bei Melle, Hannover
Homann, Joseph	25, Aug. 1862	5, July	25-11m	136		Baraboo, WI	Düttershausen bei Fulda, Kurhessen
Homberger, Maria	30, July1883	9, July	72- 6m	247	Noll	Newark, NJ	Delzberg, Fritzlar, Kurhessen
Homburg, Katharina E.	17, Apr. 1882	12, Mar.	59- 9m-19d	127		Francisco, MI	Elgershausen, Kassel, Kurhessen
Homeier, Christine Eleonora	30, Mar. 1885	13, Mar.	77	7		Oakland, CA	Bederkesa, Hannover
Homer, (Mrs)	20, Feb. 1890	23, Jan.	70- 2m-13d	126		Greenville, OH	Wolf, Hessen-Darmstadt
Homfeld, Herman	24, Dec. 1896	1, Nov.	39	831		Bland, MO	Bland, Missouri
Homfield, H.	23, Feb. 1880	3, Feb.	69	63		Dillsboro, IN	Bendorf, Hohenhaus, Lippe-Detmold
Honegger, Susanna	1, Mar. 1894	31, Jan.	41	150		Melvin, IL	Arburg, Aargau, Schweiz
Hönegger, Susanna	19, Mar. 1896	3, Mar.	72	190	Santmann	Cincinnati, OH	Schönenberg, Zürich, Schweiz
Hönemeier, Johan Friedrich	25, Mar.1872	15, Mar.	45- 9m	103		Cincinnati, OH	Kalkriese, Amt Malgarten, Hannover
Hönemeier, Theodor Johan	27, Feb. 1871	8, Feb.	10- 5m-19d	71		Cincinnati, OH	
Honen, H.	7, Nov. 1870	26, Sept	66	359		Nemota, NE	Wulsdorf, Amt Kamin, HinterPommern
Hönes, Elisabeth	21, Apr. 1892	3, Apr.	79- -15d	254	Krumm	Kendallville, IN	Ohmenhausen, Reutlingen, Württemberg
Höneß, Maria Elisabeth	20, Oct. 1887	26, Aug.	30	670	Schlegel	Bloomington, Il	Honau, Reutlingen, Württemberg
Honnen, Bertha Henrietta	28, Jan. 1878	25, Nov.	30	31		Tecumseh, NE	
Honnen, Heinrich	18, Mar. 1867	7, Feb.	16	86		Salem, NE	
Honsen, Eibel	21, Apr. 1879	5, Apr.	75	127		Platteville, WI	Campbell County, Kentucky
Hoos, Heinrich	2, May 1889	6, Apr.	48-10m-13d	286		Pittsfield, IL	Spika, Dorum, Hannover
Hoos, Johan Georg	31, Jan. 1870	3, Jan.	66	39		Pittsfield, IL	Wasenberg, Ziegenheim, Hessen-Kassel
Hopf, Dorothea	6, Oct. 1873	23, Sept	45- 9m-16d	319	Händel	White Creek, IN	Wasenberg, Ziegenhain, Hessen
Höpfner, Friederika	13, Dec. 1880	15, Nov.	79	399		Milwaukee, WI	Eisfeld, Sachsen-Meiningen
Höpner, Johanna Sophia Carolina	14, May 1891	28, Apr.	36	318	Jenerjohn	Elkport, IA	Klempnow, Vorpommern
Hoppe, August	22, July 1897	2, July	76	463		Brenham, TX	Güten, Mecklenburg-Schwerin
Hoppe, Christoph	7, Mar. 1881	18, Feb.	62- 9m- 4d	79		Columbus, OH	Colaia, Posen
Hoppe, Eduard	11, Aug. 1898	9, July	16	511		Chester, IL	Prezelle, Gartow, Hannover
Hoppe, Friedrich	15, Dec. 1892	20, Nov.	65	798		Francisco, MI	Randolph County, Illinois
Hoppe, Friedrich	19, Jan. 1899	13, Oct.	64	47		St. Paul, MN	Stodel bei Bremerhaven, Hannover
Hoppe, Friedrich Wilhelm	1, Aug. 1889	13, July	47	494		Hartford, CT	Schobin, Preußen
Hoppe, Johan J.C.	6, Oct. 1879	2, Sept	72	319		Dodgeville, IA	Putlitz, West Prienitz, Preußen
Hoppe, John Konrad	26, May 1898	18, Apr.	56	335		Oakland, CA	Diesdorf, Salzwedel, Magdeburg, Preußen
Hoppe, Karl Christian	1, May 1882	28, Mar.	34	143		Kewaunee, WI	Stotel, Leh, Hannover
Hoppe, Karolina	30, June 1873	29, Apr.	27- 8m	207	Notten	San Francisco, CA	Hammelstall, Vorpommern
Hoppe, Rosalie	28, Mar. 1881	7, Mar.	20	103		Dalton, MO	New York
Hoppen, Carolina	30, July 1877	14, July	28- 9m-25d	247	Haas	Evansville, IN	
Hoppen, Christoph	12, Apr. 1888	22, Feb.	47	238		Wyandotte, KS	Chillicothe, Ross County, Ohio
Hoppen, John C.	29, Nov. 1894	14, Nov.	30	774		Kansas City, KS	Kansas City, Kansas
Hoppenwarth, Johan	11, Dec. 1882	7, Nov.	20- 3m-16d	399		Sheboygan, WI	
Hoppmann, Karoline	23, Dec. 1886	8, Dec.	79	7	Ossenford	Schnectady, NY	
Höppner, Louise	26, Mar. 1891	22, Feb.	70- -17d	206		Wausau, WI	Hille, Minden, Preußen

Christliche Apologete Death Notices --- 1839 - 1899

Name of Deceased	Notice Date	Death Date	Age	Page	Maiden Name	Place of Death	Place of Birth
Hopstätter, Friederike	23, Jan. 1896	30, Dec.	43	62	Schulz	Ironton, OH	Lieblingroth, Nordhausen, Preußen
Hopt, Fridolin	29, Mar. 1869	9, Jan.	42	103		Pomeroy, OH	Laufen bei Rottweil, Württemberg
Horath, Martha	3, Mar. 1898	12, Feb.	24	143	Schröder	Chicago, IL	Gartz, Insel Rügen, Pommern
Hörchner, Christine	9, May 1895	16, Apr.	50	302	Reinhardt	St. Paul, MN	Fambach, Kurhessen
Hördt, Anna Maria	9, Sept 1897	14, Aug.	22	575	Guth	Mascoutah, IL	Mascoutah, Illinois
Hörer, Jacobine	7, Dec. 1874	8, Nov.	68- 1m-25d	391	Schüle	Canton, MO	Sersheim, Vaihingen, Württemberg
Hörer, Jakob Friedrich	2, Feb. 1888	14, Jan.	54	78		Canton, MO	Metterzimmern, Bösigheim, Württemberg
Hörer, Wilhelm Heinrich	28, July 1887	9, July	22	478		Canton, MO	Canton, Missouri
Höreth, Clara Sophia	20, Apr. 1863	24, Feb.	6	64		Indianapolis, IN	
Höreth, Dorothea	26, June 1865	8, June	59	104	Krebs	Indianapolis, IN	Kleestadt, Hessen
Höreth, Georg	28, Sept 1893	7, Sept	28	622		Indianapolis, IN	Indianapolis, Marion County, Indiana
Höreth, Ludwig	1, Nov. 1888	5, Oct.	86- 5m-19d	702		Indianapolis, IN	Schaffhausen, Hessen-Darmstadt
Hörger, Magdalena	9, May 1889	17, Apr.	46- -14d	302	Mack	Aurora, IL	Sontheim, Heidenheim, Württemberg
Hörger, Maria Barbara	22, Jan. 1872	12, Oct.	50	31		Aurora, IL	Sundheim an der Brentz, Württemberg
Hörhold, C.	12, Mar. 1896	5, Feb.	82	174		Lexington, TX	Kroppenstedt, Sachsen
Höning, Katharina Barbara	25, Mar. 1867	8, Mar.	68- 3m-15d	94	Fiesser	Mascoutah, IL	Haßloch, Rheinkreis Baiern
Hörker, Johan Heinrich	1, Jan. 1877	8, Dec.	79- 1m-11d	7		Bucyrus, OH	Unter-Heinrieth, Weinsberg, Württemberg
Hörl, (Mrs)	6, June 1870	15, May	43- 4m	183		Stockton, CA	Würzburg am Main, Baiern
Horlacher, Anna Barbara	30, Aug. 1869	13, Aug.	58- 3m-14d	279	Hönig	Cleveland, OH	Reingenheim, Baiern
Horlacher, Barbara	26, Nov. 1891	1, Nov.	37	766		Spokane, WA	Hall, Württemberg
Horlacher, Johannes	13, Oct. 1879	29, Sept	69	327		Cleveland, OH	Rheingönheim, Baiern
Horle, Anna Katharina	4, Aug. 1892	19, June	57	494	Walter	Boston, MA	Gras-Ellenbach, Hessen-Darmstadt
Hörle, Johannes	13, May 1852	28, Apr.	75- 2m	80		Galion, OH	Münzenheim, Baden
Hörle, Margaretha	23, May 1864	5, May	76- 4m-17d	84		Bucyrus, OH	Hawartespach, Durlach, Baden
Horn, Barbara	3, Sept 1857	21, Aug.	30	144	Groß	Newport, KY	Merzweiler, Elsaß
Horn, Catharine Elisabeth	25, Oct. 1880	5, Oct.	67- 7m-10d	343	Schäfer	Frankfort, IL	Kirchhosbach, Kurhessen
Horn, Catharine Elisabeth	18, Oct. 1880			335	Andres	New Bremen, IL	
Horn, Charles	5, Apr. 1894	12, Mar.	24- 9m- 7d	230		Buffalo, NY	
Horn, Christian	4, May 1874	4, Apr.	29- 1m	143		Ottawa, IL	
Horn, Elisa	1, Nov. 1855	17, Oct.	36	176	Wippelmann	Newport, KY	Löbenstein, Reuß
Horn, Katharina Elisabeth	23, Aug. 1894	30, July	70	550	Schwarz	Wellsville, NY	Westendorf, Amt Melle, Hannover
Horn, Louise	4, Jan. 1869	17, Dec.	51	7	Zastrow	Wausau, WI	Leiferde, Hannover
Horn, Mathilde	10, Mar. 1879	13, Feb.	24- 2m-23d	79	Beierle	Jerusalem, IA	Streton, Neumark, Preußen
Hornberg, Wilhelm	9, June 1884	13, May	15- 2m-21d	7		Laporte, IN	Wisconsin
Hornberger, Anna Maria	4, Oct. 1875	17, Sept	78	319	Forstner	Lawrenceburg, IN	Minfeld, Langen-Candel, Rheinpfalz Baiern
Hornberger, Georg Nicklaus	3, Apr. 1865	17, Mar.	76- 4m-24d	56		Lawrenceburg, IN	Steinweiler, Candel, Rheinkreis Baiern
Hornberger, Johannes	11, Jan. 1849		Inquiry	7		Defiance, OH	Minfeld bei Langkandel, Rheinkreis Baiern
Hornberger, Mic	28, Oct. 1886	31, Aug.	39	7		Batesville, IN	
Hornberger, Michael	14, Nov. 1895	15, July	91	734		Stryker, OH	
Hornberger, Rahel	17, Apr. 1890	24, Mar.	69- -18d	254	Klein	Brookville, IN	Baden
Hornecker, John	10, Mar. 1898	22, Feb.	72	158		Orgon, MO	Winden, Rheinkreis Baiern
Hornecker, Maria Katharina	26, Jan. 1899	3, Dec.	66	63	Wiedermann	Columbus, IL	Augen, Baden
Hörner, Adam	25, July 1895	4, July	68	478		Dubuque, IA	Baden
Hörner, Annie	5, Feb. 1891	17, Jan.	18-10m-17d	94		Dubuque, IA	Sherrills Mount, Dubuque County, Iowa
Horner, Johan Rudolph	27, Sept 1880	6, Sept	36	311		Vanderburg Co, IN	Schaffhausen, Schweiz
Horner, Johan Rudolph	4, Oct. 1880	6, Sept	37	319		Henderson, KY	Basel, Schweiz

Christliche Apologete Death Notices --- 1839 - 1899

Name of Deceased	Notice Date	Death Date	Age	Page	Maiden Name	Place of Death	Place of Birth
Horner, Johan Rudolph	18, Oct. 1880	6, Sept	37	335		Henderson, KY	Basel, Schweiz
Horner, Johann Heinrich	1, Aug. 1850	20, July	55	124		Evansville, IN	Basel, Schweiz
Hörner, Wilhelm	23, July 1866	30, May	19	238		Second Creek, MO	Thun, Bern, Schweiz
Hornicker, Anna Maria	9, Oct. 1865	25, Sept		164	Bruner	Cincinnati, OH	Langendenslingen, Emmendingen, Baden
Hornicker, Anna Maria	28, Feb. 1876	4, Feb.	52	71	Nußbaumer	Oregon, MO	Dattingen, Mühlheim, Baden
Horne, Georg	26, Sept 1889	31, Aug.	21-5m-11d	619		Sherrills Mount, IA	Sherrill, Iowa
Horney, Selma B.	5, Jan. 1893	1, Nov.	14	14		Sherrills Mount, IA	
Hornung, Clara Louise	26, Apr. 1875	7, Apr.	31-10m	135	Kötter	Portsmouth, OH	Kispelbur, Grüneberg, Hannover
Hornung, Karl	15, Dec. 1892	13, Nov.	33	798		Defiance, OH	Henry County, Ohio
Hornung, Magdalena	20, July 1893	25, June	80	462	Schwab	Defiance, OH	Hofrügen, Baiern
Hornung, Micklena	18, Mar. 1867	22, Feb.	63	86		Portsmouth, OH	Guntelingen, Horb, Württemberg
Hornung, Peter	9, Mar. 1854	1, Dec.	44-3m-16d	40		Poplar Ridge, OH	Thalversche, Rheinkreis Baiern
Horr, Johan Jakob	29, Oct. 1891	6, Oct.		702		Baltimore, MD	Hessen-Darmstadt
Horr, Otto	11, Jan. 1875	23, Dec.	21-9m	15		Baltimore, MD	
Hörring, Ursula	20, Dec. 1894	27, Nov.	67	822		Anaheim, CA	Württemberg
Hörsch, Johan Jakob	26, May 1892	3, May	66	334		Davenport, IA	Nehnslätten, Württemberg
Hörsemann, Caspar H.	14, Dec. 1868	17, Nov.	30-2m-16d	399		Wyandotte, KS	Lindorf, Amt Witlage, Hannover
Hörsemann, Ernst	1, Feb. 1875	3, Jan.	67-10m	39		Wyandotte, KS	Höringhausen, Amt Wittlage, Hannover
Hörsemann, Maria Elisabeth	31, Dec. 1877	6, Dec.	65-6m	423	Blase	Wyandotte, KS	Lintorf, Hannover
Hörsemann, Vinnie	4, Aug. 1898	12, July	21	495		Kansas City, KS	Kansas City, Kansas
Horßmann, Cassie	19, May 1887	27, Apr.	31	318		Kansas City, KS	Jackson County, Ohio
Horst, Elisabeth	10, Aug. 1885	5, May	77	7		Lincoln, NE	Lobenhausen, Hessen-Darmstadt
Horst, Heinrich	17, June 1852	2, May	21	100		Le Sueur, MN	Bubenhausen, Nidda, Hessen-Darmstadt
Horst, Johan	2, Apr. 1891	14, Mar.	86	222		Birmingham, PA	Badenhausen, Germany
Horst, Andreas	25, Aug. 1898	5, Aug.	79	543		Le Sueur, MN	Köngernheim an der Selz, Hessen-Darmstadt
Horst, Anna Babette	14, Aug. 1882	14, June	48	263	Fichtenmüller	Madison, NE	Langensend, Baiern
Horst, Emilie M.	29, Nov. 1880	11, Nov.	43	383		Baltimore, MD	Lebanon County, Pennsylvania
Horst, Eva Lydia	20, Dec. 1880	26, Nov.	8-11m-2d	407		Bloomington, IL	
Horst, Leonhard	13, Aug. 1883	8, July	27-4m-2d	263		Columbus, NE	Green Bay, Wisconsin
Horst, Maria E.	8, Nov. 1894	17, Oct.	44	726	Schmidt	Osceola, NE	Farmington, Washington County, Wisconsin
Hörster, Elisabeth	18, Feb. 1878	29, Jan.	36	55	Gammenthaler	Llano, TX	Irsigen, Bern, Schweiz
Hörster, Lydia	18, Feb. 1878	2, Feb.	10-5m	55		Llano, TX	
Horstmann, Anna Catharine	12, Apr. 1894	14, Mar.	23	246	Mönch	Laghery, IN	Millpoint, New York
Horstmann, Carolina Clara	24, Nov. 1884	29, Oct.	37	7	Kruse	Ft. Hunter, NY	St. Charles County, Missouri
Horstmann, Ernst	5, Nov. 1866	21, Oct.	85	385		St. Louis, MO	Hille, Minden, Preußen
Horstmann, F. (Mrs)	11, Feb. 1848	13, Jan.	34	27		Herman, MO	Bisssendorf, Hannover
Horstmann, Franz	14, July 1862	13, Apr.	21	112		New Orleans, LA	Hille, Minden, Preußen
Horstmann, Friedrich	26, Feb. 1891	27, Jan.	56	142		Union, MO	
Horstmann, Friedrich	30, June 1859	25, May	66	104		Schnectady, NY	Stemmer, Minden, Preußen
Horstmann, Friedrich	24, July 1865	17, June	50-6m	120		Herman, MO	Hille bei Minden, Westphalen
Horstmann, Gottlieb	25, Feb. 1886		71	7		Wyandotte, KS	Stemmer, Petershagen, Preußen
Horstmann, Heinrich A.	1, Dec. 1898	9, Nov.	33	767		Ft. Hunter, NY	Franklin County, Missouri
Horstmann, Heinrich C.	12, Nov. 1883	29, Oct.	43-8m-12d	367		Batesville, IN	Aschendorf, Iburg, Osnabrück, Hannover
Horstmann, Heinrich W.	25, Mar. 1867	9, Mar.	26	94		Wyandotte, KS	Hille, Minden, Preußen
Horstmann, Heinrich Wilhelm	21, Oct. 1878		72-6m-19d	335		St. Louis, MO	
Horstmann, Karl	15, Nov. 1875	26, Sept	47	367		Herman, MO	Hille, Minden, Preußen

- 218 -

Christliche Apologete Death Notices --- 1839 - 1899

Name of Deceased	Notice Date	Death Date	Age	Page	Maiden Name	Place of Death	Place of Birth
Horstmann, Karolina Wilhelmina	14, Aug. 1876	8, July	12	263		Herman, MO	Bracke, Lippe
Horstmann, Karoline	25, Dec. 1851	21, Nov.	26	208		Monroe, IL	Pennington, Indiana
Horstmann, Louise Emilie	19, Sept 1895	6, Sept	28	606		Batesville, IN	Melle, Hannover
Horstmann, Luisa	10, May 1894	21, Apr.	77	310	Jasper	Kansas City, KS	Manzingen bei Kreuznach, Rheinpreußen
Horstmann, Margaretha	25, Aug. 1879	8, Aug.	64	271	Alt	Platteville, WI	Eichhorst, Minden, Preußen
Horstmann, Maria	24, Nov. 1879	25, Oct.	87	375	Ekersberg	Herman, MO	Hille, Minden, Preußen
Horstmann, S. M. Elisabeth	22, Jan. 1877	9, Dec.	69-10m	31	Feisel	Herman, MO	Dissen, Osnabrück, Hannover
Horstmann, Wilhelmine	14, Nov. 1881	19, Sept	69- 7m-17d	367	Schütz	Bloomington, IL	Hille, Minden, Preußen
Horstmann, Wilhelmine	28, Aug. 1882	15, July	51	279	Gerding	Drake, MO	
Horstmann, Wilhelmine	6, Dec. 1875	5, Oct.	14	391		Herman, MO	
Horstmeier, Carolina Wilhelmine	27, Dec. 1888	26, Oct.	78- 6m- 6d	830	Wiese	Schnectady, NY	Südhemmern, Minden, Westphalen
Hosch, Anna Catharina	1, Nov. 1875	15, Oct.	60	351	Jaspring	Eudora, KS	Melle bei Osnabrück, Hannover
Hosch, Catharina	24, Nov. 1859	1, Nov.	44- 1m-18d	188		Ft. Riley, KS	Jigenheim, Baden
Hosch, Christina	21, Oct. 1867	5, Sept	26	334	Dösch	Danville, IL	Treisbach, Kreis Marburg, Kurhessen
Hosch, Johan	7, Aug. 1890	12, July	85	510		Danville, IL	NiederAspe, Kurhessen
Hosch, Johan Wilhelm	29, Nov. 1894	3, Nov.	23	774		Danville, IL	Danville, Illinois
Hosch, Luise	23, Jan. 1896	2, Jan.	56	62	Neuhaus	Danville, IL	Kiespe, Arnsberg, Westphalen
Hosch, Maria	25, May 1899	8, May	37	335	Kahler	Danville, IL	Untersimmtshausen, Kurhessen
Höschele, Maria	15, Nov. 1894	24, Oct.	51	742	Kilgus	Hoboken, NJ	Aichelberg, Calw, Württemberg
Hosen, Katharine	21, Jan. 1897	1, Jan.	78- 5m-25d	46	Staab	Etna, MO	Gönnheim, Rheinpfalz Baiern
Hosket, Alice	27, July 1893	1, July	33	478	Riegel	Dayton, OH	Darke County, Ohio
Hosket, Louise Charlotte	15, Sept 1879	26, Aug.	40- 2m-23d	295	Ellemund	Dayton, OH	Oldendorf, Preußen
Hoß, Maria Agnes	10, Dec. 1857	18,Nov.	32	200	Schaich	Louisville, KY	Kohlberg, Nürtingen, Württemberg
Hothem, Valtin	25, Mar. 1897	7, Mar.	72	190		Canal Dover, OH	Finkenbach, Rheinpfalz Baiern
Hotom, Charley	4, Sept 1865	30, July	19- 4m	144		St. Paul, MN	
Hottmann, David	4, Oct. 1888	31, Aug.	73	638		Enterprise, KS	
Hottmann, Johan Gottlieb	3, Jan. 1895	11, Dec.	72	14		Madison, WI	Gumbach, Schorndorf, Württemberg
Houch, Sara	1, Oct. 1877	4, Sept	39	319	Diemer	Defiance, OH	
Houdler, Augusta	24, Oct. 1881	4, Sept	70	343		Brooklyn, NY	Pommern
Hövel, Louise Henriette	19, Aug. 1878	2, Aug.	32	263	Niedringhaus	St. Louis, MO	Blasheim bei Lübbecke, Westphalen
Hövelmeier, Gerhard Heinrich	16, Aug. 1849	5, July	65	132		Laughery, IN	OsterCappeln bei Osnabrück, Hannover
Hövelmeier, Maria Engel	16, Aug. 1849	5, July	63	132		Laughery, IN	Drohne bei Osnabrück, Hannover
Hövener, Dorothea	19, Nov. 1847	14, Aug.	72	187		Delaware, OH	
Howard, Carolina	10, Dec. 1896	23, Oct.	28	798	Does	Clarington, OH	Cincinnati, Hamilton County, Ohio
Howe, Rosine	11, Aug. 1898	10, June	70	511		Poughkeepsie, NY	Burgstar, Württemberg
Howe, (Mrs)	1, May 1876	16, Apr.	44	143	Wettenhagen	Nora Springs, IA	Tolz, HinterPommern
Höwing, Martha	8, Nov. 1869	23, Oct.	24	359		Decatur, IL	
Hoy, Joahnn Gottlieb	25, July 1881	2, July	66	239		Silver Creek, NE	Wernsdorf, Sachsen-Weimar
Hoyer, Charles	3, May 1894	22, Mar.	49	294		Chicago, IL	Emmendingen, Baden
Hoyer, Katharina Maria Christine	24, Aug. 1899	5, Aug.	70	543		Morris, MN	Bohlsen, Hannover
Hoyler, Minnie	9, Sept 1897	23, Aug.	22- 1m- 9d	575		Chicago, IL	
Hubacher, Anna Maria	24, July 1882	7, July	60-11m- 4d	239	Lapp	Clarington, OH	Imsheim, Elsaß
Hubacher, Elisabeth	21, Dec. 1868	2, Dec.	82	407		Clarington, MO	Urtenen, Bern, Schweiz
Hubacher, Nikolaus	10, Nov. 1862	18, Oct.	75- 6m-12d	180		Captina, OH	Orien, Bern, Schweiz
Hube, Katharina Justine	29, Sept 1879	25, Aug.	51	311		Truxton, MO	Schönhagen, Lippe-Detmold
Hubel, John	12, Nov. 1866	16, Sept	34	366		Nashville, TN	Kircheim, Nieresheim, Württemberg

- 219 -

Christliche Apologete Death Notices --- 1839 - 1899

Name of Deceased	Notice Date	Death Date	Age	Maiden Name	Page	Place of Death	Place of Birth
Hübel, Maria	12, Nov. 1847	15, Oct.	28		183	Newark, ---	Eimsheim, Hessen
Huber, (Mrs)	2, July 1877	20, May	79		215	White Creek, IN	Hoffen, Elsaß
Huber, Adolf	3, Sept 1883	10, Aug.	40- 1m-2d		287	New York City, NY	Außerstehl bei Zürich, Schweiz
Huber, Agnes	2, Nov. 1874	19, Oct.	68- 7m- 3d	Tischer	351	Toledo, OH	Magenheim, Rheinkreis Baiern
Huber, Alice Margaretha	8, Aug. 1881	27, July	15- 9m-23d		255	Louisville, KY	
Huber, Anna	8, Feb. 1869	18, Jan.	23- 1m-16d	Moser	47	Toledo, OH	Wessen, Solothurn, Schweiz
Huber, Anna	15, Dec. 1892	18, Nov.	81	Müller	798	Jeffersonville, IN	Kappel, Zürich, Schweiz
Huber, Anna Elisabeth	7, Aug. 1871	17, July	64- 1m-26d	Rutz	255	Fond du Lac, WI	Mogelsberg, St. Gallen, Schweiz
Huber, Anna Maria	28, Apr. 1887	9, Apr.	59	Oswald	270	Minneapolis, MN	Oberaach, Thurgau, Schweiz
Huber, Auguste	9, May 1895	10, Apr.	39		302	Evansville, IN	Posey County, Indiana
Huber, Barbara	3, Nov. 1873	11, Sept	69		351	Dayton, OH	Alpirsbach, Württemberg
Huber, Barbara	24, Aug. 1899	23, July	69	Seifert	543	Mt. Vernon, IN	Gerstfelt, Baiern
Huber, Carolina	27, June 1881	31, May	21- 4m- 3d		207	Lexington, MO	Evansville, Indiana
Huber, Elisabeth	30, June 1898	10, June	77	Schmidt	415	Chicago, IL	Biedenkopf, Hessen-Darmstadt
Huber, Elisabeth	8, May 1865	31, Mar.			76	Galion, OH	
Huber, Friedrich	2, May 1870	25, Feb.	74		143	Seymour, IN	Ingolsheim, Sulz, Elsaß
Huber, Georg Friedrich	21, Dec. 1868	3, Dec.	66		407	Louisville, KY	Kochendorf, Nekarsulm, Württemberg
Huber, Gottlieb	4, Sept 1890	2, Aug.	33- - 5d		574	Covington, KY	Enzberg, Maulbronn, Württemberg
Huber, Johan Jakob	23, Jan. 1890	18, Oct.	61		62	Poughkeepsie, NY	Entzweihingen, Vaihingen, Württemberg
Huber, Johan Jakob	21, Feb. 1881	7, Feb.	61		63	Winona, MN	Wädensweil, Zürich, Schweiz
Huber, John	3, June 1872	30, Apr.	66- 5m-18d		183	Toledo, OH	
Huber, Joseph	22, Aug. 1870	20, July	69		271	Fond du Lac, WI	Magelsberg, Schweiz
Huber, Karoline	27, Apr. 1893	5, Apr.	41		270	Evansville, IN	Posey County, Indiana
Huber, Karoline Franziska	17, Mar. 1892	27, Feb.	34	Porth	174	Lexington, MO	Gaugrehweiler, Rheinpfalz Baiern
Huber, Kate	8, Nov. 1894	13, Oct.	21		726	Evansville, IN	
Huber, Katharina	11, Feb. 1892	28, Jan.	58	Leithmann	94	New Orleans, LA	Lambsheim, Rheinkreis Baiern
Huber, Louisa C.	3, Apr. 1876	17, Mar.	37- 7m-19d	Holtkamp	111	Toledo, OH	Bonnenberg, Amt Vlotho, Minden, Preußen
Huber, Magdalena	28, Aug. 1876		65	Mann	279	Louisville, KY	KleinSachsenheim, Vaihingen, Württemberg
Huber, Magdalena	7, July 1892	22, June	81	Flaig	430	Louisville, KY	Breutlingen, Baden
Huber, Sybille	29, Sept 1884	7, Sept	61	Böshens	7	Cincinnati, OH	Rissingen, Rheinkreis Baiern
Huber, Wilhelm	18, Oct. 1869	16, Sept	51		335	Cincinnati, OH	Marnheim, Rheinkreis Baiern
Huber, William	1, Dec. 1887	26, Oct.	33- 7m		766	White Creek, IN	
Hubert, Anna Christina	27, Nov. 1890	30, Oct.	71	Baul	766	Morris, MN	Singhöfen, Nassau
Hubert, Wilhelm Heinrich	14, Oct. 1867	2, Sept	47		326	Fosterburg, IL	Nassau, Nassau
Hüberter, Christina	25, Dec. 1865	27, Nov.	67		208	Madison, WI	Godenstadt, Hannover
Hubler, Barbara	14, Jan. 1867	31, Dec.	64	Herth	14	Jefferson City, MO	Bibern, Solothurn, Schweiz
Hubmann, Elisabeth	5, Dec. 1870	13, Nov.		Pückel	391	Brunswick, MO	Oberrheinbach, Oberpfalz, Baiern
Hübner, Anna	3, May 1894	8, Apr.		Eckhardt	294	Chicago, IL	Kolditz, Sachsen
Hübner, Charles G.	28, Feb. 1881	7, Nov.	49		71	Stockton, CA	Neukirch bei Bautzen, Sachsen
Hübner, Christian Friedrich	27, May 1872	7, Apr.	66- 6m-15d		175	Yellow Creek, IL	Wudarge, Kreis Satze, Preußen
Hübner, Christian Friedrich	14, June 1894	20, May	60		390	Lowell, WI	Satzig, Stettin, Pommern
Hübner, Christine	4, Feb. 1892	12, Jan.	71		78	Odebolt, IA	Damm, Prenzlau, Preußen
Hübner, Dorothea Louise	20, Aug. 1891	21, July	56-11m-20d		542	Lowell, WI	Stolzenhagen, Pommern
Hübner, Elisabeth	14, July 1884	26, June	22		7	Baltimore, MD	Baltimore, Maryland
Hubner, Emma	15, Oct. 1896	17, Sept	27	Keuer	671	Brillion, WI	Schleswig, Wisconsin
Hübner, Friedrich G.	3, Aug. 1899	14, July	51		495	Ft. Dodge, IA	Peoria, Illinois

Christliche Apologete Death Notices --- 1839 - 1899

Name of Deceased	Notice Date	Death Date	Age	Maiden Name	Page	Place of Death	Place of Birth
Hübner, Georg	9, Aug. 1849	16, July	32		128	St. Louis, MO	
Hübner, George C.	4, May 1899	26, Mar.	72		287	Alden, IA	Wiesleth, Baiern
Hübner, J.	15, July 1872	1, July	70- 3m-13d		231	Iowa City, IA	
Hübner, Johan Gottlieb	22, July 1867	6, May	57		230	Oconomowoc, WI	Berkenau, Pommern, Preußen
Hübner, Karl	7, Oct. 1886	19, Sept	54		7	Milwaukee, WI	Neudorf, Schlesien
Hübner, Karl Friedrich Nik	28, Apr. 1848		Inquiry		71	Peoria, IL	
Hübner, Karolina	7, Feb. 1895	11, Jan.	52		94	Louisville, KY	Friedland, Böhmen
Hübner, Karolina	30, June 1859	14, June	15- 8m		104	Iowa City, IA	
Hübner, Katharina	18, Nov. 1897	28, Oct.	71	Knöringer	735	Alden, IA	Mennigen, Baiern
Hübner, Louise Friedrike Henriette	10, Nov. 1892	22, Oct.	46	Vollmer	718	Grand Island, NE	Schlangen, Lippe-Detmold
Hübner, Maria Magdalena	12, May 1887	11, Apr.	68	Koch	302	Burlington, IA	Schwegenheim, Speyer, Rheinkreis Baiern
Hubner, Martin	15, Mar. 1888	17, Feb.	72		174	Danville, MN	Wels, Oesterreich
Hübner, Wilhelm	6, Apr. 1885	12, Mar.	19		7	St. Paul, NE	Dodge County, Wisconsin
Hübner, Wilhelm	5, Oct. 1885	3, Sept	20		7	Baltimore, MD	Baltimore, Maryland
Hübsch, David	18, Sept 1846		Inquiry		161	Pomeroy, OH	
Hübsch, Jacob	25, Feb. 1892	7, Jan.	83- 2m-16d		126	Hartford, WI	Seibenzell, Baiern
Hübsch, Margaretha	1, June 1874	24, Apr.	68	Knierer	175	Bradford, IN	Lindenhart, Baiern
Hübscher, Jakob	6, Apr. 1899	6, Feb.	62		222	Stryker, OH	Thayingen, Schaffhausen, Schweiz
Huch, Friedrich	16, Sept 1878	6, Aug.	83- 7m-26d		295	Lafayette, IN	Könnern, Anhalt, Preußen
Huch, Friedrich	18, Feb. 1886	23, Jan.	63		7	Lafayette, IN	Genthin, Sachsen
Huck, Friederike	15, Mar. 1860	19, Feb.	30- 8m-12d	Müller	44	Auburn, OH	
Huck, Friedrich Wilhelm Louis	10, Aug. 1885	21, July	58		7	Hoyleton, IL	Unterlübbe, Minden, Preußen
Huck, Katharine	10, Feb. 1887	17, Jan.	76	Bockstahler	94	Baresville, OH	Eichstädten, Baden
Huck, Louise	23, June 1873	27, May	40	Rithmann	199	Nashville, IL	Unterlübbe, Kreis Minden, Preußen
Huck, Maria Sophia	21, Oct. 1886	5, Oct.	73		7	Ironton, OH	Oppau, Frankenthal, Baiern
Huck, Minnie	20, Mar. 1890	18, Feb.	21-10m-16d		190	Cannelton, IN	Cannelton, Indiana
Huck, Rosina	5, Jan. 1893	11, Dec.	31- 6m- 6d	Fehlmann	14	Louisville, KY	Aarburg, Aargau, Schweiz
Hucke, Catharina	14, May 1896	19, Mar.	88		318	Wrayville, IL	Lendorf bei Kassel, Hessen-Kassel
Huckemeyer, Herman Heinrich	19, June 1876	11, May	68		199	Beaufort, MO	Bissendorf, Achelriede, Osnabrück, Hannover
Huckrieden, Sophia	9, Nov. 1854	1, June	16- 3m- 6d		180	Marthasville, MO	
Hueber, Elisabeth	19, May 1898	22, Mar.	69	Heiderscheid	319	Malta, IL	Folscheid, Luxemburg
Hueg, Wilhelm	3, Apr. 1890	27, Feb.	73		222	Boston, MA	Göttingen, Hannover
Hueg, Wilhelmina	5, Aug. 1886	21, July	66	Kummert	7	Boston, MA	Osterburg, Altmark, Magdeburg, Preußen
Huehle, Elisabeth	11, Sept 1876	24, Aug.	30	Fenstermann	295	Lansing, ----	Bippen, Hannover
Huf, Maria	17, Aug. 1893	26, July	75	Flüchiger	526	Elmore, OH	Canton Bern, Schweiz
Huff, Philipp	14, Apr. 1843	24, Feb.			59	St. Louis, MO	
Hufnagel, (Mrs)	4, June 1891	7, Mar.	85	Röder	366	Marrs, IN	Altenkranau, Schwarzenfels, Kurhessen
Hufnagel, Carolina	12, July 1880	23, June	21		223	Evansville, IN	Marrs, Indiana
Hufnagel, Elisabeth	31, July 1871	9, July	34- 9m-13d	Schmuch	247	Marrs, IN	Neumurschen, Kurhessen
Hüftle, Caroline Lavine	29, July 1893	7, May	24	Klein	414	Eustis, NE	
Hüftle, Karoline	29, Dec. 1898	16, Nov.	65		828	Eustis, NE	Nassach, Marbach, Württemberg
Hug, Caroline	28, Apr. 1879	14, Apr.	46- 6m- 7d	Zehnder	135	Covington, KY	Ettenhausen, Thurgau, Schweiz
Hug, Friedrich	24, Feb. 1887	12, Feb.	61		126	Great Bend, KS	Lauterbach bei Schramberg, Württemberg
Hügel, Anna Eva	5, Jan. 1885	18, Dec.	15		7	Boonville, IN	Warrick County, Indiana
Hügel, Barbara	14, Jan. 1886	7, Dec.	68		7	Des Moines, IA	
Hügel, Jakob	19, Feb. 1852	19, Dec.			32	Boonville, IN	Birkenfeld, Oldenburg

Christliche Apologete Death Notices --- 1839 - 1899

Name of Deceased	Notice Date	Death Date	Age	Page	Maiden Name	Place of Death	Place of Birth
Hügel, John L.	19, Oct. 1863	14, Sept	20- 4m- 4d	168	Keller	Decatur, IL	Birkenfeld, Oldenburg
Hügel, Karolina	21, Apr. 1884	10, Apr.	65	7		Boonville, IN	Schöneich, Beblingen, Württemberg
Hügel, Maria	20, Aug. 1891	28, July	50-10m- 8d	542	Wacker	Saginaw, MI	Birkenfeld, Oldenburg
Hügel, Phil. Karl	20, Mar. 1876	28, Feb.	34- 9m- 8d	95		Boonville, IN	Merenburg, Nassau
Hügelli, (Mr)	15, Mar. 1860	3, Feb.	44	44		Nashville, IL	Nashville, Illinois
Hügely, Anna Susanna	13, Oct. 1892	2, Sept	30	654	Keller	Nashville, IL	Holzhausen, Lübke, Minden, Preußen
Huggy, Charlotte	28, Sept 1893	5, Sept	63	622	Korphage	Springfield, IL	Rhein-Bischofsheim, Baden
Hügle, L.	6, Mar. 1882	9, Feb.	64	79		Des Moines, IA	Untersenn, Bern, Schweiz
Hugler, Susanna	12, Aug. 1897	15, July	48-11m- 2d	511		Osceola, NE	
Hügni, Ludwig	27, Aug. 1847	11, Aug.	77	139		Newark, ---	Liegnitz, Schlesien
Hugo, Albertine	20, Mar. 1890	27, Feb.	42	190		Yoakum, TX	Gleishorbach, RheinPfalz Baiern
Hugo, Andreas	7, Apr. 1887	20, Mar.	37	222		Cincinnati, OH	Bauer, Pommern
Hugo, Charlotte	11, Aug. 1898			511	Schulz	Arlington Heights, IL	
Hugo, Elisabeth	17, May 1888	9, Mar.	30	318		Amsterdam, NY	Schnectady, New York
Hugo, Emma	8, Oct. 1891	24, Aug.	24	654		Amsterdam, NY	Niscayuna, New York
Hugo, Fanny	10, July 1871	4, June	39	223	Fiedler	Warrenton, MO	Hohenleusen, Sachsen
Hugo, Fred.	25, Feb. 1892	30, Dec.	23	126		Amsterdam, NY	
Hugo, Friedrich	29, Jan. 1891	4, Sept	52	78		Schnectady, NY	Nerdelstadt, Preußen
Hugo, Heinrich	1, Nov. 1875	28, June	30- 3m- 6d	351		Barsons, KS	Hagenburg, Lippe-Schaumburg
Hugo, Maria	7, Apr. 1879	12, Mar.	73	111	Strecker	Warrenton, MO	Poppenweiler, Ludwigsburg, Württemberg
Hugo, Maria	20, Aug. 1891	19, July	25	542		Pittsburg, PA	Hagenburg, Lippe-Schaumburg
Hugo, Martha	17, Feb. 1887	26, Jan.	59	110	Beling	Hugosheim, TX	Texas
Hugo, Peter	22, Nov. 1894	5, Nov.	29	758		Wheeling, WV	Burghofen, Kurhessen
Hugy, Louise Charlotte	15, Dec. 1884	1, Dec.	67	7		Springfield, IL	Springfield, Illinois
Hühne, Andreas Wilhelm	23, Sept 1897	28, Aug.	62	607		Quincy, IL	Hohegeist, Braunschweig
Hühne, Sophia	12, July 1888	12, May	80	446		Chicago, IL	Schleswig
Hühnerjäger, Joseph	7, May 1891	15, Apr.	16	302		Goshen, IN	Schönfeld, Preußen
Huiras, Michael Joseph	25, June 1891	3, May	29- 2m	414		Springfield, MN	Leavenworth, Brown County, Minnesota
Huiras, Minnie	30, Apr. 1883	10, Apr.	81	143	Schneider	Sleepy Eye, MN	Buffalo, New York
Huibert, (Mrs)	13, July 1863	17, Apr.	58	112	Knauf	Mt. Vernon, IN	
Hüfik, Catharina	21, Sept 1854	8, July	71	152		St. Louis, MO	
Hüfik, Friedrich	21, Sept 1854	14, July	79	152		St. Louis, MO	
Hülsiek, Salome	19, Apr. 1894	22, Mar.	57- 6m- 5d	262		St. Paul, MN	Wurmlingen bei Tübingen, Württemberg
Hully, Louise	19, Apr. 1880	28, Mar.	18	127	Günther	Burlington, IA	Dielingen, Westphalen, Preußen
Hüls, Eva Dorothea	1, Sept 1892	17, July	72	558	Schmidt	New York City, NY	Obermerzbach, Untermainkreis, Baiern
Hülsebosch, John	29, Nov. 1869	2, Nov.	26-10m	383		Newark, NJ	Gröningen, Holland
Hülsemann, Emma L.	9, May 1895	23, Apr.	51-10m	302		Evansville, IN	
Hülsemann, Meta Elsebein	11, Mar.1872			87	Hülscher	Lake Creek, MO	Blasheim, Minden, Preußen
Hülsick, John G	20, July 1854			116		St. Louis, MO	Neunkirchen bei Melle, Hannover
Hülsmann, Karl	27, Feb. 1862	13, Feb.	52	36		St. Louis, MO	Blasheim, Preußen
Hülsmann, Margaretha Dorothea	20, Mar. 1851	4, Feb.	57	48	Koch	Des Moines, IA	Roten, Preußen
Hülsmeier, Henriette	23, Sept 1886	5, Sept	81	7		Huntingburg, IN	Dissen, Hannover
Hülsmeyer, Adolf	23, Mar. 1899	14, Feb.	29	191		Huntingburg, IN	Ladbergen, Tecklenburg, Münster, Preußen
Hulzebosch, John C.	7, May 1896	5, Apr.	71	302		Paterson, NJ	Newark, New Jersey
Humbel, Elisabeth	19, July 1875	23, June	63	231	Siegrift	Cleveland, OH	Meisterschwanden, Aargau, Schweiz
Humbold, Carl F.	24, Feb. 1887	5, Feb.		126		Oconomowoc, WI	Liebenfeld, Pommern

Christliche Apologete Death Notices --- 1839 - 1899

Name of Deceased	Notice Date	Death Date	Age	Maiden Name	Page	Place of Death	Place of Birth
Humbold, Christian Fr.	8, Sept 1879	17, Aug.	58- 2m-17d		287	Concord, WI	Grebenstein, Hessen
Humburg, Heinrich	26, Nov. 1891		51		766	Chicago, IL	Crambach, Hessen-Kassel
Humburg, Johan	2, Apr. 1896	9, Mar.	66		222	Berger, MO	Heckershausen, Hessen-Kassel
Humburg, Johan Ludwig	25, Oct. 1869	1, Oct.	62		343	Ann Arbor, MI	Karlshafen, Kurhessen
Humburg, Ottilie Christine	10, Feb. 1898	13, Jan.	62	Hartmann	95	Chicago, IL	Bentorf, Hohenhausen, Lippe-Detmold
Humfeld, Anna Maria	6, July 1893	5, June	78		430	High Hill, MO	Steinfort, Preußen
Humfeld, Catharina	29, Apr. 1872	10, Apr.	65	Mühlemann	143	Milan, IN	Bendorf, Lippe-Detmold
Humfeld, Simon C.	4, May 1893	27, Mar.	69		286	Clay Center, KS	Kannenberg bei Stargard, Preußen
Humich, Friederika Maria	20, Jan. 1873	3, Dec.		Schwarz	23	Wausau, WI	Nashville, Illinois
Hummel, Caroline	1, Apr. 1897	1, Mar.	36	Weyking	207	Warrenton, MO	Pennsylvania
Hummel, Caty	11, Apr. 1881		65- 7m- 2d		119	Lena, IL	
Hummel, Elisabeth	4, Aug. 1887	16, July	91- 6m-10d	Mueller	494	West Bend, WI	Oberhilbersheim, Hessen-Darmstadt
Hummel, Elisabeth	16, Mar. 1899	12, Feb.	70		175	West Bend, WI	Oberhilbersheim, Hessen-Darmstadt
Hummel, Elisabeth	12, May 1884	29, Apr.		Seitz	7	Enterprise, KS	Liedolsheim bei Karlsruhe, Baden
Hummel, Georg	7, Jan. 1858	8, Dec.	70		4	Rock River, WI	
Hummel, Gottlob	27, Apr. 1868	25, Mar.	38		135	Warrenton, MO	Erdmannhausen, Marbach, Württemberg
Hummel, Helena	8, Dec. 1884	13, Oct.	48		7	Beaver Dam, WI	Berlin, Preußen
Hummel, Johan Georg	27, Sept 1894	8, Sept	48		630	Jersey City, NJ	Upfingen, Urach, Württemberg
Hummel, Wilhelm	10, Mar. 1884	16, Feb.	23		7	Warrenton, MO	Cincinnati, Hamilton County, Ohio
Hummel, Wilhelm	21, Sept 1885	23, Aug.	50		7	Iron Ridge, WI	Oberhilbersheim, Hessen-Darmstadt
Hummelke, Karl	26, Mar. 1883	8, Mar.	44		103	Wichita, KS	Wendhausen, Hannover
Hummels, Maria Sophia	28, Apr. 1873	6, Apr.	31- 2m-16d	Blome	135	Petersburg, IL	Liebenau, Kreis Hofgeismar, Kurhessen
Hummerd, Rosina	2, Dec. 1897	28, Oct.	31	Breibeck	767	Pittsburg, PA	Oberaldeich bei Straubing, Baiern
Humphrey, Anna Magdalena	9, Aug. 1894	12, July	27	Joachim	518	Morrison, MO	
Hund, Emilie	13, Sept 1880	1, Sept	14- - 5d		295	Fosterburg, IL	Singhofen, Nassau
Hund, Karl	23, Aug. 1894	6, Aug.	61		550	Brighton, IL	Schönborn, Dietz, Nassau
Hund, Katharina	19, Jan. 1888	30, Nov.	75	Reuter	46	Geneseo, IL	Württemberg
Hundt, Anna Rosie	15, Sept 1887	3, Sept	68	Paasch	590	Marine City, MI	Sophienberg, Posen
Hundt, Gottlieb	6, Nov. 1882	17, Oct.	62- 6m-10d		359	Marine City, MI	Polen, Posen
Hüne, Melinda Pauline	25, Aug. 1884	11, Aug.	23		7	Burlington, IA	Pekin, Illinois
Hünecke, Geschen	26, May 1862	17, May	64		84	Cincinnati, OH	Lunsen, Braunschweig
Hünefauth, Georg M.	28, Apr. 1887	5, Apr.	71- 4m-22d		270	Pomeroy, OH	Zeiskam, Germersheim, Rheinkreis Baiern
Hünefeld, Christine	22, June 1854	21, May	30- 1m- 4d	Fiegenbaum	100	Cincinnati, OH	Ladbergen, Tecklenburg, Preußen
Hünefeld, Edward	18, Apr. 1889	16, Mar.	18		254	Huntingburg, IN	Dubois County, Indiana
Hünefeld, Elisabeth	15, June 1893	26, May	36	Feldmeier	382	Huntingburg, IN	Dubois County, Indiana
Hünefeld, Friedrich Wilhelm	12, July 1888	24, June	59		446	Huntingburg, IN	Ladbergen, Preußen
Hünefeld, Heinrich Wilhelm	21, June 1880	5, June	49- 2m- 8d		199	Huntingburg, IN	Ladbergen, Tecklenburg, Preußen
Hünefeld, Lydia	31, May 1888	8, May	32		350	Huntingburg, IN	
Hünefeld, Maria	3, Dec. 1883	29, Oct.	22		391	Huntingburg, IN	
Hünefeld, Maria Elisabeth	11, Feb. 1878	26, Jan.	45- 8m-24d	Schroerlüke	47	Huntingburg, IN	Venne, Hannover
Hünefeld, Sophia	15, Dec. 1879	26, Nov.	49- 4m-28d		399	Huntingburg, IN	Ladbergen, Tecklenburg, Preußen
Hüneke, Christine	29, Apr. 1867	14, Apr.	33-10m-23d	Ringen	134	Cincinnati, OH	Holltorf, Amt Thedinghausen, Braunschweig
Hüneke, Gesche	29, July 1852	17, July	27		124	Cincinnati, OH	Morheim, Westen, Hannover
Hüneke, Johan (Rev)	27, May 1897	7, May	70- 8m		335	Marion, OH	
Hüneke, Maria Elisa	16, Nov. 1868	25, Oct.	27- 1m-17d	Prior	367	Cincinnati, OH	
Hünerfaut, Margaretha	29, July 1852	5, July	23		124	Cincinnati, OH	Waldsheim, Rheinkreis Baiern

- 223 -

Christliche Apologete Death Notices --- 1839 - 1899

Name of Deceased	Notice Date	Death Date	Age	Page	Maiden Name	Place of Death	Place of Birth
Hünerfaut, Maria	1, June 1874	14, May	14- 4m	175	Biebinger	Pomeroy, OH	Oppau, Frankenthal , Rheinkreis Baiern
Hünerfauth, Magdalena	19, Nov. 1883	28, Oct.	53- 9m-26d	375		Pomeroy, OH	Garmauthien, Preußen
Hünerjäger, Caroline H.	29, Apr. 1897	2, Apr.	86	271	Eilert	Elkhart, IN	Dukoo, Vorpommern
Hünerjäger, Friederike Dorothea	9, Aug. 1894	14, June	82	518		Akron, NY	Schönfeld, Uckermark, Preußen
Hünerjäger, Mina	27, Feb. 1896	18, Jan.	40	142	Hensel	Akron, NY	Altenhagen, Mecklenburg-Schwerin
Hünermöhrder, Kaspar Johan Heinr.	20, Feb. 1862	14, Jan.	47	32		New Port, MI	Pumptow, Pyrtiz, Preußen
Hunholtz, Anna Regina	14, Sept 1874	28, Aug.	43	295		Beaver Dam, WI	Cappeln, Amt Dorum, Hannover
Hünken, Christine	4, July 1864	9, June	41- 6m	108	Rotscher	Platteville, WI	Lienen, Münster, Preußen
Hunsche, Friedrich	13, Nov. 1871	28, Oct.	78	367		Kennshaw, WI	Lienen, Tecklenburg, Preußen
Hunsche, Friedrich William	20, Sept 1880	28, Aug.	58- 5m-15d	303		St. Louis, MO	Lienen, Tecklenburg, Preußen
Hunsche, Wilhelm	21, Aug. 1871	1, Aug.	42	271		Edwardsville, IL	Lien, Westphalen
Hunsche, Wilhelm C.	7, Dec. 1893	5, Nov.	66	782		Kenosha, WI	Lienen, Tecklenburg, Preußen
Hunske, Eberhard Heinrich	21, Apr. 1887	30, Mar.	87	254		Edwardsville, IL	Meischbach, Oberkirchen, Baden
Hunt, Anton	15, Nov. 1875	6, Oct.	71	367		Geneseo, IL	Ober-Achern, Achern, Baden
Hunt, Carl	1, May 1890	20, Apr.	67	286		Dayton, OH	Fosterburg, Illinois
Hunt, Karl Philipp	11, Aug. 1898	23, July	30	511		Edwardsville, IL	Wäder, Wohlenker, Hannover
Hunze, Annette	14, Apr. 1892	22, Mar.	83	238	Thene	Cape Girardeau, MO	Brocklog, Hannover
Hunze, Charlotte	19, Apr. 1888	22, Mar.	72- 2m-17d	254	Schrader	Napoleon, MO	Waldeck
Hunze, Elise	19, May 1887	28, Apr.	51	318	Kiepe	Lexington, MO	Schleweke, Braunschweig
Hunze, Friedrich	7, Oct. 1867	18, Aug.	61	318		Cape Girardeau, MO	Aargau, Schweiz
Hunziker, Verena	7, Mar. 1889	10, Feb.	73	158		Humboldt, NE	Schweiz
Hunzinger, Samuel	14, Dec. 1868	27, Nov.	42- 1m-27d	399		Portsmouth, OH	Parmerbach, Kurhessen
Hüpenthal, Anna	29, Aug. 1861	22, May	73	140		Weston, MO	
Hüpfer, Annie E.	7, Feb. 1889	14, Jan.	26- -20d	94	Moon	Giard, IA	
Huppert, Balthasar	29, Mar. 1888	9, Mar.	59	206		Ft. Atkinson, WI	Gündigen, Saarbrücken, Preußen
Huppert, Clara Catharina	18, Apr. 1881	5, Apr.	69- -23d	127	Michel	Santa Claus, IN	Holzhausen a. d. Haide, Nastätten, Nassau
Huppert, Johan David	27, Dec. 1894	3, Dec.	75	836		Santa Claus, IN	Holshausen d. d. Harde, Nastätten, Nassau
Huppert, Sophia	24, Oct. 1895	7, Sept	21	686	Rohde	Duncan, NE	Jefferson, Wisconsin
Hüner, Franz Samuel Jacob	18, July 1889	22, June	66	462		Wabasha, MN	Thun, Bern, Schweiz
Hurst, (Mr)	11, May 1874	13, Apr.	84	151		St. Louis, MO	Vagenheim, Amt Mülheim, Baden
Hurst, Anton	4, Apr. 1864	11, Mar.	38	56		St. Louis, MO	Keisersberg, Elsaß
Hurst, Dorothea	11, Feb. 1892	11, Dec.	79	94	Geiger	Oregon, MO	Güarton, St. Gallen, Schweiz
Hurst, John	21, Oct. 1886	30, Sept	82	7		Portsmouth, OH	Seefelden, Mühlhausen, Baden
Hurstmann, Mary	16, Mar. 1868	24, Feb.	31- 9m	87	Kötter	Higginsville, MO	Kispeldur, Amt Grüneberg, Hannover
Huscher, Wilhelm Ferdinand	10, Oct. 1895	11, Sept	74	654		Cape Girardeau, MO	Oelnitz bei Plauen, Vogtlande, Sachsen
Huse, Wilhelm	17, Dec. 1877	28, Nov.	38	407		Clatonia, NE	Bockenem, Hannover
Husel, Zacharias	9, Sept 1852	26, Aug.	61- 3m-21d	148		St. Clair, MI	Göllenbeck, Westphalen
Husemann, Anna	27, July 1890	24, July	83	279		St. Louis, MO	Schetten, Lippe-Detmold
Husemann, Wilhelm	11, Sept 1890	21, Aug.	34- 9m-28d	590		Pittsfield, IL	Polk County, Iowa
Huser, Maria Selina	24, Oct. 1895	17, Sept	20	686		Ora Labor, IA	Mäußenheim, Elsaß
Huser, Matthias	26, Dec. 1881	16, Nov.	72- 7m-24d	415		St. Paul, MN	Babbenhausen, Minden, Preußen
Husmeyer, Friedrich	3, Nov. 1862	24, Sept	55	176		Marthasville, MO	Bergkirchen, Preußen
Husner, (Mrs)	25, May 1899	2, May	78	335	Hammelmann	Clatonia, NE	
Hussel, Friedrich	4, Dec. 1851	10, Nov.	22- 8m-18d	196		St. Clair, MI	
Hutfielder, Friedrich	2, May 1889	15, Apr.	64- 3m	286		Greenville, IN	Blasheim, Lüpke, Preußen
Huth, Catharina Maria Dorothea	6, Aug. 1896	19, July	67	511		Sioux City, IA	Weste-Sunderberg, Uelzen, Hannover

Christliche Apologete Death Notices --- 1839 - 1899

Name of Deceased	Notice Date	Death Date	Age	Page	Maiden Name	Place of Death	Place of Birth
Huth, Johann	14, Feb. 1850	21, Dec.	24	28		Maysville, KY	Bruchsal, Baden
Huth, Sophie	4, Feb. 1892	28, Dec.	85	78		Ft. Dodge, IA	
Huth, Therese	25, July 1850	16, July		120		Cincinnati, OH	
Hüther, (Mrs)	14, Feb. 1889	22, Jan.	86	110	Engel	Lansing, IA	Binsförth, Melsungen, Kurhessen
Hütsch, Richard	27, July 1899	23, June	60	479		Louisville, KY	Salmünster, Kurhessen
Hutschenreider, Meta	20, Aug. 1896	24, July	20	542		Waco, TX	Waco, Texas
Hutt, Juliana	23, Aug. 1888	13, July	82	542	Federschmidt	Danville, IL	Württemberg
Hutter, Harriet	17, Nov. 1884	31, Oct.	64	7	Spayd	Chicago, IL	Pennsylvania
Hutter, Louise	17, Mar. 1892	22, Feb.	29	174		Detroit, MI	Danville, Illinois
Hüttinger, Eva Maria	13, July 1899	26, June	74	447	Weiß	Allegheny City, PA	Dittenheim, Baiern
Hüttner, Johann Michael	4, July 1881	10, May	63	215		Allegheny City, PA	Schillingsfürst, Baiern
Hüttner, Margaretha	15, Aug. 1889	26, July	60- 2m- 9d	526	Seelich	Charles City, IA	Mergelstetten, Heidenheim, Württemberg
Huxohl, Caroline	26, Nov. 1891	23, Oct.	74	766		Charles City, IA	Kircheide, Hohenhausen, Lippe-Detmold
Huxohl, Conrad	28, July 1887	4, June	74- 1m-14d	478		Charles City, IA	Kircheide, Hohenhausen, Lippe-Detmold
Hynert, Margarethe	3, Sept 1866	6, Aug.	77	286		Cincinnati, OH	Nieder-Guda, Rothenberg, Kurhessen
Ibelmesser, Barbara	6, Apr. 1874	4, Mar.	42-10m- 4d	111		Vandalia, IL	
Ibsch, Carl	5, Mar. 1866	2, Oct.	18	78		Manitowoc, WI	Dombrowo, Preußen
Ibsch, John	10, Feb. 1859	29, Dec.	41- 6m	24		Manitowoc, WI	Domproos, Amt Krotoschyn, Preußen
Ibsen, Carsten	3, May 1880	5, Apr.	39	143		Jersey City, NJ	Achternu, Schleswig-Holstein
Ickler, Heinrich	25, July 1881	29, June	55- 4m-28d	239		Sandusky, OH	Neumorschen, Spangenberg, Kurhessen
Ickler, Heinrich	29, Sept 1887	28, Aug.	28	622		Woodbury, MN	Brent, Bruss County, Canada
Idel, August	27, Mar. 1890	10, Mar.	22	206		Drake, MO	Gasconade County, Missouri
Idel, Jetta	17, May 1894	5, Mar.	13	326		Owensville, MO	
Iding, Johan Herman	4, May 1893	13, Apr.	68	286		Defiance, OH	Landen, Hannover
Iding, Johann Gerhard	8, May 1856	1, Apr.	34	76		Poplar Ridge, OH	Landen, Osnabrück, Hannover
Iding, Margaretha	27, Oct. 1859	5, Sept	26	172		Defiance, OH	Dorum, Ostfriesland
Iff, Anna	22, Mar. 1894	26, Feb.	80	198	Käser	Moweaqua, IL	Schinznach, Aargau, Schweiz
Iff, Johannes	8, Nov. 1869	4, Oct.	80	359		Decatur, IL	
Ihben, Johan	1, June 1874	17, May	65	175		Pekin, IL	Norden, Ostfriesland
Ihben, Katharina	22, Aug. 1881	4, Aug.	38-11m	271	Neeb	Pekin, IL	Zelle, Hessen-Darmstadt
Ihben, Margarethe	7, May 1891	19, Apr.	88	302	Schmidt	Pekin, IL	Dorum, Ostfriesland
Ihle, Abraham	14, Feb. 1870			55			Edigheim, Frankenthal, Rheinpfalz Baiern
Ihle, Abraham P.	31, Jan. 1870	3, Jan.	67	39		Pomeroy, OH	Ottichheim, Rheinkreis Baiern
Ihle, Anna	8, Mar. 1894	9, Feb.	68	166	Backhaus	Cincinnati, OH	Donnersberg, Ottersberg, Hannover
Ihle, Anna Maria	7, Aug. 1890	13, July	85- 3m-29d	510	Jacobi	Pomeroy, OH	Edigheim, Rheinpfalz Baiern
Ihle, Anna Maria	18, Mar. 1842	1, Feb.	42-11m	43		Chester, OH	
Ihle, Carolina	7, July 1853	25, June	3	108		Cincinnati, OH	
Ihle, Johan Peter	4, Aug. 1892	22, July	74	494		Pomeroy, OH	Edigheim, Frankenthal, Rheinkreis Baiern
Ihle, Katharina	25, Dec. 1856	20, Nov.	17	208		Pomeroy, OH	Meigs County, Ohio
Ihle, Margarethe Elisabeth	25, Jan. 1855	26, Dec.	80	16		Pomeroy, OH	Edigheim, Frankenthal, Rheinkreis Baiern
Ihle, Michael	26, Dec. 1889	4, Dec.	66	830		Cincinnati, OH	Edigheim, Rheinkreis Baiern
Ihme, Anna	23, Feb. 1885	15, Jan.	26- 6m-19d	7		Cass Co., SD	
Ihmels, Folkert	13, Feb. 1882	22, Jan.	62	55		Ramsay, IA	Loquard, Ostfriesland
Ihne, Herman	10, Mar. 1887	11, Feb.	72	158		Humboldt, NE	Dortmund, Preußen
Ihnenfeld, Christian	7, Feb. 1895	13, Jan.	75	94		Yellow Creek, IL	Britzig, Vorpommern

Christliche Apologete Death Notices --- 1839 - 1899

Name of Deceased	Notice Date	Death Date	Age	Page	Maiden Name	Place of Death	Place of Birth
Ihnenfeld, Justina	24, Dec. 1896	28, Nov.	66	831		Yellow Creek, IL	Rosenthal, Soldin, Brandenburg
Ihrig, Georg Heinrich	27, Apr. 1893	24, Mar.	66	270		Columbus, IL	Beerfelden, Hessen-Darmstadt
Ihrig, Marie Julie	11, Jan. 1894	21, Dec.	53	30	Völbel	Brooklyn, NY	Bergzabern, Rheinpfalz Baiern
Ilkenhans, Immanuel	13, Apr. 1893	15, Mar.	62	238		Atchison, KS	Eschwegen, Hessen-Kassel
Ilkenhaus, Martha Catharina	11, Aug. 1892	24, July	64- 8m	510	Eckhardt	Atchison, KS	Eschwege, Hessen
Illert, Henriette	26, Dec. 1864	11, Dec.	18	208	Stumph	St. Louis, MO	Großzimmern, Hessen-Darmstadt
Illert, Louise	24, Mar. 1853	10, Jan.	55- 7m-10d	48		Perry, IL	Hessen-Darmstadt
Illgen, Anna Selma	16, Sept 1897	26, Aug.	37	591		Milwaukee, WI	Fraureut, Reuß
Illgen, Karl Herman	30, May 1881	28, Apr.	17	175		Milwaukee, WI	Fraureuth, Reuß
Illig, (Mr)	27, July 1854	4, July	44	120		Portsmouth, OH	Lichtenau, Bischofsheim am Rhein, Baden
Illig, (Mrs)	27, July 1854	4, July	34	120		Portsmouth, OH	Reithenau, Aargau, Schweiz
Illius, Ludwig	10, Feb. 1887	15, Dec.		94		Pirmasens, GE	
Ils, Magdalena	16, Feb. 1893	10, Jan.	59- 5m-18d	110	Großniklaus	San Francisco, CA	St. Beatenberg, Interlaken, Bern, Schweiz
Imboden, Magdalena	24, Dec. 1891	21, Nov.	75	830	Groß	Oregon, MO	Böhl, Neustadt an der Hardt, Rheinkreis Baiern
Imhof, (Mrs)	21, Mar. 1861	25, Feb.	32	48		Mascoutah, IL	Kanton Bern, Schweiz
Imhof, A. Elisabeth	17, Nov. 1873	25, Oct.	24- -12d	367		Davenport, IA	
Imhof, Edwin	29, Mar. 1888	12, Jan.	16	206		Humboldt, NE	
Imhof, Friedrich	27, June 1870	10, May	74	207		Newark, OH	Wintersingen, Basel, Schweiz
Imhof, Friedrich	19, Nov. 1857	5, Nov.	77	188		Newark, OH	Reichenbach, Basel, Schweiz
Imhof, Magdalena	7, Dec. 1874	14, Nov.	48	391	Bleuer	Rock Island, IL	Canton Solothurn, Lugeburg, Schweiz
Imhof, Peter	10, Aug. 1885	27, July	67	7		Le Sueur, MN	Landshausen, Baden
Imhoff, Ludwig	3, Feb. 1887	5, Jan.	24- 9m-10d	78		Switzer, OH	
Imle, Philipp Heinrich	29, Sept 1873	5, Sept	85- 2m- 2d	311		Marion, OH	Gündelbach, Maulbronn, Württemberg
Imly, Regina Rahel	11, Oct. 1860	5, Sept	11- 3m-15d	164		Abott, WI	
Immel, Conrad	16, Aug. 1888	3, July	75- 2m-23d	526		Marietta, OH	Marburg, Kurhessen
Immel, Elisabeth	31, Mar. 1879	13, Mar.	40- 8m- 8d	103	Grebe	Charles City, IA	Kleingladenbach, Biedenkopf, Hessen-Darmstadt
Immel, J.M.	26, Nov. 1891	30, Aug.	66	766		Oxford, IA	Crailsheim, Württemberg
Immel, Jost	14, Feb. 1889	14, Jan.	61-10m-23d	110		Forest, WI	OberDieten, Hessen-Darmstadt
Immel, Maria E.	16, May 1864	20, Apr.	23-10m	80		Washington, OH	Bebra, Kreis Rothenburg, Kurhessen
Immel, Martha Elisabeth	30, Aug. 1880	17, Aug.	70	279	Becker	Marietta, OH	Wallenstein, Homberg, Kurhessen
Immer, Andreas	2, Oct. 1882	6, Sept	54	319		Grand Ridge, IL	Sachsen
Immer, Emma M.	12, Mar. 1896	10, Feb.	34	174	Lehmann	Charles City, IA	West Albany, Wabasha County, Minnesota
Immer, Karl	12, July 1888	25, June	62	446		Spencer, IA	Ottenhausen, Erfurt, Preußen
Immerheiser, Philipp	27, Oct. 1843	21, Oct.	32	171		Cincinnati, OH	Sauerschwabenheim, Hessen
Inderlied, Regina	22, Dec. 1873	4, Nov.	40- 8m-24d	407	Kratzen	Jeffersonville, NY	Singen, Baden
Irig, Adam	11, Aug. 1887	7, July	61- 1m- 2d	510		Clayton, WI	Schellenbach, Hessen-Darmstadt
Irion, Catharina	29, Dec. 1862	8, Dec.	41- 9m- 7d	208	Benzing	Hamilton, OH	Schwenningen, Rottweil, Württemberg
Irion, Katharina	13, Nov. 1865	28, Sept	43	184		Hamilton, OH	Pirmasens, Rheinkreis Baiern
Irmiger, Rudolph	19, Oct. 1874	6, Oct.	77	335		Liberty, MO	Lenzburg, Aargau, Schweiz
Irminger, Catharina	10, May 1894	17, Apr.	63	310	Hammel	Arley, MO	Föhl, Buchenberg, Hessen-Darmstadt
Irminger, Edna	24, Dec. 1896	21, Nov.	17	831		Arley, MO	
Irminger, Susanne	1, Jan. 1877	14, Dec.	77	7	Hoppler	Liberty, MO	Mildegg, Seuzburg, Aargau, Schweiz
Irmscher, Christine	13, June 1889	16, May	74	382		Colesburg, IA	Sachsen
Irmscher, Johan David	29, Apr. 1897		84	271		Colesburg, IA	Waldkirchen, Sachsen
Irmy, Maria	11, June 1877	23, May	50	191	Hefti	St. Paul, MN	Adelbach, Glarus, Schweiz
Isaak, Bernhard	18, Nov. 1872	30, Oct.	39	375		St. Paul, MN	Rußland

Christliche Apologete Death Notices --- 1839 - 1899

Name of Deceased	Notice Date	Death Date	Age	Page	Maiden Name	Place of Death	Place of Birth
Isemann, Sophia	23, July 1896	30, June	71-6m-4d	479	Schäfer	De Soto, MO	Lippe-Detmold
Isenberg, Louisa	22, Dec. 1898	12, Nov.	65	815	Ahle	Owensville, MO	Hille, Minden, Preußen
Isermann, Carl Friedrich	10, May 1880	17, Apr.	66-6m-17d	151		Burlington, IA	Hille, Westphalen
Isermann, Maria Louise	11, Nov. 1897	7, Oct.	78	719	Beckmann	Burlington, IA	Fürstenberg, Waldeck
Iske, Christiane	5, July 1880	13, June	32-5m-22d	215		St. Louis, MO	Stadtfache an der Werra, Sachsen-Weimar
Isleib, Heinrich	6, Feb. 1890	8, Jan.	55	94		Lawrence, MA	Kaltenbach, Thurgau, Schweiz
Isler, Johannes	26, Jan. 1893	7, Jan.	26	62		Warrenton, MO	Basse, Hannover
Israel, Charles	9, Dec. 1897	14, Nov.	83	783		Lawrenceburg, IN	Lawrenceburg, Dearborn County, Indiana
Israel, Eduard	2, Oct. 1882	19, Sept	29-8m-19d	319		Lawrenceburg, IN	Augustdorf, Lippe-Detmold
Issenberg, Herman	23, Oct. 1871	19, Sept	42-1m-27d	343		Union, MO	Germany
Ista, Catharina	25, Feb. 1892	1, Feb.	43	126	Seits	St. Paul, MN	Gutmandingen, Schaffhausen, Schweiz
Ittner, Agnes	2, Apr. 1891	1, Mar.	72	222	Kehlhoff	Herman, MO	Weißbach, Vaihingen, Württemberg
Ittner, Anna M.	9, Feb. 1893	20, Jan.	72	94	Jaklitschen	Cincinnati, OH	Trautskirchen, Mark Erlbach, Baiern
Ittner, John	18, Nov. 1867	30, Oct.	46	366		Lawrenceburg, IN	Großpeppeln, Germany
Iwan, Henrietta	15, Oct. 1896	16, Sept	12	671		Beatrice, NE	Oconomowoc, Wisconsin
Iwert, Emma	1, Apr. 1886	6, Mar.	17	7		Watertown, WI	Lottien, Pommern
Iwert, Ernst	12, Apr. 1894	20, Mar.	80	246		Columbus, WI	Lottin, Pommern
Iwert, Friedrich	8, Jan. 1877	22, Dec.	59	15		Columbus, WI	Grabionne, Bromberg, Preußen
Iwert, Karoline	26, Feb. 1877	8, Feb.	60	71	Maratz	Columbus, WI	Fond du Lac, Wisconsin
Iwert, Klara	13, Apr. 1899	25, Mar.	21	238		Watertown, WI	Wissuk, Posen
Iwert, Rosine	17, Mar. 1898	1, Mar.	78	175	Meyer	Columbus, WI	Milwaukee, Wisconsin
Iwert, Wilhelm Friedrich	18, June 1896	1, June	21	399		Milwaukee, WI	Milwaukee, Wisconsin
Iwig, Catharina	11, Oct. 1888	25, Mar.	74	654			Landau, RheinPfalz Baiern
Iwohn, Henriette	5, Nov. 1896	16, Sept	12	719		Beatrice, NE	Großpeppeln, Germany
Jäbker, Anna Maria	3, Feb. 1868	27, Dec.	40	39		Nashville, IL	
Jabusch, Johan August	26, May 1892	2, May	68	334		Menominee, MI	Antonienhof, Kocieschen, Preußen
Jabusch, Johan Herman	31, Dec. 1877	11, Dec.	22	423		Osgrove, WI	Highland, Iowa County, Wisconsin
Jabusch, Ottilie	29, Oct. 1883	13, Sept		351		Menomonie, WI	
Jach, Friedrich	27, Mar. 1871	24, Feb.	62	103		Berea, OH	Bauerkuhl, Mecklenburg-Schwerin
Jäck, Catharina	15, Jan. 1866	2, Feb.	75	22	Schifferle	Saugerties, NY	Feldrenach, Neuenbürg, Württemberg
Jäckel, Elisabeth	24, Feb. 1859	28, July	76	32		Lafayette, IN	Dexheim bei Oppenheim, Hessen
Jäckel, Johanna	17, Aug. 1899	25, Feb.	83	527	Mohr	Lafayette, IN	Ehringdorf bei Weimar, Germany
Jacob, Anna	3, Apr. 1871	3, Apr.	80	111	Marte	Iowa City, IA	Schwarzenburg, Bern, Schweiz
Jacob, Carolina Maria	31, Mar. 1873	31, Mar.	31	103	Schwendker	Buffalo, NY	Bottga, Vogtland, Sachsen
Jacob, Catharina	22, Nov. 1860	7, Mar.	67	188	Unglaub	Baraboo, WI	Sohnstädt, Bieselbach, Sachsen-Weimar
Jacob, Christina Susanna	7, May 1891	8, Apr.	33	302	Helfer	Berne, MI	Bristol, Wisconsin
Jacob, Friedrich	29, Dec. 1887	25, Nov.	72	830		Berne, MI	Ahlfeld, Hannover
Jacob, Karoline Luise	13, Apr. 1899	12, Mar.	56	238	Weneke	Oasis, IA	Ahlfeld, Hannover
Jacob, Wilhelmine Elisabeth	29, Sept 1879	27, Aug.		311	Wienecke	Iowa City, IA	
Jacobs, Agnes Sophia	12, July 1888	20, June	21	446		San Jose, IL	
Jacobs, Anna Katharine	11, Aug. 1887	7, July	46-2m-1d	510	Striele	Menomonie, WI	
Jacobs, Christian	14, Apr. 1887	28, Mar.		238		Chicago, IL	
Jacobs, Ferdinand August	3, Jan. 1895	4, Dec.	17	14		Cass Co, IA	Württemberg
Jacobs, Katharina	6, Sept 1875	24, May	75-10m-2d	287	Biehler	Greenville, NJ	Jever, Oldenburg
Jacoby, Arthur H.	18, June 1891		17-2m-6d	398		Alton, IL	Langenhagen, Treptow, Greifenberg, Pommern

Christliche Apologete Death Notices --- 1839 - 1899

Name of Deceased	Notice Date	Death Date	Age	Page	Maiden Name	Place of Death	Place of Birth
Jacoby, Elisabeth	8, Aug. 1870	27, June	66-10m- 3d	255	Lust	Bucyrus, OH	Ilsfeld bei Heilbronn, Württemberg
Jacoby, Elisabeth	26, Dec. 1889	24, Nov.	71	830	Colonius	Brighton, IL	Naher, Nassau
Jacoby, Erwin	10, Mar. 1873	14, Feb.	29	79		New Albany, IN	Oberrode, Hessen-Darmstadt
Jacoby, Henry William	28, Dec. 1885	9, Dec.	66	7		Brighton, IL	Nochem, St. Goarshausen, Nassau
Jacoby, James	13, May 1852	28, Mar.	21- 1m- 3d	80		Tiffin, OH	
Jacoby, Katharina E.	25, Feb. 1897	6, Feb.	73	127	Peiter	Brighton, IL	Rochem, Nassau
Jacoby, Rebecca	9, Apr. 1896	15, Mar.	45	238	Appel	Alton, IL	
Jagels, Anna G.	20, Sept 1869	29, Aug.	41	303	Grieben	Luke Creek, MO	Bogel, Amt Zeven, Hannover
Jäger, Anna Maria	18, Apr. 1889	28, Mar.		254		Stitzer, WI	
Jäger, Charlotte	21, Sept 1863	20, May	19	152		Sheboygan, WI	Wehrheim, Nassau
Jäger, Christine K.E.	28, Jan. 1867	11, Dec.	69- -30d	30	Schäfer	De Soto, MO	
Jäger, Christoph	1, Aug. 1895	29, Apr.	81	494		Boston, MA	Ilsfeld, Besigheim, Württemberg
Jäger, Elisabeth	6, Feb. 1890	16, Jan.	70- 1m-28d	94	Helfrich	Perrysburg, OH	Wattenheim, Hessen
Jäger, Emil W. Ludiwg	18, Feb. 1897	24, Jan.	43- 9m-12d	111		Sun Prairie, WI	Roggow bei Daller, Pommern
Jäger, Friedrich	20, June 1881	8, June	42	199		Almond, WI	Hesselhorst, Baden
Jäger, Jakob	20, Dec. 1855	26, Nov.	24- 7m	204		Portsmouth, OH	Denzen, Coblenz, RheinPreußen
Jäger, John	5, Apr. 1844	21, Mar.	61	55		Delaware, OH	Heimerdingen, Leonberg, Württemberg
Jäger, John	21, May 1891	27, Apr.	69- 9m-18d	334		Perrysburg, OH	Wangen, Elsaß
Jäger, Nikolaus	23, Nov. 1899		36	751		Pomeroy, OH	Pomeroy, Ohio
Jäger, P.C.	29, Jan. 1883	8, Jan.	62	39		Sheboygan, WI	Wehrheim, Ufingen, Nassau
Jäger, Ursula	4, Dec. 1890	5, Nov.	77	782	Nägele	New Orleans, LA	Ethenheim, Baden
Jahn, Christian Friedrich	8, Nov. 1880	10, Oct.	79	359		Bay City, MI	Hohenwald, Landsberg an der Warthe, Preußen
Jahn, Hanna Louise	8, Nov. 1880	10, Oct.	79	359		Bay City, MI	Lepene, Soltiner, Preußen
Jahn, Heinrich	30, Sept 1858	21, July	21	156		Petersburg, IL	Zeigenrück, Erfurt, Preußen
Jahn, Johanna Louise	25, Dec. 1882	29, Nov.	62- 3m- 4d	415	Remus	Carrollton, MI	Korschdorf, Soltin, Brandenburg
Jahn, Marianna	18, Nov. 1878	1, Nov.	59- 6m	367	Martin	Jamestown, MO	Langenthal, Bern, Schweiz
Jahnke, Christiane	19, Oct. 1863	23, Sept	30- 7m-10d	168		Wabasha, MN	Kircheim, Württemberg
Jahnke, Wilhelm	29, May 1890	4, May	22	350		Brenham, TX	Brandenburg
Jahr, Christina	13, Feb. 1862	21, Jan.	37	28	Eler	Kewaskum, WI	Zetzweil, Magdeburg, Preußen
Jahr, Justina	17, Apr. 1865	25, Nov.	66	64		Farmington, IA	Braunshein, Sachsen-Altenburg
Jahraus, Barbara	18, Sept 1865	26, Aug.	68	152	Munch	Cincinnati, OH	Oberlustadt, Germersheim, Baiern
Jahraus, Georg	30, Mar. 1874	17, Mar.	31	103		Giard, IA	Knox County, Ohio
Jahrenhorst, Hanna Elisabeth	9, May 1861	13, Nov.	64	76		Hamilton, OH	Niederhochstadt, Rheinkreis Baiern
Jahrmarkt, August	23, Dec. 1872	7, Dec.	77- 9m-15d	415	Dellbrügge	Boody, IL	Barthausen, Preußen
Jahrmarkt, Henriette	21, July 1884	1, July	37	7		Graham, MO	Germany
Jaide, Johan J.	11, May 1868	22, Apr.		151	Krüger	East Troy, WI	Vietnitz, Preußen
Jaiser, Gottlieb Heinrich	6, Feb. 1890	12, Jan.	61	94		Beaufort, MO	Ober-Eisenhausen, Bidekop, Hessen-Darmstadt
Jaißle, Rahel Jane	6, Nov. 1890	11, Oct.	25	718		Denver, CO	Kornwestheim, Württemberg
Jaißly, (Mr)	28, Apr. 1884	26, Mar.	36- 1m-10d	7	Geier	Spencerville, OH	
Jakob, Adolf	30, Nov. 1893	10, Oct.	75	766		New Knoxville, OH	Nieder-Bipp, Bern, Schweiz
Jakob, Anna	24, Aug. 1899	13, July	25	543		Oakland, CA	San Francisco, California
Jakob, Eduard Ferdinand	26, Mar. 1877	11, Mar.	25	103		Saginaw, MI	Dane County, Wisconsin
Jakob, Elisabeth	11, June 1891	23, May	19	382		Warsau, IL	Warsau, Illinois
Jakob, Elisabeth	7, Feb. 1861	23, Jan.	22	24		Hamilton, OH	
Jakob, Emma	18, June 1866	26, May	16	198		Ora Labora, MI	
Jakob, Johan C.	13, Apr. 1893	26, Mar.	67	238		Warsaw, IL	Escenstrut, Kurhessen

Christliche Apologete Death Notices --- 1839 - 1899

Name of Deceased	Notice Date	Death Date	Age	Page	Maiden Name	Place of Death	Place of Birth
Jakob, Johanna	25, Apr. 1870	2, Apr.	68	135		Louisville, KY	Kloster-Roda, Altenburg, Sachsen
Jakob, Ludwig	1, Dec. 1879	16, Nov.	71- 2m-23d	383		Buffalo, NY	Lehmbach, Elsaß
Jakob, Philippine	12, May 1892	26, Apr.	62- 3m- 1d	302		Warsaw, IL	Hifweiler, Rheinkreis Baiern
Jakob, Wilhelmine	3, Feb. 1879	27, Dec.	65- 2m-15d	39	Denhof	Caseville, MI	Andisleben, Erfurt, Preußen
Jakobi, Jonathan	9, June 1879	22, Apr.	77- 8m- 2d	183	Hicketheier	Bucyrus, OH	Schuykill County, Pennsylvania
Jakobi, Sophie	29, Nov. 1880	3, Nov.	87	383		Crow River, MN	Bornstein, Preußen
Jakobs, Johan Christian	14, Apr. 1879	29, Mar.	24- 9m-17d	119		Nashville, IL	
Jakobs, Sophia	31, Mar. 1873	15, Jan.	26-10m	103	Ewers	Brunswick, MO	Karmon bei Schwerin, Mecklenburg-Schwerin
Jakoby, Anna Maria	24, July 1865	16, June	15	120		New Albany, IN	York County, Pennsylvania
Jakoby, Elias	29, May 1851	3, Feb.	60	88		Tiffin, OH	
Jakoby, Ludwig	13, June 1864	23, Mar.	61	96		Chester, IL	
Jammerthal, Friedrieke	25, Mar. 1886	8, Mar.	57	7	Dürr	Lemars, IA	Hochstetten, Karlsruhe, Baden
Jammerthal, Wilhelm F.	30, Jan. 1896	2, Nov.	31	78		Tacoma, WA	Hochstetten, Karlsruhe, Baden
Jandebeur, Maria Barbara	16, Dec. 1897	3, Nov.	67	799	Bockstahler	Huntingburg, IN	Baden
Jandre, Ernestine Wilhelmine	19, Apr. 1888	26, Mar.	59	254	Stephen	Milford, WI	Mesow bei Daber, Stettin, Pommern
Jandre, Franziska	29, Jan. 1883	15, Jan.	27- -14d	39	Witt	Milford, WI	Joxina, Jefferson County, Wisconsin
Jandre, Wilhelm	29, July 1897	27, June	76	479		Ft. Atkinson, WI	Mesow, Stettin, Germany
Jandrey, Ernestine	8, Dec. 1898	9, Nov.	69	783	Böck	Burlington, WI	Wangerim, Pommern
Janke, August Carl Gottlieb	31, Dec. 1896	27, Nov.	81	844		Baresville, OH	Rütznow, Stettin, Pommern
Janke, Dorothea	20, June 1881	19, May		199	Burg	Burlington, IA	
Janke, Ida Emilie	9, June 1887	24, May	4m	366		Burlington, WI	
Janle, Johannes Jakob	1, June 1863	13, Mar.	7	88		Baresville, OH	
Jann, Friedrich	1, Jan. 1883	8, Dec.	65	7		Columbus, WI	
Jann, Katharina Charlotte	2, July 1896	6, June	60	431	Hasler	Charlestown, IN	Neuhofen, West Preußen
Janning, Anna E.	8, June 1868	20, May	37	183		Pittsburg, PA	Basel, Schweiz
Jännisch, Maria	13, Aug. 1877	5, Aug.	42- 3m-18d	263	Rixse	Covington, KY	Wachendorf, Hannover
Jannsen, Maria	28, Apr. 1898	30, Mar.	72	271	Gronewald	Nokomis, IL	Voßberg, Ostfriesland
Janse, Anna	12, Sept 1889	11, Aug.	24	590		Baresville, OH	Redwing, Minnesota
Jansen, Amalie Pauline	31, July 1851	9, July	30- 8m- 7d	124	Pfannschmidt	Quincy, IL	Mühlhausen, Thüringen, Preußen
Jansen, Anna	10, Sept 1883	23, Aug.	21-10m-24d	295	Koch	Yellow Creek, IL	
Jansen, Engalina	1, Sept 1879		16- 8m-16d	279		Yellow Creek, IL	
Jansen, Engelina	12, Feb. 1891	24, Jan.	66	110	Schröder	Yellow Creek, IL	Logabirum, Ostfriesland
Jansen, Engelina	9, July 1891	24, Jan.	66	446	Schröder	Yellow Creek, IL	Logahirum, Ostfriesland
Jansen, F.	13, Oct. 1898	10, Sept	79	655		Kansas City, KS	Förstchen, Düsseldorf, Preußen
Jansen, Friedericke	21, Feb. 1876	3, Feb.	55	63		Red Bud, IL	Essens, Ostfriesland
Jansen, Friedrich Wilhelm	13, Feb. 1871	28, Jan.	56	55		Quincy, IL	Leichlingen, Solingen, Düsseldorf, RheinPreußen
Jansen, Gerhard	17, Feb. 1873	23, Jan.	65	53		Nokomis, IL	Grobstede, Oldenburg
Jansen, Henriette	15, Dec. 1848	27, Nov.	23-10m	204		Cincinnati, OH	
Jansen, John	13, Dec. 1894	1, Nov.	25	806		Wheeling, WV	Cincinnati, Hamilton County, Ohio
Jansen, Katharina E.	21, Feb. 1881	2, Feb.	63	63	Kinkel	Wyandotte, KS	Todtenau, Hessen-Darmstadt
Jansen, Tönnies	30, Aug. 1875	24, June	81	279		Bunker Hill, IL	Selverde, Reemers, Ostfriesland
Jansen, William Heinrich	21, Feb. 1870	6, Feb.	4	63		Cincinnati, OH	
Janson, (Mr)	21, Apr. 1887	11, Feb.	40	254		Edwardsville, IL	Ostfriesland
Janson, Anna Maria	15, Mar. 1888	17, Feb.	41-11m	174	Striebing	Quincy, IL	
Janson, Catharina	9, Mar. 1868	21, Feb.	76- 9m	79	Rottenberg	Quincy, IL	Leichlingen, Solingen, Preußen
Janson, Henrietta	24, Nov. 1884	9, Nov.	51	7	Steuernagel	Quincy, IL	Grünstadt, Rheinkreis Baiern

Christliche Apologete Death Notices --- 1839 - 1899

Name of Deceased	Notice Date	Death Date	Age	Maiden Name	Page	Place of Death	Place of Birth
Janson, Maria	27, May 1886	3, May	53		7	Petersburg, IL	Hessen-Kassel
Janson, Peter Johan	23, Mar. 1868	1, Mar.	61		95	Quincy, IL	Leichlingen, Solingen, Düsseldorf, Preußen
Janssen, Christina Johanna	21, Jan. 1886	2, Jan.	68		7	St. Louis, MO	Saldern, Braunschweig
Janßen, Gerhard	5, July 1869	17, June	62		215	St. Louis, MO	Schmalenfleth, Rodenkirchen, Oldenburg
Janßen, Hilke	12, Nov. 1891	13, Sept	61	Classen	734	Spokane, WA	Nauchoo, Esens, Ostfriesland
Janssen, John H.	31, May 1894	4, May	81		358	Yellow Creek, IL	Nortmoor, Hannover
Jantz, Elisabeth	21, Oct. 1897	25, Sept	75		671	Swanton, NE	Hessen-Kassel
Jantzen, Friedrich	3, Mar. 1884	17, Jan.	58		7	San Francisco, CA	Dorum, Hannover
Jantzen, Johan	7, May 1883	23, Apr.	15- 9m		151	Hoboken, NJ	
Jantzer, Philippine	22, Nov. 1894	4, Aug.	53- 7m-26d		758	New York City, NY	Steg bei Acharach, Preußen
Jantzer, Stephan	6, May 1897	15, Apr.	62		287	Sea Cliff, NY	Nilsheim, Germany
Jaquillard, Andreas	8, July 1872	23, May	27		223	Elizabeth City, NJ	
Jastram, Sophia	19, Aug. 1878	14, July	45- 1m-14d	Mernitz	263	West Point, NE	Dorf Fisege, Preußen
Jauch, J.	11, Aug. 1862	17, May	25-10m		128	Pittsfield, IL	Schwenningen, Rottweil, Württemberg
Jauch, Jakob	26, Nov. 1877	13, Nov.	76		383	Hamilton, OH	Schwenningen, Rottweil, Württemberg
Jaup, Anna Barbara	7, Feb. 1881	24, Jan.	37		47	Wabasha, MN	Dießlingen, Rottweil, Württemberg
Jaus, Johan Georg	22, Nov. 1894	27, Oct.	60		758	Morristown, MN	Hattenhofen, Göppingen, Württemberg
Jayne, Sophie	14, Sept 1893	9, Aug.	23	Jonker	590	Eldora, Hardin County, Iowa	Eldora, Hardin County, Iowa
Jeasting, Eleonora	14, Aug. 1882	1, Aug.	75- 9m	Wischmeier	263	Woodville, OH	Wimmer, Wittlage, Hannover
Jebker, Maria Eleonore	20, Nov. 1865	8, Oct.	70-11m		188	Nashville, IL	Lintorf, Hannover
Jeck, Heinrich	11, Sept 1882	7, Aug.	41- -14d		295	Pittsburg, PA	Baiersbronn, Württemberg
Jeck, Katharina	23, Nov. 1899	28, Oct.	74		751	Nashville, TN	Büdingen, Hessen-Darmstadt
Jeck, Konrad	26, May 1898	30, Apr.	75		335	Nashville, TN	Pferdsbach, Hessen
Jeck, Peter	25, Feb. 1892	24, Jan.	55- 8m-15d		126	Nashville, TN	Pferdsbach, Hessen-Darmstadt
Jeck, Wilhelmine	26, July 1880	14, July	78- 8m- 2d		239	Nashville, TN	Bindsachsen, Hessen-Darmstadt
Jecklin, Wilhelm	31, Jan. 1889	19, Dec.	20		78	Albert Lea, MN	West Bend, Wisconsin
Jede, August Wilhelm	8, Dec. 1892	27, Aug.	19		782	Rockham, SD	Sauc City, Sack County, Wisconsin
Jeffe, Leopold	22, Aug. 1881	27, July	36		271	Milwaukee, WI	Glockau bei Danzig, Germany
Jehle, Friederika	12, Dec. 1861	6, Sept	9		200	Columbus, OH	
Jeirer, Michael	1, Jan. 1877	15, Dec.	80		7	Galena, IL	Ephausen, Nagold, Württemberg
Jeise, Christoph	10, Feb. 1887	25, Jan.	85- 6m-15d		94	Moweaqua, IL	Basel, Schweiz
Jeiter, Emmanuel	8, Aug. 1895	17, July	52		510	Bucyrus, OH	Liberty Township, Crawford County, Ohio
Jeiter, Maria	15, Oct. 1891	4, Sept	66	Meck	670	Lowell, MI	Jebenhausen, Göppingen, Württemberg
Jeiter, Maria	25, Oct. 1894	2, Oct.	65	Auperle	694	Freeport, MI	Streich, Schorndorf, Württemberg
Jeklin, Johan	23, Nov. 1874	10, Nov.	72-11m- 9d		375	West Bend, WI	Scheirs, Graubünden, Schweiz
Jelle, Wilhelm	21, Nov. 1870		45- 2m-23d		375	Columbus, OH	
Jellig, Katharina	25, May 1899	9, May	69	Frühorn	335	New York City, NY	Stahlberg, Rheinpfalz Baiern
Jenisch, Anna Margaretha Heinrike	11, Feb. 1886	20, Jan.	41	Dauberschmidt	7	Decorah, IA	Dinkelsbühl, Mittelfranken, Baiern
Jenke, Maria	18, Dec. 1876	30, Nov.	20		407	Wabasha, MN	
Jenne, Friedrich Erdmann	26, Apr. 1888	2, Apr.	64		270	Valparaiso, IN	Blumenthal , Brandenburg
Jenne, John	28, Apr. 1871	7, Aug.			279	Lawrenceburg, IN	Speyer, Baiern
Jenne, Sophie	16, Dec. 1872	24, Nov.	34- 1m-21d		407	Lawrenceburg, IN	Drohne, Kreis Lübeck, Preußen
Jenner, Jacob	30, Aug. 1855	14, Aug.	57		140	West Union, OH	Erdmannshausen, Marbach, Württemberg
Jenner, Katharina	5, Jan. 1899	3, Dec.	84- 8m- 8d	Eabell	14	Bucyrus, OH	Elsaß
Jenner, Wilhelm	22, Mar. 1894		87		198	Bucyrus, OH	Erdmannshausen, Marbach, Württemberg
Jennewein, Joseph	11, Mar. 1858	25, Feb.			40	Columbus, OH	Oberwalden, Göppingen, Württemberg

- 230 -

Christliche Apologete Death Notices --- 1839 - 1899

Name of Deceased	Notice Date	Death Date	Age	Page	Maiden Name	Place of Death	Place of Birth
Jenny, Johannes	11, May 1854	12, Jan.	83-10m	70	Brun	Herman, MO	Kanton Bern, Schweiz
Jens, Elisabetha	7, Oct. 1858	21, Aug.	64- 6m	160		Stevens Point, WI	Nimmersatt, Schlesien
Jentsch, Julius J.	19, Dec. 1895	14, Nov.	39	814		Third Creek, MO	Köslin, Pommern
Jenz, Friedrich	20, Nov. 1871	22, Oct.	77-10m	375		Nashville, IL	
Jepker, Anna W. Carolina	30, Dec. 1867	11, Dec.	20-2m- 2d	414		Mt. Prairie, TX	
Jerisho, Dorothea	10, Dec. 1883	23, Nov.	37	7	Fick	St. Joseph, MO	
Jesberg, Catharina	25, Nov. 1872	2, Nov.	26	383	Hartmann	St. Joseph, MO	
Jesberg, Georg	25, Sept 1865	17, July	13-11m	156		Iowa City, IA	
Jesberg, Henriette	13, Nov. 1865	22, Oct.	38- 5m	184	Blum	Iowa City, IA	Durelsheim, Preußen
Jesberg, Katharina	19, June 1865	2, June	65	100		New Albany, IN	Wollmar, Kurhessen
Jesberg, Mary	4, Apr. 1881	13, Mar.	41- 6m-14d	111	Wieser	St. Joseph, MO	Philadelphia, Pennsylvania
Jesberg, Wiegand	31, Jan. 1861	9, Jan.	66- 1m	20		New Albany, IN	Wollmar, Marburg, Kurhessen
Jeschke, Lizzie	21, Dec. 1893	19, Nov.	34	814	Hauck	Brooklyn, NY	Kassel, Kurhessen
Jeske, Franz F.	4, May 1899	12, Apr.	56	287		Springfield, MN	Alt-Kuddezow, Hinterpommern
Jester, Wilhelmine	4, Feb. 1884	15, Jan.	44	7	Oehm	Jeffersonville, IN	Thorn, Preußen
Jetberg, Wilhelm	9, Feb. 1863	18, Oct.	14- 9m	24		New Albany, IN	
Jetheke, Maria Christina	8, Jan. 1872	7, Nov.	63	15		Chicago, IL	Stuttenheim, Sachsen-Weimar
Jetter, John	22, Sept 1873	7, Sept	51- 5m- 7d	303		Peru, IL	Ostmettingen, Balingen, Württemberg
Jeude, Johannes	7, Mar. 1870	7, Feb.	44	79		Morris, MO	Oberasphe, Hessen
Jeuter, Elisabetha	27, Aug.1857	2, Aug.	20	140	Schmelchor	Lowell, MI	Wiesloch, Baden
Jeuter, Jakob	1, July 1878	17, June	77- 7m- 6d	207		Bucyrus, OH	Rettersburg, Waiblingen, Württemberg
Joachim, Abraham	30, July 1891	3, July	18-11m- 3d	494		Morrison, MO	Chamois, Missouri
Joachim, Bertha	12, Dec. 1895	27, Nov.	26	798		Chamois, MO	Chamois, Missouri
Joachim, Elisabeth	12, Dec. 1895	18, Nov.	57	798	Rufi	Chamois, MO	Steffisburg, Bern, Schweiz
Joachim, Elmer Wihelm	12, Mar. 1891	3, Feb.	22	174		Pomeroy, OH	
Joachim, Martha Rosa	4, Feb. 1897	9, Jan.	21	79		Morrison, MO	Osage County, Missouri
Joachims, Bettge	24, May 1880	6, Apr.	35- 9m-19d	167		Secor, IL	Neuschoo, Amt Esens, Ostfriesland
Joachims, Herman	31, July 1890	7, July	30	494		Secor, IL	Neuschoo, Ostfriesland
Joachums, Anna	23, May 1889	3, May	38	334		Secor, IL	Neuscho, Esens, Ostfriesland
Jochums, Joachim B.	3, Mar. 1892	20, Jan.	83	142		Quincy, IL	Ochtersum, Ostfriesland
Jöckel, Wilhelmine Karoline	4, Dec. 1871	5, Nov.	32	391	Kuhfuß	Tecumseh, NE	Bösingfeld, Amt Sternberg, Lippe
Jockey, Louis	15, Oct. 1896	8, July	47	671		Pittsfield, IL	Monroe County, Ohio
Jockisch, Gottlieb	14, Nov. 1864	4, Oct.		184		Arenzville, IL	Haldendorf, Sachsen
Jocklisch, Johanna Christina	21, Sept 1868	28, July	56- 9m- 5d	303	Elsner	Arenzville, IL	Seifhennersdorf, Sachsen
Joekel, August	25, Sept 1890		20	622		Sterling, NE	
Joeks, Maria Emilie	13, Oct. 1898	27, Aug.	15	655		Ft. Atkinson, WI	Cottage Grove , Wisconsin
Joerg, Regina	13, Apr. 1893	24, Feb.	62	238	Schwarz	Ft. Atkinson, WI	Württemberg
Joerig, Maria	31, Jan. 1876	10, Jan.	63	39		Pekin, IL	
Johanaber, Friedrich	2, May 1870	1, Nov.	51	143		Hopewell, MO	Münster, Westphalen
Johann, Carl Wilhelm	13, Sept 1875	24, June	70	295		Cannelton, MO	Wermelskirchen, Lennep, Elberfeld, Preußen
Johann, Caroline	7, Aug. 1871	13, July	26	255	Schwartz	Boonville, IN	Kölderholt, Minden, Preußen
Johann, Lisette	14, Dec. 1893	29, Oct.	86	798	Wourth	Cannelton, IN	Wermelskirchen, Preußen
Johann, Lydia	30, Aug. 1880	11, Aug.	21- 4m- 5d	279		Evansville, IN	Evansville, Indiana
Johannaber,	17, Nov. 1892	31, Oct.	62-10m-11d	734	Meyer	Pinckney, MO	Minden, Hannover
Johannaber, Maria	25, Aug. 1873		15	271		Hopewell, MO	
Johannes, Elisabeth	11, Mar. 1878	15, Feb.	32	79	Grimmeyer	Angelica, NY	Vordorf, Amt Gifhorn, Hannover

Christliche Apologete Death Notices --- 1839 - 1899

Name of Deceased	Notice Date	Death Date	Age	Page	Maiden Name	Place of Death	Place of Birth
Johannes, Friedrich Carl	3, Nov. 1887	21, Oct.	5m	702		Angelica, NY	Allen , New York
Johannes, Jürgen Heinrich	30, Aug. 1894	7, Aug.	87	566		Caneadea, Ny	Vorsdorf, Gifhorn, Hannover
Johannes, Maria	8, Sept 1884	13, Aug.	76- 4m-10d	7		Angelica, NY	Grassel, Gifhorn, Hannover
Johannes, Maria	4, Mar. 1872	4, Feb.	65	79		Angelica, NY	Hannover
Johannessohn, Anna	17, Nov. 1898	28, Oct.	38	735	Laub	Ada, MN	Görsbach, Sachsen
Johanning, Anna Maria Katharina	20, Sept 1888	28, Aug.	32	606	Twelker	Willow Springs, KS	Port Hudson, Franklin County, Missouri
Johannsen, Anna	15, Nov. 1894	24, Oct.	25	742	Kohlhase	Sleepy Eye, MN	Brown County, Minnesota
Johannsen, Anna Sophia	26, Oct. 1899	1, Oct.	66	687	Petersen	Sleepy Eye, MN	Drey, Schleswig
Johansen, Ingwer	28, June 1888	2, May	44	414		Lake Creek, MO	Schnatebüll, Schleswig
John, Adolph	28, Nov. 1864	30, Oct.	36	192		Decatur, IL	Burchholzhausen, Preußen
John, Ernst	10, Mar. 1884	24, Feb.	71- 2m- 8d	7		Detroit, MI	Mühlhausen, Preußen
Johnle, Johann Jakob	16, May 1861	4, Apr.	34- 3m- 8d	80		Baresville, OH	Hepfigheim, Marbach, Württemberg
Johnson, Elisabeth	11, Mar. 1886	22, Feb.	22	7		Grand Rapids, MI	New York
Johnson, Jac. T.	28, Jan. 1892	5, Jan.	59	62		Mt. Olive, IL	Schwerinsdorf, Hesel, Ostfriesland
Johnson, Karoline Katharine	14, Sept 1885	31, Aug.	29	7	Pfaff	Dayton, OH	
Johonnes, Johan Heinrich	28, June 1875	10, June	71	207		Angelica, NY	Vordorf, Amt Gifhorn, Hannover
Jöhrendt, Anna Maria	23, Feb. 1880	3, Feb.	15- 9m-13d	63		Laporte, IN	
Jöhrendt, Christoph	9, June 1879	22, May	66- 1m-14d	183		Laporte, IN	
Jokisch, Edward B.	23, June 1887	20, May	33	398		Arenzville, IL	Cass County, Illinois
Jokisch, Heinrich Gottlob	30, June 1898	29, May	66	415		Boody, IL	Halbendorf, Sachsen
Jokisch, Karl August	9, Feb. 1888	31, Dec.	70	94		Arenzville, IL	Helbendorf, Sachsen
Jokisch, Karl Traugott	9, Feb. 1899	16, Jan.	77	95		Arenzville, IL	Helbendorf, Sachsen
Jokisch, Susanna	31, Jan. 1889	24, Dec.	62	78	Lehmann	Arenzville, IL	Franklin County, Pennsylvania
Jonas, Christina	12, July 1875	26, June	72	223		Laporte, IN	Kittendorf, Mecklenburg-Schwerin
Jonas, Friedrich	18, Sept 1865	26, Aug.	36-11m- 9d	152		Laporte, IN	Kittendorf, Mecklenburg-Schwerin
Jonas, Friedrich	25, Sept 1865	18, July	37	156		Laporte, IN	Kittendorf, Mecklenburg-Schwerin
Jonas, Friedrich	28, Jan. 1878	16, Jan.	32- 2m-24d	31		Laporte, IN	Kittendorf, Mecklenburg
Jonas, Friedrich Joachim	4, May 1868	25, Jan.	77	143		Newtonburg, WI	Hippendorf, Mecklenburg-Schwerin
Jonas, Katharine	7, June 1860	13, May	32	92		Pittsburg, PA	Dudenhofen, Hessen
Jonas, Louis	31, Jan. 1881	11, Jan.	23	39		Saginaw, MI	
Jonas, May Louise	26, Sept 1889	21, Aug.	24	619	Deininger	Schnectady, NY	Troy, New York
Jonas, Wilhelm	13, Mar. 1890	26, Jan.	30- 5m-22d	174		Saginaw, MI	Detroit, Wayne County, Michigan
Jones, Minnie	11, May 1899	9, Apr.	22	302	Multhaup	Lewis, IA	Warren County, Missouri
Jones, Sophia	31, May 1869	25, Mar.	76	175		Manitowoc, WI	Mecklenburg-Schwerin
Jonker, Kornelie Friederike	6, Apr. 1899		77	223	Von Stein	Eldora, IA	Kampen, Holland
Jonson, Philipp	18, Mar.1872	5, Mar.	33	95		Platteville, WI	Sobernheim, Kreuznach, RheinPreußen
Joost, Nikolaus	23, Mar. 1899	14, Feb.	80	191		Brooklyn, NY	Drangstedt, Hannover
Jordan, Friedericka	13, Mar. 1876	1, Jan.	85- 4m	87	Gebert	Mt. Pleasant, IA	Fürstenhagen, Amt Uslar, Hannover
Jordan, Georg Heinrich	24, Apr. 1871	7, Apr.	57	135		Cincinnati, OH	Holler, Woldenberg, Hannover
Jordan, Gottfried	4, Oct. 1880	12, Sept	71- 9m-17d	319		Etna, MO	Mühlbach, Hersfeld, Kurhessen
Jordan, Henry	23, June 1887	25, May	61	398		Sandusky, OH	Necklensberg, Schorndorf, Württemberg
Jordan, Katharina	13, Nov. 1890	20, Oct.	70- 7m-24d	734	Heckel	Woodland, MI	Ruppichteroth, Köln, Germany
Jordan, Lisette	14, Sept 1899	23, Aug.	77	591	Bickenbach	Mason, TX	Fußgönheim, Rheinkreis Baiern
Jordan, Nikolaus	12, May 1873	20, Apr.	36- 8m-26d	151		Marrs, TX	
Jordan, Sophia Maria	10, Aug. 1899	14, June	74	511	Heidel	Kendallville, IN	Sandfeld, Mecklenburg-Schwerin
Jordan, Stephan	6, Aug. 1883	19, July	76- 3m-11d	255		Kendallville, IN	Palmenbach, Baden

Christliche Apologete Death Notices --- 1839 - 1899

Name of Deceased	Notice Date	Death Date	Age	Maiden Name	Page	Place of Death	Place of Birth
Jordan, Wilhelm Louis	23, Apr. 1896	28, Mar.	40		270	Cincinnati, OH	Greencastle, Indiana
Jörg, Barbara	13, Oct. 1859	22, Sept	61		164	Long Point, IL	Neschikon, Zürich, Schweiz
Jörg, Jakob Heinrich	1, Jan. 1891	9, Dec.	89		14	Sandwich, IL	Gundersdorf, Herborn, Nassau
Jörgensen, Peter	23, Apr. 1891	3, Apr.	48		270	De Soto, MO	
Jörgensen, Sabine	9, Feb. 1893	17, Jan.	38	Schaumburg	94	St. Louis, MO	Hermann, Missouri
Jörger, Johan Baptist	27, Sept 1875	16, Aug.	61		311	Lancaster, NY	Graffern, Amt Bühl, Baden
Jörke, Wilhelmine	16, June 1884	20, May	53	Trumpf	7	Lancaster, NY	Gülzau, Mecklenburg-Schwerin
Jörling, Adolf H.	22, Sept 1898	3, Sept	57		607	Oregon, MO	Preußen
Jörn, Henriette	14, Mar. 1881	23, Feb.	83- 2m-15d		87	Dayton, OH	Wida, Wolgenreth, Blankenburg, Braunschweig
Jörn, Johan Heinrich Louis	8, Dec. 1887	5, Nov.	64		782	Batesville, IN	Nette, Woldenberg, Hannover
Jörs, Wilhelmine	5, Apr. 1875	21, Mar.	39		111	Chicago, IL	Liesow, Mecklenburg-Schwerin
Joseph, Elisabeth	10, June 1872	20, Apr.	33	Fuchs	191	Charlestown, IN	Nordheim, Hessen-Darmstadt
Joses, Elise	9, May 1895	19, Mar.	81	Warnes	302	Lorin, CA	Memel, Germany
Josewski, Bertha	30, Dec. 1897	13, Dec.	34	Fride	828	Crandon, SD	Dolgen, Dramburg, Pommern
Jost, Conrad	12, Sept 1870	16, Aug.	21		295	St. Louis, MO	
Jost, Fr.	4, Apr. 1881	11, Mar.	60		111	Berea, OH	Attisville, Wangen, Bern, Schweiz
Jost, Katharina	25, Apr. 1870	25, Feb.	81	Pfeifer	135	Red Bud, IL	Darmstadt, Hessen-Darmstadt
Jost, Louise C.	31, July 1890	23, June	25	Hoffmann	494	St. Louis, MO	Ueterlande, Deudesdorf, Oldenburg
Jost, Margaretha	21, Aug. 1882	4, July	16		271	Lansing, MI	
Jost, Maria	12, May 1892	22, Apr.	63		302	St. Joseph, MO	Canton Bern, Schweiz
Jostes, Charlotte Wilhelmine	27, Aug. 1896	12, Aug.	71	Diekmann	559	Boody, IL	Pekeloh, Minden, Preußen
Jostes, Wilhelm	6, May 1886	2, Apr.	48		7	Decatur, IL	Versmoldt, Halle, Preußen
Jösting, (girl)	9, Sept 1872	25, Aug.			295	San Jose, IL	
Jostus, Friedrich W.	10, Nov. 1879	19, Oct.	76		359	Boody, IL	Pekeloh, Westphalen
Jotter, Eduard Heinrich	30, Apr. 1896	31, Mar.	37		286	Warsaw, IL	Warsaw, Illinois
Joung, Friedrich Bernhard	3, Nov. 1884	4, Oct.	71		7	Almond, WI	Wernshausen, Sachsen-Meiningen
Joung, Paulina Amalie	18, Mar. 1897	14, Feb.	44	Baumann	174	Jordan, MN	Remptendorf, Reuß, Thüringen
Jourdan, Abraham	3, July 1871	6, Mar.	80		215	Marrs, IN	Walldorf, Hessen-Darmstadt
Jourdan, Catharine Elisabetha	3, Nov. 1862	12, Oct.	16-10m-15d		176	Kendallville, IN	
Jourdan, Hanna	29, July 1878	9, July	31		239	Kendallville, IN	Mahoning County, Ohio
Jourdan, Johan	28, Oct. 1878	8, Oct.	37		343	Kendallville, IN	Moser County, Pennsylvania
Juchter, Anna Margaretha	8, June 1863	25, Mar.			92	New York, NY	Delmenhorst, Hannover
Jucker, Heinrich	16, Dec. 1897	22, Nov.			799	Cincinnati, OH	Neubrunn, Turbenthal, Zürich, Schweiz
Judd, Anna Maria	20, Oct. 1898	24, Aug.	81	Flamm	670	New Albany, NY	Riederich, Urach, Württemberg
Judisch, Ludwig Ferdinand	23, July 1877	8, July	81		239	Muscatine, IA	Göritz, Prenzlow, Preußen
Juelfs, Carolina Margaretha	21, Oct. 1878	26, Sept	56	Glocke	335	Galveston, TX	Oldendorf, Hessen
Juliane, Caroline	6, Aug. 1877		71	Hänerlien	255	Kewaunee, WI	Landsberg an der Warte, Preußen
Juliar, Magdalena	30, May 1889	1, May	83- 4m-13d		350	Baraboo, WI	Sundhofen, Elsaß
Juliar, Nikolaus	24, Apr. 1882	2, Apr.	84- 2m-18d		135	Baraboo, WI	Ostheim, Elsaß
Julius, Karolina	19, Apr. 1894	30, Mar.	27		262	Stitzer, WI	Lawrence County, Ohio
Julius, Katharina	15, Mar. 1880	26, Feb.	15- 6m		87	Lancaster, WI	
Julius, Louis	1, Dec. 1884	3, Nov.	75	Fischer	7	Stitzer, WI	Schile, Berlenburg, Preußen
Julius, Louis	8, Apr. 1897	18, Mar.	67		223	Stitzer, WI	Schiller, Wichtenstein, Preußen
Julius, Louise	21, May 1883	2, May	16- 1m-13d		167	Lancaster, OH	
Julius, Louise	19, Mar. 1883		47- 4m-18d		95	Lancaster, WI	Frohnhausen, Biedenkopf, Hessen-Darmstadt
Julius, Ludwig	4, Mar. 1886	6, Feb.	83		7	Lancaster, WI	Christans Eck, Preußen

Christliche Apologete Death Notices --- 1839 - 1899

Name of Deceased	Notice Date	Death Date	Age	Maiden Name	Page	Place of Death	Place of Birth
Juncker, Katharina	7, Apr. 1884	21, Mar.	75	Wiegand	7	Cameron, MO	Frieda, Eschwe, Kurhessen
Jung, Elisabeth	31, Jan. 1895	2, Jan.	74	Ruff	78	Defiance, OH	Zweibrücken, Baiern
Jung, Heinrich Wilhelm	26, Jan. 1893	31, Dec.	13		62	Charles City, IA	
Jung, Katharine	30, Oct. 1890	14, Oct.	74	Koch	702	Louisville, KY	Pothseelberg, Rheinkreis Baiern
Jung, Amalie	17, May 1860	21, Apr.	60		80	Grand Rapids, MI	Drüber, Eimbeck, Hannover
Jung, Anna Katharine	5, Apr. 1888	11, Feb.	77- 4m- 1d		222	Charles City, IA	Gehau bei Eschwege, Kurhessen
Jung, Catharina Barbara	19, Mar. 1877	16, Feb.	77-10m- 7d		95	Chillicothe, OH	Schwegenheim, Germesheim, Rheinpfalz Baiern
Jung, Christiane Charlotte	28, Jan. 1884	12, Jan.	81		7	Wathena, KS	
Jung, Christina	2, Dec. 1852	4, Oct.	33		196	Louisville, KY	Lorsbach, Nassau
Jung, Christine	8, Feb. 1894	21, Jan.	80	Schwartz	94	Newark, NJ	Oberheinrieth, Württemberg
Jung, Christoph	23, Apr. 1883	7, Apr.	31-11m-19d		135	Scranton, PA	Lichtenau, Preußen
Jung, Conrad	28, June 1860	11, May	37		104	Louisville, KY	Abterode, Eschwegen, Kurhessen
Jung, Conrad	25, Feb. 1897	10, Feb.	72		127	St. Charles, MO	Steinmauer, Baden
Jung, Elisabeth	14, Jan. 1878	29, Dec.	71- 5m-20d		15	De Soto, MO	Sinkershausen, Hessen-Darmstadt
Jung, Eva Katharina	28, May 1877	22, Apr.	56	Schleicher	175	Farmington, WI	Wernshausen, Sachsen-Meiningen
Jung, Georg Adam	5, Oct. 1885	6, Aug.	70		7	Defiance, OH	Minfeld bei Langkandel, Rheinpfalz Baiern
Jung, Heinrich	24, Nov. 1898		69		751	South Bend, IN	Preußen
Jung, Johan Benjamin	9, Sept 1897	6, Aug.	79		575	Jordan, MN	Neuhain, Waldenburg, Schlesien
Jung, Johan Christoph	14, May 1883	30, Apr.	49- 6m-26d		159	Charles City, MO	Gehau, Kurhessen
Jung, Katharina	23, Feb. 1899	31, Jan.	58	Blankenbach	127	Charles City, IA	Königswald , Kurhessen
Jung, Konrad	11, May 1874	1, Apr.	68		151	De Soto, MO	Kreis Biedenkopf, Hessen-Darmstadt
Jung, Lisette	10, Dec. 1857	20, Oct.	34		200	Blue Island, IL	Heinsenhausen, Rheinkreis Baiern
Jung, Ludwig	13, Oct. 1898	27, Sept	86		655	Newark, NJ	Neuenberge, Ottweiler, Rheinpfalz Baiern
Jung, Lydia Emma	25, June 1896	15, May	14		415	Columbus, OH	
Jung, Margaretha	13, Jan. 1868	18, Dec.	40- 2m	Kaiser	14	Canton, MO	
Jung, Margaretha	9, Nov. 1893	11, Oct.	58		718		Erzenhausen, Kaiserslautern, Rheinkreis Baiern
Jung, Margaretha	17, Sept 1877	1, Sept	71- 3m- 4d		305	Rochester, MN	Enzwangen, Göppingen, Württemberg
Jung, Maria Anna	1, May 1871				143		Pirmasens, Rheinkreis Baiern
Jung, Maria Catharina	12, July 1888	6, June	21- 3m- 3d	Fischer	446	Minneapolis, MN	Laporte, Indiana
Jung, Nicolaus	21, Feb. 1895	11, Jan.	78		126	Muscatine, IA	Weyer, Drulingen, Elsaß
Jung, Peter	24, Mar. 1884	2, Mar.	82- 9m		7	Rochester, MN	Primasens, Rheinkreis Baiern
Jung, Rosine	25, Jan. 1894	14, Dec.	56- 7m-10d	Schemp	62	Columbus, OH	Ochsenwang, Württemberg
Jung, Wilhelmine Louise	21, June 1869	4, June	16- 3m		199	Louisville, KY	
Junge, Friedrich	11, Aug. 1884	9, June	63		7	Arlington, MI	Breddorf, Ottersberg, Hannover
Junge, H.	26, Oct. 1874	28, Sept	73		343	Monterey, WI	Eboldshausen, Hannover
Jungeblut, F.W.	7, Nov. 1895	9, Oct.	52- 9m		718	Alton, IL	Lippe-Detmold
Jünger, Christian Gottfried	13, Feb. 1896	16, Jan.	86		110	Sheboygan, WI	Lauche, Sachsen
Jünger, Christina Elisabeth	25, Oct. 1869	10, Oct.	63- 1m- 6d	Bilke	343	Sheboygan, WI	Kösen an der Saale, Preußen
Jünger, Franklin	26, Apr. 1894	7, Apr.	25		278	Columbus, WI	Columbus, Wisconsin
Jünger, Hannah W.	17, July 1882	2, July	56		231	Sheboygan, WI	Hildebrandshausen, Uckermark, Preußen
Jungermann, Karl L.	2, Oct. 1890	14, Sept	16		638	Nashville, TN	
Junghanns, Karl L. E.	23, Nov. 1899	31, Oct.	78		751	Wilmington, CA	Pommern
Jungheim, Johan	26, Nov. 1896	31, Oct.	67		766	Jerusalem, NY	Liebenau, Kurhessen
Jungheim, Katharina Elisabeth	9, July 1877	15, June	15- 8m-27d		223	Columbus, IL	
Jungheim, Louise	13, Mar. 1871	18, Jan.	31	Görtz	87	Columbus, IL	Mainz, Germany
Jungmann, Adam	8, Dec. 1892	15, Oct.	42		782	Ridgefield, WA	Westheim, Rheinpfalz Baiern

Christliche Apologete Death Notices --- 1839 - 1899

Name of Deceased	Notice Date	Death Date	Age	Maiden Name	Page	Place of Death	Place of Birth
Jungmann, Barbara	2, May 1889	3, Apr.	29- 2m-15d		286	St. Louis, MO	RheinPfalz Baiern
Jungmann, Barbara	22, Nov. 1894	20, Oct.	13- 9m-21d		758	Nauvoo, IL	
Jungmeier, Elisabeth	18, Apr. 1861	24, Mar.	27	Ochs	64	New Ulm, MN	Quentel, Amt Lichtenau, Kurhessen
Juni, Ernestine	28, Apr. 1884	8, Apr.	48- 1m-21d	Klingbeil	7	New Ulm, MN	Zearnikow, Posen
Juni, Weibicht	16, Dec. 1897		72		799	Baltimore, MD	Schweiz
Junk, Georg	18, June 1883	2, June	69		199	Pittsburg, PA	Winkbach, Marburg, Kurhessen
Junk, Juliana	20, Mar. 1882	5, Mar.	60-4m-13d	Vaas	95	Angelica, NY	Engelberg, Neuenbürg, Württemberg
Junke, Johan Heinrich	5, Dec. 1870	26, Sept	60-11m- 9d		391	San Jose, IL	Rolfsbüttel, Hannover
Junker, Anna	18, Nov. 1878	28, Oct.	67		367	Henderson, KY	Vorinholz, Bern, Schweiz
Junker, Anna Maria	9, Apr. 1877	23, Mar.	45	Mertens	119	Marrs, IN	Albig, Alzey, Werstadt, Rhein-Hessen
Junker, Georg	12, Oct. 1874	19, Sept	22		327	Newton, IA	Posey County, Indiana
Junker, Georg Elias	31, May 1880	12, May	70		175	Allegheny City, PA	Görsbach, Merseburg, Preußen
Junker, Henriette	18, Dec. 1856	5, Dec.	24	Pferdcort	204	Owatonna, MN	Liberdetmer, Preußen
Junker, Jakob	10, Nov. 1898	23, Oct.	66		719	Salem, IN	Kanton Bern, Schweiz
Junker, Jakob	31, Jan. 1895	11, Jan.	36		78		
Junker, Johannes	10, June 1858	24, May	29		92	Allegheny City, PA	Bodtenhorn, Hessen-Darmstadt
Junker, Leudicht	5, Apr. 1880	22, Jan.	63		111	San Jose, IL	Zimlisberg, Bern, Schweiz
Junker, Lorenz	13, June 1895	28, May	80		382	Pekin, IL	Kirchberg, Koblenz, Rheinpfalz Baiern
Junker, Louise	8, Dec. 1884	25, Nov.	33	Willmann	7	St. Philip, IN	
Junker, Margaretha	20, Oct. 1898	26, Sept	68	Mertens	670	Marrs, IN	Albig, Alzey, Hessen-Darmstadt
Junker, Maria	21, July 1873	26, June	65- 6m	Kellner	231	Newtonburg, WI	Urbach bei Nordhausen, Preußen
Junker, Nicholas	18, Sept 1890	15, Aug.	75- 2m-12d		606	Holt, MI	Buberg, Elsaß
Junkermann, Wilhelmine	7, Nov. 1895	24, Sept	59	Wohl	718	Quincy, IL	BadWildungen, Waldeck
Jürgens, Anna Elisabeth	24, Mar. 1892	6, Mar.	57	Pagenhart	190	Chicago, IL	Hombressen, Hofgeismar, Hessen
Jürgens, Margaretha	20, Oct. 1892	20, Sept	42	Rübling	670	Belleville, IL	Charles County, Maryland
Jürgensmeyer, August	30, July 1896	9, June	35		495	Nashville, IL	Oehnhausen, Preußen
Just, Anna Margaretha	16, Dec. 1858	23, Sept	62		200	Lansing, MI	
Justin, (Mrs)	21, Mar. 1861	24, Feb.		Baum	48	Callicoon, NY	Woonsheim, Hessen-Darmstadt
Justin, Elisabeth	6, Apr. 1885	14, Mar.	72		7	Jeffersonville, IN	Gießen, Hessen
Justin, Ludwig	24, Apr. 1890	12, Mar.	82		270	Jeffersonville, NY	Enzheim, Hessen-Darmstadt
Kaasch, Christine	11, July 1895	31, May	71- 1m- 7d	Gensman	446	Brillion, WI	Balkenhagen, Pommern
Kaatz, Michael	28, July 1873	27, June	40		239	Strongsville, OH	Großkolten, Preußen
Käbelin, Johan Georg	21, Feb. 1895	14, Jan.	89		126	Laporte, IN	Eichstetten, Emmendingen, Baden
Käberich, Martha	3, Jan. 1881	10, Dec.	13- 1m-24d		7	Charles City, IA	New Bremen, Cook County, Illinois
Kachel, Carolina	19, Sept 1889	2, Aug.	32	Kaiser	606	Philadelphia, PA	Philadelphia , Pennsylvania
Kächele, Augusta	14, Jan. 1897	26, Dec.	81	Rudin	31	Sandusky, OH	Böttingen, Württemberg
Kächele, Jakob	20, Sept 1888	19, Aug.	74		606	Sandusky, OH	Rottenacker, Donau, Ehringen, Württemberg
Kachler, Johann E.	16, Aug. 1849	21, July	60		132	Dayton, OH	Ried, Württemberg
Kadel, (Mrs)	18, Mar. 1886	16, Feb.	68		7	Cleveland, OH	Haudwebach, Runkel, Nassau
Kadel, Albert	21, Feb. 1889	7, Oct.	26- 3m-28d		126	Nashville, TN	Nashville, Tennessee
Kadel, Herman	21, Feb. 1889	6, Jan.	23- 2m-26d		126	Nashville, TN	Nashville, Tennessee
Kadolph, Carl	27, June 1895	24, May	68		414	Alden, IA	Sitzmien, Schlawe, Cöslin, Pommern
Kadow, Johan Joachim	16, Mar. 1899	14, Feb.	94		175	Osceola, NE	Strelitz, Mecklenburg-Strelitz
Kaeding, Gottfried	9, Aug. 1888	25, July	65		510	Michigan City, IN	Alt-Falkenberg, Pieritz, Pommern
Kaelber, Jakob	18, Apr. 1895	28, Mar.	75		254	Newark, NJ	Pforzheim, Baden

Christliche Apologete Death Notices --- 1839 - 1899

Name of Deceased	Notice Date	Death Date	Age	Page	Maiden Name	Place of Death	Place of Birth
Kaelke, Mina	8, Aug. 1895	17, Apr.	63	510		Golden City, MO	Grebs, Dömitz, Mecklenburg-Schwerin
Kaercher, Georg David	1, Aug. 1895	27, June	72	494		Brooklyn, NY	Canstatt, Württemberg
Kaese, August Wilhelm	15, Sept 1884	14, Aug.	54- 3m	7		San Francisco, CA	Rithmershausen, Hannover
Kaese, Friedrich	21, Apr. 1887	30, Mar.	57	254		St. Paul, MN	Rittmarshausen, Preußen
Kaetter, Katharine	24, July 1882	8, July	72- 3m-20d	239	Decker	Columbus, OH	Dauphin County, Pennsylvania
Kaffenberger, Elisabeth	30, Sept 1886	19, Aug.	68	7		Beardstown, IL	Hemsbach, Baden
Kaffenberger, Heinrich	1, Sept 1884	11, Aug.	69-11m-19d	7		Beardstown, IL	Leitershausen, Weinheim, Baden
Käffer, Henrika	21, Feb. 1861	1, Feb.	67	32		Louisville, KY	
Kahl, Angenete Engel	21, Jan. 1884	29, Dec.	66-11m-29d	7		St. Louis, MO	
Kahl, Elisabeth	29, May 1890	12, May	61- -23d	350	Strack	Charlestown, IN	Klingelbach, Naschstätte, Nassau
Kahl, Helene	3, Mar. 1898	23, Jan.	64	143	Behrens	Freyburg, TX	Neusüdende, Oldenburg
Kahl, Johannes	8, Aug. 1889	25, July	73- 4m- 3d	510		Charlestown, IN	Massenheim, Hochheim, Nassau
Kahl, Katharine Margarethe	11, Aug. 1859	28, July	23	128		Charlestown, IN	Dietenbergen, Amt Hochheim, Nassau
Kahl, L. (Mrs)	31, May 1894	9, May	72	358		Hannibal, MO	Liberty, Pennsylvania
Kahl, Wilhelmina Magdalena	19, Mar. 1877	3, Feb.	38- 9m- 6d	95	Kartum	Illinois City, IL	Adelig, Panker, Holstein
Kahle, Dietrich Heinrich	20, Aug. 1896	24, July	65	542		Beman, KS	Huhum, Hannover
Kahle, Dorothea	23, Mar. 1868	2, Mar.	76- 2m	95		Le Sueur, MN	
Kahle, Heinrich Wilhelm	18, Oct. 1880	6, Sept	39	335		Madison, IN	Mardorf, Schneeren, Hannover
Kähler, Emilie	7, July 1892	16, June	38	430	Henning	Chicago, IL	Hardenbeck, Uckermark, Preußen
Kahlo, Anna	26, Nov. 1896	17, Oct.	67	766	VonBehren	Toledo, OH	Lancaster, Ohio
Kahlo, Karl	26, Jan. 1899	1, Jan.	43	63		Defiance, OH	Defiance , Ohio
Kahlo, Orville Ewing	19, Dec. 1889	27, Nov.	10	814		Toledo, OH	Toledo, Lucas County, Ohio
Kähny, Joseph Anton	12, Jan. 1893	17, Dec.	58	30		Chicago, IL	Adelhausen, Schopfheim, Germany
Kahrs, Albert	5, Sept 1895	11, Aug.	20	574	Bohling	Lake Creek, MO	Lake Creek, Missouri
Kahrs, Anna	27, Apr. 1868	2, Apr.	23	135		Lake Creek, MO	Pettis County, Missouri
Kahrs, Dorothea	22, Nov. 1875	2, Oct.	58	375		Lake Creek, MO	
Kahrs, Gesche	12, May 1853	23, Mar.	41	76		Florence, MO	Altenhalstedt, Amt Ottersberg, Hannover
Kahrs, Herman	3, May 1894	2, Apr.	78	294		Sedalia, MO	Neuenböldstett, Otterburg, Hannover
Kahrs, John	30, Aug. 1880	3, Aug.	69- 1m-25d	279		Lake Creek, MO	Neuer-Bülstadt, Hannover
Kahrs, John L.	28, May 1896	2, May	45	350		Lake Creek, MO	Lake Creek, Missouri
Kahrs, Louis	23, May 1881	2, May	75	167		Lake Creek, MO	Altenbühlstet, Ottersberg, Hannover
Kahrs, Margaretha	27, Jan. 1859	22, Dec.	74	16	Ficken	Florence, MO	Vorwerk, Ottersberg, Billstedt, Hannover
Kahrs, Margaretha	17, July 1890	29, June	22	462	Otten	Sedalia, MO	
Kahrs, Maria	16, June 1887		59- 4m- 2d	382	Hinken	Lake Creek, MO	Altenbülstedt, Ottersberg, Hannover
Kahrs, Maria	4, June 1866	9, May	46	182		Edwardsville, IL	Neuen Bülstedt, Hannover
Kaiser, (Mr)	18, Oct. 1869	14, Sept	75- 9m	335		Santa Claus, IN	Firral, Ostfriesland
Kaiser, Andreas	11, Feb. 1897	2, Jan.	82	94		Santa Claus, IN	Fechheim, Sachsen-Coburg-Gotha
Kaiser, Andreas	6, July 1863	14, June	41	108		Santa Cruz, CA	Burghaig, Baiern
Kaiser, Anna Elisabeth	15, Mar. 1894	18, Feb.	41	182	Prüssing	Daytonville, IA	Mühlhausen, Hessen-Nassau
Kaiser, Anna Elisabeth	16, Dec. 1878	28, Nov.	54- 6m- 4d	399		Mt. Vernon, IN	Erfurt, Preußen
Kaiser, Anna Margaretha	12, Mar. 1857	5, Dec.	36	44	Steiner	Roseville, MI	Blumenroth, Sachsen-Coburg
Kaiser, August	5, May 1862	16, Apr.	71- 7m	72		Swanton, NE	Degerloch, Württemberg
Kaiser, Christian	13, Apr. 1893	21, Mar.	52	238		Redfield, SD	Sallentin, Pommern
Kaiser, Christian F.	19, Apr. 1894	25, Mar.	70	262		Swanton, NE	Dölitz bei Stargard, Pommern
Kaiser, Christine	25, Apr. 1889	23, Mar.	43- 6m-29d	270	Witt	Francisco, MI	Dölitz, Pommern
Kaiser, Christoph	20, Nov. 1890	5, Aug.	70	750			Degerloch, Württemberg

- 236 -

Name of Deceased	Notice Date	Death Date	Age	Maiden Name	Page	Place of Death	Place of Birth
Kaiser, Elisabeth	23, May 1864	24, Apr.	65- 5m- 5d	Seibold	84	Preston, CD	Beinstein, Waiblingen, Württemberg
Kaiser, Elisabeth	8, June 1899	31, Jan.	62	Welsch	367	Canton, MO	Meißenheim, Hamburg, Germany
Kaiser, Elisabeth	3, Dec. 1896	12, Nov.	60		782	Clay Center, KS	Leutsigen, Bern, Schweiz
Kaiser, Elisabeth Anna	29, Jan. 1883	13, Jan.	. 30	Land	39	Portsmouth, OH	Rohrbach, Simmen, Preußen
Kaiser, Eva Margaretha	21, Feb. 1856	31, Jan.	63- -37d	Frech	32	Roseville, MI	Degerloch, Stuttgart, Württemberg
Kaiser, Eva Maria	21, Jan. 1892	17, Nov.	67	Braun	46	Marine City, MI	Eggenhausen, Württemberg
Kaiser, Friederike	24, Jan. 1895	1, Jan.	57		62	Brooklyn, NY	Rowe bei Treptow, Hinterpommern
Kaiser, Georg L.	24, July 1890	27, June	80		478	East Troy, WI	Stübach bei Neustadt a.d. Esch, Baiern
Kaiser, Georg Wilhelm	10, Feb. 1859	27, Jan.	35		24	Madison, IN	Born bei Wiesbaden, Nassau
Kaiser, Helena	10, Nov. 1892	10, Oct.	56		718	Ellenwood, KS	Firrell, Ostfriesland
Kaiser, Herman	18, July 1889	21, June	18		462	Swanton, NE	Jefferson County, Nebraska
Kaiser, Johan Adam	13, Aug. 1883	18, June	18- 9m- 8d		263	Canton, MO	
Kaiser, Johan Jakob	28, Dec. 1899	3, Dec.	78		828	Laporte, IN	Eichstädten, Baden
Kaiser, Johanna	11, Jan. 1875	24, Dec.	27- 3m- 1d	Elbrecht	15	Appleton, MO	
Kaiser, John	31, Mar. 1884	18, Mar.	56		7	Pittsfield, IL	Oberflachs, Aargau, Schweiz
Kaiser, Karl J.	27, Oct. 1892	11, Oct.	57		686	Detroit, MI	Roseville, Michigan
Kaiser, Katharina	20, Dec. 1880	15, Oct.	46	Schrag	407	Toledo, OH	Hitzerode, Hessen-Nassau
Kaiser, Katharina E.	9, June 1898	23, May	54		367	Allegheny, PA	Brodhead, Wisconsin
Kaiser, Klara Helene	13, July 1899	8, June	23	Hintzmann	447	Swanton, NE	Florence Township, Williams County, Ohio
Kaiser, Louise	15, Oct. 1891	1, Oct.	13		670	Edon, OH	Edigheim, Rheinpfalz Baiern
Kaiser, Margaretha	21, Aug. 1851	14, June	47	Jacobi	136	Pomeroy, OH	
Kaiser, Marie Katharine	10, June 1858	5, May	66		92	Franciscoville, MI	Bockerode, Kreis Melzungen, Kurhessen
Kaiser, Martha Elisabeth	10, Oct. 1870	17, Sept	25		327	Warsaw, IL	
Kaiser, Martin	3, Oct. 1870	3, Sept	31		319	Nokomis, IL	Rütehof, Aargau, Schweiz
Kaiser, Mina	13, Sept 1888	14, aug.	18		590	Grand Rapids, MI	Plieningen, Württemberg
Kaiser, Urban	19, June 1856	17, May	64		100	Ann Arbor, MI	Vosingen, Lennex, RheinPreußen
Kaiser, Wilhelmine	14, Dec. 1885	27, Nov.	66- 3m- 5d	Karrensten	7	St. Paul, MN	
Kaitzer, Margaretha	22, Feb. 1849		Inquiry		31	Burlington, IA	
Kaitzer, Michael	22, Feb. 1849		Inquiry		31	Burlington, IA	
Kalb, Regina	1, June 1893	6, May	71	Greifenstein	350	Pittsburg, PA	Kirchberg, Württemberg
Kalberlah, Friedrich	22, Jan. 1891	1, Jan.	65		62	Chicago, IL	Walle, Hannover
Kalbfleisch, Friederike	27, Nov. 1876	6, Nov.	58- 1m-14d	Schott	383	Clarington, OH	Oberlenningen, Kirchheim, Württemberg
Kalenbach, Katharine	21, Nov. 1870	27, Oct.	27- 3m-25d	Kammrer	375	Grand Rapids, MI	
Kaletsch, John	11, Apr. 1861	15, Mar.	59- 3m		60	Burlington, IA	Ockershausen, Kurhessen
Kalien, Ferdinand	11, May 1899	9, Nov.	75		302	Faribault, MN	Workow bei Stargard, Pommern
Kalkbrenner, Ernestine	28, July 1884		24	Günther	7	Detroit, MI	Treudörschen, Marienwerder, West Preußen
Kälke, Heinrich	19, May 1887	16, Apr.	13		318	Golden City, MO	
Kallbreier, Katharina	24, Feb. 1868	6, Feb.	71		63	Mt. Vernon, IN	Seßen am Harz, Braunschweig
Kallenbach, (Mrs)	28, Nov. 1850	19, Oct.	32		192	Springfield, IL	halbendorf, Sachsen
Kallenbach, Johan Moritz	14, Dec. 1874	3, Nov.	71		399	Pittsfield, IL	Neuendorf bei Salzungen, Sachsen-Meiningen
Kallenberger, Maria Eva	9, Mar. 1854	21, Feb.	38- 8m	Haubold	40	Cincinnati, OH	Steinweiler, Rheinkreis Baiern
Kallmautzki, Johan	26, Nov. 1891	9, Nov.	78		766	Seguin, TX	Jorgenburg, Rußland
Kallmann, Johan Philipp	1, July 1897	16, May			414	Bridgeport, CT	Hochstätten, Rheinpfalz Baiern
Kalmbach, Adam	3, May 1894	23, Nov.	67		294	Francisco, MI	Schönegründ, Freudenstadt, Württemberg
Kalmbach, Anna Maria	26, Nov. 1866	31, Oct.	21- 4m-23d	Nuhfer	382	Grand Rapids, MI	
Kalmbach, Bertha	3, Sept 1883	15, Aug.	36- 7m- 2d	Benter	287	Francisco, MI	Hülsing, Amt Dorum, Hannover

Christliche Apologete Death Notices --- 1839 - 1899

Name of Deceased	Notice Date	Death Date	Age	Page	Maiden Name	Place of Death	Place of Birth
Kalmbach, Carolina	16, June 1879	19, May	22	191		Franciscoville, MI	Chelsea, Michigan
Kalmbach, Johan Georg	25, Dec. 1882	14, Nov.	26	415		Grand Rapids, MI	Pfalzgrafenweiler, Freudenstadt, Württemberg
Kalmbach, Johanna	5, Apr. 1888	13, Mar.	55- 3m- 3d	222	Rolf	Francisco, MI	Bramsche, Hannover
Kalmerten, Ernst	14, Feb. 1895	26, Jan.	78	110		Sheboygan, WI	Westphalen
Kalmerten, Sophie	21, Apr. 1898	30, Mar.	77	255	Leig	Sheboygan, WI	Westphalen
Kalmerten, Wilhelm	20, June 1861	26, May	16- 6m-10d	100		Sheboygan, WI	
Kaltenbach, Catharina	24, June 1867	11, Apr.	46	198		New York, NY	Neuhausen, Eßlingen, Württemberg
Kaltenbach, Karl	19, May 1879	29, Apr.	15-10m	159		Oregon, MO	
Kaltenbach, Karl	11, June 1883	10, May	34- -10d	191		Wheeling, WV	Selters, Hessen-Darmstadt
Kaltenbach, Karl Fr.	30, Jan. 1882	8, Jan.	71- 2m-16d	39		Wheeling, WV	Eckertshausen, Büdingen, Hessen-Darmstadt
Kaltenbach, Louise Barbara	5, July 1888	14, June	15	430		Oregon, MO	
Kaltenbach, Margaretha	2, May 1889	12, Apr.	40- 2m-23d	286	Hechler	Wheeling, WV	Georgenhausen, Hessen
Kaltenbacher, Adam	21, Jan. 1886	10, Nov.		7		New York City, NY	
Kaltenhäuser, Katharina	24, May 1888	12, Apr.	78	334	Zimmer	Des Moines, IA	Saalbrücken, Preußen
Kalter, Paul	12, Jan. 1888	8, Dec.	73	30		Dayton, OH	Lützelhausen, Kurhessen
Kaman, Wilhelmine Francisca	3, Mar. 1884	30, Jan.	60	7	Ratkens	Bay City, MI	Hamburg, Germany
Kämer, Johannes	2, May 1895	2, Mar.	88	286		Albert Lea, MN	Waldorf, Wiesloch, Baden
Kamm , Louis	4, Mar. 1897	12, Feb.	70	143		Nebraska City, NE	Redehausen, Marburg, Kurhessen
Kamm, Anna Katharina	1, Dec. 1884	12, Nov.	51	7		Baltimore, MD	Brezenacker, Württemberg
Kamm, Johannes	27, Dec. 1880	23, Nov.	55- 9m- 6d	415	Grimmel	lancaster, PA	Feßmond, Preußen
Kammann, Herman Philipp	7, Jan. 1897	5, Dec.	67	15		Huntingburg, IN	Schleswig-Holstein
Kammann, Ludwig	7, Aug. 1890	8, July	67	510		Bay City, MI	Genschmar, Lebuser, Preußen
Kammb, Anna Sophia	6, June 1870	16, Apr.	62- 2m-15d	183		Horicon, WI	Marienwalde, Arnswalde, Preußen
Kammer, Bertha	16, May 1889	7, Apr.	41	318	Schmidt	Waterford, SD	
Kammer, Philippine	6, June 1861	8, May	21	92	Welsch	Canton, MO	
Kammerer, Christine	14, Sept 1893	14, Aug.	83	590	Waik	Charles City, IA	Graben, Baden
Kammerer, Wilhelm	19, Nov. 1896	23, Oct.	86- - 4d	750		Charles City, IA	Graben, Baden
Kämmerle , (Mr)	28, Jan. 1848	17, Jan.	41- 4m	19		West Union, OH	Württemberg
Kammermeier, Catharine	24, Nov. 1862	13, Oct.	63	188	Mäle	Peru, IL	Edenkoben, Rheinpfalz Baiern
Kammet, Friedrich	21, Sept 1893	25, Aug.	15	606		Tinley Park, IL	Tinley Park, Illinois
Kammet, Heinrich	25, Apr. 1895	24, Mar.	33	270		Tinley Park, IL	New Bremen, Illinois
Kammeyer, Charlotte	19, Dec. 1889	12, Nov.	69	814	Brune	Big Spring, MO	Borgholzhausen, Halle, Preußen
Kammeyer, Wilhelm	7, Apr. 1873	28, Feb.	14- 2m- 6d	111		Herman, MO	
Kamp, Anna Sibylla	23, July 1877	6, July	23	239		Lowell, WI	Cxonia, Wisconsin
Kamp, Helena	18, Aug. 1862	19, July	67- 5m-15d	132		Watertown, WI	Cappelen, Mörs, Düsseldorf, RheinPreußen
Kamp, Helene G.	15, Aug. 1889	27, June	27	526		Lowell, WI	Ixonie, Wisconsin
Kampe, Amalie	9, Feb. 1888	4, Jan.	34	94		Rochester, MN	Plauen, Sachsen
Kampe, Anna Christina	12, Nov. 1877	2, Oct.	62	367	VonDüssen	Madison, IN	Liebenau, Hofgeismar, Kurhessen
Kampe, Ernst	7, Feb. 1889	30, Dec.	74- 3m-26d	94		St. Louis, MO	Nettelstedt, Preußen
Kampe, Johan Georg	26, Apr. 1894	1, Apr.	81	278		Madison, IN	Liebenau, Geismar, Kurhessen
Kampe, Wesley Edward	14, May 1896	12, Apr.	26	318		Madison, IN	
Kampe, Wilhelmine	18, Feb. 1884	17, Jan.		7	Pieper	St. Louis, MO	Gellenbach, Preußen
Kämper, Catharina Friederike	5, Mar. 1877	18, Feb.	41	79	Koch	St. Louis, MO	Bergholzhausen, Minden, Preußen
Kämpf, Fr.	5, Nov. 1877	8, Oct.	50- 8m-17d	359		Lansing, MI	Gussenstadt, Württemberg
Kämpfer, Heinrich Jost	7, Feb. 1845	6, Jan.	35	23		Herman, MO	
Kämpfer, Maria	27, Sept 1888	31, Aug.	57	622	Haudenschield	Switzer, OH	Kanton Bern , Schweiz

Christliche Apologete Death Notices --- 1839 - 1899

Name of Deceased	Notice Date	Death Date	Age	Maiden Name	Page	Place of Death	Place of Birth
Kämpfer, Maria Anna	24, Oct. 1895	2, Oct.	67	Roth	686	Pekin, IL	Kanton Bern, Schweiz
Kampmann, Kasper	27, Apr. 1885	11, Apr.	68		7	Warsaw, IL	Oettinghausen, Herford, Preußen
Kamps, Johan Wilhelm	17, Jan. 1895	26, Dec.	50		46	Chicago, IL	Harmengeln, Preußen
Kamus, Karl Friedrich Wilhelm	20, Aug. 1857	30, July	28		136	Lake Creek, MO	Osterholz, Amt Stade, Hannover
Kanable, A.G. Elisabeth	11, Sept 1882	25, Aug.	59- 3m-20d	Stumpenhusen	295	Dubuque, IA	Schweringen, Hannover
Kandlane, (Mr)	17, Jan. 1850	8, Nov.	44		12		Württemberg
Kanehl, Elisabeth	23, May 1895	18, Apr.	36	Berkholz	334	Oconomowoc, WI	Concord, Jefferson County, Wisconsin
Kanike, Anna	21, July 1859	28, June	26	Faber	116	Cincinnati, OH	Hastedt bei Bremen, Germany
Kanike, Heinrich	8, May 1882	25, Apr.	25		151	Newport, KY	Cincinnati, Hamilton County, Ohio
Kanike, Heinrich J.	17, Sept 1891	28, Aug.	77		606	Newport, KY	Machtsum, Hildesheim, Hannover
Kanne, Auguste	17, July 1865	16, May	40- 2m	Thide	116	Waseca, MN	
Kanne, Christiane	21, Apr. 1884	8, Apr.	63	Matthäe	7	Blooming Grove, MN	Muckwar bei Kottbus, Preußen
Kanne, Friedrich	16, June 1898	9, May	78		383	Waseca, MN	Nordhausen bei Königsberg, Neumark
Kanne, Georg Gottfried	6, May 1886	11, Apr.	88		7	Blooming Grove, MN	Nordhausen, Königsberg, Neumark, Preußen
Kanne, Justine Wilhelmine	7, Jan. 1886	17, Dec.	71	Krüger	7	Blooming Grove, MN	Mroczen, Posen
Kannengießer, Ottilie	23, July 1896	16, June	74		479	Canada, KS	
Kansler, Maria M.	28, Jan. 1897	1, Jan.	69	Mathes	62	De Soto, MO	Gallsheim, Baiern
Kantelehner, Katharina Rosina	29, Sept 1887	10, Sept	81- 4m-18d		622	Sherrills Mount, IA	Ernsbach, Ehringen, Württemberg
Kanzler, Lina	8, May 1882	8, Apr.	19- 4m-12d	Falbusch	151	Evansville, IN	Golconda, Illinois
Kanzler, Louis	31, Mar. 1884	29, Nov.	30		7	Evansville, IN	Wagenstadt, Baden
Kapel, Elisabeth	16, July 1866	8, July	70	Holderrieth	230	Covington, KY	Oelbronn, Maulbronn, Württemberg
Kapelle, (Mrs)	29, Aug. 1850	6, Aug.	22	Ekam	140	Columbus, OH	
Kapellen, Heinrich	9, Jan. 1882	16, Dec.	63 - 7d		15	Alden, IA	Aldenbach, Düsseldorf, Preußen
Kaper, Karoline	2, Sept 1886	22, Aug.	47		7	Cincinnati, OH	
Kaphahn, Margaretha	13, Sept 1880	25, Aug.	74- 7m	Katzmeyer	295	Pittsburg, PA	Grabenstetten, Urach, Württemberg
Käpke, Wilhelmine	26, Jan. 1899	6, Jan.	48	Bustrin	63	Oconomowoc, WI	Plate an der Rega, Hinterpommern
Kaplan, Johanna	21, Mar. 1870	12, Feb.	45	Janßen	95	Haddington, PA	Hooksiel, Oldenburg
Kapp, Adelina	14, July 1884	23, June	26		7	Green Bay, WI	
Kapp, Anna Maria	29, Sept 1873	11, Aug.	71		311	Brooklyn, NY	Wolfenhausen, Rottenburg, Württemberg
Kapp, Dorothea	1, Feb. 1869	2, Jan.	37- 3m-16d	Kapp	39	Ann Arbor, MI	Gültstein, Herrenberg, Württemberg
Kapp, Meta	8, Nov. 1875	12, Oct.	40- 4m	Henken	359	Williamsburg, NY	Langen, Hannover
Käppel, Barbara	30, Jan. 1882	5, Jan.	72- 9m		39	New York City, NY	Bergzabern, Rheinkreis Baiern
Käppel, Johann	22, July 1852	1, June	70		120	West Union, OH	
Kappel, John	7, June 1860	13, May	39		92	Jerusalem, NY	Schwarzburg, Schwarzburg-Sondershausen
Kappel, Katharina	16, Dec. 1886	17, Nov.	41	Gegenheimer	7	Brooklyn, NY	Havre, Frankreich
Käppeler, Friedrich	23, Jan. 1875	5, Jan.	57		31	Baraboo, WI	Hundersingen, Münsingen, Württemberg
Kappenmann, Charles M. (Rev)	26, Apr. 1880	9, Apr.	50		135	Marrs, IN	Neuhausen, Eßlingen, Württemberg
Kappenmann, Georg	21, July 1873	1, July	15		231	Henderson, KY	Vanderburg County, Indiana
Kappenmann, Johan Baptist	10, Oct. 1864	18, Sept	48		164	Mt. Vernon, IN	Pfauhausen, Eßlingen, Württemberg
Kappenmann, Ottilie Caroline	13, Jan. 1855	26, Dec.	48	Wahl	30	Marrs, IN	Cincinnati, Hamilton County, Ohio
Kappermann, Ernstina	25, Oct. 1855	1, Aug.	24	Hoffmann	172	Mt. Vernon, IN	Plangenloch, Baden
Kappermann, Johan	5, Nov. 1883	15, Oct.	26- 1m-29d		359	Mt. Vernon, IN	
Kappes, Katharina	14, June 1894	10, May	82	Schwäbel	390	Parsons, KS	Nichelbach, Odenwald, Hessen-Darmstadt
Kapphahn, Edward Francis	6, Aug. 1891	30, June	23- 1m-26d		510	Allegheny City, PA	Allegheny City, Pennsylvania
Kapphan, Sophia Rebecca	26, June 1876	27, May	36	Göber	207	Allegheny City, PA	Pittsburg, Pennsylvania
Kapphorn, Sophia Rebecca	12, June 1876	27, May	36	Göber	191	Allegheny City, PA	Pittsburg, Pennsylvania

Christliche Apologete Death Notices --- 1839 - 1899

Name of Deceased	Notice Date	Death Date	Age	Maiden Name	Page	Place of Death	Place of Birth
Kappler, Johann	1, Aug. 1850	11, July	45		124	Evansville, IN	Knittlingen, Maulbronn, Württemberg
Kappus, (Mrs)	28, July 1887	2, July	81- 3m		478	New Evans, NY	Horslach, Baden
Kaps, C.F.	19, Jan. 1860	Dec.	35		12	Des Moines, IA	
Kapsch, Barbara	21, Jan. 1867	8, Jan.	22	Schick	22	Covington, KY	Chillicothe, Ross County, Ohio
Karch, Elisabeth	31, Jan. 1895	6, Jan.	52	Scar	78	Chili, OH	Weinsberg, Holmes County, Ohio
Karch, Heinrich	13, Feb. 1890	23, Jan.	49- 2m-27d		110	Canal Dover, OH	Bischstenscheid, Baiern
Karch, Heinrich Jakob	2, Nov. 1863	20, Sept	21	Fechter	176	Blue Island, IL	Herkimer County, New York
Karch, Katharina	25, Oct. 1888	3, Oct.	75- 6m- 9d		686	Frankfort, IL	Roßbach, RheinPfalz Baiern
Kärcher, Anna	1, Nov. 1875	2, Oct.	72	Ruch	351	Highland, IL	Lauenburg, Baden
Kärcher, H.	3, Oct. 1861	16, Sept	41		160	East Troy, WI	Großheim, Kreis Büngen, Hessen
Karcher, Jakob	13, Sept 1880	21, Aug.	27		295	East Troy, WI	
Karcher, Magdalena	21, July 1879	3, July	65- 8m-13d		231	Menomonie, WI	Dürkheim an der Hard, Rheinkreis Baiern
Karcher, Michael	26, Dec. 1881	5, Oct.	23		415	Vermillion, OH	Iltersbach, Baden
Karcher, Regina	26, Mar. 1866	1, Mar.	16		102	East Troy, WI	
Karcher, Wilhelm	28, Mar. 1870	24, Feb.	51		103	East Troy, WI	Spielberg, Baden
Karg, M.	19, Feb. 1883	15, Jan.	30		63	Denver, CO	Niederkinzig, Hessen-Darmstadt
Karg, Maria Elisabeth	12, Aug. 1897	20, July	80	König	511	Baltimore, MD	Asshöllerbach, Neustadt, Hessen-Darmstadt
Karg, Nicolaus	4, Apr. 1870	8, Mar.	21- 5m-21d		111	Baltimore, MD	NiederKinzig, Hessen-Darmstadt
Karge, Eduard	21, Nov. 1881	11, Sept	58- 1m-11d		375	Chicago, IL	Fellendorf bei Lignitz, Schlesien
Karl, Catharina	29, May 1890	25, Apr.	66	Foßler	350	Enterprise, KS	Schmieheim, Ettenheim, Baden
Karl, Friederike	8, May 1876	8, Apr.	75	Pintpke	151	Crown Point, IN	Bulgarin, Preußen
Karl, Johan Hermann	22, Dec. 1862		9- 7m- 8d		204	St. Peter, MN	
Karländer, Heinrich	21, Oct. 1852	30, Sept	38		172	St. Louis, MO	Ringhausen, Preußen
Karle, Karoline	16, Aug. 1860	28, July	44	Regelmann	132	Dayton, OH	Plochingen, Eßlingen, Württemberg
Karle, Phil.	22, Oct. 1891	2, Oct.	28		686	Clearwater, MN	Germany
Karn, Eva Maria	16, June 1887	25, May	73		382	Holt, MI	Hessen-Darmstadt
Karn, Margaretha	27, June 1881	13, June	25- 5m		207	Salina, KS	
Karnatz, John C.	27, Apr. 1893	11, Feb.	64	König	270	Harrison, KS	Holzhof, Krämmen, Preußen
Karnitz, Maria Sophia	19, Feb. 1891	8, Jan.	51	Martens	126	Akron, NY	Hohenfelde, Mecklenburg-Schwerin
Karnopp, Anna Sophia	21, May 1896	30, Apr.	79	Fischer	334	Almond, WI	Zozenow, Pommern
Karnopp, Carolina	14, Dec. 1874	22, Sept	25- 8m	Tesch	399	Kewaunee, WI	Kenzlin,
Karnopp, Wilhelm	24, Oct. 1889	2, Oct.	74- -11d		686	Almond, WI	
Karow, Johanne Rosina M.	30, Apr. 1891	9, Apr.	68	Strauch	286	Columbus, WI	Friedeberg, Frankfurt a.d. Oder, Preußen
Karrenbrock, Lydia	21, July 1892	2, July	20		462	New Melle, MO	New Melle, St. Charles County, Missouri
Karrenbrock, Maria	12, May 1898	15, Apr.	57	Laumeier	303	New Melle, MO	Femosage, Missouri
Karrenbruck, Heinrich	11, Feb. 1878	19, Jan.	15- 2m-16d		47	New Melle, MO	
Karrer, (Mrs)	28, June 1888	5, June	46- 9m-27d	Becker	414	Bible Grove, IL	Albisheim an der Pfriem, Rheinkreis Baiern
Karst, Andreas	23, Apr. 1865	28, Nov.	32- 6m		68	Louisville, KY	Augsburg, Baiern
Karsten, Christian	10, Feb. 1859	17, Dec.	34		24	Schnectady, NY	
Karsten, Friedrich Gottlieb	1, June 1893	20, Apr.	82		350	Marine City, MI	Meseritz, Hinterpommern
Karsten, Immel Gerhard	18, July 1891	29, May	31		398	Pekin, IL	Nesse, Norden, Ostfriesland
Karsten, Maria	17, June 1886	15, May	49	Tews	7	Blooming Grove, MN	Buchholz, Mecklenburg-Schwerin
Karstens, Lydia S.	28, Oct. 1897	13, Oct.	28		687	Nashville, IL	Chester, Illinois
Karston, Heinrich	4, Aug. 1892	20, June			494	Milwaukee, WI	Semerow, Preußen
Karter, Anna Maria Sophia	7, May 1896	9, Apr.	76	Biker	302	Yellow Creek, IL	Bentorf, Hohenhausen, Germany
Käs, Elisabeth	29, Oct. 1896	10, Oct.	84	Fern	703	Scranton, PA	Lautenbach, Kurhessen

Christliche Apologete Death Notices --- 1839 - 1899

Name of Deceased	Notice Date	Death Date	Age	Maiden Name	Place of Death	Page	Place of Birth
Käsberg, Matthias	21, Nov. 1889	29, Oct.	65- 7m- 5d		Evansville, IN	750	Sain bei Koblenz, RheinPreußen
Kasch, Christina	14, Oct. 1886	18, Sept	78		Davenport, IA	7	Kakol, Holstein
Käse, Karl Gustav	3, May 1875	12, Feb.	26		New York City, NY	143	Bruchsal, Baden
Käse, Michael	21, July 1898	3, July	80		Scranton, PA	463	Arnshausen, Baiern
Käsemann, Maria	8, July 1867	21, Apr.	66-11m-24d		Jefferson City, MO	214	Canton Bern, Schweiz
Käser, Barbara	18, Oct. 1869		61		Decatur, IL	335	Schweiz
Kaske, Magdalena	19, Dec. 1881	30, Nov.		Müller	Chicago, IL	407	Dürkheim, RheinPfalz Baiern
Kaspari, Karoline	7, Jan. 1867	10, Dec.	59		Milwaukee, WI	6	Eichelsdorf, Kreis Nidda, Hessen-Darmstadt
Kaspary, Elisabetha	7, Oct. 1858	31, Aug.	61		Charlestown, IN	160	Diedenbergen, Amt Hochheim, Nassau
Kasper, Ursula	22, Apr. 1886	25, Mar.	37	Hauswirth	Big Stone City, SD	7	Davos, Graubünden, Schweiz
Kaß, Maria Katharina	10, Aug. 1899	2, July	55	Brockel	Pittsburg, PA	511	Schleerbach, Württemberg
Kassebaum, Charles L.	12, Mar. 1891	16, Feb.	25		St. Louis, MO	174	Farmington, Iowa
Kassebaum, Edward	13, Apr. 1899	16, Mar.	38- 1m-16d		St. Louis, MO	238	
Kassebaum, Friedrich	15, Nov. 1888	2, Oct.	70- 3m-23d		St. Louis, MO	734	Lübbecke, Westphalen
Kassebaum, Friedrich	13, Jan. 1859	28, Dec.	62- - 2d		Belleville, IL	8	Blasheim , Preußen
Kassebaum, George	28, Mar. 1881	10, Mar.	19- 2m		St. Louis, MO	103	
Kassebaum, Heinrich	26, May 1884	11, May	30- 2m-29d		St. Louis, MO	7	
Kassel, Caroline	21, Mar. 1889	19, Feb.	76	Staats	Wichita, KS	190	Lafferde, Hannover
Kassel, Christian August	2, Oct. 1876	17, Sept	57		St. Louis, MO	319	Gusta, Hannover
Kassel, Katharina M.	4, July 1889	15, June	66		Spencer, IA	430	Hittenthal, Schwarznau, Ansberg, Preußen
Kassel, William	20, Feb. 1882	2, Feb.	70		Wichita, KS	63	Germany
Kässens, Catharina	18, Oct. 1894	30, Sept	79	Amerkamps	Batesville, IN	678	Quakenbrück, Hannover
Kassing, Joseph H.	20, July 1863	5, Oct.	30		Hanging Rock, OH	116	Wehrendorf, Amt Witlage, Hannover
Kassing, Maria Louise	24, Oct. 1895	25, Sept	21		Clatonia, NE	686	Clatonia, Nebraska
Kaßling, Eduard	5, Oct. 1874	17, Sept	13- 6m		Evansville, IN	319	
Kaßling, Herman Arnold	30, June 1892	12, June	67		Evansville, IN	414	Ladbergen, Preußen
Kaßling, Lisette	5, Oct. 1874	17, Sept	49- 2m-14d	Hilgemann	Evansville, IN	319	Ladbergen, Tecklenburg, Münster, Preußen
Kaßling, Ludwig	25, Jan. 1894		68		Evansville, IN	62	Ladbergen, Tecklenburg, Hannover
Kaßling, Sophie	8, May 1890	16, Apr.	54	Schrörlücke	Evansville, IN	302	Ladbergen, Preußen
Kasso, Johan Friedrich	30, Sept 1872	1, Sept	29		Altamont, IL	319	Klein-Belitz, Bützow, Mecklenburg-Schwerin
Kassube, Albertine Wilhelmine D.	13, Sept 1855	17, Aug.	22-11m		Red Wing, MN	148	Fersetz, Kreis Templin, Potsdam, Preußen
Kassube, Otto	1, May 1871	2, Apr.	42		Minneapolis, MN	143	Preußen
Kast, Barbara	14, Apr. 1887	30, Mar.	83-11m-29d		Baresville, OH	238	Edmanhaus, Marbach, Württemberg
Kast, Georg Conrad	26, July 1875	11, July	78		Baresville, OH	239	Oberamt Maulbronn, Württemberg
Kast, Lillie	20, Aug. 1896	1, Aug.	23		Baresville, OH	542	Monroe County, Ohio
Kaste, Friedrich	18, Nov. 1886	25, Oct.	65		Alma, WI	7	Harbarnsen, Hannover
Kaste, Johanna	16, June 1887	13, May	64- 3m-29d	Ottleben	Alma, WI	382	Adenstedt, Hannover
Kasten, Augusta	22, Dec. 1884	6, Dec.	71- 2m- 3d		Lowell, WI	7	Roggow, Pommern
Kasten, Christian Friedrich	13, Jan. 1887	18, Dec.	27		Ft. Hunter, NY	30	Ft. Hunter, New York
Kästen, Elisabeth	22, Aug. 1850	15, June			Pomeroy, OH	136	
Kasten, Friedrich	28, Jan. 1878	20, Nov.	64		Lowell, WI	31	Bich, Brandenburg, Preußen
Kasten, Johanna Maria Christina	17, Oct. 1889	13, May	62	Cords	West Bend, WI	670	Gustävel, Mecklenburg-Schwerin
Kasten, M. Wilhelmina Charlotte	17, Apr. 1876	29, Feb.	24	Rathei	Ahnapee, WI	127	Glansee, HinterPommern
Kasten, Maria Elisabeth	30, Oct. 1890	9, Oct.	89- 7m- 7d		Amsterdam, NY	702	Eickhorst, Westphalen
Kasten, Wilhelm Friedrich	7, Aug. 1876	9, July	75		Ft. Hunter, NY	255	Eickhorst, Preußen
Kastendieck, Carolina	27, Feb. 1896	12, Jan.	62	Kolb	Brooklyn, NY	142	Philadelphia, Pennsylvania

Name of Deceased	Notice Date	Death Date	Age	Maiden Name	Page	Place of Death	Place of Birth
Kastens, Christine	15, Apr. 1878	16, Mar.	42- 9m- 8d	Schlozhauer	119	Lake Creek, MO	Hunteburg, Wittlage, Hannover
Kasting, Johan Fr.	13, Dec. 1888	20, Nov.	81- 1m-16d		798	Seymour, IN	Gerden, Amt Malge, Hannover
Kasting, Katharina El.	27, Nov. 1876	8, Nov.	73		383	Seymour, IN	
Kastner, Barbara	27, May 1897	10, Mar.	76		335	Minneapolis, MN	Bernstein bei Wunsiedel, Baireuth, Baiern
Kastner, Johan Christoph	21, Dec. 1874	8, Dec.	70- 8m-13d		407	Jeffersonville, NY	Bernstein bei Wunsiedel, Baiern
Kastner, Margaretha	7, Dec. 1885	20, Nov.	79-11m-13d		7	Jeffersonville, IN	
Kästner, Theodor	16, June 1879	31, May	29		191	Algona, IA	Neukalden, Mecklenburg-Schwerin
Kastning, Ernst	14, Apr. 1892	12, Mar.	72		238	Highland, IL	Meinsen, Bückeburg, Lippe-Detmold
Kästning, Heinrich	26, May 1887	2, Apr.	31		334	Highland, IL	Osage County, Missouri
Katenhusen, Carolina	29, Sept 1873	11, Sept	45-10m-20d	Hanebuth	311	Newburg, IN	Ribbesbüttel, Hannover
Kätter, Heinrich	15, Nov. 1880	2, Nov.	59- 9m-25d		367	Cincinnati, OH	Ladbergen, Münster, Preußen
Kätter, Wilhelmine Charlotte	15, Apr. 1897	14, Mar.	57	Schretter	239	Huntingburg, IN	Beyern, Germany
Kätterheinrich, Adolf Salomo	11, May 1899	19, July	49		302	New Knoxville, OH	Auglaize County, Ohio
Kätterheinrich, Adolph	4, Aug. 1887	3, May	67		494	Huntingburg, IN	Badbergen, Preußen
Kätterheinrich, Anna Maria	20, May 1897	23, Aug.	21	Prüter	319	New Knoxville, OH	Auglaize County, Ohio
Kätterheinrich, Christine Elisabeth	11, Sept 1865	30, Nov.	54- 9m	Lutherbeck	148	New Knoxville, OH	Ladbergen, Tecklenburg, Preußen
Kätterheinrich, F. W.	2, Jan. 1896	21, Nov.	52		14	Huntingburg, IN	Huntingburg, Dubois County, Indiana
Kätterheinrich, Friederike	15, Dec. 1887	11, Feb.	41		798	New Knoxville, OH	Ladbergen, Westphalen
Kätterheinrich, Herman Wilhelm	28, Feb. 1870	15, July	62- -14d		71	New Knoxville, OH	Ladbergen, Tecklenburg, Preußen
Kätterhenry, William	4, Aug. 1892	21, Jan.	40		494	Huntingburg, IN	
Kätterjohann, Herman Wilhelm	30, June 1873	11, Jan.	77		207	Red Wing, MN	Ladbergen, Tecklenburg, Münster, Preußen
Kätterjohn, Friedrich Wilhelm	11, Feb. 1897	14, July	70		94	Paducah, KY	Ladbergen, Westphalen
Kätterjohn, Gustav Adolph	28, Jan. 1884	20, June	16-10m-25d		7	Paducah, KY	
Kätterjohn, Herman H.	14, Sept 1899	18, Apr.	69		591	Huntingburg, IN	Ladbergen, Hannover
Kätterjohn, J.S.	18, Sept 1890	9, May	25		606	Evansville, IN	Newburgh, Indiana
Kätterjohn, Sophia Elisabeth	8, May 1890	19, Nov.	67	Kätter	302	Huntingburg, IN	Ladbergen, Tecklenburg, Westphalen
Kätterjohn, Wilhelm	25, May 1893	11, Sept	75- 4m		334	Huntingburg, IN	
Kattländer, Katharina	8, Dec. 1898	8, Jan.	58		783	St. Louis, MO	St. Louis, Missouri
Kattmann, Herman Heinrich	4, Oct. 1855	11, July	37- 1m-19d		160	Newark, OH	Ladbergen, Tecklenburg, Preußen
Kattmann, Maria	14, Feb. 1856	1, July	23		28	Newark, OH	
Kattner, Amand	29, Aug. 1889	8, Oct.	73- 8m-18d	Barsch	558	Paige, TX	Münsterberg, Schlesien
Kattner, Marie	2, Aug. 1894	28, June	15	Kokomoor	502	Bartlett, TX	Bordorf, Schlesien
Kätzel, Carolina Sophie	29, Nov. 1894	31, July	73- 6m		774	Santa Claus, IN	Wolbrechthausen bei Göttingen, Hannover
Kätzel, Christina Elisabeth	15, July 1867	12, Apr.	78		222	New Knoxville, OH	Diefenbach, Elsaß
Kätzel, Gottfried	30, Aug. 1875	3, Nov.	22		279	Santa Claus, IN	Auglaize County, Ohio
Kätzel, Margarethe	15, May 1882	21, Feb.	19		159	Santa Claus, IN	
Katzenberger, Wilhelm	19, Oct. 1893	25, May	82		670	Springfield, MN	
Katzmann, Martha Elisabeth	25, Nov. 1878	11, June	90		375	East Troy, WI	Gebirge Marx, Nordershausen, Kurhessen
Katzmann, Wilhelm	17, Mar. 1892	5, July	65		174	East Troy, WI	Wilsteroda, Rodenburg, Kurhessen
Katzmann, Worte Sophia	11, June 1877	8, Aug.	39		191	East Troy, WI	Wilsterode, Amt Sonira, Kurhessen
Kaufhold, Andreas	8, Aug. 1864	31, Oct.	74		128	St. Louis, MO	Freienhagen, Erfurt, Sachsen, Preußen
Kaufholz, Elisabeth	15, Nov. 1880	25, Dec.	60		367	Cleveland, OH	Lacha, Neustadt an der Haardt, Baiern
Kaufman, Joseph	19, Jan. 1893	9, Feb.	82		46	Denver, CO	Oesterreich
Kaufmann, (Mr)	21, Mar. 1861	14, May	28		48	Leavenworth, KS	Overlink bei Neustadt, Hannover
Kaufmann, (Mr)	12, June 1856	1, Feb.	69		96	St. Louis, MO	Empede, Amt Neustadt, Hannover
Kaufmann, (Mrs)	24, Apr. 1851				68	St. Joseph, MO	Empede, Amt Neustadt, Hannover

Christliche Apologete Death Notices --- 1839 - 1899

Name of Deceased	Notice Date	Death Date	Age	Maiden Name	Page	Place of Death	Place of Birth
Kaufmann, Andreas	24, Jan. 1845	1, Jan.	30		15	Cincinnati, OH	Fairfield County, Ohio
Kaufmann, Anna	30, Aug. 1880	25, July	83- 9m-29d	Plank	279	Canal Dover, OH	Berks County, Pennsylvania
Kaufmann, Christian	3, Mar. 1898	2, Feb.	47		143	Canal Dover, OH	Weinsberg, Holmes County, Ohio
Kaufmann, Edward	27, Dec. 1894	26, Nov.	25		836	Pittsfield, IL	Pittsfield, Illinois
Kaufmann, Elisabeth	8, June 1893	13, May	75- 6m-13d	Ridinger	366	Wichita, KS	Ortmertel, Baden
Kaufmann, Friedrich	7, June 1855	23, Mar.	58- 2m		92	Dayton, OH	Wettershausen, Sulz, Württemberg
Kaufmann, Heinrich A.	5, July 1894	18, June	71		438	Wrayville, IL	Derdesheim, Preußen
Kaufmann, Johan	8, Feb. 1869	17, Jan.	57		47	Warsaw, IL	Breitenbach, Amt Schliche, Kurhessen
Kaufmann, John Martin	5, Oct. 1863	3, Nov.			160	Dayton, OH	
Kaufmann, Margarethe	20, Oct. 1853	26, Sept	39		168	Warsaw,	Kurhessen
Kaufmann, Marie	9, Jan. 1871	29, Nov.	60		15	Louisville, KY	Baudenbach, Neustadt a.d. Eisch, Baiern
Kaufmann, Nora	18, Oct. 1894	18, Sept	20		678	Pittsfield, IL	Pittsfield, Illinois
Kaufmann, Sarah	18, Aug. 1862	26, July	8		132	Louisville, KY	
Kaul, Jakob	11, May 1874	12, Apr.	63		151	Milwaukee, WI	Waldbeckelheim, Coblenz, Rheinpreußen
Kaul, Jakob	2, Feb. 1899		57		79	Milwaukee, WI	Waldbeckelheim, Preußen
Kaul, Johan Gottfried	12, Aug. 1878	28, June	56		255	Baltimore, MD	Bischdorf, Schlesien
Kaul, Josephine	15, Dec. 1884	30, Nov.	11		7	Madison, NE	Montague, Michigan
Kaul, Justine	7, Apr. 1879	18, Mar.	65	Klees	111	Milwaukee, WI	Burg-Sponheim, Rheinpreußen
Kaul, Maria Barbara Margaretha	23, June 1873	31, May	40	Seckel	199	Baltimore, MD	Buchenbach, Künzelsau, Württemberg
Kaus, Carl	22, Dec. 1887	22, Nov.	14		814	Danville, MN	Danville, Blue Earth County, Minnesota
Kaus, Elisabeth	18, Dec. 1890	13, Nov.	68	Schmidt	814	Mankato, MN	Weickartshain, Grünberg, Hessen-Darmstadt
Kaus, John	19, Dec. 1881	4, Dec.	39- 1m- 7d		407	Minnesota Lake, MN	Wikardsheim, Grünberg, Hessen-Darmstadt
Kaus, John	9, Mar. 1893	24, Jan.	21		158	Mankato, MN	
Kautz, Christian	19, Oct. 1874	6, Oct.	51- -13d		335	Terre Haute, IN	Ischringen, Pforzheim, Baden
Kayser, Johan Andreas	18, Mar. 1897	11, Feb.	80		175	New York City, NY	Dieffenbach, Württemberg
Keck, Andreas	20, Mar. 1876	11, Feb.	63		95	Marrs, IN	Waldennach, Neuenbürg, Württemberg
Keck, Anna	27, Sept 1849	16, July	1- 7m		156	Manchester, MO	
Keck, Anna Maria	10, July 1890	11, June	71	Schmidt	446	Lena, IL	Haßloch, Rheinkreis Baiern
Keck, Catharina	19, Aug. 1858	24, July	55- -21d	Reinhardt	132	Cannelton, IN	Herbrechtingen, Heidenheim, Württemberg
Keck, Emeline	11, Sept 1871	13, Aug.	21- 5m- 8d		295	Marrs, IN	Vanderburg County, Indiana
Keck, Friederika	24, July 1890	27, June	78- 2m-26d	Richter	478	Pittsburg, PA	Rohrbronn, Schorndorf, Württemberg
Keck, Jacob Friedrich	4, Aug. 1873	4, July	62		247	Marrs, IN	Waldrennach, Neuenbürg, Württemberg
Keck, Jakob Friedrich	26, Nov. 1883	25, Oct.	43		383	Marrs, IN	Philadelphia County, Pennsylvania
Keck, Jakobine Rosina	11, Apr. 1895	16, Mar.		Bodamer	238	Marrs, IN	Hoefen, Neuenburg, Württemberg
Keck, Jessie Luella	29, July 1897	9, July	25		479	Chicago, IL	Aurora, Illinois
Keck, Johan Georg	20, Mar. 1876	19, Jan.	65		95	Cannelton, IN	Herbrechtingen, Heidenheim, Württemberg
Keck, John	14, May 1891	12, Apr.	77		318	St. Louis, MO	Hasloch, Rheinkreis Baiern
Keck, John Christian	21, Apr. 1892	1, Apr.	65		254	Omaha, NE	Obingen, Reutlingen, Württemberg
Keck, Joseph	21, June 1880	28, May	24- 3m		199	Omaha, NE	
Keck, Louisa	22, May 1882	8, May	16- 1m-29d	Kurtz	167	Harper, IA	Harper, Iowa
Keefer, Maria	14, May 1877		20-4m- 7d		159	Chicago, IL	Shakopee, Minnesota
Keefner, Johan	29, Nov. 1880	10, Nov.	22		383	Springfield, IL	Laineck, Oberfranken, Baiern
Keffner, Peter	10, Sept 1896	15, Aug.	56		591	Almond, WI	Weingarten, Baden
Kehl, Eduard C.	23, June 1898	7, June	30		399	Peoria, IL	Peoria, Illinois
Kehl, Elisabeth	24, Dec. 1896	1, Dec.	65	Maier	831	Jubilee, IL	Waldböckelheim, Preußen
Kehl, Sebastian	21, Aug. 1876	24, July	76- 7m-21d		271	Peoria, IL	Herzfeld, Kurhessen

Christliche Apologete Death Notices --- 1839 - 1899

Name of Deceased	Notice Date	Death Date	Age	Maiden Name	Page	Place of Death	Place of Birth
Kehler, Emma D.	2, June 1873	5, May	19- 5m- 3d		175	Worchester, MA	Cumberland, Maryland
Kehler, Johan Wilhelm	14,May 1883	23, Apr.	16- 1m- 8d		159	Meredosia, IL	
Kehm, Conrad	19, Apr. 1888	27,Mar.	45		254	Marion, OH	Hüttengesäß, Hanau, Kurhessen
Kehnlein, Luise	28, Sept 1899	1, Sept	29	Schäfer	623	Garrett, IN	Nistor, Preußen
Kehr, Georg F.	20, Nov. 1882	25, Oct.	19		375	Bridgeport, CT	Steinbach, Sachsen-Meiningen
Kehr, Johannes	25, Dec. 1876	9, Dec.	52		413	Turners Falls, MA	Steinbach, Sachsen-Meiningen
Kehrer, Barbara	12, Mar. 1891	9, Feb.	81- 9m	Burkhardt	174	Edon, OH	Williamsport, Pennsylvania
Kehrer, Georg	18, Dec. 1890	23, Nov.	80- 9m- 4d		814	Edgerton, OH	
Kehrer, Maria	23, June 1898	3, June	57		399	New York City, NY	Stuttgart, Württemberg
Kehnt, Jakob	1, Aug. 1850	21, July	31- 1m		124	Evansville, IN	Minden, Rheinkreis Baiern
Keiber, Margaretha	18, Sept 1876	3, Sept	46- 4m- 3d	Kuntz	303	Tea Creek, IN	Hallgarten, Baiern
Keil, Anna Maria	7, Oct. 1872	20, Sept	65- 1m-13d		327	Des Moines, IA	Vollkrücken, Hessen-Darmstadt
Keil, Christine	28, Jan. 1878	2, Jan.	50	Salz	31	Waseca, MN	Weißenburg, Elsaß
Keil, Eva Barbara	10, Oct. 1895	7, Sept	68		654	Hokah, MN	Baiern
Keil, Felicitas	14, Aug. 1871	28, July	32- 3m-26d		263	Des Moines, IA	
Keil, Heinrich	21, June 1880	10, May	23		199	Blooming Grove, MN	Lyons, New York
Keil, Johan Georg	30, Mar. 1874	21, Feb.	52		103	Hallens Grove, IL	Streidbach bei Jetzbach,
Keil, Johan Peter	23, Sept 1886	4, Sept	15		7	Plattsmouth, NE	Illinois
Keil, Katharina	23, Oct. 1890	1, Aug.	27	Goldfuß	686	Schnectady, NY	
Keil, Lorenz	6, May 1867	4, Feb.	65		142	Des Moines, IA	Feldkrücken, Hessen-Darmstadt
Keil, Lorenz	29, Apr. 1867	4, Feb.	66		134	Des Moines, IA	
Keil, Mary	21, July 1887	27, June		Hahn	462	New York City, NY	
Keil, Wilhelm	14, Dec. 1893	27, Nov.			798	Waseca, MN	Weißenborn, Ziegenheim, Kurhessen
Keilman, Margaretha	16, Mar. 1899	9, Feb.	63- 1m- 6d	Hocker	175	Bucyrus, OH	Konstanz, Baden
Keilmann, Anna Christina	26, Dec. 1889	7, Dec.	33		830	Cannelton, IN	Perry County, Indiana
Keilmann, Daniel	29, Jan. 1872	18, Dec.	81- 7m-22d		39	Santa Claus, IN	Iba, Rodenburg, Kurhessen
Keilmann, Jacob	27, Aug. 1883	27, July	60- 5m-29d		279	Cannelton, IN	Ida, Rodenburg, Kurhessen
Keilmann, Katharina Elisabeth	13, June 1881	16, May	50-10m		191	Cannelton, IN	Iba, Rodenburg, Kurhessen
Keinath, Christoph	1, Apr. 1897	18, Feb.	68	Knieriem	207	Cannelton, IN	
Keinath, Johan Georg	4, Sept 1851	31, July	47		144	Birmingham, PA	Grabenstätten, Württemberg
Keiper, Elisabeth	30, Jan. 1862	1, Jan.	26		20	Birmingham, PA	Grabenstetten, Urach, Württemberg
Keipfel, Elisa	7, June 1888	19, May	32- 2m	Adam	366	Charlestown, IN	Lettweiler, Baiern
Keis, Eva Elisabetha	17, Jan. 1881	9, Oct.	30- -23d	Edler	23	Marion Center, KS	Wheeling, West Virginia
Keiser, Caroline	1, Sept 1862	11, Aug.	42	Weis	140	Quincy, IL	Oberdorfe, Kreis Mülhausen, Preußen
Keiser, Elisabeth	15, Feb. 1864	22, Jan.	72		28	Cincinnati, OH	Rothenburg, Kurhessen
Keiser, Lizzie	3, Sept 1883		73	Mees	287	Portsmouth, OH	Oppau, Frankenthal , Schweiz
Keiser, Mary F.	18, May 1893	19, Apr.	23		318	Ironton, OH	Scioto County, Ohio
Keißner, Friederike	13, June 1895	20, May	28	Thiede	382	Rockham, SD	Poloski, Iowa County, Wisconsin
Keitel, Georg Michael	9, June 1873	4, May	68		183	Bushnell, IL	Blankenburg, Schwarzburg-Rudolstadt
Kek, Catharine	28, Jan. 1897	25, Dec.	87		62	Madison, IN	Hötlenbach, Künzelsau, Württemberg
Kek, Rosina Gottliebe	9, June 1862	24, May	18- 2m-14d		92	Mt. Vernon, IN	
Kelle, Karl Ludwig	9, June 1862	20, May	51- 9m-28d		92	Mt. Vernon, IN	Höfen, Neuenburg, Württemberg
Kelleman, Caroline	11, Nov. 1878	19, Oct.	63- 6m-20d		359	Schnectady, NY	Südhemmern, Preußen
Keller, (boy)	6, Aug. 1896	25, June	55		511	Oregon, MI	Preußen
Keller, (boy)	28, June 1855	27, May	7m		104	New Orleans, LA	
	28, June 1855	5, June	14d		104	New Orleans, LA	

- 244 -

Christliche Apologete Death Notices --- 1839 - 1899

Name of Deceased	Notice Date	Death Date	Age	Maiden Name	Page	Place of Death	Place of Birth
Keller, Anna	31, Oct. 1889	11, Oct.	14		702	Boonville, IN	Boonville, Indiana
Keller, Barbara	27, June 1889	10, June	40	Billau	414	Toledo, OH	Nordheim, Hessen-Darmstadt
Keller, Catharina	4, Feb. 1884	20, Jan.	81		7	St. Louis, MO	Gladenbach, Hessen
Keller, Christina	18, Mar. 1852	26, Dec.	56-10m-26d		48	Bethlehem, OH	Zaiserweiher, Württemberg
Keller, Christina	1, Mar. 1875	10, Feb.	39	Hartsler	71	Leavenworth, KS	
Keller, David	22, Dec. 1898	13, Nov.	77		815	Milwaukee, OR	
Keller, Dorothea	10, Nov. 1848	27, Aug.	19		184	Monroe, IL	New Albany, Indiana
Keller, Elisabeth	1, May 1876	6, Mar.	18		143	Cannelton, IN	
Keller, Elthy Magdalena	18, *Mar. 1897	12, Feb.	15		143	Faribault, MN	
Keller, Ernst	18, Mar. 1867	27, Feb.	36		175	Huntingburg, IN	Lengerich, Münster, Preußen
Keller, Eva	5, May 1879	13, Apr.	52- - 7d	Schneider	86	Evansville, IN	Ida, Birkenfeld, Oldenburg
Keller, Frida	4, May 1863	18, Apr.	71- 1m-26d	Müller	143	Laporte, IN	Schleitheim, Schaffhausen, Schweiz
Keller, Friederike	22, Apr. 1886	7, Apr.	70	Zehnder	72	Marion, OH	Wiedelspach, Schorndorf, Württemberg
Keller, Friederike	29, June 1885	30, May	35	Diebold	7	Aurora, IL	Sontheim a. d. Brenz, Württemberg
Keller, Friederike	31, Mar. 1859	12, Mar.	16- 4m-13d	Weckel	7	Lafayette, IN	Zickra bei Berga, Sachsen-Weimar
Keller, Georg Leonhard	16, Feb. 1854	16, Jan.	62		52	Muscatine, IA	
Keller, Heinrich C.	13, Apr. 1899	2, Mar.	66		28	Sprague, NE	Hannover
Keller, Jacob	9, June 1884	3, May	22		239	Big Stone City, SD	Sonnthausen, Elsaß
Keller, Jacob	11, Oct. 1849	6, May	53		7	Boonville, IN	
Keller, Jacob (Rev)	2, Apr. 1891	22, Jan.	77		164		
Keller, Jakob	27, Feb. 1896	16, Dec.	31		222	Clarington, OH	Bochberg, Schweiz
Keller, Johan	20, Dec. 1894	29, Nov.	44		142	Milwaukee, WI	Canton Bern, Schweiz
Keller, Johan	16, Dec. 1878	8, Dec.	61- 7m- 2d		822	Schnectady, NY	Wirchel, Bern, Schweiz
Keller, Johan Stephan	25, Dec. 1882	5, Oct.	76		399	Schulenburg, TX	Birenbach, Baiern
Keller, Johan Ulrich	25, Oct. 1875	27, May	6- 3m-13d		415	Marion, OH	Aldorf, Baiern
Keller, Johann	20, June 1864	19, May	77		343	Buffalo, NY	Gündelbach, Maulbronn, Württemberg
Keller, John	23, June 1898	26, Aug.	15		100	Aurora, IL	Sontheim a. d. Brenz, Heidenheim, Württemberg
Keller, John	13, Sept 1880	18, May	39		399	German Creek, IA	Keokuk County, Iowa
Keller, John	19, June 1865	20, May	81		295	New Albany, IN	
Keller, Joseph	14, June 1894	24, Jan.	49		100	St. Paul, MN	Buchberg, Schaffhausen, Schweiz
Keller, Joseph	25, Feb. 1892	2, Mar.	27		390	St. Paul, MN	Buchberg, Schaffhausen, Schweiz
Keller, Karl	8, Apr. 1872	10, Feb.	68		126	Boonville, IN	Marrick County, Indiana
Keller, Karl	3, Mar. 1892	3, Nov.	63- 2m- 8d		119	Evansville, IN	Birkenfeld, Oldenburg
Keller, Karl	22, Nov. 1894	23, Jan.	60		142	Oregon, MO	Germany
Keller, Katharina Elisabeth	12, Feb. 1883	26, July	26	Reichert	758	Clarington, OH	Württemberg
Keller, Katharina Sophia	16, Sept 1886	24, Dec.			55	New York City, NY	Bauernheim, Frankfurt am Main, Hessen
Keller, Louis	28, Jan. 1848	20, June			7	Boonville, IN	Birkenfeld, Oldenburg
Keller, Mamie	26, July 1888	18, Aug.			19	New York City, NY	
Keller, Margaretha	23, Oct. 1871	3, Mar.	19- 4m		478	Muscatine, IA	
Keller, Margaretha	18, Mar. 1886	20, Mar.	64- 9m-23d		343	Dayton, OH	
Keller, Margaretha Barbara	8, Apr. 1897	13, Jan.	81		7	Clatonia, NE	
Keller, Maria	7, Feb. 1889	1, Oct.	62- 6m- 6d	Jauch	223	Hamilton, OH	Weingarten, Baden
Keller, Maria	18, Oct. 1875	17, June	63	Leon	94	Summerfield, IL	Schwenigen, Rothweil, Württemberg
Keller, Maria Eva	29, June 1874	9, May	26- 1m-24d	Hecker	335	Marion, OH	Rathschein, Bern, Schweiz
Keller, Matthias	30, May 1895	27, May	74		207	Baltimore, MD	Todtmoos-Rütte, St. Blasien, Baden
Keller, Stephan	16, June 1879		55		350	Buffalo, NY	Harlachen, Baden

Christliche Apologete Death Notices --- 1839 - 1899

Name of Deceased	Notice Date	Death Date	Age	Maiden Name	Page	Place of Death	Place of Birth
Keller, Susanna	7, May 1866	18, Mar.	70		150	New York, NY	Bauernheim bei Friedberg, Hessen
Keller, Verena	21, Oct. 1872	9, Sept	73- 4m	Känzig	343	Baresville, OH	Oberbipp, Wangen, Bern, Schweiz
Kellemann, Ernst	14, Oct. 1867	17, Sept	40- 6m-15d		326	St. Paul, MN	Börninghausen, Preußen
Kellemann, Heinrich	22, Mar. 1888	24, Feb.	26- 4m-29d		190	Defiance, OH	
Kellemeier, Adolf	18, Sept 1856	30, June	35		152	Evansport, OH	Haalen zu Wersen, Preußen
Kellemeier, Bernhard	18, Sept 1856	10, July	66		152	Evansport, OH	Wersen, Westphalen, Preußen
Kellemeier, Bernhard Heinrich	26, Oct. 1868	30, Sept	54		343	Defiance, OH	Tiffin, Defiance County, Ohio
Kellemeier, Bernhardt Franklin	4, Dec. 1890	27, Oct.	23- 3m-24d		782	Stryker, OH	Wersen, Westphalen
Kellemeier, Christine	10, Nov. 1892	22, Oct.	73	Rötger	718	West Unity, OH	Wersen, Tecklenburg, Preußen
Kellemeyer, Regine M.	7, Nov. 1864	16, Oct.	73- 9m-16d	Beiderwillen	180	Defiance, OH	Klein-Latzkow, Brandenburg
Kelling, Charlotte	30, May 1889	14, May	72	Pinow	350	Oconomowoc, WI	St. Francois County, Missouri
Kellner, Catharine M.	5, Apr. 1888	11, Mar.	30	Kühling	222	Denver, CO	Tarnstädt, Amt Ottersberg, Hannover
Kellner, Sibille	25, May 1868	7, Apr.	73	Lüdemann	167	Washington, OH	
Kelly, Katharine	26, May 1892		76		334	Chicago, IL	
Kelner, Georg Heinrich	2, Apr. 1883	15, Mar.	91- 2m--14d		111	Marietta, OH	Groß-Sultrum, Rothenburg, Hannover
Kelp, Wilhelm	19, Apr. 1875	22, Mar.	42		127	Hamburg, IA	Steinfeld bei Magdeburg, Preußen
Kemler, Friedrich	6, Dec. 1849	29, Aug.			196	Galena, IL	Loger, Litten, Hannover
Kemler, Regina	3, Sept 1857	13, Aug.			144	Galena, IL	Weddewarden, Hannover
Kemmerer, Maria Amalia	3, Mar.1873	15, Feb.	31- 6m- 2d	Bühl	71	Worchester, MA	Holzhausen, Kurhessen
Kemmler, Johannes	21, Jan. 1884	29, Dec.	45		7	Fairmount, KS	Betzingen, Reutlingen, Württemberg
Kemp , Anna	21, Oct. 1886	2, Oct.	66		7	Muscatine, IA	Hammelwörden, Hannover
Kemp, Johann Heinrich	2, Aug. 1860	21, July	50		124	De Soto, MO	Heiligenfelde, Magdeburg, Preußen
Kempel, Anna Katharine	24, Feb. 1879	10, Feb.	53	Nagel	63	Schnectady, NY	Eichelsdorf, Hessen–Darmstadt
Kemper, Anna	29, Nov. 1894	16, Nov.	27	Wibbelar	774	Huntingburg, IN	Pike County, Indiana
Kemper, Anna Maria	30, Dec. 1886	12, Dec.	77	Brinkhof	7	St. Charles, MO	Blasheim, Lübbeke, Minden, Preußen
Kemper, Eberhard	26, Sept 1895	1, Sept	67		622	Huntingburg, IN	Schütdorf, Bentheim, Hannover
Kemper, Friedrich	14, July 1892	13, Apr.	23		446	St. Philip, IN	
Kemper, Friedrike	12, May 1879	28, Apr.	42-10m-17d	Kronemeier	151	Huntingburg, IN	Schüttdorf, Bentheim, Hannover
Kemper, Heinrich	25, Sept 1871	11, Sept	52- 4m		311	St. Paul, MN	Holzhausen, Minden, Preußen
Kemper, Heinrich	23, Apr. 1877	28, Mar.	36- 2m-16d		135	Marrs, IN	Posey County, Indiana
Kemper, Heinrich	12, Feb. 1883	27, Jan.	80		55	St. Charles, MO	Renkhausen, Preußen
Kemper, Herman	11, Dec. 1876	16, Sept	73		399	Herman, MO	Ladbergen bei Osnabrück, Hannover
Kemper, J.W.	22, Feb. 1894	2, Feb.	38		126	Senate Grove, MO	Franklin County, Missouri
Kemper, John Heinrich	15, Mar. 1880	25, Feb.	16		87	Marrs, IN	
Kemper, Marie	25, Aug. 1862	19, July	18-10m- 1d		136	Mt. Vernon, IN	Gellersen, Hannover
Kemper, Sophia	4, Feb. 1878	16, Jan.	73-11m-12d		39	Marrs, IN	Wintersingen, Basel, Schweiz
Kempf, Anna	20, Oct. 1862	21, Sept	61	Immhof	168	New York, NY	Diersburg, Baden
Kempf, Benedikt	9, Sept 1886	26, Aug.	85- 5m-14d		7	Brooklyn, NY	Neustadt, Sachsen
Kempf, Bertha	5, Nov. 1896	9, Oct.	64	Knauß	719	Sheboygan, WI	
Kempf, Jakob	24, Jan. 1881	5, Jan.	57- 2m- 1d		31	Bridgeport, CT	Rohrdorf, Nagold, Württemberg
Kempf, Joh. Georg	23, Nov. 1868	17, Oct.	49		375	Wathena, KS	Griffenbach, Kreis Siegen, Preußen
Kempfer, Friedrich	27, Sept 1855	10, Aug.	30- 5m- 4d		156	Bloomington, IL	Osterburg, Germany
Kempkau, Dorothea	29, Oct. 1891	10, Oct.	74		702	Nashville, TN	Grand Rapids , Illinois
Kempke, Elize	18, Apr. 1889	25, Mar.	25	Hagedorn	254	Papillion, NE	Aschaward, Kojöschen, Germany
Kenke, Friedrich Wilhelm	21, July 1887	20, June	26		462	Onida, SD	Nordhausen bei Königsberg, Preußen
Kenne, (Mrs)	11, May 1863	21, Mar.	72		76	Waseca, MN	

- 246 -

Christliche Apologete Death Notices --- 1839 - 1899

Name of Deceased	Notice Date	Death Date	Age	Maiden Name	Place of Death	Page	Place of Birth
Kenne, Julia	14, Nov. 1889	10, Oct.	60- 9m-14d	Molle	Baltimore, MD	734	Klausthal am Harz, Hannover
Kenngott, Luise	26, Jan. 1899	27, Dec.		Grimm	Newark, NJ	63	
Kenzel, Ludwig	16, Sept 1886	1, Sept	69		Oshkosh, WI	7	Blievensdorf, Neustadt, Mecklenburg-Schwerin
Keppel, Josiah	14, Nov. 1895	23, Oct.	84		Indianapolis, IN	734	Reading, Berks County, Pennsylvania
Kepper, Conrad	29, Mar. 1894	27, Feb.			Batesville, IN	214	Wolhagen, Kurhessen
Kepper, Karoline Florence	4, Sept 1882	27, Aug.	52- 1m-10d		Lawrenceburg, IN	287	Buckow bei Berlin, Preußen
Kepper, Louise	1, Nov. 1894	3, Oct.	42	Schleicher	Lawrenceburg, IN	710	Lawrenceburg, Dearborn County, Indiana
Kerber, Jakob	11, Aug. 1879	25, July	11-10m		Newport, KY	255	
Kerber, Philipp Jakob	20, May 1897	5, May	57		Newport, KY	319	Lorsch, Hessen-Darmstadt
Kercher, Luise	13, Nov. 1890	20, Oct.	30- 9m-11d	Faltenberg	Culbertson, NE	734	Sonnenberg, Germany
Kercher, Magdalena	10, Nov. 1884	24, Oct.	67-10m	Hecker	Burlington, WI	7	Münster bei Binger, Preußen
Kercher, Martin	12, Jan. 1860	25, Dec.	41		Covington, KY	8	Bieselsberg, O.A. Neuenbürg, Württemberg
Kercher, Rosina	12, May 1884	13, Apr.	64	Trautwein	St. Louis, MO	7	Weingarten, Baden
Kerding, Louisa	29, Nov. 1855	16, Sept			Baltimore, MD	192	Steuerberg, Hannover
Kerkhof, J.W.H.	27, Nov. 1876	31, Oct.	39		White Creek, IN	383	Ohio
Kerkhof, Katharina Elisabeth	18, Dec. 1876	28, Nov.	25-11m- 8d	Stockhover	White Creek, IN	407	
Kerkhof, Maria Elsabein	15, July 1852	19, May	45	Vombrucke	Rockford, IN	116	Körr, Hannover
Kerkhoff, Anna Maria	29, Sept 1892	4, Sept	68	Fink	New Palestine, IN	622	Leisel, Hessen-Darmstadt
Kerkhoff, Malinda	13, Aug. 1877	31, July	23-10m	Caspari	Indianapolis, IN	263	New Palestine, Indiana
Kerkmann, Caroline Wilhelmine	3, Mar. 1879	8, Feb.	85	Hagedorn	Mill Creek, IL	71	
Kern, Anna Maria	21, July 1892	2, July	78	Lange	Roseville, MI	462	Musbach, Elsaß
Kern, Barbara	4, Feb. 1884	3, Jan.	56	Grimmer	Baltimore, MD	7	Schönbrunn, Baiern
Kern, Charlotte	15, Nov. 1894	15, Oct.	75	Wagner	St. Louis, MO	742	Hareschausen, Hessen-Darmstadt
Kern, Emanuel	6, Sept 1880	5, Aug.	23		Aurora, IL	287	Michigan
Kern, Emanuel	20, Sept 1880	5, Aug.	29		Aurora, IL	303	Michigan
Kern, Emilie	22, June 1893	25, May	49	Wolf	Roseville, MI	398	Morehouseville, New York
Kern, Friederike	30, June 1898	17, May	29	See	Roseville, MI	415	Roseville, Michigan
Kern, Friedrich	27, Dec. 1860	31, Oct.	20- 8m		Chicago, IL	208	
Kern, Friedrich	6, Mar. 1876	10, Jan.	26		St. Louis, MO	79	
Kern, G.	15, Aug. 1864	16, July	42- 3m- 4d		Le Sueur, MN	132	Canton Bern, Schweiz
Kern, Georg	28, Nov. 1881	10, Nov.	52		Roseville, MI	383	Bechingen bei Landau, Rheinkreis Baiern
Kern, Georg Jakob	4, June 1857	2, May	12		Roseville, MI	92	
Kern, Gilbert	1, Nov. 1880	30, Aug.	44	Ganzhorn	Valparaiso, IN	351	Unterniebelsbach, Neuenburg, Württemberg
Kern, Justina	1, Mar. 1875	17, Jan.			Jeffersonville, IN	71	Kahlstadt, Dürkheim, Rheinkreis Baiern
Kern, Karl W.	17, Mar. 1884	23, Feb.			St. Louis, MO	7	Gumbrechtshoffen, Elsaß
Kern, Katharina Barbara	23, Aug. 1888	13, Aug.	76		Ironton, OH	542	Schweiz
Kern, Konrad	21, Jan. 1897	28, Dec.	66		Brighton, IA	46	Ittersbach, Pforzheim, Baden
Kern, Matthias	31, July 1882	13, July	67		Rochester, NY	247	Ellhofen, Württemberg
Kern, Peter	24, Feb. 1859	23, Jan.	63		Cedar Lake, IN	32	Nazareth, Pennsylvania
Kern, Rudolf	13, May 1897	11, Apr.	73		Crown Point, IN	303	Washtanow County, Michigan
Kern, Sarah Maria	14, July 1873	22, June	19		Valparaiso, IN	223	Hausen, Württemberg
Kern, Susanna	7, June 1880	13, May	44	Kohler	Lyona, KS	183	Reutingen, Bern, Schweiz
Kernen, Jakob	18, Apr. 1870	10, Mar.	34- 4m-22d		St. Paul, MN	127	Kitzen, Geppingen, Württemberg
Kerner, Anna	11, June 1891	22, May	32		Chicago, IL	382	Schönrade, Friedeburg, Preußen
Kernien, Caroline Sophia	3, May 1888	9, Apr.	42	Kellbach	Marion, WI	286	Menslage, Osnabrück, Hannover
Kernkamp, H.H.	3, Aug. 1868	9, July	44		Woodberrytown, MN	247	

- 247 -

Christliche Apologete Death Notices --- 1839 - 1899

Name of Deceased	Notice Date	Death Date	Age	Page	Maiden Name	Place of Death	Place of Birth
Kernkamp, Hanne Louise Wilhelmine	7, Apr. 1862	7, Mar.	35- 5m-22d	56	Albert	Stillwater, MN	Schiefelstein, Amt Hameln, Hannover
Kernkamp, Hattie Anna Luise	13, Apr. 1899	25, Feb.	29	239	Temme	St. Paul, MN	St. Paul, Minnesota
Kermann, Anton	25, July 1864	1, June	42	120		Hanging Rock, OH	Oppau, Frankenthal, Baiern
Kerm, Heinrich	8, Jan. 1866	19, Nov.	17- 4m-11d	14		Rochester, NY	
Kersch, Maria	28, Mar. 1895	9, Mar.	81	206		Madison, IN	Noldheim, Hessen-Darmstadt
Kersch, Peter	14, Mar. 1895	13, Feb.	81	174		Madison, WI	Rohrheim, Hessen-Darmstadt
Kersten, Friederike Louise	24, May 1888	7, May	35	334	Mönke	Marion, WI	Schönerade, Friedeburg, Brandenburg
Kerstetter, Samuel Lafayette	10, Aug. 1863	25, July	36- 5m- 5d	128		Baraboo, WI	
Kesch, Amalie	7, Jan. 1884	12, Dec.	39	7	Kunkel	Madison, IN	Fleschbach, Hessen-Kassel
Kesler, David W.	3, Sept 1877	15, Aug.	66	287		New Albany, IN	Marburg, Kurhessen
Kesler, Salame	2, Apr. 1896	17, Mar.	75- 3m	222	Naas	Mt. Vernon, IN	Elsaß
Kespohl, Friedrich	2, Jan. 1896	30, Nov.	75	14		Pittsfield, IL	Knetterheide, Lippe-Detmold
Kespohl, Louis	27, Mar. 1882	8, Mar.	64- 5m	103		Crow River, MN	Oerlinghausen, Lippe-Detmold
Kespohl, Wilhelmine	8, June 1899	20, May	68	367	Mühlig	Crow River, MN	Altenburg, Sachsen
Kespohl, Wilhelmine	21, Mar. 1889	12, Feb.	67	190	Kaufmann	Pittsfield, IL	
Kessel, Karolina	30, Jan. 1882	3, Jan.	68	39		Boonville, MO	Goelshausen, Baden
Kessen, Johan Herman	5, Dec. 1889	1, Nov.	81	782		Batesville, IN	Betbergen, Hannover
Kessens, Maria	19, Jan. 1854	1, Jan.	12-11m-17d	12		Pennsylvanienburg, IN	
Keßler, Anna Margaretha	10, May 1888	28, Apr.	20	302		Fairbury, IL	LaSalle County, Illinois
Keßler, Christian	8, Apr. 1878	9, Mar.	40- - 5d	111		Chicago, IL	Renroth, Nassau
Keßler, Eva Christina	4, June 1891	13, May	76- 7m- 7d	366	Holzell	Altamont, IL	Allmoshof, Rothenburg, Kurhessen
Keßler, Friedrich	8, Dec. 1887	19, Oct.	73	782		Mt. Vernon, IN	Lützelhausen, Kurhessen
Keßler, Friedrich	19, Sept 1895	27, July	80	606		Mt. Vernon, NY	Steinem, Baden
Keßler, Gustav	28, July 1898	5, July	49	479		Mt. Vernon, NY	Steinen, Baden
Keßler, Hannah	6, Mar. 1876	12, Feb.	60- 6m- 9d	79	Wilke	Chicago, IL	Sastedt, Hannover
Keßler, J. Louis	13, July 1893	24, June	45	446		Warrenton, MO	Ballwin, St. Louis County, Missouri
Keßler, Johan	13, Dec. 1888	22, Nov.	23- 2m-24d	798		Crete, NE	Jefferson County, Missouri
Keßler, Johan Heinrich	12, Dec. 1889	24, Nov.	69- 7m	798		Sprague, NE	Leisa, Biedenkopf, Hessen-Darmstadt
Keßler, Johanna Maria	8, Sept 1879	3, Aug.	36-10m-26d	287	Mahr	Baltimore, MD	Baltimore, Maryland
Keßler, Karoline	2, Feb. 1899	2, Jan.	50	79	Stähle	Chicago, IL	Winterbach, Württemberg
Keßler, Kasper	11, Aug. 1892	3, July	88	510		Madison, IN	Stangenroth, Kissingen, Baiern
Keßler, Katharina	17, May 1855	4, May	41	80		Madison, IN	Langenthal, Bern, Schweiz
Keßler, Katharine	3, Nov. 1879	23, Sept	27	351	Bopp	Ballwin, MO	
Keßler, Louis	17, Sept 1896	24, Aug.	77	607		Ballwin, MO	Frohnhausen, Hessen-Darmstadt
Keßler, Margaretha	17, Jan. 1889	27, Dec.	30- 1m-11d	46		Crete, NE	
Keßler, William	18, July 1861	21, June	25	116		Chicago, IL	Belen, Osnabrück, Hannover
Kester, Georg Friedrich	23, Nov. 1893	13, Oct.	78	750	Marks	Nerstrand, MN	Cumberland County, Pennsylvania
Kestetter, Maria Elisabeth	19, Apr. 1860		68	64	Wolf	Baraboo, WI	Oberkeinsbach, Hessen-Darmstadt
Kests, Margaretha	4, Apr. 1881	17, Mar.	61- 9m	111		Ripley, OH	
Ketels, Henry	2, Oct. 1871	18, Sept	26	319		Springfield, IL	
Ketscher, Harry	25, Nov. 1897	7, Nov.	18	751		Cincinnati, OH	Cincinnati, Hamilton County, Ohio
Kette, Anna Philippina	5, July 1855		18	108	Weber	Dayton, OH	Baltimore, Maryland
Kettelkamp, Esther	16, Feb. 1895	27, Jan.	30	111	Schneider	Nokomis, IL	Edwardsville, Illinois
Kettelkamp, George A.	3, Aug. 1885		13- 4m	7		Nokomis, IL	
Kettelkamp, Maria	7, May 1891	10, Mar.	73	302		Nokomis, IL	Lienen, Tecklenburg, Westphalen
Kettelkamp, Rudolph	27, Dec. 1888	4, Dec.	38-10m-25d	830		Nokomis, IL	Lienen, Westphalen

Christliche Apologete Death Notices --- 1839 - 1899

Name of Deceased	Notice Date	Death Date	Age	Page	Maiden Name	Place of Death	Place of Birth
Kettelkamp, Wilhelm	7, Feb. 1889	14, Jan.	78-10m-25d	94		Nokomis, IL	Lienen, Westphalen
Kettenacker, Anna Katharina	19, Feb. 1872	7, Feb.	68- 2m- 3d	63	Zimmermann	Newport, KY	Nabern, Kirchheim a.T., Württemberg
Kettenburg, Maria Friederika	1, Jan. 1866	9, Dec.	52	6		Pittsburg, PA	
Kettenburg, Wilhelm D.	7, Mar. 1870	16, Feb.	69- 4m-23d	79		Pittsburg, PA	Bremen, Germany
Kettering, Adam	1, Sept 1887	13, Aug.	79	558		Defiance, OH	Zweibrücken, Rheinkreis Baiern
Kettering, Catharina Salome	20, July 1874	5, July	58	231	Kurz	Newport, KY	Winzler, Pirmasens, Baiern
Kettering, Charlotte	16, Oct. 1856	19, Aug.	43	168		Defiance, OH	Thalfreschen, Rheinkreis Baiern
Ketterheinrich, Wilhelm A.	20, May 1886	4, May	32	7		Huntingburg, IN	Ladbergen, Tecklenburg, Preußen
Kettering, Jakob	17, Sept 1883	1, Sept	72- 5m-24d	303		Laporte, IN	Krickenbach, Kaiserslautern, RheinPfalz Baiern
Kettewacker, Michael	21, Aug. 1871	6, Aug.	66- 2m-24d	271		Newport, KY	Denkendorf, Eßlingen, Württemberg
Kettler, Jacobine Louise	3, May 1888	19, Apr.	49- 5m-18d	286	Blankenhagen	Milwaukee, WI	Worms am Rhein, Preußen
Kettner, Friedrich Wilhelm	15, Mar. 1849	13, Feb.	23	44		Cincinnati, OH	Ludwigsburg, Württemberg
Keuer, Maria Dorothea Carolina	18, Feb. 1884	27, Jan.	79	7	Leferenz	Brillion, WI	Schluton, Mecklenburg-Schwerin
Keuer, Sophie Elisabeth Johanna	3, Feb. 1873	15, Jan.	39	39	Dickelmann	Charlestown, VA	Walgenburg, Mecklenburg-Schwerin
Keup, Katharina	30, July 1896	11, July	66	495	Mühleichen	Aurora, IL	Wiesensteig, Geislingen, Württemberg
Keusch, Georg	7, Oct. 1897	1, Sept	76	639		Lansing, MI	Neuhausen an der Erms, Tübingen, Württemberg
Keylor, Maria	2, Feb. 1893	2, Jan.	54	78	Heins	Pittsfield, IL	Monroe County, Ohio
Keyser, Friederike Emilie	20, Oct. 1898	18, Aug.	83	671	Lippert	Oxford, NE	Potsdam, Preußen
Keyser, Helena Christiana	22, Dec. 1884	5, Dec.	63	7		Philadelphia, PA	Grunbach, Schorndorf, Württemberg
Keyser, J. Christian	9, July 1877	24, May	61	223		Philadelphia, PA	Grumbach, Schorndorf, Württemberg
Kibler, John	11, Dec. 1890	19, Nov.	63- 1m-16d	798		Marion, OH	Reichenberg, Backnang, Württemberg
Kibler, Karolina	28, July 1898	26, June	70	479	Keller	Marion, OH	Seisenschweier, Maulbronn, Württemberg
Kick, Christina Rosina	9, Nov. 1893	25, Oct.	68	718		Chicago, IL	Schlierbach, Württemberg
Kiebenapp, Wilhelm T.	20, May 1897	30, Apr.	73	319		Faribault, MN	Moringen, hevensen, Hannover
Kiebs, Matthias	11, Apr. 1895	9, Mar.	54- 5m- 3d	238		Moberly, MO	
Kiefer, Auguste	31, Dec. 1891	3, Dec.	81	846		Portsmouth, OH	Imshausen, Hannover
Kiefer, Elisabeth	29, Sept 1892	30, Aug.	88	622	Rosenmeyer	Portsmouth, OH	Herrenhausen bei Hannover, Hannover
Kiefer, Henry	16, July 1891	14, June	10	462		Clarington, OH	Gersdorf, Elsaß
Kiefer, Ida A.	10, Nov. 1887	18, Oct.	48	718		Portsmouth, OH	Portsmouth, Scioto County, Ohio
Kiefer, Johann	21, Jan. 1867	10, Dec.	73	22		Wheeling, IL	Dundee, Kane County, Illinois
Kiefer, Katharina	29, Nov. 1869	12, Oct.	45	383		Rushville, IL	Upgant, Marienhave, Norden, Ostfriesland
Kiefer, Maria Dorothea	5, July 1869	10, June	12- 3m	215	Beiser	Clarington, OH	Bruken, Kirchheim, Württemberg
Kiefer, Marie	18, Dec. 1856	17, Sept	21	204		Captina, OH	
Kiefer, Samuel	22, Dec. 1879	23, Nov.	13- 3m-12d	407		Clarington, OH	Monroe County, Ohio
Kiefer, Maria	6, Dec. 1875	18, Nov.	77	391		Clarington, OH	
Kiefhaber, Conrad	12, July 1894	13, June	20	454		Harper, IA	Nürnberg, Baiern
Kiefhaber, John	11, June 1877	17, May	67	191		German Creek, IA	
Kiefhaber, Lisette	22, June 1893	19, Apr.	16-10m	398	Neubold	Harper, IA	Philippsburg, Baden
Kiekenapp, Magdalena	10, Feb. 1873	20, Jan.	62	47		German Creek, IA	
Kiehl, Wilhelmine Christine	3, Dec. 1877	15, Oct.	36- 1m-13d	391		Nauvoo, IL	
Kiehm, Konrad	12, Apr. 1875	13, Mar.	68	119		Delhi, MI	Hartershausen, Hessen-Darmstadt
Kiehnbaum, Friedrich	14, July 1884	26, June	80	7		Oconomowoc, WI	Linde, Pieritz, Pommern
Kiehnbaum, Maria	16, June 1884	31, May	33	7		Oconomowoc, WI	Schönwerder, Pieritz, Pommern
Kiekenapp, Magdalena	28, Nov. 1861	4, Nov.	62	192	Martig	Cannon City, MN	Kanton Bern, Schweiz
Kiel, Elisabeth	27, Feb. 1896	3, Feb.	64	142	Feick	Montague, MI	Rimbach, Lauterbach, Hessen-Darmstadt
Kiel, Heinrich Christian August	3, Dec. 1896	2, Nov.		782		Wheeling, WV	Hammersen, Feldenhagen, Lippe-Detmold

Name of Deceased	Notice Date	Death Date	Age	Maiden Name	Page	Place of Death	Place of Birth
Kiel, Katharine	3, Dec. 1896	4, Nov.	53	Treiber	782	Wheeling, WV	Clarington, Ohio
Kieling, Daniel	5, Feb. 1891	12, Jan.	74- 7m- 1d		94	Farmington, IA	Fürstenburg, Waldeck
Kienast, (Mr)	29, Apr. 1878	3, Mar.	75		135	Watertown, WI	
Kienbaum, Heinrich F.	27, Mar. 1890	23, Feb.	14		206	Wausau, WI	
Kiene, Johan	30, June 1873	4, June			207	Lowell, WI	Canton Graubünden, Schweiz
Kiener, John	24, Nov. 1862				188	Connersville, IN	Zittswyl, Schweiz
Kieni, Domeniga	4, Mar. 1897	8, Feb.	74- 2m	Regerie	143	Parker, SD	Flimß, Graubünden, Schweiz
Kienitz, Friedrich Wilhelm	9, Dec. 1897	17, Sept	60		783	Maple Grove, MN	Prawomgsl, Bromberg, Preußen
Kienle, Jakob	30, June 1892	10, June	24		414	Newark, NJ	Wurmberg, Maulbronn, Württemberg
Kienle, Johan Jacob (Rev)	15, Feb. 1894	24, Jan.	43		110	Brenham, TX	Heimsheim, Württemberg
Kienlin, Karl August	10, Jan. 1889	14, Dec.	75		30	Edwardsville, IL	Marbach am Neckar, Württemberg
Kientz, Anna Maria	14, July 1884	26, June	62		7	Iowa City, IA	Leimen, Rheinkreis Baiern
Kientz, Matthias	2, Sept 1897	15, Aug.	66		559	St. Louis, MO	Scherzheim, Baden
Kientz, Oscar	8, July 1878	25, June	12-10m- 5d		215	St. Louis, MO	Quincy, Illinois
Kienzly, Magdalena	20, July 1874	1, July	70- -25d		231	Oregon, MO	Hoheneck, Ludwigsburg, Württemberg
Kiepe, Charlotte	25, June 1883	25, May	26- 8m	Mehring	207	Farmington, MO	
Kiepe, Katharina	2, May 1895	1, Apr.	35	Schäfer	286	Farmington, MO	Lorbach, Hessen
Kiepe, Louise	21, Sept 1868	19, Aug.		Zarges	303	Farmington, MO	
Kiepe, Rudolph	9, June 1898	19, Apr.	40		367	Farmington, MO	Farmington, St. Francois County, Missouri
Kiepert, Friederike Wilhelmine	11, May 1899	25, Apr.	63- 1m- 1d	Koch	302	Oconomowoc, WI	Friedrichsgnade, Regenwalde, Pommern
Kieppert, August F.W.	5, Mar. 1891	30, Jan.	57		158	Oconomowoc, WI	Wismar, Naugard, Germany
Kies, Bertha C.	21, May 1896	18, Apr.	49	Steeps	334	Oshkosh, WI	Paryat, Pommern
Kies, Christian Louis	15, Feb. 1894	27, Jan.	60		110	Oshkosh, WI	Schorndorf, Württemberg
Kies, Friedrich	21, Oct. 1878	7, Oct.	76		335	New Knoxville, OH	Dietenhausen, Pforzheim, Baden
Kieschke, Julius	1, Nov. 1860	11, Oct.	25		176	Cincinnati, OH	Muskau, Preußen
Kieselmanan, Jakob	16, Feb. 1874	18, Jan.			55	Williamsburg, NY	
Kieselmann, Jakob	3, Sept 1891	25, July	63		574	Jeffersonville, IN	OberNiebelsbach, Württemberg
Kieser, Maria C.	29, May 1865	22, Apr.	37	Menge	88	Cannelton, IN	Dachrieten, Preußen
Kiesling, Barbara	5, Jan. 1874	29, Nov.	75- 7m-27d		7	Farmington, IA	Grafton County, Virginia
Kieß, W.	18, Mar. 1886	14, Feb.	28-11m- 5d		7		Flacksee, Pommern
Kietzke, Amalia	16, Mar. 1899	18, Feb.	76	Kaum	175	Columbus, WI	Hoffstaedt, Krone, Preußen
Kietzke, August	5, Jan. 1885	11, Dec.	40		7	Columbus, WI	Winchester, Winnebago County, Wisconsin
Kietzke, Bertha	22, Mar. 1894	11, Feb.	39	Wegner	198	Crandon, SD	Hoffstadt, Deutschkrone, West Preußen
Kietzke, Friedrich W.	4, Mar. 1897	3, Feb.	84		143	Columbus, WI	Winchester, Winnebago County, Wisconsin
Kietzle, Bertha	7, June 1894	16, Feb.	39	Wegner	374	Crandon, SD	Rynarzerro, Schubin, Preußen
Kietzmann, Edwin Cyrus	25, Sept 1895	7, Apr.	23- 4m-26d		270	Dubuque, IA	
Kiffer, Karl Wesley	15, Sept 1887		30- 6m		590	Clarington, OH	
Kiffer, Magdalena	30, Apr. 1841	5, Apr.			67	Captina, OH	
Kihn, Charles	20, Nov. 1882	30, Sept	29		375	Schnectady, NY	Birmingham, Pennsylvania
Kilian, Anna Barbara	23, Nov. 1874	7, Oct.	70	Reinhard	375	Belleville, IL	Wollrode, Melsungen, Kurhessen
Kilian, Catharina	20, Dec. 1888	23, Nov.	70- 4m		814	New York City, NY	Niederamstadt, Hessen
Kilian, Elisabetha	22, Apr. 1858	29, Mar.	21	Doose	64	Wheeling, IL	
Kilian, Johannes	12, Aug. 1897	25, July	93		511	Belleville, IL	Wollroda, Melsungen, Kurhessen
Kilian, Mamie A.	30, May 1895	8, May	23		350	Belleville, IL	Belleville, Illinois
Kilins, Friedrich	14, July 1873	24, June	33		223	Louisville, KY	Chur, Schweiz
Kill, Wilhelmina Karolina	7, Apr. 1873	15, Mar.	38		111	Wheeling, WV	Klingen, Sachsen-Gotha

Christliche Apologete Death Notices --- 1839 - 1899

Name of Deceased	Notice Date	Death Date	Age	Page	Maiden Name	Place of Death	Place of Birth
Killian, Harry Otto	15, July 1886	12, June	14	7		Muscatine, IA	Pennsylvania
Killian, Maria	19, Jan. 1880	21, Dec.	27- 4m- 6d	23	Habegger	Jordan, MN	Beinstein, Württemberg
Killinger, Andreas Gottlob	17, Sept 1883	26, Aug.	65	303		Papillion, NE	Sherrills Mount, Iowa
Killinger, Christian Daniel	1, Nov. 1880	21, Oct.	21- -27d	351		Papillion, NE	OberSchönthal, Rachnank, Württemberg
Killinger, Dorothea	13, Oct. 1892	18, Sept	67	654		Papillion, NE	Wollroda, Amt Melsungen, Kurhessen
Kiljan, (Mr)	24, Jan. 1856		74	16		Belleville, IL	Lispenhausen, Hessen-Kassel
Kilmer, Anna Katharina	10, Aug. 1899	24, July	81	511	Sangmeister	Marietta, OH	
Kilo, Martha Maria	15, Sept 1887	23, Aug.	53	590		Chicago, IL	
Kimmel, Christ	18, Feb. 1884	31, Jan.	39	7		St. Louis, MO	
Kimmel, Johanna Louisa	18, Feb. 1897	26, Jan.	73	111	Gensel	Dayton, OH	Langensalza, Preußen
Kimmich, Christian	25, Aug. 1862	25, July	48	136		Bonn, OH	Klein-Sachsenheim, Vaihingen, Württemberg
Kimmich, Christiana	13, Nov. 1856	15, Aug.	12- 1m- 7d	184		Washington, ---	
Kimmich, Rosina	11, Aug. 1898	24, July	84- 6m- 7d	511	Schmidt	Cincinnati, OH	Bechringen, Württemberg
Kimmick, Drusilla	11, Apr. 1889		79	238		Caywood, OH	Bremen, Germany
Kimmpel, Elisabeth Katharina	21, Feb. 1870	5, Feb.	83- 7m	63	Völler	Clarington, OH	Obersorg, Amt Ahlsfeld, Hessen-Darmstadt
Kinast, Florentine	25, Feb. 1884	1, Feb.	75	7	Blasen	Watertown, WI	Reetz, Neumo, Brandenburg
Kind, Christine Friederike	16, Feb. 1888	27, Jan.	58- 3m-28d	110	Prescher	Dunkirk, NY	Gräfendorf, Neumark
Kind, Konrad	14, Mar. 1889	1, Feb.	34	174		Dunkirk, NJ	Berlin, Preußen
Kind, Wilhelm	17, Mar. 1898	6, Feb.	60	175		Dunkirk, NY	Wittenberg an der Elbe, Germany
Kinderdick, Jakob	16, June 1862	5, May	54	96		Lyons Creek, KS	
Kineriem, Anna Ch.	24, Apr. 1890	27, Mar.	65- 1m- 3d	270	Bachmann	Delhi, MI	Schwarzenhasel, Kurhessen
King, Friedrich	21, Oct. 1897	1, Oct.	66	671		Danville, IL	Luxemburg
Kinkel, August	22, Oct. 1864	22, Aug.	19- 1m-20d	172		Warsaw, IL	Frohnhausen, Hessen
Kinkel, Catharine	14, Nov. 1850	22, Sept	29	184	Dröscher	Quincy, IL	Haringhausen, Hessen-Darmstadt
Kinkel, Cora	22, Dec. 1892	2, Dec.	19- 7m- 2d	814		St. Louis, MO	
Kinkel, David	13, Dec. 1860		9- 6m	200		Quincy, IL	
Kinkel, Jacob	11, May 1863	16, Apr.	28	76		Warsaw, IL	
Kinkel, Johan	27, Feb. 1896	10, Feb.	76	142		Quincy, IL	
Kinkel, John	12, Apr. 1860	15, Mar.	64	60		Quincy, IL	
Kinkel, Louise Catharine	17, Feb. 1873	28, Jan.	66	53	Feisel	Quincy, IL	
Kinsi, Christian	5, Apr. 1844		Inquiry	55		Evansville, IN	Kaiserslautern, Rheinkreis Baiern
Kinsi, Heinrich	5, Apr. 1844		Inquiry	55			Kaiserslautern, Rheinkreis Baiern
Kinsi, Peter	5, Apr. 1844		Inquiry	55			Kaiserslautern, Rheinkreis Baiern
Kintzle, Maria	10, Oct. 1870	26, Aug.	58	327		East Troy, WI	Kaiserslautern, Baiern
Kinum, Laura Luise	13, July 1899	25, June	20	447		Schnectady, NY	Todtenau, Bindekopf, Hessen-Darmstadt
Kinum, Wilhelm	14, Jan. 1897	22, Dec.	27	31		Schnectady, NY	Dodenau, Biedenkopf, Hessen-Darmstadt
Kinvet, Gonthilda	27, Sept 1894	27, Aug.	31	630	Göppinger	Bushnell, IL	Hessen-Darmstadt
Kipp, Christine Elisabeth	5, June 1876	18, May	59	183	Stockdick	Dresden, OH	Bottingen, Emmendingen, Baden
Kipp, Heinrich	8, Mar. 1883	3, Feb.	66- 9m-11d	79		Baraboo, WI	Cleveland, Ohio
Kipp, Heinrich	24, Sept 1883	29, Aug.	67	311		Newark, OH	Ladbergen, Preußen
Kipp, Katharina Elise	20, July 1885	13, June	69	7	Bammel	Baraboo, WI	Westewein, Amt Mittingen, Hannover
Kippe, Rosine	9, Feb. 1888	12, Jan.	22- 6m-22d	94		Delhi, MI	Ladbergen, Münster, Preußen
Kirchberg, K.	16, June 1898	11, May	78	383		New Orleans, LA	Barum, Medingen, Hannover
Kirchberg, Margaretha F.	20, Mar. 1890	10, Feb.	63	190		New Orleans, LA	Buchtewyl, Elsaß
Kirchdorffer, Andreas	30, May 1881	12, May	51- 9m	175		Goshen, IN	Reurieth, Sachsen-Meiningen
Kircheis, Barbara	4, Jan. 1869	13, Nov.	22	7	Uebel	St. Louis, MO	Sufflingheim bei Bischwille, Elsaß

Christliche Apologete Death Notices -- 1839 - 1899

Name of Deceased	Notice Date	Death Date	Age	Page	Maiden Name	Place of Death	Place of Birth
Kirchenschläger, Karoline	30, Aug. 1875	5, July	16	279		Waverly, OH	Greenfield, Ohio
Kircher, Christine	10, June 1858	26, May	31- 1m- 9d	92	Bertsch	Covington, KY	Friolzheim, Leonberg, Württemberg
Kircher, Jakob	29, Oct. 1877	25, Sept	78- 4m-19d	351		Highland, IL	Windesheim, Koblenz, Preußen
Kircher, Jakob Friedrich	20, Jan. 1887	12, Dec.	63	46		Columbus, OH	Schwan, Württemberg
Kircher, Katharine	18, Mar. 1897	21, Feb.	63- 2m- 6d	175		Cincinnati, OH	Winzler, Baiern
Kirchfeld, Barbara	28, Mar. 1895	12, Feb.	65	206	Becker	Troy, NY	Kirchheim-Boland, Rheinpfalz Baiern
Kirchfeld, Julius Heinrich	12, May 1884	13, Apr.	59	7		Troy, NY	Kirchborchen, Paderborn, Minden, Preußen
Kirchgraber, Anna	13, Jan. 1879	28, Dec.	44- 9m-19d	15	Breitinger	Angelica, NY	Ehingen an der Donau, Württemberg
Kirchher, Anton	6, Dec. 1880	4, Nov.	15- 8m- 1d	391		Columbus, OH	
Kirchher, Karl Friedrich	10, Feb. 1868	7, Jan.	60	47		Peoria, IL	Schwann, Neuenbürg, Württemberg
Kirchhoefer, John	7, June 1888	10, May	72	366		Mt. Vernon, NY	Schaffheim, Hessen-Darmstadt
Kirchhoff, John	22, Jan. 1891	19, Dec.	76	62		Poughkeepsie, NY	Almenhausen, Preußen
Kirchhoff, Maria	31, Aug. 1893	23, July	75	558	Schneidewind	Poughkeepsie, NY	Werningshausen, Sachsen
Kirchner, Eva Maria	4, Mar. 1878	13, Feb.	31- 1m- 8d	71	Feldmann	Hartford, CT	Pfotz, Baiern
Kirchner, Heinrich	4, Oct. 1869	1, Sept	29	319		Ballwin, MO	
Kirchner, Wilhelm	19, Dec. 1889	21, Nov.	87	814		Harper, IA	Linn County, Pennsylvania
Kirchstein, Barbara	4, Oct. 1855	6, Sept	65	160		Huntingburg, IN	Mekenheim, Rheinpfalz Baiern
Kirckhoff, Heinrich	1, Aug. 1881	19, July	38- 4m- 9d	247		New Palestine, IN	Palestine, Hancock County, Indiana
Kirkhof, Johan Heinrich	30, Nov. 1868	10, Nov.	60	383		Seymour, IN	Gerde, Amt Berchenbrück, Hannover
Kirkhoff, Anton Friedrich	18, Sept 1882	29, Aug.	70- 8m- 3d	303		Palestine, IN	Frille bei Minden, Preußen
Kirkhoff, Karl F.	10, Oct. 1895	5, Sept	38	654		Indianapolis, IN	Frille, Minden, Preußen
Kirn, Christitiana	19, May 1892	30, Mar.	68- 4m	80		Chicago, IL	Schwandorf, Württemberg
Kirn, Magga	30, Apr. 1891	6, Apr.	25	286	Jaggi	Allegan, MI	Canton Bern, Schweiz
Kirsch, Dorothea	16, Apr. 1891	20, Mar.	45	254		Evansville, IN	
Kirsch, Peter	7, Feb. 1870	11, Jan.	43- -21d	47		Louisville, KY	Marpingen, Trier, Preußen
Kirschbaum, John Georg	24, Dec. 1877	7, Dec.		415		Baltimore, MD	Trautzkirchen, Baiern
Kirschenmann, Johannes	11, Oct. 1894	12, Sept	83	662		Bradford, IN	Lichtenau, Bischofsheim, Baden
Kirschler, Heinrich	26, May 1884	1, May	42	7		Elizabeth, NJ	Kirchardt, Baden
Kirschmann, Charlotte	19, Nov. 1891	31, Oct.	63	750	Weber	Decorah, IA	Halsmaden, Württemberg
Kirschner, Jakobine	5, Sept 1870	27, Aug.	76	287	Augenstein	Cincinnati, OH	Kieselbronn, Pforzheim, Baden
Kirschner, Johan Heinrich	6, Feb. 1890	8, Jan.	78	94		New Haven, CT	Dodenhausen, Kurhessen
Kirschner, Johannes	26, July 1894	6, July	57	486		New Haven, CT	Dodenhausen, Kurhessen
Kirschner, Louise Friederiek	5, June 1890	17, Apr.	83- 6m-24d	366	Strack	New Haven, CT	Heina, Kurhessen
Kirschner, Nellie E.	16, Jan. 1882	25, Dec.	15	23		New Haven, CT	
Kirschner, Philippine	5, May 1873	19, Apr.	35- -28d	143	Heiß	Kendallville, IN	KleinWaken, Mecklenburg-Schwerin
Kirwitz, Christina	18, Oct. 1869	30, Sept	56- 6m	335	Mätz	Jeffersonville, IN	Louisville, Jefferson County, Kentucky
Kiseselmann, Jakob	13, Dec. 1875	17, Nov.	19	399		Linton, IN	
Kisling, Emma M.	14, July 1887	24, June	25	446		Linton, IN	
Kisling, Simon	2, July 1891	24, Jan.	61	430		Sun Prairie, WI	Schweiz
Kiso, Maria Christina	5, Jan. 1880	18, Dec.	65	7	Bast	Boonville, IN	Delitz, Pommern
Kissel, Katharina	16, June 1898	31, May	58	383	Schipper	Seymour, IN	Suldesfeld, Eppingen, Baden
Kisselmann, (Mrs)	30, Mar. 1899		74	207		Dodgeville, IA	Ober-ersbach, Neuenburg, Württemberg
Kissinger, Margaretha	26, May 1879	30, Mar.	48	167	Müller	St. Louis, MO	Griesheim, Darmstadt, Hessen-Darmstadt
Kißner, Georg	5, Dec. 1845		Inquiry	195		Bethlehem, OH	Schotten, Kreis Nidda, Hessen-Darmstadt
Kist, Carolina	12, Sept 1850	10, Aug.	15-11m-19d	148		Flood Creek, IA	Bergzabern, Rheinkreis Baiern
Kister, Conrad	22, Nov. 1875	8, Nov.	45	375			

Christliche Apologete Death Notices --- 1839 - 1899

Name of Deceased	Notice Date	Death Date	Age	Page	Maiden Name	Place of Death	Place of Birth
Kistner, Johannes	9, May 1861	19, Mar.	30	76		Huntingburg, IN	Guxhaven, Amt Melsungen, Kurhessen
Kittel, Anna Margaretha	21, Oct. 1867	5, Sept	42- 9m- 3d	334	Geitz	Warsaw, IL	Markt Herrnsheim, Baiern
Kittel, Eva Margaretha	19, Nov. 1883	24, Oct.	39	375	Kittel	Warsaw, IL	Langensteinach, Mittelfranken, Baiern
Kitto, Kitto Marie M.	26, Jan. 1893	23, Dec.	24	62		Stockton, CA	Jersey City, New Jersey
Kittsteiner, Friedrich	14, June 1888	29, May	30- 6m	382		Cleveland, OH	
Kitzenberger, Katharina Barbara	27, June 1864	23, May	51	104	Kitzenberger	Jerseyville, IL	Ferrerbach, Württemberg
Klaas, Friedrich	8, Mar. 1875	22, Jan.	40	79		Third Creek, MO	
Klaaßen, (Mrs)	5, Mar. 1877	11, Feb.	73- 3m-22d	79		Hartsburg, IL	Wibelsum, Ostfriesland
Klahn, Dorothea Christina Maria	12, Mar. 1896	16, Feb.	62	174	Schröder	Freeport, MI	Laudo, Mecklenburg-Schwerin
Klähner, Anna Catharina	2, Oct. 1882	7, July	73	319		Denver, CO	
Klaiber, Anna Maria	6, Oct. 1879	19, Sept	23	319		New Albany, IN	Straßburg, Frankreich
Klaiber, Christian	29, May 1890	4, May	78- 5m	350		Denver, CO	
Klaiber, Christian Konrad	7, June 1880	25, May	21- 6m-24d	183		Chicago, IL	Schwenningen, Rottweil, Württemberg
Klaiber, Jacob	10, May 1894	19, Apr.	27	310		Nashville, IL	
Klamm, Louise	27, July 1893	23, May	63	478	Anke	Wyandotte, KS	Neuhofen, Rheinkreis Baiern
Klamm, Maria Katharine	3, Feb. 1887	15, Jan.	62	78	Brenner	Colesburg, IA	Glewitz bei Gollnow, Pommern
Klamp, Friedericke	9, Sept 1878	15, Aug.	64	287	Schwichtenberg	Colesburg, IA	Zeitland, Fürstenau, Hannover
Klamp, Mina Friederike	14, July 1892	21, May	35	446	Schenke	Colesburg, IA	Mögendorf, Neugard, Pommern
Klamp, W.	28, Jan. 1886	29, Dec.	66	7		Indianapolis, IN	Liebenau, Hofgeismar, Kurhessen
Klanke, Margaretha Elisabeth	25, June 1883	29, May	85- - 3d	207	Fommel	Valparaiso, IN	
Klapper, Celinde Christine	4, Sept 1882	17, Aug.	16	287		Valparaiso, IN	
Klapper, Johan	24, Jan. 1876	11, Jan.	42	31		Chicago, IL	Götzenheim, Hessen-Darmstadt
Klapproth, Wilhelm	27, Feb. 1896	6, Feb.	20	143		Greenville, OH	Lasfelde, Hannover
Klärig, Lorenz	4, July 1895	9, June	67	430		Greenville, OH	Erfurt, Preußen
Klarig, Wilhelm	28, Feb. 1895	2, Feb.	26	142		Greenville, OH	Darke County, Ohio
Klärig, Wilhelmine	26, Jan. 1863	30, Dec.	62	16		Greenville, OH	Erfurt, Preußen
Klark, Karl	24, Nov. 1887	2, Nov.	61- 9m	750		Marshalltown, IA	
Klatt, Charlotte	2, Jan. 1871	15, Dec.	52- 3m-14d	7	Kunde	Frankfort, IL	Wustenwitz, Preußen
Klaub, Karolina	25, Nov. 1878	24, Oct.	83- - 4d	375		Cincinnati, OH	Weißensee, Sachsen-Weimar
Klauberg, Daniel	15, Nov. 1844	2, Nov.	65	176		Batesville, IN	Solingen, Elberfeld, Preußen
Klauen, Karl	9, Sept 1872	22, June	62	295		Bloomington, IL	Krainzfeld, Meiningen, Sachsen
Klauer, Heinrich	4, Nov. 1886	13, Oct.	74	7		Vermillion, OH	Kramingfeld, Sachsen-Weimar
Klaus, Adam	20, Jan. 1873	17, Dec.	69	23		Chillicothe, OH	Obermellrich, Kreis Fritzlar, Kurhessen
Klaus, Adam	3, June 1897	8, May	75	351		Chillicothe, OH	Westheim, Baiern
Klaus, Anna	11, Feb. 1886	19, Jan.	22	7	Hellmann	Chillicothe, OH	Waverly, Ohio
Klaus, Anna Margaretha Elisabeth	3, Jan. 1889	4, Dec.	67	14	Hartbecken	Colesburg, IA	Hanenberge, Fürstenau, Hannover
Klaus, Charlotte	8, Dec. 1892	15, Nov.	77	782		Bunker Hill, IL	Guntersdorf, Preußen
Klaus, Heinrich J.	8, Dec. 1892	7, Nov.	32-11m- 5d	782		Chillicothe, OH	Chillicothe, Ross County, Ohio
Klaus, Herman Heinrich	3, July 1890	21, May	68- 7m-13d	430		Colesburg, IA	Talge, Fürstenau, Hannover
Klaus, John D.	22, July 1878	7, July	65	231		Colesburg, IA	Bippen, Amt Fürstenau, Hannover
Klaus, Karl August	7, Feb. 1895	21, Jan.	73	94		Jacksonville, IL	Rodewisch, Sachsen
Klaus, Katharina	25, Dec. 1890	1, Dec.	39	830	Gildner	Mason City, IA	Canada
Klaus, Katharine M.	11, June 1896	22, May	65	383	Krümpel	Colesburg, IA	Talgen, Fürstenau, Hannover
Klaus, Maria	2, Oct. 1871	13, Sept	65	319	Frick	Perry, IL	Nellingsheim, Rottenburg, Württemberg
Klaus, Maria Christine	2, Apr. 1891	1, Mar.	68- 4m- 1d	222	Konradi	Jacksonville, IL	Nortenstät, Nassau
Klaus, Matthias	21, Nov. 1870	27, Oct.	73- 9m-22d	375		Chillicothe, OH	Westheim, Germersheim, Rheinkreis Baiern

Christliche Apologete Death Notices --- 1839 - 1899

Name of Deceased	Notice Date	Death Date	Age	Page	Maiden Name	Place of Death	Place of Birth
Klaus, Wilhelm	28, Aug. 1882	6, Aug.		279	Evers	Bunker Hill, IL	Mattfeld, Hannover
Klausen, Emma	28, Mar. 1889	2, Mar.	26-10m-15d	206	Rutenschröer	Odebolt, IA	
Klausmeier, Maria	25, Aug. 1884	16, Aug.	43	7		Huntingburg, IN	Hamilton County, Ohio
Klausritzer, Johanna Christiana A.	20, July 1893	20, June		462	Eisbrich	Paige, TX	Kleinburg, Sachsen
Klaver, Friedrich	16, July1883	16, May	56- 8m	231		St. Louis, MO	Leer, Ostfriesland
Klebahn, Anna Katharina W.	23, Mar. 1893	28, Feb.	63	190	Lange	Cincinnati, OH	Bremen an der Weser, Germany
Klebahn, Heinrich	6, Jan. 1879	8, Dec.	22-7m	7		Cincinnati, OH	
Klebe, Christoph	22, Oct. 1883	9, Sept	68- 6m- 6d	343		Clarington, OH	Reichensachsen, Eschwege, Kurhessen
Klebe, Elisabeth	10, Mar. 1898	4, Feb.	7-	158	Böttner	Clarington, OH	Reichensachsen, Eschwege, Kurhessen
Klebe, Wilhelm Karl	14, Sept 1899	1, Sept	20	591		Clarington, OH	Monroe County, Ohio
Kleber, Georg	26, Feb. 1891	25, Jan.	78	142		Charlestown, IN	Dietenbergen, Hochheim, Nassau
Kleber, Julia Emma	2, Nov. 1899	22, Oct.	37	703	Rausch	Humboldt, NE	Monroe County, Illinois
Klebs, Johan Christian	29, Sept 1884	9, Sept	34	7		Wadena, MN	Sydowswyse, Lebuser, Brandenburg
Kledehn, Christ.	21, Oct. 1878	28, Aug.		335		Beaver Dam, WI	Girard, Kansas
Kledehn, Christian	11, Feb. 1884	25, Jan.	80	7		Beaver Dam, WI	Britzig bei Pieritz, Pommern
Kledehn, Wilhelm Friedrich	20, May 1897	30, Apr.	21	319		Beaver Dam, WI	Beaver Dam, Wisconsin
Klee, Maria Elisabeth	27, Apr. 1893	9, Apr.	71- 4m-26d	270	Märker	Scranton, PA	Pittsburg, Pennsylvania
Kleekamp, Heinrich H.	11, Jan. 1864	30, Oct.	25	8		Seymour, IN	Venne, Amt Wittage, Hannover
Kleekamp, John Friedrich	16, Feb. 1863	14, Jan.	27	28		Seymour, IN	Auernheim, Herford, Minden, Westphalen
Kleemann, Wilhelm	7, July 1892	12, June	73- 6m-19d	430		Sheffield, IA	Walle, Aurich, Ostfriesland
Kleen, Ulfert Gerd	29, Dec. 1898	1, Dec.	50	828		Macon, NE	Haussen, Friedberg, Hessen-Darmstadt
Klees, Anna Elisabeth	11, Aug. 1879	28, July	61	255	Fett	Baltimore, MD	
Klees, Daniel B.	24, Dec. 1866	30, Nov.	12-10m	414		Baltimore, MD	Harbach, Hessen-Darmstadt
Klees, Henry	12, Jan. 1880	22, Dec.	66- 8m-10d	15		Baltimore, MD	Baltimore, Maryland
Klees, John	3, June 1878	10, May	37-11m- 5d	175		Baltimore, MD	Zahn, West Preußen
Klehn, Anna Rosa	28, Mar. 1889	27, Feb.	69- -17d	206	Waldenberg	Parkston, SD	Schwenningen, Rottweil, Württemberg
Kleiber, Christian	28, Jan. 1892	6, Jan.	26	62		Chicago, IL	Bergzabern, Rheinkreis Baiern
Kleiber, Katharine	8, Sept 1884	19, Aug.	73	7	Gelbach	New Albany, IN	Bergzabern, Rheinkreis Baiern
Kleiber, Katharine	1, Sept 1884	19, Aug.	73	7	Gelbach	New Albany, IN	Bergzabern, Elsaß
Kleihauer, Anna Lucia	25, Nov. 1878		6m	375		Grant, IA	
Kleihauer, Engel Margaretha	25, Nov. 1878		5- 6m	375		Grant, IA	
Klein, (Mr)	11, Apr. 1895	14, Mar.	81	238		Blue Island, IL	Villingen, Hessen-Darmstadt
Klein, Andreas	20, Sept 1888	2, Sept	65	606		Sandwich, IL	Frohnhausen, Nassau
Klein, August	14, Feb. 1895	2, Jan.	18	110		Blue Island, IL	Blue Island, Illinois
Klein, Carolina	19, Aug. 1878	4, Aug.	15- 6m-14d	263		Boonville, IN	
Klein, Charlotte Auguste	31, Jan. 1856	29, Aug.	22	20		Ft. Wayne, IN	
Klein, Christian	24, Feb. 1873	2, Feb.	70	63		San Jose, IL	Marbach am Neckar, Württemberg
Klein, Christian	16, Aug. 1894	27, July	89	534		St. Paul, MN	Eichhorst, Minden, Preußen
Klein, Christina	14, Aug. 1890	22, July	64- 5m-13d	526	Hoffmann	New Orleans, LA	Landau, Rheinkreis Baiern
Klein, Clemens	25, Jan. 1869	2, Jan.	68- 7m-27d	31		Bushnell, IL	Engers, Rheinprovinz, Preußen
Klein, Daniel	28, July 1884	11, July	17	7		Hokah, MN	Manderbach, Nassau
Klein, Dorothea	3, May 1880	1, Apr.	74- 2m- 5d	143	Engel	Crown Point, IN	
Klein, Eleonora	8, Mar. 1888	8, Feb.		158		Chicago, IL	Sobernheim, Kreuznach, RheinPreußen
Klein, Eleonora	29, Mar. 1888	8, Feb.		206		Chicago, IL	Sobernheim, Kreuznach, RheinPreußen
Klein, Elisabeth	22, Sept 1873	4, Sept	65- 8m- 8d	303	Trapp	Blue Island, IL	Nonnenroth, Hessen-Darmstadt
Klein, Elisabeth	19, Mar. 1891	24, Feb.	66	190	Ebert	Bushnell, IL	Manderbach, Nassau

Christliche Apologete Death Notices --- 1839 - 1899

Name of Deceased	Notice Date	Death Date	Age	Maiden Name	Page	Place of Death	Place of Birth
Klein, Franz	25, Apr. 1889	21, Mar.	68- 7m- 4d		270	Schulenburg, TX	Dünnebusch, RheinPreußen
Klein, Friedrich	14, Apr. 1887	28, Mar.	79		238	Blue Island, IL	Fillingen, Hessen-Darmstadt
Klein, Friedrich Ludwig	24, Jan. 1895	4, Jan.	25		62	Chicago, IL	Chicago, Cook County, Illinois
Klein, Gottlieb	11, June 1891	24, May	87		382	Columbus, OH	Unterheimrieth, Weinsberg, Württemberg
Klein, Gustav	4, Oct. 1888	10, Sept	45- 5m		638	Owatonna, MN	Böckingen bei Heilbronn, Württemberg
Klein, Heinrich	25, Jan. 1894	1, Jan.	80		62	Salem, MN	Eikhorst, Westphalen
Klein, Heinrich	16, Dec. 1867	8, Oct.	15- 7m-13d		398	Bradford, IN	
Klein, Henrietta	16, Jan. 1890		75- 6m		46	Wapello, IA	Sachsen
Klein, Ida E.	31, Jan. 1881	2, Jan.	17		39	Bloomington, IL	
Klein, Johan Adam	16, Dec. 1886	4, Dec.	64		7	Quincy, IL	Häfnerhasloch, Württemberg
Klein, Johan Christian	2, Nov. 1899		56-10m- 7d		703	Beardstown, IL	Württemberg
Klein, Johan Heinrich	4, Aug. 1873	16, July	50		247	Booneville, IN	Zella, Amt Ziegenhain, Kurhessen
Klein, John	3, Feb. 1887	19, Nov.	23		78	Freeport, IL	
Klein, Karl	25, July 1889	28, June	3		478	Redfield, SD	Regersville, Ohio
Klein, Karoline	25, July 1889	22, June	17		478	Redfield, SD	Regersville, Ohio
Klein, Katharina	4, Apr. 1881	8, Mar.	79- 8m-13d	Hay	111	Batesville, IN	Winden, Kandel, Rheinkreis Baiern
Klein, Konrad	8, Apr. 1897	17, Mar.	71		223	Yellow Creek, IL	Hessen-Kassel
Klein, Konrad	26, July 1849	17, July	69		120	Cincinnati, OH	
Klein, Louise	23, Nov. 1893	6, Nov.	62	Kröger	750	Salem, MN	Nettelstedt, Westphalen
Klein, Magdalene	3, July 1851	14, Apr.			108	Detroit, MI	Medersheim, La Meurthe, Lothingen
Klein, Maria	18, Jan. 1894	20, Dec.	70	Hauch	46	Hokah, MN	Elschbach, Rheinpfalz Baiern
Klein, Maria	23, Nov. 1899	5, Nov.	55	Meyer	751	Pyrmont, MO	
Klein, Maria A.	7, Mar. 1895	21, Jan.	69		158	Indianapolis, IN	Obau, Baiern
Klein, Maria Agnes Louise	19, Jan. 1880	3, Jan.	76	Lillienthal	23	Quincy, IL	Dillingen, Amt Baden, Preußen
Klein, Maria Johannette	18, Jan. 1894	21, Dec.	69	Böcker	46	Austin, TX	Kratzhahn, Coblenz, Preußen
Klein, Maria Katharina	24, May 1894	28, Apr.	76	Röser	342	Bushnell, IL	Bendorf, Preußen
Klein, Martin	17, Feb. 1859	6, Feb.	22		28	Connersville, IN	Wittlensweiler, Freudenstadt, Württemberg
Klein, Mina	3, Feb. 1898	10, Jan.	74	Musey	79	New Haven, CT	Vaihingen an der Enz, Württemberg
Klein, Otto	23, Nov. 1893	25, Oct.	25		750	Redfield, SD	Ragersville, Ohio
Klein, Peter	1, Dec. 1843	23, Nov.	34		191	Cincinnati, OH	Lachen, Neustadt, Rheinkreis Baiern
Klein, Peter	8, July 1886	26, June	63		7	Austin, TX	Düneburg, RheinPreußen
Klein, Peter	11, Feb. 1842	6, Feb.	20m		23		
Klein, Robert Heinrich	9, Mar. 1885	18, Feb.	21- 1m-14d		7	Indianapolis, IN	Winkelhausen, Lennep, Düsseldorf, Preußen
Klein, Rosalie	5, Mar. 1877	12, Feb.	48	Staller	79	Sheboygan, WI	Güglingen, Württemberg
Klein, Rosina Sperli	14, Nov. 1881	23, Oct.	41		367	Cedar Lake, IN	
Klein, Wilhelm	30, July1883	17, July	16- 3m-13d		247	Chicago, IL	
Kleine, Karl	3, Nov. 1884	2, Oct.	14- 2m-26d		7	St. Paul, MN	
Kleine, Maria	20, Feb. 1882	26, Jan.	76		63	St. Paul, MN	Eichhorst, Minden, Westphalen
Kleineck, Elisabeth	25, Sept 1865	23, Aug.	32	Hamel	156	Edwardsville, IL	Kirch-Lothheim, Hessen
Kleineck, Elisabeth	2, Oct. 1865	23, Aug.	32	Hamel	160	Edwardsville, IL	Lothheim, Hessen
Kleinekemper, Maria	1, Oct. 1866		59 - 3d		318	Nashville, IL	Eininghausen, Lübbeke, Preußen
Kleiner, Anna Catharina	19, Apr. 1875	26, Mar.	72-10m-19d	Zuberbühler	127	St. Louis, MO	Herisau, Appenzell, Schweiz
Kleinert, John Michael	9, Apr. 1857	17, Mar.	44		60	Warsaw, IL	Melchershausen, Hessen-Kassel
Kleinfelder, Joseph	5, Aug. 1858	17, July	48		124	---, KS	York County, Pennsylvania
Kleinforge, Anna Wilhelmine	9, Dec. 1878	19, Nov.	16		391	Union, MO	
Kleinik, Anna Maria	20, Feb. 1896	31, Jan.	90	Reuter	126	Nokomis, IL	Itter, Hessen

- 255 -

Christliche Apologete Death Notices -- 1839 - 1899

Name of Deceased	Notice Date	Death Date	Age	Maiden Name	Page	Place of Death	Place of Birth
Kleinkamper, Hermann	6, May 1858	17, Apr.	44		72	Nashville, IL	Rödinghausen, Bünden, Preußen
Kleinke, Friedrich	19, May 1887	6, May	90		318	Chicago, IL	Neißkow, Stolpe, Köslin, Hinterpommern
Kleinke, Henriette Wilhelmine	8, Mar. 1894	3, Feb.	63	Ziske	166	Albert Lea, MN	Goschin, Danzig, Preußen
Kleinkemper, Maria	23, Apr. 1883	6, Apr.	37- - 4d		135	Crete, NE	Hille, Minden, Preußen
Kleinknecht, Barbara Rosina	19, Mar. 1891	20, Feb.	82	Tresz	190	Fairview, OH	Unterweibach, Württemberg
Kleinknecht, Caspar	27, Oct. 1873	26, Sept	68		343	Ripley, OH	Erdmanhausen, Marbach, Württemberg
Kleinknecht, Catharina	5, Apr. 1894	14, Mar.	62	Baker	230	Hoboken, NJ	New York
Kleinknecht, Margaretha	19, Dec. 1845	20, Aug.			203	Brown County, OH	Erdmannshausen, Marbach, Württemberg
Kleinlein, Georg	1, Dec. 1898	7, Nov.	29		767	Perry, IL	
Kleinschmidt, Anna Catharina	13, Feb. 1862	16, Jan.	47	Broker	28	Valley Mines, MO	Bände, Minden, Preußen
Kleinschmidt, Elisabeth	17, Feb. 1873	13, Jan.	67	Pieper	53	De Soto, MO	Jöllenbeck, Preußen
Kleinschmidt, Franz Heinrich	23, Aug. 1894	25, July	70		550	St. Louis, MO	Blasheim, Preußen
Kleinschmidt, Heinrich Friedrich Wm.	6, Sept 1888	13, Aug.	73- 9m- 2d		574	St. Louis, MO	Blasheim, Lübbeke, Minden, Preußen
Kleinschmidt, Karl	28, Jan. 1867	30, Dec.	61- -27d		30	De Soto, MO	
Kleinschmidt, Louis	24, June 1872	26, May	18		207	Nashville, IL	Franklin County, Missouri
Kleinschmidt, Louisa Emma	20, Apr. 1893	22, Mar.	29- 5m-14d	Wannewal	254	St. Louis, MO	St. Louis, Missouri
Kleinschmidt, Maria	17, Aug. 1893	22, July	67	Möller	526	St. Louis, MO	Obermehlen, Westphalen
Kleinschmidt, Maria Charlotte	1, Oct. 1857	7, Sept	50- 6m		160	Valley Mines, MO	Mehnen, Lübbeke, Kreis Minden, Preußen
Kleinschmidt, Sophia	4, June 1891	5, May	66	Krüger	366	St. Louis, MO	Blasheim, Minden, Preußen
Kleinsorgen, Johann Heinrich	24, Aug. 1854		61- 9m		136	Osage, MO	Amt Blomberg, Lippe-Detmold
Kleinsorger, Wilhelm	12, Jan. 1888	22, Nov.	56		30	Beaufort, MO	Lippe-Detmold
Kleinsorger, Wilhelmine	24, July 1871	20, June	27- 5m-10d	Meyer	239	Beaufort, MO	Herfort, Minden, Preußen
Kleinsorger, Wilhelmine	24, June 1867	23, May	72	Kuhlhenke	198	Jefferson City, MO	Lippe-Detmold
Kleinvogel, Dorothea	4, Apr. 1889	6, Mar.	73		222	Fairmount, KS	
Kleinvogel, Karl	28, Mar. 1895	11, Mar.	82		206	Lawrence, KS	Sachsen
Kleinvogel, Maria	7, Aug. 1865	29, June	50- 9m- 7d		128	Lawrence, KS	Altstedt, Sachsen-Weimar
Kleisly, Anna	14, Jan. 1884	20, Dec.	65		7	De Soto, MO	Niederwenigen, Zürich, Schweiz
Kleist, Christian	23, May 1889	5, May	89		334	Watertown, WI	Schwanebeck, Salzig, Pommern
Kleist, Christina Maria	7, Nov. 1895	16, Oct.	70	Löeskow	718	Wrayville, IL	Taschenberg, Preußen
Kleist, Johan Chr. Fr.	15, Mar. 1875	31, Jan.	55		87	Illinois City, IL	Mühlen, Preußen
Kleist, Karl	19, Feb. 1872	1, Feb.	26		63	Michigan City, IN	Chodeziejen, Preußen
Klemens, Margaretha	20, Nov. 1876	31, Oct.	74	Kyburtz	375	Walworth Co, WI	Schweiz
Klemer, Albertine Karoline	20, Aug. 1891	23, July	59- -12d	DeLatre	542	Nokomis, IL	Mandelkow bei Stettin, Pommern
Klemer, Anna Friederike	26, Jan. 1893	11, Jan.		Steffen	62	Faribault, MN	Heidelbeck, Lippe-Detmold
Klemm, Maria Sophia	8, Dec. 1853	9, Nov.	35- 2m- 7d		196	Watertown, WI	Altenrätz, Wriezen a. d. Oder, Preußen
Klemm, Dorothea Louise	25, Feb. 1892	1, Feb.	66	Radke	126	Lena, IL	Temnick, Saatzig, Pommern
Klemm, Louise	27, Oct. 1879	30, Aug.	30	Kalien	343	Wausau, WI	Sietnow, Flotow, Preußen
Klemm, Maria	4, Jan. 1864	10, Dec.	49	Hackh	4	Chicago, IL	Stuttgart, Württemberg
Klemme, Adolph	6, Apr. 1874	23, Feb.	63- 3m		111	Beaufort, MO	Oerlinghausen, Lippe-Detmold
Klemme, Elisabeth	17, June 1886	16, May	85	Brinker	7	Watkins, IA	Razig, Lippe-Detmold
Klemme, Friederike Dorothea	4, July 1895	10, June	76	Elbrechter	430	Belleville, IL	Heben, Bielefeld, Germany
Klemme, Heinrich Conrad	24, Jan. 1895	4, Jan.	70		62	Belleville, IL	Weichbild, Schildesche, Preußen
Klemme, Pauline	22, Jan. 1891	14, Dec.	27-11m-10d	Bauch	62	Pittsfield, IL	Pike County, Illinois
Klenke, Karl	3, Aug. 1899	22, July	75		495	Wausau, WI	Reinebeck, Hannover
Klenke, Louise Helene	3, Dec. 1896	11, Nov.	21		782	Wausau, WI	Oshkosh, Wisconsin
Klenske, Johan	19, Jan. 1885	3, Jan.	75		7	Ahnapee, WI	Schöneberg, Pommern

- 256 -

Christliche Apologete Death Notices --- 1839 - 1899

Name of Deceased	Notice Date	Death Date	Age	Maiden Name	Page	Place of Death	Place of Birth
Klepfer, Georg	5, June 1882	28, Apr.	80- 2m-26d		183	Buffalo, NY	Kirchheim am Neckar, Besigheim, Württemberg
Klepfer, Johan Friedrich	24, Apr. 1871	5, Apr.	75- 9m		135	Buffalo, NY	Kirchheim am Neckar, Württemberg
Klepper, Frank	16, Oct. 1890	27, Sept	25-11m-22d		670	Wilber, NE	Scioto County, Ohio
Klepper, Heinrich	27, Mar. 1865	7, Mar.	43		52	Batesville, IN	Holzhausen, Hartum, Münden, Preußen
Klepser, Katharina	19, Jan. 1880	30, Dec.	78	Maurer	23	Rochester, NY	Bodenheim, Brackenheim, Württemberg
Klepser, Regina	19, Feb. 1872	29, Jan.	54	Stierle	63	Buffalo, NY	Kirchheim am Neckar, Württemberg
Klerry, Katharine	4, June 1896	29, Apr.	53	Schöpfer	367	Muskegon, MI	Mühlenberg, Baiern
Klett, Caroline Malwine	7, May 1896	13, Apr.	54	Henning	302	Manitowoc, WI	Gransee, Potsdam, Brandenburg
Klett, Christian	17, Aug. 1874	12, July	27		263	Manitowoc, WI	Steinberg, Backnang, Württemberg
Klett, Gottlieb	5, May 1879	7, Apr.	67		143	Montague, WI	Wiesensteighof, Welzheim, Württemberg
Klett, Wilhelmina	8, June 1868	16, May	34		183	Giard, IA	Illingen, Maulbronn, Württemberg
Kletzin, Abraham	25, Oct. 1875	14, Sept	82		343	Sheboygan, WI	Weichow, Uckermark, Preußen
Klindtworth, J.J.	15, Sept 1884	23, Aug.	80		7	Mountain Lake, MN	Apensen, Hannover
Kline, Christian	17, Mar. 1887	26, Feb.	68- - 7d		174	Lindsey, OH	Baden
Kline, Worthington	9, Nov. 1885	21, Oct.	24		7	Sumersett, NE	
Klingbeil, (Mrs)	24, Nov. 1887	16, Aug.	73		750	New Ulm, MN	Putzig, Preußen
Klingberg, August	17, Nov. 1884		43		7	Enterprise, KS	Sachsen
Klinge, Maria	19, Feb. 1877	25, Jan.	27- 9m-27d	Bachmann	63	Columbus, IL	Oberdon bei Mühlhausen, Preußen
Klinge, Maria Elisabeth	25, Dec. 1865	29, Oct.	62		208	Columbus, IL	
Klinge, Saacharias	19, Feb. 1877	25, Jan.	74- 3m-10d		63	Columbus, IL	
Klingebiel, Carl G.	23, Aug. 1888	2, Aug.	69		542	Warsaw, IL	Betheln, Adessen, Hannover
Klingebiel, Eva Katharina	18, May 1899	15, Apr.	79		319	Warsaw, IL	Haak, Baden
Klingebiel, Friedrich	17, Dec. 1877	23, Nov.	40- -23d		407	Jackson, MO	Neuhof, Amt Ahlfeld, Hannover
Klingebiel, Julia	6, Aug. 1883	19, July	64- 8m- 2d	Warmbold	255	Warsaw, IL	Nettlingen, Hildesheim, Hannover
Klingel, Johannes	21, Sept 1868	19, Aug.	53		303	Warsaw, IL	Wimsheim, Leonberg, Württemberg
Klingel, Maria Eva	12, Sept 1870		63		295	Marion, OH	Oeschingen, Pforzheim, Baden
Klingelhoefer, Hanna	5, May 1884	16, Apr.	27	Burgdorf	7	Fredericksburg, TX	Llano, Mason County, Texas
Klingelhöfer, Adolph	30, June 1873	7, June	40		207	Aurora, IN	Little Rock, Arkansas
Klingelhöfer, Barbara	22, Oct. 1877	7, Oct.	68	Kirscherf	343	Lawrenceburg, IN	Birkenau, Odenwald, Hessen-Darmstadt
Klingelhöfer, Karl Ludwig Heinrich V.	7, Aug. 1882	18, July	77- 4m- 5d		255	Aurora, IN	Kirchberg bei Gießen, Hessen-Darmstadt
Klingelhöffer, August	13, May 1858	13, Apr.	15		76	Lawrenceburg, IN	Lawrenceburgh, Indiana
Klingemann, Alex	20, Apr. 1885	3, Apr.	15- 9m		7	Chester, IL	
Klingemann, Heinrich	31, July 1871	9, July	44		247	Edwardsville, IL	
Klingmann, Georg	5, Dec. 1895	4, Nov.	67-11m-20d		782	San Francisco, CA	Kleineicholz, Adelsheim, Baden
Klingwarth, Johan Friedrich	7, Jan. 1892	9, Nov.	77		14	Mt. Healthy, OH	Schleßel, Germany
Klingworth, Johan Heinrich Wilhelm	17, Feb. 1859	2, Jan.	58		28	Marietta, OH	Hannover
Klingworth, Sophia Dorothea	23, Aug. 1880	6, Aug.	59- 3m	Knone	271	Mt. Pleasant, OH	Liensburg, Hannover
Klink, Charlotte	19, Nov. 1891	22, July	77	Kittner	124	Rock River, WI	Wismar, HinterPommern, Preußen
Klink, J. G.	29, Oct. 1896	3, Oct.	71		703	Berea, OH	Cincinnati, Hamilton County, Ohio
Klink, Julia	11, Nov. 1886	20, Oct.	29	Triebel	7	Springfield, IL	Springfield, Illinois
Klink, Kunigunde	15, Feb. 1864	17, Jan.	56	Schweizer	28	Golconda, IL	Alt-Bulach, Schwarzwald, Württemberg

Christliche Apologete Death Notices --- 1839 - 1899

Name of Deceased	Notice Date	Death Date	Age	Maiden Name	Page	Place of Death	Place of Birth
Klink, Luise F.	24, Aug. 1899	4, Aug.	14		543	Chicago, IL	
Klink, Michael Friedrich	3, Aug. 1863	19, July	63- 4m- 6d		124	Golconda, IL	Alt Bulach, Caln, Württemberg
Klinkwarth, Johan	3, Sept 1883	9, Aug.	60		287	Marietta, OH	Vinkelmore, Hannover
Klintworth, Drussilla	16, Aug. 1888	1, Aug.	63- 1m-11d	Otten	526	Marietta, OH	Hepstedt, Ottersberg, Hannover
Klintworth, Friederike	9, May 1864	24, Apr.	28- 1m-24d		76	Marietta, OH	Erdmannshausen, Marbach, Württemberg
Klintworth, Margaretha	21, Mar. 1870	6, Mar.	74- 7m-17d	Mareß	95	Marietta, OH	St. Jürgens, Amt Ottersberg, Hannover
Klippel, Anna Maria	24, Jan. 1876	11, Dec.	76- 2m-18d	Schmal	31	St. Joseph, MO	Effenheim, Hessen-Darmstadt
Klippel, Anna Maria	18, Apr. 1861	31, Mar.	6- 3m-12d		64	Beardstown, IL	
Klippel, Margarethe	22, May 1876	30, Apr.	51- 8m- 2d		167	St. Joseph, MO	Steinweiler, Landau, Baiern
Klipper, (Mrs)	28, Aug. 1871	14, July	75	Ulbrand	279	Santa Claus, IN	Ilbeshausen, Hessen
Klipper, Heinrich	29, June 1885	23, May	46		7	Warsaw, IL	Niedernuff, Hessen
Klippert, John S.	2, Feb. 1874	2, July	81		39	Cannelton, IN	Crainfeld, Gießen, Hessen-Darmstadt
Klitsch, Zacharias	3, Feb. 1873	9, Jan.	44		39	Leavenworth, KS	Salzschlirf, Kurhessen
Klitz, Dorothea	8, June 1874	22, May	83		183	West Bend, WI	Neumarkt, Preußen
Klocke, Friedrich	6, Sept 1894	20, Aug.	72		582	Mt. Healthy, OH	Lippe-Detmold
Klockenga, Trienke	20, Dec. 1880	3, Dec.	5- 2m-13d		407	Emden, IL	
Klockow, Dorothea	12, Jan. 1899	26, Dec.	81		31	Galena, IL	Garwitz, Mecklenburg-Schwerin
Klockow, Heinrich W.	15, Mar. 1888	14, Feb.	19		174	Quincy, IL	Galena, Illinois
Klockow, Helmuth Karl Wilhelm	2, June 1898	16, May	58		351	Milwaukee, WI	Tützpatz, Pommern
Klockow, Ida	10, Apr. 1882	19, Mar.	82		119	Milwaukee, WI	Tützpatz, Demmin, Stettin, Vorpommern
Klockow, Johan Fr.	29, May 1876	5, May	80- 7m		175	Milwaukee, WI	Markow, Mecklenburg-Schwerin
Klockow, Maria	12, Feb. 1883	29, Jan.	53-10m- 9d	Behrendt	55	Milwaukee, WI	Golchen, Pommern
Klocksiem, Chr.	5, May 1887	11, Apr.			286	Laporte, IN	Kiddendorf, Mecklenburg-Schwerin
Klocksiem, Dorothea	20, Oct. 1898	30, Sept	80	Zese	671	Laporte, IN	Lüben, Mecklenburg-Schwerin
Klocksiem, Elisabeth	12, May 1898	24, Apr.	86		303	Milwaukee, WI	Philippshoff, Demien, Pommern
Klocksiem, Friedrich	24, Nov. 1887	3, Nov.	79		750	Milwaukee, WI	Guelz, Vorpommern
Klocksiem, Friedricka	25, Dec. 1871	2, Dec.	57	Jonas	415	Laporte, IN	Kitlendorf, Mecklenburg-Schwerin
Klocksiem, John	27, Feb. 1896	27, Jan.	82		143	Laporte, IN	Kittendorf, Mecklenburg-Schwerin
Klocksien, Elise	23, Apr. 1896	5, Mar.	18		270	Milwaukee, WI	
Klocksien, Friedrich	1, June 1899		56- 4m- 9d		351	Paton, IA	Zolkendorf, Mecklenburg-Schwerin
Klocksin, Maria	10, Apr. 1890	15, Feb.	47		238	Milwaukee, WI	Tützpatz, Vorpommern
Kloepel, Andreas (Rev)	8, Aug. 1895	4, July	35		510	Beaver Dam, WI	Freckleben, Sandersleben, Sachsen-Anhalt
Klokow, Mina	20, Feb. 1890	16, Jan.	24		126	Quincy, IL	
Kloos, Catharina	15, Mar. 1888	23, Feb.	46- - 3d	Schmidt	174	Berea, OH	Rohnhausen, Hessen
Klöpfel, Heinrich	7, Oct. 1867	20, Sept	41- 5m-13d		318	Lawrenceburg, IN	Erbenhausen, Rodenburg, Kurhessen
Klöpfel, Jacob	2, Apr. 1896	19, Feb.	72		222	Madison, IN	Baiern
Klopfenstein, Jakob	17, Nov. 1887	26, Oct.	78		734	Toledo, OH	Bärenthal, Elsaß
Klopfenstein, Salome	10, June 1886	23, May	77		7	Toledo, OH	Bärenthal, Elsaß
Klöpfer, Gottliebin Margaretha	14, Nov. 1881	1, Nov.	81- 6m- 2d	Schillinger	367	Greenville, OH	Bietigheim, Besigheim, Württemberg
Klöpfer, Immanuel Gottlob	8, June 1863	11, May	67		92	Cincinnati, OH	Winnenden, Waiblingen, Württemberg
Klopfleisch, Carl	1, Jan. 1891	23, Nov.	66		14	Brownton, MN	Esperstadt, Schwarzburg-Rudolstadt
Klopfleisch, Johan Christoph F.	20, May 1897	29, Apr.	75		319	Brownton, MN	Esperstedt, Schwarzburg-Rudolstadt
Klopp, Martha	4, Oct. 1839	27, Sept	30		159	Baltimore, MD	Gebersdorf, Kurhessen
Klöpper, Christian	24, Mar. 1879	25, Feb.	45		95	Hopewell, MO	Rahlen, Minden, Preußen
Klöpper, Heinrich	5, Sept 1889	7, Aug.	68		574	Clatonia, NE	Bückeburg, Germany
Klöpper, John	26, Oct. 1899	11, Sept	48		687	Clatonia, NE	Scioto County, Ohio

Christliche Apologete Death Notices --- 1839 - 1899

Name of Deceased	Notice Date	Death Date	Age	Page	Maiden Name	Place of Death	Place of Birth
Klöpper, Karl Heinrich	6, Oct. 1879	11, Sept	20- 1m- 2d	319		Salt Creek, NE	Scioto County, Ohio
Klöpping, W.	25, Aug. 1873	8, Aug.	46- 5m	271		Newton, IA	
Klöpping, Wilhelmine	25, Aug. 1873	Aug.	16-11m-20d	271		Newton, IA	Freeport, Illinois
Kloppmeyer, Louisa	29, Dec. 1879	29, Oct.		415	Kuhlmeier	Ft. Hunter, NY	
Klore, Georg Jakob	28, Apr. 1887	30, Mar.	63- 9m-24d	270		Decatur, IL	Malterdingen, Baden
Kloß, Christian Heinrich	11, Dec. 1871	18, Nov.	90	399		Aurora, IN	Berniz bei Schleiz, Reuß
Klossener, Elisabeth	11, Nov. 1872	28, Oct.	75	367	Klossener	Kendallville, IN	Erlenbach, Bern, Schweiz
Kloßner, Johannes	7, May 1866	1, Apr.	75	150		Kendallville, IN	
Klostermann, Albert Bennie	24, Sept 1891	30, Aug.	17-11m-15d	622		St. Paul, MN	
Klostermann, Karl Friedrich	7, Feb. 1895	17, Jan.	43	94		Louisville, KY	Lieblos, Gellhausen, Kurhessen
Klostermann, Wilhelmine Christine	21, Apr. 1892	28, Mar.	41	254	Schmidt	Louisville, KY	Louisville, Jefferson County, Kentucky
Klotz, Anna Maria	20, Feb. 1862	1, Feb.	60	32		Sherrills Mount, IA	OberRixingen, Württemberg
Klotz, Friederika	23, Oct. 1876	16, Sept	79- 8m- 8d	343	Tickemeyer	St. Louis, MO	Ruher, Amt Melle, Hannover
Klotz, Margarethe	2, May 1845	7, Apr.	62- 5m	71		St. Louis, MO	
Klotz, Rosine	23, May 1881		84- 6m-11d	167		Lancaster, NY	Oeschelbronn, Waiblingen, Württemberg
Klotz, Thomas	18, Mar. 1867	2, Mar.	75	86		Lancaster, NY	Oberschlechtbach, Württemberg
Klotzbach, Anna Martha	30, Apr. 1891	26, Mar.	86	286	Lotz	Giard, IA	Ausbach, Kurhessen
Klotzbach, Emilie	6, Dec. 1888	14, Nov.	52- 7m-15d	782	Brömse	St. Louis, MO	Floto, Minden, Preußen
Klotzbach, Heinrich August	30, Dec. 1878	3, Dec.	31- 3m- 4d	415		Newport, KY	Pfortmühle, Völkershausen, Sachsen-Weimar
Klotzbach, Henriette	20, Dec. 1888	13, Nov.	57- 8m- 4d	814	Muder	Belleville, IL	Oberdunla bei Mühlhausen, Preußen
Klotzbach, Karolina	23, Apr. 1866	5, Apr.	79- 5m-16d	134		Belleville, IL	Rodenburg, Kurhessen
Klötzien, Dorothea Wilhelmine	15, Sept 1887	23, Aug.	83-10m- 8d	590	Schmidt	Sheboygan, WI	Meichow, Uckermark, Brandenburg
Kluckhohn, Clara	1, Apr. 1872	16, Mar.	6- 7m- 8d	111		Reddick, IL	Orland, Cook County, Illinois
Kluckhohn, Friedrich August	17, Sept 1896	23, Aug.	80	607		Columbus, WI	Rentrup, Bavenhausen, Germany
Kluckhohn, Heinrich	27, July 1893	10, July	36	478		Herman, MO	Wisconsin
Kluckhohn, Louise	19, Feb. 1866	5, Oct.	52- 6m	62	Vogelmeier	Lemars, IA	Meinberg, Lippe-Detmold
Kluckhohn, Minna	18, Feb. 1897	28, Jan.	68	111	Riele	Senate Grove , MO	Bavenhausen, Lippe-Detmold
Kluckhohn, Otto	23, Nov. 1899	5, Nov.	21	751		Galena, IL	Senate Grove , Missouri
Kluckow, Phillipine Karoline	5, Jan. 1885	24, Dec.	27	7		Quincy, IL	
Klude, Franz	23, Aug. 1849	8, July		136		Davenport, IA	Hannover
Klug, Eva	18, Feb. 1884	29, Jan.	93	7	Weis	Nashville, IL	Schloß Fibbach, Sachsen-Weimar
Klug, H. Fr.	30, Mar. 1863	2, Mar.	48	52		Brooklyn, NY	Bubenburg bei Hildesheim,
Klug, Karl Ludwig	30, May 1889	3, May	77	350		Roseville, MI	Lich, Hessen
Klug, Sophia	10, July 1882	27, May	34	223	Thiemann	Chicago, IL	
Kluge, August	25, Aug. 1898	6, Aug.	49	543		Dayton, OH	Pommern
Klugel, Anna Dora	22, Oct. 1896		50	687	Merkle	Quincy, IL	Edmundhausen, Württemberg
Klukow, Bertha	31, Dec. 1891	2, Dec.	19	846		Quincy, IL	Galena, Illinois
Klukow, George	31, Dec. 1891	3, Dec.		846		Galena, IL	Quincy, Illinois
Klukow, Heinrich	12, May 1884	28, Apr.	78	7		Quincy, IL	Ruthenbach, Kriwitz, Mecklenburg-Schwerin
Klukow, Louise	17, Dec. 1891	21, Nov.	24	814		LaCrosse, WI	Quincy, Illinois
Klum, Rosina	4, May 1899	14, Apr.	19- 4m	287		Baltimore, MD	
Klump, Catharina Elisabeth	19, Jan. 1885	30, Dec.	22	7		Baltimore, MD	Hessen-Darmstadt
Klump, Georg Philipp	13, Aug. 1883	23, July	22	263		Oxford, IA	Hessen-Darmstadt
Klump, Jakob	23, June 1898	1, Apr.	74	399		Baltimore, MD	Duerm, Pforzheim, Baden
Klump, Johan Philipp	11, Aug. 1884	14, July	25	7		Peoria, IL	Hessen-Darmstadt
Klumpp, Wilhelm F.	7, Dec. 1863	2, Oct.	24	196			Kniehis, Freudenstadt, Württemberg

Christliche Apologete Death Notices --- 1839 - 1899

Name of Deceased	Notice Date	Death Date	Age	Maiden Name	Page	Place of Death	Place of Birth
Klund, Katharina	23, July 1891	19, June	52	Senn	478	West Bend, WI	Bucks, St. Gallen, Schweiz
Klund, Wolfgang W.	25, May 1893	1, May	35-10m-12d		334	Kewaskum, WI	
Klusenkam, (Mr)	14, Mar. 1881	20, Dec.	91-10m- 9d		87	Hannibal, OH	
Klüsenkam, Maria	10, Feb. 1879	29, Jan.	90- 7m- 7d		47	Hannibal, OH	
Klusmann, Frd.	20, Aug. 1883	4, Aug.	41- 8m-17d		271	Clatonia, NE	
Klusmann, Jobst Heinrich	15, May 1856	16, Apr.	35		80	Herman, MO	Jöllenbeck bei Bielefeld, Preußen
Klusmeier, Christine Charlotte	21, Sept 1854	8, July	38	Meier	152	Union, MO	Holzhausen bei Minden, Preußen
Klusmeyer, Anna May	29, Dec. 1884	14, Dec.	14		7	Big Spring, MO	Montgomery County, Missouri
Klusmeyer, Katharina	15, Feb. 1869	11, Jan.	39	Kamp	55	Union, MO	
Klüsner, Ludwig	5, Mar. 1883	15, Dec.	17- 3m		79	Dornum, CO	
Klüß, Friedrich	14, Feb. 1876	23, Jan.	48		55	Algona, IA	
Klüßmann, Johan	21, Sept 1868	3, Sept	16- 7m		303	Leavenworth, KS	Stegnitz, Preußen
Klust, Heinrich	9, Feb. 1880	15, Jan.	13-11m-15d		47	Minneapolis, MN	
Kluth, Maria	7, Apr. 1879	19, Mar.	63- 2m		111	Cottage, IA	Labenz, Lauenburg, Pommern
Knaack, Louise	19, Nov. 1891	19, Oct.	69	Palenske	750	Marion, WI	Krelzin, Vorpommern
Knaak, Carl G.	14, June 1888	23, May	56		382	Chicago, IL	
Knaap, Alice	16, Apr. 1891	2, Mar.	20		254	Springfield, IL	
Knaap, Alice	7, May 1891	2, Mar.	11		302	Springfield, IL	
Knabe, Georg	31, Dec. 1896	18, Nov.	51		844	Fairmount, KS	Kurhessen
Knabe, Heinrich	29, Oct. 1866	28, Sept	36		350	Lawrence, KS	Wölfterode, Kurhessen
Knabe, Johan Wilhelm	30, Oct. 1871	20, Sept	25- -20d		351	Vermillion, OH	Kurhessen
Knagg, Julia Dorothea	11, Apr. 1895	17, Mar.	62	Walter	238	Cleveland, OH	Breikheim, Württemberg
Knape, Wilhelmine	29, Dec. 1892	23, Nov.	60	Deppe	828	Gilead, NE	Lue, Lippe-Detmold
Knapheide, Catharine	16, June 1853	21, Nov.	58	Horstmeier	96		Lengerich, Münster, Preußen
Knapheide, Heinrich H.	4, Sept 1890	15, Aug.	66		574	Quincy, IL	Längerich, Westphalen
Knapheide, Wilhelm	16, June 1853	20, Apr.	60		96	St. Paul, MN	Linne, Münster, Preußen
Knäpmeyer, (Mr)	20, Oct. 1853	10, Sept	78		168		Rimsolo, Grünenberg, Osnabrück, Hannover
Knapp, Carl	6, Aug. 1891	11, June	66-11m- 9d		510	Elkton, SD	Heppenheim, Reisen, Hessen-Darmstadt
Knapp, Charlotte	20, Mar. 1851	2, Feb.	21- 6m	Gussenberg	48	Chester, IL	Klekamp bei Minden, Preußen
Knapp, Christian	12, Jan. 1899	20, Dec.	39		31	Chester, IL	Chester, Illinois
Knapp, Dorothea	11, Oct. 1855	31, Aug.	52		164	Chester, IL	
Knapp, Jakob	29, June 1893	3, June	68		414	Chester, IL	Burbach, Birkenfeld, Germany
Knapp, Johan Karl	14, Jan. 1886	13, Dec.	65		7	Chester, IL	Burbach, Rheinland
Knapp, Johan Karl	14, July 1892	21, June	21		446	Chester, IL	
Knapp, Julia Dorothea	25, Apr. 1895	17, Mar.	62	Walter	270	Cleveland, OH	Breikheim, Württemberg
Knapp, Karl F.	23, May 1895	6, May	38		334	Lyona, KS	Schovanz, Regenwalde, Hinterpommern
Knapp, Lillie	7, May 1896	18, Apr.	27	Eiseman	302	Galena, IL	Galena, Illinois
Knapp, Margarethe	31, Jan. 1861	7, Jan.	32	Frenzel	20	Chester, IL	
Knapp, Maria	26, Mar. 1896	1, Mar.	67	VonZung	206	Chester, IL	Wolfhagen, Hessen-Kassel
Knapp, Maria	14, July 1892	30, June	35	Geyer	446	Chester, IL	
Knapp, Maria Carolina	22, Sept 1853	2, Sept	53		152	Chester, IL	Burbach, Niederbrombach, Oldenburg
Knapp, Pauline	4, Apr. 1881	6, Mar.	28	Dressel	111	Red Bud, IL	
Knapp, Wilhelm	27, Mar. 1882	9, Mar.	47- 1m-10d		103	Defiance, OH	Crawford County, Ohio
Knappenberger, Georg	1, Sept 1859	15, Aug.	39		140	Bucyrus, OH	Schorndorf, Württemberg
Knaub, Julius	23, June 1898	29, May	73		399	Chicago, IL	Eberbach, Baden
Knauer, Simon	11, Mar. 1886	21, Feb.	84- 7m-22d		7	New Albany, IN	Buchfeld, Baiern

Christliche Apologete Death Notices --- 1839 - 1899

Name of Deceased	Notice Date	Death Date	Age	Page	Maiden Name	Place of Death	Place of Birth
Knauff, Anna Elisabeth	25, July 1889		48	478	Schmidt	St. Paul, MN	Asterode, Ziegenhain, Hessen-Kassel
Knauft, Christiana	7, June 1875		33-4m-19d	183	Ebel	St. Paul, MN	Graben, Baden
Knauft, Katherine	19, Apr. 1860		37	64	Schnittger	St. Paul, MN	Blasheim, Lübeke, Preußen
Knaug, Mina Anna	23, Aug. 1880	4, Aug.	19- 7m- 8d	271		Berea, OH	
Knaup, Anna Elisabeth	22, May 1882	5, May	69- - 28d	167	Baumann	Woodville, OH	Groß Rohrheim, Bensheim, Hessen
Knaup, Elisabeth	28, June 1875	12, June	44	207	Schweikert	Beaver Dam, WI	Großhausen, Hessen-Darmstadt
Knaup, Georg	5, May 1898	18, Apr.	28	287		Beaver Dam, WI	Watertown, Wisconsin
Knaup, Heinrich	7, July 1892	28, May	25	430		Beaver Dam, WI	Watertown, Wisconsin
Knaup, Ida Bertha	7, Feb. 1895	21, Jan.	28	94	Bröcker	Beaver Dam, WI	Westford, Wisconsin
Knaup, Lene	5, Mar. 1891	2, Jan.	17	158		Beaver Dam, WI	Beaver Dam, Wisconsin
Knaup, Louise	20, Mar. 1890	24, Feb.	30	190	Sander	Redfield, SD	Fond du Lac County, Wisconsin
Knaup, Peter	22, Jan. 1866	25, Dec.	32- 5m-10d	30		Watertown, WI	Großenhausen, Hessen-Darmstadt
Knaup, Philipp	20, Sept 1888	29, Aug.	65- 8m-23d	606		Beaver Dam, WI	Großhausen, Hessen-Darmstadt
Knaus, Anna Maria	6, Apr. 1868		74	111		Evansville, IN	
Knaus, Christian Gottlieb	2, Apr. 1877	15, Mar.	48	111		Indianapolis, IN	Schorndorf, Württemberg
Knaus, Peter	28, Jan. 1848		55	19		Evansville, IN	Pennsylvania
Knax, Martha Friederike	28, Mar. 1881	13, Dec.	21-10m-23d	103	Wendt	Vermillion, OH	Peninsula, Ottowa County, Ohio
Knebel, Gustav	9, July 1891	21, June	20-10m-15d	446		Waco, TX	
Knecht, Catharina	14, Dec. 1874	21, Nov.	76	399		Cannelton, IN	Herrbrunn, Nassau
Knecht, Franz H.	18, May 1874	21, Apr.	80	159		Canal Dover, OH	Schneisingen, Argau, Schweiz
Knecht, Johan K.	7, Dec. 1893	21, Nov.	62	782		Fosterburg, IL	Oberfischbach, Nassau
Knecht, John Harle	8, May 1882	16, Apr.	2	151		Petovskey, MI	
Knecht, Maria	24, Apr. 1882	26, Feb.	45	135	Sauerwein	Brighton, IL	Lahrscheidt, St. Goarshausen, Nassau
Kneese, H. Ferdinand	19, Aug. 1867	9, July	68	262		Fredericksburg, TX	Friedrichshagen, Kurhessen
Knehaus, Catharina Elisabeth	16, June 1887	16, May	64	382	Reckmeyer	Bushnell, IL	Bockel, Halle, Preußen
Knehaus, Heinrich	25, Sept 1890		74	622		Bushnell, IL	Borgholzhausen, Preußen
Kneip, William	23, Aug. 1888	4, Aug.	36- - 7d	542		New Albany, IN	
Kneisel, Elisabeth	16, Feb. 1854	23, Dec.	24	28		Iowa City, IA	
Kneller, Catharina	21, June 1888	27, May	87	398		Poughkeepsie, NY	
Kneller, Karl	28, Feb. 1881	16, Feb.	21	71		Poughkeepsie, NY	Poughkeepsie, New York
Knemöller, Alvina	15, June 1899	22, May	34	383		St. Louis, MO	
Knerr, Elisabeth	13, Sept 1855	2, Sept	53	148		Cincinnati, OH	Kirschbach, Rheinkreis Baiern
Knetsch, Johannes Peter	11, Oct. 1880	27, Sept	44	327		Sandwich, IL	Manderbach, Nassau
Knetsch, Philippine	1, June 1874	13, May	52	175	Hermann	Sandwich, IL	Oberscheid, Dillenburg, Nassau
Knibis, Heinrich	2, Jan. 1890	5, Dec.	69- 9m	14		Scott, WI	Bechtheim, Worms, Hessen-Darmstadt
Kniebes, Katharina	20, Dec. 1880	20, Nov.	81- 6m	407		Scott, WI	
Kniee, Elisabeth	21, Oct. 1878	20, Aug.	76	335		Sibley, MN	
Kniege, Hanna	1, Feb. 1864	5, Jan.	34	20		Warrenton, MO	Reme, Kreis Herfort, Preußen
Knieper, Elisabeth	18, May 1885	5, May	64	7	Wagner	Winchester, MO	Nügeln, Hannover
Knieper, Elisabeth Friederika	5, May 1873	18, Apr.	18	143		New Orleans, LA	Neuerieth, Sachsen-Meiningen
Knieper, Friedrich	12, Oct. 1868	15, Sept	77	327		Quincy, IL	Hindemühlen, Amt Ahlden, Hannover
Knieper, Wilhelm Friedrich	15, Apr. 1878	11, Mar.	16	119		Quincy, IL	
Knieriem, Christine	5, Feb. 1883	10, Jan.	80- 8m-29d	47		Scranton, PA	Rothenburg, Kurhessen
Knieriem, Henry	28, May 1866		27	174		St. Joseph, MO	Walburg, Amt Lichenau, Kurhessen
Knieriem, John	18, Jan. 1869	23, Dec.	45	23		Iowa City, IA	Breitenbach, Rothenburg, Kurhessen
Knierieme, John	23, June 1862	7, Apr.	19	100		Oil Creek, IN	Rothenburg Ibau, Kurhessen

Christliche Apologete Death Notices --- 1839 - 1899

Name of Deceased	Notice Date	Death Date	Age	Page	Maiden Name	Place of Death	Place of Birth
Knierim, Georg Henry	15, May 1890	15, Apr.	31	318		Danville, IL	Randall Station, Indiana
Knierim, Oscar Stuart	8, Apr. 1897	15, Mar.	22	223		Danville, IL	
Knierim, Wilhelm	10, Nov. 1887	21, Oct.	21	718		Danville, IL	
Knigge, Caroline	4, Jan. 1894	11, Dec.	45	14	Hanke	Pinckney, MO	Reme, Minden, Herfurt, Preußen
Knigge, Friederika	18, Oct. 1875	14, Aug.	77	335		Hopewell, MO	Rehme, Minden, Preußen
Knigge, Wilhelm	6, Feb. 1871	9, Jan.	73- 5m	47		Hopewell, MO	Ufel, Holtrup, Amt Floto, Minden, Preußen
Knikel, Lora Elisabeth	27, Mar. 1882	4, Mar.	20- -29d	103	Schweinfurth	Marion, OH	Marion County, Ohio
Knipmeier, Maria Elisabeth	22, Sept 1898	16, Aug.	86	607	Kölling	Warren, MO	Buer, Mülle, Hannover
Knipmeyer, Carl	23, Feb. 1874	27, Dec.	31	63		Warren, MO	
Knipmeyer, Caspar	8, Nov. 1875	22, Sept	61	359		Warren, MO	Heuel, Amt Melle, Hannover
Knipmeyer, Engel	23, Jan. 1862	8, Dec.	29	16	Tacke	Warren, MO	
Knipmeyer, Hermann	15, May 1856	18, Apr.	48	80		Warrenton, MO	Rimslo, Hannover
Knippenberg, (Mrs)	14, Feb. 1895	24, Jan.	82	110	Stork	Louisville, KY	Oberroßbach, Friedberg, Hessen-Darmstadt
Knippschield, John	22, Feb. 1864	14, Dec.	12-11m-10d	32		Carrolton, MO	
Knipschild, Georg	23, Aug. 1875	22, July	20	271		Carroll Co., MO	Carroll County, Missouri
Knipschild, Heinrich	21, Sept 1874	28, Aug.	57	303		Carroll Co., MO	Heringhausen, Hessen-Darmstadt
Knirsch, Karoline	17, Mar. 1884	20, Feb.	67	7	Feistkorn	Blue Island, IL	Ellersleben, Sachsen-Weimar
Knittel, Katharine Louise	29, June 1874	13, June	26- 2m-16d	207		Nauvoo, IL	
Knobel, Karoline	6, Oct. 1879	27, Aug.	22- -19d	319	Möhler	Pittsburg, PA	Hannover
Knoblauch, Emma	5, Oct. 1885	1, Sept	15	7		St. Louis, MO	
Knoblauch, Louise	24, Nov. 1884	17, Oct.		7		St. Louis, MO	
Knoblauch, Philippine	17, June 1897	1, June	70	383	Stephan	Duncan, NE	Rubertsweiler, Rheinkreis Baiern
Knoch, Heinrich	22, Dec. 1862	16, Oct.	18	204		Washington, OH	Oranienbaum, Anhalt Dessau, Sachsen-Anhalt
Knoch, Louise	8, Feb. 1869	9, Jan.	52	47	Rast	Wabasha, MN	Liestal, Basel, Schweiz
Knoch, Maria	9, Aug. 1888	21, July	64	510	Scheible	Smithton, MO	Wöhl, Hessen-Darmstadt
Knoche, Anna Maria	28, Apr. 1892	8, Apr.	55	270	Wißemann	Edwardsville, IL	Bederkesa, Hannover
Knoche, Johanna	26, Oct. 1885	2, Oct.		7		Oakland, CA	
Knoche, Johannes	25, Apr. 1864	1, Apr.	9	68		Warsaw, IL	
Knoche, Paulus	25, Apr. 1864	2, Apr.	4	68		Warsaw, IL	
Knoche, Rosa	9, June 1887	23, May	29	366	Schöne	Warsaw, IL	Warsaw, Illinois
Knoche, S.	20, Nov. 1882	5, Nov.	16	375		Sedalia, MO	Franklin County, Missouri
Knochel, Elisabeth	7, Jan. 1897	12, Dec.	77	15		Cleveland, OH	Segenstorf, Bern, Schweiz
Knodel, Eberhardine	22, May 1876	23, Apr.	66	167		Shelbyville, KY	Dertingen, Maulbronn, Württemberg
Knodel, Salome	30, Jan. 1862	15, Jan.	73- 3m- 8d	20		Milwaukee, WI	Stiefern, Pforzheim, Baden
Knoderer, Christina Elisabeth	6, Jan. 1859	14, Dec.	31	4		Columbus, OH	
Knödler, Christina	4, July 1870	5, June	63- 2m- 4d	215	Leilich	Louisville, KY	Schaafheim, Großumstadt, Hessen-Darmstadt
Knödler, Friedrich	26, Mar. 1877	3, Mar.	50	103		Louisville, KY	Beutelsbach, Schorndorf, Württemberg
Knödler, Katharine	16, Dec. 1897	24, Nov.	28	799		LaHarpe, IL	McDonnouch County, Illinois
Knödler, Magdalena	29, Oct. 1866	8, Sept	89	350	Bürkemeier	Louisville, KY	Beutelsbach, Schorndorf, Württemberg
Knödler, Magdalena	7, Feb. 1870	19, Jan.	78- 6m-29d	47	Roth	Louisville, KY	Beutelsbach, Schorndorf, Württemberg
Knödler, Margaretha	27, Aug. 1877	11, Aug.	52	279		Louisville, KY	Beutelsbach, Schorndorf, Württemberg
Knödler, Matthias	22, Oct. 1864	1, Oct.	54	172		Louisville, KY	Leutenbach, Waiblingen, Württemberg
Knödler, Rosina Barbara	20, Feb. 1882	4, Feb.	62- 5m- 2d	63	Schnarrenberger	Bucyrus, OH	Rennerod, Zehnhaußen, Hessen-Nassau
Knödler, Theodore	21, Oct. 1897	21, Sept	70	671	Menk	Crown Point, IN	Gumbach, Schorndorf, Württemberg
Knoedler, Johan	17, May 1888	1, May	61	318		LaHarpe, IL	Plymouth, Hancock County, Illinois
Knoedler, Maria Catharina	8, Nov. 1888	15, Oct.	28	718		LaHarpe, IL	

Christliche Apologete Death Notices --- 1839 - 1899

Name of Deceased	Notice Date	Death Date	Age	Page	Maiden Name	Place of Death	Place of Birth
Knoll, Louise Christina	27, Aug. 1883	3, Aug.	19	279		Philadelphia, PA	Wahlheim, Besigheim, Württemberg
Knoll, Minna	28, Apr. 1892	2, Apr.	37	270		Chicago, IL	Pommern
Knoll, Susanna	26, Dec. 1895		36	828	Well	Spokane, WA	Carver County, Minnesota
Knolle, Fr.	14, Mar. 1864	28, Jan.	23	44		Milan, IN	Lippe-Schaumburg
Knolle, Ida Helene	14, Apr. 1898	22, Mar.	25	239	Niebuhr	Industry, TX	Industry, Texas
Knollmeyer, Georg Simon	18, Sept 1871	3, Sept	57	303		New Haven, CT	Markt-Eisölden, Baiern
Knolmanns, Anna M.	26, July 1849	28, June		120		St. Louis, MO	
Knoop, Anna	9, Aug. 1869	5, July	74	255		Richland, MO	Brümerhof, Amt Sefen, Hannover
Knoop, Georg Lewis	29, Oct. 1877	26, Sept	15- 8m-28d	351		Lake Creek, MO	
Knoop, Johan Ludwig	22, Feb. 1864	14, Jan.	43	32		Florence, MO	Oltendorf, Amt Zevern, Hannover
Knoop, Karline	19, Aug. 1897	2, Aug.	66	527	Stemmler	Newport, KY	Matzenbach, Landstuhl, Rheinkreis Baiern
Knoop, Peter	1, Nov. 1888	13, Oct.	69	702		Newport, KY	Breddof, Ottersberg, Hannover
Knoop, Wilhelm	9, June 1892	11, May	36	366		Ada, MN	Oldendorf, Holzminden, Braunschweig
Knop, Peter	28, Nov. 1861	3, Nov.	60	192		Florence, MO	Breddof, Amt Ottersberg, Hannover
Knopf, Adam	27, Aug. 1896	29, July	88	559		St. Paul, MN	Grießbach, Elsaß
Knopf, Adam	20, Aug. 1896	29, July	88	542		St. Paul, MN	Kreisbach, Elsaß
Knopf, Heinrich	28, Jan. 1892	4, Jan.	65	62		Cleveland, OH	Fleimersheim, Alzei, Hessen-Darmstadt
Knopf, Heinrich W.	11, Oct. 1888		26	654		Deschler, OH	Cleveland, Ohio
Knopf, Jacob	30, Apr. 1896	9, Sept	77- 5m-17d	286		Cleveland, OH	Wahlheim, Hessen-Darmstadt
Knopf, Justus	20, Oct. 1859	28, May	65	168		Cleveland, OH	Wahlheim, Hessen-Darmstadt
Knopf, Karl Edward	3, July 1882	17- 1m-20d	215			Rockport, OH	
Knopf, Margaretha	7, Mar. 1881	11, Feb.	71- 1m- 7d	79	Ruch	Nerstrand, MN	Grießbach, Elsaß
Knopf, Maria Wilhelmina	27, May 1886	9, May	65	7	Moll	Cleveland, OH	Heiningen, Göppingen, Württemberg
Knopf, Peter	5, May 1859	12, Apr.	27	72		Cannon City, MN	Buffalo, New York
Knöpfle, Georg	19, Apr. 1860	25, Mar.	37	64		Santa Claus, IN	Fluorn, Oberndorf, Württemberg
Knöppel, Johannes	4, Aug. 1879	15, June	79	247		Lawrence, KS	Rosenthal, Frankenberg, Kurhessen
Knöppel, Katharina	26, Oct. 1899	5, Sept	70-10m-11d	687	Noll	Eudora, KS	Roda bei Rosenthal, Frankenberg, Hessen
Knorr, Rosina	13, Oct. 1873	30, Sept	71- -22d	327		Chicago, IL	Schlottau, Schlesien, Preußen
Knorpp, Christina	9, Aug. 1869	8, July	76	255	Schmid	De Soto, MO	Marbach, Württemberg
Knorppel, Friedrich K.	2, June 1887	8, May	17	350		Colony, KS	Baldwin City, Douglas County, Kansas
Knörr, Catharina	25, Dec. 1865	14, Nov.	23	208	Siegmeier	Woodville, OH	Herxheim am Berg, Rheinkreis Baiern
Knorr, Johan F.	7, Apr. 1879	12, Mar.	40- 2m-10d	111		Alden, IA	Großmedling, Mecklenburg-Schwerin
Knosp, Rosine Therese	25, Dec. 1882	12, Dec.	56- -23d	415	Meier	Omaha, NE	Biberach, Württemberg
Knost, Heinrich	16, Aug. 1888	2, Aug.	67	526		Rock Island, IL	Mecklenburg-Schwerin
Knost, Margaretha	20, July 1885	2, July	68	7	Hartkorn	Rock Island, IL	Baiern
Knote, Carolina	2, July 1857	19, June	22	108		Monroe, IL	Sulz, Rothenburg, Kurhessen
Knoth, (Mr)	16, June 1859	11, Apr.	63	96		Red Bud, IL	Kurhessen
Knoth, John	17, Mar. 1884	19, Jan.	58	7		Mascoutah, IL	Sulz, Kurhessen
Knülling, August	19, Jan. 1885	25, Dec.	42	7		Owatonna, MN	Norten, Hannover
Knüpfer, Gottlieb Heinrich	20, Nov. 1890	30, Oct.	64	750	Schwäbelein	Kansas City, KS	Dittersdorf bei Schleiz, Sachsen
Knupfer, Johanne M.	28, Dec. 1899	29, Nov.	74	828	Heinemann	Kansas City, KS	Vionau, Erfurt, Preußen
Knüppel, Margaretha	6, Apr. 1863	6, Mar.	35- 1m- 6d	56		Melrose, NY	Schönheim, Ziegenhain, Kurhessen
Knüttel, Johan	24, Mar. 1887	5, Mar.	62- 3m- 4d	190		Hicksville, NY	Rützts, Mecklenburg-Schwerin
Knüttel, Maria Dorothea	9, Apr. 1877		81-10m	119		Brooklyn, NY	Altenhagen, Mecklenburg
Koate, Friedrich	26, Nov. 1866	10, Nov.		382		Herman, MO	Birkhausen, Minden, Preußen
Kobel, Jane	17, Nov. 1873	2, Sept	52	367		Columbus, IL	Roxbury, Scotland

Christliche Apologete Death Notices --- 1839 - 1899

Name of Deceased	Notice Date	Death Date	Age	Page	Maiden Name	Place of Death	Place of Birth
Kobel, Lilian	19, Dec. 1895	6, Nov.	23	814		Champaign, IL	Steffenhagen, Mecklenburg-Schwerin
Kobel, Sophia	28, Jan. 1897	11, Dec.	60	62		Monticello, IL	Eichstettin, Emmendingen, Baden
Köbelin, Wilhelmine	11, Apr. 1889	12, Mar.	76	238	Haug	Laporte, IN	Pfullingen, Reutlingen, Württemberg
Kober, Anna Maria	23, Oct. 1865	8, Oct.	80- 2m	172	Heyd	Bucyrus, OH	Crawford County, Ohio
Kober, Daniel	29, Dec. 1887	10, Dec.	39	830		Galion, OH	Pennsylvania
Kober, Georg	1, May 1882	14, Apr.	63- 5m- 9d	143		Galion, OH	Falkenberg, Osterburg, Sachsen
Kober, J. H.	26, Aug. 1897	7, Aug.	61	543		Charles City, IA	Crawford County, Ohio
Kober, Maria	11, Aug. 1873	20, July	18-10m-20d	255	Hirtz	Bucyrus, OH	
Kober, Samuel	11, Aug. 1873	18, July	17- 9m-19d	255		Bucyrus, OH	
Kobetz, Crescentia	23, June 1859		10	100		St. Louis, MO	
Kobi, Andreas	30, Jan. 1896		66	78		Ora Labor, IA	Baden
Kobi, Anna Elisabeth	16, Nov. 1885	26, Oct.	42	7	Weyrauch	Des Moines, IA	Warren County, Missouri
Kobicke, Otto	11, Feb. 1886	29, Dec.	24	7		San Francisco, CA	San Francisco, California
Köbke, Johan David	14, Nov. 1881	29, Oct.	81- 4m-11d	367		Oconomowoc, WI	Sukow an der Plöne, Piritz, Pommern
Koch , Friedrich Johan	28, Mar. 1895	9, Mar.	76	206		Warrenton, MO	Valdorf, Herford, Preußen
Koch , Sophie	11, Apr. 1895	24, Mar.	64	238	Moor	Zion, OH	Großeneixen, Mecklenburg-Schwerin
Koch, (Mrs)	15, June 1863	5, May	40- 4m-13d	96	Tölke	Union, MO	Lippe-Detmold
Koch, Adolph	7, July 1879	9, June	23- 7m- 7d	215		Sioux Falls, SD	Großfurra, Schwarzburg-Sondershausen
Koch, Alwine	16, June 1898	2, June	34	383		Sheboygan, WI	Mosel, Germany
Koch, Anna	4, Jan. 1875	27, Nov.	81- 1m-28d	7	Rothmeier	Plattsmouth, NE	Schwegenheim, Germersheim, Rheinkreis Baiern
Koch, Anna Barbara	22, Mar. 1880	Mar.	46	95	Ludwig	Howard, NE	Niederdunlau, Mühlhausen, Erfurt, Thüringen
Koch, Anna Catharina	14, May 1896	25, Apr.	62	318		Quincy, IL	Bielefeld, Westphalen
Koch, Anna M.	23, Mar. 1899	5, Feb.	79	191	Münch	Indianapolis, IN	Niederlust, Rheinpfalz Baiern
Koch, Anna Maria	5, Mar. 1896	7, Feb.		158	Stein	Ridgefield, WA	Holzhausen, Sulz, Württemberg
Koch, Anna Maria	28, Feb. 1876	28, Jan.	53- 6m- 3d	71		Red Wing, MN	
Koch, Anna Sibila	23, Mar. 1893	17, Feb.	64	190		Burlington, IA	Schwegenheim, Rheinpfalz Baiern
Koch, Barbara	4, Apr. 1889	16, Mar.	66-11m-18d	222		Jefferson City, MO	Untersteinach, Weidenberg, Baiern
Koch, Christian	3, Mar. 1884	15, Feb.	58- 9m-20d	7		San Antonio, TX	Berg, Ebersbach, Nassau
Koch, Christina	26, Mar. 1896	21, Feb.	62	206	Wallieser	Mt. Pleasant, IA	Kleinsachsenheim, Württemberg
Koch, Christoph	7, Feb. 1850	20, Jan.	58	24		Chillicothe, OH	Rheinpfalz Baiern
Koch, Conrad	16, Dec. 1852	9, Nov.	41-10m-14d	204		Portsmouth, OH	Imbshausen, Hannover
Koch, Elisabeth	18, Mar.1872	28, Feb.	28	95	Hohmann	Buffalo, NY	Neckargemünd, Baden
Koch, Elisabeth	18, June 1883		31	199	Werly	Canton, MO	Lagrange, Missouri
Koch, Elisabeth	28, Apr. 1859	4, Apr.	23- 3m	68	Weil	Quincy, IL	
Koch, Elisabeth	26, July 1860	30, June	16- 4m	120		New Knoxville, OH	
Koch, Elisabeth Catharine	28, Mar. 1864	19, Feb.	38	52	Reinheimer	Brooklyn, NY	Russelheim, Hessen-Darmstadt
Koch, Elise Katharina	3, Apr. 1890	14, Feb.	58	222	Bartels	Brooklyn, NY	Ottendorf, Stade, Hannover
Koch, Emil	14, Aug. 1882	11, July	22- 1m- 1d	263		Chicago, IL	Gudersdorf, Preußen
Koch, Emilie Catharina	22, Mar. 1880	15, Jan.	22- 1m	95		Jersey City, NJ	
Koch, Emma	28, Jan. 1897	7, Jan.	21	62		Bloomington, IL	Bloomington, Illinois
Koch, Fr. Wilhelm	15, Mar. 1880	22, Feb.	51- 7m	87		Quincy, IL	Heben, Westphalen
Koch, Franz Heinrich	16, June 1887	28, May	80	382		New Melle, MO	Drantum, Hannover
Koch, Friederike	13, Mar. 1882	22, Feb.	74-10m-15d	87	Schelak	Marine City, MI	Preußen
Koch, Friederike	27, Sept 1875	23, Aug.	17- 1m	311		Mt. Pleasant, IA	
Koch, Friedrich	1, Dec. 1898	31, Oct.	82	767		LaCrosse, WI	Groß-Furra, Schwarzburg-Sondershausen
Koch, Friedrich C.	2, Mar. 1899	2, Feb.	20	143		Saginaw, MI	Saginaw, Michigan

Christliche Apologete Death Notices --- 1839 - 1899

Name of Deceased	Notice Date	Death Date	Age	Page	Maiden Name	Place of Death	Place of Birth
Koch, Friedrich W.	13, July 1863	25, May	19- 5m-23d	112		LaCrosse, WI	St. Louis, Missouri
Koch, Friedrich W.	10, June 1878	11, May	29	183		Union, MO	Hollenbach, Künzelsau, Württemberg
Koch, Georg	27, Oct. 1884	1, Oct.	61- 8m-18d	7		Giard, IA	
Koch, Georg Albert	24, Nov. 1887	4, Nov.	16- 9m- 6d	750		Waco, TX	
Koch, Gustav Adolph	26, May 1879	13, May		167		Quincy, IL	
Koch, Heinrich	3, May 1894	1, Apr.	43	294		Kansas City, MO	Osage Bluff, Cole County, Missouri
Koch, Heinrich	18, Nov. 1872	19, Oct.	67	375		Hebron, IA	Bostedt, Schleswig-Holstein
Koch, Heinrich D.	15, Mar. 1880	10, Feb.	80	86		Hopewell, MO	Silixen, Lippe
Koch, Heinrich Friedrich	2, July 1896	3, June	48	431		Almond, WI	Langensalza, Thüringen
Koch, Helena	11, July 1864	20, June	9	112		Cincinnati, OH	
Koch, Herman A. (Rev)	25, Mar. 1897	13, Mar.	68	184		Chicago, IL	Lohmerfeld, Preußen
Koch, Herman Heinrich	15, Mar. 1888	5, Feb.		174		Baltimore, MD	Bruchmühlen, Hannover
Koch, Ida	21, Aug. 1882		58- 2m-15d	271	Lorenz	Milwaukee, WI	Kantzow, Mecklenburg
Koch, J. Mathilde	29, Sept 1879	13, Sept	23-11m- 3d	311		San Antonio, TX	Petersburg, Mecklenburg-Strelitz
Koch, Johan	11, Aug. 1884	23, Feb.	65- 4m-13d	7		Milwaukee, WI	Thüringen
Koch, Johan Andreas	14, May 1891		83-10m	318		New York City, NY	
Koch, Johan Benjamin	17, Nov. 1862	26, Oct.	3- 7m-14d	184		Defiance, OH	
Koch, Johan Friedrich	4, Feb. 1892	10, Jan.	58	78		Mt. Pleasant, IA	Hefingen, Leonberg, Württemberg
Koch, Johan Heinrich	23, Mar. 1899	13, Feb.	82	191		Pekin, IL	Badersleben, Preußen
Koch, Johan Nikolaus	10, Dec. 1896	14, Nov.	69	798		Edwardsville, IL	Mühlhausen, Elsaß
Koch, Johan Peter	30, June 1887	11, June	78	414		Morrison, MO	Döhlau bei Hof, Baiern
Koch, Johan Wilhelm	8, Dec. 1887	10, Nov.	59	782		Quincy, IL	Dittelsheim am Rhein, Preußen
Koch, Johan Wilhelm	23, May 1864	30, Apr.	11- 6m-14d	84		Red Wing, MN	
Koch, Johanna	25, Nov. 1858	21, Oct.	41	188		LaCrosse, WI	Großfurra, Schwarzburg-Sondershausen
Koch, John	8, Feb. 1894	9, Jan.	80	94		Bucyrus, OH	Lycoming County, Pennsylvania
Koch, Karolina	28, Jan. 1886	9, Jan.	19	7		Yellow Creek, IL	Jo Davis County, Illinois
Koch, Katharina Maria Dorothea	10, Feb. 1887	17, Jan.	56	94	Pätzhorn	Milwaukee, WI	Altenebstorf, Hannover
Koch, Lena	23, May 1870	26, Apr.	18- 2m- 9d	167		Red Wing, MN	
Koch, Magdalena	10, Apr. 1882	19, Mar.	53	119	Heberly	Loran, IL	Haferschlacht, Württemberg
Koch, Margaretha	30, Oct. 1856	8, Oct.	60- 8m	176	Götz	Red Wing, MN	Hildesheim, Hessen-Darmstadt
Koch, Margaretha	6, Feb. 1890	19, Jan.	76-11m- 6d	94	Stoppler	Seymour, IN	Wallroth, Kurhessen
Koch, Maria	24, Sept 1896	22, Aug.	69	623	Rheinfranke	Plattsville, NE	Haßloch bei Neustatt an der Hard, Germany
Koch, Maria Barbara	11, Nov. 1886	25, Oct.	83	7	Ruchnart	Poughkeepsie, NY	Weißenburg, Elsaß
Koch, Maria Sophia	15, Apr. 1897	10, Mar.	85	239	Ahrens	Kendallville, IN	Damkow bei Wismar, Mecklenburg-Schwerin
Koch, Marie	26, Oct. 1874	14, Oct.	22	343		Giard, IA	
Koch, Matthäus	10, Feb. 1873	20, Jan.	57- 9m-15d	47		Danville, IL	Winterlingen, Valingen, Württemberg
Koch, Metta	18, May 1885	27, Apr.	64	7	Blome	Peoria, IL	Osterholz bei Bremen, Germany
Koch, Pauline	9, Apr. 1866	21, Mar.	9	118		Sheboygan, WI	
Koch, Rosa	17, Aug. 1893	17, July	67	526	Faußer	Jersey City, NJ	Tübingen, Württemberg
Koch, Rosina	20, Oct. 1862			168		Cole County, MO	
Koch, Sarah	10, May 1894	10, Apr.	71	310	Jung	Bucyrus, OH	Lycoming County, Pennsylvania
Koch, Sarah	21, May 1847	29, Apr.	34- 8m-20d	83		Woodville, OH	
Koch, Simon	10, Jan. 1856		61	8		Pekin, IL	Ostfriesland
Koch, Sophia	7, Aug. 1851	18, June	50	128		Portsmouth, OH	
Koch, Sophia	4, Feb. 1878	26, Dec.	51- -16d	39		Bayonne, NJ	
Koch, Sophie Charlotte	18, Mar. 1897	14, Feb.	73	175		Pinckney, MO	Langenholzhausen, Lippe-Detmold

Name of Deceased	Notice Date	Death Date	Age	Page	Maiden Name	Place of Death	Place of Birth
Koch, Susanna	10, Jan. 1876	10, Dec.	21	15	Groß	Bucyrus, OH	Crawford County, Ohio
Koch, Theresa Mathilde	15, May 1882	20, Apr.	20- 6m-28d	159		Plymouth, WI	Mössingen, Rottenburg, Württemberg
Koch, Ursula	26, May 1862	9, May	28	84		Portsmouth, OH	
Koch, Walburga	24, Jan. 1871		62- 8m	31		Leland, MI	
Koch, Wilhelm	13, Oct. 1859	23, Sept.	39	164		LaCrosse, WI	Gleisenau, Würzburg, Baiern
Koch, Wilhelm	19, Mar. 1896	10, Feb.	77	190		Plymouth, WI	Breitungen, Sachsen
Koch, Wilhelm	9, Apr. 1866	25, Mar.	12	118		Sheboygan, WI	
Koch, Wilhelm	5, July 1875	18, June	21- 4m-14d	215		Brooklyn, NY	
Koch, Wilhelmine	27, Oct. 1879	4, Oct.	32	343		Union, MO	Löhne, Herford, Minden, Westphalen
Koch, Willie Heinrich	6, Nov. 1890	2, Oct.	12	718		Almond, WI	Almond, Wisconsin
Kochenberger, Georg	4, Feb. 1878	22, Dec.	65	39		Bland, MO	
Köcher, Katharina	27, Nov. 1876	23, Oct.	77- 9m-10d	383		Salem, MN	Kammer, Bückeburg, Lippe-Schaumburg
Kocher, Maria Elisabeth	10, Jan. 1895	10, Dec.	35	30	Häßler	Los Angeles, CA	Syracuse, New York
Köchle, Caroline	25, Feb. 1892	28, Jan.	57	126	Richter	Brenham, TX	Bransge bei Löbau, Sachsen
Köchle, Eduard	27, Aug. 1877	10, Aug.	18-10m- 1d	279		Cleveland, OH	
Ködding, Anna Elisabeth	13, Dec. 1894	14, Nov.	79	806	Stahl	Wakefield, NY	Mechsscheide, Kurhessen
Ködding, Justus	4, Oct. 1860		21	160		Mt. Vernon, IN	
Ködding, Nicolaus	28, Oct. 1872	24, Aug.	40- - 4d	351		Schnectady, NY	Huntshausen, Hessen-Kassel
Koeble, Fr.	29, July 1878	9, July	26	239		Dallas City, IL	Hegensberg, Eßlingen, Württemberg
Koebrich, Georg	9, Oct. 1890	14, Sept	16- 8m-16d	654		Charles City, IA	Charles City, Iowa
Koedding, Georg Wilhelm	19, May 1879	2, May	15	159		Schnectady, NY	
Koedelhan, Amalia	26, Dec. 1889	1, Dec.	81	830	Schultz	Jordan, MN	Ludwigslust, Mecklenburg-Schwerin
Koehler, Conrad	8, Dec. 1887	28, Oct.	22	782		Lawrence, KS	Germany
Koeller, Friedrich	13, Feb. 1890	17, Jan.	54	110		Berne, MI	Neustadt an der Haardt, Rheinkreis Baiern
Koeller, Christian	20, Oct. 1898	15, Sept	85	670		Peoria, IL	Lippe-Detmold
Koelsch, Anna Maria	17, Dec. 1877	23, Nov.	58	407	Weinbrenner	Chicago, IL	Lanzenbrück, Hachenburg, Nassau
Koeneke, Louise Katharina	3, Nov. 1887	5, Oct.	40	702	Hackmann	Arenzville, IL	Arenzville, Illinois
Koepke, Anna	6, Mar. 1882	14, Jan.	80-11m- 2d	79		Algona, IA	Büsso, Köslin, Hinterpommern
Koepke, Johanna	8, Nov. 1888	21, Aug.	46	718	Acker	Whittemore, IA	HinterPommern
Koerner, Alfred Leopold	12, Sept 1881	19, Aug.	3- 8m-19d	295		Sleepy Eye, MN	
Koerner, Matthias	6, Jan. 1887	15, Dec.	56	14		Crandon, SD	Oderheim, Hessen-Darmstadt
Koerper, Michael	1, Dec. 1879	10, Nov.	44	383		Milwaukee, WI	Germersheim, Baiern
Koger, Johan Ernst	4, July 1889		78	430		Flood Creek, IA	Augen, Baden
Koger, Johan Ernst	11, July 1889	15, June	78- -16d	446		Charles City, IA	Baden
Köhl, (Mr)	30, Dec. 1867	14, Dec.	75- 5m- 3d	414		East Troy, WI	Zaberfeld, Brackenheim, Württemberg
Köhl, (Mrs)	8, Jan. 1866	12, Dec.	59	14		Bucyrus, OH	Hohenstraßen, Württemberg
Kohl, Dorothea	23, May 1889	2, May	80- 6m- 3d	334	Müller	LaCrosse, WI	Matzdorf, HinterPommern
Kohl, Jakob	31, Aug. 1899	5, Aug.	64	559		New Albany, IN	Dresel, Hessen-Darmstadt
Kohl, Katharina	4, Nov. 1878	23, Sept	42	351	Zeilmann	New Albany, IN	Haag, Oberfranken, Baiern
Köhl, Philipp	2, Jan. 1871	14, Sept	67	7		Carver, MN	
Köhl, Rosina	7, Apr. 1862	17, Mar.	71	56		East Troy, WI	Zaverfeld, Brackenheim, Württemberg
Kohl, Sarah Anna	11, May 1899	17, Apr.	81	302		Baltimore, MD	Pennsylvania
Kohl, Wilhelmine	16, May 1861	19, Apr.	37	80		East Troy, WI	Schiffelbein, Pommern
Kohlberg, Elisabeth	24, May 1860	9, May	37	84	Leje	Cincinnati, OH	Rehmsfeld, Homburg, Kurhessen
Kohlberg, Joseph	30, Mar. 1874	17, Mar.	50	103		Covington, KY	Herstelle, Preußen
Köhle, Gottlieb	28, Dec. 1893	7, Dec.	77	828		LaCrosse, WI	Emmigen, Nagold, Württemberg

Christliche Apologete Death Notices --- 1839 - 1899

Name of Deceased	Notice Date	Death Date	Age	Maiden Name	Place of Death	Page	Place of Birth
Kohlenberger, Christina	26, Jan. 1863	9, Jan.	27- 1m- 6d		Edgerton, OH	16	Brackenheim, Württemberg
Kohler, Andreas	5, Aug. 1878	30, June	79- -25d		Ripley, OH	247	Hausen ob Verena, Tuttlingen, Württemberg
Köhler, Anna	9, Feb. 1880	30, Jan.	50	Sauser	Covington, KY	47	Speckelbach, Amweiler, Baiern
Köhler, Anna Maria	1, June 1874	16, Apr.	68	Kabold	Bradford, IN	175	Loffen, Bern, Schweiz
Köhler, Barbara	15, May 1882	22, Apr.	73		Eudora, KS	159	Aufhausen, Geißlingen, Württemberg
Köhler, Barbara	20, Dec. 1888	20, Nov.	49-11m	Ströhle	Rochester, NY	814	
Köhler, Barbara	21, June 1855	24, May	50		Rochester, NY	100	Gengenbach, Kinzigthal, Baden
Köhler, Caroline	16, July 1877	24, June	40- 4m		St. Johns, MI	231	
Köhler, Caroline	30, Dec. 1886	2, Dec.		Weber	Fredericksburg, TX	7	
Köhler, Christian	21, Apr. 1892	4, Apr.	76- 5m- 5d		Louisville, KY	254	Bönnigheim, Besigheim, Württemberg
Köhler, Christian	14, June 1880	9, May	65		Beaver Dam, MN	191	Groß Ehrenberg, Soldin, Brandenburg
Köhler, Christian	12, July 1880	9, May	65		Beaver Dam, WI	223	Groß Ehrenberg, Soldin, Brandenburg
Köhler, Christina	7, Oct. 1858	16, Sept	15- 7m-26d		Rochester, NY	160	
Köhler, Conrad	17, July 1865	3, June	56		Bristol, IN	116	Hausen, Zabergäu, Württemberg
Köhler, Elisabeth	23, Nov. 1863	9, Oct.	61- 4m		West Union, OH	188	
Köhler, Elisabeth	31, Aug. 1874	13, Aug.	15- 9m		St. Louis, MO	279	Berlin, Preußen
Köhler, Emilie	9, June 1892	12, May	65		Zumbro Falls, MN	366	Ostramonta, Merseburg, Preußen
Köhler, Eva S.	3, Oct. 1889	10, Sept	71- 7m-16d		Papillion, NE	638	Beutelsbach, Württemberg
Köhler, Friederika	25, Feb. 1897	8, Feb.	77		Louisville, KY	127	Tapinau bei Königsberg, Preußen
Köhler, Gustav Moritz	30, June 1873	5, June	54		Worchester, MA	207	Harrison County, Indiana
Köhler, Heinrich	12, June 1871	13, Apr.	24		Bradford, IN	191	Schmalkalden in der Aue,
Köhler, Heinrich Wilhelm	15, Mar. 1894	26, Feb.	76		Clearwater, MN	182	Oerie, Calenberg, Hannover
Köhler, Hinr.	17, Feb. 1887	25, Jan.	78		Lemars, IA	110	Hardt bei Neustadt, Rheinkreis Baiern
Köhler, Jakob	5, June 1865	10, May	20		St. Johns, MI	92	Kaiserslautern, Germany
Köhler, Jakob	10, Nov. 1887	25, Oct.	76		Freeport, IL	718	Oeric, Amt Kalenburg, Hannover
Köhler, Johan Conrad	17, Feb. 1868	19, Dec.	65- 1m-20d		Pomeroy, OH	55	Leibenstadt, Adelsheim, Baden
Köhler, Johan Michael	26, Nov. 1896	17, Oct.	77		Boelus, NE	766	
Köhler, Johann G	20, Jan. 1853	18, Nov.	18- 4m-20d		New Albany, IN	12	Floyd County, Indiana
Köhler, Johannes	18, Nov. 1897	2, Nov.	41		New Albany, IN	735	
Köhler, John	3, Aug. 1874	9, July	18- 8m- 4d		St. Joseph, MO	247	
Köhler, Juliana	29, Nov. 1888	22, Oct.	86- 4m	Ehresmann	DeWitt, MI	766	Hart bei Neustadt, Baiern
Köhler, Juliane	5, Mar. 1891	11, Feb.	50- -12d	Berg	New Melle, MO	158	Warren County, Missouri
Köhler, Karl	12, Jan. 1880	27, Dec.	82- 3m-23d		Flood Creek, IA	15	Ehrenberg, Kreis Soldin, Brandenburg
Köhler, Karl Wilhelm	22, Apr. 1878	1, Apr.	34- 6m- 7d		Fond du Lac, WI	127	
Köhler, Karoline	4, Aug. 1898	18, May	83		Schnectady, NY	495	Bremen, Germany
Köhler, Karoline Susanna	28, Apr. 1887	10, Apr.			DeWitt, MI	270	Bingham Twp, Clinton County, Michigan
Köhler, Katharina Elisabeth	26, June 1882	29, May	30- -28d	Löber	New York City, NY	207	Rabertshausen, Hessen-Darmstadt
Köhler, Lydia	21, Feb. 1876	10, Jan.	17-11m-18d		Lemars, IA	63	
Köhler, Maria	7, Jan. 1884	19, Dec.	27		Salina, KS	7	Wills County, Illinois
Köhler, Maria Elisabeth	24, July 1876	22, June	77	Schünemann	Flood Creek, IA	239	Amt Bernstein, Preußen
Köhler, Rosine Chr.	5, May 1884	23, Apr.	23	Reif	Scranton, PA	7	Dornstettin, Freudenstadt, Württemberg
Köhler, Salome	14, June 1880	15, May	85- -24d		Sandusky, OH	191	Blankenloch, Karlsruhe, Baden
Köhler, Samuel Louis	20, Dec. 1894	24, Nov.	34		Lemars, IA	822	Galena, Illinois
Köhler, W.	11, May 1899	20, Apr.	90-11m-17d		Papillion, NE	302	Rettgenstädt, Merseburg, Preußen
Köhlerschmidt, Henry	23, Dec. 1897	22, Nov.	75		Baltimore, MD	815	Oberlangenstadt, Oberfranken, Baiern
Kohlhaase, Christian J.	23, Apr. 1896	3, Apr.	36		Sleepy Eye, MN	270	Hilpernhausen, Hessen

Christliche Apologete Death Notices --- 1839 - 1899

Name of Deceased	Notice Date	Death Date	Age	Maiden Name	Page	Place of Death	Place of Birth
Kohlhase, Johan	23, May 1889	12, May	23		334	Sleepy Eye, MN	Milford, Brown County, Minnesota
Kohlhase, Maria	9, June 1892	16, May	20		366	Sleepy Eye, MN	Home, Brown County, Minnesota
Kohlhase, Maria	2, Feb. 1893	1, Jan.	58	Schade	78	Sleepy Eye, MN	Kohlhausen, Kurhessen
Kohlhasse, Heinrich	9, Apr. 1877	10, Feb.			119	Sleepy Eye, MN	
Kohlhepp, Henriette	20, Oct. 1873	9, Oct.	24		335	Cottleville, MO	Schlüctern, Kurhessen
Köhli, Christian	10, Mar. 1898	10, Feb.	79	Hilberg	158	Gladbrook, IA	Kul–, Bern, Schweiz
Kohlmann, (Mrs)	16, Feb. 1888	27, Jan.	70		110	New York City, NY	Hude, Oldenburg
Kohlmann, Barbara	8, Mar. 1894	31, Jan.	86	Reister	166	New Albany, IN	Stein, Baden
Kohlmann, Heinrich	31, July 1846		Inquiry		123	Sigarne, IA	
Kohlmeier, Wilhelm	26, Sept 1850	17, Aug.	53- - 1d		156	Chester, IL	Eisbergen bei Minden, Preußen
Kohls, C.W.	28, Apr. 1892	27, Mar.	76		270	Wheatland, WI	Volzkow, Koslin, Pommern
Kohls, Christian Friedrich Wilhelm	30, Oct. 1890	3, Oct.	58		702	Brownton, MN	Boltenhagen, Köslin, Pommern
Kohlstäst, Friederike Katharine L.	25, Oct. 1875	8, Oct.	76- 7m-27d		343	Yellow Creek, IL	Bistrup, Lippe-Detmold
Kohlstedt, Emma Louise	7, May 1896	10, Apr.	26		302	Minneapolis, MN	Buffalo, Wright County, Minnesota
Kohn, Katharine	27, July 1893	24, June	39	Häffner	478	Columbus, OH	Kuppishausen, Württemberg
Kohn, Rebekka	13, Sept 1875	19, Aug.	32- 9m-13d	Nuding	295	Columbus, OH	
Köhn, Wilhelm	9, Dec. 1897	16, Nov.	45		783	Milwaukee, WI	Bartow, Vorpommern
Kohne, Carolina Louise	28, Feb. 1895	28, Jan.	57	Wiebling	142	Toledo, OH	Hannover
Köhnemann, Emilie F. W.	23, May 1895	23, Apr.	40	Wessow	334	Ballwin, MO	Preis, Pommern
Köhnhorst, Sophia Maria Louisa	25, Jan. 1869	8, Jan.	26	Brinkmeyer	31	Evansville, IN	Cincinnati, Hamilton County, Ohio
Kohnke, Frank K.	10, Aug. 1893	22, July	39		510	Allegan, MI	Rommelsburg, Preußen
Köhnke, Friederike	22, May 1882	3, May	72		167	Honey Creek, WI	
Kohring, Charlotte	3, Mar. 1892	5, Feb.	75	Weghorst	142	Owatonna, MN	Brokum, Hannover
Kohring, Gerhard	21, Apr. 1887	31, Mar.	66		254	Owatonna, MN	Hagewede, Lemförde, Hannover
Kohrs, Cord	21, July 1862	3, July	20- 9m-15d		116	Pettes Co, MO	Pettes County, Missouri
Koke, Christine Wilhelmine	11, Mar. 1897	20, Feb.	67		158	New Orleans, LA	Westphalen
Kokemor, Johann Heinrich	5, May 1862	19, Mar.	23- -20d	Lange	72	Santa Claus, IN	Drone, Dielingen, Preußen
Kokomar, Johannes	14, Oct. 1858	8, Sept	54		164	Santa Claus, IN	Dielingen, Münden, Preußen
Kokomoor, Lucinde	12, Oct. 1899	18, Sept	39		655	Santa Claus, IN	Santa Claus, Indiana
Kolb, Emma	6, Nov. 1882	23, Oct.	15-11m-25d		359	Mt. Vernon, NY	
Kolb, Genoveva	31, Dec. 1896	6, Dec.	64	Zimmermann	844	Mt. Vernon, NY	
Kolb, Gottlieb	5, Apr. 1875	27, Feb.	36- 2m-11d		111	Clayton, WI	Tettnang, Württemberg
Kolb, Jakob	6, Feb. 1890	14, Jan.	72- 3m-29d		94	Baltimore, MD	Weiler, Schorndorf, Württemberg
Kolb, Jost Heinrich	17, Jan. 1889	21, Dec.	64		46	Sandwich, IL	Bahnbrücken, Bretten, Baden
Kolb, Katharina	30, Mar. 1893	8, Mar.	60	Widman	206	Jersey City, NJ	Breitscheid, Hessen-Nassau
Kolb, Margaretha	28, Nov. 1889	29, Oct.	66	Kerbs	766	Rush Lake, WI	Feuerbach, Stuttgart, Württemberg
Kolb, Philipp	8, Nov. 1860	16, Sept	33- 1m- 6d		180	Kassath, OH	Keffenoh, Elsaß
Kolbe, (Mrs)	20, Nov. 1865	27, Oct.	60- 3m		188	Red Wing, MN	Babenhausen, Hessen-Darmstadt
Kolbe, Anna Barbara	1, Mar. 1869	13, Feb.	80	Glein	71	Cincinnati, OH	Heinbach, Spangenberg, Kurhessen
Kolbe, August	18, Aug. 1862	17, June	49		132	New Albany, IN	Kleinfahnern, Sachsen-Coburg-Gotha
Kolbe, Clara	8, Dec. 1887	18, Nov.	15		782	Rochester, MN	
Kolbe, Dorothea Maria	2, Apr. 1877	4, Mar.	76- 2m-18d		111	Marine City, MI	Pakulent bei Greifenhagen, Preußen
Kolbe, Elisabeth	23, Feb. 1874	10, Feb.	63	Kolmar	63	Cincinnati, OH	Ellenbach, Rodenburg, Kurhessen
Kolbe, Georg	20, Jan. 1887	3, Jan.			46	Council Grove, KS	
Kolbe, Henriette Caroline	28, Apr. 1873	15, Apr.	25- 7m	Lesemann	135	Leavenworth, MN	Hannover, Lake County, Indiana
Kolbe, Hermann	17, Jan. 1856	4, Jan.	65		12	Cincinnati, OH	Niedergode, Amt Rothenburg, Hessen-Kassel

Christliche Apologete Death Notices --- 1839 - 1899

Name of Deceased	Notice Date	Death Date	Age	Maiden Name	Page	Place of Death	Place of Birth
Kolbe, Johan H.	4, Jan. 1875	22, Nov.	7		7	Mineola, MN	Indiana
Kolbe, Johan W. F.	29, Sept 1887	6, Sept	22- 3m-24d		622	Rochester, MN	Mt. Pleasant, Wabasha County, Minnesota
Kolbe, Katharina	16, May 1861	14, Apr.	20- 6m		80	Cincinnati, OH	
Kolbe, Martin	28, Apr. 1898	7, Apr.	65- 1m-11d		271	Rochester, MN	Niederhut, Kurhessen
Kolbe, Werner	24, July 1882	10, June	83		239	Rochester, MN	Niedemgude, Rodenburg, Kurhessen
Kolbe, Werner	30, Nov. 1868	3, Nov.	69		383	Cincinnati, OH	Nieder-Gude, Kurhessen
Kolbenschlag, Franz Gerhard	9, Nov. 1893	3, Aug.	63- 2m-29d		718	Newark, NJ	Königsbach, Germany
Kolberg, Christian	8, June 1899	9, May	74		367	Sheboygan, WI	Mark Brandenburg, Preußen
Kolbus, Martha M.	7, Jan. 1897	3, Nov.	21		15	Garden City, KS	Lafayette County, Missouri
Kölke, Mina	6, June 1895	17, Apr.	63		366	Golden City, MO	Grebs, Dürwitz, Mecklenburg-Schwerin
Koll, Heinrich	25, Sept 1846		Inquiry		165	St. Louis, MO	Odenhausen, Grümberg, Hessen-Darmstadt
Kollas, Anna Katharina	13, Oct. 1884	16, Sept	56	Fey	7	St. Louis, MO	Wehrheim, Wiesbaden, Nassau
Kollas, Mary	9, May 1881	23, Apr.	16- 4m-20d		151	St. Louis, MO	Wehrheim, Nassau
Kollath, Ernestine Wilhelmine H.	29, Apr. 1886	3, Apr.	51		7	Wausau, WI	Wangeritz, Naugard, Preußen
Kollensberg, Anna	29, Mar. 1888	29, Feb.	59	Maas	206	Santa Claus, IN	Schledehausen, Osnabrück, Hannover
Köller, Anna Elisabeth	3, Mar. 1884	16, Feb.	36	Butt	7	Secor, IL	Oldenburg
Koller, Anna Franciska	30, Nov. 1863	29, Oct.	329	Wichmann	192	LaCrosse, WI	Dobern, Benzen, Kreis Leibaer, Böhmen
Köller, Caroline Wilhelmine A.	27, June 1870	2, May	49	Rischel	207	New Haven, CT	Gransee, Brandenburg, Preußen
Koller, Catharine	12, Sept 1889	23, Aug.	82- 1m	Elsholz	590	Le Sueur, MN	
Köller, Christine Wilhelmine Louise	20, Apr. 1874	31, Mar.	64- 9m-17d	Bremer	127	Secor, IL	Thale bei Pyrmont, Waldeck
Kölling, Anna Elisabeth	16, Mar. 1893	10, Feb.	85	Assum	174	Warren, MO	Amsterdam, Holland
Kölling, Dina	19, May 1887	28, Apr.	58		318	Oregon, MO	Lotte, Westphalen
Kölling, Ernst	28, Jan. 1878	13, Jan.	69- 3m		31	Warren, MO	Buer, Amt Melle, Hannover
Kölling, Friedrich	5, Oct. 1893	6, Sept	75-11m-19d		638	Evansville, IN	Oeringsen bei Minden, Preußen
Kölling, Katharina Justine	29, Sept 1879	23, Aug.	21- 4d	Hube	311	Truxton, MO	
Kölling, Louise	22, Sept 1853	12, Aug.	31-11m-13d		152	Evansville, IN	
Kölling, Louise	31, Jan. 1870	17, Dec.	16		39	Warren, MO	Warren County, Missouri
Kölling, Maria	19, Nov. 1891	27, Oct.	79	Kurtz	750	Evansville, IN	Schareich, Württemberg
Kölling, Maria	11, May 1893	7, Apr.	36	Bebermeier	302	Warren, MO	Warren County, Missouri
Kölling, Maria Elisabeth	10, July 1890	18, June	66	Tismeyer	446	Warren, MO	Burr, Melle, Hannover
Kölling, Matthias	14, Aug. 1865	25, June	19		132	Warrenton, MO	
Kölling, Wilhelmine	5, July 1888	1, June	42- 8m-22d	Düwel	430	Hopewell, MO	
Kollmann, (Mr)	15, Apr. 1872		76		127	Athens, NE	Fokenga, Ostfriesland
Kollmann, Gerhard J.	26, Feb. 1872	5, Feb.	73		71	Tecumseh, NE	Friel, Amt Stickhausen, Ostfriesland
Kollmer, Christiana	28, Dec. 1868	7, Dec.	74- 5m-24d		415	Delaware, OH	Eßlingen, Württemberg
Kollmer, Friederika	10, Jan. 1876	15, Dec.	52	Pfeifer	15	Kossuth, OH	Bernhbach, Neuenbürg, Württemberg
Kolmeier, Marie	11, Feb. 1858	20, Jan.	29- 3m	Breimer	24	Kingston, IL	Heugel, Osnabrück, Hannover
Kolms, Friedrich	27, June 1870	1, June	71		207	Sand Creek, MN	Heinersdorf, Liegnitz, Preußen
Kolnsberg, Heinrich	6, Mar. 1871	1, Feb.	49-11m		79	Santa Claus, IN	Erichshagen, Amt Wälven, Hannover
Kolpke, Wilhelm Fr.	15, Sept 1879	26, Aug.	29		295	Nebraska City, NE	Petersdorf, Mecklenburg-Strelitz
Kölsch, Daniel	9, Oct. 1890	7, Sept	80		654	Chicago, IL	Neunkhausen, Hachenburg, Nassau
Kölsch, Ludwig	9, Apr. 1866		18		118	Chicago, IL	
Koltermann, Elisabeth	2, June 1879	7, May	23- 3m- 7d	Shincke	175	Papillion, NE	Stevenson, Canada
Kölz, Johan Gottlieb	5, Feb. 1891	26, Dec.	62		94	Sherrills Mount, IA	Beinstein, Weiblingen, Württemberg
Konantz, John	25, Oct. 1894	25, Sept	68		694	Wichita, KS	Hohenzollern, Württemberg
Konantz, Rosa	16, Aug. 1880	28, July	51	Siebert	263	Parsons Creek, KS	

Christliche Apologete Death Notices --- 1839 - 1899

Name of Deceased	Notice Date	Death Date	Age	Page	Maiden Name	Place of Death	Place of Birth
Köneke, Charles A.	19, June 1890	8, June	55	398	Dickhuth	St. Louis, MO	Zeven, Germany
Köneke, Johanna Maria	26, June 1851	3, June	17- 7m-11d	104		Quincy, IL	Zeven, Hannover
Köneke, Karl	29, Apr. 1872	8, Apr.	63- 1m- 6d	143		St. Charles, MO	Buckhorn, Valingbostel, Hannover
Köneke, Katharina	6, Sept 1894	21, Aug.	88	582		St. Charles, MO	Kenzing, Baden
Köneke, Pauline	6, Sept 1894	16, Aug.	64	582	Linnemann	St. Louis, MO	Falldorf, Westphalen
Könemann, Christine Louise	27, Dec. 1888	7, Dec.	77	830	Haly	Farmington, MO	
Könemann, Louise Wilhelmine	9, Mar. 1863		18	40		St. Louis, MO	
König , Heinrich	15, Nov. 1894	22, Oct.	73	742		Galena, IL	Rohrbach , Germany
König, August	11, Apr. 1881		22	119		Chicago, IL	Chicago, Cook County, Illinois
König, August	30, Sept 1872	28, Aug.	13- -26d	319		Concordia, MO	
König, Charlotte Friederike	18, Aug. 1879		65- 1m- 2d	263	Mohr	Marine City, MI	Güstow, OstPreußen
König, Dina	18, May 1893	20, Apr.	33	318		Yonkers, NY	Gochsen, Württemberg
König, Friedrich	27, Apr. 1893	11, Apr.	90	270		New Orleans, LA	Benekenhagen, Mecklenburg-Schwerin
König, Friedrich	18, Feb. 1878	19, Jan.	27- 1m-23d	55		Schnectady, NY	Liebenau, Hannover
König, Heinrich	20, July 1854	21, June	59	116		St. Louis, MO	Buer, Hannover
König, Herman	26, Mar. 1891	28, Feb.	79	206		Bland, MO	Ride, Sicke, Hannover
König, Joachim	22, Oct. 1896	10, Sept	66	687		Kline, IA	Wernitz, Magdeburg, Preußen
König, Johan Wilhelm	7, Apr. 1873	13, Mar.	63- 5m- 9d	111		Marine City, MI	Wekkuhn, Amt Weizenburg, Preußen
König, Johnnie	12, Jan. 1888	13, Nov.	3-10m-17d	30		Bland, MO	
König, Katharina Dorothea Elis.	14, Oct. 1878	5, Sept	75	327	Mewes	Flint Creek, IA	Breitenfeld, Magdeburg, Preußen
König, Katharina Magdalena	20, Apr. 1899	22, Mar.		255	Kühl	Muscatine, IA	Barg, Dithmarschen, Schleswig-Holstein
König, Katharine	13, Nov. 1890	29, Oct.	32- 7m- 5d	734	Peters	St. Louis, MO	Mascoutah, Illinois
König, Louisa Dorothea	17, Mar. 1887	3, Mar.	35	174	Langhorst	Covington, KY	Mt. Pleasant, Hamilton County, Ohio
König, Louise	9, Jan. 1882	30, Nov.	32	15	Burmann	Schnectady, NY	Hille, Minden, Preußen
König, Ludwig J. J.	19, Dec. 1895	1, Dec.	81	814		Fredericksburg, TX	Gelbensande, Mecklenburg-Schwerin
König, Margaretha	13, Dec. 1888	22, Nov.	48	798	Früh	Crandon, SD	Queckborn, Gießen, Hessen-Darmstadt
König, Margaretha	3, Jan. 1861	24, Dec.	64	4	Sieck	St. Louis, MO	Buer, Hannover
König, Maria	2, June 1887	29, Apr.	86	350	Bachmann	Clayton, WI	Corbussen, Sachsen-Altenburg
König, Maria Eva	6, Apr. 1885	16, Mar.	51	7	Frantz	Philadelphia, PA	Oberamt Gaildorf, Württemberg
König, Martha	7, Dec. 1893	7, Nov.	23- 2m-21d	782	Schrumpf	Appleton, WI	
König, Oscar Franklin	3, May 1888	9, Apr.	16	286		LaCrosse, WI	St. Joe, Missouri
König, Philippine	1, Dec. 1873	18, Nov.		383	Scheidt	Cincinnati, OH	Kaiserslautern
König, Sophia	3, May 1875	14, Apr.	18	143		Chicago, IL	
König, Valentin	7, Feb. 1881	29, Dec.	48	47		New York City, NY	Schwarza, Preußen
Königfeld, Katharina	3, Dec. 1877	19, Nov.	60	391		Perrysburg, OH	Dalheim, Hessen
Königshof, H. Menken	8, Feb. 1855	Aug.	46	24		St. Louis, MO	Nasse, Amt Bährum, Hannover
Königstein, Jakob	22, Feb. 1894	31, Jan.	57	126		Bloomington, IL	Kusell, Harsbach, Baiern
Köning, Bernhard Albert	2, Aug. 1849	7, July	39	124		St. Louis, MO	Fenne bei Feren, Hannover
Koninszeski, Theophilia	8, Mar. 1888	8, Feb.	74- 2m- 6d	158		St. Louis, MO	Lubna, Kaiserthum, Oesterreich
Könning, Maria	6, Aug. 1847	24, July	1	127		St. Louis, MO	
Konold, Georg Friedrich	20, Aug. 1866	18, July	55	270	Gerken	Cannelton, IN	Bohlheim, Heidenheim, Württemberg
Konow, Mary	27, Apr. 1899	28, Mar.	55	271		Owensville, MO	Liezum, Blumenthal, Hannover
Konrad, Anna C.	19, Mar. 1883	3, Mar.	26- 5m- 7d	95		Covington, KY	Covington, Kenton County, Kentucky
Konrad, Heinrich	23, July1883	4, July	28	239		Covington, KY	Pirmasens, Rheinkreis Baiern
Konrad, Johan Heinrich Ludwig	22, Dec. 1887	5, Dec.	81- -27d	814		Mankato, MN	Werden, Pommern
Konrad, Louise	17, Feb. 1879	4, Feb.	62- 8m-26d	55	Helmstätter	Covington, KY	Pirmasens, Rheinpfalz Baiern

Christliche Apologete Death Notices -- 1839 - 1899

Name of Deceased	Notice Date	Death Date	Age	Maiden Name	Page	Place of Death	Place of Birth
Kopenbring, Friedrich Wilhelm	19, Nov. 1877		67- 4m-15d		375	Concordia, MO	Tenhausen, Kreis Herfort, Westphalen
Kopenbrink, Katharina	7, June 1875	25, May	33		183	Concordia, MO	Wallenbrück, Minden, Preußen
Kopenhagen, Elisabeth	8, May 1890	13, Apr.	30- 5m-15d	Mahler	302	Lexington, TX	
Kopenhagen, Louis	5, May 1892	27, Mar.	40		286	Lexington, TX	Preußen
Koperz, Michael	6, Sept 1875	16, Aug.	8- -19d		287	Indianola, TX	
Kopf, Jakob	28, Jan. 1892	27, Dec.	71		62	West Bend, WI	Guntersblum bei Mainz, Hessen-Darmstadt
Köpfel, Sophie	2, Sept 1872	1, Aug.	70	Batke	287	Manitowoc, WI	Stettin, Pommern
Kopieske, Johan Friedrich	20, July 1874	27, June	56		231	Blooming Grove, MN	Thurow, Neu-Stettin, Pommern, Preußen
Köpke, Charlotte	11, Mar. 1886	25, Feb.	85		7	Grand Rapids, MI	Hartensdorf, Preußen
Köpke, Dorothea	28, Nov. 1895	10, Nov.	70		766	Laporte, IN	Adamshof, Mecklenburg-Schwerin
Köpke, Johanna Friederika	25, Aug. 1884	7, Aug.	41- 2m-20d	Schröder	7	Watertown, WI	Zühlsdorf, in der Neumark, Preußen
Köpke, Karl F.	31, Dec. 1877	12, Dec.	59- -15d		423	Kewaskum, WI	Farbezin, Kreis Naugard, Hinterpommern
Köpke, Michael	21, Dec. 1893	28, Nov.	86- 6m		814	Watertown, WI	Suchow a.d. Plöne, Pieritz, Pommern
Koplin, Johan Friedrich	16, Nov. 1893	18, Oct.	45		734	Princeton, WI	Marienberg, Brandenburg
Koplitz, Emilie	25, Feb. 1892	31, Jan.	66	Stenzel	126	Oshkosh, WI	Trebitsch, Bromberg, Posen
Koplitz, Joseph	25, Sept 1890	29, Aug.	69		622	Oshkosh, WI	Hedesheim, Koblenz, Preußen
Kopp, Anna	5, June 1865	18, May	63- 9m		92	Ann Arbor, MI	Rohrau, Herrenberg, Württemberg
Kopp, Anna	19, Feb. 1877	3, Feb.	74- 3m-25d	Rieger	63	Rock River, WI	Mergelstetten, Württemberg
Kopp, Anna Sophia	27, Feb. 1871	9, Feb.	19- 5m-27d		71	Bucyrus, OH	New Braunfels, Texas
Kopp, August Friedrich	2, June 1887	12, May	83		350	Lexington, TX	Heiligensee, Brandenburg
Kopp, Daniel	29, Dec. 1873	7, Dec.	46- 8m-27d		415	Muscatine, IA	Rheinheim, Hessen-Darmstadt
Kopp, Elisabeth	11, Apr. 1889	21, Mar.	79	Jenni	238	Watertown, WI	Oberholz bei Münzingen, Bern, Schweiz
Kopp, Gertrude	26, June 1890	21, May	31-11m-10d	Brings	414	St. Paul, MN	St. Paul, Minnesota
Kopp, Henriette	19, Mar. 1891	27, Jan.	55	Westerheide	190	Los Angeles, CA	Bielefeld, Preußen
Kopp, Margaretha	19, Aug. 1878		76- 9m-12d	Stegemann	263	Newark, NJ	Göppingen, Württemberg
Kopp, Maria	1, Dec. 1873	8, Nov.	85	Steiner	383	Woodville, OH	Leimiswyl, Bern, Schweiz
Kopp, Maria	11, Feb. 1897	13, Jan.	62- 9m-14d	Meyer	94	Newark, NJ	Baiern
Köpp, Maria	10, June 1886	3, May	16- 3m-19d		7	Milwaukee, WI	
Kopp, Rudolph	1, Nov. 1860	9, Sept	49		176	Watertown, WI	Thun, Bern, Schweiz
Koppe, Carl August	21, Mar. 1895	27, Feb.			190	Galion, OH	Dodenau, Biedenkopf, Hessen-Darmstadt
Köppe, Christian	1, Dec. 1848		Inquiry		195	St. Louis, MO	Bückeburg, Minden, Preußen
Koppenbrink, A. Catharina Elsabein	13, Jan. 1873	11, Dec.	58	Gieselmann	15	Concordia, MO	Minden, Preußen
Koppert, Elisabeth	7, Oct. 1867	27, Aug.	56-10m-11d		318	Zanesville, OH	
Koppert, Helene M.	15, Nov. 1875	27, Sept	47	Loffert	367	Newark, OH	West Virginia
Koppert, Johan Phil.	16, Jan. 1871	1, Jan.	63		23	Newark, OH	Walldorf, Amt Wiesloch, Baden
Koppinger, Mary	23, Nov. 1874	5, Nov.	15- 1m-24d		375	Nora Springs, IA	Dorchester, Alamakee County, Iowa
Koppler, Wilhelm	28, Mar. 1895	5, Mar.	58		206	Evansville, IN	Louisville, Jefferson County, Kentucky
Kopplien, Albert	11, July 1895	25, June	34		446	Sterling, NE	Zuchomühlen, Arnswalde, Preußen
Kopplien, Johanna Henriette	27, Feb. 1896	8, Feb.	67	Röhl	143	Sterling, NE	Zuchomühlen, Hochzeit, Arnswalde, Preußen
Kopplin, Arthur Emil	4, Jan. 1894	8, Dec.	19		14	Crandon, SD	Princeton, Green Lake County, Wisconsin
Kopplin, Auguste Albertine Wilh.	16, Feb. 1874	29, Jan.	52		55	Beaver Dam, WI	Denkahus, Arnswalde, Neumark, Preußen
Kopplin, Georg Emil	11, Nov. 1897	18, Oct.	21		719	Beaver Dam, WI	Loft Lake, Wisconsin
Kopplin, Hubert Theodor	18, May 1899	25, Apr.	21		319	Crandon, SD	Calmus, Dodge County, Wisconsin
Kopplin, Johanna	28, June 1888	2, June	71		414	Beaver Dam, WI	Schulzendorf, Arnswalde, Neumark
Kopplin, Julius	24, June 1897	6, June	48		399	Crandon, SD	Marienberg, Arnswalde, Germany
Kopplin, K.L.	15, Oct. 1877	19, Sept	63		335	Beaver Dam, WI	Marzdorf, Bromberg, Neumark, Preußen

Name of Deceased	Notice Date	Death Date	Age	Maiden Name	Page	Place of Death	Place of Birth
Kopplin, Lene	25, Feb. 1892	21, Jan.	19	Deglow	126	Beaver Dam, WI	Fountain Prairie, Columbia County, Wisconsin
Kopplin, Leo	21, Apr. 1892	23, Mar.	77		254	Beaver Dam, WI	Neu-Hölge, Arnswalde, Neumark
Kopplin, Ludwig H.	24, Aug. 1885	5, Aug.	13		7	Beaver Dam, WI	
Kopplin, Wilhelm August Friedrich	6, Aug. 1877	12, July	43-10m-10d		255	Tecumseh, NE	Springe, Arnswalde, Preußen
Köpsel, Amalie	22, May 1890	27, Apr.	66	Leißner	334	Guadalupe Valley, TX	Kulm, West Preußen
Köpsel, Carolina	14, July 1879	27, June	78- 3m		223	Seguin, TX	Posen
Köpsel, Ida	6, Dec. 1894	10, Nov.	26- 5m-13d		790	Milwaukee, WI	
Köpsel, Johan Daniel	9, Dec. 1886	22, Nov.	87		7	Manitowoc, WI	Borntien, Pommern
Köpsel, Johanna	18, Nov. 1878	1, Nov.	71		367	Milwaukee, WI	Plantikow, Hinterpommern
Köpsel, Robert	7, Nov. 1895	16, Oct.	32		718	Kansas City, KS	Liberty , Wisconsin
Köpsel, Wilhelmina	27, Feb. 1862	5, Feb.	18-10m-18d		36	Manitowoc, WI	Görke, Greifenberg, Hinterpommern
Korb, Eduard	24, July 1890	30, June	62		478	Brillion, WI	Reuß
Körber, Conrad	23, Dec. 1872	10, Nov.	74		415	Nemaha, NE	Colenfeld, Hannover
Kordian, Gottlieb	21, May 1883	9, May	84		167	Beaver Dam, WI	Schönfeld, Preußen
Korf, Catharina	13, Sept 1869	25, Aug.	30	Wolf	295	St. Joseph, MO	St. Louis, Missouri
Korf, Emilie	30, Nov. 1893	25, Oct.	28		766	Bushton, KS	Hoyleton, Illinois
Korf, Friedrich	16, June 1884	6, May	60		7	Chase, KS	Alferdisen, Lippe-Detmold
Korf, Friedrich	2, June 1884	6, May	60		7	Chase, KS	Aferdisen, Lippe-Detmold
Korf, Friedrich Wilhelm	13, July 1899	24, May	82		447	Huntsville, KS	Alverdissen, Sternberg, Lippe-Detmold
Korf, Louise C.	22, Sept 1879	31, Aug.	19- 3m-27d	Schlake	303	Salt Creek, NE	Birdinghausen, Westphalen
Korf, Margaretha	26, Oct. 1874	17, Sept	44	Weber	343	Nashville, IL	Unterspach, Hall, Württemberg
Korf, Sophia	5, June 1882	4, May	42 - 5d	Bergmann	183	Newton, IA	Maienberg, Lippe-Detmold
Korf, Sophia	19, June 1865	25, Jan.	40	Austermann	100	Marthasville, MO	Detmold, Lippe
Korfhage, A. F. (Rev)	12, Jan. 1899	5, Dec.	79		30	Kansas City, MO	Holzhausen, Westphalen
Korfhage, Amalie	2, Feb. 1863	4, Jan.	28	Keese	20	St. Paul, MN	Rauschenwasser, Bofinden, Hannover
Korfhage, Friederike	15, Mar. 1888	16, Feb.	87	Grambeck	174	St. Paul, MN	Börninghausen, Preußen
Korfhage, Friedrich	7, Sept 1854	12, Aug.	74		144	St. Paul, MN	Holzhausen, Lübbecke, Minden, Preußen
Korfhage, Friedrich	17, Apr. 1865		27		64	St. Paul, MN	Holzhausen, Preußen
Korfhage, Ida Luise	23, Feb. 1899	25, Dec.	35	Spekeen	127	St. Paul, MN	Waukesha, Wisconsin
Korfhage, J.H. Gottlieb	28, Nov. 1864	28, Sept	37- 4m		192	St. Paul, MN	Holzhausen, Preußen
Korfhage, Johan Friedrich	23, Feb. 1880	5, Feb.	65		63	St. Paul, MN	Holzhausen, Lübbecke, Minden, Preußen
Korfhage, Wilhelm	29, Jan. 1877	4, Jan.	72- 2m		39	Salem, MN	Holzhausen, Lübbeke, Minden, Preußen
Korfhage, Wilhelm	28, Sept 1899	17, Aug.	65		623	St. Paul, MN	Börninghausen, Westphalen
Kork, Heinrich	12, May 1884	27, Apr.	63		7	Kenosha, WI	an der Nordsee, Holland
Kork, Lisetta	13, Aug. 1877	3, Aug.	41	Weiler	263	Cincinnati, OH	Durlach, Baden
Korn, Johanna	19, Mar. 1883	27, Feb.	24	Bartrof	95	Llano, TX	Biberach, Württemberg
Kornemann, Franz Christoph	20, Nov. 1871	22, Oct.	57		375	Liberty, MO	Weitesingen, Kreis Wolfhagen, Kurhessen
Kornemann, Marie Katharine	28, Apr. 1879	25, Mar.	56- 2m- 6d		135	Liberty, MO	Weitesingen, Volkmarsen, Hessen-Kassel
Körner, Anna Maria	4, June 1877	14, May	52	Guth	183	Santa Claus, IN	Zierolshofen, Rhein-bischofsheim, Baden
Körner, Catharine Philippine	23, Aug. 1864	4, Aug.			136	Charlestown, IN	Mensfelden, Nassau
Körner, Christian	28, Sept 1885	9, Aug.	63- -15d		311	Madison, IN	Owen bei Kirchheim, Württemberg
Körner, Christina	14, Sept 1885	11, Aug.	76		7	Madison, IN	Owie, Württemberg
Körner, Georg Jakob	15, Nov. 1875	26, Sept	18-10m- 3d		367	Edgerton, OH	
Körner, Gottlieb David	28, May 1883	6, May	52- 5m- 6d		175	Edgerton, OH	Affalterbach, Marbach, Württemberg
Körner, Johan Jacob	25, Mar. 1897	3, Mar.	80		190	Kansas City, KS	Holzhausen, Bischofsheim, Baden
Körner, Joseph	12, Sept 1864	7, July	30		148	Charlestown, IN	Klosterlobenfeld, Neckar-Gmünd, Baden

Christliche Apologete Death Notices --- 1839 - 1899

Name of Deceased	Notice Date	Death Date	Age	Page	Maiden Name	Place of Death	Place of Birth
Körner, Katharina	3, Mar. 1884	11, Feb.	43- -2d	7	Stiehl	Mt. Vernon, IN	Milford Township, Defiance County, Ohio
Körner, Samuel Benjamin	20, Jan. 1898	31, Dec.	24	47		Edon, OH	Poplar Ridge, Henry County, Ohio
Körner, Sophie	1, May 1876		31	143	Rennollet	Edgerton, OH	Mosebeck, Lippe-Detmold
Körner, Wilhelmine	12, July 1880	21, June	66	223		Yellow Creek, IL	Garrensee, Preußen
Kornetzki, William	20, Nov. 1882	26, Oct.	37	375		Troy, NY	Oberfleude, Hessen-Darmstadt
Kornmann, Heinrich	12, Apr. 1888	18, Feb.	70	238		Allegheny City, PA	Niederkinzig, Hessen-Darmstadt
Korp, M.	5, Feb. 1883	15, Jan.	30	47		Denver, CO	Schledehausen, Osnabrück, Hannover
Kors, J. Maria E.	5, Feb.1847	27, Dec.	36	23	Hemminghaus	Beardstown, IL	Perrysburg, Ohio
Korschland, Maria Ellen	27, Sept 1888	21, Aug.	30	622	Schneider	Toledo, OH	Rosberg bei Zeitz, Preußen
Körst, Johan Gottlob	9, Nov. 1874		62-10m- 8d	359		Galena, IL	Gottingen, Hannover
Kort, August	30, Apr. 1857	15, Mar.	54	72		Schnectady, NY	Esek, Kreis Trier, Preußen
Kortel, J.	12, Dec. 1864	24, Sept		200		Waverly, OH	Vahrenholz, Lippe-Detmold
Kortemeyer, Charlotte	14, Feb. 1881	14, Nov.	66- 6m-10d	55		Sherrills Mount, IA	Slakow, Stalpe, Preußen
Korth, Friedrich	3, Aug. 1899	11, July	79	495		Peoria, IL	
Korthhauer, Friedrich	3, July 1851	17, June		108		Louisville, KY	
Kortlang, Heinrich Anton	19, Aug. 1897	27, July	83	527		Freyburg, TX	Langwarden, Burhave, Oldenburg
Kortlang, Margarethe Christine	23, Dec. 1897	21, Nov.	61	815	Oeltjen	Freyburg, TX	Langwarden, Oldenburg
Körtner, Pauline Friederike A.	24, Apr. 1890	14, Mar.	61	270	Meier	Yellow Creek, IL	Biesen, Detmold, Lippe-Detmold
Kortz, Johan Joseph Ernst F.	16, Apr. 1866	24, Mar.	47	126		Lansing, MI	Goldenbov, Mecklenburg-Schwerin
Korzer, Friedrich	20, Nov. 1882	Aug.	16-10m	375		Crete, NE	
Korzer, Hannah Carolina Augusta	20, Nov. 1882	19, Sept	48	375	Karo	Crete, NE	
Kosbab, Carl	18, Sept 1890	4, Sept	54	606		Toledo, OH	Friedeberg in der Neumark, Preußen
Kösmeyer, Christine	21, July 1879	2, July	73	231	Buhrmester	Burlington, IA	Banzig, Stolp, Hinterpommern
Kosmeyer, Heinrich Gottlieb	29, July 1886	15, July	76	7		Burlington, IA	Dankersen, Minden, Preußen
Kössel, Leonora	24, Sept 1896	12, Aug.	52	623	Grökel	Chicago, IL	Dankersen, Minden, Preußen
Koßmann, Charlotte	26, July 1894	30, June	34	486	Jäger	Scranton, PA	Arnstadt, Germany
Koßmann, Heinrich	9, Mar. 1899	2, Feb.	60	159		Troy, NY	Alsheim, Hessen
Kossube, Sophia	21, Dec. 1868	7, Nov.	76- 2m	407	Fischer	Red Wing, MN	Jamekan, Posen
Kossug, Emilie	4, Jan. 1894	12, Dec.	29	14	Streicher	Detroit, MI	Fürstenwerder, Brandenburg, Preußen
Kost, Adam	15, Sept 1848	14, July	54	151		Quincy, IL	Detroit, Wayne County, Michigan
Kost, Anna Dora	29, Aug. 1881	12, Aug.	18	279		Quincy, IL	
Kost, Anna Dorothea	13, June 1889	23, May	88	382	Heß	Quincy, IL	Ober-Dorlau, Erfurt, Preußen
Kost, Catharine Elisabeth	31, July 1851	27, June	19- 2m- 6d	124		Quincy, IL	Oberdorlau bei Mühlhausen, Preußen
Kost, Eduard Adam	24, Jan. 1870	3, Dec.	5- 6m-21d	31		St. Joseph, MO	Mascoutah, Illinois
Kost, Johan Georg (Rev)	9, June 1892	10, May	66	366		St. Joseph, MO	Oberdoria, Mühlhausen, Erfurt, Preußen
Kost, Johan Heinrich	26, Mar. 1896	8, Mar.	69	206		Quincy, IL	Oberdorlau, Preußen
Köster, Augusta Josephine	22, Dec. 1898	21, Nov.	49	815	Mann	Beardstown, IL	Beardstown, Illinois
Köster, Catharina	29, Apr. 1897	28, Mar.	71	271		Hamilton Co, OH	Edigheim, Baiern
Köster, Dorothea	12, Nov. 1847	10, Oct.	20	183		New Orleans, LA	
Köster, Heinrich	11, Nov. 1886	15, Oct.	54	7		Topeka, KS	Deisen, Hofgeismar, Hessen-Nassau
Köster, Herman	9, Mar. 1874	17, Feb.	47- 9m -6d	79		Piqua, OH	Nordhorn, Hannover
Koster, Johan	6, June 1895	24, Mar.	76- 6m-24d	366		Hamilton Co, OH	Buchhausen, Hannover
Köster, Johan G.	26, Jan. 1880	10, Jan.	30	31		Pomeroy, OH	
Köster, John	28, Sept 1893	5, Sept	55- 2m	622		Macon, NE	Alten Tanko, Mecklenburg-Schwerin
Köster, Margaretha	18, Apr. 1864	3, Mar.		64		Pomeroy, OH	
Köster, Maria Engel	28, Sept 1863	6, Sept	74	156	Kilvit	Seymour, IN	Haltern, Amt Osnabrück, Hannover

Christliche Apologete Death Notices — 1839 - 1899

Name of Deceased	Notice Date	Death Date	Age	Page	Maiden Name	Place of Death	Place of Birth
Köster, Minna	10, May 1888	4, Apr.	23	302	Kuhn	Nerstrand, MN	Goodhue County, Minnesota
Köster, Sophie	18, Sept 1882	6, Sept	19-5m-5d	303		Pomeroy, OH	
Köthe, Alwina	4, Dec. 1865	1, Nov.	15-7m	196		Hokah, MN	Großfurra, Schwarzburg-Sondershausen
Kothe, Heinrich	12, Feb. 1891	20, Jan.	68	110		Enterprise, KS	
Köthe, Johan Friedrich Christoph	1, Apr. 1886	14, Mar.	78	7		LaCrosse, WI	Großenfura, Schwarzburg-Sondershausen
Köthe, Maria Albertina	8, Aug. 1870	2, July	29	255	Rebe	Hokah, MN	Mobro bei Colberg, HinterPommern
Köthe, Maria Sophia	2, July 1877	19, June	68-7m-19d	215	Marolden	LaCrosse, WI	
Köthe, Oskar	16, June 1884	30, May	48	7		Hokah, MN	Großenfura, Schwarzburg-Sondershausen
Kothemann, Charlotte	9, June 1884	23, May	40	7	Topp	Indianapolis, IN	Blomberg, Lippe-Detmold
Kothert, Wilhelm	27, Sept 1888	24, Sept	77-5m-13d	622		Huntingburg, IN	Barnau, Vörder, Engter, Hannover
Kotpeter, Rudolph	12, Nov. 1847	12, June	34	183	Bramwischer	New Orleans, LA	
Kötter, Clara Maria	6, Sept 1894	28, Nov.	82	582		Ironton, OH	Buhr, Hannover
Kötter, Emilie Mathilde	3, Jan. 1876	31, May	17	7		Ironton, OH	Portsmouth, Ohio
Kötter, Ernst Heinrich	27, June 1870	16, Jan.	53	207		Portsmouth, OH	Bur, Hannover
Kötter, Johan Friedrich	18, Feb. 1886	17, Jan.	75	7		Ironton, OH	Buhr, Hannover
Kötter, Maria	5, Mar. 1847	3, Nov.	39	39		Cincinnati, OH	Holzhausen, Amt Gröneberg, Hannover
Kötter, Maria Elisabeth	22, Jan. 1852	25, June	31-8m-15d	16		Waverly, OH	
Kötter, Sophie	16, July 1866	19, July	14	230		Cincinnati, OH	
Kötter, Wilhelm	7, Aug. 1851	30, Oct.	32	128		Portsmouth, OH	
Kotterheinrich, Elisabetha	19, Nov. 1857	1, Feb.	15	188		Knoxville, OH	Ladbergen, Tecklenburg, Preußen
Kotterheinrich, Elsebein	19, Feb. 1883	20, Apr.	68	63	König	New Knoxville, OH	Ladbergen, Tecklenburg, Hannover
Kotterheinrich, Ernst	5, May 1887	18, Nov.	64-1m	286		Evansville, IN	Ladbergen, Tecklenburg, Westphalen
Kotterheinrich, J.H.W.	9, Dec. 1886	26, Apr.	76	7		New Knoxville, OH	Atlantic Ocean
Kotterheinrich, John Wilhelm	12, June 1865	12, Feb.	26	96		New Knoxville, OH	Ladbergen, Preußen
Kötterjohann, Anna Christina	2, Mar. 1874	14, Nov.	74-11m	71		Red Wing, MN	Ladbergen, Tecklenburg, Münster, Preußen
Kötterjohann, Heinrich Adolph	30, Nov. 1885	10, Jan.	65-3m-10d	7		Huntingburg, IN	Ladbergen, Preußen
Kötterjöhann, Herman J.	2, Feb. 1888	10, Feb.	75	78		Huntingburg, IN	
Kötterjöhann, Louise	3, Mar.1873	13, Apr.	23	71	Hartke	Huntingburg, IN	
Kottmann, Karoline Sophia	29, Apr. 1878	18, July	19	135		Lena, IL	Stephenson County, Illinois
Kottmeier, Heinrich Karl	4, Aug. 1898	18, Aug.	49	495		St. Louis, MO	Börninghausen, Preußen
Kottmeier, Louise	30, Sept 1858	27, Mar.	32	156		Union, MO	Möllbergen, Kreis Minden, Preußen
Kottmeyer, Emilie	1, May 1882	16, Mar.	18	143		Drake, MO	
Kottmeyer, Herman	24, Apr. 1871	26, Nov.	17-8m-2d	135		Union, MO	
Kowalk, Bertha Karolina	17, Feb. 1898	21, May	32	111		Bay City, MI	Darsin, Pommern
Kowalk, Charlotte	13, Dec. 1880	22, Nov.	56-10m	399	Marutz	Allegan, MI	Viartlum, Pommern
Kowalk, Hannah	16, June 1898	13, July	48	383		Fremont, OH	Preußen
Kowalk, Michael	15, Dec. 1892	5, June	29	798		Allegan, MI	Allegan, Michigan
Kraas, Christoph K.	14, Aug. 1846	7, Oct.	1-7m-7d	131		Lawrenceburg, IN	Rockport, Ohio
Kraas, Louisa C.	3, July 1890	22, Dec.	33	430	Mack	DeWitt, MI	
Kraas, Louise	27, Oct. 1853	29, Sept	33	172		Lawrenceburg, IN	Rimsloh, Amt Melle, Hannover
Kraas, Wilhelm F.	4, Feb. 1884	25, Mar.	34	7		Greenville, OH	Lawrenceburg, Dearborn County, Indiana
Kraatz, Ella	24, Oct. 1889	5, Apr.	29-9d	686	Jürke	Akron, NY	
Kraatz, Johanna	17, Apr. 1882	29, July	21-11m-2d	127		Akron, NY	
Kraatz, Karl Heinrich	28, Apr. 1898	19, Jan.	71	271		Akron, NY	
Kraatz, Maria	19, Oct. 1893		56-5d	670	Bohr	Akron, NY	Bliesekow, Mecklenburg-Schwerin
Krabbe, Johan Heinrich	17, Feb. 1873			53		St. Louis, MO	Blisekow, Mecklenburg-Schwerin

Christliche Apologete Death Notices --- 1839 - 1899

Name of Deceased	Notice Date	Death Date	Age	Maiden Name	Page	Place of Death	Place of Birth
Krackhart, Dorothea	1, Aug. 1881	13, July	53- 3m	Lug	247	Newburg, IN	Kirchheim, Grünstadt, Rheinpfalz Baiern
Kraemer, Michael	28, Apr. 1879	4, Apr.	67- 4m		135	Summerfield, IL	Häbenheim, Hessen
Kraft, Anna Maria	27, Dec. 1888	4, Dec.	50		830	Louisville, KY	Hertenhausen, Weihers, Baiern
Kräft, Caroline	2, Dec. 1867	11, Nov.	34- -10d		382	Schnectady, NY	Grießen, Hannover
Kraft, D.B.	25, Nov. 1867	21, Oct.	56		374	Goliad, TX	Böblingen, Württemberg
Kraft, Gottlieb	1, Dec. 1898	6, Nov.	57		767	Berea, OH	Großkottors, Preußen
Kraft, Heinrich	10, Feb. 1868	22, Jan.	31		47	Edwardsville, IL	Marienhagen, Hessen-Darmstadt
Kraft, Herman Heinrich	29, Jan. 1891	26, Sept	55		78	Schnectady, NY	Oberlübbe, Minden, Preußen
Kraft, Jacob	22, Nov. 1888	29, Oct.	60- 3m-14d		750	Spencerville, OH	Hopsigheim, Marbach, Württemberg
Kraft, Jakobine	16, Jan. 1896	22, Dec.	77		46	Newark, NJ	Diedlingen, Pforzheim, Baden
Kraft, Johan	28, Sept 1874	1, Sept	48		311	Berea, OH	Mischke, Posen, Preußen
Kraft, Johan Michael	28, July 1879	2, July	75	Ohde	239	New Haven, CT	Breitenholz, Herrenberg, Württemberg
Kraft, Julie	27, Sept 1888	27, Aug.	32		622	Denton, TX	Herman , Wisconsin
Kraft, Louise	18, May 1893	20, Apr.	75	Kühlman	318	Berea, OH	Sawadamühl, Czarnikau, Preußen
Kraft, Louise	25, Feb. 1892	18, Jan.	69	Boneß	126	Oconomowoc, WI	Büssow bei Kollberg, Preußen
Kraft, Louise	27, Jan. 1887	29, Dec.	65		62	Waco, TX	Basel, Schweiz
Kraft, Louise	18, Aug. 1873	6, July	23- 2m-15d	Schulz	263	Scranton, PA	
Kraft, Martin Friedrich	29, Oct. 1891	5, Oct.	82		702	Oconomowoc, WI	Drosedow bei Kolberg, Preußen
Kraft, Philippine	6, June 1881	12, May	35- 9m- 4d	Zimmermann	183	New Knoxville, OH	Marion County, Ohio
Kraft, Susanna	23, May 1895	29, Apr.	43	Genheimer	334	Bethel, MO	Meigs County, Ohio
Kraft, Susanna Margaretha	8, Oct. 1877	9, Sept	65		327	New York City, NY	Zuzenhausen, Baden
Krah, Salomine	23, July 1891	1, July	78	Ruch	478	Stryker, OH	
Krähling, Katharine	17, Aug. 1868	24, July	23	Koch	263	Warsaw, IL	Deinrode, Kurhessen
Krainhop,	19, Aug. 1852	21, July	4-10m- 7d		136	Pekin, IL	
Kraiß, Michael	14, June 1894	12, May	15		390	Chicago, IL	
Kramer, Anna	22, Dec. 1873	3, Dec.	41		407	Schnectady, NY	Schrötinghausen, Minden, Preußen
Kramer, Anna Klara	12, Sept 1870	15, Aug.	49	Korring	295	Sherrills Mount, IA	
Kramer, Anna Martha	13, Oct. 1859	7, Sept	78		164	Spring Lake, OH	Dalbke, Amt Hohnhausen, Lippe-Detmold
Kramer, Anna Sophia	10, June 1872	22, May	80		191	Summerfield, IL	Kriesheim an der Brem, Rheinpfalz Baiern
Krämer, Barbara	2, Mar. 1874	14, Feb.	63	Seitz	71	New York City, NY	Afulderbach, Hessen-Darmstadt
Kramer, Bertha	15, Sept 1892	9, Aug.	27	Feuruch	590	Indianapolis, IN	
Kramer, Casper	26, July 1880	17, June	79- 8m- 7d		239	Bushnell, IL	New York City, New York
Kramer, Charlie	8, Apr. 1886	20, Mar.	25		7	Golden City, MO	Kastdorf, Preußen
Krämer, Christina	12, Nov. 1896	27, Sept	89	Wiegand	734	Cleveland, OH	Blankenloch, Karlsruhe, Baden
Kramer, Christine	5, May 1898	31, Mar.	77- 6m-11d	Rausch	287	St. Louis, MO	
Krämer, Ella	28, Oct. 1886	17, Sept	17		7	Galena, IL	Gräfenhausen, Neuenburg, Württemberg
Krämer, Ezekiel	10, Oct. 1861	17, Aug.	26	Leiners	164	San Jose, IL	Ostfriesland
Kramer, Fanny	27, Mar. 1890	27, Feb.	71		206	Saginaw, MI	
Kramer, Georg	22, July 1867	26, May	13- 7m		230	Hanging Rock, OH	Niederwalmenach, St. Goarshausen, Nassau
Krämer, Georg	13, Oct. 1862	30, Aug.	20		164	Brighton, IL	Dalbke, Hohnhausen, Lippe-Detmold
Krämer, Georg Philipp	29, June 1885	25, May	69		7	Hokah, MN	Leimershofen, Bielefeld, Minden, Preußen
Krämer, Hans Heinrich	31, May 1869	22, Mar.	84		175	Batesville, IN	Mandelsheim, Marbach, Württemberg
Krämer, Henry	18, Sept 1876		54- 6m		303	Oregon, MO	Gräfenhausen, Neuenburg, Württemberg
Krämer, Jakob Friedrich	20, Dec. 1894	19, Nov.	72		822	Galena, IL	Ober-Hallau, Schaffhausen, Schweiz
Krämer, Johann	22, June 1863	5, June	49		100	Louisville, KY	
Kramer, Johann Jakob	8, Sept 1862	20, Aug.	64- 6m-20d		144		

Christliche Apologete Death Notices --- 1839 - 1899

Name of Deceased	Notice Date	Death Date	Age	Page	Maiden Name	Place of Death	Place of Birth
Kramer, John L.	15, Mar. 1894	18, Feb.	32	182	Reis	Bushnell, IL	New York
Krämer, Katharine	6, June 1895	20, May	65	366		Chillicothe, OH	Albisheim, Rheinpfalz Baiern
Kramer, Margaretha	12, Nov. 1891	25, Oct.	72- 6m	734	Stegner	Hokah, MN	Baiern
Krämer, Martin	29, Dec. 1898	16, Nov.	75	828		Algona, WI	Preußen
Krämer, Peter	29, Apr. 1872	3, Apr.	43- 8m	143		Saginaw, MI	Reichelsheim, Lindenfeld, Hessen-Darmstadt
Krämer, Sophia	25, Apr. 1889	3, Apr.	54	270	Hellmann	Chillicothe, OH	Niederlustadt, Rheinkreis Baiern
Krämer, Sophie	8, Apr. 1878	21, Feb.	61- -10d	111	Klopp	Lawrence, KS	Freisbach, Germersheim, Baiern
Kramms, Johan	5, Mar. 1883	8, Feb.	68	79		Seguin, TX	Küderich, Nassau
Kramms, Mathilde	28, May 1883	6, May	28	175		Seguin, TX	New Braunfels, Texas
Kramp, Johan Georg	7, June 1888	22, May	63	366		Louisville, KY	
Kranig, Johanna	4, June 1857	8, Apr.	22	92		Detroit, MI	Gleebronn, Württemberg
Kranz, Friedrich	2, Mar. 1868	25, Jan.	50-10m-21d	71		Muscatine, IA	Lindhorst, Prenzlow, Brandenburg, Preußen
Kranz, Maria	17, Apr. 1876	29, Mar.	59- -26d	127	Zielesch	Illinois City, IL	Potsdam, Preußen
Kranz, Mina Anna	6, Sept 1880	4, Aug.	19- 7m- 8d	287		Berea, OH	
Kranz, Sadie Karoline	14, Sept 1899	1, Sept	22- 7m- 6d	591		Wrayville, IL	
Kränz, Stephan	12, Jan. 1874	16, Nov.	52	15		Prairie Creek, MN	Polagever, Braunsberg, Posen, Preußen
Kränz, Stephan	15, Dec. 1873	16, Nov.		399		Prairie Creek, MN	Kreis Posen, Preußen
Kranzlin, Maria	28, Apr. 1884	1, Apr.	61	7		Schnectady, NY	Zurenten, Mecklenburg-Schwerin
Kräper, Lisette	21, Sept 1893	27, Aug.	30-10m-10d	606	Mahns	Golconda, IL	
Krapf, Anna	17, Dec. 1896	17, Nov.	50	814	Reckmann	Frankfort, IL	Tessendorf, Mecklenburg-Schwerin
Krapf, Anna Martha	12, Oct. 1893	15, Sept	79	654	Lange	Peotone, Il	Königswald, Sondra, Rothenburg, Kurhessen
Krapf, Wilhelmine Johanna Louise	6, Dec. 1888	11, Nov.	20	782	Bettenhausen	Frankfort, IL	New Lenox, Illinois
Krapohl, Gerhard	21, Feb. 1895	29, Jan.	87	126	Stricker	Saginaw, MI	Düsseldorf, Preußen
Krapohl, Johann	10, Apr. 1856	14, Mar.		60		Roseville, MI	Mürmeln, Grevendroich, Düsseldorf, Preußen
Krapp, Maria Margaretha	28, May 1883	19, May	79- -21d	175	Engel	Cincinnati, OH	Schaafheim, Umstadt, Hessen
Kräschel, Anna Franzisca	10, July 1871		27	223	Sandmann	Boody, IL	Grochau, Schlesien
Kraß, Karoline	21, May 1877	1, Apr.	82	166		Seymour, IN	Linsburg, Amt Welpe, Preußen
Krassin, Christian T.	15, May 1876	23, Apr.	59-10m- 4d	159		Waseca, MN	Radwonke, Posen, Preußen
Krassin, Wilhelm Martin	25, June 1877	1, June	56- 7m- 5d	207		Waseca, MN	
Krassine, Gottlieb	21, Mar. 1861	7, Feb.	73	48		Warsica, MN	Postolitz, Preußen
Krätsch, Bertha	23, Jan. 1875	1, Jan.	22- -29d	31	Wüst	Des Moines, IA	
Kratt, Anna Maria	3, July 1890	12, June	71	430		Rochester, NY	Schweningen, Württemberg
Kratt, Christine	6, May 1867	29, Mar.	26	142	Bächtler	Pittsburg, PA	Pittsburg, Pennsylvania
Kratt, Elostina Henriette	29, June 1885	4, June	33	7	Pferdiot	Pittsburg, PA	
Krättli, George	2, Nov. 1899	12, Oct.	18	703		Senate Grove, MO	Stony Hill, Gasconda County, Missouri
Kratz, Anna Katharina	2, Oct. 1882	13, Sept	53	319	Weber	New Palestine, IN	Eberhausen, Alsfeld, Kurhessen
Kratz, Conrad	27, Oct. 1879	10, Oct.	25- 1m- 7d	343		New Palestine, IN	
Kratz, Heinrich	23, Feb. 1880	2, Feb.	28- 7m-20d	63		New Palestine, IN	
Kratz, Jakob	10, Sept 1883	31, Aug.	66- 1m- 4d	295	Bachmann	New Palestine, IN	Burgemeinden, Hessen-Darmstadt
Kratzer, Regine Dorothea	11, Sept 1868	26, Apr.	65-10m-18d	151		Jeffersonville, NY	Gochsheim, Baden
Krätzmeyer, Christina	13, Sept 1855	3, Sept	33	148		Pennsylvanienburg, IN	
Kraus, Adam	9, Dec. 1886		59	7		Etna, MO	
Kraus, David	19, Nov. 1877	26, Oct.	68	375		Brooklyn, NY	
Kraus, Dorothea	25, Aug. 1873	5, Aug.	72-11m	271		Chicago, IL	
Kraus, Elisabeth S.	12, Nov. 1877	25, Oct.	14- 9m- 3d	367		Marion, OH	
Kraus, Henry	4, July 1895	17, June	71	430		Canaan, IN	Edenkoben, Baiern

Christliche Apologete Death Notices --- 1839 - 1899

Name of Deceased	Notice Date	Death Date	Age	Page	Maiden Name	Place of Death	Place of Birth
Kraus, Margaretha	12, May 1873	25, Feb.	62	151	Reis	Brooklyn, NY	Mehlbach, Rheinpfalz Baiern
Kraus, Margaretha	19, Dec. 1864	15, Oct.	30- 4m-10d	204	Hoffmann	Fairmount, KS	Harmgtam, Häfen Momert,
Kraus, Wilhelm	24, Dec. 1847		Inquiry	207		Quincy, IL	Eckenhagen, Walbrel, Germany
Krause, Adolph	17, May 1869	20, Apr.	23	159		Charles City, IA	
Krause, Albert	4, May 1863	15, Apr.	19- -17d	72		Chicago, IL	
Krause, Anna Christine	18, Aug. 1879	30, July	80- -20d	263	Gede	Portland, WI	Treptow, Pommern
Krause, August	16, Apr. 1896	1, Apr.	67	254		Spencer, IA	Garin, Pommern
Krause, Caroline	25, Aug. 1879	6, Aug.	68- 5m-26d	271		Chicago, IL	
Krause, Christian	28, Nov. 1870	9, Nov.	77	383	Humboldt	Watertown, WI	Lekow, Kreis Schiefelstein, Stettin, Preußen
Krause, Christina	28, July 1892		82	478		Sterling, NE	Schönfeld bei Amswalde, Preußen
Krause, Christine Louise	28, Apr. 1892	28, Mar.	75	270		Oconomowoc, WI	Klebow bei Stettin, Pommern
Krause, Emil	29, Apr. 1878	5, Apr.		135		Portland, WI	
Krause, Ernestine	13, Mar. 1890	8, Feb.	66- 1m-20d	174	Albrecht	Sun Prairie, WI	Shönow, Pyritz, Pommern
Krause, Friederike	28, Sept 1899	23, Aug.	47	623		Spencer, IA	Gendelien, Germany
Krause, Friedrich	1, Feb. 1894	29, Dec.	36	78		Waseca, MN	Marquette County, Wisconsin
Krause, Friedrich	29, Sept 1887	26, Aug.	2- -15d	622		Dover, MN	
Krause, Henrietta Friedericka	28, Feb. 1876	7, Feb.		71	Völtz	Red Wing, MN	Jastchembo, West Preußen
Krause, Henriette	22, Dec. 1884	2, Dec.	71	7		Green Bay, WI	Born, Dramberg, Pommern
Krause, Henriette Antonette Sophia	11, Nov. 1878	16, Oct.	58	359	Naß	Red Wing, MN	Petershagen, Kofelina, Kolberg, Germany
Krause, Julius	4, Feb. 1892	11, Jan.	54	78		Ada, MN	OstPreußen
Krause, Justina	28, Jan. 1892	25, Dec.	72	62	Romanowsky	Charles City, IA	
Krause, Karolina	4, Dec. 1882	21, Nov.	36- 6m- 8d	391	Koch	Charles City, IA	Pinnow, Mecklenburg-Schwerin
Krause, Regina	11, Sept 1871	28, June	45- 1m-13d	295	Nack	Polk City, IA	
Krause, Rosalia	12, Nov. 1896	26, Sept	72	734	Richter	Pasadena, CA	Langendorf bei Weisenfels, Preußen
Krause, Wilhelm	19, May 1898	1, May	85	319		Ada, MN	Nüttenhagen bei Labes, Germany
Krause, Wilhelm	14, Dec. 1885	27, Nov.	60	7		Portland, WI	Trepton bei Stargart, Germany
Krause, Wilhelm	7, Mar. 1895	18, Feb.	72	158		Sun Prairie, WI	Garz, Pieritz, Pommern
Krause, Wilhelm	24, Mar. 1873	1, Jan.	13- - 9d	95		Rochester, MN	
Krause, Wilhelmine Auguste Emiiie	14, Nov. 1881	31, Oct.	27	367	Völz	Red Wing, MN	Falkenberg, Pommern
Krauß, Carolina	15, Oct. 1896	19, Sept	72	671	Reineke	White Creek, IN	Hakenberg, Brandenburg
Krauß, Sophia Katharina	9, June 1898	9, May	78	367		Marion, OH	Mächtersheim, Speyer, Rheinpfalz Baiern
Krauße, Berthold	8, Aug. 1864	25, June	53	128		Rock River, WI	Waldenburg bei Breslau, Schlesien
Krausse, Johann Friedrich	16, June 1859	13, May	48	96		West Chicago, IL	Altenschlawe, Kreis Schlawe, Preußen
Krause, Karolina	28, July 1859	27, June		120		Waterloo, MI	
Kraut, Anna Martha	20, Mar. 1865	7, Feb.	26- 3m	48	Lampe	Iowa City, IA	Niedernoff, Fritzlar, Kurhessen
Kraut, Carolina Friederike	20, June 1895	23, May	61	398		Louisville, KY	Louisville, Jefferson County, Kentucky
Kraut, Simon	6, July 1863	16, May	24- 3m-24d	108		Iowa City, IA	Troken, Erforth, Homberg, Kurhessen
Krauter, Anna Maria	28, Sept 1854	31, Aug.	49	156	Knaus	Lawrenceburg, IN	Streich, Schorndorf, Württemberg
Krauter, Christian	14, Apr. 1898	18, Mar.	72	239		Louisville, KY	Stuttgart, Württemberg
Krauter, Christina Katharina	5, Mar. 1877	10, Feb.	60- 3m- 4d	79	Börner	Bucyrus, OH	Hartmannsweiler, Waiblingen, Württemberg
Krauter, David	26, Jan. 1854	27, Sept	21	16		Louisville, KY	
Krauter, Gottlieb	21, July 1892		39	462		Bucyrus, OH	Leutenbach, Waiblingen, Württemberg
Krauter, Johan	1, Jan. 1877	7, Dec.	49- 4m- 2d	7		Bucyrus, OH	Leutenbach, Waiblingen, Württemberg
Krauter, Joseph A.	17, Nov. 1898	19, Oct.	17- 6m-25d	735		Bucyrus, OH	
Krauter, Maria	14, Aug. 1846	3, Aug.	5- 2m- 7d	131		Lawrenceburg, IN	
Krauter, Rosina	20, May 1897	9, Apr.	83	319	Rieke	Quincy, IL	Elscheid, Schlesien

Christliche Apologete Death Notices --- 1839 - 1899

Name of Deceased	Notice Date	Death Date	Age	Maiden Name	Page	Place of Death	Place of Birth
Krautter, Johan	8, Oct. 1877	22, Sept	76		327	Lawrenceburg, IN	Streich, Schorndorf, Württemberg
Krebs, August	13, Oct. 1898	10, Sept	41		655	Akron, OH	Schmelwitz bei Schweitnitz, Schlesien
Krebs, August	6, Oct. 1892	10, Sept	74		638	St. Louis, MO	
Krebs, Carl Friedrich Ernst	23, Sept 1897	2, Sept	82		607	San Francisco, CA	Wyke, Insel Föhr, Schleswig-Holstein
Krebs, Catharina	23, June 1887	24, May	31		398	Madison, IN	Madison, Indiana
Krebs, Christine M.	16, June 1853	13, Apr.	23		96	Fond du Lac, WI	Oberwelden, Göppingen, Württemberg
Krebs, Jakobine	21, Oct. 1886	8, Sept	51- 4m-11d	Wägner	7	Eureka, WI	Winterbach, Schorndorf, Württemberg
Krebs, Johan Jakob	8, July 1897	18, June	53		431	St. Louis, MO	Bühl-Watenwyl, Bern, Schweiz
Krebs, Louisa	5, Oct. 1874	4, Sept	22- 3m-30d	Williams	319	Oceola, WI	
Krebs, Louise Elisabeth	25, July 1881	27, June	35	Otto	239	Eureka, WI	Richfield, Washington County, Wisconsin
Krebs, Ludwig	14, Nov. 1870	8, Oct.	80- 9m-23d		367		Kefenach, Sulz, Schweiz
Krebs, Margaretha Eva	23, Aug. 1880	28, July	89-10m		271	Eureka, WI	Keffenach, Elsaß
Krebs, Michael	16, June 1887	28, May	69- 7m-24d		382	Eureka, WI	Kerstenach, Elsaß
Krebs, Rudolf	20, Oct. 1873	1, Oct.	21		335	Bloomington, IL	
Krebs, Valentin	19, Apr. 1844		Inquiry		63	Madison, IN	Kleestadt,
Kreckmann, Lillie Cordelia	3, Nov. 1887	10, Oct.	17- 3m-10d		702	Rochester, NY	
Kreding, Johan	29, Sept 1873	28, Aug.	56- 6m-12d		311	Marble Rock, IA	Weitin, Mecklenburg-Strelitz
Kreeb, Catharina Dorothea	12, Mar. 1866	15, Feb.	67		86	Bucyrus, OH	Lorch, Württemberg
Krehbiel, Anna Maria Elisabeth	31, Mar. 1898	6, Mar.	72	Haacke	207	Cincinnati, OH	Schweningdorf, Germany
Krehbiel, Christian	29, Apr. 1878	7, Apr.	70- 2m		135	Warsaw, IL	
Krehbiel, Jakob	24, July 1890	19, July	63		465	Saginaw, MI	Wachenheim, Hessen-Darmstadt
Krei, Anna	18, Oct. 1875	24, Sept	16		335	Kahoka, MO	Clarke County, Missouri
Krei, Joachim	5, Nov. 1877	20, Oct.	71		359	Kendallville, IN	Gieren, Amt Griewitz, Mecklenburg-Schwerin
Kreider, Dorothea	26, Dec. 1895	5, Dec.	73	Ditzel	828	Louisville, KY	Biedingen, Hessen
Kreie, Louisa	6, May 1886	10, Apr.	62		7	Mt. Vernon, IN	Lichtenberg, Salder, Braunschweig
Kreimann, Friedrich	15, Mar. 1875	3, Feb.	43		87	Brillion, WI	Marienhoff, Teterow, Mecklenburg-Schwerin
Kreimann, Johan	26, Jan. 1874	9, Jan.	46- 2m- 5d		31	Charlestown, WI	Marienhoff, Teterow, Mecklenburg-Schwerin
Kreinhagen, Anna Elisa	18, Feb. 1878	1, Feb.	25- 6m- 1d	Ewers	55	White Creek, IN	Buffalo, New York
Kreinhagen, Friedrich Wilhelm	7, May 1866	1, May	23- 4m		150	Seymour, IN	
Kreinhagen, Wilhelm G.	18, Mar. 1886	20, Feb.	75		7	White Creek, IN	Engster bei Osnabrück, Hannover
Kreinhop, Johan Heinrich	26, June 1876	11, June	69		207	Quincy, IL	Fegehart, Oldenburg
Kreinhop, Magdalena	24, Jan. 1876	15, Dec.	57	Mick	31	Quincy, IL	Elsaß
Kreinhop, Maria Elisabeth	11, Feb. 1867	8, Jan.	45- 5m- 4d		46	Columbus, IL	Hessen-Darmstadt
Kreipke, Anna Margaretha	23, Apr. 1896	25, Mar.	85-11m-24d	Röder	270	Marrs, IN	Altkronau, Kurhessen
Kreis, Jacob	27, Dec. 1860	25, Nov.			208	Michigan City, IN	Weiler, Elsaß
Kreis, Katharina	5, Nov. 1866	9, Oct.	44	Braun	385	Davenport, IA	Niederfaulheim, Hessen-Darmstadt
Kreischer, Katharina	4, Mar. 1867	6, Jan.	53- 8m-24d		70	Galion, OH	Somerset County, Pennsylvania
Kreisle, Louise	19, Aug. 1886	5, Aug.	35- 1m-27d	Bommer	7	Cincinnati, OH	
Kreitler, Elisabeth	14, Apr. 1879	24, Mar.	44	Walter	119	New Rochelle, NY	New York
Kreitmann, Johan Friedrich	7, Feb. 1876	18, Jan.	76		47	Newton, IA	Sulz am Neckar, Württemberg
Kreitner, (Mr)	26, Oct. 1885	12, Oct.	60		7	Sterling, NE	Binzen, Lörrach, Baden
Kreitner, Anna	1, Sept 1873	11, July		Hascher	279	Milan, IN	Merklingen, Blaubeuern, Württemberg
Krell, Anna Elisabeth	23, Dec. 1897	5, Dec.	72	Schäfer	815	Freeport, IL	Süß, Rothenburg, Germany
Kremer, Maria	10, Apr. 1890	19, Mar.	51	Müller	238	Chicago, IL	
Kremer, Theresea	23, Jan. 1890	30, Dec.	41		62	Keokuk, IA	
Kremke, Albert	15, Apr. 1897	20, Mar.	62		239	Jansen, NE	Schaprode, Insel Rügen, Pommern

Christliche Apologete Death Notices --- 1839 - 1899

Name of Deceased	Notice Date	Death Date	Age	Page	Maiden Name	Place of Death	Place of Birth
Kremling, Konradine	3, Mar. 1898	11, Feb.	76	143	Harms	Arlington, NE	Uepfingen, Solder, Braunschweig
Krempel, Anna Maria	15, Mar. 1888	13, Feb.	73- -27d	174	Schmidt	Allegheny City, PA	Kreuznach, RheinPreußen
Krempel, Franz Jacob	22, Mar. 1894	23, Feb.	84	198		Allegheny City, PA	Kreuznach, RheinPreußen
Krenkel, Conrad	19, May 1884	27, Apr.	59-4m	7		Defiance, OH	Semd, Hessen-Darmstadt
Krentz, Carl F.A.	22, Dec. 1873	24, Nov.	46	407		Berea, OH	
Krenzel, Anna	20, Mar. 1876	18, Dec.	55	95	Papen	Lake Creek, MO	Grasdorf, Hannover
Krenzlin, Johan	3, Nov. 1892	8, Oct.	62-11-20d	702		Schnectady, NY	Mecklenburg-Schwerin
Kres, Sophia	11, Sept 1890	8, Aug.	15	590		St. Paul, MN	
Kreß, Andreas	6, Mar. 1846	20, Jan.	40- 3m-15d	39		Galena, OH	Elm, Kurhessen
Kreß, Christina	7, July 1862	20, June	35-11m-14d	108	Essinger	Sherrills Mount, IA	Weiden, Sulz, Württemberg
Kreß, Clara	24, July 1882	6, June	26	239	Putnam	Dubuque, IA	
Kreß, Eduard (Rev)	19, Oct. 1899	30, Sept	55- 5m-19d	671			Wildentaube, Reuß
Kreß, Eduard (Rev)	12, Oct. 1899	30, Sept	55	649			Reuß
Kreß, Emma	31, May 1888	13, May	34	350	Miller	Lawrence, MA	Falkenheim, Preußen
Kreß, Henry S.	31, Dec. 1896	5, Dec.	47	844		Red Wing, MN	Dubuque, Iowa
Kreß, Johanna Ernestina	9, Jan. 1890	21, Dec.	62	30	Kassube	Red Wing, MN	Hewitz, Brandenburg
Kreß, Johannes Nikolaus	7, Mar. 1895	8, Feb.	69	158		Red Wing, MN	Motgers, Schlüctern, Kurhessen
Kresse, Barbara	21, Nov. 1889	6, Oct.	27	750	Löffler	Cameron, MO	Clay County, Missouri
Kresse, Georg	16, Sept 1867	30, Aug.	45	294		Oshkosh, WI	Corbussen, Sachsen-Altenburg
Kresse, Karl	30, Mar. 1893	16, Feb.	76	206		Cameron, MO	Zeitz, Sachsen
Kresse, Laura	7, July 1887	22, June	65	430	Selle	Cameron, MO	Mannsdorf bei Zeitz, Merseburg, Sachsen
Kretsching, Johanne	21, Apr. 1892	17, Mar.	26	254		Beatrice, NE	Pertellen, OstPreußen
Kretzmeier, Heinrich	27, Nov. 1890	31, Oct.	40	766		Brookville, IN	
Kretzmeier, Maria	10, Nov. 1898	17, Oct.	69	719	Busch	Lawrenceville, IN	SüdWeyhe, Syke, Hannover
Kretzmeier, Wilhelm Friedrich	19, Jan. 1888	22, Dec.	25	46		Lawrenceville, IN	Weisburg, Indiana
Kretzmeyer, Dorothea	13, Feb. 1882	25, Jan.	59- - 28d	55		Batesville, IN	Klein-Branbs, Hannover
Kretzmeyer, Friedrich	26, Sept 1895	9, Sept	73	622		Batesville, IN	Schnören, Hannover
Kreudel, Henriette	18, Apr. 1889	19, Mar.	82	254		Freeport, IL	Varenholz, Lippe-Detmold
Kreuske, Dorothea Louise	19, Mar. 1896	26, Feb.	87	190		Faribault, MN	Wallersdorf bei Freienwalde, Pommern
Kreutel, Johan M.	23, Nov. 1885	3, Nov.	71- -17d	7		Freeport, IL	Büchenbronn, Pforzheim, Baden
Kreuter, Christina	25, Mar. 1897	1, Mar.	68	190	Fritsch	Bloomington, IL	Germany
Kreutz, Elisabeth	15, Jan. 1891	25, Dec.	24- -21d	46	Bettin	Lexington, MO	Lafayette County, Missouri
Kreuz, Heinrich	8, Oct. 1891	30, Aug.	29	654		Waseca, MN	Würgendorf, Westphalen
Kreuzer, Heinrich	13, Feb. 1882	21, Jan.	22- 9m-11d	55		Indianapolis, IN	Indianapolis, Marion County, Indiana
Kreuzer, Johan	17, July 1876	1, July	22	231		Indianapolis, IN	Markt Ipsheim bei Winsheim, Baiern
Kreuzer, Johann Christoph	14, Oct. 1852	21, Sept	36	168		Cincinnati, OH	
Kreuzinger, Heinrich	3, July 1846			107		Evansville, IN	
Krichbaum, Anna Catharina	6, Mar. 1856	21, Jan.	78	40	Wirtenberg	Burlington, IA	Oberhausen, Lichtenberg, Hessen-Darmstadt
Krichtbaum, Anna Margaretha	15, May 1851	10, Apr.	52- 9m	80	Hölzheimer	Laughery, IN	Lambertheim, Hessen-Darmstadt
Krieg, Anna Maria	11, June 1896	26, May		383	Diehm	Cincinnati, OH	
Krieg, Elisabeth	14, Aug. 1882	28, July	85- 5m-26d	263	Walter	Metamoras, OH	Beuren, Nürtingen, Württemberg
Krieg, Johan Friedrich	9, Aug. 1880	28, July	70-10m-27d	255		Cincinnati, OH	Anweiler, RheinPfalz Baiern
Kriege, Ernst	28, Mar. 1870	3, Mar.	60	103		Edwardsville, IL	Lienen, Tecklenburg, Preußen
Kriege, Marie Louise	3, Dec. 1883	20, Nov.	71	391	Niemeier	Edwardsville, IL	Laher, Hannover
Kriegel, Agnes	30, Aug. 1894	6, Aug.	36	566	Surky	Corperas Cove, TX	Meschwitz, Sachsen
Krieger, Elisabeth	1, Jan. 1852	2, Oct.		4		Cleveland, OH	Winsingen, Baiern

Christliche Apologete Death Notices --- 1839 - 1899

Name of Deceased	Notice Date	Death Date	Age	Page	Maiden Name	Place of Death	Place of Birth
Krieger, Elisabeth	8, Mar. 1875	3, Feb.	71	79	Domer	Edgerton, OH	Pennsylvania
Krieger, Louis	25, Feb. 1884	7, Feb.	55	7		St. Paul, MN	Blasheim, Preußen
Kriegmann, Johan	17, June 1897	22, May	75	383		Pekin, IL	Norden, Ostfriesland
Kriegsmann, Anna Catharine	12, Mar. 1891	15, Feb.	51	174	Grünsfelder	Pekin, IL	Reilingen, Schwetzingen, Baden
Krienke, Edward August	21, May 1891	13, Apr.	21	334		Sleepy Eye, MN	Fountain Prairie, Wisconsin
Kriesbach, Christian	22, Sept 1853	9, June	21	152		Sandusky, OH	Asch, Kreis Eger, Böhmen
Kriese, Ottilie Bertha W.	12, Dec. 1889	21, Nov.	22	798		Green Bay, WI	Caro, Hinterpommern
Kieser, Wilhelm	23, May 1895	25, Apr.	58	334		Rosendale, WI	Labenz, Pommern
Kriete, Charlotte	30, Sept 1897	9, Sept	87	623	Küter	Owensville, MO	Minden, Preußen
Kriete, Heinrich	18, May 1885	1, May	80	7		Drake, MO	Häverstädt, Minden, Preußen
Krill, Elisabeth Margaretha	20, May 1872	30, Apr.	73	167	Saam	Edgerton, OH	Oberbach, Amt Weilburg, Nassau
Krill, Emma Rebecca	23, May 1870	9, May	8- 6m-22d	167		Edgerton, OH	Allegan, Michigan
Krill, Johan	12, Sept 1889	19, Aug.	65- 7m-25d	590		Stryker, OH	Gaudernbach, Runkel, Hessen-Nassau
Krimbill, Maria Ursula	15, May 1865	26, Apr.		80	Urban	Cedar Lake, IN	Elsaß
Krimmeyer, Elisabeth	22, Dec. 1887	23, Nov.	74	814	Achilles	Angelica, NY	Vollbuttel, Gifforn, Hannover
Krimmeyer, Johan Heinrich	7, June 1875	29, May	65	183		Angelica, NY	Vordorf, Amt Gifhorn, Hannover
Krinn, (Miss)	2, May 1864	25, Mar.	24- 7m-17d	72		Dresden, OH	Hocking County, Ohio
Kritemeier, Karl	2, May 1889	13, Apr.	47	286		Nashville, IL	Schathorst bei Lübeck, Germany
Kritemeyer, Julia	30, Mar. 1899	7, Mar.		207	Fergen	Nashville, IL	Elberfeld, RheinPreußen
Kritsoh, Barbara	13, Dec. 1880	9, Nov.	28-11m- 1d	399	Gömmel	Indianapolis, IN	
Kriwitz, Ella Louise	31, Oct. 1881	13, Oct.	14- 4m-19d	351		Kendallville, IN	
Kröckel, Barbara	17, Mar. 1892	26, Feb.	79	174		New York City, NY	Oberlin, Sachsen-Meiningen
Kröcker, Bessie	5, Aug. 1878	9, July	12- 2m	247		Muscatine, IA	
Kroeck, Adam	8, Sept 1892	22, Aug.	18	574		Lexington, MO	
Kroell, Georg	4, Oct. 1888	7, Sept	62	638		Lena, IL	Süß, Rothenburg, Germany
Kroft, Felix	8, Aug. 1881	16, July		255		Wabasha, MN	Kaltenwesten, Besigheim, Württemberg
Krogbien, Johan Gottlieb	10, Oct. 1889	14, Sept	69	654		New Rochelle, NY	
Kröger, Johan Heinrich	22, Dec. 1887	24, Nov.	18	814		Ft. Hunter, NY	Ft. Hunter, New York
Krohm, Elisabeth	14, Oct. 1878	21, Sept	22	327		Concordia, MO	
Kröhme, Christoph	25, Apr. 1864	9, Apr.	61	68		Louisville, KY	Schledehausen, Osnabrück, Hannover
Krohn, Dorothea	29, Nov. 1888	8, Nov.	82	766	Baatz	Crandon, SD	Zedlin, Pommern
Krohn, Emma	9, July1883	14, June	11- 8m- 2d	223		Frederick, SD	
Krohn, Friedrich	22, May 1882	6, May	19-11m- 1d	167		Almond, WI	Prust, Pommern
Krohn, Johanne	1, Sept 1887	9, Aug.	84	558	Zimmdas	Almond, WI	
Kroll, Christoph	29, May 1890	27, Apr.	68	350		Montague, MI	Hamianke, Kalmer, Posen
Kroll, Henriette	4, Apr. 1889	5, Mar.	74- 2m-10d	222		Oakland, CA	Karlsruhe, Baden
Kroll, Henriette	2, May 1889	5, Mar.	74- 2m-10d	286		Oakland, CA	Karlsruhe, Baden
Kroll, J.	21, Dec. 1893	24, Nov.	72-10m-12d	814		Arlington, MN	Germany
Kroll, Louise	21, Dec. 1893	30, Nov.	77- 9m- 1d	814		Arlington, MN	
Kroll, Maria	26, Mar. 1883	7, Mar.	61- 5m	103	Schewe	Lincoln, NE	Howish, Mecklenburg-Schwerin
Kroll, Maria	14, Oct. 1872	4, Sept	17- 8m-19d	335		St. Joseph, MO	
Krome, Wilhelm	9, Mar. 1863	16, Jan.	21- 9m	40		Cincinnati, OH	Cincinnati, Hamilton County, Ohio
Kromer, Martin	15, Aug. 1861	11, July	24	132		New Haven, CT	Harthausen, Preußen
Krömling, Heinrich	29, Apr. 1897	23, Mar.	82	271		Quincy, IL	Evesen, Schabern, Braunschweig
Kromminga, Margaretha	16, July 1891	7, June	67- 4m-15d	462	Gröneveld	Emden, IL	Hilkenburg, Ostfriesland
Kröner, Jakobine	10, Nov. 1887	20, Oct.	57- - 7d	718	Emrich	Columbus, OH	Mauchenheim, Baiem

Christliche Apologete Death Notices --- 1839 - 1899

Name of Deceased	Notice Date	Death Date	Age	Page	Maiden Name	Place of Death	Place of Birth
Kronert, Carl	12, Nov. 1866	26, Oct.	51	366		Chicago, IL	Feuerbach, Baiern
Krönlein, Maria Katharina	27, Mar. 1871		43	103		Nokomis, IL	Chicago, Cook County, Illinois
Kroon, Georg	21, May 1891	6, May	12	334		Chicago, IL	Osterdeich, Ostfriesland
Kroon, John	7, Mar. 1881			79		Chicago, IL	
Kropf, Elisabeth	23, July1883	11, July	17	239		Vermillion, OH	Schwarzen-Eck, Bern, Schweiz
Kropp, August	31, Dec. 1877	29, Nov.	32	423		Herman, MO	Almena, Sternberg, Lippe-Detmold
Kropp, Ernst August	15, July 1886	1, June	7- 7m-18d	7		Nebraska City, NE	
Kropp, Georg	5, Sept 1889	10, Aug.	26	574		Nebraska City, NE	
Krosinsky, Friederike Wilhelmine	1, Dec. 1887	21, Oct.	87	766		Stillwater, MN	Prenzlow, Preußen
Krück, Maria	25, Dec. 1890	6, Dec.	25- 1m- 6d	830		Portsmouth, OH	
Krückmann, Karolina	2, Mar. 1874		7- -22d	71		Burlington, WI	
Krückmann, Klara	21, Nov. 1881	2, Nov.	71	375	Wenner	Kenosha, WI	Frönnenberg, Westphalen
Krueger, Elisabeth	14, Oct. 1886	27, Sept	19	7		Wrayville, IL	Drury Twp, Rock Island County, Illinois
Krueger, Karoline	5, May 1898	9, Apr.	50	287	Wagner	Ballwin, MO	Gladenbach, Biedenkopf, Preußen
Krueger, Lulu Henrietta	26, May 1898	3, May	22	335		Topeka, KS	Cincinnati, Hamilton County, Ohio
Krug, John	5, Dec. 1881	16, Nov.	72- -29d	391		Wheeling, WV	Reichensachsen, Kurhessen
Krug, Juliane	5, Aug. 1878	16, July	76	247	Faupel	Wheeling, WV	Reichensachsen, Hessen
Krug, Katharine	3, Feb. 1879	14, Jan.	69	39	Meier	Forest, WI	Kleingladenbach, Hessen-Darmstadt
Krug, Konrad	9, Feb. 1899	13, Jan.	66	95		Charles City, IA	Udenhausen, Hessen-Darmstadt
Krüger, (Mrs)	14, Jan. 1878		66- 8m- 7d	15	Gauger	Kewaunee, WI	Wartikow bei Berlin, Preußen
Krüger, Anna	27, Sept 1875	10, Aug.	33	311	Ottmans	Nashville, IL	
Krüger, Anna	23, May 1895	10, Apr.	23	334		Ballwin, MO	
Krüger, Anna P.	21, Apr. 1887	12, Jan.	23	254	Flater	Milwaukee, WI	Sommerfeld, Krossen, Brandenburg
Krüger, Anton Ludwig	3, Apr. 1882	20, Mar.	78	111		Beaufort, MO	Lippe-Detmold
Krüger, Bertha Augusta Friedrike	21, Feb. 1895	23, Jan.	43	126	Käcker	Kewaunee, WI	Woldenburg, Pommern
Krüger, Carl Friedrich	21, June 1875	8, June	43	199		Clayton, WI	Iowa
Krüger, Carolina	27, Nov. 1882	23, Sept	28	383	Horstmann	Hoyleton, IL	Franklin County, Missouri
Krüger, Carolina Maria	16, May 1889	4, Mar.	64-10m	318	Meyer	Schnectady, NY	Hille, Minden, Preußen
Krüger, Caroline	5, Aug. 1878	13, July	53	247	Weidemann	Wheeling, WV	Justow bei Stettin, Pommern
Krüger, Caroline	26, Feb. 1872	13, Dec.		71	Schenke	Colesburg, IA	Hannover
Krüger, Catharina Maria	2, Oct. 1876	16, Sept	87- 9m	319		Schnectady, NY	Hille, Preußen
Krüger, Charlotte	6, June 1895	10, May	69	366	Varias	Muscatine, IA	Barten Amtsfreiheit, Germany
Krüger, Christian	23, Dec. 1897	4, Dec.	79	815		Sun Prairie, WI	Güterberg, Brandenburg
Krüger, Christian	8, Nov. 1888	11, Oct.	42	718		Fond du Lac, WI	Saatzig, HinterPommern
Krüger, Christina	8, Sept 1887	10, Aug.	69- 5m-26d	574	Schmidt	Fond du Lac, WI	Stück, Mecklenburg-Schwerin
Krüger, Dorothea	20, Apr. 1885	7, Apr.	74- 4m-17d	7		Cincinnati, OH	
Krüger, Dorothea Maria Johanna	21, Jan. 1884		59	7	Schuldt	Detroit, MI	Günz, Vorpommern
Krüger, Elisabeth	19, Jan. 1885	28, Dec.	40	7	Steckert	Evansville, IN	Wachenheim, Baiern
Kruger, Emilia	18, May 1899	30, Mar.	18	319		Forest, WI	Forest, Fond du Lac County, Wisconsin
Krüger, F.W.	16, May 1864	2, Mar.	50	80		Rush Creek, IL	Bitkow, Brandenburg, Preußen
Krüger, Fr.	25, Feb. 1878	8, Feb.	69	63		Kewaunee, WI	Wetelwitz, Köslin, Pommern
Krüger, Frank	10, May 1888	6, Mar.	41	302		Colesburg, IA	Schaale, Tecklenburg, Preußen
Krüger, Frd.	18, Nov. 1886	23, Oct.	79	7		Washington, MN	Köslin, Pommern
Krüger, Friedrich	13, May 1867	10, Apr.	60	150		Schnectady, NY	Bünte, Kreis Minden, Preußen
Krüger, H.	3, Jan. 1895	6, Dec.	80	14		Garner, IA	
Krüger, Heinrich	8, Aug. 1889	4, July	67	510		St. Louis, MO	Hille, Preußen

- 281 -

Christliche Apologete Death Notices --- 1839 - 1899

Name of Deceased	Notice Date	Death Date	Age	Maiden Name	Place of Death	Page	Place of Birth
Krüger, Heinrich	18, Apr. 1881	31, Mar.	42- 2m- 8d		Beaufort, MO	127	Greenwood Prairie,
Krüger, Helene	3, Oct. 1889	5, Sept	15- 9m- 2d		Wrayville, IL	638	Sulzfeld, Eppingen, Baden
Krüger, Herman	9, Mar. 1885	28, Nov.	6- 7m-11d		Menominee, MI	7	Brallentheim bei Stargard, Pommern
Krüger, Herman Julius	27, Apr. 1893	23, Mar.	22		Rochester, MN	270	Witzmütz, Stettin, Preußen
Krüger, Johan	17, Sept 1877	18, Aug.	63		Henderson, KY	305	Planich bei Kreuznach, Preußen
Krüger, Johan Friedrich	12, Dec. 1895	17, Nov.	74		Clarington, OH	798	Görnin, Vorpommern
Krüger, Johan Gottfried	2, Sept 1872	8, Aug.	61		Kenosha, WI	287	Rinarzewo, Posen, Preußen
Kruger, Johan Philipp	23, Oct. 1876		57-10m-10d		Summerfield, IL	343	Parchim, Mecklenburg-Schwerin
Krüger, Johanna	3, Oct. 1881	28, Aug.	70		Danville, IL	319	Hille, Minden, Preußen
Krüger, Karl	19, Apr. 1875	17, Mar.	56		New Braunfels, TX	127	Plaunich, Hessen-Darmstadt
Krüger, Karl Julius	6, Dec. 1894	3, Nov.	86		Michigan City, IN	790	
Krüger, Karoline Marie Luise	15, Dec. 1898	15, Nov.	44	Reimler	Schnectady, NY	799	
Krüger, Katharina	29, Sept 1873	4, Sept		Miller	Summerfield, IL	311	Pommern
Krüger, Katharina	31, July 1876	14, July	25-10m-26d	Litzenberger	Newburg, IN	247	
Krüger, Louisa	2, Dec. 1872	2, Dec.	71		Schnectady, NY	391	
Krüger, Louise	10, Dec. 1891	16, Nov.	88	Gutzmer	Maine, WI	798	Forest, Fond du Lac County, Wisconsin
Krüger, Ludwig Heinrich Herman	26, Sept 1895	27, Aug.	24		Stevens Point, WI	622	Idar, Birkenfeld, Germany
Krüger, Margaretha	27, Sept 1880	14, Sept	91- 5m- 4d	Helder	Evansville, IN	311	Louisville, Jefferson County, Kentucky
Krüger, Maria	24, May 1880	20, Apr.	30- 5m-15d	Hugo	Parsons, KS	167	Schlepkow, Prenzlau, Potsdam, Preußen
Krüger, Maria	29, Apr. 1886	4, Apr.	75	Witte	Illinois City, IL	7	Lulle, Fürstenau, Hannover
Krüger, Maria Elisabeth	3, Sept 1896	10, Aug.	60	Löffers	Colesburg, IA	575	Yancowo, Kolmar, Posen
Krüger, Michael	2, Feb. 1899	30, Dec.	84		Milwaukee, WI	79	Industry, Texas
Krüger, Mina	12, May 1898	11, Apr.	23		Perry, TX	303	Freeport, Illinois
Krüger, Simon	22, Sept 1884	30, Aug.	29		Garner, IA	7	Essern, Dübenau, Hannover
Krüger, Sophia Caroline	21, May 1896		58	Kuhlmann	Waltersburg, IL	334	
Krüger, Susanna	16, June 1884	19, May	81		Tacoma, WA	7	
Kruger, W.	20, Mar. 1865		29		Fond du Lac, WI	48	Rogzow, Preußen
Krüger, Wilhelm Friedrich August	3, July 1882	17, June	51		Marine Mills, MN	215	Brüsewitz bei Stargard, Pommern
Krüger, Wilhelm J.M.	19, Jan. 1893	29, Dec.	37-11m-21d		Milwaukee, WI	46	Rothensier, Stettin, Pommern
Krüger, Wilhelmine	10, May 1888	19, Apr.	68	Schröder	Seguin, TX	302	Rynarzewo, Posen
Krügerherm, Friedrich	20, Jan. 1898	20, Dec.	74		Parsons, KS	47	Schwelentrup, Sternberg, Lippe-Detmold
Krughoff, Anna	11, Apr. 1895	20, Mar.	30	Barthelsmeyer	Hoyleton, IL	238	Neu-Minden, Illinois
Krük, Alla	17, Mar. 1892	17, Feb.	24		Portsmouth, OH	174	
Krull, Christian Friedrich	5, Mar. 1883	14, Feb.	61- 3m-17d		Cosby, MO	79	Wöbbelin, Mecklenburg
Krull, Friedrich	31, May 1888	4, May	61-11m- 9d		Crete, NE	350	Wöbbelin, Mecklenburg-Schwerin
Krull, Ida	24, Nov. 1884	26, Oct.	18- 9m-14d		Cameron, MO	7	
Krull, Johan	24, Apr. 1890	25, Mar.	61- 3m- 1d		Cosby, MO	270	Webelin, Neustadt, Mecklenburg-Schwerin
Krull, Karl	15, Nov. 1888	16, Oct.	65- 4m-15d		Lincoln, NE	734	Wöbbelin, Mecklenburg-Schwerin
Krumenauer, Karl	25, Apr. 1895	27, Mar.	83		Honey Creek, WI	270	Oberbraunbach, Birkenfeld, Germany
Krumenauer, Sophia	11, Apr. 1895	16, Mar.	75		Honey Creek, WI	238	Höhnebach, Rothenburg an der Fulda, Kurhessen
Krumey, Margaretha Elisabeth	12, July 1880	22, June	31- 1m	Petri	Quincy, IL	223	
Krümling, Johan Gottfried	23, Oct. 1890	24, Sept	60		Toledo, OH	686	Emden bei Magdeburg, Preußen
Krümling, Johan Heinrich	2, Nov. 1885	19, Oct.	22		Toledo, OH	7	
Krümling, Sarah Craft	12, July 1894	13, June	35		Toledo, OH	454	Wapakoneta, Auglaize County, Ohio
Krumm, Dorothea	23, May 1850	14, Jan.	34			84	Württemberg
Krumm, Johan Jakob	19, June 1871	28, Apr.	65		German Creek, IA	199	Omenhausen, Reutlingen, Württemberg

Christliche Apologete Death Notices --- 1839 - 1899

Name of Deceased	Notice Date	Death Date	Age	Maiden Name	Page	Place of Death	Place of Birth
Krumm, John	31, May 1860	27, Apr.	23- 5m-20d		88	German Creek, IA	
Krumm, Magdalena	2, June 1887	11, May	70		350	Harper, IA	Schaafheim, Hessen-Darmstadt
Krumme, Dorothea	27, Mar. 1865	26, Feb.	41- 6m-12d	Dreyer	52	St. Joseph, MO	Lübenau, Hannover
Krumme, Heinrich	23, Oct. 1871	1, Aug.	28		343	St. Joseph, MO	
Krummel, Friedrich	12, Apr. 1888	15, Mar.	88- 2m- 9d		238	Nokomis, IL	Vöhl, Hessen-Darmstadt
Krummel, Johan Reinhard	8, Feb. 1894	9, Jan.	77		94	Batesville, IN	Winzlen, Zweibrücken, Rheinpfalz Baiern
Krümmel, Katharina	26, Sept 1889	20, Aug.	31- 8m-21d	Broening	619	Baltimore, MD	Baltimore, Maryland
Krümmling, Christian G.	19, June 1890	25, May	56		398	Toledo, OH	Emden bei Magdeburg, Preußen
Krumnow, Friedrich C.	9, June 1884	3, May	33		7	Graffyville, TX	Flathof, Brandenburg
Krümpel, Anna Adelheid	2, Apr. 1896	14, Mar.	93	Hartbeke	222	Garner, IA	Talgen, Büppen, Fürstenau, Hannover
Krümpel, Elisabeth	17, Mar. 1879	28, Feb.	77- 4m-13d		87	Colesburg, IA	Bechtel, Hannover
Krümpel, H.	22, Nov. 1860	28, Oct.	61		188	Sherrills Mount, IA	Bippen, Hannover
Krümpel, Herman Diedrich	3, July 1890	3, June	88		430	Colesburg, IA	Hannover
Krümpel, Johan Herman	21, Jan. 1884	5, Jan.	84- 6m		7	Garner, IA	Talgen, Bübben, Fürstenau, Hannover
Krumrei, Michael	7, Dec. 1868	21, Nov.	65		391	Berea, OH	Großkotten, Preußen
Krumrey, Andreas	26, Apr. 1875	8, Mar.	35		135	Quincy, IL	Württemberg
Krumsick, Fr. Ernst	4, Oct. 1869	16, Sept	51		319	Nashville, IL	Alverdissen, Lippe-Detmold
Krumsick, Katharina	24, May 1888	5, May	63	Kopp	334	Nashville, IL	Oberamt Heidenheim, Württemberg
Krumsick, Louise Julaine	11, Apr. 1870	27, Mar.	32-10m-27d	Ohstedt	119	Nashville, IL	Gustedt, Hannover
Krumsick, Maria Louise	28, Apr. 1879	5, Apr.	16- 9m-29d		135	Nashville, IL	
Krumwiede, Abigail	18, Dec. 1882	4, Dec.	59		407	Chester, IL	
Krumwiede, Maria	5, Apr. 1869	25, Jan.	62	Andermann	111	Chester, IL	Bossel, Amt Nienburg, Hannover
Krumwiede, Wilhelm	17, Aug. 1863	11, July	14		132	Chester, IL	Stöckse, Amt Nienburg, Hannover
Kruschke, Anna Regina	8, Nov. 1894	16, Oct.	72		726	Beaver Dam, WI	Megow, Pieritz, Pommern
Kruschke, Gottlieb	14, Dec. 1874	29, Nov.	56		399	Beaver Dam, WI	Schwachenwalde, Arnswalde, Preußen
Kruse, (Mrs)	20, May 1897	13, Apr.	91		319	Salem, MN	Halen, Minden, Preußen
Kruse, Anna	19, June 1865	3, May	81	Buthmann	100	Smithton, MO	Neuenbüelstedt, Amt Ottersberg, Hannover
Kruse, Annetta	9, Feb. 1899	18, Jan.	69- 3m-15d	Windler	95	Smithton, MO	Worpendorf, Germany
Kruse, Christian	4, Apr. 1861	5, Mar.	37		56	Arenzville, IL	Bruchmühlen, Amt Grönenberg, Hannover
Kruse, Christian	27, Nov. 1876	21, Oct.	64		383	Salem, MN	Hahlen, Minden, Preußen
Kruse, Elisabeth	27, Nov. 1882	5, Nov.	49- 9m-24d	Kätterheinrich	383	New Knoxville, OH	Ladbergen, Tecklenburg, Preußen
Kruse, Enne	30, Dec. 1872	17, Dec.	20-11m-17d		423	Mascoutah, IL	Extum, Amt Auerich, Hannover
Kruse, Ernst A.	12, Nov. 1847	2, Sept	32		183	New Orleans, LA	
Kruse, Franziska	29, Oct. 1883	27, Sept	65- 9m-14d	Meyer	351	Dalton, MO	Freiburg, Baden
Kruse, Georg	1, Sept 1884	16, Aug.	84- 2m- 9d		7	Peoria, IL	Wehner, Ostfriesland
Kruse, Gerhard Heinrich	8, Nov. 1855	13, Sept	49- 5m		180	Sidney, OH	Ladbergen, Tecklenburg, Preußen
Kruse, Gerjert	4, June 1877	11, May	59- 3m		183	Mascoutah, IL	Kleinhafen bei Emden, Ostfriesland
Kruse, Heinrich	2, Oct. 1856	29, Aug.	54		160	Marthasville, MO	Riemsloh, Amt Gröningen, Hannover
Kruse, Heinrich	22, Dec. 1873	29, Nov.	59		407	Brunswick, MO	Friedewald, Minden, Preußen
Kruse, Heinrich Hans Friedrich	16, May 1895	27, Apr.	53		318	Columbus, WI	Gamehl, Buckoff, Mecklenburg-Schwerin
Kruse, Heinrich Wilhelm	16, May 1861	15, Apr.	7- 5m- 6d		80	New Knoxville, OH	
Kruse, Hey Allack	13, Aug. 1877	17, July	61		263	Arenzville, IL	Ostdahl, Ostfriesland
Kruse, Jemina	31, Dec. 1866	4, Dec.	37	Reinhardt	422	Santa Claus, IN	Bork County, North Carolina
Kruse, Joh. Joachim	28, Jan. 1867	30, Dec.	83- 4m		30	Smithton, MO	Horstedt, Amt Ottersberg, Hannover
Kruse, Johan Dietrich	30, Nov. 1874	25, Oct.	56		383	Smithton, MO	Neuenbilstädt, Odersberg, Hannover
Kruse, Johan Heinrich	16, Nov. 1893	31, Oct.	70		734	Smithton, MO	Neuenbolsstett, Hannover

- 283 -

Christliche Apologete Death Notices --- 1839 - 1899

Name of Deceased	Notice Date	Death Date	Age	Maiden Name	Place of Death	Page	Place of Birth
Kruse, Johanna	9, June 1898	21, May	98	Giese	Auburn, IN	367	Rothmanshagen, Preußen
Kruse, Katharine	28, Jan. 1884	6, Jan.	63	Riemann	St. Louis, MO	7	Bur, Melle, Hannover
Kruse, Katharine	7, Jan. 1858	4, Nov.	68- 4m		Arenzville, IL	4	Reinslo, Hannover
Kruse, Margaretha	10, Mar. 1898	16, Feb.	53	Kahrs	Sedalia, MO	159	Lake Creek, Pettis County, Missouri
Kruse, Margaretha	12, Dec. 1881	17, Nov.	16		Sedalia, MO	399	
Kruse, Maria	24, Aug. 1885	10, Aug.	26- -23d		Mascoutah, IL	7	Buhr, Amt Grönenberg, Hannover
Kruse, Maria Elisabeth	9, Apr. 1866	17, Jan.	83	Henscher	Arenzville, IL	118	
Kruse, Sonora	19, Nov. 1877	5, Nov.	14- 2m- 3d		Brunswick, MO	375	Norden, Ostfriesland
Kruse, Wübke	14, Mar. 1889	4, Feb.	71-10m-20d	Thölen	Greensburg, KS	174	Ladbergen, Tecklenburg, Preußen
Krusenklaus, Christina	21, Apr. 1884	25, Mar.	60- 6m- 9d	Hülsmeier	Huntingburg, IN	7	Ladbergen, Tecklenburg, Preußen
Krusenklaus, Heinrich Wilhelm	10, Sept 1891		69		Huntingburg, IN	590	Gultzow, Mecklenburg-Schwerin
Krusse, Caroline	5, July 1894	19, May	62	Biedermann	Poughkeepsie, NY	438	Bartholomew County, Indiana
Kruwel, Anna Maria	21, Apr. 1873	24, Mar.	20	Hartmann	Seymour, IN	127	Bartholomew County, Indiana
Kruwel, Emilie Charlotte	25, Oct. 1869	22, Sept	26	Stockhofer	Seymour, IN	343	Osnabrück, Hannover
Kruwel, Johann Adam	2, June 1859	6, May	40- 4m-18d		Rockford, IN	88	Jeggen, Amt Osnabrück, Hannover
Kruwel, Johann Heinrich	5, Dec. 1861	12, Nov.	67		Seymour, IN	196	Engter, Amt Vörden, Hannover
Kruwel, Maria	19, Dec. 1864	27, Nov.	60	Schmersal	Columbus, IN	204	Bartholomew County, Indiana
Kruwel, Maria Emma	17, Jan. 1895	23, Dec.	21		White Creek, IN	46	Liedolsheim, Baden
Kubach, Christian	10, Oct. 1881	7, Sept	73		Milwaukee, WI	327	
Kubach, Ludwig	23, July 1891	6, June	25		Enterprise, KS	478	
Kuball, Wilhelmine Albertine H.	25, Feb. 1892	22, Jan.	70	Seils	Baraboo, WI	126	Reinwasser, Rummelsburg, Pommern
Kübbeler, Johan Joseph	7, Nov. 1889	20, Oct.	21		Toledo, OH	718	Sabbath Rest, Pennsylvania
Kube, Elisabetha	12, Jan. 1863	8, Nov.	56	Hilmes	Nauvoo, IL	8	Raudenhausen, Kurhessen
Kubitz, Otto	17, Oct. 1889	15, Sept	43- 4m-23d		Chicago, IL	670	Safin, Lauenburg, Pommern
Kübler, Anna	11, Oct. 1855	7, Sept	51	Surbeck	Laporte, IN	164	Sieblingen, Schaffhausen, Schweiz
Kübler, Anna	16, Jan. 1890	27, Dec.	59- 9m-17d	Wanner	Laporte, IN	46	Schleitheim, Schaffhausen, Schweiz
Kübler, Anna Barbara	4, Mar. 1897	14, Feb.	75	Decker	Honey Creek, WI	143	Oberstetten, Württemberg
Kübler, Charles	30, Dec. 1886	31, Oct.	68		Los Angeles, CA	7	Mainhardt, Württemberg
Kübler, Christian	6, Oct. 1892	4, Sept	60		Friendship, WI	638	Hornberg, Württemberg
Kübler, Eva Maria	25, Sept 1890		82-11m- 7d	Kalmbach	Mankato, MN	622	Zundorf, Rangold, Württemberg
Kübler, Friedrich	21, Jan. 1892	2, Jan.	64			46	Michelstadt, Hessen-Darmstadt
Kübler, Gertrud	7, Apr. 1862	24, Feb.	24	Schlee	Ann Arbor, MI	56	Waldorf, Nagold, Württemberg
Kübler, Gottl. Fr.	21, Jan. 1848	29, Dec.	39- - 4d		West Baltimore, MD	15	Oberamt Backnang, Württemberg
Kübler, Ida	23, July 1891	14, June	21		Toledo, OH	478	Toledo, Lucas County, Ohio
Kübler, Jacob	11, Sept 1882	17, Aug.	76		Dunkirk, NY	295	Siblingen, Schaffhausen, Schweiz
Kübler, Jakob	28, Nov. 1870	29, Oct.	42			383	Sipplingen, Schaffhausen, Schweiz
Kübler, Johan Christian	2, Dec. 1867	12, Oct.	87- 4m-27d		Menomonie, WI	382	Ittenberg, Backnang, Württemberg
Kübler, Johan Georg	3, Feb. 1868	14, Jan.	24		Fond du Lac, WI	39	Hornberg, Calw, Württemberg
Kübler, Johan Gottlieb	27, June 1895	6, June	75		Honey Creek, WI	414	Göppingen, Württemberg
Kübler, Johannes	12, Mar. 1877	23, Feb.	76		Wyandotte, KS	87	Oberheinrieth, Württemberg
Kübler, Magd.	6, Sept 1869	16, Aug.	68		Toledo, OH	287	Sieblingen, Schaffhausen, Schweiz
Kübler, Maria	8, Aug. 1881	26, July	74	Fischer	Wyandotte, KS	255	Affaltrach, Weinsberg, Württemberg
Kübler, Marie	26, Jan. 1885	10, Sept	27		Stockton, CA	7	Palermo, Doniphan County, Kansas
Kübler, Rosina Katharina	18, Nov. 1886	5, Nov.	82	Jordan	Poughkeepsie, NY	7	Burgstall, Marbach, Württemberg
Küch, Konrad	4, Sept 1876	13, July	24- 9m-27d		New Bremen, IL	287	Königswald, Rothenburg, Kurhessen
Kuchen, Katharina	6, Dec. 1880	15, Nov.	64	Deboben	Dayton, OH	391	Dittelsheim, Hessen-Darmstadt

Christliche Apologete Death Notices --- 1839 - 1899

Name of Deceased	Notice Date	Death Date	Age	Page	Maiden Name	Place of Death	Place of Birth
Kuchenbecker, Meta	3, Apr. 1890	27, Feb.	79- 8m- 1d	222	Woltmann	Brooklyn, NY	Lübberstedt, Hagen, Hannover
Kuchenbeiser, Katharina	8, Feb. 1894	5, Jan.	72	94	Hoovert	San Jose, CA	Saarbrücken, Preußen
Küchenmeister, Joachim	8, Apr. 1867	20, Mar.	44- -29d	110		Laporte, IN	Jürgenshagen, Mecklenburg-Schwerin
Küchmann, Maria	24, Jan. 1881	7, Jan.	76- -25d	31	Siebert	Muscatine, IA	Gatensberg, Fritzlar, Kurhessen
Kuck, Anna	6, Jan. 1879	14, Dec.	17- 9m- 9d	7		Charles City, IA	Lansing, Allamakee County, Iowa
Kuck, Anna Maria Elisabetha	9, Apr. 1857	21, Mar.	48	60		Sidney, OH	Ladbergen, Tecklenburg, Preußen
Kuck, Christina Elisabeth	23, Feb. 1874	6, Feb.	55	63	Sundermann	Huntingburg, IN	Ladbergen, Münster, Preußen
Kück, Elisabeth Dorothea	22, July 1858	4, July	33- 7m- 6d	116	Beihl	Wheeling, VA	Münchhof, Kreis Rezart, Baiern
Kuck, Heinrich	2, Feb. 1863	10, Oct.	23	20		Lansing, MI	Adolfsdorf, Amt Lilienthal, Hannover
Kuck, Herman W.	13, Feb. 1896	5, Jan.	86	110		Huntingburg, IN	Preußen
Kück, Katharina	20, Oct. 1848	22, Sept	22- 7m	172		Marietta, OH	
Kück, Meta	24, May 1880	10, May	33	167	Bischof	Beaver Falls, MN	Meierdamm, Achim, Hannover
Kück, Metha	2, Mar. 1893		28	142	Bürfeind	North Redwood, MN	Schloßdorf, Blinnthal, Germany
Kück, Sophia	24, Apr. 1882	5, Apr.	63- 3m-10d	135		Marietta, OH	Hannover
Kück, Wilhelm	12, Oct. 1899	29, Aug.	51	655		Holland, IN	Dubois County, Indiana
Kuckenbeißer, Katharina	24, Jan. 1889	9, Jan.	63	62	Pfeifer	Cincinnati, OH	Karlsruhe, Baden
Kückenmeister, Rosina	12, June 1876		48	191	Stolze	Rock River, WI	Lichteneigen, Sachsen
Kücker, Heinrich	8, June 1893	21, May	74	366		Kewaunee, WI	Lappenow, Preußen
Kücker, Juliane Jakobine	7, Apr. 1879	2, Mar.	78	111	Kohler	Nauvoo, IL	Bönnigheim, Besigheim, Württemberg
Kuebler, Rosina	20, May 1886	28, Feb.	61	7		San Francisco, CA	Meinhardt, Württemberg
Kuecker, Dietrich	18, Dec. 1871	3, Dec.	74	407		Red Bud, IL	
Kuehl, Catharine	10, Sept 1891	21, Aug.	87	590	Gruemmer	Crown Point, IN	Lensahn, Holstein
Kuehl, Christian Wilhelm J.	2, Feb. 1888	8, Jan.	54- 7m-18d	78		Creston, IN	Hohenstein, Gut Farve, Schleswig-Holstein
Kueker, Heinrich	14, Mar. 1870	25, Feb.	70	87		Nauvoo, IL	
Kuerner, Christine Louise	26, Sept 1881	7, Sept	48	311	Siebrecht	Wheeling, WV	
Kuerner, Roseline	8, May 1882	15, Apr.	18- 1m-27d	151		Wheeling, WV	
Kues, Doris	31, July 1865	30, Apr.	17- 1m	124		New Orleans, LA	
Küf, John	23, Aug. 1860	12, Aug.	43	136	Herzog	Marietta, OH	Schlußdorf, Amt Ottersberg, Hannover
Kufahl, Otto	18, Aug. 1892	27, July	25	526		Watertown, WI	Tribus bei Treptow an der Rega, Pommern
Küfer, Heinrich	19, May 1892	23, Apr.	19- 3m- 2d	80		Captina, OH	Captina, Monroe County, Ohio
Kugel, Friedrich	24, Jan. 1881	1, Jan.	50	31		Storm Lake, IA	
Kugele, Margaretha	5, Apr. 1888	14, Mar.	67	222		Dayton, OH	Plech, Baiern
Kuhbach, Conrad	22, May 1882	6, May	57	167		Enterprise, KS	Liebolsheim, Baden
Kuhe, Katharina B.	16, Dec. 1897	26, Nov.	88	799	Aupperle	Kramer, NE	Birken-Weißbuch, Württemberg
Kuhfuß, Christ.	2, Jan. 1896	9, Dec.	73	14		Herman, MO	Bösingfeld, Lippe-Detmold
Kuhfuß, Friedrich	19, Dec. 1864	14, Oct.	53	204		Hopewell, MO	Bösingfeld, Amt Sternberg, Lippe
Kuhfuß, Friedrich	19, Dec. 1864	23, Nov.	17	204		Hopewell, MO	Bösingfeld, Amt Sternberg, Lippe
Kuhl, Johanna Henrietta	21, Jan. 1897	28, Nov.	82	46	Scheffler	Beaver Dam, WI	Schönrade, Friedeberg, Neumark
Kuhl, Augusta	5, Feb. 1883	28, Dec.	64	47	Moldenhauer	Marshall, WI	Blankensien, Neumark, Preußen
Kuhl, Carl Friedrich	25, June 1891	13, May	68	414		Beaver Dam, WI	Siede, Neumark
Kuhl, Christian Heinrich	1, Jan. 1847	17, Sept	9d	3		Beardstown, IL	
Kuhl, Elisabeth	1, Jan. 1872	2, Dec.	85- 6m	7		Beardstown, IL	Bindsachsen, Hessen-Darmstadt
Kuhl, Emilie	3, June 1872	5, May	17- 1m-20d	183		Warrenton, MO	Quincy, Illinois
Kuhl, Georg	14, Sept 1893	21, Aug.	86	590		Beardstown, IL	Hessen-Darmstadt
Kühl, Gustav Adolph	10, Dec. 1896	7, Nov.	23-11m-23d	798		Tomah, WI	Adrian, Wisconsin
Kühl, Heinrich	14, June 1888	24, May	19-10m-25d	382		Tomah, WI	

Christliche Apologete Death Notices --- 1839 - 1899

Name of Deceased	Notice Date	Death Date	Age	Page	Maiden Name	Place of Death	Place of Birth
Kuhl, Heinrich Conrad	1, Jan. 1847	4, Sept	1-11m-21d	3	Schuppan	Beardstown, IL	Neudorf bei Zittau, Sachsen
Kuhl, Henriette	6, Oct. 1892	9, Nov.	78	638		Burlington, IA	Bindsachsen, Büdington, Hessen-Darmstadt
Kuhl, Johan Georg	26, Nov. 1891	9, Nov.	61	766		Pekin, IL	Bindsachsen, Hessen-Darmstadt
Kuhl, Johan Georg	22, Mar. 1869	6, Mar.	59	95		Beardstown, IL	Neu Gintersdorf, Sachsen
Kuhl, Johanne Christiane	2, Aug. 1849	8, July	30	124		Beardstown, IL	Eglosheim, Württemberg
Kühl, Katharine Maria	9, July 1891	8, June	64	446	Kraft	Wheeling, WV	Roggow bei Daber, Pommern
Kühl, Leantina W.	20, Aug. 1896		62	543	Kasten	Lowell, WI	
Kuhl, Margaretha	27, Dec. 1888	14, Dec.	22-4m-8d	830		Allegheny City, PA	Lohra, Marburg, Preußen
Kuhl, Michael Friedrich	16, Feb. 1888	29, Jan.	73-11m-14d	110		Sun Prairie, WI	Pomtoff, Peritz, Pommern
Kühl, Reinhart	27, Dec. 1880	29, Nov.	25	415		Warren, OH	
Kühl, Wilhelm	13, Jan. 1887	16, Dec.	67- 7m	30		Stockton, CA	Hessen-Darmstadt
Kühl, William Christian	27, Apr. 1863	14, Mar.	12- 2m	68		Stockton, CA	
Kühlborn, Heinrich	15, Nov. 1875	9, Oct.	39-10m-23d	367		Clarington, OH	Nieste, Oberkaufungen, Hessen-Kassel
Kühle, Christian Ludwig	25, Apr. 1895		78	270		Cleveland, OH	Doderstadt, Hannover
Kühle, Eduard	17, Sept 1877	10, Aug.	18-10m- 1d	305		Cleveland, OH	
Kühle, Ferd.	5, Apr. 1875	21, Mar.	76- 3m-14d	111	Dorrges	Jackson, MO	Alt-Gandersheim, Braunschweig
Kühle, Hanna	28, Apr. 1898	2, Apr.	72- 7m- 7d	271	Heyer	Gordonville, MO	Bierbergen, Beina, Hannover
Kuhlenkamp, Maria Catharina	17, Feb. 1887	27, Jan.	29	110		Brighton, IL	Red Bud, Monroe County, Illinois
Kuehler, Johan Wilhelm	25, Feb. 1886	6, Jan.	88	7		Parker, SD	Westfelden, Solingen, Preußen
Kuehler, Maria Katharine	28, Aug. 1890	30, July	85	558	Funke	Waconda, SD	Witzhelden, Düsseldorf, Preußen
Kühlin, Wilhelm	18, Sept 1882	5, Sept	48	303		St. Paul, MN	Isenkirch, Marienwerder, Preußen
Kühling, Daniel	1, Jan. 1872	22, Nov.	24	7		De Soto, MO	Madison County, Missouri
Kuhlman, Wilhelm	24, Nov. 1892	31, Oct.	39	750		Allegan, MI	Preußen
Kuhlmann, Anna	10, Feb. 1879	14, Dec.	20 - 7m	47		Berea, OH	Filehne, Posen, Preußen
Kuhlmann, Anna Margarethe Elis.	29, Oct. 1896	2, Oct.	59	703	Kleine	Colesburg, IA	Settrup, Fürstenau, Hannover
Kuhlmann, Caroline L.E.	11, July 1881	19, June	54- 4m- 3d	223	Hiller	Lowell, WI	Großenmarpe, Blomberg, Lippe-Detmold
Kuhlmann, Caroline Wilhelmine	19, Apr. 1894		36	262	Fehling	Lowell, WI	Clyman, Dodge County, Wisconsin
Kuhlmann, Emma Amalia	26, June 1890	7, June	8m- 3d	414		Lowell, WI	
Kuhlmann, Georg	4, Mar. 1886		68	7		Weston, MO	Rothewald, Neustatt, Preußen
Kuhlmann, Herman Dietrich	23, Feb. 1893	3, Feb.	62	126		Colesburg, IA	Vechtel, Bippen, Hannover
Kuhlmann, Johan Heinrich	25, Feb. 1886	13, Feb.	68	7		Lowell, WI	Großenmarpe, Lippe-Detmold
Kuhlmann, Johan Samuel	25, Aug. 1892	17, July	71- 7m-15d	542		Vermillion, OH	Zawada bei Filchen, Posen
Kuhlmann, Sophia	24, Dec. 1891	25, Nov.	65- 2m	830		Galena, IL	
Kuhlmann, Sophie	7, Nov. 1881	3, Oct.	62-11m-23d	359	Dierking	Weston, MO	Rodewald, Neustadt, Hannover
Kuhlmann, Wilhelmina	9, Dec. 1881	19, Nov.	31	196		Milan, IN	Exter, Preußen
Kühlmann, Wilhelmine Ernestine	9, Mar. 1899	31, Dec.	64	159	Thom	Vermillion, OH	Felehn, Preußen
Kuhm, Mathilda	10, Oct. 1895	25, Sept	25	654	Dürigg	Cleveland, OH	Powhatan, Belmont County, Ohio
Kuhn , Christian	15, Feb. 1894	12, Jan.	81	110		Baresville, OH	Canton St. Gallen, Schweiz
Kühn , Katharina	28, Apr. 1898	1, Apr.	73	271	Tempel	Bradford, IN	Hohheim, Nassau
Kuhn, Adam	10, Nov. 1884	26, Oct.	54- -17d	7		Jersey City, NJ	Niedernurph, Kurhessen
Kuhn, Anna	19, Nov. 1866	28, Oct.	70	374	Egele	German Creek, IA	St. Antonien, Graubünden, Schweiz
Kuhn, Elisabetha	26, Feb. 1857	3, Dec.	64	36		Louisville, KY	Nassau
Kühn, Emma Lydia	13, Apr. 1893	18, Mar.	15	238		Bay City, MI	Bay City, Michigan
Kühn, Friederike Wilhelmine	20, July 1885	1, July	49	7	Neumann	Watertown, WI	Collin, Stettin, Pommern
Kuhn, Friedrich	15, Aug. 1889	19, July		526		Kramer, NE	
Kühn, Hanna Charlotte	4, Apr. 1881	9, Mar.	44	111	Rachudt	Lena, IL	Rehwinkel, Preußen

Christliche Apologete Death Notices --- 1839 - 1899

Name of Deceased	Notice Date	Death Date	Age	Page	Maiden Name	Place of Death	Place of Birth
Kuhn, Henriette	21, June 1880	5, June	25	199	Hund	Bay City, MI	St. Clair County, Michigan
Kuhn, Jacob G.	31, Jan. 1876	4, Jan.	66	39		Newark, NJ	Oberbrun, Elsaß
Kühn, Johan	16, Sept 1897	2, Sept	76	591		Newport, KY	Höringen, Kaiserslautern, Baiern
Kuhn, Justus	26, Jan. 1899	18, Dec.	66	63		Tappan, NY	Niederuff, Nassau
Kühn, Katharina Magdalena	11, May 1893	11, Apr.	70- 8m-25d	302		Newport, KY	Wintzlen, Pirmasens, Baiern
Kuhn, Katharine B.	6, Jan. 1898	26, Nov.	88	15	Aupperle	Kramer, NE	Birken-Weißbuch, Württemberg
Kuhn, Margarethe	29, Oct. 1896		84	703		Newark, NJ	Gaisberg, Baiern
Kuhn, Meta	13, Sept 1875	30, Aug.	21	295		Rock Island, IL	Viotho, Preußen
Kuhn, Wilhelm	2, June 1884	14, May	58	7		Cannon River, MN	Westphalen
Kühna, Maria	19, June 1882	2, June	58	199		West Bend, WI	Wolfsheim, Hessen-Darmstadt
Kühnau, Elisabeth	20, Oct. 1887	4, Oct.	24- 5m-28d	670		West Bend, WI	Granville, Wisconsin
Kühne, Conrad	11, Jan. 1849		Inquiry	7		Parksville, MO	Klaunen, Amt Penne, Hannover
Kuhne, Friederika	12, Dec. 1895	28, Oct.	60	798	Stolting	Warren, MO	Meiernberg, Lippe-Detmold
Kuhne, Friederika	9, Jan. 1896	28, Oct.	60	30	Rolting	Warren, MO	Meiernberg, Lippe-Detmold
Kuhne, Heinrich	14, Dec. 1893	31, Oct.	92- 6m-28d	798		Randolph, KS	Westphalen
Kuhne, Henrietta	3, June 1872	1, May	66	183		Randolph, KS	Gohfeld, Minden, Preußen
Kühne, Karl	21, Dec. 1863	30, Nov.	39	204		Galena, IL	Bildshausen, Hannover
Kühne, Karl	12, Oct. 1899	19, July	59	655		Honey Creek, WI	Berlin, Germany
Kühnemund, Christine	17, Mar. 1898	27, Feb.	82	175		Ironton, OH	Hannover
Kühner, Karl	5, Mar. 1896	10, Feb.	70	158		St. Louis, MO	Kusen, Rheinpfalz Baiern
Kühner, Katharina	26, May 1892	11, May	56- 2m-26d	334	Büttner	St. Louis, MO	Kusel, Rheinkreis Baiern
Kühnle, Christine	8, May 1856	12, Apr.	62	76	Warenberg	Ann Arbor, MI	Hohenlohe-Oehringen, Germany
Kühnlein, Friedrich	9, Apr. 1883	23, Mar.	17- 4m-17d	119		Springfield, IL	St. Louis, Missouri
Kuhrke, Louisa	9, Nov. 1893	29, Sept	67	718	Gerth	Clearwater, MN	Preußen
Kuhrt, (Mrs)	11, Dec. 1882	16, Nov.	69- 5m-23d	399	Koplin	Maine, WI	Benatzen, Soldin, Neumark
Kuhrt, Christoph	28, July 1879	3, July	76	239		Wausau, WI	Plönzig, Pieritz, Pommern
Kuhrt, Elisabeth	7, May 1891	18, Apr.	75	302	Lanz	Grantfork, IL	Walterswyl, Draxelwald, Bern, Schweiz
Kuhrt, Wilhelm	6, Aug. 1877	12, July	33	255		Wausau, WI	Cratzen, Soldine, Neumark, Preußen
Kuhrts, Joachim	18, Apr. 1881	1, Apr.	64	127		Ellis Grove, IL	Brunau, Altmark, Preußen
Kuhrtz, Anna Dorothea	28, June 1888	15, June	72- 9m- 3d	414	Schultz	Ellis Grove, IL	Heiligenfelde, Sachsen
Kuhrtz, Elisabeth	23, Oct. 1882	18, Sept	27- 6m-18d	343	Rurödi	Ellis Grove, IL	Perry County, Illinois
Kuk, Maria	16, June 1879	31, May	42	191	Maier	Charles City, IA	Canton Bern, Schweiz
Küker, (Mrs)	9, June 1862	18, May		92	Schneermann	Red Bud, IL	Scharl, Neustadt am Rübenberge, Hannover
Küker, Louisa	12, Apr. 1880	26, Mar.	78- 9m	119	Peters	Eudora, KS	Klostermeierhause, Neustadt, Hannover
Kükert, Peter	12, July 1888	14, June	56	446		Poughkeepsie, NY	Krottelbach, RheinPfalz Baiern
Kulenkamp, Heinrich	21, Nov. 1881	4, Nov.	51	375		Brighton, IL	Hofenmohr, Cruchhausen, Hannover
Kuler, (Mr)	5, July 1894	28, May	82	438		Le Sueur, MN	Segeber, Germany
Kull, Friedrich J.	26, Nov. 1896	9, Sept	71	766		Green Bay, WI	Rieth, Vaihingen, Württemberg
Küllmar, Martin	19, Sept 1895	2, Sept	22	606		New Rochelle, NY	Haddamar, Fritzlar, Kurhessen
Küllmer, Heinrich	12, May 1884	19, Apr.	64- 4m- 8d	7		Brownhelm, OH	Kornberg, Sondra, Kurhessen
Kulmer, Friedrich	30, Aug. 1880	26, July	52- 1m-15d	279		Laporte, IN	Wolkenzien, Mecklenburg-Strelitz
Kumle, Wilhelm	25, Feb. 1884	12, Feb.	41- 6m-10d	7		Chicago, IL	Walterdingen, Baden
Kumm, Louise	21, Apr. 1879	28, Mar.	37- -18d	127	Klingbeil	New Ulm, MN	Butzig, Bromberg, Preußen
Kummer, Barbara	24, July 1871	24, June	63- 2m- 3d	239		Hoboken, NJ	
Kummer, Elisabeth	13, Feb. 1862	21, Dec.	70- 3m	28		Baresville, OH	
Kummer, Henrietta	23, May 1895	29, Apr.	86	334		Bloomington, IL	Sasfinn, Laumburg, Pommern

- 287 -

Christliche Apologete Death Notices --- 1839 - 1899

Name of Deceased	Notice Date	Death Date	Age	Maiden Name	Page	Place of Death	Place of Birth
Kummer, Sophia	7, Apr. 1873	9, Mar.	73- 1m-24d	Dammeyer	111	St. Louis, MO	Repmer, Braunschweig
Kümmerle, Justina Katharina	4, Apr. 1870	23, Jan.	59	Schilling	111	Higginsport, OH	Stetten, Brackenheim, Württemberg
Kumpf, Barbara	17, Mar. 1898	12, Feb.	75	Bauer	175	Pekin, IL	Heppinheim, Hessen-Darmstadt
Kumpf, Karl Philipp	2, Jan. 1865	3, Dec.	55- 3m-24d		4	Poland, IN	Neckarbischofsheim bei Sinsheim, Baden
Kumpf, Maria Elisabeth	7, June 1869	10, May	31	Immig	183	Waterloo, IA	Elfershausen, Amt Melsungen, Kurhessen
Kumpf, Sophia	30, July 1877	15, July	66- 3m-28d		247	Terre Haute, IN	Neckar-Bischofsheim, Baden
Kundel, Carl	1, Aug. 1861	2, May	13		124	Dayton, OH	
Kundel, Peter	1, Aug. 1861	26, June	50		124	Dayton, OH	Hangenweißenheim, Worms, Hessen-Darmstadt
Kundert, Anna	1, Apr. 1878	6, Mar.	63- 1m-16d		103	St. Louis, MO	Canton Glarus, Schweiz
Kundert, Fridolin	1, Jan. 1872	8, Dec.	71		7	Highland, IL	Bilten, Glarus, Schweiz
Kunerth, Ignatz	24, Apr. 1882	8, Mar.	75		135	Minneapolis, MN	Bosdorf, Teschen, Böhmen
Kunerth-Hinkel, Anna	13, Sept 1894	4, Aug.	58		598	LaCrosse, WI	Ebersdorf, Bensen, Böhmen
Kunitz, Christina	29, Apr. 1858	29, Mar.	20- -16d		68	Madison, IN	Gute Rärdorf, Holstein
Kunkel, Anna	22, Jan. 1861	13, Dec.	75	Müller	16	Oregon, MO	Pennsylvania
Kunkel, Carolina	29, Aug. 1889	9, Aug.	77- 3m-22d	Nothdurft	558	Gordonville, MO	Groß-Rüden, Hannover
Kunkel, Friedrich	24, May 1875	21, Apr.	66		167	Madison, IN	Flörschbach, Bieber, Hessen
Kunkel, Georg	31, Mar. 1862		50		52	Cape Girardeau, MO	
Kunkel, Michael	20, Dec. 1869	1, Dec.	53		407	Lawrenceburg, IN	Floisbach, Kurhessen
Kunkel, Sophie	21, June 1888	1, June	76- 4m-16d	Hoffmann	398	Madison, IN	Florsbach, Bibber, Kurhessen
Kunnerth, Franziska	30, Dec. 1897	3, Dec.	45	Tietze	828	LaCrosse, WI	Oberebersdorf, Bensen, Leipa, Böhmen
Kunsmann, Rebekka	9, Sept 1858	2, Aug.	75		144	Ripley, OH	Stein, Amt Bretten, Baden
Künsting, Friederike	15, Sept 1892	2, Sept	58		590	Elmore, OH	Hannover
Künsting, Friedrich W.	28, Aug. 1871	28, July	76- 6m		279	Woodville, OH	Exter, Preußen
Künsting, Wilhelmine	5, Jan. 1885	13, Dec.	80	Sack	7	Elmore, OH	Boneberg, Preußen
Kuntz, Anna Maria	21, Feb. 1876	29, Jan.	77	Schneider	63	Sherrills Mount, IA	Weiboldshausen, Schweinfurt, Baiern
Kuntz, Barbara	15, Mar. 1888	5, Feb.	48- -27d		174	Batesville, IN	Laghery, Indiana
Kuntz, Catharina	17, June 1897	15, May	42		383	Quincy, Illinois	Quincy, Illinois
Kuntz, Elisabetha	23, Nov. 1868	3, Oct.	36- 5m- 5d	Haas	375	Dubuque, IA	Chambersburg, Pennsylvania
Kuntz, Heinrich	18, Sept 1882	26, Aug.	78- - 4d		303	Batesville, IN	Niederbronn, Elsaß
Kuntz, Jacob	15, Nov. 1894	5, Oct.	65		742	Dubuque, IA	Utica, New York
Kuntz, Johannes	1, May 1876	13, Apr.	75		143	Sherrills Mount, IA	Dosenheim, Elsaß
Kuntz, Katharina S.	10, Aug. 1885	28, July	81	Knerr	7	Batesville, IN	Niederborn, Elsaß
Kuntz, Louise	7, Feb. 1895	15, Jan.	61	Landeck	94	Minneapolis, MN	Graumenz, Neustettin, Hinterpommern
Kuntz, Margaretha	31, Jan. 1870	5, Dec.	31	Christofel	39	Greencastle, IN	Landau, Rheinpfalz Baiern
Kuntz, Peter	7, July 1892	30, May	59		430	Sherrills Mount, IA	Pennsylvania
Kuntz, Rosa	20, Mar. 1890	19, Feb.	11-11m- 9d		190	Columbus, IL	McKee Township, Adams County, Illinois
Kuntz, Wilhelm	17, Mar. 1890	17, Mar.	83- 5m- 3d		254	Columbus, IL	Ittlingen, Epingen, Baden
Küntzle, Henriette	7, Apr. 1862	9, Mar.	19		56	East Troy, WI	
Kuntzmann, Maria	12, Jan. 1885	27, Dec.	60- 6m- 6d	Reiners	7	Chicago, IL	Wittmund, Ostfriesland
Kunz, Abraham	12, Oct. 1868	4, Aug.	33		327	Rock River, WI	
Kunz, Amanda	18, Feb. 1886	29, Jan.	21		7	Etna, MO	
Kunz, Anna Maria	8, Nov. 1869		41	Bertram	359	St. Charles, MO	Spenger, Minden, Preußen
Kunz, Carl	16, Apr. 1866		26	Schäper	126	Perry, IL	Pittsburg, Pennsylvania
Kunz, E.	18, Oct. 1880	26, Sept	66- 1m-24d		335	Winona, MN	St. Gallen, Schweiz
Kunz, Evaline S.	22, Apr. 1878	19, 8m- 4d			127	German Creek, IA	
Kunz, Heinrich	7, Mar. 1861	16, Feb.	59- 7m-22d		40	Newport, KY	Winzelen, Pirmasenz, Baiern

- 288 -

Christliche Apologete Death Notices --- 1839 - 1899

Name of Deceased	Notice Date	Death Date	Age	Page	Maiden Name	Place of Death	Place of Birth
Kunz, Heinrich	2, Apr. 1877	9, Mar.	33- 5m- 2d	111		Columbus, IL	Winzeln, Pirmasenz, Baiern
Kunz, Heinrich Philipp	16, Feb. 1885	22, Jan.	61	7		Huntingburg, IN	Stuckwelles, Coblenz, Germany
Kunz, Johan Adam	8, Sept 1892	16, Aug.	69	574		Watertown, WI	Stäfa, Zürich, Schweiz
Kunz, Johannes	1, Dec. 1892	13, Nov.	74	766		Chicago, IL	Weinzlen, Pirmasenz, Baiern
Kunz, Margaretha	13, Apr. 1885	23, Mar.	81- 2m- 7d	7	Wagner	Newport, KY	Obertshausen, Simmern, RheinPreußen
Kunz, Peter	14, Feb. 1876	22, Jan.	46	55		Defiance, OH	
Kunz, Philippine	26, Nov. 1866	4, Nov.	14	382		Warren, MO	
Kunz, Samuel Washington	27, Nov. 1882		28	383		New Albany, IN	Newport, Campbell County, Kentucky
Kunz, Wilhelm Friedrich	5, Nov. 1896	23, Sept	85	719		Beaver Dam, WI	Schönow, Pyritz, Pommern
Kunze, Augusta	27, Apr. 1874	3, Apr.	26- 4m-25d	135	Bilge	Milwaukee, WI	Kerst, Colberg, Pommern
Kunze, Carl	29, Jan. 1883	9, Jan.	72- -19d	39		Spring, TX	Sagan, Liegnitz, Schlesien
Kunze, Christiana	30, July1883	19, July	71- 8m	247	Budig	Rose Hill, TX	Sagan, Liegnitz, Schlesien
Kunze, Friedrich Herman	28, Oct. 1897	11, Sept	71	687		Hartford, CT	Attenburg, Sachsen
Künzel, (Mrs)	7, June 1869	27, May	64	183		Covington, KY	Altenstaig, Nagold, Württemberg
Künzel, (Mrs)	14, June 1869	27, May	64	191		Covington, KY	Altenstaig, Nagold, Württemberg
Künzler, Christian	31, Oct. 1870	12, Sept	46- -27d	351		Mt. Vernon, IN	St. Margaretha, St. Gallen, Schweiz
Künzler, Elisabeth	1, July 1867	6, June	31- 9m- 2d	206	Schmalz	Mt. Vernon, IN	
Kunzmann, Georg	12, Apr. 1894	30, Mar.	68	246		Louisville, KY	Bocklet bei Kissingen, Baiern
Kunzmann, Karolina	8, Jan. 1877	22, Dec.	72- 9m- 4d	15		Pittsburg, PA	Graben, Karlsruhe, Baden
Kunzy, Johan	14, Nov. 1881		66	367		Delaware, OH	Steinenberg, Schorndorf, Württemberg
Kupfer, Hanna Christiana	18, Dec. 1882	29, Nov.	68	407		Wheeling, WV	Stöcken bei Werdau, Sachsen-Weimar
Kupfer, Karl Gottlob	17, Feb. 1873		69	53		Wheeling, WV	Katzendorf, Amt Berga, Sachsen-Weimar
Küpfer, Magdalena	15, Mar. 1860	9, Feb.	84- 1m-21d	44		Spring Lake, IL	Markirche, Elsaß
Kupp, Wilhelm	5, Aug. 1886	20, July	85	7		Aurora, IN	Stadthausen, Baden
Küppers, Herman	30, Aug. 1869	28, July	60	279		Alton, IL	Repelen, Preußen
Kuppinger, Johan Adam	10, Jan. 1895	7, Dec.	65	30		Mason City, IA	Neulsheim, Baden
Kuppinger, M.E.	22, Dec. 1879	21, Nov.	48-11m- 2d	407	Naas	Nora Springs, IA	Hessen-Darmstadt
Kuppinger, M.E.	5, Jan. 1880	21, Nov.	48-11m- 2d	7	Naas	Nora Springs, IA	König, Hessen-Darmstadt
Kürner, Anna C.	16, June 1892	25, May	59	382	Finsel	Wheeling, WV	
Kürner, Edward Ferdinand	23, July 1891	21, June	21-10m- 5d	478		Wheeling, WV	Wheeling, West Virginia
Kurpp, Johan	25, July 1870	3, July	64	239		Seymour, IN	Baumter, Osnabrück, Hannover
Kurrelmeier, Agnes Lisette	14, July 1884	26, June	18	7		St. Paul, MN	Westerkappeln, Preußen
Kurrelmeier, Louise	17, Mar. 1884		12- 5m	7		St. Paul, MN	
Kurrelmeier, Louise	14, July 1884	May		7		St. Paul, MN	
Kurrelmeier, Marie Elise	24, Oct. 1881	10, Oct.	20- 2m-28d	343		St. Paul, MN	Westerkappeln, Preußen
Kurrle, Eva Katharina	24, Sept 1877	30, Aug.	70- -16d	311		Kendallville, IN	Gündelbach, Maulbronn, Württemberg
Kurrle, Georg	27, July 1868	14, July	21	239		Kendallville, IN	Columbiana County, Ohio
Kurrle, Johan Christoph	24, Sept 1877	29, Aug.		311		Kendallville, IN	Stetten, Cannstatt, Württemberg
Kürschner, Ursula	25, Feb. 1892	29, Jan.	60	126		Cincinnati, OH	Appelzell, Schweiz
Kürst, Wilhemine Friederike	30, Mar. 1893	20, Feb.	76	206	Beier	West Point, NE	Zeitz bei Leipzig, Sachsen
Kurt, Adolph	14, Feb. 1889	25, Jan.	44	110		Duncan, NE	Roggwyl, Bern, Schweiz
Kurth, Barbara	22, Apr. 1897	12, Mar.	52 3m- 7d	255	Cadonau	Portland, OR	Waltensburg, Graubünden, Schweiz
Kurth, Emma Helena	5, Nov. 1883	7, Oct.	13- 9m-17d	359		Maine, WI	
Kurth, Friedrike	21, Dec. 1885	28, Nov.	82	7	Naß	Laporte, IN	Mögenhal, Hinterpommern
Kurth, Johan	9, Feb. 1893	23, Jan.	83	94		Highland, Il	Rütschleben, Arwanger, Bern, Schweiz
Kurth, Ursula	22, Apr. 1897	17, Feb.		255		Portland, OR	

Christliche Apologete Death Notices --- 1839 - 1899

Name of Deceased	Notice Date	Death Date	Age	Page	Maiden Name	Place of Death	Place of Birth
Kurtz, Anna Magdalena	5, June 1890	27, Apr.	79	366	Stern	Bloomington, IL	Morsbach, Künzelsau, Württemberg
Kurtz, Elisabeth	3, June 1867	13, May	71	174		Lafayette, IN	Frohnhausen, Preußen
Kurtz, Emilie	1, Nov. 1880		22- 9m	351	Zschiesche	Brenham, TX	Bautzmühle bei Grothenheim, Sachsen
Kurtz, Friedrich	6, Feb. 1846	16, Jan.	51-10m-24d	23		Delaware, OH	Oberamt Schorndorf, Württemberg
Kurtz, Friedrich	13, Aug. 1891	26, July	34	526		Jamestown, MO	Wichtrach, Bern, Schweiz
Kurtz, Georg Ahab	6, Mar. 1890	29, Jan.	22- 1m-19d	158		Lincoln, NE	Washington County, Iowa
Kurtz, Heinrich	21, Dec. 1893	25, Nov.	69	814		Delhi, MI	Geismar, Kurhessen
Kurtz, Johan	30, Aug. 1888	2, Aug.	68- 7m- 3d	558		Peotone, IL	Jesingen, Kirchheim a. d. Teck, Württemberg
Kurtz, Johan	11, June 1877	27, May	52	191		Clearwater, MN	Jessingen, Württemberg
Kurtz, Johan	1, Nov. 1880		65	351		Brenham, TX	
Kurtz, Johannes	25, Mar. 1858	16, Jan.	75- 6m	48		Captina, OH	Wechingen, Bern, Schweiz
Kurtz, Magd. Dorothea	2, Mar. 1868	24, Jan.	80	71	Schmitt	Clarington, OH	Lüchau, Hannover
Kurtz, Maria Anna	25, May 1899	23, Apr.	66	335	Ruter	Lafayette, IN	Gulf of Mexico,
Kurtz, Martha Anna	4, Mar. 1886	16, Feb.	27- - 4d	7		Lake Creek, MO	
Kurtz, Susanna	30, Oct. 1882	8, Oct.	52	351	Wolf	Rocky Hill, TX	Groß Golle, Posen, Preußen
Kurtz, Wilhelm	28, Apr. 1887	6, Apr.	34	270		Rocky, TX	Posen
Kurtz, Wilhelmine	11, May 1868	13, Apr.	68	151	Piper	Flint Creek, IA	Lennup, Düsseldorf, Preußen
Kurz, Anna Sophia	3, Mar.1873	28, Jan.	26- 9m	71	Remagen	Louisville, KY	Hemmerich, Neuwied, Preußen
Kurz, Charles	30, May 1895	26, Mar.	49	350		Troy, NY	Menningen, Württemberg
Kurz, Christina	12, Nov. 1883		16- 8m- 6d	367		Montrose, MN	
Kurz, Friederike	20, Jan. 1873	25, Dec.	69	23	Hardmann	Salem, MN	Türrenzimmern, Brockenheim, Württemberg
Kurz, Friedrich	28, Aug. 1890	30, July	37- 2m-13d	558		Rochester, NY	Buck, Waiblingen, Württemberg
Kurz, Jakob	6, Mar. 1882	6, Feb.	23- -29d	79		Clearwater, MN	
Kurz, Johan David	4, June 1866	16, May	43- 8m	182		Seymour, IN	Elbronn, Maulbronn, Württemberg
Kurz, Katharina	22, Jan. 1883	15, Dec.	18- 6m-21d	31		Clearwater, MN	
Kurz, Louise	15, Mar. 1880	26, Feb.	20- 4m-26d	87		Salem, MN	Waterloo, Jefferson County, Wisconsin
Kurz, Maria Lizzie	12, May 1884	25, Apr.	22	7		Clearwater, MN	St. Cloud, Minnesota
Kurz, Regina	10, Sept 1857	28, Aug.	61	148	Tritt	Delaware, OH	Aichschieß, Schorndorf, Württemberg
Kurz, Rosa Elisabeth	2, Mar. 1893	8, Feb.	28	142		St. Joseph, MO	Mundelsheim, Marbach, Württemberg
Kurzen, Louise	24, Oct. 1895	25, Sept	32	686	Schreyer	Kramer, NE	Neuchatel, Schweiz
Kuse, Henriette Caroline Charlotte	28, Feb. 1870	12, Feb.	33- 8m-14d	71	Niedringhaus	Warsaw, IL	Lübbecke, Preußen
Küsel, Wilhelm	25, Oct. 1888	28, Sept	30-10m-19d	686		Fontanelle, IA	Gandelin, Germany
Kusian, (Mrs)	23, Dec. 1867	8, Dec.	45- 2m-16d	406		Defiance, OH	Neuhaldensleben, Magdeburg, Preußen
Küssinger, Johanna	27, Aug. 1877	10, Aug.	18- 4m- 5d	279		Freeport, IL	
Küster, Augusta Friederike	30, Mar. 1874	15, Mar.	45	103	Reiske	Giard, IA	HinterPommern
Küster, Dorette	29, Oct. 1891	22, Sept	17	702		Thomas Co, KS	Cass County, Iowa
Kuster, Johan	21, July 1879	9, July	85- 8m	231		Batesville, IN	Brienz, Bern, Schweiz
Kuster, John	15, Mar. 1880	25, Feb.	55- 7m	87		Batesville, IN	
Kusterer, Christina	19, Jan. 1863	26, Dec.	40- 4m-26d	12	Kalmbach	Grand Rapids, MI	Pfalzgrafenweiler, Freudenstadt, Württemberg
Kusterer, Henriette	5, May 1884	24, Mar.	52	7	Diterick	Baltimore, MD	Oberkaufungen, Hessen-Kassel
Kusterer, Jakob	25, May 1899	5, May	68	335		Baltimore, MD	Schwarzenberg, Württemberg
Küstermeyer, Heinrich E.	17, Sept 1891	5, Aug.	25	606		Higginsville, MO	Lippe-Detmold
Küther, Albert Ferdinand	30, Oct. 1890	1, Oct.	32	702		Milwaukee, WI	Plantiko, Naugardt, Preußen
Kutler, Rosina	9, July 1877	31, May	33	223	Pfeiffer	Dubuque, IA	Charlesmouth, Dubuque County, Iowa
Kutzbach, Friedrich Wilhelm	14, July 1862		37- 8m-17d	112		Iowa City, IA	Meichow, Angermünden, Potsdam, Preußen
Kyburtz, Dorlisces	12, Feb. 1866	20, Jan.	17	54		East Troy, WI	Wallworth County, Wisconsin

Name of Deceased	Notice Date	Death Date	Age	Maiden Name	Page	Place of Death	Place of Birth
Kyburtz, Friedrich	24, Nov. 1892	31, Oct.	83		750	East Troy, WI	Oberendfeld, Aarau, Schweiz
Kyburtz, Louise	10, Apr. 1876	25, Mar.	55	Lehmann	118	East Troy, WI	Hannover
Kyburz, Daniel	20, Feb. 1862	22, Jan.	84		32	East Troy, WI	Ober-Entfelden, Aargau, Schweiz
Laabs, Martin	15, Mar. 1888		80- 6m-7d		174	Lansing, IA	Sindars, Pommern
Laabs, Wilhelmine	25, Apr. 1895	26, Mar.	89	Pagel	270	Oshkosh, WI	Nateflitz, Pommern
Laage, Carolina	16, Aug. 1875	23, July	19		263	Industry, TX	Bastrop, Texas
Laas, Hanna Malvina	7, Apr. 1859	21, Feb.	22		56	Detroit, MI	
Laas, Leopold (Rev)	19, Dec. 1870				407	Schnectady, NY	Wehrheim, Nassau
Labanta, Amalia	23, Apr. 1883	9, Apr.	64- 4m	May	135	St. Joseph, MO	
Labbo, Wilhelmine	6, Apr. 1868	20, Mar.	82		111	Boonville, MO	
Laber, Elisabeth	14, Oct. 1878		74- 8m-20d	Plath	327	Mill Creek, IL	
Lachtrup, Carolina Agnes	26, Feb. 1891	26, Dec.	27		142	Schnectady, NY	
Lacker, Barbara	9, Feb. 1880	9, Feb.	11- 6m-23d		47	Bay City, MI	Sammerheim, Baiern
Lacker, Michael	28, Mar. 1895	25, Aug.	80- 2m		206	Kochville, MI	
Lacker, Salome	18, Sept 1846		40		161	Philadelphia, PA	
Lackore, Sophia	17, Jan. 1876	2, Jan.	86	Seibert	23	Garner, IA	Ellweiler, Preußen
Lader, Johan	10, Mar. 1898	14, Feb.	63		159	Mankato, MN	Volerdingen, Lothringen
Läderich, Louise	13, Oct. 1892	7, Sept	57		654	San Jose, CA	Elsaß
Ladner, J.	19, July 1849	25, June	67- 1m- 2d		116	Buckhill, OH	
Ladwig, Johanna Chr.	7, Aug. 1890	17, July	54- 3m	Hachmann	510	Sun Prairie, WI	Santien, Brandenburg
Lafon, Elisa	28, May 1866	14, Apr.	80		174	Summerfield, IL	
Lafontaine, (Mr)	21, Feb. 1856	10, Jan.			32	Mascoutah, IL	
Lafranz, Carsten	7, June 1849		Inquiry		91	Canton, MO	
Lafrenz, (Mrs)	6, Aug. 1877	22, July	64		255	Lake Creek, MO	Willstedt, Hannover
Lafrenz, Elisabeth	13, June 1895	10, May	67	Obländer	382	Etna, MO	Zuzenhausen, Sinsheim, Baden
Lafrenz, Joachim Heinrich	19, June 1876	1, June	68		199	Etna, MO	Bansdorf, Insel Fehmern, Holstein
Lafrenz, Maria A.	22, Dec. 1898	13, Nov.	49	Eiermann	815	Etna, MO	Ober-Gimmbern, Baden
Lafrenz, Milta	2, Aug. 1855	27, May	40		124	Canton, MO	Bremerhafen, Germany
Lagemann, Dorothea	22, Aug. 1881	14, July	59	Klein	271	Chicago, IL	Mecklenburg-Schwerin
Läger, (Mrs)	18, Oct. 1880	21, Sept	50	Renshausen	335	Hooker, NE	Kurhessen
Läger, Catharina	3, Jan. 1876	7, Dec.	26	Dell	7	Miller Co, MO	Warren County, Missouri
Läger, Eduard	23, Feb. 1880	9, Feb.	20-11m		63	Huntingburg, IN	Huntingburg, Indiana
Läger, Friedrich	9, Sept 1897	23, Aug.	66		575	Sterling, NE	Sonneborn, Lippe-Detmold
Läger, Martha Amalia	20, Apr. 1899	20, Mar.	84	Jürgens	255	Boonville, IN	Blickershausen, Witzenhausen, Hessen-Kassel
Lagemann, Rudolph Wilhelm	31, Mar. 1884	5, Mar.	63		7	Fosterburg, IL	Tecklenburg, Westphalen
LaHann, Mary	19, Sept 1889	3, Aug.	59	Eppele	606	Galesburg, IL	Baden
Lahlker, Louise	18, Aug. 1879	23, Aug.	40		263	St. Paul, MN	Blasenheim, Lübbeke, Preußen
Lahm, Philippine	4, Sept 1871	14, June	55	Nobis	287	Canal Dover, OH	Ranzweiler, Rheinkreis Baiern
Lahm, Wilhelmine	12, July 1875	1, Sept	53- 6m-14d	Müller	223	Canal Dover, OH	Ranzweiler, Baiern
Lähn, Friedrich	10, Oct. 1861	14, June	39		164	Baraboo, WI	Großlasch, Grabow, Mecklenburg-Schwerin
Lahne, Wilhelmine	28, June 1875	12, Mar.	53- 6m-14d	Müller	207	Canal Dover, OH	Ranzweiler, Baiern
Lahr, Ulrich	18, Apr. 1895	22, Nov.	84		254	Lafayette, IN	Weinheim, Hessen-Darmstadt
Lahrmann, Sophie	17, Jan. 1889	12, June	71		46		Chemnitz, Altenburg, Sachsen
Lahrmann, Heinrich (Rev)	23, July 1891		68- 3m-19d		478	Keokuk, IA	Lintorf, Wittlage, Hannover
Lahrmann, Johan H.	7, Nov. 1889		81- 2m-15d		718	Greenville, OH	Belm, Hannover

Christliche Apologete Death Notices --- 1839 - 1899

Name of Deceased	Notice Date	Death Date	Age	Maiden Name	Page	Place of Death	Place of Birth
Lahmann, Maria Elisabeth	7, Oct. 1878	9, Sept	78		319	Boonville, MO	Lintorf, Wittlage, Hannover
Lai, Lisette	26, July 1888	3, July	67- 8m		478	Chicago, IL	
Laib, Johan Martin	7, Mar. 1895	6, Feb.	70		158	Galena, IL	Metzinger, Württemberg
Laib, Katharina	29, June 1899	14, June	76		415	Galena, IL	Metingen, Württemberg
Laible, Barbara	11, Mar. 1897	17, Feb.	59	Glöckler	159	Chicago, IL	Albeck, Ulm, Württemberg
Laible, Christian	8, Aug. 1895	18, July	74		510	Freeport, IL	Bittenfeld, Weiblingen, Württemberg
Laible, Lea	23, Dec. 1872	30, Oct.	21-10m- 7d		415	Freeport, IL	
Laible, Lea	27, Jan. 1873	30, Oct.	21-10m- 7d		31	Freeport, IL	
Laier, Jacob	30, Aug. 1894	14, Aug.	68		566	Freeport, MI	Steinbach, Backnang, Württemberg
Lais, Gustav F.	10, Jan. 1895	2, Dec.	28		30	Elizabeth, NJ	Zürich, Schweiz
Laitner, Bertha Augusta	30, July 1891	24, June	21		494	Detroit, MI	
Lalk, (Mrs)	7, Oct. 1886	4, Sept	30	Suenkel	7	Morrison, MO	
Lalk, Kurth Heinrich	20, June 1889	25, May	76		398	Ft. Atkinson, WI	Gehrenberg, Blomberg, Lippe-Detmold
Lalk, Maria Elisabeth	9, Apr. 1877	5, Mar.	22	Sünkel	119	Drake, MO	
Lalk, Mary	29, Jan. 1891	3, Jan.	36	Nollmann	78	St. Louis, MO	
Lalk, Wilhelmine	31, Aug. 1899	11, Aug.	50	Krug	559	Ada, MN	Lüdershof, Blumberg, Germany
Lalk, Wilhelmine	10, Mar. 1884	23, Feb.	83	Thermann	7	Red Wing, MN	Pfermeke, Lippe-Detmold
Lamberecht, Augusta Amelia	23, Feb. 1899	27, Dec.	35- 4m-16d	Schmidt	127	Ripon, WI	Arnswalde, Germany
Lambkin, Elisabeth	7, Jan. 1884	27, Nov.	55		7	Sidney, OH	
Lambrecht, Anna	26, Nov. 1896	4, Nov.	44	Lüttge	766	Kenosha, WI	Vinau, Sachsen
Lambrecht, Emma Louise	2, Sept 1897	26, July	20		559	Bay City, MI	Bay City, Michigan
Lambrecht, Karl	16, Mar. 1885	25, Feb.	29		7	Bedford, IN	Klein-Wißeck, Wirsetz, Bromberg, Posen
Lambrecht, Robert Ludwig	22, July 1886	30, June	27		7	Sleepy Eye, MN	Freundsthal, West Preußen
Lameli, Peter	11, Mar. 1886	8, Feb.	39		7		Sandusky County, Ohio
Lämle, Magdalena	4, Nov. 1886	18, Oct.	58		7	Chillicothe, OH	
Lämli, Dorothea	11, Feb. 1886	17, Jan.	82		7	Chillicothe, OH	
Lamm, Elisabeth	8, Dec. 1879	23, Nov.	58	Böhm	391	Ripley, OH	Murr, Marbach, Württemberg
Lämmer, Johan	8, Feb. 1875	8, Jan.	81		47	Blue Island, IL	Breunings, Schwarzenfels, Kurhessen
Lammers, Adolph	29, Apr. 1878	16, Apr.	65		135	Huntingburg, IN	Hachborn, Kreis Marburg, Kurhessen
Lammers, Anna Maria	5, Apr. 1869	18, Mar.	22	Wellmeier	111	Huntingburg, IN	Ladbergen, Preußen
Lammers, Daniel Adolph	1, Mar. 1894	8, Feb.	19		150	Boonville, IN	Dubois County, Indiana
Lammers, Elisabeth	15, Oct. 1891	19, Sept	59	Daßmann	670	New York City, NY	Holland, Indiana
Lammers, Emilie Josephine	17, Mar. 1887	13, Feb.	33	Hauck	174	Highland, IL	Brusterbeck, Westphalen
Lammers, Johan Wilhelm	29, May 1882	15, May	74- 9m-19d		175	New Ulm, MN	St. Genevieve, Missouri
Lammers, Katharina Wilhelmine	8, Jan. 1866	18, Dec.	51	Oelyeclaus	14	Cincinnati, OH	Ladbergen, Tecklenburg, Preußen
Lammers, Maria	9, May 1895	14, Mar.	65	Gottschämmer	302	St. Louis, MO	Lengerich, Preußen
Lammers, Maria	11, July 1889	18, June	46- 9m- 5d	Hemmer	446	Boonville, IN	Götzenheim, Hessen
Lammers, Maria Elisabeth	27, Jan. 1879	7, Jan.	31	Steinkamp	31	Huntingburg, IN	Holland, Indiana
Lammers, Wilhelm	21, Feb. 1895	29, Jan.	76		126	Huntingburg, IN	Ladbergen, Tecklenburg, Preußen
Lammers, William	28, Nov. 1889	6, Nov.	26		766	Fairfax, MN	
Lammert, Bonne Look	21, Sept 1899	5, Sept	66		607	Peoria, IL	Ostfriesland
Lammert, Friederike	6, Sept 1860	3, Aug.	45		144	Sheboygan, WI	Lünen, Münster, Preußen
Lammert, Johan Christoph	16, Feb. 1899		74- 4m-29d		111	Chicago, IL	Astrugg, Osnabrück, Hannover
Lammes, Oliver Louis	7, July 1898	8, June	14		431	Huntingburg, IN	Holland, Indiana
Lamp, Friedrich	16, Aug. 1888	20, Feb.	56- 7m-12d		526	Rochester, MN	Mecklenburg-Schwerin
Lämp, Johan Michael G.	21, June 1869	3, June	34		199	Rochester, NY	Mecklenburg-Schwerin

Name of Deceased	Notice Date	Death Date	Age	Maiden Name	Page	Place of Death	Place of Birth
Lampart, Maria	21, May 1877	4, May	62	Rue	166	Louisville, KY	Freiburg, Baden
Lampe, Christian	21, July 1884	5, July	76-10m-17d		7	Angelica, NY	Gamsen, Gifhorn, Hannover
Lampe, Friedrich Wilhelm	18, Feb. 1886	30, Jan.	45		7	Sheboygan, WI	Grischow, Treptow an der Tolensen, Preußen
Lampe, Heinrich	22, July 1886	6, July	57		7	St. Paul, MN	Boitzenburg, Mecklenburg-Schwerin
Lampe, Maria	9, July 1891	1, June	85	Bühring	446	Angelica, NY	Grossen, Oesingen, Hannover
Lampert, Anna Katharina	14, Feb. 1889	19, Jan.	69		110	Oshkosh, WI	Fläsch, Graubünden, Schweiz
Lampert, Bartholomäus (Rev)	25, Aug. 1898	7, Aug.	52		543	Chicago, IL	Mayfield, Wisconsin
Lampert, Christian	3, Mar. 1884	7, Feb.	68		7	Oshkosh, WI	Kur, Graubündten, Schweiz
Lampert, Louise	19, Aug. 1886	4, Aug.	30	Stotzer	7	Chicago, IL	Büren, Bern, Schweiz
Lampert, Margaretha	12, June 1890	7, May	84		382	Oshkosh, WI	Fläsch, Graubünden, Schweiz
Lampert, Matthias	7, Aug. 1876	12, July	37		255	Chicago, IL	Fläsch, Graubünden, Schweiz
Lamping, Elisabeth	23, Feb. 1874	2, Feb.	27		63	Lawrenceburg, IN	Mutterstadt, Rheinkreis Baiern
Lamping, Katharina	7, Oct. 1867	5, Sept	18	Koch	318	Lawrenceburg, IN	Höchstenburg, Hagenburg, Nassau
Lamping, Ludwig	21, June 1860	8, May	45- 6m-24d		100	Lawrenceburg, IN	Düste, Hannover
Land, Franz	23, Nov. 1863	7, Nov.	43		188	Portsmouth, OH	Rohrbach, Simmern, Coblenz, RheinPreußen
Lander, Jacob	12, Feb. 1891	19, Jan.	91- 6m-26d		110	Marietta, OH	Mannheim, Baiern
Lander, Johanna	24, Jan. 1881	6, Jan.	83	Sahlin	31	Marietta, OH	
Lander, Katharine	30, Mar. 1885	7, Mar.	78	Heine	7	Marietta, OH	Gundersweiler, Rheinkreis Baiern
Lander, Philippine	28, Jan. 1848	29, Dec.	18		19	West Union, OH	
Lander, Robert	12, Feb. 1877	14, Dec.	79-10m- 1d		55	Marietta, OH	Marnheim, Baiern
Landes, (Mrs)	27, May 1867	30, Apr.	63	Vogt	166	Ann Arbor, MI	Rohrbach, Schwarzburg-Rudolstadt
Landes, Elisabeth	7, Feb. 1861	20, Nov.	20- - 4d		24	Ann Arbor, MI	
Landes, Katharina	9, Sept 1858	22, Aug.	65- 9m-20d		144	Waterloo, MI	
Ländes, Katharina	2, Apr. 1857	18, Feb.	12- 6m		56	Ann Arbor, MI	
Landes, Lydia	8, July 1886	19, June	77	Drückenmüller	7	Francisco, MI	Barrocks County, Pennsylvania
Landes, Magdalena	14, Oct. 1858	19, Sept			164	Waterloo, MI	
Landgrebe, Anna Christina	2, Sept 1878	3, Aug.	64	Fischer	279	Decatur, IL	Albshausen, Kurhessen
Landgrebe, Jakob	23, Dec. 1897	13, Oct.	85		815	Moweaqua, IL	Grebenau, Mehlsungen, Kurhessen
Landherr, Johan Georg	8, Jan. 1877	21, Dec.	48- 4m- 8d		15	Rochester, ---	Neuweiler, Württemberg
Landolt, Antonia Wilhelmina	16, June 1887		66		382	Chicago, IL	Wien, Oesterreich
Landolt, Catharina Mathilda	8, Feb. 1855		31		24	St. Louis, MO	Zürich, Schweiz
Landrick, Anna	24, Mar. 1887	4, Mar.	40	Vaupel	190	Sandusky, OH	Besse, Fritzlar, Kurhessen
Landwehr, Anna Maria Elisabeth	9, Mar. 1899	3, Jan.	83	Bonse	159	Owensville, MO	Engern, Minden, Preußen
Landwehr, Bernhard Heinrich	9, Oct. 1840	30, Sept	17- 5m-27d		159		Melle, Hannover
Landwehr, Casper Heinrich	30, June 1892	9, June	83		414	Warren, MO	Warren County, Missouri
Landwehr, Georg	7, Mar. 1870	26, Jan.	36		79	Warren, MO	Eidinksen, Minden, Preußen
Landwehr, Louise	15, Mar. 1894	11, Feb.	67	Wegner	182	Pinckneyville, IL	Auenstein, Württemberg
Lang, (Mrs)	15, Oct. 1883	25, Sept	67	Rode	335	Minneapolis, MN	Walldorf, Baden
Lang, Adam	17, Nov. 1879	1, Nov.	78		367	St. Louis, MO	Spencerville, Allen County, Ohio
Lang, Allen	2, Nov. 1874	6, Oct.	20- 6m-10d		351	Kossuth, OH	Weinzerlein, Baiern
Lang, Andreas	21, Jan. 1897	19, Dec.	74		46	Beaver Dam, WI	Dieburg, Hessen-Darmstadt
Lang, Andreas Joseph	29, Apr. 1858	12, Apr.	26		68	New Albany, IN	Reichenbach, Hessen
Lang, Anna M.	3, June 1878	7, May	41- 2m-29d	Ludolph	175	Chicago, IL	Eringshausen, Homburg, Hessen-Darmstadt
Lang, Anna Maria	9, Mar. 1854	23, Aug.			40	Indianapolis, IN	
Lang, August	19, Jan. 1863	21, Oct.	19		12	Poughkeepsie, NY	
Lang, Carl	9, Aug. 1875	7, June	37		255	Eden, NY	

Christliche Apologete Death Notices --- 1839 - 1899

Name of Deceased	Notice Date	Death Date	Age	Page	Maiden Name	Place of Death	Place of Birth
Lang, Christian M.	19, Jan. 1863	29, Aug.	47	12		Poughkeepsie, NY	Blaubeuren, Württemberg
Lang, Christiane	6, July 1874	21, May	62- 3m-19d	215	Beesmer	Poughkeepsie, NY	
Lang, Christina	16, Oct. 1865	4, Sept	51- 3m- 4d	168	Kapp	Seymour, IN	Heumaden, Württemberg
Lang, Christina	9, Apr. 1883		85- 8m- 3d	119		St. Louis, MO	
Lang, Donat Peter	24, July 1871	5, July	48- 2m- 6d	239		Louisville, KY	Biel, Mühlheim, Baden
Lang, Dora	4, Apr. 1895	17, Mar.	26	222		Mt. Olive, IL	Macoupin County, Illinois
Lang, Elisabeth	22, Mar. 1888	28, Feb.	43	190		Danville, IL	UnterSemdHaufa, Marburg, Kurhessen
Lang, Elisabeth	25, Oct. 1888	3, Oct.	59	686	Anweiler	Columbus, OH	Nusloch, Heidelberg, Baden
Lang, Elisabeth	4, Mar. 1897	19, Jan.	69	143	Sauer	Jeffersonville, IN	Germany
Lang, Erhard	28, Nov. 1861	1, Nov.	29	192		Manchester, MO	Ettenheim, Kreis OberRhein, Baden
Lang, Friederika	4, Mar. 1897	8, Feb.	80	143	Miller	Spencerville, OH	Eidingen, Pforzheim, Baden
Lang, Friedrich	1, Mar. 1894	4, Feb.	85	150		Waymansville, IN	Heumaden, Stuttgart, Württemberg
Lang, Georg	10, May 1894	23, Apr.	16	310		Mt. Vernon, IN	
Lang, Georg Jacob Friedrich	12, Nov. 1891	15, Sept	73- 5m-20d	734		Eden, NY	Blanckenloch, Baden
Lang, Gottlieb	19, Apr. 1894	5, Apr.	61	262		Danville, IL	Württemberg
Lang, Henry	5, Jan. 1899	15, Nov.	79	14		Ft. Lupton, CO	Germany
Lang, Jakob	23, Oct. 1882	8, Oct.	64	343		Minneapolis, MN	Oberstendfeld, Marbach , Württemberg
Lang, Jakob	2, Oct. 1882	4, Sept	68-10m-20d	319		Julietta, IN	HinterBreitenhann, Feuchtwang, Baiern
Lang, Johan	27, Dec. 1888	10, Nov.	50-11m-11d	830		Dunkirk, NY	Winnenden, Württemberg
Lang, Johan Christoph	23, Apr. 1865	27, Mar.	72- 6m-12d	68		Louisville, KY	Marbach, Kurhessen
Lang, Johann	4, July 1881	11, Apr.	53	215		Alton, IL	Darmstadt, Hessen-Darmstadt
Lang, John	11, Sept 1871	13, May	60	295		Graham, MO	Nordhausen, Brackenheim, Württemberg
Lang, Juliana S.	21, Dec. 1874	23, Nov.	62- 2m-16d	407		Kossuth, OH	Marietta, Ohio
Lang, Karl	10, June 1886	8, May	18	7		Marietta, OH	Baden
Lang, Karl	5, May 1892	17, Apr.	47	286		Mt. Vernon, IN	Büssig, Karlsruhe, Baden
Lang, Karl August	26, Feb. 1877	14, Jan.	57	71		Mt. Vernon, IN	
Lang, Lydia Pauline	9, June 1887		15- 9m	366		Cleveland, OH	
Lang, M.	1, May 1856	13, Apr.		72		Poughkeepsie, NY	
Lang, Margaretha	1, Sept 1887	7, Aug.	35	558	Ries	Mt. Vernon, IN	Oberschüpf, Bocksberg, Baden
Lang, Margaretha El.	21, Aug. 1876	2, Aug.	55	271		Mt. Vernon, IN	Büchig, Karlsruhe, Baden
Lang, Maria D.	1, Feb. 1864	17, Jan.	36	20	Reicherd	Marietta, OH	Kuppingen, Württemberg
Lang, Maria E.	17, Mar. 1887	24, Feb.	51	174	Neeb	Indianapolis, IN	Zell, Hessen-Darmstadt
Lang, Maria Elisabeth	29, Jan. 1891	8, Jan.	82	78	Jung	Geneseo, IL	Miesebach, Landau, Rheinkreis Baiern
Lang, Martin	15, Apr. 1858	23, Mar.	43	60		Dunkirk, NY	Plankenloch, Baden
Lang, Philipp	2, Aug. 1888	3, July	63	494		New York City, NY	Alzei, Kurhessen
Lang, Rahel Augusta	21, Dec. 1868	1, Dec.	17	407		Detroit, MI	Rosenthal, Kreis Sittau, Sachsen
Lang, Rosalie	3, Feb. 1887	11, Jan.	20	78		Dunkirk, NY	
Lang, Theobald	26, Apr. 1869	7, Apr.	42	135		Marietta, OH	Selchenbach, Rheinkreis Baiern
Lang, Wilhelmine	20, Apr. 1893	29, Mar.	85	254	Koch	De Soto, MO	
Langacker, Margaretha	5, Jan. 1885	13, Dec.	20	7		Baresville, OH	Canton Bern, Schweiz
Langbauer, Rosalia L.	14, June 1894	9, May	9	390		Almond, WI	Almond, Wisconsin
Langbecker, Karl Christlieb	6, Apr. 1899	9, Mar.	78	223		Baraboo, WI	Dittersdorf bei Fallenburg, Preußen
Lange, Adam	30, July 1896	12, July	83	495		Springfield, IL	Besse, Wetzlar, Kurhessen
Lange, Catharina	25, Aug. 1892	20, July	36	542	Koch	Brooklyn, NY	
Lange, Christian Friedrich	31, Aug. 1899	9, Aug.	74	559		Maple Grove, MN	Gesuw, Pommern
Lange, E. Karoline	27, Oct. 1884	10, Oct.	56	7	Blessin	Lowell, WI	Blankensee, Pommern

Name of Deceased	Notice Date	Death Date	Age	Page	Maiden Name	Place of Death	Place of Birth
Lange, Emilie Alwine	9, Sept 1897	15, Aug.	43	575	Röhr	West Superior, WI	Rothenberger, Sachsen, Preußen
Lange, Emma Karoline	1, May 1882	16, Apr.	16-11m-25d	143		Corcoran, MN	
Lange, F.	23, Feb. 1860	3, Feb.	23	32		Captina, OH	
Lange, Franz Joachim	17, Oct. 1889	25, Sept	66	670		Roseville, MI	Witzeze bei Büchen, Germany
Lange, Friedrich	19, May 1859	3, May	66	80		Columbus, WI	Lauckstadt, Preußen
Lange, Friedrich H.	31, Jan. 1881	11, Jan.	56	39		Bloomington, IL	Friedrichshagen, Greifswalde, Preußen
Lange, Friedrich W.	9, Aug. 1894	10, June	35- 6m- 6d	518		Schnectady, NY	Hille, Minden, Preußen
Lange, Gottlieb	20, Oct. 1873	25, Aug.	39	335		Columbus, WI	Hohengrape, Kreis Soldin, Pommern
Lange, Heinrich	26, Nov. 1866	5, Oct.	55	382		Second Creek, MO	Belle, Amt Schieden, Lippe-Detmold
Lange, Heinrich	22, Jan. 1872	29, Dec.	67	31		Frankfort, IL	Tesmendorf, Mecklenburg-Schwerin
Lange, Heinrich	26, July 1894	27, June	33	486		Saginaw, MI	Saginaw, Michigan
Lange, Heinrich	6, Nov. 1882	20, Oct.	20	359		Eudora, KS	
Lange, J. Bernhardt	12, July 1880	25, June	36	223		Cleveland, OH	Ebersdorf, Sachsen
Lange, Jacob	14, Nov. 1870	1, Oct.		367		Clarington, OH	Datterode, Kreis Eschwegen, Kurhessen
Lange, John T.	19, Jan. 1893	21, Dec.	54	46		Brooklyn, NY	Bokel-Ahausen, Rotenberg, Hannover
Lange, Karl	1, Jan. 1883	3, Dec.	20	7		Columbus, WI	Hohengrafen, Neumark, Preußen
Lange, Karoline Wilhelmine H.	18, Apr. 1895	28, Mar.	65	254	Walter	Maple Grove, MN	Schwennenz, Pommern
Lange, Katharina	19, May 1848		Inquiry	83		New Orleans, LA	Westerkappeln, Preußen
Lange, Katharina	23, Sept 1852	14, Sept		156		Buffalo, NY	
Lange, Katharina E.	21, Aug. 1876	6, Aug.	82- 3m-24d	271	Lange	New Orleans, LA	Kappeln, Westphalen
Lange, Katharine	29, Sept 1873	9, Sept	33- 7m-16d	311		Bunker Hill, IL	Uppendorf, Westphalen
Lange, Louis	9, Mar. 1893	4, Feb.	25	158		Fairmount, KS	
Lange, Louise	17, Nov. 1884	27, Oct.	89	7	Hinze	Columbus, WI	Hohengrafen, Soldien, Preußen
Lange, Magdalena	29, May 1882	19, Apr.	67- 5m-22d	175	Wehrnert	Petersburg, IL	Dissen, Gudensburg, Fritzlar, Hessen
Lange, Maria S.H.	2, Feb. 1874	30, Dec.	33- 2m-28d	39	Hülsmann	New Orleans, LA	
Lange, Ottilie Wilhelmine	21, Jan. 1897	15, Dec.	53	47	Krempin	Beaver Dam, WI	Schmarfendorf, Uckermark, Brandenburg
Lange, Sophia	29, May 1856	15, May	4- 4m	88		Chicago, IL	
Lange, Sophia Maria	21, June 1894	27, May	49	406	Barklage	Halstead, KS	Westerscheps, Oldenburg
Lange, Sophie	19, May 1884	14, Apr.	73	7	Schiefer	Frankfort, IL	Neubuckow, Mecklenburg-Schwerin
Lange, Theodor Rudolph	31, Jan. 1881	26, Dec.	41- 2m-25d	39		Secor, IL	Neubrück bei Frankfurt a. Oder, Preußen
Lange, Wilhelm	6, July 1899	12, Feb.	85	431		De Soto, MO	Blasheim, Lübeck, Preußen
Lange, Wilhelm	5, May 1898	16, Apr.	68	287		Evansville, IN	Rodenberg, Hannover
Lange, Wilhelm	31, Jan. 1876	9, Jan.	51- 9m	39		Lowell, WI	Gottberg, Preußen
Lange, Wilhelmine	20, Dec. 1894	1, Dec.	50	822	Dohmann	Chicago, IL	Benzien, Pommern
Langebrake, Christine	25, Mar. 1878	11, Mar.	29- 9m-27d	95	Schrölüke	Newport, KY	Ladbergen, Münster, Preußen
Langebrake, Ernst Friedrich	27, Aug. 1896	27, July	34	559		Huntingburg, IN	Pike County, Indiana
Langebrake, Ernst Heinrich	11, Nov. 1878	14, Oct.	35- 8m- 4d	359		New Orleans, LA	Baldbergen, Münster, Preußen
Langebrake, Friederike	29, Jan. 1872	8, Jan.	13	39		Newport, KY	Ladbergen, Tecklenburg, Preußen
Langebrake, Hanna Sophia	1, June 1899	25, Apr.	69	351	Esmeier	Huntingburg, IN	Ladbergen, Preußen
Langebrake, Herman Heinrich	31, Mar. 1873	6, Mar.	63	103		Huntingburg, IN	Ladbergen, Tecklenburg, Münster, Preußen
Langebrake, Wilhelm	19, July 1880	27, June	60- 1m-17d	231		Huntingburg, IN	Ladbergen, Tecklenburg, Preußen
Langebrake, Wilhelm Ernst	25, Nov. 1897	15, Oct.	33	751		Huntingburg, IN	Dubois County, Indiana
Langenbracke, Elsbeth	8, Dec. 1859	4, Nov.	44	196		Huntingburg, IN	Ladbergen, Tecklenburg, Preußen
Langenbrake, Elisabeth	4, Feb. 1897	12, Jan.	47	79	Schäfer	Newport, KY	Newport, Campbell County, Kentucky
Langenbrake, Friederika Franziska	12, Apr. 1875	26, Mar.	16	119		Huntingburg, IN	
Langenbrake, Heinrich Wilhelm	22, Oct. 1883	10, Oct.	15- 7m-21d	343		Newport, KY	Evansville, Indiana

Christliche Apologete Death Notices --- 1839 - 1899

Name of Deceased	Notice Date	Death Date	Age	Maiden Name	Page	Place of Death	Place of Birth
Langenbrake, Maria Louise	14, May 1896	26, Apr.	24	Beumann	318	Newport, KY	Newport, Campbell County, Kentucky
Langendörder, Ernestine Wilhelmine	4, Jan. 1864	23, Nov.	35- 5m		4	Herman, MO	Barensen bei Göttingen, Hannover
Langendorf, Georg	31, May 1855	9, May	27		88	Warsaw, IL	Marienhagen, Vöhl, Hessen-Darmstadt
Langendorfer, Johan A.	30, Mar. 1874	10, Feb.	52		103	Giard, IA	Weingarten, Baden
Langendörfer, Maria Katharina	11, Sept 1876	16, Aug.	50	Eckmann	295	Clayton, IA	Weingarten, Baden
Langer, Alphonse	10, Jan. 1895	24, Dec.	22-10m-12d		30	St. Paul, MN	
Langer, Frank Henry	10, Jan. 1895	24, Dec.	19-10m-24d		30	St. Paul, MN	
Langer, Karl	5, Apr. 1888	18, Mar.	74		222	Dalton, MO	Lüneburg, Hannover
Langguth, Gertrud	30, Mar. 1893	9, Mar.	80	Reuter	206	Paterson, NJ	Krefeld, Preußen
Langhoff, Sophia	25, Feb. 1897	28, Jan.	18		127	Lamberton, MN	Selma Twp, Cottonwood County, Minnesota
Langhorst, Anna	15, Jan. 1872	1, Jan.	59	VonderAh	23	Baltimore, MD	Rathen, Minden, Preußen
Langhorst, Anna Margaretha	5, Feb. 1857	25, Jan.	58		24	Cincinnati, OH	Specken, Diepholtz, Hannover
Langhorst, Auguste Wilhelmine L.	7, Feb. 1881	21, Jan.	50-10m- 8d	Willes	47	Mt. Pleasant, OH	Lavelslohr, Diepenau, Hannover
Langhorst, Heinrich	28, May 1896	9, May	76		350	Mt. Healthy, OH	Mariendrebber, Diepholz, Hannover
Langhorst, Wilhelm	23, Jan. 1890	7, Jan.	46- 8m-27d		62	Baltimore, MD	Baltimore, Maryland
Langschied, Hermann	20, Apr. 1868	23, Mar.	62		127	Louisville, KY	Altendietz, Nassau
Langwasser, Adam	7, Feb. 1881	29, Sept	55- 6m		47	New York City, NY	Nußbach, Baiern
Langwasser, Margaretha	20, Mar. 1890	2, Mar.	63	Molter	190	New York City, NY	Hauptstuhl, Baiern
Lanius, Caroline Mathilde	1, Dec. 1887	6, Nov.	22	Thomas	766	Edon, OH	Canton, Williams County, Ohio
Lanius, Emilie Margaretha	6, Mar. 1890	15, Feb.	11		158	Edgerton, OH	Defiance County, Ohio
Lanius, Johannes	10, Jan. 1895	19, Dec.	66		30	Edon, OH	Breitenbach, Wetzlar, Coblenz, Preußen
Lanius, Sarah E.	25, Oct. 1888	3, Oct.	20-11m- 9d		686	Edon, OH	Richland, Crawford County, Ohio
Lanius, Wilhelm Salomo	20, Oct. 1887	30, Sept	23- 6m- 6d		670	Edon, OH	Galion, Ohio
Lann, Maria Christina	9, Nov. 1893	12, Oct.	75	Relke	718	Chicago, IL	Zierenberg, Kurhessen
Lannert, Wilhelmine	3, Dec. 1857	18, Nov.		Weinel	196	Bellesville, IL	
Lantes, David	17, Dec. 1891	19, Nov.	63		814	Francisco, MI	Seneca County, New York
Lantes, Jakob	25, Feb. 1884	9, Feb.	76		7	Francisco, MI	Rockland, Pennsylvania
Lantes, Martin	31, Oct. 1881	7, Oct.	79-11m- 3d	Stephan	351	Francisco, MI	Rockland, Berks County, Pennsylvania
Lantis, Jesaias	24, Nov. 1862	30, Oct.	71-10m-22d	Hubacher	188	Ann Arbor, MI	
Lantz, Maria	17, Apr. 1865	16, Mar.	17- 4m		64	Washington, OH	
Lanz, B.	4, May 1868		12		143	Baresville, OH	
Lapell, Henriette	25, Apr. 1881	9, Apr.	81	Blum	135	Valparaiso, IN	Kreisheimfeld, Hessen
Lapp, A.	20, July 1899	29, June	71		463	Alton, IL	
Lapp, Anna	18, Aug. 1892	24, July	24	Jakob	526	Chicago, IL	Zehna, Güstrow, Mecklenburg-Schwerin
Lapp, Christoph	17, Jan. 1889	15, Dec.	64		46	Cleveland, OH	Gersdorf, Werth, Elsaß
Lapp, Elisabeth	29, July 1897	7, July	75	Stephan	479	Clarington, OH	Canton Bern, Schweiz
Lapp, Elisabeth	27, Oct. 1887	4, Oct.	71-10m-22d	Hubacher	686	Clarington, OH	Düsselbach, Baiern
Lapp, Elisabeth	3, Feb. 1898	14, Jan.	64		79	Cleveland, OH	Jacobsheim, Buchsweiler, Elsaß
Lapp, Georg	4, July 1881	28, May	66- 1m-29d		215	Clarington, OH	Wolferode, Kirchhain, Preußen
Lapp, Johan Konrad	7, Sept 1899	11, Aug.	64		575	Peoria, IL	
Lapp, Johannes	29, Dec. 1862	7, Nov.	24		208	Captina, OH	
Lapp, Maria Elisa	24, Aug. 1899	5, Aug.	28	Spring	543	Clarington, OH	Reutige, Bern, Schweiz
Lapp, Michael	21, Mar. 1889	20, Feb.	75- 3m- 8d		190	Clarington, OH	Emsheim, Elsaß
Läpple, Maria	23, Aug. 1875	5, Aug.	27- 3m-12d		271	Allegan, MI	Bittenfeld, Waiblingen, Württemberg
Lappnow, Friederika Louise	19, Nov. 1891	28, Oct.	80		750	Crow River, MN	Libso, Pommern
Larkin, Elise	14, Feb. 1895	24, Jan.	43	Hunziker	110	Brooklyn, NY	Kirchleerau, Schweiz

Christliche Apologete Death Notices --- 1839 - 1899

Name of Deceased	Notice Date	Death Date	Age	Page	Maiden Name	Place of Death	Place of Birth
Larwig, M.	18, Jan. 1864	23, Dec.	32	12		Valley Mines, MO	Fulda, Kurhessen
Lasch, Anna Regina	12, Apr. 1869	23, Mar.	77	119		Oconomowoc, WI	Fürstensee bei Stargard, Pommern
Lasch, Elisabeth	23, Feb. 1899	11, Jan.	70	127	Stein	Louisville, KY	Neu-Mühl, Kork, Baden
Lasch, Johan	13, Feb. 1871	31, Jan.	57-10m-9d	55		New Albany, IN	Scherzheim, Baden
Läsch, Maria Elisabeth	6, Aug. 1883	19, July	88-5m-20d	255	Mololf	Charles City, IA	Liebenthal, Preußen
Laske, Carl	6, June 1889	19, May	79	366		Burlington, WI	Pritzlaff, Pommern
Laske, Charlotte Friederike	7, Nov. 1889	14, Oct.	78	718	Kröner	Burlington, WI	Labenz, Hinterpommern
Laskowsky, Anna Christine	16, Dec. 1897	6, Nov.	33	799	Bauer	Dallas, TX	Wolfsöldern, Marbach, Württemberg
Laßke, Philipp H.	25, June 1891	2, June	16- 7m- 1d	414		Lyona, KS	
Lätje, Heinrich	2, Apr. 1866	28, Feb.	62	110		Appleton, MO	Klein-Heidorn, Hannover
Lattermann, Gottlieb	16, Sept 1852	14, Aug.	46- 1m- 8d	152		Portsmouth, OH	
Latzke, Johanna Wilhelmina	1, May 1882	14, Apr.	43	143		Lyona, KS	Stockhoff bei Greifenberg, Pommern
Lau, Anna	31, Jan. 1895	21, Dec.	28	78	Heller	Green Bay, WI	Green Bay, Wisconsin
Lau, Christian	20, Sept 1894	30, Aug.	65- 5m-20d	614		Klemme, IA	Pribinow, Mecklenburg-Schwerin
Lau, Maria	24, Nov. 1892	7, Aug.	26	750	Traub	Waverly, OH	Ross County, Ohio
Laubach, Louise	2, Nov. 1863	15, Oct.	19- 9m-14d	176	Barth	St. Louis, MO	
Laube, Robert	14, Nov. 1889	21, Oct.		734		San Bernardino, CA	Otterstedt, Schlesien
Laubenberger, John	6, Aug. 1891	15, July	81	510		Brooklyn, NY	Emmingen, Baden
Laubenberger, Maria Josephine	26, Mar. 1891	19, Feb.	71	206	Guirß	Brooklyn, NY	Emmingen, Baden
Lauberheimer, F. C.	16, June 1898	27, Apr.	72	383		Council Bluffs, IA	
Laubersheimer, Friedrich Christian	28, July 1898	27, Apr.	72	479		Council Bluffs, IA	
Laubscher, Christian	21, Dec. 1885	2, Dec.	73- 9m-20d	7		Evansville, IN	Tauffelen, Nidau, Bern, Schweiz
Laubscher, Emma	9, Aug. 1888	10, July	23- 1m-26d	510		Evansville, IN	
Laubscher, Johan Rudolf	19, Feb. 1891	26, Jan.	77	126		Evansville, IN	Kanton Bern, Schweiz
Laubscher, Maria Elisabeth	9, Sept 1886	13, Aug.	34	7		Salem, IN	Vanderburgh County, Indiana
Laubschier, Maria	30, Aug. 1860	31, July	28	140		Santa Claus, IN	Künitz, O.A. Bern, Schweiz
Laubschter, Johann Rudolph	26, Dec. 1861	26, Oct.	20	208		Boonville, IN	Neuenburg, Schweiz
Lauche, Dorothea	22, Oct. 1877	9, Oct.	43- 5m-13d	343	Mangold	Waverly, OH	
Lauche, Johan Benjamin	1, Nov. 1880	9, Oct.	57- 5m- 7d	351		Waverly, OH	
Laucher, Friedrich	19, Apr. 1894	29, Mar.	67	262		San Francisco, CA	Grünstädt, Preußen
Laudemann, Maria	6, Apr. 1868	22, Mar.	20	111	Bayer	Hamilton, OH	Sankt Gotthart, Göppingen, Württemberg
Laudermann, Georg	28, May 1866	12, May	15	174		Hamilton, OH	Hamilton, Butler County, Ohio
Lauenroth, Christian Friedrich	13, June 1895	25, May	19	382		Burlington, IA	Hamilton, Butler County, Ohio
Lauenroth, Christoph	25, May 1885	10, May	55	7		Burlington, IA	Segerde, Wahferlingen, Magdeburg, Preußen
Lauer, Christine	27, Apr. 1868	11, Apr.	38	135	Huberter	Madison, WI	Paine, Hannover
Lauer, Clara Amelia	15, Dec. 1892	16, Nov.	23	798		Cannelton, IN	Perry County, Indiana
Lauer, Grace S.	31, Oct. 1895	27, Sept	22	702		Ft. Atkinson, WI	
Lauer, Gustav A.	14, Feb. 1889	27, Dec.	20	110		Chicago, IL	Freiburg, Baden
Lauer, Katharina	11, July 1889	18, June	27	446	Born	Baltimore, MD	Kurhessen
Lauer, Peter	12, Oct. 1893	4, Sept	66	654		Cannelton, IN	Weiler, Kreuznach, RheinPreußen
Laufenberger, Chleopha	9, Mar. 1899	21, Feb.	79	159	Degen	Faribault, MN	Gerstheim, Elsaß
Laufer, Johannes	24, May 1855	1, May	53-11m	84		Wapello, IA	Malmsheim, Leonberg, Württemberg
Laufer, John M.	1, July 1886	22, June	57	7		Louisville, KY	Malmsheim, Leonberg, Württemberg
Laufer, Katharina	29, Aug. 1850	13, Aug.	17- 9m	140		Louisville, KY	
Laufer, Louise	10, May 1855	21, Apr.	52	76		Burlington, IA	Mallemsheim, Württemberg
Laufer, Veronika	31, July 1890	7, July	70- 9m	494	Neeracher	Seymour, IN	Dielsdorf, Zürich, Schweiz

Christliche Apologete Death Notices --- 1839 - 1899

Name of Deceased	Notice Date	Death Date	Age	Page	Maiden Name	Place of Death	Place of Birth
Laumann, Christian Friedrich	2, Mar. 1868	6, Feb.	22	71		Chicago, IL	Beutelsbach, Schorndorf, Württemberg
Laun, Anna Christina	19, June 1882	2, June	69- 9m-19d	199	Vogt	Bremen, IL	Rockenfüs, Kurhessen
Laun, Christitian	12, May 1884	24, Apr.	75	7		Bremen, IL	Stadthosbach, Eschwege, Kurhessen
Laupscher, Maria	5, Jan. 1863	22, Nov.	20-10m	4		Boonville, IN	
Lausch, Joseph	6, Apr. 1885	18, Mar.	64	7		St. Paul, MN	Zduny, Krotoschin, Posen
Laussau, Anna Christina	16, Jan. 1890	1, Jan.	32	46		Chicago, IL	
Lautenschläger, Katharina	15, Oct. 1877	27, Sept	46- 6m-10d	335	Weiß	Schumway, IL	Oberacker, Amt Bretten, Baden
Lautenschlager, Marie Magdalena	17, June 1886	25, Mar.	71	7	Hotz	Mocasin, IL	Germany
Lauter, Judith	26, May 1887	28, Apr.	81	334		Newark, NJ	Steinbach, Eslingen, Württemberg
Lauterbach, Elise	19, Jan. 1899	11, Dec.	71	47	Isking	Indianapolis, IN	Hersfeld, Kurhessen
Lauterbach, Johan	11, Apr. 1881	11, Mar.	68	119		Keokuk, IA	Ruggendorf, Oberfranken, Baiern
Lauterbach, Johan Wilhelm	26, Oct. 1893	18, Sept	69	686		Columbus, OH	Kleinenglis, Hessen-Kassel
Lauterbach, Karl	11, Apr. 1895	15, Mar.	67	238		Indianapolis, IN	Hausen, Oberaula, Kurhessen
Lauterbach, Karl	7, Aug. 1890	20, July	13	510		Farmington, IA	
Laux, Anna Maria	26, Dec. 1895	26, Nov.	68	828	Schneider	Blooming Grove, MN	Bell, Koblenz, RheinPreußen
Laux, Anna Marie	20, Sept 1894	3, Sept	71- 6m- 4d	614	Musbach	Lemars, IA	Reusten, Herrenberg, Württemberg
Laux, Catharine	1, Nov. 1869	13, Sept	25-10m-23d	351	Kieser	Alton, IL	Notzingen, Kirchheim, Württemberg
Laux, Georg J.	22, Dec. 1879	3, Dec.	25- 5m-15d	407		Lemars, IA	Cedar Lake, Indiana
Laux, Johanna Emilie	27, May 1886	26, Apr.	46	7		Brighton, IL	Rußdorf, Sachsen
Laux, Maria Catharina	1, Oct. 1877	12, Sept	49	319	Schäfer	Alton, IL	Singhofen, Nassau
Laux, Philipp A.	13, June 1889	18, May	61- 1m- 5d	382		Brighton, IL	Hunsel, Nassau
Laux, Stephen	13, Apr. 1874	27, Mar.	49- 5m	119		Cedar Lake, IN	Reusten, Herrenberg, Württemberg
Laux, Wilhelm	12, May 1873	14, Apr.	31	151		Lincoln, NE	Singenhofen, Amt Nassau, Nassau
Lauzinger, John J.	6, Feb. 1890	7, Jan.	59	94		Billings, MO	Netschal, Glarus, Schweiz
Lawbert, Joseph	8, May 1882	6, Apr.	76- 9m	151		Columbus, OH	Lancaster County, Pennsylvania
Lay, Johan Heinrich	13, July 1893	17, June	89- 2m-10d	446	Kolb	Bushton, KS	Bingen am Rhein, Germany
Lay, Katharina	6, Sept 1888	16, Aug.	80	574		Bushton, KS	Monabach, Coblenz, Preußen
Lay, Maria Catharina	10, May 1894	17, Apr.	21	310		West Bend, WI	Wayne, Washington County, Wisconsin
Lay, Sophia	11, Mar. 1886	24, Feb.	17	7		Kewaskum, WI	
Layer, Barbara	13, Jan. 1843	28, Dec.	62	7		Louisville, KY	
Layher, Frank	6, Sept 1849		Inquiry	143		Greenfield, OH	Aichelbach, Backnang, Württemberg
Lebermann, Friederike	28, Jan. 1897	11, Jan.	64	62	Webner	Milwaukee, WI	Kirchberg, Marbach, Württemberg
Lebermann, Margaretha	1, Feb. 1875	9, Jan.	81-10m-21d	39	Heidenreich	Sandwich, IL	Semmling, Cammien, Pommern
Lebold, Catharina	29, Mar. 1888	2, Mar.	69	206	Rang	Bucyrus, OH	Grünstein, Baireuth, Oberfranken, Baiern
Lechleitner, Anna Maria	12, May 1898	13, Apr.	67	303	Stähle	New York City, NY	Hessen-Darmstadt
Lechner, Amalia	12, May 1892		30	302	Frankenstein	Parker, SD	Isingen, Württemberg
Lechtreck, Fannie	11, May 1899	24, Apr.	26	302		St. Louis, MO	Neustadt bei Danzig, West Preußen
Ledendecker, Heinrich	6, Mar. 1871		55	79		Pinckneyville, IL	St. Louis, Missouri
Leder, Albert	10, June 1872	12- 7m-25d		191		Leavenworth, MN	Markendorf, Rödinghausen, Bünde, Preußen
Leder, Barbara	16, Feb. 1888	22, Jan.	73	110	Hilbolt	Highland, IL	Cherentown, Lesuer County,
Leder, Christine	2, Jan. 1896	30, Oct.	60	14	Haman	Lamberton, MN	Schiedsnacht, Aargau, Schweiz
Leder, Emil	10, June 1872	12, Feb.	10-11m- 5d	191		Leavenworth, MN	Hannover
Leder, Philipp	24, May 1894	13, Apr.		342		Springfield, MN	Cherentown, Lesuer County
Lederer, Maria	12, May 1884	25, Apr.	54	7		Allegheny City, PA	Mountain Lake, Minnesota
Ledrich, Emil	15, Dec. 1898	26, Nov.	19	799		Pittsburg, PA	Sulz am Neckar, Württemberg
Ledtermann, Friedrich	20, May 1878		67	159		Pekin, IL	Bärenthal, Lothringen
							Dannheim bei Landau, Baiern

Christliche Apologete Death Notices --- 1839 - 1899

Name of Deceased	Notice Date	Death Date	Age	Maiden Name	Page	Place of Death	Place of Birth
Lee, Dorothea	17, Dec. 1877	1, Dec.	38		407	Warsaw, IL	
Lee, John Wilhelm	14, Sept 1863	7, Aug.			148	Clayton, IA	
Leecker, Sophie	21, Mar. 1889	8, Mar.	75- 1m		190	Dalton, MO	Osnabrück, Hannover
Leffert, Bertha Alwina	7, May 1896	22, Apr.	31	Wagner	302	Bridgeport, CT	Broterode, Hessen-Kassel
Lefholz, Wilhelmine	16, June 1892	19, May	61- 2m	Brakmann	382	Pinckney, MO	Löhne, Minden, Preußen
Lefmann, Franz	28, Sept 1863	27, July	23		156	Union, MO	Burchholzhausen, Preußen
Legel, John	12, Aug. 1858	14, June	28		128	Lansing, MI	New York
Leger, Louis	21, Apr. 1887	2, Apr.	57		254	Covington, KY	Neuschatel, Schweiz
Legler, Elisabeth Crescentia	6, Mar. 1876	21, Feb.	63- 6m	Landolt	79	Wyandotte, KS	
Lehberger, Maria	19, Dec. 1895	3, Dec.	63	Tausend	814	Pittsburg, PA	Saarbrücken, Germany
Lehling, Peter	29, Nov. 1894	25, Oct.	61		774	Emden, IL	Larrelt, Emden, Ostfriesland
Lehman, Anna Barbara	5, Feb. 1891	7, Jan.	52- 3m-27d	Nehf	94	Chicago, IL	Archshofen, Mergentheim, Württemberg
Lehman, Augusta Maria	3, Mar. 1892	29, Jan.	21		142	Ripon, WI	Ripon, Wisconsin
Lehman, John	9, Jan. 1882	24, Nov.	49		15	Florence, KS	Mickelweyer, Elsaß
Lehmann, Anna Elisabeth	14, July 1892	26, Apr.	83- -28d	Schmidt	446	Schenectady, NY	Lora, Hessen
Lehmann, Elisabeth	11, May 1899	14, Feb.	81	Hauter	302	Wheeling, IL	Obersebach, Weißenburg, Frankreich
Lehmann, Elisabeth	30, Nov. 1874	29, Oct.	55- 1m	Köhler	383	Edgerton, OH	Blankenloch, Karlsruhe, Baden
Lehmann, Frank	2, Nov. 1893		29- 2m-11d		702	Ripon, WI	Ripon, Wisconsin
Lehmann, Friedericka Louisa	8, Oct. 1896	2, Sept	76	Weden	655	Ripon, WI	Parlin bei Massow, Stettin, Pommern
Lehmann, Friederike	12, Jan. 1885		28	Wurster	7	Francisco, MI	Schänfach, Freudenstadt, Württemberg
Lehmann, Georg	21, Feb. 1895	29, Jan.	77		126	Schenectady, NY	Marburg, Hessen-Darmstadt
Lehmann, Georg	29, June 1874	13, June	73		207	Wheeling, IL	Gerstheim, Elsaß
Lehmann, Jakob	30, Sept 1872	5, July	21		319	Altamont, IL	Indiana
Lehmann, Johan Adam	31, Mar. 1887	17, Mar.	77		206	Altamont, IL	Ransbach, Rheinkreis Baiern
Lehmann, Johan Gottlieb	27, Feb. 1865	28, Oct.	40		36	Wabasha, MN	Kleingurau, Falkenberg, Preußen
Lehmann, Johan W. F.	21, Apr. 1892	16, Mar.	65		254	Taegesville, WI	Friederich der Große, Brandenburg
Lehmann, Johanna Eva Rosina	19, Sept 1870	30, Aug.	69- 6m-13d	Gutgahr	303	Buckley, IL	Kößlitz, Sachsen, Preußen
Lehmann, John	5, Nov. 1891	16, Oct.	73		718	Halstead, KS	Domenick, Neckarsulm, Württemberg
Lehmann, John	9, Aug. 1894	21, July	59- -24d		518	Indianapolis, IN	Worb, Bern, Schweiz
Lehmann, Joseph	4, Aug. 1892	26, June	39		494	Altamont, IL	St. Joseph County, Indiana
Lehmann, Louise Friedrike	16, Nov. 1885	29, Oct.	58	Schulz	7	Denver, CO	Godow bei Waren , Mecklenburg-Schwerin
Lehmann, Ludwig A.	16, June 1884	17, May	74		7	Freeport, IL	Kosendorf, Potsdam, Brandenburg
Lehmann, Maria	20, Apr. 1899	11, Mar.	74	Schuß	255	Philadelphia, PA	Kälberbach, Gerabronn, Württemberg
Lehmann, Maria	13, Feb. 1871	23, Jan.	25- 9m -2d	Lehmann	55	Trenton, IL	Dann, Baiern
Lehmann, Phil.	26, Aug. 1897	25, July	62		543	Chicago, IL	Dürenenzen, Elsaß
Lehmann, Rosine	19, Feb. 1891	17, Jan.	64	Hemminger	126	New York City, NY	Kirchheim a. T. , Württemberg
Lehmann, Sibilla	1, Oct. 1896	19, Aug.	79	Mattes	639	Howard, NE	Holzhausen, Sulz a. Neckar, Württemberg
Lehmann, Susanna	15, Dec. 1873	29, Nov.	68		399	Summerfield, IL	Kriegsheim a. d. Brem, Worms, Rheinpfalz Baiern
Lehmann, Susanna	13, Dec. 1880	22, Nov.	29		399	Farmington, IA	Klokuk, Iowa
Lehmberg, Sophia	13, May 1878	25, Mar.	54-11m	Kreye	151	Llano, TX	Broistädt, Braunschweig
Lehmkuhl, Adelheid	16, Oct. 1871	18, Sept	25		335	Newton, WI	Fahrenhorst, Amt Syke, Hannover
Lehmkuhl, Johan Dietrich	23, Nov. 1893	7, Nov.	76		750	Manitowoc, WI	Kloster Selder, Hannover
Lehmkuhl, Johann	13, July 1854	22, June	11- 7m- 4d		112	Manitowoc, WI	
Lehmkuhl, Margarethe	8, Dec. 1898	19, Nov.	81		783	Manitowoc, WI	Bremen, Hannover
Lehne, Christian Heinrich	13, Feb. 1871	5, Jan.	73		55	Alton, IL	Drammfeld bei Göttingen, Hannover
Lehne, Georg	6, Apr. 1863	15, Mar.	18		56	Alton, IL	Holtland, Stickhausen, Ostfriesland

- 299 -

Christliche Apologete Death Notices --- 1839 - 1899

Name of Deceased	Notice Date	Death Date	Age	Page	Maiden Name	Place of Death	Place of Birth
Lehne, Imke	4, July 1870	7, June	71	215	DeBurr	Alton, IL	Norden, Amt Norden, Ostfriesland
Lehne, Juliana Anna	19, Oct. 1899	22, Sept	50	671	Brenner	Springfield, IL	St. Louis, Missouri
Lehne, Louise Leonore	17, May 1894	26, Apr.	23	326		Alton, IL	
Lehne, Magdalene	22, May 1871	1, May	28	167		Sleepy Eye, MN	Schwerrinsdorf, Stickhausen, Ostfriesland
Lehnert, Ida Christine	6, July 1893	19, June	29	430		Le Sueur, MN	LeSueur, Minnesota
Lehnert, John	28, July 1898	1, July	67	479		Le Sueur, MN	Wittelshofen, Dingelspiel, Baiern
Lehnhoff, Eduard Fr.	3, Feb. 1887	18, Jan.	23	78		Dalton, MO	St. Charles, Missouri
Lehnhoff, Heinrich	10, Feb. 1887	23, Jan.	89	94		Dalton, MO	Roth bei Mühlheim an der Ruhr, Preußen
Lehnhoff, Wilhelm Herman	28, Jan. 1884	27, Dec.	56	7		Dalton, MO	Haarzopf, Mühlheim an der Ruhr, RheinPreußen
Lehning, Adam	27, Oct. 1892	9, Oct.	49	686		Columbus, OH	Merkenfritz, Hessen-Darmstadt
Lehning, Emma A.	10, Dec. 1896	25, Nov.		798		Columbus, OH	Bern, Schweiz
Lehning, Katharina	29, Mar. 1888	8, Mar.	78	206	Jäger	Chillicothe, OH	Fleschenbach, Hessen-Darmstadt
Lehr, Andreas Moritz	23, Feb. 1860	28, Jan.	53	32		Saginaw, MI	Merenburg, Nassau
Lehrman, Karoline	14, May 1877	1, May	49	159		Fond du Lac, WI	Friedeberg, Brandenburg, Preußen
Leibrand, Friedrich	30, Dec. 1867	7, Dec.	13- 6m- 7d	414		Shakopee, MN	Künzelsau, Württemberg
Leibrand, Jakobine	31, Mar. 1873	5, Mar.	81- 7m-27d	103	Weigel	Canal Dover, OH	Gundelbach, Maulbronn, Württemberg
Leibrand, Rosina	9, Sept 1886	19, Aug.	55	7	Zentzler	Jordan, MN	Künzelsau, Württemberg
Leibnitz, Margaretha	3, June 1878	15, May	51-10m-15d	175	Schurr	Waseca, MN	Oberwälden, Göppingen, Württemberg
Leibrand, Margarethe	29, July 1878	9, July	67- 8m	239	Eisenbrey	Sandwich, IL	Gündelbach, Marbach, Württemberg
Leibrock, Dan	16, Apr. 1877	15, Mar.	50	127		Ripley, OH	Ellenbrunnen, Rheinkreis Baiern
Leibrock, Eva Magdalena	11, Nov. 1897	23, Sept	79	719	Schuster	Mascoutah, IL	Haßloch, Neustadt a. d. Haardt, Germany
Leibrock, Johan Philipp	6, Aug. 1891	10, July	80	510		Mascoutah, IL	Haßloch, Rheinpfalz Baiern
Leibrock, Katharina	14, Sept 1868	19, Aug.	57- 1m- 3d	295		Mascoutah, IL	Hasloch, Rheinpfalz Baiern
Leiby, Benjamin	6, Apr. 1863	1, Feb.		56		Valparaiso, IN	Berks County, Pennsylvania
Leichtmann, David	5, July 1869	14, June	40- 6m-21d	215		Baltimore, MD	Reichenbach, Schlesien, Preußen
Leidheiser, Anna	15, Oct. 1877	16, Sept	23- 3m- 4d	335	Reinhart	Vermillion, OH	Brownheim, Ohio
Leidolph, Elisa	26, May 1873	29, Apr.	21	167	Höhnemeyer	Cincinnati, OH	Calkreise, Hannover
Leidolph, Margaretha	31, Jan. 1876	3, Jan.	33- 1m- 1d	39	Goepfer	Cincinnati, OH	Meinberg bei Schweinfurth, Baiern
Leienberger, Karolina	10, Feb. 1879	21, Jan.	56	47	Hummel	West Bend, WI	Wolfsheim, Hessen-Darmstadt
Leiendecker, Elisabeth	9, Sept 1886	25, Aug.	43- 4m-11d	7	König	Canal Dover, OH	Tuscarawas County, Ohio
Leiendecker, Philipp	22, Oct. 1883	4, Oct.	44- 5m-12d	343		Canal Dover, OH	Finkenbach, RheinPfalz Baiern
Leiendecker, Valtin	20, Sept 1880	6, Sept	24- 5m-15d	303		Delaware, OH	
Leifer, (Mr)	11, May 1854	26, Jan.	64	70		Captina, OH	Görsdorf, Niederrhein, Frankreich
Leifer, Magdalena	4, Apr. 1861	23, Mar.	69	56		Captina, OH	
Leifest, Lydia	27, Nov. 1876	26, Oct.	11- 3m-21d	383		Llano, TX	
Leifeste, August	9, Aug. 1888	20, July	44	510		Llano, TX	Broistedt, Braunschweig
Leifeste, August	19, July 1894	25, June	82	470		Hedwigs Hill, TX	Broistedt, Braunschweig
Leifeste, Elisabeth	5, Feb. 1883	11, Dec.	66	47		Llano, TX	Broistedt, Braunschweig
Leifeste, Emma	25, Nov. 1878	4, Nov.	18- 3m-27d	375		Llano, TX	
Leifeste, Johan Friedrich	20, Aug. 1896	30, July	75	543		Hedwigs Hill, TX	Breustadt, Germany
Leifeste, Mina	17, Mar. 1879	24, Feb.	21- 3m-17d	87		Llano, TX	
Leifester, Christoph	9, Dec. 1897	11, Nov.	83	783		Hedwigs Hill, TX	Breistadt, Braunschweig
Leifester, Margaretha	31, May 1875	8, May	40	175	Reinhart	Mason, TX	Orb, Baiern
Leimbach, Barbara	22, Mar. 1888	27, Feb.	69- 8m	190	Rudolph	Harper, IA	Hosbach, Kurhessen
Leimbach, Elisabeth	18, Sept 1865	13, Aug.		152		German Creek, IA	
Leimbach, Georg	26, June 1876	6, June	27- 6m	207		German Creek, IA	

- 300 -

Christliche Apologete Death Notices --- 1839 - 1899

Name of Deceased	Notice Date	Death Date	Age	Maiden Name	Place of Death	Page	Place of Birth
Leimbrock, Katie	1, June 1899	25, Apr.	52	Riske	Swanton, NE	351	Hannover
Leinbach, Killian	24, May 1894	7, Apr.	77		Harper, IA	342	Kurhessen
Leindorf, Franz	22, July 1878	18, June	40- 6m- 3d		Summit, WI	231	Alt-Damerow, Germany
Leindorf, Franz	5, Aug. 1878	18, June	40- 6m- 3d		Summit, WI	247	Alt-Damerow, Germany
Leindorf, Franz E.	3, May 1880	1, Mar.	12- 6m- 1d		Wonowoi, WI	143	
Leinert, Andreas	29, July 1852	8, June			Pittsburg, PA	124	Kanton St. Gallen, Schweiz
Leinike, Wilhelm	26, Jan. 1880	11, Jan.	61		Newport, KY	31	Kornbach, Waldeck
Leininger, Jakob	13, Oct. 1879	24, Aug.	33- - 2d			327	Cincinnati, Hamilton County, Ohio
Leininger, Johan Georg	24, Jan. 1889	6, Jan.	80		Cincinnati, OH	62	Steinweiler, Rheinkreis Baiern
Leininger, Maria Anna	25, Sept 1846	7, Sept	29- 3m-20d		Cincinnati, OH	165	
Leinken, Theresia	17, Oct. 1864	27, Sept	21	Butz	Indianapolis, IN	168	Baden
Leins, Friedrika Sophia Emilia	12, Feb. 1877	16, Jan.	54	Seeger	Aurora, IL	55	Herrenalb, Neuenbürg, Württemberg
Leins, Isidor	21, Apr. 1898	31, Mar.	74		Aurora, IL	255	Eutingen, Horb, Württemberg
Leins, Manda Louisa	4, May 1893	25, Mar.	24		Kendallville, IN	286	Wayne Township, Noble County, Ohio
Leipprandt, Engel Maria Dora	13, Nov. 1890	12, Oct.	54	Hofschmidt	Berne, MI	734	Klein-Heydorn, Hannover
Leiprand, Jonathan	12, July 1875	25, June	67		Sandwich, IL	223	Gündelbach, Maulbronn, Württemberg
Leischen, Barbara	30, July1883	5, July	43-11m- 9d	Stauffocher	Warsaw, IL	247	Matt, Glarus, Schweiz
Leiseman, Gustine	10, Dec. 1891	17, Oct.	63-11m-15d	Wandtke	Beaver Dam, WI	798	Grunke, Stolp, Pommern
Leiseman, Mathilde	29, May 1890	25, Apr.	22- 1m- 2d		Beaver Dam, WI	350	
Leisemann, Wilhelm	31, Oct. 1895	4, Oct.	67		Beaver Dam, WI	702	Pommern
Leiser, Anna	28, Apr. 1887	4, Apr.	37		Chicago, IL	270	
Leiser, Henriette	31, Oct. 1895	7, Sept	28	Peppel	Ada, MN	702	
Leiser, Johan	22, Sept 1879	5, Sept	85- 4m- 7d		Cannelton, IN	303	Arnsheim, Hessen-Darmstadt
Leitelt, Christine	5, Nov. 1891	18, Oct.	56	Lehmann	Grand Rapids, MI	718	Peterzell, Oberndorf, Württemberg
Leiter, Anna	30, May 1881		46	Rörich	Howard, NE	175	Tschirnischen, Schöngerg, Mähren, Oesterreich
Leitheißer, (boy)	31, Aug. 1874	4, Aug.	11- 9m-19d		Vermillion, OH	279	
Leitheißer, Catharina	31, Aug. 1874	5, Aug.	30- 5m-20d	Schellhauß	Vermillion, OH	279	Lambsheim, RheinPfalz Baiern
Leithmann, David	12, Nov. 1883	2, Oct.	36		New Orleans, LA	367	West Preußen
Leitner, Mina	19, Mar. 1883	24, Feb.	41-11m- 4d	Behrent	St. Louis, MO	95	Schwalbach, Weinsberg, Württemberg
Leitz, Christian	8, Feb. 1894	21, Jan.	71		Bucyrus, OH	94	Michelstadt, Odenwald, Hessen-Darmstadt
Leitz, Marie	11, Dec. 1882	20, Nov.	47-11m-15d	Rexroth	Bucyrus, OH	399	Bleidelsheim, Marbach, Württemberg
Leize, Gottlieb	15, Sept 1887	13, Aug.	30		Waco, NE	590	Forest City, Winnebago County, Iowa
Lekore, Ellen	30, Aug. 1880	25, July	19- 5m- 7d		Concord, IA	279	Seevis, Graubünden, Schweiz
Lembach, Elisabeth	25, Aug. 1884	8, Aug.	76	Johanni	Highland, IL	7	Meienfeld, Graubünden, Schweiz
Lembach, Johan Georg	28, Feb. 1889	8, Feb.	80- 4m- 7d		Highland, IL	142	Liennen, Tecklenburg, Preußen
Lemberg, Jakob	17, Dec. 1847	18, Sept	40		Monroe, IL	203	Wetzen, Winzen a. d. Luhe, Hannover
Lemcke, Jürgen Heinrich	6, Sept 1894	22, Aug.	82	Rakow	Madison, WI	582	Faulenbentz, Pommern
Lemcke, Wilhelmine Friedrike	7, Dec. 1885	5, Nov.	49		Milwaukee, WI	7	
Lemkau, Anna Elisabeth	21, May 1896		37- -22d	Hartmann	Muscatine, IA	334	Freiburg, Hannover
Lemkau, Johan	3, June 1886	17, May	72- 3m-26d		Muscatine, IA	7	Drewitz, Pommern
Lemke, Albert J.	4, Jan. 1894	3, Dec.	60		Milwaukee, WI	14	Benton, Carver County, Minnesota
Lemke, Anna	17, June 1886	23, May	25	Bitzer	Brownton, MN	7	Lützow, Ukemark
Lemke, Friedrich	29, Aug. 1889	12, Aug.	79- 3m-20d		Sheboygan, WI	558	Modgarben, Preußen
Lemke, Henrietta	10, Apr. 1876	29, Mar.	53		Boston Highlands, MA	118	Eldorado, Wisconsin
Lemke, Martha	5, Apr. 1894	15, Feb.	17		Van Dyne, WI	230	
Lemke, Martin	8, Dec. 1898	18, Nov.	78		Alden, IA	783	Robe, Treptow an der Rebe, Germany

Christliche Apologete Death Notices --- 1839 - 1899

Name of Deceased	Notice Date	Death Date	Age	Maiden Name	Page	Place of Death	Place of Birth
Lemm, Sophie	26, Jan. 1874	20, Sept	72	Thiele	31	Wabasha, MN	Dannenberg, Hannover
Lemmer, Bete	2, Mar. 1885	31, Jan.	66		7	Minneapolis, MN	Goldberg, Schlesien
Lemmler, Josephine	27, Sept 1888	27, Aug.	30	Reichert	622	Boston, MA	Rastatt, Baden
Lemmler, Maria Elisabeth	1, Jan. 1891	12, Oct.	66- 7m-12d	Seitz	14	Boston, MA	Leimen, Baden
Lengacher, Magdalena	26, Jan. 1885	13, Dec.	20		7	Baresville, OH	Canton Bern, Schweiz
Lenger, Louise	12, Nov. 1896	20, Oct.	33	Süllwold	734	Mt. Vernon, MO	Bendorf, Lippe-Detmold
Lenhard, Albertine Katharina	29, Dec. 1884	13, Dec.	24	Schwendener	7	Enterprise, KS	Henau bei St. Gallen, Schweiz
Lenhart, Anna Emilie Elisabeth	15, Oct. 1883	17, Sept	21- 5m-11d	Gohs	335	Mascoutah, IL	Mascoutah, Illinois
Lenhart, Magdalena	25, Aug. 1892	17, July	78		542	Canal Dover, OH	Somerset County, Pennsylvania
Lenker, Jones A.	2, Nov. 1885	12, Oct.	26		7	Nebraska City, NE	Dauphin County, Pennsylvania
Lennet, Magdalena	21, Jan. 1897	26, Dec.	80	Iwel	47	Baltimore, MD	Rheinschdorf bei Weißsendorf, Baiem
Lent, Elisabeth	12, Jan. 1860	4, Dec.	35		8		
Lentow, Johan	6, Nov. 1890	22, Oct.	91		718	Warrenton, MO	Lieben, Mecklenburg-Schwerin
Lentow, Johan	14, May 1896	20, Apr.	60		318	Warrenton, MO	Marlo, Mecklenburg
Lentz, Adam	4, June 1866	27, Nov.	55		182	Perry, IL	Eckhardsborn, Hessen-Darmstadt
Lentz, Daniel	3, Mar. 1898	12, Feb.	79		143	Philadelphia, PA	Schneith, Württemberg
Lentz, Elisabeth	4, June 1866	19, May	37		182	Perry, IL	Sparksbrücken, Hessen-Darmstadt
Lentz, Friederika	2, June 1898	9, May	77	Miller	351	Philadelphia, PA	Serrisheim, Württemberg
Lentz, Friedrike	9, Feb. 1893	5, Jan.	63	Schwegler	94	Cleveland, OH	Beutelsbach, Schorndorf, Württemberg
Lentz, Heinrich	21, Apr. 1892	29, Mar.	87		254	Eudora, KS	Reichsachsen, Kurhessen
Lentz, Karl Friedrich	14, Dec. 1885		64- 7m-21d		7	Mankato, MN	Pflugrode, Naugarde, Pommern
Lentz, Kate	30, May 1895	17, Apr.			350	Philadelphia, PA	
Lentz, Margaretha	21, Mar. 1889	26, Feb.	53-10m- 7d	Schmitt	190	Larned, KS	bei Worms, Hessen-Darmstadt
Lentz, Rosina	16, June 1898	23, May	70		383	Lancaster, NY	Weiler, Württemberg
Lentz, Salome	5, June 1890	9, May	66	Brumm	366	Nashville, MI	Petersbach, Elsaß
Lentzner, Hanna C.	10, Mar. 1879	3, Feb.	91- -20d		79	Menomonie, WI	Unterkosker, Schleitz, Sachsen
Lenz, (Mrs)	28, Dec. 1874	9, Dec.	70-11m-11d	Schlee	415	Canal Dover, OH	Durrweiler, Freudenstadt, Württemberg
Lenz, Anna	11, Feb. 1897	15, Jan.	70	Beck	94	Summerfield, IL	Amsterdam, Holland
Lenz, Barbara	3, Nov. 1887	12, Oct.	16- 1m-14d		702	Rochester, NY	
Lenz, David	11, July 1895	11, June	78		446	Akron, NY	Kleebrunn, Brackenheim, Württemberg
Lenz, Dorothea	23, May 1870	18, Apr.	77		167	Canal Dover, OH	Rohrdorf, Nagold, Württemberg
Lenz, Elisabeth	22, Feb. 1894	24, Dec.			126	Quincy, IL	Hageloch, Tübingen, Württemberg
Lenz, Emma Maria F.	27, July 1893	4, July		Sidow	478	Beaver Dam, WI	
Lenz, Fr.	6, Sept 1894	19, Aug.	82		582	Lansing, IA	Neberar, Preußen
Lenz, Georg Heinrich	21, Nov. 1889	28, Oct.	59- 6m- 1d		750	Danforth, IL	Schlitz, Lauterbach, Hessen-Darmstadt
Lenz, Gertrude	8, Mar. 1888	8, Feb.	71- 9m-24d	Vaubel	158	Eudora, KS	Richen-Sachsen, Kurhessen
Lenz, Henriette	25, May 1899	27, Apr.	75		335	Minneapolis, MN	Straduhn bei Schönlanke, Germany
Lenz, Henriette	9, Apr. 1883	28, Mar.	69- 2m-18d		119	Minnesota Lake, MN	Sandschönau, Pommern
Lenz, Ida	30, Nov. 1893	10, Nov.	21		766	Terre Haute, IN	Indianapolis, Marion County, Indiana
Lenz, Johan Friedrich	26, June 1882	8, June	82- 5m		207	Canal Dover, OH	Rordorf, Nagold, Württemberg
Lenz, Leopold (Rev)	11, Nov. 1867	29, Sept	32		358	New Orleans, LA	Baiem
Lenz, Maria	24, Mar. 1892	29, Jan.	17- 5m- 6d	Bauer	190	Milwaukee, WI	
Lenz, Maria Catharina	23, Feb. 1874	3, Feb.	55- - 5d	Schiller	63	Indianapolis, IN	Schnaith, Schorndorf, Württemberg
Lenz, Mina	24, May 1869	16, Apr.	18- 6m		167	Watertown, WI	
Leonard, Johan	21, July 1898	26, June	77		463	Bible Grove, IL	Haßloch an der Haardt, Rheinkreis Baiem
Leonhard , Anna Maria	25, Apr. 1895	31, Mar.	15		270	Stuttgart, AR	Staunton, Macoupin County, Illinois

Christliche Apologete Death Notices --- 1839 - 1899

Name of Deceased	Notice Date	Death Date	Age	Page	Maiden Name	Place of Death	Place of Birth
Leonhard, Elisabeth	10, Sept 1883	18, Aug.	75-11m-10d	295	Schuhmann	Meredosia, IL	Sulzbach, Baden
Leonhard, John H.	28, Feb. 1876	4, Feb.	59-11m-12d	71		Golconda, IL	Biskirchen, Wetzlar, Rheinpreußen
Leonhard, Maria	24, June 1886	21, May	64	7	Roth	Marietta, OH	Marnheim, Rheinkreis Baiern
Leonhard, Maria Elisabeth	28, Jan. 1897	25, Dec.	76	62	Scheurer	Farina, IL	Haßloch bei Neustatt an der Hard, Baiern
Leonhard, Michael	9, Nov. 1893	10, Oct.	73	718		Arenzville, IL	Sulzbach, Weinheim, Baden
Leonhardt, Elisabeth	9, June 1859	19, Apr.		92		Terre Haute, IN	
Leonhardt, J.C.	20, Dec. 1894	17, Nov.	37	822		Brooklyn, NY	Steilsfurt bei Sinsheim, Baden
Leonhardt, Maria	9, June 1859	15, Apr.	10- 4m- 5d	92		Terre Haute, IN	
Leonhardt, Valentin	16, July1883	22, June	73- 3m-22d	231		Meredosia, IL	Baden
Leonhart, Anna Maria	3, Nov. 1873	3, Oct.	19	351		Pittsburg, PA	Weißweil, Amt Kenzingen, Baden
Leonhart, Elisabeth	4, Aug. 1884	22, July	70	7		Chicago, IL	Mallerdingen, Baden
Leonhart, Katharine	4, May 1899	19, Mar.	75	287	Ehrold	Marion, OH	Hessen
Leonhart, Margaretha	16, Oct. 1876	25, Sept	21	335		Marion, OH	
Leors, Louise	23, Aug. 1888	20, July	24- 5m-18d	542		Harper, IA	
Lepper , Anna Elisabeth	3, Oct. 1889	18, Sept	48	638	Nordheim	Newport, KY	Gehhaus, Sachsen-Weimar
Lepper, Christian Eduard	19, Feb. 1877	23, Jan.	18- -14d	63		Allegheny City, PA	
Lepper, Georg Friedrich	24, Dec. 1896	29, Nov.	25	831		Allegheny City, PA	Pittsburg, Pennsylvania
Lepper, Maria	29, Dec. 1887	17, Dec.	68	830	Metzler	Galion, OH	Schlebach, Hessen-Darmstadt
Lepper, Paul	19, May 1879	26, Apr.	45	159		Pittsburg, PA	Eubach, Melsungen, Kurhessen
Leppert, Andreas	25, Apr. 1881	20, Mar.	56	135		Lansing Ridge, IA	Kitzingen, Baiern
Leppert, Barbara	3, Feb. 1879	4, Jan.	55	39	Hurst	Manito, IL	Sputterzell, Lahr, Baden
Leppert, Barbara	20, Mar. 1876	26, Feb.	34	95	Urban	Pomeroy, OH	Allmansweyer, Baden
Leppert, Carl	13, May 1886	13, Apr.	29	7		Lansing, IA	French Creek, Allamakee County, Iowa
Leppert, Elisabeth	11, Oct. 1880	14, Sept	41- 7m-14d	327	Meyer	Brooklyn, NY	Berwangen, Baden
Leppert, Johann	21, Apr. 1853	29, Mar.	49	64		Pomeroy, OH	Allmansweier, Baden
Leppert, Johannes	3, Feb. 1859	8, Jan.	81	20		Pomeroy, OH	Almansweyer, Lahr, Baden
Leppert, John	2, Feb. 1893	31, Dec.	82	78		Pomeroy, OH	Annan Weiler, Lahr, Baden
Leppert, Maria Christine	25, May 1899	14, Apr.	73	335	Fick	Lake City, MN	Mecklenburg
Leppert, Mathilde	11, July 1889	17, June	20- 3m-10d	446		Lansing, IA	
Leppert, Wilhelm	3, Oct. 1864	24, July	25-10m	160		Winchester, VA	
Leppert, Wilhelmine	20, Apr. 1868	23, Mar.	24- 5m-14d	127	Schäfer	Will County, IL	
Leppien, John	7, Mar. 1889	16, Jan.	80- 1m-11d	158		New Redwood, MN	Mecklenburg-Schwerin
Lepple, Wilhelmine	15, Nov. 1888	22, Oct.	31- -15d	734	Ohnmeiß	Eudora, KS	Wangen, Kannstatt, Württemberg
Lerch, Katharina	11, July 1850	25, May	45	112		Jennings County, IN	Nordheim, Bensheim, Hessen-Darmstadt
Lescher, Konrad	2, Aug. 1849	4, July	52- 5m- 3d	124		St. Louis, MO	Weingardten, Baiern
Lesemann, Heinrich	30, Jan. 1862	2, Jan.	60-10m- 3d	20		Nashville, IL	Volberdingsen bei Minden, Preußen
Lesemann, Sophia M. Elisabeth	30, Dec. 1867	10, Dec.	25- 4m- 6d	414	Grote	Nashville, IL	
Leser, Anna Maria	19, Oct. 1863		78- 1m- 9d	168	Baumann	Booneville, IL	Reitenau, Aargau, Schweiz
Leser, Jakobina	7, Apr. 1873	11, Mar.	36- -18d	111	Siegel	Booneville, IL	Birkenfeld, Oldenburg
Lesin, Wilhelmine	17, Dec. 1866	24, Nov.	21	406	Schwarz	Lowell, WI	Brietzig, Kreis Pyritz, Pommern
Lesser, Katharina	26, Mar. 1896	29, Feb.	70	206		Newark, NJ	Schabbach, Baden
Lesz, Margaretha	12, June 1871	18, May	39- - 8d	191	Meule	Boonville, MO	Aue bei Durlach, Baden
Letterle, Margaretha Elisabeth	21, July 1876	14, Dec.	21	63	Frank	Louisville, KY	Louisville, Jefferson County, Kentucky
Lettow, Wilhelmine	6, June 1889	16, May	77	366		Manitowoc, WI	Schönhausen bei Naugard, Pommern
Leuenberger, Andreas	24, Jan. 1871	11, Nov.	48	31		Saginaw, MI	Ursenbach, Bern, Schweiz
Leuenberger, Carolina	21, July 1892	29, June	23	462		Kochville, MI	Kochville, Saginaw County, Michigan

Christliche Apologete Death Notices --- 1839 - 1899

Name of Deceased	Notice Date	Death Date	Age	Page	Maiden Name	Place of Death	Place of Birth
Leuenberger, Jakob	9, Jan. 1882	28,Nov.	61-10m	15		Rochester, MN	Melchnau, Bern, Schweiz
Leuenberger, Jakob	19, Dec. 1881	28,Nov.	61-10m	407		Rochester, MN	Welchnau, Bern, Schweiz
Leuenberger, Jakob	21, Mar. 1895	28, Feb.	66-10m-28d	190		Des Moines, IA	Bern, Schweiz
Leukering, Louise	21, Sept 1885	20, Aug.	65- 1m-13d	7	Resing	Golconda, IL	Wohlstreck, Barnstorf, Diepholz, Hannover
Leukering, Wilhelm	26, Mar. 1891	23, Feb.	72	206		Golconda, IL	Wetschen, Diepholz, Hannover
Leukring, Emilie	18, Sept 1882	21, Aug.	20- 1m-16d	303	Arensmann	Golconda, IL	Massac County, Illinois
Leukroth, Gotthold	10, May 1875	22, Apr.	52	151		Mt. Vernon, IN	Wöllmirstädt bei Wiehe, Preußen
Leuschner, Julius Herman	19, July 1894	13, June	71	470		Perry, TX	Fürstenau, Schlesien
Leuschner, Maria	6, Nov. 1882	9, Oct.	26	359		Peyton, TX	Industry, Austin County, Texas
Leverenz, Gertrud	8, Dec. 1879	18, Nov.	65- 5m-10d	391	Bierschenk	New Bremen, IL	Wichmannshausen, Kurhessen
Leverenz, Maria Dorothea	29, Dec. 1884	1, Dec.	80 - 9m	7	Keuer	Brillion, WI	Jordensdorf, Mecklenburg-Schwerin
Levi, Daniel Julius	23, Apr. 1891	22, Mar.	43	270		Sleepy Eye, MN	Heigerloh, Württemberg
Levings, (Dr)	25, Jan. 1849	9, Jan.	52	16		Cincinnati, OH	
Lewandowski, Robert	9, Mar. 1899	5, Feb.	27	159		Watertown, WI	Waterloo, Wisconsin
Leweke, (Mrs)	7, Apr. 1879	16, Mar.	84	111	Reker	Drake, MO	Kleinmark, Lippe-Detmold
Leweke, Conrad	21, Mar. 1895	26, Feb.	89	190		Allegan, MI	Vahlhausen, Preußen
Leweke, Dorothea	29, Dec. 1884	11, Dec.	33	7	Dendel	Allegan, MI	Roseville, Michigan
Leweke, Fr. Christoph	4, Feb. 1884	19, Jan.	80	7		Drake, MO	Belle, Lippe-Detmold
Leweke, Heinrich	27, Aug. 1896	23, July	22	559		Drake, MO	Gasconade County, Missouri
Leweke, Sophie	12, Apr. 1880	17, Mar.	70	119	Begemann	Allegan, WI	Leopoldsthal, Amt Horn, Lippe-Detmold
Leweke, Wilhelm F.	19, Dec. 1895	22, Nov.	33	814		Altamont, IL	Drake, Gasconade County, Missouri
Ley, Elisabeth	17, Mar. 1892	21, Feb.	76	174	Meyer	Burlington, IA	Weingarten, Durlach, Baden
Leyrer, Wilhelmine	19, July 1888	25, June	23	462		Bay City, MI	Kirchberg, Marbach, Württemberg
Lezerich, Anna Christina	22, Mar. 1880	5, Mar.	71	95		Chicago, IL	Sand, Wohlhagen, Naumburg, Kurhessen
Licey, Henry	15, Jan. 1891	28, Dec.	48	46		Chicago, IL	Effity, Lancaster County, Pennsylvania
Lich, Anna Elisabeth	9, Feb. 1863	16, Jan.	51	24	Strudel	Louisville, KY	Bußbach, Kreis Friedberg, Hessen
Lich, Maggie	2, Feb. 1893	4, Jan.	34	78	Steinhauer	New Albany, IN	Harrison County, Indiana
Licht, Jakob	23, Dec. 1897		65	815		Burt, IA	Cincinnati, Hamilton County, Ohio
Lichte, Anna Christina	24, Apr. 1876	6, Feb.	53	135		St. Louis, MO	Minden, Preußen
Lichte, Christopher	14, Apr. 1873	18, Jan.	77	119		Hopewell, MO	Gofeld, Kreis Herford, Minden, Preußen
Lichte, Christopher	22, Feb. 1875	1, Jan.	38	63		Herman, MO	Gofeld, Kreis Herford, Minden, Preußen
Lichte, Elisabeth	20, June 1870	27, Mar.	75- 3m-15d	199	Ellermann	Hopewell, MO	Rehme, Minden, Preußen
Lichte, Heinrich	21, Aug. 1871	May		271		Red Wing, MN	Gohfeld, Amt Vlotho, Minden, Preußen
Lichte, Heinrich	31, Aug. 1893	14, Aug.	76	558		Big Spring, MO	Jafeld, Minden, Preußen
Lichte, J.	8, May 1871	14, Apr.		151		Weston, MO	Rämlag, Zürich, Schweiz
Lichte, Johan Friedrich	22, Mar. 1875	18, Feb.	25- 2m	95		Red Wing, MN	
Lichte, Louise Karoline Charlotte	20, Oct. 1898	19, Sept	83	671	Rolfmeyer	Herman, MO	Edinghausen, Germany
Lichtenberg, Johan Julius	14, Feb. 1895	21, Jan.	23	110		Pinckney, MO	Summerfield, Illinois
Lichtenberg, Louise	18, Jan. 1894	1, Jan.	73	46	Freitag	Pinckney, MO	Falldorf, Minden, Preußen
Lichtenberg, Louise	11, Oct. 1875	26, Aug.	23	327	Scholl	Herman, MO	Ischbringen, Baden
Lichtenberger, Anna Maria	29, Mar. 1888	7, Mar.	81- 6m	206	Hettron	New York City, NY	Wollmatingen, Konstanz, Baden
Lichtensteiger, Maria Agnes	10, Aug. 1899	19, July	86	511	Reutinger	Wapello, IA	Burlington, Racine County, Wisconsin
Lichtfeld, Heinrich	24, Nov. 1887	1, Nov.	19	750		Eldora, IA	
Lichthardt, Mathilda Adalie	1, Dec. 1873	8, Nov.	12	383		Grand Ridge, IL	
Lichtsinn, Heinrich	27, Jan. 1898	25, Dec.	84	63		Cincinnati, OH	Eldagsen, Petershagen, Minden, Preußen
Lichtsinn, Louisa	27, Jan. 1898	8, Jan.		63	Hesselmeier	Cincinnati, OH	Drohne, Dilinge, Raden, Hannover

Christliche Apologete Death Notices --- 1839 - 1899

Name of Deceased	Notice Date	Death Date	Age	Page	Maiden Name	Place of Death	Place of Birth
Lickel, Friedrich Wilhelm	28, Oct. 1872	22, Sept	19-10m-24d	351		Lancaster, WI	Dorf Elsof, Wittgenstein, Preußen
Lickel, Johan Georg	16, Dec. 1878	18, Nov.	63- 2m- 1d	399		Lancaster, WI	Ellenboro, Grand County, Wisconsin
Lickel, Louis	26, May 1879	12, May	24- 1m	167		Lancaster, WI	Hay Creek, Minnesota
Lidgerding, Willie	26, Sept 1895	28, Aug.	21	622		Red Wing, MN	Rockford, Iowa
Lidike, Friedrich Wilhelm	26, Aug. 1897		18	543		Klemme, IA	Bleichenbach, Hessen-Darmstadt
Liebegott, Georg	9, Nov. 1885	27, Oct.	67- 9m-21d	7		Louisville, KY	Louisville, Jefferson County, Kentucky
Liebegott, Heinrich	8, Apr. 1897	15, Mar.	43	223		Louisville, KY	Stockheim, Büdingen, Hessen-Darmstadt
Liebegott, Katharina	13, Oct. 1879	25, Sept	54	327	Ormbriester	Louisville, KY	Covington, Kenton County, Kentucky
Liebegott, Louise	26, Sept 1895	24, Aug.	36	622	Genzheimer	Louisville, KY	Stralsund, Preußen
Liebenow, Christian Gottfried	25, Aug. 1879	5, Aug.	90- 8m-14d	271		Manitowoc, WI	Eschelbach, Baden
Liebenstein, Christoph	15, Aug. 1889	25, July	55	526		Yellow Creek, IL	
Liebenstein, Emilie	11, Dec. 1871	19, Nov.	4- 7m- 3d	399		Polk City, IA	
Liebenstein, Georg Burkhard	14, Sept 1899	26, Aug.	67	591		Sherrills Mount, IA	Eschelbach, Baden
Liebenstein, John	12, Jan. 1899	11, Dec.	21	31		Pearl City, IL	Loran, Stephenson County, Illinois
Liebenstein, Louisa	17, Dec. 1891	12, Nov.	79- 2m-18d	814	Krüger	Sherman, WI	Sulsfeld, Eppingen, Baden
Liebenstein, Maria	16, Feb. 1874	27, Dec.	26	55	Mahle	Des Moines, IA	Dahlberg, Schwerin, Mecklenburg-Schwerin
Liebenstein, Philipp	7, Sept 1899	13, Aug.	87	575		Scott, WI	Stebach, Eppingen, Baden
Liebenstein, Philipp	11, Dec. 1871	17, Nov.	29- 5m- 2d	399		Polk City, IA	Eschenbach, Baden
Liebenstein, Susanna	10, Apr. 1871	28, Feb.		119	Tiller	Giard, IA	Daisbach, Amt Sinsheim, Baden
Lieberenz, Dorothea	20, Nov. 1876	31, Oct.	51	375	Michaelius	Kendallville, IN	Drüsedau, Kreis Osterburg, Preußen
Liebergesell, Herman	11, May 1893	20, Apr.	24	302		Yellow Creek, IL	Stephenson County, Illinois
Liebhart, H.	31, Jan. 1895			65		Cincinnati, OH	
Liebhart, Henry	20, Aug. 1891	9, July	36	542		Covington, KY	Saugerties, New York
Liebig, Elisabeth	3, May 1869	16, Apr.	85- 2m	143	Schwebel	Quincy, IL	Lichtenstein
Liebig, Mina Hopper	16, July 1896	21, June	40- 3m-13d	463		Council Bluffs, IA	
Liechte, Crescentia	14, Mar. 1870	24, Dec.	30- 6m-17d	87	Sauter	Weston, MO	Liggeringen, Amt Constanz, Baden
Lieder, Karl Friedrich	12, Jan. 1880	24, Dec.	60- 8m- 7d	15		Newport, KY	Fraustadt, Posen, Preußen
Liehr, Anna Katharina	7, Feb. 1889	4, Jan.	18-10m- 8d	94		Pittsfield, IL	
Lienhard, Louise	17, Mar. 1898	1, Mar.	65	175	Kleiner	Highland, IL	Suhr, Aargau, Schweiz
Lienschmidt, J. Christoph	20, Oct. 1853	11, Sept	63	168		Marthasville, MO	Valdo, Minden, Preußen
Liephard, John	21, Jan. 1878	8, Jan.	58	23		Goshen, IN	Gensungen, Kurhessen
Liepper, John	22, Mar. 1875	18, Feb.	14	95		Wabasha, MN	
Liermann, August	11, June 1891	22, Apr.	69- 5m-19d	382		Menomonie, WI	Cramorsdorf, Stettin, Preußen
Liermann, Carl Friedrich Wilhelm	2, May 1895	12, Apr.	42	286		Crandon, SD	Wisbu, Pommern
Liermann, Friedrich W.	1, May 1882	15, Apr.	66- 1m- 7d	143		Iron Ridge, WI	Plantikow, Naugard, Pommern
Liermann, Georg	7, Nov. 1881	17, Oct.	66	359		Lexington, MO	Hugsweyer, Amt Lahr, Baden
Lies, Johan	12, Dec. 1861	16, Nov.	22	200		Chipmonkooly, WI	
Liesberg, Elisabeth	26, Apr. 1894	30, Mar.	72	278	Blumberg	Scioto Co, OH	Fräulein Steinfort, Mecklenburg-Schwerin
Liese, Mathilde	27, Dec. 1880	18, Nov.	12- 6m-17d	415		Concordia, MO	Wisconsin
Liese, Wilhelm	8, July 1878	22, June	60	215		Concordia, MO	Drewitz bei Küstrin, Preußen
Lieseberg, Joachim Heinrich	15, July 1878	26, June	56	223		Portsmouth, OH	Upahl, Mecklenburg-Schwerin
Lieske, Auguste	26, Sept 1895	3, Sept	38	622	Arndt	Duluth, MN	Grünister, Bromberg, Germany
Liesner, Sophie	27, Nov. 1876	8, Nov.	69	383	Retzlaff	Milwaukee, WI	Freienwalde, Pommern
Liestermann, Anna Elisabeth	4, May 1868	20, Mar.	64-11m-24d	143		Defiance, OH	Hundesburg, Magdeburg, Preußen
Lietzke, Dorothea L. H.	14, Apr. 1896	14, Apr.	81	318	Larenz	DeWitt, MI	Muttain, Pommern
Lietzow, Karl August	26, Sept 1889	16, July	43	619		Oshkosh, WI	Manow, Pommern

Christliche Apologete Death Notices --- 1839 - 1899

Name of Deceased	Notice Date	Death Date	Age	Maiden Name	Place of Death	Page	Place of Birth
Likert, Anna Maria	9, Mar. 1899	15, Feb.	38	Peterson	San Diego, CA	159	Harris, Schleswig-Holstein
Lilie, Johan	3, Aug. 1868	13, June	59- 3m-16d		Angelica, NY	247	Lasebüttel, Amt Gifhorn, Hannover
Liljegren, John	14, Feb. 1895	16, Jan.	75		Pittsburg, PA	110	Schweden
Liller, (Mrs)	9, June 1879	8, Apr.	61- 1m		New Boston, OH	183	
Liller, Adam	22, Dec. 1862	26, Oct.	6- 1m		Cincinnati, OH	204	Steinweiler, Rheinpfalz Baiern
Liller, Michael	20, Apr. 1899	3, Apr.	75		Cincinnati, OH	255	Scioto County, Ohio
Lillich, Adam	17, June 1886	27, Feb.	41		Wyandotte, KS	7	Lichtenau, Baden
Lillich, Andreas	10, Jan. 1889	28, Dec.	84- 7m- 5d		Armourdale, KS	30	Hessen-Darmstadt
Lillich, Anna Maria	5, Mar. 1896	11, Feb.	77	Staff	Kansas City, KS	158	
Lillich, Caspar	10, Apr. 1871	23, Feb.	19- 4m-28d		Wyandotte, KS	119	
Lillie, Christian	30, Oct. 1876	13, Oct.	78- 2m- 4d		Lafayette, MN	351	Rothenmehle, Amt Giffhorn, Hannover
Lilly, Catharina Maria	23, Sept 1886	20, Aug.	50	Schrader	Angelica, NY	7	Dannenbüttel, Hannover
Lilly, Dorothea	17, Sept 1891	11, Aug.	79		Angelica, NY	606	Bordorf, Giffhorn, Hannover
Limburg, Lena	8, Oct. 1891	14, Sept	31	Fink	Buffalo, NY	654	Boston Center, Erie County, New York
Limle, Carl Fr.	22, Nov. 1860	4, Nov.	21		Chillicothe, OH	188	Ross County, Ohio
Linbach, Jakob	14, Aug. 1846		Inquiry		Warrenton, MO	131	Krumbach, Hessen
Linck, Anna Maria	12, May 1879	26, Apr.	23- - 3d	Kloprin	Newport, KY	151	
Linck, Emma Maria	7, Mar. 1889	8, Feb.	24		Columbus, WI	158	
Linck, Katy	30, Nov. 1868	11, Nov.	18- 7m-22d		Cincinnati, OH	383	St. Goar am Rhein, Preußen
Lindauer, Jakob	21, Dec. 1885	5, Dec.	81- 5m- 3d		Newark, NJ	7	Ruppertshofen, Faildorf, Württemberg
Linde, Gottfried	12, Jan. 1899	21, Dec.	78		Beaver Dam, WI	31	Britzig bei Piritz, Germany
Lindeke, Carolina Wilhelmina	23, Apr. 1891	26, Mar.	57	Gerth	St. Paul, MN	270	Posen
Lindemann, (Mr)	11, Mar. 1867	6, Jan.	68		Hudson City, NJ	78	Vegesack bei Bremen, Germany
Lindemann, Auguste	18, Dec. 1890	30, Nov.	26	Fiesches	Industry, TX	814	
Lindemann, Heinrich	9, Dec. 1872	14, Nov.	47- 8m-18d		Bunker Hill, IL	399	Sauingen, Braunschweig
Lindemann, Johan	9, June 1887	17, May	18		Pittsfield, IL	366	Pittsfield, Illinois
Lindemann, John	31, Mar. 1862	5, Mar.	52		Wapello, IA	52	Amt Bathbergen, Hannover
Lindemann, Karolina	21, Jan. 1892	13, Dec.	62		Chicago, IL	46	Neizow, Pommern
Lindenmeier, Johan Jakob	23, Mar. 1899	13, Feb.	82	Ternod	Otisco, IN	191	Leitershausen, Weinheim, Baden
Linder, Theresa	6, Oct. 1873	5, Sept	14		Le Sueur, MN	319	Le Sueur, Minnesota
Linders, Casper H.	11, Mar. 1878	26, Feb.	60		Red Bud, IL	79	Hüttenhausen, Herford, Westphalen
Lindhorst, Klara Maria	31, Aug. 1899	13, Aug.	86	Siek	St. Louis, MO	559	Melle bei Osnabrück, Hannover
Lindlove, Wilhelm	13, June 1864	26, Jan.	46		Manitowoc, WI	96	
Lindner, C. Richard	28, Apr. 1892	5, Apr.	33		Paige, TX	270	Längefeld, Sachsen
Lindner, Georg Lehnhardt	16, Feb. 1893	27, Jan.	79		Kendallville, IN	110	Oberöstheim, Baiern
Lindner, Karoline Friederike	13, July 1899	2, June	73		Zwickau, GE	447	
Lindner, Maria	28, Apr. 1873	7, Apr.	62	Achtelstätter	Perrysburg, OH	135	Uhlmet, Baiern
Lindner, Maria Elisabeth	11, May 1893	10, Apr.	73	Simon	Bay City, MI	302	Unterdireckheim, Württemberg
Lindner, Rosina	29, Mar. 1894	9, Mar.	70		Kendallville, IN	214	Rommburg, Württemberg
Lindorfer, Karolina	9, July 1877	4, June	41- 2m- 8d	Daihle	Kendallville, IN	223	Thomsdorf, Preußen
Lindow, Friedrich	29, June 1899	5, June	51		Detroit, MI	415	Thomsdorf, Brandenburg
Lindow, Justine	7, Feb. 1895	15, Jan.	73		Detroit, MI	94	Tiffin Township, Defiance County, Ohio
Linebrink, Elon	23, Jan. 1896	7, Oct.	24	Rengert	Stryker, OH	62	Sandusky County, Ohio
Linebrink, Heinrich	11, Feb. 1884	23, Jan.	43		Stryker, OH	7	Reme, Minden, Preußen
Linenschmidt, Christina	13, Sept 1894	19, Aug.	61		Denton, TX	598	
Linghardt, J.	12, Jan. 1885	12, Dec.	50		Chicago, IL	7	

Christliche Apologete Death Notices --- 1839 - 1899

Name of Deceased	Notice Date	Death Date	Age	Page	Maiden Name	Place of Death	Place of Birth
Link, C.	20, Apr. 1899		87	255		Wellsville, NY	Ergenbrechtweiler, Württemberg
Link, Caspar	19, Aug. 1878	30, July	65	263		Bay City, MI	Baiern
Link, Christian	13, Aug. 1883	24, July	55	263		Chicago, IL	Schwenningen, Rottweil, Württemberg
Link, Christian Wilhelm	16, Feb. 1860	4, Feb.	46	28		Newport, KY	St. Goar, Koblenz, Preußen
Link, Emilie	9, Apr. 1866	17, Mar.	22	118	Meyer	Columbus, WI	Ligan, Neu-Markischen, Brandenburg
Link, F.	2, June 1879	16, May	79- -24d	175		Columbus, WI	Blievensdorf, Neustadt, Mecklenburg-Schwerin
Link, Georg	10, Apr. 1882	29, Mar.	23	119		Newport, KY	Newport, Campbell County, Kentucky
Link, Herman L.	28, Nov. 1881		66	383		Buffalo, NY	Cimerzelle bei Fulda, Preußen
Link, Jakob	30, Mar. 1893	5, Oct.	83	206		Crow River, MN	Droßingen, Tuttlingen, Württemberg
Link, Johan Friedrich	17, Dec. 1891	4, Mar.	60	814		Columbus, WI	Grünwettersbach, Durlach, Baden
Link, John	25, May 1893	22, Nov.	32	334		Columbus, WI	Elba, Wisconsin
Link, Katharina	29, Mar. 1880	30, Apr.	78	103		Montrose, MN	Blievensdorf, Mecklenburg-Schwerin
Link, Margaretha	15, Sept 1887	15, Mar.	58	590	Rau	Newport, KY	Kalmbach, Württemberg
Link, Mina Sophia	23, Jan. 1875	22, Aug.	19	31		Columbus, WI	Cincinnati, Hamilton County, Ohio
Link, Wilhelmina	6, Nov. 1882	15, Oct.	15- 6m	359		Pittsburg, PA	
Linn, Johannes	6, Oct. 1884	4, Aug.	72	7		Danville, IL	Reifelbach, Baiern
Linne, Elisabetha	22, Sept 1862	30, Aug.	44- 9m-16d	152	Paulus	Danville, IL	Münchhausen, Kreis Marburg, Kurhessen
Linne, Jacob	14, Nov. 1889	9, Oct.	51	734		West Unity, OH	Münchhausen, Marburg, Kurhessen
Linnebrink, Ludwig	1, Oct. 1883	26, Aug.	76- 5m-20d	319		Burlington, IA	Baumde, Germany
Linnemann, Maria	17, June 1897	30, Apr.	51	383	Wurster	St. Louis, MO	Warsaw, Illinois
Linnemann, Maria	27, July 1868	2, July	60	239		Burlington, IA	
Linnemann, Philipp Wilhelm Ernst	28, Sept 1893	30, Aug.	64	622		St. Louis, MO	Cappeln, Lippe-Detmold
Linnemann, Xavier	27, May 1878	13, May	77- 2m-14d	167		Marthasville, MO	Kenzing, Baden
Linnenschmidt, Friedrika	4, Nov. 1867	15, Sept	67	350	Brandt	Pinckney, MO	Valldorf, Minden, Preußen
Linnenschmidt, Herman Heinrich	3, Dec. 1891	17, Oct.	59- 7m- 2d	782		Concordia, MO	Waldorf, Minden, Preußen
Linse, Mathilda	6, Dec. 1880	18, Nov.	12- 6m-17d	391		Galena, IL	Wisconsin
Linsemeyer, Christina	6, Mar. 1865	13, Jan.	39- 3m- 6d	40	Traub	Chicago, IL	Nordheim, Brakenheim, Württemberg
Linsenmeier, Louise	25, Dec. 1876	3, Dec.	12	413		Fond du Lac, WI	
Linsenmeyer, Gottlieb	1, Jan. 1891	7, Dec.	66	14		Winona, MN	Stetten, Württemberg
Lint, (Mr)	11, July 1889	19, Mar.	72- 9m	446		Edon, OH	Berlin, Preußen
Lint, Samuel	18, Jan. 1894	26, Dec.	77	46		Ironton, OH	Somerset County, Pennsylvania
Lintner, Friedrich	6, Feb. 1890	16, Jan.	64	94		Madison, IN	Holzhort, Baiern
Lionhardt, Bernhardt	20, Nov. 1890	13, Oct.	79	750		Perry, IL	Berghampten, Genkenbach, Baden
Lipcaman, Oliver Samuel	3, Mar. 1898	2, Jan.	22	143		Sandusky, OH	Perry, Illinois
Liphardt, Heinrich	9, May 1881	14, Apr.	52	151		Chicago, IL	Ziegelhütte, Mittelhof, Felsberg, Preußen
Liphardt, Karl	26, Jan. 1899	29, Dec.	39	63		South Bend, IN	Benthen, Mecklenburg-Schwerin
Liphart, Eduard	15, Dec. 1879	2, Dec.	16	399		South Bend, IN	
Liphart, Konrad	15, Dec. 1898	23, Nov.	65	799		Brighton, IL	Jensingen, Kurhessen
Lipolt, Frank	25, Apr. 1881	6, Mar.	39	135		St. Louis, MO	
Lipp, Ernst	12, Sept 1850	12, July	31	148		Jersey City, NJ	Längerich, Preußen
Lipp, Rosa	6, Nov. 1890	3, Apr.	34- 6m	718		Madison, IN	Stammheim, Württemberg
Lippert, Christian	18, May 1863	30, Mar.	79	80		Michigan City, IN	Bodenheim, Brackenheim, Württemberg
Lippert, Sarah	3, Sept 1896	7, Aug.	26- 5m-13d	575	Steinke	Fairfax, MN	Osnabrück, Hannover
Lippmann, Karl Rudolph	20, Jan. 1898	2, Jan.	79	47		Brighton, IL	Wolfersdorf, Sachsen-Weimar
Lippold, Gottfried	18, Oct. 1869	12, Sept	64	335		Bunker Hill, IL	Klein-Falke bei Gera, Reuß, Sachsen
Lippoldt, Christiane	13, Mar. 1890	21, Feb.	75	174	Neumark		

Christliche Apologete Death Notices --- 1839 - 1899

Name of Deceased	Notice Date	Death Date	Age	Page	Maiden Name	Place of Death	Place of Birth
Lippoldt, Henrietta	22, Sept 1898	26, Aug.	67	607		Bunker Hill, IL	Rußdorf, Sachsen-Weimar
Lippot, Christina Juliana	24, Oct. 1850	11, Sept	55- 3m	172		Madison, IN	Oberamt Besigheim, Württemberg
Lips, Anna Martha	28, Aug. 1882	17, July	81	279	Damm	Etna, MO	Niedervollmar bei Kassel, Kurhessen
Lips, Elisabeth	28, Nov. 1870	27, Oct.	38	383		East Prairie, MN	Boßhard aus Seebach, Zürich, Schweiz
Lips, Friedrich	14, Sept 1874	1, Aug.	72- 5m-18d	295		Etna, MO	Niederuf, Hessen
Lips, Karl	11, Nov. 1897			719		Nerstrand, MN	
Lips, Wilhelm	7, Sept 1899	19, Aug.	41	575		Cannon River, MN	Ost-Prairie, Minnesota
Lisch, Louise	3, Jan. 1881	15, Dec.	25-10m	7		Salem, MN	
Lischer, Christina	8, Dec. 1892	9, Nov.	86	782	Diedrisch	St. Paul, MN	Weingarten, Rheinkreis Baiern
Lischer, Dorothea	25, Mar. 1867	5, Mar.	70- 3m-14d	94	Dietrich	Mascoutah, IL	Weingarten, Rheinkreis Baiern
Lischer, Friedrich	6, Sept 1855	23, July	36	144		Red Bud, IL	Weingarten, Baiern
Lischer, Martin	5, Feb. 1872	26, Dec.	70- 4m- 2d	47		Nashville, IL	Weingarten, Germersheim, Rheinkreis Baiem
Lischer, Peter	12, May 1892	24, Apr.	67	302		Mascoutah, IL	Weingarten, Rheinkreis Baiern
Litke, David	16, July 1891	16, June	70	462		Alta Vista, KS	
Litsch, Karolina	7, Nov. 1881		67	359	Bogda	Chicago, IL	Wossow, Lauenberg, Pommern
Littau, Anna Louise Julie	28, June 1888	24, May	62	414		Montague, MI	Thorn, West Preußen
Littau, Heinrich	20, July 1885	5, July	61-10m- 9d	7		Montague, MI	Teschendorf, West Preußen
Litzel, Barbara	28, Mar. 1861	17, Feb.	67	52		Belleville, IL	
Lizrodt, Dorothea	31, Oct. 1881	12, Oct.	59-11m-12d	351	Klug	Davenport, IA	Schloßvippach, Sachsen-Weimar
Lizrodt, Johan Ludwig	1, Dec. 1892	26, Oct.	74	766		Davenport, IA	Schloß Vipbach, Sachsen-Weimar
Lizrodt, Maria Amalia	26, Dec. 1889		14- -21d	830		Des Moines, IA	Burlington, Iowa
Lizrodt, Wilhelm	21, July 1879	19, June	35	231		Davenport, IA	Schloß-Bippach, Sachsen-Weimar
Loarts, Georg	22, June 1893	19, May	55	398		Alton, IL	Remers, Ostfriesland
Löb, Johannes	12, Sept 1861	24, Aug.	58	148		Newport, KY	Gehaus, Sachsen-Weimar
Löbe , Hulda	6, Jan. 1898	21, Dec.	34	15	Kahnt	West Bend, WI	Trenton, Washington County, Wisconsin
Lobeck, Louise	29, Jan. 1866	30, Dec.	28-10m-24d	38		Portland, WI	Liebenow, Kreis Arnswalde, Preußen
Löbenstein, Christina	7, Jan. 1892	13, Nov.	57-11m	14		Schnectady, NY	Oberdurlach, Preußen
Lober, Barbara	21, Nov. 1864	24, Oct.	34- 7m-24d	188	Maurer	Perrysburg, OH	Ulrichsberg, Oehringen, Württemberg
Lober, Maria	28, July 1873		66- 2m	239	Reiser	Perrysburg, OH	Weckhof, Württemberg
Löber, Theodor A.	29, Apr. 1897	11, Apr.	31	271		Chicago, IL	Chicago, Cook County, Illinois
Löber, Wilhelmine Henriette	30, Sept 1897	2, Sept	77	623	Wüsteman	Ft. Dodge, IA	Schloß Biebach, Sachsen-Weimar
Löbermann, Maria Anna	7, Oct. 1886	12, Sept	57- 9m- 2d	7		Rossville, OH	
Löbermann, Wilhelm	8, Apr. 1886	6, Mar.	29- -27d	7		Darke Co, OH	Bingen, Baden
Loch, Charlotte	6, Dec. 1875	8, Nov.	46- 2m-15d	391	Hils	Brooklyn, NY	Ließbach, Hessen-Darmstadt
Loch, Elisabeth	18, Nov. 1872	1, Nov.	69	375	Wild	Boonville, IN	Idar, Birkenfeld, Oldenburg
Loch, Katharine	17, Aug. 1899	16, July	90- 6m- 7d	527	Becker	Concordia, MO	St. Wendel, RheinPreußen
Loch, Philipp	19, Feb. 1877	1, Feb.	75- -21d	63		Boonville, IN	Idar, Birkenfeld, Oldenburg
Locher, Karl D.	2, Oct. 1890	17, Sept	60	638		Portsmouth, OH	Heßlach bei Stuttgart, Württemberg
Lochmann, Christine	23, Sept 1897	6, Sept	59	607	Rätz	Oshkosh, WI	Gondelsheim, Baden
Lochmann, Jacob	28, Aug. 1890	1, July	81	558		Oshkosh, WI	Mettenheim, RheinPreußen
Locke, Johan	11, Jan. 1839			8			
Löckle, Friedrich	17, Dec. 1896	14, Nov.	59	814		Junction City, KS	Winnenden, Oberweiblinglen, Württemberg
Lockwood, Caroline	5, Sept 1881	20, Aug.	23- 7m	287	Thoele	St. Paul, MN	
Loddenkemper, Anna	30, Mar. 1899	7, Mar.	45	207	Nuhfer	Piqua, OH	Tübingen, Württemberg
Loeb, Herman	2, Apr. 1896	20- 7m-11d		222		Muscatine, IA	Muscatine, Iowa
Loeb, Katharina	14, Aug. 1882	17, July	77	263	Leopold	Newport, KY	Gehaus, Sachsen-Weimar

Christliche Apologete Death Notices --- 1839 - 1899

Name of Deceased	Notice Date	Death Date	Age	Maiden Name	Page	Place of Death	Place of Birth
Loebe, Johanna Justine	27, Aug. 1877	4, Aug.	38- 6m-27d	Zschregner	279	Fillmore, WI	Jonaswalde, Sachsen-Altenburg
Loebe, Michael	16, July1883	27, June	52- 5m-16d		231	West Bend, WI	Altkirchen, Sachsen-Altenburg
Loeber, Friedrich Christian	1, Sept 1887	16, Aug.	68		558	Ft. Dodge, IA	Schloß Viebach, Sachsen-Weimar
Loeh, Etje Johanna	21, Sept 1893	24, July	46	Spinker	606	San Jose, IL	Marienhof, Ostfriesland
Loehpolth, Peter Ludwig	8, Dec. 1884	26, Oct.	73		7	Bucyrus, OH	Plieningen, Württemberg
Loehr, Johan Jacob	30, July 1891	8, June	69-11m- 5d		494	Newport, KY	Möttau, Weilenburg, Nassau
Loenhardt, Maria	10, June 1886	21, May	64	Roth	7	Marietta, OH	Mannheim, Baden
Loese, Wilhelmine	25, Aug. 1887	7, Aug.	23-10m- 3d		542	Minneapolis, MN	
Loetz, Emma F. M. B.	2, June 1898	2, May	25	Piehl	351	Kenosha, WI	Gremersdorf, Pommern
Loew, Carrie Sophia	19, Dec. 1881	24, Nov.	26- 9m-29d	Kluckhohn	407	Lemars, IA	Cedar Lake , Iowa
Loew, Margaretha	27, Dec. 1880	11, Dec.	24	Portmann	415	Clarington, OH	Ohio County, West Virginia
Loew, Margaretha	6, Mar. 1882	8, Feb.	27- 9m		79	Allegan, MI	
Loew, Regina Dorothea	25, Apr. 1861	8, Apr.	37		68	Captina, OH	Brucken, Kirchheim, Württemberg
Loew, Ruben	21, Nov. 1881	28, Oct.	26-10m-11d		375	Lemars, IA	Clarington, Monroe County, Ohio
Loewe, Christian Friedrich	14, Oct. 1872	26, Sept	23		335	Nashville, IL	Nille, Kreis Minden, Preußen
Löffers, Anna Gertrud	22, May 1882	3, May	71	Harbecken	167	Colesburg, IA	Hanenberge, Fürstenau, Hannover
Löffers, Emma	17, Aug. 1874	22, July	2- 7m		263	Colesburg, IA	
Löffers, Johan Gerhard	6, Aug. 1896	17, July	76		511	Colesburg, IA	Lulle, Fürstenau, Hannover
Löffers, Maria	17, Aug. 1874	28, July	13- 9m		263	Colesburg, IA	
Löffers, Willie	17, Aug. 1874	26, July	5- 8m		263	Colesburg, IA	
Löffler, Catharina	16, Sept 1852	6, Aug.	51		152	Waverly, OH	
Löffler, Elisabeth	18, Mar. 1897	29, Jan.	65	Gonser	175	Cameron, MO	Duslingen, Tübingen, Württemberg
Lofrens, (Mr)	25, June 1857	12, May	47		104	Florence, MO	Femen Island, Dänemark
Logemann, Casten Albert	30, May 1870	29, Apr.	83- 6m-22d		175	Lawrenceburg, IN	
Logemann, Johanna	22, Dec. 1873	1, Dec.	33		407	Roberts, IL	Amt Trittoff, Holstein
Löher, Johan Heinrich	15, July 1858	21, June	10- 6m-10d		112	Danville, IL	
Lohm, Herman	23, Apr. 1896	21, Mar.	41		270	Fond du Lac, WI	Denso, Templin, Potsdam, Preußen
Lohmann, Caroline	16, Feb. 1893	10, Jan.	92		110	Champaign, IL	Hannover
Lohmann, Franz	11, June 1896	23, Jan.	54		383	Geneseo, IL	Breidenbon bei Maßdorf, Sachsen
Lohmann, Friedrich	27, Mar. 1876	29, Feb.	51		103	Schnectady, NY	Griesen, Hannover
Lohmann, Louis	8, Jan. 1883	13, Dec.	55-10m-22d		15	Milwaukee, WI	
Lohmann, Sophie	20, Sept 1880	5, Sept	55		303	Milwaukee, WI	Gießen an der Lahn, Hessen-Darmstadt
Lohmans, Rosina	1, Jan. 1847	4, Sept	1-11m-21d		3	Beardstown, IL	
Lohmeier, Maria	7, Dec. 1885	29, Sept	28- 5m-16d		7	Peoria, IL	
Lohmolder, John W.	29, Nov. 1894	10, Nov.	53- 3m- 8d		774	Allegan, MI	Altendorf
Lohmolder, Karoline	17, Jan. 1895	28, Dec.	36	Dendel	46	Allegan, MI	Roseville, Michigan
Löhr, Conrad	30, Sept 1858	8, Sept	48		156	Woodville, OH	Seeheim, Hessen-Darmstadt
Löhr, Elisabeth	19, Apr. 1888	26, Mar.	64	Willig	254	Newport, KY	Gräfeneck, Weilburg, Nassau
Löhr, Leopold	2, Jan. 1871		17- 5m- 6d		7	St. Louis, MO	Lippe-Detmold
Löhr, Peter	21, Nov. 1881	6, Nov.	31		375	Danville, IL	
Löhr, Philipp	10, Nov. 1879	29, Oct.	70		359	Chicago, IL	Altenkirchen, Nassau
Löhr, Phillip	6, Oct. 1887		65- 7m - 7d		638	New York City, NY	Westerburg, Nassau
Löhr, Susanna	22, Dec. 1873	Dec.	53- 1m- 1d		407	Danville, IL	Mammelzen, Rheinkreis Baiern
Löhr, Wilhelm	11, Dec. 1890	25, Nov.	28- 9m-13d		798	Newport, KY	Friedrichsruh, Württemberg
Lohrberg, Carolina Anna	17, Feb. 1873	15, Jan.	21- 1m-27d	Renzenhausen	53	Allegan, MI	Youngstown, Mahoning County, Ohio
Lohrberg, Magdalena	6, Oct. 1884	19, Sept	52- 4m-20d		7	Allegan, MI	

Christliche Apologete Death Notices --- 1839 - 1899

Name of Deceased	Notice Date	Death Date	Age	Page	Maiden Name	Place of Death	Place of Birth
Löhrding, Elva	14, Jan. 1886	22, Dec.	5	7		Peace Creek, KS	
Lohrey, Margaretha	29, Oct. 1857	8, Oct.		176		New York City, NY	
Lohmann, John	1, Mar. 1894	6, Feb.	87	150		Kendallville, IN	Bastedow, Mecklenburg-Schwerin
Lohmann, Margaretha	27, Sept 1869	19, Aug.	63	311		Cambridge, IN	Engler bei Osnabrück, Hannover
Lohse, Carrie	31, Aug. 1893	1, Aug.	35- 9m-11d	558	Strüben	Boonville, MO	
Lokenvitz, Christopher	4, Aug. 1887	23, July	88	494		Grand Ridge, IL	Rappin, Insel Rügen, Pommern
Lokenvitz, Margaretha Eleonore	2, Dec. 1897	18, Nov.	90- 3m-21d	767		Charles City, IA	
Lölf, August	26, May 1873	29, Mar.		167		Warren, MO	Stamen, Lippe-Detmold
Lolker, Heinrich	31, Mar. 1873	1, Mar.	24	103		St. Louis, MO	Horden, Ostfriesland
Lommler, Katharina	24, Apr. 1890	31, Mar.	81- -11d	270		Pittsburg, PA	Nassau
Longan, Elisabeth	3, Sept 1891	22- 3m-29d		574	Burges	Jamestown, MO	
Longe, Maria	9, Nov. 1874	18, Oct.	35	359	Bleßmann	York, NE	Ziegenhagen, Hessen-Kassel
Look, Bonne M.	21, Apr. 1898	1, Apr.	34	255		Peoria, IL	Limestone Twp, Peoria County, Illinois
Look, Bonne Moritz	4, Aug. 1873	11, May	80- 4m-12d	247		Peoria, IL	Ostdörp, Ostfriesland
Look, Ibe	8, May 1876	6, Apr.	51- -26d	151		Pekin, IL	Menstede, Ostfriesland
Look, Katharina	10, Jan. 1856	15, Dec.	30-10m	8		Pekin, IL	Ostfriesland
Look, Lammert Bonne	5, Oct. 1899	5, Sept	66	639		Peoria, IL	Ostfriesland
Look, Lena	25, Apr. 1889	27, Mar.	57	270	Steen	Pekin, IL	Grimersum, Ostfriesland
Look, Tebbe Bonnen	27, Dec. 1860	12, Dec.	41	208		Pekin, IL	Arle, Ost Friesland, Hannover
Loomis, Mathilde Louise Jokisch	9, July1883	28, Apr.	29- 1m	223		Arenzville, IL	
Loos, Friedrich	12, Jan. 1899	23, Dec.	62	31		Detroit, MI	Kalma, Gumbinnen, OstPreußen
Loos, Ludwig	28, Dec. 1893		56	828		Pittsburg, PA	Calbach, Hessen-Darmstadt
Loose, Emilie	30, Apr. 1877	11, Apr.	19	143		Milwaukee, WI	
Loose, Heinrich Wilhelm	29, Sept 1879	8, Sept	52	311		Milwaukee, WI	Schwerin, Mecklenburg-Schwerin
Loose, Henriette	3, Oct. 1881	22, Aug.	44- 5m-24d	319	Henning	Columbus, OH	Oberdorla, Mühlhausen, Erfurt, Preußen
Loose, Julia	2, Dec. 1878		16	383		Galena, IL	
Loose, Karl	4, Aug. 1879	17, July	54-11m	247		Galena, IL	Friedrichsruhe, Mecklenburg-Schwerin
Loose, Magdalena	25, Sept 1856	26, Aug.	63- 8m	156		Milwaukee, WI	Mecklenburg-Schwerin
Loose, Wilhelm	6, Sept 1849		Inquiry	144		Westport, MO	
Lopp, Johan	29, Sept 1887	17, Aug.	30-11m-15d	622		Beaufort, MO	St. Louis, Missouri
Lorberg, August	16, Mar. 1899	14, Feb.	74	175		Portsmouth, OH	Imshausen bei Nordheim, Hannover
Lörcher, Margarine	31, Aug. 1866	4, Nov.	30	422	Groß	Roxbury, MA	Adelsdorf, Baiern
Loren, Katharine	3, Aug. 1893	13, July	55	494		Edon, OH	Gomberth, Kurhessen
Lorentz, Magdalena	27, Dec. 1880	10, Dec.	65-11m-17d	415	Nippert	Clarington, OH	Görsdorf, Wörth, Elsaß
Lorentz, Michael	26, Sept 1889	28, Aug.	80	619		Clarington, OH	Görßdorf, Wörth, Elsaß
Lorenz, Elisabeth	19, Apr. 1880	4, Apr.	33- -29d	127	Rindfuß	Allegheny City, PA	
Lorenz, Emma	22, Dec. 1873	1, Dec.	14- -14d	407		Geneseo, IL	
Lorenz, Friedrich	13, Apr. 1899	20, Mar.	16	239		Mason, TX	Simonsville, Texas
Lorenz, Johan Fürchtegott	10, Oct. 1895	17, Sept	62	654		Detroit, MI	Zeunitz, Sachsen
Lorenz, Sophia	17, Mar. 1884	25, Feb.	68	7	Hagen	Blooming Grove, MN	Mecklenburg-Schwerin
Lorenzen, Julius	19, Feb. 1891	21, Jan.	30	126		New York City, NY	Flensburg, Schleswig
Lorey, Anna	16, June 1859	17, Apr.	38	96		Spring Lake, OH	Columbian County, Ohio
Lorey, Heinrich	10, Nov. 1892	26, Oct.	78	718		Edon, OH	Burgbracht, Hessen-Darmstadt
Loris, Catharina	21, Sept 1868	21, July	28- 1m	303	Kirckhof	Alton, IL	
Lorsch, Jakob H.	7, Dec. 1893	17, Nov.		782		Alton, IL	Attenhausen, Germany
Lörtscher, David	30, May 1864	13, May	49- 4m-17d	88		Wabasha, MN	Oberwyl, Bern, Schweiz

- 310 -

Christliche Apologete Death Notices --- 1839 - 1899

Name of Deceased	Notice Date	Death Date	Age	Page	Maiden Name	Place of Death	Place of Birth
Lösch, Adam	26, Nov. 1877	25, Sept	38	383		Defiance, OH	
Losch, Anna Maria	23, Apr. 1891	31, Mar.	50- 5m	270	Schmidt	Brooklyn, NY	Isingen, Sulz, Württemberg
Lösch, C.H.	21, Jan. 1884	20, Nov.	51	7		Mountain Lake, MN	Baden-Baden, Baden
Lösch, Emma Louise	7, Aug. 1882	17, July	21	255		Brooklyn, NY	Williamsburg, New York
Lösch, Johan	3, July 1882	17, June	82- 1m-13d	215			Hemsbach, Weinheim, Baden
Lösch, Katharina	28, Jan. 1878	14, Dec.	81- 4m- 9d	31	Nichwitz	Lancaster, NY	Hemsbach, Weinheim, Baden
Lösch, Margaretha	12, May 1892	13, Apr.	83	302	Hofrichter	Defiance, OH	Daisbach, Sinsheim, Baden
Löscher, Christiane Rosine	6, Apr. 1899	11, Mar.	62	223	Schmidt	Hartford, CT	Brücklar, Reuß, Sachsen
Löscher, Friedrich August	8, June 1893	10, May	56	366		Hartford, CT	Hohenleuben, Gera, Reuß
Loscher, Margaretha	30, Nov. 1885	29, Oct.	69	7		Allegheny City, PA	
Lose, Maria	12, Sept 1861	9, Aug.	25	148	Klappmeyer	Wyandotte, KS	
Losen, Samuel	11, May 1854	18, Apr.	29	70		Mobile, AL	
Löser, Johan Karl	30, June 1884	3, June	56	7		Woodville, WI	Buntarn, Marienwerder, Preußen
Lossner, Carl August	26, Aug. 1886	2, Aug.	87	7		Madison, WI	Oschatz, Sachsen
Lotes, Anna Katharine	18, June 1896	28, May	73	399		Hokah, MN	Baiern
Loth, Johan Friedrich	24, May 1888	12, May	72	334		De Soto, MO	Siedenbollentin, Pommern
Lother, Charlotte Karolina Wil.	12, Sept 1881	24, Aug.	45- 6m-12d	295	Fischer	Watertown, WI	Beerwalde, Preußen
Lother, Dorothea Sophie	15, Mar. 1880	12, Feb.	74- 5m-12d	86		De Soto, MN	Billerbeck bei Arenswalde, Pommern
Lothes, Ulrich	27, Oct. 1887	14, Oct.	56-10m-29d	686		Pittsburg, PA	Born, Baiern
Lott, Heinrich	12, Mar. 1891	16, Feb.	62	174		Edon, OH	Vonhausen, Büdingen, Germany
Lott, Johannes	3, Dec. 1891	15, Nov.	69	782		Holt, MI	Vonhausen, Biedingen, Hessen-Darmstadt
Lott, Karolina	14, Aug. 1882	20, July	20- 3m-20d	263		Lansing, MI	
Lott, Louise	8, Feb. 1869	13, Jan.	49	47		Lansing, MI	Vonhausen, Hessen-Darmstadt
Lott, Margaretha	28, June 1875	26, May	76	207	Papst	Delhi, MI	Vonhausen, Büdingen, Hessen-Darmstadt
Lottes, John	10, Feb. 1898	23, Jan.	78	95		Hokah, MN	Baiern
Lottes, John B.	23, Mar. 1893		25- 5m-16d	190		Hokah, MN	Houston County, Minnesota
Lottmann, Wilhelm B.	12, May 1892		70	302		Stockton, CA	Emden, Ostfriesland
Lotz, Dorothea	18, June 1847	11, May		99		Beardstown, IL	Plebsheim, NiederRhein, Frankreich
Lotz, Elisabeth	17, July 1890	27, June	39- 6m- 4d	462		Boody, IL	Groß-Eichen, Hessen-Darmstadt
Lotz, Henriette	17, Oct. 1889	27, Aug.	74- 7m-12d	670	Meier	Angelica, NY	Rübbesbüttel, Giffhorn, Hannover
Lotz, John	11, May 1874	21, Apr.	53	151		Rochester, NY	Freiending, Nassau
Lotz, Maria Katharina	3, Nov. 1879	8, Oct.	29	351	Noblet	Oregon, MO	China, St. Clair County, Michigan
Louis, Clara Emma	28, Dec. 1885	16, Dec.	12- 9m- 3d	7		Wheeling, WV	
Louis, Daniel	25, Jan. 1855	10, Jan.	37-11m	16		Wheeling, VA	Langenbach, Rheinkreis Baiern
Louis, Theodore B.	25, Nov. 1886	5, Sept	49	7		Baltimore, MD	Lengerich, Hannover
Lovekin, Anna Christina	21, June 1849	1, May	60	100		Madison, IN	Solingen, Düsseldorf, Preußen
Löw, Barbara	14, Apr. 1879	29, Mar.	38- 2m-19d	119	Otto	Clarington, OH	Reichensachsen, Eschwege, Kurhessen
Löw, Christian	15, Nov. 1888	16, Oct.	94- 5m- 3d	734		Clarington, OH	Brucken, Kirchheim, Württemberg
Löw, Dorothea	4, May 1874	12, Apr.	79- 3m- 3d	143	Beisser	Clarington, OH	Brucken, Kirchheim a. d. Teck, Württemberg
Löw, Johannes	26, May 1887	28, Apr.	76- 5m-17d	334		Quincy, IL	
Löw, Margaretha	9, Nov. 1868	Oct.	18	359		Clarington, OH	
Löwe, Chr.	7, Oct. 1858	20, Aug.	34	160	Horstmann	Herman, MO	Süthnormann bei Minden, Preußen
Löwe, Christian	8, Feb. 1894		71- 6m-10d	94		Senate Grove, MO	Südhemmen, Westphalen
Lowe, Elisabeth	22, Apr. 1872	3, Apr.	40	135	Anthes	Boonville, IN	Heimbach, Trier, Preußen
Löwer, Julia Dorothea	3, May 1894	15, Apr.	75	294		Chicago, IL	Altona bei Hamburg, Germany
Löwer, Martha Elisabeth	24, Aug. 1854	12, July	32	136		Detroit, MI	Lutzelwitz, Kurhessen

Christliche Apologete Death Notices --- 1839 - 1899

Name of Deceased	Notice Date	Death Date	Age	Maiden Name	Page	Place of Death	Place of Birth
Lowmiller, Daniel Henry	23, Apr. 1896		58		270	Bucyrus, OH	Union County, Pennsylvania
Lowrenz, Otto	18, Feb. 1886	24, Jan.	68		7	Burlington, IA	Stolpe, Köslin, Pommern
Loxold, Peter Ludwig	17, Nov. 1884	26, Oct.	73		7	Bucyrus, OH	Plieningen, Württemberg
Lübbing, Greetje	30, Nov. 1885	22, Oct.	75		7	Bible Grove, IL	Oldersum, Emden, Ostfriesland
Lübeke, Sophia	24, Jan. 1889	18, Dec.	75		62	Corning, ---	Kreuz, Naugard, Pommern
Lubenow, Fr. Ferdinand	1, Jan. 1866	27, Nov.	32		6	Wheatland, WI	Schrievelbein, Preußen
Lübke, Aug. Friedrich Wilhelm	18, Nov. 1867	15, Oct.	22		366	Milwaukee, WI	Schwirsen bei Kamin, Hinterpommern
Lübke, Emilie	1, Aug. 1895	15, July	77	Burow	494	Milwaukee, WI	Zemlin, Pommern
Lübke, Johan	9, Jan. 1882	27, Nov.	76- 6m- 2d		15	Greenfield, WI	Schönhagen, Neugrad, Pommern
Lübke, Karl	14, Nov. 1870		22		367	Milwaukee, WI	Schwirsim bei Kamin, HinterPommern
Lübke, Maria	19, Aug. 1852	6, Aug.	21-11m-25d		136	Milwaukee, WI	
Lübkemann, John Friedrich	27, Mar. 1890	2, Mar.	74- 4m-10d		206	Pittsfield, IL	Minden, Preußen
Lübker, Christian	25, Jan. 1894	15, Dec.			62	Bunker Hill, IL	
Lucas, Georg	9, Nov. 1863	10, Sept	41		180	Chester, IL	Ellershausen, Amt Göttingen, Hannover
Lucas, John	26, Oct. 1874	18, Sept	21		343	Milwaukee, WI	Milwaukee, Wisconsin
Lüchau, Gesche	22, July 1897	4, July	63	Augustin	463	Ada, MN	Bu-ehude, Hannover
Lüchau, John Peter	24, Jan. 1895	4, Jan.	58		62	Ada, MN	Hagen bei Stade, Germany
Luchsinger, Katharine	5, Mar. 1896	16, Feb.	60	Schreiber	158	Lansing, IA	Unterwalden, Schweiz
Lucht, Julie	4, June 1891	6, May	28		366	Troy, NY	Troy , New York
Lück, Auguste	24, Jan. 1895	9, Dec.	80	Böcker	62	Mt. Vernon, MO	
Lück, Karl	12, May 1873	23, Apr.	57-11m-7d		151	Petersburg, IL	Friedricksdorf, Hofgeismar, Kurhessen
Luck, Karl Friedrich	4, July 1881	13, June	42		215	Danville, IL	Kletzke, Brandenburg
Luckau, Friedrich	2, Apr. 1891	22, Feb.	49		222	Ada, MN	Hagen bei Stade, Hannover
Lücke, Theodor L.	31, Aug. 1899	14, Aug.	25		559	Lemars, IA	Waukon, Allamakee County, Iowa
Lückemann, Philipp	30, June 1898	21, May	75		415	Pinckney, MO	Steinhagen, Herford, Westphalen
Lückemeier, Christoph	1, Sept 1873	27, July	70		279	Morrison, MO	Rehme, Minden, Preußen
Lückemeyer, Friederike	20, Sept 1860	31, July			152	Marthasville, MO	Rehme , Preußen
Lucken, Wübke	7, Apr. 1879	17, Mar.	21		111	Petersburg, IL	
Lücker, Karl Ludwig	18, Feb. 1878		67- 7m-21d		55	Hoyleton, IL	Isenstädt, Minden, Preußen
Luckerman, Christian Friedrich	8, Dec. 1892	6, Nov.	24		782		Giard, Clayton County, Iowa
Luckerman, Christian Friedrich	30, Mar. 1893	9, Mar.	71		206		Rohden, Minden, Germany
Luckermann, John	20, Apr. 1874	3, Apr.	26		127	Los Angeles, CA	Pittsburg, Pennsylvania
Luckermann, Louise Charlotte	30, Mar. 1874		15		103	Giard, IA	Iowa
Lücking, Benjamin Franklin	20, June 1895	31, May	28- 3m-19d		398	Giard, IA	
Lücking, Emma	12, May 1898	26, Apr.	19		303	Fosterburg, IL	
Luckmann, Louise	10, Apr. 1871	2, Feb.	65- -16d		119	Fosterburg, IL	
Lucko, Ferdinand F. Johannes	9, Nov. 1885	21, Oct.	39		7	Rockford, MN	Dassow, Mecklenburg-Schwerin
Luckow, Charlotte Sophie	16, June 1873	28, May	34		191	Industry, TX	Oldenburg
Lucksinger, Christina	27, Mar. 1890	19, Feb.	59- -23d		206	Watertown, WI	Zachan, Kreis Sadzig, Pommern
Ludau, Johan	24, Nov. 1873	4, Nov.	46		375	Beaufort, MO	Schwieberdingen, Ludwigsburg, Württemberg
Lüdde, Friedrich	8, Jan. 1877	21, Nov.	20		15	Liberty, MO	Zimmern, Adelsheim, Baden
Lüdde, Heinrich	30, Oct. 1876	13, Oct.	34		351	Angelica, NY	Gamsen, Amt Giffhorn, Hannover
Lüdde, Peter	26, Feb. 1883	13, Jan.	64- 5m		71	Angelica, NY	Gamsen, Amt Giffhorn, Hannover
Lüdde, Peter	5, Feb. 1883	13, Jan.	64- 5m		47	Warsaw, IL	Dain, Roda, Frankenberg, Kurhessen
Lüdecke, Friedrich	9, Feb. 1899	23, Jan.	75		95	Warsaw, IL	Roda, Frankenberg, Kurhessen
Lüdeke, Hedwig	30, Dec. 1897	7, Dec.	60	Zinn	828	Klemme, IA	Großfurra, Schwarzburg-Sondershausen
						Klemme, IA	Philippsthal, Kurhessen

- 312 -

Christliche Apologete Death Notices --- 1839 - 1899

Name of Deceased	Place of Birth	Place of Death	Maiden Name	Page	Age	Death Date	Notice Date
Lüdeke, Karl	Großfurra, Schwarzburg-Sondershausen	Freeport, IL		180	27- 3m- 7d	25, Sept	7, Nov. 1864
Lüdersen, Johanna Friederike	Amthaben, Bielefeld, Preußen	Truxton, MO	Holtkamp	687	75	2, Oct.	26, Oct. 1899
Lüdge, Ernst	Lagesbüttel, Amt Gifhorn, Hannover	Chicago, IL		168	19	14, July	17, Oct. 1864
Lüdgerding, Anna Sophia	Stedersdorf, Amt Meinersen, Hannover	Red Wing, MN	Sandelmann	407	52- 3m- 4d	24, Nov.	18, Dec. 1871
Lüdke, Carl	Marin, Mecklenburg-Schwerin	Milwaukee, WI		30	78	21, Nov.	8, Jan. 1891
Lüdke, Dorothea	Kankelfitz, Regenwalde, Preußen	Oconomowoc, WI		238	80- 3m-16d	20, Mar.	11, Apr. 1895
Lüdke, Dorothea Maria	Groß Wachlin, Germany	Great Bend, KS	Schröder	279	62	9, Aug.	29, Aug. 1881
Lüdke, Friedrich Wilhelm	Schinschkoff, West Preußen	West Point, NE		828	65	20, Nov.	29, Dec. 1898
Lüdke, Friedrich Wilhelm	Weitenhagen, Germany	Great Bend, KS		415	61	9, Dec.	26, Dec. 1881
Lüdke, Marie	Zimdasse, Treptow an der Rega, Hinterpommern	Day Co, SD	Berg	750	75- 5m	14, Oct.	21, Nov. 1889
Lüdke, Martin	Schwetz, West Preußen	West Point, NE		335	74	25, Sept	15, Oct. 1883
Lüdke, Theodor	Posen	West Point, NE		383	27- 7m-13d	8, Nov.	27, Nov. 1882
Ludolff, Ch. J.	Roseland, Illinois	Blue Island, IL		46	21- 9m-10d	20, Jan. 1887	
Ludolph, Clara	Winona, Minnesota	Minneapolis, MN	Schröder	30	27	19, Dec.	12, Jan. 1888
Lüdtke, Caroline Albertine		Beaver Dam, WI		103	18- 9m	21, Feb.	26, Mar. 1877
Lüdtke, Maria Elisabeth		Beaver Dam, WI		71	16- 5m-16d	28, Jan.	26, Feb. 1877
Ludwig, Andreas	Zuzenhausen, Sinsheim, Baden	Bushnell, IL		31	42- 4m-13d	7, Jan.	27, Jan. 1868
Ludwig, Anna Eva		Peoria, IL	Ludwig	111	39- -22d	24, Mar.	6, Apr. 1874
Ludwig, Catharina	Monchzell bei Heidelberg, Preußen	Bushnell, IL	Fiederer	295	46	21, Aug.	13, Sept 1875
Ludwig, Celia	Madison, Indiana	Belleville, IL	Winkler	398	24	23, May	23, June 1892
Ludwig, Georg	Zuzenhausen bei Heidelberg, Baden	Bushnell, IL		87	76-10m	16, Feb.	13, Mar. 1882
Ludwig, Georg Friedrich	Zuzenhausen, Sinsheim, Baden	Bushnell, IL		319	58	22, Sept	7, Oct. 1878
Ludwig, Georg M.	Zuzenhausen, Sinsheim, Baden	Arlington, NE		7	72	20, Oct.	4, Nov. 1886
Ludwig, Gustav	Zuzenhausen, Baden	Bushnell, IL		124	17- 5m-18d	11, July	31, July 1865
Ludwig, Helena	Wolferode, Rauschenburg, Kirchheim, Kurhessen	Secor, IL		335	71	5, Oct.	21, Oct. 1878
Ludwig, Johan Heinrich	Thraisa, Kurhessen	Chicago, IL		622	54	2, Sept	28, Sept 1893
Ludwig, Johanna	Konradswaldau, Schlesien	Akron, OH		494	72	15, July	4, Aug. 1892
Ludwig, Johanna Caroline	Adersbach, Amt Sinsheim, Baden	Bushnell, IL		287	49- 3m-26d	15, Aug.	6, Sept 1869
Ludwig, John L.	Bridgeton, New Jersey	Philadelphia, PA		558	27- 6m- 3d	15, July	27, Aug. 1891
Ludwig, Karoline	Grünwetterspach, Baden	Buffalo, NY	Schmidt	367	84- 6m-24d	27, Apr.	12, Nov. 1883
Ludwig, Katharina	Mölsheim, Hochfelden, Elsaß	Farina, IL	Heyer	14	80- - 8d	19, Dec.	7, Jan. 1892
Ludwig, Katharina	Hochfrankenheim, Elsaß	Bible Grove, IL	Lenz	95	46- 5m-21d	3, Mar.	19, Mar. 1883
Ludwig, Katharina Elisabeth	Secor, Illinois	Peoria, IL		366	17	20, Apr.	4, June 1891
Ludwig, Katharine	Lichtenstein, Baiern	Cincinnati, OH	Oesper	846	79	11, Dec.	31, Dec. 1891
Ludwig, Louise	Linsburg, Amt Wölbe, Hannover	Santa Claus, IN	Hoffmeyer	80	36	19, Mar.	16, May 1861
Ludwig, Louise C.		Chicago, IL	Kunkel	231	28	22, June	16, July 1877
Ludwig, Lydia	Moweaqua, Illinois	Los Angeles, CA	Baab	239	33	13, Mar.	13, Apr. 1899
Ludwig, Maria Catharina	Obertiefenbach, Nastetten, Nassau	Huntingburg, IN		391	81- 4m-22d	23, Nov.	9, Dec. 1878
Ludwig, Maria Mathilda	Flatbranch Township, Shelby County, Illinois	Moweaqua, IL		198	21	23, Jan.	22, Mar. 1894
Ludwig, Mina Magdalena	Lawrenceburg, Indiana	Chicago, IL	Kunkel	295	24	17, Aug.	11, Sept 1871
Ludwig, Tillie	Chicago, Cook County, Illinois	Chicago, IL		550	26	1, Aug.	23, Aug. 1894
Ludwig, Wilhelmina	Rapkow, Neu-Vorpommern, Preußen	Laporte, IN	Rehsen	23	69	7, Jan.	21, Jan. 1878
Luebke, Pauline	Farmington, Wisconsin	Milwaukee, WI	Kuechenmeister	158	36	15, Feb.	7, Mar. 1889
Luecke, Georg F.P.	Centerville, Wisconsin	Storm Lake, IA	Kunkel	526	25	14, July	15, Aug. 1889
Luedke, Wilhelmine	Zinskowo, Preußen	Crandon, SD	Hiller	350	70	2, May	2, June 1887
Luelf, Lisette		Truxton, MO	Schuster	191	23	7, May	16, June 1879

Christliche Apologete Death Notices -- 1839 - 1899

Name of Deceased	Notice Date	Death Date	Age	Page	Maiden Name	Place of Death	Place of Birth
Luetye, H.	13, Mar. 1882	17, Feb.	40	87		Cape Girardeau, MO	Kleinheidorn, Hannover
Lühr, (Mrs)	15, May 1890	28, Apr.	67	318			Borum, Hannover
Lühr, Emma Karoline	12, July 1894	4, June	32	454	Koebbemann	Lansing, IA	Schalen, Preußen
Lühr, Johan Heinrich	23, Nov. 1885	1, Nov.	67- 7m-22d	7		Lansing, IA	Emmendorf, Baiern
Lühring, Carolina Maria	16, Aug. 1849		42	132		Laughery, IN	Hille, Münden, Preußen
Lühring, Christian	2, Sept 1872	5, Aug.	66	287		Henderson, MN	
Lührs, Wilhelmine	23, Jan. 1875	21, Dec.	38	31	VonHollnufer	Piqua, OH	Deinste, Hannover
Luikard, Jakob	17, July 1890	27, May	83	462		Hannibal, OH	Brücken, Kirchheim, Württemberg
Luikart, John	16, June 1862	7, May	21	96		Baresville, OH	
Luikart, Juliane	24, Dec. 1857	13, Nov.	15	208		Baresville, OH	
Luikart, Rosa	2, Mar. 1899	19, Jan.	52	143	Schaffer	Hannibal, OH	Monroe County, Ohio
Luikhart, Elisabeth	3, Dec. 1883	12, Nov.	75	391		Baresville, OH	Bietzwiel, Solothurn, Schweiz
Luithly, Louis	20, Apr. 1874	7, Apr.	58	127		German Creek, IA	Ulm, Württemberg
Lukemeier, Katharina	3, Aug. 1893	19, July	65	494	Krohme	Huntingburg, IN	Schledehausen, Osnabrück, Hannover
Lüker, Maria Charl.	16, Nov. 1868	29, Oct.	50	367		Nashville, ---	Tenthein, Preußen
Lülf, Sophia	26, Apr. 1875	10, Mar.	37	135		Warren, MO	Lüdenhausen, Hohenhausen, Lippe-Detmold
Lumpe, Eckhardt	23, May 1861	13, Apr.	11- 6m	84		Muscatine, IA	
Lumpe, Heinrich	9, Apr. 1883	15, Mar.	65	119		Muscatine, IA	Nedernürsa, Fritzlar, Kurhessen
Lumpe, Martha Elisabeth	11, Sept 1890	22, Aug.	70-10m-24d	590	Bräutigam	Muscatine, IA	Geismar, Fritzlar, Hessen
Lundy, Maria	9, Nov. 1893	10, Sept	32	718	Schmitt	Osceola, NE	
Lünebring, Wilhelm	31, July 1846		Inquiry	123		Woodville, OH	
Lünebrink, (Mrs)	13, June 1850	8, May	40	96		Woodville, OH	
Lünemann, Georg Wilhelm	28, June 1849	18, June	30	104		Louisville, KY	Hagenburg, Bückeburg, Lippe-Schaumburg
Lünemann, Wilhelmine Louise	18, Oct. 1875	27, Sept	62- 6m-24d	335		St. Paul, MN	Lienen, Tecklenburg, Preußen
Lünemeyer, Louise	11, Jan. 1849	22, Dec.	29	8		St. Louis, MO	Melle, Hannover
Lung, Catharina	28, Sept 1893	7, Sept	61	622		Toledo, OH	Forchtenberg, Oehringen, Württemberg
Lüning, Anna Dorothea	1, Mar. 1875	19, Dec.	74	71	Scheffler	Rochester, MN	Gembitz-Hauland, Czarnilau, Posen, Preußen
Lüneburg, Anna Maria	21, Mar. 1895	2, Mar.	85- 3m-20d	190		Milwaukee, WI	Krusenhagen, Mecklenburg-Schwerin
Lunte, Anna Marie Luise	23, Mar. 1899	31, Jan.	74	191	Busch	Seymour, IN	Hüllhorst, Lübbecke, Preußen
Lüppen, Katharina	25, Dec. 1882	4, Dec.	67- 4m-16d	415	Smith	Pekin, IL	Hammschweren, Ostfriesland
Lurker, Christina	3, Feb. 1887	16, Jan.	44	78	Wimpelberg	Marrs, IN	Mühlheim a. d. Ruhr, Düsseldorf, RheinPreußen
Lurker, Lorenz	15, June 1899	25, May	85	383		Marrs, IN	Griesheim, Offenburg, Baden
Lürs, Johan Dietrich	5, June 1890	5, May	57- 4m-10d	366		Hebron, IA	Weihe, Syke, Hannover
Lürs, Mary	31, Jan. 1876	8, Jan.	16	39		Hebron, IA	Hebron, Adair County, Iowa
Lust, Johan	29, Mar. 1888	3, Mar.	25- 5m- 7d	206		Champaign, IL	
Lüte, Jakob	27, Aug. 1866	23, July	64	278		Allegheny City, PA	Rüdelswille, Bern, Schweiz
Luth, Augusta	11, Nov. 1897	29, Sept	87	719	Kastner	Burlington, IA	Dormesheim, Baden
Luth, Georg Bernhard	17, Jan. 1889	6, Dec.	34- 3m	46		Hicksville, NY	
Luth, Heinrich L.	29, Jan. 1877	10, Jan.	71	39		Burlington, IA	Spiesen, Ottweiler, Preußen
Luth, Katharina Margaretha	7, July 1887	24, May	60	430	Wesendorf	Brooklyn, NY	Quakenbrück, Hannover
Lüthe, Barbara	9, May 1870	24, Apr.	58- 4m-16d	151	Tätwiller	Allegheny City, PA	Hölstein, Basel, Schweiz
Lütje, Justine	9, Nov. 1893	17, Oct.	84	718	Schwiering	Appleton, WI	Winzlar, Rehburg, Hannover
Lütjens, Gesche	17, July 1890	30, June	77	462	Kruse	Smithton, MO	Neuenböhlstet, Hannover
Lütjens, Johannes H.	19, Mar. 1877	20, Feb.	71	95		Smithton, MO	Hostet, Ottersberg, Hannover
Lütjens, Meta	15, Dec. 1862	14, Nov.	25	200	Wahlers	Florence, MO	
Lütke, Friedrich	20, Jan. 1879	17, Dec.	12	23		Wausau, WI	Lübsow, Greifenburg, Stettin, Preußen

Christliche Apologete Death Notices --- 1839 - 1899

Name of Deceased	Notice Date	Death Date	Age	Page	Maiden Name	Place of Death	Place of Birth
Lutterot, Christine	16, July1883	29, June	79-3m	231		Yellow Creek, IL	Betheln, Gronau, Hannover
Lüttge, Charles C.	16, Feb. 1893	14, Jan.	22	110		San Bernardino, CA	Arlington Heights, Illinois
Lutz, Anna	11, Mar. 1886	26, Feb.	67	7		New York City, NY	St. Gallen, Schweiz
Lutz, Auguste	1, Dec. 1873	14, Nov.	37	383	Duwald	Geneseo, IL	Wolfenbüttel, Hannover
Lutz, Barbara	13, Oct. 1898	26, Sept	69	655	Gompert	Chicago, IL	Mittlenzweiler, Freudenstadt, Württemberg
Lutz, Barbara	31, Jan. 1889	7, Jan.	61-11m- 3d	78	Schneider	Dayton, OH	Oberamtstadt, Hessen-Darmstadt
Lutz, Barbara	28, Sept 1899	13, Sept	74	623		Pittsfield, IL	Ohmbach, Hessen-Darmstadt
Lutz, Christian Johan	7, Feb. 1881	20, Jan.	65	47		Hartford, CT	Ludwigsburg, Württemberg
Lutz, Christina	19, July 1849	9, July	21	116		Cincinnati, OH	
Lutz, Emilie	27, Oct. 1892	27, Sept	18	686		New Haven, CT	
Lutz, Friedrike Wilhelmine Rosalie	4, Aug. 1879		59	247	Krauß	Hartford, CT	München, Baiern
Lutz, Heinrich	15, Aug. 1889	23, July	23- - 9d	526		Odebolt, IA	Kefenrode, Büdingen, Hessen-Darmstadt
Lutz, Heinrich W.	31, May 1894	10, May	16- 8m-11d	358		Ellis Grove, Il	
Lutz, Jacob	3, Dec. 1896	22, Oct.	63	782		New York City, NY	Württemberg
Lutz, Johan G.	14, Dec. 1885	30, Nov.	54	7		Madison, IN	Oeschingen, Rothenburg, Württemberg
Lutz, Johan Georg (Rev)	17, Aug. 1899	20, July	82	527		Elizabeth, NJ	Osterdingen, Rothenburg am Neckar, Germany
Lutz, Johannes	14, June 1875	25, May	87- -26d	191		Pittsfield, IL	Langfeld, Niederklingen, Hessen-Darmstadt
Lutz, Johannes	5, July 1875	25, May	89	215		Pittsfield, IL	Langfeld, Niederklingen, Hessen-Darmstadt
Lutz, John Charles	24, May 1888	30, Apr.	23	334		Scranton, PA	Pittston, Pennsylvania
Lutz, Karolina	25, Nov. 1897	6, Nov.	37	751	Witte	Boonville, IN	Warrick County, Indiana
Lutz, Leonhard	4, Jan. 1894	29, Nov.	87	14		Pittsfield, IL	Niederklingen, Hessen-Darmstadt
Lutz, Magdalene	21, Sept 1899	25, Aug.	83-9m	607	Fritsch	Scranton, PA	Hesselhurst, Kehl, Baden
Lutz, Margaretha	30, Jan. 1890	29, Dec.	67-11m-28d	78	Lipps	Brooklyn, NY	Weißenburg, Elsaß
Lutz, Maria	10, May 1894	12, Apr.	79	310	Wehlen	Francisco, MI	Ost Cocalico, Lancaster Co., Pennsylvania
Lutz, Maria Elisabeth	21, Oct. 1858	6, Sept	73- 6m	168	Petre	Scranton, PA	Umstadt, Germany
Lutz, Michael	19, Feb. 1891	31, Jan.	89- 6m	126		Dayton, OH	Eckartsweier, Kehl, Baden
Lutz, Pauline	14, May 1877	16, Apr.	23	159		Scranton, PA	Dayton, Montgomery County, Ohio
Lutz, Rosine Margarethe	4, July 1889	4, June	52	430	Sonn	Newark, NJ	Köngen, Eßlingen, Württemberg
Lutz, Rudolph	2, Apr. 1891	2, Feb.	22	222		San Jose, IL	
Lux, Elisabeth	11, Aug. 1898	11, July	69	511	Hautz	San Jose, IL	Williams Valley, Schuylkill Co., Pennsylvania
Lux, Friedrich	16, Sept 1886	26, Aug.	64	7		Spring Lake, IL	Hatten, Elsaß
Lux, Salome	15, Nov. 1860	10, Oct.	63- 3m	184		Lansing, IA	Hatten, Elsaß
Luxinger, Martin	10, Dec. 1896	3, Nov.	53	798			Matt, Glarus, Schweiz
Maag, (Mrs)	17, Apr. 1871	28, Mar.	66	127		Westfield, WI	Gelfershausen, Kreis Rodenburg, Kurhessen
Maag, J.F.	24, Oct. 1895	24, Sept	84	686		Le Sueur, MN	Neunkirch, Schaffhausen, Schweiz
Maag, Sophia	21, Feb. 1870	25, Jan.	27	63	Schlimme	Jackson, MO	Groß-Rhäden, Amt Bockenem, Hannover
Maahs, Auguste Karoline	25, June 1883	29, May	42	207		Montague, MI	Rosenow, Naugard, Stettin, Preußen
Maak, Johan Heinrich	15, Apr. 1878	8, Mar.	28-11m-20d	119		Victor, IA	Olze, Braunschweig
Maas, (Mrs)	14, Apr. 1859	29, Mar.	42	60	Wrede	Angelica, NY	Schöningen, Braunschweig
Maas, Albert	17, Oct. 1889	13, Sept	42	670		Hebron, IA	Nehmer bei Kolberg, Köslin, Pommern
Maas, Andreas	12, Mar. 1883	15, Feb.	78- 4m-20d	87		Burlington, WI	Odenbüttel, Hannover
Maas, B.D.	15, June 1893	6, May	63	382		Keokuk, IA	Holland
Maas, Bertha Charlotte Sophia	31, Jan. 1881	8, Jan.	59- 1m	39	Schultz	Sun Prairie, WI	Leppin, Köslin, Schieferbein, Pommern
Maas, Carl Fr. W.	19, June 1890	24, May	67- 4d	398		Sun Prairie, WI	Belzdrey, Schiefelbein, Preußen
Maas, Elisabeth	17, Aug. 1874	29, July	65	263		New Orleans, LA	Freden, Kreis Ahaus, Westphalen

Christliche Apologete Death Notices --- 1839 - 1899

Name of Deceased	Notice Date	Death Date	Age	Maiden Name	Page	Place of Death	Place of Birth
Maas, Friedrike M.	14, Dec. 1885	29, Nov.	47	Sanner	7	Louisville, KY	Bönnigheim, Bessigheim, Württemberg
Maas, Heinrich	8, Mar. 1880	14, Feb.	74		79	Albert Lea, MN	Fitzdorf, Insel Fehmarn, Holstein
Maas, Heinrich	24, Oct. 1870	5, Oct.	61		343	New Orleans, LA	Lembeck, Preußen
Maas, Juliana	21, Nov. 1895	14, Oct.	66	Zezak	750	Arlington, MN	Greifenberg, Pommern
Maas, Maria Elisabeth	23, Dec. 1872	2, Dec.	69		415	Boody, IL	Greishalle, Vörsmold, Preußen
Maas, Mathias	25, Dec. 1876	2, Sept	56- 3m-15d		413	Frankfurt am Main, GE	
Maas, Wilhelm	15, July 1886	3, July	91- 5m- 7d		7	Marshall, WI	Neuleib, Schwievelbein, Pommern
Maas, Wilhelmine	11, June 1896	9, May	60	Steffen	383	Milwaukee, WI	Mäsow, Pommern
Maaß, J.B.	4, Dec. 1890	16, Nov.	47- 4m		782	St. Paul, MN	Bittsburg, RheinPreußen
Machelis, Maria	23, Apr. 1883	5, Apr.	56- -15d	Kersen	135	Evansville, IN	Arock, Preußen
Mächnig, (Mr)	13, Apr. 1874	13, Mar.	63		119	Wabasha, MN	Muhlwich bei Falkenberg, Oppeln, Preußen
Mächtel, Wilhelmine	7, Aug. 1865	12, July	35		128	Chillicothe, OH	Kernbach, Baden
Mack, (Mrs)	31, Oct. 1870	22, Sept	46- 7m-14d	Krieger	351	Lansing, MI	Neustadt a.d. Hardt, Rheinkreis Baiern
Mack, Adam	6, Aug. 1896	10, July	73		511	Bucyrus, OH	Elsenhausen, Göppingen, Württemberg
Mack, Gottlieb	6, Dec. 1849	15, Nov.	24- 4m		196	Delaware, OH	
Mack, Heinrich W.	31, Mar. 1879	7, Mar.	26- 9m-10d		103	Marion, OH	Marion County, Ohio
Mack, Jakob Friedrich	5, May 1892	14, Apr.	59		286	Lafayette, IN	Neckerdenslingen, Württemberg
Mack, Johan	27, Oct. 1879		69		343	Cleveland, OH	Württemberg
Mack, John Wesley	7, Feb. 1895	15, Jan.	22		94	Cleveland, OH	Clinton County, Michigan
Mack, Katharine	24, Nov. 1884	8, Sept	66	Stumpf	7	Sidney, OH	Hessen-Darmstadt
Mack, Magdalena	18, Oct. 1855	28, Sept	27- 6m		168	Gordonville, MO	Bernbach, Neuenbürg, Württemberg
Mack, Margaretha	6, Dec. 1849	7, Sept	50- 6m- 8d		196	Delaware, OH	
Mack, Maria Carolina	4, Aug. 1879	23, July	29-11m-27d	Schwarz	247	Marion, OH	
Mack, Peter	6, May 1878	5, Apr.	27- 5m- 8d		143	Marion, OH	
Mack, Philipp	24, Jan. 1895	2, Jan.	61		62	Clarington, OH	Weilheim an der Teck, Württemberg
Mack, Rosina Christiana	11, June 1896	26, May	62	Jeiter	383	Bucyrus, OH	Liberty Township, Crawford County, Ohio
Mack, Stephan	13, May 1867		78- 3m-11d		150	Marion, OH	Roßwaag, Vaihingen an der Enz, Württemberg
Mack, Wilhelm	29, Nov. 1894	11, Oct.	74		774	DeWitt, MI	Großingersheim, Backnang, Württemberg
Macke, Emma	13, Apr. 1893	24, Mar.	32	Kühle	238	Gordonville, MO	Gordonville, Missouri
Macke, Lena	9, Oct. 1882	17, Sept	18- 9m-26d	Ahrens	327	Jackson, MO	
MacWaters, Anna Elisabeth	28, July 1873	4, July	32	Baldes	239	Milwaukee, WI	Keidelheim, Alt-Simmern, Preußen
Madaus, Maria Friederike	17, Mar. 1887	29, Jan.	54- 9m-25d	Wendt	174	Columbus, WI	Goldabe, Mecklenburg-Schwerin
Mader, Carl	19, Dec. 1870	19, Nov.	46- 2m-27d		407	Henderson, MN	Stanschen, Schlesien, Preußen
Mader, Dora	26, Feb. 1891	29, Nov.	17		142	Schnectady, NY	
Mader, Jakob	4, Nov. 1852	20, Oct.	72- 5m		180	Lawrenceburg, IN	
Mader, Johanna	17, Feb. 1879	25, Jan.	36- -22d	Roß	55	Schnectady, NY	Oberhorn, Elsaß
Mader, john	30, Oct. 1871	26, Sept	66		351	Greenfield, IL	Pfullingen, Reutlingen, Württemberg
Mader, Louise	24, Dec. 1891	29, Nov.	83		830	Greenfield, OH	Sindelfingen, Württemberg
Mäder, Louise	17, Sept 1891	27, Aug.	26	Kernlamp	606	Arlington, MN	Woodbury, Washington County, Minnesota
Mäder, Sophie	28, Feb. 1895	22, Jan.	73	Quilling	142	Arlington, MN	Dallin, Brandenburg
Mädke, Friedrich A. G.	17, Jan. 1895	8, Dec.	35		46	Ahnapee, WI	Ahnapee, Kewaunee County, Wisconsin
Madlung, Friedrich Wilhelm	6, Jan. 1879	18, Dec.	26		7	Freeport, IL	East Troy, Wisconsin
Maeder, Amalia	27, Dec. 1888	8, Dec.	61- 7m-24d	Heyland	830	Bucyrus, OH	Schwarzburg-Rudolstadt
Maedle, Wilhelmina Friederike	17, Mar.1873	24, Feb.	44	Frömming	87	Ahnapee, WI	Zerlin, Pommern
Maeker, Johan	31, May 1875	12, May	78- 2m-20d		175	Mountain Lake, MN	Wathschendorf, Mecklenburg-Schwerin
Mägdly, Katharina	27, Aug. 1847	21, June	37		139	Delaware, OH	

Christliche Apologete Death Notices --- 1839 - 1899

Name of Deceased	Notice Date	Death Date	Age	Page	Maiden Name	Place of Death	Place of Birth
Magdsick, Emma	25, Nov. 1872	3, Oct.	16- 4m- 4d	383		Chicago, IL	Steinweiler, Rheinpfalz Baiern
Mägely, Anna Maria	22, Apr. 1872	5, Feb.	76-11m-23d	135	Hauck	New Boston, OH	Kindenhein, Rheinkreis Baiern
Magerkurth, Caroline	11, Feb. 1892	19, Jan.	79	94	Fischer	Salina, KS	Kindenhein, Rheinkreis Baiern
Magley, Elisabeth	26, Nov. 1896	9, Oct.	66	766		Columbia City, IN	Oberbipp, Bern, Schweiz
Mägley, Joseph	14, June 1875	22, May	26- 2m-23d	191		Cincinnati, OH	
Mäglin, Maria Magdalena	28, Jan. 1892	4, Jan.	82	62	Wurst	Norwich, KS	Niederbronn, Elsaß
Mägly, Jakob	25, June 1891	25, May	70- 2m-17d	414		San Jose, CA	Steinweiler, Rheinkreis Baiern
Mägly, Jakob	6, Dec. 1875	28, Sept	81	391		Cincinnati, OH	Steinweiler, Rheinpfalz Baiern
Magnus, Catharina	3, Feb. 1887	10, Jan.	70	78	Wetz	Cibolo, TX	Ofenbach, Nassau
Magnus, Jakob	7, Aug. 1876	24, June	81	255		Terre Haute, IN	
Magnus, Sophia	17, Jan. 1870	26, Dec.	65	23		Blue Island, IL	Treho, Mecklenburg-Schwerin
Magsig, Emilie	3, Nov. 1887	8, Oct.	24- 8m-21d	702	Rothert	Elmore, OH	
Magsig, Friedrich August	6, Jan. 1898	8, Dec.	73	15		Elliston, OH	Grapitz bei Cöstlin, Pommern
Mahl, Johan Friedrich	14, Jan. 1892	15, Dec.		30		Amsterdam, NY	Anklam, Preußen
Mähl, Karl	11, May 1899	18, Apr.	83	302		Bracken, TX	Griefswald, Pommern
Mahle, Elenora Mathilda	3, Feb. 1898	16, Jan.	37- 4m-26d	79		Belleville, IL	Warsaw, Illinois
Mahler, Charlotte	24, Mar. 1892	16, Feb.	44	190	Wagner	Le Sueur, MN	Indiana
Mahler, Christian Friedrich	4, Apr. 1889	16, Mar.	67	222		Duncan, NE	Nordleda, Otterndorf, Hannover
Mahler, Dietrich Heinrich Christian	25, Feb. 1886	5, Feb.	94	7		Aurora, IN	Bühren, Neustadt am Rüdenberg, Hannover
Mahler, Emma	18, Apr. 1881	3, Apr.	18- 7m-10d	127		Dallas, TX	Württemberg
Mähler, Gottlob	23, Nov. 1885	14, Oct.	60	7		Philadelphia, PA	Mariensee, Amt Neustadt, Hannover
Mahler, Louise	17, Sept 1857	16, Aug.	65	152		Aurora, IN	Hannover
Mahler, William	30, Aug. 1894	26, July	69-11m	566		Aurora, IN	
Mahnke, Gesche	26, Sept 1846	21, July	22- 5m-15d	155		Pettes Co, MO	
Mahnke, Hanna Christina	24, May 1880	23, Apr.	64- 8m-19d	167	Bruchwitz	Grand Rapids, IL	Wehrheim, Ussingen, Nassau
Mahnken, Edward	15, Oct. 1896	23, Sept	18	671		Lutman, MO	
Mai, Friedrich	1, Nov. 1875	27, Sept	50	351		Brunswick, MO	Barton, Washington County, Wisconsin
Mai, Sophia	9, Apr. 1866	21, Mar.	29-11m	118		Columbus, IL	Irrendorf, Württemberg
Maichele, Ludwig	3, Aug. 1885	19, July	18	7		Iron Ridge, WI	Mildenberg am Main, Baiern
Maier, (Mr)	13, Oct. 1879	25, Sept	65- 7m- 5d	327		Jerusalem, IA	Württemberg
Maier, Anna Maria	6, July 1899	12, June	57	431	Farrenkopf	Wathena, KS	Schönau, Baiern
Maier, Christina	11, Oct. 1849	4, Aug.	43	164		Herman, MO	
Maier, Elisabeth	8, Oct. 1896	27, Aug.	69	655	Weber	Edon, OH	
Maier, Emilie	24, Jan. 1876	11, Dec.	30- 9m	31	Rüdiger	Poughkeepsie, NY	Kalldorf, Lippe
Maier, Friedrich H.	29, Nov. 1869	12, Nov.	81- 2m-14d	383		Kossuth, OH	Allmersbach, Marbach, Württemberg
Maier, Gottlieb	22, Dec. 1879	29, Nov.	43	407		Philadelphia, PA	
Maier, Gottlob	18, Mar. 1886	20, Jan.	23- 1m-20d	7		Ottowa, KS	Sandusky City, Ohio
Maier, Jakob	9, Apr. 1883	24, Mar.	36	119		Edgerton, OH	Schweigern, Brackenheim, Württemberg
Maier, Jakob	4, June 1857	16, May	16	92		Waverly, OH	Sieglingen, Nekarsulm, Württemberg
Maier, Johan Jakob	26, Mar. 1877	23, Feb.	76	103		Mt. Vernon, IN	Schornbach, Schorndorf, Württemberg
Maier, Katharina	12, Nov. 1866	28, Sept	46- 6m-10d	366		Union, MO	Leonberg, Württemberg
Maier, Katharina Dorothea	1, Mar. 1894	10, Feb.	79	150	Fischer	Bucyrus, OH	Elmendingen, Pforzheim, Baden
Maier, Rosina	21, Feb. 1876	24, Jan.	71	63	Lyon	Poughkeepsie, NY	Württemberg
Maier, Rosine	26, Apr. 1888	6, Feb.	69	270		Marion, OH	Degerloch, Stuttgart, Württemberg
Maier, Sophie	3, Sept 1891	4, Aug.	72	574	Haselmaier	Anaheim, CA	
Maier, Wilhelm	14, Feb. 1895	26, Jan.	58	110		Louisville, KY	

Christliche Apologete Death Notices -- 1839 - 1899

Name of Deceased	Notice Date	Death Date	Age	Page	Maiden Name	Place of Death	Place of Birth
Maier, Wilhelmine Charlotte	5, Dec. 1870	6, Nov.	70	391	Brand	Spencerville, OH	Rodenberg, Krankenhagen, Lippe-Schaumburg
Mainz, Anna Catharine	23, Nov. 1863	4, Oct.	32	188	Hugo	Wheeling, WV	Burchhofen, Kreis Eschwege, Kurhessen
Mainz, Elisabeth	18, Dec. 1876	4, Dec.	32- 1m-21d	407	Klebe	Clarington, OH	Reichensachsen, Kurhessen
Maisch, Joseph Benjamin	26, Aug. 1897	1, Aug.	27	543		Washington, MN	Washington County, Minnesota
Maisch, Stephan	31, Oct. 1895	26, Sept	74	702		Washington, MN	Kaih, Herrenberg, Württemberg
Maisenzahl, Maria	16, June 1873	3, June	38- 7m- 6d	191		Marion, OH	Nöttingen, Pforzheim, Baden
Majer, Sebastian	12, Oct. 1868		60	327		Edgerton, OH	Friedrichsthal, Karlsruhe, Baden
Mak, Karolina	15, Oct. 1857		60	168		Marion, OH	Marion County, Ohio
Make, Anna Maria	21, Apr. 1873	20, Aug.	16	127	Hartmann	Seymour, IN	Engder, Hannover
Make, Johan Friedrich	6, June 1870	26, Mar.	60	183		Seymour, IN	Eichter, Amt Föde, Hannover
Malakowsky, Auguste	8, Oct. 1896	19, May	70	655	Knoop	Ada, MN	
Malakowsky, Elise	7, Apr. 1892	16, Sept	44- -10d	222		Ada, MN	Stramehl bei Labes, Pommern
Malenke, Friedrich	25, Feb. 1892	12, Mar.	34	126		Winona, MN	AltDamero, Hinterpommern
Malick, Joseph	14, Apr. 1887	31, Jan.	54	238		Beaver Dam, WI	Glauscha, Schlesien
Malik, Rosa	6, June 1895	29, Mar.	84	366		Beaver Dam, WI	Riewe, Wartenberg, Schlesien
Mall, Johan Chr.	27, Nov. 1890	18, May	92	766		Jeffersonville, NY	Westhofen, Elsaß
Mall, Louise	19, Dec. 1895	6, Nov.	77	814	Beel	Clay Center, KS	Söllingen, Baden
Mall, Louise	2, Jan. 1896	26, Nov.	37	14	Beeh	Clay Center, KS	Söllingen, Baden
Mall, Mary	23, May 1881	26, Nov.	37	167	Damm	Graham, MO	Jeffersonville, Sullivan County, New York
Malle, Johan	14, Aug. 1871	1, Aug.	24-11m- 6d	263		Des Moines, IA	
Mallo, Michael	27, May 1897	1, May	19	335		Philadelphia, PA	Melsheim, Elsaß
Mallot, Friedrich	22, Apr. 1872	17, Mar.	53	135		Faribault, MN	Satzig, Stettin, Preußen
Malisch, Sebastian	7, Apr. 1879	21, Mar.	57	111		Burlington, IA	Westhausen, Meiningen, Sachsen-Meiningen
Malott, Dorothea Louise	9, June 1887	8, May	76- -20d	366		Faribault, MN	Pansin, Pommern
Maloun, Elisabeth	27, Aug. 1883			279	Schröder	Baltimore, MD	Elsfleth, Oldenburg
Malsch, Anna Katharina Friederike	19, Oct. 1899	24, Sept	74	671	Harm	Burlington, WI	Großbanko, Mecklenburg
Malsch, Barbara Elisabeth	21, Feb. 1881	21, Jan.	59	63		Burlington, WI	Wereshausen, Sachsen-Meiningen
Malsch, Martha	22, Nov. 1888	7, Nov.	77	750		Burlington, WI	Lyons,
Malüg, Christian	6, Mar. 1890	20, Feb.	16	158		Milwaukee, WI	Mellen, Pommern
Malüg, Johanna Maria Fr.	5, Aug. 1886	14, July	63	7		Milwaukee, WI	Premslaff, Pommern
Malwitz, Maria	22, July 1886	5, July	68	7	Wobig	Ft. Dodge, IA	Tornow, Saizig, Pommern
Mammen, Sievertje Janßen	27, Apr. 1899	12, Apr.	72	271	Müller	Emden, IL	Groothusen, Emden, Ostfriesland
Mampe, Edie	22, Aug. 1893	31, July	65- 3m-29d	542		Hokah, MN	Hokah, Houston County, Minnesota
Mamrow, Louisa Dorothea	21, Sept 1893	15, Aug.	15	606	Schwampe	Kendallville, IN	Wayne Township, Noble County, Indiana
Manche, Johannes	9, Feb. 1854	6, Jan.	25	24		Palestine, IN	Aperoth, Hessen-Darmstadt
Mandel, Maria	9, Feb. 1899	22, Jan.	43	95	Schade	Sleepy Eye, MN	Kurhessen
Manderie, Peter	1, Dec. 1873	17, Sept	70	383		Cincinnati, OH	Siltz, Anweiler, Rheinkreis Baiern
Manderscheid, Christian	9, Mar. 1893	11, Feb.	54	158		Lansing, IA	Baiern
Manderscheid, Magdalena	23, Aug. 1894	31, July	86	550	Hirth	Lansing, IA	Hockenheim, Baden
Manderscheid, Maria Magdalena	18, Aug. 1892	30, July	83	526		Lansing, IA	Allamakee County, Iowa
Mandler, Johannes	9, Oct. 1871	24, Sept	16	327		Wathena, KS	Rehof, Marienwerder, Preußen
Manecke, Sophia Christina	20, Dec. 1888	12, Nov.	32	814	Hölscher	Huntingburg, IN	Ladbergen, Tecklenburg, Münster, Preußen
Mangel, Friederike	12, June 1882	28, Apr.	25	191	Dauwen	Huntingburg, IN	Lengerich, Tecklenburg, Preußen
Mangel, Sophia Friederike	7, Apr. 1892	5, Mar.	72	222	Katterjohn	Huntingburg, IN	
Mangels, Catharina	11, Sept 1851	20, Aug.	33	148	Thöle	Quincy, IL	
Mangels, Heinrich	5, Jan. 1893	27, Nov.	81	14		Huntsville, KS	Diepstäd, Hannover

Christliche Apologete Death Notices --- 1839 - 1899

Name of Deceased	Notice Date	Death Date	Age	Maiden Name	Page	Place of Death	Place of Birth
Mangels, Maria	20, Dec. 1844	1, Dec.	36	Sannmann	196	New Orleans, LA	Besenbrücken, Hannover
Mangels, Nicolaus	4, Oct. 1869	14, Sept	60		319		Zeven, Bremen, Hannover
Mangels, Wilhelmine	16, Apr. 1883	17, Mar.	65	Kurz	127	Etna, MO	Zuzenhausen, Baden
Mangels, Wilhelmine	26, Oct. 1854	15, Sept	29	Borgard	172	Perry, IL	Minden, Preußen
Mangold, Christian Wilhelm	27, May 1872	13, May	74- 3m-27d		175	San Jose, IL	Westgrauhsen, Schwarzburg-Sondershausen
Mangold, Christine	30, Mar. 1874	13, Mar.	63		103	San Jose, IL	Schwarzburg-Sondershausen
Manhardt, Maria Walburga	20, Feb. 1871	3, Nov.	57	Spindler	63	German Creek, IA	Beuren, Nürtingen, Württemberg
Manke, Augusta	9, June 1898	9, May	40		367	Larned, KS	Kreiskaslin, Pommern
Mankel, Andreas	20, Aug. 1877	1, Aug.			271	Danville, IL	Nieder-Aspeh, Marburg, Kurhessen
Mankowske, Minna	9, June 1884	13, May	43		7	Spring Lake, ---	Schubin, Posen
Mann, (Mr)	8, Apr. 1886	13, Mar.	71		7	Beardstown, IL	Schammelsberg, Oberfranken, Baiem
Mann, (Mrs)	21, Jan. 1884	7, Dec.	42	Schmidt	7	St. Louis, MO	
Mann, Anna Barbara	9, May 1895	21, Apr.	74	Sesselmann	302	Beardstown, IL	Höferangen, Germany
Mann, Anna Katharina	12, Jan. 1863	24, Dec.	43- 3m-15d		8	Louisville, KY	Nußdorf, Württemberg
Mann, Anna Maria	2, Sept 1867	19, Aug.	63	Mondinger	278	St. Louis, MO	Eltingen, Leonberg, Württemberg
Mann, Barbara	19, July 1880	30, June	87	Berner	231	New Metamoras, OH	Hammen, Sachsen-Meiningen
Mann, Christina Magdalena	16, Mar. 1893	24, Feb.	79		174	Fairmount, KS	KleinSachsenheim, Vaihingen, Württemberg
Mann, David	28, Jan. 1884	9, Jan.	60		7	Freeport, IL	Schwanenbeck bei Zachan, Saatzig, Pommern
Mann, Elisabeth Dorothea	1, Jan. 1883	11, Nov.	78	Keil	7	Clayton, IA	Feldkrüken, Schotten, Hessen-Darmstadt
Mann, Friedrich	10, Dec. 1883	12, Nov.	66		7	New Albany, IN	Weißbach, Leonberg, Württemberg
Mann, Jakob	17, Aug. 1885	26, July	58		7	St. Paul, MN	Ditzingen, Leonberg, Württemberg
Mann, Jakob	26, Oct. 1863	19, July	23		172	Defiance, OH	Niederalben, Preußen
Mann, Johan Jakob	9, July 1877	3, June	36		223	St. Louis, MO	Eslingen, Württemberg
Mann, Johannes	13, Sept 1894	25, Aug.	76- 4m-21d		598	Giard, IA	Bußenborn, Hessen-Darmstadt
Mann, John	21, Nov. 1881	3, Nov.	71- 9m		375	Giard, IA	Busenborn, Schotten, Hessen-Darmstadt
Mann, Katharina	29, Oct. 1896	8, Oct.	79	Repp	703	Giard, IA	Busenborn, Schotten, Hessen-Darmstadt
Mann, Maria Katharina	4, Apr. 1864	2, Mar.			56	St. Paul, MN	Rieberg, Minden, Preußen
Mann, Nikolaus	11, July 1861	1, June	83		112	Baresville, OH	Rauhenstein, Sachsen-Meiningen
Mann, Philipp	13, May 1867	9, Apr.	59		150	German Creek, IA	Kleinsachsenheim, Vaihingen, Württemberg
Männel, Wilhelmina Christiana	28, Jan. 1892	3, Jan.	80	Lenk	62	Lawrence, MA	Schönheide, Sachsen
Mannhardt, Johan	18, Aug. 1884	6, July	68		7	Mt. Pleasant, IA	Beuren, Württemberg
Mannhardt, Rosina	14, Jan. 1858	4, Dec.	15- 3m		8	Burlington, IA	
Mannherz, Anna	7, Jan. 1892	16, Dec.	70-10m-11d	Süsholz	14	Sedalia, MO	Oberhannover, Montgomery Co., Pennsylvania
Mannherz, Georg	28, July 1892	9, July	74		478	Sedalia, MO	Münzersheim, Bretten, Baden
Mannherz, George Washington	5, Dec. 1870	3, Nov.	15		391	Smithton, MO	
Manns, Friedrich	17, Oct. 1889	26, Sept	69- 8m- 5d		670	Pittsburg, PA	Rothenburg, Kurhessen
Manske, Friedrich Wilhelm	2, Feb. 1899	2, Jan.	62		79	Milwaukee, WI	Piritz, Pommern
Manß, Martha	25, May 1893	3, May	20		334	Bushton, KS	Louisville, Jefferson County, Kentucky
Manßen, Heie Wilke	4, Oct. 1888	18, Sept	73		638	Golconda, IL	Aurich, Altendorf, Ostfriesland
Manßen, Jakob	21, Nov. 1889	24, Oct.	48		750	Waltersburg, IL	Plaggenburg, Aurich, Ostfriesland
Manßen, Johan Heie	26, Nov. 1896	13, Oct.	43		766	Waltersburg, IL	Plaggenburg, Aurich, Hannover
Mantey, Maria Pauline Leonora	26, Aug. 1886	1, Aug.	19		7	Lexington, MO	Lincoln, Benton County, Missouri
Mantz, Anna Catharina	2, Feb. 1874	5, Jan.	81	Sälzer	39	Pittsfield, IL	Holzburg, Kurhessen
Mantz, Heinrich	31, May 1849	26, Apr.	49		88	New Albany, IN	Fehr-Altdorf, Zürich, Schweiz
Mantz, Wilhelm	5, Oct. 1874	19, Aug.	81- 3m- 3d		319	Pittsfield, IL	
Mäntzinger, Katharina	26, Dec. 1895	19, Nov.	70	Fuhrmann	828	New Albany, IN	Haih, Baiem

Name of Deceased	Notice Date	Death Date	Age	Maiden Name	Page	Place of Death	Place of Birth
Manus, Remde	27, Sept 1888	11, Sept	41- -2d	Böning	622	Emden, IL	Riegsterhamrich, Ostfriesland
Manz, Jakob	24, July 1865	June			120	New York, NY	Untenheim, Hessen-Darmstadt
Marben, Katharina Magdalena	22, Nov. 1894	27, July	71		758	Portland, OR	Stelle, Hannover
Marburger, Anna Barbara	1, Dec. 1887	9, Nov.	16		766	Allegheny City, PA	Allegheny City, Pennsylvania
Marburger, John	9, Mar. 1893	11, Feb.	70		158	Allegheny City, PA	Oberamholz bei Kassel, Kurhessen
Märckel, Katharina	12, May 1879	21, Apr.	76-11m-21d		151	Boonville, MO	Hessen-Darmstadt
Marcoot, Martin	11, Mar. 1867	15, Nov.			78	Highland, IL	Klosters, Graubünden, Schweiz
Marder, Anna	1, Aug. 1864	11, July	60		124	Madison, IN	Feldberg, Amt Müllheim, Baden
Mardorf, Anna Elisabeth	11, Feb. 1892	15, Jan.	64	Ide	94	Big Spring, MO	Schelbach, Homberg, Kurhessen
Margoot, Agnes	16, Aug. 1875	16, July	58	Risch	263	Highland, IL	Waldensburg, Graubünden, Schweiz
Margraf, Johan	14, Apr. 1887	24, Mar.	75		238	Cincinnati, OH	Borken, Kurhessen
Mark, Conrad	30, Sept 1886	18, Sept	87		7	Wilton, IA	Melgershausen, Kurhessen
Mark, Henrietta	9, Apr. 1891	11, Mar.	76	Kimpel	238	Lincoln, NE	Gießen,
Mark, Johan Berthold	4, Mar. 1867	27, Jan.	50-10m		70	Muscatine, IA	Melgershausen, Amt Felsberg, Kurhessen
Mark, Konrad	3, Dec. 1866	16, Nov.	19- 5m-20d		390	Buffalo, NY	
Mark, Maria Magdalena	6, June 1861	11, May	8- 7m- 8d		92	Wilton, IA	
Mark, Sophie	23, Dec. 1878	3, Dec.	30-11m	Schott	407	Muscatine, IA	Schaffheim, Hessen-Darmstadt
Märkel, Conr.	9, June 1848	28, Mar.	65- -14d		96	Mascoutah, IL	York County, Pennsylvania
Markel, Georg	21, Apr. 1887	31, Mar.	73-10m-27d		254	LaCrosse, WI	Cleveland, Ohio
Market, Katharina	29, Dec. 1898	29, Nov.	46	Döring	828	Marion, OH	Großalmerode, Witzenhausen, Kurhessen
Market, Sophia	3, Nov. 1884	9, Oct.	68- 9m- 3d		7	Marion, OH	Humberg, Kurhessen
Markgraf, Katharina Elisabeth	5, Dec. 1889	11, Nov.	81- 5m	Treudorf	782	Cincinnati, OH	Newark, New Jersey
Markhart, Margaret	31, Oct. 1895	7, Oct.	30	Gössel	702	Newark, NJ	Rehme, Minden, Preußen
Marks, Friederike	7, May 1877	20, Apr.	61		151	Hopewell, MO	
Marks, Friedrich	18, Oct. 1875	31, Aug.	18		335	Hopewell, MO	Dominke, Pommern
Marks, Friedrich Wilhelm	12, Jan. 1888	21, Dec.	65		30	Neshkora, WI	
Marks, Friedrike	10, Feb. 1879	28, Jan.	32- 4m	Schwengerdt	47	Morrison, MO	
Marks, Hanna	7, July 1879	23, May	20	Stöber	215	Platteville, WI	Hazelgreen, Wisconsin
Marks, Henrietta	30, Apr. 1891	11, Mar.	76	Kimpel	286	Lincoln, NE	Gießen,
Marks, Karl	17, Mar. 1884	26, Feb.	75		7	Hopewell, MO	Rehme, Minden, Preußen
Markt, Anna Maria	11, Mar. 1878	19, Feb.	69	Hauerin	79	Oregon, MO	Augen, Baden
Markut, Katharina Dorothea	22, Aug. 1861	26, July	14- 3m- 5d		136	Highland, IL	
Märky, Lisette	1, Sept 1892	14, Aug.	16- 6m-20d		558	Pepin, IL	
Marmer, Maria	5, May 1873	9, Apr.		Stein	143	Cannelton, IN	Niedergrund, Ahlsfeld, Hessen-Darmstadt
Marmor,	12, Oct. 1893	27, Aug.	78		654	Cannelton, IN	Mondzingen, Kreuznach, Koblenz, Preußen
Marmor, Friedrich	3, July 1882	9, June	45		215	Cannelton, IN	Monsingen, Preußen
Marmor, Samuel	17, Jan. 1895	13, Oct.	23		46	Cannelton, IN	Perry County, Indiana
Marmor, Sarah Catharina	14, Feb. 1889	17, Jan.	76		110	Cannelton, IN	Monzingen, Koblenz, Preußen
Marold, Friedrich	13, May 1886	17, Apr.	56		7	Wathena, KS	Walpersweil, Nidau, Bern, Schweiz
Marolf, Anna	4, Apr. 1881	16, Mar.	52	Roth	111	Wathena, KS	Walwertswyl, Bern, Schweiz
Marolf, Benedikt	1, Aug. 1870	30, June			247	Wathena, KS	Walperwil, Nidau, Bern, Schweiz
Marolf, Friedrich	14, Dec. 1885	29, Nov.	25		7	Wathena, KS	
Marolf, Peter	14, Oct. 1872	31, Aug.	84		335	St. Joseph, MO	Walpersweil, Bern, Schweiz
Maronde, Friedrich	13, Nov. 1871	17, Oct.			367	Victoria, TX	Seidel bei Koslin, Pommern
Marotz, Christina Wilhelmina	1, Aug. 1895	24, Feb.	81	Voigt	494	Washington, MN	Natzlow, Belgard, Hinterpommern
Marotz, Wilhelm	16, Aug. 1875	18, July	22		263	Columbus, WI	Königsdorf, Bromberg, Preußen

Christliche Apologete Death Notices --- 1839 - 1899

Name of Deceased	Notice Date	Death Date	Age	Maiden Name	Page	Place of Death	Place of Birth
Marqua, Emma Louise	28, Dec. 1885	15, Dec.	19		7	Cincinnati, OH	Cincinnati, Hamilton County, Ohio
Marqua, Maria A.	13, Apr. 1893		75	Mägli	238	Cincinnati, OH	Landau , Rheinpfalz Baiern
Marquard, Eva Elisabeth	31, Mar. 1879	12, Mar.	72		103	Rochester, MN	Elmshausen, Hessen-Darmstadt
Marquard, Martha	23, Feb. 1880	31, Dec.	13- 5m-21d		63	Columbus, OH	
Marquard, Matilda	23, Feb. 1880	31, Dec.	10		63	Columbus, OH	
Marquardt, Albert	1, Sept 1892	14, Aug.	11- 5m- 8d		558	Turtle Mount, ---	
Marquardt, Anna M.	4, Oct. 1869	14, Sept	78	Heilemann	319	Lawrenceburg, IN	Hochdorf, Vaihingen, Württemberg
Marquardt, August	9, Dec. 1897	18, Nov.	64		783	Chicago, IL	Großsachsenheim, Vaihingen, Württemberg
Marquardt, Auguste	19, Sept 1850	24, Aug.	35		152	Dayton, OH	
Marquardt, C. F.	18, Aug. 1898	16, July	66		527	Sleepy Eye, MN	Paminn, Arnswald, Germany
Marquardt, Elisabeth	8, Nov. 1880	6, Oct.	40-10m-25d	Schleffel	359	Columbus, OH	
Marquardt, Emma	31, Jan. 1881	13, Jan.	14		39	Iowa City, IA	Iowa City, Iowa
Marquardt, Fritz	18, June 1896	3, June	56		399	Rutersville, TX	Quardenschönfeld, Mecklenburg-Strelitz
Marquardt, Jakob	3, Apr. 1846		Inquiry		55	Dayton, OH	Elmshausen, Hessen-Darmstadt
Marquardt, Johan Friedrich	8, Jan. 1891	9, Dec.	10		30	Pepin, IL	
Marquardt, Johan Michael	6, Apr. 1868	17, Mar.	65- 7m		111	Watertown, WI	Lukatz bei Filehne, Czarnikau, Preußen
Marquardt, John	22, Nov. 1875	2, Nov.			375	Rochester, MN	Elmshausen, Hessen-Darmstadt
Marquardt, Katharina	2, June 1898	8, May	78		351	Dayton, OH	Greifenstein, Wetzlar, Koblenz, Preußen
Marquardt, Margaretha	22, Apr. 1897	28, Mar.	71		255	Lawrence, MA	Asch, Oesterreich
Marquardt, Maria	16, Nov. 1885	20, Oct.	58	Laamann	7	Jeffersonville, IN	Rampe, Mecklenburg-Schwerin
Marquardt, Maria	14, Sept 1885	30, Aug.	32	Ewinger	7	Burlington, IA	Landel, Rheinpfalz Baiern
Marquardt, Maria Anna	20, Dec. 1880	13, Nov.	31- 7m-20d	Lampert	407	Madison, SD	Elmshausen, Hessen-Darmstadt
Marquardt, Maria Emily	7, June 1888	17, May	17		366	Pepin, WI	Nelson, Buffalo County, Wisconsin
Marquardt, Philipp	28, July 1898	11, July	65		479	Des Moines, IA	Emshausen, Hessen-Darmstadt
Marquardt, Philipp	31, Oct. 1895	10, Oct.	81		702	Dayton, OH	Elmshausen, Bensheim, Hessen-Darmstadt
Marquart, Edward	16, June 1887	19, May	5m		382	Pepin, WI	Beeffslough, Buf. County, Wisconsin
Marquart, Louise	12, Oct. 1893	9, Sept	86	Zimmermann	654	Watertown, WI	Neumark
Marrett, Carolina	18, Oct. 1875	28, Sept	20		335	Louisville, KY	Jefferson County, Kentucky
Marschall, Anna Gertraud	10, Sept 1883	19, Aug.	73		295	Washington, MN	Lumbach, Rothenburg, Kurhessen
Marschall, Gelasea	5, Dec. 1895	12, Nov.	53	Riemenschneider	782	Valley City, ND	Bambach, Kurhessen
Marschall, Jakob	18, Aug. 1898	31, July	93		527	Washington, MN	Baumbach, Kurhessen
Marschel, Fritz	13, Sept 1849		Inquiry		147	Hartford, IN	
Marsmann, Peter H.	15, Jan. 1891	13, Dec.	43- 2m- 5d		46	Brazil, IN	Rothenhagen, Preußen
Martel, Julia	24, Mar. 1879	27, Feb.	24	Schneider	95	Platteville, WI	
Marten, Carl	20, Dec. 1869		51		407	Milwaukee, WI	Wismar, Preußen
Marten, Heinrich	7, June 1888	24, May	22- -16d		366	Milwaukee, WI	
Marten, Karoline	19, Mar. 1896	2, Mar.	68- 8m-22d	Hacker	190	Berea, OH	Stinitz, Dramburg, Preußen
Marten, Maria	6, Apr. 1885	18, Jan.	76	Rathmann	7	Hannibal, MO	Barkow, Neustadt, Mecklenburg-Schwerin
Marten, Wilhelmina	19, Aug. 1897	21, July	14		527	Berea, OH	Berea, Ohio
Martens, Anna Dorothea	2, Mar. 1899	31, Jan.	48	Schröder	143	Denison, IA	Thielen, Schleswig-Holstein
Martens, Heinrich	24, Aug. 1893	27, July	66		542	Schnectady, NY	Mecklenburg-Schwerin
Martens, Herman	1, Oct. 1883	10, Aug.			319	Neuschoo, ---	
Martens, Karl	4, Nov. 1897	13, Oct.	70		703	LaCrosse, WI	Enzow, Lanenburg, Köslin, Preußen
Martens, Meta	12, Apr. 1888	5, Mar.	20- 3m- 4d		238	San Francisco, CA	Westerscheps, Oldenburg
Martenstein, Anna	26, Nov. 1883	11, Nov.	79		383	Lawrenceburg, IN	Lippe-Detmold
Martenstein, Anna Maria	2, Aug. 1849	14, July	45		124	Lawrenceburg, IN	

Christliche Apologete Death Notices --- 1839 - 1899

Name of Deceased	Notice Date	Death Date	Age	Page	Maiden Name	Place of Death	Place of Birth
Martenstein, Otis	2, Apr. 1866	26, Jan.	6- 8m	110		San Francisco, CA	Mülchi, Fraubrunnen, Bern, Schweiz
Marti, Adam	9, Apr. 1896	19, Mar.	73	238		Kochville, MI	
Marti, Adam	18, Oct. 1880			335		Bay City, MI	
Marti, Elisabeth	28, Feb. 1870	26, Jan.	48	71	Geiser	Milwaukee, WI	Othmarsingen, Aargau, Schweiz
Marti, Jakob	16, June 1892	29, May	65	382		Kochville, MI	Mühche, Fraubrunner, Bern, Schweiz
Marti, Margaretha	18, Oct. 1880	23, Aug.	56	335		Bay City, MI	Meriswyl, Bern, Schweiz
Marti, Mary	4, Oct. 1880	23, Aug.	56	319		Bay City, MI	Meriswyl, Bern, Schweiz
Marti, Sophia	24, Mar. 1892	1, Mar.	30	190	Hasse	Kochville, MI	Kochville, Saginaw County, Michigan
Martin , Johan Heinrich	23, Sept 1897	29, Aug.	57	607		Fairlawn, NJ	Freutendorf, Baselland, Schweiz
Martin, Andreas	1, Mar. 1894	31, Jan.		150		Marrs, IN	Mars Township, Posey County, Indiana
Martin, Auguste Elisabeth	10, Aug. 1899	27, June	41	511	Nahrung	Lemars, IA	St. Joseph, Missouri
Martin, Barbara	17, Mar. 1853	23, Feb.	51- 4m	44		New York, NY	Ittlingen bei Heidelberg, Baden
Martin, Christine	15, Jan. 1891	8, Dec.	76	46	Kautz	Higginsport, OH	Ispringen, Baden
Martin, Dorothea	6, Apr. 1885	16, Mar.	40	7		Chicago, IL	Reinfahrtshausen, Waldeck
Martin, Elisa Charlotte	2, Aug. 1894	18, July		502	Dörr	Marrs, IN	Terre Haute, Indiana
Martin, Ferdinand	16, May 1889	9, Apr.	69	318		Higginsport, OH	Ruppertsberg, Baiern
Martin, Friedrich	27, Oct. 1892	6, Oct.	63	686		Berea, OH	Schonwahl, Preußen
Martin, Gottlieb	22, Jan. 1883	28, Nov.	79	31		Industry, TX	Reifland, Sachsen
Martin, Heinrich Wilhelm	20, June 1889	3, June	23	398		Canton, MO	Canton, Missouri
Martin, Jeanette Marie	23, Aug. 1894	2, Aug.	50	550	Meyer	Brenham, TX	Berschwil, Schlothurn, Schweiz
Martin, Johanne Rosina	23, Sept 1867	31, Aug.	63	302		Industry, TX	Reifland, Sachsen
Martin, John	21, Dec. 1863	29, July	72	204		Lansing, MI	Grünstadt, Hannover
Martin, John	25, Oct. 1875	27, Sept	21	343		St. Louis, MO	
Martin, John J.	22, Nov. 1875	18, Oct.	36	375		Marrs, IN	Posey County, Indiana
Martin, Joseph	30, June 1898	9, June	71	415		Cannon River, MN	Schweiz
Martin, Karoline	2, June 1884	4, May	20	7		Marrs, IN	Posey County, Indiana
Martin, Ludwig	28, Jan. 1897	3, Jan.	75	62		Almond, WI	Retzerau, Mecklenburg
Martin, Maggie	22, Nov. 1880	25, Oct.	22-10m-28d	375		Jeffersonville, IN	
Martin, Maria Christina	15, Dec. 1892	27, Oct.	76	798		Marrs, IN	Höfen, Neuburg, Württemberg
Martin, Peter	29, July 1886	11, July	76	7		Warsaw, IL	Miesenbach, Landstuhl, Rheinkreis Baiern
Martin, Peter	17, Dec. 1883	25, Nov.	74	7		Schnectady, NY	Katzenfurth, Wetzlar, Preußen
Martin, Rose	2, Feb. 1880	10, Jan.	17- 4m-29d	39		Mt. Vernon, IN	
Martin, Sebastian	10, Sept 1847	23, July	13	147		Warsaw, IL	
Martin, Wilhelmine Charlotte	7, Apr. 1884	16, Mar.	68	7	Kuhlbörsch	Portsmouth, OH	Katzenfurth, Wetzlar, Koblenz, Preußen
Marting, Georg Heinrich	29, Jan. 1877	6, Jan.	18	39		Ironton, OH	Oldendorf, Melle, Hannover
Marting, Heinrich Wilhelm	3, June 1897		70	351		Portsmouth, OH	Oldendorf bei Osnabrück, Hannover
Marting, Johan Heinrich	3, June 1897	1, May	80	351		Portsmouth, OH	
Marting, Karl Heinrich	18, June 1877	28, May		199		Portsmouth, OH	Gut Ostenwaldt, Melle, Hannover
Marting, Maria Elsabein	5, Mar. 1877	16, Feb.	58	79	Knöper	Greenville, OH	Greenville, Ohio
Martini, H. Paul	4, Apr. 1895	6, Mar.	28	222		Bloomington, IL	Bloomington, Illinois
Marton, Emma Maria	30, Nov. 1885	3, Nov.	28	7	Frenzel	Saginaw, MI	Milchi, Amt Frauenbrunnen, Bern, Schweiz
Marty, Elisabeth	14, Dec. 1863	18, Oct.	62	200	Schnell	Sherrills Mount, IA	Matt, Glarus, Schweiz
Marty, Johannes	29, Apr. 1872	14, Apr.	51	143		Sherrills Mount, IA	Schweiz
Marty, Maria	16, Dec. 1897	22, Nov.	75	799		Newport, KY	Cincinnati, Hamilton County, Ohio
Martz, Amanda Rosa	16, July1883	23, June	30	231	Großkordt	Newport, KY	Matzenbach, Rheinkreis Baiern
Martz, Charlotte	10, Sept 1891	28, July	67	590	Stemler	Newport, KY	

Christliche Apologete Death Notices --- 1839 - 1899

Name of Deceased	Notice Date	Death Date	Age	Page	Maiden Name	Place of Death	Place of Birth
Martz, Lizzie	11, Mar. 1886	27, Feb.	30	7	Bettinger	Boonville, IN	Warwick County, Indiana
Martz, Nikolaus	24, Apr. 1890	16, Mar.	49	270		Long Island City, NY	Werensberg, Rheinpfalz Baiern
Marx, Barbara	4, Oct. 1880	9, Sept	28- 1m- 9d	319	Mehne	Almond, WI	
März, Catharina	16, Feb. 1888	24, Jan.	77- 3m	110		Cleveland, OH	Urtene, Bern, Schweiz
Marzahn, Wilhelm	13, July 1893	27, June	73	446		Waseca, MN	Dobberpfuhl, Neumark
Masche, Emilie Henriette A.	7, Jan. 1892	18, Dec.	35	14	Krüger	Lowell, WI	Weitenhagen, Pommern
Masemann, Johan A.	10, Dec. 1896	14, Nov.	74	798		Platteville, WI	Martfeld, Hannover
Maski, Johan	24, Mar. 1892	1, Mar.	48	190		Milwaukee, WI	Zellowo, Posen
Mason, Fanny Emilie	13, Aug. 1896	18, July	24	527		Cincinnati, OH	New Albany , Indiana
Maßbrook, Ella Laura	3, Dec. 1883	9, Nov.		391	Forger	Pittsburg, PA	
Massemann, Anna	24, Jan. 1881	26, Dec.	65	31	Cordts	Platteville, WI	Langenhausen, Gnardenburg, Hannover
Massinger, Maria	12, Oct. 1899	10, Sept	49	655		Portland, OR	Grünstadt, Rheinpfalz Baiern
Mast, Anna	28, Mar. 1895	4, Mar.	49	206	Zwahlen	Seattle, WA	Aechanmatt, Bern, Schweiz
Mast, Maria A.	5, May 1879	20, Apr.	34- 5m- 7d	143		Quincy, IL	Mühlhausen, Preußen
Math, Katharina	18, June 1847	31, Oct.	55- 3m	99			
Mathäi, Wilhelm	13, Sept 1869	22, Aug.	67	295		Louisville, KY	Marburg, Kurhessen
Mathe, Johan	23, Mar. 1899	1, Mar.	87	191		Kewaunee, WI	Prachardiz, Oesterreich
Matheis, Philipp	20, Nov. 1882	3, Nov.	28	375		Charlestown, IN	Bettweiler, Baiern
Mathes, Elisabeth	3, June 1886	19, Apr.	53	7		St. Paul, MN	Langula, Sachsen
Mathes, Elisabeth	17, June 1886	19, May	53	7		St. Paul, MN	Langula, Sachsen
Mathes, Ernestine	15, June 1893	25, May	56	382	Wegner	St. Paul, MN	Groß-Benz, Stettin, Pommern
Mathes, Georg Louis	16, Feb. 1885	1, Feb.	26	7		St. Paul, MN	
Matheus, Louise	17, Aug. 1868	3, Aug.	20	263	Koch	New Albany, IN	
Mathews, Karoline	25, May 1899	24, Apr.	68	335	Lünig	Panola, MN	Nakel, Bromberg, Pommern
Mathews, Wilhelm	31, Jan. 1895	17, Dec.	70	78		Mason City, IA	Posen
Mathias, Henry	31, July 1890	15, May	61	494		Aurora, IN	OberEbbenfeld, Kurhessen
Mathis, Johan	19, Nov. 1883	20, Oct.	45	375		Nashville, TN	Trimnus, Graubünden, Schweiz
Mathwig, A. Chr.	4, Oct. 1894	1, Sept	81- 3m-14d	646	Kühn	Ripon, WI	Ansfelde, Scharnika, Posen
Mathwig, Minna	3, Feb. 1887	12, Jan.	53	78	Erbe	Owatonna, MN	Filehne, Czarnikau, Bromberg, Posen
Matins, Lina	3, May 1875	13, Apr.	11	143		Kenaunee, WI	
Matins, Theresia	3, May 1875	15, Apr.	17	143		Kenaunee, WI	
Matten, Johan Bernard	26, Jan. 1885	7, Jan.	81- 4m-28d	7		Humboldt, NE	Lulle, Bippen, Hannover
Matter, Jacob	28, Jan. 1892	10, Jan.	72- 5m-16d	62		Louisville, KY	Wickersheim, Elsaß
Matter, Johan Martin	8, Feb. 1869	15, Jan.	41	47		Chicago, IL	Metzeral, Haut-Rhin, Frankreich
Matter, Maria	17, Nov. 1884	3, Nov.	70	7	Hoff	Louisville, KY	Gottesheim, Elsaß
Mattern, Amalia	19, May 1898	11, Apr.	63	319	Friedrichs	Brooklyn, NY	Barmen, Westphalen
Mattern, Anna Maria	29, Mar. 1860	8, Feb.	63	52		Louisville, KY	Landau, Baiern
Mattern, Christian	13, Mar. 1890	13, Feb.	35	174		St. Louis, MO	Neuwied, Koblenz, Preußen
Mattern, Heinrich	17, Apr. 1865	14, Jan.	75- 6m	64		Appleton, MO	Oberrosbach, Hessen
Mattes, Jakob	23, May 1870	1, Apr.	25	167		New Haven, CT	Eßlingen, Württemberg
Mattes, Louise S.	6, May 1886	6, Apr.	22	7	Jahn	Decatur, IL	Boody, Illinois
Matthäiw, Wilhelm	27, Sept 1875	30, Aug.	16	311		Delhi, MI	Pittsburg, Pennsylvania
Mattheis, Christian	1, Apr. 1897	28, Feb.	79	207		St. Paul, MN	Langtafel, Nauerdt, Pommern
Matthern, Katharina	18, Aug. 1859	2, Aug.	37	132		New Albany, IN	Eltmann, Baiern
Matthews, Gottlieb	23, Nov. 1885	7, Nov.	63- 5m- 9d	7		Menominee, MI	Radun, Preußen
Matthews, Heinrich	14, July 1884	29, June	17	7		Menomonie, WI	

Christliche Apologete Death Notices --- 1839 - 1899

Name of Deceased	Notice Date	Death Date	Age	Maiden Name	Page	Place of Death	Place of Birth
Matusch, Karl Conrad	16, Apr. 1891	23, Mar.	63		254	Redfield, SD	Arnswalde, Frankfurt an der Oder, Preußen
Matz, Anna Maria	29, May 1876	10, May	47- 6m- 6d	Harmeier	175	Portsmouth, OH	Stribe, Wittlage, Osnabrück, Hannover
Mätz, Georg	20, July 1854	1, July	33		116	St. Louis, MO	Kehl, Baden
Matzate, Waldemar Wm. Daniel	5, July 1888	16, June	27		430	Brenham, TX	Berlin, Preußen
Matzen, Abelohm	31, Jan. 1881	1, Jan.	48		39	Cedar Lake, IN	Sophienhau, Hohne, Schleswig
Matzinger, Joseph	1, Apr. 1872	12, Mar.	30-11m-30d		111	Toledo, OH	Schaffhausen, Schweiz
Matzke, Ernestine	10, Feb. 1873	15, Jan.	48	Paul	47	Wausau, WI	Dolfersbruch, Marienwalde, Preußen
Mau, Caroline	9, May 1895	8, Apr.	67	Walter	302	Lena, IL	Succow an der Ina, Saatzig, Pommern
Mau, Christian Friedrich	4, July 1881	11, June	79		215	Watertown, WI	Collin bei Stargart, Pommern
Mau, David	7, Apr. 1884	9, Jan.	60		7	Freeport, IL	Schwanenbeck, Zachan, Saatzig, Pommern
Mau, Maria	13, Apr. 1899	13, Mar.	72	Tietzer	239	Marine City, MI	Treptow, Pommern
Mauck, Dorothea	6, Mar. 1890	10, Feb.	33-10m-18d	Gagel	158	Louisville, KY	
Mauer, Marie Elisabeth	21, Oct. 1897	26, Sept	76	Roth	671	Stitzer, WI	Sachsen-Meiningen
Mauk, Herman	11, Feb. 1878	28, Jan.	41		47	Milwaukee, WI	Greifenberg, Pommern
Mauken, Anna	12, Nov. 1847	7, Sept	20		183	New Orleans, LA	
Maul , Magdalena	11, Oct. 1860	14, Sept	40- 4m-26d	Claus	164	Portsmouth, OH	Westheim, Baiern
Maul, Adolph	20, Sept 1869	3, Sept	23		303	St. Louis, MO	
Maul, Anna Elisabeth	7, Oct. 1872	6, Sept	71-10m- 6d	Eckhart	327	Washington, IL	Niedernaula, Kreis Hersfeld, Kurhessen
Maul, Conrad	22, Jan. 1891	3, Jan.	91- 6m- 3d		62	Peoria, IL	Hilberhausen, Hirsfled, Kurhessen
Maul, Heinrich	20, Apr. 1885	29, Mar.	40		7	Chillicothe, OH	Chillicothe, Ross County, Ohio
Maul, John	16, Jan. 1890	24, Dec.	56- 3m-24d		46	Portsmouth, OH	Albersheim an der Brim, Rheinkreis Baiern
Maul, Margaretha	9, Aug. 1855	29, July	61		128	Portsmouth, OH	Albisheim an der Pfrimm, Rheinpfalz Baiern
Maul, Martin	27, July 1893	23, June	79- 5m- 9d		478	Newport, KY	Albisheim, Baiern
Mäule, Christoph	4, Mar. 1886	17, Feb.	85		7	St. Philip, IN	Au, Baden
Mäule, Gottfried	21, Apr. 1884	21, Mar.	77		7	Jamestown, MO	Aue bei Durlach, Baden
Maule, Othilde	22, June 1899	21, May	64	Warschko	399	Portsmouth, OH	Oppau, Rheinpfalz Baiern
Mauler, Heinrich	28, June 1860	9, June	23		104	Jacksonville, IL	Hunawilu, Oberrhein, Colmar, Frankreich
Maull, Carl Ludwig	5, Aug. 1897	22, July	54		495	St. Louis, MO	Nohfelden, Berkenfeld, RheinPreußen
Maunter, Katharine	11, Feb. 1892	11, Jan.	52		94	Madison Lake, MN	Bomberg, Kurhessen
Maurer, (Mrs)	7, June 1869	23, May	36	Reck	183	Brooklyn, NY	Kurhessen
Maurer, Anna Maria	22, Dec. 1879	30, Nov.	43	Schmidt	407	Marrs, IN	Pennsylvania
Maurer, Babette	11, Mar. 1897	17, Feb.	38		159	St. Louis, MO	Schweiz
Maurer, Benjamin	14, June 1880	31, May	45		191	New Orleans, LA	New Orleans, Louisiana
Maurer, Edwin	5, July 1888	3, June	23		430	Great Bend, KS	Pike County, Illinois
Maurer, Elisabeth	24, July 1890	21, June	30-10m-15d	Brechtelsbauer	478	Saginaw, MI	Saginaw, Michigan
Maurer, Elisabeth Margaretha	11, Mar. 1897	12, Dec.	75	Rost	159	Green Bay, WI	Soxmeining an der Saale, Germany
Maurer, Friederike	16, May 1895	20, Apr.	72	Hammer	318	Elizabeth, NJ	Künzelau, Württemberg
Maurer, Georg	29, Oct. 1896	8, Oct.	72		703	Elkton, SD	Schwabsburg, Hessen-Darmstadt
Maurer, Georg	23, Feb. 1893	30, Jan.	18- 1m-11d		126	Green Bay, WI	
Maurer, John	19, Oct. 1863	4, Sept	38		168	Lancaster, WI	Nordheim, Sachsen-Meiningen
Maurer, Kathrine	19, Aug. 1897	21, July	78	Oswald	527	New Orleans, LA	Baiern
Maurer, Leonhart	12, Nov. 1841	20, Aug.			179	New Orleans, LA	
Maurer, Ursula	30, Nov. 1863	27, Aug.	60		192	Calhoun, IL	Ottenheim bei Lahr, Baden
Maurer, Wilhelm Heinrich August	25, Aug. 1892	2, Aug.	22		542	Perrysburg, OH	Brooklyn, New York
Maurer, Wilhelmine Louise	18, May 1863	22, Apr.	18	Beker	80	Calhoun, IL	Chillicothe, Ohio
Maurin, Elisabeth	7, Dec. 1885	20, Oct.	63	Großkopf	7	Ft. Hunter, NY	Unterschwarzen, Baden

Christliche Apologete Death Notices --- 1839 - 1899

Name of Deceased	Notice Date	Death Date	Age	Page	Maiden Name	Place of Death	Place of Birth
Maus, Caroline	18, Oct. 1880	28, Sept	43	335		New Orleans, LA	Frankenhausen, Nordhausen, Sachsen
Maus, Margaretha	28, Sept 1863	2, Aug.	37-2m-16d	156	Seibert		Münchhof, Hochspeier, Baiern
Maus, Wilhelm	9, June 1859	29, Apr.	9- -11d	92			
Mausehund, Andreas	22, Jan. 1883	4, Jan.	50-1m-25d	31		St. Louis, MO	Seifertshausen, Rothenburg, Kurhessen
Mausehund, Catharina	27, Nov. 1882	2, Nov.	52-5m-13d	383	Sippel	St. Louis, MO	Königswald, Kurhessen
Mausehund, Heinrich	28, June 1888	27, May	49-6m-3d	414		St. Louis, MO	Seifertshausen, Rotenburg, Kurhessen
Mausehund, Johannes	24, Sept 1878	28, Aug.	52-10m-12d	303		St. Louis, MO	Seifertshausen, Rotenburg, Kurhessen
Mausehund, Katharine	14, July 1892	25, June	50	446	Berge	St. Louis, MO	Seifertshausen, Kurhessen
Maußen, Johan Heie	5, Nov. 1896	13, Oct.	43	719		Waltersburg, IL	Plaggenburg, Aurich, Hannover
Maußhardt, Johanna	16, Oct. 1871	2, Oct.	34	335	Heitlinger	Pinckneyville, IL	Rohrbach, Amt Eppingen, Baden
Maute, Barbara	16, Nov. 1885	4, Nov.	30-3m-16d	7		Pittsburg, PA	Pfäffingen, Balingen, Württemberg
Maute, Christian	18, May 1899	20, Apr.	38	319	Eisele	Chicago, IL	Petersdorf, Schleswig-Holstein
Mauth, Eva Barbara	3, Sept 1883	31, July	48-1m	287	Herr	Hartford, CT	Marolds-Weißbach, Ebern, Baiern
Mautner, Katharine	23, Dec. 1878	1, Dec.	74-7m-6d	407		Sleepy Eye, MN	Millefels, Baiern
Maves, Dalbert	11, Aug. 1892	23, July	17	510		Freeport, IL	Iowa
Maxeiner, Katharina	4, Mar. 1897	11, Feb.	57	143	Krämer	Nokomis, IL	Kaßdorf, Nassau
May , Philipp P.	2, Mar. 1899	14, Jan.	73	143		Walnut, KS	Nassau
May, Elisabeth	12, Dec. 1864	15, Oct.	29	200	Kaiser	Brunswick, MO	Leutzingen, Bern, Schweiz
May, Elisabeth Christina	17, Feb. 1898	14, Jan.	75	111	Groß	Quincy, IL	Mihlen, Nagstätten, Nassau
May, Heinrich	19, Dec. 1895	14, Nov.	66	814		Ft. Atkinson, WI	Waldien, Baden
May, Heinrich Leopold	3, Jan. 1881	20, Dec.	53	7		Dalton, MO	Wehrheim, Usingen, Nassau
May, Jennie Susanna	13, Oct. 1898	3, Aug.	24	655		Cannelton, IN	
Maybach, Magdalena Katharina	14, Jan. 1886	21, Dec.	68	7	Hoffmann	Quincy, IL	Gelding, Halle, Württemberg
Maybach, Michael	21, Nov. 1889	24, Oct.	68	750		Quincy, IL	Selz, Württemberg
Mayer, Albert	13, Feb. 1896	23, Jan.	54	110		Kansas City, KS	Leonberg, Württemberg
Mayer, Barbara	21, July 1859	7, June	79-8m-22d	116		Canal Dover, OH	Canton Bern, Schweiz
Mayer, Carolina	28, Nov. 1881	20, Oct.	75	383		Industry, TX	Westerwald, Schaumburg, Kurhessen
Mayer, Catharina	21, July 1862	18, June	64	116		Ann Arbor, MI	Nufringen, Herrenberg, Württemberg
Mayer, Emily Margaretha Lisette	12, July 1894	8, June	24	454		New York City, NY	
Mayer, Emma	7, Jan. 1886	19, Nov.	17-6m-19d	7		Marion, OH	
Mayer, Georg J.	5, Jan. 1893	7, Dec.	21	14		Hebron, IA	Hebron , Iowa
Mayer, Henry	24, Aug. 1868	23, July	18	271		Oregon, MO	Quincy, Illinois
Mayer, Isaak	14, Apr. 1873	26, Mar.	31-1m-20d	119		Marion, OH	
Mayer, Jakob	17, Aug. 1868	21, July	72	263		Broken Sword, NY	Leutenbach, Waiblingen, Württemberg
Mayer, Jakob	24, July 1846		Inquiry	119		Circleville, OH	Mergentheim, Württemberg
Mayer, Johann Christian	31, Aug. 1863	15, June	24	140		Bucyrus, OH	Leidenbach, Waiblingen, Württemberg
Mayer, Johanna Sophia Caroline	4, Sept 1882		54	287	Cinram	Valparaiso, IN	Latfert, Hannover
Mayer, John	13, June 1895	26, May	26	382		Marietta, OH	Fearing Twp, Washington County, Ohio
Mayer, John A.	16, Feb. 1899	17, Jan.	71	111		Minneapolis, MN	Nierstein, Hessen-Darmstadt
Mayer, Jürchen	28, June 1860	9, May	48	104		Chester, IL	Dänschendorf, Insel Fehmarn, Dänemark
Mayer, Karl Friedrich	1, May 1890	12, Apr.	64-8m-29d	286		Marion, OH	Nöttingen, Pforzheim, Baden
Mayer, Katharina	7, July 1879	22, June	29	215	Pausch	Poughkeepsie, NY	Baiern
Mayer, Konrad	24, Nov. 1879	26, Oct.	59	375		Peoria, IL	Aasen, Donaueschingen, Baden
Mayer, Lena	7, Jan. 1886	8, Dec.	27-1m-4d	7		Marion, OH	
Mayer, Luise	14, Aug. 1840	7, Aug.	5m-4d	127			
Mayer, Magdalena	31, Mar. 1873	13, Mar.	37	103	Michel	Goshen, IN	Kanton Bern, Schweiz

Christliche Apologete Death Notices --- 1839 - 1899

Name of Deceased	Notice Date	Death Date	Age	Maiden Name	Page	Place of Death	Place of Birth
Mayer, Margaretha	21, June 1869	7, June	62	Hilbert	199	Buffalo, NY	Freinsheim, Rheinkreis Baiern
Mayer, Margaretha	26, July 1849	11, July	32		120	St. Louis, MO	
Mayer, Maria	9, June 1879		58- 3m-29d		183	Marshall, IL	Elmendingen, Pforzheim, Baden
Mayer, Matthias	12, Mar. 1866	23, Jan.	21		86	Buffalo, NY	Erie County, New York
Mayer, Rosine	5, Nov. 1891	17, Oct.	42	Rudel	718	Waconda, SD	
Mayer, Susanna	20, Feb. 1882	4, Feb.	43- 1m- 4d		63	Hoboken, NJ	Nowgorod, Rußland
Mayer, Willie	7, Jan. 1886	12, Dec.	20- 2m- 8d		7	Marion, OH	
Mayers, Anna Maria	5, Sept 1864	15, Aug.	26- 7m- 2d	Becker	144	Boonville, IN	Sandusky County, Ohio
Mayforth, Valentin	19, Oct. 1874	29, Sept	60		335	Jersey City, NJ	Madelungen, Sachsen-Weimar
Maynard, August	18, Mar. 1897	27, Feb.	80		175	Bay City, MI	Sachsen
Mayor, Philipp	7, Nov. 1870	20, Oct.	79		359	Louisville, KY	Rommelhausen, Hessen-Darmstadt
McBride, Laura	13, Jan. 1887	25, Dec.	25	Weidmann	30	Pomeroy, OH	Indianapolis, Marion County, Indiana
McCarrel, Maria Rosina	26, Nov. 1891	25, Oct.	66	Weidner	766	Brighton, IL	Zickera, Sachsen-Weimar
McCrimmon, Mathilde F.	8, July 1886	8, June	29	Klippel	7	Portland, OR	Springfield, Illinois
McVaughton, Henriette	12, June 1890	28, May	33- 9m-10d	Kaspohl	382	Crow River, MN	St. Paul, Minnesota
Mechau, Helena	14, Dec. 1885	24, Nov.	53	Breuer	7	White Cloud, KS	Bronsfeld, Schleiden, Aachen, Preußen
Mechler, Anna Maria	17, Dec. 1896	12, Nov.	63		814	Toledo, OH	Luzern, Schweiz
Meck, Joseph	11, Apr. 1895	11, Mar.	76- 3m		238	New York City, NY	Baiern
Mecke, Minna	4, June 1896	26, Apr.	23		367	Burlington, IA	Wiedlingsweil, Freudenstadt, Württemberg
Meckel, Maria	24, Apr. 1890		51	Kuchler	270	Cincinnati, OH	Dänemark
Meckelson, Christian	31, Oct. 1889	7, Oct.	48- 5m- 9d		702	Burlington, IA	Knoxville, Ohio
Meckstroht, Ernst August	20, Mar. 1890	21, Feb.	42- 1m-29d		190	Le Sueur, MN	Ladbergen, Tecklenburg, Preußen
Meckstroth, Anna C.	19, Apr. 1880	3, Apr.	65		127	Le Sueur, MN	Hillersheim, Trier, Preußen
Meckstroth, Clara	14, Apr. 1879	6, Mar.	37	Hohm	119	Le Sueur, MN	
Meckstroth, H.H.	12, Apr. 1888	22, Mar.	43- 8m- 5d		238	Le Sueur, MN	Auglaize County, Ohio
Meckstroth, Heinrich	29, Dec. 1884	19, Nov.	43		7	New Knoxville, OH	New Knoxville, Auglaize County, Ohio
Meckstroth, Herman	20, Nov. 1871	3, Nov.	25- 1m-23d		375	New Knoxville, OH	
Meckstroth, Sophia Wilhelmine	1, Nov. 1880	12, Oct.	40- 2m-24d	Drenker	351	New Knoxville, OH	Minden, Preußen
Medaus, Joseph	31, May 1869		35- 4m- 5d		175	Effingham, IL	Milback, Mecklenburg-Schwerin
Meecker, Elisabeth	8, May 1890	18, Apr.	39- 4m-11d	Lapp	302	Clarington, OH	Monroe County, Ohio
Mees, Christina	25, Sept 1871	1, Aug.	63		311	Chillicothe, OH	Niederlustadt, Rheinpfalz Baiern
Mees, Christina	16, Oct. 1871	1, Aug.	63	Mulder	335	Chillicothe, OH	Niederlustadt, Rheinpfalz Baiern
Mees, Niklaus	24, May 1894	2, May	71		342	Rockford, IA	Altenstein, Baiern
Meese, Wilhelmine	4, Aug. 1873		80		247	Quincy, IL	Schötmar, Lippe-Detmold
Meeß, Maria Juliana	17, Mar.1873	22, Feb.	53- 7m- 3d	Hoffmann	87	Flood Creek, IA	Elpersheim, Mergentheim, Württemberg
Meetz, Friedrich	15, Nov. 1894	24, Oct.	77		742	Davenport, IA	Süsel, Holstein
Meetz, Sophia Elise	1, Mar. 1894	31, Jan.	72	Megebier	150	Davenport, IA	Winterhagen, Holstein
Mehl, A.	1, Dec. 1898	7, Nov.	70		767	Pittsfield, IL	Bosolshausen, Elsaß
Mehl, Elisabeth	9, Mar. 1885	17, Feb.	58		7	Pittsfield, IL	Rhumbach, Rheinpfalz Baiern
Mehl, Elisabeth	14,May 1883	17, Apr.	70-10m-12d	Roth	159	Clarington, OH	Ober-Sulzbach, Elsaß
Mehl, Georg	23, Sept 1872	23, Aug.	78- - 9d		311	Mt. Vernon, IN	Bußweiler bei Straßburg, Elsaß
Mehl, Georg	5, June 1865	20, Jan.	30- 3m-20d		92	Clarington, OH	Imsheim, Elsaß
Mehl, Georg	19, May 1884	1, May	81		7	Clarington, OH	Imsheim, Elsaß
Mehl, Maria	11, Jan. 1864	13, Dec.	73- 9m		8	Washington, OH	Urweiler, Ober-Elsaß, Frankreich
Mehl, Maria	3, Feb. 1887	14, Jan.	68	Domin	78	Cibolo, TX	Lazann, Pommern
Mehlbach, Bernhard	17, May 1894	30, Apr.	75		326	Dayton, OH	Mardorf, Hamberg, Kurhessen

Christliche Apologete Death Notices --- 1839 - 1899

Name of Deceased	Notice Date	Death Date	Age	Page	Maiden Name	Place of Death	Place of Birth
Mehler, Catharina	24, Nov. 1862	29, Sept	52	188	Linn	Birmingham, PA	Reifelbach, Cusel, Rheinkreis Baiern
Mehne, Georg	14, Dec. 1885	23, Nov.	28	7		Almond, WI	Eckartsweier, Kork, Baden
Mehnert, Reinhart	9, Feb. 1888	9, Jan.	23	94		Bay City, MI	St. Clair County, Michigan
Mehrhof, Carolina Maria	11, Oct. 1888	23, Sept	65	654		Cider Grove, MO	Nord Hemmern, Hannover
Mehrhoff, Heinrich	7, July 1898	13, June	81	431		Senate Grove, MO	Hemmern, Preußen
Mehrstedt, Dorothea	26, Feb. 1852	29, Jan.	32- 8m-28d	36		Quincy, IL	Mühlhausen, Preußen
Meichle, Theresa	1, July 1897	10, June	68	414	Gies	West Bend, WI	Dittesfeld, Rheinkreis Baiern
Meider, Barbara	8, Aug. 1861	8, July	67	128		Ripley, OH	Zeiskam, Germersheim, Baiern
Meidinger, Christine	1, May 1882	3, Apr.	70	143	Kohler	Wathena, KS	Dürrenzimmern, Brackenheim, Württemberg
Meidinger, Johan Friedrich	13, Sept 1894	28, Aug.	89- - 8d	598		Wathena, KS	Neuberg, Brackenheim, Württemberg
Meidinger, Ottillia	30, Nov. 1885	12, Nov.	16	7		Walthena, KS	
Meier, (Mrs)	15, Jan. 1891	19, Dec.	102-8m-10d	46	Westermann	Lemars, IA	Fererl, Stiekhausen, Ostfriesland
Meier, (Mrs)	9, June 1898		87	367		New Ulm, MN	Hannover
Meier, Adam	19, July 1869	2, July	45	231		Defiance, OH	Lehnsweiler, Landau, Rheinkreis Baiern
Meier, Adam	1, May 1876	8, Apr.	73- 5m	143		Bucyrus, OH	Schornbach, Schorndorf, Württemberg
Meier, Anna	30, Sept 1878	18, Sept	66	311	Rieder	Blue Island, IL	Rothenfluh, Baselland, Schweiz
Meier, Anna	30, Jan. 1896	5, Jan.	75	78	Wylenmann	Paterson, NJ	Wyla, Zürich, Schweiz
Meier, Anna Friedrike	24, Feb. 1879	9, Feb.	22	63	Witthaus	Morrison, MO	Warren County, Missouri
Meier, Anna Maria	20, Mar. 1865	1, Mar.	66- 5m	48	Warmbrod	Defiance, OH	Niedersteinmauer, Zürich, Schweiz
Meier, Anna Maria	20, Nov. 1871	26, Sept	84	375		St. Louis, MO	Kanton Zürich, Schweiz
Meier, Anton	17, Nov. 1884	30, Oct.	37- 2m-23d	7		Ann Arbor, MI	Hart am Bodensee, Oesterreich
Meier, Barbara	5, Feb. 1857	18, Jan.	24	24	Ochs	Chicago, IL	Arnsbach, Homberg, Hessen-Kassel
Meier, C.	19, July 1888	21, June	77	462		St. Louis, MO	Preußen
Meier, Charles Friedrich	27, Jan. 1879	12, Jan.	17	31		Sandwich, IL	Baraboo, Wisconsin
Meier, Christian	26, May 1853	28, Mar.	61	84			Nordhämmern bei Münden, Preußen
Meier, Christian	25, Nov. 1878	20, Oct.	70	375		Sherrills Mount, IA	
Meier, Christine	15, Sept 1884	29, Aug.	69	7	Bleidorn	Junction City, KS	Minderheide, Minden, Preußen
Meier, Christine	20, Mar. 1882	4, Mar.	44	95	Bitter	--, IL	Holtum, Hannover
Meier, Dietrich	13, Aug. 1883	26, July	67- 1m- 1d	263		Muscatine, IA	Drachenburg, Nienburg, Hannover
Meier, Dietrich Heinrich Wilhelm	1, June 1874	9, May	21	175		Concordia, MO	Krumbach, Hessen
Meier, Dorothea	26, Mar. 1866	23, Jan.	27-10m-11d	102		Shakopee, MN	Vitschu, Mecklenburg-Schwerin
Meier, Elise	31, July 1876	17, July	22- 7m	247	Hoffmann	Galena, IL	Ersan, Schötmer, Lippe-Detmold
Meier, Friederike	20, Dec. 1875	1, Dec.	75	407		Bay City, MI	Grabiana, Wirsitz, Preußen
Meier, Friedrich	21, Apr. 1892	12, Feb.	71	254		Columbus, IL	Hasbergen bei Bremen, Germany
Meier, Friedrich Ludwig	13, Jan. 1898	28, Dec.	24	31		Mankato, MN	Scanikow, Zürich, Schweiz
Meier, Gesina	19, July 1860	3, July	45	116	Wittenberg	Cincinnati, OH	Fürstensee, Kreis Pyritzer, Preußen
Meier, Gustav	29, Oct. 1896	7, Oct.	52	703		Medford, OK	Ripley County, Indiana
Meier, H.	16, Dec. 1867	7, Nov.	19- 7m- 2d	398		Columbus, WI	Ripley County, Indiana
Meier, Heinrich	5, Jan. 1874	27, Nov.	17- 3m-21d	7		Batesville, IN	Stolpe, Köslin, Hinterpommern
Meier, Jane	5, Jan. 1874	1, Dec.	52- -26d	7		Batesville, IN	Randolph County, Illinois
Meier, Johan	7, Apr. 1879	21, Mar.	42	111		Clayton, IA	Reichenbach, Heppenheim, Hessen
Meier, Johan	21, May 1896	24, Mar.	14	334		Chester, IL	Hannover
Meier, Johan	24, Feb. 1879	7, Feb.	53	63		Blue Island, IL	Dörnberg, Preußen
Meier, Johann	20, Apr. 1863	10, Mar.	54	64		Highland, IL	
Meier, Johann H.C.	3, Dec. 1847	28, July	30	195		Perry County, MO	
Meier, Johanna Friederika	4, Feb. 1867	25, Nov.		38	Schulze	Junction City, KS	

Christliche Apologete Death Notices --- 1839 - 1899

Name of Deceased	Notice Date	Death Date	Age	Page	Maiden Name	Place of Death	Place of Birth
Meier, Johanna Friederike	19, Jan. 1888	13, Dec.	73- 6m- 3d	46		Columbus, IL	Ersan, Schötmer, Lippe-Detmold
Meier, Karolina	16, Jan. 1871	30, Dec.	78- 4m-14d	23	Bährens	Cincinnati, OH	Erichshagen bei Nienburg, Hannover
Meier, Katharina	3, Nov. 1898	15, Oct.	67	703	Köcher	St. Paul, MN	Nothurm, Minden, Preußen
Meier, Katharine	10, June 1886	21, May	71	7	Schwalm	Cannelton, IN	Riebelsdorf, Kurhessen
Meier, Lena	14, June 1860	12, May	39- 3m	96		Dayton, OH	Mahndorf, Braunschweig
Meier, Louis Josef	2, Nov. 1885	16, Oct.		7		Nashville, IL	North Prairie,
Meier, Louise	24, Apr. 1856	4, Apr.	37	68	Müller	Furnace, OH	Mölschbacher, Wattweiler, Rheinkreis Baiern
Meier, Louise	14, Feb. 1870	21, Nov.	76	55		Schnectady, NY	Minden, Preußen
Meier, Louise	17, Sept 1866	2, Sept		302		Batesville, OH	
Meier, Ludwig Ernst	25, June 1891	3, June	57	414		Giard, IA	Köslin, Pommern
Meier, Lydia	12, Nov. 1891	22, Oct.	30	734	Schneider	Waco, TX	Indianapolis, Marion County, Indiana
Meier, Magdalena	13, Aug. 1883	19, July	57	263		St. Louis, MO	Altenheim, Baden
Meier, Maria	11, Feb. 1878	24, Jan.	53- 7m-16d	47		Goshen, IN	Enderingen, Herrenberg, Württemberg
Meier, Maria	27, Apr. 1885		51	7	Kalthoff	Hopewell, MO	Braunfels, Coblenz, Preußen
Meier, Maria	31, May 1894	6, May	33	358	Cohen	Perry, TX	Castellet County, Missouri
Meier, Maria Louisa	23, Mar. 1893	14, Feb.	81- 2m	190	Degen	Nerstrand, MN	Gerstheim, Elsaß
Meier, Marie Elisabeth	4, Aug. 1898	4, Apr.	50	495	Horstmann	Schnectady, NY	Nord-Haman, Minden, Preußen
Meier, Mary	24, Feb. 1873	29, Jan.	19	63	Klöpper	Batesville, IN	Indiana
Meier, Peter H.	28, June 1880	26, May	70- 4m-15d	207		Holton, KS	Rotenburg, Hannover
Meier, Susanne	2, Feb. 1899	10, Jan.	73	79	DeWein	Boonville, IN	Nieder-Horenbach, Rheinpfalz Baiern
Meier, Wilhelm	4, May 1899	7, Apr.	80	287		Decorah, IA	Engelsheim, Württemberg
Meier, Wilhelm	23, Feb. 1863		23	32		Greencastle, IN	Braunschweig
Meier, Wilhelm	26, Mar. 1866		17	102		Shakopee, MN	
Meier, Wilhelmine	16, Nov. 1863	24, Sept	34	184	Rühl	Baltimore, MD	Großbeeren, Preußen
Meier, Wilhelmine	3, Feb. 1853	4, Jan.	37- 6m	20		St. Louis, MO	
Meier, Zacharias	6, Mar. 1851	28, Jan.	51	40		Lexington, MO	Drüber, Amt Einbeck, Hannover
Meierbachtol, Charlotte	21, Feb. 1881	4, Feb.	40	63		Le Sueur, MN	Bövörde, Polle, Hannover
Meierbick, Anna Barbara	26, Mar. 1866	22, Feb.	40	102	Fick	Valley, IA	Delau, Baiern
Meierdierk, Bernhard H.	13, June 1861	27, May	20	96		German Creek, IA	Fehr bei Vegesack, Hannover
Meierding, (son)	7, Nov. 1881		13- 1m-25d	359		New Ulm, MN	
Meierdirks, Heinrich	23, May 1850	5, Apr.		84		German Creek, IA	Hannover
Meierhofer, Rosa	30, Apr. 1891	3, Apr.	20	286	Ewald	Toledo, OH	Zachinzin, Lauenburg, Hinterpommern
Meierkort, W.	30, May 1881	22, Jan.	52	175		Warren, MO	Stemmern, Lippe-Detmold
Meiers, Christoph	24, Feb. 1879	5, Jan.	78	63		Flint Creek, IA	Westerop, Amt Raden, Preußen
Meiers, Maria	31, May 1880	30, Mar.	70	175	Unland	Dodgeville, IA	Raber, Amt Wittlage, Hannover
Meim, Katharina	17, Jan. 1876	28, Dec.	73	23	Schnarenberger	Bucyrus, OH	Leutenbach, Waiblingen, Württemberg
Meincke, Maria	26, Jan. 1888	3, Jan.	78	62	Wiegers	Red Wing, MN	Neu-Kloster, Hannover
Meincke, Mary	18, May 1863	27, Apr.	28- 2m	80	Detje	Red Wing, MN	Nottensdorf, Amt Horneburg, Hannover
Meinders, George J.	8, Sept 1898	3, Aug.	25- 5m-19d	575		Piqua, OH	
Meine, Anton	13, Nov. 1865	18, Oct.	55	184		Warren, MO	Lippe
Meine, Heinrich	10, July 1865	15, Apr.	23	112		Warrenton, MO	Meiersberg, Lippe-Detmold
Meine, Karolina	9, July1883	20, June	70	223	Fieth	Warren, MO	Minden, Preußen
Meine, Louise	19, Mar. 1866	24, Feb.	23	94		Lawrence, KS	Federwarden, Oldenburg
Meinecke, Friedrich August	27, Nov. 1890	2, Nov.	62	766		Bunker Hill, IL	
Meinen, Elke	23, Jan. 1875	2, Jan.	32- 4m-11d	31		Pekin, IL	Strackholt, Ostfriesland
Meinen, Epke	19, Mar. 1883	1, Feb.	42	95		Pekin, IL	

Christliche Apologete Death Notices --- 1839 - 1899

Name of Deceased	Notice Date	Death Date	Age	Page	Maiden Name	Place of Death	Place of Birth
Meinhard, Maria	2, Apr. 1877	21, Mar.	73	111		Toledo, OH	Winterstadt, Hessen-Darmstadt
Meinhart, Philipp	9, Mar. 1863	8, Jan.	22	40		Toledo, OH	Weiterstadt, Hessen-Darmstadt
Meining, Sophia	18, Sept 1890	9, Aug.	83- 7m- 2d	606	Gottschalk	Laporte, IN	Titzpatz, Demin, Preußen
Meinke, Peter	1, Sept 1884	15, Aug.	74	7		Red Wing, MN	Nuttensdorf, Hannover
Meinzer, Barbara	21, Nov. 1895	1, Nov.	70	750	Schäfer	Nokomis, IL	Brikenweisbach, Württemberg
Meinzer, Emma Virginia	9, Oct. 1876	19, Sept	58	327	Lang	Pittsburg, PA	Graben, Karlsruhe, Baden
Meinzer, Johan	8, Apr. 1897	21, Mar.	72	223		Nokomis, IL	Hochstetten, Karlsruhe, Baden
Meinzer, Katharina	27, Nov. 1882	7, Nov.	72- 6m-22d	383	Leyse	Austin, TX	Albesheim,
Meinzer, Margaretha	1, June 1874	21, Apr.	76- 5m	175		Greenfield, WI	Deutsch-Neureit bei Karlsruhe, Germany
Meinzer, Philipp	27, Sept 1894	25, Aug.	77	630		Austin, TX	
Meisch, Emma E.	16, Aug. 1894	12, July	39- 1m-17d	534		Ballwin, MO	Herfurth, Preußen
Meise, Friedrich Wilhelm	14, Nov. 1870	27, Oct.	79- 4m	367		Quincy, IL	Lockhausen, Schöttmar, Lippe-Detmold
Meise, Hanna Charlotte	28, May 1877	23, Apr.	42- 4m-29d	175	Hollmann	Union, MO	Emmenhausen, Lippe-Detmold
Meise, Wilhelmine	12, Feb. 1883	29, Jan.	31- 4m-13d	55	Niemann	Beaufort, MO	Lockhausen, Amt Schödmer, Lippe
Meisen, F.W.L.	23, June 1848		Inquiry	103		Quincy, IL	Basel, Schweiz
Meisenheimer, Francis	21, Sept 1868	12, Aug.	41	303	Wunderlich	Wathena, KS	
Meisenheimer, Wilhelm	7, Jan. 1892	30, Nov.	37- 5m	14		Brighton, IL	
Meiser, Adam	13, Feb. 1890	25, Jan.	85	110		Oregon, MO	
Meiser, Georg	16, Feb. 1863	1, Jan.	25	28		Bellville, IL	
Meiser, Louise Johanna	19, Sept 1889	27, Aug.	48	606	Dickhut	Quincy, IL	Quincy, Illinois
Meissenheimer, Phil	12, June 1871	11, May	67- 1m-28d	191		Alton, IL	Gensungen, Bingen, Hessen-Darmstadt
Meißer, Katharina B.	31, Aug. 1868	12, Aug.	33	279	Dickhut	Quincy, IL	
Meißner, Anna Margaretha	19, July 1888	1, June	66	462		Redfield, SD	Treffort, Mühlhausen, Erfurt, Preußen
Meißner, Carl Heinrich	19, Jan. 1893	24, Dec.	80	46		Lawrence, MA	Langenwetzendorf, Reuß
Meißner, Christine Herm.	21, Jan. 1897	5, Dec.	54	47	Lippold	Milwaukee, WI	Frauenrath bei Werden, Sachsen
Meister, Anna Katharina	11, July 1881	20, June	78- 1m-20d	223	Fuhrmann	Louisville, KY	Oberfranken, Baiern
Meister, Johan Leonhard	28, Apr. 1887	7, Mar.	83	270		Louisville, KY	Haag bei Beyreuth, Baiern
Meitzner, Maria	3, Mar. 1887	17, Feb.	26	142	Peters	Brillion, WI	Waukesha, Wisconsin
Meixner, Franz	31, July 1871	10, July	76	247		Madison, WI	Tattenitz, Hohenstadt, Olmütz, Oesterreich
Meixner, Joseph	16, May 1861	25, Apr.	25	80		Columbus, WI	Tattenitz, Oesterreich
Meixner, Rosalie	11, Nov. 1886	12, Oct.	82	7	Fränzel	Sun Prairie, WI	Tattenitz, Hohenstadt, Mähren, Oesterreich
Mekstroh, Herman Heinrich	13, Jan. 1898	6, Dec.	85	31		Le Seuer, MN	Ladbergen, Tecklenburg, Preußen
Melbourn, Helena Elisabeth	21, Sept 1868	15, July	33- 9m	303	Rose	San Francisco, CA	Riga, Rußland
Melcher, Bertha	10, Apr. 1876	6, Mar.	24	118		Milwaukee, WI	
Melcher, Christine	27, June 1895	4, June	47	414	Winkler	Bushnell, IL	Zusenhausen, Baden
Melcher, Georg	22, July 1897		86-10m-23d	463		Mankato, MN	Altrüdnitz, Brandenburg
Melcher, Sylvanus G.	22, Mar. 1894	1, Mar.	24	198		Charles City, IA	Floyd County, Iowa
Melchior, Charlotte Henriette S.	21, Oct. 1867	12, Sept	65- 6m-10d	334	Schulze	New Haven, CT	Schlesien
Melis, Gottfried John	27, Jan. 1873	11, Jan.	75-11m	31		Bonn, OH	Dennstedt, Erfurt, Langensalza, Preußen
Melkersmann, Rudolph	18, Feb. 1878	2, Feb.	52	55		Boonville, MO	Mella, Hannover
Melkesmann, Caroline	4, May 1854	8, Feb.	54	72		St. Charles, MO	Dilingdorf, Hannover
Melkesmann, Friedrich	4, May 1854	10, Feb.	54	72		St. Charles, MO	Dilingdorf, Hannover
Mell, Dorothea	23, Oct. 1882	2, Oct.	72- -27d	343	Glitzing	Chicago, IL	Großbelow, Anklam, Preußen
Mell, Emilie Friedrieke	18, Jan. 1869	27, Dec.	22- 2m-21d	23	Frey	Chicago, IL	
Menchow, Sybille	14, Apr. 1862	23, Mar.	46	60	Tendick	Jacksonville, IL	
Menewisch, Hermann H.	26, July 1849	4, July		120		St. Louis, MO	Blüyn, Kreis Moers, Düsseldorf, Preußen

Christliche Apologete Death Notices -- 1839 - 1899

Name of Deceased	Notice Date	Death Date	Age	Page	Maiden Name	Place of Death	Place of Birth
Meng, Ernestine	21, June 1869	25, May	23	199	Gummig	Columbus, KS	Breslau, Preußen
Menge, Adolph	28, Jan. 1886	12, Jan.	65	7		Elizabeth, NJ	Hagen, Lippe-Schaumburg
Menge, Christine	28, Dec. 1899	17, Nov.	73	828	Rudolph	Newark, NJ	Waldangelloch, Baden
Menge, Johannette	15, Dec. 1873	10, Oct.	73	399	Kraft	Bonn, OH	Bleichenbach, Amt Ottenberg, Hessen
Mengedod, Ernst & Wilhelmine	13, Sept 1849		Inquiry	147		Victoria, TX	Masbruch, Lippe-Detmold
Mengel, Jakob	4, Apr. 1895	8, Mar.	35	222		Scranton, PA	Ross, Monroe County, Pennsylvania
Mengel, Johannes	12, Jan. 1893	20, Dec.	49	30		Danville, IL	Hachkorn, Marburg, Kurhessen
Mengel, Maria	30, Jan. 1871	20, Dec.	51	39		New York City, NY	Ochshausen bei Kassel, Kurhessen
Mengels, David	5, Jan. 1899	10, Oct.	42	14		Huntsville, KS	Clark County, Missouri
Mengensdorf, Julius	18, Mar. 1886	7, Mar.	52	7		Akron, OH	Wiesloch, Baden
Menger, Adelheid	4, Apr. 1889	16, Mar.	64- 2m-18d	222	Ehlers	Delhi, MI	Westerwisch, Thedighausen, Braunschweig
Menger, Henry Adolph	2, Feb. 1863		3- 2m-10d	20		Holt, MI	
Menger, Jakok	12, Nov. 1896	21, Oct.	76	734		Lawrence, KS	Dittelsheim, Hessen-Darmstadt
Menger, Louise	23, Dec. 1872	21, Nov.	32	415	Eberbach	Lawrence, KS	Philadelphia, Pennsylvania
Menger, Sophia	12, July 1880	3, May	3m	223		Lawrence, KS	
Menger, Wilhelm F. Sigel	2, Feb. 1863	16, Dec.	78	20		Lawrence, KS	
Menges, John	21, Dec. 1893	21, Nov.	85- 7m-14d	814		Stockton, CA	Landau, Baiern
Menk, Anna Elisabeth	30, Aug. 1880	13, July	68	279	Jung	Pittsburg, PA	Liedenscheid, Nassau
Menke, J. Friedrich	24, May 1869	11, Feb.	66	167		Herman, MO	Diebruck, Minden, Preußen
Menke, Johanna Wilhelmine	20, Aug. 1896	27, July	21- 6m- 8d	543	Flehr	Berger, MO	Herfort, Germany
Menkel, Johan	22, Apr. 1897	23, Mar.	33	255		Beardstown, IL	Mühlhausen, Sachsen
Menken, Wilhelmine	4, Nov. 1886	13, Oct.	66- 5m-16d	7	Meyer	Berger, MO	
Mense, Joachim	25, Jan. 1869	19, Dec.	72	31		Melrose, NY	Liessan, Mecklenburg-Schwerin
Mensinaer, Chr.	13, May 1886	27, Apr.	59	7		Pittsburg, PA	Schmie, Württemberg
Mensing, Anna Katharina	9, May 1895	24, Apr.	82	302	Ortbring	Francisco, MI	Grothe bei Buddergen, Hannover
Mensing, Christine	5, Nov. 1891	15, Oct.	79- 8m-25d	718	Niehoff	Cincinnati, OH	Gebhardhagen, Wolfenbüttel, Braunschweig
Mensing, Heinrich	23, June 1892	8, June	76	398		Cincinnati, OH	Hannover City, Hannover
Mensing, Maria	14, Nov. 1889	27, Oct.	28	734		Cincinnati, OH	Bremen, Germany
Mensinger, (Mrs)	18, Apr. 1861	2, Apr.	83	64		Pittsburg, PA	Schniehe, Maulbronn, Württemberg
Mensinger, Caroline	21, July 1887	27, June	56- 7m	462		Pittsburg, PA	
Mental, Johan Heinrich	27, Jan. 1898	4, Jan.	43	63		Elliston, OH	Raboldshausen, Kurhessen
Mentemeyer, Catharina Elisabetha	23, July 1857	30, June	64	120	Milatz	Springfield, IL	Haarlem, Holland
Mentler, Barbara	25, Jan. 1869	25, Dec.	73	31		New York, NY	
Mentz, Adelheid	1, Feb. 1894	18, Jan.	58- 4m-28d	78	Ebeling	Altamont, IL	Webster, Hannover
Mentze, Heinrich Wilhelm	19, Oct. 1899	8, Feb.	61	671		Truxton, MO	Halle, Minden, Preußen
Mentzer, Jacob	7, Aug. 1882	18, July	70	255		Moweaqua, IL	Engenheim, Elsaß
Menz, Johan	18, Sept 1890	4, Aug.	60	606		St. Paul, MN	Fambach, Schmalkalden, Hessen-Kassel
Menz, Margaretha	4, Sept 1865	14, Aug.	27	144		Cannon City, MN	Fambach, Kurhessen
Menzemer, Christoph	26, Dec. 1889	6, Dec.	71	830		Allegheny City, PA	Gondelsheim, Baden
Menzer, Lydia Maria	23, Oct. 1882	27, Sept	70	343	Schulz	Eudora, KS	Lexington, Missouri
Menzinger, Andreas	15, Dec. 1873	2, Dec.	76	399		New Albany, IN	Liensingen, Maulbronn, Württemberg
Menzinger, Catharina	8, Dec. 1892	15, Nov.	73	782	Matern	Pittsburg, PA	Gladenbach, Hessen
Menzinger, Gottlieb	14, July 1884	30, June		7		New Albany, IN	Lenzingen, Maulbronn, Württemberg
Menzinger, Jakob	1, Apr. 1897	7, Mar.		207		Pittsburg, PA	Maulbronn, Württemberg
Menzli, Sophia	18, Nov. 1878	29, Oct.	67-10m-28d	367	Schmith	Carrolton, MO	Weisenheim am Berg, Rheinkreis Baiern
Mergel, Friedrich Wilhelm	4, Apr. 1870	25, Feb.	55	111		St. Cloud, MN	Bovenden, Hannover

Christliche Apologete Death Notices --- 1839 - 1899

Name of Deceased	Notice Date	Death Date	Age	Maiden Name	Page	Place of Death	Place of Birth
Merkel, August	25, Aug. 1892	19, July	64		542	Springfield, IL	Germany
Merkel, Barbara	18, Oct. 1860	1, Oct.	40	Trippel	168	Urbana, IL	Schaafheim, Dieburg, Hessen
Merkel, Caroline	21, June 1894	3, June	65		406	Brooklyn, NY	Oberndorf, Rheinkreis Baiern
Merkel, John Kaspar	10, Sept 1891	2, Feb.	79	Schumacher	590	Mascoutah, IL	Schaafheim, Dieburg, Hessen-Darmstadt
Merkel, Karolina	5, Apr. 1880	19, Mar.	22- 6m- 8d	Meyer	111	St. Louis, MO	Auerbach, Hessen-Darmstadt
Merkel, Peter	12, Dec. 1870	6, Nov.	41- 4m-23d		399	Eudora, KS	New York
Merkel, Peter	14, Sept 1885	21, June	19		7	Brooklyn, NY	Passin, Mecklenburg-Schwerin
Merkel, Sophia	5, Mar. 1891	8, Feb.	58	Baustigan	158	Watertown, WI	Schwieberdingen, Württemberg
Merkelbach, Rosine	4, Feb. 1884	16, Jan.	51	Wagner	7	Blue Island, IL	Groß Asbach, Brackenheim, Württemberg
Merker, Ernestina Regina	3, Mar. 1859	29, Jan.			36	Ripley, OH	Quincy, Illinois
Merker, Pauline Friederike	2, Sept 1886	18, Aug.	30	Speckhard	7	Quincy, IL	Jettenburg, Tübingen, Württemberg
Merkle, Anna Maria	9, Dec. 1897	6, Nov.	48	Dürr	783	Bucyrus, OH	Lengerich, Westphalen
Merkle, Charlotte	16, Apr. 1896	25, Mar.	32	Kienemann	254	Kansas City, KS	Beinstein, Waiblingen, Württemberg
Merkle, Dorothea	20, Nov. 1876	14, Oct.	75	Allmendinger	375	Franciscoville, MI	Michelau, Württemberg
Merkle, Friedrich	31, Mar. 1887	14, Mar.	77		206	Bucyrus, OH	Beinstein, Württemberg
Merkle, Johan Jakob	28, Oct. 1878	15, Sept	75		343	Francisco, MI	
Merkle, John	17, Oct. 1861	29, Sept	40- -23d		168	Richmond, IN	
Merkle, Margaretha	24, Aug. 1885	4, Aug.	77	Finder	7	Algona, IA	Feldtennah, Neuenbürg, Württemberg
Merks, Elisabeth	2, Mar. 1868	6, Feb.	20	Colonkus	71	Alton, IL	
Merks, Johan	17, Apr. 1876	28, Mar.	63		127	Alton, IL	Reinhardts, Kurhessen
Mermann, Anna Martha	9, Nov. 1863	9, Oct.	61		180	Watertown, WI	
Mermann, Emma	22, Oct. 1857	29, Sept	29- 9m		172	Chicago, IL	Zehopan, Sachsen
Mermann, Peter	14, May 1877		73- 8m		159	Minneapolis, MN	Mörs, Rheinpreußen
Merrill, Anna Barbara	11, Mar. 1897	10, Feb.	51	Ell	159	Klemme, IA	Union County, Ohio
Mersch, Elisabeth	6, Mar. 1882	12, Feb.	76	Gähring	79	Nashville, TN	Calw, Württemberg
Merschrod, Jacob	9, Apr. 1877	24, Mar.	26		119	Wheeling, WV	Liederbach, Hessen
Merschrod, Katharine	9, July 1891	2, June	68	Klee	446	Wheeling, WV	Liederbach, Hessen
Mersfelder, Jakob	15, May 1890	6, Apr.	55		318	Newark, NJ	Niedereisenbach, RheinPreußen
Mersfelder, Philippine	2, Sept 1886	19, Aug.	42- 5m-21d		7	Newark, NJ	Bockenberg, Baiern
Merten, B. F.	7, Sept 1899	18, Aug.	52		575	Charles City, IA	Colesburg, Iowa
Merten, Catharine M.	17, Jan. 1895	29, Dec.	77- 3m- 5d	Klaus	46	Galena, IL	Bippen, Fürstenau, Hannover
Merten, Herman	17, May 1875	21, Apr.	23		159	Milwaukee, WI	Hildebrandshausen, Brinzlau, Preußen
Merten, Herman Friedrich (Rev)	10, Mar. 1898	2, Feb.	78		158	Garner, IA	Halen, Münster, Preußen
Merten, Lydia K.	30, July 1891	30, June	25	Schaub	494	Galena, IL	Lancaster, Grant County, Wisconsin
Mertens, Christina	21, Sept 1874	30, Aug.	24- 4m- 6d	Ficken	303	Marshalltown, IA	Ederwecht, Oldenburg
Mertens, Christoph	16, Feb. 1880	30, Dec.	46- 8m		55	Bloomington, IL	Riebau, Magdeburg, Preußen
Mertens, Joachim Christian	22, June 1899	6, June	90		399	Milwaukee, WI	Gentzkow, Mecklenburg-Strelitz
Mertens, Johan Christian	25, Apr. 1895	4, Apr.	74		270	Gladbrook, IA	Danickhorst, Oldenburg
Mertens, Johann	27, July 1854		47		120	Weston, MO	Ewinger, Alt-Preußen, Preußen
Mertens, Mathilde	30, Oct. 1890	28, Sept	17		702	Grand Rapids, MI	Grand Rapids, Michigan
Merthisheimer, Ph.	22, Nov. 1880		80		375	Sedalia, MO	Heppenheim a. d. Wiese,
Mertisheimer, (Mrs)	14, May 1891	17, Apr.	80		318	Sedalia, MO	Hessen-Darmstadt
Merz, Carl Wilhelm	4, Nov. 1872	16, Oct.	16		359	Bloomington, IL	
Merz, Georg	27, Apr. 1868	29, Mar.	40		135	Angelica, NY	Großeichen, Gießen, Hessen-Darmstadt
Merz, Johan Caspar	28, Apr. 1884	31, Mar.	61		7	Burlington, IA	Beinstein, Waiblingen, Württemberg
Merz, Katharina	21, Jan. 1858	25, Dec.	30	Schneider	12	Saginaw, MI	Randen beim Zollhause, Baden

Christliche Apologete Death Notices --- 1839 - 1899

Name of Deceased	Notice Date	Death Date	Age	Page	Maiden Name	Place of Death	Place of Birth
Merz, Louise	5, Dec. 1864	17, Oct.	24- 6m-21d	196	Rohn	Beardstown, IL	Menzikon, Aargau, Schweiz
Merz, Melchior	1, Aug. 1881	16, July	40	247		Eudora, KS	Beinstein, Waiblingen, Württemberg
Merz, Wilhelmine Auguste	10, Mar. 1873	28, Feb.	49	79		Bloomington, IL	Benton County, Iowa
Messer, Anna Margaretha Elisabeth	2, Nov. 1885	10, Oct.	12- 6m	7		Odebolt, IA	Nöwen, Dramburg, Pommern
Messer, Auguste Franziska	19, June 1890		33	398	Mattke	Baraboo, WI	Hersfeld, Hessen-Kassel
Messer, Ernstina	21, May 1877	25, Apr.		166		Louisville, KY	Hirschfeld, Kurhessen
Messer, Georg	19, Apr. 1855	2, Mar.	67	64		Louisville, KY	Gispersleben bei Erfurt, Sachsen
Messer, Wilhelm Gotthard	8, June 1893	12, May	78- 6m-12d	366		Caledonia, WI	Andersbein, Düring, Preußen
Messer, Wilhelmine	17, Sept 1891	28, July	78- 3m- 4d	606		Caledonia, WI	Andisleben, Erfurt, Sachsen
Messer, Wilhelmine	22, Oct. 1891	29, July	78	686	Gerlach	Baraboo, WI	Andersleben, Sachsen
Messer, Wilhelmine	10, Sept 1891	29, July	78	590	Gerlach	Baraboo, WI	Marktflecken, Blech, Baiern
Messerer, Elisabeth	21, Feb. 1889	6, Feb.	87- 5m	126	Ruckdeschel	Ironton, OH	Markblech, Baiern
Messerer, Friedrich	9, Jan. 1871	22, Dec.	75	15		Portsmouth, OH	
Messerer, Friedrich	22, Jan. 1861	Dec.	2	16		Furnace, OH	
Messerer, Georg	16, Mar. 1899	18, Feb.	73	175		Wheelersburg, OH	Markt Plach, Baiern
Messerly, F.	8, Oct. 1877	19, Sept	39- 5m	327		Ft. Dodge, IA	
Messerschmidt, Anna Catharina	31, Oct. 1889	4, Oct.	40	702	Schaub	East Troy, WI	Spring Prairie, Walworth County, Wisconsin
Messerschmidt, Anna Rosina	30, Mar. 1885	12, Mar.	72	7	Sus	Higginsport, OH	Kälberbach, Gerabronn, Württemberg
Messerschmidt, August	25, Feb. 1858	21, Dec.	42	32		Lexington, MO	Drüber, Eimbeck, Hannover
Messerschmidt, Catharina	7, July 1884	22, June		7		St. Paul, MN	Fambach, Kurhessen
Messerschmidt, Johan Georg	19, Jan. 1863	26, Dec.	29- 2m-12d	12		Cincinnati, OH	Kalderbach, Gerabronn, Württemberg
Messerschmidt, Johan Michael	16, Nov. 1893	20, Oct.	81	734		Higginsport, OH	Oberstetten, Gerabronn, Württemberg
Messerschmidt, Louise	24, Mar. 1879	18, Feb.	40- 9m- 8d	95		Ackley, IA	Langenhagen, Hannover
Messerschmidt, Maria	22, Sept 1879	6, Sept	37- 8m-22d	303	Eichelstein	Cincinnati, OH	Pomeroy, Ohio
Messing, Johan Georg	15, Sept 1887	25, Aug.	60	590		Chicago, IL	Friedrichroda, Sachsen-Gotha
Meßmer, August	30, Mar. 1885	11, Mar.	72	7		Charlestown, IN	Zunsweier, Ossenburg, Baden
Meßmer, Carolina	6, Apr. 1885	22, Mar.	54	7	Becker	Ft. Atkinson, WI	Nieder-Eschbach, Hessen-Darmstadt
Meßmer, Karoline	26, May 1898	17, Apr.	40	335	Hilgärtner	Newport, KY	Newport, Campbell County, Kentucky
Meßner, Apollonia	24, Dec. 1891	19, Nov.	81	830	Drexler	Cannelton, IN	Herbrectingen, Heidenheim, Württemberg
Meßner, Katharina	27, Nov. 1882	31, Oct.	83	383		S. Cayuga, CD	Troßingen, Württemberg
Mester, Karl H.A.	24, Jan. 1876	6, Jan.	65	31		Quincy, IL	Melle, Amt Grönenberg, Hannover
Mester, Louise	6, June 1850	23, Apr.	39- 3m	92		Quincy, IL	Herford, Kreis Münden, Preußen
Mestwarp, Sophia	26, July 1849	28, June	15	120		St. Louis, MO	
Metler, August	26, Aug. 1858	27, July	33	136		Poughkeepsie, NY	Gehofen, Kreis Angerhausen, Preußen
Mette, Heinrich	24, July 1851	29, June	41	120		St. Louis, MO	Cappeln, Westphalen, Preußen
Mette, Johanne	6, Aug. 1877	12, July	36- 2m- 8d	255	Schuppan	St. Louis, MO	Ebersbach, Sachsen
Mettler, August	16, Mar. 1863	23, Feb.	57	44		Saugerties, NY	Gehofen, Kreis Sangerhausen, Preußen
Mettler, August Friedrich	16, Sept 1858	27, July	32	148		Saugerties, NY	Gehofen, Kreis Sangershausen, Preußen
Mettler, Maria Magdalena	17, Feb. 1879	27, Jan.	73- 4m	55		Saugerties, NY	
Metz, Elisabeth	20, Apr. 1874	31, Mar.	69	127	Fischer	Wheeling, IL	Linkenheim, Baden
Metz, Georg	13, Sept 1844	20, Aug.	63	140		St. Louis, MO	
Metz, (Mr)	1, July 1858	17, Feb.	70	104		Dunkirk, NY	Blankenloch, Baden
Metz, Anna	25, Nov. 1886	10, Sept	13-11m- 1d	7		Allegheny, PA	
Metz, Anna Catharina	27, May 1897	5, May	74	335	Kensley	Quincy, IL	P-feld, Württemberg
Metz, Anna Elisabeth	11, Aug. 1887	22, July	89- 9m-29d	510	Haxel	Des Moines, IA	Marienfels, Nastetten, Nassau
Metz, Anna Margaretha	27, July 1854		40	120	Fischbach	Dayton, OH	Greifenstein, Kreis Wetzlar, Preußen

Christliche Apologete Death Notices --- 1839 - 1899

Name of Deceased	Notice Date	Death Date	Age	Page	Maiden Name	Place of Death	Place of Birth
Metz, Catharina	14, Apr. 1892	25, Mar.	28	238	Klein	Boonville, IN	Indiana
Metz, Elisabeth	5, Dec. 1870	14, Nov.	19- 4m- 2d	391		Des Moines, IA	Warsaw, Illinois
Metz, Elisabetha	21, Feb. 1850	14, Nov.	66	32		St. Louis, MO	Kehl, Baden
Metz, Emil	6, Nov. 1882	23, Sept	21	359		Quincy, IL	
Metz, Eva Rosina	14, Aug. 1882	30, July	74- 1m-28d	263	Rink	De Soto, MO	Jockgrimm bei Kandel, Rheinpfalz Baiern
Metz, Franz Michael	22, May 1871	6, May	63- 7m- 8d	167		De Soto, MO	Jockgrimm, Langen-Kandel, Rheinkreis Baiern
Metz, Friedrich	11, Mar. 1867	7, Feb.	48-11m- 5d	78		Galion, OH	Lindolsheim, Baden
Metz, Georg	24, Mar. 1884	21, Feb.	79- 3m-12d	7		Chicago, IL	Lindolsheim, Baden
Metz, Heinrich	1, Apr. 1897	21, Feb.	51	207		Rockham, SD	Bürgeln, Hessen-Nassau
Metz, Heinrich	19, May 1879	22, Apr.	27	159		St. Paul, MN	St. Louis, Missouri
Metz, Jakob	5, Apr. 1888	16, Mar.	43	222		St. Louis, MO	Jockrimm, RheinPfalz Baiern
Metz, John Andreas	8, Oct. 1866	16, Sept	76- 7m- 2d	326		Burlington, IA	Marienfels, Amt Nasteten, Nassau
Metz, Katharina	16, Feb. 1899	27, Jan.	65	111	Helwer	Boonville, IN	Greenville, Ohio
Metz, Louis	25, July 1864	24, June	28	120		Wheeling, IL	Detroit, Wayne County, Michigan
Metz, Louise	25, Nov. 1886	13, Oct.	18- 6m- 9d	7		Allegheny, PA	
Metz, Margaretha	27, Aug. 1866	9, Aug.	82	278		Cincinnati, OH	Diernbach, Baiern
Metz, Maria	24, Mar. 1892	29, Feb.	31	190	Statz	Salina, KS	Löwenthal, Davis County, Kansas
Metz, Sophia	1, May 1890	25, Mar.	28	286	Seitz	Boonville, IN	
Metz, Wilhelm	25, Dec. 1865	8, Dec.		208		St. Paul, MN	Wallenbrik, Preußen
Metz, Wilhelm	12, May 1873	28, Apr.	51	151		Quincy, IL	Marienfels, Nassau
Metzger, Aaron Christian	11, Mar. 1886	25, Feb.	13	7			
Metzger, Barbara	17, Sept 1891	11, Aug.	78	606	Stomm	Garrett, IN	Elsins, Baden
Metzger, Conrad	8, Aug. 1881	13, July	68- -19d	255		Jeffersonville, NY	Gambach, Hessen-Darmstadt
Metzger, Dorothea Maria	20, Jan. 1879	31, Dec.	79	23	Golumer	Woodbury, MN	Oberheldron, Preußen
Metzger, Heinrich	27, Feb. 1896	27, Jan.	68	143		Dayton, OH	Allendorf, Wetzlar, Coblenz, Preußen
Metzger, Heinrich Jakob	6, Oct. 1873	2, Sept	73	319		St. Paul, MN	Leubingen, Preußen
Metzger, Jakob	28, Mar. 1895	3, Mar.	80	206		Gratiot Co, MI	Rheinsburg, Rheinkreis Baiern
Metzger, Katharina Maria	17, Nov. 1892	25, Oct.	17	734		Jeffersonville, NY	Jeffersonville, Sullivan County, New York
Metzger, Lulu Katharine	12, Apr. 1894	20, mar.	15	246		Columbus, OH	Columbus, Franklin County, Ohio
Metzger, Margaretha	10, Dec. 1891	16, Sept	78	798	Lipps	Brooklyn, NY	Queck, Hessen
Metzger, Mary	24, Apr. 1882	6, Apr.	28	135		Portsmouth, OH	Portsmouth, Scioto County, Ohio
Metzger, Philipp	7, Feb. 1895	17, Jan.	48	94		Jeffersonville, NY	Gambach, Hessen
Metzger, Philipp Heinrich	28, Dec. 1874	21, Nov.	79	415		Dayton, OH	Greifenstein, Wetzlar, Koblenz, Preußen
Metzger, Philippine	1, Oct. 1883	12, Aug.	74- 5m-15d	319		Marion, OH	Graben, Karlsruhe, Baden
Metzger, Rosina	22, Dec. 1892	2, Dec.	70	814	Schaub	Dayton, OH	Neckartenzlingen, Nürtingen, Württemberg
Metzger, Wilhelm	6, June 1881	13, Apr.	28-11m- 9d	183		New Knoxville, OH	Marion County, Ohio
Metzler, Conrad	10, Jan. 1876	2, Oct.	62- 4m-20d	15		Evansville, IN	Langstadt, Dieburg, Hessen-Darmstadt
Metzler, Leonhard	17, July 1856	27, June	10	116		Evansville, IN	Langstadt, Dieburg, Hessen-Darmstadt
Metzler, Margaretha	2, Mar. 1893	8, Feb.	75	142		Evansville, IN	Langstadt, Hessen-Darmstadt
Metzner, Henriette	1, July 1886	23, May	62	7	Saalmüller	Wheeling, WV	Huldburg, Sachsen-Meiningen
Metzner, Hulda Blanch	2, Mar. 1899	8, Feb.	19	143		Wheeling, WV	
Metzner, Maria	25, Nov. 1842		Inquiry	187		Wheeling, VA	
Metzner, Oscar	26, July 1888	12, July		478		Jordan, MN	Hirzbach, Leutenberg, Schwarzburg-Rudolstadt
Metzner, Philipp	28, Apr. 1884	11, Apr.	51	7		Wheeling, WV	Hellburg, Sachsen-Meiningen
Meule, Barbara	7, Feb. 1870	20, Jan.	49	47	Kaupein	Marrs, IN	
Meule, Friedrike	27, Dec. 1855	4, Oct.		208		Boonville, MO	Grünwetterbach, Baden

Christliche Apologete Death Notices --- 1839 - 1899

Name of Deceased	Notice Date	Death Date	Age	Maiden Name	Page	Place of Death	Place of Birth
Meuselbach, Magdalena Maria	6, Dec. 1869	16, Nov.	11- 7m- 6d		391	Rushville, IL	Lippstadt, Westphalen, Preußen
Meußer, Carl	26, May 1873	18, Apr.	63		167	Grandview, IN	Taschenberg bei Prenzlauw, Preußen
Mewes, Auguste	10, Feb. 1879	19, Jan.	25	Kleist	47	Illinois City, IL	Breitenstein, Brandenburg
Mewis, Johan Wilhelm	29, Mar. 1894	5, Mar.	29		214	Charles City, IA	Drury Township, Rock Island County, Illinois
Mewis, Maria Friederike Christine	5, July 1894	17, June	27	Krüger	438	Wrayville, IL	Lippe-Detmold
Meyer , Amalie	3, July 1851				108	St. Louis, MO	Rummelsburg, Pommern
Meyer, Heinrich	3, Nov. 1887	11, Oct.	73		702	Big Stone, SD	
Meyer, (Mr)	26, June 1840				99	Wheeling, VA	
Meyer, Albert N.	27, Aug. 1891	31, July	60- 3m-17d		558	Seymour, IN	Bremen, Germany
Meyer, Anna	16, July 1896	18, June	86	Boschen	463	Lake Creek, MO	Tarnstead, Sevin, Hannover
Meyer, Anna	22, Dec. 1898	28, Nov.	50	Kruse	815	Sedalia, MO	Morgan County, Missouri
Meyer, Anna	22, Mar. 1894	31, Jan.	64	Hencken	198	New York City, NY	Langen, Hannover
Meyer, Anna	1, Aug. 1895	4, July	29-10m		494	Buffalo, NY	
Meyer, Anna Christina	14, June 1880	22, May	68- - 6d	Pienow	191	Oconomowoc, WI	Kleinlotzkow, Soldin, Brandenburg
Meyer, Anna Christine	31, Jan. 1881	29, Dec.	82	Luers	39	Shelby, IA	Sudweihe, Syke, Hannover
Meyer, Anna Dorothea	23, May 1881	12, Apr.	70	Riechers	167	Bremen, GE	
Meyer, Anna Margaretha	7, Apr. 1892	16, Mar.	89- 3m- 9d	Timken	222	Dayton, OH	Altenbücken, Hoya, Hannover
Meyer, Anna Maria	15, Jan. 1891	29, Dec.	79- 6m-12d	Roller	46	Great Bend, KS	Kopingen, Hermbern, Württemberg
Meyer, Anna Maria	1, Aug. 1889	30, June	79- 7m- 1d		494	St. Louis, MO	Kanton Aargau, Schweiz
Meyer, Anna Maria Charlotte	28, Apr. 1887	9, Apr.	78	Janböcke	270	Wyandotte, KS	Dissen, Hannover
Meyer, Anton	2, Dec. 1878	6, Nov.	64-10m		383	St. Louis, MO	Bremen, Germany
Meyer, Anton	1, Apr. 1872	10, Feb.	17-11m-29d		111	Alton, IL	
Meyer, August	5, Apr. 1888	15, Mar.	22		222	Dalton, MO	Dalton, Missouri
Meyer, August	30, Dec. 1886	4, Dec.	23		7	Halstead, KS	Garlow, Hannover
Meyer, August	14, Mar. 1881	13, Feb.	20- 6m-17d		87	Jersey City, NJ	
Meyer, Barbara	27, Jan. 1898	31, Dec.	56	Schmidt	63	Rochester, NY	Zinsheim, Baden
Meyer, Barbara	26, Mar. 1866	28, July	33		102	Pleasant Hill, OH	
Meyer, Becke	28, Aug. 1871	10, Dec.	37	Henken	279	New York City, NY	Langen, Amt Peterkese, Hannover
Meyer, Bertha	26, Dec. 1889	6, Jan.	34-10m	Fleckhammer	830	Newark, NJ	Pforzheim, Baden
Meyer, Betty	18, Feb. 1878	18, July	60- 7m- 8d		55	Concordia, MO	
Meyer, Carl Gottfried	15, Aug. 1881	2, Mar.	59- 4m-15d		263	Ledlars, IA	Gehofen, Merseburg, Preußen
Meyer, Carolina	26, Jan. 1880	14, Nov.	14- - 2d	Spaar	31	Oshkosh, WI	Neumark, Preußen
Meyer, Caroline	7, Apr. 1853				56	Terre Haute, IN	
Meyer, Caroline E.	1, Dec. 1879	28, Jan.	24	Maag	383	Le Sueur, MN	St. Paul, Minnesota
Meyer, Catharina Henriette	9, Mar. 1893	23, Apr.	56	Kolosz	158	Dalton, MO	Wehrheim, Ussingen, Nassau
Meyer, Catharine	4, June 1896	23, Jan.	78	Freiburger	367	Burlington, IA	Leineck, Baiern
Meyer, Ch.	24, Feb. 1887	11, Oct.	19		126	Sedalia, MO	
Meyer, Charlotte	28, Oct. 1878	25, June	81- 6m		343	Hopewell, MO	Reme, Herfort, Minden, Preußen
Meyer, Charlotte	13, July 1899	8, Sept	68	Kasper	447	Lawrenceville, IN	Blanken, Münden, Preußen
Meyer, Christian	5, Oct. 1874	4, Nov.	36-10m-27d		319	New Orleans, LA	Lesse, Braunschweig
Meyer, Christina	4, Dec. 1865	2, Feb.	48		196	Terre Haute, IN	Mühlheim am Bach, Württemberg
Meyer, Christina	23, Feb. 1863	22, Oct.	51- 1m- 8d	Grannemann	32	Herman, MO	Nordhemmern, Minden, Preußen
Meyer, Christina	30, Nov. 1893	29, Oct.	68		766	Boody, IL	Lobmachtersen, Braunschweig
Meyer, Christina	17, Dec. 1857			Dennig	204	Marion, OH	Elmendingen, Baden
Meyer, Christine	21, May 1883	1, May	43- 4m- 6d	Rothfuß	167	Golconda, IL	Oberlengenhardt, Neuenbürg, Württemberg
Meyer, Christine	20, Sept 1869	5, Aug.	61- 1m- 1d	Horstmann	303	Herman, MO	Friedewalde, Minden, Preußen

Christliche Apologete Death Notices --- 1839 - 1899

Name of Deceased	Notice Date	Death Date	Age	Page	Maiden Name	Place of Death	Place of Birth
Meyer, Christine	18, Feb. 1867	2, Jan.	73	54		Chester, IL	Canton Bern, Schweiz
Meyer, Christine	10, July 1882	23, June	70- 6m- 6d	223	Dotterer	Yates Place, NY	Berwangen, Baden
Meyer, Christine Mathilda	2, Feb. 1893	16, Jan.	30	78		Eudora, KS	Pettis County, Missouri
Meyer, Christoph	15, Feb. 1875	2, Feb.	65- 2m-13d	55		Lake Creek, MO	Ostereistädt, Amt Seven, Hannover
Meyer, Christoph	8, Jan. 1891	11, Dec.	48	30		Jordan, MN	Höfferingen, Hannover
Meyer, Cora F. E.	12, Jan. 1899	18, Dec.	14	31		Herman, MO	Herman, Missouri
Meyer, Daniel	9, Apr. 1877	14, Mar.	12	119		Ballwin, MO	
Meyer, Daniel August	17, May 1869	26, Apr.	2- 3m	159		New Orleans, LA	
Meyer, Diethelm	31, Jan. 1895	5, Jan.	76	78		Hannibal, MO	Neuenkirch, Schaffhausen, Schweiz
Meyer, Dominick	31, Oct. 1881	23, Sept	72	351		Burlington, IA	Dumersheim, Baden
Meyer, Dorothea	16, Feb. 1899	3, Jan.	97	111		Crown Point, IN	Lemgo, Lippe-Detmold
Meyer, Dorothea	2, Nov. 1874	25, Sept	45	351	Stele	Flint Creek, IA	Hoenzollen, Schweiz
Meyer, Dorothea Maria	31, Dec. 1877	30, Nov.	76	423		Salem, MN	Friedewald, Preußen
Meyer, Eberhardina	28, Jan. 1858	3, Jan.	44	16	Mußgang	Des Moines, IA	
Meyer, Eduard F.	23, Oct. 1882	5, Oct.	21- 8m-16d	343		Sedalia, MO	St. Louis, Missouri
Meyer, Elisabeth	20, Feb. 1882	12, Jan.	32- 3m-14d	63	Bohl	Marietta, OH	Wachenheim a. d. Hardt, RheinPfalz Baiern
Meyer, Elisabeth	6, Apr. 1899	15, Mar.	75	223	Schmidt	Chicago, IL	Waldgermes, Wetzlar, Hessen-Darmstadt
Meyer, Elisabeth	9, Jan. 1890	13, Dec.	62	30	Renner	Buffalo, NY	Schnellersdorf, Sulzbach, Baiern
Meyer, Elisabeth	17, Apr. 1890	11, Mar.	67	254	Volz	New York City, NY	Herschberg, Baiern
Meyer, Elisabeth	11, Sept 1890	7, Aug.	68	590		Scranton, PA	Laibach, Kurhessen
Meyer, Elisabeth	13, Dec. 1849	4, Nov.	30	200		Evansport, OH	
Meyer, Elisabeth Christina Charl.	22, Nov. 1894	28, Oct.	39	758	Schulte	Dalton, MO	Holzhausen, Minden, Westphalen
Meyer, Elisabetha	30, Apr. 1857	1, Apr.	48	72	Roth	St. Charles, MO	Ramholz, Kurhessen
Meyer, Emilie	7, Sept 1893	13, Aug.		574	Graf	Crandon, SD	Weißenhöhe, Wirsitz, Preußen
Meyer, Emilie	21, June 1880	18, Apr.	27- 8m-20d	199		Cincinnati, OH	
Meyer, Emma Katharina	1, June 1899	16, Mar.	40	351	Stellter	Seymour, IN	Charlestown, Indiana
Meyer, Emma V.	31, Aug. 1899	19, Aug.	57	559	Neighley	Herman, MO	Catasauqua, Lehigh County, Pennsylvania
Meyer, Engel	25, Apr. 1861	8, Feb.	68- 4m	68		Columbus, WI	Nord-Hemmen, Preußen
Meyer, Erdmann	10, Sept 1866	8, June	83	294		Nashville, IL	Slarren, Preußen
Meyer, Ernst Fr. Wilhelm	4, Aug. 1898	19, July	80	495		Batesville, IN	Vollmerdingsten, Minden, Preußen
Meyer, Evangeline	28, Oct. 1886	15, Oct.	32	7	Arnold	Great Bend, KS	
Meyer, F.H.	15, Jan. 1877	23, Dec.	23- 1m- 2d	23		Wyandotte, KS	
Meyer, F.W.	8, Jan. 1872	20, Nov.	69	15		Quincy, IL	Dissen, Hannover
Meyer, Florenz	18, June 1891	25, May	74- 6m	398		New Haven, CT	Hagen, Bielefeld, Westphalen
Meyer, Fr.	12, Nov. 1877	14, Oct.	40	367		Union, MO	Calw, Württemberg
Meyer, Fr. W. (Rev)	4, Apr. 1861	13, Mar.	23- 2m-13d	56		Boonville, MO	
Meyer, Frank	3, Mar. 1892	28, Dec.	25	142		Champaign, IL	Cedar Lake, Indiana
Meyer, Fredy	13, Dec. 1875	16, Nov.	9-11m	399		Hebron, IA	Gehoven, Preußen
Meyer, Friederike	15, Apr. 1872	26, Mar.	75- 3m- 1d	127		Muscatine, IA	Mechantien, Pommern
Meyer, Friedrich	18, Aug. 1892	3, July	65	526		Milwaukee, WI	Mechentien, Pommern
Meyer, Friedrich	4, Aug. 1892	3, July	65	494		Milwaukee, WI	Dörverden, Verden, Hannover
Meyer, Friedrich Dietrich Jobst	28, Oct. 1886	10, Oct.	70	7		Dayton, OH	Barnstorf, Diepholz, Hannover
Meyer, Friedrich Heinrich	13, Dec. 1888	20, Nov.	69	798		Muscatine, IA	Neuglashagen, Mecklenburg-Schwerin
Meyer, Friedrich Johan	26, Dec. 1895	20, Nov.	72	828		Schnectady, NY	Neckardenzingen, Württemberg
Meyer, Friedrike	16, Feb. 1893	31, Jan.	64	110		Scranton, PA	
Meyer, Georg Heinrich	17, July 1876	17, June	27	231		New Orleans, LA	New Orleans, Louisiana

Christliche Apologete Death Notices --- 1839 - 1899

Name of Deceased	Notice Date	Death Date	Age	Page	Maiden Name	Place of Death	Place of Birth
Meyer, Gottlieb	13, Apr. 1899	18, Mar.	55	239		Bison, KS	Schoren bei Thun, Bern, Schweiz
Meyer, H.W.	29, Mar. 1880	4, Mar.	71	103		Le Sueur, MN	Westerkappeln, Tecklenburg, Preußen
Meyer, Hanna Margarethe	15, Sept 1862	1, Aug.	51	148	Fischer	Bucyrus, OH	Rudersberg, Welzheim, Württemberg
Meyer, Heinericke Christina	1, Sept 1862	17, Aug.	29- 9m-21d	140	Blinzinger	Evansville, IN	Willsbach, Weinsberg, Württemberg
Meyer, Heinrich	1, Jan. 1872	9, Sept	62	7		Herman, MO	Holzhausen, Gertung, Minden, Preußen
Meyer, Heinrich	8, May 1890	19, Apr.	26	302		Yoakum, TX	Varel, Schweiburg, Oldenburg
Meyer, Heinrich	11, July 1864	26, June	40- 2m- 9d	112		Cincinnati, OH	Regensdorf, Zürich, Schweiz
Meyer, Heinrich	12, Sept 1889	23, Aug.	60	590		Chicago, IL	Weichersbach, Kurhessen
Meyer, Heinrich	23, Aug. 1888	10, Aug.	29	542		Terre Haute, IN	Zobbenitz, Braunschweig
Meyer, Heinrich	3, May 1888	12, Apr.	70- 2m-12d	286		Boody, IL	Beinum, Hannover
Meyer, Heinrich	10, July 1865	29, Apr.	56- 2m	112		Scranton, PA	Harle, Kurhessen
Meyer, Heinrich	27, June 1895	8, June	68	414		Wrayville, IL	Hannover
Meyer, Heinrich	4, Dec. 1876	25, Oct.	54- 7m-13d	391		Great Bend, KS	
Meyer, Heinrich	30, Aug. 1880	7, Aug.	12- 6m-12d	279		Hays City, KS	
Meyer, Heinrich Jakob	6, Sept 1844		Inquiry	136		Ft. Wayne, IN	Lienen, Tecklenburg, Preußen
Meyer, Heinrich L.	17, Dec. 1891	8, Nov.	55	814		Norwich, KS	Gellenbeck, Lübbecke, Minden, Westphalen
Meyer, Heinrich Wilhelm	12, Jan. 1863	19, Sept	22	8		Warren Co., MO	Franklin County, Missouri
Meyer, Helene Friederike	24, June 1886	22, Apr.	11-11m- 2d	7		Blue Island, IL	
Meyer, Henriette	19, Mar. 1891	25, Feb.	60- 8m-27d	190		Baltimore, MD	Holzhausen , Westphalen
Meyer, Henriette	1, Feb. 1894	4, Jan.	75	78		Chicago, IL	Berlin , Preußen
Meyer, Henry	4, Aug. 1892	10, July		494		Chicago, IL	
Meyer, Henry C.	18, Aug. 1898	3, Aug.	60	527		St. Louis, MO	Halem bei Minden, Preußen
Meyer, Henry Friedrich	2, Jan. 1882	14, Dec.	39- 1m	7		Dalton, MO	Eisbergen, Hansberge, Preußen
Meyer, Herman	13, Sept 1888	17, Aug.	51- 6m- 6d	590		Big Spring, MO	Künsebeck, Halle, Westphalen
Meyer, Herman	11, July 1895	9, June	83	446		Salisbury, MO	Radtsiek, Lippe-Detmold
Meyer, Herman H.	24, Nov. 1898	17, Oct.	69	751		Bible Grove, IL	Ostfriesland
Meyer, Ilse Ch.	24, Apr. 1882	10, Apr.	61- 1m-21d	135	Wißmer	St. Louis, MO	Wallenbrück, Westphalen
Meyer, Jacob	15, Feb. 1875	21, Jan.	69	55		Fredericksburg, TX	Kirchdorf, Hannover
Meyer, Jacob	11, Nov. 1878	10, Oct.	68- 8m-22d	359		Edgerton, OH	Friedrichsthal, Karlsruhe, Baden
Meyer, Jacob	25, July 1895	1, July	77	478		Marion, OH	Almendingen, Baden
Meyer, Jakob	7, Oct. 1872	9, Sept	39	327		Boonville, MO	Kanton Solothurn, Schweiz
Meyer, Jakob	25, May 1899	28, Apr.	87	335		Brenham, TX	Berschwyl, Schweiz
Meyer, Jakobine	14, Sept 1899	15, Aug.	72-11m-28d	591	Kinzlin	Cosby, MO	Nebringen, Herrenberg, Württemberg
Meyer, Johan	17, Sept 1891	18, Aug.	50	606		Chicago, IL	Briest, Potsdam, Preußen
Meyer, Johan	16, Mar. 1874	25, Feb.	73- 7m	87		Herman, MO	Marbach, Württemberg
Meyer, Johan Adolph	15, Oct. 1896		74	671		White Cloud, KS	Lotte, Westphalen
Meyer, Johan Christoph	10, Sept 1883	25, Aug.	61- 9m- 6d	295		Faribault, MN	Riehe, Rodenberg, Kurhessen
Meyer, Johan Friedrich	29, July 1878	7, July	45	239		Concordia, MO	Drackenburg, Nienburg, Hannover
Meyer, Johan Friedrich	28, June 1888	28, Apr.	12	414		Brooklyn, NY	
Meyer, Johan Herman Heinrich	2, Dec. 1872	12, Nov.	23	391		New Haven, MO	Schülske, Bielefeld, Minden, Preußen
Meyer, Johan Jacob	8, Dec. 1892	5, Oct.	63	782		Halton, ND	Kuppingen, Württemberg
Meyer, Johan Jürgen	25, Dec. 1882	24, Nov.	71	415		Halstead, KS	Moltzen, Ueltzen, Hannover
Meyer, Johann	5, Aug. 1867	1, July	49	246		Schnectady, NY	Eickhorst, Preußen
Meyer, Johann C.	20, Dec. 1860	17, Nov.	38	204		Marthasville, MO	Rehme , Preußen
Meyer, Johann Georg	6, Mar. 1862	12- 5m-10d		40		Boonville, IN	
Meyer, Johanna	1, Dec. 1887	17, Feb.	82	766	Sievert	Lexington, MO	Immensen, Einbeck, Hannover

Christliche Apologete Death Notices --- 1839 - 1899

Name of Deceased	Notice Date	Death Date	Age	Page	Maiden Name	Place of Death	Place of Birth
Meyer, Johanna	9, July 1896	18, June	88	447	Meyer	Webster, SD	Pflugrad, Neumark, Hinterpommern
Meyer, Johanna Carolina	29, Jan. 1857	22, Nov.		20		Albany, NY	
Meyer, Johannes	19, June 1876	21, May	87-10m-21d	199		Great Bend, KS	Kleinbockenheim, Grünstadt, Rheinpfalz Baiern
Meyer, Johannes	1, Feb. 1864	1, Dec.	70	20		Baresville, OH	Blauenstein, Thun, Bern, Schweiz
Meyer, Johannes	23, Oct. 1871	6, Oct.	76-6m-26d	343		Blue Island, IL	Itingen, Sispach, Basel, Schweiz
Meyer, John	30, Sept 1897	5, Aug.	52	623		Blue Island, IL	Crete, Illinois
Meyer, John Edward	24, June 1886	15, Apr.	5- 1m-19d	7		Blue Island, IL	
Meyer, John Gerhart	10, Nov. 1873	17, Oct.	49	359		Huntingburg, IN	Gerde, Hannover
Meyer, John J.	3, May 1875	24, Mar.	25	143		Scranton, PA	Scranton, Pennsylvania
Meyer, John William	15, Jan. 1877	10, Dec.	19-10m-12d	23		Great Bend, KS	
Meyer, Karl August	16, June 1873	27, May	61- 9m	191		Oconomowoc, WI	Fürstensee, Pommern
Meyer, Karl Conrad	9, June 1873	21, Apr.	48	183		E. Pennfield, NY	Bartfeld, Hannover
Meyer, Karl Friedrich	20, Dec. 1869	10, Nov.	75	407		Indianapolis, IN	Dankersen, Minden, Preußen
Meyer, Karl Friedrich August	4, Nov. 1867	14, Oct.	48	350		Blue Island, IL	Hartum, Minden, Preußen
Meyer, Karl Wesley	23, Aug. 1869	20, June	1	271		Wyandotte, KS	
Meyer, Karoline Maria	28, Jan. 1892	30, Dec.	65	62	Roggenfuß	Columbus, OH	Hille , Westphalen
Meyer, Katharina	7, Feb. 1881	6, Jan.		47		New York City, NY	Graben, Karlsruhe, Baden
Meyer, Katharina	6, Jan. 1879	16, Dec.	13- 5m-27d	7		Columbus, IL	
Meyer, Katharina E.	2, Oct. 1876	5, Sept		319	Noll	Concordia, MO	Roda, Frankenburg, Kurhessen
Meyer, Katharina Mathilde	23, Feb. 1874	26, Dec.	13- 8m- 3d	63		Oregon, MO	Quincy, Illinois
Meyer, Laura Annette	24, June 1886	6, May	16- 1m-23d	7		Blue Island, IL	Sandridge,
Meyer, Leonhart	17, Mar.1873	16, Feb.	68	87		Newark, NJ	
Meyer, Lisetta	26, Apr. 1888	3, Apr.	19- 4m-20d	270		Milwaukee, WI	
Meyer, Lizzie Louise	31, Oct. 1895	30, Sept	32	702		Buffalo, NY	
Meyer, Lizzie M.	3, Aug. 1885	14, July	16	7		Giard, IA	
Meyer, Louis	1, Sept 1898	13, Aug.	80	559		Ironton, OH	Zweibrücken, Baiem
Meyer, Louise	14, Mar. 1895	12, Feb.	62	174	Thoms	Capac, MI	Briest, Angermünde, Preußen
Meyer, Louise	9, Mar. 1854	1, Feb.	22	40	Berghorn	Herman, MO	Eichhorst, Münden, Preußen
Meyer, Louise	10, July 1876	11, June	23	223		Oregon, MO	Quincy, Illinois
Meyer, Louise Dorothea	24, Jan. 1876	6, Jan.	21- 2m-20d	31	Rufe	Brunswick, MO	Osage County,
Meyer, Maggie	2, Nov. 1885	20, Oct.	37	7	Stutheit	Lincoln, NE	New Bremen, Auglaize County, Ohio
Meyer, Maggie	23, Feb. 1888	31, Jan.	34	126		Newport, KY	Newport, Campbell County, Kentucky
Meyer, Margaretha	1, Feb. 1875	14, Jan.	67	39		Chicago, IL	Schleitheim, Schaffhausen, Schweiz
Meyer, Margaretha	13, Oct. 1884	22, Sept	34- 8m-17d	7	Weber	Columbus, NE	Groß-Busing, Hessen-Darmstadt
Meyer, Margaretha	10, Jan. 1895	11, Dec.	64	30	Busch	St. Paul, MN	Hannover
Meyer, Margaretha R.M	23, Nov. 1899	25, Oct.	69	751		Newport, KY	
Meyer, Maria	30, Aug. 1869	30, July	59	279	Fiehn	Bonn, OH	Atzsang, Oberfranken, Baiem
Meyer, Maria	24, Aug. 1874	5, Aug.	34	273	Niemeyer	Concordia, MO	Zeven, Hannover
Meyer, Maria	20, Feb. 1890	21, Jan.	58	126		New York City, NY	St. Louis, Missouri
Meyer, Maria	10, Dec. 1877	24, Nov.		399	Rölling	Oregon, MO	Hessen-Darmstadt
Meyer, Maria	5, Nov. 1847	12, Sept	45	179	Elsenbein	Herman, MO	Bur, Hannover
Meyer, Maria	20, Dec. 1855	9, Nov.	15-11m- 2d	204		Washington Co, OH	Minden,
Meyer, Maria	31, Oct. 1870	20, Oct.	31- -14d	351	Wehner	Cincinnati, OH	
Meyer, Maria Anna	29, Nov. 1888	10, Nov.	21- 9m- 8d	766		Batesville, IN	Laughery, Indiana
Meyer, Maria Anna	28, Feb. 1856	21, Jan.	38	36		Highland, IL	Baden
Meyer, Maria Barbara	13, Dec. 1869	20, Nov.	78- 1m- 9d	399	Klein	Calhoun, IL	Kleinbeckenheim, Rheinkreis Baiem

Christliche Apologete Death Notices --- 1839 - 1899

Name of Deceased	Notice Date	Death Date	Age	Page	Maiden Name	Place of Death	Place of Birth
Meyer, Maria Elisabeth	26, Feb. 1883	3, Feb.	69	71	Hilsick	Summerfield, IL	Neuenkirchen bei Melle, Hannover
Meyer, Maria Margarethe	26, June 1890	30, May	93	414		Red Wing, MN	Hannover
Meyer, Marie	20, Apr. 1893	27, Mar.	73	254		Lemars, IA	Bodendorf, Preußen
Meyer, Meta	28, May 1891	9, May	61	350	Kattenhorn	Jersey City, NJ	Scharmbah bei Bremen, Germany
Meyer, Meta	22, Dec. 1887	5, Dec.	47	814	Hasselmann	Baltimore, MD	Lage, Lippe-Detmold
Meyer, Michael	4, July 1895	1, June	58	430		Evansville, IN	Klingen, Rheinkreis Baiern
Meyer, Minna	23, June 1862	24, May	39	100		Decatur, IL	Lebanon, Pennsylvania
Meyer, Minnie	26, Apr. 1888	27, Mar.	16	270		Madison, WI	Buckley, Illinois
Meyer, Pauline	26, Oct. 1899	30, Sept	25	687		Lexington, MO	Hopewell, Warren County, Missouri
Meyer, Pauline	2, Nov. 1899	12, Oct.	61	703	Lucks	Belleville, IL	Schwetz, Marienberg, Preußen
Meyer, Rebecca	1, Sept 1898	21, Aug.	45	559	Geften	Lutman, MO	Hannover
Meyer, Regina	6, June 1864	14, Mar.		92	Koch	New Haven, CT	Kirchentellinsfurth, Tübingen, Württemberg
Meyer, Rosina	14, Oct. 1872	24, Sept	64	335	Gügel	Waverly, OH	Freistett, Baden
Meyer, Rosine	15, Mar. 1875	23, Feb.	28- 9m-16d	87		Marion, OH	Marion County, Ohio
Meyer, Siemtje	14, Feb. 1895	11, Jan.	47	110	Nanninga	San Jose, IL	Pewsum, Emden, Ostfriesland
Meyer, Sophia	19, July 1849	27, June	41	116		Cincinnati, OH	Diebholz, Hannover
Meyer, Sophia	18, Dec. 1871	8, Dec.	18	407	Krehe	Covington, KY	Uffenheim, Baiern
Meyer, Sophia Maria	18, Apr. 1895	23, Mar.	39	254	Frevert	Odebolt, IA	Cedar Lake, Indiana
Meyer, Valentin	21, May 1891	22, Apr.	70- 7m-14d	334		Emden, IL	Oberalben bei Kusel, Rheinkreis Baiern
Meyer, Wilhelm	13, July 1899	18, June	77- 6m	447		Scranton, PA	Fischbach, Rheinkreis Baiern
Meyer, Wilhelm	23, Aug. 1880	30, July	40	271		Oregon, MO	Wayne County, Ohio
Meyer, Wilhelm Anton Dietrich	13, Apr. 1899	6, Mar.	64	239		Concordia, MO	Drakenburg, Nienburg a. d. Weser, Hannover
Meyer, Wilhelm Dietrich	11, July 1895	13, June	22	446		Covington, KY	Seymour, Indiana
Meyer, Wilhelmine Christina A.	3, Feb. 1898	14, Jan.	22-10m-29d	79	Waack	Columbus, IL	Bindendorf, Germany
Meyer, William	14, Sept 1863	1, July	27	148		Fond du Lac, WI	
Meyerdirks, Catharine	3, Jan. 1850	10, Nov.	48	4		St. Louis, MO	
Meyerford, J. Martha	28, Jan. 1878	23, Dec.	18- -18d	31		Warren, MO	
Meyerhoff, Johan	29, Mar. 1869	5, Mar.	48	103		Hudson City, NJ	Osterholz, Preußen
Meyerhoff, Johanna	5, Jan. 1874	15, Sept	68	7		Adams Co, IA	
Meyerotto, Dietrich	17, Apr. 1865	2, Mar.		64		St. Louis, MO	Rehme, Preußen
Meyers, Elisabeth	9, Feb. 1893	14, Jan.	85- 5m- 4d	94	Schwarz	Bucyrus, OH	Birgmansweiler, Weilingen, Württemberg
Meyers, Ellen Margaretha	15, Aug. 1889	18, July	25	526	Hildebrandt	Etna, MO	Cass County, Illinois
Meyers, Georg	21, Sept 1893	4, Sept	37	606		San Antonio, TX	Baltimore, Maryland
Meyers, Ida	10, Jan. 1895	13, Dec.	33- 7m-26d	30	Wiebusch	Brenham, TX	
Meyers, Johan Friedrich	13, Oct. 1887	18, Aug.	38	654		Wichita, KS	Lebanon, Illinois
Meyers, Regula	24, Mar. 1892	3, Mar.	89	190	Hauenstein	New Orleans, LA	Ober-Endingen, Aargau, Schweiz
Meyn, Claus Jakob	18, June 1877	9, June	48	199		Chicago, IL	Meldorf, Schleswig-Holstein
Meyn, Francis	28, Oct. 1886		8- 7m- 7d	7		Chicago, IL	
Meyn, Heinrich	5, Sept 1889	11, Aug.	23	574		Tacoma, WA	
Meyn, Karolina	8, May 1882	11, Apr.	19- 8m-29d	151		Howard, NE	Cedar Lake , Indiana
Meytrott, Charles	31, Oct. 1895	8, Oct.	54	702		New York City, NY	Richelsdorf, Kurhessen
Meytrott, John Justis	3, Nov. 1892	4, Oct.	22	702		New York City, NY	New York
Meytrott, Martha Katharina	14, Aug. 1890	25, July	42- -19d	526	Stehl	New York City, NY	
Michael, Barbara	4, Jan. 1894	27, Nov.	69	14	Dunkel	Edon, OH	Dauphin County, Pennsylvania
Michael, Elenora	6, Sept 1860	15, Aug.	54	144	Werner	Fond du Lac, WI	Zeesewitz, Sachsen
Michael, Enos	20, Mar. 1890	25, Feb.	65- 3m-21d	190		Edgerton, OH	Susquehannah Twp., Dauphin Co., Pennsylvania

Christliche Apologete Death Notices --- 1839 - 1899

Name of Deceased	Notice Date	Death Date	Age	Maiden Name	Page	Place of Death	Place of Birth
Michael, Gottlob	26, Dec. 1864	6, Dec.	75		208	Fond du Lac, WI	Zetzritz bei Rochlitz, Sachsen
Michael, Hanna Rosina	27, Dec. 1860	8, Dec.	45	Thalheim	208	Fond du Lac, WI	Aschersheim, Sachsen
Michael, Henriette F. Y.	7, Feb. 1895	10, Jan.	65	Richter	94	Parker, SD	Ronneburg, Sachsen-Altenburg
Michael, Johan Heinrich	18, June 1896	31, May	71		399	Parker, SD	Waltersdorf a. d. Elster, Sachsen-Weimar
Michael, Johanna	25, Dec. 1882	7, Dec.	40		415	Hannibal, MO	Phanzlo, Demmin, Pommern
Michael, Josua	11, Aug. 1884	31, July	53		7	Edgerton, OH	Harrisburg, Pennsylvania
Michael, Magdalena	30, Mar. 1874	22, Feb.	75		103	Edgerton, OH	Packstein County, Pennsylvania
Michael, Maria Anna	19, Dec. 1881	1, Nov.	28- 9m-21d	Kröner	407	Columbus, OH	Columbus, Franklin County, Ohio
Michael, Marie	16, Nov. 1863		36		184	Brokrill, IN	Dauphyn County, Pennsylvania
Michael, Philipp	11, Apr. 1870	21, Mar.	69		119	Edgerton, OH	Pennsylvania
Michael, Wilhelmine	15, May 1882	29, Apr.	29		159	Chicago, IL	Fraureuth, Sachsen
Michaelis, Friedrich	12, Nov. 1841		Inquiry		179	St. Louis, MO	Wihe bei Erfurt,
Michaelis, Johan Friedrich	24, Dec. 1896	26, Oct.	79		831	Jordan, MN	Hudemühlen, Hannover
Michaelis, Maria	18, July 1895	27, June	75	Eilers	462	Jordan, MN	Eickloh, Ahlden, Hannover
Michaelis, Mathilda	14, Apr. 1898	22, Mar.	20		239	Valley City, ND	Silver Lake, Renfrew, Ontario, Canada
Michel, Anna Katharina	18, May 1885	27, Apr.	66		7	Santa Claus, IN	Holzhausen, Nester, Nassau
Michel, Anna Katharina	23, May 1881	14, Apr.	27	Schaup	167	Edon, OH	Wills County, Ohio
Michel, Anna Katharina Sophia	15, Jan. 1891	28, Dec.	76	Möller	46	Chicago, IL	Löhlbach bei Frankenberg, Kurhessen
Michel, Christina Dorothea	20, June 1889	19, May	58- 5m-17d	Weiß	398	Saginaw, MI	Ochsenbach, Brackenheim, Württemberg
Michel, Elisabeth	20, Sept 1855	23, Aug.	70		152	Huntingburg, IN	Holzhausen an der Heyd, Nastetten, Nassau
Michel, Elisabeth	23, Apr. 1866	16, Feb.	70		134	Allegheny City, PA	Bümpliz, Bern, Schweiz
Michel, Ernestina	30, Apr. 1891	11, Apr.	26- 1m-27d	Schäfer	286	Indianapolis, IN	
Michel, Friedrich	9, Oct. 1882	2, Sept	50- 6m- 7d		327	Saginaw, MI	Kirchberg, Sachsen
Michel, Heinrich	29, Sept 1862	2, Sept	79		156	Huntingburg, IN	Kemel, Amt Schwalbach, Nassau
Michel, Henriette	6, June 1870	17, May	23	Grandlienart	183	Goshen, IN	Frutigen, Bern, Schweiz
Michel, John G.	29, Oct. 1896	25, Sept	26		703	San Francisco, CA	Goshen, Indiana
Michel, Kaspar	16, Aug. 1894	26, July	73		534	Graham, MO	Briens, Bern, Schweiz
Michel, Margaretha	12, Jan. 1874	15, Dec.	46	Huggler	15	Oregon, MO	Briez, Bern, Schweiz
Michel, Maria	5, Feb. 1857	21, Jan.	42	Klanke	24	Pennsylvaniaburg, MD	Witlage, Hannover
Michel, Maria Sophia	25, Oct. 1880	5, Oct.	47- 1m- 1d	Albers	343	Batesville, IN	Stühren, Hannover
Michel, Matthäus	25, May 1899	22, Apr.	80		335	Lawrenceville, IN	Brenz, Bern, Schweiz
Michel, Matthäus	23, Nov. 1868	6, Nov.	74- 1m		375	Batesville, IN	Schweiz
Michel, Michael	25, June 1857	18, May	33		104	Rochester, NY	
Michel, Salomo	23, May 1864	8, Mar.	30		84	Edgerton, OH	Dauphin County, Pennsylvania
Michel, Wilhelm	1, Oct. 1883	8, Sept	62		319	Santa Claus, IN	Holzhausen auf der Heide, Nastetten, Nassau
Michel, Wilhelm	5, Aug. 1886	15, July	18		7	Graham, MO	
Michelfelder, Maria	30, Jan. 1871	14, Jan.	31		39	New York City, NY	Duslingen, Württemberg
Michelson, Margaretha	27, Aug. 1877		45	Gretschel	279	Cincinnati, OH	Baiern
Miehle, Louisa	8, July 1897	19, June	65- 8m		431	Evansville, IN	Birlefeld, Oldenburg
Mielke, Emma	14, Sept 1893	23, Aug.	31	Adam	590	Chicago, IL	Chicago, Cook County, Illinois
Mielke, Gottlieb	5, Oct. 1893	13, Sept	44		638	Harrington, WA	West Preußen
Miener, Anna	17, July 1890	4, July	31- 6m- 3d	Backer	462	Pekin, IL	Wiesens, Aurich, Ostfriesland
Miener, Heinrich	14, Apr. 1887	26, Mar.	72		238	Summerfield, IL	Wollrode, Kurhessen
Mieras, Charlotte	20, Sept 1875	31, Aug.	51		303		Lepenhusen, Friesland, Holland
Mierke, Paulina Christiana	9, Feb. 1893	3, Jan.	25		94	Owatonna, MN	Wheeling, Rice County, Minnesota
Mierke, Wilhelm Friedrich August	15, Nov. 1894	18, Oct.	56		742	Blooming Grove, MN	Stettin, Pommern

Christliche Apologete Death Notices --- 1839 - 1899

Name of Deceased	Notice Date	Death Date	Age	Maiden Name	Page	Place of Death	Place of Birth
Miesegans, August	4, Nov. 1897	9, Oct.	38		703	Freyburg, TX	Oldenburg Stadt, Oldenburg
Miläger, A.F.	16, Aug. 1880	18, July	57- 3m-11d		263	Kenosha, WI	Gumminshof, Pommern
Mild, Carolina	7, Oct. 1872	8, Sept	15- 9m-10d		327	St. Louis, MO	Altenheim, Baden
Mild, Johan	9, Oct. 1882	7, Sept	72- 5m-12d		327	St. Louis, MO	Altheim, Baden
Mild, Ursula	2, Sept 1886	8, Aug.	76	Fink	7	St. Louis, MO	Paris, Ohio
Mildenberger, Emma	19, Dec. 1864	20, Nov.	25		204	Rushville, IL	Schmiedhachenbach, Preußen
Mildenberger, Jacob	11, July 1870	17, June	46		223	Rushville, IL	Sienhagenbach, St. Wendel, Trier, Preußen
Mildenberger, Maria	29, July 1878	29, June	60		239	Rushville, IL	Bockerade, Kurhessen
Mildner, August J.	9, Sept 1897	12, Aug.	54		575	Warsaw, IL	Lancaster County, Pennsylvania
Miles, Katharina	5, Jan. 1874	23, Dec.	80		7	Freeport, IL	Neustadt an der Saale, Baiern
Milhaus, Margarethe	11, Mar. 1852	21, Feb.	38-11m-17d	Christ	44	Terre Haute, IN	Diebach, Hessen-Darmstadt
Milhaus, Nikolaus	18, Mar. 1852	6, Feb.	75		48	Bethlehem, OH	Steinbach, Salzungen, Sachsen-Meiningen
Mike, Carl	5, Apr. 1888	19, Mar.	45		222	Greenfield, MA	Sternbach, Sachsen
Mike, Fritz	12, Jan. 1893	3, Dec.	43		30	Greenfield, MA	Budo, Stolper, Köslin, Hinterpommern
Mike, Johan Theodor Ludwig	19, Dec. 1889	22, Nov.	55- 5m- 8d		814	Kansas City, KS	Bunzlau, Schlesien
Mike, Julius	14, Apr. 1892	28, Mar.	76		238	Greenfield, MA	Zilsdorf, Arnswalde, Preußen
Mike, Wilhelm	2, May 1895		48		286	Ripon, WI	Gummin, Pommern
Milleger, Anna Maria	5, July 1880	13, June	62- 3m-21d	Miller	215	Kenosha, WI	Beutelsbach, Württemberg
Millenberg, Maria Katharina	20, Nov. 1882	30, Oct.	57- 7m		375	Baltimore, MD	
Miller, (son of Adam)	24, Sept 1841	10, Sept			151	Mt. Gilead, ---	Hessen-Darmstadt
Miller, Adam	26, Oct. 1885	17, Sept	72		7	San Francisco, CA	Diedelsheim, Bretten, Baden
Miller, Albert	18, Oct. 1888	17, Aug.	6m-27d		670	Scranton, PA	Weitaroda, Kurhessen
Miller, Andreas	3, Nov. 1887	17, Sept	44		702	Charlestown, IN	Lachen, Neustadt a. d. Haardt, Rheinkreis Baiern
Miller, Anna Barbara	24, July 1890		55- 3m	Borschel	478	Iowa City, IA	Zeidloff, Unterfranken, Baiern
Miller, Anna Margaretha	14, Sept 1874	30, Aug.	57	Klein	295	Cincinnati, OH	Zwesten, Fritzlar, Kurhessen
Miller, Anna Margarethe	3, June 1897	4, May	75- 3m-16d		351	Philadelphia, PA	
Miller, Anna Maria	7, Jan. 1878	9, Dec.	68- 9m		7	Muscatine, IA	Bremen,
Miller, Anna Maria	1, Nov. 1855	18, Oct.	7- 5m-24d		176	Rockford, IN	Arenshorst, Osterkappeln, Hannover
Miller, Anna Maria Adelheid	20, Dec. 1869	27, Nov.	62	Ahrens	407	De Soto, MO	Köthenberg, Oberndorf, Württemberg
Miller, Anna Maria Clara	2, May 1895	2, Apr.	75		286	White Creek, IN	Jackson County, Indiana
Miller, Barbara	15, Mar. 1869	26, Feb.	28	Habrer	87	Allegan, MI	Fuezen, Baden
Miller, Barbara	13, Mar. 1856	15, Feb.	21		44	Rockford, IN	Klein-Luckow, Kreis Prenzlau, Preußen
Miller, Benedikt	26, July 1880	10, July	51		239	Altamont, IL	
Miller, Bertha	15, July 1867			Giermann	222	Lancaster, NY	Braunschweig
Miller, Bessy May	12, July 1888	22, June	15- 4m-13d		446	Atchison, KS	Riegersdorf, Schlesien
Miller, Carolina	5, Feb. 1877	18, Jan.	60- 8m-15d	Willi	47	Windsor, WI	Huntingburg, Dubois County, Indiana
Miller, Caroline E.	13, May 1897	22, Apr.	74		303	Evansville, IN	
Miller, Caroline Linda	14, June 1894	11, May	40		390	Enterprise, IL	Crailsheim, Württemberg
Miller, Catharina	24, Jan. 1871	6, Jan.	32- 4m-11d		31	Cincinnati, OH	Rechtebach, Eschwege, Hessen-Kassel
Miller, Catharina Maria	22, Sept 1884	5, Sept	71		7	Troy, NY	Sonnenberg, Wiesbaden, Nassau
Miller, Christian	16, Apr. 1891	24, Feb.	74- 1m-28d		254	New Metamoras, OH	Eichenroth, Lauterbach, Hessen-Darmstadt
Miller, Christian	25, Feb. 1897	9, Feb.	72		127	Crown Point, IN	Kirchhosbach, Bischhausen, Kurhessen
Miller, Christina	2, Sept 1878	21, Aug.	77		279	Seymour, IN	Wollenhausen, Nieda, Hessen-Darmstadt
Miller, Christine	30, Oct. 1871	18, Sept	46	Jackel	351	Alton, IL	
Miller, Christine	28, Apr. 1898	6, Apr.	77	Knierim	271	Monroefield, OH	
Miller, Conrad	8, July 1886	4, June	69		7	Ft. Hunter, NY	

Christliche Apologete Death Notices --- 1839 - 1899

Name of Deceased	Notice Date	Death Date	Age	Maiden Name	Page	Place of Death	Place of Birth
Miller, Daniel	29, July 1872	25, June	76		247	De Soto, MO	Schmidtlottheim, Vöhle, Hessen-Darmstadt
Miller, Daniel C.	27, Jan. 1887	14, Jan.	50		62	Farmington, MO	St. Genevieve County, Missouri
Miller, David	7, May 1877	11, Apr.	42- 7m-25d		151	Salem, MN	Canton Bern, Schweiz
Miller, Dietrich	26, Dec. 1895	4, Dec.	67		828	Seymour, IN	Brokloh, Wölge, Hannover
Miller, Elisabeth	1, Mar. 1875	9, Feb.	38	Partenheimer	71	Brusnwick, MO	Waldböckelheim, Kreuznach, Rheinpreußen
Miller, Elisabeth	22, Nov. 1894	9, Oct.	53	Meyer	758	Evansville, IN	Eninger, Württemberg
Miller, Elisabetha	28, Dec. 1854	24, Oct.	18- -27d		208	Captina, OH	
Miller, Emma Louise	8, Nov. 1888	9, Oct.	26		718	Alton, IL	Alton, Illinois
Miller, Emma Louise	11, Jan. 1875	17, Dec.	14		15	Cincinnati, OH	
Miller, Ernestine Wilhelmine C.	3, Nov. 1892	8, Oct.	41	Block	702	Lyona, KS	Alt Damerow, Saatzig, Hinterpommern
Miller, Ernst Wilhem Herman	21, Aug. 1876	29, July	56		271	Henderson, KY	Bertelsdorf bei Reichenbach, Schlesien
Miller, Frank	16, Oct. 1890	11, Sept	72- 9m-16d		670	Oakland, CA	Riechen-Dieburg, Hessen-Darmstadt
Miller, Frank	27, Aug. 1896	23, July	25		559	Tallula, IL	Petersburg, Illinois
Miller, Fred.	28, Sept 1893	9, Aug.	59		622	Lincoln, NE	Tengern, Lübke, Preußen
Miller, Friedrich	15, Oct. 1883	24, Sept	68		335	Ironton, OH	Melchbachhof, Zweibrücken, Schweiz
Miller, Friedrich	9, Apr. 1891	19, Mar.	65		238	Louisville, KY	Ingweiler bei Straßburg, Elsaß
Miller, Friedrich	17, Mar. 1892	11, Jan.	78		174		Richstein, Preußen
Miller, Friedrich Wilhelm	21, Apr. 1873	28, Feb.	14		127	Seymour, IN	Indianapolis, Marion County, Indiana
Miller, Friedrich Wilhelm	6, Oct. 1879	5, July	17		319	Oakland, CA	Milwaukee, Wisconsin
Miller, George J.	31, July 1890	13, July	31- 4m-21d		494	St. Paul, MN	
Miller, Grötje	8, Jan. 1872	3, Dec.	56	Mahnken	15	Trenton, IL	
Miller, Hanna	6, Apr. 1899	4, Mar.	51	Bensinger	223	Bucyrus, OH	Schuylkill County, Pennsylvania
Miller, Hanna Elisabeth	28, Jan. 1892	2, Jan.	61	Keil	62	Decatur, IL	Hickersdorf, Hessen-Darmstadt
Miller, Heinrich	11, Dec. 1882	2, Nov.	82		399	St. Ansgar, IA	Streit, Braunschweig
Miller, Heinrich	24, Nov. 1887	17, Oct.	32		750	Lyona, KS	Canada
Miller, Helena	4, Apr. 1889	8, Mar.	63	Kammerer	222	Troy, NY	Nordstädt, Fillingen, Baden
Miller, Henrietta	9, June 1887	26, May	22		366	Burlington, IA	Rock Spring, Iowa
Miller, Henry	8, Apr. 1886	11, Mar.	13		7	Terre Haute, IN	
Miller, Henry F.	11, Jan. 1894	22, Dec.	24- 1m-21d		30	Farmington, IA	
Miller, Hermann	28, Nov. 1864	16, Sept	18		192	West Bend, WI	
Miller, Hermina Gesina	5, July 1894	13, June	18- 6m-22d		438		
Miller, Jak.	9, Nov. 1868	4, Oct.	37- 2m- 9d		359	Clarington, OH	Steinweiler, Germersheim, Rheinkreis Baiern
Miller, Jakob	31, May 1875	25, Apr.	39		175	Bushnell, IL	New York
Miller, Jakob Heinrich	9, Aug. 1849	13, July			128	Smooth Prairie, ---	Nordhausen, Nassau
Miller, Johan	12, Mar. 1891	20, Feb.	68		174	Warsaw, IL	Bethlehem, Pennsylvania
Miller, Johan Adam	11, Apr. 1881	16, Mar.	75		119	Galion, OH	Pisdorf, Elsaß
Miller, Johan Dietrich	16, Sept 1872	27, Aug.	77		303	Newport, KY	Gehaus, Sachsen-Weimar
Miller, Johan Georg	26, July 1894	3, July	68		486	Bucyrus, OH	Hohenstaufen, Württemberg
Miller, Johan Karl	27, Sept 1894	26, Aug.	42		630	Scranton, PA	Allenbach, RheinPreußen
Miller, Johann	14, Apr. 1853	7, Mar.	57		60	Captina, OH	Kanton Bern, Schweiz
Miller, Johann Friedrich	15, Dec. 1859	6, Dec.	9		200	Indianapolis, IN	
Miller, Johann Philipp	21, July 1862	11, May	20		116	Seymour, IN	Cincinnati, Ohio
Miller, John	31, Dec. 1883	3, Dec.	17- 7m- 3d		7	Iowa City, IA	
Miller, Karl	15, Mar. 1880	29, Feb.	79		87	Seymour, IN	Sonnenberg, Nassau
Miller, Katharina	24, Aug. 1874	9, Aug.	32		273	Cincinnati, OH	Bergbach, Bergzabern, Rheinpfalz Baiern
Miller, Katharina	9, Feb. 1880	24, Jan.	29	Boller	47	Evansville, IN	Evansville, Indiana

Christliche Apologete Death Notices --- 1839 - 1899

Name of Deceased	Notice Date	Death Date	Age	Page	Maiden Name	Place of Death	Place of Birth
Miller, Katharine	25, June 1883	27, May	81- 3m- 3d	207	Grieshauer	Summerfield, IL	Hohenhaslach, Württemberg
Miller, Katharine	28, Apr. 1884	23, June	68- -16d	7	Nagel	Brooklyn, NY	Karlsruhe, Baden
Miller, Katharine Elisabeth	2, July 1877	14, June	55	215	Wittekindt	Quincy, IL	Bischhausen, Eschwinge, Hessen-Kassel
Miller, Konrad	9, Mar. 1885	14, Feb.	61	7		Metamoras, OH	
Miller, Leonidas Hamline	26, July 1839	19, July	1- 2m-16d	119		Cincinnati, OH	
Miller, Lillie	11, May 1899	10, Mar.	27	302	Bach	St. Paul, MN	Woodbury, Minnesota
Miller, Lizzie	25, Sept 1882	31, Aug.	22- 6m-10d	311		Bucyrus, OH	Crawford County, Ohio
Miller, Lizzie	22, May 1890	4, May	35-11m	334	Meyer	Scranton, PA	Radsitz, West Preußen
Miller, Louise	1, Nov. 1880	5, Oct.	90	351		Rochester, MN	Freisteinau, Lauderbach, Hessen-Darmstadt
Miller, Luise	29, Dec. 1898	4, Oct.	72	828	Grob	Moberly, MO	Freisteinau, Hessen-Darmstadt
Miller, Luise	12, Jan. 1899	4, Oct.	75	31		Moberly, MO	Cincinnati, Hamilton County, Ohio
Miller, Lydia Louise	18, Apr. 1895		32- 6m-21d	254	Meyer	Seymour, IN	
Miller, Lydia Paulina	25, Oct. 1888	3, Oct.	27-10m- 2d	686	Bäuerle	Columbus, OH	Ilsfeld, Besigheim, Württemberg
Miller, Magdalena	13, Jan. 1868	1, Jan.	60	14	Jäger	Fremont, IN	Berlenbach, Weißenburg, Elsaß
Miller, Magdalena	22, Oct. 1891	3, Oct.	85	686	Walter	Bushnell, IL	
Miller, Magdalena Christine	12, June 1876	15, May	14- 5m	191		Edwardsville, IL	Sprentlingen, Hessen-Darmstadt
Miller, Margaretha	27, Dec. 1860	11, Dec.	60- 4m-24d	208	Haan	Hamilton, OH	
Miller, Margaretha	12, Jan. 1893	9, Dec.	93	30		Pomeroy, OH	Breitingen, Sachsen
Miller, Maria	21, May 1896	25, Apr.	72	334	Kipping	Lawrence, MA	Osnabrück, Hannover
Miller, Maria Engel	31, Oct. 1895	5, Oct.	81- 5m-21d	702	Stammbosch	White Creek, IN	Geschweiler, Baden
Miller, Maria Josepha	25, July 1895	30, June	67	478	Schwerer	Warsaw, IL	Knoxville, Illinois
Miller, Maria Katharina	1, May 1890	9, Apr.	26	286	Burger	Jamestown, MO	Schweiz
Miller, Marie	20, Nov. 1890	23, Oct.	84-10m-12d	750		Crow River, MN	
Miller, Marie Mathilde	14, Oct. 1852	17, Sept	7- 8m	168		Quincy, IL	Elsaß
Miller, Martin	24, Dec. 1896	5, Dec.	49	831		New Orleans, LA	
Miller, Martin August	14, Oct. 1872	11, Sept		335		St. Joseph, MO	
Miller, Mary Elisabeth	9, May 1881	23, Apr.	45	151		St. Louis, MO	
Miller, Michael	3, Apr. 1865		41	56		Dunkirk, NY	Korb, Waiblingen, Württemberg
Miller, Minna Gesina	19, July 1894	13, June	18-6m-22d	470		Chicago, IL	
Miller, Pauline	17, Mar. 1898	20, Feb.	23	175	Melk	Morris, MN	Germany
Miller, Peter	3, Aug. 1893	9, July	66	494		Evansville, IN	Birgenau, Hessen-Darmstadt
Miller, Sarah Virginia	10, Aug. 1893	21, July	27	510	Phillipp	Beardstown, IL	Wheeling, West Virginia
Miller, Sophia Alwine	28, Mar. 1895	18, Mar.	26	206	Brakebusch	Highland, IL	
Miller, Sophia Helene Maria	2, Sept 1897	27, Apr.	83	559		New York City, NY	Lembach, Weißenburg, Elsaß
Miller, Sophie	26, Jan. 1899	29, Dec.	70	63	Bey	Clarington, OH	
Miller, Wilhelm	24, Oct. 1881	7, Oct.	20	343		Brighton, IL	Coll County, Missouri
Miller, Wilhelm F.	26, Feb. 1872	10, Feb.	24	71		Lyons Creek, KS	Falkenheim, Preußen
Miller, Willie	8, Sept 1887	17, Aug.	29	574		Lawrence, MA	Kassel, Kurhessen
Millhaus , Wilhelmine	16, Dec. 1858	15, Nov.	33	200	Koch	Marshall, IL	
Millhaus, Katharina	5, Feb. 1847	8, Oct.	67	23		Delaware, OH	
Millhause, Catharina	17, Dec. 1857	25, Nov.	10-10m- 9d	204		Marshall, IL	Guttschin, Brandenburg
Milling, Julius	27, Feb. 1890	5, Jan.	38	142	Lieben	Perry, TX	Gorjost, Cüstrin an der Oder, Preußen
Militz, Albertine	20, Apr. 1885	6, Apr.	76	7		Watertown, WI	Bellgard, Preußen
Milly, Ida Johanna Emilie	29, Aug.1895	26, June		558		Red Wing, MN	
Milo, Heinrich	27, Feb. 1882	12, Feb.	11- 8m	71		Spring, TX	
Milo, Louise Wilhelmine	20, Feb. 1882	29, Jan.	21- -26d	63		Spring, TX	

- 342 -

Christliche Apologete Death Notices --- 1839 - 1899

Name of Deceased	Notice Date	Death Date	Age	Maiden Name	Page	Place of Death	Place of Birth
Mils, Sarah	2, Jan. 1890	17, Dec.	46	Schmiker	14	Santa Claus, IN	Kanton Bern, Schweiz
Mischler, Anna	3, Nov. 1898	29, Sept	88	Tischer	703	Baresville, OH	Hille, Preußen
Minden, Maria	25, Nov. 1872	3, Nov.	64	Düwel	383	St. Louis, MO	Windumer, Altendeich, Ostfriesland
Miner, Konrad	23, Mar. 1899	24, Feb.	42		191	Emden, IL	Wirsitz, Posen
Minich, Clara A. L.	18, June 1891	11, May	19		398	Chicago, IL	Kurhessen
Minkel, Heinrich	24, Feb. 1879		57		63	San Jose, CA	Epfendach, Neckarbischofsheim, Baden
Minkel, John A.	16, Nov. 1863	27, May			184	Rochester, NY	
Minor, August	5, Dec. 1889	11, Nov.	20		782	Dalton, MO	
Minor, Heinrich	14, Oct. 1878	23, Sept	52		327	Brunswick, MO	Braubach, Nassau
Minor, Louisa	19, Dec. 1889	3, Dec.	23- 4m		814	Dalton, MO	
Minor, Mary Christina	29, Oct. 1896	3, Oct.	26		703	Dalton, MO	Dalton, Missouri
Minske, Friedrich Wilhelm	8, Oct. 1891	13, Sept	62		654	Waseca, MN	Belgen, Brandenburg
Minske, Johann	26, Dec. 1861	2, Dec.	57		208	Morristown, MN	Blankenfelde, Preußen
Minske, Juliana	26, Mar. 1896	22, Feb.	83	Noack	206	Waseca, MN	Nordhausen bei Königsberg, Neumark
Minstermann, Dorothea	27, Sept 1849	4, Sept	46		156	St. Louis, MO	Bollhagen, Bücheburg, Lippe-Schaumburg
Mintner, Anna	14, May 1896	8, Apr.	86	Schwendner	318	Kewaskum, WI	Buchs, Werdenberg, St. Gallen, Schweiz
Minzel, Andreas	12, July 1844		Inquiry		103	Henry County, OH	Heiligersdorf, Untermainkreis, Baiern
Minzel, Caroline	10, May 1894	19, Apr.	77	Ruf	310	Defiance, OH	Zweibrücken, Baiern
Minzenmeier, Johan Andreas	7, Feb. 1889	7, Dec.	64		94	Jeffersonville, IN	Rothenberg, Cannstadt, Württemberg
Mirker, Katharina	1, Apr. 1878	13, Feb.	76- -13d		103	Ripley, OH	Niederhofen, Brackenheim, Württemberg
Mische, C.	2, Apr. 1857	5, Jan.	59		56	Warren, MO	
Mische, C. (Mrs)	2, Apr. 1857	12, Mar.	47		56	Warren, MO	
Mische, Friedrich	13, July 1863	11, June			112	Warrenton, MO	Alverdissen, Lippe-Detmold
Mischke, Amalie	4, Apr. 1881	17, Mar.	59	Sucker	111	Yankton, SD	Memmingen, Baiern
Mischky, Carl Fr.	12, Apr. 1894	4, Mar.	70		246	Ahn, NE	Wisbuhr, Manow, Pommern
Mischler, Christian	28, Dec. 1893	11, Dec.			828	Jamestown, MO	Ruggesberg, Bern, Schweiz
Mischler, Samuel	16, Feb. 1899		88		111	Hannibal, OH	Kanton Bern, Schweiz
Mischnick, August	23, July 1896	30, June	65		479	Elmore, OH	Rummelsburg, Pommern
Mißner, Johanna	18, Oct. 1894	2, Oct.	64		678	Platteville, WI	Schönfeld, Preußen
Mißner, Julius	16, Mar. 1893	28, Feb.	67		174	Platteville, WI	Zadow , Preußen
Mitchel, Elisa	22, Feb. 1875	31, Jan.	20- 8m- 5d	Keck	63	Lostant, MO	St. Louis, Missouri
Mitchel, Margarethe	27, Aug. 1896	31, July	77	Busch	559	Rochester, NY	Gießbach, Baden
Mitchel, Sophie	21, Feb. 1870	6, Feb.	17		63	Rochester, NY	
Mitsch, Johan Phil.	12, Oct. 1899	20, Aug.	76		655	Honey Creek, WI	Leibenstadt, Adeisheim, Baden
Mitsch, Johanna Christine	11, Jan. 1894	15, Dec.	63	Noll	30	East Troy, WI	Sulzfeld, Epinger, Baden
Mittelhäuser, Wilhelm	13, Nov. 1876	19, Oct.	55		367	St. Louis, MO	Wilster, Holstein
Mittelsdorf, Anna Katharina	12, Aug. 1886	26, July	75	Trautwetter	7	East Troy, WI	Wieldprechtsroda, Sachsen-Meiningen
Mittelsdorf, Paul	16, July 1891	9, June	85		462	East Troy, WI	Wilbrechtroda, Sachsen-Meiningen
Mittelstädt, (Mrs)	4, Nov. 1878	5, Oct.	78- 8m- 2d		351	Watertown, WI	Collin, Preußen
Mittelstadt, Christian Friedrich	10, June 1867	26, Mar.	73- 5m-20d		182	Oconomowoc, WI	Collin, Pommern
Mittelstädt, Wilhem	15, Aug. 1864	24, May	24- 9m-16d		132	Oconomowoc, WI	Cölin, Kreis Pieriz, Pommern, Preußen
Mittendorf, Adam Heinrich	12, July 1869	22, June	70		223	Furnace, OH	Wester Oldendorf, Grönenberg, Hannover
Mittendorf, Carolina	22, Apr. 1872	28, Mar.	24- 3m-11d	Grannemann	135	Morrison Station, ---	
Mittendorf, Catharina Elisabeth	15, June 1874	30, May	64- 2m	Obermiller	191	Webster, OH	WesterOldendorf, Amt Melle, Hannover
Mittendorf, Georg	1, Nov. 1875	11, Oct.	36		351	Morrison, MO	Ohio
Mittendorf, Johan Heinrich	9, Nov. 1885	26, Oct.	72		7	Portsmouth, OH	Oltendorf, Grünenberg, Hannover

Christliche Apologete Death Notices --- 1839 - 1899

Name of Deceased	Notice Date	Death Date	Age	Page	Maiden Name	Place of Death	Place of Birth
Mitzel, Susanna Eleonora	21, Mar. 1881	1, Mar.	41- 5m-23d	95	Henning	Detroit, MI	Neuwartsch, Preußen
Mitzkus, Jakob	12, Apr. 1888	8, Mar.	77	238		San Francisco, CA	Labiau, Königsberg, Preußen
Mitzkus, Rosina	11, Sept 1890	10, July	79	590		San Francisco, CA	Colmar, Posen
Mitzner, Gottlieb	20, Apr. 1874	8, Apr.	29	127		Buffalo, NY	Grabowka, Preußen
Mix, Franz Ferdinand	15, Apr. 1886	22, Mar.	12- 4m-12d	7		Oak Lake, SD	
Mix, Herman Gustav	4, Sept 1876	3, Aug.	33	287		Milwaukee, WI	Danzig, Preußen
Moadinger, Joh. Ul.	12, Sept 1864	7, Aug.	60	148		New York, NY	Stempfelbach, Württemberg
Moak, Eva	19, July 1888	31, May	38- 4m-21d	462	Helwig	Lancaster, NY	
Moak, Peter Philipp	15, Mar. 1888	12, Feb.		174		Lancaster, NY	Zweibrücken, Rheinkreis Baiern
Möbus, Heinrich	26, Dec. 1889	8, Dec.	66	830		Troy, NY	Langendorf, Kurhessen
Möchnig, Caroline	16, Apr. 1891	10, Mar.	81- -24d	254	Hirsch	Zumbro Falls, MN	Terinze, Falkenburg, Oppen, Schlesien
Möchnig, Friedrich Wilhelm	25, Oct. 1888	10, Oct.	18- 6m	686		Zumbro Falls, MN	West Albany, Wabasha County, Minnesota
Möchnig, Johan Carl	18, Oct. 1888	24, Sept	16- 7m-22d	670		Zumbro Falls, MN	
Möcke, Georg Friedrich	30, June 1892	9, May	62	414		Greenfield, MA	Wernshausen, Sachsen-Meiningen
Mockler, Karolina	28, Aug. 1876	27, July	57- 1m	279	Klein	Baraboo, WI	Böckingen, Württemberg
Modar, Friedrich Johan	24, Apr. 1890	31, Mar.	16- 5m-19d	270		Wheeling, WV	Wheeling, West Virginia
Moehle, Conradine	25, July 1889		68- 6m-10d	478	Bierschwale	Willow, TX	Gadenstedt, Hannover
Moellenberndt, Wilhelm	14, May 1891	11, Apr.	41	318		Paige, TX	Fayette County, Texas
Moeller, Abraham	13, Aug. 1883	20, July	19-11m- 8d	263		Red Bud, IL	
Moeller, August	18, Mar.1872	28, Feb.	38- 5m	95		Red Bud, IL	
Moeller, Benjamin	18, Dec. 1890	24, Oct.	16	814		Milwaukee, WI	Petersdorf, Insel Fehmarn, Dänemark
Moeller, Catharine	1, Sept 1879	20, June	40- 9m	279	Julier	Baraboo, WI	Milwaukee, Wisconsin
Moeller, Ernestine	23, Dec. 1886	22, Nov.	32	7		Jordan, MN	Ostheim, Elsaß
Moeller, Ernst	24, Jan. 1881		48	31		Industry, TX	Windhagen, Lippe-Schaumburg
Moeller, Heinrich	10, Feb. 1887	21, Jan.	58	94		Grand Island, NE	Schleswig-Holstein
Moeller, John	19, June 1890	24, May	63- 8m-28d	398		New Bremen, IL	Röckenfus, Rotenburg, Kurhessen
Moeller, Maria Catharina	3, May 1875	13, Apr.	55	143	Hammann	Chicago, IL	Rostock, Mecklenburg-Schwerin
Moeyer, Anna E.	22, Sept 1898	27, Apr.	53	607		Waco, NE	Jöllenbeck, Westphalen
Mogke, Karl	19, Jan. 1863	18, Sept		12		Dunkirk, NY	
Mogke, Weymand	19, Jan. 1863	16, Nov.	77- 5m	12		Dunkirk, NY	
Mogler, (Mr)	11, Jan. 1869	19, Dec.	47- 7m-28d	15		Blooming Grove, MN	Kernbach, Kurhessen
Mogler, Friederika	28, May 1877	3, May	57	175		Baraboo, WI	Beginnen, Heilbronn, Württemberg
Mohland, Juliane Wilhelmine	2, Feb. 1899	2, Jan.	83	79	Luers	Harper, IA	Schluchtern, Baden
Mohland, Martin	27, June 1881	15, May	77	207		German Creek, IA	Teckleburg, Preußen
Möhle, Christian	10, July 1882	19, June	36- -25d	223		Wapello, IA	Neukirchen, Ottendorf, Hannover
Möhle, Dorothea	17, Feb. 1879	1, Feb.	32- 5m-30d	55	Dippe	Wapello, IA	Hille, Minden, Preußen
Möhle, Friedrich	4, Oct. 1860	9, Aug.	26	160		Wapello, IA	Bösgenfeld, Sternberg, Lippe-Detmold
Möhle, Friedrich W.	13, Oct. 1859	22, Sept	59	164		Wapello, IA	Hile bei Preußisch Minden, Preußen
Möhle, Johan Gottfried	29, May 1890	3, May	74	350		Fredericksburg, TX	Hille, Minden, Preußen
Möhle, Maria	3, Aug. 1885	16, June	31	7	Stiehl	Fredericksburg, TX	Watigenstet, Hannover
Möhlemann, Christian	1, Nov. 1875	1, Oct.	52	351		Indianapolis, IN	Fredericksburg, Gillespie County, Texas
Möhlmann, Anna	3, July 1865	1, May	15	108		De Soto, MO	Schweiz
Mohn, Gustav Adolph	27, Dec. 1888	15, Dec.	33	830		Akron, OH	Oberau bei Meißen, Sachsen
Mohn, Wilhelm	4, Sept 1882	21, Aug.	62	287		Chicago, IL	Bernstein, Preußen
Mohns, Dietrich	3, July 1851	15, June	6- 6m	108		Louisville, KY	
Mohns, Enore	5, July 1849	25, June	59	108		Louisville, KY	Bückeburg, Lippe-Schaumburg

- 344 -

Christliche Apologete Death Notices --- 1839 - 1899

Name of Deceased	Notice Date	Death Date	Age	Page	Maiden Name	Place of Death	Place of Birth
Mohns, Ernstine	2, Sept 1897	6, Aug.	75	559		Chicago, IL	Warsin, Pommern
Mohns, Friedrich	7, Nov. 1895	15, Oct.	75	718		Seymour, IL	Hagenburg, Lippe-Schaumburg
Mohns, Heinrich Wilhelm	3, July 1851	18, June	37	108		Louisville, KY	
Mohns, Henriette	12, May 1887	15, Apr.	59	302	Hintzen	New Albany, IN	
Mohns, Louise F.	6, May 1878	4, Apr.	21- -21d	143	Rausch	Louisville, KY	
Mohns, Marie Louise	3, July 1851	25, June	6m	108		Louisville, KY	
Mohns, Sarah	10, July 1851	12, June	8- 3m	112		Louisville, KY	
Mohr, Anna Martha	14, Mar. 1895	20, Feb.	79	174	Eckert	Honey Creek, WI	Krauthausen, Sontra, Hessen-Kassel
Mohr, Ceßny	15, Nov. 1880	5, Sept	25- 9m- 5d	367	Kuns	Etna, MO	Watertown, Wisconsin
Mohr, Charlotte Henriette	13, Jan. 1898	23, Dec.	47	31	Breidenstein	Etna, MO	Page County, Virginia
Mohr, Elisabeth	19, Sept 1889	24, Aug.	46	606	Kleinschrot	Freeport, IL	Adelshofen, Offenheim, Baiern
Mohr, Elisabeth	12, Jan. 1863	12, Dec.		8		East Troy, WI	
Mohr, Engel	27, Apr. 1893	18, Mar.	74	270		Waco, NE	Holzhausen, Eschwege, Kurhessen
Mohr, Georg	12, Nov. 1891	3, Oct.	72	734		Lee, IL	Schlitz, Hessen-Darmstadt
Mohr, Heinrich	27, Feb. 1851	10, Jan.	42- 1m-27d	36			Glückstadt bei Hamburg, Germany
Mohr, Johann	10, Nov. 1848		Inquiry	183		Red Bud, IL	
Mohr, Johanna	16, Jan. 1890	6, Dec.	69	46		Etna, MO	Weiler, Pforzheim, Baden
Mohr, John	27, Sept 1855	10, Sept	29	156		Seneca Falls, NY	Hering, Kreis Dieburg, Hessen-Darmstadt
Mohr, John	16, June 1862	26, May	47	96		East Troy, WI	Wülfterode, Kreis Rodenburg, Kurhessen
Mohr, Karl Johan	12, Nov. 1891	15, Sept	46-11m-23d	734		Freeport, IL	Bießen, Baiern
Mohr, Katharina	26, Aug. 1878	13, July	76	271		Philadelphia, PA	Meißenheim, Homburg, Hessen
Moldenhauer, Augusta	9, Mar. 1899	8, Feb.	83- 5m- 9d	159		Sandusky, OH	
Moldenhauer, Friedrich	20, Jan. 1879	8, Jan.	34	23		Chicago, IL	Charbrow, Köslin, Preußen
Moldenhauer, Henriette Char.	5, Dec. 1889	5, Nov.	69- 8m-15d	782	Magsig	Delhi, MI	Krobitz, Keßlien, Preußen
Moldenhauer, Johan	1, Dec. 1898	16, Nov.	77	767		Sandusky, OH	Lauenburger, Pommern
Moldenhauer, Louise	26, Mar. 1877	12, Mar.	40	103	Henske	Sun Prairie, WI	Sabes, Pyritz, Pommern, Preußen
Moldenhauer, Wilhelmine	1, July 1878	27, May	61- 2m-17d	207	Kassube	Detroit, MI	Görschwalde, Brandenburg, Preußen
Molder, Elisabeth	26, Oct. 1885	11, Oct.	23	7	Grob	Vermillion, OH	Braunhelm, Lorain County, Ohio
Molder, Konrad	22, June 1899	1, May	70	399		Vermillion, OH	Altenkirchen, Baiern
Molhagen, Carolina	7, Mar. 1864	23, Dec.	28	40		Dickinson Co, KA	Serwest, Brandenburg, Preußen
Moll, Heinrich A.	11, Feb. 1886	17, Dec.	27	7		Evansville, IN	Vanderburg County, Indiana
Moll, Heinrich Jakob	20, Oct. 1873	23, Sept	72	335		Columbus, WI	Kalsow, Mecklenburg-Schwerin
Möll, Jakob	28, Oct. 1878	7, Oct.		343		Marrs, IN	Buhlbronn, Schorndorf, Württemberg
Moll, Walter K.	29, June 1899	6, June	20	415		Evansville, IN	
Möllenbruck, H.	31, Oct. 1881	16, Oct.	49	351		Olmstead, OH	Hüsde, Amt Wittlage, Hannover
Mollenhauer, Anna	23, Mar. 1899	28, Feb.	31	191	Kramberg	Columbus, IL	Adams County, Illinois
Mollenhauer, August	7, July 1884	21, June	62- 6m	7		Owatonna, MN	Westerhof, Hannover
Mollenhauer, Sophia	8, Feb. 1869	26, Oct.	79	47	Bode	Etna, MO	Binder, Hildesheim, Hannover
Möllenkamp, Heinrich R.	12, June 1882	24, Apr.	59	191		Huntingburg, IN	Kassel, Tecklenburg, Münster, Preußen
Möller, August Heinrich	31, Mar. 1898	8, Mar.	74	207		Morrison, MO	Begoldshausen, Minden, Preußen
Möller, Auguste	24, June 1886	31, May	16	7		Papillion, NE	
Möller, Carl H. Ch.	25, Dec. 1876	7, Dec.	49	413		Chicago, IL	Volkenhagen, Mecklenburg-Schwerin
Möller, Carl Heinrich Wilhelm	30, July 1891	28, June	14- 1m- 3d	494		Wilber, NE	Alswede, Lübeck, Westphalen
Möller, Daniel Carl Christian	19, Aug. 1886	25, July	48	7		Berea, OH	Volksdorf, Grimmen, Stralsund, Preußen
Möller, Elisabeth	16, Oct. 1876	2, Oct.	18- 1m-16d	335		St. Paul, MN	
Möller, Emilie	14, Dec. 1885	29, Nov.	33	7	Kräuter	Chicago, IL	Bloomington, Illinois

Christliche Apologete Death Notices --- 1839 - 1899

Name of Deceased	Place of Death	Maiden Name	Page	Age	Death Date	Notice Date	Place of Birth
Möller, Engel Christine	Shakopee, MN	Witt	104	45	2, July	26, June 1865	Großinbrode, Schleswig-Holstein
Möller, Fletcher	Jordan, MN		239	21- 3m- 1d	1, Mar.	25, July 1881	
Möller, Friedrich	Marine City, MI		111	24- 2m-13d	7, Apr. 1873	7, Apr. 1873	Alt-Karin, Neu Buckow, Mecklenburg-Schwerin
Möller, Friedrich	St. Louis, MO		607	69	5, Sept	21, Sept 1899	Lippe-Detmold
Möller, Friedrich Karl	Decatur, IL		52	27	17, Feb.	31, Mar. 1862	Meitze, Amt Bissendorf, Hannover
Möller, Georg	Boonville, IN		192		30, Oct.	27, Nov. 1856	
Möller, Heinrich	Industry, TX		828	66	19, Oct.	26, Dec. 1895	Wendhaken, Lippe-Schaumburg
Möller, Heinrich	St. Paul, MN		142	60	9, Feb.	3, Mar. 1892	
Möller, Johanna Charlotte	Oklahoma City, OK	Bürger	262	39	28, Mar.	19, Apr. 1894	Bruchhausen, Höxter, Westphalen
Möller, Katharina	Baraboo, WI	Juliar	223	40- 9m	20, June	14, July 1879	Ostheim, Elsaß
Möller, Wilhelm	Jordan, MN		383	48	19, May	11, June 1896	Zietel, Holstein
Möller, Wilhelmina	Ellis Grove, MO		7	34	7, Nov.	1, Dec. 1884	St. Louis, Missouri
Molzahn, Albert A.E.	Bristol, WI		686	37	5, Oct.	24, Oct. 1895	Buchholz bei Belgard, Pommern
Molzen, Martha E.	New York City, NY		486		22, June	26, July 1894	Quaret, Schleswig
Molzen, Peter	New York City, NY		318	47	6, Mar.	14, May 1891	Quarrs, Schleswig
Molzow, Maria	Washington, MN		303	71	19, Apr.	12, May 1898	Stefenhagen, Germany
Momberg, Adam Conrad	Cincinnati, OH		7	30	6, Jan.	21, Jan. 1886	Green Twp., Hamilton County, Ohio
Momberg, Anna Elisabeth	Cincinnati, OH	Winter	143	85- 3m- 5d	6, Feb.	3, Mar. 1898	Dissen, Kurhessen
Momberg, Anna Martha	Wyandotte, KS	Götze	103	58	12, Mar.	26, Mar. 1877	Kirchberg, Kurhessen
Momberg, Louisa	Cincinnati, OH	Rühl	783	46	19, Nov.	9, Dec. 1897	Neuenheim, Hessen-Darmstadt
Momberger, (Mr)	Cannelton, IN		100	26		22, June 1854	Zeilbach, Hessen
Mönch, Konrad	Ft. Hunter, NY		438	62	12, June	5, July 1894	Dens, Kurhessen
Mönch, Philipp	Ripley, OH		359	43- -27d	8, Oct.	5, Nov. 1877	
Mönch, Susanna	Ft. Hunter, NY	Lehr	7	43	13, Oct.	11, Nov. 1886	E. Penn Twp, Carbon County, Pennsylvania
Monde, Wilhelmina	Springfield, MN	Sawadda	735	64	14, Oct.	18, Nov. 1897	Neidenburg, OstPreußen
Monhard, Margaretha	Sheboygan, WI	Schorer	383	40	19, Sept	27, Nov. 1871	Wangen, Bern, Schweiz
Monk, John C.	Kendallville, IN		127	24	18, Mar.	21, Apr. 1879	Milwaulkee, Wisconsin
Mönnig, Christian	Pinckneyville, IL		271	71-10m-14d	30, June	21, Aug. 1871	Hoteln, Amt Ruthe, Hannover
Monsees, Martin	Smithton, MO		158	87	12, Feb.	5, Mar. 1896	Hüttendorf, Ottersberg, Hannover
Monsees, Trina	Smithton, MO		238	87	24, Mar.	13, Apr. 1893	Hüttendorf, Ottersberg, Hannover
Monses, Catharine A.	Sedalia, MO		558	44	6, Aug.	27, Aug. 1891	St. Louis, Missouri
Montandon, Albert	Highland, IL		415	38	11, June	30, June 1898	Kleinwaben, Schweiz
Monz, John	Elkport, IA		214	67	19, Feb.	29, Mar. 1894	Seiningen, Wurttemberg
Moog, Louis Heinrich	Baraboo, WI		263	12- 9m-25d	20, July	17, Aug. 1874	
Moog, Maria K.	Baraboo, WI	Schmidt	174	56	17, Feb.	12, Mar. 1896	Dillheim, Coblenz, Preußen
Moog, Valentin	Cameron, MO		286	67	20, Mar.	1, May 1890	Wintzenbach, Sellz, Elsaß
Moogler, Johan Michael	Baraboo, WI		414	73	10, June	30, June 1892	Bökingen, Heilbronn, Württemberg
Moor, Emma	Quincy, IL	Dasbach	686	24- 7m- 8d	12, Oct.	27, Oct. 1887	Quincy, Illinois
Moor, John	Sandwich, IL		184	23	22, Oct.	13, Nov. 1865	Schlitz bei Fulda, Hessen-Darmstadt
Moosdorf, Minna	Perry, TX	Ohde	7	26	3, Nov.	24, Nov. 1884	
Mooser, Johannes	Captina, OH		176	60	8, Oct.	1, Nov. 1849	
Mooty, Gustav	Lincoln, NE		279	39		29, Aug. 1870	
Morack, Anna P.	Mason City, IA		94	21- 1m-15d	14, Jan.	9, Feb. 1888	Lenzburg an der Warte, Berlin, Brandenburg
Morack, Anna P.	Mason City, IA	Rudd	174	21- 1m-15d	14, Jan.	15, Mar. 1888	Landsberg, Brandenburg
Morack, Caroline	Charles City, IA		62	58	29, Dec.	23, Jan. 1896	Schainart, Hammer, Sternberg, Germany
Moran, Laura	Omaha, NE		254	14- 1m- 8d	16, Mar.	19, Apr. 1888	

- 346 -

Christliche Apologete Death Notices --- 1839 - 1899

Name of Deceased	Notice Date	Death Date	Age	Page	Maiden Name	Place of Death	Place of Birth
Morawetz, Alois	31, Aug. 1874	30, July	41	279		Hannibal, MO	Chotzen, Böhmen
Morbach, Joseph	5, Jan. 1863	13, Nov.	35	4		Canal Dover, OH	
Mordt, Karl Heinrich	4, June 1896	16, May	53	367		Truxton, MO	Stemmen, Lippe-Detmold
Morge, Elisabeth	1, Oct. 1896	21, Aug.	69	639		New Albany, IN	Dosenheim, Elsaß
Morge, Elisabeth	29, Mar. 1888	7, Mar.	40	206	Gutbub	New Albany, IN	
Morgenstern, Ehrgott Lebrech	19, Aug. 1886	21, Mar.	88	7		Lexington, KY	Schellenberg, Sachsen
Mori, Karoline	10, May 1869		30	151	Renkert	Sherrills Mount, IA	
Mori, Karoline	17, May 1869		30	159	Renkert	Sherrills Mount, IA	
Morig, Herman Heinrich	9, Jan. 1882	25, Dec.	30	15		Colesburg, IA	Ohrtermersch, Fürstenau, Hannover
Moritz, Anna F.	17, Nov. 1892	29, Oct.	70	734		Quincy, IL	Rickenthal, Brandenburg
Moritz, Franz August	11, Apr. 1895		56	238		Drake, MO	Addernhausen, Hever, Oldenburg
Moritz, Friedrich Wilhelm	17, June 1897	27, May	73	383		Quincy, IL	Zachhow, Zelten an der Oder, Preußen
Moritz, Friedrich Wilhelm	5, May 1873	27, Mar.	69- 2m-24d	143		Michigan City, IN	Nienhagen, Hannover
Morloch, Christian	15, Mar. 1880	29, Feb.	18-10m	87		Mt. Vernon, IN	
Morloch, Christian	15, Mar. 1880	4, Mar.	45- 6m	87		Mt. Vernon, IN	
Morlock, Anna Christina	9, Apr. 1883	14, Mar.	73- 8m-20d	119		Mascoutah, IL	Sachssenflur, Boxberg, Baden
Morlock, Anna Maria	18, Mar. 1897	12, Feb.	19	175		Jordan, MN	Jordan, Minnesota
Morlock, Catharine	4, July 1861	3, May	18- 7m-25d	108	Lang	Mt. Vernon, IN	
Morlock, Christian	27, June 1870	2, June	62	207		Mt. Vernon, IN	Stein, Amt Bretten, Baden
Morlock, Georg Balthasar	8, Jan. 1883	21, Dec.	71- 7m- 1d	15		Lancaster, MO	Weißach, Württemberg
Morlock, Jacob	8, Dec. 1887	11, Nov.	80	782		Mascoutah, IL	Böhl, RheinPfalz Baiern
Morlock, John	2, Apr. 1896	24, Feb.	43	222		Mascoutah, IL	St. Clair County, Illinois
Morlock, Katharina Louisa	1, Feb. 1869	6, Jan.	59- 1m-15d	39		Mt. Vernon, IN	Wünschberg, Rheinkreis Baiern
Morlock, Maria	6, July 1899	9, June	26	431	Reipp	Toledo, OH	Elmore , Ohio
Morlock, Philippine	22, Apr. 1872	30, Mar.	59- 4m-8d	135	Wagner	Mascoutah, IL	Behl bei Neustadt an der Haardt,
Morlok, Friederike	28, Aug. 1882	25, July	34	279	Baumann	Jordan, MN	Remptendorf, Reuß
Morlok, Friederike	7, Aug. 1882	25, July	34	255	Baumann	Jordan, MN	
Morlok, Jakob Heinrich	4, Oct. 1888	22, Sept	51- 7m	638		Perrysburg, OH	Löchgau, Besigheim, Württemberg
Mormann, Philippina	28, Apr. 1898	21, Mar.	73	271	Weber	Hamilton, OH	Schönau, Rheinkreis Baiern
Morrell, Margaretha Elisabetha	20, Oct. 1862	24, Sept	21- 6m	168		Petersburg, IL	Kelze, Hofgeismar, Kurhessen
Morsbach, Johan	22, Jan. 1883	31, Dec.	75	31		Butlerville, ---	Ratingen bei Düsseldorf, Preußen
Morsch, Ernstine	26, Mar. 1877	5, Mar.	70	103	Brandner	Sandwich, IL	Rinklingen, Baden
Morsch, Justina	5, July 1880	18, June	50	215	Morsch	Sandwich, IL	Rinklingen, Baden
Morwitz, Walter A.	17, Mar. 1892		23	174		Springfield, IL	Springfield, Illinois
Mörz, Christine	25, June 1896	9, May	73	415	Walter	Green Bay, WI	Linkenheim, Baden
Mosabach, Jos.	10, Jan. 1876	16, Dec.	20- 1m	15		Columbus, TX	Rabbs Creek, Austin County, Texas
Mosebach, Caspar	11, Mar. 1897	31, Dec.	74	159		Scranton, PA	Oberdünzebach, Eschwege, Hessen-Nassau
Moser, Anna Maria	1, Sept 1898	13, Aug.	59	559	Wälde	Toledo, OH	Gudach, Baden
Möser, Charlotte	31, Dec. 1877	10, Dec.	42	423	Dreher	Belleville, IL	Annweiler, Rheinkreis Baiern
Möser, Christina	26, Oct. 1874	8, Oct.	60- 7m- 1d	343	Steffin	Toledo, OH	
Moser, Christina E.	17, July 1865	16, June	70	116		Toledo, OH	Edenkoden, Rheinkreis Baiern
Moser, Friedrich	20, July 1854	4, July	22- 9m	116		Toledo, OH	Messen, Solothurn, Schweiz
Moser, Jakob	30, Aug. 1880	6, July	59	279		Toledo, OH	Thierachem, Bern, Schweiz
Moser, Jakob	5, Dec. 1889	28, Oct.	34- 2m- 8d	782		Vermillion, OH	Schweikheim, Waiblingen, Württemberg
Moser, Ludwig	14, Jan. 1892	14, Dec.	45	30		Brooklyn, NY	Plum Tope, Alleghany County, Pennsylvania
Moser, Margaretha Josephine	5, Mar. 1896	5, Feb.	48	158		Covington, KY	

Christliche Apologete Death Notices --- 1839 - 1899

Name of Deceased	Notice Date	Death Date	Age	Page	Maiden Name	Place of Death	Place of Birth
Moser, Philipp Jakob	1, Apr. 1858	11, Mar.	64	52		Toledo, OH	Eslenkoben, Rheinkreis Baiern
Moses, Appolonia	25, Aug. 1879	9, Aug.	79-11m-16d	271	Hartmann	Boston, MA	Ilbesheim bei Kirchheim, Rheinkreis Baiern
Moses, Friedrich	1, Dec. 1873	23, Oct.	73- 4m	383		Boston Highlands, MA	Ilbesheim, Baiern
Mosimann, Christian	10, Dec. 1866		55	398		Baresville, OH	Hutlingen, Bern, Schweiz
Mosler, Georg	17, Nov. 1859	2, Sept	49	184		New Albany, IN	Dettweiler, NiederRhein, Zabern, Frankreich
Mosler, Katharina	5, Apr. 1860	27, Dec.	16- 2m	56	Köhler	New Albany, NY	
Moßbacker, Heinrich	5, Aug. 1852	4, June	35	128		Newark, NJ	Deidesheim, Neustadt an der Hardt, Germany
Mosseler, (son of Friedrich)	16, Apr. 1883	13, Feb.	17- 3m- 3d	127		Bradford, IN	Harrison County, Indiana
Moßler, Margaretha	14, Jan. 1886	12, Dec.	80	7		Bradford, IN	Hangweiler, Pfalzburg, Lothringen
Mößner, Amalie	17, Feb. 1898	27, Jan.	50	111	Walter	Scranton, PA	Eckartsweier, Baden
Mößner, Katharina	11, Oct. 1894	25, Sept		662		Philadelphia, PA	Feuerberbach, Württemberg
Möste, Johan Herman	28, Jan. 1892	5, Jan.	62	62		Colesburg, IA	Heneberg, Hannover
Motzfeld, Wilhelm	16, Feb. 1893	13, Jan.	80	110		Garrett, IN	Alpenrod, Hessen-Nassau
Motzkus, Carolina	25, July 1889	5, June	68- 1m-19d	478	Kischkowitz	New Orleans, LA	Quwaren, Insterburg, Gumbinnen, Preußen
Moude, John	23, Sept 1897	5, Sept	70	607		Springfield, MN	Falkenberg, Schlesien
Moyer, Anna	27, Apr. 1893	26, Mar.	31	270	Link	Philadelphia, PA	Rainham, Ontario, Canada
Moyer, Louise	13, Aug. 1896	28, June	39	527	Boger	Junction City, KS	Geary County, Kansas
Muck, Charlotte	7, June 1888		69- -25d	366		Weston, MO	Honelle, Rheinkreis Baiern
Muck, Joseph	25, Apr. 1895	11, Mar.	76- 3m	270		New York City, NY	Baiern
Muck, Margaretha	22, Nov. 1880	19, Sept	58	375		New York City, NY	Lauf bei Nürnberg, Baiern
Mücke, Johanna Augusta	25, Mar. 1886	12, Feb.	57	7	Schultz	Lemars, IA	Golgowitz, Glogau, Germany
Mückenheim, Wilhelm H.J.	19, Jan. 1885	4, Jan.	83-11m-17d	7		Freeport, IL	Walkenried, Braunschweig
Mucker, Georg	12, Apr. 1888	25, Mar.	17- 5m- 4d	238		Allegheny City, PA	Allegheny City, Pennsylvania
Müdeking, Sophia Kohring	23, July 1896		45	479		Owatonna, MN	Hagevede, Hannover
Muder, Anna Elisabeth	26, Apr. 1860	6, Apr.		68		Macoutah, IL	
Muder, Georg	24, Jan. 1881	5, Jan.	80- - 8d	31		Belleville, IL	Oberdorla, Erfurt, Preußen
Muder, Maria	14, Feb. 1870	21, Jan.	22- 8m	55		Madison, IN	Oberdorlau, Preußen
Muders, Jakob	20, Oct. 1892	25, Sept	32	670		Cameron, MO	Clay County, Missouri
Muehlenbrock, Sophia	26, July 1875	4, May	63	239	Linnemann	Omaha, NE	Kleinemarge, Lippe-Detmold
Mueller, Christina	27, Jan. 1887	21, Dec.	65- 6m-26d	62	Zwickel	Indianapolis, IN	Müllerstadt, Rheinkreis Baiern
Mueller, Dorothea	1, Sept 1887	11, Aug.	71	558		Redfield, SD	Wickshausen, Hessen-Darmstadt
Mueller, Emilie L.	31, Aug. 1874	15, Aug.	27	279	Hartmann	Cincinnati, OH	
Mueller, Gust. Wilhelm	22, Mar. 1888	19, Feb.	28	190		Crandon, SD	Squaw Grove, DeKalb County, Illinois
Mueller, Heinrich	18, Feb. 1886	17, Dec.	78	7		Burlington, IA	Odenhausen, Rabenau, Hessen
Mueller, Juliana	14, Jan. 1886		31	7	Reipeld	Evansville, IN	Warwick County, Indiana
Mueller, Juliana	28, Jan. 1886		31	7	Reicheld	Evansville, IN	Warwick County, Indiana
Mugford, Elisabeth	7, Oct. 1897	25, July	57	639	Helmich	Lutman, MO	Pinckney, Missouri
Muhl, Christoph	1, Mar. 1888	17, Jan.	76	142		Bloomington, IL	Brunau, Salzwedel, Magdeburg, Preußen
Muhl, Gertrud	25, Oct. 1875	6, Oct.	33	343		Schnectady, NY	Oberaula, Kurhessen
Mühlaus, Christina	11, Aug. 1884	13, July	63	7	Schneider	Clarksville, IL	Matesheim, Leonberg, Württemberg
Mühlaus, Christina	25, Aug. 1884	13, July	63	7	Schneider	Clarksville, IL	Matesheim, Leonberg, Württemberg
Mühlbauer, L.	17, Mar. 1892	16, Feb.	64	174		Duluth, MN	München, Baiern
Mühleisen, Caroline	2, Mar. 1893	8, Dec.	14	142		Philadelphia, PA	
Mühleisen, Clara Hattie	2, Mar. 1893	1, Jan.	8- 3m	142		Philadelphia, PA	
Mühleisen, Flora Anna	2, Mar. 1893	9, Dec.	5- 6m	142		Philadelphia, PA	
Muhleman, Jacob	18, Feb. 1897	24, Jan.	74	111		Baresville, OH	Steffisburg, Bern, Schweiz

Christliche Apologete Death Notices --- 1839 - 1899

Name of Deceased	Notice Date	Death Date	Age	Page	Maiden Name	Place of Death	Place of Birth
Mühlemann, Andreas	12, Sept 1845	24, Apr.		147			Schweiz
Mühlemann, Anna	16, June 1859	15, May	75-10m-18d	96			Canton Bern, Schweiz
Mühlemann, Anna Elise	19, Sept 1850	3, Sept	40- 3m	152			Schweiz
Mühlemann, Anna Margaretha	4, Aug. 1884	15, July	81	7		Buckhill, OH	Rosenthal, Frankenberg, Kurhessen
Mühlemann, Barbara	11, Mar. 1867		81	78	Schwarz	Evansville, IN	Canton Bern, Schweiz
Mühlemann, Catharina	19, Apr. 1880	30, Mar.	75- 4m- 5d	127	Stucki	Baresville, IN	Heimburg, Bern, Schweiz
Mühlemann, Elisabeth	31, Mar. 1898	26, Feb.	78	207	Zink	Hannibal, OH	Niederbipp, Bern, Schweiz
Mühlemann, Fr.	7, Apr. 1884	15, Mar.	71	7		Hannibal, OH	Steffisburg, Thun, Bern, Schweiz
Mühlemann, Henry R.	18, Oct. 1894	5, July	46	678		Baresville, OH	
Mühlemann, Jacob	20, Apr. 1885	6, Apr.	83	7		Baresville, OH	Heimberg, Bern, Schweiz
Mühlemann, Jakob	2, May 1845	26, Feb.	66- 9m	71		Captina, OH	Kanton Bern, Schweiz
Mühlemann, Johan	13, Mar. 1882	20, Feb.	77- 6m	87		Baresville, OH	Großwyl, Seeberg, Bern, Schweiz
Mühlemann, Johan Gottfried	21, May 1896	30, Apr.	69	334		Baresville, OH	Heimberg, Bern, Schweiz
Mühlemann, John	15, Oct. 1891	24, Sept	87	670		Baresville, OH	Heimberg, Bern, Schweiz
Mühlemann, Josephina	9, June 1859	4, Mar.	16	92		Baresville, OH	
Mühlemann, Louise Rosina	3, Apr. 1865	18, Feb.	23	56		Baresville, OH	
Mühlemann, Margaretha Magdalena	12, Mar. 1896	13, Feb.	65	174	Anschutz	Baresville, OH	Alleghany County, Pennsylvania
Mühlemann, Margarethe	11, Mar. 1852	25, Dec.	42	44		Evansville, IN	Oldenburg
Mühlemann, Maria Anna	15, Apr. 1878	27, Mar.	50	119		Baresville, OH	Humberg, Bern, Schweiz
Mühlemann, Maria Arminta	22, Mar. 1880	4, Mar.	20-11m- 4d	95		Hannibal, OH	Monroe County, Ohio
Mühlemann, Susanna	9, June 1879	12, May	64- 2m	183	Fischer	Hannibal, OH	
Mühlenbein, Friederika	14, Aug. 1890	9, June	71	526	Balke	St. Philip, ND	Golenbach, Holzmünden, Braunschweig
Mühlenbern, Friedrich Wilhelm	4, Oct. 1875	28, Aug.	56	319		Marrs, IN	Hummersen, Schwalenberg, Lippe-Detmold
Mühlenbrock, Anna Maria	6, July 1893	10, June	77	430	Resch	Falls City, NE	Chur, Graubünden, Schweiz
Mühlenbrock, Heinrich Ludwig (Rev)	23, Feb. 1899	1, Jan.	80-10m	126		Council Bluffs, IA	Klein-Marpe, Lippe-Detmold
Mühlenbrock, Sophie	24, May 1875	4, May	63	167		Omaha, NE	Rheinmark, Blomberg, Lippe-Detmold
Mühlenstein, Karolina Friederika	20, Aug. 1883	3, Aug.	71- 5m-24d	271		Pittsburg, PA	Mühltroff, Sachsen
Mühlhaus, Catharina	13, July 1868	8, June	32	223	Kroll	Galena, IL	Wangen, Cannstadt, Württemberg
Mühlhaus, John	14, Sept 1893	7, Aug.	81	590		Galena, IL	Neuterhausen, Rothenburg, Kurhessen
Mühlhaus, John	9, Jan. 1871	24, Dec.	55- 2m- 9d	15		Marion, OH	
Mühlhaus, Luise	1, Sept 1884	13, July	63	7	Schneider	Clarksville, IL	Malmsheim, Leonberg, Württemberg
Mühlheim, Lisette	21, Jan. 1892	8, Dec.	71	46	Pauls	Nashville, IL	Sollingen, Preußen
Mühlheim, Maria	20, Nov. 1871	28, Oct.	36	375	Ellinger	Allegan, MI	Thalmessing, Baiern
Mühlig, Anna	23, May 1889	3, May	54	334	Pombitzky	Lawrence, MA	Terschliegel, Posen
Mühius, Franz Friedrich	31, May 1888	17, Apr.	68	350		West Bend, WI	Gera, Reuß
Mühlke, Emilie	13, Apr. 1899	19, Mar.	75	239	Volland	Chicago, IL	Buttstädt, Sachsen-Weimar
Mühlleitner, Balthes	2, June 1892	28, Feb.	69	350		Marine City, MI	Süßwing, Baiern
Mühlmann, Anna Maria	29, Apr. 1886	12, Apr.	64	7	Zink	Baresville, OH	Niederbipp, Bern, Schweiz
Mühlmann, Johan Dietrich	17, Aug. 1874	11, July	68- 8m	263		Evansville, IN	Westenstäte bei Oldenburg, Oldenburg
Muhs, Augusta	23, Feb. 1880	22, Jan.	38- 6m	63	Krüger	New Ulm, MN	
Mulfinger, Anna Maria	2, June 1892	10, May	70- 4m-12d	350	Schlothauer	Chicago, IL	Oppershausen, Thüringen
Mulfinger, Elisabeth	4, Dec. 1856	21, Nov.	34	196	Neeb	Pekin, IL	Neunheim, Hessen-Darmstadt
Mulfinger, Elise	5, May 1853	13, Apr.	7- - 6d	72		Milwaukee, WI	
Mulfinger, Johannes Michael	17, Feb. 1859	30, Jan.	77-10m- 1d	28		Lawrenceburg, IN	Nenzenheim, Amt Uffenheim, Baiern
Mulfinger, Karoline Christine	22, Dec. 1843	15, Dec.	25	203	Schlothauer	Lawrenceburg, IN	Obershausen, Langensalza, Preußen
Mulfinger, Rosanna	29, Oct. 1847	18, Oct.	25	175		Pittsburg, PA	

Christliche Apologete Death Notices -- 1839 - 1899

Name of Deceased	Notice Date	Death Date	Age	Maiden Name	Page	Place of Death	Place of Birth
Mulfinger, Wilhelm	29, Oct. 1847	18, Oct.	1-10m		175	Pittsburg, PA	
Mulford, Katharina	24, Oct. 1881	29, Sept	44		343	Bridgeport, CT	
Müller, (Mr)	28, Feb. 1856	24, Jan.	33		36	Highland, IL	
Müller, (Mrs)	10, July 1856	29, June	33		112	Brookville, IN	
Müller, A. Maria	28, Oct. 1852	8, Oct.			176	Toledo, OH	
Müller, Adolph L.	26, Nov. 1896	15, Oct.	22		766	San Francisco, CA	San Francisco, California
Müller, Albert	23, Oct. 1882	12, Oct.	17		343	Louisville, KY	Louisville, Jefferson County, Kentucky
Müller, Amelia L.	17, Dec. 1883	4, Dec.	58	Renschahaus	7	Seymour, IN	Imbshausen, Hannover
Müller, Andreas	19, Sept 1845	2, Sept			151	St. Louis, MO	
Müller, Andreas	28, Oct. 1852	5, Oct.			176	Toledo, OH	
Müller, Anna	26, Oct. 1885	28, Sept		Keller	7	Aurora, IN	Sontheim a. d. Brenz, Heidenheim, Württemberg
Müller, Anna	16, Feb. 1880	3, Feb.	50-7m		55	St. Louis, MO	Thayingen, Schaffhausen, Schweiz
Müller, Anna	10, June 1897	4, May	81	Nolt	367	Peoria, IL	Surhausen, Emden, Ostfriesland
Müller, Anna	16, Sept 1897	27, Aug.	75		591	New York City, NY	Schöneberg bei Kiel, Germany
Müller, Anna	12, Jan. 1899	13, Dec.	88		31	Highland, IL	Oberkulm, Aargau, Schweiz
Müller, Anna	10, Oct. 1895	17, Sept	49-7m-23d		654	Berea, OH	Schaffhausen, Schweiz
Müller, Anna	20, Aug. 1896	21, July	31	Seibel	543	Fond du Lac, WI	Thephetah, Wisconsin
Müller, Anna	27, Sept 1869	24, Aug.	11		311	Wathena, KS	Hümme, Kurhessen
Müller, Anna Elisabeth	24, Sept 1891	8, Sept	79	Brohmann	622	Geneseo, IL	Angern, Magdeburg, Preußen
Müller, Anna Katharina	3, Aug. 1885	19, June	47	Fleer	7	Mt. Pleasant, IA	Enger, Herford, Minden, Preußen
Müller, Anna Katharina	17, Mar. 1887	4, Mar.	79	Steinmetz	174	Roseville, MI	Körner, Sachsen-Gotha
Müller, Anna Margaretha	24, Sept 1896	9, Sept	68	Schwarz	623	Oshkosh, WI	Klein-Gladenbach, Hessen-Darmstadt
Müller, Anna Maria Elisabeth	22, Feb. 1875	25, Jan.		Schröder	63	Herman, MO	Osnabrück, Hannover
Müller, August	19, May 1884	28, Apr.	23-7m-28d		7	Angelica, NY	Wellsville, Alleghany County, New York
Müller, August C.	1, Mar. 1894	1, Feb.	57		150	San Francisco, CA	Sulz, Mecklenburg-Schwerin
Müller, August Ferdinand	3, Apr. 1890	12, Mar.	47-7m-12d		222	Marietta, OH	Lasberg, Preußen
Müller, Augusta	6, Dec. 1888	27, Oct.	30	Fick	782	St. Joseph, MO	Harnfelde bei Stargard, Pommern
Müller, Augusta	16, July 1896	27, June	96		463	Wellsville, NY	Hannover
Müller, Auguste	12, May 1884	21, Apr.	47	Bauersfeld	7	Aurora, IL	Schwarzberg, Schwarzburg-Rudolstadt
Müller, Auguste	10, Oct. 1881	21, Sept	15-11m-14d		327	Olmstead, OH	Grethen, Dürkheim, Rheinpfalz Baiern
Müller, Barbara	14, May 1891	24, Mar.	70	Dietz	318	Bloomington, IL	Aligham County, Maryland
Müller, Benedict	4, Feb. 1892	5, Jan.	60		78	Wellman, IA	Stegeberg, Preußen
Müller, Carl	14, Apr. 1873	11, Mar.	41		119	Oshkosh, WI	Lasberg, Pommern
Müller, Carl Friedrich	17, Oct. 1889	17, Sept	54		670	Milwaukee, WI	Tramberg, Pommern
Müller, Carl Gottlieb	5, June 1890		91		366	Appleton, WI	Jettenborg, Backnang, Württemberg
Müller, Carolina	4, Oct. 1888	20, July	34	Schmiedkal	638	Portland, OR	Mecklenburg-Schwerin
Müller, Carolina Friedrika	25, June 1896	16, May	53	Rubinstein	415	Benton Co, IA	
Müller, Caroline	22, May 1865	15, Apr.	51-4m-17d	Beilke	84	Chicago, IL	
Müller, Caspar	27, May 1867	25, Apr.	47		166	Milwaukee, WI	Alsfeld, Hessen-Darmstadt
Müller, Catharina	27, Feb. 1890	13, Jan.	53	Cordes	142	Sedalia, MO	Wilstedt, Ottersberg, Hannover
Müller, Catharina	13, May 1872	30, Apr.	33	Scheubli	159	Allegheny City, PA	
Müller, Charlotte	7, June 1880	16, May	28	Koller	183	Woodville, OH	Dreidorf, Posen, Preußen
Müller, Charlotte	1, Mar. 1894	1, Feb.	72	Hartmann	150	Clatonia, NE	Barntrup, Lippe-Detmold
Müller, Charlotte	14, Jan. 1878	10, Dec.	52-11m-15d		15	Hopewell, MO	Minden, Preußen
Müller, Charlotte	25, Apr. 1895	71-9m-27d			270	Chicago, IL	Kirchdorf, Hannover
Müller, Christian	13, Apr. 1874	22, Mar.	75		119	Charles City, IA	Lauchrüden, Sachsen-Weimar

Christliche Apologete Death Notices --- 1839 - 1899

Name of Deceased	Notice Date	Death Date	Age	Maiden Name	Page	Place of Death	Place of Birth
Müller, Christian	1, Apr. 1886	12, Mar.	66		7	Nebraska City, NE	Kettenbach, Weh, Nassau
Müller, Christian	9, Sept 1886	17, Aug.	74- 5m-30d		7	Defiance, OH	Hamburg, Germany
Müller, Christian Friedrich	23, Aug. 1880	8, Aug.	76-11m		271	Louisiana, MO	Asperg, Ludwigsburg, Württemberg
Müller, Christian Friedrich	21, Nov. 1881	8, Aug.	76-11m		375	Chicago, IL	Asperg, Ludwigsburg, Württemberg
Müller, Christian Gottlob	12, Apr. 1894	19, Mar.	64		246	Pittsburg, PA	Asperg, Württemberg
Müller, Christiana	25, Dec. 1876	7, Dec.	64	Hendrich	413	New Albany, IN	Tennstädt, Langensalza, Erfurt, Preußen
Müller, Christina	9, June 1898	19, May	80	Schlittenhart	367		Elmendingen, Pforzheim, Baden
Müller, Christina	9, Aug. 1849	22, July	37		128	Chicago, IL	Asperg, Württemberg
Müller, Christine	18, Oct. 1888	30, Aug.	78	Schnell	670	Burlington, IA	
Müller, Christine Louise	8, Mar. 1880	21, Jan.	27	Geule	79	Portsmouth, OH	Geismar, Hessen
Müller, Christine Louise	22, Jan. 1872	15, Sept	14		31	Hopewell, MO	
Müller, Christoph	4, Apr. 1864	10, Jan.			56	Poughkeepsie, NY	Würm bie Pforzheim, Baden
Müller, Conrad	12, May 1862	6, Apr.	19		72	Golconda, IL	Ströhen, Varel, Amt Sulingen, Hannover
Müller, Daniel	23, Oct. 1871	28, Sept	63		343	Milwaukee, WI	Kulm, Aargau, Schweiz
Müller, Daniel W.	23, Nov. 1885	23, Oct.	62- 9m-25d		7	Morgantown, IN	Reihstein, Arnsberg, Germany
Müller, David	1, Feb. 1875	8, Jan.	43		39	Cape Girardeau, MO	Leidersweilen, Preußen
Müller, David	4, Aug. 1879	10, July	47		247	Iowa City, IA	
Müller, Dierk Harms	14, Mar. 1895	13, Feb.	59		174	Petersburg, IL	Ochtelburg, Aurich, Ostfriesland
Müller, Dietrich	13, May 1878	30, Apr.	37		151	St. Louis, MO	Benton County, Missouri
Müller, Dietrich	29, Apr. 1897	1, Apr.	89		271	Chicago, IL	Liebenau, Hannover
Müller, Dietrich Heinrich Wilhelm	5, Nov. 1896	12, Oct.	67		719	Colesburg, IA	Husum, Nienburg, Hannover
Müller, Edward Arthur	25, Nov. 1886	29, Oct.	23		7	Milwaukee, WI	
Müller, Elisabeth	20, Sept 1860	12, July			152	Baresville, OH	
Müller, Elisabeth	24, Sept 1878	3, Sept	90	Berg	303	Laporte, IN	Groß-Floto, Mecklenburg-Schwerin
Müller, Elisabeth	21, July 1887	19, June	58	Kehm	462	Arenzville, IL	Mennings, Hessen-Darmstadt
Müller, Elisabeth	11, Mar. 1878	19, Feb.	73		79	Clarington, OH	Stätesburg, Bern, Schweiz
Müller, Elisabeth	17, Mar. 1892	1, Feb.	27		174	Sandwich, IL	Sandwich, Illinois
Müller, Emma	21, Nov. 1895	7, Nov.	33	Strüben	750	Boonville, MO	St. Charles County, Missouri
Müller, Emma Carolina Friederka	16, Aug. 1894	10, July	29	Wegner	534	Milwaukee, WI	Milwaukee, Wisconsin
Müller, Engel Sophia	20, July 1874	5, July	89	Steinhoff	231	Windsor, WI	Streut, Braunschweig
Müller, Ernestine Pauline	3, Nov. 1892	16, Oct.	41	Hornfischer	702	Cleveland, OH	Netzschkau, Sachsen
Müller, Ernst	1, July 1886	16, June	66- 9m-26d		7	Windsor, WI	Stroit, Braunschweig
Müller, Ernst August	6, Jan. 1898	18, Dec.	94		15	Industry, TX	Fallersleben, Hannover
Müller, Fr.	16, Feb. 1863	27, Dec.	21		28	Waseca, MN	Mecklenburg-Schwerin
Müller, Frauke	7, Dec. 1893	13, Nov.	69	Gerdes	782	Oakford, IL	Zwischenbergen, Aurich, Ostfriesland
Müller, Friederike	16, June 1862	25, May	56		96	Wausau, WI	Hermelsdorf, Naugard, Hinterpommern
Müller, Friedrich	5, Apr. 1860	8, Mar.	24		56	Fond du Lac, WI	Sulz, Mecklenburg-Schwerin
Müller, Friedrich August	20, Feb. 1896	16, Jan.	49		126	St. Charles, MN	Flöha, Sachsen
Müller, Friedrich Karl	2, June 1892	4, May	83		350	Marine City, MI	Altenkarrin, Mecklenburg-Schwerin
Müller, Friedrich Wilhelm	7, Nov. 1889	25, Sept	71		718	Brooklyn, NY	Schleussingen, Preußen
Müller, Georg	10, Sept 1896	2, July	70		591	Arenzville, IL	Ecklofstein, Baiern
Müller, Georg	6, May 1867	5, Apr.	23		142	Pittsburg, PA	Bärenthal, Elsaß
Müller, Georg	17, Apr. 1890	19, Mar.	54-10m-19d		254	Body, IL	Sellnrod, Hessen
Müller, Georg	22, Dec. 1873	4, Nov.	62- 8m-27d		407	Lansing, IA	
Müller, Georg Louis	7, May 1891	15, Apr.	15		302	Pittsburg, PA	
Müller, Gerhard Heinrich	18, Apr. 1895	23, Mar.	64		254	Grand Island, NE	Lehmden, Oldenburg

- 351 -

Christliche Apologete Death Notices --- 1839 - 1899

Name of Deceased	Notice Date	Death Date	Age	Page	Maiden Name	Place of Death	Place of Birth
Müller, H.	11, Jan. 1894	14, Dec.	46	30	Blette	Farmington, IA	St. Louis, Missouri
Müller, Hannah	26, Apr. 1880	30, Mar.	33- 5m	135		St. Louis, MO	St. Louis, Missouri
Müller, Hartmann	1, May 1871	5, Apr.	71- -26d	143		Evansville, IN	Josbach, Kreis Kirchheim, Kurhessen
Müller, Heinrich	4, June 1877	22, May	47	183		Angelica, NY	Heiferde, Amt Gifhorn, Hannover
Müller, Heinrich	9, Dec. 1872	11, Nov.	79	399		Detroit, MI	Wolfskirchen, Elsaß
Müller, Heinrich	2, Aug. 1855	29, Apr.	56	124		Farmington, IA	
Müller, Heinrich Konrad	11, Jan. 1864	5, Dec.	50	8		Belmont, MO	Großschwülper, Hannover
Müller, Helene	14, Mar. 1889	21, Feb.	55	174		New York City, NY	Kölbe bei Marburg, Kurhessen
Müller, Henriette	16, Feb. 1863	28, Dec.	20- - 2d	28		Waseca, MN	
Müller, Herman	12, Dec. 1881	29, Nov.	17	399		Great Bend, KS	Waldeck
Müller, Herman	26, Dec. 1881	29, Nov.	27	415		Great Bend, KS	Waldeck
Müller, Isaak	7, Nov. 1870	17, Oct.	70- 9m	359		New York City, NY	Druntheim, Norway
Müller, J.	25, Mar. 1886	18, Feb.	81-10m-11d	7		Custer Co., NE	Sechshelden, Tillenburg, Nassau
Müller, J.F.	4, Aug. 1887	14, July	59	494		Dalton, MO	Heppenheim, Hessen-Darmstadt
Müller, Jac.	27, May 1867	1, May	80-9m-20d	166		Ann Arbor, MI	Reichenbach, Bern, Schweiz
Müller, Jakob	13, Aug. 1866	24, July	71-2m-12d	262		Cannelton, IN	Becklekews, Preußen
Müller, Jakob	21, Oct. 1872	1, Oct.	60	343		Galion, OH	Pennsylvania
Müller, Johan	17, Aug. 1893	29, July	73	526		Columbus, WI	Wulfsaal, Mecklenburg-Schwerin
Müller, Johan	14, Mar. 1889	16, Feb.	78	174		Higginsville, MO	Drewitz, Brandenburg
Müller, Johan	29, July 1897	30, June	73	479		Jerusalem, NY	Mecklenburg-Schwerin
Müller, Johan Dietrich F.W.	29, Oct. 1877	30, Sept	70- 5m- 8d	351		Woodville, OH	Schlesingen, Amt Wolpe,
Müller, Johan Dietrich Gerdes	6, Nov. 1890	18, Oct.	19	718		Chicago, IL	Chicago, Cook County, Illinois
Müller, Johan F.A.	20, Sept 1888	29, Aug.	84- 7m-10d	606		Maine, WI	Schönwalde, Pommern
Müller, Johan Friedrich	16, Apr. 1883	25, Mar.	78- 1m- 3d	127		Roseville, MI	Körner, Sachsen-Gotha
Müller, Johan G.	7, Jan. 1897	13, Dec.	35	15		Chillicothe, OH	Oettlingen, Lörrach, Baden
Müller, Johan Heinrich	15, Nov. 1888	5, Oct.	74	734		White Creek, IN	Ostercappeln bei Osnabrück, Hannover
Müller, Johan Jakob	4, July 1895	15, June	68	430		Delaware, OH	Affalterbach, Marbach, Württemberg
Müller, Johan Jakob	21, Oct. 1867	7, Oct.	55	334		Ft. Wayne, IN	Niederbipp, Bern, Schweiz
Müller, Johann	20, Sept 1849	23, Aug.	1- 2m	152		Milwaukee, WI	
Müller, Johann Friedrich	27, Jan. 1859	13, Jan.	31	16		Freeport, IL	Birkenau, Hessen-Darmstadt
Müller, Johannes	30, May 1889	14, May	64	350		Newport, KY	Gehaus, Sachsen
Müller, Johannes Nicolaus	15, June 1874	31, May	78-8m-19d	191		Geneseo, IL	Canton Druling, Löthringen, Frankreich
Müller, John	19, Apr. 1869	27, Mar.	53	127		Alton, IL	Freiensteinau, Hessen-Darmstadt
Müller, John Conrad	4, July 1861	June	6- 4m-14d	108		Philadelphia, PA	
Müller, John H.	1, Mar. 1888	21, Dec.	56	142		Chester, IL	Celle, Hannover
Müller, Jost Heinrich	24, Nov. 1873	10, Nov.	62	375	Boden	Sandwich, IL	Sechshelden, Amt Dillenburg, Nassau
Müller, Julia	4, May 1899	15, Apr.	75- 8m-22d	287	Boyn	West Bend, WI	Lichtenberg, Salder, Braunschweig
Müller, Juliana	2, Sept 1886	13, Aug.	63	7		Dover Center, MN	Plaue, Sachsen
Müller, Karl	20, June 1881	4, June	61	199		Manitowoc, WI	Pommern
Müller, Karoline	15, Apr. 1897	7, Mar.	53	239	Dittmann	Cincinnati, OH	Sieglingen, Neckarsulm, Württemberg
Müller, Katharina	18, Aug. 1892	25, July	82	526	Walther	Lincoln, NE	Birlenbach bei Weißenburg, Elsaß
Müller, Katharina	1, Oct. 1891	15, Sept	75	638		Arlington Heights, IL	Alfdorf, Welzheim, Württemberg
Müller, Katharina	8, Oct. 1891	16, Sept	35	654	Schnitzler	Louisville, KY	Dubois County, Indiana
Müller, Katharina	2, June 1887	5, May	72- 2m	350		Clearwater, MN	Weschlauter, Baiern
Müller, Katharina	14, Apr. 1884	15, Mar.	25	7		Cannelton, IN	Cannelton, Indiana
Müller, Katharina	16, Aug. 1880	16, July	70	263	Weiß	Batesville, IN	Pistorf, Elsaß

Christliche Apologete Death Notices --- 1839 - 1899

Name of Deceased	Notice Date	Death Date	Age	Page	Maiden Name	Place of Death	Place of Birth
Müller, Katharina E.	3, June 1878	17, May	32- 2m-10d	175	Sachs	Evansville, IN	Heimbach, Ziegenhain, Kurhessen
Müller, Katharine Christine	4, Oct. 1888	17, Sept	87- 6m-22d	638	Schwarz	Marion, OH	Marion, Ohio
Müller, Katharine Juliana	6, June 1895	17, May	17	366	Folte	Kansas City, KS	Hammelwerden, Bremen, Germany
Müller, Katie	18, Nov. 1897	20, Oct.	44	735		Pittsburg, PA	Pittsburg, Pennsylvania
Müller, Konrad	13, Nov. 1876	29, Oct.	44	367		Cincinnati, OH	Brokeloh, Hannover
Müller, Louis Wilhelm	4, July 1881	18, June	55- 1m- 6d	215		Lena, IL	Grötzingen, Durlach, Baden
Müller, Louise	3, Dec. 1883	19, Nov.	83- 7m-17d	391	Beerwald	Burlington, WI	Schiefelbein, Pommern
Müller, Louise Rosine	2, Mar. 1893	16, Feb.	64	142	Betz	Cincinnati, OH	Poppenweiler, Ludwigsburg, Württemberg
Müller, Louise Wilhelmina	13, Oct. 1879	25, Sept	36	327	Thann	Metropolis, IL	Fähne, Osnabrück, Hannover
Müller, Lydia	25, Apr. 1895	27, Mar.	41	270		Canton, OH	Wheeling, West Virginia
Müller, Magdalena	8, Nov. 1888	16, Oct.	46	718		Hoboken, NJ	Langweil, RheinPfalz Baiern
Müller, Magdalena Dorothea	20, Mar. 1890	19, Feb.	77	190	Schneider	New York City, NY	Kindelsau, Württemberg
Müller, Maggie	4, June 1883	7, May	22- 5m	183	Langlitz	San Francisco, CA	Louisville, Jefferson County, Kentucky
Müller, Margaretha	22, June 1868	1, June	72	199		Cannelton, IL	Munzingen, Kreis Kreuznach, Preußen
Müller, Margaretha	25, Nov. 1878	17, Oct.	39- - 9d	375		Louisville, KY	Windecken bei Hanau, Kurhessen
Müller, Margaretha	25, Oct. 1894	5, Oct.	52	694	Bäuerle	Baltimore, MD	Essingen, Aalen, Württemberg
Müller, Margarethe	25, July 1881	7, July	45- 8m	239		Evansville, IN	Pittsburg, Pennsylvania
Müller, Maria	7, Aug. 1890	21, July	30- 8m-10d	510	Ehlert	Altamont, IL	Second Creek, Gasconade County, Missouri
Müller, Maria	28, May 1883	26, Apr.	76-10m- 4d	175	Scheifele	Clayton, IA	Wustenrieth, Welzheim, Württemberg
Müller, Maria	12, July 1869	25, May	47- 1m-25d	223	Schärtle	Canton, MO	Tiefenmath, Welzheim, Württemberg
Müller, Maria	23, May 1889	22, Apr.	76- 5m-18d	334	Hartwig	Roseville, MI	Alt-Karin, Mecklenburg-Schwerin
Müller, Maria	17, June 1878	14, Apr.	13- 1m-10d	191		St. Charles, MN	
Müller, Maria	18, Sept 1890	26, Aug.	67-11m- 2d	606		Defiance, OH	
Müller, Maria Elisabeth	19, Apr. 1894	1, Apr.	53	262		Rochester, NY	Bischhausen, Kurhessen
Müller, Maria Elisabeth	27, Nov. 1865	6, Nov.	65	192		Detroit, MI	Hirschland, Elsaß
Müller, Maria Wilhelmina	3, June 1878	19, Apr.	56	175	Bode	Wathena, KS	Hülme, Hofgeismar, Kurhessen
Müller, Martha Elisabeth	12, Feb. 1872	18, Jan.	30	55	Vorhaur	Wilton, IA	Geißmar, Kurhessen
Müller, Martin	15, Nov. 1880		58	367		Louisville, KY	Bräunlingen, Donau-Eschingen, Baden
Müller, Mathilde Karolina	16, Apr. 1883	3, Apr.	32	127		St. Paul, MN	St. Paul, Minnesota
Müller, Michael	25, Feb. 1886	4, Feb.	75	7		Lincoln, NE	Claiburn, Weißenburg, Straßburg, Elsaß
Müller, Mollie	4, Aug. 1892	9, July	17	494		Ironton, OH	Wheelersburg, Scioto County, Ohio
Müller, Nancy	17, June 1897	4, May	81	383	Nolt	Howard, NE	Surhausen, Emden, Ostfriesland
Müller, Ottilie	3, Apr. 1876	15, Mar.	33	111	Grim	Laporte, IN	Kerkingen, Neresheim, Württemberg
Müller, Otto Ferdinand	29, Mar. 1880	11, Mar.	14- 4m- 2d	103		Arlington, MN	
Müller, Paul	20, Dec. 1894	18, Oct.	73	822		Canton, MO	Debeke, Wössitz, Preußen
Müller, Phil. Jakob	2, May 1895	7, Apr.	69	286			Böchingen bei Landau, Rheinpfalz Baiern
Müller, Philippine	5, Mar. 1896		39	158			Kreuznach,
Müller, Rebekka	13, Oct. 1898	24, Sept	67	655	Bertsch	Newark, NJ	Hohenwertersbach, Durlach, Baden
Müller, Regina	16, July 1877	20, June	79	231	Berfinger	Smithton, MO	Wetach, Zürich, Schweiz
Müller, Rosalia	9, Sept 1878		57- 6w	287	Goltz	Waseca, MN	Kamönke, Posen, Preußen
Müller, Rosine	4, July 1861	2, June	22- 7m-23d	108	Hermann	Mt. Vernon, IN	Hinterdiegelberg, Backnang, Württemberg
Müller, Rupina	28, Nov. 1889	28, Oct.	70	766	Zuckschwerdt	Cleveland, OH	Herzogsweiler, Württemberg
Müller, Sarah	17, Oct. 1889	27, Aug.		670		Morris, MN	Leonardsville, Minnesota
Müller, Sibylle	27, Nov. 1882	2, Nov.	60	383	Hege	Lancaster, MO	Haßloch, Rheinpfalz Baiern
Müller, Sophia	16, Dec. 1867	27, Nov.	37	398	Knüttel	Jerusalem, NY	Rüst, Kapptihn, Mecklenburg-Schwerin
Müller, Theresia	30, June 1892	4, June	80	414		Brooklyn, NY	Nußbach, Baden

Christliche Apologete Death Notices --- 1839 - 1899

Name of Deceased	Notice Date	Death Date	Age	Page	Maiden Name	Place of Death	Place of Birth
Müller, Thomas	14, Feb. 1881	1, Feb.	20	55		Greenville, OH	Quebec, Canada
Müller, Ulrich	15, Feb. 1894	20, Jan.	91	110		Arlington Heights, IL	Alsdorf, Württemberg
Müller, Veronika	9, Jan. 1865	30, Nov.	62	8		Chicago, IL	Demingen, Württemberg
Müller, Wilhelm	18, Sept 1865	28, Aug.	34	152		Jackson, MO	Brokeloh, Hannover
Müller, Wilhelm	26, Mar. 1866	1, Mar.	52	102		Marine City, MI	Sembach, Baiern
Müller, Wilhelm Georg Heinrich	11, Feb. 1892	9, Jan.	17	94		Milwaukee, WI	Milwaukee, Wisconsin
Müller, Wilhelm Martin	8, Mar. 1894	18, Jan.	21	166		Chicago, IL	Chicago, Cook County, Illinois
Müller, Wilhelmine	31, Mar. 1898	24, Feb.	59	207	Fenske	Arlington, MN	Witton, Marienwerder, West Preußen
Mullin, William	17, May 1869	1, May	58	159		Boiling Springs, PA	
Mulvaney, Christina	4, Feb. 1897	12, Dec.	38	79	Holz	New Albany, IN	
Mummenthaler, Friedrich	22, Oct. 1883	1, Oct.	76- 2m- 6d	343		Toledo, OH	Langenthal, Bern, Schweiz
Mumprecht, Friedrich	29, Dec. 1887	8, Dec.	31	830		Cincinnati, OH	Bern, Schweiz
Münch, Anna Marie	21, Dec. 1885	1, Dec.	48	7	Sigmund	New York City, NY	Weißbach, Baden
Münch, Friederike	6, Mar. 1865	3, Feb.	36	40	Bagel	Sheboygan, WI	Poreb bei Putlitz, Potsdam, Preußen
Munch, Heinrich	24, Sept 1891	24, Aug.	51	622		Algona, IA	Frankfurt am Main, Preußen
Münch, Heinrich	12, May 1892	28, Mar.	80	302		New Orleans, LA	Münzberg, Germany
Münch, Johan Peter	19, Sept 1870	19, Aug.	78- 4m-10d	303		Higginsport, OH	Niederluststadt, Germersheim, Rheinkreis Baiern
Münch, Karl	16, Apr. 1877	23- 5m-10d	23- 5m-10d	127	III	Sheboygan, WI	
Münch, Wilhelmina	25, Dec. 1890	8, Nov.	46	830	Ziehfuß	New York City, NY	Johannesburg, OstPreußen
Münchenhagen, Johanne	30, Mar. 1893	11, Mar.	71	206	Rüs	Louisville, KY	Urach, Urach, Württemberg
Mund, Friedrike J. Wilhelmine	18, Mar. 1878	25- 7m-24d	25- 7m-24d	87	Vogt	Manitowoc, WI	Wasdow, Mecklenburg-Schwerin
Mund, Gottfried	11, Jan. 1894	13, Dec.	84	30		Manitowoc, WI	
Mund, Heinrich	30, Mar. 1868	27, Jan.	55	103		Newtonburg, WI	Gersbach, Nordhausen, Preußen
Mund, Henrietta	20, Jan. 1898	13, Dec.	65	47	Baule	Hedwigs Hill, TX	Nördlingen, Peine, Hannover
Mund, Karl	11, Oct. 1880	25, Sept	10-10m- 7d	327		Fillmore, WI	
Mund, Sophie	30, May 1861	9, May	53- 5m-23d	88	Junker	Manitowoc, WI	Eikost, Preußen
Mundfahl, Marie	12, Dec. 1861	24, Nov.		200		Schnectady, NY	Kirschheim, Germany
Mundorf, Margarethe	3, June 1897	2, May	67	351	Junker	Marshall, IL	Eikhast, Minden, Preußen
Mundsahl, Christian	23, Feb. 1893	29, Jan.	65	126		Schnectady, NY	Bretleben, Preußen
Mundt, Auguste	2, Feb. 1885	7, Jan.	44	7	Weinreich	Kewaskum, WI	
Mundt, Ludwig August	24, Mar. 1892	1, Mar.	53- 4m- 7d	190		Scranton, PA	Teldau, Boizenburg, Mecklenburg-Schwerin
Mundt, Wilhelm	17, Nov. 1884	27, Oct.	70	7		Onatonna, MN	Wohlen, Bern, Schweiz
Münger, Christian	17, June 1878	1, June	32	191		Bay City, MI	Braunsfeld, Pommern
Munsch, Dorothe	26, Sept 1895	7, Sept	59- 1m-25d	622	Megow	Bay City, MI	Detroit, Wayne County, Michigan
Munsch, Karl Johannes	16, May 1889	24, Apr.	31	318		Bay City, MI	Buchs, St. Gallen, Schweiz
Müntener, Heinrich	19, Sept 1889		56- 2m-19d	606		Berne, MI	Buchs, St. Gallen, Schweiz
Müntener, Johan	21, Jan. 1892	20, Dec.	79	46		Kewaskum, WI	East Saginaw, Michigan
Müntner, Georg	18, Dec. 1882	27, Nov.	18- 8m- 5d	407		Caseville, MI	Galena, Illinois
Muntz, Emma H. C.	20, June 1895	26, May	34	398		Dubuque, IA	Schorndorf, Württemberg
Muntz, Erhart	21, May 1891	2, May	71	334		Dubuque, IA	
Muntz, Georg	19, Apr. 1880	22, Mar.	61	127		Mt. Vernon, IN	
Muntzinger, Fronia	29, Dec. 1884	3, Dec.	27- 9m-14d	7		Marion, OH	
Munz, Johan Georg	21, June 1888	26, May	66	398		Farmington, IA	Lustnau bei Tübingen, Württemberg
Munz, Maria	2, Feb. 1893	3, Jan.	56	78	Stecker	Lansing, IA	
Munz, Maria Anna	16, Sept 1897	25, Aug.	38	591		Lansing, IA	French Creek, Iowa
Münzdorf, Elisabeth	7, Feb. 1870	18, Jan.	56- -13d	47	Clobes	Allegheny City, PA	Hesserode, Amt Felsberg, Kurhessen

Christliche Apologete Death Notices --- 1839 - 1899

Name of Deceased	Notice Date	Death Date	Age	Maiden Name	Page	Place of Death	Place of Birth
Munzel, Elisabeth Katharina	25, Mar. 1886	6, Mar.	67	Buxmann	7	Quincy, IL	Reinheim, Dieburg, Hessen-Darmstadt
Münzel, Wesley	30, June 1884	15, May	24-11m-15d		7	Defiance, OH	Burlington, Iowa
Münzemeier, Anna Elisa	3, Feb. 1898	26, Dec.	39	Dewein	79	Dallas City, IL	Affinghausen, Bruchhausen, Hannover
Münzemeier, Anna Maria	17, May 1894	28, Apr.	66	Kilmeier	326	Charlestown, IN	Rodenberg, Kanstatt, Württemberg
Münzenmayer, Wilhelm Gottlieb	6, June 1889	26, May	60-7m-15d		366	Charlestown, IN	Hegensberg, Eßlingen, Germany
Münzenmeier, Margaretha C.	20, Aug. 1896	18, July	79		543	Dallas City, IL	Rothenberg, Kannstadt, Württemberg
Münzenmeyer, Gottlieb	18, Feb. 1858	26, Jan.	36		28	Charlestown, IN	Olnhausen, Neckarsulm, Württemberg
Münzler, Andreas G.	19, Apr. 1888	29, Mar.	78-2m-26d	Hornung	254	Industry, TX	Unterkessach, Adelsheim, Baden
Münzler, Christiana	14, Nov. 1881	8, Oct.	58		367	Industry, TX	Kumheim, Oberrhein, Elsaß
Murbach, Jakob	29, Apr. 1872				143	Winona, MN	Künheim, Elsaß
Murbach, Jakob	15, Sept 1879	25, Aug.	80		295	Jordan, MN	Fountain City, Wisconsin
Murbach, Katharina	29, Aug. 1881	1, Aug.	25	Raetz	279	Winona, MN	Kunheim, Elsaß
Murbach, Maria Magdalena	29, May 1882	7, May	52-7m	Hanhardt	175	Winona, MN	Kumheim, Oberrhein, Elsaß
Murbacher, Jacob	15, Apr. 1872	10, Mar.	40		127	Winona, MN	Pretzier, Mecklenburg-Schwerin
Murjahn, Mina	23, Feb. 1880	29, Jan.	17		63	Allegan, WI	Eutingen, Pforzheim, Baden
Mürle, Eva	17, Nov. 1879	25, Oct.	74-8m-18d		367	New Knoxville, OH	Neuhausen, Frauenfeld, Thurgau, Schweiz
Murri, Maria	27, Dec. 1888	4, Dec.	30	König	830	Topeka, KS	Sandhofen, Baden
Murst, Margaretha	20, Dec. 1888	3, Dec.	45		814	Newport, KY	Beierheim, Baden
Musbach, Christine	24, Feb. 1873	24, Jan.	19-8m		63	Cedar Lake, IN	Baiernheim, Baden
Musbach, Karl Friedrich	27, Apr. 1893	6, Apr.	33		270	Crown Point, IN	
Musch, Johanna	10, Nov. 1873	22, Oct.	50		359	Bloomington, IL	
Musch, Maria K.	5, Nov. 1891	22, Oct.	39	Ritter	718	Boody, IL	Terre Haute, Indiana
Muser, Anna Maria	14, Jan. 1886	19, Dec.	59-11m-16d	Meder	7	Sun Prairie, WI	Feldberg, Mühlheim, Baden
Muser, Christina	12, June 1882	22, May	22		191	Sun Prairie, WI	Mühlheim, Baden
Musgat, Emma	17, May 1875	23, Mar.	49	Reinhart	159	Fond du Lac, WI	Querfurth, Preußen
Musgat, Emma	3, May 1875	23, Mar.	49		143	Fond du Lac, WI	Oberfeld, Germany
Mußbach, Johan Georg	29, Aug. 1870	13, Aug.	67		279	Cedar Lake, IN	Reusten, Herrenberg, Württemberg
Müsse, Wilhelmine Carolina	10, May 1888	26, Mar.	39		302	St. Paul, MN	Sohl bei Diedenshausen, Westphalen
Musselmann, Magdalena	7, July 1898	12, June	26		431	Freeport, IL	Woodbine, Illinois
Mussemann, Anna	10, Jan. 1881	26, Dec.	65	Cordts	15	Platteville, WI	Langenhausen, Gnardeburg, Bremervörde,
Mußkopf, Elisabeth	24, Aug. 1885	10, Aug.	79	Sämet	7	Brookville, IN	Rischweiler, Baiern
Müßmann, Wilhelm	17, Aug. 1885	30, July	22		7	Petersburg, IL	
Muth, Angelika Elisabeth	1, May 1871	24, Mar.	51	Aschenbrenner	143	Evansville, IN	Schwarzenfels, Kreis Schlüctern, Kurhessen
Muth, Anna Katharina	9, Mar. 1899	8, Feb.	91	Hartmann	158	Evansville, IN	Rosenthal, Kurhessen
Muth, Anna Maria	26, Feb. 1872	2, Feb.	12-7m-5d		71	Davenport, IA	
Muth, Catharina M.	26, Feb. 1872	14, Feb.	9-6m-7d		71	Davenport, IA	
Muth, Conrad	5, Oct. 1874		65-7m		319	Evansville, IN	Mottgers, Schwarzenfels, Kurhessen
Muth, Conrad	22, Aug. 1881	21, July	32-11m-5d		271	Evansville, IN	Evansville, , Indiana
Muth, Eva Barbara	10, July 1890	18, June	72-1m-14d		446	Evansville, IN	Eberbach, Württemberg
Muth, Gottlieb Wilhelm	26, Feb. 1872	31, Jan.	3-3m		71	Davenport, IA	
Muth, Johan	21, May 1896	26, Apr.	78		334	Evansville, IN	Starbretz, Hessen-Darmstadt
Muth, Johan William	4, Aug. 1879	17, July	39-9m-4d		247	Evansville, IN	Mottgers, Schlüctern, Kurhessen
Muth, John C.	17, Nov. 1892	19, Oct.	20-10m-27d		734	Evansville, IN	
Muth, Julia Pauline	26, Feb. 1872	29, Jan.	7-4m-8d		71	Davenport, IA	
Muth, Julius August	26, Feb. 1872	31, Jan.	5-4m-26d		71	Davenport, IA	
Muth, Katharina	5, May 1892	8, Apr.	63	Muth	286	Davenport, IA	Selle, Preußen

Christliche Apologete Death Notices --- 1839 - 1899

Name of Deceased	Notice Date	Death Date	Age	Page	Maiden Name	Place of Death	Place of Birth
Muth, Maria	20, July 1893	27, June	60	462		Giard, IA	Todtenhausen, Germany
Muth, Nicolaus	11, Mar. 1878	18, Feb.	36- 5m- 2d	79		Evansville, IN	Lycoming County, Pennsylvania
Mutschler, Elisabeth	14, May 1877	14, Apr.	65- 5m- 3d	159		Marion, OH	Unterhausen, Reutlingen, Württemberg
Mutschler, Johan Jakob	17, May 1894	5, Apr.	84- -12d	326		Center Point, IA	Herrgottsheim, Baden
Mutschler, Joseph	15, Dec. 1884	29, Nov.	68- 6m- 1d	7		Louisville, KY	Herrgottsheim, Baden
Mutschler, Juliana	25, Oct. 1888		68- 8m	686		Louisville, KY	
Mutschmann, Carl	8, Nov. 1855	29, Sept		180		Galena, IL	Steppach, Heckstadt, Baiern
Mutter, Seraphim	26, May 1898	24, Apr.	66	335		Toledo, OH	Altenschwand, Säcklingen, Baden
Mütze, Anna Maria	23, July 1896		38	479	Kraft	Chicago, IL	Carroll County, Maryland
Mütze, Henriette	20, Jan. 1898	13, Dec.	39	47		Chicago, IL	Reading, Pennsylvania
Mütze, Karolina	22, Feb. 1894	3, Feb.	42	126	Auer	Chicago, IL	Manchester, Carroll County, Maryland
Myers, Johan Karl	14, July 1892	26, May	59	446		Schnectady, NY	Mecklenburg-Schwerin
Naab, Magdalena	10, Sept 1877	13, Aug.	84- 6m-26d	295		Etna, MO	Göanheim, Dürkheim, Rheinpfalz Baiern
Naas, Jakob	12, Feb. 1877	31, Dec.	65	55		Mt. Vernon, IN	Sesenheim, Bischweiler, Elsaß
Nabe, Dorothea	22, May 1865	8, Mar.	43	84		Cape Girardeau, MO	Drätzen,
Nabe, Heinrich	22, May 1865	23, Oct.	53	84		Cape Girardeau, MO	Heimern, Amt Ilten, Hannover
Nachtrieb, Anna Maria	7, May 1883	20, Apr.	59- 6m-12d	151	Fehr	Buffalo, NY	Kirchhart, Baden
Nachtrieb, Emma	15, Sept 1884	8, Aug.	22	7		Evansville, IN	Detroit, Wayne County, Michigan
Nachtrieb, Friedrich	16, Oct. 1876	15, Sept	45- 7m-12d	335		San Francisco, CA	
Nachtrieb, Friedrich Louis	18, Aug. 1879	3, Aug.	19- 1m-12d	263		Galion, OH	
Nachtrieb, Georg	21, July 1862	2, May	26	116		Woodville, OH	Brezenacker, Waiblingen, Württemberg
Nachtrieb, Gottlob (Rev)	28, Feb. 1895	7, Feb.	72	142		Indianapolis, IN	Brenzenaker, Waiblingen, Württemberg
Nachtrieb, Joh. Gottlob	14, Feb. 1876	28, Jan.	16	55		Berea, OH	Sandusky City, Ohio
Nachtrieb, Johan Friedrich	13, May 1886	13, Apr.	45	7		Chicago, IL	Waiblingen, Württemberg
Nachtrieb, Johan Georg	21, Sept 1899	18, Aug.	71	607		Minneapolis, MN	Bözenacker, Waiblingen, Württemberg
Nachtrieb, Johan Georg	7, Sept 1899	18, Aug.	71	575		Buffalo, NY	Birkmannsweiler, Württemberg
Nachtrieb, Johan Georg	2, Sept 1878	13, Aug.	28- 6m-11d	279		Blissfield, MI	
Nachtrieb, Johan Jakob	4, Aug. 1884	2, July	64- 5m-17d	7		Blissfield, MI	Brezenacker, Waiblingen, Württemberg
Nachtrieb, Karl	6, June 1895	29, Mar.	65	366		Derby, KS	Volkartsmühle, Brezenacker, Württemberg
Nachtrieb, Paulina	29, Oct. 1877	10, Oct.	34- 6m-25d	351	Schnepple	Galion, OH	Weinnenden, Waiblingen, Württemberg
Nachtrieb, Sarah Rebecca	3, Nov. 1892	7, Oct.	38	702		San Francisco, CA	Bethlehem, Ohio
Nachtrieb, Thirza Rebecca	8, Apr. 1897	17, Mar.	31	223		Minneapolis, MN	Galion, Ohio
Nacke, Christian	3, Mar.1873	7, Jan.		71		Beaver Falls, MN	Abberbüttel, Hannover
Naffe, Adam Edward	25, Feb. 1884	29, Jan.	18	7		White Creek, IN	Canada
Nafziger, Elisabeth	20, July 1893	9, June	78	462		Peoria, IL	Liebenauer Hofe bei Worms, Rheinpfalz Baiern
Nagel, Anton	11, Sept 1890	21, Aug.	94	590		Arlington Heights, IL	Bergholschang, Preußen
Nagel, Cäcilia	3, June 1878	9, May	64- 1m- 9d	175		Seguin, TX	Bruchsal, Baden
Nagel, Catharina	7, Mar. 1881	9, Feb.	59- 3m-20d	79	Prosch	Dalton, MO	Karow, Mecklenburg-Schwerin
Nagel, Claus Johan	4, Feb. 1892	16, Jan.	71	78		Wichita, KS	Süderdithmarschen bei Marne, Holstein
Nagel, Eberhard	22, Sept 1898	4, Sept	70	607		Montrose, MN	Hoheneck, Württemberg
Nagel, Ed.	27, Sept 1894	27, Aug.	27	630		Arlington Heights, IL	Elk Grove, Illinois
Nagel, Elisabeth	7, Feb. 1889	24, Dec.	37- 2m-19d	94	Reutzel	Odebolt, IA	Kefenrode, Hessen-Darmstadt
Nagel, Heinrich	26, Nov. 1891	3, Nov.	80- 1m-20d	766		Brighton, IL	Mennichhüffen, Bünde, Westphalen
Nagel, Henry	28, July 1879	14, July	18- 1m- 1d	239		Crow River, MN	
Nagel, Hulda	24, Jan. 1889	26, Dec.	34	62	Kaiser	Belmont, TX	Blanco County, Texas

Christliche Apologete Death Notices --- 1839 - 1899

Name of Deceased	Notice Date	Death Date	Age	Page	Maiden Name	Place of Death	Place of Birth
Nagel, Johan Martin	22, Jan. 1877	2, Jan.	52	31		Louisville, KY	Degenschlacht, Tübingen, Württemberg
Nagel, Johannes	28, Jan. 1886	12, Jan.	79	7		Seguin, TX	Bruchsal, Baden
Nagel, John	4, Aug. 1887	13, July	65	494		Dalton, MO	Altenstadt, Hessen-Darmstadt
Nagel, John	3, Sept 1896	13, Aug.	73	575		Arlington Heights, IL	Ansgete, Overissel, Holland
Nagel, Katharina	17, Aug. 1899	30, July	74	527	Knarr	Baltimore, MD	Baiern
Nagel, Ludwig	27, May 1867	9, May	49- 5m-20d	166		Poland, IN	Großsachsenheim, Vaihingen, Württemberg
Nagel, Margaretha	1, Sept 1887	19, Aug.	77- 3m	558	Wörz	Jersey City, NJ	Graben, Baden
Nägele, Christian Wilhelm	8, Sept 1859	7, Aug.	51- 1m-19d	144		Tiffin, OH	Waiblingen, Württemberg
Nagler, August	17, Oct. 1870	13, Sept	37- 2m-13d	335		Grand Rapids, MI	Ransbach bei Plauen, Sachsen
Nagler, Caroline	15, June 1893	22, May	67	382	Chemnitz	Freeport, MI	Plauen, Sachsen
Nagler, Hannah	16, Jan. 1871	6, Dec.	77	23	Purfürst	Grand Rapids, MI	Ransbach bei Plauen, Sachsen
Nahrung, Ursula	5, Mar. 1877	16, Feb.	21	79		Wathena, KS	Dußlingen, Tübingen, Württemberg
Namendorf, Friedrich	3, May 1894	14, Apr.	30	294		Dayton, OH	Richmond, Indiana
Nardheim, David Franklin	11, Dec. 1890	1, Nov.	21- 7m- 7d	798		Newport, KY	
Naß, August	22, Apr. 1886	28, Jan.	47	7		Maine, WI	Hohenschanau, Pommern
Naß, Friedrich	31, Mar. 1884	12, Mar.	68-11m-25d	7		Clintonville, WI	Farbezin bei Neugart, Pommern
Naß, Johan	3, Dec. 1883	25, Oct.	71	391		Maine, WI	Hohenschönau, Pommern
Nast, Ernst Theodor	1, Nov. 1839	25, Oct.	15m-15d	175			
Nast, Heinrich	23, Jan. 1896	4, Jan.	81	62		Cincinnati, OH	Kleinheubach am Main, Baiern
Nast, Sarah	21, Jan. 1884	19, Dec.	35	6	McDermott	Wellington, OH	Whitly, Canada
Nast, Susanna	28, July 1892	8, July	43	478	Zink	Cincinnati, OH	Kleinheubach, Baiern
Nast, Wilhelm (Rev Dr)	25, May 1899	16, May	92	321		Cincinnati, OH	
Nastke, Wilhelm	14, Mar. 1895	20, Feb.	63	174		Detroit, MI	Poplotz, Stolp, Hinterpommern
Näthing, Johannes	26, July 1860	12, July	54	120		Allegheny City, PA	Jesingen, Kirchheim an der Teck, Württemberg
Natzke, Jakob	5, May 1884	18, Apr.	62	7		Galesburg, IA	
Natzkie, Dorothea	20, Mar. 1890	22, Feb.	82- 4m	190	Korth	Peoria, IL	Schlakow, Hinterpommern
Nau, Henry	25, Jan. 1894	6, Dec.	66	62		Berea, OH	Marburg, Kurhessen
Naumann, Anna Maria	21, July 1898	6, July	88	463	Kuhl	Mandota, IL	Bindsachsen, Hessen-Darmstadt
Naumann, Caroline	18, Apr. 1850	17, Feb.	23- 3m	64		Springfield, IL	Oberlausitz, Sachsen
Naumann, Elisabeth	9, Mar. 1893	5, Feb.	66	158	Heckle	St. Paul, MN	Schlatt, Baden
Naumann, Heinrich	28, July 1848			123		Williams County, OH	Mittelseemen, Hessen-Darmstadt
Naumann, Henriette Elisabeth	1, Dec. 1862	29, Oct.	4-11m	192		Beardstown, IL	
Naumann, John	30, June 1887	11, June	69	414		Berea, OH	Beuern, Gießen, Hessen-Darmstadt
Naumann, Lydia	16, Feb. 1880	31, Jan.	15	55		Quincy, IL	St. Louis, Missouri
Naumann, Maria Catharina	27, Apr. 1863	27, Feb.	30- 4m-17d	68		Beardstown, IL	Wayne County, Ohio
Naumann, Maria Katharina	13, Apr. 1863	27, Feb.	30- 4m-17d	60		Beardstown, IL	Wayne County, Ohio
Naurath, Elisabeth	18, Oct. 1888	27, Aug.	43	670	Isemann	Burlington, IA	Harten, Hiller, Preußen
Nayler, Johan Georg	16, Oct. 1865	24, Sept	78	168		Irwing, MI	Reesbach, Sachsen
Neckel, Catharina	21, Oct. 1852			172		Beardstown, IL	
Neef, (Mrs)	9, Jan. 1865	27, Dec.	69- 4m	8	Wagner	Bucyrus, OH	Möhringen auf den Fildern, Württemberg
Neef, Anna	31, Dec. 1883	5, Dec.	35- 4m-12d	7		Hooker, NE	
Neef, Antje	31, Dec. 1883	17, Dec.	36	7	Oltmanns	Pekin, IL	Ochtersum, Ostfriesland
Neef, Freerk Janssen	25, Apr. 1889	3, Apr.	48	270		Pekin, IL	Loquard, Ostfriesland
Neef, Herman	31, Dec. 1883	4, Dec.	47-11m	7		Hooker, NE	Ostfriesland
Neef, Jakob	9, Aug. 1875	19, July	26- 6m-28d	255		Galion, OH	
Neeman, Sibetje	17, May 1875	28, Apr.	30	159	Kruse	New Ulm, MN	

- 357 -

Christliche Apologete Death Notices --- 1839 - 1899

Name of Deceased	Notice Date	Death Date	Age	Page	Maiden Name	Place of Death	Place of Birth
Neese, Emil	17, Nov. 1873	1, Nov.	31	367		Freeport, IL	Heesten, Amt Horn, Lippe-Detmold
Neese, Katharina Margaretha	13, Sept 1894	12, Aug.	47	598	Gerkes	Drake, MO	Lison, Blumenthal, Hannover
Neff, Christina	26, Feb. 1877	12, Feb.	61	71		Hamilton, OH	Hornberg, Baden
Neff, Dorothea	25, Feb. 1884	28, Jan.	52	7		Bucyrus, OH	Hepurn Twp, Lycoming County, Pennsylvania
Neff, Gottlob	15, Nov. 1875	2, Oct.	57	367		Galion, OH	Philadelphia, Pennsylvania
Neff, Jonathan	5, Jan. 1899	9, Dec.	66	14		Bucyrus, OH	Lycoming County, Pennsylvania
Neff, Lorenz	18, June 1857	23, Apr.	70	100		Burlington, IA	Möhringen, Amt Stuttgart, Württemberg
Neff, Louis Conrad	17, Aug. 1893	25, July	24	526		Louisville, KY	Louisville, Jefferson County, Kentucky
Neff, Louisa	3, Dec. 1896	16, Nov.	38	782	Weinbrecht	Terre Haute, IN	Greencastle, Indiana
Neff, Louise	7, Aug. 1865	19, Apr.	9- 2m	128		Louisville, KY	
Neff, Maria Magdalena	22, Mar. 1880	16, Feb.	60- 2m-28d	95	Hammel	Sutton, NE	Chrainthal, Württemberg
Neff, Rosina	13, Dec. 1894	22, Nov.	61	806	Hagmann	Louisville, KY	Hechtel, Mergentheim, Württemberg
Neff, Sophia Mathilde	26, Oct. 1899	5, Oct.		687		Bucyrus, OH	Holmes Township, Crawford County, Ohio
Negele, Charles F.	30, July 1896	29, June		495		Vermillion, OH	Isingen, Kirchheim, Württemberg
Nehf, Henry	19, Jan. 1899	19, Dec.	32	47		Terre Haute, IN	Württemberg
Nehf, Johan Heinrich	19, May 1898	21, Apr.	63	319		Johnsonville, IL	Württemberg
Nehf, Johannes Matthias	27, Oct. 1892	4, Oct.	65	686		Menomonie, WI	Archshofen, Mergentheim, Württemberg
Nehls, Anna	26, Apr. 1894	10, Apr.	94	278		Platteville, WI	Padingbüttel, Hannover
Nehls, Anna Helena	13, Mar. 1865	18, Jan.	8- 7m-15d	44		Platteville, WI	
Nehls, Carl Friedrich Wesley	5, Aug. 1897	6, July	19	495		Platteville, WI	Platteville, Wisconsin
Nehls, Edward	8, Feb. 1894	2, Jan.	21	94		Dubuque, IA	Platteville, Wisconsin
Nehls, Ella Helena	31, July 1890	11, July	14	494		Platteville, WI	Platteville, Grant County, Wisconsin
Nehls, F.C.	7, Jan. 1892	8, Dec.	18	14		Ripon, WI	East Rosenthal, Fond du Lac Co., Wisconsin
Nehls, Gustav	7, Feb. 1881	20, Dec.	58	47		East Troy, WI	Beinhagen, Pommern
Nehls, Hulda Louise Karolina	12, May 1898	18, Apr.	20	303		Honey Creek, WI	Waterford, Racine County, Wisconsin
Nehls, Johan Friedrich	24, Nov. 1898	25, Oct.	67	751		Platteville, WI	Sievern, Lehe, Hannover
Nehls, Luise S. J.	20, July 1899	14, May	78	463	Hasse	Honey Creek, WI	Pommern
Nehrdich, Johan	12, Nov. 1896	25, Sept	75	734		Troy, NY	Heerda, Berka an der Werra, Sachsen-Weimar
Nehring, Wilhelmine	27, May 1886	5, May	34	7	Doppert	Milwaukee, WI	Leuschentin, Vorpommern
Nehs, Elisabeth	3, Apr. 1890	15, Feb.	54	222		Jackson, IL	Mansfield, New Jersey
Neibich, Carl August	1, Apr. 1856	11, Apr.	25- 1m	72		Baltimore, MD	Schwarzenberg, Neuenburg, Württemberg
Neibich, Katharina	17, Sept 1896	17, Aug.	72	607	Kusterer	Baltimore, MD	Schwarzenberg, Neuenburg, Württemberg
Neibich, Philipp Jacob	7, Jan. 1892	19, Dec.	68	14		Baltimore, MD	Schwarzenberg, Neuenburg, Württemberg
Neibich, Virginia Regina	7, Dec. 1885	13, Nov.	11	7		Baltimore, MD	
Neidhart, Katharina	13, Dec. 1888	22, Nov.	71- 1m-28d	798	Mack	Marion, OH	Roßwaag, Vaihingen, Württemberg
Neiger, Magdalena	18, Apr. 1861	27, Mar.	75	64		Canal Dover, OH	Ober-Hasli, Bern, Schweiz
Nein, Margaetha	20, Apr. 1885	23, Mar.	86- - 9d	7	Emrich	Metamoras, OH	Bleichenbach, Ottenberg, Hessen-Darmstadt
Neithast, Heinrich Jakob	2, Nov. 1899	11, Sept	55	703		Columbus, OH	Schaffhausen, Schweiz
Neitsch, Carl August	19, Oct. 1885	3, Oct.	27	7		Industry, TX	Lagrange, Texas
Neitzel, Gottlob Michael F.	26, Feb. 1883	11, Feb.	70	71		Milwaukee, WI	Folbenz bei Massow, Pommern
Neitzel, Johanna	28, July 1887	2, July	59	478	Knappke	Baraboo, WI	Treptow , Pommern
Neitzel, Laura W.	30, Mar. 1899	1, Mar.	17	207		Baraboo, WI	
Nell, Georg	13, Aug. 1883	12, July	43	263		Rushville, IL	Dillenburg, Nassau
Nell, Lena	7, Nov. 1881	22, Oct.	18- -19d	359		Rushville, IL	Dillenburg, Nassau
Neller, Heinrich G. A.	26, July 1894	28, June	65	486		DeWitt, MI	Hochfelden, Sachsen-Meiningen
Nelson, Carolina	23, May 1861	4, May	37	84		Galion, OH	

Name of Deceased	Notice Date	Death Date	Age	Page	Maiden Name	Place of Death	Place of Birth
Nendel, Helena	26, Sept 1895	24, Aug.	31	622	Rommel	Evansville, IN	Steinbach, Hallenberg, Germany
Nerk, Friedrich	2, May 1889	12, Apr.	61- 2m-22d	286		Pittsburg, PA	Heilbronn, Württemberg
Nesemann, Louise	25, Apr. 1895	25, Mar.	77	270	Kuzke	Swanton, NE	Kollin bei Stargardt, Pommern
Nesper, Karoline	20, Apr. 1899	16, Mar.	76	255	Uebelmesser	Philadelphia, PA	Backnang, Württemberg
Nesselrodt, Andreas	21, Apr. 1879	9, Apr.	64- 7m	127		Golconda, IL	Heerda bei Berka, Sachsen-Weimar
Nesselrodt, Anna M.	21, Apr. 1879	5, Apr.	63- 9m	127	Schuchart	Golconda, IL	Hausbreitenbach, Sachsen-Weimar
Nest, Marie	16, Feb. 1880	13, Jan.	17	55		Wheeling, WV	Warlin, NeuBrandenburg, Mecklenburg-Strelitz
Nest, Sophia	30, Apr. 1896	18, Mar.	76	286		Wheeling, WV	Berlin, Mecklenburg-Strelitz
Nestle, Georg A.	11, Feb. 1897	16, Jan.	65	94		Cleveland, OH	Rohrdorf, Württemberg
Nestler, Anna	13, Sept 1894	18, Aug.	66	598	Käfer	Pierceville, IN	Schweningen, Württemberg
Nestler, August Herman	6, Mar. 1876	13, Feb.	20	79		Cincinnati, OH	Cincinnati, Hamilton County, Ohio
Nestler, Carl August	27, July 1885	13, July	63	7		Nashville, TN	Steinbach bei Annaberg, Sachsen
Nestler, Emil	4, Apr. 1864	18, Mar.	11	56		Cincinnati, OH	
Nestler, Friedrieke Eberhardine	24, May 1875	10, May	52	167	Cortes	Cincinnati, OH	Moekgröningen, Württemberg
Nestler, Karolina	15, Mar. 1880	29, Feb.	44- 5m-16d	87	Altemöller	Cincinnati, OH	Stettingen, Preußen
Neth, Conrad	16, Dec. 1878	1, Nov.	23	399		Liberty, MO	Oeschingen, Rottenburg, Württemberg
Neth, Georg	10, Sept 1891	18, Aug.	92	590		Greenville, OH	Mössingen, Rottenburg, Württemberg
Neth, Georg	24, Sept 1891	18, Aug.	92	622		Covington, OH	Mössingen, Rottenburg, Württemberg
Neth, Margaretha Magdalena	15, Feb. 1894	7, Jan.	74	110	Möck	Arley, MO	Willmandingen, Württemberg
Neth, Mary	25, Aug. 1884	3, Aug.	45	7	Holland	Kearney, MO	
Neth, Mary	22, Sept 1884	3, Aug.	35	7	Holland	Kearney, MO	
Nething, Anna Barbara	30, Mar. 1863	23, Feb.	74	52	Pfänder	Baresville, OH	Beuren, Nürtlingen, Württemberg
Netzscher, Nikolaus	24, Nov. 1843		Inquiry	187		Chillicothe, OH	Großbieberau, Hessen-Darmstadt
Netzscher, Franz	16, Sept 1842		Inquiry	147		Chillicothe, OH	Hessen-Darmstadt
Netzscher, Ludwig	16, Sept 1842		Inquiry	147		Chillicothe, OH	Hessen-Darmstadt
Netzscher, Nicolaus	16, Sept 1842		Inquiry	147		Chillicothe, OH	Hessen-Darmstadt
Neu , Heinrich	16, June 1892	27, May	91-3m- 7d	382		Baltimore, MD	Rheinkreis Baiern
Neu, Amanda Wilhelmina	24, Dec. 1877	6, Dec.	26	415	Heitbrink	St. Louis, MO	
Neu, Georg Friedrich	16, Sept 1886	16, Aug.	66	7		Mt. Vernon, NY	Hoffheim, Sinsheim, Baden
Neu, Georg H.	26, July 1880	10, July	26	239		New Rochelle, NY	
Neu, Wilhelmine	31, Dec. 1883	11, Dec.	24	7		Mt. Vernon, NY	New York
Neubauer, Caroline	22, Dec. 1892	28, Nov.	74	814	Nenninger	Schnectady, NY	Langenau, Oberfranken, Baiern
Neubauer, Charlotte Sophia	21, Aug. 1876	26, July	80- 7m-15d	271		Washington, MN	Großbenz, Naugardt, Pommern, Preußen
Neubauer, Wilhelm	27, June 1881	8, June	59- 9m-26d	207		Marietta, OH	Großbentz, Naugard, Altstettin, Preußen
Neubeck, Johan W.	27, June 1881	15, June	55- 7m-25d	207		Schnectady, NY	Stein am Kocher, Baden
Neuber, Louisa	5, June 1876	19, May	38	183	Kessler	Schnectady, NY	Neukirchen bei Kirchheim, Kurhessen
Neuber, Margaretha	25, Sept 1876	21, Aug.	76	311		Columbus, OH	Magstadt, Böblingen, Württemberg
Neubig, Christian M.	11, June 1891	14, May	60	382		Columbus, OH	Brettach, Neckarsulm, Württemberg
Neubig, Rosina	9, June 1887	23, May	49	366	Klein	Kansas City, KS	Kochersteinsfeld, Württemberg
Neudeck, Elise	20, Apr. 1899	22, Mar.	75	255	Abke	Wyandotte, KS	Stemshorn, Lemförde, Hannover
Neudeck, Ernestine	11, Aug. 1873	20, July	62- 5m-11d	255	Stengel	Fairmount, KS	Trebitsch, Neumark, Preußen
Neudeck, Friedrich	21, Jan. 1884	30, Dec.	73	7		Kansas City, KS	Posen-Charni, Preußen
Neudeck, Herman	16, Mar. 1899	14, Feb.	55	175		Wittens, OH	Schanikow, Posen
Neudeck, Katharina	29, Jan. 1877	11, Dec.	33-11m-27d	39		Fairmount, KS	
Neudeck, Wilhelm F.	1, Dec. 1879	15, Nov.	19	383	Arnold	St. Joseph, MO	Elsaß
Neudorff, Anna Maria	29, Jan. 1891		58	78			

Christliche Apologete Death Notices --- 1839 - 1899

Name of Deceased	Notice Date	Death Date	Age	Page	Maiden Name	Place of Death	Place of Birth
Neudorff, Clara Lisette	25, Feb. 1892	6, Feb.	30	126	Fiegenbaum	St. Joseph, MO	Wapello, Iowa
Neuendorf, Dorothea	21, Sept 1893	18, Aug.	81	606	Kulow	Sun Prairie, WI	Neuenkirchen, Mecklenburg-Strelitz
Neuendorf, Maria Sophia Johanna	25, June 1891		68- 2m-25d	414	Wilck	Moorheads, PA	Sharpszow, Mecklenburg-Schwerin
Neuer, Eva Maria	20, June 1861	5, June	83-10m-17d	100	Staller	Galion, OH	Berks County, Pennsylvania
Neufer, Christian	13, Sept 1894	18, Aug.	82- 6m	598		Chillicothe, OH	Mähringen bei Stuttgart, Württemberg
Neuffer, Margaretha	21, Nov. 1895	3, Nov.	81	750	Günther		Möhringen bei Stuttgart, Württemberg
Neuhardt, E.	8, Dec. 1884	6, Oct.		7		Pirmasens, GE	Nothweila, RheinPfalz Baiern
Neuhart, Anna Katharina	20, June 1889	4, June	77- 7m-26d	398	Beppler	New Palestine, IN	Dannenrod, Hessen-Darmstadt
Neuhart, Carolina	19, Oct. 1868	3, Oct.	22- 3m- 4d	335		Wheeling, VA	
Neuhart, David	7, May 1891	15, Apr.	80- 8m-14d	302		St. Paul, MN	Rumbach, Rheinpfalz Baiern
Neuhart, David	26, May 1892	5, May	42	334		St. Paul, MN	Washington County, Ohio
Neuhart, Georg Jak.	4, Mar. 1886	4, Dec.	69- 6m	7		Nothweiler, GE	
Neuhart, Georg Jakob	21, Jan. 1886	4, Dec.	69- 6m	7		Rothweiler, GE	
Neuhart, Heinrich	27, Aug. 1896	11, Aug.	42	559		Indianapolis, IN	Ohio
Neuhart, Katharina	22, May 1890	4, May	67	334	Schaub	Woodsfield, OH	Altenkirchen, Wetzlar, Koblenz, Preußen
Neuhart, Magdalena	16, Sept 1886	8, July	77	7	Brubach	St. Paul, MN	Rumbach, RheinPfalz Baiern
Neuhaus, Johanna	20, Nov. 1882	6, Oct.	30	375	Ruck	Schnectady, NY	
Neuhaus, Margaretha	23, Jan. 1882	3, Jan.	62	31	Allman	New Albany, IN	Wilderswiel, Interlaken, Schweiz
Neuhausen, Helene	15, Mar. 1888	18, Feb.	40-11m-27d	174	Koch	Bible Grove, IL	Mölsfeldt, Schleswig
Neukom, Friederika	2, Aug. 1894	11, July	60	502	Engelhard	Terre Haute, IN	Roswak, Vaihingen, Württemberg
Neukom, Theolinde Martha	4, May 1885	12, Apr.	13	7		Terre Haute, IN	
Neukomm, Maria	17, Feb. 1898	3, Jan.	43	111		Toledo, OH	Müllenberg, Bern, Schweiz
Neuling, Wilhelm	29, Oct. 1877	31, Aug.	59	351		Florence, IL	Velgau, Sachsen, Preußen
Neuman, Margaretha	9, Feb. 1885	18, Jan.	48	7	Brunnemeier	Bay City, MI	Gungenhausen, Baiern
Neumann, (Mrs)	26, Dec. 1870	5, Dec.	44	415		Rockford, MN	Radekow, Pommern, Preußen
Neumann, (Mrs)	5, Sept 1850	15, Aug.	35	144		Williams County, OH	Hessen-Darmstadt
Neumann, Anna	10, Feb. 1887	22, Jan.	66	94	Kaiser	Crandon, SD	Thalheim, Aargau, Schweiz
Neumann, Anna Augusta	19, Jan. 1899	28, Dec.	22	47		Prospect Park, CA	Prospect Park, Los Angeles, California
Neumann, Anna Sophia	30, May 1889	15, May	78	350	Howig	Austin, TX	Scheiblersburg, Landsberg., Brandenburg
Neumann, Augusta Maria	7, Oct. 1897	9, Sept	52	639	Megow	Cincinnati, OH	Pemmerensdorf, Stettin a. d. Oder, Germany
Neumann, Christina	8, July 1886	18, June	58	7	Droßmann	Scottville, NE	Welkenwichke, Russisch-Polen
Neumann, Dorothea Sophia	20, Dec. 1880	27, Nov.	77- -18d	407		Juda, WI	Dölitz, Preußen
Neumann, Elisabeth	10, Feb. 1873		40	47		New Orleans, LA	Zürich, Schweiz
Neumann, Friedrich Ferd.	1, Mar. 1875	2, Feb.	62	71		San Antonio, TX	Stoeben, Pommern
Neumann, Gottfried	14, May 1891	13, Apr.	38	318		St. Paul, MN	Wabasha County, Wisconsin
Neumann, Gottlieb	13, Feb. 1890	7, Jan.	65- 3m- 7d	110		St. Paul, MN	Preußen
Neumann, Johan Gottlieb	29, Jan. 1891	2, Jan.	79- 6m	78		Elmore, MN	
Neumann, Johannes	8, Apr. 1886	17, Mar.	75- 1m-16d	7		Edon, OH	Mittel-Semen, Nidau, Hessen-Darmstadt
Neumann, Johannes	2, Nov. 1885	7, Oct.	62	7		Perry, TX	Growitz, Preußen
Neumann, Joseph	10, Sept 1896	8, Aug.	60	591		Rutersville, TX	Lusdorf bei Friedland, Oesterreich
Neumann, Maria Sophia	9, Nov. 1885	17, Sept	34	7	Rutenschröer	Huntingburg, IN	Hamilton County, Ohio
Neumann, Philipp	21, May 1891	7, Apr.	73-10m-15d	334		New Metamoras, OH	Salters, Hessen-Darmstadt
Neumann, Rosina	26, Oct. 1885	6, Oct.	61	7	Schieber	Mt. Vernon, IN	Fornsbach, Backnang, Württemberg
Neumeier, Amalia	23, Apr. 1883	5, Apr.	54	135		Pekin, IL	Wapello, Iowa
Neumeier, Caroline Friedrike	27, July 1893	8, July	22	478		Gladbrook, IA	
Neumeier, Johan	1, Nov. 1869	20, Sept	43	351		Jackson, MO	Berndorf, Waldeck

Christliche Apologete Death Notices --- 1839 - 1899

Name of Deceased	Notice Date	Death Date	Age	Maiden Name	Page	Place of Death	Place of Birth
Neumeier, Klara Peine	28, Dec. 1893	5, Dec.	15		828	Indianapolis, IN	Indianapolis, Marion County, Indiana
Neumeier, Maria	29, June 1863	27, May	40- 8m		104	Jackson, MO	Berndorf, Eisenberg, Waldeck
Neumeister, Maria	16, Dec. 1867	7, Nov.	32		398	Wapello, IA	
Neumetz, Wilhelmina	14, Mar. 1861	14, Feb.	30	Kannenberg	44	Cedar Lake, IN	Großmellen bei Köslin, Preußen
Neumeyer, John	19, Oct. 1899	12, Sept	40		671	Lutman, MO	Morgan County, Missouri
Neumeyer, Karl	3, Oct. 1870	30, Aug.	16		319	Jackson, MO	
Neumiller, Maria	3, Jan. 1876	15, Dec.	63	Pothmann	7	Davenport, IA	Herdeke, Westphalen, Preußen
Neumüller, Peter	8, Nov. 1894	17, Oct.	84		726	Davenport, IA	Rothenwerth, Baiern
Neun, (Mr)	19, July 1869	4, May	70		231	Bonn, OH	Bleichenbach, Ottenberg, Hessen-Darmstadt
Neuschler, Julia Katharina	7, Jan. 1892	8, Dec.	32	Rohrbacher	14	Sandusky, OH	Erie County, Ohio
Neusperlie, Franciska Fannie	12, Sept 1889	25, Aug.	86- 3m-27d		590	Baresville, OH	Lauden County, West Virginia
Neustel, Heinrich	10, Sept 1896	18, Aug.	70		591	Brownton, MN	Sulzbach am Kocher, Gauldorf, Württemberg
Neustel, Heinrich	7, Mar. 1881	16, Feb.	24		79	Glencoe, MN	Kronhütte, Welzheim, Württemberg
New , John	16, Feb. 1899	19, Jan.	73		111	New Rochelle, NY	Hoffenheim bei Sinsheim, Baden
New , Harry	10, May 1894	10, Apr.	13		310	New Rochelle, NY	New Rochelle, New York
New , Peter	18, Feb. 1897	22, Jan.	69		111	Baltimore, MD	Laufersweiler, Coblenz, Preußen
Newman, John	5, Jan. 1899	3, Dec.	73		14	Junction City, KS	Newmanstown, Pennsylvania
Ney, Maria A.	25, Aug. 1853	12, Aug.	19- 9m		136	Defiance, OH	
Neyer, Christina	16, Sept 1858	24, July	26		148	Poland, IN	Hombressen, Hofgeismar, Kurhessen
Niaus, Johann	2, Aug. 1849	3, July	51- 4m		124	St. Louis, MO	Wenterswick, Gelderland, Holland
Nicholson, Maria	22, Sept 1898	26, Aug.	64		607	Norwich, KS	Schleswig-Holstein
Nichter, Bonifacius	23, July 1891	2, July	83- 3m- 8d		478	Stryker, OH	Unterstork, Kurhessen
Nickel, A.	4, Apr. 1864	28, Feb.	34		56	Iowa City, IA	
Nickel, Friedrich	25, Nov. 1842		Inquiry		187	Jefferson Barraks, MO	OberAuerbach bei Zweibrücken,
Nickenbach, Verona Barbara	26, Jan. 1863	9, Dec.	75- 7m-27d		16	Newark, OH	Margel, Baden
Nicklas, Anna Katharina	31, Jan. 1889	5, Jan.	80- 5m-28d	Bitsch	78	Platteville, WI	Lenabach, Hessen-Darmstadt
Nicklas, Augusta	25, Nov. 1878	26, Oct.	17		375	West Pensaukee, WI	Kleinsilber, Neumark, Preußen
Nicklas, Jakob	31, Mar. 1873	3, Jan.	21- 2m		103	Platteville, WI	
Nickles, Anna	21, June 1875	24, May	74	Graden	199	Boonville, MO	Siselen, Bern, Schweiz
Nickles, Maria	12, Jan. 1893	16, Dec.	70	Groß	30	Jamestown, MO	Wolperswyl, Nidau, Bern, Schweiz
Nickles, Peter	26, Apr. 1869	15, Mar.	78-6m		135	Boonville, MO	Bühl, Bern, Schweiz
Nicolai, Bertha	24, June 1897	20, May	30-10m-25d	Markgraf	399	LaCrosse, WI	Scheldon, Monroe County, Wisconsin
Nicolai, Friederike	21, July 1892	6, July	79	Mann	462	Indianapolis, IN	Wohnheim, Hessen-Darmstadt
Nicolai, Karl Ludwig	26, June 1871	9, June	54		207	Indianapolis, IN	Essingen bei Landau, Rheinkreis Baiern
Nicolaisen, Heinrich Harke	29, Dec. 1892	6, Dec.	59- -11d		828	Cleveland, OH	
Niebel, Christian	5, June 1865	1, Apr.	72- 4m- 6d		92	Zanesville, OH	
Niebel, Heinrich	12, Oct. 1863		28- - 3d		164		
Niebel, Maria Barbara	27, Feb. 1882	5, Feb.	22	Stortz	71	Caseville, MI	Meridian, Ingh. County, Michigan
Niebeling, Wilhelmina	31, May 1880	15, May	74	Koch	175	Decatur, IL	Rückert, Hünfeld, Kurhessen
Niebling, Johan	31, Mar. 1879	7, Mar.	34		103	Garden Grove, IA	Denchingen, Baden
Niebuhr, Anna	21, Jan. 1886	30, Dec.	64	Bolhöfer	7	Pittsfield, IL	Bexten, Schörmar, Lippe-Detmold
Niebuhr, Elisabeth	30, Sept 1867	11, Sept	77		310	Louisville, KY	St. Einöde, Rheinkreis Baiern
Niebuhr, Fr. W.	8, May 1890	18, Apr.	78- 3m- 6d		302	Brenham, TX	Brome, Hannover
Niebuhr, John F.	12, July 1880	23, June	82- 4m		223	Warrenton, MO	
Niedecker, Emilie	24, Nov. 1879	15, Oct.	27	Schneider	375	San Jose, CA	Germany, Ft. Atkinson, Wisconsin
Niedenführ, Ernst Friedrich	3, Apr. 1882	11, Mar.	49		111	Meredosia, IL	Haberdorf, Schlesien, Preußen

Name of Deceased	Notice Date	Death Date	Age	Page	Maiden Name	Place of Death	Place of Birth
Niederführ, Helene	29, May 1890	29, Apr.	84- 2m-10d	350	Stache	Great Bend, KS	Habendorf, Schlesien
Niederführ, Karl Wilhelm	1, Apr. 1872	29, Feb.	72	111		Pittsfield, IL	Habendorf bei Reichenbach, Schlesien
Nieder, Friedrich	5, Apr. 1880	19, Mar.	63- 1m-12d	111		Cincinnati, OH	Marheim, Rheinkreis Baiern
Nieder, Georg	30, Oct. 1890	14, Oct.	70	702		Cincinnati, OH	Marenheim, Rheinpfalz Baiern
Nieder, Katharina	16, Jan. 1890		70	46	Roth	Cincinnati, OH	Marnheim, Baiern
Nieder, Magdalena	13, Oct. 1898	13, Sept	70	655	Stüber	Cincinnati, OH	Rüßlingen, Rheinpfalz Baiern
Niederauer, Anna Maria	4, Dec. 1871	14, Nov.	19	391		Cincinnati, OH	Stettin, Rheinkreis Baiern
Niederauer, Catharina	11, Oct. 1875	28, Sept	25	327	Keller	Hamilton, OH	Cincinnati, Hamilton County, Ohio
Niederauer, John	25, May 1893		33	334		Brooklyn, NY	New York
Niederbröker, Margaretha	17, Feb. 1868	1, Feb.	22	55	Iwig	Hamilton, OH	Welsheim, Rheinkreis Baiern
Niederbröker, Friedrich	28, Mar. 1864	7, Nov.	22	52		Herman, MO	Rödinghausen, Bünde, Preußen
Niedergerke, Elisabeth	17, Apr. 1890	26, Mar.	27	254	Joachim	Morrison, MO	Osage County, Missouri
Niederjohann, Florentine	12, Mar. 1866	23, Feb.	42- 5m- 8d	86	Kölling	Warren, MO	
Niederjohann, Herman Heinrich	15, Dec. 1898	11, Nov.	90	799		Truxton, MO	Heuel, Melle, Hannover
Niedermeyer, Clara Ida	18, Aug. 1884	26, July	22- 8m-23d	7	Frenzel	Bloomington, IL	
Niedermeyer, Clara Ida	8, Sept 1884	26, July	22- 8m-23d	7	Frenzel	Bloomington, IL	
Niedermeyer, David	2, Feb. 1874	10, Jan.	21	39		Decatur, IL	Clark County, Missouri
Niedermeyer, Jacob	4, Feb. 1892	8, Jan.	72- 3m- 8d	78		Hokah, MN	Knitlingen, Maulbronn, Württemberg
Niedermeyer, Karoline	16, Feb. 1899	26, Jan.	45	111		Bloomington, IL	Arenzville, Illinois
Niedermeyer, Lena	5, June 1890	30, Apr.	35	366	Neff	Bloomington, IL	Danvers Township, Illinois
Niedernjohan, (girl)	13, July 1854	27, May	4	112		St. Charles, MO	
Niedfelt, Anna Elisabeth	17, May 1894	17, Apr.	26	326	Greife	Denver, CO	Franklin County, Missouri
Niedhamer, Barbara	28, Apr. 1884	5, Apr.	68- 5m- 5d	7	Armbruster	Ann Arbor, MI	Dettlingen, Siegmaringen, Hohenzollern
Nieding, Margaretha	7, Oct. 1878	24, Sept	49- 7m-17d	319	Häußner	Vermilion, OH	Heenes, Kurhessen
Niedringhaus, Walter C.	4, Feb. 1886	17, Jan.	19	7		St. Louis, MO	St. Louis, Missouri
Niedringhaus, Wilhelm	5, Jan. 1863	15, Dec.	60	4		St. Louis, MO	Blaßheim, Preußen
Niedringhaus, Wilhelmine Charlotte	11, July 1889	19, June	35	446		St. Louis, MO	Blasheim, Lübbeke, Minden, Westphalen
Niehaus, Adelheid	30, Jan. 1871	14, Jan.	60- 5m-13d	39	Hünecke	New Albany, IN	Morsum, Amt Westen, Hannover
Niehaus, Anna Maria	13, July 1893	24, May	77	446	Quebbeman	New Albany, IN	Achman, Hannover
Niehaus, Anna Maria Sophia	25, Jan. 1894	27, Dec.	64	62	Bahrmann	Seymour, IN	Essen, Oldenburg
Niehaus, Christina C.	23, May 1895	27, Apr.	88	334	Muntz	Salem, IN	Württemberg
Niehaus, Friedrich Ludwig	9, Feb. 1880	21, Jan.	71- 3m-23d	47		New Albany, IN	Osterbinde, Amt Freudenburg, Hannover
Niehaus, Friedrich Wilhelm	24, Apr. 1876	1, Apr.	58	135		Seymour, IN	Schwarzdorf, OsterKappeln, Wittlage, Hannover
Niehaus, Gerhard	11, Mar. 1858	13, Feb.	55	40		New Albany, IN	Osterbinden, Amt Freudenberg, Hannover
Niehaus, Johan Heinrich	10, Jan. 1881	25, Dec.	74-10m-12d	15		Evansville, IN	Amtshut, Hannover
Niehaus, Ludwig	30, June 1879	25, May	67	207		Truxton, MO	Flackenholz, Hannover
Niehaus, Maria	13, Sept 1869	6, Aug.	28- 9m-10d	295	Otto	Evansville, IN	Püffort, Gerdo, Amt Bersenbrück, Hannover
Niehaus, Sarah Mathilda	2, Feb. 1885	19, Jan.	24	7	Schultz	Mt. Olive, IL	Macoupin County, Illinois
Niehaus, Seigse	25, Feb. 1892	3, Feb.	56	126	VanBeest	Warrenton, MO	Geurkum, Holland
Niehaus, Sophia	14, Feb. 1881	26, Jan.	51	55		Menominee, MI	Altwedel, Neumark
Niehaus, Wilhelm J.	4, Sept 1890	31, July	38- 9m-12d	574		Seymour, IN	Grassy Fork, Jackson County, Indiana
Niehl, Margaretha	5, Mar. 1877	10, Feb.	66	79		Portsmouth, OH	Mössingen, Rottenburg, Württemberg
Niehus, Sophia	21, June 1894	25, Apr.	82	406	Wenthe	Warren, MO	Egge, Hamel, Hannover
Niels, Sophie	29, Oct. 1896		82- - 1d	703	Konrad	Gladbrook, IA	Barnskono, Pommern
Niemand, Barbara	21, Apr. 1859	7, Mar.	62	64		Baraboo, WI	
Niemand, Peter	13, Mar. 1862	6, Feb.	64- 2m	44		Baraboo, WI	

Christliche Apologete Death Notices --- 1839 - 1899

Name of Deceased	Notice Date	Death Date	Age	Maiden Name	Page	Place of Death	Place of Birth
Niemann, Catharina E.	12, Oct. 1874	5, Sept	18- 8m-17d		327	White Creek, IN	
Niemann, Ernestine	25, Mar.1872	17, Dec.	18- 6m-17d		103	Roseville, MI	
Niemann, Friedrich Johan	3, Dec. 1896	28, Oct.	71		782	Roseville, MI	Hofgrabow, Mecklenburg-Schwerin
Niemann, Heinrich	1, July 1897	7, May	77		414	Marine City, MI	Kleinlees, Mecklenburg-Schwerin
Niemann, Heinrich	12, Mar. 1877	18, Feb.	18		87	Roseville, MI	
Niemann, Henry	10, Apr. 1882	8, Mar.	33		119	Drake, MO	Emmenhausen, Oerlinghausen, Lippe-Detmold
Niemann, Johan A.	31, July 1876	12, July	63- 6m-27d		247	Covington, KY	Bramsche, Hannover
Niemann, Johan Heinrich	10, Feb. 1868	20, Jan.	69-11m		47	Seymour, IN	Fenne, Hannover
Niemann, Johann	14, Oct. 1858	31, Aug.	65		164	Monroe, IL	Kirchdorf, Ostfriesland
Niemann, Karoline	16, Aug. 1875	28, July	35	Tonne	263	Seymour, IN	Cincinnati, Hamilton County, Ohio
Niemann, Karoline	6, Apr. 1899	8, Mar.	60	Sievers	223	San Diego, CA	Borstel, Wiesen, Hannover
Niemann, Katharina	30, Aug. 1888	31, July	82		558	Newport, KY	Schlehausen, Osnabrück, Hannover
Niemann, Maria	13, Feb. 1896	30, Jan.	63	Buck	110	Mt. Healthy, OH	Gramberg, Selehausen, Osnabrück, Hannover
Niemann, Maria	13, Dec. 1855	17, Nov.	42		200	Herman, MO	Nordhemmern bei Minden, Preußen
Niemann, Maria	22, Oct. 1883	17, Sept	21	Kern	343	Montague, MI	Erin, Macomb County, Michigan
Niemann, Maria E.	22, Apr. 1867	27, Mar.	57- 8m	Klekamp	126	Seymour, IN	Fenne, Hannover
Niemann, Sophia	22, June 1899	29, Apr.	68	Niebuhr	399	Roseville, MI	Gräwen, Mecklenburg-Schwerin
Niemann, Wilhelm F.	8, Nov. 1894	12, Oct.	48		726	Seymour, IN	Seymour, Indiana
Niemeier, Christian	20, Oct. 1898	28, Sept	67		671	Rochester, MN	Nienberg, Germany
Niemeier, Daniel	3, Jan. 1895	10, Dec.	75		14	Salem, MN	Nordheim, Hannover
Niemeier, Emma	16, Feb. 1885	16, Jan.	23- 9m-25d	Dewitz	7	Mayville, SD	
Niemeier, Georg S.	5, Oct. 1874	19, Sept	16- 8m-14d		319	Rochester, MN	Rochester, Minnesota
Niemeier, Helena	26, May 1898		65-10m-11d	Herber	335	Rochester, MN	Lehrbach, Hessen-Darmstadt
Niemeier, Henriette Dorothea	8, Feb. 1875	2, Jan.	17- 9m-28d		47	St. Paul, MN	Dakota County, Minnesota
Niemeier, Katharina M.	10, Sept 1847	25, Aug.	60		147	Madison, IN	
Niemeier, Martha Sophia	8, Feb. 1875	12, Jan.	16- 5m-10d		47	St. Paul, MN	Dakota County, Minnesota
Niemeyer, Aug.	17, Jan. 1889	31, Dec.	64- 4m-22d		46	Hopewell, MO	Laßbruch, Lippe-Detmold
Niemeyer, C.	11, Apr. 1889	21, Mar.	49- 9m-10d		238	Hopewell, MO	Meierberg, Lippe-Detmold
Niemeyer, Caroline Conradine	7, Dec. 1893	7, Nov.	73	Wesemann	782	Quincy, IL	Ottenstein, Braunschweig
Niemeyer, Christian	8, Feb. 1875	17, Jan.	59- - 3d		47	Quincy, IL	Wahlbruck, Amt Polle, Hannover
Niemeyer, Christine	21, Apr. 1859	3, Apr.		Noltensmeyer	64	Marthasville, MO	
Niemeyer, Friedrich	16, June 1873	26, May	65		191	Quincy, IL	Vollbruch, Hannover
Niemeyer, Herman Heinrich	26, Nov. 1891	20, Oct.	21		766	Rockham, SD	Troy, Sac County, Wisconsin
Niemeyer, Wilhelm	19, Oct. 1874	16, Sept	50		335	Warren, MO	Goldbeck, Rinteln, Lippe-Schaumburg
Niemüller, Christine Elise	27, Jan. 1879	6, Jan.	18		31	Huntingburg, IN	
Niemüller, Maria Louise	20, Mar. 1890	26, Feb.	40-11m- 1d		190	Junction City, KS	Dubois County, Indiana
Nienaber, Wilhelm	22, Aug. 1881	7, Aug.	57		271	St. Paul, MN	Riemsloh, Hannover
Nienas, Martha	20, May 1897	21, Apr.	20- 1m-18d		319	Holmes, ND	
Nienhueser, Karl	9, Nov. 1868	6, Oct.			359	St. Paul, MN	
Nienhüser, Regina	30, Aug. 1869	7, Aug.	27	Funk	279	St. Paul, MN	St. Louis, Missouri
Nienhüser, Sophie Friederike	3, Nov. 1859	13, Oct.	35	Hilgemann	176	St. Paul, MN	Lünen, Teklenburg, Münster, Preußen
Nientker, Rebekka	29, Feb. 1864	6, Feb.	39- 3m		36	Decatur, IL	Lebanon, Lebanon County, Pennsylvania
Nieper, Adolf	8, Jan. 1883	18, Dec.	55- - 1d		15	Cannelton, IN	Gifhorn, Hannover
Nieper, Maria Sophia Henrietta	6, Sept 1894	7, Aug.	67	Fricke	582	Cannelton, IN	Platendorf, Gifhorn, Hannover
Niepoth, Anna Katharina	14, Nov. 1889	17, Oct.	62	Pfifferling	734	Detroit, MI	Schlitz, Lauterbach, Hessen-Darmstadt
Niepoth, Friedrich Christian	4, May 1893	9, Apr.	73		286	Detroit, MI	Willofs, Schlitz, Hessen

Christliche Apologete Death Notices --- 1839 - 1899

Name of Deceased	Notice Date	Death Date	Age	Maiden Name	Page	Place of Death	Place of Birth
Niepoth, Georg F.C.	5, Feb. 1891	5, Jan.	42		94	Detroit, MI	Detroit, Wayne County, Michigan
Nieppold, Lydia	11, Apr. 1870	23, Mar.	16-11m-27d		119	Washington, MN	St. Paul , Minnesota
Niermeyer, Lydia Elisabeth	19, May 1898		20- 3m		319	Columbus, OH	Columbus, Franklin County, Ohio
Nies, Georg	19, Aug. 1878	31, July			263	Dallas, TX	Neu-Isenburg, Preußen
Nieß, Christina	27, Aug. 1883	8, Aug.	69- 7m-13d		279	Matamoras, OH	Oberseemen, Hessen-Darmstadt
Nieß, Johannes Wilhelm	19, Mar. 1896	1, Mar.	84		190	Monroefield, OH	Obersaamen, Nieda, Hessen-Darmstadt
Niet, (Mr)	13, May 1867	29, Mar.	69- 5m-22d		150	Brooklyn, NY	Dissen, Amt Iburg, Osnabrück, Hannover
Nietenhöfer, Antke	14, June 1880	20, May		Saathoff	191	New Fountain, TX	Ostersande, Ostfriesland
Niethammer, J.G.	19, Mar. 1857	16, Feb.	39		48	Ann Arbor, MI	Unterjettingen, Herrenberg, Württemberg
Nietz, Paul	21, Sept 1893	22, Aug.	17		606	Toledo, OH	Berlin, Preußen
Nievar, Jacob	19, Oct. 1893	23, Sept	91		670	Quincy, IL	Zabern, Rheinpfalz Baiern
Nievar, John	9, Mar. 1863		27		40	Pekin, IL	
Nievar, Katharina	27, Dec. 1880	12, Dec.	73		415	Pekin, IL	Rohdt bei Neustadt an der Hardt,
Nigg, Elisabeth	21, Mar. 1881	27, Feb.	52	Michel	95	Oregon, MO	Brienz, Bern, Schweiz
Nigg, Wolfgang	12, Dec. 1881	16, Nov.	64- 8m		399	Canton, MO	Gersau, Schwyz, Schweiz
Nihaus, Maria Elisa	8, Dec. 1859	14, Oct.	45		196	Seymour, IN	Belm, Hannover
Nikola, Katharina	11, Dec. 1876	23, Oct.	73	Wilms	399	Petersburg, IL	Zäselberg, Baiern
Nill, Margaretha	5, Mar. 1877	10, Feb.	66		79	Portsmouth, OH	Mössingen, Rottenburg, Württemberg
Nimphie, Franz Heinrich	22, May 1890	22, Apr.	70- 8m- 8d		334	Duffield, MI	Schünsdorf, Mecklenburg
Nims, Johannes	3, June 1878		62		175	Red Wing, MN	Witu, Pommern
Nimz, Augustine	19, Dec. 1895	24, Nov.	71	Lebert	814	Fond du Lac, WI	Waldo, Rummelsburg, Köslin, Preußen
Ninas, Emil F.	20, Aug. 1896	31, July	54		543	Kansas City, MO	Ilowe bei Pudewitz, Posen
Ninas, Mathilde	20, Feb. 1871	26, Jan.	24	Stünkel	63	Freedom, MO	
Ningler, (Mrs)	18, July 1864	25, June	27- 6m- 7d		116	Chester, IL	Rucheim, Speier, Baiern
Nippert, Anna Catharina	23, July 1896	26, May	75	Schlägel	479	Baraboo, WI	Hainbach, Spangenberg, Kurhessen
Nippert, Anna Maria	25, Apr. 1861	27, Jan.	17- 1m-24d		68	Baraboo, WI	
Nippert, Elise	11, Aug. 1898	21, July			511	Cincinnati, OH	Karlsruhe, Baden
Nippert, Eva Margaretha	10, Apr. 1856	18, Mar.	55- 2m-24d		60	Baraboo, WI	Lehnbach, Weißenburg, Elsaß
Nippert, Gottfried	6, Mar. 1882	19, Feb.	70		79	Portsmouth, OH	Gersdorf, Elsaß
Nippert, John	30, Aug. 1880	26, July	28- 8m		279	Washington, MN	Pittsburg, Pennsylvania
Nippert, Ludwig (Rev)	30, Aug. 1894	17, Aug.	69- 6m		566	Baraboo, WI	Görsdorf, Elsaß
Nippert, Meta	7, Oct. 1858	26, Aug.		Duntze	160		Bremen, Germany
Nippert, Michael	20, June 1864	25, May	70- 2m		100	Baraboo, WI	Gersdorf, Weißenburg, Elsaß
Nippert, Michael L.	24, Mar. 1887	6, Mar.	52		190	Baraboo, WI	Captina, Ohio
Nippert, Philipp	12, Jan. 1874	19, Dec.	59		15	Baraboo, WI	Gordorff, Wörth, Elsaß
Nippert, Salome	18, June 1883	3, June	65		199	Portsmouth, OH	Gestdorf, Elsaß
Nippold, Anna Martha	27, Nov. 1890	7, Nov.	67	Zulaaf	766	South Bend, IN	Josbach, Hessen-Kassel
Nippold, Gotthilf	18, May 1893	27, Apr.	82		318	Washington, MN	Langula, Preußen
Nippold, Wilhelm J.	20, Jan. 1887	9, Jan.	37- 7m-12d		46	Le Sueur, MN	
Nippoldt, Anna Christina	21, Nov. 1861	23, Sept	54	Bang	188	Stillwater, MN	Langula, Preußen
Nippoldt, Catharina Elisabeth	26, May 1887	30, Apr.	38	Biedighäuser	334	Washington, MN	Dudenau, Hessen-Darmstadt
Nirk, Elisabeth	16, Mar. 1893	28, Feb.	75	Schneider	174	Pittsburg, PA	Glatten, Württemberg
Nisperly, (boy)	9, Aug. 1849	May	11		128	Buckhill, OH	
Nisperly, Rosina	9, Aug. 1849	12, July	22- 7m		128	Buckhill, OH	
Nisson, Niß	19, Sept 1895	16, Aug.	52		606	Klemme, IA	Munkbramp, Flensburg, Schleswig-Holstein
Nitsch, Johan Wilhelm	19, Jan. 1874	15, Dec.	55		23	Chicago, IL	Einberg, Sachsen-Coburg

Christliche Apologete Death Notices --- 1839 - 1899

Name of Deceased	Death Date	Age	Maiden Name	Page	Place of Death	Place of Birth	Notice Date
Nitsch, Katharina	8, Feb.	66- 1m-19d	Nuhr	63	Chicago, IL	Sachsen-Meiningen	20, Feb. 1882
Nitsch, Peter August	16, Aug.	44		671	Cincinnati, OH	Steegnerwerder, Preußen	20, Oct. 1898
Nitzel, Henry	8, Oct.	48		343	Sandwich, IL	Frohnhausen, Amt Dillenburg, Nassau	26, Oct. 1868
Nitzsche, Anna Friederike	3, Dec.	24-10m- 9d		7	Cedar Lake, IN	Sand Ridge, Cook County, Indiana	22, Dec. 1884
Nitzsche, Johan August	16, Dec.	73		62	Crown Point, IN	Tirschheim, Sachsen	28, Jan. 1892
Nix, Katharina	11, Feb.	13- 4m- 7d	Hoffmann	87	Carmi, IL		15, Mar. 1880
Nixel, Maria Barbara	26, Jan.	87		110	Columbus, OH		13, Feb. 1890
Noack, Carl Erdmann	17, Mar.	80	Kastner	222	Waseca, MN	Nordhausen bei Königsberg, Neumark	7, Apr. 1892
Noblet, Alexander	27, July	26		279	East Troy, WI	St. Clair County, Michigan	31, Aug. 1874
Noblet, Johannes	21, Oct.	24		383	East Troy, WI	St. Clair County, Michigan	28, Nov. 1870
Noblet, Joseph	5, Oct.	88		836	Honey Creek, WI	Elsaß	27, Dec. 1894
Noblet, Salome	26, Apr.	71- 5m- 2d		7	Milwaukee, WI	Baiern	12, May 1884
Noe, Lizzie	12, Dec.	42- 2m-28d	Knaup	31	Oshkosh, WI	Hessen-Darmstadt	13, Jan. 1898
Noe, Michael				12	Sandusky, OH	Homburg, Zweibrücken, Rheinkreis Baiern	17, Jan. 1856
Noe, Michael	30, July	48		542	Elizabeth, NJ	Baden	25, Aug. 1892
Noftz, Louise	13, Dec.	33	Schulz	7	Toledo, OH	Bünden, Münden, Preußen	4, Jan. 1875
Nohls, Nikolaus	16, Nov.	66		391	Platteville, WI	Pardingbüttel, Amt Dorum, Hannover	6, Dec. 1869
Nohr, Esther Susanna Karolina	18, Jan.	16		207	Ripon, WI	Marion , Wisconsin	31, Mar. 1898
Nohr, Franz	23, Aug.	42		639	New York City, NY	Gerbstedt, Sachsen	5, Oct. 1899
Nohr, Heinrich	23, Mar.	18		7	Oshkosh, WI	Eldorado, Fond du Lac County, Wisconsin	8, Apr. 1886
Nohr, Johan Friedrich	15, Jan.	74		142	Marion, WI	Klein~Justin bei Cammin, Pommern	2, Mar. 1893
Nohr, Nellie Sophie	13, June	14		494	Marion, WI	Oshkosh, Wisconsin	31, July 1890
Nol, Heinrich	4, Nov.	17- 8m-19d		375	East Troy, WI		24, Nov. 1879
Nol, Louis	6, Oct.	21- 6m-26d		375	East Troy, WI		24, Nov. 1879
Noldenmeier, August	19, Apr.	54- 4m		151	Washington, MN	Duttenhausen, Alberdissen, Lippe-Detmold	8, May 1882
Noldensmeier, John Fr.	10, Feb.	84- 3m		103	Morrison, MO	Vlotho, Minden, Preußen	27, Mar. 1876
Noldensmeier, John Fr.	10, Feb.	84- 3m		79	Morrison, MO	Vlöhte, Preußen	6, Mar. 1876
Nolf, Gottlieb	6, Nov.	74		750	Cleveland, OH	Großgartach, Württemberg	24, Nov. 1892
Nolfensmeier, Heinrich	29, Dec.	42- 7m		55	Morrison, MO	Vlotho, Minden, Preußen	15, Feb. 1875
Nölke, (Mr)	19, Oct.	68		359	Seymour, IN	Venne, Amt Wittlage, Hannover	6, Nov. 1876
Nölke, Maria	1, Aug.	62		271	Seymour, IN	Fenne, Hannover	20, Aug. 1877
Nölker, Heinrich F.	4, May	69		191	Seymour, IN	Vorwald, Venne, Hannover	16, June 1873
Nölker, Maria Engel	22, July	76-11m		542	Seymour, IN	Fenne, Hannover	20, Aug. 1891
Noll, Conrad	4, Oct.	74		192	Lawrence, KS	Baden, Kurhessen	27, Nov. 1865
Noll, Elisabeth	24, Mar.	82		143	Baresville, OH	Ebertsheim, Rheinkreis Baiern	2, May 1870
Noll, Elisabeth	18, Oct.	40		184	Cincinnati, OH	Sulzfeld, Amt Eppingen, Baden	10, Nov. 1848
Noll, Friedrich Christoph	17, June	55		215	Waterford, WI	Sulzfeld, Eppingen, Baden	4, July 1881
Noll, Friedrich Eberhard	26, Jan.	86		55	Waterford, WI		14, Feb. 1881
Noll, Hanida		10		83	St. Louis, MO		21, May 1847
Noll, Heinrich	28, Oct.	55		7	East Troy, WI	Hönebach, Rodenburg, Kurhessen	17, Nov. 1884
Noll, Heinrich	27, Dec.	70		63	St. Louis, MO	Odenhausen, Hessen-Darmstadt	22, Feb. 1869
Noll, Johannes	12, Oct.	76		180	Batesville, OH	Franklin County, Pennsylvania	10, Nov. 1862
Noll, Katharine Elisabeth	16, Apr.	63	Fiehler	302	East Troy, WI	Hannebach, Rodenburg, Kurhessen	11, May 1893
Noll, Margaretha	14, May	68	Hoffmann	88	Lawrence, KS	Roda, Kurhessen	2, June 1862
Noll, Maria A.	7, Mar.	42- 9m-14d	Tüscher	103	Baresville, OH	Monroe County, Ohio	28, Mar. 1870
Noll, Wilhelmine	20, Nov.	26- 2m	Busching	4	Quincy, IL	Harrinestedt, Amt Holzenau, Hannover	5, Jan. 1854

Christliche Apologete Death Notices --- 1839 - 1899

Name of Deceased	Notice Date	Death Date	Age	Page	Maiden Name	Place of Death	Place of Birth
Nolle, Friedrich August	18, Oct. 1860	4, Sept	17	168		Golconda, IL	Bitterfeld, Merseburg, Preußen
Nolle, Johan Gottlob	15, May 1876	26, Apr.	66	159		Golconda, IL	Bitterfeld, Merseburg, Preußen
Nolle, Wilhelm	17, Apr. 1882	31, Mar.	45-3m-12d	127		Pinckneyville, IL	Buhr, Amt Melle, Hannover
Nölsch, (Mr)	29, Apr. 1897	7, Apr.	78	271		Springfield, IL	Donauwörth, Germany
Nölsch, Clara Elisabeth	20, Nov. 1882	25, Oct.	19-7m-28d	375		Oregon, MO	Otto County, Nebraska
Nölsch, Elisabeth Margaretha	16, June 1859	15, May	74	96	Gerber	Arenzville, IL	Göppingen, Württemberg
Nölsch, Gottlieb	25, June 1896	30, May	74	415		Emden, IL	Dürnau, Göppingen, Württemberg
Nölsch, Helene	28, July 1898	1, July	82	479		Springfield, IL	
Nölsch, Johannes	18, Mar. 1878	1, Mar.	72	87		Oregon, MO	Dürnau, Göppingen, Württemberg
Nölsch, Anna	3, Aug. 1893	14, July	67	494	Falner	Beardstown, IL	Sandreit, Oberfranken, Baiern
Nölsch, Dorothea Catharina	31, Oct. 1864	24, Sept	33	176	Lotz	Arenzville, IL	Plopsheim, Elsaß
Nolt, Friederike	26, June 1890	27, May	39-5m-17d	414		Clintonville, WI	
Nolte, Anna Martha	28, Oct. 1878	8, Oct.	39	343	Humburg	Herman, MO	Krumbach, Hessen-Kassel
Nolte, Christitian	3, Feb. 1879	10, Jan.	54	39		Nashville, IL	Dankersen, Minden, Preußen
Nolte, Friedrich	30, Apr. 1891	23, Mar.	79	286		Nashville, IL	Holzhausen, Minden, Preußen
Nolte, Friedrich	25, Sept 1851	5, Apr.	40	156		Platteville, WI	Lichtenberg, Falder, Braunschweig
Nolte, Maria	24, May 1869	29, Apr.	62-2m-3d	167	Schäfer	Herman, MO	Waldeck
Nolte, Sophia	25, Sept 1851	22, Aug.	14-8m	156		Platteville, WI	
Nolte, Wilhelmina	21, Jan. 1892	9, Dec.	78	46		Nashville, IL	Holzhausen, Minden, Preußen
Noltemeier, Friedrich	16, Feb. 1893	29, Jan.	62	110		St. Paul, MN	Lippe-Detmold
Noltemeier, Cornelia	22, Sept 1879	20, Aug.	31	303	Haubt	Morrison, MO	
Noltensmeier, August	2, Feb. 1874	14, Jan.	16	39		Gasconade Co, MO	
Noltensmeier, August	7, Apr. 1873	6, Feb.		111		Herman, MO	
Noltensmeier, Charlotte	3, Feb. 1873	9, Jan.	40	39	Hoberg	Herman, MO	Vlotho, Minden, Preußen
Noltensmeier, Christina Hedwig	23, Feb. 1863	28, Dec.	64-8m	32		Herman, MO	Waldorf, Kreis Herfort, Preußen
Noltensmeier, Friedrich	3, Feb. 1873	22, Dec.	45	39		Herman, MO	Vlotho, Minden, Preußen
Noltensmeier, Johan David	10, Apr. 1876	15, Feb.	16	118		Herman, MO	
Noltensmeier, Louis	12, Mar. 1866	2, Oct.	30	86		Herman, MO	Flote, Minden, Preußen
Noltensmeier, Maria Louisa	25, May 1874	22, Apr.	26-9m	167	Merhof	Herman, MO	Nord Hemmen, Minden, Preußen
Noltensmeier, Wilhelmine	20, Sept 1869	23, Aug.	23	303	Forderhase	Herman, MO	Malle, St. Charles County, Missouri
Nolter, Amalie	17, Mar. 1879	1, Mar.	58-25d	87		Chicago, IL	Schokken, Posen, Preußen
Nolting , Anna Dorothea	3, Sept 1896	4, Aug.	44	575	Werbach	Salisbury, MO	Milwaukee, Wisconsin
Nolting, Anna Maria	13, Mar. 1890	28, Dec.	42	174	Kallmeier	Mankato, MN	Hannover
Nolting, Anna Maria Engel	5, May 1898	15, Apr.	85	287	Nolting	Lamberton, MN	Gofeld, Minden, Preußen
Nolting, August Ludwig	16, Sept 1886	3, Sept	79	7		Higginsville, MO	Hunfeld, Lippe-Detmold
Nolting, Christoph	26, Jan. 1860			16		Warren, MO	Sternberg, Lippe
Nolting, Friederike Elisabeth	28, Aug. 1890	14, Aug.	76-1m-9d	558	Winter	Wapello, IA	
Nolting, Friedrich	2, May 1870	27, Mar.	34-3m-21d	143		Terre Haute, IN	
Nolting, Johan Fr. Wilhelm	28, May 1891	5, May	64	350		Yellow Creek, IL	Stemmen, Lippe-Detmold
Nolting, Johan Heinrich	18, May 1868	17, Apr.	58-7m-4d	159		Herman, MO	Boneberg, Flote, Minden, Herford, Preußen
Nolting, Louis	29, June 1899	29, May	23-10m-1d	415		Warrenton, MO	
Nolting, Maria	21, Jan. 1878	28, Dec.	33-6m-17d	23	Hoff	Brunswick, MO	
Nolting, Wilhelm	18, Aug. 1892	19, July	66	526		Dalton, MO	Eisbergen, Minden, Preußen
Nolting, Wilhelmine	26, Apr. 1869	17, Mar.	41	135		Union, MO	Golfeld, Herford, Minden, Preußen
Noltner, Wilhelm	15, Nov. 1894	7, Oct.	27	742		Ft. Hunter, NY	
Nonemacher, John	20, May 1878	15, Apr.	69	159		Plain City, OH	Germany

Christliche Apologete Death Notices --- 1839 - 1899

Name of Deceased	Notice Date	Death Date	Age	Page	Maiden Name	Place of Death	Place of Birth
Nonnemacher, Leopold	1, June 1863	18, May	32	88		Columbus, OH	Osterburg, Adelsheim, Baden
Nonnweiler, Catharina	30, Jan. 1862	5, Jan.	27- 5m-20d	20	Gemlich	Boonville, IN	Kirchheim an der Eck, Rheinpfalz Baiern
Nonnweiler, Karl	29, Nov. 1860	31, Oct.		192		Boonville, IN	Birkenfeld, Oldenburg
Nonnweiler, Maria Elisabeth	5, Dec. 1861	9, Nov.	75	196	Heidrich	Boonville, IN	Reichenbach, Preußen
Nonweiler, Anna Maria	14, Dec. 1893	25, Nov.	62	798	Gemlich	Boonville, IN	Kirchheim an der Eck, Rheinpfalz Baiern
Nonweiler, Catharina	16, Oct. 1876	1, Oct.	16- 6m-23d	335		Boonville, IN	
Nonweiler, Elisabeth	19, July 1894	1, June	70	470	Nonweiler	Garner, IA	Eisen, Bärzenfeld, Germany
Nonweiler, Jacobine	9, Jan. 1846	16, Dec.	38	7	Dieterich	Evansville, IN	Birkenfeld, Oldenburg
Nonweiler, Louisa	26, Apr. 1860	29, Mar.	15	68		Boonville, IN	
Nonweiler, Louise	4, Dec. 1876	17, Nov.	33- 6m- 1d	391	Breyer	Boonville, IN	Grünenwettersbach, Durlach, Baden
Norden, Anna Sophia	14, Jan. 1897	9, Dec.	35- 8m-19d	31	Meincke	Boelus, NE	Bendingbostel, Hannover
Nordheim, Andreas	21, Dec. 1893	15, Oct.	57- 9m-18d	814		Newport, KY	Gehaus, Langenfeld, Sachsen-Weimar
Nordheim, Johan A.	19, Apr. 1875	5, Apr.	75	127		Newport, KY	Gehaus, Lengsfeld, Sachsen-Eisenach
Nordheim, Johannes Michael	30, Dec. 1886	13, Dec.	55	7		Newport, KY	Gehaus, Lengsfeld, Sachsen-Weimar
Nordheim, Maria	1, Apr. 1886	19, Mar.	86	7		Newport, KY	Mengerinkhausen, Arolzen, Waldeck
Nordhop, Anna	13, Feb. 1871	31, Jan.	23	55		Pennsylvanienburg, IN	Sunmansville, Ripley County, Indiana
Nordhop, Curt Albert	23, June 1892	6, June	73	398		Batesville, IN	Hannover
Nordhop, Hanna Wilhelmina Charl.	13, Apr. 1899	9, Mar.	68	239	Kley	Lawrenceville, IN	Lämmershausen, Bielefeld, Preußen
Nordhop, J.	24, Oct. 1889	2, Sept	39- - 9d	686		Lawrenceburg, IN	
Nordmann, Bertha	29, Nov. 1875	14, Nov.		383	Kutzki	St. Paul, MN	Wangrein, Pommern, Preußen
Nörenberg. F.	23, Oct. 1871	16, Sept	48	343		Lowell, WI	Schwachenwalde, Pommern
Nöring, Katharina	21, June 1894	15, May	64	406	Ball	Victor, IA	Württemberg
Nörnberg, Franz W.	11, Nov. 1878	25, Oct.	15	359		Milwaukee, WI	Belgard, Pommern
Nortop, Maria	17, Dec. 1877		50	407	Mahler	Lawrenceburg, IN	Bühren, Amt Neustadt, Hannover
Nostadt, Friederike	9, Dec. 1878	19, Nov.	66	391		Dayton, OH	Heilbronn, Württemberg
Noth, Adam	17, Feb. 1879	2, Feb.	32	55		New York City, NY	
Noth, Catharine	19, Jan. 1893	22, Nov.	44	46	Powley	New York City, NY	New York
Nothdurft, Julius	18, Aug. 1873	26, July	70	263		Jackson, MO	Rhüden, Hannover
Nothdurft, Minna	26, Aug. 1858	20, July	17	136	Kühle	Jackson, MO	
Nothdurft, Sophie	30, Nov. 1868	22, Sept	58	383		Jackson, OH	GroßRüden, Braunschweig
Nothdurst, H.D.	5, Aug. 1872	3, July	39	255		Jackson, MO	GroßRhüden, Bockenem, Hannover
Nothard, Elisabeth M.	26, Oct. 1899	1, Oct.	61	687	Lenz	Rochester, NY	Eschelbronn, Baden
Nothardt, Maria	9, July 1877	10, June		223	Malthauer	Philadelphia, PA	Baden
Nothnagel, Anna Catharina	26, Jan. 1880	4, Jan.	45- 4m-19d	31	Rathjen	Carrollton, MO	Sittensen, Zeven, Hannover
Noting, Auguste Emilia	28, Apr. 1898	22, Mar.	29	271		Caldwell, TX	PineOak, Bastrop County, Texas
Notten, Ehlert	13, Apr. 1874	23, Mar.	73- 6m	119		Francisco, MI	Windsor, England
Notten, John	13, Mar. 1876	28, Feb.	75	87		Francisco, MI	Windsor, England
Notten, Maria	18, Nov. 1878	12, Oct.	71	367	Kruse	Francisco, MI	Hemke, Hannover
Notter, Wilhelm	16, Jan. 1882	30, Dec.	42- 7m- 7d	23		Francisco, MI	New York
Notter, Friederike	6, Feb. 1862	30, Dec.	50- 1m-19d	24		Quincy, IL	Rottmannsberg, Württemberg
Notter, Johann David	23, Aug. 1849	14, July	39	136		Quincy, IL	Neustadt, Württemberg
Notter, John Michael	27, Sept 1875		60	311		Quincy, IL	Neustadt, Waiblingen, Württemberg
Nötzel, Wilhelmine	17, July 1876	7, July		231	Reske	Watertown, WI	Dobberpful, Pommern
Nought, Lena	11, Aug. 1887	17, July	26	510	Stremmel	Bushnell, IL	
Nowacke, Karl August	17, Apr. 1890	25, Mar.	59	254		Cincinati, OH	Brieg, Schlesien
Nuber, Johan Jakob	19, Dec. 1889	5, Dec.	51	814		Columbus, OH	Markstadt, Beblingen, Württemberg

Christliche Apologete Death Notices -- 1839 - 1899

Name of Deceased	Notice Date	Death Date	Age	Maiden Name	Page	Place of Death	Place of Birth
Nüchter, Joseph	28, Dec. 1854	30, Nov.	49		208	West Unity, OH	Unterstorch, Hessen
Nuelsen, Dorothea	16, Aug. 1888	29, July	68-4m-22d	Daiß	526	Cincinnati, OH	Mittelbrüden, Backnang, Württemberg
Nuenke, Wilhelmine	28, Mar. 1895	7, Mar.	73	Krenzin	206	Bay City, MI	Nemitz, Pommern
Nuhfer, Anna Eva	8, Apr. 1852	26, Mar.	68- 8m		60	Woodville, OH	Dirmstein, Rheinkreis Baiern
Nuhfer, Helena Catharina	29, Feb. 1864	5, Feb.	13-11m		36	Detroit, MI	Galion, Crawford County, Ohio
Nuhfer, Julie A.	21, Feb. 1889	23, Feb.	22- 6m-16d	Gerken	126	Elmore, OH	Woodville, Ohio
Nuhfer, Louise	14, July 1879	27, June	65	Jung	223	Perrysburg, OH	Erlebrunn, Pirmasenz, Rheinkreis Baiern
Nuhn, Anna Margaretha	2, Dec. 1886	28, Oct.	79	Bätz	7	Topeka, KS	Nieder-Aula, Herschfeld, Kurhessen
Null, Emma	16, May 1881	15, Apr.	22	Kreutz	159	Lexington, MO	Indiana
Nülsen, Anna Marie	27, Aug. 1896	10, Aug.	75	Pinger	559	St. Louis, MO	Framersheim, Hessen-Darmstadt
Nülsen, Marie Louise	18, Aug. 1884	3, July	31		7	Philadelphia, PA	Bremen, Germany
Nülsen, Mina	17, Sept 1866	2, Sept	22		302	Alton, IL	
Nunamaker, John (Mrs)	6, June 1895	13, Apr.	89		366	Waco, TX	Wittenberg, Germany
Nungesser, Anna Margaretha	18, Aug. 1892	25, June		Barth	526		Umstadt, Germany
Nungeßer, Friedrich	13, Mar. 1871	16, Feb.	19- 6m-12d		87	Farmington, MI	Westbend, Washington County, Wisconsin
Nungesser, John W.	4, Aug. 1873	10, July	65		247	West Bend, WI	Klein Umstadt, Hessen-Darmstadt
Nünke, Friedrich Wilhelm Heinrich	13, Nov. 1890	30, Oct.	82		734	Bay City, MI	Rezenhagen, Pommern
Nunning, Maria	19, Aug. 1878	2, Aug.	26	Blier	263	St. Joseph, MO	
Nusperlin, Jakob	30, Nov. 1874	11, Nov.	75		383	Baresville, OH	Kanton Bern, Schweiz
Nußbaum, Benjamin F.	24, Aug. 1863	20, July	19		136	Monroe, IA	Allen County, Ohio
Nußbaum, Isaak Z.	24, Aug. 1863	1, Aug.	23		136	Monroe, IA	Richland County, Ohio
Nußbäumer, Charlotte	12, Mar. 1896	17, Feb.	92	Landow	174	Montague, MI	Müllrose, Frankfurt, Preußen
Nüsse, Luise	16, Feb. 1899	21, Jan.	26	Bauer	111	Rock Island, IL	Preußen
Nustadt, Philipp	14, Mar. 1861	15, Feb.	28		44	Dayton, OH	Oberramstadt, Hessen-Darmstadt
Nützer, Charlotte	31, Jan. 1895	30, Dec.	66	Wentland	78	Brooklyn, NY	Sengelburg, West Preußen
Nützmann, Albert Karl Wilhelm	28, Nov. 1889	28, Oct.	36		766	Morrison, MO	Klüß auf der Insel Rügen, Pommern
Nützmann, Christoph	24, June 1897	19, May	81		399	Highland, IL	Karnitz, auf Rügen, Germany
Nützmann, Margaretha	5, May 1892	15, Apr.	83		286	St. Paul, MN	
Nyfeler, Anna	17, Aug. 1893	16, July	37		526	Los Angeles, CA	Hutwyl, Bern, Schweiz
Obel, Anna Margareha	9, Nov. 1863	8, Oct.	23		180	Covington, KY	Holzhausen, Nassau
Obel, Heinrich	22, Nov. 1880	9, Nov.	60		375	Covington, KY	Holzhausen, Nastätten, Nassau
Obel, Margaretha	3, Apr. 1890	11, Mar.	80		222	Covington, KY	
Obel, Peter	20, Dec. 1880		68		407	Covington, KY	Holzhausen, Nassau
Obenhaus, Carolina Katharina Char.	29, Dec. 1892	26, Nov.	76	Schäfer	828	Freyburg, TX	Kappell, Lippe-Detmold
Obenhaus, Louise	11, Aug. 1879	29, July	22		255	Columbus, TX	Columbus, Texas
Oberbeck, Johanna	21, Dec. 1874	22, Nov.	41- 7m-13d		407	Appleton, MO	Neuhof, Lamspringe, Ahlfeldt, Hannover
Oberbeck, Ludwig	8, Mar. 1888	9, Feb.	68		158	Sheboygan, WI	Goslar, Hannover
Oberdeck, Elisabeth	9, July 1891	11, June	46	Ockel	446	Wheeling, WV	Selters, Hessen
Oberer, Elisabeth	13, Aug. 1883	26, July	39- 1m-20d	Kramer	263	Hokah, MN	Winterbach bei Zweibrücken, Baiern
Oberhellmann, Josephine Louise	6, Feb. 1871	13, Jan.	19- 1m- 1d		47	St. Louis, MO	St. Louis, Missouri
Obering, Emma	15, Feb. 1869	26, Dec.	30- -15d	Portzig	55	St. Charles, MO	Altenburg, Sachsen
Oberle, Matthew	19, Jan. 1885	13, Dec.	27		7	Bakersfield, CA	Bedford, Indiana
Oberling, Anna	2, June 1887	10, May	58- 4m-18d		350	Grand Rapids, MI	Kleekampf, Mecklenburg-Schwerin
Obermeier, Wilhelm	15, Apr. 1897	22, Mar.	54		239	Senate Grove, MO	Feßmold, Harle, Minden, Preußen
Obermeyer, Friedrich W.H.R.	25, July 1870	2, July	27		239	St. Louis, MO	Holzhausen, Lübbecke, Preußen

Name of Deceased	Notice Date	Death Date	Age	Maiden Name	Page	Place of Death	Place of Birth
Oberst, Johan	29, Apr. 1872	2, Apr.	16- 2m		143	Wheeling, IL	Unteröwisheim, Bruchsal, Baden
Oberst, Maria	17, Apr. 1876	1, Mar.	66		127	Toledo, OH	Gersbach, Amt Schopfheim, Baden
Obert, Sophia	19, Sept 1881	1, Sept	64		303	Quincy, IL	Herringhaus, Hessen-Darmstadt
Obländer, Georg	10, Dec. 1877	19, Nov.	50-11m-18d		399	Bushnell, IL	Zuzenhausen, Baden
Obländer, Heinrich	14, May 1896	15, Apr.	54		318	Chicago, IL	Zuzenhausen, Sinsheim, Baden
Oblinger, Susanne	27, July 1863	13, June	81		120	Dayton, OH	Virginia
Ochele, Joachim H.	22, May 1865	6, Apr.	48		84	Schnectady, NY	Streng, Güstrow, Mecklenburg-Schwerin
Ochs, Anna	28, Nov. 1870		24-11m- 2d	Fischer	383	Chicago, IL	
Ochs, Anna Martha	13, Nov. 1871	5, Oct.	72-10m-10d	Fink	367	Chicago, IL	
Ochs, Conrad	9, Feb. 1885	23, Jan.	79		7	Chicago, IL	Arnsbach, Kurhessen
Ochs, Georg	8, Apr. 1897	20, Mar.	19- 3m-28d		223	Chicago, IL	Arnsbach, Kurhessen
Ochs, Jakob Friedrich	5, Sept 1889	22, July	67		574	New Haven, CT	Feldrenach, Neuenburg, Württemberg
Ochs, Katharina	20, July 1899	23, June	69- 3m-13d	Gebhardt	463	New Haven, CT	Raumbach, Meisenheim am Rhein, Preußen
Ochs, Lisette H.	6, Aug. 1896	19, July	69	König	511	Fredericksburg, TX	Obersteinbach, Hallenberg, Preußen
Ochs, Nikolaus	21, Sept 1885	30, Aug.	69		7	Fredericksburg, TX	Imenach, Coblenz, RheinPreußen
Ochs, Valentin	26, Mar. 1883	7, Mar.	73		103	Charlestown, IN	bei Worms, Hessen
Ochsen, Friederika	28, Mar. 1870	3, Mar.	29- 7m- 2d	Schwiering	103	Appleton, MO	Winzlar, Amt Stolzna, Hannover
Ocks, Matthias	23, June 1879	13, June	78		199	Pomeroy, OH	Hahn, Koblenz, Rheinpreußen
Odenwald, Heinrich	4, Dec. 1871	23, Oct.	7- 8m		391	Jordan, MN	
Odenwald, William	23, Apr. 1866		15		134	Allegheny City, PA	
Odewald, Johan	30, Aug. 1875	11, Aug.	52		279	Jordan, MN	Golshausen, Amt Bretten, Baden
Oech, Anna Maria	24, May 1880	23, Apr.	67-11m-17d		167	Winona, MN	Leudershausen, Baden
Oech, Ellen	17, June 1886	16, May	32	Augustin	7	Winona, MN	Rickway, Ohio
Oech, Johan Friedrich	30, Dec. 1886	27, Nov.	78		7	Winona, MN	Leidershausen, Baden
Oechler, Sophia M.	27, Aug. 1891	29, July	17- 8m		558	Brooklyn, NY	
Oechsle, Anna Maria	30, June 1898	3, June	29		415	Peoria, IL	Peoria, Illinois
Oechsle, Matthias	28, Aug. 1882	4, Aug.	61		279	Peoria, IL	Klingenstein, Blaubeuren, Württemberg
Oechsle, Ursula	12, Feb. 1883	17, Jan.	58		55	Peoria, IL	Klingenstein, Blaubeuren, Württemberg
Oeckel, Carl	19, Aug. 1897	22, July	61	Meier	527	San Jose, CA	Husburghausen, Sachsen
Oeckel, Friederike	8, Feb. 1894	18, Jan.	64	Ulrich	94	San Jose, CA	Marienkirch, Elsaß
Oeder, Maria	11, Oct. 1894	25, Aug.	58		662	Althof, SD	Philadelphia, Pennsylvania
Oehlenschläger, Kunigunda	11, Mar.1872	21, Feb.	42-11m- 3d		87	Terre Haute, IN	Kirchenreinbach, Nürnberg, Baiern
Oehler, Magdalena	18, Nov. 1872	29, Oct.	29- 4m-27d	Becker	375	Buffalo, NY	Kratzingen, Baden
Oehlkers, Adelheid	29, Oct. 1841		Inquiry		171	Marietta, OH	
Oehlmann, Carl	9, Apr. 1891	15, Mar.	68		238	Derby, IA	Hannover
Oehlschläger, Conrad	31, July 1871	2, July	59		247	Jackson, MO	Brockeloh, Amt Wölpe, Hannover
Oehlschläger, Dorothea	7, Sept 1863	25, July	53-11m- 5d	Schrader	144	Jackson, MO	Brokoloch, Amt Wölpe, Hannover
Oehlschläger, Henrietta	15, Nov. 1888	27, Oct.	79		734	Burlington, IA	Weingarten, Baden
Oehlschläger, J.H.F.	31, May 1880	26, Apr.	49		175	Lexington, MO	Suderbruch, Nienburg, Hannover
Oehms, Margaretha	23, Apr. 1891	28, Mar.		Zeitner	270	Alma, KS	
Oehrle, (Mr)	21, Sept 1863	26, Aug.	38		152	Lawrence, KS	Dehausen, Rohden, Waldeck
Oeksen, Friedrich	4, Nov. 1897	11, Oct.	78		703	Appleton, MO	Lindingworth, Hannover
Oelerich, Anna Maria	2, July 1896	12, June	46		431	Brooklyn, NY	Breddorf, Amt Ottersberg, Hannover
Oelfers, Anna	26, Feb. 1852	17, Jan.	69- 1m		36	Marietta, OH	Kirchtimken, Ottersberg, Hannover
Oelkers, Hermann	13, Oct. 1859	27, Sept	72- 3m-23d		164	Marietta, OH	Cincinnati, Hamilton County, Ohio
Oelrich, Lulu	20, Mar. 1890		15- -16d		190	Quincy, IL	

Christliche Apologete Death Notices -- 1839 - 1899

Name of Deceased	Notice Date	Death Date	Age	Page	Maiden Name	Place of Death	Place of Birth
Oelrichs, Heinrich	26, July 1849	23, June	28	120		St. Louis, MO	Tarmstadt, Hannover
Oemke, Dorothea	4, Dec. 1890	29, Oct.	57- 9m-12d	782			
Oemke, Hannah Dora Sophia	27, Oct. 1892	19, Sept	27- 4m- 9d	686		Kendallville, IN	
Oemke, Lizzie	4, Dec. 1890	7, Aug.		782			
Oertel, Mina	13, Mar. 1876	13, Feb.	40- 3m- 4d	87	Staatz	Lyona, KS	Damerow, Naugard, Pommern
Oertel, Reinhold Theodor August	8, June 1874	18, May	23	183		Scranton, PA	
Oeschger, Ignatz	25, Feb. 1878	30, Dec.	68- -22d	63		St. Gallen, ---	Gansingen, Aargau, Schweiz
Oesper, Johan	22, Apr. 1886	7, Apr.	67	7		Cincinnati, OH	Lichtenstein, Baiern
Oesper, John	17, Nov. 1887	31, Oct.	39- 9m-23d	734		Cincinnati, OH	Cincinnati, Hamilton County, Ohio
Oesper, Peter	4, Dec. 1890		73	782		Cincinnati, OH	Lichtenstein, Ebern, Unterfranken, Baiern
Oester, Margaretha	11, Oct. 1894	30, Aug.	43	662	Trachsel	Bethany, OR	Rohrbach-Frutigen, Bern, Schweiz
Oesterhaus, Friederike	23, Feb. 1899	26, Jan.	44	127	Busch	Junction City, KS	
Oesterhaus, Philippine	5, Jan. 1899	6, Dec.	78	14	Blanke	Junction City, KS	Sylbach, Schöttma, Lippe-Detmold
Oesterle, Andreas	3, May 1894	22, Mar.	47	294		Francisco, MI	Röth, Freudenstadt, Württemberg
Oesterle, Anna Margaretha	4, Feb. 1886	15, Jan.	24-11m- 6d	7		Grand Rapids, MI	Grand Rapids, Michigan
Oesterle, Eva Catharina	5, Oct. 1885	12, Sept	52	7	Hertlein	Grand Rapids, MI	Wölchingen, Baden
Oesterle, Friedrich	30, Apr. 1891	26, Mar.	57	286		Grand Rapids, MI	Pfalzgrafenweiler, Freudenstadt, Württemberg
Oesterle, Katharina	7, July 1892	15, June	70	430	Kalmbach	Francisco, MI	Röth, Freudenstadt, Württemberg
Oesterreich, Ferdinand	18, Feb. 1897	11, Oct.	75	111		Brownton, MN	Driesen, Posen
Oestreich, Jakob	21, Nov. 1864	27, Mar.	24- 7m-16d	188		Edgerton, OH	
Oestreich, Peter	18, Apr. 1881	26, June	64- 2m- 7d	127		Edon, OH	Gedern, Niedau, Hessen-Darmstadt
Oestrich, Katharina Elisabeth	10, July 1890	6, Aug.	75	446		Edgerton, OH	Gedern, Hessen-Darmstadt
Oeth, Elisabeth	10, Sept 1891	22, Oct.	42	590		St. Philip, IN	Bergzabern, Rheinpfalz Baiern
Oeth, Karl	15, Nov. 1894	26, Apr.	77-11m- 3d	742		Marrs, IN	Niederingelheim, Hessen-Darmstadt
Oeth, Maria Catharina	9, May 1889	13, Sept	27-11m-10d	302	Storck	Atchinson, KS	Canton, Missouri
Oetherer, Johan Adam	14, Oct. 1886	20, Sept	67	7		Jeffersonville, IN	Ottmausreuth, Baiern
Oetjens, Cassens	10, Oct. 1861	29, Apr.	57	164		St. Louis, MO	Bremerhafen, Germany
Oetliker, Johan	16, May 1889	18, Mar.	67-10m	318		Rochester, NY	Zosingen, Aargau, Schweiz
Oetterer, Barbara	14, Apr. 1879	26, Oct.	14	119		Jeffersonville, IN	Jeffersonville, Indiana
Oetting, Emma Luise	22, Nov. 1894	6, Dec.	66	758	Zahlmann	Jeffersonville, IN	Kreußen, Baiern
Oetting, Fred August	19, Jan. 1899	1, Aug.	24	47	Frewert	Pinckney, MO	Pinckney, Warren County, Missouri
Oetting, John Dietrich	27, Aug. 1877	24, Jan.	18- 4m	279		Batesville, IN	
Oetting, Simon Dietrich	7, Feb. 1876	2, Sept	58	47		Batesville, IN	Wormsen, Amt Uchte, Hannover
Ofel, Wilhelmina	25, Nov. 1878	2, Sept	72	375	Spellmann	Herman, MO	
Offel, Wilhelm	5, Sept 1881	5, Nov.	49	287		Hopewell, MO	Sternberg, Lippe-Detmold
Offel, Wilhelmine Catharine	19, Sept 1864	29, Aug.	28- 7m	152		Warrenton, MO	Bega, Lippe-Detmold
Offeld, Richard C.	29, July 1878	28, June	30	239		Holden, MO	Bösengfeld, Lippe-Detmold
Offenheiser, Caroline	30, Dec. 1867	11, Dec.	41	414	Schiemann	Schnectady, NY	Deutschrone, West Preußen
Offenheiser, Dorothea	31, Aug. 1868	15, Aug.	9m	279		Schnectady, NY	Neuenhagen, Freienwalde a.O., Preußen
Offenheiser, Eddie	31, Aug. 1868	10, Aug.	3- 7m	279		Schnectady, NY	
Offermann, Elisabeth	19, Apr. 1888	27, Mar.	55	254	Grisson	St. Louis, MO	
Offermann, Jakob Friedrich	30, July 1891	29, June	63	494		St. Louis, MO	Oggersheim, Rheinkreis Baiern
Oge, Caroline	19, Dec. 1889	5, Nov.	72	814		Dodgeville, IA	Isensee, Osten, Hannover
Ohde, Wilhelm	8, Sept 1887	14, Aug.	34- -20d	574	Becker	Denton, TX	Neu Ruppien, Brandenburg
Ohl, August	18, Dec. 1890	25, Nov.	68	814		Roseville, MI	Schwarzburg-Sondershausen

Name of Deceased	Notice Date	Death Date	Age	Page	Maiden Name	Place of Death	Place of Birth
Ohle, Christian Ludwig	8, Sept 1884	26, Aug.	80	7		Berea, OH	Bodenfelde, Hannover
Ohle, Eleonore	1, June 1899	4, May	68	351	Bühl	Berea, OH	Künzelsau, Württemberg
Ohle, Elisabeth	24, June 1872	26, May	63- -17d	207		Berea, OH	Bodenfelde, Amt Rienofer, Hannover
Ohlendorf, Sophie Louise	25, Dec. 1882	30, Nov.	58-8m-1d	415	Hulka	Weston, MO	Mariensee, Neustadt am Rübenberge, Hannover
Ohlf, Heinrich T.	21, July 1898	24, June	59	463		Omaha, NE	Neumünster, Holstein
Ohlinger, Catharina	10, Nov. 1887	29, Sept	77	718	Wessauer	Pomeroy, OH	Edigheim, Frankenthal, Baiern
Ohlinger, H.	29, Jan. 1866	2, Dec.	56-4m-18d	38		Pomeroy, OH	Edigheim, Frankenthal, Baiern
Ohlinger, Hanna	11, Oct. 1888	31, Aug.	79-4m-16d	654		Delhi, MI	
Ohlinger, Heinrich	19, Feb. 1866	2, Dec.	56-4m-18d	62		Pomeroy, OH	Edigheim, Preußen
Ohlinger, Louise	5, Aug. 1897	26, June	38	495	Artz	Elmore, OH	Rice Township, Sandusky County, Ohio
Ohm, Otto Johan Ferdinand	12, Nov. 1896	20, Oct.	20	734		Swanton, NE	Pribbernow, Pommern
Ohm, Wilhelmina	12, Dec. 1881	23, Nov.	72	399	Voltmann	Dunkirk, NY	
Ohmstede, Christian	23, Feb. 1893	19, Jan.	79	126		Industry, TX	Wadders, Oldenburg
Ohnacker, Rudolph	23, Oct. 1890	28, Sept	96-10m-11d	686		Berea, OH	Griesheim, Worms, Hessen-Darmstadt
Ohning, Elisabeth	31, Mar. 1887	14, Mar.	73- 2m-14d	206	Witter	Sherrills Mount, IA	Hasmarsheim, Mosbach, Baden
Okel, Conrad	23, July 1891	30, June	71- 6m- 9d	478		Wheeling, WV	Selters, Hessen
Okel, Dorothea	12, Mar. 1877	20, Feb.	55	87		Wheeling, WV	Bleichenbach, Hessen
Oldenborg, Carl Friedrich Wilhelm	13, Feb. 1896	9, Jan.	59	110	Neun	Montgomery Co, IA	Beenz, Brandenburg
Oldenburg, (Mrs)	6, Mar. 1871		39-4m-15d	79	Richter	Friendship, WI	Annenwalde, Brandenburg, Preußen
Oldenburg, August	5, Mar. 1896	30, Jan.	46	158		Nasewaupee, WI	Regenwalde, Pommern
Oldenburg, Caroline	19, Jan. 1885	30, Dec.	32- 8m-23d	7	Heiden	Dotyville, WI	Gnewekow, Pommern
Oldenburg, Christian F. A.	3, June 1897	16, May	65	351		Dotyville, WI	Beenz bei Beutel, Templin, Preußen
Oldenburg, Franklin Benjamin	15, Feb. 1894	26, Jan.	21	110		Milwaukee, WI	Milwaukee, Wisconsin
Oldenburg, Friederike Wilhelmine H.	3, Jan. 1895	6, Dec.	77	14		Beaver Dam, WI	Riegenhagen, Pommern
Oldenburg, Gerhard	26, June 1890	7, June	74	414		Green Bay, WI	Friederichstadt, Schleswig-Holstein
Oldenburg, Karl	17, Jan. 1881	23, Dec.	71	23		Milwaukee, WI	Neuendorf, Vorpommern
Oldenburg, Margarete	5, Oct. 1899	15, Sept	67	639	Berner	Green Bay, WI	Elna, Mecklenburg
Oldenburg, Maria	1, Apr. 1886	17, Mar.	28	7	Zitlow	LaCrosse, WI	LaCrescent, Houston County, Minnesota
Oldenburg, Maria	15, Nov. 1894	23, Oct.	68	742	Grote	Fond du Lac, WI	Bading, Brandenburg
Oldenburg, Maria	22, Feb. 1894	30, Jan.	80	126	Heiden	Milwaukee, WI	Burow, Pommern
Oldenburg, Mathilda	20, Jan. 1898	24, Dec.	60	47	Matthies	Montgomery Co, IA	Dansow, Germany
Oldenburg, Sophie	24, Feb. 1873		41	63	Wolf	Hokah, MN	Kittendorf, Mecklenburg-Schwerin
Oldenhage, Hermann	1, Aug. 1864		24	124		Francisco, MI	Ladbergen, Amt Osnabrück, Hannover
Oldenhage, Johan Herman	30, Apr. 1896	12, Apr.	82	286		Francisco, MI	Große Minmelage, Bersenbrück, Hannover
Oldenhage, Margaretha A.	28, Feb. 1881	21, Jan.	65- 5m- 1d	71	Grönloh	Francisco, MI	Langen, Baldbergen, Hannover
Olfers, Voske	11, Aug. 1884		75-8m-22d	7	Janion	Secor, IL	
Olgart, Wilhelmine	12, Mar. 1891	20, Feb.	81	174		Newport, KY	Westenburg, Nassau
Olhaber, John D.	15, Dec. 1887	27, Nov.	80	798		Marietta, OH	Remenau, Dilm, Apesen, Hannover
Olhaber, Katharina	26, Aug. 1878	25, July	69	271	Duden	Marietta, OH	Groß-Wördenstadt, Amt Zeven, Hannover
Oliver, Arabella	21, July 1884	26, June	35	7	Kissel	Greenville, OH	Greenville, Darke County, Ohio
Oliver, Maria	29, May 1890	9, May	49	350	Wilkens	Le Sueur, MN	Harmar, Ohio
Ollhoff, Maria	25, July 1889	9, July	37- 1m- 1d	478		Woodbine, KS	
Ollhoff, Martin Friedrich	28, Apr. 1879	13, Apr.	26- 1m-26d	135		Lyona, KS	
Ollhoff, Peter	13, June 1881	11, May	80- 6m	191		Lyona, KS	Pommern
Olmesdahl, Johann Gerhard	20, Sept 1849	20, Aug.	58	152		Milwaukee, WI	Düßberg am Rhein,
Olschke, Friedrich	10, May 1869	23, Apr.	38	151		Louisville, KY	Braunsrode, Eckelsbergen, Preußen

Christliche Apologete Death Notices --- 1839 - 1899

Name of Deceased	Notice Date	Death Date	Age	Page	Maiden Name	Place of Death	Place of Birth
Olsen, Ole Christian	13, Jan. 1898	27, Dec.	27	31	Heuermann	Sleepy Eye, MN	Mangstrup, Schleswig
Oltmann Setje-Eilers, A. Maria Sophia	8, Dec. 1898		78	783		Gladbrook, IA	Edewecht, Oldenburg
Oltmann, John	25, Feb. 1878	28, Jan.	62	63		Faribault, MN	Etzel, Ostfriesland
Omelia, Anna	27, Jan. 1898	29, Dec.	30	63	Jauch	Chicago, IL	Oden, Marion County, Illinois
Ommert, Tillie	6, Dec. 1894	4, Nov.	22	790		Quincy, IL	
Onacker, Anna Maria	26, Apr. 1894	6, Apr.	85- -27d	278		Berea, OH	Ginsheim, Hessen-Darmstadt
Onnen, Kassen	22, Oct. 1877	2, Oct.	21- -12d	343		San Jose, IL	Neuschoo, Ostfriesland
Onts, John	19, Feb. 1891	20, Jan.	15	126		Graham, MO	Nodaway County, Missouri
Opel, Margaretha	26, Jan. 1885	11, Jan.	87- 8m-22d	7	Kiesling	Jefferson City, MO	Stobersreuth, Baiern
Opitz, Wilhelmine	20, Dec. 1888	28, Nov.	48	814	Hallbauer	Chicago, IL	Rohrbach, Ebingen, Baden
Opp, (Mrs)	23, Mar. 1863	2, Mar.	77	48		Milan, IN	Eiselthum, Rheinkreis Baiern
Opp, Anton	20, July 1899	29, June	80	463		Cincinnati, OH	Freimersheim, Alzey, Hessen-Darmstadt
Opp, Barbara	22, Sept 1843	16, Sept	28- 8m-6d	151		Lawrenceburg, IN	Gundersheim, Hessen
Opp, Barbara	10, May 1849	14, Apr.	22	76	Dexheimer	Lawrenceburg, IN	
Opp, Karl	14, Mar. 1895	17, Feb.	49	174		Mt. Olive, IL	Breitenbrunn, Sachsen
Opp, Kunigunde	20, Oct. 1884	9, Sept		7	Lautner	Pinckneyville, IL	Wolfsbach, Baiern
Opp, Maria	9, Feb. 1888	19, Jan.	66	94	Hesselmeier	Farmers Retreat, IN	Drohne, Dilgen, Roden, Preußen
Opp, Maria	28, Oct. 1852	10, Oct.	23	176	Zimmermann	Lawrenceburg, IN	König, Hessen-Darmstadt
Opp, Maria	22, Feb. 1875	31, Jan.	60	63	Beckmann	Pinckneyville, IL	Steinlar, Hannover
Oppel, Barbara	9, May 1889	23, Apr.	67	302	Heinlein	Bradford, IN	Utzmannsbach, Greifenbach, Baiern
Oppel, Johan	5, Apr. 1894	28, Nov.	69	230		Bradford, IN	Velden, Mittelfranken, Baiern
Ordwein, Heinrich	19, Aug. 1878	5, Aug.	13	263		Frankfort, IL	Green Garden, Illinois
Orr, Katharine	9, Sept 1897	15, Aug.	56	575	Ruckdäschel	Chicago, IL	Grünstein, Berneck, Oberfranken, Baiern
Ort, Lydia	10, July 1876	31, May	76- 2m	223		Allegheny City, PA	
Ortgier, Anna L.	19, Dec. 1881	25, Nov.	63- 5m- 7d	407	Brüning	St. Louis, MO	Besenbrück bei Gehrde, Hannover
Ortgier, Anna S.	26, Dec. 1881	25, Nov.	63	415	Brüning	St. Louis, MO	Besenbrück bei Gehrde, Hannover
Orth, Anna Maria	3, June 1872	19, May	51- 4m-5d	183	Balke	Davenport, IA	Dünne, Westphalen
Orth, David	7, May 1883	2, Apr.	28-10m-27d	151		Warsaw, IL	Butler County, Ohio
Orth, Karl Johan	16, June 1898	19, May	74- 6m-18d	383		Frankfort, IL	
Orth, Susanna	24, Aug. 1874		51- 2m-17d	273			
Orth, W.	28, Jan. 1884	10, Jan.	61- 8m- 8d	7		Warsaw, IL	
Ortmann, Carl	3, Nov. 1862	8, Oct.		176		Edwardsville, IL	Pfeddersheim, Worms, Hessen
Ortmann, Margaretha	21, May 1866	25, Apr.	28	166		Brunswick, MO	Lychen, Dembline, Meklenburg, Preußen
Ortmeier, Friederika Justina	2, May 1881	9, Apr.	70- 7m-12d	143	Kluckhohn	Cedar Lake, IN	Fürstenau, Hannover
Ortmeyer, Charlotte	25, June 1894	23, Dec.	43	62	Frevert	Crown Point, IN	Bavenhausen, Lippe-Detmold
Ortmeyer, Simon	11, Oct. 1875	21, Sept	68	327		Cedar Lake, IN	Asendorf, Lippe-Detmold
Ortwein, Helena	28, June 1875	8, June	66	207		Frankfort, IL	Bavenhausen, Lippe-Detmold
Ortwein, Karolina	6, Nov. 1882	19, Oct.	38	359	Albring	Sleepy Eye, MN	Binswangen, Neckarsulm, Württemberg
Orum, Friedrike Wilhelmine	27, Nov. 1882	7, Nov.	36	383	Kupfer	Wheeling, WV	Ostfriesland
Oschwald, Philippine	29, Oct. 1857	4, Sept	34	176	Brengel	Sacramento, CA	Katzendorf, Sachsen-Weimar
Osmers, Bruno	12, Jan. 1874	30, Nov.	34	15		Decatur, IL	Baden, Hannover
Osmers, Gretha	10, Mar. 1887	20, Feb.	73- 6m	158	Elmers	Decatur, IL	Baden, Hannover
Osmers, Harry	27, June 1895	8, May	36	414		Decatur, IL	St. Louis, Missouri
Osmers, Johan	26, Jan. 1893	28, Dec.	78	62		Decatur, IL	Baden, Hannover
Osmeyer, Ludwig	17, May 1875	26, Apr.	41- 9m	159		Scioto, OH	Minden, Preußen
Ossenforth, Carl Heinrich	13, May 1897	9, Mar.	31	303		Amsterdam, NY	

Christliche Apologete Death Notices --- 1839 - 1899

Name of Deceased	Notice Date	Death Date	Age	Page	Maiden Name	Place of Death	Place of Birth
Oßmann, Katharina	20, Aug. 1866	25, July	33- 2m-26d	270	Hooker	Bucyrus, OH	Auerbach, Durlach, Baden
Ostadt, Catharina	28, Sept 1874	13, Sept	84- 8m- 3d	311	Braun	Portsmouth, OH	Straßburg, Pennsylvania
Oster, Jakob	10, Sept 1891	7, July	64	590		New York City, NY	Steinsfort, Baden
Osterhage, Sophia	16, Mar. 1893	16, Feb.	81	174		Lyman, IA	Luhe, Brake, Lippe-Detmold
Osterhagen, Mina	4, Aug. 1862	18, July	47- 7m	124		Blue Island, IL	Höllenberg, Lippe-Detmold
Osterhagen, Simon	5, Nov. 1865	10, Oct.	57	180		Blue Island, IL	Talle, Amt Hohenhausen, Lippe-Detmold
Osterlow, Heinrich	27, Sept 1860	4, Sept	43	156		Manitowoc, WI	
Ostermann, Elisabeth	26, July 1860	8, July	38	120	Woode	Pomeroy, OH	Edigheim, Baiern
Ostermeier, Anna K.	15, Nov. 1888	18, Oct.	60- 8m- 1d	734	Stump	New Palestine, IN	Ansheim, Ahlsfeld, Kurhessen
Ostermeier, Carl G.	8, Sept 1887	15, Aug.	67	574		New Palestine, IN	Wietersheim, Minden, Preußen
Osthof, Maria	21, Dec. 1874	18, Nov.	38- 7m	407	Ledermann	Sherrills Mount, IA	
Osting, Maria	4, Apr. 1881	6, Mar.	81	111	Tangemann	Batesville, IN	Varneß, Goldenstedt, Vechta, Oldenburg
Ostinger, Meint	30, July 1857	9, June	53	124		German Creek, IA	Hoogesand, Gröningen, Holland
Ostreicher, Georg	20, Sept 1860	7, Sept	33	152		Iowa City, IA	Kreutzheim, Württemberg
Oswald, Friedrich	30, Aug. 1855	14, Aug.	68	140		Chillicothe, OH	Heppenheim, Hessen-Darmstadt
Oswald, Johan Heinrich	2, July1883	9, June	62	215		Greenfield, OH	Herßdorf, Sachsen-Meiningen
Oswald, Katharina	27, May 1872	24, Apr.	83	175	Dakermann	Chillicothe, OH	Großmedelsheim, Baiern
Otchen, Bernhardt	26, Dec. 1870	7, Nov.	56	415		Marine City, MI	Oldenburg
Oijen, Dorothea	4, Oct. 1855	29, Aug.	44	160		Bellriver, MI	Klein Odweiler, Baiern
Otte, Christina	11, Oct. 1869	18, Sept	21- 1m-20d	327	Wiegand	Calhoun, MO	Chicago County, Wisconsin
Ott , Franz	6, Apr. 1899	13, Mar.	79	223		St. Louis, MO	Karlstadt, Rheinpfalz Baiern
Ott, Anna	11, Oct. 1894	10, Sept	33	662		St. Louis, MO	St. Louis, Missouri
Ott, Anna Maria	14, Mar. 1895	14, Feb.	70	174	Meyer	DeWitt, MI	Möhringen, Tübingen, Württemberg
Ott, Carolina	19, Sept 1889	10, July		606	Schuler	Schnectady, NY	Hoffenheim, Baden
Ott, Christian	3, Nov. 1884	21, Oct.	64	7		Albert Lea, MN	Bechigen, Bern, Schweiz
Ott, Edward	4, Mar.1872	13, Jan.	17- -22d	79		Herman, MO	
Ott, Eva Elisabeth	25, Feb. 1892	13, Jan.	53	127		Troy, NY	Birchheim, Kurhessen
Ott, Heinrich	28, Oct. 1897	9, Oct.	54	687		Louisville, KY	Oberbischingen, Ehingen, Germany
Ott, Heinrich	4, Mar.1872	22, Jan.	18- 8m-16d	79		Herman, MO	
Ott, Henriette	18, July 1895	28, June	69	462	Hoffmann	Herman, MO	Barntrup, Lippe-Detmold
Ott, Jakob	22, Apr. 1867	20, Jan.	59	126		Booneville, MO	Bückelsberg, Sulz, Württemberg
Ott, Johan	14, Nov. 1895	20, Oct.	44	734		Albert Lea, MN	Hausen, Bern, Schweiz
Ott, Johan Martin	22, Dec. 1892	10, Nov.	71	814		DeWitt, MI	Möhringen, Tübingen, Württemberg
Ott, Johanna	28, June 1888	12, June	21-11m-18d	414		Louisville, KY	Riederich, Württemberg
Ott, Johanna	5, Dec. 1889	26, Oct.	62	782		Los Angeles, CA	Alzei, Hessen
Ott, Johannes	2, Feb. 1885	18, Jan.	81	7		Ellis Grove, IL	Wallpereuth, Münchberg, Baiern
Ott, Louis	5, Aug. 1886	19, July		7		Louisville, KY	Oberdischingen, Egnen, Württemberg
Ott, Louise Wilhelmine	29, Mar. 1894	15, Mar.	42	214	Horstmann	St. Joseph, MO	Franklin County, Missouri
Ott, Ludwig	20, Oct. 1898	13, Sept	42	671		Bland, MO	Gasconade County, Missouri
Ott, Margaretha	24, Apr. 1890	1, Apr.	64- 9m	270	Ufer	Nebraska City, NE	Brünig, Bern, Schweiz
Ott, Maria Magdalena	14, Oct. 1878		59- 3m- 8d	327	Müller	Albert Lea, MN	Polen
Ott, Nikolaus	15, May 1882	14, Apr.	65	159		Albert Lea, MN	Vehingen, Sieringen, Bern, Schweiz
Ott, Theodora	10, May 1894	24, Apr.	88	310		Louisville, KY	Ober-Dischingen, Ehlingen, Württemberg
Otte , Karl F. G.	16, Feb. 1899	26, Jan.	79- 4m-22d	111		Oconomowoc, WI	Schlesien, Stettin, Pommern
Otte, Heinrich	3, Feb. 1879	26, Dec.	59- 4m- 8d	39		Brunswick, MO	Esselsee, Hannover
Otte, Karolina	30, June 1898	3, June	59	415	Bröler	Owensville, MO	Thalle, Lippe-Detmold

Christliche Apologete Death Notices --- 1839 - 1899

Name of Deceased	Notice Date	Death Date	Age	Maiden Name	Page	Place of Death	Place of Birth
Otte, Maria	24, Feb. 1859	1, Dec.	46- 2m	Julius	32	Cedar Lake, IN	Ingeln, Hannover
Ottemeier, Sophie	2, Dec. 1897	26, Oct.	65		767	Sitzer, WI	Schiller, Witchenstein, Preußen
Otten, Adelheid	30, Apr. 1866	14, Apr.	83	Ringen	142	Marietta, OH	Hepstedt, Amt Ottersberg, Hannover
Otten, Anna	28, July 1898	6, July	83		479	St. Paul, MN	Hannover
Otten, Anna Katharina	24, Apr. 1890	1, Apr.	88		270	Boonville, MO	Amtshefen, Hannover
Otten, Caroline M.C.	7, Oct. 1878	18, Sept	36- 5m-10d	Becker	319	Covington, KY	Holzhausen, Minden, Preußen
Otten, Claus	1, June 1863	2, May	75- 8m-13d		88	Marietta, OH	Gramstedt, Amt Zeven, Hannover
Otten, Georg H.	21, Mar. 1889	25, Feb.	23- -14d		190	Sedalia, MO	Kansas City, Missouri
Otten, Heinrich	19, Dec. 1889	20, Nov.	60- 5m		814	Sedalia, MO	Brüttendorf, Zeven, Hannover
Otten, Heinrich	30, June 1853	10, June	72		104	Marietta, OH	Granstätt, Hannover
Otten, Johan Heinrich	10, Nov. 1898	20, Oct.	66		719	Covington, KY	Vorwerk, Zeven, Hannover
Otten, Johanna	30, July 1891	20, June	61	Westermann	494	Boonville, MO	Waldprechtsweiler, Baden
Otten, John	11, Apr. 1895	16, Mar.	69		238	Boonville, MO	Hannover
Otten, Maria Elisabeth	21, Dec. 1868	29, Nov.	30- 8m-27d	Reiners	407	Cincinnati, OH	Seckenhausen, Brinkum, Hannover
Otten, Martin	3, Nov. 1873	12, Oct.	30- 5m- 7d		351	Hochheim, TX	Aurich, Oldendorf, Ostfriesland
Otten, Ziefer Martins	30, June 1879	12, June	65		207	Hochheim, TX	Westersander, Ostfriesland
Otterbein, Conrad	7, Aug. 1846	19, June	22- 5m		127	Walnut Creek, IA	Obernomer, Hessen-Darmstadt
Ottersberg, John	19, Jan. 1863	7, Dec.	34		12	Salem, NE	Spetzerfehn, Timmel, Ostfriesland
Otterstein, Friederike	31, Dec. 1877	2, Dec.	32- 7m	Müller	423	--, WI	Werben, Pommern, Preußen
Ottes, Wilhelmina	24, Apr. 1882	15, Feb.	69- 5m		135	Jersey City, NJ	Wartenheim, Rheinpfalz Baiern
Ottmanns, Gesche Margaretha	21, July 1884	23, June	68- 1m	Clarksen	7	Emden, IL	Hegemerten, Essens, Ostfriesland
Otto, (Mr)	5, Mar. 1883	4, Feb.	73- 4m-29d		79	Eureka, WI	Wambeck, Hannover
Otto, Anna	17, Nov. 1873	30, Sept	63- 2m-22d	Fresen	367	Colesburg, IA	Alt-Brunzlar, Kurhessen
Otto, Anna Maria	22, Oct. 1883	3, Oct.	85- 5m-15d	Bauer	343	Canal Dover, OH	Wildenfels, Sachsen
Otto, Auguste Rosalie	4, May 1899	13, Apr.	57	Bodenschatz	287	Milwaukee, WI	
Otto, Bertha Emma Emilie	21, July 1887	5, July	13		462	Kenosha, WI	
Otto, Charlotte	21, Nov. 1889	17, Oct.	65	Conrad	750	Sheboygan, WI	Wanning, Brandenburg
Otto, Christian	28, Jan. 1897	27, Dec.	65		62	Milwaukee, WI	Crivitz, Mecklenburg-Schwerin
Otto, Christian	23, June 1879	30, May	21- 5m-22d		199	Kewaunee, WI	
Otto, Dietrich	28, Nov. 1895	9, Sept	57		766	Evansville, IN	Greeresen, Germany
Otto, Friedrich	9, Feb. 1885	10, Nov.	58		7	Allmuth, WI	Blumberg, Preußen
Otto, Georg	12, Sept 1881	15, Aug.	66- 6m-17d		295	Clarington, OH	Reichensachsen, Kurhessen
Otto, Heinrich	13, Sept 1888	12, Aug.	86		590	Burlington, IA	Osnabrück, Hannover
Otto, Helena	30, Sept 1858	6, Aug.	38		156	Rock River, WI	Ludwigslust, Mecklenburg
Otto, Johanna Sophia Carolina	21, Apr. 1887	19, Mar.	78- 5m- 4d	Bunzendahl	254	Rush Lake, WI	Scharmbeck, Hannover
Otto, Karl	3, Feb. 1887	11, Jan.	32-10m-11d		78	Switzer, OH	
Otto, Margaretha Elisabetha	13, Apr. 1854	6, Mar.	51- -20d	Rolf	60	German Creek, IA	Belm bei Osnabrück, Hannover
Otto, Maria	20, Apr. 1874	2, Apr.			127	Papillion, NE	Gebese, Sachsen, Preußen
Otto, Sabina	17, May 1888	28, Apr.	72- -14d	Knieriem	318	Switzer, OH	Eschwege, Kurhessen
Otto, Sophie	17, June 1852	30, May	36		100	Milwaukee, WI	Pittitz, Preußen
Otto, Wilhelmine Friederike	7, Mar. 1889	6, Feb.	66	Ortmann	158	Appleton, WI	Rignow, Soldin, Neumark
Otzenberger, August	18, Dec. 1882	2, Dec.	38		407	Wathena, KS	
Otzenberger, Ida	18, Apr. 1889	26, Mar.	29- 9m-28d	Lehmann	254	Wathena, KS	
Outs, Betge	6, Feb. 1882	23, Jan.	70	Telenga	47	Graham, MO	Emden, Ostfriesland
Outs, John	5, Jan. 1893	10, Dec.	44		14	Graham, MO	Emden, Ostfriesland
Overbeck, Emilie Amalia	21, Jan. 1886	28, Dec.	24		7	Ahnapee, WI	Lake Mills, Jefferson County, Wisconsin

Christliche Apologete Death Notices --- 1839 - 1899

Name of Deceased	Notice Date	Death Date	Age	Page	Maiden Name	Place of Death	Place of Birth
Overbeck, Georg Walter	4, May 1899	11, Apr.	22	287		Algoma, WI	Algoma, Wisconsin
Overbeck, Wilhelm	23, Nov. 1863	17, Aug.	27	188		Lake Mills, WI	Versmold, Halle, Minden, Preußen
Oxen, (Mrs)	12, May 1873	22, Apr.	25	151	Wills	Appleton, MO	
Oylheiesr, Elisabeth	9, Jan. 1865	17, Nov.		8		Rochester, NY	Baden
Paalhorn, Louisa	22, Oct. 1896	25, Sept	38	687	Gegenheimer	Vermillion, OH	Ittersbach, Pforzheim, Baden
Paap, Dorothea	8, Oct. 1896	18, Sept	60	655		Nebraska City, NE	Volkshagen, Mecklenburg-Schwerin
Paap, Frank Friedrich	28, Jan. 1886	11, Jan.	17- 7m-11d	7		Nebraska City, NE	
Paap, Friedrich D.	18, Aug. 1879	4, Aug.	69- - 9d	263		Nebraska City, NE	Steinhausen, Mecklenburg-Schwerin
Paap, Maria	20, Apr. 1893		82	254		Plattsmouth, NE	Mecklenburg-Schwerin
Paap, Wilhelm	20, Oct. 1892		43-11m-23d	670		Plattsmouth, NE	Teschow, Mecklenburg-Schwerin
Paar, Maria Katharina	14, May 1891	26, Apr.	83	318	Spangenberg	Warsaw, IL	Bründersen, Wolfhagen, Kurhessen
Paas, Friedrich Wilhelm	13, June 1895	8, May	22	382		San Jose, IL	San Jose, Illinois
Paas, Katharina	25, Dec. 1890	25, Nov.	53- 7m-15d	830		San Jose, IL	Brockterbeck, Arensberg, Preußen
Pabst, Doris	7, Feb. 1889	16, Jan.	54- 9m	94	Borges	New York City, NY	Neuenburg, Hannover
Pabst, Emil	27, Apr. 1899	31, Mar.	56	271		South Bend, IN	Sachsen
Pabst, Heinrich Jacob	21, Feb. 1870	9, Dec.	17	63		St. Louis, MO	
Pace, Anna Marie	19, Mar. 1896	21, Feb.	73	190		Waco, TX	Voegesheim, Mühlheim, Baden
Padberg, Friedrich	19, Mar. 1883	23, Feb.	54- - 2d	95		Petersburg, IL	Landau, Waldeck
Pade, August	21, Sept 1854	3, July	36	152		Union, MO	Borgholzhausen, Minden, Preußen
Pade, Elisabeth	21, Sept 1854	4, July	44	152	Kottmeier	Union, MO	Eichen, Mölle, Hannover
Padei, Sophia	16, Feb. 1860	5, Jan.	40	28		Rochester, NY	Gerden, Hannover
Paeper, Caroline	6, Mar. 1871	13, Feb.		79	Rinow	Valparaiso, IN	Neuenkirchen, Insel Rügen, Pommern
Pagel, Benjamin George Edward	16, Oct. 1890	24, Sept	10- 2m-15d	670		Laporte, IN	
Pagel, (Mrs)	7, Jan. 1886	20, Dec.	71	7	Jäger	San Francisco, CA	Dargitz, Preußen
Pagel, Anna Catharina	31, July 1865	9, June		124		Burlington, WI	
Pagel, Anna Catharina Friedrike	6, Dec. 1880	12, Nov.	72	391	Harm	Alden, IA	Großspankow, Mecklenburg-Schwerin
Pagel, Ernst	16, Mar. 1885	23, Jan.	24	7		Eldorado, WI	Eldorado, Fond du Lac County, Wisconsin
Pagel, Johan Gottfried	18, Aug. 1892	22, July	93- 7m-24d	526		Laporte, IN	Neu Werder bei Colberg, Pommern
Pagel, Marie	18, Aug. 1898	31, July	63	527		Akron, OH	Zwidorf, Mecklenburg-Schwerin
Pagels, Johanna	17, July 1890	25, June	52	462		Chicago, IL	Duckow, Preußen
Pagenhart, Gertrud Elisabeth	23, Feb. 1888	28, Jan.	82	126		Chicago, IL	Westuffeln, Kurhessen
Pagenhart, Johan Georg	26, May 1873	5, May	69	167		Montrose, MN	Hombressen, Hofgeismar, Kurhessen
Pagenkopf, Carolina	1, Aug. 1895	27, June	38	494	Horsch	Blooming Grove, MN	Naugardt, Pommern
Pagenkopf, Friedrich	13, Oct. 1884	22, Sept	65	7		St. Louis, MO	Neu Mühl, Kork, Baden
Pahl, Barbara	14, Apr. 1898	24, Mar.	52	239		Bushton, KS	Meinersfeld, Lippe-Detmold
Pahl, Caroline Wilhelmine D.	17, May 1894	13, Apr.	81	326	Gerwes	St. Louis, MO	Alt Waldmoden, Hannover
Pahl, Henry	21, Feb. 1895	19, Jan.	51	126		St. Louis, MO	Ziegelhirt, Liebenburg, Hannover
Pahl, Louise	30, June 1862		46	104		Hopewell, MO	Gohfeld, Herford, Minden, Preußen
Pahmeyer, Johan Heinrich	11, Mar. 1872	12, Jan.	78	87		Laporte, IN	Kittendorf, Mecklenburg-Schwerin
Pahrmann, Johannes	9, Feb. 1885	25, Jan.	65	7		Cincinnati, OH	Hollenstedt, Hannover
Paland, August	18, Aug. 1892	4, Aug.	59	527		Los Angeles, CA	Bütow, Hinterpommern
Pallas, Maria	20, Feb. 1890	10, Jan.	88	126		Staunton, IL	Staunton, Illinois
Panhorst, Carolina	22, Oct. 1883	30, Sept	19	343		Staunton, IL	Lengerich, Preußen
Panhorst, Wilhelm Bernard	28, July 1879	23, June	51	239		Caseville, MI	Mecklenburg-Schwerin
Pann, Johan	11, Dec. 1871	8, Nov.	86	399			Mecklenburg-Schwerin

Christliche Apologete Death Notices --- 1839 - 1899

Name of Deceased	Notice Date	Death Date	Age	Page	Maiden Name	Place of Death	Place of Birth
Pannwitt, Maria	19, Dec. 1895	27, Nov.	70	814	Höppner	Bible Grove, IL	Wiendorf, Schwann, Mecklenburg-Schwerin
Panzer, Bertha Maria Charlotte	24, Mar. 1887	28, Feb.	33- 2m-22d	190	Fick	Park Ridge, IL	Gazigar, Lauenburg, Preußen
Panzlau, Emma	30, Apr. 1891	1, Apr.	22	286	Göttler	Menominee, MI	Pittsfield, Brown County, Wisconsin
Pape, Carl	10, Apr. 1882	23, Mar.	17- 3m-28d	119		Clayton, WI	Neenah, Wisconsin
Pape, Carl W.	2, Oct. 1876	13, Sept	20	319		Bloomington, IL	St. Louis, Missouri
Pape, Christine	22, Dec. 1884	25, Nov.	39-10m-20d	7	Heß	Clayton, WI	Straßeberbach, Dillenburg, Nassau
Pape, Christoph	29, June 1868	10, Sept	49	207		Industry, TX	Hannover
Pape, Heinrich	22, Mar. 1888	22, Jan.	58	190		Caywood, OH	
Pape, Maria	25, Mar. 1897	9, Feb.	78	190	Drewes	Bloomington, IL	Lippe-Detmold
Päpe, Maria E.	27, Oct. 1884	25, Sept	51- 4m-20d	7	Eifler	Marietta, OH	Cedern, Birkenfeld, Oldenburg
Pape, Wilhelm	29, Dec. 1862	25, Nov.	53	208		Bloomington, IL	Humfeld, Lippe-Detmold
Papen, Fritz	20, July 1874	3, July		231		Lake Creek, MO	
Papen, John F.	8, Apr. 1878	4, Mar.	37- -23d	111		Sedalia, MO	Pettis County, Missouri
Papen, Katharina M. Wilhelmina	12, Apr. 1894	18, Mar.	72	246		Sedalia, MO	Wenden, Wölpen, Hannover
Papenfuß, Heinrich Herman R.	25, Nov. 1897	8, Nov.	28	751		Pearl City, IL	Schlawe, Pommern
Papke, Anna	6, Sept 1894	5, Aug.	20	582	Krippner	Meriden, MN	Meriden, Steele County, Minnesota
Pappe, Sophia	16, Nov. 1868	29, Oct.	44	367		Peoria, IL	Hilchenfeld, Amt Sicar, Hannover
Pappen, Johan Heinrich	30, Nov. 1874	31, Oct.	65	383		Sedalia, MO	Graasdorf, Odersberg, Hannover
Papst, Elisabeth	26, Jan. 1863	6, Nov.	44	16		Oregon, MO	Grumbach bei Gießen, Kurhessen
Parker, Lydia	7, Sept 1893	19, Aug.	67	574	Keller	Akron, OH	Berks County, Ohio
Parmenter, Louise	29, Mar. 1894	12, Mar.	31	214	Pierstorff	Madison, WI	Middleton, Wisconsin
Parret, Eva	20, Dec. 1880	16, Nov.	31- 5m- 9d	407	Siegel	Boonville, IN	Newburg, Indiana
Paschen, Friedrich	19, Aug. 1897	2, Aug.	68	527		Baraboo, WI	Neuhoff, Freistadt, Mecklenburg-Schwerin
Paschen, J. Alb.	26, May 1873	21, Apr.	52-10m	167		Brunswick, MO	Spellen bei der Weser, Düsseldorf, Preußen
Paschen, John	26, Apr. 1869	6, Apr.	54	135		Baraboo, WI	Neuhof, Neustadt, Mecklenburg-Schwerin
Paschold, Sophie	21, Jan. 1886	23, Dec.	44	7	Wixforth	Sterling, NE	Iselhort bei Gütersloh, Westphalen
Pasewalk, Johanna Friederike	31, Dec. 1891	10, Dec.	70	846	Toltzmann	Manitowoc, WI	Pflugrade, Pommern
Passauer, Catharina	29, Aug. 1861	27, July	19	140		Cincinnati, OH	
Päth, Herman	26, July 1894	23, June	42	486		DeWitt, MI	Stolp, Hinterpommern
Pätow, August F.	8, Sept 1884	23, Aug.	84	7		Roseville, MI	Warlitz, Mecklenburg-Schwerin
Patow, Emma	30, Sept 1886	5, Sept	29	7	Geinitz	Roseville, MI	Forestport, New York
Pätow, Henry	27, Dec. 1880	23, Nov.	11- 8m-11d	415		Freeport, IL	
Pätow, Wilhelm	20, Dec. 1880	26, Nov.	52	407		Roseville, MI	Gammelin, Nagenow, Mecklenburg-Schwerin
Patzig, Carl	17, Nov. 1879	26, Oct.	64- -25d	367	Wawarowsky	Lemars, IA	Sachsen
Paul , Johan F.	24, Nov. 1898	9, Oct.	88	751		Quincy, IL	Nitzbach, Rheinpfalz Baiern
Paul , Lisette	8, July 1897	15, June	47	431	Kohlhase	Summerfield, IL	Plau, Mecklenburg-Schwerin
Paul, Anna	9, Apr. 1896	16, Mar.	85	238	Rigg	Quincy, IL	Malix, Graubünden, Schweiz
Paul, Anna	26, Jan. 1863	30, Oct.	25	16	Iff	Jerseyville, IL	Kanton Aargau, Schweiz
Paul, Anna	2, Mar. 1863	30, Oct.	25	36	Iff	Carlinville, IL	Kanton Aargau, Schweiz
Paul, Anna Katharine	25, Aug. 1898	12, Aug.	71	543		Nashville, IL	Homber, Kurhessen
Paul, Catharine Elisabeth	30, Oct. 1876	16, Oct.	58	351		Alton, IL	Senghofen, Nassau
Paul, Emma	18, Aug. 1898	29, July	24	527		Webster, SD	Sleepy Eye , Minnesota
Paul, Jakob	30, Mar. 1868	17, Jan.	67	103		Boonville, IN	Klingen, Bergzabern, Rheinpfalz Baiern
Paul, Johan	23, Feb. 1888	3, Feb.	29- 3m	126		Alton, IL	
Paul, Johan Georg	13, Dec. 1869	21, Oct.	55	399		Alton, IL	Singhofen, Amt Nassau, Nassau
Paul, Johan Gottlob	2, May 1881	14, Apr.	65	143		Wilton, IA	Laubenheim bei Bautzen, Sachsen

- 376 -

Christliche Apologete Death Notices --- 1839 - 1899

Name of Deceased	Notice Date	Death Date	Age	Page	Maiden Name	Place of Death	Place of Birth
Paul, Katharina Barbara	11, Nov. 1867	17, Oct.	65- 3m- 4d	358		Boonville, IN	Klingen, Bergzabern, Rheinkreis Baiern
Paul, Katharine	23, Jan. 1875	5, Jan.	51	31	Lippla	Lena, IL	Märzheim, Landau, Rheinkreis Baiern
Paul, Margarethe	16, May 1861	11, Apr.	22	80	Herner	Jerseyville, IL	Remels, Ostfriesland
Paul, Mina	7, Sept 1899	18, Aug.	55	575	VonderMeden	Brighton, IL	Schwerin
Paul, Mina	23, Dec. 1886	1, Dec.	68	7	Weber	Henderson, KY	Singhofen, Nassau
Paul, Phil. H.	14, Mar. 1864	Dec.	57	44		Alton, IL	Ansbach, Hessen-Nassau
Pauli, Elisabeth	16, July 1896	24, June	81	463	Brand	St. Louis, MO	Zeullingen, Baden
Pauli, Franciska	3, Dec. 1866	10, Nov.	80	390		New Orleans, LA	Berea, Ohio
Pauli, Lydia	18, July 1895	23, June	17	462	Weinreich	Chicago, IL	Wehrheim, Nassau
Pauli, Wilhelm	30, Aug. 1894	25, July	77	566		St. Louis, MO	Thronitz bei Litzen, Sachsen
Pauli, Wilhelmine	21, May 1891	30, Apr.	55	334	Fiedler	Chicago, IL	Einbeck, Hannover
Pauling, Friedericke A.	1, Aug. 1881	9, July	59	247	Engelbrecht	Falls Mission, TX	Schwarmstädt, Hannover
Pauling, Johan Friedrich	8, June 1874	18, May	66- 1m-25d	183		Concordia, MO	Espark, Neustadt am Rüberg, Hannover
Pauling, Katharina Dorothea	2, Sept 1872	23, July	67	287	Dierking	Concordia, MO	Limer, Hannover
Pauling, Otto	25, Jan. 1894	7, Dec.	39	62		Los Angeles, CA	Glowno, Posen
Pauling, Pauline	28, July 1884	10, July	41	7	Ninas	Concordia, MO	Rheinkreis Baiern
Paull, John	9, Jan. 1896	15, Dec.	73	30		Louisville, KY	Gifhorn, Hannover
Paulmann, Elisabeth	3, May 1875	20, Mar.	85	143		Angelica, NY	West Preußen
Paulsen, Henriette	28, Dec. 1899	9, Dec.	82	828	Lemke	New Ulm, MN	Röst, Holstein
Paulssen, Johan Ch.	18, Aug. 1898	11, July	79	527		New Ulm, MN	Morrisons Cove, Huntington Co., Pennsylvania
Paulus, Johan	31, Mar. 1887	15, Mar.	80	206		Goshen, IN	Münschenhausen, Marburg, Kurhessen
Paulus, Kasper	28, Nov. 1870	3, Nov.	78	383		Danville, IL	Lozi, Rußland
Pauly, Emilie	10, May 1875	26, Apr.	27	151	Heilmann	St. Louis, MO	Nieder-Bierbach, Hessen-Darmstadt
Pauly, Friederika	20, Aug. 1891	21, July	69	542		Crow River, MN	Schleswig
Paustian, Margaretha	7, Jan. 1897	30, Nov.	75	15		Cameron, MO	Dobern, Böhmen
Pautler, (Mr)	8, Apr. 1872	5, Mar.	60- 6m	119		LaCrosse, WI	
Pautler, (Mr)	10, Apr. 1876	22, Mar.	56- 6m-14d	118		LaCrosse, WI	
Pautz, Bertha Wilhelmine C.	3, Nov. 1892	17, Sept	19	702		Jordan, MN	Waldenburg, Regenwald, Hinterpommern
Pautz, Carl	25, Jan. 1869	23, Dec.	76	31		Liberty, WI	Pommern
Pautz, Ferdinand	22, Aug. 1870	5, Aug.	33- 6m-27d	271		Manitowoc, WI	
Pechert, Margaretha	27, May 1842		Inquiry	83		Lacone, IN	
Pedig, Amalia	23, Dec. 1878	2, Dec.	29	407		Morrison, MO	
Peetz, Maria	17, June 1897	8, May	59	383	Fetzer	Aurora, IL	Amon-Schönbrunn, Baiern
Pegelow, Sophie	4, June 1891	23, Apr.		366	Schütt	Silver Creek, NY	Preußen
Pegelow, Ferdinand	31, Mar. 1873		33	103		Chicago, IL	Wolfshagen bei Köslin, HinterPommern
Peglow, Friedrich	14, Nov. 1861	23, Oct.	49	184		Laporte, IN	Lipen, Mecklenburg-Schwerin
Peglow, Friedrike Maria	20, Nov. 1882	3, Nov.	45	375	Batzloff	Laporte, IN	Hohenmoko, Demin , Preußen
Peglow, Heinrich	28, Jan. 1897	11, Jan.		63		Laporte, IN	Liepen, Mecklenburg-Schwerin
Peglow, Karl	10, Mar.1873	16, Feb.		79		Laporte, IN	Liegen, Malichin, Mecklenburg-Schwerin
Pehle, Adolph	2, Aug. 1869	27, June	23	247		Herman, MO	Börringhausen, Lippe
Pehle, Heinrich F.	11, July 1889	19, May	51	446		New Haven, MO	Franklin County, Missouri
Pehle, Karl	25, Mar. 1886	8, Feb.		7		Herman, MO	Schuckenbaum, Oerlinghausen, Lippe-Detmold
Pehle, Louise	18, Nov. 1852	20, Aug.	21	188	Meyer	Herman, MO	Nordhammern, Minden, Westphalen
Peifer, Conrad	26, Nov. 1857	30, Oct.	17	192		Vandalia, IL	
Peik, Conrad	26, July 1888	28, June	49	478		Brownton, MN	Stemmen, Lippe-Detmold
Peik, Friederika Dorothea Louise	18, Jan. 1894	20, Dec.	79	46	Hanke	Brownton, MN	Silixen, Lippe-Detmold

Christliche Apologete Death Notices --- 1839 - 1899

Name of Deceased	Notice Date	Death Date	Age	Maiden Name	Place of Death	Page	Place of Birth
Peik, Friedrich Carl	28, May 1896	5, May	19		Brownton, MN	350	Sumter, Minnesota
Pein, Sophie	31, Oct. 1881	7, Oct.	29	Lorenz	Clayton, WI	351	Klocksin, Mecklenburg-Schwerin
Peisch, Christian	26, Apr. 1894		57		Des Moines, IA	278	Mittelgründe, Hessen-Darmstadt
Peisch, H.	11, Mar. 1867	19, Feb.	68		German Creek, IA	78	Wiedrunes, Kreis Nieda, Hessen-Darmstadt
Peisch, Katharine	8, July 1872	17, June	67	Meininger	Etna, MO	223	Mittelgründen, Nidda, Hessen-Darmstadt
Peitsmann, H.	20, Jan. 1868	30, Dec.	60		Giard, IA	22	Westphalen
Pelser, Emilia Charlotte	6, Oct. 1892	5, Sept	39	Göttlish	Boonville, IN	638	New Jersey
Peltier, E.	22, July 1897	6, July	46		Indianapolis, IN	463	Frankreich
Peltzer, Fr.	11, June 1883	17, May	57			191	
Penning, Anna Hendrika	19, Apr. 1894	19, Mar.	30	Fecht	Alton, IL	262	
Penzold, Eduard	21, Mar. 1895	26, Feb.	66		Chicago, IL	190	Neumark bei Reichenbach, Germany
Peper, Benjamin	8, Nov. 1894	22, Oct.	36		Nokomis, IL	726	Schwerinsdorf, Ostfriesland
Peper, Johan Cord	21, Jan. 1884	3, Dec.	75		Schnectady, NY	7	Eikhorst, Minden, Preußen
Peper, Johny	23, June 1862				New York, NY	100	
Pepmiller, Heinrich	18, Sept 1890	29, Aug.	76		Boonville, IN	606	Liemke bei Preuß, Münden, Preußen
Pepper, Carolina Maria	4, Mar.1872	23, Jan.	22- 6m-23d		Schnectady, NY	79	
Pepper, Caroline Marie	25, Aug. 1892	1, Aug.	76- 1m- 5d	Grannemann	Schnectady, NY	542	Lavelsloh, Hannover
Pepper, Christian	6, May 1897	17, Apr.	78		Schnectady, NY	287	Eikhorst, Minden, Preußen
Pepper, Christine	21, July 1879	2, July	23- 3m-28d	Feldmann	Louisville, KY	231	Karlsruh, Baden
Pepper, Edward Christian	6, May 1886	19, Apr.	30		Schnectady, NY	7	Glenville, New York
Pepper, Friedrich Johan	31, Dec. 1877	5, Dec.	48-11m-17d		Schnectady, NY	423	Eickhorst, Preußen
Pepper, Friedrich Wilhelm	10, June 1878	22, May	66- 1m-26d		Schnectady, NY	183	
Pepper, Herman	14, Mar. 1889	14, Feb.	28- 4m-17d		Nokomis, IL	174	Schwerinsdorf, Ostfriesland
Pepper, Herman	31, May 1880	17, Apr.	72		Schnectady, NY	175	Eickhorst, Preußen
Pepper, Louis	10, Dec. 1896	9, Nov.	72		Schnectady, NY	798	Eickhorst, Minden, Preußen
Pepper, Louisa	24, June 1872	31, May	64		Schnectady, NY	207	Eickhorst, Minden, Preußen
Pepper, Maria	11, June 1883	25, Mar.	61	Danneberg	Schnectady, NY	191	Hille, Minden, Preußen
Pepper, Maria Louisa Carolina	22, Jan. 1872	9, Nov.	17- -5m-15d		Schnectady, NY	31	
Pepper, Maria Louise	10, May 1894	29, Mar.	71	Dannenberg	Schnectady, NY	310	Hille, Minden, Preußen
Peppor, Charles	24, Sept 1883	1, Sept	31- 4m-23d		South Bend, IN	311	Rambien, Vorpommern
Peppor, Maria	13, Oct. 1892	11, Sept	40		Chicago, IL	654	Schleswig, Schleswig-Holstein
Pergande, Karl Friedrich	26, Nov. 1877	7, Nov.	22		Buffalo, NY	383	Christfeld bei Schlochau, West Preußen
Perlick, Friedrike Caroline	26, May 1879	21, Apr.	59- 3m- 6d	Marzahn	Beaver Dam, WI	167	
Perschbacher, Elisa Catharina	31, Dec. 1877	12, Dec.	38	Bohland	Kewaskum, WI	423	Schaafheim, Hessen
Perschbacher, N. J.	14, Sept 1899	24, Aug.	71		Kewaskum, WI	591	Golditz, Sachsen
Persohn, Albertina Augusta	3, Nov. 1887	20, Oct.	11		Brillion, WI	702	Brillion, Wisconsin
Persohn, Joachim	30, Oct. 1890	1, Oct.	77-10m- 8d		Brillion, WI	702	Neuendorf, Pommern
Pestdorf, Christian	8, Oct. 1857	13, Sept	29		Baltimore, MD	164	Catharinenford, Sachsen
Pestorf, Marie	26, June 1890	9, June	61- 5m-17d		Baltimore, MD	414	Rierenford, Kurhessen
Peter, Amanda	10, Mar. 1898	13, Feb.	16		Milwaukee, WI	159	Milwaukee, Wisconsin
Peter, Barbara	14, Sept 1854	22, Aug.	34		Rockford, IN	148	
Peter, Barbara	18, May 1874	30, Apr.	47- 2m-16d		Jacksonville, IL	159	Kanton Zürich, Schweiz
Peter, Christian	2, Oct. 1876	24, Aug.	50- 6m-18d		St. Louis, MO	319	Blasheim, Lübbeke, Westphalen
Peter, Christian	12, Apr. 1894	24, Mar.	71		Elizabeth, NJ	246	Elsaß
Peter, Emilie	26, Mar. 1896	11, Mar.	52	Becker	Crandon, SD	206	Pommern
Peter, Friedrich	29, Dec. 1873	29, Oct.	56		Kendallville, IN	415	Bernien, Kriwitz, Mecklenburg-Schwerin

Christliche Apologete Death Notices --- 1839 - 1899

Name of Deceased	Notice Date	Death Date	Age	Maiden Name	Page	Place of Death	Place of Birth
Peter, Friedrich	23, Oct. 1846		Inquiry		181	Mt. Vernon, IN	Homburg, Hessen
Peter, Johan	6, May 1867	15, Apr.	40		142	Green Bay, WI	Mecklenburg-Schwerin
Peter, Johannes	6, Nov. 1876	20, Aug.			359	San Francisco, CA	Unterschlatt, Thurgau, Schweiz
Peter, John	30, Apr. 1883	11, Apr.	39- -18d		143	Woodville, OH	Wädenschwil, Zürich, Schweiz
Peter, Katharina	1, Apr. 1886	10, Mar.	84	Haas	7	Bushnell, IL	Sechshelden, Dillenburg, Nassau
Peter, Katharina	28, Jan. 1878	26, Dec.	49	Brinker	31	Lasalle, IL	Sterzhausen, Kurhessen
Peter, Louis Karl	5, Oct. 1899	4, Sept	20		639	New York City, NY	New York
Peter, Margaretha	22, Jan. 1883	28, Dec.	43	Bolly	31	San Francisco, CA	Beringen, Schaffhausen, Schweiz
Peter, Margaretha	9, Aug. 1894	5, July	78- 1m- 6d	Hörner	518	Elizabeth, NJ	Dörnbach, Rheinpfalz Baiern
Peter, Margaretha	2, June 1873	9, May	18- 2m-15d		175	Minneapolis, MN	St. Paul, Minnesota
Peter, Margaretha Barbara	29, Dec. 1898	6, Nov.	74	Vogel	828	Seymour, IN	Hähnlein, Hessen-Darmstadt
Peter, Susanna	30, Sept 1858	8, Sept	17-10m- 4d		156	Rockford, IN	
Peter, Wilhelm	28, Jan. 1842		Inquiry		15	---, IL	
Petering, Martha D.	13, July 1893	26, June	23	Meyer	446	Concordia, MO	
Peterke, Ella Sophia	15, Aug. 1889	28, June	25- 7m-19d	Zörb	526	Ahnapee, WI	
Peterrein, Johan F.A.	31, May 1888	30, Apr.	18		350	Beaver Falls, MN	Sleepy Eye, Minnesota
Peterreins, Justine Wilhelmine	4, Oct. 1888	24, Aug.	25- 4m- 3d		638	Beaver Falls, MN	Wabasha County, Minnesota
Peters, Anna	19, Oct. 1893	13, Sept	27	Schröder	670	Owensville, MO	Gasconade County, Missouri
Peters, Anna Katharine	12, July 1880	22, June	43	Knüttel	223	Lancaster, MO	Hessen-Darmstadt
Peters, Augusta	29, Apr. 1897	10, Apr.	19		271	Denison, IA	Süderditmarschen, Holstein
Peters, Barbara	20, July 1874	29, June	79		231	Elizabeth, NJ	Weißlingen, Elsaß
Peters, Bernardina	29, Oct. 1866	3, Sept	45- 6m		350	Marthasville, MO	Leden, Tecklenburg, Münster, Preußen
Peters, Elisabeth	7, May 1883	17, Apr.	74	Spruth	151		Butow, Mecklenburg-Schwerin
Peters, Elisabeth	18, Jan. 1894	19, Dec.	61- 2m- 1d		46	Waco, NE	Leer, Hannover
Peters, Emilie	24, Oct. 1889	25, Sept	49	Frey	686	Milwaukee, WI	Huffelde, Hinterpommern
Peters, Ernst Heinrich	1, Sept 1887	22, Aug.	88- 5m- 4d		558	Cincinnati, OH	Lienen, Westphalen
Peters, Ferdinand	17, Aug. 1868	26, June	51		263	Marthasville, MO	Magdeburg,
Peters, Friedrich	22, Dec. 1887	4, Dec.	82		814	Scranton, PA	Bissendorf, Hannover
Peters, Friedrich Wilhelm	23, Oct. 1856				172	Jefferson City, MO	Borkhorst, Amt Halle, Minden, Preußen
Peters, J. Conrad	18, Oct. 1880	28, Sept	67		335	Altamont, IL	
Peters, Johan	27, July 1899	8, July	48		479	LaCrosse, WI	Tonden, Schleswig-Holstein
Peters, Julius S.	12, Apr. 1888	28, Mar.	13- 3m- 8d		238	Hopewell, MO	
Peters, Karl	8, Dec. 1898	21, Nov.	69		783	Akron, NY	Gülzon, Stavenhagen, Mecklenburg-Schwerin
Peters, Karl J. F.	19, May 1898	20, Apr.	63		319	Pepin, WI	Mertensdorf, Brandenburg
Peters, Karl Nikolaus	13, July 1899	20, June	60		447	Golden City, MO	St. Clair County, Illinois
Peters, Konrad Ch.	13, Jan. 1898	13, Nov.	29		31	Waco, TX	Waco, Texas
Peters, Kundel	2, Mar. 1863	14, Jan.	29	Braunsreiter	36	Highland, IL	
Peters, Louisa	13, Aug. 1883	28, July	45-11m-17d	Kling	263	Woodville, OH	Bremen, Germany
Peters, Maria Friederika	17, Nov. 1898	24, Oct.	28		735	Golden City, MO	St. Clair County, Illinois
Peters, Oscar	16, July 1896	9, June	23		463	Waco, TX	Waco, Texas
Peters, Rudolph	10, Feb. 1898	19, Jan.	88		95	Elmore, OH	Wald, Zürich, Schweiz
Peters, Sophia	12, June 1890	24, May	60		382	Dietrich, IL	Mecklenburg-Schwerin
Peters, Wilhelmine	8, Dec. 1884	25, Nov.	23		7	Elmore, OH	Brinkhof, Pommern
Petersen, Augustine	15, June 1854	2, June		Buscher	96	Cincinnati, OH	Bremen, Germany
Petersen, Christian	7, Nov. 1864	23, Sept	45- 1m-13d		180	Defiance, OH	Halsen, Minden, Preußen
Petersen, Heinrich	9, Dec. 1897	15, Nov.	71		783	Bushton, KS	Schleswig-Holstein

Christliche Apologete Death Notices --- 1839 - 1899

Name of Deceased	Notice Date	Death Date	Age	Maiden Name	Page	Place of Death	Place of Birth
Petersen, Hulda	5, May 1887	18, Apr.	28	Marquardt	286	Sleepy Eye, MN	Retz, Arnswalde, Neumark, Preußen
Petersen, J. Christian	22, Oct. 1866	4, Oct.	66		342	Cincinnati, OH	Rechtenfleht, Amt Hagen, Hannover
Petersen, Johann D.	15, Jan. 1841		Inquiry		7	Markheim, CD	
Petersen, Margaretha	30, Apr. 1883	11, Apr.	30		143	Fond du Lac, WI	Lindholm, Schleswig-Holstein
Petersen, Mathilda Maria	19, Oct. 1899	6, Oct.	44		671	Nashville, TN	Flensburg, Germany
Petersmeyer, Caroline	25, Dec. 1876	27, Nov.	36- 6m	Ortmeyer	413	Cannon, MN	Barbenhausen, Lippe-Detmold
Petersmeyer, Wilhelmine Dorothea	5, Oct. 1893	5, Sept	42	Meyer	638	Nerstrand, MN	Marthasville, Warren County, Missouri
Peterson, Anna	1, June 1899	27, Apr.	39	Behne	351	Stryker, OH	Barleben, Sachsen
Peterson, Christina	18, June 1847		25- 5m-20d		99	Evansport, OH	
Peterson, Marie	11, Apr. 1889	22, Mar.	74	Bornemann	238	Denver, CO	Katharienenheit, Eiderstätt, Schleswig-Holstein
Petersonn, Sophia	4, Mar. 1886	19, Feb.	72	Hagenböck	7	Cincinnati, OH	Stolzenau, Hannover
Peth, Carolina Regina	17, Aug. 1863	14, July	44- 8m-23d	Moldenhauer	132	Sandusky, OH	Schönwal, Kreis Stolp, Preußen
Peth, Wilhelmina Friederika	9, Apr. 1877	3, Mar.	45	Borlesch	119	Canaan, MO	Bixow, Stolpe, Köslin, HinterPommern
Petmiller, Maria Louisa	11, Dec. 1890	9, Nov.	77	Schreiber	798	Boonville, ---	Uffen, Minden, Westphalen
Petri, (girl)	18, Dec. 1871	27, Nov.	7		407	Dayton, OH	
Petri, Carolina	26, June 1882	10, June	44	Miller	207	Galion, OH	Pistorf, Drulingen, Elsaß
Petri, Dina	7, July 1884	24, June		Schultheis	7	Quincy, IL	Marjos, Kurhessen
Petri, Moses	18, Dec. 1871	27, Nov.	43		407	Dayton, OH	Berks County, Pennsylvania
Petri, Wilhelm Christian	27, July 1899	5, July	34		479	St. Louis, MO	Lawrenceville, Indiana
Petrich, Maria A.	16, Nov. 1893	28, Oct.	30	Hager	734	Morgan, MN	Winnebago County, Wisconsin
Petrich, Rudolph	20, Nov. 1890	12, Sept	35- 1m-12d		750	Meriden, MN	
Petrie, Anna Louisa	27, Sept 1894	6, Sept	24		630	Wichita, KS	Lawrenceville, Indiana
Petrie, Kaspar	29, Sept 1884	12, Sept	70		7	Mt. Vernon, NY	Sinsheim, Württemberg
Petrowski, Lena	28, May 1883	8, May	12- 6m-11d		7	Menomonie, WI	
Petry, Elisabeth	24, Oct. 1881	15, Oct.			343	Shelbyville, KY	
Petry, J.C.	18, Aug. 1862	2, Aug.	47		132	Louisville, KY	Zweibrücken, Rheinkreis Baiern
Petry, Louis	13, Apr. 1899	14, Mar.	44		239	Lemars, IA	Hessen-Darmstadt
Petter , Catharine	28, Feb. 1895	11, Jan.	64	Messerschmidt	142	Minneapolis, MN	Fambach, Kurhessen
Petter, Louise	26, May 1884	7, May	19		7	St. Paul, Minnesota	St. Paul, Minnesota
Petter, Rebekka Dorothea	29, Aug. 1889		86- 5m-25d		558	St. Paul, MN	Fambach, Kurhessen
Petter, Verena	25, Sept 1865	23, Aug.	54	Galtsche	156	Woodville, OH	Obereinach, Aargau, Schweiz
Petter, Wilhelm	19, Apr. 1894	24, Mar.	67		262	Minneapolis, MN	Fambach, Kurhessen
Petterman, Henriette	14, Feb. 1895	24, Jan.	46	Riechers	110	Covington, KY	Cincinnati, Hamilton County, Ohio
Petzhold, Wilhelm Edward	20, Oct. 1898	23, Sept	21		671	Ellis Grove, IL	Ellis Grove, Illinois
Petzinger, Dorothea	10, Aug. 1863	13, June	18		128	Burlington, IN	Langenheim, Friedberg, Hessen-Darmstadt
Petzke, Daniel Heinrich Gottfried	9, May 1889	5, Apr.	78		302	Kenosha, WI	Müttrin, Köslin, Pommern
Petzke, Friederika	24, July 1890	3, June	53	Zybell	478	Kenosha, WI	Zodtkow, Belgard, Hinterpommern
Petzinger, Elisabeth	5, June 1871	8, Feb.	48	Kopp	183	Pleasant Grove, IA	Zügenberg, Hessen-Darmstadt
Peuscher, Christina	25, Apr. 1881	31, Mar.	43	Diefenbach	135	Valparaiso, IN	
Pfaff, Andreas	20, Feb. 1896	26, Jan.	84- -14d		126	St. Paul, MN	
Pfaff, Elisabeth Margaretha	23, Dec. 1872	7, Nov.	70	Klösner	415	Dayton, OH	Katzenfurth, Wetzlar, Koblenz, Preußen
Pfaff, Jessie Ames	11, May 1899	7, Apr.	19		302	Salem, MN	Menomonie, Wisconsin
Pfaff, Johannes	22, May 1876	4, May	52- 6m-15d		167	Springfield, IL	
Pfaff, Katharina	1, July 1897	3, June	83	Decklar	414	St. Paul, MN	Quirnbach, Rheinpfalz Baiern
Pfaff, Phil.	18, Sept 1890	24, Aug.	71		606	Scranton, PA	Aslar, Coblenz, Preußen
Pfaff, Sophia Theresia	25, Aug. 1898	29, July	76	Schlicher	543	Berea, OH	Fischbach, Rheinpfalz Baiern

Christliche Apologete Death Notices --- 1839 - 1899

Name of Deceased	Notice Date	Death Date	Age	Page	Maiden Name	Place of Death	Place of Birth
Pfaff, Wilhelm	26, Jan. 1863	30, Dec.	18	16		Dayton, OH	Ehringshausen, RheinPreußen
Pfaffenbach, Franz	9, June 1879	20, May	34	183		Chicago, IL	Elbersdorf, Kurhessen
Pfaffenberg, Catharina	15, Feb. 1864	24, Jan.	67	28	Kramp	Seymour, IN	Betzmannberg, Kuhlenbach, Baiern
Pfaffenberger, Andreas	28, Apr. 1892	11, Mar.	93-11m-20d	270		Seymour, IN	Forstlahm, Kuhlmbach, Baiern
Pfaffenberger, Elisabeth	6, Feb. 1871	16, Jan.	58	47		Seymour, IN	Baiern
Pfaffenberger, Joseph	12, Jan. 1863	3, Dec.	24-11m-15d	8		Seymour, IN	Pittsburg, Pennsylvania
Pfaffenberger, Louise	20, Mar. 1876	2, Mar.	58	95		Seymour, IN	Liinsburg, Amt Welpe, Hannover
Pfaffenberger, Maria	20, Apr. 1854	6, Apr.		64		Rockford, IN	
Pfäffle, Anna Katharina	1, Dec. 1892	28, Oct.	41	766	Schröder	Aurora, IL	Salzungen, Sachsen-Weimar
Pfäffle, Johan Dietrich	26, Jan. 1880	12, Jan.	83- -11d	31		Aurora, IL	Gemmingen, Baden
Pfäffle, Sophie	22, Dec. 1873	8, Dec.	42	407		Aurora, IL	Bornum, Braunschweig
Pfankuchen, Konrad	24, May 1888	12, May	66	334		Madison, WI	Heiligenrode, Hessen-Kassel
Pfannekuchen, Otto Carl Heinrich	11, Feb. 1897	22, Jan.	59	94		Ritzville, WA	Braunschweig
Pfannschmidt, Eva Elisabeth	18, June 1877	2, June	83	199		Quincy, IL	Mühlhausen, Thüringen
Pfannschmidt, Herman Christian	4, May 1899	18, Apr.	74	287		Quincy, IL	Mühlhausen, Thüringen
Pfanschmidt, Charlotte	24, Nov. 1898	24, Oct.	72	751	Meise	Quincy, IL	Schötmar, Preußen
Pfarr, Philipp	14, Apr. 1848	10, Feb.	65- 5m	63		St. Charles, MO	Lampsheim, Rheinkreis Baiern
Päthscher, Louise	26, Jan. 1874		33- 7m-20d	31	Kind	Osceola, OH	
Pfeffer, Pauline Friederike	27, July 1899	9, July	53	479	Mitbauer	Stitzer, WI	Zeitz, Sachsen
Pfefferle, Katharina	19, Sept 1870	5, Sept	40	303	Wagner	Piqua, OH	Königsbach, Baden
Pfeifer, Adam	25, Sept 1871	4, Sept	68	311		Mt. Vernon, IN	Miesenbach bei Landstuhl, Rheinkreis Baiern
Pfeifer, Anna	3, Apr. 1882	18, Feb.	76- 1m-26d	111	Strauth	Fond du Lac, WI	Klein-Gladenbach, Hessen-Darmstadt
Pfeifer, Anna	15, Apr. 1852		31	64	Eßlinger	Dubuque, IA	Weiden, Sulz, Württemberg
Pfeifer, Anna Maria	12, Oct. 1863	21, Sept	80- -20d	164		Chillicothe, OH	Lambertheim, Heppenheim, Hessen-Darmstadt
Pfeifer, Anton	2, Apr. 1877	9, Mar.	47- 3m-11d	111		Indianapolis, IN	Hochsaal, Waldshut, Baden
Pfeifer, Carolina	19, June 1871	21, May	14- -23d	199		Furnace, OH	
Pfeifer, Caroline	16, May 1889	14, Apr.	84- 1m- 8d	318		Rochester, NY	Stahlberg, Rheinkreis Baiern
Pfeifer, Christina	26, July 1880	6, July	76- 8m-11d	239	Hooß	Indianapolis, IN	Kleinsachsenheim, Württemberg
Pfeifer, Elisabetha	1, Oct. 1857	12, Aug.	64	160		Mt. Vernon, IN	Bonweiler, Rheinkreis Baiern
Pfeifer, Eva	21, Nov. 1881	22, Oct.	75- 9m- 7d	375		Scranton, PA	Rothenburg, Kurhessen
Pfeifer, Friedrich	13, Sept 1880	28, Aug.	54	295		Wyandotte, KS	Alsenberg, Calw, Württemberg
Pfeifer, Hanna Sophia	7, May 1891	2, Apr.	52- 1m-16d	302		Wheeling, WV	Kleinkundorf, Sachsen-Weimar
Pfeifer, Heinrich	10, Jan. 1876	24, Dec.	74- 3m-18d	15		Forest, WI	Niedereisenhausen, Hessen-Darmstadt
Pfeifer, Jakob	3, Apr. 1846		Inquiry	55		Cincinnati, OH	RheinBischofsheim, Baden
Pfeifer, Johan	13, Jan. 1887	17, Dec.	72	30		St. Paul, MN	Widem, Neckarsulm, Württemberg
Pfeifer, Johan Heinrich	12, Mar. 1883	27, Feb.	55-11m	87		Wheeling, WV	Kleinreinsdorf, Reuß
Pfeifer, Johanna Louisa	18, Feb. 1858	18, Dec.	15	28		German Creek, IA	Kleinsachsenheim, Vaihingen, Württemberg
Pfeifer, Louise	28, Aug. 1871	9, July	46- 1m	279	Freistein	Quincy, IL	Wieda, Braunschweig
Pfeifer, Maria Elisabeth	18, Feb. 1858	17, Jan.	13	28		German Creek, IA	Kleinsachsenheim, Vaihingen, Württemberg
Pfeifer, Maria Emilie	16, Mar. 1899	18, Feb.	47	175		Piqua, OH	Sidney, Shelby County, Ohio
Pfeifer, Nikolaus	25, Oct. 1880	6, Oct.	57	343		Chillicothe, OH	Lumbertheim, Hessen-Darmstadt
Pfeifer, Paulus	5, Dec. 1861	21, Oct.		196		Baltimore, MD	
Pfeiff, Conrad	12, Apr. 1875	24, Mar.	64- 5m-11d	119		Burlington, IA	Geilshausen, Hessen
Pfeiff, Johan Heinrich	6, Feb. 1896	29, Dec.	88	94		Burlington, IA	Geilshausen, Hessen-Darmstadt
Pfeiffer, Barbara	7, Jan. 1884	21, Dec.	63	7	Hering	Indianapolis, IN	Schweigersdorf, Baiern
Pfeiffer, Christoph	26, Mar. 1866	8, Mar.	31	102		Marietta, OH	Kleinsachsenheim, Vaihingen, Württemberg

Christliche Apologete Death Notices -- 1839 - 1899

Name of Deceased	Notice Date	Death Date	Age	Page	Maiden Name	Place of Death	Place of Birth
Pfeiffer, Elisabeth	16, Feb. 1893	14, Jan.	75	110	Ebel	Burlington, IA	Ebelsheim, Rheinkreis Baiern
Pfeiffer, Elisabeth	30, June 1898	3, June	74	415	Miller	Marrs, IN	Winzenbach, Elsaß
Pfeiffer, Emilie Karoline	3, Mar. 1887	9, Feb.	16	142		Quincy, IL	Quincy, Illinois
Pfeiffer, Georg	2, Mar. 1893	10, Feb.	67	142		Cincinnati, OH	Rheinzabern, Rheinpfalz Baiern
Pfeiffer, Gottlob	25, Apr. 1861	14, Mar.	11- 5m- 4d	68		German Creek, IA	Kleinsachsenheim, Vaihingen, Württemberg
Pfeiffer, Jakob Friedrich	28, Jan. 1886	6, Jan.	74	7		Mt. Pleasant, IA	KleinSachsenheim, Vaihingen, Württemberg
Pfeiffer, Karl	13, May 1897	9, Apr.	71	303		Quincy, IL	Wilda, Braunschweig
Pfeiffer, Katharine	13, Aug. 1847	31, July	22	131		Indianapolis, IN	Sonnenberg bei Wiesbaden, Nassau
Pfeiffer, Lena	24, Mar. 1887	2, Mar.	24	190	Thöle	St. Paul, MN	Dakota County, Minnesota
Pfeiffer, Lena	4, Sept 1876	2, Aug.		287	Vick	Chicago, IL	Hamburg, Germany
Pfeiffer, Lydia	9, Jan. 1890	14, Dec.	25	30	Benz	Charles City, IA	Palatine, Cook County, Illinois
Pfeiffer, Margaretha	19, Feb. 1891	11, Jan.		126		Mt. Vernon, IN	Oberschüpp, Boxberg, Baden
Pfeiffer, Maria Agnes	5, Mar. 1891	1, Feb.	73	158	Meyer	Mt. Pleasant, IA	Kleinsachsenheim, Vaihingen, Württemberg
Pfeiffer, Maria Anna	29, June 1874	14, June	25- 6m	207	Himmler	Terre Haute, IN	
Pfeiffer, Maria Catharina	1, July 1878	19, June	58- 9m	207		Terre Haute, IN	Widdern, Neckars-Ulm, Württemberg
Pfeiffer, Martin	6, Oct. 1887	31, Aug.	80-11m-24d	638		Charles City, IA	Bergfelden, Sulz, Württemberg
Pfeiffer, Peter	14, June 1849	16, May	38	96		Pomeroy, OH	Edigheim, Rheinkreis Baiern
Pfeiffer, Sarah	13, Sept 1880	20, July	43	295	Esch	Charlestown, IN	Holmes County, Ohio
Pfeiffer, Sophia	9, Sept 1886	25, Aug.	35	7	Sekander	Charles City, IA	Mecklenburg-Schwerin
Pfeiffer, Walter Louis	9, Feb. 1893	10, Jan.	23	94		Owatonna, MN	Jonesboro, Grand County, Indiana
Pfeil, (child)	23, Sept 1852	6, Sept		156		Buffalo, NY	
Pfeil, Margaretha Barbara	5, Sept 1895	13, Aug.	82	574	Schneider	Pittsburg, PA	Darmstadt, Hessen-Darmstadt
Pfeil, Maria	23, Sept 1852	9, Sept		156		Buffalo, NY	
Pfeil, Maria Magdalena	26, Mar. 1891	1, Mar.	35	206	Hierholzer	Bracken, tX	Comal County, Texas
Pferdeort, Doris Sophia	29, May 1851	6, Apr.	44- -21d	88		Pittsburg, PA	Lippe-Detmold
Pferdeort, August	6, Aug. 1866	28, Jan.	39	254		Monroe Co, OH	Center County, Pennsylvania
Pfetscher, Israel	11, Mar. 1897	19, Feb.	79	159	Reiff	Galion, OH	Hamilton, Butler County, Ohio
Pfetzing, Bertha E.	26, Jan. 1893	28, Dec.	31	62	Koch	Hamilton, OH	
Pfetzinger, Barbara	23, Apr. 1883	1, Apr.		135		Greenville, OH	
Pfeufer, Anna Barbara	9, Sept 1858	23, Aug.	67	144		Laughery, IN	Kleinlangheim, Baiern
Pfeute, Fritz	12, July 1894	18, June	31	454		New Ulm, MN	Guggesberg, Bern, Schweiz
Pfiffner, Lydia	3, Sept 1883	9, Aug.	18- 7m-26d	287		Delaware, OH	
Pfister, Elisabeth	4, June 1891	19, May	56	366	Weick	Cincinnati, OH	Bischofsheim, Baden
Pfister, Eva	15, Aug. 1889	27, July	59	526	Bindner	Aurora, IL	Wittenweiher, Baden
Pfister, Heinrich	22, Aug. 1895	31, July	75	542		Aurora, IL	Heidenheim, Württemberg
Pfister, Maria Dorothea	29, Nov. 1869	26- 1m-16d		383	Kompst	Madison, IN	Niederdorla, Mühlhausen, Preußen
Pfläging, Katharine	5, Aug. 1886	19, July	57	7		Omaha, NE	Friesenheim, Laar, Baden
Pflaume, Heinrich	25, Feb. 1897	15, Jan.	65	127		Arlington, MN	Falldorf bei Floda, Westphalen
Pflaumer, (girl)	16, Oct. 1871		12- 5m	335		Hills Fork, ---	
Pfleiderer, Katharine	4, Aug. 1898	14, July	70	495	Rösch	Saginaw, MI	Stuttgart, Württemberg
Pfleiderer, Louise	17, Nov. 1873	8, Aug.	65	367		Louisville, KY	Bönnigheim, Besigheim, Württemberg
Pflieger, Elisabeth	5, Jan. 1854	12, Aug.	25- 7m	4		Columbus, OH	Dauphin County, Ohio
Pflückhahn, Auguste	9, Apr. 1866	8, Feb.		118		Wyandotte, KS	
Pflückhahn, Dorothea	16, Oct. 1876	26, Sept	65-11m	335		Wyandotte, KS	
Pflug, Anna Margaretha	21, Aug. 1871	28, July	81	271		Marine City, MI	Joelsheim, Elsaß
Pflug, Georg P.	27, Oct. 1879	13, Oct.	51- 1m-28d	343		Pittsburg, PA	Oberbeschdorf, Elsaß

- 382 -

Christliche Apologete Death Notices --- 1839 - 1899

Name of Deceased	Notice Date	Death Date	Age	Maiden Name	Page	Place of Death	Place of Birth
Pflug, Johan	21, Feb. 1870	Jan.	18		63	Birmingham, PA	Barchfeld, Schmalkalden, Kurhessen
Pflug, Margaretha Elisabeth	21, Feb. 1870	3, Feb.	35	Erbe	63	Birmingham, PA	Oberseebach, Weißenburg, Elsaß
Pflug, Martin	14, Apr. 1873	20, Mar.	83- 8m-18d		119	Marine City, MI	Rochester, New York
Pfluger, Anna Frida	27, Jan. 1898	18, Dec.	21		63	Rochester, NY	Bremen, Germany
Pflüger, Elise Johanna	31, Jan. 1895	6, Jan.	83	Rasch	78	Covington, KY	Bremen, Germany
Pflüger, Ferdinand	11, Mar. 1886	25, Feb.	42		7	Covington, KY	Bremen, Germany
Pflüger, Georg Gottfried	8, June 1893	17, May	51		366	Covington, KY	Scheng-Lengsfeld, Kurhessen
Pfroeder, Elisabeth	26, May 1892	4, May	61	Messer	334	St. Louis, MO	Thüringen, Württemberg
Pfrömder, (Mr)	18, Feb. 1897	14, Jan.	71		111	St. Louis, MO	Emmerdingen, Baden
Pfrommer, Gottlieb	25, Sept 1871	30, Aug.	69- 6m-27d		311	Marion, OH	Bringhausen, Kurhessen
Pfuhl, Gertraud	2, Apr. 1866	27, Jan.	66		110	Lafayette, IN	
Pfuhl, John	4, Feb. 1886	6, Jan.	90		7	Lafayette, IN	
Pfund, Jakob	25, June 1896	8, June	46		415	Hamilton, OH	Lenk, Ober-Simmenthal, Bern, Schweiz
Pfund, Maria	3, Jan. 1895	7, Dec.	32		14	Oak Park, IL	Canton Bern, Schweiz
Pfundheller, Bertha	19, Nov. 1891	24, Oct.	44		750	Rockford, IA	Plettmin, Pommern
Pfundheller, Franz	2, Jan. 1890	11, Dec.	24		14	Hebron, IA	Milwaukee, Wisconsin
Pfundheller, Heinrich	12, Feb. 1891	20, Jan.	73		110	Flood Creek, IA	Rehmer bei Colberg, Pommern
Pfundheller, Maria	19, Mar. 1883		62- 8m- 6d	Gaulke	95	Flood Creek, IA	Nessin bei Kolburg, Pommern
Pfundheller, Mathilda	21, June 1880	5, June	19		199	Flood Creek, IA	
Phetzing, Alfred A.	4, Mar. 1897	1, Feb.	43		143	San Francisco, CA	Pomeroy, Meigs County, Ohio
Phetzing, Katharine	26, Dec. 1895	13, Nov.	37	Gabel	828	Lexington, MO	Millersburg, Indiana
Phetzing, Salome Katharine	12, June 1846	1, June	11m-14d		95	Lawrenceburg, IN	
Philipp, Louise	22, Mar. 1888	16, Feb.	28	Piehler	190	Beardstown, IL	Wheeling, West Virginia
Phillips, August	15, May 1890	21, Apr.	69		318	Toledo, OH	Lauenburg, Preußen
Phinster, Johan	18, Feb. 1884	1, Feb.	54		7	Bible Grove, IL	Krosern, Sachsen-Altenburg
Piederit, Caroline	21, June 1880	26, Mar.	30		199	Yellow Creek, IL	Langenholzhausen, Lippe-Detmold
Piederit, Charlotte	19, Feb. 1872	2, Feb.	74	Stock	63	Warrenton, MO	Hohenhausen, Lippe-Detmold
Piederit, Charlotte Carolina	29, Mar. 1888	23, Feb.	18		206	Yellow Creek, IL	
Piederit, Simon	19, Feb. 1877	31, Jan.	40		63	Yellow Creek, IL	Langenholzhausen, Vahrenholz, Lippe-Detmold
Piehler, Anna	8, Oct. 1896	20, Sept	38- 3m-23d	Greiner	655	St. Louis, MO	Burlington, Iowa
Piehler, Hugo	14, July 1898	9, June	12		447	Burlington, IA	Emden, Illinois
Piehler, Karl	14, Apr. 1898	21, Mar.	82		239	Wheeling, WV	Kulmitzsch, Weidau, Sachsen-Weimar
Piehn, Maria Dorothea	7, Mar. 1870	13, Jan.	40		79	Springfield, IL	Kölzow, Mecklenburg-Schwerin
Piepenburg, Ernestine	26, July 1894	7, July	58		486	Lemars, IA	Wangerien, Germany
Pieper, Anna Maria	28, Dec. 1893	15, Nov.			828	Warner, MO	Renkhausen, Bühne, Preußen
Pierstorff, Louise	22, Sept 1898	5, Sept	68	Frahm	607	Madison, WI	Mettel, Mecklenburg-Schwerin
Pietrowski, Friedrich	28, Apr. 1887	17, Apr.	65-11m-12d		270	Menomonie, WI	Peterkau, Rosenberg, Preußen
Pietsch, Ernestine	6, Oct. 1887	23, Sept	45	Krüger	638	Wrayville, IL	Schleykon, Ukermark
Pietsch, Johannes	16, Feb. 1860	27, Jan.	19- 6m- 6d		28	Lakeport, OH	
Pigolowske, August	24, Oct. 1889	14, Sept	35	Dagit	686	Montague, MI	Ostroßke, Posen
Pilgrim, Elisabeth	8, Mar. 1875	26, Feb.	30- 4m-24d		79	Summerfield, IL	
Piltz, Johan Wilhelm	18, Oct. 1894	17, Sept	76		678	Dalton, MO	Brennungstein, Preußen
Piltz, Maria Elisabeth	27, Dec. 1869	14, Nov.	48	Fieselmann	415	Brunswick, MO	Hille, Minden, Preußen
Pingel, Christian	2, Oct. 1876	14, Sept	62		319	DeWitt, MI	Domfühl, Mecklenburg-Schwerin
Pingel, Emma Mathilde	27, June 1889	25, Apr.	18		414	DeWitt, MI	Riley, Clinton County, Michigan
Pinger, Adam	20, Nov. 1871	31, Oct.	59		375	Cincinnati, OH	Framersheim, Alzei, Hessen-Darmstadt

Christliche Apologete Death Notices --- 1839 - 1899

Name of Deceased	Notice Date	Death Date	Age	Page	Maiden Name	Place of Death	Place of Birth
Pinger, Anton	21, Mar. 1881	27, Feb.	66- 2m- 4d	95		Columbus, OH	Framershausen, Alzei, Hessen-Darmstadt
Pinger, Apollonia	25, Feb. 1867	5, Feb.	52	62		Cincinnati, OH	Bechtingen bei Landau, Rheinkreis Baiern
Pinger, Caroline	22, Feb. 1875	8, Feb.	52	63	Helwig	St. Joseph, MO	Wilmenroth, Nassau
Pinger, Charles	13, May 1886	17, Apr.	24- -19d	7		Minneapolis, MN	
Pinger, Christian	10, Apr. 1871	21, Mar.	86- 6m-13d	119		St. Joseph, MO	Bechtelsheim, Hessen-Darmstadt
Pinger, Emilie	11, Feb. 1884	23, Jan.	56	7		St. Joseph, MO	
Pinger, Jacob	16, Oct. 1890	7, Sept	74- 4m-14d	670		Peoria, IL	Framersheim, Hessen-Darmstadt
Pinger, Magdalene	6, May 1852	23, Apr.	57	76	Metzger	Cincinnati, OH	Odernheim, Hessen-Darmstadt
Pinger, Maria	21, Jan. 1884	25, Dec.	60	7		Peoria, IL	Rheinkreis Baiern
Pinger, Maria Elisabeth	9, May 1850	17, Apr.	2- 6m	76		Cincinnati, OH	
Pinger, Minnie	2, Dec. 1886	11, Nov.	24	7	Sauerwein	St. Joseph, MO	
Pinger, Sarah	3, July 1876	1, June	61	215	Bottenberg	Columbus, OH	
Pinger, Willie	28, June 1875	11, June	18- 9m- 9d	207		St. Joseph, MO	
Pinnow, Dorothea Luise	23, Nov. 1899	9, Nov.	76- -11d	751	Elske	Oconomowoc, WI	Warsin, Vorpommern
Pinnschmidt, Conrad	21,May 1883	12, Mar.	60	167		Baltimore, MD	Schönstadt, Marburg, Kurhessen
Pinow, Gottlieb	3, Nov. 1887	11, Oct.	65	702		Oconomowoc, WI	Kleinlotzkow, Brandenburg
Pinschmidt, Conrad	13, Aug. 1896	10, July	34	527		Baltimore, MD	Baltimore, Maryland
Pinschmiedt, Katharina	21, Nov. 1864	4, Sept	23	188		Baltimore, MD	Schönstadt, Kurhessen
Piper, August	6, July 1899	29, May	80	431		St. Louis, MO	Melle, Germany
Piper, Maria Katharina	2, July 1891	9, June	69	430		Sidney, OH	Hessen-Darmstadt
Pistor, Charlotte Louise	16, Sept 1886	24, Aug.	54- 8m- 9d	7	Thurmann	Lawrence, KS	Lippstadt, Westphalen
Pistorius, Catharina	2, May 1895	7, Apr.	33	286	Bohlander	Moweaqua, IL	New Memphis, Illinois
Pistorius, Franky	19, Jan. 1874	21, Dec.	3	23		Burlington, IA	
Pistorius, Rosa	19, Jan. 1874	16, Dec.	22- 7m-16d	23	Hofmeier	Burlington, IA	
Pistorius, Sophie	31, Oct. 1881	14, Oct.	38- 3m-20d	351	Hofmeier	Burlington, IA	
Pitmeier, Barbara	3, Dec. 1866	13, Nov.	34	390		Evansville, IN	
Pitschmann, Lina	4, Jan. 1894	13, Dec.	27	14	Brandt	Brenham, TX	Bear Creek, Harris County, Texas
Pitt, Mina	3, Apr. 1890	4, Mar.	26-10m-16d	222	Bartels	Kewaskum, WI	Klein-Sabow, Hinterpommern
Plagemann, Elisabeth	13, May 1872	5, Apr.	41- 2m-22d	159	Köhler	Waseca, MN	Alt-Rüdnitz, Preußen
Plagge, Wilhelm	22, Apr. 1872	10, Mar.	60	135		Jackson, MO	Bornumhausen, Seesen, Braunschweig
Plamböck, Pauline	15, Nov. 1888	16, Oct.	68	734	Klasen	Laporte, IN	Teterow, Mecklenburg-Schwerin
Planert, Caroline	6, Sept 1880	25, Aug.	27	287	Illefeld	Green Bay, WI	Mecklenburg-Strelitz
Planet, Louise	10, June 1858	13, Apr.	66	92		Terre Haute, IN	
Plank , Sophia Wilhemina Auguste	26, Oct. 1893		35	686		Warsaw, IL	Eutmersleben, Sachsen
Plank, Adam	5, Dec. 1864	6, Nov.	46	196		Canton, MO	Zwingenberg, Hessen
Plank, Alvine Sophia Maria	16, July 1896	28, June	36	463		Warsaw, IL	Alt-Mersleben, Sachsen
Plank, Dora	22, Oct. 1891	19, Sept	54	686	Ortlepp	Chicago, IL	Friedrichroda, Sachsen-Gotha
Plank, Jakob	25, Apr. 1864	13, Mar.	16	68		Lewis Co, MO	
Plank, James	16, Nov. 1874	3, Nov.	30	367		Giard, IA	
Plank, William Henry	24, May 1855	18, Apr.	16- 5m-21d	84		Monona, IA	
Plant, Sophia	23, June 1898	5, June	37	399	Krüger	West Superior, WI	Mandschaunk, Pennsylvania
Plapperd, Maria	15, Nov. 1869	30, Sept	44	367		Des Moines, IA	Reichholzheim, Hessen-Darmstadt
Plaswirth, Arnoldine	7, Apr. 1892	20, Mar.	67	222	Lange	New Orleans, LA	Westerkappeln, Münster, Preußen
Plaswirth, Peter	13, Aug. 1896	8, July	76	527		New Orleans, LA	Beckrum bei Neukirchen, Westphalen
Plate, Anna Sophia	7, July 1892	6, June	65	430	Meyer	Jersey City, NJ	Neudorf, Braunschweig
Plate, Georg	28, July 1898	10, July	17	479		Crandon, SD	Chicago, Cook County, Illinois

Christliche Apologete Death Notices --- 1839 - 1899

Name of Deceased	Notice Date	Death Date	Age	Page	Maiden Name	Place of Death	Place of Birth
Plate, Heinrich	4, Feb. 1892	22, Dec.	85	78		Newark, NJ	Varel, Oldenburg
Plate, Heinrich Dietrich	19, Mar. 1896	18, Sept	58	190		Arlington, NJ	Varrel, Oldenburg
Plate, Margaretha	31, Oct. 1864	20, Aug.	14- 7m- 7d	176		New York, NY	
Plath, Annie	14, Oct. 1886	19, Sept	18	7		Schnectady, NY	Hille, Minden, Preußen
Plath, Caroline	16, Mar. 1893	23, Feb.		174	Schwentker	Schnectady, NY	
Plath, Hattie Louisa	31, Dec. 1891	16, June	17- 5m	846		Schnectady, NY	
Platt, Albert	16, July 1891	27, June	52	462		Crow River, MN	Buchhorscht, Hinterpommern
Platt, Louise	23, June 1898	21, Apr.	41	399	Voltz	Elgin, IL	Rothheim bei Gießen, Hessen
Platt, Maria Magdalena	8, Sept 1879	25, July	68	287	Dudenhöfer	Bradford, IN	Radheim, Gießen, Hessen-Darmstadt
Platte, Rankin Wilhelm	11, May 1893	20, Apr.	71- 5m-16d	302		San Francisco, CA	Oldersum, Hannover
Platz, Andreas	18, Jan. 1894	25, Dec.	62	46		Delaware, OH	Maylhammer, Rheinpfalz Baiern
Platz, Maria	23, Aug. 1875	3, July	50	271		New York City, NY	Schönstein, Kurhessen
Plautz, Albert J.W.	8, Feb. 1875	11, Jan.	20- 5m-11d	47		Oconto, WI	
Plautz, Charlotte	23, Dec. 1897	1, Dec.	86	815	Apenfuß	Chase, WI	Felingsdorf, Pommern
Plautz, Johan Gottlieb	10, Dec. 1883	21, Nov.	72- 5m-10d	7		Green Bay, WI	Rützow, Pommern
Plentl, Martha	7, Apr. 1892	9, Mar.		222	Thülemeyer	Freyburg, TX	
Pletsch, Anna Elisabeth	9, Aug. 1888	24, July	58- 9m- 1d	510	Immel	Columbus, OH	Schiffelbach, Kurhessen
Pletsch, August	27, Aug. 1896	30, July	51	559		Rochester, NY	Hochstetten, Baden
Pletsch, Johannes	22, Aug. 1850	2, Aug.		136		Pittsburg, PA	
Pletsch, Martin	22, Aug. 1850	2, Aug.		136		Pittsburg, PA	
Pletscher, J. C.	23, Feb. 1899	28, Jan.	50	127		Galion, OH	
Pletzing, John (Rev)	4, Oct. 1894	21, Aug.	79- 9m- 8d	646		Lexington, MO	Stärkselshausen, Rothenburg, Kurhessen
Plier, Matthias	29, July 1867	3, July	24	238		German Creek, IA	Part, Arlon, Belgium
Plinke, Conrad F.	9, Jan. 1865	17, Oct.	35	8		Ahnapee, WI	Ostermunzel, Amt Wenzdorf, Hannover
Plitt, Georg	10, Feb. 1898	30, Nov.	76	95		Wapello, IA	Bidenkopf, Hessen-Darmstadt
Plitt, Rosa Marie	10, Feb. 1898	2, Jan.	73	95		Wapello, IA	Kanton Bern, Schweiz
Pitzkow, Emilie	9, Nov. 1893	7, Sept	61	718		Wausau, WI	Pommern
Ploch, August P.	8, Mar. 1875	20, Feb.	23	79		Cannelton, IN	Cincinnati, Hamilton County, Ohio
Ploch, Casper	28, Jan. 1892	1, Jan.	70- 8m-29d	62		Cannelton, IN	Lindenstruth, Hessen-Darmstadt
Ploch, Casper	7, Dec. 1863	2, Oct.	18- 8m- 5d	196		Cannelton, IN	Lindenstruth, Hessen-Darmstadt
Ploch, Georg	18, May 1874	30, Apr.	83	159		Cannelton, IN	Bernshausen, Kreis Alsfeld, Hessen
Ploch, Heinrich	25, July 1864	5, May	20-11m	120		Cannelton, IN	Niederohmen, Kreis Grünberg, Hessen
Ploch, Johannes	15, Feb. 1894	23, Jan.	78	110		Cannelton, IN	Lindenstruth, Hessen-Darmstadt
Plocher, Thomas & Jakob	29, May 1840		Inquiry	83		Pittsburg, PA	Holzhausen am Neckar, Sulz, Württemberg
Plock, Dorothea Elisabeth	12, Aug. 1897	5, July	78	511	Drathring	Burlington, IA	Pelefritz, Gardelegen, Magdeburg, Preußen
Plock, Heinrich	3, Oct. 1895	28, Aug.	80	638		Burlington, IA	Zobbenitz, Braunschweig
Ploeger, Friedrich Wilhelm	29, Apr. 1886	4, Apr.	53	7		Concordia, MO	Hegen bei Bielefeld, Westphalen
Ploetz, Bertha	4, Aug. 1884	17, July		7	Ulrich	Le Sueur, MN	Fischenhagen, Kamin, Pommern
Plotow, Louis	7, Oct. 1878	28, Sept	66	319		Lawrenceburg, IN	Berlin, Preußen
Plüddemann, Karoline F. W.	3, Aug. 1893	15, June	56	494	Kolbe	Marine City, MI	Greifenhagen, Pommern
Plümer, Franziska	28, July 1898	19, June		479	Leimkühler	Owensville, MO	Dissen, Westphalen
Plünneke, Conrad (Rev)	17, June 1897	13, May	78	382		Hedwigs Hill, TX	Klein-Lafferde, Peine, Hannover
Plünneke, Elise	23, Dec. 1878	2, Dec.	23	407	Bradenberg	Llano, TX	Evansville, Indiana
Plünneke, Sophie	27, Jan. 1898	9, Jan.	74	63	Leifester	Hedwigs Hill, TX	Breistedt, Salders, Braunschweig
Pochert, Friedrich Wilhelm	1, May 1871	26, Mar.	72	143		Detroit, MI	Goldlaudern bei Suhl, Preußen
Poertner, Anna Maria	4, Oct. 1880	23, Aug.	26	319		Milwaukee, WI	Milwaukee, Wisconsin

Christliche Apologete Death Notices --- 1839 - 1899

Name of Deceased	Notice Date	Death Date	Age	Page	Maiden Name	Place of Death	Place of Birth
Pofahl, Friederike Wilhelmine	6, Apr. 1899	12, Mar.	77	223	Zibell	Bristol, WI	Burzlaff, Belgard, Preußen
Poggenpohl, Anna Maria	6, Nov. 1882	24, Oct.	62	359	Herchenhahn	Iowa City, IA	Ober-Elßbach, Baiern
Pohle, Carolina	11, Apr. 1864	21, Mar.	23-2m	60	Berg	Cattelsville, MO	
Pohle, Louisa Friederika	1, Dec. 1887	8, Nov.	16- 6m-14d	766		Pittsburg, PA	Flein, Heilbronn, Württemberg
Pohle, Sophia	15, Mar. 1888	10, Feb.	42	174	Bayer	Pittsburg, PA	Feldheim, Hausberga, Minden, Preußen
Pöhler, Christina	17, Nov. 1879	28, Oct.	59	367	Schröder	Nashville, IL	Hille, Minden, Preußen
Pohlman, Christian	1, Sept 1887	13, July	58- 6m-13d	558		Schnectady, NY	
Pohlman, Elisabetha	12, July 1849	26, June	50	112		St. Louis, MO	
Pohlmann, Christian Eduard	19, Sept 1889	27, Mar.	21	606		Amsterdam, NY	
Pohlmann, Fr.	22, Apr. 1897	9, Mar.	80	255		Drake, MO	Lippe-Detmold
Pohlmann, Heinrich	4, July 1870	22, June	21	215		Berea, OH	Hagenburg, Lippe-Schaumburg
Pöhlmann, Simon Wilhelm	11, June 1883	20, May	45	191		Jacksonville, IL	Kulmbach, Oberfranken, Baiern
Pohlmann, Sophia	31, May 1869	7, Feb.	19	175	Thiele	Manitowoc, WI	Cedarburgh, Wisconsin
Poland, Elisabeth	20, Dec. 1888	3, Dec.	24- - 9d	814	Döffinger	Cincinnati, OH	Cincinnati, Hamilton County, Ohio
Polesky, Katharina	24, Dec. 1891	27, Nov.	42	830	Guntle	Kewaskum, WI	Barton, Washington County, Wisconsin
Poley, Bernhard	3, Dec. 1896	18, Sept	21	782		Tomah, WI	Tomah, Wisconsin
Pollack, Fr.	2, June 1862	10, Apr.	24	88		Oshkosh, WI	
Pollo, Friederike	4, June 1891	20, Apr.	72-8m- 2d	366	Schulz	Silver Creek, NY	Barko, Preußen
Pollow, Carolina	28, Dec. 1893	4, Dec.	58	828	Steffenhagen	Bloomington, IL	Basbal, Mecklenburg-Schwerin
Pollow, Christine	28, Apr. 1879	7, Apr.	76	135	Lübner	Milwaukee, WI	Letzin, Vorpommern, Preußen
Pollow, Heinrich Robert	27, July 1899	8, July	30	479		Milwaukee, WI	Milwaukee, Wisconsin
Pollow, Johan Christoph	27, Jan. 1873	5, Jan.	71- 9m-28d	31		Milwaukee, WI	Rosemarsow, Kreis Demmin, Pommern
Polster, Johan	19, July 1880		43	231		Baxter Springs, KS	Ungarn
Polster, Johan Georg	25, Sept 1890	30, Aug.	68	622		Warrenton, MO	Oberschützen, Ungarn
Polter, Catharine	4, June 1883	17, May	29- 5m-27d	183	Lipphart	Sandusky, OH	Sandusky, Ohio
Polzien, Friederike	1, May 1882	6, Apr.	55- 2m- 2d	382	Hackhardt	Kenosha, WI	Zadkow, Pommern
Polzien, Herman	8, Dec. 1884	25, Nov.	25	7		Kenosha, WI	Zadtkow, Pommern
Pommrenke, Bertha	13, Sept 1888	21, Aug.	22	590		Junction City, KS	Replin, Pommern
Ponath, Auguste Albertine	29, Apr. 1894	12, Mar.	55	214		Lyona, KS	Witzmitz bei Gräfenberg, Pommern
Ponath, Herman	19, Oct. 1885	5, Oct.	23	7		Cincinnati, OH	Alt-Döbritz, Pommern
Pontius, Louise	29, Nov. 1890	15, Nov.	66	383	Becher	Cincinnati, OH	Hermsdorf bei Waldbrunn, RheinPreußen
Poock, Louis	16, June 1892	30, May	86- -18d	382		Fredericksburg, TX	Hamel an der Weser, Hannover
Poorman, Friedrich	4, May 1899	10, Mar.	72	287		Pekin, IL	Mecklenburg-Schwerin
Pope, Maria Catharina	16, Jan. 1871	21, Dec.	72-9m- 6d	23	Wehrmann	Warren, MO	Schönhagen, Sternberg, Lippe-Detmold
Popke, Friedrich Wilhelm	1, Jan. 1877	7, Dec.	70- 2m	7		White Hall, MI	Neuenburg, Amt Solden, Preußen
Popp, Christina Magdalena	30, June 1859	13, June	31- 1m-23d	104	Mayer	Allegheny City, PA	Unterhambach, Weinsberg, Württemberg
Popp, H.C.	19, Apr. 1880	22, Mar.	68	127		Kewaunee, WI	Semeron, Köslin, Pommern
Popp, Henriette	28, Dec. 1868	17, Dec.	49	415	Haas	Allegheny City, PA	Schönbach, Amt Herrburn, Nassau
Popp, Henriette	11, Jan. 1869			15			
Popp, Johan	15, July 1886	25, June	82	7		Kewaunee, WI	Ritzenhagen, Labes, Stettin, Hinterpommern
Popp, Johan Nepomuck	1, May 1890	12, Apr.	77- - 5d	286		Blue Island, IL	Albertsdorf, Böhmen
Popp, John	18, Nov. 1867	20, Oct.	52- -18d	366		Allegheny City, PA	Kirchberg, Gerabronn, Württemberg
Popp, Wilhelmine	10, Mar. 1884	20, Feb.	36	7	Martins	Kewaunee, WI	Köslin, Vorpommern
Poppe, Louisa	10, Mar.1873	21, Feb.	61	79	Fischer	Batesville, IN	Linsburg, Hannover
Poppy, Friedrich	6, May 1872	3, Apr.	73	151		Kendallville, IN	Wolbrechtshausen, Hannover
Porath, Albertine	5, Sept 1889	16, Aug.	41	574		Storm Lake, IA	Hermalsdorf, Naugard, Preußen

Christliche Apologete Death Notices --- 1839 - 1899

Name of Deceased	Notice Date	Death Date	Age	Maiden Name	Page	Place of Death	Place of Birth
Porath, Ferdinand	5, Apr. 1894	20, Feb.	83		230	Blackberry, OH	Pommern
Poreb, Sophie	13, Apr. 1885	26, Mar.	83	Harm	7	Burlington, WI	Großböskow, Mecklenburg-Schwerin
Porr, Katharina	14, Oct. 1858	6, Sept	22		164	St. Joseph, MO	Duckroh, Pfalz, Baiern
Porth, Dorothea	29, Aug. 1881	23, July	64	Miller	279		Papenwerder, Potsdam, Preußen
Porth, Gottfried	28, Oct. 1878	13, Oct.	60		343	Sleepy Eye, MN	Templin, Preußen
Portier, Marie Justine	6, Mar. 1882	24, Feb.	46- 8m-15d	Klein	79	Cincinnati, OH	Ottmarsheim, Marbach, Württemberg
Portmann, Anna	11, June 1883	19, May	64	Rubi	191	Vermillion, OH	Steffensburg, Bern, Schweiz
Portmann, Johan	28, Mar. 1889	1, Mar.	70- 3m-13d		206	Vermillion, OH	Steffysburg, Bern, Schweiz
Pörtner, Christine	26, Dec. 1881	14, Oct.	83- 6m- 2d	Krüger	415	Albert Lea, MN	Schönfeld, Arnswalde, Preußen
Pörtner, Gertrud	26, Jan. 1885	8, Jan.	54	Blässer	7	Milwaukee, WI	Esselborn, Hessen-Darmstadt
Portzig, Julius	9, Sept 1872		25		295	St. Charles, MO	St. Charles County, Missouri
Portzig, Louis Wilhelm	10, June 1897		29		367	St. Charles, MO	
Post, Anna Maria Elsabein	7, Jan. 1858	31, Mar.	22- 2m	Kleinschmidt	4	St. Louis, MO	Mehnen, Lübbeke, Minden, Preußen
Postel, Andreas	31, Oct. 1850	29, Nov.	40- - 2d		176	Mascoutah, IL	Haßloch, Baiern
Postel, Anna Maria	13, Mar. 1882	15, Sept	62	Leininger	87	Cincinnati, OH	Steinweiler, RheinPfalz Baiern
Postel, Anna Maria	22, Dec. 1887	5, Mar.	64-11m-23d	Eisenmeier	814	Mascoutah, IL	Haßloch, RheinPfalz Baiern
Postel, Katharine	13, Sept 1894	4, Dec.	81	Hauck	598	Jeffersonville, IN	Ingelheim bei Landau, Germany
Poth, Catharina	12, Aug. 1867	11, Aug.	48	Eck	254	Jerseyville, IL	Großzimmern, Kreis Dieburg, Hessen
Poth, Elisabeth	9, Apr. 1877	19, July	76- - 9d		119	Pittsburg, PA	Homberg, Rheinkreis Baiern
Poth, Jakob	4, Apr. 1870	17, Mar.	71- 7m		111	Birmingham, PA	Arnbach, Zweibrücken, Rheinkreis Baiern
Pottebaum, Henry Fr.	14, Nov. 1889	2, Mar.			734	Little Rock, AR	Mecklenburg-Schwerin
Potthast, Heinrich Fr. Christian	1, Oct. 1883	21, Oct.	55- 3m-16d		319	Berger, MO	Bösenfeld, Lippe-Detmold
Pötting, Christina	1, May 1876	25, Aug.	82- 9m		143	Morrison, MO	
Pötting, Elisabeth	7, July 1898	9, Apr.	55	Panhorst	431	Senate Grove, MO	Hemmern, Minden, Preußen
Pötting, Katharina	3, Nov. 1898	12, June	71		703	St. Louis, MO	Bergholzhausen, Halle, Minden, Preußen
Pötting, Louise	2, Dec. 1878	16, Oct.	26- 6m-19d	Ulricht	383	St. Louis, MO	Hildesheim, Hannover
Pottratz, Elisabeth	28, July 1892	31, Oct.	60	Jahr	478	Michigan City, IN	Königsdorf, Flatow, West Preußen
Powals, Otto	28, July 1898	28, June	15		479	Ft. Atkinson, Wisconsin	Ft. Atkinson, Wisconsin
Powers, James	25, Apr. 1895	17, June	81		270	Austin, TX	Ireland
Prächter, Johannes	13, Feb. 1896	24, Mar.	68		110	Woodington, OH	Obermoos, Hessen-Darmstadt
Praeger, Henriette	26, Mar. 1891	30, Dec.	22	Filigus	206	Brillion, WI	Waukesha, Wisconsin
Prahl, Carolina	29, Oct. 1866	28, Jan.	58		350	Chicago, IL	
Prahl, Johan	22, Nov. 1875	19, Oct.	49		375	Tomah, WI	Petzien, Kreis Flatow, West Preußen
Prange, Christian	8, May 1865	22, Oct.	58		76	German Creek, IA	
Prange, Mary	2, Oct. 1876	9, Mar.	34		319	Jordan, MN	Dankersen, Minden, Preußen
Prange, Salla	6, Dec. 1875	9, Sept	37		391	Chicago, IL	
Prante, Wilhelm August	13, Jan. 1887	18, Nov.	34		30	Quincy, IL	Wülferheide, Schötmar, Lippe-Detmold
Prapernau, Karl	4, Oct. 1880	31, Dec.	40		319	Illinois City, IL	Lindhorst, Preußen
Prasse, Johan Karl Gottlob	7, Jan. 1884	31, Aug.	69		7	Roseville, MI	Langenpeilau, Reichenbach, Schlesien
Prätz, Elisabeth	20, Jan. 1879	20, Dec.	85-10m- 2d		23	St. Paul, MN	Hundelshausen, Kurhessen
Prech, Georg	13, May 1872	5, Jan.	46- 5m-20d		159	Terre Haute, IN	Ackersbach bei Sinsheim, Baden
Prechel, Wilhelmina	7, Feb. 1895	24, Apr.	65	Stelljes	223	Waseca, MN	Radewonke, Posen
Pregge, Anna	6, Apr. 1899	11, Dec.	68	Meyer	167	Sedalia, MO	Hüttenbusch, Lilienthor, Hannover
Pregge, Anna	26, May 1879	15, Mar.	29	Kirchner	174	Sedalia, MO	Morgan County, Missouri
Preine, Caroline Christine	12, Mar. 1891	5, May	33	Lang	135	Minneapolis, MN	Weinsberg, Württemberg
Preine, Rosie	24, Apr. 1882	17, Feb.	24			Minneapolis, MN	Auenstein, Marbach, Württemberg

Christliche Apologete Death Notices --- 1839 - 1899

Name of Deceased	Notice Date	Death Date	Age	Maiden Name	Page	Place of Death	Place of Birth
Prell, Henriette	29, Nov. 1888	25, Oct.	70	Lumer	766	Troy, NY	Gera, Reuß
Prescher, Alice	4, Aug. 1879	8, July	18- 7m-22d		247	Dunkirk, NY	
Prescher, Caroline	20, Sept 1880	18, Aug.	51- 6m- 7d	Köble	303	Dunkirk, NY	Badien, Schönfließ in der Neumark, Preußen
Prescher, Karl	17, July 1876		27		231	Dunkirk, NY	Petzing, Schönfließ in der Neumark, Preußen
Preß, Bertha	18, July 1895	2, July	65	Wohlleben	462	Jersey City, NJ	Kreuznach, Preußen
Presser, Louis	28, Oct. 1897	26, Sept	36		687	Milwaukee, WI	Odenbach, Rheinpfalz Baiern
Preßler, Anna Katharina	9, June 1884	22, May	76	Wiegand	7	St. Paul, MN	Hundelshausen, Mitzenhausen, Kurhessen
Prestmüller, Franz Johan	4, Aug. 1873	25, May	14		247	Belleville, IL	
Presuhn, Wilhelmine Auguste E.	8, May 1890	19, Apr.	26	Feske	302	Bridgewater, SD	Falkenburg, Piritz, Pommern
Presun, Emma	17, Nov. 1898	22, Oct.	24- 5m	Feske	735	Parker, SD	
Pretz, Caroline Wilhelmine	5, July 1888	8, June	24	Volkel	430	Evansville, IN	
Pretzer, (Mrs)	7, June 1869	10, May	62- 2m-10d	Kemke	183	Rochester, MN	Grambin, Ufermünde, Vorpommern, Preußen
Pretzer, Luisa	22, Oct. 1896	15, Sept	42	Struckmeier	687	Clatonia, NE	Obernkirchen, Rindel, Hessen
Pretzer, Luisa	8, Oct. 1896		42- 7m-13d	Struckmeier	655	Clatonia, NE	Oberkirchen, Rindel, Hessen
Pretzinger, Jacobina	17, May 1855	23, Apr.	40	Helber	80	West Union, OH	Herzogweiler, Freudenstadt, Württemberg
Pretzinger, Johan Philip	12, Dec. 1889	16, Oct.	79		798	Burtonsville, KY	Heiterbach, Nagold, Württemberg
Pretzinger, John Martin	27, Jan. 1887	10, Jan.	79		62	Greenville, OH	Haiterbach, Württemberg
Pretzinger, Salomon	1, Dec. 1862	8, Oct.	24		192	Euphemia, OH	Greenville, Ohio
Pretzinger, Wilhelmina	29, Dec. 1859	11, Nov.	25		208	Ripley, OH	
Pretzler, Wilhelm	24, Feb. 1887	31, Jan.	80- 3m-22d		126	Mt. Carmel, IL	Gailsdorf, Württemberg
Preuß, John Friedrich	31, Dec. 1883	12, Dec.	68		7	Los Angeles, CA	Oberschönau, Kurhessen
Preußner, Karoline	3, Nov. 1862	31, Aug.	45	Hasenjeger	176	Marthasville, MO	Deme, Rehme, Minden, Preußen
Pribbenow, Carl Ferdinand	25, Feb. 1858	1, Feb.	23		32	Columbus, WI	Alt-Stettin, Preußen
Pribbenow, Ferdinand	26, Dec. 1889	20, Nov.	26		830	Nora Springs, IA	Windsor, Dane County, Wisconsin
Priebe, Augusta	16, Mar. 1899	5, Jan.	69	Jahnke	175	Birschville, MN	Groß-Solnawi, Bromberg, Preußen
Priebe, Ferdinand	22, Mar. 1880	5, Mar.	34- 1m- 1d		95	Minneapolis, MN	
Priebe, Heinrich Fr.	7, July 1884	22, June	29		7	Mankato, MN	Alt-Salzdorf, Bromberg, Posen
Priebe, Maria Christina	23, July 1877	19, June	78	Münchow	239	Baltimore, MD	Vorwerk, Amt Belgard, Preußen
Priebe, Michael	9, Nov. 1893	23, Oct.	69		718	Detroit, MI	Thiergart, West Preußen
Prielipp, Louise	15, Apr. 1897		47- 7m	Malwitz	239	Garner, IA	Tornow, Pommern
Priem, Emma Maria	13, July 1891	19, June	24		526	Columbus, WI	Farmington, Wisconsin
Priem, Wilhelmine	8, July 1897	14, June	65	Fritz	431	Columbus, WI	Kollin, Pieritz, Pommern
Pries, Heinrich John	18, May 1893	27, Apr.	79		318	Altamont, IL	Sterenz, Güstrow, Mecklenburg-Schwerin
Prieß, Charlotte	11, Aug. 1898	27, July	79- 3m-24d	Martinson	511	Altamont, IL	Piermont, Preußen
Priester, Katharine	20, Jan. 1887	18, Dec.	54	Süß	46	Los Angeles, CA	Hessen-Darmstadt
Prigge, Anna	31, Aug. 1863	3, Aug.	17		140	Sheboygan, WI	
Prigge, Catharina	10, Feb. 1873	15, Jan.	24- 1m-22d	Corleis	47	Winona, MN	Ifsendorf, Hannover
Prigge, Elisabeth	24, May 1894	25, Apr.	78	Lümpmann	342	Sheboygan, WI	Kirchwalseda, Rothenburg, Germany
Prigge, Johan Fr.	3, Aug. 1874	13, July	63- 7m-15d		247	Sheboygan, WI	Rodenburg, Hannover
Primster, G. A.	24, Sept 1896	28, Aug.	30		623	Los Angeles, CA	Marybourgh, Queensland, Australia
Prinzing, J. H. H.	22, Apr. 1897	27, Mar.	36		255	Brenham, TX	Houston, Texas
Priode, Eva	27, Oct. 1892	28, Aug.	77		686	Cincinnati, OH	Lambsheim, Baiern
Priode, Eva Catharina	11, Aug. 1862	20, July	58		128	Pomeroy, OH	Edichheim, Rheinkreis Baiern
Priode, Jakob	16, Apr. 1891	7, Mar.	86		254	Pomeroy, OH	Edigheim, Frankenthal, Rheinkreis Baiern
Prior, Chr. W.	14, July 1873	4, July	59- 7m- 8d		223	Cincinnati, OH	Krefinghausen, Schledehausen, Hannover
Probant, Wilhelmine	7, May 1891	20, Apr.	78		302	Chicago, IL	Hinterpommern

Christliche Apologete Death Notices --- 1839 - 1899

Name of Deceased	Notice Date	Death Date	Age	Page	Maiden Name	Place of Death	Place of Birth
Probst, Karl	19, July 1894	27, June	14	470		St. Paul, MN	Schaffhausen, Schweiz
Prochnow, August Friedrich	11, July 1881	14, June	31	223		Waco, TX	Ziegenhagen, Saatzig, Stettin, Preußen
Prodehl, Wilhelmine Ernestine	27, Oct. 1873	7, Oct.	27	343	Frädrich	Beaver Falls, MN	Falkenwalde, Pommern
Profke, Dorothea	7, Sept 1893	24, Aug.	92- 9m-13d	574		Chicago, IL	Schneidemühl, Posen
Prop, Maria	7, May 1883	18, Apr.	84- -26d	151		Cedar Lake, IN	Pensien, Mecklenburg-Schwerin
Propst, Franz J.	6, Feb. 1896	19, Oct.	81	94		Jefferson City, MO	Canton Solothurn, Schweiz
Prötz, Georg	29, Oct. 1866	7, Sept	50	350		Central City, IL	Hundelshausen, Witzenhausen, Kurhessen
Prötz, Georg Peter	12, May 1862	30, Mar.		76		St. Louis, MO	Hundelshausen, Kurhessen
Prötz, Heinrich	11, June 1877	26, May	55- 9m-20d	191		St. Paul, MN	Hundelshausen, Witzenhausen, Kurhessen
Prötz, Heinrich	7, May 1866	25, Apr.	11- 2m-13d	150		St. Louis, MO	St. Louis, Missouri
Prötz, Margaretha	13, Feb. 1882	11, Jan.	60- 3m-15d	55		St. Paul, MN	
Prundocsky, Mary	11, Feb. 1878	23, Jan.		47		Chicago, IL	
Prüß, Johan K. F.	16, Apr. 1891	27, Mar.	45	254		Berea, OH	Eichholz, Franzburg, Vorpommern
Prüßmann, Johan Heinrich	3, Dec. 1883	2, Nov.	63	391		Oregon, MO	Mecklenburg-Schwerin
Prüßner, Christoph	7, Sept 1893		60	574		Reddick, Il	Bashagen, Lippe-Detmold
Prüßner, Friederika Wilhelmina C.	14, Apr. 1873	25, Mar.	45	119	Süllwald	New Haven, MO	Vlotho, Kreis Herford, Minden, Preußen
Prüßner, Friedrich	24, Aug. 1868	4, Aug.	49	271		Union, MO	Rehme, Preußen
Prüßner, Heinrich	4, Apr. 1895	6, Mar.	28	222		Norton, IL	Norton Town, Kankokee County, Illinois
Prüßner, Sophia	12, Jan. 1874	24, Dec.	39-10m- 6d	15	Hänke	Grand Prairie, IL	
Prüter, Catharina L.C.	2, Sept 1878	16, Aug.	66- 4m-22d	279	Jarchow	Wabasha, MN	Wustrow, Neubuckow, Mecklenburg-Schwerin
Prüter, Dorothea	16, Apr. 1896	29, Mar.	59	254	Saß	Jansen, NE	Clausdorf, Mecklenburg-Schwerin
Prüter, Jochen	16, Apr. 1891	21, Mar.	84	254		Zumbro Falls, MN	Neubucko, Mecklenburg-Schwerin
Pucklitsch, Christiana Ernestine	12, Mar. 1891	10, Feb.	50	174	Zschegner	Lawrence, MA	Langenwetzendorf, Elsaß
Pucklitsch, Gustav Adolph	6, Oct. 1887	16, Sept	43	638		Lawrence, MA	Langenwetzendorf, Sachsen
Pucklitsch, Olga Louisa	11, Aug. 1898	4, July	27	511		Cincinnati, OH	Frankfurt a. Main, Preußen
Pudig, Carl	5, July 1888	10, June	79	430		Elizabeth, NJ	Maveln, Preußen
Pullmann, Elisabeth	16, June 1898	8, May	73	383	Draser	Kendallville, IN	Großzimmern, Hessen
Pullmann, Susanna Elisabeth	25, Mar. 1886	8, Mar.	93- 3m-10d	7		Toledo, OH	Großzimmern, Hessen-Darmstadt
Puls, Christina D.	7, Apr. 1887	10, Mar.	73- 2m-21d	222	Schuldt	Allegan, MI	Goldnitz, Mecklenburg-Schwerin
Pungs, Angelica	27, Oct. 1873	10, Oct.	64	343	Quack	Detroit, MI	
Purmeister, Karl	12, May 1879	14, Apr.	52	151		Mainville, OH	Wittenburg, Mecklenburg-Schwerin
Pustmiller, Louise	18, Mar. 1872	3, Mar.	19	95		Belleville, IL	Franklin County, Missouri
Pustmüller, August W.	13, Sept 1894	13, Aug.	65-11m-21d	598		Belleville, IL	Halle, Minden, Preußen
Pustmüller, Emilie Clara	5, May 1892	7, Apr.	30- 5m-11d	286	Heidel	Belleville, IL	St. Joseph, Missouri
Pustmüller, Karolina Emma	2, Feb. 1885	17, Jan.	17- 5m-24d	7		Belleville, IL	
Pustmüller, Louis	5, Sept 1895	13, Aug.	37	574		Belleville, IL	Franklin County, Missouri
Puvogel, Dietrich	16, Sept 1852	2, Sept	39	152		Cincinnati, OH	Horstedt, Thedinghausen, Braunschweig
Quaas, Melchior	20, Jan. 1879	31, Dec.	55- 6m	23		West Bend, WI	Schwantwitz, Sachsen-Altenburg
Quade, Katharine	10, Dec. 1883	14, Nov.		7		Bear Creek, TX	
Quade, Samuel	11, July 1895	9, June	59	446		Houston, TX	Gruntowitz, Vongrowitz, Posen
Qualman, Heinrich Jochen	3, Oct. 1895	11, Sept	74	638		New Rochelle, NY	Mecklenburg-Schwerin
Quandt, (Mrs)	18, Aug. 1898	27, May	55	527	Blumrik	New Ulm, MN	Karishof, Ukermark
Quandt, Christian	6, Jan. 1887	15, Nov.	86	14		Lowell, WI	Mecklenburg-Schwerin
Quandt, Christine	10, Mar. 1879	18, Feb.	69	79	Drester	New Ulm, MN	Schönefeld bei Prenzlau, Preußen
Quandt, Louis	25, Feb. 1884	29, Jan.	29	7		Los Angeles, CA	Conitz, West Preußen

Christliche Apologete Death Notices --- 1839 - 1899

Name of Deceased	Notice Date	Death Date	Age	Page	Maiden Name	Place of Death	Place of Birth
Quandt, Maria	4, Jan. 1894	14, Dec.	67	14	Gerth	Galion, OH	Hohensolms, Wetzlar, Preußen
Quattländer, Maria	2, Nov. 1885	13, Oct.	82- 7m-16d	7	Schlenber	Brooklyn, NY	Schwenningen, Württemberg
Quattländer, Maria Louise	29, Nov. 1875	11, Nov.	37- 7m-20d	383	Ackermann	Brooklyn, NY	New York City, New York
Quattländer, Paul	25, June 1866	12, Mar.	69	206		New York, NY	Schwenningen, Württemberg
Quattländer, Sophia Friederike	19, July 1894	26, June	51	470	Horn	Buffalo, NY	Württemberg
Quebbemann, Heinrich	24, June 1897	4, June	72	399		Bradford, IN	Osnabrück, Hannover
Quebbemann, Margarethe	10, July 1865	15, May	34- 6m- 3d	112	Moßler	Bradford, IN	Derwiller, Frankreich
Quellmalz, (Mrs)	23, Dec. 1858	19, Oct.	34	204	Breunemann	Golconda, IL	Knox County, Ohio
Queren, Ernst Friedrich	24, Aug. 1885	4, Aug.	42-10m-14d	7		Hoyleton, IL	Hädinghausen, Hannover
Quilling, Johan	30, Aug. 1875	29, July	57	279		Menomonie, WI	Dallmien, Potsdam, Preußen
Quinzer, Adam	5, Mar. 1896	8, Feb.	65	158		Mt. Vernon, IN	Baden
Raab, Elisabeth	30, Sept 1886	11, Sept	72	7	Jäkel	Lafayette, IN	Texheim, Hessen
Raab, Franz	23, May 1889	6, May	75- 9m	334		Grand Ridge, IL	Etlingen, Baden
Raab, Jacob	1, Oct. 1891	8, Sept	64- 1m- 7d	638		Allegan, MI	Thüngen, Baiern
Raab, Jakob	15, Nov. 1894	2, Oct.	74	742		Lafayette, IN	Linswald, Wächtersbach, Kurhessen
Raab, Lydia	23, Aug. 1880	6, Aug.	19	271		Allegan, MI	Salem, Allegan County, Michigan
Raab, Veronika	8, Nov. 1888	16, Oct.	89- 6m-10d	718	Hoffmann	Allegan, MI	Thüngen, Karlstadt, Baiern
Raab, Wilhelm	4, Feb. 1884	21, Jan.	30	7		Bradford, IN	Heumaden, Stuttgart, Württemberg
Raabe, Margaretha	4, June 1877	16, May	70- 9m	183	Dewein	Mascoutah, IL	Langenkandel, Rheinkreis Baiern
Raabe, Wilhelm	8, Apr. 1897	19, Mar.	83	223		Mascoutah, IL	Albshausen bei Marburg, Kurhessen
Raake, Friedrich	20, Sept 1880	10, July	13	303		Bradford, IN	
Raake, Louise	20, Sept 1880	19, July	7	303		Bradford, IN	
Raas, Christine	21, Jan. 1886	26, Sept	36	7	Gucker	Rochester, NY	Messingen, Rothenburg, Württemberg
Raasch, Emilie	21, June 1880	6, June	23	199		Chicago, IL	
Rabe, (Mr)	5, Aug. 1878	29, May	66	247		Illinois City, IL	
Rabe, Augusta Sophia	3, Jan. 1889	12, Dec.	41- 8m-24d	14	Pfeil	San Antonio, TX	Elberfeld, Germany
Rabe, Catharina	29, Sept 1879	7, July	32- 7m	311	Welle	Newark, NJ	
Rabe, Catharina Luise	8, Apr. 1897	21, Mar.	38	223	Leistikow	Lena, IL	Buena Vista , Illinois
Rabe, Hannah	9, July 1891	16, June		446	Rödel	Wheeling, WV	Waltersdorf, Sachsen-Weimar
Rabe, Minna	14, Mar. 1889	15, Feb.	17- 3m-15d	174		Odebolt, IA	
Rabe, Wilhelmine	28, Mar. 1889	15, Feb.	17- 3m-15d	206		Odebolt, IA	
Rabel, Friederike	17, Jan. 1876	2, Jan.	23	23	Luikhart	Clarington, OH	Sulzberger, Kirchheim a. d. Teck, Württemberg
Rabel, Johan	16, Feb. 1885	2, Feb.	29	7		Baresville, OH	Marshall County, West Virginia
Rabel, Johannes	14, Aug. 1851	26, July		132		Captina, OH	Brucken, Kirchheim, Württemberg
Rabenson, Catharina	2, Apr. 1877	13, Mar.	80	111	Hübner	Glencoe, MN	Germantown, Bucks County, Pennsylvania
Rabenstein, Heinrich	19, July 1888	28, June	69	462		Cincinnati, OH	Seibothenreuth, Oberfranken, Baiern
Rabenstein, Louis	4, Oct. 1875	9, Sept	16- 8m- 1d	319		Milan, IN	
Raber, Philipp	31, May 1849		Inquiry	87		New Albany, IN	
Rabewolt, Michael	6, Oct. 1887	4, Sept	53- 1m- 7d	638		Salina, KS	Blankenloch, Baden
Rabich, Johanna M. Wilhelmina	17, Jan. 1870	5, Dec.	34- 1m-23d	23	Hartmann	Cape Girardeau, MO	Mechtshausen, Hannover
Rabold, Wilhelm	11, Feb. 1884	9, Jan.	74	7		Wapello, IA	Ilm, Preußen
Racho, Eduard Heinrich	23, June 1884	11, May	15- 6m-17d	7		Detroit, MI	
Racho, Rahel Augusta	4, Jan. 1869			7	Lang		
Rachow, Wilhelm	30, May 1889	11, May	36	350		Milwaukee, WI	Friebzeß, Vorpommern
Rachwitz, Friederike	28, May 1896	19, Apr.	69	350	Schirmer	Marine City, MI	Friederichswald, Preußen

Christliche Apologete Death Notices --- 1839 - 1899

Name of Deceased	Notice Date	Death Date	Age	Page	Maiden Name	Place of Death	Place of Birth
Räck, August Heinrich	11, Mar. 1897	8, Feb.	37	159		Waco, TX	Seidlitz, Preußen
Racke, Friedrich	1, Nov. 1875	30, Sept	73- 4m- 5d	351		Bradford, IN	
Racke, Louise	28, Mar. 1861	18, Feb.	20- 9m	52	Rosenbach	Topeka, KS	Marienfeld, Nassau
Racke, Rosina Friedrike	24, Jan. 1881	10, Dec.		31		Bradford, IN	
Rackemann, Charlotte	14, Apr. 1898	24, Mar.	70	239	Krumsick	Watertown, WI	Alverdissen, Lippe-Detmold
Rackemann, Eduard	1, Aug. 1889	24, June	20	494		Watertown, WI	Watertown, Wisconsin
Rackow, Johan Gottlieb	16, July 1877	25, June	70	231		Wausau, WI	Weisenfeld, Naugart, Pommern, Preußen
Radeke, Karl	20, Feb. 1896	28, Jan.	65	126		Clearwater, MN	Flieth, Preußen
Radeloff, Christian Friedrich	28, Mar. 1864	12, Mar.	14	52	Schön	Louisville, KY	Burg, Magdeburg, Preußen
Rademacher, Andye	11, May 1874	22, Apr.		151		Muddy Creek, NE	Firret, Amt Stükhausen, Ostfriesland
Rademacher, Katharina	26, Mar. 1896	8, Mar.	16	206		Michigan City, IN	Marienhausen, Hessen-Nassau
Rademacher, Nanke Ulfert	1, Dec. 1892	3, Nov.	17	766		Emden, IL	Emden, Illinois
Radert, Friedrich	11, Feb. 1848		Inquiry	27		New Orleans, LA	
Rades, Louise	20, July 1893	23, June	60	462	Bork	Sun Prairie, WI	Satzig, Pommern
Rades, Maria	18, Dec. 1890	25, Nov.	28	814		Sun Prairie, WI	Watertown, Wisconsin
Rades, Otto	6, June 1881	20, May	17	183		Sun Prairie, WI	
Radicke, Heinrich	23, Nov. 1868	5, Nov.	47-10m-18d	375		Marine City, MI	Standemin, Pommern, Preußen
Radii, August Ferdinand	26, July 1894	2, July	74	486		Kewaunee, WI	Arnzwalden, Brandenburg
Radike, Anna Wilhelmina	18, Nov. 1872	9, Oct.	14- 9m-18d	375		Marine City, MI	Stolzenberg, Preußen
Radike, Gustav	28, July 1873	27, May	27- 4m- 6d	239		Marine City, MI	Grasse, Preußen
Radix, Dorothea	7, Mar. 1889	13, Jan.	35- 4m	158		Lyona, KS	
Radke, Charlotte	1, Sept 1898	11, Aug.	78	559		Watertown, WI	Nemmin, Pommern
Radke, Christian Friedrich	14, Sept 1893	13, Aug.	65	590		Albert Lea, MN	Schlagentin, Arnswalde, Neumark
Radke, Erich Helmuth	9, June 1898	22, May	16	367		Beaver Dam, WI	Concord, Jefferson County, Wisconsin
Radke, Johanna Sophia	20, Oct. 1873	3, Sept	45	335	Lange	Columbus, WI	Hohengrape, Kreis Soldin, Pommern
Radke, Wilhelm Friedrich	1, Dec. 1887	24, Oct.	15	766		Albert Lea, MN	
Radloff, Ernst	20, Oct. 1898	2, Oct.	21	671		Billion, WI	New Holstein, Calumet County, Wisconsin
Radloff, Friderika	28, Feb. 1889	21, Jan.	71	142	Kruhs	Brillion, WI	Samon, Mecklenburg-Schwerin
Radloff, Friedrich	27, July 1893	12, June	63	478		Appleton, WI	Kicker, Pommern
Radne, Louis	29, Oct. 1891		17- 8m-24d	702		Escanabe, MI	Eton, Brown County, Wisconsin
Radspinner, Anna Maria	29, Dec. 1887	14, Dec.	82	830	Müller	Aurora, IN	Mandach, Baiem
Radspinner, Michael	19, Feb. 1857	2, Feb.		32		Beaver Dam, WI	Maubach, Baiem
Radtke, Hubert Erwin	9, July 1896	19, June	21	447		Kewaunee, WI	Concord, Wisconsin
Radue, Auguste	13, Dec. 1888	22, Nov.	58- 7m-10d	798	Garder	Ripon, WI	Arnswalde, Brandenburg
Radünzel, Johanna Luise	16, Feb. 1899	27, Dec.	79	111	Weber	Industry, TX	Arnswalde, Germany
Raeke, Heinrich Ernst Friedrich	3, Feb. 1898	5, Jan.	68	79		Industry, TX	Isenbüttel, Gifhorn, Hannover
Raeke, Sophia Maria Dorothea	4, Aug. 1887		56	494	Müller	Berne, MI	Isenbüttel, Gifhorn, Hannover
Raether, Emma Mathilde	12, July 1888	4, June	20	446		Winona, MN	Concord, Wisconsin
Raetz, Lydia Regula	20, Sept 1880		13-11m	303		Winona, MN	Fountain City, Minnesota
Raetz, Sophia Emilie	27, Mar. 1882	6, Mar.	23- 4m	103	Meyer	Lake Creek, MO	Lüthberge, Osnabrück, Hannover
Rages, Anna	22, Feb. 1875		62	63		Bremen, GE	Deichshausen, Amt Berne, Germany
Rahe, Berend Dietrich	25, Feb. 1878			63		Blue Island, IL	Heiligen Muschel, Rheinkreis Baiem
Rahm, Carl	13, Sept 1855	2, Sept		148		Oakford, IL	
Rahmann, Albert Janson	22, Oct. 1891	5, Oct.	26	686		Watertown, WI	Zeven, Hannover
Rahn, Anna	2, Apr. 1891	11, Mar.	42	222	Budde	Watertown, WI	
Rahn, Bertha A.F.	20, July 1885	14, June	27	7	Schulz	Milwaukee, WI	Milwaukee, Wisconsin

Name of Deceased	Notice Date	Death Date	Age	Maiden Name	Page	Place of Death	Place of Birth
Rahn, Friederika	21, Mar. 1895	19, Feb.	76- 5m		190	Berea, OH	Neuvorpommern, Stralsund, Preußen
Rahn, Karl	25, Apr. 1895	20, Mar.	67		270	Berea, OH	Neuvorpommern, Stralsund, Preußen
Rahn, Karl	16, Mar. 1899	11, Feb.	75		175	Minneapolis, MN	Stettin, Pommern
Rahn, Margaretha	19, Aug. 1867	16, July	73		262	Aurora, IL	Markbechofen, Baiern
Rahn, Wilhelmine	5, Oct. 1874		54		319	Watertown, WI	
Rähr, Heinrich Friedrich	1, Dec. 1892	11, Oct.	40		766	Wellsville, NY	Wellsville, New York
Rahskopf, Maria	2, Mar. 1885	4, Feb.		Bürklie	7	Batavia, WI	Olungen, Elsaß
Raich, Caroline	19, Jan. 1885	26, Dec.	23- 3m-21d		7	Warsaw, IL	Warsaw, Illinois
Raich, Marie Ellen	24, Feb. 1879	8, Feb.	18		63	Warsaw, IL	Warsaw, Illinois
Raihle, Friederike	17, Feb. 1887	25, Jan.	57	Silcher	110	Mankato, MN	Rommelshausen, Württemberg
Raihle, Johan	5, Jan. 1899	8, Dec.	71		14	Mankato, MN	Großheppach, Waiblingen, Württemberg
Raisch, Anna Maria	10, Nov. 1892	7, Oct.	69		718	Troy, NY	Thailfingen, Württemberg
Raisch, Johannes	9, Oct. 1865	1, July	58		164	Cincinnati, OH	Eltingen, Leonberg, Württemberg
Raiser, Gabriel	11, Apr. 1864	9, Mar.	26		60	Arenzville, IL	Pliezhausen, Tübingen, Württemberg
Raiser, Johan	12, Oct. 1893	16, Sept	82		654	Columbus, OH	Bechtholt, Baiern
Raisig, Johan Martin	30, May 1881	9, May	62		175	Nora Springs, IA	Biberach am Neckar, Württemberg
Raitz, Anna	2, Nov. 1874	20, Oct.	54- 2m- 3d	Moser	351	Toledo, OH	Messen, Solothurn, Schweiz
Rajes, Christian	22, May 1876	2, May	68		167	Lake Creek, MO	England
Räke, Mathilde	10, Mar. 1884	22, Feb.	26	Lütge	7	Industry, TX	Fallersleben, Preußen
Rakow, Friedrike Louise	3, Dec. 1883	1, Nov.	71- 6m		391	Maine, WI	Faulenbenz, Pommern
Rakow, Johan Friedrich	30, Jan. 1896	12, Jan.	62		78	Taegesville, WI	Wittenfelde, Naugard, Stettin, Preußen
Rakow, Johan Gottlieb	6, Aug. 1877	25, June	70		255	Wausau, WI	Sadelberg, Preußen
Rakow, Johanna Carolina Emilie	4, Apr. 1881	16, Mar.	39- 2m-14d	Backhaus	111	Lena, IL	Faulenbenz, Pommern, Preußen
Rakow, John Gottfried	16, Mar. 1863	4, Feb.	25		44	Wausau, WI	
Ralph, Christine	23, Dec. 1897	30, Nov.	13		815	Council Bluffs, IA	
Ralph, Daniel	23, Dec. 1897	17, Nov.	20		815	Council Bluffs, IA	
Ramer, Lina Bertha	5, May 1884	11, Apr.	33	Brand	7	Mountain Lake, MN	Silma, Cottonwood County, Minnesota
Ramhorst, Johan Heinrich	25, Dec. 1882	5, Dec.	47- 3m- 1d		415	New York City, NY	Fersmold, Westphalen
Ramin, Friedrich	20, Dec. 1875	3, Dec.	46		407	New Ulm, MN	
Rammel, Emma	21, May 1896	29, Apr.	31	Schäfer	334	Almond, WI	Almond, Portage County, Wisconsin
Rammel, Otto	4, Aug. 1898	17, July	34		495	Almond, WI	Eldorado, Wisconsin
Rammel, W.	11, Jan. 1894	7, Dec.	76		30	Almond, WI	Sangerhausen, Magdeburg, Sachsen
Rammers, Adolph	6, Apr. 1872	2, Mar.			111	Louisville, KY	
Rammers, Magdalena	5, Apr. 1869	20, Mar.	32- 7m-10d	Laufer	111	Louisville, KY	Molmsheim, Leonburg, Württemberg
Rammes, Louis	2, Aug. 1849	8, July	43		124	St. Louis, MO	
Rammes, Louis (Mrs)	2, Aug. 1849	14, July			124	St. Louis, MO	
Rammes, Maria	2, Aug. 1849	2, July	40		124	St. Louis, MO	
Rampag, Catharine	27, Dec. 1875	10, Dec.	29	Pfaff	415	Minneapolis, MN	Quirnbach bei Cusel, Rheinkreis Baiern
Rampag, Christian	16, Mar. 1899	2, Feb.	73		175	Minneapolis, MN	Lehsen, Mecklenburg-Schwerin
Ramser, Rosina	27, Feb. 1865	13, Jan.	34	Arn	36	San Francisco, CA	Alleghany County, Pennsylvania
Ramspot, Sarah	15, Oct. 1891	8, Sept	84		670	Madison, IN	Friesenheim, Baden
Randels, Charles J.	28, Sept 1899	26, Aug.	42		623	Stryker, OH	Columbiana County, Ohio
Ranft, Katharina	3, Feb. 1898	8, Jan.	57	Trautmüller	79	Newark, NJ	Schwarbach, Baiern
Range, Catharine Elisabeth	22, Jan. 1883	12, Dec.	69	Seibel	31	Ft. Dodge, IA	Mandem, Eder, Waldeck
Rank, Adolf	20, Sept 1875	5, Sept	19		303	Francisco, MI	Waterloo, Canada
Rankin, Anna Yotter	18, Mar. 1897	28, Jan.	51		175	Ft. Madison, IA	Franklin Center, Lee County, Iowa

Christliche Apologete Death Notices --- 1839 - 1899

Name of Deceased	Notice Date	Death Date	Age	Maiden Name	Place of Death	Page	Place of Birth
Ransom, Albert	29, Dec. 1879	10, Dec.	17-3m		Clearwater, MN	415	Eutingen, Pforzheim, Baden
Ransom, Elise	1, Nov. 1860	12, Oct.	29	Weinacht	Milan, IN	176	
Ransom, Fredi	29, Dec. 1879	2, Nov.	12-9m		Clearwater, MN	415	
Ransom, Tille	29, Dec. 1879	29, Nov.	15-3m		Clearwater, MN	415	
Ransom, Willi	29, Dec. 1879	30, Nov.	5-2m		Clearwater, MN	415	
Rapp, Dorothea	10, Mar. 1887	20, Feb.	60	Kais	Spencerville, OH	158	Bergzabern, Baiern
Rapp, Fr.	1, Sept 1884	21, Aug.	50- -5d		Cincinnati, OH	7	Canton Bergzabern, Rheinpfalz Baiern
Rapp, Friedrich J.	11, Oct. 1888	18, Sept	68-1m-18d		Indianapolis, IN	654	
Rapp, Johan	8, July 1897	22, June	81		San Jose, IL	431	Tiefengrün, Baiern
Rapp, Johann	4, Aug. 1859	22, July	24		Cincinnati, OH	124	Steinweiler, Rheinkreis Baiern
Rapp, Katharina	9, Apr. 1877	22, Mar.	48-10m	Dick	San Jose, IL	119	Esens, Ostfriesland
Rapp, Margaretha	30, July 1857	15, July	39	Leininger	Cincinnati, OH	124	Weaverly, Pike County, Ohio
Rapp, Margaretha	16, Mar. 1874	22, Feb.	23	Barkmeyer	San Jose, IL	87	Eutingen, Baiern
Rapp, Maria	24, Oct. 1881	1, Oct.	25- -4d	Börnschein	Spencerville, OH	343	Hesselweder, Kurhessen
Rapp, Matthias	18, Aug. 1887	3, Aug.	69		Indianapolis, IN	526	Niederwenigen, Regensberg, Zürich, Schweiz
Rapp, Sophia Christina	28, Dec. 1874	12, Dec.	52	Gans	Wathena, KS	415	Miesenbach bei Landstuhl, Baiern
Rapp, Veronica	19, Mar. 1877	25, Feb.	55	Meyer	Wheeling, WV	95	
Raquet, Catharine	15, Nov. 1869	16, Oct.	60-6m-23d		Farmington, WI	367	Klein Jestin, Köslin, Pommern
Rasch, Barbara	19, July 1869	5, July	33	Unglaub	Peru, IL	231	New Orleans, Louisiana
Rasch, Friedrich	8, Mar. 1875	1, Feb.	41		Covington, KY	79	Bremen, Germany
Rasch, Klara	10, Nov. 1892	18, Oct.	40		Cincinnati, OH	718	Falldorf, Westphalen, Preußen
Rasch, Ludwig Theodor	2, Sept 1897	14, Aug.	61		Burlington, IA	559	Scholerten, Steinbrücken, Hannover
Rasche, Anna Margaretha	1, Jan. 1877	18, Dec.	71		Gordonville, MO	7	Gordonville, Cape Girardeau County, Missouri
Rasche, Christine Johanna	26, Oct. 1899	17, Aug.	76	Deneke	Jackson, MO	687	Bippen, Hannover
Rasche, Maria	11, Sept 1890	15, Aug.	21		Metropolis, IL	590	Exter, Westphalen
Rasche, Maria	16, Sept 1878	18, July		Nordemann	Burlington, IA	295	
Rasche, Wilhelm	13, Apr. 1885	28, Mar.	74		Philadelphia, PA	7	Neuhoff, Stolp, Pommern
Rascher, C.	4, Dec. 1871	11, Nov.	38		Chicago, IL	391	Stawanger, Norway
Raschke, Otto	9, Jan. 1882	22, Dec.	31		Baltimore, MD	15	Uphusum, Schleswig-Holstein
Rasmussen, Axel	28, July 1879	11, July	28		Sioux City, IA	239	
Rasmussen, Maria	23, June 1892	18, May	37	Gutschmidt	Brenham, TX	398	Mörsch, Baden
Rast, Sohie	15, Apr. 1872	22, Jan.	46		Louisville, KY	127	
Raststetter, Katharina	17, Mar. 1879	17, Feb.	68-4m-4d	Martin	Pepin, WI	87	Manitowoc, Wisconsin
Rätcke, Rudolph	3, Jan. 1895	14, Dec.	39-3m-14d		Almond, WI	14	Gibbert, Mecklenburg-Schwerin
Rath, Carl J.F.	19, June 1890	22, May	32		Auburn, IN	398	Rottmanshagen, Pommern, Preußen
Rath, Charlotte	19, Nov. 1877	10, Sept	66	Weden	Kendallville, IN	375	Wattmanshagen, Mecklenburg-Schwerin
Rath, F.	14, June 1875	22, May	35-4m-22d		Kewaunee, WI	191	Zarnkow, Mecklenburg-Schwerin
Rath, Johan	22, Sept 1884	7, Sept	58		Oshkosh, WI	7	Nordhemmern, Preußen
Rath, Maria Elisabeth Dorothea	25, Apr. 1895	3, Apr.	67	Hansen	St. Louis, MO	270	
Rathemeyer, Louis	5, Oct. 1874	11, Aug.	35-2m-10d		Sheboygan, WI	319	Streelohagen, Preußen
Rathenmacher, Sophia Wilhelmina	17, Aug. 1854	24, June	47	Bähr	Cincinnati, OH	132	Oldendorf, Amt Zeven, Hannover
Rathgens, Christian Dietrich	5, Nov. 1841		Inquiry		Jordan, MN	175	Lawrenceburg, Dearborn County, Indiana
Rathloff, Louise	26, Feb. 1877	10, Feb.	48-11m-15d		Salt Creek, NE	71	Preußen
Ratje, Johan Heinrich	7, Dec. 1874	13, Nov.	50		Salt Creek, NE	391	
Ratjen, Herman	31, Mar. 1898	5, Mar.	19		Lawrenceburg, IN	207	
Ratloff, Friederika	25, Oct. 1875	27, Sept	65-9m	Meier	Mankato, MN	343	

Christliche Apologete Death Notices -- 1839 - 1899

Name of Deceased	Notice Date	Death Date	Age	Page	Maiden Name	Place of Death	Place of Birth
Rattay, Anna	16, May 1861	19, Mar.		80		Oshkosh, WI	Romanshoff, Bromberg, Posen, Preußen
Rattay, Joseph	8, Dec. 1879	28, Oct. 1879	48- 1m-28d	391		Hays City, KS	Romanshof, Posen, Preußen
Rattstead, Louise	2, July 1896	11, June	63	431		Sheboygan, WI	
Rätzer, Friederike	5, Jan. 1874	31, Oct.	72	7		Marbach, ---	Pleidelsheim,
Rau, Margaretha	5, Nov. 1896		77-10m-18d	719	Nummerich	Belleville, IL	Escholbrücken, Hessen-Darmstadt
Rau, Philipp	4, May 1899	8, Apr.	73	287		Cannelton, IN	Wieseck, Hessen-Nassau
Rau, Anna Elisabeth	5, May 1873	11, Mar.	46	143	Siegfried	Cannelton, IN	Caltern, Kreis Marburg, Kurhessen
Rau, Anna Elisabeth	18, Apr. 1889	28, Mar.	25- -14d	254		Forest, WI	Forest, Wisconsin
Rau, Christiana	20, Jan. 1879	12, Nov.	15- -21d	23		Pittsburg, PA	
Rau, David	15, Jan. 1852	30, Dec.	41-9m-20d	12		Louisville, KY	Winnenden, Württemberg
Rau, Elisabeth	3, Feb. 1879	11, Jan.	52-11m	39	Seibel	Forest, WI	Kleingladenbach, Biedenkopf, Hessen-Darmstadt
Rau, Henry	18, Apr. 1889		28- 5m-24d	254		Forest, WI	Forest, Wisconsin
Rau, Johan	12, Nov. 1891	20, Oct.	33	734		Fond du Lac, WI	Forest, Fond du Lac County, Wisconsin
Rau, Katharina	11, Oct. 1875	6, Sept	76	327	Minch	Cannelton, IN	Leigestern, Kreis Gießen, Hessen
Rau, Lydia Catharina	26, Sept 1889	31, Aug.	14	619		Chicago, IL	Chicago, Cook County, Illinois
Rau, Margaret	28, Mar. 1895	8, Mar.	65	206		Portsmouth, OH	Oberschmitten, Biedingen, Hessen-Darmstadt
Rau, Margaretha	18, Oct. 1888	3, Aug.	18	670		Jeffersonville, IN	
Rau, Margaretha	13, Dec. 1888	3, Aug.	18	798		Jeffersonville, IN	
Rau, Maria Katharina	9, July 1877	14, June	37	223	Rescher	Jeffersonville, IN	Bickenbach, Hessen-Darmstadt
Rau, Philipp	6, Apr. 1893	11, Mar.	103- 5m-27d	222		Cannelton, IN	Wüßeck, Gießen, Hessen-Darmstadt
Räuber, Gertrude	3, Oct. 1895	10, Sept	63	638	Geier	Philadelphia, PA	Adelschorf bei Nürnberg, Baiern
Rauch, Johan Georg	10, Mar. 1887	20, Feb.	68	158		Rochester, NY	Baiern
Rauch, Philippine	11, May 1863	11, May	50	76		Philadelphia, PA	Graben bei Karlsruhe, Baden
Rauch, Rudolph	15, Nov. 1875	3, Nov.	46	367		Chicago, IL	Schramberg, Oberndorf, Württemberg
Rauch, Sophie	22, Feb. 1869	31, Dec.	38- 8m-17d	63	Baab	Philadelphia, PA	Freinsheim, Rheinkreis Baiern
Raue, Emilie	9, Feb. 1899	20, Jan.	74	95	Lüben	Watertown, WI	Wittenwalde, Preußen
Rauh, Franziska	5, Aug. 1886	9, July	28	7	Weiß	Cannelton, IN	Spencer County, Indiana
Rauh, Louise	17, Aug. 1890	24, Mar.	36-10m-23d	254		Detroit, MI	Pittsburg, Pennsylvania
Rauh, Rosina	23, Jan. 1882	8, Jan.	38-10m-11d	31	Haas	Hannibal, MO	Württemberg
Rauler, Christian	20, Oct. 1898	27, Sept	72	671		Lansing, MI	Elshausen, Württemberg
Raus, Ursual	8, Apr. 1852	13, Mar.	54	60	Anselm	Weston, MO	Altenheim am Rhein, Baden
Rausch, Andreas	22, Oct. 1896	18, Sept	25	687		Madison, IN	
Rausch, Anna Maria	1, Aug. 1881	16, July	74- 5m-17d	247		Angelica, NY	Alleghany County, New York
Rausch, Anna Maria	4, Nov. 1878	2, Oct.	51	351	Landwehrs	Warrenton, MO	
Rausch, Carolina	3, Aug. 1893	5, July	55-11m- 3d	494	Feuerstein	Madison, IN	Berg, Trükingen, Elsaß
Rausch, Ehrhardt	28, Oct. 1858	5, Oct.	39	172		Mt. Vernon, IN	Kleinschwartzbach, Oberfranken, Baiern
Rausch, Friederike Dorothea	17, Mar. 1892	25, Jan.	68	174		Angelica, NY	Caneadea, New York
Rausch, Friedrich B.	18, Oct. 1875	24, Sept	22	335		Warrenton, MO	Artern, Preußen
Rausch, Georg	7, Apr. 1873	17, Mar.	75	111		Madison, IN	
Rausch, Johan Christian	23, Apr. 1891	21, Dec.	70	270		Galena, IL	Arlern, Sanderhausen, Merseburg, Sachsen
Rausch, Johanna Eleonora	9, Jan. 1890	14, Jan.	73	30	Kluhs	Jordan, MN	Plomehl, Strehlen, Germany
Rausch, Katharina	12, Feb. 1883	13, Dec.	35	55	Bodenschatz	Santa Claus, IN	Kleinschwarzenbach, Baiern
Rausch, Katharina	27, Dec. 1875	22, Nov.	76	415	Schiffmann	Evansville, IN	Hessen-Darmstadt
Rausch, Michael	17, Dec. 1891			814	Schmid	Madison, IN	Holzhausen, Hausfurth, Baiern
Rausch, Susanna	11, July 1881	11, June	67	223		Madison, IN	Holzhausen , Baiern
Rauschkolb, Anna Lydia	21, Jan. 1886	17, Dec.	25	7	Hüne	Belleville, IL	Canton, Missouri

Christliche Apologete Death Notices --- 1839 - 1899

Name of Deceased	Notice Date	Death Date	Age	Maiden Name	Page	Place of Death	Place of Birth
Rauschkolb, Ludwig	23, Nov. 1863	1, Nov.	46		188	Belleville, IL	Wachenheim a. d. Pfrimm, Hessen-Darmstadt
Rausenberger, Anna M.	4, Aug. 1884	20, July	70		7	Philadelphia, PA	Nusringen, Württemberg
Rausenberger, George Henry	13, Nov. 1882	22, Oct.	29		367	Philadelphia, PA	
Rausenberger, Louisa	3, June 1872	18, Apr.	27-10m-18d		183	Philadelphia, PA	
Rautenburg, Louise	21, Feb. 1876	28, Jan.	78	Recke	63	Rock River, WI	Sellin, Neu-Mark, Frankfurt, Preußen
Ravenstein, Albert W.	13, Dec. 1894	12, Nov.	72-10m		806	Norwich, KS	Kampen, Ostfriesland
Ray, Nikolaus	11, Apr. 1895	8, Mar.	54		238	Mankato, MN	Elsaß
Rebber, Louise	22, Mar. 1869	27, Feb.	26- 9m	Tormmöhlen	95	Huntingburg, IN	Jackson County, Indiana
Rebber, Luisa	9, Jan. 1896	21, Dec.	60	Mönch	30	Terre Haute, IN	Hessen-Kassel
Rebber, Martin	18, May 1885	23, Apr.			7	Terre Haute, IN	
Rebell, Henrietta	3, May 1894	5, Apr.	39		294	Bloomington, IL	Neddesite, Jasmond auf Rügen, Germany
Reber, Elias	25, Sept 1865	27, Aug.	44		156		
Reber, Louise	5, June 1882	11, May	36- 8m-10d	Seibold	183	Bucyrus, OH	Leutenbach, Waiblingen, Württemberg
Rebermeier, Christine	8, Dec. 1859	30, Sept	72		196	Warrenton, MO	Alberdißen, Lippe
Rech, Katharina	30, Mar. 1885	7, Mar.	80		7	Beaufort, MO	Niedermoor, Rheinkreis Baiern
Rechfus, Maria	3, Mar. 1884	27, Dec.	62	Klett	7	Clayton, IA	Illingen, Maulbronn, Württemberg
Rechfuß, Karl Gustav Theodore	18, Apr. 1881	31, Mar.	55		127	Giard, IA	Tuttlingen an der Donau, Württemberg
Rechman, Wilhelm	23, Jan. 1890	8, Nov.	29		62	Belknap, IL	Wähaus, Hannover
Reckenberger, Maria E.	15, Oct. 1896	21, Sept	70	Meyer	671	Baltimore, MD	Etzelheim, Baiern
Recker, Friedrich	15, June 1893	25, May	69		382	Boonville, IN	Birkenfeld, Oldenburg
Recker, H.	4, Jan. 1875	6, Dec.	53		7	St. Paul, MN	Augustdorf, Behringen, Lippe-Detmold
Reckmeier, Maria	12, Feb. 1857	22, Jan.		Hartwig	28	Farmington, IA	Blasheim, Lübbeke, Minden, Preußen
Reckmeyer, (Mrs)	17, Nov. 1892	16, Sept	63		734	Quincy, IL	Herford, Preußen
Reckmeyer, Emilie	9, Feb. 1899	1, Jan.	66		95	Boonville, MO	Bokel, Bielefeld, Minden, Preußen
Reckmeyer, Friedrich	13, Dec. 1894	21, Nov.	66		806	Farmington, IA	Halle , Preußen
Reckmeyer, Heinrich Hermann	2, Oct. 1851	1, Sept	57		160	Union, MO	Bockel, Kreis Halle, Preußen
Recktenwald, Anna	11, Aug. 1879	25, July	81- 9m-27d		255	Auburn, IN	Elsaß
Reckterwalt, (Mr)	3, Mar.1873	15, Jan.	69		71	Ft. Wayne, IN	Marbingen, Metz, Lothringen
Reddinger, Sophia Sus.	6, Apr. 1899	1, Mar.	73	Stier	223	Quincy, IL	Rappenau, Baden
Redecker, Johan Friedrich	24, Nov. 1898	3, Nov.	64		751	Lawrenceville, IN	Teggen, Osnabrück, Hannover
Redecker, Victoria	9, Feb. 1888	22, Jan.	48	Bremmer	94	Rock Island, IL	Baiern
Redeker, Charlotte	22, Mar. 1880	2, Mar.	47- 7m-22d	Halsenberg	95	Morrison, MO	Werste, Eideinghausen, Minden, Preußen
Redeker, Sophie	5, May 1853	7, Feb.	36		72		Liedenhausen, Lippe
Redika, J.H.	20, Apr. 1874	30, Mar.	48- 6m		127	Morrison, MO	Bremen, Minden, Herford, Preußen
Redinger, Georg Peter	6, Sept 1875	10, Aug.	69- 9m-10d		287	Topeka, KS	Lützelsachsen bei Weinheim,
Redinger, Johannes	24, Jan. 1876	9, Jan.	34-10m		31	Warsaw, IL	
Redmann, Michael	14, Feb. 1881	9, Jan.	55- 7m-27d		55	New Ulm, MN	Neuhöfen, Bromberg, Posen
Redwillm, Johan Wilhelm	14, Aug. 1871	27, July	65- 6m		263	Le Sueur, MN	Ladbergen, Tecklenburg, Westphalen
Reed, Daniel	18, June 1883	3, June	64		199	Nebraska City, NE	Pennsylvania
Reed, Margaretha	5, Oct. 1893	5, Sept	22	Benz	638	Marion, OH	Big Island Townshp, Marion County, Ohio
Reeder, Hanna Carolina	28, Feb. 1889	30, Jan.	36	Schulz	142	Anaheim, CA	Lottin bei Neu-Stettin, HinterPommern
Reeker, Caroline	22, Feb. 1894	25, Jan.	59	Koch	126	Pittsfield, IL	Ketterheide, Schottmer, Lippe-Detmold
Reeker, Simon August Adolph	22, Mar. 1888	18, Feb.	64		190	Pittsfield, IL	Knetterheide, Schottmar, Lippe-Detmold
Rees, Heinrich	8, Nov. 1888	8, Oct.	69		718	Indianapolis, IN	Picken, Herbom, Nassau
Rees, Katharina	4, Feb. 1892	1, Jan.		Stolz	78	Indianapolis, IN	Pecken, Nassau
Reesch, Salome Louise	20, Apr. 1874	6, Apr.	14- 5m-11d		127	Galion, OH	

Christliche Apologete Death Notices --- 1839 - 1899

Name of Deceased	Notice Date	Death Date	Age	Maiden Name	Page	Place of Death	Place of Birth
Reese, Anna Elisabeth	5, Dec. 1889	31, Oct.	80	Brinkmann	782	Terre Haute, IN	Kirchheim, Langenholz, Lippe-Detmold
Reese, Emma	18, Oct. 1888	24, Sept	28	Moldenhauer	670	Milwaukee, WI	Watertown, Wisconsin
Reese, Maria Friedrike	31, Oct. 1895	16, Oct.	65	Kunow	702	Milwaukee, WI	
Reese, Simon J.	11, Apr. 1881	10, Mar.	78-10m- 3d		119	Terre Haute, IN	Pillenbruch, Hohenhausen, Lippe-Detmold
Reese, Sophia	21, Mar. 1889	26, Feb.	66	Kordemann	190	Pittsfield, IL	Horn, Lippe-Detmold
Reetz, Carl Joachim	18, Oct. 1894	26, Aug.	78		678	Seattle, WA	Anklam, Pommern
Reetz, Karl August	29, June 1899	8, June	64		415	West Point, NE	Wriezen an der Oder, Brandenburg
Reetz, Wilhelmine	1, June 1874	30, Apr.	40	Gertshow	175	Rockford, MN	Zettemin, Stettin, Preußen
Refeld, Maria	19, May 1879	4, May	58-10m-15d	Brandt	159	Schnectady, NY	Einbeck, Hannover
Regal, August C.	5, Jan. 1899	24, Nov.	34		15	Chase, WI	Johannesthal, Wersitz, Posen
Regal, August Carl	11, Apr. 1889	18, Mar.	42		238	Green Bay, WI	Djumjonik, Posen
Regal, Edward G.	13, Feb. 1896	1, Jan.	22		110	Chase , Wisconsin	Chase , Wisconsin
Regal, Gottfried	4, Feb. 1884	8, Jan.	47		7	Green Bay, WI	Falkenmühle, Preußen
Regitz, Louis	3, July 1865	7, June	35		108	Ft. Wayne, IN	Carlsbrunn, Preußen
Rehbehn, Christina	30, June 1887	5, Mar.	70-11m-27d	Reichhardt	414	Muscatine, IA	Schwabstedt, Husum, Schleswig-Holstein
Rehbein, August	6, Apr. 1885	18, Mar.	75- 1m-21d		7	St. Paul, MN	Gällin, Pommern
Rehbein, Wilhelmine	20, May 1897	3, May	80	Priebe	319	Manitowoc, WI	Pommern
Rehberger, Gertrud	26, Feb. 1877	10, Feb.	78-10m-24d	Kleinschmidt	71	Baltimore, MD	Hessen-Darmstadt
Rehkop, Heinrich Chr. August	8, Apr. 1886	23, Mar.	25		7	Concordia, MO	Colefeld, Osterode, Hannover
Rehling, Carl Wilhelm	17, Dec. 1891	22, Nov.	75		814	Decatur, IN	Bückeburg, Lippe-Detmold
Rehls, Julia Anna	31, Jan. 1889	17, Jan.	27- 1m- 7d		78	Platteville, WI	Platteville, Wisconsin
Rehm, Catharina	1, Sept 1862	24, July	30- 4m- 9d	Buße	140	Newark, OH	Lambach, Baiern
Rehm, Karl	13, Jan. 1873	12, Dec.	36		15	Galena, IL	Büchauer, Württemberg
Rehm, Magdalena	3, May 1860	15, Apr.	30	Mayer	72	Ann Arbor, MI	Nufringen, Herrenberg, Württemberg
Rehs, Christoph	4, Aug. 1892	30, June	48		494	Ironton, OH	Bebra, Rodenburg, Kurhessen
Rehs, Conrad	20, July 1863	22, May	23- 5m-16d		116	Portsmouth, OH	Bäbra Rotenburg, Kurhessen
Reiber, Anna Catharina	12, Jan. 1874	23, Dec.	43- 4m	Vögelin	15	San Jose, IL	Reilingen, Baden
Reiber, Anna Maria	10, Feb. 1879	28, Jan.	20		47	Portsmouth, OH	Sidney, Shelby County, Ohio
Reiber, Elisabeth	14, Apr. 1859	5, Mar.	53		60	Rockford, IN	Lettweiler, Rheinkreis Baiern
Reiber, Emma	3, Jan. 1881	17, Dec.	19- 1m-26d		7	Marietta, OH	Hanging Rock, Ohio
Reiber, Gesche Margaretha	11, June 1891	25, May	67	Bollmann	382	Columbus, OH	Schwarmen, Westen, Hannover
Reibert, Adam	21, May 1896	5, May	54		334	St. Louis, MO	Coshocton County, Ohio
Reich, Anna R.	19, Oct. 1863	26, July	42		168	New Knoxville, OH	Pennsylvania
Reich, Emilie	8, Dec. 1879	15, Nov.	15		391	West Point, NE	
Reich, Gertrude Elisabeth	10, Nov. 1862	5, Oct.	25	Roß	180	Warsau, IL	Vockerode, Melsungen, Kurhessen
Reichardt, Cotula	21, Apr. 1898	25, Mar.	78	Goll	255	Marietta, OH	Weilheim, Kirchheim, Württemberg
Reichardt, Elisabeth	13, Apr. 1893	15, Mar.	69	Bock	238	Tinley Park, IL	Rohra, Sachsen-Weimar
Reichardt, Emma Karolina	1, Mar. 1894	1, Feb.	24	Wieting	150	Brillion, WI	Charlestown, Wisconsin
Reichardt, Georg	15, June 1893	25, May	37		382	Indianapolis, IN	Marietta, Ohio
Reichardt, Johannes	27, Jan. 1898	5, Jan.	77		63	Indianapolis, IN	Kupingen, Herrenberg, Württemberg
Reichardt, Katharina	2, Apr. 1896	17, Mar.	52	Caflisch	222	Brillion, WI	Schweiz
Reichardt, Wilhelm Heinrich	24, Nov. 1884	19, Oct.	20		7	Brillion, WI	Maple Grove, Wisconsin
Reichart, Margaretha	1, Jan. 1877	4, Dec.	76	Schiller	7	New Bremen, IL	Schloßvippach, Sachsen-Weimar
Reiche , Johanna Rosina	30, June 1859	25, May	38-11m-10d		104	Madison, WI	
Reiche, Carl Friedrich Wilhelm	20, Apr. 1863	4, Mar.	15		64	Columbus, WI	Leipzig,
Reiche, Dina	11, July 1881	21, June	26	Schröder	223	Great Bend, KS	Barver, Diepholz, Hannover

Christliche Apologete Death Notices --- 1839 - 1899

Name of Deceased	Notice Date	Death Date	Age	Maiden Name	Page	Place of Death	Place of Birth
Reiche, W.F.	19, Mar. 1866	23, Feb.	41		94	Madison, WI	Bresen, Sachsen
Reichele, (Mrs)	9, Feb. 1874	20, Jan.		Werner	47	Chillicothe, OH	
Reichelt, Gottlieb	18, Apr. 1889	20, Mar.	74		254	Evansville, IN	Neugersdorf, Sachsen
Reichelt, Philippine	19, Apr. 1888		63	Senn	254	Evansville, IN	Mehlbach, Rheinkreis Baiern
Reichen, Rosina	25, Apr. 1895	25, Mar.	20		270	Portland, OR	Adelboden, Frutigen, Bern, Schweiz
Reichenbach, Emilie Rosine	10, Dec. 1883	15, Nov.	24- 8m- 2d	Müller	7	Philadelphia, PA	
Reichenecker, Anna Maria	21, May 1891	31, Mar.	34- 9m		334	Rochester, NY	Neuhausen an der Ems, Württemberg
Reichenecker, Michael	14, Aug. 1856	14, July	52		132	Rochester, NY	
Reichenegger, Anna Maria	23, Apr. 1891	31, Mar.	34- 9m		270	Rochester, NY	Neuhausen an der Ems, Württemberg
Reichert, Barbara	12, June 1882	26, May	71- 6m-22d		191	Delaware, OH	Horheim, Württemberg
Reichert, Barbara	29, Apr. 1858	6, Apr.	70- 4m	Hoff	68	Milan, IN	Krießheim, Elsaß
Reichert, Caroline	23, Dec. 1867	28, Nov.	27	Graff	406	Delaware, OH	Häfnerhaßloch, Brackenheim, Württemberg
Reichert, Gottfried	25, Nov. 1858	2, Nov.	30- 8m- 1d		188	Allegheny City, PA	Rohrdorf, Nagold, Württemberg
Reichert, Johan	20, Dec. 1875	30, Nov.	59-10m- 6d		407	Jeffersonville, NY	Thailfingen, Herrenberg, Württemberg
Reichert, Juliane	21, July 1862	8, May	39- 3m- 4d		116	Bushnell, IL	
Reichert, Maria	24, Jan. 1889		64- 1m-28d		62	Brookville, IN	Kries, Brumpt, Elsaß
Reichert, Tobias Fr.	6, Oct. 1879	23, Sept			319		Illingen, Maulbronn, Württemberg
Reichhard, Enoch	29, Nov. 1880	13, Nov.	83- 9m-11d		383	New Bremen, IL	Schloß Vippach, Sachsen-Weimar
Reichhardt, Friedrich	22, Nov. 1888	3, Nov.	72- 9m-15d		750	Mt. Vernon, IN	Backnang, Württemberg
Reichhardt, Magdalena	3, Jan. 1889	28, Nov.	84- 1m-12d		14	Mt. Vernon, IN	Fornsbach, Backnang, Württemberg
Reichmann, Christian	2, Mar. 1899	30, Jan.	80		143	Holt, MI	Illingen, Maulbronn, Württemberg
Reichmann, Johan Fr.	22, Feb. 1875	30, Jan.	65- - 5d		63	St. Joseph, MO	Dillenburg, Nassau
Reichmann, Karoline Amalie	17, Sept 1857	17, May	42	Schlegel	152	St. Joseph, MO	Pirna, Sachsen
Reichmann, Katharina	22, July 1897	3, July	68		463	Lansing, MI	Malstatt Saarbrücken, Rheinpfalz Baiern
Reichow, Augusta Louisa	5, Dec. 1881		22		391	Washington, MN	
Reichstadt, Joseph	29, Mar. 1880		51- 1m-15d		103	Salem, ---	Winzeln, Oberndorf, Württemberg
Reidel, Katharina	23, Jan. 1875	24, Dec.	51- 2m-14d	Hoch	31	Giard, IA	Biebelsheim, Wöllstein, Hessen-Darmstadt
Reidenbach, Emma	2, Apr. 1883	16, Mar.	28	Munk	111	Goshen, IN	
Reidenbach, Heinrich	25, Jan. 1864	25, Nov.	20- -11d		16	Kendallville, IN	Kirchroth, Meißenheim, Homburg, Hessen
Reidenbach, Philipp	14, Nov. 1881	18, Oct.	61		367	Kendallville, IN	Marburg,
Reidt, Peter	15, Jan. 1852	7, Dec.	33-10m-17d		12	Baltimore, MD	Germany
Reif, Magdalena	19, Aug. 1897	9, July	77	Gabels	527	Chillicothe, OH	
Reif, (Mr)	2, Aug. 1869				247	Sarkelville, ---	
Reif, Anna Mathilda	6, May 1872		15- 2m-26d		151	Hamilton, OH	Hamilton, Butler County, Ohio
Reif, Christina	25, Feb. 1892	5, Feb.	75- 8m- 5d	Koch	127	Dodgeville, IA	Schwegenheim, Germersheim, Baiern
Reif, Franz	9, Oct. 1871	8, Sept	61		327	Flint Creek, IA	Lachen, Neustadt a. d. Haardt, Rheinpfalz Baiern
Reif, Georg Adam	30, Mar. 1885	9, Mar.	78		7	Freeport, IL	Stein, Bretten, Baden
Reif, George	13, Dec. 1880	24, Nov.	9		399	West Side, IA	San Jose, Illinois
Reif, Johan	15, Dec. 1873	24, Nov.	63		399	Chillicothe, OH	Lachen, Baiern
Reif, Johan Conrad	13, Dec. 1880	27, Nov.	3		399	West Side, IA	Arcadia, Iowa
Reif, Katharina	9, June 1848		42	Fürst	96	Circleville, OH	Zeiskano bei Landau, Baiern
Reif, Ph.	31, May 1869	24, Apr.	61- -10d		175	Ironton, OH	Sciotoville, Scioto County, Ohio
Reif, Rosa	1, Sept 1892	5, Aug.	21		558	Burlington, IA	Lancaster County, Pennsylvania
Reiff, Fanny	31, May 1880	9, May	76- 1m-24d		175	Hamilton, OH	Unterhausen, Reutlingen, Württemberg
Reiff, Maria Agnes	5, Aug. 1897	15, July	69		495	Hamilton, OH	Baden
Reih, Elisabeth	11, Oct. 1860	25, Jan.	56- 6m-11d		164	Lexington, MI	

- 397 -

Christliche Apologete Death Notices --- 1839 - 1899

Name of Deceased	Notice Date	Death Date	Age	Page	Maiden Name	Place of Death	Place of Birth
Reiher, Sophia	10, Oct. 1895	14, Sept	35	654	Hülskämper	Detroit, MI	Detroit, Wayne County, Michigan
Reil, Catharine Maria	9, Sept 1872	6, Aug.	45	295		Washington, ---	Menslage, Osnabrück, Hannover
Reilein, Tillie	5, Jan. 1899	8, Dec.	31	15		Aurora, IL	
Reim, Karolina	7, Nov. 1861	25, Oct.	19- 5m-30d	180		Cincinnati, OH	
Reiman, Marie	2, Nov. 1874	21, Oct.	26	351		Chicago, IL	
Reimbold, Catharina Elisabeth	1, May 1876	14, Apr.	41	143	Reitz	Lansing, IA	Ober-Appenfeldt, Kurhessen
Reimer, Jürchen P.F.	26, Jan. 1860	10, Jan.	17	16		Chester, IL	Petersdorf, Fehmern Island, Dänemark
Reimer, Margaretha	5, May 1879	16, Apr.	28- 6m- 7d	143	Becker	Evansville, IN	Chester, Illinois
Reimer, Maria Sophia	8, June 1899	19, May	39	367	Dannenbrink	Chester, IL	Randolph County, Illinois
Reimer, Sophia	14, Feb. 1876	23, Jan.	20	55		Chester, IL	Rediwitz, Pommern
Reimers, Charlotte	22, July 1897	31, May		463	Zimmermann	Eldora, IA	Holstein
Reimers, Reimer	31, May 1888	11, May	69	350		Eldora, IA	
Reimler, Anna	6, Dec. 1894	30, Oct.	42	790	Revier	Baltimore, MD	Emden, Ostfriesland
Reimler, Christine Maria	24, Aug. 1893	24, July	65	542	Buddenbohm	Baltimore, MD	Minden, Preußen
Rein , John Conrad	26, Apr. 1860	14, Mar.	72-10m-15d	68		Baresville, OH	Oeschingen, Schwarzwald, Württemberg
Rein, A.	28, Sept 1893	6, Sept	26	622		Los Angeles, CA	Lorn, Marburg, Germany
Rein, Gottliebin	24, May 1875	28, Apr.	82- 5m-11d	167		Burlington, IA	Horheim, Württemberg
Rein, Katharina	9, Dec. 1878	18, Nov.	31	391	Klostermann	Louisville, KY	Markedel, Amt Hanau, Kurhessen
Reinbe, Joachim	29, Nov. 1869	8, Oct.	64- 9m-19d	383		LaCrosse, WI	
Reineberg, Dorothea	17, Mar. 1892	14, Feb.	64	174	Albers	Indianapolis, IN	Amte-Bassum, Hannover
Reineberg, Johan Heinrich	12, Dec. 1881	25, Nov.	77	399		Indianapolis, IN	Wildeshausen, Oldenburg
Reineberg, Katharina Maria	27, Jan. 1879	8, Jan.	29-10m-15d	31		Aurora, IN	Milan, Ripley County, Indiana
Reineberg, Maria	4, July 1889	12, June	37	430	Reichart	Indianapolis, IN	Marietta, Ohio
Reineberg, Richard D.	20, July 1885	5, July	33	7		Junction City, KS	
Reineberg, Wilhelmina	29, Oct. 1891	9, Oct.	26	702	Dieterich	Indianapolis, IN	
Reinecke, Emilie	26, July 1880	16, July	16- 4m-12d	239		Indianapolis, IN	
Reineke, August	2, Nov. 1899	17, Oct.	61	703		Flood Creek, IA	Buche bei Lemjo, Lippe-Detmold
Reineke, Conrad	10, Nov. 1884	16, Oct.	64	7		Farmington, IA	Wehningen, Ruthe, Hannover
Reineke, Conrad	15, Sept 1862	21, Aug.	52	148		Morristown, MN	Göderingen, Hannover
Reineke, Fr.	30, Aug. 1875	23, July	71- 3m- 8d	279		Altamont, IL	Daberkow, Kreis Demmin, Preußen
Reineke, Hannah L.S.	20, July 1893	26, June	74	462	Lücke	Pittsfield, IL	Werl, Schottener, Lippe-Detmold
Reineke, Hulda Emma	30, Mar. 1893	6, Feb.	13	206		Blooming Grove, MN	Blooming Grove, Minnesota
Reineke, Katharine Elisabeth	1, Sept 1887	2, Aug.	30- 1m-20d	558	Reckmeyer	Farmington, IA	
Reineke, Simon F.	12, Nov. 1896	15, Oct.	84	734		Pittsfield, IL	Herrscherheide, Lippe-Detmold
Reineker, Leontine M.	19, Sept 1864	31, Aug.	32- 2m- 7d	152	Bert	Quincy, IL	North Sea, Atlantic Ocean
Reineking, Albertine	3, July 1890	22, May	46	430	Nizle	Storm Lake, IA	
Reiners, Heinrich	6, Oct. 1879	20, Sept	32- 5m-20d	319		Santa Claus, IN	Ripley County, Indiana
Reiners, Johan Heinrich	24, Apr. 1890	3, Apr.	79	270		Santa Claus, IN	Vahmesch, Goldenstedt, Vechta, Oldenburg
Reiners, John	14, Apr. 1862		17- 4m	60		Santa Claus, IN	Ripley County, Indiana
Reiners, Wilhelm	8, Oct. 1877	24, Sept	28	327		Chicago, IL	Kuschern, Preußen
Reinet, Maria	25, Dec. 1890	1, Dec.	77- 5m- 7d	830	Lehmann	Milwaukee, WI	Horheim, Vaihingen, Württemberg
Reinfrank, Daniel	7, July 1898	12, June	79	431		Des Moines, IA	Pfeddersheim, Germany
Reinhard, Alexander	1, Aug. 1895	11, July	74	494		Allegheny City, PA	Makbreit, Baiern
Reinhard, Anna Margarethe	8, Nov. 1880	22, Oct.	52	359	Förster	Blooming Grove, MN	Angermünde, Ukermark, Potsdam, Preußen
Reinhard, Gottfried	17, July 1876	8, June	54	231			
Reinhard, Heinrich	24, Sept 1841	17, Sept	5	151			

Christliche Apologete Death Notices --- 1839 - 1899

Name of Deceased	Notice Date	Death Date	Age	Maiden Name	Page	Place of Death	Place of Birth
Reinhard, Maria	21, Oct. 1872	3, Oct.	37		343	New Haven, CT	Sindelfinden, Württemberg
Reinhard, Regina	26, Nov. 1847	19, Sept			191	Boonville, IN	
Reinhardt, (boy)	22, Oct. 1841	Sept	4		167	Cincinnati, OH	
Reinhardt, Anna	11, May 1899	4, Apr.	61	Auwärter	302	Akron, NY	Heidelberg, Württemberg
Reinhardt, August	17, Nov. 1884	28, Oct.			7	Woodbury, MN	
Reinhardt, Christoph Otto	10, Nov. 1862	19, Oct.	9- -3d		180	Golconda, IL	Waverly, Ohio
Reinhardt, Daniel Friedrich	3, Jan. 1881	19, Dec.	22- 9m- 7d		7	Waverly, OH	Oeritz, Falling-Bostel, Hannover
Reinhardt, Dorothea Maria	24, June 1897	30, May	62		399	Le Sueur, MN	
Reinhardt, Emilie	20, Aug. 1891	10, July	18		542	Kansas City, KS	
Reinhardt, Friedrich	1, June 1893	7, May	70		350	Allegan, MI	Battenfeld, Hessen-Darmstadt
Reinhardt, Friedrich	8, June 1893	7, May	70		366	Allegan, MI	Battenfeld, Hessen-Darmstadt
Reinhardt, Jakob	6, Apr. 1868	16, Mar.	45		111	Allegan, MI	RheinPreußen
Reinhardt, Johannes H.	3, Mar. 1884	1, Dec.	66- 4m-12d		7	San Jose, CA	Illfach, Elsaß
Reinhardt, John	7, Jan. 1884	15, Dec.	57		7	Kendallville, IN	Heenes, Kurhessen
Reinhardt, Karl W.	10, Apr. 1876	18, Mar.	17- 2m		118	Le Sueur, MN	
Reinhardt, Louise	31, Mar. 1898	2, Mar.	21	Klemm	207	Mason City, IA	Happenbach, Württemberg
Reinhardt, Maria	22, Oct. 1841	Oct.	18m		167	Cincinnati, OH	
Reinhardt, Rosela	24, Nov. 1892	19, Oct.	70		750	San Jose, CA	Mühlhausen, Elsaß
Reinhardt, Wilhelm	9, July 1891	19, June	56		446	Pekin, IL	Wollrode, Melsungen, Kurhessen
Reinhardt, Wilhelm Heinrich	10, Nov. 1884	19, Oct.	20		7	Brillion, WI	Maple Grove, Wisconsin
Reinhart, (Mrs)	7, Oct. 1897	3, Sept	77		639	Laporte, IN	Knorrendorf, Mecklenburg-Schwerin
Reinhart, (Mrs)	10, Oct. 1864	25, Sept	63		164	Seymour, IN	
Reinhart, Amalie	5, May 1879	1, Apr.	38	Mulfinger	143	Pekin, IL	Lawrenceburg, Ripley County, Indiana
Reinhart, Anna Martha	19, Apr. 1880	30, Mar.	58		127	Kendallville, IN	Heenes, Kreis Hersfeld, Kurhessen
Reinhart, Christian	17, Mar.1873	24, Feb.	22- 6m		87	Lowell, WI	Fleins, Graubünden, Schweiz
Reinhart, David	1, Mar. 1855	2, Feb.	56		36	Waukegan, IL	Vogelsberg, Sachsen-Weimar
Reinhart, Dorothea	29, July 1852	9, July	41- 6m		124	Cincinnati, OH	Ehringshagen, Amt Wülbe, Hannover
Reinhart, Johan	6, Feb. 1882	23, Jan.	50- 3m		47	Laporte, IN	Kasdorf, Mecklenburg-Schwerin
Reinhart, Johannes	31, May 1888	4, May	56- 1m- 4d		350	Kendallville, IN	Gerterode, Hessen
Reinhart, Justus	30, Mar. 1893	1, Mar.	30		206	Blooming Grove, MN	North Lake, Waukesha County, Wisconsin
Reinhart, Louis	14, Aug. 1856	3, July	6- 6m		132	Covington, KY	
Reinhart, Maria	23, Feb. 1885	10, Feb.	98	Bacherts	7	Laporte, IN	Ritzerau, Mecklenburg-Schwerin
Reinhart, Maria Elisabeth	11, May 1868	24, Mar.	44		151	Waverly, OH	Frankenhausen, Schwarzburg-Rudolstadt
Reinhart, Susanna Maria	29, May 1876	12,May	66- 7m- 6d		175	Washington, MN	Fambach, Schmalkalden, Kurhessen
Reinhart, Wilhelm	11, Aug. 1887	18, July	27		510	Wheeling, WV	Monroe County, Ohio
Reinheimer, Daniel	4, Nov. 1897	18, Sept	83		703	Sheboygan, WI	Wolfstein, Baiern
Reinheimer, Regina	24, Sept 1878	15, Aug.	57- 9m- 4d	Imlin	303	Scott, WI	Gündelbach, Maulbronn, Württemberg
Reinhold, Karl	14, Apr. 1884	22, Mar.			7	Dalton, MO	
Reinick, Elisabeth	4, Aug. 1879	11, July	50- 3m- 5d	Dahlem	247	Fond du Lac, WI	Wiesbaden, Hessen-Nassau
Reinicker, F.J.	5, Dec. 1889	19, Nov.	64		782	St. Paul, MN	Mühlhausen, Thüringen, Sachsen
Reinig, Maria	31, May 1888	30, Apr.	39	Amrhein	350	Saginaw, MI	Ruppertenrod, Hessen-Darmstadt
Reining, Conrad	16, Feb. 1860	21, Dec.	65		28	Beardstown, IL	Reuters, Lauterbach, Hessen-Darmstadt
Reining, Conrad	19, Jan. 1880	18, Dec.	56		23	Arenzville, IL	Reutersch, Lauterbach, Hessen
Reinke, Heinrich	9, May 1895	16, Apr.	77		302	Batesville, IN	Lienen, Bracke, Lippe-Detmold
Reinken, Maria Louisa	13, Nov. 1876	21, Oct.	75- 6m		367	Schnectady, NY	Eickhorst, Preußen
Reinken, Maria Louisa	22, Jan. 1877	21, Oct.	75- 6m	Woellner	31	Schnectady, NY	Eickhorst, Preußen

Christliche Apologete Death Notices --- 1839 - 1899

Name of Deceased	Notice Date	Death Date	Age	Page	Maiden Name	Place of Death	Place of Birth
Reinkens, Carolina Maria	27, Jan. 1887	12, Jan.	55	62	Schwenker	Columbus, OH	Hille, Minden, Preußen
Reinkens, Hattie Elisabeth	20, Nov. 1882	25, Sept	22	375	Pepper	Schenectady, NY	Waterfield, Albany County, New York
Reinkens, Herman	6, June 1870	15, Apr.	68	183		Schenectady, NY	Eichhorst, Minden, Preußen
Reinkens, Johan Heinrich	28, June 1875	16, May	13- 6m	207		Columbus, OH	
Reinkins, Marie Louise Fr.	6, Aug. 1896	9, July	73- 8m-12d	511	Lückens	Schenectady, NY	Eickhorst, Minden, Preußen
Reinkins, Sophie Henriette	3, Jan. 1895	9, Dec.	61	14	Brandhorst	Schenectady, NY	Hille, Minden, Preußen
Reinl, Barbara	7, May 1896	10, Apr.	62	302		Waterbury, CT	Walterdorf bei Wien, Oesterreich
Reinmels, Johanna Henrietta	3, Feb. 1873	2, Jan.	49	39		New York City, NY	
Reinmuth, Johan	9, Dec. 1872	24, Nov.	80	399		Hebron, IA	Neunkirchen, Amt Eberbach, Baden
Reinmuth, Johan Adam	2, May 1895	8, Apr.	69	286		Hebron, IA	Neukirchen, Baden
Reinmuth, John	22, Jan. 1861	18, Dec.	2	16		Des Moines, IA	
Reinsch, Augusta	28, Mar. 1881	9, Mar.	56	103		Danville, IL	
Reinschild, Helena	20, Jan. 1898	12, Dec.	40	47		Los Angeles, CA	
Reinschild, John	24, July 1856	29, June	10	120		Pomeroy, OH	Dresden, Sachsen
Reinsdorf, Julius	31, Dec. 1877	19, Dec.	43	423		Sandwich, IL	Burg bei Magdeburg, Preußen
Reinsdorf, Katharina	22, Jan. 1866	26, Dec.	35	30	Hechler	Aurora, IL	Gelmersbach, Württemberg
Reinwald, Elisabeth	8, June 1874	21, May	71	183		Marietta, OH	Schwaigern, Brackenheim, Württemberg
Reinwald, Johan Jakob	6, May 1878	31, Mar.	71- 5m- 5d	143		Marietta, OH	Schweigern, Brackenheim, Württemberg
Reis, Maria	8, Dec. 1892	12, Nov.	62	782	Fuhrmann	Louisville, KY	Melsheim, Elsaß
Reischel, Wilhelmina	26, Mar. 1877	2, Mar.	50	103	Schwertfeger	St. Joseph, MO	
Reischer, Catharina	26, July 1880	30, May	68- 4m-14d	239	Mühlhaus	Delaware, OH	Diebach, Hessen-Darmstadt
Reisener, Heinrich	25, Apr. 1881	6, Apr.	73-10m-28d	135		Farmington, IA	Pyrmont, Waldeck
Reiser, Johannes	8, Mar. 1869	21, Feb.	79	79		Waterloo, IA	Heimisweil, Bern, Schweiz
Reisner, (Mrs)	3, Mar. 1879	9, Feb.	85	71	Kruse	Farmington, IA	Werfleih, Oldenburg
Reisner, Marie	9, July 1883	23, June	64	223	König	Farmington, IA	
Reisner, Minnie	6, Nov. 1876	7, Oct.	20	359		Farmington, IA	Farmington, Iowa
Reiß, Bertha	23, May 1895	27, Mar.	42	334	Ziemann	Milwaukee, WI	Meßdorf, Pommern
Reißer, Paul Christian	20, Dec. 1860	8, Nov.	40	204		Dayton, OH	Oberamt Leonberg, Württemberg
Reißner, Catharina	31, Jan. 1889	5, Dec.	65	78		Davenport, IA	Baden
Reister, John	10, Dec. 1883	27, Nov.	66	7		New Albany, IN	Stein, Baden
Reister, Regina	9, Mar. 1899	11, Jan.	74	159	Schleehausen	New Albany, IN	Hasloch bei Stuttgart, Württemberg
Reiter, (Mrs)	15, Nov. 1869	31, Oct.	57	367	Ohto	Belleville, IL	Usingen, Nassau
Reiter, Adam	14, Aug. 1865	10, July	58	132		Portsmouth, OH	Oppau, Rheinkreis Baiern
Reiter, Agathe	24, July 1882	10, July	76	239		Portsmouth, OH	Hättesheim, Baden
Reiter, Anna Maria	9, Mar. 1854	24, Jan.	8	40		Pomeroy, OH	
Reiter, Christina	2, Aug. 1849	28, June	14	124		St. Louis, MO	
Reiter, John	11, July 1864	3, May	46	112		Canton, MO	Kreutzwertheim, Baden
Reith, Luise Maria	26, Oct. 1899	24, Sept	77	687		San Jose, CA	Meißenheim, Baden
Reith, Sophie Maria Friedrike	19, Oct. 1893	19, Sept	67	670	Hartwig	Akron, NY	Gaazerhof, Mecklenburg-Schwerin
Reithmeier, Wilhelm H.	1, May 1876	19, Mar.	33	143		Ironton, OH	Etna-Furnace, Lawrence County, Ohio
Reitmeyer, Katharina	13, Mar. 1890	21, Feb.	78- 1m-24d	174	Gospel	Portsmouth, OH	Fladder-Lohhausen, Holdorf, Oldenburg
Reitmeyer, Wilhelm	26, July 1880		62	239		Portsmouth, OH	Hundeburg, Hannover
Reitz, (Mrs)	4, Dec. 1851	24, Oct.	69-11m-19d	196		Monroe, IL	Gelnhausen, Amt Bieber, Hessen
Reitz, Adam	2, June 1862	18, Mar.	21-7w-2d	88		Red Bud, IL	
Reitz, Elisabeth	24, June 1852	1, June	35	104	Geiger	Marthasville, MO	Bieber bei Gelnhausen, Kurhessen
Reitz, Georg	5, Feb. 1852	15, Dec.	41- 8m- 8d	24		Monroe, IL	Gelnhausen, Amt Bieber, Kurhessen

Christliche Apologete Death Notices --- 1839 - 1899

Name of Deceased	Notice Date	Death Date	Age	Page	Maiden Name	Place of Death	Place of Birth
Reitz, Nicolaus	19, Jan. 1893	25, Dec.	80	46		Monticello, KS	Biber, Gelnhausen, Kurhessen
Reitze, Henry	23, June 1898	7, May	68	399		Denver, CO	Haddamar, Fritzlar, Kurhessen
Reitzel, Louise	5, Apr. 1860	17, Jan.	32	56	Feißel	Kingston, IL	
Rekopp, Wilhelmine	3, Nov. 1873	17, Oct.	22-3m	351		Concordia, MO	Mt. Vernon, Posey County, Indiana
Reller, Catharina E.	6, Oct. 1873	11, Sept	14-7m	319		Centreville, NE	
Reller, Heinrich C.	4, May 1899	2, Mar.	62	287		Sprague, NE	Hannover
Rellstab, Theodor	22, Aug. 1895	6, Aug.	36	542		New Rochelle, NY	Neuenkirch, Schaffhausen, Schweiz
Remagen, Bertha C.	21, May 1877	3, Jan.	14	166		Louisville, KY	Jefferson County, Kentucky
Remagen, Fr.	7, Feb. 1881	14, Jan.	69-6m-11d	47		Louisville, KY	Oberhinnrich, Neuwied, Koblenz, Preußen
Reman, Maria	31, July 1876	17, July	31	247	Bähr	New Ulm, MN	Korganke, Kreis Flatow, Preußen
Rembold, Jakob Wilhelm	15, Dec. 1887	28, Nov.	27	798		Santa Claus, IN	Spencer County, Indiana
Remer, Ida	20, June 1895	1, June	35	398	Gralapp	Lemars, IA	Friendship, Fond du Lac County, Wisconsin
Remer, Karoline	17, Mar. 1898	21, Feb.	35	175	Hilmer	Lemars, IA	Waldeck
Remerscheid, Friedrich Karl	1, Nov. 1888	9, Oct.	65- -19d	702		Burlington, IA	Schellenbach, Kumersbach, Köln, Preußen
Remert, Ferdinand	26, Apr. 1860		54	68		Lancaster, WI	Wilberg, Lippe-Detmold
Remling, (Mrs)	5, Mar. 1866	2, Feb.	56	78		Etna, MO	Bräustedt, Braunschweig
Remmer, Nettie	22, Jan. 1883	15, Dec.	13	31		Friendship, WI	
Remmert, Karoline Wilhelmine H.	31, Dec. 1896	9, Dec.	44	844	Brockmann	Bushton, KS	Kolstett, Lippe-Detmold
Remmert, Wilhelmine	2, May 1881	19, Apr.	73-8m	143		Lancaster, WI	Bavenhausen, Lippe-Detmold
Remond, Anna	27, Mar. 1871	23, Feb.	34-7m-13d	103	Jüni	Blooming Grove, MN	Mühlebach, Bern, Schweiz
Remond, Samuel	28, July 1862	8, May	6- -7d	120		Morristown, MN	
Remund, Anna	28, Feb. 1889	5, Feb.	62	142	Baumgardner	Blooming Grove, MN	Rapperwill, Uetlingen, Bern, Schweiz
Remund, Barbara	16, June 1873	24, May	78	191	Niederhauser	Blooming Grove, MN	Eggiwyl, Langnau, Bern, Schweiz
Remund, Elisabeth	23, Feb. 1874	6, Feb.	31-6m-12d	63	Neuhardt	Blooming Grove, MN	Monroe County, Ohio
Remund, Johan	27, Dec. 1894	26, Nov.	64	836		Wilmot, SD	Buttenried, Munteberg, Bern, Schweiz
Remund, Samuel	17, Aug. 1868	3, Aug.	62	263		Wilton, MN	Mühlenberg, Laupen, Bern, Schweiz
Remund, Ursulene	26, Jan. 1899		54	63	Schneke	Blooming Grove, MN	Daffosdörfle, Graubünden, Schweiz
Remus, Emilie Karoline Friederike	6, Apr. 1899	15, Mar.	23	223		Bristol, WI	Klein-Krösin, Belgard, Preußen
Rendelmann, Sophie	11, Sept 1871	15, Aug.	74	295		Groefes?, IL	Magdeburg, Preußen
Renebohm, Antoinette	11, Jan. 1875	22, Dec.	22	15		Chicago, IL	Bremen, Germany
Renike, Margaretha	20, Dec. 1855	1, Dec.	45- -29d	204	Medjen	Indianapolis, IN	Erichshof, Amt Sicke, Hannover
Renke, Louise	6, Aug. 1866	14, July	75	254		Cincinnati, OH	Reibersdorf, Sachsen
Renken, Jurgen J.	5, Jan. 1893	18, Dec.	89	14		Alden, IA	Ostfriesland
Renkert, John	29, Dec. 1862	4, Nov.	20	208		Sherrills Mount, IA	Sherrill's Mound, Iowa
Renkert, Matthäus	4, Jan. 1894	20, Nov.		14		Sherrills Mount, IA	Menge, Freiburg, Baden
Rennabohm, Dorothea	6, Oct. 1898	5, Aug.	84	639	Freudenreich	Blue Island, IL	Bremen, Germany
Rennebohm, Heinrich F.C.	24, July 1871	30, June	57	239		Chicago, IL	Hohe, Braunschweig
Renner, (Mrs)	2, Jan. 1896	6, Dec.	70	14	Lobricht	Delaware, OH	Hessen-Darmstadt
Renner, Conrad	1, Apr. 1872	16, Mar.	74	111		Des Moines, IA	
Renner, Eva Barbara	7, Jan. 1867	4, Dec.	64-8m-5d	6		Delaware, OH	Roßwag, Vaihingen, Württemberg
Renner, Johanna Christine	26, Dec. 1889	8, Dec.	64	830	Collmer	Delaware, OH	Roßwag, Vaihingen, Württemberg
Renner, Johannes	16, Nov. 1854	15, Oct.	31-11m-24d	184		Clayton, IA	Starmstadt, Rheinkreis Baiern
Renner, Karoline	7, July 1887	19, June	24-1m-27d	430		Delaware, OH	Delaware, Ohio
Renner, Katharina	2, May 1870	14, Apr.	31-6m-8d	143	Rupp	Lawrenceburg, IN	Mutterstadt, Rheinkreis Baiern
Renner, Katharina	30, Dec. 1867	19, Nov.	69-1m-19d	414	Kecke	Batesville, IN	Schaureihen, Rheinkreis Baiern
Renner, Peter	6, Nov. 1882	16, Oct.	47	359		Vandyne, WI	Obenau, Köln, Preußen

Christliche Apologete Death Notices — 1839 - 1899

Name of Deceased	Notice Date	Death Date	Age	Maiden Name	Page	Place of Death	Place of Birth
Renner, Wilhelm	7, Aug. 1890	10, July	60		510	Lawrenceburg, IN	Dannstadt, Ludwigshafen, Rheinpfalz Baiern
Rennert, Henrietta	17, June 1886	1, June		Fleeth	7	New York City, NY	Norden, Ostfriesland
Rennman, Johan Dietrich	25, Aug. 1887	9, Aug.	30		542		Elsfleth, Oldenburg
Renollet, Maria	25, Dec. 1876	24, Nov.	73	Odon	413	Edgerton, OH	Ludweiler, Preußen
Renschenhaus, Hanna	3, July 1871	18, June	74	Koch	215	Portsmouth, OH	Imshausen, Hannover
Renschenhaus, Heinrich	23, Sept 1858	15, June	26-8m-9d		152	Scioto Co, OH	
Renschenhaus, Wilhelm	14, Jan. 1897	16, Dec.	74		31	Wheelersburg, OH	Imitshausen, Hannover
Renschler, Anna	17, Oct. 1881		71- -19d	Schnierle	335	Nauvoo, IL	Schornbach, Württemberg
Renschler, Georg Friedrich	19, Apr. 1880	9, Mar.	75- - 8d		127	Bethlehem, OH	Grünwettersbach, Durlach, Baden
Renschler, Georg Friedrich	3, May 1880	9, Mar.	75- - 8d		143	Bethlehem, OH	Grünwettersbach, Durlach, Baden
Renschler, Johan Michael	4, Aug. 1887	24, May	82		494		Schornbach, Württemberg
Renshaw, Lena	25, Apr. 1895	5, Apr.	40- -10d	Appenzeller	270	Louisville, KY	Cincinnati, Hamilton County, Ohio
Rentsch, Anna Katharine	21, Mar. 1889	3, Mar.	63-9m	Fölzsing	190	Wheeling, WV	Landenhausen, Hessen
Rentschler, John	16, Apr. 1896	24, Mar.	38		254	Marion, OH	Marion County, Ohio
Rentschler, Wilhelmine	2, May 1889	12, Apr.	67- 1m-25d	Wurst	286		Heimsheim, Leonberg, Württemberg
Rentz, Andreas	7,May 1883	19, Apr.	59- 1m-10d		151	Troy, NY	Emmingen, Nagold, Württemberg
Rentz, Barbara	15, Mar. 1888	9, Feb.	87- 7m-17d	Dangel	174	Clarington, OH	Oberamt Kirchheim, Württemberg
Rentz, Edward G.	20, Oct. 1887	1, Oct.	25- 2m-28d		670	Washington, MN	
Rentz, Gottlieb	20, Jan. 1879	30, Dec.	35		23	Woodbury, MN	
Rentz, John George	5, Mar. 1883	14, Feb.	21- 4m- 1d		79	Troy, NY	Perouse, Leonberg, Württemberg
Rentz, Maria	14, Feb. 1889		82- 7m	Jordan	110	Washington, MN	Troy, New York
Rentz, Samuel	15, Feb. 1894	30, Dec.	28		110	Washington, MN	Serres, Maulbronn, Württemberg
Rentz, Wilhelm	7, July 1898	25, May	39		431	St. Paul, MN	Aston, Washington County, Minnesota
Renz, Anna	6, Aug. 1883	19, July	49	Schweizer	255	Hobart, IN	Ober-Sielmingen, Württemberg
Renz, Charlotte	2, July1883	1, June	36- 3m- 3d	Kuhlmann	215	Greenville, OH	Hemingen, Hammel, Hannover
Renz, Conrad	12, June 1871	24, May	29		191	Greenville, OH	Emmingen, Nagold, Württemberg
Renz, Elisabeth	3, Jan. 1881	21, Dec.	76- 3m-10d	Smith	7	Peoria, IL	Pennsylvania
Renz, Friederike	14, June 1894	15, May	17- 4m-14d		390	Bracken, TX	
Renz, Jakob	7, Dec. 1874	23, Nov.	76- 8m-15d		391	Clarington, OH	Unterlenningen, Kirchheim, Württemberg
Renz, Jakob	18, Mar. 1867	13, Feb.	65		86	Washington, MN	Perouse, Württemberg
Renz, Sophia	30, Mar. 1885	13, Feb.	63	Almann	7	Wyandotte, KS	Canton Bern, Schweiz
Renziehausen, (Mrs)	11, Oct. 1869	11, Sept	43- 2m-17d		327	Allegan, MI	Bramsche, Hannover
Renziehausen, Christian	20, Feb. 1896	26, Jan.	75		126	Allegan, MI	Eboldshausen, Westerhof, Hannover
Renziehausen, H. Louisa Amalia	22, Aug. 1889	25, July	69- 4m-10d	Löhrberg	542	Allegan, MI	Ebolshausen, Hannover
Renziehausen, Louise	10, Oct. 1881	23, Sept	55- 7m-26d		327	Giard, IA	Imtshausen, Westerhof, Hannover
Renziehausen, Sarah	9, June 1873	13, Apr.	19- 4m-19d		183	Allegan, MI	
Renziehausen, Sarah	16, June 1879	23, May	28		191	Allegan, MI	
Renzihausen, Heinrich Ludwig	27, Jan. 1898	31, Dec.	80		63	Giard, IA	Ebolshausen, Hannover
Repp, Heinrich	19, June 1871	28, May	25		199	Baltimore, MD	
Repp, Margaretha	19, Jan. 1880	27, Nov.	62- 5m-23d	Mai	23	Baltimore, MD	Stockheim, Hessen
Reps, Margaretha	18, Apr. 1881	17, Mar.	61- 9m	Wolf	127	Ripley, OH	Oberkeinsbach, Hessen-Darmstadt
Rerroth, Adam	8, Feb. 1855	10, Jan.	22- 9m-22d		24	Galion, OH	Gettysburg, Pennsylvania
Reßler, Sarah Viola	4, Oct. 1894	11, Sept	29		646	Oshkosh, WI	Spring Prairie, Dane County, Wisconsin
Reth, Maria Katharina	4, Oct. 1875	24, Sept	71	Schneider	319	Davenport, IA	Oeschingen, Rottenburg, Württemberg
Reth, Wilhelm	16, Nov. 1874	22, Oct.	21		367	Liberty, MO	Oeschingen, Rottenburg, Württemberg
Rethemeyer, Sophie	19, Sept 1861	18, Aug.	24	Friedrichs	152	Herman, MO	

Christliche Apologete Death Notices --- 1839 - 1899

Name of Deceased	Notice Date	Death Date	Age	Maiden Name	Page	Place of Death	Place of Birth
Rethhammel, Louisa	7, Apr. 1887	10, Mar.	65	Johnske	222	Decorah, IA	Pommern
Rethmüller, Christian Tobias	21, Oct. 1872		21		343	Cedar Lake, IN	Gilstein, Württemberg
Rethwilm, Marie Elsbein	15, June 1874	28, May	70	Sundermann	191	Le Sueur, MN	Ladbergen, Tecklenburg, Münster, Preußen
Retteker, Anna	13, Sept 1869	22, Aug.	13		295	Jefferson City, MO	
Retteker, Bertha	13, Sept 1869	22, Aug.	11		295	Jefferson City, MO	
Rettelsdorfer, Thekla	5, Jan. 1880	8, Dec.	65		7	New Haven, CT	Kurzendorf, Oesterreich
Rettmeyer, Heinrich	13, Oct. 1892	26, Sept	70		654	Sherrills Mount, IA	Hildesheim, Hannover
Retz, Johan Georg	23, June 1887	3, June	78		398	Lena, IL	Oberamt Eringen, Württemberg
Retzel, Catharina	11, Oct. 1849	19, Aug.	53		164	Knoxville, OH	Erkartsweiler bei Straßburg,
Retzer, Jakob	13, Mar. 1846	25, Feb.	75		43	Cincinnati, OH	
Reubelt, Lavinia	15, May 1865	2, Apr.	46	Orwig	80	Greencastle, IN	Orwigsburg, Pennsylvania
Reuff, Rosine	20, May 1897	27, Mar.	62		319	New York City, NY	Dornsteihen, Freudenstadt, Württemberg
Reuhl, Georg	31, Jan. 1895	15, Jan.	75		78	Brooklyn, NY	Holzheim, Hessen-Darmstadt
Reuhse, Catharina Elisabeth	8, Dec. 1879	20, Nov.	38	Koch	391	Falls Mission, TX	Alberode, Eschwege, Kurhessen
Reum, Anna Maria	3, Aug. 1885	13, July	84	Ardus	7	Decorah, IA	Frauen Breitungen, Sachsen-Meiningen
Reum, Georg Heinrich Carl	23, May 1895	23, Apr.	52		334	Greenfield, MA	Steinbach, Sachsen-Meiningen
Reum, Maria Christiana	28, Feb. 1895	26, Jan.	21	Heineck	142	Greenfield, MA	
Reunig, Conrad	7, July 1879	20, June	75- 2m- 4d		215	Saginaw, MI	Ruppertenrod, Grünberg, Hessen
Reunig, Margarethe	16, Sept 1878	30, Aug.	73-10m- 2d		295	Saginaw, MI	Ruppertenrod, Hessen-Darmstadt
Reuper, Wilhelmine	9, Nov. 1868	15, Oct.	24- 1m-27d	Rephagen	359	Mascoutah, IL	Dammwalde, Mecklenburg-Schwerin
Reupert, Franz	2, Oct. 1871	9, Sept	40- 5m- 8d		319	Mascoutah, IL	Alum, Amt Wolfenbüttel, Braunschweig
Reupmann, Anna	16, Aug. 1880	25, July	83- 9m-29d	Plank	263	Canal Dover, OH	Berks County, Pennsylvania
Reusch, Friedrich	28, Aug. 1876	11, Aug.	65		279	Angelica, NY	Neuhausen an der Ems, Urach, Württemberg
Reusch, Georg	21, Oct. 1897	1, Sept	76		671	Lansing, MI	Neuhausen a. d. Ems, Tübingen, Württemberg
Reusch, Johannes	12, May 1898	15, Apr.	91		303	San Francisco, CA	Neuhausen, Urach, Württemberg
Reusch, Margaret	17, Sept 1896	25, Aug.	83	Fritz	607	Wellsville, NY	Neuhausen, Württemberg
Reusch, Rosina	8, June 1874	8, May	67		183	Ionia, MI	Neuhausen, Urach, Württemberg
Reuß, Friedrich Wilhelm	24, May 1888		12		334	New York City, NY	
Reuß, Herman A.	8, Dec. 1887		32		782	Atchison, KS	Brunsen, Braunschweig
Reuß, Theodor	19, Mar. 1883	16, Feb.			95	Waco, TX	
Reuß, Willy Alfred	20, Sept 1888	7, Sept	18- 6m-26d		606	Sun Prairie, WI	Windsor, Wisconsin
Reusse, Maria Sibilla	10, Feb. 1873	7, Dec.	71		47	Martin, TX	Wipperrode, Kreis Eschwegen, Kurhessen
Reußer, C.	16, Feb. 1893	26, Jan.	58		110	Vermillion, OH	Steffisburg, Thun, Schweiz
Reusser, Johan Friedrich	17, Nov. 1898	18, Oct.	17		735	Vermillion, OH	Mansfield, Ohio
Reutepohler, Margaretha E.	6, Sept 1875	21, Aug.	26	Kunz	287	Huntingburg, IN	Newport, Campbell County, Kentucky
Reutepohler, Maria	4, Aug. 1892	29, June	68	Deppe	494	Huntingburg, IN	Osnabrück, Hannover
Reuter, Anna	28,May 1883	4, May	31- 4m-13d	Kinnie	175	Portland, OR	Chur, Graubünden, Schweiz
Reuter, Elisabeth	25, Jan. 1894	6, Jan.	82	Scheerer	62	Warsaw, IL	Lölbach, Kurhessen
Reuter, Elisabeth	11, Aug. 1892	17, June	56	Schuchmann	510	Quincy, IL	
Reuter, Hulda Esther	5, Nov. 1883	17, Oct.	7- 5m-27d		359	Delhi, MI	
Reuter, Johan Wilhelm	2, Sept 1878	16, Aug.	54		279	Houston, TX	Lieberhausen, Rheinpreußen
Reuter, John	17, Apr. 1865	1, Apr.	65- 1m- 7d		64	St. Louis, MO	Altenhain am Rhein, Baden
Reuter, John Michael	17, Feb. 1887	13, Jan.	59		110	St. Louis, MO	Altenheim, Baden
Reuter, Karl Wilhelm	14, Sept 1899	21, Aug.			591	Dayton, OH	Greifenstein, Wetzlar, Koblenz, Preußen
Reuter, Katharina	18, Oct. 1875	25, Sept		Mentzinger	335	New Albany, IN	Liensingen, Maulbronn, Württemberg
Reuter, Magdalena	3, Aug. 1899	17, July	63	Becker	495	Dayton, OH	Greifenstein, Preußen

Christliche Apologete Death Notices --- 1839 - 1899

Name of Deceased	Notice Date	Death Date	Age	Page	Maiden Name	Place of Death	Place of Birth
Reuter, Maria Magdalena	13, Feb. 1871	18, Jan.	66	55	Rinkel	St. Louis, MO	Altenheim, Baden
Reuter, Marie	23, Oct. 1890	10, Sept	20	686		Storm Lake, IA	Clayton County, Iowa
Reuter, Philipp Conrad	6, May 1872	20, Apr.	61-10m- 1d	151		Belleville, IL	Oberlaucken, Amt Ufingen, Nassau
Reuter, Charlotte Louise Karoline	28, July 1892	12, July	19	478		Pekin, IL	Clarenthal, Saarbrücken, Rheinpfalz Baiern
Reutlinger, Anna M.	17, Sept 1891	16, Aug.	31	606	Hölscher	Evansville, IN	Evansville, Indiana
Reutner, Johan	1, Nov. 1894	8, Oct.	81	710		Hobart, IN	Degersheim, Baiern
Reuwer, Katharina	18, Oct. 1888	30, Sept	48	670		Perry, TX	
Rewalt, Maria	31, Jan. 1895	3, Jan.	67	78	Eger	Montrose, MN	Stripo, Hinterpommern
Rexer, Georg Friedrich	24, Feb. 1879	8, Feb.	73	63		Golconda, IL	Sommenhardt, Calw, Württemberg
Rexroth, Anna Maria	22, Mar. 1894		88	198	Rittmann	Bucyrus, OH	Obermutschelbach, Pforzheim, Baden
Rexroth, Daniel	23, Jan. 1882	28, Dec.	28-10m-20d	31		Galion, OH	Crawford County, Ohio
Rexroth, Johan Nikolaus	29, July 1867	17, June	67	238		Bucyrus, OH	Erbach, Hessen
Rexse, Dorothea	1, Oct. 1847	4, Sept	30-10m-23d	159		Cincinnati, OH	
Rey, Catharina	22, Oct. 1866	6, Oct.	35- 8m- 2d	342	Schmidt	Detroit, MI	Eichen, Amt Windecken, Kurhessen
Reyer, Friederika	17, Apr. 1876	25, Mar.	70- 7m-27d	127		Nashville, TN	Rothenburg an der Fulda, Kurhessen
Reyer, Wilhelm	17, Apr. 1882	22, Mar.	78- 5m	127		Nashville, TN	Rothenburg, Kurhessen
Rheim, William	16, May 1889	25, Apr.	60	318		Burlington, WI	Wernshausen, Meiningen, Sachsen-Meiningen
Rhein, Andreas Lincoln	10, Nov. 1887	22, Oct.	23	718		Woodbury, MN	St. Paul, Minnesota
Rhein, Friedrich	15, Jan. 1841		Inquiry	7		Waterloo, Canada	Nechterbach, , Baiern
Rhein, Wilhelmine	23, June 1887	4, June	26	398	Leithauser	St. Paul, MN	Vambach, Kurhessen
Rheinfranck, Mina	20, Feb. 1890	21, Jan.	61	126		Sterling, NE	Eßtorf, Hannover
Rheinfrank, A. Maria	3, Oct. 1889	13, Sept	50- 6m-11d	638	Lochbaum	Portsmouth, OH	RheinPfalz Baiern
Rheinfrank, Ida Mathilde	30, Apr. 1891	17, Mar.	13	286		Milwaukee, WI	
Rheinfrank, Jakob	12, Dec. 1895	4, Nov.	61	798		Dubuque, IA	Horheim, Vaihingen, Württemberg
Rheinfrank, Jennie Thusnelde	14, June 1888	30, May	11- 4m- 6d	382		Dubuque, IA	Dubuque, Dubuque County, Iowa
Rheinfrank, Lydia	9, June 1887	19, May	51	366	VandenBruck	Dubuque, IA	Wesel am Rhein, Germany
Rheinfrank, Lydia	9, Feb. 1888	18, Jan.	30	94		Milwaukee, WI	Milwaukee, Wisconsin
Rheinfrank, Lydia Amanda	28, May 1896	3, May	23	350		Dubuque, IA	Dubuque, Iowa
Rheinfrank, Philipp J.	20, Sept 1894	12, Aug.	82	614		Plattsmouth, NE	Haßloch, Hunstadt a. d. Haardt, Rheinkreis Baiern
Rheinschield, John	21, Nov. 1864	7, Nov.	12- 4m-15d	188		Pomeroy, OH	Appau, Frankenthal, Rheinkreis Baiern
Rheinschild, Georg	31, Jan. 1881	15, Jan.	60	39		Pomeroy, OH	Pittsburg, Pennsylvania
Rheinschild, Maria Katharina	22, Nov. 1894	1, Nov.	50	758	Findling	Indianapolis, IN	Heichelheim, Sachsen-Weimar
Rheinschild, Sibylla	12, Apr. 1880	9, Mar.	60	119	Dürick	Pomeroy, OH	Staufenberg, Gernsbach, Baden
Rheinschmidt, Christoph	10, Mar. 1898	4, Feb.	70	159		Burlington, IA	Missouri
Rhiter, Katharina Barbara	24, Dec. 1891	15, Nov.	20	830	Sauer	Huntsville, KS	Wahren, Mecklenburg-Schwerin
Rhoda, Sophia	20, Dec. 1888	24, Nov.	54	814	DeJungh	Laporte, IN	
Rhode, Anna Maria	5, June 1871	22, Mar.		183			
Rhode, Emma	14, July 1898	20, June	25	447		Chicago, IL	Chicago, Cook County, Illinois
Rhode, Louis	26, Apr. 1894	26, Mar.	65	278		Laporte, IN	Mecklenburg-Schwerin
Rhode, Wilhelm	9, Nov. 1893	17, Oct.	29	718		Laporte, IN	
Rhodes, Anna C.	11, Apr. 1881	10, Feb.	20	119		Indianapolis, IN	Jefferson County, Indiana
Rhyner, Johan Heinrich	15, Dec. 1887	13, Nov.	18	798		Oshkosh, WI	
Ribbe, Catharina	26, May 1887	26, Apr.	78	334	VanHoren	Chillicothe, OH	Tholen, Zeeland, Holland
Ribel, Maria	23, June 1879	6, June	40	199		Pomeroy, OH	Meigs County, Ohio
Richard, Charlotte Sophia	14, Mar. 1895	23, Feb.	85	174	Bütow	Brownton, MN	Cölpin bei Treptow a.d. Rega, Pommern
Richard, David	8, July 1878		91	215		Lawrenceville, IN	Odelshofen, Kalk, Baden

Christliche Apologete Death Notices --- 1839 - 1899

Name of Deceased	Notice Date	Death Date	Age	Maiden Name	Page	Place of Death	Place of Birth
Richard, Ferdinand	23, Feb. 1863	7, Jan.	18		32	Ahnapee, WI	Bellbock, Treptow, Pommern
Richard, Friedrich Wilhelm	27, Oct. 1879	10, Oct.	68- 1m-16d		343	Glencoe, MN	Trepton a. R., Pommern, Preußen
Richard, Wilhelm	2, Oct. 1865	9, Aug.	25- 5m-17d		160	Ahnapee, WI	Harlem, Minden, Preußen
Richmann, Caroline	28, Aug. 1882	11, Aug.	50- 6m- 9d	Meier	279	St. Louis, MO	
Richmond, Amalia	2, Mar. 1885	12, Feb.	23	Vogt	7	Chicago, IL	
Richner, Wilhelm August	30, Jan. 1896	18, Dec.	15		78	Rochester, NY	Rochester, New York
Richter, August	1, Oct. 1891	13, Sept	53		638	Jersey City, NJ	Sempsenberg, Sachsen
Richter, Emilie Amalie	19, Jan. 1874	28, Dec.	53	Best	23	Grand Ridge, IL	Berlin, Preußen
Richter, Herman	9, Apr. 1883	23, Mar.	64- 2m		119	Platteville, WI	Berlin, Preußen
Richter, Karoline	10, Jan. 1895	11, Dec.	85		30	Scranton, PA	Kotbus, Preußen
Richter, Katharina E.	1, June 1874	5, May	75	Aldrup	175	St. Paul, MN	Lünen, Warendorf, Münster, Preußen
Richter, Mathilde	30, Dec. 1897	29, Nov.	14		828	Newark, NJ	
Richter, Max	19, Mar. 1883	6, Feb.	33		95	Fond du Lac, WI	Naumburg, Sachsen, Preußen
Richter, Theresia	11, Aug. 1898	30, July	66		511	Mt. Olive, IL	Rittersgrün, Sachsen
Richterberg, Friederike Luise	19, Oct. 1899	22, Aug.	71		671	Truxton, MO	Lüderhausen, Lippe-Detmold
Richterberg, Henriette	12, Apr. 1888	21, Mar.	36		238	Warren, MO	Kirchdorf bei Aurich, Ostfriesland
Richterberg, Simon Friedrich	8, Nov. 1875	23, Sept	61		359	Warren, MO	Lüdenhausen, Hohenhausen, Lippe-Detmold
Richters, Meta	22, Oct. 1883	29, Sept	26		343	Muscatine, IA	Oede-quarter-moore, Hannover
Rick, Rosine	15, Mar. 1880	5, Jan.			86	Wallula, WA	Hegenlohe, Schorndorf, Württemberg
Ricke, Charlotte	22, May 1876	25, Apr.	21		167	Drake, MO	
Ricke, Friedrich	8, Jan. 1891	20, Nov.	71		30	Reddick, IL	BahenHausen, Hohenhausen, Lippe-Detmold
Ricke, Johan Heinrich	22, Dec. 1862	23, Aug.	17- 8m		204	St. Peter, MN	Schledehausen, Osnabrück, Hannover
Rickert, John	9, June 1898	16, May	29		367	Aurora, IL	Laporte, Indiana
Rickert, Sophia	29, Jan. 1883	5, Jan.	65		39	Mankato, MN	Fahrbein, Mecklenburg-Schwerin
Rickhoff, Wilhelm Heinrich	28, Dec. 1893	2, Dec.	17		828	Arlington Heights, IL	Arlington Heights, Illinois
Rickle, Felix	15, Jan. 1852	28, Dec.	54		12	Toledo, OH	
Rickus, Marie	20, Apr. 1899		72	Sheldon	255	Farmington, MO	South Carolina
Ridder, Adolph	29, Nov. 1894	5, Nov.	55		774	Flood Creek, IA	Hörstmar, Lage, Lippe-Detmold
Riebe, Johan M.	2, Oct. 1865	28, Aug.	40		160	Cedar Lake, IN	Sassen, Preußen
Riebe, Maria	31, May 1880	13, Mar.	83	Schumacher	175	Dalton, MO	Sachsen, Grimmen, Preußen
Riebe, Sophia Dorothea Johanna	14, Apr. 1859	26, Sept	24		60	Cedar Lake, IN	Sassen, Pommern
Riebel, Katharine	25, Feb. 1897	12, Dec.	84- 6m-24d	Geyer	127	Pomeroy, OH	Dürmstein, Grünstein, Rheinkreis Baiern
Riebel, Peter	10, Jan. 1881		72- 6m		15	Pomeroy, OH	Edigheim, Frankenthal, Rheinkreis Baiern
Riebeling, Nicolaus	4, Aug. 1892	25, July	82		494	Decatur, IL	Wasenburg, Kurhessen
Riebeth, Johan Gottlieb	19, May 1884	16, Apr.	68		7	Minneapolis, MN	Iduny, Schlesien
Riechemeier, Elisabeth	19, Aug. 1858	9, July	33- 2m- 3d	Hepp	132	Cannelton, IN	Emmershausen, Aschaffenburg, Baiern
Riechenmeyer, H.W.	11, Aug. 1887	24, July	35		510	Lafayette, IN	Indianapolis, Marion County, Indiana
Riechers, Carolina	8, Feb. 1875	20, Jan.	19		47	Newport, KY	Indianapolis, Marion County, Indiana
Riechers, Elisa	22, May 1871	6, May	18- 4m-26d		167	Newport, KY	Cincinnati, Hamilton County, Ohio
Riechers, Friedrich	2, Nov. 1874	14, Oct.	56		351	Nebraska City, NE	Westerlinden, Braunschweig
Riechers, Henriette	11, Feb. 1886	24, Jan.	64		7	Newport, KY	Zahler, Braunschweig
Riechers, Karl	16, Jan. 1896	29, Dec.	80		46	Newport, KY	Hohenasel, Salder, Braunschweig
Riechers, Laura Pauline	8, July 1897	16, June	17		431	Humboldt, NE	
Riechers, Lydia Henriette	17, Feb. 1898	27, Jan.	21		111	Humboldt, NE	
Riechers, Wilhelmine	26, Apr. 1888	7, Apr.	64	Schnake	270	Newport, KY	Emmenhausen, Hannover
Riechmann, Christian	17, Mar. 1892	24, Feb.	69		174	St. Louis, MO	Hartum, Hartum, Minden, Preußen

Christliche Apologete Death Notices -- 1839 - 1899

Name of Deceased	Notice Date	Death Date	Age	Page	Maiden Name	Place of Death	Place of Birth
Riechmann, Emilie	4, May 1885	16, Apr.	29-11m-21d	7		St. Louis, MO	
Rieckert, Barbara Rosina	11, June 1896	13, May	65	383	Bühler	Michigan City, IN	Bad bei Mainhardt, Württemberg
Ried, Carl	24, Apr. 1840	1, Apr.		63			
Ried, Konrad	18, Nov. 1897	2, Nov.	81	735		Davenport, IA	Bernhausen, Kurhessen
Ried, Margaretha	11, Aug. 1884	24, July	55- -16d	7	Frank	Brooklyn, NY	Wendelstein, Baiern
Riedel, Anna Barbara	17, Aug. 1885	31, July	73	7		Madison, IN	Neudorf, Baiern
Riedel, Anna Maria	23, June 1873	27, May	61	199	Michel	Dawn, MO	Reinheim, Darmstadt, Hessen-Darmstadt
Riedel, Gottfried Friedrich	28, May 1866	17, Apr.	61	174		Delaware, OH	Heutingsheim, Ludwigsburg, Württemberg
Riedel, Johanna Christine	9, Aug. 1869	16, July	48- 6m- 6d	255		Delaware, OH	Illingen, Maulbronn, Württemberg
Riedel, Martin	8, May 1890	26, Mar.	80	302		Madison, IN	Herbersdorf, Erbach, Baiern
Rieder, Anna Margaretha	3, Feb. 1879	30, Nov.	43-10m-21d	39	Meister	Brunswick, MO	Kohlbühl bei Neila, Baiern
Riedinger, Adam	3, Aug. 1899	27, June	77	495		Quincy, IL	Mirdelstein, Moosbach, Germany
Riedinger, Eva K.	27, Feb. 1862	11, Feb.	55- 1m-18d	36	Bauter	Havana, IL	Bitzel-Sachsen, Amt Weinheim, Baden
Riedinger, Christian	12, Apr. 1875	26, Mar.	66- 5m-18d	119		Vernon, IL	Gerstheim, Elsaß
Riedinger, Elisabeth	9, Feb. 1885	15, Jan.	65-10m- 8d	7		Vernon, IL	Genstheim, Elsaß
Riedlinger, Maria Salome	4, July 1861	17, June	70	108		Wheeling, VA	Elsaß
Riedlinger, Philipp	5, May 1859	18, July	71	72		Wheeling, IL	Thaldorf, Ravensburg, Württemberg
Riedmann, Joseph	19, Dec. 1895	10, Nov.	36	814		Valley City, ND	Belmont County, Ohio
Rieff, Clara Virginia	20, Jan. 1887	25, Dec.	29	46		Columbus, OH	Licking County, Ohio
Rieff, Maria Anna	19, Dec. 1870	7, Oct.	20	407		Newark, OH	
Riege, Anna	8, Dec. 1887	1, Nov.	24- 7m-10d	782		Platteville, WI	
Riege, John	27, Sept 1894	6, Sept	70	630		Danville, IL	Nieder-Aspen, Kurhessen
Rieger, Anna Barbara	28, Aug. 1871	17, July	41	279	Ruffi	Brunswick, MO	Steffisburg, Bern, Schweiz
Rieger, J. Friedrich	25, May 1893	16, Apr.	53	334		Akron, OH	Niederweiler, Millheim, Baden
Rieger, John	25, Oct. 1894	6, Sept	70	694		Danville, IL	Nieder-Aspen, Kurhessen
Rieger, Margaretha	20, Jan. 1879	23, Dec.	64- 3m- 9d	23	Geiger	Pittsburg, PA	Kronach, Baiern
Riegert, Anna Barbara	8, Jan. 1877	15, Nov.	28	15	Bauer	Keokuk, IA	Waldmanshofen, Württemberg
Riehl, Elisabeth	20, June 1861	15, Apr.	56	100		Buffalo, NY	
Riehle, Christina	31, May 1869	10, May	35	175	Mack	Marion, OH	
Riehle, Georg	14, Aug. 1865	6, July	41	132		Terre Haute, IN	Marion County, Ohio
Riehle, Gottfried	7, Sept 1854	21, Aug.	57	144		Bethlehem, OH	Schnaith, Schorndorf, Württemberg
Riehle, Jakob	4, Aug. 1862			124		Cincinnati, OH	
Riehle, Maria	26, Apr. 1849	22, Mar.	23	68	Wieder	Cincinnati, OH	Obernilford, Pennsylvania
Riehms, August	23, Mar. 1883	19, Mar.	54	135		Bushnell, IL	Hamburg, Germany
Rieke, Friederike	25, Mar. 1878	18, Feb.	64- 7m-16d	95	Stapperfenne	Norton, IL	Bega, Lippe-Detmold
Rieke, Friedrich	25, June 1896	19, May	39	415		Drake, MO	Gasconade County, Missouri
Rieke, Friedrich	17, Jan. 1889	27, Dec.	67-10m-22d	46		Drake, MO	Hensdorf, Lippe-Detmold
Rieke, Hanna	18, Oct. 1875		45- 2m-20d	335	Freitag	Drake, MO	Telle, Amt Hohnhausen, Lippe
Rieke, Heinrich	20, July 1868	1, May	52	231		Cedar Lake, IN	Bavenhausen, Hohenhausen, Lippe-Detmold
Rieke, Johan H.F.	7, Apr. 1879	17, Mar.	83- 1m	111		Sleepy Eye, MN	Osterkappeln, Amt Wittlage, Hannover
Rieke, Wilhelmine	5, Feb. 1877	22, Dec.	25	47	Meyer	Drake, MO	Franklin County, Missouri
Riekert, Johann Leonhard	29, Mar. 1860	26, Feb.	37	52		Michigan City, IN	Auenstein, Marbach, Württemberg
Riele, Anna Katharina Gertrud	13, May 1897	12, Apr.	90	303	Burke	Fairfax, MN	Wulften, Schledehausen, Osnabrück, Hannover
Rielin, Georg	7, Aug. 1865	6, July	41- 1m-26d	128		Clarksville, IL	
Rieling, Anna Barbara	24, Oct. 1881	9, Oct.	79- 6m- 9d	343	Eisele	Fillmore, WI	Duslingen, Tüblingen, Württemberg
Riemann, Florentina	27, Jan. 1879	18, Dec.	66	31		Jacksonville, IL	Bur, Amt Melle, Hannover

Christliche Apologete Death Notices --- 1839 - 1899

Name of Deceased	Notice Date	Death Date	Age	Page	Maiden Name	Place of Death	Place of Birth
Riemann, Franz	18, Dec. 1871	19, Nov.	56	407		Meredosia, IL	Buer, Amt Melle, Hannover
Riemann, Heinrich W.	19, Nov. 1877	29, Oct.	32	375		Jacksonville, IL	
Riemann, Maria Elisabeth	27, Jan. 1879	3, Jan.	58	31	Kienker	Jacksonville, IL	Bur, Amt Melle, Hannover
Riemenschneider, Adolf	20, Apr. 1893		21	254		Francisco, MI	Sylvan Township, Washtenaw Co., Michigan
Riemenschneider, Anna B.	21, Aug. 1890	31, July	58	542	Freiberger	Francisco, MI	Eckerweiler, Rothenburg, Württemberg
Riemenschneider, Anna Maria	15, Oct. 1883	30, Sept	83	335	Nicklaus	Indianapolis, IN	Kanton Bern, Schweiz
Riemenschneider, Anna Maria	22, Oct. 1883	30, Sept	63	343	Nicklaus	Indianapolis, IN	Kanton Bern, Schweiz
Riemenschneider, Caroline Amalia	28, June 1894	8, June	39	422		St. Joseph, MO	
Riemenschneider, Christian	7, May 1866	10, Mar.	62	150		Baraboo, WI	Binsferd, Kurhessen
Riemenschneider, Christina Cath.	21, June 1860	20, May	34	100	Kaiser	Franciscoville, MI	Degerloch, Stuttgart, Württemberg
Riemenschneider, Conrad	11, Dec. 1865	2, Nov.	75	200		Pittsburg, PA	Eubach, Kreis Melsungen, Kurhessen
Riemenschneider, E.F.W. (Mrs)	9, Aug. 1849	11, July		128	Stivarius	Smooth Prairie, ---	Horn, Lippe-Detmold
Riemenschneider, Elisabeth	6, Sept 1869	9, Aug.	61-11m- 1d	287	Ronshausen	Baraboo, WI	
Riemenschneider, Eva Katharina	16, Sept 1897	30, Aug.	63	591	Grießbach	Francisco, MI	Asch, Böhmen
Riemenschneider, Hanna Christine	1, Dec. 1879	19, Oct.	22- 9m-22d	383		Francisco, MI	Sylvan, Washtenaw County, Michigan
Riemenschneider, Heinrich	17, Mar. 1887	16, Feb.	68	174		St. Joseph, MO	Eubach, Kurhessen
Riemenschneider, Helene	17, Aug. 1863	18, June	15- 2m	132		Ludwigsburg, GE	
Riemenschneider, Johan	2, Apr. 1891	11, Mar.	77	222		Francisco, MI	Oberwöllrich, Fritzlar, Kurhessen
Riemenschneider, John Conrad	14, Aug. 1882	2, July	60	263		Allegheny City, PA	Altmorschen, Spangenberg, Kurhessen
Riemenschneider, Justus	24, Mar. 1873	1, Mar.	54	95		Sandusky, OH	Rothenburg, Kurhessen
Riemenschneider, Katharina Elis.	22, May 1856	8, May	27	84		Sandusky, OH	Besse, Amt Gundersberg, Kurhessen
Riemenschneider, Maria	15, Apr. 1897	29, Mar.	77	239		Francisco, MI	Ober-Möllrich, Fritzlar, Kurhessen
Riemenschneider, Maria	12, May 1892	8, Apr.	73	302		St. Joseph, MO	Hüne, Hofgeismar, Hessen-Kassel
Riemenschneider, Martha Elis.	19, Sept 1864	7, Aug.	71	152		Pittsburg, PA	Altmorschen, Spangenberg, Kurhessen
Riemer, Charlotte	29, Apr. 1897	27, Mar.	70- 1m-12d	271	Radlof	Sheboygan, WI	Wolfhagen, Preußen
Riemer, Herman Johannes	22, May 1890	26, Apr.	22- 6m-12d	334		Sheboygan, WI	Sheboygan Falls, Wisconsin
Riepe, Ida	26, Jan. 1893	27, Dec.	21- 5m- 2d	62		St. Louis, MO	
Riepe, Nellie	11, Aug. 1884	23, July	15- - 2d	7		St. Louis, MO	
Riepe, Wilhelm	27, May 1878	12, May	29- 6m- 8d	167		St. Louis, MO	
Rierchen, August	24, Aug. 1885	8, Aug.	25	7		Wathena, KS	Sawade, Schlesien
Ries , Catharina	27, Mar. 1890	18, Feb.	66	206	Stahlman	Goodrich, MI	Glashütten, Baireuth, Franken, Baiem
Ries, Adam	29, Apr. 1897	2, Mar.	79	271		New Albany, IN	Steinsfurth, Zinsheim, Baden
Ries, Georg	4, July 1895	30, May	76	430		Mt. Vernon, IN	Oberschüpf, Boxberg, Baden
Ries, Katharina	9, Mar. 1899	16, Feb.	76	159	Wärner	Mt. Vernon, IN	Oberschüpf, Boxberg, Baden
Ries, Margaretha	16, Aug. 1849	3, July	22	132		Dayton, OH	Edelfingen, Württemberg
Ries, Stephan	10, Apr. 1890	8, Mar.	65- 7m-22d	238		Goodrich, MI	Glashütten, Baireuth, Franken, Baiem
Ries, Thomas	26, Dec. 1889	19, Oct.	60- 4m-14d	830		Mt. Vernon, IN	Oberschüpf, Boxberg, Baden
Riese, Johan	21, Aug. 1890	23, June	66- - 9d	542		Sylvester, WI	Körthzin, Germany
Riesenbeck, Adolph Moritz	30, Mar. 1893	9, Mar.	72	206		Huntingburg, IN	Tecklenburg, Preußen
Riesenbeck, Phena	23, Jan. 1890	31, Dec.	40	62		Baraboo, WI	Illinois
Rieser, Marie	6, July 1874	19, June	66- 7m- 5d	215		Baresville, OH	Kisen, Bern, Schweiz
Rieß, Heinrich	22, Aug. 1881	16, July	80	271		Edon, OH	Lützelwig, Homberg, Kurhessen
Rieß, Sarah Jane	10, Dec. 1877	18, Nov.	20	399		Kendallville, IN	Wawaka, Indiana
Rieth, Friedrich	8, July 1878	19, June	51-10m-25d	215		Garfield, IL	Erfurt, Weißensee, Ottenhausen, Preußen
Rieth, Sarah	27, Aug. 1891	25, July	49	558		Canal Dover, OH	Bedford, Coschocton County, Ohio
Riethmiller, Maria Katharina	3, Jan. 1895	2, Dec.	77	14	Breitling	Crown Point, IN	Kuppingen, Herrenberg, Württemberg

Christliche Apologete Death Notices -- 1839 - 1899

Name of Deceased	Notice Date	Death Date	Age	Maiden Name	Place of Death	Page	Place of Birth
Riethmiller, Tobias	25, Feb. 1892	1, Feb.	73		Crown Point, IN	127	Gültstein, Herrenberg, Württemberg
Riethmüller, Karl	17, Feb. 1868	26, Jan.	13		Valparaiso, IN	55	
Rietmann, Wilhelm G. H.	7, Mar. 1895	31, Jan.	53		Lake City, MN	158	Schledehausen, Osnabrück, Hannover
Rietz, August Fr.	14, Feb. 1881	4, Feb.	18		Blue Island, IL	55	Regenwald, Stettin, Hinterpommern
Riexinger, Maria	21, Jan. 1897	27, Dec.	45- -26d	Sachse	New York City, NY	47	Niederuff, Kurhessen
Rigert, Anna Maria	23, June 1879	8, June	58		Pomeroy, OH	199	Euerdorf, Lichtenau, Baiern
Rigges, Dorothea	3, July 1882	18, May	45- 2m-14d	Grammes	Cleveland, OH	215	Cusel, Rheinkreis Baiern
Rigler, Anna Barbara	10, Feb. 1898	15, Jan.	69		Newton, KS	95	Reutlingen, Württemberg
Rigler, C.	13, Sept 1894	15, Aug.	69		Newton, KS	598	Bingarten, Baiern
Rilling, Jakob	18, Jan. 1875	23, Dec.	46- 3m- 1d		West Bend, WI	23	Tübingen, Württemberg
Rilling, Martin	12, Mar. 1891	15, Feb.	92		West Bend, WI	174	Tübingen, Schwarzwald, Württemberg
Rinder, F. (Rev)	12, Mar. 1896	16, Feb.	56		Chicago, IL	174	Libbin, VorPommern
Rinder, Friederike	30, Aug. 1888	8, Aug.	78		Sun Prairie, WI	558	---kow, Demmin, Stettin, Preußen
Rinder, Joachim	5, Feb. 1883	9, Jan.	76- 2m		Nora Springs, IA	47	Lebin a. d. Trulense, Pommern
Rinder, Johan Friedrich	9, Dec. 1897	19, Nov.	94		Madison, WI	783	Tetzleben, Stettin, Pommern
Rinder, John	29, Oct. 1877	11, Oct.	43		Flood Creek, IA	351	Lebien, Preußen
Rinder, Louise	15, Nov. 1894	28, Sept	84	Höpner	Nora Springs, IA	742	Mecklenburg
Rindfeld, (Mr)	7, May 1883		67		Cedar Lake, IN	151	
Ring, Gottlieb	13, Mar. 1865	28, Jan.	48- 5m- 6d		Fremont, OH	44	Röthenbuch, Oberndorf, Württemberg
Ringe, Louise Conradina	17, Mar. 1892	19, Feb.	59	Brandes	Vandalia, IL	174	Cramme, Salder, Braunschweig
Ringel, Heinrich	25, June 1883	28, May	70		Algona, IA	207	Hoheneggelsen, Hannover
Ringel, Julia	6, Sept 1888	13, Aug.	76- 4m- 6d		Dubuque, IA	574	Schellerton, Hannover
Ringen, Adelheid	9, Oct. 1876	3, Sept	52	Timken	Smithton, MO	327	Tarnstedt, Ottersberg, Hannover
Ringen, Cord	29, Aug. 1861	19, June	30		Pettes Co, MO	140	Breddorf, Amt Ottersberg, Hannover
Ringen, Corett	13, Dec. 1839	13, Nov.	2- 1m-23d			195	
Ringen, Gretchen	20, Mar. 1876	4, Mar.	70	Mahnken	Lake Creek, MO	95	Oftertemke, Amt Ottersberg, Hannover
Ringen, Margaretha	14, Dec. 1893		84- 4m		Sedalia, MO	798	Glenstätt, Zeven, Hannover
Ringen, Margarethe	13, Aug. 1896	11, June	60	Höhns	Lake Creek, MO	527	Taken, Ottersberg, Hannover
Ringen, Tebeka	19, Dec. 1881	29, Nov.	80-11m-28d	Vag	Newport, KY	407	Hanstadt, Amt Zeven, Hannover
Ringler, Georg	11, Apr. 1881	24, Mar.	21		Danville, IL	119	Bromskirch, Preußen
Ringler, Maria	14, Apr. 1889	24, Jan.	63	Müller	Danville, IL	110	Bromskirchen, Battenberg, Hessen-Darmstadt
Ringling, Bertha Caroline Henriette	10, Aug. 1893	14, July	24	Zink	Willow Creek, WI	510	Zakenzin, Lauenburg, Germany
Ringwald, Andreas	10, Oct. 1895	12, Sept	27		Pittsburg, PA	654	Pfeffingen, Bahlingen, Württemberg
Riniker, Anna Maria	3, Nov. 1884	13, Oct.	73	Steiner	Covington, KY	7	Sand, Baden
Riniker, Georg F.	5, Oct. 1885	28, July	28		Covington, KY	7	Sidney, Shelby County, Ohio
Rininsland, Catharina	22, Jan. 1877	31, Dec.	34	Lapp	Peoria, IL	31	Wolferode, Kirchhain, Kurhessen
Rinke, Johan Georg	21, Feb. 1870	7, Feb.	69- 6m-13d		Cincinnati, OH	63	Ellsching, Schlesien
Rinkel, Anna E.	12, Nov. 1896	8, Oct.	34	Köneke	Bunker Hill, IL	734	Beardstown, Illinois
Rinkel, Christian	31, July 1865	19, Sept	28		Berea, OH	124	Neudorf, Amt Gifhorn, Hannover
Rinkel, Josephine Christine	12, Aug. 1886	24, July	23		Warsaw, IL	7	
Rinkel, Katharina	2, Aug. 1849	23, June	49		St. Louis, MO	124	
Rinkel, Louise	15, Oct. 1891	16, Sept	30	Müller	Cannelton, IN	670	Westheim, Baiern
Rinkel, Margaretha	19, Sept 1870	29, Aug.	20	Rohrscheib	Booneville, IN	303	
Rinkel, Maria	22, Jan. 1861	2, Jan.	38- 4m-26d		Edgerton, OH	16	
Rinkel, Michael	13, Apr. 1893	20, Mar.	66		Warsaw, IL	238	Altenheim, Osenburg, Baden
Rinkenberg, Katharine	9, Sept 1867	13, Aug.	23	Beckerle	Blue Island, IL	286	

Christliche Apologete Death Notices --- 1839 - 1899

Name of Deceased	Notice Date	Death Date	Age	Page	Maiden Name	Place of Death	Place of Birth
Rinkenberger, Anna Maria	2, Jan. 1862	10, Dec.	30	4	Beckley	Cedar Lake, IN	New York
Rinkenberger, Christian	5, Dec. 1895	9, Nov.	69	782		Blue Island, IL	Schwiebendingen, Württemberg
Rinkenberger, Ludwig	2, Apr. 1883	16, Mar.	51	111		Chicago, IL	Schwieberdingen, Württemberg
Rinker, Christian	3, Mar. 1898	14, Feb.	88	143		Grand Ridge, IL	Leudenbach, Waiblingen, Württemberg
Rinker, Jessie	19, Jan. 1888	27, Dec.	46	46	Lichthardt	Great Bend, KS	
Rinker, Sabine	24, Mar. 1884	3, Mar.	66	7	Keser	Grand Ridge, IL	Winterbach, Schorndorf, Württemberg
Rinker, Wilhelmine	25, May 1893	5, May	45	334	Sundermann	Grand Ridge, IL	Lehmkuhlen, Lippe-Detmold
Rinne, Caroline	24, Nov. 1887	5, Nov.	54-10m- 6d	750	Busch	Seymour, IN	Hüllhorst, Lübecke, Minden, Preußen
Rintelmann, Carl	17, Sept 1891	25, Aug.	82- 1m-20d	606		Milwaukee, WI	Steinbude, Lippe-Schaumburg
Rintelmann, Emma	8, Jan. 1872	26, Nov.	26	15	Weinreich	Milwaukee, WI	Gatterstatt, Kreis Querfurt, Preußen
Ripberger, Eva	17, Aug. 1854	10, July	44	132		Chicago, IL	Schwetzingen, Baden
Ripp, Barbara	22, Aug. 1870	2, Aug.	43- 9m	271		Bernadotte, IL	Niederbrun, Elsaß
Rippberger, Karl Ignatz	17, Oct. 1881	25, Aug.	41	335		Prairieville, MN	Mannheim, Baden
Rippberger, Maria	24, June 1886	28, May	74- 4m- 1d	7	Spernagel	Elgin, IL	Schwetzinger, Baden
Rippen, Sebastian W.	24, Jan. 1895	5, Dec.	53	62		St. Louis, MO	Friedeberg, Wittmund, Ostfriesland
Rippentrob, Johanna	3, Jan. 1881	8, Dec.	64- 4m-16d	7	Blume	Jordan, MN	Bredenbeck, Hannover
Risenigger, Anton	7, Oct. 1867	15, Aug.	42- 6m	318		Hebron, IA	Roth, Baiern
Riser, Emilie	13, May 1886	21, Mar.		7	Rethhammel	Decorah, IA	
Risius, Jakob	2, Sept 1886	17, Aug.	39	7		Pekin, IL	Jemgum, Ostfriesland
Risius, Sarah B.	7, Sept 1874	24, Aug.	20- 3m-11d	287		Pekin, IL	Jengum, Ostfriesland
Riske, Elisabeth	10, Mar. 1887	22, Feb.	63	158	Sudbrock	New Melle, MO	Melle, Hannover
Riske, Jobst H.	20, Oct. 1898	18, Sept	77	671		Warrenton, MO	Melle, Hannover
Risser, Amelie	2, Feb. 1880	1, Jan.	23	39		Henry County, IA	
Risser, Barbara	27, Mar. 1876	24, Feb.	62-10m-19d	103	Brubacher	Dubuque, IA	Alpesheim, Rheinkreis Baiern
Risser, Jacob	18, Oct. 1875	18, Sept	70	335		Dubuque, IA	Kobsburg, Baiern
Risser, Sara M.	16, Apr. 1857	6, Mar.	18	64	Krehbiel	Farmington, IA	Butler County, Ohio
Ristau, Dorothea	17, Sept 1891	20, Aug.	77	606		New Ulm, MN	Deutsch-Ruhden, Preußen
Ristau, Elisabeth	3, Oct. 1889	26, Aug.	26	638	Volz	Duluth, MN	Plankstadt bei Schwätzingen, Baden
Ristau, Karl	10, Mar. 1898	4, Feb.	35	159		Duluth, MN	Sittnow, Preußen
Ristig, (Mr)	25, Dec. 1865	9, Nov.	57	208		Jackson, MO	Harisch, Amt Bokenem,
Ristig, (Mrs)	25, Dec. 1865	28, Nov.	55	208		Jackson, MO	
Ritchel, Birgitta	23, Jan. 1862	27, Dec.	16	16		Chipmonkooly, WI	Dobern, Kreis Leitmeritz, Böhmen
Ritschand, John	21, Jan. 1892	Dec.	62	46		Cullman, AL	Thun, Bern, Schweiz
Ritschard, Ulrich	2, May 1870	12, Mar.	69	143		Watertown, WI	Oberhofen, Thun, Bern, Schweiz
Ritschel, Florian	16, Apr. 1877	31, Mar.	75	127		LaCrosse, WI	
Ritschel, Johann	26, July 1860	27, June	31	120		LaCrosse, WI	Dobern, Tetschen, Böhmen
Ritschel, Theresia	24, Mar. 1879	27, Feb.	75	95		LaCrosse, WI	Bresen, Böhmen
Ritt, Caroline	13, Sept 1869	26, Aug.	58	295	Hofmann	Evansville, IN	Denzlingen, Emmerdingen, Baden
Rite, Anna Katharina	2, Mar. 1899	29, Dec.	82-10m-13d	143	Wittich	Jeffersonville, IN	Werkel, Fritzlar, Kurhessen
Ritter, Adam	7, Jan. 1878	14, Dec.	56	7		Quincy, IL	Mühlhausen, Hessen-Darmstadt
Ritter, Emilie	28, June 1869	4, June	43- 2m-17d	207		Wheeling, WV	Kulmitzsch, Berga, Neustadt, Sachsen-Weimar
Ritter, Jakob	13, June 1870	6, Apr.	55	191		Furnace, OH	Hombressen, Kurhessen
Ritter, John C.	4, Apr. 1895	10, Mar.	22	222		Pinckney, MO	Hopewell
Ritter, Joseph H.	2, Feb. 1880	10, Jan.	78- 1m	39		Warrenton, MO	Caldorf, Vahrenholz, Lippe-Detmold
Ritter, Julia	12, Jan. 1874	21, Sept	34	15	Miller	Wheeling, WV	
Ritter, Julia	26, Jan. 1874	21, Dec.	34	15	Miller	Wheeling, WV	

Christliche Apologete Death Notices --- 1839 - 1899

Name of Deceased	Notice Date	Death Date	Age	Maiden Name	Page	Place of Death	Place of Birth
Ritter, Karl August	21, Nov. 1881	8, Nov.	64- 9m- 3d		375	Wheeling, WV	Culmischs, Sachsen-Weimar
Ritter, Karl Julius	12, Apr. 1880	23, Mar.	13		119	Higginsville, MO	Warren County, Missouri
Ritter, Katharina	27, Oct. 1887	8, Oct.	78	Fritzensmeier	686	Concordia, MO	Valldeup, Lippe-Detmold
Ritter, Lena	23, June 1892	25, May	57- -26d	Meierle	398	New York City, NY	Detnang, Württemberg
Ritter, Maria	26, July 1880	6, July	80- 6m		239	Dayton, OH	
Ritter, Simon Philip August	5, Jan. 1893		60		14	Higginsville, MO	Lürdessen, Brake , Lippe-Detmold
Ritterbusch, August Wilhelm	27, Feb. 1890	23, Jan.	18		142	Bland, MO	
Rittinger, J. Wilhelm	26, Mar. 1877	11, Mar.	38- 5m-14d		103	Geneseo, IL	Straußdorf, Sachsen
Rittinger, Katharina	30, July 1847	2, July	36		123	Glasboro, NJ	Württemberg
Rittinger, Sarah Elisabeth	18, Apr. 1889	17, Mar.	17		254	Freeport, MI	Bowne Township, Kent County, Michigan
Ritz, Albert	15, Mar. 1888	15, Feb.	14		174	Newport, KY	
Ritz, Anna Margaretha	26, Dec. 1889	11, Nov.	70-10m-14d	Reumann	830	Seymour, IN	Schafhausen, Sachsen-Weimar
Ritz, Verona	23, Aug. 1869	3, Aug.	58		271	Toledo, OH	Inkwyl, Wangen, Bern, Schweiz
Ritzenthaler, Louise	23, Jan. 1862	24, Dec.		Göres	16	Defiance, OH	
Ritzenthaler, Maria E.	6, May 1886	11, Apr.	16		7		Wauseon, Ohio
Ritzhaupt, Johanna Elisabeth	21, Oct. 1872	24, Sept	28	Lang	343	New Knoxville, OH	Nordhausen, Brackenheim, Württemberg
Ritzkofski, John	17, Aug. 1899	12, July	20		527	Mankato, MN	
Ritzmann, Albertine	20, May 1878	6, May	54		159	Aurora, IN	Mutterstadt, Rheinpfalz Baiern
Ritzmann, Anna	14, Jan. 1892	4, Dec.	69	Griesel	30	Buffalo, NY	Wilchingen, Schweiz
Ritzmann, Anna Barbara	2, June 1898	8, May	71		351	Columbus, OH	Ochswang, Kirchheim, Württemberg
Rixe, Katharina Maria	19, Mar. 1896	3, Mar.	83	Schröders	190	Cincinnati, OH	Melle, Hannover
Rixse, Anna	26, July 1849	14, July	26	Kück	120	Cincinnati, OH	Adelsdorf, Hannover
Rixse, Catharina	19, July 1849	9, July	30		116	Cincinnati, OH	Westkirchen, Preußen
Rixse, Franz	13, June 1870	25, May	59- 5m-27d		191	Cincinnati, OH	Wachendorf, Amt Syke, Hannover
Rixse, Friedrich Heinrich	17, July 1865	29, June	57		116	Cincinnati, OH	Wachendorf, Amt Syke, Hannover
Rixse, Georg	25, July 1870	3, July	18- 2m- 3d		239	Cincinnati, OH	
Rixse, Marie	9, Feb. 1874	30, Jan.	44	Fornau	47	Covington, KY	Dielingen, Preußen
Rixse, Sophia	14, Apr. 1862	17, Mar.	41	Lohstroh	60	Huntingburg, IN	Maaslingen, Petershagen, Minden, Preußen
Roady, Louise Elisabeth	2, Aug. 1875	25, June	25- 4m- 3d	Iff	247	Boody, IL	Basel, Schweiz
Robe, Sophia Louisa	20, Apr. 1893	22, Mar.	63- 6m-12d	Dallman	254	Liberty Grove, WI	Ussentien, Pommern
Roberding, Christina	8, Jan. 1883	15, Dec.	82- 1m	Niemann	15	New Knoxville, OH	Todtenhausen, Preußen
Robert, Maria L.	27, Feb. 1896	24, Jan.	77	Asshemeier	143	Baltimore, MD	Holland
Robert, Wilhelm	20, Apr. 1885	4, Apr.	82		7	Baltimore, MD	Portugal
Robertgreve, Ludwig	7, Apr. 1873	22, Mar.	11- 3m-14d		111	Cleveland, OH	
Roberts, Emeline Elisabeth	7, Apr. 1887	21, Mar.	39		222	Lena, IL	Galena, Illinois
Robertson, Rosette	26, Jan. 1863	14, Dec.	36	Holzer	16	New Knoxville, OH	Erlenbach, Amt Wimmis, Bern, Schweiz
Robeson, Anna Barbara	30, Aug. 1880	11, Aug.	35	Lay	279	St. Louis, MO	
Robinson, John	23, Sept 1897	5, Sept	86		607	Fairfax, MN	Loughbircklan, County Down, Ireland
Robinson, Marie	7, Oct. 1897	24, Aug.	26- 8m	Haag	639	Scranton, PA	
Roblet, Christoph	5, July 1860	14, June	17- 9m-22d		108	Newport, MI	
Rocke, Frances	13, June 1895	7, May	34	Schwarzentrüber	382	Farmington, IA	Charleston, Lee County, Iowa
Röckel, Hermann	27, Feb. 1865	12, Jan.	38		36	Peoria, IL	Hamburg, Hannover
Rockenfuß, Ludwig Christian	19, Nov. 1877	26, Oct.	58		375	Lake Creek, MO	Hille, Minden, Preußen
Röcker, Agatha	25, Mar. 1886	28, Feb.	64	Binder	7	Delhi, MI	Schwarzwald, Herrenberg, Württemberg
Röcker, Maria Sophia	20, Aug. 1866	5, July	55	Mannsperger	270	Watertown, WI	Adelshofen, Baden
Rocktischler, Christina Barbara	14, Sept 1885	27, Aug.	77	Zorn	7	Portsmouth, OH	Oberleisstadt, Rheinkreis Baiern

Christliche Apologete Death Notices --- 1839 - 1899

Name of Deceased	Notice Date	Death Date	Age	Maiden Name	Page	Place of Death	Place of Birth
Rockzien, Maria	29, Sept 1898	13, Sept	81		623	Charles City, IA	Zittow, Mecklenburg-Schwerin
Rockzien, Wilhelm	25, Mar. 1897	4, Mar.	78		190	Charles City, IA	Medow, Mecklenburg-Schwerin
Rode, Anton Friedrich Gottlieb	12, Apr. 1894	1, Mar.	70		246	Washington, MN	Lippe-Schaumburg
Rode, Friedrich	6, May 1878	19, Apr.	78		143	Bloomington, IL	
Rode, Karoline	17, Feb. 1879	29, Jan.	40- 2m-54d	Fritze	55	Fredericksburg, TX	Dillenburg, Nassau
Rode, Mathilde	31, Dec. 1883	5, Dec.	13		7	Chicago, IL	
Rödecker, Heinrich Wilhelm	19, Oct. 1893	26, Sept	17		670	Pennington, IN	Pennington, Decatur County, Indiana
Rodekohr, Dorothea	4, Feb. 1892	13, Jan.	68	Wicken	78	Lake Creek, MO	Schweringen, Hannover
Rödel, Elisabeth	13, July 1863	14, Apr.		Schreiber	112	Mt. Vernon, IN	
Rödelsberger, Valentin	6, May 1878	20, Apr.	60		143	Alaidon, MI	Heubach, Hessen-Darmstadt
Rodemeyer, August (Rev)	27, July 1899	1, July	62		472	Thalweil, SW	Vegesack, Bremen, Germany
Rodenbeck, Caroline	24, Nov. 1873	5, Nov.	25-11m- 3d	Miller	375	Pekin, IL	
Rodenbeek, Elisabeth	28, Mar. 1895	3, Mar.	63	Ledtermann	206	Pekin, IL	Massillon, Ohio
Rodenberg, Eduard Dietrich	21, Jan. 1884	17, Dec.	20		7	St. Louis, MO	Cape Girardeau County, Missouri
Rodenberger, Elise	29, Mar. 1888	2, Mar.	28-11m-18d	Schultze	206	Ellis Grove, IL	Chambersburg, Pennsylvania
Rodenheber, John	18, May 1863	Aug.	23		80	Piqua, OH	Zweibrücken, Rheinkreis Baiern
Rodenstein, Elisabeth	9, Oct. 1890	14, Sept	53		654		Nordeck, Marburg, Kurhessen
Röder, Anna K.	1, Sept 1879		67	Schäfer	279	Bloomington, IL	Zielsdorf, Neumark an der Oder, Preußen
Röder, August	11, May 1874		44		151	Beaver Dam, WI	Gornitz, Schönlanke, Scharikan, Posen
Röder, August	19, Jan. 1893	22, Dec.	55		46	Tomah, WI	Krummfließ, West Preußen
Röder, August Ferdinand	4, July 1889	13, June	72		430	Berne, MI	Lübeck, Minden, Preußen
Röder, Charlotte	2, Dec. 1897	11, Nov.	51	Tegeler	767	Ballwin, MO	Prüzeldorf,
Röder, Chr.	1, Nov. 1875	15, Oct.	65		351	Tomah, WI	Döhnsen, Weser, Braunschweig
Röder, Ernestine	17, May 1855	25, Apr.	35- 5m	Brunner	80	Evansville, IN	Baltimore, Maryland
Röder, Jakob Peter	13, June 1870	19, Apr.	33		191	Baltimore, MD	Landerstadt, Mittelfranken, Baiern
Röder, Kaspar	7, Apr. 1884	22, Mar.	78		7	Batesville, IN	Urach, Württemberg
Röder, Maria Katharina	24, May 1894	10, May	66	Schöllhammer	342	Cincinnati, OH	Himmelforden, Hannover
Röder, Rebekka	4, June 1896	19, May	56- 2m-24d	Offermann	367	St. Louis, MO	Zülsdorf, Arenswalde,
Röder, Sophia Christina	10, Jan. 1881	6, Dec.	71	Kart	15	Wausau, WI	Zülsdorf, Arenswalde,
Röder, Sophia Christina	31, Jan. 1881	6, Dec.	71	Kartholz	39	Wausau, WI	Seesen, Braunschweig
Röder, Theodor	16, Jan. 1890	30, Nov.	70		46	Evansville, IN	Norteck, Kreis Marbach, Kurhessen
Röder, Wilhelm	20, Jan. 1859	1, Jan.	17		12	Bloomington, IL	Zühlzdorf, Neumark
Röder, Wilhelm Herman	15, Oct. 1896	26, Sept	65		671	Taegesville, WI	Siebbentuch, Lippe-Detmold
Rodewald, Karl	29, July 1878	24, June	52- 4m-22d		239	Rushville, IL	Saarbrücken, Preußen
Rodgers, Elisabeth	3, June 1878	25, Apr.	64- 3m-20d	Blatter	175	Golconda, IL	Stevenhagen, Mecklenburg-Schwerin
Rody, Dorothea	25, Jan. 1864	28, Dec.	66		16	Laporte, IN	Rastede, Oldenburg
Roeben, Gerd Heinrich	26, Aug. 1878	9, Aug.	56-10m- 4d		271	Schulenburg, TX	Adelshofen, Baden
Roecker, Andreas	2, Sept 1878	24, July	77- 4m- 2d		279	Oshkosh, WI	Neustadt an der Orla, Sachsen-Weimar
Roedel, Friederika	8, Jan. 1883	9, Dec.	60	Herdwig	15	Francisco, MI	
Roehl, Victor	29, Dec. 1884	18, July	4- 7m		7	Fond du Lac, WI	Sulz, Nagold, Württemberg
Roehm, Johan Jakob	5, Apr. 1875	27, Feb.	72		111	Ripley, OH	Windheim, Minden, Preußen
Roelfs, Dietrike	21, July 1873	23, June	16- 8m-20d		231	Pekin, IL	Nürnberg, Baiern
Roemke, Conrad D.	26, Jan. 1880	5, Jan.	75- 5m-17d		31	Burlington, IA	Leopoldshafen, Baden
Roesch, Anna Elisabeth	16, June 1898		75- 9m-15d	Hügelschasser	383	Lawrenceburg, IN	Obernzenn, Mittelfranken, Baiern
Roesch, Johan Adam	30, Aug. 1894	2, Aug.	70		566	Brooklyn, NY	
Roesch, Lorenz	16, Apr. 1877	19, Mar.			127	Lawrenceburg, IN	

Christliche Apologete Death Notices -- 1839 - 1899

Name of Deceased	Notice Date	Death Date	Age	Page	Maiden Name	Place of Death	Place of Birth
Roesener, Jakob	1, Nov. 1880	14, Oct.	17-11m-12d	351		Marrs, IN	Posey County, Indiana
Roesler, Charles	21, Mar. 1889	6, Mar.	72	190		Junction City, KS	Berlinchen, Preußen
Roeßler, Auguste Wilhelmine	2, Feb. 1888	8, Jan.	73	78	Sommer	Junction City, KS	
Röfert, Christina	7, Nov. 1881	25, Oct.	80-7m	359		Indianapolis, IN	Frille, Minden, Preußen
Röfert, Friedrich W.	8, Aug. 1864	18, July	33	128		Indianapolis, IN	Frille, Preußen
Röfert, Heinrich	28, May 1891	8, May	91	350		Indianapolis, IN	Meins bei Bückeburg, Germany
Röfert, Maria	28, Nov. 1881	10, Nov.	59- 5m-23d	383	Sichting	Golconda, IL	Berga, Nordhausen am Harz, Preußen
Röfflen, Dorothea	7, Dec. 1874	9, Nov.	60	391	Bardill	Golconda, IL	Jenatz, Graubünden, Schweiz
Röffler, Jakob	20, Apr. 1885	31, Mar.	83	7		Golconda, IL	Valzeina, Graubünden, Schweiz
Rogers, Amalie	17, Aug. 1885	19, July	33	7	Beck	Los Angeles, CA	Quincy, Illinois
Rogers, Anna Sophia	31, Dec. 1891	6, Dec.	34	846	Kunst	Bushnell, IL	Wesenstedt, Hannover
Rogers, Georg	22, July 1897	24, June	64	463		Farmington, IA	Bruchhausen, Hannover
Rogers, Leonora	11, Feb. 1892	22, Jan.	59	94	Bäsmann	Bushnell, IL	Hastbergen, Hoya, Hannover
Rogers, Mary	26, Jan. 1885	1, Jan.	17	7		Golconda, IL	
Rogers, William	26, Jan. 1885	Dec.	15	7		Golconda, IL	
Rogge, Anna	12, May 1898	13, Apr.	72	303	Rütemann	Alton, IL	Oldenburg
Rogge, Augusta	28, Oct. 1897	13, Sept	51	687	Gray	Fond du Lac, WI	Neuenburg, Brandenburg
Rogge, Johanna	3, Apr. 1890	25, Feb.	68	222		Alton, IL	Meinike, Fedderwarden, Oldenburg
Rogge, Johanna	20, Mar. 1890	25, Feb.	68	190	Meinike	Lawrence, KS	Fedderwarden, Oldenburg
Roggenfüs, Carl August	3, Feb. 1853	6, Jan.		20		Laporte, IN	Hille, Münden, Preußen
Roggenfuß, Friedrich W.	28, Feb. 1889	7, Feb.	27- 2m- 9d	142		Warrenton, MO	
Roggenfuß, Margaretha	6, Oct. 1848	24, Aug.	63	164		St. Louis, MO	Hille, Preußen
Roggensuß, Marie J.	7, Mar. 1889	13, Feb.	69	158	Backhaus	Warrenton, MO	Linthrop, Tecklenburg, Hannover
Roggensuß, Heinrich	12, May 1892	29, Jan.	76- 4m-17d	302		St. Charles, MO	Hille, Minden, Preußen
Rohde, Albert	2, Jan. 1882	17, Dec.	13-10m-17d	7		Laporte, IN	
Rohde, Auguste Ottilie	19, May 1898	21, Apr.	37	319		Lowell, WI	Watertown, Wisconsin
Rohde, Elisa	3, Oct. 1881	17, Sept	25	319		Lena, IL	Rohrmoos, Oberburg, Bern, Schweiz
Rohde, Hermuth Joh.	23, Sept 1872	3, Sept	72	311		Laporte, IN	Iwenack, Steffenhagen, Mecklenburg-Schwerin
Rohde, Martha	23, Aug. 1894	1, July	43	550	Heppel	Houston, TX	Retterrode, Hessen-Nassau
Rohde, Sophia Ernestine Friedr.	29, May 1890	29, Apr.	46	350	Wollbrandt	East Troy, WI	Beggerow, Pommern
Rohde, Wilhelmine Louise F.	5, Sept 1895	9, Aug.	77	574	Lehmann	Giard, IA	Mentin, Mecklenburg-Schwerin
Rohe, Wilhelmine	14, Sept 1885	30, Aug.	77	7		Chillicothe, OH	Hauterode, Preußen
Roherer, Margaretha	18, Nov. 1872	1, Nov.	18	375		Beaver Dam, WI	
Rohkop, Lydia M.	30, Dec. 1897	10, Dec.	35	828	Engelmann	Concordia, MO	Lexington, Missouri
Röhl, Gottfried	4, Aug. 1898	14, July	77	495		Watertown, WI	Kortenhagen, Germany
Röhl, Gottlieb	25, Nov. 1897	2, Nov.	68- 6m- 9d	751		Bridgewater, IA	Langehagen bei Colberg, Pommern
Röhl, Maria	16, Jan. 1882	2, Jan.	59	23	Schulz	Watertown, WI	Sinzlow, Stettin, Preußen
Rohleder, Agnes	26, Feb. 1883	27, Dec.	37- 2m- 2d	71		Springfield, IL	Hohenleuben, Sachsen
Rohleder, Georg	29, Mar. 1894	7, Mar.	76	214		East Troy, WI	Simanshofen, Lauh, Baiern
Rohleder, Maria	16, June 1898	25, May	67	383	Bartholomäus	Honey Creek, WI	Hönebach, Rotenburg, Kurhessen
Rohlfing, Adolph Friedrich	16, Apr. 1896	24, Mar.	22	254		Grand Ridge, IL	Grand Rapids, Illinois
Rohlfing, Anna Katharina	4, Feb. 1878	18, Jan.	37	39		New Haven, MO	Franklin County, Missouri
Rohlfing, Friedrich	29, Mar. 1888	27, Feb.	52	206		Grand Ridge, IL	Heimsen, Windheim, Preußen
Rohlfing, Johan Heinrich	23, July 1883	6, June	31	239		Altamont, IL	New Melle, Missouri
Rohlfing, Louis	16, Dec. 1872	23, Nov.	54- 4m- 2d	407		Herman, MO	NordHemmen, Minden, Preußen
Rohlfing, Lydia	3, Nov. 1879	16, Oct.	20	351	Spreckelmeier	Herman, MO	

Christliche Apologete Death Notices --- 1839 - 1899

Name of Deceased	Notice Date	Death Date	Age	Maiden Name	Page	Place of Death	Place of Birth
Rohlfing, Maria	14, Mar. 1881	23, Feb.	29- 8m	Voß	87	Nashville, IL	Senate Grove, Missouri
Rohlfing, Mathilde	2, July 1896	16, June	40	Stöppelmann	431	Senate Grove, MO	Nordhemmen, Minden, Preußen
Rohlfing, Wilhelm	2, Oct. 1865	13, Aug.	24		160	Herman, MO	Sulz, Nagold, Württemberg
Röhm, Christina Magdalena	11, Sept 1871	21, July	82	Dürr	295	Higginsport, OH	Nordheim, Brackenheim, Württemberg
Rohmeyer, Wilhelm	24, Aug. 1885	11, Aug.	32		7	Marietta, OH	Beardstown, Illinois
Rohn, Auguste Rosalie	5, Mar. 1891	4, Feb.	32- 6m- 3d	Mechen	158	Beardstown, IL	Niederohmen, Laubach, Hessen-Darmstadt
Rohn, Elisabeth	25, Jan. 1894	29, Dec.	84	Langohr	62	Beardstown, IL	Stockhäuser Hof, Laubach, Hessen-Darmstadt
Rohn, Heinrich	21, May 1891	21, Apr.	85- 8m		334	Beardstown, IL	
Rohn, Maria	7, May 1877	13, Apr.	26	Jotisch	151	Beardstown, IL	
Rohner, Frieda	10, June 1897	15, May	22		367	Hoboken, NJ	Canton Appenzell, Schweiz
Rohr , Anna Barbara	4, May 1893	8, Mar.	62		286	St. Joseph, MO	Kurtenberg, Bern, Schweiz
Röhr, Friedrich A.	18, Aug. 1887	16, July	48		526	Bushton, KS	Olbersleben, Sachsen-Weimar
Röhr, Heinrich	16, July 1896	20, June	78		463	Wellsville, NY	Hannover
Röhr, Hugo Ernst	2, Nov. 1893		10		702	Bushton, KS	Rice County, Kansas
Rohr, Johan	5, Mar. 1891	23, Jan.	70		158	St. Joseph, MO	Hohnzenschiel, Aarau, Schweiz
Rohr, Louisa	8, June 1874	2, May	16 - -18d		183	Junction Falls, NY	
Rohr, Susanna	30, Sept 1886	15, Sept	68		7	Milwaukee, WI	Canton Aargau, Schweiz
Rohrbach, Johan Adam	15, Sept 1892	17, Aug.	48-10m- 9d		590	Paterson, NJ	
Rohrbach, Johanne Wilhelmine	23, Feb. 1888	27, Jan.	36	Müller	126	Paterson, NJ	Elberfeld, RheinPreußen
Rohrbach, Margaretha	8, Aug. 1881	21, July	19	Fischer	255	Wyandotte, KS	Estrich, Nassau
Rohrbacher, Anna Barbara	12, Nov. 1847	3, Oct.			183	New Orleans, LA	
Rohrbacher, Johann	12, Nov. 1847	7, Sept	32		183	New Orleans, LA	
Rohrbacher, Margaretha	12, Nov. 1847	25, Aug.	25		183	New Orleans, LA	
Rohrer, Heinrich	7, Dec. 1885	15, Nov.	64		7	Beaver Dam, WI	St. Gallen, Schweiz
Rohrhasser, Heinrich	11, Dec. 1871	17, Nov.	41		399	Toledo, OH	Behringen, Schaffhausen, Schweiz
Röhrich, J.G.	24, July 1882	30, June	71- 1m-19d		239	Fredericksburg, TX	
Röhrs, Cord Wilhelm	12, Nov. 1896	23, Oct.	63		734	New York City, NY	Osterwede, Hannover
Rohrscheib, Andreas	11, Sept 1890	11, Aug.	27		590	Huntingburg, IN	
Rohrscheib, Johan Jacob	5, Mar. 1891	3, Feb.	76		158	Huntingburg, IN	Westheim, Rheinpfalz Baiern
Rohrscheib, Philipp	23, July1883	2, July	38- 4m-23d		239	Boonville, IN	Westheim, Rheinpfalz Baiern
Rohs, Benjamin F.	25, Feb. 1897	1, Jan.	25		127	Burlington, IA	Canton, Lewis County, Missouri
Rohs, Friederike	25, Feb. 1897	2, Feb.	59	Klaus	127	Burlington, IA	Oberdürkheim, Württemberg
Rohwedder, Anna Katharina	25, Apr. 1881	9, Apr.	53	Brill	135	Valparaiso, IN	Reichenbach, Kurhessen
Rojahn, Maria	2, Nov. 1893	12, Aug.			702	Quincy, IL	
Rolbitzki, Johan	24, Apr. 1882	9, Apr.	62- 7m-21d		135	Buffalo, NY	Konesin, West Preußen
Rolf, Maria A.	10, Oct. 1881	5, Sept	77- 8m-25d	Kruse	327	Francisco, MI	Brunschedt, Hannover
Rolfing, Anna Christina	7, Sept 1874	6, Aug.	60-10m-11d	Meier	287	Salem, —	Hahlen, Hartum, Minden, Preußen
Rolfing, Carolina	15, Oct. 1891	12, Sept	60	Korfhage	670	St. Paul, MN	Berninghausen, Minden, Preußen
Rolfing, Josephine	5, Jan. 1863	15, Nov.	5- 3m- 3d		4	St. Paul, MN	
Rolfing, Luise Anna	11, May 1899	16, Mar.		Busch	302	St. Paul, MN	Ft. Madison, Iowa
Rolfing, Maria	15, Nov. 1869	25, Oct.	77		367	St. Paul, MN	Hahlen, Hartum, Minden, Preußen
Rolfing, Maria	18, Mar. 1897	20, Feb.	71	Kurrelmeier	175	St. Paul, MN	Westerkappeln, Preußen
Rolfing, Maria	5, Jan. 1863	21, Nov.	13		4	St. Paul, MN	
Rolfing, Sophie Martha	23, Feb. 1888		18- 5m-14d		126	Nashville, IL	Addieville, Washington County, Illinois
Rolfing, Heinrich	26, Jan. 1888	16, Dec.	20- 2m- 3d		62	Bensonville, IL	
Rölfs, Henriette	19, Nov. 1896	30, Oct.	70	Schliep	750	Bushton, KS	Felde, Ostfriesland

- 413 -

Christliche Apologete Death Notices --- 1839 - 1899

Name of Deceased	Notice Date	Death Date	Age	Page	Maiden Name	Place of Death	Place of Birth
Rolfs, R.	7, Nov. 1881	20, Sept	60	359	VanderVelde	Rice Co, KS	Wenden, Rückhausen, Ostfriesland
Rölfs, Trientge D.	1, Dec. 1892	14, Nov.	67	766		Pekin, IL	Hanswehrum, Ostfriesland
Roll, Heinrich	8, Mar. 1869	27, Dec.	70	79		St. Louis, MO	Odenhausen, Grünberg, Hessen-Darmstadt
Roll, Jacob	13, Dec. 1875	26, Nov.	69	399		St. Louis, MO	Ebersheim, Grünstadt, Rheinkreis Baiern
Röll, Maria Sophia	1, June 1899	21, Apr.	33	351		Huntingburg, IN	Santa Claus, Indiana
Röll, Sophia	9, Oct. 1876	16, Sept	39	327	Kätzel	Santa Claus, IN	Waynesburgh, Star County, Ohio
Roller, Albert	12, Apr. 1869	15, Mar.	35	119		Boonville, IN	Nethene, Geldern, Holland
Roller, Enandine	19, Jan. 1863	1, Jan.	35	12		Evansville, IN	Neede, Holland
Roller, Eva Maria	26, June 1890	13, May	68-10m-23d	414	Ehneß	Brookville, IN	Wath bullag,
Roller, Gerhard	30, Dec. 1867	26, Nov.	44	414		Boonville, IN	Neete, Gelterland, Holland
Roller, Heinrich	3, Aug. 1863	4, July	34	124		Evansville, IN	Gellerland, Holland
Roller, Henriette	13, Aug. 1891	17, July	61	526	Bockhorst	Boonville, IN	Heppen, Bielefeld, Minden, Preußen
Roller, Johan Georg	4, May 1885	15, Apr.	82	7		Mt. Olive, IL	Maistem, Calw, Württemberg
Roller, John	1, June 1868	25, Apr.	32	175		Boonville, IN	Nethene, Geldern, Holland
Roller, Katharina	12, June 1865	21, May	29	96	Oue	Evansville, IN	Osnabrück, Hannover
Roloff, August	23, Feb. 1880	21, Jan.	61	63		Crow River, MN	Radow, Preußen
Roloff, Louise	10, Mar. 1884	28, Feb.	66-10m- 9d	7		Montrose, MN	Hoffelde, Pommern
Romanus, Friederika	1, Jan. 1891	23, Nov.	70	14		Golconda, IL	Roitzsch, Preußen
Romanus, Gottfried	16, June 1884	7, Apr.	61- 4m-24d	7		Golconda, IL	Laue, Bitterfeld, Preußen
Rombold, Friederika C.	14, June 1894	17, May	23	390	Schauner	Wichita, KS	Evansville, Indiana
Römer, Anna	27, May 1886	26, Mar.	18	7		Baltimore, MD	
Römer, Anna Dorothea	7, Feb. 1870	18, Dec.	40	47	Jökel	Warrenton, MO	Höckersdorf, Grünberg, Hessen-Darmstadt
Römer, Augusta Maria Charlotte	29, May 1890	4, May	29	350	Last	Winona, MN	Schlackow, Schlawo, Pommern
Römer, Emma	8, Mar. 1894	10, Feb.	26	166	Andres	Tinley Park, IL	Orland, Illinois
Römer, Ida	3, Feb. 1898	26, Dec.	31	79	Huff	Baltimore, MD	Mogilno, Posen
Römer, Johan	28, Mar. 1895	27, Feb.	49	206		Baltimore, MD	Gutenborn, Kurhessen
Römer, John	25, Aug. 1873	4, Aug.	20	271		Newark, NJ	
Römer, Katharina	29, Oct. 1896	28, Sept	83- 7m-11d	703	Ubrich	Evansville, IN	Oberbeisheim, Humberg, Kurhessen
Römer, Peter	1, Oct. 1896	15, Sept	82	639		Evansville, IN	Sangorshausen, Nassau
Römer, Wilhelm	30, Jan. 1882	12, Jan.	78- 8m-25d	39		New Bremen, IL	Stadthosbach, Eschwe, Kurhessen
Rometsch, August Gottfried	16, Dec. 1897	27, Nov.	76	799		Philadelphia, PA	Sulz am Neckar, Württemberg
Rometsch, Kunigunde	14, Dec. 1885	19, Nov.	47	7	Heuschmid	Newark, NJ	Schelklingen, Württemberg
Rometsch, Wilhelmine Henriette	7, May 1891	7, Apr.	75	302	Stähli	Philadelphia, PA	Alpiersbach, Württemberg
Romkey, Franklin Konrad	29, Dec. 1898	28, Nov.	41	828		Toledo, OH	Defiance , Ohio
Römling, Catharina Barbara	18, Feb. 1886		70	7	Rothe	Etna, MO	Ellerstadt, Baiern
Römling, Heinrich	6, Sept 1894	28, July	52	582		Etna, MO	Woltwiese, Braunschweig
Römling, Heinrich M.	13, Apr. 1885	24, Mar.	76	7		Etna, MO	Woltwiesche, Saldern, Braunschweig
Römling, Lizzie	21, Jan. 1892	4, Nov.	18	46		Etna, MO	Etna, Missouri
Romoser, Samuel Heinrich	12, Dec. 1889	18, Nov.	15- 8m-28d	798		Marion, OH	Marion County, Ohio
Rompag, Henriette	10, Aug. 1893	22, July	60	510	Essenwein	Minneapolis, MN	Neustadt, Mecklenburg-Schwerin
Ronde, Friedrich Karl	8, Nov. 1880	24, Oct.	62- 7m	359		Allegan, MI	Schwollenberg, Preußen
Rongers, Heinrich	6, Sept 1849	16, Aug.	22	144		Milwaukee, WI	Wesel, RheinPreußen
Rönicke, Johanna	1, Sept 1853	31, July	52	140		Detroit, MI	Kranichborn, Sachsen-Weimar
Roning, (Mrs)	21, Apr. 1879	3, Feb.	33	127	Stieckmann	Herman, MO	Edinghausen, Minden, Preußen
Rönke, Wilhelmine	13, Jan. 1868	25, Dec.	40- 4m-12d	14	Grässmann	North Evans, NY	Neuenkirchen, Wittenburg, Mecklenburg-Schwerin
Ronshausen, Catharina E.	1, Dec. 1873	14, Aug.	74-10m-15d	383	Ekel	Pittsburg, PA	Altmorschen, Melsungen, Kurhessen

Christliche Apologete Death Notices --- 1839 - 1899

Name of Deceased	Notice Date	Death Date	Age	Page	Maiden Name	Place of Death	Place of Birth
Ronshausen, Conrad	1, July 1897	11, June	76	414		Monroefield, OH	Eschwa, Nördua, Hessen
Ronshausen, George	29, Nov. 1860	24, Sept	37	192		Pittsburg, PA	Atmorschen, Melsbungen, Kurhessen
Ronshausen, Margarethe	28, July 1862	17, July	21- 5m-20d	120	Schneider	Pittsburg, PA	Pittsburg, Pennsylvania
Rooney, Elisabeth	25, Aug. 1873	7, Aug.	36- 4m-10d	271	Ringel	Chicago, IL	
Roos, (Mrs)	20, May 1886	26, Apr.	79- 2m	7		Cold Spring, KY	Thomashardt, Schorndorf, Württemberg
Roos, Clara	14, Dec. 1868	14, Nov.		399		Wapello, IA	
Roos, Elisabeth	21, June 1875	26, May	77	199	Bauer	Baresville, OH	Rumbach, Rheinkreis Baiern
Roos, Jennie	13, Oct. 1887	6, Sept	19- 2m	654		Wapello, IA	
Roos, Katharine	26, Dec. 1895	30, Nov.	78	828	Hüsing	Cleveland, OH	Berlgingen, Kieselau, Württemberg
Roos, Leonhard	8, June 1868	14, May	40	183		Wapello, IA	Hohenstaufen, Göppingen, Württemberg
Roos, Maria Rosina Margaretha	3, Sept 1896	5, Aug.	68	575	Hafner	Mt. Vernon, IN	Kupferzell, Oehringen, Württemberg
Roos, Michael	29, Mar. 1894	4, Mar.	72	214		Wapello, IA	Hohenstaufen, Göppingen, Württemberg
Roos, Michael	26, Sept 1850	5, Sept	57- 2m	156		Captina, OH	Rombach, Rheinkreis Baiern
Roose, Friedrich Wilhelm	30, Jan. 1846	12, Jan.	45	19		St. Louis, MO	Neukirchen, Amt Krönenberg, Hannover
Roose, Louise Maria	10, July 1882	10, May	17- 3m-19d	223		Chicago, IL	
Roper, Marie Philippine Johanne	26, Mar. 1891	9, Jan.	39	206	Gentz	Amsterdam, NY	Johannishof , Preußen
Röpke, Justina	23, Sept 1872	30, Aug.	52- -27d	311		St. Paul, MN	Moschütz, Bromberg, Preußen
Röpken, Casten	18, July 1889	15, June	77- 4m- 5d	462		Dayton, OH	Thedinghausen bei Bremen, Brandenburg
Röpken, Margaretha	29, May 1876	29, Apr.	41	175		Dayton, OH	Thedingshausen, Braunschweig
Roppel, Caspar	7, Nov. 1895	27, Sept	60	718		Webster City, IA	Kurhessen
Rörich, Carolina	16, Nov. 1885	25, Oct.	52	7		Fredericksburg, TX	Glesendorf, Preußen
Röring, Johan Gerhard	20, Sept 1860	31, July	36	152		Danville, IL	Mammelzen, Altenkirchen, Preußen
Rörling, Eduard	15, Apr. 1897	29, Mar.	68	239		Scranton, PA	Löbnitz an der Linde, Cöhlen, Sachsen
Rösch, Adam	5, July 1875	19, June	74	215		Buffalo, NY	Blankenloch, Baden
Rösch, Christina	8, Dec. 1873	3, Nov.	70	391	Ulrizi	Buffalo, NY	Leopoldshafen, Baden
Rösch, Kunigunda	22, Jan. 1872	30, Dec.	64- 7m-17d	31	Flaach	Weston, MO	Wölflingen, Zürich, Schweiz
Rösch, Salome	1, July 1886	17, June	75	7	Kamerer	Galion, OH	Graben, Baden
Rösch, William Conrad	4, Feb. 1886	16, Jan.	29	7		Stockton, CA	Gomaringen, Reutlingen, Württemberg
Röscher, Caroline	15, Mar. 1875	17, Feb.	44	87	Dörres	Petersburg, IL	Negenbam, Braunschweig
Röscher, Katharina	25, Aug. 1887	21, July	40	542	Humberger	Jeffersonville, IN	Diedenbergen, Nassau
Rose, Carl	14, Jan. 1848	21, Dec.	24	11		St. Louis, MO	Neuenkirchen bei Mellau, Hannover
Rose, Catharine	23, June 1862	27, May	67	100		New York, NY	
Rose, Friedrich	8, Apr. 1897	11, Mar.	79	223		Chicago, IL	Mecklenburg-Schwerin
Rose, Henriette Wilhelmine	22, Sept 1898	13, Aug.	64	607	Ulm	Sleepy Eye, MN	Giesenau bei Landesberg, Preußen
Rose, Johanna	2, July 1896	13, June	62	431	Wilde	Rockham, SD	Kratzik bei Neu-Wedel, Neumark
Rose, Johanna Katharine	13, Jan. 1887	29, Dec.	87- 2m-26d	30	Einbrink	St. Louis, MO	
Rose, Martha	13, Mar. 1890	14, Feb.	19- - 7d	174		Milwaukee, WI	GroßOttersleben, Sachsen
Rose, Sophia	26, Jan. 1893	27, Dec.	71	62	Behnke	Kendallville, IN	Glasewitz, Mecklenburg-Schwerin
Rose, Wilhelm	23, June 1862	20, May	69	100		New York, NY	Neuenkirchen bei Mella,
Rose, Wilhelm Friedrich	7, Sept 1899	20, Aug.	36	575		Rockham, SD	Neumark
Rosebach, John William	13, Aug. 1883	16, June	75- 6m-16d	263		Newton, IA	Marienfels, Nastätten, Nassau
Rosemeier, Jakobine Dorette A.	6, Oct. 1879	14, Aug.	11- 2m-16d	319		Springfield, IL	
Rosenau, Caroline	9, Feb. 1885	17, Jan.	58- 5m-17d	7	Molsuch	Elysian, MN	Jankindorf, Kollmar, West Preußen
Rosenbaum, Karl	9, June 1873	11, Apr.	19	183		Brenham, TX	Wehden, Kreis Lübbeke, Minden, Preußen
Rösener, Caroline	19, Sept 1850	22, July	29- 3m-14d	152		Cincinnati, OH	Zesmelin, Minden, Preußen
Rosenkranz, Carolina	29, July 1886	13, July	38	7	Fritz	Laporte, IN	Mittelsdorf, Schorndorf, Württemberg

Christliche Apologete Death Notices --- 1839 - 1899

Name of Deceased	Notice Date	Death Date	Age	Page	Maiden Name	Place of Death	Place of Birth
Rosenlieb, Katharina	9, July 1891	4, May	33- 11m-13d	446	Heythem	New Metamoras, OH	Perry Township, Monroe County, Ohio
Rosenow, Ernestina	28, Feb. 1881	8, Feb.	56	71	Großkreutz	Washington, MN	Grosbentz, Naugard, Pommern
Rosenow, Friedrich	6, Oct. 1892	4, Sept	18	638		Brownton, MN	Braunsberg, Naugard, Pommern
Rosenow, W.	11, Dec. 1890		15- 1m	798		Washington, MO	
Rosenoy, Christian F.	14, Jan. 1897	29, Oct.	78	31		Woodbury, MN	Kannenberg, Germany
Rosenstiel, Henry	4, Aug. 1898	23, June	70	495		Lena, IL	
Rosenstiel, Jakob	21, Sept 1863	31, Aug.	70- 1m-22d	152		Freeport, IL	Großvora, Schwarzburg-Sondershausen
Rosenthal, Carolina Henriette	29, Dec. 1873	10, Dec.	37- 2m-17d	415		Blooming Grove, MN	
Rosenthal, Catharina	24, Feb. 1887	19, Jan.	44	126		Chester, IL	Georgetown, Illinois
Roser, Christian	30, June 1884	17, June	82	7		Baraboo, WI	Pirmasenz, Rheinkreis Baiern
Roser, Dorothea Katharine	10, July 1890	21, June	85- 1m-19d	446	Hunsenger	Bethel, MO	Hatter, Elsaß
Roser, Hulda Ephrosina	17, Mar. 1892	22, Feb.	30	175	Ristau	Baraboo, WI	Freedom, Wisconsin
Röser, Katharina	31, Aug. 1893	16, July	75	558	Düffort	Hebron, IA	Elsaß
Roser, Laura	5, July 1894	31, May	30	438	Zwalina	New York City, NY	Liebenmiel, West Preußen
Röser, Peter	26, July 1894	4, June	80	486		Hebron, IA	Bettweiler, Frankreich
Roser, Samuel G.	28, Apr. 1887	8, Apr.	22	270		Baraboo, WI	Freedom, Sauk County, Wisconsin
Rosher, Ernst August	8, June 1893	18, May	66	366		Pekin, IL	Siechendorf Löbau, Sachsen
Roske, Helena Rosa	11, Jan. 1894	5, Dec.	18	30		Rock Island, IL	Flint, Michigan
Rösler, (Mrs)	24, Sept 1878	24, July	85	303	Gräver	Wilton, MN	Radwonke, Preußen
Rösler, Ferdinand	27, June 1861	1, June	16	104		Michigan City, IN	
Rosono, Wilhelmine Auguste H.	24, Sept 1878	5, Sept	32- 1m- 3d	303	Voigt	Washington, MN	Bramonsdorf, Hinterpommern
Roß, Anna Margaretha	10, Sept 1896		27	591		Columbus, OH	
Roß, Anna Martha	19, Apr. 1880	1, Apr.		127	Klebe	Warsaw, IL	Bokerode, Kurhessen
Roß, Conrad	14, Mar. 1895	9, Feb.	59	174		Baltimore, MD	Aldenbloß, Oberfranken, Baiern
Roß, David	18, June 1891	27, May	54	398		St. Louis, MO	Griesheim, Hessen-Darmstadt
Roß, Johan	13, Apr. 1885	22, Mar.	85- 5m- 7d	7		Charlestown, IN	Nordheim, Hessen-Darmstadt
Roß, Johann L.	26, July 1849	12, July	40	120		Cincinnati, OH	
Roß, John Valentin	2, Dec. 1878	14, Nov.	44	383		Canton, MO	Viernau, Preußen
Roß, Katharina	19, Nov. 1883	6, Oct.	78- 7m-11d	375	Brenner	San Francisco, CA	Altmorschen, Melsungen, Kurhessen
Roß, Katharina	8, Mar. 1849	25, Feb.	43	40		Cincinnati, OH	Elsaß
Roß, Lydia	28, Mar. 1895	19, Jan.	24	206		Albert Lea, MN	
Roß, P.	18, Apr. 1861	7, Apr.	62	64		Rochester, NY	
Roß, Sophia	31, Dec. 1891	4, Dec.	86	846	Heußner	Frankfort, IL	Königswalde, Kurhessen
Roß, Susanna M.	12, July 1849	26, June		112	Mufinger	Lawrenceburg, IN	
Rössiger, Wilhelmine	26, Jan. 1885	18, Dec.	48	7	Rappsilber	Golconda, IL	
Rößle, Friedrich Wilhelm	2, Apr. 1883	19, Mar.	63	111		Allegheny City, PA	Niemeck, Sachsen
Rößle, Johan Friedrich	7, Apr. 1879	20, Mar.	82	111		Freeport, MI	Gelmersbach, Weinsberg, Württemberg
Rößle, Rosina	15, Jan. 1866	14, Dec.	37	22	Baierbach	Allegheny City, PA	Damm, Ludwigsburg, Württemberg
Rößler, Ida Emilie	30, Mar. 1893	14, Mar.	18	206		Pittsburg, PA	Eschenau, Württemberg
Rößler, Margaretha	8, Mar. 1880	15, Feb.	56	79		Chicago, IL	Daisbach, Baden
Roßmann, Karl	27, Apr. 1885	10, Apr.	61	7		Stryker, OH	Leschwitz, Liegnitz, Schlesien
Rößner, Anna Christina	16, Aug. 1894	14, Jan.	17-11m- 6d	534		Marrs, IN	
Rößner, Christina	1, Feb. 1894	14, Jan.	69- 9m-19d	78		Marrs, IN	Neukirchen, Rheinpfalz Baiern
Rößner, Georg	1, Aug. 1870	13, July	57- 4m	247		Marrs, IN	Neuhimschbach, Kaiserslautern, Rheinkreis Baiern
Rößner, Georg W.	5, Aug. 1886	8, July	25	7		Pomeroy, OH	Cincinnati, Hamilton County, Ohio
Rößner, Heinrich	4, June 1891	5, Apr.	51	366		Marrs, IN	Richmond, Virginia

Christliche Apologete Death Notices --- 1839 - 1899

Name of Deceased	Notice Date	Death Date	Age	Page	Maiden Name	Place of Death	Place of Birth
Rößner, Magdalena	26, Apr. 1875	2, Apr.	60	135	Herrer	Marrs, IN	Metterzimmern, Besigheim, Württemberg
Rost, Elisabeth Maria	6, Feb. 1871	3, Jan.	66	47	Lindemann	Mt. Vernon, IN	Zweibrücken, Rheinpfalz Baiern
Rost, Maria	9, Nov. 1874	29, Oct.	58	359		Lafayette, IN	Gröninger bei Ludwigsburg, Württemberg
Rost, Martha	14, May 1883	1, Mar.	27- 9m- 7d	159		Wilton, IA	
Rosteberg, Louise	23, Jan. 1882	12, Nov.	58	31		Baltimore, MD	Spanbeck, Hannover
Rostock, Elisabeth	26, Apr. 1894	10, Mar.	64	278		Oregon, MO	Eichtersheim, Wisloch, Baden
Rostock, Elisabeth	29, Mar. 1894	10, Mar.	64	214		Oregon, MO	
Rostock, Eva Catharina	30, Nov. 1893	3, Nov.	82	766			Wilbingen, Baden
Rotert, (son of Heinrich Herman)	17, Dec. 1857	20, Sept	18m	204		Henderson, MN	
Rotert, Anna Maria	2, Dec. 1872	3, Nov.	17- 7m-20d	391		Wyandotte, KS	Franklin County, Missouri
Rotert, Catharine Bernardine	14, July 1853	5, June	23	112	Uhlenhake	Union, MO	Lienen, Tecklenburg, Preußen
Rotert, Eduard	30, Oct. 1882	16, Oct.	27- 1m- 6d	351		St. Paul, MN	
Rotert, Friedrich	17, Dec. 1857	1, Nov.	65	204		Henderson, MN	Fenne, Amt Witlage, Hannover
Rotert, Herman	29, June 1899	6, June	73	415		Kansas City, KS	Venne, Wittlage, Hannover
Rotert, Johan Heinrich	16, Dec. 1872	14, Nov.	49	407		Quincy, IL	Fenne, Amt Witlage, Hannover
Rotert, Katharina Maria	17, Dec. 1857	19, Sept	65	204		Henderson, MN	Fenne, Amt Witlage, Hannover
Rotert, Maria	18, Dec. 1876	1, Dec.	40	407	Wallenbrock	Quincy, IL	WesterKappeln, Tecklenburg, Münster, Preußen
Rotert, Wilhelmina	6, Jan. 1873	6, Dec.	38	7	Meyer	Wyandotte, KS	Dissen, Hannover
Rötger, Adolph Heinrich	13, May 1867	1, Apr.	77- 7m	150		Defiance, OH	
Roth, Louise	8, Aug. 1889	18, July	75- 3m-18d	510	Böshenz	Anaheim, CA	Lobenheim am Berg, RheinPfalz Baiern
Roth, (boy)	9, Apr. 1857	23, Mar.	2	60		East Evans, NY	
Roth, (Mrs)	4, Feb. 1867		46-10m-12d	38	Böshenz	Summerfield, IL	Rüffingen, Baiern
Roth, Adam	22, June 1863	22, May	21	100		Chicago, IL	
Roth, Adele	29, Dec. 1887	7, Nov.	10- 6m	830		Milwaukee, WI	Milwaukee, Wisconsin
Roth, Adelia	7, Dec. 1885	17, Nov.	7	7		Watertown, WI	
Roth, Albert	26, Jan. 1885	5, Jan.	21- 1m-27d	7		Milwaukee, WI	
Roth, Anna Elisabeth	11, Aug. 1892	18, July	80	510	Mees	Boonville, IN	Westheim, Germersheim, Rheinpfalz Baiern
Roth, Anna Margaretha	28, Mar. 1870	13, Mar.	51	103	Benstein	Newark, OH	Jossa, Kurhessen
Roth, Benedikt	15, May 1882	11, Apr.	59	159		Cedar Co, NE	Niederbipp, Wangen, Bern, Schweiz
Roth, Benedikt	2, June 1884	18, May	22	7		Norfolk, NE	
Roth, Christian	17, Feb. 1873	4, Jan.	63- 1m-18d	53		Cannon City, MN	Marnheim, Rheinkreis Baiern
Roth, Christian	8, Nov. 1880	22, Oct.	63- 2m-15d	359		Marietta, OH	Marnheim, Rheinkreis Baiern
Roth, Christian	14, June 1860	16, May	78	96		Bonn, OH	Warrenheim, Bolanden, Rheinkreis Baiern
Roth, Elisabeth	13, May 1852	20, Feb.	70	80		Des Moines, IA	Neuhof, Rheinkreis Baiern
Roth, Elisabeth	3, Mar. 1873	12, Feb.	33	71	Seibert	Jeffersonville, IN	Floyd County, Indiana
Roth, Elisabeth	27, June 1864	12, June	16- 6m-26d	104		Evansville, IN	
Roth, Elise	5, Oct. 1874	21, Aug.	24	319	Kühne	Ironton, OH	Homgressen, Kurhessen
Roth, Emilie Auguste	25, June 1883	29, May	14	207		Watertown, WI	
Roth, Franz	4, Oct. 1888	22, Sept	26	638		Ironton, OH	Triebes, Sachsen
Roth, Friederike	15, Sept 1879	13, Aug.	26	295		Jeffersonville, IN	Ober-Niebelsbach, Neuenbürg, Württemberg
Roth, Friederike Wilhelmine	26, May 1887	30, Apr.	44	334	Schröder	Oconomowoc, WI	Zachan, Pommern
Roth, Georg	21, June 1880	31, May	29	199		LaCrosse, WI	Washington County, Ohio
Roth, George	19, Jan. 1880	4, Jan.	47-10m- 5d	23		Carlton, MO	
Roth, Heinrich	29, Sept 1892	9, Sept	71- 1m-21d	622			Marnheim, Rheinpfalz Baiern
Roth, Jac. H.	4, May 1885	31, Mar.	45-10m-28d	7		Airesville, OH	Württemberg
Roth, Jacob	29, May 1890	8, May	75	350		Herman, MO	Kanton Bern, Schweiz

Christliche Apologete Death Notices --- 1839 - 1899

Name of Deceased	Notice Date	Death Date	Age	Page	Maiden Name	Place of Death	Place of Birth
Roth, Jakob	31, Mar. 1862	14, Jan.	33- 4m-24d	52		Columbia City, IN	Canton Bern, Schweiz
Roth, Jakob	4, Feb. 1867		21	38		Summerfield, IL	
Roth, Jakob	24, Mar. 1892	31, Jan.	76	191		Faribault, MN	Marnheim, Rheinkreis Baiern
Roth, Jakob B.	12, Dec. 1889	17, Sept	46- 7m- 5d	798		Los Angeles, CA	Lee County, Iowa
Roth, Jakob G.	5, Oct. 1899	7, Sept	63	639		Boonville, IN	Rheinpfalz Baiern
Roth, Johan	5, Jan. 1885	19, Dec.	65	7		Warsaw, IL	Mavenheim, RheinPfalz Baiern
Roth, Johan	15, Jan. 1891	22, Dec.	66- -21d	46		Huntingburg, IN	
Roth, Johann Jacob	27, Dec. 1860	12, Dec.	5- 3m- 6d	208		Watertown, WI	
Roth, Johannes	25, Sept 1871	28, Aug.	26- 7m	311		Faribault, MN	
Roth, Johnnie	20, Aug. 1891	19, June	20	542		Huntingburg, IN	
Roth, Joseph	23, Apr. 1865	3, Mar.	63	68		Vermillion, OH	Schwarzenbach, Amt Bühl, Baden
Roth, Karl	23, Oct. 1882	24, Sept		343		Ironton, OH	Triebes, Reuß-Schleiz
Roth, Katharina	7, July 1892	19, May	64	430	Veth	Nebraska City, NE	Holzhausen, Siger, Westphalen
Roth, L.	16, Mar. 1893	21, Feb.	73	174		Evansville, IN	Langstadt, Hessen-Darmstadt
Roth, Louise	7, Dec. 1874	18, Nov.	19	391	Mack	Columbus, WI	Jörendorf, Mecklenburg-Schwerin
Roth, Margaretha	28, Oct. 1897	29, Sept	57	687		Galena, IL	Lanschreden a. d. Werra, Sachsen-Weimar
Roth, Margaretha	10, Mar. 1898	12, Feb.	78	159	Dietz	Jeffersonville, IN	Wenings, Hessen
Roth, Maria	19, Dec. 1864	27, Nov.	77- 6m	204	Staufer	Bonn, OH	Ungstein, Dürfheim, Rheinkreis Baiern
Roth, Maria	3, Mar. 1884	11, Feb.	70	7	Hert	Jefferson City, MO	Bibern, Solothurn, Schweiz
Roth, Maria	31, Aug. 1893	13, Aug.	62- 11m-18d	558	Niemeier	Huntingburg, IN	Offerten, Minden, Preußen
Roth, Maria	2, June 1873	14, May	36- 2m-17d	175	Landauer	Cleveland, OH	Crailsheim, Württemberg
Roth, Maria M.	10, May 1875	4, Apr.	29- 5m- 3d	151	Spach	Poughkeepsie, NY	
Roth, Maria M.	16, June 1898	28, May	28	383	Conrad	St. Louis, MO	Oberschlesien, Germany
Roth, Marietta	6, May 1872	11, Apr.	21- 3m- 3d	151	Ziegler	Marrs, IN	Posey County, Indiana
Roth, Michael	21, June 1880	17, May	65	199		Milwaukee, WI	Hasser, Elsaß
Roth, Peter	5, July 1888	18, May	31	430		Faribault, MN	
Roth, Philipp	1, Mar. 1894	7, Feb.	77	150		Jeffersonville, IN	Hessen-Darmstadt
Roth, Philipp Lorenz	25, May 1899	2, May	59	335		Boonville, IN	Pike County, Ohio
Roth, Rosina	20, Jan. 1887	29, Dec.	66	46		Clay Center, KS	
Roth, Sophia Christina	23, July 1896	28, June	45	479	Hildebrandt	Faribault, MN	Hevensen, Hannover
Roth, Therese	24, June 1897	8, June	64	399		Scranton, PA	Fulda, Kurhessen
Rothe, Dorothea	6, Mar. 1890	26, Jan.	63	158	Seidel	Troy, NY	Döbeln, Sachsen
Röthemeyer, Maria	8, Mar. 1860	6, Jan.	42	40	Meyer	Herman, MO	Nord-Hemmen, Hartum, Preußen
Rothert, Anna Maria	21, Mar. 1881	13, Feb.	44-10m	95	Evers	Elmore, OH	
Rothert, Bertha	18, Apr. 1889	27, Mar.	13-11m- 8d	254		Elmore, OH	Elmore, Ohio
Rothert, Carolina Louisa	2, Apr. 1896	7, Mar.	19	222		Boonville, IN	Holland, Indiana
Rothert, Christian	17, Mar. 1848			47		New Orleans, LA	Westphalen
Rothert, Christian F.	14, Nov. 1895	9, Oct.	78	734		Huntingburg, IN	Barnau, Hannover
Rothert, Elisabeth	9, Apr. 1896	11, Mar.	43	238	Steinkamp	Elmore, OH	Woodville Township, Sandusky County, Ohio
Rothert, Gottfried Daniel	13, Oct. 1862	7, Aug.	12	164		Huntingburg, IN	
Rothert, Henriette Florentine	31, Jan. 1856	20, Sept	22	20	Gelhaus	Carrolton, LA	Bahrenholz, Lippe-Detmold
Rothert, Katharine Helene	27, Aug. 1891	28, July	78	558	Wibbeler	Huntingburg, IN	Goldenstädt, Oldenburg
Rothert, Louise	14, Aug. 1876	14, July	29	263	Laker	Herman, MO	
Rothert, Marie	17, Nov. 1859		25- -14d	184	Kruse	St. Louis, MO	Misdorf, Amt Grönnenberg, Hannover
Rothert, Sophie	7, Dec. 1885	26, Nov.	29	7	Bemmes	Huntingburg, IN	Cincinnati, Hamilton County, Ohio
Rothert, Wilhelm	18, Oct. 1888		77- 5m-13d	670		Huntingburg, IN	Barnau, Vörder, Engter, Hannover

Christliche Apologete Death Notices --- 1839 - 1899

Name of Deceased	Notice Date	Death Date	Age	Page	Maiden Name	Place of Death	Place of Birth
Rothfuß, Margaretha	11, May 1893	10, Apr.	23- 1m-13d	302		Newark, NJ	Achim, Hannover
Rothhaar, Elisabeth	5, Oct. 1885	8, Sept	84	7		New Haven, CT	
Rothkopf, Anna Maria	16, Aug. 1849	5, July	12- 9m	132		Cincinnati, OH	Amt Gröneberg, Hannover
Rothkopf, Charles Henry	14, June 1888	31, May	17	382		Cincinnati, OH	Cincinnati, Hamilton County, Ohio
Rothkopf, Elisabeth	11, Jan. 1875	2, Jan.	68	15	Sickermann	Cincinnati, OH	Bönnen, Hannover
Rothkopf, H. Friedrich	8, Mar. 1855	5, Aug.	24	40		St. Paul, MN	Hovel, Amt Gronenberg, Hannover
Rothkopf, Johan Heinrich	31, Aug. 1874	13, Aug.	68	279		Cincinnati, OH	Hoyel, Amt Gröneberg, Hannover
Rothmann, Caroline	20, Aug. 1883	30, July	65- 4m-21d	271	Herzer	New Orleans, LA	Württemberg
Rothweiler, Charlotte	16, May 1881	3, May	36	159	Groß	Cleveland, OH	Brighton, Ohio
Rothweiler, Christopher	30, Dec. 1886	17, Dec.	57	7		Newport, KY	Berghausen, Baden
Rothweiler, Elisabeth	30, Dec. 1878	13, Dec.	74-10m- 8d	415		Amherst, OH	Wössingen, Baden
Rothweiler, Robert	17, Jan. 1881	1, Nov.	31	23		Clearwater, MN	Berghausen, Durlach, Baden
Rotien, Amanda	4, Oct. 1875	11, Sept	21	319	Hoppe	Francisco, MI	New York City, New York
Rott, Magdalena	1, Feb. 1875	6, Jan.	64- 8m	39	Fingbohne	New Haven, CT	Straßburg, Frankreich
Röttger, Daniel	1, Mar. 1875	17, Feb.	84	71		Newport, KY	Luttrum, Wohldenburg, Hannover
Röttger, Daniel	15, Mar. 1875	17, Feb.	34	71		Newport, KY	Luttrum, Wohldenburg, Hannover
Röttger, Friedrich	18, June 1857	30, May	83	100		Newport, KY	Luttrum, Wohldenberg, Hannover
Röttger, Heinrich	19, Oct. 1899	24, Sept	59	671		Newport, KY	Luttrum, Wohldenberg, Hannover
Röttger, Lina	4, Mar. 1886	20, Feb.	71	7	Reth	Newport, KY	Segeberg, Schleswig-Holstein
Röttger, Maria	16, Nov. 1863	29, Oct.	65- 1m	184		Newport, KY	Luttrum, Amt Wohldenberg, Hannover
Röttgers, Anna Katharina	10, June 1872	26, May	27- 1m-11d	191	Heider	Brighton, IL	Wermelskirchen, Düsseldorf, Preußen
Röttig, Catharina	11, Dec. 1876	11, Nov.	49-10m	399	Schur	Marrs, IN	Posey County, Indiana
Rottler, Anna Mathilde	12, Sept 1881	25, Aug.	63- 3m-23d	295	Falk	Galena, IL	Orsoy, RheinPreußen
Rottler, Johan C.	9, June 1884	19, May	15- 1m	7		Galena, IL	Duningen, Rottweil, Württemberg
Rottler, John W.	1, Mar. 1880	11, Feb.		71		Galena, IL	
Rottstedt, Bertha	13, Oct. 1892	12, Sept	30	654	Sellheim	Sheboygan, WI	Sheboygan Falls, Wisconsin
Rottstedt, Heinrich	8, Oct. 1896	6, Sept	36	655		Sheboygan, WI	
Rousch, Sophia	19, June 1890	30, Apr.	32	398	Betz	Pomeroy, OH	
Rousche, (Mrs)	23, Feb. 1888	25, Jan.		126	Nichlas	Stitzer, WI	Schweiz
Rubbe, Katharina	24, Oct. 1895	6, Oct.	78	686		McGirks, MO	Borgholzhausen, Preußen
Rübeling, Franklin	8, Jan. 1872	16, Dec.	30	15		Boody, IL	Manchester, Missouri
Rubensdörfer, Georg Michael	29, Nov. 1860	16, Nov.	43	192		Chicago, IL	Bullerswagen, Krailsheim, Württemberg
Rubert, Maria	25, Feb. 1858	31, Jan.		32	Irwin	Marshall, IL	Pennsylvania
Rubin, Benjamin August	29, July 1886	14, June	11	7		Lyona, KS	Davis County, Kansas
Rubin, Clara Lisette	13, Oct. 1887	19, Sept	14	654		Junction City, KS	Lyons Creek, Davis County, Kansas
Rubin, Harry Edmund	21, Dec. 1893	3, Dec.	23	814		Junction City, KS	Davis County, Kansas
Rubin, Wilhelmina	23, Feb. 1885	1, Feb.	45	7	Henning	Lyona, KS	Servirst, Brandenburg
Rubow, Louisa	10, May 1880	26, Mar.	25	151	Pieper	Sibley, IA	Altenhagen, Schlawe, Köslin, Hinterpommern
Rubsch, Anna Maria	17, Aug. 1885	31, July	41	7	Schwebel	Terre Haute, IN	Oberscharbach, Hessen
Ruby, Barbara	1, May 1882	14, Apr.	73	143	Niergart	Baresville, OH	Blumenstein, Thun, Bern, Schweiz
Ruch, Henriette	7, Aug. 1876	26, July	76	255	Bonke	Bloomington, IL	Jelesen, Kreis Nolv, HinterPommern
Ruch, Pauline Emilie	7, May 1896	20, Apr.	20	302	Schönig	Bushton, KS	Pine Creek, Muscatine County, Iowa
Ruchti, Maria	17, Mar. 1892	26, Feb.	64	175	Wälti	Newton, IA	Biglen, Bern, Schweiz
Ruckdeschel, Lorenz	15, Sept 1884	24, Aug.	64	7		Aurora, IL	Hof, Baiern
Rückel, Carolina Wilhelmina	9, Apr. 1896		73	238	Wilde	Lowell, WI	Pommin, Neumark
Ruckelshausen, Bertha	14, Apr. 1887	28, Mar.	22	238	Mayer	Topeka, KS	Wallerstädten, Groß-Gerau, Hessen

Name of Deceased	Place of Birth	Place of Death	Maiden Name	Page	Age	Death Date	Notice Date
Ruckenbrodt, Christina	Jebenhausen, Württemberg	Burlington, IA	Almendinger	223	50	12, Mar.	6, Apr. 1899
Rücker, Elisabeth	Brady Township, Williams County, Ohio	Stryker, OH	Mayer	798	35	13, Oct.	12, Dec. 1895
Rückert, Auguste Louise	Kremshof bei Stargard, Pommern	Oshkosh, WI	Stübbe	222	56	3, Mar.	6, Apr. 1893
Rückert, Catharina	Niederhausen, Hessen-Darmstadt	Higginsville, MO	Ruppel	7	55	14, Oct.	4, Nov. 1886
Rückheim, Rosa	Ducherow, Anklam, Preußen	Chicago, IL		126	17	23, Jan.	20, Feb. 1890
Ruckle, Katharina		Hummel, PA		399	64	25, Aug.	14, Dec. 1868
Rückli, Anna Maira	Canton Bern, Schweiz	Toledo, OH		686	82	2, Aug.	23, Oct. 1890
Rudat, Daniel	Daupeken, Insterburg, Germany	Duncan, NE		287	79	9, Apr.	4, May 1899
Rudat, Karl	Dobelen, OstPreußen	Duncan, NE		254	79	18, Mar.	16, Apr. 1896
Rüdde, Christian	Gamsen, Amt Giffhorn, Hannover	Angelica, NY		367	62- 5m		13, Nov. 1876
Rudel, Christian		Lena, IL		143	90	4, Feb.	2, Mar. 1899
Rudel, Friederike	Schweigem, Brackenheim, Württemberg	Yellow Creek, IL	Behringer	798	74	9, Nov.	15, Dec. 1887
Rudel, Jakob	Schweigem, Württemberg	Freeport, IL		156	20	5, July	25, Sept 1865
Rudenberg, Maria	Hugsweier, Baden	Kendallville, IN		196	23	23, Oct.	4, Dec. 1865
Ruder, Friedrich	Berea, Ohio	Delaware, OH		703	78	21, Sept	2, Nov. 1899
Ruder, Henry		Berea, OH		190	24	26, Feb.	19, Mar. 1896
Rudert, Katharina Dorothea	Burbach bei Saarbrücken, Preußen	Louisville, KY	Stephan	119	43- 5m-18d	20, Mar.	11, Apr. 1881
Rudginski, Auguste Mathilde	Albrechtsdorf, Rosenberg, Preußen	Menominee, MI		375	16		22, Nov. 1880
Rudi, Johannes	Canton Bern, Schweiz	Baresville, OH		55	67	10, Dec.	13, Feb. 1871
Rüdiger, Friedrich		Baltimore, MD		144	19- 6m-28d	11, Aug.	7, Sept 1863
Rüdiger, Maria Rosine	Polen, Gera, Preußen	Baltimore, MD	Eberhard	151	64	14, Mar.	9, May 1881
Rüdiger, Marie Elisabeth	Sandusky, Ohio	Sandusky, OH	Liphart	607	41	31, Aug.	22, Sept 1898
Rudin, Robert	Basel, Schweiz	New York City, NY		782	26	13, Nov.	3, Dec. 1896
Rudolf, Wiibald	Grimmelshofen, Baden	Cohaktah, MI		207	62	23, May	29, June 1874
Rudolph, Adelheid		Mt. Vernon, NY		40	3	Dec.	7, Mar. 1861
Rudolph, Amalia Wilhelmine	Kottbus, Brandenburg	Chicago, IL	Elias	846	69	12, Dec.	31, Dec. 1891
Rudolph, Anna Catharina	Ellenbach, Rothenburg, Kurhessen	Pittsburg, PA	Gilfert	278	75	14, July	27, Aug. 1866
Rudolph, Anna Margaretha	Altenaronau, Schwarzenfels, Kurhessen	Cedar Lake, IN	Ulrich	247	69- 7m- 7d	13, July	31, July 1882
Rudolph, Carl	Hosbach, Bischhausen, Kurhessen	German Creek, IA		79	44	30, Jan.	6, Mar. 1876
Rudolph, Ernst Heinrich	Pagenkopp, Naugard, Pommern	Kenosha, WI		271	58- -17d	7, Aug.	20, Aug. 1883
Rudolph, Georg Julius		Newport, KY		287	17	4, July	8, Sept 1873
Rudolph, Jacob Georg	West Creek, Lake County, Indiana	Junction City, KS		686	24	3, Oct.	24, Oct. 1895
Rudolph, Jakob	Ritheim, Aargau, Schweiz	Columbus, OH		144	45		7, Sept 1863
Rudolph, Louise		Mt. Vernon, NY		40	9	Dec.	7, Mar. 1861
Rudolph, Louise Henriette	Saaleck a. S. , Sachsen	Cedar Lake, IN	Gehre	206	68- 9m-24d	17, Mar.	29, Mar. 1888
Rudolph, Maria Barbara	Ross Station, Lake County, Indiana	Cedar Lake, IN	Dietrich	415	32	2, Dec.	27, Dec. 1880
Rudolph, Mary		Mt. Vernon, NY		119	13- 8m-16d	28, Mar.	14, Apr. 1879
Rudolph, Sophie		Mt. Vernon, NY		40	6	Dec.	7, Mar. 1861
Rudolph, Susanna	Westmort County, Pennsylvania	Bucyrus, OH	Nelson	30	70- 2m		14, Jan. 1892
Rudolph, Valentin	Louisville, Jefferson County, Kentucky	Cedar Lake, IN		183	28	7, May	9, June 1873
Rudolph, Valentin	Nieder-Ellenbach, Kurhessen	Chicago, IL		670	71	30, Sept	17, Oct. 1889
Rudolphf, Friederike	Fraheide, Pommern	Kenosha, WI		7	52	4, Apr.	20, Apr. 1885
Rüdt, Georg		New York City, NY		622	27- 8m - 4d	7, Sept	29, Sept 1887
Rudy, Johann (Rev)	Schweiz	---, NY		43	51	8, Feb.	18, Mar. 1842
Rued, Emilie	Stillwater, Minnesota	Beaver Falls, MN	Beltz	7	28	14, Jan.	4, Feb. 1886
Ruedy, Johann	Gächlingen, Schaffhausen, Schweiz	Linden, MO		366	59	17, Oct.	18, Nov. 1867

Christliche Apologete Death Notices --- 1839 - 1899

Name of Deceased	Notice Date	Death Date	Age	Page	Maiden Name	Place of Death	Place of Birth
Ruedy, Margarethe	29, June 1874	18, May	67- 7m-12d	207	Müller	Nebraska City, NE	Gächlingen, Schaffhausen, Schweiz
Ruehl, Andreas	19, Oct. 1885	6, Oct.	32	7		Cincinnati, OH	
Ruehle, Franziska	30, June 1898	3, June	69- 2m-24d	415	Hasler	Chicago, IL	Wiel, Kensingen, Baden
Ruehle, Katharina	7, Feb. 1876	16, Jan.	77- 8m- 2d	47		Marion, OH	Zinsweiler, Elsaß
Ruehle, Valentin	14, Nov. 1864	1, Sept	22	184		Allegan, MI	Langendeinbach, Baden
Ruehmkorf, Heinrich Friedrich Wm.	21, Apr. 1887	7, Apr.	65-11m- 7d	254		Red Bud, IL	Hotteln, Ruthe, Hannover
Ruepke, Christina	10, June 1886	10, May	63- -13d	7		Indianapolis, IN	
Ruetz, Christina	17, Sept 1866	18, Aug.	80	302	Dalo	Muscatine, IA	Pommern
Ruf, Johann Martin	20, Sept 1860	4, Sept	31	152		Nauvoo, IL	
Ruf, Johannes	18, Jan. 1864	27, Nov.	43	12			Attisbyl, Bern, Schweiz
Ruf, Joseph	18, Jan. 1894	17, Dec.	83	46		Atchinson, KS	Reuthe, Emmendingen, Baden
Ruf, Leopold	5, May 1887	23, Mar.	47	286		Tappan, NY	Baden-Baden, Baden
Ruf, Susanna M.	20, Oct. 1853	2, Sept	59- 8m-25d	168		Defiance, OH	Oberauerbach, Baiern
Rüfenacht, Gottlieb	18, June 1896	5, June	26	399		Newport, KY	Heimenhausen, Bern, Schweiz
Rüfener, Elisabeth	8, Nov. 1894	10, Oct.	48	726	Lorentz	Washington Co, OH	
Ruff, Johanna	20, Jan. 1873	20, Sept	72	23		Indianapolis, IN	Hemingen, Württemberg
Ruffener, Elisabeth	6, Apr. 1899	5, Mar.	57	223	Ruby	Hannibal, OH	Monroe County, Ohio
Ruffi, Samuel	28, Oct. 1867	11, Oct.	33- 8m	342		Osage, MO	Steffenburg, Bern, Schweiz
Ruffler, Johann	14, Apr. 1862	20, Mar.	20- -19d	60		Golconda, IL	Börtigen, Graubünden, Schweiz
Ruffner, Samuel	15, June 1899		82	383		Hannibal, OH	Kanton Bern, Schweiz
Rufi, A.	4, May 1863	14, Jan.	23	72		Brunswick, MO	Steffisburg, Bern, Schweiz
Rufi, Anna Christina	13, Nov. 1882	19, Oct.	14- 4m-29d	367		Morrison, MO	
Rufi, Christina	22, Mar. 1880	2, Mar.	36	95		Morrison, MO	
Rufle, Friedrich	16, Nov. 1863	27, Oct.	29-11m	184	Peter	Rochester, NY	
Rufner, Anna	14, Dec. 1885	29, Nov.	73	7		Baresville, OH	Kanton Aargau, Schweiz
Ruge, (Mrs)	15, Mar. 1869	3, Feb.	43	87		Williamsburg, NY	Radelfingen, Bern, Schweiz
Rüger, Agnes	25, Nov. 1897	26, Oct.	77	751		Pomeroy, OH	Langwarden, Oldenburg
Rüger, Andreas	7, Sept 1893	11, Aug.	78	574		Pomeroy, OH	Eichberg-Weismann, Baiern
Rüger, Gertrud	24, Nov. 1884	11, Nov.	61	7	Mengel	Danville, IL	Eichberg, Baiern
Rügge, Louis	9, Apr. 1891	20, Mar.	26	238		Drake, MO	Stertshausen, Marburg, Kurhessen
Rügge, Maria	18, July 1889	23, June	21- 4m-16d	462		Drake, MO	Drake, Missouri
Rügge, Michael	26, Apr. 1880	13, Apr.	75- - 9d	135		Arena, WI	Drake, Missouri
Ruh, Katharine	12, Jan. 1893	15, Dec.	53	30	Schäfer	South Bend, IN	Pritzig, Pommern
Ruh, Therese	30, Nov. 1868	13, Nov.	63	383		Nashville, TN	Liverpool, Ohio
Ruhaak, Gretje	27, Dec. 1888	10, Nov.	70	830	Peppinga	Norwich, KS	Gudmadingen, Amt Radolfzell, Baden
Rühl, Andreas	20, July 1854	4, July	57	116		Cincinnati, OH	Norden, Ostfriesland
Rühl, Elisabeth	28, Sept 1899	12, Sept	71	623	Kriechbaum	Bucyrus, OH	Nauheim, Gießen, Hessen-Darmstadt
Rühl, Johann	12, Mar. 1883	21, Feb.	30	87		Lawrence, KS	Reichenbach, Hessen-Darmstadt
Rühl, Johanna	18, Feb. 1897	21, Jan.	78	111	Rückert	Baltimore, MD	Nauheim, Hessen-Darmstadt
Rühl, Katharine	19, May 1879	30, Apr.	58- 8m-27d	159	Feth	Cincinnati, OH	Flachslanden, Mittelfranken, Baiern
Rühl, Ludwig	12, May 1892	14, Apr.	73	302		Cincinnati, OH	Naunheim, Gießen, Hessen-Darmstadt
Rühl, Sophie Henriette	24, Mar. 1884	8, Mar.	61- 9m- 6d	7	Imhäuser	Cincinnati, OH	Naunheim, Gießen, Hessen-Darmstadt
Rühle, Georg	13, Dec. 1869	21, Nov.	62	399		Detroit, MI	Friedewald, Preußen
Rühle, Jakob	25, June 1877	30, May	73	207		Montrey, MI	Langensteinbach, Durlach, Baden
Rühle, Katharina	27, Nov. 1890	6, Nov.	76- 1m-21d	766		Allegan, MI	Langensteinbach, Durlach, Baden
Rühle, Katharina	1, Sept 1853	23, July	71	140		Detroit, MI	Langensteinbach, Baden

Christliche Apologete Death Notices --- 1839 - 1899

Name of Deceased	Notice Date	Death Date	Age	Page	Maiden Name	Place of Death	Place of Birth
Rühle, Katharina	13, Feb. 1882	19, Jan.	63	55	Maus	Evansville, IN	Weil, Lörrach, Baden
Rühle, Katharina B.	21, June 1869	26, May	63	199	Rerscherten	Detroit, MI	Youngstown, Ohio
Rühle, Maria Anna	23, Nov. 1885	5, Nov.	35	7	Renziehausen	Allegan, MI	
Rühle, Samuel	29, July 1886	11, July	16	7		Bucyrus, OH	Brake, Lippe-Detmold
Rühmkorf, Sophia	19, Jan. 1885	3, Jan.	55	7	Sanders	Red Bud, IL	Zettlin bei Treptow an der Rega, Pommern
Ruhnke, August L.	22, Sept 1887	31, Aug.	22	606		Lyona, KS	Zettlin bei Treptow an der Rega, Pommern
Ruhnke, Johan	22, Jan. 1891	2, Jan.	67	62		Woodbine, KS	Zettlin bei Treptow an der Rega, Pommern
Ruhnke, Maria	22, Sept 1887	29, Aug.	20	606		Lyona, KS	Recksheim, Rheinkreis Baiern
Ruhser, Elisabeth	12, Feb. 1891	18, Jan.	80	110	Krick	Toledo, OH	Hastadt, Elsaß
Ruhstuhl, (Mrs)	30, Mar. 1863	24, Feb.	36	52		St. Louis, MO	Rannstadt, Oteburg, Hessen-Darmstadt
Rullmann, Christiana	3, Nov. 1879	3, Oct.	47	351	Jung	Wathena, KS	Haßloch, Neustadt a. d. Haardt, Rheinkreis Baiern
Rumer, Bernhardt	28, Nov. 1895	7, Nov.	66	766		Mascoutah, IL	Washington County, Illinois
Rumig, Christine	30, July 1896	11, July	37- 2m- 7d	495	Hoffmann	Nashville, IL	Trumbull County, Ohio
Rummel, Heinrich	25, Jan. 1855	2, Jan.	43- 5m	16		Pomeroy, OH	Kreisbach, Baiern
Rummel, Maria Engelina	3, Feb. 1898	26, Dec.	85	79	Klopp	Burlington, KS	Schwarza, Schleusingen, Preußen
Rumpel, Christoph	18, Oct. 1855	21, Sept	37	168		Union, MO	Bergfelden, Sulz am Neckar, Württemberg
Rumpel, Jakob	24, Aug. 1874	24, July	24- 3m-19d	273	Dreyer	Sherrills Mount, IA	Hannover
Rumpf, Charlotte	17, Dec. 1883	8, Sept	63	7	Ode	Spraytown, IN	Gabelitz, Mecklenburg
Rumpf, Maria	16, Apr. 1877	24, Mar.	27	127	Droß	Baraboo, WI	Allendorf auf der Ulm, Preußen
Rumpf, Maria Christina	27, Mar. 1882	6, Mar.	67- 8m - 2d	103		Dayton, OH	Allendorf auf der Ulm, Wetzlar, Coblenz, Preußen
Rumpf, Peter	22, Oct. 1896	9, Sept	84	687		Dayton, OH	
Rumpf, Rosine	9, June 1859	9, Mar.	5-11m	92		Dayton, OH	Allendorf auf der Ulm, Koblenz, Preußen
Rumpf, Wilhelm	15, June 1893		48	382		Dayton, OH	Loburg, Sachsen
Rumpf, Wilhelm Chr. Ferdinand	13, Sept 1888	23, Aug.	67	590		Seguin, TX	Gnevzow, Demin, Preußen
Rümpler, Anna Maria Sophia	5, Jan. 1899	4, Dec.	85	15	Rathsak	Goshen, IN	Herzogweiler, Württemberg
Rümpler, Catharine	17, Mar. 1853	2, Feb.	51- 8m	44		Greenville, OH	Gremmentin, Pommern
Rümpler, W.	18, Aug. 1879	5, Aug.	66- 2m-22d	263		Goshen, IN	Gramentin, Pommern
Rümpler, Wilhelm	5, Apr. 1888	16, Mar.	40	222		Goshen, IN	Pietz, Brandenburg
Rundorff, Karolina	9, Oct. 1882	19, Sept	67- 3m-15d	327	Klee	Burlington, IA	Hofen, Waiblingen, Württemberg
Runft, Dorothea	29, Oct. 1891	2, Oct.	47	702	Eckardt	Reinbeck, IA	Kirchberg, Marbach, Württemberg
Rung , Friederika Seyfert-Rötsch	24, Mar. 1892	21, Feb.	69	191		Oregon, MO	Riestedt bei Eisleben, Preußen
Runge, Carl Friedrich	24, Sept 1857	7, Sept	29	156		Springfield, IL	
Runge, Christian	15, Oct. 1847	8, Oct.	42- 4m- 2d	167		Cincinnati, OH	Hannover
Runge, Elisabeth	8, Dec. 1853	8, Nov.	42	196		Cincinnati, OH	Barlt, Holstein
Runge, Fr.	7, Feb. 1889	15, Jan.	68-10m-24d	94		Nokomis, IL	Baarlt, Holstein
Runge, Maria Elisabeth	17, Jan. 1876	5, Jan.	40- 3m-20d	23	Welkämper	White Creek, IN	Ballendas, Schweiz
Runge, Mathilde	11, Feb. 1892	9, Nov.	71- 4m-26d	94	Ahrens	Nokomis, IL	Ellenbach, Rheinpfalz Baiern
Runger, Richard	23, Aug. 1888	29, July	68	542		Cincinnati, OH	Jacksonville, Illinois
Runk, John Jakob	1, Jan. 1891	13, Nov.	84	14		Indianapolis, IN	Grolsheim, Hessen-Darmstadt
Runkel, Anna Magdalena	29, July 1886	15, July	27	7	Lampert	Jacksonville, IL	Hessen-Darmstadt
Runkel, Quirin	6, Sept 1875	15, Aug.	56	287		Burlington, IA	Truxton, Missouri
Runkel, S.	28, Feb. 1870	24, Jan.	82	71		East Troy, WI	Leopoldsthal, Horn, Preußen
Runte, Charlotte	12, Aug. 1886	27, July	27	7		Warren, MO	Ravenhorst, Pommern
Runte, Wilhelmine	4, May 1893	14, Apr.	82	286	Begemann	Allegan, MI	Müsnow, Pommern
Rüntzel, Wilhelm	26, Jan. 1885	9, Jan.	55	7		Montague, MI	
Rüntzel, Wilhelmine	29, Apr. 1897	5, Feb.	67	271		Montague, MI	

Christliche Apologete Death Notices --- 1839 - 1899

Name of Deceased	Notice Date	Death Date	Age	Page	Maiden Name	Place of Death	Place of Birth
Rüntzel, Wilhelmine	2, Aug. 1894	13, July	64- -26d	502		New York City, NY	Klozin, Pommern
Ruoff, Barbara	30, Aug. 1888	30, Aug.	78-8m-18d	558	Fritz	Hamilton, OH	Dürm, Pforzheim, Baden
Ruoff, Christina	24, Aug. 1885	8, July	76	7	Binder	Stockton, CA	Herrenberg, Württemberg
Rupel, John	23, Feb. 1860	23, Nov.	27	32		Lexington, MI	
Ruply, Reinhardt	24, Dec. 1896	2, Dec.	73	831		San Francisco, CA	Hallau bei Schaffhausen, Schweiz
Rupnow, Gottfried	29, Nov. 1880	13, Nov.	53- 6m- 2d	383		Portland, WI	Brandenburg
Rupp, Barbara	27, Feb. 1896	5, Feb.	67	143	Kübler		Schweiz
Rupp, Lorenz	13, Mar. 1890	14, Feb.	71	174		Moberly, MO	Heidelbach, Hessen
Rupp, Salome	12, Dec. 1889	10, Nov.	64- 3m-22d	798	Wolf	Moberly, MO	Steinstelz, Elsaß
Ruppel, Anna Gehla	29, June 1885	11, June	76	7	Otter	Chillicothe, OH	Oberhaun bei Hersfeld, Kurhessen
Ruppel, Friederika	15, Dec. 1898	17, Nov.	63-10m-16d	799		Ft. Dodge, IA	Baden
Ruppel, Heinrich	4, July 1870	3, June	59	215		Ballwin, MO	Guntzenau, Hessen-Darmstadt
Rüppel, Heinrich	11, Sept 1882	24, Aug.	64-10m- 7d	295		New York City, NY	Kassel, Kurhessen
Rüppel, Herman	14, Jan. 1886	13, Dec.	30	7		New York City, NY	New York City, New York
Ruppel, Johan	11, Oct. 1869	26, Sept	65	327		Detroit, MI	Windecken, Kurhessen
Ruppel, K. Jacob	22, Oct. 1883	22, Oct.	43	343		Greenfield, OH	Oberhaun bei Hersfeld, Kurhessen
Ruppel, Margaretha	30, July 1891	14, June	77	494		Ballwin, MO	
Rupprecht, F.G.	28, Nov. 1881		37- 7m-12d	383		Wilber, NE	
Rupprecht, Justine	29, Mar. 1888	29, Feb.	78	206	Sucker	Laporte, IN	Menningen, Baiern
Rupprecht, Louise Juliana	1, Sept 1862	11, Aug.	37- 8m- 9d	140	Graf	Columbus, IN	Jaxthausen, Neckarsulm, Württemberg
Rupprecht, Catharine	30, Apr. 1891	3, Apr.	66	286	Bühler	Cleveland, OH	Sigrisvill, Bern, Schweiz
Rupprecht, Friedrich	12, Aug. 1872	13, Mar.	23	263		Cleveland, OH	Laupen, Bern, Schweiz
Rupprecht, Jacob	17, Apr. 1890	18, Sept	76	254		Newark, NJ	Memmingen, Baiern
Rupprecht, Jakob	5, Oct. 1899	12, Apr.	81	639		Cleveland, OH	Laupen, Bern, Schweiz
Rupprecht, Susanna	7, May 1891	6, Sept	35	302	Müller	Cleveland, OH	Cleveland, Cuyahoga County, Ohio
Ruröde, Friedrich	24, Oct. 1889	19, Dec.	21	686		Chester, IL	
Rürode, Maria	20, Jan. 1873	6, Oct.	73	23		Chester, IL	Eilvese, Amt Wölpke, Hannover
Ruröde, Simon Daniel	24, Oct. 1889	6, Oct.	19- -26d	686		Chester, IL	
Rüsch, Carolina	2, Feb. 1874	6, Jan.	40	39	Steffen	Kendallville, IN	Rützenfeld, Stettin, Preußen
Rüsch, Maria	25, Oct. 1894	5, Oct.	46	694	Bolliger	Auburn, IN	Baden, Aargau, Schweiz
Rüscher, Eduard	25, May 1893	30, Apr.	46	334		Columbus, OH	Hildburghausen, Sachsen-Meiningen
Rüscher, Heinrich G.	12, Mar. 1896	19, Feb.	67	175		Jersey City, NJ	Waddens, Oldenburg
Ruske, Anna Sophia	29, Mar. 1894	5, Mar.	47	214	Strutz	Oconomowoc, WI	Dölitz bei Pyritz, Pommern
Ruske, Heinrich Albert	30, Apr. 1896	12, Apr.	65	286		Indianapolis, IN	Wusseken, Preußen
Rußbolt, Wilhelm	14, May 1877	30, Apr.	81	159		Bible Grove, IL	Viegest, Mecklenburg-Schwerin
Russer, Mathilde	7, Jan. 1886	7, Dec.	40- 6m-22d	7	Lechler	Cleveland, OH	Wasserallfenig, Württemberg
Rustedt, Margaretha	28, Apr. 1884	14, Apr.	60- 2m	7		Williamsburg, NY	Aiten bei Bremen, Germany
Rutenschröer, Ernst	25, Aug. 1887	10, Aug.	71- 9m-11d	542		Cincinnati, OH	Längerich, Preußen
Rutenschröer, Heinrich Johan	14, July 1887	22, June	10	446		Cincinnati, OH	Bissingen, Hohenzollern, Hechingen, Preußen
Rutenschröer, Maria	2, June 1898	14, May	32	351	Bender	Cincinnati, OH	Hille, Minden, Preußen
Rutenschröm, Karoline	18, Sept 1876	29, Aug.	25	303	Kruse	Ft. Hunter, NY	Ladbergen, Tecklenburg, Münster, Preußen
Rüter, Caroline Maria Elisabeth	1, Mar. 1888	24, Jan.	80	142	Krietemeier	Cincinnati, OH	
Ruterschroer, Sophia Elisabeth	16, Feb. 1899	27, Jan.	85	111	Kuck	Defiance, OH	
Rütger, Louis	2, June 1862	1, May	18	88		Stryker, OH	
Ruth, Adam	5, June 1890	19, May	79	366		East Liberty, PA	Ulmit, Kusel, Baiern
Ruth, Christina	26, Dec. 1895	8, Dec.	58	828	Schmidt		Rimbach, Hessen-Darmstadt

Christliche Apologete Death Notices --- 1839 - 1899

Name of Deceased	Notice Date	Death Date	Age	Page	Maiden Name	Place of Death	Place of Birth
Ruth, Georg	1, Jan. 1891	13, Nov.	85	14		Brooklyn, NY	Bruchköbel, Hanau, Kurhessen
Ruth, Helene	26, May 1892	29, Apr.	33	334	Scherzer	Columbus, OH	Lowell, Kent County, Michigan
Ruth, Katharina	14, Feb. 1881	8, Jan.	74- -17d	55	Hildt	Brooklyn, NY	Bruchkebel, Kurhessen
Ruth, Louis	14, Nov. 1895	11, Sept	21	734		Stryker, OH	Brady Township, Williams County, Ohio
Ruth, Ludwig	26, Nov. 1866	29, Oct.		382		Etna, MO	Elstadt, Baiern
Ruth, Maria Elisabeth	4, Dec. 1890	1, Nov.	79	782	Hebel	Stryker, OH	Welchweiler, Wollstein, Baiern
Ruth, Maria Eva	13, Oct. 1884	27, Sept	75	7	Matthies	Etna, MO	Ellerstadt, Rheinkreis Baiern
Ruth, Valentin	24, Aug. 1885	30, July	74	7		Etna, MO	Ellerstadt, Baiern
Rütherhenke, Franz	12, Nov. 1857	12, Oct.	41	184		Rich Fountain, MO	Belle, Lippe
Rutter, Friedrich	26, May 1879	17, Apr.	43-10m-4d	167		Syracuse, NY	Hille, Minden, Preußen
Rutz, Anna	26, Jan. 1893	8, Jan.	68	62	Tischhauser	Highland, IL	St. Gallen, Schweiz
Rutz, Gallus	18, Feb. 1886	21, Jan.	83	7		Highland, IL	Buchs, St. Callen, Schwciz
Rutzatz, Friedrich	4, Oct. 1894	8, Sept	84	646		Redfield, SD	Wolldisch, Tychow, Cöslin, Hinterpommern
Rutzatz, Karoline	29, June 1899	14, June	80	415	Kiekow	Redfield, SD	Zahnfanz bei Belgard, Pommern
Ruwaledt, Wilhelmine	24, Feb. 1879	11, Feb.	38	63		St. Louis, MO	Woltersdorf, Sachsen-Weimar
Ruwe, Herman	16, June 1879	30, Apr.	58	191		Truxton, MO	Westhovel, Riemsloh, Melle, Hannover
Ruwold, Sophie	15, Oct. 1877	7, Sept	15- 1m-11d	335		St. Louis, MO	
Ruwoldt, Wilhelmine	17, Mar. 1879	11, Feb.	38	87	Geyer	St. Louis, MO	Woltersdorf, Sachsen-Weimar
Ryan, Katharina	30, Jan. 1882	29, Dec.	22	39	Helwig	Newport, KY	Pomeroy, Ohio
Ryland, W. (Rev)	6, Mar. 1846	19, Jan.	76	39		Galena, OH	
Ryniker, Anna	7, Jan. 1886	18, Dec.	18	7		Quincy, IL	Quincy, Illinois
Ryniker, Lina	17, Dec. 1891	26, Nov.	22	814		Chicago, IL	Quincy, Illinois
Ryniker, Louise	26, July 1880	27, June	29	239	Freistein	Quincy, IL	St. Louis , Missouri
Ryniker, Samuel	3, Nov. 1892	11, Oct.	47	702		Quincy, IL	Schinznach, Schweiz
Saak, Friedrich	13, Aug. 1857	25, July	58	132		Cedar Lake, IN	Barvenhausen, Lippe
Saak, Henriette	23, Aug. 1869	6, Aug.	65	271		Cedar Lake, IN	Kirchhaide, Amt Hohnhausen, Lippe
Saak, Sophia Catharina	18, Nov. 1872	26, Oct.	73	375	Begemann	Lancaster, WI	Hellierg, Hohnhausen, Lippe-Detmold
Saal, Andreas	22, Feb. 1849	11, Jan.	25- 7m	32		Cincinnati, OH	
Saal, Magdalena	23, Feb. 1888	24, Dec.	64	126	Dahl	San Francisco, CA	Bergzabern, RheinPfalz Baiern
Saalfeld, Wilhelm	4, Aug. 1892	23, June		494		Portland, OR	Balthausen bei Erfurt, Sachsen
Saalmann, Christian	29, May 1865	29, Aug.		88		Cannelton, IN	
Saatkamp, August Wilhelm	15, Nov. 1880	2, Nov.	16- 5m-20d	367		Huntingburg, IN	Pike County, Indiana
Saatkamp, Ernst L.	19, July 1880	1, July	18- 4m	231		Huntingburg, IN	Pike County, Indiana
Saatkamp, Herman Heinrich	8, Nov. 1880	23, Oct.	63- 6m- 2d	359		Huntingburg, IN	Ladbergen, Tecklenburg, Preußen
Sabboth, Anna Rebecca	1, Aug. 1895	25, June	22	494	Lemkau	Muscatine, IA	Hammelwörden, Freiburg, Hannover
Sachs, Friedrich	23, Apr. 1891	5, Apr.	76	270		Arlington Heights, IL	Gießenthal, Pommern
Saeger, Katharina	24, Apr. 1890	1, Apr.	92- 2m- 7d	270	Katz	Francisco, MI	Hochdorf, Horb, Württemberg
Saegesser, Friedrich	1, Aug. 1895	5, July	44- 4m- 4d	494		St. Louis, MO	Zechlingen, Baselland, Schweiz
Sagehorn, Heinrich	2, May 1895	31, Mar.	70	286		San Francisco, CA	Fischerhude, Hannover
Säger, Maria	21, Feb. 1895	29, Jan.	54	126	Notten	Francisco, MI	New York City, New York
Sägesser, Lydia Emilie	21, Apr. 1898	1, Mar.	65	255		Quincy, IL	Springfield, Illinois
Sailer, Johan Gottfried	18, Feb. 1886	6, Feb.	55- 2m-5d	7		Scranton, PA	Glems, Urach, Württemberg
Sakel, Maria E.	14, Sept 1893	29, Aug.	68	590		Huntingburg, IN	Bokeln, Halle, Preußen
Salathe, Augusta Hermine	13, July 1899	18, June	19	447	Todrank	New York City, NY	
Salewski, Martin	8, Mar. 1894	14, Feb.	38	166		Menominee, MI	Kleinbrausen, Marienwarter, West Preußen

Christliche Apologete Death Notices --- 1839 - 1899

Name of Deceased	Notice Date	Death Date	Age	Page	Maiden Name	Place of Death	Place of Birth
Salewski, Martin	16, Jan. 1882	11, Dec.	80	23		Menominee, MI	Peterkau, Rosenberg, Germany
Sallenbach, Johan Jakob	26, May 1873	10, May	29	167		Galena, IL	Canton Zürich, Schweiz
Salomon, August	26, Oct. 1893	25, Sept	39	686		Chicago, IL	Eichwerder, Frankfurt, Brandenburg
Salow, Marie	10, May 1894	29, Mar.	68- 4m-18d	310		Schnectady, NY	Todtenhausen, Minden, Preußen
Salz, Elisabeth	25, Mar. 1886	8, Mar.	61	7		Mascoutah, IL	
Salzer, Anna Maria	4, Feb. 1886	14, Jan.	70	7		Rochester, NY	
Salzer, Marie	2, May 1864	14, Apr.	12	72		Chicago, IL	
Salzer, Minnie	27, Apr. 1893	6, Apr.	25- 3m-28d	270		LaCrosse, WI	
Salzer, Sebastian	13, Mar. 1862	21, Feb.	49	44		Rochester, NY	Neuhausen, Württemberg
Salzgeber, Maggie	25, May 1893	20, Apr.	21	334		Columbus, OH	Columbus, Franklin County, Ohio
Salzkorn, Christina	13, Nov. 1882	31, Oct.	64	367		Lena, IL	Schwarzburg bei Sondershausen, Germany
Salzmann, Georg Ludwig	12, Sept 1870	28, Aug.	22	295		Chicago, IL	Lottenmühle, Kaltensundheim, Sachsen-Weimar
Salzmann, Johannes	24, Oct. 1870	6, Oct.	74- 7m- 4d	343		Arena, WI	Benerode, Amt Münden, Hannover
Salzsieder, Maria Dorothea	22, May 1882	1, May	66- 1m- 4d	167	Hunt	Brooklyn, NY	Kölleda, Sachsen, Preußen
Sáman, Elisabeth	31, Dec. 1883	9, Dec.	73	7	Baumann	Batavia, WI	Gintelbach, Maulbronn, Württemberg
Sámann, Wilhelmine	10, June 1867	10, May	40	182	Lenz	Delaware, OH	Beutelsbach, Schorndorf, Württemberg
Samm, Dorothea	4, Apr. 1870	8, Feb.	71	111		Manitowoc, WI	Dorstfeld, Westphalen
Samm, Wilhelmine	13, Mar. 1876	25, Feb.	73	87	Mancher	Manitowoc, WI	Elberfeld,
Sammet, Christina Magdalena	23, Nov. 1899	23, Oct.	69	751	Spöhrle	Champaign, IL	Marbach, Württemberg
Sampen, Albertine H.	1, Jan. 1877	9, Dec.	30	7		Hartsburg, IL	Hamswerum, Ostfriesland
Sampen, Trinthe	25, Feb. 1892	27, Jan.	82	127	Adams	Emden, IL	Rysum, Ostfriesland
Sampson, (Mrs)	5, May 1887	17, Apr.	77	286		Colesburg, IA	Bonnte, Hannover
Sámpson, Christine	19, Dec. 1870	22, Nov.	32	407	Gatz	Charles City, IA	Bergfelden, Württemberg
Sampson, Friedrich	17, Jan. 1876	28, Dec.	45	23		Charles City, IA	
Sampson, Friedrich Christoph	13, Sept 1880	24, Aug.	71	295		Colesburg, IA	Bonte bei Osnabrück, Hannover
Samsel, Charlotte	20, Oct. 1859	16, Aug.	20	168		Crow River, MN	
Samsel, Jakob	17, June 1867	13, May	67- 7m-26d	190		Crow River, MN	Schellweiler, Baiern
Samsen, Anna Maria	12, Nov. 1857	20, Sept	56	184	Hartmann	Woodville, OH	Wittlage-Hundenburg, Hannover
Samson, Jeannette	28, Jan. 1884	16, Dec.	35	7	Krahlmann	Toledo, OH	Wenner, Ostfriesland
Samson, Ludwig	19, Mar. 1877	28, Feb.	75	95		Toledo, OH	Hannover
Samuels, Rosette M.	28, May 1896	19, Apr.	27	350	Paul	Peoria, IL	Fosterburg, Illinois
Sand, Friedrich Heinrich	6, Oct. 1873	18, Aug.	76	319		Portsmouth, OH	Hettstedt, Mansfeld, Merseburg, Preußen
Sander, Anna	7, Sept 1893	18, Aug.	75	574		Mt. Healthy, OH	Aschen, Diepholz, Hannover
Sander, Anna C.	23, Feb. 1888	20, Jan.	73-10m-10d	126		Arlington, MN	Filehne, Bromberg, Preußen
Sander, Friedrich	17, June 1878	23, May	65-11m-12d	191		Henderson, MN	Volstein, Bromberg, Preußen
Sander, Heinrich	22, Dec. 1892	27, Aug.	34	814		Gordonville, MO	Cape Girardeau County, Missouri
Sänder, Lorenz	31, Dec. 1883	13, Dec.	69	7		St. Louis, MO	Kohlstatt, Rheinkreis Baiern
Sander, Maria	21, Feb. 1850	3, Feb.	34	32		Mt. Healthy, OH	Schwölper, Braunschweig
Sander, Wilhelmine	22, Feb. 1875	14, Jan.	29	63	Kühnemund	Ironton, OH	Kleinwechsung, Sachsen
Sanders, Everd	28, May 1896	11, May	87	350		Ironton, OH	Oberisel, Kellterland, Holland
Sanders, Geretge	29, June 1874	14, Apr.	67	207	Tysen	Ironton, OH	Hatten, Holland
Sanders, Herman	7, Mar. 1870	16, Feb.	29	79		Furnace, OH	Hatten, Getteland, Holland
Sanders, Johanna	7, Mar. 1870	16, Feb.	32	79		Furnace, OH	Hatten, Getteland, Holland
Sanders, Rosina	28, Nov. 1889	31, Oct.	64	766	Kern	Ironton, OH	Rochester, New York
Sanders, Sophia	28, Nov. 1895	5, Nov.	46- 2m-15d	766	Fischer	Ironton, OH	
Sanders, Wilhelmina	5, Sept 1895	12, Aug.	58	574	Weber	Rose Hill, TX	Krumbach, Preußen

Christliche Apologete Death Notices --- 1839 - 1899

Name of Deceased	Death Date	Age	Maiden Name	Page	Notice Date	Place of Death	Place of Birth
Sandford, Louis	26, Mar.	16		167	26, May 1873	Osage, MO	Cole County, Missouri
Sandfort, Wilhelmine	24, Mar.	68	Frauenhof	68	25, Apr. 1861	Osage, MO	Hilden, Düsseldorf, Preußen
Sandler, Julie		Inquiry		83	23, May 1849	Marion, OH	
Sandman, Amalia		82	Zimmermann	734	14, Nov. 1895	Morgan, MN	Reddewitz, Penkum, Stettin, Pommern
Sandmann, Carl	30, June	71- 3m-19d		231	17, July 1882	New Ulm, MN	Nadrense, Stettin, Preußen
Sandmann, Mary	7, Sept	24		183	12, Nov. 1847	New Orleans, LA	
Sandmeier, Friedrich	9, Mar.	65		238	10, Apr. 1890	Yellow Creek, IL	Almena, Varenholz, Lippe-Detmold
Sandmeier, Jakob Wilhelm	10, Aug.	23		279	1, Sept 1873	Covington, KY	Newalton, Kentucky
Sandmeier, Julia	14, Apr.	22		287	4, May 1899	Pearl City, IL	Galena, Illinois
Sandmeyer, Caroline M.L.	10, Jan.	65	Young	191	24, Mar. 1892	Topeka, KS	
Sandrock, Katharine Elisabeth	29, July	86- 2m	Meyer	7	19, Aug. 1886	Wheeling, WV	Hille, Münden, Preußen
Sandry, August	28, June	63		462	17, July 1890	Lansing, IA	
Sandwoß, Wilhelm	11, Feb.	65		142	2, Mar. 1893	Cape Girardeau, MO	Schweiz
Sanford, C.W.	24, Dec.	39- -14d	Müller	7	7, Jan. 1884	New Albany, IN	Hakenstedt, Hannover
Sanger, Catharina	12, Feb.	62- 3m-27d	Enzen	71	28, Feb. 1870	Bucyrus, OH	
Sanger, Elisabetha	10, Feb.		Burckhardt	36	29, Feb. 1864	Galion, OH	Lycoming County, Pennsylvania
Sanger, Georg	27, Aug.	85		590	15, Sept 1892	Bucyrus, OH	Württemberg
Sangmeister, Anna Maria	21, Apr.	62	Sangmeister	319	18, May 1899	Frankfort, IL	Königswald, Rodenburg, Kurhessen
Sangmeister, Anna Martha	22, Nov.	84- 1m	Ulrich	814	17, Dec. 1891	Frankfort, IL	Königswalde, Kurhessen
Sangmeister, Barbara Elisabeth	29, Dec.	86	Bettenhausen	63	28, Jan. 1897	Frankfort, IL	Königswals, Kurhessen
Sangmeister, Christian	12, Nov.	80		7	2, Dec. 1886	Frankfort, IL	Königswalde, Kurhessen
Sangmeister, Conrad	25, Oct.	79		734	16, Nov. 1893	Frankfort, IL	Königswalde, Kurhessen
Sangmeister, John	23, Aug.	62		7	22, Sept 1884	Metamoras, OH	Lispenhausen, Rodenburg, Kurhessen
Sangmeister, Maria	4, Jan.	39	Sprenger	23	19, Jan. 1880	Frankfort, IL	Königswald, Rodenburg, Kurhessen
Sanman, Brunhein	25, Dec.	2- -1d		24	9, Jan. 1854	Peoria, IL	
Santer, Catharine	29, Aug.	39- 6m	Schäfer	188	24, Nov. 1853	St. Louis, MO	Reibach, Dieburg, Hessen-Darmstadt
Santer, Charley	17, Apr.	7- 1m		76	8, May 1865	Carver, MN	
Santer, Friedrich	1, Feb.	62		55	12, Feb. 1872	Cincinnati, OH	Braunschweig
Santschie, Maria		21	Bühner	351	29, Oct. 1883	Madison, IN	Signau, Bern, Schweiz
Sargel, Malinde	1, Oct.	31	Kramer	671	21, Oct. 1897	Galion, OH	Crawford County, Ohio
Sartor, Christina	13, Mar.	22	Wolf	222	2, Apr. 1896	Auburn, IN	Heßlar, Hessen-Kassel
Saß, Friedrich	5, Apr.	76		286	30, Apr. 1891	Arlington Heights, IL	Gießenthal, Pommern
Saß, Johan Gottlieb	19, Nov.	82- 5m		415	28, Dec. 1874	Sleepy Eye, MN	Alten Fließ in der Neumark, Preußen
Saß, Wilhelmine	4, Jan.	67	Wenzel	126	22, Feb. 1894	Arlington Heights, IL	Geblershoff, Pommern
Saßmanshausen, Heinrich	9, Nov.	19		383	29, Nov. 1875	San Jose, TX	Berkenfehl, Wittgenstein, Preußen
Saßmanshausen, Lisette	14, Mar.	28-11m-14d	Seiler	111	2, Apr. 1877	Danville, TX	
Saßmanshausen, Ludwig	21, June	54		454	12, July 1894	Bracken, TX	Herbershausen, Wittgenstein, Germany
Saßmanshausen, Maria Elisabeth	21, Oct.	15		359	8, Nov. 1875	San Jose, IL	Birkenfehl, Wittgenstein, Preußen
Satorius, Gretje	5, Apr.	80	Rahmann	319	18, May 1899	Petersburg, IL	Obschet, Ostfriesland
Sattler, Adolf	15, Nov.	21		790	6, Dec. 1894	Indianapolis, IN	St. Joseph, Missouri
Sattler, Carrie	27, Oct.	18		734	14, Nov. 1895	Indianapolis, IN	Indianapolis, Marion County, Indiana
Sattler, Christina	23, July	76	Ebinger	542	22, Aug. 1895	Lee, IL	Wiesenbach, Baden
Satuer, Mathilda	28, Nov.	22- 4m-28d		415	25, Dec. 1882	Warsaw, IL	Warsaw, Illinois
Sauer, Adam	23, Nov.	70- 3m		399	15, Dec. 1879	Brooklyn, NY	Ottrau, Kurhessen
Sauer, Anna Kunigunde	28, Sept	62- 7m		335	18, Oct. 1880	Brooklyn, NY	Otterau, Kurhessen
Sauer, Anna Maria	8, Jan.	14		7	4, Feb. 1886	Drake, MO	

Christliche Apologete Death Notices --- 1839 - 1899

Name of Deceased	Notice Date	Death Date	Age	Maiden Name	Place of Death	Page	Place of Birth
Sauer, Barbara	14, Mar. 1895		69	Heubeck	Madison, WI	174	Vestenbergs, Gereuth, Oberfranken, Baiern
Sauer, Christian	28, Mar. 1895	9, Mar.	69		Madison, IN	206	Kaffenroth, Büdingen, Baiern
Sauer, Dorothea	11, Nov. 1858	3, Sept	28		Hanging Rock, OH	180	Ströhen, Amt Ehrenburg, Hannover
Sauer, Elisabeth	8, Apr. 1897	17, Mar.	68	Waldschmidt	Sandwich, IL	223	Frohnhausen, Dillenburg, Nassau
Sauer, H. (Rev)	24, Dec. 1896	13, Nov.	42		Sandwich, IL	831	Northville, Illinois
Sauer, H. Wilhelm	4, Dec. 1871				Heckerstown, MD	391	
Sauer, Jacobine E.	20, Apr. 1893	11, Mar.	68- 2m		Boston, MA	254	Groß-Backnau, Württemberg
Sauer, Johan Adam	18, June 1877	5, June	21		Morrisania, NY	199	Uttrau, Kurhessen
Sauer, Johan Heinrich	13, Nov. 1871	29, Oct.	76- 4m-15d		Marion, OH	367	Marburg, Hessen
Sauer, John	25, Nov. 1897	26, Oct.	19		Earlville, IL	751	
Sauer, Joseph	15, Feb. 1894	8, Jan.	72		Owensville, MO	110	Urloffen, Baden
Sauer, Peter	12, May 1873	20, Apr.	73		Portsmouth, OH	151	Hergershausen, Rothenburg, Kurhessen
Sauer, Valentin	3, May 1860	17, Apr.	73		Newport, MI	72	Donseits, Rheinkreis Baiern
Sauerbier, Friedrich	11, Feb. 1892	25, Jan.	88		St. Paul, MN	94	Schwenemünde, Germany
Sauerbrey, Louise	23, July1883	7, July	65- 2m-27d	Spoth	Canal Dover, OH	239	Königsberg, Preußen
Sauerwein, Anna Maria	3, Apr. 1865	15, Mar.	62	Blickhahn	Mascoutah, IL	56	Spitzaltheim, Dieburg, Hessen-Darmstadt
Sauerwein, Christina	3, Mar.1873	26, Dec.	21	Wöll	Alton, IL	71	
Sauerwein, Elisabeth	17, Apr. 1876	29, Mar.	22	Möll	Alton, IL	127	Indiana
Sauerwein, Elisabeth	21, Aug. 1876	29, Mar.	22	Wöll	Alton, IL	271	Indiana
Sauerwein, Maria Elisabeth	4, May 1868	3, Apr.	44	Weber	Brighton, IL	143	Biberheim, RheinPreußen
Säuferer, Mathilde	29, Sept 1884	16, Sept	24		Blooming Grove, MN	7	
Säufferer, Emilie H.	13, Dec. 1894	23, Oct.	35	Schütte	Blooming Grove, MN	806	Warsaw, Rice County, Minnesota
Saugel, Maria	16, May 1881	24, Apr.	21		Farmington, IA	159	Etna, Ohio
Saul, Marie Elisabeth	22, Feb. 1875	23, Jan.	73		Nauvoo, IL	63	Langenla bei Mühlhausen, Preußen
Saumweber, Johannes	11, Mar.1872	23, Feb.	68		Philadelphia, PA	87	Ried bei Bählingen, Baiern
Saumweber, Juliane	10, Mar.1873	17, Feb.	64	Hertlä	Philadelphia, PA	79	Fellheim, Baiern
Saupe, Maria	3, May 1888	27, Mar.	73- 7m		Madison, IN	286	Windhorst, Hannover
Sauß, Christian	23, Mar. 1893	27, Feb.	57		Oakfield, NY	190	Mecklenburg-Schwerin
Sauter, (Mr)	10, Jan. 1861	16, Dec.	35		Red Bud, IL	8	Thalfingen, Herrenberg, Württemberg
Sauter, Anna Maria	4, Nov. 1858	21, Oct.	33-11m-14d	Haller	Davenport, IA	176	Aldingen, Württemberg
Sauter, Benjamin Franklin	25, Aug. 1892	4, Aug.	21		Warsaw, IL	542	Boody, Illinois
Sauter, Caroline	7, May 1866	2, Apr.	15- 4m-15d		Warsaw, IL	150	
Sauter, Charles	21, Aug. 1882	4, Aug.	16		Benton, MN	271	
Sauter, Christiana	28, Apr. 1859	31, Mar.	32	Kim	Cedar Lake, IN	68	Untergetigen, Herrenberg, Württemberg
Sauter, Ernst	18, Apr. 1895	24, Mar.	63		Brownton, MN	254	Gondelscheim, Bretten, Baden
Sauter, Georg	17, Aug. 1854	18, July	39		Cedar Lake, IN	132	Reusten , Württemberg
Sauter, Georg Paul	27, Aug. 1877	2, Aug.	67- 8m- 5d		Warsaw, IL	279	
Sauter, Heinricka	1, Nov. 1894	14, Oct.	68		Berea, OH	710	Erkenbuchtsweiler, Nürtlingen, Württemberg Preußen
Sauter, Henriette	21, Feb. 1876	19, Jan.	34	Schewe	Benton, MN	63	
Sauter, Jacob	18, Oct. 1875	25, Sept	64		Summerfield, IL	335	Neustadt an der Haardt,
Sauter, Jacob	13, Aug. 1857	14, July	62		Carver, MN	132	Deidelsheim, Baden
Sauter, Jakob	20, Oct. 1853	24, Sept	13		Rochester, NY	168	
Sauter, Johan Michael	13, Mar. 1876	24, Feb.	27		Cedar Lake, IN	87	White Creek, Lock County, Indiana
Sauter, Johan Michael	29, June 1874	15, June	49- 9m-23d		Cedar Lake, IN	207	Reusten, Herrenberg, Württemberg
Sauter, Justina	14, Apr. 1862	27, Jan.	62-11m	Burkhardt	Benton, MN	60	Gundelsheim, Amt Bretten, Baden
Sauter, Katie	15, Jan. 1883	23, Dec.	25- 2m-25d		Brownton, MN	23	

Christliche Apologete Death Notices --- 1839 - 1899

Name of Deceased	Notice Date	Death Date	Age	Maiden Name	Page	Place of Death	Place of Birth
Sauter, Lisetta	9, Feb. 1885	30, Jan.	73		7	Brooklyn, NY	
Sauter, Maria Eleonore	29, July 1886	12, July	29	Rinkel	7	Warsaw, IL	Warsaw, Illinois
Sauter, Minna	27, Oct. 1884	2, Oct.	37- 4m- 8d	Hügel	7	Des Moines, IA	
Sauter, Monika	26, Mar. 1896	8, Mar.	78	Huber	206	Warsaw, IL	Waltersweier, Offenbach, Baden
Sauter, Anna Maria	15, May 1876	28, Apr.	53	Gaus	159	Cedar Lake, IN	Reusten, Herrenberg, Württemberg
Sauter, Dorothea	19, Mar. 1883	19, Feb.	71		95	Cedar Lake, IN	Reusten, Herrenberg, Württemberg
Sauter, Gottlieb	15, Aug. 1864	13, June	26		132	Cedar Lake, IN	Reusten, Herrenberg, Württemberg
Sauter, Gottlieb	20, July 1899	28, June	84		463	Crown Point, IN	Reusten, Herrenberg, Württemberg
Sauter, Ida B.	21, Apr. 1887	8, Apr.	30	Neimetz	254	Scotia, NE	
Sauter, Jakob	5, Oct. 1893	8, Sept	70		638	Waverly, OH	Emingen, Württemberg
Sauter, Johan Martin	28, Dec. 1893	3, Dec.	70		828	Crown Point, IN	Reusten, Hernber, Württemberg
Sauter, Johannes	12, May 1884	27, Apr.	37		7	Aurora, IL	Schopfloch, Württemberg
Sauter, Maria	30, Mar. 1893	6, Mar.	61		206	Crown Point, IN	Langwedel, Verden, Hannover
Sauter, Maria	27, Apr. 1885	11, Apr.			7	St. Paul, NE	Lake County, Indiana
Saxer, (Mrs)	25, Apr. 1889	22, Mar.	74		270	Pittsfield, IL	Worms, Germany
Saxer, Anna Catharina	8, June 1874	4, May	61	Prior	183	Perry, IL	Merstadt, Worms, Hessen-Darmstadt
Saxer, Frank	15, Dec. 1892	14, Sept	22		798	Springfield, IL	Springfield, Illinois
Saxer, Georg Wilhelm	21, Sept 1899	16, July	15		607	Springfield, IL	Springfield, Illinois
Saxer, Johan Martin	17, Jan. 1870	14, Dec.	42- 5m- 2d	Ill	23	Perry, IL	Pfifflichheim, Worms, Hessen
Saxer, Johannes	2, Aug. 1888	7, July	75- 2m-26d		494	Pittsfield, IL	Pifigheim bei Worms, Preußen
Schaaf, Johanna Rosina	26, Nov. 1877	31, Oct.	71	Böhner	383	Santa Claus, IN	Laufen am Neckar, Besigheim, Württemberg
Schaad, Friedrich	4, July 1895	26, Apr.	24		430	Covington, KY	Bamberg, Oberfranken, Baiern
Schaad, Johann Gottlieb	30, Oct. 1840		Inquiry		171	Columbus, OH	Rudersberg, Welzheim, Württemberg
Schaad, Luise Katharina	27, June 1864		17		104	Indianapolis, IN	Weiler zum Stein, Marbach, Württemberg
Schaad, Mathilde	6, Sept 1860	22, Aug.	30	Rudolf	144	New Albany, IN	Sachsen-Gotha, Germany
Schaade, Johann	18, Aug. 1859	3, Aug.	44		132	St. Louis, MO	Richelsdorf, Rothenburg, Kurhessen
Schaaf, Anna Christina	18, June 1877	2, June	65	Koch	199	Columbus, OH	Ellenhausen bei Marburg, Preußen
Schaaf, Elisabeth	4, Oct. 1855			Born	160	Indianapolis, IN	Zell, Alsfeld, Hessen-Darmstadt
Schaaf, Jakob	14, May 1857	5, Apr.	23		80	Huntingburg, IN	Lauffen am Neckar, Württemberg
Schaaf, Jakob	24, July 1882	29, June	71		239	Red Wing, MN	Lauffen, Württemberg
Schaaf, Johan Jakob	25, Sept 1882	21, Aug.	76- 2m- 7d		311	Santa Claus, IN	Laufen am Neckar, Besigheim, Württemberg
Schaal, (Mrs)	19, Apr. 1880	30, Mar.	89- 4m-21d		127	Bucyrus, OH	
Schaal, Christiane	21, Mar. 1895	1, Feb.	78		190	Troy, NY	Grunbach, Württemberg
Schaal, Friederike	9, Dec. 1872	15, Nov.	49	Rapp	399	Santa Claus, IN	Haubersbraun, Schorndorf, Württemberg
Schaal, Joh. Fr.	2, Oct. 1871	16, Sept	70- 1m-20d		319	Bucyrus, OH	Ruthersberg, Welsheim, Württemberg
Schaal, Johan Georg	18, May 1899	13, Apr.	79		319	Jamestown, MO	Mannheim, Germany
Schaal, Johanna	8, Dec. 1879	22, Nov.	53	Kämmer	391	Santa Claus, IN	Heilsberg, Remda, Sachsen-Weimar
Schaal, Margaretha	10, Nov. 1879	26, Oct.	56- 6m- 7d	Speer	359	Bay City, MI	Kübeheim an Rhein, Germany
Schaal, Philipp	29, Jan. 1877	2, Jan.	64- 7m		39	Bay City, MI	Waldhausen, Wertheim, Baden
Schaal, Susanna	30, Oct. 1871	5, Oct.	49	Herschberger	351	Bucyrus, OH	Lancaster County, Pennsylvania
Schaar, Mathilde	6, Dec. 1894	8, Nov.	22	Ebert	790	Menomonie, WI	Henderson, Sipley County, Minnesota
Schaarmann, Christian	1, May 1876	10, Apr.	86- 5m-26d		143	Clarington, OH	Ulrichstein, Schotten, Hessen
Schäbbel, Emma Albertine	11, Nov. 1897	10, Oct.	32	Kutzner	719	South Bend, IN	Stolp, Pommern
Schaberg, (Mr)	27, Apr. 1863	1, Apr.	44		68	Warrenton, MO	Wesen, Kreis Tecklenburg, Preußen
Schaberg, (Mrs)	27, Apr. 1863	2, Apr.	52		68	Warrenton, MO	Wesen, Kreis Tecklenburg, Preußen
Schaberg, Johan H.	4, May 1893	12, Apr.	101		286	New Melle, MO	Wersen, Westphalen

Christliche Apologete Death Notices --- 1839 - 1899

Name of Deceased	Notice Date	Death Date	Age	Maiden Name	Page	Place of Death	Place of Birth
Schaberg, Sophia	25, Nov. 1867	8, Nov.	30		374	Quincy, IL	Linen, Tecklenburg, Preußen
Schächerr, Christina Friederike	4, Sept 1882	16, Aug.	61	Kimmick	287	Dayton, OH	Kleinsachsenheim, Württemberg
Schack, Sophia	18, Sept 1890	24, Aug.	73	Dörr	606	Kansas City, KS	Sonnenberg, Nassau
Schacke, Friedricka	4, Apr. 1895	17, Mar.	83	Kuhfuß	222	Pinckney, MO	Ludenhausen, Lippe-Detmold
Schacke, Johan Kurt	20, Feb. 1890	28, Jan.	81- 2m-13d		126	Hopewell, MO	Hunfeld, Lippe-Detmold
Schad, Christina	15, Apr. 1867	31, Mar.	43	Weißhaar	118	Indianapolis, IN	Weiler zum Stein, Marbach, Württemberg
Schad, Gottlieb	16, Aug. 1880	2, Aug.	57- 4m-25d		263	Indianapolis, IN	Weiler zum Stein, Marbach, Württemberg
Schad, Matthäus	20, Dec. 1880	29, Nov.	59- 3m- 6d		407	Indianapolis, IN	Weiler zum Stein, Marbach, Württemberg
Schade, Anna Barbara	27, Jan. 1873	14, Dec.	72		31	Leavenworth, MN	Stärkgloß, Kurhessen
Schade, Elisabeth	17, Jan. 1889	29, Dec.	76		46	LaCrosse, WI	Nurenberg, Baiern
Schade, Johannes	14, Dec. 1874	24, Nov.	71		399	East Troy, WI	Henebach, Kurhessen
Schadewald, August Friedrich	27, June 1881	11, June	20- 1m-25d		207	Maple Grove, MN	Plönnzig-Pyritz, Preußen
Schadewald, Karl Friedrich Wm.	4, Mar. 1886	19, Feb.	54		7	Milwaukee, WI	Großenhagen, Naugard, Pommern
Schadh, Katharina	4, May 1863	18, Apr.	22		72	St. Louis, MO	
Schädle, Alois	12, Jan. 1893	25, Nov.	75- 4m-20d		30	Boston, MA	Jelingen, Baden
Schaefer, John L.	14, July 1884	16, June			6	Fond du Lac, WI	Kernbach, Marburg, Kurhessen
Schaeffer, Johan Michael	10, Apr. 1890	11, Feb.			238	Pinckneyville, IL	Thaifingen, Herrenberg, Württemberg
Schaekler, John David	29, Oct. 1883	2, Oct.	46- 3m- 6d		351	Kenosha, WI	Rommelshausen, Württemberg
Schaeper, Wilhelmine	12, Feb. 1891	20, Jan.	64- 4m		110	Warren, MO	Lotta, Minden, Preußen
Schäfer, (Mr)	19, Aug. 1878	21, July	66- 5m- 6d	Meyer	263	Cape Girardeau, MO	Rodehim v.d. Höhe, Bilwill, Hessen-Darmstadt
Schäfer, (Mrs)	12, May 1873	26, Apr.	60- 5m	Teiton	151	Cleveland, OH	Wieseck, Gießen, Hessen-Darmstadt
Schäfer, (Mrs)	24, Feb. 1873	8, Feb.	35	Wilkening	63	Goshen, IN	Hemeringen, Amt Hameln, Hannover
Schäfer, Adam	30, Nov. 1874	12, Nov.			383	Baresville, OH	
Schäfer, Agnes Rosine	12, Oct. 1868	27, Sept	52	Riedinger	327	Galena, IL	Dutzlingen, Tübingen, Württemberg
Schäfer, Anna	9, Nov. 1863	22, Oct.	79		180	Madison, IN	
Schäfer, Anna Christine Charlotte	18, Oct. 1860	23, Sept	63- 5m- 4d		168	Herman, MO	Flote, Minden, Preußen
Schäfer, Anna Eva	10, Sept 1866	18, Aug.	67- 6m		294	Quincy, IL	Niederkeinsbach, Erbach, Hessen-Darmstadt
Schäfer, Anna Maria	22, June 1863	29, May	21		100	Madison, IN	Eltingen, Leonberg, Württemberg
Schäfer, Anna Maria	30, July 1891	4, June	34	Willmann	494	Albina, OR	Rußland
Schäfer, Augustina Dorothea L.	5, Aug. 1897	8, July	59	Giese	495	Macon, NE	Uchtenhagen, Pommern
Schäfer, Balthasar	5, Mar. 1891	29, Dec.	80		158	Cleveland, OH	Oppenroth, Gießen, Hessen-Darmstadt
Schäfer, Barbara	25, Mar. 1858	11, Jan.	75		48	Baresville, OH	Brucken, Kirchheim, Württemberg
Schäfer, Barbara	18, June 1883	2, May	78	Müller	199	Clearwater, MN	Weilerbach, Baiern
Schäfer, Beata Catharina Judith	22, Oct. 1866	29, Aug.	15		342	Galena, IL	Basel, Schweiz
Schäfer, Catharina Friederike	9, Jan. 1896	6, Dec.	42	Schäfer	30	Farmington, MO	St. Francois County, Missouri
Schäfer, Christina	15, Nov. 1855	6, Oct.	36		184	Evansport, OH	Hartum bei Münden, Preußen
Schäfer, Christoph Bernhardt	10, Dec. 1896	18, Nov.	46		798	Peoria, IL	Heimsheim, Leonberg, Württemberg
Schäfer, Conrad	14, Aug. 1882		75		263	Baltimore, MD	Niedermittlau bei Kassel, Kurhessen
Schäfer, Daniel	18, Aug. 1873	26, July	35- 6m-18d		263	Burlington, IA	Kesselbach, Grünberg, Hessen-Darmstadt
Schäfer, David	10, Apr. 1846		Inquiry		59		Leutenbach bei Winnenden, Württemberg
Schäfer, Doretchen	23, June 1862				100	New York, NY	
Schäfer, Edward Henry	4, June 1896	22, Apr.	19	Junker	367	Flora, MN	Flora, Renville County, Minnesota
Schäfer, Elisabeth	24, Dec. 1891	19, Nov.	67	Rau	830	Allegheny City, PA	Bottehorn, Biedekopf, Hessen-Darmstadt
Schäfer, Elisabeth	29, Jan. 1866	23, Dec.			38	Boonville, IN	Lora, Kreis Marburg, Kurhessen
Schäfer, Elisabeth	24, July 1882	20, May	23- 8m-11d	Schäfer	239	Roberts, IL	Wohra, Rauschenberg, Kurhessen
Schäfer, Elisabeth	28, Feb. 1881	2, Feb.	69- 9m-17d	Vogel	71	Chillicothe, OH	Freisbach, RheinPfalz Baiern

Christliche Apologete Death Notices --- 1839 - 1899

Name of Deceased	Notice Date	Death Date	Age	Maiden Name	Place of Death	Page	Place of Birth
Schäfer, Elisabeth	10, May 1888	14, Apr.	23		St. Louis, MO	302	Elbersfeld, Preußen
Schäfer, Elisabeth	3, Mar. 1884	14, Feb.	64	Klattern	Cape Girardeau, MO	7	
Schäfer, Elisabeth Katharina	22, Sept 1898	25, Aug.	33	Grünewaldt	Lincoln, NE	607	Sarotaf, Rußland
Schäfer, Emma	11, Feb. 1884	25, Jan.	27		Beaver Falls, MN	7	Cincinnati, Hamilton County, Ohio
Schäfer, Emma	28, Dec. 1885	1, Dec.	24- 7m	Schantz	Jersey City, NJ	7	Poughkeepsie, New York
Schäfer, Georg	24, May 1855	3, May	68- 3m- 1d		Chillicothe, OH	84	Schwegenheim, Rheinkreis Baiern
Schäfer, Georg	3, Sept 1877	16, Aug.	45- 3m- 3d		Goshen, IN	287	Ottenstein, Braunschweig
Schäfer, Georg	6, Dec. 1875	19, Nov.	21		Quincy, IL	391	
Schäfer, Georg	25, Oct. 1880	26, Aug.	59- 4m-19d		Lemars, IA	343	Eltingen, Leonberg, Württemberg
Schäfer, Gottlieb	20, Feb. 1862	11, Jan.	39		Madison, IN	32	Harthum, Germany
Schäfer, H. Gottlieb	20, Oct. 1898	22, Sept	77		Lansing, MI	671	Schlierbach, Jesberg, Kurhessen
Schäfer, Heinrich	17, Apr. 1890	27, Mar.	67 1m 10d		Dayton, OH	254	Kaltendorf, Garteleben, Preußen
Schäfer, Heinrich Christoph Wm.	23, June 1892	22, May	66		Denver, CO	398	Müdersbach, Wetzlar, Preußen
Schäfer, Helena Karolina	10, Feb. 1898	19, Jan.	26	Gellermann	Orlando, OK	95	Marrina Mills, Minnesota
Schäfer, Helene	9, Aug. 1888	22, Jan.	53- 7m-22d	Brickwedel	New York City, NY	510	Drangstedt, Hannover
Schäfer, Jakob	26, Mar. 1891	4, Mar.	85		Clarington, OH	206	Brucken, Kirchheim an der Teck, Württemberg
Schäfer, Jakob	30, June 1859	13, June	39		Madison, IN	104	Eldingen, Leonberg, Württemberg
Schäfer, Jakob	2, Nov. 1874	4, Oct.	48- 9m-25d		Allegheny City, PA	351	Müdersbach, Wetzlar, Preußen
Schäfer, Johan	27, Jan. 1879	10, Jan.	68		Quincy, IL	31	Hedheim, Biedingen, Hessen-Darmstadt
Schäfer, Johan	3, Mar.1873	12, Feb.	26		Baltimore, MD	71	
Schäfer, Johan Bernard	18, Mar.1872	19, Jan.	56- 5m-19d		Warsaw, IL	95	Lauter, Nassau
Schäfer, Johan Conrad	4, Feb. 1897	23, Nov.	66		New York City, NY	79	Evansville, Indiana
Schäfer, Johan David	9, June 1898	14, May	31		Boonville, IN	367	Rommershausen, Treysa, Kurhessen
Schäfer, Johan Heinrich	19, Feb. 1877	31, Jan.	86		Deep River, IA	63	Engter, Vörden, Hannover
Schäfer, Johan Heinrich	24, Jan. 1889	25, Dec.	60- 5m-19d		Beaver Falls, MN	62	Kernbach, Marburg, Kurhessen
Schäfer, Johan Ludwig	8, Aug. 1870	25, June	71		Ulster, IA	255	Flocke, Kreis Minden, Preußen
Schäfer, Johann	19, May 1859	3, May	25- 4m-28d		Herman, MO	80	Erlenhausen, Rotenburg, Kurhessen
Schäfer, Johann	4, Nov. 1842				Pittsburg, PA	175	
Schäfer, Johann	5, Aug. 1852	25, June	24		Portsmouth, OH	128	
Schäfer, Johannes	28, May 1857	12, Apr.	61		Perry, IL	88	Ossen bei Worms, Hessen-Darmstadt
Schäfer, Johannes	24, May 1880	29, Apr.	76- 2m-14d		Allegheny City, PA	167	Walddorf, Württemberg
Schäfer, Juliane	17, Nov. 1898	18, Oct.	76		Berne, MI	735	Kesselbach, Hessen-Nassau
Schäfer, Karl Gottlieb	7, July 1887	18, June	61		Berne, MI	430	Göhe, Böhmen
Schäfer, Kasper Heinrich	18, May 1874	8, May	73- 8m		Newport, KY	159	Oldendorf bei Melle, Hannover
Schäfer, Katharina	8, Nov. 1875	1, Oct.	67-10m-10d	Ensinger	Clarington, OH	359	Brucken, Kirchheim an der Teck, Württemberg
Schäfer, Katharina	27, Jan. 1887	7, Jan.	61	Schnaithman	McPherson, KS	62	Hanweiler, Waiblingen, Württemberg
Schäfer, Katharina	6, Apr. 1885	6, Mar.	84		Flood Creek, IA	7	Warzenbach, Marburg, Kurhessen
Schäfer, Katharina	22, Apr. 1878	7, Apr.	61- 3m-13d	Mittendorf	Newport, KY	127	Oldendorf bei Melle, Hannover
Schäfer, Katharina	2, Nov. 1874	8, Oct.	40 - 9d	Steinmetz	Muscatine, IA	351	Niedermöllich, Kurhessen
Schäfer, Katharina	31, Mar. 1898	15, Feb.	84	Klaus	Quincy, IL	207	Biedinger, Hessen-Darmstadt
Schäfer, Katharine	16, Feb. 1854	25, Jan.			Newburg, IN	28	
Schäfer, Katharine	1, Nov. 1880	12, Oct.	66- 8m		Galena, IL	351	
Schäfer, M.	10, Apr. 1882	23, Mar.	40		Palatine, IL	119	Elsaß
Schäfer, Margaret	15, Mar. 1875	14, Jan.	84- 7m-18d	Beckmann	Edgerton, OH	87	Dauphin County, Pennsylvania
Schäfer, Margarethe	29, Dec. 1887	4, Dec.	64- 9m	Götzinger	Rochester, NY	830	Stein, Germany
Schäfer, Maria	16, Aug. 1894	18, July	21		Auburn, IN	534	Nister bei Hachenburg, Germany

- 430 -

Christliche Apologete Death Notices --- 1839 - 1899

Name of Deceased	Death Date	Age	Maiden Name	Page	Place of Death	Place of Birth	Notice Date
Schäfer, Maria	23, July	51	Merker	7	Olive Branch, NE	Godien, Mecklenburg-Schwerin	12, Aug. 1886
Schäfer, Maria Elisabeth	7, Feb.	63		175	Quincy, IL	Chambersburg, Pennsylvania	18, Mar. 1897
Schäfer, Maria Katharina	15, Jan.	82	Scheer	79	Bloomington, IL	Lauterbach, Hessen-Darmstadt	2, Feb. 1899
Schäfer, Peter Johan	7, Nov.	59		766	Watertown, WI	Kurhessen	27, Nov. 1890
Schäfer, Phil.	22, Nov.	69- 3m-25d		399	Farmington, IA	Goldhausen, Waldeck	13, Dec. 1880
Schäfer, Philipp	2, Nov.	73		766	Champaign, IL	Gießen, Hessen-Darmstadt	28, Nov. 1895
Schäfer, Priscilla	19, Feb.	23	Steiger	175	Wheeling, WV	Switzer Township, Monroe County, Ohio	18, Mar. 1897
Schäfer, Regina		45	Schäffer	7	Higginsport, OH	Deidesheim, Rheinkreis Baiern	26, May 1884
Schäfer, Rosine	27, July	85	Jung	263	Cleveland, OH	Osweil, Ludwigsburg, Württemberg	16, Aug. 1880
Schäfer, Samuel	16, Sept	61-11m- 6d		343	Fremont, IN	Susquehanna, Pennsylvania	22, Oct. 1877
Schäfer, Sophia	8, July	69- 2m-23d	Jakob	494	Louisville, KY	Roder, Sachsen	3, Aug. 1893
Schäfer, Sophia	4, July	73	Vöhr	463	Melvin, IL	Ellenrode, Krankenberg, Kurhessen	22, July 1897
Schäfer, Susanna		62	Weber	79	Edon, OH	Dauphin County, Pennsylvania	8, Mar. 1880
Schäfer, Wendel	7, May	87		7	Quincy, IL	Brenschbach, Hessen-Darmstadt	25, May 1885
Schäfer, Wilhelm	2, Feb.	35- 7m-11d		63	Farmington, MO	Fredricktown, Madison County, Missouri	19, Feb. 1883
Schäfer, Wilhelmine	21, Aug.	34	Schneider	606	Canton, MO	Canton , Missouri	19, Sept 1889
Schäfermeier, Friedrich	12, Jan.			32	Charlestown, IN	Lippe-Detmold	22, Feb. 1864
Schäffer, Christopher	30, Apr.	70		334	Odebolt, IA	Uentze, Brandenburg	22, May 1890
Schäffer, Georg Peter	29, June	57		223	Chillicothe, OH	Schwengenheim, Rheinkreis Baiern	12, July 1875
Schäffer, Killian	21, Mar.	72		239	Rochester, NY	Wentheim, Baden	15, Apr. 1897
Schäffer, Ursula	2, Aug.	26- 1m-15d	Jauch	132	Hamilton, OH	Schwenningen , Württemberg	14, Aug. 1856
Schäffler, Johan Heinrich	23, Aug.	73- 3m- 7d		606	Creighton, NE	Hoffenheim bei Sinsheim, Baden	19, Sept 1889
Schaffner, (girl)	21, June	10		231	Herman, MO		18, July 1870
Schaffner, Adele Eveline	13, July	36	Glimm	511	New York City, NY	New York City, New York	6, Aug. 1896
Schaffner, Anna	22, Apr.	13		167	Herman, MO		24, May 1875
Schaffner, Barbara	30, July	78-10m- 4d		558	Rochester, NY	Anweiler, Rheinkreis Baiern	29, Aug. 1889
Schaffner, Elisabeth	4, Apr.	76	Mangauld	143	Herman, MO	Susach, Basel, Schweiz	3, May 1880
schaffner, Friedrich	18, Dec.	83		14	Rochester, NY	Elsaß	4, Jan. 1894
Schaffner, Friedrich Johan	12, May	14- 9m-18d		167	Herman, MO		26, May 1873
Schaffner, Gottlieb	23, Mar.	37		7	Chicago, IL	Canton Aargau, Schweiz	8, Apr. 1886
Schaffner, Heinrich	20, Oct.	70		703	Berger, MO	Sissach, Baselland, Schweiz	4, Nov. 1897
Schaffner, Jakob	1, Apr.	86		143	Herman, MO	Wintersingen, Baselland, Schweiz	3, May 1880
Schaffner, Johan	10, Jan.	43		39	Ellis Grove, IL	Plobsheim, Elsaß	29, Jan. 1883
Schaffner, Martin	21, June	34		231	Herman, MO	Sisak, Basel, Schweiz	18, July 1870
Schaffnit, Anna Margaretha	2, Apr.	19- 2m-10d		127	Perry, IL		19, Apr. 1880
Schaffnit, Martin Jakob	14, Feb.	79	Merz	223	Perry, TX	Bernsbach, Hessen	8, Apr. 1897
Schaffold, Franz	18, Aug.	42- 2m-24d		311	Jonia, MI	Hechingen, Hohenzollern	27, Sept 1880
Schäffsky, Philipp	3, Aug.	62		263	Oregon, MO	Celle, Hannover	18, Aug. 1879
Schafstall, Bernhardine	4, May	50	Pellmeyer	92	Rockford, IN	Lienen, Preußen	5, June 1856
Schafstall, Charles	4, Feb.	23		126	Seymour, IN	Jackson County, Indiana	23, Feb. 1893
Schafstall, Johan H.	13, Dec.	69		62	Cameron, MO	Hunteburg, Wittlage, Hannover	26, Jan. 1893
Schaible, Andreas	7, Jan.	80		7	Jeffersonville, NY	Warih, Nagold, Württemberg	28, Jan. 1886
Schaible, Barbara	20, Nov.			204	Troy, NY	Feldstadt, Münsingen, Württemberg	22, Dec. 1862
Schaible, Christian	16, Oct.			790	Troy, NY	Neuweiler, Württemberg	6, Dec. 1894
Schaible, G.F.		Inquiry		83	Marion, OH		23, May 1849
Schaible, John	5, Mar.	71		223	Freeport, MI	Insthal, Württemberg	6, Apr. 1899

Christliche Apologete Death Notices --- 1839 - 1899

Name of Deceased	Notice Date	Death Date	Age	Maiden Name	Page	Place of Death	Place of Birth
Schaible, Maria Katharine	5, July 1888	9, June	83- 2m-10d	Schweikhardt	430	Allegheny City, PA	Vittinsweiler, Freudenstadt, Württemberg
Schaible, Rosine	24, Mar. 1887	9, Mar.	68- 5m	Schreber	190	Philadelphia, PA	Aach, Freudenstadt, Württemberg
Schaibli, Elisabeth	8, Feb. 1875	12, Jan.	57- 5m-27d		47	Melrose, NY	Wibermuth, Preußen
Schait, Johan Conrad	4, July 1881	30, June	69- 4m-20d		215	Cannelton, IN	Kressebuch, Thurgau, Schweiz
Schäkel, Margaretha	20, Feb. 1890	2, Feb.	32- 9m-11d	Kernkamp	126	Alexandria, MN	St. Louis, Missouri
Schalk, Elisabeth	19, Aug. 1897	18, July	64		527	Bay City, MI	Baden
Schalk, Johan	30, Nov. 1874	14, Nov.	42- 4m- 3d		383	Charlestown, IN	Mansheim, Worms, Hessen-Darmstadt
Schalk, Johan Friedrich	4, Apr. 1870	26, Feb.	10- 9m		111	La Motte, MO	
Schalk, Johan Friedrich	31, Mar. 1873	14, Mar.			103	LaMotte, MO	
Schalker, Johan	25, Apr. 1881	9, Apr.	63		135	Weston, MO	Wülflingen, Zürich, Schweiz
Schall, Anton	4, Mar.1872	13, Feb.	66		79	Winnamac, IN	Hirschau, Rottenburg, Württemberg
Schaller, (Mrs)	2, June 1879	11, May	73-4m-11d	Hensel	175	Red Bud, IL	Haßloch, Rheinkreis Baiern
Schaller, Elisabeth	28, July 1887	1, July	46	Emerig	478	New Metamoras, OH	Bleichenbach, Hessen-Darmstadt
Schaller, Johan	1, June 1893	11, May	65		350	Salem, OR	Canton Bern, Schweiz
Schambach, Anna M.	7, Mar. 1889		60	Rene	158	Charlestown, IN	Rhein-Dürkheim bei Worms, Germany
Schambach, Jakob	3, Jan. 1881	5, Dec.	81		7	Tea Creek, IN	Nordheim bei Worms, Hessen-Darmstadt
Schambach, Valentin	24, May 1855	17, Mar.	78		84	Rockford, IN	Nordheim, Hessen-Darmstadt
Schambei, Angelika	15, Mar. 1894	24, Feb.	80	Stierlin	182	Cincinnati, OH	Schaffhausen, Schweiz
Schamber, Augusta	22, Oct. 1883	28, Sept	40- 1m-25d	Zugschwerd	343	Spraytown, IN	
Schamberger, Helena Barbara	15, Dec. 1884	17, Nov.	63	Leibold	7	Nashville, TN	Elpersheim, Mergentheim, Württemberg
Schambers, Johann	9, Apr. 1883	28, Mar.	77- 7m		119	Cincinnati, OH	
Schamburg, Anna	18, Apr. 1889	27, Mar.	25	Bieringer	254	Boonville, MO	
Schanbacher, Christina	19, Jan. 1885	31, Dec.	85		7	Troy, NY	Grunbach, Schorndorf, Württemberg
Schandelmeier, Eddy	4, Sept 1882	10, Aug.	15		287	Louisville, KY	Louisville, Jefferson County, Kentucky
Schandelmeier, Georg	25, Apr. 1895	26, Mar.	59		270	Louisville, KY	Weißweil, Kenzingen, Baden
Schandelmeyer, Georg	17, Feb. 1887		22		110	Louisville, KY	Louisville, Jefferson County, Kentucky
Schang, Anton	29, May 1865	8, Nov.	37		88	Philadelphia, PA	Ravensburg, Württemberg
Schank, Eucharius	8, Sept 1887	20, Aug.			574	Chicago, IL	Obrigheim, Mosbach, Baden
Schank, Heinrich	25, Feb. 1897	13, Jan.	80		127	Cannelton, IN	Soberntheim, Coblenz, Preußen
Schank, Margaretha	18, Oct. 1875	19, Sept	74	Leonhard	335	Louisville, KY	Zösen, Oldenburg
Schank, Philipp	6, Sept 1894	22, July	59		582	Scranton, PA	agielert, Preußen
Schanß, Adam	29, July 1897	7, July	58		479	Buffalo, NY	Eckweiler, RheinPreußen
Schantschi, Anna	31, Jan. 1881	11, Jan.	60	Bühlen	39	Madison, IN	Ringoldswyll, Bern, Schweiz
Schantz, Amalia Augusta	16, June 1892	26, May	56	Schuppan	382	Jersey City, NJ	Lomatsch, Sachsen
Schantz, Edward G.	25, June 1891	5, June	21- 2m- 2d		414	Jersey City, NJ	
Schantz, Katharina	15, Mar. 1880	24, Feb.	78	Sulz	87	Jersey City, NJ	Mössingen, Württemberg
Schanz, Barbara	15, Sept 1892	29, July	58	Pfeifer	590	New York City, NY	Schonberg, Hessen-Darmstadt
Schanz, Peter	4, Feb. 1878	25, Dec.	79		39	Jersey City, NJ	Mössingen, Rottenburg, Württemberg
Schanz, Philipp	27, Feb. 1851	2, Dec.	37		36		Sundheim bei Kehl, Baden
Schapbach, Kunigunde Margaret	5, Sept 1861	24, Aug.	61	Weber	144	Lawrenceburg, IN	Kleinhieb, Baiern
Schaper, Amalia	21, July 1898	23, June	67	Lutteroth	463		Bethlen, Gronau, Hannover
Schäper, Anna	11, Apr. 1895	7, Mar.	49	Ihtys	238	Warren, MO	Baltimore, Maryland
Schäper, Anna Maria	18, Nov. 1858	3, Nov.	63	Kiel	184	St. Charles, MO	Spenge, Kreis Herfort, Preußen
Schaper, Auguste	1, Nov. 1894	6, Oct.	26		710	Seguin, TX	Guadalupe County, Texas
Schaper, Ernst	26, Apr. 1880	5, Apr.	44	Merz	135	Fredericksburg, TX	Almstedt, Amt Binten, Hannover
Schaper, Friedrich	25, Oct. 1894	27, Sept	73		694	Yellow Creek, IL	Meiborsen, Hannover

Christliche Apologete Death Notices --- 1839 - 1899

Name of Deceased	Notice Date	Death Date	Age	Page	Maiden Name	Place of Death	Place of Birth
Schaper, Henriette	26, Apr. 1875	14, Mar.	38- 2m	135		Warren, MO	Amsterdam, Holland
Schaper, Herman	10, Nov. 1873	20, Sept	17	359		Warren, MO	
Schäper, Hermann H.	30, Mar. 1863	4, Mar.	78	52		Warrenton, MO	Spenge, Kreis Herford, Preußen
Schäper, Julia	3, Aug. 1868	11, July	40	247	Sandfos	Warren, MO	Holle, Amt Wollenberg, Hannover
Schäper, Louis	1, Jan. 1877	5, Dec.	22	7		Warren, MO	Lincoln County, Missouri
Schapira, Isaac	25, Sept 1890			622		Bridgeport, CT	Rußland
Schäppi, Adelheid	30, Apr. 1883	8, Apr.	61	143	Rinderknect	Chicago, IL	Zürich, Schweiz
Schärer, Eduard	12, June 1882	26, May	5	191		Tappan, NY	Ulster, Zürich, Schweiz
Schärer, Emil	5, Oct. 1893	28, Aug.	24-11m	638		North Vale, NJ	
Schärer, Regine Helene	27, May 1897	4, May	67	335	Wenerich	Hartford, CT	
Scharf, Adam	11, Aug. 1879	6, July	22	255		Newton, IA	Monroe, Iowa
Scharf, Michael Adam	7, June 1888	25, Apr.	66- 6m	366		Stryker, OH	Aichschieß, Eßlingen, Württemberg
Scharf, Philipp	5, Oct. 1863	7, Sept	12	160		New Albany, IN	Harrison County, Indiana
Scharff, Maria Augusta	31, Dec. 1896	29, Nov.	75	844	Feliche	Mt. Vernon, NY	Dunduff, Germany
Schärger, Eva Maria	3, Oct. 1881	11, Sept	79	319	Probst	Cleveland, OH	Wetteringen a. d. Tauber, Rothenburg, Baiern
Scharl, Louise Henriette	22, Oct. 1883	8, Oct.	36	343	Hunfeld	Dillsborough, IN	
Scharlach, Charlotte Marie	3, Sept 1891	11, Aug.	22	574		Perry, TX	Industry, Texas
Scharmann, Elisabeth	4, Dec. 1890	12, Nov.	67- -16d	782	Tomer	Clarington, OH	Eineutshausen, Hessen-Darmstadt
Scharmann, Juliana	17, Mar. 1879	28, Feb.	80-10m-22d	87	Kimbel	Clarington, OH	Hopfengarten, Hessen-Darmstadt
Scharnhorst, Katharina Dor.	1, Nov. 1869	27, Sept	75	351		German Creek, IA	Rodewald, Amt Neustadt, Hannover
Scharnikau, Johan	20, July 1899	22, June	65	463		Kramer, NE	Schornikau, Sachsen
Scharnke, Emilie	1, June 1899	18, Apr.	75	351	Häfer	Baraboo, WI	Fraustadt, Preußen
Scharnke, Ernestine	18, May 1874	24, Apr.	62- 4m-19d	159	Ulke	Baraboo, WI	Breslau, Schlesien, Preußen
Scharnke, Ernst	13, Jan. 1873	25, Dec.	60	15		Baraboo, WI	Lübchen, Schlesien
Scharnke, Friedrich Wilhelm	15, Nov. 1888	26, Sept	67- -31d	734		Ablemans, WI	Lübchen, Kölben, Buhrau, Breslau, Posen
Scharpf, Mary	14, Apr. 1892	24, Mar.	62	238		Champaign, IL	Hemlingsweiler, Aalen, Württemberg
Scharpf, Rosina	7, Oct. 1886	13, Sept	61	7	Schilpp	Springfield, IL	Württemberg
Scharr, Anna	1, Feb. 1875	12, Jan.	14	39		St. Croix, WI	Pepin, Wisconsin
Scharr, John Ulrich	30, Jan. 1890	10, Jan.	63	78		St. Paul, MN	Vaihingen, Stuttgart, Württemberg
Scharr, Rosine	17, Mar. 1898	20, Feb.	68- 3m-16d	175		Prescott, WI	Herzogweiler, Freudenstadt, Württemberg
Scharrer, Kunigunda	8, Sept 1879	5, Aug.	61	287	Bracher	Bradford, IN	Ellenbach, Baiern
Schärtel, John	28, June 1880	12, June	50-11m- 1d	207		Caseville, MI	Oberreichenbach, Herzogenaurach, Baiern
Schaßberger, Friederike	22, Nov. 1888	19, Oct.	36	750	Müller	Grand Rapids, MI	Ilsfeld, Besigheim, Württemberg
Schath, Margaretha	11, Feb. 1892	16, Jan.	79	94	Grob	Alton, IL	Freisteinhau, Hessen-Darmstadt
Schath, Peter	4, Sept 1890	13, Aug.	80- 8m- 3d	574	Valentin	Alton, IL	
Schatt, Emma	30, Nov. 1893	27, Sept	25	766		Menominee, MI	Eaton, Brown County, Wisconsin
Schatt, Maria	31, Jan. 1870		39	39		Marysville, CA	
Schatz, Eva	4, Feb. 1886	30, Dec.	76	7	Steinmüller	Pomeroy, OH	Mersch, Frankenthal, Rheinkreis Baiern
Schatz, Eva	3, Sept 1847	7, Apr.	11m-21d	143		Pomeroy, OH	
Schatz, Markus	25, May 1863	29, Mar.	38	84		Brunswick, MO	Wahlwies, Amt Stockach, Baden
Schatz, Martha	27, Oct. 1862		6	172		St. Joseph, MO	
Schaub, Anna Christina	8, Jan. 1883	7, Dec.	57	15	Grünewald	Honey Creek, WI	Hönebach, Rotenburg, Hessen
Schaub, Caspar	21, July 1887	15, June	55	462			Hühnebach, Rothenberg, Kurhessen
Schaub, Catharina	26, Nov. 1857	22, Oct.	24	192	Schwarz	East Troy, WI	Hünebach, Kurhessen
Schaub, Catharina Barbara	14, June 1875	11, May	76- 5m-23d	191	Bintz	Pittsfield, IL	Rumbach, Rheinkreis Baiern
Schaub, Clara Esther	26, Aug. 1897	10, Aug.	14	543		Colesburg, IA	Galena, Illinois

Christliche Apologete Death Notices --- 1839 - 1899

Name of Deceased	Notice Date	Death Date	Age	Page	Maiden Name	Place of Death	Place of Birth
Schaub, D.H.	22, Mar. 1888	19, Feb.	52	190		Miltonsburg, OH	Monroe County, Ohio
Schaub, David	24, Mar. 1884	9, Mar.	82	7		Pittsfield, IL	Rumbach, Rheinkreis Baiern
Schaub, El.	3, Nov. 1879	11, Oct.	78	351		Matamoras, OH	Rothweil, Baiern
Schaub, Elisabeth	20, July 1893	29, June	54	462	Dauber	Honey Creek, WI	Höhnebach, Rothenburg, Kurhessen
Schaub, Georg Jakob	11, Jan. 1864	8, Dec.	91	8		Washington, OH	Rumbach, Rheinkreis Baiern
Schaub, Hannah Sophia	5, May 1887	19, Apr.	89	286	Miller	Iowa City, IA	Ahfeld, Hannover
Schaub, Heinrich	27, Nov. 1876	22, Sept	60	383		Wabasha, MN	Kurhessen
Schaub, Heinrich Otto	24, Nov. 1873	4, Nov.	24	375		East Troy, WI	Höhnebach, Kurhessen
Schaub, Jacob	24, Aug. 1854	13, Aug.		136		Wheeling, VA	Rombach, Baiern
Schaub, Johan	7, Dec. 1893	16, Nov.	69	782		East Troy, WI	Höhnebach, Rothenburg, Hessen
Schaub, John Michael	12, May 1873	17, Apr.	70	151		Bonn, OH	Rumbach, Zweibrücken, Rheinkreis Baiern
Schaub, Karolina	26, Nov. 1896	3, Nov.	32	766	Schaal	LaCrosse, WI	Zuffenllausen, Württemberg
Schaub, Katharina Elisabeth	20, Dec. 1880			407	Heck		
Schaub, Maria Elisabeth	29, Oct. 1891	3, Oct.	79- 1m-21d	702	Stoehr	New Metamoras, OH	Rumbach, Rheinkreis Baiern
Schaub, Philipp Jakob	3, June 1886	9, May	63	7		Stitzer, WI	Holzappel, Nassau
Schaub, Rosena	15, Mar. 1888	16, Feb.	20	174		Galena, IL	
Schaub, Rosette	11, May 1893	13, Apr.	26	302		East Troy, WI	Spring Prairie, Walworth County, Wisconsin
Schaub, Rosina	22, Mar. 1875	12, Feb.	48- 9m- 8d	95	Gatz	Altamont, IL	Canton Baselland, Sitzach, Schweiz
Schauberger, Carolina	2, Feb. 1874	6, Jan.	32	39	Schelke	Madison, IN	Liebenau, Kurhessen
Schauberger, Maria Sophia	27, Sept 1888	2, Aug.	17	622		Oil Creek, IN	Perry County, Indiana
Schäuble, Samuel	14, Sept 1863	20, July	28	148		Chicago, IL	
Schaud, Carl	15, Aug. 1850	2, Aug.	32	132		Columbus, OH	Baden
Schauer, Mathilde Wilhelmine	14, June 1888	20, May	38	382	Schmidt	Arlington, MN	Klein-Wiesnöske, Flatow, Preußen
Schaumburg, Johan Michael	13, July 1899	24, May	77	447		Bison, KS	Hessen-Kassel
Schaumel, Anna Margaretha	30, Apr. 1891	1, Apr.	89	286	Roß	Batesville, IN	Müstelgau, Oberfranken, Baiern
Schauner, John	20, Aug. 1883	1, Aug.	75- 5m-15d	271		Wichita, KS	Nüsen, Flandern, Zeeland, Holland
Schaup, Anna Katharina	26, Mar. 1896	2, Mar.	76	206	Feld	Edon, OH	Altmerschen, Meltzungen, Preußen
Schaup, John	21, Nov. 1864		20- 5m-21d	188		Edgerton, OH	
Schaup, Peter	17, May 1894	25, Apr.	76	326		Edon, OH	
Schaupp, Gottlob	19, May 1891	24, Feb.	42- 7m-12d	190		Santa Rosa, CA	Altenkirchen, Wetzlar, Koblenz, Preußen
Schaupp, Maria Anna	4, Nov. 1858	13, Oct.	63-10m-15d	176		Greenville, OH	Reutlingen, Württemberg
Schawe, Maria	26, Feb. 1883	5, Feb.	36	71	Horstmann	St. Louis, MO	Neuhausen an der Ems, Urach, Württemberg
Schawener, Elisabeth	17, Oct. 1864	21, Sept	50- 1m- 6d	168		Evansville, IN	Ladbergen, Preußen
Schawner, Susanna	6, Feb. 1862	25, Jan.	54	24		Evansville, IN	Eiland gues, Kapelle, Seeland, Holland
Schearer, Margaretha	26, Feb. 1891	24, Jan.	56	142	Waltz	Crown Point, IN	Mainz, Hessen
Scheble, Casper	17, May 1888	21, Apr.	63	318		Moweaqua, IL	Dischingen, Neresheim, Württemberg
Scheck, Dorothea	30, Jan. 1882	7, Jan.	68- 6m	39	Hermann	Glencoe, MN	Bützow, Mecklenburg-Schwerin
Scheck, John	13, Apr. 1885	13, Mar.	14- 1m	7		Evansville, IN	
Scheck, Margaretha	13, Apr. 1899	22, Feb.	65	239	Schäffer	Evansville, IN	Lohra, Kurhessen
Scheel, (Mr)	28, June 1860	28, Apr.	39	104		Monterey, WI	Dölitz, Pieritz, Preußen
Scheel, August F. C.	27, June 1895	26, May	66	414		St. Paul, MN	Crammunsdorf, Pommern
Scheel, Juliana Magdalena	25, Sept 1876	11, Sept	31- 5m- 5d	311	Brodrecht	Galena, IL	Wörstadt, Kreis Alzey, Hessen
Scheel, Karl	28, Sept 1893	4, Sept	79	622		Galena, IL	Daaden, Preußen
Scheel, Theresa	6, Oct. 1887	19, Sept	63	638	Ammann	Galena, IL	Rißstissen, Württemberg
Scheele, Anna Philippine	26, Mar. 1891	26, Feb.	67	206	Dresing	St. Louis, MO	Essen, Hannover
Scheele, Joh.	21, July 1848		Inquiry	119		Cincinnati, OH	Hannover

Christliche Apologete Death Notices --- 1839 - 1899

Name of Deceased	Notice Date	Death Date	Age	Page	Maiden Name	Place of Death	Place of Birth
Scheelhorn, Maria	13, Nov. 1876	17, Oct.	23	367	Huber	Mt. Vernon, IN	Posey County, Indiana
Scheer, Conrad	16, Dec. 1878	27, Nov.	60- 8m- 8d	399		Crow River, MN	Reichenbach bei Wetzburg, Baiern
Scheer, Maria	21, May 1877	20, Apr.	26	166	Kölling	Warren, MO	Lincoln County, Missouri
Scheer, Maria	24, Jan. 1850	14, Nov.		16		Marthasville, MO	
Scheerbaum, Johan Friedrich	25, Dec. 1876	12, Nov.		413		Mt. Vernon, IN	Amt Wittlage, Hannover
Scheerer, Anton Herman	28, Apr. 1898	4, Apr.	11	271		Grand Ridge, IL	Farm Ridge, Illinois
Scheerer, Heinrich A.	8, May 1876	16, Apr.	42	151		Grand Rapids, MI	Karlsruhe, Baden
Scheffel, Johan Heinrich August	15, Dec. 1898	2, Dec.	64	799		Louisville, KY	Flarchheim, Langensalza, Erfurt, Preußen
Scheffler, Hulda	29, Aug.1895	10, Aug.	42	558		Los Angeles, CA	Stackel, Germany
Scheffler, Pauline	24, Aug. 1885	27, June	53	7	Kiefer		Neckars-Ulm, Württemberg
Schehrer, Carolina	5, Dec. 1861	10, Nov.	15- 9m- 4d	196		Toledo, OH	
Schehrer, Elisabeth	4, Jan. 1875	20, Dec.	51- 1m-26d	7	VonGunten	Toledo, OH	Sigrisweil, Thun, Bern, Schweiz
Scheibe, Anna	28, Apr. 1887	6, Apr.	71- 7m	270	Möller	Grand Island, NE	Voightshagen, Pommern
Scheibe, Dorothea	20, Nov. 1890	30, Oct.	41- -27d	750	Pagel	Burlington, WI	Groß-Bankow, Mecklenburg-Schwerin
Scheibe, John	16, May 1895	23, Apr.	78	318		Grand Island, NE	Voigshagen, Pommern
Scheibe, Lena	7, Oct. 1886	17, Sept	15- 6m	7		West Point, NE	
Scheibel, Emilie	22, Nov. 1894	26, Oct.	50	758	Funke	Paterson, NJ	Waldbröll, Köln, Preußen
Scheibele, Catharina An.	10, Feb. 1887	24, Jan.	77	94		Marietta, OH	Seifertshausen, Rodenburg, Hessen-Kassel
Scheible, Anna Maria	4, Dec. 1865	17, Nov.	62- 6m	196		Washington, OH	Goldekenten, Liestal, Basel, Schweiz
Scheible, Christine	19, Feb. 1883	12, Jan.	88- -21d	63		Derinda, IL	
Scheible, Louise	10, Feb. 1873	17, Jan.	61- 2m-27d	47	Frank	Callicoon, NY	Calmbach, Neuenbürg, Württemberg
Scheible, Martin	4, Apr. 1889	11, Mar.	89	222		Marietta, OH	Kanton Bern , Schweiz
Scheible, Susanne	16, Sept 1878	17, Aug.	21- 2m-17d	295		New Knoxville, OH	Allen County, Ohio
Scheibner, Barbara	11, Sept 1865		41	148		Indianapolis, IN	Obernbreit, Baiern
Scheibner, Caspar	20, Sept 1880	12, Aug.	66- 2m- 9d	303		Ripley, OH	
Scheibner, Gottlieb	6, Feb. 1882	13, Jan.	62	47		Indianapolis, IN	
Scheid, Bertha	8, Oct. 1883	30, Aug.	22- 1m-13d	327	Schmidt	Fillmore, WI	Großfilber, Pommern
Scheider, Karoline	6, Apr. 1899	9, Mar.	77	223	Braatz	Lena, IL	Pommern
Scheider, Lena	2, Nov. 1899	4, Oct.	42	703	Foß	Lena, IL	
Scheidt, Adam	21, Sept 1874	1, Sept	28	303		Cincinnati, OH	Volmersweiler, Rheinpfalz Baiern
Scheidt, Herman	27, Jan. 1887	24, Dec.	34	62		St. Louis, MO	St. Louis, Missouri
Scheidt, Katharina Margartha	19, Oct. 1893	26, Sept		670	Leuthäuser	Cincinnati, OH	Biebesheim, Hessen-Darmstadt
Scheidt, Louisa	21, Jan. 1884	30, Dec.	64	7	Hensel	Cincinnati, OH	
Scheidt, Maria Anna	13, Oct. 1873	25, Sept	53	327	Reihn	Cincinnati, OH	Bibbigheim, Rheinpfalz Baiern
Scheifele, Dorothea	10, July 1856	26, June	54- 4m	112		Chicago, IL	Blaubeuren, Württemberg
Scheifele, Gottlieb Friedrich	6, July 1893	13, June		430		Philadelphia, PA	Plüderhausen, Welzheim, Württemberg
Scheiffele, Catharina	1, Jan. 1891	3, Dec.	61	14		Chicago, IL	Chicago, Cook County, Illinois
Scheiffele, Heinrich	17, Nov. 1887	24, Oct.	26	734		Chicago, IL	Blankenbach, Rodenburg, Hessen
Schein, Conrad	4, Sept 1882	7, Aug.	39- 3m-22d	287		Oshkosh, WI	Blankenbach, Reutershausen, Hessen
Schein, Cornelius	2, May 1895	5, Apr.		286		Ripon, WI	Blankenbach, Kurhessen
Schein, Dorothea	4, Nov. 1867	9, Oct.	64- 8m-28d	350		East Troy, WI	Romanshorn, Kreßibuch, Thurgau, Schweiz
Scheit, Elisabeth	14, Oct. 1872	8, Sept	18-10m-10d	335	Knecht	Louisville, KY	Marion County, Ohio
Scheiveley, Philippine	11, Oct. 1880	24, Sept		327		New Knoxville, OH	Licking County, Ohio
Scheively, Susanna Elisabeth	24, Nov. 1879	2, Nov.	18-10m- 4d	375	Gräßle	New Knoxville, OH	Portsmouth, Scioto County, Ohio
Schela, John Wilhelm	16, Mar. 1899	9, Feb.	25	175		Portsmouth, OH	Liebau, Sachsen-Meiningen
Schelhorn, Anna Maria	12, May 1884	27, Apr.	77	7		Marrs, IN	

Christliche Apologete Death Notices --- 1839 - 1899

Name of Deceased	Notice Date	Death Date	Age	Page	Maiden Name	Place of Death	Place of Birth
Schelhorn, Eleonora M.	5, Nov. 1883	9, Oct.	58	359	Schierbaum	Mt. Vernon, IN	Linde Haide, Barkhausen, Wittenberg, Hannover
Schelhorn, Katharina	3, Sept 1896	14, Aug.	27	575		Mt. Vernon, IN	Mt. Vernon, Indiana
Schelke, Maria Sophia	23, Apr. 1896	31, Mar.	83	270	Austermuhler	Madison, IN	Liebenau, Kurhessen
Schell, Anna Barbara	7, Jan. 1897	17, Dec.	50	15	Frey	Chicago, IL	Reilingen, Schwezingen, Baden
Schell, Catharina	9, Aug. 1860	9, July	61	128		Chicago, IL	Driedorf, Nassau
Schell, Christiane	26, Oct. 1854	27, Aug.	27	172	Scharpf	Lafayette, IN	Schlierbach, Göppingen, Württemberg
Schell, Francisca	12, Apr. 1880	30, Mar.	77	119		Boston, MA	Jelingen, Baden
Schell, Georg Michael	9, Mar. 1868	5, Feb.	69-11m- 5d	79		Roxbury, MA	
Schell, Louis	15, Apr. 1878	13, Mar.	46	119		Schumway, IL	Höpfingen, Walldürn, Baden
Schellang, Elisabeth	6, July 1899	15, June	76- 4m	431	Hollinger	New Orleans, LA	Amweiler, Rheinpfalz Baiern
Scheller, Maria Rosina	14, Aug. 1890	23, July	43- 2m-15d	526	Hellwig	Mt. Olive, IL	Kainsdorf bei Zwickau, Sachsen
Schellhaas, Eva	26, Apr. 1880	9, Mar.	60- 5m- 2d	135	Reinmüller	Kendallville, IN	Kadus, Hersfeld, Kurhessen
Schellhaas, Georg	17, Jan. 1876	1, Jan.	68	23		Kendallville, IN	Nentershausen, Rotenburg, Kurhessen
Schellhardt, Lizzie	1, Mar. 1875	4, Jan.	71	71	Toggenburger	Des Moines, IA	
Schellhase, Georg	20, Jan. 1898	4, Jan.	74	47		Allegheny, PA	Reichensachsen, Kurhessen
Schellhase, Karl	22, Nov. 1860	9, Nov.	71	188		Wheeling, VA	Reichensachsen, Kurhessen
Schellhorn, Georg	11, Sept 1871	5, Aug.	62- 9m- 3d	295		Marrs, IN	Verdamberg, Neustadt, Coburg, Baiern
Schelling, Barbara	18, Mar. 1897	15, Feb.	80- -10d	175		San Francisco, CA	Schluchtern, Württemberg
Schelling, Katharina	23, Oct. 1882	5, Oct.	55	343		New York City, NY	Oberamt Maulbronn, Württemberg
Schelling, Wilhelm	1, May 1890	4, Apr.	85	286		Redfield, SD	Hohenzollern-Sigmaringen, Württemberg
Schellinger, Diosco	28, Aug. 1882	10, Aug.	51	279		Sheboygan, WI	Ballwin, Missouri
Schelp, Friedrich	3, Dec. 1896	31, Oct.	36	782		St. Louis, MO	Hagen bei Pyrmont, Waldeck
Schelp, Maria	22, Nov. 1888	4, Nov.	63- 1m- 9d	750	Kleinsorge	Ballwin, MO	Ballwin, Missouri
Schelp, Mathilde	11, Aug. 1898	23, July	44	511		Ballwin, MO	
Schelper, Charles Theodor	30, July 1857	10, June	4- 1m-22d	124		Terre Haute, IN	
Schelper, Emilie	9, May 1895	10, Apr.	88	302		Chicago, IL	
Schembera, Sophia	21, May 1896	20, Apr.	34	334	Müller	Sun Prairie, WI	Windsor, Dane County, Wisconsin
Schembora, Florian	9, May 1895	20, Apr.	85	302		Sun Prairie, WI	Schönwald, Olmütz, Mähren, Oesterreich
Schemet, Carolina	26, July 1894	24, June	66	486	Stahl	Evansville, IN	Lomersheim, Vaihingen, Württemberg
Schemet, Louis	18, Apr. 1889	29, Mar.	66- 2m- 6d	254		Evansville, IN	Perouse, Leonberg, Württemberg
Schemet, Louisa	5, Nov. 1883	20, Sept	20	359		Evansville, IN	Evansville, Indiana
Schemgber, Katharina Maria	27, Nov. 1856	10, Oct.	47	192	Niehaus	Moscow, OH	Neuenkirchen, Melle, Gröneberg, Preußen
Schemp, Barbara	5, Mar. 1891	12, Feb.	15	158		Greenfield, MA	Irgendorf, Bonndorf, Baden
Schemp, Johan Michael	29, May 1865	4, May	26	88		Philadelphia, PA	Ochsenwann, Württemberg
Schemp, Margaretha	23, Aug. 1875	13, June	75- 7m- 8d	271		Philadelphia, PA	
Schenck, Christina	24, Aug. 1893	10, July	33	542	Winkler	New York City, NY	Mönzheim, Leonberg, Württemberg
Schendel, Augusta	24, Mar. 1879	27, Feb.	20	95		Minneapolis, MN	Greenwood, Hennepin County, Minnesota
Schendel, Christoph	18, Apr. 1895	27, Mar.	82	254		Greenwood, MN	Schlonawo, Posen
Schendel, Emilie Augusta Louisa	15, Sept 1887	18, Aug.	25	590	Zacho	Renville, MN	Greifenberg, Stettin, Pommern
Schenk , Lizzie	11, Feb. 1892	28, Dec.	31	94	Amrheim	Milwaukee, WI	Baltimore, Maryland
Schenk, (Mrs)	8, Nov. 1894	5, Oct.	93	726		Beaver Dam, WI	Stolzenberg bei Landsberg, Pommern
Schenk, Anna	7, Apr. 1862	10, Feb.	19	56	Schenk	Columbus, OH	Urwissen, Zürich, Schweiz
Schenk, Anna K.	5, Jan. 1874	16, Nov.	66-11m	7		Flint Creek, IA	Sondelfingen, Urach, Württemberg
Schenk, Anna Maria	17, Feb. 1879	29, Jan.	54	55	Naab	Chicago, IL	Schwabsburg, Oppenheim, Hessen
Schenk, Casper	22, Oct. 1896	20, Sept	70- 1m	687		Lincoln, NE	
Schenk, Eva Maria	9, June 1873	26, May	27	183	Wagner	Columbus, OH	Württemberg

Christliche Apologete Death Notices --- 1839 - 1899

Name of Deceased	Notice Date	Death Date	Age	Page	Maiden Name	Place of Death	Place of Birth
Schenk, Florentine	3, Jan. 1895	6, Dec.		14	Bold	Beatrice, NE	West Preußen
Schenk, Jakob	6, Dec. 1880	1, Nov.	78- 2m-10d	391		Columbus, OH	Uhwiesen, Zürich, Schweiz
Schenk, Jakob	24, Feb. 1873	1, Feb.	31- 1m-21d	63		Columbus, OH	Uhwiesen, Zürich, Schweiz
Schenk, Maria	27, June 1895	4, May	79	414	Meister	Columbus, OH	Uhwiesen, Zürich, Schweiz
Schenk, Sophia	26, May 1887	28, Apr.	39	334	Fey	Milwaukee, WI	Simmern, Coblenz, Germany
Schenke, Anna K.G.	4, Mar. 1886	16, Feb.	89- 1m	7	Krümpel	Colesburg, IA	Talge, Bippen, Fürstenau, Hannover
Schenke, Bernhard	8, May 1876	18, Apr.	65	151		Colesburg, IA	Setrup, Amt Fürstenau, Hannover
Schenke, Elisabeth	28, Jan. 1892	7, Jan.	72	62		Colesburg, IA	Settrup, Fürstenau, Hannover
Schenkel, (Mrs)	27, Nov. 1882	29, Sept	71- 1m-15d	383		San Francisco, CA	Mecklenburg-Schwerin
Schennerlein, Johan Gottlob	4, Aug. 1879	16, July	44	247		Wheeling, WV	Dörtendorf, Sachsen-Weimar
Schennerlein, Maria	28, Jan. 1884		25	7	Kaltenbach	Wheeling, WV	Monroe County, Ohio
Schepfer, Anna	2, Nov. 1893	29, Sept	39	702	Steinmann	Paterson, NJ	NiederUrnen, Schweiz
Schepmann, Heinrich	28, Jan. 1867	18, Nov.	19	30		Seymour, IN	Arenshort, Hannover
Scheppelmann, Friedrich	30, Jan. 1871	31, Dec.	6- 1m	39		Fairbury, IL	
Scheppli, Anna Marie	16, May 1895	12, Apr.	73	318		Colesburg, IA	Baden
Scherb, Georg	11, Feb. 1892	11, Jan.	83- 1m-29d	94		Brazil, IN	Kleinhabersdorf, Ausbach, Rezat, Baiern
Scherb, Katharina Elisabeth	27, Jan. 1887	13, Jan.	55	62	Heck	Greenville, OH	Haßloch, RheinPfalz Baiern
Scherb, Philipp Peter	29, Nov. 1880	30, Oct.	64- 1m- 2d	383		Richmond, IN	Gomersheim, RheinPfalz Baiern
Scherer, Anna Margaretha	6, Oct. 1892	11, Sept	56	638	Reitz	Santa Rosa, CA	Hessen
Scherer, Christina	22, Dec. 1887	7, Dec.	77	814		Lafayette, IN	Fürnsaal, Sulz, Württemberg
Scherer, Gertrude	14, Sept 1885	23, Aug.	70	7	Wagner	Rock Island, IL	Osthofen, Hessen-Darmstadt
Scherer, Jacob	30, July 1877	25, June	84-10m-16d	247		Galion, OH	Oberamt Reutlingen, Württemberg
Scherer, Jakob	22, Dec. 1853	7, Oct.	42	204		Washington Co, OH	Dittweiler bei Humburg, Rheinkreis Baiern
Scherer, Joseph	18, Jan. 1864	9, Dec.	48	12		St. Louis, MO	Collmar, Elsaß
Scherer, Katharina	28, July 1848	13, May	39	123		Marietta, OH	Ohmbach, Rheinkreis Baiern
Scherer, Katharina	7, July 1848	13, May	39	112		Marietta, OH	Linken, Rheinkreis Baiern
Scherer, Maria	17, Jan. 1876	27, Dec.	34	23	Hunven	Galion, OH	Lycoming County, Pennsylvania
Scherf, Christian Wilhelm	5, Apr. 1888	18, Mar.	70	222		Baraboo, WI	Lobenstein, Reuß
Scherf, Christine	5, Oct. 1899	4, Sept	50	639	Grosch	Elizabeth, NJ	Württemberg
Scherf, Henriette	24, Mar. 1887		72	190	Becher	Columbus, OH	Oberheimsdorf, Sachsen
Scherf, Louise Margarethe	5, Nov. 1896	12, Oct.	45	719	Schwarz	Elizabeth, NJ	Elizabeth, New Jersey
Scherff, Heinrich	7, Jan. 1892	15, Dec.	74- 8m-15d	14		Brooklyn, NY	Oberfülzen, Rheinkreis Baiern
Scherff, Regina	30, Jan. 1896	21, Dec.	78	78	Dackermann	Brooklyn, NY	Speyer, Rheinpfalz Baiern
Scherer, Karl	6, Mar. 1882	13, Feb.	16	79		Decatur, IL	
Schermann, Klara Louise C.	28, Jan. 1892	30, Dec.	22	62	Dreseler	Batesville, IN	Schrödinghausen, Oldendorf, Westphalen
Schemikau, Anna Maria	15, Mar. 1880	22, Feb.	16- 6m-13d	86		Defiance, OH	
Scherpf, Emilie L.	19, Apr. 1888	13, Feb.	29	254	Seifert	Brooklyn, NY	New York City, New York
Scherr, Georg	20, Feb. 1862	17, Jan.	58	32		Warren, MO	Ibbenbüren, Tecklenburg, Preußen
Scherrer, Frank	8, Apr. 1897		72	223		Santa Rosa, CA	Unterhegenthal, Aargau, Schweiz
Scherrer, Philipp	27, Nov. 1882	11, Nov.	69- 5m	383		Rock Island, IL	Osthofen, Rheinpfalz Baiern
Scherringhausen, Heinrich	6, Dec. 1888	29, Oct.	56-10m- 4d	782		Arlington Heights, IL	Stamke, Burke, Hannover
Schertz, Helena	5, Feb. 1891	13, Jan.	40	94	Seiler	Cibolo, TX	Guadalupe County, Texas
Schertzer, Johan Balthasar	23, Sept 1886	29, Aug.	64	7		Columbus, OH	Dückendorf, Burghaßler, Baiern
Scherzer, Anna Katharina	22, Sept 1879	26, Aug.	44	303	Gertz	Wyandotte, KS	Bischofsheim, Oberbach, Baiern
Scherzer, Elisabeth	20, Oct. 1898	7, Sept	77	671	Emrich	Columbus, OH	Mankenheim, Rheinpfalz Baiern
Scherzinger, Mathias	24, Nov. 1887	26, Oct.	66	750		Santa Claus, IN	Hinterstraß-Märgen, Freiburg, Baden

Christliche Apologete Death Notices --- 1839 - 1899

Name of Deceased	Notice Date	Death Date	Age	Page	Maiden Name	Place of Death	Place of Birth
Schessow, Johan	26, Apr. 1888	3, Apr.	89	270		Lyona, KS	Kollmann bei Greiffenberg, Hinterpommern
Scheu, Georg	3, Aug. 1885	18, July	32	7		Cincinnati, OH	Cincinnati, Hamilton County, Ohio
Scheu, Ludwig	26, June 1882	13, June	48	207		Louisville, KY	Lautern, Rheinkreis Baiern
Scheu, Philippine	6, Feb. 1896	7, Jan.	68	94	Schenkel	Louisville, KY	Rodsellberg, Rheinpfalz Baiern
Scheuer, Anna Maria Theresia	22, May 1876	4, May	49	167	Molock	Etna, MO	Obergimpen, Baden
Scheuerman, Anna Maria	25, Aug. 1884	29, July	57	7		Ironton, OH	Oppau, Frankenthal, Rheinkreis Baiern
Scheuermann, (boy)	2, Nov. 1863	7, Oct.	7	176		Newport, MI	
Scheuermann, (Mr)	4, June 1877	21, May	71	183		Fairbault, MN	Winweiler bei Kaiserslautern, Baiern
Scheuermann, Anna Maria	25, Nov. 1872	28, Oct.	75- 1m-20d	383		Portsmouth, OH	Oppau, Frankenthal, Rheinkreis Baiern
Scheuermann, Anton	31, Mar. 1853	22, Feb.	28	52		Mt. Vernon, IN	
Scheuermann, Michal	11, Nov. 1878	24, Oct.	86- 6m	359		Portsmouth, OH	Oppau, Rheinkreis Baiern
Scheuermann, Peter	28, May 1896	3, May	73	350		Ironton, OH	Oppau, Baiern
Scheuermann, Philippine	13, Dec. 1860	20, Nov.	26- 6m	200		Terre Haute, IN	Katzebach in der Pfalz, Baiern
Scheufler, Justus	19, July 1894	18, June	73	470		Allegheny, PA	Morschen, Spengenberg, Kurhessen
Scheufler, Minna	2, Mar. 1893	4, Feb.	17	142		Cleveland, OH	
Scheur, Johannes	2, Feb. 1860	1, Jan.	49	20		Mt. Vernon, IN	Dudenhofen, Hessen-Darmstadt
Scheurer, Georg	23, Mar. 1899	1, Mar.	73	191		Bloomington, IL	Hasloch, Baiern
Scheurer, Katharina	13, Nov. 1882	27, Oct.	77- 2m-10d	367		Mt. Vernon, NY	
Schewe, Amilie Friederika	5, Aug. 1897	6, July	68	495	Zimmermann	Ripon, WI	Pammin bei Arnswalde, Neumark
Schewe, Friedrich W.	18, Mar. 1886	25, Feb.	39	7		St. Louis, MO	Löhne, Herford, Preußen
Schewe, Louise	20, Feb. 1896	2, Feb.	81	126	Stiegemann	St. Louis, MO	Herford, Hannover
Schewe, Marie	11, Apr. 1889	10, Mar.	33	238	Schneider	Sleepy Eye, MN	Buffalo, New York
Schewe, Wilhelm	14, Jan. 1867	5, Dec.	51	14		St. Louis, MO	Zweigel, Preußen
Scheydt, Nanie	11, Dec. 1890	16, Sept	15	798		Terre Haute, IN	Derendingen, Württemberg
Scheytt, Johan Gottfried	5, Nov. 1883	1, Oct.	37	359		Terre Haute, IN	Oberderdingen, Württemberg
Schickler, Adam	26, Sept 1895	7, Sept	68	622		Brighton, IL	Notzingen, Württemberg
Schickler, Theresa	25, Dec. 1882	25, Nov.	57	415		Fosterburg, IL	Bahde, Oldenburg
Schieber, Christine	30, May 1895	17, May	68	350	Heckenleiwle	Bucyrus, OH	Columbiana County, Ohio
Schieber, Christoph	10, Jan. 1889	21, Dec.	68- 9m-17d	30		Bucyrus, OH	Steinbach, Backnang, Württemberg
Schieber, Gottlieb	3, July 1865	18, June	41- 9m- 8d	108		Bucyrus, OH	
Schieber, Jakob	6, Nov. 1882	15, Sept	60	359		Peyton, TX	Württemberg
Schieber, John Fr.	3, Sept 1896	21, July	65	575		Mt. Vernon, IN	Fornsbach, Bachnang, Württemberg
Schieber, Lydia	10, Mar. 1898	11, Feb.	78	159	Herschberger	Bucyrus, OH	Lancaster County, Pennsylvania
Schieber, Magdalena	10, Oct. 1889	25, Sept	90- 5m- 3d	654		Bucyrus, OH	Oberamt Backnang, Württemberg
Schieber, Sarah Jane	5, Dec. 1881	17, Nov.	24- -10d	391		Bucyrus, OH	
Schieber, Wilhelm	23, Jan. 1875	4, Jan.	14	31		Mt. Vernon, IN	
Schiebold, Josephine	10, Apr. 1871	20, Mar.	55	119		Toledo, OH	
Schieck, Adam	16, Apr. 1891	31, Mar.	77- 2m-10d	254		Seguin, TX	Ouwal, Böhmen
Schieck, Johanne Elisabeth	21, Jan. 1897	30, Dec.	85	47	Schütze	Seguin, TX	Sebach, Sachsen-Meiningen
Schied, Maria Anna	26, Mar. 1896	19, Dec.	43	206	Tienken	New York City, NY	Bad Flensburg, Schlesien
Schieding, Margaretha E.	30, Nov. 1885	5, Nov.	82	7		Turners Falls, MA	New York City, New York
Schiefelbein, Albertine	11, Mar. 1897	21, Feb.	79	159	Lübke	Bristol, WI	Steinbach, Sachsen-Meiningen
Schiefelbein, Christian	25, Aug. 1898	7, Aug.	73	543		Panola, MN	Meltsow, Treptow, Germany
Schiefelbein, Johanne	21, Apr. 1892	2, Apr.	61	254	Pauke	Stillwater, MN	Jakobsdorf, Pommern
Schiefelbein, John Michael	3, Oct. 1895	6, Sept	53	638		Lansing, IA	Schönfeld , Pommern; Lebehnke, Pommern
Schiefer, Rosine	18, Jan. 1864	11, Nov.	64- 7m	12	Krauter	Brokensword, OH	Oeschelbronn, Waiblingen, Württemberg

Christliche Apologete Death Notices --- 1839 - 1899

Name of Deceased	Notice Date	Death Date	Age	Maiden Name	Page	Place of Death	Place of Birth
Schiel, Heinrich	13, July 1899	20, June	73	Jäger	447	Nashville, TN	Bondenbach, Birkenfeld, Germany
Schiel, Paulina	25, Dec. 1890	30, Nov.	60- 1m-29d	Reidt	830	Nashville, TN	Sachsen-Altenburg
Schiela, Christina	18, Aug. 1898	1, Aug.	70		527	Mt. Vernon, IN	Neukirchen, Kurhessen
Schiela, Karl	6, Dec. 1880	20, Nov.	59- 7m		391	Mt. Vernon, IN	Oberliederbach, Nassau
Schied, Conrad	11, Nov. 1858	18, Oct.	39		180	Hanging Rock, OH	Udenhausen, Hofgeismar, Kurhessen
Schiele, Mary	8, Mar. 1869	18, Feb.	25	Dreßler	79	Portsmouth, OH	Pomeroy, Ohio
Schier, Friedrich	1, Dec. 1892	12, Oct.	66		766	Wellsville, NY	Meinerse, Hannover
Schier, Maria Louise	1, Oct. 1883	9, Sept	52- 1m-23d		319	Angelica, NY	
Schierbaum, Edwin	18, Dec. 1890	6, Oct.	15- 9m		814	Santa Claus, IN	Spencer County, Indiana
Schierbaum, Friedrich Wilhelm	14, Oct. 1886	27, Sept	32		7	Santa Claus, IN	Spencer County, Indiana
Schierbaum, Georg W.	14, July 1898	20, June	42		447	New Melle, MO	New Melle, Missouri
Schierbaum, Josephine	18, May 1885	19, Apr.	24- 9m-21d	Retzel	7	Santa Claus, IN	
Schierbaum, Katharina	1, Oct. 1883	9, Sept	38	Günther	319	Santa Claus, IN	Dearborn County, Indiana
Schierenberg, Conrad	15, Feb. 1849		Inquiry		27	Warrentown, MO	
Schierling, Maria	17, Jan. 1895	1, Jan.	35	Ulrich	46	Indianapolis, IN	Columbus, Bartholomew County, Indiana
Schierling, Nicholaus	5, Jan. 1899	15, Dec.	69		15	Indianapolis, IN	Haßfurt, Baiern
Schießer, Katharina	19, Dec. 1889	24, Nov.	42	Zimmermann	814	Ahnapee, WI	Canton Glarus, Schweiz
Schiewe, Ludolph	29, Sept 1898	10, Sept	13		623	Portland, OR	Wenglewer-Hauland, Russisch-Polen
Schiff, Anna Maria	28, Apr. 1879	11, Apr.	55	Meier	135	Champaign, IL	Schmiedheim, Ettenheim, Baden
Schiff, Anna Maria	2, June 1879	11, Apr.	55	Meier	175	Champaign, IL	Schmieheim, Ettenheim, Baden
Schiffmann, Eva	23, June 1879	30, May	68	Schmidt	199	Marrs, IN	Algesheim, Bingen, Hessen-Darmstadt
Schiffmann, John	20, Dec. 1880	28, Nov.	69		407	Marrs, IN	Niederingelheim, Bingen, Hessen-Darmstadt
Schiffmann, Louise	4, Feb. 1848		Inquiry		23	St. Louis, MO	
Schikle, Ernst Immanuel	12, July 1855	15, June	4- 2m- 4d		112	Poughkeepsie, NY	
Schilder, Katharine Augustine	18, Jan. 1894	25, Dec.	34	Vogel	46	Chillicothe, OH	Columbus, Franklin County, Ohio
Schildknecht, Martin	2, Oct. 1846		26		169	Belleville, IL	Großniedesheim, Rheinkreis Baiern
Schilge, Philipp	21, June 1894	2, June	71		406	Charlestown, IN	Massenheim, Hochheim, Nassau
Schilinger, Susanna	23, June 1892	4, May	74	Rüsti	398	Rochester, NY	Malterdingen, Baden
Schilke, Katharina Sophie	15, Mar. 1894	7, Feb.	72	Jung	182	Charlestown, IN	Wasssenheim, Hochheim, Nassau
Schill, Georg	2, May 1895	13, Apr.	74		286	Toledo, OH	Gillstein, Hermberg, Württemberg
Schilling, Catharine	20, Aug. 1883	16, July	75-10m- 9d	Lücker	271	Troy, NY	Krumstadt, Hessen-Darmstadt
Schilling, Christian	30, Oct. 1890	10, Oct.	71- -19d		702	St. Paul, MN	Langenholzhausen, Lippe-Detmold
Schilling, Elisabeth	25, Feb. 1897	5, Jan.	63	Licker	127	Troy, NY	Krumstadt, Hessen-Darmstadt
Schilling, Engel	19, Sept 1889	25, Aug.	76- 3m	Paulsmeyer	606	Hopewell, MO	Eidinghausen, Minden, Preußen
Schilling, Georg	12, Jan. 1874	11, Dec.	12- 3m-24d		15	Woodbury, MN	
Schilling, Jette	19, Sept 1861	18, Aug.			152	Watertown, WI	
Schilling, Johan Heinrich	7, Oct. 1878	20, Sept	66		319	Washington, MN	Carldorf, Vahrenholz, Lippe-Detmold
Schilling, Karl Wilhelm	6, Mar. 1862	12, Feb.	18- 1m- 4d		40	Batesville, IN	
Schilling, Katharina	15, Nov. 1869	29, Oct.	43	Oster	367	Prescott, WI	Neustein, Herrenberg, Württemberg
Schilling, Maria	16, June 1873	30, May	44	Richter	191	St. Paul, MN	Lienen, Warrendorf, Münster, Preußen
Schilling, Philipp	5, Mar. 1877	19, Feb.	41		79	Brillion, WI	Bischofsheim, Hessen
Schilling, Rosina	10, Oct. 1864	29, May	5- 5m	Deutsch	164	Schnectady, NY	
Schilling, Simon Conrad	30, Nov. 1863	5, July			192	St. Paul, MN	
Schilling, Sophie	18, Oct. 1869	18- 8m-23d			335	St. Paul, MN	
Schilling, Wilhelm	4, May 1874	17, Mar.	16- 8m-12d		143	Galena, IL	
Schilling, Wilhelm Heinrich	23, Apr. 1891	20, Mar.	17- 2m-16d		270	Brillion, WI	

Christliche Apologete Death Notices -- 1839 - 1899

Name of Deceased	Notice Date	Death Date	Age	Page	Maiden Name	Place of Death	Place of Birth
Schilling, Wilhelmina	20, Sept 1894	23, Aug.	20	614		Galena, IL	Galena, Illinois
Schilpp, Johan David	6, Feb. 1896	19, Jan.	78	94		Oregon, MO	Steinheim, Morbach, Württemberg
Schiltz, Magdalena	18, Oct. 1894	30, Sept	88	678	Kilner	Ann Arbor, MI	Beinstein, Waiblingen, Württemberg
Schilz, Jacob Friedrich	5, Mar. 1883	19, Feb.	78- 6m-26d	79		Ann Arbor, MI	Beinstein, Waiblingen, Württemberg
Schimmel, Anna Christina	10, Oct. 1895	30, Aug.	23	654		Evansville, IN	Evansville, Indiana
Schimmel, (child)	16, May 1870	26, Apr.	10d	159		LaCrosse, WI	
Schimmel, Brigitte	16, Feb. 1888	19, Jan.	81- 5m- 9d	110		Minneapolis, MN	Losdorf, Böhmen
Schimmel, Carolina	7, Aug. 1871	11, July	18	255		Evansville, IN	Evansville, Indiana
Schimmel, Charley	7, Nov. 1895	23, Oct.	46	718		Evansville, IN	Evansville, Indiana
Schimmel, J.	11, May 1874	12, Apr.	62	151		LaCrosse, WI	Dobern, Böhmen
Schimmel, J. Maria	26, July 1888	30, June	68- -10d	478	Reichardt	New Bremen, IL	Schloß Vippach, Sachsen-Weimar
Schimmel, Theresia	16, May 1870	26, Apr.	21	159	Pautler	LaCrosse, WI	Böhmen
Schimmelpfennig, Anna	14,May 1883	27, Apr.	14- 7m-25d	159		Oconomowoc, WI	
Schimmelpfennig, Johan	7, Dec. 1874		84	391		Oconomowoc, WI	Stargo, Pommern, Preußen
Schimmelpfennig, Johanna M.	26, Jan. 1899	10, Jan.	55	63	Hübner	Oconomowoc, WI	Kankelfitz, Regenwalde, Pommern
Schimmelpfennig, Lydia	12, July 1888	11, June	13	446		Oconomowoc, WI	
Schimmelpfennig, Wilhelm F.	11, July 1895	17, June	24	446		Oconomowoc, WI	Monterey, Waukesha County, Wisconsin
Schimmet, Louis J.	28, Jan. 1897	11, Jan.	47	63		Evansville, IN	Pernsa, Germany
Schimming, Gustav Rudolph	21, Oct. 1897		44	671		Arlington Heights, IL	Arnswalde, Brandenburg
Schindel, Emil	30, Sept 1878	29, Aug.	13	311		Minneapolis, MN	Greenwood, Minnesota
Schindel, Henriette Emma	9, Dec. 1886	13, Nov.	16- 1m-18d	7		Crow River, MN	
Schindler, Anna M.	5, Aug. 1897	12, July	58	495	Hertlein	Grand Rapids, MI	Wölchingen, Boxberg, Baden
Schindler, Barbara	20, Feb. 1890	30, Jan.	76	126		Cleveland, OH	Lauferswyl, Signau, Bern, Schweiz
Schipbach, Anna	6, June 1889	19, May	62- 1m- 7d	366	Zürcher	Highland, IL	Thun, Bern, Schweiz
Schipner, Joseph	29, June 1899	11, June	75	415		Chicago, IL	Fulda, Hannover
Schipper, Margaretha	15, Feb. 1864	11, Jan.	58-11m-22d	28	Taaties	Quincy, IL	Ost-Friesland, Hannover
Schippner, Henriette	7, July 1887	15, June	63	430	Funkler	Chicago, IL	Breitenbach, Schwarzburg-Sondershausen
Schirmacher, Carl	28, July 1884	30, June		7		Spring Lake, WI	Elbing, Schubin, Bromberg, Preußen
Schirmann, Philipp	7, Nov. 1895	18, Oct.	74	718		Chicago, IL	Edenkowen, Rheinpfalz Baiern
Schirmer, Amelia	17, Sept 1877	28, Aug.	13	305		Mt. Vernon, NY	New Rochelle, New York
Schirmer, Emil J.	1, Dec. 1884	13, Nov.	38- 4m	7		Philadelphia, PA	Pirmasens, Rheinkreis Baiern
Schirmer, Georg	28, Dec. 1893		58	828		New Rochelle, NY	Landau, Rheinpfalz Baiern
Schirmer, Joseph E.	19, June 1890	11, Jan.	25	398		Wichita, KS	Warmbach, Baden
Schittenhelm, Wilhelmina Christ. Elis.	4, Feb. 1892	19, Jan.	64	78	Beyer	Philadelphia, PA	Braunlage, Braunschweig
Schkenker, Christian	11, Aug. 1879	16, July	46- 6m-19d	255		Hamilton, OH	Schwenningen, Rottweil, Württemberg
Schlabach, Anna Dorothea	27, Jan. 1898	7, Jan.	33-11m-15d	63	Leidel	Hokah, MN	Winona County, Minnesota
Schlag, Emilie	27, June 1895	5, June	41	414	Kuhl	Honey Creek, WI	Losloven, Preußen
Schlag, Emma	7, Mar. 1895	3, Feb.	14	158		Honey Creek, WI	Honey Creek, Wisconsin
Schlage, Ferdinand	26, Jan. 1885	7, Jan.	63	7		Ahnapee, WI	Zirk, Hinterpommern
Schlägel, Peter	6, July 1893	8, June	89	430		Pomeroy, OH	Edigheim, Rheinkreis Baiern
Schläger, Johan	24, Mar. 1892	4, Mar.	78	191		Scranton, PA	Wilstedt, Kehl, Baden
Schläger, Maria	12, Aug. 1886	26, July	60	7	Färber	Scranton, PA	Willstädt, Baden
Schlapbach, Jakob	14, Nov. 1889	18, Oct.	83- 2m- 7d	734		Jamestown, MO	Steffisburg, Bern, Schweiz
Schlapbach, Peter	4, May 1885	20, Apr.	77	7		Clarington, OH	Staffisburg, Bern, Schweiz
Schlarb, Christine	5, Oct. 1893	18, Aug.		638	Reister	Pomeroy, OH	
Schlattman, Johan Eduard	22, Aug. 1895	16, July	39	542		St. Paul, MN	St. Louis, Missouri

Christliche Apologete Death Notices --- 1839 - 1899

Name of Deceased	Notice Date	Death Date	Age	Maiden Name	Page	Place of Death	Place of Birth
Schlattmann, Karoline	2, Dec. 1897	4, Nov.	41	Schmidt	767	Morris, MN	Laporte, Indiana
Schlattmann, Karoline Florentine	22, Jan. 1883	21, Dec.	12- 8m-13d		31	St. Paul, MN	
Schlattmann, Kasper Heinrich	3, Mar. 1898	30, Jan.	76		143	St. Paul, MN	Oberbauerschaft, Preußen
Schlattmann, Wilhelmine Sophia	30, Jan. 1882		14- 6m- 5d		39	St. Paul, MN	
Schlaudt, Christina E.S.	26, Nov. 1891	8, Nov.	73	Pape	766	Lawrenceburg, IN	Westerberg, Ranroth, Nassau
Schlaut, Philipp Georg	22, Feb. 1894	14, Jan.	82		126	Lawrenceburg, IN	Westerberg, Zenroth, Germany
Schlechemaier, Louis	24, Mar. 1892	23, Feb.	28		191	Junction City, KS	Württemberg
Schlecht, Elisabeth	12, Sept 1870		59	Renschler	295	Marion, OH	Grünwettersbach, Durlach, Baden
Schlecht, Elisabeth	4, Oct. 1880	5, Aug.	35	Fuchs	319	Marion, OH	Marion County, Ohio
Schlechter, Anna Maria	5, May 1873		71- 2m-22d		143	Vermillion, OH	Benningen, Ludwigsburg, Württemberg
Schlechter, Johan G.	7, Nov. 1889	27, Sept	51		718	Vermillion, OH	Stecken, Ludwigsburg, Württemberg
Schlechter, Johan Georg	2, June 1873		71- 9m-16d		175	Vermillion, OH	Murr, Marbach, Württemberg
Schlee, Barbara	5, Aug. 1886	16, July	78	Beutler	7	Lansing, MI	Waldorf, Nagold, Württemberg
Schlee, Margaretha	31, Jan. 1895	11, Jan.	51	Mack	78	Lansing, MI	Rockport, Ohio
Schleef, Johan Friedrich	4, July 1889	9, June	79-11m-10d		430	Beaufort, MO	Floto, Germany
Schleehenbecker, Caroline	15, Mar. 1888	15, Feb.	41- 9m-15d	Schendler	174	Greenville, OH	Bucyrus, Ohio
Schlegel, Andreas	28, Sept 1854	7, Sept			156	Chicago, IL	Grabs, St. Gallen, Schweiz
Schlegel, August	21, Oct. 1872	21, Sept	72		343	Le Sueur, MN	Wechselburg, Sachsen
Schlegel, Elisabetha	7, May 1857	18, Apr.	48		76	Pomeroy, OH	Edigheim, Rheinkreis Baiern
Schlegel, Emilie	11, Feb. 1897	11, Jan.	47		94	Le Sueur, MN	Remptendorf, Reis-Greitz, Sachsen
Schlegel, Emma Christine	29, Jan. 1883	4, Jan.	21- 2m-17d		39	Le Sueur, MN	
Schlegel, Ernst Ferdinand	23, June 1873	2, June	21		199	Le Sueur, MN	Watertown, Wisconsin
Schlegel, Johan	14, Apr. 1884	24, Mar.	75		7	Platteville, WI	Ranz, Severn, St. Gallen, Schweiz
Schlegel, Johann Rudolph	23, Aug. 1860	14, Aug.	23		136	Dover, OH	Kirchthurnen, Seftingen, Bern, Schweiz
Schlegel, Johanna	18, Mar. 1897	14, Feb.	72	Blank	175	Bethany, OR	Wurzbach bei Logenstein, Germany
Schlegel, Joseph Herman	2, Dec. 1897	4, Nov.	55		767	Los Angeles, CA	Frickingen, Ueberlingen, Baden
Schlegel, Maria E.	5, Apr. 1880	20, Mar.	75	Stahlecker	111	Bloomington, IL	Honau, Reutlingen, Württemberg
Schlegel, Maria M. Engel	2, May 1870	27, Mar.	19- 3m	Kuhlmann	143	Le Sueur, MN	Wehe, Minden, Preußen
Schlegel, Rosine Johanna	29, Sept 1884	6, Sept	72	Lintner	7	Le Sueur, MN	Altschila, Sachsen
Schlegel, Wilhelm	2, Sept 1897	31, July	58		559	Topeka, KS	Fleetwood, Berks County, Pennsylvania
Schlegel, Wilhelm	8, June 1893	14, May	63		366	Le Sueur, MN	Wecheselburg, Sachsen
Schlei, Emil Eduard	4, Aug. 1898	16, July	18		495	Klemme, IA	Germantown, Hancock County, Iowa
Schlei, Friedrich	14, Apr. 1898	26, Mar.	58		239	Klemme, IA	Karmonsdorf, Hinterpommern
Schleicher, Adelia Jeanette	30, Nov. 1893	11, Oct.	25	Schlechteweg	766	Lawrenceburg, IN	
Schleicher, Catharina	19, May 1892	15, Mar.		Stütz	80	Roxbury, MA	Lingesfeld, Sachsen-Weimar
Schleicher, Elisabeth	6, Nov. 1871	9, Oct.	74- 4m- 6d		359	Lawrenceburg, IN	Lengsfeld, Sachsen-Weimar
Schleicher, Georg C.	5, Jan. 1899	5, Dec.	73		15	Peoria, IL	Lengsfeld, Sachsen-Weimar
Schleicher, Henriette	22, Nov. 1880	25, Oct.	58- 2m	Schlechtweg	375	Boston, MA	Langsfeld, Eisenach, Sachsen-Weimar
Schleicher, J. Adam	20, Aug. 1896	30, July	76		543	Boston, MA	Langsfeld, Sachsen-Weimar
Schleicher, John Adam	18, Aug. 1898	4, Aug.	76		527	Lawrenceburg, IN	Lengsfeld, Sachsen-Weimar
Schleicher, Justin Christian	22, Oct. 1866	5, Oct.	71		342	Lawrenceburg, IN	Stadtlensfeld, Sachsen-Weimar
Schleicher, Tillie	30, July 1896	9, July	36		495	Indianapolis, IN	Lawrenceburg, Dearborn County, Indiana
Schleier, Magdalena	11, Aug. 1884	28, July	85	Link	7	Toledo, OH	Oberacker, Baden
Schleifer, Louis	3, May 1880	10, Mar.	46- 7m- 2d		143	Kansas City, MO	Hochenburg, Nassau
Schleifer, Wilhelm	16, Oct. 1876	2, Oct.	23- 1m-22d		335	Wyandotte, KS	
Schleister, Catharina	27, Aug. 1896	8, Aug.	66		559	Kansas City, MO	Düsseldorf, Preußen

Christliche Apologete Death Notices --- 1839 - 1899

Name of Deceased	Notice Date	Death Date	Age	Page	Maiden Name	Place of Death	Place of Birth
Schlemmer, Heinrich	12, July 1875	9, Apr.	2	223		Pittsfield, IL	New York City, New York
Schlenker, Anna	1, June 1893	12, Apr.	17	350		New York City, NY	Schwenningen, Rothweil, Württemberg
Schlenker, Christian	10, May 1888	25, Apr.	55	302		Toledo, OH	Herzoganbuchei, Bern, Schweiz
Schlenker, Elisabeth	6, Apr. 1893	9, Nov.	62	222	Kummer	Toledo, OH	Clayton County, Iowa
Schlenker, Martha	28, Dec. 1893	29, Nov.	29	828		Des Moines, IA	Weißenheim, Lahr, Baden
Schlenker, Theobald	24, July 1890	28, June	63	478		Des Moines, IA	Bächingen, Baiern
Schlenberger, Leonard	18, Aug. 1892	11, July	55	527		Allentown, PA	Hille, Minden, Preußen
Schlensker, Karolina W.S.	11, Sept 1882	18, June	30	295		Schenectady, NY	Grisen, Hannover
Schlensker, Louise	9, Apr. 1896	9, Mar.	66- 9m-21d	238	Lohmann	Schenectady, NY	Nord-Hemmern, Minden, Preußen
Schlensker, Maria Louise	28, July 1884	12, July	38	7	Horstmann	Schenectady, NY	Wilstadt, Baden
Schlenz, Anna Maria	20, Dec. 1875	2, Nov.	45	407	Hetzel	Scranton, PA	Willstädt, Baden
Schlenz, David	23, July 1896	3, July	58- 6m	479		Scranton, PA	Kirchheim a.T., Württemberg
Schlenz, Jeanna M.	7, July 1887	20, June	21- 8m-10d	430		Defiance, OH	Meklesch, Osnabrück, Hannover
Schlenz, Rosine	20, Mar. 1871	1, Mar.	65- 7m	95		Cincinnati, OH	Nasse bei Wertheim, Baden
Schleselmann, Katharina Dorothea	6, Oct. 1898	19, Sept	80	639	Wellmer	St. Louis, MO	
Schlesmann, Anna Barbara	8, Nov. 1888	16, Oct.	83	718	Doersch	New York City, NY	Riemberg bei Goldberg, Schlesien
Schleten, Louise	1, June 1893	1, May	40	350	Bertsch	Tulare, CA	Bosdorf, Hessen
Schlettner, Ernestine	7, Dec. 1893	14, Nov.	45	782	Ernst	Armourdale, KS	Rahden, Preußen
Schleuning, Catharina Elisabeth	21, Apr. 1887	6, Apr.	52	254	Michel	Scranton, PA	Mittelbrüden, Württemberg
Schleuning, Dorothea	25, July 1889	28, June	62	478		Pittsburg, PA	Oesterwethe, Versmold, Halle, Preußen
Schlichenmeyer, Friederike	22, July 1897	4, June	73	463	Rieger	Lincoln, NE	
Schlichte, Heinrich Wilhelm	29, Oct. 1866	20, Sept	45- 6m-25d	350		Decatur, IL	
Schlichters, Hannah Amalia	16, June 1862	10, May	14- 4m-12d	96		Decatur, IL	
Schlichters, Henriette Elisabeth	16, June 1862	28, Apr.	6-1m	96		Decatur, IL	
Schlichters, Laura Augusta	16, June 1862	6, Jan.	5m-16d	96		Decatur, IL	
Schlichters, Wilhelm Lewis	16, June 1862	13, May	8- 2m	96		Decatur, IL	
Schlick, Alvin	20, Feb. 1890	13, Dec.	13- 4m-19d	126		St. Paul, MN	Andeas-Berg am Harze, Preußen
Schlick, August	8, Dec. 1873	18, Nov.	49	391		Waco, TX	Sachsen-Coburg-Gotha
Schlick, Charles Gottlieb	13, Apr. 1893	17, Mar.	54	238		Brooklyn, NY	Clausthal am Harz, Hannover
Schlick, Karl Friedrich Wilhelm	14, Feb. 1889	11, Dec.	68	110		Charles City, IA	Oppenweiler, Bachnang, Württemberg
Schliepf, Jacob	14, Apr. 1859	17, Mar.	64	60		Newark, NJ	Klein-Rhüden, Braunschweig
Schlimme, H. Philipp	19, Jan. 1874	27, Dec.	75	23		Jackson, MO	
Schlimme, Maria	20, Nov. 1851	8, Oct.	45	188		Jackson, MO	Jefferkorn, Zürich, Schweiz
Schlinger, Anna	3, Apr. 1876		61	111	Drechsler	Elizabeth, NJ	Hille, Minden, Preußen
Schlinger, Caroline	12, Mar. 1883	13, Feb.	74	87		Nashville, IL	Hille, Minden, Preußen
Schlinger, Johan Cordt	20, Dec. 1880	23, Nov.	81- 2m- 3d	407		Nashville, IL	
Schlinger, Julie	13, June 1864	30, May		96	Westenkühler	St. Charles, MO	Westerkappeln, Preußen
Schlinger, Katharina Agnesa	27, Dec. 1894	24, Nov.	68	836	Glatze	San Jose, CA	
Schlinger, Maria	3, Nov. 1892	14, Oct.	41- 9m-10d	702		Nashville, IL	Schweiz
Schlinger, Thomas	3, Dec. 1891	11, Nov.	78	782		Elizabeth, NJ	Burgholzhausen, Preußen
Schlingmann, J.H. Philipp	31, July 1871		44- 7m- 4d	247		Decatur, IL	
Schlitz, Louis	30, Aug. 1894	28, July	21- 1m	566		Milwaukee, WI	Spenge, Kreis Herford, Westphalen
Schlobohm, Margaretha	2, Feb. 1885	4, Sept	36	7	Meyer	Marietta, OH	Römershausen, Ziegenhain, Kurhessen
Schloemann, Elisabeth	3, July 1871	16, June	53-10m	215	Schaeper	Warren, MO	Eichendorf, Amt Ottersberg, Hannover
Schlöffel, Martha Elisabeth	16, May 1889	27, Apr.	80	318		Columbus, OH	
Schlohn, Anna	8, June 1863	20, Mar.	75	92		Washington, OH	

- 442 -

Christliche Apologete Death Notices --- 1839 - 1899

Name of Deceased	Notice Date	Death Date	Age	Maiden Name	Page	Place of Death	Place of Birth
Schlohn, Jakob	15, Mar. 1875	1, Mar.	75- 6m		87	Bonn, OH	Ottersberg, Hannover
Schlohn, Margaretha	10, Apr. 1871	24, Feb.	60	Rauch	119	Bonn, OH	Nothweiler, Dahn, Rheinkreis Baiern
Schlömann, (Mrs)	8, May 1865	16, Apr.	70		76	Second Creek, MO	Jöllenbeck, Bielefeld, Minden, Preußen
Schlömann, Heinrich	5, Nov. 1857	18, Oct.	36		180	Herman, MO	Jöllenbeck bei Bielefeld, Westphalen
Schlömann, Heinrich	13, Dec. 1855	12, Oct.	61		200	Herman, MO	Jöllenbeck bei Bielefeld, Preußen
Schlosser, Wilhelm	14, Jan. 1858	4, Oct.	10- 3m		8	Schnectady, NY	Mühlhausen, Preußen
Schlothauer, Anna Margaretha	5, June 1851	21, May	54		92	St. Louis, MO	
Schlothauer, Johann Adam	9, Dec. 1842	4, Dec.	15- 9m		195	Lawrenceburg, IN	Mülhausen, Sachsen
Schlothauer, Johann Michael	8, Oct. 1841	16, Sept	59		159	Lawrenceburg, IN	Kalkobus bei Hersfeld, Kurhessen
Schlott, Anna Margaretha	16, Sept 1878	25, July	45	Heyer	295	Black River, OH	Grabin, Mecklenburg-Schwerin
Schlottmann, Carolina	15, Aug. 1864	20, July	55- 7m-28d		132	Newport, MI	
Schlottmann, Christian	18, Apr. 1864	18, Feb.	21- -18d		64	Newport, MI	
Schlottmann, Friedrich	14, Mar. 1889	16, Feb.	86		174	Marine City, MI	Benzin, Mecklenburg-Schwerin
Schlotzhauer, Maria Christina	18, July 1845	4, June	50		115	Pilot Grove, MO	Hessen-Philippsthal, Hessen
Schlotzhauer, Rudolph	25, Mar. 1867		74		94	Booneville, MO	Philippsthal, Kurhessen
Schlüchter, Anna Maria	14, Apr. 1873		71- 2m-22d		119	Vermillion, OH	Neckar-Beitingen, Ludwigsburg, Württemberg
Schluckebier, Emilie Emma	17, Apr. 1890	17, Mar.	28- 4m-22d	Bliese	254	Milwaukee, WI	Milwaukee, Wisconsin
Schlüder, Friedrich	2, Aug. 1869	15, July	66- 8m		247	Le Sueur, MN	Großrüden, Amt Bilderlahe, Hannover
Schluesing, Wilhelm Friedrich	8, Dec. 1887	6, Oct.	23- 3m-14d		782	Lake Creek, MO	
Schlueter, Ernst Karl	19, Jan. 1885	28, Dec.	60		7	St. Louis, MO	Lübbeke, Minden, Preußen
Schlund, Johan	7, June 1894	19, Apr.	71- 3m		374	North Vale, NJ	Baiern
Schlundt, J. Joachim Christian Fr.	28, Apr. 1892	11, Apr.	69		270	Madison, WI	Basedow, Mecklenburg-Schwerin
Schlung, Marie	21, June 1894	28, May	70	Söder	406	Charles City, IA	Ober-Riden, Witzenhausen, Kurhessen
Schlunt, Anna Maria	6, Apr. 1868	16, Mar.	58- 9m		111	Hudson City, NJ	Sutersdorf, Baiern
Schlupp, Benjamin	13, Oct. 1848	30, Aug.	32		168	Sangag, IA	
Schlupp, Maria	7, Apr. 1892	10, Mar.	68		222	Jamestown, MO	Kuttighofen, Solothurn, Schweiz
Schlüsing, Catharina M.	9, Oct. 1890	21, July	47- 3m- 8d	Müller	654	Lake Creek, MO	Benton County, Missouri
Schlüsing, Katharina Margaretha	21, Apr. 1879	19, Mar.	38	Fitschen	127	Lake Creek, MO	New Orleans, Louisiana
Schlüsing, Margaretha	21, Mar. 1895	18, Feb.	87	Mahnken	190	Lake Creek, Mo	Sevin, Hannover
Schlüsing, Maria Anna	14, Sept 1893	24, Aug.	45	Lasrenz	590	Lake Creek, MO	New Orleans, Louisiana
Schlüssel, A. Caroline Wilhelmine	21, Jan. 1878	9, Jan.	14		23	Ahnapee, WI	Glansee, Treptow an der Rega, Hinterpommern
Schlüssel, Caroline Friederike	2, Sept 1886	16, Aug.	56	Butzlaff	7	Ahnapee, WI	Glansen, Pommern
Schlüssel, Wilhelm	22, Oct. 1896	3, Sept	2m		687	Ahnapee, WI	
Schlüsselmann, Claus	31, Jan. 1895	16, Jan.	81		78	St. Louis, MO	Zeven, Hannover
Schlüsser, Sophia	2, Nov. 1899	6, Oct.	63	Engelbath	703	Brooklyn, NY	Rastede, Oldenburg
Schlüter, Amanda Georgine	7, Aug. 1871	1, June	32	Hoffmann	255	Schnectady, NY	Sachsen-Gotha
Schlüter, Carl Heinrich	3, Nov. 1892	10, Oct.	76		702	Alton, IL	Disselbruch, Lippe-Detmold
Schluter, Caroline	22, Nov. 1875	25, Oct.	16		375	Schnectady, NY	
Schlüter, Christian F.A.	18, Sept 1882	15, Aug.	64		303	Schnectady, NY	Hille, Minden, Preußen
Schlüter, Christine	31, Mar. 1862	8, Mar.	24		52	Cape Girardeau, MO	
Schlüter, Christoph	1, Aug. 1881	21, Mar.	69		247	Boody, IL	Lewe, Amt Liebenburg, Hannover
Schlüter, Ernst	13, Jan. 1868	26, Dec.	20- 3m		14	Decatur, IL	
Schlüter, Friedrich Christian	20, May 1897	73- 4m-24d			319	Gordonville, MO	Groß-Rhüden, Hannover
Schlüter, H. F.	9, May 1895	4, Apr.	38- 1m-17d		302	Gordonville, MO	Gordonville, Missouri
Schlüter, Johann Heinrich	17, May 1855	29, Mar.	57		80	Rockford, IN	Hunteburg, Amt Wittlage, Hannover
Schlüter, Karoline Wilhelmine H.	17, Mar. 1898	13, Feb.	63- 5m-18d	Brockmeier	175	Schnectady, NY	Hille, Minden, Preußen

Christliche Apologete Death Notices --- 1839 - 1899

Name of Deceased	Notice Date	Death Date	Age	Maiden Name	Page	Place of Death	Place of Birth
Schlüter, Louis	22, June 1893	1, June	30		398	St. Louis, MO	St. Louis, Missouri
Schlüter, Louisa	18, May 1874	2, May	41- -22d	Uphoff	159	Schnectady, NY	Hille, Minden, Preußen
Schlüter, Maria	5, Mar. 1883	4, Feb.	80- 5m-30d		79	Le Sueur, MN	Groß Rüden, Hannover
Schlüter, Sophie	8, May 1876	7, Apr.	36		151	Indianapolis, IN	Germany
Schlüter, Verene	20, Jan. 1879	26, Dec.	36	Maag	23	Le Sueur, MN	Neuenkirch, Schaffhausen, Schweiz
Schlüter, Wilhelm Heinrich	4, Feb. 1886	15, Jan.	49		7	Le Sueur, MN	Groß-Rüden, Bilderlahe, Hannover
Schlüter, Gottlieb	30, Mar. 1899	12, Jan.	53		207	Pasadena, CA	Oldenbrücken, Germany
Schlüter, Johan Eduard	30, Aug. 1888	3, Aug.	29		558	Enterprise, KS	Lesueur, Minnesota
Schlüter, Ulrike Luise Mathilda	6, Apr. 1899	18, Mar.	61	Backhaus	223	Milwaukee, WI	Daber, Naugart, Pommern
Schmadel, Ferdinand	12, Feb. 1872	21, Jan.	31		55	Poughkeepsie, NY	Gackenau, Baden
Schmäh, Philippine	28, May 1883	9, May	44- 9m		175	Troy, NY	Berzhain, Nassau
Schmahl, Anna Gertraud	10, Feb. 1868	10, Jan.	74-11m-19d	Pickhardt	47	Cannelton, IL	Hückeswagen, Lennep, Preußen
Schmahl, August	19, June 1882	13, May	56		199	Cannelton, IN	Bornfeld, Preußen
Schmahl, Jakob	4, Aug. 1892	8, July	70		494	Aurora, IL	Ingenheim, Bingen, Hessen
Schmahl, Katharine	14, Mar. 1864	29, Jan.	18-11m-13d		44	Wheeling, IL	Sodus, Wayne County, New York
Schmahl, Robert	13, Nov. 1856	20, Sept	21		184	Cannelton, IN	Bornfeld, Preußen
Schmalhof, Wilhelm	8, Mar. 1875	7, Feb.	54		79	Cannelton, IN	Bornfeld, Hückeswagen, Lennep, Preußen
Schmalhof, Katharine	28, Jan. 1897	29, Dec.	85		63	Boston, MA	Breitenheim, Hessen
Schmalz, Carolina	24, July 1890	6, July	26	Knieper	478	Brenham, TX	New Orleans, Louisiana
Schmalz, Christian	16, Feb. 1874	27, Jan.	45		55	St. Paul, MN	Schildach, Baden
Schmalz, Edmund	6, Dec. 1888	28, Oct.	36- 5m-25d		782	New Orleans, LA	Gehren, Thüringen
Schmalz, Friedrich Julius	31, Dec. 1883	2, Dec.	63		7	New Orleans, LA	Gehren, Schwarzburg-Sondershausen
Schmalz, Karolina	9, Jan. 1896	16, Dec.	75	Quade	30	Bay City, MI	Jankosko, Posen
Schmalzhof, Heinrich	23, June 1862	24, Apr.	25		100	Freeport, IL	Schwaigern, Württemberg
Schmauß, Georg	15, Dec. 1873	29, Nov.	66- 3m-22d		399	Perrysburg, OH	Amöneburg, Kurhessen
Schmechel, Emilie Helena	25, Feb. 1892	3, Feb.	20		127	Decatur, IL	Decatur, Illinois
Schmechel, Ottilia Carolina	8, Jan. 1891	11, Dec.	20- 1m- 9d		30	Decatur, IL	Decatur, Illinois
Schmechel, Wilhelmine Maria	6, July 1893	12, June	26		430	Decatur, IL	Decatur, Illinois
Schmecker, Louisa	2, Sept 1858	20, Aug.		Quebe	140	Newport, KY	Halden, Dilien, Preußen
Schmeidel, Sophia	26, Jan. 1893	4, Jan.	79		62	Grand Rapids, MI	Techentien, Mecklenburg
Schmeidel, Joseph	4, Oct. 1894	11, Sept	74- 5m-24d		646	Hennepin Co, MN	
Schmelcher, Carolina	22, Jan. 1883	1, Jan.	24	Hellriegel	31	Irwing, MI	Canada
Schmelcher, Jakob	13, Jan. 1898	2, Dec.	91		31	Freeport, IL	Wißloch, Baden
Schmelcher, Katharina	2, Apr. 1883	19, Mar.	37	Schmidt	111	Irwing, MI	Yeats County, New York
Schmell, Catharina	25, Aug. 1884	2, Aug.	63- 5m- 7d		7	Edgerton, OH	Wisselbach, Baiern
Schmell, Christian	22, Mar. 1875	26, Feb.	63- 2m- 4d		95	Edgerton, OH	Trier, Rheinpreußen
Schmell, Johan	30, Mar. 1874	14, Mar.	70		103	Grand Rapids, MI	Mecklenburg-Schwerin
Schmicker, Wilhelm	21, Oct. 1886	8, Oct.	39		7	Santa Claus, IN	
Schmid, Adam	5, Mar. 1896	16, Feb.	66		158	New Point, MO	Nahburn, Württemberg
Schmid, Anna Margretha	24, Jan. 1881	5, Dec.	81	Hirsch	31	Chicago, IL	Equarhofen, Mittel-Franken, Baiern
Schmid, Carl	27, Dec. 1894	7, Oct.	38		836	Minneapolis, MN	Mötzingen, Württemberg
Schmid, Catharina	5, June 1890	25, Apr.	68	Blank	366	De Soto, MO	Minsfelden, Nassau
Schmid, Christina	27, Apr. 1893	29, Mar.	76	Bischof	270	Bay City, MI	Hunzholz, Württemberg
Schmid, Gottlieb Jakob	10, Mar. 1887	21, Feb.	75- 1m- 9d		158	De Soto, MO	Marbach, Neckar, Württemberg
Schmid, John Ulrich	17, Mar. 1892	13, Feb.	71		175	Chicago, IL	Brütten, Winterthur, Zürich, Schweiz
Schmid, Julie Caroline	24, Jan. 1889	10, Jan.	35	Schilling	62	New York City, NY	

Name of Deceased	Notice Date	Death Date	Age	Page	Maiden Name	Place of Death	Place of Birth
Schmid, Karl Heinrich	6, Sept 1880	13, Aug.	21- 5m	287		New Knoxville, OH	New York
Schmid, Karoline Sophia	3, June 1886	12, May	27	7	Wieling	Brillion, WI	New York
Schmid, Karoline Sophia	17, June 1886	12, May	27	7	Wieting	Brillion, WI	
Schmid, Louise	26, Apr. 1875	30,Mar.	35	135	Bucher	Rochester, NY	Niederhasle, Schweiz
Schmid, M. Magdalena	1, Nov. 1860	5, Oct.	18- 3m-21d	176		Dayton, OH	
Schmid, Nikolaus	31, Jan. 1876	14, Jan.	31	39		Cincinnati, OH	Landau, Rheinkreis Baiern
Schmid, Peter	8, Mar. 1869	17, Feb.	46	79		New Rochelle, NY	Oberndorf bei Braunfels, Preußen
Schmid, Philipp	29, Aug. 1881	14, Aug.	66	279		Allegan, MI	Düngen bei Würzburg, Baiern
Schmid, Simond	15, June 1899	28, May	81	383		Canal Dover, OH	Endingen, Aargau, Schweiz
Schmid, Sophia Henriette	10, June 1886	23, May	80	7	Schlemann	Chicago, IL	Zelle, Hannover
Schmidel, Adelheid	23, Jan. 1875	13, Jan.	48	31		Cincinnati, OH	Bruckhausen, Bruckhausen, Hannover
Schmidlap, Johan C.	2, Mar. 1885	20, Feb.	60	7		Madison, IN	Kleenbrunn, Maulbronn, Württemberg
Schmidlap, Rosina	27, Apr. 1885	2, Apr.	44	7	Siegloch	Madison, IN	Zuffenhausen, Ludwigsburg, Württemberg
Schmidlapp, Heinrich	3, Sept 1883	8, Aug.	50	287		Madison, IN	Hamilton County, Ohio
Schmidlapp, Johan David	6, Apr. 1868	20, Mar.	76- 2m-20d	111		Madison, IN	Kleebronn, Brackenheim, Württemberg
Schmidli, Franz X.	16, Dec. 1886	20, Nov.	74	7		Cannelton, IN	Wölflingsweil, Aarau, Schweiz
Schmidt, (Mrs)	18, Mar. 1852	1, Mar.		48	Laib	Bellesville, IL	Burgstall, Marbach, Württemberg
Schmidt, Adam	29, June 1885	3, June	80	7		Quincy, IL	Gorzheim, Weinheim, Hessen-Darmstadt
Schmidt, Adam	20, Apr. 1885	6, Apr.	75- 4m-22d	7		Franklin Co., IN	
Schmidt, Agnes	6, Feb. 1890	20, Jan.	38	94	Cassio	Louisville, KY	Louisville, Jefferson County, Kentucky
Schmidt, Agnes Elisabeth	24, May 1894	28, Apr.	15	342		Sheboygan, WI	Sheboygan, Wisconsin
Schmidt, Albertine Wilhelmine	27, July 1893	15, June	60	478	Fick	Sandusky, OH	Lupow, Stolp, Keßlien, Preußen
Schmidt, Amalia	14, Jan. 1886	15, Nov.	30	7		New York City, NY	New York City, New York
Schmidt, Andreas	10, Mar. 1887	21, Feb.	49	158		Bible Grove, IL	Huerup bei Flensburg, Schleswig
Schmidt, Anna	22, Sept 1884	25, Aug.	19	7		Summerfield, IL	Summerfield, Illinois
Schmidt, Anna	13, Oct. 1892	26, Aug.	53	654	Krämer	Summerfield, IL	bei München, Baiern
Schmidt, Anna Adelheid	26, July 1894	20, June	76- 7m-25d	486	Wilmers	Chicago, IL	Schale bei Ibbenbühren, Westphalen
Schmidt, Anna Elisabeth	17, Nov. 1898	1, Nov.	59	735	Krug	Charles City, IA	Niederdieten, Biedenkopf, Hessen
Schmidt, Anna Elise	19, Mar. 1877	3, Mar.	30- - 9d	95	Wetjen	Hokah, MN	Kirchweih, Sieke, Hannover
Schmidt, Anna Ernestine	4, Sept 1890	10, Aug.	64- 9m-10d	574	Kurzeg	Berea, OH	Filehne, Bromberg, Preußen
Schmidt, Anna Gertrud	25, Aug. 1862	26, July	65- - 8d	136		Mascoutah, IL	Ost-Friesland, Hannover
Schmidt, Anna Julia Elisabeth	30, Apr. 1896	3, Apr.	4_ 9m	286		Oregon, MO	
Schmidt, Anna Julia Elisabeth	21, May 1896	3, Apr.	47- 9m	334		Oregon, MO	
Schmidt, Anna Katharina	4, May 1885	19, Apr.	36	7	Well	Brownton, MN	Schönberg, Dietz, Nassau
Schmidt, Anna Margaretha	26, Dec. 1889	18, Nov.	66	830	Zimmermann	Mt. Vernon, IN	Spitzaltheim, Hessen-Darmstadt
Schmidt, Anna Margaretha	10, Dec. 1877	19, Nov.	17	399	Hofferberth	Brooklyn, NY	Wallbach, Hessen-Darmstadt
Schmidt, Anna Maria	24, Sept 1847		25	155	Stiegler	St. Louis, MO	Himmelskron, Berneck, Baiern
Schmidt, Anna Maria	24, Dec. 1896	2, Dec.	85	831	Ott	Lafayette, IN	Gleisweiler, Baiern
Schmidt, Anna Maria	31, Mar. 1862	5, Mar.	36-10m	52		St. Paul, MN	
Schmidt, Anna Phil.	25, Oct. 1875	4, Sept	64	343	Saathof	St. Louis, MO	Sulsbach, Nassau
Schmidt, Antie	16, Apr. 1877		70	127		Summerfield, IL	Lingum, Ostfriesland
Schmidt, August	2, Sept 1878	15, Aug.	65- 7m- 2d	279		Oshkosh, WI	Bötzen, Schaumburg, Hessen
Schmidt, August	27, Feb. 1890	5, Feb.	67- 7m-26d	142		St. Louis, MO	Liebertswolkwitz, Sachsen
Schmidt, August	19, Jan. 1893	15, Dec.	45	46		Chicago, IL	Obernrf, Fritzlar, Hessen
Schmidt, August	5, Feb. 1883	7, Jan.	61- -19d	47		Maine, WI	
Schmidt, August Ferd.	30, Dec. 1897	5, Dec.	48	828		Swanton, NE	Hohenheide bei Rosenfelde, Pommern

- 445 -

Christliche Apologete Death Notices --- 1839 - 1899

Name of Deceased	Notice Date	Death Date	Age	Page	Maiden Name	Place of Death	Place of Birth
Schmidt, August Martin	5, Dec. 1889	8, Nov.	70- 1m-15d	782		Elkton, SD	Filehne, Bromberg, Preußen
Schmidt, Augusta	3, Aug. 1899	10, July	64	495	Vieregge	Berea, OH	Lippe-Detmold
Schmidt, Auguste	24, July 1876	4, July	22	239		Berea, Ohio	Berea, Ohio
Schmidt, Auguste Wilhelmine	22, Mar. 1888	4, Feb.	33	190	Paschke	Akron, NY	Buffalo, New York
Schmidt, Balthasar	28, July 1892	5, July	82	478		Evansville, IN	Rotheim, Hessen-Darmstadt
Schmidt, Barbara	15, Dec. 1887	23, Nov.	79- 5m-26d	798	Schneider	Summerfield, IL	Schmalfeld, Baiern
Schmidt, Carl	21, Jan. 1897	10, Nov.	19	47		Portland, OR	Portland, Oregon
Schmidt, Caroline	6, May 1872	14, Apr.	26- 3m	151	Link	Freeport, IL	Adelmannsfelden, Württemberg
Schmidt, Caroline	14, May 1896	12, Apr.	74	318	Witt	Morris, MN	Neukirchen, VorPommern
Schmidt, Caroline	21, Jan. 1897	19, Sept	37	47	Hummel	Portland, OR	Eldorado County, California
Schmidt, Caroline Wilhelmine	31, Oct. 1895	8, Oct.	62	702	Buck	Burlington, WI	Rietzig, Hinterpommern
Schmidt, Catharina	16, Aug. 1860	17, July	32	132	Veit	Kingston, IL	
Schmidt, Catharina Sophia	13, Sept 1888	24, Aug.		590	Huenecke	Cincinnati, OH	Marsen, Hannover
Schmidt, Charles	15, Jan. 1891	25, Dec.	10	46		Oregon, MO	
Schmidt, Charles Christian	11, Apr. 1870	9, Feb.	27	119		Pomeroy, OH	Stepenitz, OstPriegnitz, Preußen
Schmidt, Charlotte	12, Jan. 1899	18, Dec.	67	31		New York City, NY	Frankenthal, Rheinkreis Baiern
Schmidt, Charlotte	1, June 1863	8, May	12-10m-24d	88		Grand Rapids, MI	
Schmidt, Christian	3, July 1876	8, Apr.	59	215		Pomeroy, OH	Stepenitz, Ostbrechnitz, Preußen
Schmidt, Christian	23, Mar. 1899	26, Feb.	46	191		Ellis Grove, IL	
Schmidt, Christian Gotthilf	12, Sept 1881	22, Aug.	41	295		Hartford, CT	Brickla, Reuß-Greiz
Schmidt, Christina Friederike	19, Jan. 1899	7, Dec.	93	47	Eisenlohr	De Soto, MO	Oberamt Marbach, Württemberg
Schmidt, Christine	6, Feb. 1862	17, Jan.	73- 4m- 8d	24	Haßler	Detroit, MI	Sasen bei Raboldshausen, Kurhessen
Schmidt, Christine Margaretha	30, Aug. 1888	17, Aug.	70- 2m-13d	558	Jäger	Spencerville, OH	Heimerdingen, Leonberg, Württemberg
Schmidt, Christoph Johan	28, Aug. 1876	10, Aug.	73	279		Lancaster, NY	Dahlen, Friedland, Mecklenburg-Strelitz
Schmidt, Dicks	7, Jan. 1884		80	7		Lebanon, IL	Etzel, Wittmund, Hannover
Schmidt, Dora	4, Jan. 1894	22, Nov.	42	14	Cook	Stryker, OH	West Unity, Ohio
Schmidt, Dora K.	8, Sept 1898	20, July	51	575	Behlendorf	Chicago, IL	Hannover
Schmidt, Dorothea Charlotte M.	12, July 1894	19, June	58- 4m-25d	454	Fieger	Pomeroy, OH	Schöningen, Oslar, Hannover
Schmidt, Dorothea Elisabeth	20, Oct. 1879	5, Oct.	64- 6m-29d	335		Nashville, TN	Rodenburg, Kurhessen
Schmidt, Dorothea Maria Louise	18, May 1885	10, Apr.	50	7	Müller	Merrill, WI	Buchholz, Stargard, Pommern
Schmidt, Dorothea Sophia	4, Mar. 1852	16, Feb.	29- -14d	40	Grube	Defiance, OH	
Schmidt, Eduard	5, Sept 1870	11, Aug.	26- 9m	287		Swan Creek, NE	Hohenhaide, Dramburg, Cöslin, Preußen
Schmidt, Eduard	28, Aug. 1876	15, Aug.	51	279		St. Paul, MN	Poblitz, Preußen
Schmidt, Edward August	10, Nov. 1898	20, Oct.	19	719		Morris, MN	St. Paul, Minnesota
Schmidt, Elena	11, Oct. 1894	30, July	40	662	Combs	Stryker, OH	Williams County, Ohio
Schmidt, Elisabeth	5, Feb. 1883	19, Jan.	68- -29d	47	Frank	Dillsboro, IN	Rücklesreuth, Münchberg, Zell, Baiern
Schmidt, Elisabeth	17, Jan. 1889	3, Jan.	79	46		Danville, IL	Warzenbach, Marburg, Kurhessen
Schmidt, Elisabeth	21, June 1860		28	100	Heiß	New York	
Schmidt, Elisabeth Karoline	30, Jan. 1890	7, Jan.	22- 8m-24d	78		Wheeling, WV	
Schmidt, Elise	17, Jan. 1889	25, Dec.	71	46	Uhrwieler	Danville, IL	Arwangen, Bern, Schweiz
Schmidt, Emil	21, Nov. 1895	10, Oct.	23	750		Detroit, MI	New York
Schmidt, Emil	9, Mar. 1893	2, Feb.	57- 5m	158		Nashville, IL	Nassau
Schmidt, Emma	8, Oct. 1891	17, Sept	31	654	Huber	Louisville, KY	Louisville, Jefferson County, Kentucky
Schmidt, Emma	4, June 1891	8, May	27	366	Weitmann	Pittsburg, PA	Indianapolis, Marion County, Indiana
Schmidt, Emma	26, Sept 1889	25, Aug.	17- 4m	619		Forest, WI	Empire, Wisconsin
Schmidt, Emma	18, July 1895	23, June	20	462	Thiele	Pittsfield, IL	Perry, Illinois

Christliche Apologete Death Notices --- 1839 - 1899

Name of Deceased	Notice Date	Death Date	Age	Page	Maiden Name	Place of Death	Place of Birth
Schmidt, Emma Dorothea	27, Dec. 1888	7, Dec.	21	830		Toledo, OH	Toledo, Lucas County, Ohio
Schmidt, Eva	7, Sept 1868	12, Aug.	57	287		Lawrence, KS	Neubrunn, Baiern
Schmidt, Eva	10, Sept 1896	21, Aug.	82	591		New York City, NY	
Schmidt, Ferdinand	24, Mar. 1884	12, Mar.	73- 3m- 2d	7		Burlington, WI	Schievelbein, Pommern
Schmidt, Fr.	13, June 1895	24, Mar.	84	382		Detroit, MI	Gardedegen, Magdeburg, Preußen
Schmidt, Friederike	12, Apr. 1894	19, Mar.	38- 3m-23d	246	Seefled	Milwaukee, WI	
Schmidt, Friederike Louise C.	21, May 1891	20, Apr.	64	334	Schowitzke	Long Island City, NY	Zossen, Brandenburg
Schmidt, Friedrich	20, Nov. 1871	3, Sept	66	375		Third Creek, MO	Neuenkirchen, Mecklenburg-Strelitz
Schmidt, Friedrich	22, Mar. 1894	1, Mar.	74	198		Louisville, KY	Feldberg, Mecklenburg-Strelitz
Schmidt, Friedrich	1, June 1899	5, May	78	351		Louisville, KY	Freiendrietz, Nassau
Schmidt, Friedrich	11, Oct. 1869	11, Sept	38	327		Berea, OH	Filehne, Preußen
Schmidt, Friedrich	17, Aug. 1863	21, June	26	132		Ft. Atkinson, WI	
Schmidt, Friedrich	30, Mar. 1874	13, Mar.	12	103		San Jose, IL	
Schmidt, Friedrich Heinrich	17, Aug. 1863	20, July	39- 4m-12d	132		Kendallville, IN	
Schmidt, Georg	7, June 1880	22, May	80- 3m-14d	183		Giard, IA	Rohrau, Herrenberg, Württemberg
Schmidt, Georg	14, July 1853		6- 6m-10d	112		Woodville, OH	
Schmidt, Georg C.	10, July 1876	23, May	52	223		Bradford, IN	Marxheim, Nassau
Schmidt, Georg Friedrich	20, Dec. 1860	21, Nov.	52	204		De Soto, MO	Marbach am Neckar, Württemberg
Schmidt, Gertrud Karolina	4, July 1881	8, June	71	215	Linds	Louisville, KY	Schwarzenfels, Schlichten, Kurhessen
Schmidt, Hanna Louise	15, Oct. 1883	3, Oct.	57- 3m-10d	335	Radike	Milwaukee, WI	Sültshagen, Hinterpommern
Schmidt, Heinrich	31, Dec. 1891	3, Dec.	77- 7m	846		Bensenville, IL	Landesbergen, Germany
Schmidt, Heinrich	5, Sept 1895	2, July	53	574		Nauvoo, IL	Zimmerschied, Nassau
Schmidt, Heinrich	19, Jan. 1893	10, Dec.	69	46		Waco, TX	Mecklenburg-Schwerin
Schmidt, Heinrich	24, Mar. 1873	6, Mar.	57	95		Second Creek, MO	Lippe-Detmold
Schmidt, Heinrich	26, Sept 1881	29, Aug.	21- 3m- 7d	311		New Orleans, LA	
Schmidt, Helena	8, Nov. 1880		30- 1m- 6d	359		Kenwill County, MN	Galena, Illinois
Schmidt, Henriette	23, Aug. 1869	4, Aug.	35-11m	271		Geißler	Wredenhagen, Mecklenburg-Schwerin
Schmidt, Henriette	23, Jan. 1890	27, Dec.	51	62	Zeidler	Muscatine, IA	Nieder-Gläsersdorf, Schlesien
Schmidt, Henriette Vickotine	17, Sept 1891	18, Aug.	22	606		New Orleans, LA	New Orleans, Louisiana
Schmidt, Herman F.	30, Apr. 1891	3, Apr.	48	286		Minneapolis, MN	Posen
Schmidt, Ivy Gertrud	30, Jan. 1896	29, Nov.	22	78		Stryker, OH	West Unity, Ohio
Schmidt, J. (Mrs)	5, Nov. 1865	8, Oct.	54	180	Netscher	Chillicothe, OH	Groß Bieberau, Hessen-Darmstadt
Schmidt, J. Gottlieb Ferdinand	26, May 1898	25, Apr.	71	335		Menomonie, WI	Plälicow, Germany
Schmidt, Jacob	3, Aug. 1863	25, Feb.	78	124		Clayton, IA	Kippenheim, Amt Ettenheim, Baden
Schmidt, Jacob Fr.	2, Feb. 1885	12, Jan.	Inquiry	7		Summerfield, IL	Waldgrehweiler, Rogenhausen, Rheinpfalz Baiern
Schmidt, Jakob	8, Feb. 1849		55	23		Pittsburg, PA	Gerolsheim, Frankenthal, Rheinkreis Baiern
Schmidt, Jakob	15, Jan. 1866	4, Dec.	23-11m-21d	22		Delaware, OH	Teinach, Württemberg
Schmidt, Jakob	16, Nov. 1874	22, Oct.	1-11m-16d	367		Allegan, MI	Thüngen, Baiern
Schmidt, Jakob	21, June 1869	11, Apr.	62	199		Summerfield, IL	
Schmidt, Joh.	16, Sept 1872	22, Aug.	78	303		Chillicothe, OH	
Schmidt, Johan	23, Feb. 1899	4, Feb.	66	127		Danville, IL	Lampertheim, Hessen-Darmstadt
Schmidt, Johan	27, Jan. 1879	6, Jan.	81	31		Lafayette, IN	Berner-Oberland, Schweiz
Schmidt, Johan	23, Dec. 1878	20, Nov.	39- 9m-11d	407		Colesburg, IA	Hannover
Schmidt, Johan	5, Dec. 1881	18, Nov.	81	391		Ellis Grove, IL	
Schmidt, Johan Friedrich	23, Dec. 1897	15, Nov.	54	815		Dayton, OH	Robber, Wittlage, Hannover
Schmidt, Johan Friedrich	2, July 1891	6, June		430		Cincinnati, OH	Landau, Rheinkreis Baiern

Christliche Apologete Death Notices --- 1839 - 1899

Name of Deceased	Notice Date	Death Date	Age	Maiden Name	Page	Place of Death	Place of Birth
Schmidt, Johan Friedrich	5, July 1875	4, June	65		215	Dayton, OH	Sachsen-Coburg
Schmidt, Johan G.	25, Oct. 1869	25, Sept	50- 4m-19d		343	Lafayette, IN	Stein, Bretten, Baden
Schmidt, Johan Georg	15, Nov. 1888	21, Sept	85		734	Tappan, NY	Liederbach, Kurhessen
Schmidt, Johan Georg	3, Mar. 1898	10, Feb.	79		143	Wheelersburg, OH	Lorenzen, Elsaß
Schmidt, Johan Georg Gottlieb	1, Jan. 1891	23, Nov.	76		14	Big Stone City, SD	Zieten, Vorpommern
Schmidt, Johan Gottfried	11, Sept 1890	23, Mar.	75- 2m-21d		590	South Park, MN	Hemberg, Nassau
Schmidt, Johan Heinrich Otto	7, Jan. 1886	8, Dec.	83		7	Arlington Heights, IL	Auenolter, Stolzenau, Hannover
Schmidt, Johan Louis	26, Jan. 1880	14, Dec.	62- 1m- 3d		31	Sandusky, OH	Bergtheim, Arnstein, Baiern
Schmidt, Johan N.	6, Dec. 1888	20, Oct.	59		782	Brooklyn, NY	Scharnau bei Würzburg, Baiern
Schmidt, Johan Philipp	26, July 1869	12, July	78		239	Charlestown, IN	Münzfelden, Nassau
Schmidt, Johan Wilhelm	1, Sept 1884	15, Aug.	74		7	Fosterburg, IL	Hemberg, Nassau
Schmidt, Johan Wolfgang	21, Jan. 1886	2, Jan.	83		7	Louisville, KY	Berneck, Gefrees, Baiern
Schmidt, Johann Christoph	28, Mar. 1861	16, Mar.	58		52	De Soto, MO	Marbach am Neckar, Württemberg
Schmidt, Johanna	31, May 1875	26, Apr.	59	Rebbeling	175	Newark, NJ	Eimbeck, Hannover
Schmidt, Johanna Friederike W.	3, Jan. 1895	5, Dec.	66	Generich	14	Menomonie, WI	Breitenfelde, Naugard, Stettin, Preußen
Schmidt, Johanne	25, Mar. 1897	9, Mar.	37		190	Louisville, KY	Louisville, Jefferson County, Kentucky
Schmidt, Johannes	25, Jan. 1864	May	49		16	Galion, OH	Hoben Salms, Koblenz, Wetzlar, Preußen
Schmidt, Johannes	31, Mar. 1887	12, Mar.	78		206	Chillicothe, OH	Dilheim, Wetzlar, Koblenz, Preußen
Schmidt, John	19, Aug. 1878	6, Aug.	39		263	Chillicothe, Ross County, Ohio	Chillicothe, Ross County, Ohio
Schmidt, John	28, June 1894	12, June	48		422	Danville, IL	Matzenbach, Kurhessen
Schmidt, John	2, Nov. 1893	16, Oct.	67		702	Rose Hill, TX	Mecklenburg-Schwerin
Schmidt, John	3, Aug. 1885	9, July	60		7	Graham, MO	Nassau
Schmidt, John L.	13, Nov. 1871	28, Oct.	33		367	Huntingburg, IN	
Schmidt, Joseph	14, Jan. 1878	17, Dec.	56		15	Menomonie, WI	
Schmidt, Joseph	24, July 1865	2, Apr.	18- 6m		120	Batesville, IN	
Schmidt, Joseph	3, Nov. 1892	7, Oct.	26		702	New York City, NY	
Schmidt, Josephine	20, June 1881	7, June	47- 5m		199	Galena, IL	
Schmidt, Juliane	29, Oct. 1857	17, Oct.	49	Schönhalz	176	Wheeling, VA	Oberndorf, Württemberg
Schmidt, Jürgen	14, Feb. 1889	20, Apr.	54- 1m-17d		110	Pierce City, MO	Strebendorf, Asfeld, Hessen-Darmstadt
Schmidt, Jürgen G.	1, Sept 1898	13, July	82		559	Clatonia, NE	Aurich, Ostfriesland
Schmidt, Karl	12, May 1898	21, Apr.	54		303	Cortland, NE	Röchenstädt, Ostfriesland
Schmidt, Karl	14, Mar. 1889	22, Feb.	32		174	Morrison, MO	Brietzig bei Piritz, Pommern
Schmidt, Karl	7, June 1880	24, May	57		183	Schnectady, NY	Belleville, Illinois
Schmidt, Karl	1, June 1880	28, Apr.	65		175	Bucyrus, OH	Preußen
Schmidt, Karl Friedrich	4, Sept 1876	26, July	76		287	Milwaukee, WI	Siegelsbrück, HinterPommern
Schmidt, Karl Wilhelm	16, June 1898	14, May	96		383	Swanton, NE	Swanton, Nebraska
Schmidt, Karoline	18, July 1895	23, June	67	Radke	462	Bedford, IN	Zeglinewo, Preußen
Schmidt, Katharina	6, Dec. 1888	30, Oct.	54	Will	782	Rose Hill, TX	Zarrendorf, Boitzenburg, Mecklenburg-Schwerin
Schmidt, Katharina	25, Nov. 1878	5, Nov.	36	Krug	375	Forest, WI	Niederndieter, Biedenkopf, Hessen-Darmstadt
Schmidt, Katharina	14, Feb. 1870	26, Jan.	83		55	Woodville, OH	Bahlingen, Amt Emmendingen, Baden
Schmidt, Katharina	9, Dec. 1886	20, Oct.	54	Jäger	7	Winona, MN	Uttershausen, Fitzlar, Kurhessen
Schmidt, Katharina	5, Nov. 1866	19, Oct.	83- 6m-19d		385	Chillicothe, OH	Dermstein, Hessen-Darmstadt
Schmidt, Katharina	5, May 1892	12, Apr.	76	Leicht	286	Mt. Vernon, IN	Obermutschelbach, Baden
Schmidt, Katharina	5, Feb. 1891	22, Dec.	66	Kuhnle	94	Cincinnati, OH	
Schmidt, Katharina Elisabeth	20, June 1889	2, May	34	Wenderoth	398	Newton, IA	Melchershausen, Melsungen, Hessen-Kassel
Schmidt, Katharine	17, Mar. 1853	16, Feb.			44	New York, NY	

Christliche Apologete Death Notices --- 1839 - 1899

Name of Deceased	Notice Date	Death Date	Age	Maiden Name	Page	Place of Death	Place of Birth
Schmidt, Klara	27, Oct. 1884	23, Sept	38	Schmal	7	Buffalo, NY	Eichloch, Hessen-Darmstadt
Schmidt, Konrad	3, Mar. 1892	20, Jan.	82		142	Freeport, MI	Kulmbach, Rheinkreis Baiern
Schmidt, Kunigunda	12, June 1871	23, May	37- 4m-12d	Karl	191	Yellow Creek, IL	Reicharts, Schlüchtern, Kurhessen
Schmidt, Kunigunde	31, Dec. 1883	18, Dec.	41	Rieß	7	Baltimore, MD	Frauenaurach, Baiern
Schmidt, Lena	26, Mar. 1896	18, Feb.	32	Wolker	206	New York City, NY	Achtelsbach, Brekenfeld, Oldenburg
Schmidt, Lizzie	20, Sept 1894	10, Aug.	41		614	Nauvoo, IL	Des Moines County, Iowa
Schmidt, Lorenz	5, Feb. 1891	14, Jan.	59		94	Bible Grove, IL	Angeln, Schleswig
Schmidt, Louisa Emma	26, Aug. 1867		15- 6m-12d		270	Golconda, IL	
Schmidt, Louise	21, Dec. 1893	24, Nov.	87	Miller	814	Nashville, IL	Rudolstadt, Thüringen
Schmidt, Louise	6, Mar. 1890	4, Feb.	21	Friedrich	158	Los Angeles, CA	Wisconsin
Schmidt, Magdalena	28, Dec. 1885	25, Nov.	64- 5m- 4d		7	Giard, IA	Küppenheimweiler, Ettenheim, Baden
Schmidt, Mamie	16, June 1898	25, May	19- 2m		383	Chicago, IL	
Schmidt, Margaretha	3, Sept 1896	29, July	69	Dollkopf	575	New York City, NY	Mark Elbach, Mittelfranken, Baiern
Schmidt, Margaretha	3, Feb. 1898	16, Jan.	60	Geisel	79	Nashville, IL	Cincinnati, Hamilton County, Ohio
Schmidt, Margaretha	26, May 1898	28, Mar.	80		335	Batesville, IN	Aschaffenburg, Baiern
Schmidt, Margaretha	27, May 1878	30, Apr.	60	Oesper	167	Third Creek, MO	Lichtenstein, Baiern
Schmidt, Margaretha	1, July 1897		65	Herboldsheimer	414	Danville, IL	Lenkersheim, Baiern
Schmidt, Margaretha	6, Jan. 1873	3, Dec.	47	Raab	7	Allegan, MI	Thüngen, Baiern
Schmidt, Margaretha	14, June 1894	7, May	86	Jacoby	390	Baltimore, MD	
Schmidt, Maria	27, Nov. 1882	10, Nov.	77	Klesner	383	Baraboo, WI	Katzenfort, Wetzlar, Koblenz, Preußen
Schmidt, Maria	27, Nov. 1882	9, Nov.	78	Weiler	383	Greenville, OH	Heutesheim, Rheinbischofsheim, Baden
Schmidt, Maria	19, Feb. 1883	25, Jan.	23	Pfeiffer	63	Cincinnati, OH	Cincinnati, Hamilton County, Ohio
Schmidt, Maria	5, Oct. 1885	1, Sept	74	Kador	7	Peoria, IL	Breßwitz, Mecklenburg-Strelitz
Schmidt, Maria	29, Mar. 1888	10, Feb.	56	Dunker	206	Detroit, MI	Glarin, Mecklenburg-Schwerin
Schmidt, Maria	27, Mar. 1882	5, Mar.	58		103	St. Paul, MN	Mascoutah, Illinois
Schmidt, Maria	6, Aug. 1847	24, July	1		127	St. Louis, MO	
Schmidt, Maria Catharine	1, June 1893	24, Apr.	53	Helm	350	New York City, NY	Aßlar, Wetzlar, Preußen
Schmidt, Maria Eleonore	7, Oct. 1872	13, Aug.	47	Blumenkamp	327	Dayton, OH	Kabber, Amt Witlage, Hannover
Schmidt, Maria Katharine	26, May 1887	3, May	51	Faller	334	Milwaukee, WI	Pittsburg, Pennsylvania
Schmidt, Maria Magdalena	21, July 1887	25, June	84- 2m-21d		462	St. Louis, MO	Fahringen, Sulz, Württemberg
Schmidt, Maria Wilhelmina	7, Apr. 1879	28, Feb.	62	Diekhof	111	Drake, MO	Schötmar, Lippe-Detmold
Schmidt, Marianna Elisabeth	29, July 1872	6, July	43- 5m- 3d		247	Louisville, KY	Mesfelden, Amt Linberg, Nassau
Schmidt, Mary	15, Dec. 1892		44		798	Grass Lake, MI	Wittenberg, Germany
Schmidt, Mary	4, May 1885	4, Apr.	18		7	Detroit, MI	
Schmidt, Michael	16, Nov. 1874	27, Oct.	16		367	Summerfield, IL	
Schmidt, Mina	3, May 1888	21, Mar.	32	Hehmann	286	Kansas City, KS	Lengerich, Tecklenburg, Preußen
Schmidt, Nellie	18, Aug. 1892	27, July	21		527	Newark, NJ	
Schmidt, Nikolaus	25, May 1899	8, Apr.	34		335	Bible Grove, IL	Dänemark
Schmidt, Ottilie	17, Apr. 1882		24		127	Berea, OH	Henderson, Minnesota
Schmidt, Philipp	21, Mar. 1864	1, Jan.	51		48	St. Louis, MO	Poggenhausen, Helburg, Sachsen-Meiningen
Schmidt, Philipp	28, Dec. 1899	11, Dec.	70- 9m- 9d		828	Osceola, NE	Straßburg, Elsaß
Schmidt, Philipp	1, Apr. 1852	Feb.			56	St. Louis, MO	Homberg, Nassau
Schmidt, Philipp August	12, Nov. 1896	10, Oct.	17		734	Swanton, NE	
Schmidt, Philipp Heinrich	1, Apr. 1897		86- 5m-12d	Alton	207	New York City, NY	
Schmidt, Philippine	8, Sept 1887	18, Aug.	76		574	Freeport, MI	Dörsdorf, Nassau
Schmidt, Regina	28, Mar. 1895	7, Mar.	65		206	Evansville, IN	Gaugrehweiler, Baiern
							Steiger,

Name of Deceased	Notice Date	Death Date	Age	Page	Maiden Name	Place of Death	Place of Birth
Schmidt, Robert	1, Dec. 1884	10, Nov.	26	7	Bäuerle	Wabasha, MN	Milwaukee, Wisconsin
Schmidt, Rosina	30, Aug. 1875	10, Aug.	52- 7m-16d	279		Columbus, OH	Heiningen, Backnang, Württemberg
Schmidt, Rosina	2, Dec. 1872	2, Nov.	23	391		St. Louis, MO	
Schmidt, Samuel	17, Apr. 1865	27, Mar.	31	64		Baltimore, MD	Darmstadt, Hessen-Darmstadt
Schmidt, Sophia	29, June 1874	12, June	30	207	Ave	Chicago, IL	Overrother, Hannover
Schmidt, Sophia Christina	7, Oct. 1878	18, Sept	39- 9m- 2d	319	Hewer	Danville, MN	Schladen, Hannover
Schmidt, Sophia Maria	1, Feb. 1875	14, Jan.	84	39		Indianapolis, IN	Widdershausen bei Sulz am Neckar,
Schmidt, Sophie	16, June 1898	21, Apr.	77	383	Aliot	New York City, NY	Biel, Bern, Schweiz
Schmidt, Stephan	5, Aug. 1878	7, July	68	247		Marietta, OH	Vorderweidenthal, Rheinkreis Baiern
Schmidt, Susanna	25, July 1881	7, July	60	239		Ellis Grove, IL	Schweiz
Schmidt, Tebecka	19, Feb. 1883	12, Jan.	63	63	Postels	Great Bend, KS	Milstadt, Hannover
Schmidt, Theophilus	17, Aug. 1893	26, July	41	526		Berea, OH	Ronhausen, Kurhessen
Schmidt, Theresia	19, May 1898	24, Apr.	70	319	Gnad	Brooklyn, NY	Merscheid, Preußen
Schmidt, Vernea	29, July 1878	14, July	44	239	Schlittler	Brunswick, MO	Niederurnen, Glarus, Schweiz
Schmidt, Victor	2, Apr. 1883	19, Mar.	38	111		St. Paul, MN	Sachsen-Gotha
Schmidt, Wilhelm	27, July 1863	4, June	29	120		Ft. Atkinson, WI	Cölpin, Frankfurt a. d. Oder, Brandenburg
Schmidt, Wilhelm	18, Sept 1882	29, Aug.	67- 4m-20d	303		Swan Creek, NE	Stettin, Hinterpommern
Schmidt, Wilhelm	11, Nov. 1852	12, Sept	67	184		Milwaukee, WI	
Schmidt, Wilhelm	26, Jan. 1874	3, Jan.		31		Watertown, WI	
Schmidt, Wilhelmina	4, Feb. 1858	15, Jan.	23-11m	20		Buffalo, NY	Chemnitz, Sachsen
Schmidt, Wilhelmine	21, July 1884	18, June	72- 4m	7		Swanton, NE	Milizwinkel, Brandenburg
Schmidt, Wilhelmine E.	20, May 1886	26, Apr.	31- -19d	7	Witt	Pittsburg, PA	Dölitz, Pommern
Schmidt, William Gottlob F.	7, Sept 1863	20, Aug.	27- 1m- 16d	144		Spring Prairie, WI	Winnenden, Württemberg
Schmidter, Amalia	23, Feb. 1899	27, Jan.	78	127	Mannert	East Troy, WI	Itenburg, Hessen-Darmstadt
Schmidter, Lydia	12, Jan. 1863	15, Dec.	5- 3m	8		East Troy, WI	
Schmidter, Magdalena	12, Jan. 1863	17, Dec.	16	8		Madison, IN	Boston, Massachuetts
Schmidtlag, Sophia	12, Feb. 1872	29, Jan.	72	55		Furnace, OH	Tiefenbach, Maulbronn, Württemberg
Schmidts, (Mr)	14, Feb. 1861	10, Jan.	79- -5d	28		Furnace, OH	Otweiler, Elsaß
Schmidts, (Mrs)	14, Feb. 1861	18, Jan.	71- -24d	28		Furnace, OH	Lorenzen, Elsaß
Schmidtt, Anna M.	21, Aug. 1851	24, June	57	136		Pekin, IL	
Schmidtt, Christina	29, Aug. 1850	28, June	19- 6m	140		Effingham, IL	Württemberg
Schmied, (Mrs)	15, Jan. 1866	28, Sept	65	22		Manitowoc, WI	Adams County, Illinois
Schmied, A.	14, July 1853	21, June	37	112		Quincy, IL	Lockhausen, Schöpner, Lippe-Detmold
Schmiedeskamp, Louise	17, Aug. 1885		28	7	Kling	Union, MO	Morgan County, Missouri
Schmiedeskamp, Philipp	29, May 1871	26, Apr.	51	175		Great Bend, KS	Alfermiffen, Lippe-Detmold
Schmiedt, Anna	16, Oct. 1876	22, Aug.	22- 9m	335	Gährs	Warren, MO	Hessen-Darmstadt
Schmiedt, Dorothea Wilhelmina M.	5, Feb. 1872	2, Jan.	36-11m- 1d	47	Humberg	St. Louis, MO	
Schmiermund, John	31, Mar. 1887	4, Mar.	60	206		St. Louis, MO	Bomde, Wittlage, Hannover
Schmiermund, Sophie	26, Mar. 1883	13, Mar.	43- - 1d	103	Schmidt	Santa Claus, IN	Dieligen, Preußen
Schmiker, Anna Maria	4, July 1895	17, June	77	430	Bredhold	Santa Claus, IN	Bebra, Amt Rothenburg, Kurhessen
Schmiker, Henriette	15, July 1878	27, June	44	223	Günter	Marietta, OH	
Schminke, Justus	14, Mar. 1864	6, Nov.	33	44		Huntingburg, IN	Bahlingen, Amt Emmendingen, Baden
Schmirke, Anna Margaretha Sarah	3, Dec. 1883	17, Nov.	15- 6m-13d	391		Woodville, OH	Rußdorf, Rheinkreis Baiern
Schmit, Johannes	28, Mar. 1870	22, Feb.	61	103		Ripley Co, IN	Erbes, Pettesheim, Hessen-Darmstadt
Schmit, Katharine	7, Feb. 1850	22, Jan.	21	24			
Schmith, Catharina	28, July 1879	11, July	76	239	Korell	Woodville, OH	

Christliche Apologete Death Notices --- 1839 - 1899

Name of Deceased	Notice Date	Death Date	Age	Maiden Name	Place of Death	Page	Place of Birth
Schmith, Elisabeth	1, Oct. 1877	30, Sept	59- 8m-10d	Jungmann	Muscatine, IA	319	Besigheim, Württemberg
Schmith, Gottlieb	3, July 1871	31, May	41- 9m-20d		Rockford, MN	215	Canton Bern, Schweiz
Schmith, Johan	19, July 1894	28, June	73		Le Sueur, MN	470	
Schmith, John	27, Jan. 1873	27, Dec.	70- 6m- 2d		Sherrills Mount, IA	31	Hackmatt, Elsaß
Schmith, Margaretha	8, Nov. 1880	24, Oct.	64- 3m-16d	Paul	Woodville, OH	359	Hessen-Kassel
Schmith, Wilhelm H.	16, Mar. 1885	17, Feb.	46		Newport, KY	7	Romrod, Hessen-Darmstadt
Schmiths, August	15, Dec. 1884	21, Nov.	38		Indianapolis, IN	7	Elberfeld, Germany
Schmitt, (Mrs)	11, June 1896	5, May	25	Bulsterbaum	Philipsburg, TX	383	Marxheim, Nassau
Schmitt, Anna	4, July 1889	10, May	65- 8m- 3d	Westenberger	Bradford, IN	430	
Schmitt, Auguste	27, July 1868	18, Apr.			Newtonburg, WI	239	
Schmitt, Bertha	21, Nov. 1889	15, Oct.	30	Roßenau	Creston, IA	750	
Schmitt, Catharina	5, Sept 1889	16, Aug.	83	Weikesser	Seguin, TX	574	Ziegenhain, Kurhessen
Schmitt, Christine	24, Feb. 1887	9, Jan.	62		Portsmouth, OH	126	Lorenzen, Elsaß
Schmitt, Elisabeth	20, Mar. 1882	19, Feb.	77		Daytonville, IA	95	Maxweiler, Neuenburg a. d. Donau, Baiern
Schmitt, Elisabeth	15, Mar. 1880	27, Feb.	62- 9m-27d	Herschberger	Beaver Dam, WI	87	
Schmitt, Georg Wilhelm	22, July 1878	7, July	49- 6m-27d		Seguin, TX	231	Ziegenhain, Oberhessen, Hessen
Schmitt, Hannah	28, July 1884	6, July	60	Kidney	St. Louis, MO	7	Bucks County, Pennsylvania
Schmitt, Joh. Philipp	17, Nov. 1859	8, Oct.	59		Edwardsville, IL	184	Vöhl, Hessen-Darmstadt
Schmitt, Johan Heinrich	5, Aug. 1886	22, July	75		New Orleans, LA	7	Hattenhausen, Minden, Preußen
Schmitt, Johannes	27, Sept 1849	17, July	79		Manchester, MO	156	Haßloch, Rheinpfalz Baiern
Schmitt, Johannes	2, June 1898	5, May	89		Seguin, TX	351	Ziegenhain, Hessen-Nassau
Schmitt, John Wesley	15, Sept 1879	28, Aug.	14- 2m-11d		Santa Claus, IN	295	Spencer County, Indiana
Schmitt, K.	29, Aug. 1850	28, June	64		Pekin, IL	140	Ostfriesland
Schmitt, Lorenz	20, May 1867	20, Apr.	54		Lansing, MI	158	Burgheim, Elsaß
Schmitt, Maria	21, May 1896	5, May	25	Bulsterbaum		334	Elberfeld, Germany
Schmitt, Maria Margaretha	7, Aug. 1890		81-11m- 8d	Herlemann	Quincy, IL	510	Großbieberau, Hessen-Darmstadt
Schmitt, Michael	19, May 1879	25, Apr.	78		Lawrence, KS	159	Sachsenflur, Amt Boxberg, Baden
Schmitt, Philipp	23, Oct. 1882	16, Sept	47- 6m- 1d		Chester, OH	343	Pittsburg, Pennsylvania
Schmitt, R.	11, Oct. 1888	18, Sept	82		Giard, IA	654	Neugardheim, Truchtersheim, Elsaß
Schmitt, Valentin	25, Apr. 1895	16, Mar.	78		Santa Claus, IN	270	Zell, Benschheim, Hessen
Schmitt, Werner	28, Feb. 1889	1, Feb.	69		Cameron, MO	142	Esselborn, Rhein-Hessen
Schmitts, Susanna	20, Apr. 1885	2, Apr.	76	Gonder	Palestine, IN	7	Oberglan, Homberg, Hessen-Darmstadt
Schmitz, Alice	19, Dec. 1895	29, Nov.	25	Wesler	Chicago, IL	814	Lawrenceburg, Dearborn County, Indiana
Schmitz, Julius	9, Sept 1897	27, Aug.	67		Cleveland, OH	575	Elberfeld, Preußen
Schmock, Johanna	26, May 1862	7, Apr.	57		Newport, MI	84	Poratz, Brandenburg, Preußen
Schmoker, Auguste Charlotte	11, Apr. 1895	5, Mar.	26	Bastian	Ft. Dodge, IA	238	Iroquois County, Illinois
Schmokro, Anna	5, June 1882	3, May	28	Twarz	New Frankford, MO	183	Weisal, Niederlausitz, Germany
Schmoll, Heinrich	15, July 1858				Muscatine, IA	112	Kehrenbach, Mehlsburg, Kurhessen
Schmollinger, Johan Martin	12, Feb. 1877	27, Jan.	52		Aurora, IL	55	Breitenholz, Herrenberg, Württemberg
Schmolsmeier, Caspar	16, Aug. 1849	11, July	34-10m-17d		Laughery, IN	132	Quemheim, Münden, Preußen
Schmoock, Anna Maria	2, Apr. 1891	8, Mar.	56-10m-14d	Panter	Louisville, KY	222	Neßlared, Baden
Schmook, Friederike	22, Dec. 1887		75	Giese	Chicago, IL	814	
Schmoker, Caroline Henr. Auguste	25, Nov. 1858	15, Oct.	37	Schiffmann	Red Bud, IL	188	Schötmer, Lippe-Detmold
Schmuck, Ferd.	18, Sept 1876	29, Aug.	54		Quincy, IL	303	Germany
Schmuck, Johan A.	8, Oct. 1896	13, Sept	77		Red Bud, IL	655	Ueberlingen am Bodensee, BAden
Schmuck, Maria	27, Apr. 1885	3, Apr.	58	Buser	Red Bud, IL	7	

- 451 -

Christliche Apologete Death Notices --- 1839 - 1899

Name of Deceased	Notice Date	Death Date	Age	Maiden Name	Page	Place of Death	Place of Birth
Schmucker, Karoline	22, May 1882	8, May	26	Richter	167	West Unity, OH	West Unity, Ohio
Schmutz, Rosine	17, Aug. 1893	23, July	41	Küginbühl	526	Sedalia, MO	Canton Bern, Schweiz
Schmutzler, Emma Mathilde	10, June 1886	29, Apr.	15		7	Watertown, WI	Watertown, Wisconsin
Schmutzler, Emma Sophia	22, June 1899	20, May	32	Meyer	399	Prospect Park, CA	Cedar Lake, Indiana
Schmutzler, Friedrich	15, Jan. 1872		23		23	Watertown, WI	
Schmutzler, Friedrich Wilhelm	11, Apr. 1895	18, Mar.	63		238	Watertown, WI	Greiz, Vogtland, Sachsen
Schmutzler, Leopold	31, Oct. 1889	2, Oct.	70-10m-13d		702	Watertown, WI	Watertown, Wisconsin
Schmutzler, Priscilla	23, June 1887	1, June	22	Herbst	398	Watertown, WI	Watertown, Wisconsin
Schnaar, Margaretha	16, Aug. 1894	23, July	64	Leidorf	534	Bushnell, IL	Marburg, Kurhessen
Schnabel, Anna Caroline	27, Nov. 1882	14, Nov.	30	Traub	383	Indianapolis, IN	Indianapolis, Marion County, Indiana
Schnabel, Barbara	21, Dec. 1893	27, Nov.	74	Distel	814	Indianapolis, IN	Ruith, Stuttgart, Württemberg
Schnabel, Johan	12, July 1880	13, June	64- 1m- 8d		223	Indianapolis, IN	Geradstettin, Schorndorf, Württemberg
Schnäbele, Helene	12, Apr. 1880				119	Alton, IL	
Schnäbely, Eva Elisabeth	10, Dec. 1896	15, Nov.	60	Gerhardt	798	Bucyrus, OH	Baden
Schnäck, Christoph F.	31, Dec. 1866	10, Dec.	77		422	Seymour, IN	Osweil, Ludwigsburg, Württemberg
Schnack, Dorothea Margaretha	12, Mar. 1896	10, Feb.	62		175	Los Angeles, CA	Wißmassen, Pfön, Preußen
Schnackenberg, Ella	23, Feb. 1880	4, Feb.			63	German Creek, IA	
Schnackenberg, Maria Friederika	26, Apr. 1880	30, Mar.	69	Siebe	135	German Creek, IA	Zeven, Hannover
Schnaidt, Anna	30, Oct. 1882	15, Oct.	82- 9m	Uehlinger	351	St. Paul, MN	Neuenkirchen, Schaffhausen, Schweiz
Schnaitter, Hattie Sarah	3, July 1890	9, June	14		430	Toledo, OH	Toledo, Lucas County, Ohio
Schnake, Christine Louise	14, June 1869	18, Apr.	26		191	Nashville, IL	Unterlübbe, Minden, Preußen
Schnake, Elisabeth	24, June 1872	10, May	64	Weihe	207	Nashville, IL	Eichhorst, Minden, Preußen
Schnakenberg, Johan	27, Aug. 1891	28, July	77		558	Harper, IA	NeuenBülstedt, Ottersberg, Hannover
Schnakenberg, John Diederich	22, Dec. 1898	25, Nov.	87		815	Harper, IA	Neuen-Bülsted, Ottersberg, Hannover
Schnarrenberger, Christiane	30, Aug. 1855	2, Aug.	30-11m		140	Cincinnati, OH	Schmieden, Kannstadt, Württemberg
Schnarrenberger, Louise	16, May 1864	3, May	28- 6m	Bosse	80	Cincinnati, OH	Dielingen, Amt Lamphöre, Preußen
Schnasse, Edward	29, Apr. 1878	13, Apr.	41- 5m- 1d	Köhler	135	Central City, NE	Heiden, Lage, Lippe-Detmold
Schnasse, Emma Augusta	20, Apr. 1893	22, Mar.	27	Rössing	254	Boelus, NE	East Troy, Walwoth County, Wisconsin
Schnasse, Louise Friedrike	25, Apr. 1895		58		270	Howard, NE	Heiden bei Lage, Lippe-Detmold
Schnaufer, Friederika	5, Jan. 1899	28, Nov.	87- 1m-24d		15	Allegheny City, PA	Nicklingen, Württemberg
Schnaufer, Friedrich	24, Jan. 1881	4, Jan.	80		31	Allegheny City, PA	Malmsheim, Württemberg
Schnaufer, Maria	19, Nov. 1847	25, Oct.	29		187	Marietta, OH	
Schnebeli, Anna Elisabeth	27, Mar. 1890	6, Mar.	15- 2m- 9d		206	Bucyrus, OH	Lebanon County, Pennsylvania
Schnebeli, David	8, May 1890	23, Apr.	57- 5m-25d		302	Bucyrus, OH	Osweil, Ludwigsburg, Württemberg
Schneck, (Mr)	9, June 1884	15, May	57		7	Huntingburg, IN	
Schneck, Amelia	12, Mar. 1896	4, Feb.	22		175	Schnectady, NY	
Schneck, Beatrice	13, Apr. 1893	21, Mar.	10		238	Seymour, IN	
Schneck, Carl	25, Feb. 1897	3, Feb.	40		127	Seymour, IN	Jeffersonville, Indiana
Schneck, Christina	26, May 1873	9, May	58	Almentinger	167	Milwaukee, WI	Horrheim, Vaihingen, Württemberg
Schneck, Heinrich Peter	19, May 1884	1, May	25		7	Huntingburg, IN	
Schneck, Jakob	4, July 1895	11, June	81		430	Milwaukee, WI	Breitenholz, Herrenberg, Württemberg
Schneck, John C.	28, May 1891	3, May	24- 9m- 2d		350	Seymour, IN	Seymour, Indiana
Schneck, John J.	30, Apr. 1891	21, Feb.	46-10m-27d		286	Milwaukee, WI	New York
Schneckenberg, Johann	31, Oct. 1850	7, July	80- 5m		176	Keokuk County, IA	
Schnee, Dorothea Elisabeth	21, June 1875	30, May	85- 1m-11d	Bröning	199	Louisville, KY	
Schneesche, Emilie	19, Sept 1870	4, Sept	25	Pietröschke	303	Chicago, IL	HinterPommern

- 452 -

Christliche Apologete Death Notices --- 1839 - 1899

Name of Deceased	Notice Date	Death Date	Age	Page	Maiden Name	Place of Death	Place of Birth
Schneider, Adam	9, Nov. 1874	15, Oct.	65	359		Bradford, IN	Hienerd, Zweibrücken, Rheinpfalz Baiern
Schneider, Anna	28, Apr. 1884	6, Apr.		7	Winkler	Eudora, KS	Hilterfingen an Thuner See, Bern, Schweiz
Schneider, Anna	29, Aug. 1870	5, Aug.	49	279	Koch	Nauvoo, IL	Holzhausen, Hessen-Darmstadt
Schneider, Anna	5, Oct. 1893	19, Sept	25- -19d	638	Gräber	Minneapolis, MN	Radwonke, Bromberg, Preußen
Schneider, Anna Carolina	21, Sept 1874	9, Sept	55	303	Buschow	Michigan City, IN	Imsheim, Elsaß
Schneider, Anna Katharina	11, May 1893	15, Apr.	67	302	Schuler	New Albany, IN	Freisbach, Rheinpfalz Baiern
Schneider, Anna M.	16, Feb. 1899	13, Jan.	65	111	Vogel	Chillicothe, OH	Bützberg, Arwangen, Bern, Schweiz
Schneider, Anna Maria	12, July 1875	27, June	46	223	Hug	Bible Grove, IL	Münsterberg, Schlesien
Schneider, Anna Maria	9, Apr. 1891	10, Mar.	71	238	Neumann	Michigan City, IN	Lellbach, Preußen
Schneider, Anna Maria	1, Dec. 1884	12, Nov.	73	7	Kreischer	Edwardsville, IL	Michigan City, Indiana
Schneider, Anton	5, June 1876	6, May	22	183		Michigan City, IN	Berea, Ohio
Schneider, Arthur L.	9, Dec. 1897	9, Nov.	17	783		Dunkirk, NY	Stamheim, Calw, Württemberg
Schneider, Barbara	17, July 1890	17, June	77- 7m-16d	462		Kansas City, MO	
Schneider, Barbara	10, Sept 1891	1, Aug.		590		Waco, TX	Indianapolis, Marion County, Indiana
Schneider, Carl August	26, Sept 1881	11, Sept	18	311		Marrs, IN	Vanderburgh County, Indiana
Schneider, Carolina	29, Apr. 1897	6, Apr.	36	271	Ruch	Pomeroy, OH	Chester Twp., Meigs County, Ohio
Schneider, Catharina	4, Feb. 1892	19, Dec.	50	78	Genheimer	Birmingham, PA	Gundernhausen, Starkenburg, Hessen
Schneider, Catharina Elisabetha	24, Nov. 1862	18, Oct.	82	188		Troy, NY	Wallernhausen, Hessen-Darmstadt
Schneider, Catharina Margaretha	24, Nov. 1873	10, Nov.	45	375		Mt. Vernon, NY	Kornwestheim, Ludwigsburg, Württemberg
Schneider, Catharine	9, Jan. 1890	8, Dec.	70	30	Roth	Minneapolis, MN	Pennsylvania
Schneider, Catharine	13, Dec. 1880	12, Nov.	65- 8m	399		Berea, OH	
Schneider, Charles	15, Mar. 1894	23, Feb.	25- -23d	182		Parker, SD	
Schneider, Christ. Jakob	9, Dec. 1897	2, Nov.	67	783	Müller	Atchinson, KS	Zweibrücken, Rheinpfalz Baiern
Schneider, Christina	29, Dec. 1884	16, Dec.	79	7		Marrs, IN	Wülflingen, Zürich, Schweiz
Schneider, Christina	24, Feb. 1873	24, Jan.	16- 2m-22d	63		Ft. Atkinson, WI	
Schneider, Christine	26, June 1882	22, May	57-11m-12d	207	Huppert	Sacramento, CA	Gündigen, Saarbrücken, Trier, Preußen
Schneider, Christine	21, Apr. 1892	19, Mar.	88- 5m-16d	254	Kallerbach	Cincinnati, OH	Schmieheim bei Lahr, Baden
Schneider, Christine Barbara	8, Nov. 1844		40	172		Lowell, WI	Linsenhofen, Nürtingen, Württemberg
Schneider, Christine M.	7, Mar. 1889	12, Feb.	87	158	Huppert	Syracuse, NY	Giedingen, Saarbrücken, Trier, Preußen
Schneider, Dorothea	24, May 1880	3, Apr.	69- 2m-30d	167	Motzer	St. Louis, MO	Reusten, Württemberg
Schneider, Dorothea Maria	29, Apr. 1872	4, Apr.	54- 3m-20d	143	Rott	Paige, TX	Bramsche, Amt Föhren, Hannover
Schneider, Eduard (Rev)	25, Dec. 1890	1, Dec.	80	830	Brück	Galion, OH	Thürnen, Basel, Schweiz
Schneider, Elisabeth	11, Sept 1876	14, Aug.	83- 9m-10d	295		Marion, OH	Großerda, Kreis Wetzlar, Coblenz, Preußen
Schneider, Elisabeth	1, Oct. 1883		73- 2m- 2d	319	Leonhard	Nauvoo, IL	Eisingen, Pforzheim, Baden
Schneider, Elisabeth	21, Aug. 1851	1, Aug.	55	136		Nauvoo, IL	Raden, Münden, Preußen
Schneider, Elisabeth	30, May 1895	14, Apr.	45	350		Eudora, KS	Nauvoo, Illinois
Schneider, Elisabeth	5, July 1888	18, June		430		Marrs, IN	Westphalen
Schneider, Elisabeth	30, May 1895	1, May	32- 3m- 1d	350	Zilch	Canton, IL	
Schneider, Emilie	30, July 1857	24, June	10	124		Booneville, IN	
Schneider, Eva	20, Nov. 1876	5, Nov.	78-11m-20d	375	Helder	Chillicothe, OH	Idar, Birkenfeld, Oldenburg
Schneider, Eva Katharina	23, Feb. 1885	10, Feb.	78	7	Kochem	Boonville, IN	Schwegenheim, Germersheim, Rheinpfalz Baiern
Schneider, Eva Louisa	5, Oct. 1868	29, Aug.	13	319		Golconda, IL	
Schneider, F.W.	1, Nov. 1875	17, Oct.	62	351		Michigan City, IN	KleinBallhausen, Thüringen
Schneider, Fr. Wilhelm	13, Mar. 1876		62	87		Edwardsville, IL	Neuwedel, Preußen
Schneider, Franziska	11, Mar.1872	17, Feb.	62	87	Pfeffer	Galena, IL	Bieringen, Württemberg
Schneider, Franziska	20, Sept 1894	12, Aug.	64	614			Obersbach, Baden

Christliche Apologete Death Notices --- 1839 - 1899

Name of Deceased	Notice Date	Death Date	Age	Page	Maiden Name	Place of Death	Place of Birth
Schneider, Friederike	23, Aug. 1869	3, Aug.	31	271	Büker	Saginaw, MI	Augustdorf, Lippe-Detmold
Schneider, Friedrich	22, Apr. 1897	15, Mar.	63	255		Fairmount, KS	Armenburg, Hessen-Darmstadt
Schneider, Friedrich	26, May 1873	25, Apr.	55	167		Louisville, KY	Enzheim, Hessen-Darmstadt
Schneider, Friedrich	9, Jan. 1871	19, Dec.	63	15		Buffalo, NY	Schwabweiler, Sulz, Elsaß
Schneider, Friedrich	1, Dec. 1887	26, Oct.	67	766		Albert Lea, MN	Vasbeck, Waldeck
Schneider, Friedrich Wilhelm	20, Apr. 1899	25, Mar.	85	255		Stitzer, WI	Karlsruhe, Baden
Schneider, G. Jakob	25, Apr. 1895	27, Mar.	85	270		Chillicothe, OH	Freisbach, Germersheim, Rheinpfalz Baiern
Schneider, Georg	13, Oct. 1859		60	164		Germany, WI	Güdingen, Saarbrücken, Preußen
Schneider, Georg	16, Feb. 1899	1, Feb.	87	111		Dotyville, WI	Zweibrücken, Rheinkreis Baiern
Schneider, Georg J.	31, Mar. 1887	17, Mar.	60	206		Ft. Atkinson, WI	Giedingen, Sarbrücken, Trier, RheinPreußen
Schneider, Gustav	16, Dec. 1897	27, Nov.	82-11m- 2d	799		Baltimore, MD	Klauer, Sachsen
Schneider, Heinrich	22, Feb. 1894	19, Jan.	79	126		Canton, MO	Graubergen bei Osnabrück, Hannover
Schneider, Heinrich	16, Aug. 1860	2, Aug.	46	132		Elizabeth City, NJ	Berghausen bei Berleburg, Preußen
Schneider, Heinrich	30, Mar. 1868	11, Mar.	30	103		Galion, OH	Galion, Crawford County, Ohio
Schneider, Heinrich	22, Nov. 1855	1, Oct.	21	188		Perry, IL	Dodenau, Hessen-Darmstadt
Schneider, Heinrich	18, Feb. 1886	27, Jan.	74	7		Pittsfield, IL	Dodenau, Hessen-Darmstadt
Schneider, Heinrich	14, July 1898	24, May	75	447		Columbus, OH	Grünerwettersbach, Baden
Schneider, Henriette	16, Apr. 1883	21, Mar.	69-11m-11d	127		Wichita, KS	Dillenburg, Nassau
Schneider, Herman	22, Nov. 1894	31, Oct.	82	758		Giard, IA	Relwehausen, Homberg, Kurhessen
Schneider, J. Georg	17, Nov. 1853	30, Oct.	74- 1m-26d	184		Birmingham, PA	Starkenburg, Reinheim, Hessen
Schneider, J.F.	3, Apr. 1882	7, Mar.	70	111		Smithton, MO	Rumbach, RheinPfalz Baiern
Schneider, Jac. Peter	18, Mar. 1858	3, Mar.	32	44		Chillicothe, OH	Friesbach, Rheinkreis Baiern
Schneider, Jacob	7, Oct. 1872	23, Sept	63-10m-10d	327		Blue Island, IL	Münchsweiler, Zweibrücken, Rheinkreis Baiern
Schneider, Jakob	24, Nov. 1879	15, Oct.	23- 4m-20d	375		San Jose, CA	Germany, Ft. Atkinson, Wisconsin
Schneider, Jakob	26, Feb. 1891	8, Feb.	94	142		Evansville, IN	Ida, Birkenfels, Oldenburg
Schneider, Jakob	11, Dec. 1882	5, Nov.	84- 2m-13d	399		Rainham, CD	Niederlinxweiler, Preußen
Schneider, Jakob	28, May 1877	22, Mar.	72	175		Liestal, ----	Thürnen, Basel, Schweiz
Schneider, Jakomina	9, July 1891	15, June	67	446	Smidt	Bible Grove, IL	Oldersum, Emden, Hannover
Schneider, Johan	25, June 1883	15, May	66- 7m- 6d	207		Burlington, IA	Casdorf, Homberg, Kurhessen
Schneider, Johan	21, Oct. 1897	7, Sept	69	671		Drake, MO	Kanton Bern, Schweiz
Schneider, Johan Carl	25, Apr. 1889	23, Mar.	64	270		Peoria, IL	Nachhallenbach, Wedel, Trier, Preußen
Schneider, Johan Heinrich	28, May 1883	26, Apr.	75	175		Nauvoo, IL	Weidenhausen, Kurhessen
Schneider, Johan Heinrich	30, July 1891	30, May	69	494		Sleepy Eye, MN	Westphalen
Schneider, Johan M.	10, Nov. 1873	3, Oct.	37- 1m- 3d	359		Syracuse, NY	
Schneider, John	28, Nov. 1864	4, Nov.	51- -16d	192		West Bend, WI	Linsenhofen, Nürtingen, Württemberg
Schneider, John J.	28, Aug. 1882	4, Aug.	58- 5m-10d	279		Marietta, OH	Baiingen, Ludwigsburg, Württemberg
Schneider, John Wesley	18, Jan. 1875	30, Dec.	50	23		Burlington, IA	Kriegsfeld, Rheinkreis Baiern
Schneider, Jonas	4, Jan. 1864	7, July	22	4		Rochester, NY	Arfeld, Kreis Wittgenstein, Preußen
Schneider, Karl	31, May 1844		Inquiry	87		Fairplay, WI	Schorndorf, Württemberg
Schneider, Karl	13, May 1886	22, Apr.	29- 1m- 4d	7		Herman, MO	Sparneck bei Münchberg, Baiern
Schneider, Karl Johan	5, Nov. 1891	14, Oct.	72	718		Evansville, IN	Allentown, Pennsylvania
							Tuscarawas County, Ohio
							Idar, Birkenfeld, Oldenburg

Christliche Apologete Death Notices --- 1839 - 1899

Name of Deceased	Notice Date	Death Date	Age	Page	Maiden Name	Place of Death	Place of Birth
Schneider, Karoline	19, Aug. 1878	31, July	62	263	Rind	Blue Island, IL	Niedermoor, Rheinpfalz Baiern
Schneider, Karoline	18, July 1895	1, July	57	462	Topt	Waco, TX	Blomberg, Lippe-Detmold
Schneider, Katharina	26, Jan. 1893	19, Dec.	28	62	Schäfer	Garrett, IN	Nister bei Hachenburg, Germany
Schneider, Katharina	12, Jan. 1885	5, Dec.	70	7		Louisville, KY	Brenzheim, Hessen-Darmstadt
Schneider, Katharina	8, Sept 1884	11, Aug.	63	7	Naurer	Jersey City, NJ	Niederdorf, Hessen-Kassel
Schneider, Katharina	25, Dec. 1846	27, Oct.	21- 1m-15d	207		Galion, OH	Hohensolms, RheinPreußen
Schneider, Katharina	1, Sept 1892	11, July	67	558	Noll	Jersey City, NJ	Niedernorf, Hessen
Schneider, Katharina	2, Mar. 1899	5, Feb.	73	143	Goller	Newport, KY	Bayreuth, Baiern
Schneider, Katharina	20, Aug. 1841	3, Aug.	22	131		Pittsburg, PA	
Schneider, Katharina Barbara	18, Nov. 1897	29, Oct.	76	735	Hahn	Redfield, SD	Linsenhosen, Müsingen, Württemberg
Schneider, Katharina Barbara	25, Sept 1890	28, Aug.	77- 1m- 3d	622	Voisin	Ellis Grove, IL	Ruchheim, Rheinkreis Baiern
Schneider, Katharina E.	28, Nov. 1845	1, Nov.	52	191		New York, NY	
Schneider, Katharina Maria	13, Jan. 1859	1, Jan.	72	8		Warren, MO	
Schneider, Katharine	12, Dec. 1870	17, Nov.	70	399		Winona, MN	
Schneider, Katharine	27, May 1878	28, Apr.	36	167	Brunner	Eudora, KS	
Schneider, Katharine Elisabeth	17, Dec. 1896	19, Nov.	82	814	Feisel	Pittsfield, IL	Dodenau, Hessen-Darmstadt
Schneider, Lizzie	27, Aug. 1877	2, Aug.	12	279		New Albany, IN	
Schneider, Louis	3, Aug. 1899	10, July	47	495		Rochester, NY	New York City, New York
Schneider, Louisa	3, Feb. 1859	10, Jan.	60	20		Bridgeport, CT	Nordheim, Württemberg
Schneider, Louise	20, July 1893	22, June	87	462	Hahn	Bradford, IN	Schorndorf, Württemberg
Schneider, Louise	21, Feb. 1876	3, Feb.	20	63		Mt. Vernon, NY	Mt. Vernon, New York
Schneider, Louise	15, Apr. 1886	31, Mar.	43	7	Schulz	Gladbrook, IA	Grapzow, Preußen
Schneider, Louise Auguste	28, Feb. 1889	16, Jan.	20	142		Brooklyn, NY	Brooklyn, New York
Schneider, Louise C.	25, Apr. 1881	22, Feb.	35- 1m-11d	135	Schilz	Ann Arbor, MI	
Schneider, Louise Maria	8, July 1897	26, May	53	431	Schwartz	Columbus, OH	Columbus, Franklin County, Ohio
Schneider, Ludwig	31, May 1844		Inquiry	87		Fairplay, WI	
Schneider, Luzia Dorothea	19, Jan. 1860	22, Dec.	34-11m-14d	12	Wrede	Platteville, WI	Dorum, Hannover
Schneider, Magdalena	25, Apr. 1870	25, Mar.	51	135		Gasconade Co, MO	Canton Bern, Schweiz
Schneider, Magdalena Augusta	30, July 1896		70	495	Merkle	Columbus, OH	Rudersberg, Welzheim, Württemberg
Schneider, Margaretha	26, Mar. 1891	2, Feb.	78	206	Fritz	Brooklyn, NY	Kanton Wolfstein, Rheinpfalz Baiern
Schneider, Margaretha	17, Nov. 1898	21, Oct.	88	735		Pittsburg, PA	Mittelbrunn, Rheinkreis Baiern
Schneider, Margaretha	29, July 1867	16, July	57	238	Genheimer	Marietta, OH	Oppau, Rheinkreis Baiern
Schneider, Margaretha	12, Jan. 1860	16, Dec.	28	8	Schulte	Oregon, MO	
Schneider, Margaretha	8, June 1899		72	367	Seiler	Bracken, TX	Manderbach, Nassau
Schneider, Margarethe	28, Mar. 1870	7, Mar.	70	103	Simon	Berea, OH	Reimershausen, Marburg, Kurhessen
Schneider, Maria	22, July 1897	6, July	64	463	Gegner	Boonville, MO	Erlangen, Mittelfranken, Baiern
Schneider, Maria	3, Jan. 1876	14, Dec.	23	7		Canton, MO	Chillicothe, Ross County, Ohio
Schneider, Maria	18, Aug. 1873	13, July	30	263	Hasenpflug	Chillicothe, OH	
Schneider, Maria Anna	3, Nov. 1887	5, Oct.	67	702	Henkel	Chillicothe, OH	Muttersbach, Gießen, Hessen-Darmstadt
Schneider, Maria Anna	9, June 1898	17, May	35	367	Severinghaus	Berea, OH	Batesville, Indiana
Schneider, Maria Barbara	5, Aug. 1878	17, July	65-10m	247	Rilling	West Bend, WI	Dußlingen, Tübingen, Württemberg
Schneider, Maria Elisabeth	7, June 1875	9, May	54	183		Canton, MO	
Schneider, Maria Eva	1, Sept 1879	31, July	41- 5m-24d	279	Haller	Syracuse, NY	Lafargeville, Jefferson County, New York
Schneider, Maria Friedrike	3, Feb. 1853	11, Dec.		20	Klein	Oregon, MO	Kriegsfled, Rheinkreis Baiern
Schneider, Maria Genofefa	17, Nov. 1887		68	734	Feger	Lancaster, WI	
Schneider, Maria Genofefa	22, Sept 1887	27, Aug.	67- 7m-30d	606	Feger	Lancaster, WI	Fernach, Oberkirch, Baden

- 455 -

Christliche Apologete Death Notices --- 1839 - 1899

Name of Deceased	Notice Date	Death Date	Age	Page	Maiden Name	Place of Death	Place of Birth
Schneider, Maria L.	14, Jan. 1897	27, Dec.	26	31		Newport, KY	Cleveland, Ohio
Schneider, Maria Magdalena	1, Apr. 1897	7, Mar.	66	207	Stark	Platteville, WI	Hillesheim, Hessen-Darmstadt
Schneider, Maria Magdalena	5, Apr. 1875	13, Mar.	18	111		Marrs, IN	Vanderburg County, Indiana
Schneider, Maria Philppine	12, Apr. 1869	20, Mar.	70	119	Schäfer	Galena, IL	Haßloch, Neustadt a. d. Haardt, Rheinkreis Baiern
Schneider, Martha	8, Oct. 1891	16, Sept	31	654	Vater	St. Louis, MO	Preuswitz, Nieder-Schlesien, Preußen
Schneider, Martha Helena	7, Jan. 1884	11, Dec.	23	7		Dubuque, IA	Plattville, Grant County, Wisconsin
Schneider, Matthias	23, Aug. 1869	1, Aug.	36	271		Saginaw, MI	Randen bei Blumberg, Donaueschingen, Baden
Schneider, Paulina	23, Feb. 1863	30, Jan.	30	32	Eller	Farmington, IA	Zedoweil, Merseburg, Preußen
Schneider, Peter	14, July 1887	21, June	86	446		Dayton, OH	Oberamstadt, Darmstadt, Hessen-Darmstadt
Schneider, Peter	11, June 1883	30, May	70	191		Louisville, KY	Kaiserslautern, Rheinkreis Baiern
Schneider, Peter	13, Jan. 1873	17, Nov.	66	15		Evansville, IN	Schwarzenburg, Bern, Schweiz
Schneider, Peter	7, Feb. 1889	9, Jan.	74- 7m- 8d	94		Nokomis, IL	Cappeln,
Schneider, Peter Franz	2, May 1895	17, Apr.	69- 6m- 5d	286		Eudora, KS	Hohen-Solms, Preußen
Schneider, Phil. J. M.	24, Sept 1896	7, Sept	88	623		Nokomis, IL	Dillenburg, Nassau
Schneider, Philipp	29, May 1890	4, May	47- 1m-27d	350		Ellis Grove, IL	Edwardsville, Madison County, Illinois
Schneider, Philipp	14, Apr. 1873	10, Mar.	63- -20d	119		Chillicothe, OH	Ruchheim, Rheinkreis Baiern
Schneider, Philipp	2, Mar. 1893	10, Feb.	80	142		Oregon, MO	Osthafen, Hessen-Darmstadt
Schneider, Philipp	15, June 1893	16, May	85- 4m- 2d	382		North Vale, NJ	Kreiffeld, Baiern
Schneider, Philipp	15, June 1893	6, Apr.	67	382		Chillicothe, OH	Hessen
Schneider, Philipp	20, Oct. 1862	3, Oct.	14	168		Chillicothe, OH	
Schneider, Philipp	24, Feb. 1873	19, Jan.	2- 3m	63		Marrs, IN	
Schneider, Philipp G.	3, Oct. 1889	11, Sept	68	638	Gärtler	New Albany, IN	Dossenheim, Elsaß
Schneider, Philippine	2, May 1881	10, Apr.	68	143		Smithton, MO	Rumbach, RheinPfalz Baiern
Schneider, Rosalie	30, Jan. 1871	2, Dec.	28	39		San Francisco, CA	Elsach, Elsaß
Schneider, Rosetta	28, Oct. 1886	29, Sept	18	7		Sandusky, OH	Michelbach, Nassau
Schneider, Rosine	28, Sept 1899	26, Aug.	76- - 8d	623		Perry, TX	Rümlingen, Baselland, Schweiz
Schneider, Samuel	22, Oct. 1877	23, Sept	33- 3m- 8d	343		Marion, OH	Marion County, Ohio
Schneider, Sophie Helene	25, Feb. 1892	15, Jan.	25	127		Brooklyn, NY	Brooklyn, New York
Schneider, Susanna	19, Jan. 1888	25, Dec.	60	46	Strack	Burlington, IA	Lebanon County, Pennsylvania
Schneider, Susanna	19, Jan. 1893	22, Dec.	74-11m- 4d	46		Chicago, IL	
Schneider, Susie	28, July 1887	10, July	33	478		Chillicothe, OH	
Schneider, Theresia	24, Mar. 1879	8, Mar.	57	95	Klausmann	St. Louis, MO	Schnellingen, Hasloch, Baden
Schneider, Theresia	30, Mar. 1899	22, Feb.	68	207		Grand Rapids, MI	Affenberg, Baden
Schneider, W.	7, June 1880	20, May	41- 6m- 9d	183		Ft. Atkinson, WI	Güdingen, Saarbrücken, Preußen
Schneider, Wilhelm	17, Aug. 1863	2, Aug.	64- 1m- 2d	132		Marietta, OH	Roden, Minden, Preußen
Schneider, Willie	24, Aug. 1893	31, July	59	542		Victoria, TX	Hinterpommern
Schnek, Eberhardina	20, Jan. 1873	18, Dec.	76	23	Rupp	Seymour, IN	Marbach, Württemberg
Schnell, Anna Emilie	16, Apr. 1883	28, Mar.	21- 7m	127		Chicago, IL	Henderson, Siply County, Minnesota
Schnell, Carl	16, Jan. 1896	28, Dec.	41	46		Covington, KY	Bischweiler, Elsaß
Schnell, Charlotte	7, Nov. 1870	15, Oct.	32	359	Orns	Kentucky, IA	Mecklenburg-Schwerin
Schnell, Georg	25, Sept 1846		Inquiry	165		St. Louis, MO	Odenhausen, Grümberg, Hessen-Darmstadt
Schnell, Johannes	19, Mar. 1891	1, Mar.	58- 5m- 8d	190		Chicago, IL	Niedervorschütz,
Schnell, Paul	28, Sept	28, Sept	64	359		Peoria, IL	Kurhessen
Schnell, Peter	21, Nov. 1864	21- 8m-12d	188			Edgerton, OH	
Schnelle, Johanne	10, Mar. 1879	20, Feb.	69- 6m-19d	79	Bertram	Salem, IN	Grenisheim, Gandersheim, Braunschweig
Schnelle, Louise	26, May 1879	7, May	33- 2m- 1d	167	Gläser	Columbus, IL	Columbus, Illinois

Christliche Apologete Death Notices --- 1839 - 1899

Name of Deceased	Notice Date	Death Date	Age	Maiden Name	Page	Place of Death	Place of Birth
Schnepf, Louise Katharina	18, Dec. 1890	23, Oct.	78-10m-12d		814	Boston, MA	Baden
Schnepple, Max	7, Sept 1863	11, Aug.	17		144	Buffalo, NY	Winnenden, Württemberg
Schnert, Catharina	17, Sept 1857	15, Aug.	21		152	Monroe, IL	Schlierbach, Hessen-Darmstadt
Schnert, Johan Peter	12, Sept 1881	23, Aug.	82-11m- 6d		295	San Jose, IL	Schlierbach, Umstadt, Hessen-Darmstadt
Schnieder, Maria	9, Aug. 1869	8, July	52	Hillan	255	New Haven, CT	Herringhausen, Wittlage, Osnabrück, Hannover
Schniederjohann, Conrad	26, Nov. 1866	21, Sept			382	Herman, MO	Lienen, Tecklenburg, Westphalen, Preußen
Schniederjohann, Katharina	26, Nov. 1866	17, Sept		Laig	382	Herman, MO	
Schniep, Louise	12, Dec. 1870	23, Nov.	60		399	Winona, MN	Oberbergen, Schorndorf, Württemberg
Schniepp, Elisabeth	18, Nov. 1897	30, Oct.	25	Nönmann	735	Bible Grove, IL	
Schnierle, Christina Magdalena	8, Oct. 1896	17, Sept	75- 8m-24d	Roller	655	St. Louis, MO	Maistem, Calw, Württemberg
Schnierle, Christine	11, Oct. 1880	28, Aug.	45- 8m-10d	Weller	327	Golconda, IL	Adelberg, Schorndorf, Württemberg
Schnierle, Michael	17, Dec. 1896	19, Nov.	70		814	Belleville, IL	Altburg, Calw, Württemberg
Schnietker, Maria Henriette	17, Sept 1877	31, Aug.	41		305	Seymour, IN	Ewinghaus, Hannover
Schnipp, Johan Michael	30, Sept 1867	12, Sept	65		310	Fountain City, WI	Oberwelter, Schorndorf, Württemberg
Schnitger, Anna Maria Luise	12, Mar. 1896	26, Feb.	82- 5m- 4d	Ruth	175	Watertown, WI	Dedinghausen, Lippe-Detmold
Schnitger, Herman Friedrich	5, Apr. 1894	12, Mar.	76		230	Watertown, WI	Wendlinghausen, Lippe-Detmold
Schnitker, Christian	29, Sept 1879	6, Sept	28-10m-12d		311	Hoyleton, IL	Hartum, Minden, Preußen
Schnitker, Eddie	1, Apr. 1886	14, Mar.	19		7	St. Paul, MN	Waseca County, Minnesota
Schnitker, Louis	14, Apr. 1892	24, Mar.	24		238	Red Wing, MN	Redwing, Minnesota
Schnitger, Wilhelmine	5, Feb. 1891	17, Jan.	55	Kellermann	94	St. Paul, MN	Bördinghausen, Minden, Preußen
Schnittker, Charlotte	7, July 1848		Inquiry		111	St. Louis, MO	Blasheim, Preußen
Schnizler, Barbara	4, Feb. 1892	13, Jan.	73	Kleinhardt	78	Alexandria, KY	Döttingen, Württemberg
Schnizler, Christoph	19, Nov. 1877	1, Nov.	61- 5m-16d		375	Newport, KY	Dettingen, Urach, Württemberg
Schnögelsberger, Louise	31, Mar. 1879	16, Mar.	31- 1m- 1d	Steinmiller	103	Galion, OH	Ratchen, Gießen, Hessen-Darmstadt
Schnökenberg, Maria	11, Oct. 1849	28, Aug.	72		164	German Creek, IA	Hannover
Schnörr, Eva Barbara	22, Oct. 1877	18, Sept	30	Steiner	343	Marrs, IN	Vanderburgh County, Indiana
Schnuckel, Johan Friedrich	31, Mar. 1898	7, Mar.	37		207	Odebolt, IA	Princeton, Bureau County, Illinois
Schnücker, Christian	25, June 1857	15, May	26-11m		104	Mt. Vernon, IN	Metzhausen, Hessen
Schnur, Anna Elisabeth	24, Apr. 1890	5, Apr.	66	Kalbfleisch	270	Jamestown, MO	Neu-Hattendorf, Ziegenhain, Kurhessen
Schnur, Christina	7, June 1860	21, May	38		92	Mt. Vernon, IN	
Schnur, Dorothea	3, July 1846		19	Schneider	107	Evansville, IN	Danter, Baiem
Schnur, Georg Heinrich	5, Aug. 1852	11, July	63		128	Mt. Vernon, IN	Harpertshausen, Dieburg, Hessen-Darmstadt
Schnur, Johan Georg	15, June 1899	13, Apr.	79		383	Jamestown, MO	Mannheim, Germany
Schnur, Leonhard	3, Nov. 1859	25, Sept	75		176	Mt. Vernon, IN	Dudenhofen, Hessen
Schnur, Louisa	19, Jan. 1885	28, Dec.	25		7	Mt. Vernon, IN	Mars Township, Posey County, Indiana
Schnur, Maria Louisa	2, June 1887	1, May	23	Fogas	350	Mt. Vernon, IN	Mt. Vernon, Indiana
Schnur, Philipp	19, Feb. 1866	20, Jan.	42- 5m-15d		62	Evansville, IN	Düdenhofen, Hessen
Schnurr, Anna Maria	14, May 1877	14, Apr.	76- 8m-19d	Kraft	159	Galion, OH	Hohensolms, Wetzlar, Preußen
Schnute, Harry Eduard	17, Sept 1883	18, July	7- 8m-18d		303	St. Louis, MO	
Schnute, Heinrich	22, Dec. 1873	18, Nov.	43		407	St. Louis, MO	Nettelstadt, Preußen
Schnute, John Heinrich Friedrich	26, Oct. 1885	8, Sept	22- -12d		7	St. Louis, MO	
Schnute, Lydia Mathilde	17, Sept 1883	31, July	10-10m		303	St. Louis, MO	
Schob, Friedrich Traugott	14, Aug. 1882	26, July	58		263	Marietta, OH	Döschwitz bei Zeita, Preußen
Schobe, Johan Jacob	3, Nov. 1862	21, Oct.	70		176	Cincinnati, OH	Basel, Schweiz
Schobert, Johan	18, Jan. 1894	11, Dec.	76		46	Papillion, NE	Lanzendorf, Baiem
Schoch, (Mrs)	29, Apr. 1858	12, Apr.	26		68	Freeport, IL	

Christliche Apologete Death Notices --- 1839 - 1899

Name of Deceased	Notice Date	Death Date	Age	Page	Maiden Name	Place of Death	Place of Birth
Schoch, Barbara Fröhlich	31, Mar. 1898	6, Mar.	66	207	Weber	Clay Center, KS	Bretzingen, Geildorf, Württemberg
Schoch, Peter	21, Jan. 1897	31, Dec.	79	47		Yellow Creek, IL	Ausweiler, RheinPreußen
Schock, Christina	28, July 1892	31, May	56	478	Biebenderser	Delaware, OH	Groß-Glattbach, Wachingen, Württemberg
Schöder, Karolina	3, May 1888	22, Apr.	36-10m	286	Weißensee	Allegheny City, PA	Barmen, RheinPreußen
Schöderlein, Leonhardt	17, Mar. 1879	1, Mar.	60- 2m	87		Aurora, IN	Brandt, Grunzenhausen, Baiern
Schoeberlein, Maria Sibilla	15, Dec. 1873	28, Nov.	14- 8m-15d	399		Aurora, IL	
Schoen, Ludwig	13, Aug. 1891	1, Aug.	73	526		Marion, OH	Ernsbach, Oehringen, Württemberg
Schoen, Marianne	4, June 1883	20, May	48	183		Lancaster, NY	Elsaß
Schoenig, Dorothea Amalia	20, Sept 1888	23, Aug.	42- 9m-11d	606	Schultze	Wilton, IA	Beeser, Preußen
Schoening, Carl Hugo	30, May 1895	6, May	15	350		Beaver Falls, MN	Flora, Renville County, Minnesota
Schoening, Moriz	25, Dec. 1876	22, Nov.	39- 8m	413		Brunswick, MO	Radsiek, Schwallenberg, Lippe-Detmold
Schoepflin, Georg Jakob	27, Sept 1888	15, Aug.	22	622		Brooklyn, NY	Barlingen, Emmendingen, Baden
Schoeppel, Margaretha	3, Mar.1873	20, Jan.	67	71	Moret	Chester, IL	Wandelhofen, Baireuth, Baiern
Schoewe, Louise	24, May 1894	3, May	75	342		Brownton, MN	Germany
Schöf, Margaretha	26, Jan. 1854	6, Jan.	31	16	Häuser	Newburg, IN	Römershausen, Hessen
Schöffel, Jakob	22, Apr. 1872	9, Apr.	57	135		Chillicothe, OH	Schaffhausen, Emmendingen, Baden
Scholer, Maria Barbara	26, Jan. 1888	29, Dec.	60	62	Hurst	Zumbro Falls, MN	Vogesheim, Mühlheim, Baden
Schölkopf, Johan Martin	18, Mar. 1897	17, Jan.	72	175		Ft. Atkinson, WI	Geißlingen, Württemberg
Scholl, Caroline	12, Apr. 1894	23, Feb.	42	246	Ziske	Troy, NY	Waschin, Preußen
Scholl, Christian	20, Oct. 1887	5, Oct.	66- 4m-28d	670		Hopewell, MO	Wurmberg, Württemberg
Scholl, Elisabeth	6, Feb. 1882	25, Jan.	77	47		Watertown, WI	Siglingen, Württemberg
Scholl, Friedrich	18, June 1891	29, May	60- 5m	398		Storm Lake, IA	Roßwag, Württemberg
Scholl, Johan Adam	2, May 1895	13, Apr.	88	286		Chillicothe, OH	Meckheim, Germany
Scholl, Johan Ludwig	2, Jan. 1896	3, Dec.	84	14		Baltimore, MD	Sippersfeld, Kaiserslautern, Baiem
Scholl, Maria Elisabeth	12, Feb. 1891	19, Jan.	66- 7m-23d	110	Schneider	Montpelier, WI	Niederschelden, Preußen
Scholl, Maria Magdalena	7, Sept 1899	21, Aug.	92	575	Pommert	Chillicothe, OH	Baummenthal, Baden
Scholl, Wilhelmine	13, Nov. 1882	4, Oct.	13- 1m-14d	367		Storm Lake, IA	KleinGlattbach, Vaihingen, Württemberg
Schollenberger, Johanna C.	28, Apr. 1887	6, Apr.	85	270	Pfeifer	Marietta, OH	KleinSachsenheim, Vaihingen, Württemberg
Schollenberger, Philipp Jakob	8, Apr. 1870	24, July	68- 4m-23d	255		Marietta, OH	KleinSachsenheim, Vaihingen, Württemberg
Scholler, Margaretha	10, Apr. 1882	17, Mar.	74	119		Madison, IN	Links, Bischofsheim, Baden
Scholler, Wilhelm	16, Sept 1852	June	21	152		St. Louis, MO	Osnabrück, Hannover
Schöllhammer, Sibylla	11, Dec. 1865	24, Oct.		200		Clayton, IA	GroßDeinbach, Württemberg
Scholz, Johan Karl	29, Aug. 1889	12, Aug.	66	558		Emden, IL	Liegnitz, Schlesien
Scholz, Maria	29, Nov. 1894	3, Nov.	64	774		Emden, IL	Hessen-Darmstadt
Schömborg, Maria	30, June 1892	4, June	74	414	Porthis	Sun Prairie, WI	Tatenitz, Hohenstadt, Mähren, Oesterreich
Schomburg, Elisa	9, Feb. 1874	27, Jan.	27	47	Stegelmann	Detroit, MI	Tegelstorf, Holstein
Schompert, Katharina M.	14, June 1844	30, May	48	91		Evansport, OH	
Schön, Catharina	18, June 1877	31, May	27	199	Berends	Danbury, CT	Leer, Ostfriesland
Schönberg, Caroline	15, Mar. 1888	28, Dec.	44	174		Arlington, MN	riedland, West Preußen
Schönberger, (Mr)	1, Aug. 1889	25, June	73	494		Marine, MN	Hessen-Darmstadt
Schönberger, Anna Christina	12, Feb. 1877	15, Jan.	36	55	Steigewald	Lawrenceburg, IN	
Schönberger, Emma	5, Jan. 1885	25, Dec.	17- 1m-28d	7		Lawrenceburg, IN	
Schöne, Caroline	26, Mar. 1866	12, Mar.	27- 7m-8d	102		Summerfield, IL	
Schöne, David	6, Nov. 1882	9, Oct.	28- 7m-21d	359		Sandusky, OH	Bebra, Hessen-Kassel
Schöne, Heinrich J.	13, Oct. 1892	23, Aug.	34	654		Summerfield, IL	High Prairie, Randolph County, Illinois
Schöne, Jakob	27, Nov. 1876	13, Nov.	41	383		Summerfield, IL	Großesehn, Ostfriesland

Christliche Apologete Death Notices --- 1839 - 1899

Name of Deceased	Notice Date	Death Date	Age	Page	Maiden Name	Place of Death	Place of Birth
Schöne, Margaretha	26, Nov. 1883	8, Nov.	82	383	Rahmann	Summerfield, IL	Timmel, Amt Aurich, Hannover
Schone, Pauline	18, Aug. 1862	21, July	10	132		Louisville, KY	
Schone, Peter	1, Mar. 1875	15, Feb.	79- 6m	71		Summerfield, IL	Amt Aurich, Ostfriesland
Schönebaum, Emma	9, Apr. 1891	25, Mar.		238		Warrenton, MO	Warren County, Missouri
Schönebaum, Ernst	6, Sept 1880	17, Aug.	52- 6m- 6d	287		Warrenton, MO	Oehnhausen, Minden, Preußen
Schönebaum, Henriette	27, Dec. 1888	29, Nov.	55- 7m-29d	830	Meierkord	Warrenton, MO	Stemmen, Lippe-Detmold
Schönebaum, Mina	19, Feb. 1891	1, Feb.	25	126		Warrenton, MO	Warren County, Missouri
Schonecker, Heinrich	28, Dec. 1854	27, Nov.	35	208		Huntingburg, IN	
Schönemann, Dorothea	18, May 1885	22, Apr.	64	7		Sterling, NE	Sanbeck, Potsdam, Preußen
Schöner, Karoline	24, Aug. 1899	7, Aug.	37	543		Warsaw, IL	Warsaw, Illinois
Schöner, Katharina	22, Dec. 1898	16, Nov.	80	815		Warsaw, IL	Rothmannsberg, Württemberg
Schöner, Mich.	22, Dec. 1862	30, Nov.	40	204		Warsaw, IL	
Schöneweis, Friedrich	9, Aug. 1860		21	128		Petersburg, IL	
Schöneweis, Johan Friedrich	17, Jan. 1881	2, Jan.	62- -28d	23		Petersburg, IL	Goddelsheim, Waldeck
Schönfeld, Elisabeth	2, Jan. 1896	7, Dec.	40	14	Koch	Pekin, IL	Sheboygan, Wisconsin
Schönhardt, Christ.	4, Nov. 1897	7, Oct.	36	703		Danville, IL	Fünfbrunn, Württemberg
Schönheim, Louise Susanna	18, Feb. 1886	15, Jan.	53	7	Zimmer	Mt. vernon, NY	Billingen, Hessen-Darmstadt
Schönig, Johan	26, May 1898	18, Apr.	82	335		Bushton, KS	Sarah bei Ahrens, Spöck, Holstein
Schönig, Lorenzo Elmore Marco	2, Mar. 1899	1, Feb.	15	143		Burlington, IA	Decatur, Illinois
Schöning, Emilia Albertine	9, July 1896	8, June	48	447	Stelter	Flora, MN	Ruhnau, Bromberg, Germany
Schönlober, Anna Maria	13, Oct. 1892	29, Aug.	73	654		West Bend, WI	Atiergen, Göppingen, Württemberg
Schonscheck, Esther Justine	25, Apr. 1889	23, Mar.	77- 9m-10d	270		Chicago, IL	Posilge, Stuhm, Preußen
Schönthaler, Christine	1, Sept 1898	3, Aug.	80	559	Noser	Spencerville, OH	Feldremoch, Neuenburg, Württemberg
Schönthaler, Friedrika Jacobina	4, Nov. 1878	20, Oct.	67	351		New Knoxville, OH	Heimendingen, Leonberg, Württemberg
Schönthaler, Henry	25, Aug. 1862		29	136		Delaware, OH	
Schönthaler, Ludwig F.	21, July 1884	24, June	67	7		Spencerville, OH	Feldrennach, Neuenbürg, Württemberg
Schönthaler, Michael	30, Apr. 1847	12, Mar.	34	71			Feldrennig, Neuenburg, Württemberg
Schönthaler, Philipp	25, Aug. 1862		25	136		Delaware, OH	
Schönwetter, Augustine Wilhel.	24, Oct. 1895	9, Oct.	67	686	Gebhart	Columbus, WI	Piräm, Neumark
Schoo, Heinrich	30, Dec. 1897	3, Dec.	19	828		Decorah, IA	Canoe Township, Iowa
Schoolmann, Victor Heinrich J.	23, Apr. 1883	30, Mar.	72	135		New Orleans, LA	Berum, Ostfriesland
Schopenhorst, Anna Katharina	9, July 1866	12, Apr.		222	Brandt	Hopewell, MO	Falldorf, Amt Floto, Herford, Preußen
Schöpf, Anna Catharine	7, Mar. 1881	2, Feb.	42-10m-14d	79	Strobel	Halstead, KS	
Schöpf, Friederike	20, June 1895	30, May	78	398	Heriegel	Brooklyn, NY	Roßwag, Vaihingen a.d. Enz, Württemberg
Schöpflin, Barbara	11, Oct. 1880	6, Aug.	13	327		Brooklyn, NY	Westphalen
Schöpflin, Georg Jakob	7, Apr. 1884	15, Mar.	51	7		Chester, IL	Behlingen, Emendingen, Baden
Schöpflin, Katharine	4, Dec. 1876	22, Nov.	69	391	Staüblin	Brooklyn, NY	Bahlingen, Baden
Schopmeyer, Friedrich	13, Dec. 1849	1, Oct.		200		Evansport, OH	
Schöppe, Friedrich Ferdinand	26, Dec. 1881	6, Dec.		415		Cleveland, OH	Lintengreutz, Werda, Sachsen-Weimar
Schoppe, Johan H.	8, Oct. 1896	6, Aug.	72	655	Wienand	Decatur, IL	Hombressen, Kurhessen
Schoppe, Sabine	25, Aug. 1873	10, July	38	271	Hißgen	Decatur, IL	Freinsheim, Neustadt, Baiern
Schöppel, Katharina	19, Jan. 1863	10, Dec.	31-6m-30d	12	Wüstlich	Chester, IL	Burg Brebach, Baiem
Schoppelrey, Susanna Maria	19, May 1898	12, Apr.	77	319		Boston, MA	Burg Brebach, Baiem
Schoppelrey, Thomas	13, Apr. 1899	23, Mar.	78	239		Boston, MA	Ladbergen, Tecklenburg, Preußen
Schoppenhorst, Christina	15, Dec. 1892	16, Nov.	71- 2m- 1d	798	Heunroth	Huntingburg, IN	Poland, Indiana
Schoppenhorst, Franz Philipp	19, Mar. 1877	10, Jan.	8-10m	95		Bucyrus, OH	

- 459 -

Christliche Apologete Death Notices --- 1839 - 1899

Name of Deceased	Notice Date	Death Date	Age	Page	Maiden Name	Place of Death	Place of Birth
Schoppenhorst, Herman Heinrich	25, Apr. 1889	31, Mar.	70- 2m- 9d	270		Huntingburg, IN	Ladbergen, Preußen
Schoppenhorst, Johan	27, Aug. 1877	11, Aug.	24	279		Louisville, KY	Louisville, Jefferson County, Kentucky
Schoppenhorst, Johan	13, Aug. 1891	21, July	67- 7m-27d	526		Louisville, KY	Ladbergen, Münster, Preußen
Schoppenhorst, Maria	28, Apr. 1862		53	68	Peterjohann	Marthasville, MO	Ladbergen, Tecklenburg, Münster, Preußen
Schoppenhorst, Maria	10, Apr. 1876	25, Mar.	24- 9m- 4d	118		Huntingburg, IN	Dubois County, Indiana
Schoppenhorst, Sophia	19, Mar. 1877	9, Oct.	23- 6m-28d	95		Bucyrus, OH	Louisville, Jefferson County, Kentucky
Schoppenhorst, Sophia Elisabeth	10, Nov. 1892	21, Oct.	63	718	Mismeier	Louisville, KY	Ladbergen, Tecklenburg, Preußen
Schoppenhorst, Wilhelm	22, Sept 1884	29, Aug.	70-11m-22d	7		Hopewell, MO	Ladbergen, Tecklenburg, Münster, Preußen
Schöppler, Josephine	26, Oct. 1874	23, Sept		343	Schmeidel	Carver Co., MN	Wien, Oesterreich
Schoppmeier, Friedrich	2, Oct. 1876	15, Sept	23	319		Schnectady, NY	
Schoppmeier, Louisa	25, Sept 1876	23, Aug.	16	311		Schnectady, NY	
Schoppmeier, Richard	22, July 1867	30, June	20-10m-13d	230		Defiance, OH	Defiance County, Ohio
Schöpvel, Johann	23, Sept 1858	1, Sept	54- 4m-26d	152		Chester, IL	Nemansräuth, Baiern
Schorb, Rosina	4, Aug. 1873	13, July	24- 9m-16d	247		Burlington, WI	Trais Corner, Milwaukee County, Wisconsin
Schorer, Alma	23, July1883	2, July	9	239		New Haven, CT	
Schorling, Elisabeth	29, July 1886	7, July	67	7	Blaufarber	Oregon, MO	Lindorf, Wittlage, Hannover
Schormann, Anna Klara	1, Jan. 1852	23, Nov.	64-10m- 3d	4	Schleunings	Captina, OH	Ulrichstein, Hessen-Darmstadt
Schörmann, Maria Elisabeth	28, May 1877	19, Apr.	74	175	Stiegemeier	Stryker, OH	Tecklenburg, Münster, Preußen
Schorn, Mathilda	8, Oct. 1891	16, Sept	31	654		St. Paul, MN	
Schorri, Johannes	13, Sept 1894	13, July	53	598		Evansville, IN	Aarberg, Bern, Schweiz
Schort, Catharina	18, June 1891	23, May	36	398		Scranton, PA	Birkenfeld, Oldenburg
Schösser, (Mrs)	23, May 1864	13, Apr.	70	84		Lyons Creek, KS	Valkenberg, Naugart, Pommern
Schossow, Anna Bertha	6, Apr. 1893	17, Mar.	37	222	Degen	Lena, IL	Penkun, Randow, Pommern
Schott, Anna Christine	24, May 1894	2, May	73	342	Paul	Hokah, MN	Oberhaun, Hersfeld, Hessen
Schott, Anna Katharine	26, June 1871	7, June	43	207	Schäfer	Marietta, OH	Unterhaun, Kreis Hirschfeld, Kurhessen
Schott, Anna Margaretha	29, Nov. 1869	26, Sept	23	383		Chastity, IA	Wichmanshausen, Kurhessen
Schott, Barbara	9, Sept 1886	27, Aug.	30- 8m-27d	7	Schmidt	Marion, OH	Neulußheim, Schwetzingen, Baden
Schott, Friedrich Heinrich	27, Mar. 1890	4, Mar.	23- 1m-12d	206		Edgerton, OH	Elmore, Ohio
Schott, Heinrich	19, Jan. 1880	4, Jan.	65	23		Marietta, OH	Weißenbach, Hünfeld, Fulda, Preußen
Schott, Johan	1, Nov. 1888	6, Oct.	71	702		Cannelton, IN	Münchhausen, Kurhessen
Schott, Johan Heinrich	22, Aug. 1895	7, Aug.	74	542		Hokah, MN	Kurhessen
Schott, Johan Jacob	16, Apr. 1891	20, Mar.	64	254		LaCarne, OH	Neulußheim, Schwetzingen, Baden
Schott, John C.	17, Dec. 1891	19, Nov.	85- 2m- 8d	814		Muscatine, IA	Seenheim, Uffenheim, Baiern
Schott, Katharine	12, Dec. 1889	15, Nov.	66- 2m- 15d	798		Cannelton, IN	UnterSimmshausen, Marburg, Hessen
Schott, Maria Barbara	8, Sept 1879	25, Aug.	68- 2m-20d	287	Winkler	Muscatine, IA	Petersaurach, Baiern
Schott, Maria Elisabeth	1, Oct. 1866	13, Sept	41	318		Alton, IL	
Schott, Wilhelm Heinrich	11, Aug. 1892	14, July	12	510		Edon, OH	Milford Township, Defiance County, Ohio
Schöttel, Barbara	21, Mar. 1864	19, Feb.	70- 3m-17d	48		St. Paul, MN	Wolfisheim bei Strasburg, Frankreich
Schöttler, August Christian	27, June 1895	1, June	63	414		Denison, IA	Milow, Brandenburg
Schöttler, Elisabetha	5, July 1849	19, June	12- 7m	108		St. Louis, MO	Spitzaltheim, Hessen-Darmstadt
Schöttler, Magdalena	26, July 1849	25, June	39	120		St. Louis, MO	Kerschon, Köslin, HinterPommern
Schöwe, (Mr)	11, Oct. 1875	25, Sept	72- 2m	327	Heinsch	Sandusky, OH	Lauenburg, Pommern
Schöwe, Caroline Charlotte	8, May 1882	21, Apr.	80	151		Sandusky, OH	Weingarten, Durlach, Baden
Schöwe, Christina Wilhelmina	19, July 1880	3, July	42	231		Sandusky, OH	Voshüt, Bernt, Preußen
Schöwe, Gottlieb	10, Apr. 1890	4, Mar.	75	238		Brownton, MN	Stolp, Hinterpommern
Schöwe, Johanna	9, Mar. 1899	5, Feb.	66	159	Knuth	Sandusky, OH	

Christliche Apologete Death Notices --- 1839 - 1899

Name of Deceased	Notice Date	Death Date	Age	Maiden Name	Page	Place of Death	Place of Birth
Schöwe, Karoline	21, Jan. 1897		48	Sengstock	47	Sandusky, OH	Maslow, Cöslin, Preußen
Schowengerdt, Amalia	12, Feb. 1883	25, Jan.	35- -28d	Schake	55	Hopewell, MO	Humfeld, Bega, Lippe-Detmold
Schowengerdt, Friedrich	11, May 1899	10, Apr.	83		302	Independence, MO	Linen, Preußen
Schowengerdt, Johan	1, Nov. 1888	11, Oct.	40		702	Morrison, MO	Hopewell, Missouri
Schowengerdt, Leise	29, Mar. 1888	28, Feb.	70	Determann	206	Kansas City, MO	Lengerich, Tecklenburg, Preußen
Schowengerdt, Lisette Wilhelmine	30, Mar. 1868	28, Feb.		Husmeier	103	Herman, MO	Marthasville, Warren County, Missouri
Schowengerdt, Maria	19, Dec. 1861	21, Aug.	79		204	Marthasville, MO	Lienen, Kreis Münster, Preußen
Schowengert, Sophia Katharina	16, Nov. 1868	9, Oct.	20		367	San Jose, IL	Hopewell, Warren County, Missouri
Schrack, Christian	25, Dec. 1890		71		830	Portsmouth, OH	Württemberg
Schrack, Manassa	2, Dec. 1867	16, Nov.	22- 5m-18d		382	Canal Dover, OH	
Schrade, Johan Georg	26, Nov. 1883	11, Nov.	80		383	Aurora, IL	Neuffen, Württemberg
Schrade, Luise Elisabeth	9, Feb. 1899	15, Jan.	55	Weber	95	Chicago, IL	Heidelberg, Germany
Schrade, Maria	5, Jan. 1899	25, Nov.	57	Kehrer	15	Newark, NJ	Dernach, Tübingen, Württemberg
Schrader, Christian Wilhelm	30, Nov. 1885		17- 2m		7	Cape Girardeau, MO	
Schräder, Conrad	7, Oct. 1897	16, Sept	82		639	Indianapolis, IN	Schötmar, Lippe-Detmold
Schrader, Dietrich	4, May 1899	13, Apr.	66		287	Cape Girardeau, MO	Brokoloh, Hannover
Schrader, Dorothea	23, Oct. 1856	18, Sept	13- -14d		172	Canadea, NY	
Schrader, Ernst Wilhelm	12, June 1865	6, Apr.	21- 1m-16d		96	Lawrenceburg, IN	
Schrader, Friedrich	6, Dec. 1888	12, Nov.	71		782	Hochheim, TX	Hannover
Schrader, Friedrich William	3, Aug. 1868	30, June	28		247	Marysville, CA	
Schrader, H.	10, May 1888	30, Mar.	80		302	Caneadea, NY	Vollbüttel, Giffhorn, Hannover
Schrader, Heinrich	4, July 1864	20, May	23		108	Caneadea, NY	Vollbüttel, Amt Gißhorn, Hannover
Schrader, Heinrich	26, Oct. 1899	25, Sept	60		687	New Ulm, MN	Gamsen, Gifhorn, Hannover
Schrader, Heinrich Ludwig	3, May 1875	14, Apr.	74- 4m		143	Lawrenceburg, IN	Wesbeck, Neustadt, Hannover
Schrader, Helene	7, Oct. 1897	20, Aug.	57		639	San Francisco, CA	Edewecht, Germany
Schrader, Judith	17, Jan. 1889	27, Dec.	68-10m- 2d	Meier	46	Lawrenceburg, IN	Eldingen, Württemberg
Schrader, Karoline Friederika	12, June 1876	29, Apr.			191	St. Louis, MO	
Schrader, Karoline Wilhelmine	17, Aug. 1885	2, Aug.	66	Meil	7	Hochheim, TX	Wendhausen, Hildesheim, Hannover
Schrader, Maria	19, July 1894	23, June	57	Otto	470	Huntsville, KS	Hannover
Schrader, Maria Engel	31, May 1894	5, May	79	Hackmann	358	St. Louis, MO	Venne, Osnabrück, Hannover
Schrader, Mina	21, Jan. 1897	27, Dec.	49	Fahrweg	47	Cape Girardeau, MO	Altenau, Westphalen
Schrader, Sabina Dorothea	31, Aug. 1868	14, Aug.	59	Aikele	279	Aurora, IN	Neuffen, Württemberg
Schrader, William	25, May 1885	5, May	75		7	St. Louis, MO	Bofzen, Holzminden, Braunschweig
Schräer, Anna Ch. E.	22, Mar. 1869	7, Mar.	62- 1m- 4d	Christopher	95	Huntingburg, IN	Ladbergen, Münster, Preußen
Schrag, Anna	9, May 1889	13, Mar.	27- 8m-14d	Hartnagel	302	Belleville, IL	Belleville, Illinois
Schrag, Anna Katharina	2, Oct. 1890	12, Sept	67- 3m- 3d	Jäger	638	Portsmouth, OH	Denzen, Koblenz, RheinPreußen
Schrage, Anton Friedrich	17, Jan. 1895	25, Dec.	84- 5m-18d		46	Quincy, IL	Fortheim, Lübeck, Münden, Preußen
Schrage, Karoline Maria	13, Apr. 1885	26, Mar.	76	Thiemann	7	Quincy, IL	Hille, Minden, Preußen
Schräher, Herman Wilhelm	4, Nov. 1872	14, Oct.	69- 4m- 1d		359	Huntingburg, IN	
Schram, Heinrich	20, Jan. 1887	5, Jan.	25- 3m		46	Clay Center, KS	
Schram, Johan C.	13, Jan. 1887	19, Dec.	84		30	Marietta, OH	
Schram, Katharina Chr.	22, Dec. 1862	27, Nov.	84	Besinger	204	Washington, OH	Hölznen, Weinsberg, Württemberg
Schramm, Adolph	8, Oct. 1866	6, Aug.	25		326	San Francisco, CA	Hölzern, Weinsberg, Württemberg
Schramm, Anna Catharina	14, June 1880		17- 6m		191	Clay Center, KS	Cappeln, Schleswig
Schramm, Barbara	25, July 1864	11, June	46		120	Elizabeth City, NJ	Elsaß
Schramm, Bertha	4, July 1870		12		215	New Ulm, MN	Brown County, Minnesota

Christliche Apologete Death Notices --- 1839 - 1899

Name of Deceased	Notice Date	Death Date	Age	Page	Maiden Name	Place of Death	Place of Birth
Schramm, Conr.	22, Feb. 1869	26, Jan.	57	63		Wapello, IA	Markt-Plech, Baiern
Schramm, Elisabeth Margaretha	17, Oct. 1864	22, Sept	11	168		Bonn, OH	
Schramm, Emma	14, June 1880		13	191		Clay Center, KS	
Schramm, Heinrich	17, Feb. 1879	31, Jan.	42	55		Rushville, IL	Manderbach, Dillenburg, Nassau
Schramm, Henry	26, June 1890	31, May	58	414		Clay Center, KS	Schamader, Witgenstein, Preußen
Schramm, Ida	11, Nov. 1878	27, Oct.	12- 8m-21d	359		New York City, NY	
Schramm, Karl Ludwig	21, Sept 1899	29, Aug.	68	607		Fairfax, MN	Weißenhöh, Posen
Schramm, Ludwig	3, Aug. 1893	21, May	67	494		New York City, NY	Pommern
Schramm, Margaretha Barbara	17, Mar.1873	19, Jan.	74	87	Farmbauer	Portsmouth, OH	Blech, Bängerts, Baiern
Schramm, Maria Margaretha	13, Nov. 1890	13, Oct.	89	734	Kunzenheimer	Mt. Vernon, MO	Ziegenfeld, Ebrm, Baiern
Schramm, Peter	18, July 1861	2, July	68	116		Rushville, IL	Manderbach, Amt Dillenburg, Nassau
Schramm, Sarah	18, Mar. 1878	27, Feb.	20- 9m- 2d	87		Rushville, IL	Quincy, Illinois
Schranz, Elisabeth	27, Oct. 1892	7, Oct.	33	686		Warrenton, MO	Elmendingen, Pforzheim, Baden
Schratt, Christina	7, Oct. 1878	14, Sept	84- 7m	319	Diebold	Marion, OH	Sonnenfeld, Sachsen-Coburg
Schrauder, J. Johannes	22, Oct. 1857	20, July	26- -28d	172		Brooklyn, NY	
Schreck, (Mrs)	26, Sept 1850	9, Aug.		156		---, MO	
Schreck, Arnold	15, Mar. 1860	27, Feb.	7- 4m-12d	44		Mascoutah, IL	
Schreck, Heinrich	11, Sept 1882	16, Aug.	72- 8m-15d	295		Weston, MO	Lotte, Tecklenburg, Münster, Preußen
Schreck, Louis Sam.	5, Sept 1881	10, Aug.	13	287		St. Louis, MO	Weston, Missouri
Schreck, Maria E.	8, Sept 1884	6, Aug.	81- 9m-27d	7	Böhmer	Weston, MO	Lotte, Tecklenburg, Münster, Preußen
Schreiber, Carrie	2, Dec. 1886	10, Nov.	21	7		St. Joseph, MO	Floyd County, Indiana
Schreiber, Elisabeth	11, July 1889		58- 8m- 5d	446		Madison, WI	Enshusen, Germany
Schreiber, Emma	28, June 1894	5, June	24	422	Hackbarl	Bristol, WI	Salem Twp, Kenosha County, Wisconsin
Schreiber, Ferd. Louis	25, Oct. 1869	7, Oct.	15- 8m-29d	343		Sturgeon Bay, WI	
Schreiber, H.L.	30, June 1879	14, June	18- -11d	207		St. Joseph, MO	
Schreiber, Juliana Magdalena	11, Jan. 1864	3, Dec.	13	8		Louisville, KY	
Schreiber, Karl	19, June 1876	17, May	53- 3m-14d	199		Ahnapee, WI	Karlshafen, Kurhessen
Schreiber, Katharina	12, June 1871	3, May	69	191	Findling	Pomeroy, OH	Oppau, Frankenthal, Baiern
Schreiber, Magdalena	13, May 1886	17, Apr.	76	7	Huber	New Albany, IN	Berghausen, Durlach, Baden
Schreiber, Magdalena	18, Apr. 1895	18, Feb.	68-10m	254		Ahnapee, WI	
Schreiber, Maria	20, Aug. 1883	16, July	58	271	Bogen	New York City, NY	Dirmstein, RheinPfalz Baiern
Schreiber, Maria Magdalena	16, Apr. 1891	19, Mar.	27	254		St. Joseph, MO	Floyd County, Indiana
Schreiber, Martin	7, May 1891	26, Mar.	60- -29d	302		Sully Co, SD	Nußdorf bei Landau, Rheinkreis Baiern
Schreiber, Philipp	8, Aug. 1864	26, May	22	128		Pomeroy, OH	
Schreiber, Sebastian	19, July 1888	2, July	63	462		Madison, WI	Gumbelstadt, Sachsen-Meiningen
Schreiber, Wilhelm	20, May 1878		68	159		---, NY	Rheinkreis Baiern
Schreiber, Wilhelmina	20, Sept 1894	27, Aug.	35	614	Martin	Marrs, IN	Posey County, Indiana
Schreier, John G.	2, July 1896	5, June	76	431		Delaware, OH	Oberamt Marbach, Württemberg
Schreier, Karoline Friederike	24, Nov. 1892	10, Nov.	66	750	Schneider	Delaware, OH	Veihingen a. d. Enz, Württemberg
Schreiner, (Mrs)	12, Dec. 1864	13, Oct.		200	Lütje	Appleton, MO	
Schreiner, Amelia Bertha	13, Apr. 1899	23, Mar.	20	239		Whitewater, MO	Appleton, Missouri
Schreiner, Catharina	15, June 1868	6, May	58	191		Appleton, MO	Rottheim, Hessen-Darmstadt
Schreiner, Ida Bertha	14, July 1898	2, June	53	447	Gentsch	Appleton, MO	
Schreiner, John	5, Aug. 1878	2, July	54- 7m- 9d	247		Sleepy Eye, MN	Kersterhausen, Kurhessen
Schreiner, Karl	14, Jan. 1884	26, Dec.	23	7		China, MI	
Schreiner, Lizzie Laura	24, Dec. 1896	30, Nov.	13	831		Wadena, MN	Wadena, Minnesota

Christliche Apologete Death Notices --- 1839 - 1899

Name of Deceased	Notice Date	Death Date	Age	Maiden Name	Page	Place of Death	Place of Birth
Schreiner, Margaretha	17, Mar. 1898	11, Feb.	70	Groll	175	Marine City, MI	Hessen-Darmstadt
Schreiner, Mathilda	29, Sept 1898	30, Aug.	23		623	Appleton, MO	Appleton, Missouri
Schreitle, Anna Maria	3, Oct. 1889	28, Aug.	61	Wezel	638	Long Island City, NY	Waldorf, Tübingen, Württemberg
Schrey, Anna Maria	31, Oct. 1870	21, Sept	27- 9m		351	Lansing, MI	Volz aus Walddorf, Nagold, Württemberg
Schrey, Margaretha	20, Sept 1880		58		303	DeWitt, MI	Ober-Riexingen, Württemberg
Schreyer, Carolina	25, Oct. 1855	29, Sept	28- 8m-13d		172	Delaware, OH	Storndorf, Hessen-Darmstadt
Schrickel, Katharina	3, June 1872	25, Apr.	50	Kraft	183	Wheeling, WV	Burgstall, Marbach, Württemberg
Schrieber, Heva Margaretha	1, Nov. 1880	15, Oct.	54	Fink	351	Falls County, TX	Witlagen, Hannover
Schriefer, Friedrich	7, Nov. 1861	24, Aug.	36		180	Santa Claus, IN	
Schriefer, Melville	28, July 1892	21, May		Harris	478	Santa Claus, IN	Ripley County, Ohio
Schriever, Elisabeth	6, Oct. 1898	21, Aug.	49	Vortmann	639	Santa Claus, IN	Harmhausen, Oldenburg
Schriever, Johann	31, July 1865	2, Jan.	24		124	New Orleans, LA	Germersheim, Rheinkreis Baiern
Schröck, Christian	18, Oct. 1849		Inquiry		167	New York, NY	Germersheim, Rheinkreis Baiern
Schröck, Michael	18, Oct. 1849		Inquiry		167	New York, NY	Belle, Schieder, Lippe-Detmold
Schröder, (Mrs)	29, Nov. 1875	8, Aug.			383	Canaan, MO	Maßfeld, Sachsen-Meiningen
Schröder, Amalia	6, Jan. 1887	23, Dec.	58	Kiesewetter	14	Michigan City, IN	Dölitz, Piritz, Pommern
Schröder, Anna Christine	9, May 1889	25, Apr.	71- 7m-10d	Zabel	302	Watertown, WI	Spika Neuenfelde, Dorum, Hannover
Schröder, Anna Dorothea	15, Apr. 1858		42- 5m	Hennings	60	Platteville, WI	Rittmannshausen, Kurhessen
Schröder, Anna Maria Elisabeth	24, May 1880	7, May	45	Hoßbach	167	Altamont, IL	
Schröder, Anna Maria Florentina	28, Oct. 1878	10, Oct.	21	Wehmeier	343	Herman, MO	Rostock, Mecklenburg-Schwerin
Schröder, August	4, Aug. 1887	19, July	59-10m-22d		494	Marion, OH	Hustätt, Nenndorf, Stolzenau, Hannover
Schröder, Carl	7, June 1855	7, Mar.	34		92	Mt. Vernon, IN	Reben, Minden, Preußen
Schröder, Carl Friedrich	1, Sept 1879	18, Aug.	43		279	New Haven, MO	
Schröder, Catharina	15, Jan. 1866	13, Oct.	36		22	Effingham, IL	
Schröder, Catharina	4, Mar. 1878	12, Feb.	42- 9m-23d		71	South Bend, IN	Fürstenau, Hannover
Schröder, Charlotte	30, Apr. 1857	26, Mar.	40	Moritz	72	Nashville, IL	Schwachenwalde, Brandenburg
Schröder, Christian Friedrich	4, Mar. 1897	1, Feb.	47		143	Limestone, OH	Beckstadt, Hannover
Schröder, Christopher	9, June 1884	3, Apr.	62		7	San Jose, CA	Langerick, Westphalen
Schröder, Dina	24, Jan. 1895	27, Nov.	33	Linemann	62	Red Oak, MO	Blumberg, Pommern
Schröder, Dora Sophia	21, Sept 1899	1, Sept	59	Lambrecht	607	Rockham, SD	Schieder, Lippe-Detmold
Schröder, Dorothea	18, Feb. 1867	21, Jan.	73- 3m		54	Second Creek, MO	Balge, Amt Nienburg, Hannover
Schröder, Dorothea Elisabeth	15, Feb. 1875	21, Jan.	52- 5m-24d	Harms	55	Lake Creek, MO	
Schröder, Dorothea Emilie	3, Apr. 1865	13, Mar.	12- 8m-17d		56	Platteville, WI	Diestelow, Mecklenburg-Schwerin
Schröder, Elisabeth	16, May 1895	8, Apr.	72	Lehmann	318	Bay City, MI	Buffalo, New York
Schröder, Eliza Anna	24, June 1897	11, May	43		399	Kline, IA	Grünau bei Hirschberg, Schlesien
Schröder, Emanuel	25, Oct. 1869	8, Oct.	48- 6m-12d		343	Williamsburg, NY	Grickstang, Schabien, OstPreußen
Schröder, Emilie	9, Jan. 1890	18, Dec.	66	Schaudin	30	Enterprise, KS	Laporte, Indiana
Schröder, Emma	12, Dec. 1895	15, Nov.	35		798	Laporte, IN	
Schröder, Emma Alvine	3, May 1888	20, Apr.	16- 2m- 4d		286	Milwaukee, WI	Vanderburg County, Indiana
Schröder, Emma Clara	14, Nov. 1881	26, Oct.	14		367	Salem, IN	Zachen, Salzig, Pommern
Schröder, Ernst Wilhelm	17, Mar. 1892	18, Feb.	78		175	Lowell, WI	Sukow bei Parchim, Baiern
Schröder, F. Charles W.	12, June 1890	22, May	58- 6m		382	Swanton, NE	
Schröder, F. Wilhelm	24, July 1865	2, Apr.			120	Vandalia, IL	
Schröder, Felicitas	20, Jan. 1887	25, Dec.	60- 3m-29d	Bens	46	Marion, OH	Altwiesloch, Baden
Schröder, Fr. Chr.	2, Feb. 1880	9, Jan.	72		39	Third Creek, MO	Belle, Amt Schiede, Lippe-Detmold
Schröder, Friedrich	20, Sept 1860	27, Aug.	54		152	Lena, IL	Oppurg, Sachsen-Weimar

Christliche Apologete Death Notices --- 1839 - 1899

Name of Deceased	Notice Date	Death Date	Age	Maiden Name	Page	Place of Death	Place of Birth
Schröder, Friedrich	21, Aug. 1890	20, May	82	Friedeberg	542	Brillion, WI	Insel Rügen, Pommern
Schröder, Gesina	6, Apr. 1874	25, Mar.	25- 5m		111	Peoria, IL	Oldenburg, Oldenburg
Schröder, H.C.D.	5, May 1887	20, Apr.	79-4m-28d		286	Platteville, WI	Nordholz, Spika, Dorum, Hannover
Schröder, Heinrich	12, Nov. 1847	2, Sept	68		183	New Orleans, LA	
Schröder, Heinrich	29, Aug. 1870	21, Mar.	15- -10d		279	Lake Creek, MO	
Schröder, Heinrich Carl	11, Jan. 1894	19, Dec.	80		30	Dodgeville, IA	Mennighüffen, Herford, Preußen
Schröder, Heinrich Ernst	23, Sept 1897	2, Sept	74		607	Pinckney, MO	Reme, Minden, Preußen
Schröder, Henry	5, Apr. 1894	13, Mar.	48		230	Burlington, IA	Flint Creek, Iowa
Schröder, Herman	2, Nov. 1893	25, Sept	86		702	Peoria, IL	Hude, Oldenburg
Schröder, Johan	12, Apr. 1894	19, Mar.	40		246	Roseville, MI	Zachan, Pommern
Schröder, Johan August	1, Mar. 1894	2, Feb.	54		150	Madison, WI	Quasal, Mecklenburg-Schwerin
Schröder, Johan Friedrich Christian	9, May 1895	16, Apr.	76		302	Detroit, MI	Teppingen, Solta, Hannover
Schröder, Johan Heinrich	10, Jan. 1895	13, Dec.	60		30	Portland, OR	Carle, Hoia, Hannover
Schröder, Johan Heinrich	4, Apr. 1895	28, Feb.	76		222	Lake Creek, MO	Falkenwalde, Uckermark, Preußen
Schröder, Johanna	30, Apr. 1877	22, Mar.	47	Müller	143	Danville, MN	
Schröder, Johanna Charlotte	30, Nov. 1893	5, Oct.	71-11m- 9d		766	Ripon, WI	
Schröder, John	20, Apr. 1893	23, Apr.	80		254	Pittsburg, PA	Elsfleth, Oldenburg
Schröder, John Rudolph	20, Nov. 1890	8, Sept	68		750	Dennis, MO	Hannover
Schröder, Karl August	7, Aug. 1876	17, July	56		255	Mountain Lake, MN	Eichberg, Bromberg, Preußen
Schröder, Katharina	26, Jan. 1899	1, Jan.	79	Humberg	63	Pittsburg, PA	Mischheid, Ziegenheim, Kurhessen
Schröder, Katharina	31, May 1880	24, Apr.	54	Döhrheiter	175	Dodgeville, IA	Ruherberg, Salzwedel, Preußen
Schröder, Katharina	21, Aug. 1876	1, Aug.	48	Ehrig	271	Bunker Hill, IL	Högsdorf, Holstein
Schröder, Louise	17, Jan. 1895	17, Dec.	48	Kei	46	Peace Creek, KS	
Schröder, Ludwig	16, Nov. 1893	13, Oct.	58		734	Perry, TX	Patzig auf der Insel Rügen, Pommern
Schröder, Magdalena	12, Sept 1870	1, Aug.	22		295	Des Moines, IA	
Schröder, Maria	12, Sept 1870	30, Aug.	18- 6m-20d		295	Aurora, IL	
Schröder, Maria	15, May 1876	27, Apr.			159	New York City, NY	
Schröder, Maria Elisabeth	9, Mar. 1885	23, Feb.	57- 8m-23d	Ströder	7	Blue Island, IL	Niederdorla, Mühlhausen, Thüringen
Schröder, Martha Elisabeth	17, Mar.1873	5, Mar.	15- 6m-15d		87	Blue Island, IL	
Schröder, Mathilde	21, Feb. 1881	19, Jan.	16-10m-12d		63	Roseville, MI	
Schröder, Nancy	31, Dec. 1877	18, Nov.	39		423	Salem, IN	
Schröder, Rudolph	29, Sept 1898	5, Sept	51		623	Brooklyn, NY	Coose, Pommern
Schröder, Simon J.	17, Dec. 1896	29, Nov.	44		814	Bushton, KS	Des Moines County, Iowa
Schröder, Wilhelm	19, May 1887	2, May	71- 5m-16d		318	Green Bay, WI	
Schröder, Wilhelm	19, Sept 1895	27, Aug.	26		606	Milwaukee, WI	Zachau, Satzig, Pommern
Schröder, Wilhelm Ernst	24, Dec. 1891	4, Dec.	50		830	Madison, WI	Roßnow, Hinterpommern, Preußen
Schröder, Wilhelmine	19, Apr. 1875	23, Mar.	50- 7m-13d	Karl	127	Victor, IA	
Schröder, Wilhelmine	24, Oct. 1895	25, Sept	14- 6m		686	Taegesville, WI	Schönberg, Neuburg, Württemberg
Schrodt, Barbara	5, Oct. 1899	11, Sept		Kuster	639	Cincinnati, OH	Stift Quernheim, Minden, Preußen
Schroeckel, John	27, June 1881	31, May	22- 6m- 6d		207	Wheeling, WV	Farsin, Hinterpommern
Schroeder, Elisabeth	17, Nov. 1884	29, Oct.	64		7	Burlington, IA	
Schroeder, Friederike	19, May 1898	29, Apr.	36	Gimm	319	Blackberry, OH	Kallstadt, Baiern
Schroeder, Louise	31, Dec. 1883	15, Dec.	26	Zittinger	7	Baltimore, MD	Iowa City, Iowa
Schroeder, Richard	17, July 1882	21, June	35- 5m-29d		231	Scranton, PA	
Schroeder, Rosa Anna	3, Mar. 1884	4, Jan.	30		7	Victor, IA	
Schröer, Dina Sophia	7, July 1898	12, June	50	Fellwisch	431	Huntingburg, IN	Dubois County, Indiana

Christliche Apologete Death Notices --- 1839 - 1899

Name of Deceased	Notice Date	Death Date	Age	Maiden Name	Page	Place of Death	Place of Birth
Schröer, Emma M.	31, Aug. 1893	15, July	23		558	Cullman, AL	Huntingburg, Indiana
Schröer, Johann Wilhelm	21, June 1855	1, June	39- 5m		100	Rockford, IL	Lenchrich, Tecklenburg, Preußen
Schröer, Maria Elisabeth	15, Mar. 1880	28, Feb.	70- 3m	Schoppenhorst	87	Cincinnati, OH	Ladbergen, Tecklenburg, Preußen
Schröerlöke, Herman Wilhelm	6, May 1872	29, Mar.	19- 1m-13d		151	Sidney, OH	
Schroerlucke, Francis	6, Dec. 1894	3, Nov.	23		790	Evansville, IN	Evansville, Indiana
Schroh, Magdalena	14, Apr. 1898	11, Mar.	59		239	Poughkeepsie, NY	Kaiserslautern, Rheinpfalz Baiern
Schröleke, Wilhelm	4, Aug. 1879	7, July	62		247	Louisville, KY	
Schrölike, Anna Christina Elsabina	25, Aug. 1879	29, July	90- -11d		271	Madison, IN	Ladbergen, Tecklenburg, Preußen
Schrolike, Wilhelm F.	18, June 1877	29, May	11		199	Madison, IN	Madison, Indiana
Schrölleke, Heinrich	5, May 1892	13, Apr.	48		286	Boonville, IN	Ladbergen, Preußen
Schrölüke, Wilhelm	29, Aug. 1861	1, Aug.	70		140	Huntingburg, IN	Ladbergen, Tecklenburg, Preußen
Schrölürke, Anna Maria Elisabeth	6, May 1872	18, Apr.	80- 6m-10d	Stork	151	Huntingburg, IN	Ladbergen, Tecklenburg, Germany
Schrop, Maria	8, Dec. 1884	21, Nov.	70	Giesler	7	South Bend, IN	Berks County, Pennsylvania
Schrör, Heinrich	10, Oct. 1889	27, Sept	80- 5m-27d		654	Cincinnati, OH	Ladbergen, Tecklenburg, Münster, Preußen
Schrörike, Adolph Wilhelm	16, Oct. 1890	22, Sept	78		670	Huntingburg, IN	Ladbergen, Tecklenburg, Preußen
Schrörlüke, Anna Elsebein	17, Mar. 1879	19, Feb.	64-10m- 4d	Stieneker	87	Huntingburg, IN	Ladbergen, Tecklenburg, Preußen
Schrörluke, Carrie	6, Oct. 1898	21, Sept	25		639	Evansville, IN	Evansville, Indiana
Schrörluke, Ida Alice	9, Dec. 1897	22, Nov.	17- 9m- 6d		783	Evansville, IN	
Schrot, Friedrich	25, Jan. 1894	2, Jan.	72		62	Marion, OH	Elmerdingen, Baden
Schröter, Christian	18, Dec. 1890	17, Nov.	72		814	Evansville, IN	Kanton Bern, Schweiz
Schröter, Ernestine	16, Nov. 1885	30, Oct.	69	Grunzert	7	Charles City, IA	Lichtenau, Sachsen-Weimar
Schröter, Hanna	13, Oct. 1873	23, Sept	10- 1m-19d		327	Henderson, IN	
Schröter, Johan	10, Nov. 1892	21, Oct.	31	Fryhofer	718	Evansville, IN	Vanderburgh County, Indiana
Schröter, Maria	19, Oct. 1899	30, Sept	59		671	Salem, IN	Seymour, Indiana
Schröter, Ulrich	26, Oct. 1899	28, Sept	73		687	Salem, IN	Schwarzburg, Walleren, Schweiz
Schroth, Anna Rosina	11, Aug. 1892	11, July	60		510	Nashville, IL	Romanshof bei Czarnikau, Posen
Schroth, Cathie	26, July 1875	10,May	13		239	Poughkeepsie, NY	
Schroth, Dorothea	19, Feb. 1883	30, Jan.	82- -26d		63	Altamont, IL	Haag, Oehringen, Württemberg
Schroth, Jakob	13, Oct. 1892	9, Aug.	59		654	Poughkeepsie, NY	Kaiserslautern, Rheinpfalz Baiern
Schroth, John Andreas	28, May 1857	1, May	38		88	Buffalo, NY	Hohenstein, Besigheim, Württemberg
Schroth, Philipp	28, May 1877	4, May	16- -24d		175	Altamont, IL	Washington County, Illinois
Schrotter, Elisabeth	13, Jan. 1873	27, Nov.	79- 4m	Zwahlen	15	Evansville, IN	
Schrubbe, Kalr Friedrich Wilhelm	14, July 1898	26, June	63		447	Decorah, IA	Mötzelfitz, Pommern
Schruff, A.	24, Nov. 1859	11, Nov.	35		188	Louisville, KY	
Schrupp, Auguste Emilie	27, Apr. 1899	2, Apr.	32	Furch	271	Arlington, MN	Henderson, Sibley County, Minnesota
Schruth, John Ernst	19, Nov. 1883	27, Oct.	63		375	Wabasha, MN	Lüthow, Mecklenburg-Schwerin
Schu, Elisabeth	8, Jan. 1891	15, Dec.	82	Leibig	30	Greenville, OH	Sanct Ilgen, Baden
Schuart, Maria Christiana	14, Dec. 1863	11, Nov.	23	Karr	200	Quincy, IL	Zeugenhausen, Amt Sinsheim, Baden
Schübel, Friedrich Imanuel	22, Oct. 1866	22, Sept	45		342	Marine City, MI	Goldlauter, Preußen
Schubert, Elisabeth	16, Aug. 1875	6, July	46	Henne	263	Highland, IL	Canton Bern, Schweiz
Schubert, Hanna Sophia	19, Nov. 1883	25, Oct.	62- 1m- 1d	Zom	375	Wheeling, WV	KleinKundorf, Sachsen-Weimar
Schubert, J.	25, Nov. 1878	12, Nov.	50-10m- 6d		375	St. Joseph, MO	Neu Waldo, Schlesien
Schubert, Karl	23, June 1898	27, May	82		399	Wheeling, WV	Kleinkundorf, Sachsen-Weimar
Schuch, Johannes	27, Sept 1869	14, Aug.	46- 4m-11d		311	Louisville, KY	Niederaula, Kurhessen
Schuchard, Emma	28, Apr. 1879	16, Feb.	12- 9m		135	Boston, MA	
Schuchard, Georg	2, Apr. 1866	12, Jan.	36-10m		110	San Francisco, CA	

Christliche Apologete Death Notices — 1839 - 1899

Name of Deceased	Notice Date	Death Date	Age	Page	Maiden Name	Place of Death	Place of Birth
Schuchardt, Martin	6, Mar. 1882	8, Feb.	79	79		Golconda, IL	Eisenach, Sachsen-Weimar
Schuchardt, Wilhelmine	27, Aug. 1891	6, Aug.	60	558	Sedebier	New Orleans, LA	Pelkeloh, Westphalen
Schuchart, Anna Barbara	19, Mar. 1883	3, Mar.	76- -10d	95		Columbus, IL	Gutten, Mühlhausen, Erfurt, Preußen
Schuchmann, Elisabeth Margaret	7, Dec. 1863	22, Nov.	32	196	Röder	Mascoutah, IL	Groß-Bieberau, Dieburg, Hessen-Darmstadt
Schuchmann, Elisabeth Margaret	3, Feb. 1879	14, Jan.	60- 5m- 5d	39	Waldhaus	Mill Creek, IL	Ueberau, Hessen
Schuchmann, Elisabeth Margaret	24, Mar. 1879	14, Jan.	60	95	Waldhaus	Mill Creek, IL	Hessen
Schuchmann, Heinrich	24, May 1880	24, Apr.	69	167		Quincy, IL	Hansen, Lichtenberg, Hessen-Darmstadt
Schuchmann, John	23, Jan. 1890	15, Dec.	69	62		Mascoutah, IL	Hessen-Darmstadt
Schuchmann, Lucinda Emilie	11, June 1891	17, Apr.	32	382	Joesting	San Jose, IL	Cass County, Illinois
Schuchmann, Melchior	16, Apr. 1866	31, Mar.	49- 5m- 1d	126		St. Louis, MO	Illingen, Ebingen, Baden
Schuck, Georg	28, Nov. 1889	31, Oct.	77	766		New Knoxville, OH	Baiern
Schudel, Anna	23, Aug. 1875	17, July	73	271	Bletscher	Boody, IL	Schleitheim, Schweiz
Schudel, Caroline	10, July 1871	23, June	35-10m	223	Scheffe	Louisville, KY	Rieschwille, Zweibrücken, Baiern
Schueler, Julia A.	30, Jan. 1882	6, Jan.	38-11m-17d	39	Becker	Allegheny City, PA	Nußloch bei Heidelberg, Baden
Schuerger, Johan Georg	22, Nov. 1869	30, Oct.	66	375		Cleveland, OH	Wheeling, West Virginia
Schueman, John H.	29, Mar. 1888	3, Feb.	88	206		Stryker, OH	
Schuermeier, William	25, Mar. 1886	2, Mar.		7		Los Angeles, CA	Kappeln, Tecklenburg, Westphalen
Schuette, Johan Carl	28, Jan. 1886	29, Dec.	42	7		Blooming Grove, MN	
Schuetz, Karl Christian	9, May 1895	11, Apr.	24	302		Humboldt, NE	Louisenthal, Plathe, Regenwalde, Preußen
Schugard, J.C.	26, June 1890	29, May	57	414		Portland, OR	Hessen-Darmstadt
Schuh, Caroline	8, July 1897	13, June	42	431	Pfender	Freeport, IL	Württemberg
Schuh, Christian	19, Apr. 1880	7, Apr.	66- 4m- 7d	127		Greenville, OH	Nagold, Nagold, Württemberg
Schuh, Dorothea	1, Apr. 1886	21, Feb.	60- 8m-21d	7	Armbruster	Bern, MI	24-Hoef, Oberndorf, Württemberg
Schuh, Jakob Heinrich	18, June 1883	2, June	77	199		Greenville, OH	Niedergola, Kurhessen
Schuh, Johannes	13, Sept 1869	14, Aug.	46- 4m-11d	295		Louisville, KY	Klammer, Marienwerder, West Preußen
Schuh, Justine	27, June 1889	2, May	44	414		Berne, MI	Minsheim, Baiern
Schuh, Margaretha	29, May 1871	15, May	56	175	Engelhart	Caseville, MI	
Schuhard, Johan Georg	31, Oct. 1870	15, Oct.	65	351		Golconda, IL	
Schuhbrink, Christine	25, Feb. 1897	3, Feb.	72	127	Schachschneider	Detroit, MI	Thiergartz, Rosenberg, Germany
Schuhkraft, Catharine	15, Feb. 1894	12, Jan.	83	110	Frank	Quincy, IL	Weinsberg, Württemberg
Schuhmacher, Charlotte	7, May 1896	15, Mar.	63	302	Winter	Drake, MO	Detmold, Lippe-Detmold
Schuhmacher, Friederike	31, Oct. 1870	14, Oct.	31	351		Louisville, KY	
Schuhmacher, Heinrich	29, Nov. 1875	9, Nov.	35- 3m- 2d	383		New York City, NY	Iprump, Delmenhorst, Oldenburg
Schuldt, Fr.	7, July 1898	10, June	74	431		Klemme, IA	Altona, Mecklenburg-Schwerin
Schuldt, Hanna Maria	17, Mar. 1898	24, Feb.	72	175	Müller	Columbus, WI	Wulfsuhl, Mecklenburg-Schwerin
Schuldt, J.	30, June 1887	10, June	65	414		Colesburg, IA	Eldenau, Mecklenburg-Schwerin
Schuldt, Ludwig	9, June 1887	22, May	27	366		Colesburg, IA	Eldena, Mecklenburg-Schwerin
Schuldt, M. Friederika Karolina	4, Sept 1890	17, Aug.	56	574	Bergwart	Detroit, MI	Lassentin, Pommern
Schuldt, Sophia	13, Oct. 1892	15, Sept	64	654	Schütt	Colesburg, IA	Eldena, Mecklenburg-Schwerin
Schüle, Katharin	6, Apr. 1874	17, Mar.	34- 2m-17d	111		Goshen, IN	
Schüler, Adam	20, Mar. 1890	7, Feb.	54	190		Allegheny City, PA	Spangenburg, Melsungen, Kurhessen
Schuler, Agnes	3, Apr. 1846	23, Feb.	58- 4m	55		Woodville, OH	Oberamt Bahlingen, Württemberg
Schuler, Albert	5, May 1898	31, Mar.	29	287		Garner, IA	Giard, Iowa
Schuler, Andreas	24, Sept 1891	23, Aug.	74	622		Sheboygan, WI	Württemberg
Schuler, Andreas	30, Aug. 1855	14, July	4- 4m-21d	140		Cedar Lake, IN	
Schuler, Anna Maria	16, Apr. 1857	31, Mar.	39	64		Galena, IL	Kehl, Baden

- 466 -

Christliche Apologete Death Notices --- 1839 - 1899

Name of Deceased	Notice Date	Death Date	Age	Maiden Name	Page	Place of Death	Place of Birth
Schuler, Emma	5, Feb. 1883	8, Jan.	22- 3m-21d		47	Garner, IA	Blue Island, Illinois
Schuler, Emma	11, June 1883	25, May	20-9m-28d		191	Garner, IA	
Schuler, Georg	30, Aug. 1855	14, July	6- 6m-14d		140	Cedar Lake, IN	
Schuler, Johan Georg	23, Apr. 1877	6, Apr.	51		135	Wathena, KS	Kilchberg, Tübingen, Württemberg
Schuler, Julia	11, June 1883		5m		191	Garner, IA	
Schuler, Justina	12, May 1892		56-10m- 5d		302	Crow River, MN	Duningen, Rottweil, Württemberg
Schuler, Karolina	1, May 1882	4, Apr.	23	Marolf	143	Wathena, KS	Doniphan County, Kansas
Schuler, Karoline	6, Sept 1860	16, Aug.	9		144	Watertown, WI	
Schüler, Katharina	15, Aug. 1861	21, July	74- 4m- 21d	Dietrich	132	Oshkosh, WI	Mandeln, Amt Dillenburg, Nassau
Schuler, Luise	13, Oct. 1873	29, Sept	90	Eisenbeis	327	Galena, IL	Kehl, Baden
Schüler, Maria Elisabeth	29, July 1878	15, July	42	Lepper	239	Allegheny City, PA	Eubach, Kurhessen
Schuler, Martin	27, Jan. 1898	27, Nov.	74- 2m- 5d		63	Hannover, MN	Waldorf, Nagold, Württemberg
Schuler, Ruben	26, Apr. 1894	2, Apr.	64		278	New Knoxville, OH	Lehigh County, Pennsylvania
Schüler, Wilhelm H.	6, Aug. 1883	16, July	15-11m-16d		255	Pittsburg, PA	Wollmershausen, Crailsheim, Württemberg
Schüke, Ferdinand Rudolph	9, Oct. 1890	20, Sept	30- 2m-18d		654	Decatur, IL	Alentia, West Preußen
Schulmann, Caroline	9, Feb. 1874	21, Jan.	70	Eckhoff	47	New Orleans, LA	Morfelden, Großgerau, Hessen-Darmstadt
Schulmeier, Heinrich	15, Apr. 1886	1, Apr.	74		7	Terre Haute, IN	Dalsheim, Hessen-Darmstadt
Schulmerich, Gertrud	29, July 1897	30, June	70- 8m		479	New York City, NY	Drestsethe, Hagen, Hannover
Schult, Anna	19, June 1890	27, May	33	Stark	398	Milwaukee, WI	Steinenbronn, Stuttgart, Württemberg
Schult, Christine	2, May 1889	19, Apr.	52	Quade	286	Ann Arbor, MI	Ohrte, Fürstenau, Hannover
Schulte, A. Margaretha Elsebein	23, June 1898	2, June	83	Van Talge	399	Colesburg, IA	St. Paul, Minnesota
Schulte, Anna	24, Nov. 1887	3, Sept	24-10m- 7d		750	San Jose, CA	Jastrow, West Preußen
Schülte, August W.	18, Feb. 1897	14, Jan.	78		111	Bastrop, TX	Settrup, Amt Fürstenau, Hannover
Schulte, Bernhard H.	19, Apr. 1880	11, Mar.	70		127	Colesburg, IA	Hahnenberg, Fürstenau, Hannover
Schulte, Bernhardt	8, Aug. 1889	21, June	67- 4m		510	San Jose, CA	
Schulte, Daniel	27, Mar. 1890	27, Feb.	40		206	Oregon, MO	Hollen, Ostfriesland
Schulte, Dietrich	14, Apr. 1862	6, Mar.	20 - 6d		60	Alton, IL	
Schulte, Harm R.	5, Dec. 1889	6, Nov.	60		782	Oregon, MO	Ohrte, Amt Fürstenau, Pippen, Preußen
Schulte, Heinrich	12, Jan. 1860	1, Dec.	20-2m-14d		8	Oregon, MO	Verden, Osnabrück, Hannover
Schulte, Henry H.	13, Dec. 1869	21, Nov.	29		399	Oregon, MO	Ohrte, Beppen, Fürstenau, Hannover
Schulte, Hermann Heinrich	15, Sept 1848	13, Aug.			152	Pennsylvanienburg, IN	
Schulte, Johan Herman	24, Feb. 1887	24, Jan.	77	Vollrath	126	Humboldt, NE	Ohrte, Bippen, Fürstenau, Hannover
Schulte, John	11, May 1863	5, Apr.	25- 5m-26d		76	Oregon, MO	Remels, Ostfriesland
Schulte, Katharina	29, June 1863	20, May	47- 4m		104	Oregon, MO	
Schulte, Lena	2, Feb. 1893	8, Jan.	65	Miller	78	Alton, IL	Schittdorf, Hannover
Schulte-Wieking, Aleida	10, Mar. 1898	11, Feb.	61	Schrapp	159	Jeffersonville, IN	Sieringhoch, Hannover
Schultewieking, Lambert	15, Oct. 1891	3, Sept	57- -12d		670	Jeffersonville, IN	Ziegelhütten, Neuenkronau, Kurhessen
Schultheis, (Mr)	1, May 1856	5, Apr.	68		72	Quincy, IL	Burgsponheim, Kreuznach, Elsaß
Schultheis, Elisabeth	26, Jan. 1899	7, Jan.	76	Vollrath	63	Columbus, IL	Rheinkreis Baiern
Schultheis, Magdalena	19, Mar. 1883	11, Feb.	68	Mengert	95	Quincy, IL	Rheinkreis Baiern
Schultheis, Magdalena	9, Apr. 1883	11, Feb.	68	Wengert	119	Quincy, IL	Steinenberg, Schorndorf, Württemberg
Schultheiß, Christoph	28, June 1849		Inquiry		103	New York, NY	
Schultheiß, Elisabeth	26, July 1849	8, July	40		120	Cincinnati, OH	Steinenberg, Schorndorf, Württemberg
Schultheiß, Gottlieb	27, May 1852	14, Sept	47		88	New York, NY	Steinau, Kurhessen
Schultheiß, Maria Catharina	2, Jan. 1851	10, Dec.	34-10m		4	Quincy, IL	Bad, Vorpommern
Schulthieße, Karl	28, July 1887	17, July	36		478	Milwaukee, WI	

Christliche Apologete Death Notices --- 1839 - 1899

Name of Deceased	Notice Date	Death Date	Age	Page	Maiden Name	Place of Death	Place of Birth
Schulthieße, Martin	7, July 1887	10, June	72- 3m-25d	430		Hastings, NE	Marjos, Kurhessen
Schultz , Christian	23, Nov. 1893	4, Oct.	72	750		Merrill, WI	Romanshof, Bromberg, Preußen
Schultz, Albertine	13, Nov. 1890	18, Mar.	38- 4m-13d	734	Schwerenzke	Faribault, MN	
Schultz, Anna Elisabeth	12, June 1882	25, May	62- - 7d	191		Scranton, PA	Vockerothe, Kurhessen
Schultz, Anna Maria	13, Oct. 1892	20, Sept	28	654		Colesburg, IA	
Schultz, Anna Regina	28, Apr. 1879	13, Apr.	45	135	Hertel	Beaver Dam, WI	Pritzig, Piritz, Pommern
Schultz, August	24, Nov. 1892	7, Nov.	69	750		Mt. Olive, IL	Vitz bei Kistrin, Preußen
Schultz, August	13, Sept 1849		Inquiry	147		Hartford, IN	Heisebeck, Hessen-Kassel
Schultz, Auguste Amalie	11, July 1881	14, June	19	223		Oregon, MO	Mroczen, West Preußen
Schultz, Auguste Marie Caroline	15, Apr. 1897	28, Mar.	75	239	Müller	Laporte, IN	Waren, Mecklenburg-Schwerin
Schultz, Barbara Anna	24, Apr. 1890	16, Mar.	76- 1m-26d	270		Burlington, IA	Darmstadt, Hessen-Darmstadt
Schultz, Carl	4, Nov. 1872	4, Oct.	28	359		Oshkosh, WI	Jakobsdorf, Kreis Naugard, Preußen
Schultz, Caroline	23, May 1895	4, May	71	334	Silberstoff	Laporte, IN	Breidenfeld, Mecklenburg-Schwerin
Schultz, Caroline	29, Oct. 1896	23, Sept	72	703		Merrill, WI	Romanshof, Bromberg, Preußen
Schultz, Carrie	25, Aug. 1887	2, July	13	542		Lyona, KS	Tavistock, Ontario, Canada
Schultz, Charlotte	23, July1883	25, June	94	239	Sauer	Mt. Olive, IL	Witz bei Landsbeyer, Preußen
Schultz, Christoph H.	31, July 1851	18, May	33- 1m- 9d	124		Philadelphia, PA	
Schultz, Dorothea	12, Oct. 1874	29, Aug.	60	327	Brockmann	Penn's Station, PA	
Schultz, Elisabeth	3, Oct. 1889	1, Sept	20	638		Detroit, MI	Zewelin in der Uckermark, Preußen
Schultz, Elisabeth	10, Dec. 1896	21, Nov.	77	798	Majen	Laporte, IN	Waaren, Mecklenburg-Schwerin
Schultz, Elisabeth	14, Sept 1899	3, Aug.	34	591	Kretzmeyer	Batesville, IN	Lawrenceville, Indiana
Schultz, Emma	3, Jan. 1881	7, Dec.	20	7.		Denver, CO	
Schultz, Ernestine Wilhelmine	19, Apr. 1869	29, Mar.	47- - 2d	127	Zimmermann	Sheboygan, WI	Schönermark, Schwedt, Preußen
Schultz, Ernst	26, Oct. 1899	15, Sept	24	687		Webster, SD	Brotzen, Deutsch Krone, West Preußen
Schultz, Ferdinand	1, Aug. 1895	26, June	45	494		Fremont, NE	Bockau, Preußen
Schultz, Ferdinand	16, Dec. 1852	7, Nov.	30	204		Aurora, ---	
Schultz, Friederika	16, Mar. 1899	16, Feb.	75	175	Meister	Burlington, WI	Schilton, Tromburg, Germany
Schultz, Gottfried	18, Feb. 1886	3, Feb.	63	7		Wood Lake, NE	Hoffstädt, Deutsch-Krone, West Preußen
Schultz, Gustav	13, Dec. 1894	17, Nov.	34	806		Laporte, IN	Germany
Schultz, Heinrich	9, Jan. 1896	7, Dec.	72	30		Laporte, IN	Schwarzdorf, Mecklenburg-Schwerin
Schultz, Heinrich Jakob	26, May 1879	18, Mar.	38	167		Dodgeville, IA	Cornau, Salzwedel, Magdeburg, Preußen
Schultz, Johan	22, Oct. 1883	18, Sept	53- 1m-25d	343		Brillion, WI	Wieschenholland, Kolmar, Posen
Schultz, Johan Georg	6, June 1889	19, May	78- 1m-15d	366		Appleton, WI	Dammersitz, Pommern
Schultz, Johan Joachim Theodor	30, July 1891	4, July	67	494		Bland, MO	Wolkenzien, Mecklenburg-Strelitz
Schultz, Karl	28, Nov. 1889	29, Oct.	70	766		Berne, MI	Raddatz, Hinterpommern
Schultz, Katharina	28, Apr. 1898	3, Mar.	56	271	Miller	Sandwich, Il	Sechshelden, Nassau
Schultz, Katharine	12, Apr. 1875	21, Feb.	19- 7m- 7d	119	Bettenhausen	LeMond, IL	Königswald, Rathenburg, Kurhessen
Schultz, Lina Bertha	21, Apr. 1898	18, Mar.	26	255	Becker	Bland, MO	Senate Grove, Missouri
Schultz, Margaretha	18, Oct. 1888	1, Sept	34	670	Geiger	Maine, WI	Oshkosh, Wisconsin
Schultz, Maria	27, July 1885		81	7	Müller	Greensburg, IN	Hannover
Schultz, Maria Anna	4, Feb. 1892	15, Jan.	33- 1m-24d	78	Zinman	Milwaukee, WI	
Schultz, Maria Dorothea	19, Oct. 1874	28, Aug.	60	335	Brockmann	Pittsburg, PA	Semmensdorf, Preußen
Schultz, Maria Magdalena	23, Aug. 1894	31, July	79	550	Unrau	Wessington Springs, SD	Schleswig
Schultz, Maria Sophia Dorothea	23, May 1895	30, Apr.	71	334	Blumberg	Batesville, IN	Freulein, Steinfurt, Mecklenburg-Schwerin
Schultz, Rosina	17, June 1897	25, May	48	383	Wilke	Anaheim, CA	Berndorf, Waldeck
Schultz, Thomas	21, Apr. 1848		27	66		---, IL	Hamburg, Germany

Christliche Apologete Death Notices --- 1839 - 1899

Name of Deceased	Notice Date	Death Date	Age	Maiden Name	Place of Death	Place of Birth
Schultz, Wilhelm F.	24, Oct. 1895	28, Sept	78		Anaheim, CA	Waldeck
Schultz, Wilhelm Friedrich	2, May 1889	1, Apr.	38		Berne, MI	Lottin bei Neu-Stettin, Pommern
Schultz, Wilhelmine	4, June 1883	22, May	33- 4m-26d		Gladbrook, IA	Udorf, Preußen
Schultze, Anna Caroline	26, Sept 1895	8, Aug.	19	Gethmann	Warren, MO	Warren County, Missouri
Schultze, Anna Maria	6, Apr. 1893	4, Mar.	32		Warren, MO	Warren County, Missouri
Schultze, Elisabeth	25, July 1895	24, June		Schmidt	Baltimore, MD	Hessen-Darmstadt
Schultze, Georg Johan	8, Jan. 1891	13, Dec.	59- - 7d		Ellis Grove, IL	Berndorf, Eisenberg, Waldeck
Schultze, Georg Richard	28, Nov. 1895	31, Oct.	31		Mt. Vernon, MO	Appleton, Bollinger County, Missouri
Schultze, John Heinrich	31, Aug. 1893	22, Aug.	74- 3m-11d		Pinckneyville, IL	Wieze an der Aller, Hannover
Schultze, Karl Heinrich	26, Jan. 1893	2, Jan.	26		Warren, MO	Warren County, Missouri
Schultze, Reneta	16, Nov. 1893	18, Oct.	65		Michigan City, IN	Meiwald, Hirschberg, Schlesien
Schultze, Wilhelmine	12, Oct. 1899	19, Sept	54	Planko	Buffalo, NY	Eulenkrug, Mecklenburg-Strelitz
Schulz, (Mrs)	4, Aug. 1879	16, July	79		Beaver Falls, MN	Repcke, Hannover
Schulz, Andreas	30, Apr. 1896	13, Apr.	73		Ballwin, MO	Nonnenweier, Lahr, Baden
Schulz, Andreas	22, Nov. 1888		78		Oshkosh, WI	Romannsdorf, Posen
Schulz, Andreas	5, Apr. 1860	31, Jan.	87		Fond du Lac, WI	New Ulm, Posen, Preußen
Schulz, Andreas Albert	22, July 1878	10, July	21		Oshkosh, WI	Blackwolf, Wisconsin
Schulz, Anna Catharina	30, June 1892	3, June	75		Ballwin, MO	Hottingen, Lörrach, Baden
Schulz, Anna Elisabeth	21, Mar. 1881	24, Feb.	58-10m-14d		Wheeling, WV	Ulfen, Rodenberg, Kurhessen
Schulz, Anna Margaretha	11, Oct. 1880	21, Sept	71- 5m	Ferna	San Jose, CA	Heldburg, Sachsen-Meiningen
Schulz, August	17, Aug. 1874	21, July	60		Detroit, MI	Kröxen, Marienwerder, West Preußen
Schulz, Auguste	21, Mar. 1895	28, Feb.	24	Pech	Elkport, IA	Bernsee, Preußen
Schulz, Bertha Antonia Rosilie	17, May 1894	28, Apr.	50	Kuhlmann	Berne, MI	Caseville, Michigan
Schulz, Bertha Mathilde Luise	16, Feb. 1888	21, Jan.	20		St. Paul, MN	Blaßheim, Minden, Preußen
Schulz, Carl	1, Aug. 1889	17, July	75-10m- 7d		Wheeling, VA	Lauenförde, Hannover
Schulz, Carl	9, Aug. 1855	23, July	51- 6m		Pembina Co, SD	Gerbstädt, Preußen
Schulz, Carl	31, Oct. 1881	5, Oct.	62- 8m		Valley City, ND	Neu-Stettin, Pommern
Schulz, Carl W.	17, Apr. 1890	28, Mar.	63		Stryker, OH	Tiffintown, Defiance County, Ohio
Schulz, Charles Wesley	7, Nov. 1889	4, Oct.	19		Clayton, WI	Corkenhagen, Pommern
Schulz, Charlotte	22, July 1878	1, July	71- 3m-23d	Radoechel	Laporte, IN	Schwasdorf, Mecklenburg-Schwerin
Schulz, Christian	6, Mar. 1890	9, Feb.	69- 4m-25d		Marshall, WI	Mincheu, Neuwedel, in der Neumark, Preußen
Schulz, Christiane	14, Jan. 1886	19, Dec.	70-11m-19d	Bernhagen	Le Sueur, MN	Adenbüttel, Hannover
Schulz, Conradine	5, Nov. 1896		67	Maa	Clerno, WI	Saaps, Pommern
Schulz, Dorothea Louise	30, Nov. 1893	21, Oct.	75-11m- 1d	Strutz	Emden, IL	
Schulz, Eddie	27, Sept 1888	6, Sept	15- 9m-11d		St. Louis, MO	
Schulz, Elisabetha	2, Aug. 1849	28, June	27		Brooklyn, NY	Edewecht, Oldenburg
Schulz, Elise Catharine	12, Nov. 1896	29, Oct.	40	Fiefstück	Chicago, IL	Griesheim, Baden
Schulz, Emilie Caroline	24, Mar. 1862	15, Dec.	21- 5m	Hipp	Milwaukee, WI	Groß-Daberkow, Mecklenburg-Strelitz
Schulz, Georg	17, Aug. 1874	1, Aug.	38		Mankato, MN	Kleinsonnenberg, Riesenburg, West Preußen
Schulz, Gottlob	3, Sept 1896	11, Aug.	60		Rockford, MN	Schwerin, Mecklenburg-Schwerin
Schulz, Hartwig	2, Mar. 1874	8, Feb.	50		Sherman, WI	Oberfischbach, Geildorf, Württemberg
Schulz, Heinrich	24, Apr. 1890	24, Jan.	58-1m-17d		Ellis Grove, IL	
Schulz, Heinrich	18, July 1870	19, May	28- 4m-13d		Akron, NY	Hohenfelde, Doberaan, Mecklenburg-Schwerin
Schulz, Helene Dorothea	1, Feb. 1894	23, Dec.	51	Maltens	Kewaskum, WI	Kewaskum, Wisconsin
Schulz, Henriette Wilhelmina U.	4, Apr. 1895	8, Mar.	26		Lena, IL	Unhausen, Eschwege, Hessen
Schulz, Henry	22, Jan. 1883	6, Dec.	66			

Christliche Apologete Death Notices --- 1839 - 1899

Name of Deceased	Notice Date	Death Date	Age	Page	Maiden Name	Place of Death	Place of Birth
Schulz, Johan	5, Aug. 1897	7, July	75	495		Portsmouth, OH	Güstrow, Mecklenburg-Schwerin
Schulz, Johan	11, July 1895	19, May	97	446		Rochester, NY	Rauh, Mecklenburg-Schwerin
Schulz, Johan Christian	26, Oct. 1874	Sept	75- 5m- 1d	343		Cannon River, MN	Poelitz, Mecklenburg-Schwerin
Schulz, Johan Friedrich	6, Jan. 1873	17, Dec.	65	7		Defiance, OH	Schönfeld, Kreis Steinthal, Magdeburg, Preußen
Schulz, Johan Friedrich	1, Sept 1879	16, Aug.	54	279		Detroit, MI	Kröchendorf, Potsdam, Preußen
Schulz, Johan Friedrich	13, Dec. 1894	16, Nov.	68	806		Bloomington, IL	Mechau, Osterburg, Preußen
Schulz, Johanna	28, Feb. 1881	4, Feb.	32	71	Dubke	Lake Mills, WI	Zettlin, Stolp, Pommern
Schulz, Johanne Louise	18, Apr. 1864	21, Feb.	37	64			
Schulz, Johannes	4, June 1883	19, May	65- 2m- 4d	183		Laporte, IN	Schwasdorf, Worn, Mecklenburg-Schwerin
Schulz, Julia	24, Jan. 1895	5, Jan.	55	62	Lüpke	Milwaukee, WI	Massow, Pommern
Schulz, Justine	13, June 1889	2, May	44	382		Berne, MI	Klammer, Marienwerder, West Preußen
Schulz, Karl	31, Mar. 1862	10, Mar.	19	52		Sandusky, OH	
Schulz, Karl Friedrich	14, Apr. 1898	24, Mar.	69- 4m-24d	239	Meier	Rochester, MN	Zorndorf, Brandenburg
Schulz, Karolina Helena Dorothea	11, Apr. 1881	15, Mar.	63-11m-23d	119	Luckmann	Jewells Prairie, IL	Pommern
Schulz, Katharine Elisabeth	19, Sept 1861	28, Aug.	85	152		Pennsylvanienburg, IN	Neuenkirchen, Hannover
Schulz, Lizzie	28, Jan. 1892	31, Dec.	24	62		Crow River, MN	New York
Schulz, Margaretha	6, Jan. 1873	8, Dec.	48	7		San Jose, CA	Windhorst, Hannover
Schulz, Maria	11, Mar. 1897	4, Feb.	66	159	Foß	Lansing, MI	Jennehof, Mecklenburg-Schwerin
Schulz, Maria	11, July 1895	14, June	82	446		Rochester, NY	Köthen, Mecklenburg-Schwerin
Schulz, Maria	11, Nov. 1878	23, Oct.	48	359	Deutsch	Bloomington, MO	Binde, Magdeburg, Preußen
Schulz, Maria	18, Nov. 1878	23, Oct.	48	367	Deutsch	Bloomington, IL	Binde, Magdeburg, Preußen
Schulz, Maria	13, Jan. 1859	26, Dec.	22	8		Rochester, NY	Württemberg
Schulz, Maria Elisabeth	21, June 1875	6, June	58	199	Stek	Lena, IL	Boonville, New York
Schulz, Marie	21, Nov. 1881	5, Nov.	18- 2m- 2d	375		Crow River, MN	Freedom, Sauk County, Wisconsin
Schulz, Sarah Katharina	7, Feb. 1881	27, Jan.	12-11m- 2d	47	Fischbeck	Freeport, IL	Dangel, Magdeburg, Preußen
Schulz, Sophie	29, Sept 1862	1, Sept	52	156	Bagans	Nauvoo, IL	Schönwerder, Pommern
Schulz, Sophie Dorothea	8, Jan. 1891	11, Dec.	58	30		Columbus, WI	Weisenbach, Witzenhausen, Hessen-Kassel
Schulz, Wilhelm Georg	12, Oct. 1874	27, Aug.	48	327		Scranton, PA	Belgard, Pommern
Schulz, Wilhelmina Loretta Auguste	2, Dec. 1897	14, Nov.	73	767	Priebe	Valley City, ND	Brodzen, Krone, West Preußen
Schulz, Wilhelmine	11, Dec. 1890	10, July	69- 9m	798	Teske	Wood Lake, NE	Kossowo, Hinterpommern
Schulz, William C.	22, Oct. 1891	12, June	28	686		Schnectady, NY	Karoline, Posen
Schulze, Albertine Karoline W.	14, July 1892	18, May	40	446	Ferch	Waseca, MN	Simonsville, Mason County, Texas
Schulze, Amalie	4, June 1883		22	183	Burgdorf	Llano, TX	Winsen, Hannover
Schulze, Anna Maria	9, Nov. 1863	9, Sept	69	180		Chester, IL	
Schulze, Anna Marie	8, May 1890	20, Apr.	66- 3m	302		Baltimore, MD	Steinbach, Backnang, Württemberg
Schulze, Carl	26, Dec. 1889	3, Dec.	87	830		Rutersville, TX	
Schulze, Friedericke	12, Nov. 1896	24, Sept	69	734	Möll	Jamestown, MO	Müncheberg, Brandenburg
Schulze, Friedrich	2, June 1887	16, May	89	350		St. Paul, MN	Spenge, Preußen
Schulze, Friedrich Wilhelm	23, Dec. 1897	28, Nov.		815		Watertown, WI	Hildenhausen, Preußen
Schulze, H. Heinrich	6, Feb. 1882	7, Jan.		47		Warren, MO	Bretten, Baden
Schulze, Hanna Elisabeth	10, May 1860	24, Apr.	26	76	Punge	Warrenton, MO	
Schulze, Johanna Regina	14, Dec. 1893	18, Nov.	50	798	Göelzle	San Diego, CA	Salzwedel, Magdeburg, Preußen
Schulze, John	15, Apr. 1886	22, Mar.	21- - 4d	7		Chester, IL	Holzhausen, Preußen
Schulze, Karl G.	14, Aug. 1876	28, July	75	263		Nauvoo, IL	Parchem, Preußen
Schulze, Louise	21, Sept 1874	9, Sept	49	303	Korghage	St. Paul, MN	
Schulze, Maria	31, Jan. 1895	6, Jan.	53	78	Strock	Cleveland, OH	

Christliche Apologete Death Notices --- 1839 - 1899

Name of Deceased	Notice Date	Death Date	Age	Maiden Name	Page	Place of Death	Place of Birth
Schulze, Maria Margaretha	21, June 1894	1, June	31	Burgdorf	406	Beaver Creek, TX	Mason County, Texas
Schulze, Wilhelm Heinrich	23, Feb. 1880	28, Jan.	27- 3m-21d		63	Jamestown, MO	Evansville, Indiana
Schumacher, Andrew	25, May 1893	20, Apr.	32		334	Perrysburg, OH	Perrysburg, Ohio
Schumacher, Anna Christina	25, Mar. 1878	22, Feb.	67	Küster	95	St. Paul, MN	Heischeid, Waldbröl, Cöln, Preußen
Schumacher, Anna Maria	25, Mar. 1897	13, Feb.	71	Schaffner	190	Toledo, OH	Wintersingen, Baselland, Schweiz
Schumacher, August	30, Mar. 1874	2, Mar.	54- 7m-13d		103	Nebraska City, NE	Oberdorf, Hannover
Schumacher, Auguste	14, Dec. 1874	28, Nov.	25- 2m		399	Kenosha, WI	Gumminshof, Treptow an der Rega, Preußen
Schumacher, Casten	24, Apr. 1876	4, Apr.	79		135	Brooklyn, NY	Bordenfleth, Oldenburg
Schumacher, Christian	21, July 1873	25, June	59		231	Milwaukee, WI	Drosedow, Pommern
Schumacher, Edward	26, Mar. 1891	2, Feb.	19		206	Schnectady, NY	Schnectady, New York
Schumacher, Friedrich	5, Mar. 1883	3, Feb.	81- 2m-24d		79	Carrolton, MI	Nirx, Mecklenburg-Schwerin
Schumacher, Gottlieb	1, Dec. 1898	11, Nov.	80- 2m-20d		767	Kenosha, WI	Pinno, Pommern
Schumacher, Heinrich	23, June 1873	2, May	14-11m-12d		199	Marine City, MI	
Schumacher, Henry G.	11, Sept 1882	28, July	21		295	Schnectady, NY	Roxbury, Massachuetts
Schumacher, Ida	23, June 1873	10, Apr.	9- 7m- 5d		199	Marine City, MI	
Schumacher, Johan Heinrich	17, Nov. 1898	27, Oct.	83		735	Waltersburg, IL	Windhorst, Bicken, Hoja, Hannover
Schumacher, Johan M.	11, Mar. 1897	18, Feb.	57		159	Akron, OH	Oberkochen, Aalen, Württemberg
Schumacher, Karl	25, Dec. 1882	2, Dec.	71		415	Dunkirk, NY	Großen-Plasten, Mecklenburg-Schwerin
Schumacher, Karl	19, Jan. 1893	26, Nov.	81		46	Drake, MO	Reme, Germany
Schumacher, Laura	2, Nov. 1885	15, Oct.	37	Dühmke	7	Brooklyn, NY	Preußen
Schumacher, Lina	23, June 1873	3, Apr.	7- 8m-16d		199	Marine City, MI	
Schumacher, Louisa	23, June 1873	15, Apr.	3- 7m-14d		199	Marine City, MI	
Schumacher, Mallritta	19, Feb. 1866	30, Dec.			62	New York, NY	Gauspe, Oldenburg
Schumacher, Margaretha	27, Mar. 1871	1, Mar.	76- -14d		103	Golconda, IL	Amt Hoya, Hannover
Schumacher, Maria	4, Jan. 1875	22, Dec.	53-10m- 3d		7	Kenosha, WI	Gummin Treptow an der Rega, Stettin, Preußen
Schumacher, Maria	19, Aug. 1897		60- 7m		527	Brooklyn, NY	
Schumacher, Meta	25, Feb. 1886	5, Feb.	82	Lenz	7	Brooklyn, NY	Lemwerder, Oldenburg
Schumacher, Sophie	14, Apr. 1873	22, Mar.	18- 3m-16d		119	Marine City, MI	Doberan, Mecklenburg-Schwerin
Schumacher, Sophie Christiane E.	14, Dec. 1893		59	Schulz	798	Milwaukee, WI	Daberkow, Mecklenburg
Schumacher, Ulrich	4, Jan. 1894	18, Oct.	60		14	Beman, KS	Hobsern, Oberland, Bern, Schweiz
Schumacher, Wilhelm Albert	11, May 1893	8, Mar.	15		302	Milwaukee, WI	
Schumacher, Wilhelmine Louise H.	2, Apr. 1896	8, Mar.	27	Kasdorf	222	Allegheny City, PA	Lindenfled, Pommern
Schumäker, Johan Heinrich	16, Jan. 1882	1, Jan.	21		23	Allegheny, PA	Alleghany City, Pennsylvania
Schumaker, Wilhelm	4, July 1895	7, June	66		430	Arenzville, IL	Ströhen, Raden, Preußen
Schumann, Adam	3, Nov. 1887	1, Oct.	69		702	New Ulm, MN	Sulzbach, Baden
Schumann, Christoph	25, June 1883	3, June	75- -19d		207	Chicago, IL	Runau, Bromberg, Preußen
Schumann, Ernst	23, Feb. 1885	9, Feb.	66		7	Delaware, OH	Geisenheim, Sachsen-Altenburg
Schumann, Franz	11, Oct. 1888	13, Sept	29- 9m- 8d		654	Delaware, OH	Bischweiler, Elsaß
Schumann, Henriette Wilhelmine	25, Dec. 1865	6, Dec.	22- -16d	Schwab	208	Madison, IN	
Schumann, J.	20, Mar. 1882	29, Jan.	74- 7m- 4d		95	Sheboygan, WI	Gustow, Uckermark, Preußen
Schumann, John	1, Apr. 1897	11, Mar.	61		207	Aurora, IL	Threner, Norden, Hannover
Schumann, Katharine	5, Aug. 1867	26, June	41	Löb	246	Arenzville, IL	Henschbach, Amt Weinheim, Baden
Schumann, Maria	31, July 1882	8, July	26- 6m- 3d	Jakobs	247	Cincinnati, OH	Wisconsin
Schumann, Theodor (Rev)	21, Mar. 1895	24, Feb.	46- 6m-11d		190	Roseville, MI	Delhi Township, Hamilton County, Ohio
Schumann, Wilhelm Friedrich Ed.	27, Feb. 1896	3, Feb.	49		143	Storm Lake, IA	Schönwalde, Naugard, Preußen
Schumann, Wilhelmine	21,May 1883	7, May	67		167	Milwaukee, WI	Klein-Wachlin, Hinterpommern

Christliche Apologete Death Notices --- 1839 - 1899

Name of Deceased	Notice Date	Death Date	Age	Page	Maiden Name	Place of Death	Place of Birth
Schumpe, Johan Konrad	22, June 1899	27, May	87	399		Wheelersburg, OH	Oldendorf, Melle, Hannover
Schumpe, Maria Isabella	22, June 1899	28,May	84	399	Marting	Wheelersburg, OH	Oldendorf, Melle, Hannover
Schünemann, Gottlieb	1, Sept 1898	6, Aug.	82	559		Watertown, WI	Fürstensee, Pommern
Schünemann, Louise	30, Dec. 1872	10, Dec.	58- 1m	423	Pinnow	Oconomowoc, WI	Neumark, Pommern
Schünemann, Luise	18, May 1899	28, Apr.	53	319	Krüger	Eldora, IA	Altsteinort, Schlawe, Pommern
Schünemann, Wilhelm	24, Mar. 1887	12, Mar.	53- 2m- 9d	190		Flood Creek, IA	Jago, Pommern
Schünemann, Wilhelmine	3, Oct. 1895	12, Sept	58	638		Oklahoma City, OK	Abtshagen, Pommern
Schunk, Catharine	28, Apr. 1873	14, Apr.	56	135	Hoffmann	Marine City, MI	Waldmohr, Rheinkreis Baiern
Schunk, Friedrich (Rev)	9, Jan. 1871	9, Dec.	37	15		Marion City, MI	Canton Waldmohr, Baiern
Schunk, Georg	7, Aug. 1882	18, July	15-10m- 5d	255		Toledo, OH	
Schunk, Karoline	9, Apr. 1883	19, Mar.	36- 7m- 2d	119	Nuhser	Toledo, OH	Woodville, Ohio
Schunk, Katharina	14, Aug. 1890	23, July	82	526	Böttler	Toledo, OH	Waldmohr, Zweibrücken, Baiern
Schunk, Michael	4, Feb. 1878	9, Jan.	61- 1m-22d	39		Marine City, MI	Waldmohr, Rheinpfalz Baiern
Schunk, Theobald	13, July 1874	13, June	69- 4m- 5d	223		Marine City, MI	Waldmohr, Rheinkreis Baiern
Schuppan, Emilie	26, May 1892	20, Mar.	38	334	Brodbeck	Houston, TX	
Schuppan, Georg E. (Dr)	1, Sept 1892	1, July		558	Gätschef	Hoboken, NJ	
Schuppann, (Mrs)	21, Feb. 1881	5, Feb.	39	63		Warrenton, MO	Jamestown, Moniteau County, Missouri
Schuppann, Herman	22, Oct. 1891	1, Oct.	51	686		Warrenton, MO	Zittau, Sachsen
Schuppel, Katharina	11, Nov. 1878	19, Oct.	84- 3m-25d	359		Galion, OH	Gaiberg, Baden
Schuppener, Eduard Christian	27, Feb. 1896	9, Feb.	22	143		Stitzer, WI	Liberty, Grant County, Wisconsin
Schuppert, Katharina Barbara	11, Nov. 1858	30, Oct.	57	180		Ripley, OH	Niederhofen, Württemberg
Schuppner, Eduard Christian	19, Mar. 1896	9, Feb.	22	190		Stitzer, WI	Liberty, Grant County, Wisconsin
Schuppner, Katharine	17, Nov. 1879	31, Oct.	51- 4m-22d	367	Limper	Lancaster, WI	Orfeld, Wittgenstein, Preußen
Schüring, Elisabeth	3, Oct. 1870	10, Aug.	78- 9m-28d	319	Vollmer	Kossuth, OH	Ehlbronn, Maulbronn, Württemberg
Schürle, Rosine	13, Mar. 1890	23, Feb.	36	174	Reber	Clay Center, KS	Michelfled, Hall, Württemberg
Schürmann, Abraham	16, Sept 1858	27, Aug.	19- 4m-21d	148		Defiance, IN	
Schürmann, Maria	24, Sept 1857	9, Aug.	21	156		Evansport, OH	Stark County, Ohio
Schürmeier, Carl	16, Feb. 1888	19, Jan.	78-10m	110		Warrenton, MO	Jofeld, Preußen
Schürmeier, Caroline	31, July 1890	13, July	62- 6m- 3d	494	Wenzel	St. Paul, MN	Arendsee, Altmark, Preußen
Schürmeier, Charles F.	31, July 1890	13, July	22- 8m- 5d	494		St. Paul, MN	
Schürmeier, Charlotte Engel	31, Dec. 1883	3, Dec.	72	7	Stickdom	Warrenton, MO	Gofeld, Minden, Preußen
Schürmeier, Louise	16, Mar. 1874	16, Feb.	72	87	Göcker	Charlestown, IN	Gerspielhilder, Amt Iburg, Hannover
Schürmeier, Maria	12, Apr. 1894	16, Mar.	43	246	Koester	St. Paul, MN	Bartholomew County, Indiana
Schürmeyer, C.	10, Feb. 1887	23, Jan.		94		St. Paul, MN	Holzhausen, Minden, Preußen
Schürmeyer, Heinrich	4, July 1881	18, June	70- 5m	215		St. Charles, MO	Minden, Preußen
Schürmeyer, Louise	26, Jan. 1880	29, Dec.	68- 9m	31	Nolting	Warrenton, MO	Jöllenbeck, Minden, Preußen
Schurr, Christina	25, Nov. 1858	8, Nov.		188		Paris, IL	Ulm, Württemberg
Schurran, Traugott	14, Feb. 1861	1, Feb.	64	28		Poughkeepsie, NY	Lammatzsch, Sachsen
Schurter, Maria Anna	11, Apr. 1895	26, Jan.	40	238	Frey	New York City, NY	Gonkensweil, Aargau, Schweiz
Schüßler, Anna Maria	22, Oct. 1877	21, Sept	75	343	Wenz	Galena, IL	Neuenburg, Württemberg
Schüßler, August Heinrich	1, Aug. 1895	12, July	21	494		Hedwigs Hill, TX	Cherry Spring, Gillespie County, Texas
Schüßler, Johan Michael	8, June 1874	26, May	76- 6m-13d	183		Galena, IL	Schwann, Neuenbürg, Württemberg
Schüßler, Valentin	7, Jan. 1892	6, Dec.	55- 9m	14		Newark, NJ	Pferdsdorf, Sachsen-Weimar
Schuster, (Mrs)	12, Nov. 1866	1, Sept		366	Hoffmeier	Marthasville, MO	Ibenbühren, Tecklenburg, Münster, Preußen
Schuster, Christian	31, Jan. 1895	5, Jan.	77	78		Cullman, AL	Schwarzenburg, Bern, Schweiz
Schuster, Christine	23, June 1884	5, June	86	7	Hehe	Dayton, OH	Lundorf, Wittlage, Hannover

Christliche Apologete Death Notices --- 1839 - 1899

Name of Deceased	Notice Date	Death Date	Age	Page	Maiden Name	Place of Death	Place of Birth
Schuster, Elisabeth	31, Dec. 1891	14, Dec.	74- 5m-15d	846	Nolte	Dayton, OH	Hargenfeld, Wittlage, Osnabrück, Hannover
Schuster, Georg	30, Nov. 1874	15, Oct.	21	383		Cincinnati, OH	Lawrenceburg, Dearborn County, Indiana
Schuster, Gottlieb	29, Sept 1848	13, Sept	18	160		Portsmouth, OH	
Schuster, Gottlieb	1, Nov. 1894	8, Oct.	68	710		Cincinnati, OH	Neu Krausendorf, Schlesien
Schuster, Heinrich	24, Jan. 1876	21, Dec.	47	31		Warren Co. MO	Tecklenburg, Preußen
Schuster, Jakob	14, Apr. 1892	24, Mar.	64	238		Fairview, OH	Heidingsheim, Württemberg
Schuster, Johan Friedrich	15, Apr. 1867	2, Apr.	39- 6m-23d	118		Dayton, OH	Rabbes, Amt Wittlage, Hannover
Schuster, Johan Georg	14, Mar. 1889	27, Jan.	65	174		Etna, MO	Heutingsheim, Württemberg
Schuster, Johan Jakob	10, Jan. 1895	15, Dec.	41	30		McKeesport, PA	Allegheny, Pennsylvania
Schuster, Josephine	29, Aug.1895	8, July	53	558		Rochester, MN	Lörra bei Adelhausen, Baden
Schuster, Katharina	5, Dec. 1895	11, Nov.	32	782	Zimmermann	Cleveland, OH	Wachenheim a. d. Haardt, Rheinpfalz Baiern
Schuster, Mary L.	18, Dec. 1865	1, Nov.	18- 5m- 7d	204		Canton, MO	
Schuster, Regina	16, Oct. 1871	9, Aug.	53	335		Hills Fork, ——	
Schuster, Wilhelm F.	7, Aug. 1890	15, July	33- 2m-21d	510		Cincinnati, OH	Möhringen, Stuttgart, Württemberg
Schute, Maria Juliana	27, May 1886	6, May	78	7	Mayer	Allegan, MI	Adams County, Ohio
Schuth, Maria Theresa	13, Sept 1894	26, Aug.	69	598	Markert	Pepin, WI	Hamburg, Germany
Schuth, Wilhelm	5, Jan. 1893	20, Dec.	42	14		Chicago, IL	Bischofsheim, Baiern
Schutrum, Katharine Elisabeth	23, Oct. 1876	5, Oct.	79	343		Buffalo, NY	Janritz, Pommern
Schutt, Bertha	13, Sept 1894	13, Aug.	67	598		Menominee, MI	Kurhessen
Schutt, Elisabeth	15, Sept 1873	10, Aug.	69- 6m	295	Begerow	Newark, NJ	Dorgerns, Stolp, Hinterpommern
Schütt, Johan Heinrich	24, Aug. 1874	13, July	66	273		Allegan, MI	
Schutt, Mina	18, Feb. 1878	29, Jan.	19- 8m- 8d	55		Davenport, IA	Hamburg,
Schütte, Augusta	28, Mar. 1889	4, Mar.	66	206		Faribault, MN	
Schütte, Auguste Karol. Henriette	7, Feb. 1870	23, Nov.	19- 2m- 6d	47		Blooming Grove, MN	Böckingen, Heilbronn, Württemberg
Schütte, Dorothea	1, July 1897	24, May	85	414	Gallisch	Waltersburg, IL	Jeglitz, Preußen
Schütte, Elisabeth	3, May 1894	8, Apr.	67	294	Freiberg	Eudora, KS	Bensen, Bruckhausen, Hannover
Schütte, Friedrike Wilhelmine	4, May 1868	6, Apr.	48-10m-14d	143	Fromming	Morristown, MN	Baireuth, Baiern
Schütte, Henriette	15, Aug. 1889	27, July	35- 9m-17d	526	Säufferer	Blooming Grove, MN	Unheim, Lades, HinterPommern
Schütte, Karl F.	23, July1883	23, June	70	239		Blooming Grove, MN	Clay County, Illinois
Schütte, Maria	23, Nov. 1885	3, Nov.	50	7	VonBehren	Schnectady, NY	Machwitz bei Platte, Preußen
Schütten, Anna	22, Sept 1884	30, Aug.	68	7		Papillion, NE	Hille, Minden, Preußen
Schütten, Katharine	2, Aug. 1880	2, July	29-10m-24d	247		Beardstown, IL	Vluhn, Preußen
Schütterle, D.	23, Jan. 1882	30, Dec.	40	31		Jackson, MO	Vluyn, Geldern, Düsseldorf, Preußen
Schütterle, Michael	14, Feb. 1881	17, Jan.	60	55		Schulenburg, TX	Basbäck, Hannover
Schüttler, Christian	6, Sept 1888	17, Aug.	60- 8m-22d	574		Farmington, MO	Kehl, Baden
Schüttler, Georg	31, Dec. 1883	6, Dec.	19- 4m-12d	7		Farmington, MO	Flechtdorf, Waldeck
Schüttler, Louisa Christina	5, July 1888	17, June	14- - 7d	430		Farmington, MO	
Schüttler, Wilhelm	27, Nov. 1856	13, Nov.	29	192		Milwaukee, WI	Niedereschbach, Hessen-Darmstadt
Schütz, Anna	15, June 1868	23, May	60	191		Mt. Vernon, IN	Dissen, Hannover
Schütz, Anna	16, Dec. 1872	20, Oct.	87	407	Preuß	Warrenton, MO	
Schütz, Anna Maria	26, Apr. 1875	6, Mar.	54	135	Münchenbach	Peru, IL	Eisern, Wilgersdorf, Siegen, Westphalen
Schütz, Anna Maria	28, Feb. 1861	22, Jan.	81	36	Wagner	Newark, OH	Altbulach, Caln, Württemberg
Schütz, Barbara	7, Aug. 1846	17, Mar.	62	127		Monroe Co, ---	
Schütz, Christian Friedrich	9, May 1881		62	151		Lancaster, NY	Linzingen, Maulbronn, Württemberg
Schütz, Ernst	22, Nov. 1855	2, Nov.	25	188		Mascoutah, IL	Zielenzig, Sternberg, Preußen
Schütz, Georg	18, May 1885	27, Apr.	68	7		Brighton, IL	Langensulzbach, Straßburg, Elsaß

Christliche Apologete Death Notices --- 1839 - 1899

Name of Deceased	Notice Date	Death Date	Age	Maiden Name	Page	Place of Death	Place of Birth
Schütz, Heinrich	30, Aug. 1880	30, July	65		279	Baraboo, WI	Katzenfurth, Coblenz, Wetzlau, Preußen
Schutz, Herman	28, Jan. 1897	7, Jan.	76- 5m-17d		63	Belleville, IL	Wilnsdorf, Westphalen
Schütz, John	2, Aug. 1869	29, June	21		247	Peru, IL	
Schütz, Katharina	2, Nov. 1899	20, Oct.	26	Seiles	703	Humboldt, NE	Kanton Bern, Schweiz
Schütz, Lucy	18, June 1896	27, May	17		399	Humboldt, NE	Humboldt, Nebraska
Schütz, Margarethe	14, Feb. 1889	15, Jan.	45- 7m	Züpach	110	Duncan, NE	Böttigen, Bern, Schweiz
Schütz, Maria Henriette	25, Nov. 1897	27, Oct.	62	Hepp	751	Boonville, IN	Birkenfeld, Oldenburg
Schütz, Martin	16, Feb. 1863	24, Jan.	41		28	Chillicothe, OH	Lampertheim, Hessen
Schütz, Nicholas	30, Oct. 1890	10, Oct.	71- 7m-14d		702	Boonville, IN	Velsrod, Bürgenfeld, Oldenburg
Schütz, Otto Henry	20, Apr. 1899	8, Mar.	30		255	Moweaqua, IL	Bloomington, Illinois
Schüze, Elisa	29, Oct. 1877		12- 5m		351	Tecumseh, NE	
Schuze, Friedrich	8, Sept 1887	1, Aug.	65		574	Chester, IL	Witze, Winsen, Hannover
Schwab, Elisabeth	11, July 1895	23, June	62	Suppes	446	Boody, IL	Stockhausen, Grünberg, Hessen-Darmstadt
Schwab, Abraham	6, Aug. 1857	20, June	31- 6m		128		Seefelen, Bern, Schweiz
Schwab, Barbara	17, Mar. 1879	23, Feb.	29	Liller	87	Columbus, OH	
Schwab, Catharina	20, Jan. 1859	10, Sept	33		12	Louisville, KY	Herznacht, Aargau, Schweiz
Schwab, Christian	17, Jan. 1876	17, Dec.	27		23	Pekin, IL	Bindsachsen, Kreis Büdingen, Hessen
Schwab, Friederike Wilhelmine	15, Nov. 1880	26, Oct.	76	Kurtz	367	Madison, IN	Großglattbach, Vaihingen, Württemberg
Schwab, Friedrich	9, Oct. 1890	10, Sept	80- 3m-16d		654	Cincinnati, OH	Rheinbischofsheim, Baden
Schwab, Jakob	18, June 1877	8, Apr.	75		199	Madison, IN	Niederoderbach, Rheinkreis Baiern
Schwab, Katharina	13, Feb. 1896	25, Jan.	79	Stephan	110	Cincinnati, OH	Memprechtshofen, Baden
Schwab, Maria Magdalena	24, Mar. 1884	2, Mar.	45	Hoch	7	Hochheim, TX	Ober-Schönau, Schmalkalden, Kurhessen
Schwab, Maria Magdalena	30, Apr. 1891	13, Apr.	78- 5m-26d		286	Cincinnati, OH	Memprechtshofen, Baden
Schwab, Paul	18, Mar. 1852	4, Mar.	44- 1m-26d		48	Cincinnati, OH	Rheinbischofsheim, Baden
Schwab, Sarah	17, Sept 1866	2, Sept	21		302	Cincinnati, OH	
Schwaben, Friederika	13, Dec. 1860	23, Nov.	25	Dendel	200	Erie, MI	
Schwaben, Rosina	25, Nov. 1858	5, Nov.	37		188	Newport, MI	Rosenfeld, Sulz, Württemberg
Schwaberow, Emilie Augusta	3, Sept 1891	7, Aug.	33- 6m		574	Roseville, MI	Ulm, Württemberg
Schwaberow, Friedrich Karl	18, Apr. 1895	19, Mar.	84		254	Marine City, MI	Stramehl, Brenzlau, Preußen
Schwabron, Dorothea	21, Jan. 1867	24, Dec.	50	Polz	22	Marine City, MI	Pritzier, Mecklenburg-Schwerin
Schwaderer, Christina	24, Jan. 1873	7, Feb.		Lachenmeyer	63	Marion, OH	Schwechow, Haggenhow, Mecklenburg-Schwerin
Schwaderer, Gottlieb	1, Nov. 1869	20, Sept	45- 6m-13d		351	Grand Rapids, MI	Marbach, Backnang, Württemberg
Schwaderer, Hiob	7, Oct. 1872	19, Sept	85- 5m- 2d		327	Marion, OH	Oppelsbohm, Württemberg
Schwaderer, Jakob	23, Feb. 1899	27, Jan.	86		127	Marion, OH	Marbach, Backnang, Württemberg
Schwager, Johan	29, Aug.1895	29, July	75		558	Toledo, OH	Marbach, Backnang, Württemberg
Schwager, Maria Catharina	16, June 1862	31, May	34- 4m-29d	Allgeyer	96	Toledo, OH	Lochenbach, Baiern
Schwahlen, Barbara	1, Sept 1892	19, July	82	Aebische	558	Evansville, IN	Deiningen, Wallenstein, Baiern
Schwakenberg, Dietrich	22, Mar. 1875	2, Mar.			95	German Creek, IA	Canton Bern, Schweiz
Schwalm, Maria Magdalena	17, Nov. 1887	27, Oct.	29	Leischner	734	Sioux City, IA	Illinois
Schwambach, Amalia	25, Jan. 1864	6, Jan.	23	Thomas	16	Cannelton, IN	Wermelskirchen, Kreis Lennep, RheinPreußen
Schwambach, Rosa Katharina	20, Jan. 1873	1, Jan.	35- 2m-19d	Ritt	23	Evansville, IN	Denzlingen bei Freiburg, Breisgau, Baden
Schwambeck, Christian	29, July 1878	16, July	40		239	Wheeling, IL	Berenshagen, Buckow, Mecklenburg-Schwerin
Schwander, Barbara	7, Dec. 1885	13, Nov.	84		7	Newport, KY	
Schwandner, Caroline	12, Apr. 1894	19, Mar.	80	Bossert	246	Brillion, WI	Göbrücken, Pforzheim, Baden
Schwanebeck, Joachim G.	10, Aug. 1868	4, July	60		255	Portland, WI	Hohen-Luckow, Luckow, Mecklenburg-Schwerin
Schwanebeck, Sophia J.W.	18, June 1891	23, May	82		398	Watertown, WI	Gerdeshagen, Mecklenburg-Schwerin

Christliche Apologete Death Notices --- 1839 - 1899

Name of Deceased	Notice Date	Death Date	Age	Page	Maiden Name	Place of Death	Place of Birth
Schwaninger, Adam	18, Aug. 1898	25, July	63	527		Jeffersonville, IN	Gutmandingen, Schaffhausen, Schweiz
Schwaninger, Caspar	21, Oct. 1867	29, Sept	31	334		Chicago, IL	Gunsmadingen, Schaffhausen, Schweiz
Schwaninger, Jakob	2, Mar. 1874	10, Feb.	81	71		Jeffersonville, IN	Gundmardingen, Schaffhausen, Schweiz
Schwanke, Christian	8, July 1897	29, May	71	431		Klemme, IA	Garwitz, Mecklenburg-Schwerin
Schwanke, Anna Caroline	6, Nov. 1890	18, Oct.	72	718		Ft. Atkinson, WI	Komanchen, Posen
Schwanke, Friedrich August	20, July 1899	15, Mar.	63	463		Ft. Atkinson, WI	Mutlef, Bromberg, Germany
Schwantes, Friedrich	25, May 1893	4, May	63	334		Oconomowoc, WI	Mötzelfitz, Pommern
Schwantes, M. Friedrike Caroline	15, Nov. 1894	20, Oct.	66	742		Colesburg, IA	Dumadel, Pommern
Schwardo, John	23, Feb. 1874	11, Jan.	43	63	Frei	Kendallville, IN	Kleyenlosch, Mecklenburg-Schwerin
Schwark, Charlotte	3, Mar. 1887	11, Feb.	56	142		Geneseo, IL	Memsheim, Baiern
Schwarto, Louisa	14, May 1891		70-10m- 5d	318			Mecklenburg-Schwerin
Schwartz, Catharine	25, Aug. 1887	12, Aug.	63	542	Schmidt	Cincinnati, OH	Saarbrücken, RheinPreußen
Schwartz, Dorothea	23, May 1870	24, Apr.	83- 7m-19d	167	Alberding	Newport, KY	Notenstadt, Amt Ehrenburg, Hannover
Schwartz, Elisabeth	20, Oct. 1879	5, Oct.	31	335		Mt. Vernon, IN	Ueberau, Hessen-Darmstadt
Schwartz, Franz	2, Aug. 1880	20, July	43- 2m	247		Mt. Vernon, IN	Weimar, Sachsen
Schwartz, Friedrich	12, May 1898	15, Apr.	93	303		Beaver Dam, WI	Brietzig bei Piritz, Pommern
Schwartz, Georg	28, Oct. 1872	23, Sept	57	351		Marietta, OH	Rothenzimmern, Sulz, Württemberg
Schwartz, Jakob	18, Dec. 1876	3, Dec.	66	407		Pomeroy, OH	Oppau, Rheinkreis Baiern
Schwartz, Johan	14, Mar. 1889	16, Feb.	49	174		Sandusky, OH	Jürgenstorf, Stavenhagen, Mecklenburg-Schwerin
Schwartz, Julia Christina	1, Dec. 1879	18, Nov.	51- 8m- 4d	383	Bischoff	Minneapolis, MN	Sigmarswangen, Sulz am Neckar, Württemberg
Schwartz, Lena	15, June 1893	26, May	34	382		Danville, IL	Bremen, Germany
Schwartz, Louisa	26, May 1898	2, May	87	335	Pophal	Taegesville, WI	Kannenberg bei Freienwalde, Pommern
Schwartz, Maria	17, Aug. 1885	2, Aug.	61	7	Baumgärtner	Marietta, OH	KleinSachsenheim, Vaihnigen, Württemberg
Schwartz, Martha Anna	8, June 1874		13- 9m-26d	183		Baresville, OH	
Schwartz, Pauline	27, May 1858	23, Apr.	14	84		Marshall, IL	Oberschönthal, Backnang, Württemberg
Schwartz, Sophie	8, Apr. 1897	22, Mar.	57	223	Müller	New York City, NY	Herisau, Appenzell, Schweiz
Schwartz, Wilhelm	14, Apr. 1887	27, Mar.	40	238		Danville, IL	Warzenbach, Kurhessen
Schwartze, (Mr)	20, Sept 1860	3, Aug.	66	152		Marthasville, MO	Rehme , Preußen
Schwartze, Louise	15, Jan. 1852	20, Aug.	37- 4m	12		Marietta, OH	Birgkirchen, Preußen
Schwartzmann, Dina	23, Dec. 1852	29, Nov.	13	208		Woodville, OH	Woodville,
Schwartz, Andreas	29, Jan. 1847	24, Dec.	68-11m-14d	19		---, NY	
Schwarz, Anna Elisabeth	30, Nov. 1868	28, Oct.	30- - 7d	383	Ochs	Cannon River, MN	Arnsbach, Kurhessen
Schwarz, Anna Elisabeth	14, Aug. 1876	27, July	55	263	Hahn	Lansing, IA	Gunzendorf, Baiern
Schwarz, August D.F.	22, May 1890	3, May	77- -28d	334		Maine, WI	Vogtshagen, Pommern
Schwarz, Auguste Emilie	2, Feb. 1899	3, Jan.	69-10m-25d	79	Pezold	Milwaukee, WI	Eibenstock, Vogtland, Sachsen
Schwarz, Barbara	14, Dec. 1874	26, Nov.		399		East Troy, WI	
Schwarz, Bertha Emilie	15, Oct. 1896	19, Sept	23	671	Greiner	Philadelphia, PA	Philadelphia, Pennsylvania
Schwarz, Carolina	5, Sept 1895	30, July	73	574	Mann	Baresville, OH	Rauenstein, Sachsen-Meiningen
Schwarz, Caroline	16, June 1853	21, Mar.		96		Mt. Vernon, IN	
Schwarz, Christian	10, Oct. 1889	19, Sept	73- 9m- 4d	654		Elizabeth, NJ	Röddenau, Kurhessen
Schwarz, Christian Friedrich	23, June 1884	29, Apr.	76	7		Maine, WI	Pflugrode, Pommern
Schwarz, Christoph	11, Mar. 1878	21, Feb.	34	79		Portsmouth, OH	Monroe County, Ohio
Schwarz, Conrad	24, Sept 1896	7, Sept	78	623		Baresville, OH	Zweingen, Vaihingen, Württemberg
Schwarz, Elisabeth	24, June 1852	3, June	38	104	Danker	Marietta, OH	Tüschendorf, Ottersberg, Hannover
Schwarz, Elisabeth	8, May 1876	5, Apr.	58	151		Cleveland, OH	Gegenstdorf, Bern, Schweiz
Schwarz, Elisabeth	16, June 1884	25, May	75	7	Eiselstein	Cincinnati, OH	Appau, Rheinkreis Baiern

Christliche Apologete Death Notices -- 1839 - 1899

Name of Deceased	Notice Date	Death Date	Age	Page	Maiden Name	Place of Death	Place of Birth
Schwarz, Elisabeth	25, Oct. 1888	30, Aug.	73	686	Gelzer	Angelica, NY	Mainbach, Baiern
Schwarz, Elisabeth	6, Feb. 1851	13, Jan.		24	Diegel	Buckhill, OH	
Schwarz, Friedrich August	10, Feb. 1859	10, Nov.	57	24		Waukegan, IL	Usingen, Nassau
Schwarz, Georg H.	2, Feb. 1893	6, Jan.	20	78		Ironton, OH	Greenup County, Kentucky
Schwarz, Georg J.	9, May 1881	15, Apr.	68- 2m- 7d	151		Angelica, NY	Minbach, Baiern
Schwarz, Heinrich	1, Mar. 1869	14, Feb.	15	71		Elizabeth, NJ	
Schwarz, J. (Mrs)	11, Sept 1865	20, Aug.	57	148		Port Clinton, OH	Kittendorf, Mecklenburg-Schwerin
Schwarz, Jacob	22, Oct. 1866	5, Oct.	61	342		Goshen, IN	Mutterstadt, Rheinkreis Baiern
Schwarz, Jakob	6, Mar. 1890	11, Feb.	12	158		Ironton, OH	Baresville, Monroe County, Ohio
Schwarz, Jakob	24, Dec. 1877	7, Dec.	64- 6m -5d	415		Marrs, IN	Wangen, Elsaß
Schwarz, Johanna Wilhelmina	17, Nov. 1879	25, Oct.	22	367	Gentz	Kenosha, WI	Sträkentin, Pommern
Schwarz, Johannes	21, Oct. 1867	18, Sept	48	334		Danville, IL	Warzebach, Kreis Marburg, Kurhessen
Schwarz, Katharina	4, Feb. 1867	21, Jan.	56- 6m- 7d	38	Stang	Goshen, IN	Gommersheim, Rheinkreis Baiern
Schwarz, Katharina	14, Jan. 1892	12, Dec.	60	30	Heinz	Hannibal, OH	Oldenburg, Hannover
Schwarz, Katharine	1, July 1872	10, June	32	215		Piqua, OH	Flecken, Kleebronn, Brackenheim, Württemberg
Schwarz, Lydia Christine	1, June 1874	20, May	14	175		Buffalo, NY	Buffalo, New York
Schwarz, Margaretha	10, Sept 1891	5, Aug.	58	590	Werner	St. Philip, IN	Rechtenbach, Bergzabern, Rheinpfalz Baiern
Schwarz, Margaretha	19, Oct. 1893	27, Sept	67- 3m- 6d	670		St. Louis, MO	Schwarzenberg an der Saale, Baiern
Schwarz, Maria	17, Feb. 1868		58	55	Kehl	East Troy, WI	Hönebach, Rothenburg, Kurhessen
Schwarz, Maria	4, Mar. 1897	7, Jan.	90	143	Pagendorf	Beaver Dam, WI	Großmellen, Pommern
Schwarz, Maria	17, Feb. 1873	26, Jan.	24- 3m- 6d	53	Martin	Baresville, OH	Wheeling, West Virginia
Schwarz, Mathilda	21, Nov. 1895	23, Oct.	39	750	Sehbrecht	Clarksville, IL	Oberschönthal, Backnang, Württemberg
Schwarz, Michael	30, May 1870	11, May	67- -28d	175		Pomeroy, OH	
Schwarz, Michael	29, July 1852		47	124		Pomeroy, OH	
Schwarz, Minnie	4, May 1893	6, Apr.	16	286		Blue Island, IL	Birrhart, Aargau, Schweiz
Schwarz, Susanna	5, July 1849	3, Apr.	63	108		Buckhill, OH	Württemberg
Schwarz, Valentin	16, Apr. 1847	11, Nov.	14- 8m	63		Pomeroy, OH	Obba, Rheinkreis Baiern
Schwarz, Wilhelm	8, June 1863	9, May	2- 9m- 9d	92		Elizabeth, NJ	
Schwarz, Wilhelmina	6, Dec. 1888	17, Nov.	59	782	Tillmann	Cannelton, IN	Bliedinghausen, Remscheid, Köln, Preußen
Schwarze, Anna Maria	30, June 1879	24, May	16	207		Truxton, MO	Spenge, Herfort, Preußen
Schwarze, Friedrich	8, June 1899	1, May	85	367		Warren, MO	Vlotho, Harford, Germany
Schwarze, Friedrich	15, Feb. 1894	26, Jan.	67	110		Brownton, MN	Sprenge, Herford, Preußen
Schwarze, Herman	19, June 1890	13, May	64- 4m-13d	398		Truxton, MO	Spengen, Herfort, Preußen
Schwarze, Katharina	4, May 1885	7, Apr.	68	7	Hafersick	Warrenton, MO	Mißwalden bei Königsberg, Preußen
Schwarzrock, Rud.	3, Nov. 1898	23, Sept	19- 2m- 1d	703		Baltimore, MD	Gutach, Baden
Schwarzwälder, (Mrs)	4, Aug. 1887	20, May		494		Yonkers, NY	Sulz am Necker, Württemberg
Schwarzwälder, Augusta	19, May 1898	22, Apr.	73	319		Boston, MA	Friedrichshoff, Stettin, Pommern
Schwebs, Auguste	19, Sept 1889	23, Aug.	15- -13d	606		Sun Prairie, WI	Altlußheim, Amt Schwetzingen, Baden
Schwechheimer, Elisabeth	8, June 1863	27, Mar.	48	92	Nagel	Canal Dover, OH	
Schweder, William	5, Jan. 1893	25, Nov.	22- 9m	14		Akron, NJ	Lancaster County, Pennsylvania
Schwedes, Jakob	30, Oct. 1876	10, Oct.	16- 6m-25d	351		Nauvoo, IL	Schlaitdorf, Tübingen, Württemberg
Schwegheimer, Anna Maria	5, Oct. 1868	10, Sept	33	319	Löffler	Canal Dover, OH	Pennsylvania
Schweigert, Georg	1, Aug. 1861	10, July	55	124		Seymour, IN	Heidelberg, Baden
Schweigert, Johann	27, June 1861	8, June	47- 4m- 6d	104		St. Charles, MO	Winzeln, Oberndorf, Württemberg
Schweikert, Valentin	20, Aug. 1896	21, June	69	543		Brooklyn, NY	Wisloch, Baden
Schweikert, Veronika	28, Feb. 1870	9, Feb.	72	71	Schweinfurth	Oregon, MO	

Christliche Apologete Death Notices --- 1839 - 1899

Name of Deceased	Notice Date	Death Date	Age	Page	Maiden Name	Place of Death	Place of Birth
Schweinforth, Anna Maria	13, May 1867	4, Apr.	50	150	Gaberdiel	Spencerville, OH	Wisloch, Baden
Schweinfurt,	8, Apr. 1886	9, Mar.	33- -4d	7		Rockport, IN	
Schweinfurth, Christina	18, May 1885	30, Apr.	65	7	Bühler	Francisco, MI	Wilferdingen, Durlach, Baden
Schweinfurth, Eva	25, Apr. 1864	8, Apr.	29- -20d	68	Benz	Marion, OH	Altwiesloch, Wiesloch, Baden
Schweinfurth, Katharina	31, May 1869	6, Feb.	80	175		Marion, OH	Wiesloch, Baden
Schweinfurth, Louisa	23, Mar. 1893	1, Mar.	56	190	Benz	Marion, OH	Altwiesloch, Baden
Schweinfurth, Louise	23, May 1881	9, May	21-4m-23d	167		Marion, OH	Dresden, Ohio
Schweinfurth, Peter	11, May 1893	21, Apr.	79	302		Francisco, MI	Wisloch, Baden
Schweinfurth, Philipp	12, Nov. 1896	24, Oct.	70	734		Galion, OH	Wiesloch, Baden
Schweither, Paul Samuel (Rev)	20, Jan. 1898	11, Dec.	54	47		München, GE	Leonberg, Stuttgart, Württemberg
Schweitzer, Anna Christina	13, May 1897	23, Apr.	74	303	Dick	San Jose, IL	Tiefenbrin bei Hoff, Baiern
Schweitzer, Catharina	12, Sept 1850	1, Aug.		148		Burlington, ---	
Schweitzer, Georg	14, Apr. 1859	1, Apr.	23- 5m-22d	60		Greenville, OH	Obermoß, Hessen-Darmstadt
Schweitzer, Heinrich Gottlieb	10, Aug. 1893	20, July	81	510		San Jose, IL	Kaltenthal, Stuttgart, Württemberg
Schweitzer, John	15, May 1890	15, Apr.	88	318		Swanton, NE	Wanzer, Bern, Schweiz
Schweitzer, Karl	5, Apr. 1880	3, Mar.	22- 1m-13d	111		San Jose, IL	Canton Bern, Schweiz
Schweitzer, Lucy	19, Mar. 1896	26, Feb.	34	190	Muhl	Peoria, IL	Bloomington, Illinois
Schweizer, Anna Barbara	26, Dec. 1881	27, Nov.	79- 2m	415		Swan Creek, NE	Langenthal, Bern, Schweiz
Schweizer, Barthol.	11, June 1857	28, May	57	96		Cincinnati, OH	Obermos, Hessen-Darmstadt
Schweizer, Christina	19, Dec. 1870	28, Nov.	30	407	Langebrake	Evansville, IN	Ladbergen, Tecklenburg, Preußen
Schweizer, Daniel	7, Dec. 1874	14, Nov.	67	391		Valparaiso, IN	Obersielmingen, Stuttgart, Württemberg
Schweizer, Elisabeth	29, July 1886	1, July	42	7	Inabnet	Denton, TX	Canton Bern, Schweiz
Schweizer, Johan Adam	11, July 1889	16, June	55- 2m-16d	446		Evansville, IN	Hirschlanden, Baden
Schweizer, Maria Franziska	27, Jan. 1873	22, Dec.	26- 5m	31	Eckhart	Evansville, IN	Großwinternheim, Hessen-Darmstadt
Schweizer, Ursula	7, June 1888	19, May	87	366	Schweizer	Milwaukee, WI	Dahlhof, Württemberg
Schwemmer, Christian	6, Apr. 1874	27, Mar.	72- 6m	111		Dunkirk, NY	Plau, Mecklenburg-Schwerin
Schwemmer, Friedrich	7, Sept 1863	4, July	29- - 9d	144		Dunkirk, NY	Stadt Blau, Mecklenburg-Schwerin
Schwemmer, Louisa	19, Jan. 1874	6, Jan.	72	23		Dunkirk, NY	Wahlstorff, Mecklenburg-Schwerin
Schwenck, Karl	13, Jan. 1879	19, Dec.	29-7m-19d	15		Brooklyn, NY	Lech bei Gießen, Hessen
Schwenicke, Bertha	28, Nov. 1870		48	383	Pfeifer	Chicago, IL	Potsdam, Preußen
Schwenk, Anna Maria	29, Nov. 1875	8, Aug.	23	383	Engel	Louisville, KY	
Schwenk, John Wilhelm	21, June 1880	1, June	31- 1m-24d	199		Louisville, KY	Mansfelden, Limburg, Nassau
Schwenk, Katharina	24, Jan. 1881	15, Dec.	52	31		Louisville, KY	Huntingburg, Indiana
Schwenker, Anna M.	21, Nov. 1864	21, Oct.	20	188	Mankehaus	Cannelton, IN	Hille, Minden, Preußen
Schwenker, August Ferdinand	15, Dec. 1898	24, Nov.	75	799		Schnectady, NY	Hille, Minden, Preußen
Schwenker, Carolina Maria	6, Jan. 1853	15, Dec.	22	4	Brockmeier	Schnectady, NY	Hille, Preußen
Schwenker, Caroline Marie L.	2, Oct. 1890	31, Aug.	22- 3m-28d	638		Amsterdam, NY	
Schwenker, Georg	26, July 1855	17, June	53	120		Mobile, AL	Legelshurst, Baden
Schwenker, Heinrich A.	19, Sept 1889	2, Aug.	54	606		Amsterdam, NY	Hille, Minden, Preußen
Schwenker, Wilhelm H.	6, July 1899	16, June	63- 5m-27d	431		Schnectady, NY	
Schwenkert, Christine M.	26, Feb. 1877	6, Feb.	31- 5m- 4d	71	Weil	Golconda, IL	Muldenstein, Bitterfeld, Preußen
Schwenkert, Elisabeth	12, Feb. 1877	17, Jan.	71- 2m	55		Evansville, IN	Hille, Hartum, Minden, Preußen
Schwenkert, Friedrich	17, Apr. 1865	4, Jan.	63	64		Schnectady, NY	Hille, Minden, Preußen
Schwenker, Friedrich Wilhelm	18, Mar. 1878	19, Feb.	30- 2m-22d	87		Schnectady, NY	Hille, Minden, Preußen
Schwenker, Georg Edward	29, June 1899	31, May	27	415		Anaheim, CA	Evansville, Indiana
Schwentker, Karl	26, June 1856	19, May	22- 3m-13d	104		Schnectady, NY	Hille, Minden, Preußen

Christliche Apologete Death Notices -- 1839 - 1899

Name of Deceased	Notice Date	Death Date	Age	Page	Maiden Name	Place of Death	Place of Birth
Schwentker, Maria Elisabeth	29, May 1876	12, May	76	175		Schnectady, NY	Hille, Preußen
Schwentker, Maria M.	4, May 1893	7, Apr.	47	286		Anaheim, CA	Cincinnati, Hamilton County, Ohio
Schwentker, Wilhelm	16, May 1889	19, Apr.	22- 7m	318		Anaheim, CA	Santa Claus, Indiana
Schweppe, Amalie	25, Feb. 1884	11, Feb.		7		Port Hudson, MO	Werl, Schlötmar, Lippe-Detmold
Schweppe, Jobst Barthold Heinr.	16, Aug. 1894	27, June	68	534		Beaufort, MO	Wart, Schöttmar, Lippe-Detmold
Schweppe, Maria	15, May 1876	3, May	60	159		Ft. Dodge, IA	Herfort, Preußen
Schwerdt, Heinrich Friedrich	16, Feb. 1874	4, Sept	23	55		Hopewell, MO	Rehme, Minden, Preußen
Schwerin, Friedrich	21, Feb. 1895	24, Jan.	80	126		Montrose, MN	Mecklenburg-Schwerin
Schwerin, Maria Friederike	15, Dec. 1887	25, Nov.	63- 3m-14d	798	Gropmann	Montrose, MN	Penslin, Mecklenburg-Schwerin
Schwert, Elisabeth	14, Mar. 1889	20, Feb.	14	174		Galion, OH	Richland County, Ohio
Schwert, Maria Dorothea	13, July 1893	16, June	77	446	Strauch	Galion, OH	Thaleischweiler, Pirmasens, Rheinkreis Baiern
Schwert, Maria Dorothea	13, Jan. 1898	26, Dec.	26	31		Galion, OH	
Schwertfeger, (Mr)	7, Feb. 1870	21, Jan.	75	47		Batesville, IN	Balsehle, Hannover
Schwertfeger, Karl	10, Jan. 1870	1, Dec.	73- 8m	15		Batesville, IN	Retlingen, Hannover
Schwerzrock, Wilhelmine	7, May 1896	23, Mar.	44	302	Jobs	Baltimore, MD	Miswalde, OstPreußen
Schwichtenberg, Friedrich	29, June 1893	29, May	74	414		Elkport, IA	Nauwalde, Pommern
Schwichtenberg, Heinrich	12, Jan. 1880	25, Dec.	27	15		Concord, IA	Rosine County, Wisconsin
Schwichtenberg, Karoline Frieder.	18, Sept 1876	29, Aug.	45	303	Nickolei	Allegan, MI	Leibchel, Preußen
Schwichtenberg, Wilhelmine	27, Mar. 1890	9, Mar.	36	206	Lübke	Milwaukee, WI	Schwirsen bei Kammin, Hinterpommern
Schwieghusen, Heinrich	3, Apr. 1876	17, Mar.	66	111		Oshkosh, WI	Friedland, Mecklenburg-Strelitz
Schwien, (Mr)	18, Nov. 1867	12, Oct.	67	366		Davenport, IA	Steinbusch, Amt Plön, Holstein
Schwier, Bertha	26, Oct. 1899	12, Oct.	17	687		Chester, IL	Roma, Randolph County, Indiana
Schwier, Heinrich Wilhelm	26, July 1880	13, July	60	239		Schnectady, NY	Friedewalde, Preußen
Schwieson, Louise	10, Jan. 1895	23, Dec.	64	30	Lange	Columbus, WI	Teßmannsdorf, Mecklenburg-Schwerin
Schwietert, Friedrich	19, Mar. 1891	27, Feb.	63	190		Warrenton, MO	Bersenbrück, Hannover
Schwind, C. Heinrich	21, Nov. 1895	31, Oct.	71	750		Springfield, IL	Kleingarten, Hessen-Darmstadt
Schwind, Martha	15, Dec. 1884	3, Dec.	63	7	Gerk	Perrysburg, OH	Munzenheim, Elsaß
Schwinger, Henry	5, Oct. 1893	7, Sept	72	638		Enterprise, KS	Germany
Schwinger, Katharine	12, Nov. 1896	17, Oct.	54	734		Enterprise, KS	Wittenweier, Baden
Schwinn, Georg (Rev)	12, Aug. 1897	24, July	64	511		Evansville, IN	Niederbeerbach, Beisheim, Hessen-Darmstadt
Schwinn, Maria Dorothea	26, Dec. 1881	6, Dec.	79- 9m- 4d	415	Stein	Davenport, IA	Stadtbeck, Amt Plöen, Schleswig-Holstein
Schwinn, Matthäus	11, July 1864	20, June	37	112		Galena, IL	Metlingen, Baiern
Schwir, Heinrich	1, Feb. 1864	3, Jan.	22- 3m-15d	20		Schnectady, NY	Friedewald, Minden, Preußen
Schwitzgöbel, Benjamin	13, Apr. 1893	13, Mar.	18	238		Holt, MI	
Schwitzgöbel, Jakob	4, Aug. 1892	17, July	75	494		Holt, MI	Neuhofen, Rheinkreis Baiern
Schwitzgöbel, Margaretha	2, Dec. 1897	29, Oct.	81	767	Provo	Holt, MI	Neuhofen, Speyer, Rheinkreis Baiern
Schwoedes, Maria Catharina	3, Jan. 1881	13, Nov.	19	7		Nauvoo, IL	Lancaster County, Pennsylvania
Schwoerer, Anna M.	27, June 1895	1, June	23- 8m-20d	414		Dallas City, IL	
Schwope, Caroline	2, Jan. 1865	1, Sept	33	4		Columbus, KS	Nikoline, Schlesien, Preußen
Schwope, Gottlob	4, Jan. 1864	26, Apr.	22- 4m-20d	4		Columbus, KS	Nickoliene, Kreis Falkenberg, Schlesien
Schwope, Johan Georg	13, Dec. 1888	22, Nov.	86	798	Bönz	Wathena, KS	Heidersdorf, Schlesien
Schwope, Johanna	29, June 1885	12, June	50	7		Wathena, KS	Hohenfelde, Schleswig-Holstein
Schwope, Johanne Eleonore	25, Mar. 1886	11, Mar.	80	7	Linder	Wathena, KS	Nikoline, Falkenberg, Schlesien
Schwope, Mathilde Lydia	13, Dec. 1894		16- 5m	806		Wathena, KS	Donophan County, Kansas
Scoles, Minnie	16, Sept 1897	29, Aug.	37- 9m	591	Achilles	Caneadea, NY	
Scott, Emilia	3, May 1894	5, Apr.	27	294	Wieser	Albert Lea, MN	Rickerel Lake, Minnesota

Christliche Apologete Death Notices --- 1839 - 1899

Name of Deceased	Notice Date	Death Date	Age	Page	Maiden Name	Place of Death	Place of Birth
Sczuck, Marie P.L.	14, June 1888	11, May	52- 5m-16d	382	Drafz	Menomonie, WI	Zirwinz, Pommern
Seaman, Karolina	27, Jan. 1879	1, Jan.	37	31	Busching		Jörnhorst, Hannover
Sebastian, Georg	29, Oct. 1857	7, Oct.		176		West Baltimore, MD	Zernitsch, Sachsen-Altenburg
Sebich, Louise Wilhelmine	19, Jan. 1863	25, Dec.	20-11m-17d	12	Herdis	Galena, IL	
Seck, (Mrs)	20, Mar. 1871		56	95		Frankfurt, ---	
Seddelmeyer, Maria Magdalena	20, Aug. 1847	1, Aug.	1- -10d	135		St. Louis, MO	
See , Johan Jochen Friedrich	1, July 1897	5, May	68	414		Roseville, MI	Drieberg, Mecklenburg-Schwerin
See, Dorothea Sophia	13, Oct. 1898	20, Aug.	70	655	Knief	Roseville, MI	Preußen
Seebach, Ehrenfried	3, June 1897	1, May	89	351		Red Wing, MN	Wesel am Rhein, Germany
Seebach, Margarethe	22, Dec. 1873	30, Oct.	35	407	Wilhelmi	St. Paul, MN	Langenschwalbach, Nassau
Seebeck, Erich Friedrich	21, Jan. 1884	26, Dec.	30	7		Le Sueur, MN	Midlun, Dorum, Hannover
Seebeck, Helena Katharina	22, July 1897	29, Mar.	75	463	Rüsch	Le Sueur, MN	
Seebeck, Johan Heinrich	8, Dec. 1884	11, Nov.	72-10m-17d	7		Le Sueur, MN	
Seeberger, Emilie	10, Feb. 1898	26, Jan.	31	95	Langbein	Chicago, IL	Spika, Daran, Hannover
Seebich, John	23, June 1898	12, May	69	399		St. Paul, MN	Chicago, Cook County, Illinois
Seefeld, Dorothea	5, Apr. 1888	19, Mar.	66- 1m-1d	222	Tews	Milwaukee, WI	Mergelstetten, Heidenheim, Württemberg
Seefeld, Karl	4, Nov. 1878	17, Oct.	37	351		Milwaukee, WI	Plantikow, Naugard, Pommern
Seefeld, Peter	13, May 1867	5, Mar.	76	150		Milwaukee, WI	Blandikow, Pommern
Seefeld, Sophia R.	9, Mar. 1899	12, Feb.	67	159	Spittler	Milwaukee, WI	Plantikow, Himmterpommern, Preußen
Seefeld, Wilhelm	2, Jan. 1890	14, Dec.	44	14		Milwaukee, WI	Cannstatt, Württemberg
Seefeld, Wilhemine	1, June 1899	19, May	77	351	Tews	Milwaukee, WI	Radum, Preußen
Seefeldt, Wilhelm	23, Jan. 1875	2, Oct.	55	31		Milwaukee, WI	Plankekow, Pommern
Seeger, Johan Jacob	20, Apr. 1893	28, Mar.	64	254		Francisco, MI	Plantilow, Stettin, Pommern, Preußen
Seeger, Johanna	1, Aug. 1864	17, July	83	124	Gräßle	Chicago, IL	UnterJettingen, Herrenberg, Württemberg
Seeger, Martin	18, Oct. 1888	9, Sept	84	670		Lyona, KS	Herrenalb, Württemberg
Seegers, Karl Heinrich	15, Sept 1892	27, Aug.	16	590		Cincinnati, OH	Gustin an der Plant, Pommern
Seegrist, Ames	22, Aug. 1870	3, Aug.	22-10m-22d	271		Centreville, NE	Hannover
Seeheld, Dorothea Elisabeth	6, Mar. 1865	9, Feb.	77	40		Milwaukee, WI	
Seeheld, Gottlieb	9, Feb. 1863	21, Jan.	37- 6m-28d	24		Milwaukee, WI	Plantikow, Hinterpommern
Seekamp, Dorothea	6, Sept 1855	18, Aug.	58- 8m	144	Weslaus	Covington, KY	Blantikow, HinterPommern, Preußen
Seekamp, Elisabeth	23, Sept 1852	30, Aug.	50	156	Böse	Aurora, ---	Bruckhaus, Hannover
Seekamp, Harm	22, May 1865	4, May	66	84		Cincinnati, OH	Anheim, OberBremen, Hannover
Seekamp, Louise A.	12, Mar. 1896	25, Feb.	64	175		Indianapolis, IN	Hemelingen, Amt Achim, Hannover
Seekamp, Minnie	14, Sept 1885	23, Aug.	12- - 3d	7		Covington, KY	Sachsen
Seekatz, Karoline	7, Sept 1899	12, Aug.	49	575		Lawrenceburg, IN	
Sekatz, Maria Katharine	24, Dec. 1896	4, Dec.	76	831	Link	Lawrenceburg, IN	Newport, Campbell County, Kentucky
Seel, August	27, Aug. 1877	9, Aug.	57- - 2d	279		Columbus, OH	Westerburg, Nassau
Seemann, Georg	7, July 1884	21, June	47	7		Humboldt, NE	
Seemann, Johanna Margaretha Elis.	19, Oct. 1893	5, Oct.	77	670	Bornemann	Louisville, KY	Auggen, Mühlheim, Baden
Seemann, Katharina Rosina	28, Jan. 1897	10, Jan.	62	63	Strecker	Hamilton, OH	Gestendorf, Preußen
Seemann, Maria	10, Dec. 1866	12, Nov.	19-10m	398			Rielingshausen, Marbach, Württemberg
Seewald, Karl	9, Mar. 1899	17, Feb.	70	159		Troy, NY	Arnsdorf, Preußen
Segelken, Cord	29, Oct. 1841	23, Aug.	25- 6m	171		Marietta, OH	
Seger, Carl	10, Feb. 1873	31, Dec.	63- 2m	47		German Creek, IA	Ippingen, Baden
Seger, Karoline	7, July 1884	24, June	58- 5m	7		Harper, IA	Lette, Tecklenburg, Münster, Preußen
Seger, Theresia	5, Sept 1850	1, Aug.	26- 6m	144		Louisville, KY	Wassenweiler bei Breisach, Baden

Christliche Apologete Death Notices --- 1839 - 1899

Name of Deceased	Notice Date	Death Date	Age	Page	Maiden Name	Place of Death	Place of Birth
Sehl, Pauline	20, July 1868		24	231	Winter	Ottumwa, IA	Warren County, Missouri
Sehlhorst, Dorothea	28, Mar. 1870	9, Mar.	74	103		Appleton, MO	Meitze, Amt Bissendorf, Hannover
Sehnert, Elisabeth	31, Oct. 1895	28, Sept	92	702	Hüner	Pekin, IL	Hersfeld, Hessen
Sehnert, Katharina	11, Mar. 1897	18, Feb.	87	159	Sauerwein	Bible Grove, IL	Scharfheim, Hessen-Darmstadt
Sehnert, Margaretha	24, Feb. 1887	5, Feb.	74	126	Hirt	Pekin, IL	Schlierbach, Hessen-Darmstadt
Sehnert, Susanna	23, Aug. 1875	28, July	28	271	Herdy	Bible Grove, IL	St. Clair County, Illinois
Seib, Esther W.	27, Mar. 1890	8, Mar.	25- 8m-16d	206	Walter	New York City, NY	
Seib, Georg	25, May 1893	9, Apr.	56	334		New York City, NY	Lambrecht, Rheinpfalz Baiern
Seibel, Anna	22, Mar. 1888	4, Jan.	26- 4m- 8d	190	Schmidt	Forest, WI	Forest, Wisconsin
Seibel, Christina	16, May 1895	9, Apr.	66	318	Epple	Montrose, MN	Oberliningen, Württemberg
Seibel, Dorothea Elisabeth	2, May 1870		73	143	Jung	Pittsburg, PA	Liebenscheid, Marienberg, Nassau
Seibel, Elisa	23, July 1891	25, June	25	478	Müller	Fond du Lac, WI	Forest, Wisconsin
Seibel, Elisabeth	18, May 1885	26, Apr.	62	7		Bremen, IL	Weisenhassel, Kurhessen
Seibel, Eva	3, Apr. 1882	29, Nov.	80	111		Fond du Lac, WI	Klein-Gladenbach, Hessen-Darmstadt
Seibel, Eva Elisabeth	19, Dec. 1895	12, Nov.	67	814	Pfeifer	Fond du Lac, WI	Kleinkladenbach, Hessen-Darmstadt
Seibel, Johannes Georg	16, Feb. 1880	2, Feb.	64- - 2d	55		New Bremen, IL	Mandern, Eder, Waldeck
Seibel, Kath. Johanna Henrietta	19, Feb. 1891	17, Jan.	20	126		Fond du Lac, WI	Forest, Wisconsin
Seibel, Theresia	10, Mar. 1879		27-10m	79	Steiner	Philippsburg, OH	Montgomery County, Ohio
Seibert, Adam	17, July 1882	1, June	90- -17d	231		Garner, IA	Ellweiler, Preußen
Seibert, John Emil	14, Mar. 1864	6, Feb.	16-10m- 6d	44		New Albany, IN	
Seibert, Ludwig	27, Oct. 1853	12, Oct.	20-11m	172		Jeffersonville, IN	
Seibert, Magdalena	28, Apr. 1887	27, Mar.	83- 4m-26d	270	Mosmann	Jeffersonville, IN	Mausweiler, Elsaß
Seibert, Maria C.	22, Mar. 1894	26, Feb.	48	198		Berea, OH	Veltheim, Zürich, Schweiz
Seibert, Martin	13, Jan. 1898	13, Dec.	74	31		Jeffersonville, IN	Niedermordau, Hessen-Darmstadt
Seibert, Rosette	3, Mar. 1879	4, Feb.	22	71	Lekore		Chicago, Cook County, Illinois
Seibold, Amalia	9, May 1881	21, Apr.	27- 7m-26d	151		Papillion, NE	Maquon River, Opoukee County, Wisconsin
Seibold, Christine	10, Jan. 1895		71	30	Krauter	Bucyrus, OH	Leutenbach, Waiblingen, Württemberg
Seibold, Emilie	30, May 1881	21, Apr.	27- 7m-26d	175		Papillion, NE	Maquon River, Ozaukee County, Wisconsin
Seibold, Emma Johanna	28, July 1873	13, June	13- 7m- 9d	239		Bucyrus, OH	
Seibold, Friedrich	8, Oct. 1877	5, Sept	61-10m- 6d	327		Le Sueur, MN	Fellbach, Cannstatt, Stuttgart, Württemberg
Seibold, Friedrich	14, July 1873	1, July	21- 8m- 9d	223		Bucyrus, OH	Leutenbach, Waiblingen, Württemberg
Seibold, Jacob	23, Apr. 1883	2, Apr.	87- -29d	135		Canal Dover, OH	Nufringen, Herrenberg, Württemberg
Seibold, Jacob Friedrich	23, Dec. 1886	1, Dec.	68	7		Bucyrus, OH	Bittenfeld, Waiblingen, Württemberg
Seibold, Peter	27, Jan. 1873	7, Jan.	71	31		Wheeling, WV	Schmieden, Cannstadt, Württemberg
Seibold, Sophia Catharina	28, July 1873	13, June	11- -20d	239		Bucyrus, OH	
Seidel, Christina	17, June 1886	15, May	85-10m-21d	7		Sterling, IL	Klein-Glettbach, Württemberg
Seidel, Christine Barbara	11, June 1883	11, May	69	191		Sterling, IL	Schwiberdingen, Ludwigsburg, Württemberg
Seidel, Franz	29, Oct. 1883	16, Oct.	37- 8m- 8d	351		Canal Dover, OH	Wünschbarsdorf, Reuß
Seidel, Franz Joseph	30, Aug. 1869	14, Aug.	55	279		Winona, MN	Birkigt bei Tetschen, Böhmen
Seidel, Friederike	20, Oct. 1884	26, Sept	43	7		Draese, MN	Schönlanke, Scharniko, Preußen
Seidel, Friederike	29, Apr. 1886	17, Apr.	66	7		Watertown, WI	Oedersdorf, Reuß-Schleiz
Seidel, Friedrich Ernst	26, Dec. 1881	28, Nov.	61- 9m- 6d	415		Buffalo, NY	Döbeln, Sachsen
Seidel, Gottlieb	14, Dec. 1885	17, Nov.	78- 2m	7		Sterling, IL	Württemberg
Seidel, Julius Friedrich (Rev)	1, Feb. 1894	30, Dec.	65	78		Baltimore, MD	Döbeln, Sachsen
Seidel, Therese	2, June 1892	12, May	74	350		Winona, MN	Kulm bei Tetschen, Böhmen
Seidelmann, Louis	1, Feb. 1869	3, Dec.	36	39		Industry, TX	Seehausen, Altmark, Preußen

Christliche Apologete Death Notices --- 1839 - 1899

Name of Deceased	Notice Date	Death Date	Age	Maiden Name	Page	Place of Death	Place of Birth
Seidenspinner, Caroline Louise	3, May 1894	17, Mar.	36	Aubert	294	Cincinnati, OH	Liemersbach, Backnang, Württemberg
Seidler, Friedrich	21, Aug. 1890	25, July	9		542	Minneapolis, MN	
Seidler, Henriette	29, Aug. 1889	26, July	70- 6m- 3d	Witte	558	Wrayville, IL	Latokow, Prinzlau, Preußen
Seidler, Martha	27, June 1895	12, May	23		414	Minneapolis, MN	Schönlanke, Preußen
Seidler, Paul Herman	21, Aug. 1890	6, Aug.	16		542	Minneapolis, MN	Winona, Minnesota
Seidler, Willie	21, Aug. 1890	31, July	5		542	Minneapolis, MN	
Seidlitz, Luise	23, Mar. 1899	23, Jan.	30	Rohweder	191	Winona, MN	Winona, Minnesota
Seif, Catharina	19, Jan. 1888	23, Dec.	57	Pister	46	Galion, OH	Nußlach, Baden
Seif, Harriet	11, Oct. 1860	21, Sept	22- 7m-22d	Olshaus	164	Galion, OH	
Seif, Margaretha	21, Nov. 1864	25, Sept	68- 7m- 3d		188	Galion, OH	Langensteinbach, Durlach, Baden
Seif, Michael	11, Aug. 1873	13, July	53- 9m-27d		255	Galion, OH	Langensteinbach, Durlach, Baden
Seif, Michael	4, Aug. 1873	13, July	53- 9m-27d		247	Galion, OH	Baden
Seif, Noah	5, Dec. 1861	21, Nov.	14- 8m-28d		196	Galion, OH	
Seif, Samuel	24, Feb. 1873	24, Jan.	18- 2m		63	Galion, OH	
Seif, Sophia	21, Sept 1863	1, Sept	11- 5m-21d		152	Galion, OH	
Seif, Sophie	4, Sept 1871	19, Aug.	54- 4m-12d	Neyer	287	Galion, OH	
Seifert, Antonie	28, Dec. 1868	7, Dec.	23		415	Milan, IN	Weißendorf, Reuß-Schleiz
Seifert, Auguste J.	20, June 1895	30, May	66	Finke	398	Lawrence, MA	Preßwitz a. d. Saale, Schwarzburg-Rudolstadt
Seifert, Caroline	2, Oct. 1865	6, Aug.	29		160	Herman, MO	Weingarten, Baden
Seifert, Christian Friedrich	17, Jan. 1870	23, Dec.	63		23	Milan, IN	Weißendorf, Reuß-Schleiz
Seifert, Dorothea M.	11, Nov. 1867	17, Sept	40	Zürn	358	Melrose, NY	Reusten, Württemberg
Seifert, Edward Heinrich	3, Nov. 1884	24, Oct.	19m		7	Lemars, IA	
Seifert, Elizabeth Dorothea	28, Nov. 1895	6, Nov.	19		766	Lexington, TX	Lexington, Lee County, Texas
Seifert, Gottlieb	14, June 1880	21, May	47- 9m-14d		191	Brooklyn, NY	Lindenheim, Baden
Seifert, Heinrich J.	26, Oct. 1899		81		687	Pittsburg, PA	Waltershausen, Sachsen
Seifert, Hermann Ludwig	25, July 1861	22, June	25		120	Milan, IN	Weißendorf, Reuß-Schleiz
Seifert, Johanna	5, Mar. 1896	27, Jan.	80	Bergner	158	Cannelton, IN	Tabtis, Sachsen-Weimar
Seifert, John	27, Nov. 1890	7, Oct.	64		766	Marrs, IN	Gesfeld a.d. Rhöne, Germany
Seifert, Karl Edward	1, Feb. 1894	8, Jan.	16-10m- 6d		78	Marrs, IN	
Seifert, Katharina	22, Sept 1887	2, Sept	43		606	Nashville, TN	Niederweisel, Hessen-Darmstadt
Seifert, Maria	26, Jan. 1893	29, Dec.	82		62	New Rochelle, NY	Oberbrücken, Backnang, Württemberg
Seifert, Maria	3, Nov. 1884	22, Oct.	33	Resner	7	Lemars, IA	Posey County, Indiana
Seifert, Selma	28, Oct. 1897	2, Oct.	19		687	Milwaukee, WI	
Seifert, Wilhelm	20, Oct. 1898	27, Sept	80		671	New Rochelle, NY	Sulzbach, Backnang, Württemberg
Seifferer, Lydia Emma	15, Dec. 1892	18, Nov.	26		798	Blooming Grove, MN	Conweiler, Neuenburg, Württemberg
Seifried, Christina	21, Jan. 1886	26, Dec.	79	Faut	7	Jeffersonville, IN	Nunmis, Württemberg
Seifried, Friedrich	25, Dec. 1865	16, Nov.	64- 9m-14d		208	Jeffersonville, IN	Rottweil, Württemberg
Seifritz, Josephina	28, Jan. 1878	5, Jan.	82		31	Poughkeepsie, NY	Rottenburg bei Dresden, Sachsen
Seiler, Louise	19, May 1887	30, Apr.	74	Stark	318	Poughkeepsie, NY	
Seiler, Carl	20, Sept 1880	17, July	3		303	Bradford, IN	
Seiler, Christian	13, Jan. 1898	23, Dec.	71		31	Bradford, IN	Bönigen, Bern, Schweiz
Seiler, Christian	19, Mar. 1857	13, Feb.	56		48	New Albany, IN	Bönerken, Schweiz
Seiler, Georg F.	24, Aug. 1893	18, July	70		542	Rochester, MN	Erfurt, Sachsen
Seiler, Helene	13, Aug. 1891	20, June	69	Stock	526	Zumbro Falls, MN	Greweiler bei Kaiserslautern, Preußen
Seiler, Henry J.	20, Sept 1880	17, July	11		303	Bradford, IN	
Seiler, Katharina	9, July 1896	7, June	73	Hermann	447	Minneapolis, MN	Basel, Schweiz

Christliche Apologete Death Notices --- 1839 - 1899

Name of Deceased	Notice Date	Death Date	Age	Maiden Name	Page	Place of Death	Place of Birth
Seiler, Magdalena	1, Jan. 1877	18, Dec.	69	ZurSchmiede	7	Bradford, IN	Wildersweil, Bern, Schweiz
Seiler, Margaretha	22, Jan. 1891	3, Jan.	27		62	Pittsburg, PA	Pittsburg, Pennsylvania
Seiler, Maria	2, June 1887	10, May	23- 5m-14d	Junker	350	Evansville, IN	Vanderburgh County, Indiana
Seimer, (Mrs)	12, Sept 1850	31, May	51		148	St. Louis, MO	Osnabrück, Hannover
Seipel, Johanna	15, July 1886	1, July	75- 3m-16d	Dörtzner	7	Newark, NJ	Jena, Sachsen-Weimar
Seipel, Wilhelm	4, Dec. 1890	7, Nov.	81		782	Newark, NJ	Allendorf an der Werra, Kurhessen
Seiter, Elisabeth	5, Apr. 1894		42- 6m-16d	Almendinger	230	Marion, OH	Bethlehem, Marion County, Ohio
Seiter, Heinrich	1, Aug. 1864	3, July	22		124	Marion, OH	Marion County, Ohio
Seiter, Jakob	17, July 1865	6, Apr.	19		116	Marion, OH	Marion County, Ohio
Seiter, Johannes	24, Sept 1878	22, Aug.	65- 7m-21d		303	Marion, OH	Elmendingen, Pforzheim, Baden
Seiter, Magdalena	2, Feb. 1880	20, Jan.	87- 1m-18d	Drollinger	39	Marion, OH	Ellmendingen, Baden
Seiter, Margaretha	1, Mar. 1894	12, Feb.	75	Klingel	150	Marion, OH	Erschöningen, Pforzheim, Württemberg
Seiter, Maria	9, Sept 1852	30, July	36- 6m-16d		148	Delaware, OH	
Seiter, Wilhelm	26, Apr. 1880	4, Apr.	28- 3m-14d		135	New Knoxville, OH	
Seits, Barbara	17, Mar. 1873		36	Rausch	87	Seymour, IN	Madison, Indiana
Seitz, Adam	14, Dec. 1868	2, Oct.	32		399	Boonville, IN	Weißenheim am Berg, Dürkheim, Baiern
Seitz, Anna Dorothea	24, Oct. 1895	22, Sept	80	Neumann	686	Boonville, IN	Weisenheim am Berg, Reinfalls, Baiern
Seitz, Catharina	25, Mar. 1858	1, Mar.	67		48	New Albany, IN	Niedermos, Landerbas, Hessen-Darmstadt
Seitz, Elisabeth	23, May 1864	12, Feb.	8		84	Bradford, IN	
Seitz, Jacob	26, Apr. 1888	21, Mar.	41		270	Boonville, IN	
Seitz, Katharina	23, May 1864	29, Jan.	12		84	Bradford, IN	
Seitz, Lorenz	30, Sept 1878	13, Sept	59- 5m-24d		311	Boonville, IN	Weißenheim am Berg, Rheinkreis Baiern
Seitz, Louise	1, Sept 1887	10, Aug.	36	Flohri	558	Boonville, IN	Sulzfeld, Baden
Seitz, Louise	20, Nov. 1876	18, Oct.	25-11m-15d	Hügel	375	Boonville, IN	
Seitz, Philipp	23, May 1864	29, Jan.	16		84	Bradford, IN	
Seiz, Philipp	13, Nov. 1882	26, May	90		367	Louisville, KY	Bergheim, Niedau, Hessen-Darmstadt
Selig, Auguste	14, Oct. 1872	5, Sept	48	Anton	335	Milwaukee, WI	Drosedow, Mecklenburg-Strelitz
Selig, Friederike	10, Mar. 1873	17, Feb.	78	Henning	79	Madison, WI	Metzingen, Württemberg
Selig, Wilhelm	9, July 1866	6, June	60		222	Baresville, OH	Rokenzitz, Kreis Rotenburg, Kurhessen
Selke, Ernestine	28, Apr. 1884		40	Zank	7	Morrison, MO	Lauenburg, Pommern
Selke, Herman Ferdinand	21, May 1891	1, May	56		334	Morrison, MO	Stemeitz, Schlave, Pommern
Sell, Anna Rosina	18, June 1891	18, May	49- - 9d	Stolper	398	Wausau, WI	
Sell, Gustav W.	28, May 1891		27		350	Renville, MN	Zozenow, Regenwalde, Pommern
Sell, Gustav W.	7, May 1891		27		302	Renville, MN	Regenwald, Zozenow, Pommern
Sell, Johan Friedrich	19, June 1890	16, May	76		398	Maine, WI	Falkenberg, Piritz, Pommern
Sell, Johanna Louise	14, Nov. 1881	30, Oct.	82		367	Algona, CD	Blumenfelde, Friedeberg, Preußen
Sell, Wilhelmine Julie	13, June 1881		26- 7m- 4d	Krassin	191	Waseca, MN	Justin bei Plat an der Reg, Germany
Sellam, Wilhelm	15, Sept 1879	13, Aug.	58		295	Sleepy Eye, MN	Semrow, Schiefelbein, Preußen
Selle, Heinrich	7, July 1887	19, June	67		430	Cameron, MO	Merseburg, Sachsen
Selle, Johanna Rebecca	14, Dec. 1874	18, Nov.	78		399	Liberty, MO	Stolpenheim, Sachsen, Preußen
Sellheim, Wilhelmine	20, June 1895	21, May	76	Liebzeit	398	Sheboygan, WI	Falkenwalde, Ukermark, Brandenburg
Sellin, Henriette Maria Louise	28, Jan. 1892	6, Jan.	60		62	Lyona, KS	Justin bei Plat an der Reg, Germany
Sellmann, Marie	24, June 1858	11, May	21		100	Baltimore, MD	
Sellnow, Anna	18, Aug. 1898	7, July	55		527	Whitewater, WI	Ponigtow, Piritz, Pommern
Sellnow, Christian	23, Mar. 1874	5, Mar.	62- -25d		95	Swan Creek, NE	Dönlitz, Kreis Pyritz, Pommern
Semke, Clara	20, June 1889	19, May	22- 3m	Intermill	398	Harrison, KS	

Christliche Apologete Death Notices — 1839 - 1899

Name of Deceased	Notice Date	Death Date	Age	Page	Maiden Name	Place of Death	Place of Birth
Semler, Anna Maria	11, Nov. 1886	13, Oct.	61- 5m- 8d	7	Dietrich	Iowa City, IA	Gensungen, Kurhessen
Semmler, Georg	4, Feb. 1892	6, Jan.	72	78		Wellman, IA	Gensungen, Kurhessen
Semmler, Johan Heinrich	20, Nov. 1871		81- 2m-11d	375		Mascoutah, IL	Nordstadt, Nassau
Semmler, Nicolaus	28, July 1887	7, July	74- 3m-10d	478			Heineberg, Kurhessen
Senft, August	17, June 1878	20, Apr.	13- 1m- 4d	191		Ahnapee, WI	
Senft, Elisabeth	17, June 1878	21, Apr.	5- 5m-11d	191		Ahnapee, WI	
Senft, Emilie	17, June 1878	21, Apr.	10- 9m-28d	191		Ahnapee, WI	
Senft, Friedrich	17, June 1878	2, May	9- 5m- 9d	191		Ahnapee, WI	
Senft, Heinrich	17, June 1878	1, May	2- 3m-13d	191		Ahnapee, WI	
Senft, Maria	9, Jan. 1896	3, Dec.	52	30	Knuth	Sturgeon Bay, WI	Posen
Senft, Maria	17, June 1878	21, Apr.	12- - 8d	191		Ahnapee, WI	
Senft, Wilhelm	17, June 1878	21, Apr.	4- 1m-21d	191		Ahnapee, WI	
Senftleben, Anna Hattie	26, Mar. 1883		16	103		Chicago, IL	Berlin, Preußen
Seng, Anna Elisabeth	1, Mar. 1880	31, Jan.	64	71	Pfeifer	Peoria, IL	Niederjossa, Ziegenhain, Kurhessen
Seng, Anna Katharina Elisabeth	28, Mar. 1881	4, Mar.	15- 2m-12d	103		Secor, IL	Oberjossa, Ziegenhain, Kurhessen
Seng, Conrad	14, Apr. 1879	3, Apr.	64- 3m- 4d	119		Secor, IL	Tazewell County, Illinois
Seng, Sebastian	29, Jan. 1891	26, Dec.	49- 2m- 8d	78		Wilber, NE	Oberjoßa, Kreis Ziegenhain, Kurhessen
Seng, Wilhelm	5, May 1859	6, Apr.	33	72		Peoria, IL	Buchs, St. Gallen, Schweiz
Senn, (Mrs)	4, Apr. 1870	9, Mar.	76	111	Rohrer	Rock River, WI	Altendorf, St. Gallen, Schweiz
Senn, Andreas	24, Mar. 1879	7, Mar.	52	95		Fillmore, WI	Ashforth, Fond du Lac County, Wisconsin
Senn, Anna	1, Nov. 1875	14, Oct.	21- 7m-12d	351		Rock River, WI	Ashford, Fond du Lac County, Wisconsin
Senn, Anna	25, June 1877	24, May	23	207	Gantenhein	Elmore, WI	Oberamt Thun, Schweiz
Senn, Barbara	21, Dec. 1874	23, Sept	73	407		Ft. Dodge, IA	Ashford, Fond du Lac County, Wisconsin
Senn, Barbara	17, Jan. 1876	18, Dec.	26	23		Rock River, WI	Canton St. Gallen, Schweiz
Senn, Barbara	15, Nov. 1894	19, Oct.	82	742		Oshkosh, WI	
Senn, Barbara	8, Jan. 1866	16, Oct.		14		Lyons Creek, KS	
Senn, Christian	6, Sept 1894	11, Aug.	74	582		West Bend, WI	Altendorf, St. Gallen, Schweiz
Senn, Christian	27, Nov. 1882	10, Nov.	67	383		Enterprise, KS	Buchs, St. Gallen, Schweiz
Senn, Christian	14, July 1879	2, July	20- 9m-11d	223		Fillmore, WI	Ashford, Wisconsin
Senn, Dorothea	16, Sept 1852		15- 6m	152		St. Louis, MO	Schweiz
Senn, Elise H.	20, Sept 1888	2, Sept	36	606	Nix	Oshkosh, WI	Bleeker, Fulton County, New York
Senn, Ida Margaretha	3, Dec. 1896	25, Sept	20	782		Green Bay, WI	Green Bay, Wisconsin
Senn, Johan	27, Nov. 1876	31, Oct.	80- -21d	383		Rock River, WI	Buchs, St. Gallen, Schweiz
Senn, Johannes	24, Aug. 1885	28, July	70	7		Kewaskum, WI	Altendorf, St. Gallen, Schweiz
Senn, Johannes	14, Sept 1885	28, July	60	7		Kewaskum, WI	Altendorf, St. Gallen, Schweiz
Senn, Leonhard	27, Feb. 1865	13, Jan.	19	36		Lyons Creek, KS	Kanton St. Gallen, Schweiz
Senn, Magdalena	1, Oct. 1857	30, Aug.	29	160	Kutscher	German Creek, IA	Eberdingen, Vaihingen, Württemberg
Senn, Minnie	18, Oct. 1888	25, Aug.	4- 9m-13d	670		Scranton, PA	
Senn, Nicolaus	10, May 1888	20, Apr.	82- 3m-26d	302		West Bend, WI	Buchs, St. Gallen, Schweiz
Senn, Sophia	8, Mar. 1880	20, Feb.	31- 3m-26d	79	Findeisen	Green Bay, WI	New Franken, Brown County, Wisconsin
Senn, Wolfgang	19, July 1880		79- 6m-17d	231		Barton, WI	Buchs, St. Gallen, Schweiz
Seprecht, Caroline	10, June 1858	11, May	13- 9m- 2d	92		Monroe, MI	
Serber, Margaretha Josephina	11, Jan. 1875	27, Nov.	20	15	Dilk	Madison, IN	
Sette, Dorothea Elisabeth	11, Mar. 1897	22, Feb.	82	159	Hensel	Lowell, WI	Warnick, Preußen
Sette, Louise Mathilde	22, Jan. 1891	3, Dec.	22	62	Jede	Rockham, SD	Sac City, Sac County, Wisconsin
Sette, Lydia	26, Nov. 1883	3, Nov.	16	383		Owatonna, MN	Owatonna, Minnesota

Christliche Apologete Death Notices --- 1839 - 1899

Name of Deceased	Notice Date	Death Date	Age	Page	Maiden Name	Place of Death	Place of Birth
Sette, Wilhelmina Augusta	22, Apr. 1897	31, Mar.	70	255	Franz	Owatonna, MN	Ziger, Brandenburg
Setzekorn, Anna Dorothea	20, Dec. 1869	29, Nov.	66	407	Weber	Mascoutah, IL	Oberdoral, Mühlhausen, Preußen
Setzekorn, Heinrich	24, Feb. 1879	29, Dec.	45- 5m- 2d	63		Pinckneyville, IL	Oberdoria, Mühlhausen, Preußen
Setzekorn, Louise	11, Mar.1872	33- 8m- 2d		87	Lümpkemeier	Mascoutah, IL	Holzhausen, Minden, Preußen
Setzkom, Martin	21, Feb. 1856	7, Jan.	19- 7m	32		Mascoutah, IL	
Setzkom, Wilhelm	27, Mar. 1890	6, Mar.	59- 7m- 5d	206		St. Louis, MO	Oberdalla, Mühlhausen, Preußen
Seuberlich, Carl Gottlieb	30, Oct. 1846	3, Sept	34	185		Ft. Wayne, IN	Oberlausitz, Sachsen
Seubert, Anna Barbara	27, Oct. 1887	14, Oct.	58	686	Haas	Galena, IL	Mühlhausen, Baiern
Seubert, Edward	15, Mar. 1888	14, Feb.	16	174		Galena, IL	
Seubert, Katharine Elisabeth	7, Jan. 1884	15, Dec.	25	7		Galena, IL	
Seufferle, Juliana	20, Jan. 1898	27, Dec.	68	47	Bauschilicher	Sandusky, OH	Auerbach, Durlach, Baden
Seuser, Johan Wilhelm	14, Jan. 1897	23, Nov.	74	31		Bison, KS	Herdesdorf, RheinPreußen
Sever, Maria	29, Dec. 1898	26, Nov.	84	828	Korfhage	St. Paul, MN	Holzhausen, Hannover
Severing, Christine	16, Mar. 1874	25, Feb.	71	87		Wheeling, WV	Lauenfelde, Hannover
Severing, Johan Heinrich	9, June 1879	13, May	77	183		Wheeling, WV	Lauenförde, Inofer, Hannover
Severinghaus, Johan Dietrich	9, July1883	24, June	80- 4m-22d	223		Batesville, IN	
Severinghaus, Philippine W.	11, June 1891	26, May	24	382	Schneider	Evansville, IN	Mt. Vernon, Indiana
Sewald, Maria	7, Apr. 1873	18, Mar.	79	111	Schulz	Wabasha, MN	Baumgarten, Oppel, Preußen
Sewing, Johan H.	24, Mar. 1884	8, Feb.	62	7		Council Bluffs, IA	
Sexauer, Georg Jakob	22, Dec. 1873	25, Nov.	49	407		Des Moines, IA	Ober-Schafhausen, Baden
Sexauer, Maria Magdalena	30, June 1884	14, June	56	7	Maier	Greenfield, OH	Eichstetten, Emmendingen, Baden
Sexauer, Tobias	21, Apr. 1898	27, Mar.	86	255		Cincinnati, OH	Bischoffingen, Baden
Seybold, Friedrich	24, Mar. 1848	Inquiry		51		Ann Arbor, MI	Beutelsbach, Württemberg
Seybold, Sibylla K.	9, Sept 1897	4, Aug.	82	575		Wheeling, WV	Unterlubach, Württemberg
Seyboldt, Katharine	26, Sept 1895	31, Aug.	55	622	Kroll	Defiance, OH	Reihingen, Ludwigsburg, Württemberg
Seyfarth, Charles H.	14, July 1898	1, May	27	447		Brooklyn, NY	Leominster, Massachuetts
Seyfarth, Johan Friedrich Karl	16, Mar. 1885	24, Feb.	64	7		Lawrence, MA	Preßwitz, Könitz, Schwarzburg-Rudolstadt
Seyfer, Johan Fr.	1, Jan. 1891	25, Nov.	76- 6m-12d	14		Decatur, IL	Kirchberg, Marbach, Württemberg
Seyfer, Johan Friedrich	12, Aug. 1878	18, July	85- 8m-15d	255		Oregon, MO	Kirchberg, Marbach, Württemberg
Seyfert, Catharina	23, Mar. 1893	5, Mar.	58	190	Kirchen	Pittsburg, PA	Friesenheim, Baden
Seyler, Philippine E.	29, July 1886	7, July	79	7		Oshkosh, WI	Osterbrücken, Kaiserslautern, Rheinkreis Baiern
Shäfer, Katharine Christine	21, Feb. 1889	28, Feb.	66-11m-20d	126	Maier	Allegheny City, PA	Frauenzimmern, Brackenheim, Württemberg
Shafer, William H.L.	11, Jan. 1894	11, Dec.	32	30		Fairmount, KS	
Sharpe, Dorothea K.	12, Jan. 1888	2, Nov.	43	30		Arlington, MN	Schernhof, Brandenburg
Sheriff, Elias	6, Oct. 1887	21, Sept	68	638		Chicago, IL	Dauphin County, Pennsylvania
Sherwood, Amelia Theresia	3, May 1888	12, Apr.	24	286	Keck	Harper, IA	Harper, Iowa
Shieber, Georg	4, June 1883	9, May	33- 3m-20d	183		Bucyrus, OH	Crawford County, Ohio
Shiro, Carl	10, Mar.1873	26, Jan.	53	79		Farmington, IA	Klein Laferde, Hannover
Shlyster, Peter	10, Mar. 1884	6, Feb.	50	7		Dalton, MO	Südfend, Holland
Shupp, Maria	19, Sept 1895	27, Aug.	48	606	Weik	Greenville, OH	Liverpool, Medina County, Ohio
Sibert, Johan	11, Feb. 1892	19, Jan.	75	95		Dallas City, IL	Weißenhasel, Rotenburg, Kurhessen
Sick, Herman Heinrich	27, Apr. 1899	22, Mar.	67	271		Batesville, IN	Hettinghausen, Osnabrück, Hannover
Sick, Michael	13, Aug. 1891	6, July	73	526		Vermillion, OH	Riedheim, Baiern
Sickbert, Elise	9, Apr. 1891	14, Mar.	57	238	Schmidt	Edwardsville, IL	Lienen, Westphalen
Sickmann, Heinrich	3, June 1878	5, May	64	175		Flint Creek, IA	Bielefeld, Minden, Preußen
Sickmann, Herman Adolph	17, Mar. 1892	10, Jan.	72	175		Beaufort, MO	Lürdiken, Lippe-Detmold

- 484 -

Christliche Apologete Death Notices --- 1839 - 1899

Name of Deceased	Notice Date	Death Date	Age	Page	Maiden Name	Place of Death	Place of Birth
Sidow, Herman C.F.	23, May 1889	25, Apr.	33-1m- 4d	334		Milwaukee, WI	Jacktion, Warlington County, Wisconsin
Siebeking, (Mrs)	16, June 1879	31, May	78	191		Schnectady, NY	Hille, Preußen
Siebels, John	29, Sept 1887	10, Sept	47	622		Pekin, IL	Esens, Dünom, Oldenburg
Sieben, Joseph	4, June 1877	3, May	20- 4m	183		Geneseo, IL	
Siebens, Johanna Carolina	16, Jan. 1896	17, Dec.	37	46	Vogt	Pekin, IL	Kenosha, Wisconsin
Sieber, Johan	1, May 1876	16, Apr.	63	143		Baltimore, MD	Kastel-Neustadt, Baiern
Sieber, Margaretha	1, Sept 1892	13, Aug.	70	558		Baltimore, MD	Losan, Oberfranken, Baiern
Siebering, August	25, Nov. 1852	29, Oct.	26	192		Wheeling, VA	
Siebert, Elisabeth	26, Mar. 1891	3, Mar.	88- 3m-14d	206		Ballwin, MO	
Siebert, Heinrich	16, Oct. 1846	16, Aug.	10m	177		Woodville, OH	
Siebert, Heinrich Gerhard	14, Dec. 1874	20, Nov.	71	399		Perrysburg, OH	Schledehausen, Osnabrück, Hannover
Siebert, John Volkman	13, May 1886	20, Apr.	86	7		Clarington, OH	Immenrode, Schwarzburg-Rudolstadt
Siebert, Maria	8, Sept 1862	14, Aug.	63- 4m- 9d	144		Captina, OH	Großenfahren, Schwarzburg-Sondershausen
Siebert, Sophie	6, Nov. 1871	21, Sept	29- - 5d	359	Albers	Clarington, OH	Lübenhausen, Hessen-Darmstadt
Siebirt, Hanna Wilina	12, Dec. 1864	22, Nov.	53	200		Alton, IL	Wittlage, Amt Osnabrück, Hannover
Siebrasse, A. Margaret Elisabeth	1, Apr. 1872	3, Mar.	72- 5m- 5d	111		Red Wing, MN	Schildesche, Bielefeld, Westphalen, Preußen
Siebrasse, Gottlieb	19, June 1876	3, June	43	199		Red Wing, MN	Schildesche, Preußen
Siebrasse, Hanna	30, July 1857	8, July		124	Borkermann	Red Wing, MN	Schildesche, Münden, Preußen
Siebrasse, Katharina Wilhelmine	11, May 1868	20, Apr.	30- 1m- 7d	151	Külter	Red Wing, MN	Burgholzhausen, Minden, Preußen
Siebrecht, Emilie	30, Dec. 1878	3, Dec.	18	415	Prestin	Roberts, IL	Champaign , Illinois
Siebrecht, Friederike	30, June 1892	8, June	71	414	Haack	Redfield, SD	Zaas, Trenate, Insel Rügen, Pommern
Siebrecht, H.W.	12, Mar. 1857	24, Feb.	51	44		Wheeling, VA	Eschenhausen, Amt Uslar, Hannover
Siebrecht, Johan Christian	25, Oct. 1875	7, Oct.	68	343		Allegan, MI	Hohenstädt, Hannover
Siebrecht, Maria Christina	17, Apr. 1890	26, Mar.	79	254	Sohnreich	Allegan, MI	Eboldhausen, Hannover
Sieckert, Emma Emilie	31, Oct. 1895	9, Oct.	32	702	Redmann	Springfield, MN	Sibley County, Minnesota
Siedecker, J.	19, Dec. 1870	29, Aug.		407		Ironton, OH	Barndolf, Waldeck
Siedentop, Catharina	30, Dec. 1878	5, Dec.	49-11m-29d	415	Köhler	Angelica, NY	Rolfsbüttel, Hannover
Siederling, Johan Friedrich	29, Dec. 1862	16, Oct.	27- 7m- 3d	208		Kendallville, IN	
Siefers, Heinrich	13, Mar. 1890	30, Jan.	70	174		Beaufort, MO	Amelpatzen, Hannover
Siefert, August	29, Nov. 1880	3, Nov.	23- 7m	383		Montague, MI	
Siefert, Ferdinand	16, Sept 1897	14, Aug.	73	591		Montague, MI	Blumenthal, Frankfurt a. Oder, Preußen
Siefert, Sophia	18, Nov. 1878	24, Oct.	48	367		Toledo, OH	Mecklenburg-Schwerin
Sieg, Georg	11, Mar. 1886	15, Feb.	23- 2m-17d	7	Schmidt	Peace Creek, KS	Missouri
Sieg, Johan	15, Sept 1884	8, Aug.	32	7		Bedford, IN	Biedingen, Baiern
Siegel, (Mrs)	22, Apr. 1897	20, Mar.	72	94	Kern	Laporte, IN	
Siegel, Dorothea	4, Oct. 1875	13, Sept	36- 7m-12d	7	Gemlich	Boonville, IN	Kircheim an der Eck, Rheinpfalz Baiern
Siegel, Ernestine	22, June 1893	6, May	35	255	Tauber	Bertha, MN	Schönhain, Germany
Siegel, Friedrich	22, Sept 1848	29, Aug.	48- 5m-21d	319		Boonville, IN	Meckenbach, Homburg, Hessen
Siegel, Friedrich	27, Dec. 1888	24, Nov.	54	398		Boonville, IN	Birkenfeld, Oldenburg
Siegel, Georg	5, Oct. 1885	16, Sept	62	156		Farmington, WI	Trebula, Altenburg, Sachsen
Siegel, Karl Friedrich	14, Dec. 1885	29, Nov.	18- 2m-20d	830		Louisville, KY	
Siegel, Karoline	7, Feb. 1895	9, Jan.	58	7		Louisville, KY	Kaiserswalde, Posen
Siegel, Margaretha	8, Jan. 1872	23, Dec.	73	15	Diedrich	Boonville, MO	Birkenfeld, Oldenburg
Siegel, Margarethe	13, May 1867	14, Apr.	37- 8m-14d	150	Lercher	Booneville, IN	Kön, Württemberg
Siegel, Martin	23, Jan. 1890	9, Jan.	64	62		Laporte, IN	Oberdorf, Baiern
Siegel, Peter	11, Feb. 1878	27, Jan.	51- 9m-13d	47		Boonville, IN	Meckenbach, Homburg, Hessen

Christliche Apologete Death Notices --- 1839 - 1899

Name of Deceased	Notice Date	Death Date	Age	Maiden Name	Place of Death	Page	Place of Birth
Siegel, Philipp	18, Aug. 1884	6, Aug.	66- 5m-12d		Warrenton, MO	7	Kerzenheim, Rheinkreis Baiern
Siegel, Philipp	14, Mar. 1895	18, Feb.	73		Evansville, IN	174	Meckenbach, Germany
Siegel, Sophia	26, Sept 1895	3, Sept	78	Sachsenräder	West Bend, WI	622	Großtauschwitz, Sachsen-Altenburg
Siegel, Wilhelmina	8, Dec. 1898	19, Nov.	64	Seefeld	Kewaskum, WI	783	Plantiko, Naugard, Pommern
Siegenthaler, Alfred Friedrich	10, Mar. 1898	3, Feb.	59		Logan, OR	159	Siegnau, Bern, Schweiz
Siegenthaler, Katharine	15, Nov. 1894	22, Oct.	70	Wolf	Nashville, TN	742	Niederhausbergen, Elsaß
Siegenthaler, Lorenz	9, Aug. 1888	15, July	61- 5m-18d		Nashville, TN	510	Straßburg, Elsaß
Siegenthaler, Louis Ph.	18, Jan. 1894	25, Dec.	29		Nashville, TN	46	Augusta, Kentucky
Siegesmund, Johan Gottlieb	19, Feb. 1877	28, Jan.	87- -20d		Chillicothe, OH	63	Schlefien, Preußen
Siegfried, Sophia	24, Mar. 1887	1, Mar.	61	Tidel	Cannelton, IN	190	Triebes, Reuß-Schleiz, Sachsen
Siegler, Elisabeth	19, Jan. 1874	4, Jan.	60		Newark, NJ	23	Spielberg, Württemberg
Siegmund, Martin	5, Oct. 1899	5, Aug.	76		New York City, NY	639	Lohrbach, Baden
Siegner, Conrad	7, Nov. 1895	18, Oct.	59- 5m- 5d		East Liberty, PA	718	Rensfeld, Hessen
Siegrist, Barbara	27, July 1868	3, July	73		Toledo, OH	239	Britnau, Aargau, Schweiz
Siegrist, Eva Maria	25, May 1893	5, May	34	Schönhardt	Mt. Vernon, MO	334	Fünfbrunnen, Nagold, Württemberg
Siekbert, Wilhelm	4, Dec. 1876	26, Oct.			Edwardsville, IL	391	Linn, Tecklenburg, Preußen
Siemann, Maria	3, Sept 1877	17, Aug.	57- 3m-16d	Kammann	Menomonie, MI	287	Oppershausen, Celle, Hannover
Siemäntel, Margarethe	15, May 1871	21, Apr.	49		Lawrenceburg, IN	159	Oberdachsten, Baiern
Siemer, August	17, Aug. 1893	29, July	67		Mt. Healthy, OH	526	Wagenfeld, Hannover
Siemer, Heinrich	12, July 1849		Inquiry		Cincinnati, OH	111	
Siemon, Catharine	22, Aug. 1861	10, Aug.	41		Wheeling, VA	136	Kirchhasbach, Bischhausen, Kurhessen
Siemon, Dorothea E.	30, Jan. 1871	6, Dec.	45		Wheeling, WV	39	Cincinnati, Hamilton County, Ohio
Siemon, Georg	11, May 1874	15, Mar.	21		Decatur, IL	151	Sterbfritz, Kurhessen
Siemon, John N.	20, Jan. 1873	6, Jan.	36		Allegheny City, PA	23	Weisenhasel, Rodenburg, Kurhessen
Siering, Anna Martha	18, Jan. 1894		46	Sandrock	Altamont, IL	46	Zuthämmern, Minden, Preußen
Sieveking, Christina	28, Oct. 1872	16, Oct.	50		New Albany, IN	351	Tengern, Lübbecke, Minden, Preußen
Sieveking, Fr. W.	14, Dec. 1885	23, Nov.	76		New Albany, IN	7	Abecke, Hannover
Sievers, Anna	5, Jan. 1899	25, Nov.	80	Wiedekind	Quincy, IL	15	Oldenburg, Holstein
Sievers, Catharina Christina H.	26, Jan. 1880	6, Jan.	33- -16d	Stark	Winona, MN	31	
Sievers, Detleff	28, Sept 1899	28, Aug.	62		Pittsburg, KS	623	Hajen, Gronde, Hannover
Sievers, Friederike	10, Sept 1896	18, Aug.	67		Beaufort, MO	591	
Sievert, Hugo	20, June 1889	9, May	15- 1m- 9d		Rochester, MN	398	Tenngern, Schnahorst, Preußen
Sieweking, Chr. Ludwig	21, Jan. 1858	23, Dec.	80		New Albany, IN	12	Hemmersdorf bei Görlitz, Schlesien
Sigismund, Johan Karl Gottlieb F.	4, Jan. 1894	3, Dec.	76		Chillicothe, OH	14	Botenheim, Brackenheim, Württemberg
Sigloch, Elisabeth Katharina	4, Oct. 1894	1, Sept	71	Keppler	Cincinnati, OH	646	New York
Sigmund, Heinrich Wilhelm	4, Feb. 1878	18, Jan.	22- 7m		Melrose, NY	39	Veltheim, Zürich, Schweiz
Sigrist, (Mrs)	10, Apr. 1890	24, Mar.	93- 3m	Freyhofer	Redington, IN	238	Veltheim, Katon Zürich, Schweiz
Sigrist, Susanna	20, Apr. 1854	31, Mar.	49- 4m-19d		Arlington Heights, IL	64	NiederRatzenhausen, Elsaß
Sigwalt, Barbara	8, Sept 1892	16, Aug.	57		Chillicothe, OH	574	Denckendorf, Eßlingen, Württemberg
Silber, Christina	13, June 1850	1, May	41		New Orleans, LA	96	Württemberg
Silber, Friedrich	12, June 1851	23, May	26		Cannelton, IN	96	Cannelton, Indiana
Silbereiser, Lydia	24, Nov. 1887	25, Oct.	16		Mankato, MN	750	Erbachhof, Waiblingen, Württemberg
Silcher, Ernst August	12, Dec. 1895	17, Nov.	30		Toledo, OH	798	Oskofen, Pommern
Sill, Augusta	15, Nov. 1894	15, Oct.	64		Nauvoo, IL	742	Lichtel, Mergentheim, Württemberg
Siller, Sophia	1, June 1854	12, May		Hochhalter	De Soto, MO	88	Canton Aargau, Schweiz
Simen, Anna	28, Oct. 1886	9, Oct.	66	Frei		7	

Christliche Apologete Death Notices --- 1839 - 1899

Name of Deceased	Notice Date	Death Date	Age	Page	Maiden Name	Place of Death	Place of Birth
Simen, Elisabeth	27, Jan. 1879	2, Jan.	64	31	Amsler	De Soto, MN	Schinznach, Aargau, Schweiz
Simmermacher, Maria Magdalena	11, Mar. 1897	18, Feb.	73	159	Birti	Peoria, IL	Weilbach, Baiern
Simmersbach, Karl	6, Apr. 1863	9, Jan.	25	56		Louisville, KY	Treysa, Kurhessen
Simon , Mamie B.	19, Jan. 1899	30, Oct.	27	47		Decatur, IL	
Simon, Anna	7, Nov. 1889	4, Oct.	64- 2m- 8d	718	Budensky	Burlington, IA	Reichenberg, Böhmen
Simon, August	25, Apr. 1881	11, Apr.	21- 2m-23d	135		St. Louis, MO	
Simon, Dorothea	14, Oct. 1872	10, Sept	48	335	Geschow	Milwaukee, WI	Woltenzin, Mecklenburg-Strelitz
Simon, Emma	21, June 1875	8, June	17- 2m-17d	199		Cincinnati, OH	Ihringshausen, Kreis Wezlar, Preußen
Simon, Henriette	8, Nov. 1869	22, Oct.	58	359	Diel	Baraboo, WI	Merzweiler, Unter-Elsaß, Frankreich
Simon, Katharina	25, Apr. 1870	13, Jan.	52	135	Groß	Decatur, IL	
Simon, Katharina	16, June 1859	13, May	74	96		Spring Lake, OH	
Simon, Katie	31, Aug. 1899		30	559		Ironton, OH	Wheelersburg, Ohio
Simon, Margaretha Elisabeth	21, Nov. 1861	15, Sept	16	188		Lansing, MI	New York
Simon, Maria	26, Feb. 1877	9, Feb.	27- 6m	71	Fiedler	Meredosia, IL	Reuters, Hessen-Darmstadt
Simon, Sophie	3, Mar. 1898	8, Feb.	75-10m-23d	143	Neuser	Cleveland, OH	Wimpfen, Württemberg
Simon, Susanna	15, Apr. 1886	26, Mar.	67	7		Llano, TX	Nassau
Simons, Georg H. (Rev)	9, Feb. 1899	31, Jan.	59	89			Nordfriesland
Simons, Georg Heinrich	27, Apr. 1899	1, Feb.	58- 6m-25d	270		Newark, NJ	Nebel auf Amrum, Nordfriesland
Simons, John Franklin	28, Sept 1899	31, Aug.	26- 6m-23d	623		Brooklyn, NY	LaPorte, Indiana
Simons, Martha	12, May 1887	23, Apr.	24	302	Muhlitner	Adair, MI	St. Clair County, Michigan
Sindel, Friederike	27, Jan. 1887	9, Jan.	29	62	Schiefer	Columbus, OH	Feuerbach bei Stuttgart, Württemberg
Sindorf, Jacob	18, Sept 1876	2, Sept	16	303		Milwaukee, WI	
Sindorf, Maria Katharina	12, Jan. 1893	20, Dec.	66	30	Klumb	Milwaukee, WI	Buttenbach, RheinPreußen
Sinell, Emma	10, Oct. 1889	14, Sept	16- 2m-14d	654		Le Sueur, MN	
Singer, E.	10, Dec. 1883	30, Oct.	83	7		Pittsburg, PA	Franken, Germany
Single, Christine	6, July 1893	11, June	80	430	Bleicher	Baltimore, MD	Rosenfeld, Württemberg
Singley, Friedrich	21, Nov. 1864	22, Aug.	26	188		Baltimore, MD	
Sinn, Anna Maria	25, May 1885	5, May	78	7	Weinheimer	Canton, MO	Landau, RheinPfalz Baiern
Sinn, Anna Maria	14, May 1883	17, Apr.	43- 6m- 8d	159	Volmer	Quincy, IL	Landau, Rheinkreis Baiern
Sinn, Margaretha	21, May 1883	17, Mar.	44	167	Volmer	Quincy, IL	Zeiskam bei Landau, Rheinkreis Baiern
Sinn, Theobald	29, May 1856	26, Apr.	65	88		Newark, NJ	
Sinn, Theobald	30, May 1864	9, Dec.		88			
Sinndorf, Georg	25, Apr. 1889	1, Apr.	26	270		Milwaukee, WI	Milwaukee, Wisconsin
Sinnert, Wilhelm	11, Aug. 1862		23	128		Havana, IL	Schlürbach, Dieburg, Hessen-Darmstadt
Sinning, Margaretha	12, Nov. 1896	20, Oct.	27	734		Toledo, OH	Ersrode, Hessen-Kassel
Sinram, Anna Maria	14,May 1883	17, Mar.	43- 6m- 8d	159	Volmer	Brooklyn, NY	Baden
Sinram, Anna Maria	21,May 1883	17, Mar.	44	167	Volmer	Brooklyn, NY	Baden
Sinram, Maria Elisabeth	9, May 1895	12, Mar.	56	302		Newark, NJ	Hille, Minden, Preußen
Sinskey, F.W.	1, Aug. 1889	26, June	21	494		Des Moines, IA	
Sinsky, Emma	7, Mar. 1895	28, Nov.	14	159		Des Moines, IA	
Sipf, Anna Margaretha	9, May 1881	25, Apr.	38- 7m-23d	151	Modenbach	Indianapolis, IN	Preußen
Sipf, Francis	30, June 1859	6, June	45-11m- 9d	104		Louisville, KY	Kleinheubach, Aschaffenburg, Baiern
Sipfle, Anna Elisabeth	8, Apr. 1886	24, Mar.	51	7	Döring	Pekin, IL	Nieder-Vorschütz, Hessen-Kassel
Sippel, Adam	12, July 1894	23, June	77	454		Tinley Park, IL	Königswald, Rotenburg, Kurhessen
Sippel, Anna Christina	29, Oct. 1877	7, Oct.	60	351	Bettenhausen	Bremen, IL	Königswalde, Rothenburg, Kurhessen
Sippel, Anna Elisabeth	21, Feb. 1889	21, Jan.	78-11m-11d	126	Hartung	New Bremen, IL	Jermerode, Kurhessen
Sippel, Barbara	31, Aug. 1899	10, Aug.	55	559	Sangmeister	Charles City, IA	Königswald, Rodenburg, Kurhessen

Name of Deceased	Notice Date	Death Date	Age	Page	Maiden Name	Place of Death	Place of Birth
Sippel, Catharina	19, Jan. 1880	9, Dec.	83- 2m- 2d	23		Baltimore, MD	
Sippel, Christian	19, Dec. 1881	21, Nov.	72- 3m-17d	407		New Bremen, IL	Schemmer, Eschwe, Kurhessen
Sippel, Christian	26, Aug. 1867	7, Aug.	74	270		New Bremen, IL	Königswald, Kurhessen
Sippel, David	19, Dec. 1881	8, Dec.	64	407		Warrenton, MO	
Sippel, Heinrich	28, Apr. 1873		36	135		New Bremen, IL	Königswald, Kurhessen
Sippel, Heinrich	14, Jan. 1886		12- 8m- 5d	7		Charles City, IA	
Sippel, John	5, Sept 1861	20, Aug.	12- 7m-29d	144		Blue Island, IL	
Sippel, Magdalena	25, Oct. 1894	15, Sept	72	694	Bischoff	Jeffersonville, NY	Dießen, Iburg, Hannover
Sippel, Margaretha	18, Apr. 1895	27, Mar.	66	254	Moßmeyer	Belleville, IL	Oberdachstetten, Mittelfranken, Baiern
Sippel, Wilhelm	31, Oct. 1889	13, Oct.	44- 7m-13d	702		Charles City, IA	Königswald, Germany
Sipple, Margaretha	16, Mar. 1885	13, Feb.	35	7	Mall	Jeffersonville, IN	Callicoon,
Sitler, Victoria	18, Jan. 1894	19, Dec.	86	46	Schuh	Nebraska City, NE	Biel bei Offenburg, Baden
Sitterly, Sophia Catharina	3, Feb. 1868	10, Jan.	14	39		Milwaukee, WI	
Sittermann, Anna Katharina	16, Nov. 1893	22, Oct.	83	734		Beaufort, MO	Dießen, Iburg, Hannover
Sittermann, Caspar	1, Aug. 1895	9, July	94- 5m- 7d	494		Beaufort, MO	Dissen, Iburg, Hannover
Sittermann, Heinrich J.	21, Oct. 1886	25, Sept	36	7		Wyandotte, KS	Franklin County, Missouri
Sittler, Anna Elisabeth	16, June 1892	28, Apr.	76	382	Glöser	Columbus, IL	Dodenau, Battenberg, Hessen-Darmstadt
Sittler, Charlotte Wilhelmine	20, Aug. 1896	28, July	43	543	Bicker	Moberly, MO	Ehrsen, Schötmar, Lippe-Detmold
Sittler, Chr.	7, July 1873	4, June	74	215	Zacharias	Columbus, IL	Hüttenthal, Preußen
Sittler, Johan	29, Jan. 1866	23, Dec.	75	38		Perry, IL	Schwarzenau, Amt Perleberg, Preußen
Sittler, Johan Jost	23, Oct. 1871	2, Oct.	69	343		Quincy, IL	Dodenau, Battenberg, Hessen-Darmstadt
Sittler, Johan Julius (Rev)	7, July 1898	12, June	50	431		Moberly, MO	Mill Creek near Quincy, Illinois
Sittler, John Eduard	9, Dec. 1897	19, Nov.	44	783		Moberly, MO	Millrose, Adams County, Illinois
Sitz, John Wilhelm	20, Mar. 1865	27, Jan.	38	48		Davenport, IA	Rattey, Preußen
Sitzler, Elisabeth	18, Aug. 1892	20, July	85	527	Bühler	Fallport, MI	Nußloch, Baden
Sitzler, Walburga	18, May 1863	7, Apr.	46- 3m	80	Haselwander	Rochester, NY	Wehr, Seckingen, Baden
Siwer, Georg	27, Apr. 1868	28, Jan.	54	135		Angelica, NY	Celle, Hannover
Skaer, Jakob W.	25, Dec. 1882	27, Nov.	57	415		Chicago, IL	Merksheim, Homburg, Hessen
Skär, Luise Barbara	5, Jan. 1899	18, Nov.	38	15		Chicago, IL	Chicago, Cook County, Illinois
Skär, Philipp	22, Feb. 1894	3, Feb.	43	126		Nokomis, Il	Merxheim, Miessenheim, RheinPreußen
Skär, Rosa	9, Dec. 1897	19, Nov.	42	783	Schulze	Nokomis, Il	Nashville, Illinois
Sleeter, Clara	4, May 1893	31, Mar.	18	286		Boody, IL	Boody, Macon County, Illinois
Sleeter, John H.	13, Jan. 1898	19, Dec.	48	31		Council Bluffs, IA	Decatur, Macon County, Illinois
Sleeter, Marie Louise	20, Aug. 1896	21, July	23	543		Schnectady, NY	Schnectady, New York
Sleyster, (Mrs)	22, Sept 1898	4, Sept	52	607	Wegner	Dalton, MO	Werblitz, Soldin, Preußen
Sleyster, Gerret	18, Nov. 1886	4, Nov.	51	7		Dalton, MO	Zutphen, Gelderland, Holland
Slobohm, Hannah	1, Dec. 1887	28, Oct.	19	766		Caywood, OH	
Slobohm, Johan Peter	15, Sept 1879	16, Dec.	30- 4m-19d	295		Marietta, OH	Bremen, Germany
Slobohm, John	20, Dec. 1888	28, July	81	814		Caywood, OH	Emsdorf, Hannover
Slobohm, Martha	6, July 1893	30, Apr.	83	430	Bolin	Marietta, OH	
Slobohm, Rosa	2, Apr. 1883	2, Nov.		111		Marietta, OH	
Slyter, Loyd	23, Aug. 1880	4, Aug.	13- 6m	271		Hebron, IA	
Smidt, Engelke Jansen	18, Jan. 1894	7, Dec.	76	46		Kramer, NE	Grimesum, Ostfriesland
Smith, Anna Katharina	11, Nov. 1872	24, Sept	88	367	Ruprecht	San Jose, IL	Grafenberg, Oberfranken, Baiern
Smith, Barbara	10, Dec. 1896		73	798	Weimer	Canton, OH	Württemberg
Smith, Catharine	23, Nov. 1863	2, Nov.	33	188	Hübschmann	Pekin, IL	Strahlenfels, Grävenberg, Baiern

Christliche Apologete Death Notices --- 1839 - 1899

Name of Deceased	Notice Date	Death Date	Age	Maiden Name	Page	Place of Death	Place of Birth
Smith, Elisabeth	30, June 1862	9, June	36		104	Pekin, IL	Loquard, Ost-Friesland, Hannover
Smith, Friedrich C.	25, Dec. 1890	4, Dec.	61		830	Pekin, IL	Hansverum, Ostfriesland
Smith, Georg	7, May 1883	23, Mar.	28- 3m- 4d		151	Kearney, MO	Morgan County, Missouri
Smith, Hannah Louise	3, Sept 1883	25, July	77- 9m-26d	Ratz	287	Milwaukee, WI	Vischow, Preußen
Smith, Heinrich	2, June 1859	5, May	37- 2m		88	Pekin, IL	Hamswerum, Amt Gretzziel, Hannover
Smith, Heinrich Friedrich	2, June 1898	21, Apr.	32		351	Pekin, IL	Pekin, Illinois
Smith, Katharina	25, Nov. 1897	4, Nov.	65- 9m- 2d	Rochholz	751	San Jose, IL	Beckgraben, Kuhmbach, Baiern
Smith, Margaretha	2, May 1861	14, Apr.	65		72	Pekin, IL	Wirdum, Ostfriesland, Hannover
Smith, Maria	24, Aug. 1885	7, Aug.	61		7	De Soto, MN	Sachsen-Altenburg
Smith, Michael	7, Sept 1893	7, Aug.	69		574	Greenfield, PA	Württemberg
Smith, Rosa	8, Nov. 1888	16, Sept	18- -12d		718	San Jose, IL	Jonesville, New Jersey
Smith, Sophie	12, Oct. 1868	1, Sept	68		327	Wheeling, ---	
Smith, Theis	26, Sept 1870	12, Sept	43		311	Pekin, IL	Hamswehrum, Ostfriesland, Preußen
Sniram, Maria Elisabeth	4, Apr. 1895	12, Mar.	56		222	Newark, NJ	Hille, Minden, Preußen
Snure, Catharina M.	22, Apr. 1867	18, Mar.	16-11m-24d	Schott	126	Hokah, MN	Cruspis, Kreis Hersfeld, Kurhessen
Soehler, August	29, May 1882	16, May	64- 4m-27d		175	Owatonna, MN	Löwenstadt, Amt Salder, Braunschweig
Soerhof, Sophia	12, Apr. 1869	27, Mar.	21- 9m-13d	Weibusch	119	Piqua, OH	Helmstedt, Hannover
Söhle, Carolina	12, Sept 1889	10, Aug.	71- -22d	Wöltje	590	Appleton,	Witzlar, Rehburg, Hannover
Söhler, Emilie	7, Apr. 1892	12, Mar.	34	Mathwig	222	Owatonna, MN	Watertown, Wisconsin
Söhler, Pauline	13, Sept 1869	9, Aug.	18- -21d		295	Blooming Grove, MN	Böckingen, Heilbronn, Württemberg
Sohm, (Mr)	19, July 1875	30, June	70- 1m-25d		231		Rütscheln, Lozwil, Bern, Schweiz
Sohm, Henriette Friederike	28, Feb. 1895	26, Jan.	64	Kapiski	142	Le Sueur, MN	Jakobshausen, Schwersien, Pommern
Sohm, Katharina	15, Nov. 1869	29, Oct.	72	Reme	367	Le Sueur, MN	Matiswill, Aarwangen, Bern, Schweiz
Sohm, Katharina	14, Dec. 1863	6, Nov.			200	Le Sueur, MN	
Sohm, Ulrich	12, Dec. 1864	5, Oct.	26- 1m-23d		200	Le Sueur, MN	Rischelen, Bern, Schweiz
Sohn, Sophie	2, Jan. 1882	12, Dec.	50- 3m- 7d	Zahn	7	Michigan City, IN	Panschen, Hagen, Mecklenburg-Schwerin
Soland, Jakob	11, Feb. 1897	29, Dec.	87		94	Farmington, IA	Schweiz
Soland, Maria Louise	7, July 1898	6, June	34	Bohlander	431	Boody, IL	New Memphis, Illinois
Soland, Susanne	15, May 1871	18, Apr.	50	Bertsch	159	Nauvoo, IL	Dürrenaesch, Culm, Aargau, Schweiz
Soland, Verone	11, Jan. 1864	29, Nov.	36	Frey	8	Warsaw, IL	Biberstein, Aargau, Schweiz
Söllhamer, Sophia	30, Oct. 1856	21, Sept	74		176	Dayton, OH	Lancaster County, Pennsylvania
Solms, Elisabeth	4, Dec. 1882	15, Nov.	70	Kattmann	391	New York City, NY	Ladbergen, Tecklenburg, Preußen
Solms, Heinrich W.	24, Mar. 1892	9, Mar.	78		191	New York City, NY	Ladbergen, Westphalen
Sölter, Louise	23, Dec. 1872	29, Nov.		Hugen	415	St. Louis, MO	
Soltwedel, J. Friedrich Christian	2, Feb. 1888	1, Jan.	82-10m-26d		78	Altamont, IL	Kloster Dobbertien, Mecklenburg-Schwerin
Soltwedel, Louisa Karoline	18, Sept 1882	75- 6m- 8d		Bruen	303	Altamont, IL	Debin, Dobertin, Mecklenburg-Schwerin
Sommer, Amalie Auguste	7, Dec. 1893	25, Sept	40		782	Waseca, MN	Princton, Wisconsin
Sommer, Anna M.	13, June 1861	12, May	67		96	Zanesville, OH	
Sommer, Friedrich	7, Dec. 1885	11, Nov.	64		7	Cannon River, MN	Steinhausen, Mecklenburg-Schwerin
Sommer, Friedrich	7, June 1875	19, May	24		183	Prairie Creek, MN	
Sommer, Rosina	18, Oct. 1875		46	Schulz	335	Faribault, MN	Steinhusen, Mecklenburg-Schwerin
Sommer, Susanna	12, May 1892	20, Apr.	49		302	Berea, OH	Rohrbach, Sinsheim, Baden
Sommerfeld, Gottfried	11, Feb. 1884	26, Jan.	73- 6m-18d		7	Sleepy Eye, MN	Klorin, Pyritz, Stettin, Hinterpommern
Sommerhalder, Rudolph	12, Jan. 1885	17, Dec.	72- 3m- 1d		7	Nauvoo, IL	Guntenschwyl, Aargau, Schweiz
Sommerhalter, Johan Jacob	8, July 1878	9, June	78- 4m-14d		215		Langenthal, Bern, Schweiz
Sommermeier, Charlotte	3, Oct. 1870	16, July	57		319	Industry, TX	Riga, Rußland

Christliche Apologete Death Notices --- 1839 - 1899

Name of Deceased	Notice Date	Death Date	Age	Page	Maiden Name	Place of Death	Place of Birth
Sommermeyer, Christian	12, Feb. 1883	21, Jan.	70	55		Industry, TX	Weferlingen, Preußen
Sommermeyer, Maria	27, Jan. 1859	9, Jan.	20- 6m- 2d	16		Ripley, OH	Western-Cappeln, Preußen
Sommers, Maria Barbara	13, Aug. 1883	4, July	73	263		Cleveland, OH	Seibottenberg, Württemberg
Sondermann, Ferdinand	8, July 1897	19, June	84	431		St. Joseph, MO	Stendal, Altmark, Magdeburg, Preußen
Sondermann, Sophia Charlotte	21, Feb. 1889	3, Feb.	76	126	Herwig	Kansas City, MO	Iserheide, Windheim, Minden, Preußen
Sondermann, Wilhelm	12, July 1888	21, June	56	446		Quincy, IL	Schöttmer, Lippe-Detmold
Song, Johan Karl	15, Jan. 1877	25, Dec.	76- 8m-18d	23		Pinckneyville, IL	Allenbach, Rheinpreußen
Sonn, Christoph Friedrich	18, May 1863	19, Apr.	65- 7m- 7d	80		Newark, NJ	Köngen, Württemberg
Sonn, Johan C.	2, Aug. 1888	12, July	58	494		Newark, NJ	Köngen, Eßlingen, Württemberg
Sonnefeld, Catharina Margaretha	1, Apr. 1878	27, Feb.	69- 4m-15d	103	Aman	Terre Haute, IN	Großsachsenheim, Vaihingen, Württemberg
Sonnefeld, Franz Heinrich	27, Jan. 1868	10, Jan.	63	31		Terre Haute, IN	Wester-Kappeln, Tecklenburg, Preußen
Sonnefeld, Heinrich	19, Feb. 1877	31, Jan.	34- 3m- 2d	63		Terre Haute, IN	WesterCappeln, Kreis Münster, Preußen
Sonnefeld, Katharina	13, Nov. 1851	12, Sept	59- 5m- 8d	184			Westerkappeln, Tecklenburg, Preußen
Sonnefeld, Maria Elisabeth	12, May 1879	20, Apr.	81- 3m-18d	151	Ahlemeiers	Terre Haute, IN	Wester-Cappeln, Tecklenburg, Preußen
Sonnefeld, Wilhelm	6, Dec. 1869	5, Oct.	77- 9m-25d	391		Terre Haute, IN	Tramp, Kreis Prenzlau, Preußen
Sonnemann, Christoph	22, Oct. 1866	29, Sept	64	342		Sheboygan, WI	
Sonntag, Anna	10, Nov. 1879		40- 1m	359	Schultz	Scranton, PA	Beddenhausen, Sachsen-Meiningen
Sorg, John	22, May 1865	7, May	43	84		Poughkeepsie, NY	Leitenburg, Schwarzburg-Rudolstadt
Sorgel, Richard	28, Apr. 1898	31, Mar.	46	271		Faribault, MN	
Sorgenfrei, Henrietta	25, Mar. 1886	5, Mar.	24	7		Kendallville, IN	
Sörhof, Margaretha	21, Oct. 1872	12, Sept		343		Piqua, OH	Homste, Amt Hasefeld, Hannover
Sotorius, Johanne	16, Apr. 1891	24, Feb.	40- 6m-11d	254	Haverkamp	Oakford, IL	Oldenburg
Sowasch, Nikolaus	24, Aug. 1885	12, Aug.	86	7		Spraytown, IN	Oppau, Frankenthal, Rheinkreis Baiern
Sowasch, Sophia	13, Feb. 1862	28, Jan.	55	28	Heinz	Furnace, OH	Opau, Frankenthal, Rheinkreis Baiern
Spach, Gertrude	25, Feb. 1886		68	7	Gosmann	Poughkeepsie, NY	Hessen-Kassel
Spade, Anna Maria	23, Mar. 1893	7, Mar.	78	190	Fry	Goshen, IN	York county, Pennsylvania
Spaits, Maria	31, May 1888	4, May	82	350	Krebs	Manito, IL	Baiern
Spaits, Susanna	13, Dec. 1869	18, Oct.	35	399		Mantro, IL	
Spalinger, Andreas	28, July 1887	2, July	70	478		Sheboygan, WI	Marthalen, Zürich, Schweiz
Spalinger, Pauline	12, July 1888	26, June	30	446	Kuhfuß	Sheboygan, WI	Sheboygan Falls, Wisconsin
Spanagel, Maria Catharina	5, Mar. 1857	14, Feb.	34	40	Weikel	Pomeroy, OH	Sandhofen, Baden
Spang, Friedrich	23, Jan. 1882	4, Jan.	41- 3m-11d	31		Woodbury, MN	Ober-Fischbach, Gaildorf, Württemberg
Spangenberg, Louise	13, Aug. 1883	28, July	23- 3m-10d	263		Colesburg, IA	Chicago, Cook County, Illinois
Spangenberg, Maria	26, Dec. 1881	9, Dec.	76	415	Brandenburger	Colesburg, IA	Kröpelin, Mecklenburg-Schwerin
Spangenberg, Sophia	19, Mar. 1883	3, Mar.	51	95		Colesburg, IA	Bankow, Mecklenburg-Schwerin
Späth, Elisabeth	24, Dec. 1883	1, Dec.	72	7	Schwalm	Lawrence, KS	Hessen-Kassel
Spatholdt, Maria	21, Dec. 1893	30, Nov.	66	814	Nehls	Chicago, IL	Grimmen, Germany
Spatholt, Heinrich	31, Jan. 1895	4, Nov.	64	78		Chicago, IL	Sahl, Stralsund
Späyd, Henriette	28, June 1894	8, June	55	422	Riebel	Toledo, OH	Juniata County, Pennsylvania
Specht, Anna Maria	31, May 1888	14, May	30-10m	350		San Jose, IL	Hille, Minden, Preußen
Specht, Elisabeth	21, Mar. 1889	26, Feb.	65	190	Niermeier	Altamont, IL	Herborn, Nassau
Specht, Elisabeth C.	9, June 1887	8, May	30	366		Quincy, IL	Maniteau, Mason County, Illinois
Specht, Elisabeth Rebekka	1, Dec. 1884	10, Nov.	23	7		Sedalia, MO	Dodenau, Battenberg, Hessen-Darmstadt
Specht, Friedrich August	26, June 1890	5, June	56	414		Quincy, IL	
Specht, Johan	18, July 1870	7, May	21- 3m- 4d	231		San Jose, IL	
Specht, John H.	23, Apr. 1896	2, Apr.	76	270		Bible Grove, IL	Engter, Osnabrück, Hannover

Christliche Apologete Death Notices --- 1839 - 1899

Name of Deceased	Notice Date	Death Date	Age	Maiden Name	Page	Place of Death	Place of Birth
Specht, Katharina	21, Feb. 1870	21, Dec.	31- 9m- 7d	Nicklaus	63	San Jose, IL	New York City, New York
Specht, Magdalena	7, May 1891	27, Mar.	66- -18d	Wilking	302	San Jose, IL	Mehlbach, Rheinkreis Baiern
Speck, Margaretha Elisabeth	5, Apr. 1894		77	Melder	230	Galion, OH	Graben, Baden
Speck, Naoma	13, May 1878	24, Apr.	24- 6m-29d	Markle	151	LaCrosse, WI	
Speckhard, Leonhard	13, June 1889	31, May	68		382	Quincy, IL	Stetten, Brackenheim, Württemberg
Speckien, Ludwig Karl Otto	15, Mar. 1869	3, Feb.	34		87	Kendallville, IN	Klasewitz, Güstron, Mecklenburg-Schwerin
Speckin, Louise	16, Mar. 1874	26, Feb.	63		87	Goshen, IN	Glaßwitz, Güstrow, Mecklenburg-Schwerin
Speckman, Hanna Caroline L.	1, Aug. 1889	7, July	61	Sasse	494	Sleepy Eye, MN	Alten-Fließ bei Friedeberg, Brandenburg
Speckmann, Amalia	7, Mar. 1895	2, Feb.	57	Miller	158	Golconda, IL	Marion, Ohio
Speckmann, Anna Maria	28, May 1891	6, May	73	Sollmann	350	Denver, CO	Icker, Hannover
Speckmann, Anna Maria	18, July 1864	20, June			116	Newport, KY	
Speckmann, H. Georg	12, June 1890	26, Apr.	40		382	Metropolis, IL	Newport, Campbell County, Kentucky
Speckmann, Heinrich Friedrich	4, Aug. 1892	7, July	64		494	Newport, KY	Barnsdorf, Hannover
Speckmann, Heinrich Wilhelm	8, May 1876	9, Apr.	20		151	Newport, KY	
Speckmann, J.G.	5, June 1890	29, Apr.	65		366	Winona, MN	Riede, Syke, Hannover
Speckmann, Johan	4, June 1866	11, May	70-11m-20d		182	Winona, MN	Riede, Amt Lüpe, Hannover
Speckmann, Johan H.	31, Jan. 1881	14, Jan.	36- 1m- 4d		39	Newport, KY	Franklin County, Indiana
Speckmann, Lydia E.	20, Aug. 1877	1, Aug.	21		271	Winona, MN	St. Paul , Minnesota
Speer, Friederike	14, July 1898	13, June	40		447	Baltimore, MD	Eggenstein, Baden
Speich, Barbara	21, Aug. 1876	5, Aug.	54		271	Minneapolis, MN	Luchsingen, Glarus, Schweiz
Speich, Magdalena	14, May 1877	30, Apr.	13- 6m-12d		159	Minneapolis, MN	Luchsingen, Glarus, Schweiz
Speidel, Katharina E.	12, Nov. 1891	17, Oct.	55	Lenz	734	Cannelton, IN	Niederohmen, Hessen-Darmstadt
Speiser, Barbara	27, Feb. 1890	11, Jan.	78- 2m-29d		142	Cincinnati, OH	Etlingen, Württemberg
Speiser, David	9, Feb. 1899	18, Jan.	72		95	Humboldt, NE	Kehl, Baden
Speiser, Georg	2, Feb. 1880	5, Jan.	78		39	Cincinnati, OH	Kembach, Baden
Spellman, Ida Lydia	10, Nov. 1884	29, Oct.	20		7	Olive Branch, NE	Scioto County, Ohio
Spellmann, Anna Marie	22, Apr. 1878	4, Apr.		Schäfer	127	Crete, NE	Wittlage, Hannover
Spellmann, Herman	25, Sept 1876	12, Sept	57- 3m		311	Crete, NE	Nordhausen, Osnabrück, Hannover
Spellmann, Margaretha	11, Mar. 1872	17, Feb.	86- 7w	Sieck	87	Lincoln, NE	Osnabrück, Hannover
Spellmann, Maria Elise	5, Sept 1895	19, Aug.	39		574	Kramer, NE	Scioto County, Ohio
Spenner, Anna Catharine	12, Mar. 1896	8, Feb.	63- 5m-24d	Schmidt	175	Lyona, KS	Gotha, Sachsen
Sperley, Jacob	3, Mar. 1892	5, Feb.	59		142	Crown Point, IN	Göggingen, Gemünd, Württemberg
Sperling, Charles	22, May 1890	19, Apr.	70		334	Akron, NY	Scharpso, Mecklenburg-Schwerin
Sperry, Lena	14, Dec. 1893	20, Nov.	17		798	Cincinnati, OH	Cincinnati, Hamilton County, Ohio
Sperry, Louise	2, Nov. 1885	19, Oct.	14- 4m		7	Cincinnati, OH	
Sperry, Margaretha	4, Feb. 1897	12, Jan.	38	Rühl	79	Cincinnati, OH	Cincinnati, Hamilton County, Ohio
Spertzel, Eva	25, July 1850	2, June	57-11m- 9d		120	Louisville, KY	
Spertzel, Johan	25, Sept 1865	26, Aug.	36- 1m-23d		156	Louisville, KY	Zeitloffs, Baiern
Sperzel, Louise Friederika	8, Sept 1859	10, Aug.	28- 8m-16d	Laufer	144	Louisville, KY	
Spicker, (Mr)	2, Nov. 1854	28, Aug.	43		176	Waukegan, IL	Ostfriesland
Spicker, Henriette	27, Nov. 1876	7, Nov.	39		383	Colesburg, IA	Petzin, Kreis Flatow, Preußen
Spicker, Johan Heinrich	17, Nov. 1862	28, Oct.	50- 7m-16d		184	Seymour, IN	Birrendorf, Osnabrück, Hannover
Spicker, Louisa	10, Nov. 1887	25, Oct.	88	Lange	718	Flood Creek, IA	Posen
Spicker, M. Margaretha Dorothea	22, Dec. 1862	25, Nov.	42- 5m-27d		204	Seymour, IN	Icker, Belm, Amt Osnabrück, Hannover
Spiegel, Catharina Charlotte	26, Nov. 1883	7, Nov.	53	Cramer	383	Beardstown, IL	Kirchlenken, Minden, Preußen
Spiegel, Sophia	11, Feb. 1842	4, Feb.	54		23	Cincinnati, OH	

Christliche Apologete Death Notices --- 1839 - 1899

Name of Deceased	Notice Date	Death Date	Age	Page	Maiden Name	Place of Death	Place of Birth
Spielmann, Heinrich	1, Jan. 1866	6, Dec.	18	6		St. Charles, MO	Wayne, Washington County, Wisconsin
Spielmann, Anna Maria	5, Mar. 1883	26, Jan.	72- 9m-12d	79		Lamville, IL	Bindsachsen, Hessen-Darmstadt
Spielmann, Clara Elisabeth	23, Feb. 1854	11, Jan.	57	32		Clayton County, MO	Rabel, Amt Wietlage, Hannover
Spielmann, John	22, Apr. 1872		29	135		Faribault, MN	Soffield, Portage County, Ohio
Spielmann, Katharina	3, Aug. 1899	12, July	76- 5m-19d	495	Mohn	Rochester, MN	Hersingen, Elsaß
Spielmann, Ludwg Benedikt	10, Aug. 1863	25, June	82	128		Hazel Green, WI	Neckardenzlingen, Nürlingen, Württemberg
Spies, Anna Margaretha	7, Jan. 1858	3, Dec.		4		Platteville, WI	Wremen, Hannover
Spies, Georg	18, Aug. 1879	4, Aug.	36-10m-16d	263		Lancaster, PA	Perry County, Pennsylvania
Spieß, Maria Magdalena	12, Dec. 1864	7, Oct.	49- 9m-29d	200	Benner	Platteville, WI	Elhof, Wittgenstein, Arensberg, Preußen
Spilker, August	14, Sept 1893	16, Aug.	74	590		Mt. Vernon, MO	Kirchdornberg, Westphalen
Spilker, Friederike Louise	29, June 1893	6, June	72	414	Wenke	Mt. Vernon, MO	Melle, Gröneberg, Hannover
Spilker, Margaretha	6, May 1897		57	287	Schmidt	St. Louis, MO	Rheinpfalz Baiern
Spille, Gerd	18, May 1874	22, Apr.	19- 6m-20d	159		Sandridge, IL	
Spinck, Johan	25, Oct. 1888	4, Oct.	77- 3m-11d	686		Aurora, IL	Wursten, Padig-Püttel, Hannover
Spinger, Maria	22, June 1899	24, Apr.	67	399	Tautz	Beman, KS	Neurode, Schlesien
Spiniker, Johan H.	24, May 1888	27, Apr.	70	334		San Jose, IL	Meinhaf, Ostfriesland
Spink, A.H.	29, Sept 1887	12, Sept	72	622		Platteville, WI	Dorum, Hannover
Spink, Alice E.	12, Sept 1889	9, July	9- 3m-17d	590		Platteville, WI	Smelser, Wisconsin
Spink, Friedrich August	10, Nov. 1892	19, Sept	14- 9m- 9d	718		Platteville, WI	
Spink, George A.	4, July 1895	7, June	32- 6m- 9d	430		Platteville, WI	
Spink, Johanna Luise	5, Oct. 1899	27, Aug.	32	639		Aurora, IL	Aurora, Illinois
Spink, John E.	2, June 1892	11, May	73- 3m-12d	350		Platteville, WI	Dorum, Hannover
Spinler, John	26, June 1871	31, Mar.	71- 3m	207		Herman, MO	Meisprach, Basel, Schweiz
Spinner, Adam	6, Oct. 1887	14, Sept	28	638		Santa Claus, IN	
Spinner, Margaretha	27, Mar. 1890	4, Mar.	64	206	Michel	Santa Claus, IN	Brüns, Bern, Schweiz
Spinter, Margarethe	22, Apr. 1897	5, Apr.	75	255	Dauen	San Jose, IL	Marienhafe, Ostfriesland
Spitze, Katharina Maria	6, Jan. 1887	15, Dec.	41	14	Deitzel	Edwardsville, IL	Marienhagen, Vöhl, Hessen-Darmstadt
Spitzle, Joseph Friedrich	30, Mar. 1885	2, Mar.	54	7		Brighton, KS	Ober-Utzwyl, St. Gallen, Schweiz
Spitznagel, Elisabeth	28, Apr. 1887	13, Apr.	28	270	Koelsch	Cincinnati, OH	Cincinnati, Hamilton County, Ohio
Splitgerber, Friedrich	30, Mar. 1893	2, Mar.	83	206		Storm Lake, IA	Russel, Pommern
Splitter, Maria	4, May 1863	15, Apr.	20	72	Senn	Hokah, MN	
Splitzgerber, Dorothea	16, Aug. 1894	30, July	64	534	Riewen	Bedford, IN	Broden, Posen
Spohr, Elisabeth	17, July 1890	2, July	58- 3m-24d	462	Schuster	Dayton, OH	Rapper, Hannover
Sponagel, Johan	22, Oct. 1896	30, Sept	36	687		Indianapolis, IN	Mannheim, Baden
Sponsel, Georg	20, Feb. 1882	19, Jan.	17- 7m-14d	63		Hartford, CT	
Spörri, Marie Magdalena	31, May 1894	9, May	64	358	Müller	Enterprise, KS	Hittlingen, Zürich, Schweiz
Spray, Sabina Adelheid	27, Dec. 1880	12, Dec.	23-10m- 1d	415	Meyer	Seymour, IN	Cincinnati, Hamilton County, Ohio
Spreckelmeier, A. Maria Charlotte	3, Sept 1896	14, Aug.	63- 7m-26d	575	Müller	Berger, MO	Mehnen, Blasheim, Minden, Preußen
Spreckelmeyer, Johan Friedrich	4, Apr. 1895	12, Mar.	83	222		Bergen, MO	Bergholzhausen, Bielefeld, Westphalen
Spreen, John Henry	9, Feb. 1880	26, Jan.	70- 9m-17d	47		Baltimore, MD	Lübbenstedt, Lübbeke, Minden, Preußen
Spreen, Kaspar Heinrich G.	2, Apr. 1877		33	111		Seymour, IN	Blaßheim, Minden, Preußen
Spreen, Margaretha Charlotte	4, Sept 1890	12, Aug.	73- 5m-12d	574	Wleke	Seymour, IN	Oldendorf, Minden, Preußen
Spreen, Maria	6, May 1886		71- 1m- 3d	7		Seymour, IN	Blasheim, Lübbecke, Westphalen
Spreider, Magdalena	3, Aug. 1863	4, June	50	124	Geiger	Farmington, IA	Sevelen, St. Gallen, Schweiz
Spreiter, Christian	24, Dec. 1866	7, Nov.	60	414		Kewaskum, WI	Sefelen, Mertenber, St. Gallen, Schweiz
Spreng, Barbara	24, Jan. 1876	9, Jan.	54- 2m- 8d	31	Dewein	St. Louis, MO	LangenKandel, Rheinpfalz Baiern

Christliche Apologete Death Notices --- 1839 - 1899

Name of Deceased	Notice Date	Death Date	Age	Page	Maiden Name	Place of Death	Place of Birth
Sprenger, Anna Rosina	13, Dec. 1875	20, Nov.	74	399	Volkmann	Topeka, KS	Langenblau, Schlesien, Preußen
Sprenger, Karl	27, Mar. 1876	29, Feb.	53	103		Schnectady, NY	Eikhorst, Preußen
Sprenger, Wilhelmine	14, Oct. 1886	29, Sept	43	7		Chicago, IL	Justow, Brandenburg
Sprenn, Christian	2, Nov. 1874	23, Oct.	62-11m- 9d	351		White Creek, IN	Blasheim, Preußen
Sprich, Adelheid	20, Jan. 1879	9, Dec.	30- 8m- 8d	23	Ehlers	Belvedere, MN	Kleinfreulenbrik, Hannover
Spriesterbach, John Adolph	11, June 1891	15, May	33-11m- 8d	382		Mascoutah, IL	
Spriestersbach, David	13, Nov. 1871	24, Oct.	16- 7m	367		Mascoutah, IL	
Spriestersbach, Johan Melchior	20, Apr. 1899	9, Feb.	77	255		Mascoutah, IL	Attenhausen, Nassau
Spring, Albertina	2, Apr. 1866	28, Feb.	14	110		Baresville, OH	
Spring, Elisabeth	30, Apr. 1866	19, Mar.	38- 6m- 9d	142		Baresville, OH	Blumenstein, Bern, Schweiz
Spring, Elisabeth	30, Mar. 1863	13, Jan.	8	52		Baresville, OH	
Spring, Karl August	30, Mar. 1863	4, Jan.	7	52		Baresville, OH	
Spring, Maria	3, Nov. 1879	16, Oct.	42	351	Zimmermann	Oregon, MO	Rederswill, Bern, Schweiz
Spring, Maria	24, Nov. 1879	10, Nov.	16- 5m- 6d	375		Graham, MO	Goldewil, Bern, Schweiz
Spring, Maria Karolina	30, Mar. 1863	13, Jan.	3	52		Baresville, OH	
Spring, Rosina	30, Mar. 1863	22, Jan.	5	52		Baresville, OH	
Spring, Samuel	9, Feb. 1888	20, Jan.		94		Graham, MO	Thun, Schwedi, Bern, Schweiz
Spring, Susanna Katharina	11, Jan. 1894		80	30	Spring	Baresville, OH	Reutigen, Bern, Schweiz
Springborn, Johan Chr. W.	24, Mar. 1873	9, Mar.	66	95		Kenosha, WI	Glienk, Mecklenburg-Schwerin
Springer, Elisabeth	23, Aug. 1894		87- 2m	550		Minneapolis, MN	Heimertshausen, Hessen-Darmstadt
Springer, Gottlieb	24, Feb. 1873	11, Sept	71- -15d	63		Alma, KS	Langenbielau, Schlesien, Preußen
Springer, Jakob	8, Oct. 1877	6, Sept	51- 1m-27d	327		Minneola, MN	Neftenbach, Zürich, Schweiz
Springer, Katharina	5, Feb. 1866	3, Jan.	55	46	Giesler	LaCrosse, WI	Volken, Zürich, Schweiz
Springer, Louis	12, May 1884	24, Apr.	80	7		St. Paul, MN	Kirdorf, Hessen-Darmstadt
Spröhnle, Lucy	7, Mar. 1864	24, Feb.	27	40		St. Louis, MO	
Sproß, Karl	21, Jan. 1897	26, Nov.	32	47		Dallas, TX	Texas
Sprute, Heinrich	6, Dec. 1894	17, Nov.	75	790		Salem, MN	Schönemark, Detmold, Lippe-Detmold
Spuhleder, (Mr)	25, Nov. 1878	25, Oct.	67	375		Illinois City, IL	
Staak, Erdmann	2, Sept 1878	22, Aug.	26	279		New York City, NY	Grammentin, Pommern
Staalz, Augusta W.K.	7, Jan. 1878	18, Dec.	36- 4m-25d	7	Krause	Lyona, KS	Regenwald, Stettin, Pommern, Preußen
Staatz, August F.	20, Mar. 1882	10, Feb.	72- 1m- 7d	95		Lyona, KS	Zicke, Stettin, Hinterpommern
Staatz, C.F.	18, July 1889	25, June	77-10m- 2d	462		Lyona, KS	Zickert bei Naugard, Preußen
Staatz, Catharina	17, Apr. 1871	30, Mar.	29-11m-14d	127	Biegert	Lyons Creek, KS	Ichenheim, Baden
Staatz, Friedrich W.	25, Aug. 1887	1, Aug.	48	542		Lyona, KS	Trieloff bei Greifenberg, Pommern
Staatz, Hedwig Clara	8, Sept 1887	13, Aug.	15	574		Lyona, KS	Dickinson County, Kansas
Staatz, J. F.	8, Sept 1898	10, Aug.	61	575		Enterprise, KS	Schwessow, Preußen
Staatz, Karl W.	25, Aug. 1887	7, Aug.	54	542		Lyona, KS	Lensin, Treptow an der Rega, Pommern
Staatz, Maria	25, Mar. 1858	6, Feb.	23	48	Rekken	Kansas Falls, KS	
Staatz, Pauline Auguste	27, Oct. 1887	16, Sept	49	686	Knies	Lyona, KS	Uebbenhagen, Stettin, Hinterpommern
Staatz, Wilhelmina	5, Dec. 1870		55	391	Wallow	Lyons Creek, KS	Trögloff, Kreis Greifenberg, Preußen
Stäbe, Louis	28, May 1877	8, May	16-10m	175		Houston, TX	
Stabenau, Anna Elisabeth	8, Sept 1884	19, July	57	7	Kamm	Dalton, MO	Posen
Stabenow, Carl Friedrich	7, Jan. 1886	13, Dec.	60	7		Ft. Atkinson, WI	Fürstenau, Arnswalde, Brandenburg
Stabnow, Wilhelm F.	17, Mar. 1892	20, Feb.	36	175		Ft. Atkinson, WI	Arnswalde, Brandenburg
Städele, Anna	21, Aug. 1876	25, July	43	271	Gisler	Jersey City, NJ	Flaach, Zürich, Schweiz
Städeli, Heinrich	5, Oct. 1885	20, Sept	20	7		Melrose, NJ	Ufter, Zürich, Schweiz

Christliche Apologete Death Notices --- 1839 - 1899

Name of Deceased	Notice Date	Death Date	Age	Page	Maiden Name	Place of Death	Place of Birth
Städeli, Johannes	18, Oct. 1888	5, Oct.	25	670	Stadtmann	New York City, NY	Dann bei Mühlhausen, Frankreich
Städeli, Rosine	28, Sept 1893	22, July	57	622		New York City, NY	Lindach, Gmünd, Württemberg
Stadelmeyer, (Mrs)	27, June 1870	13, May	39-10m-24d	207	Krieg	Colesburg, IA	Lanste, Amt Syke, Hannover
Stadtlander, Anna Katharina	13, Aug. 1866	8, July	17	262		Second Creek, MO	Markt Erlbach, Baiern
Stadtler, Eva Barbara	12, Nov. 1877	25, Oct.	57	367	Heubeck	Philadelphia, PA	
Staff, Dorothea	13, Jan. 1873	10, Dec.	30	15	König	Columbus, IL	
Staff, Georg	19, Nov. 1896	22, Oct.	61	750		Quincy, IL	Marjoß, Kurhessen
Staffer, Heinrich	21, Nov. 1870	29, Oct.	79- 7m-16d	375		Charles City, IA	Amt Osnabrück, Hannover
Stafhorst, Maria D.	18, July 1889	26, June	40- 7m-12d	462	Gauding	Greenville, OH	Lawrenceburg, Dearborn County, Indiana
Stahl, (Mr)	30, Oct. 1871	11, Oct.	66-11m-11d	351		Calhoun, IL	Aslar, Koblenz, Preußen
Stahl, Anna	24, Mar. 1887	1, Mar.	25	190		Cleveland, OH	Weißach, Vaihingen, Württemberg
Stahl, Anna	17, Apr. 1876	1, Apr.	31- 4m-13d	127	Creborn	Muscatine, IA	
Stahl, Anna Elisabeth	2, Aug. 1888	2, July	82	494		Mt. Vernon, NY	Mescheide, Kurhessen
Stahl, Brigitta	25, June 1891	8, June	48	414		Scranton, PA	
Stahl, Christina	21, May 1896	30, Apr.	27	334		Salem, IN	Vanderburgh County, Indiana
Stahl, Dietrich	15, Apr. 1858	8, Feb.	81	60		Jackson County, IN	Eschtorf, Stolzenau, Hannover
Stahl, Dorothea	15, Dec. 1892	14, Nov.	79	798	Kies	Springfield, IL	Ellmendingen, Baden
Stahl, Elisabeth	3, Feb. 1873	13, Jan.	17	39	Renth	Effingham, IL	
Stahl, Friederika	16, Oct. 1882	24, Sept	84	335	Dargo	Houston, TX	Kuhwinkel bei Perleberg, Preußen
Stahl, Friedrich	20, Dec. 1875	2, Dec.	8-11m- 4d	407		Red Bud, IL	
Stahl, Gottlob	16, Apr. 1883	1, Apr.	49	127		Evansville, IN	Lomersheim, Maulbronn, Württemberg
Stahl, Ippe Janssen	9, Mar. 1874	13, Feb.	21	79		Red Bud, IL	Tannenhausen, Aurich, Ostfriesland
Stahl, John H.	23, Feb. 1893	4, Feb.	78	126		Springfield, IL	Aslar, Wetzlar, Preußen
Stahl, Katharina Barbara	20, Aug. 1896	30, July	72	543		Berea, OH	Oettingen, Lörach, Baden
Stahl, Mäntie	9, Feb. 1880	26, Apr.	55	47	Tohlen	Red Bud, IL	Amt Aurich, Ostfriesland
Stahl, Margaretha	7, July 1873	9, June	43	215	Fischer	Canal Dover, OH	Gräfenberg, Grafenburg, Baiern
Stahlberg, J. Friedrich Theodor	6, Sept 1880	17, Aug.	53- 8m- 7d	287		Laporte, IN	Kittendorf, Mecklenburg-Schwerin
Stähle, Georg	11, Oct. 1855	31, Aug.	30	164		Laporte, IN	Schwenningen, Rothweil, Württemberg
Stahle, J.	28, Jan. 1897	5, Jan.	69	63		San Francisco, CA	Frankenberg, Hessen
Stahle, Maria	18, July 1889	16, June	65	462	Limpert	San Jose, CA	Hanau bei Frankfurt am Main, Germany
Stahlhut, Ernst	14, Mar. 1889	23, Feb.	89- 8m	174		St. Charles, MO	Merbeck, Lippe-Schaumburg
Stahlhut, (daughter of Sophia)	26, July 1849	30, June	25	120		St. Louis, MO	
Stahlhuth, (son of Friedrich)	26, July 1849	30, June	27	120		St. Louis, MO	
Stahlhuth, Clara Emma Olga	20, July 1893	13, June	27	462	Herzog	St. Louis, MO	Danzig, Germany
Stahlhuth, Sophia	26, July 1849	29, June	54	120		St. Louis, MO	
Stähli, Kasper	29, Nov. 1880	16, Sept	74	383		Denver, MO	Brienz, Bern, Schweiz
Stahmann, Ludwig	4, Aug. 1873	23, June	6-10m-15d	247		Cincinnati, OH	Unterlenningen, Kirchheim, Württemberg
Staib, Anna Magdalena	15, Mar. 1880	23, Feb.	58- 4m-18d	87	Rentz	Clarington, OH	Batesville, Indiana
Staiger, Maria	24, Mar. 1892	26, Feb.	26	191		Batesville, IN	Wahlprechtshausen, Hannover
Stake, Wilhelm	7, Oct. 1878	20, Sept	40- 8m-16d	319		Marion, OH	Emden, Ostfriesland
Stamm, Johanna	17, Jan. 1876	24, Dec.	63	23	Marinesse	Milwaukee, WI	Hannover, Hannover
Stamm, Karl Heinrich	6, Jan. 1887	3, Dec.	76	14		Milwaukee, WI	Schwerin, Mecklenburg-Schwerin
Stamm, Maria	27, Sept 1894	21, Aug.	69	630		Geneseo, IL	Leidendorf, Sachsen-Coburg
Stammberger, Johan G.S.	12, Dec. 1881	14, Nov.	81- 1m	399		Milwaukee, WI	
Stampp, Julia	13, Jan. 1887	19, Dec.	44	30	Protzmann	Milwaukee, WI	
Stampp, Michael	2, Oct. 1890	31, Aug.	45- 9m-13d	638		Milwaukee, WI	Gimbsheim, Hessen-Darmstadt

Name of Deceased	Notice Date	Death Date	Age	Maiden Name	Page	Place of Death	Place of Birth
Standemann, Jacob	16, May 1881	27, Apr.	83		159	Quincy, IL	Stetten, RheinPfalz Baiern
Stange, Anna Rebekka	18, July 1895	21, June	28	Büschlen	462	Bay City, MI	Huron County, Canada
Stange, Karl	24, Feb. 1879	26, Jan.			63	Bay City, MI	
Stange, Louise Anna	2, Sept 1886	28, July	19- 3m-12d		7	Bay City, MI	
Stange, Pauline	8, July 1878	21, June	15		215	Bay City, MI	Bay City, Michigan
Stange, Wilhelmine	25, Apr. 1895	30, Mar.	65	Hellmer	270	Bay City, MI	Sonnenthin, Preußen
Stangor, Wilhelmine	6, Oct. 1887	17, Sept	67	Rennack	638	Chicago, IL	Tauenzin, Lauenburg, Köslin, Pommern
Stapfer, Elisabeth	14, Jan. 1884	1, Jan.	86		7	Charles City, IA	Osnabrück, Hannover
Stapper, Elisabeth	3, Mar. 1898	8, Feb.	63	Marolf	143	Pueblo, CO	Kanton Bern, Schweiz
Starch, Anna Maria	21, June 1880	10, May	55	Porsche	199	LaCrosse, WI	Oberedersdorf, Bensen, Böhmen
Starch, Brigitta	26, Mar. 1883	14, Mar.	65		103	Shelby, WI	Dobern, Leippan, Böhmen
Starch, Stephan	2, Feb. 1899	31, Dec.	75		79	LaCrosse, WI	Oberebersdorf bei Benson, Böhmen
Stark, Gottlieb	20, Nov. 1890	2, Oct.	73		750	Lansing, IA	Unterbrieden, Backnang, Württemberg
Stark, Albertine	16, Mar. 1885	26, Feb.	49	Bremer	7	Lansing, IA	Triebus bei Treptow an der Raga, Preußen
Stark, Augustina Christiana	22, Apr. 1872				135	Indianapolis, IN	Sulz am Neckar, Württemberg
Stark, Christiana Rosina	16, Sept 1852	5, Aug.	69		152	Aurora, ----	Hundersingen, Württemberg
Stark, Friederika	16, Apr. 1896	6, Mar.	82		254	Faribault, MN	Kröß, Oldenburg, Holstein
Stark, Friedrich Karl	14, Apr. 1898	20, Mar.	64		239	Greenfield, MA	Gadun, Mecklenburg-Schwerin
Stark, H.W.	26, Dec. 1870	29, Nov.	56		415	Peterson, IA	Oldenburg, Holstein
Stark, Heinrich Karl	14, June 1880	28, May	42- 7m-21d		191	Winona, MN	Oldenburg, Holstein
Stark, Karl Friedrich Gustav	22, Apr. 1897	1, Apr.	16		255	Columbus, WI	Portland, Dodge County, Wisconsin
Stark, Karoline Barbara	2, Aug. 1894	3, July	69		502	Boston, MA	Hedelfingen, Canstatt, Württemberg
Stark, Leona	1, Nov. 1888	4, Oct.	55		702	Indianapolis, IN	Bozsingen, Württemberg
Stark, Louis	21, Sept 1885	11, Aug.	24		7	Greenfield, MA	
Stark, Louise	1, Oct. 1891	6, Sept	60		638	Philadelphia, PA	Marltröningen, Württemberg
Stark, Maria	24, Feb. 1868	31, Jan.	48- 6m	Wille	63	Dorchester, IA	Lichtenstein
Stark, Rosine	24, Oct. 1889	27, Sept	23		686	Golconda, IL	
Stark, Sophia C.	8, July 1872	21, June	50- 6m-12d		223	Indianapolis, IN	Sulz am Neckar, Württemberg
Stark, Wilhelmine	28, Jan. 1886	15, Jan.	40		7	Greenfield, MA	Mecklenburg-Schwerin
Starks, Wilhelmine	18, July 1895	28, June	71	Lorenz	462	Lowell, WI	Uckermark, Germany
Starks, Friedrich A.	11, Sept 1890	17, Aug.	95- 2m-18d		590	Graham, MO	Plugrade, Pommern
Start, Augustina Christiana	8, Apr. 1872	18, Mar.	55- -13d		119	Indianapolis, IN	Sulz am Neckar, Württemberg
Staub, Albert	16, Jan. 1896	25, Dec.	24		46	Portland, OR	Wärdenweil, Zürich, Schweiz
Staub, Felix	25, Feb. 1867		38		62	Nashville, TN	Trimms, Graubünden, Schweiz
Staub, Georg	11, Sept 1876	23, Aug.	62		295	Louisville, KY	Heubach, Umstadt, Dieburg, Hessen-Darmstadt
Staub, Jacob	10, Feb. 1887	19, Jan.	20		94	Nashville, TN	
Staub, Johan	17, Dec. 1891	24, Nov.	68		814	New York City, NY	Ellingerode, Hessen-Kassel
Staub, Johan Felix	8, Apr. 1897	31, Jan.	32- 4m		223	Nashville, TN	Nashville, Tennessee
Staub, John Henry	1, Jan. 1891	16, Nov.	81		14	Spencerville, OH	Semd, Hessen-Darmstadt
Staub, Michael	10, July 1882	13, June	67		223	Walnut Creek, IA	Zuzendorf, Elsaß
Stäubli, Theodor Gottlob J. (Rev)	7, Nov. 1895	7, Oct.	55		718	Columbus, WI	Horgen, Zürich, Schweiz
Stauch, Samuel	11, June 1883	22, Apr.	80- 6m-19d		191	Allegheny City, PA	Pennsylvania
Staud, Jakob	23, Mar. 1868	7, Mar.	12		95	Quincy, IL	
Staudermann, Peter	13, Sept 1888	17, Aug.	60- 8m- 9d		590	Putnam County, OH	Setten, Kirchheimboland, Baiern
Staufer, Christian	17, Oct. 1845		Inquiry		167		Soltalhof, Neustadt a. d. Haardt, Rheinkreis Baiern
Staufer, David	14, Dec. 1893	23, Nov.	80		798	Clarington, OH	

Christliche Apologete Death Notices --- 1839 - 1899

Name of Deceased	Death Date	Age	Page	Maiden Name	Place of Death	Place of Birth
Staufer, Gottfried	10, June	22- 6m	223		Clarington, OH	Monroe County, Ohio
Stauffacher, Barbara	11, Nov.	67-10m-11d	391		Warsaw, IL	Matt, Glarus, Schweiz
Stauffer, Anna	12, Oct.	68- 6m-12d	702	Burri	Clarington, OH	Burgdorf, Bern, Schweiz
Stauffer, Charles C.	4, July	25	494		Topeka, KS	Laupen, Bern, Schweiz
Stauffer, Nikolaus	27, Apr.	74- 7m- 9d	159		Clarington, OH	Oberwyl, Bern, Schweiz
Stäup, Christian	7, Nov.	40	196		Saline Coal Mines, IL	Marienberg, Nassau
Stauß, Christiana	4, Mar.	54	111	Wöchner	Pittsburg, PA	Rockum, Blumenthal, Hannover
Staut, Barbara	9, Feb.	63	158		Allegheny, PA	Annabils, Glarus, Schweiz
Stautermann, Barbara	6, Jan.	57	55	Schäfer	Columbus, IL	Freimersheim, Hessen-Darmstadt
Stautermann, Maria	6, Mar.	66	222		Quincy, IL	Setten, Kirchheimboland, Baiern
Stecher, Anton	31, Aug.	72	156		Pennsylvanienburg, IN	Atter bei Osnabrück, Hannover
Stecher, Caroline Wilhelmine Elise	16, Mar.	82-10m-13d	135	Nietit	White Creek, IN	Hörsten, Osnabrück, Hannover
Stecher, Catharina	26, May	16-11m-15d	191		Batesville, IN	Ripley County, Indiana
Stecher, Johan Heinrich	26, Sept	28- 8m-12d	327		Batesville, IN	Ripley County, Indiana
Stecher, Johann Gerhard	27, Nov.	40	208		Pennsylvanienburg, IN	Atter bei Osnabrück, Hannover
Stecher, Louise	25, Sept	17	164		Cincinnati, OH	
Steck, Anna Maria	27, Nov.	77	7	Walz	Buffalo, NY	Bernhausen, Stuttgart, Württemberg
Steck, Gottlieb	25, Feb.	82	190		Brenham, TX	Neu Ulm, Friedeberg, Neumark
Steck, Johan David	18, Jan.	62	95		West Union, OH	Möhringen, Stuttgart, Württemberg
Steck, Sophia	8, Sept	57	623	Tetterling	Buffalo, NY	Freienwalde, Preußen
Steckeling, Augusta	9, July	17	247		Milwaukee, WI	Malskoy, HinterPommern
Steckmann, Heinrich	29, Sept	34- -26d	327		Sandusky, OH	Detmold, Lippe-Detmold
Stedtfeld, Rudolph	24, Feb.	60	7		Evansville, IN	Untereisisheim, Heilbronn, Württemberg
Steeb, Johanna Margaretha	28, Oct.	44- 7m-10d	8	Neuffer	Newark, NJ	
Steege, Anna Sophia Louise Fr.	4, Dec.	40	414	Buß	Milwaukee, WI	Pommern
Steenken, Auguste Luise	31, Oct.	15- 2m-19d	127		Covington, KY	Görke, Pommern
Steeps, (Mrs)	25, Oct.	77-11m	375		Oshkosh, WI	Kamorsdorf, Neugard, Pommern
Steeps, Gustav Franz Wilhelm	2, Nov.	19	351		Oshkosh, WI	Klößke, West Preußen
Steeps, Johan	14, Oct.	80	703		Oshkosh, WI	
Steeps, Louise Pauline	26, Nov.	67	798	Kickhöfer	Oshkosh, WI	
Steffen, August	18, June	45	446		Oconomowoc, WI	Gasconade County, Missouri
Steffen, August	28, June	49	124		Swan Creek, NE	Augustdorf, Lippe-Detmold
Steffen, Elisabeth Maria	4, Aug.	40	559	Zeitz	Morrison, MO	Crampin, Mecklenburg-Schwerin
Steffen, Friedrich	9, Oct.	77	7		Drake, MO	Augustdorf, Lippe-Detmold
Steffen, Helene	19, Dec.	42	15		Roseville, MI	Gasconade County, Missouri
Steffen, Henriette	7, Jan.	67	78	Isenberg	Owensville, MO	Köln am Rhein, Preußen
Steffen, Josephine Malinde	9, May	58	351	Brinkmann	Drake, MO	Bulsten, Melle, Hannover
Steffen, Karl Theodor	27, Jan.	66	158		St. Joseph, MO	Chicago, Cook County, Illinois
Steffen, Konrad Heinrich	8, Sept	89	623		Warren, MO	Uphausen, Amt Achim, Hannover
Steffen, Sophia Katharine	14, July	18	239	Henkhaus	Herman, MO	Morsum, Westen, Hannover
Steffens, Gesine	24, Jan.	67	47	Meinken	Cincinnati, OH	Jo Davis County, Illinois
Steffens, Johan Heinrich	2, Dec.	44- -22d	407		Cincinnati, OH	Wallhalben, Rheinpfalz Baiern
Steffens, Louis Philipp	11, Dec.	19- 4m- 8d	15		Norfolk, NE	
Steffens, Maria	8, Feb.	68	158	Fuchs	Laporte, IN	
Steffer, Elwine Marie	16, Dec.	18- 8m-22d	7	Müller	Arlington, MN	Vandsburg, West Preußen
Steffer, Johan	16, May	81	383		Arlington, MN	

Christliche Apologete Death Notices --- 1839 - 1899

Name of Deceased	Notice Date	Death Date	Age	Page	Maiden Name	Place of Death	Place of Birth
Steffler, Lydia	1, Aug. 1889	3, June	11-11m-18d	494		Ida Grove, IA	
Stegelmann, Detler H.	8, Sept 1884	18, Aug.	69- 6m	7		Fremont, NE	Kiel, Schleswig-Holstein
Stegelmann, Elisabeth Catharina	29, Nov. 1888	27, Oct.	67- 3m-21d	766		Fremont, NE	KleinFlembeck, Kiel, Schleswig-Holstein
Stegelmann, Gottfried Christian	23, Aug. 1894	28, July	33	550		West Point, NE	Mühlbrock, Schleswig-Holstein
Stegmann, Louis	30, July1883	19, July	31- 3m	247		St. Paul, MN	
Stegner, Elisabeth	30, May 1895	6, May	68	350	Stegner	Fairbault, MN	Ebersdorf bei Coburg, Sachsen
Stegner, Elise Jane	6, Dec. 1855	29, Oct.	3- 7m-15d	196		Pennsylvanienburg, IN	
Stegner, Emilie Floredin	12, Jan. 1885	23, Dec.	9	7		Newport, KY	
Stegner, Friedrich Daniel	22, Dec. 1887	23, Nov.	20	814		Newport, KY	
Stegner, Gottfried	21, Mar. 1889	4, Mar.	64- 4m-16d	190		Clarington, OH	Neuville, Elsaß
Stegner, Thomas	6, Dec. 1855	12, Oct.	12- 3m	196		Pennsylvanienburg, IN	
Stehenberger, Michael	24, Aug. 1854	9, Apr.	47	136		Jefferson City, MO	Efferding bei Linz, Austria
Stehl, Barbara Cath. Wilhelmine	10, Nov. 1853	19, Oct.	12- 2m-23d	180		New York, NY	
Stehl, Georg C.	28, Nov. 1895	23, Oct.	81	766		New York City, NY	Soden, Kurhessen
Stehl, Maria Elisabeth	19, Aug. 1897	26, May	77	527	Gundlach	New York City, NY	Allendorf, Kurhessen
Stehle, Emilie	27, Dec. 1894	1, Nov.	38	836		Clatonia, NE	
Stehle, John	14, Sept 1863	20, Aug.	44- 7m-10d	148		Dunkirk, NY	Schwenningen, Württemberg
Stehr, Elisabeth	26, May 1892	1, May	46	334	Treiber	Baraboo, WI	Iowa
Stehr, John	27, Jan. 1898	9, Dec.	68	63		Baraboo, WI	Hessen-Darmstadt
Steib, Karl Ludwig	4, Nov. 1878	21, Oct.	73- 5m-17d	351		West Unity, OH	Bissingen a.d. Teck, Württemberg
Steierberg, Karoline	28, May 1896	7, May	56	350	Lange	Cannon River, MN	Pole, Springe, Hannover
Steiernagel, Joseph	19, Jan. 1880	3, Jan.	20- 2m	23		Allegheny City, PA	Alleghany City, Pennsylvania
Steigele, Barbara	16, June 1887	21, May	78	382		Chicago, IL	Gebingen, Württemberg
Steiger, (Mrs)	21, Mar. 1864	14, Dec.	28	48		Batesville, IN	
Steiger, Barbara	23, Apr. 1883	4, Apr.	30- 4m-15d	135	Schäfer	Batesville, IN	Ohio
Steiger, Ignatz	31, July 1865	19, July	37- 5m-18d	124		Brookville, IN	Hirschau, Württemberg
Steiger, Katharina B.	6, Dec. 1888	17, Oct.	18- 8m-19d	782		Madison, IN	Lawrenceburg, Indiana
Steigerwald, Anna E.	5, Aug. 1872	17, July	33	255	Muther	Madison, IN	Oberdurlach, Preußen
Steigerwald, Catharina	25, June 1866	8, June	42-11m-14d	206	Gantschir	Lawrenceburg, IN	Partenstein, Rheinkreis Baiern
Steigerwald, Johan	8, July 1878	24, June	72	215		Buffalo, NY	Dassel, Hannover
Steigerwald, Johanna	5, Oct. 1893	7, Sept	38	638	Borgmann	Madison, IN	
Steigerwald, John William	5, June 1865	Mar.	20- 5m	92		Lawrenceburg, IN	
Steigewald, Christine	15, Mar. 1888	19, Feb.	76- 8m-11d	174	Imhof	Brooklyn, NY	Bortenstein am Main, Baiern
Stein, Henry	16, Jan. 1896	20, Nov.	12	46		Newport, KY	Newport, Kentucky
Stein, Julia	20, June 1895	29, May	37	398	Berey	Henderson, KY	Covington, Kenton County, Kentucky
Stein, Anna Catharina	17, Mar. 1879	1, Mar.	56	87	Leiser	Boonville, MO	Hessen-Darmstadt
Stein, Anton	25, Dec. 1851	7, Oct.	42	208		Terre Haute, IN	Riesel, Preußen
Stein, Caroline	12, May 1887	1, May	33	302	Sezer	Boelus, NE	Mühlheim, Sulz am Neckar, Württemberg
Stein, Friedrich	13, Aug. 1896	14, July	52	527		Cameron, MO	Wettesingen, Volkmarshausen, Hessen-Kassel
Stein, Friedrich Wilhelm	25, Aug. 1879	13, July	71	271		Covington, KY	Bellheim, Rheinkreis Baiern
Stein, Georg Carl	24, Apr. 1890	3, Apr.	26- 7m- 1d	270		Liberty, MO	Wettesingen, Kurhessen
Stein, Heinrich	13, Apr. 1863			60		Liberty, MO	Wettesingen, Kurhessen
Stein, Johannes	13, Apr. 1863			60		Liberty, MO	
Stein, Katharina	28, Apr. 1848		Inquiry	71	Seng	Tazwell County, IL	Perry County, Indiana
Stein, Margaretha	27, Aug. 1877	10, Aug.	22-10m-20d	279		Henderson, KY	Zozenbach, Hessen-Darmstadt
Stein, Nicolaus	27, Dec. 1894	18, Nov.	86- 6m-10d	836		Terre Haute, IN	

Christliche Apologete Death Notices --- 1839 - 1899

Name of Deceased	Notice Date	Death Date	Age	Page	Maiden Name	Place of Death	Place of Birth
Stein, Phil. (Rev)	18, Sept 1876	1, Sept	28	303		New Albany, IN	Osthofen, Hessen-Darmstadt
Stein, Philipp	29, Aug. 1870	5, Aug.	63- 4m-20d	279		Cannelton, IN	Canton Bern, Schweiz
Steinagel, Anna M.	9, Apr. 1891	3, Mar.	68- 4m- 4d	238	Muhri	Cannelton, IN	
Steinbach, (girl)	7, Aug. 1882	24, May		255		Wadena, MN	
Steinbach, Anna Louise	7, Aug. 1882	11, July	14	255		Wadena, MN	
Steinbach, Christine	19, Feb. 1891	5, Dec.	63	126		New York City, NY	Gießen, Hessen-Darmstadt
Steinbach, David	12, Nov. 1883	24, Oct.	29	367		Wadena, MN	Beotha, Todd County, Minnesota
Steinbach, Elisabeth	13, Aug. 1896	2, July	74	527	Wenig	Lansing, IA	Malsfeld, Kurhessen
Steinbach, Frank Hugo	16, Feb. 1885	2, Feb.	21	7		Wadena, MN	Dodge County, Wisconsin
Steinbach, Friedrich August	7, Aug. 1882	19, July	3- 5m-20d	255		Wadena, MN	
Steinbach, Katharina	12, Apr. 1869	24, Mar.	14- 5m-20d	119		Waterloo, IA	Summerhill, Cambria County, Pennsylvania
Steinbach, Minna Emilie	11, Apr. 1889	8, Mar.	25	238	Masoni	White City, KS	Leipzig, Sachsen
Steinbeck, Anna	8, Sept 1887		19- 8m- 6d	574		Chester, IL	
Steinbeck, Herman	10, Aug. 1893	12, July	69	510		Chester, IL	Preußen
Steinbeck, Katharina Maria	15, Oct. 1896	6, Sept	67	671	Gerecke	Chester, IL	Boxberg, Hannover
Steinbeck, Sophie	18, July 1870	25, June	37	231	Meyer	Chester, IL	Lütteringhausen, Preußen
Steinbock, Amalie	18, Mar.1872	3, Mar.	47	95	Ehlies	Philadelphia, PA	Lawrenceburg, Indiana
Steinbock, Marie Luise	17, Aug. 1899	4, Aug.	27-10m	527		Lawrenceburg, IN	Limritz, Preußen
Steinborn, Ferdinand	27, Mar. 1890	14, Feb.	42	206		Arlington, MN	Meoczen, Preußen
Steinborn, Karolina Ernestine	2, Aug. 1894	9, July	36	502	Link	Arlington, MN	Hohenschwarz, Oberfranken, Baiern
Steinbrecher, Konrad	24, Feb. 1887	26, Jan.	73	126		Hamilton, OH	Taschendorf, Baiern
Steinbrecher, Margaretha	21, May 1896	20, Apr.	84	334	Dingfelder	Hamilton, OH	Messen, Saraton, Rußland
Steinbrecher, Maria	23, July1883	8, July	36- 6m-21d	239	Betz	Burlington, IA	Zuzenhausen, Baden
Steinbrenner, Georg Michael	18, Mar. 1897	19, Feb.	73	175		Cleveland, OH	Seneca County, Ohio
Steinbrenner, Katharine	24, Mar. 1887	7, Mar.	16	190		Spencerville, OH	Bebra, Rothenburg, Kurhessen
Steinbrenner, Magdalena	6, Dec. 1880	22, Nov.	60	391	Killmer	Cleveland, OH	Reichenbach, Bensheim, Hessen-Darmstadt
Steinbrenner, Maria Sophia	30, Aug. 1888	10, Aug.	41	558	Trodt	Spencerville, OH	Wilhelmshaven, Greifswald, Pommern
Steinbrink, Auguste	29, Oct. 1896	21, Sept	38	703		Elgin, IL	Saalfeld, Königsberg, Preußen
Steinecke, Louisa	21, June 1888	6, June	74	398		New Knoxville, OH	Pfarpichel, Burtzwells, Oesterreich
Steiner, (Mr)	1, Dec. 1879	9, Nov.	61- 2m	383		Third Creek, MO	Bartenbach, Göppingen, Württemberg
Steiner, Anna	16, June 1879	3, May	85	191	Schurr	Hartford, WI	Dürrenäsch, Aargau, Schweiz
Steiner, Arnold	1, May 1890	29, Mar.	60- 2m-15d	286		Lemars, IA	
Steiner, Carolina	23, Apr. 1865	24, Mar.	15- 2m	68		Oregon, MO	
Steiner, Carolina Sophia Eleone	25, Jan. 1869	18, Dec.	30	31	Knolle	Industry, TX	Krebshagen, Bückeburg, Lippe-Schaumburg
Steiner, Ernstine Henrietta	1, Aug. 1881	16, July	62- 2m-24d	247	Wilhelm	New Albany, IN	Kleutsch, Frankenstein, Schlesien
Steiner, Heinrich	15, Sept 1884	2, Sept	69	7		Dayton, OH	Erlenbach, Kandel, RheinPfalz Baiern
Steiner, Heinrich	23, Feb. 1899	25, Jan.	82	127		San Jose, CA	Pfungen, Zürich, Schweiz
Steiner, Ida	6, Oct. 1892	10, Sept		638		Columbus, OH	Neila, Baiern
Steiner, Ida Elisabeth	21, July 1898	2, July	16	463		Marrs, IN	Posey County, Indiana
Steiner, Johan	19, July 1880	21, June	86	231		Lake Creek, MO	Wallern, Oesterreich
Steiner, Johan Gottfried	10, Apr. 1890	4, Feb.	72	238			Seifersdorf, Schweidnitz, Schlesien
Steiner, Johan Nikolaus	10, Feb. 1898	15, Jan.	83	95		Marrs, IN	Sachsen-Coburg
Steiner, John	14, Mar. 1889	15, Feb.	70	174		West Bend, WI	Oberwalden, Göppingen, Württemberg
Steiner, Margaretha	20, Sept 1849	12, Aug.	32	152		Mt. Vernon, IN	Thaan, Neustadt an der Haide, Sachsen-Coburg
Steiner, Maria	31, Oct. 1895	23, Sept	84	702	Metz	Cincinnati, OH	Dierbach, Rheinpfalz Baiern
Steiner, Maria	8, Sept 1892	22, Aug.	20	574		Lafayette, IN	

Christliche Apologete Death Notices --- 1839 - 1899

Name of Deceased	Notice Date	Death Date	Age	Maiden Name	Page	Place of Death	Place of Birth
Steiner, Maria Elisabeth	6, Feb. 1871	18, Jan.	70	Steiner	47	Cincinnati, OH	Erlenbach, Rheinkreis Baiern
Steiner, Maria Magdalena	27, Feb. 1890	6, Feb.	20		142	Bland, MO	Jefferson City, Missouri
Steiner, Mattheus	1, Dec. 1879	8, Nov.	19- 8m-26d		383	Third Creek, MO	
Steiner, Philipp Jakob	8, June 1854	24, May	52		92	Cincinnati, OH	Erlenbach, Rheinkreis Baiern
Steiner, Rosine	23, Feb. 1863	3, Feb.	40		32	Herman, MO	Oberwälden, Göppingen, Württemberg
Steiner, Susanna Eleonora	26, Sept 1881	12, Aug.			311	Philadelphia, PA	
Steiner, Susanna Salomea	12, Apr. 1875	15, Mar.	52	Gerter	119	San Jose, CA	Pfungen, Zürich, Schweiz
Steingräber, Friedrich	6, Feb. 1890	31, Oct.	52		94	Dallas City, IL	Stolpe, Pommern
Steingräber, Hermina	2, Aug. 1894	10, July	56	Krampig	502	Dallas City, IL	Stolp, Pommern
Steingrube, Heinrich	14, June 1894	13, May	25		390	Walonda, SD	Elze, Hannover
Steinhage, John	7, Feb. 1876	25, Jan.	75		47	Edwardsville, IL	
Steinhage, Maria Elisabeth	12, Oct. 1863	6, Aug.	64		164	Edwardsville, IL	Daubendocke, Schledehausen, Hannover
Steinhagen, Louise	23, Mar. 1868	4, Mar.	68		95	Louisville, KY	Erlinghausen, Lippe-Detmold
Steinhauer, Anna M. L.	23, Apr. 1866	20, Feb.		Krüger	134	Schenectady, NY	Welferdinsen, Preußen
Steinhauer, Anna Maria	16, Mar. 1854	23, Feb.	25		44	Vandalia, IL	
Steinhauer, Elisabeth	7, June 1869	17, May	45	Hildebrant	183	New Albany, IN	Niederweisel, Hessen
Steinhauer, Heinrich	17, Nov. 1898	28, Sept	83		735	Schenectady, NY	Westphalen
Steinhauer, Konrad	17, Jan. 1881	22, Dec.	54		23	New Albany, IN	Fauerbach, Hessen
Steinhauer, Maria E.	12, June 1876	11, May	73- 6m		191	Fayette Co., IL	
Steinhauer, Maria Elisabeth	21, Jan. 1884	26, Sept	38	Hugo	7	Schenectady, NY	Netelstadt, Lippe-Detmold
Steinhauer, Michael	23, Nov. 1868	10, Nov.	57		375	Vandalia, IL	
Steinhauer, Wilhelmine	28, Apr. 1884	9, Mar.	56	Lehmann	7	Schenectady, NY	Berg, Magdeburg, Preußen
Steinhaus, Elisabeth Katharina	23, Feb. 1893	27, Jan.	38	Bambai	126	Culbertson, NE	Zell, Hannover
Steinhäuser, Anna Maria	4, June 1896	19, May	69	Löb	367	Newport, KY	Gehaus, Sachsen-Weimar
Steinhäuser, Johan	14, Jan. 1884	26, Dec.	65- 3m- 3d		7	Newport, KY	Gehaus, Sachsen-Weimar
Steinhäußer, John	4, Dec. 1882	26, -5m-22d	26- -5m-22d		391	Newport, KY	Newport, Campbell County, Kentucky
Steinhelfer, Barbara	16, Apr. 1891	25, Mar.	61- 6m-24d		254	Galion, OH	Pfullingen, Württemberg
Steinhelfer, Christoph	18, Oct. 1888	30, Sept	68- 7m-16d	König	670	Galion, OH	Satteldorf, Kreitzheim, Württemberg
Steinhelper, Catharina	5, Sept 1889	15, Aug.	59- 6m-15d		574	Greenville, OH	Ofterdingen, Rottenburg, Württemberg
Steinhilber, Johan Georg	29, Nov. 1869	28, Mar.	53- 3m-13d		383	Crow River, MN	Westmoreland County, Pennsylvania
Steinhilfer, Lydia	30, Dec. 1872	6, Dec.	49	Karck	423	Bucyrus, OH	Osterdingen, Rottenburg, Württemberg
Steinhöfer, Anna	4, Mar. 1858	7, Feb.	48	Nill	36	St. Anthony, MN	Nemersdorf, Verneck, Baiern
Steininger, Anna Margaretha	7, June 1875	21, May	74	Hörnlein	183	Jefferson City, MO	Jefferson City, Missouri
Steininger, Emilie	16, Oct. 1890	28, Sept	35- 6m-20d	Bauer	670	Herman, MO	Eveding, Oesterreich
Steininger, Julia	18, Nov. 1878	26, Sept	33- 5m		367	Osage, MO	
Steininger, Katharina	3, June 1867	12, May	33- 2m- 4d	Holzbeierlein	174	Jefferson City, MO	Eichhammer, Pegnitz, Baiern
Steininger, Margaretha	16, Feb. 1874		41	Holzbeierlein	55	Jefferson City, MO	Eichhammer, Baiern
Steininger, Margaretha	16, Dec. 1886	27, Nov.		Hehenbeyer	7	Jefferson City, MO	
Steinkamp, Charlotte	1, Apr. 1867	4, Mar.	24- 8m-13d		102	Piqua, OH	
Steinkamp, Christian Johann	19, Mar. 1883		61		95	Greenville, OH	Stotel, Hannover
Steinkamp, Conrad	20, May 1886	29, Apr.	38		7	Elmore, OH	
Steinkamp, Frank	14, Mar. 1895	16, Jan.	73		174	Kansas City, MO	Blasheim bei Lübeke, Preußen
Steinkamp, Friedrich	23, Apr. 1865	26, Mar.	62- 5m-27d		68	Greenville, OH	Rechtensteth, Amt Hagen, Hannover
Steinkamp, Friedrich	20, July 1893	1, July	77		462	Huntingburg, IN	Venne, Osnabrück, Hannover
Steinkamp, Heinrich	12, Aug. 1872	24, July	82		263	Woodville, OH	Fenne bei Osnbrück, Hannover
Steinkamp, Heinrich Friedrich G.	6, July 1899	27, May	34		431	Salem, MN	Bünde, Germany

Christliche Apologete Death Notices --- 1839 - 1899

Name of Deceased	Notice Date	Death Date	Age	Page	Maiden Name	Place of Death	Place of Birth
Steinkamp, Herman	24, Nov. 1887	6, Nov.	40	750		Seymour, IN	Dudleytown, Jackson County, Indiana
Steinkamp, Johan Friedrich	27, Oct. 1879	8, Oct.	62	343		Woodville, OH	Venne, Amt Wittlage, Hannover
Steinkamp, Katharine	24, Mar. 1873	7, Feb.	27-11m- 7d	95	Battaglia	Liberty, MO	
Steinkamp, Louis Albert	3, May 1894	14, Apr.	25- 7m-30d	294		White Creek, IN	Wester-Kappeln, Preußen
Steinkamp, Maria	28, Jan. 1867	18, Dec.	51	30		Liberty, MO	
Steinkamp, Maria	14, Mar. 1895	24, Feb.	38	174		Huntingburg, IN	
Steinkamp, Maria Engel	24, July 1865	7, July	77	120	Topien	Woodville, OH	Venne, Amt Wittlage, Hannover
Steinkamp, Maria Engel	23, Apr. 1866	2, Apr.	19	134		Woodville, OH	Sandusky County, Ohio
Steinkamp, Minnie	5, June 1890	14, May	18- 7m-29d	366		White Creek, IN	
Steinkamp, Peter	9, Feb. 1863	28, Jan.		24		Woodville, OH	
Steinkampf, Charlotte	12, Nov. 1877	27, Oct.	79	367		Greenville, IN	Notel, Hannover
Steinke, Anna Emilie	7, Apr. 1884	10, Mar.	29- 5m- 5d	7		York, NE	Driesen, Preußen
Steinke, Friedrich	17, May 1888	1, May	72- 8m-24d	318		Sheboygan, WI	Schweiz, Marienwerder, Preußen
Steinko, Martha	29, Dec. 1892	28, Nov.	19	828		Blue Island, IL	Strahlsund an der Ostee, Pommern
Steinkrüger, Charles	14, July 1887	3, May	57	446		Petersburg, IL	Herford, Minden, Preußen
Steinkrüger, Julia	21, Apr. 1884	28, Mar.		7	Niemann	Petersburg, IL	Emmenhausen, Lippe-Detmold
Steinkrüger, Maria	25, Apr. 1870	4, Mar.	37	135		Petersburg, IL	Spengen, Westphalen, Preußen
Steinle, John	2, Feb. 1888	17, Jan.	63	78		Scranton, PA	Mittelbrunn, Goldorf, Württemberg
Steinle, Katharine	30, July 1896	9, July		495	Will	Scranton, PA	Hasenhof, Württemberg
Steinley, Rebekka	19, May 1884	3, May	22	7		Wyandotte, KS	
Steinmann, Henry	28, Apr. 1873	28, Mar.	55	135		Petersburg, IL	Zwischenbergen, Aurich, Ostfriesland
Steinmeier, Friedrich	12, July 1894	22, May	84	454		Burlington, IA	Lehmkulle, Lippe-Detmold
Steinmeier, Louise	5, Jan. 1863	7, Dec.	66	4		Jackson City, KS	Brakelsick am Schwalenberg, Lippe-Detmold
Steinmeier, Wilhelmina	4, Sept 1871	18, Aug.	80-11m-18d	287		Farmington, IA	Holzhausen bei Pirmont, Waldeck
Steinmetz, Conrad	20, Aug. 1896	76- 5m-28d		543		Muscatine, IA	Niedermellrich, Melsungen, Hessen-Kassel
Steinmetz, Elisabeth	22, Apr. 1897	3, Apr.	79	255	Stocke	Bridgeport, CT	Großanpach, Rheinpfalz Baiern
Steinmetz, Georg	30, June 1879	15, June	49	207		Chicago, IL	Waldkappel, Kurhessen
Steinmetz, John H.	9, Sept 1886	22, Aug.	25- 6m-17d	7		Muscatine, IA	
Steinmetz, Louis	17, Aug. 1899	3, Aug.	39	527		Long Island City, NY	Künbach, Baden
Steinmetz, Peter	22, June 1893	26, May	57	398		Keokuk, IA	Osthofen, Hessen-Darmstadt
Steinmeyer, Anna	24, Dec. 1891	1, Dec.	72	830	Stets	Wichita, KS	Hastadt bei Bremen, Germany
Steinmeyer, Carl (Mrs)	21, Jan. 1892		72- 8m-13d	46			
Steinmeyer, Conradine Louise	26, Oct. 1874	6, Oct.	63- 2m	343		Burlington, IA	Talle, Lippe-Detmold
Steinmeyer, Jobst Heinrich	7, Mar. 1895	6, Feb.	81	159		Clatonia, NE	Lockhausen, Hannover
Steinmiller, Margaretha	21, Oct. 1872	26, Sept	90	343	Sauer	Pomeroy, OH	Darmstadt, Hessen-Darmstadt
Steip, Maria Anna	29, Oct. 1891	8, Oct.	85- 9m- 4d	702	Walz	West Unity, OH	Lissingen, Württemberg
Steller, Emma Rebecca	17, Mar. 1887		29	174	Pepper	Schnectady, NY	Glenville, New York
Stelling, Carsten Nicolaus	24, May 1860	9, Feb.	43- 1m	84		San Francisco, CA	Dingen, Amt Dorum, Hannover
Stellmacher, Louisa	26, Mar. 1891	28, Feb.	77- 3m-24d	206	Zihm	Ripon, WI	Hitzdorf, Arnswalde, Preußen
Stellter, Christian	8, Nov. 1894	15, Oct.	71	726		Seymour, IN	Waldwischen, Braunschweig
Stellter, Margaretha	19, May 1873	10, Apr.	66	159		Chicago, IL	Duddenhausen, Hannover
Stellter, Wilhelmine Juliane F.	7, July 1892	11, June	60	430	Behrens	Seymour, IN	Waldwiese, Braunschweig
Stelten, Henrietta	18, Nov. 1878	10, Oct.	33	367	Kraft	Berea, OH	Eichenberg, Preußen
Stelz, Heinrich	19, Apr. 1880	29, Mar.	55	127		Wausau, WI	Ostheim bei Windecken, Kurhessen
Stelz, Louisa	8, Jan. 1891	18, Dec.	76	30	Krommüller	Louisville, KY	Oberamt Backnang, Württemberg
Stelzing, Paul	6, Jan. 1868	24, Dec.	56	6		Summerfield, IL	Rothenburg, Kurhessen

- 500 -

Christliche Apologete Death Notices --- 1839 - 1899

Name of Deceased	Notice Date	Death Date	Age	Page	Maiden Name	Place of Death	Place of Birth
Stelzriebe, Louise Christine	17, Nov. 1887	24, Oct.	29- 3m-24d	734	Krüger	Hoyleton, IL	Matzenbach, Rheinkreis Baiern
Stemler, Charlotte	13, Oct. 1892	14, Sept	90	654	Kuntz	Newport, KY	Ispringen, Pforzheim, Baden
Stemmler, Johan Georg	11, Oct. 1880	22, Sept	64- 7m-28d	327		New Knoxville, OH	Messershausen, Gerlachsheim, Baden
Stempel, Eva Gertraud	29, May 1876	9, May	44	175		Carrollton, MO	Jeffersonville, Sullivan County, New York
Stengel, Anna	18, May 1874	2, Apr.	24-10m-13d	159		Jeffersonville, NY	Kirchsembach, Mittelfranken, Baiern
Stengel, Catharine	2, Feb. 1874	20, Jan.	72	39		Saginaw, MI	Güntersberg, Pommern
Stengel, Ferdinand August	15, Nov. 1894	29, Oct.	27	742		Watertown, WI	Dannefels, Rheinpfalz Baiern
Stengel, Friedrich	16, Sept 1897	15, July	82	591		Jeffersonville, NY	Neulen, Baiern
Stengel, Friedrich	23, Feb. 1899	27, Jan.	73	127		Baltimore, MD	Jeffersonville, Sullivan County, New York
Stengel, Heinrich	29, Sept 1898	19, Aug.	44	623		Jeffersonville, NY	
Stengel, Maria	7, Apr. 1887	5, Mar.	36- 1m-25d	222	Pfeiffer	Jeffersonville, NY	Rafenstein, Pommern
Stengel, Wilhelm	22, May 1882	4, May	39	167		Watertown, WI	Maria, Ungarn
Stenzel, Martin	7, June 1888		62- 7m	366		St. Louis, MO	Lauffen am Neckar, Besigheim, Württemberg
Stephan, Andreas	4, Aug. 1898	5, July	68	495		Los Angeles, CA	Neuen Brunslahr, Hessen
Stephan, Anna Elisabeth	18, June 1891	27, May	72	398		Muscatine, IA	Burbach bei Saarbrücken, Preußen
Stephan, Carl	19, Jan. 1880	27, Dec.	79	23		Louisville, KY	Des Moines, Iowa
Stephan, Christine	24, Oct. 1870	2, Sept	21- 1m	343	Cassel	Warsaw, IL	Lembach, Weißenburg, Elsaß
Stephan, Daniel	8, Dec. 1853	19, Oct.	43	196		Defiance, OH	Altwid, RheinPreußen
Stephan, Friedrich Wilhelm	9, Aug. 1894	29, June	73	518		Quincy, IL	Görsdorf, Werth, Elsaß
Stephan, Georg	21, July 1859	9, July	76	116		Captina, OH	
Stephan, Georg	19, May 1884	1, May	43- 4m	7		Defiance, OH	
Stephan, Georg Friedrich	7, Sept 1868	30, July	74	287		Clarington, OH	Gerstdorf, Elsaß
Stephan, Johan	8, Jan. 1891	7, Dec.	60	30		Clarington, OH	Switzer County,
Stephan, Johan Michael	17, Feb. 1859	29, Jan.	78	28		Captina, OH	Görßdorf, Werth, Elsaß
Stephan, Johannetta	2, Feb. 1880	31, Dec.	66	39		German Creek, IA	Katzenellenbogen, Nassau
Stephan, John	26, Feb. 1877	6, Feb.	41	71		Bloomington, IL	Rautenhausen, Rodenburg, Kurhessen
Stephan, Karl	10, Nov. 1873	15, Oct.	43- -12d	359		Louisville, KY	Burbach, Preußen
Stephan, Karoline Rosa	16, Sept 1886	27, Aug.	24	7		Clarington, OH	
Stephan, Katharine Elisabeth	20, May 1867	14, Apr.	74	158	Walter	Clarington, OH	Gustdorf, Elsaß
Stephan, Louise	12, Nov. 1857	24, Aug.	42	184		Louisville, KY	Burbach bei Saarbrücken, Preußen
Stephan, Magdalena	9, June 1862	1, May	66	92		Cincinnati, OH	Bischofsheim, Baden
Stephan, Margaretha Maria	22, Aug. 1870	27, July	64	271	Dörr	Louisville, KY	Burbach bei Saarbrücken, Preußen
Stephan, Philipp	17, Apr. 1890	22, Mar.	79- 9m- 1d	254		Louisville, KY	Burbach, Saarbrücken, Preußen
Stephan, Rosina	15, May 1876	24, Apr.	41- 4m-26d	159	Wetzel	San Jose, CA	Sickenhausen, Reutlingen, Württemberg
Stephan, Sabine	24, Feb. 1879	28, Jan.	83- 6m-13d	63	Vogt	Clarington, OH	Görsdorf, Wörth, Elsaß
Stephan, Sarah	15, Jan. 1872	22, Dec.	33	23		Portsmouth, OH	Monroe County, Ohio
Stephan, Sarah Jane	13, Apr. 1899	6, Mar.	35	239		Wheeling, WV	Monroe County, Ohio
Stephann, Catharina Elisabeth	12, Oct. 1874	24, Sept	65- -24d	327	Wolf	Warsaw, IL	Beuern, Kreis Gießen, Hessen
Stephens, Christoph	27, Aug. 1866	1, July	63- 9m-19d	278		Warsaw, IL	Großenbuseck, Gießsen, Hessen-Darmstadt
Stern, Katharina	20, July 1899	2, July	48	463	Inboden	Allegheny, PA	Womrath, Koblenz, Germany
Stern, Charles	28, Jan. 1886	7, Jan.	14	7		Fond du Lac, WI	
Stern, Katharina	8, July 1886	17, May	33	7	Christnagel	Fond du Lac, WI	Washington, Wisconsin
Stern, Katharina	3, Aug. 1885	20, July	48- -26d	7	Münchdorf	Allegheny City, PA	Kurhessen
Stern, Katharina	17, Aug. 1885	20, July	48- -26d	7	Münzdorf	Allegheny City, PA	Kurhessen
Stern, Pauline	24, Jan. 1895	17, Dec.	26	62	Löffler	Cameron, MO	Clay County, Missouri
Sternberg, (Mrs)	27, Nov. 1876	4, Oct.	76	383	Rabe	Chester, IL	Luther, Neustadt, Hannover

Christliche Apologete Death Notices -- 1839 - 1899

Name of Deceased	Notice Date	Death Date	Age	Maiden Name	Page	Place of Death	Place of Birth
Sternberg, Dorothea Maria	25, Feb. 1892	1, Feb.	72	Neiemeyer	127	Chester, IL	Wölpe, Hannover
Sternberg, Friedrich	3, July 1890	16, June	68- 8m- 6d		430	Chester, IL	Wolpe, Hannover
Sternberg, John Friedrich	17, Feb. 1898	24, Jan.	39		111	Chester, IL	Randolph County, Illinois
Sternberg, Wilhelm	15, Apr. 1872		46- 5m-26d		127	Chester, IL	Nepker, Hannover
Sternemann, Maria	21, Mar. 1881	4, Feb.	64- 1m- 9d		95	St. Louis, MO	Canton Aargau, Schweiz
Sternke, Johanna Louise	15, Dec. 1873	19, Nov.	55	Siedow	399	Watertown, WI	Plönzig, Stettin, Preußen
Sternke, Wilhelmine	18, May 1899	26, Jan.	74	Krüger	319	Ft. Atkinson, WI	Plagow, Answalde, Preußen
Stets, Melusine	14, Apr. 1879	17, Feb.	67		119	Herman, MO	Lüneburg, Hannover
Stetter, (Mrs Georg)	4, Sept 1882	18, Aug.			287	Galena, IL	
Stetter, Georg	27, June 1895	9, June	76		414	Brush Creek, IA	Memmingen, Baiern
Stetter, Jakob	13, Sept 1869	11, Aug.	74-10m-23d		295	Poughkeepsie, NY	Steinbach, Backnang, Württemberg
Stetter, John	20, Oct. 1887	4, Oct.	65		670	Defiance, OH	Arlesried, Neuburg, Baiern
Stetzelberger, Margaretha	1, Apr. 1897	6, Mar.	72	Mayer	207	Rochester, NY	Neidenstein, Baden
Stetzler, Friedrika	24, Feb. 1859	10, Jan.	40		32	Woodville, OH	Sindholzheim, Baden
Stetzler, Rosina	24, Feb. 1859	5, Jan.	16		32	Woodville, OH	Sindholzheim, Baden
Steube, Anna Martha	3, Nov. 1873	9, Sept	72- 7m- 6d	Schmelz	351	Dayton, OH	Nausis, Amt Rotenburg, Kurhessen
Steube, Christoph	15, Mar. 1894	17, Feb.	68		182	Peoria, IL	Pferdsdorf, Sachsen-Weimar
Steuber, Johan Christoph	25, May 1885	28, Mar.			7	Newark, NJ	Enzklösterle, Neuenbürg, Württemberg
Steublein, Elisabeth	30, July 1891	8, June	59	Meyer	494	---, PA	Kirchdorf, Seftigen, Bern, Schweiz
Steuerwald, Ernst	5, Oct. 1899	7, Sept	20		639	West Bend, WI	Batavia, Sheboygan County, Wisconsin
Steuerwald, Magdalena	25, May 1885	25, Apr.	67- 4m-15d	Claus	7	Newburg, WI	Allwig bei Allzey, Hessen-Darmstadt
Steurer, Caroline	31, May 1880	7, May	17		175	New York City, NY	Melrose,
Steurer, Charles	9, Apr. 1866	19, Dec.	7		118	Melrose, NY	
Steurer, David	16, June 1873	2, June	40		191	Melrose, NY	
Steurer, Georg	3, Dec. 1866	27, July	69- 1m- 4d		390	Mt. Vernon, IN	Leutesheim, Baden
Steurer, Michael	6, Oct. 1873	22, Sept	50		319	Mt. Vernon, IN	Neumühlen, Amt Korck, Baden
Stevan, Mathilda Rebekka	25, June 1891	27, May	21		414	Clarington, OH	Leutesheim, Baden
Steve, A.M.	20, Sept 1855	2, Aug.	18		152	Chicago, IL	
Steward, Louise	28, Apr. 1887	15, Apr.	20- 4m-26d	Klußmeier	270	Big Spring, MO	Ansterdam, Holland
Stey, David	14, Apr. 1853	6, Nov.	1- 1m-13d		60	Defiance, OH	Montgomery County, Missouri
Stey, Immanuel	14, Apr. 1853	6, Oct.	13- 2m- 7d		60	Defiance, OH	
Stey, Samuel	14, Apr. 1853	30, Oct.	3- 3m- 6d		60	Defiance, OH	
Stich, Eva	22, June 1854	2, Mar.	32- 5m-18d	Beckel	100	Fond du Lac, WI	Heltersberg, Rheinkreis Baiern
Stich, Georg	9, Feb. 1893	12, Jan.	72		94	Cleveland, OH	Ergersheim, Ufenheim, Baiern
Stichmeyer, Heinrich	25, Feb. 1878	7, Feb.	73-11m		63	Hopewell, MO	Eidinghausen, Minden, Preußen
Stickler, Elisabeth	7, Aug. 1865	29, June	21	Kaiser	128	Danville, IL	
Stickler, Georg	23, Feb. 1880	21, Jan.	58		63	Danville, IL	Brettenfeld, Gerabronn, Württemberg
Stickmann, August A.	12, Nov. 1896	12, Oct.	29		734	Pittsfield, IL	Pittsfield, Illinois
Stickney, Maria Anna	31, Aug. 1899	15, Aug.	36	Herz	559	Charles City, IA	Mayville, Wisconsin
Stickrath, Paul	2, Apr. 1857	16, Mar.	60		56	Marietta, OH	Siebertshausen, Hessen
Stief, Anna	8, May 1865	17, Apr.	35	Thien	76	Freeport, IL	Gnägenbrücken, Hannover
Stiefel, (child)	24, July 1846	7, June	7m		119	Cincinnati, OH	
Stiefel, Lydia	20, Feb. 1896		32	Mack	126	Bucyrus, OH	
Stiefel, Wilhelmine Christine	24, July 1846	8, June	23-10m- 5d		119	Cincinnati, OH	Lylens Township, Crawford County, Ohio
Stiegelmeyer, Johanna	24, Mar. 1892	26, Feb.	79-11m- 2d	Spilker	191	Van Horne, IA	Hüssen, Bünde, Herford, Westphalen
Stiegelmeyer, Johanna	7, Apr. 1892	26, Feb.	79-11m- 2d	Spilker	222	Van Horne, IA	Hüssen, Bünde, Herford, Westphalen

Name of Deceased	Notice Date	Death Date	Age	Maiden Name	Page	Place of Death	Place of Birth
Stiegelmeyer, Jürgen H.	16, Apr. 1896	6, Mar.	88		254	Van Horne, IA	Werfen, Westphalen
Stieghorst, Heinrich Christoph	29, July 1872	20, May	65		247	Second Creek, MO	Lehmershagen, Amt Heepen, Preußen
Stiegler, Maria Elisabeth	2, July 1896	14, June	60	Wiegand	431	Louisville, KY	Nössel, Rede, Hessen-Kassel
Stieglitz, Elisabeth	18, Dec. 1856	1, Nov.	15- 1m-17d		204	Louisville, KY	Oberroßbach, Friedberg, Hessen-Darmstadt
Stieglitz, Johannes	3, Jan. 1889	18, Nov.	57		14	Newton, IA	Felsberg, Kassel, Kurhessen
Stiegmann, Dorothea	5, Aug. 1886	25, May	61	Pann	7	Berne, MI	Alt Pannekow, Mecklenburg-Schwerin
Stieh, Gottfried	10, Apr. 1882	2, Mar.	81- 4m-19d		119	Grove, NY	Webenheim, Rheinkreis Baiern
Stiehl, Elisabeth Philippine	20, Feb. 1882	27, Jan.	77- -25d	Brenner	63	Nashville, TN	Mersenheim, Homburg, Hessen
Stiehl, Ferdinand	13, Dec. 1869	31, Oct.	33- -17d		399	Mt. Vernon, IN	Meißenheim, Homburg, Hessen
Stiehl, Georg Daniel	10, July 1876	11, June	27		223	Montana, WI	Gottelsheim, Germany
Stiehl, Johan Heinrich	27, Dec. 1880	27, Nov.	66- 3m-15d		415	Fredericksburg, TX	Höringhausen, Hessen
Stiehl, Johan Philipp	11, Nov. 1878	16, Oct.	73		359	Mt. Vernon, IN	Lieberbach, Nassau
Stiehl, Johanna	5, Feb. 1891	5, Jan.	38	Kneese	94	Fredericksburg, TX	Fredericksburg, Gillespie County, Texas
Stiehl, Louise	9, Jan. 1865	13, Dec.	21-10m- 4d		8	Mt. Vernon, IN	Mt. Vernon, Posey County, Indiana
Stiehl, Maria	11, Apr. 1861	6, Mar.	13- 5m-27d		60	Mt. Vernon, IN	
Stiehl, Otto	20, Oct. 1898	4, Aug.	21		671	San Antonio, TX	Fryburg, Fayette County, Texas
Stiehl, Wilhelmine	26, Apr. 1888	23, Mar.	35	Velau	270	Garner, IA	Glasin, Mecklenburg-Schwerin
Stiehr, Anna Maria	22, Aug. 1895	20, July	60	Röver	542	Fond du Lac, WI	Lüneburg, Hannover
Stieler, Heinrich	21, Jan. 1886	31, Dec.	70		7	Baltimore, MD	Lobenhausen, Hessen-Darmstadt
Stienecke, Louise	11, Aug. 1898	24, July	27		511	Garner, IA	Detmold, Franklin County, Missouri
Stieneke, Wilhelm	23, Dec. 1886	2, Dec.	77- 1m-22d		7	Garner, IA	Ladbergen, Tecklenburg, Preußen
Stier, Elisabeth	8, Feb. 1894	10, Dec.	61	Schaul	94	Quincy, IL	Lorbach , Baden
Stier, Friederika	9, June 1859	20, May	39		92	Defiance, OH	Giesewold, Verliehausen, Hannover
Stier, John Georg	2, June 1862	29, Apr.	48		88	Defiance, OH	Eschelbronn, Kreis Neckar, Baden
Stierle, Anna	17, Mar. 1892	20, Feb.	66	Rohr	175	Rochester, NY	Hundsichwyl, Aargau, Schweiz
Stierle, Christina Catharina	25, Sept 1876	8, Sept	71- 9m-17d	Alber	311	DeWitt, MI	Untereichen, Stuttgart, Württemberg
Stierle, Johan Georg	14, Apr. 1879	1, Apr.	73- 6m		119	Dewitt, MI	Uneraichen, Stuttgart, Württemberg
Stierle, Samuel	28, Mar. 1889	1, Mar.	62		206	Rochester, NY	Reuß a. Reuß, Aargau, Schweiz
Stierlin, Bernhardt	24, Feb. 1887	31, Dec.	72		126	Cincinnati, OH	Schaffhausen, Schweiz
Sterling, Cora Elise	27, May 1897	9, May	16		335	Freyburg, TX	Grassville, Bastrup County, Texas
Stieß, Wilhelm Lorenz	2, Mar. 1899	2, Feb.	39		143	Cincinnati, OH	Dürmenz, Württemberg
Stiesus, Sophia	24, May 1894	25, Apr.	81	Wenthe	342	Kendallville, IN	Harmel, Hannover
Stigner, David	9, Oct. 1871	31, Aug.	62- 5m		327	Scranton, PA	Hannover, Pennsylvania
Still, Andreas	9, July 1896	26, May	72		447		
Stille, Heinrich	19, Mar. 1883	25, Feb.	47- 3m-28d		95	Garner, IA	Floto, Minden, Preußen
Stille, Herman Heinrich	17, June 1878	3, June	17- 8m-15d		191	Garner, IA	Warren County, Missouri
Stillon, Margaretha	21, Apr. 1884	5, Apr.	63	Hoppmann	7	Staunton, IL	Hohenmar, Aschendorf, Hannover
Stilz, Johan	20, Aug. 1891	24, July	70- 2m-17d		542	Edwards Co, IL	Langenthal, Keuznach, Koblenz, Preußen
Stilz, Anna M.	23, Oct. 1882	10, Oct.	35		343	Louisville, KY	Jefferson County, Kentucky
Stilz, Carolina Ernestina	28, May 1896	8, May	82	Dettmer	350	Louisville, KY	Lickwege, Oberkirchen, Hessen
Stilz, Charlotte	15, Dec. 1884	25, Nov.	66	Mai	7	Cannelton, IN	Sobernheim, Kreuznach, Preußen
Stilz, Christina	9, June 1884	24, May	60	Knödler	7	Louisville, KY	Beutelsbach, Württemberg
Stilz, Conrad	16, Oct. 1871	1, Oct.	49- 7m-19d		335	Charlestown, ---	Schnaith, Schorndorf, Württemberg
Stilz, Johan Gottfried	2, Jan. 1882	6, Dec.	33		7	Indianapolis, IN	Schnaith, Schorndorf, Württemberg
Stilz, Joseph	25, Sept 1851	20, Aug.	31		156	Louisville, KY	
Stilz, Maria Magdalena	22, Mar. 1888	24, Feb.	72- 2m- 6d	Metzger	190	West Salem, IL	Westheim, Germersheim, Rheinkreis Baiern

Name of Deceased	Notice Date	Death Date	Age	Maiden Name	Page	Place of Death	Place of Birth
Stilz, Melinda C.	22, Mar. 1894	24, Feb.	34		198	Louisville, KY	Louisville, Jefferson County, Kentucky
Stilz, Wilhelm F.	16, Feb. 1888	14, Jan.	34- 9m- 9d		110	Indianapolis, IN	
Stilz, Wilhelm Heinrich	10, Nov. 1884	23, Oct.	36		7	Louisville, KY	Charlestown , Indiana
Stingel, Christina	22, Mar. 1888	18, Feb.	67		190	Saginaw, MI	Laufen, Bahlingen, Württemberg
Stingel, Friederike Christine	16, June 1892	21, May	45	Neff	382	Saginaw, MI	Buffalo, New York
Stinnker, Henriette	19, Mar. 1877	8, Feb.	82	Jostmeier	95	Bucyrus, OH	Brachterbeck, Tecklenburg, Minden, Preußen
Stirzel, Charlotte Henriette	12, Dec. 1895	15, Nov.	81	Osterwald	798	Mankato, MN	Bretsch, Osterburg, Magdeburg, Preußen
Stirzel, Daniel	8, Aug. 1870	18, July	60		255	De Soto, MO	Sachsen-Meiningen
Stirzel, Leonhard	6, Apr. 1885	17, Feb.	40- 2m-26d		7	De Soto, MN	
Stirzel, Verena	8, Nov. 1860	25, Oct.	33		180	De Soto, MO	Conter, Graubündten, Schweiz
Stitzer, Maria	23, Feb. 1888	29, Jan.	42	Mathis	126	Stitzer, WI	Philadelphia, Pennsylvania
Stöber, Elisabeth	5, Feb. 1891	16, Jan.	73	Spas	94	Platteville, WI	Hoengeda bei Mühlhausen, Preußen
Stöber, Heinrich W.	24, May 1894	25, Apr.	83- 1m-14d	Lestemann	342	Charles City, IA	Allenhausen, Schwarzburg-Sondershausen
Stock, Andrew	24, June 1886	14, June	56		7	Lowell, WI	Massachuetts
Stock, Anna Margaretha	10, Sept 1896	28, July	20	Weinberger	591	Stryker, OH	
Stock, Anna Marie	11, May 1893	23, Apr.			302	Schnectady, NY	Lanzenhain, Hessen
Stock, Caroline Hannah	26, Mar. 1891	19, Feb.	64		206	Warren, MO	Egge, Hameln, Hannover
Stock, Heinrich	21, Feb. 1876	19, Jan.	17		63	Schnectady, NY	
Stock, Johan Georg	6, Oct. 1884	1, Sept	67		7	Schnectady, NY	Langenheim, Hessen-Darmstadt
Stock, Maria	17, Mar.1873	24, Feb.	81	Heins	87	Lowell, WI	Baiern
Stock, Maria	15, Dec. 1879	4, Nov.	17		399	Warren, MO	
Stock, Martha Johanna	23, Mar. 1893	23, Feb.	17		190	Lowell, WI	Lowell, Wisconsin
Stock, Peter	16, Mar. 1863	3, Feb.	68- 6m- 9d		44	Watertown, WI	Oberndorf, Obermorschel, Baiern
Stock, Wilhelm	9, Apr. 1891	9, Jan.	67		238	Truxton, MO	Bäsingfeld, Lippe-Detmold
Stockdieck, Heinrich	4, May 1854	17, Apr.	44		72	Newark, OH	Ladbergen, Tecklenburg, Preußen
Stockdieck, Maria	16, Oct. 1865	2, Oct.	75		168	Zanesville, OH	Ladbergen, Tecklenburg, Preußen
Stocke, Barbara	3, Sept 1866	15, Aug.	50- 6m		286	St. Louis, MO	Siebeldingen, Rheinkreis Baiern
Stocker, Anna	27, May 1886	24, Apr.	41	Esdorn	7	Saginaw, MI	Schwarme bei Bremen, Germany
Stöcker, Catharina	28, Oct. 1872	30, Sept	48		351	Oshkosh, WI	Schweiz
Stöcker, Georg	19, Feb. 1883	26, Jan.	22- 9m-26d		63	Saginaw, MI	
Stöcker, Ida	23, Aug. 1894	22, June	23- 9m-18d	Firkus	550	Bay City, MI	Bay City, Michigan
Stöcker, J. Heinrich	9, Nov. 1885	5, Oct.	77		7	Corder, MO	Buer, Grünberg, Hannover
Stocker, Magdalena	21, Dec. 1874	13, Nov.	80- - 4d	Burri	407	Cleveland, OH	Bollingen, Obersimmenthal, Bern, Schweiz
Stocker, Maria	21, Dec. 1885	21, Nov.	72		7	Saginaw, MI	Thalheim, Tuttlingen, Württemberg
Stockers, Maria	7, Dec. 1868	12, Nov.		Steffen	391	Bradford, IN	Lengerich, Tecklenburg, Münster, Preußen
Stockhofer, Johan Friedrich	13, Aug. 1877	14, July	73		263	White Creek, IN	Hannover
Stockhover, Johan Friedrich	16, Sept 1897	16, Aug.	48- 5m-28d		591	White Creek, IN	
Stockhover, Katharina Elisabeth	8, Sept 1887	26, July	69	Kreinhagen	574	White Creek, IN	
Stockinger, Katharina	27, Oct. 1892	3, Oct.	81	Beckmann	686	Batesville, IN	Engter bei Osnabrück, Hannover
Stocklausen, Johan	22, Mar. 1888	15, Feb.	74		190	Pittsfield, IL	Fusgenheim, Frankenthal, Rheinpfalz Baiern
Stocklausen, Margaretha	2, Aug. 1888	7, July	67		494	Pittsfield, IL	Weigensheim, Württemberg
Stöckle, Johanette	3, Feb. 1879	11, Dec.	57-10m	Noll	39	Brunswick, MO	Bauschlott bei Pforzheim, Baden
Stöckle, Johannes	6, May 1872	22, Mar.	62		151	Kendallville, IN	
Stöckly, Karl	19, Jan. 1863		20		12	Troy, NY	Waldhausen, Welzheim, Württemberg
Stöckly, Elisabeth	13, Sept 1894	28, July	89	Hild	598	Troy, NY	Gundelsheim, Baden
Stoetzel, Henry	24, Jan. 1881	23, Dec.	56		31	Valparaiso, IN	Bruchkobel, Hanau, Germany

Name of Deceased	Notice Date	Death Date	Age	Page	Maiden Name	Place of Death	Place of Birth
Stoffers, Johan Friedrich	15, June 1893	23, Mar.	61	382		Morris, MN	Schleswig-Holstein
Stoffregen, Johan Friedrich	17, Apr. 1865	2, Mar.	74	64		Jackson, MO	Salzdepfer, Amt Hildesheim, Hannover
Stoffregen, Johanna Maria	28, Feb. 1876	9, Feb.	78	71	Klages	Jackson Station, IL	Schlem, Lammspringe, Hannover
Stoffregen, Lydia	28, June 1880			207		St. Louis, MO	
Stoffregen, Lydia Margaretha	7, June 1880	9, May	20- 6m-15d	183		St. Louis, MO	Jackson, Missouri
Stoft, Lydia	29, Oct. 1891	30, Sept	17- 5m-25d	702		Omaha, NE	
Stöhlein, Susanna	2, Apr. 1896	1, Mar.	59	222		Baltimore, MD	Aschbach, Germany
Stöhler, Elisabeth	27, Jan. 1898	21, Dec.	69	63	Rezacher	Paterson, NJ	Wettingen, Aargau, Schweiz
Stöhr, Christian	15, Jan. 1866	11, May	71	22		New York, NY	
Stöhr, Margaretha	31, Aug. 1893	4, Aug.	68	558		Terre Haute, IN	Schrießheim, Baden
Stöhr, Rosine	15, Jan. 1866	28, Nov.	73	22		New York, NY	
Stöhrs, Pauline L.	27, Oct. 1883	25, Sept	59	686	Keinath	Jersey City, NJ	
Stok, Christian	21, Sept 1863	18, July	27	152		Perrysburg, OH	Kupferzell, Oehringen, Württemberg
Stoke, Henry Adam	3, Jan. 1895	9, Dec.	69	14		Pittsburg, PA	Groß-Karlbach, Rheinkreis Baiern
Stoke, Katharina	1, Nov. 1894	3, Oct.	71	710	Storck	Pittsburg, PA	waisenheim am Sand, Rheinkreis Baiern
Stökli, (Mr)	17, Mar. 1879	4, Mar.	67	87		Troy, NY	Gundelsheim, Baden
Stolberg, Johann Martin	17, Jan. 1845		Inquiry	11		St. Louis, MO	Türingen, Mühlhausen, Oberdorla, Preußen
Stoll, Anna Maria	7, July 1873	21, June	42	215	Lampert	Milan, IN	Mutterstadt, Rheinkreis Baiern
Stoll, Caspar	7, Mar. 1864	12, Oct.	47	40		Booneville, MO	Gutmadingen, Schaffhausen, Schweiz
Stoll, Catharina	11, Jan. 1894	18, Dec.	59	30	Traxel	Milan, IN	Viningen, Rheinkreis Baiern
Stoll, Christine	6, Apr. 1893	1, Mar.	67	222	Schmoll	Jerusalem, NY	Northeim, Brockenheim, Württemberg
Stoll, Elisabeth	25, Aug. 1887	18, July	45	542	Diehl	DeWitt, MI	Stark County, Ohio
Stoll, Florentine	29, Dec. 1873	2, Dec.	43	415		New Ulm, MN	Posen, Preußen
Stoll, Heinrich	8, Feb. 1869	27, Dec.	70	47		St. Louis, MO	Odenhausen, Grünberg, Hessen-Darmstadt
Stoll, Heinrich	11, Jan. 1864	17, Aug.	19- 6m-11d	8		West Cleveland, OH	Gautenbach, Amt Runkel, Nassau
Stoll, Jakob	12, Sept 1870	14, Aug.	57	295		New Ulm, MN	Posen, Preußen
Stoll, Johan Friedrich	7, July 1884	12, June	69	7		Detroit, MI	Pasenau, Mecklenburg-Strelitz
Stoll, Johan Martin	8, Oct. 1877		73- 6m	327		Milan, IN	Asbach, Mosbach, Baden
Stoll, Johanna	20, Apr. 1893	64- 9m-25d		254	Schulz	Milwaukee, WI	Wulgensien, Mecklenburg-Strelitz
Stoll, Johannes	29, Dec. 1873	3, Dec.	68- - 9d	415		Cleveland, OH	Scherz, Brugg, Aargau, Schweiz
Stoll, Juliana	24, Nov. 1873	3, Nov.	44- 7m-16d	375	Bertfin	Concordia, MO	Vollnitz, Posen, Preußen
Stoll, Kasper	9, Mar. 1899	3, Feb.	68	159		Lansing, MI	Scherz, Brüg, Schweiz
Stoll, Katharina Elisabeth	27, July 1899	30, June	74	479	Acker	Louisville, KY	Alberweiler bei Landau, Baiern
Stoll, Louise	7, Aug. 1865	8, May	13- -20d	128		Louisville, KY	
Stoll, Margaretha	16, Jan. 1890	15, Dec.	86- 1m-15d	46	Büchler	Milwaukee, WI	Laufahr, Aargau, Schweiz
Stoll, Margaretha	12, Jan. 1893	15, Dec.	53	30	Harbeck	Akron, OH	Oldenburg
Stoll, Maria	30, Mar. 1899	26, Feb.	48	207	Stoll	Woodville, OH	Osterfingen, Schaffhausen, Schweiz
Stoll, Maria	26, Sept 1889	27, Aug.	63- 1m	619	Frechtel	Woodville, OH	Fraukenberg, Baiern
Stoll, Maria	9, Feb. 1860	13, Jan.		24		Mascoutah, IL	
Stoll, Maria Dorothea	28, Jan. 1897	7, Jan.	44	63	Hufnagel	Bloomington, IL	Baiern
Stoll, Maria Elisa	7, Apr. 1859	14, Mar.	26	56		New Haven, CT	
Stoll, Maria Katharina	1, Oct. 1866	25, Aug.	45- 5m- 4d	318	Rank	Woodville, OH	
Stoll, Marie A.	1, July 1897	26, May	77	414		Schnectady, NY	Wehrstädten, Baden
Stoll, Philipp	20, Nov. 1851	22, Oct.	41	188		Brunswick, MO	Kochdorf, Württemberg
Stollberg, Anna	25, June 1866	23, Apr.	38	206		Toledo, OH	Bermbach, Amt Idstein, Nassau
Stollberg, Christel	19, July 1894	29, June	75	470		Toledo, OH	Frankenhausen, Schwarzburg-Rudolstadt

Christliche Apologete Death Notices — 1839 - 1899

Name of Deceased	Notice Date	Death Date	Age	Maiden Name	Page	Place of Death	Place of Birth
Stollberg, Friedrich	3, Nov. 1879	17, July	43		351	Lancaster, NY	Langensalza, Preußen
Stollberg, Johann Heinrich	6, Sept 1849	5, July	37- 6m-2d		144	Belleville, IL	Oberdürbau, Preußen
Stollberg, Maria E.	4, June 1896	13, May	58		367	Toledo, OH	
Stolle, Maria	29, Oct. 1866	4, Oct.	52		350	Golconda, IL	
Stoller, Samuel	22, Nov. 1894	23, Oct.	71		758	Bethany, OR	Rohrbach-Frutigen, Bern, Schweiz
Stollsteimer, Adam Fr.	30, Nov. 1885	14, Nov.	74		7	Ann Arbor, MI	Obereichen, Württemberg
Stollsteimer, Magdalena	16, June 1887	30, May	68	Armbruster	382	Ann Arbor, MI	Dettingen, Glatt, Hohenzollern
Stolß, Regina	17, June 1858	6, Mar.	69	Riehs	96	Louisville, KY	Brackenheim, Württemberg
Stolte, Franz	14, Jan. 1884	30, Dec.	84		7	Port Hudson, MO	Brokhagen, West Preußen
Stolte, Friedrich Ludwig	23, June 1898	26, May	21		399	Waco, TX	Wendhagen, Lippe-Schaumburg
Stolte, Herman	30, Dec. 1878	9, Dec.	63		415	Union, MO	
Stolte, Rudolph	15, Oct. 1883	28, Sept	59		335	Edwardsville, IL	Lengerich, Westphalen, Preußen
Stolty, Christina	14, Aug. 1876	9, July	71		263	Champaign, IL	Hannover
Stolz, Elisabeth	14, July 1887	1, July	65		446	Dayton, OH	Mehringen a. d. Filden, Stuttgart, Württemberg
Stolz, Elisabeth	2, Sept 1897	16, Aug.	57	Vetter	559	Louisville, KY	Philippsburg, Pennsylvania
Stolz, Friederike	16, Sept 1872	9, Aug.	70		303	Higginsport, OH	Möhringen, Stuttgart, Württemberg
Stolz, Friedrich	18, May 1899	25, Apr.	66- 9m		319	Waseca, MN	Mariendorf, Posen
Stolz, Georg	24, Feb. 1873	2, Feb.	35		63	New York City, NY	Koppenheim, Baden
Stolz, Henriette	18, Feb. 1867	4, Dec.	75-11m-20d		54	Wausau, WI	Kolberg, Preußen
Stolz, Isaak	19, June 1890	29, May	28		398	Dayton, OH	Möhringen a. d.Fildern, Stuttgart, Württemberg
Stolz, Jacob	9, Mar. 1863	27, Jan.	58		40	Bradford, IN	Columbia County, Ohio
Stolz, Johan	5, Sept 1870	2, Aug.	46- 2m		287	Williamsburg, NY	Hertenhausen, Weiers, Baiern
Stolzen, Margaretha	10, Mar. 1848	23, Feb.	47- 8m-16d		43	Pittsburg, PA	
Stolzenbach, Anna Katharina	24, Apr. 1882	7, Apr.	37		135	Pittsburg, PA	Pittsburg, Pennsylvania
Stolzenbach, Karl	5, Apr. 1880	19, Feb.	34-10m-22d		111	Mascoutah, IL	Homberg, Kurhessen
Stölzing, Friederike Louise	9, Apr. 1857	18, Sept	2- -10d		60	Boonville, IN	Rotenburg, Kurhessen
Stonweiler, Philipp	28, Nov. 1864	9, June	72		192	Terre Haute, IN	Birkenfeld, Oldenburg
Stör, Sophia	9, June 1859				92		
Storch, Adelheid	28, Dec. 1899	8, Dec.	72	Plagge	828	Cincinnati, OH	Dalves, Fürstenau, Hannover
Storch, Dietrich	11, Feb. 1884	26, Jan.	25- 7m-22d		7	Covington, KY	Germany
Storch, Ludwig H.	19, Feb. 1877	6, Feb.	15		63	Covington, KY	
Storck, Christina	6, Dec. 1875	18, Nov.	30- 5m-20d	Finck	391	Evansville, IN	Louisville, Jefferson County, Kentucky
Storck, Vinzens	2, Sept 1867	19, Aug.	56		278	LaCrosse, WI	Ober-Ebersdorf, Böhmen
Störing, Pauline	28, Dec. 1874	8, Nov.	23	Richter	415	Waterville, MN	
Stork, (boy)	24, July 1871	23, June	8m		239	Louisville, KY	
Stork, A. Wilhelm	21, June 1880	31, May	58- 1m-19d		199	Huntingburg, IN	Ladbergen, Tecklenburg, Preußen
Stork, Barbara	16, June 1898	29, Apr.	73	Miller	383	Edon, OH	Allerheiligen, Hessen-Darmstadt
Stork, Barbara	24, July 1871	26, June	29	Eberli	239	Louisville, KY	
Stork, Carl Eduard	21, Jan. 1884	30, Dec.	23		7	Evansville, IN	
Stork, Caroline	20, Nov. 1871	14, Oct.	16-11m- 9d		375	Warren, MO	
Stork, Dorothea	26, July 1875	26, June	35		239	Giddings, TX	Seehausen, Altmark, Preußen
Stork, Friedrich L.	11, Mar. 1897	7, Feb.	46		159	Huntingburg, IN	Dubois County, Indiana
Stork, Jesse K.	25, Aug. 1898	24, June	23		543	Huntingburg, IN	Evansville, Indiana
Stork, Johan Heinrich	24, Jan. 1889	2, Jan.	30		62	Evansville, IN	
Stork, Johannes	26, Nov. 1883	10, Nov.	62- 1m-17d		383	Edgerton, OH	Allerheiligen, Hessen-Darmstadt
Störk, Maria	29, June 1893	15, June	44	Weiß	414	Saginaw, MI	Rohrbach, Baden

Christliche Apologete Death Notices --- 1839 - 1899

Name of Deceased	Place of Birth	Place of Death	Maiden Name	Page	Age	Death Date	Notice Date
Stork, Phebe Teressia	Defiance County, Ohio	West Unity, OH		239	16	27, Mar.	15, Apr. 1897
Stork, Sophia	Ladbergen, Tecklenburg, Westphalen	Evansville, IN	Hölscher	46	63	30, Dec.	20, Jan. 1887
Stork, Sophia E.	Evansville, Indiana	Evansville, IN		206	32	12, Mar.	31, Mar. 1887
Störker, Clara Maria Elisabeth	Grüneberg, Bürer, Osnabrück, Hannover	Concordia, MO		7	51- 9m- 3d	18, Dec.	7, Jan. 1878
Störker, Maria	Markendorf, Germany	New Melle, MO	Pößer	607	80	17, June	22, Sept 1898
Storm, Albertine	Arensberg bei Treptow, Hinterpommern	Maine, WI	Woller	191	60	23, Apr.	11, June 1883
Storm, Johan	Zimdorsi, Pommern	Taegesville, WI		78	58	14, Jan.	30, Jan. 1896
Storm, Maria	Gützlaffshagen, Pommern	Maine, WI		142	46	8, Feb.	3, Mar. 1887
Storm, Peter	Borgsthagen, Pommern	Vandyne, WI		167	81	1, May	22, May 1882
Störmer, Henriette	Evansville, Indiana	Wichita, KS		95	15	14, Feb.	19, Mar. 1877
Stortz, Anna Maria	Steinbach, Backnang, Württemberg	Berne, MI	Oppen	766	61	6, Nov.	28, Nov. 1889
Stortz, Anna Maria	Freudenstadt, Württemberg	Berne, MI	Niebel	30	33	17, Dec.	11, Jan. 1894
Story, L.		Waco, TX		247		26, June	5, Aug. 1878
Störz, Wilhelm	hausen, Hessen-Nassau	Akron, OH		798	48	19, Nov.	10, Dec. 1891
Störzbach, Bennie		Burlington, IA		95	10- 8m-21d	8, Jan.	10, Feb. 1898
Stötzel, Amalie	Bafenhausen, Hohenhausen, Lippe-Detmold	Cedar Lake, IN	Rieke	72	36	9, Apr.	2, May 1864
Stötzel, Johan W.	Walpersdorf, Siegen, Westphalen	Chicago, IL		159	75	3, Feb.	7, Mar. 1895
Stough, Hannah		Sherrills Mount, IA		124	50	15, July	5, Aug. 1858
Stout, Maria	Württemberg	New York City, NY	Haar	351	45- 2m	9, Oct.	30, Oct. 1876
Strack, Auguste Charlotte		Hoboken, NJ		215	15- 4m-21d	10, June	5, July 1880
Strack, Caroline	Baiern	Tappan, NY	Heß	399	49	25, Nov.	11, Dec. 1882
Strack, Louis	Mittelfischbach, Nassau	Bland, MO		415	74	28, Apr.	25, June 1896
Strack, Margaretha	Worfelden, Hessen-Darmstadt	New Albany, IN	Hartmann	351	57	30, Mar.	3, June 1897
Strack, Maria Elisa	Steinsberg, Amt Diez, Nassau	Charlestown, IN		132	62	27, July	19, Aug. 1858
Strack, Peter	Mittelfrischbach, Nassau	Bland, MO		78	70	7, Jan.	31, Jan. 1889
Strack, Ph. Fr. Chr.	Mittelfischbach, Rastätten, Nassau	Brighton, IL		7	59	3, Oct.	9, Nov. 1885
Strack, Wilhelmine	Billerbeck, Amt Schieder, Lippe-Detmold	Gasconade Co, MO	Müller	191	43	10, Mar.	13, June 1870
Strackmann, Heinrich	Kudenhausen, Münden, Preußen	Lyons Creek, KS		303	45	24, Aug.	16, Sept 1872
Strähle, Christiane	OberLeuningen, Württemberg	Industry, TX		302	64	9, June	23, Sept 1867
Strähley, R.	Cincinnati, Hamilton County, Ohio	Cincinnati, OH	Oesper	622	52	2, Sept	29, Sept 1892
Strahley, Sophia Rosamunda	Wilerbrock, Stab Lorch, Welzheim, Württemberg	Cincinnati, OH	Bühner	39	66	14, Jan.	30, Jan. 1871
Straizer, Johanne	Guben, Preußen	Bloomington, IL		164	72		9, Oct 1865
Strak, Heinrich Peter		Charlestown, IN		295	15	29, Aug.	12, Sept 1870
Stram, Rosina	Zinalshofen, Kork, Baden	Swanton, NE	Ebs	718	42	14, Oct.	10, Nov. 1887
Strasburg, Louise Wilhelmina	Radewig, Stettin, Preußen	Wadena, MN	Zimmermann	191	60	1, June	16, June 1879
Straßburg, Friedrich	Sommerdorf, Pommern	Wadena, MN		7	73	14, Mar.	31, Mar. 1884
Straßburg, Lydia		Lexington, MO		95	2- 7m-15d	7, Mar.	24, Mar. 1879
Straßburg, Rosina	Untertürkheim, Württemberg	Louisville, KY	Kiefer	134	45- 5m-20d	10, Apr.	29, Apr. 1867
Straßburg, Sarah B.	Reading, Pennsylvania	Louisville, KY	Dißler	270	80	28, Mar.	23, Apr. 1896
Straßburger, Christina	Sandusky, Ohio	Edgerton, OH	Löhmann	351	27- 8m-19d	6, Oct.	1, Nov. 1869
Straßer, (Mr)	Guben, Kreis Guben, Preußen	Bloomington, IL		196	75-10m- 8d	8, Nov.	7, Dec. 1863
Straßer, Jakob	Nußbaumen, Thurgau, Schweiz	Toledo, OH		135	34		24, Apr. 1871
Strathmann, Arnold Carl	Salzufen, Lippe-Detmold	St. Louis, MO		158	69	24, Jan.	5, Mar. 1891
Strathmann, Caroline	Salzuflen, Lippe-Detmold	St. Louis, MO	Epmeier	142	71- 8m-20d	6, Feb.	1, Mar. 1888
Strathmann, Dorothea Henrietta	Gütersloh, Westphalen, Preußen	Dayton, OH	Barkey	127	61	12, Mar.	15, Apr. 1872
Strathmann, Gustav Adolph	Lippe-Detmold	Dayton, OH		39	35	9, Dec.	1, Feb. 1869

Christliche Apologete Death Notices -- 1839 - 1899

Name of Deceased	Notice Date	Death Date	Age	Page	Maiden Name	Place of Death	Place of Birth
Strathmann, Karl Adolph	20, Dec. 1880	22, Oct.	40	407	Maas	St. Louis, MO	Salzufeln, Lippe-Detmold
Strathmann, Mary	11, Dec. 1882	22, Nov.	56-11m	399		Hoboken, NJ	Ostfriesland
Strathmann, Sarah Josephine	9, Apr. 1891	20, Feb.	21	238	Schäper	Warren, MO	Indian Camp,
Stratmann, F.W.	29, Sept 1862	25, Aug.	35	156		Warren, MO	Spenge, Kreis Herford, Preußen
Strats, Christine	9, Feb. 1860	30, Jan.	35	24		St. Louis, MO	
Straub, Daniel	7, Aug. 1876	23, July	59	255		Red Wing, MN	Grötzingen, Nürtingen, Württemberg
Straub, Friederike	26, Jan. 1888	5, Jan.	71- 6m-19d	62	Hunt	Baltimore, MD	Reuß-Lobenstein
Straub, Karolina Gottliebin	9, June 1898	9, May	81	367	Kühnle	Lansing, MI	Komthal, Württemberg
Straub, Mathilde	11, Nov. 1878	25, Oct.	75	359		Goshen, IN	Virginia
Straub, Michael	8, Sept 1879	24, Aug.	74	287		Burlington, IA	Tschirschen, Graubünden, Schweiz
Straub, Roman	18, Jan. 1894	21, Dec.	88	46		Goshen, IN	Lenzkirch, Baden
Strauch, Johannes	28, Nov. 1895	3, Nov.	80	766		Clarington, OH	Busenborn, Hessen
Strauch, Maria	25, July 1861	14, July	21	120		Louisville, KY	Monroe County, Ohio
Strauk, Margaretha	10, Nov. 1892	27, Sept	33	718	Stelz	Milwaukee, WI	
Strauß, Charles	29, Dec. 1887	2, Dec.	19	830		Mt. Vernon, NY	
Strauß, Heinrich	28, Apr. 1879	6, Apr.	51	135		Chicago, IL	Göxe, Wennigsen, Hannover
Strauß, Peter	23, Mar. 1899	13, Feb.	70	191		New York City, NY	Müsenbach, Rheinkreis Baiern
Straußer, Elisabeth	14, Apr. 1879	19, Mar.	87-10m-26d	119	Steiger	St. Louis, MO	Canton St. Gallen, Schweiz
Strebel, Eva Barbara	11, Aug. 1892	6, July	72- 8m-15d	510	Eschenbacher	Arlington, MN	Frauenthal, Mergentheim, Württemberg
Strebel, Georg Adam	8, Sept 1898	17, July	80	575		Arlington, MN	Niedersteinach, Mergentheim, Württemberg
Strecker, Christian	26, July 1880	30, June	63- -13d	239		Warrenton, MO	Poppenweiler, Württemberg
Strecker, Christina	19, Dec. 1889	23, Nov.	74- 1m- 5d	814	Rau	Marietta, OH	Höfen, Waiblingen, Württemberg
Strecker, Johannes	22, Jan. 1891	30, Dec.	58	62		Marietta, OH	Rielinghausen, Marbach, Württemberg
Strecker, Katharina	13, June 1895	10, May	53	382	Lander	Marietta, OH	Fearing Township, Washington County, Ohio
Strecker, Sallie	11, Feb. 1886	22, Jan.	50	7	Kiefer	Hamilton, OH	Gersdorf, Elsaß
Streder, Peter	16, Mar. 1863	25, Feb.	26- 6m-25d	44		Monroe, IA	Villbach, Nassau
Streever, Heinrich F.	11, June 1896	18, May	76	383		Schnectady, NY	Eisberg, Minden, Preußen
Strehle, Louis	16, Feb. 1880	6, Nov.	51	55		Bloomington, IL	Kirchberg, Württemberg
Strehler, Auguste	17, Aug. 1893	28, July	70	526	König	Crow River, MN	Dombrowska, Posen
Strehler, Carl Ludwig	3, Aug. 1893	18, July	69	494		Crow River, MN	Klein-Saamoklius, Posen
Strehler, Louise	10, Mar. 1884	22, Feb.	44	7	Schrank	Montrose, MN	Romanshof, Posen
Strehlmann, Katharina	29, Mar. 1880	4, Mar.	71	103		Third Creek, MO	Bokost, Halle, Minden, Preußen
Strehlow, Ernestine	6, Apr. 1885	11, Mar.	68- 1m- 9d	7		Blumfield, WI	Lansbergerhollander, Brandenburg
Strei, Gottlieb	5, Mar. 1896	17, Feb.	60- 5m- 9d	158		Kenosha, WI	
Strei, Ottilie	18, Feb. 1897	2, Feb.	32	111	Fenske	Kenosha, WI	Bristol, Kenosha County, Wisconsin
Streicher, Gustav	6, June 1895	30, Apr.	36	366		Detroit, MI	San Francisco, California
Streicher, Juliana	26, Dec. 1861	29, Nov.	33- 8m- 7d	208		Detroit, MI	Langen-Steinbach bei Karlsruhe, Baden
Streicher, Sophie	15, June 1863	22, May	39- 4m- 7d	96	Kort	Detroit, MI	Schwerin, Mecklenburg-Schwerin
Streip, Christina	9, Feb. 1888	19, Jan.	24	94		Bucyrus, OH	
Streit, Christian	14, Feb. 1881	30, Jan.	72	55		Wausau, WI	Wolkow, Hinterpommern
Strelow, Karoline	1, Dec. 1887	3, Sept	56	766	Ewert	Wausau, WI	Neureisen bei Kolberg, Preußen
Stremel, Maria Elisabeth	23, June 1884	30, May	80- 4m	7		Almond, WI	Vitz, , Brandenburg
Stremmel, Friederika	22, Mar. 1880	22, Feb.	69- 6m- 5d	95	Feuring	Bucyrus, OH	
Stremmel, Georg	16, Feb. 1885	31, Jan.	51	7		Rushville, IL	Dillenburg, Nassau
Streng, Johan Wilhelm	16, Feb. 1860	30, Jan.	59- 5m	28		Columbus, OH	Daisbach, Baden
Streng, Susanna	2, Apr. 1877	28, Feb.	72	111		Columbus, OH	Deißbach, Baden

Christliche Apologete Death Notices -- 1839 - 1899

Name of Deceased	Notice Date	Death Date	Age	Page	Maiden Name	Place of Death	Place of Birth
Streßmann, Johan Friedrich	29, Dec. 1898	15, Nov.	80	828		Jerusalem, NY	Langworden, Oldenburg
Strey, Augustine	15, Mar. 1888		44- 2m-18d	174	Wedig	Crow River, MN	Lipjo, Pommern
Stricker, Bernhard	10, May 1869	15, Apr.	59- 2m-13d	151		Waverly, OH	Culte, Waldeck
Stricker, Bernhard	17, May 1869	15, Apr.	59- 2m-13d	159		Waverly, OH	Culte, Waldeck
Stricker, Rosina	13, Dec. 1880	31, Oct.	44- -21d	399	Bandel	Murray Co, MN	Unter-Uhrbach, Württemberg
Strickler, Margaretha	1, Oct. 1866	31, Aug.		318		Galion, OH	
Strickrott, Anna Maria	23, June 1879	3, June	62	199	Strauß	Waverly, OH	Niederbösa, Schwarzburg-Sondershausen
Strickrott, Christoph	18, Feb. 1886	27, Jan.	74	7		Chillicothe, OH	Frömstädt, Sachsen
Striebel, Joseph	4, Sept 1890	17, Aug.	37	574		Garner, IA	Saßbach, Achen, Baden
Striede, Philipine	17, Nov. 1859	22, Sept		184		Schnectady, NY	Eisbergen, Minden, Preußen
Striefler, David	24, Feb. 1873	30, Dec.	37	63		Buffalo, NY	
Strienz, Anna M.	21, Dec. 1893	30, Nov.	84	814	Roller	Greenville, OH	Oberjettingen, Württemberg
Strietelmeier, Maria Elisa	6, June 1870	17, May	51- 4m-21d	183	Büsenmeier	Cincinnati, OH	Lede, Tecklenburg, Münster, Preußen
Striethorst, Anna Maria	27, Oct. 1853	4, Oct.	31-11m-21d	172	Thimann	Lawrenceburg, IN	Sanheim, Hannover
Striethorst, Barbara	14, May 1896	13, Apr.	71	318	Schneider	Louisville, KY	Benzheim, Hessen-Darmstadt
Striethorst, Emma R.	9, June 1887	21, May	30	366		Louisville, KY	Lawrenceburg, Dearborn County, Indiana
Striethorst, Franz Wilhelm	8, Dec. 1892	6, Nov.	69	782		Lawrenceburg, IN	Hogel, Gröneberg, Hannover
Striffler, Anna	22, Mar. 1888	21, Feb.	30	190		Flood Creek, IA	Wien, Oesterreich
Striffler, Leonard	8, Dec. 1887	16, Nov.	54	782		Flood Creek, IA	Wörmutzhausen, Württemberg
Striffler, Maria Barbara	21, Sept 1885	25, July	71	7		Flood Creek, IA	Baiern
Stritemeyer, Friedrich	15, Sept 1859	29, Aug.	31	148		Warren, MO	Linnen, Warrendorf, Münster, Preußen
Strobel, Anna	24, May 1894		82	342	Max	Mound City, MO	Leopoldsgrün, Hof, Baiern
Strobel, Cosena Helena Friedrike	13, Oct. 1873	20, Dec.	41-11m	327	Brunken	Evansville, IN	
Strobel, Georg Jakob	24, Mar. 1873	23, Feb.	60	95		Lansing, MI	Oberrixingen, Vaihingen, Württemberg
Strobel, Helena	13, Oct. 1873	11, Sept	21- 6m-13d	327		Evansville, IN	
Strobel, Jakob Ludwig	10, Nov. 1892	12, Oct.	75	718		Evansville, IN	Zaberfeld, Brackenfeld, Württemberg
Strobel, John	4, June 1891	28, Apr.	68	366		Indianapolis, IN	Zauberfeld, Württemberg
Strobel, Maria Magdalena	29, Dec. 1892	10, Dec.	59	828		Indianapolis, IN	Philadelphia, Pennsylvania
Ströbel, Matthäus	21, Sept 1868	4, Sept	57	303		Jefferson City, MO	Ruzenmoos, Oesterreich
Strobel, Rosina	3, July 1882	16, Sept	28- 3m-14d	215		Evansville, IN	Vanderburgh County, Indiana
Stroben, Dorothea	5, Oct. 1874	16, Sept	63- 2m- 5d	319		Lansing, MI	Bissingen, Württemberg
Stroh, Elisabeth	11, Dec. 1882	20, Oct.	75- - 2d	399	Dürrstein	Brooklyn, NY	Eiwigheim, Baden
Stroh, Johan	13, Feb. 1896	23, Jan.	76	110		Warsaw, IL	Gabenheim, Preußen
Stroh, Katharine E.	3, June 1872	19, May	50	183	Dietsch	Buffalo, NY	Calw, Württemberg
Stroh, Sarah	29, Mar. 1860	3, Mar.	38	52		Auburn, IN	
Strohäcker, Balthasar	28, May 1896	20, Apr.	25	350		Logan, OR	Württemberg
Strohecker, Nikolaus	1, Apr. 1897	19, Feb.	65	207		Logan, OR	Unterferingen, Württemberg
Stroheker, Christine	4, Sept 1876	8, Aug.	47	287		Galveston, TX	Plieningen, Württemberg
Strohkirch, Wilhelm	16, Nov. 1893	4, Sept	64	734		Fosterburg, IL	Nochen, St. Vershausen, Nassau
Strohm, Eden L.	6, Aug. 1877	21, July	22	255		Newport, KY	Sellersville, Pennsylvania
Strohm, Franz	11, Sept 1890	16, Aug.	34	590		Cincinnati, OH	Freiburg, Baden
Strohm, John	30, Sept 1886	15, Sept	63	7		Freeport, IL	Aldingen, Speichingen, Württemberg
Strohm, Maria	5, Aug. 1872	26, June	48	255	Löb	Newport, KY	Gehaus, Sachsen-Weimar
Strohmann, Dorothea	16, Apr. 1896	10, Mar.	78	254	Hahn	Louisville, KY	Zeitlauf, Baiern
Strohmeier, Christina Eleonora	21, Jan. 1858	22, Dec.	87	12	Blanke	Pomeroy, OH	Niedernwöhren, Hagen, Lippe-Schaumburg
Strohmeier, Engel M. Dorothea	7, Oct. 1867	23, Aug.	69	318	Bartels	Cannelton, IL	Pohlhagen, Hagenburg, Lippe-Schaumburg

Christliche Apologete Death Notices --- 1839 - 1899

Name of Deceased	Notice Date	Death Date	Age	Page	Maiden Name	Place of Death	Place of Birth
Strohmeier, Gottlieb	6, Apr. 1868	25, Feb.	66- 2m	111		Cannelton, IL	Nordsehl, Lippe-Schaumburg
Strohmeier, Sophia	30, Mar. 1874	4, Jan.	35	103	Dahmer	Pomeroy, OH	Langenheim, Hessen-Darmstadt
Ströhmer, Friederika Carolina	4, May 1893	4, Apr.	75	286	Mielke	Fond du Lac, WI	Treblin, Rummelsburg, Germany
Strohmeyer, Fr.	22, Dec. 1884	17, Oct.	75	7		Rive County, KS	Lippe-Schaumburg
Strömberg, Uthilla	12, June 1856	20, May	51	96	Nilsen	Jefferson City, MO	Grammartstorp, Blekinge, Schweden
Strömer, Johan August	21,May 1883	29, Apr.	59	167		Fond du Lac, WI	Neuhof bei Treplin, Pommern
Strothmann, Hanna	12, Aug. 1878	21, May	70	255		Wapello, IA	
Strott, Lydia	13, Jan. 1898		70- 6m- 6d	31	Cogel	Galena, IL	Württemberg
Strott, Nicholas	21, Dec. 1893	1, Dec.	78	814		Galena, IL	Hannau, Hessen-Kassel
Strott, Nikolaus	8, Sept 1848		Inquiry	147		Pittsburg, PA	
Strott, Wilhelm Nast	29, Sept 1879	13, Sept	30- 5m	311		Galena, IL	
Strub, J. Rudolph	25, May 1893	1, May	74	334		Toledo, OH	Läufelfingen, Baselland, Schweiz
Strübe, Karl	20, Jan. 1853	7, Jan.	2- 6m- 3d	12		Schnectady, NY	
Strubler, Barbara	22, Feb. 1875	26, Jan.	79	63		Chicago, IL	Sundhausen, Elsaß
Strubler, Fr.	23, Oct. 1865	27, Sept	65	172		Wheeling, IL	
Struchen, Eduard	5, Oct. 1885	9, Aug.	15- 1m- 6d	7		Evansville, IN	
Struchtenmeier, Dorothea	24, Jan. 1876	26, Dec.	55	31	Hoßmann	Warrenton, MO	Lemgo, Lippe-Detmold
Struckmann, Wilhelm	14, July 1862	2, June	20- 3m	112		Milan, IN	
Struckmeyer, Anna Rosina	10, Apr. 1882	13, Mar.	56	119	Fuhrmann	Wabasha, MN	Herdersdorf, Schlesien, Preußen
Structmeyer, August	17, Jan. 1889	23, Dec.	47	46		Clatonia, NE	Obernkirchen, Rindeln, Hessen
Strunk, Anna Margaretha	6, Aug. 1896	17, July	74	511	Seng	Peoria, IL	Oberjossa, Hessen-Nassau
Strunk, F.C. Chr.	25, Feb. 1892	12, Dec.	67- 3m-16d	127		Peoria, IL	Belle, Lippe-Detmold
Strüwe, Lena	6, Feb. 1896	18, Dec.	16	94		Beaufort, MO	Port Hudson, Missouri
Stubaus, Andreas	21, Feb. 1889	1, Feb.	22	126		Baraboo, WI	Westfield, Wisconsin
Stubaus, Peter	20, Feb. 1890	26, Jan.	82- 3m-23d	126		Baraboo, WI	Hessen-Darmstadt
Stubbe, Johan Wilhelm	26, Nov. 1896	14, Oct.	75	766		Berlin, WI	Klein Lups, Posen
Stüber, Anna Maria	20, Aug. 1866	5, Aug.	58	270	Unrath	Evansport, OH	Reimersweiler, Schorndorf, Württemberg
Stuber, Catharina	20, Feb. 1871	4,Feb.	31- 6m	63	Naumann	Edgerton, OH	Mittel Seemen, Nidda, Hessen-Darmstadt
Stüber, Christina	6, Mar. 1856	1, Feb.	39	40		Evansport, OH	Vonzuhoff, Württemberg
Stüber, Johan Georg	22, Sept 1887	20, Aug.	72- 5m-17d	606		West Unity, OH	Weiler Walchems, Backnang, Württemberg
Stüber, Ludwig	7, Nov. 1864	1, Sept	22	180		Defiance, OH	Waldrems, Backnang, Württemberg
Stübich, Lena	14, Dec. 1885	27, Nov.	35	7	Marschal	Sandusky, OH	Sandusky, Ohio
Stucke, Carl Heinrich	18, Apr. 1895	22, Mar.	76	254		Indianapolis, IN	Minden, Preußen
Stückemann, Morris	27, Apr. 1874	8, Apr.	2- 8m	135		Jacksonville, IL	
Stuckenbröker, Magdalena	27, Oct. 1873	27, May	18	343		Second Creek, MO	
Stücker, Karolina	4, Feb. 1886	17, Jan.	62	7	Berson	Louisville, KY	Tiefenbach, Lützenstein, Elsaß
Stückler, Katharina	26, Oct. 1899	29, Sept	76	687	Seibel	Chicago, IL	Oberfelden, Hannau, Kurhessen
Stucky, Christian	26, May 1884	29, Apr.	76	7		Elizabeth, NJ	Murmos, Worb, Bern, Schweiz
Stucky, Christina	1, May 1890	10, Apr.	81-10m-18d	286	Lentz	Elizabeth, NJ	Bicklau, Bern, Schweiz
Studheid, Metta Margaretha	14, July 1873	25, June	85	223	Niehaus	---, IA	Rehden, Diepholz, Preußen
Stuehr, Fr.	26, July 1888	5, July	57	478		Cleveland, OH	Gehrden, Hannover
Stüffe, Dorothea	18, Aug. 1879	29, July	64- 9m-15d	263		Allegheny City, PA	Niedersachswerfen, Hohenstein, Hannover
Stuhaus, Sophie	9, Feb. 1874	21, Jan.	68	47		Baraboo, WI	Gundenhausen, Hessen-Darmstadt
Stuhl, Rudolphine	17, May 1894	8, Feb.	76	326		Sidney, KS	
Stühmeier, Maria Elisabeth	5, Dec. 1895	13, Nov.	75	782	Meier	Pinckney, MO	Eidinghausen, Minden, Preußen
Stühmeyer, Heinrich	11, Mar. 1878	7, Feb.	73-11m	79		Hopewell, MO	Eidinghausen, Minden, Preußen

Christliche Apologete Death Notices --- 1839 - 1899

Name of Deceased	Notice Date	Death Date	Age	Page	Maiden Name	Place of Death	Place of Birth
Stuhr, Joachim	13, Apr. 1899	25, Mar.	60- 2m-18d	239		Wrayville, IL	Breddorf, Hannover
Stührmann, Anna	21, Mar. 1895	22, Jan.	74	190	Bäschen	Santa Claus, IN	Altendorf, Grünenberg, Hannover
Stührmann, Johan	6, Dec. 1875	10, Nov.	60	391		Santa Claus, IN	Oldendorf, Amt Zesen, Hannover
Stührmann, Johan	10, Jan. 1876	10, Nov.	60	391		Santa Claus, IN	Metemien, Mecklenburg-Strelitz
Stuht, Friedrich	5, Aug. 1872	5, July	56	255		East Troy, WI	Diemen, Germany
Stuht, Rudolphine	15, Mar. 1894	8, Feb.	76	182	Toms	East Troy, WI	
Stükemann, Catharina	1, Mar. 1855	12, Jan.		36	Knopp	St. Joseph, MO	
Stukenbröker, Friedrich W.	21, July 1898	4, July	84	463		Bland, MO	Wulfer, Schöttmar, Lippe-Detmold
Stukenbröker, Helena	21, Jan. 1892	30, Dec.	50	46	Amlick	Owensville, MO	Bahntrop, Lippe-Detmold
Stükenholz, Friedrich August	26, Dec. 1895	25, Nov.	64	828		Nebraska City, NE	Herford, Westphalen
Stulken, Dietrich	25, Jan. 1869	26, Dec.	68	31		Edwardsville, IL	Kummifade, Amt Vrrel, Oldenburg
Stullken, Caroline	23, Sept 1886	11, Sept	55	7	Smith	Edwardsville, IL	Marienhagen, Böhl, Hessen-Darmstadt
Stullken, Johan	2, Mar. 1885	16, Feb.	58	7		Edwardsville, IL	Fordel, Oldenburg
Stullken, Katharina	23, Nov. 1874	8, Nov.	36- 8m-10d	375	Schmidt	Edwardsville, IL	Martenhagen, Böhl, Hessen-Darmstadt
Stullken, Margaretha	28, Apr. 1879	12, Apr.	78- 8m- 2d	135		Nashville, IL	Wieselstedte, Oldenburg
Stullken, Otto	27, Feb. 1896	21, Jan.	19	143		Bison, KS	Nokomis, Illinois
Stultz, Maria Elisabeth	9, Sept 1897	21, June	85	575		New York City, NY	Kippenheim am Rhein, Baden
Stulz, Johan Jakob	22, Dec. 1892		72	814		Enterprise, KS	Schmieheim bei Lahr, Baden
Stumberg, Aletta	21, Mar. 1870	2, Mar.	38	95		Pekin, IL	Riesum, Amt Emden, Ostfriesland
Stump, Daniel	20, May 1897	3, May	64	319		Galion, OH	Pennsylvania
Stump, Klara	15, June 1899	30, May	20	383		Galion, OH	
Stump, Martin	5, Jan. 1880	18, Dec.	74- 9m- 9d	7		Galion, OH	Betzingen, Reutlingen, Württemberg
Stumpe, Adolf	30, June 1862	11, June	13	104		Decatur, IL	
Stumpe, Caspar Henry	23, June 1862	7, June	24-11m	100		Decatur, IL	
Stumpe, Louise	21, Nov. 1861	6, Nov.	14- 7m-10d	188		Decatur, IL	
Stumpf, Adam	30, Oct. 1871	6, Oct.	41- -12d	351		Petersburg, IL	Schrecksbach, Ziegenheim, Kurhessen
Stumpf, Andreas	25, June 1891	4, June	59- 8m- 4d	414		Buffalo, NY	Unter-Schwarzach, Baden
Stumpf, Catharina Barbara	31, July 1865	13, June	58	124		Red Wing, MN	Mark Selbitz, Baiern
Stumpf, Johan Georg	14, Jan. 1897	20, Dec.	71	31		Buffalo, NY	Unterschwarzach, Baden
Stumpf, Karl	15, June 1854	24, May	31- 9m	96		Portsmouth, OH	Würzburg, Baiern
Stumpf, Karl Johan	18, Nov. 1886	22, Oct.	84	7		Red Wing, MN	Bruck, Hof, Baiern
Stumpf, Katharina	4, Aug. 1892	14, July	29	494	Rummer	Bischof, IL	Handschuchsheim, Baden
Stumpf, Margaret	14, Nov. 1895	26, Oct.	27	734		Buffalo, NY	Buffalo, New York
Stumpf, Philipp Ernst	2, Mar. 1863	11, Feb.	23- 3m	36		Red Wing, MN	Bruck, Baiern
Stumpf, Sophia	5, Oct. 1899	2, Sept	66	639	Meier	Buffalo, NY	Eschenfelden, Baiern
Stumpfmeyer, Conrad	4, Feb. 1897		72	79		Cincinnati, OH	Fürth, Baiern
Stumph, Elisabeth	21, Sept 1863	6, Sept	43	152		Indianapolis, IN	Arnsheim, Kreis Alsfeld, Hannover
Stünkel, Heinrich D.	1, Jan. 1877	5, Dec.	69	7		Concordia, MO	Schwarmstedt, Bissendorf, Hannover
Stünkel, Rebekka	12, Feb. 1866	24, Jan.	49	54		Freedom, MO	Schwormstedt, Bissendorf, Hannover
Sturhahn, Christine Friedrike	21, Nov. 1895	1, Nov.	66	750	Busekrus	Seymour, IN	Waldorf, Westphalen
Sturm, Elisabeth	20, Feb. 1871	29, Jan.	59- 2m-27d	63	Baumann	Enterprise, KS	Annweiler, Rheinkreis Baiern
Sturm, Lina Barbara	15, June 1893	29, May	15	382		Berne, MI	Hüsingen, Baden
Sturm, Maria	30, Jan. 1890	6, Jan.	61	78	Eckelkam	Lincoln, NE	Lahr, Hannover
Sturm, Mary	29, Jan. 1891	17, Dec.	20	78		Evansville, IN	
Stürmer, Heinrich	3, Nov. 1862	24, Sept	28	176		Lyona, KS	Schlierbach, Frißlar, Kurhessen
Stürmer, Johanna	21, Nov. 1881	30, Oct.	47- - 4d	375	Günther		Schönfeld, Amt Ferchow, VorPommern

Christliche Apologete Death Notices --- 1839 - 1899

Name of Deceased	Notice Date	Death Date	Age	Page	Maiden Name	Place of Death	Place of Birth
Stürmer, Louisa	26, Apr. 1894	6, Apr.	52	278	Witte	Elkton, SD	Petznick, Piritz, Preußen
Stürnagel, Clara	20, Apr. 1893	21, Mar.	17	254		Belleville, IL	Belleville, Illinois
Sturtz, Anna Maria	25, May 1893	29, Mar.	21	334	Behnke	Chicago, IL	Chicago, Cook County, Illinois
Sturtz, Gottlieb	15, May 1846		Inquiry	79		St. Louis, MO	
Stüssi, Johan Jakob	11, May 1899	19, Apr.	58	302		Cameron, MO	Linththale, Glarus, Schweiz
Stüßy, Andreas	19, Apr. 1869	30, Mar.	63- 3m-18d	127		Allegheny City, PA	Riedern, Glarus, Schweiz
Stute, Ernst Herman Friedrich	15, July 1886	30, June	35	7		Industry, TX	Schleptrup, Bersenbrück, Germany
Stuter, Maria Elisa	23, Apr. 1865	29, Mar.	27- 5m-22d	68	Kaufmann	Cleveland, OH	
Stutheit,	5, Apr. 1894			230	Spellmann		Ohio
Stutheit, Caroline Louise	29, June 1893	6, June	68	414	Mörker	Lincoln, NE	
Stutheit, H. W.	4, Aug. 1898	5, July	74	495		Kramer, NE	Hannover
Stutt, Wilhelm	26, May 1848		Inquiry	87		St. Louis, MO	
Stutz, (Mrs)	20, Feb. 1862	25, Jan.	68- -14d	32		Red Bud, IL	
Stutz, Christine	27, July 1899	10, June	81	479	Ladwig	Marientte, WI	Sulz am Neckar, Württemberg
Stutz, Jacob	5, Feb. 1877	10, Jan.	61	47		Pinckneyville, IL	Zollnick, Marienwerder, West Preußen
Stutz, Margaretha	28, June 1875	12, June	54	207	Schad	Pinckneyville, IL	Sulz am Neckar, Württemberg
Stutzmann, Annie	17, Nov. 1892	2, Aug.	30	734		Washington, MN	Südmarswangen, Sulz, Württemberg
Stutzmann, Katharina	4, Sept 1865	29, July	36- 5m	144		St. Paul, MN	Woodbury, Washington County, Minnesota
Stutzmann, Peter	19, Dec. 1870	3, Dec.	82	407		St. Paul, MN	
Stüwe, Dorothea Henr. Georgine	30, June 1892	9, June	14	414		Stevens Point, WI	Steinbach, Kreis Wendel, Preußen
Stüwe, Friedrich	28, Oct. 1878	21, Sept	64- 3m- 2d	343		Fond du Lac, WI	Osceola, Fond du Lac County, Wisconsin
Stüwe, Johanna Sophia Caroline	22, Sept 1884	3, Sept	68	7		Fond du Lac, WI	
Sucher, Katharina	27, Oct. 1859	5, Oct.	45	172	Kurz	Defiance, OH	Kraak, Mecklenburg-Schwerin
Sudbrock, Casper Heinrich	23, June 1892	2, June	79	398		Davenport, IA	Waldrems, Backnang, Württemberg
Sudbrock, Franz H.	27, Oct. 1892	3, Oct.	59	686		New Melle, MO	Hannover
Sudbrock, Kasper	7, Sept 1893	15, July	77	574		Belleville, IL	Buer, Melle, Hannover
Sudbrock, Katharina	4, Dec. 1876	16, Nov.	61- 1m-14d	391	Weseler	San Jose, IL	Borninghausen, Lübeck, Preußen
Sudbrock, Klara Maria	20, June 1861	30, May	39	100	Marting	Furnace, OH	Holsen, Bünde, Preußen
Sudbrock, Lidya	8, Sept 1892		16- - 5d	574		New Melle, MO	Oldendorf, Amt Melle, Hannover
Sudbrük, Cl. Elisabeth	7, Feb. 1889	11, Jan.	60	94	Hamburger	New Melle, MO	
Südmeier, Maria	26, May 1853	31, Mar.	28	84		Warren, MO	Melle, Hannover
Südmessen, Catharina Maria	1, July 1886	14, June	72	7	Trampe	Warren, MO	Hille, Preußen
Sugg, Ursula	24, Oct. 1870			343	Tobler	Wabasha, MN	Osnabrück, Hannover
Suhmutzler, Sophia	12, Aug. 1897	17, July	67	511	Orlaminder	Watertown, WI	Schönengrund, Appenzell, Schweiz
Suhr, Dorothea Johanna	30, Sept 1897	30, Aug.	19	623		Rochester, NY	Oedersdorf, Elsaß
Suhre, Katharina	18, Mar. 1878	6, Feb.	75	87		St. James, NE	Bremen, Germany
Suhre, Lisette	13, Nov. 1851	17, Oct.	17- 9m- 9d	184		Warren, NE	Lienen bei Osnabrück, Hannover
Suhree, Katharina	4, Mar. 1878	6, Feb.	75	71		St. James, NE	Lienen, Tecklenburg, Preußen
Sullivan, Maria Caroline Johanna	9, Jan. 1890	18, Dec.	27	30	Koch	Quincy, IL	Bienen bei Osnabrück, Hannover
Sulzer, Elisabeth	17, Mar. 1884	24, Feb.	46	7	Brück	Galion, OH	Galion, Ohio
Summermeier, Wilhelmine	11, Mar. 1858	16, Feb.	49- 2m-14d	40		Ripley, OH	Western-Cappeln, Preußen
Sumner, Charles	23, Mar. 1874		63	95			Boston, Massachuetts
Sumnicht, Louise	16, June 1879		23	191	Lange	Lowell, WI	
Sump, Wilhelmine	4, Feb. 1897	16, Jan.	58	79	Heiden	Duncan, NE	Großennamroh, Mecklenburg-Strelitz
Sund, Maria	16, Nov. 1885	16, Oct.	78	7		Harrison, KS	Papenhagen, Pommern
Sundermann, (Mrs)	10, June 1886	25, May	50	7		Colesburg, IA	Dalum, Bippen, Hannover

Christliche Apologete Death Notices --- 1839 - 1899

Name of Deceased	Notice Date	Death Date	Age	Maiden Name	Page	Place of Death	Place of Birth
Sundermann, Anna Elisabeth	4, Mar.1872	7, Feb.	65	Kuck	79	Le Sueur, MN	Ladbergen, Tecklenburg, Preußen
Sundermann, Carolina Sophia L.	20, Mar. 1890	22, Feb.	51	Müller	190	Crown Point, IN	Huxol, Hohenhausen, Lippe-Detmold
Sundermann, Friedrich	18, May 1863	20, Mar.	19		80	Peru, IL	Hohnhausen, Lippe-Detmold
Sundermann, J. Herman Heinrich	23, July 1896	1, July	67		479	Colesburg, IA	Dalum, Bippen, Fürstenau, Hannover
Sundermann, Sophia	18, May 1863	30, Mar.	35	Stock	80	Peru, IL	Hohnhausen, Lippe-Detmold
Sundermann, Wilhelmine	1, Aug. 1881	28, June	83		247	Jerusalem, IA	Bavenhausen, Hohenhausen, Lippe-Detmold
Sundermeier, Friederike	29, Dec. 1879	14, Dec.	14- 7m		415	Morrison, MO	
Sünkel, (Mr)	4, June 1866	4, May	75		182	Union, MO	Lippe-Detmold
Sünkel, Karl Friedrich Wilhelm	2, Sept 1897	8, Aug.	57		559	St. Louis, MO	
Süpfle, Elisabeth	31, Dec. 1877	15, Dec.	82	Bauer	423	Walburg, IN	Schwarzenberg, Neuenbürg, Württemberg
Supper, Anna Maria	23, Mar. 1868	3, Mar.	46	Siegele	95	Detroit, MI	Münchingen, Leonberg, Württemberg
Surbek, Nanette	6, Oct. 1884	21, Aug.	21		7		Oberhallau,
Süß, Herman	27, Jan. 1898	6, Jan.	55		63	San Diego, CA	Schwarzenberg, Sachsen
Süß, Philippine	17, May 1894	20, Apr.	52		326	Minneapolis, MN	Graben, Baden
Sussick, Friedrich Wilhelm	14, Nov. 1889	6, Oct.	43- 9m-14d		734	Newark, NJ	Herford, Westphalen
Sussick, Friedrich Wilhelm	28, Nov. 1889	6, Oct.	44		766	Newark, NJ	Herford, Westphalen
Suter, John	14, Mar. 1881	9, Feb.	51-10m-14d		87	Hannibal, OH	Monroe County, Ohio
Suter, Maria Mag.	15, Nov. 1888	25, Oct.	54- 4m-20d	Walter	734	Allegheny City, PA	Schaffhausen, Schweiz
Sutherland, Ella	30, July1883	27, June	26	Rensinhausen	247	Allegan, MI	Allegan, Michigan
Sutro, Elisabeth	2, Oct. 1865	11, Sept		Merz	160	Indianapolis, IN	
Sutter, Abraham	23, Nov. 1863	13, Aug.	19		188	Baresville, OH	Monroe County, Ohio
Sutter, Christine	19, Dec. 1881	1, Dec.	31	Preiß	407	St. Louis, MO	St. Louis County, Missouri
Sutter, D.	22, Feb. 1849	26, Jan.	49		32	Buckhill, OH	Schweiz
Sutter, Elisabeth	1, Jan. 1883	4, Dec.	80	Kaiser	7	McGregor, IA	Canton Aargau, Schweiz
Sutter, Gottfried	13, Nov. 1876	20, Oct.	52		367	Swanville, NE	Imbegoven, Kreis Bonn, Preußen
Sutter, Jacob	28, Oct. 1867	15, Oct.	20		342	St. Louis, MO	
Sutter, Johan	28, Apr. 1898	29, Mar.	92		271	Giard, IA	Kanton Bern, Schweiz
Sutter, Johan Samuel	21, Sept 1893	4, Sept	71		606	Altamont, IL	Baren, Bern, Schweiz
Sutter, John	2, Dec. 1867	21, Nov.	52- 8m-19d		382	St. Louis, MO	Altenheim, Baden
Sutter, Katharine	1, Apr. 1897	13, Mar.	67	Kilian	207	St. Louis, MO	Wallrode, Melsungen, Kurhessen
Sutter, Magdalena	15, July 1867	28, June	75		222	Allegheny City, PA	Rugelsried, Bern, Schweiz
Sutter, Rosina	10, Sept 1896	15, Aug.	70- 7m	Sträuli	591	Houston, TX	Wedenschweil, Schweiz
Sutter, Salomon	30, Mar. 1863	22, Dec.	23		52	Batesville, OH	Monroe County, Ohio
Sutter, Ursula	13, Nov. 1856	16, Oct.	36	Anselm	184	St. Louis, MO	Altenheim am Rhein, Germany
Sütterlin, Anna Maria	24, Mar. 1892	8, Feb.	83- 6m	Weler	191	Steuben Co, IN	Buggingen, Baden
Sütterlin, Minna	14, Apr. 1898	11, Mar.	51	Meyer	239	Graham, MO	St. Louis, Missouri
Süwer, Adam Heinrich	24, Sept 1877	3, Sept	75- 4m		311	Salem, MN	Brackhausen, Amt Witlage, Hannover
Swahlen, Christian	27, May 1872	29, Apr.	76		175	Boonville, IN	Wahlem, Schwarzenburg, Bern, Schweiz
Sweney, Maria A.	4, Nov. 1878	9, Oct.	64- 8m-12d		351	Warrenton, MO	Oberkirchen, Baden
Swieter, Warner	18, Aug. 1898	28, July	32		527	Pasadena, CA	Hannover
Swirzinski, (Mrs)	19, June 1882	6, June	71- 6m-26d		199	Eureka, WI	Karmieke bei Driesen, Germany
Symne, Emilie	7, Apr. 1884	18, Mar.	36- 6m-14d	Klein	7	Cincinnati, OH	Lista, OstPreußen
Synwold, Johan H.W.	3, July 1871	30, May	12		215	Chicago, IL	
Taaties, Edelt	15, Feb. 1869	30, Jan.	58		55	Rushville, IL	Halbemond, Berum, Ostfriesland
Tabbert, Wilhelimine	26, Mar. 1891	12, Jan.	71- 3m-24d	Klingbeil	206	Ripon, WI	Plagow, Neumarkt, Preußen

Christliche Apologete Death Notices --- 1839 - 1899

Name of Deceased	Notice Date	Death Date	Age	Page	Maiden Name	Place of Death	Place of Birth
Tackenberg, Charles	28, May 1896	15, Apr.	29	350		Burlington, IA	Kingston, Iowa
Tackenberg, Heinrich	18, Oct. 1888	8, Sept	50	670		Dodgeville, IA	Westerkappel, Tecklenburg, Preußen
Taffe, Katharina	3, Mar. 1884	15, Feb.	70	7		Louisville, KY	Liefe, Trier, Germany
Talmon, Mathilda	25, Feb. 1886	6, Feb.	25- 9m- 4d	7	Boger	Junction City, KS	Davis County, Kansas
Tamm, Katharina	1, Jan. 1883	30, Nov.	42	7	Neuhardt	Waseca, MN	
Tank, Friedrich	21, May 1896	24, Apr.	78	334		Bristol, WI	Linde, Pieritz, Pommern
Tanner, Elisabeth	21, Jan. 1886	5, Nov.	34	7	Trachsel	Highland, IL	Oberey zu Röthenbach, Schweiz
Tanner, Elisabeth	2, Feb. 1885	13, Jan.	67	7	Stocke	Cedar Lake, IN	Kanton Bern, Indiana
Tanner, Elizabeth	6, June 1895	21, May	50- 1m-17d	366	Kurth	Lincoln, NE	Rütscheln, Bern, Schweiz
Tanner, Ella	30, Jan. 1890	13, Jan.	30-10m- 8d	78	Schuh	Toledo, OH	Wood County, Ohio
Tanner, Georg	11, Aug. 1898	6, July	73	511		Toledo, OH	Siblingen, Schaffhausen, Schweiz
Tanner, Katharina	26, Sept 1864	7, Sept	38	156	Homberger	Lawrenceburg, IN	Steinweiler, Landau, Rheinpfalz Baiern
Tanner, Maria Antoinette	4, July 1881		25	215	König	Toledo, OH	Toledo, Lucas County, Ohio
Tanner, Susanna	23, June 1879	3, June	43-11m-20d	199		Highland, IL	Diemtigen, Bern, Schweiz
Tännler, Anna Louisa	2, July 1877	19, May	17- 4m	215		Highland, IL	
Tantau, Katharina	2, Sept 1886	25, July	68- 7m-15d	7	Theuerkauf	San Jose, CA	Burg, Insel Femern, Schleswig
Tantau, Matthäus	6, June 1881	29, Apr.	65-11m-29d	183	Bermet	San Francisco, CA	Iges, Graubünden, Schweiz
Täntz, Barbara	19, Sept 1881	26, Aug.	76- 9m-20d	303	Reimann	Highland, IL	Salzbrunn bei Breslau, Schlesien
Täntz, Karoline Pauline	23, June 1892	30, May	65	398		Muskegon, MI	Mehna, Sachsen-Altenburg
Tanz, Gottfried	25, Nov. 1897	6, Nov.	77	751		West Bend, WI	Hohenwalde, Püritz, Preußen
Tappe, Louise	30, June 1892	5, June	32-11m	414	Fischer	Sleepy Eye, MN	
Tarnow, Auguste	23, Jan. 1875	7, Jan.	17-10m-21d	31		Chicago, IL	
Tarnow, Elisabeth	16, Sept 1878	25, Aug.	41	295	Milke	Wadena, MN	Dreidorf, Wirsitz, Preußen
Tarnow, John	29, Oct. 1866	19, Oct.	72	350		Chicago, IL	Pitnitz, Vor-Pommern, Preußen
Tarnow, John C.	17, July 1882	28, June	46- 7m-24d	415		Chicago, IL	Prusdorf, Franzburg, Preußen
Tatman, Carrie	21, May 1896	19, Apr.	25	334	Diehl	Dayton, OH	Dayton, Montgomery County, Ohio
Tausch, Karoline	13, Jan. 1898	6, Dec.	29	31	Bracht	Corder, MO	Lincoln County, Missouri
Tebben, Geschke	3, Mar. 1873	15, Feb.	61	71	Hellmann	San Jose, IL	Nenndorf, Amt Esens, Ostfriesland
Tebel, Franz Heinrich	17, Nov. 1843	23, Oct.	22	183		St. Louis, MO	Neukirchen, Osnabrück, Hannover
Tebel, Friedrich Wilhelm	17, Nov. 1843	1, Oct.	28	183		St. Louis, MO	Neukirchen, Osnabrück, Hannover
Tebel, Heinrich	20, Aug. 1847	23, July	5	135		St. Louis, MO	
Tebel, Katharina	5, Apr. 1844	18, Mar.	18	55		New Orleans, LA	
Tecklenburg, Friedrich Wilhelm	8, Sept 1873		47	287		Mascoutah, IL	Bückeburg, Lippe-Schaumburg
Tecklenburg, Johan Friedrich C.	1, Sept 1898	28, July	69	559		Summerfield, IL	Schei, Lippe-Schaumburg
Tecklenburg, Sophie M.	25, Dec. 1882	22, Nov.	44	415		Summerfield, IL	Linne, Westphalen
Teelen, Peter	2, Jan. 1896	14, Dec.	38	14		Pittsburg, PA	Düsberg, Hochfeld, RheinPreußen
Tegeler, Bernhardt	15, Nov. 1894		42- 6m-21d	742		Oklahoma City, OK	Mosebeck, Detmold, Lippe-Detmold
Tegeler, Line Henriette D.	8, Aug. 1889	19, July	20	510		Charles City, IA	Lippe-Detmold
Tegmeier, Ernst Heinrich	8, Nov. 1875	24, Oct.	43	359		Davenport, IA	Lippe-Detmold
Tegtmeier, Elisabeth	26, May 1887	23, Mar.	19	334		Oil Creek, IN	Evansville, Indiana
Tegtmeier, Heinrich	12, Jan. 1899	20, Dec.	87	31		Evansville, IN	Großenberkel, Hammeln, Hannover
Tegtmeier, Katharina	9, Feb. 1880	24, Jan.	33	47	Hermann	St. Paul, MN	New Orleans, Louisiana
Tegtmeier, Wilhelm	6, Feb. 1890	20, Jan.	58	94		Dotyville, WI	Oldendorf, Preußen
Teichmöller, Johan Georg	31, Jan. 1881	21, Jan.	51- 5m	39		Newport, KY	Völkershausen, Vach, Sachsen-Weimar
Teichmüller, Heinrich	9, May 1895	57- 7m-29d		302		Muscatine, IA	Wölferbütt, Sachsen-Weimar
Teising, Emilie	13, Mar. 1876	3, Mar.	20	87		Cincinnati, OH	Cincinnati, Hamilton County, Ohio

- 514 -

Christliche Apologete Death Notices --- 1839 - 1899

Name of Deceased	Notice Date	Death Date	Age	Page	Maiden Name	Place of Death	Place of Birth
Telenium, Martin	29, Apr. 1886	5, Apr.	67	7		Buffalo, NY	Winterswyk, Holland
Tellejohann, Herman J.	16, Feb. 1888	10, Jan.	75	110		Huntingburg, IN	Ladbergen, Preußen
Tellejohn, Elisabeth	11, May 1899	29, Mar.	83	302		Huntingburg, IN	Ladbergen, Preußen
Tellejohn, Louis	25, Apr. 1895	26, Mar.	42	270		Huntingburg, IN	Pike County, Indiana
Tellkamp, Dorothea Therese	3, Aug. 1885	11, July	39	7	Hemmer	St. Louis, MO	Diepholz, Hannover
Temagen, Maria Katharina	1, Jan. 1883	23, Nov.	59	7	Hustadt	Louisville, KY	
Tembel, Elisabeth	2, Apr. 1896	24, Feb.	40	222	Müller	Bradford, IN	Harrison County, Indiana
Tembück, Anna	23, Jan. 1875	15, Dec.	64	31	Tendick	Jacksonville, IL	Vluyn, Moers, Düsseldorf, Preußen
Temke, Maria	6, Apr. 1893	17, Mar.	77	222	Gusmar	Brillion, WI	Mecklenburg-Schwerin
Temme, Anna Maria Louise	1, Apr. 1872	16, Mar.	59- 2m-16d	111	Krieger	St. Paul, MN	Mehnsen bei Blasheim, Preußen
Temme, Ludwig	30, Mar. 1885	14, Mar.	68- 9m- 2d	7		St. Paul, MN	Mehmen bei Blasheim, Preußen
Temme, Wilhelm	20, Dec. 1875	27, Nov.	23- 3m-20d	407		St. Paul, MN	
Tempel, Catharina	22, Aug. 1850	26, July		136		New Albany, IN	
Tempel, Conrad	22, Nov. 1875	26, Oct.	82	375		Bradford, IN	
Tempel, Eleonora	28, July 1884	11, July	58	7	Habig	Bradford, IN	Katzenellenborgen, Nassau
Tempel, Luise	22, Aug. 1850	1, Aug.	16- 1m-24d	136		New Albany, IN	
Tempel, Lydia J.	22, Oct. 1877	5, Oct.	21- 6m-13d	343	Ketterjohn	Huntingburg, IN	
Tempel, Sophia Henriette	30, Apr. 1877	8, Apr.	48-10m	143		Hopewell, MO	Bega, Lippe-Detmold
Tempelmann, August	25, Sept 1890	22, July	36	622		Kenosha, WI	Belbock, Treptow a.d. Rega, Preußen
Tempelmann, Gottlieb Johannes	23, Nov. 1899	23, Oct.	76	751		Kenosha, WI	Domadel, Pommern
Tems, Katharina	28, Jan. 1892	5, Jan.	57	62	Schlappner	Louisville, KY	Alterschlirf, Hessen-Darmstadt
Tendick, Anna Johanna	25, Apr. 1889	22, Mar.	20-11m-22d	270		Jacksonville, IL	Flühn, Möhrs, RheinPreußen
Tendick, Dietrich	27, Jan. 1898	8, Jan.	78	63		Jacksonville, IL	Flüen, Preußen
Tendick, Gottfried	24, Oct. 1895	20, Sept	70	686		Jacksonville, IL	Blüyn, RheinPreußen
Tendick, Gottfried	6, June 1895	21, May	65	366		Jacksonville, IL	Rheinpreußen
Tendick, Johan	17, Feb. 1887	27, Jan.	75	110		Jacksonville, IL	Vluin, Düsseldorf, Preußen
Tendick, Johanna	24, Dec. 1891	21, Nov.	83	830	Strucken	Jacksonville, IL	Vluyn, RheinPreußen
Tendick, Peter	26, May 1884	9, May	26	7		Jacksonville, IL	Jacksonville, Illinois
Tendick, Sophia	2, Nov. 1893	19, Oct.	81	702	Voortmann	Jacksonville, IL	Huntgen, Morsch, RheinPreußen
Tenwinkel, Heinrich	28, Feb. 1895	8, Dec.	77	142		Detroit, MI	Krehfeld, Rheinpreußen
Tenz, Dorthe	20, Nov. 1876	16, Sept	30	375	Lembach	Highland, IL	
Tepel, Heinrich	22, May 1871		78- - 2d	167		St. Paul, MN	Spenge, Preußen
Tepel, Louise	26, July 1849	30, June	12- 6m	120		St. Louis, MO	
Tepel, Maria Elisabeth	13, Mar. 1871	20, Feb.	67- 5m	87	Kerksieck	St. Paul, MN	Neuenkirchen, Melle, Osnabrück, Hannover
Terhufen, Sibilla	7, Aug. 1876	23, July	58	255	Kamp	Sun Prairie, WI	Kapellen, Kreis Mörs, Preußen
TerVeer, Herman	3, Dec. 1891	5, Nov.	17	782		St. Louis, MO	St. Louis, Missouri
Tesch, Bertha	27, Feb. 1890	19, Jan.	20- 1m- 7d	142		Beauford, MN	
Tesch, Christine Maria	22, June 1893	4, June	68	398	Timm	Brillion, WI	Techlin, Mecklenburg
Tesch, Wilhelmine	29, Aug. 1870	25, July	40- -12d	279	Timm	Charlestown, WI	Deerben, Mecklenburg-Schwerin
Teske, Anna Regine	29, Oct. 1891	15, Oct.	82	702		Watertown, WI	Banskenow, Piritz, Pommern
Teske, Eveline	16, July 1896	23, June	54	463	Werner	Nebraska City, NE	Derzow, Selden, Frankfurt a. d. Oder, Preußen
Teske, John Fr.	14, Nov. 1889	21, Oct.	73	734		Watertown, WI	klein-Küssow, Pieritz, Pommern
Tesno, Christian	22, May 1890	15, Apr.	57	334		Akron, NY	Teterow, Mecklenburg-Schwerin
Teß, Fr.	21, Feb. 1895	25, Jan.	53	126		Almond, WI	Kenzlin, Pommern
Tesserat, Catharina	2, Nov. 1874	17, Oct.	70	351		Pekin, IL	Elsaß
Tetzlaff, Albertine	17, June 1872	19, May	36- 5m- 4d	199	Popp	Kewaunee, WI	Petershaben, HinterPommern

Christliche Apologete Death Notices --- 1839 - 1899

Name of Deceased	Notice Date	Death Date	Age	Page	Maiden Name	Place of Death	Place of Birth
Tetzlaff, Lesetta	10, Aug. 1893	30, June	22	510	Bastian	Menominee, MI	Suko, Mecklenburg-Schwerin
Tetzlaff, Maria	16, Mar. 1893	19, Feb.	52	174	Springborn	Kenosha, WI	Hildebrandshagen, Pommern
Teuber, Carl	20, Oct. 1884	17, Sept	36	7		Michigan City, IN	Schubin, Posen
Teufel, Alene	26, Nov. 1866	9, Nov.		382	Reulenberger	Saginaw, MI	
Teufel, Anna Maria	17, Jan. 1889		73	46	Werner	Rochester, NY	Bahndorf, Herrenberg, Württemberg
Teufel, Friedrich	26, May 1884	30, Apr.	64	7		Saginaw, MI	Vondorf, Württemberg
Teufel, Johanna	27, Mar. 1882	7, Jan.	89- 4m-12d	103		Kochville, MI	Bondorf, Herrenberg, Württemberg
Teuffell, Friedrich	29, Jan. 1872	11, Jan.	54	39			Bohndorf, Württemberg
Teuscher, Christian	30, Aug. 1894	6, Aug.	54	566		Harper, IA	Derstätten, Bern, Schweiz
Teuscher, Jakobine	17, Mar. 1898	30, Jan.	67	175		Troy, NY	Königsbach, Durlach, Baden
Teuscher, Susanna Katharina	18, Apr. 1895	26, Mar.	59	254	Reber	Bucyrus, OH	Allmenden, Bern, Schweiz
Tews, August	11, Feb. 1897	13, Jan.	43	94		Kochville, MI	Brünken, Stettin, Germany
Tews, August	15, Aug. 1881	22, July	24	263		Milwaukee, WI	Daber, Preußen
Tews, Carl F. G.	20, June 1895	28, May	72	398		Milwaukee, WI	Plantikow, Naugard, Pommern
Tews, Maria Louise	23, Dec. 1897	6, Dec.	82	815	Kloß	Bay City, MI	Pommern
Tews, Michael	24, Feb. 1873	3, Feb.	61	63		Detroit, MI	Brünken, Stettin, Preußen
Teyson, Franziska	24, Apr. 1882	6, Apr.	50- 2m	135	Setzer	Hokah, MN	Reizenhain, Böhmen
Thalenhorst, Anna Margaretha	21, Feb. 1895	28, Jan.	31	126		Panola, MN	Stillwater, Minnesota
Thalenhorst, Casper Heinrich	19, Apr. 1888		53	254		Stillwater, MN	Stift Quernheim, Bünde, Preußen
Thalenhorst, Karl	10, Feb. 1898	8, Dec.	28	95		Wapello, IA	Des Moines, Iowa
Thalenhorst, Louise Maria	21, Apr. 1892	4, Apr.	23	254		Stillwater, MN	Panola, Chisago County, Minnesota
Thalheim, Frank	2, Aug. 1880	1, July	19	247		Great Bend, KS	Fond du Lac, Wisconsin
Thalheim, Friedrich	1, Jan. 1891	7, Dec.	25- 3m-14d	14		Friendship, WI	
Thalheim, Henry Louis	30, Jan. 1862	23, Dec.	9	20		Fond du Lac, WI	Mayville, Wisconsin
Thalheim, Karl	26, May 1879	22, Apr.	59- 4m-10d	167		Great Bend, KS	Sachsen
Thalmann, Anna Elisabeth	7, Apr. 1859	27, Mar.	27	56	Grein	Indianapolis, IN	Zell, Hessen-Darmstadt
Thalmann, Elisabeth	4, Dec. 1882	21, Nov.	84- 8m-25d	391	Schupp	Indianapolis, IN	Eschlikon, Thurgau, Schweiz
Thalmann, Isaak	8, May 1876	24, Apr.	82	151		Indianapolis, IN	Wieszikon, Thurgau, Schweiz
Thauer, Anna Margaretha	19, Oct. 1893	1, Oct.	51	670	Sommer	Watertown, WI	Hollenstein, Oberpfalz, Baiern
Thauer, Christine	7, Oct. 1897	8, Sept	35	639	Burger	Watertown, WI	Clyman, Wisconsin
Thauer, Georg	23, Dec. 1897	2, Dec.	37- 5m-24d	815			
Thauer, Lena	8, Dec. 1892	14, Nov.	29	782		Chicago, IL	Waukesha, Wisconsin
Thauer, Nicolaus	18, Oct. 1888	20, Sept	77	670		Watertown, WI	Sachsen-Coburg
Thayer, Beany	4, Mar. 1872	12, Feb.	23	79	Enz	Kenosha, WI	Mußbach, Rheinkreis Baiern
Thede, M.	11, Apr. 1881	26, Mar.	62	119	Schwarz	Columbus, WI	Goldebee, Wismar, Mecklenburg-Schwerin
Thedrahn, Herman	25, Aug. 1884	29, July	56- 5m- 9d	7		St. Paul, NE	Hassendorf bei Entin, Oldenburg
Thee, Caroline	9, Apr. 1896	16, Sept	65	238	Habsmeyer	Boonville, MO	Rehme, Minden, Preußen
Thee, Herman	8, Oct. 1896	22, Feb.		655		Pinckney, MO	Hopewell, Missouri
Thee, Louise	2, June 1873	15, May	61	175	Koch	Jefferson City, MO	Rehme, Minden, Preußen
Thee, Luise Christine	1, June 1899	20, Feb.	33	351	Wehking	Nashville, IL	Nord Prairie,
Thee, Margaretha	3, Mar. 1879	27, Apr.	30	71	Brinkmeier	Morrison, MO	
Thee, Wilhelm	16, May 1889	4, Apr.	62	318		Hopewell, MO	
Theel, Friederike	20, Apr. 1885	5, Oct.	67	7		Colesburg, IA	Hackenwalde bei Golnow, Pommern
Thees, Christina	18, Nov. 1897	1, Feb.	50	735		Washington, MN	Indianapolis, Marion County, Indiana
Thees, Dorothea Barbara	17, Mar. 1853	18, Apr.	30- 1m-13d	44	Frenz	Rondout, NY	Schwäbisch Hall, Württemberg
Thees, Herman	13, May 1886			7		Washington, MN	Brunsbrock, Verden, Hannover

Christliche Apologete Death Notices --- 1839 - 1899

Name of Deceased	Notice Date	Death Date	Age	Page	Maiden Name	Place of Death	Place of Birth
Theis, Anna Elisabeth	27, July 1893		68	478		Waseca, MN	Wisheim, Fimmen, Coblenz, Preußen
Theis, John C.	9, Aug. 1855	25, July	51	128		Louisville, KY	Hohenroth, Nassau
Theis, Katharina	13, Aug. 1891	27, June	16- -11d	526		Columbus, OH	Coshocton County, Ohio
Theis, Maria Louisa	13, Dec. 1839	2, Dec.	1- 9m-12d	195			
Theisinger, Peter	3, Oct. 1889	4, Sept	63	638		Detroit, MI	Alsbrücken, Kaiserslautern, RheinPfalz Baiern
Theiß, Catharina	13, Oct. 1879	13, Sept	35	327		Newport, KY	Cincinnati, Hamilton County, Ohio
Theiß, Johannes	9, Nov. 1863	2, Sept	20	180		Santa Claus, IN	Hameln, Hannover
Theiß, Louis	9, June 1898	21, May	39	367		Madison, WI	Rehweiler, Kusel, Baiern
Theiß, Peter	26, Apr. 1880	13, Apr.	80- 7m-19d	135		Newport, KY	Bandseckow, Pommern
Theobald, Auguste	30, Nov. 1893	31, Oct.	41	766	Freitag	Bay City, MI	Lachen, Neustadt a. d. Hardt, Rheinpfalz Baiern
Theobald, Elisabeth	8, Oct. 1891	2, Sept	64	654	Roos	San Jose, IL	Schenklengsfeld, Hersfeld, Kurhessen
Theobald, Elisabeth	17, Feb. 1873	12, Jan.	27-11m- 8d	53	Heußner	De Soto, MO	Lachen bei Neustadt, Rheinpfalz Baiern
Theobald, Johan	9, Apr. 1896	11, Mar.	70	238		San Jose, IL	Baden
Theuerkauf, Catharina	25, Feb. 1892	31, Jan.	67	127		San Jose, CA	Darmstadt, Hessen-Darmstadt
Theuerkauf, Elise	16, Jan. 1896	20, Dec.	58	46	Miller	San Francisco, CA	Niederingelheim, Bingen, Hessen
Theuerkauf, Maria Catharina	12, July 1860	9, May	75	112	Roos	San Francisco, CA	Nieder Ingelheim, Hessen-Darmstadt
Theuerkauf, Matthias	3, May 1844	16, Apr.	56	71		New Orleans, LA	Wattawa, Prag, Oesterreich
Theuerl, Wolfgang	11, Aug. 1884	20, July	64	7		Morrison, MO	Hirnach, Preußen
Theuerli, Wilhelmine	28, Aug. 1890	30, July	62	558	Bleit	Morrison, MO	Germany
Theurer, Auguste	26, Oct. 1899	15, Sept	58	687	Papkey	Montague, MI	
Theyson,	8, May 1882			151			
Thias, Anna Maria Wilhelmine	24, Aug. 1899	4, July	89	543		Seymour, IN	Rothenfeld, Hannover
Thias, Friedrich Wilhelm	22, Mar. 1894	25, Feb.	81	198		Seymour, IN	Heidland, Dissen, Hannover
Thias, Heinrich	1, June 1874	18, Apr.	37	151		Giard, IA	Rothenfelde, Dissen, Hannover
Thias, Heinrich	11, May 1874	18, Apr.	37	151		Giard, IA	Osterbrück, Hannover
Thias, Wilhelm	28, July 1898	7, June	68	479		Jeffersonville, IN	Hilder, Osnabrück, Hannover
Thiede, Anna Sophie	25, Dec. 1871	7, Dec.	60	415		Columbus, WI	Horst, Kreis Degenwalde, Preußen
Thiede, Sophie A.	21, Nov. 1870	2, Nov.	23	375	Theede	Columbus, WI	Zoldebee, Mecklenburg-Schwerin
Thiekötter, Christoph	4, Apr. 1881	16, Mar.	72-11m- 8d	111		Beaufort, MO	
Thiel, Anna	10, June 1897	14, May	68	367	Pompe	LaCrosse, WI	Kleinschecken, Böhmen
Thiel, August	21, July 1887		42	462		Wadena, MN	Leinakel, Posen
Thiel, Charlotte Sophia	10, Sept 1896	22, Aug.	87	591	Waibl	Bertha, MN	Pommern
Thiel, Karl Friedrich	25, Sept 1876	8, Sept	66	311		Flood Creek, IA	Dobberspfuhl, HinterPommern
Thiel, Mathilde	15, Oct. 1866	26, Aug.		334		Wausau, WI	Annille, Posen, Preußen
Thiel, Wilhelm	6, May 1872	5, Apr.	37- 6m	151	Wait	Flood Creek, IA	Wietstock, Kreis Kammin, Preußen
Thiel, Wilhelm	5, Nov. 1896	21, Sept	57	719		Guadalupe Valley, TX	Germany
Thielbar, Gesche Margaretha	15, July 1872	16, June	81	231		Washington, IL	Sülstadt, Amt Bruckhausen, Hannover
Thielbar, Johan Friedrich	4, July 1889	7, Apr.	73- 5m-18d	430		Peoria, IL	Heiligenfelde, Syke, Hannover
Thiele, Adolph	3, Aug. 1893	19, July	35	494		Fredericksburg, TX	Fredericksburg, Gillespie County, Texas
Thiele, Franz	2, June 1862	17, May	3	88		Breckinridge, WI	
Thiele, Heinrich	7, July 1887	9, June	71	430		Manitowoc, WI	Steinhude, Lippe-Schaumburg
Thiele, Heinrich Carl	10, Jan. 1889		27	30		Manitowoc, WI	Newton, Wisconsin
Thiele, Joseph	2, June 1862	17, May	1- 2m	88		Breckinridge, WI	
Thiele, Reinhart	11, Jan. 1894	28, Nov.	30	30		Springfield, MN	Reinsdorf bei Waldheim, Sachsen
Thiele, Wilhelm	11, Nov. 1852	11, Sept	29- 6m	184		Chicago, IL	Shönerstadt, Sachsen
Thielemann, Johan Andreas	26, Aug. 1878	8, Aug.	86	271		Milwaukee, WI	Immenrode, Hannover

- 517 -

Christliche Apologete Death Notices --- 1839 - 1899

Name of Deceased	Notice Date	Death Date	Age	Maiden Name	Page	Place of Death	Place of Birth
Thieling, Rosine	22, Dec. 1873	21, Nov.	30	Seffke	407	St. Paul, MN	Segelhorst, Kurhessen
Thielke, (Mrs)	11, Mar. 1878	18, Feb.	63- 9m-18d		79	Watertown, WI	Mecklenburg-Schwerin
Thiemann, Dorothea Maria	19, Jan. 1874	30, Dec.	16- 5m		23	Concordia, MO	
Thiemann, Georg	23, May 1864	19, Mar.	17- -20d		84	Oregon, MO	Lafayette County, Missouri
Thiemann, Johann	27, July 1854	30, June	25		120	Dayton, OH	Morsum, Amt Westen, Hannover
Thiemann, Jürgen Heinrich	31, Oct. 1889	30, Sept	81		702	Concordia, MO	Rodewalt, Neustadt am Rünnenberg, Hannover
Thiemann, Karl	29, Apr. 1897	3, Apr.	81		271	Montague, MI	Giesmansdorf, Schlesien
Thiemann, Maria Elise	1, Apr. 1897	13, Mar.	32	Jansen	207	Concordia, MO	Hannover
Thiemann, Martha	21, Mar. 1889	21, Feb.	28-11m-21d		271	Montague, MI	
Thiemann, Sophie Wilhelmine	19, Aug. 1886	29, July	67-10m-27d	Windeknecht	207	Montague, MI	Böhme, Zelle, Hannover
Thiergart, August Samuel	20, Aug. 1891		68	Baar	190	Concordia, MO	Groß-Sobrost, Gerbauen, Preußen
Thies, Anna	11, July 1889	15, June	17- 8m-20d		542	New Orleans, LA	
Thies, August Ludwig	14, Mar. 1895	15, Feb.			446	Pepin, WI	
Thies, Hanna F.W.	11, Jan. 1894	19, Dec.	58	Stahlberg	174	Chicago, IL	Buchholz, Bissendorf, Hannover
Thies, John H.	11, Mar. 1897	30, Jan.	73		30	Chester, IL	Heepen bei Bielefeld, Preußen
Thies, Meiner	7, June 1869	13, Apr.	63		159	Chester, IL	Bockhorst, Halle, Preußen
Thiesing, Heinrich Friedrich	27, Jan. 1873	11, Jan.	51		183	Red Bud, IL	Amt Aurich, Ostfriesland
Thiesing, Katharine Elise	27, Apr. 1899	10, Mar.	80		31	Cincinnati, OH	Haldem, Kreis Lübekke, Preußen
Thiesing, Sophia Elisabeth	7, July 1898	8, June	49		271	Covington, KY	Quackenbrück, Hannover
Thinnel, Wilhelmine	14, Dec. 1868	29, Nov.	45	Bleßer	431	Covington, KY	Covington, Kenton County, Kentucky
Thöle, Bernhart	18, Feb. 1897	19, Jan.	39		399	East Troy, WI	Eselborn, Hessen-Darmstadt
Thöle, Heinrich	23, Apr. 1877	6, Apr.	56		111	Mason City, IA	Caspelbiben, Hannover
Thöle, Karl Heinrich	12, Jan. 1899	2, Dec.	77		135	Quincy, IL	Schale, Tecklenburg, Münster, Preußen
Thoma, Johanna Friederike E.	21, May 1896	22, Apr.	57	Wolfram	31	St. Paul, MN	Blasheim, Minden, Preußen
Thomas, Auguste	12, July 1880	24, June		Vollmer	334	Jordan, MN	Rauschengesees, Reuß
Thomas, Eduard C.	6, Sept 1888	7, Aug.	25		223	Austin, TX	
Thomas, Franz Heinrich	23, Nov. 1863	18, Oct.	76- 6m		574	Quincy, IL	Quincy, Illinois
Thomas, Helene	1, Aug. 1889	9, July	36- 8m-13d		188	Belleville, IL	Rödiekhausen, Minden, Preußen
Thomas, Johan Chr.	3, Sept 1877	7, Aug.	75- 8m- 8d		494	Beardstown, IL	Musbach, Neustadt a. d. Hardt, RheinPfalz Baiern
Thomas, Johan Christian	23, Jan. 1875	9, Jan.	43		287	San Francisco, CA	Allendorf a. Werra, Kurhessen
Thomas, Karl (Mrs)	3, Oct. 1895	31, Aug.	34	Reetz	31	Quincy, IL	
Thomas, Karolina	28, July 1879	14, July	65	Müller	638	Greenwood, MN	Germany
Thomas, Katharina	23, Mar. 1874	4, Mar.	34- 3m-23d	Schneider	239	Cannelton, IN	Wermelskirchen, Rheinpreußen
Thomas, Maria	10, Mar.1873	6, Feb.	76- 1m-19d		95	Edgerton, OH	Crawford County, Ohio
Thomas, Maria	23, Apr. 1877	4, Mar.	22- 9m-19d		79	Edgerton, OH	Summerset County, Pennsylvania
Thomas, Michael	12, May 1879	21, Apr.	71- 2m-21d	Oeth	135	Marrs, IN	Posey County, Indiana
Thomas, Rosalie	28, Sept 1854	23, Aug.	16		151	Llano, TX	Göbelshausen, Wetzlar, Köln, Preußen
Thomas, Wilhelm	3, Dec. 1866	9, Sept	58		156	Cannelton, IN	Wermelskirchen, Lennep, Preußen
Thomen, Ursula	8, Jan. 1857	21, Dec.	69	Dettwiller	390	Beaver Creek, IL	Reigoldswyl, Basel, Schweiz
Thomer, Georg	1, Jan. 1852	10, Dec.	39- 7m-18d		8	Cincinnati, OH	Einighausen, Hessen-Darmstadt
Thomer, Katharine	20, July 1854	9, July	41- 9m- 4d		4	Cincinnati, OH	Einardshausen, Hessen-Darmstadt
Thomman, Martin	14, Jan. 1892				116	Kansas City, MO	Sisach, Baselland, Schweiz
Thoms, Caroline	24, Jan. 1856	1, Jan.	29	Knoke	30	Indianapolis, IN	Liensburg, Amt Wölze, Hannover
Thoms, Friedrich Wilhelm	21, Mar. 1895	1, Mar.	71		16	Indianapolis, IN	Schneeren, Hannover
Thomsen, Anna Katharina	10, Feb. 1898	14, Jan.	72	Martensen	190	Bloomington, IL	Ellingstadt, Schleswig-Holstein
Thomson, Arthur	23, May 1864	31, Mar.	28		95	Madison, IN	

Christliche Apologete Death Notices --- 1839 - 1899

Name of Deceased	Notice Date	Death Date	Age	Maiden Name	Place of Death	Page	Place of Birth
Thönen, Elisabeth	20, Sept 1880	13, Aug.	43- 9m-13d	Lengacker	Hannibal, OH	303	Allmanden, Erlenbach, Bern, Schweiz
Thoreiter, Philipp	7, Dec. 1863	11, Nov.	35- 9m-27d		Defiance, OH	196	Wendelsheim, Hessen-Darmstadt
Thorn, Johanette	4, Dec. 1890	12, Nov.	70- 6m-14d	Diefenbach	New Albany, IN	782	NiederFischbach, Nassau
Thorreuter, Agnes	6, Oct. 1873	22, Sept	82	Klaus	Defiance, OH	319	Vendersheim, Alsfeld, Hessen
Thorreuter, David Johannes	28, Mar. 1870	15, Feb.	79		Defiance, OH	103	Wendelsheim, Hessen
Thorreuter, David Johannes	21, Mar. 1870	15, Feb.	80		Defiance, OH	95	
Thorwegen, Maria	25, Dec. 1876	26, Nov.	63- 6m	Groß	Green Bay, WI	413	Mecklenburg-Schwerin
Thos, Heinrich Edwin	1, July 1872	6, June	11- 9m- 4d		Arenzville, IL	215	
Thrams, Amanda	22, Dec. 1898	22, Nov.	33	Priebbenow	Hector, MN	815	Keslin, Hinterpommern
Thrams, Heinrich	28, Oct. 1886		88		Nora Springs, IA	7	
Thran, Maria	21, Feb. 1881		34- -28d		Covington, KY	63	Cincinnati, Hamilton County, Ohio
Thränert, H.	7, Oct. 1872	15, Sept	48		Milan, IN	327	Udestedt, Sachsen-Weimar
Thuernau, Henriette	5, Mar. 1891	5, Feb.	54	Reckwart	Owatonna, Mn	158	Ringel, Hannover
Thul, Wilhelmine	11, July 1870	22, May	18	Bogus	St. Louis, MO	223	
Thum, Christina	25, June 1866	5, June	47	Amann	Dunkirk, NY	206	Baisingen, Württemberg
Thumm, Adam	23, Apr. 1883		67		Dunkirk, NY	135	Ober-Riexingen, Vaihingen, Württemberg
Thumm, Margaretha	12, Nov. 1866	18, Sept	44		Nashville, TN	366	
Thürauf, Michael	21, Dec. 1868		46		Iowa City, IA	407	Winsheim, Baiern
Thürk, Carolina	25, Feb. 1892		51	Hauser	Chicago, IL	127	Züssow, Greifswald, Pommern
Thürnau, Friedrich	6, June 1895	3, May	27		Owatonna, MN	366	Aurora, Steel County, Minnesota
Thust, Emilie	9, Apr. 1891	8, Feb.	32	Lübke	Storm Lake, IA	238	
Tickötter, Verona	22, Oct. 1891	29, July	71	Meyer	Drake, MO	686	Canton Zürich, Schweiz
Tiedemann, Anna Rebecca	1, Aug. 1895	6, July	38	Toborg	Muscatine, IA	494	Oederquart, Freiburg, Hannover
Tiedemann, Claus	22, Feb. 1894	25, Dec.	83		Muscatine, IA	126	Oederquart, Hannover
Tiedemann, Sophia	9, Sept 1872	15, Aug.	22		St. Charles, MO	295	Koppendorf, Amt Uchte, Hannover
Tiedge, Caroline	28, Jan. 1884	4, Jan.	65	Rasche	Peace Creek, KS	7	Rützlingen, Preußen
Tiefenthal, Luise	4, Feb. 1867	15, Jan.	40		Allegan, MI	38	Hückeswagen, Preußen
Tiegs, Herman	27, Oct. 1887	27, Sept	14		Lyona, KS	686	Davis County, Kansas
Tiegs, Robert	22, Aug. 1889	3, Aug.	11-11m- 2d		Lyona, KS	542	
Tiemann, Auguste	25, Mar. 1897	19, Feb.	71	Horstmann	Seguin, TX	190	Oppendorf, Lübeke, Westphalen
Tiemann, Caroline W. Sophia	17, Aug. 1868	27, July	21-11m		Schnectady, NY	263	Südhemmern, Preußen
Tiemann, Emil Gerhard	20, June 1881	29, May	16- 9m-25d		St. Charles, MO	199	
Tiemann, Fr.	18, Oct. 1860	18, June	58		Table Rock, NE	168	Germany
Tiemann, Friedrich Christian	25, Mar. 1897	3, Mar.	24		St. Charles, MO	190	St. Charles, Missouri
Tiemann, Friedrich Wilhelm	15, Oct. 1866	19, Aug.	40		Meredosia, IL	334	Büscherhaide, Oldendorf, Minden, Preußen
Tiemann, Friedrich Wilhelm	11, Dec. 1871	7, Sept	64		Schnectady, NY	399	Südhemmern, Minden, Preußen
Tiemann, Henrietta	14, Feb. 1895	8, Jan.	46	Meyer	Perry, TX	110	
Tiemann, John H.	5, Sept 1895	16, Aug.	37		Warrenton, MO	574	St. Charles County, Missouri
Tiemann, Louise	1, Dec. 1892	7, Nov.	80	Brandhorst	Schnectady, NY	766	Hille, Minden, Preußen
Tiemann, Wilhelm	26, Nov. 1896	14, Oct.	81		Perry, TX	766	Oldendorf, Lüpke, Preußen
Tiemens, Christian Gottfried	7, Dec. 1885	9, Nov.	64		New Orleans, LA	7	Oldenburg
Tienken, Carsten	22, Sept 1892	23, Aug.	60		Quincy, IL	606	
Tienken, Catharina C.H.	3, June 1878		14- 8m- 8d		Brooklyn, NY	175	
Tienken, Johan Herman	27, June 1895	18, May	77		New York City, NY	414	Detersdorf, Oldenburg
Tiesing, (boy)	30, Nov. 1868	Nov.			Cincinnati, OH	383	
Tiesing, Rebekka	3, Sept 1877	23, Aug.	44-10m- 6d	Hüneke	Louisville, KY	287	Morsum, Hannover

Christliche Apologete Death Notices --- 1839 - 1899

Name of Deceased	Notice Date	Death Date	Age	Page	Maiden Name	Place of Death	Place of Birth
Tieste, Heinrich Louis	19, June 1856	23, May	9-11m-23d	100		Indianapolis, IN	List, Hannover
Tieste, Karoline	29, Apr. 1878	10, Apr.	62- 5m- 2d	135		Nashville, TN	Hagenburg, Hannover
Tieste, Louis	20, Oct. 1879	3, Oct.	60- 6m-18d	335		Nashville, TN	Mölle, Amt Grönberg, Hannover
Tieste, Sophia	1, Nov. 1855	30, Sept	39- 5m	176		Indianapolis, IN	Regbez, Potsdam, Brandenburg
Tietz, Friederike	10, Apr. 1890	21, Mar.	71	238	Köhler	Roseville, MI	Friedrichswalde, Brandenburg
Tietz, Heinrich	23, Mar. 1899	19, Jan.	57	191		Marine City, MI	
Tietz, Maria	16, Nov. 1885	19, Oct.	60- 9m-11d	7	Loose	Milwaukee, WI	Dobern, Leipa, Böhmen
Tietze, Franz	17, Apr. 1882	25, Feb.	29- 4m-10d	127		LaCrosse, WI	Dobern, Böhmen
Tietze, Franz	20, Nov. 1876	7, Nov.	56- 9m- 3d	375		LaCrosse, WI	Milwaukee, Wisconsin
Tietze, Gustav	11, Oct. 1880	23, Sept	22	327		Milwaukee, WI	Neschwitz, Tetschen, Leiteneritz, Böhmen
Tietze, Theresia	28, Apr. 1898	10, Apr.	79	271	Seidel	LaCrosse, WI	Radewig, Feldmark, Herford, Preußen
tilker, Anna Maria Elisa	26, Jan. 1880		66	31	Wittenbröder	Golconda, IL	Bliedinghausen, Remscheid, Köln, Preußen
Tillmann, Friedrich Wilhelm	28, Oct. 1897	1, Oct.	71	687		Canton, MO	Unna, Preußen
Tillmann, Gustav	16, Oct. 1865	19, Sept	23- 5m	168		Waukegan, WI	Des Moines, Iowa
Tillmann, Gustav A.	27, Apr. 1893	20, Mar.	27	270		Wapello, IA	Hebron, Adam County, Iowa
Tillmann, Johan Wilhelm	29, Dec. 1892	9, Dec.	24	828		Jacksonville, IL	Lüttringhausen, Preußen
Tillmann, Katharine	27, Nov. 1865		65- 8m-17d	192		Waukegan, WI	Weipelhausen, Schweinfurt, Baiern
Tillmann, Maria	21, Dec. 1868	25, Nov.	29- -10d	407	Heß	St. Paul, MN	Schnectady, New York
Timann, Mary	13, Mar. 1882	7, Feb.	27	87	Schwenler	Schnectady, NY	Westercappeln, Preußen
Timans, Mina	6, Dec. 1888	11, Nov.	67	782	Lange	New Orleans, LA	Bremen, Germany
Timke, Meta Maria	11, Dec. 1871	30, Oct.	36	399	Weber	Brunswick, MO	Locum, Hannover
Timken, Dorothea	12, Sept 1850	21, July	33	148		St. Louis, MO	Pettis County, Missouri
Timken, Friedrich Eduard	15, Nov. 1888	16, Sept	32	734		Lacrosse, KS	Tarmste, Amt Otterberg, Hannover
Timken, Herman	16, May 1870	7, Apr.	35	159		Lake Creek, MO	Farmstedt, Amt Ottersberg, Hannover
Timken, Jakob	7, Jan. 1867	5, Dec.	85- 8m	6		Lake Creek, Mo	
Timken, Karl	22, Oct. 1883	24, Sept		343		Dallas, TX	
Timm, August	23, June 1898	29, May	86	399		Bay City, MI	Mecklenburg-Schwerin
Timm, Bertha Laura	21, Feb. 1895	27, Jan.	22	126		Bay City, MI	Bay City, Michigan
Timm, Caroline	20, May 1872		52	167	Miller	Lyons Creek, KS	Kirchhagen, Treptow a. d. Rega, Pommern
Timm, Franz	8, Sept 1887	21, Aug.	25	574		Lyona, KS	Dickinson County, Kansas
Timm, Friederika	18, Nov. 1872	15, Oct.		375		Bay City, MI	
Timm, G.C.	2, June 1873	15, May	40	175		Charlestown, WI	Suckow bei Teterow, Mecklenburg-Schwerin
Timm, Maria	7, Feb. 1895	5, Jan.	81	94	Kracht	Bay City, MI	Vietschow, Mecklenburg-Schwerin
Timm, Maria	8, Mar. 1878	3, Mar.	18- 4m- 3d	111		Brillion, WI	Holstein
Timm, Robert J.	28, May 1891	8, May	25	350		Osceola, NE	Schleswig, Vandevoort County, Wisconsin
Timm, Robert J.	11, June 1891	8, May	25	382		Brillion, WI	Schleswig, Vandevoort County, Wisconsin
Timm, Sophia	26, Mar. 1891	25, Jan.	78	206	Lemke	Brillion, WI	Mecklenburg-Schwerin
Timmel, Conrad	26, July 1888	3, July	75- 2m-23d	478		Marietta, OH	Marburg, Kurhessen
Timmerberg, Anna M.L.	1, Aug. 1895	9, July	60	494	Obernolte	Warrenton, MO	Aeckster, Vlothe, Minden, Preußen
Timmermann, Margarethe	16, May 1870	25, Apr.	46	159		Batesville, IN	Hespe, Amt Stadthagen, Hannover
Timmermann, Wilke	2, Jan. 1890	5, Dec.	74	14		Pleasant Valley, IA	Oldenburg
Timpner, Katharine	11, June 1883	6, May	55- 1m-19d	191	Weingarth	Pinckneyville, IL	Bledesbach bei Kassel, RheinPfalz Baiern
Tindick, Gottlieb	5, May 1898	22, Mar.	78	287		Quincy, IL	Hürstgen, RheinPreußen
Tinken, Heinrich	4, Dec. 1882	1, Nov.	59- 2m- 9d	391		Aurora, IN	Hagen, Hannover
Tinken, Margaretha	6, Apr. 1863	3, Mar.	41	56	Hein	Melrose, NY	Rechtenstecht, Hannover
Tinne, Maria	18, Mar. 1878	3, Mar.	18- 4m- 3d	87		Brillion, WI	

Christliche Apologete Death Notices --- 1839 - 1899

Name of Deceased	Notice Date	Death Date	Age	Page	Maiden Name	Place of Death	Place of Birth
Tintelnot, Heinrich	30, Dec. 1872	10, Dec.	63	423		Salem, MN	Ballenberg, Amt Horn, Lippe-Detmold
Tintelnot, Louisa Maria	7, Aug. 1890	18, July	69	510	Warweg	St. Paul, MN	Heiligenkirchen, Lippe-Detmold
Tipp, (Mrs)	7, Mar. 1881	19, Feb.	31- -19d	79	Burmerster	Hays City, KS	
Tisbelde, Ulrich Edward	20, June 1881	6, June	73-8m-18d	199		Secor, IL	Westerhold, Amt Essen, Ostfriesland
Tischendorf, Anna Sophia	8, June 1899		56	367	Reiners	Santa Claus, IN	Ripley County, Indiana
Tischendorf, Christiane	3, Dec. 1857	18, Oct.	57	196	Büttner	Santa Claus, IN	
Tischendorf, Heinrich E.	21, Oct. 1886	2, Oct.	19	7		Santa Claus, IN	Thörntan, Sachsen-Weimar
Tischendorf, Johan Gottfried	16, July 1896	19, May	74	463		Santa Claus, IN	Pausa, Sachsen
Tischendorf, Johanna	30, Apr. 1891	6, Apr.	63	286		Santa Claus, IN	Santa Claus, Indiana
Tischendorf, John	9, May 1889	22, Apr.	25	302		Santa Claus, IN	Diebes, Reuß-Schleiz
Tischendorf, Wilhelmina	15, Jan. 1857	15, Dec.	29	12	Dietell	Huntingburg, IN	
Tischer, Henry	6, Oct. 1884	9, Sept	20	7		Baresville, OH	
Tischer, Philippina	5, Mar. 1896	7, Feb.	84	158	Meinknecht	Baresville, OH	Iptingen, Vaihingen, Württemberg
Tischer, Samuel	2, July 1896	1, May	44	431		Baresville, OH	Monroe County, Ohio
Tischhauser, Katharina	4, Mar. 1886	4, Feb.	88	7		Sherrills Mount, IA	Schweiz
Tischhauser, Katharine	16, Apr. 1891	18, Mar.	73	254	Schmit	Sherrills Mount, IA	Elenbach, Rheinkreis Baiern
Tischhauser, Matthias	13, Oct. 1892	8, Aug.	71	654		Sherrills Mount, IA	Sevelen, St. Gallen, Schweiz
Tischhauser, Nicolaus	20, July 1854	3, July	51	116		Highland, IL	Sevlen, Werdenberg, St. Gallen
Tisserat, Peter	8, Nov. 1869	16, Sept	65	359		Petersburg, IL	Anster a Bourges, Frankreich
Tites, Ernst Friedrich	19, Dec. 1881	25, Nov.	72- 8m-25d	407		Ft. Dodge, IA	Hoya a. d. Weser, Hannover
Titze, Dorothea	15, Apr. 1878	23, Mar.	55	119		Minneapolis, MN	GroßRosen, Preußen
Titze, Eleonora	29, Sept 1873	27, Aug.	84	311		Minneapolis, MN	Kampern, Schlesien, Preußen
Többen, Maria	17, Mar. 1892	17, Feb.	29	175	Kuhlmann	Mason City, IA	Vechtel, Fürstenau, Hannover
Tobelmann, C.S.	22, Apr. 1886	7, Mar.	89	7		Delmenhorst, GE	
Tobelmann, Friedrich	17, Apr. 1876	30, Mar.	48- 9m- 3d	127		New Orleans, LA	Rahden, Minden, Preußen
Toberan, Elisabeth	18, Mar. 1878	20, Feb.	73-11m	87		Stryker, OH	Wesen, Tecklenburg, Münster, Preußen
Toberen, Eliza	23, Feb. 1885	30, Dec.	44	7		Stryker, OH	
Tobert, Henrietta	9, Mar. 1899	11, Feb.	87	159	Simmling	Ironton, OH	Wenderswick, Holland
Tobias, Elisabeth	19, Oct. 1885	26, Sept	73- 4m- 3d	7		Washington, IL	Oberamt Neubirg, Württemberg
Tobias, Heinrich E.	1, Jan. 1891	8, Dec.	18 - -25d	14		Bunker Hill, IL	
Tobler, Anna Maria	26, July 1888	30, June	40- 6m	478	Zuberbühler	Harrison, KS	Herisau, Appenzell, Schweiz
Tobrock, Anna M. Louisa	26, Jan. 1860	4, Aug.	12	16		Seymour, IN	
Tobrocke, Anna Maria Elisabeth	4, Feb. 1897	10, Jan.	76	79	Kreinhagen	White Creek, IN	Engter bei Osnabrück, Hannover
Tobüren, Friedrich	28, Nov. 1850	10, Oct.	48	192		Evansport, OH	Wesen, Tecklenburg, Preußen
Tobüren, Heinrich A.	30, Aug. 1855	29, July	46	140		Evansport, OH	Wehrsen, Preußen
Tochtermann, Margarethe	24, Feb. 1868		43	63		Oregon, MO	Feutigen, Bern, Schweiz
Todd, Joseph H.	29, Oct. 1896	27, Sept	53	703		Oshkosh, WI	Huddersfield, England
Todrank, Johann J. Wilhelm	17, Jan. 1861	30, Nov.	59	12		Huntingburg, IN	Künsebeck, Halle, Minden, Preußen
Tödt, Anna	3, Apr. 1871		71- 2m- 5d	111		Troy, NY	Rendsburg, Holstein
Todt, Daniel	3, Dec. 1877	15, Nov.	74- 5m	391		Iowa City, IA	Niederstein, Elsaß
Todt, Magdalena	28,May 1883	16, May	77	175	Birkelbacher	Iowa City, IA	Niedersteinbach bei Weißenburg, Elsaß
Tödtemann, Christina	19, Jan. 1880	2, Jan.	31	23	Keßler	St. Peters, MO	St. Charles County, Missouri
Tödtemann, Emilie	26, May 1892	1, May	76- 9m- 4d	334	Friedrich	St. Louis, MO	Hameln, Hannover
Tödtli, Anna	16, July1883	24, June	81- 6m-16d	231		Fillmore, WI	Leuchningen, St. Gallen, Schweiz
Toedt, Sophie	1, Dec. 1887	11, Oct.	52	766		Schnectady, NY	Reußburg, Holstein
Toelle, Maria L.	30, Nov. 1885	4, Nov.	78- 5m-22d	7		Galion, OH	Hombressen, Hofgeismar, Kurhessen

Christliche Apologete Death Notices -- 1839 - 1899

Name of Deceased	Notice Date	Death Date	Age	Page	Maiden Name	Place of Death	Place of Birth
Toener, Ernst	21, Mar. 1870	1, Mar.	57	95		Alton, IL	Lienen, Münster, Westphalen, Preußen
Toenjes, Wilhelm Rudolf	8, Apr. 1886	19, Mar.	67	7		Huntingburg, IN	Lienen, Münster, Preußen
Toffe, (Mrs)	9, Sept 1858	4, Aug.	24- 4m- 4d	144		Chester, IL	
Tolin, Elisabeth	12, Feb. 1891	20, Jan.	29-11m	110	Schulze	Jeffersonville, IN	Jeffersonville, Indiana
Tölke, Anna Margaretha	27, Oct. 1873	8, Aug.	61- 5m-27d	343	Oeterer	Jeffersonville, IN	Ahausen, Preußen
Tölke, Caroline	20, Nov. 1856	12, Oct.	25	188	Vilbergs	Ironton, OH	Altena bei Iserlohn, Westphalen, Preußen
Tölke, Friederike	24, Aug. 1854	19, July	66	136	Grotensohn	Beaufort, MO	
Tölke, Johan August	25, Feb. 1892	12, Jan.	29	127	Reuters	Union, MO	Beaufort, Franklin County, Missouri
Tölke, Johan Christoph	24, Aug. 1854	21, July	67	136		Drake, MO	Ohrlinghausen, Lippe-Detmold
Tölke, Johan Heinrich	28, Apr. 1898	9, Mar.	34	271		Union, MO	
Tölke, Johanna Henriette	12, Feb. 1866	9, Jan.	38	54		Beaufort, MO	
Tölke, Lydia	9, Feb. 1880	17, Jan.	20	47	Brinkmeyer	Union, MO	
Tölker, Karl August	1, Mar. 1875	9, Feb.	42	71		Beaufort, MO	Warren County, Missouri
Tölle, Amalia	3, June 1872	8, Apr.	75	183		Beaufort, MO	Lippe
Tolle, Catharina Wilhelmina	19, Nov. 1857	28, Oct.	54	188	Rahmans	Second Creek, MO	Henstrup, Lippe-Detmold
Tölle, Heinrich	2, Oct. 1882	16, Aug.	81- 6m	319		Huntingburg, IN	Fersmold, Holle, Hannover
Tölle, Herman	12, June 1876	21, May	18	191		Pittsburg, PA	Humbreksen, Hofgeismar, Hessen-Kassel
Tölle, Karolina	28, Apr. 1898	6, Apr.	61	271	Knipmeier	Warren Co, MO	
Tölle, Wilhelm	28, Nov. 1864	27, Sept	16-11m-18d	192		White Cloud, KS	Hannover
Tollmann, Anna M. Margaretha	27, Mar. 1890	4, Mar.	24-11m- 2d	206	Gerken	Poland, IN	Indiana
Toltzmann, Maria	1, Jan. 1877	17, Dec.	19	7		Warren, MO	Indian Camp, Warren County, Missouri
Toltzmann, Wm. Friedrich August	21, Sept 1863	2, May	19	152		Manitowoc, WI	Milwaukee, Wisconsin
Tom, Henriette D.	20, Feb. 1871	28, Jan.	36	63	Buchweizen	Milwaukee, WI	Matzdorf, Preußen
Tomas, Philipp Adam	8, Dec. 1879		16- 6m-27d	391		Charles City, IA	Schmalenhagen, Pommern
Toms, Friedrich	2, May 1881	7, Apr.	31	143		Farmington, WI	Ashfort, Wisconsin
Tomson, Katie	2, Dec. 1897	30, Oct.	25	767	Binz	Iron Ridge, WI	Uckermark, Preußen
Töne, Anna	11, Oct. 1894	25, Sept	89	662	Hartmann	Marion, OH	Marion County, Ohio
Töne, Christian	12, Sept 1861	22, Aug.	21	148		Harper, IA	St. Antonien, Graubünden, Schweiz
Töne, Johan	14, May 1883	24, Apr.	78	159		German Creek, IA	St. Antöni, Graubünden, Schweiz
Tonne, Heinrich	27, Feb. 1882	21, Jan.	40	71		Harper, IA	St. Antonen, Graubündten, Schweiz
Tonnemacher, Margarethe	31, Jan. 1861	9, Jan.	52	20		Roseville, MI	Seymour, Indiana
Tönnies, Charles Gustav	11, Aug. 1892	29, June	34	510		Cincinnati, OH	
Tönnings, Heinrich C.	6, June 1889	16, May	57	366		Bloomington, IL	Helfern, Preußen
Töpfer, Anna Elisabeth	9, May 1895	2, Apr.	66	302		Pekin, IL	Dingelstädt, Preußen
Töpfer, Catharina	13, Dec. 1888	9, Sept	50 - 6d	798	Bookel	Charles City, IA	Singlis, Broken, Hessen-Kassel
Töpfer, Conrad	15, Apr. 1897	26, Mar.	78	239		Charles City, IA	Heltra, Eschwe, Kurhessen
Töpfer, Minna	5, Mar. 1896	12, Feb.	27	158	Gruhn	Charles City, IA	Bremen, Cook County, Illinois
Topp, Anna M.	14, Dec. 1885	23, Nov.		7		Wheeling, WV	Neu-Kampenau, OstPreußen
Topp, Christine	3, Nov. 1898	11, Sept	75	703	Vespermann	Wheeling, WV	Hohenbüchen, Braunschweig
Topp, Christopher	20, Apr. 1899	3, Mar.	71	255		Honey Creek, WI	Bülow, Mecklenburg-Schwerin
Topp, Clara Sophie	29, Aug. 1861	27, July	21- 8m- 3d	140		Indianapolis, IN	Blomberg, Lippe-Detmold
Topp, Fr.	23, June 1879	9, June	53	199		Columbus, WI	Neubrenz, Mecklenburg-Schwerin
Topp, Johanna Maria	18, Apr. 1895		55	254	Gebhardt	Indianapolis, IN	Sulbitz, Naila, Baiern
Topp, Karl Konrad	22, Jan. 1852	3, Dec.	52- 9m	16		Indianapolis, IN	Blomberg, Lippe-Detmold
Topp, Maria	25, Nov. 1872	30, Oct.	69	383	Kruse	Columbus, WI	Kermien, Grabow, Mecklenburg-Schwerin
Topp, Wilhelmine	20, Sept 1849	10, Aug.	33	152	Whemeyer	Wheeling, VA	Hannover

Christliche Apologete Death Notices --- 1839 - 1899

Name of Deceased	Notice Date	Death Date	Age	Page	Maiden Name	Place of Death	Place of Birth
Torley, Albertine	28, Oct. 1858	26, Sept	19	172		Des Moines, IA	Wermmelskirchen, Preußen
Torley, Friedrich	7, Feb. 1889	11, Jan.	80	94		West Point, IA	Neustadt, Schwarzburg, Preußen
Tormöhlen, Anna	22, Nov. 1894		30	758	Busch	Seymour, IN	Seymour, Indiana
Tormöhlen, Johan Gerhard	17, Aug. 1899	7, July	68	527		Huntingburg, IN	Wittlage, Hannover
Törne, Karl H.M.	27, July 1893	8, July	35	478		Oconomowoc, WI	Marchin, Mecklenburg-Schwerin
Törner, Anna Maria	6, May 1878	10, Apr.	70- 7m-14d	143		Indianapolis, IN	Landrighausen, Hannover
Torney, Johan	12, June 1890	26, May	75- 4m-16d	382		Sheboygan, WI	
Tostrick, Katharina Elisabeth	12, Nov. 1847	25, Aug.	34	183		New Orleans, LA	Ringen, Preußen
Tostrick, Wilhelm	19, Apr. 1849	24, Mar.	35	64		New Orleans, LA	
Tostrick, Wilhelm	26, Apr. 1849	24, Mar.		68		New Orleans, LA	
Trachsel, Rudolf	25, Feb. 1867	3, Feb.	37	62		Santa Claus, IN	Ruggisberg, Amt Seftigen, Bern, Schweiz
Tracht, Heinrich	14, July 1887	15, June	44	446		Drake, MO	Hessen-Darmstadt
Trachte, Dorothea J.	20, Feb. 1890	3, Feb.	74	126	Schäfer	Watertown, WI	Sommerfell, Lippe-Detmold
Trachte, Franz Friedr. Christoph	4, May 1893	2, Apr.	82	286		Watertown, WI	
Trachti, Maria	3, Aug. 1893	13, July	37	494	Vincen	Bertha, MN	
Tracy, Elisabeth	11, Aug. 1879	21, July	24- 3m-24d	255	Neun	New Matamoras, OH	Watertown, Wisconsin
Taeder, Albert Bernhard	1, Sept 1884	15, Aug.	35	7		Lemars, IA	Lees Run, Washington County, Ohio
Taeger, Friedrich W.	21, Nov. 1889	15, Oct.	60	750		Kansas City, MO	Zewitz, Lauenburg, Cöslin, Pommern
Träger, Bertha	28, May 1896		20	350		Kansas City, MO	Freiburg, Sachsen
Träger, Christine Louise	9, June 1884	22, May	58	7		Waterloo, WI	Michigan
Träger, Elisabeth Katharine	28, Apr. 1879	10, Apr.	46-10m- 3d	135	Strohsacker	Glencoe, MN	Lauchstädt bei Wollenberg, Preußen
Träger, Johan Andreas	13, Oct. 1879	28, Sept	95- 4m-10d	327		Woodbury, MN	Erkenbrechtsweiler, Nürtingen, Württemberg
Träger, Karl (Rev)	5, May 1898	12, Feb.	71	287		Perry, TX	Weißenschirmbach, Merseburg, Preußen
Trageser, Heinrich	10, July 1890	28, June	86	446		Marietta, OH	Freiburg an der Unstrut, Germany
Trägler, Magdalena	19, Oct. 1899	22, Sept	79	671		Quincy, IL	Baiern
Tram, Maria	6, Sept 1860	16, Aug.	60	144		St. Paul, MN	Bern, Schweiz
Tramm, Carolina	17, Feb. 1873	28, Jan.	39-11m-25d	53	Priebe	St. Paul, MN	Slonave, Schubin, Bromberg, Posen, Preußen
Tramm, Daniel	20, Nov. 1882		82	375		Northfield, MN	Nakel, Preußen
Tramm, Michael	30, Oct. 1890	9, Oct.	59	702		Nordfield, MN	Nakel, Bromberg, Posen
Tramp, Friedrich	1, Sept 1879	8, Aug.	65	279		Bloomington, IL	Warren, Mecklenburg-Schwerin
Trampe, August Wilhelm	9, July 1896	29, May	57	447		Waltersburg, IL	Lavelsloh, Dübenau, Hannover
Trampe, Louise	17, Jan. 1895	15, Dec.	45-10m- 3d	46	Schlüter	Schnectady, NY	Hille, Minden, Preußen
Trampe, Sophia Maria	19, Dec. 1881	23, Nov.	17	407		Golconda, IL	Massac County, Illinois
Trams, Wilhelmine	31, Jan. 1895	7, Jan.	63	78		Brownton, MN	Preußen
Trank, Ernstina	29, Oct. 1877	17, Sept	17- 3m- 7d	351		Tecumseh, NE	
Tränker, Conrad	27, June 1889	19, May	44	414		Delaware, OH	Queck, Lauterbach, Hessen
Transier, Joseph	16, Aug. 1849	2, June	25- 6m	132		Laughery, IN	Mundach, Rheinkreis Baiern
Transmeier, Herman	15, July 1878			223		Eudora, KS	Lippe-Detmold
Trantow, Christian	14, Feb. 1881	1, Feb.	64- 1m- 7d	55		Wausau, WI	Kniphow bei Massow, Pommern
Trapp, Helena Maria	22, Jan. 1891	9, Dec.	19- 5m-15d	62		Kenaunee, WI	
Trapp, Karl Ludwig	28, May 1877	17, Apr.	73- 3m-28d	175		Cooperstown, WI	Glötzin, Preußen
Trapp, Maria	7, June 1888	13, May	26-11m- 5d	366		Charlestown, ---	
Trappe, Andreas H.	1, Nov. 1880	9, Oct.	14- 4m-12d	351		Giard, IA	Giard, Iowa
Trappe, Hanna	11, Nov. 1858	8, Sept	39	180		Hanging Rock, OH	Eboldshausen, Westerhoff, Hannover
Traser, Christine	18, July 1895	15, June	82	462	Grinig	Dallas City, IL	Stockstadt am Rhein, Preußen
Traser, Johann Ewald	12, Mar. 1883	17, Feb.	70	87		Nauvoo, IL	Arheiligen, Darmstadt, Hessen-Darmstadt

Name of Deceased	Notice Date	Death Date	Age	Page	Maiden Name	Place of Death	Place of Birth
Traser, Karoline	25, June 1883	16, May	35	207	Soland	Nauvoo, IL	Reinach, Aargau, Schweiz
Traub, Amalia	20, Jan. 1879	4, Jan.	38- 2m-22d	23	Breunig	Indianapolis, IN	Cincinnati, Hamilton County, Ohio
Traub, Carl	6, Mar. 1882	20, Feb.	48- -11d	79		Indianapolis, IN	Canton Zürich, Schweiz
Traub, Elisabeth	13, Aug. 1877	29, July	65- 6m-17d	263	Schwarz	Indianapolis, IN	Senzach, Zürich, Schweiz
Traub, Georg Adam	11, Nov. 1878	17, Oct.	82	359		Waverly, OH	Razbach, Weinsberg, Württemberg
Traub, Georg Adam	24, Nov. 1892	15, Aug.	23	750		Waverly, OH	Ross County, Ohio
Traub, Jakob	24, July 1882		71	239		Indianapolis, IN	Schnatt, Schorndorf, Württemberg
Traub, Johann Tobias	22, Sept 1862	27, Aug.	23- 7m- 2d	152		Indianapolis, IN	Seuzach, Zürich, Schweiz
Traub, Karl	10, Feb. 1898	23, Dec.	67	95		Chillicothe, OH	Germany
Traub, Katharina	8, Sept 1879	10, Aug.	34- 6m- 2d	287	Schneider	Syracuse, NY	
Traub, Margarethe	10, Jan. 1895	3, Dec.	75	30	Weber	Indianapolis, IN	Schnaith, Schorndorf, Württemberg
Traub, Rosina Katharina	24, May 1880	23, Apr.	77	167	Dietrich	Waverly, OH	Bretzfeld, Weinberg, Württemberg
Traub, Sophia	3, May 1869	10, Apr.	20- 2m- 2d	143		Indianapolis, IN	
Traumer, Sophia	18, Jan. 1864	29, Dec.	38	12	Schelper	Louisville, KY	Boventen, Hannover
Traunburg, Louise	7, Feb. 1895	18, Jan.	61	94	Zühlke	Columbus, WI	Insel Wollin, Germany
Trautig, Carolina	4, Nov. 1872	17, Oct.	19- 2m	359		Pittsburg, PA	
Trautig, Magdalena	28, Jan. 1878	13, Jan.	51	31	Kuhlbührs	Pittsburg, PA	Katzenfurth bei Wetzlar, Preußen
Trautmann, Elisabeth	14, Apr. 1887	11, Mar.	78	238	Röcken	Indianapolis, IN	Rheinkreis Baiem
Trautmann, Katharine	3, Nov. 1898	12, Oct.	62	703		Chicago, IL	Plieningen, Württemberg
Trautmann, Louis	1, Feb. 1864	10, Jan.	19- 2m- 4d	20		Batesville, OH	Erbach, Homburg, Baiem
Trautmann, Theobald	2, Mar. 1893	29, Jan.	90	142		Ironton, OH	Baiem
Trauwinkel, Louisa	7, Jan. 1878	11, Dec.		7	Green	Morrison, MO	
Traxel, Philippina	18, Jan. 1894	23, Dec.	81	46	Allman	Milan, IN	Vinningen, Baiem
Trebesch, Christine	1, Jan. 1891	4, Dec.	73-11m-20d	14	Sohn	Detroit, MI	Klinkow, Prenzlau, Brandenburg
Trebesch, Friedrich	13, June 1881	7, May	64- 7m-14d	191		Detroit, MI	Schönwerder, Potsdam, Preußen
Tredup, Friederike	27, Sept 1875	11, Aug.	25	311	Wegner	Milwaukee, WI	Tellin, Kreis Demmin, Pommern, Preußen
Treffinger, (Mr)	3, Feb. 1879	13, Jan.	77	39		East Troy, WI	Diefenbach, Maulbronn, Württemberg
Treffinger, Elisabeth	26, Sept 1889		87	619	Straser	East Troy, WI	Zaberfeld, Brakenheim, Württemberg
Treffinger, Ludwig	6, Jan. 1868	20, Dec.	8	6		East Troy, WI	
Trefz, Elisabeth	22, Nov. 1855	24, Oct.	26- 5m-11d	188		Ripley, OH	Niederhofen, Brackenheim, Württemberg
Trefz, Johann Jakob	23, Dec. 1858	15, Nov.	51- 4m- 1d	204		Ripley, OH	Backnen, Württemberg
Trefz, Rebekka	17, Mar. 1879	23, Feb.	83- 1m- 6d	87	Brodt	Louisville, KY	Großaspach, Backnang, Württemberg
Treiber, Catharina	14, Apr. 1879	25, Mar.	66- 1m-16d	119	Eyer	Clarington, OH	Wingen, Weißenburg, Elsaß
Treiber, Catharina	25, May 1862	17, May	64- -25d	136	Benz	Philadelphia, PA	Kisselbronn, Pforzheim, Baden
Treiber, Dorothea	7, July 1892	12, June	76	430	Walther	Clarington, OH	Görstdof, Wörth, Elsaß
Treiber, Johan Wilhelm	17, Oct. 1881	29, Sept	74- 5m-26d	335		Jefferonville, IN	Neckar-Gröningen, Ludwigsburg, Württemberg
Treiber, Josephine	13, Dec. 1849	5, Nov.	16- 5m	200		Philadelphia, PA	Dietenhaus, Baden
Treiber, Louis	2, Nov. 1874	29, Aug.		351		Des Moines, IA	Lembach, Weißenburg, Elsaß
Treiber, Ludwig	15, Sept 1848	12, Mar.	65- 6m	152		Captina, OH	Lehmbach, Weissenburg, Rheinkreis Baiem
Treiber, Ludwig	14, Feb. 1881	7, Jan.	71- -15d	55		Clarington, OH	Lembach, Weißenburg, Elsaß
Treiber, Michael	25, Oct. 1880	19, Sept	70-11m-14d	343		Clarington, OH	Lembach, Weißenburg, Elsaß
Treiber, Sophia	30, June 1884	26, May	73- 7m-13d	7	Minch	Sauk City, WI	Lembach, Weisenburg, Elsaß
Treibs, Jacob	6, Nov. 1876	17, Aug.	48	359		Fredericksburg, TX	Kirchberg, Coblenz, Rheinpreußen
Treibs, Katharine	28, Dec. 1899	2, Dec.	63	828	Durst	Fredericksburg, TX	Dettenhausen, Tübingen, Württemberg
Treider, Margaretha	1, May 1865	8, Apr.	52	72	Zapf	Jeffersonville, IN	Zaunsweier, Offenburg, Baden
Treitle, Katharine	20, Dec. 1888	27, Nov.	67- 4m- 2d	814	Pfäffle	Chicago, IL	Diedelsheim, Baden

Christliche Apologete Death Notices --- 1839 - 1899

Name of Deceased	Notice Date	Death Date	Age	Maiden Name	Page	Place of Death	Place of Birth
Trelle, Heinrich	18, Sept 1882	16, Aug.	81- 6m		303	Pittsburg, PA	Humbreksen, Hofgeismar, Hessen-Kassel
Treuer, Maria Anna	1, Nov. 1869	30, Aug.	80		351	Newburyport, MA	Langensteinbach, Baden
Treusch, Georg Peter	7, Mar. 1881	16, Feb.	49		79	Brooklyn, NY	Sandhofen bei Mannheim, Baden
Treuschel, Anna Maria	7, July 1898	6, June	53	Lober	431	Toledo, OH	Ulrichsberg, Württemberg
Treuschel, Barbara	26, May 1898	6, May	63	Straßel	335	Toledo, OH	Offendorf, Elsaß
Treuschel, Catharina Elisabeth	21, Mar. 1889	27, Feb.	62- 1m- 3d	Zaenger	190	Toledo, OH	Wangen, Elsaß
Treuschel, Michel	9, Dec. 1897	1, Nov.	75		783	Toledo, OH	Wangen, Elsaß
Treuter, Georg	28, Feb. 1895	15, Jan.	62		142	New Albany, IN	Zehnacker, Elsaß
Treutle, Elisabeth	23, Nov. 1874	8, Nov.	32		375	Brenham, TX	Bretten, Baden
Treyz, Louise Friederike	18, June 1891	22, May	71		398	Brooklyn, NY	Böblingen, Württemberg
Tribbe, Heinrich	8, Aug. 1864	20, July	58		128	Quincy, IL	Hunteburg, Amt Wittlage, Hannover
Tribbe, Heinrich	22, Aug. 1861	26, June	26- 7m- 2d		136	Quincy, IL	
Tribbe, Johann Friedrich	9, Aug. 1849	13, July	31		128	Quincy, IL	
Tribold, Willie	18, Nov. 1872		8		375	St. Paul, MN	
Trickart, Friedrich Rudolf	23, Dec. 1897	16, Nov.	20		815	Morrison, MO	Launburg, Pommern
Trickart, Wilhelm Martin	21, Oct. 1897	26, Sept	17		671	Morrison, MO	Lauenburg, Pommern
Triebold, Wilhelmine Caroline J. C.	3, Jan. 1895	11, Dec.	74	Oehler	14	Washington, MN	Passinghausen-Hemeringen, Hannover
Trier, Jakob	24, July 1890	27, June	48		478	Stockton, CA	Backweiler, Hörnbach, Rheinpfalz Baiern
Trierweiler, Johan	28, July 1879	6, July	57- 6m		239	Flood Creek, IA	Tarforst, Preußen
Trietsch, Elisa Barbara	11, Oct. 1860	18, Aug.	40		164	Defiance, OH	
Trietsch, Herman	1, Nov. 1894	4, Oct.	21		710	Denton, TX	Wieblingen, Baden
Trietsch, Katharina	16, Mar. 1899	17, Feb.	63	Wacher	175	Denton, TX	Wüblingen, Baden
Trietsch, Peter	14, Jan. 1897	1, Dec.	41		31	Denton, TX	Wieblingen, Baden
Triller, Jakob	20, Apr. 1868	17, Mar.	69		127	Poughkeepsie, NY	Hetzelrode, Kreis Eschwegen, Kurhessen
Trischmann, J.W.	5, Nov. 1891	2, Oct.	71		718	Wellman, IA	Mosheim, Kurhessen
Troeger, Georg Friedrich	7, Sept 1874	22, Aug.	82-10m- 8d		287	Sandwich, IL	Neuwied, Rheinpreußen
Tröger, (Mrs)	29, July 1852	19, May	29		124	Clayton, IA	Seiblitz, Baiern
Tropf, Christina	25, Jan. 1864	20, Dec.	70- 3m		16	Galion, OH	Leibolsheim, Amt Karlsruhe, Baden
Tropf, Georg Fr.	8, May 1865	9, Mar.	77		76	Galion, OH	
Trost, Caroline Friederike	29, Dec. 1887	10, Dec.	53	Handmann	830	East Troy, WI	Volksdorf, Preußen
Trost, Elisabeth	15, Nov. 1869	13, Oct.	34	Rahm	367	Mascoutah, IL	Schaffhausen,
Trottier, (Mrs)	13, July 1854	13, Apr.	28- 1m-24d		112	Poland, IN	
Trou, Maria	3, Feb. 1887	20, Jan.	14		78	Marrs, IN	
Troyer, Samuel	5, Jan. 1863	16, Nov.	19- 6m- 2d		4	Huntingburg, IN	
Truckleß, Christina	5, June 1851	21, Apr.	30- 3m		92	Indianapolis, IN	Langenhagen, Pommern
Truettner, Wilhelmine	30, Apr. 1896	30, Mar.	40	Block	286	Manitowoc, WI	Hohenshülsen, Petershein, Hessen-Darmstadt
Trumler, Georg	11, Mar. 1858	13, Feb.	68		40	Waverly, OH	Posey County, Indiana
Trümpe, Anna Wilhelmine	24, Sept 1877	14, Nov.	22	Fellemende	311	Mt. Vernon, IN	Schellenbach, Hessen-Darmstadt
Trumpfheller, William	23, July 1891	25, June	68		478	Brooklyn, NY	
Trumpfhiller, Kate	23, Nov. 1863	2, Aug.	15- 7m		188	New York, NY	
Trümpler, Maria Elisabeth	23, Nov. 1885	5, Sept	85	Freytag	7	Manchester, IA	Gorsleben, Merseburg, Preußen
Trumpp, Michael	13, Feb. 1896	27, Jan.	43		110	Clay Center, KS	Hornberg, Württemberg
Trus, Carolina	4, June 1891	15, May	39	Stroh	366	Moberly, MO	Dietenhausen, Weilburg, Hessen-Nassau
Trus, Elisabeth	30, Mar. 1874	26, Jan.	39	Busch	103	Danville, IL	Wendorf, Kreis Wetzlar, Preußen
Trus, John	22, Jan. 1891	9, Dec.	24		62	Danville, IL	Danville, Illinois
Trus, Michael	25, Feb. 1897	5, Feb.	68		127	Danville, IL	Niederasphä, Marburg, Hessen

Christliche Apologete Death Notices --- 1839 - 1899

Name of Deceased	Notice Date	Death Date	Age	Page	Maiden Name	Place of Death	Place of Birth
Trus, Wilhelm E.	17, Jan. 1889	20, Dec.	19	46		Danville, IL	
Trüter, Katharina Sophie	30, Dec. 1897	10, Dec.	71	828	Ernstmeyer	Mt. Healthy, OH	Hackenmüssen, Hohenhausen, Lippe-Detmold
Trüttner, Friedrich	22, May 1890	4, May	78- - 9d	334		Manitowoc, WI	Sieden bei Borstel, Hannover
Trüttner, Friedrich	12, Sept 1864	25, Aug.	20-11m	148		Manitowoc, WI	
Tschabold, Katharina	31, Dec. 1896	15, Oct.	80	844		Kendallville, IN	
Tscharner, Anna Catharina	25, Sept 1890	6, Sept	83- - 6d	622		Milwaukee, WI	Malaus, Graubünden, Schweiz
Tschiche, Wilhelm	13, Apr. 1893	17, Mar.	60	238		Nokomis, IL	Guhrau, Schlesien
Tschoepe, Friederike	8, Aug. 1870	19, July	65- 2m	255	Barunke	Rock River, WI	Großglogau, Schlesien, Preußen
Tschöpe, Anton	25, May 1899	4, May	88	335		West Bend, WI	Breslau, Germany
Tschöpe, Emilie	6, May 1897	19, Apr.	54	287		West Bend, WI	Münsterberg, Schlesien
Tschopp, Anna	2, Nov. 1863	3, Oct.	67	176		Herman, MO	Ziefen, Schweiz
Tschopp, Bernhard	8, Mar. 1860	6, Jan.	72	40		Herman, MO	Zofen, Basel, Schweiz
Tschudy, Lucy	8, Oct. 1877	16, Sept	24- 9m-4d	327		Harper, IA	
Tschumper, Berthold	2, Oct. 1876	12, Aug.	38	319		Hokah, MN	Trubbach, St. Gallen, Schweiz
Tubach, Peter	2, Apr. 1896	3, Mar.	82	222		Baresville, OH	Bern, Schweiz
Tubbesing, Anna M.	9, Feb. 1899	16, Jan.	50	95	Kück	Red Wing, MN	Adolfsdorf bei Bremen, Germany
Tubbesing, Georg H.	29, Sept 1898	12, Sept	31	623		St. Paul, Minnesota	St. Paul, Minnesota
Tubbesing, Johan Wilhelm	3, June 1897		84- 5m	351		Red Wing, MN	Schröttinghausen-Werther, Halle, Westphalen
Tubesing, Addie Marie	10, Jan. 1889	30, Dec.	18- 6m- 9d	30		Red Wing, MN	Red Wing, Minnesota
Tubesing, Margarethe	13, Feb. 1890	21, Jan.	42	110	Vogt	Red Wing, MN	
Tuchter, Dierk	23, Mar. 1868	10, Mar.	51	95		Jeffersonville, NY	Bookhorn, Oldenburg
Tucker, Aminda	17, Sept 1877	23, Aug.	37	305	Hoch	Hochheim, TX	
Tuffli, Anna Maria	26, June 1890	19, May	58	414	Steidling	San Antonio, TX	Klamps, Württemberg
Tuffli, Karoline	9, Jan. 1871	29, Dec.	46- 9m- 4d	15		Highland, IL	Baden
Tügel, Friedrich	11, Sept 1865	29, May	61	148		Schnectady, NY	Eickhost, Minden, Preußen
Tügel, Maria	22, Sept 1884	8, Sept	70	7	Aspelmeier	Schnectady, NY	Hille, Minden, Preußen
Tuininga, Trintje	17, Feb. 1898	28, Jan.	84	111	DeHaan	Hokah, MN	Harlingen, Friesien, Holland
Tuker, Joh.	25, Aug. 1873		70	271		Elkader, IA	
Tünker, Barbara	13, Apr. 1899	16, Mar.	64	239	Vetter	Bunker Hill, IL	Darmstadt, Hessen-Darmstadt
Tüscher, (Mrs)	26, May 1873	25, Mar.	70	167		Hannibal, MO	Biezwyl, Bucheggberg, Solothurn, Schweiz
Tüscher, Elisabeth	27, Dec. 1849	13, Dec.	57	208		Buckhill, OH	Schweiz
Tüscher, Georg Christian	28, Apr. 1862	2, Apr.	70- 7m-28d	68		Marietta, OH	Leun, Kreis Wetzlar, Preußen
Tüscher, Jacob	5, July 1860	23, Apr.	84	108		Baresville, OH	Bern, Schweiz
Tuschhoff, Anna Maria	1, Jan. 1883	2, Dec.	70	7		Cape Girardeau, MO	
Tuschhoff, Rosine	2, Mar. 1885	14, Feb.	34	7	Schultze	Appleton, WI	Appleton, Cape Girardeau County, Missouri
Tuschinsky, Johan	24, Dec. 1896	13, Nov.	81	831		San Francisco, CA	
Tuschoff, Carolina	18, Mar.1872	16, Feb.	19	95	Gieseke	Appleton, MO	Cape Girardeau County, Missouri
Tushof, Maria	13, Mar. 1882	16, Feb.	68- 5m-21d	87	Richter	Cape Girardeau, MO	Nordenbeck, Waldeck
Tuxhorn, Gebke G.	6, Aug. 1891	16, July	58-10m-18d	510	Willms	Humboldt, NE	Germany
Twente, Katharina Elisabeth	13, Jan. 1879	24, Dec.	78	15		Huntingburg, IN	Lenge—-, Tecklenburg, Preußen
Uchtmann, Heinrich Fr.	29, Dec. 1884	5, Dec.	21	7		Santa Claus, IN	Cincinnati, Hamilton County, Ohio
Uchtmann, Louisa	28, Apr. 1873	1, Apr.	18- 4m-28d	135		Santa Claus, IN	Cincinnati, Hamilton County, Ohio
Ucken, Wilhelmina	5, Apr. 1880	11, Mar.	29-10m-19d	111	Spinker	San Jose, IL	Marienhafen, Ostfriesland
Uckermann, Franz Salis	23, Feb. 1899	11, Jan.	75	127		White Creek, IN	Wolfwyl, Solothurn, Schweiz
Uckert, Meta	5, Mar. 1896	19, Jan.	68	158	Seekamp	Covington, KY	Hemlingen, Hannover

Christliche Apologete Death Notices --- 1839 - 1899

Name of Deceased	Notice Date	Death Date	Age	Page	Maiden Name	Place of Death	Place of Birth
Uebele, Albert G.	24, Jan. 1895	4, Jan.	24	62		Wheatland, WI	Kirchberg, Württemberg
Uebele, Gottfried	13, Oct. 1898	19, Sept	36- 4m	655		Eustis, NE	Spawissen, Göppingen, Württemberg
Uebele, Rosina	30, Dec. 1872	9, Dec.	54	423	Alt	Madison, IN	Stetten, Brackenheim, Württemberg
Uebelmesser, Henriette	10, Oct. 1870	18, Sept	51	327	Ziegeler	Vandalia, IL	Windesheim, RheinPreußen
Ueber, Anna Elisabeth	19, July 1888	4, July	69- 4m- 8d	462	Edel	New Orleans, LA	Sauerschwabenheim, Hessen-Darmstadt
Ueber, Jakob (Rev)	23, Sept 1897	5, Sept	76	607		New Orleans, LA	
Ueber, Maria Elisabeth	3, Feb. 1879	5, Jan.	48- 1m- 8d	39	Stroh	New Orleans, LA	Jagow, Pyritz, Preußen
Uecker, Christian	29, July 1878	27, June	65-11m- 3d	239		Milford, WI	Rädlow, Greifswald, Vorpommern
Uecker, Johannes Friedrich	17, Apr. 1882	2, Apr.	72	127		Laporte, IN	Wrangelsburg, Neu-Vorpommern, Preußen
Uecker, Sophia Magd. Friederika	7, June 1880	23, May	76- 3m- 1d	183	Debahn	Laporte, IN	Glashütten, Schopfheim, Baden
Uehle, Verena	9, Jan. 1882	22, Dec.	59	15	Wild	Vermillion, OH	Neunkirch, Schaffhausen, Schweiz
Uehlinger, Katharine	6, Jan. 1887	25, Dec.	81	14		Plattsmouth, NE	
Uehrly, (boy)	26, Sept 1861	27, Aug.	4- 8m- 9d	156		Sandusky, OH	Zülsdorf, Neumark
Uehrly, (boy)	26, Sept 1861	12, Sept	2- 9m-19d	156		Sandusky, OH	Ringenwald, Frankfurt a.d. Oder, Preußen
Ueker, Wilhelm	5, Sept 1895	11, Aug.	73- 8m	574		Ripon, WI	Neunkirch, Schaffhausen, Schweiz
Uekert, Carl Friedrich	28, Dec. 1893	2, Dec.	70	828		Covington, KY	
Uelinger, Johan Ulrich	8, June 1868		71	183		Linden, MO	
Uhden, Catharina Dorothea	1, Oct. 1891	29, July	81- 9m-24d	638	Leibbrandt	Papillion, NE	Harbke bei Holmstedt, Preußen
Uhe, Andreas	7, July 1879	13, June	70- 8m- 4d	215		Papillion, NE	Garbke, Halbersleben, Preußen
Uhe, Friederika	2, Nov. 1893	10, Oct.	83	702	Baumgarten	Papillion, NE	
Uhe, Heinrich	7, Oct. 1886	4, Sept	10-10m	7		Papillion, NE	Esbach, Württemberg
Uhl, Karl	13, Oct. 1887	24, Sept	23	654		Baltimore, MD	Rottweil, Württemberg
Uhl, Math. (Dr)	4, Jan. 1894	18, Dec.	85	14		LaCrosse, WI	
Uhl, Matthäus E.	10, Jan. 1895	24, Dec.	19- 8m-10d	30		St. Paul, MN	Ladbergen, Tecklenburg, Preußen
Uhlenhake, Christine	27, Sept 1869	5, Sept	39- 6m	311	Radwillm	Le Sueur, MN	Hof, Marienberg, Nassau
Uhr, Ida	12, May 1892	12, Apr.	72-10m- 4d	302	Schütz	Bracken, TX	Marienberg, Nassau
Uhr, Johan Heinrich	9, May 1881	20, Apr.	72- 1m-14d	151		Danville, TX	
Uhri, Anna	18, Sept 1890	12, Aug.	37	606	Holischek	Humboldt, NE	Eckarsweier, Kork, Baden
Uhri, Barbara	25, Feb. 1886	8, Feb.	58	7	Lutz	Humboldt, NE	
Uhri, Georg	26, Jan. 1880	10, Jan.	27- 1m-10d	31		Humboldt, NE	
Uhrlettig, Anna	14, Mar. 1895	7, Feb.	57	174	King	Honey Creek, WI	Wildprechtsrode, Meiningen, Sachsen-Meiningen
Uhrlettig, Anna Katharine	10, Mar. 1887	10, Feb.	56	158		Honey Creek, WI	Wildprechtroda, Sachsen-Meiningen
Uhrlettig, Johan Casp.	6, Aug. 1883	20, June	50- 7m-20d	255		East Troy, WI	Maienhafen, Amt Berum, Ostfriesland
Ufers, Foke Peter	24, May 1880	28, Apr.	70- - 6d	167		Secor, IL	Maienhofen, Berum, Ostfriesland
Ufers, Peter	31, May 1880	13, May	41- 4m- 6d	175		Secor, IL	Karlsruhe, Baden
Ullmer, Sophia	17, Aug. 1893	2, Aug.	63	526	Förster	Jersey City, NJ	Königswald, Kreis Rotenburg, Kurhessen
Ulrich, George	29, June 1868	5, June	71	207		New Bremen, IL	Green-Garden, Illinois
Ulrich, Johannes Conrad	23, July 1896	24, June	18	479		Frankfort, IL	Unverbach, Baiern
Ulrich, Joseph Anton	17, Jan. 1881	23, Nov.	63- 6m- 2d	23		Nerstrand, MN	Columbus, Bartholomew County, Indiana
Ullrich, Katharina	21, Oct. 1872	7, Oct.	19	343		Seymour, IN	Guadalupe County, Texas
Ullrich, Rosa	24, May 1894	7, May	40	342	Dammann	Seguin, TX	Ceylon, Landsberg a. d. Warthe, Brandenburg
Ulm, Caroline Wilhelmine	23, May 1889	28, Apr.	82	334	Wiegand	Sleepy Eye, MN	Giesenau, Preußen
Ulm, Ferdinand	13, Dec. 1869	14, Nov.	69	399		Columbus, WI	Stembach, Backnang, Württemberg
Ulmer, Adam	8, Feb. 1855	14, Jan.	35-11m-17d	24		Galion, OH	Neuhausen, Württemberg
Ulmer, Anna Maria	24, Jan. 1881	10, Jan.	69	31		Louisville, KY	Mehringen, Urach, Württemberg
Ulmer, Daniel	15, Jan. 1872	21, Dec.	62	23		Louisville, KY	

Christliche Apologete Death Notices --- 1839 - 1899

Name of Deceased	Notice Date	Death Date	Age	Page	Maiden Name	Place of Death	Place of Birth
Ulmer, Eduard	3, Mar. 1887	13, Feb.	20	142		Quincy, IL	Bond County, Illinois
Ulmer, Elisabeth	28, Apr. 1853	28, Mar.	70- -15d	68			Aich, Nürtingen, Württemberg
Ulmer, Friederike	8, Nov. 1880	16, Oct.	28	359			Steinbach, Backnang, Württemberg
Ulrich, Anna	24, Nov. 1887	15, Oct.	72- 6m- 9d	750	Krieg	Monona, IA	Mutterstadt, Baiern
Ulrich, Anna	13, Jan. 1873	16, Nov.	55- 4m	15	Schrötter	Evansville, IN	
Ulrich, Charles Theodor	23, Oct. 1882	13, Oct.	14- -19d	343		Columbus, IN	
Ulrich, Conrad	24, Nov. 1887	1, Nov.	74- - 9d	750		Monona, IA	Mutterstadt, Baiern
Ulrich, Dorothea	22, Aug. 1881	9, Aug.	46	271	Mahler	Cameron, MO	Buhren, Neustadt an Rumenberg, Hannover
Ulrich, Elisabeth	11, Apr. 1889	17, Mar.	74	238	Kurtz	Lafayette, IN	Rehweiler, RheinPfalz Baiern
Ulrich, Friederike Louise	21, Mar. 1889	8, Mar.	78	190		Le Sueur, MN	Dorfhagen, Cammin, Pommern
Ulrich, Friedrich	3, Mar. 1884	4, Feb.	65	7		Jackson, MO	Beerel, Braunschweig
Ulrich, Herman	1, Apr. 1897		16	207		Gordonville, MO	
Ulrich, Johan	20, Dec. 1875	6, Dec.	20	407		DuQuoin, IL	
Ulrich, Johan Georg	6, May 1897	13, Apr.	65	287		Pevione, IL	Königswald, Rottenburg, Kurhessen
Ulrich, Johan Georg	13, Mar. 1871	11, Feb.	78- 7m- 5d	87		Arenzville, IL	Neuhoff, Amt Weben, Nassau
Ulrich, Johanna	24, Feb. 1887	29, Jan.	57- 1m-23d	126	Jäger	Indianapolis, IN	Widdem, Neckarsulm, Württemberg
Ulrich, Johannes	18, Oct. 1875	26, Sept	85	335		Greenville, OH	Chester County, Pennsylvania
Ulrich, Johannes	23, Nov. 1854	22, Oct.	68	188		Newark, NJ	Allenwollenburg, Kurhessen
Ulrich, Julie	23, Mar. 1874	12, Mar.	40	95	Schnell	Covington, KY	Bischweiler, Elsaß
Ulrich, Karl	16, Feb. 1893	6, Jan.	69	110		Covington, KY	Markirch, Elsaß
Ulrich, Karl Gotthelf	12, May 1884	27, Apr.	74	7		Le Sueur, MN	Greifenberg, Pommern
Ulrich, Katharina	16, May 1889	3, Dec.	69	318	Miller	Schnectady, NY	Gotho, Sachsen-Meiningen
Ulrich, Katharina Dorothea	2, May 1870	18, Apr.	62	143	Miller	Dresden, OH	Botenheim, Brackenheim, Württemberg
Ulrich, Katharina Elisabeth	26, May 1884	7, May	78- 1m-25d	7		Cameron, MO	Speier, Mutterstadt, Rheinkreis Baiern
Ulrich, Maria	21, Apr. 1898	1, Apr.	86	255	Funk	Cannon River, MN	Neustadt, Mecklenburg-Schwerin
Ulrich, Maria	16, May 1889	30, Apr.	34	318	Lang	Le Sueur, MN	St. Paul, Minnesota
Ulrich, Maria Christina	28, Mar. 1881	24, Feb.	52- 5m-23d	103	Steeb	Cleveland, OH	Untereißesheim, Württemberg
Ulrich, Maria Elisabeth	7, Jan. 1858	19, Dec.	30	4	Ritzmann	Milan, IN	Mutterstadt, Baiern
Ulrich, Maria Katharina	29, Nov. 1860	7, Nov.	50	192	Braun	Milan, IN	Gengheim, Baiern
Ulrich, Martha Elisabeth	9, May 1870	22, Apr.		151	Res	Bremen, IL	Königswalde, Kurhessen
Ulrich, Martin Heinrich	2, Aug. 1888	15, July	71- 1m-23d	494		Le Sueur, MN	Greifenberg, Pommern
Ulrich, Peter	24, Aug. 1854	31, July	52	136		Aurora, IN	Mutterstadt, Speier, Rheinkreis Baiern
Umdenstock, Maria Magdalena	14, Oct. 1872	14, Sept	71	335		Pekin, IL	Mittelweiher, Elsaß
Umdenstock, Matthias	19, Nov. 1857	5, Nov.	62	188		Pekin, IL	Mittelmeyer, Elsaß
Umlang, Adolph	20, Aug. 1877		32	271		Giddings, TX	Brätz, Posen, Preußen
Ummer, Ferdinand	27, June 1895	13, May	42	414		Greenfield, MA	Genooka, Polen
Unewehr, Elisabeth	22, Oct. 1864	27, Sept	24- 5m	172	Uphaus	Batesville, IN	Schledhausen, Osnabrück, Hannover
Unewehr, Maria Engel	19, Jan. 1888	30, Nov.	75	46		Batesville, IN	Altluſheim, Amt Schwetzingen, Baden
Unger, Maria	23, June 1873	13, May	58	199	Stephan	Terre Haute, IN	Rothfelden, Nagold, Württemberg
Ungericht, David	18, Aug. 1898	30, July	70	527		Greenville, OH	Rothfelden, Nagold, Württemberg
Ungericht, Simon Christian	10, Sept 1883	22, Aug.	62- 6m-17d	295		Greenville, OH	Zürich, Schweiz
Unholz, August	31, Mar. 1898	2, Mar.	55	207		Champaign, IL	
Unholz, Lulu	4, Dec. 1890	9, Nov.	15	782		Champaign, IL	
Unholz, Magdalena	6, Feb. 1871	14, Jan.	60	47	Scherer	Belleville, IL	Alpis, Affoltern, Zürich, Schweiz
Unland, Emma	17, Nov. 1884	26, Oct.	17	7		Dayton, OH	
Unland, Julia Anna	12, Feb. 1857	10, Jan.	24	28	Wiegel	Arenzville, IL	

Christliche Apologete Death Notices --- 1839 - 1899

Name of Deceased	Notice Date	Death Date	Age	Maiden Name	Page	Place of Death	Place of Birth
Unland, Maria	15, Oct. 1891	23, Sept	80	Karls	670	Arenzville, IL	Wimmer, Osnabrück, Wittlage, Hannover
Unland, Nellie	15, May 1890	29, Apr.	19		318	Swanton, NE	
Unland, Philippina	4, May 1899	6, Apr.	60	Ludwig	287	Arlington, NE	Zuzenhausen, Sinsheim, Baden
Untied, Hermann Heinrich	21, Jan. 1867	21, Dec.	51		22	Newark, OH	Ladbergen, Kreis Münster, Preußen
Untied, Susanne	20, Nov. 1882	18, Oct.	26		375	Newark, OH	Dresden, Muskingum County, Ohio
Unverzagt, Anton	28, Sept 1874	21, Aug.	49		311	Alton, IL	
Unverzagt, Elisabeth	17, Apr. 1890	27, Mar.	23	Maxeiner	254	Bunker Hill, IL	Weiler zum Stein, Marbach, Württemberg
Unverzagt, Louise	2, Feb. 1885	18, Jan.	57- 8m-15d		7	Indianapolis, IN	
Unverzagt, Maria	1, Nov. 1855	30, Sept		Bäker	176	Indianapolis, IN	Lüdenhausen, Lippe-Detmold
Unverzagt, Wilhelmina	21, Nov. 1870	4, Sept	32-11m	Petersmeier	375	Hopewell, MO	Bönnigheim, Besigheim, Württemberg
Unz, Christian	16, Aug. 1844				124	Louisville, KY	Wallenbrücker, Mark, Westphalen
Uphaus, A.M.J.	29, June 1893	31, May	66		414	Concordia, MO	Ahe, Amt Verden, Hannover
Uphaus, Anna Maria	19, Aug. 1878	27, July	52	Igelmann	263	Batesville, OH	Werder, Preußen
Uphaus, Anna Maria	26, May 1879	8, May	55		167	Concordia, MO	Eye, Amt Verden, Hannover
Uphaus, Elisabeth	19, July 1849	9, July	31		116	Cincinnati, OH	Werther, Kreis Halle, Minden, Preußen
Uphaus, Heinrich	23, Nov. 1868	24, Sept	88		375	Freedom, MO	Ostrup bei Osnabrück, Hannover
Uphaus, Johan Friedrich	31, Dec. 1883	11, Dec.	72		7	Batesville, IN	Spange, Herford, Minden, Preußen
Uphaus, Katharina	17, Sept 1883	26, Aug.	60		303	Concordia, MO	Lafayette County, Missouri
Uphaus, Katharina	9, Aug. 1875	17, July	26		255		Asturb, Neunkirchen, Verden, Hannover
Uphaus, Maria Elisabeth	19, May 1859		79- 9m	Knolenberg	80	Laughery, IN	Spange, Minden, Preußen
Uphaus, Peter Heinrich	24, Aug. 1899	31, July	81		543	Concordia, MO	Mühlhausen, Sachsen, Preußen
Urbach, Anna Regina	13, Aug. 1877	30, June	74	Göbeln	263	Glencoe, MN	Großlangheim, Baiern
Urban, Elisabeth	9, Dec. 1878	13, Nov.	44	Seiferling	391	Baltimore, MD	Uebigau, Sachsen
Urban, Friedrich David	15, Dec. 1892	11, Nov.	73-11m- 3d		798	Cannelton, IN	
Urbanike, Charles H.	18, June 1891	25, May	24- 8m- 4d		398	Brenham, TX	Bielitz, Schlesien
Urbantke, Friedrich	22, Nov. 1875	28, Oct.	77		375	Industry, TX	Bönigen, Interlaken, Bern, Schweiz
Urfer, Christian	23, Feb. 1893	20, Jan.	33		126	LaCrosse, WI	Dunkirk, New York
Urmey, Christina	27, June 1889	22, May	35		414	Dunkirk, NY	Brakelsiecke, Lippe-Detmold
Use, Friedrich	5, Feb. 1866	20, Jan.	30		46	Freeport, IL	Roggow, Pommern
Utech, Friedrike	14, Jan. 1884	13, Dec.	75- 6m-21d	Falk	7	Lemars, IA	Ruhnow bei Wangerin, Pommern
Utech, Karl	6, Feb. 1882	15, Jan.	17- 4m- 4d		47	Lemars, IA	Lienen, Tecklenburg, Preußen
Utlant, Ernst Fr.	18, Dec. 1876	26, Nov.	34- 3m- 8d		407	Highland, IL	Edwardsville, Illinois
Utlaut, August	6, May 1897	3, Apr.	44		287	Highland, IL	
Utlaut, Eberhard	10, Sept 1883	29, Aug.	85		295	Highland, MS	
Utlaut, Friedrich Wilhelm August	31, Aug. 1893	12, Aug.	17-5m-29d		558	Highland, IL	Lienen, Tecklenburg, Preußen
Utlaut, Katharina	31, Mar. 1879	2, Mar.	68		103	Highland, IL	Lienen, Tecklenburg, Preußen
Utlernt, Katharine	17, Mar. 1879	2, Mar.	68		87	Highland, IL	Sontheim an der Brenz, Württemberg
Utz, Barbara	16, Oct. 1871	20, Sept		Keller	335	Chicago, IL	Winterfingen, Basel, Schweiz
Utzinger, Barbara	15, Mar. 1880	3, Mar.	73- 9m	Graf	87	New York City, NY	
Uzinger, Mathilda	19, Sept 1895	2, Sept	24-7m-21d	Artz	606	Tea Creek, IN	
Vaihinger, Gottliebe	7, Apr. 1879	19, Mar.	70- -19d	Meier	111	New Ulm, MN	Mergelstetten, Heidenheim, Württemberg
Valet, Adam	24, Jan. 1871	5, Dec.	82- 5m		31	Herman, MO	Ochsenburg, Württemberg
Valtes, Margaretha	11, Jan. 1864	17, Nov.	55	Sack	8	Milwaukee, WI	Heichelheim, Hessen-Darmstadt
VanAllmen, Christ	14, Sept 1899	28, Aug.	70		591	Oregon, MO	Interlacken, Schweiz
VanBeunning, Johan	27, Sept 1875	3, Sept	26		311	San Jose, IL	Repersterlaurich, Aurich, Ostfriesland

Christliche Apologete Death Notices --- 1839 - 1899

Name of Deceased	Notice Date	Death Date	Age	Maiden Name	Place of Death	Page	Place of Birth
VanBönning, Hinderk	31, Aug. 1868	31, July	49- 7m- 9d		San Jose, IL	279	Gandreson, Amt Emden, Ostfriesland
VanderSloot, Martin	25, Feb. 1892	25, Jan.	63- 4m-15d		Keokuk, IA	127	Holland
VanderVelde, Föke	11, Feb. 1878	11, Jan.	81		San Jose, IL	47	Wirden, Ostfriesland
VanderVelde, Franke	20, Nov. 1865	4, Oct.	65	Luptes	Pekin, IL	188	Pensum, Ostfriesland
VanDyke, Johannes F.	4, Oct. 1880	14, Sept	86- 5m-27d		Pekin, IL	319	Virdum, Ostfriesland
VanEßen, Johan Heinrich	4, Apr. 1881	17, Mar.	68-11m-19d		Harrison, KS	111	Dover, Delaware
VanHoorn, Geerdt	10, Nov. 1898	22, Oct.	76		Sea Cliff, NY	719	Vielstädt, Oldenburg
VanHorn, Trintje	19, Oct. 1893	3, Oct.	72	Ohling	Pekin, IL	670	Oldersun, Emden, Ostfriesland
VanLoon, (3 children)	2, Jan. 1896				Pekin, IL	14	Borsum, Emden, Hannover
VanLoon, Albertje	19, Mar. 1877	7, Dec.	74	Tünninge	Hokah, MN	95	Wyuldum, Holland
VanLoon, Lena	20, Mar. 1890	17, Feb.	42		LaCrosse, WI	190	New Hartford, Winona County, Minnesota
VanTalge, Katharina Maria A.	23, June 1887	20, May	19	Severding	LaCrosse, WI	398	Hannover
Varregut, Anna	6, Sept 1888	18, Aug.	68	Marolf	Colesburg, IA	574	Walperswyl, Bern, Schweiz
Varwig, Charles Gustav	7, Mar. 1881	15, Feb.	47-10m		St. Joseph, MO	79	
Varwig, Heinrich	5, May 1892	29, Mar.	31- 8m		St. Louis, MO	286	Dissen, Hannover
Vast, Paul	13, Dec. 1888	1, Dec.	65		Macon, NE	798	Ravengiersburg, RheinPreußen
Vasterling, Heinrich	5, Feb. 1872	8, Jan.	67		Llano, TX	47	
Väth, Jakob	13, Mar. 1865	8, Jan.	24- 8m- 6d		Le Sueur, MN	44	Karbach, Baiern
Vatkin, Maria	23, Feb. 1899	23, Jan.	77	Prepper	Madison, IN	127	Settin, Preußen
Vaupel, Clara	4, Feb. 1858	4, Nov.	36	Clutinger	Blue Island, IL	20	
	22, Nov. 1888			Vaupel		750	
Vaupel, Anna Barbara	27, Oct. 1862	27, Aug.	69- 3m-11d		Mt. Vernon, IN	172	Harrison County, Indiana
Vaupel, Katharina Elisabeth	28, Feb. 1876	5, Feb.	79		Captina, OH	71	Rheinsachsen, Eschwege, Kurhessen
Veal, Hattie	1, Aug. 1889	15, July	19	Heise	Lena, IL	494	Reichensachsen, Kurhessen
Veeck, Elisabeth	24, May 1888	22, Apr.	48	Seitz	Michigan City, IN	334	Michigan City, Indiana
Veeck, Jakobina	24, Aug. 1899	4, Aug.	64	Nonweiler	Boonville, IN	543	Birkenfeld, Oldenburg
Veeck, Katharina	17, Dec. 1857	15, Oct.	66	Halle	Boonville, IN	204	Mackenroth, Birkenfeld, Oldenburg
Veeck, Magdalena	8, Apr. 1886	26, Mar.	31	Roth	Boonville, IN	7	Warrick County, Indiana
Veeck, Nicolaus B.	11, Feb. 1884	28, Jan.	36		Boonville, IN	7	Boonville, Warrick County, Indiana
Veek, Karl	5, Aug. 1878	20, July	25- 2m-22d		Boonville, IN	247	Warrick County, Indiana
Veek, Karolina	4, Dec. 1876	20, Nov.	21- -23d	Gerhart	Boonville, IN	391	Port Washington, Tuscarawas County, Ohio
Veek, Karoline	20, Apr. 1874	3, Apr.	49	Hepp	Boonville, IN	127	Birkenfeld, Oldenburg
Veek, Katharina Friederika	16, Aug. 1894	28, July	70	Seitz	Boonville, IN	534	Weisenheim am Berg, Baiern
Veek, Ludwig	12, Mar. 1883	26, Feb.	23-10m- 3d		Boonville, IN	87	Warrick County, Indiana
Veh, Magdalena	11, June 1866	15, Jan.	42	Roth	Peninsula, ---	190	Weibhausen, Offenheim, Baiern
Vehlewald, Ferdinand	28, June 1894	15, June	70		Morrison, MO	422	Holzhausen, Westphalen
Veigtling, Margaretha	23, June 1898	28, May	81	Jakobs	Lansing, MI	399	Obermodern, Elsaß
Veit, Johannes	17, Apr. 1890	27, Mar.	66		Chillicothe, OH	254	GroßBettlingen, Nürtingen, Württemberg
Veith, Anna Elisabeth	11, June 1891	11, May	75-10m-11d	Kambecher	Columbus, IL	382	Totenau, Hessen-Darmstadt
Veith, Johan	13, Feb. 1896	11, Dec.	78		Quincy, IL	110	Todtenau, Hessen-Darmstadt
Veith, Katie	8, May 1890	24, Apr.	15- 5m-22d		New Orleans, LA	302	New Orleans, Louisiana
Velde, Heinrich	23, Dec. 1872	28, Nov.	35		Pekin, IL	415	Wirdummer-Neuland, Ostfriesland
Velte, Elisabet	7, July 1853	13, June	21- 2m-20d		Bethlehem, OH	108	
Velte, Jakob Friedrich	13, June 1864	19, May	72- 2m-17d		Grand Rapids, MI	96	Münchingen, Leonberg, Württemberg
Velte, Johanna	25, Dec. 1865	9, Dec.	45	Schwarz	Woodland, OH	208	Münchingen, Leonberg, Württemberg
Velte, Rosina Maria	18, Feb. 1867	22, Jan.	72- 8m		Grand Rapids, MI	54	Münchingen, Württemberg

Christliche Apologete Death Notices --- 1839 - 1899

Name of Deceased	Notice Date	Death Date	Age	Maiden Name	Page	Place of Death	Place of Birth
Veninga, Anna Elisabeth	2, Dec. 1897		79	Eckhoff	767	St. Louis, MO	Arle, Ostfriesland
Venneberg, Heinrich	8, Apr. 1878	19, Feb.	14- 3m- 6d		111	Sheboygan, WI	
Venneberg, Karl	30, June 1892	6, June	61		414	Sheboygan, WI	Damlos, Holstein
Vennekolt, Emma Sophia	11, Sept 1890	23, Aug.	30	Krüger	590	Flood Creek, IA	Allamakee County, Iowa
Vennekolt, Heinrich Anton	12, May 1862		44- 3m-12d		76	Freeport, IL	Berlin, Preußen
Vennekolt, Henriette	13, Apr. 1874	26, Mar.	17- 7m		119	Flood Creek, IA	Yellow Creek, Stephenson County, Illinois
Vennemann, Christina Elisabeth	28, Nov. 1889		72	Feldwisch	766	Huntingburg, IN	Ladbergen, Tecklenburg, Münster, Preußen
Vennemann, Georg Daniel	14, Apr. 1879		6- 5m-19d		119	Huntingburg, IN	
Vennemann, Johan Heinrich	29, Jan. 1866	6, Jan.	24- - 6d		38	Huntingburg, IN	
Vennemann, Johan Heinrich	8, Oct. 1891	20, Sept	20		654	Huntingburg, IN	
Venninger, Wilhelmina	3, Dec. 1891	27, Oct.	35	Wilke	782	Boonville, IN	Posey County, Indiana
Veragut, (Mr)	30, Mar. 1868	25, Feb.			103	St. Joseph, MO	Thusis, Graubünden, Schweiz
Veraguth, Anna Marie	3, Feb. 1898	18, Dec.	26		79	St. Joseph, MO	St. Joseph, Missouri
Verclaß, Christine	16, Nov. 1874		51		367	Schnectady, NY	Horst, Holstein
Vernia, Emma	23, Jan. 1882	24, Nov.	22	Sieveking	31	New Albany, IN	
Versemann, Louisa	17, Feb. 1898	26, Jan.	69	Rotefeld	111	Kansas City, KS	Osnabrück, Hannover
Vertein, Maria	14, Nov. 1889	7, Sept	15-11m-22d		734	Baraboo, WI	Westfield, Wisconsin
Vesper, Alma Huldina	2, July 1891		44		430	Topeka, KS	Mengelsdorf, Schlesien
Vesper, Barbara	23, Apr. 1896	17, Mar.	50- 4m-18d	Oehlschläger	270	Topeka, KS	Langenbrand, Württemberg
Vesper, Elisabeth E.	24, Dec. 1896	18, Oct.	42	Brose	831	Canton, MO	Quincy, Illinois
Vesper, Maria	11, June 1866	15, May	40		190	Canton, MO	Niederwerden, Waldeck
Vespermann, Emma	5, July 1888	28, May	21		430	Walsh Co, SD	Windsor, Dana County, Wisconsin
Vespermann, Johan	5, Apr. 1894	17, Feb.	22		230	Sun Prairie, WI	Windsor, Wisconsin
Vespermann, Sophia	10, Jan. 1889	11, Dec.	40- 9m-18d	Rinder	30	Sun Prairie, WI	Lebbin, Demmin, Preußen
Vetsch, Apollonia	9, Sept 1886	15, Aug.	54- 4m- 7d		7	Junction City, KS	Buchs, Werdenberg, St. Gallen, Schweiz
Vetsch, Caspar	30, Jan. 1890	5, Jan.	76- 7m- 2d		78	Hokah, MN	Grab, St. Gallen, Schweiz
Vetsch, Elisabeth	7, Feb. 1881	21, Jan.	61	Berger	47	Davenport, IA	Sennwald, Werdenberg, St. Gallen, Schweiz
Vetsch, Elisabeth	4, Jan. 1894	30, Nov.	81	Schlegel	14	Plattsmouth, NE	Azmoos, St. Gallen, Schweiz
Vetter, Carl	1, Oct. 1877	30, Aug.	24- 9m-17d		319	Wabasha, MN	Halltesburg, Pennsylvania
Vetter, Fritz	8, June 1893	21, Apr.	39		366	Big Spring, MO	Bonneberg, Minden, Preußen
Vetter, Karl Fr. Wilhelm	25, Feb. 1878	1, Feb.	27- 5m- 9d		63	Hopewell, MO	Valldorf, Herford, Preußen
Vetter, Karoline Catharine	7, Sept 1893	7, Aug.			574	Belleville, IL	Belleville, Illinois
Vetter, Louis	16, June 1873	29, May	39- 4m-29d		191	Birmingham, PA	Dietlingen, Baden
Vetter, Luigarte	6, Mar. 1890	12, Feb.	61		158	Pittsburg, PA	Dietlingen, Pforzheim, Baden
Vetter, Margaretha	23, Feb. 1863	5, Feb.	70- -10d		32	Louisville, KY	Ditielheim, Hessen
Vetter, Mina M.	28, Mar. 1889	27, Feb.	19- 5m		206	Belleville, IL	
Vetter, Philipp	23, Mar. 1874	21, Dec.	77-10m- 9d		95	Louisville, KY	Weingarten, Durlach, Baden
Vetter, Samuel	2, June 1873	10, May	55- 5m-18d		175	Birmingham, PA	Eggenstein, Baden
Vetter, Samuel	16, Apr. 1857	20, Mar.	8- 9m-15d		64	Birmingham, PA	
Vetting, Bertha	14, June 1888	14, May	24	Gelbke	382	Manitowoc, WI	Manitowoc, Wisconsin
Veyhle, Magdalene	20, Oct. 1887	25, Sept	76- 8m	Kübler	670	Pittsburg, PA	Böchgand, Württemberg
Vicinus, Caroline Magdalene	6, Mar. 1882	10, Feb.	15		79	Rochester, NY	Rochester, New York
Vick, Elisa Maria	7, June 1869	28, Apr.	18- 6m		183	Fond du Lac, WI	
Vick, Fritz	8, Apr. 1886	16, Mar.	21		7	Milwaukee, WI	Milwaukee, Wisconsin
Vick, Joachim	25, Apr. 1895	6, Apr.	81		270	Milwaukee, WI	Milwaukee, Wisconsin
Vicker, Richard	7, May 1883	22, Apr.	39		151	Brunswick, MO	Wendelsdorf, Mecklenburg-Schwerin

Christliche Apologete Death Notices --- 1839 - 1899

Name of Deceased	Notice Date	Death Date	Age	Page	Maiden Name	Place of Death	Place of Birth
Viehmann, Anna Catharina	7, July 1892	11, Feb.	53	430	Wölf	Rushville, NE	Elnrode, Jesberg, Fritzlar, Kurhessen
Viehmeyer, Henriette	3, Mar. 1884	14, Apr.	35- 4m	7	Eiffert	St. Louis, MO	
Vieht, Hanna	23, May 1864	18, Apr.	32	84		Warrenton, MO	
Vielbig, V.K.	15, May 1871		24- 9m-12d	159	Uehlin	Peterson, IA	
Vierkamp, Wilhelm Karl	26, June 1890	4, June	12	414		Nerstrand, MN	Wheeling, Rice County, Minnesota
Vierkant, Karl	24, Aug. 1899	2, Aug.	61	543		Cannon River, MN	Göttingen, Hannover
Vieth, Amalia	3, Nov. 1879	16, Oct.	66	351		Hopewell, MO	Humfeld, Amt Alberdissen, Lippe-Detmold
Vieth, August W.	30, Mar. 1899	6, Mar.	84	207		Sterling, NE	Bösingfeld, Lippe-Detmold
Vieth, Friederika Seyfert-Rötsch	7, Apr. 1892	9, Mar.	84-10m	222		Warren, MO	Meierberg, Lippe-Detmold
Vieth, Friederike Sophia	1, Sept 1887	14, Aug.	58	558	Böger	Warren, MO	Bößingfeld, Aßmissen, Lippe-Detmold
Vieth, Friedrich	6, July 1893	15, June	27	430		Newton, IA	
Vieth, Heinrich	11, May 1893	7, Apr.	86	302		Pinckney, MO	Bösingfeld, Lippe-Detmold
Vieth, Herman	20, Jan. 1873	8, Nov.	34	23		Warren, MO	Allmano, Lippe-Detmold
Vieth, Johan Heinrich	28, Oct. 1886		21- 3m-19d	7		Newton, IA	Warren County, Missouri
Vieth, Lydia	18, Jan. 1894	19, Dec.	40	46	Dothage	Pinckney, MO	
Vieth, Sophie	18, Nov. 1858	2, Oct.		184		Warren, MO	Heidelbeck, Lippe-Detmold
Vieths, Christiana	24, May 1869	17, Apr.	39- 6m-16d	167	Schneider	Cincinnati, OH	Neuwied, Preußen
Vieths, Johan Dietrich	15, Oct. 1866	16, Sept	53	334		Cincinnati, OH	Wingersen, Amt Hasefeld, Hannover
Vifel, Jacob	29, Aug. 1870	31, July	41	279		New York City, NY	Remingsheim, Rottenburg, Württemberg
Vincenz, F.D.	28, Mar. 1889	4, Mar.	86- 2m	206		Alexandria, MN	Gleina bei Freiburg an der Unstrut, Sachsen
Virenkes, Joseph	1, Jan. 1847	27, Sept	1- 6m	3		Beardstown, IL	
Visel, Rosalie C.	2, Feb. 1899	13, Jan.	76	79	Weiß	New Haven, CT	
Vissering, Peter Gerhard	17, Sept 1891	13, Aug.	77	606		Alton, IL	Riepe, Aurich, Ostfriesland
Vitt, Paul	17, Jan. 1889	24, Nov.	48- 1m	46		St. Louis, MO	Seifertshausen, Rotenburg, Kurhessen
Vittmer, Johann	30, Aug. 1860	30, July	45	140		Lansing, MI	Timk, Amt Ottersberg, Hannover
Vocke, Caroline	8, Sept 1887	14, Aug.	76- 4m-13d	574	Budling	Madison, WI	Blooming Grove, Wisconsin
Voegt, Heinrich	4, Aug. 1892	29, May	38	494		Nashville, TN	Nashville, Tennessee
Voelbel, Henry	28, Apr. 1884	16, Mar.	32	7		Brooklyn, NY	Bergzabern, Baiern
Voelkel, Johannes Heinrich	3, Aug. 1863	5, July	68	124		Evansville, IN	Ruckersfeld, Kreis Siegen, Preußen
Voelkel, Magdalena	7, Apr. 1873	9, Mar.	39	111	Geming	Mascoutah, IL	Haßloch, Rheinkreis Baiern
Voelkel, Philipp Peter	13, Mar. 1882	15, Feb.	79- 3m-24d	87		Mascoutah, IL	Haßloch, Rheinkreis Baiern
Voge, Friedrich Michael	19, Aug. 1897	26, June	83	527		Blooming Grove, MN	Ziegenhagen, Satzig, Pommern
Voge, Maria Magdalena	10, Jan. 1895		41	30	Lips	Blooming Grove, MN	Canton Zürich, Schweiz
Voge, Louise	1, June 1893	28, Apr.	32	350	Meierheinrich	Tacoma, NE	Summersell, Lippe-Detmold
Voge, Maria	26, Aug. 1878	6, Aug.	59	271	Kühndopp	Cannon River, MN	West Preußen
Vogel, Maria Dorothea	21, Mar. 1895	4, Mar.	68	190	Kretzmeier	Chillicothe, OH	Hannover
Vogel, Albert	22, Nov. 1880	9, Nov.	32	375		Storm Lake, IA	Canton Aargau, Schweiz
Vogel, Barbara	15, June 1854	22, May	27	96	Wetzel	Galena, IL	Metzingen, Württemberg
Vogel, Christian	28, Dec. 1899	24, Nov.	77	828		Chillicothe, OH	Hähnlein, Hessen-Darmstadt
Vogel, Emilie Louise	26, Feb. 1883	2, Feb.	23- 2m-25d	71		Santa Claus, IN	Spencer County, Indiana
Vogel, George	20, Aug. 1896	8, June	77	543		Brooklyn, NY	Orb, Baiern
Vogel, Gesine Friederike	12, Jan. 1885	20, Dec.	61	7	Klaver	St. Louis, MO	Leer, Ostfriesland
Vogel, Heinrich	17, June 1886	30, May	70	7		Cannelton, IN	Obergruppenbach, Besigheim, Württemberg
Vogel, Heinrich	30, July 1877	27, June	33- 6m-17d	247		Pittsburg, PA	Pittsburg, Pennsylvania
Vogel, Johan G.	14, Oct. 1878	21, Sept	55- 9m-17d	327		Santa Claus, IN	OberUrbach, Württemberg
Vogel, Johan Georg	18, Apr. 1895	23, Mar.	79	254		San Francisco, CA	Schaffhausen, Schweiz

Christliche Apologete Death Notices --- 1839 - 1899

Name of Deceased	Notice Date	Death Date	Age	Maiden Name	Page	Place of Death	Place of Birth
Vogel, Julie	26, Apr. 1855	23, Mar.	6		68	Piqua, OH	
Vogel, Katharina	24, Feb. 1879	2, Feb.	70- -22d	Mahler	63	Louisville, KY	Wahenheim bei der Hard, Rheinkreis Baiern
Vogel, Katharina	16, Feb. 1899	18, Jan.	74	Bauer	111	Cannelton, IN	Gruppenbach, Württemberg
Vogel, Louise Charlotte Marie	10, June 1897	18, May	68	Wiebusch	367	St. Louis, MO	Minden, Westphalen
Vogel, Samuel	28, Feb. 1889	23, Jan.	86- 5m-23d		142	Mound City, MO	Kölligen, Aargau, Schweiz
Vogel, Sigmund	22, Dec. 1892		76- - 4d		814	St. Louis, MO	Germany
Vögele, Wilhelm	19, July 1849		Inquiry		115	Monroe, OH	Elsaß
Vogeley, Catharine	1, Nov. 1894	12, Oct.	76	Schneider	710	Pittsburg, PA	Gundesheim, Hessen-Darmstadt
Vogeley, Conrad	8, Oct. 1883	24, Sept	67		327	Pittsburg, PA	Melsungen, Hessen-Kassel
Vogeley, Robert	19, Dec. 1889	1, Dec.	33-10m-21d		814	Pittsburg, PA	Pittsburg, Pennsylvania
Vogelgesang, Abelana	18, Feb. 1897	1, Jan.	93	Thomas	111	Pekin, IL	Essingen bei Landau, Rheinkreis Baiern
Vogelgesang, Michael	13, Oct. 1887	25, Sept	40		654	Pekin, IL	Damheim bei Landau, Baiern
Vogelsang, Anna M.	22, Nov. 1888	5, Nov.	69		750	Ironton, OH	Desde, Preußen
Vogelsang, Carl H.	21, June 1888	2, June	69		398	Ironton, OH	Südlengern, Germany
Vogelsang, Maria	28, Jan. 1892	1, Jan.	48	Trapp	62	Ironton, OH	Mt. Vernon Furnace, Lawrence County, Ohio
Vogelsang, Maria	28, May 1877	3, May	83- 6m	Seger	175	Cannon River, MN	Friesen, Baden
Voges, Heinrich	21, Sept 1893	25, Aug.	53		606	Perry, TX	Haueshausen, Sandersheim, Braunschweig
Vogler, Christine	14, Nov. 1889	25, Oct.		Ebert	734	Warsaw, IL	Maunterbach, Delleburg, Nassau
Vogler, Ferdinand	5, Dec. 1889		49		782	St. Louis, MO	Insterburg, Gumbinnen, OstPreußen
Vogler, Friedrich Wilhelm	16, Jan. 1871	20, Nov.	43		23	Burlington, IA	Memke, Salzwedel, Magdeburg, Preußen
Vogt, Anna Margaretha	4, Dec. 1890	17, Nov.	68- 6m	Hag	782	Red Wing, MN	Streichenthal, Mergentheim, Württemberg
Vogt, Catharina	26, Sept 1881				311	Philadelphia, PA	
Vogt, Elisabeth	6, May 1897	31, Mar.	79	Köhne	287	Lamberton, MN	
Vogt, Emma	19, Oct. 1893	30, Sept	31		670	Burlington, IA	Burlington, Iowa
Vogt, Friedrich Wilhelm	14, Apr. 1873	26, Mar.	50- 6m-24d		119	Cincinnati, OH	Treptow, Pommern
Vogt, Gustav	21, Jan. 1897	31, Dec.	49		47	Chicago, IL	Remingen, Aargau, Schweiz
Vogt, Ida Bertha	17, Jan. 1895	30, Dec.	17		46	Grand Rapids, MI	Wildenthierbach, Gerrebron, Württemberg
Vogt, Johan Philipp	12, Jan. 1893	12, Dec.	81		30	Red Wing, MN	Basel, Schweiz
Vogt, Joseph	20, Mar. 1882	7, Mar.	58- 2m- 7d		95	Nashville, TN	
Vogt, Louis	31, July 1865	3, June			124	Le Sueur, MN	Remigen, Aargau, Schweiz
Vogt, Louise	5, Oct. 1885	14, Sept	13		7	Grand Rapids, MI	
Vogt, Mary Jane	11, Sept 1876	25, Aug.	17- 4m-13d		295	Nashville, TN	Oak Creek, Wisconsin
Vogt, Minna	6, Dec. 1888	13, Nov.	31-10m-13d		782	Red Wing, MN	Lembrock, Hannover
Vogt, Sophia	1, Aug. 1895	10, July	53	Bente	494	Cincinnati, OH	Dartz, Pommern
Vogt, Wilhelmine	8, Dec. 1873		34		391	Le Sueur, MN	Kremkau, Gardeleben, Magdeburg, Preußen
Vogtländer, Dorothea	17, Apr. 1890	23, Mar.	68	Gürs	254	Baresville, OH	
Vögte, Elisabeth	1, Apr. 1886	7, Mar.	71	Tüscher	7	Highland, IL	Hessen-Darmstadt
Vögte, Katharine	30, Mar. 1885	20, Jan.	75		7	St. Louis, MO	
Vogtli, Karoline	28, June 1875	16, May	29	Knelle	207	Jackson, MO	Cape Girardeau, Missouri
Vogus, Dorothea	25, Oct. 1875	29, Sept	22	Schrader	343	Jackson, IL	
Vogus, Rosine	29, June 1874	28, May	41-11m-16d	Nabe	207	Scranton, PA	Pfullingen, Reutlingen, Württemberg
Vohrer, Jakob	21, June 1880	6, May	43- 8m		199	Scranton, PA	Pfullingen, Württemberg
Vohrer, Maria	28, June 1888	3, June	53- 8m- 9d	Fischer	414	Chicago, IL	Wittlingen, Urach, Württemberg
Vöhringer, John	26, Jan. 1888	6, Jan.	49		62	Manchester, MO	
Vohs, (Mrs)	27, Sept 1849	23, July	35		156	Herman, MO	Hilte bei Osnabrück, Hannover
Vohs, Chr. Wilhelmine Charlotte	30, Mar. 1868	11, Feb.	41	Meyer	103		

Christliche Apologete Death Notices --- 1839 - 1899

Name of Deceased	Notice Date	Death Date	Age	Page	Maiden Name	Place of Death	Place of Birth
Vohs, Heinrich Friedrich Wilhelm	2, Feb. 1899	16, Jan.	73	79		Berger, MO	Hörste, Halle, Westphalen
Vohs, Johann	3, May 1860	12, Apr.	36	72		Pomeroy, OH	Kremdendorf, Ostpriegnitz, Preußen
Vohs, Ludwig	27, Sept 1849	19, July	40	156		Manchester, MO	
Vohs, Ludwig (Mrs)	27, Sept 1849	23, July		156		Manchester, MO	
Voige, Catharina	20, Jan. 1873	5, Jan.	36- 6m	23	Faber	Newport, KY	
Voight, Frank Willie	18, Jan. 1894	12, Dec.	23- 8m	46		Cincinnati, OH	
Voigt, Carl	2, June 1873	19, May	56	175		Milwaukee, WI	Rogzow, Stettin, Pommern
Voigt, Carl Gustav	10, Mar. 1884	24, Feb.	55	7		Pekin, IL	Weida, Sachsen-Weimar
Voigt, Carl Heinrich Gottlieb	27, July 1868	8, July	50	239		Manitowoc, WI	Temploo, Pommern, Preußen
Voigt, Carolina	13, June 1895	16, May	77	382	Brandenburg	Manitowoc, WI	Witzmitz, Pommern
Voigt, Franz Heinrich Wilhelm	13, Aug. 1896	25, July	52	527		Cincinnati, OH	Bremen, Germany
Voigt, Hermann	30, Dec. 1867	21, Dec.	18	414		Cincinnati, OH	Bremen, Germany
Voigt, Maria	21, June 1888	8, June	37	398	Starck	Milwaukee, WI	
Voigt, Wilhelmine	3, Mar. 1898	15, Feb.	51	143	Nützmann	Chicago, IL	Treptow an der Tolenz, Pommern
Voigtländer, Christian	5, Dec. 1895	30, Oct.	74	782		Detroit, MI	Lindstädt, Sachsen
Voisin, Jakob	5, Nov. 1857	22, Sept	16- 8m	180		Chester, IL	
Voisin, Samuel	23, Sept 1867	6, Sept	53	302		Belleville, IL	Rucheim, Rheinkreis Baiern
Voisin, Samuel	2, Apr. 1866	9, Mar.	17	110		Belleville, IL	
Voisin, Susanna Elisabeth	9, Sept 1867	28, Aug.	53	286	Voisin	Belleville, IL	Ruckheim, Baiern
Volbrecht, Maria	18, Apr. 1881	19, Mar.	42	127	Wilhelm	Nokomis, IL	Meineringhausen, Korbach, Wisenberg, Waldeck
Volk, Anna Alvine	16, July 1896	31, May	23	463		Vermilion, OH	Henrietta, Lorain County, Ohio
Volk, Michael	12, June 1865	4, Oct.	27	96		Des Moines, IA	Kramersteterhof, Dinkelsbuhl, Baiern
Volk, Mina Katharina	15, Jan. 1877	29, Dec.	66	23	Brunner	Newton, IA	Geisbühl, Crailsheim, Württemberg
Völkel, Anna	26, Mar. 1877	5, Mar.	21- 6m-21d	103	Bertloch	Belleville, IL	Mascoutah, Illinois
Völkel, Anna Margaretha	19, Apr. 1888	26, Mar.	64	254	Moser	Belleville, IL	RheinPfalz Baiern
Völkel, Louise	8, June 1893		58- 5m	366	Stünkel	Evansville, IN	Germany
Völkel, Maria El.	14, Aug. 1865	31, July	65- -22d	132		Evansville, IN	Rückersfeld, Preußen
Völker, Christian	27, Feb. 1882	8, Feb.	15- - 5d	71		Marine City, MI	
Völker, Dorothea	24, May 1860	23, Apr.	64	84		Watertown, WI	
Völker, E. J.	9, Dec. 1878		18- 3m	391		Flood Creek, IA	
Völker, Fr.	17, July 1865	14, May	28	116		Watertown, WI	
Völker, Heinrich	20, July 1874	7, July	33- 8m- 7d	231		Fillmore, MI	Leonberg, Württemberg
Völker, Johan Gottlieb	25, May 1874	6, May	45	167		Flood Creek, IA	Zählsdorf, Arnswalde, Frankfurt, Preußen
Völker, Johannes	28, July 1887	15, Feb.	68	478		New York City, NY	Niedermoxstadt, Hessen-Darmstadt
Völker, Karl	4, Feb. 1848		Inquiry	23		Monroe County, IL	Einertshausen, Hungen, Hessen
Völker, Karl Heinrich	23, July 1866	2, July	45	238		Wheeling, WV	Einartshausen, Hessen-Darmstadt
Völker, Michael	21, Oct. 1872	19, Sept	71	343		Watertown, WI	
Völker, Sophia Christine	30, Dec. 1897	6, Dec.	69	828	Witte	Marine City, MI	Sachsen-Gotha
Völkers, Elisabeth	2, Jan. 1851	16, Nov.	34	4	Rothenbeck	Wheeling, VA	
Volkland, Otto	12, Aug. 1878	13, July	22	255		Great Bend, KS	
Volkland, Robert	16, Apr. 1877	4, Apr.	22- 5m- 3d	127		Fond du Lac, WI	Plymouth, Wisconsin
Volkland, Wilhelm	20, Dec. 1888	3, Dec.	62	814		Bushton, KS	Sußenborn, Sachsen-Weimar
Volkman, Ferdinand August	5, Apr. 1894	11, Mar.	44	230		Watertown, WI	Tribus, Treptow an der Rega, Pommern
Volkmann, Auguste Johanna L.	7, Apr. 1879	26, Mar.	33- 4m	111		Lyona, KS	
Volkmann, Caroline	13, Feb. 1882	27, Jan.	37	55	Timm	Lyona, KS	Kirchhagen, Treptow an der Rega, Pommern
Volkmann, Dorothea	12, Mar. 1896	24, Feb.	91	175		Lyona, KS	Hoff bei Camin, Pommern

Christliche Apologete Death Notices --- 1839 - 1899

Name of Deceased	Notice Date	Death Date	Age	Maiden Name	Place of Death	Page	Place of Birth
Volkmann, Maria Caroline	16, Jan. 1896	25, Dec.	64	Hoppe	Watertown, WI	46	Tribus, Treptow a. d. Rega, Pommern
Volkmann, Martin	3, Apr. 1871	28, Feb.	73- 1m- 7d		Lyons Creek, KS	111	Zedlin, Treptow a.d. Rega, Stettin, Pommern
Volkmann, Wilhelm Julius	21, June 1888	8, June	6- 4m-17d		Watertown, WI	398	
Volkmann, Wilhelm Theodor	4, Nov. 1878	15, Oct.	38		Lyona, KS	351	Mittelhagen, Stettin, Pommern
Voll, Amalia	14, June 1894	16, May	70	Bork	Baraboo, WI	390	Baldenburg, West Preußen
Voll, Katharina Elisabeth	21, Dec. 1893	15, Nov.	70	Deichmüller	Newport, KY	814	Völkershausen, Sachsen-Weimar
Voller, John	10, Jan. 1884	27, Feb.	20- 1m-17d		Evansville, IN	7	
Voller, Maria Elisabeth	4, Feb. 1886	13, Jan.	23	Völkel	Evansville, IN	7	Evansville, Indiana
Vollmer, Heinrich	18, Feb. 1897	16, Jan.	76		Kline, IA	111	Hüttenhausen, Minden, Preußen
Vollmer, Heinrich	29, Oct. 1883	23, Sept	71		Camden, IN	351	Humburg, Baiern
Vollmer, Herman	23, Mar. 1874	11, Mar.	73		Marshall, WI	95	Bielefeld, Preußen
Vollmer, Jakob Friedrich	1, Sept 1859	16, Aug.	39		Hamilton, OH	140	Gräfenhausen, Württemberg
Vollmer, Johan Thomas	11, Jan. 1894	16, Dec.	62		Cincinnati, OH	30	Olnhausen, Neckarsulm, Württemberg
Vollmer, Johannes	13, Apr. 1863	22, Mar.	68		Lafayette, IN	60	Unterhausen, Reutlingen, Württemberg
Vollrath, Michael	11, Sept 1851	28, July	75- 2m-10d		Quincy, IL	148	
Vollrath, Valentin	28, Jan. 1897	30, Dec.	76		Edwardsville, IL	63	Sponheim, Germany
Vollriede, Dorothea	15, July 1878	15, Apr.	58- 3m	Blum	Flint Creek, IA	223	
Volmer, Anna Maria	29, Jan. 1877	11, Jan.	79- -17d	Hofmeier	Decatur, IL	39	Lippinghausen, Herfort, Preußen
Volmer, Louis	7, Oct. 1872	25, Aug.	37		Etna, MO	327	Wheeling , West Virginia
Voltmann, Sarah	27, Feb. 1896	28, Jan.	59		Ossian, IN	143	Germany
Voltz, Christian	13, July 1899	12, May	79		Cleveland, OH	447	Stammheim, Württemberg
Volz, Barbara	27, Mar. 1865	7, Mar.	41- 1m-17d		Eudora, KS	52	Lafayette, Allen County, Indiana
Volz, Jakob Friedrich	30, Aug. 1880	11, Aug.	22		Spencerville, OH	279	Semd, Dieburg, Hessen-Darmstadt
Volz, Maria	6, Sept 1869	29, July	58- 3m-15d	Staub	New York City, NY	287	
Volz, Ottilia	13, Oct. 1873	23, July	77		Ft. Wayne, IN	327	
Volz, Susanna	6, Apr. 1863	10, Mar.	25- 4m- 8d		Oregon, MO	56	Baltimore, Maryland
VonAllmen, Barbara Großniklaus	23, June 1892	25, May	67		New Orleans, LA	398	St. Beatenberg, Bern, Schweiz
VonAlt, John	10, Apr. 1890	2, Mar.	54-11m-15d		Vandalia, IL	238	Eichelheim, Hessen-Darmstadt
VonArx, (Mr)	27, Apr. 1874	26, Mar.	52- 5m-20d		San Bernardino, CA	135	Nießlingen, Sobothum, Schweiz
VonAspern, John J.	8, May 1890	19, Apr.	58-11m-22d		Schenectady, NY	302	Heide , Holstein
VonBehren, Carolina Marie	19, June 1890	8, Apr.	53- 9m	Schwentker	Defiance, OH	398	Hille , Minden, Preußen
VonBehren, Caroline	29, Dec. 1873	16, Dec.	22		Burlington, IA	415	Evansport, Defiance County, Ohio
VonBehren, Fr.	31, Jan. 1881	15, Jan.	66- 8m-10d		Toledo, OH	39	Hartum, Minden, Preußen
VonBehren, Ida Emilie	6, Jan. 1898	14, Dec.	21		Evansport, OH	15	Peabody, Kansas
VonBehren, Margaretha	12, Apr. 1849	18, Mar.	30- 6m		Galena, IL	60	Schalkendorf bei Straßburg, Frankreich
VonBerg, Leonhard	4, Apr. 1889	12, Feb.	17- 8m-18d		Alton, IL	222	Charles City, Iowa
VonBergen, Elisabeth	18, Aug. 1862	15, July	15- 3m		Marietta, OH	132	Hausen, Hasle, Bern, Schweiz
VonBergen, Katharina	13, July 1854	30, June	28	Danker	Schnectady, NY	112	Tüschendorf, Amt Ottersberg, Hannover
VonBuhren, Caroline	8, June 1893	19, May	57- 4m-25d		Madison, IN	366	Hille , Minden, Preußen
VonBuren, Maria Nancy	15, Nov. 1855	6, Nov.	23- 1m-20d		Blue Island, IL	184	Hellberg, Amt Hohnhausen, Lippe-Detmold
Vondenberg, Caroline	1, June 1863	10, May	36		Schnectady, NY	88	Hille, Minden, Preußen
VonderAhe, Louise	16, July 1896	6, June	22- 9m- 3d		Rud Bud, IL	463	Aurich, Ostfriesland
VonderGrant, Harm Harms	1, Dec. 1859	6, Oct.	47		Los Angeles, CA	192	Elmshorn, Schleswig-Holstein
VonderLohe, Amanda G. H.	6, Feb. 1896	1, Jan.	30	Warnke	Madison, IN	94	Liebenau, Kurhessen
VonDissen, Phil.	16, Mar. 1893	30, Jan.	75		Tallula, IL	174	Ochtelburg, Ostfriesland
VonDornum, Hinrika	23, Aug. 1894	25, July	62	Müller		550	

Christliche Apologete Death Notices --- 1839 - 1899

Name of Deceased	Notice Date	Death Date	Age	Page	Maiden Name	Place of Death	Place of Birth
VonDran, Karl	21, Sept 1863	23, May	28	152		Milwaukee, WI	Stollberg, Preußen
VonGalena, Dora	10, Nov. 1887	22, Oct.	67	718		Rushville, NE	Frankfort am Main, Hessen
VonGlahn, Christopher	2, Apr. 1896	16, Feb.		222		Stockton, CA	
VonGlahn, Wilhelmina	23, Oct. 1876	20, Aug.	30	343		Brooklyn, NY	Hannover
VonGunten, Johan	7, Sept 1868	8, Aug.	59	287		Toledo, OH	Schwanden, Bern, Schweiz
VonHardt, Elsie	5, Mar. 1896	10, Feb.	15	158		Warrenton, MO	St. Louis, Missouri
VonHove, Harm	30, Aug. 1880	1, July	37- 8m	279		Crete, NE	Emden, Ostfriesland
VonOertzen, Louise	30, Apr. 1883	14, Apr.	30- 3m-20d	143	Antonsen	Le Sueur, MN	Cape Girardeau County, Missouri
VonSanders, Friedrich Wilhelm	14, Dec. 1863	2, Dec.	82	200		St. Charles, MO	Preußen
Vonsien, W.	29, Apr. 1897	7, Apr.	64	271		Waseca, MN	AltKrantzlien, Mecklenburg-Schwerin
VonUxküll, Olga	1, Nov. 1875	10, Sept	37	351		Frankfurt, ---	Sulz am Neckar, Preußen
Vorchers, Wilhelm	21, June 1875	9, Apr.	39	199		San Francisco, CA	Leithorst, Hannover
Vorderbrügge, Maria Charlotte	14, Nov. 1889	21, Oct.	66	734	Langenkamp	Pinckneyville, IL	Oesterweg, Halle, Westphalen
Vorlesch, Henriette	8, July 1878	28, May	25	215		Bland, MO	Güsebitz, Kreis Stolp, Preußen
Vornkahl, Johanna L.	30, May 1850	2, Mar.	67	88		Jackson, MO	Bierl, Braunschweig
Vorsbrink, Johan Herman	12, Dec. 1864	1, Dec.	60	200		Seymour, IN	Gerde, Hannover
Vörsner, Georg	13, Mar. 1890	4, Feb.	76- 9m- 8d	174		Menomonie, WI	Württemberg
Vortmann, Catharina Elisabeth	10, Feb. 1873	19, Jan.	66- 5m- 2d	47	Aring	Santa Claus, IN	WesterOldendorf, Melle, Hannover
Vortmann, Herman Gerhard	19, Feb. 1857	7, Nov.	45	32		Huntingburg, IN	Mienlage, Badbergen, Hannover
Vos, Elisabeth	23, Dec. 1897	6, Dec.	54	815	Schneider	Russell, KS	Rußland
Voshage, Friedrich	28, Jan. 1897	31, Dec.	66	63		Belvidere, IL	Fahrbruck, Hannover
Vosinek, Frank	9, Mar. 1885	12, Feb.	52-11m-20d	7		Jordan, MN	Böhmen
Voskamp, Johanna Christiana	22, Sept 1887	8, Sept	55	606	Hildebrandt	Industry, TX	Wittenberg, Preußen
Vosmer, Catharina	8, May 1890	17, Apr.	74- 3m- 6d	302	Willis	Covington, KY	Lavelsloh, Diepenau, Hannover
Vosmer, Magdalena Louise	19, Sept 1881	29, Aug.	41- -10d	303	Pflüger	Covington, KY	Bremen, Germany
Voß, Chr. Wilhelm	2, July 1891	8, June	59 -6m- 4d	430		Holt, MI	Poppenhagen, Preußen
Voß, Christian	15, June 1863	20, Mar.	29	96		Union, MO	
Voß, Dietrich F.	31, May 1880	3, Apr.	66- 9m-13d	175		Kansas City, MO	Hilter, Hannover
Voß, Elisabeth	9, Apr. 1883	5, Feb.	30- 2m-17d	119	Heigel	Neenah, WI	
Voß, Eva	15, Apr. 1882	8, Apr.	34- 6m-29d	159		Wyandotte, KS	Clay County, Missouri
Voß, Friederika	6, Aug. 1896	13, July	28	511	Weden	Detroit, MI	Zetemien, Preußen
Voß, Friedrich	16, Feb. 1899	20, Jan.	73	111		Albert Lea, MN	Kreen, Stettin, Pommern
Voß, Hanna Maria	27, June 1889	18, May	33	414	Debald	Hokah, MN	Allenburg, Canada
Voß, Herman Wilhelm	23, July 1896	3, June	63	479		Rochester, MN	Holstein
Voß, Louisa Catharina	13, Sept 1888	14, Aug.	74- 6m-25d	590	Horstmann	Kansas City, MO	Westbarthausen, Hannover
Voß, Mamie C.S.	8, Feb. 1894	14, Jan.	18- 9m-28d	94		Kansas City, KS	Kansas City, Kansas
Voß, Maria	14, Apr. 1873	16, Mar.	27	119	Meyer	Wyandotte, KS	Franklin County, Missouri
Voß, Maria	6, Sept 1849	1, July		144		Belleville, IL	
Voß, Sophie	4, Mar. 1867	14, Feb.	68	70	Bose	Chicago, IL	Dösewitz, Pommern
Voß, Wilhelm	28, Aug. 1890	13, Feb.	61	558		Almond, NY	Rothmühl, Germany
Vosselmann, Maria Magdalena	13, Dec. 1894	12, Nov.	48	806		Brooklyn, NY	
Waaser, Rosina	18, Mar. 1867	5, Feb.	46- 6m-20d	86	Jordan	Ann Arbor, MI	Oetisheim, Maulbronn, Württemberg
Waber, Magdalena	4, Dec. 1890	14, Oct.	37	782		Cleveland, OH	Homberg, Bern, Schweiz
Wachlin, Bertha Auguste	23, June 1892	29, May	37	398	Schröder	Chicago, IL	
Wachsmuth, Anna	20, Feb. 1882	23, Jan.		63	Fritze	New York City, NY	Breine, Kurhessen

- 536 -

Christliche Apologete Death Notices --- 1839 - 1899

Name of Deceased	Notice Date	Death Date	Age	Page	Maiden Name	Place of Death	Place of Birth
Wachsmuth, Anna Maria	4, Dec. 1871	10, Sept	46- 6m-17d	391	Luther	Bremen, IL	Denstedt, Langensalza, Preußen
Wachsmuth, Louise Anna D.	28, Oct. 1897	9, Oct.	48	687	Buchholz	New York City, NY	Hannover Stadt, Hannover
Wachstedter, Christina	21, Sept 1854	10, Sept	22	152		Indianapolis, IN	Kleinsachsenheim, Württemberg
Wächter, Anna Gertrude	15, June 1899	20, May	83	383	Schumacher	Poughkeepsie, NY	
Wächter, Georg	11, Apr. 1895	22, Mar.	84	238		Zion, OH	Martin, Büschweiler, Elsaß
Wächter, John Nicolaus	24, Sept 1878	8, Sept	61	303		Poughkeepsie, NY	Michelbach, Koblenz, Preußen
Wächter, Theresia	13, July 1893	8, June	82	446		Baltimore, MD	
Wächtler, Victoria	29, Mar. 1894	9, Feb.	63	214	Weiß	Springfield, MN	Seeg, Baiern
Wackenhut, Anna	9, May 1864	14, Mar.	32- 6m- 2d	76	Rüfli	Newark, NJ	Langenau, Bern, Schweiz
Wacker, Carl F.	28, Mar. 1895	20, Feb.	44	206		Troy, NY	Grunbach, Württemberg
Wacker, F.	3, Oct. 1861	11, Sept	41- 6m	160		Troy, NY	Grunbach, Schorndorf, Württemberg
Wacker, Johan Philipp	20, Sept 1869	10, Aug.	65	303		Berea, OH	Weinheim a. d. B., Baden
Wacker, Louise	26, May 1873	6, May	49- -14d	167	Schlehauf	Geneva, NY	Häsloch, Stuttgart, Württemberg
Wacker, Margaretha	18, Jan. 1875	18, Dec.	50- 8m-24d	23		Cleveland, OH	Michelbach, Gerabronn, Württemberg
Wacker, Margaretha	29, Dec. 1884	12, Dec.	69	7	Weidner	Kansas City, MO	Lauterbach, Hessen
Wacker, Maria Elisabeth	6, Feb. 1871	7, Jan.	64	47		Giard, IA	
Wacker, Philipp (Rev)	15, Apr. 1897	11, Mar.	58-11m-12d	238		Charles City, IA	Weinheim, Baden
Wackwitz, Carl Wilhelm	25, July 1864	31, May	30	120		St. Joseph, MO	Neustadt bei Dresden, Sachsen
Wackwitz, Karl	11, July 1864	31, May		112		Marietta, OH	
Wagenblast, Regina	3, Jan. 1895	13, Dec.	66	14	Knödler	Crown Point, IN	Seifertshofen, Gaildorf, Württemberg
Wagener, Anna Koranda	6, Oct. 1898	6, Sept	86	639	Becker	Cosby, MO	Eisenrod, Niedau, Hessen-Darmstadt
Wagenknecht, Friederike	25, Feb. 1897	31, Jan.	77	127	Wolter	Buffalo, NY	Sulten, Mecklenburg-Schwerin
Wagner, Adelgunde	12, Nov. 1896	22, Aug.	62	734	Schmidt	Waltersburg, MO	Philipsburg, Pennsylvania
Wagner, Anna Louisa	11, Mar. 1897	17, Feb.	24	159		Waltersburg, IL	Pope County, Illinois
Wagner, Anna Maria	21, July 1862	8, July	36- 7m-27d	116		Beardstown, IL	Holzburg, Neukirchen, Ziegenhain, Kurhessen
Wagner, Anna Maria	12, Mar. 1896	22, Feb.	32- 9m	175	Amende	Culbertson, NE	Frank, Rußland
Wagner, Caroline	4, Feb. 1892	12, Jan.	75	78	Wadisch	Quincy, IL	Grünstadt, Rheinpfalz Baiern
Wagner, Caspar	29, May 1871	17, May	47	175		Baltimore, MD	Mittel-Gründau, Hessen-Darmstadt
Wagner, Catharina Elisabeth	6, Sept 1894	2, Aug.	19	582		Baltimore, MD	Baltimore, Maryland
Wagner, Christian	15, Mar. 1849	17, Feb.	21- 8m	44		West Union, OH	
Wagner, Christina	7, June 1875	21, May	20	183	Heimbach	Indianapolis, IN	Indianapolis, Marion County, Indiana
Wagner, Christina	21, Oct. 1867	2, Oct.	63	334		Mt. Vernon, IN	Auä bei Karlsruhe, Baden
Wagner, Conrad	22, Aug. 1895	17, July	87- 2m-25d	542		Geneseo, IL	Großenbusiek, Hessen-Darmstadt
Wagner, Dorothea	29, May 1882	16, May	73-10m-25d	175		Belleville, IL	Weinheim bei Alzei, Baiern
Wagner, Elisabeth	10, Dec. 1891	15, Nov.	25	798		Allegheny City, PA	Kirchvers, Hessen-Nassau
Wagner, Elisabeth	15, Jan. 1891	29, Dec.	71- 8m-18d	46		Rock Island, IL	
Wagner, Emilie	17, Aug. 1893		35	526	Wener	Nebraska City, NE	Pitzelwitz, Brandenburg
Wagner, Emilie Mina	18, Nov. 1897	30, Oct.	20	735		Cincinnati, OH	Cincinnati, Hamilton County, Ohio
Wagner, Emma	7, Mar. 1895	12, Feb.	29	159		Gladbrook, IA	Johnson County, Iowa
Wagner, Ernst Christian Heinrich	14, Sept 1893	16, Aug.	82	590		Stockton, CA	Hannover
Wagner, Friedrich	28, Mar. 1864	27, Dec.	33	52		St. Joseph, MO	Satteldorf, Krailsheim, Württemberg
Wagner, Friedrich	10, Mar. 1898	9, Feb.	68	159		Woodland, MI	Höfingen, Leonberg, Württemberg
Wagner, Friedrich	8, Apr. 1872	11, Mar.	15-11m	119		Pittsfield, IL	Perry, Pike County, Illinois
Wagner, Heinrich	14, Dec. 1885	28, Nov.	78	7		Le Sueur, MN	Winslo bei Pirmasenz, Rheinkreis Baiern
Wagner, Heinrich	4, Jan. 1869	17, Dec.	80	7		Vandalia, IL	
Wagner, Henriette	7, Apr. 1892	20, Mar.	36	222	Dyer	Golconda, IL	Louisville, Jefferson County, Kentucky

Christliche Apologete Death Notices --- 1839 - 1899

Name of Deceased	Notice Date	Death Date	Age	Page	Maiden Name	Place of Death	Place of Birth
Wagner, Jane	8, Feb. 1894	18, Jan.	55	94	Vernolt	Kline, IA	Emkirch, Zell, Coblenz, Preußen
Wagner, Joh. Ph.	30, Dec. 1886	30, Nov.	70	7		Seguin, TX	Kanton Bern, Schweiz
Wagner, Johan	9, Aug. 1880	17, July	61	255		Schnectady, NY	Heinebach, Melsungen, Kurhessen
Wagner, Johan	13, Apr. 1899	25, Mar.	78	239		Waltersburg, IL	Inchirch, RheinPreußen
Wagner, Johan Daniel	16, Mar. 1893	17, Feb.	71	174		Seguin, TX	Schwieberdingen, Ludwigsburg, Württemberg
Wagner, Johan Georg	25, May 1874	2, May	75	167		Blue Island, IL	Brakelsieck, Schwalenberg, Lippe-Detmold
Wagner, Johanna Friederike Elise	3, Mar. 1892		64	142	Riecke	Crown Point, IN	Eschenroth, Schotten, Hessen-Darmstadt
Wagner, Johannes	10, May 1869	27, Apr.	61	151		St. Joseph, MO	Alburtis, Berks County, Pennsylvania
Wagner, Johannes	28, Mar. 1895	4, Mar.	83	206		Terre Haute, IN	Atzenheim, Hessen-Darmstadt
Wagner, Johannes	25, Nov. 1867	22, Oct.	56	374		Flint Creek, IA	Schöneberg, Baiern
Wagner, John	9, May 1861	2, Mar.	49	76		Perry, IL	
Wagner, John	27, Jan. 1873	6, Nov.	17	31		Golconda, IL	Pope County, Illinois
Wagner, Julia	25, Apr. 1889	8, Mar.	34	270	Densch	Golconda, IL	Golconda, Illinois
Wagner, Karolina	16, Mar. 1893	24, Feb.	85	174	Betz	Geneseo, IL	Münster am Stein, Baiern
Wagner, Karolina	21, June 1875	11, May	40	199	Drescher	La Grange, MO	
Wagner, Katharina	1, Nov. 1860	17, Sept	55- -25d	176	Benz	Hanging Rock, OH	Kirchard, Sinsheim, Baden
Wagner, Katharina	27, Apr. 1885	23, Mar.	74	7	Wolfraum	Cannelton, IN	Breitenau, Hessen-Kassel
Wagner, Katharina	20, July 1893	26, June	82	462	Baum	Ballwin, MO	Hardenest, Preußen
Wagner, Katharine	3, Nov. 1898	16, Oct.	78-4m-26d	703	Stegmeier	Warsaw, IL	Bartholomä, Gemünd, Württemberg
Wagner, Lisetta	23, May 1895	4, May	44	334	Pauls	Ballwin, MO	
Wagner, Louis	10, May 1894	22, Apr.	45	310		Baltimore, MD	Pfedelbach, Württemberg
Wagner, Louise	9, Aug. 1880	17, July	57	255		Le Sueur, MN	Winsli, Pirmasens, Baiern
Wagner, Louise J.	21, Feb. 1895	18, Jan.	44	126	Schmidt	Pittsfield, IL	Perry, Illinois
Wagner, Magdalena	30, May 1895	9, May	66	350	Haas	St. Louis, MO	Altenheim, Baden
Wagner, Magdalene	14, Apr. 1873	24, Mar.	81- -20d	119		Golconda, IL	Heinebach, Melsungen, Kurhessen
Wagner, Maria	24, July 1890	8, June	70-4m	478	Schmidt	Dodgeville, IA	Kesselbach, Gießen, Hessen-Darmstadt
Wagner, Maria	11, May 1899	30, Mar.	82	302	Dirfeld	Rochester, NY	Codsiesen, Posen
Wagner, Maria Apollonia	10, Apr. 1890		44	238	Hirt	Scranton, PA	Obenbreit, Baiern
Wagner, Peter	8, June 1874	29, Apr.	39	183		Flint Creek, IA	Kesselbach, Geisen, Hessen-Darmstadt
Wagner, Peter	30, Dec. 1867	22, Sept	67	414		Belleville, IL	Grießfeld, Rheinkreis Baiern
Wagner, Peter	9, July 1896	13, June	72	447		Victoria, TX	Nassau
Wagner, Philipp	31, May 1875	12, May	74	175		Ballwin, MO	Gladenbach, Biedenkopf, Hessen-Darmstadt
Wagner, Phillipine	8, Sept 1892	13, Aug.	26	574	Zinnecker	Chillicothe, OH	Pirmasens, Rheinkreis Baiern
Wagner, Rebekka	4, Jan. 1894	3, Dec.	80	14	Sell	Terre Haute, IN	Berks County, Pennsylvania
Wagner, Sophia	12, Mar. 1896	23, Feb.	72	175	Kemmet	Chicago, IL	Dürrenbichig, Baden
Wagner, Wilhelmine	14, Nov. 1881	21, Oct.	27	367		Aurora, IL	Belleville, Illinois
Wagstaf, Mathilde	5, Mar. 1883	11, Feb.	20-1m-10d	79	Bokus	St. Louis, MO	
Wahl, Carl Heinrich	17, Sept 1896	19, Aug.	22	607		Saginaw, MI	Cleveland, Ohio
Wahl, Christoph F.H.	2, Aug. 1880	19, July	38- -15d	247		Red Wing, MN	Jaenack, Mecklenburg-Schwerin
Wahl, Friedrich W.	7, Oct. 1897	16, Sept	19	639		Indianapolis, IN	Indianapolis, Marion County, Indiana
Wahl, Georg Adam	7, Jan. 1858	6, Dec.	58	4		Evansville, IN	Walterrems, Backnang, Württemberg
Wahl, Johan Gottlieb	14, Jan. 1892	16, Dec.	80	30		Marietta, OH	Wahldriems, Württemberg
Wahl, Karolina Dorothea Rosalie	19, Feb. 1872	30, Jan.	55-6m-10d	63	Dürr	Evansville, IN	Stuttgart, Württemberg
Wahl, Katharina	7, Aug. 1851	27, June		128		Dayton, OH	Backnang, Württemberg
Wahl, Margarethe	27, Mar. 1890	12, Feb.	60-10m-26d	206		San Jose, IL	Allershausen, Lauterbach, Hessen-Darmstadt
Wahl, Maria	30, Dec. 1886	8, Dec.	38	7	Gilbert	Seattle, WA	Funckstadt, Hessen-Darmstadt

Christliche Apologete Death Notices --- 1839 - 1899

Name of Deceased	Notice Date	Death Date	Age	Page	Maiden Name	Place of Death	Place of Birth
Wahlemeier, Benjamin	28, Jan. 1897	31, Dec.	26	63	Beutel	Kansas City, KS	Kansas City, Kansas
Wahlenmaier, Anna Maria	29, Dec. 1873	3, Dec.	61	415		Wyandotte, KS	Buhlbronn, Württemberg
Wahlenmaier, J. Wilhelm	27, Apr. 1885	4, Apr.	39	7		Wyandotte, KS	Asperglen, Schorndorf, Württemberg
Wahler, Martha	17, Jan. 1889	26, Dec.	78	46	Röhers	Lake Creek, MO	Steinfeld, Hannover
Wahlers, Friedrich	3, Mar. 1884	18, Feb.	76-5m	7		Lake Creek, MO	Steinfeld, Otterbach, Hannover
Wahlers, Gesche	17, Sept 1896	5, Aug.	75-2m	607	Bluhm	Lake Creek, MO	Bülsted, Ottersberg, Hannover
Wahlers, Johan Dietrich	11, May 1874	14, Apr.	70	151		Lake Creek, MO	Steinfeld, Amt Ottersberg, Hannover
Wahlers, Maria	20, Nov. 1876	6, Nov.	26- -24d	375		Lake Creek, MO	
Wahner, Katharina	12, Apr. 1869	27, Feb.	68	119		Seymour, IN	Nordheim, Hessen-Darmstadt
Wahner, Nicolaus	23, Apr. 1866	2, Feb.	36	134		Seymour, IN	Northeim, Hessen-Darmstadt
Wahrenbrock, Louise	23, June 1898	10, May	55	399	Eggers	Concordia, MS	Weißenburg, Elsaß
Wahrenburg, Gustav Wilhelm Karl	24, June 1897	12, May	48	399		Lafayette, IN	Altenplathow, Preußen
Wahssik, Johan Herman	27, Sept 1888	23, Aug.	18	622		Piqua, OH	Piqua, Miami County, Ohio
Waibel, Friedrich	18, Jan. 1894	11, Dec.	45	46		Covington, KY	Basel, Schweiz
Waible, Christian	1, Dec. 1898	5, Nov.	68	767		Mt. Pleasant, IA	Germany
Waida, Rosina	19, Sept 1895	28, Aug.	87	606		Lansing, IA	Kirchenkirnberg, Welzheim, Württemberg
Waide, Karl	23, June 1884	6, June	56	7		Lansing, IA	Kirnberg, Welzheim, Württemberg
Waisner, Georg	1, Aug. 1881	29, June	60-7m	247		Milwaukee, WI	Sulz am Neckar, Württemberg
Walbow, Wilhelmine	17, July 1882	6, June	66-3m-21d	231	Hain	Garner, IA	
Walbrandt, Theodor J.	4, Mar. 1886	15, Feb.	44	7		Honey Creek, WI	Wolrich bei Jarne, Pommern
Waldbaum, Herman	1, June 1863	16, May	77	88		Nashville, IL	Spenge, Kreis Herford, Minden, Preußen
Waldemayer, Edward A.	11, Dec. 1890	17, Nov.	23-8m-29d	798		Newport, KY	
Walden, Auguste	28, Apr. 1887	15, Apr.	26	270		Fairmount, KS	
Walder, Louise	29, Dec. 1884	29, Nov.	43-1m-4d	7	König	---, NY	Hinweil, Zürich, Schweiz
Waldhaus, Heinrich	19, Apr. 1875	17, Mar.	84-2m-21d	127		Columbus, IL	Unbrau, Hessen-Darmstadt
Waldheim, Louise	12, Mar. 1891	15, Feb.	71	174	Laring	Baltimore, MD	Mengershausen, Hannover
Waldmann, Anna	25, Mar.1872	8, Feb.	76-11m- 2d	103		Etna, MO	Axtet, Amt Hagen, Hannover
Waldmeier, Wilhelm	22, Sept 1887	6, Aug.	14	606		Topeka, KS	Topeka, Kansas
Waldow, Caroline	29, Jan. 1891	8, Jan.	43	78	Frommel	Buffalo, NY	Kirchberg, Preußen
Waldow, Ufred	18, May 1863	28, Mar.	35	80		De Soto, MO	Malmö, Schweden
Waldschmidt, (Mrs)	11, May 1874	27, Mar.	68	151		Elizabeth City, IL	Frohnhausen, Dillenburg, Nassau
Waldschmidt, Katharina	1, Feb. 1894	28, Dec.	52	78	Röder	Roberts, IL	Speckswinkel, Neustadt, Kirchhain, Kurhessen
Waldschmidt, Philippina	4, May 1874	27, Mar.	68	143		Earl, IL	Frohnhausen, Dillenburg, Nassau
Walkenhast, Maria M.	6, Dec. 1880	12, Nov.	71-1m-19d	391		Concordia, MO	Pennsylvania
Walkenhorst, Johanna Matilde	8, Aug. 1895	20, July	44	510	Küster	Concordia, MO	Concordia, Missouri
Walkenhorst, Louise	6, Mar. 1890	31, Jan.	32	158	Sullivan	Concordia, MO	North Carolina
Walker, Bertha A. E.	9, Apr. 1896	19, Mar.	42	238	Schwaab	Louisville, KY	
Walker, David	5, Jan. 1874	24, Dec.	49-5m	7		Cincinnati, OH	Lustnau, Tübingen, Württemberg
Walker, Maggie K.M.	31, May 1888	21, May	25-5m-18d	350		Covington, KY	Covington, Kenton County, Kentucky
Walker, Mathilde	5, July 1869	8, June	35	215	Courtz	Flint Creek, IA	Wermelskirchen, Düsseldorf, Preußen
Wallbaum, August	21, Feb. 1895	19, Jan.	81	126		Charles City, IA	Stemmen, Lippe-Detmold
Wallbrandt, Wilhelm Heinrich	17, Jan. 1881	26, Dec.	76	23		Spring Prairie, WI	Mecklenburg
Wallenbrock, Dorothea	26, July 1860	1, July	30	120	Holstein	Warsaw, IL	Bockerode, Melsungen, Kurhessen
Wallenbrock, Ernst Heinrich	6, July 1893	11, June	21	430		St. Charles, MO	St. Charles, Missouri
Wallenbrock, Theresia	2, Sept 1858	31, July	21	140	Bertsche	Warsaw, IL	Dürrenasch, Aargau, Schweiz
Wallenbruck, Wilhelm	4, Oct. 1894	4, Sept	19	646		St. Louis, MO	St. Charles County, Missouri

Christliche Apologete Death Notices -- 1839 - 1899

Name of Deceased	Notice Date	Death Date	Age	Page	Maiden Name	Place of Death	Place of Birth
Waller, Anton	22, Aug. 1881	15, July	78	271		Chicago, IL	Hirlingen, Rottenburg, Württemberg
Waller, Antonie	20, Oct. 1884	3, Oct.	71- 4m-28d	7		Chicago, IL	Hirlingen, Rottenburg am Neckar, Württemberg
Wallich, Magdalena	11, Jan. 1894	14, Dec.	89	30		Berea, OH	Prum, Trier, Preußen
Walliser, Christina Magdalena	4, Nov. 1867	19, Sept	79	350	Metzger	Walnut Creek, IA	Kleinsachsenheim, Vaihingen, Württemberg
Wallisser, Georg	21, June 1894	1, June	66	406		Aurora, IL	Sontheim a. d. Brenz, Heidenheim, Württemberg
Wallner, Maria Magdalena	10, Oct. 1881	22, Sept	73	327		Louisville, KY	Mackrebel, Hanau, Kurhessen
Wallon, Abraham Louis	21, Feb. 1889	5, Feb.	82	126		Newark, NJ	Friedrichsdorf, Homburg v. d. Heide, Germany
Walrave, Jakobus	25, Dec. 1876	1, Dec.	62	413		Evansville, IN	Cuttendyke, Leeland, Holland
Wallschläger, Johan	2, Nov. 1899	4, Sept	77	703		Manitowoc, WI	Hagen, Pommern
Walrave, Clasina	5, Jan. 1863	12, Dec.	22- 5m	4		Evansville, IN	Klontinge, Seeland, Holland
Walser, Roman	26, Oct. 1893	28, Sept	73	686		Batesville, IN	Fuchsburg, Baden
Walsmann, Heinrich E.	2, May 1870	19, Apr.	48	143		St. Charles, MO	Walsen, Amt Diepholz, Hannover
Waltemath, Heinrich	13, Mar. 1882	13, Feb.		87		Akron, OH	
Walter, (Mrs)	10, Feb. 1887	14, Jan.	75	94		Jersey City, NJ	
Walter, A. Katharina Wilhelmina	10, June 1867	17, Mar.	24- 4m- 5d	182		Golconda, IL	Plaggenburg, Hannover
Walter, Almuth Harmes	13, Jan. 1887	19, Dec.	73- 8m	30	Renken	Golconda, IL	Ostersande, Aurich, Hannover
Walter, Anna Catharina	30, Mar. 1874	9, Mar.	31- 2m-27d	103	Lehmann	Golconda, IL	Berka an der Werra, Sachsen-Weimar
Walter, Anna Elisabeth	20, Sept 1888	23, Aug.	80- 6m-16d	606	Diehl	Canton, MO	Zeilbach, Alsfeld, Hessen
Walter, Anna Friederike	27, Jan. 1873	6, Dec.	61	31	Müller	Golconda, IL	Pfalzdorf, Amt Aurich, Ostfriesland
Walter, Anna Maria	28, Feb. 1876	3, Feb.	66	71	Rodewald	Golconda, IL	Sandhorst, Amt Aurich, Ostfriesland
Walter, Anna Maria	5, Sept 1895	20, Aug.	63- 4m	574	Bartholomeß	Scranton, PA	Ostheim, Oberfranken, Baiern
Walter, Anna Maria	19, June 1882	4, June	63- 4m- 2d	199		Scranton, PA	Eckartsweiher, Baden
Walter, Anna Maria	8, Oct. 1896	1, Sept	78	655	Hinners	Elmore, OH	Hannover
Walter, Barbara	21, July 1892		44	462	Hoffmann	Canton, MO	Fernau bei Suhl, Preußen
Walter, Benedikt	12, May 1843		Inquiry	75		Monroe Co, OH	Urselen, Münsingen, Bern, Schweiz
Walter, Bertha	22, Dec. 1887	18, Nov.	19	814		Perry, TX	Fredericksburg, Gillespie County, Texas
Walter, Bonifazius	7, June 1869	13, May	65	183		Melrose, NY	Katzenthal, Baden
Walter, Catharina	5, Dec. 1895	15, Nov.	68	782	Lindner	Odebolt, IA	Brandt bei Wohnzüttel, Baiern
Walter, Catharina Barbara	8, Feb. 1875	20, Jan.	27-10m-28d	47	Blatter	Golconda, IL	Pope County, Illinois
Walter, Christoph	15, Sept 1879	28, Aug.		295		Bucyrus, OH	Grötzingen, Baden
Walter, Daniel	31, Jan. 1881	8, Jan.	74	39		Golconda, IL	Plagenburg, Aurich, Hannover
Walter, Eduard	12, June 1876	8, Apr.	20	191		West Chester Co, NY	Melrose, West Chester County, New York
Walter, Elisabeth	17, Apr. 1882	27, Mar.	41- 2m-21d	127	Staiger	Danbury, CT	Metzingen, Urach, Württemberg
Walter, Elisabeth	27, Nov. 1890	2, Nov.	32	766		Waltersburg, IL	Butler County, Pennsylvania
Walter, Elisabeth	28, Oct. 1872	9, Aug.	65-10m- 2d	351	Dall	Bucyrus, OH	Grötzingen, Baden
Walter, Emilie	5, July 1894	13, June	23	438	Schlegel	Le Sueur, MN	Scott County, Minnesota
Walter, Emilie	14, Feb. 1889	23, Jan.	24	110	Walter	Golconda, IL	Pope County, Illinois
Walter, Eva	8, June 1863	24, Mar.	81	92		New York, NY	Lembach, Weissenberg, Elsaß
Walter, Eva	28, Feb. 1870		61	71		Baresville, OH	
Walter, Eva Katharine	25, Jan. 1869	27, Dec.	55- - 4d	31	Hägelin	Waverly, OH	Freistett, Baden
Walter, Friedrich	17, Sept 1891	12, Aug.	21	606			Monroe County, Ohio
Walter, Friedrich Jakob	11, May 1863	21, Apr.	65	76		Golconda, IL	Plagenburg, Ost-Friesland, Hannover
Walter, Georg	17, July 1890	26, June	79	462		Canton, MO	Eckezweier, Baden
Walter, Heinrich	15, Oct. 1866	2, Aug.		334		Golconda, IL	
Walter, Ida Pauline	6, June 1895	21, May	19	366		Clarington, OH	Switzerland Twp, Monroe County, Ohio
Walter, Ilse Dorothea	21, Jan. 1892	17, Dec.	70	46	Wiedenroth	Angelica, NY	Abensen, Hannover

Christliche Apologete Death Notices --- 1839 - 1899

Name of Deceased	Notice Date	Death Date	Age	Page	Maiden Name	Place of Death	Place of Birth
Walter, Johan	19, Nov. 1883	1, Nov.	72-11m-22d	375		Almond, WI	Eckartsweier, Kork, Baden
Walter, Johan Friedrich	21, June 1875	28, Apr.	60	199		Wabasha, MN	Briesenhorst, Landsberg A.d.W., Preußen
Walter, Johan Ludwig	17, Aug. 1893	25, July	84	526		Elmore, OH	Unter-Urbach, Schorndorf, Württemberg
Walter, Johanna Friederika	11, Mar. 1867	22, Feb.	36- 5m- 3d	78		Golconda, IL	
Walter, Katharina	28, Sept 1893	29, July	76	622	Knapp	New York City, NY	Muckenthal, Baden
Walter, Katharine	26, Jan. 1885	2, Jan.	33	7	Nesselrod	Golconda, IL	Heerda bei Berga, Sachsen-Weimar
Walter, Louise Katharina	25, Feb. 1878	9, Feb.	31- -12d	63	Blatter	Golconda, IL	
Walter, Maria	22, Oct. 1857	21, Sept		172	Kafets	Mt. Vernon, IN	Dausenberg, Kaiserslautern, Rheinkreis Baiern
Walter, Maria Anna	4, Oct. 1880	3, Sept	53- 8m-11d	319	Grüner	Scranton, PA	Weilderstadt, Württemberg
Walter, Maria Ernestina	20, Sept 1869	19, Aug.	25- 4m	303	Stumpf	Golconda, IL	Reitzsch bei Bitterfeld, Preußen
Walter, Maria Magdalena	25, Feb. 1878	3, Feb.	61	63		Golconda, IL	Plagenburg, Amt Aurich, Hannover
Walter, Nikolaus	2, Apr. 1883	15, Mar.	74- 1m- 6d	111		Golconda, IL	Plaggenburg, Amt Aurich, Hannover
Walter, Peter	12, June 1890	23, May	67	382		Empire Prairie, MO	Oppau, Frankenthal, Rheinpfalz Baiern
Walter, Rosa	5, May 1892	12, Apr.		286	Steinle	Scranton, PA	Hasenhof, Württemberg
Walter, Rose	16, Nov. 1899	31, Jan.	32	111	Loose	Milwaukee, WI	Milwaukee, Wisconsin
Walter, Thomas	21, Jan. 1897	14, Dec.	73	47		Mt. Vernon, IN	Dainbach, Boxberg, Baden
Walter, Ursula	8, Feb. 1869	14, Jan.	69- 4m- 9d	47		Shakopee, MN	Insheim, Frankreich
Walter, Wesley	28, Feb. 1895	3, Feb.	42	142		Elmore, OH	Woodville Township, Sandusky County, Ohio
Walter, Wilhelm	4, Jan. 1894	10, Dec.	71	14		Chicago, IL	Löningen, Schaffhausen, Schweiz
Walter, Wilhelmine	19, May 1873	5, May	81	159		Nauvoo, IL	Mistelgau bei Baireuth, Baiern
Walther, Charles	21, July 1863	19, June	19	116		Canton, MO	
Walther, Elisabeth	12, June 1890	16, May	66	382	Kübler	Chicago, IL	Siblingen, Schaffhausen, Schweiz
Walther, Fred.	19, Aug. 1897	12, June	79	527		De Soto, MN	Bouxbille, Elsaß
Walther, Jacob	3, May 1888	6, Apr.	65- 9m-19d	286		Almond, WI	Hohnhurst, Baden
Walther, Johanne S.	27, Mar. 1865	13, Feb.	49	52	Aeschbacher	St. Joseph, MO	Seedorf, Zürich, Schweiz
Walther, Maria Barbara	28, Feb. 1889	29, Dec.	19	142		Cameron, MO	Willmendingen, Reutlingen, Württemberg
Walther, Mathilda	10, Nov. 1879	13, Oct.	34- 6m	359		Quincy, IL	Louisville, Jefferson County, Kentucky
Walther, Sal.	14, Jan. 1848	18, Dec.		11		St. Louis, MO	Sontheim, Baden
Walther, Thekla	14, Oct. 1878	29, Sept	58	327	Purg	Quincy, IL	Plauen, Sachsen
Waltz, Jakob	28, Aug. 1871	12, Aug.	23	279		Birmingham, PA	
Waltz, John	10, Aug. 1863	6, Apr.		128		Baraboo, WI	
Walz, Christina	5, July 1860		14- 2m-12d	108		Hazel Green, WI	
Walz, John	2, Aug. 1880	12, July	22-10m-25d	247		Sherrills Mount, IA	
Walz, Marie Ellen	19, Jan. 1863	4, Jan.	13	12		Baraboo, WI	
Walz, Simon	13, Apr. 1874	5, Mar.	79- 6m- 6d	119		Baraboo, WI	
Wamer, Friederika	19, Feb. 1891	27, Jan.	65	126	Zeller	Pittsburg, PA	Berks County, Pennsylvania
Wandmacher, Catharine	14, Apr. 1873	26, Feb.	35- 4m- 3d	119	Meinike	Red Wing, MN	Massenbach, Brackenheim, Württemberg
Wangelin, Ida	2, Dec. 1897	28, Oct.	30	767	Meisner	Chicago, IL	Nortensdorf, Hannover
Wangemann, Julius	6, Sept 1888	10, Aug.	71- 1m-20d	574		Watertown, WI	Manitowoc, Wisconsin
Wangemann, Susanna	5, Apr. 1888	17, Mar.	59-10m- 2d	222	Schildt	Watertown, WI	Bienstedt, Sachsen
Wangemann, Theresia	22, Oct. 1864		46	172	Granil	Oconomowoc, WI	Oberhellingen, Sachsen-Meiningen
Wanke, Johanna	13, Dec. 1860	25, Oct.	66- 4m- 1d	200		Baresville, OH	Dallstedt,
Wanneburger, Charlotte	14, Apr. 1887	12, Mar.	32	238		Paige, TX	Hohenfluß, Mähren, Germany
Wanner, (Mrs)	11, Feb. 1886	27, Jan.	85	7	Denger	Laporte, IN	Industry, Texas
Wanner, Anna	14, Sept 1863	8, Aug.	22- 4m- 8d	148	Hilti	Highland, IL	Schleitheim, Schaffhausen, Schweiz
Wanner, Clara	12, Oct. 1893	18, Sept	16	654		St. Louis, MO	

Christliche Apologete Death Notices --- 1839 - 1899

Name of Deceased	Notice Date	Death Date	Age	Page	Maiden Name	Place of Death	Place of Birth
Wanner, Friedrich W.	1, Sept 1879	11, Aug.	19- 1m-15d	279		Chicago, IL	Bodenweiler, Arnsbach, Baiern
Wanner, Georg Michael	11, Sept 1882	10, Aug.	55- -20d	295		Pittsburg, PA	Schleitheim, Schaffhausen, Schweiz
Wanner, Kasper	28, Apr. 1898	6, Apr.	72	271		Laporte, IN	Rütschelen, Arwangen, Bern, Schweiz
Wanner, Maria	3, Nov. 1873	5, Oct.	31	351	Keller	Brunswick, MO	Steinfurth, Sinsheim, Württemberg
Wanner, Peter	6, Oct. 1892	2, Sept	40	638		Marion, OH	Schleitheim, Schaffhausen, Schweiz
Wanner, Theresa	4, Nov. 1858	21, Oct.	30- 8m-15d	176	Meyer	Laporte, IN	Schleitheim, Schaffhausen, Schweiz
Wanner, Verena	25, Apr. 1881	8, Apr.	46- 9m-28d	135	Stamm	Laporte, IN	Schwaßdorf, Mecklenburg-Schwerin
Wanner, Wilhelmina	30, Sept 1886		44	7	Brückmann	Laporte, IN	
Wannewetsch, Veronika	6, Feb. 1882	7, Dec.		47		Baltimore, MD	
Wantzig, Katharina	16, Dec. 1878	27, Nov.	40-11m- 2d	399	Mayer	Stryker, OH	Sandusky, Ohio
Wanzig, Jacob	1, Apr. 1886	25, Jan.	64	7		Stryker, OH	Schweikhausen, Hagenau, Elsaß
Wappler, Katharina	12, Feb. 1891	6, Nov.	39- 7m-20d	110		De Soto, MO	
Wardmann, Elisabeth	6, Sept 1869	6, Aug.	20- 5m	287	Spritersbach	Mascoutah, IL	
Warg, Karl	24, May 1860	5, May	29	84		Chicago, IL	Dorfstadt, Sachsen
Warly, Anna	31, July 1865	18, July	67	124		Canton, MO	Canton Graubündten, Schweiz
Warner, Barbara	8, Jan. 1891	24, Dec.	50	30	Gerisch	Warsaw, IL	Pittsburg, Pennsylvania
Warner, Friederika	12, Mar. 1891	27, Jan.	65	174	Zeller	Pittsburg, PA	Massenbach, Brackenheim, Württemberg
Warner, Julia A.	7, Oct. 1886	22, Sept	68	7	Grill	Blue Island, IL	Niederalben, RheinPreußen
Warner, Peter	20, Jan. 1887	17, Dec.	74- 8m-15d	46		Blue Island, IL	Kernweiler, RheinPreußen
Warning, Maria	5, Apr. 1860	30, Jan.	77	56		Seymour, IN	Storhe, Vörden, Hannover
Warnke, Jürgen	9, May 1895	14, Apr.	81	302		Lake Creek, MO	Sevin, Hannover
Warnke, Maria Karoline	20, Apr. 1899	10, Mar.	19	255		Woodbury, MN	
Warnken, Herman	19, July 1894	22, May	64	470		Troy, NY	Greblingen bei Bremen, Germany
Warnken, John	18, Jan. 1875	28, Dec.	21	23		Lake Creek, MO	
Warnow, Johan Christian	17, June 1886	27, May	65- 4m-26d	7		New Bremen, IL	Herzberg, Mecklenburg-Schwerin
Warns, Ella	16, Mar. 1893	13, Feb.	31	174	Hemminger	Toledo, OH	Bay City, Michigan
Warns, Henriette	20, Oct. 1887	1, Oct.	54-10m-21d	670	Aden	Toledo, OH	
Warns, John	27, May 1878	6, May	22- 2m-18d	167		Perrysburg, OH	
Warnstedt, Josephine	25, June 1883	27, May	23- 2m-14d	207		New Orleans, LA	
Warweg, Philipp	19, May 1859	21, Apr.	48	80		Lowell, WI	Thalhausen, Amt Horn, Lippe-Detmold
Waschel, Eva	5, Dec. 1895	6, Nov.	83	782	Schäfer	Newark, NJ	
Waschink, Georg	9, Mar. 1874	17, Feb.	36- 5m-13d	79		Piqua, OH	Bockholt, Hannover
Waschko, John	7, Aug. 1851	25, June	42	128		Portsmouth, OH	
Waschner, Petronelle	1, Apr. 1872	15, Mar.	14- 2m- 3d	111		Toledo, OH	Toledo, Ohio
Waser, Gottfried	11, May 1899	20, Apr.	57	302		Indianapolis, IN	Großbottwar, Württemberg
Wasmund, Christian	8, Dec. 1892	8, Nov.	87- 3m-11d	782		Lafayette, IN	Pritzier-Wolgast, Pommern
Wassermann, Johanna Dorothea	29, Dec. 1862	31, Oct.	48	208	Hagemann	Peoria, IL	Fellbach, Cannstedt, Württemberg
Wassermann, Maria	23, Mar. 1874	7, Mar.		95		Saginaw, MI	Wallenberg, Mecklenburg-Schwerin
Waßmann, Anna Maria	20, June 1881	13, May	84- 8m	199	Reimeier	Boonville, MO	Hille, Minden, Preußen
Waßmann, Karl Heinrich	6, Apr. 1874	8, Mar.	73	111		Boonville, MO	
Waßmann, Kaspar	2, Feb. 1874	7, Jan.	63- 2m-11d	39		Le Sueur, MN	Schwelen, Preußen
Waßmann, Sarah	15, Aug. 1870	18, June	57	263		Le Sueur, MN	Alleghany County, New York
Wattenweilir, Elisabeth	7, Nov. 1881	24, Oct.	61	359	Gauschi	Concordia, MO	Rinnag, Bern, Schweiz
Wätzig, Wilhelmine	15, Dec. 1898	27, Nov.	39- 7m-14d	799	Lorenz	Chicago, IL	Freiberg, Sachsen
Weaver, Johan Joseph	7, June 1869	22, May	27	183		Evansville, IN	Evansville, Indiana
Weaver, Margaretha	27, Apr. 1893	9, Apr.	70	270	Schäfer	Edon, OH	Dauphin County, Pennsylvania

- 542 -

Christliche Apologete Death Notices --- 1839 - 1899

Name of Deceased	Notice Date	Death Date	Age	Maiden Name	Page	Place of Death	Place of Birth
Webbelmann, Maria	6, Oct. 1862	13, Sept	26		160	Rush Creek, MO	Minden, Preußen
Webel, Wilhelm	30, Mar. 1874	1, Mar.	35		103	Perry, IL	Großniedesheim, Frananthal, Rheinkreis Baiern
Weber, Adam	6, Nov. 1846		Inquiry		189	Baltimore, MD	Oberamt Backnang, Württemberg
Weber, Adam	10, July 1846		Inquiry		111	Baltimore, MD	
Weber, Adelhaid	23, Dec. 1852	9, Sept	32	Böschen	208	Marietta, OH	Bredorf, Amt Ottensberg, Hannover
Weber, Agnes	28, Nov. 1881	29, Sept	47	Carstensen	383	Fond du Lac, WI	Lindholm, Schleswig-Holstein
Weber, Agnes	14, Nov. 1881	29, Sept	47	Carstensen	367	Fond du Lac, WI	Lindwurm, Schleswig-Holstein
Weber, Andreas	19, Dec. 1881	21, Nov.	50-11m		407	Boston, MA	Göhlshausen bei Bretten, Baden
Weber, Anna	5, Sept 1895	18, Mar.	81	Haselei	574	Madison, WI	Germany
Weber, Anna	14, Apr. 1859	16, Mar.	12- 6m-24d		60	Spring Lake, OH	
Weber, Anna Berta Johanna	15, Mar. 1894	21, Feb.	17		182	Canal Dover, OH	
Weber, Anna Friederika	16, July1883	2, July	50- 4m	Braun	231	New Bremen, IL	Sundhausen bei Langensalza, Preußen
Weber, Anna Johanna	29, May 1865		29	Hartmann	88	Covington, KY	Bremen,
Weber, Anna Katharina	4, Jan. 1894	24, Nov.	69	Reiter	14	Berne, MI	Holmich, Koblenz, Simmern, Preußen
Weber, Anna M.	15, Oct. 1896	9, Sept	74	Oelkers	671	Marietta, OH	Breddorf, Ottersberg, Hannover
Weber, Anna Margaretha	15, Jan. 1857	16, Dec.	72- 6m-16d	Bänter	12	Dayton, OH	Holzhausen, Amt Greiffenstein, Preußen
Weber, August	28, July 1879	30, June	29- 4m- 4d		239	New Albany, IN	Hessen-Nassau
Weber, Barbara	22, Feb. 1894	28, Jan.	63-11m-22d	Rocke	126	Mascoutah, IL	Aschbacherhof, Kaiserslautern, Rheinpfalz Baiern
Weber, Barbara	29, Dec. 1862	25, Nov.	39- -27d		208	Toledo, OH	Wilklingen, Schaffhausen, Schweiz
Weber, Carolina	31, Mar. 1859	25, Dec.	13		52	Canal Dover, OH	
Weber, Caroline	31, Mar. 1859	25, Dec.	14		52	Masillon, OH	
Weber, Caroline Magdalena	18, Nov. 1872		48- 2m-19d	Hagemann	375	Bloomington, IL	
Weber, Dorothea	15, Nov. 1875	9, Oct.	13		367	Jeffersonville, NY	Callicoon, Sullivan County, New York
Weber, Elisabeth Katharina Maria	23, June 1879	6, June	22- 7m-13d		199	New Palestine, IN	
Weber, Elisabeth Katharine	19, Feb. 1883	22, Jan.	76		63	Iowa City, IA	Freudenstein, Maulbronn, Württemberg
Weber, Elise Henriette	14, Sept 1885	26, Aug.	11		7	Mascoutah, IL	
Weber, Emil	31, May 1880	14, May	28		175	Chicago, IL	
Weber, Emilie	28, Feb. 1876	11, Feb.	21- 7m-17d	Willis	71	Newport, KY	
Weber, Ernestine	6, Dec. 1894	18, Nov.	37		790	Cincinnati, OH	Bonbaden, Koblenz, Württemberg
Weber, Eva	10, May 1894	7, Apr.	87- 3m- 7d	Seibel	310	Fond du Lac, WI	Wiesenbach, Hessen-Darmstadt
Weber, Ferdinand	23, Oct. 1890	9, Oct.	19-11m- 9d		686	New Palestine, IN	New Palestine , Indiana
Weber, Fr.	14, July 1859	2, July	60- 8m		112	Indianapolis, IN	
Weber, Frank	14, Mar. 1889	19, Feb.	22		174	Wausau, WI	New York
Weber, Franz	3, Aug. 1899	13, June	70		495	New York City, NY	
Weber, Franz G.	20, Dec. 1888	7, Dec.	50-11m-19d		814	Kansas City, MO	
Weber, Friederike	12, Mar. 1896	21, Feb.	45	Reichert	175	New Albany, IN	Düttenberg, Hochheim, Nassau
Weber, Friedrich	20, July 1885	9, July	60- 8m		7	Mankato, MN	Ottmansheim, Württemberg
Weber, Friedrich	23, Mar. 1868	5, Feb.			95	Indianapolis, IN	Schnait, Schorndorf, Württemberg
Weber, Friedrich	8, Dec. 1892	7, Nov.	46		782	Lafayette, IN	Arnswalde, Preußen
Weber, Friedrike	8, Oct. 1883	18, Sept	60- 8m -1d		327	Canal Dover, OH	Magdeburg, Preußen
Weber, G. Friedrich	7, June 1888	18, May	69		366	Bunker Hill, IL	Hohenacker, Waiblingen, Württemberg
Weber, Georg	14, Apr. 1887	27, Mar.	75-10m- 5d		238	Fond du Lac, WI	Unter-Asbach, Hall, Württemberg
Weber, Georg	6, Apr. 1893	20, Mar.			222	Pekin, IL	Kleingladenbach, Biedenkopf, Hessen-Darmstadt
Weber, Georg Johan	31, Mar. 1898	6, Mar.	72		207	Edon, OH	Hergetshausen, Hessen-Darmstadt
Weber, Gerhard Heinrich	7, Apr. 1879	19, Mar.	44		111	Wyandotte, KS	Weiler zum Stein, Marbach, Württemberg
Weber, Gertrud	24, Oct. 1870	18, Sept	44		343	Evansville, IN	Hördinghausen, Wittlage, Hannover
							Fischbach bei Hochspeier, Rheinkreis Baiern

- 543 -

Christliche Apologete Death Notices --- 1839 - 1899

Name of Deceased	Notice Date	Death Date	Age	Page	Maiden Name	Place of Death	Place of Birth
Weber, Gottfried	15, Oct. 1877	20, Sept	73	335		Madison, WI	Gertzlow, Pommern
Weber, Gottfried Hermann	6, Feb. 1862	29, Dec.	33	24		Monona, IA	Staad bei Constanz, Baden
Weber, Heinrich	31, Mar. 1873	8, Mar.	49	103		Mascoutah, IL	Litzenhausen, Gelnhausen, Kurhessen
Weber, Heinrich	20, Feb. 1882	4, Feb.	54 -4m	63		Kearney, MO	Aargau, Kulm, Schweiz
Weber, Heinrich	9, Mar. 1874	28, Jan.	75- 3m	79		Boston Highlands, MA	Baiern
Weber, Helena	7, July 1898	20, June	69	431	Völker	Terre Haute, IN	Bergen, Hessen-Nassau
Weber, Herman	2, Aug. 1875	11, July	26- 7m	247		Crete, NE	Amt Diepholz, Hannover
Weber, Jacob	9, Oct. 1890	26, Sept	75- 4m-13d	654		Edgerton, OH	Susquehannah Twp, Dauphin Co., Pennsylvania
Weber, Jacob	14, Dec. 1874	9, Nov.	79	399		Liberty, MO	Menziken, Kulm, Aargau, Schweiz
Weber, Jacob	3, Feb. 1873	1, Jan.	22- 9m	39		Liberty, NY	
Weber, Jakob	28, Feb. 1889	2, Feb.	70	142		Toledo, OH	Siblingen, Schafhausen, Schweiz
Weber, Jakob	1, Apr. 1878	13, Mar.	70- 7m	103		Belleville, IL	Canton Aargau, Schweiz
Weber, Jakob	10, Mar. 1879	14, Feb.		79		Roseville, MI	
Weber, Janna E.	13, Jan. 1898	20, Dec.	35	31	Smidt	Kramer, NE	Osterhusen, Ostfriesland
Weber, Joachim Christian N.	1, Sept 1879	13, Aug.	74	279		Dotyville, WI	Meßlin, Mecklenburg–Schwerin
Weber, Johan C.	6, June 1881	1, May	36- 2m- 3d	183		Buffalo, NY	Buffalo, New York
Weber, Johan Elias	23, Oct. 1890	29, Sept	69- 7m-22d	686		Evansville, IN	Unter-Eifesheim, Heilbronn, Württemberg
Weber, Johan Georg Heinrich	22, Oct. 1877	10, Sept	61- 1m	343		Wapello, IA	Steinsdorf, Schwarzburg-Rudolstadt
Weber, Johan Jost	15, Oct. 1891	24, Sept	51- 5m-21d	670		Wathena, KS	Leisa, Lindenkopf, Hessen-Darmstadt
Weber, Johan Martin	8, Mar. 1894	8, Feb.	75	166		Bushnell, IL	Baden
Weber, Johannes	25, Feb. 1884	29, Jan.	18	7		Edgerton, OH	Milford, Defiance County, Ohio
Weber, Johannes	3, May 1875	18, Apr.	68	143		Toledo, OH	Ottisloye, Bern, Schweiz
Weber, Johannette	2, Aug. 1875	7, July	26- 5m-25d	247		Louisville, KY	Klingenbach, Nassau
Weber, John	20, Mar. 1890	17, Feb.	25	190		Cameron, MO	Clay County, Missouri
Weber, John	26, Mar. 1891	2, Mar.	22-10m	206		New Palestine, IN	
Weber, Jost Friedrich	14, July 1892	13, June	60- 2m	446		Kansas City, MO	Hörtinghausen, Wittlage, Hannover
Weber, Julia	1, Sept 1879	19, Aug.		279		Chicago, IL	Diedelsheim, Bretten, Baden
Weber, Justus	14, Nov. 1889	25, Sept	57- 9m- 9d	734		New Bremen, IL	Heyerode, Kurhessen
Weber, Karl	5, Jan. 1893	12, Dec.	69	14		Flood Creek, IA	Giesenbrügge, Soldin, Germany
Weber, Karl	25, June 1883	1, June	25	207		Canal Dover, OH	Canal Dover, Ohio
Weber, Karl F.	3, June 1897	21, Apr.	23	351		Columbus, OH	Lafayette, Indiana
Weber, Karl Martin	2, Nov. 1899	13, Oct.	80	703		Marietta, OH	Frankenburg, Lilienthal, Hannover
Weber, Karolina	20, Sept 1860	18, Aug.	33	152	Längen	Steuben Co, IN	Serfelden, Müllheim, Baden
Weber, Katharina	11, Sept 1865	27, Aug.		148		Highland, IL	
Weber, Katharina Margaretha	20, Aug. 1891	17, July	64	542	Colonius	Brighton, IL	Lierschied, St. Goarshausen, Nassau
Weber, Katharine	30, June 1887	4, June		414	Koch	New Albany, IN	Diebenbergen, Nassau
Weber, Louisa	22, Mar. 1894	20, Feb.	39	198	Reif	Burlington, IA	Dodgeville, Iowa
Weber, Louise	29, Sept 1873	15, Sept	30	311		Nauvoo, IL	Louisville, Jefferson County, Kentucky
Weber, Louise	22, July 1878	13, July	27- 3m-20d	231	Nolte	Nashville, IL	
Weber, Louise Henriette	24, Aug. 1885	6, Aug.	16-10m-27d	7		Mascoutah, IL	
Weber, Margaretha	21, Oct. 1878	1, Oct.	36	335	Reif	Wapello, IA	Coshocton County, Ohio
Weber, Maria	11, May 1874	5, Apr.	39- 5m	151	Gebker	Nashville, IL	Lintorf, Amt Wittlage, Hannover
Weber, Maria	2, Oct. 1851	9, Sept	21	160	Stirnberg	Chester, IL	Steinke, Amt Wölpe, Hannover
Weber, Maria	21, Nov. 1895	31, Oct.	62	750	Hammel	Kearney, MO	Giesen, Hessen-Darmstadt
Weber, Maria	5, June 1851	8, May	53- 8m- 6d	92	Brunner	Weston, MO	Kulm, Aargau, Schweiz
Weber, Maria	15, Dec. 1892	26, Nov.	68	798	Hirt	Boonville, IN	Melheim, Baiern

Christliche Apologete Death Notices --- 1839 - 1899

Name of Deceased	Notice Date	Death Date	Age	Page	Maiden Name	Place of Death	Place of Birth
Weber, Maria	31, Mar. 1859	14, Mar.	17- 5m-15d	52		Canal Dover, OH	
Weber, Maria	2, Aug. 1860		63	124		Boston, MA	
Weber, Maria A.	4, Feb. 1892	17, Jan.	63	78		Bushnell, IL	Vockawind, Ebern, Baiern
Weber, Maria Elisabeth	17, Apr. 1876	28, Mar.	68	127		Newport, KY	Eiserfeld, Preußen
Weber, Maria Theresa	6, Dec. 1894	21, Nov.	70	790	Geismeier	Chicago, IL	Friedrichshafen, Württemberg
Weber, Martin	26, Dec. 1889	6, Dec.	71	830		Chicago, IL	Buggingen, Müllheim, Baden
Weber, Mathes	30, Dec. 1897	25, Nov.	80	828		Quincy, IL	Welsheim, Württemberg
Weber, Missouri	9, Nov. 1868	26, Sept	22	359	Schwinny	St. Louis, MO	
Weber, Phil B.	13, May 1886	26, Apr.	52	359		Berea, OH	Dautenzell, Mosbach, Baden
Weber, Phil.	30, July 1877	5, July	39- 4m- 8d	7		Pekin, IL	
Weber, Philipp	1, Jan. 1891	12, Dec.	64	247		Iowa City, IA	Haselbrun, Mittelstadt, Hessen-Darmstadt
Weber, Philipp	11, Feb. 1892	20, Jan.	87	14		Dayton, OH	Holzhausen, Wetzlar, Preußen
Weber, Roselea	14, Jan. 1897	28, Dec.	52	95		Wathena, KS	Preußen
Weber, Samuel	24, Nov. 1892	19, Oct.	76- 8m- 5d	31	Weiß	Nauvoo, IL	Canton Aargau , Schweiz
Weber, Sophia	26, Nov. 1866	11, Mar.	48	750		Evansville, IN	Neuenstadt am Kocher, Württemberg
Weber, Sophia L.	10, Sept 1883	15, Aug.	71	102	Fischbach	Dayton, OH	Greifenstein, Wetzlar, Preußen
Weber, Sophie Dorothea	28, July 1884	11, July	66	295	Horn	Philadelphia, PA	Lobenstein, Reuß
Weber, Susanna	15, Dec. 1892	22, Nov.	74	7	Meier	Brighton, IL	Bradtelen, Basel, Schweiz
Weber, Theresa	10, Oct. 1861	17, Sept	7	798		Chicago, IL	
Weber, Thomas	10, Aug. 1868	7, July	66- 4m	164		Columbus, ---	Grissenbach, Ahrensberg, Westphalen, Preußen
Weber, Wilhelm	14, Jan. 1892	18, Dec.	35	255		Brooklyn, NY	Ludwigsthal, Württemberg
Weber, Wilhelm	1, Feb. 1894	6, Jan.	78- 8m	30		Philadelphia, PA	Lobenstein, Reuß
Weber, Wilhelm	25, Feb. 1884	5, Feb.	27-11m- 7d	78		Edgerton, OH	
Weber, Wilhelm Heinrich	16, June 1859	12, Apr.	16- 5m-28d	7		Spring Lake, OH	
Weber, Wilhelmina	1, Sept 1898	8, July	68	96		New York City, NY	Blattenhott, Württemberg
Weber, Wilhelmine Catharina	7, Jan. 1867	22, Nov.	34	559	Pehle	Herman, MO	Lippe-Detmold
Weber, William Adam	19, May 1884	29, Apr.	20	6		Mt. Vernon, NY	New York
Weber, William H.	26, Dec. 1864	9, Oct.	27	7		Fond du Lac, WI	Kleingladenbach, Biedenkopf, Hessen-Darmstadt
Wecht, Chrisitiana Margaretha	19, Jan. 1854	29, Nov.	16- 2m	208		Charlestown, IN	
Wechter, Maria Elisa	25, Aug. 1853	12, Aug.	7- 1m	12		Poughkeepsie, NY	
Weckel, Johan Georg	6, Oct. 1887	10, Sept	89- 6m- 6d	136		Dayton, OH	Neuhausen, Sachsen-Meiningen
Weckel, Maria Rosina	3, Oct. 1845	19, Sept		638		Dayton, OH	
Weckerle, Lydia	21, Apr. 1879	27, Mar.	20	159		Milwaukee, WI	Pittsburg, Pennsylvania
Weckerle, M. Aloisa	12, May 1859		38	127		Pittsburg, PA	Edelstettin, Rogenburg, Baiern
Weckerling, Johanna	25, Feb. 1884	7, Feb.		76	Taschner	Lowell, KS	Jütel, Braunschweig
Weckmann, Johannes	6, Mar. 1856	9, Feb.	45- 5m- 6d	7		Des Moines, IA	Langenselbold, Kurhessen
Weckstroth, (Mr)	25, Mar. 1886	25, Feb.	75	40		New Knoxville, OH	Ladbergen, Tecklenburg, Münster, Preußen
Weddig, Magdalena	16, June 1898	28, May	63	7	Guntly	West Bend, WI	Burgerau, St. Gallen, Schweiz
Weddig, Regina	4, Nov. 1886	11, Oct.	38	383	Hoch	San Francisco, CA	Grewenhausen, Württemberg
Wedeking, (Mrs)	5, Apr. 1894		84	7	Hoffmeier		Linsburg, Hannover
Wedeking, Christian	9, Feb. 1888	17, Jan.	81	230		Santa Claus, IN	Liesburg, Wolpen, Hannover
Wedeking, Johan Ernst	11, Aug. 1887	30, July	81	94		Metropolis, IL	Balge, Nienburg, Hannover
Wedeking, Louise	8, Jan. 1866	12, Dec.	16	510		Santa Claus, IN	
Wedeward, Wilhelmina	24, June 1897	28, May	49- 2m	14		Sun Prairie, WI	Blumberg, Stettin, Preußen
Wedewart, Wilhelmine	19, Oct. 1893	2, Sept	39- 7m-26d	399	Frank	Ahnapee, WI	Grünz, Randow, Stettin,
Wedgen, H.	13, Oct. 1862	20, Aug.	22- 4m- 2d	670		Hokah, MN	

Christliche Apologete Death Notices --- 1839 - 1899

Name of Deceased	Notice Date	Death Date	Age	Page	Maiden Name	Place of Death	Place of Birth
Weehler, W.	15, Mar. 1888	17, Feb.	54	174		Miltonsburg, OH	Gamshurst, Baden
Weerdgarals, Auguste	19, Jan. 1880	16, Dec.	21	23	Walther	Eldora, IA	
Weerts, Weert Wessels	20, Dec. 1880	13, Dec.	55	407		Alton, WI	Filzum, Stickhausen, Preußen
Weerts, Wesley Adolph	7, Jan. 1886	21, Dec.	25- 8m- 8d	7		Alton, IL	
Wege, Heinrich Friedrich Wilhelm	14, Apr. 1887	31, Mar.	19	238		Schnectady, NY	Steinbrink, Uchte, Hannover
Wegel, Friedrike	29, Mar. 1869	26, Feb.	38	103	Läsch	Fond du Lac, WI	
Wegener, Ernst	26, July 1888	18, June	60	478		Detroit, MI	Falkenwalde, Uckermark, Preußen
Wegener, Fr.	18, May 1885	4, May	81	7		Higginsville, MO	Gohfeld, Erfurt, Minden, Preußen
Wegener, Mathilde	17, Dec. 1896	25, Nov.	25	814		Detroit, MI	Roseville, Macomb County, Michigan
Weger, Anna Barbara	29, June 1885	21, Apr.	50- 9m	7	Becker	Portland, OR	Birden, Schweiz
Wegerle, Johanne Elisabeth	19, Mar. 1896	2, Feb.	55	190	Reinwald	Columbus, OH	Oberamt Brackenheim, Württemberg
Wegmann, Catharina E.	27, Feb. 1890	29, Jan.	55	142	Harmel	Tulare, CA	
Wegmann, Dorothea	7, Apr. 1848		Inquiry	59	Klein	St. Louis, MO	Orza, Wirtheim, Baden
Wegmann, Nannette	22, Mar. 1888	22, Feb.	52	190	Isler	Bridgeport, CT	Holland
Wegner, Anna	14, Apr. 1879	2, Apr.	36	119	Brunk	Columbus, WI	Brietzig, Pieritz, Stettin, Preußen
Wegner, Anna Maria Christina	3, July 1871	11, June	67- 9m	215	Behrendsmeier	Hopewell, MO	Godfeld, Münden, Preußen
Wegner, Anna Maria Sophia	5, Nov. 1883	19, Oct.	57- 2m- 2d	359		Michigan City, IN	Großwildberg, Demin, Pommern
Wegner, August	7, Nov. 1895	6, Oct.	72	718		Alden, IA	Triglof, Greifenberg, Stettin, Pommern
Wegner, August	1, Jan. 1883	1, Dec.	55- 2m	7		Milwaukee, WI	Treptow an der Talensee, Pommern
Wegner, August Friedrich	6, May 1897	6, Apr.	73	287		Dundee, IL	Suto, Piritz, Pommern
Wegner, August T.	9, Mar. 1893	14, Feb.	53	158		Burt, IA	Sagow , Pommern
Wegner, Auguste	22, Jan. 1883	2, Jan.	19- -16d	31		Alden, IA	Naugard, Stettin, Preußen
Wegner, Carl	17, Nov. 1873	29, Oct.	57- 7m-24d	367		Michigan City, IN	Treptow, Stettin, Preußen
Wegner, Christian	25, Oct. 1875	23, Sept	51- 5m- 9d	343		Laporte, IN	Klein-Plasten, Mecklenburg-Schwerin
Wegner, Dorothea	4, Jan. 1864	3, Dec.	39	4		Laporte, IN	Mecklenburg
Wegner, Dorothea Louisa	30, Mar. 1885	15, Mar.	74	7	Goetsch	St. Paul, MN	Plantikow, Pommern
Wegner, Eke Gerrets	27, Aug. 1891		44	558	Weiß	Valley City, ND	Westerende, Aurich, Hannover
Wegner, Emma Maria	22, Nov. 1888	31, Oct.	31-10m- 6d	750	Achen	Frederick, SD	Orion, Richland County, Wisconsin
Wegner, Friederike	6, Oct. 1884	12, Sept	69	7		Crandon, SD	Greifenberg, Stettin, Pommern
Wegner, Hanna Henriette	23, May 1895	20, Apr.	72	334	Schmidt	Eldorado, WI	Radelfitz, Pommern
Wegner, Ida	19, May 1873	30, Apr.	37	159	Dumke	Columbus, WI	Rassee, Pommern
Wegner, Johan Friedrich Wilhelm	8, Sept 1879	7, Aug.	67- 5m-10d	287		Almond, WI	Schirsen, Kammin, Stettin, Pommern
Wegner, Johanna	23, Apr. 1896	17, Mar.	57	270	Vielhak	Kewaunee, WI	Wahren, Mecklenburg-Schwerin
Wegner, Karl Ludwig	20, Apr. 1874	24, Mar.	75	127		Chicago, IL	
Wegner, Minna	11, Feb. 1897	19, Jan.	77	94	Rickoff	Milwaukee, WI	Wismar, Mecklenburg-Schwerin
Wegst, Georg	3, Oct. 1895	9, Sept	24	638		Philadelphia, PA	Philadelphia, Pennsylvania
Wegst, Jacob F.	26, July 1894	24, June	70	486		Philadelphia, PA	Dunnstetten, Württemberg
Wegst, Margaretha	1, Dec. 1892	15, Nov.	64- -18d	766	Schempp	Philadelphia, PA	
Wehe, Anna	15, June 1874	29, May	15- 5m	191		Aurora, IN	
Wehinger, Juliana	12, May 1879	27, Apr.	65	151	Dehaven	Lansing, IA	Summit County, Ohio
Wehl, Theodor	13, Jan. 1868	24, Dec.	37	14		East Troy, WI	Zelle, Hannover
Wehle, Maria	11, Oct. 1880	30, Sept	40- 1m- 8d	327	Traub	Indianapolis, IN	Seizach, Zürich, Schweiz
Wehle, Maria	1, Nov. 1880	30, Sept	40- 1m- 8d	351	Traub		Seizach, Zürich, Schweiz
Wehmann, Johanna Margaretha	19, Oct. 1885	25, Sept	71	7	Wiebens	Brooklyn, NY	
Wehmeier, Anna Maria Dorothea	7, Mar. 1870	11, Feb.	94	79	Rettger	Furnace, OH	Alswete, Preußen
Wehmeier, Auguste	29, Mar. 1894	4, Mar.	59	214		Chicago, IL	Bielefeld, Westphalen

Christliche Apologete Death Notices --- 1839 - 1899

Name of Deceased	Notice Date	Death Date	Age	Maiden Name	Page	Place of Death	Place of Birth
Wehmeier, Maria	11, Apr. 1881	4, Mar.	35- 6m- 3d	Stephan	119	Herman, MO	Augustdorf, Detmold, Lippe-Detmold
Wehmer, August	20, Dec. 1888	17, Nov.	30		814	Lacrosse, KS	Hille, Minden, Westphalen
Wehmer, Christian	5, Feb. 1877	4, Jan.	75		47	Herman, MO	Holzhausen, Minden, Preußen
Wehmer, Maria	15, Oct. 1883	27, Sept	72- 8m-15d	Rethemeier	335	Berger, MO	Nordhämmen, Minden, Preußen
Wehmeyer, Friedrich	11, Apr. 1861	20, Mar.	60		60	Marthasville, MO	Vlotho, Minden, Preußen
Wehmeyer, Heinrich August	29, Oct. 1891	13, Oct.	48		702	Jamestown, MO	
Wehmeyer, Margaretha	19, Nov. 1896	26, Oct.	66		750	Bloomington, IL	Doerpling, Holstein
Wehmeyer, Simon	2, Mar. 1868	5, Jan.	40		71	Hoyleton, IL	
Wehmheuer, Anna Amalia	10, Dec. 1891	16, Nov.	30	Leweke	798	Napoleon, MO	Gasconade County, Missouri
Wehmhöner, Friedrich Gustav	17, Feb. 1873	28, Jan.			53	Second Creek, MO	Jöllenbeck, Bielefeld, Preußen
Wehmhöner, Johan Friedrich	2, Mar. 1899	29, Jan.	71		143	Drake, MO	Nieder-Zollenbeck, Germany
Wehmüller, Wilhelm	5, Nov. 1877	7, Oct.	67		359	Herman, MO	Halle, Minden, Preußen
Wehn, Heinrich	27, Oct. 1887	8, Oct.	60		686	Baltimore, MD	Biedenkopf, Hessen-Darmstadt
Wehn, Elisabeth	21, Juńe 1855	2, June	20		100	Baltimore, MD	
Wehn, Georg	30, Nov. 1868	13, Oct.	18- 2m-13d		383	Baltimore, MD	Baltimore, Maryland
Wehner, Johan Gottlieb	24, Jan. 1881	3, Jan.	68		31	San Jose, ---	Freiburg, Schlesien
Wehnes, Elisabeth	23, Apr. 1877	12, Feb.	73	Faust	135	Bay City, MI	Bernsberg, Alsfeld, Hessen-Darmstadt
Wehnes, Elisabeth	13, Apr. 1893	16, Mar.	57		238	Akron, OH	Lehrbach, Alsfeld, Hessen-Darmstadt
Wehning, Gertraut	9, May 1864	18, Mar.	43	Maul	76	Bradford, IN	Giegenbach Hoff, Weiers, Baiern
Wehr, Maria Magdalena	4, Jan. 1869	10, Dec.	22- 6m-18d		7	Madison, IN	Eltingen, Leonberg, Württemberg
Wehring, Wilhelmine	25, Feb. 1884	11, Feb.	38	Homburg	7	Brenham, TX	
Wehrle, Elisabeth	13, Sept 1894	22, Aug.	88		598	Pekin, IL	Friesenheim, Baden
Wehrle, Maria	6, Oct. 1887	18, Aug.	51	Wirz	638	Cleveland, OH	Arau, Schweiz
Wehrli, Gottlieb	30, May 1889	12, May	70		350	Indianapolis, IN	Großheben, Württemberg
Wehrli, Rudolph	5, May 1873	31, Mar.	87		143	Wheeling, IL	Köttingen, Aargau, Schweiz
Wehrman, Anna Katharina	10, May 1894		35- 6m- 9d	Vollrath	310	Edwardsville, IL	Belleville, Illinois
Wehrmann, Christian	22, Jan. 1861	18, Dec.	65		16	Warren, MO	Schönhagen, Amt Sternberg, Lippe
Wehrmann, Conrad	2, Oct. 1876	1, Sept	33		319	Warren, MO	Schönhagen, Lippe-Detmold
Wehrmann, Friedrich	12, Oct. 1868	7, Sept	27		327	Warren, MO	Schönhagen, Lippe-Detmold
Wehrmann, Heinrich	25, Sept 1890	24, Aug.	53- 4m		622	Truxton, MO	Schönhagne, Sternberg, Lippe-Detmold
Wehrmann, Karoline	22, Dec. 1898	18, Nov.	82	Drünert	815	Higginsville, MO	Wiebusch, Lippe-Detmold
Wehrmann, Wilhelm	30, Dec. 1878	26, Nov.	54- -26d		415	Eldora, WI	Ruhler bei Schwepper, Hannover
Wehrung, Heinrich	16, Sept 1897	21, Aug.	87		591	Pomeroy, OH	Paderborn, Elsaß
Wehrung, Katharina	26, May 1879	1, May	59	Kreider	167	Pomeroy, OH	Baldrunn, Niederrhein, Elsaß
Weiaus, Anna	25, Feb. 1884	15, Feb.	47		7	Lawrence, KS	Jackelsdorf, Böhmen
Weibel, Anna Maria	12, Apr. 1888		66- 1m- 1d	Thomann	238	Eudora, KS	Tennicken, Baselland, Schweiz
Weibel, Friedrich	25, May 1899	23, Apr.	78		335	Eudora, KS	Bekten, Baselland, Schweiz
Weible, Christoph	28, Oct. 1878	12, Oct.	47		343	Talleyrand, IA	Württemberg
Weichbrodt, Wilhelmine	26, Jan. 1899	10, Jan.	59	Kummer	63	Bloomington, IL	Garbro, Lauenburg, Preußen
Weichemeier, Simeon	28, Nov. 1881	27, Oct.	14- - 9d		383	Galion, OH	
Weid, A.	3, Dec. 1857	31, Oct.			196	Rochester, NY	
Weide, Hubert	27, Mar. 1876	14, Mar.	15		103		
Weide, Maria	12, Sept 1881	28, Aug.	43	Winderfeld	295	Waco, TX	Barby bei Magdaburg, Preußen
Weidemaier, Anna Margaretha	26, Apr. 1894	1, Apr.	84	Bechtin	278	Galion, OH	Beilingen, Baden
Weideman, Daniel	4, Feb. 1858	15, Jan.	47		20	Petersburg, IL	Kelze, Hofgeismar, Kurhessen
Weidemann, Alfred	18, Feb. 1842		Inquiry		27	Wheeling, VA	

- 547 -

Christliche Apologete Death Notices --- 1839 - 1899

Name of Deceased	Notice Date	Death Date	Age	Page	Maiden Name	Place of Death	Place of Birth
Weidemann, Johanette	11, Feb. 1867	30, Nov.	58- 6m	46		Petersburg, IL	Hofgeismar, Hessen
Weidemann, Peter	11, Aug. 1862	13, July	22	128		Memphis, TN	
Weidemeier, Samuel David	15, July 1878	25, May	10- 5m-15d	223		Galion, OH	
Weidemeier, Simeon	19, Dec. 1881	27, Oct.	14- - 9d	407		Galion, OH	
Weidemyer, Adolph	14, Apr. 1879	4, Mar.	65	119		Rockdale, MD	Groß-Roggerhausen, Kurhessen
Weidenbach, Heinrich	6, Nov. 1871	30, July	47	359		Santa Claus, IN	Unterrixingen a. d. Enz, Vaihingen, Württemberg
Weidensee, Ottilie	1, Apr. 1872	16, Mar.	42	111	Keißner	Bushnell, IL	Blankenburg, Schwarzburg-Rudolstadt
Weidmann, Jakob	8, June 1863	20, Feb.	18	92		Long Point, IL	Stadel, Zürich, Schweiz
Weidmann, John Georg	2, Apr. 1877	24, Feb.	21- 2m	111		Indianapolis, IN	
Weidmayer, Christine	26, Oct. 1899	26, Sept	60	687	Diegel	Galion, OH	Crawford County, Ohio
Weidnauer, Wilhelmina	24, Nov. 1873	18, Oct.	17-11m-28d	375		Chillicothe, OH	Greenfield, Highland County, Ohio
Weidner, Georg Michael	25, Nov. 1878	3, Nov.	53	375		Portsmouth, OH	Sulzdorf, Württemberg
Weidner, Johan Michael	1, May 1865	12, Mar.	7- 1m-10d	72		Portsmouth, OH	
Weidner, John G.	23, Feb. 1893	1, Feb.	65-11m-14d	126		Bunker Hill, IL	Zickra bei Weida, Sachsen-Weimar
Weidner, Joseph Heinrich	1, May 1865	23, Feb.	5-10m	72		Portsmouth, OH	
Weidner, Louis Jakob	1, May 1865	20, Feb.	8m-15d	72		Portsmouth, OH	
Weidner, Maria Elisabeth	1, May 1865	14, Aug.	3- 9m	72		Portsmouth, OH	
Weidner, Maria Magdalena	28, Jan. 1884	27, Dec.	51	7		Ida Grove, IA	Gündringen, Horb, Württemberg
Weidner, Maria Magdalena	1, May 1865	5, Mar.	2- 7m	72		Portsmouth, OH	
Weidt, Catharina Margaretha	7, May 1857	27, Mar.	55	76		Rochester, NY	
Weidt, Dorothea Friedr. Augusta	25, May 1893	5, May	55	334	Bückmann	Colesburg, IA	Ziersdorf, Mecklenburg-Schwerin
Weidt, George J.	27, Aug. 1896	2, Aug.	77	559		Cheyenne, WY	Mecklenburg-Schwerin
Weierbacher, Franz	29, Nov. 1860	30, Sept	47	192		Boonville, IN	Heimbach, St. Wennel, Rheinkreis Baiern
Weiershäuser, Elisabeth	9, Nov. 1893	30, Sept	78	718	Siegfried	Cannelton, IN	Marburg, Kurhessen
Weifert, Barbara	15, Mar. 1894	8, Jan.	90	182		New York City, NY	Württemberg
Weiffenbach, Catharine	17, July 1865	Feb.	37- 7m	116		New York, NY	
Weiffenbach, Maria	6, Mar. 1890	12, Feb.	18- - 2d	158		Boody, IL	
Weiffenbach, Wilhelmine	25, May 1874	28, Apr.	60	167	Baumann	Hudson City, NJ	Suttgart, Württemberg
Weigand, Agnes	25, Apr. 1889	2, Apr.	49	270	Pampel	Perry, TX	Deisel, Kurhessen
Weigand, Peter	30, June 1892	11, June	*	414		Warsaw, IL	Damshausen, Hessen-Darmstadt
Weigel, (Mrs)	22, Jan. 1866	7, Nov.	77	30		Chester, IL	Baireuth, Baiern
Weigel, Catharina	6, Oct. 1884	20, Sept	64	7	Hesse	Harrison, KS	Rennerdehausen, Hessen-Darmstadt
Weigel, Johan Peter	14, Dec. 1893	17, Nov.	78	798		Ellis Grove, Il	Grafenthal, Baiern
Weigel, Johann Adam	24, Mar. 1862	15, Feb.	19- 7m	48		Chester, IL	
Weigel, John Georg	21, Feb. 1870	21, Jan.	23	63		Ellis Grove, IL	Ellis Grove, Randolph County, Illinois
Weigel, Margaretha	21, Feb. 1870	19, Jan.	57	63	Zeischel	Ellis Grove, IL	Ober-Preuswitz, Ober-Franken, Baiern
Weigel, Philipp Jakob	30, Jan. 1846		Inquiry	19		Marietta, OH	Derdingen, Maulbronn, Württemberg
Weigle, Anna Katharina	9, May 1889		59	302		Denver, CO	Württemberg
Weih, Magdalena	6, Apr. 1874	6, Mar.	78	111	Leimstoll	Cincinnati, OH	Vorstettin, Dreisam, Freiburg, Baden
Weihe, Ludwig	11, Oct. 1849	24, June	50	164		Des Moines, IA	Hessen-Kassel
Weihnacht, Margaretha	15, May 1890	20, Apr.	82-10m-16d	318	Zwickel	Red Wing, MN	Mutterstadt, Rheinkreis Baiern
Weihrauch, Anna Margaretha	1, Feb. 1894	7, Jan.	75	78	Walter	Des Moines, IA	Bellau, Hessen
Weihrauch, Dorothea	21, Apr. 1887	11, Apr.	59	254	Reinhardt	Cincinnati, OH	Kloster Mariensee, Hannover
Weihrauch, Johannes	12, May 1887	29, Apr.	71	302		Cincinnati, OH	Alleuthshausen, Homburg, Kurhessen
Weik, Catharina	21, July 1887	2, July	78- 7m	462		Cincinnati, OH	Hopen, Baden
Weik, Karl	20, Dec. 1869	9, Nov.	30	407		Cincinnati, OH	Rheinbischofsheim bei Kehl, Baden

Christliche Apologete Death Notices --- 1839 - 1899

Name of Deceased	Notice Date	Death Date	Age	Maiden Name	Page	Place of Death	Place of Birth
Weik, Karl	11, Aug. 1873	18, July	70		255	Cincinnati, OH	Bischofsheim, Baden
Weik, Wilhelm Friedrich	18, Apr. 1889	29, Mar.	29		254	Jersey City, NJ	Graben, Baden
Weil, August	25, Apr. 1895	12, Feb.	60		270	Golconda, IL	Muldenstein, Merseburg, Germany
Weil, Christiane M.	11, Jan. 1869	23, Dec.	31- 4m- 8d	Weigele	15	Lafayette, IN	Schlierbach, Göppingen, Württemberg
Weil, Elisabeth	10, Feb. 1873	20, Jan.	78	Caspar	47	Baltimore, MD	Hettsassen, Grünberg, Hessen-Darmstadt
Weil, Heinrich	19, Mar. 1891	25, Feb.	67-8m-29d		190	Baltimore, MD	Grünberg, Hessen-Darmstadt
Weil, Johannes	13, Nov. 1871	29, Oct.	63		367	Lafayette, IN	Seckbach, Kurhessen
Weil, Maria Anna Elisabeth	14, July 1873	26, June	31	Dresser	223	Golconda, IL	Pittsburg, Pennsylvania
Weilage, J.H.	19, Feb. 1877	28, Jan.	52		63	Crete, NE	Hannover
Weilage, Marie	10, Dec. 1883	22, Nov.	26- 3m	Fischer	7	Crete, NE	Good Faram, Grandy County, Illinois
Weiland, Elise	3, Sept 1877	7, Aug.	31	Kern	287	San Francisco, CA	Eberstadt, Hessen-Darmstadt
Weiland, Gottlieb Adolph Franz	1, Dec. 1879	18, Nov.	71-6m		383	Jamestown, MO	Lauterbach, Rheinpreußen
Weiland, Marianna	15, Apr. 1878	30, Mar.	30	Bauer	119	Jamestown, MO	
Weiland, Sophia	20, July 1885	23, June	73	Scheerer	7	Milwaukee, WI	Freudenberg, Westphalen
Weiland, Ytje J.	26, May 1873	26, Apr.	26- 5m-16d		167	Pekin, IL	Risum, Ostfriesland
Weilbrenner, Carolina	4, Aug. 1873	10, July	51-10m- 3d	Ries	247	Mt. Vernon, IN	Oberschüpf, Boxberg, Baden
Weilbrenner, Elisa	25, Aug. 1873	6, Aug.	17		271	Mt. Vernon, IN	
Weilbrenner, Friedrich	17, Mar. 1892	4, Jan.	33		175	Mt. Vernon, IN	Mt. Vernon , Indiana
Weilbrenner, Georg Michael	20, Oct. 1898	1, Oct.	74		671	Mt. Vernon, IN	Oberschüpf, Boxberg, Baden
Weiler, Erhardt	30, Dec. 1872	9, Dec.	71		423	Richmond, IN	Leidersheim, Amt Bischofsheim, Baden
Weimar, Johannes	20, May 1878	7, May	90		159	Lawrenceburg, IN	Lützel, Amt Bieber, Kurhessen
Weimer, Wilhelmine	14, Mar. 1895	7, Feb.	45	Winkelmann	174	Detroit, MI	Ukamark, Brandenburg
Wein, Victoria	24, Nov. 1884	4, Nov.	28- - 4d	Ansmann	7	Nashville, IL	Waldaschaff, Baiern
Weinacht, Abraham	16, Mar. 1863	24, Feb.	19-11m		44	Milan, IN	Mutterstadt, Rheinkreis Baiern
Weinacht, Andreas	3, Feb. 1868	21, Jan.	59		39	Milan, IN	Mutterstadt, Rheinkreis Baiern
Weinacht, John	2, Oct. 1865	23, Aug.	26		160	Milan, IN	
Weinand, Christina	19, Oct. 1885	20, Sept	51		7	Saugerties, NY	Gudensburg, Germany
Weinand, Elisabet	23, Mar. 1863	6, Feb.	16- 9m-29d		48	Pittsfield, IL	
Weinand, Heinrich	17, Mar. 1892	8, Feb.	87- 6m- 6d		175	Warren, MO	Gudensberg, Fritzlar, Kurhessen
Weinauge, August	7, Apr. 1884	23, Mar.	67		7	Lancaster, NY	Langensalza, Erfurt, Preußen
Weinauge, Marie Louise	5, May 1879	21, Mar.	62- 4m-24d	Thal	143	Lancaster, WI	lengensalza, Preußen
Weinbrecht, Emma Sophia	26, Jan. 1888	8, Jan.	19		62	Terre Haute, IN	Greencastle, Indiana
Weinbrecht, H.	17, Oct. 1881	5, Oct.	56-10m-27d		335	Terre Haute, IN	Stein, Bretten, Baden
Weinbrecht, Wilhelmine Carolina	23, Feb. 1888	30, Jan.	26		126	Terre Haute, IN	Greencastle, Indiana
Weinel, Georg	4, Apr. 1870	3, Mar.	72		111	Belleville, IL	Merkheim, Homburg, Hessen
Weinel, Georg Peter	25, Apr. 1864	1, Apr.	35		68	Belleville, IL	Merxheim, Homburg, Hessen
Weinel, Heinrich	27, July 1863	26, June	22		120	Belleville, IL	
Weinel, Louise	29, Aug. 1861	17, June	21- 4m		140	Belleville, IL	
Weiner, Theresa	24, Mar. 1887	8, Mar.	29		190	Madison, WI	Freiburg, Sachsen
Weingärtner, Joseph	31, Mar. 1887	31, Jan.	77		206	New York City, NY	Aidesheim, Württemberg
Weingärtner, Margaretha	12, Sept 1881	20, Aug.	66- 6m		295	New York City, NY	Weidenthal, Neustadt, Rheinkreis Baiern
Weinhardt, Justine	18, Aug. 1862	19, July	17	Jordan	132	Greencastle, IN	Fürstenhagen, Amt Uslar, Hannover
Weinreich, Carl	7, Feb. 1876	16, Jan.	70		47	Milwaukee, WI	Bretleben, Sachsen
Weinreich, Dorothea	30, Apr. 1877	11, Apr.	69		143	Milwaukee, WI	Katharinenrieth, Preußen
Weinreich, Gertrud	4, Mar. 1897	11, Feb.	56	Bläser	143	Chicago, IL	Esselborn, Hessen-Darmstadt
Weinreich, Karl Franklin	12, Dec. 1889	17, Nov.	14		798	Chicago, IL	Blue Island, Illinois

Christliche Apologete Death Notices --- 1839 - 1899

Name of Deceased	Notice Date	Death Date	Age	Page	Maiden Name	Place of Death	Place of Birth
Weinreich, Karl Gottfried (Rev)	20, Dec. 1894	30, Nov.	56	822			Rathe , Sachsen
Weinrich, Anna Clara	6, Nov. 1890	19, Oct.	32	718		Geneseo, IL	Geneseo, Illinois
Weinsheimer, Margaretha	23, Sept 1886	7, Sept	72	7		Galena, IL	Rocksheim, Kreuznach, Koblenz, Preußen
Weir , Maria Augusta	24, Dec. 1896	4, Nov.	38	831	Kienitz	Minneapolis, MN	Canada
Weirather, Franz	14, June 1894	16, May	65	390		Keokuk, IA	Zuzenhausen, Baden
Weirather, Sophia	3, Dec. 1896	16, Oct.	69	782	Passer	Keokuk, IA	Kleinhöll, Mecklenburg
Weirather, Sophie	26, Nov. 1896	16, Oct.	69	766	Passer	Keokuk, IA	Kleinhöll, Mecklenburg
Weirauch, Georg	19, July 1869	27, June	18	231		Des Moines, IA	
Weirich, Friedrich F. J.	24, June 1897	19, May	73	399		Owensville, MO	Mecklenburg-Schwerin
Weirith, Marie Katharine	16, Jan. 1890	29, Dec.	65	46		Youngstown, OH	Herbach, Herborn, Dillenburg, Nassau
Weis, Anna Rosina	8, Sept 1884	19, Aug.	67	7		Wathena, KS	
Weis, Catharina	29, Dec. 1879	9, Sept	9	415		Sheldon, IA	
Weis, Catharina Elisabeth	8, Dec. 1859	9, Nov.	48- 2m	196		Kingston, IL	
Weis, Elisabeth	29, Dec. 1879	15, Oct.	11	415		Sheldon, IA	
Weis, Heinrich	23, July 1866	3, July	18-11m- 8d	238		Piqua, OH	Piqua, Ohio
Weis, Johan Jakob	23, July 1891	27, June	76	478		Ballwin, MO	Altenheim, Baden
Weis, Johannes	17, Dec. 1877	6, Nov.	77	407		Stryker, OH	Beierthal, Baden
Weis, Karolina	28, June 1869	13, June		207	Eisele	Cincinnati, OH	Waiblingen, Württemberg
Weis, M.	27, Jan. 1887	11, Jan.	46	62		Swanton, NE	Baiern
Weisbrod, Christine	27, Aug. 1877	9, Aug.	53- 1m-10d	279	Vögele	Algona, IA	Reilingen, Schwetzingen, Mannheim, Baden
Weisbrod, Johan Jakob	20, Apr. 1899	22, Mar.	81	255		Fenton, IA	Reilingen, Baden
Weisbrodt, Johan	18, Nov. 1872			375			
Weiser, Maria	29, Dec. 1879	7, Dec.	85- 4m-27d	415	Schröder	Fargo, ND	Berks County, Pennsylvania
Weiser, Wilhelm	17, Apr. 1882	20, Mar.	49	127		Albert Lea, MN	Schmielinghausen, Waldeck
Weishaar, Rosina Dorothea	17, Feb. 1887	12, Jan.	87- - 5d	110	Stahl	Indianapolis, IN	Weiler zum Stein, Marbach, Württemberg
Weiß, (Mrs)	21, June 1860	15, May	27	100	Zinkhan	Warsaw, IL	Breitenbach, Schlichtern, Hessen
Weiß, Adelheid	13, May 1897	21, Apr.	82	303	Beitzel	Galion, OH	Schweiz
Weiß, Andreas	6, Oct. 1879	30, Aug.	17- - 4d	319		Roberts, IL	Westerende, Aurich, Ostfriesland
Weiß, Anna	11, June 1883	22, May	47	191		St. Louis, MO	Canton Zürich, Schweiz
Weiß, Barbara	11, Feb. 1858	10, Dec.	31	24	Weißlogel	Warsaw, IL	Deidisheim, Bischofsheim, Baden
Weiß, Barbara	21, Mar. 1870	2, Mar.	61- 1m-25d	95		Lawrence, KS	Guxhagen, Kurhessen
Weiß, Calvin	30, May 1895	29, Apr.	20	350		Mt. Vernon, MO	Deutsch-Hugel, Illinois
Weiß, Christina	24, Jan. 1889	20, Dec.	81- -11d	62	Schilling	Ballwin, MO	Brackheim, Württemberg
Weiß, Christoph	26, Aug. 1878	3, Aug.	36	271		Quincy, IL	Oberdorla bei Mühlhausen, Preußen
Weiß, Dinah Aletta	1, Dec. 1898	12, Nov.	70	767	Schröder	Valley City, ND	Horst bei Groß-Midlum, Ostfriesland
Weiß, Ellen	1, Apr. 1897	14, Mar.	30	207		Quincy, IL	
Weiß, Emil	28, Nov. 1895	9, Nov.	23	766		Cleveland, OH	Bremen, Germany
Weiß, Ernst	19, Oct. 1899	17, Sept	29	671		Cleveland, OH	Lahr, Baden
Weiß, Jerad	3, Nov. 1887		82	702		Galion, OH	Montgomery County, Pennsylvania
Weiß, Johan	7, July 1873	12, June	44	215		Piqua, OH	Culmbach, Baiern
Weiß, Johan Georg	15, Mar. 1894	25, Feb.	77	182		Denison, IA	Horbburg, Elsaß
Weiß, Johan Michael	4, Oct. 1888	10, Sept	64	638		Quincy, IL	Oberdorlau, Mühlhausen, Erfurt, Preußen
Weiß, Katharine	18, Nov. 1897	2, Nov.	69	735	Wahl	Cleveland, OH	Althengheit, Württemberg
Weiß, Konrad	31, Aug. 1854	1, Aug.	26	140		Cincinnati, OH	Baireuth, Baiern
Weiß, Ottilie M.	16, July 1891	23, June	29- 8m-25d	462		Quincy, IL	
Weiß, W.	29, July 1867	13, July	22	238		Piqua, OH	Piqua, Miami County, Ohio

Christliche Apologete Death Notices --- 1839 - 1899

Name of Deceased	Notice Date	Death Date	Age	Maiden Name	Page	Place of Death	Place of Birth
Weiß, Wilhelm	19, Apr. 1880	1, Apr.	56- 7m-12d		127	Roberts, IL	Norden, Ostfriesland
Weiß, Wilhelm Heinrich	17, Sept 1896	24, Aug.	29		607	Mt. Vernon, MO	St. Clair County, Illinois
Weißenbach, Christian	30, May 1881	14, May	57- 3m-24d		175	Morrison, MO	Neunheilingen, Langensalza, Erfurt, Preußen
Weißenbach, Maria Katharina	19, May 1879	7, May			159	Morrison, MO	
Weißenborn, Bernard Heinrich	25, Nov. 1897	5, Nov.	81		751	Cleveland, OH	Osnabrück, Hannover
Weißenborn, Joh. Martin	21, July 1859	28, June	68- 4m- 6d		116	Belleville, IL	Felchta, Preußen
Weissenborn, Magdalena	24, Oct. 1889	4, Oct.	80	Rieder	686	Cleveland, OH	St. Stephan, Simmenthal, Bern, Schweiz
Weißenborn, Magdalena	17, Sept 1891	18, Aug.	41	Weiß	606	Cleveland, OH	Alt-Hengstett, Calw, Württemberg
Weißenfluch, Heinrich	19, Aug. 1897	30, July	58		527	Golden City, MO	Bern, Schweiz
Weißenfluh, Anna	21, Apr. 1898	28, Mar.	18		255	Golden City, MO	Boppelsen, Zürich, Schweiz
Weißenfluh, Heinrich	9, Sept 1897	30, July	58		575	Golden City, MO	Bern, Schweiz
Weißer, Katharine	18, Oct. 1860	4, Sept		Hürdner	168	Ann Arbor, MI	Beilstein, O.A. Marbach, Württemberg
Weissert, Catharina	25, May 1885	4, May	59	Ott	7	Brooklyn, NY	Vaihingen, Württemberg
Weißheim, Elisabeth	6, Apr. 1863	7, Mar.	80- 4m		56	Frederick City, MO	Ostheim, Windecken, Hanau, Kurhessen
Weißlocke, Barbara	31, May 1855	1, Apr.	50- 4m		88	Warsaw, IL	
Weißmüller, Barbara	22, Apr. 1886	30, Mar.	76	Stier	7	Stryker, OH	Eserbrunnen, Offenheim, Baden
Weißmüller, Regina Margaretha	21, Nov. 1845	18, Oct.	57- - 1d		187	Brunersburg, ---	
Weißschuh, Maria Agnes	23, Apr. 1891	1, Apr.	67- 7m	Spätt	270	Orange City, IA	Gündelbach, Württemberg
Weist, August Wilhelm Robert	13, Nov. 1890	25, Oct.	71		734	Cincinnati, OH	Seifersdorf, Schönau, Preußen
Weist, Maria	11, July 1889	22, June	27		446	Cincinnati, OH	Lancaster, New York
Weit, Karl	1, Oct. 1891	22, Aug.	88		638	Bushton, KS	Esterup, Hannover
Weitkamp, Christine Elisabeth	11, Feb. 1892	10, Dec.	72	Katter	95	Huntingburg, IN	Ladbergen, Tecklenburg, Preußen
Weitkamp, Herman Wilhelm	17, May 1888	22, Apr.	83		318	Huntingburg, IN	Lattbergen, Tecklenburg, Preußen
Weitkamp, Herman Wilhelm	20, Feb. 1882	2, Feb.	31-10m- 1d		63	Huntingburg, IN	Dubois County, Indiana
Weitkamp, Johan Heinrich	7, Feb. 1881	15, Jan.	64- -12d		47	Huntingburg, IN	Ladbergen, Tecklenburg, Preußen
Weitkamp, Maria E.	29, Aug.1895	12, Aug.	81		558	Huntingburg, IN	Ladbergen, Tecklenburg, Preußen
Weitkamp, Wilhelmina Sophia	27, Apr. 1893	12, Apr.	25	Hünefeld	270	Huntingburg, IN	
Weitling, Dorothea	2, Feb. 1880	23, Dec.	45- 6m-23d	Baab	39	Illinois City, IL	
Weitmann, Margaretha	24, May 1869	23, Mar.	60	Hauter	167	Wapello, IA	
Weitze, August Christian Konrad	31, Aug. 1899	23, July	21		559	Charles City, IA	Pfalzweier, Pfalzburg, Elsaß
Weixler, J.P.	12, May 1884	14, Apr.	85		7	Boston, MA	Mitchell County, Iowa
Weizenbauer, Caroline	19, Feb. 1872	1, Nov.	65	Bauer	63	Jeffersonville, NY	Bremen, Germany
Welb, Ernst	12, Nov. 1847	2, Sept	25		183	New Orleans, LA	Baiern
Welb, Friedrich	26, Mar. 1847	9, Feb.	23		51	New Orleans, LA	
Welke, Christiana	8, Sept 1887	16, Aug.	54	Klienert	574	Rochester, MN	Linnenn, Preußen
Welke, Henrietta	8, Aug. 1881	8, July	43	Krüger	255	Rochester, MN	Grassa, Falkenberg, Oppeln, Schlesien
Welker, Anna Maria	2, Sept 1872	1, Aug.	17- 7m-17d		287	Birmingham, PA	Gunbitz, Hauland, Bromberg, Preußen
Well, Johan Peter	4, Apr. 1881	13, Mar.	66		111	Glencoe, MN	
Well, Katharina	26, Dec. 1895	21, Sept	58	Hartz	828	Spokane, WA	Kärdorf, Nassau
Wellbrock, Martin Heinrich	21, June 1894	1, June	21		406	Peoria, IL	Germany
Welle, Elias	29, Sept 1879	23, July	27- 3m		311	Newark, NJ	
Welle, Thomas	12, Mar. 1857	4, Feb.	45		44	Newark, NJ	Wolffach, Baden
Welle, William	8, Nov. 1880	18, Oct.	23-11m		359	Newark, NJ	
Wellemeier, Heinrich Wilhelm	4, Aug. 1862	19, July	49		124	Huntingburg, IN	Ladbergen, Preußen
Wellemeyer, Anna Maria Louise	11, Aug. 1884	13, July	68		6	St. Louis, MO	Ankum, Besenbrück, Hannover
Wellemeyer, Heinrich F.	31, Aug. 1899	12, Aug.	77		559	Garner, IA	Hannover

Christliche Apologete Death Notices -- 1839 - 1899

Name of Deceased	Notice Date	Death Date	Age	Page	Maiden Name	Place of Death	Place of Birth
Wellemeyer, Heinrich Wilhelm	10, Dec. 1896	17, Nov.	79	798		St. Louis, MO	Kasinn, Halle, Preußen
Wellemeyer, Johanna Kath. Marg.	11, Oct. 1880	27, Sept	56- 2m-23d	327	Lagemann	Huntingburg, IN	Gaste bei Osnabrück, Hannover
Wellemeyer, Johanna Kath. Maria	25, Oct. 1880	27, Sept	56- 2m-23d	343	Lagemann	Huntingburg, IN	Gaste bei Osnabrück, Hannover
Wellemeyer, Maria Elisabeth	11, Jan. 1864	23, Nov.	61	8		St. Louis, MO	Burgholzhausen, Kreis Halle, Preußen
Wellemeyer, Marie Elisabeth	4, Jan. 1864	24, Nov.	61	4		St. Louis, MO	Burgholzhausen, Kreis Halle, Preußen
Wellemeyer, William	10, Sept 1891	31, July	74	590		Huntingburg, IN	Ladbergen, Münster, Preußen
Wellenreiter, Karl	16, Feb. 1899	15, Jan.	66	111		Chillicothe, OH	Oberbergen, Baden
Weller, Anna Maria	3, Nov. 1887	16, Oct.	85	702	Hägeläu	Bland, MO	Oberbergen, Schorndorf, Württemberg
Weller, Dorothea	22, Mar. 1860	14, Feb.	28	48	Wohlmacher	Laporte, IN	Roßbach, Baiern
Weller, Friederike	12, July 1894	1, June	81	454	Schaaf	Santa Claus, IN	Lauffen a. N., Besigheim, Württemberg
Weller, Friedrich	23, Mar. 1868	15- 3m- 3d		95		Salem, IN	
Weller, Georg	25, Aug. 1892	9, Aug.	71	542		Boyne City, WI	Geildorf, Württemberg
Weller, Johan Georg	20, Apr. 1868	24, Mar.	36	127		Second Creek, MO	Adelberg, Schorndorf, Württemberg
Weller, Johan Georg	19, Nov. 1877	23, Oct.	78	375		Bland, MO	Bairek, Schorndorf, Württemberg
Weller, Johan Jacob	2, June 1873	14, May	65	175		Santa Claus, IN	Lembach, Marbach, Württemberg
Weller, Johan Jakob	27, Oct. 1887	16, Sept		686		Bland, MO	Adelberg, Schorndorf, Württemberg
Weller, Johannes	26, July 1860	9, July	65	120		Newport, KY	Beyreck, Schorndorf, Württemberg
Weller, Karolina Katharina	13, Jan. 1898	8, Dec.	37	31	Koltmeyer	Owensville, MO	Shotwell, Franklin County, Missouri
Weller, Katharina	29, Jan. 1883	3, Jan.	56-10m- 7d	39	Meyer	Bridgeport, CT	Michelbach, Gaildorf, Württemberg
Weller, Magdalena	16, Aug. 1875	5, July	71- - 8d	263	Kraft	Indian Creek, MO	Diegelsberge, Göppingen, Württemberg
Wellers, Allerrich	2, Aug. 1855	25, June	44	124		Platteville, WI	Wulsdorf, Amt Bremerleke, Hannover
Wellers, Wilhelmina	17, Mar. 1887	13, Feb.	76	174	Meier	Platteville, WI	Waddewarden, Minsen, Oldenburg
Wellers, Wilhelmina	31, Mar. 1887	13, Feb.	76	206	Meier	Platteville, WI	Weddewarden, Dorum, Hannover
Welling, Henriette	16, Sept 1878	7, Aug.	68	295	Vogt	Warren, MO	Riemschloh, Amt Melle, Hannover
Wellmann, Friedrich Heinrich Carl	11, Oct. 1888		49	654		Brenham, TX	Haldem, Preußen
Wellmann, Heinrich C.	26, Sept 1889	2, Sept	88-10m	619		Lansing, MI	Bünde, Herford, Minden, Preußen
Wellmann, Henry	14, July 1898	7, June	53	447		New Orleans, LA	Wehdem, Germany
Wellmeier, Joh. Matth.	1, Apr. 1852	Dec.		56		St. Louis, MO	Burgholzhausen, Preußen
Wellner, Maria	31, Oct. 1889	7, Aug.	56	702	Schöneweis	Park Ridge, NJ	Obernorgel, Germany
Wellpott, Karl H.W.	6, Dec. 1888	23, Oct.	47- 6m-27d	782		St. Louis, MO	OberMehnen, Westphalen
Welmes, Amalia	7, July 1898	10, June	10m-10d	431		Minonk, IL	
Welp, Heinrich	5, June 1876	5, May	40	183		New Orleans, LA	Lienen, Preußen
Welp, Katharina	26, July 1894	10, July	80- 6m-15d	486		New Orleans, LA	
Welsch, Georg	2, Apr. 1877	15, Nov.	66	111		Quincy, IL	Geckenbach, Maisenheim, Homburg, Hessen
Welsch, Johan	22, Dec. 1892	9, Dec.	69	814		Marion, OH	Roßwag, Vaihingen, Württemberg
Welti, Margaretha	3, May 1888	14, Apr.	44- 6m	286		South Bend, IN	Unterseen, Bern, Schweiz
Welty, Florence	22, Apr. 1897	3, Apr.	25	255	Goller	Peoria, IL	Peoria, Illinois
Weltzien, Ellen L.	4, Jan. 1894	11, Dec.	33	14		South Bend, IN	
Werner, Christian	12, Nov. 1847	4, Sept	26	183		New Orleans, LA	
Wemüller, Katharina Maria	8, Apr. 1867		57	110	Lohmeyer	Herman, MO	Berghausen, Bergholzhausen, Halle, Preußen
Wende , Bertha Emma	12, May 1898	15, Apr.	44	303	Schroer	St. Louis, MO	Warmen, RheinPreußen
Wende, Heinrich W.	27, Feb. 1890	19, Jan.	43- -19d	142		Nashville, IL	Buchhold, Lippe-Schaumburg
Wendel, Charlotte	3, Feb. 1879	14, Jan.	45- 2m-23d	39		Brooklyn, NY	Schönborn, Rheinkreis Baiern
Wendel, Christina	25, July 1895	5, July	45	478	Whittmann	Wood, IA	Hainweihe, Baiern
Wendel, Edward	9, June 1887	19, May	18- 3m-24d	366		Lansing, MI	
Wendel, Heinrich	3, Sept 1891	5, Aug.	57	574		Rochester, NY	Rockenhausen, Rheinkreis Baiern

Christliche Apologete Death Notices --- 1839 - 1899

Name of Deceased	Notice Date	Death Date	Age	Page	Maiden Name	Place of Death	Place of Birth
Wendel, Katharine Sophie	29, Dec. 1884	17, Dec.	37	7	Otterstedt	Brooklyn, NY	Groß-Sottrum, Hannover
Wendel, Kunigunde	21, Apr. 1898	26, Mar.	85	255	Heublein	Elkport, IA	Schmölz, Baiern
Wendelken, Caroline	20, Apr. 1874	30, Mar.		127	Fischer	Marietta, OH	
Wendelken, Frank Louis	12, Mar. 1883	31, Jan.	29-11m-21d	87		Le Sueur, MN	Marietta, Ohio
Wendelken, Johan	4, Jan. 1894	7, Dec.	77	14		Elkton, SD	Ottersberg, Hannover
Wendelken, Margaretha Adelheid	28, May 1896	8, May	71	350	Kück	Marietta, OH	Hüttendorf, Ottersberg, Hannover
Wender, Rebekka	21, Sept 1854	16, Aug.	70-11m	152		Ohio City,	
Wendland, Dorothea Sophia	16, July 1896	15, June	75	463	Branko	Owatonna, MN	Dölitz bei Stargard, Pommern
Wendland, Gottfried	18, Mar. 1878	2, Mar.	59- 3m-12d	87		Wabasha, MN	Kopplin,Stargard, Pommern, Preußen
Wendland, Herman Friedrich	18, July 1889	24, June	16- 1m-26d	462		Swanton, NE	
Wendland, Wilhelm	25, Sept 1882	21, Aug.	45-11m- 2d	311		Swan Creek, NE	Repplin-Dölitz, Pommern
Wendler, Emilie	10, Aug. 1899	23, July	59	511		Grand Rapids, MI	Polnedo, West Preußen
Wendler, Emma L.	8, Oct. 1891	15, Sept	22	654		Elmore, OH	Woodville, Sandusky County, Ohio
Wendler, Wilhelm	9, Oct. 1890	18, Sept	40	654		St. Louis, MO	Engter, Hannover
Wending, Jakob	4, Nov. 1867	8, Oct.	35	350		Walnut Creek, IA	Ohio
Wending, Wilhelmina	11, June 1896	21, Apr.	60	383	Hauswald	Halstead, KS	Lummitz, Sachsen
Wendorf, August	2, Sept 1886	14, Aug.	58	7		Portland, OR	Uckermark, Preußen
Wendorf, Eduard	20, Aug. 1866	13, July	39	270		Manitowoc, WI	Pommern
Wendt, Albert	28, Apr. 1884	1, Apr.	11- 2m	7		Wausau, WI	
Wendt, Anna	1, May 1890	11, Apr.		286		Lowell, WI	Lowell, Wisconsin
Wendt, August	9, Feb. 1888	6, Jan.	17	94		Wausau, WI	Kannenberg, Stettin, Pommern
Wendt, Auguste	21, Mar. 1881		29	95		Albert Lea, MN	Rogow, Stargard, Pommern
Wendt, Auguste	1, Oct. 1866	11, Sept	34	318	Lütke	Green Bay, WI	Zukofshof, Pommern
Wendt, Carl	24, Jan. 1895	22, Oct.	21	62		Lexington, MO	
Wendt, Caroline	14, Feb. 1895	21, Jan.	73	110	Palau	Detroit, MI	Teschendorf bei Riesenburg, West Preußen
Wendt, Catharina M.	2, Feb. 1885	16, Jan.	21	7		Newport, KY	Newport, Campbell County, Kentucky
Wendt, Daniel	4, Feb. 1884	8, Jan.	77	7		Parker, SD	Treptow an der Rega, Hinterpommern
Wendt, Elisabeth	5, Apr. 1875	7, Mar.	72- 7m-17d	111	Kloot	Columbus, WI	Stramens, Neukloster, Mecklenburg-Schwerin
Wendt, Friederika	1, July 1872	5, June	36	215	Schwarz	Sandusky, OH	Kittendorf, Mecklenburg-Schwerin
Wendt, Friedrich	3, Nov. 1898	26, Oct.	57	703		Newport, KY	Cincinnati, Hamilton County, Ohio
Wendt, Helene	30, Sept 1897	4, Sept	34	623	Dühn	Parker, SD	Ahnapee, Kewaunee County, Wisconsin
Wendt, Herman	9, Nov. 1874	13, Oct.		359		St. Charles, MO	Baden, Amt Achim, Hannover
Wendt, Johan Ferd.	3, June 1872	14, May	72	183		Cleveland, OH	Wilhelmsfelde, Preußen
Wendt, Johan Friedrich	4, Feb. 1892	18, Dec.	77	78		Madison, WI	Altendorf, Dobberlin, Mecklenburg-Schwerin
Wendt, Johan Wilhelm	4, Nov. 1897	28, Sept	45	703		Canada, KS	Altenhagen, Pommern
Wendt, Karl	24, Jan. 1895	22, Oct.	21	62		St. Louis, MO	
Wendt, Karl Franz	12, Apr. 1888	14, Mar.	52	238	Ringen	Wausau, WI	Kattenhof, Naugard, Pommern
Wendt, Katharine	6, May 1897	17, Apr.	68	287		Newport, KY	Beddorf, Hannover
Wendt, Louis C.	1, May 1882	14, Apr.	30	143		Newport, KY	Cincinnati, Hamilton County, Ohio
Wendt, Maria	25, Mar. 1897	19, Feb.	70-8m-24d	190	Hols	Taylor, MI	Alt Torpen, Neuenburg, Mecklenburg
Wendt, Maria	26, June 1890	27, May	61- 1m-12d	414		Lowell, WI	Turow, Mecklenburg-Schwerin
Wendt, Maria	22, Aug. 1895	5, Aug.	45- 4m	542	Strutz	Watertown, WI	Dölitz, Pommern
Wendt, Maria Ilsabein	10, Oct. 1864	2, Oct.	78- 5m	164	Bödicker	Covington, KY	Halden, Dielingen, Preußen
Wendt, Maria Wilhelmine	11, Aug. 1884	28, July	18- 7m- 9d	7		Wausau, WI	
Wendt, Michael	28, July 1898	29, June	75	479		Ft. Atkinson, WI	Jakobshagen, Salzig, Germany
Wendt, Samuel C.	6, July 1893	31, May	33-10m-20d	430		Newport, KY	Cincinnati, Hamilton County, Ohio

Christliche Apologete Death Notices -- 1839 - 1899

Name of Deceased	Notice Date	Death Date	Age	Page	Maiden Name	Place of Death	Place of Birth
Wendt, Sophia	27, Sept 1894	15, Aug.	73	630	Meinke	Honey Creek, WI	Brunnen, Mecklenburg-Strelitz
Wendt, Sophie	2, Jan. 1890	10, Dec.	55	14	Holst	Columbus, WI	Blowatz, Redentheim, Mecklenburg-Schwerin
Wendt, Wilhelm	18, June 1896	18, Apr.	63	399		Parker, SD	Voigtshagen, Treptow a. d. Rega, Hinterpommern
Wendt, Wilhelm	23, Nov. 1885	9, Nov.	24	7		Lowell, WI	Watertown, Wisconsin
Wendte, H.	8, June 1868	9, Apr.	46- 5m	183		Chester, IL	
Wendtorf, (Mr)	23, Sept 1886	8, Sept	46	7		Arlington Heights, IL	Krempern, Schleswig-Holstein
Wendtorf, Magnus	30, Sept 1886	8, Sept	46	7		Welington Heights, IL	Neustadt, Holstein
Wengenroth, Karl	7, Apr. 1892	19, Mar.	32- 7m- 5d	222		Peoria, IL	Langenberg bei Bonn, RheinPreußen
Wenger, Albrecht	15, Oct. 1877	17, Sept		335		Vermillion, OH	Canton Bern, Schweiz
Wenig, (Mr)	18, Mar.1872	25, Jan.	75-10m	95		Waterloo, IA	Malsfeld, Kreis Melzungen, Kurhessen
Wenig, Friedrich	10, Feb. 1887	16, Jan.	66	94		Lansing, IA	Malsfeld, Hessen
Wening, Christian G.	14, Sept 1885	23, Aug.	64	7		Marietta, OH	Großhasbach, Ansbach, Baiern
Wenisch, Auguste	7, Feb. 1876	6, Jan.	30- 8m-12d	47	Bahret	Poughkeepsie, NY	
Wenke, Georg	15, Dec. 1862	14, Oct.		200		Baraboo, WI	
Wennagel, Johan	30, Sept 1897	17, Aug.	75	623		Liberty, ----	Lichtenfels, Württemberg
Wennagel, K.	5, June 1890	16, May	19	366		East Liberty, PA	Pittsburg, Pennsylvania
Wenneker, Clemens	25, Dec. 1871		44	415		St. Louis, MO	Lengerich, Münster, Preußen
Wenneker, Heinrich D.	13, Oct. 1887	25, Sept	32	654		St. Louis, MO	St. Louis, Missouri
Wenner, Anna Barbara	22, Oct. 1891	25, Aug.	71	686	Schuler	Vinton, IA	Endingen bei Balingen, Württemberg
Wenner, Margaretha	28, Dec. 1854	9, Dec.	17-10m- 8d	208		Cincinnati, OH	
Wenner, Michael	10, Mar. 1848	28, Feb.	46	43		Cincinnati, OH	
Wenning, A.	31, May 1888	30, Apr.	68	350		Bradford, IN	
Wensel, Philipp	20, July 1868	3, July	25- 9m	231		Jacksonville, IL	OberSeitwitz, Pegnitz, Oberfranken, Baiern
Wente, Caroline	6, Apr. 1874	2, Mar.	23	111	Sternberg	Nashville, IL	
Wente, Caroline W.	22, July 1897	4, July	72	463	Schwartze	Chester, IL	Eilsen, Bückeberg, Germany
Wenthe, Johan Christoph	10, July 1876	24, June	77	223		Sheboygan, WI	Escher, Oberkirchen, Hessen
Wenthe, Sophia	26, June 1865	15, May		104	Wimpner	Sheboygan, WI	
Wentz, Anton	13, Nov. 1865		43	184		Dunkirk, NY	Feichingen, Spaichingen, Württemberg
Wentz, Karl	14, Jan. 1897	20, Dec.	17d	31		Eustis, NE	
Wentzel, Anna	27, Apr. 1885	15, Apr.	20	7	Röder	Evansville, IN	Evansville, Indiana
Wentzel, Friedrich	28, Apr. 1892	9, Apr.	15	270		Evansville, IN	
Wenz, Johannes	27, Apr. 1893	20, Mar.	70	270		Aurora, IL	Söllingen, Durlach, Baden
Wenz, Christina	12, Dec. 1895	14, Nov.	70	798	Berg	Springfield, IL	Oberstetten, Württemberg
Wenz, Christoph	1, Dec. 1884	14, Nov.	59- 9m- 1d	7		Springfield, IL	Gräfenhausen, Neuenburg, Württemberg
Wenz, Heinrich	16, Aug. 1894		60	534		Cannon Falls, MN	Blickershausen, Wizenhausen, Kurhessen
Wenzel, Katharina Barbara	20, Mar. 1865	24, Jan.	62	48	Friehelin	Colesburg, IA	Solingen, Amt Durlach, Baden
Wenzel, Margaretha	7, Apr. 1873	9, Mar.	30	111	Krimpel	Birmingham, PA	Alleghany County, Pennsylvania
Wenz, Maria Magdalena	20, Oct. 1853	24, Sept	21- 5m-16d	168	Kreinbill	Watertown, WI	Dürmünzenheim, Elsaß
Wenz, Martha	11, May 1854	28, Apr.	6- 7m	70		Poughkeepsie, NY	
Wenzel, Anna Christiane	20, Jan. 1868	2, Jan.	41- 9m-26d	22	Fima	Frederick City, MD	Herleshausen, Kurhessen
Wenzel, Anna Christiane	24, Feb. 1868	2, Jan.	41	63		Frederick City, MD	
Wenzel, Caroline	24, June 1867	1, June	23- 2m-20d	198	Heilmann	Quincy, IL	Quincy, Illinois
Wenzel, Caroline	5, Sept 1881	23, July	65- 3m- 7d	287		St. Louis, MO	Uft, Posen
Wenzel, Christian	20, Feb. 1882	4, Feb.	82- 2m- 9d	63		St. Louis, MO	Panko bei Berlin, Preußen
Wenzel, Ehrenfried	5, Nov. 1877	15, Oct.	87- 3m-13d	359		Bloomington, IL	Otterwitz, Sachsen
Wenzel, Elisabeth Margaretha	26, Oct. 1893	11, Aug.	76- 4m-23d	686	Liebig	Quincy, IL	

Christliche Apologete Death Notices --- 1839 - 1899

Name of Deceased	Notice Date	Death Date	Age	Maiden Name	Page	Place of Death	Place of Birth
Wenzel, John	9, Mar. 1893	4, Feb.	77		158	Quincy, IL	Reibach, Hessen-Darmstadt
Wenzel, Louis	27, Aug. 1896	24, July	62		559	Louisville, KY	Büdingen, Hessen-Darmstadt
Wenziker, Rudolph	1, Oct. 1866	12, Aug.	69		318	Covington, IN	Niederwenningen, Zürich, Schweiz
Weppner, Christina Elisabeth	6, Nov. 1876	24, Sept	41		359	San Francisco, CA	Spangenberg, Kurhessen
Werdin, John L.	22, Feb. 1875	25, Jan.	44-10m-15d		63	Blooming Grove, MN	Zachasberg, Posen, Preußen
Werfelmann, Dietrich	11, June 1891	15, May	76		382	Bland, MO	Lemke, Nienburg, Hannover
Werges, Anna Maria	23, Feb. 1893	26, Jan.	35	Lüdersen	126	Warren, MO	Hopewell, Warren County, Missouri
Werk, Anna Lydia	2, Nov. 1893	12, Oct.	31	VonBerg	702	Charles City, IA	Hazle Green, Wisconsin
Werk, Johanna Christiana	31, July 1882	15, July	73	Bensch	247	Rose Hill, TX	Vorbruch, Friedeberg, Frankfurt a. Oder, Preußen
Werkmeister, August	6, Jan. 1879	10, Nov.	18		7	Alleghany City, PA	Alleghany City, Pennsylvania
Werkmeister, Heinrich	3, Sept 1891	8, Aug.	78- 2m- 1d		574	Alleghany City, PA	Heierothe, Sondra, Rothenburg, Kurhessen
Werkmeister, Johan	6, May 1886	18, Mar.	47		7	New Metamoras, OH	Königswald, Kurhessen
Werle, Johann	20, Nov. 1851	16, Oct.	54		188	Canton, MO	Kanton Graubünden, Schweiz
Werle, Juliana	26, Oct. 1885	6, Sept	58	Schilling	7	Milwaukee, WI	Bischofsheim, Hessen-Darmstadt
Werle, Magdalena	30, Oct. 1890	11, Oct.	70	Belz	702	Chester, IL	Kanton Graubünden, Schweiz
Werle, Wilhelm	27, Apr. 1893	26, Mar.			270	Milwaukee, WI	Welgesheim, Hessen-Darmstadt
Werly, Barbara	4, Feb. 1878	30, Dec.	24		39	Canton, MO	
Werly, Peter	7, July 1884	11, June	82		7	Canton, MO	Prettigau, Graubünden, Schweiz
Wermann, Eddie Darwin	25, Feb. 1892	7, Feb.	20		127	Sheboygan, WI	
Wernecke, Auguste	4, Sept 1865	20, Aug.	65	Koch	144	Freeport, IL	Großfurra, Schwarzburg-Sondershausen
Wernecke, Eleonora Wilhelmine	10, Nov. 1879	21, Oct.	57	Wettig	359	Covington, KY	Neustadt am Rübenberg, Hannover
Wernecke, Friedrich	10, Dec. 1877	18, Nov.	53- 1m- 5d		399	Manitowoc, WI	Uftringen am Harz, Preußen
Wernecke, Louise	25, July 1895	7, July	50- 8m- 7d	Zaak	478	Lemars, IA	Stemmen, Fahrenholz, Lippe-Detmold
Wernecke, Wilhelm Joh. Christian	15, Dec. 1892	17, Nov.	66		798	Manitowoc, WI	Ufdrungen bei Stölberg im Harz, Sachsen
Werneke, (daughter)	19, July 1860		3		116	Newtonburg, WI	
Werneke, (son)	19, July 1860		13		116	Newtonburg, WI	
Werneke, (son)	19, July 1860		7		116	Newtonburg, WI	
Werneke, Mathilda Jane	4, Nov. 1867	15, Sept	6		350	Yellow Creek, IL	
Werneke, Mina Katharina	29, Jan. 1877	16, Jan.	19		39	Lena, IL	Verden, Margarten, Preußen
Werneke, William Carl	2, Jan. 1890	11, Dec.	18- 8m- 6d		14	West Unity, OH	Stephenson County, Illinois
Wernemann, Catharina	15, Mar. 1875	11, Feb.	69	Delbrügge	87	Defiance, OH	Linen, Warendorf, Preußen
Wernemann, Heinrich	13, June 1881	11, May	83-10m- 4d		191	Huntingburg, IN	Lengerich, Tecklenburg, Preußen
Wernemeier, Louise	15, Apr. 1886	31, Mar.	38	Schulte	7	Rochester, OH	Cincinnati, Hamilton County, Ohio
Werner, (Mrs)	7, June 1869	13, May	69	Lange	183	Golconda, IL	Rosenthal, Mecklenburg-Schwerin
Werner, Adam	13, Mar. 1876	13, Feb.	32		87	Woodville, OH	Heinebach, Melsungen, Kurhessen
Werner, Andreas	2, Nov. 1863	1, July	29- 9m-21d		176	Plattsmouth, NE	Sulz am Neckar, Württemberg
Werner, Anna	3, Dec. 1891	7, Nov.	31	Stuckmann	782	Brighton, IL	Leck, Schleswig
Werner, Anna Maria	14, Sept 1893	17, Aug.	34	Harthausen	590	Pomeroy, OH	Fosterburg, Illinois
Werner, Appolonia	21, Dec. 1893	26, Nov.		Pflaum	814	Pomeroy, OH	Weinheim, Baden
Werner, Augusta	10, Jan. 1889	17, Dec.	62- 4m-24d		30	Eldora, IA	
Werner, Auguste	30, Oct. 1882	26, Sept	43	Bormann	351	Winona, MN	Rosenthal, Brandenburg
Werner, Barbara	4, Dec. 1876	20, Nov.	72- 2m	Haselmayer	391	Greenville, OH	Rothfelden, Nagold, Württemberg
Werner, Barbara E.	25, Mar. 1872	10, Mar.	62		103	Golconda, IL	
Werner, Bertha Martha	10, Sept 1891	9, Aug.	16		590	Sun Prairie, WI	Sun Prairie, Dane County, Wisconsin
Werner, Carolina	17, Apr. 1890	19, Mar.	59- 5m- 4d	Vos	254	Nebraska City, NE	Schildberg, Brandenburg
Werner, Caroline	26, Jan. 1888	2, Jan.	78	Clink	62	Plattsmouth, NE	Dertzow, Brandenburg

Christliche Apologete Death Notices --- 1839 - 1899

Name of Deceased	Notice Date	Death Date	Age	Page	Maiden Name	Place of Death	Place of Birth
Werner, Catharina Barbara	20, Feb. 1890	30, Jan.	20- 6m- 6d	126		Greenville, OH	Ebershardt, Nagold, Württemberg
Werner, Catharina Elisabetha	3, Nov. 1862	29, Sept	61- 8m	176	Fig	Wesley, OH	Vöhl, Itter, Hessen-Darmstadt
Werner, Christian Friedrich	3, Jan. 1881	28, Nov.	52	7		Cameron, MO	Laienhain, Sachsen
Werner, Christine Justine F.	10, Dec. 1896	14, Oct.	77	798	Geißer	Brighton, IL	Freudenstadt, Württemberg
Werner, Christoph	18, Nov. 1897	31, Oct.	72	735		Cincinnati, OH	Langen, Starlenburg, Hessen
Werner, Conrad	13, Oct. 1887	1, Oct.	63	654		Jacksonville, IL	Kuxhagen, Kurhessen
Werner, Dorothea	8, Mar. 1880	23, Feb.	62	79	Ranchberg	Milwaukee, WI	Doppelfuhl, Vorpommern
Werner, Elisabeth Friederika	13, June 1889	23, May	15- 3m-23d	382		Golconda, IL	
Werner, Ernestine	8, May 1890	8, Apr.	76- 2m	302	Pohlmann	Saginaw, MI	Blankensee, Preußen
Werner, Ferdinand	8, Aug. 1881	7, July	81	255		Saginaw, MI	Bergenhorst a. d. Warde, Preußen
Werner, Fr.	20, Jan. 1887	30, Oct.	79	46		Etna, MO	Hövingshausen, Hessen
Werner, Friederike	17, Oct. 1889	20, Sept		670	Bekendorf	Rose Hill, TX	
Werner, Friedrich	24, Sept 1878	5, Sept	37	303		Sun Prairie, WI	Fürstensee, Pyritz, Preußen
Werner, Georg	29, Dec. 1879	15, Dec.	55	415		St. Paul, MN	Wundertshausen, Kurhessen
Werner, Heinrich	2, Dec. 1867	4, Oct.	34	382		Industry, TX	Ussen, Amt Liebenberg, Hannover
Werner, J.A.	17, Apr. 1865	14, Mar.	61	64		Danbury, OH	Sulz am Neckar, Württemberg
Werner, Jakob	26, Jan. 1893	9, Jan.	87	62		Greenville, OH	Ebershardt, Nagold, Württemberg
Werner, Jakob	23, Aug. 1888	8, Aug.	52	542		Lansing, MI	Friedrichsroda, Sachsen
Werner, Jakob	5, Nov. 1877	10, Oct.	16	359		Ahnapee, WI	
Werner, Johan Adam	14, Nov. 1895	9, Oct.	72	734		Waltersburg, IL	Heinebach, Melsungen, Kurhessen
Werner, Johan Friedrich	17, Feb. 1873	24, Jan.	58	53		Golconda, IL	Heinebach, Melsungen, Kurhessen
Werner, Karl (Rev)	18, Aug. 1898	20, July	37	527		Sterling, NE	Naulin, Pyritz, Pommern
Werner, Karl Fr.	26, Sept 1881	7, Sept	80	311		Galena, IL	Wesenstein bei Dresden, Preußen
Werner, Karolina	28, July 1879	10, July	29	239	Pinnow	Nebraska City, NE	Pitzerwitz, Soldin, Brandenburg, Preußen
Werner, Katharina	22, Feb. 1869	6, Feb.	24- 2m- 5d	63	Helwig	Lancaster, NY	
Werner, Louise	9, Aug. 1888	24, July	38	510	Dietz	Lansing, MI	Eßlinger, Württemberg
Werner, Maria Magdalena	30, Sept 1872			319		Baltimore, MD	
Werner, Marie	21, Apr. 1892	28, Dec.	38	254	Tietze	LaCrosse, WI	Dobern, Bensen, Böhmen
Werner, Minnie A.	21, Jan. 1897	26, May	31	47		Des Moines, IA	Cincinnati, Hamilton County, Ohio
Werner, Rosina	9, June 1879	4, Feb.	68	183	Remmig	Marrs, IN	Rechtenbach, Rheinpfalz Baiern
Werner, Wilhelm	3, Mar. 1898	22, Nov.	61	143		Orlando, OK	Fürstensee, Pommern
Werner, Wilhelm Friedrich	16, Dec. 1886	22, Sept	15	7		Golconda, IL	
Wernicke, Carl Friedrich	6, Oct. 1884		20	7	Steiner	Lemars, IA	Freeport, Illinois
Wernicke, Mathilda Jane	18, Nov. 1867		6	366			
Wernke, Johan Ernst	5, Apr. 1888	1, Mar.	81	222		Lemars, IA	Groß-Furra, Schwarzburg-Sondershausen
Wernke, Johan Friedrich	8, Sept 1892	14, Aug.	76	574		Santa Claus, IN	Horsten, Vörden, Hannover
Wernke, Katharina Elisabeth	17, Jan. 1856	28, Dec.	48- 6m	12		Huntingburg, IN	Astrup, Amt Vörden, Hannover
Wernke, Michael	26, Oct. 1893	13, Sept	75	686		Washington, MN	Radolin, Bromberg, Preußen
Wernli, Adolf Heinrich	16, May 1889	20, Apr.	29- 7m-25d	318		Lemars, IA	Iola, Waseca County, Wisconsin
Wernli, Anna Maria	7, Jan. 1867	16, Dec.	30	6		Milwaukee, WI	Dürrenäsch, Aargau, Schweiz
Wernli, Eduard Friedrich	27, Nov. 1882	10, Nov.	9- 8m- 3d	383		Lemars, IA	
Wernli, Louisa Dorothea	27, Nov. 1882	5, Aug.	12- 9m	383		Lemars, IA	
Werre, August H.	12, Mar. 1883		25- -20d	87		Nashville, IL	Randolph County, Illinois
Werre, Karl	25, Oct. 1875	4, Oct.	42	343		Chester, IL	Rethem, Hannover
Werren, Maria	3, Oct. 1895	19, Aug.	68	638		Danville, IL	
Werron, John	9, Nov. 1893	23, Oct.	74	718		Baraboo, WI	Lambertheim, Hessen-Darmstadt

Christliche Apologete Death Notices --- 1839 - 1899

Name of Deceased	Notice Date	Death Date	Age	Page	Maiden Name	Place of Death	Place of Birth
Werron, Philippine	15, Oct. 1857	14, Sept	40	168	Gräser	Baraboo, WI	Mackenroth, Birkenfeld, Oldenburg
Werry, Catharina	24, Sept 1878	7, Sept	55- 1m-28d	303	Veek	Boonville, IN	Ellweiler, Birkenfeld, Oldenburg
Werry, Charles	1, Sept 1887	16, Aug.	60	558		Booneville, IN	New York
Wertag, Louise M.	8, Jan. 1891	6, Dec.	26	30	Moser	Brooklyn, NY	Michigan City, Indiana
Werth, Clara Agnes A.	11, May 1893	17, Apr.	17	302		San Diego, CA	Leisewald, Kurhessen
Werth, Heinrich	8, Oct. 1883	2, Sept	49- 2m-15d	327		New York City, NY	Leville, Ohio
Werth, Mary Dorothea	13, July 1899	18, June	45	447	Feth	Los Angeles, CA	Gorkow bei Löcknitz, Pommern
Werth, Wilhelm	6, May 1897	12, Apr.	68	287		Neenah, WI	Altbunicksiel, Ostfriesland
Wertz, Beatta	30, Apr. 1896	1, Apr.	72	286	Bott	Alton, IL	Cartlow, Pommern
Wertzler, Maria C. F.	21, Dec. 1893	26, Nov.	45	814	Arndt	Chicago, IL	Elze, Amt Metnersen, Hannover
Wesche, Christina	14, Apr. 1862	26, Mar.	82	60	Heuer	Watertown, WI	Bremen, Germany
Wesely, Frank	4, Jan. 1894	7, Dec.	39- 1m-22d	14		Portage, WI	Lahde, Minden, Preußen
Wesemann, Charlotte Louisa	23, Dec. 1897	30, Nov.	68	815	Sackhof	Mt. Pleasant, IA	Thalamt, Piermont, Waldeck
Wesemann, Christian	27, Dec. 1875	1, Nov.	57	415		Bushnell, IL	Hagen, Waldeck
Wesemann, Heinrich	15, June 1899	20, May	76	383		Newark, NJ	Cassebruch, Hagen bei Bremen, Germany
Wesemann, Meta	9, Dec. 1886	25, Nov.	62- 8m-17d	7		Newark, NJ	Baden
Wesenbeck, Elisabeth Regina	11, June 1877	10, May	45	191	Noll	East Troy, NY	
Wesenberg, Albert	4, Jan. 1864	28, Nov.		4		Fond du Lac, WI	Zarben, Hinterpommern
Wesenberg, Johannes	31, Aug. 1868	13, Aug.	73	279		Fond du Lac, WI	Zarben, Treptow an der Rega, Hinterpommern
Wesenberg, Karl	19, Jan. 1880	16, Nov.	61	23		Alden, IA	
Wesenberg, Mathilda Maria	18, June 1891	8, May	13- 5m	398		Dovos, IA	Robe , Pommern
Wesenberg, Sophie	22, Sept 1887	23, Aug.	44	606	Kasten	Big Stone City, SD	Schönemark, Angermünde, Brandenburg
Wesener, Wilhelmine	29, Apr. 1897	7, Apr.	65	271	Duckerl	Oshkosh, WI	Crawford County, Ohio
Weske, Elisabeth	11, Oct. 1875	30, Aug.		327	Köhler	Detroit, MI	New York
Weske, Sophie Emma	24, Nov. 1873	26, Oct.	23- 5m-12d	375	Ellinger	Allegan, MI	Michelbach, Koblenz, Rheinpreußen
Wesler, Christian	10, June 1878	30, May	43	183		Lawrenceburg, IN	Michelbach, Altenkirchen, Coblenz, Preußen
Wesler, Maria Margaretha	16, Apr. 1877	26, Mar.	74	127		Lawrenceburg, IN	Mutterstadt, Rheinkreis Baiern
Wessa, Elisabeth	29, Nov. 1888	7, Nov.	78	766	Zwickel	Lawrenceburg, IN	Mutterstadt, Baiern
Wessa, Jakob	14, July 1862	13, Dec.	23- 6m	112		Milan, IN	Vechtel, Lippen, Hannover
Wessel, (Mrs)	13, May 1886	18, Apr.	79	7		Colesburg, IA	Vechtel, Fürstenau, Hannover
Wessel, Albert	18, Aug. 1884	27, July	78-10m-28d	7		Colesburg, IA	Astrup, Schledehausen, Hannover
Wessel, Anna Maria	23, Apr. 1891	26, Mar.	70	270	Prior	Huntingburg, IN	Etna Furnace, Ohio
Wessel, Carolina	25, Mar. 1886	1, Mar.	32	7	Reithmeier	Portsmouth, OH	Hille, Minden, Preußen
Wessel, Christian Ludwig	10, Oct. 1864	25, June	21	164		Schnectady, NY	Vechel, Bippen, Hannover
Wessel, Herman Bernard	29, Nov. 1894	8, Nov.	56	774		Colesburg, IA	Vehrte, Belm, Osnabrück, Hannover
Wessel, Johan Friedrich	18, July 1864	24, June	47- 3m-23d	116		Huntingburg, IN	Bechtel, Bippen, Fürstenau, Hannover
Wessel, Katharina Maria	13, Jan. 1887	22, Dec.	76	30	Hartbecke	Colesburg, IA	Rush Creek, Illinois
Wessel, Lea	25, Nov. 1878	11, Nov.	21- -19d	375	Irmscher	Schnectady, NY	Hille, Preußen
Wessel, Margaretha	19, May 1879	14, Mar.	72-11m	159	Glindmeier	Chase, KS	Huntingburg, Indiana
Wesseler, Karoline	9, Dec. 1886	18, Nov.	29	7	Niemüller	Wheeling, WV	
West, Susanne	17, Nov. 1884	3, Nov.	81- 4m-18d	7		Emden, IL	Gwienesum, Ostfriesland
Westen, Folina	27, June 1895	31, May	44	414	Miners	Jeffersonville, IN	Lemförde, Hannover
Westenberg, Gerhard F. H.	21, Dec. 1874	5, Dec.	61	407		Jeffersonville, IN	Wagenfeld, Diepholz, Hannover
Westenberg, Sophia Dorothea F.	6, Dec. 1894	11, Nov.	73	790	Finkenstadt	Bradford, IN	Herenhausen, Weihers, Baiern
Westenberger, Anna	25, Apr. 1870	28, Mar.	53- 5m-19d	135	Hartmann	Clarksville, TN	Marxheim, Hochheim, Nassau
Westenberger, Johan	2, Dec. 1886	7, Nov.	69	7			

Christliche Apologete Death Notices -- 1839 - 1899

Name of Deceased	Notice Date	Death Date	Age	Maiden Name	Page	Place of Death	Place of Birth
Westenkühler, Herman Heinrich	1, Nov. 1869	11, Sept	93		351	St. Charles, MO	Wester Kappeln, Münster, Preußen
Westerfeld, Karolina Sophia	4, Apr. 1881	16, Mar.	25- 3m-12d	Rogenfüß	111	St. Charles, MO	
Westerhaus, Anna Maria	25, Oct. 1880	6, Oct.	77	Brandt	343	Concordia, OH	Wallenbrück, Herford, Minden, Preußen
Westermann, Friedrich	23, Sept 1867	19, Aug.	58		302	Cedar Lake, IN	Varel, Amt Inlingen, Hannover
Westermann, John H.	13, July 1899	28, June	82		447	Newton, IL	Oldenburg
Westermayer, Wilhelm	8, Nov. 1844				172	New Orleans, LA	Rehne, Minden, Preußen
Westfahl, Helena	23, Oct. 1871	7, Oct.	7		343	Oregon, MO	
Westfahl, Martha	23, Oct. 1871	4, Oct.	5		343	Oregon, MO	
Westfahl, Rudolph	18, Sept 1876	25, Aug.	38		303	Chicago, IL	
Westmeyer, Clara	4, May 1893	25, Mar.	18- 6m		286	Peoria, IL	
Westmeyer, Margaretha	10, June 1886	17, May	42	Riedinger	7	Peoria, IL	Franklin County, Indiana
Weston, Johan A.	8, Oct. 1896	15, Sept	74		655	Red Bud, IL	Baiern
Westpal, Anna	18, July 1889	11, May	5- 9m		462	Morris, MN	
Westpal, Christian	18, July 1889	20, May	2- 7m		462	Morris, MN	
Westpal, Emil	18, July 1889	19, May	1- 4m		462	Morris, MN	
Westphal, Friedrika	10, Jan. 1870	20, Dec.	34	Lehmbek	15	Kendallville, IN	Rothmanshagen, Stettin, Preußen
Westphal, Karl Heinrich	29, Nov. 1894	12, Nov.	60		774	Marine City, MI	Stolzenberg , Hinterpommern
Westphal, Ludwig August	9, May 1881	30, Mar.	16- 4m- 8d		151	Wyandotte, KS	
Westphal, Wihelm Friedrich	29, July 1886	14, July	31		7	Paige, TX	
Westrup, Arnold	25, Aug. 1862	29, July	70		136	Batesville, IN	Westrup, Amt Malgarten, Hannover
Westrup, Elisabeth	15, Mar. 1875	26, Feb.	74	Schulz	87	Lyons Creek, KS	Horsten, Malgarten, Hannover
Westrup, Heinrich Rudolph	30, Jan. 1896	8, Jan.	61		78	Lyona, KS	Hörsten, Hannover
Westrup, William	8, Sept 1887	18, Aug.	26		574	Lyona, KS	Davis County, Kansas
Wetbrau, Louis	28, Nov. 1864	6, Aug.	20		192	St. Paul, MN	
Weth, Johan Leonhard	26, Oct. 1885	12, Oct.	58		7	Kenosha, WI	Steinbach, Wiedsheim, Baiern
Wetjen, Johan Heinrich	28, Mar. 1870	26, Feb.	54		103	Hokah, MN	Lahausen, Hannover
Wetjen, Louisa	3, Aug. 1885	8, July	18- 8m- 5d		7	Hokah, MN	
Wetstein, Barbara	27, Nov. 1890	2, Nov.	47	Meierhofer	766	Toledo, OH	Weihach, Zürich, Schweiz
Wetstein, Henriette	21, Nov. 1889	26, Oct.	70	Kiefer	750	Louisville, KY	Unter-Dürkheim, Cannstatt, Württemberg
Wetstein, Jakob	20, Mar. 1876	13, Jan.	63		95	Louisville, KY	Veltheim, Zürich, Schweiz
Wetstein, Louise	21, Sept 1854	2, Sept	5-10m- 9d		152	Ohio City,	
Wetterau, Maria	6, July 1893	8, June	19	Beyer	430	Honey Creek, WI	Germany
Wettmann, Heinrich	26, Oct. 1874	19, Sept	41- 6m		343	San Francisco, CA	Goddelau, Hessen-Darmstadt
Wettrau, Maria	4, Nov. 1867	18, Oct.	46		350	East Troy, WI	Esselborn, Hessen-Darmstadt
Wetz, Johan Georg	23, Aug. 1888	1, Aug.	60- 2m- 9d		542	Cibolo, TX	Offenbach, Nassau
Wetz, Margaretha	14, Mar. 1881	22, Feb.	74	Meckel	87	Danville, TX	Bicke, Herborn, Nassau
Wetzel, Andreas	29, Mar. 1888	13, Mar.	74		206	Santa Claus, IN	Beaver County, Pennsylvania
Wetzel, Anna	15, June 1899	24, Apr.	76	Meinhardt	383	San Jose, IL	Roßberg, Oberfranken, Germany
Wetzel, Barbara	2, Apr. 1891	8, Mar.	76	Ulmer	222	Santa Claus, IN	Württemberg
Wetzel, Carolina	18, Oct. 1860	7, Oct.	71		168	Galena, IL	Metzingen, Urach, Württemberg
Wetzel, Emma	2, June 1879	11, May	20		175	Chicago, IL	Wheeling, Cook County, Illinois
Wetzel, Eva Elisabeth	4, May 1874	15, Apr.	26	Hahn	143	Kendallville, IN	Salzberg, Kreis Homburg, Kurhessen
Wetzel, Karl G.	13, Feb. 1882	26, Jan.	46		55	Chicago, IL	Schwarzburg-Rudolstadt
Wetzel, Louis	25, Apr. 1889	23, Mar.	57		270	Pittsfield, IL	Berleburg, Westphalen
Wetzel, Ludwig	2, Mar. 1885	31, Jan.	21		7	Pittsfield, IL	Berleburg, Witgenstein, Preußen
Wetzel, Magdalena	2, Sept 1872	13, Aug.	33	Strubler	287	Chicago, IL	Lake County, Illinois

Christliche Apologete Death Notices --- 1839 - 1899

Name of Deceased	Notice Date	Death Date	Age	Page	Maiden Name	Place of Death	Place of Birth
Wetzel, Margaretha	3, Apr. 1876	4, Mar.	52	111	Hauck	Bushnell, IL	Rohrbach, Landau, Rheinkreis Baiern
Wetzel, Peter	15, Oct. 1896	31, Aug.	75	671		Santa Claus, IN	Beaver County, Pennsylvania
Wetzel, Sarah	17, May 1849	15, Mar.		78		Rodaway, MO	
Wetzler, Katharine	11, Feb. 1886	14, Jan.	29	7	Fuchs	San Francisco, CA	Sacramento, California
Wexelberg, Catharine	10, Mar. 1884	11, Feb.	67	7	Kirschner	Blue Island, IL	Kieselborne, Baden
Wey, Jakob	5, July 1849			108		Bloomington, IL	Sommerset, Sommerset Co., Pennsylvania
Weyand, Johanna Elisabeth	27, Feb. 1896	26, Jan.	28	143	Mühlberger	Scranton, PA	Königsbrunn, Württemberg
Weyant, Karoline Wilhelmine	14, June 1894	22, May	38	390	Westpfahl	Scranton, PA	West Hamilton, Canada
Weyer, Catharina	14, July 1862	20, June	68	112	Alexander	Boonville, IN	Klingen, Bergzabern, Rheinpfalz, Baiern
Weyerbacher, Helene	27, Feb. 1896	31, Jan.	83	143	Breetz	Kansas City, KS	Berne Township, Fairfield County, Ohio
Weyrauch, Peter	20, Oct. 1892	25, Sept	79	670		Des Moines, IA	Bullau, Hessen
Weznar, Wilhelm	29, Jan. 1883	5, Jan.	68	39		Menominee, MI	Holland
Whearley, Amanda	24, Aug. 1885	29, July	31-11m- 6d	7	Reinsch	Danville, IL	New York
When, Helena	12, June 1871	30, May	43	191	Debus	Baltimore, MD	Josbach, Kurhessen
Wherret, William	1, July 1852	5, May	80- 4m-5d	108		Columbia, IN	
Whipps, Katharine	3, Nov. 1884	18, Oct.	54	7		Jordan, MN	Pennsylvania
White, Alma	10, Nov. 1898	22, Oct.	18	719		Boonville, IN	
White, Charles	1, Oct. 1891	22, Aug.	88	638		Bushton, KS	Esterup, Hannover
White, Mary	11, Nov. 1886	27, Oct.	20- 9m- 6d	7	Licey	Chicago, IL	
Whitlack, Anna	6, Apr. 1863	18, Feb.	22	56	Wurster	Farmington, IA	Cleveland, Ohio
Whitlock, (Mrs)	21, Oct. 1878	8, Sept	77- - 3d	335		Farmington, IA	Holzhausen bei Pirmont, Waldeck
Whitlock, Catharine	9, May 1861	13, Apr.	28- - 8d	76	Reckmeier	Farmington, IA	Bockel, Amt Halle, Preußen
Whitlock, Charles	18, May 1899	19, Feb.	65	319		Burlington, IA	Waldeck
Whitlock, Minna	3, Mar. 1884	5, Feb.	52	7		Farmington, IA	Holzhausen, Waldeck
Whitmer, Christine	30, June 1898	8, June	77	415	Januwein	St. Louis, MO	Eler-Eichen, Baiern
Wibbeler, Christine Sarah	5, Mar. 1891	3, Feb.	23	158		Huntingburg, IN	
Wibbeler, Elisabeth	10, May 1880		38- 5m-11d	151	Hemmer	Huntingburg, IN	Ladbergen, Tecklenburg, Preußen
Wibbeler, Heinrich	15, Dec. 1892	24, Nov.	62	798		Huntingburg, IN	Ladbergen, Tecklenburg, Preußen
Wibbeler, Herman Heinrich	15, Aug. 1889	19, July	77- 5m-19d	526		Huntingburg, IN	Ladbergen, Tecklenburg, Münster, Preußen
Wibbeler, Louis Benjamin	8, Oct. 1891	17, Sept	25	654		Huntingburg, IN	
Wibbeler, Sophia	16, May 1889	16, Apr.	56	318	Feldwisch	Huntingburg, IN	Knoxville, Ohio
Wibbing, Julia	17, Oct. 1889	29, July	31	670	Harpstrite	Summerfield, IL	
Wibbing, Julia Harpstrite	7, Nov. 1889	29, July	30	718		Bridgeport, CT	
Wibel, Ernst	28, July 1892	13, June	17	478		Woodville, OH	Straßburg, Elsaß
Wibkin, Maria	24, Aug. 1854	9, Aug.	44	136		St. Paul, MN	Schessinghausen, Amt Wölpe, Hannover
Wich, Ernestina	27, Mar. 1876	21, Feb.	50	103	Heidner	Milwaukee, WI	Verwalde, Preußen
Wich, Gustav	7, Apr. 1887	24, Mar.	28- 8m- 2d	222		Milwaukee, WI	West Bend, Wisconsin
Wich, Johan Heinrich	29, July 1897	8, June	72	479		New York City, NY	Kronach, Oberfranken, Baiern
Wichelhaus, Margaretha	5, July 1894	8, Apr.	79	438	Kirchheis	Florence, MO	Wilschstedt, Amt Ottersberg, Hannover
Wichen, Gesche	28, June 1855	23, May	22- 3m	104	Ficken	Lawrenceburg, IN	Münden, Rheinkreis Baiern
Wicher, (Mrs)	25, June 1866	12, June	70	206		Newport, KY	Dielingen, Kreis Lübbecke, Preußen
Wichert, Herman	10, June 1872	30, May	33	191		Halstead, KS	Munershausen, Lilienfeld, Hannover
Wichmann, Anna	28, Jan. 1886	10, Jan.		7		Peoria, IL	Wüstenland, Oldenburg
Wichmann, Anna	11, Feb. 1884	22, Jan.	70	7			
Wichmann, Anna Catharina	14, July 1887	28, June	30	446	Scheffel	Milwaukee, WI	DeinRode, Hessen-Kassel
Wichmann, Carolina Emma	20, Nov. 1890	2, Nov.	28- 1m-10d	750		White Creek, IN	

Christliche Apologete Death Notices --- 1839 - 1899

Name of Deceased	Notice Date	Death Date	Age	Page	Maiden Name	Place of Death	Place of Birth
Wichmann, Claus Hermann	10, Oct. 1864	21, Sept		164		Seymour, IN	Arnshorst, Amt Wittage, Hannover
Wichmann, Elise	13, Dec. 1888	18, Nov.	64- 8m-15d	798		Galena, IL	Weddeworden, Dorum, Hannover
Wichmann, Emma Maria	5, Nov. 1891	24, Sept		718		St. Paul, MN	
Wichmann, Friedrich	18, Jan. 1875	1, Jan.	43	23		Oshkosh, WI	Walsrode, Hannover
Wichmann, Johann Heinrich	20, Jan. 1859	2, Jan.	28-7m	12		Rockford, IN	
Wichmann, John	12, Sept 1881	27, Aug.	52	295		Galena, IL	Wremen, Hannover
Wichmann, Maria Elisabeth	11, Dec. 1865	15, Nov.	14	200	Kerkhof	Seymour, IN	Bartholomew County, Indiana
Wichmann, Mete	3, Oct. 1889	8, Sept	46	638	Backenhus	Peoria, IL	Bornhorst, Oldenburg
Wichmann, Theodor	16, Feb. 1885	22, Jan.	29	7		Oconomowoc, WI	Blumberg, Pieritz, Pommern
Wichner, Margaretha	17, Dec. 1847	15, July	38	203		Defiance, OH	
Wicht, Christina Margaretha	18, Oct. 1875	3, Oct.	68	335		Charlestown, IN	Hefdrich, Amt Istein, Nassau
Wicht, Peter H.	26, July 1869	1, July	28- 2m-19d	239		Charlestown, IN	Hefrich, Amt Idstein, Nassau
Wichterman, Samuel	6, Oct. 1892	7, Sept	77	638		Clarington, OH	Kirchthurnen, Bern, Schweiz
Wichtermann, Elisabeth	22, July 1886	8, July	37	7		Clarington, OH	Monroe County, Ohio
Wichtermann, Margaretha	9, Apr. 1896		79	238	Lapp	Clarington, OH	Imbsheim, Elsaß
Wichtermann, Samuel	29, Dec. 1862	7, Nov.	22	208		Captina, OH	
Wick, Andreas	2, Nov. 1885	16, Oct.	74	7		Columbus, OH	Hopenheim, Hessen-Darmstadt
Wick, Timotheus	30, Aug. 1869	13, Aug.	55	279		Dunkirk, NY	Ehningen, Reutlingen, Württemberg
Wickardt, Elisabeth Friederike	5, Dec. 1889	10, Nov.	55	782		Blue Island, IL	Gebsee bei Erfurt, Preußen
Wicke, Carl	30, June 1887		62- 4m- 3d	414		Davenport, IA	Holzminden, Braunschweig
Wicke, Christiana	17, Nov. 1887	28, Oct.	76	734	Lucan	Baltimore, MD	Zierenberg, Hessen-Kassel
Wicke, Friedrich	30, Dec. 1897	13, Dec.	81	828		Baltimore, MD	Waltershausen, Kurhessen
Wickel, Rosina	30, Oct. 1840	20, Aug.	20	171		Wheeling, VA	
Wickmann, Maria Margaretha	13, June 1850	20, May	56	96		Jackson County, IN	Arenshorst, Hannover
Widemann, Andreas	25, Jan. 1869	12, Jan.	46-10m-27d	31		Batesville, IN	Gries, Brumpt, Elsaß
Widmann, Anna Kunigunda	11, Feb. 1867	14, Dec.	36	46	Friedmann	New Haven, CT	Redwitz, Lichtenfels, Baiern
Widmann, Anna Maria	1, Dec. 1887	25, Aug.	71	766		Albert Lea, MN	Herbrectingen, Württemberg
Widmann, Christian	18, Dec. 1865	7, Nov.	70	204		Ora Labora, MI	
Widmann, Christian L.	22, June 1863	3, June	32- 6m-26d	100		Chillicothe, OH	Murr, Marbach, Württemberg
Widmann, Friedrike	8, Jan. 1883	26, Dec.	78- 3m	15		Philadelphia, PA	Feuerbach, Stuttgart, Württemberg
Widmann, Georg	3, May 1894	6, Apr.	50	294		Albert Lea, MN	Herbrechtigen, Heidenheim, Württemberg
Widmann, Gottlob	1, Dec. 1884	22, Oct.	26	7		Warrenton, MO	Kornwestheim, Württemberg
Widmann, Katharina	25, Apr. 1895	24, Feb.	23	270		Albert Lea, MN	Washington County, Wisconsin
Widmeier, Jacob Friedrich	20, Apr. 1874	23, Mar.	75	127		Huntingburg, IN	Benningen, Württemberg
Widmeier, Philippine	20, Apr. 1874	25, Mar.	67	127	Hoffmann	Huntingburg, IN	Machenheim, Baiern
Widmer, Gabriel	21, Sept 1899	3, Sept	72	607		Bay City, MI	Kanton Aargau, Schweiz
Widmer, Georg	10, Jan. 1895	21, Dec.	64	30		Cincinnati, OH	Aistaig, Württemberg
Widmer, Karl	25, Oct. 1888	13, Sept	32	686		Berne, MI	Rochester, New York
Wiebe, Conrad	23, Feb. 1893	3, Feb.	59	126		Huntingburg, IN	Bühren, Neustadt, Germany
Wiebe, Katharina Anna	19, Mar. 1883	6, Mar.	49- - 6d	95	Holzhauer	Newport, KY	Sulz, Rotenburg, Kurhessen
Wiebe, Wilhelm H.	12, July 1894	5, June	67	454		Newport, KY	Büchern, Neustadt, Hannover
Wieben, Anna	24, Dec. 1896	5, Dec.	38	831	Thompson	Grand Ridge, IL	Schleswig-Holstein
Wiebusch, Adolph	6, Sept 1888	16, Aug.	33	574		Waco, TX	Waco, Texas
Wiebusch, Augusta H.	5, Sept 1881	22, Aug.	30	287	Brandes	Waco, TX	Bramsche bei Osnabrück, Hannover
Wiebusch, Dorothea	1, June 1899	14, Apr.	53	351	Heidorn	Perry, TX	Rehburg, Hannover
Wiebusch, E.G.	18, Aug. 1887	26, July	65	526		Waco, TX	Haßbergen bei Osnabrück, Hannover

Christliche Apologete Death Notices --- 1839 - 1899

Name of Deceased	Notice Date	Death Date	Age	Page	Maiden Name	Place of Death	Place of Birth
Wiechart, Charlotte	16, July 1877	7, July	71	231		Newport, KY	Levern, Lübbeke, Preußen
Wiechen, Catharina	18, Mar. 1867	18, Feb.	74	86		Lake Creek, MO	Schweringen, Amt Hoya, Hannover
Wiechen, Dorothea	10, May 1894	15, Apr.	69	310	Bult	Lake Creek, MO	Nieburg, Lebenau, Hannover
Wiechen, Friedrich	11, June 1857	15, Jan.	64	96		Florence, MO	Lohe, Nienburg, Hannover
Wiechers, Heinrich	21, June 1855	5, June	53- 7m	100		Cincinnati, OH	Dillingen, Kreis Lübecke, Preußen
Wiechmann, Eva	19, Mar. 1877	2, Mar.	23-9m-10d	95	Kappes	Jeffersonville, NY	Callikoon, Sullivan County, New York
Wiechmann, Johan Anton	7, Nov. 1895	17, Oct.	54	718		Peoria, IL	Oldenburg, Oldenburg
Wieck, Emma Anna	13, Mar. 1890	17, Feb.	17-10m- 2d	174		Chicago, IL	Chicago, Cook County, Illinois
Wieck, Johan Friedrich	9, June 1887	25, May	50	366		Chicago, IL	Groß-Perlin, Lauenburg, Koeslin, Pommern
Wiedel, John	4, Apr. 1889	12, Mar.	57	222		Waco, NE	Breitenbrück, Baiern
Wiedemann,	15, June 1893	19, May	73	382	Schwartz	Dodgeville, IA	Bünde, Herford, Preußen
Wiedemann, Barbara	24, Jan. 1895	5, Jan.	74	62	Richerd	Batesville, IN	Brund, Elsaß
Wiedemann, Georg Friedrich	12, Feb. 1883	29, Jan.	79- 5m-26d	55		Columbus, ---	Eichstetten, Baden
Wiedenhöft, Gottlob Heinrich	26, Jan. 1893	7, Jan.	51- 3m- 7d	62		Quincy, IL	Ahmsen, Lippe-Detmold
Wiedemann, Herman	16, June 1887		75	382		Dodgeville, IA	Bünde, Herford, Preußen
Wiedemann, Maria	29, Mar. 1880	26, Feb.	50- 5m	103		Roberts, IL	
Wiedenheft, Karl Friedrich	17, Nov. 1879	31, Oct.	66-10m-21d	367		Sandusky, OH	Reitz, Stolp, Preußen
Wiedenhöft, Albert	8, Sept 1887	14, July	30	574		Sandusky, OH	Lupow, Stolp, Hinterpommern
Wiedenhöft, Maria Carolina	5, May 1887	24, Apr.	74	286	Truhn	Sandusky, OH	Losow, Cöslin, Hinterpommern
Wieder, Louise	26, July 1888	9, July	38- 7m-18d	478	Mudra	Rutersville, TX	Byylo bei Spreneberg, Brandenburg
Wieder, Maria	19, Jan. 1885	3, Dec.	76	7	Jäckel	Stryker, OH	Mitesheim, Elsaß
Wiederholt, Ludwig	17, Aug. 1899	22, July	75	527		Mt. Vernon, NY	Trockenerforth, Kurhessen
Wiedler, Emma Beel	11, Aug. 1887	24, July	28	510		Chillicothe, OH	
Wiedler, Johan	19, Nov. 1891	25, Oct.	63	750		Enterprise, KS	Hagenbuch, Schweiz
Wiedmann, Charlotte Justine	2, Mar. 1874		32	71	Vahlenkamp	Pittsfield, IL	Ahmsen, Lippe-Detmold
Wiedmann, Maria Katharina	16, Jan. 1896	26, Dec.	71	46	Walter	Cincinnati, OH	Lorch, Welzheim, Württemberg
Wiedmer, Bernhard	9, Jan. 1882	18, Dec.	28	15		Blue Island, IL	Brittenau, Argau, Schweiz
Wiegand, Adam	27, Apr. 1863	29, Mar.	20	68		Calhoun, IL	
Wiegand, Adolph Clamor	7, Mar. 1870	14, Feb.	62- -25d	79		Clearwater, MN	Osnabrück, Hannover
Wiegand, Heinrich	15, May 1882	4, Mar.	65	159		Calhoun Co, IL	Mansfeld, Hessen
Wiegand, Johan	14, Feb. 1881	24, Jan.	79	55		Brighton, IL	Schenklengsfeld, Hersfeld, Kurhessen
Wiegand, Johan Adam	4, Aug. 1873	5, July	88- 6m- 4d	247		Calhoun, IL	Heenes, Kreis Hersfeld, Kurhessen
Wiegand, Louis	6, Oct. 1892	20, Sept	60	638	Gildehaus	Clearwater, MN	Hannover
Wiegand, Margaretha Maria	20, Mar. 1871	2, Mar.	64	95	Reis	Clearwater, MN	Dissen, Amt Iburg, Hannover
Wiegand, Margarethe	30, May 1895	4, Apr.	67	350	Stutz	New Orleans, LA	Darmstadt, Hessen-Darmstadt
Wiegand, Marie	18, Aug. 1887	30, July	25	526	Tischer	San Francisco, CA	Dellsberg, Bern, Schweiz
Wiegand, Martha Elisabeth	12, Aug. 1867	23, July	46	254	Grest	Calhoun, IL	Mülsungen, Rodenburg, Kurhessen
Wiegand, Mary E.	20, Apr. 1899	20, Mar.	51	255		Clearwater, MN	Schweiz
Wiegand, Peter	17, June 1858	5, June	25	96		Lexington, MO	
Wiegand, William	27, Apr. 1863	9, Mar.	22	68		Calhoun, IL	
Wiegard, Bertha	24, Jan. 1889	21, Dec.	12-11m-16d	62		St. Paul, MN	St. Paul, Minnesota
Wiegel, Lorenz	26, Sept 1861	22, Aug.	25- 6m-19d	156		Sandusky, OH	
Wiegmann, Heinrich (Rev)	17, Sept 1896	22, Aug.	80- 6m- 6d	607		DeWitt, MI	Hörringhausen, Wittlage, Hannover
Wiegmann, Karl	16, Aug. 1888	29, June	15	526		Lansing, MI	Delhi, Michigan
Wiegmann, Margaretha	12, Apr. 1894		78	246	Diehl	Holt, MI	Nordheim, Hessen-Darmstadt
Wiegner, Friederika	3, July 1882	9, June	72-10m-16d	215		Defiance, OH	Mollenberg, Mecklenburg-Schwerin

Christliche Apologete Death Notices -- 1839 - 1899

Name of Deceased	Notice Date	Death Date	Age	Page	Maiden Name	Place of Death	Place of Birth
Wiegner, Jo. Leonhardt	13, Sept 1849	5, Aug.	35- 9m	148		Columbus, OH	Baiern
Wieh, Ernestina	13, Mar. 1876	21, Feb.	50	87	Heidner	Milwaukee, WI	Verwalde, Preußen
Wiehmann, Maria	6, Dec. 1844	27, Sept	27- 8m	188		Woodville, OH	
Wieland, Amalie	10, Apr. 1876		35- 6m-25d	118		Boonville, MO	Lautenbach, Köln, Preußen
Wieland, Anna Carolina	11, Apr. 1895		76	238	Gernhart	Emden, IL	Bruchhausen, Germany
Wieland, Elisabeth	20, Oct. 1887	29, Sept	82- 2m-27d	670	Bechtler	Pittsburg, PA	Brötzingen, Pforzheim, Baden
Wieland, Heinrich	26, Aug. 1897	6, Aug.	75	543		Duluth, MN	Württemberg
Wieland, Johann Gottlieb	17, Apr. 1856	24, Mar.	63- 3m- 5d	64		Buffalo, NY	Unterbrüden, Backnang, Württemberg
Wieland, Johannes	29, May 1890	27, Apr.	82- 9m-24d	350		Pittsburg, PA	Oberbrüden, Backnang, Württemberg
Wieland, Karolina	11, Mar. 1897	2, Feb.	31	159	Haith	Lansing, MI	Württemberg
Wieland, Maria Friedrike	21, Nov. 1895	3, Nov.	36	750	Wiedenhöfer	Duluth, MN	Oberkochen, Württemberg
Wieland, Rosina Christine	23, Jan. 1862		34-10m-18d	16		Defiance, OH	Waldrims, Backnang, Württemberg
Wiemann, Elisa	2, Aug. 1875	15, July	53	247	Krumsik	Watertown, WI	Alvertissen, Lippe-Detmold
Wiemann, Heinrich	3, Aug. 1874	6, July	62- 9m-14d	247		Watertown, WI	Bentrop, Vega, Lippe-Detmold
Wiemann, Heinrich Friedrich Christ.	8, Sept 1898	1, Apr.	75	575		Arlington, MN	Vollsten, Rieteln, Kurhessen
Wiemann, Louise Henriette	21, Nov. 1895	22, Oct.	60	750	Meier	--, MN	Rumbeck, Rinteln, Kurhessen
Wiemann, Wilhelmine	16, Dec. 1867	15, Sept	53	398	Wissmann	Second Creek, MO	Herford, Lippe-Detmold
Wiemeier, Maria E.	2, Apr. 1877	9, Mar.	66	111	Bahrt	Union, MO	Behm, Osnabrück, Hannover
Wiemer, Charlotte Sophia	26, Nov. 1896	9, Nov.	71	766	Kremer	San Jose, IL	Gütersloh, Wiedenbrück, Minden, Preußen
Wiemeyer, Johan Heinrich	5, Jan. 1899	8, Dec.	51	15		Senate Grove, MO	Belm, Hannover
Wienand, Johan Georg	23, June 1879	24, Apr.	77- 7m- 7d	199		Decatur, IL	Hombressen, Kurhessen
Wienand, Karl Wilhelm	3, Nov. 1873	16, Oct.	46	351		Terre Haute, IN	Hombressen, Kurhessen
Wienand, Wilhelmine	8, May 1890	9, Apr.	77	302		Industry, TX	Barmen,
Wienefeld, Anna Barbara	19, Dec. 1889	19, Nov.	70	814		Industry, TX	Barmen, Wupperthal, Germany
Wienefeld, Elisabeth	11, Sept 1865	26, Aug.	65	148	Busch	Dayton, OH	Wallenstein, Humberg, Kurhessen
Wieneke, Heinrich	15, Feb. 1875	29, Jan.	50- 5m-15d	55	Steube	Dayton, OH	Naufis, Kurhessen
Wieneke, Friedrich	17, Oct. 1870	29, Sept	75	335		Dayton, OH	Grebenhagen, Kurhessen
Wieneke, Lisette	12, Apr. 1869	19, Mar.	49	119		Edwardsville, IL	Lienen, Tecklenburg, Preußen
Wiener, Maria	27, Dec. 1888	27, Nov.	37- 1m-17d	830	Niemann	Nokomis, IL	Lienen, Westphalen
Wiener, Margaretha	15, May 1876	1, May	26-10m- 3d	159		Edwardsville, IL	Nordcampen, Preußen
	17, Apr. 1890	2, Mar.	83- 3m	254		Waterville, OH	Guttenheim, Baiern
Wierwille, Louis	24, Mar. 1879		8- 1m- 8d	95		Golconda, IL	
Wiese, Anna	7, Mar. 1864	10, Feb.	41	40	Kintwort	Roseville, MI	Nartauen bei Achen, Hannover
Wiese, Christopher	3, Apr. 1890	8, Mar.	56	222		Quincy, IL	Pommern
Wiese, Emma Albertine	6, Jan. 1898	16, Dec.	24	15		Hokah, MN	Hokah, Houston County, Minnesota
Wiese, Johanna	6, Oct. 1892	15, Sept	71	639	Schmidt	Winamoc, IN	Samoczyn, Posen
Wiese, Maria	12, Mar. 1891	1, Feb.	27	174	Wilkowsky	Kewaunee, WI	Gibson, Manitowoc County, Wisconsin
Wiese, Maria	3, Sept 1891	13, Aug.	72	574	Schnurstein	Kewaunee, WI	Alt-Kentzlin, Stettin, Preußen
Wiese, Maria Louise	8, Oct. 1891	12, Sept	59	654	Breek	Ft. Hunter, NY	Hille, Minden, Preußen
Wiesel, Alvine	17, Mar. 1884	6, Feb.		7		Hartford, CT	
Wiesemann, Fred W.	12, July 1894	18, June	63	454		St. Louis, MO	Phele, Germany
Wiesemann, John	11, Aug. 1898	18, July	72	511		Osceola, NE	Affholden, Waldeck
Wiesemann, Louise	21, Jan. 1897	22, Dec.	67	47	Späth	Hedwigs Hill, TX	Mattemühlen, Herborn, Nassau
Wiesemann, Maria	10, Sept 1866	27, Aug.	30	294	Gläser	St. Louis, MO	Bromskirchen, Hessen-Darmstadt
Wieser, Anna Maria	6, Sept 1860	14, Aug.	54- 2m-16d	144	Osterheld	Camden Point, MO	Hochspeier, Kaiserslautern, Baiern
Wieser, Elisabeth	12, Sept 1864		74- 9m	148		New York, NY	Neustadt an der Hard, Rheinpfalz Baiern

Christliche Apologete Death Notices --- 1839 - 1899

Name of Deceased	Maiden Name	Place of Death	Place of Birth	Page	Age	Death Date	Notice Date
Wieser, John		St. Louis, MO	Hammer, Schlesien	124		22, July	4, Aug. 1862
Wiesner, Anna Rosine		Holt, MI	Schweiz	127	94	3, Feb.	25, Feb. 1892
Wieß, Anna		Lancaster, MO		23	67- 6m-12d	1, Jan.	17, Jan. 1881
Wiethoff, Heinrich Wilhelm	Schuch	Seymour, IN	Tinnen, Tecklenburg, Preußen	110	56	17, Dec.	14, Feb. 1895
Wieties, Minnie			Olndorf, Ostfriesland	222		7, Mar.	4, Apr. 1895
Wieties, Ufka		Springfield, IL	Ostfriesland	7	61	22, Sept	7, Oct. 1886
Wieting, Heinrich		Brillion, WI		46	20- 3m- 1d	23, Dec.	19, Jan. 1888
Wieting, Heinrich C.		Crandon, SD	Charlestown, Calumet County, Wisconsin	350	15	8, May	30, May 1895
Wieting, Joachim		Brillion, WI	Suckow, Mecklenburg-Schwerin	319	71	29, Apr.	20, May 1897
Wieting, Joachim		Sheboygan, WI	Suctow, Mecklenburg-Schwerin	167	69	10, Apr.	25, May 1868
Wieting, Karoline M.	Bastian	Charlestown, IN	Sukow, Mecklenburg-Schwerin	7	81- 1m	13, Dec.	3, Jan. 1881
Wieting, Lena		Crandon, SD	Charleston, Wisconsin	463	17	5, July	21, July 1898
Wieting, Martha Maria		Brillion, WI		127	17- 9m- 5d	27, Mar.	16, Apr. 1883
Wieting, Ottilie		Perry, TX		511	32	19, July	12, Aug. 1897
Wieting, William		Charlestown, WI		23	17- 2m-20d	30, Dec.	20, Jan. 1873
Wievel, Cardel		Huntingburg, IN	Ibbenbühren, Tecklenburg, Westphalen	72		4, Mar.	1, May 1851
Wigand, Heinrich		Giard, IA	Homberg, Hessen-Kassel	143	80	8, Feb.	3, Mar. 1898
Wihler, Caroline Francis		New Metamoras, OH	Summit Township, Monroe County, Ohio	766	24- 2m- 7d	30, Aug.	27, Nov. 1890
Wiker, (Mr)		Melbourne, IA	Mendode, Illinois	183	19	7, May	8, June 1874
Wilbers, Elisabeth Magdalena	Dehner	Covington, KY	Covington, Kenton County, Kentucky	703	32	1, Oct.	4, Nov. 1897
Wilboog, Magnus		Brooklyn, NY	Westratorp, Schweden	462	53	17, June	20, July 1893
Wilbort, Valentin		Carroll, OH	Germany	31	86	29, Dec.	27, Jan. 1879
Wild, Catharina	Struth	Newark, NJ	Lauterbach, Hessen-Darmstadt	14	75- 3m	24, Nov.	1, Jan. 1891
Wild, Carrie	Netting	Liberty, PA	Isingen, Irchheim an der Teck, Württemberg	350	48	12, May	28, May 1891
Wild, Elisabeth	Baldinger	Hoboken, NJ	Kanton Aargau, Schweiz	63	74	24, Dec.	27, Jan. 1898
Wild, Georg		Pekin, IL	Theiningen, Baden	32	38	25, Jan.	25, Feb. 1858
Wild, Joseph		Marrs, IN	Posey County, Indiana	7	15	17, Dec.	2, Jan. 1882
Wild, Marie		New Orleans, LA	Schlüchtern, Hessen	367	53	3, Nov.	18, Nov. 1878
Wildberger, Wilhelmina Katharina	Kaufmann	St. Louis, MO	St. Louis, Missouri	62	40	22, Dec.	25, Jan. 1894
Wildbeyer, John		Nebraska City, NE	Neunkirch, Schaffhausen, Schweiz	574	63- -28d	13, Aug.	5, Sept 1889
Wilde, Gustav		New Orleans, LA	Schlühtern, Preußen	638	37	10, Sept	2, Oct. 1890
Wilde, Hanna Luise		Lincoln, NE	Döitz bei Stargart, Piritz, Pommern	30	64- 8m-24d	15, Dec.	12, Jan. 1888
Wilde, Louise		Wausau, WI	Bammin, Walde, Preußen	207	89		27, June 1881
Wilden, Mathilde Elisabetha		Vandalia, IL	Richland County, Ohio	180	24	18, Oct.	5, Nov. 1857
Widermann, Johan Michael		Marietta, OH	Reinsbronn, Württemberg	151	46- 5m- 1d	28, Apr.	8, May 1882
Widermuth, Johan David		Pomeroy, OH	Rielingshausen, Marbach, Württemberg	398	68- 2m-21d	18, Nov.	10, Dec. 1866
Widermuth, Magdalene	Hoffmann	Pomeroy, OH	Ridgshausen, Marbach, Württemberg	7	84	23, Mar.	15, Apr. 1886
Wildin, (Mr)		Vandalia, IL		16	58		22, Jan. 1857
Wildy, Jacobine E.		Lenzburg, IL	Feuerbach, Stuttgart, Württemberg	222	61	27, Feb.	6, Apr. 1893
Wiley, Isaac W.		Foochow, CN	Lewistown, Pennsylvania	4	59		1, Dec. 1884
Wifort, Maria	Lenger	Jeffersonville, NY	Rockport, Ohio	254	27	24, Mar.	18, Apr. 1889
Wilharm, Luise		Scranton, PA	Germany	590	31	11, Aug.	11, Sept 1890
Wilhauer, Andreas		Sidney, OH	Morrow County, Ohio	407	45	9, Dec.	19, Dec. 1881
Wilhelm, Christian		Rochester, NY	Hohengeren, Württemberg	398	41	30, May	18, June 1891
Wilhelm, Christoph		Marion, OH	Hambach, Heppenheim, Hessen-Darmstadt	334	66	8, May	24, May 1888
Wilhelm, Elisabeth		Hokah, MN	Kemmerothe, Hersfeld, Kurhessen	639	66	11, Sept	6, Oct. 1892

Name of Deceased	Notice Date	Death Date	Age	Page	Maiden Name	Place of Death	Place of Birth
Wilhelm, Katharine Christine	27, Oct. 1892	4, Oct.	32	686	Hopperich	Columbus, OH	Crawford County, Ohio
Wilhelmi, Adolph	27, Apr. 1874	7, Apr.	30-6m	135		St. Paul, MN	
Wilhelmi, Friedrich	22, Aug. 1881	6, Aug.	72- 4m	271		St. Paul, MN	Burg, Schwalbach, Nassau
Wilhelmi, Georg W.	28, Mar. 1895	1, Mar.	19	206		Wrayville, IL	Pine Creek, Iowa
Wilhelmi, Susanna K.	24, Nov. 1884	6, Nov.	69	7	Henritzy	St. Paul, MN	Hettenheim, Schwalbach, Hessen-Darmstadt
Wilke , Joachim	9, Mar. 1893	11, Feb.	74	158		Garrett, IN	Magdeburg, Germany
Wilke , Catharina	25, Mar. 1858	11, Feb.	56	48	Kuhlmann	Warsaw, IL	Westerkappeln, Tecklenburg, Preußen
Wilke , Heinrich	17, Jan. 1856	21, Dec.	18- 2m- 7d	12		Woodville, OH	
Wilke, (girl)	17, Jan. 1856	20, Nov.		12		Woodville, OH	
Wilke, (Mr)	4, Mar. 1852	1, Feb.	44	40		Nauvoo, IL	
Wilke, (Mrs)	20, Nov. 1851	22, Oct.	67	188	Buschen	Nauvoo, IL	Bledeln, Hannover
Wilke, Anna	4, Nov. 1852	19, Aug.		180		Indianapolis, IN	
Wilke, August Albert	13, Jan. 1879	15, Dec.	45	15		Olive Branch, NE	Diepholz, Hannover
Wilke, Caroline	3, Apr. 1890	15, Mar.	44	222	Behnke	Elmore, OH	Stuppendorf, Mecklenburg-Schwerin
Wilke, Christina	14, Apr. 1887	17, Mar.	84	238	Leenhart	Alida, KS	Bledeln, Ruthe, Hannover
Wilke, Christine	31, Mar. 1887		84	206	Leenhart	Junction City, KS	Bledeln, Ruthe, Hannover
Wilke, Christine G.	1, July 1897	7, June	27	414	Helmer	Dallas, IL	Peoria, Illinois
Wilke, Dina	12, Sept 1861	12, Aug.	40	148	Heinstedt	Sherrills Mount, IA	Hoben-Eggelsen, Steinbrück, Hannover
Wilke, Dorothea	27, Sept 1880	15, Sept	63- 1m-22d	311		Boonville, IN	Lichtenberg, Braunschweig
Wilke, Elisabeth	18, Mar. 1867			86		Etna, MO	Vokerode, Hessen-Kassel
Wilke, Elisabeth	4, July 1895	13, June	73	430	Loose	San Jose, CA	Mecklenburg-Schwerin
Wilke, Emilie	18, Aug. 1892	29, July	38- 3m-15d	526	Mühlemann	San Jose, CA	Buckhill Bottom, Monroe County, Ohio
Wilke, Georg Jakob	6, Apr. 1899	15, Mar.	16	223		Boonville, IN	Boonville, Indiana
Wilke, Gerhart	7, Jan. 1884	13, Dec.	85	7		Woodville, OH	Fenna, Hannover
Wilke, Heinrich	23, July 1891	1, July	79- 3m- 2d	478		Milwaukee, WI	Pichow, Mecklenburg-Schwerin
Wilke, Heinrich	9, Feb. 1863	12, Feb.	19- -24d	40		Boonville, IN	Lebenstätt, Braunschweig
Wilke, Johan Heinrich	25, Dec. 1876	13, Dec.	66- 9m- 4d	413		Boonville, IN	Lebenstedt, Amt Salder, Braunschweig
Wilke, Sophia	17, Jan. 1856	9, Dec.	4	12		Woodville, OH	
Wilke, Sophie	10, Dec. 1883	20, Nov.	69- 7m	7		Mt. Vernon, NY	Eckhoff, Mecklenburg-Schwerin
Wilken, Auguste Wilhelmine Emilie	15, Sept 1879	16, Aug.	21	295	Böcker	Petersburg, IL	Landridge, Menard County, Illinois
Wilken, Helena	23, Dec. 1886	12, Dec.	84	7		Chicago, IL	Vorpommern
Wilken, Herman	17, May 1894	20, Apr.	57	326		Haskins, NE	Vorpommern
Wilken, Herman Fr.	28, June 1894	7, June	17	422		Macon, NE	Petersburg, Illinois
Wilken, Jochem Friedrich Heinrich	18, Dec. 1876	4, Dec.	67	407		Mt. Vernon, NY	Jarchow, Mecklenburg-Schwerin
Wilkenning, (Mr)	16, Feb. 1893	28, Jan.	66	110		Appleton, MO	Winzlau, Reburg, Hannover
Wilkens, Heinrich	28, May 1857	9, May	42- 5m	88		Bloomingdale, NY	Fischerhude, Hannover
Wilkens, Louise	13, Dec. 1855	19, Nov.	20	200		Toledo, OH	Woodville, Ohio
Wilkens, Wilhelm Gerard	28, Sept 1893	1, Sept	38	622		Guthrie, IL	Essens, Ostfriesland
Wiker, Mina	17, Apr. 1865	25, Mar.	21	64	Unnewehr	Batesville, IN	Franklin County, Indiana
Wilkonske, Ida Friedrike Karolina	26, May 1898	4, May	55	335	Kopieske	Morristown, MN	Turow , Pommern
Wilkowske, Hulda	12, Apr. 1888	1, Mar.	34- 9m	238		Blooming Grove, MN	Posen
Wilkowsky, Caroline	7, June 1875	21, May	37	183	Krüger	Kenaunee, WI	Rochzow, Pommern, Preußen
Will, August	29, Mar. 1894	19, Feb.	50	214	Kiepe	Almond, WI	Sesenburg, Sarzig, Pommern
Will, Christine	17, Apr. 1890	16, Mar.	57	254	Kübler	Cape Girardeau, MO	Birndorf, Germany
Will, Anna Catharina	19, June 1882	27, May	38- - 7d	199		Louisville, KY	Ettweiler, Nagold, Württemberg
Will, Anna Elisabeth	29, June 1868	5, June	60- 6m -1d	207	Krick	Columbus, OH	Niedercleen, Kreis Wetzlar, Preußen

Christliche Apologete Death Notices --- 1839 - 1899

Name of Deceased	Notice Date	Death Date	Age	Page	Maiden Name	Place of Death	Place of Birth
Will, Anna Maria	28, Aug. 1876	9, July	86	279		Louisville, KY	Mensfelden, Limburg, Nassau
Will, August Friedrich	13, Feb. 1896	21, Jan.	38	110		Bridgewater, IA	
Will, Barbara	28, Mar. 1889	27, Feb.	42	206	Dold	Hartford, CT	Tuttlingen, Württemberg
Will, Caroline	28, Apr. 1884	12, Apr.	22	7	Hamann	Cape Girardeau, MO	
Will, Christine Gottliebe	15, Dec. 1887	17, Nov.	62	798		Galena, IL	Heilbronn, Württemberg
Will, Eleonora	5, June 1882	28, Apr.	65- 7m	183		Cape Girardeau, MO	Rothheim, Hessen-Darmstadt
Will, Elisabeth	15, Jan. 1883	29, Dec.	25	23	Ullrich	Cape Girardeau, MO	
Will, Friederike	27, June 1889		52	414		Silver Creek, NY	Brilwitz, Mecklenburg-Strelitz
Will, Hanna A.	21, July 1892	16, June	22	462	Rogge	Alton, IL	
Will, Henriette Katharina	20, Apr. 1893	23, Mar.	76-10m-12d	254	Göbel	Louisville, KY	Menzfelten, Limburg, Nassau
Will, Louise	11, Feb. 1886	15, Jan.	37- 1m- 9d	7	Horn	Almond, WI	Branberg, Neumark, Preußen
Will, Philipp	31, Jan. 1861	12, Jan.	69	20		Charlestown, IN	Münsfeld, Nassau
Wille, (Mr)	18, Oct. 1869		83	335		Edwardsville, IL	
Wille, Eleonore	28, July 1862	21, June		120		Chicago, IL	
Wille, Friedrich	23, Oct. 1871	23, Sept	51	343		Milwaukee, WI	Benz, HinterPommern
Wille, John C.	27, Mar. 1890	27, Feb.	63	206		Oregon, MO	
Wille, Martha	13, Mar. 1890	24, Feb.	70	174	Mühlhaus	Chicago, IL	Wolstein, Witzenhausen, Kurhessen
Willenbacher, Johan	21, Oct. 1886	25, Aug.	26	7		New York City, NY	
Willenbrock, Heinrich Georg	24, Feb. 1887	17, Jan.	14- 8m-23d	126		Brooklyn, NY	
Willenmeyer, Louis	16, Nov. 1874		44	367		Schnectady, NY	Minden, Preußen
Willer, Elisabeth	6, Sept 1888	15, Aug.	79	574	Piderit	Waukow, IA	Langenholzhausen, Lippe
Willer-Piederit, Friedrich	2, Sept 1886	22, July	79- 2m	7		Ludlow, IA	Langenholzhausen, Lippe-Detmold
Willers, August E.	27, Aug. 1891	10, Aug.	73- 4m-21d	558		Lawrenceburg, IN	Braunschweig
Willers, Dierks	8, July 1867	8, June	72	214		Houston, TX	Westerholt, Oldenburg
Willes, Friedrich Wilhelm	18, Aug. 1873	31, July	17- 4m-13d	263		Cincinnati, OH	
Williams, Elisabeth	12, Jan. 1899	21, Dec.	71	31		Chicago, IL	Lothringen
Williams, Jakob	21, July 1892	11, May	71	462		Charlestown, ---	Omseldingen, Bern, Schweiz
Willis, Heinrich	9, Mar. 1863	22, Feb.	22- 4m- 3d	40		Cincinnati, OH	Lavelsloh, Hannover
Wilkom, Phillippina	4, Mar. 1886	22, Feb.	40- 1m-28d	7	Adam	Seymour, IN	Lettweiler, RheinPfalz Baiern
Willmann, Heinrich	19, Oct. 1893	30, Sept	31	670		Braken, TX	Comal County, Texas
Willmann, Louisa Verena	30, July 1891	5, July	61	494	Widmer	New York City, NY	Canton Aargau, Schweiz
Willmann, Maria	9, Oct. 1876	19, Sept	31	327	Klußmeyer	Ballwin, MO	Franklin County, Missouri
Wilms, Antje	24, Jan. 1895	16, Dec.	65	62	Pree	Quincy, IL	Westerholt, Ostfriesland
Wilms, Behrend	11, Aug. 1898			511		Quincy, IL	
Wilms, Eduard	15, Feb. 1864	19, Jan.	10- 2m-26d	28		Quincy, IL	Quincy, Illinois
Wilms, Emma Johanna	6, Dec. 1894	13, Nov.	37	790		Quincy, IL	RheinPreußen
Wilms, Johan Heinrich	7, Oct. 1872	22, Sept	66	327		Quincy, IL	Neukirchen, RheinPreußen
Wilms, Karoline	27, Jan. 1887	7, Jan.	72	62	Hammacher	Quincy, IL	Rehme, Westphalen
Wilmsmeyer, Christian	22, Aug. 1881	6, Aug.	79	271		Hopewell, MO	Reme, Minden, Preußen
Wilmsmeyer, Heinrich	22, Oct. 1878	13, Oct.	69	343		Hopewell, MO	
Wilmsmeyer, Henriette	5, July 1888	17, June	89- 3m	430		Hopewell, MO	Blankenbach, Reutershausen, Kurhessen
Wils, Anna Dorothea	30, Apr. 1847	5, Apr.	27- 8m- 5d	71	Stunz	New York, NY	
Wilske, Fritz	7, Sept 1893	1, Aug.	16	574		Champaign, IL	
Wilsmann, Ella	13, Dec. 1894	1, Oct.	19	806		Santa Claus, IN	
Wilso, August	5, June 1890	16, Apr.	39	366		St. Paul, MN	Krebsfelde, Preußen
Wilso, Rosa	10, June 1897	16, May	14	367		St. Paul, MN	St. Paul, Minnesota

Christliche Apologete Death Notices --- 1839 - 1899

Name of Deceased	Notice Date	Death Date	Age	Page	Maiden Name	Place of Death	Place of Birth
Wilson, Anna Martha	23, Sept 1886	8, Sept	43	7	Sippel	Frankfort, IL	Königswalde, Kurhessen
Wilson, Bertha	7, Jan. 1886	10, Dec.	26	7	Bade	Lexington, TX	Austin County, Texas
Wilson, Christian Conrad	18, Oct. 1888	1, Oct.	26	670		Frankfort, IL	
Wilson, Clara Emma	15, Oct. 1896	23, Sept	17	671	Regal	Chase, WI	'Orland, Cook County, Illinois
Wilson, Wilhelm Friedrich	4, Oct. 1888	19, Sept	21	638		Frankfort, IL	
Wilson, Willie	18, Oct. 1888	18, Sept		670		Frankfort, IL	St. Joseph, Missouri
Wiltz, Emilie	27, June 1889	24, Feb.	38- 5m-11d	414	Mögly	San Jose, CA	
Wily, John	22, July 1878	1, June	16	231		Oregon, MO	
Wimmer, Eva	3, May 1880	9, Apr.	60-4m-26d	143	Hilt	Indianapolis, IN	Pfalzwippelsbach, Hessen-Darmstadt
Wimmer, Xavier	17, Mar. 1884	24, Feb.	62	7		Indianapolis, IN	
Wimpelberg, Johan	10, May 1894	8, Apr.		310		Marrs, IN	Meidrich, RheinPreußen
Wimpelberg, Margaret Berthina	28, Jan. 1897	4, Jan.	82	63	Lindermann	Marrs, IN	Alstaden, Mühlhausen a. d. Ruhr, Germany
Wincher, Robert	13, June 1895	9, Apr.	18- 1m-12d	382		Wheeling, WV	Wheeling, West Virginia
Wind, (Mrs)	9, Nov. 1854	21, Oct.	45	180	Seiler	Lawrenceburg, IN	Sulz, Elsaß
Windels, Pia Margaretha	10, Nov. 1879	20, Oct.	25- 7m	359		Brooklyn, NY	New York
Windelspecht, Gottfried	9, Oct. 1882	10, Sept	68	327		Cleveland, OH	Kochersteinfeld, Neckarsulm, Württemberg
Windhorst, Heinrich	14, Jan. 1892	25, Dec.	59	30		Senate Grove, MO	Minderheide, Minden, Preußen
Windhorst, Maria Margaretha E.	18, July 1870			231	Meyer	Herman, MO	Friedewalde, Minden, Preußen
Windhorst, Sophie Elise	7, Mar. 1881	16, Feb.	22	79	Leubering	Golconda, IL	Massac County, Illinois
Windhorst, Willie	21, Apr. 1898	31, Mar.	19	255		Indianapolis, IN	Indianapolis, Marion County, Indiana
Windmeyer, Karoline	17, Dec. 1866	3, Dec.	37	406		Warren, MO	
Windmöller, Anna Maria	10, May 1888	15, Apr.	80	302	Schachtzig	Edwardsville, IL	Biehlerfeld, Germany
Windmöller, Katharine	31, Dec. 1891	11, Dec.	32	846	Eckmann	Cincinnati, OH	Birlenbach, Elsaß
Windmüller, Catharina El.	26, July 1849	30, June	36	120		St. Louis, MO	
Windmüller, Wilhelm	19, Mar. 1883		73- 9m-22d	95		Edwardsville, IL	Blasheim, Lübbeke, Preußen
Wineke, Heinrich C.S.	3, Jan. 1870	26, Nov.	63- 7m-20d	7		Dubuque, IA	Lösgenfeld, Sternberg, Lippe-Detmold
Wing, Maria Christina	29, Oct. 1877	4, Oct.	19- 1m-22d	351		Woodville, OH	Sandusky County, Ohio
Wingeier, John	15, Oct. 1896	15, Sept	42	671		Cleveland, OH	Bern, Schweiz
Winger, Augusta	22, May 1882	29, Apr.	36-10m-14d	167	Koepke	Petosbey, MI	Belien, Königsberg, Preußen
Winke, Maria Christina	22, Oct. 1891	5, Oct.	77	686	Hesser	Baraboo, WI	
Winkel, Wilhelm H.	23, Nov. 1874	4, Nov.	21- 6m- 7d	375		Beardstown, IL	
Winkel, Ernst	12, June 1871	1, May	20	191		Fredericksburg, TX	Friederichsburg, Gillespie County, Texas
Winkel, Fritz	19, July 1894	1, June	66	470		Ballinger, TX	Stettendorf, Hannover
Winkel, Heinrich	17, July 1890	23, June	21	462		Brenham, TX	Fredericksburg, Gillespie County, Texas
Winkel, Louise	8, Oct. 1896	56- -23d		655	Frosch	Elmore, OH	Nieneburg, Germany
Winkelhage, Maria Wilhelmine	24, July 1890	21, June	34	478	Jokisch	Arenzville, IL	Beardstown, Illinois
Winkelhake, Eleonore	8, Oct. 1883	15, Sept	88- 7m	327		Beardstown, IL	Polhagen, Lippe-Schaumburg
Winkelhake, Heinrich	9, Feb. 1885	24, Jan.	60	7		Beardstown, IL	Wittlage, Hannover
Winkelhake, Louisa	28, Apr. 1859	6, Apr.	28	68	Meyer	Beardstown, IL	Osterkappeln, Amt Wittlage, Hannover
Winkelhake, Maria	7, Feb. 1876	25, Jan.	48-11m-30d	47	Christianer	Beardstown, IL	Haberfeld, Amt Wittlage, Hannover
Winkelmann, August	18, May 1899	15, Mar.	79	319		Roseville, MI	Rossow, Brandenburg
Winkelmann, Charlotte	13, Oct. 1898	31, Aug.	76	655	Koppelmann	Roseville, MI	Rossow, Brandenburg
Winkelmann, Heinrich	9, May 1895	25, Apr.	65	302		Chicago, IL	Föhren, Hannover
Winkelmeyer, Georg H.	4, Dec. 1871	12, Nov.	46- 5m-27d	391		Boonville, MO	
Winkler, Alice Friederika	14, July 1887	29, May	23	446	Eisenmayer	Summerfield, IL	Summerfield, Illinois
Winkler, Amalie	22, Dec. 1892	19, Nov.	66	814	Weiß	Detroit, MI	Osterbruck, Braunschweig

Christliche Apologete Death Notices --- 1839 - 1899

Name of Deceased	Notice Date	Death Date	Age	Page	Maiden Name	Place of Death	Place of Birth
Winkler, Anna Maria	6, Aug. 1896	10, July	91	511	Groß	Bushnell, IL	Ober-Hohf bei Zinsheim, Baden
Winkler, Barbara	12, Jan. 1899	30, Nov.	33	31	Rumer	Mascoutah, IL	Mascoutah, Illinois
Winkler, Carl	8, Nov. 1888	10, Oct.	22- 7m-23d	718		Lincoln, NE	Hannibal, Monroe County, Ohio
Winkler, Carolina	29, Sept 1887	30, Aug.	36	622	Rudlaff	Ida Grove, IA	Sachsen, Thüringen
Winkler, Dorothea E.	17, Sept 1896	17, Aug.	60	607	Meißner	Gordonville, MO	Ober-Dorla, Mühlhausen, Thüringen
Winkler, Edward	6, Oct. 1884	22, Sept	22	7		Summerfield, IL	
Winkler, Elisabeth	25, June 1883	3, June	48- 2m- 5d	207	Gimlin	Canal Dover, OH	
Winkler, Emil	15, May 1876	14, Apr.	27	159		Brooklyn, NY	Tiefenfurt, Schlesien
Winkler, Franz Anton	26, Sept 1895	6, Sept	80	622		Newark, NJ	Niedereschbach, Hessen-Darmstadt
Winkler, Henriette	15, May 1890	29, Mar.	70	318		New York City, NY	
Winkler, Joseph	20, May 1872	1, May	52- 3m	167		Batesville, OH	Blumenstein, Thun, Bern, Schweiz
Winkler, Joseph H.	26, Apr. 1888	7, Apr.	89	270		Bushnell, IL	Zuzenhausen, Baden
Winkler, Karolina	24, Mar. 1879	24, Jan.	41	95	Bickel	Newark, NJ	Heilbronn, Württemberg
Winkler, Leopold	10, Jan. 1889	6, Dec.	17- 6m	30		New Rochelle, NY	
Winkler, Louise	16, June 1879	28, May	33	191		Newark, NJ	Wülfingen, Zürich, Schweiz
Winkler, Maria	17, May 1894	23, apr.	52	326	Werle	Bushnell, IL	Baiern
Winkler, Maria Elisabeth	10, Aug. 1885	22, July	24- 3m-12d	7	Wünsch	Jackson, MO	
Winkler, Oskar	17, Jan. 1876		11	23		Summerfield, IL	
Winkler, Wilhelm	6, Apr. 1893	14, Mar.	59	222		Gordonville, MO	Strupitz bei torgau, Sachsen
Winkler, Wilhelm Friedrich	7, Sept 1899	18, Aug.	78	575		Burlington, IA	Dahlen, Sachsen
Winscher, Virginia Friederike	5, Apr. 1888	15, Mar.	22- 3m	222		Wheeling, WV	
Winstel, Edward W.	11, Apr. 1895	19, Mar.	19	238		Newport, KY	Newport, Cambell County, Kentucky
Winstel, John A.	13, Apr. 1893	29, Mar.		238		Newport, KY	Heinau, Rheinkreis Baiern
Winstel, Rosina	28, Oct. 1872	12, Oct.	26- 2m	351		Newport, KY	Cincinnati, Hamilton County, Ohio
Winter, F.C.	4, Feb. 1892	14, Jan.	73	78		Kansas City, KS	Nordhemern, Minden, Preußen
Winter, Amalia	17, June 1886	26, Apr.	67- 3m-11d	7	Kannengießer	Beaver Creek, MN	Büle, Hannover
Winter, Barbara	31, Mar. 1898	Feb.	83	207		San Francisco, CA	Neuhausen, Urach, Württemberg
Winter, Barbara	14, Apr. 1884	16, Mar.	44	7	Mueller	Great Bend, KS	
Winter, Carl V.	15, Aug. 1864	24, June	28- 4m-16d	132		Lawrenceburg, IN	Sinsleben, Mansfelder, Preußen
Winter, Catharina B.	30, Nov. 1893	11, Oct.	72	766	Meder	Cedar Lake, IN	Elsaß
Winter, Christian F.	19, Dec. 1864	29, July	23- 6m-15d	204		Yellow Creek, IL	Sinsleben, Mansfelder, Sachsen, Preußen
Winter, Christoph	20, Nov. 1890	27, Oct.	72- 9m-13d	750		Warren, MO	Meinberg, Lippe-Detmold
Winter, Dorothea	3, July 1871	1, June	24- 4m-12d	215	Druenert	Warrenton, MO	
Winter, Dorothea W.C.	4, Apr. 1889	27, Feb.	60- 6m- 9d	222	Nolting	Cannelton, IN	Alverdissen, Lippe-Detmold
Winter, Ernst Christoph	13, Oct. 1898	6, Sept	78	655		Ridgeway, IA	Hebershausen, Witzenhausen, Kurhessen
Winter, F. Ernst	8, Nov. 1880	2, Sept	76	359		Yellow Creek, IL	Nertingen, Lörrach, Baden
Winter, Friederike	28, May 1891	16, Apr.	74	350	Leumann	Muscatine, IA	Meinberg, Lippe-Detmold
Winter, Friedrich	13, May 1867	1, Apr.	79	150		Wapello, IA	
Winter, Friedrich Ludwig	14, Aug. 1871	14, July	58- 4m-28d	263		Warren, MO	Rinteln, Kurhessen
Winter, Heinrich	21, Jan. 1886	4, Jan.	66	7		Warren, MO	Hummerbruck, Alverdissen, Lippe-Detmold
Winter, Heinrich	23, Jan. 1862	19, Dec.	43	16		Warren, MO	
Winter, Heinrich Christian	12, Apr. 1860	16, Mar.	41	60		Wapello, IA	Humerbruch, Bösingfeld, Lippe-Detmold
Winter, Heinrich Justus	28, Feb. 1861	23, Jan.	38	36		Cannelton, IN	Hebenshausen, Witzenhausen, Kurhessen
Winter, Jakob	23, May 1881	6, May	55	167		Great Bend, KS	Dithelsheim, Hessen-Darmstadt
Winter, Johannes	13, Oct. 1887	13, Sept	51-11m-23d	654		San Jose, CA	Neuhausen a. d. Erms, Urach, Württemberg
Winter, Johannes	10, Mar. 1848		Inquiry	43		Ripley Co, IN	Bintzen, Lörach, Baden

Christliche Apologete Death Notices --- 1839 - 1899

Name of Deceased	Notice Date	Death Date	Age	Page	Maiden Name	Place of Death	Place of Birth
Winter, John	21, May 1857	18, Apr.	58	84		Kingston, IL	Pommern
Winter, John Friedrich	28, Nov. 1864	15, Aug.	34	192		West Bend, WI	Dillingen, Preußen
Winter, Margaretha	30, Mar. 1868	10, Mar.	45	103	Hänsel	Milan, IN	Nordhemern, Minden, Preußen
Winter, Margaretha E.	4, Feb. 1892	14, Jan.	77	78	VonBehren	Kansas City, KS	Warren County, Missouri
Winter, Maria	17, Aug. 1868	23, June	50	263		Wapello, IA	Obereggenen, Amt Mühlheim, Baden
Winter, Maria B.	28, Nov. 1864	3, Sept	48- 6m-25d	192		Clayton, IA	Münden, Baiern
Winter, Maria Elisabeth	9, July 1866	12, June	70	222			Wellerode, Kurhessen
Winter, Maria Emilie	1, Sept 1892	17, Aug.	64	558	Kurg	St. Paul, MN	Neukirchen, Kosel, Baiern
Winter, Peter	11, Mar. 1858	2, Feb.	49	40		Perry, IL	Schwarzach, Baden
Winter, Robert	29, Jan. 1877	28, Dec.	19	39		Chicago, IL	Schwarzach, Baden
Winter, Robert	2, Mar. 1893	1, Feb.	66- 9m	142		Chicago, IL	Stemmen, Amt Fahrenholz, Lippe-Detmold
Winter, Sophia Louise	3, Feb. 1868	13, Jan.	58- 7m- 8d	39	Klemmen	Wapello, IA	Lippe-Detmold
Winter, Wilhelmine	10, Sept 1896		73	591	Ute	Wapello, IA	Kruberg, Bracke, Lippe-Detmold
Winter, Wilhelmine Christine	21, May 1896	22, Apr.	85	334	Brackemeyer	Truxton, MO	Egg Harbor City, New Jersey
Winterberg, Caroline	27, Feb. 1890	22, Jan.	19	142		Brooklyn, NY	Karlshaven, Kurhessen
Winterberg, Johan Georg	27, Feb. 1890	1, Jan.	60	142		Brooklyn, NY	Egg Harbor City, New Jersey
Winterberg, Lizzie A.	28, Jan. 1892	4, Jan.	25	62		Brooklyn, NY	Auerbach, Hessen-Darmstadt
Winterstein, Caspar	29, Jan. 1866	1, Dec.	43	38		Louisville, KY	Ettmansweiler, Nagold, Württemberg
Winterstein, Eva M.	29, Jan. 1866	17, Dec.	38	38	Kübler	Louisville, KY	Holzluken, Baiern
Winterstein, Margaretha Barbara	29, Dec. 1887	28, Oct.	74	830	Pecher	Louisville, KY	Auerbach, Hessen-Darmstadt
Winterstein, Philipp	29, Dec. 1859	9, Dec.	47	208		Louisville, KY	Langendorf, Weißenfels, Merseburg, Preußen
Wintroup, A.L.	23, Feb. 1885	15, Jan.	51	7	Richter	Wilmington, CA	Canton Thurgau, Schweiz
Wintsch, Susanna	20, Mar. 1871	24, Feb.	34- 9m	95	Wohnlich	Newark, NJ	
Winter, Caroline	7, Mar. 1895	6, Feb.	56	159	Pflieger	Philadelphia, PA	Cincinnati, Hamilton County, Ohio
Winzinger, Clara	28, Nov. 1895	6, Nov.	27	766	Voigt	Cincinnati, OH	Bargheim, Schaffhausen, Schweiz
Winzeler, Matthias	27, Nov. 1882	29, Oct.	83	383		Toledo, OH	Zimmerwald, Bern, Schweiz
Winzenried, Anna Maria	31, Jan. 1876	10, Jan.	59-10m-13d	39	Streit	Toledo, OH	Velp, Bern, Schweiz
Winzenried, Benedikt	4, Feb. 1892	3, Jan.	77	78		Toledo, OH	Breswitz, Mecklenburg-Strelitz
Winzenried, Ellen	1, Mar. 1880	3, Feb.	29	71	Schmidt	Schulenburg, TX	Gugesberg, Bern, Schweiz
Winzenried, Margarethe	7, Aug. 1882	11, July	59- 3m- 1d	255	Suter	Toledo, OH	Barzheim, Schaffhausen, Schweiz
Winzler, Anna	15, Apr. 1886	29, Mar.		7		Toledo, OH	Schweiz
Winzler, Anna	14, July 1887	29, June	82	446		Perrysburg, OH	Perrysburg, Ohio
Winzler, Emma	10, Apr. 1882	26, Mar.	27- 3m-15d	119		Perrysburg, OH	Baierthal, Baden
Wipfler, Franz	12, Jan. 1863	3, July	34	8		Williamsburg, NY	Gehoffen, Sachsen, Thüringen
Wippach, Bernard	17, Dec. 1877	29, Nov.	55- 4m	407		Cannelton, IN	Wersen, Preußen
Wippermann, Katharina	22, Dec. 1887	30, Nov.	85	814	Hauerbruch	Rapids, NY	Warren County, Missouri
Wippermann, Lydia Wilhelmine	3, Dec. 1891	6, Nov.	22	782		Pinckney, MO	York County, Pennsylvania
Wire, Daniel	2, June 1873	13, May	74	175		Columbus, OH	Little York, Pennsylvania
Wire, Michael	17, Aug. 1863	12, July	69- -22d	132		Ft. Atkinson, WI	Lancaster, Pennsylvania
Wire, Nancy	10, Jan. 1861	20, Dec.	62	8		Ft. Atkinson, WI	Lemgo, Lippe
Wirte, Simon Heinrich	14, Feb. 1881	27, Sept	75	55		Flint Creek, IA	Richland County, Wisconsin
Wirth, Friedrich J. C.	31, May 1894	6, May	36	358		Dubuque, IA	
Wirth, Johann Michael	10, Mar. 1843	7, Mar.	47	39		Lawrenceburg, IN	
Wirth, Karolina	6, Feb. 1882	15, Jan.	57	47	Braun	Marion, OH	Backnang, Württemberg
Wirtner, Balthas	28, Jan. 1892	4, Jan.	65	62		St. Joseph, MO	Schweningen, Rottweil, Württemberg
Wischhusen, Katharina Lucia	24, July 1882	26, June	73- 5m	239	Mehrtens	Hoboken, NJ	

Christliche Apologete Death Notices --- 1839 - 1899

Name of Deceased	Notice Date	Death Date	Age	Page	Maiden Name	Place of Death	Place of Birth
Wischmeier, Clara	25, May 1893	8, May	71	334	Weber	New Melle, MO	Kesselbach, Hessen-Darmstadt
Wischmeier, Elisabeth	7, Apr. 1879	28, Feb.	38	111	Wagner	Dodgeville, IA	
Wiskow, Ernestine Wilhelmine	1, Dec. 1873	15, Nov.	19	383		Oshkosh, WI	
Wiskow, Ferdinand	11, June 1877		22	191		Oshkosh, WI	
Wiskow, Wilhelm	28, Oct. 1872	29, Sept	15	351		Oshkosh, WI	
Wismeyer, Georg Leonhard	30, Mar. 1874	16, Mar.	23	103		Hamilton, OH	Hamilton, Butler County, Ohio
Wisner, Hans	1, Oct. 1883	11, Sept	7	319		Eldora, IA	
Wisner, Louisa	8, Aug. 1889	3, July	40	510	Ackermann	Naumburg, NY	North East, Iowa
Wisner, Otto	1, Oct. 1883	11, Sept	9	319		Eldora, IA	
Wissinger, Anna Marie	16, Oct. 1865	29, Sept	18- 2m-12d	168		Sidney, OH	
Wißmann, August	11, Dec. 1890	10, Oct.	63- -13d	798		Marine City, MI	Poratz, Ukermark, Preußen
Wißmann, Georg	5, Aug. 1886	6, July	71	7		Waco, NE	Rölbach, Klingenberg, Baiern
Wißmann, Karl	25, Nov. 1867	18, Oct.	26	374		Goliad, TX	Baiern
Wissmann, Katharina Barbara	16, June 1887	26, May	31	382		Pittsburg, PA	Pfeffingen, Balingen, Württemberg
Wißmann, Marie	25, Nov. 1867	20, Oct.		374	Klafke	Goliad, TX	
Wissmann, Wilhelm	6, Apr. 1899	11, Mar.	19	223		Hedwigs Hill, TX	Frederiksburg, Texas
Wißmann, Wilhelm Konrad	11, July 1898	11, July	17	511		Pittsburg, PA	Pittsburg, Pennsylvania
Wißmeier, Anna	29, May 1882	10, May	54- 1m-11d	175		Hamilton, OH	Whettenhoffen, Baiern
Witekan, Elisabeth	8, Apr. 1886		96-10m-23d	7	Yogel	Adams Co, IL	Rausenburg, Preußen
Withaus, Marie Elisabeth	5, May 1853	18, Mar.	20- 1m	72	Suhre	Marthasville, MO	Lienen, Münster, Preußen
Withoff, Robert E.	2, Feb. 1893	10, Jan.	24	78		Seymour, IN	Cincinnati, Hamilton County, Ohio
Witlinger, Anna	27, Jan. 1887	11, Jan.	62	62	Straup	Sedalia, MO	Dürinau, Göppingen, Württemberg
Witt, Ludwig	25, Aug. 1892	27, July	79	542		Michigan City, IN	Zanzkow, Demin, Preußen
Witt, Wilhelm Friedrich	1, Sept 1892	14, Aug.	20- 1m	558		Enterprise, KS	Bates, Illinois
Witt, Anna Marie	25, May 1893	25, Apr.	25	334		Enterprise, KS	Springfield, Illinois
Witt, Charlotte	19, Sept 1889	26, Aug.	78	606	Fust	Chicago, IL	Radebur, Anclam, Pommern
Witt, Christian Friedrich	23, Nov. 1885	20, Oct.	45	7		Swanton, NE	Dölitz, Pommern
Witt, Emma	12, Mar. 1891	31, Jan.	22	174	Heyden	Milwaukee, WI	
Witt, F.C.	11, July 1889	22, June	48- 9m	446		Chicago, IL	Ducherow, Vorpommern
Witt, Johanna Maria	13, June 1895	14, May	73	382	Bartel	Michigan City, IN	Seltz, Demmin, Pommern
Witt, Joseph H.	8, May 1871	10, Apr.	47	151		Canton, MO	Kiel, Schleswig-Holstein
Wittbäcker, Sophie Dorothea	25, Apr. 1889	3, Apr.	73	270		Schulenburg, TX	Bremen, Germany
Witte, Amalia Charlotte	14, Sept 1885	30, Aug.	49	7	Henneberg	Arlington, MN	Valdorf, Herford, Preußen
Witte, August Wilhelm Adolf	29, Mar. 1888	17, Mar.	47	206		Cincinnati, OH	Remmighausen, Lippe
Witte, Carolina	13, May 1872	24, Apr.	45	159	Liscow	Muscatine, IA	Uckermark, Preußen
Witte, Charles Henry	3, Dec. 1896	20, Nov.	34	782		Cincinnati, OH	Cincinnati, Hamilton County, Ohio
Witte, Elisabeth	26, Aug. 1858	8, Aug.	54	136	Gerbes	Cincinnati, OH	Meinsfeld, Amt Detmold, Lippe
Witte, Emma	10, Sept 1896	8, Aug.	33	591		New York City, NY	Dunkirk, New York
Witte, K. Chr.	16, Feb. 1893	22, Jan.	65	110		Arlington, MN	Lemgo, Lippe-Detmold
Witte, Karl F.	21, Aug. 1882	10, Aug.	54- 6m-13d	271		Cincinnati, OH	Remighausen, Lippe-Detmold
Witte, Karl Friedrich	29, Sept 1892	7, Aug.	21	622		Cincinnati, OH	Cincinnati, Hamilton County, Ohio
Witte, M.	31, Oct. 1864	13, Sept	53	176		Watertown, WI	Dölitz, Stettin, Pommern, Preußen
Wittemeier, Caroline	18, Jan. 1864	17, Nov.		12	Hacke	Schnectady, NY	Hille, Minden, Preußen
Wittemeier, K. H. Ludwig	5, Feb. 1866	23, Dec.	33	46		Schnectady, NY	Hille, Preußen
Wittemeier, Maria	11, Sept 1865	2, July	29	148	Schlenzker	Schnectady, NY	Hille, Minden, Preußen
Wittemeyer, Maria Elisabeth	12, Aug. 1878	15, July	49	255	Brück	Ft. Hunter, NY	Hille, Preußen

Christliche Apologete Death Notices --- 1839 - 1899

Name of Deceased	Notice Date	Death Date	Age	Maiden Name	Place of Death	Page	Place of Birth
Witten, Anna Margaretha	21, Jan. 1878	28, Dec.	36	Maier	Sherrills Mount, IA	23	Pennsylvania
Wittenbach, Christian	3, Nov. 1873	14, Oct.	69		Morrison, MO	351	Gerzensee, Seftingen, Bern, Schweiz
Wittenbach, Karl	21, Apr. 1862	12, Mar.	22-9m		Herman, MO	64	Canton Bern, Schweiz
Wittenbach, Maria	22, Mar. 1875	10, Mar.	64		German, MO	95	Steffisburg am Thunersee, Bern, Schweiz
Wittenbacher, (Mrs)	20, Aug. 1877	28, July	78- 5m- 8d		St. Joseph, MO	271	Carsdorf, Merseburg, Sachsen, Preußen
Wittenberg, Christine	2, May 1861	24, Mar.	19	Märthesheimer	Independence, MO	72	
Wittenberg, Maria Amalie	19, May 1884	2, May	88- -16d	Höpke	Peoria, IL	7	
Wittenberger, Maria Christine	4, May 1899		39	Schulze	Jamestown, MO	287	Jamestown, Missouri
Wittenburg, Johan Christian	22, Feb. 1894	5, Dec.	76		Milwaukee, WI	126	Zarchlin, Mecklenburg
Wittenfeld, Franziska	5, May 1884	14, Apr.	76	Türk	Belleville, IL	7	Burghagel, Lauingen, Baiern
Wittenfeld, Friederike	16, Aug. 1869	30, July	62	Meier	Belleville, IL	263	Dietz, Kreis Minden, Preußen
Wittenfeld, W.	30, Apr. 1883	15, Apr.	82		Belleville, IL	143	Vehlage, Lübeke, Preußen
Witter, Anna Margaretha	11, Feb. 1878	28, Dec.	36- 6m-11d	Mayer	Sherrills Mount, IA	47	Pennsylvania
Witter, Christina	3, May 1860	29, Mar.	16		Sherrills Mount, IA	72	Gasmesheim, Mosbach, Baden
Witter, Elisabeth	5, Jan. 1885	20, Dec.	46- 8m- 7d	Trefz	Sherrills Mount, IA	7	Neulußheim, Schwetzingen, Baden
Witter, Elisabeth	24, May 1860	30, Apr.	18		Sherrills Mount, IA	84	Hasmesheim, Mosbach, Baden
Witter, Katharina Elisabeth	3, Aug. 1874	6, July	60- 5m- 1d	Peter	Sherrills Mount, IA	247	Haßmersheim bei Mosbach, Baden
Witter, Katie	25, July 1895	30, June	25		Dubuque, IA	478	Baden
Witter, Margaretha	26, Aug. 1886	10, Aug.	19- 2m-15d		Sherrills Mount, IA	7	Neulusheim, Schwetzingen, Baden
Witter, Regina	4, Mar. 1886	7, Feb.	20		Sherrills Mount, IA	7	NeuLosheim, Schwetzingen, Baden
Witfeld, Anna	2, Mar. 1863	8, Feb.	24		Jacksonville, IL	36	Möhrs, RheinPreußen
Witthaus, Christina	22, Sept 1848	26, Aug.	20	Schröer	Marthasville, MO	156	
Witthaus, Elisa B.J.	10, Apr. 1876	14, Feb.	18		Herman, MO	118	Bega, Lippe-Detmold
Witthaus, Friederike	24, Feb. 1879	7, Feb.	50	Krone	Morrison, MO	63	Franklin County, Missouri
Witthaus, Gustav	1, Dec. 1887	2, Nov.	23		Mt. Vernon, MO	766	Bielefeld,
Witthaus, Hannah	18, May 1868	22, Apr.	32- 3m-21d	Beumer	Herman, MO	159	Vlotho, Minden, Preußen
Witthaus, Heinrich	17, June 1878	2, June	57- 6m-21d		Morrison, MO	191	Valdorf, Minden, Preußen
Witthaus, Heinrich Herman	25, Feb. 1892	23, Jan.	64		Mt. Vernon, MO	127	
Witthaus, Martha	3, June 1878	29, Apr.	18- 2m-28d		Morrison, MO	175	
Witthaus, Seraphine E.	3, May 1875	24, Feb.	14- 7m-26d		Herman, MO	143	
Witthaus, Sophie	18, Jan. 1869	26, Dec.	32- - 3d	Saatmann	Herman, MO	23	Marthasville, Warren County, Missouri
Witthaus, Wilhelmine	16, Mar. 1874	19, Feb.		Huckriede	Herman, MO	87	Hannover
Witthof, Heinrich	20, Aug. 1896	18, July	77		Indianapolis, IN	543	
Witthöft, Hanna	8, Jan. 1883	10, Dec.	16- 3m-20d		Indianapolis, IN	15	Hintersee, Pommern, Preußen
Witthuhn, Friedrich L.D.	10, Jan. 1876	18, Dec.	69-10m		Brillion Mission, WI	15	Mecklenburg-Schwerin
Witthuhn, M. Charlotte Christine	18, Mar. 1878	25, Feb.	70	Wolter	Clayton, WI	87	Bebra, Hessen-Kassel
Wittich, Georg	27, Aug. 1896	26, July	69		Auburn, IN	559	Mannheim, Baden
Wittig, Elisabeth Franziska	29, June 1893	1, June	39		Saginaw, MI	414	Sachsen
Wittig, Johannes	21, Jan. 1897	26, Dec.	51		Saginaw, MI	47	Breslau, Schlesien
Wittig, John R.	13, Oct. 1887	25, Sept	60		Hartford, CT	654	Hersfeld, Kurhessen
Wittler, Catharina	5, June 1871	21, May	38-11m	Gerst	St. Louis, MO	183	Bremen, Germany
Wittler, Johan Dietrich	6, Mar. 1865	13, Feb.	60		Birden, IA	40	Pleasant Plains, Sangamon County, Illinois
Wittlinger, Andreas	19, Jan. 1880	1, Jan.	18- 7m-12d		Sedalia, MO	23	
Wittlinger, Gustav	4, Aug. 1862	3, July			Delaware, OH	124	Bahlingen, Baden
Wittmann, (Mrs)	3, Nov. 1884	14, Oct.	42		Cleveland, OH	7	
Wittmann, Anna Barbara	21, Sept 1868		59- 5m		Williamsburg, NY	303	Büttelbronn, MittelFranken, Baiern

Christliche Apologete Death Notices --- 1839 - 1899

Name of Deceased	Notice Date	Death Date	Age	Page	Maiden Name	Place of Death	Place of Birth
Wittmann, Anna Margaretha	19, July 1888	22, June	56	462	Ziegler	Columbus, OH	Spies, Baiern
Wittmann, Carl	12, Dec. 1889	13, Nov.	54	798		St. Louis, MO	Sachsen
Wittmann, Christiane Philippine	12, June 1856	18, May	22- 2m-10d	96		Mt. Vernon, IN	Höfen, Neuenbürg, Württemberg
Wittmann, Dorothea	27, Dec. 1894	28, Nov.	66	836	Schwenk	Brooklyn, NY	Schömberg, Freudenstadt, Württemberg
Wittmann, Friedrich	7, July 1892	11, June	48	430		Almond, WI	Altkenzin, Vorpommern
Wittmann, Johan Georg	12, Dec. 1895	17, Sept	78	798		New York City, NY	Hüszing, Heidenheim, Baiern
Wittmann, Louise Catharina	1, Feb. 1875	10, Jan.	27- 7m-13d	39	Hirn	San Francisco, CA	New York
Wittmann, Maria	24, Apr. 1882	2, Apr.	38- 3m	135	Schwille	St. Louis, MO	Pfullingen, Reutlingen, Württemberg
Wittmann, Regina	28, Dec. 1868	2, Dec.	23	415	Hirn	Williamsburg, NY	
Wittmann, Rudolph	13, Oct. 1879	24, Sept		327		St. Louis, MO	
Wittmer,	1, Aug. 1881			247			
Wittmer, Jakob	2, Dec. 1897	24, Oct.	65	767		Elkton, SD	Jebsheim, Elsaß
Wittmer, Philippine	27, July 1899	7, July	75	479	Lebeck	Vermillion, OH	
Wittmershaus, (Mrs)	25, Jan. 1869	2, Jan.	80	31		Bushnell, IL	
Wittmershaus, Johan Heinr. Philipp	6, Dec. 1888	17, Nov.	69-11m-25d	782		Big Springs, NE	Huntington, Blair County, Pennsylvania
Wittmeyer, Anna M.	24, Sept 1896	6, Sept	71	623	Windel	Higginsville, MO	Binnen, Hannover
Wittmeyer, Gottlob	30, Nov. 1893	3, Nov.	75- 7m-15d	766		Higginsville, MO	Ildingen, Leonberg, Württemberg
Wittner, Emma	28, Apr. 1884	10, Apr.	13	7		Ash Lake, MN	Eldingen, Leonberg, Württemberg
Witzel, Anna Elisabeth	6, Apr. 1899	11, Jan.	75	223	Georg	St. Paul, MN	Deerfield, Lake County, Illinois
Witzel, C. E.	13, Jan. 1879	25, Dec.	73- 3m	15		Flood Creek, IA	Rabelshausen, Kurhessen
Witzel, Heinrich	23, Oct. 1876	18, Sept	66	343		Arena, WI	Hannover
Witzig, Rudolph	3, Aug. 1893	14, July	63	494		Columbus, OH	Uschlag, Hannover
Wiwart, (Mr)	6, June 1864	8, Apr.	45	92		Lawrence, KS	Ohwiesen, Zürich, Schweiz
Wobschall, Ernst Friedrich Wm.	2, June 1892	29, Apr.	70	350		Waseca, MN	Elbing, Preußen
Wockenfus, Emilie Henriette	26, Sept 1889	28, Aug.	37	619	Rahn	Winona, MN	Colmar, Bromberg, Posen
Wocosin, Johan Carl	25, Nov. 1872	8, Nov.	54	383		Victor, IA	Groß-Strellin, Germany
Wocosin, Maria	16, Dec. 1872	23, Nov.	48	407		Victor, IA	Weizenhagen, Greifswalde, Preußen
Wode, Anton	1, Aug. 1889	29, June	63	494		Pomeroy, OH	Wusterusen, Stralsund, Preußen
Wode, Emma Helena	27, Apr. 1885	9, Apr.	15	7		Berea, OH	Oppau, Frankenthal, Baiern
Wode, Margaretha Elisabeth	21, Oct. 1872	29, Sept	72	343	Hermann	Pomeroy, OH	Berea, Ohio
Wode, Valentin	5, Jan. 1893	8, Dec.	65	14		Berea, OH	Edigheim, Baiern
Woefle, Johannes	26, Apr. 1888	6, Apr.	73- 7m- 8d	270		Boody, IL	Oppau, Frankenthal, Rheinkreis Baiern
Woefle, Joseph Anton	3, Apr. 1890	4, Feb.	64	222		Terre Haute, IN	Frankenried, Baiern
Woerpel, Dorothea Louise	12, July 1888	12, June	75	446	Brüßow	Sun Prairie, WI	Warsin, Pyritz, Pommern
Wöhl, Johan Wilhelm	21, Apr. 1898	31, Mar.	28	255		Detroit, MI	Greenfield Township, Michigan
Wöhl, Karoline	23, July 1891	28, June	25- 1m-20d	478	Zimmermann	Detroit, MI	Casko, St. Clair County, Michigan
Wöhl, Luise Dorothea	13, Apr. 1899	9, Mar.	68	239	Voß	Detroit, MI	Gottmannsförde, Mecklenburg-Schwerin
Wöhl, Wilhelmine	14, Apr. 1898	14, Mar.	73	239	Platt	Detroit, MI	Weltsien, Mecklenburg-Schwerin
Wohlbeck, Johan H.	24, July 1876	9, July	45	239		Lake Creek, MO	Ostereistädt, Hannover
Wohlbeck, John	22, Mar. 1888	13, Jan.	18	190		Lake Creek, MO	
Wohlberg, Wilhelm	22, Apr. 1897	26, Mar.	77	255		Chicago, IL	Holtmanshof, Rothenburg, Hannover
Wohlberg, Wilhelmine	14, Mar. 1870	23, Feb.	16	87		Chicago, IL	
Wöhleke, (Mrs)	17, Sept 1866	17, Aug.	32	302		Cape Girardeau, MO	
Wöhler, Auguste	16, June 1859	27, Apr.		96	Hippe	Henderson, MN	Engern, Lippe-Detmold
Wöhlert, Christian	2, Feb. 1874	17, Jan.	65	39		Wheeling, WV	Cammerdorn, Hannover
Wohlfahrt, Barbara	6, Aug. 1857	3, July	18	128		Marion, OH	

Christliche Apologete Death Notices --- 1839 - 1899

Name of Deceased	Notice Date	Death Date	Age	Page	Maiden Name	Place of Death	Place of Birth
Wohlfahrt, Catharine	10, July 1882	16, June	63- 4m-21d	223		Burlington, IA	Langenberg, Gerabronn, Württemberg
Wohlfahrt, Christian	13, Apr. 1885	25, Mar.	72	7		Burlington, IA	Ingelfingen, Württemberg
Wohlfahrt, Emil	11, Feb. 1892	23, Dec.	16	95		Yonkers, NY	Eßlingen, Württemberg
Wohlfahrt, Gottlieb	1, Feb. 1875	9, Jan.	77- 8m-20d	39		Marion, OH	Oberbrüden, Backnang, Württemberg
Wohlfahrt, Margaretha	18, Nov. 1886	8, Sept	79- 7m-10d	7		Marion, OH	Oberbrüden, Württemberg
Wohltmann, Christoph	20, Oct. 1898	12, Aug.	77	671		Brooklyn, NY	Selstedt, Hannover
Wohltmann, Margaretha Gesina	16, Nov. 1893	27, Oct.	70	734	Kroosch	Brooklyn, NY	Netz, Hannover
Wöhr, Maria Magdalena	27, Apr. 1885	10, Apr.	63	7	Wandel	Concordia, MO	Eldingen, Leonberg, Württemberg
Wöhr, Michael	22, Apr. 1886	28, Mar.	71	7		Concordia, MO	Eltingen, Leonberg, Württemberg
Wöhm, Dorothea	16, Dec. 1897	22, Nov.	74	799		Baltimore, MD	Biedenkopf, Hessen-Darmstadt
Wöhm, Heinrich	26, Dec. 1895	29, Nov.	75	828		Baltimore, MD	Hessen-Darmstadt
Woidel, Emma Louise	8, Dec. 1892	8, Nov.	21	782		Columbus, WI	Atlantic Ocean,
Woite, Olga	6, Apr. 1893	17, Mar.		222		Chicago, IL	
Woite, Wilhelmina	10, Dec. 1891	16, Nov.	42	798	Harder	Chicago, IL	Lutzin bei Stettin, Pommern
Wolbrink, Christiana	23, Apr. 1896	25, Feb.	43	270	Kuhn	Edwardsville, IL	Pine Oak, Madison County, Illinois
Wöleke, Wilhelm	8, June 1899	19, May	73	367		Cape Girardeau, MO	Marienthal, Helmstadt, Braunschweig
Wolf, Johanna Sybille	13, Dec. 1894	25, Nov.	64	806		Indianapolis, IN	Erfurt, Sachsen
Wolf, (Mrs)	28, Oct. 1897	4, July	80	687	Wanzil	West Unity, OH	Schweighausen, Elsaß
Wolf, Albin (Rev)	25, June 1896	4, May	41	415		Zwickau, GE	
Wolf, Anna	24, Apr. 1876	23, Mar.	26	135	Platt	Bradford, IN	Harrison County, Indiana
Wolf, Anna Margaretha	6, Nov. 1846	22, Sept	35- 3m	189		Washington, IA	
Wolf, Barbara	24, June 1886	4, June	73	7	Wenzel	Quincy, IL	Reibach, Hessen-Darmstadt
Wolf, Carolina	11, Oct. 1888	25, Aug.	90-10m-10d	654	Salznan	Defiance, OH	Ober-Auerbach, Zweibrücken, Baiern
Wolf, Catharina M.	4, Mar. 1858	28, Jan.	37	36		New Albany, IN	Melsheim, Elsaß
Wolf, Christian F.	30, Mar. 1885	11, Mar.	34- 3m-20d	7		Indianapolis, IN	Schorndorf, Württemberg
Wolf, Christian Friedrich	7, Sept 1893	2, Aug.	74	574		New Albany, IN	Scharndorf, Württemberg
Wolf, Christina Maria Ida	27, June 1881	13, June	22- 8m-15d	207		West Bend, WI	
Wolf, Daniel	3, Jan. 1881	1, Dec.	72- 3m- 1d	7		Dubuque, IA	Mittelbach, Zweibrücken, Rheinkreis Baiern
Wolf, Daniel	8, Apr. 1886	5, Mar.	85- 8m-17d	7		Defiance, OH	Ober-Auerbach, Contwig, Baiern
Wolf, Elisabeth	13, Nov. 1890	25, Oct.	63	734	Sonner	Warsaw, IL	Urloffen, Offenburg, Baden
Wolf, Elisabeth	20, Oct. 1859	29, Sept	42- 1m-11d	168	Yäckel	Red Wing, MN	Homberg, Kurhessen
Wolf, Elisabeth	20, Apr. 1854	24, Mar.	20	64		Poplar Ridge, OH	
Wolf, Elisabeth	1, Mar. 1875	1, Feb.	20	71	Wenning	Bradford, IN	
Wolf, Elisabeth	21, Dec. 1885	1, Dec.	78- 6m	7		Cleveland, OH	
Wolf, Elisabetha	27, Apr. 1868	13, Apr.	66	135		Defiance, OH	Oberorbach, Zweibrücken, Rheinkreis Baiern
Wolf, Friedrich	30, Nov. 1893	6, Oct.	78	766		Stryker, OH	Schweighausen, Hageman, Elsaß
Wolf, Georg	30, Sept 1878	29, Aug.	30	311		Bradford, IN	Harrison County, Indiana
Wolf, Georg L.	25, Dec. 1865	2, Dec.	33	208		New Albany, IN	Weil im Schönbuch, Böblingen, Württemberg
Wolf, Georg P.	4, June 1857	21, Feb.	41- 6m- 9d	92		Cannon City, MN	Kitzingen, Baiern
Wolf, Gottlieb	31, May 1869	12, May	35- 3m	175		Ann Arbor, MI	Poppenweiler, Ludwigsburg, Württemberg
Wolf, Gustav	28, Aug. 1882	16, July	59	279		Brenham, TX	
Wolf, Helena Susanna	9, Feb. 1888	31, Dec.	81	94	Burgraf	Bay City, MI	Wetzendorf, Sachsen
Wolf, Henrietta Gerard	20, Sept 1888	21, Aug.	49	606		Menasha, WI	
Wolf, Johan	16, Apr. 1877	23, Mar.	69	127		Ahnapee, WI	Rüting, Grevismühlen, Mecklenburg-Schwerin
Wolf, Johan	14, Dec. 1874	23, Nov.	60- 4m-28d	399		Marine City, MI	Großentischo, Mecklenburg-Schwerin
Wolf, Johan	27, Oct. 1879	28, July	65	343		Cleveland, OH	Mecklenburg-Strelitz

Christliche Apologete Death Notices --- 1839 - 1899

Name of Deceased	Notice Date	Death Date	Age	Page	Maiden Name	Place of Death	Place of Birth
Wolf, Johan J.	9, Mar. 1893	7, Feb.	85	158		Quincy, IL	Hessen-Darmstadt
Wolf, Johannes	9, Nov. 1863	20, Sept	34	180		Madison, IN	
Wolf, Johannes	7, Dec. 1863	20, Sept	34	196		Madison, IN	
Wolf, Jonathan	26, Nov. 1877	8, Nov.	67- 6m-21d	383		Watertown, WI	
Wolf, Joseph	13, Jan. 1853	18, Oct.	41	8		Louisville, KY	
Wolf, Karl	29, Sept 1879	9, Sept	22	311		Warsaw, IL	Warsaw, Illinois
Wolf, Kate	24, July 1882	6, July	21- 6m- 2d	239		Woodville, OH	
Wolf, Katharina	2, Apr. 1896	16, Feb.	51	222	Yunker	Elmore, OH	Rice Township, Sandusky County, Ohio
Wolf, Katharina	12, Mar. 1883	20, Feb.	56- 8m-10d	87	Krieger	Woodville, OH	Hattmatt, Elsaß
Wolf, Louis	26, Dec. 1881	12, Dec.	28	415		Chicago, IL	Beutelsbach, Schorndorf, Württemberg
Wolf, Ludwig	29, Aug. 1881	4, Aug.	83-10m	279		Defiance, OH	Zweibrücken, Baiern
Wolf, Maria	13, Dec. 1888	1, Dec.	39	798	Fliesbach	Warsaw, IL	Halle an der Saale, Sachsen
Wolf, Maria Katharine	17, Dec. 1883	6, Dec.	72	7	Ulrich	New Albany, IN	Schorndorf, Württemberg
Wolf, Martin	31, Jan. 1889	11, Jan.	59	78		Berne, MI	Frauenberg, Angermünde, Potsdam, Preußen
Wolf, Michael	29, Mar. 1888	28, Feb.	68- 7m- 3d	206		Elmore, OH	Hattmot, Zebrau, Elsaß
Wolf, Peter J.	2, Feb. 1880	21, Jan.	25	39		Warsaw, IL	Warsaw, Illinois
Wolf, Philipp	30, Aug. 1855	23, July	83- 6m	140		Poplar Ridge, OH	
Wolf, Robert	20, Dec. 1880	6, Sept	23	407		San Jose, IL	
Wolf, Sophia	19, Apr. 1880	28, Mar.	65- 3m	127		Marine City, MI	
Wolf, William	8, Sept 1879	27, July	15	287		Bradford, IN	
Wolfänger, Katharina	2, June 1887	21, May		350		Cincinnati, OH	Eldingen, Württemberg
Wölfel, Magdalena	21, June 1849	9, May	17	100		Madison, IN	
Wolfer, Christina	6, Dec. 1894	31, Oct.	79	790	Kleinfelder	Cincinnati, OH	Siebeldingen, Rheinpfalz Baiern
Wolfer, Leonhart	25, May 1893	29, Apr.	79	334		Richmond, IN	Württemberg
Wolfert, Andreas	29, June 1893	30, May	56	414		Marietta, OH	Mannheim, Baden
Wolfert, Friederike	16, Oct. 1865	1, Oct.	38	168		Cincinnati, OH	Neuenstetten, Baden
Wolfert, Johannes	28, Apr. 1853	28, Mar.	55-10m-28d	68		Delaware, OH	Illingen, Maulbronn, Württemberg
Wolfert, Philipp	26, Feb. 1872	31, Jan.	80- 4m	71		Bonn, OH	Neunstettin, Kreutheim, Baden
Wolff, (Mr)	12, Nov. 1847	Sept		183		New Orleans, LA	
Wolfgang, Emma Louisa	8, May 1890	13, Apr.	26- 2m	302		Evansville, IN	
Wölfle, Anna Magdalena	31, Mar. 1887	8, Mar.	58- 3m-10d	206	Kuntzman	Terre Haute, IN	Westheim, Rheinkreis Baiern
Wölfle, Christina Barbara	9, Aug. 1880	27, July	63	255	Stäbler	Decatur, IL	Echterdingen, Stuttgart, Württemberg
Wolfram, Christoph	1, Dec. 1898	7, Nov.	71	767		Belleville, IL	Eulach, Sachsen-Weimar
Wolfram, Friedrich	24, Jan. 1889	25, Dec.	29- -26d	62		Belleville, IL	Belleville, Illinois
Wolfram, Jakob	13, Sept 1875	30, Aug.	37- -10d	295		Weldon Springs, ---	
Wolfram, Maria	7, Apr. 1887	21, Feb.	67	222		St. Louis, MO	
Wolfrum, Nikolaus	8, Feb. 1875	24, Jan.	61	47		Cottleville, MO	
Wolfrum, Johan Peter	21, Dec. 1893	27, Nov.	73	814		Pittsburg, PA	Töpen, Baiern
Wolgast, Johanna Friederike	10, Apr. 1890		28	238	Wilke	Lancaster, NY	Reihersdorf bei Templin, Preußen
Wolkenhauer, Caroline	7, Apr. 1892	14, Mar.	76	222		Cannon River, MN	
Wolkenhauer, Heinrich	2, Jan. 1871	10, Dec.	64	7		Cannon City, MN	Dunsun, Neustadt am Rübenberg, Hannover
Wöll, (Mrs)	12, Jan. 1874		58	15		Alton, IL	
Wöll, Heinrich	3, Mar. 1873		26	71		Alton, IL	
Wöll, Maria Sophia	14, Oct. 1858	22, Dec.		164	Pulck	Alton, IL	Schönborn, Amt Diez, Nassau
Wollbrink, Anna Maria	21, Apr. 1887	22, Sept	70	254	Glaskars	Edwardsville, IL	Engel, West Preußen
Wollbrink, Herman Heinrich	4, Dec. 1890	15, Nov.	76- 2m-15d	782		Edwardsville, IL	Eickum, Minden, Westphalen

Christliche Apologete Death Notices -- 1839 - 1899

Name of Deceased	Notice Date	Death Date	Age	Page	Maiden Name	Place of Death	Place of Birth
Wollenzien, Dorothea	29, Jan. 1883	12, Jan.	42	39	Stolzenburg	Louisville, KY	Brohn, Mecklenburg-Strelitz
Wollenzien, Heinrich	8, Oct. 1891	15, Sept	49-11m-15d	654		Louisville, KY	Brom, Mecklenburg-Strelitz
Wollenzin, Augusta	4, Nov. 1886	11, Oct.	53-10m-24d	7		Vernon, WI	Bärwalde, in der Neumark, Preußen
Wolter, Dorothea	7, Dec. 1874	23, Oct.	72	391	Schröder	Wausau, WI	Treptow an der Rega, Pommern
Wolter, Ferdinand	5, Sept 1864	16, Aug.		144		Atlanta, GA	
Wolter, Maria	17, June 1867	13, May	57	190		Wausau, WI	Kohlberg, Hinterpommern, Preußen
Wolter, Martin	29, July 1872	11, July	36	247		Wausau, WI	Treptow a. d. Rega, Stettin, Preußen
Wolfart, Margaretha	29, Nov. 1869	24, Sept	70	383		Wausau, WI	Großingersheim, Marbach, Württemberg
Woltmann, Maria	22, June 1893	24, May	20	398			Clark County, Missouri
Wolpert, Elisabeth	22, Apr. 1897	3, Apr.	75	255	Voisin	Emden, IL	Ruchheim, Baiern
Wolter, Amalie	24, Mar. 1879	1, Mar.	58- -25d	95		Belleville, IL	Schokken, Posen, Preußen
Wolter, Johan Friedrich	25, Oct. 1894	7, Oct.	58	694		Chicago, IL	Lettnien bei Prieritz, Pommern
Wolter, Johanna Louise	15, Mar. 1880	21, Feb.	79	86	Rohrbeck	Beaver Dam, WI	Mecho, Pommern
Wolter, Maria	16, Apr. 1877	10, Mar.	64	127	Schulz	Beaver Dam, WI	Brietzig bei Piritz, Pommern
Wolter, Samuel	27, Dec. 1869	9, Dec.	56- 8m-26d	415		Beaver Dam, WI	Lettnin, Pommern
Wolters, Margaretha	11, Oct. 1869	21, Aug.	29	327	Cordes	Smithton, MO	Witstadt, Amt Ottersberg, Hannover
Wolterstorff, Amalia	17, Feb. 1887	27, Jan.	63	110	Wenzel	Washington, MN	Arendsen, Altmark, Preußen
Wöltje, Karoline	24, Nov. 1873	3, Nov.	72	375	Wilkening	Appleton, MO	Winzlar, Amt Reburg, Hannover
Wöltje, Louisa	2, July 1891	5, June	47	430	Möhle	Appleton, WI	Sehlen, Hannover
Woltjen, Herman	28, June 1888	18, May	47	414		Brooklyn, NY	Iprump, Delmenhorst, Oldenburg
Woltmann, Sarah	26, Mar. 1896	24, Feb.	91	206		Lyona, KS	Hoff bei Camin, Pommern
Woodbridge, Frances Ph. Karoline	27, Jan. 1898		81	63	Gehring	LaCrosse, WI	Baiern
Woodbridge, Martin	19, Jan. 1885	18, Dec.	71	7		LaCrosse, WI	Madrid, St. Lawrence County, New York
Woodchick, Anna	2, Apr. 1896		65	222	Malick	Beaver Dam, WI	Glausche, Schlesien
Woode, Maria	22, Oct. 1896	2, Oct.	76	687		Pomeroy, OH	Unnstein, Rheinpfalz Baiern
Woode, Michael	6, Nov. 1890	7, Oct.	88	718		Pomeroy, OH	Oppau, Frankenthal, Baiern
Woodke, Henriette	17, May 1888	18, Apr.	85	318	Otto	Lemars, IA	Groß Jestin bei Colberg, Hinterpommern
Woodke, Johan	5, Jan. 1899	5, Dec.	74	15		Lemars, IA	Groß,Jestin, Hinterpommern
Woodrich, Anna Maria	2, Feb. 1885	12, Jan.	52	7	Lange	Brooklyn, NY	Bockel, Hannover
Woodrich, Anna Maria	2, Mar. 1885			7		Appleton, WI	
Woost, Heinrich	31, May 1869	16, May	32	175		Covington, KY	
Woost, Johanna	13, Feb. 1890	21, Jan.	46- 5m-16d	110		Cincinnati, OH	
Woost, Louise	1, Sept 1898	24, Sept	25	559	Scharrellmann	Pekin, IL	
Worick, Elisabeth	8, Oct. 1857	12, July	75	164	MacKesson	Freeport, IL	Northumberland County, Pennsylvania
Wörlitz, Augusta	4, Aug. 1884	21, Apr.	65	7		Plattsmouth, NE	Sachsen
Worm, Julius	26, May 1887	9, Nov.	63	334		Milwaukee, WI	Karpich, Neumark, Preußen
Wörner, Catharina	21, Dec. 1885			7		Pekin, IL	Schwaigheim, Waiblingen, Württemberg
Wörner, Friedrich	9, Sept 1858	24- 6m- 8d		144	Liedle	Des Moines, IA	
Wörner, Georg Heinrich	14, June 1855	4, Apr.	24	96		Pittsburg, PA	
Wörner, Henry	27, Apr. 1868	10, Apr.	66	135		Junction City, KS	Flein, Heilbronn, Württemberg
Wörner, Hulda	1, Sept 1898	4, Aug.	34	559		Fredericksburg, TX	Fredericksburg, Gillespie County, Texas
Wörner, Johanna	23, Mar. 1899	28, Feb.	25	191	Friederich	Pittsburg, PA	Flein bei Heilbronn, Württemberg
Wörner, Katharina	16, June 1873	21, May	65	191	Forster	Pittsburg, PA	Flein, Heilbronn, Württemberg
Worten, Charlotte	15, Jan. 1883	23, Dec.	76- 9m-21d	23	Forster	Davenport, IA	Loxten, Westphalen
Worth, Anton	17, May 1894	21, Apr.	73	326	Hagemeier	Cincinnati, OH	Dundenheim, Baden
Wörther, Johann Caspar	27, May 1858	12, May	41	84		Manchester, MO	Kleinheubach, Untermainkeise, Germany
	20, May 1852	31, Mar.	43- -25d	84			

Christliche Apologete Death Notices --- 1839 - 1899

Name of Deceased	Notice Date	Death Date	Age	Page	Maiden Name	Place of Death	Place of Birth
Wörz, A.K.	8, Sept 1892	20, Aug.	47	574		Salina, KS	Hannweiler, Waiblingen, Württemberg
Wörz, Heinrich	2, Aug. 1869	5, July	78	247		Melrose, NY	Hartford, Connecticut
Wörz, Martha Minnie	29, June 1899	13, June	17	415		Brooklyn, NY	Sulz am Neckar, Württemberg
Wösner, Georg	9, Mar. 1885	20, Feb.	85	7		Boston, MN	Sulz am Neckar, Württemberg
Wößner, Elisabeth	30, May 1864	11, Apr.	62	88	Kreitmann	East Troy, WI	Lonnerbecke, Hannover
Wöste, Adina B.	28, Apr. 1887	9, Apr.	16	270		Colesburg, IA	Brockhorst, Kreis Halle, Preußen
Wöstmann, Friedrich	5, July 1849	15, June	28- 6m	108		St. Louis, MO	
Wotring, Anna Maria Elisabeth	5, Feb. 1866	12, Dec.	19- 4m- 2d	46		Delaware, OH	Klempzow, Hinterpommern, Preußen
Wrase, Johan	19, Aug. 1878	25, July	74- 9m-15d	263		Brunswick, MO	Speckenholz, Hannover
Wrede, Heinrich	18, June 1891	19, May	58	398		Odebolt, IA	Anderten, Hannover
Wrede, Katharine Dorothea	12, Jan. 1888	18, Dec.	51- 7m-16d	30	Greve	Creston, IN	Auglaize County, Ohio
Wright, Elisabeth	2, Jan. 1890	27, Nov.	55	14	Geyer	New Knoxville, OH	Campen, Ostfriesland
Wübben, Beerentje Garrels	2, Dec. 1897	24, Oct.	60	767	Bruns	Pekin, IL	Wattenberg, Namslau, Schlesien
Wudschick, Michael	7, July 1887	24, June	68	430		Beaver Dam, WI	Sumiswald, Trachselwald, Bern, Schweiz
Wuetherich, Christian	10, Mar. 1873	21, Feb.	66- 9m-15d	79		Covington, IN	Längerich, Preußen
Wühlert, Katharine	1, Dec. 1887	8, Nov.	80	766	Ruthenschröer	Wheeling, WV	Ovelgönne, Hannover
Wulf, Johan Heinrich	18, Apr. 1889	7, Mar.	67	254		Mt. Vernon, IN	Posey County, Indiana
Wulf, Karolina Margaretha	7, Oct. 1897	17, Sept	35	639	Schreiber	Mt. Vernon, IN	Forestville, Door County, Wisconsin
Wulf, Louise	31, Oct. 1889	8, Oct.	13	702		Muscatine, IA	Holstein, Ditmarschen, Koog, Germany
Wulf, Peter Friedrich	28, Aug. 1890	5, Aug.	35	558		Morris, MN	Enger, Westphalen
Wulfmeier, Herman H.	20, Nov. 1890	28, Oct.	73	750		Quincy, IL	
Wulfmeyer, Lydia Augusta	19, Sept 1881	30, Aug.	17	303		Quincy, IL	
Wulfrum, Maria	9, May 1870	21, Apr.	40-11m- 3d	151	Siegel	Birmingham, PA	Nielingen, Amt Karlsruh, Baden
Wulzen, Arthur F.	25, Oct. 1894	9, Oct.	20	694		Berea, OH	Nashville, Tennessee
Wulzen, Eddy	26, Dec. 1870	3- 1m-15d	3- 1m-15d	415		Bradford, IN	
Wundenberg, Catharina Elisabeth	29, Apr. 1886	10, Apr.	36	7	Pohlmann	New Orleans, LA	New Orleans, Louisiana
Wunderlich, (Mrs)	24, May 1855			84			
Wunderlich, Ehrhardt Friedrich	21, Feb. 1895	5, Feb.	65- - 3d	126		Chicago, IL	Rüßdorf, Sachsen-Weimar
Wunderlich, Margaretha	6, Oct. 1892	23, Aug.	82- 4m-25d	639	Miller		Baiern
Wunderlich, Maria	10, Jan. 1876	31, Dec.	23	15	Keßler		Warsaw, Illinois
Wunderlich, Otto	28, Apr. 1873	23, Mar.	32- 6m	135		New York City, NY	Tober, Schwarzburg-Sondershausen
Wunderlich, Otto	14, Apr. 1873	23, Mar.	32- 6m	119		New York City, NY	Toba, Schwarzburg-Sondershausen
Wunsch, Johannes	19, Oct. 1899	8, Sept	76	671		Greenfield, MA	Tiefenbach, Baden
Wünsch, Maria Friederika	20, Nov. 1856	27, Oct.	64	188		St. Clair, MI	Nöstlingen, Baiern
Wünscher, Emilie	11, May 1893	24, Mar.	50	302	Meinhardt	Wheeling, WV	Triebes, Reuß
Wünscher, Johanna Dorothea	29, Apr. 1886	12, Apr.	79	7	Kobe	Wheeling, WV	Eckartsberge, Naumburg a. d. Saale, Preußen
Wüppermann, Karl Ch.	14, Oct. 1852	25, Sept	53- 1m- 9d	168		Buffalo, NY	
Würfel, Anna J.	10, Aug. 1885	24, July	22	7	Fuchs	Jeffersonville, IN	Otisco, Clark County, Indiana
Würfel, Christiana	19, July 1875	3, July	73- 1m- 3d	231	Olbert	Toledo, OH	Rohrbach, Amt Simsheim, Baden
Würfel, Christina	29, Aug. 1889	6, Aug.	62	558	Dörflinger	Jeffersonville, IN	Blankenloch, Baden
Würfel, Elisabeth	31, Mar. 1873	4, Mar.	39- -15d	103	Weber	Toledo, OH	
Würfel, Georg A.	24, May 1875	2, May	42- 1m	167		Toledo, OH	Rohrbach, Sinsheim, Baden
Würfel, Georg John	25, Nov. 1872	8, Nov.	15- 6m	383		Toledo, OH	Rohrbach, Sinsheim, Baden
Würfel, Johan Georg	26, Dec. 1889	11, Dec.	84	830		Toledo, OH	Jeffersonville, Indiana
Würfel, Marie Emilie	12, Jan. 1885	25, Dec.	35	7	Treiber	Jeffersonville, IN	Rohrbach, Sinsheim, Baden
Würfel, Martin	24, July 1890	4, July	45	478		Jeffersonville, IN	

Christliche Apologete Death Notices --- 1839 - 1899

Name of Deceased	Notice Date	Death Date	Age	Maiden Name	Page	Place of Death	Place of Birth
Würker, Friedrich	6, May 1897	9, Apr.	71		287	Alton, IL	Mahlen, Meeseburg, Preußen
Wurm, Wilhelm	6, Jan. 1898	20, Dec.	55		15	Berea, OH	Glashütte bei Czarnikau, Preußen
Wurmnest, Anna E.	20, May 1886	20, Apr.	19-11m-18d		7	Secor, IL	Washington, Illinois
Wurmnest, Anna Katharina	23, May 1895	7, May	64	Maul	334	Peoria, IL	Niederaula , Kurhessen
Wurmnest, Johan	6, June 1895	19, May	53- 9m		366	Peoria, IL	Unterhaun, Kurhessen
Wurst, Gottlieb Christian	24, July 1882	10, July	48- 8m-21d		239	Quincy, IL	Sulzbach, Weinsberg, Württemberg
Wurst, Karl Friedrich	14, June 1860	27, Apr.			96	Elizabeth City, NJ	Bubenorbis, Hall, Württemberg
Wurst, Katharina	6, May 1872	19, Dec.	70		151	Green Bay, WI	Aichelberg, Württemberg
Wurst, Katharine	17, Aug. 1863	15, July	13-10m		132	Elizabeth, NJ	
Wurster, Balthasar	7, Apr. 1879	22, Feb.	61- 4m-12d		111	West Point, IA	Albisheim, Rheinpfalz Baiern
Wurster, Charles Wilhelm	30, Aug. 1875	14, Aug.	22		279	Farmington, IA	Lee County, Iowa
Wurster, Christina	22, Nov. 1880	31, Oct.	59- 5m-11d	Lauer	375	Golconda, IL	Zuweiler, Nagold, Württemberg
Wurster, Christina	13, Dec. 1880	31, Oct.	59- 5m-11d	Bauer	399	Golconda, IL	Zuweiler, Nagold, Württemberg
Wurster, Elisabeth	18, Mar. 1858	23, Feb.	25	Roth	44	Farmington, IA	Marnheim, Bolanden, Baiern
Wurster, Friedricka	4, Feb. 1884	17, Jan.	59	Kalmbach	7	Francisco, MI	Schönengründ, Freudenstadt, Württemberg
Wurster, Jakob	10, May 1875	21, Apr.	22		151	Golconda, IL	Louisville, Jefferson County, Kentucky
Wurster, Jakob Friedrich	9, Feb. 1880	22, Jan.	65- 7m- 8d		47	Golconda, IL	Beinberg, Amt Neuenbürg, Württemberg
Wurster, John J.	25, Mar. 1878	11, Mar.	62		95	Buffalo, NY	Hirschau, Württemberg
Wurster, Karl Friedrich	30, Jan. 1882	18, Jan.	27- -10d		39	Terre Haute, IN	Harrisburg, Pennsylvania
Wurster, Katharina	23, Mar. 1899	25, Feb.	19		191	Terre Haute, IN	
Wurster, Margaretha	28, Jan. 1878	23, Dec.	61- 3m-18d		31	West Point, IA	Rogendorf, Stadtsteinach, Baiern
Wurster, Margaretha	22, Jan. 1891	22, Dec.	79		62	Grand Rapids, MI	Freudenstadt, Württemberg
Wurster, Robert	17, Feb. 1879	30, Jan.	15-10m-27d		55	Buffalo, NY	
Wurster, Rosina Katharina	8, Dec. 1887	22, Nov.	30		782	Terre Haute, IN	Ann Arbor, Michigan
Wurster, Wilhelmina Katharina	14, Mar. 1881	19, Feb.	62	Scheller	87	Lancaster, NY	Gerabronn, Württemberg
Würtele, Johannes	7, Dec. 1863	1, Nov.	16		196	West Point, NY	
Würterle, Anna Maria	21, June 1894	26, May	81		406	Clay Center, KS	Strümschelbach, Waiblingen, Württemberg
Würthner, Erhard	9, Apr. 1877	26, Mar.	83-10m-22d		119	Louisville, KY	Zovenroth, Württemberg
Würtner, Christine	7, Nov. 1881	16, Oct.	54- 9m-21d		359	St. Joseph, MO	Schwenningen, Rothweil, Württemberg
Würtner, M.	18, Oct. 1869	28, Sept	66-11m- 6d	Meyer	335	Dunkirk, NY	Wenningen, Rottweil, Württemberg
	10, Sept 1866	May			294		
Würtner, Martin	27, Aug. 1866	Aug.	43		278	Buffalo, NY	Schwenningen, Rottweil, Württemberg
Würtz, Katharina	20, Feb. 1882	20, Jan.	81		63	New York City, NY	Herrenberg, Württemberg
Würtz, Maria	21, Sept 1854	15, July	63		152	Louisville, KY	Lorbach, Hessen-Darmstadt
Wurzel, Maria Christina	23, Aug. 1875	6, Aug.	63	Mayer	271	Detroit, MI	Standel, Brandenburg, Preußen
Wurzel, Wilhelm	3, Jan. 1876	17, Dec.	66		7	Roseville, MI	Kumere, Preußen
Wussow, Wilhelm	14, Feb. 1895	31, Dec.	66		110	Ballwin, MO	Pommern
Wüst, Christiana	29, Aug. 1889	13, Aug.	62	Seidel	558	Moberly, MO	Schleußweiler, Backnang, Württemberg
Wüst, Dorothea	20, Aug. 1896	2, Aug.	86	Mayer	543	Spencerville, OH	Ellmendingen, Baden
Wüst, Emma	3, Oct. 1881	14, Sept	26- 6m-11d		319	Danville, TX	Comal County, Texas
Wüst, Georg	1, June 1899	14, May	17		351	Cibolo, TX	
Wüst, Georg F.	31, Mar. 1884	13, Mar.	82- 8m- 6d		7	Spencerville, OH	Ellmendingen, Baden
Wüst, Heinrich	17, July 1882	6, July	74		231	Cincinnati, OH	Erlenbach, Kandel, Rheinkreis Baiern
Wüst, Johan Adam	17, June 1897	19, May	91- 5m- 4d		383	Bracken, TX	Berzhahn, Rennerod, Nassau
Wüst, Johan Nicholas	19, Feb. 1891	26, Jan.	78- 7m-12d		126	Cosby, MO	Sachsenhausen, Wertheim, Baden
Wüst, Samuel	7, Sept 1893	18, Aug.	69		574	Chicago, IL	Berrhard, Schweiz

Christliche Apologete Death Notices --- 1839 - 1899

Name of Deceased	Notice Date	Age	Death Date	Page	Maiden Name	Place of Death	Place of Birth
Wusterhausen, Wilhelm	11, Aug. 1887	50	23, July	510		Paige, TX	Diethoff bei Magdeburg, Preußen
Wüstermann, Friedrich	9, Aug. 1880	29	26, July	255		Henderson, KY	Berka bei Sondershausen, Sachsen
Wütherich, Anna	20, Sept 1888	44	18, Aug.	606		Danville, IL	Bern , Schweiz
Wütherich, Christina	22, Aug. 1889	82- 3m-25d	31, July	542	Minter	Danville, IL	Canton Bern, Schweiz
Wütherich, Franz Friedrich	19, Dec. 1864	26- 7m-16d	16, Aug.	204		Covington, MO	
Wütherich, Ida	15, July 1886	21- 5m	22, June	7		Danville, IL	
Wüthrich, Elisa	16, May 1889	40- -14d	30, Apr.	318	Zürcher	Chili, OH	Canton Bern, Schweiz
Wütig, H.	1, Oct. 1866			318		Blue Island, IL	
Wyland, Dorothea	27, July 1885	80	8, Sept	7	Stoffel	Jamestown, MO	Reininghausen, Jomersbach, Köln, Preußen
Wys, Christian	25, Nov. 1858	48	28, Sept	188		Jefferson City, MO	Gerzense, Bern, Schweiz
Wyß, Carl Wilhelm	2, July 1891	19	14, June	430		Jamestown, MO	
Wyß, Caroline	7, Apr. 1892	32	11, Mar.	222	Gertsch	Halstead, KS	Canton Bern, Schweiz
Wyß, Christoph	12, Dec. 1864	30	13, Oct.	200		Jefferson City, MO	Gerzensee, Bern, Schweiz
Wyß, Elisabeth	6, Dec. 1880	73- 1m- 4d	15, Nov.	391		Jamestown, MO	Wisterig, Bern, Schweiz
Wyß, Elisabeth	6, Apr. 1885	68	23, Mar.	7	Mergter	Halstead, KS	
Wyß, Fanny	3, June 1897	22	23, Apr.	351	Bieri	Lowell, WI	Oberlangenegg, Bern, Schweiz
Wyß, Gottlieb	6, Oct. 1892	41	2, Sept	639		Halstead, KS	Regesburg, Bern, Schweiz
Wyß, Sarah Louise	31, Jan. 1895	13	22, Dec.	78		Jefferson City, MO	Lafayette bei Lexington, Missouri
Wyttenbach, Christian	11, Aug. 1892	80- 8m-12d	26, July	510		Santa Claus, IN	Kirchdorf, Bern, Schweiz
Wyttenbach, Christian	6, Aug. 1857	24	30, July	128		Huntingburg, IN	Bern, Schweiz
Wyttenbach, Karl Heinrich	27, Aug. 1866	20	4, May	278		Santa Claus, IN	Pennsylvaniaburg, Indiana
Wyttenbach, Katharina	1, June 1863	52	23, Jan.	88	Moster	Santa Claus, IN	Canton Bern, Schweiz
Wyttenbach, Maria Ilsabein	16, Feb. 1893	58	19, Aug.	110	Meyer	Santa Claus, IN	Oldendorf, Preußen
Wyttenbach, Maria Louise	17, Sept 1866	45	17, Feb.	302	Degeder	Santa Claus, IN	Drohne, Dielingen, Preußen
Wyttenbach, Rosina	12, Mar. 1877	69- 7m-15d	3, Dec.	87	Sutter	Morrison, MO	Büren, Bern, Schweiz
Xander, John	29, Dec. 1873	39	5, Feb.	415		Troy, NY	Grunbach, Schorndorf, Württemberg
Xander, Sara Louise	25, Feb. 1884	16- 6m- 3d	25, July	7		Troy, NY	Troy, New York
Xander, Sophia	13, Aug. 1877	45	14, Oct.	263		Troy, NY	Obergrombach, Baden
Yada, Karl Friedrich	27, Nov. 1890	41	23, Aug.	766		Rockham, SD	Lowell, Dodge County, Wisconsin
Yaisley, Elisabeth	5, Sept 1895	34	8, Aug.	574	Löffel	Spencerville, OH	Crawford County, Ohio
Yantz, Peter	17, Sept 1896	85	21, Mar.	607		Swanton, NE	Kirberg, Elsaß
Yeasting, Georg	16, Apr. 1891	16	13, Sept	254		Elmore, OH	Woodville, Ohio
Yeiter, Friedrich	30, Oct. 1882	56	13, Oct.	351		Irwing, IL	Rettersburg, Waiblingen, Württemberg
Yeiter, Friedrich	27, Nov. 1882	56	27, Dec.	383		Irwing, MI	Rettersburg, Waiblingen, Württemberg
Yester, Lydia	21, Jan. 1897	48	6, Feb.	47		Jeffersonville, IN	Leidershausen, Baden
Yetter, Catharina Barbara	8, Mar. 1894	69	23, Oct.	166	Schmidt	Oregon, MO	Nabern a. d. Teck, Kirchheim, Württemberg
Yetter, John	21, Nov. 1870	12- 6m	1, Feb.	375		Oregon, MO	
Yobst, Catharine	7, Mar. 1895	36	30, Apr.	159	Einwächter	Baltimore, MD	Baltimore, Maryland
Yockel, Karoline	25, May 1899	56	21, June	335		New York City, NY	Odenheim, Rheinkreis Baiern
Yockey, Philipp	13, July 1893	76	20, Aug.	446		Southland, IA	Rheinkreis Baiern
Yoh, Conrad	7, Sept 1874			287		Baltimore, MD	
Yokel, Peter	29, Dec. 1873	54	14, Dec.	415		Omaha, NE	
Yokisch, Karl Gotthelf	6, Apr. 1874	53	11, Mar.	111		Arenzville, IL	Halbendorf, Sachsen
York, Heinrich	23, Aug. 1888	82- 7m-13d	6, Aug.	542		Pekin, IL	Hochfeldern, Zürich, Schweiz

Christliche Apologete Death Notices --- 1839 - 1899

Name of Deceased	Notice Date	Death Date	Age	Maiden Name	Page	Place of Death	Place of Birth
Yoss, Elisabeth	1, Apr. 1858	1, Mar.	77	Lugenbühl	52	East Troy, WI	Zaziwyl, Bern, Schweiz
Yost, Charlotte Sarah	26, Jan. 1885	6, Dec.	11- 8m-19d		7	Stockton, CA	
Yost, Philipp Karl	14, Sept 1893	16, Aug.	28- 9m-18d		590	St. Louis, MO	Ludwigshafen, Rheinpfalz Baiern
Yotter, Otto	25, Oct. 1894	14, June	18		694	Halstead, KS	Ottawa County, Ohio
Youch, Emma R.	20, Jan. 1898	5, Nov.	19		47	Elmore, OH	Owatonna, Steel County, Minnesota
Young, Benjamin Franklin	20, June 1889	8, June	7		398	Le Sueur, MN	Detweiler bei Straßburg, Elsaß
Young, Catharine	9, Apr. 1891	16, Mar.	86		238	Bushnell, IL	Grenitz, Baiern
Young, Conrad	29, Mar. 1880	3, Mar.	58		103	Summerfield, IL	Monroe, Jasper County, Iowa
Young, Georg D.	30, Aug. 1875	8, Aug.	18		279	Bloomington, IL	
Young, Jakob	6, Dec. 1880	27, Oct.	39		391	Lemars, IA	
Young, Katharina	28, Apr. 1892	12, Apr.	60	Roche	270	Warsaw, IL	Kaiserslautern, Rheinkreis Baiern
Young, Louise C.	25, Sept 1882	23, Aug.	19- 3m-14d		311	Cincinnati, OH	Cincinnati, Hamilton County, Ohio
Young, Maggie	12, May 1892		24- 3m-24d	Zülch	302	Jersey City, NJ	
Young, Maria	19, Dec. 1895	25, Oct.	65- 5m-25d	Besler	814	Louisville, KY	Kircheim, Württemberg
Young, Theodore	14, July 1887		57		446	Galion, OH	Hohensolms, Wetzlar, Coblenz, Preußen
Youssy, Elisabeth	24, Sept 1896	23, Aug.	78	Muhlemann	623	Baresville, OH	Thun, Bern, Schweiz
Yung, Elisabeth	1, July 1886	14, June	81		7	Galion, OH	Reimershausen, Hessen
Yünger, G. Bernhard	10, May 1875	20, Apr.	54	Simon	151	Rochester, MN	Laucha a.d. Unstrut, Preußen
Yüngert, Georg	20, Dec. 1880	22, Nov.	50- 9m		407	Pittsburg, PA	Gersfeld, Baiern
Yunke, Dorothea	5, Dec. 1889	23, Oct.	80	Salgmann	782	Angelica, NY	Lehndorf, Braunschweig
Yunker, Charlie	28, Apr. 1892	30, Mar.	20		270	Elmore, OH	Sandusky County, Ohio
Yunker, Heinrich Adam	12, Feb. 1891	16, Jan.	16		110	Elmore, OH	Fremont, Ohio
Yust, Christine	16, Dec. 1897	24, Nov.	76	Becher	799	Canton, MO	Grafenheimchen, Sachsen
Zabel, Caroline	31, Dec. 1883	11, Dec.	78- -22d	Teßner	7	Tomah, WI	Posen
Zabel, Christian Friedrich	27, Jan. 1898	25, Jan.	72		63	Swanton, NE	Döitz, Piritz, Pommern
Zabel, Eleonore	24, Mar. 1892	4, Mar.	78	Weiß	191	Perry, TX	Germany
Zabel, Friedrich W.	14, Apr. 1887	18, Mar.	29		238	Pepin, WI	Oconomowoc, Wisconsin
Zabel, Peter	20, Nov. 1876	27, Oct.	77		375	New Braunfels, TX	Kulm, Marienwerder, Posen
Zabel, Wilhelmine	26, Sept 1895	10, Sept	66	Buchholz	622	Chicago, IL	Bremzo, Pommern
Zabler, Johanna Friederike	20, Aug. 1896	23, July	80	Bolgrin	543	Burlington, WI	Schiefelbein, Pommern
Zachari, Karl	28, Apr. 1898	6, Apr.	76		271	Louisville, KY	Rothe bei Erfurt, Preußen
Zachari, Minna	11, June 1891	19, May	61- 6m-15d	Schütt	382	Louisville, KY	Lübz, Mecklenburg-Schwerin
Zachari, Walter	2, Oct. 1890	6, Sept	28- 1m- 9d		638	Louisville, KY	
Zachmann, (Mrs)	19, Oct. 1874	1, Oct.	31- 5m-15d		335	Marion, OH	
Zachmann, Gertrude	19, Dec. 1889	12, Nov.	68	Kaufmann	814	Chicago, IL	Breidau, Kurhessen
Zachmann, Regina	24, Jan. 1871	9, Jan.	27- 1m-26d	Knieriem	31	Marion, OH	
Zagelmeier, Christian	9, July 1866	27, June		Britsch	222	Detroit, MI	Obristenfeld, Marbach, Württemberg
Zagelmeier, Friedrich Jakob	27, Mar. 1890	4, Mar.	33		206	Grand Rapids, MI	Detroit, Wayne County, Michigan
Zagelmeier, Johan David	26, June 1882	29, May	69		207	Allegan, MI	Oberstendfeld, Marbach, Württemberg
Zagelmeier, Karolina F.	7, May 1883	6, Apr.	22		151	Grand Rapids, MI	Detroit, Wayne County, Michigan
Zahn, Anna	27, Oct. 1884	12, Aug.	7		7	Troy, NY	Schweiz
Zahn, Barbara	3, June 1897	10, May	67	Zeitner	351	Chicago, IL	Großenau, Baiern
Zahn, Johan	11, Sept 1871	26, July	29		295	Arenzville, IL	Ohio
Zahn, Margaretha	18, Oct. 1894	24, Sept	69	Hohenstein	678	Canton, MO	Brackenheim, Württemberg
Zahn, Margaretha	19, Aug. 1878	3, Aug.	19		263	Canton, MO	Pike County, Ohio

Christliche Apologete Death Notices --- 1839 - 1899

Name of Deceased	Notice Date	Death Date	Age	Page	Maiden Name	Place of Death	Place of Birth
Zahn, Philippine	9, Jan. 1871	4, Dec.		15	Dentz	San Francisco, CA	Lowell, Ohio
Zahn, Sophie Marie Dorothea	25, Feb. 1884	20, Dec.	64	7	Barner	Rochester, MN	Petersdorf, Mecklenburg
Zahn, Wilhelm	4, Sept 1876	25, July	20	287		Canton, MO	
Zahnd, Rosine	31, Mar. 1887	19, Mar.	47	206	Pfeuti	Rushville, NE	Gugisberg, Bern, Schweiz
Zahner, Rosa	7, Dec. 1893	8, Nov.	85	782	Mesey	Louisville, KY	Murten, Schweiz
Zähninger, Karolina	18, July 1895	28, June	69	462		Indianapolis, IN	Kenzingen, Baden
Zahmdt, Albert	14, June 1894	26, May	19	390		Chicago, IL	
Zaiser, Anna Maria	29, Oct. 1896	7, May	64	703	Burg	Burlington, IA	Hergesweiler, Bergzaber, Rheinpfalz Baiern
Zaiser, Christian	11, Aug. 1879	12, July	85- 8m- 5d	255		Burlington, IA	Schweigern, Brackenheim, Württemberg
Zaiser, Christian	16, Feb. 1888	25, Jan.	68	110		Burlington, IA	Schweigern, Brackenheim, Württemberg
Zander, Carl	4, Feb. 1884	20, Jan.	71	7		Charles City, IA	Bergen, Sachsen
Zander, Christian	29, Aug. 1889	5, Aug.	78	558		Quincy, IL	Osteburg, Altmark, Sachsen
Zander, Frieda	30, Dec. 1897	2, Dec.	22	828		Chicago, IL	Chicago, Cook County, Illinois
Zander, Hans Georg	22, May 1876	2, May	62	167		Quincy, IL	Boock, Preußen
Zander, Julius Christian	27, Feb. 1896	5, Feb.	52	143		Charles City, IA	Neukirchen, Sachsen
Zander, Karl	17, July 1882	4, July	62- 3m-14d	231		Chicago, IL	Strabund, Pommern
Zander, Ursula	4, Feb. 1884	17, Jan.	76	7	Weber	Watertown, WI	Adelhausen, Baden
Zander, Walther William	28, Dec. 1899		19- 2m	828		Chicago, IL	Chicago, Cook County, Illinois
Zang, Jakob	10, Mar. 1898	5, Feb.	78	159		Chester, IL	Allenbach, Preußen
Zänger, Elisabeth	31, Jan. 1881	12, Jan.	24-11m	39		Perrysburg, OH	Hirschberg, Reuß
Zänger, Henriette	16, Mar. 1893	13, Feb.	69	174		Columbus, OH	Wangen, Elsaß
Zänger, Johan Fr.	25, Nov. 1897	20, Oct.	70	751		Toledo, OH	Ripley County, Indiana
Zangmeister, Louise	20, July 1893	2, July	44	462	Krummel	Indianapolis, IN	Radolfzell, Baden
Zapf, Barbara	22, Aug. 1845	10, June	74	135			
Zapf, Elisabeth	19, Apr. 1875		23-11m- 8d	127	Werner	Pomeroy, OH	
Zapf, Johan Michael	17, June 1897	12, May	61	383		Cincinnati, OH	Hühnehof, Baiern
Zapf, John Frank	13, Apr. 1893		18-11m- 2d	238		Detroit, MI	
Zapf, Leonard	25, Oct. 1894	29, Aug.	74	694		Detroit, MI	Streitau, Baden
Zapp, Andreas	7, Sept 1899	4, Aug.	64	575		Mascoutah, IL	Haßloch, Neustadt a. d. Haard, Preußen
Zapp, Gertrud	12, Oct. 1899	14, Sept	62	655	Kurz	Belleville, IL	Mußbach, Rheinkreis Baiern
Zapp, Heinrich	10, Apr. 1890	16, Mar.	29- 1m-17d	238		Mascoutah, IL	Mascoutah, Illinois
Zarn, Friedrich	22, Mar. 1875	4, Feb.	66- 4m- 9d	95		Rochester, MN	Mecklenburg-Schwerin
Zarndt, Hannah Sophia	6, Aug. 1877	30, June	34	255	Conver	Chicago, IL	Dahlen, Mecklenburg-Schwerin
Zarndt, Maria	22, Feb. 1875	6, Feb.	73- 4m- 6d	63		Chicago, IL	Wendischhapen, Mecklenburg-Schwerin
Zarnicke, Julie	2, Dec. 1878	15, Nov.		383	Baumgarten	Burlington, WI	Mecklenburg-Schwerin
Zarth, Johanna Martha Gertrud	5, Jan. 1899	9, Nov.	17	15		Gonzales, TX	Germany
Zartmann, Adam	14, Feb. 1856	3, Feb.	14	28		Newark, OH	Linville, Licking County, Ohio
Zartmann, Josua	28, Jan. 1892	11, Dec.	75	62		Columbus, OH	Gleefort, Perry County, Ohio
Zartmann, Lydia	30, June 1887	8, June	68- 6m- 8d	414		Columbus, OH	Somerset, Perry County, Ohio
Zarwel, Johanna Louise	19, Feb. 1891	9, Jan.		126	Berg	Beaver Dam, WI	Dölitz, Pommern
Zarwel, Mathilde	2, Feb. 1893	13, Jan.	30	78	Grunert	Beaver Dam, WI	Watertown, Wisconsin
Zarwel, Wilhelm Friedrich	1, Sept 1892	4, Aug.	46	558		Beaver Dam, WI	Döritz, Pommern
Zarwell, Chr. Fr.	22, Nov. 1880	4, Nov.	55	375		Beaver Dam, WI	Doelitz, Pieritz, Pommern
Zarwell, Ida Friederike	19, Jan. 1885	5, Jan.	32-10m-20d	7	Grunert	Beaver Dam, WI	Watertown, Wisconsin
Zaske, Johan	18, Oct. 1894	22, Sept	45	678	Maier	Morgan, MN	Friedericksberg, Marienwerder, West Preußen
Zaubig, (Mrs)	2, Nov. 1868		83	351		Edgerton, OH	Sachsen

Christliche Apologete Death Notices --- 1839 - 1899

Name of Deceased	Notice Date	Death Date	Age	Maiden Name	Place of Death	Page	Place of Birth
Zeber, Katharina	9, Nov. 1863	18, Oct.	32-10m- 5d		Evansville, IN	180	Rosenthal, Hessen-Kassel
Zech, Jennie	16, Dec. 1897	6, Nov.	20		Lincoln, NE	799	
Zech, Johannes	29, Oct. 1877	29, Sept	48- 4m- 8d		Secor, IL	351	Weißensee, Sachsen, Preußen
Zede, Louise	9, June 1887	6, May	45	Gurke	Macon, NE	366	Schwanenbeck, Pommern
Zeeb, Mina	19, Feb. 1891	28, Jan.	33	Schlüter	Newark, NJ	126	Uelzen, Hannover
Zeh, Alexander	29, May 1882	15, May	60- 2m-12d		Cincinnati, OH	175	Nördlingen, Germany
Zeh, Barbara	21, July 1884	9, July	73	Giegold	Dillsboro, MO	7	Baiern
Zeh, Edward Albert	26, Jan. 1885		20- 5m-26d		Antelop, CA	7	
Zeh, Gottfried	24, Feb. 1879	10, Jan.	55- 3m-16d		San Francisco, CA	63	Liebesbrunn, Württemberg
Zeh, Johann Gustav	14, July 1859	23, June	83		Milan, IN	112	Münchenreit, Sachsen
Zehnder, Caroline Friedrika	11, Feb. 1867	17, Jan.	35		Salem, MN	46	Winnenden, Württemberg
Zehnder, Rosine	6, Aug. 1883	18, July	46- 1m-28d	Kaufmann	Pittsburg, PA	255	Thun, Bern, Schweiz
Zehner, Jeanette	21, May 1896	2, May	61-10m		Scranton, PA	334	Klein-Altenstetten, RheinPreußen
Zehnter, Sophia	5, Jan. 1880	10, Dec.	36- 6m- 9d	Patzwalg	Pittsburg, PA	7	Wenthagen, Lippe-Schaumburg
Zehringer, Franz Xavier	10, Jan. 1895	19, Dec.	44		Indianapolis, IN	30	Kenzingen, Baden
Zehringer, Landolin	21, Apr. 1873	28, Mar.	55- 6m		Indianapolis, IN	127	Bleichheim, Amt Kinzingen, Baden
Zeidler, (Mr)	18, Dec. 1882	3, Dec.	84- 4m		Lansing, IA	407	Raußensteig, Oberfranken, Baiern
Zeidler, Heinrich	10, May 1888	24, Apr.	57		Lansing, IA	302	Oberfranken, Baiern
Zeidler, Otto	3, Mar. 1887	14, Feb.		Brandt	Clearwater, MN	142	Colonie Brinks, Marienwerder, Preußen
Zeidler, Rosina	5, Nov. 1883	7, Oct.	52	Jackson	Clearwater, MN	359	Braumburg, West Preußen
Zeidler, Samuel Allen	25, Mar. 1897	28, Feb.	31- 8m-13d		Muscatine, IA	190	
Zeidtler, Johan Gottlieb	8, Sept 1887	26, Aug.	81		Burlington, IA	574	Peichau, Schlesien
Zeiher, Gottfried	6, Oct. 1873	7, Sept	26		Indianapolis, IN	319	Grünbach, Schorndorf, Württemberg
Zeilbeer, Barbara	12, May 1898	21, Apr.	73	Hofmänner	Grand Island, NE	303	Buchs, St. Gallen, Schweiz
Zeilmann, Anna	28, Aug. 1882	7, Aug.	76	Fuhrmann	New Albany, IN	279	Haag bei Baireuth, Baiern
Zeilmann, Johan	3, Apr. 1876	9, Mar.	79		New Albany, IN	111	Plößen, Baiern
Zeilmann, Samuel	20, Oct. 1879	7, Oct.	56		New Albany, IN	335	Meßelgau bei Baireuth, Baiern
Zeinert, Albert August	29, Oct. 1891	5, Oct.	19		Appleton, WI	702	
Zeiser, Johann	30, Mar. 1854	17, Mar.	19		Delaware, OH	52	Eßlingen, Württemberg
Zeitler, Johanna Dorothea	10, Mar. 1879	8, Feb.	67- 5m-29d	Woywode	Burlington, WI	79	Kriegheim, Lüben, Preußen
Zeitz, Elisabeth	16, Oct. 1890	23, Sept	60	Bender	Moweaqua, IL	670	Hermershausen, Germany
Zeitz, Herman	13, Aug. 1883	25, July	57- 1m-29d		Moweaqua, IL	263	Kaldern, Marburg, Kurhessen
Zekalla, Johan	9, Feb. 1899	14, Jan.	44		Beaver Dam, WI	95	Niederschlesien, Namslau, Germany
Zekalla, Mary	4, Feb. 1886	18, Jan.	20-10m- 7d		Beaver Dam, WI	7	
Zeller, (Mr)	28, Feb. 1861	4, Jan.			Germantown, OH	36	
Zeller, (Mrs)	28, Feb. 1861	13, Jan.			Germantown, OH	36	
Zeller, Andreas	29, June 1899	5, May	81		Boelus, NE	415	Holzhausen, Sulz, Württemberg
Zeller, Ernst Gottlieb	5, Mar. 1896	18, Feb.	56		Chicago, IL	158	Hohenstaufen, Göppingen, Württemberg
Zeller, Josephine	4, May 1899	19, Mar.	75		Cannelton, IN	287	Großeislingen, Württemberg
Zellmann, Christian L.	18, May 1874	2, May	67	Dreible	West Bend, WI	159	Zimmerhausen, Pommern
Zellmer, Christian Ludwig	1, June 1874	5, May	43		Oshkosh, WI	175	Romanshoff, Posen, Preußen
Zellmer, Christian Theodore	29, Feb. 1864	4, Dec.	5- 5m- 3d		Oshkosh, WI	36	
Zellmer, Johan Gottlieb	26, Oct. 1893	28, Sept	65		Oshkosh, WI	686	Romanshof, Preußen
Zellmer, Johanna Caroline	30, Apr. 1883	7, Apr.	20-9m-12d		Oshkosh, WI	143	Oshkosh, Wisconsin
Zellmer, John F.	10, Oct. 1895	15, Sept	42		Oshkosh, WI	654	Blackwolf, Winnebago County, Wisconsin
Zellmer, Pauline	2, May 1889	3, Apr.	25		Oshkosh, WI	286	Oshkosh, Wisconsin

Christliche Apologete Death Notices --- 1839 - 1899

Name of Deceased	Notice Date	Death Date	Age	Page	Maiden Name	Place of Death	Place of Birth
Zensler, Christina	14, Apr. 1892	24, Mar.	63	238		Cincinnati, OH	Oberreggen, Baden
Zeratzki, Wilhelmine	4, June 1883	18, May	35	183	Stutz	Menominee, MI	West Preußen
Zeratzky, Johanna	18, May 1885	25, Apr.	32	7	Wilki	Menominee, MI	Pommern
Zeratzky, Louise	29, Oct. 1891	4, Oct.	70	702	Panzlau	Menominee, MI	Fabian, Rosenberg, Marienwerder, West Preußen
Zergiebel, Charles Philipp	23, Aug. 1869	18- 7m-15d		271		Mt. Vernon, IN	
Zerley, Margaretha	20, Sept 1880	29, Aug.	49- 5m	303		Woodville, OH	York County, Pennsylvania
Zeugin, Georg	2, Mar. 1893	13, Feb.	68	142		Berger, MO	Duingen, Bern, Schweiz
Zich, Johanna Juliane	24, Jan. 1889	19, Sept	38	62	Seibert	Brenham, TX	Lenker, Holland
Zick, Johan Julius	4, Nov. 1897		48	703		Brillion, WI	Schosierten, Neu Stettin, Hinterpommern
Zick, Martin Christoph	11, Apr. 1895	20, Mar.	76	238		Brillion, WI	Gramenz, Hinterpommern
Zickgraff, Anna Barbara	9, Dec. 1886	17, Nov.	68	7		Delhi, MI	Rheingenheim, Rheinpfalz Baiern
Ziebarth, Henry B.	27, Oct. 1884	11, Sept	15- 2m	7		Rockford, MN	
Ziebarth, Ida	15, Mar. 1888	1, Feb.	18- 4m-12d	174		Crow River, MN	Wright County, Minnesota
Ziebarth, Johan Friedrich	1, May 1890	13, Apr.	87- 5m- 2d	286		Crow River, MN	Letschien, Brandenburg
Ziebarth, Theodor	6, May 1886	24, Mar.	58	7		Montrose, MN	Kleinmarwitz, Brandenburg
Ziebell, Daniel	17, Sept 1891	7, Aug.	93- 7m- 3d	606		Wausau, WI	
Ziebell, Wilhelmine	20, Oct. 1879	27, Sept	76	335	Vinner	Wausau, WI	Fehlingsdorf, Pommern
Ziefle, John G.	1, Aug. 1864		22	124		Francisco, MI	Schönengründ, Freudenstadt, Württemberg
Ziegan, Maria Anna	17, Feb. 1887	24, Jan.	70	110	Knoch	Detroit, MI	Lauterbach, Hessen-Darmstadt
Ziegebein, Louise	17, Oct. 1870	26, Sept	54- - 8d	335	Hambe	Pekin, IL	Osterlinde, Braunschweig
Ziegel, Elisabeth	12, June 1871	13, May	60-10m-20d	191		Boonville, MO	Offenburg, Baden
Ziegelmeier, Herman Heinrich	4, July 1864	13, Mar.	37	108		Arenzville, IL	Schledehausen, Amt Osnabrück, Hannover
Ziegenbein, Ernst	18, Mar.1872	1, Mar.	65	95		Manito, IL	Westerlinde, Braunschweig
Ziegenbein, Julius	9, Feb. 1863	8, Jan.	48- - 8d	24		Milan, IN	Westerlinde, Braunschweig
Ziegenbein, Sophia	21, Mar. 1870	9, Feb.	37	95	Wöll	Alton, IL	Kördorf, Amt Nassau, Nassau
Ziegenbein, Ulricke	18, Aug. 1892	5, July	48	527	Heuer	Brighton, IL	Spiegarden, Treptow a. d. Rega, Hinterpommern
Ziegenbein, Wilhelm	20, July 1899	7, July	71	463		Brighton, IL	Bokenem, Hannover
Ziegenfelder, Anna Barbara	29, June 1885	30, Apr.	75- 8m-21d	7	Weißbrodt	Stockton, CA	
Zieglar, Emma	31, Dec. 1877	26, Nov.	19-10m- 7d	423		Giard, IA	Giard, Clayton County, Iowa
Ziegler, Anna Catharina	17, May 1888	1, May	24-10m-14d	318	Schade	Pittsburg, PA	Pittsburg, Pennsylvania
Ziegler, Anna Chr.	26, June 1890	1, June	74	414		Scranton, PA	Großalmardoe, Kurhessen
Ziegler, Anna Elisabeth	6, Oct. 1892	12, Sept	49	639		Scranton, PA	Großalbenrode, Kurhessen
Ziegler, Catharina	20, Mar. 1871	6, Mar.	67	95		Pinckneyville, IL	
Ziegler, Christine Marie	28, Nov. 1895	5, Nov.	61	766		Hamline, MN	Twiste, Waldeck
Ziegler, Elisabeth	6, Oct. 1898	12, Sept	71	639	Müller	Greenfield, MA	Salzungen, Sachsen-Meiningen
Ziegler, Franz	10, Sept 1877	18, July	72- 1m	295		Scranton, PA	
Ziegler, Georg	27, Dec. 1875	30, Nov.	58	415		Marrs, IN	Altengronau, Schwarzenfels, Kurhessen
Ziegler, Georg	8, Dec. 1892	13, Nov.	49	782		Highland, IL	Oberamt Sulz, Württemberg
Ziegler, Georg	18, Nov. 1872			375		Giard, IA	Eschelbronn, Baden
Ziegler, Gottfried	31, Aug. 1854	16, Aug.	51	140		Indianapolis, IN	Urach, Württemberg
Ziegler, Jakob Fr.	25, Dec. 1882	4, Dec.	55- 9m-29d	415		Brooklyn, NY	Bessingen, Kirchheim an der Teck, Preußen
Ziegler, John	9, Aug. 1888	24, July	42	510		St. Philip, IN	
Ziegler, Katharina	30, June 1898	2, June	52	415	Binder	New York City, NY	Metzingen, Württemberg
Ziegler, Katharina	4, May 1893	4, Apr.	67	286	Koch	Beman, KS	Weingarten, Baden
Ziegler, Louise	10, Mar. 1898	13, Feb.	35	159	Korf	Posey Co, IN	Evansville, Indiana
Ziegler, Ludwig	27, Oct. 1887	17, Sept	24	686		Lyona, KS	Rohrbach bei Heidelberg, Baden

Christliche Apologete Death Notices --- 1839 - 1899

Name of Deceased	Maiden Name	Place of Death	Page	Age	Death Date	Notice Date	Place of Birth
Ziegler, Philippine		Hickory Branch, IN	128	15- 6m-16d	10, July	10, Aug. 1863	Eisterheim, Amt Wisloch, Baden
Ziegler, Sophia	Schweigert	St. Joseph, MO	164		14, Sept	13, Oct. 1862	Epfenbach, Simmsheim, Baden
Ziegler, Wilhelm		Rochester, NY	622	56	20, Aug.	29, Sept 1887	Riedlingen a. d. Donau, Württemberg
Zieman, Katharina	Wagner	Philadelphia, PA	351	69	21, Oct.	3, Nov. 1873	Blantikow, Hinterpommern, Preußen
Ziemann, Dorothea Luise	Seefeld	Milwaukee, WI	375	61- 7m- 2d	19, Oct.	19, Nov. 1877	
Ziemann, Eduard		Philadelphia, PA	463	20- 3m-17d	11, June	16, July 1896	
Ziemann, Sophia		Mascoutah, IL	176	72	23, Oct.	3, Nov. 1859	Briesenhorst, Brandenburg
Zieme, Johanna Louise	Ringewalt	Crown Point, IN	238	91	20, Mar.	9, Apr. 1896	Gützlaffshagen, Hinterpommern
Ziemer, Martha Maria Magdalena		Wausau, WI	782	24- 6m-14d	14, Nov.	8, Dec. 1892	Wausau, Wisconsin
Ziemer, Martin		Minneola, MN	366	61	12, May	9, June 1887	Carsbaum, Pommern
Ziemer, Richard G.A.		Wausau, WI	814	27	20, Nov.	21, Dec. 1893	AltMarin, Hinterpommern
Ziemer, Wilhelm Friedrich		Wausau, WI	7	50	29, July	12, Aug. 1886	Buchhorst, Amt Belgard, HinterPommern
Ziemer, Wilhelmine	Strey	Crow River, MN	126	58	14, Dec.	23, Feb. 1888	Bischofsheim, Baden
Ziemer, Wilhelmine Henriette		Rockford, MN	335	13	11, Sept	17, Oct. 1870	Bischofsheim, Baden
Zier, Eva Magdalena		Oakland, CA	415	87	26, May	30, June 1898	Lindheim, Hessen-Darmstadt
Zier, John			42	39	1, Feb.	15, Mar. 1860	Lindheim, Hessen-Darmstadt
Zier, Kilian		Jeffersonville, NY	118	65- 3m- 2d	20, Mar.	10, Apr. 1876	Cincinnati, Hamilton County, Ohio
Zier, Maria	Kaisner	Jeffersonville, NY	55	70	27, Jan.	14, Feb. 1876	Neuenstein, Oehringen, Württemberg
Zierer, Elisabeth Dorothea		Batesville, IN	415	20	29, May	29, June 1899	Unter-Steinbach, Oehringen, Württemberg
Zierer, Johan Christian		Covington, KY	127	79- -18d	26, Mar.	21, Apr. 1879	Mölsheim, Hessen-Darmstadt
Zierer, Katharina	Hilkert	Covington, KY	527	81	30, July	13, Aug. 1896	Königsberg, OstPreußen
Zieres, Jakob		Jeffersonville, NY	415	75-11m- 7d	10, Dec.	30, Dec. 1878	Comal County, Texas
Ziese, Karl		Crown Point, IN	687	25	2, Oct.	26, Oct. 1899	
Zieshang, Ida		Braken, TX	710	22	2, Oct.	1, Nov. 1894	Kohlsdorf bei Neuße, Preußen
Zietlow, Karl August		Peoria, IL	112	37- 5m- 1d	13, May	10, July 1865	Höfen, Neuenbürg, Württemberg
Zigan, Johan Franz		Detroit, MI	334	70	5, May	21, May 1891	Neuhimspach, Baiern
Zigler, Katharina Barbara		Marrs, IN	7	62	23, July	4, Aug. 1884	
Zilch, Louise	Rösner	Evansville, IN	494	54-11m- 1d	8, July	1, Aug. 1889	Blathe, Pommern
Zilch, Philipp		Marrs, IN	702	23	7, Oct.	1, Nov. 1888	Kleineichen, Hessen
Zillmann, Anna Dorothea Helena L.		Iron Ridge, WI	71	81- -23d	13, Feb.	1, Mar. 1880	Summenthien, Arnswalde, Brandenburg
Zimmer, (son)		San Jose, IL	295	3m	24, Aug.	9, Sept 1872	Landsberg, Frankfurt a.d. Oder, Brandenburg
Zimmer, Caspar		Boody, IL	14	31-11m- 2d		2, Jan. 1890	
Zimmer, Christine	Schimming	Oconomowoc, WI	294	76	9, Apr.	3, May 1894	Rothbach, Elsaß
Zimmer, Ebina H.		San Jose, IL	295	41	24, Aug.	9, Sept 1872	Brietzig bei Pyritz, Pommern
Zimmer, Friedrich W.F.		Beaver Dam, WI	702	76- -12d	30, Sept	31, Oct. 1889	Zinsheim, Baden
Zimmer, Johan		San Jose, CA	766	24	20, Oct.	28, Nov. 1889	Rumbach, Rheinkreis Baiern
Zimmer, Michael (Rev)		Mishawaka, IN	590	73- 9m	20, Aug.	15, Sept 1887	Unter-Hallau, Schaffhausen, Schweiz
Zimmer, Wilhelmine	Schmidt	Beaver Dam, WI	262	49	28, Mar.	19, Apr. 1894	Altheim, Hessen-Darmstadt
Zimmerer, Anton		San Jose, CA	7	45	30, July	18, Nov. 1886	Moutier, Bern, Schweiz
Zimmerli, Elisabeth	Schaub	Clarington, OH	23	66- 4m-21d	31, Dec.	17, Jan. 1876	Bunker Hill, Illinois
Zimmerli, Heinrich		Topeka, KS	399	27	29, Nov.	11, Dec. 1882	
Zimmermann, Adam		Mt. Vernon, IN	222	73	10, Feb.	7, Apr. 1892	Bunker Hill, Illinois
Zimmermann, Adelie	Pagnard	St. Joseph, MO	446	46	12, June	14, July 1887	
Zimmermann, Almt		Marine City, MI	279	19	21, July	30, Aug. 1875	Bunker Hill, Illinois
Zimmermann, Anna		Bunker Hill, IL	782	13-11m-25d	11, Nov.	8, Dec. 1887	
Zimmermann, Anna A.		Bunker Hill, IL	367	24- 1m- 3d	19, Oct.	15, Nov. 1880	

Christliche Apologete Death Notices --- 1839 - 1899

Name of Deceased	Notice Date	Death Date	Age	Page	Maiden Name	Place of Death	Place of Birth
Zimmermann, Anna Margaretha	3, Jan. 1876	5, Dec.	61	7	Simon	Edgerton, OH	Kindheim, Grünstadt, Pfalz, Baiern
Zimmermann, August F.	4, Mar. 1897	29, Jan.	71	143		Tacoma, WA	Radewitz, Pommern
Zimmermann, Barbara	7, Oct. 1872	19, Sept	56- 8m-19d	327	Schöttel	St. Paul, MN	Straßburg, Elsaß
Zimmermann, Barbara	19, Nov. 1896	21, Oct.	70- 11m-16d	750	Miller	Bucyrus, OH	Geiberg, Baden
Zimmermann, Charles	17, Sept 1877	7, Aug.	18-11m- 6d	305		Iowa City, IA	
Zimmermann, Christian	20, July 1893	13, June	77-10m	462		Iowa City, IA	Canton Bern, Schweiz
Zimmermann, Christiana	28, Apr. 1892	13, Feb.	66	270	Schmelsley	Ft. Madison, IA	Benningheim, Württemberg
Zimmermann, Christiane	3, Dec. 1883	19, Nov.	30	391		Chicago, IL	Elias Brunnen bei Lobenstein, Elsaß
Zimmermann, David Philipp	17, Dec. 1891	25, Nov.	37	814		Boody, IL	Perry, Pike County, Illinois
Zimmermann, Eduard	20, Aug. 1866		46	270		St. Paul, MN	Straßburg, Frankreich
Zimmermann, Elisabeth	13, May 1852	Nov.	72	80	Ziegler	Des Moines, IA	Nabern, Kirchheim, Württemberg
Zimmermann, Elisabeth	16, June 1892	31, May	57	382		Edon, OH	Gründenwald, Bern, Schweiz
Zimmermann, Elisabeth	21, June 1869	29, May	74- 1m	199	Schmidt	Wathena, KS	Wattenweil, Bern, Schweiz
Zimmermann, Elisabeth	23, Nov. 1893	17, Oct.	66	750	Buchtler	Papillion, NE	Berneck, Baiern
Zimmermann, Emilie	1, June 1863		4	88		Newport, MI	
Zimmermann, Ernst	25, June 1877	4, June	13	207		Lafayette, MN	Gartz, Pommern
Zimmermann, Eva	29, July 1897	26, June	71	479	Köllner	Kendallville, IN	Wiesenthal, Sachsen-Weimar
Zimmermann, Friederike	11, Sept 1882	26, Aug.	35	295	Schmidthenner	Bradford, IN	Harrison County, Indiana
Zimmermann, Friedrich	9, Apr. 1891	14, Mar.	62	238		Oconomowoc, WI	Schönnenwerder, Piritz, Pommern
Zimmermann, Friedrich	8, Mar. 1894	18, Feb.	74	166		Oconomowoc, WI	Lebehn, Arnswalde, Brandenburg
Zimmermann, G. W.	5, July 1894	26, May	57	438		Pittsfield, IL	Perry , Illinois
Zimmermann, Georg	15, Jan. 1891	16, Dec.	73	46		Grand Ridge, IL	Grünstein, Berneck, Oberfranken, Baiern
Zimmermann, Georg	30, Apr. 1877	28, Mar.	66- 9m-18d	143		Bradford, IN	
Zimmermann, Georg Friedrich	17, Aug. 1874	2, Aug.	74	263		Philadelphia, PA	Schwabbach, Weinsberg, Württemberg
Zimmermann, Gottlieb	9, Aug. 1875		38- 5m-27d	255		Yorktown, IL	Kanton Luzern, Schweiz
Zimmermann, Hieronymus	4, Apr. 1864	7, Mar.	68	56		Osage Bluff, MO	
Zimmermann, Ida	15, Aug. 1889	27, July	17- 2m- 6d	526		Nokomis, IL	
Zimmermann, J.C. Henriette	21, Dec. 1885	2, Dec.	62	7	Brandes	Baldwin, MO	Vallstedt, Braunschweig
Zimmermann, Johan	16, Jan. 1896	28, Dec.	78	46		Kendallville, IN	Bern, Schweiz
Zimmermann, Johann	7, June 1855	21, May	57	92		Lawrenceburg, IN	König, Schemberg, Hessen-Darmstadt
Zimmermann, John	21, Jan. 1897	8, Dec.	65	47		Mt. Vernon, IN	Alheim, Hessen-Darmstadt
Zimmermann, John Friedrich	10, Dec. 1857	17, Nov.		200		Newport, MI	Potsdam, Preußen
Zimmermann, Katharina	10, Feb. 1879	24, Jan.	73-10m-21d	47	Ruwer	Sandwich, IL	Nanzenbach, Nassau
Zimmermann, Katharina	5, Aug. 1872	4, July	19	255	Dick	Bradford, IN	
Zimmermann, Konrad	4, Nov. 1897	15, Oct.	86	703		Earlville, IL	Betra, Glatt, Hohenzollern
Zimmermann, Louise	1, June 1863		6	88		Newport, MI	
Zimmermann, Magdalena	6, Sept 1869	11, Aug.	32	287	Pfäffle	Aurora, IL	
Zimmermann, Maria	4, Feb. 1878	23, Dec.	75-10m- 9d	39		Marine City, MI	Schönfeld, Preußen
Zimmermann, Maria Christina	5, Mar. 1883	12, Feb.	73- 8m- 3d	79	Schäfer	Farmington, MO	Waldeck
Zimmermann, Rosina	5, May 1859	8, Mar.	43- 9m-25d	72	Moritz	Kennyon, MN	Bruchsal, Baden
Zimmermann, Sarah Emma	26, Dec. 1895	28, Nov.	30	828		Kramer, NE	Rock Grove, Illinois
Zimmermann, Susanna Katharina	11, Apr. 1864	25, Mar.	40-10m-11d	60		Kendallville, IN	Canton Bern, Schweiz
Zimmermann, Valentin	18, May 1899	26, Apr.	75	319		Ironton, OH	Ramsen, Rheinpfalz Baiern
Zimmermann, Wilhelm	27, Apr. 1885	7, Apr.	57	7		Dover Center, MN	Lanenbrugge, Dramburg, Köslin, Preußen
Zimmermann, Wilhelm	26, Oct. 1899	9, Oct.	74	687		Mt. Vernon, IN	Bornheim, Hessen-Darmstadt
Zimmerschied, Anna Maria	8, Mar. 1894	21, Feb.	81	166	Wüst	Edwardsville, IL	Dornbach, Nassau

Christliche Apologete Death Notices --- 1839 - 1899

Name of Deceased	Notice Date	Death Date	Age	Maiden Name	Page	Place of Death	Place of Birth
Zimmerschied, Caroline	3, Sept 1883	16, Aug.	24		287	Topeka, KS	Zimmerscheid, Nassau
Zimmerschied, Georg	10, Dec. 1891		19- 1m-10d		798	Edwardsville, IL	
Zimmerschied, Johan Wilhelm	22, Jan. 1883	5, Jan.	75- 9m-16d		31	Edwardsville, IL	Kemenau, Nassau
Zingg, Heinrich	3, Dec. 1866	12, Oct.	22- 7m-21d		390	Washington, IA	
Zink, (Mrs)	18, Apr. 1864	13, Feb.	74-11m		64	Captina, OH	Oberlipp, Bern, Schweiz
Zink, Anna Barbara	15, Dec. 1873	29, Nov.	65- 4m	Stämpfli	399	Perrysburg, OH	Wenge, Schupfen, Bern, Schweiz
Zink, August	21, Dec. 1874	6, Nov.	18		407	Brooklyn, NY	Wellerode, Kreis Kassel, Kurhessen
Zink, Joseph	5, Aug. 1852	20, July	64- 7m		128	Captina, OH	Canton Bern, Schweiz
Zink, Katharina	23, Sept 1858	8, Sept	45		152	Manchester, MO	Kleinheubach, Baiern
Zinn, Philippine	4, Feb. 1886	13, Dec.	70		7	Lena, IL	Weidenheim, Hirschfeld, Kurhessen
Zinnecker, Ludwig	17, Feb. 1887	28, Dec.			110	Pirmasens, GE	
Zinßer, Barbara	4, Feb. 1886	17, Nov.	27	Reich	7		Vierundzwanzighöfe, Oberndorf, Württemberg
Zipf, Elisabeth	16, June 1879	20, May	68- 5m- 2d		191	Newark, NJ	Schweinsberg, Kirchhain, Kurhessen
Zipfel, Rosine	1, Oct. 1891	30, Aug.	78	Büttner	638	Lawrence, MA	Langenwetzendorf, Reuß
Zipperle, Johannes	27, July 1863	18, June	36		120	Indianapolis, IN	Teufringen, Böblingen, Württemberg
Zirzon, Carolina	21, Nov. 1870	22, Oct.	40	Maier	375	Chicago, IL	Bartow, Kreis Demmin, Preußen
Zische, August Martin	15, Dec. 1892	21, Nov.	72- 1m-22d		798	Fremont, OH	Alt-Malskow, Hinterpommern
Zischke, Johan Friedrich	25, Sept 1882	11, Sept	65		311	Sandusky, OH	Luzow, Nolz, Hinterpommern
Zischke, Wilhelm Friedrich	4, May 1893	9, Apr.	42		286	DeWitt, MI	Lupow bei Stolb, Pommern
Ziske, Caroline Auguste W.	14, Feb. 1889	20- 1m-17d			110	Berea, Ohio	Berea, Ohio
Zielmann, Johan Friedrich	24, June 1897	8, June	62		399	Menomonie, WI	Petznick, Pommern
Zitterell, Matthias	4, May 1893	12, Apr.	65		286	Boody, IL	Obervaihingen, Reutlingen, Württemberg
Zitinger, Georg Con.	3, Feb. 1887	31, Dec.	53		78	Baltimore, MD	Höchst, Hessen-Darmstadt
Zittlosen, Martin	25, Oct. 1888	25, Aug.	52- 7m- 3d		686	St. Louis, MO	Lemwerder, Oldenburg
Zittlosen, Martin	27, May 1886	19, Apr.	14-10m-22d		7	St. Louis, MO	
Zittrell, Maria Elisabeth	24, Mar. 1884	4, Mar.	25		7	Boody, IL	Sangamon County, Illinois
Zobel, Anna Margaretha	1, Sept 1879	17, Aug.	48	Hahn	279	Warsaw, IL	Lipprichshausen, Baiern
Zogg, Matthäus	25, Sept 1856	27, Aug.	24- 6m		156	New Haven, CT	Grabs, St. Gallen, Schweiz
Zöller, Abraham	7, Sept 1893	15, Aug.	67		574	Yonkers, NY	Pfaffenschwabenheim, Hessen
Zoller, Daniel	7, July 1884	17, June	59		7	Rochester, NY	Hohengeren, Schorndorf, Württemberg
Zöller, Elisabeth	17, Mar. 1892	26, Jan.	58	Diefenthäler	175	Yonkers, NY	Spießheim, Rhein-Hessen
Zoller, Friederike	23, Oct. 1882	10, Oct.	58	Wilhelm	343	Rochester, NY	Hohengehren, Schorndorf, Württemberg
Zöller, Maria Rosalia	10, Apr. 1882	11, Mar.	69		119	Milwaukee, WI	
Zollinger, Heinrich	26, Feb. 1866	29, Dec.	57		70	Jeffersonville, IN	Egg, Zürich, Schweiz
Zöllinger, Maria	10, Oct. 1881	27, Aug.	11		327	Cedar Lake, IN	
Zollmann, Georg Wilhelm	4, Oct. 1888	10, Sept	14		638	De Soto, MO	
Zollmann, Philipp	13, Mar. 1882	25, Jan.	79-11m-21d		87	De Soto, MO	Mensfelden, Limberg, Nassau
Zollmann, Philipp Christian	12, Dec. 1895	25, Nov.	57		798	De Soto, MO	Mensfelden, Nassau
Zollmann, Philippina	22, Nov. 1880	6, Nov.	70- 1m- 1d		375	De Soto, MO	Mansfelden, Limburg, Nassau
Zorbach, Katharina	28, Sept 1899	16, Sept	95		623	Baltimore, MD	Kleinwallstadt, Kurhessen
Zorn, Elisabeth	27, Nov. 1890	2, Nov.	44- 2m- 3d	Boese	766	Burlington, WI	Lawrenceburg, Dearborn County, Indiana
Zorn, Jakob	28, Jan. 1858	11, Jan.	41		16	Chillicothe, OH	Oberiustadt, Rheinpfalz Baiern
Zörn, Katharina	29, Mar. 1888	3, Mar.	61		206	Houston, TX	Edenkoben, Baiern
Zorn, Maria Margaretha	23, Mar. 1893	14, Feb.	69	Koch	190	Burlington, IA	Schwegenheim, Rheinpfalz Baiern
Zornd, Martha	4, Nov. 1886	14, Oct.			7	Chicago, IL	
Zosel, Karoline Wilhelmine	5, Mar. 1891	2, Feb.	55- -18d	Reinhart	158	Wadena, MN	Sednitz, Sachsen

Christliche Apologete Death Notices --- 1839 - 1899

Name of Deceased	Notice Date	Death Date	Age	Page	Maiden Name	Place of Death	Place of Birth
Zosel, Lebrecht	20, Aug. 1883	9, July	48	271		Wadena, MN	Soloant, Sachsen
Zotz, Karl	24, Feb. 1873		22- 3m-17d	63		Buffalo, NY	
Zschiegner, Maria Regina	10, Oct. 1889	12, Sept	83	654	Steinmerkel	West Bend, WI	Wüstenfalke, Reuß
Zschigner, Johan Heinr. Ferdinand	4, Nov. 1897	6, Oct.	71-10m-11d	703		McKeesport, PA	Dörtendorf, Sachsen
Zuber, Anna	28, Jan. 1897	22, Dec.	53	63	Morf	St. Louis, MO	Wangen, Zürich, Schweiz
Zuber, Anna S.	7, Jan. 1892	3, Dec.	63	14		Brooklyn, NY	Eberstadt, Baden
Zuber, Bartholomäus	28, Feb. 1895	29, Jan.	81	142		Spencerville, OH	Baierthal, Wiesloh, Baden
Zuber, Margaretha	19, Jan. 1863	27, Dec.	52	12	Arnold	Williamsburg, NY	Neuenheim, Amt Heidelberg, Baden
Zuchholdt, Bertha	24, May 1880	2, May	23- 4m- 7d	167		Jamestown, MO	Jamestown, Missouri
Zuchholdt, Wilhelmina	23, Mar. 1893	3, Mar.	57- 2m-14d	190	Nolting	Jamestown, MO	Behme am Salzwerk, Minden, Preußen
Zuck, Samuel	14, Feb. 1870	7, Jan.	51	55		Seymour, IN	Pennsylvania
Zulik, Karl	4, June 1896	17, May	74	367		Humboldt, NE	Podmaklan, Böhmen
Zumm, Dorothea Sophia	24, July 1882	8, July	62	239	Zühlsdorf	Beaver Dam, WI	Großschönfeld, Pommern
Zundel, Rosa	28, Oct. 1878	15, Oct.	20	343		New York City, NY	New York City, New York
Zundel, Rosa	1, June 1893	5, May	74	350	Pfunderer	Brooklyn, NY	Heilbronn, Württemberg
Zürcher, John	12, Mar. 1857	6, Feb.	57- 9m	44		Nashville, IL	Frutigen, Bern, Schweiz
Zürcher, Karl	19, Feb. 1877	28, Jan.	28- 8m-18d	63		Vermillion, OH	Trub, Bern, Schweiz
Zürcher, Ursula	16, Apr. 1896	13, Mar.	67- 1m-23d	254	Häs	Weigand, NE	Weisenheim, Lahr, Baden
Züricher, Elisa	18, Apr. 1870	23, Feb.	62	127		Columbus, IL	Orbe, Waadt, Schweiz
ZurJakobsmühlen, Brün	4, Mar. 1886	1, Jan.		7		Bremen, ---	
ZurJakobsmühlen, Heinrich	27, July 1854	23, June	32	120		Dayton, OH	Holtorff, Thedinghausen, Braunschweig
ZurMegede, Adelheid	12, Dec. 1864	23, Nov.	58	200		Jefferson City, MO	Soest, Arensberg, Preußen
Zürn, Agnes	19, Oct. 1868	3, Oct.	71	335	Mozer	Melrose, NY	Kusterdingen bei Tübingen, Württemberg
Zürm, Conrad	4, Sept 1846		Inquiry	153		New York, NY	Oberamt Tübingen, Württemberg
Zurschmiede, Ulrich	12, June 1871	9, May	50	191		Bradford, IN	Wildersweil, Bern, Schweiz
Zuspann, John	8, Apr. 1878	15, Dec.	49- 3m-15d	111		Quincy, IL	Breiningweiler, Rheinkreis Baiern
Zvinden, Gottfried	10, Nov. 1892	21, Oct.	34	718		Evansville, IN	Schwarzenburg, Bern, Schweiz
Zwahlen, Charles	26, Oct. 1893	6, Oct.	54	686		Michigan City, IN	Interlaken, Bern, Schweiz
Zwahlen, Johann	10, Apr. 1856	17, Mar.	79	60		Boonville, IN	Oberamt Schwarzburg, Bern, Schweiz
Zwahr, Friedrike C.D.	23, Feb. 1893	3, Feb.	48	126	Bollmann	Brenham, TX	Wertin, Mecklenburg-Strelitz
Zweifel, Jacob	24, Sept 1891	4, Sept	42	622		Algona, IA	Leuthal, Schweiz
Zweig, Maria Magdalena	22, Nov. 1888	8, Nov.	58	750	Lehmann	Mt. Vernon, IN	Gorsleben, Preußen
Zweihaus, Friedrich	5, Jan. 1863	15, Dec.	60- 9m	4		St. Louis, MO	Rödinghaus, Preußen
Zwick, Emma Carolina	21, Nov. 1881	4, Nov.	12-10m	375		Wabasha, MN	
Zwick, Julie	6, Jan. 1879	20, Dec.	40- 3m-13d	7	Taxis	Covington, KY	Maulbronn, Württemberg
Zwick, Louise	15, Oct. 1866	5, Aug.		334		Hamilton, OH	New York
Zwick, Maria	1, Jan. 1866	15, Nov.	51	6	Fritsche	Hamilton, OH	Heselhurst, Baden
Zwick, Rosine	17, Aug. 1899	28, July	51	527	Ruff	Hamilton, OH	Hamilton, Butler County, Ohio
Zwickel, Jakob	19, Aug. 1872	31, July	60	271		Milan, IN	Mutterstadt, Rheinkreis Baiern
Zwickel, Margaretha Elisabeth	30, Jan. 1890	3, Jan.	69	78	Feth	Lawrenceburg, IN	Schaurenheim, Baiern
Zwiefel, Anna Margaretha	12, Feb. 1877		79- 3m- 8d	55		Warsaw, IL	Naunheim, Hessen-Darmstadt
Zweig, Maria Magdalena	4, May 1874	11, Mar.	65- 5m	143	Oberriether	Futton, IN	Buchheim, Baden
Zwingeisen, Theresia	14, Jan. 1867	28, Nov.	34	14	König	Williamsburg, NY	Dobell, Neuenburg, Württemberg
Zwingli, Christine	17, Dec. 1896	18, Nov.	72	814	Graber	Graham, MO	Sigriswyl, Bern, Schweiz
Zysset, Magdalena							

www.ingramcontent.com/pod-product-compliance
Lightning Source LLC
Chambersburg PA
CBHW080407270326
41929CB00018B/2934